W9-DEJ-620

CHILTON®

EUROPEAN SERVICE MANUAL 2012 EDITION VOLUME II

BMW MERCEDES-BENZ VOLVO

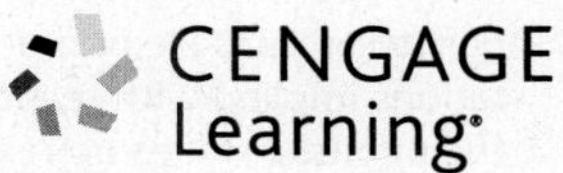

Australia • Brazil • Japan • Korea • Mexico • Singapore • Spain • United Kingdom • United States

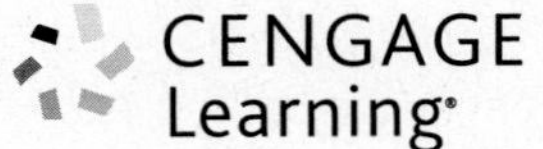

CHILTON®
European Service Manual
2012 Edition
Volume II
BMW, Mercedes-Benz, Volvo

Vice President,
Technology & Trades Professional
Business Unit
Gregory L. Clayton
Publisher:
David Koontz
Director of Marketing:
Beth A. Lutz
Senior Production Director:
Wendy Troeger
Production Manager:
Sherondra Thedford
Senior Marketing Manager:
Jennifer Barbic
Associate Marketing Manager:
Rachael Torres
Chilton Content Specialist:
Paula Baillie
Graphical Designer:
Melinda Possinger
Art Director:
Benj Gleeksman
Sr. Content Project Manager:
William Tubbert
Senior Editors:
Eugene F. Hannon, Jr., A.S.E.
Tracy Junker
Ryan Lee Price
Richard J. Rivele
Christine L. Sheeky
Editors:
Jim Bailey
Julia Gillis
Steven D. Junker, A.S.E.
Will Kesseler
Jonathon Wallace
Kyla White

ISBN-13: 978-1-2854-7111-2
ISBN-10: 1-2854-7111-3
ISSN: 2161-7872

Chilton
5 Maxwell Drive
Clifton Park, NY 12065-2919
USA

Cengage Learning is a leading provider of customized learning solutions with office locations around the globe, including Singapore, the United Kingdom, Australia, Mexico, Brazil, and Japan. Locate your local office at: **international.cengage.com/region**

Chilton products are represented in Canada by Nelson Education, Ltd.

NOTICE TO THE READER

Publisher does not warrant or guarantee any of the products described herein or perform any independent analysis in connection with any of the product information contained herein. Publisher does not assume, and expressly disclaims, any obligation to obtain and include information other than that provided to it by the manufacturer.

The reader is expressly warned to consider and adopt all safety precautions that might be indicated by the activities described herein and to avoid all potential hazards. By following the instructions contained herein, the reader willingly assumes all risks in connection with such instructions.

The publisher makes no representations or warranties of any kind, including but not limited to, the warranties of fitness for particular purpose or merchantability, nor are any such representations implied with respect to the material set forth herein, and the publisher takes no responsibility with respect to such material. The publisher shall not be liable for any special, consequential, or exemplary damages resulting, in whole or part, from the readers' use of, or reliance upon, this material.

Printed in the United States of America
1 2 3 4 5 6 7 XX 17 16 15 14 13

Contents

Sections

Model Index

USING THIS INFORMATION

Organization

To find where a particular model section or procedure is located, look in the Table of Contents. Main topics are listed with the page number on which they may be found. Following the main topics is an alphabetical listing of all of the procedures within the section and their page numbers.

Manufacturer and Model Coverage

This product covers 2011-2012 European models that are produced in sufficient quantities to warrant coverage, and which have technical content available from the vehicle manufacturers before our publication date. Although this information is as complete as possible at the time of publication, some manufacturers may make changes which cannot be included here. While striving for total accuracy, the publisher cannot assume responsibility for any errors, changes, or omissions that may occur in the compilation of this data.

Part Numbers and Special Tools

Part numbers and special tools are recommended by the publisher and vehicle manufacturer to perform specific jobs. Before substituting any part or tool for the one recommended, you must be completely satisfied that neither your personal safety, nor the performance of the vehicle will be endangered.

ACKNOWLEDGEMENT

The publisher would like to express appreciation to the following vehicle manufacturers for their assistance in producing this manual: BMW of North America, LLC, Mercedes-Benz USA, LLC, Volvo Cars of North America, LLC.

PRECAUTIONS

Before servicing any vehicle, please be sure to read all of the following precautions, which deal with personal safety, prevention of component damage, and important points to take into consideration when servicing a motor vehicle:

- Always wear safety glasses or goggles when drilling, cutting, grinding or prying.
- Steel-toed work shoes should be worn when working with heavy parts. Pockets should not be used for carrying tools. A slip or fall can drive a screwdriver into your body.
- Work surfaces, including tools and the floor should be kept clean of grease, oil or other slippery material.
- When working around moving parts, don't wear loose clothing. Long hair should be tied back under a hat or cap, or in a hair net.
- Always use tools only for the purpose for which they were designed. Never pry with a screwdriver.
- Keep a fire extinguisher and first aid kit handy.
- Always properly support the vehicle with approved stands or lift.
- Always have adequate ventilation when working with chemicals or hazardous material.
- Carbon monoxide is colorless, odorless and dangerous. If it is necessary to operate the engine with vehicle in a closed area such as a garage, always use an exhaust collector to vent the exhaust gases outside the closed area.
- When draining coolant, keep in mind that small children and some pets are attracted by ethylene glycol antifreeze, and are quite likely to drink any left in an open container, or in puddles on the ground. This will prove fatal in sufficient quantity. Always drain the coolant into a sealable container.
- To avoid personal injury, do not remove the coolant pressure relief cap while the engine is operating or hot. The cooling system is under pressure; steam and hot liquid can come out forcefully when the cap is loosened slightly. Failure to follow these instructions may result in personal injury. The coolant must be recovered in a suitable, clean container for reuse. If the coolant is contaminated it must be recycled or disposed of correctly.
- When carrying out maintenance on the starting system be aware that heavy gauge leads are connected directly to the battery. Make sure the protective caps are in place when maintenance is completed. Failure to follow these instructions may result in personal injury.
- Do not remove any part of the engine emission control system. Operating the engine without the engine emission control system will reduce fuel economy and engine ventilation. This will weaken engine performance and shorten engine life. It is also a violation of Federal law.
- Due to environmental concerns, when the air conditioning system is drained, the refrigerant must be collected using refrigerant recovery/recycling equipment. Federal law requires that refrigerant be recovered into appropriate recovery equipment and the process be conducted by qualified technicians who have been certified by an approved organization, such as MACS, ASI, etc. Use of a recovery machine dedicated to the appropriate refrigerant is necessary to reduce the possibility of oil and refrigerant incompatibility concerns. Refer to the instructions provided by the equipment manufacturer when removing refrigerant from or charging the air conditioning system.
- Always disconnect the battery ground when working on or around the electrical system.
- Batteries contain sulfuric acid. Avoid contact with skin, eyes, or clothing. Also, shield your eyes when working near batteries to protect against possible splashing of the acid solution. In case of acid contact with skin or eyes, flush immediately with water for a minimum of 15 minutes and get prompt medical attention. If acid is swallowed, call a physician immediately. Failure to follow these instructions may result in personal injury.
- Batteries normally produce explosive gases. Therefore, do not allow flames, sparks or lighted substances to come near the battery. When charging or working near a battery, always shield your face and protect your eyes. Always provide ventilation. Failure to follow these instructions may result in personal injury.

• When lifting a battery, excessive pressure on the end walls could cause acid to spew through the vent caps, resulting in personal injury, damage to the vehicle or battery. Lift with a battery carrier or with your hands on opposite corners. Failure to follow these instructions may result in personal injury.

• Observe all applicable safety precautions when working around fuel. Whenever servicing the fuel system, always work in a well-ventilated area. Do not allow fuel spray or vapors to come in contact with a spark, open flame, or excessive heat (a hot drop light, for example). Keep a dry chemical fire extinguisher near the work area. Always keep fuel in a container specifically designed for fuel storage; also, always properly seal fuel containers to avoid the possibility of fire or explosion. Do not smoke or carry lighted tobacco or open flame of any type when working on or near any fuel-related components.

• Fuel injection systems often remain pressurized, even after the engine has been turned OFF. The fuel system pressure must be relieved before disconnecting any fuel lines. Failure to do so may result in fire and/or personal injury.

• The evaporative emissions system contains fuel vapor and condensed fuel vapor. Although not present in large quantities, it still presents the danger of explosion or fire. Disconnect the battery ground cable from the battery to minimize the possibility of an electrical spark occurring, possibly causing a fire or explosion if fuel vapor or liquid fuel is present in the area. Failure to follow these instructions can result in personal injury.

• The EPA warns that prolonged contact with used engine oil may cause a number of skin disorders, including cancer! You should make every effort to minimize your exposure to used engine oil. Protective gloves should be worn when changing oil. Wash your hands and any other exposed skin areas as soon as possible after exposure to used engine oil. Soap and water, or waterless hand cleaner should be used.

• Some vehicles are equipped with an air bag system, often referred to as a Supplemental Restraint System (SRS) or Supplemental Inflatable Restraint (SIR) system. The system must be disabled before performing service on or around system components, steering column, instrument panel components, wiring and sensors. Failure to follow safety and disabling procedures could result in accidental air bag deployment, possible personal injury and unnecessary system repairs.

• Always wear safety goggles when working with, or around, the air bag system. When carrying a non-deployed air bag, be sure the bag and trim cover are pointed away from your body. When placing a non-deployed air bag on a work surface, always face the bag and trim cover upward, away from the surface. This will reduce the motion of the module if it is accidentally deployed.

• Electronic modules are sensitive to electrical charges. The ABS module can be damaged if exposed to these charges.

• Brake pads and shoes may contain asbestos, which has been determined to be a cancer-causing agent. Never clean brake surfaces with compressed air. Avoid inhaling brake dust. Clean all brake surfaces with a commercially available brake cleaning fluid.

• When replacing brake pads, shoes, discs or drums, replace them as complete axle sets.

• When servicing drum brakes, disassemble and assemble one side at a time, leaving the remaining side intact for reference.

• Brake fluid often contains polyglycol ethers and polyglycols. Avoid contact with the eyes and wash your hands thoroughly after handling brake fluid. If you do get brake fluid in your eyes, flush your eyes with clean, running water for 15 minutes. If eye irritation persists, or if you have taken brake fluid internally, immediately seek medical assistance.

• Clean, high quality brake fluid from a sealed container is essential to the safe and proper operation of the brake system. You should always buy the correct type of brake fluid for your vehicle. If the brake fluid becomes contaminated, completely flush the system with new fluid. Never reuse any brake fluid. Any brake fluid that is removed from the system should be discarded. Also, do not allow any brake fluid to come in contact with a painted or plastic surface; it will damage the paint.

• Never operate the engine without the proper amount and type of engine oil; doing so will result in severe engine damage.

• Timing belt maintenance is extremely important! Many models utilize an interference- type, non freewheeling engine. If the timing belt breaks, the valves in the cylinder head may strike the pistons, causing potentially serious (also time-consuming and expensive) engine damage.

• Disconnecting the negative battery cable on some vehicles may interfere with the functions of the on-board computer system(s) and may require the computer to undergo a relearning process once the negative battery cable is reconnected.

• Steering and suspension fasteners are critical parts because they affect performance of vital components and systems and their failure can result in major service expense. They must be replaced with the same grade or part number or an equivalent part if replacement is necessary. Do not use a replacement part of lesser quality or substitute design. Torque values must be used as specified during reassembly.

BMW

1 Series • M1

1

SPECIFICATIONS AND MAINTENANCE CHARTS

ENGINE AND VEHICLE IDENTIFICATION

Engine						
Code	Liters (cc)	Cu. In.	Cyl.	Fuel Sys.	Engine Type	Eng. Mfg.
N52B30	3.0 (2996)	183	6	Siemens MSV80	DOHC	BMW
N54B30	3.0 (2979)	181	6	Siemens MSD81	DOHC	BMW
N55B30	3.0 (2979)	181	6	Siemens MSD81	DOHC	BMW

Model Year	
Code ①	Year
B	2011
C	2012

NA: Not Available

DOHC: Double Overhead Camshaft

SOHC: Single Overhead Camshaft

① 10th digit of the Vehicle Identification Number (VIN)

71112_BMW1_C0001

GENERAL ENGINE SPECIFICATIONS

Year	Body Type	Model	Engine Displacement Liters (cc)	Engine ID/VIN	Fuel System Type	Net Horsepower @ rpm	Net Torque @ rpm (ft. lbs.)	Bore x Stroke (in.)	Com-pression Ratio	Oil Pressure @ rpm
2011	E82	128i Coupe	3.0 (2996)	N52B30	Siemens MSV80	230@6500	200@2750	3.35x3.46	10.7:1	7.3@idle
	E88	128i Convertible	3.0 (2996)	N52B30	Siemens MSV80	230@6500	200@2750	3.35x3.46	10.7:1	7.3@idle
	E82	135i Coupe	3.0 (2979)	N54B30	Siemens MSD80	306@5800	400@1400	3.27x3.49	10.2:1	21.8@idle
	E88	135i Convertible	3.0 (2979)	N54B30	Siemens MSD80	306@5800	400@1400	3.27x3.49	10.2:1	21.8@idle
	E82	135i Coupe	3.0 (2979)	N55B30	Siemens MSD80	300@5800	300@1400	3.31x3.53	10.2:1	21.8@idle
	E88	135i Convertible	3.0 (2979)	N55B30	Siemens MSD80	300@5800	300@1400	3.31x3.53	10.2:1	21.8@idle
2012	E82	128i Coupe	3.0 (2996)	N52B30	Siemens MSV80	230@6500	200@2750	3.35x3.46	10.7:1	7.3@idle
	E88	128i Convertible	3.0 (2996)	N52B30	Siemens MSV80	230@6500	200@2750	3.35x3.46	10.7:1	7.3@idle
	E82	135i Coupe	3.0 (2979)	N55B30	Siemens MSD80	300@5800	300@1400	3.31x3.53	10.2:1	21.8@idle
	E88	135i Convertible	3.0 (2979)	N55B30	Siemens MSD80	300@5800	300@1400	3.31x3.53	10.2:1	21.8@idle

71112_BMW1_C0002

ENGINE TUNE-UP SPECIFICATIONS

Year	Engine Displacement Liters (cc)	Engine ID/VIN	Spark Plug Gap (in.)	Ignition Timing (deg.)		Fuel Pump (psi)	Idle Speed (rpm)		Valve Clearance	
				MT	AT		MT	AT	In.	Ex.
2011	3.0 (2996)	N52B30	①	②	②	70-76	②	②	HYD	HYD
	3.0 (2979)	N54B30	①	②	②	70-76	②	②	HYD	HYD
	3.0 (2979)	N55B30	①	②	②	70-76	②	②	HYD	HYD
2011	3.0 (2996)	N52B30	①	②	②	70-76	②	②	HYD	HYD
	3.0 (2979)	N55B30	①	②	②	70-76	②	②	HYD	HYD

HYD: Hydraulic

NA: Not applicable

NOTE: The Vehicle Emission Control Information label reflects specification changes during production and must be used if they differ from this chart.

① Three mass and four-mass electrodes cannot be adjusted

Dual mass electrodes: 0.035-0.039 inches

All others: 0.028-0.031 inches

② Controlled by the Engine Control Module (ECM) and cannot be adjusted

71112_BMW1_C0003

CAPACITIES

Year	Body Type	Model	Engine Displacement Liters (cc)	Engine ID/VIN	Engine Oil with Filter (qts.)	Transmission (pts.) 6-Spd	Transmission (pts.) Auto.	Drive Axle Front (pts.)	Drive Axle Rear (pts.)	Fuel Tank (gal.)	Cooling System (qts.)
2011	E82	128i Coupe	3.0 (2996)	N52B30	6.9	①	②	NA	③	14.0	④
	E88	128i Convertible	3.0 (2996)	N52B30	6.9	①	②	NA	③	14.0	④
	E82	135i Coupe	3.0 (2979)	N54B30	6.9	①	②	NA	③	16.1	④
	E88	135i Coupe	3.0 (2979)	N54B30	6.9	①	②	NA	③	16.1	④
	E82	135i Coupe	3.0 (2979)	N55B30	6.9	①	②	NA	③	14.0	④
	E88	135i Coupe	3.0 (2979)	N55B30	6.9	①	②	NA	③	14.0	④
2012	E82	128i Coupe	3.0 (2996)	N52B30	6.9	①	②	NA	③	14.0	④
	E88	128i Convertible	3.0 (2996)	N52B30	6.9	①	②	NA	③	14.0	④
	E82	135i Coupe	3.0 (2979)	N55B30	6.9	①	②	NA	③	14.0	④
	E88	135i Coupe	3.0 (2979)	N55B30	6.9	①	②	NA	③	14.0	④

NA: Not applicable.

NS: Not specified by the manufacturer.

NOTE: All capacities are approximate. Add fluid gradually and ensure a proper fluid level is obtained. Capacities given are service, not overhaul capacities

① GS6-17BG/DG Transmission 3.6 pts.

② GA6L45R Transmission: 13.2 refill/20.2 total fill

③ 168L differential: 1.7 pts.
188L differential: 2.2 pts.
215 L differential: 2.6 pts.

④ M/T: 8.7 qts., A/T 8.9 qts.

71112_BMW1_C0004

FLUID SPECIFICATIONS

Year	Model	Engine Displ. Liters	Engine Oil	Man. Trans.	Auto. Trans.	Rear Drive Axle	Power Steering Fluid	Brake Master Cylinder	Cooling System
2011	128i Coupe	3.0	5W-30	①	ATF M1375.4	②	Dexron III	DOT 4	BMW Long Life Coolant
	128i Convertible	3.0	5W-30	①	ATF M1375.4	②	Dexron III	DOT 4	BMW Long Life Coolant
	135i Coupe	3.0	5W-30	①	ATF M1375.4	②	Dexron III	DOT 4	BMW Long Life Coolant
	135i Convertible	3.0	5W-30	①	ATF M1375.4	②	Dexron III	DOT 4	BMW Long Life Coolant
2012	128i Coupe	3.0	5W-30	①	ATF M1375.4	②	Dexron III	DOT 4	BMW Long Life Coolant
	128i Convertible	3.0	5W-30	①	ATF M1375.4	②	Dexron III	DOT 4	BMW Long Life Coolant
	135i Coupe	3.0	5W-30	①	ATF M1375.4	②	Dexron III	DOT 4	BMW Long Life Coolant
	135i Convertible	3.0	5W-30	①	ATF M1375.4	②	Dexron III	DOT 4	BMW Long Life Coolant

① Yellow Label: MTF-LT-1 or MTF-LT-2
Green Label: Synthetic Mobil SCH630
6-Speed: MTF-LT-3
No label: MIL-L-2105

② Limited slip: SAF-XJ. Non-limited slip: SAF-XO

71112_BMW1_C0005

VALVE SPECIFICATIONS

Year	Engine Displacement Liters (cc)	Engine ID/VIN	Seat Angle (deg.)	Face Angle (deg.)	Spring Test Pressure (lbs. @ in.)	Spring Installed Height (in.)	Stem-to-Guide Clearance (in.) Intake	Stem-to-Guide Clearance (in.) Exhaust	Stem Diameter (in.) Intake	Stem Diameter (in.) Exhaust
2011	3.0 (2996)	N52B30	①	45	NS	NS	② 0.0197	② 0.0197	0.0234-0.0235	0.0234-0.0235
	3.0 (2979)	N54B30	①	45	NS	NS	② 0.0197	② 0.0197	0.0234-0.0235	0.0234-0.0235
	3.0 (2979)	N55B30	③	45	NS	NS	NS	NS	0.1947-0.1953	0.2343-0.2349
2012	3.0 (2996)	N52B30	①	45	NS	NS	② 0.0197	② 0.0197	0.0234-0.0235	0.0234-0.0235
	3.0 (2979)	N55B30	③	45	NS	NS	NS	NS	0.1947-0.1953	0.2343-0.2349

NS: Not specified by the manufacturer

① Valve seat angle: 45 degrees
Correction angle outside: 15 degrees
Correction angle inside: 60 degrees

② To measure: Insert a new valve into guide with end of valve flush with end of guide.
Use a dial indicator to measure axial valve head movement.

③ Valve seat angle: 45 degrees
Correction angle outside: 35 degrees
Correction a
Correction angle inner, inlet valve: 65 degrees

71112_BMW1_C0006

CAMSHAFT SPECIFICATIONS

All measurements in inches unless noted

Year	Engine Displacement Liters (cc)	Engine Code/ID	Journal Dia.	Brg. Oil Clearance	Shaft End-play	Circle Runout	Lobe Height Intake	Lobe Height Exhaust
2011	3.0 (2996)	N52B30	NS	NS	0.0007-0.0063	0.0021-0.0038	NS	NS
	3.0 (2979)	N54B30	NS	NS	0.0007-0.0063	0.0021-0.0038	NS	NS
	3.0 (2979)	N55B30	NS	NS	NS	NS	NS	NS

NS: Not specified by the manufacturer

71112_BMW1_C0007

CRANKSHAFT AND CONNECTING ROD SPECIFICATIONS

All measurements are given in inches.

Year	Engine Displacement Liters (cc)	Engine ID/VIN	Crankshaft Main Brg. Journal Dia.	Crankshaft Main Brg. Oil Clearance	Crankshaft Shaft End-play	Crankshaft Thrust on No.	Connecting Rod Journal Diameter	Connecting Rod Oil Clearance	Connecting Rod Side Clearance
2011	3.0 (2996)	N52B30	①	0.0007-0.0023	0.0031-0.0064	NS	1.7706-1.7712	0.0007-0.0022	NS
	3.0 (2979)	N54B30	②	0.0007-0.0017	0.0024-0.0098	NS	1.9682-2.0742	0.0007-0.0023	NS
	3.0 (2979)	N55B30	③	0.00079-0.0018	0.0059	NS	2.1102-2.1108	NS	NS
2012	3.0 (2996)	N52B30	①	0.0007-0.0023	0.0031-0.0064	NS	1.7706-1.7712	0.0007-0.0022	NS
	3.0 (2979)	N55B30	③	0.00079-0.0018	0.0059	NS	2.1102-2.1108	NS	NS

NS: Not specified by the manufacturer

① Standard yellow 2.3615-2.3618 inches
Standard green: 2.3613-2.3615 inches
Standard white: 2.3611-2.3613 inches

② Designation S1: 2.1837-2.1839 inches
Designation S2: 2.1834-2.1836 inches
Designation S3: 2.1832-2.1834 inches

③ Identification mark S/1: 2.2040-2.2041
Identification mark S/2: 2.2038-2.2040
Identification mark S/3: 2.2035-2.2037

71112_BMW1_C0008

PISTON AND RING SPECIFICATIONS

All measurements are given in inches

Year	Engine Displacement Liters (cc)	Engine ID/VIN	Piston Clearance	Ring Gap Top Compression	Ring Gap Bottom Compression	Ring Gap Oil Control	Ring Side Clearance Top Compression	Ring Side Clearance Bottom Compression	Ring Side Clearance Oil Control
2011	3.0 (2996)	N52B30	0.0004-0.0016	0.0078-0.0157	0.0078-0.0157	0.0078-0.0177	0.0008-0.0024	0.0008-0.0024	0.0005-0.0023
	3.0 (2979)	N54B30	①	0.0071-0.0130	0.0118-0.0197	NS	0.0008-0.0024	0.0008-0.0024	NS
	3.0 (2979)	N55B30	②	③	③	NS	③	③	NS
2012	3.0 (2996)	N52B30	0.0004-0.0016	0.0078-0.0157	0.0078-0.0157	0.0078-0.0177	0.0008-0.0024	0.0008-0.0024	0.0005-0.0023
	3.0 (2979)	N55B30	②	③	③	NS	③	③	NS

NS: Not specified by the manufacturer

① New Piston: 0.000-0.001
Used Piston: 0.0007-0.0018

② New Piston: 0.000-0.001
Used Piston: 0.0007-0.0031

③ 1st groove end clearance: 0.0059-0.0118
1st groove axial clearance: 0.00078-0.0024
2nd groove end clearance: 0.0118-0.0197
2nd groove axial clearance: 0.0006-0.0024
3rd groove end clearance: 0.0078-0.0354
3rd groove axial clearance: not measureable

71112_BMW1_C0009

TORQUE SPECIFICATIONS

All readings in ft. lbs.

Year	Engine Displacement Liters (cc)	Engine ID/VIN	Cylinder Head Bolts	Main Bearing Bolts	Rod Bearing Bolts	Crankshaft Damper Bolts	Flywheel Bolts	Manifold Intake	Manifold Exhaust	Spark Plugs	Lug Nut
2011	3.0 (2996)	N52B30	①	②	③	302	④	⑤	⑥	⑦	89
	3.0 (2979)	N54B30	⑧	⑨	③	18.5	⑩	⑤	⑥	⑦	89
	3.0 (2979)	N55B30	⑪	⑨	⑫	⑬	⑭	⑤	⑥	⑦	89
2012	3.0 (2996)	N52B30	①	②	③	302	④	⑤	⑥	⑦	89
	3.0 (2979)	N55B30	⑪	⑨	⑫	⑬	⑭	⑤	⑥	⑦	89

NA: Not applicable

NS: Not specified by the manufacturer

① Cast iron block. Replace, wash and oil bolts
Step 1: 22 ft. lbs.
Step 2: 90 degrees
Step 3: 90 degrees

② Cast iron block. Replace, wash and oil bolts
Step 1: 14.8 ft. lbs.
Step 2: 50 degrees

③ Replace, wash and oil connecting rod bolts
Step 1: 14.8 ft. lbs.
Step 2: 70 degrees

④ New micro-encapsulated screws:
Automatic transmission: 88 ft. lbs.
Manual transmission: 77.4 ft. lbs.

⑤ All M6 fasteners: 88 inch lbs.
All M7 fasteners: 11 ft. lbs.
All M8 fasteners: 16 ft. lbs.

⑥ Coat with Molykkote HSC compound or equivalent
All M6 fasteners: 88 inch lbs.
All M7 fasteners: 14.8 ft. lbs.

⑦ M12x1.25:14.8-19.1 ft. lbs.
M14x1.25: 21.4-24.3 ft. lbs.

⑧ Always use new bolts.
Step 1: Tighten bolts 1-10 (M11) to 22 ft. lbs.
Step 2: Tighten bolts 11-14 (M9) to 22 ft. lbs.
Step 3: Tighten bolts 1-14 90 degrees
Step 4: Tighten bolts 1-10 (M11) 90 degrees
Step 5: Tighten bolts 1-14 45 degrees

⑨ Always use new bolts.
Step 1: 14.8 ft. lbs.
Step 2: 70 degrees

⑩ Always use new bolts.
Automatic transmission:
Step 1: 22.2 ft. lbs.
Step 2: 92.5ft. lbs.
Manual transmission: 88.8 ft. lbs.

⑪ M9x170 and M11x173: Use new bolts
Step 1: 22 ft. lbs.
Step 2: 90 degrees
Step 3: 180 degrees
M9x30 and M9x70: 22 ft. lbs.

⑫ Replace, wash and oil connecting rod bolts
Step 1: 14.8 ft. lbs.
Step 2: 180 degrees

⑬ Replace and lightly oil screw and thread
Step 1: 74 ft. lbs.
Step 2: 270 degrees

⑭ Replace scrws: 44 ft. lbs. + 45 degrees

71112_BMW1_C0010

WHEEL ALIGNMENT

Year	Model		Caster Range (+/-Deg.)	Caster Preferred Setting (Deg.)	Camber Range (+/-Deg.)	Camber Preferred Setting (Deg.)	Toe-in (Deg.)	Steering Axis Inclination (Deg.)
2011	1 Series	Front	0.15	0	0.25	-0.20	0.26 +/- 0.06	—
		Rear	—	—	0.08	-1.50	0.30 +/- 0.06	—
	135is	Front	0.15	0	0.25	-0.46	0.26 +/- 0.06	—
		Rear	—	—	0.08	-1.83	0.18 +/- 0.06	—
2012	1 Series	Front	0.15	0	0.25	-0.20	0.26 +/- 0.06	—
		Rear	—	—	0.08	-1.50	0.30 +/- 0.06	—
	135is	Front	0.15	0	0.25	-0.46	0.26 +/- 0.06	—
		Rear	—	—	0.08	-1.83	0.18 +/- 0.06	—

NOTE: Load vehicle with 150 lbs. on the front seats, 150 lbs on the rear seats and 46 lbs in the trunk with a full fuel tank.

71112_BMW1_C0011

TIRE, WHEEL AND BALL JOINT SPECIFICATIONS

Year	Model	OEM Tires Standard	OEM Tires Optional	Tire Pressures (psi) Front	Tire Pressures (psi) Rear	Wheel Size	Ball Joint Inspection	Lugnut Torque (ft. lbs.)
2011	128i Coupe	P205/50R17	P225/45R17	①	①	NA	NA	89
	128i Convertible	P205/55R16	②	①	①	NA	NA	89
	135i Coupe	P205/50R17	③	①	①	NA	NA	89
	135i Convertible	P205/50R17	③	①	①	NA	NA	89
2012	128i Coupe	P205/50R17	P225/45R17	①	①	NA	NA	89
	128i Convertible	P205/55R16	②	①	①	NA	NA	89
	135i Coupe	P205/50R17	③	①	①	NA	NA	89
	135i Convertible	P205/50R17	③	①	①	NA	NA	89

① See door sticker.
② Front: P205/50R17
Rear: P225/45R17
③ Front: P215/40R18
Rear: P245/35R18

71112_BMW1_C0012

BRAKE SPECIFICATIONS

All measurements in inches unless noted

Year	Body Type	Model		Brake Disc Original Thickness	Brake Disc Minimum Thickness	Brake Disc Maximum Runout	Minimum Lining Thickness Front	Minimum Lining Thickness Rear	Brake Caliper Bracket Bolts (ft. lbs.)	Brake Caliper Mounting Bolts (ft. lbs.)
2011	E82	128i Coupe	F	①	②	NS	④	NA	81	⑤
			R	③	②	NS	NA	④	48	⑤
	E88	128i Convertible	F	①	②	NS	④	NA	81	⑤
			R	③	②	NS	NA	④	48	⑤
	E82	135i Coupe	F	①	②	NS	④	NA	81	⑤
			R	③	②	NS	NA	④	48	⑤
	E88	135i Convertible	F	①	②	NS	④	NA	81	⑤
			R	③	②	NS	NA	④	48	⑤
2012	E82	128i Coupe	F	①	②	NS	④	NA	81	⑤
			R	③	②	NS	NA	④	48	⑤
	E88	128i Convertible	F	①	②	NS	④	NA	81	⑤
			R	③	②	NS	NA	④	48	⑤
	E82	135i Coupe	F	①	②	NS	④	NA	81	⑤
			R	③	②	NS	NA	④	48	⑤
	E88	135i Convertible	F	①	②	NS	④	NA	81	⑤
			R	③	②	NS	NA	④	48	⑤

NOTE: Do not machine M3 or perforated brake discs.
NA: Not applicable
NS: Not specified by the manufacturer
F: Front
R: Rear
① Diameter x Thickness in inches
13.18x1.01
12.87x0.936
11.70x0.936
② Minimum thickness is stamped in the brake disk shell
Maximum machining limit per side: 0.315 inches
③ Diameter x Thickness in inches.
12.63x0.858
11.70x0.780
④ Minimum lining thickness is determined by the Condition Based Service system.
⑤ Socket head cap screw: 22 ft. lbs.
Hexagon screw: 26 ft. lbs.

71112_BMW1_C0013

SCHEDULED MAINTENANCE INTERVALS
BMW—1 SERIES

TO BE SERVICED	TYPE OF SERVICE	SERVICE INTERVALS			
		INITIAL 1200 MILES	OIL SERVICE	INSPECTION I	INSPECTION II
Brake & clutch fluids	S/I			✓	✓
Brake & clutch fluids	R	every two years			
Brake pads & discs	S/I			✓	✓
Catalytic converter & shielding	S/I	✓		✓	✓
Cooling system	S/I	✓		✓	✓
Engine (check for leakage)	S/I	✓			
Engine air cleaner element	R				✓
Engine coolant	R	every two years			
Engine drive belts	S/I				✓
Engine oil	R				
Engine oil & filter	R		✓	✓	✓
Exhaust pipe & muffler	S/I			✓	✓
Fuel filter (California)	R				✓
Fuel, vapor lines & fuel cap	S/I	✓		✓	✓
Intake air dust separators (M/T)	S/I				✓
Maintenance Indicators	Reset		✓	✓	✓
OBD system for codes	S/I	✓		✓	✓
Oil level	S/I	✓			
Oxygen sensor	R	every 100,000 miles			
Parking brake system	S/I			✓	✓
Power steering system	S/I			✓	✓
Rear axle fluid	S/I			✓	✓
Rear axle fluid	R		✓		
Spark plugs (3.0L N52B30 engine)	R	every 100,000 miles			
Spark plugs (3.0L N54B30 engine)	R	every 45,000 miles			
Steering play, suspension track rods, front axle joints, steering linkage & joint disc	S/I			✓	✓
Throttle linkage	S/I			✓	✓
Transmission fluid/oil	S/I			✓	
Transmission fluid/oil	R				✓
Wheel centering hubs	S/I			✓	✓

71112_BMW1_C0014

PRECAUTIONS

Before servicing any vehicle, please be sure to read all of the following precautions, which deal with personal safety, prevention of component damage, and important points to take into consideration when servicing a motor vehicle:

- Never open, service or drain the radiator or cooling system when the engine is hot; serious burns can occur from the steam and hot coolant.
- Observe all applicable safety precautions when working around fuel. Whenever servicing the fuel system, always work in a well-ventilated area. Do not allow fuel spray or vapors to come in contact with a spark, open flame, or excessive heat (a hot drop light, for example). Keep a dry chemical fire extinguisher near the work area. Always keep fuel in a container specifically designed for fuel storage; also, always properly seal fuel containers to avoid the possibility of fire or explosion. Refer to the additional fuel system precautions later in this section.
- Fuel injection systems often remain pressurized, even after the engine has been turned **OFF**. The fuel system pressure must be relieved before disconnecting any fuel lines. Failure to do so may result in fire and/or personal injury.
- Brake fluid often contains polyglycol ethers and polyglycols. Avoid contact with the eyes and wash your hands thoroughly after handling brake fluid. If you do get brake fluid in your eyes, flush your eyes with clean, running water for 15 minutes. If eye irritation persists, or if you have taken brake fluid internally, IMMEDIATELY seek medical assistance.
- The EPA warns that prolonged contact with used engine oil may cause a number of skin disorders, including cancer. You should make every effort to minimize your exposure to used engine oil. Protective gloves should be worn when changing oil. Wash your hands and any other exposed skin areas as soon as possible after exposure to used engine oil. Soap and water, or waterless hand cleaner should be used.
- All new vehicles are now equipped with an air bag system, often referred to as a Supplemental Restraint System (SRS) or Supplemental Inflatable Restraint (SIR) system. The system must be disabled before performing service on or around system components, steering column, instrument panel components, wiring and sensors. Failure to follow safety and disabling procedures could result in accidental air bag deployment, possible personal injury and unnecessary system repairs.
- Always wear safety goggles when working with, or around, the air bag system. When carrying a non-deployed air bag, be sure the bag and trim cover are pointed away from your body. When placing a non-deployed air bag on a work surface, always face the bag and trim cover upward, away from the surface. This will reduce the motion of the module if it is accidentally deployed. Refer to the additional air bag system precautions later in this section.
- Clean, high quality brake fluid from a sealed container is essential to the safe and proper operation of the brake system. You should always buy the correct type of brake fluid for your vehicle. If the brake fluid becomes contaminated, completely flush the system with new fluid. Never reuse any brake fluid. Any brake fluid that is removed from the system should be discarded. Also, do not allow any brake fluid to come in contact with a painted surface; it will damage the paint.
- Never operate the engine without the proper amount and type of engine oil; doing so WILL result in severe engine damage.
- Timing belt maintenance is extremely important. Many models utilize an interference-type, non-freewheeling engine. If the timing belt breaks, the valves in the cylinder head may strike the pistons, causing potentially serious (also time-consuming and expensive) engine damage. Refer to the maintenance interval charts for the recommended replacement interval for the timing belt, and to the timing belt section for belt replacement and inspection.
- Disconnecting the negative battery cable on some vehicles may interfere with the functions of the on-board computer system(s) and may require the computer to undergo a relearning process once the negative battery cable is reconnected.
- When servicing drum brakes, only disassemble and assemble one side at a time, leaving the remaining side intact for reference.
- Only an MVAC-trained, EPA-certified automotive technician should service the air conditioning system or its components.

BRAKES — ANTI-LOCK BRAKE SYSTEM (ABS)

GENERAL INFORMATION

PRECAUTIONS

- Certain components within the ABS system are not intended to be serviced or repaired individually.
- Do not use rubber hoses or other parts not specifically specified for and ABS system. When using repair kits, replace all parts included in the kit. Partial or incorrect repair may lead to functional problems and require the replacement of components.
- Lubricate rubber parts with clean, fresh brake fluid to ease assembly. Do not use shop air to clean parts; damage to rubber components may result.
- Use only DOT 3 brake fluid from an unopened container.
- If any hydraulic component or line is removed or replaced, it may be necessary to bleed the entire system.
- A clean repair area is essential. Always clean the reservoir and cap thoroughly before removing the cap. The slightest amount of dirt in the fluid may plug an orifice and impair the system function. Perform repairs after components have been thoroughly cleaned; use only denatured alcohol to clean components. Do not allow ABS components to come into contact with any substance containing mineral oil; this includes used shop rags.
- The Anti-Lock control unit is a microprocessor similar to other computer units in the vehicle. Ensure that the ignition switch is **OFF** before removing or installing controller harnesses. Avoid static electricity discharge at or near the controller.
- If any arc welding is to be done on the vehicle, the control unit should be unplugged before welding operations begin.

SPEED SENSORS

REMOVAL & INSTALLATION

Front

1. Raise and safely support the vehicle securely on jackstands.
2. Raise and safely support the vehicle.
3. Remove the wheel.
4. Open plug housing.
5. Disconnect plug connection.
6. Feed brake pad sensor out of holders.
7. Press clip together and detach brake pad sensor in direction of arrow from brake pad.

To install:

8. Make sure clip and brake pad sensor are correctly seated in brake pad.
9. Check for proper ABS system function.

Rear

1. Raise and safely support the vehicle securely on jackstands.
2. Raise and safely support the vehicle.
3. Remove the wheel.
4. Slacken nut.
5. Pull wheel arch trim gently to one side.
6. Disengage cable from holders.
7. Disconnect plug connection.
8. Disengage cable from holders.
9. Detach brake pad wear sensor in direction of arrow from brake caliper.

To install:

10. Ensure proper locking of the plug connector and proper seating of the cable in the brackets.
11. Make sure holders and brake pad wear sensor are correctly seated in brake caliper.
12. Check for proper ABS system function.

BRAKES — BLEEDING THE BRAKE SYSTEM

BLEEDING PROCEDURE

BLEEDING PROCEDURE

Rear Axle Circuit

1. Disconnect retaining tabs and remove the master cylinder cover.
2. Connect a brake bleeding tool with a maximum 29 PSI (2 Bar) filling pressure.
3. Connect bleeder hose with collecting tray to bleeder valve on rear right brake caliper.
4. Bleed right brake caliper. After completing routine, press brake pedal 5 times to floor; clear and bubble-free brake fluid must flow out.
5. Close bleed valve.
6. Repeat procedure at rear left.
7. Disconnect the brake bleeding tool and remove from the master cylinder.
8. Check and adjust the brake fluid level.
9. Inspect the rubber seal in the brake fluid master cylinder cap. Replace as necessary.

Front Axle Circuit

1. Disconnect retaining tabs and remove the master cylinder cover.
2. Connect a brake bleeding tool with a maximum 29 PSI (2 Bar) filling pressure.
3. Connect bleeder hose with collecting tray to bleeder valve on front right brake caliper.
4. Bleed right front brake caliper. After completing routine, press brake pedal 5 times to floor, clear and bubble-free brake fluid must flow out.
5. Close bleed valve.
6. Repeat procedure at front left.
7. Disconnect the brake bleeding tool and remove from the master cylinder.
8. Check and adjust the brake fluid level.
9. Inspect the rubber seal in the brake fluid master cylinder cap. Replace as necessary.

FLUID FILL PROCEDURE

➡A second person is needed to help carry out this work.

1. Disconnect retaining tabs and remove the master cylinder cover.
2. Connect a brake bleeding tool with a maximum 29 PSI (2 Bar) filling pressure.
3. Flushing brake system completely.
4. Connect bleeder hose with collecting tray to bleeder valve on rear right brake caliper.
5. Open bleeder valve and purge until clear, bubble-free brake fluid emerges.
6. Close bleed valve.
7. Follow same procedure on rear left, front right and front left wheel brake.
8. Disconnect the brake bleeding tool and remove from the master cylinder.
9. Check and adjust the brake fluid level.
10. Inspect the rubber seal in the brake fluid master cylinder cap. Replace as necessary.

BRAKES — FRONT DISC BRAKES

CAUTION

Dust and dirt accumulating on brake parts during normal use may contain asbestos fibers from production or aftermarket brake linings. Breathing excessive concentrations of asbestos fibers can cause serious bodily harm. Exercise care when servicing brake parts. Do not sand or grind brake lining unless equipment used is designed to contain the dust residue. Do not clean brake parts with compressed air or by dry brushing. Cleaning should be done by dampening the brake components with a fine mist of water, then wiping the brake components clean with a dampened cloth. Dispose of cloth and all residue containing asbestos fibers in an impermeable container with the appropriate label. Follow practices prescribed by the Occupational Safety and Health Administration (OSHA) and the Environmental Protection Agency (EPA) for the handling, processing, and disposing of dust or debris that may contain asbestos fibers.

BRAKE CALIPER

REMOVAL & INSTALLATION

Brembo Caliper

See Figures 1 and 2.

1. Before servicing the vehicle, refer to the precautions.
2. Remove wheels.
3. Remove front brake pad sensor.
4. Press clutch pedal down to floor and secure with pedal support.

WARNING

The pedal support may only be released when the brake lines are reconnected. This prevents brake fluid from emerging from the expansion tank and air from entering the system when the brake lines are opened.

5. If necessary, pull brake hose out of holder.

➡Grip brake hose at square head to prevent connecting piece from turning in retaining bracket.

6. Disconnect brake hose from brake line.
7. Detach brake hose from brake caliper.

⁂ WARNING

Never twist brake hose when installing it and avoid all contact with parts attached rigidly to the body.

8. Move wheels into straight-ahead position.
9. Release bolts and pull off brake caliper with brake anchor plate towards rear.
10. Pull brake pads off guide pins and remove.

➡In the event of one-sided brake pad wear, do not change brake pads round.

11. Observe minimum thickness of brake pads.

To install:

12. Installation is the reverse of removal.
13. Clean brake pads, brake caliper and guide pins.
14. Do not grease backs of brake pads sleeve.
15. Brake pads must be correctly seated on guide pins.
16. Do not grease brake pads and guides with anti-squeak paste.
17. Clean contact surface of brake pistons.

➡First tighten brake hose on brake caliper.

18. Tighten bolts/nuts to specification as follows:
    - Brake line screws / union screws: 9 ft. lbs. (12 Nm)
    - Brake hose to caliper: 18 ft. lbs. (24 Nm)
    - Caliper to mount (Replace screws): 81 ft. lbs. (110 Nm)

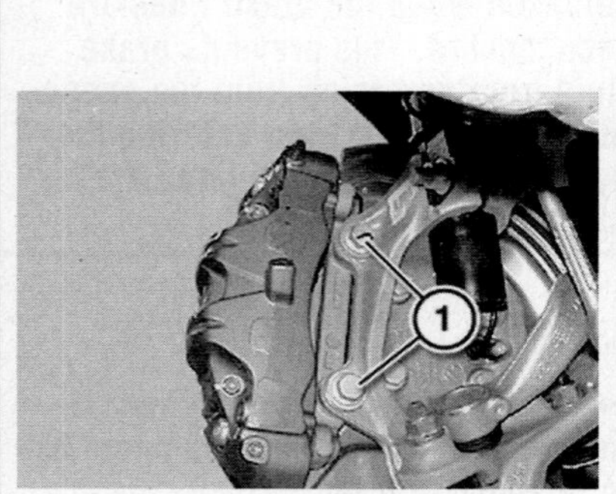

Fig. 1 Release bolts (1) and pull off brake caliper with brake anchor plate towards rear

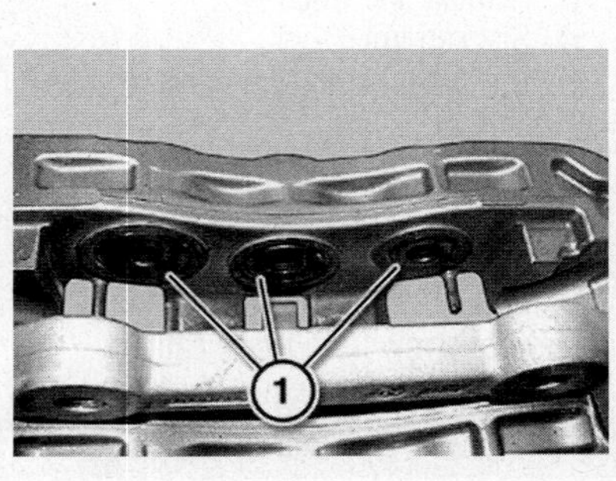

Fig. 2 Clean contact surface (1) of brake pistons

➡The brake pad wear sensor must be replaced once it has been removed (brake pad wear sensor loses its retention capability in the brake pad). If a brake pad sensor that has already been ground has to be replaced even though the minimum brake pad thickness has not yet been reached, you must observe the following: The new sliding contact must be filed down with a file to the same length as the ground sliding contact.

Teves Caliper

See Figures 3 and 4.

1. Before servicing the vehicle, refer to the precautions.
2. Remove wheels
3. Remove brake pad wear sensor

⁂ WARNING

The brake pad wear sensor must be replaced once it has been removed (brake pad wear sensor loses its retention capability in the brake pad).

4. Disconnect brake hose from brake caliper.
5. Disconnect brake hose from brake line.
6. Disconnect brake hose from holder.
7. Lift out retaining spring.
8. Remove plastic plugs.
9. Remove guide bolts and lift out brake caliper towards rear of vehicle.

To install:

10. Clean contact face of brake piston and apply a thin coating of anti-squeak compound.
11. Clean contact faces of brake pad hammer heads/brake caliper housing and coat with anti-squeak compound.
12. Clean contact face of brake caliper and apply a thin coating of anti-squeak compound.
13. Clean brake carrier at hammerhead guides and apply a thin coating of anti-squeak compound.
14. Clean guide bolts only; do not grease. Check threads.

➡Replace all guide bolts which are not in perfect condition.

15. Install brake caliper. Replace the guide bolts and tighten to 22 ft. lbs. (30 Nm) on all others.

⁂ WARNING

Never twist brake hose when installing it and avoid all contact with parts attached rigidly to the body.

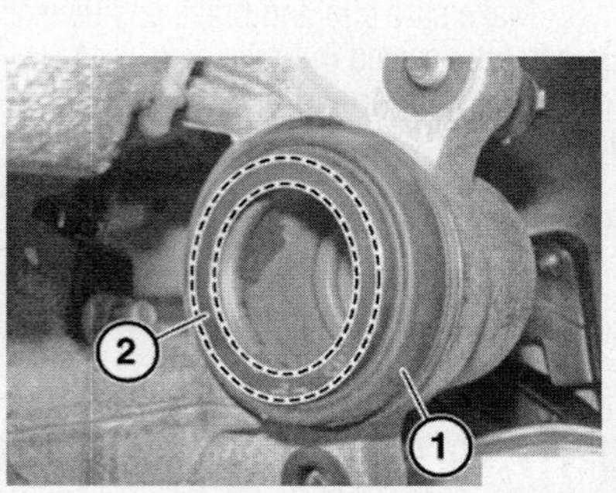

Fig. 3 Clean contact face (2) of brake piston and apply a thin coating of anti-squeak compound

Fig. 4 Clean contact faces (1) of brake pad hammer heads/brake caliper housing and coat with anti-squeak compound

16. Connect brake hose to brake caliper. Tighten to 18 ft. lbs. (24 Nm).
17. Connect brake hose to brake line. Tighten to 12 ft. lbs. (17 Nm).
18. Connect brake hose to holder.
19. Install plastic plugs.
20. Install the retaining spring.
21. Install the brake pad wear sensor.
22. Check and fill brake fluid to proper level.
23. Bleed the brake system.
24. Install the wheels.

DISC BRAKE PADS

REMOVAL & INSTALLATION

Brembo Caliper

See Figures 5 through 7.

1. Before servicing the vehicle, refer to the precautions.
2. Remove the caliper and suspend it out of the way using wire.

➡Do not allow brake caliper to hang from the brake hose.

3. Turn piston fully back with special tool 34 1 050.

WARNING

When pressing down piston, note brake fluid level in expansion tank.

4. Pull brake pads off guide pins and remove.

➡In the event of one-sided brake pad wear, do not change brake pads round.

To install:

5. Installation is the reverse of removal.

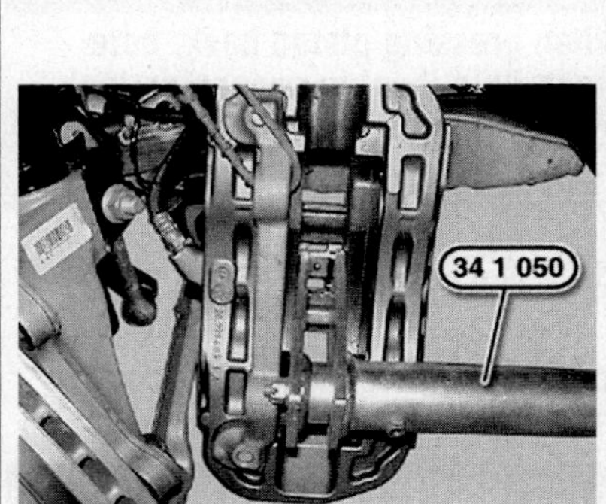

Fig. 5 Turn piston fully back with special tool 34 1 050

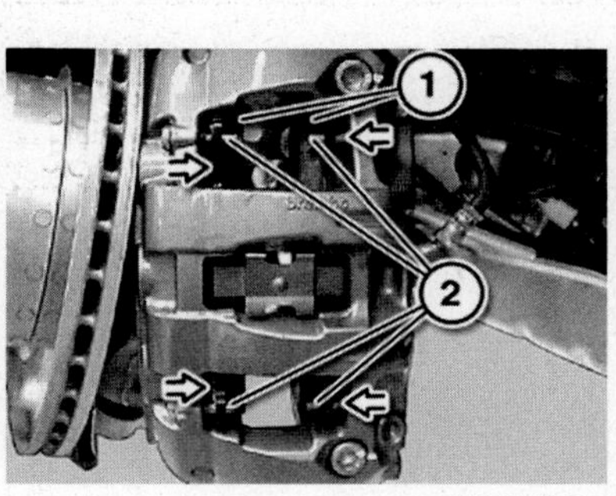

Fig. 6 Pull brake pads (1) off guide pins (2) and remove

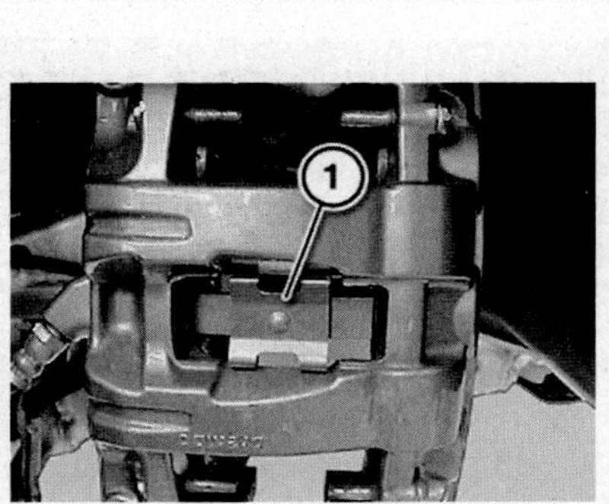

Fig. 7 Replace expanding spring (1).

6. Check minimum thickness of brake pads and brake disc. Replace components as necessary.
7. Clean brake pads, brake caliper and guide pins.
8. Do not grease backs of brake pads sleeve.
9. Brake pads must be correctly seated on guide pins.

WARNING

New brake pads may only be installed if the brake disc thickness is greater than or equal to the minimum brake disc thickness.

10. Clean contact surface of brake pistons.

➡The brake pad wear sensor must be replaced once it has been removed (brake pad wear sensor loses its retention capability in the brake pad). If a brake pad sensor that has already been ground has to be replaced even though the minimum brake pad thickness has not yet been reached, you must observe the following: The new sliding contact must be filed down with a file to the same length as the ground sliding contact.

11. Replace expanding spring.
12. When installing new brake pads at front and rear axles, brake fluid level must be brought up to "MAX" marking.
13. Fully depress brake pedal several times so that brake pads contact brake discs.
14. When replacing pads, reset the maintenance reminder.

Teves Caliper

See Figures 8 and 9.

1. Before servicing the vehicle, refer to the precautions.
2. Remove the caliper and suspend it out of the way using wire.

➡Do not allow brake caliper to hang from the brake hose.

3. Remove the brake pads.

To install:

4. Press brake piston fully back with special tool 34 1 050.

WARNING

When pressing piston back, note brake fluid level in expansion tank. Overflowing brake fluid will damage the paintwork.

5. Check dust sleeve for damage and replace if necessary.
6. Clean contact face of brake piston and apply a thin coating of anti-squeak compound.

WARNING

Dust sleeve must not come into contact with anti-squeak compound as this may cause the dust sleeve to swell.

7. Clean contact face of brake caliper and apply a thin coating of anti-squeak compound.
8. Clean hammerhead guides and apply a thin coating of anti-squeak compound.
9. Replace the lining retaining springs, as necessary.
10. Clean contact face of brake carrier and apply a thin coating of anti-squeak compound.

22205_BMWC_G0012

Fig. 8 Remove lining retaining springs (1), as necessary

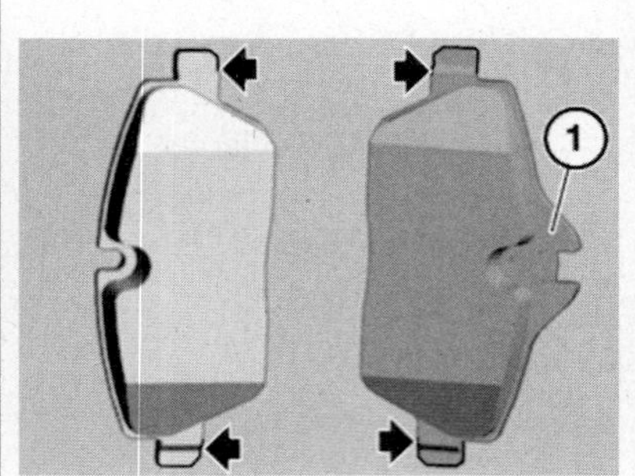

22205_BMWC_G0011

Fig. 9 Brake pad with indentation (1) is intended for accommodating the brake pad wear sensor and must be fitted on the piston side

11. Install the new brake pads.

➡Brake pad with indentation is intended for accommodating the brake pad wear sensor and must be fitted on the piston side.

12. Install the caliper.
13. Check and fill brake fluid to proper level.
14. Fully depress brake pedal several times so that brake linings contact brake discs.

➡When replacing pads, reset CBS display in accordance with factory specification.

15. Install the wheels.

⁂ CAUTION

Dust and dirt accumulating on brake parts during normal use may contain asbestos fibers from production or aftermarket brake linings. Breathing excessive concentrations of asbestos fibers can cause serious bodily harm. Exercise care when servicing brake parts. Do not sand or grind brake lining unless equipment used is designed to contain the dust residue. Do not clean brake parts with compressed air or by dry brushing. Cleaning should be done by dampening the brake components with a fine mist of water, then wiping the brake components clean with a dampened cloth. Dispose of cloth and all residue containing asbestos fibers in an impermeable container with the appropriate label. Follow practices prescribed by the Occupational Safety and Health Administration (OSHA) and the Environmental Protection Agency (EPA) for the handling, processing, and disposing of dust or debris that may contain asbestos fibers.

BRAKE CALIPER

REMOVAL & INSTALLATION

1. Before servicing the vehicle, refer to the precautions.
2. Remove wheels.
3. Remove brake pad wear sensor (right side only).

⁂ WARNING

The brake pad wear sensor must be replaced once it has been removed (brake pad wear sensor loses its retention capability in the brake pad).

4. Disconnect brake hose from brake caliper.
5. Disconnect brake hose from brake line.
6. Disconnect brake hose from holder.
7. Lift out retaining spring.
8. Remove plastic plugs.
9. Remove guide bolts and lift out brake caliper towards rear of vehicle.

To install:

10. Clean guide bolts only; do not grease. Check threads.

➡Replace all guide bolts which are not in perfect condition.

11. Install brake caliper. Replace the guide bolts and tighten to 22 ft. lbs. (30 Nm).

⁂ WARNING

Never twist brake hose when installing it and avoid all contact with parts attached rigidly to the body.

12. Connect brake hose to brake caliper. Tighten to 18 ft. lbs. (24 Nm).
13. Connect brake hose to brake line. Tighten to 12 ft. lbs. (17 Nm).
14. Install plastic plugs.
15. Install the retaining spring.
16. Install the brake pad wear sensor.
17. Check and fill brake fluid to proper level.
18. Bleed the brake system.
19. Install the wheels.

DISC BRAKE PADS

REMOVAL & INSTALLATION

See Figure 8.

1. Before servicing the vehicle, refer to the precautions.
2. Remove the caliper and suspend it out of the way using wire.

➡Do not allow brake caliper to hang from the brake hose.

3. Remove the brake pads.

To install:

4. Press brake piston fully back with special tool 34 1 050.

⁂ WARNING

When pressing piston back, note brake fluid level in expansion tank. Overflowing brake fluid will damage the paintwork.

5. Check dust sleeve for damage and replace if necessary.
6. Clean contact face of brake piston and apply a thin coating of anti-squeak compound.

⁂ WARNING

Dust sleeve must not come into contact with anti-squeak compound as this may cause the dust sleeve to swell.

7. Clean contact face of brake caliper and apply a thin coating of anti-squeak compound.

8. Clean hammerhead guides and apply a thin coating of anti-squeak compound.

9. Replace the lining retaining springs, as necessary.

10. Clean contact face of brake carrier and apply a thin coating of anti-squeak compound.

11. Install the new brake pads.

➡Brake pad with indentation is intended for accommodating the brake pad wear sensor and must be fitted on the piston side.

12. Install the caliper.

13. Check and fill brake fluid to proper level.

14. Fully depress brake pedal several times so that brake linings contact brake discs.

➡When replacing pads, reset CBS display in accordance with factory specification.

15. Install the wheels.

BRAKES — PARKING BRAKE

PARKING BRAKE CABLES

ADJUSTMENT

See Figure 10.

1. Before servicing the vehicle, refer to the precautions.
2. Perform inspection in the following manner:
   a. When 1st ratchet is engaged, no braking force should be exerted.
   b. The difference in wheel circumferential forces between the left and right wheels may deviate by max. 30 % from the greater value (when measured on brake analyzer).
   c. Braking with locked wheels must be possible with the parking brake.
   d. The parking brake must be reset if the actuation stroke is greater than 10 teeth.

➡Accurate adjustment of the parking brake is only possible if the parking brake Bowden cables and all moving parts on the parking brake move easily and function correctly.

3. Setting instruction for brake shoes (basic setting):
   a. Disconnect gaiter for parking brake pry.
   b. Lock adjuster unit (ASZE).
   c. Actuate parking brake pry. Screw in special tool 32 1 030 partially. Press stop of adjusting spring back to such an extent that retaining hook engages in stop.
   d. Completely unscrew one wheel stud on each rear wheel.
   e. Turn wheel until adjustment screw is visible in tapped hole.
   f. Turn adjusting screw with a screwdriver until the wheel is no longer able to turn. Then release 185 dia. duo-servo brake 8 notches or release 160 dia. duo-servo brake 9 notches.
   g. Unlock adjuster unit (ASZE).
   h. Pry out restraining hook with a suitable screwdriver.

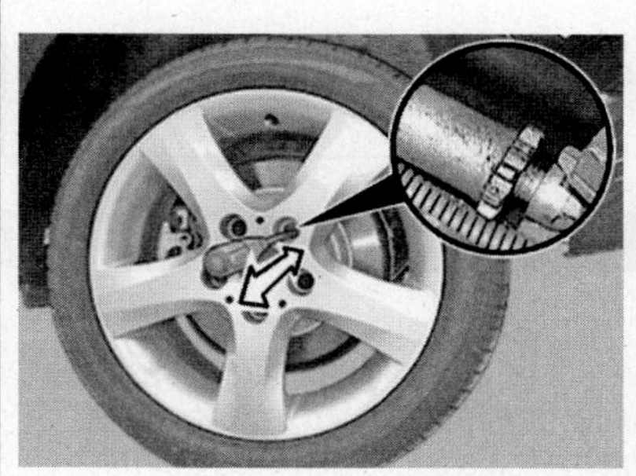

Fig. 10 Turn wheel until adjustment screw is visible in tapped hole

   i. Restraining hook must detach from stop of adjusting spring.
4. Setting instruction for parking brake Bowden cables:
   a. The parking brake pry must be applied 5 times to approximately 90 lbs. (400 N) actuating force.
   b. With the parking brake removed and the transmission in **N** position, the brake force should have reached 34 lbs. (150 N) as measured on a brake analyzer.
   c. With the parking brake on the 1st tooth, there should be no increase in braking force. However, the indicator lamp can be lit.
   d. With the parking brake on the 2nd tooth, the indicator lamp must be lit.
   e. With the parking brake on the 3rd tooth, there should be an increase in braking force.
   f. With the parking brake on the 5th tooth, the brake force must have reached 90 lbs. (400 N).
5. If new pads are installed, perform the pad break in procedure:
   a. At approximately 25 MPH (40 km/h) apply parking brake pry until a braking effect can be felt.
   b. Pull parking brake pry to next notch and drive on for approximately 1320 feet (quarter mile).
   c. If necessary, repeat braking-in procedure.
   d. Allow brake to cool down sufficiently.

PARKING BRAKE SHOES

REMOVAL & INSTALLATION

See Figures 11 and 12.

1. Before servicing the vehicle, refer to the precautions.
2. Remove rear brake disc.
3. Actuate parking brake pry. Screw in special tool 32 1 030 partially. Press stop of adjusting spring back to such an extent that retaining hook engages in stop.
4. Disconnect return upper spring with brake spring pliers.
5. Disconnect return lower spring with brake spring pliers.
6. Turn clamping pins with special tool 34 4 000 through 90° and disconnect. Remove brake shoes.

To install:

7. Install brake shoes.
8. Turn clamping pins with special tool 34 4 000 through 90° to lock.

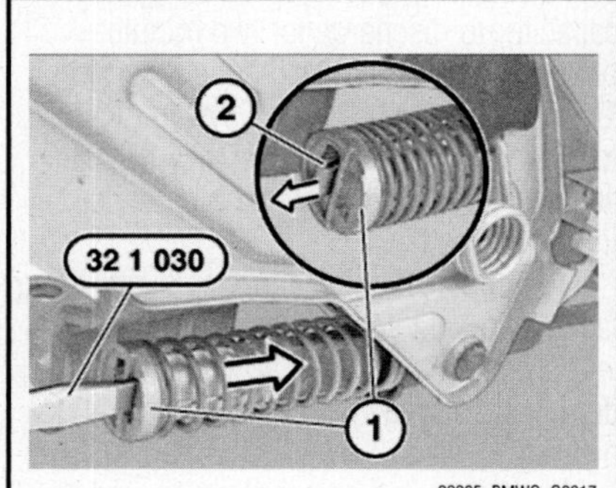

Fig. 11 Actuate parking brake pry. Screw in special tool 32 1 030 partially. Press stop (1) of adjusting spring back to such an extent that retaining hook (2) engages in stop (1)

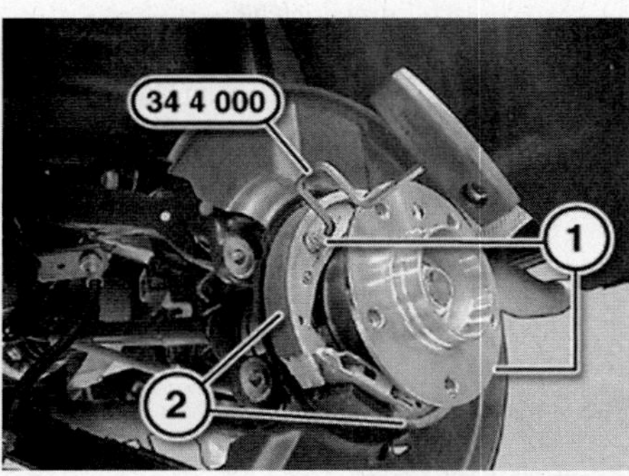

22205_BMWC_G0021

Fig. 12 Turn clamping pins (1) with special tool 34 4 000 through 90°and disconnect. Remove brake shoes (2)

9. Check and if necessary replace return springs.
10. Connect return lower spring with brake spring pliers.
11. Connect return upper spring with brake spring pliers.

➡Pay attention to installation position of adjustment screw.

12. Apply a thin coat of grease to bush and screw threads.
13. Pry out restraining hook with a suitable screwdriver.
14. Restraining hook must detach from stop of adjusting spring.
15. Install rear brake disc.
16. Adjusting parking brake.

CHASSIS ELECTRICAL

AIR BAG (SUPPLEMENTAL RESTRAINT SYSTEM)

GENERAL INFORMATION

CAUTION

These vehicles are equipped with an air bag system. The system must be disarmed before performing service on, or around, system components, the steering column, instrument panel components, wiring and sensors. Failure to follow the safety precautions and the disarming procedure could result in accidental air bag deployment, possible injury and unnecessary system repairs.

SERVICE PRECAUTIONS

Disconnect and isolate the battery negative cable before beginning any airbag system component diagnosis, testing, removal, or installation procedures. Allow system capacitor to discharge for two minutes before beginning any component service. This will disable the airbag system. Failure to disable the airbag system may result in accidental airbag deployment, personal injury, or death.

Do not place an intact undeployed airbag face down on a solid surface. The airbag will propel into the air if accidentally deployed and may result in personal injury or death.

When carrying or handling an undeployed airbag, the trim side (face) of the airbag should be pointing towards the body to minimize possibility of injury if accidental deployment occurs. Failure to do this may result in personal injury or death.

Replace airbag system components with OEM replacement parts. Substitute parts may appear interchangeable, but internal differences may result in inferior occupant protection. Failure to do so may result in occupant personal injury or death.

Wear safety glasses, rubber gloves, and long sleeved clothing when cleaning powder residue from vehicle after an airbag deployment. Powder residue emitted from a deployed airbag can cause skin irritation. Flush affected area with cool water if irritation is experienced. If nasal or throat irritation is experienced, exit the vehicle for fresh air until the irritation ceases. If irritation continues, see a physician.

Do not use a replacement airbag that is not in the original packaging. This may result in improper deployment, personal injury, or death.

The factory installed fasteners, screws and bolts used to fasten airbag components have a special coating and are specifically designed for the airbag system. Do not use substitute fasteners. Use only original equipment fasteners listed in the parts catalog when fastener replacement is required.

During, and following, any child restraint anchor service, due to impact event or vehicle repair, carefully inspect all mounting hardware, tether straps, and anchors for proper installation, operation, or damage. If a child restraint anchor is found damaged in any way, the anchor must be replaced. Failure to do this may result in personal injury or death.

Deployed and non-deployed airbags may or may not have live pyrotechnic material within the airbag inflator.

Do not dispose of driver/passenger/curtain airbags or seat belt tensioners unless you are sure of complete deployment. Refer to the Hazardous Substance Control System for proper disposal.

Dispose of deployed airbags and tensioners consistent with state, provincial, local, and federal regulations.

After any airbag component testing or service, do not connect the battery negative cable. Personal injury or death may result if the system test is not performed first.

If the vehicle is equipped with the Occupant Classification System (OCS), do not connect the battery negative cable before performing the OCS Verification Test using the scan tool and the appropriate diagnostic information. Personal injury or death may result if the system test is not performed properly.

Never replace both the Occupant Restraint Controller (ORC) and the Occupant Classification Module (OCM) at the same time. If both require replacement, replace one, then perform the Airbag System test before replacing the other.

Both the ORC and the OCM store Occupant Classification System (OCS) calibration data, which they transfer to one another when one of them is replaced. If both are replaced at the same time, an irreversible fault will be set in both modules and the OCS may malfunction and cause personal injury or death.

If equipped with OCS, the Seat Weight Sensor is a sensitive, calibrated unit and must be handled carefully. Do not drop or handle roughly. If dropped or damaged, replace with another sensor. Failure to do so may result in occupant injury or death.

If equipped with OCS, the front passenger seat must be handled carefully as well. When removing the seat, be careful when setting on floor not to drop. If dropped, the sensor may be inoperative, could result in occupant injury, or possibly death.

If equipped with OCS, when the passenger front seat is on the floor, no one should sit in the front passenger seat. This uneven force may damage the sensing ability of the seat weight sensors. If sat on and damaged, the sensor may be inoperative, could result in occupant injury, or possibly death.

DISARMING THE SYSTEM

1. Before servicing the vehicle, refer to the precautions.
2. Place the ignition switch in the **OFF**-position.
3. Disconnect the negative battery terminal and cover the battery terminal to prevent accidental contact.
4. Once the battery has been disconnected, wait for a period of approximately 10 minutes allowing the capacitor in the control unit to discharge.

ARMING THE SYSTEM

When repairs are completed, connect the negative battery cable.

CLOCKSPRING CENTERING

Connect vehicle to BMW diagnosis system. Select and carry out steering angle sensor adjustment under Service functions.

DRIVE TRAIN

AXLE HOUSING

REMOVAL & INSTALLATION

See Figure 13.

1. Before servicing the vehicle, refer to the precautions.
2. Remove propeller shaft from rear differential.
3. Remove output shaft from rear differential at both ends and tie back.

WARNING

Observe gap between special tool 33 4 420 and dust plates. To avoid grinding noises, make sure the dust plates are not bent.

4. Support rear differential with workshop jack and special tool 33 4 420.
5. Remove bolts.
6. Remove nut and remove screw towards rear.
7. Slowly lower workshop jack and remove rear differential towards rear.

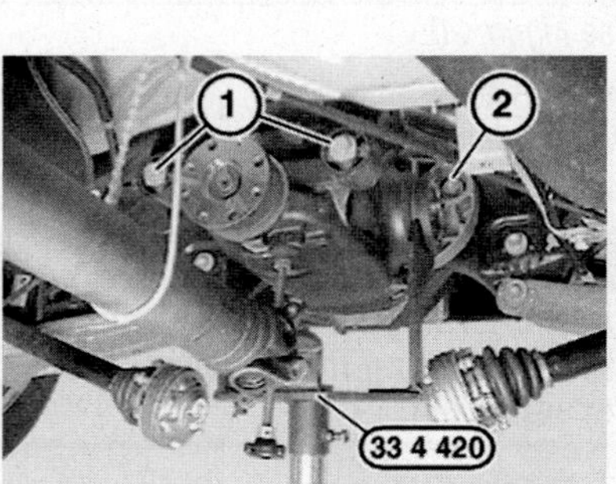

22205_BMWC_G0091

Fig. 13 Differential mounting bolt (1) and nut (2)

To install:

WARNING

Adhere to the following installation sequence in order to prevent distortion of the rear differential during installation and thereby avoid potential complaints about noise.

8. Install rear differential with workshop jack and special tool 33 4 420.
9. Insert bolts but do not tighten down.
10. Insert screw from rear and replace nut but do not tighten down.
11. Lower workshop jack.
12. Tighten fasteners to specification.
    - Rear Differential-to-Carrier M12: 74 ft. lbs. (100 Nm)
    - Rear Differential-to-Carrier M14: 122 ft. lbs. (165 Nm)
    - Crankshaft damper M12: 74 ft. lbs. (100 Nm)
13. Check rear differential oil level, correct if necessary.

DRIVESHAFT

REMOVAL & INSTALLATION

Rear

See Figures 14 through 18.

1. Before servicing the vehicle, refer to the precautions.
2. Remove underbody protection.
3. Remove complete exhaust system.
4. Remove heat shields.
5. Remove and discard the ZNS bolts at the transmission end of the driveshaft.
6. Slacken screws (1) and using a suitable tool (2), secure propeller shaft at centre universal joint against turning.
7. Remove screws of centre mount fully only after opening insert nut.
8. Release insert nut against direction of travel in clockwise direction with special tools 33 5 040 and 33 5 070.

WARNING

The hexagonal flange nut must not be used for bracing. Failure to comply with this instruction may result in serious damage to the rear differential.

9. Remove retaining clip and seal.
10. Remove insert nut.

To install:

11. Installation is the reverse of removal.
12. Retaining clip, seal and insert nut must be replaced.
13. Before installing propeller shaft, clean insert collar on flange nut and spline teeth on bevel pinion. Fill insert collar with grease.
14. Clean thread of joint hub to remove adhesive residues.
15. Clean hub teeth, then coat with grease.

WARNING

Thread of joint hub must not be fouled with grease.

16. Place insert nut with seal in insert collar of flange nut.
17. Install retaining clip.

WARNING

Adhere without fail to installation and screw-fastening sequence:

- Install propeller shaft to transmission
- Install propeller shaft to rear differential
- Install centre mount
- Tighten insert nut
- Tighten flexible disc to transmission

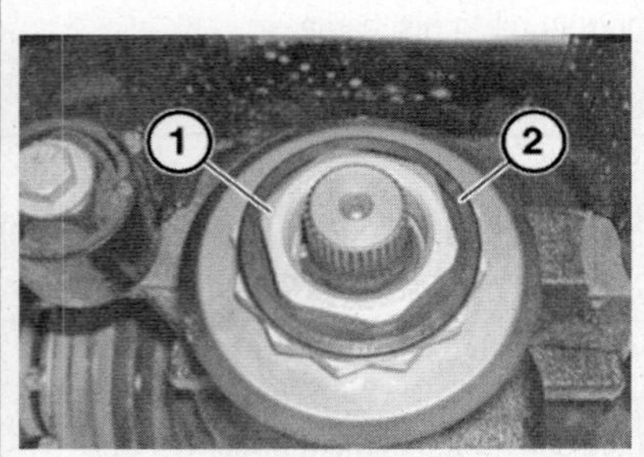

Fig. 14 Place insert nut (1) with seal in insert collar of flange nut and install retaining clip (2)

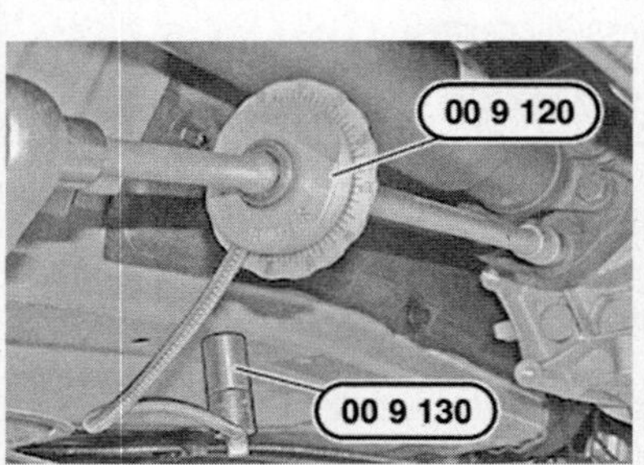

Fig. 16 Secure special tool angle of rotation 00 9 120 with magnet 00 9 130 to underbody and continue bolting according to angle of rotation

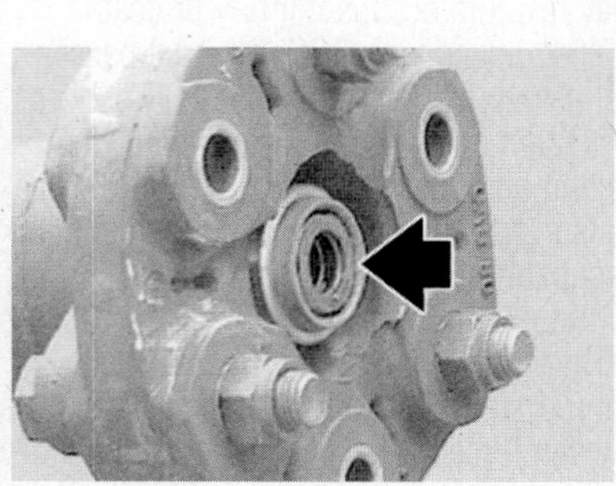

Fig. 18 Check centering mount and if necessary, replace damaged centering mount and apply grease

- Tighten centre mount

18. Join propeller shaft to transmission
    a. Replace ZNS bolts and self-locking nuts.
    b. Grip mounting bolts of flexible disc at nuts and tighten down by way of bolts.
    c. Secure special tool angle of rotation 00 9 120 with magnet 00 9 130 to underbody and continue bolting according to angle of rotation..
    d. Tighten down screws/bolts to specified torque:
    - M10 x 10.9: 15 ft. lbs. (20 Nm) plus an additional 90°rotation
    - M10 x 10.9 screw with ribbed teeth: 30 ft. lbs. (40 Nm) 45°rotation
    - M12 x 10.9: 41 ft. lbs. (55 Nm) plus an additional 90°rotation
19. Join propeller shaft to rear differential.
    a. Slide propeller shaft as far as it will go onto insert nut and secure.
    b. Secure propeller shaft at centre universal joint against turning with a tire iron.

WARNING

The hexagonal flange nut must not be used for bracing. Failure to comply with this instruction may result in serious damage to the rear differential.

➡Insert nut must be screwed into place within 5 minutes.

20. Tighten propeller shaft plugged into rear differential (insert nut) to 56 ft. lbs. (77 Nm).
21. Install centre mount.
    a. Check centering mount and if necessary, replace damaged centering mount and apply grease.
    b. Tighten center mount to body to 16 ft. lbs. (21 Nm)

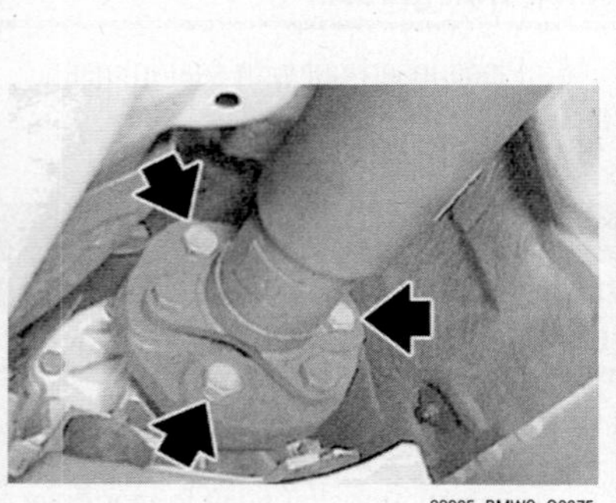

Fig. 15 Replace ZNS bolts and self-locking nuts

Fig. 17 Slide propeller shaft (1) as far as it will go onto insert nut and secure. The hexagonal flange nut (2) must not be used for bracing

REAR AXLE FLUID

DRAIN & REFILL

See Figure 19.

1. Before servicing the vehicle, refer to the precautions.

➡The oil does not need to be changed in rear differentials carrying the "Life-Time-Oil" sticker.

2. Drive vehicle until rear differential is at normal operating temperature.
3. Raise and support vehicle.
4. Open plug.
5. Drain and dispose of differential oil.
6. Add differential oil up to lower edge of opening for screw plug.
7. Replace screw plug with a new one and tighten to 44 ft. lbs. (60 Nm).
8. Lower the vehicle.

REAR HALFSHAFT

REMOVAL & INSTALLATION

See Figure 20.

1. Before servicing the vehicle, refer to the precautions.
2. Remove rear wheel.

WARNING

Expand turning lock sufficiently to avoid damaging thread when releasing collar nut.

3. Remove collar nut, activate handbrake for this purpose.
4. On the left side, remove strut if necessary.
5. On the left side, lower exhaust system in rear area.

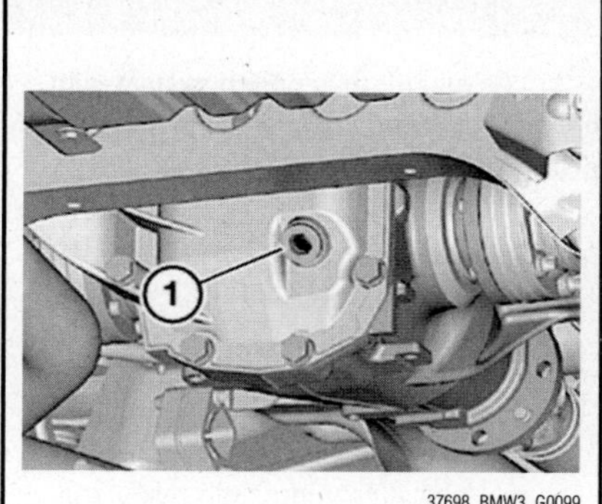

Fig. 19 Open plug (1)

6. Remove bolts and remove with washers.

7. Press output shaft off drive flange using a suitable tool; if necessary, raise wheel carrier with workshop jack approximately 20 mm.

To install:

8. Before installing output shaft, make sure that drive flange is fully engaged in rear differential.

9. Replace bolts and washers and tighten to specification.

- M8: 38 ft. lbs. (52 Nm)
- M10 ZNS3: 52 ft. lbs. (70 Nm)

10. Replace collar nut, oil collar nut/wheel bearing contact surface only and tighten to specification.

- M27: 311 ft. lbs. (420 Nm)
- M24: 185 ft. lbs. (250 Nm)

WARNING

No oil permitted on thread of shaft journal or collar nut.

11. Secure collar nut by positive peening on flat areas of output shaft.

12. Check that output shaft is correctly seated in rear differential.

13. On the left side, raise exhaust system in rear area.

14. On the left side, install strut if necessary.

15. Install rear wheel.

PINION OIL SEAL

REMOVAL & INSTALLATION

See Figures 21 through 23.

1. Before servicing the vehicle, refer to the precautions.

2. Remove propeller shaft.

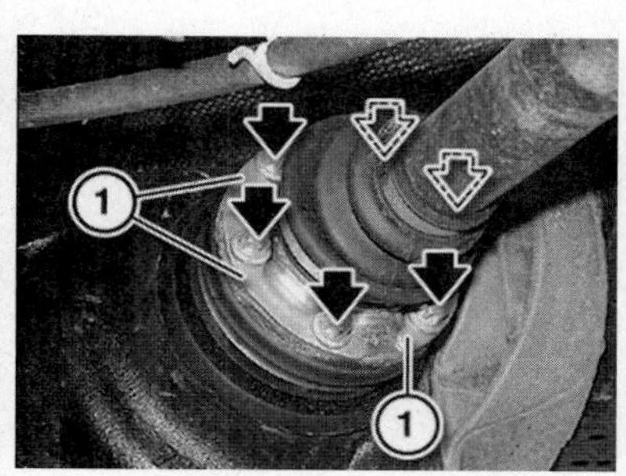

Fig. 20 Remove bolts and remove with washers (1)

3. Remove retaining clip and insert nut with diaphragm seal.

4. Mark position of flange nut to bevel pinion.

5. Release flange nut with special tools 33 5 050 and 33 5 070; to do so, grip bevel pinion with special tools 33 5 060 and 33 5 070.

6. Withdraw shaft seal with special tool 00 5 010.

To install:

7. Coat sealing lips of new shaft seal and sealing face of bevel pinion with differential oil.

8. Drive in shaft seal with special tool 33 5 080.

9. Clean bevel pinion thoroughly to remove remnants of screw-locking agent.

10. Check dust cover for damage, replace if necessary.

WARNING

Clean flange nut thoroughly to remove remnants of grease and screw-locking agent.

Fig. 21 Remove retaining clip (1) and insert nut (2) with diaphragm seal

Fig. 22 Drive in shaft seal with special tool 33 5 080

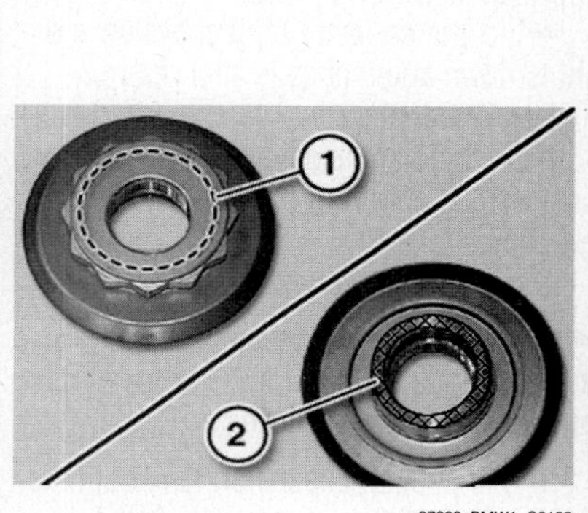

Fig. 23 Pack collar insert (1) of flange nut with grease and apply a thin coating of grease to shaded area (2) of flange nut

11. Pack collar insert of flange nut with grease.

12. Apply a thin coating of grease to shaded area of flange nut.

13. Coat at least four thread turns of flange nut with "DREI BOND adhesive type 1385".

WARNING

In order to avoid damaging the rear differential, do not under any circumstances tighten down the flange nut beyond the marker point of the bevel pinion.

14. Place insert nut with diaphragm seal in flange nut.

15. Install retaining clip.

16. Correct rear differential fluid level.

ENGINE COOLING

ENGINE COOLANT

BLEEDING

See Figure 00.

1. Before servicing the vehicle, refer to the precautions.

➡Do not open the coolant expansion tank cap during the venting procedure.

2. Connect battery charger.
3. Switch **ON** ignition.
4. Set heater to maximum temperature and turn fan down to lowest speed.
5. Press accelerator pedal for 10 seconds to floor. Engine must not be started.
6. The venting procedure is started when the accelerator pedal is pressed and takes approximately 12 minutes.

➡Electric coolant pump activates and shuts down automatically after approximately 12 minutes.

7. Fill coolant expansion tank until the float rises 0.234 in. (6mm) above the expansion tank rim.
8. Check cooling system for leaks.

➡If venting has to be carried out again, leave ignition key removed for approximately 3 minutes.

9. Fill coolant expansion tank until the float rises 0.234 in. (6mm) above the expansion tank rim again.

⁂ WARNING

Fill the expansion tank in this manner only when bleeding the cooling system.

DRAIN & REFILL

N52 Engine

1. Before servicing the vehicle, refer to the precautions.

⁂ CAUTION

Only work on the cooling system when the engine has cooled down!

⁂ WARNING

Some vehicles use a Lifetime coolant. If removing radiator, oil-coolant heat exchanger or transmission oil cooler, do not reuse drained coolant. Use only recommended coolant and observe mixture ratio (antifreeze/water).

2. Remove front underbody protection
3. Open cap on coolant expansion tank.
4. Unlock lugs on front axle carrier and remove radiator cover in direction of arrow.
5. If fitted, release drain plugs on radiator at bottom. On coolant radiators which do not have a drain plug, remove coolant hose.
6. Drain, catch and dispose of coolant.
7. Replace sealing rings and tighten to 24 inch lbs. (3 Nm).
8. Unfasten and detach coolant hose from thermostat housing.
9. Drain, catch and recycle coolant.
10. Slowly fill the cooling system with the recommended coolant in the proper mixture ratio.
    a. Open vent screw.
    b. Slowly fill coolant expansion tank up to lower edge of filler neck with recommended coolant.
    c. Observe mixture ratio.
    d. Close vent screw until bubble-free coolant emerges.
    e. Have a cleaning cloth ready and mop up emerging coolant.
    f. Close cap on expansion tank.
11. Perform the bleeding procedure.
12. Check cooling system for leaks.

N54 Engine

1. Before servicing the vehicle, refer to the precautions.

⁂ CAUTION

Only work on the cooling system when the engine has cooled down!

⁂ WARNING

Some vehicles use a Lifetime coolant. If removing radiator, oil-coolant heat exchanger or transmission oil cooler, do not reuse drained coolant. Use only recommended coolant and observe mixture ratio (antifreeze/water).

2. Remove the intercooler.
3. Open cap on coolant expansion tank.
4. If fitted, release drain plugs on radiator at bottom. On coolant radiators which do not have a drain plug, remove coolant hose.
5. Drain, catch and dispose of coolant.
6. Replace sealing rings and tighten to 24 inch lbs. (3 Nm).
7. Unfasten and detach coolant hose from thermostat housing.
8. Drain, catch and recycle coolant.

To install:

9. Slowly fill the cooling system with the recommended coolant in the proper mixture ratio.
    a. Open vent screw.
    b. Slowly fill coolant expansion tank up to lower edge of filler neck with recommended coolant.
    c. Observe mixture ratio.
    d. Close vent screw until bubble-free coolant emerges.
    e. Have a cleaning cloth ready and mop up emerging coolant.
    f. Close cap on expansion tank.
10. Perform the bleeding procedure.
11. Check cooling system for leaks.

N55 Engine

Draining:

⁂ CAUTION

Only carry out repair work on the cooling system after the engine has cooled down.

⁂ WARNING

Never reuse used coolant.

⁂ WARNING

When replacing and removing components which rely on the corrosion protection effect of the coolant, it is essential to change the coolant. The cooling system must therefore be drained and refilled.

⁂ WARNING

In the case of other removal work involving the draining of part quantities of coolant, replace these quantities which have been drained with new coolant.

⁂ WARNING

Use only recommended coolant.

⁂ WARNING

Observe mixture ratio.

⁂ CAUTION

Wear safety goggles.

⁂ CAUTION

Wear protective gloves.

WARNING

For dirt contamination of the cooling system (e.g. by engine oil), the cooling system must be rinsed with water until all dirt contamination is removed.

CAUTION

Risk of skidding due to coolant on the floor.

1. Catch and dispose of drained coolant in drip tray (1) and if necessary special tool 00 2 0303 (universal hydraulic lifting equipment).
2. Remove charge air cooler.
3. Open sealing cap (1) on coolant expansion tank (2).

➡When installing, close sealing cap (1) until the arrow marks line up.

4. Open coolant drain plug (1).
5. Drain, catch and dispose of coolant.

➡When installing, replace sealing ring.

6. Unfasten and detach coolant hose (1) from thermostat housing.
7. Drain, catch and dispose of coolant.

Adding Coolant:

WARNING

Use only recommended coolant.

WARNING

Observe mixture ratio.

WARNING

Observe capacities.

WARNING

Observe bleeding instructions without fail.

8. Visually inspect cooling system for tightness.
9. Check all the coolant hoses before filling the cooling system with the vacuum filling unit.

➡If necessary, replace damaged and porous coolant hoses.

Prerequisites:

10. Cooling system expansion tank must be empty.
11. There must be sufficiently premixed coolant in the filling unit container, 1 - 2 liters more than the vehicle filling capacity.
    a. Use only recommended coolant.
    b. Observe mixture ratio.
    c. Observe capacities.
12. Position the filling unit container at the same height as the coolant expansion tank.
13. Compressed-air connection with 6 bar pressure present.
14. Set vehicle heater to maximum temperature.

Filling Procedure:

15. Connect filler unit to Y adapter 17 0 113 to adapter connection (x).
16. Shutoff valves (A) and (B) of the filling unit (1) must be closed. (X) Expansion tank connection.
17. Connect venturi nozzle (1) to filling unit (2). (X) Expansion tank connection.
18. Connect compressed air (1).
19. Open shutoff valve (B).
    a. The venturi nozzle produces a flow noise.
20. Then open shutoff valve (A) until the filling hose (1) is free of bubbles.
21. Close shutoff valve (A) again. The filling hose (1) is vented in this way.
22. Shutoff valve (B) remains open. Generate vacuum in coolant system for approx. 2 minutes. The end vacuum is reached at a vacuum of -0.7 to -0.95 bar. Green scale on the vacuum meter.

➡The coolant hoses contract during vacuum build-up.

23. Then close shutoff valve (B) again.
24. Both shutoff valves (A) and (B) must be closed. Then seal Venturi nozzle (1).
25. The cooling system must hold the vacuum for 30 seconds. If the needle in the vacuum meter falls, this indicates a leak in the cooling system.
26. If the vacuum remains constant, proceed with filling.
27. In event of leaks, check cooling system for leaks.

WARNING

There must be sufficiently premixed coolant in the filling unit container: 1 -2 liters more than the vehicle filling capacity.

WARNING

Position the filling unit container at the same height as the coolant expansion tank.

28. Shut-off valve (B) remains closed during the filling process.
29. To fill the cooling system, open shutoff valve (A) to filling unit container.
30. Coolant is now added.
31. The filling procedure is finished when the needle in the vacuum meter is at 0 bar or no longer falls.
32. If necessary, reduce remaining vacuum. Open shutoff valve (B) to do so.
33. Remove filling unit with adapter from expansion tank.
34. Adjust coolant level to max.
35. Close coolant expansion tank.

ELECTRIC ENGINE FAN

REMOVAL & INSTALLATION

See Figures 24 and 25.

1. Before servicing the vehicle, refer to the precautions.
2. Read out fault memory of DME control unit.
3. Remove intake duct.
4. On automatic transmission vehicles, remove front underbody protection
5. Disconnect the cooler for automatic transmission from fan cowl.
6. Unlock plug and remove.
7. Disconnect line from fan cowl.
8. Disconnect cable strap from fan cowl.
9. Remove bolt.
10. Unlock catch.
11. Remove fan cowl towards top.

To install:

12. Install fan cowl.
13. Lock catch in the opposite direction of arrow.
14. Install bolt and tighten securely.
15. Connect cable strap to fan cowl.
16. Clip line to fan cowl.
17. Lock plug.
18. On automatic transmission vehicles, connect the cooler for automatic transmission to fan cowl.

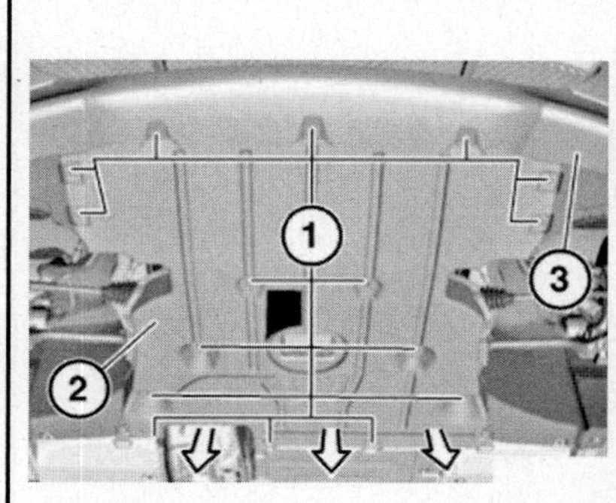

Fig. 24 Release screws (1) and pull underbody protection (2) forward under bumper trim (3)

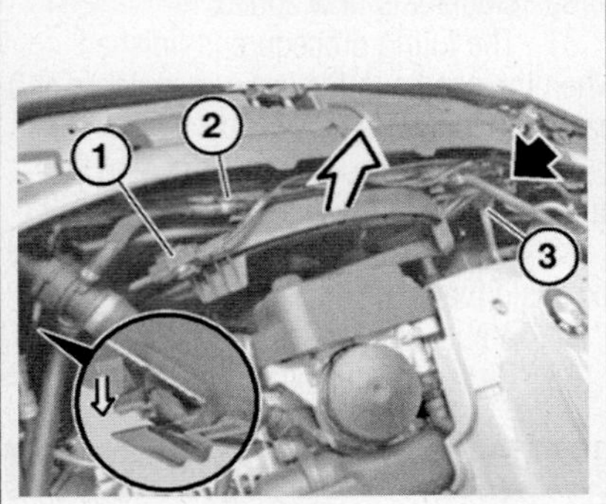

Fig. 25 Engine fan assembly showing plug (1), line (2) and cable strap (3)

19. Install front underbody protection.
20. Install intake duct.
21. Clear the fault memory.

RADIATOR

REMOVAL & INSTALLATION

N51 Engine

See Figures 26 and 27.

1. Remove intake duct.
2. Remove intake filter housing.
3. Remove fan cowl.
4. Drain coolant.
5. Unlock coolant hoses and detach.
6. If equipped, remove heat exchanger for automatic transmission fluid.
7. Automatic only: Release bolt and detach hose (1).
8. Release screws.
9. Carefully feed out radiator (1) towards top and remove.

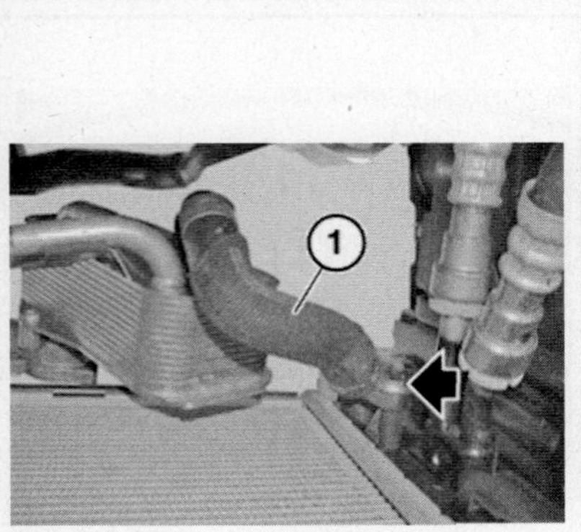

Fig. 26 Detaching hose (1)

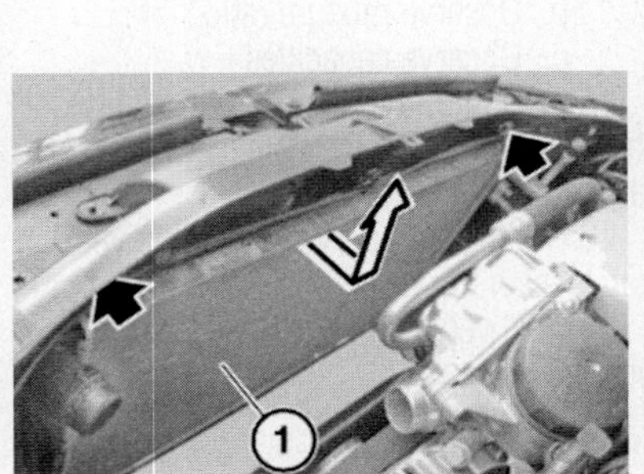

Fig. 27 Removing radiator (1)

➡**Illustration shows N54.**

To install:

To install, reverse the removal procedure.

N52 Engine

See Figure 28.

⁂ WARNING

Only perform this work after engine has cooled down.

1. Remove intake duct.
2. Remove intake filter housing.
3. Remove fan cowl.
4. Drain coolant.
5. Unlock coolant hoses and detach.
6. Automatic transmission only: Release bolt and detach hose (1).
7. Release screws.
8. Tightening torque: 40 inch lbs. (4.5 Nm)
9. Remove radiator (1) towards top.

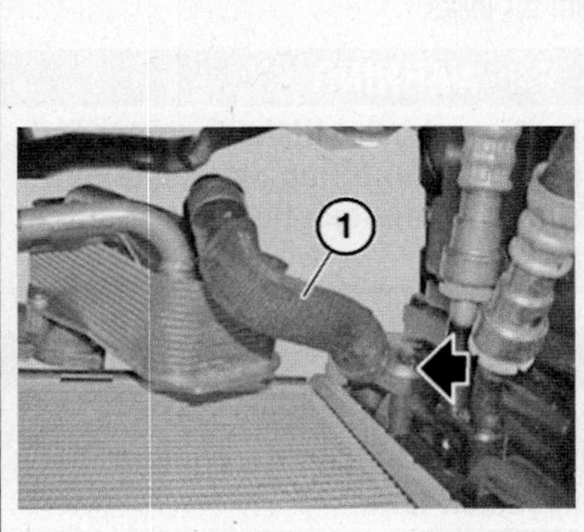

Fig. 28 Releasing bolt and detaching hose (1)

To install:

To install, reverse the removal procedure.

N55 Engine

See Figures 29 and 30.

⁂ CAUTION

Only perform this repair work after engine has cooled down.

1. Remove fan cowl.
2. Drain coolant.
3. Unlock coolant hoses and detach.
4. Only automatic or twin-clutch gearbox: Release bolt (1) and detaching hose (2).
5. Release screws.
   a. Tightening torque: 40 inch lbs. (4.5 Nm).
6. Carefully feed out radiator (1) towards top and remove.

To install:

To install, reverse the removal procedure.

7. Check for system leaks.

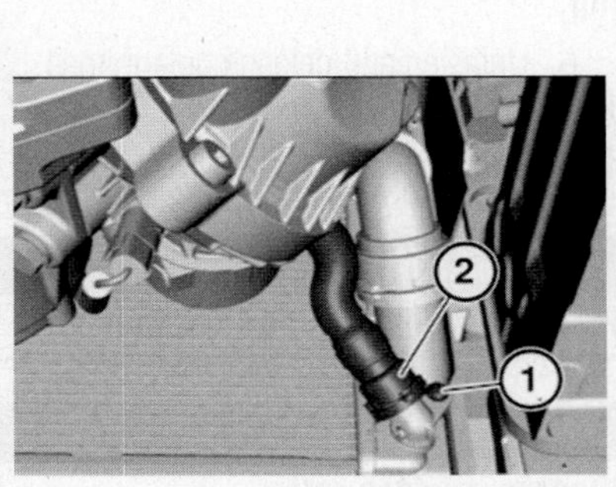

Fig. 29 Releasing bolt (1) and detaching hose (2)

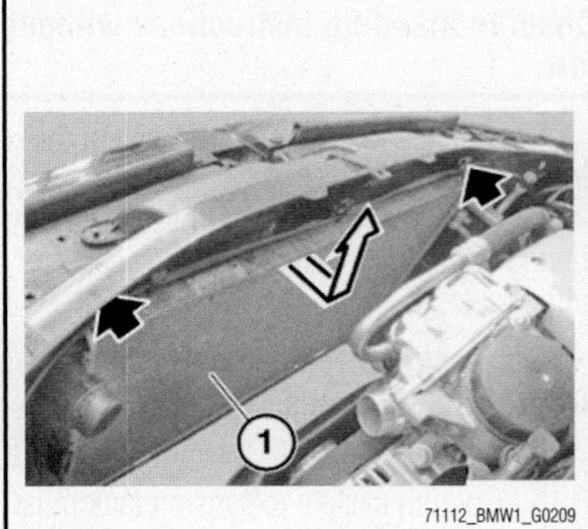

Fig. 30 Removing radiator (1)

THERMOSTAT

REMOVAL & INSTALLATION

See Figures 31 and 32.

1. Before servicing the vehicle, refer to the precautions.
2. Remove the underbody protection.
3. Drain and recycle the coolant.
4. Remove hose clips.
5. Remove coolant hoses.
6. Unlock and detach coolant hoses.
7. Disconnect plug connection.
8. Remove bolts.
9. Remove coolant thermostat.

To install:

10. Installation is the reverse of removal.
11. Tighten hose clamps/bolts to specification as follows:

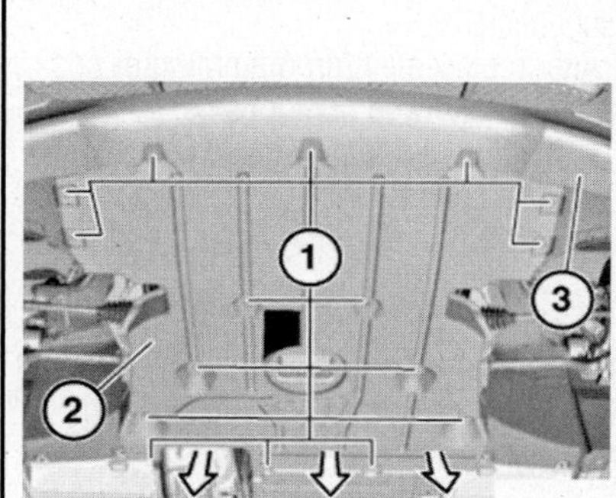

Fig. 31 Release screws (1) and pull underbody protection (2) forward under bumper trim (3)

- Coolant thermostat to electric water pump: 80 inch lbs. (9 Nm)
- Coolant hose between coolant thermostat and electric water pump: 27 inch lbs. (3 Nm)
- Coolant hose (from cylinder head) to coolant thermostat: 27 inch lbs. (3 Nm)

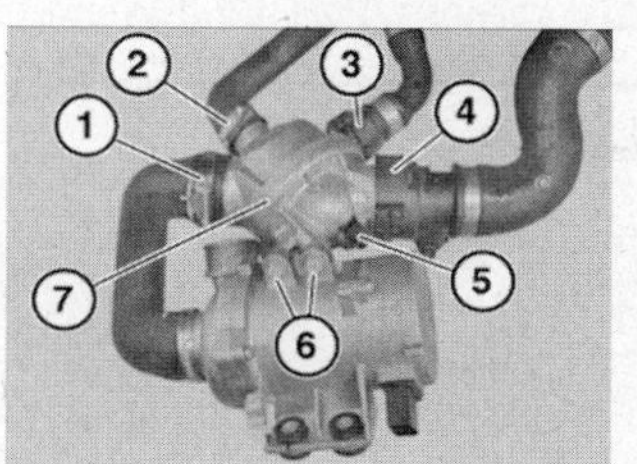

Fig. 32 Thermostat assembly

12. Fill and vent cooling system and check for leaks.

WATER PUMP

REMOVAL & INSTALLATION

See Figure 33.

⁂ WARNING

Aluminum-magnesium material. No steel fasteners may be used due to the threat of electrochemical corrosion. A magnesium crankcase requires aluminum fasteners exclusively. Aluminum fasteners must be replaced each time they are removed. The end faces of aluminum fasteners are painted blue for purposes of identification. Torque specifications and torque angles must be observed for risk of damage.

⁂ WARNING

If a water pump that has already been operated is reused, it must be filled with coolant immediately after removal.

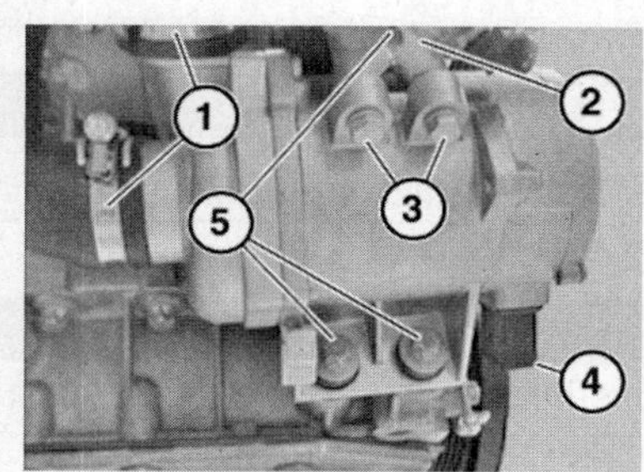

Fig. 33 Water pump assembly

1. Before servicing the vehicle, refer to the precautions.
2. Remove coolant thermostat.
3. Remove hose clamps.
4. Remove coolant hoses.
5. Disconnect plug connection.
6. Remove bolts and discard aluminum bolts.
7. Remove electric water pump.

To install:

⁂ WARNING

If the electric water pump is reused, it must be rotated one turn due to the breakaway torque at the blade wheels.

8. Install electric water pump.
9. Install new bolts and tighten to 7 ft. lbs. (10 Nm) plus 90° additional rotation.
10. Connect plug connection.
11. Install coolant hoses.
12. Fasten hose clamps.
13. Install coolant thermostat.

BATTERY

REMOVAL & INSTALLATION

See Figures 34 and 35.

✱✱ WARNING

If the ignition is not turned OFF when the battery is disconnected, fault memories may be set in some control units.

- There is a danger of mixing up battery leads: If the battery positive and negative leads are the same color and you are in doubt, follow the polarity to the battery, then mark and cover the leads.
- On vehicles with radio code: After disconnecting the battery, the radio code must be re-entered. Therefore obtain the radio code card from the customer beforehand. Note stored stations and restore them after connecting the battery.
- Stored settings of the on-board computer and clock will also be lost.
- All available central keys must be recoded for cars with first generation infrared transmitter locking systems.

✱✱ WARNING

Do not under any circumstances use force to pull/lever off Intelligent Battery Sensor (IBS).

1. Open rear lid and remove luggage compartment floor trim.
2. Loosen negative battery lead nut.
3. Disconnect battery negative lead and secure at side.
4. Remove the power distributor.
   a. Release screws and remove bracket.
   b. Disconnect plug connection.
   c. If necessary, release wiring harness fasteners from power distributor.
   d. Open covers and release nuts underneath.
   e. Press locking brackets downwards and unclip.
   f. If necessary, using a screwdriver, expand locking bracket at lower end and clip out.
   g. Remove power distributor towards top.
5. Detach vent in direction of arrow.
6. Open cover and slacken nut underneath.

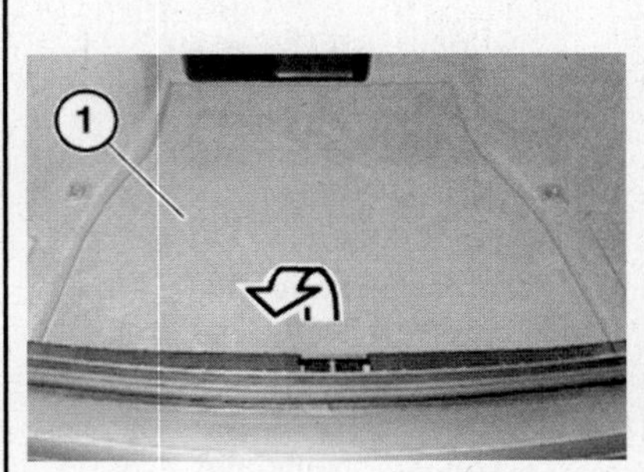

Fig. 34 Open rear lid and remove luggage compartment floor trim (1)

7. Detach safety battery terminal towards top, lay to one side and secure.
8. Release threaded pin and remove with holder.
9. Remove battery towards right side.

To install:

10. Installation is the reverse of removal.
11. Make sure battery is correctly seated in its fixture.
   - Distribution box: 11 ft. lbs. (15 Nm)
   - Rollover protection, battery (bar) to luggage compartment tray: 71 inch lbs. (8 Nm)
   - Battery positive lead, battery negative lead, safety battery terminal, IBS: 48 inch lbs. (5 Nm)
12. On vehicles with intelligent battery sensor (IBS), register battery replacement and read out fault memory, clear if necessary.

BATTERY RECONNECT/RELEARN PROCEDURE

After disconnecting/connecting battery some systems may be restricted and individual settings may be lost. Settings or activations must be carried out, depending on the equipment specification.

Active Front Steering

Adjustment of the active front steering must be carried out:

- After adjustment work on the front axle/steering
- After all mechanical work on the steering system
- After the battery has been disconnected or electrical plug connections on the steering column switch cluster have been disconnected

After replacement/programming or coding of the following components:

- Steering column switch cluster
- DSC control unit
- Active front steering control unit
- ARS control unit

Connect vehicle to BMW diagnosis system. Select and carry out initial operation/adjustment for active front steering under Service functions.

Sliding Sunroof

Initialization of the sliding sunroof comprises normalization and then learning of the characteristic curve. The mechanical end positions are recorded and stored during normalization. The characteristic curve is learnt immediately after normalization. When the characteristic curve is learned, the mechanical closing forces of the slide/tilt sunroof are recorded and stored

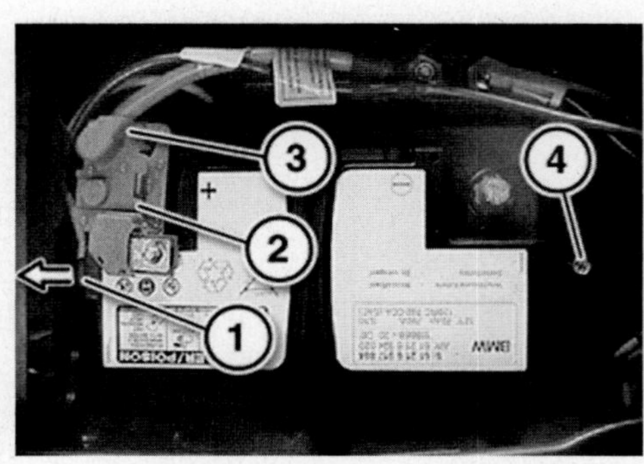

Fig. 35 Battery connections

for correct operation of the anti-trapping mechanism.

Carry out an initialization:

- If the slide/tilt sunroof has been mechanically moved by means of the emergency actuator
- In the event of malfunctions, e.g. no one-touch function, no opening or no comfort function possible
- After disengagement of the drive unit
- After work is carried out on the mechanism of the slide/tilt sunroof
- After the control unit has been replaced

WARNING

There is no anti-trapping protection during initialization.

Normalization

See Figure 36.

1. Press and hold the switch in the "Lift" direction
2. In the event of delayed starting or sudden stopping of the slide/tilt sunroof, continue pressing the switch in the "Lift" direction
3. After reaching the lift end position, keep the switch pressed for approximately 15 seconds further.
4. Normalization is completed when the slide/tilt sunroof in lift end position presses again briefly upward.

Learning Characteristic Curve

1. After normalization, keep switch pressed in "Lift" direction.
2. The slide/tilt sunroof stops for 5 seconds in the final raise position after normalization. It then moves into the "Closed" position (learning of the "Closing from raising" curve).

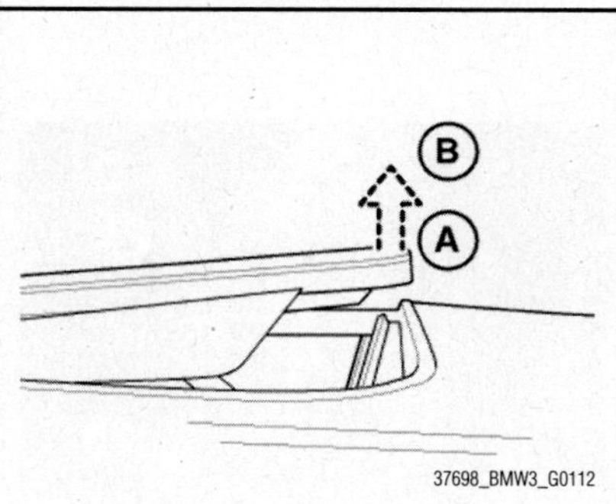

Fig. 36 Normalization is completed when the slide/tilt sunroof in lift end position (A) presses again briefly in the direction of position (B)

3. The slide/tilt sunroof then moves into the "Open" end position and immediately back into the "Closed" position (learning of the "Closing" curve).
4. Release switch.

➡The entire operation lasts approximately 75 seconds. Learning of the curve is terminated when the switch is released. If the switch is released prematurely, the entire procedure must be repeated. Upon completion of successful initialization, the corresponding messages in the check control and the control display go out.

5. Carry out function check (tip function, anti-trapping protection and, if necessary, comfort function).

Power Windows

WARNING

There is no anti-trapping protection during initialization.

An initialization must be performed:

- In the event of malfunctions, e.g. no one-touch control function, no opening or if available no comfort function is possible
- After the power window drive has been replaced
- After work is carried out on the power window mechanism
- If necessary, after an open circuit, e.g. disconnection of the battery or disconnection of the power supply to the door
- After the door window glass has been removed and installed or replaced
- After adjustment work on the door window glass
- After adjustment work on the convertible top
- After replacement of seals

Initialization is performed on the power window switch of the relevant door.

- The ignition switch must be ON
- Doors and windows closed
- Sufficient battery voltage; connect charger if necessary

Initialization comprises erasure of the previous initialization and re-initialization.

Erasure of Initialization

1. Open door window glass fully
2. Actuate power window switch in "Open" position (second switch position) and hold down for between 15 and 20 seconds. This clears initialization of the power window. Anti-trapping protection and one-touch control (toll) function are inactive.
3. Check whether one-touch control (toll) function is inactive, otherwise repeat procedure.

Reinitialization

1. Close door window completely.
2. After upper end position is reached, interrupt actuation of power window switch and then hold switch again for approximately 1 second in "Close" position (second switch position).
3. Open door window glass fully.
4. After upper end position is reached, interrupt actuation of power window switch and then hold switch again for approximately 1 second in "Open" position (second switch position).
5. Close door window completely.
6. After upper end position is reached, interrupt actuation of power window switch and then hold switch again for approximately 1 second in "Close" position (second switch position).
7. Carry out function check (one-touch control function, anti-trapping protection and, if necessary, comfort function).

➡The power windows can also be initialized by connecting the vehicle to BMW diagnosis system.

Mirror with Compass

If may be necessary to calibrate the compass if:

- The vehicle battery has been disconnected for an extended period of time
- "C" appears in compass display
- There is no compass display

Setting Magnetic Deflection Zone

See Figure 37.

1. Switch ignition on.
2. Using a suitable tool, press pushbut-

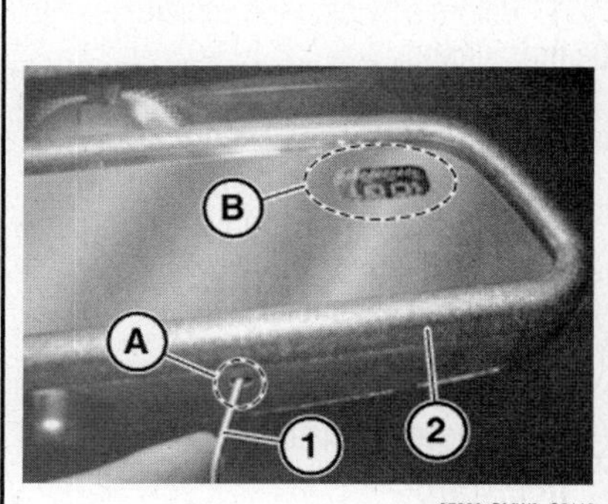

Fig. 37 Using a suitable tool (1), press pushbutton in area (A) of mirror (2) until a number appears in compass display (B)

ton on mirror until a number appears in compass display.

3. Press pushbutton repeatedly until number of desired zone appears.
4. Wait until direction display appears.
5. Magnetic deflection zone is now set.

Calibrating Compass:

See Figure 38.

1. Switch ignition on.
2. Using a suitable tool, press pushbutton on mirror until "C" appears in compass display.
3. Drive vehicle 2–3 times in a circle at approximately 10 mph.
4. Calibration process is completed when direction display appears.

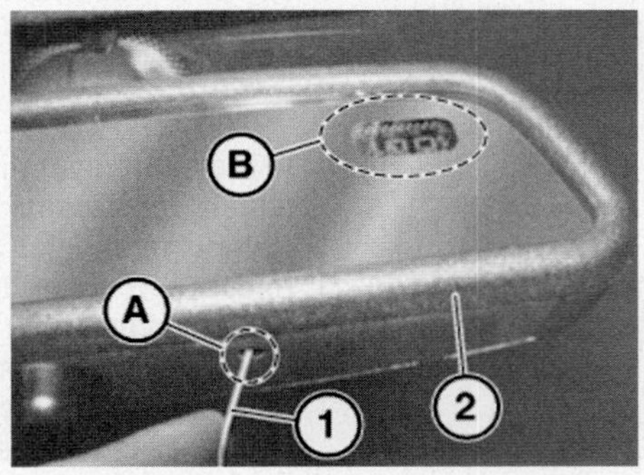

Fig. 38 Using a suitable tool (1), press pushbutton in area (A) of mirror (2) until "C" appears in compass display (B)

ENGINE ELECTRICAL

CHARGING SYSTEM

ALTERNATOR

REMOVAL & INSTALLATION

N52 Engine

See Figure 39.

WARNING

Aluminum-magnesium materials. No steel bolts/bolts may be used due to the threat of electrochemical corrosion. A magnesium crankcase requires aluminum bolts/bolts exclusively. Aluminum bolts/bolts must be replaced each time they are Removed. The end faces of aluminum bolts/bolts are painted blue for the purposes of reliable identification. Jointing torque and angle of rotation must be observed without fail (risk of damage).

1. Before servicing the vehicle, refer to the precautions.
2. Disconnect the negative battery cable.
3. Remove intake filter housing.
4. Remove alternator drive belt.
5. Unlock plug and remove.
6. Remove nut and disconnect B+ wire.
7. Remove aluminum bolts and discard.
8. Remove alternator.

To install:

9. Installation is the reverse of removal.
10. Tighten bolts/nuts to specification as follows:
    - Alternator lead to alternator: 14 ft. lbs. (19 Nm)
    - Alternator to crankcase: 89 inch lbs. (10 Nm) plus an additional 180° rotation
11. Clear fault codes.

Fig. 39 Alternator (3), mounting bolts (arrows), B+ wire (1) and plug (2)

N54 and N55 Engines

See Figures 40 and 41.

1. Before servicing the vehicle, refer to the precautions.
2. Disconnect the negative battery cable.
3. Remove charge air duct.
4. Remove alternator drive belt. on
5. Remove the A/C compressor and place to one side.

➡Do not disconnect refrigerant lines from compressor.

6. Remove bolts a few turns until bracket is loose. Do not remove bracket.

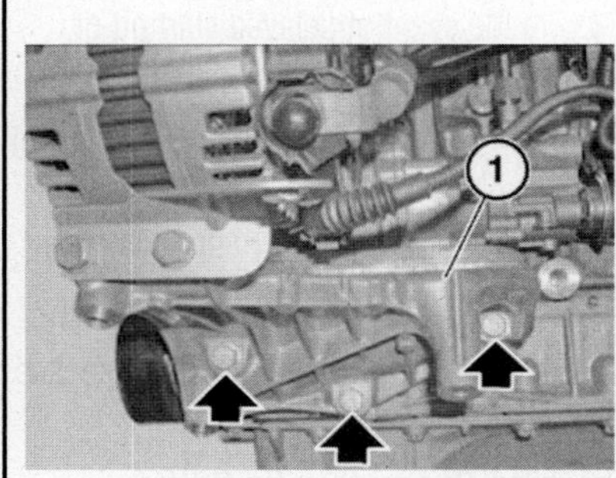

Fig. 40 Remove bolts a few turns until bracket (1) is loose. Do not remove bracket

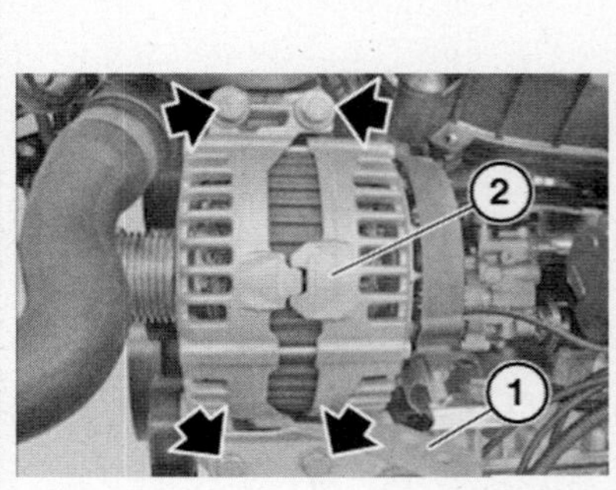

Fig. 41 Remove bracket (1) and alternator (2)

7. Unlock plug and remove.
8. Remove protective cap and Remove nut underneath.
9. Disconnect B+ wire.
10. Remove bracket and alternator.

To install:

11. Installation is the reverse of removal.
12. Tighten bolts/nuts to specification as follows:
    - Bracket, A/C compressor to lower crankcase: 14 ft. lbs. (19 Nm)
    - Alternator lead to alternator: 14 ft. lbs. (19 Nm)
    - Alternator to crankcase: 14 ft. lbs. (19 Nm)
13. Clear fault codes.

ENGINE ELECTRICAL

IGNITION SYSTEM

FIRING ORDERS

See Figure 42.

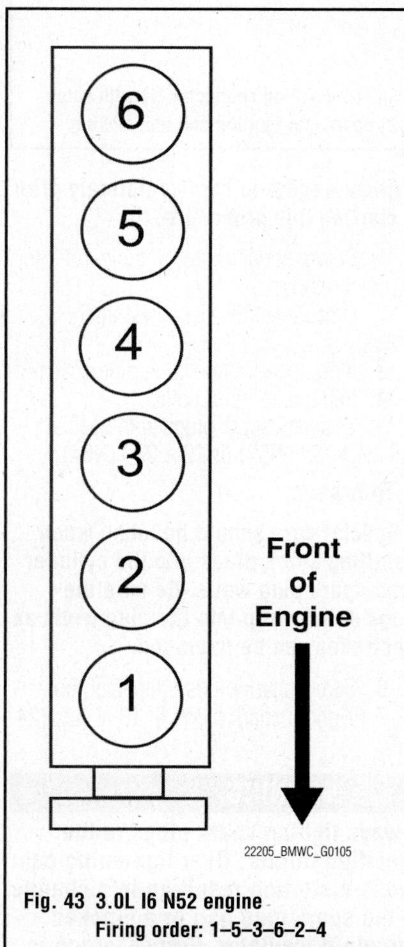

Fig. 43 3.0L I6 N52 engine Firing order: 1–5–3–6–2–4 Distributorless ignition system

IGNITION COIL

REMOVAL & INSTALLATION

N51 and N52 Engines

See Figures 43 and 44.

1. Read out the fault memory of the DME control unit.
2. Check stored fault messages and process procedure.
3. Switch off ignition.
4. Remove ignition coil cover.
5. Ignition coils must not be contaminated by fuel.
6. The resistance of the silicone material is reduced significantly by contact with fuel, which may cause the ignition coil to fail.
7. The silicone tube of the spark plug connector is coated with talc to reduce the pulling forces. The silicone tube must NOT be oiled or greased. This would greatly reduce the durability of the silicone material, which can lead to a malfunction of the ignition coil.
8. Unlock plug catch (1) of ignition coil (2) and disconnect plug.
9. Slowly pull the ignition coil (1) up and out without jerking it.

➡There is a possibility that the silicone tube will tear and therefore be destroyed.

➡This procedure is applicable to all ignition coils.

To install:

To install, reverse the removal procedure noting the following.

10. Position the ignition coil (1) and gently push it to the limit position, if necessary by twisting it back and forth slightly. Then check anti-twist lock.
11. The rubber cap must completely surround the sealing collar of the cylinder head cover.

➡If rubber parts are squashed, the ignition coil can slip out again during engine operation.

12. Push connector (1) with connector catch (2) open onto ignition coil.
13. Carefully close connector catch (2) in direction of arrow.
14. The connector must be positioned on the counter piece with hardly any gaps when the locking lever is being closed. In the process, the cheeks of the lever are positioned inside the counter piece.

➡The locking lever can become deformed if it is not installed correctly. This means that there is no longer a safety lock on the plug connection. As a result, the connector can slip out during engine operation (loose contact, misfiring).

15. The connector fastener must snap into place without great effort.
16. Delete fault memory.

N55 Engine

See Figures 45 and 46.

1. Read out the fault memory of the DME control unit.
2. Check stored fault messages and process procedure.
3. Switch off ignition.
4. Remove rear ignition coil cover.

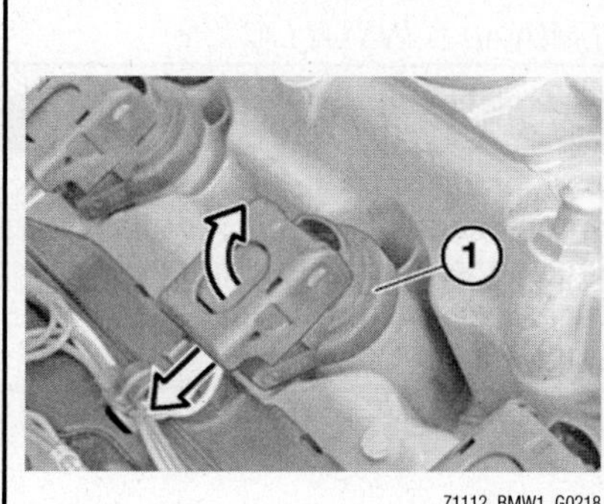

Fig. 43 Unlocking plug catch (1) of ignition coil and removing

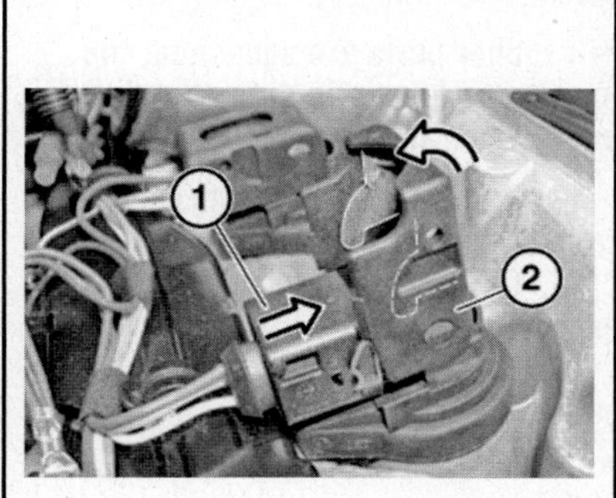

Fig. 44 Pushing connector (1) and closing connector catch (2)

WARNING

Ignition coils must not be contaminated by fuel.

WARNING

The resistance of the silicone material is reduced significantly by contact with fuel, which may cause the ignition coil to fail.

WARNING

The silicone tube of the spark plug connector is coated with talc to reduce the pulling forces. The silicone tube must NOT be oiled or greased. This would greatly reduce the durability of the silicone material, which can lead to a malfunction of the ignition coil.

5. Release oxygen sensor connector (1) from bracket.
6. Release screw (2).
7. Put cable clip aside.
8. Unlock plug catch (1) of ignition coil (2) and disconnect plug.
9. Pull out the ignition coil (2) slowly in a smooth upwards movement.

➡There is a possibility that the silicone tube will tear and therefore be destroyed.

10. This procedure is applicable to all ignition coils.

To install:

11. Position the ignition coil and gently push it to the limit position, if necessary by twisting it back and forth slightly. Then check anti-twist lock.
12. The rubber cap must completely surround the sealing collar of the cylinder head cover.

➡If rubber parts are squashed, the ignition coil can slip out again during engine operation.

13. Push connector (1) with connector catch (2) open onto ignition coil.
14. Carefully close connector catch (2) in direction of arrow.
15. The connector catch must snap into place without great effort.

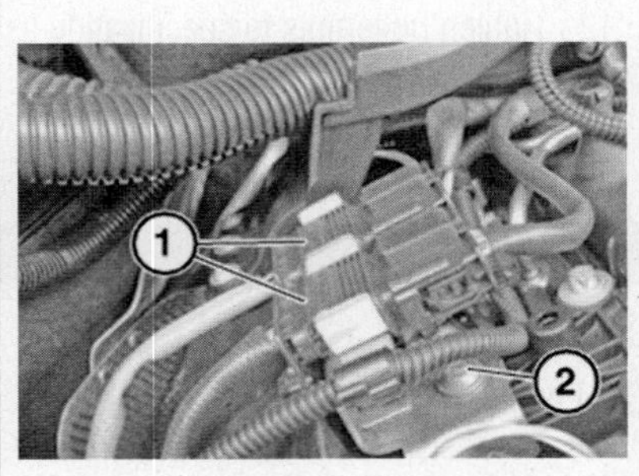

Fig. 45 Releasing oxygen sensor connector (1) and releasing screw (2)

16. The connector must be positioned on the counter piece with hardly any gaps when the locking lever is being closed. In the process, the cheeks of the lever are positioned inside the counter piece.

➡The locking lever can become deformed if it is not installed correctly. This means that there is no longer a safety lock on the plug connection. As a result, the connector can slip out during engine operation (loose contact, misfiring).

➡Delete fault memory.

17. Assemble engine.

IGNITION TIMING

INSPECTION & ADJUSTMENT

The ignition timing is controlled by the Digital Motor Electronics (DME). No adjustments are necessary.

SPARK PLUGS

REMOVAL & INSTALLATION

WARNING

Spark plugs must be replaced with the same type/number spark plug as the original. If another spark plug is substituted, damage may result.

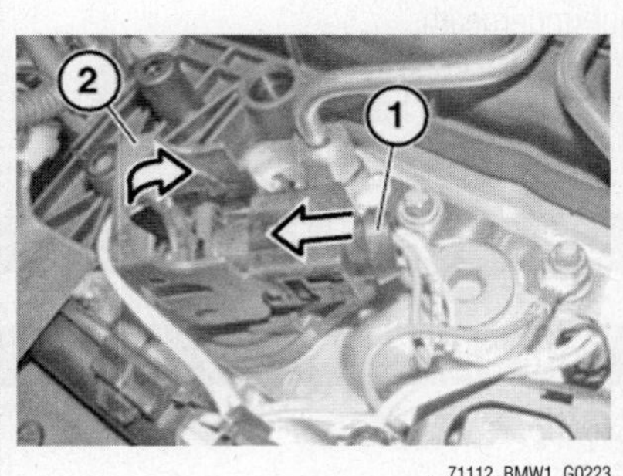

Fig. 46 Pushing connector (1) with catch (2) open onto ignition coil and closing

➡Allow engine to cool completely prior to starting this procedure.

1. Before servicing the vehicle, refer to the precautions.
2. Disconnect the negative battery cable.
3. If equipped, removal engine cover.
4. Remove ignition coils.
5. Unscrew spark plugs with special tool 12 1 171 (N52) or 12 1 220 (N54).

To install:

➡Special care should be taken when installing spark plugs into the cylinder head spark plug wells. Be sure the plugs do not drop into the plug wells as electrodes can be damaged.

6. Screw spark plugs in special tool.
7. Tighten spark plugs to 18 ft. lbs. (24 Nm).

WARNING

Always tighten spark plugs to the specified torque. Over tightening can cause distortion resulting in a change in the spark plug gap or a cracked porcelain insulator. Proper torque is especially important in the case of aluminum cylinder heads.

8. Install ignition coils.
9. If equipped, install engine cover.
10. Connect the negative battery cable.

ENGINE ELECTRICAL

STARTER

REMOVAL & INSTALLATION

See Figure 47.

⁂ WARNING

Aluminum-magnesium materials. No steel bolts/bolts may be used due to the threat of electrochemical corrosion. A magnesium crankcase requires aluminum bolts/bolts exclusively.

Aluminum bolts/bolts must be replaced each time they are Removed. The end faces of aluminum bolts/bolts are painted blue for the purposes of reliable identification. Jointing torque and angle of rotation must be observed without fail (risk of damage).

1. Before servicing the vehicle, refer to the precautions.
2. Disconnect the negative battery cable.
3. Remove intake air manifold.
4. Unlock plug and remove.
5. Remove the B+ cable from the starter.
6. Remove and discard the starter mounting bolts.
7. Remove starter motor.

To install:

8. Check starter pinion and ring gear for damage, replace damaged parts if necessary.
9. Install starter motor.
10. Install the starter mounting bolts and tighten to specification.
    - M10x85: 15 ft. lbs. (20 Nm) plus an additional 180° rotation
    - M10x30: 15 ft. lbs. (20 Nm) plus an additional 90° rotation
11. Install the B+ cable from the starter and tighten nut to 10 ft. lbs. (13 Nm).
12. Unlock plug and Install.
13. Install intake air manifold
14. Connect the negative battery cable.

TESTING

1. Before servicing the vehicle, refer to the precautions.
2. Inspect the battery for proper charge.
3. Check for proper tension on the accessory ribbed V-belts.
4. Inspect the battery terminal cables and connections for looseness, damage or corrosion and repair as necessary.

Fig. 47 Starter mounting bolt locations

5. Inspect the starter cables and connections for looseness, damage or corrosion and repair as necessary.
6. Inspect for a solid ground connection between engine and body and repair as necessary.
7. Connect a STAR DIAGNOSIS tool and read out DME fault memory.

ENGINE MECHANICAL

➡Disconnecting the negative battery cable may interfere with the functions of the on board computer systems and may require the computer to undergo a relearning process, once the negative battery cable is reconnected.

Before servicing any vehicle, please be sure to read all of the following precautions, which deal with personal safety, prevention of component damage, and important points to take into consideration when servicing a motor vehicle:

- Never open, service or drain the radiator or cooling system when the engine is hot; serious burns can occur from the steam and hot coolant.
- Observe all applicable safety precautions when working around fuel. Whenever servicing the item, always work in a well-ventilated area. Do not allow fuel spray or vapors to come in contact with a spark, open flame, or excessive heat (a hot drop light, for example). Keep a dry chemical fire extinguisher near the work area. Always keep fuel in a container specifically designed for fuel storage; also, always properly seal fuel containers to avoid the possibility of fire or explosion. Refer to the additional fuel system precautions later in this section.
- Fuel injection systems often remain pressurized, even after the engine has been turned **OFF**. The fuel system pressure must be relieved before disconnecting any fuel lines. Failure to do so may result in fire and/or personal injury.
- Brake fluid often contains polyglycol ethers and polyglycols. Avoid contact with the eyes and wash your hands thoroughly after handling brake fluid. If you do get brake fluid in your eyes, flush your eyes with clean, running water for 15 minutes. If eye irritation persists, or if you have taken brake fluid internally, IMMEDIATELY seek medical assistance.
- The EPA warns that prolonged contact with used engine oil may cause a number of skin disorders, including cancer. You should make every effort to minimize your exposure to used engine oil. Protective gloves should be worn when changing oil. Wash your hands and any other exposed skin areas as soon as possible after exposure to used engine oil. Soap and water, or waterless hand cleaner should be used.
- All new vehicles are now equipped with an air bag system, often referred to as a Supplemental Restraint System (SRS) or Supplemental Inflatable Restraint (SIR) system. The system must be disabled before performing service on or around system components, steering column, instrument panel components, wiring and sensors. Failure to follow safety and disabling procedures could result in accidental air bag deployment, possible personal injury and unnecessary system repairs.
- Always wear safety goggles when working with, or around, the air bag system. When carrying a non-deployed air bag, be sure the bag and trim cover are pointed away from your body. When placing a non-deployed air bag on a work surface, always face the bag and trim cover upward, away from the surface. This will reduce the motion of the module if it is accidentally deployed. Refer to the additional air bag system precautions later in this section.
- Clean, high quality brake fluid from a sealed container is essential to the safe and

proper operation of the brake system. You should always buy the correct type of brake fluid for your vehicle. If the brake fluid becomes contaminated, completely flush the system with new fluid. Never reuse any brake fluid. Any brake fluid that is removed from the system should be discarded. Also, do not allow any brake fluid to come in contact with a painted surface; it will damage the paint.

- Never operate the engine without the proper amount and type of engine oil; doing so WILL result in severe engine damage.
- Timing belt maintenance is extremely important. Many models utilize an interference-type, non-freewheeling engine. If the timing belt breaks, the valves in the cylinder head may strike the pistons, causing potentially serious (also time-consuming and expensive) engine damage. Refer to the maintenance interval charts for the recommended replacement interval for the timing belt, and to the timing belt section for belt replacement and inspection.
- Disconnecting the negative battery cable on some vehicles may interfere with the functions of the on-board computer system(s) and may require the computer to undergo a relearning process once the negative battery cable is reconnected.
- When servicing drum brakes, only disassemble and assemble one side at a time, leaving the remaining side intact for reference.
- Only an MVAC-trained, EPA-certified automotive technician should service the air conditioning system or its components.

ACCESSORY DRIVE BELT SYSTEM

ADJUSTMENT

The belt tension is maintained by an automatic tensioner. No adjustment is possible.

BELT ROUTINGS

See Figures 48 through 50.

INSPECTION

Inspect the drive belt for signs of glazing or cracking. A glazed belt will be perfectly smooth from slippage, while a good belt will have a slight texture of fabric visible. Cracks will usually start at the inner edge of the belt and run outward. All worn or damaged drive belts should be replaced immediately.

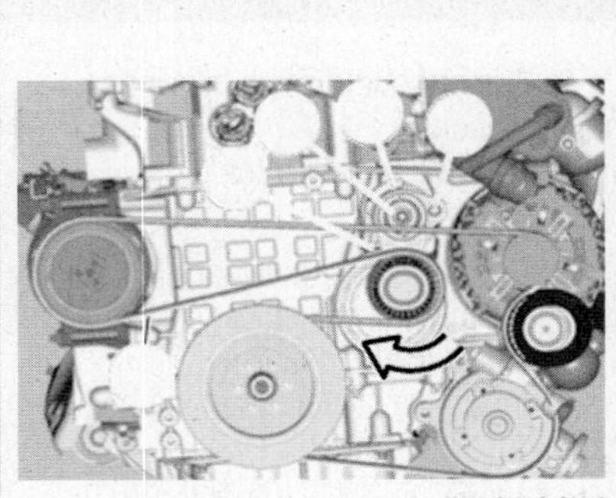
22205_BMWC_G0113

Fig. 48 Accessory belt routing—N52 engine

REMOVAL & INSTALLATION

N52 Engine

See Figure 51.

WARNING

Aluminum-magnesium materials. No steel bolts/bolts may be used due to the threat of electrochemical corrosion. A magnesium crankcase requires aluminum bolts/bolts exclusively.

Aluminum bolts/bolts must be replaced each time they are Removed. The end faces of aluminum bolts/bolts are painted blue for the purposes of reliable identification. Jointing torque and angle of rotation must be observed without fail (risk of damage).

1. Before servicing the vehicle, refer to the precautions.

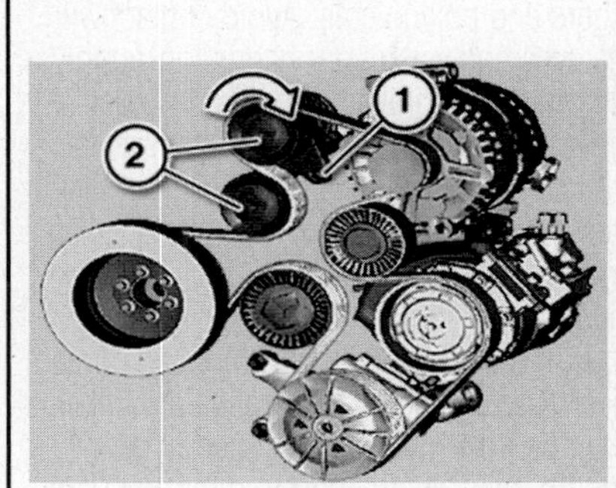

22205_BMWC_G0186

Fig. 49 Accessory belt routing—N54 engine

2. Remove fan cowl with electric fan
3. Mark the direction of rotation of the drive belt if it is to be reused.
4. Turn belt tensioner clockwise until bore is flush on housing.
5. By holding belt tensioner under tension, the load is removed from tensioning pulley.
6. Secure belt tensioner with special tool 11 3 340.
7. Remove drive belt upwards.
8. Check drive belt for correct installation position and, if reusing, observe direction of rotation.

N54 Engine

See Figure 52.

➡Mark the direction of rotation of the drive belt if it is to be reused. Depending on the build date (version), the idler pulleys can be fitted with and without grooves.

1. Before servicing the vehicle, refer to the precautions.
2. Remove fan cowl.
3. Remove hose clip.
4. Remove quick-connect fastener 90°on boost pressure pipe.
5. Pull off air hose.
6. Disconnect line from holder.
7. Remove coolant hose from holder.
8. Remove screw.
9. Fold air duct down.

➡Do not remove air duct.

10. Turn belt tensioner until bore is flush on housing.
11. Secure belt tensioner in place with special tool 11 3 340.
12. Remove drive belt (1).

To install:

13. Install belt in the previously marked direction if reusing the old belt.
14. Pretension tensioning pulley.
15. Remove special tool 11 3 340.
16. On boost pressure pipe, bring lock back 90°into installation position.
17. Recirculated air hose must audibly snap into place.
18. Check that drive belt for is in correct installation position.

N55 Engine

See Figure 53.

1. Remove fan cowl with electric fan.
2. Mark the direction of travel of the drive belt if it is to be reused.
3. Turn belt tensioner (1) in direction of arrow until belt tensioner bore hole (2)is flush on crankcase.

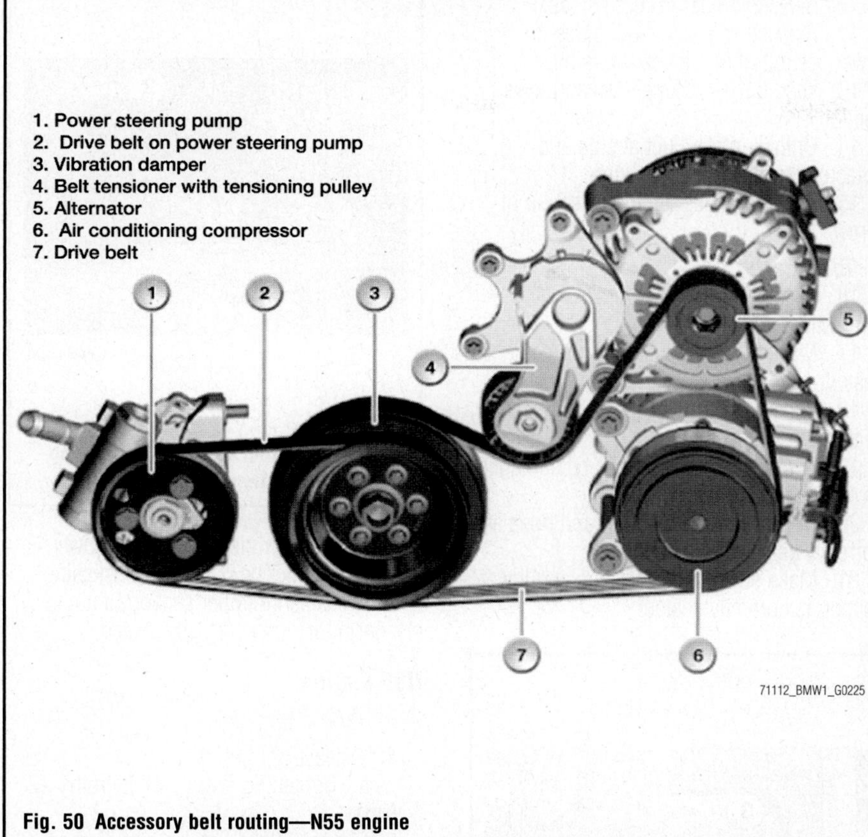

Fig. 50 Accessory belt routing—N55 engine

4. Hold belt tensioner (1) under tension.
5. Secure special tool 11 0 390.
6. Remove drive belt (3).

To install:

To install, reverse the removal procedure noting the following.

7. Check drive belt for correct installation position and, if reusing, observe direction of travel.

Fig. 51 Secure belt tensioner with special tool 11 3 340

Drive Belt Tensioner

N55 Engine

See Figure 54.

1. Remove drive belt.
2. Remove special tool 11 0 390.
3. Remove cover from deflecting element.
4. Release screw (1) on belt tensioner.
   a. Tightening torque: 28 ft. lbs. (38 Nm).

Fig. 52 Turn belt tensioner (1) until bore is flush on housing

Fig. 53 Turning belt tensioner (1), identifying bore hole (2) and removing drive belt (3)

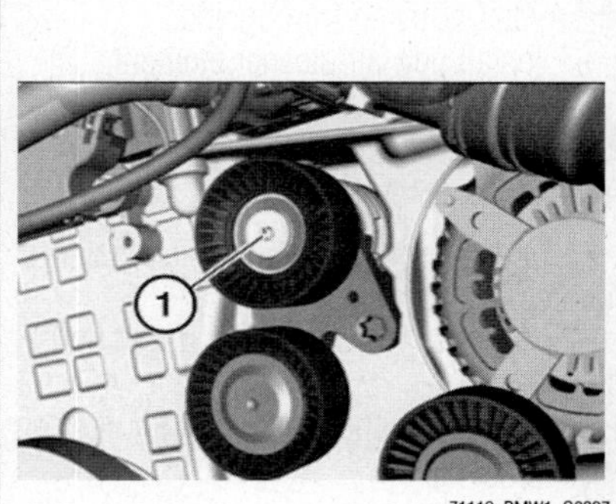

Fig. 54 Releasing screw (1) and removing belt tensioner

To install:

To install, reverse the removal procedure.

AIR CLEANER

REMOVAL & INSTALLATION

N52 Engine

See Figure 55.

1. Before servicing the vehicle, refer to the precautions.
2. Unlock plug and remove.
3. Release clamp and detach air intake hose.
4. Unlock air intake hose sideways and detach.
5. Release bolts.
6. Remove intake filter housing towards top.

To install:

7. Installation is the reverse of removal.

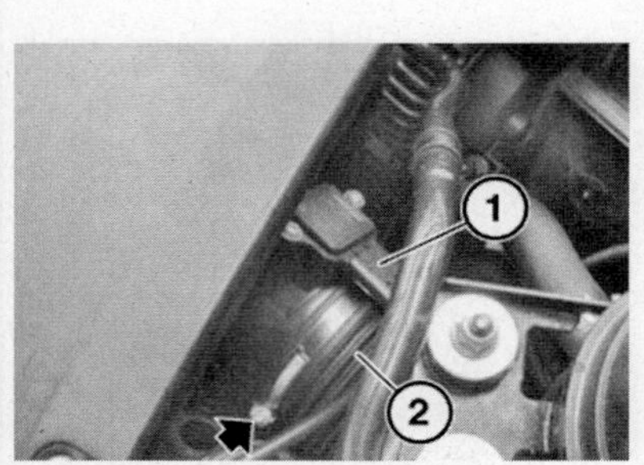

Fig. 55 Unlock air intake hose (1) sideways and detach, release screws and remove top section (2) of intake filter housing

8. Clean upper and lower sections of intake filter housing from inside.
9. Install new air cleaner element.

N54 Engine

See Figures 56 through 58.

1. Before servicing the vehicle, refer to the precautions.
2. Remove fasteners from upper housing.
3. Remove upper section of air cleaner housing.
4. Release holder.
5. Release catches.
6. Remove right cover.
7. Remove the left cover in same way as right cover.
8. Release cable holder and remove hose from cover.
9. Press detent lugs.
10. Release cable strip in direction of arrow from lower section of air cleaner housing.

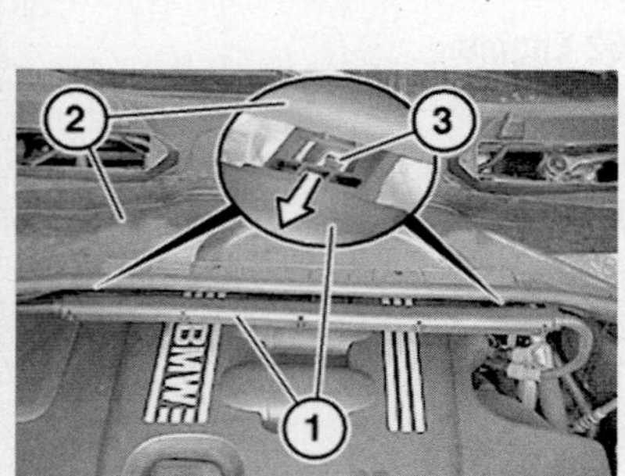

Fig. 56 Press detent lugs (3) and release cable strip (1) from lower section of air cleaner housing (2)

11. Release holder on both sides.
12. Release screw on both sides on lower section of air cleaner housing.
13. Feed out air cleaner housing lower section.
14. Unlock intake duct at side and detach from air cleaner housing.
15. Remove intake duct in direction of arrow.

To install:

16. Installation is the reverse of removal.
17. Make sure cable strip is correctly seated.
18. Make sure right cover is correctly seated.
19. Retaining lugs must not be damaged or missing.
20. Make sure cable holder and hose are correctly seated in opening.
21. Make sure air cleaner housing lower section is correctly seated.

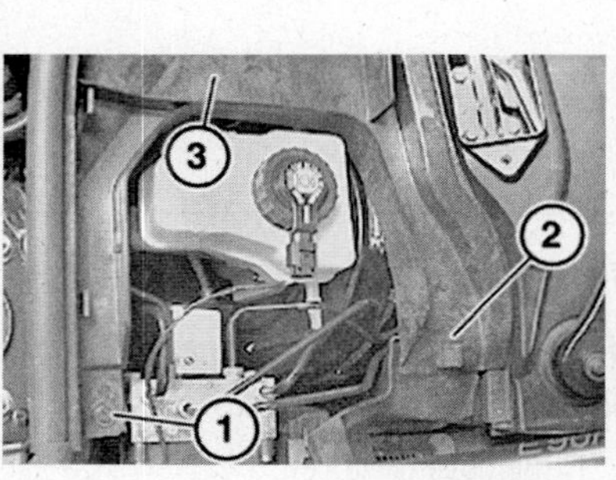

Fig. 57 Release holder (2) and screw (1) on both sides on lower section of air cleaner housing (3).

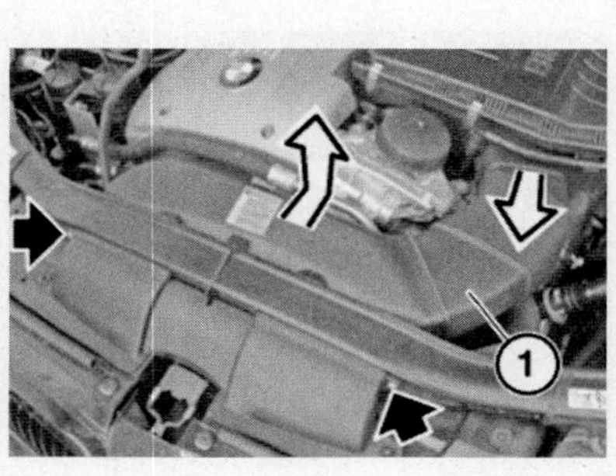

Fig. 58 Unlock intake duct (1) at side and detach from air cleaner housing

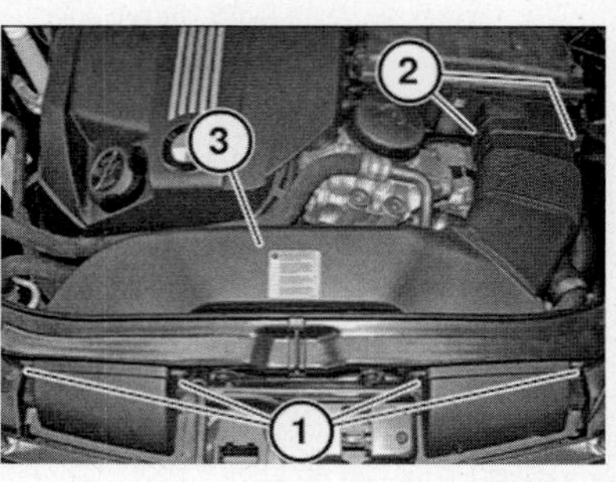

Fig. 59 Releasing screws (1), unlocking clamps (2) and removing intake port (3)

22. Seal of air cleaner housing lower section must not be damaged or missing.
23. Make sure upper section of air cleaner housing is correctly seated.

N55 Engine

See Figure 59.

1. Release screws (1).
   a. Tightening torque: 17 inch lbs. (2 Nm).
2. Unlock intake port on side clamps (2) and pull off the air filter housing.
3. Remove intake port (3).

To install:

To install, reverse the removal procedure.

CAMSHAFT & BEARINGS

REMOVAL & INSTALLATION

N51, N52 and N54 Engines

See Figures 60 through 72.

WARNING

Aluminum bolts/bolts must be replaced each time they are Removed. The end faces of aluminum bolts/bolts are painted blue for the purposes of reliable identification. Jointing torque and angle of rotation must be observed without fail (risk of damage).

1. Before servicing the vehicle, refer to the precautions.
2. Remove valve cover.
3. Remove the underbody protection.
4. Check the camshaft timing.
   a. Remove fastener.
   b. Rotate crankshaft at central bolt into TDC position.

c. Slide special tool 11 0 300 into special tool bore and secure crankshaft.

⁂ WARNING

On vehicles with optional extra SA205 (automatic transmission), there is a large bore for the TDC position shortly before the special tool bore. This bore can be confused with the special tool bore.

d. If the flywheel is secured in the correct special tool bore with special tool 11 0 300, the engine can no longer be moved at the central bolt.

e. With 1st cylinder in firing TDC position, cams of inlet camshaft at 1st cylinder point upwards at an angle.

f. The timings are correct when the part numbers on the inlet and exhaust camshafts point upwards.

g. With 1st cylinder in firing TDC position, cams of exhaust camshaft at 6th cylinder point downwards at an angle.

h. Cam follower is not actuated.

➡When the engine is installed, the position of the exhaust camshaft for the timing can only be checked with a mirror.

i. Secure special tool 11 4 283 to cylinder head with bolts.

➡Fit special tool 11 4 282 underneath on side of inlet camshaft.

j. Mount special tool 11 4 281 on inlet and exhaust camshafts.

5. Remove inlet and exhaust adjustment units.

a. Remove chain tensioner.

b. Remove central bolts on inlet and exhaust adjustment units.

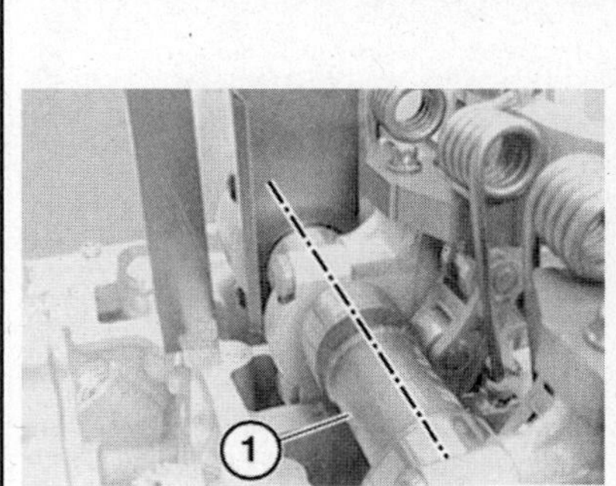

22205_BMWC_G0117

Fig. 60 With 1st cylinder in firing TDC position, cams of inlet camshaft (1) at 1st cylinder point upwards at an angle

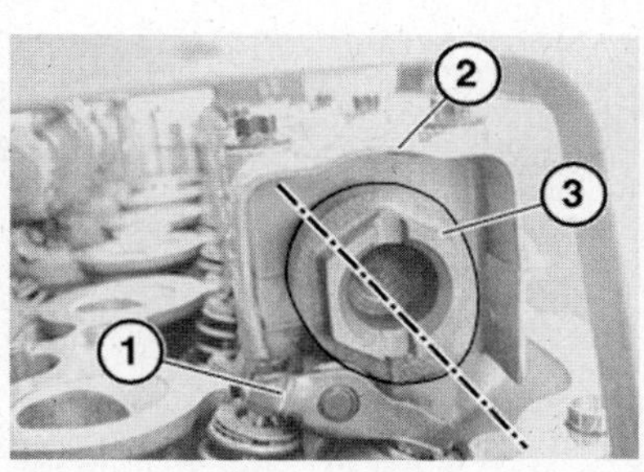

22205_BMWC_G0118

Fig. 61 With 1st cylinder in firing TDC position, cams of exhaust camshaft (3) at 6th cylinder point downwards at an angle

c. Remove exhaust adjustment unit from exhaust camshaft.

d. Remove inlet adjustment unit from inlet camshaft.

⁂ WARNING

Inlet and exhaust adjustment units are different. VANOS is marked with AUS/EX for the exhaust camshaft and EIN/IN for the inlet camshaft.

e. If necessary, move eccentric shaft on twin surface to minimum lift.

➡Oil spray nozzle must be removed from 3rd cylinder. During removal make a note of installation position of oil spray nozzle.

f. Secure special tool 11 4 270 with gripping pliers to guide block.

⁂ WARNING

Special tool 11 4 270 is only secured to guide block (2). Adjusting the gripping pliers (3) on special tool 11 4 270 is not permitted.

g. Secure both bearing pins (2) in torsion springs with knurled screw (1) of special tool 11 4 270. Press special tool 11 4 270 as far as it will go.

h. Remove screw of torsion spring.

➡To avoid jamming of screw with torsion spring, it is necessary when releasing screw to relieve the pretension on special tool 11 4 270 uniformly.

i. Relieve tension on torsion spring with special tool 11 4 270.

➡Metal lug cannot be disassembled and must not be removed.

j. Press torsion spring apart at positions. Remove torsion spring towards top.

k. Place all components in clean and neat order in special tool 11 4 481.

⁂ WARNING

All components must be reinstalled in the same positions in an engine which has already been in use.

l. Remove bolts on guide block.

m. Place all guide blocks in neat order in special tool 11 4 481.

n. Lift out intermediate rocker arms (2).

o. Place all intermediate rocker arms in neat order in special tool 11 4 481.

⁂ WARNING

All intermediate rocker arms are classified and must be reinstalled in the same positions in an engine which has already been in use.

6. Remove inlet camshaft.

➡All bearing caps are marked with numbers from 1 to 6. Bearing cap is a thrust bearing.

a. Remove bolts on bearing caps 1 to 6.

b. Set all bearing caps down in special tool 11 4 481 in a tidy and orderly fashion.

c. Remove inlet camshaft towards top.

⁂ WARNING

Markings of inlet and exhaust camshafts are different. Mixing up the inlet and exhaust camshaft will result in engine damage.

7. Remove exhaust camshaft.

a. The screw connection of the bearing banks must be Removed from the outside inwards.

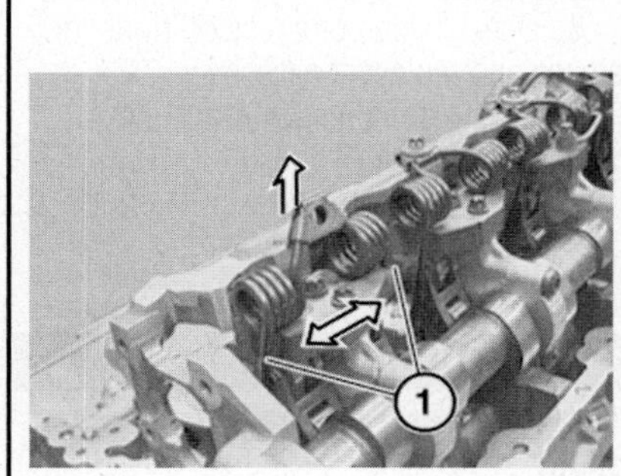

22205_BMWC_G0126

Fig. 62 Press torsion spring apart at positions (1)

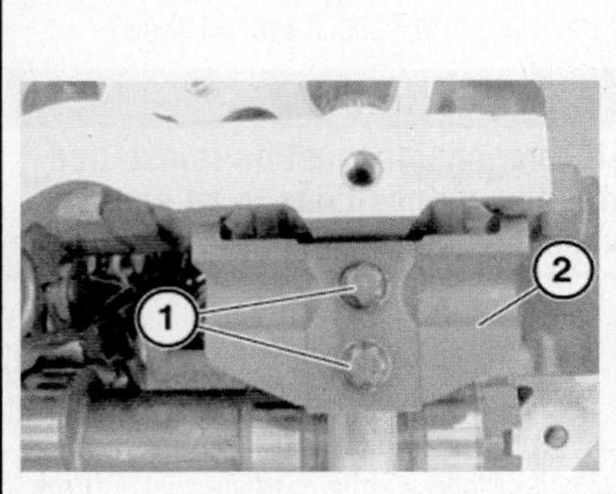

Fig. 63 Remove bolts (1) on guide block (2)

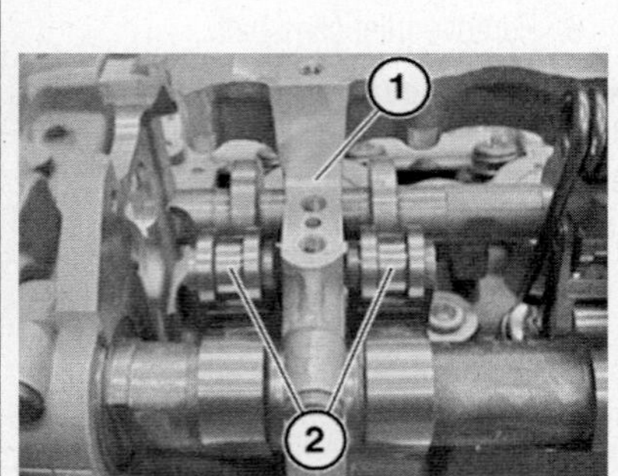

Fig. 64 Lift out intermediate rocker arms (2)

b. Lift out upper and lower bearing banks with exhaust camshaft.

c. Remove upper bearing bank.

d. Remove exhaust camshaft from lower bearing bank.

To install:

8. Check plain compression rings for damage and replace if necessary.

a. Plain compression rings are engaged at joint.

b. Press plain compression rings apart upwards and downwards and removed towards front.

WARNING

Plain compression rings can easily break.

9. Install exhaust camshaft.

a. Mounting bearing bank. Pre-install special tool 11 4 462 on cylinder no. 2.

b. Insert special tool 11 4 463 in screw connection of valve cover.

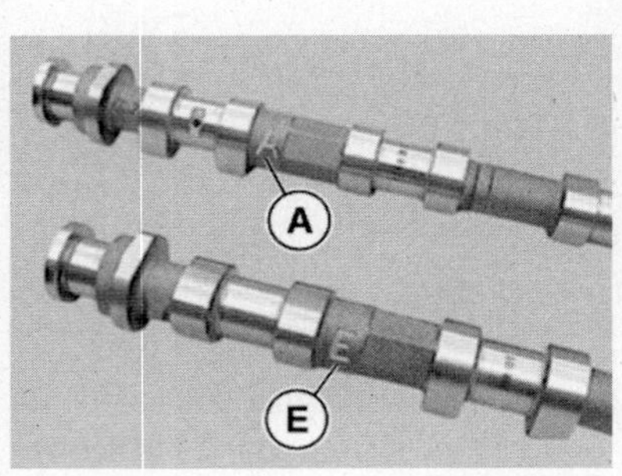

Fig. 65 Markings of inlet and exhaust camshafts are different. Mixing up the inlet (E) and exhaust (A) camshaft will result in engine damage

➡Special tool 11 4 463 is a special screw.

c. Press down cam followers on cylinder no. 2 with spindle nut of special tool 11 4 462.

d. Before mounting the exhaust camshaft on the correct cam follower seat, pay attention to the hydraulic valve clearance adjustment element and the valve.

e. Position lower bearing bank with exhaust camshaft cam followers.

f. Align exhaust camshaft so that cylinder nos. 2 and 4 are at valve overlap and the cams on cylinder No. 1 point upwards at an angle. Part number on twin surface of exhaust camshaft points upwards.

WARNING

There must be no adhesive residues in the cylinder head tapped holes.

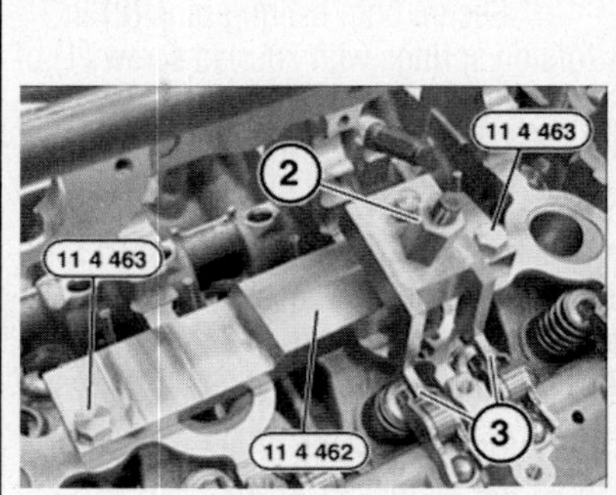

Fig. 66 Press down cam followers (3) on cylinder no. 2 with spindle nut (2) of special tool 11 4 462

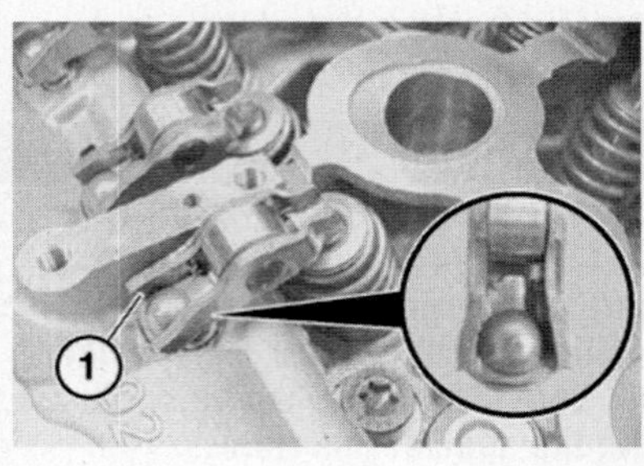

Fig. 67 Before mounting the exhaust camshaft on the correct cam follower seat (1), pay attention to the hydraulic valve clearance adjustment element and the valve

g. Clean tapped holes.

h. Fit upper bearing bank. Insert bolts dry and tension down upper bearing bank with exhaust camshaft at bearing points 3 and 5 through a½bolt turn.

i. Join exhaust camshaft to upper and lower bearing banks with torque wrench from inside outwards to 6 ft. lbs. (8 Nm).

j. Remove all bolts of upper bearing bank from outside inwards by 90°.

k. Upper and lower bearing banks must be aligned to each other at ground surfaces (1 and 2).

Make sure that the thrust piece and the legs of special tools 11 4 461 rest on the milled surfaces.

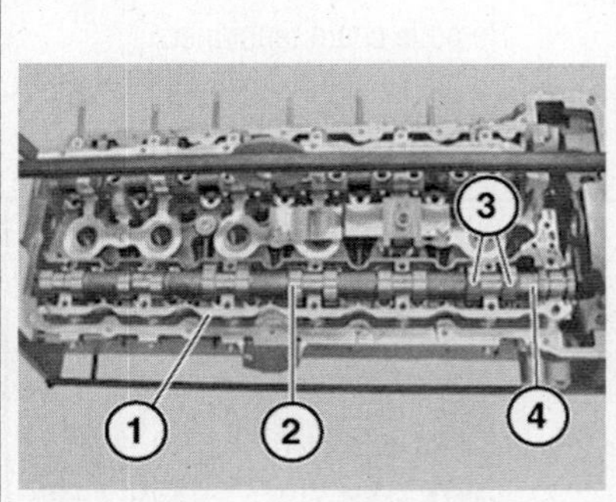

Fig. 68 Position lower bearing bank (1) with exhaust camshaft (2) cam followers. Align exhaust camshaft (2) so that cylinder nos. 2 and 4 are at valve overlap and the cams (3) on cylinder No. 1 point upwards at an angle. Part number (4) on twin surface of exhaust camshaft (2) points upwards

➡Schematic depiction of special tool 11 4 461 at upper bearing bank and lower bearing bank.

Pretension all special tools 11 4 461 with special tool 11 4 350 only.

l. Tighten screw on thrust piece to 13 inch lbs. (2 Nm).

m. Position special tool 11 4 461 over screw connection of bearing banks.

n. Make sure that the legs rest exactly on the ground surfaces of the upper bearing bank and lower bearing bank.

o. Initially tighten screw of special tool 11 4 461 to ground surfaces of upper bearing bank and lower bearing bank.

p. Tighten bolts on thrust piece to 13 inch lbs. (2 Nm).

WARNING

Set special tool 11 4 350 to 13 inch lbs. (2 Nm).

q. Pretension all special tools 11 4 461 with special tool 11 4 350 only.

r. Mount special tools 11 4 461 with screw to inside of cylinder head.

s. Mount special tool 11 4 461 with screw facing outwards on cylinder no. 2.

t. Position special tools 11 4 461 so that screw connections of bearing bank are easily accessible.

u. Insert bolts dry. Tighten upper and lower bearing banks bolts from inside outwards with special tool 00 9 120 to 6 ft. lbs. (8Nm) plus an additional 60° of rotation.

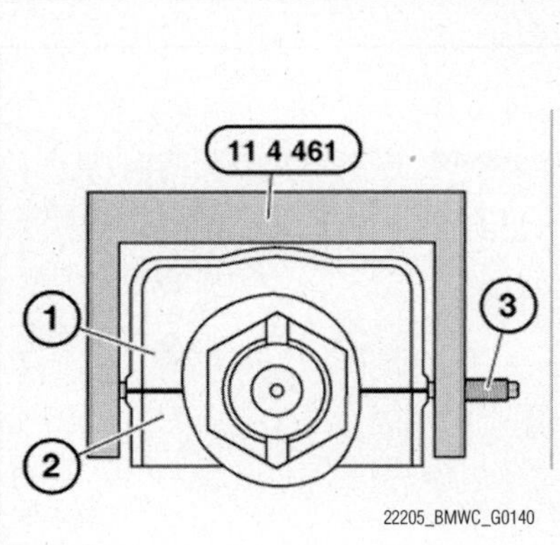

Fig. 69 Schematic depiction of special tool 11 4 461 at upper bearing bank (1) and lower bearing bank (2)

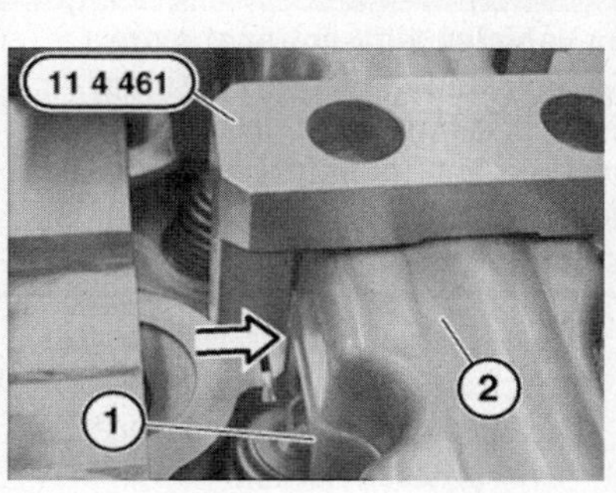

Fig. 70 Position special tool 11 4 461 over screw connection of bearing banks. Make sure that the legs rest exactly on the ground surfaces of the upper bearing bank (2) and lower bearing bank (1)

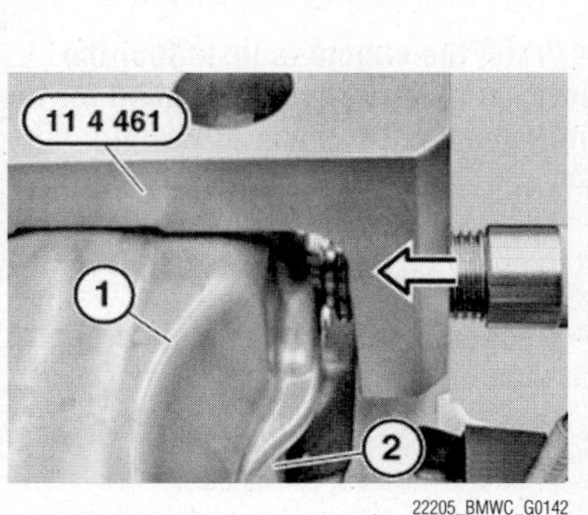

Fig. 71 Initially tighten screw of special tool 11 4 461 to ground surfaces of upper bearing bank (1) and lower bearing bank (2)

WARNING

Remove special tool 11 4 461 only when exhaust camshaft screw connection is completed.

10. Install inlet camshaft.

a. Clean all bearing points and lubricate with oil.

b. Insert inlet camshaft so that part number on twin surface points upwards.

c. Position inlet camshaft so that cams point upwards at an angle.

d. Connect special tool 11 4 281 to twin surface.

e. Tighten bearing bolts to 7 ft. lbs. (9 Nm).

11. Install intermediate prys.

a. Mixing up the guide blocks will cause the engine to suffer idle-speed fluctuations. This will result in maladjustment of uniform distribution.

b. All contact surfaces of guide block must be clean and free from oil and grease. If necessary, clean contact surfaces.

c. Mixing up the intermediate rocker arms will cause the engine to suffer idle-speed fluctuations.

d. All contact surfaces must be clean and free from oil and grease. If necessary, clean contact surfaces.

e. All intermediate rocker arms are classified and must be reinstalled in the same positions in an engine which has already been in use.

f. Before installing intermediate prys, make sure cam followers are correctly positioned.

g. Install intermediate prys.

h. Fit guide block cleanly into opening. Tighten bolts hand-tight.

i. Check that intermediate rocker arms are in correct installation position.

j. Remove bolts by a ¼ turn.

k. Secure special tool 11 4 450 to bolt connection of eccentric shaft.

l. Turn eccentric pry on special tool 11 4 450.

m. Guide block is now pre-tensioned. Insert bolts of guide blocks and tighten to 7 ft. lbs. (10 Nm).

n. At cylinder no. 3, the guide block can be pre-installed with one screw (internal) only.

o. Oil spray nozzle is fitted only after torsion spring has been installed.

p. Install torsion spring on guide block.

q. Insert torsion spring in intermediate pry.

r. Check that cam follower is in correct installation position.

s. Secure special tool 11 4 270 with gripping pliers to guide block.

➡Replace torsion spring if metal lug is faulty.

t. Secure both bearing pins in torsion springs with knurled screw of special tool 11 4 270.

u. Check torsion spring on intermediate pry to ensure correct installation position.

v. Press special tool 11 4 270 as far as it will go.

w. Insert screw of torsion spring and tighten to 7 ft. lbs. (10 Nm).

x. To avoid jamming of screw with torsion spring, it is necessary when inserting screw to increase pretension on special tool 11 4 270 uniformly.

y. Remove special tool 11 4 270.

z. At cylinder no. 3, adjust oil spray nozzle so that oil spray points precisely towards spline teeth.

aa. Insert screw with oil spray nozzle (external) and tighten to 7 ft. lbs. (10 Nm)..

12. Install inlet and exhaust adjustment units.

a. To facilitate installation of the inlet and exhaust adjustment units, turn the sensor gears at the opening downwards.

WARNING

Do not mixing up the inlet and exhaust adjustment units. VANOS is marked with AUS/EX for the exhaust camshaft and EIN/IN for the inlet camshaft. Sensor gears can be fitted alternatively.

b. Position inlet and exhaust adjustment units on camshafts.

c. Insert new central bolts but do not tighten until after valve timing is checked. Grip inlet and exhaust camshafts at dihedron when tightening. Tighten bolts to 15 ft. lbs. (20 Nm) plus an additional 180° rotation.

13. Check valve timing.

a. Install special tool 11 4 280 to secure the central bolts on the inlet and exhaust adjustment units and camshafts.

b. Press clamping rail by hand against guide rail and make sure timing chain is guided in clamping rail.

c. Rotate crankshaft at central bolt into TDC position.

d. Slide special tool 11 0 300 into special tool bore and secure crankshaft.

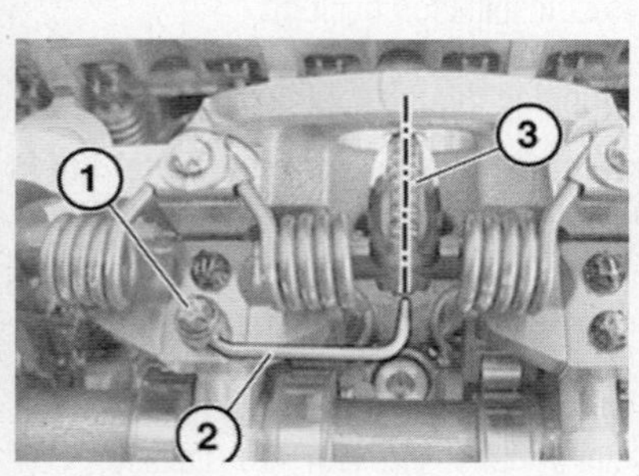

Fig. 72 At cylinder no. 3, adjust oil spray nozzle (2) so that oil spray points precisely towards spline teeth (3). Insert screw (1) with oil spray nozzle (2) (external)

WARNING

On vehicles with optional extra SA205 (automatic transmission), there is a large bore for the TDC position shortly before the special tool bore. This bore can be confused with the special tool bore.

e. If the flywheel is secured in the correct special tool bore with special tool 11 0 300, the engine can no longer be moved at the central bolt.

f. With 1st cylinder in firing TDC position, cams of inlet camshaft at 1st cylinder point upwards at an angle.

g. The timings are correct when the part numbers on the inlet and exhaust camshafts point upwards.

h. With 1st cylinder in firing TDC position, cams of exhaust camshaft at 6th cylinder point downwards at an angle.

i. Cam follower is not actuated.

➡When the engine is installed, the position of the exhaust camshaft for the timing can only be checked with a mirror.

j. Secure special tool 11 4 283 to cylinder head with bolts.

➡Fit special tool 11 4 282 underneath on side of inlet camshaft.

k. Mount special tool 11 4 281 on inlet and exhaust camshafts.

l. Make sure the chain tensioner is Removed.

m. Turn sensor gears (2) until locating pins (1) on special tool 11 4 290 match up.

n. Slide on special tool 11 4 290.

o. Secure special tool 11 4 290 with bolts (1).

p. Screw special tool 11 9 340 into cylinder head.

q. Pretension timing chain with special tool 00 9 250 to 0.6 Nm.

r. Secure both central bolts of inlet and exhaust adjustment units with special tool 00 9 120 to inlet and exhaust camshafts. Tighten bolts to 15 ft. lbs. (20 Nm) plus an additional 180° rotation.

14. Install the chain tensioner.

15. Install fastener with bore facing outwards.

N55 Engines

Exhaust

See Figures 73 through 78.

1. Remove cylinder head cover.

2. Remove all ignition coils and injector shafts.

3. Remove exhaust camshaft adjuster.

4. Adjust valve timing.

5. Position special tool 11 7 100 on cylinder 2.

6. Hand-tighten special tool 11 7 100 with special tool 11 8 552.

➡Graphic without bearing strip.

7. Screw in roller cam follower at 2nd cylinder using spindle nut of special tool 11 7 100 to end stop.

8. Release screw connection on bearing strip in sequence from 15 to 1.

9. Remove upper bearing strip (1).

➡The upper and lower bearing strips (1) can also be lifted out completely with exhaust camshaft.

10. Remove exhaust camshaft (1) from bearing strip in direction of arrow.

11. Set down exhaust camshaft (1) on special tool.

12. Marks of intake and exhaust camshafts are different.

13. Mixing up the intake and exhaust camshaft will result in engine damage.

a. A = Exhaust camshaft.

b. E = Intake camshaft

➡Plain rectangular compression rings (1) can easily break.

14. Plain rectangular compression rings (1) are engaged at joint.

15. Press plain rectangular compression rings (1) apart upwards and downwards and removed towards front.

➡When installing, modify plain rectangular compression ring on new exhaust camshaft.

16. Removal on engine:

Fig. 73 Screwing in roller cam follower at 2nd cylinder using spindle nut of special tool to end stop

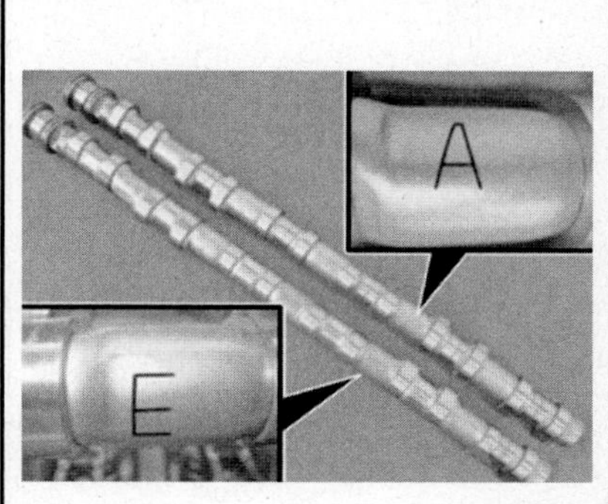

Fig. 74 Identifying intake and exhaust markers

a. Set engine to ignition TDC at cylinder No. 1.

17. Removed cylinder head:

a. When using special tool 11 9 000, it will be necessary to remove the aluminum strip.

To install:

18. Before mounting the exhaust camshaft, ensure the correct fit of the rocker arm (1) on the hydraulic valve clearance compensating element and the valve.

19. See roller cam followers.

20. Mount bearing strip.

a. Pre install special tool 11 7 100 on cylinder No. 2.

➡Special tool 11 8 552 is a special screw.

b. Press down rocker arms on cylinder No. 2 with spindle nut of special tool 11 7 100.

21. Insert exhaust camshaft so that none of the latching mechanisms for the plain rectangular compression rings (1) point to a bearing cap joint.

22. Centre latch mechanism of the plain rectangular compression rings with the bearing cap.

23. Insert exhaust camshaft so that the data code (1) on the mounting flats faces up.

➡Graphic of intake camshaft.

24. The cam (1) at cylinder 6 points downward at an angle.

WARNING

There must be no oil residues in the cylinder head threaded holes.

WARNING

Clean threaded holes.

25. Fit upper bearing strip (1).

26. Insert bolts dry.

27. Join exhaust camshaft to lower and upper bearing strips (1) with torque wrench (2) to 8 Nm in sequential order from 1 to 15.

28. Release all screws of upper bearing strip (1) from outside inwards by 90°.

➡Upper and lower bearing strips must be aligned to each other at ground surfaces (1 and 2).

29. Make sure that the synchronizing key and the shanks of special tools 11 4 461 rest on the milled surfaces.

➡Schematic diagram of special tool 11 8 553 at upper bearing strip (1) and lower bearing strip (2).

➡Preload all special tools 11 8 553with special tool 11 4 350 only.

WARNING

Tighten screw (3) on synchronizing key to 2 Nm.

30. Position special tool 11 8 553 over screw connection of bearing strips.

31. Make sure that the shanks rest exactly on the ground surfaces of the upper bearing strip (2) and lower bearing strip (1).

32. Initially tighten screw of special tool 11 8 553 to ground surfaces of upper bearing strip (1) and lower bearing strip (2).

WARNING

Tighten screws on synchronizing key to 2 Nm.

Fig. 75 Ensuring correct fit of the rocker arm (1)

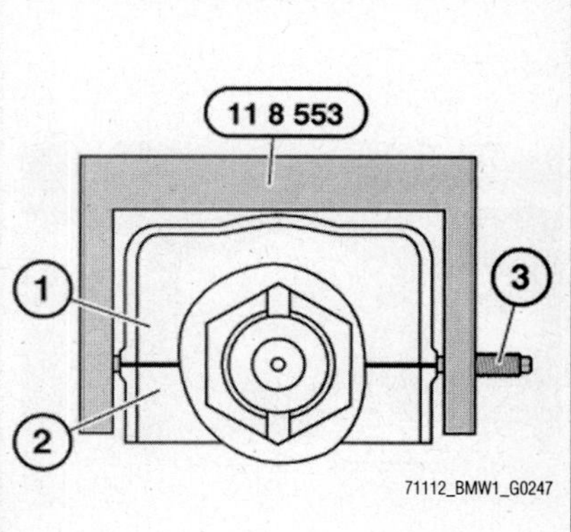

Fig. 76 Identifying upper (1) and lower (2) bearing strip with special tools and screw (3)

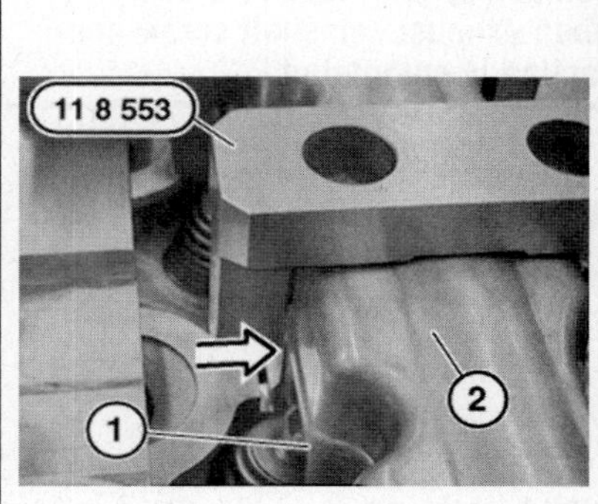

Fig. 77 Making sure shanks rest exactly on ground surfaces of the upper (2) and lower (1) bearing strip

WARNING

Set special tool 11 8 553 to 2 Nm.

WARNING

Preload all special tools 11 8 553 with special tool 11 4 350 only.

33. Mount special tools 11 8 553 to inside of cylinder head with pressure bolt.

34. Mount special tool 11 8 553 on cylinder no. 2 with pressure bolt facing outward.

35. Position special tools 11 8 553 so that screw connections (2) of bearing strip are easily accessible.

36. Tighten top and bottom bearing strip with special tool 00 9 120.

a. Tightening torque: 71 inch lbs. (8 Nm) + 60°

Fig. 78 Tightening bearing strips

WARNING

Remove special tool 11 8 553 only when exhaust camshaft screw connection is completed.

37. Assemble engine.

INTAKE

See Figures 79 through 84.

1. Remove cylinder head cover.
2. Remove intake adjuster.
3. Remove intermediate lever.
4. Adjust valve timing.

➡All bearing caps are identified with numbers from 1 to 6.

5. The front bearing cap is a thrust bearing and does not have an identification.
6. Release screws on thrust bearing cover.
7. Release screws on all bearing caps 1 to 6.
8. Set all bearing caps down in special tool 11 4 481 in a neat and orderly fashion.
9. Remove intake camshaft (2) towards top.

➡When installing, clean all bearing positions and lubricate with oil.

10. Check plain rectangular compression rings (1) for damage.

WARNING

Plain rectangular compression rings (1) can easily break.

11. Plain rectangular compression rings (1) are engaged at joint.
12. Press plain rectangular compression rings (1) apart upwards and downwards and removed towards front.

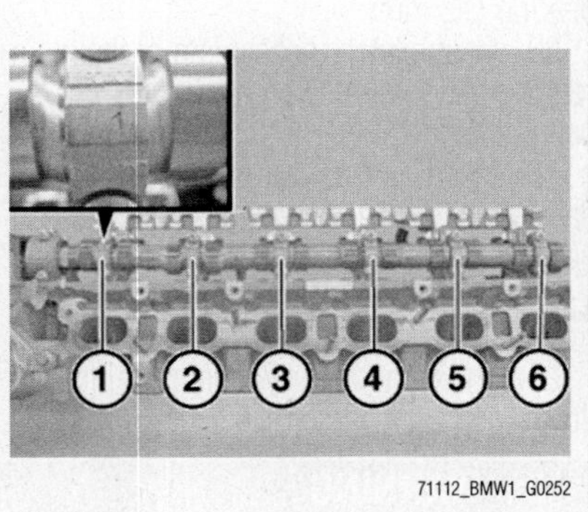

Fig. 79 Releasing screws on bearing caps 1-6

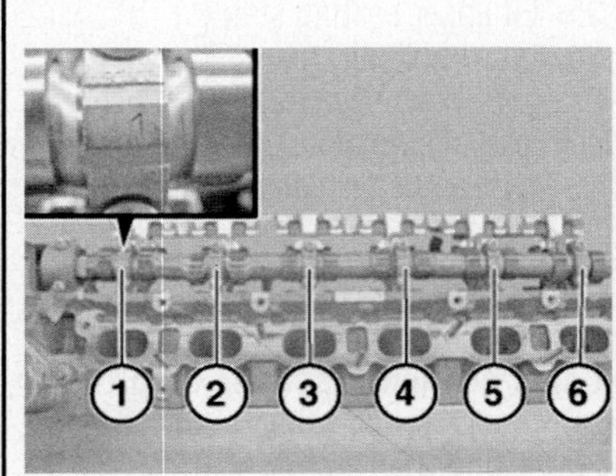

Fig. 80 Removing intake camshaft (2) and checking plain rectangular compression rings (1)

➡When installing, install plain rectangular compression ring on new intake camshaft.

13. Marks of intake and exhaust camshafts are different.
14. Mixing up the intake and exhaust camshaft will result in engine damage.
    a. A: Exhaust camshaft.
    b. E: Intake camshaft
15. Install intake camshaft so that the latch mechanism of the plain rectangular compression rings (1) does not point to a contact point of the bearing cap
16. Centre latch mechanism of the plain rectangular compression rings with the bearing cap.

➡Image of the exhaust camshaft.

17. Insert intake camshaft so that data code on mounting flats points upwards.
18. Position intake camshaft (1) so that cams point upwards at an angle and to the left.

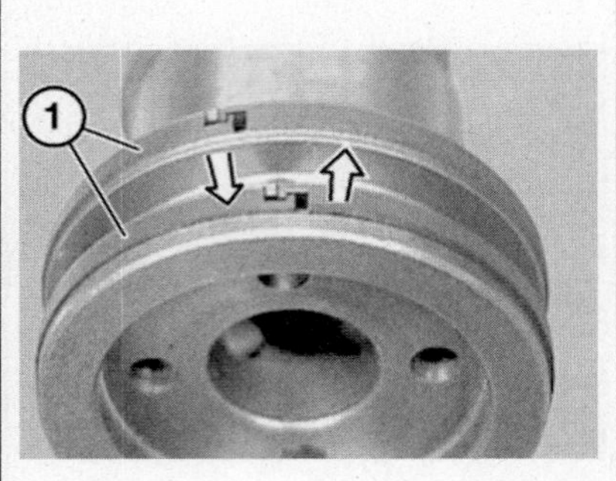

Fig. 81 Pressing plain rectangular compression rings (1) apart upwards and downwards and removing towards front

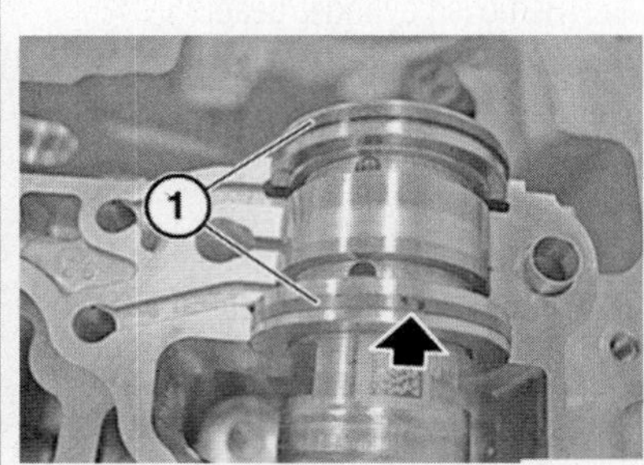

Fig. 82 Installing intake camshaft so that the latch mechanism of the plain rectangular compression rings (1) does not point to a contact point of the bearing cap

➡All bearing caps are identified with numbers from 1 to 6.

19. The front bearing cap is a thrust bearing and does not have an identification.
20. Insert screws on all bearing caps 1 to 6.
21. Insert screws on thrust bearing cover.
    a. Tightening torque: 75 inch lbs. (8.5 Nm).
22. Assemble engine.

CRANKSHAFT FRONT SEAL

REMOVAL & INSTALLATION

See Figures 85 through 89.

1. Before servicing the vehicle, refer to the precautions.
2. Remove crankshaft damper

WARNING

Do not Remove central bolt. If the central bolt is Removed, the sprocket

71112_BMW1_G0256

Fig. 83 Positioning intake camshaft (1)

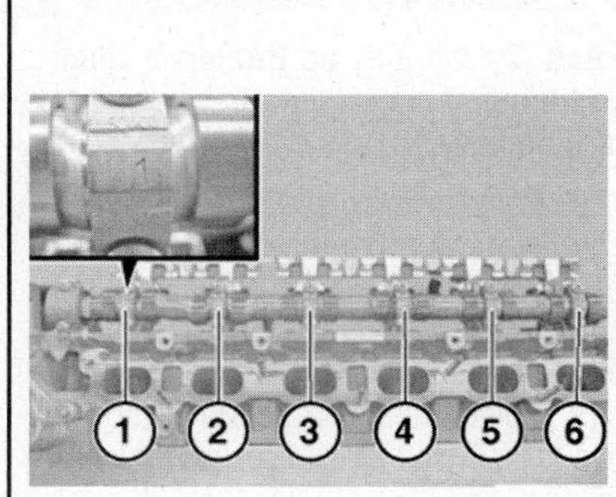

71112_BMW1_G0257

Fig. 84 Installing bearing caps in order 1-6

wheels of the timing chain and the oil pump will no longer be non-positively connected to the crankshaft. Inlet and exhaust camshafts can turn in relation to crankshaft.

3. Turn back special tool 11 9 222.
4. Push special tool 11 9 221 onto crankshaft.

➡When bolts are tightened down (special tool 11 9 224), crankshaft seal is pressed inwards approximately 1 mm and thus slackened for subsequent removal.

5. Insert bolts (special tool 11 9 224) and tighten down to approximately 15 ft. lbs. (20 Nm).
6. Screw special tool 11 0 371 to 59 ft. lbs. (80 Nm) into crankshaft seal.
7. Screw in spindle 11 0 372.
8. Remove crankshaft seal from housing.

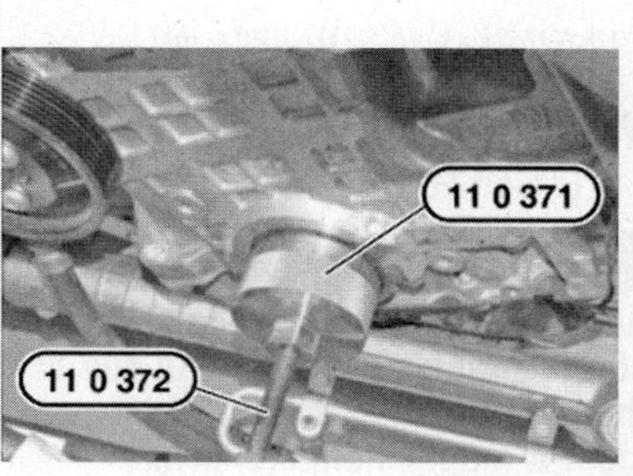

22205_BMWC_G0146

Fig. 85 Screw special tool 11 0 371 to 59 ft. lbs. (80 Nm) into crankshaft seal. Screw in spindle 11 0 372.

➡Repeat the operation several times if necessary.

9. Carefully saw open crankshaft seal at cutting line.
10. Remove crankshaft seal from special tool 11 0 371.

To install:

WARNING

The following text describes installation and sealing between the engine block and crankshaft seal.

The engine block will not be leak proof at the outside of the crankshaft seal if you fail to comply with the individual work steps and the work sequence.

11. Clean sealing surface and degrease thoroughly in area of housing partition.
12. Apply a light coat of oil to running surface of crankshaft seal.

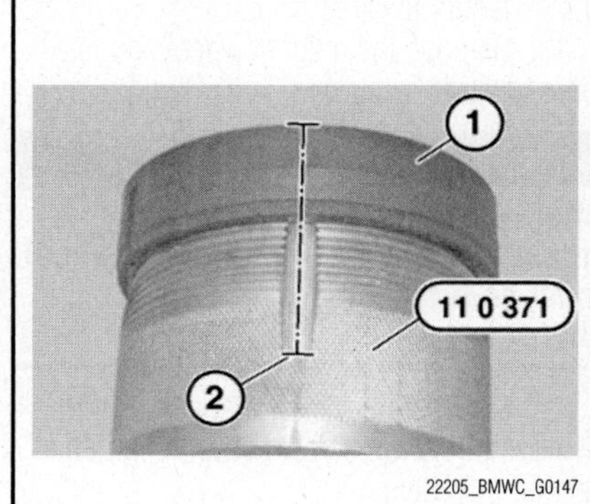

22205_BMWC_G0147

Fig. 86 Carefully saw open crankshaft seal (1) at cutting line (2)

13. Screw special tool 11 9 232 with bolts (special tool 11 9 234) to crankshaft.

➡Support sleeve is supplied with crankshaft seal.

14. When crankshaft seal is installed, only support sleeve may be used as a slip sleeve.
15. Crankshaft seal has a groove on both left and right sides.

WARNING

After installation, the grooves must be filled with sealing compound.

➡The required parts are available from the BMW Parts Service.

16. Remove screw caps from injector.
17. Screw on metering needle.
18. Insert piston for pressing out. Injector contains the sealing compound Loctite, manufacturer's number 128357. Bottle contains the primer Loctite, manufacturer's number 171000.
19. Push support sleeve with crankshaft seal onto special tool 11 9 232.

WARNING

Support sleeve remains on special tool 11 9 232, until crankshaft seal is drawn in.

20. Align groove centrally to housing partition.
21. Coat both grooves on crankshaft seal with Loctite primer, manufacturer's number 171000, and expose to air for approximately one minute.
22. Draw in crankshaft seal with special tool 11 9 231 in conjunction with special tool 11 9 233 until flush.
23. Before filling with sealing compound, moisten brush with Loctite primer, manufacturer's number 171000. Insert brush as far as possible into grooves on crankshaft seal in order to coat housing partition on engine block.
24. Using injector, fill both grooves flush with Loctite® sealing compound, manufacturer's number 128357.

➡Loctite® primer, manufacturer's number 171000, binds the Loctite sealing compound, manufacturer's number 128357, and prevents leakage.

25. Coat surface of sealing compound in both grooves with Loctite® primer, manufacturer's number 171000.
26. Install crankshaft damper.

Fig. 87 Draw in crankshaft seal with special tool 11 9 231 in conjunction with special tool 11 9 233 until flush

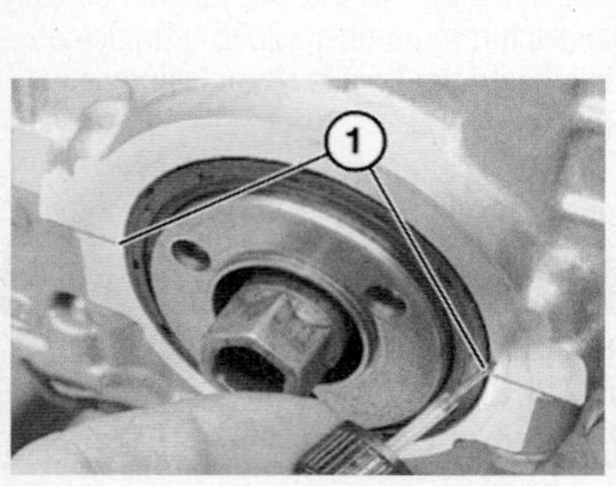

Fig. 88 Insert brush as far as possible into grooves (1) on crankshaft seal in order to coat housing partition on engine block

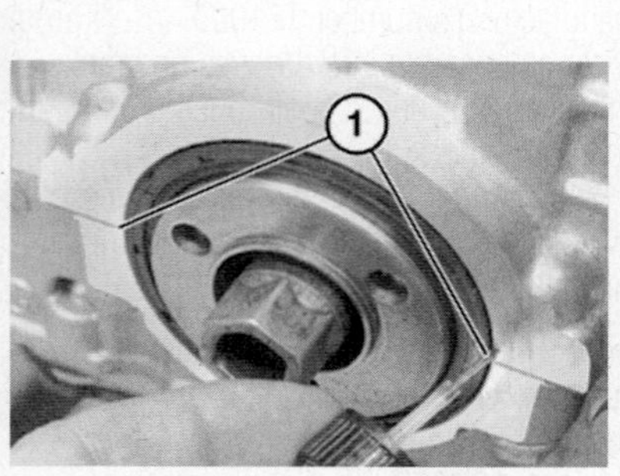

Fig. 89 Using injector (2), fill both grooves (3) flush with Loctite sealing compound, manufacturer's number 128357

CYLINDER HEAD

REMOVAL & INSTALLATION

N51, N52 and N54 Engines

See Figures 90 through 94.

WARNING

Aluminum-magnesium material. No steel fasteners may be used due to the threat of electrochemical corrosion. A magnesium crankcase requires aluminum fasteners exclusively. Aluminum fasteners must be replaced each time they are removed. The end faces of aluminum fasteners are painted blue for purposes of identification. Torque specifications and torque angles must be observed for risk of damage.

1. Before servicing the vehicle, refer to the precautions.
2. Drain the cooling system.
3. Drain the engine oil.
4. Relieve the fuel system pressure.
5. Remove the exhaust system.
6. Remove the exhaust manifolds.
7. Remove the intake manifold.
8. Remove the coolant hoses from cylinder head.
9. Remove the valve cover.
10. Remove the inlet and exhaust adjustment unit.

WARNING

If the timing chain is stored in the gear case, the crankshaft must not be rotated. Only during assembly can the timing chain be lifted out.

11. Remove the timing chain module and fasteners.
12. Remove the eccentric shaft sensor and fasteners towards front.
13. Remove the magnet wheel and fastener towards front.

WARNING

After removing, secure magnet wheel in a plastic bag. Magnet wheel must be protected against metal chips.

14. Pretension eccentric shaft upwards. Remove mini stop screw between first and second cylinders

WARNING

Secure bolt (2) with a gripper against falling down.

Fig. 90 Remove bolts (2) for eccentric shaft sensor (1)

15. Remove and discard bolt (2).

➡Bolt (2) can only be Removed when the timing chain module is pressed forward slightly.

16. Remove and discard bolts (1).
17. Remove and discard M10 cylinder head bolts (1) with special tool 11 8 580.
18. Remove and discard M9 cylinder head bolts (2) with special tool 11 4 420.
19. Remove and discard M9 cylinder head bolts (1 and 3) with special tool 11 4 420.
20. Remove and discard M10 cylinder head bolts (2) with special tool 11 8 580 from outside inwards.

WARNING

All cylinder head bolts must be replaced.

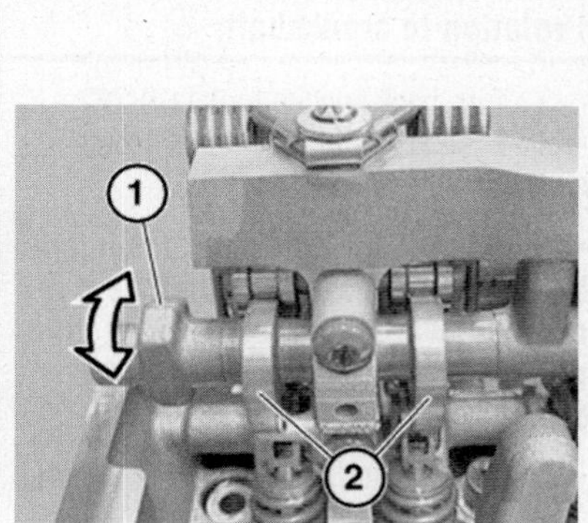

Fig. 91 Pretension eccentric shaft (1) upwards. Remove stop screw between 1st and 2nd cylinders (2)

21. Secure special tool 11 0 320 with existing valve cover bolts (1). Tighten to 7 ft. lbs. (9 Nm).

⁂ WARNING

Do not rest cylinder head on sealing surface.

22. Insert special tool 11 4 430 into bores.

To install:

Install bolts 1-10 with special tool No. 115190. Install bolts 11-14 with special tool No. 114420.

Torque following the tightening sequence as follows:

- Step 1: Tighten bolts 1-14 to 22 ft. lbs. (30 Nm)
- Step 2: Tighten bolts 1-14 an additional 90 degrees
- Step 3: Tighten bolts 1-10 an additional 90 degrees
- Step 4: Tighten bolts 1-14 an additional 45 degrees

23. The balance of installation is the reverse of the removal procedure.
24. Fill the cooling system.
25. Start the engine and check for leaks.

N55 Engines

See Figures 95 through 101.

⁂ WARNING

Fit new cylinder head bolts.

⁂ WARNING

Do not wash off bolt coating.

⁂ WARNING

Lightly oil washer on the contact surfaces (both sides).

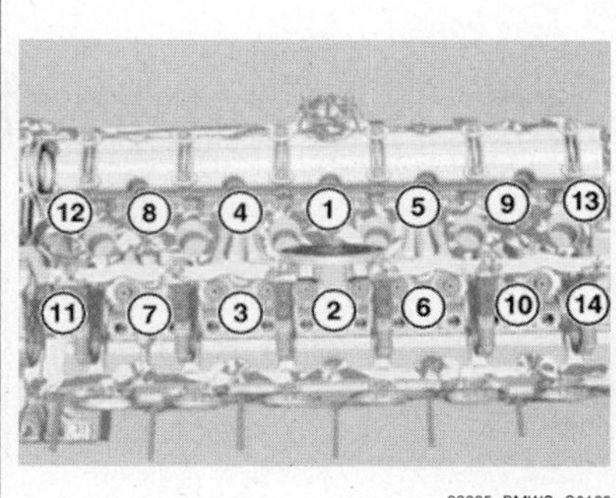

Fig. 93 Cylinder head bolt torque sequence—N52 engine

⁂ WARNING

There must be no coolant, water or engine oil in the blind holes.

1. Remove exhaust system.
2. Drain coolant.
3. Drain engine oil.
4. Remove engine.
5. Mount engine on assembly stand.
6. Remove intake plenum.
7. Remove exhaust turbocharger with integrated exhaust manifold.
8. Detach coolant hoses from cylinder head.
9. Remove intake and exhaust camshaft adjusters.

➡If the timing chain is stowed in the gear case, the crankshaft must no longer be rotated.

10. Release screws (1).
11. Unclip timing chain module (2) at separation point (3) and remove towards top.

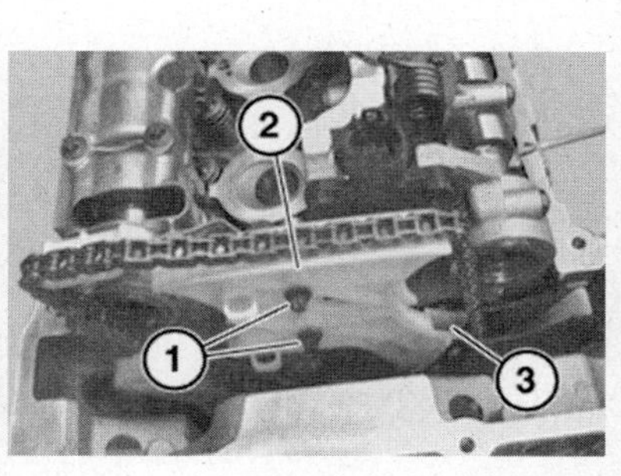

Fig. 95 Releasing screws (1), unclipping timing chain module (2) at separation point (3) and removing towards top

12. Set down timing chain.

➡Graphic shows N52.

➡Bolt (2) can only be released when the timing chain module is pressed forward slightly.

13. Release screws (1).
    a. Tightening torque: 16 ft. lbs. (22 Nm).
14. Release screw (2).
    a. Tightening torque: 16 ft. lbs. (22 Nm).
15. Release cylinder head bolts in sequence 14 to 11 with special tool 11 4 420.
16. Release cylinder head bolts in sequence 10 to 1 with special tool 11 8 580.

➡Picture shows intermediate lever and exhaust camshaft removed.

17. Secure special tool 11 0 320 with bolts (1).

Fig. 92 Insert special tool 11 4 430 into bores.

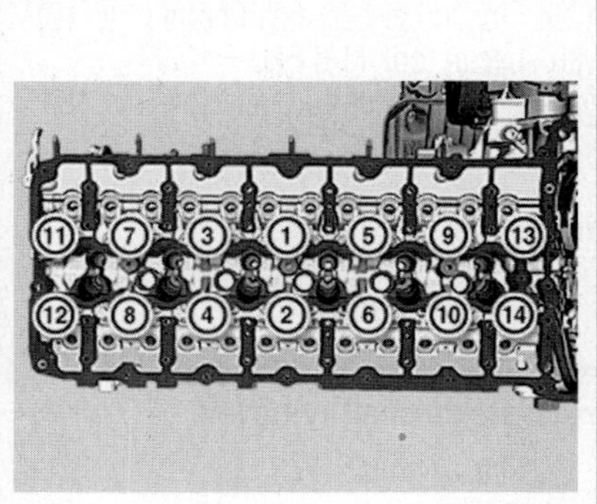

Fig. 94 Cylinder head bolt torque sequence—N54 engine

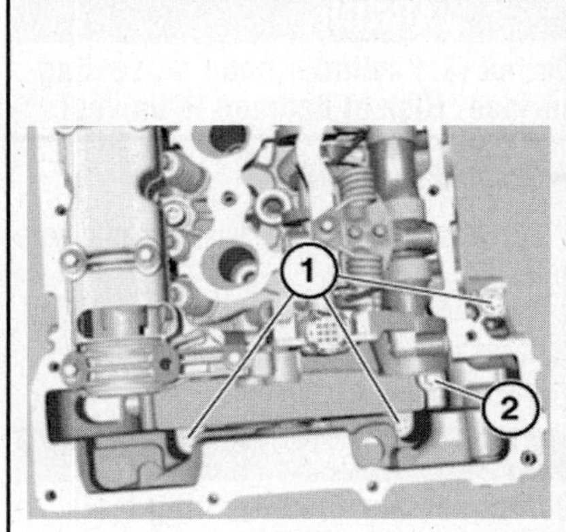

Fig. 96 Releasing screws (1 and 2)

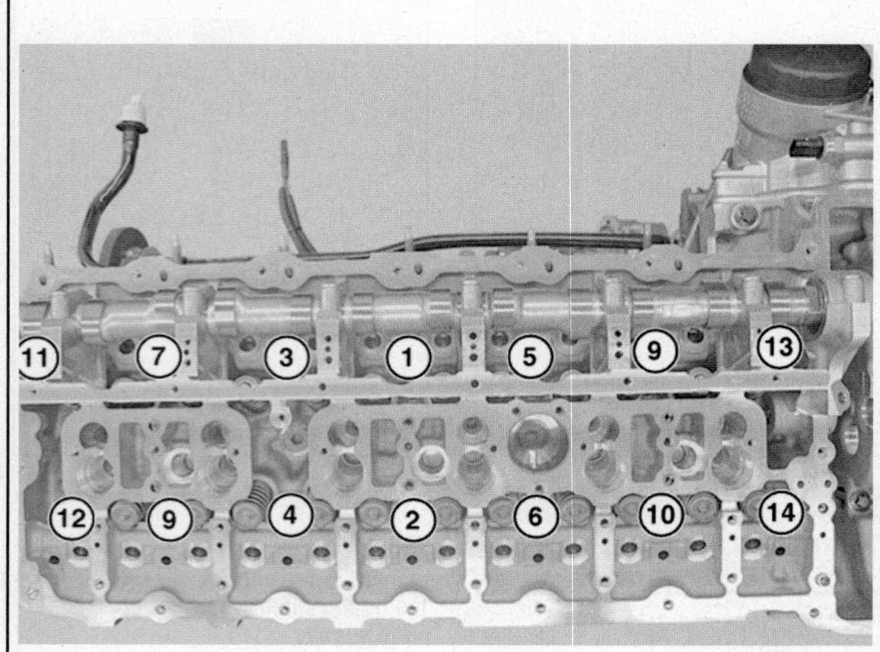

Fig. 97 Releasing cylinder head bolts in sequence 14-11 with special tool 11 4 420 and 10-1 with special tool 11 8 580

a. Tightening torque: 75 inch lbs. (8.5 Nm)

⁂ CAUTION

Removing and install cylinder head with a second person helping.

⁂ WARNING

Weight of cylinder head with add-on parts is approx. 40 kg.

⁂ WARNING

Do not rest cylinder head on sealing surface. Risk of damage to valves!

➡Graphic shows N52.

18. Insert 11 4 430 special tool into bore holes.
19. Remove coarse residues on sealing surfaces with special tool 11 4 471 from cylinder head and crankcase.

⁂ WARNING

Do not use any metal-cutting tools.

20. Remove fine residues on sealing surfaces with special tool 11 4 472 from cylinder head and crankcase.

⁂ WARNING

Do not use any metal-cutting tools.

⁂ WARNING

There must be no coolant, water or engine oil in the pocket holes.

21. Clean all blind holes.

To install:

22. Replace cylinder head gasket.
23. Fit new cylinder head bolts.
24. Insert cylinder head bolts (1 to 10) with special tool 11 8 580.
    a. Tightening torque: 22 ft. lbs. (30 Nm) + 90° + 180°.
25. Insert cylinder head bolts (11 to 14) with special tool 11 4 420.
    a. Tightening torque: 22 ft. lbs. (30 Nm) + 90° + 180°.

➡Picture shows intermediate lever and exhaust camshaft removed.

26. Insert bolts (1).
    a. Tightening torque: 16 ft. lbs. (22 Nm).
27. Insert bolt (2).
    a. Tightening torque: 16 ft. lbs. (22 Nm).
28. Assemble engine.

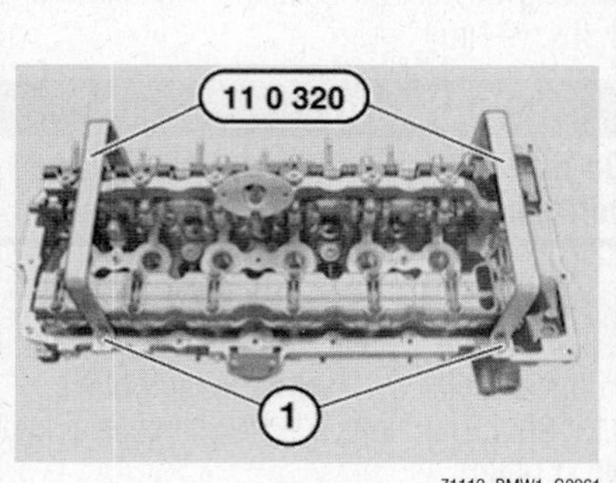

Fig. 98 Securing special tool with bolts (1) and removing cylinder head

Fig. 99 Inserting 11 4 430 special tool into bore holes

EXHAUST MANIFOLD

REMOVAL & INSTALLATION

N51 Engine

Front

See Figure 102.

1. Remove rear exhaust manifold.

➡The oxygen sensors are in danger of being damaged when the exhaust manifolds are removed and installed.

2. Remove control sensor from cylinders 1 to 3.
3. Remove monitor sensor from cylinders 1 to 3.
4. Unscrew nuts.
5. Remove exhaust manifold (1).

➡When installing, clean sealing faces and replace seals.

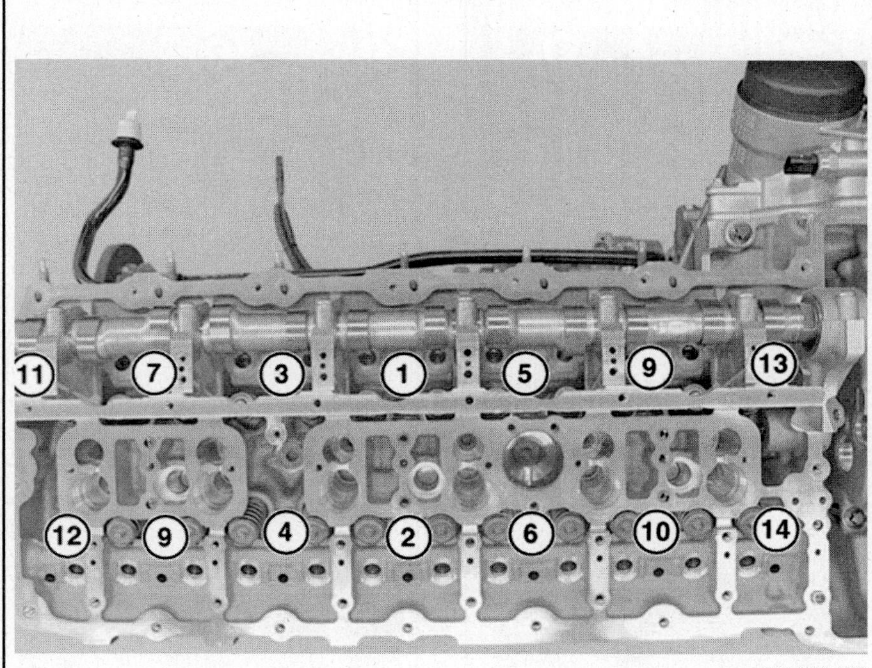

Fig. 100 Inserting cylinder head bolts (1-10) with special tool and tightening and then inserting cylinder head bolts (11-14) and tightening

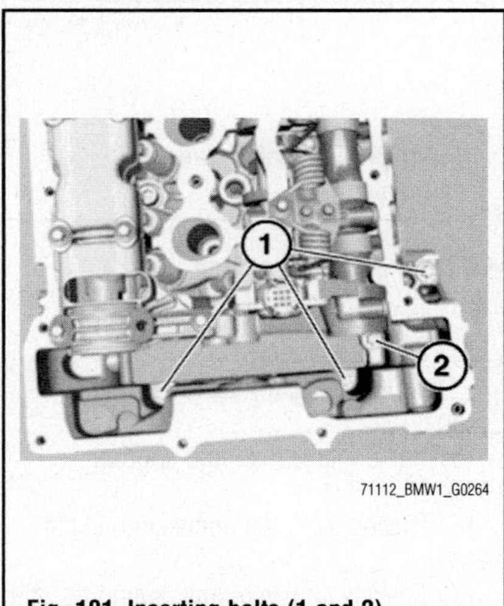

Fig. 101 Inserting bolts (1 and 2)

6. Replace nuts.
   a. Tightening torque: 15 ft. lbs. (20 Nm).

To install:

To install, reverse the removal procedure.

7. Check exhaust system for leaks.

Rear

See Figure 103.

1. Remove front underbody protection.

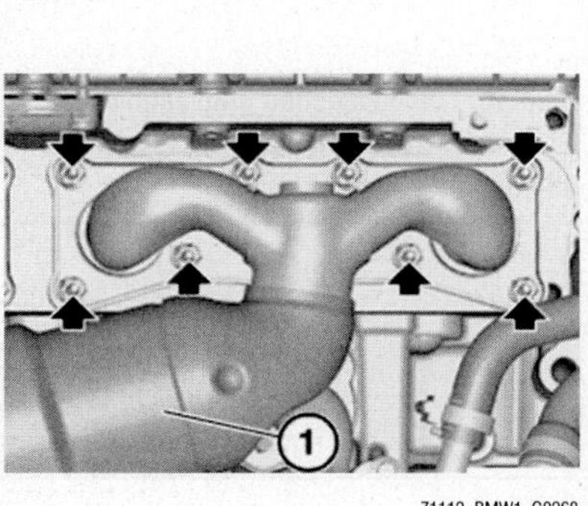

Fig. 102 Removing front exhaust manifold (1)

2. Remove rear underbody protection.
3. Remove complete exhaust system.
4. Remove lower section of microfilter housing.
5. Remove acoustic cover.

➡The oxygen sensors are in danger of being damaged when the exhaust manifolds are removed and installed.

6. Remove control sensor from cylinders 4 to 6.

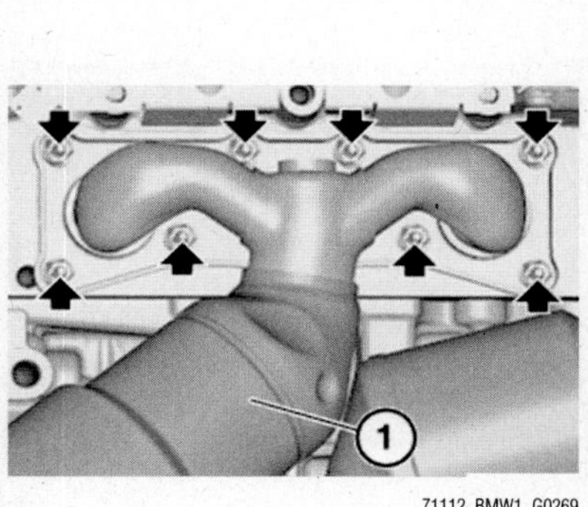

Fig. 103 Removing rear exhaust manifold (1)

7. Remove monitor sensor from cylinders 4 to 6.
8. Unscrew nuts.
9. Remove exhaust manifold (1).

➡When installing, clean sealing faces and replace seals.

10. Replace nuts.
    a. Tightening torque: 15 ft. lbs. (20 Nm).

To install:

To install, reverse the removal procedure.

11. Check exhaust system for leaks.

N52 Engine

See Figures 104 and 105.

1. Before servicing the vehicle, refer to the precautions.
2. Remove the ignition coil cover.
3. Remove the coolant expansion tank.
4. Remove the underbody protection.
5. Remove the complete exhaust system.

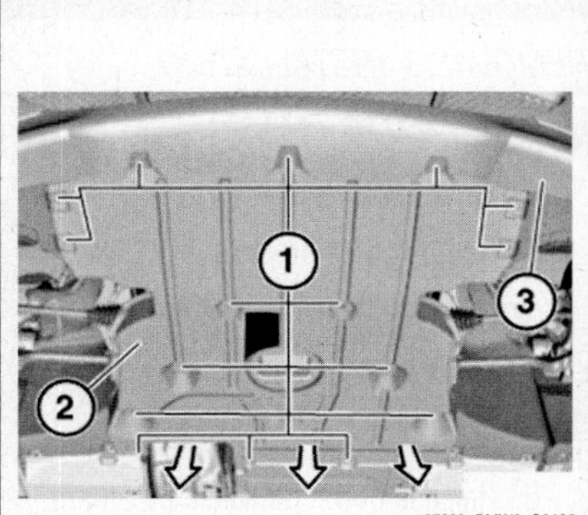

Fig. 104 Release screws (1) and pull underbody protection (2) forward under bumper trim (3)

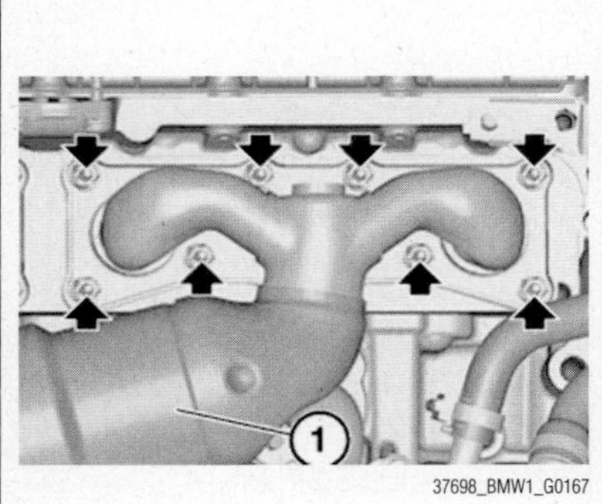

Fig. 105 Exhaust manifold (1) fastener locations (arrows)

6. Remove the oxygen sensor plug from cylinders number 4 and 6 and remove the exhaust assembly.
7. Remove the manifold for cylinders number 1 and 3 downwards.
8. Remove the manifold for cylinders number 4 and 6 downwards.

To install:

9. Remove the old gasket from the cylinder head and exhaust manifold and replace the gasket. The gasket beads face the exhaust manifolds.
10. Installation is the reverse of removal.
11. Coat screw connections with CRC copper paste.
12. Install new nuts and tighten the exhaust manifolds to 15 ft. lbs. (20 Nm).

N54 and N55 Engines

The N54 and N55 exhaust manifold is an integral part of the turbocharger assembly and is not serviced separately.

INTAKE MANIFOLD

REMOVAL & INSTALLATION

N51 Engine

See Figures 106 through 110.

1. Remove tension strut.
2. Remove suction filter housing.
3. Remove engine cover.
4. Open holder (2).
5. Disconnect plug connection (1) under manifold.
6. Release both crankcase breathers (3).
7. Disconnect plug connection (1).
8. Disconnect plug connection (3).
9. Release bolts (4).
10. Detach engine wiring harness (2) from manifold and lay to one side.

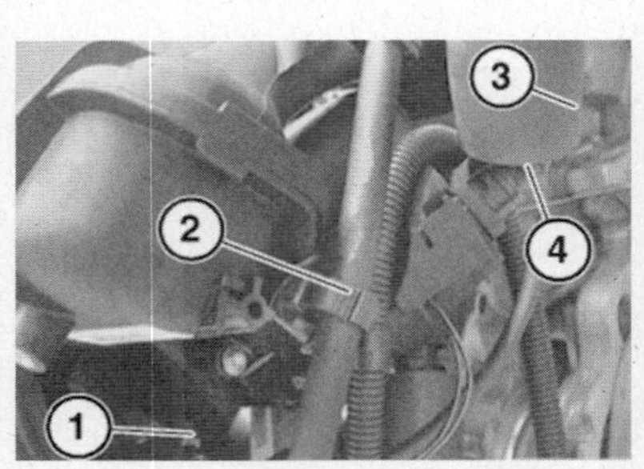

Fig. 106 Opening holder (2), disconnecting plug connection (1) and releasing both crankcase breathers (3)

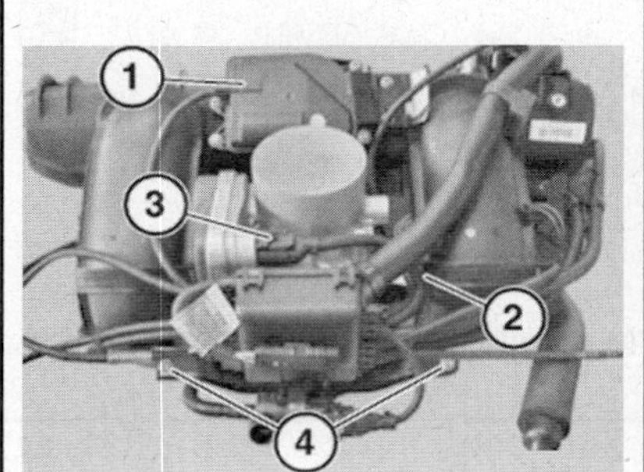

Fig. 107 Disconnecting plug connections (1 and 3), releasing bolts (4) and detaching engine wiring harness (3)

11. Disconnect plug connection (1) on oil pressure switch.
12. Release fuel rail (2) and lay to one side.

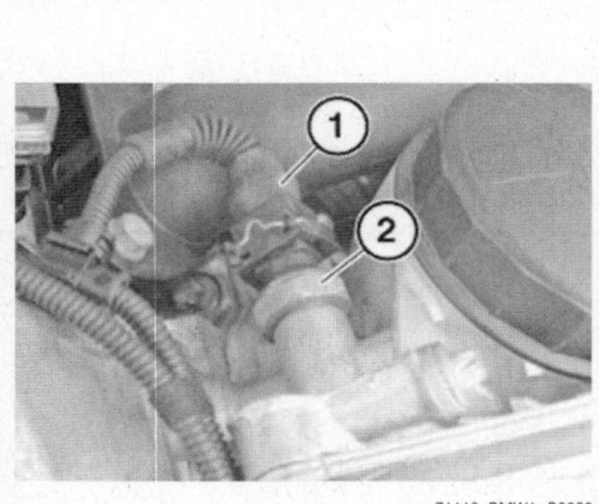

Fig. 108 Disconnecting plug connection (1) on oil pressure switch

Fig. 109 Releasing fuel rail (2) and screw (1) and unscrewing nuts (3)

Fig. 110 Disconnecting plug connection (1)

➡Do not detach fuel line.

13. Release screw (1).
14. Unscrew nuts (3).
    a. Tightening torque: 11 ft. lbs. (15 Nm).
15. Raise intake manifold approx. 10 cm.
16. Disconnect plug connection (1) at bottom.
17. Release tank vent line behind throttle valve assembly.

To install:

To install, reverse the removal procedure.

➡Replace all seals.

N52 Engine

See Figures 111 through 119.

1. Before servicing the vehicle, refer to the precautions.
2. Remove the tension strut.

⁂ WARNING

Driving without the tension strut is not permitted as otherwise the body may be damaged. Tension strut screws must be tightened to torque and then tightened down with special tool 00 9 120.

⁂ WARNING

Catch and seal of cover must not be damaged. Even a minimally damaged cover may result in water leaking in; if necessary, replace cover.

a. Remove cover and release screw underneath.

b. Version 1: Turn cover (with notch) approximately 45° counterclockwise

c. Version 2: Snap out cover (without notch) in upward direction

⁂ WARNING

Grommet must not be pulled out of bulkhead because this eliminates the possibility of correct feeding in when installed.

d. Release screw.

e. Grip grommet and pull out tension strut in direction of arrow.

3. Remove intake filter housing.
4. Remove ignition coil cover.
5. Disconnect vacuum lines as shown
6. Unscrew nuts.
7. Place oil reservoir in direction of arrow to one side.
8. Release rubber holders from guide.
9. Disconnect plug connection.
10. Unclip line from line holder.
11. Open cable duct.
12. Expose lines.
13. Lay cable duct (upper and lower sections) to one side.

➡The lines shown do not have to be detached in order to remove the air intake manifold.

14. Unfasten hose clip.
15. Detach clean-air gaiter at position in direction of arrow and remove.
16. Disconnect plug connection.

⁂ WARNING

Cover fitting with suitable apparatus to prevent objects getting into it.

17. Release screw.
18. Unclip fuel line at position from holder.

1. Line
2. Line
3. Line
4. Cable duct

37698_BMW1_G0171

Fig. 111 These lines do not have to be detached in order to remove the air intake manifold

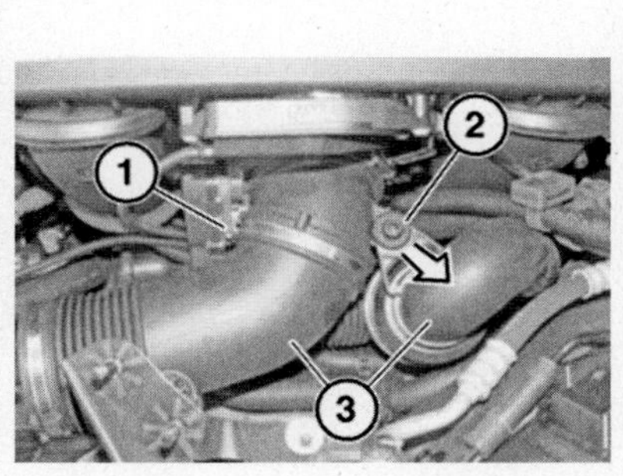

37698_BMW1_G0172

Fig. 112 Unfasten hose clip (1), detach clean-air gaiter (3) at position (2) in direction of arrow and remove

19. Disconnect plug connection and lay to one side.
20. Unclip lines at positions.
21. Remove plug connections.

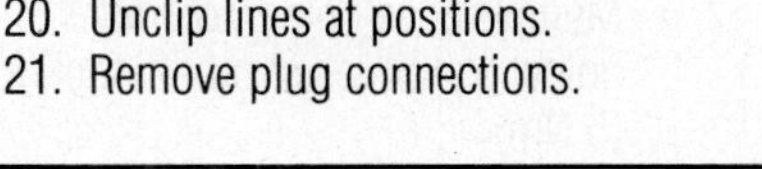

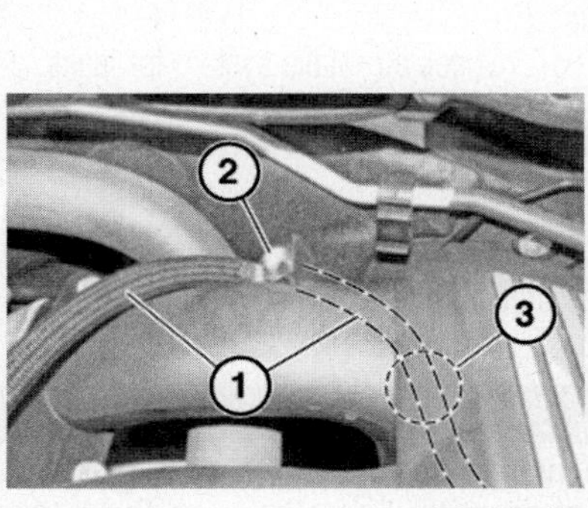

37698_BMW1_G0174

Fig. 113 Release screw (2) and unclip fuel line (1) at position (3) from holder.

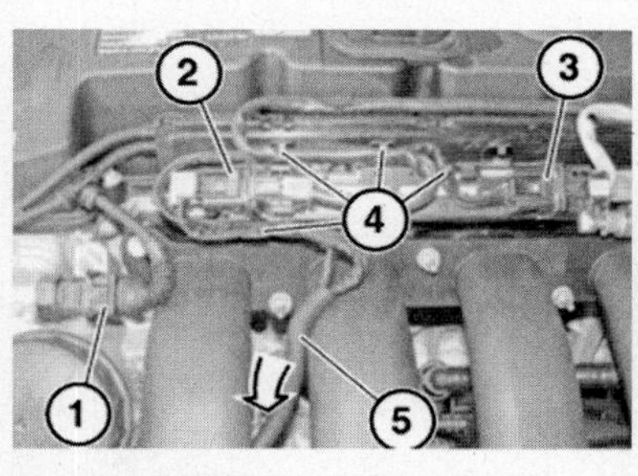

1. Plug connection
2. Plug connection
3. Plug connection
4. Line clips
5. Lines

37698_BMW1_G0175

Fig. 114 Disconnect plug connection, unclip lines and lay both lines between intake ducts (direction of arrow) downwards

22. Lay both lines between intake ducts (direction of arrow) downwards.
23. Release screws (1).
24. Lay cable duct (2) with bracket (3) and engine wiring harness to one side.
25. Unfasten intake manifold screws and nuts as shown.
26. Expose air intake manifold in following work steps, as shown:

a. Raise air intake manifold approximately 2–4 In. (5–10 cm).

b. Turn air intake manifold at front through 45°.

➡The following plug connections and connections are located below the intake ducts.

27. Disconnect plug connections.
28. Release engine ventilation connections.
29. Release tank venting connection.
30. Disconnect air intake manifold in upward direction.

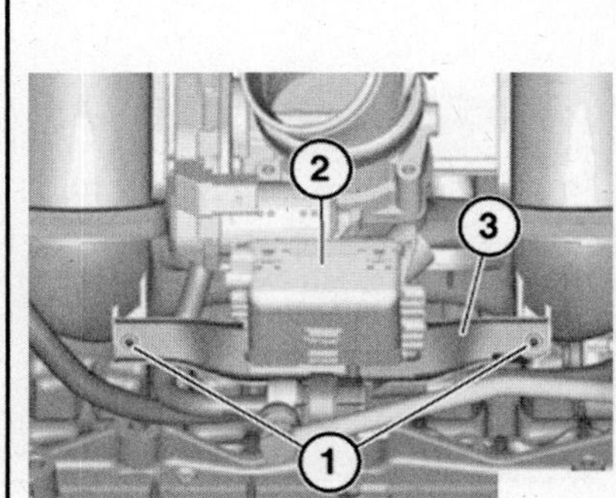

37698_BMW1_G0176

Fig. 115 Release screws (1) and lay cable duct (2) with bracket (3) and engine wiring harness to one side

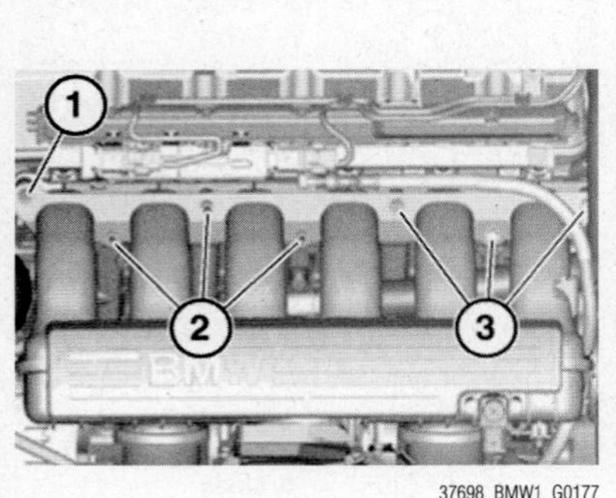

Fig. 116 Unfasten intake manifold screws (1 and 3) and nuts (2)

WARNING

Cover intake entries with suitable apparatus to prevent objects getting into them.

To install:

31. Installation is the reverse of removal.
32. Replace self-locking nuts.
33. Replace all seals and gaskets.
34. Sealing faces must be free from oil and grease.
35. Tighten bolts/nuts to specification as follows:
    - Air intake manifold to cylinder head: 11 ft. lbs. (15 Nm)
    - Clean-air gaiter to connection, throttle valve assembly: 27 inch lbs. (3 Nm)
    - Fuel line to intake manifold: 53 inch lbs. (6 Nm)
    - Holder, engine wiring harness, to intake manifold: 71 inch lbs. (8 Nm)

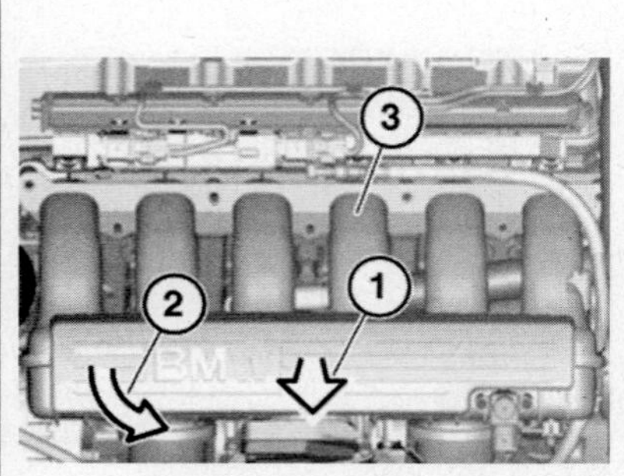

Fig. 117 Raise air intake manifold (3) approximately 2–4 In. (5–10 cm) (1) and turn air intake manifold at front through 45° (2)

Fig. 118 Disconnect plug connections (2) and release engine ventilation connections (1)

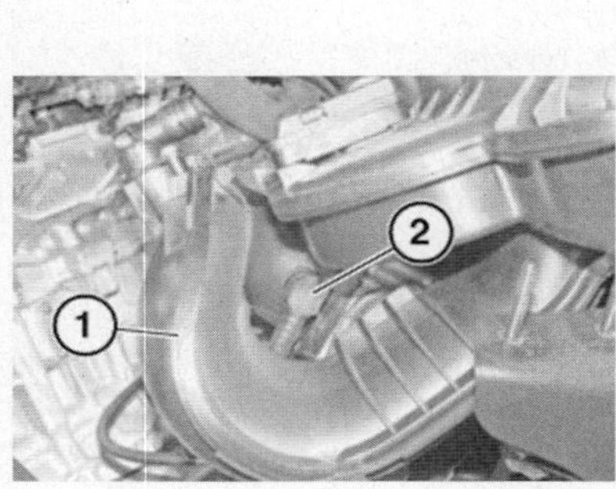

Fig. 119 Release tank venting connection (2) and disconnect air intake manifold (1) in upward direction

- Multipurpose holder to body / holder for oil reservoir: 45 inch lbs. (5 Nm)

36. Connections must snap audibly into place!
37. Check air intake system for leaks.

N54 Engine

See Figures 120 through 127.

1. Before servicing the vehicle, refer to the precautions.
2. Remove the tension strut.

WARNING

Driving without the tension strut is not permitted as otherwise the body may be damaged. Tension strut screws must be tightened to torque and then tightened down with special tool 00 9 120.

WARNING

Catch and seal of cover must not be damaged. Even a minimally damaged cover may result in water leaking in; if necessary, replace cover.

a. Remove cover and release screw underneath.
b. Version 1: Turn cover (with notch) approximately 45° counterclockwise
c. Version 2: Snap out cover (without notch) in upward direction

WARNING

Grommet must not be pulled out of bulkhead because this eliminates the possibility of correct feeding in when installed.

d. Release screw.
e. Grip grommet and pull out tension strut in direction of arrow.

3. Remove intake filter housing.

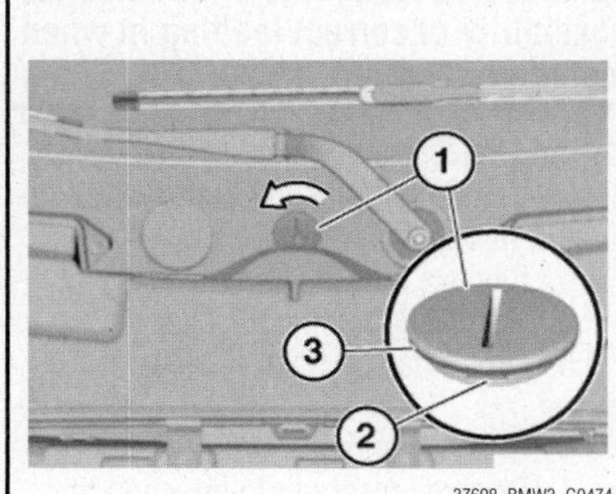

Fig. 120 Catch (2) and seal (3) of cover (1) must not be damaged

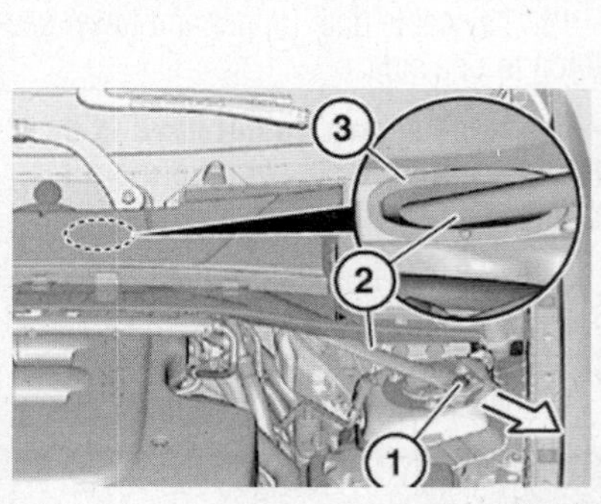

Fig. 121 Release screw (1), grip grommet (3) and pull out tension strut (2) in direction of arrow

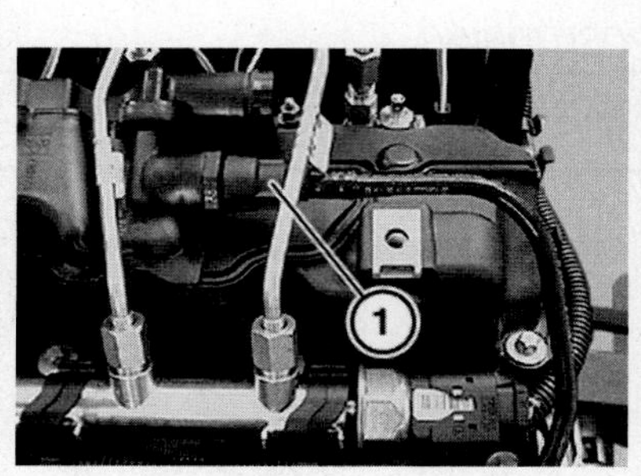

Fig. 122 Detach crankcase breather (1) at cylinder head cover

4. Detach crankcase breather at cylinder head cover.
5. Pull off vacuum hose.
6. Detach tank vent valve from mounting.
7. Release hose and lay to one side.
8. Disconnect plug connection on oil pressure switch.
9. Release retainers on fuel rail and place to one side.
10. Disconnect plug connection.

➡Do not detach fuel line.

11. Unscrew nuts as shown.
12. Release screw as shown.
13. Raise intake air manifold.
14. Release screws.
15. Place cable duct to one side.
16. Cut cable tie (1).
17. Disconnect plug connection (2).

To install:

18. Installation is the reverse of removal.
19. Replace all seals.

Fig. 123 Pull off vacuum hose (1), detach tank vent valve (2) from mounting and release hose (3) and lay to one side

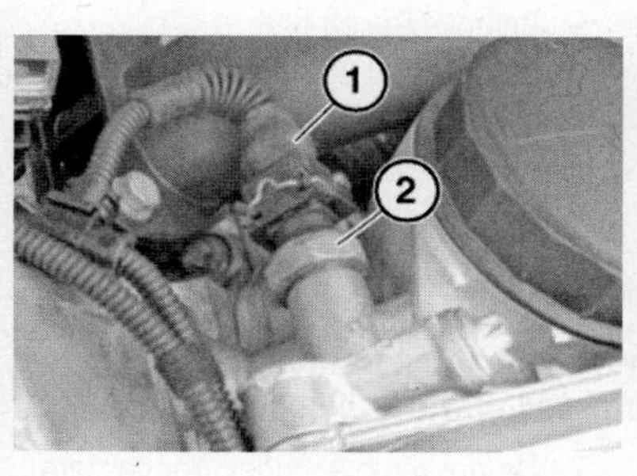

Fig. 124 Disconnect plug connection (1) on oil pressure switch (2)

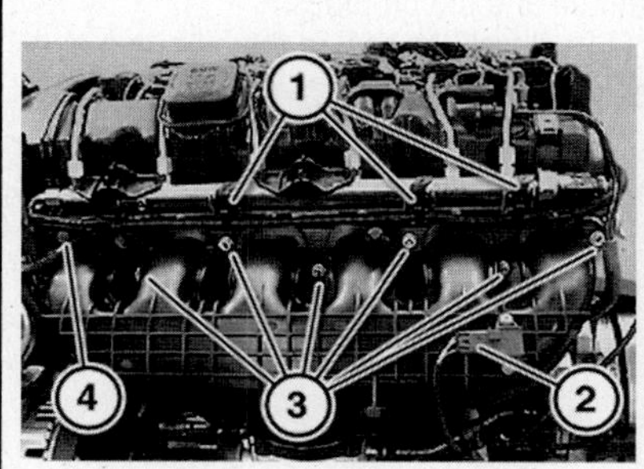

Fig. 125 Disconnect plug connection (1) on oil pressure switch (2)

20. Tighten air intake manifold to cylinder head fasteners to 11 ft. lbs. (15 Nm)
21. Check for leaks.

OIL PAN

REMOVAL & INSTALLATION

See Figures 128 and 129.

⁂ WARNING

Aluminum-magnesium material. No steel fasteners may be used due to the threat of electrochemical corrosion. A magnesium crankcase requires aluminum fasteners exclusively. Aluminum fasteners must be replaced each time they are removed. The end faces of aluminum fasteners are painted blue for purposes of identification. Torque specifications and torque angles must be observed for risk of damage.

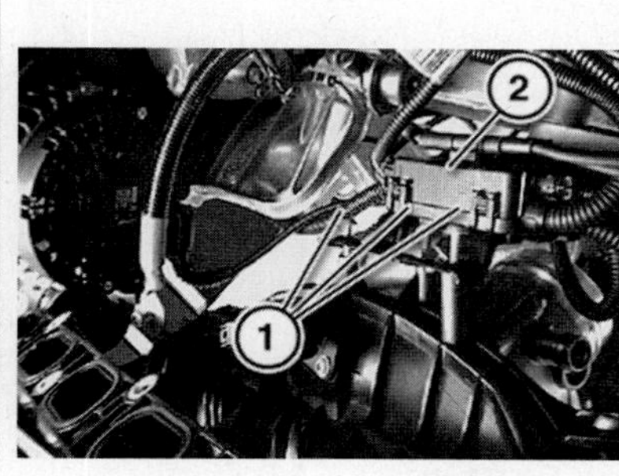

Fig. 126 Release screws (1) and place cable duct (2) to one side

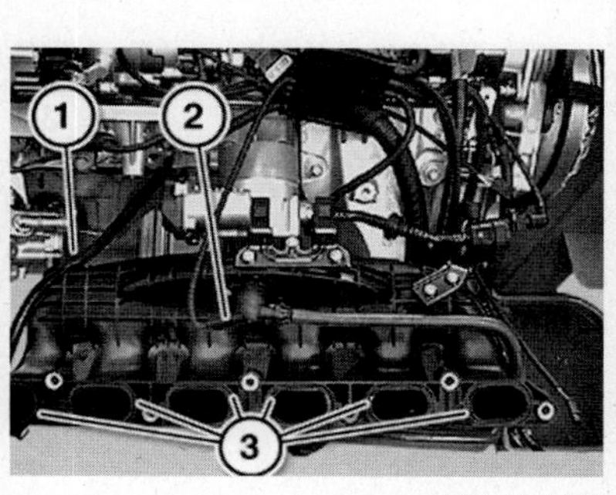

Fig. 127 Cut cable tie (1) and disconnect plug connection (2)

1. Before servicing the vehicle, refer to the precautions.
2. Install engine support tool or equivalent.
3. Disconnect the negative battery cable.
4. Remove the lower front axle.
5. Drain and recycle the engine oil.
6. On vehicles equipped with automatic transmission, oil lines must be detached from the engine oil pan.
7. Unclip electric leads of monitor sensors from holder.
8. Disconnect the electrical leads, as shown.
9. Remove the two bolts securing oil pan to transmission.
10. Remove the oil return hose.
11. Remove oil pan bolts and remove the oil pan.
12. If necessary, remove oil level sensor bolts and oil level sensor.

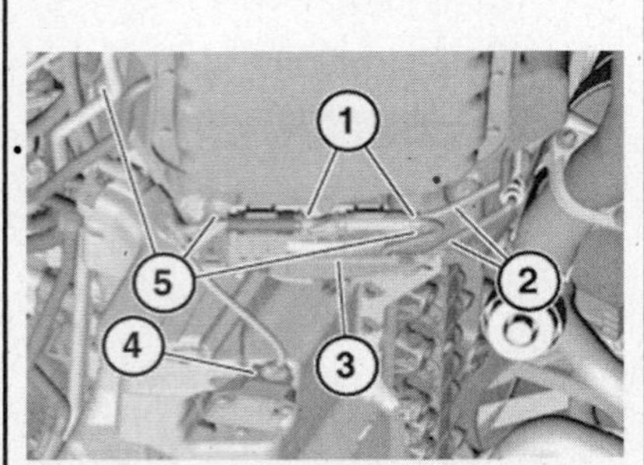

Fig. 128 Disconnecting the electrical leads

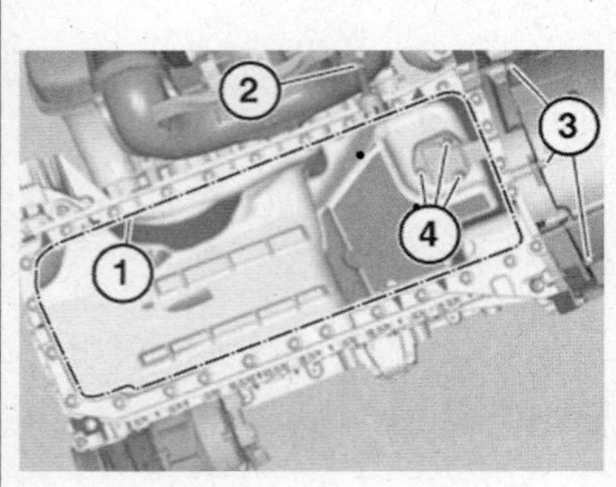

Fig. 129 Oil pan bolts (1), oil return hose (2), transmission bolts (3) and oil level sensor (4)

To install

13. Clean the mounting surfaces and install a new gasket and all seals.

WARNING

There must be no adhesive residues in the oil pan retaining threads. Clean retaining threads.

14. Install oil pan.
15. Replace all aluminum fasteners and tighten 70 inch lbs (8 Nm) plus an additional 90° rotation
16. Installation is the reverse of removal.
17. Fill the engine with oil.
18. Start the engine and check for leaks.

OIL PUMP

REMOVAL & INSTALLATION

See Figure 130.

1. Before servicing the vehicle, refer to the precautions.
2. Disconnect the negative battery cable.
3. Remove the oil pan.
4. Remove the oil pump intake pipe fasteners and oil pump intake pipe, pull towards transmission.
5. Remove the oil pump pulley bolt.
6. Remove the oil pump mounting bolts.

➡Timing chain of triangular drive is pressed upwards by chain tensioner.

7. Do not remove pulley from assembly.
8. Remove the oil pump pulley, pull towards front of engine bay.
9. Remove the oil pump.

To install

10. Check the seals on the oil pipes and replace it if necessary. Lubricate the seals with oil and the oil pipes.
11. Check the seal in the oil pump and replace it if necessary.
12. Align twin surface on oil pump to sprocket wheel.
13. Replace all aluminum fasteners and tighten to specification.
    - Oil pump to bedplate: 25 ft. lbs. (34 Nm) plus an additional 180° rotation
    - Chain module to crankcase and oil pump 35 inch lbs. (4 Nm) plus an additional 45° rotation
    - Pulley to oil pump: 15 ft. lbs. (20 Nm) plus an additional 45° rotation
    - Intake pipe to bedplate: 35 inch lbs. (4 Nm) plus an additional 100° rotation
14. Installation is the reverse of removal.
15. Fill the engine with oil.
16. Start the engine and check for leaks.

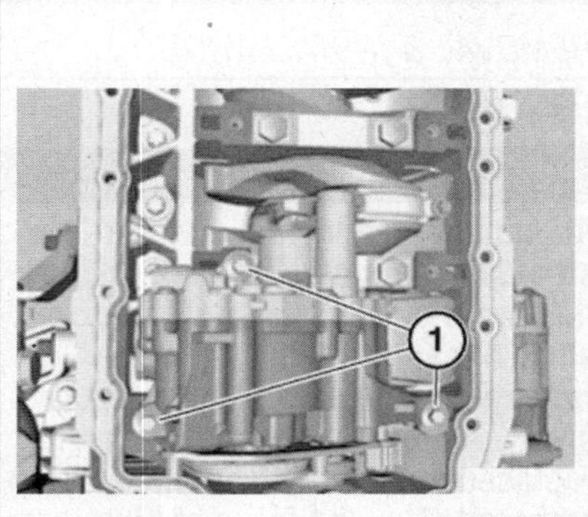

Fig. 130 Oil pump mounting bolts (1)

PISTONS & RINGS

POSITIONING

See Figures 131 through 134.

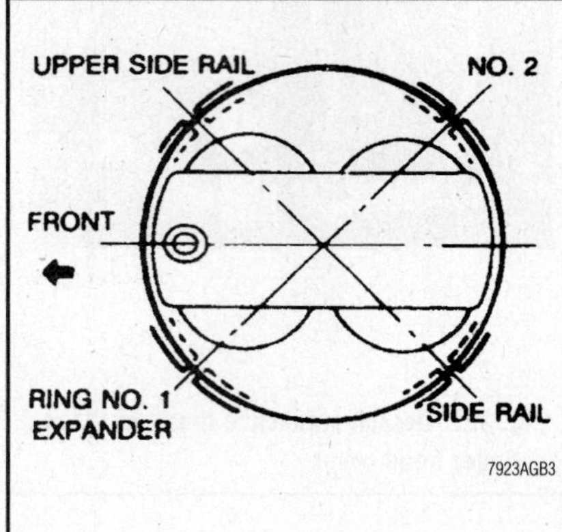

Fig. 131 Piston ring end-gap spacing—N52 and N54 Engines

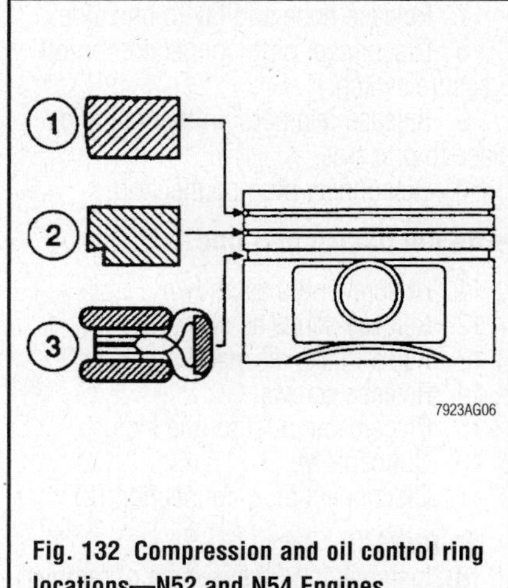

Fig. 132 Compression and oil control ring locations—N52 and N54 Engines

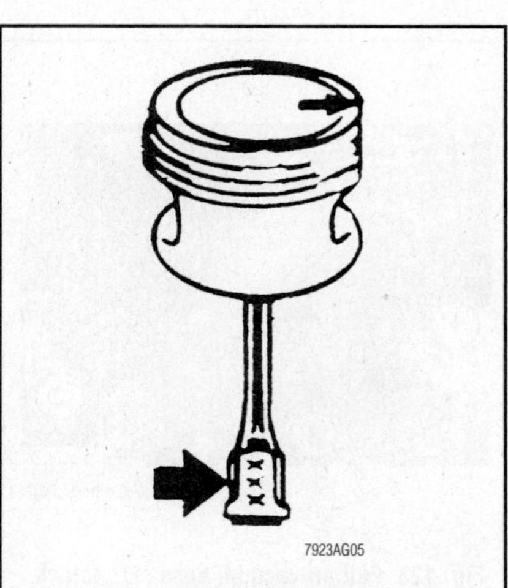

Fig. 133 Connecting rod-to-piston positioning—N52 and N54 Engines

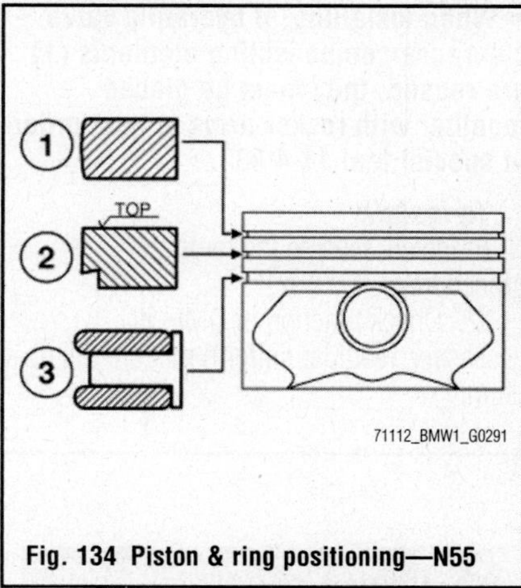

Fig. 134 Piston & ring positioning—N55

ROCKER ARMS

REMOVAL & INSTALLATION

N51 Engine

See Figures 135 and 136.

1. Remove cylinder head cover.
2. Remove intermediate lever.
3. Remove exhaust camshaft.

✲✲ WARNING

Rocker arms (1) are divided into bearing categories.

✲✲ WARNING

The tolerance classes are designated as illustrated with numbers from 1 to 5.

✲✲ WARNING

Already used rocker arms (1) may only be reused in the same position.

4. Detach roller cam followers (1) from HVCA element and remove.
5. Set all roller cam followers down in special tool 11 4 480 in a tidy and orderly fashion.

➡Before installing exhaust camshaft and intermediate lever, make sure roller cam followers are correctly seated.

6. Remove HVCA element in direction of arrow.

➡When installing, if the HVC elements are to be reused, set them down in special tool 11 4 480 in a tidy and orderly fashion with the roller cam followers.

To install:

To install, reverse the removal procedure.

7. Check function of DME; if necessary, readjust uniform mixture distribution.

N55 Engine

See Figures 137 through 141.

1. Remove cylinder head cover.
2. Remove intermediate lever.
3. Remove exhaust camshaft.

✲✲ WARNING

Roller cam followers (1) on intake side are divided into bearing classes.

✲✲ WARNING

The tolerance classes are marked according to the graphic in numbers from 1 to 5.

✲✲ WARNING

Already used roller cam followers (1) may only be reused in the same position.

4. Loosen and remove roller cam followers (1) from hydraulic valve clearance compensating element.
5. Place all roller cam followers (1) in neat order on special tool 11 4 481.

➡Prior to installation of intermediate levers, ensure proper installation position of roller cam followers (1).

6. Classification of roller cam follower intake.
   a. Standard: Number 3. standard.
   b. Number 2. slow idle.
   c. Number 4. fast idle.
7. In case of repair: rough idling speed.
   a. Repair: 1
   b. Number 1. slow speed in idle.

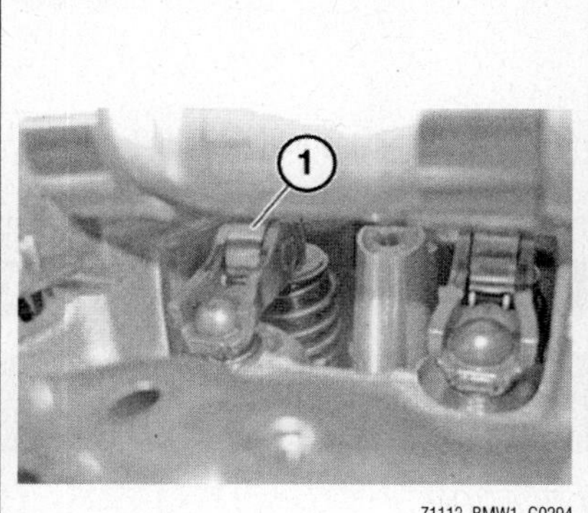

Fig. 137 Identifying cam followers (1)

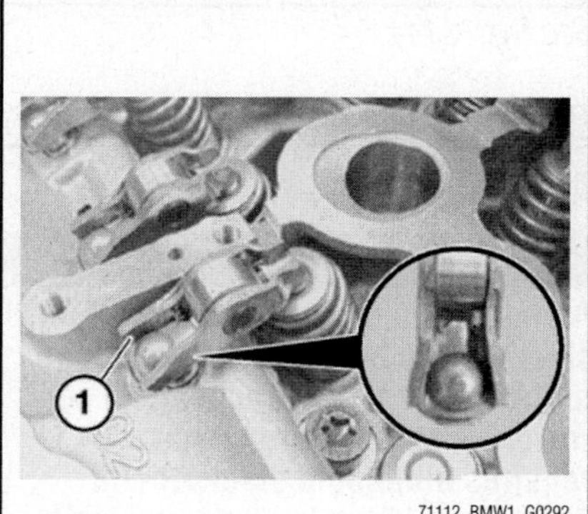

Fig. 135 Identifying rocker arms (1)

Fig. 136 Removing HVCE element in direction of arrow

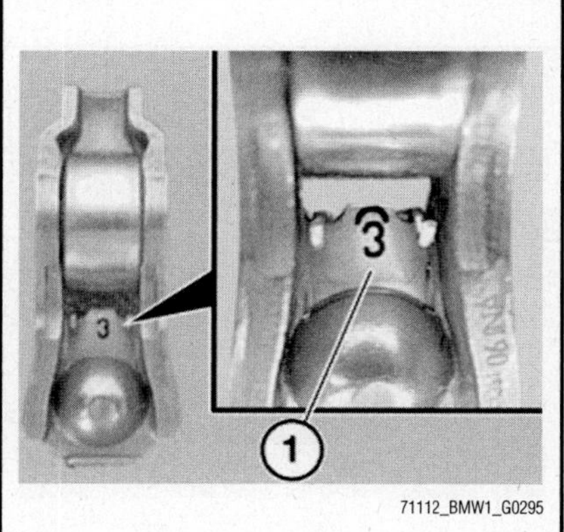

Fig. 138 Identifying roller classification

c. Number 5. high speed in idle.

8. Loosen and remove roller cam followers (1) on exhaust side from hydraulic valve clearance compensating element.

9. Place all roller cam followers (1) in neat order on special tool 11 4 482 .

➡Prior to installation of exhaust camshaft, ensure proper installation position of roller cam followers (1).

10. Remove hydraulic valve clearance compensating element (1) on intake side in direction of arrow.

➡When installing, if hydraulic valve clearance compensating elements (1) are reused, they must be placed together with rocker arms in neat order in special tool 11 4 481.

11. Remove hydraulic valve clearance compensating element (1) on exhaust side in direction of arrow.

➡When installing, if hydraulic valve clearance compensating elements (1) are reused, they must be placed together with rocker arms in neat order in special tool 11 4 482.

To install:

To install, reverse the removal procedure.

12. Check function of DME; if necessary, readjust uniform mixture distribution.

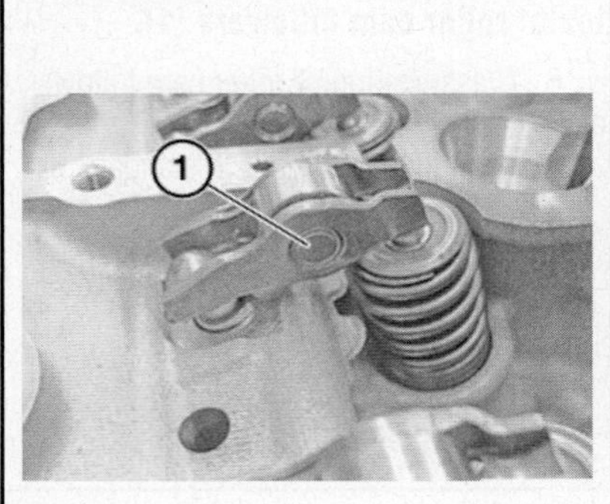

Fig. 139 Removing roller cam followers (1) on exhaust side

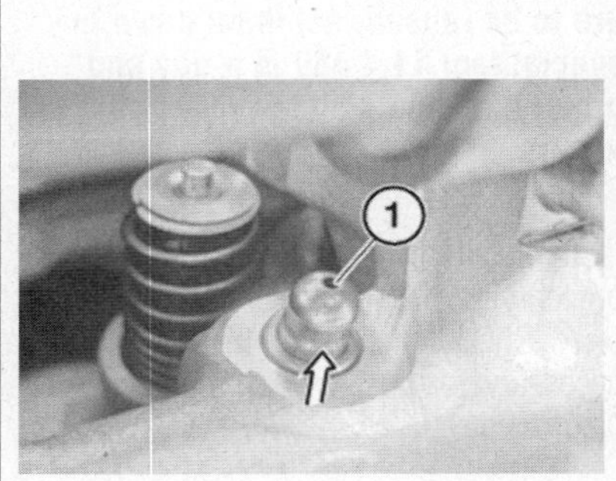

Fig. 140 Removing hydraulic valve clearance compensating element (1) on intake side

Fig. 141 Removing hydraulic valve clearance compensating element (1) on exhaust side

ENGINE PERFORMANCE & EMISSION CONTROLS

CAMSHAFT POSITION (CMP) SENSOR

LOCATION

See Figures 142 and 143.

REMOVAL & INSTALLATION

1. Before servicing the vehicle, refer to the precautions.

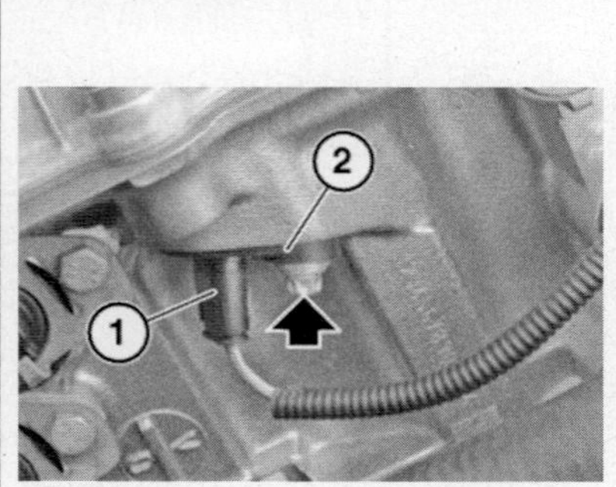

Fig. 142 Intake CMP sensor (2) and connector (1) location— N52 and N54 engines

2. Read out fault memory of DME control unit; if necessary, work through test schedules
3. Switch ignition **OFF**.
4. Remove radiator cover.
5. Remove plug connector and pull off.
6. Remove screw.
7. Remove pulse generator.

To install:

8. Installation is the reverse of removal.

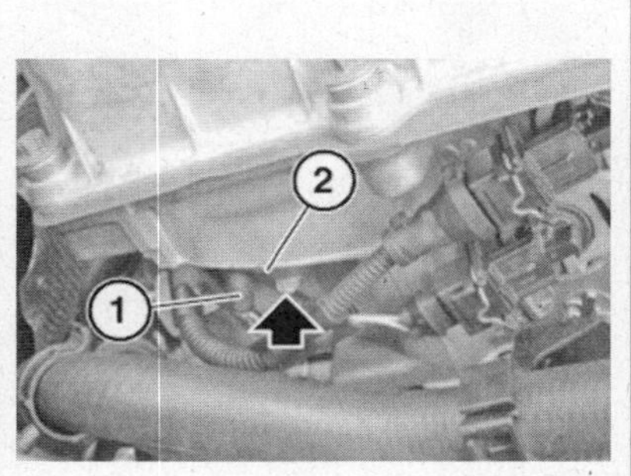

Fig. 143 Exhaust CMP sensor (2) and connector (1) location— N52 and N54 engines

9. If equipped, replace sealing ring and coat with antiseize agent.
10. Tighten sensor to 7 ft. lbs. (9 Nm).
11. Check for stored fault messages, rectify faults and clear the fault memory.

CRANKSHAFT POSITION (CKP) SENSOR

LOCATION

See Figure 144.

REMOVAL & INSTALLATION

N51, N52 and N54 Engines

⁂ WARNING

Aluminum-magnesium materials. No steel screws/bolts may be used due to the threat of electrochemical corrosion. A magnesium crankcase requires aluminum screws/bolts exclusively. Aluminum screws/bolts must be replaced each time they are Removed. The end faces of aluminum screws/bolts are painted blue for the purposes of reliable identification. Jointing torque and angle of

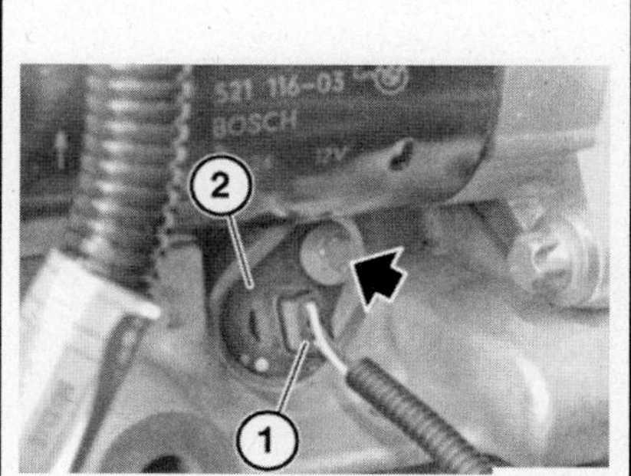

22205_BMWC_G0236

Fig. 144 CKP sensor (2) and connector (1) location— N52 and N54 engines

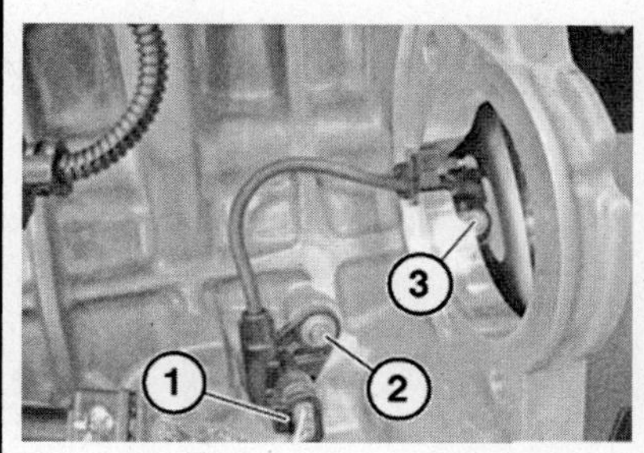

71112_BMW1_G0314

Fig. 145 Unlocking connector (1), releasing screws (2 and 3) and removing sensor

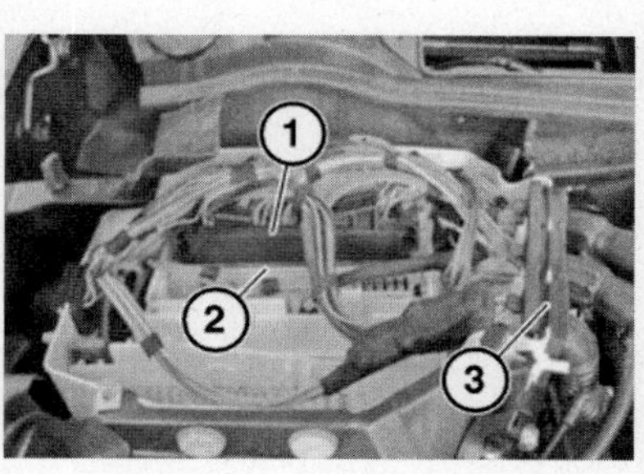

22205_BMWC_G0237

Fig. 146 DME control unit (2), connector (1) and cover (3) location

rotation must be observed without fail (risk of damage).

1. Before servicing the vehicle, refer to the precautions.
2. Read out fault memory of DME control unit; if necessary, work through test schedules
3. Switch ignition **OFF**.
4. Remove intake air manifold.
5. Disconnect plug
6. Disconnect the crankshaft pulse generator.
7. Remove and discard the aluminum bolts.
8. Remove pulse generator from crankcase.

To install:

9. Replace sealing ring.
10. Install pulse generator to crankcase.
11. Using new aluminum bolts, tighten to 2 ft. lbs (3 Nm) plus an additional 45° of rotation.
12. Connect the crankshaft pulse generator.
13. Install intake air manifold.

N55 Engines

See Figure 145.

1. Read out the fault memory of the DME control unit.
2. Switch off ignition.
3. Remove starter motor.
4. Unlock connector (1) and remove.
5. Release screw (2).
   a. Tightening torque 13 62 6AZ.
6. Remove connector housing from crankcase.
7. Release screw (3).
   a. Tightening torque 13 62 7AZ.
8. Pull pulse sensor from crankcase and remove.

To install:

To install, reverse the removal procedure noting the following.

9. During installation of pulse sensor make sure that guide pin (1) of pulse sensor is inserted in guiding groove (2) of crankcase.
10. Assemble engine.
11. Check stored fault message.
12. Delete fault memory.

DIGITAL MOTOR ELECTRONIC (DME) CONTROL UNIT

LOCATION

See Figure 146.

REMOVAL & INSTALLATION

1. Before servicing the vehicle, refer to the precautions.
2. Read out fault memory of DME control unit; if necessary, work through test schedules
3. Switch ignition **OFF**.
4. Disconnect the negative battery cable.
5. Remove the air filter housing.
6. Unlock fasteners from below and slide upwards approximately 0.39 in. (10 mm).
7. Unlock locks.
8. Remove cover.
9. Unlock plug and remove.
10. Unlock control unit and remove towards top.

To install:

11. Installation is the reverse of removal.
12. Note device identification number and coding.
13. As necessary, code and program the new control unit.
14. Check for stored fault messages, rectify faults and clear the fault memory.

RESET

Using the STAR DIAGNOSIS tool, reprogram the control unit.

ENGINE COOLANT TEMPERATURE (ECT) SENSOR

LOCATION

See Figures 147 and 148.

REMOVAL & INSTALLATION

N52 Engine

1. Before servicing the vehicle, refer to the precautions.
2. Read out fault memory of DME control unit; if necessary, work through test schedules
3. Switch ignition **OFF**.

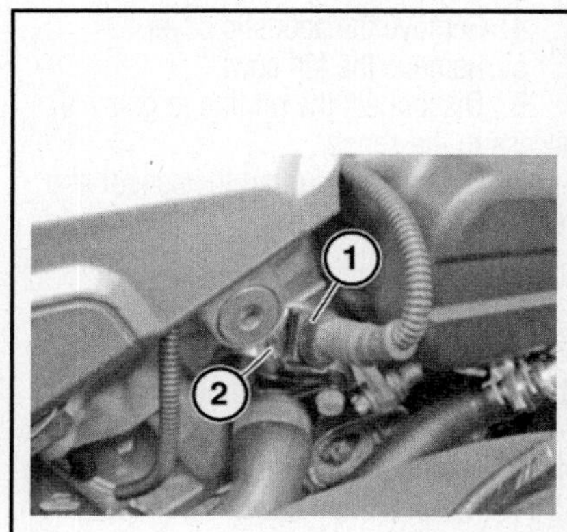

29246_BMWC_G0064

Fig. 147 ECT location—N52 engine

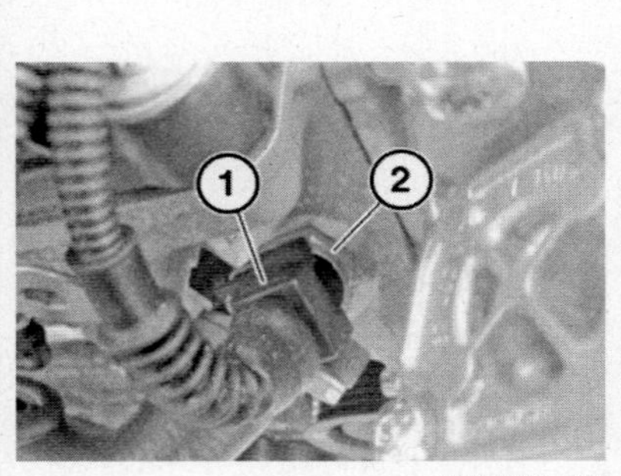

Fig. 148 ECT sensor (2) and connector (1) location—N54 engine

4. Though you can avoid it, for easier access, remove the intake duct.
5. Unlock the plug on the sensor (1) and remove it.
6. Remove the temperature sensor (2).

To install:

7. Reposition the sensor and lock the plug.
8. After returning the temperature sensor back to its position, make sure to vent the cooling system and check for leaks.
9. If necessary, top off the coolant in the reservoir.
10. Check for stored fault messages, rectify faults and clear the fault memory.

N54 Engine

See Figure 149.

1. Before servicing the vehicle, refer to the precautions.
2. Read out fault memory of DME control unit; if necessary, work through test schedules
3. Switch ignition **OFF**.
4. Remove the acoustic cover.
5. Remove the fan cowl.
6. Disconnect the oil line to gain access to the sensor.
7. Unlock the plug on the sensor and remove it.
8. Remove the temperature sensor.

To install:

9. Install the sensor and tighten to 10 ft. lbs. (14 Nm). Lock the plug.
10. Connect the oil line using new O-rings and tighten to 14 ft. lbs. (19 Nm).
11. Install the fan cowl.
12. Install the acoustic cover.
13. After returning the temperature sensor back to its position, make sure to vent the cooling system and check for leaks.

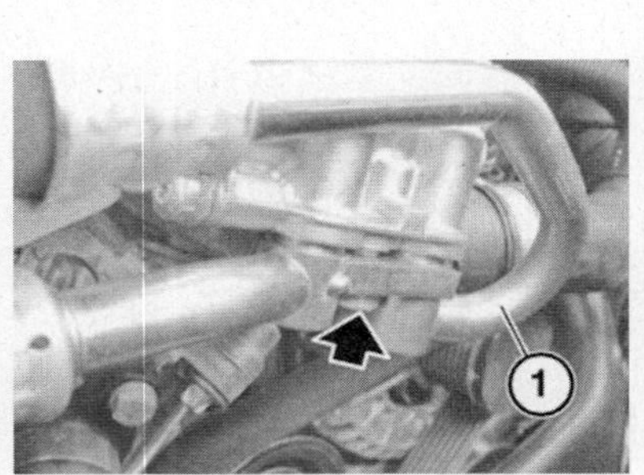

Fig. 149 Disconnect the oil line (1) to gain access to the sensor

14. If necessary, top off the coolant in the reservoir.
15. Check for stored fault messages, rectify faults and clear the fault memory.

ENGINE OIL TEMPERATURE (EOT) SENSOR

LOCATION

See Figure 150.

REMOVAL & INSTALLATION

See Figures 151 through 153.

1. Before servicing the vehicle, refer to the precautions.
2. Remove front underbody protection and as necessary reinforcement plate.
3. Drain and recycle the engine oil.
4. Unlock plug and remove the sensor.

To install:

5. Clean sealing face on oil sump.
6. Replace seal on oil level sensor.

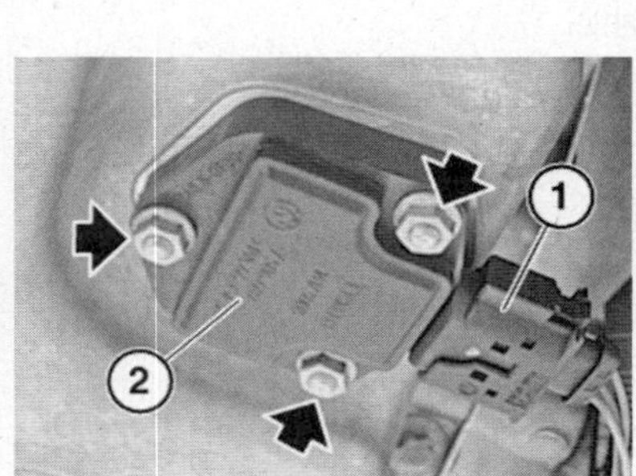

Fig. 150 Oil level and temperature sensor (2) and plug (1)

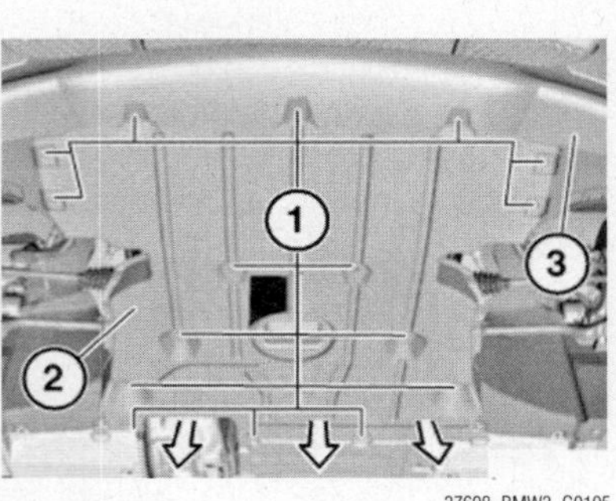

Fig. 151 Release screws (1) and pull underbody protection (2) forward under bumper trim (3)—except M3

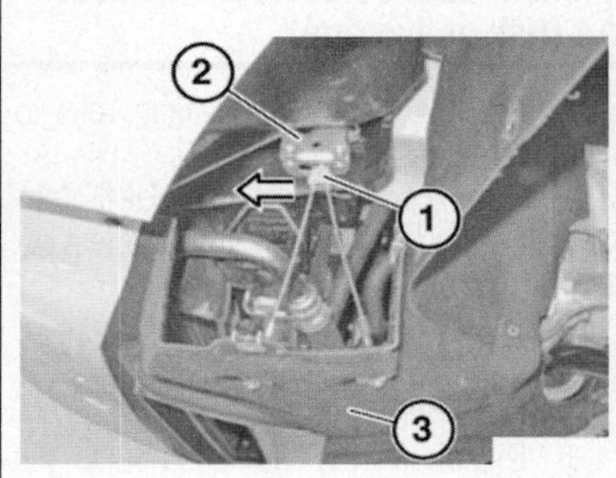

Fig. 152 Turn catch (1) on cable through 90° and disengage in direction of arrow from bracket (2) on both sides. Pull underbody protection (3) forwards under bumper trim and remove—M3

7. Tighten the bolts to 72 inch lbs. (8 Nm).

⁂ WARNING

An excessively low torque value will result in oil leaks. An excessively high torque value will result in damage to the oil level sensor.

8. Refill engine with oil.

HEATED OXYGEN (HO2S) SENSOR

LOCATION

See Figures 154 and 155.

REMOVAL & INSTALLATION

1. Before servicing the vehicle, refer to the precautions.
2. Read out fault memory of DME control unit; if necessary, work through test schedules

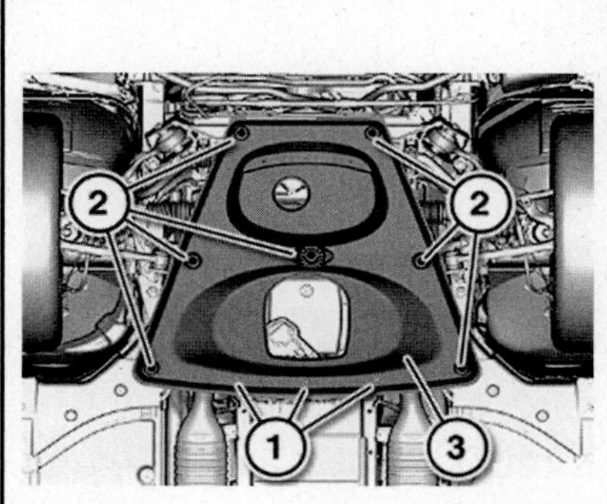

Fig. 153 Release screws (1), release screws (2) and remove reinforcement plate (3)—M3

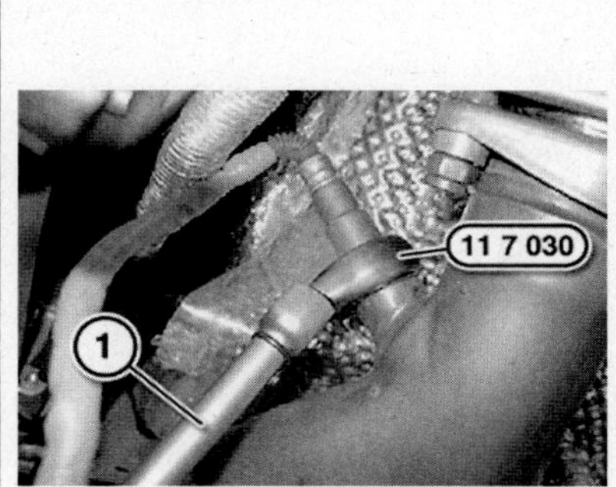

Fig. 154 HO2S sensor location—left side

3. Switch ignition **OFF**.
4. Remove the exhaust system.
5. Disconnect the plug connection from the sensors.
6. Disconnect the oxygen sensor from cylinders 4 to 6.
7. The oxygen sensor at cylinders 1 to 3 is accessible from above without the exhaust system having to be removed.

To install:

8. The threads of a new oxygen sensors are already coated with an anti-seize compound. If an oxygen sensor is to be used again, apply a thin and even coat of an anti-seize compound to the thread only.

WARNING

Do not clean the oxygen sensor section which protrudes into the exhaust line and ensure that it avoids all contact with any lubricants.

Fig. 155 HO2S sensor location—right side

➡Observe cable routing of the oxygen sensor so it doesn't interfere with any other system or the exhaust pipes.

9. Tighten sensor to 37 ft. lbs. (50 Nm).
10. Connect the oxygen sensors and their respective cables.
    - The cable color for the sensor that leads to cylinders 1 to 3 is black.
    - The cable color for the sensor that leads to cylinders 4 to 6 is gray.
11. Connect the plug connection to the sensors.
12. Check for stored fault messages, rectify faults and clear the fault memory.

INTAKE AIR TEMPERATURE (IAT)/MASS AIRFLOW (MAF) SENSOR

LOCATION

See Figure 156.

REMOVAL & INSTALLATION

N52 Engine

1. Before servicing the vehicle, refer to the precautions.
2. Read out fault memory of DME control unit; if necessary, work through test schedules
3. Switch ignition **OFF**.
4. Remove the bolts that hold the sensor in place.
5. Unlock the plug and remove it.
6. Pull the mass airflow sensor out of the upper section of the intake filter housing.

To install:

7. Replace the sensor, screw it down and connect the plug-in connector.

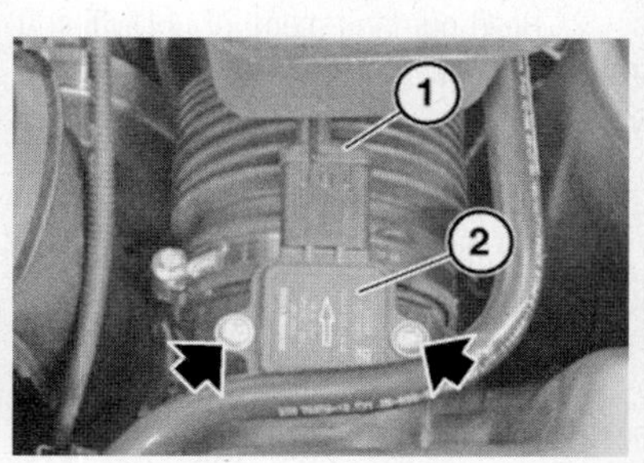

Fig. 156 MAF/IAT sensor location– N52 engine

8. Check stored fault messages.
9. Rectify faults.
10. Check for stored fault messages, rectify faults and clear the fault memory.

KNOCK SENSOR (KS)

LOCATION

See Figure 157.

REMOVAL & INSTALLATION

N52 and N54 Engines

WARNING

No steel bolts or bolts may be used due to the threat of electrochemical corrosion. A magnesium crankcase requires aluminum bolts and bolts exclusively. The end of the aluminum bolts and bolts are painted blue for the purposes of reliable identification.

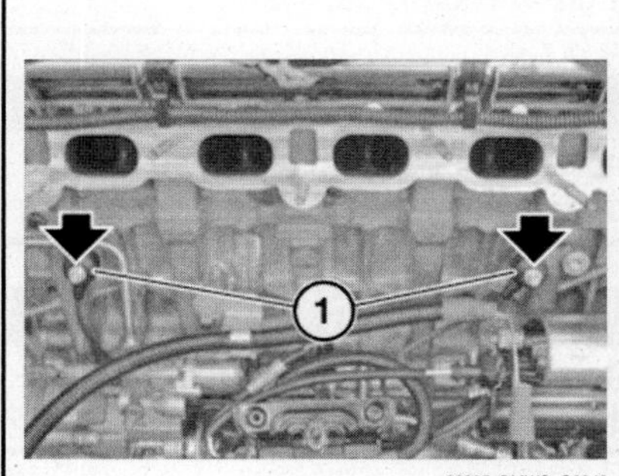

Fig. 157 KS sensor location— N52 and N54 engine

1. Before servicing the vehicle, refer to the precautions.
2. Read out fault memory of DME control unit; if necessary, work through test schedules
3. Switch ignition **OFF**.
4. Disconnect the battery.
5. Remove the air intake manifold.
6. Unlock the plug connection and remove it.
7. Unscrew the bolts on both knock sensors and remove the sensors.

To install:

8. Clean the support face of the knock sensors on engine block.
9. Tighten knock sensor to 15 ft. lbs. (21 Nm).
10. Install the bolts on both knock sensors to replace the sensors.
11. Check for stored fault messages, rectify faults and clear the fault memory.

N55 Engines

See Figures 158 and 159.

WARNING

Disconnect negative battery terminal (risk of fire due to short-circuiting on removal).

WARNING

Electric fuel pump starts up automatically when door is opened!

WARNING

Carry out installation work on fuel system only with coolant temperature below 40 °C.

WARNING

Adhere to conditions of absolute cleanliness when working on the high-pressure fuel system.

WARNING

Introduced contaminants can cause malfunctions in the system!

WARNING

Do not allow any dirt particles or foreign bodies to get into the system.

WARNING

Remove all traces of dirt contamination before removing lines or separate components.

WARNING

Use only fluff-free cloths.

WARNING

Seal all fuel system openings with protective caps or plugs.

WARNING

Aluminum screws/bolts must be replaced each time they are released.

WARNING

Aluminum screws/bolts are permitted with and without color coding (blue).

WARNING

For reliable identification: Jointing torque and angle of rotation must be observed without fail (risk of damage).

1. Read out the fault memory of the DME control unit.
2. Switch off ignition.
3. Remove intake plenum.
4. Unlock connector (1) and remove.
5. Unlock and detach fuel line.
6. Catch and dispose of escaping fuel.
7. Seal fuel lines with special tools 13 5 281 and 13 5 282 .
8. Slacken nut (1).
9. Close off fuel line connection of high-pressure pump with a matching plug from special tool set 32 1 270.
10. Release screw.

➡When installing, replace aluminum screw.

11. Remove feed line .
12. Seal feed line with matching plug from special tool kit 32 1 270.
13. Unlock connector (1) and remove.
14. Release screws on both knock sensors (1) and remove knock sensors (1).

➡When installing, replace aluminum screws.

a. Tightening torque: 16 ft. lbs. (21.5 Nm).

To install:

To install, reverse the removal procedure noting the following.

15. Clean contact surface of knock sensors on engine block.
16. Pre-install feed line (3).
    a. In so doing, tighten screw connection hand-tight only (it must still be possible to move the line at the holder).

Fig. 158 Unlocking connector (1) and removing

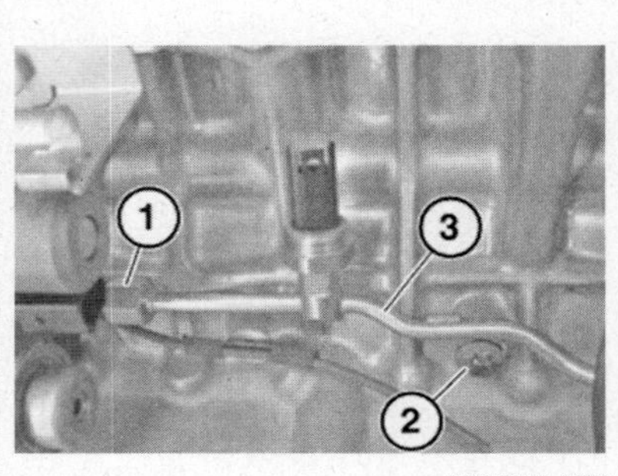

Fig. 159 Installing feed line (3), tightening nut (1) and screw (2)

WARNING

Sequence of screw connection must be observed.

b. Tighten nut (1). Tightening torque: 20-24 ft. lbs. (27-33 Nm).
c. Tighten screw (2). Replace aluminum screw. Tightening torque: 44 inch lbs. (5 Nm) + 90° + 15°.

17. Reassemble the vehicle.
18. Check stored fault messages.
19. Delete fault memory.

MANIFOLD ABSOLUTE PRESSURE (MAP) SENSOR

LOCATION

See Figure 160.

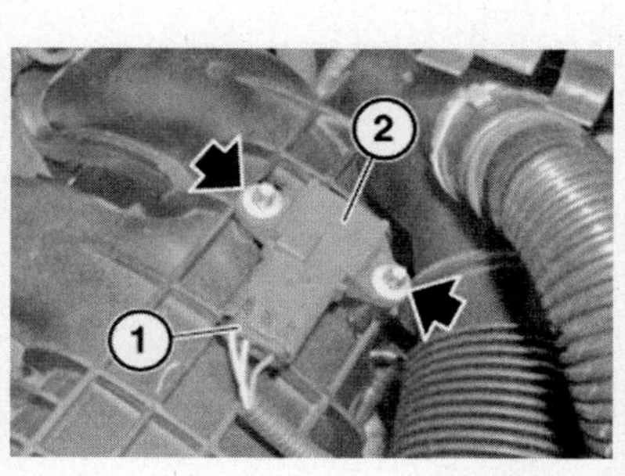

Fig. 160 MAP sensor location. Plug (1) suction pressure sensor (2)—N54 Engine

REMOVAL & INSTALLATION

N54 Engine

1. Before servicing the vehicle, refer to the precautions.

➡The installation location of the suction pressure sensor is at the rear end of the intake air manifold.

2. Read out fault memory of DME control unit; if necessary, work through test schedules
3. Switch ignition **OFF**.
4. Remove air filter housing.
5. Unlock plug and remove.
6. Release screws and pull suction pressure sensor out of intake air housing.

To install:

7. Installation is the reverse of removal.
8. Check sealing ring for damage, replace if necessary.
9. When installing, coat sealing ring with suitable antiseize agent.
10. Tighten screws to 36 inch lbs. (3.5 Nm).
11. Check stored fault messages and clear the fault memory.

THROTTLE POSITION SENSOR (TPS)

LOCATION

See Figure 161.

REMOVAL & INSTALLATION

1. Before servicing the vehicle, refer to the precautions.
2. Read out fault memory of DME control unit; if necessary, work through test schedules
3. Switch ignition **OFF**.

Fig. 161 TPS sensor (2) and connector (1) location– N52 and N54 engines

4. Remove air intake hose.
5. Unlock plug and remove.
6. Remove throttle assembly.

To install:

7. Replace sealing ring of throttle assembly.
8. Install throttle assembly. Tighten bolts to 6 ft. lbs. (9 Nm).
9. Install air intake hose.
10. Check for stored fault messages, rectify faults and clear the fault memory.

FUEL — GASOLINE FUEL INJECTION SYSTEM

FUEL SYSTEM SERVICE PRECAUTIONS

Safety is the most important factor when performing not only fuel system maintenance but any type of maintenance. Failure to conduct maintenance and repairs in a safe manner may result in serious personal injury or death. Maintenance and testing of the vehicle's fuel system components can be accomplished safely and effectively by adhering to the following rules and guidelines.

- To avoid the possibility of fire and personal injury, always disconnect the negative battery cable unless the repair or test procedure requires that battery voltage be applied.
- Always relieve the fuel system pressure prior to disconnecting any fuel system component (injector, fuel rail, pressure regulator, etc.), fitting or fuel line connection. Exercise extreme caution whenever relieving fuel system pressure to avoid exposing skin, face and eyes to fuel spray. Please be advised that fuel under pressure may penetrate the skin or any part of the body that it contacts.
- Always place a shop towel or cloth around the fitting or connection prior to loosening to absorb any excess fuel due to spillage. Ensure that all fuel spillage (should it occur) is quickly removed from engine surfaces. Ensure that all fuel soaked cloths or towels are deposited into a suitable waste container.
- Always keep a dry chemical (Class B) fire extinguisher near the work area.
- Do not allow fuel spray or fuel vapors to come into contact with a spark or open flame.
- Always use a back-up wrench when loosening and tightening fuel line connection fittings. This will prevent unnecessary stress and torsion to fuel line piping.
- Always replace worn fuel fitting O-rings with new Do not substitute fuel hose or equivalent where fuel pipe is installed.

Before servicing the vehicle, make sure to also refer to the precautions in the beginning of this section as well.

RELIEVING FUEL SYSTEM PRESSURE

To relieve the pressure in the system, locate fuel pump relay located on the cowl. The relay can sometimes be distinguished by the orange color of the housing. Unplug and remove the relay, and place it in a safe location. With the fuel pump relay removed, start the engine and operate it until it stalls. Crank the engine for 10 seconds after it stalls to remove any residual pressure.

FUEL FILTER

REMOVAL & INSTALLATION

The fuel filter is an integral component of the fuel level/fuel pump assembly in the fuel tank and is not normally serviced.

FUEL PUMP MODULE

REMOVAL & INSTALLATION

See Figures 162 through 165.

The fuel tank should not be filled more than ⅓ of the total fuel tank capacity to prevent fuel leakage during fuel level sending unit removal. If the fuel tank is filled beyond this level, the fuel level must be reduced using an approved fuel removal device.

1. Before servicing the vehicle, refer to the precautions.
2. Relive the fuel system pressure and disconnect the negative battery cable.
3. Drain the fuel, if filled beyond ⅓ of the capacity of the fuel tank. Drain the fuel tank enough to prevent spillage when removing the pump using an approved fuel removal device.

➡The fuel level sending unit must be removed through the top of the fuel tank, thus the location of the fuel tank determines whether the fuel level sending unit is accessed by removal of the rear seat, or removal of the trim panels in the trunk.

4. Remove the rear seat to access the top of the fuel tank.

➡On models which require removal of the rear seat, the insulation mat under the seat must be cut in a "U" shape to allow the insulation to be folded up to access the top of the fuel tank.

5. Remove the fasteners securing the metal cover located above the fuel tank, and remove the cover.
6. Remove the electrical connector at the top of the combination fuel level sending unit and fuel level sending unit assembly.
7. Remove the fuel feed and return lines.
8. Match mark the combination fuel level sending unit and fuel level sending unit assembly to the fuel tank to ensure proper installation during reassembly.
9. Use tool No. 16-1-020 to loosen the sealing ring in a counterclockwise direction.
10. With the seal ring removed, lift the fuel level sending unit assembly out of the fuel tank.

To install:

➡Always use a new seal or gasket when installing the fuel level sending unit or fuel level gauge sending unit assembly.

11. Install the fuel level sending unit into the fuel tank taking care not to bend or damage the fuel sending unit assembly.
12. Fit screw cap without using a tool and tighten hand-tight.
13. Then tighten screw cap with special tool 16 1 020 until notch points to marking.
14. The balance of the assembly is in reverse order of disassembly.
15. Connect the negative battery cable.
16. Once the vehicle is started, check for leaks. If a strong fuel odor is present, or any fuel leakage is noted, stop the engine immediately and repair as necessary.

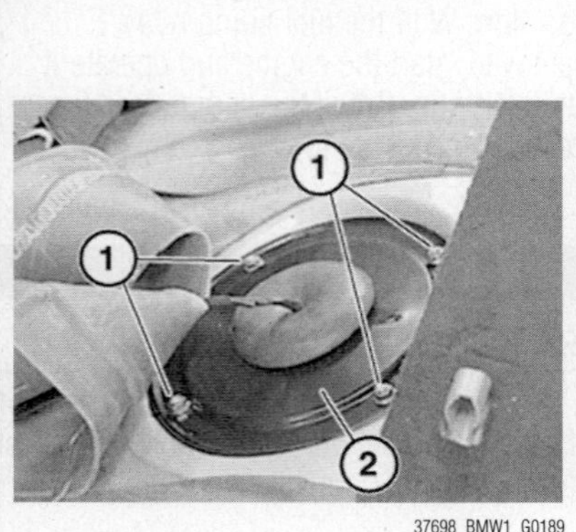

Fig. 162 Remove the fasteners (1) securing the metal cover (2) located above the fuel tank

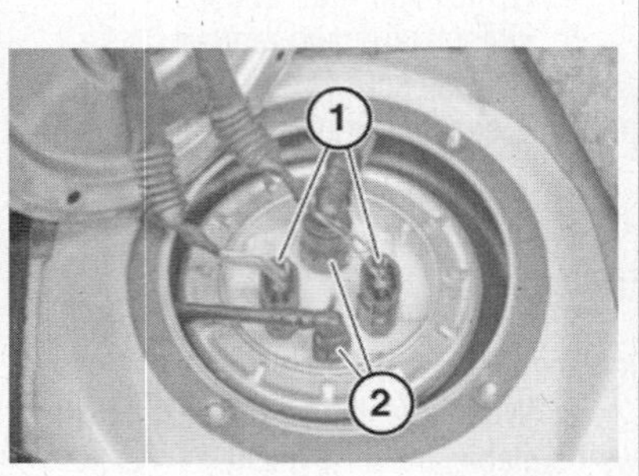

Fig. 163 Remove the electrical connector (1) and the fuel feed and return lines (2)

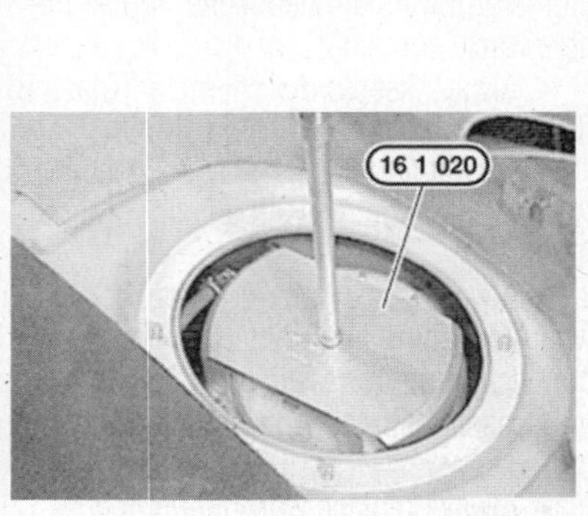

Fig. 164 Use tool No. 16-1-020 to loosen the sealing ring in a counterclockwise direction

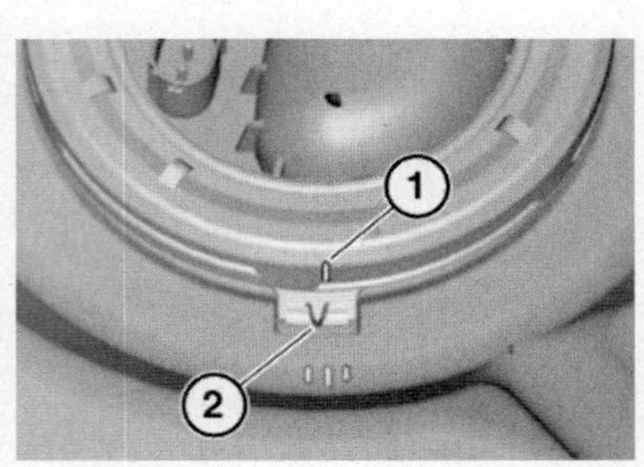

Fig. 165 Then tighten screw cap with special tool 16 1 020 until notch (1) points to marking (2)

N54 Engine (High Pressure Pump)

See Figures 166 and 167.

1. Before servicing the vehicle, refer to the precautions.
2. Disconnect battery negative terminal.

⁂ WARNING

Electric fuel pump starts up automatically each time door is opened.

3. Remove intake air manifold.
4. Unlock plug and remove.
5. Unlock and detach fuel line.
6. Catch and dispose of escaping fuel.
7. Seal fuel lines with special tools 13 5 281 and 13 5 282.
8. Remove nut, remove bolt and remove feed line.
9. Seal feed line with matching plug from special tool kit 32 1 270.

⁂ WARNING

Wear full face guard and protective gloves.

10. Remove nut, slacken nut, unscrew bolt and disconnect high-pressure line.
11. Seal connections of high-pressure line with matching plugs from special tool kit 32 1 270.
12. Seal fuel line connections of high-pressure pump with matching plugs from special tool kit 32 1 270.
13. Remove screws with special tool 11 8 610.
14. Disconnect high-pressure pump and remove.

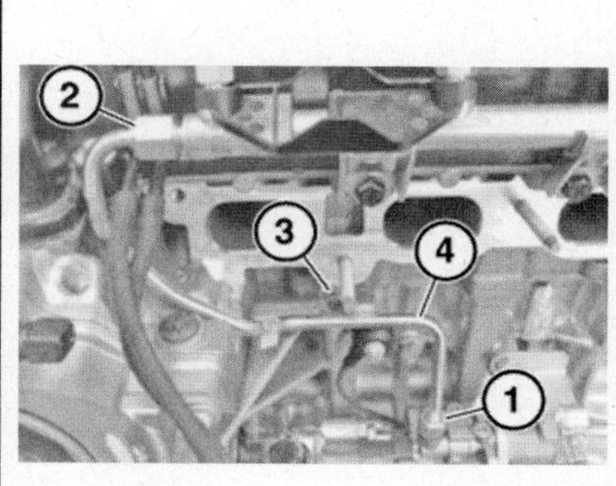

Fig. 166 Remove nut (1), slacken nut (2), unscrew bolt (3) and disconnect high-pressure line (4)

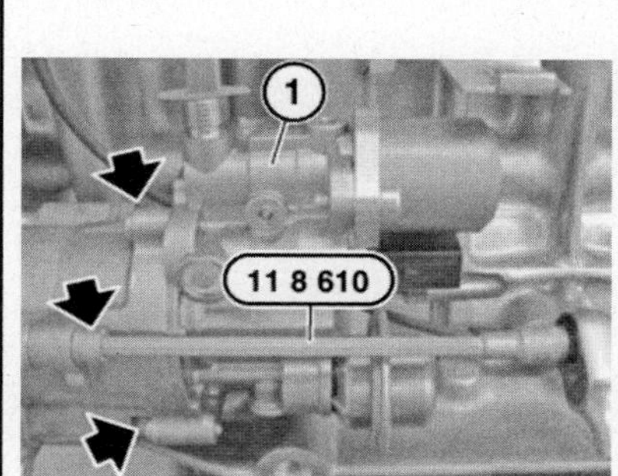

Fig. 167 Remove screws with special tool 11 8 610

➡Engine oil can escape when pump is detached; have a cleaning cloth ready.

To install:

15. Replace sealing ring and clean contact faces.
16. When installing, turn high-pressure pump until bores for screws are flush.
17. Tighten screws of high-pressure pump with special tool 11 8 610 hand-tight only. It must still be possible to turn the high-pressure pump at the flange. This prevents twisting when high-pressure line is tightened.

➡Copper seals that may be fitted on the high-pressure line are no longer needed and must be removed. If reusing pressure line, lightly grease threads of pressure connections. Threads of new pressure lines are already coated.

18. Pre-install high-pressure line. Tighten screw connections hand-tight only. You must still be able to move the high-pressure line at the holder.
19. Only when high-pressure pump has if necessary turned into position and is thus pre-installed without twisting with high pressure-line should screws of high-pressure pump be tightened down with special tool 11 8 610. Tighten to 7 ft. lbs. (9 Nm).
20. Follow sequence of screw connections:
    - Coat with transmission oil. Tighten down nut with special tool 13 5 020 to 22 ft. lbs. (30 Nm).
    - Coat with transmission oil. Tighten nut to 22 ft. lbs. (30 Nm).
    - Tighten down screw for holder to 10 ft. lbs. (13 Nm).

➡Feed lines with soldered holder must be replaced by new version with Elastomeric clamp holder. Observe installation position of fuel low-pressure sensor. Lines for solenoid switches are laid behind fuel line.

21. Install feed line. In so doing, tighten screw connection hand-tight only
22. Follow sequence of screw connections:
    - Coat with transmission oil and tighten down nut with special tool 13 5 020 to 22 ft. lbs. (30 Nm).
    - Replace aluminum screw, coat with transmission oil and tighten to 8 ft. lbs. (10 Nm) plus an additional 90° of rotation.
23. Once the vehicle is started, check for leaks. If a strong fuel odor is present, or any fuel leakage is noted, stop the engine immediately and repair as necessary.

FUEL RAIL & INJECTORS

REMOVAL & INSTALLATION

N52 Engine

See Figures 168 through 170.

1. Before servicing the vehicle, refer to the precautions.
2. Read out fault memory of DME control unit; if necessary, work through test schedules
3. Switch ignition **OFF**.
4. Remove clean air pipe.
5. Remove ignition coil cover.
6. If necessary, unclip plug connection from holder and disconnect. Unclip wiring harnesses from holder and connector strip. Disconnect holder from injection pipe.
7. Remove protective cap from compressed air valve. Connect compressed air line to compressed air valve. Blow fuel back into tank with a short blast of compressed air maximum of 43 PSI (3 bar).
8. Unlock and detach fuel line.
9. Disconnect connector strip.
10. Remove injection pipe.
11. Seal fuel hose with special tool 13 5 281.
12. Pry out retainers and pull fuel injectors out of injection pipe.

To install:

13. Replace sealing rings on fuel injectors and coat with anti-friction rubber coating.
14. Install injectors and capture with retainers.
15. Remove special tool 13 5 281.
16. Install injection pipe.
17. Connect connector strip in reverse direction of arrow.
18. Connect fuel line and lock.
19. Install ignition coil cover.
20. Install clean air pipe.

Fig. 168 Connect compressed air line to compressed air valve. Blow fuel back into tank with a short blast of compressed air maximum of 43 PSI (3 bar)

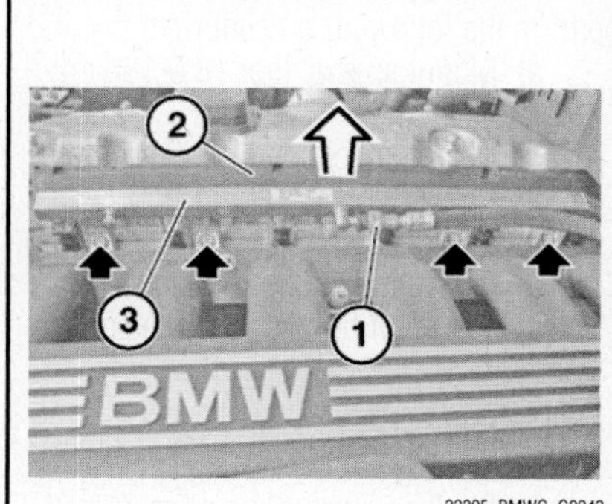

Fig. 169 Unlock and detach fuel line (1), detach connector strip (2), remove injection pipe (3).

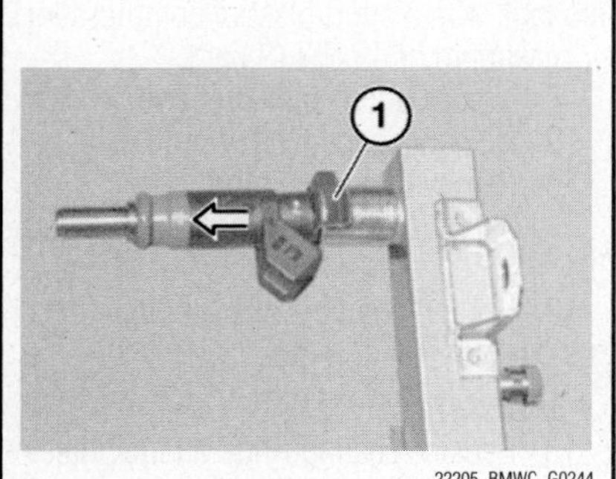

Fig. 170 Pry out retainers (1) and pull fuel injectors out of injection pipe

21. Check for stored fault messages, rectify faults and clear the fault memory.

N54 Engine

See Figures 171 through 177.

1. Before servicing the vehicle, refer to the precautions.
2. Read out fault memory of DME control unit; if necessary, work through test schedules
3. Switch ignition **OFF**.
4. Remove the pressure line at the injector.
    a. Unlock plug and remove.
    b. Remove screw and remove holding-down element.
    c. Remove injector.

⁂ WARNING

If several injectors are removed, ensure that each injector is reinstalled in its original location (cylinder). Mark injectors.

5. If the injector is stuck in its bore, perform the following procedure to free it:
    a. Mount special tool 13 0 180 on injector.
    b. Mount special tool 13 5 250.
    c. Carefully knock out injector with special tools 13 0 180 and 13 5 250.
    d. After removing, fit protective caps to injector tip and fuel line connection.

To install:

6. Installing a used fuel injector:
    a. Replace uncoupling element and the PTFE sealing ring.

⁂ WARNING

A PTFE seal which has been heated once by engine operation must be replaced before the fuel injector is reinstalled.

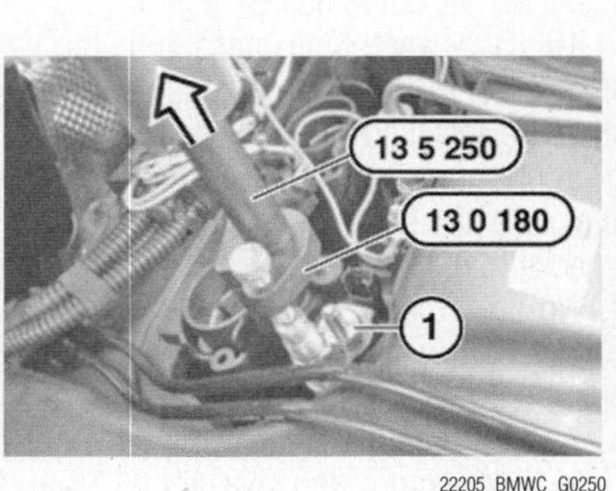

Fig. 171 Carefully knock out injector (1) with special tools 13 0 180 and 13 5 250

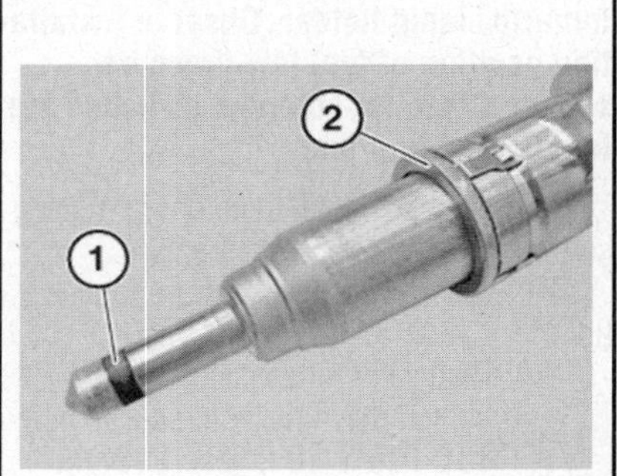

Fig. 172 Uncoupling element (2) and the PTFE sealing ring (1)

b. Before replacing PTFE sealing ring, make sure hands and work surface are clean and free of oil.

Avoid mechanical contact with injector tip.

c. Remove PTFE sealing ring with special tool 13 0 191 from injector.

d. Use a lint-free cloth only to remove combustion residues from cylindrical part of injector tip (do not use ultrasound or other tools/agents).

⁂ WARNING

Do not clean injector tip.

e. Slide new PTFE sealing ring onto mounting taper 13 0 195.

f. Use fingers and mounting taper 13 0 195 to slide PTFE sealing ring onto injector.

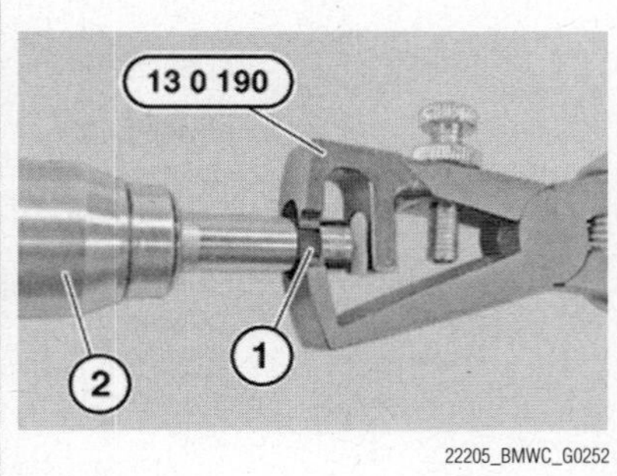

Fig. 173 Remove PTFE sealing ring (1) with special tool 13 0 191 from injector (2)

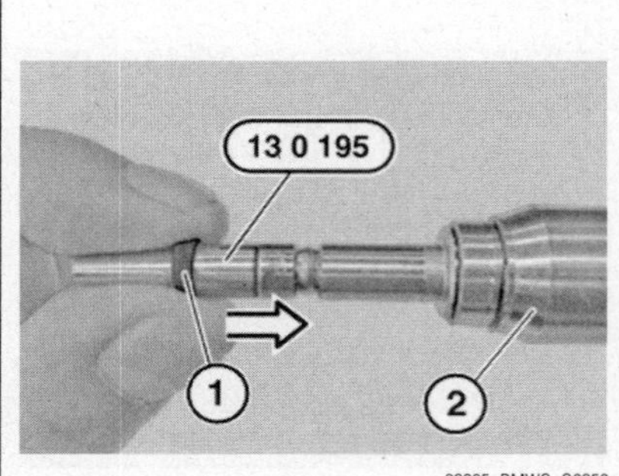

Fig. 174 Use fingers and mounting taper 13 0 195 to slide PTFE sealing ring (1) onto injector (2)

➡Do not use fingernails to slide PTFE sealing ring on. Do not use any lubricating agents. The sealing ring is expanded when slid on.

g. To bring the expanded PTFE sealing ring to its installation dimension, slide three mounting sleeves with decreasing diameters onto the injector.

h. Slide mounting sleeve with large opening first onto injector. Do not use any lubricating agents.

i. First slide mounting sleeve 13 0 192 (large diameter) onto injector. Then slide mounting sleeve 13 0 193 (medium diameter) onto injector. Finally, press injector into mounting sleeve 13 0 194 (small diameter).

⁂ WARNING

Install injector within 10 minutes or slide on protective cap as the PTFE sealing ring swells up.

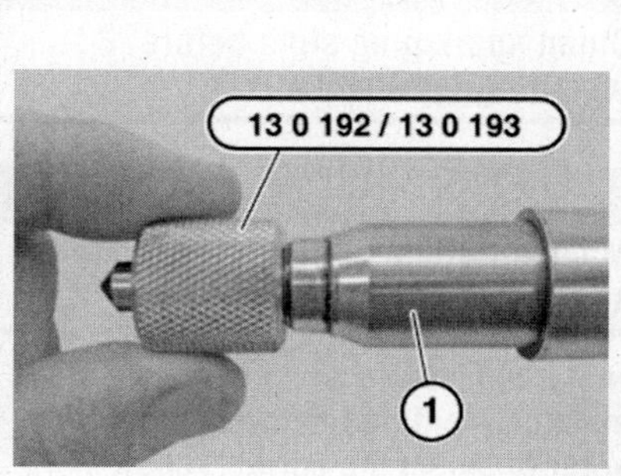

22205_BMWC_G0254

Fig. 175 To bring the expanded PTFE sealing ring to its installation dimension, slide three mounting sleeves with decreasing diameters onto the injector

7. Installing a new injector:
   a. Use a new uncoupling element.
   b. Remove protective cap from injector tip max. 10 min. before installation (PTFE sealing ring swells up).
8. Before installing injector in engines that have been run:
   a. Clean contact surfaces of uncoupling elements in cylinder head.
   b. Clean injector bore: To do so, preferably slide injector without uncoupling element but with new PTFE sealing ring in and out of injector bores several times.
   c. The PTFE sealing ring must then be replaced.
   d. Replace uncoupling element.

WARNING

An injector adjustment must be carried out if an injector is replaced or changed on the cylinder side.

Injector adjustment is carried out with the aid of a so-called adjustment value. The adjustment value is printed in two blocks of three digits on the injector. The adjustment value must be read off before installation.

9. Enter the adjustment value according to the installation position (cylinder) of the injector.

WARNING

If injector adjustment is not carried out, the engine may run roughly or fail to start.

10. Install injector and holding-down element. Make sure holding-down element is correctly seated.

WARNING

Tighten screw hand-tight only so that holding-down element is slack and if necessary injector can still be turned.

11. Connect contact plug.

➡Copper seals that may be fitted on the pressure lines are no longer needed and must be removed.

12. Connect pressure line, tightening nuts hand-tight only in the process.

WARNING

Connect pressure line without tension only.

13. To ensure distortion-free installation of the pressure line and to avoid damaging the thread, it must be possible for both nuts to be screwed on easily by hand.
14. If the nuts cannot be screwed on easily by hand, the injector must if necessary be turned a little.
15. Turn injector if necessary until nuts on pressure line can be easily screwed on by hand.
16. Tighten nuts on pressure line hand-tight.
17. Then tighten down screw for holding-down element to 10 ft. lbs. (13 Nm).
18. Adhere to tightening sequence:
    - First tighten down nut on injector
    - Then tighten down nut on high-pressure rail
19. When tightening nut on injector, grip hexagon head of injector with wrench.
20. Coat screw connection with transmission oil. Tighten down nuts with special tool 37 1 151 to 19 ft. lbs. (25 Nm).
21. Using a BMW DIS Tester perform the injector adjustment:
22. Check fuel system for leaks.
23. Check for stored fault messages, rectify faults and clear the fault memory.

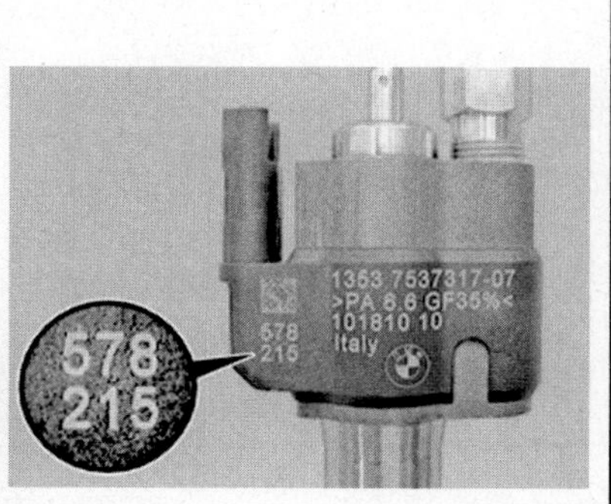

22205_BMWC_G0255

Fig. 176 The adjustment value is printed in two blocks of three digits on the injector. The adjustment value must be read off before installation

22205_BMWC_G0256

Fig. 177 Make sure holding-down element (1) is correctly seated

N55 Engine

See Figures 178 and 179.

WARNING

Fuel, oil and dirt particles may get into your eyes.

CAUTION

Wear full face guard and protective gloves.

WARNING

Observe warning on cylinder head cover.

WARNING

Disconnect negative battery terminal (risk of fire due to short circuit on removal).

WARNING

Carry out installation work on fuel system only with coolant temperature below 40 °C.

WARNING

Electric fuel pump starts up automatically when door is opened!

WARNING

Fuel can emerge spontaneously at high velocity from the fuel injectors!

WARNING

To reduce the fuel pressure, place rag over fuel injector and carefully tap against the fuel injector with a spanner.

CAUTION

There is a risk of injury if the fuel pressure is not reduced.

WARNING

Before removing the injectors, clean or vacuum off injector slots.

WARNING

There are two different injector versions for the N55 engine.

WARNING

A mixed installation of the components (hold-down device, spark plug shafts, injectors, cylinder heads, and screws) between the two hold-down device versions is not possible/permitted.

WARNING

Compliance with the following notes regarding the removal of the injectors is absolutely mandatory:

WARNING

Injectors may be pulled out with a maximum tensile force of 2000 N and twisted only to 6 Nm (torsion movement). If these values are exceeded, the injectors must be replaced!

WARNING

When assembling, it is essential to adhere to screwing sequences and tightening torques!

WARNING

Failure to comply with this requirement may result in leaks.

WARNING

Adhere to conditions of absolute cleanliness when working on the high-pressure fuel system.

WARNING

Introduced contaminants can cause malfunctions in the system.

WARNING

Do not allow any dirt particles or foreign bodies to get into the system.

WARNING

Remove all traces of dirt before removing lines or separate components.

WARNING

Use only fluff-free cloths.

WARNING

Seal all fuel system openings with protective caps or plugs.

WARNING

High pressure lines may be rescrewed a maximum of 10 times.

WARNING

Carry out engine cleaning/washing only with ignition coil cover fitted.

WARNING

No water may penetrate into injector slots and corrosion between injectors and cylinder head must be prevented.

WARNING

Prior to removing injectors, remove the ignition coil of the corresponding cylinder.

WARNING

Ignition coils must not become coated with fuel.

WARNING

The resistance of the silicone material is reduced significantly by contact with fuel, which may cause the ignition coil to fail. It is therefore essential to protect the spark plug slot against ingress of fuel with a cloth.

WARNING

Clean spark plug slots before installing ignition coils.

WARNING

Make sure the spark plug slot is absolutely clean.

➡The hold-down device version must be identified beforehand in order to select the correct repair instructions.

➡Remove acoustic cover

The bottom hold down device version can be found on the electromagnetic compatibility panel (1) installed about the injectors. (Up to engine number 14407684.)

The top hold-down device version can be found on the hold-down device installed on top (1). (From engine number 14407685.)

FUEL TANK

REMOVAL & INSTALLATION

See Figures 180 through 184.

1. Before servicing the vehicle, refer to the precautions.
2. Remove the supply fuel pump module.
3. Release hose clamp and detach fuel filler hose.
4. Unlock quick-release fastener (1) and detach vent line (2) from holder (3).
5. Heavily support the fuel tank.
6. Unfasten nut as shown.
7. Release screws for tightening straps on left and right and remove tightening straps.

71112_BMW1_G0340

Fig. 178 Identifying bottom hold down device version on the electromagnetic compatibility panel (1) above the injectors

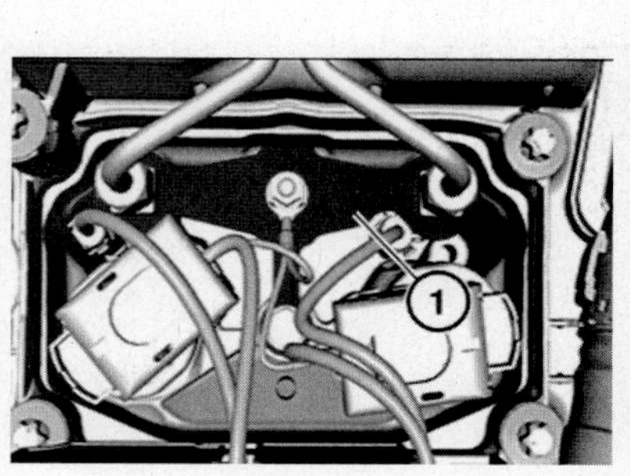

71112_BMW1_G0341

Fig. 179 Identifying top hold down device version on the hold down device installed on top (1)

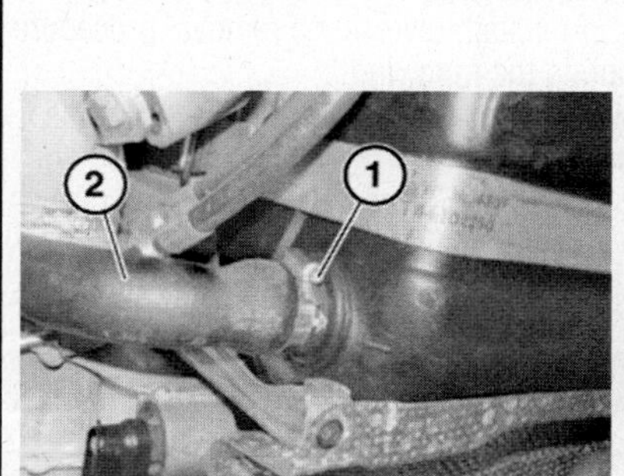

37698_BMW3_G0569

Fig. 180 Release hose clamp (1) and detach fuel filler hose (2)

⁂ WARNING

Carefully feed the vent line through the body when lowering the fuel tank.

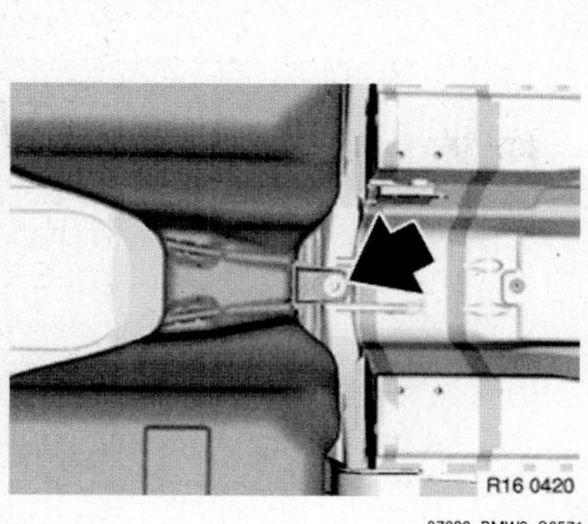

37698_BMW3_G0571

Fig. 182 Unfasten nut

37698_BMW3_G0572

Fig. 183 Release screws for tightening straps on left and right and remove tightening straps

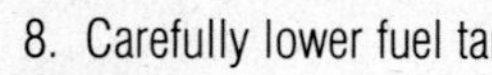

8. Carefully lower fuel tank.

To install:

9. Installation is the reverse of removal.

⁂ WARNING

Note rubber mount with spacer bush. Wide collar on spacer bush points to screw head.

10. Tighten bolts/nuts to specification as follows:
    - Fuel tank to body (Replace self locking nuts): 14 ft. lbs. (19 Nm)
    - Tension strap to body: 14 ft. lbs. (19 Nm)
    - Hose clamps: 36 inch lbs. (4 Nm)

THROTTLE BODY

REMOVAL & INSTALLATION

N51 and N52 Engines

See Figure 185.

1. Before servicing the vehicle, refer to the precautions.
2. Read out fault memory of DME control unit; if necessary, work through test schedules
3. Switch ignition **OFF**.
4. Remove air intake hose.
5. Unlock and disconnect line, then unlock connector and remove.
6. Remove throttle assembly

To install:

7. Installation is the reverse of removal.
8. Replace sealing ring of throttle assembly.
9. Install throttle assembly. Tighten bolts to 71 inch lbs. (8 Nm).
10. Install air intake hose.
11. Check for stored fault messages, rectify faults and clear the fault memory.

N55 Engine

See Figures 186 through 188.

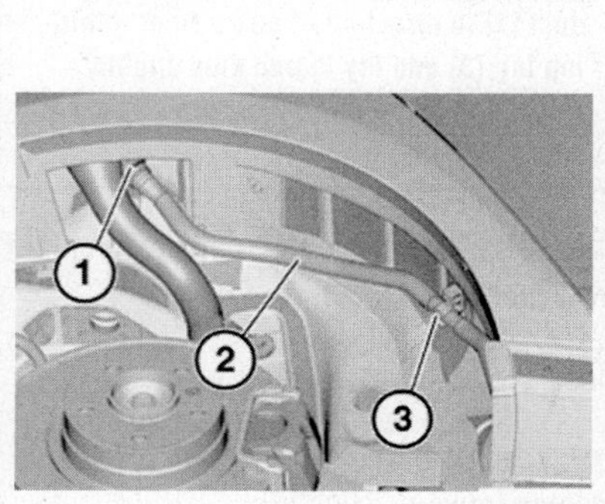

37698_BMW3_G0570

Fig. 181 Unlock quick-release fastener (1) and detach vent line (2) from holder (3)

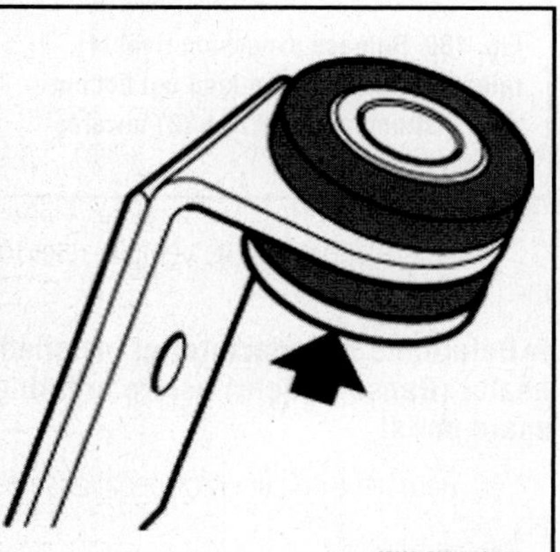

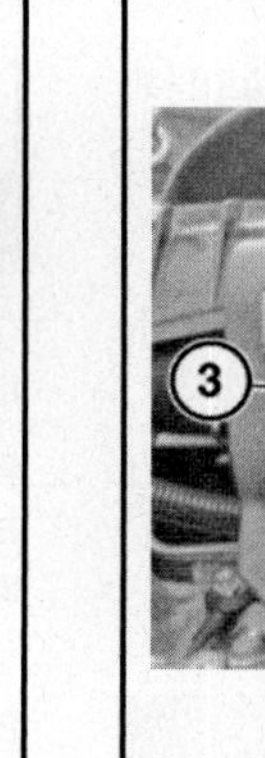

37698_BMW3_G0573

Fig. 184 Note rubber mount with spacer bush. Wide collar on spacer bush points to screw head

37698_BMW1_G0193

Fig. 185 Unlock and disconnect line (1), unlock connector (2) and remove throttle assembly (3)

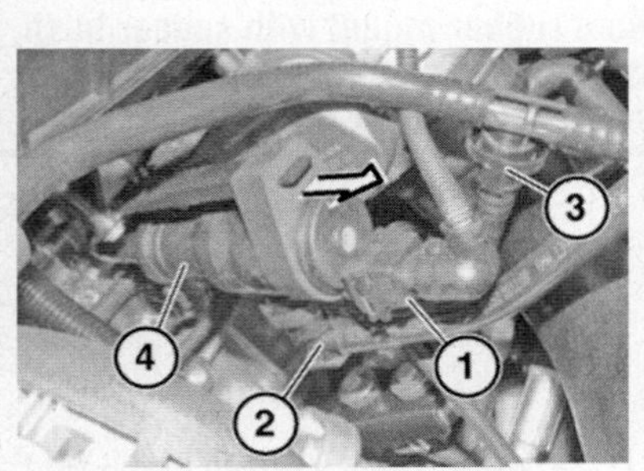

Fig. 186 Unlocking and removing connector (1), unlocking and disconnecting hoses (2 and 3) and removing tank vent valve (4)

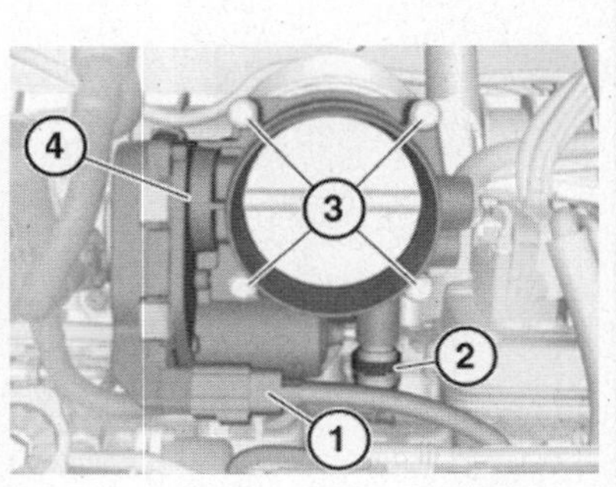

Fig. 187 Unlocking and removing connector (1), releasing screws (3), unlocking and removing tank ventilation line (2) and removing throttle body (4)

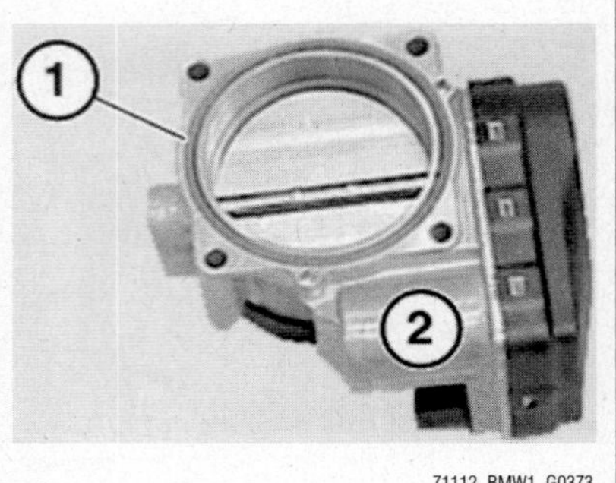

Fig. 188 Replacing sealing ring (1) of throttle body (2)

1. Switch off ignition.
2. Remove rear charge-air duct.
3. Unlock connector (1) and remove.
4. Unlock and disconnect hoses (2) and (3).
5. Remove tank vent valve (4) from holder in the direction of arrow and place aside.
6. Unlock connector (1) and remove.
7. Release screws (3).
8. Partially remove throttle body (4) and unlock tank ventilation line (2) and remove.
   a. Tightening torque 13 54 1AZ.
9. Remove throttle body (4).

To install:

To install, reverse the removal procedure noting the following.

10. Replace sealing ring (1) of throttle body (2).
11. Check stored fault message.
12. Delete fault memory.

HEATING & AIR CONDITIONING SYSTEM

BLOWER MOTOR

REMOVAL & INSTALLATION

See Figures 189 through 191.

1. Before servicing the vehicle, refer to the precautions.
2. Remove trim for instrument panel at bottom right.
3. Detach right foot well heating duct in direction of arrow from retaining lug and lay to one side slightly. Prior to installation, Make sure clip is correctly seated.
4. Unfasten plug connection and disconnect.
5. Raise plastic lug slightly and turn fan in direction of arrow.
6. Remove fan from fan shell.

To install:

7. Installation is the reverse of removal.
8. If necessary, raise lug slightly and screw in fan counterclockwise.
9. Make sure fan is correctly seated in fan shell.
10. Check exact position of lug.

HEATER CORE

REMOVAL & INSTALLATION

See Figures 192 through 197.

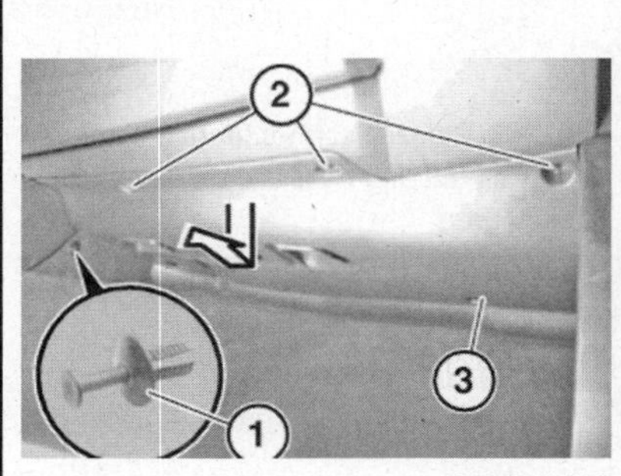

Fig. 189 Release expansion rivet (1), release screws (2) and feed out bottom right instrument panel trim (3) towards bottom front

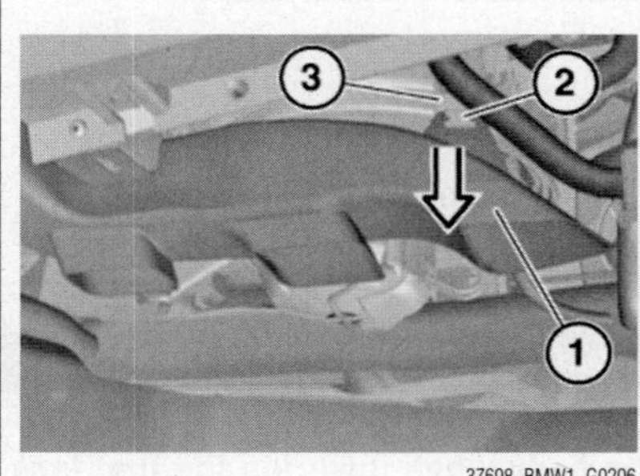

Fig. 190 Detach right foot well heating duct (1) in direction of arrow from retaining lug (3) and lay to one side slightly. Prior to installation, make sure clip (2) is correctly seated

1. Before servicing the vehicle, refer to the precautions.

➡Determine manufacturer of installed heater (Denso or Behr) before ordering spare parts!

2. Remove trim panel for pedal assembly.
3. Remove heater unit.
4. Release screws.
5. Slide rubber grommet with foam seal forward slightly.
6. Carefully feed pipe holder with pipes past rubber grommet.
7. If necessary, remove coolant hose.
8. Release screws and remove cover.
9. Release screws and slide screw clamps forwards slightly.
10. Remove pipes from heater core.

To install:

11. Installation is the reverse of removal.

1. Plug connection 4. Fan
2. Plastic lug 5. Fan shell
3. Lug
37698_BMW1_G0207

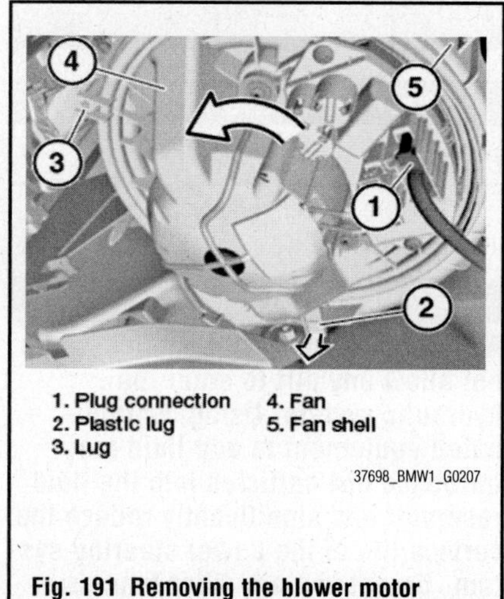

Fig. 191 Removing the blower motor

1. Screw 3. Expander rivets
2. Screw 4. Panel
37698_BMW1_G0128

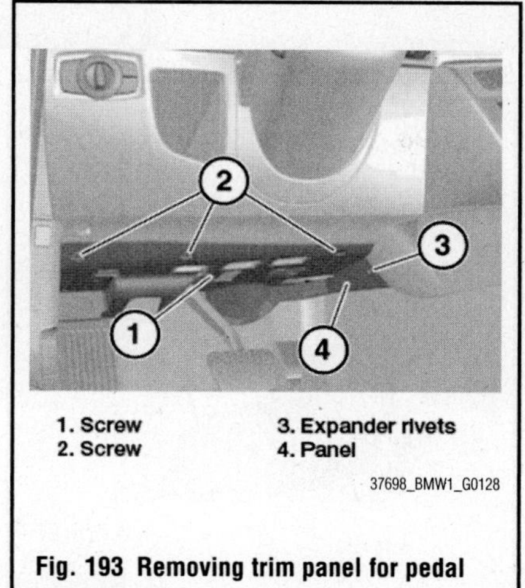

Fig. 193 Removing trim panel for pedal assembly

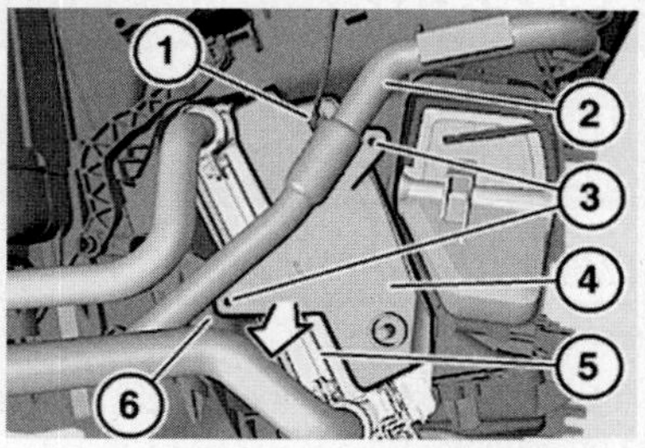

1. Plug connections (Diesel only)
2. Coolant hose
3. Screws
4. Auxiliary heater (Diesel only)
5. Heater (Diesel only)
6. Heater/air conditioner (Diesel only)
37698_BMW1_G0195

Fig. 195 If necessary, remove coolant hose, release screws and remove cover

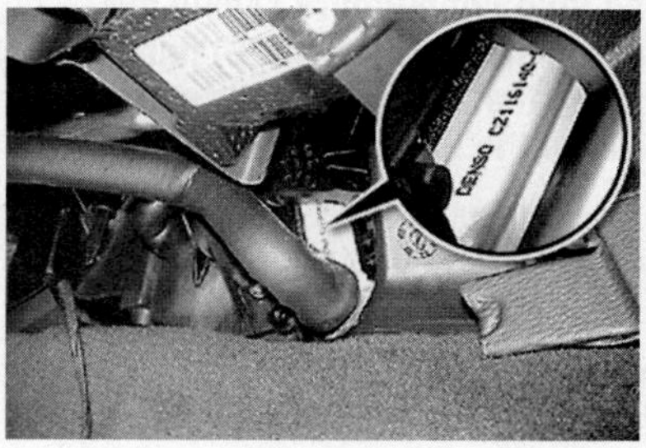

37698_BMW1_G0198

Fig. 192 Determine manufacturer of installed heater (Denso or Behr) before ordering spare parts

1. Screws 3. Pipe holder
2. Rubber grommet 4. Pipes
37698_BMW1_G0194

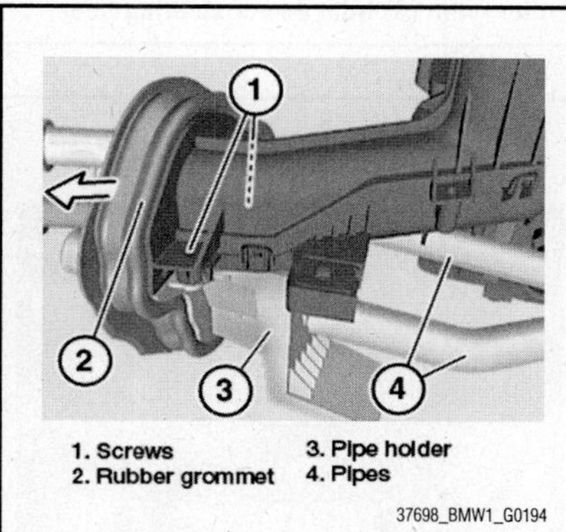

Fig. 194 Release screws, slide rubber grommet with foam seal forward slightly and carefully feed pipe holder with pipes past rubber grommet

1. Screws 3. Pipes
2. Screw clamps 4. Heater core
37698_BMW1_G0196

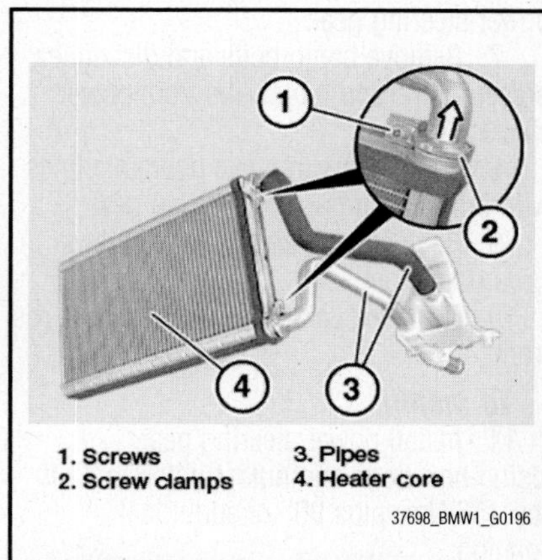

Fig. 196 Release screws, slide screw clamps forwards slightly and remove pipes from heater core

12. When installing, make sure that the return-flow connection (larger opening) marked with a black dot is positioned at the top.

⁂ WARNING

Inflow connection may only be positioned at the bottom.

13. Replace sealing rings. Coat sealing rings with antiseize agent. Make sure sealing rings are correctly seated.
14. If necessary, replace rubber grommet and/or foam seal.
15. Make sure rubber grommet is correctly seated on pipe holder.
16. Check system for proper operation.

37698_BMW1_G0197

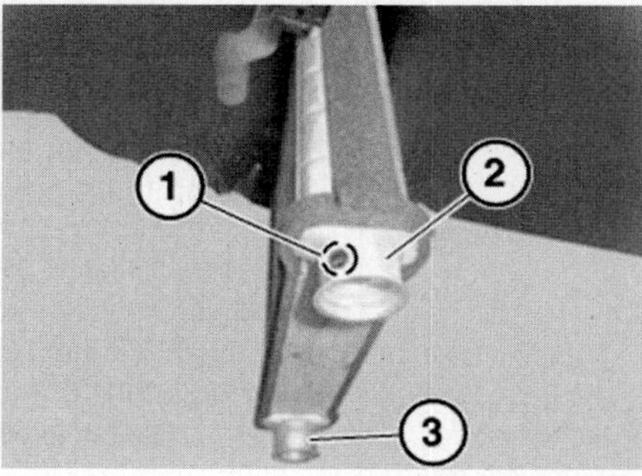

Fig. 197 When installing, make sure that the return-flow connection (2) (larger opening) marked with a black dot (1) is positioned at the top

STEERING

POWER RACK & PINION STEERING GEAR

REMOVAL & INSTALLATION

See Figures 198 through 200.

1. Before servicing the vehicle, refer to the precautions.
2. Draw off and dispose of hydraulic fluid from fluid reservoir
3. Remove front underbody protection.
4. Remove both tie rod ends from ball joint.
5. Remove lower steering spindle from power steering gear
6. If necessary, remove heat shield from power steering gear.
7. Remove banjo bolts and disconnect pressure line and return line from power steering gear.
8. If necessary, remove hydraulic lines with bracket from power steering gear.
9. Remove nuts and remove screws towards bottom.
10. Remove power steering gear towards front.

To install:

11. Install power steering gear.
Using new bolts and nuts, tighten to 41 ft. lbs. (56 Nm) plus 90° of additional rotation.
12. Install hydraulic lines with bracket to power steering gear.
13. Replace all sealing rings.
14. Connect pressure line and return line from power steering gear. Tighten pressure line to 22 ft. lbs. (30 Nm) and return line to 26 ft. lbs. (35 Nm).

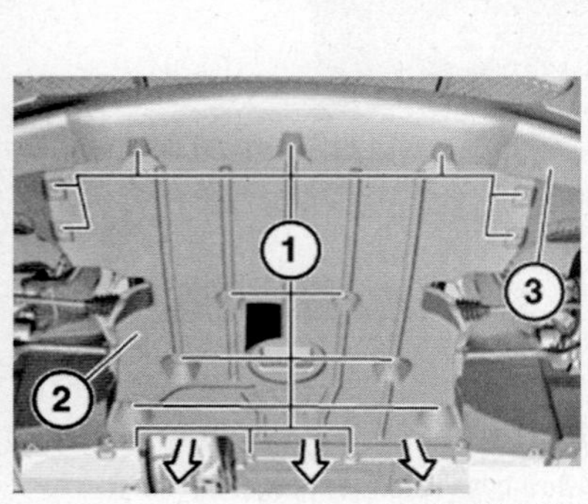

Fig. 198 Release screws (1) and pull underbody protection (2) forward under bumper trim (3)

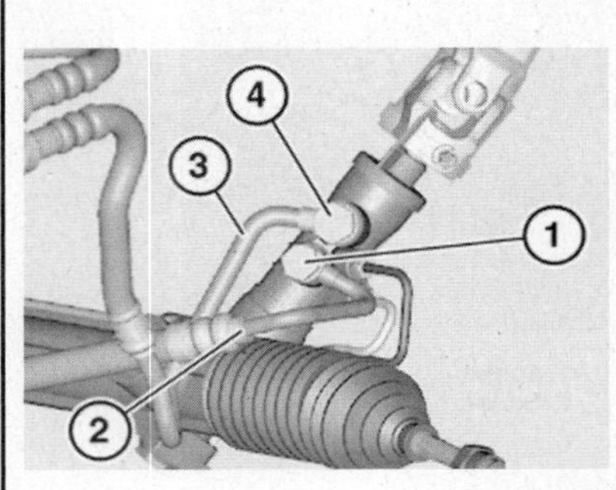

Fig. 199 Remove banjo bolts (1 and 4), then disconnect pressure line (2) and return line (3) from power steering gear

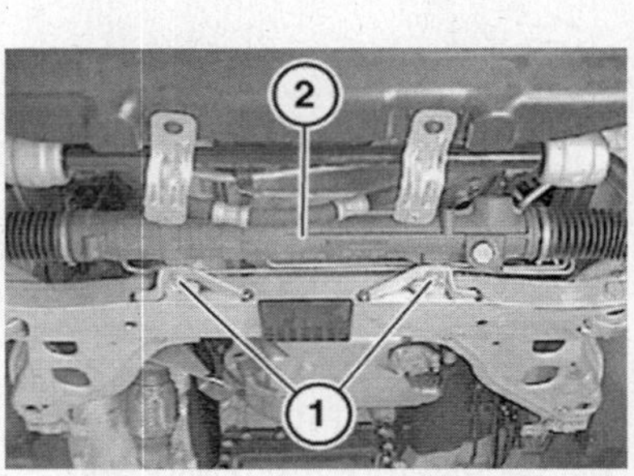

Fig. 200 Remove nuts and remove screws (1) towards bottom, then remove power steering gear (2) towards front

⁂ WARNING

Make sure hydraulic lines are laid without tension and with sufficient spacing to adjoining components.

15. Install heat shield on power steering gear.
16. Install lower steering spindle on power steering gear
17. Install both tie rod ends on ball joint.
18. Install front underbody protection.
19. Fill and bleed hydraulic system.
20. Check pipe connections for leaks.
21. Perform chassis alignment check.
22. Carry out steering angle sensor adjustment.

POWER STEERING PUMP

BLEEDING

1. Before servicing the vehicle, refer to the precautions.

⁂ WARNING

Adhere to the utmost cleanliness. Do not allow any dirt to enter the hydraulic system. Using contaminated equipment to add fluid may introduce dirt particles into the fluid reservoir and significantly reduce the service life of the power steering system. Do not use any filler funnels or similar.

➡The fill level may only be checked or adjusted when the engine is stopped. The fluid temperature should be approximately 68°F (20°C) here. Ensure that the cap is fully screwed in prior to the fill level check.

2. Thoroughly clean fluid reservoir and its immediate surroundings
3. Check and correct fill level.

➡The fill level can come to rest above the MAX mark when the engine is at normal operating temperature. This is dictated by the design in that the marking on the dipstick is referred to a fluid temperature of 68°F (20°C). With the engine at normal operating temperature (approximately 122–140°F (50–60°C) fluid temperature adjust a fill height 0.39 in. (10 mm) above the MAX mark. Do not under any circumstances draw off the fluid to the MAX mark when the engine is at normal operating temperature.

4. Start engine.
5. Turn steering wheel left and right twice in each case up to full lock; if necessary, top up hydraulic fluid (e.g. if hydraulic system is completely drained).
6. Move steering wheel to straight-ahead position and turn off engine.
7. Check and correct fill level with engine stopped.
8. Check hydraulic system for leaks.

REMOVAL & INSTALLATION

See Figures 198, 201 and 202.

⁂ WARNING

Aluminum-magnesium materials. No steel screws/bolts may be used due

to the threat of electrochemical corrosion. A magnesium crankcase requires aluminum screws/bolts exclusively.

Aluminum screws/bolts must be replaced each time they are Removed. The end faces of aluminum screws/bolts are painted blue for the purposes of reliable identification. Jointing torque and angle of rotation must be observed without fail (risk of damage).

1. Before servicing the vehicle, refer to the precautions.
2. Draw off and dispose of hydraulic fluid from fluid reservoir.
3. Remove intake filter housing.
4. Remove belt pulley.
5. Remove front underbody protection.
6. Remove radiator seal.
7. Remove hose clamp and detach suction line from vane pump.
8. Remove bolt and remove bracket with refrigerant line.
9. Remove screws.
10. Remove banjo bolt and disconnect pressure line.
11. Remove bolts and remove vane pump towards bottom.

To install:

12. Markings on suction line and vane pump connection must match up.
13. Replace aluminum screws.
14. Replace all sealing rings.
15. Make sure pressure line and return lines are laid without tension and with sufficient spacing to adjoining components. Tighten pressure line to 22 ft. lbs. (30 Nm) and return line to 26 ft. lbs. (35 Nm).
16. Tighten pump fasteners to specification as follows:
    - Secure vane pump with screws
    - Tighten side screws to 18 inch lbs. (2 Nm)
    - Tighten front screws to 18 inch lbs. (2 Nm)
    - Tighten down front screws to 15 ft. lbs. (20 Nm) plus an additional 90° rotation
    - Remove screws at side and check screw fastening points for gap freedom
    - Tighten down side screws to 15 ft. lbs. (20 Nm) plus an additional 90° rotation
17. Fill and bleed hydraulic system
18. Check pipe connections for leaks.

22205_BMWC_G0280

Fig. 201 Hose clamp (1) and suction line (2)

22205_BMWC_G0281

Fig. 202 Pressure line banjo bolt (1) and pump mounting bolts

FLUID FILL PROCEDURE

WARNING

Adhere to the utmost cleanliness. Do not allow any dirt to enter the hydraulic system. Using contaminated equipment to add fluid may introduce dirt particles into the fluid reservoir and significantly reduce the service life of the power steering system. Do not use any filler funnels or similar.

➡The fill level may only be checked or adjusted when the engine is stopped. The fluid temperature should be approximately 68°F (20°C) here. Ensure that the cap is fully screwed in prior to the fill level check.

1. Thoroughly clean fluid reservoir and its immediate surroundings
2. Check and correct fill level.

➡The fill level can come to rest above the MAX mark when the engine is at normal operating temperature. This is dictated by the design in that the marking on the dipstick is referred to a fluid temperature of 68°F (20°C). With the engine at normal operating temperature (approximately 122–140°F (50–60°C) fluid temperature adjust a fill height 0.39 in. (10 mm) above the MAX mark. Do not under any circumstances draw off the fluid to the MAX mark when the engine is at normal operating temperature.

3. Bleed the system.

KNUCKLE & SPINDLE

REMOVAL & INSTALLATION

See Figure 203.

1. Before servicing the vehicle, refer to the precautions.
2. Remove front brake disk.
3. Remove front wheel speed sensor.
4. If necessary, remove jointed rod of ride-height sensor from control arm.
5. Slacken control arm bolt connection on front axle carrier in order to prevent control arm rubber mount from being elongated.
6. Remove control arm from steering knuckle.
7. Remove tie rod end from steering knuckle.
8. Remove strut from steering knuckle.
9. Support steering knuckle with workshop jack and a suitable mounting.
10. Remove nut, remove holder and remove screw.
11. Spread steering knuckle with special tool 31 2 230.
12. Lower workshop jack and remove steering knuckle.

To install:

13. Keep press fit of swivel gearing and spring strut in lower area clean and free from oil and grease.
14. Expand steering knuckle with special tool 31 2 230, align by way of gap to positioning pins on back of spring strut and raise up to stop.
15. Make sure steering knuckle contacts stop correctly.
16. Replace self-locking nut.
17. Install the nut, holder and screw. Tighten to 60 ft. lbs. (81 Nm).

➡Screw head must point in direction of travel.

WARNING

Check sensor head and line from pulse generator prior to installation for external damage, replacing if necessary.

18. The remainder of the installation is the reverse of removal.
19. Perform chassis alignment check.
20. Carry out steering angle sensor adjustment/adjustment for active front steering.

LOWER BALL JOINTS

REMOVAL & INSTALLATION

See Figures 204 and 205.

1. Remove coil spring at rear.
2. If necessary, remove jointed rod of ride-height sensor from camber arm bracket.
3. Remove rear shock absorber from rubber mount.
4. Remove camber arm from wheel carrier.
5. Remove trailing arm from wheel carrier.
6. Pull out and remove ball joint with special tools 33 4 465 , 33 4 466 , 33 4 475 , 33 4 474 and 33 4 482 .

To install:

7. Push in new ball joint until it stops using special tools 33 4 481 , 33 4 474 , 33 4 475 , 33 4 466 and 33 4 465 .
8. Perform chassis alignment check.

33 4 481
33 4 475
33 4 465
33 4 474
33 4 466
71112_BMW1_G0405

Fig. 205 Installing ball joint

LOWER CONTROL ARMS

REMOVAL & INSTALLATION

See Figures 206 and 207.

1. Before servicing the vehicle, refer to the precautions.
2. Remove front wheel.
3. Remove front underbody protection.
4. If necessary, remove jointed rod of ride-height sensor from control arm.
5. Remove lower ball joint nut; if necessary, grip at Torx® socket (T40).
6. Remove lower control arm nut. Remove screw towards front.
7. If necessary remove bracket with ride-height sensor.
8. Remove control arm.

To install:

9. Install control arm.

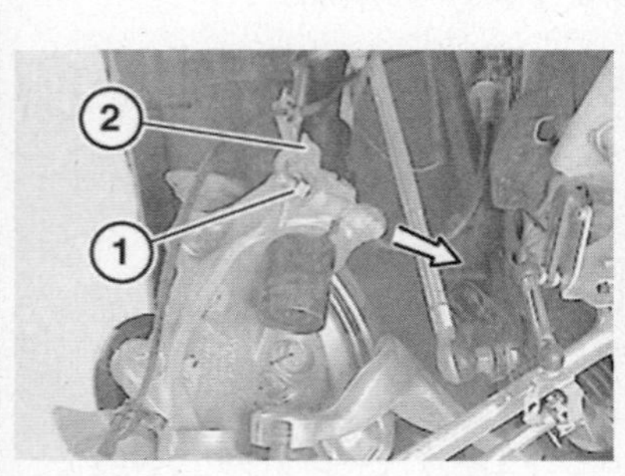

Fig. 203 Remove nut (1), remove holder (2) and remove screw

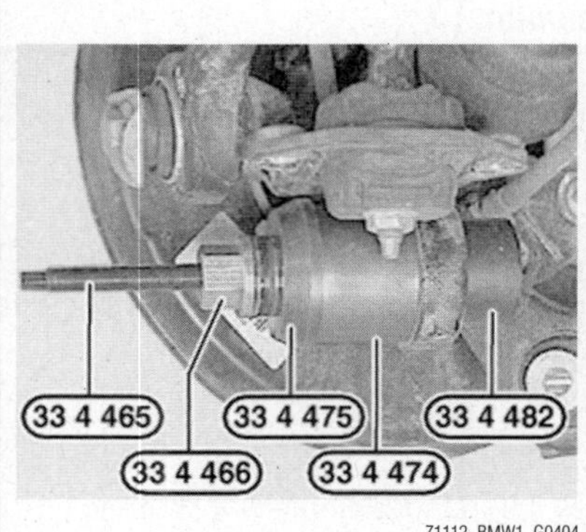

Fig. 204 Removing ball joint

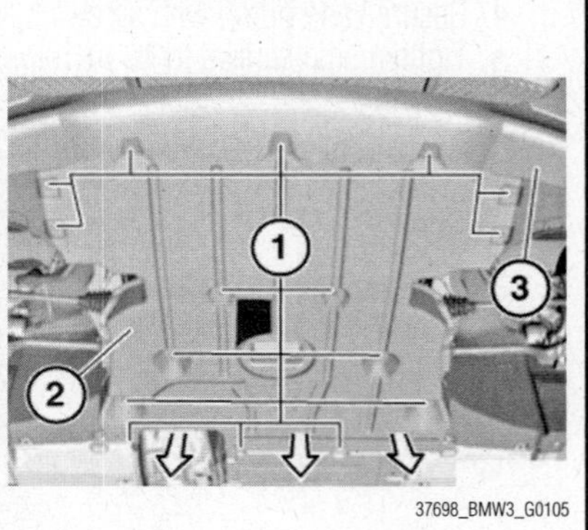

Fig. 206 Release screws (1) and pull underbody protection (2) forward under bumper trim (3)

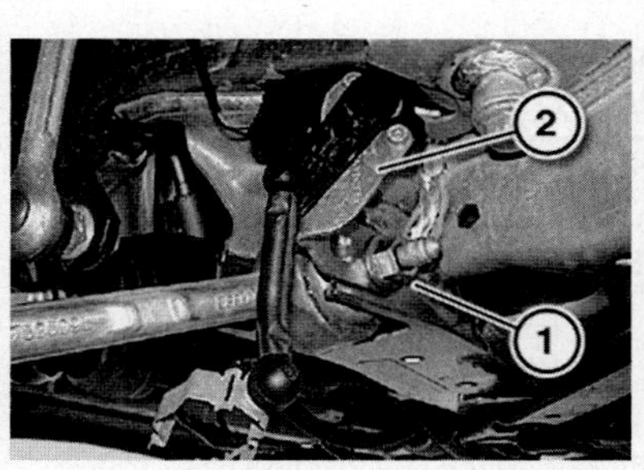

22205_BMWC_G0292

Fig. 207 Remove nut (1), then remove screw towards front. If necessary remove bracket (2) with ride-height sensor

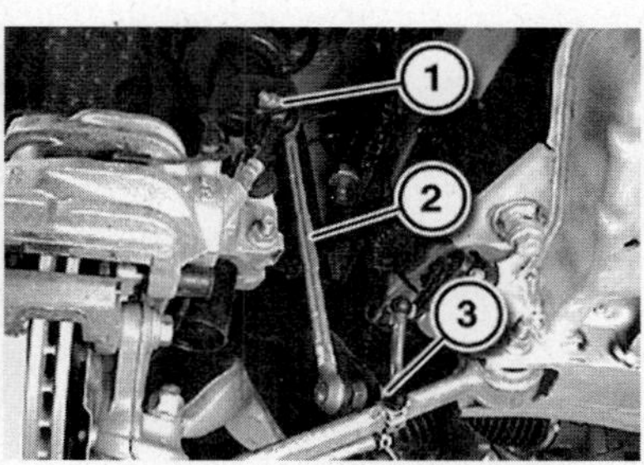

22205_BMWC_G0296

Fig. 208 Remove nut (1) and remove bracket for brake hose. Remove nut (3) and remove stabilizer link (2)

➡Screw head must point in direction of travel. Replace self-locking nut.

10. Temporarily tighten down bolt and nut. Once the vehicle is lowered to normal ride height, finish tightening to 50 ft. lbs. (68 Nm) plus an additional 90° rotation.
11. Keep control arm to ball joint connection clean and free from oil and grease.
12. Replace self-locking nut and tighten to 122 ft. lbs. (165 Nm).
13. Perform chassis alignment check.
14. Carry out steering angle sensor adjustment/adjustment for active front steering.MacPherson Strut

STABILIZER BAR (SWAY BAR) & LINKS

REMOVAL & INSTALLATION

Stabilizer Bar

See Figures 208 and 209.

1. Before servicing the vehicle, refer to the precautions.
2. Remove front underbody protection.
3. Remove stabilizer link on both sides from stabilizer.
4. Remove bolts and remove brackets.
5. Remove nuts; if necessary, grip screws after repair.
6. Remove stabilizer; if necessary, press off front axle carrier with a suitable tool.

To install:

7. If studs are damaged, repair as follows:
   a. Remove bolt.
   b. Raise locking nut in area of bore and detach from front axle carrier.
   c. Drive out studs in upwards direction and remove/feed out through an opening in front axle carrier.
   d. Insert new screws from above.
8. Check both rubber mounts for damage, replace if necessary.
9. Install stabilizer and secure with brackets.
10. Replace locking nut and tighten temporarily. Once vehicle is at normal ride height, tighten to 50 ft. lbs. (68 Nm) plus an additional 90° rotation.

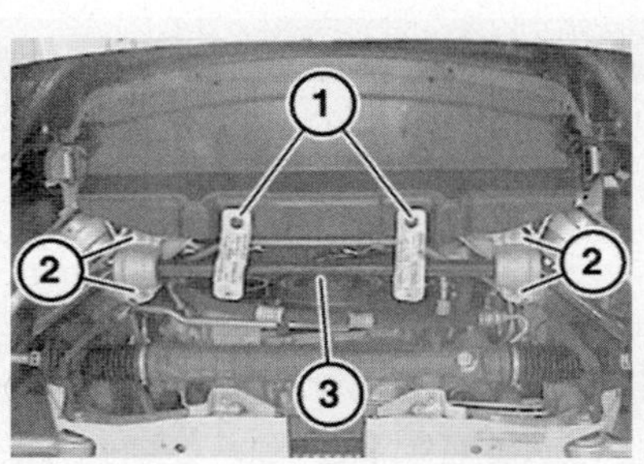

22205_BMWC_G0297

Fig. 209 Remove bolts (1) and remove brackets. Remove nuts (2); if necessary, grip screws after repair. Remove stabilizer (3)

⁂ WARNING

To avoid complaints being made by the customer about noise (e.g. grating), set the car on its wheels and tighten down the stabilizer mounting to specified torque.

11. Connect stabilizer link on both sides from stabilizer. Tighten nuts to 43 ft. lbs. (58 Nm).
12. Install front underbody protection.

STRUTS

REMOVAL & INSTALLATION

See Figure 210.

1. Before servicing the vehicle, refer to the precautions.
2. Remove front wheel.
3. Remove stabilizer link from spring strut.
4. Disconnect plug connection for pulse generator and expose line up to holder on spring strut.
5. Disconnect plug connection for brake pad sensor and expose line up to brake caliper.
6. Remove front brake disc.
7. If necessary, remove jointed rod of ride-height sensor from control arm.
8. Slacken control arm bolt connection on front axle carrier in order to prevent control arm rubber mount from being damaged.
9. Remove control arm from steering knuckle.
10. Remove tie rod end from steering knuckle.
11. Remove tension strut from steering knuckle.

⁂ WARNING

Secure spring strut against falling out.

12. Remove tension strut (on spring strut dome) and mark position of threaded pins to wheel arch.
13. Remove nuts and remove spring strut with steering knuckle towards bottom.

To install:

14. If necessary, replace faulty sealing washer.

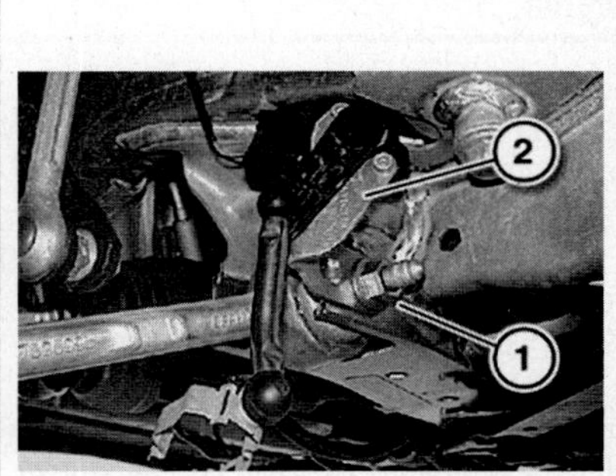

22205_BMWC_G0292

Fig. 210 Sealing washer (1) and plate insert (2)

15. Clean contact surface in spring strut dome.
16. Align spring strut using centering pin to bore in wheel arch or studs to wheel arch and push upwards.
17. Replace self-locking nuts and tighten to 25 ft. lbs. (34 Nm).
18. The remainder of the installation is the reverse of removal.
19. Perform chassis alignment check.
20. Carry out steering angle sensor adjustment/adjustment for active front steering.

WHEEL HUBS & BEARINGS

ADJUSTMENT

Wheel bearings cannot be adjusted. The front wheel bearings are pressed into the hub and are not available separately. If a front wheel bearing is in need of replacement, it is replaces as a unit with the hub.

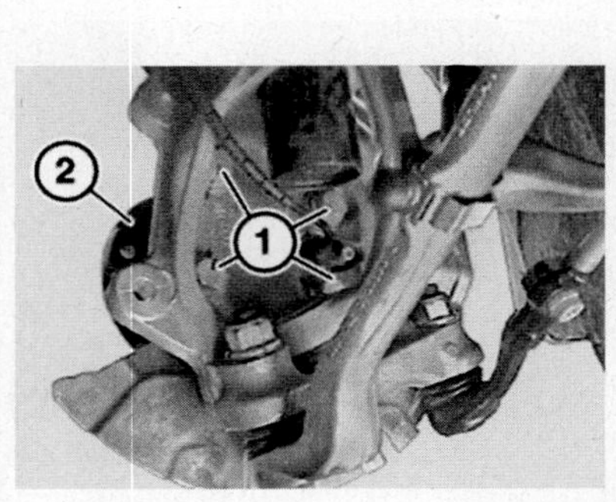

Fig. 211 Remove bolts (1) and press wheel bearing (2) off steering knuckle with a suitable tool

REMOVAL, PACKING, & INSTALLATION

See Figure 211.

1. Before servicing the vehicle, refer to the precautions.
2. Remove brake disk.
3. Remove bolts.
4. Press wheel bearing off steering knuckle with a suitable tool.

To install:

5. When reusing the wheel bearing, recut all the threads in the wheel bearing.
6. Keep contact surface of steering knuckle and wheel bearing clean and free from oil and grease.
7. Replace microencapsulated screws and tighten to 81 ft. lbs. (110 Nm).

SUSPENSION — REAR SUSPENSION

COIL SPRINGS

REMOVAL & INSTALLATION

See Figures 212 and 213.

1. Before servicing the vehicle, refer to the precautions.
2. Remove rear wheel.
3. Insert lower spring plate 33 5 012 centrally into coil spring and turn to lowest coil guide spindles 33 5 013, 33 5 014, 33 5 015 from below through camber arm and lower spring plate 33 5 012.
4. Insert upper spring plate 33 5 011 sideways into coil spring and turn to uppermost coil.

WARNING

Make sure spindle (hexagon) is correctly seated in upper spring plate 33 5 011. pull spindle 33 5 013 downwards.

5. Align special tools 33 5 011, 33 5 012, 33 5 013, 33 5 014, 33 5 015 centrally to obtain the biggest possible contact surface on the coil spring.
6. Check installation position of special tools 33 5 011, 33 5 012 and 33 5 013, 33 5 014, 33 5 015, correct if necessary.
7. Tension coil spring using special tools 33 5 016 and 33 5 020, gripping spindle of spring tensioner with special tool 33 5 017 in the process.
8. Remove coil spring upwards.

To install:

9. Bottom end of coil spring must be flush with opening of spring plate 33 5 012.

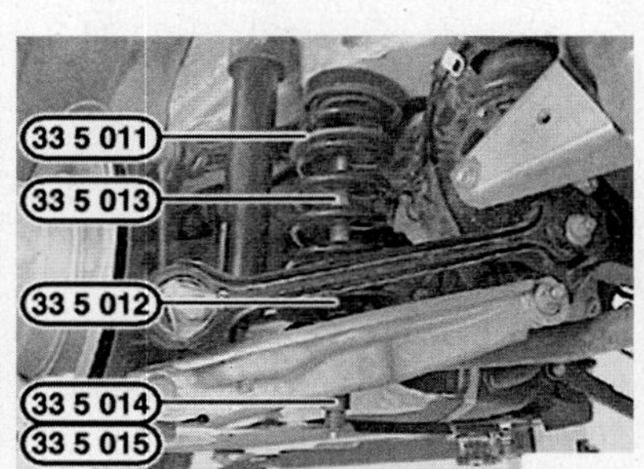

Fig. 212 Align special tools 33 5 011, 33 5 012, 33 5 013, 33 5 014, 33 5 015 centrally to obtain the biggest possible contact surface on the coil spring

10. Check spring mounts for damage, replace if necessary.
11. Remove spring plate and position with upper spring pad on coil spring.

➡Upper spring pad must come into contact with end of coil spring.

12. Lower spring pad must be positively seated in the designated receptacle in the camber arm
   a. Lower spring pad must come into contact with end of coil spring.
   b. Lower spring pad must rest flush on last coil.
13. Align coil spring by way of spring plate to opening in side member and relieve tension.

Fig. 213 Lower spring pad must be positively seated in the designated receptacle in the camber arm. The spring pad must come into contact with end of coil spring (arrow) and must rest flush on last coil (broken line)

14. Remove special tools 33 5 011, 33 5 012 and 33 5 013, 33 5 014, 33 5 015.
15. Check headlight adjustment, correct if necessary.

CONTROL LINKS

REMOVAL & INSTALLATION

Trailing Arm

See Figure 214.

1. Before servicing the vehicle, refer to the precautions.
2. Remove rear wheel.
3. Remove nuts.
4. Unscrew bolts.

5. Remove trailing arm downwards.
6. Note insertion direction of bolts.
7. Replace self-locking nuts and tighten temporarily.
8. Lower vehicle to normal ride height and tighten bolts to 74 ft. lbs. (100 Nm).
9. Perform chassis alignment check.

Upper Control Arm

See Figures 214 and 215.

1. Before servicing the vehicle, refer to the precautions.
2. Remove rear wheel.
3. Remove bolt.
4. Remove nut and remove screw towards front.
5. Unclip line holder for pulse generator or brake pad sensor on control arm.
6. Remove control arm.

To install:

7. Install control arm.

WARNING

Make sure during installation that in the connection area to the wheel carrier the tapered end of the bearing bushing (of the rubber mount) points in the direction of the wheel carrier.

8. Install control arm to rear axle carrier bolt and point head in direction of travel.
9. Replace self-locking nut and tighten to 74 ft. lbs. (100 Nm).
10. If necessary, raise brake disk in drive flange area with workshop jack.
11. Replace control arm to wheel carrier bolt and tighten temporarily. Fully tighten the bolt once the vehicle is at ride height to 74 ft. lbs. (100 Nm) plus 90° additional rotation.

22205_BMWC_G0300

Fig. 215 Make sure during installation that in the connection area to the wheel carrier the tapered end of the bearing bushing (of the rubber mount) points in the direction of the wheel carrier

12. Perform chassis alignment check.

STABILIZER BAR & LINKS

REMOVAL & INSTALLATION

See Figures 216 and 217.

1. Before servicing the vehicle, refer to the precautions.
2. Remove both rear coil springs.
3. Remove left control arm on wheel carrier.
4. Remove both stabilizer links from stabilizer.
5. Lower rear axle carrier.
6. Remove bolts and remove both rubber mounts from stabilizer.
7. Turn stabilizer and remove sideways.

To install:

8. Check both rubber mounts for damage, replace if necessary.

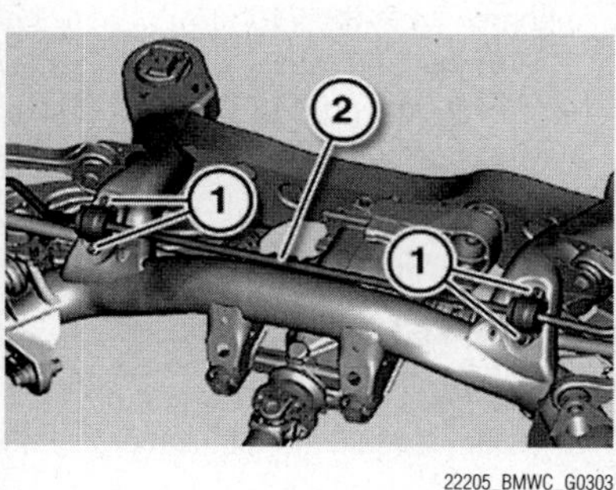

22205_BMWC_G0303

Fig. 217 Stabilizer bar (2) and mounting bolts (1)

9. Tightening fasteners to specification.
   - Retaining bracket, stabilizer bar to rear axle support: 16 ft. lbs. (21 Nm)
   - Stabilizer link to stabilizer: 43 ft. lbs. (58 Nm)
   - Stabilizer link to wheel carrier: 16 ft. lbs. (21 Nm)
10. Raise rear axle carrier.
11. Install both rear coil springs.
12. Install left control arm on wheel carrier.
13. Bleed braking system.

TRAILING ARMS

REMOVAL & INSTALLATION

See Figure 218.

➡If the trailing arm is detached from the rear axle support/wheel carrier, it is necessary after reinstallation to carry out a wheel/chassis alignment check.

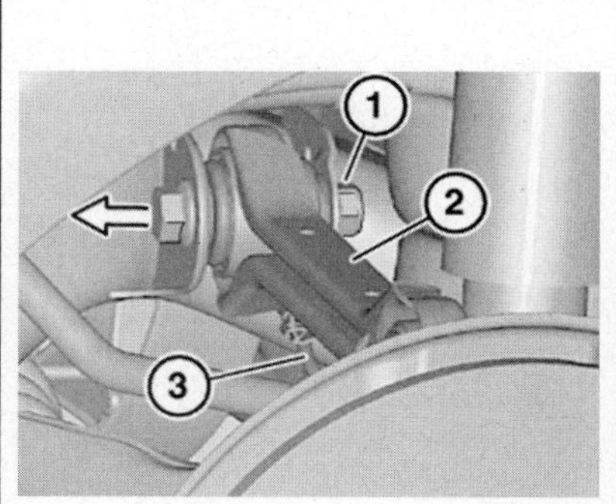

22205_BMWC_G0301

Fig. 214 Remove nut (1), remove control arm (2) and line holder (3) for pulse generator

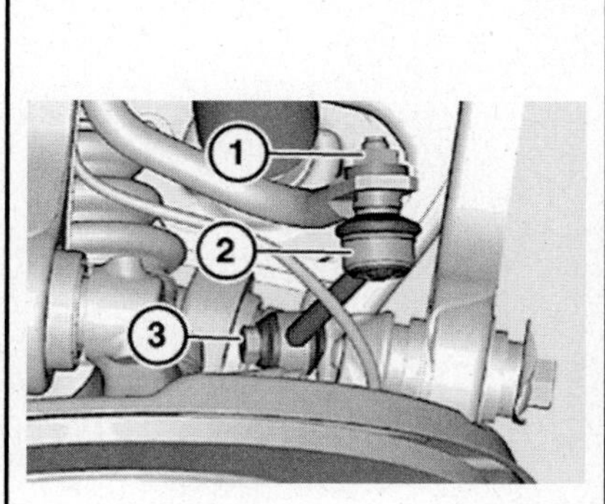

22205_BMWC_G0304

Fig. 216 Stabilizer link (2) and mounting nut (1) and bolt (3)

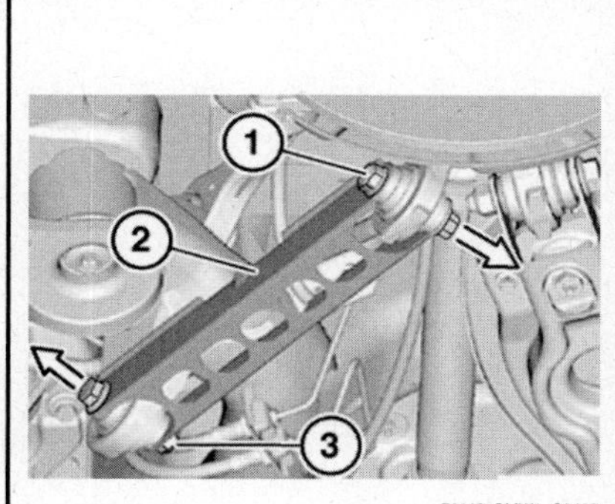

71112_BMW1_G0406

Fig. 218 Releasing nuts (1, 3) and removing trailing arm (2)

1. Release nuts (1, 3).
   a. Tightening torque (on rear axle support): 74 ft. lbs. (100 Nm).
   b. Tightening torque (on wheel carrier): 74 ft. lbs. (100 Nm).
2. Unscrew bolts.
3. Remove trailing arm (2) downward.

➡Note insertion direction of bolts.

➡Replace self-locking nuts.

To install:

To install, reverse the removal procedure.

WHEEL HUBS & BEARINGS

ADJUSTMENT

Wheel bearings cannot be adjusted. The rear bearings must be replaced as a unit and never be reused once removed.

REMOVAL, REPACKING, & INSTALLATION

See Figures 219 and 220.

1. Before servicing the vehicle, refer to the precautions.
2. Remove drive flange of rear axle shaft.
3. Remove output shaft.
4. Remove brake disk.
5. Remove pulse generator.

WARNING

Check sensor head and line from pulse generator prior to installation for external damage, replacing if necessary.

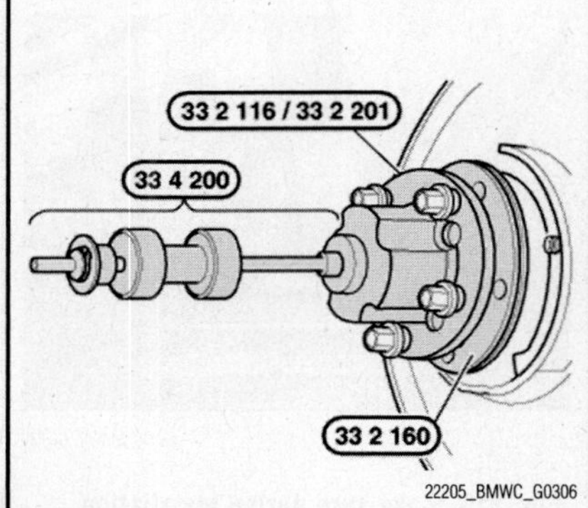

Fig. 219 Force drive flange with special tools 33 2 116 / 33 2 201, 33 2 160, 33 4 200 and 5 wheel bolts out of wheel bearing

6. Force drive flange with special tools 33 2 116 / 33 2 201, 33 2 160, 33 4 200 and 5 wheel bolts out of wheel bearing.

➡Rounded inside edge of special tool 33 2 160 must point to drive flange.

7. Press retaining ring together using pliers and remove.
8. Pull out wheel bearing with special tools 33 4 041, 33 4 042, 33 4 031, 33 4 048 and 33 4 043.

To install:

9. Install retaining ring.
10. Check seating of retaining ring, correct if necessary.
11. Draw in new wheel bearing with special tools 33 4 041, 33 4 042, 33 4 049, 33 4 047 and 33 4 043.

Fig. 220 Pull out wheel bearing with special tools 33 4 041, 33 4 042, 33 4 031, 33 4 048 and 33 4 043

WARNING

Do not reuse old wheel bearing! The wheel bearing is destroyed when the drive flange is removed and cannot be reused.

12. Replace wheel bearing.
13. Install output shaft.
14. Oil drive flange lightly and attach to splines of output shaft.
15. Draw drive flange into wheel bearing.
16. Install brake disk.
17. Install pulse generator.
18. Adjust handbrake.

BMW

3 Series • M3

2

SPECIFICATIONS AND MAINTENANCE CHARTS

ENGINE AND VEHICLE IDENTIFICATION

Engine					
Code	Liters (cc)	Cyl.	Fuel Sys.	Engine Type	Eng. Mfg.
N26	2.0 (1996)	4	Siemens MS70	DOHC	BMW
M57T2D30	3.0 (2993)	6	DDE6	DOHC	BMW
N51B30A	3.0 (2993)	6	Siemens MS70	DOHC	BMW
N52	3.0 (2993)	6	Siemens MS70	DOHC	BMW
N54B30	3.0 (2979)	6	Siemens MS70	DOHC	BMW
S65B40A	4.0 (3999)	8	Siemens MS60	DOHC	BMW

Model Year	
Code ①	Year
B	2011
C	2012

NA: Not Available

DOHC: Double Overhead Camshaft

SOHC: Single Overhead Camshaft

① 10th digit of the Vehicle Identification Number (VIN)

71112_BMW3_C0001

GENERAL ENGINE SPECIFICATIONS

Year	Model	Engine Displacement Liters (cc)	Engine ID/VIN	Net Horsepower @ rpm	Net Torque @ rpm (ft. lbs.)	Bore x Stroke (in.)	Compression Ratio	Oil Pressure @ rpm
2011	3 Series	3.0 (2996)	N52B30A	230@6500	200@2750	3.35x3.46	10.7:1	7.3@idle
		3.0 (2996)	N52	230@6500	200@2750	3.35x3.46	10.2:1	7.3@idle
		3.0 (2993)	M57D30A	265@4400	425@1750	3.31x3.54	16.5:1	18.85@idle
		3.0 (2979)	N54B30	306@5800	400@1400	3.27x3.49	10.2:1	21.8@idle
		4.0 (3999)	S65B40A	414@8300	400@1400	3.62x2.96	12.0:1	14.5@idle
2012	3 Series	2.0 (1986)	N26/N20	240@5000	260@1250	3.31x3.53	10.0:1	NA
		3.0 (2996)	N52B30A	230@6500	200@2750	3.35x3.46	10.7:1	7.3@idle
		3.0 (2996)	N52	230@6500	200@2750	3.35x3.46	10.2:1	7.3@idle
		3.0 (2993)	M57D30A	265@4400	425@1750	3.31x3.54	16.5:1	18.85@idle
		3.0 (2979)	N54B30	306@5800	400@1400	3.27x3.49	10.2:1	21.8@idle
		4.0 (3999)	S65B40A	414@8300	400@1400	3.62x2.96	12.0:1	14.5@idle

71112_BMW3_C0002

ENGINE TUNE-UP SPECIFICATIONS

Year	Engine Displacement Liters (cc)	Engine ID/VIN	Spark Plug Gap (in.)	Ignition Timing (deg.) MT	Ignition Timing (deg.) AT	Fuel Pump (psi)	Idle Speed (rpm) MT	Idle Speed (rpm) AT	Valve Clearance In.	Valve Clearance Ex.
2011	3.0 (2993)	M57D30A	NA	NA	NA	51-54	NA	800	HYD	HYD
	3.0 (2996)	N52B30	①	②	②	70-76	②	②	HYD	HYD
	3.0 (2979)	N54B30	①	②	②	70-76	②	②	HYD	HYD
	4.0 (3999)	S65B40	①	②	②	48-54	②	②	HYD	HYD
2012	3.0 (2993)	M57D30	NA	NA	NA	51-54	NA	800	HYD	HYD
	2.0 (1986)	N20/N26	NA	②	②	NA	②	②	HYD	HYD
	3.0 (2996)	N52B30	①	②	②	70-76	②	②	HYD	HYD
	3.0 (2979)	N54B30	①	②	②	70-76	②	②	HYD	HYD
	4.0 (3999)	S65B40	①	②	②	48-54	②	②	HYD	HYD

HYD: Hydraulic

NA: Not applicable

NOTE: The Vehicle Emission Control Information label reflects specification changes during production and must be used if they differ from this chart.

① Three mass and four-mass electrodes cannot be adjusted

Dual mass electrodes: 0.035-0.039 inches

All others: 0.028-0.031 inches

② Controlled by the Engine Control Module (ECM) and cannot be adjusted

71112_BMW3_C0003

CAPACITIES

Year	Body Type	Model	Engine Displacement Liters (cc)	Engine ID/VIN	Engine Oil with Filter (qts.)	Transmission (pts.) 6-Spd	Transmission (pts.) Auto.	Drive Axle Front (pts.)	Drive Axle Rear (pts.)	Fuel Tank (gal.)	Cooling System (qts.)
2011	E93	328Ci Convertible	3.0 (2996)	N52B30	6.9	①	②	NA	③	16.1	④
	E92	328i Coupe	3.0 (2996)	N52B30	6.9	①	②	NA	③	16.1	④
	E90	328i Sedan	3.0 (2996)	N52B30	6.9	①	②	NA	③	16.1	④
	E91	328i Wagon	3.0 (2996)	N52B30	6.9	①	②	NA	③	16.1	④
	E92	328xi Coupe	3.0 (2996)	N52B30	6.9	①	②	1.3	③	16.1	④
	E91	328xi Wagon	3.0 (2996)	N52B30	6.9	①	②	1.3	③	16.1	④
	E93	335Ci Convertible	3.0 (2979)	N54B30	6.9	①	②	NA	③	16.1	④
	E90	335d Sedan	3.0 (2993)	M57D30	8.2	NA	19.2	NA	③	16.1	NS
	E92	335i Coupe	3.0 (2979)	N54B30	6.9	①	②	NA	③	16.1	④
	E90	335i Sedan	3.0 (2979)	N54B30	6.9	①	②	NA	③	16.1	④
	E90	335xi Coupe	3.0 (2979)	N54B30	6.9	①	②	1.3	③	16.1	④
	E93	M3 Convertible	4.0 (3999)	S65B40	9.3	3.2	NA	NA	2.6	16.6	12.2
	E92	M3 Coupe	4.0 (3999)	S65B40	9.3	3.2	NA	NA	2.6	16.6	12.2
	E90	M3 Sedan	4.0 (3999)	S65B40	9.3	3.2	NA	NA	2.6	16.6	12.2
2012	E93	328Ci Convertible	3.0 (2996)	N52B30	6.9	①	②	NA	③	16.1	④
	E92	328i Coupe	3.0 (2996)	N52B30	6.9	①	②	NA	③	16.1	④
	E90	328i Sedan	3.0 (2996)	N52B30	6.9	①	②	NA	③	16.1	④
	E91	328i Wagon	3.0 (2996)	N52B30	6.9	①	②	NA	③	16.1	④
	E92	328xi Coupe	3.0 (2996)	N52B30	6.9	①	②	1.3	③	16.1	④
	E91	328xi Wagon	3.0 (2996)	N52B30	6.9	①	②	1.3	③	16.1	④
	E93	335Ci Convertible	3.0 (2979)	N54B30	6.9	①	②	NA	③	16.1	④
	E90	335d Sedan	3.0 (2993)	M57D30	8.2	NA	19.2	NA	③	16.1	NS
	E92	335i Coupe	3.0 (2979)	N54B30	6.9	①	②	NA	③	16.1	④
	E90	335i Sedan	3.0 (2979)	N54B30	6.9	①	②	NA	③	16.1	④
	E90	335xi Coupe	3.0 (2979)	N54B30	6.9	①	②	1.3	③	16.1	④
	E93	M3 Convertible	4.0 (3999)	S65B40	9.3	3.2	NA	NA	2.6	16.6	12.2
	E92	M3 Coupe	4.0 (3999)	S65B40	9.3	3.2	NA	NA	2.6	16.6	12.2
	E90	M3 Sedan	4.0 (3999)	S65B40	9.3	3.2	NA	NA	2.6	16.6	12.2
	F30	328i Sedan	2.0 (1986)	N20/N26	5.3	①	NA	NA	③	16.1	12.2

NA: Not applicable.

NS: Not specified by the manufacturer.

NOTE: All capacities are approximate. Add fluid gradually and ensure a proper fluid level is obtained. Capacities given are service, not overhaul capacities

① GS6-37BZ/DZ / MECH Transmission: 3.18 pts.
E53 GS6-53DZ/BZ / MECH Transmission 3.18 pts.
GS6-17BG/DG / MECH Transmission 2.76 pts.

② GA6HP19Z Transmission: 19-21.2 pts.
GA6L45R Transmission: 19.0 pts.

③ 168L differential: 1.7 pts.
188L differential: 2.2 pts.
215 L differential: 2.6 pts.

④ M/T: 8.7 qts., A/T 8.9 qts.

71112_BMW3_C0004

FLUID SPECIFICATIONS

Year	Body Type	Model	Engine Displ. Liters	Engine Oil	Man. Trans.	Auto. Trans.	Drive Axle Front	Drive Axle Rear	Transfer Case	Power Steering Fluid	Brake Master Cylinder	Cooling System
2011	E93	328i Convertible	3.0 (2996)	5W-30	①	ATF M1375.4	NA	②	NA	Dexron III	DOT 4	BMW Long Life Coolant
	E92	328i Coupe	3.0 (2996)	5W-30	①	ATF M1375.4	NA	②	NA	Dexron III	DOT 4	BMW Long Life Coolant
	E90	328i Sedan	3.0 (2996)	5W-30	①	ATF M1375.4	NA	②	NA	Dexron III	DOT 4	BMW Long Life Coolant
	E91	328i Wagon	3.0 (2996)	5W-30	①	ATF M1375.4	NA	②	NA	Dexron III	DOT 4	BMW Long Life Coolant
	E92	328xi Coupe	3.0 (2996)	5W-30	①	ATF M1375.4	SAF-XJ	SAF-XJ	TF08970	Dexron III	DOT 4	BMW Long Life Coolant
	E91	328xi Wagon	3.0 (2996)	5W-30	①	ATF M1375.4	SAF-XJ	SAF-XJ	TF08970	Dexron III	DOT 4	BMW Long Life Coolant
	E93	335i Convertible	3.0 (2979)	5W-30	①	ATF M1375.4	NA	②	NA	Dexron III	DOT 4	BMW Long Life Coolant
	E90	335d Sedan	3.0 (2993)	5W-30	NA	ATF M1375.4	NA	②	NA	Dexron III	DOT 4	BMW Long Life Coolant
	E92	335i Coupe	3.0 (2979)	5W-30	①	ATF M1375.4	NA	②	NA	Dexron III	DOT 4	BMW Long Life Coolant
	E90	335i Sedan	3.0 (2979)	5W-30	①	ATF M1375.4	NA	②	NA	Dexron III	DOT 4	BMW Long Life Coolant
	E92	335xi Coupe	3.0 (2979)	5W-30	①	ATF M1375.4	SAF-XJ	SAF-XJ	TF08970	Dexron III	DOT 4	BMW Long Life Coolant
	E93	M3 Convertible	4.0 (3999)	10W-60	DCTF-1 Pentose	NA	NA	②	NA	Dexron III	DOT 4	BMW Long Life Coolant
	E92	M3 Coupe	4.0 (3999)	10W-60	DCTF-1 Pentose	NA	NA	②	NA	Dexron III	DOT 4	BMW Long Life Coolant
	E90	M3 Sedan	4.0 (3999)	10W-60	DCTF-1 Pentose	NA	NA	②	NA	Dexron III	DOT 4	BMW Long Life Coolant
2012	E93	328i Convertible	3.0 (2996)	5W-30	①	ATF M1375.4	NA	②	NA	Dexron III	DOT 4	BMW Long Life Coolant
	E92	328i Coupe	3.0 (2996)	5W-30	①	ATF M1375.4	NA	②	NA	Dexron III	DOT 4	BMW Long Life Coolant
	E90	328i Sedan	3.0 (2996)	5W-30	①	ATF M1375.4	NA	②	NA	Dexron III	DOT 4	BMW Long Life Coolant
	E91	328i Wagon	3.0 (2996)	5W-30	①	ATF M1375.4	NA	②	NA	Dexron III	DOT 4	BMW Long Life Coolant
	E92	328xi Coupe	3.0 (2996)	5W-30	①	ATF M1375.4	SAF-XJ	SAF-XJ	TF08970	Dexron III	DOT 4	BMW Long Life Coolant
	E91	328xi Wagon	3.0 (2996)	5W-30	①	ATF M1375.4	SAF-XJ	SAF-XJ	TF08970	Dexron III	DOT 4	BMW Long Life Coolant
	E93	335i Convertible	3.0 (2979)	5W-30	①	ATF M1375.4	NA	②	NA	Dexron III	DOT 4	BMW Long Life Coolant
	E90	335d Sedan	3.0 (2993)	5W-30	NA	ATF M1375.4	NA	②	NA	Dexron III	DOT 4	BMW Long Life Coolant
	E92	335i Coupe	3.0 (2979)	5W-30	①	ATF M1375.4	NA	②	NA	Dexron III	DOT 4	BMW Long Life Coolant
	E90	335i Sedan	3.0 (2979)	5W-30	①	ATF M1375.4	NA	②	NA	Dexron III	DOT 4	BMW Long Life Coolant
	E92	335xi Coupe	3.0 (2979)	5W-30	①	ATF M1375.4	SAF-XJ	SAF-XJ	TF08970	Dexron III	DOT 4	BMW Long Life Coolant
	E93	M3 Convertible	4.0 (3999)	10W-60	DCTF-1 Pentose	NA	NA	②	NA	Dexron III	DOT 4	BMW Long Life Coolant
	E92	M3 Coupe	4.0 (3999)	10W-60	DCTF-1 Pentose	NA	NA	②	NA	Dexron III	DOT 4	BMW Long Life Coolant
	E90	M3 Sedan	4.0 (3999)	10W-60	DCTF-1 Pentose	NA	NA	②	NA	Dexron III	DOT 4	BMW Long Life Coolant
	F30	328i Sedan	2.0 (1986)	5W-30	①	ATF M1375.4	NA	②	NA	Dexron III	DOT 4	BMW Long Life Coolant

NA: Not applicable

DOT: Department Of Transpotation

① Orange Label: Dexron AFT
Green Label: Synthetic Mobil SCH630
Yellow Label: MTF-LT-1 or MTF-LT-2
6-Speed: MTF-LT-3
No label: MIL-L-2105

② Limited slip: SAF-XJ. Non-limited slip: SAF-XO

71112_BMW3_C0005

VALVE SPECIFICATIONS

Year	Engine Displacement Liters (cc)	Engine ID/VIN	Seat Angle (deg.)	Face Angle (deg.)	Spring Test Pressure (lbs. @ in.)	Spring Installed Height (in.)	Stem-to-Guide Clearance (in.)		Stem Diameter (in.)	
							Intake	Exhaust	Intake	Exhaust
2011	3.0 (2993)	M57D30	①	45	NS	NS	② 0.0195	② 0.0195	0.0230-0.0231	0.0230-0.0231
	3.0 (2996)	N52B30	①	45	NS	NS	② 0.0197	② 0.0197	0.0234-0.0235	0.0234-0.0235
	3.0 (2979)	N54B30	①	45	NS	NS	② 0.0197	② 0.0197	0.0234-0.0235	0.0234-0.0235
	4.0 (3999)	S65B40	①	45	NS	NS	NS	NS	NS	NS
2012	3.0 (2993)	M57D30	①	45	NS	NS	② 0.0195	② 0.0195	0.0230-0.0231	0.0230-0.0231
	3.0 (2996)	N52B30	①	45	NS	NS	② 0.0197	② 0.0197	0.0234-0.0235	0.0234-0.0235
	3.0 (2979)	N54B30	①	45	NS	NS	② 0.0197	② 0.0197	0.0234-0.0235	0.0234-0.0235
	4.0 (3999)	S65B40	①	45	NS	NS	NS	NS	NS	NS
	2.0 (1986)	N20/N26	③	45	NA	NA	② 0.0195	② 0.0195	0.195-0.1960	0.2339-0.2344

NS: Not specified by the manufacturer

① Valve seat angle: 45 degrees
Correction angle outside: 15 degrees
Correction angle inside: 60 degrees

② To measure: Insert a new valve into guide
with end of valve flush with end of guide.
Use a dial indicator to measure axial valve head movement.

③ Valve seat angle: 45 degrees
Correction angle outside: 35 degrees
Correction angle inside, exhaust: 60 degrees
Correction angle inside, intake: 65 degrees

71112_BMW3_C0006

CAMSHAFT SPECIFICATIONS

All measurements in inches unless noted

Year	Engine Displacement Liters (cc)	Engine Code/ID	Journal Dia.	Brg. Oil Clearance	Shaft End-play	Circle Runout	Lobe Height Intake	Lobe Height Exhaust
2011	3.0 (2993)	M57D30	NS	NS	0.0058-0.0128	0.0018-0.0034	NS	NS
	3.0 (2996)	N52B30	NS	NS	0.0007-0.0063	0.0021-0.0038	NS	NS
	3.0 (2979)	N54B30	NS	NS	0.0007-0.0063	0.0021-0.0038	NS	NS
	4.0 (3999)	S65B40	NS	NS	0.0039-0.0067	0.0010-0.0026	NS	NS
2012	3.0 (2993)	M57D30	NS	NS	0.0058-0.0128	0.0018-0.0034	NS	NS
	3.0 (2996)	N52B30	NS	NS	0.0007-0.0063	0.0021-0.0038	NS	NS
	3.0 (2979)	N54B30	NS	NS	0.0007-0.0063	0.0021-0.0038	NS	NS
	4.0 (3999)	S65B40	NS	NS	0.0039-0.0067	0.0010-0.0026	NS	NS
	2.0 (1986)	N20/ N26	NS	NS	NS	NS	NS	NS

NS: Not specified by the manufacturer

71112_BMW3_C0007

CRANKSHAFT AND CONNECTING ROD SPECIFICATIONS

All measurements are given in inches.

Year	Engine Displacement Liters (cc)	Engine ID/VIN	Crankshaft Main Brg. Journal Dia.	Crankshaft Main Brg. Oil Clearance	Crankshaft Shaft End-play	Crankshaft Thrust on No.	Connecting Rod Journal Diameter	Connecting Rod Oil Clearance	Connecting Rod Side Clearance
2011	3.0 (2993)	M57D30	①	0.0007-0.0017	0.0023-0.0081	NS	1.7540-1.7546	0.0005-0.0019	NS
	3.0 (2996)	N52B30	②	0.0007-0.0023	0.0031-0.0064	NS	1.7706-1.7712	0.0007-0.0022	NS
	3.0 (2979)	N54B30	③	0.0007-0.0017	0.0024-0.0098	NS	1.9682-2.0742	0.0007-0.0023	NS
	4.0 (3999)	S65B40	④	NS	NS	NS	NS	NS	NS
2012	3.0 (2993)	M57D30	①	0.0007-0.0017	0.0023-0.0081	NS	1.7540-1.7546	0.0005-0.0019	NS
	3.0 (2996)	N52B30	②	0.0007-0.0023	0.0031-0.0064	NS	1.7706-1.7712	0.0007-0.0022	NS
	3.0 (2979)	N54B30	③	0.0007-0.0017	0.0024-0.0098	NS	1.9682-2.0742	0.0007-0.0023	NS
	4.0 (3999)	S65B40	④	NS	NS	NS	NS	NS	NS
	2.0 (1986)	N20/N26	⑤	0.0008-0.002	NS	NS	2.1102-2.1108	NS	NS

NS: Not specified by the manufacturer

① Designation S1: 2.5346-2.5349 inches
Designation S2: 2.5344-2.5346 inches
Designation S31: 2.5342-2.5344 inches

② Standard yellow 2.3615-2.3618 inches
Standard green: 2.3613-2.3615 inches
Standard white: 2.3611-2.3613 inches

③ Designation S1: 2.1837-2.1839 inches
Designation S2: 2.1834-2.1836 inches
Designation S3: 2.1832-2.1834 inches

④ Designation Y: 2.3393-2.3396 inches
Designation G: 2.3391-2.3393 inches
Designation V: 2.3388-2.3390 inches

⑤ Designation S/1: 1.9676-1.9678
Designation S/2: 1.9674-1.9675
Designation S/3: 1.9673-1.9677

71112_BMW3_C0008

PISTON AND RING SPECIFICATIONS

All measurements are given in inches

Year	Engine Displacement Liters (cc)	Engine ID/VIN	Piston Clearance	Ring Gap Top Compression	Ring Gap Bottom Compression	Ring Gap Oil Control	Ring Side Clearance Top Compression	Ring Side Clearance Bottom Compression	Ring Side Clearance Oil Control
2011	3.0 (2993)	M57D30	0.0014-0.0028	0.0066-0.0117	0.0117-0.0175	0.0078-0.0156	0.0046-0.0062	0.0027-0.0042	0.0011-0.0027
	3.0 (2996)	N52B30	0.0004-0.0016	0.0078-0.0157	0.0078-0.0157	0.0078-0.0177	0.0008-0.0024	0.0008-0.0024	0.0005-0.0023
	3.0 (2979)	N54B30	①	0.0071-0.0130	0.0118-0.0197	NS	0.0008-0.0024	0.0008-0.0024	NS
	4.0 (3999)	S65B40	①	0.0059-0.0117	0.0156-0.0234	0.0039-0.0117	0.0007-0.0023	0.0007-0.0023	NS
2012	3.0 (2993)	M57D30	0.0014-0.0028	0.0066-0.0117	0.0117-0.0175	0.0078-0.0156	0.0046-0.0062	0.0027-0.0042	0.0011-0.0027
	3.0 (2996)	N52B30	0.0004-0.0016	0.0078-0.0157	0.0078-0.0157	0.0078-0.0177	0.0008-0.0024	0.0008-0.0024	0.0005-0.0023
	3.0 (2979)	N54B30	①	0.0071-0.0130	0.0118-0.0197	NS	0.0008-0.0024	0.0008-0.0024	NS
	4.0 (3999)	S65B40	①	0.0059-0.0117	0.0156-0.0234	0.0039-0.0117	0.0007-0.0023	0.0007-0.0023	NS
	2.0 (1986)	N20/ N26	②	0.0059-0.0118	NS	④	④	NS	NS

NS: Not specified by the manufacturer

① New Piston: 0.000-0.001
Used Piston: 0.0007.0.0018

② New Pistion: 0.0004-.0011
Used Piston: 0.0008-0.0019

③ 1st groove end clearance: 0.0059-0.0118
2nd groove end clearance: 0.0118-0.0197
3rd groove end clearance: 0.0079-0.0354

④ 1st groove side clearance: 0.0012-0.0031
2nd groove side clearance: 0.0008-0.0024
3rd groove side clearance: can not be measured

71112_BMW3_C0009

TORQUE SPECIFICATIONS

All readings in ft. lbs.

Year	Engine Displacement Liters (cc)	Engine ID/VIN	Cylinder Head Bolts	Main Bearing Bolts	Rod Bearing Bolts	Crankshaft Damper Bolts	Flywheel Bolts	Manifold Intake	Manifold Exhaust	Spark Plugs	Lug Nut
2011	3.0 (2996)	N52B30	①	②	③	302	④	⑤	⑥	⑦	89
	3.0 (2979)	N54B30	⑧	⑨	③	18.5	⑩	⑤	⑥	⑦	89
	3.0 (2993)	M57D30	⑪	⑫	③	⑬	89	⑭	⑥	NA	89
	4.0 (3999)	S65B40	⑮	⑯	⑰	⑱	78	⑲	19	⑦	89
2012	3.0 (2996)	N52B30	①	②	③	302	④	⑤	⑥	⑦	89
	3.0 (2979)	N54B30	⑧	⑨	③	18.5	⑩	⑤	⑥	⑦	89
	3.0 (2993)	M57D30	⑪	⑫	③	⑬	89	⑭	⑥	NA	89
	4.0 (3999)	S65B40	⑮	⑯	⑰	⑱	78	⑲	19	⑦	89
	2.0 (1986)	N20/N26	⑳	㉑	㉒	㉓	㉔	11	㉕	⑦	103

NA: Not applicable

NS: Not specified by the manufacturer

① Cast iron block. Replace, wash and oil bolts
Step 1: 22 ft. lbs.
Step 2: 90 degrees
Step 3: 90 degrees

② Cast iron block. Replace, wash and oil bolts
Step 1: 14.8 ft. lbs.
Step 2: 50 degrees

③ Replace, wash and oil connecting rod bolts
Step 1: 14.8 ft. lbs.
Step 2: 70 degrees

④ New micro-encapsulated screws:
Automatic transmission: 88 ft. lbs.
Manual transmission: 77.4 ft. lbs.

⑤ All M6 fasteners: 88 inch lbs.
All M7 fasteners: 11 ft. lbs.
All M8 fasteners: 16 ft. lbs.

⑥ Coat with Molykkote HSC compound or equivalent
All M6 fasteners: 88 inch lbs.
All M7 fasteners: 14.8 ft. lbs.

⑦ M12x1.25:14.8-19.1 ft. lbs.
M14x1.25: 21.4-24.3 ft. lbs.

⑧ Always use new bolts.
Step 1: Tighten bolts 1-10 (M11) to 22 ft. lbs.
Step 2: Tighten bolts 11-14 (M9) to 22 ft. lbs.
Step 3: Tighten bolts 1-14 90 degrees
Step 4: Tighten bolts 1-10 (M11) 90 degrees
Step 5: Tighten bolts 1-14 45 degrees

⑨ Always use new bolts.
Step 1: 14.8 ft. lbs.
Step 2: 70 degrees

⑩ Always use new bolts.
Automatic transmission:
Step 1: 22.2 ft. lbs.
Step 2: 92.5ft. lbs.
Manual transmission: 88.8 ft. lbs.

⑪ Always use new bolts.
Step 1: Tighten bolts to 59 ft. lbs.
Step 2: Loosen all bolts 180 degrees from outside inw
Step 3: Tighten bolts to 37 ft. lbs.
Step 4: Tighten bolts an additional 90 degrees
Step 5: Tighten bolts an additional 90 degrees

⑫ Always use new bolts.
Step 1: Tighten bolts to 37 ft. lbs.
Step 2: Tighten bolts an additional 90 degrees

⑬ Always use new bolts.
Step 1: Tighten bolts to 30 ft. lbs.
Step 2: Tighten bolts an additional 120 degrees

⑭ M6x42: 6 ft. lbs.
M7: 10 ft. lbs.

⑮ Replace, wash and oil bolts
Step 1: Tighten bolts to 30 ft. lbs.
Step 2: Tighten bolts an additional 90 degrees
Step 3: Tighten bolts an additional 90 degrees

⑯ See main bearing toruqe sequence

⑰ Replace, wash and oil connecting rod bolts
Step 1: Tighten bolts to 5 ft. lbs.
Step 2: Tighten bolts to 15 ft. lbs.
Step 3: Tighten bolts an additional 130 degrees
Step 4: Fully loosen bolts
Step 5: Perform this sequence two additional times

⑱ Replace, wash and oil connecting rod bolts
Step 1: Tighten bolts to 45 ft. lbs.
Step 4: Tighten bolts an additional 40 degrees
Step 3: Tighten bolts an additional 40 degrees

⑲ Manifold to throttle valve clamp: 9 inch lbs.
Boot to manifold clamp: 36 inch lbs.

⑳ Always use new bolts.
M11x179: 22 ft. lbs. + 90 degrees + 180 degree
M9x173: 22 ft. lbs. + 90 degrees + 180 degrees
M9x30 & M9x70: 16 ft. lbs.

㉑ Replace bolts.
Step 1: Tighten bolts 14.75 ft. lbs.
Step 2: Tighten bolts and additional 90 degrees

㉒ Replace, wash and oil screws.
Step 1: Tighten bolts 14.75 ft. lbs.
Step 2: Tighten bolts and additional 140 degree

㉓ Replace bolt. Lightly oil bolt and thread.
Step 1: Tighten bolts to 74 ft. lbs.
Step 2: Tighten bolts an additional 270 degrees

㉔ Replace screws.
Step 1: Tighten screws to 44 ft. lbs.
Step 2: Tighten an additional 45 degrees

㉕ Replace nuts.
M6: 7 ft. lbs.
M7: 11 ft. lbs.
M8: 17 ft. lbs.

㉖ M12x1.25: 14.75-19 ft. lbs.
M14x1.25: 20-24 ft. lbs.

71112_BMW3_C0010

WHEEL ALIGNMENT

Year	Model		Caster Range (+/-Deg.)	Caster Preferred Setting (Deg.)	Camber Range (+/-Deg.)	Camber Preferred Setting (Deg.)	Toe-in (Deg.)	Steering Axis Inclination (Deg.)
2011	3 Series ①	F	0.15	0	0.25	-0.18	0.14 +/- 0.10	—
		R	—	—	0.15	-1.30	0.18 +/- 0.06	—
	3 Series ②	F	0.15	0	0.20	-0.33	0.14 +/- 0.10	—
		R	—	—	0.15	-1.50	0.18 +/- 0.06	—
	3 Series ③	F	0.15	0	0.20	3	0.14 +/- 0.10	—
		R	—	—	0.15	-1.20	0.18 +/- 0.06	—
2012	3 Series ①	F	0.15	0	0.25	-0.18	0.14 +/- 0.10	—
		R	—	—	0.15	-1.30	0.18 +/- 0.06	—
	3 Series ②	F	0.15	0	0.20	-0.33	0.14 +/- 0.10	—
		R	—	—	0.15	-1.50	0.18 +/- 0.06	—
	3 Series ③	F	0.15	0	0.20	3	0.14 +/- 0.10	—
		R	—	—	0.15	-1.20	0.18 +/- 0.06	—

NOTE: Load vehicle with 150 lbs. on the front seats, 150 lbs on the rear seats and 46 lbs in the trunk with a full fuel tank.

① Standard suspension

② Sport suspension

③ Rough road package

④ 535xi Sport Wagon: 0.18+/- 0.10.
Except 535xi Sport Wagon: 0.08+/- 0.10.

71112_BMW3_C0011

TIRE, WHEEL AND BALL JOINT SPECIFICATIONS

Year	Model	OEM Tires Standard	OEM Tires Optional	Tire Pressures (psi) Front	Tire Pressures (psi) Rear	Wheel Size	Ball Joint Inspection	Lugnut Torque (ft. lbs.)
2011	328	P205/55R16	①	②	②	NA	NA	89
	335	P225/45R17	③	②	②	NA	NA	89
	M3	③	③	②	②	NA	NA	89
2012	328	P205/55R16	①	②	②	NA	NA	89
	335	P225/45R17	③	②	②	NA	NA	89
	M3	③	③	②	②	NA	NA	89

① P225/45R17, P255/40R17

② See door sticker.

③ Front: P225/40R18, P225/35R19
Rear: P225/35R18, P225/30R19

71112_BMW3_C0012

BRAKE SPECIFICATIONS

All measurements in inches unless noted

Year	Model		Brake Disc Original Thickness	Brake Disc Minimum Thickness	Brake Disc Maximum Runout	Minimum Lining Thickness Front	Minimum Lining Thickness Rear	Brake Caliper Bracket Bolts (ft. lbs.)	Brake Caliper Mounting Bolts (ft. lbs.)
2011	328Ci Convertible	F	①	②	NS	0.118	NA	81	⑤
		R	③	②	NS	NA	④	48	⑤
	328i Coupe, Sedan	F	①	②	NS	0.118	NA	81	⑤
	& Wagon	R	③	②	NS	NA	④	48	⑤
	328xi Coupe &	F	①	②	NS	0.118	NA	81	⑤
	Wagon	R	③	②	NS	NA	④	48	⑤
	335Ci Convertible	F	①	②	NS	0.118	NA	81	⑤
		R	③	②	NS	NA	④	48	⑤
	335d Sedan	F	①	②	NS	0.118	NA	81	⑤
		R	③	②	NS	NA	④	48	⑤
	335i Coupe & Sedan	F	①	②	NS	0.118	NA	81	⑤
		R	③	②	NS	NA	④	48	⑤
	335xi Coupe	F	①	②	NS	0.118	NA	81	⑤
		R	③	②	NS	NA	④	48	⑤
	M3 Convertible,	F	①	②	NS	0.118	NA	81	⑤
	Coupe & Sedan	R	③	②	NS	NA	④	48	⑤
2012	328Ci Convertible	F	①	②	NS	0.118	NA	81	⑤
		R	③	②	NS	NA	④	48	⑤
	328i Coupe, Sedan	F	①	②	NS	0.118	NA	81	⑤
	& Wagon	R	③	②	NS	NA	④	48	⑤
	328xi Coupe &	F	①	②	NS	0.118	NA	81	⑤
	Wagon	R	③	②	NS	NA	④	48	⑤
	335Ci Convertible	F	①	②	NS	0.118	NA	81	⑤
		R	③	②	NS	NA	④	48	⑤
	335d Sedan	F	①	②	NS	0.118	NA	81	⑤
		R	③	②	NS	NA	④	48	⑤
	335i Coupe & Sedan	F	①	②	NS	0.118	NA	81	⑤
		R	③	②	NS	NA	④	48	⑤
	335xi Coupe	F	①	②	NS	0.118	NA	81	⑤
		R	③	②	NS	NA	④	48	⑤
	M3 Convertible	F	①	②	NS	0.118	NA	81	⑤
		R	③	②	NS	NA	④	48	⑤
	M3 Convertible,	F	①	②	NS	0.118	NA	81	⑤
	Coupe & Sedan	R	③	②	NS	NA	④	48	⑤

NOTE: Do not machine M3 or perforated brake discs.

NA: Not applicable

NS: Not specified by the manufacturer

F: Front

R: Rear

① Diameter x Thickness in inches

14.04x1.17

13.57x1.17

13.18x1.01

12.87x0.936

12.16x0.936

11.70x0.936

11.38x0.858

② Minimum thickness is stamped in the brake disk shell

Maximum machining limit per side: 0.315 inches

③ Diameter x Thickness in inches.

13.65x0.936

13.01x0.858

12.63x0.858

11.70x0.780

11.54x0.390

④ Rear brake pad wear limit: 0.118 inches

Parking brake shoe wear limit: 0.059 inches

⑤ Socket head cap screw: 22 ft. lbs.

Hexagon screw: 26

71112_BMW3_C0013

SCHEDULED MAINTENANCE INTERVALS
BMW—3 SERIES

TO BE SERVICED	TYPE OF SERVICE	SERVICE INTERVALS: INITIAL 1200 MILES	OIL SERVICE	INSPECTION I	INSPECTION II
Brake & clutch fluids	S/I			✓	✓
Brake & clutch fluids	R	every two years			
Brake pads & discs	S/I			✓	✓
Catalytic converter & shielding	S/I	✓		✓	✓
Cooling system	S/I	✓		✓	✓
Engine (check for leakage)	S/I	✓			
Engine air cleaner element	R				✓
Engine coolant	R	every two years			
Engine drive belts	S/I				✓
Engine oil	R				
Engine oil & filter	R		✓	✓	✓
Exhaust pipe & muffler	S/I	✓		✓	✓
Fuel filter (California)	R				✓
Fuel, vapor lines & fuel cap	S/I	✓		✓	✓
Intake air dust separators (M/T)	S/I				✓
Maintenance Indicators	Reset		✓	✓	✓
OBD system for codes	S/I	✓		✓	✓
Oil level	S/I	✓			
Oxygen sensor	R	every 100,000 miles			
Parking brake system	S/I			✓	✓
Power steering system	S/I			✓	✓
Rear axle fluid	S/I			✓	✓
Rear axle fluid	R		✓		✓
Spark plugs (3.0L N52B30 engine)	R	every 100,000 miles			
Spark plugs (3.0L N54B30 engine)	R	every 45,000 miles			
Steering play, suspension track rods, front axle joints, steering linkage & joint	S/I			✓	✓
Throttle linkage	S/I			✓	✓
Transmission fluid/oil	S/I			✓	
Transmission fluid/oil	R				✓
Wheel centering hubs	S/I			✓	✓

71112_BMW3_C0014

PRECAUTIONS

Before servicing any vehicle, please be sure to read all of the following precautions, which deal with personal safety, prevention of component damage, and important points to take into consideration when servicing a motor vehicle:

- Never open, service or drain the radiator or cooling system when the engine is hot; serious burns can occur from the steam and hot coolant.
- Observe all applicable safety precautions when working around fuel. Whenever servicing the fuel system, always work in a well-ventilated area. Do not allow fuel spray or vapors to come in contact with a spark, open flame, or excessive heat (a hot drop light, for example). Keep a dry chemical fire extinguisher near the work area. Always keep fuel in a container specifically designed for fuel storage; also, always properly seal fuel containers to avoid the possibility of fire or explosion. Refer to the additional fuel system precautions later in this section.
- Fuel injection systems often remain pressurized, even after the engine has been turned **OFF**. The fuel system pressure must be relieved before disconnecting any fuel lines. Failure to do so may result in fire and/or personal injury.
- Brake fluid often contains polyglycol ethers and polyglycols. Avoid contact with the eyes and wash your hands thoroughly after handling brake fluid. If you do get brake fluid in your eyes, flush your eyes with clean, running water for 15 minutes. If eye irritation persists, or if you have taken brake fluid internally, IMMEDIATELY seek medical assistance.
- The EPA warns that prolonged contact with used engine oil may cause a number of skin disorders, including cancer. You should make every effort to minimize your exposure to used engine oil. Protective gloves should be worn when changing oil. Wash your hands and any other exposed skin areas as soon as possible after exposure to used engine oil. Soap and water, or waterless hand cleaner should be used.
- All new vehicles are now equipped with an air bag system, often referred to as a Supplemental Restraint System (SRS) or Supplemental Inflatable Restraint (SIR) system. The system must be disabled before performing service on or around system components, steering column, instrument panel components, wiring and sensors. Failure to follow safety and disabling procedures could result in accidental air bag deployment, possible personal injury and unnecessary system repairs.
- Always wear safety goggles when working with, or around, the air bag system. When carrying a non-deployed air bag, be sure the bag and trim cover are pointed away from your body. When placing a non-deployed air bag on a work surface, always face the bag and trim cover upward, away from the surface. This will reduce the motion of the module if it is accidentally deployed. Refer to the additional air bag system precautions later in this section.
- Clean, high quality brake fluid from a sealed container is essential to the safe and proper operation of the brake system. You should always buy the correct type of brake fluid for your vehicle. If the brake fluid becomes contaminated, completely flush the system with new fluid. Never reuse any brake fluid. Any brake fluid that is removed from the system should be discarded. Also, do not allow any brake fluid to come in contact with a painted surface; it will damage the paint.
- Never operate the engine without the proper amount and type of engine oil; doing so WILL result in severe engine damage.
- Timing belt maintenance is extremely important. Many models utilize an interference-type, non-freewheeling engine. If the timing belt breaks, the valves in the cylinder head may strike the pistons, causing potentially serious (also time-consuming and expensive) engine damage. Refer to the maintenance interval charts for the recommended replacement interval for the timing belt, and to the timing belt section for belt replacement and inspection.
- Disconnecting the negative battery cable on some vehicles may interfere with the functions of the on-board computer system(s) and may require the computer to undergo a relearning process once the negative battery cable is reconnected.
- When servicing drum brakes, only disassemble and assemble one side at a time, leaving the remaining side intact for reference.
- Only an MVAC-trained, EPA-certified automotive technician should service the air conditioning system or its components.

BRAKES

ANTI-LOCK BRAKE SYSTEM (ABS)

GENERAL INFORMATION

PRECAUTIONS

- Certain components within the ABS system are not intended to be serviced or repaired individually.
- Do not use rubber hoses or other parts not specifically specified for and ABS system. When using repair kits, replace all parts included in the kit. Partial or incorrect repair may lead to functional problems and require the replacement of components.
- Lubricate rubber parts with clean, fresh brake fluid to ease assembly. Do not use shop air to clean parts; damage to rubber components may result.
- Use only DOT 3 brake fluid from an unopened container.
- If any hydraulic component or line is removed or replaced, it may be necessary to bleed the entire system.
- A clean repair area is essential. Always clean the reservoir and cap thoroughly before removing the cap. The slightest amount of dirt in the fluid may plug an orifice and impair the system function. Perform repairs after components have been thoroughly cleaned; use only denatured alcohol to clean components. Do not allow ABS components to come into contact with any substance containing mineral oil; this includes used shop rags.
- The Anti-Lock control unit is a microprocessor similar to other computer units in the vehicle. Ensure that the ignition switch is **OFF** before removing or installing controller harnesses. Avoid static electricity discharge at or near the controller.
- If any arc welding is to be done on the vehicle, the control unit should be unplugged before welding operations begin.

SPEED SENSORS

REMOVAL & INSTALLATION

Front

See Figure 1.

1. Raise and safely support the vehicle securely on jackstands.
2. Remove the front wheel.
3. Open plug housing, pull plug connection out of bracket and disconnect.
4. Pull cable with rubber grommet out of bracket on spring strut.

Fig. 1 Front speed sensor location

5. Remove hexagon socket head cap screw and pull wheel speed sensor out of bore.

To install:

6. Clean bore hole for speed sensor and grease with Staburags NBU 12/K lubricating grease.

7. Install the sensor and tighten the cap screw to 6 ft. lbs. (8 Nm).

8. Install the front wheel if removed and lower the vehicle.

9. Check for proper ABS system function.

Rear

See Figure 2.

1. Raise and safely support the vehicle securely on jackstands.
2. Remove the rear wheel.
3. Open plug housing, pull plug connection out of bracket and disconnect.
4. Pull cable with rubber grommet out of bracket on spring strut.
5. Remove hexagon socket head cap screw and pull wheel speed sensor out of bore.

To install:

6. Clean bore hole for speed sensor and grease with Staburags NBU 12/K lubricating grease.

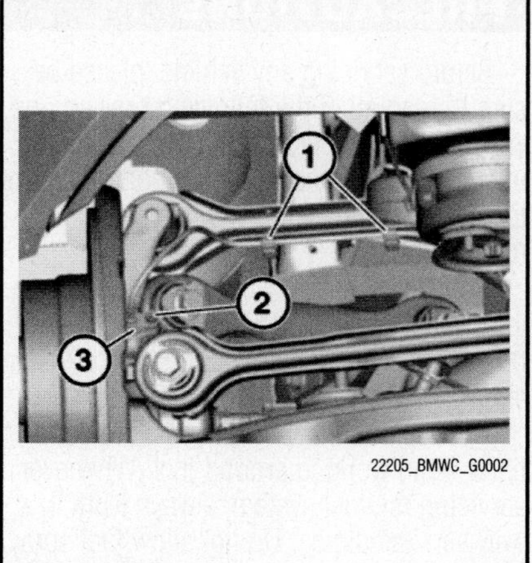

Fig. 2 Rear speed sensor location

7. Install the sensor and tighten the cap screw to 6 ft. lbs. (8 Nm).
8. Install the rear wheel if removed and lower the vehicle.
9. Check for proper ABS system function.

BRAKES — BLEEDING THE BRAKE SYSTEM

BLEEDING PROCEDURE

BLEEDING PROCEDURE

Rear Axle Circuit

1. Disconnect retaining tabs and remove the master cylinder cover.
2. Connect a brake bleeding tool with a maximum 29 PSI (2 Bar) filling pressure.
3. Connect bleeder hose with collecting tray to bleeder valve on rear right brake caliper.
4. Bleed right brake caliper. After completing routine, press brake pedal 5 times to floor; clear and bubble-free brake fluid must flow out.
5. Close bleed valve.
6. Repeat procedure at rear left.
7. Disconnect the brake bleeding tool and remove from the master cylinder.
8. Check and adjust the brake fluid level.
9. Inspect the rubber seal in the brake fluid master cylinder cap. Replace as necessary.

Front Axle Circuit

1. Disconnect retaining tabs and remove the master cylinder cover.
2. Connect a brake bleeding tool with a maximum 29 PSI (2 Bar) filling pressure.
3. Connect bleeder hose with collecting tray to bleeder valve on front right brake caliper.
4. Bleed right front brake caliper. After completing routine, press brake pedal 5 times to floor, clear and bubble-free brake fluid must flow out.
5. Close bleed valve.
6. Repeat procedure at front left.
7. Disconnect the brake bleeding tool and remove from the master cylinder.
8. Check and adjust the brake fluid level.
9. Inspect the rubber seal in the brake fluid master cylinder cap. Replace as necessary.

FLUID FILL PROCEDURE

Flushing

➡A second person is needed to help carry out this work.

1. Disconnect retaining tabs and remove the master cylinder cover.
2. Connect a brake bleeding tool with a maximum 29 PSI (2 Bar) filling pressure.
3. Flushing brake system completely.
4. Connect bleeder hose with collecting tray to bleeder valve on rear right brake caliper.
5. Open bleeder valve and purge until clear, bubble-free brake fluid emerges.
6. Close bleed valve.
7. Follow same procedure on rear left, front right and front left wheel brake.
8. Disconnect the brake bleeding tool and remove from the master cylinder.
9. Check and adjust the brake fluid level.
10. Inspect the rubber seal in the brake fluid master cylinder cap. Replace as necessary.

⁂ CAUTION

Dust and dirt accumulating on brake parts during normal use may contain asbestos fibers from production or aftermarket brake linings. Breathing excessive concentrations of asbestos fibers can cause serious bodily harm. Exercise care when servicing brake parts. Do not sand or grind brake lining unless equipment used is designed to contain the dust residue. Do not clean brake parts with compressed air or by dry brushing. Cleaning should be done by dampening the brake components with a fine mist of water, then wiping the brake components clean with a dampened cloth. Dispose of cloth and all residue containing asbestos fibers in an impermeable container with the appropriate label. Follow practices prescribed by the Occupational Safety and Health Administration (OSHA) and the Environmental Protection Agency (EPA) for the handling, processing, and disposing of dust or debris that may contain asbestos fibers.

BRAKE CALIPER

REMOVAL & INSTALLATION

Brembo Caliper

1. Before servicing the vehicle, refer to the precautions.
2. Remove wheels.
3. Remove front brake pad sensor.
4. Press clutch pedal down to floor and secure with pedal support.

⁂ WARNING

The pedal support may only be released when the brake lines are reconnected. This prevents brake fluid from emerging from the expansion tank and air from entering the system when the brake lines are opened.

5. If necessary, pull brake hose out of holder.

➡Grip brake hose at square headto prevent connecting piece from turning in retaining bracket.

6. Disconnect brake hose from brake line.
7. Detach brake hose from brake caliper.

⁂ WARNING

Never twist brake hose when installing it and avoid all contact with parts attached rigidly to the body.

8. Move wheels into straight-ahead position.
9. Release bolts and pull off brake caliper with brake anchor plate towards rear.
10. Pull brake pads off guide pins and remove.

➡In the event of one-sided brake pad wear, do not change brake pads round.

11. Observe minimum thickness of brake pads.

To install:

12. To install, reverse the removal procedure.
13. Clean brake pads, brake caliper and guide pins.
14. Do not grease backs of brake pads sleeve.
15. Brake pads must be correctly seated on guide pins.
16. Do not grease brake pads and guides with anti-squeak paste.
17. Clean contact surface of brake pistons.

➡First tighten brake hose on brake caliper.

18. Tighten bolts/nuts to specification as follows:
    - Brake line screws / union screws: 9 ft. lbs. (12 Nm)
    - Blue union screw connection M3: 12 ft. lbs. (17 Nm)
    - Brake hose to caliper: 18 ft. lbs. (24 Nm)
    - Caliper to mount (Replace screws): 81 ft. lbs. (110 Nm)

➡The brake pad wear sensor must be replaced once it has been removed (brake pad wear sensor loses its retention capability in the brake pad). If a brake pad sensor that has already been ground has to be replaced even though the minimum brake pad thickness has not yet been reached, you must observe the following: The new sliding contact must be filed down with a file to the same length as the ground sliding contact.

Teves Caliper

1. Before servicing the vehicle, refer to the precautions.
2. Remove wheels
3. Remove brake pad wear sensor

⁂ WARNING

The brake pad wear sensor must be replaced once it has been removed (brake pad wear sensor loses its retention capability in the brake pad).

4. Disconnect brake hose to brake caliper.
5. Disconnect brake hose to brake line.
6. Disconnect brake hose to holder.
7. Lift out retaining spring.
8. Remove plastic plugs.
9. Remove guide bolts and lift out brake caliper towards rear of vehicle.

To install:

10. Clean contact face of brake piston and apply a thin coating of anti-squeak compound.
11. Clean contact faces of brake pad hammer heads/brake caliper housing and coat with anti-squeak compound.
12. Clean contact face of brake caliper and apply a thin coating of anti-squeak compound.
13. Clean brake carrier at hammerhead guides and apply a thin coating of anti-squeak compound.
14. Clean guide bolts only; do not grease. Check threads.

➡Replace all guide bolts which are not in perfect condition.

15. Install brake caliper. Replace the guide bolts and tighten to 26 ft. lbs. (35 Nm) on E90 and 22 ft. lbs. (30 Nm) on all others.

⁂ WARNING

Never twist brake hose when installing it and avoid all contact with parts attached rigidly to the body.

16. Connect brake hose to brake caliper. Tighten to 18 ft. lbs. (24 Nm).
17. Connect brake hose to brake line. Tighten to 8 ft. lbs. (12 Nm) on E90 series.
18. Connect brake hose to holder.
19. Install plastic plugs.
20. Install the retaining spring.
21. Install the brake pad wear sensor.
22. Check and fill brake fluid to proper level.
23. Bleed the brake system.
24. Install the wheels.

DISC BRAKE PADS

REMOVAL & INSTALLATION

Brembo Caliper

See Figure 3.

1. Before servicing the vehicle, refer to the precautions.
2. Remove the caliper and suspend it out of the way using wire.

➡Do not allow brake caliper to hang from the brake hose.

3. Turn piston fully back with special tool 34 1 050.

⁂ WARNING

When pressing down piston, note brake fluid level in expansion tank.

4. Pull brake pads off guide pins and remove.

➡In the event of one-sided brake pad wear, do not change brake pads round.

To install:

5. To install, reverse the removal procedure.
6. Check minimum thickness of brake pads and brake disc. Replace components as necessary.
7. Clean brake pads, brake caliper and guide pins.
8. Do not grease backs of brake pads sleeve.
9. Brake pads must be correctly seated on guide pins.

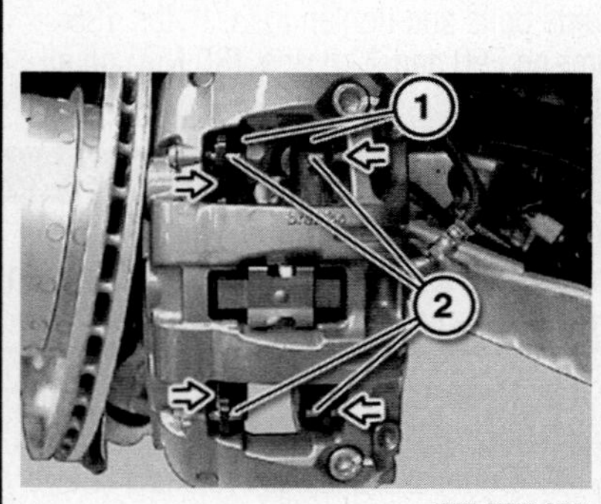

Fig. 3 Pull brake pads off guide pins and remove

⁂ WARNING

New brake pads may only be installed if the brake disc thickness is greater than or equal to the minimum brake disc thickness.

10. Clean contact surface of brake pistons.

➡The brake pad wear sensor must be replaced once it has been removed (brake pad wear sensor loses its retention capability in the brake pad). If a brake pad sensor that has already been ground has to be replaced even though the minimum brake pad thickness has not yet been reached, you must observe the following: The new sliding contact must be filed down with a file to the same length as the ground sliding contact.

11. Replace expanding spring.
12. When installing new brake pads at front and rear axles, brake fluid level must be brought up to "MAX" marking.
13. Fully depress brake pedal several times so that brake pads contact brake discs.
14. When replacing pads, reset the maintenance reminder.

Teves Caliper

See Figure 4.

1. Before servicing the vehicle, refer to the precautions.
2. Remove the caliper and suspend it out of the way using wire.

➡Do not allow brake caliper to hang from the brake hose.

3. Remove the brake pads.

To install:

4. Press brake piston fully back with special tool 34 1 050.

⁂ WARNING

When pressing piston back, note brake fluid level in expansion tank. Overflowing brake fluid will damage the paintwork.

5. Check dust sleeve for damage and replace if necessary.
6. Clean contact face of brake piston and apply a thin coating of anti-squeak compound.

Fig. 4 Remove lining retaining springs, as necessary

⁂ WARNING

Dust sleeve must not come into contact with anti-squeak compound as this may cause the dust sleeve to swell.

7. Clean contact face of brake caliper and apply a thin coating of anti-squeak compound.
8. Clean hammerhead guides and apply a thin coating of anti-squeak compound.
9. Replace the lining retaining springs, as necessary.
10. Clean contact face of brake carrier and apply a thin coating of anti-squeak compound.
11. Install the new brake pads.

➡Brake pad with indentation is intended for accommodating the brake pad wear sensor and must be fitted on the piston side.

12. Install the caliper.
13. Check and fill brake fluid to proper level.
14. Fully depress brake pedal several times so that brake linings contact brake discs.

➡When replacing pads, reset CBS display in accordance with factory specification.

15. Install the wheels.

BRAKES

REAR DISC BRAKES

⁂ CAUTION

Dust and dirt accumulating on brake parts during normal use may contain asbestos fibers from production or aftermarket brake linings. Breathing excessive concentrations of asbestos fibers can cause serious bodily harm. Exercise care when servicing brake parts. Do not sand or grind brake lining unless equipment used is designed to contain the dust residue. Do not clean brake parts with compressed air or by dry brushing. Cleaning should be done by dampening the brake components with a fine mist of water, then wiping the brake components clean with a dampened cloth. Dispose of cloth and all residue containing asbestos fibers in an impermeable container with the appropriate label. Follow practices prescribed by the Occupational Safety and Health Administration (OSHA) and the Environmental Protection Agency (EPA) for the handling, processing, and disposing of dust or debris that may contain asbestos fibers.

BRAKE CALIPER

REMOVAL & INSTALLATION

See Figure 5.

1. Before servicing the vehicle, refer to the precautions.
2. Remove wheels.
3. Remove brake pad wear sensor (right side only).

⁂ WARNING

The brake pad wear sensor must be replaced once it has been removed (brake pad wear sensor loses its retention capability in the brake pad).

4. Disconnect brake hose to brake caliper.
5. Disconnect brake hose to brake line.
6. Disconnect brake hose to holder.
7. Lift out retaining spring.
8. Remove plastic plugs.
9. Remove guide bolts and lift out brake caliper towards rear of vehicle.

Fig. 5 Retaining spring

To install:

10. Clean guide bolts only; do not grease. Check threads.

➡Replace all guide bolts which are not in perfect condition.

11. Install brake caliper. Replace the guide bolts and tighten to 26 ft. lbs. (35 Nm) on E90 and 22 ft. lbs. (30 Nm) on all others.

⁂ WARNING

Never twist brake hose when installing it and avoid all contact with parts attached rigidly to the body.

12. Connect brake hose to brake caliper. Tighten to 18 ft. lbs. (24 Nm).
13. Connect brake hose to brake line. Tighten to 8 ft. lbs. (12 Nm) on E90 series and 12 ft. lbs. (17 Nm) on E60 series.
14. Install plastic plugs.
15. Install the retaining spring.
16. Install the brake pad wear sensor.
17. Check and fill brake fluid to proper level.
18. Bleed the brake system.
19. Install the wheels.

DISC BRAKE PADS

REMOVAL & INSTALLATION

1. Before servicing the vehicle, refer to the precautions.
2. Remove the caliper and suspend it out of the way using wire.

➡Do not allow brake caliper to hang from the brake hose.

3. Remove the brake pads.

To install:

4. Press brake piston fully back with special tool 34 1 050.

⁂ WARNING

When pressing piston back, note brake fluid level in expansion tank. Overflowing brake fluid will damage the paintwork.

5. Check dust sleeve for damage and replace if necessary.
6. Clean contact face of brake piston and apply a thin coating of anti-squeak compound.

⁂ WARNING

Dust sleeve must not come into contact with anti-squeak compound as this may cause the dust sleeve to swell.

7. Clean contact face of brake caliper and apply a thin coating of anti-squeak compound.
8. Clean hammerhead guides and apply a thin coating of anti-squeak compound.
9. Replace the lining retaining springs, as necessary.
10. Clean contact face of brake carrier and apply a thin coating of anti-squeak compound.
11. Install the new brake pads.

➡Brake pad with indentation is intended for accommodating the brake pad wear sensor and must be fitted on the piston side.

12. Install the caliper.
13. Check and fill brake fluid to proper level.
14. Fully depress brake pedal several times so that brake linings contact brake discs.

➡When replacing pads, reset CBS display in accordance with factory specification.

15. Install the wheels.

PARKING BRAKE CABLES

ADJUSTMENT

1. Before servicing the vehicle, refer to the precautions.
2. Perform inspection in the following manner:
   a. When 1st ratchet is engaged, no braking force should be exerted.
   b. The difference in wheel circumferential forces between the left and right wheels may deviate by max. 30% from the greater value (when measured on brake analyzer).
   c. Braking with locked wheels must be possible with the parking brake.
   d. The parking brake must be reset if the actuation stroke is greater than 10 teeth.

➡Accurate adjustment of the parking brake is only possible if the parking brake Bowden cables and all moving parts on the parking brake move easily and function correctly.

3. Setting instruction for brake shoes (basic setting):
   a. Disconnect gaiter for parking brake pry.
   b. Lock adjuster unit (ASZE).
   c. Actuate parking brake pry. Screw in special tool 32 1 030 partially. Press stop of adjusting spring back to such an extent that retaining hook engages in stop.
   d. Completely unscrew one wheel stud on each rear wheel.
   e. Turn wheel until adjustment screw is visible in tapped hole.
   f. Turn adjusting screw with a screwdriver until the wheel is no longer able to turn. Then Remove the adjusting screw 8 notches.
   g. Unlock adjuster unit (ASZE).
   h. Pry out restraining hook with a suitable screwdriver.
   i. Restraining hook must detach from stop of adjusting spring.
4. Setting instruction for parking brake Bowden cables:
   a. The parking brake pry must be applied 5 times to approximately 90 lbs. (400 N) actuating force.
   b. With the parking brake removed and the transmission in **N** position, the brake force should have reached 34 lbs. (150 N) as measured on a brake analyzer.
   c. With the parking brake on the 1st tooth, there should be no increase in braking force. However, the indicator lamp can be lit.
   d. With the parking brake on the 2nd tooth, the indicator lamp must be lit.
   e. With the parking brake on the 3rd tooth, there should be an increase in braking force.
   f. With the parking brake on the 5th tooth, the brake force must have reached 90 lbs. (400 N).
5. If new pads are installed, perform the pad break in procedure:
   a. At approximately 25 MPH (40 km/h) apply parking brake pry until a braking effect can be felt.
   b. Pull parking brake pry to next notch and drive on for approximately 1320 feet (quarter mile).
   c. If necessary, repeat braking-in procedure.
   d. Allow brake to cool down sufficiently.

REMOVAL & INSTALLATION

See Figures 6 and 7.

1. Remove airbag control unit.

Lock adjuster unit (ASZE):

2. Actuate parking brake lever. Connect special tool 32 1 030. Press stop of adjusting spring to such an extent that retaining hook engages in stop.
3. Press retainer in balance arm forward in direction of arrow.
4. Detach handbrake Bowden cables from balance arm.
5. Release screw and remove holder. Tightening torque: 6 ft. lbs. (8 Nm)

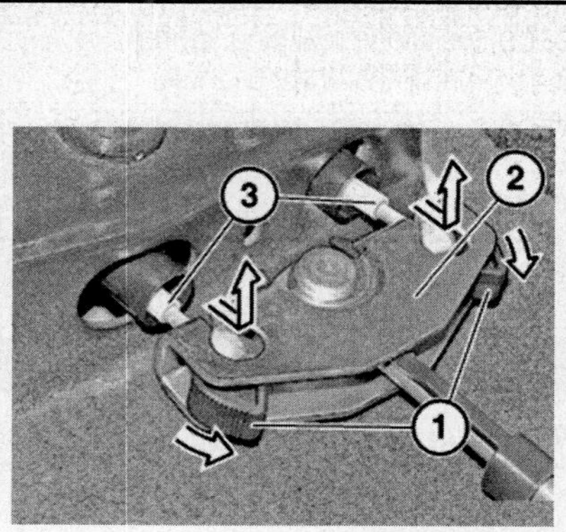

Fig. 6 Pressing retainer in balance arm to detach Bowden cables

➡To release the parking brake Bowden cable from the expander lock, it is necessary to remove the brake disc.

6. Release one wheel stud.
7. Bring wheel into position (tapped hole turned down approx. 20° from horizontal). (F=direction of travel) Tightening torque: 89 ft. lbs. (120 Nm)

➡Reinstall wheel stud only after handbrake has been adjusted.

8. Nipple and expander lock are visible through tapped hole.
9. Push in core of handbrake cable in direction of expander lock as far as it will go and grip firmly.
10. Press nipple downwards through tapped hole with a screwdriver.
11. Pull handbrake cables out of wheel carrier.
12. Disconnect handbrake cables from holders.
13. Pull handbrake cables towards rear out of guide tube.

To install:

To install, reverse the removal procedure noting the following.

14. Insert handbrake cable into brake carrier/brake guard plate. Sleeve must be inserted up to stop.
15. Nipple of handbrake cable must audibly snap into place in expander lock.

PARKING BRAKE SHOES

REMOVAL & INSTALLATION

1. Before servicing the vehicle, refer to the precautions.

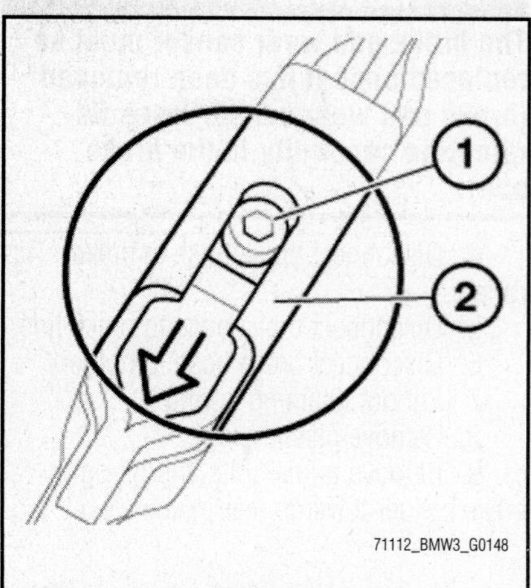

Fig. 7 Identifying nipple and expander lock

2. Remove rear brake disc.

3. Actuate parking brake pry. Screw in special tool 32 1 030 partially. Press stop of adjusting spring back to such an extent that retaining hook engages in stop.

4. Disconnect return upper spring with brake spring pliers.

5. Disconnect return lower spring with brake spring pliers.

6. Turn clamping pins with special tool 34 4 000 through 90° and disconnect.

Remove brake shoes.

To install:

7. Install brake shoes.

8. Turn clamping pins with special tool 34 4 000 through 90° to lock.

9. Check and if necessary replace return springs.

10. Connect return lower spring with brake spring pliers.

11. Connect return upper spring with brake spring pliers.

➡Pay attention to installation position of adjustment screw.

12. Apply a thin coat of grease to bush and screw threads.

13. Pry out restraining hook with a suitable screwdriver.

14. Restraining hook must detach from stop of adjusting spring.

15. Install rear brake disc.

16. Adjusting parking brake.

CHASSIS ELECTRICAL

AIR BAG (SUPPLEMENTAL RESTRAINT SYSTEM)

GENERAL INFORMATION

✲✲ CAUTION

These vehicles are equipped with an air bag system. The system must be disarmed before performing service on, or around, system components, the steering column, instrument panel components, wiring and sensors. Failure to follow the safety precautions and the disarming procedure could result in accidental air bag deployment, possible injury and unnecessary system repairs.

SERVICE PRECAUTIONS

Disconnect and isolate the battery negative cable before beginning any airbag system component diagnosis, testing, removal, or installation procedures. Allow system capacitor to discharge for two minutes before beginning any component service. This will disable the airbag system. Failure to disable the airbag system may result in accidental airbag deployment, personal injury, or death.

Do not place an intact undeployed airbag face down on a solid surface. The airbag will propel into the air if accidentally deployed and may result in personal injury or death.

When carrying or handling an undeployed airbag, the trim side (face) of the airbag should be pointing towards the body to minimize possibility of injury if accidental deployment occurs. Failure to do this may result in personal injury or death.

Replace airbag system components with OEM replacement parts. Substitute parts may appear interchangeable, but internal differences may result in inferior occupant protection. Failure to do so may result in occupant personal injury or death.

Wear safety glasses, rubber gloves, and long sleeved clothing when cleaning powder residue from vehicle after an airbag deployment. Powder residue emitted from a deployed airbag can cause skin irritation. Flush affected area with cool water if irritation is experienced. If nasal or throat irritation is experienced, exit the vehicle for fresh air until the irritation ceases. If irritation continues, see a physician.

Do not use a replacement airbag that is not in the original packaging. This may result in improper deployment, personal injury, or death.

The factory installed fasteners, screws and bolts used to fasten airbag components have a special coating and are specifically designed for the airbag system. Do not use substitute fasteners. Use only original equipment fasteners listed in the parts catalog when fastener replacement is required.

During, and following, any child restraint anchor service, due to impact event or vehicle repair, carefully inspect all mounting hardware, tether straps, and anchors for proper installation, operation, or damage. If a child restraint anchor is found damaged in any way, the anchor must be replaced. Failure to do this may result in personal injury or death.

Deployed and non-deployed airbags may or may not have live pyrotechnic material within the airbag inflator.

Do not dispose of driver/passenger/curtain airbags or seat belt tensioners unless you are sure of complete deployment. Refer to the Hazardous Substance Control System for proper disposal.

Dispose of deployed airbags and tensioners consistent with state, provincial, local, and federal regulations.

After any airbag component testing or service, do not connect the battery negative cable. Personal injury or death may result if the system test is not performed first.

If the vehicle is equipped with the Occupant Classification System (OCS), do not connect the battery negative cable before performing the OCS Verification Test using the scan tool and the appropriate diagnostic information. Personal injury or death may result if the system test is not performed properly.

Never replace both the Occupant Restraint Controller (ORC) and the Occupant Classification Module (OCM) at the same time. If both require replacement, replace one, then perform the Airbag System test before replacing the other.

Both the ORC and the OCM store Occupant Classification System (OCS) calibration data, which they transfer to one another when one of them is replaced. If both are replaced at the same time, an irreversible fault will be set in both modules and the OCS may malfunction and cause personal injury or death.

If equipped with OCS, the Seat Weight Sensor is a sensitive, calibrated unit and must be handled carefully. Do not drop or handle roughly. If dropped or damaged, replace with another sensor. Failure to do so may result in occupant injury or death.

If equipped with OCS, the front passenger seat must be handled carefully as well. When removing the seat, be careful when setting on floor not to drop. If dropped, the sensor may be inoperative, could result in occupant injury, or possibly death.

If equipped with OCS, when the passenger front seat is on the floor, no one should sit in the front passenger seat. This uneven force may damage the sensing ability of the seat weight sensors. If sat on and damaged, the sensor may be inoperative, could result in occupant injury, or possibly death.

DISARMING THE SYSTEM

1. Before servicing the vehicle, refer to the precautions.

2. Place the ignition switch in the **OFF**-position.

3. Disconnect the negative battery terminal and cover the battery terminal to prevent accidental contact.

4. Once the battery has been disconnected, wait for a period of approximately 10 minutes allowing the capacitor in the control unit to discharge.

ARMING THE SYSTEM

When repairs are completed, connect the negative battery cable.

DRIVE TRAIN

AUTOMATIC TRANSMISSION FLUID

DRAIN AND REFILL

GA6HP19Z and GA6HP26Z Transmissions

1. Before servicing the vehicle, refer to the precautions.
2. Raise and support vehicle.
3. Undo filler plug.
4. Top up transmission fluid until it emerges from filling orifice.
5. Start engine.
6. Replenish transmission fluid until it emerges from filling orifice.
7. Replace sealing ring.
8. Screw in filler plug and tighten to 26 ft. lbs. (35 Nm).
9. Press brake pedal to floor and shift through all gears several times at idle speed. Then shift to "P" position (Park).
10. Check fluid level.
    a. Connect BMW Diagnosis and Information System (DIS) to vehicle.
    b. Call up Service functions (drive).
    c. Carry out fluid level check in accordance with instructions.

GA6L45R Transmission

1. Before servicing the vehicle, refer to the precautions.
2. Raise and support vehicle.
3. Remove exhaust system bracket.
4. Undo filler plug.
5. Top up transmission fluid until it emerges from filling orifice.
6. Start engine.
7. Replenish transmission fluid until it emerges from filling orifice.
8. Replace sealing ring.
9. Screw in filler plug and tighten to 14 ft. lbs. (19 Nm).
10. Press brake pedal to floor and shift through all gears several times at idle speed. Then shift to "P" position (Park).
11. Check fluid level.
    a. Connect BMW Diagnosis and Information System (DIS) to vehicle.
    b. Call up Service functions (drive).
    c. Carry out fluid level check in accordance with instructions.

FILTER REPLACEMENT

GA6L45R Transmission

1. Before servicing the vehicle, refer to the precautions.
2. Raise and support the vehicle.
3. Remove rear underbody protection:
4. Single-part underbody protection, except AWD.
    a. Release screws.
    b. Pull underbody protection in direction of arrow out of bracket.
5. Single-part underbody protection, AWD.
    a. Release screws.
    b. Remove underbody protection downwards.
6. Two-part underbody protection
    a. Release screws.
    b. Detach underbody protection from bracket and remove.
7. Remove exhaust system bracket from transmission.
8. Remove oil drain plug.
9. Drain automatic transmission fluid.
10. Unscrew all bolts.
11. Remove transmission sump.
12. Remove gasket from transmission sump.
13. Remove transmission oil filter with a suitable tool.
14. Pull transmission oil filter gasket out of housing with special tools 24 4 390 and 13 5 250.

To install:

15. Drive transmission filter gasket into housing with special tool 24 4 400.
16. Clean sealing faces and groove with a cloth.
17. Insert new gasket in transmission sump groove.

WARNING

Do not degrease transmission sump with cleaning agent.

18. Clean sump magnet and check for metal filings/borings.
19. The gasket is correctly installed when it is engaged in the locating openings of the transmission sump.
20. Screw in bolts (1 to 17) in specified order until bolt heads make contact.
21. Tighten bolts/nuts to specification as follows:
    - Oil pan bolts: 96 inch lbs. (10 Nm).
    - Oil drain plug (replace) metal oil pan: 108 inch lbs. (12 Nm)
    - Oil drain plug (replace) metal oil pan: 96 inch lbs. (10 Nm)

FRONT AXLE HOUSING

REMOVAL & INSTALLATION

See Figures 8 and 9.

1. Before servicing the vehicle, refer to the precautions.
2. Secure engine in installation position to prevent it from falling down.

➡Adhere to the utmost cleanliness. Do not allow any dirt to enter the hydraulic system. Seal off hydraulic lines with plugs.

3. Draw off and dispose of hydraulic fluid from fluid reservoir
4. Disconnect pressure line from vane pump.
5. Disconnect return line from cooling coil.
6. Drain and dispose of front differential oil.
7. Remove left output shaft.
8. Press right output shaft approximately 2.34–2.73 (6–7 cm) out of front differential.
9. Remove propeller shaft from front differential.
10. Lower front axle carrier.

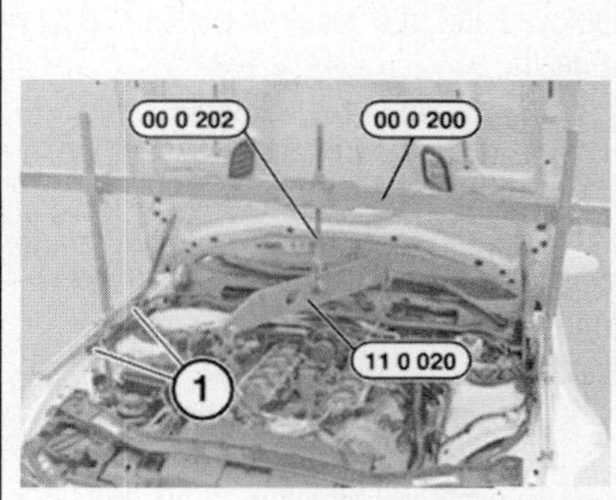

Fig. 8 Secure engine in installation position

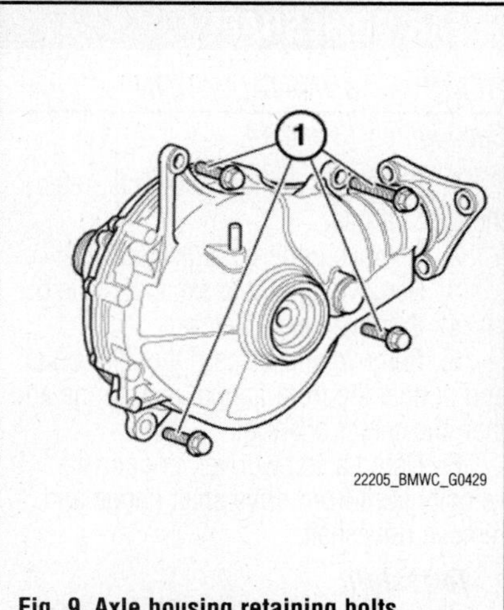

Fig. 9 Axle housing retaining bolts

⁂ WARNING

Grip front differential firmly while releasing last bolt in order to avoid damage caused by the differential falling.

11. If necessary, disconnect hydraulic lines from oil sump.
12. Remove screws.
13. Detach front differential from oil sump and remove towards rear.

➡If replacing the axle housing, replace the output flange to ensure a clean seal on the transfer case.

To install:

14. To install, reverse the removal procedure.
15. Replace O-ring if necessary. Coat O-ring with front differential oil.
16. Tighten front axle final drive to engine oil pan bolt to 48 ft. lbs. (65 Nm).
17. Fill and bleed hydraulic system.
18. Check pipe connections for leaks.
19. Fill with front differential oil.
20. Check transfer case oil level, correct if necessary.
21. Carry out steering angle sensor adjustment.

FRONT HALFSHAFT

REMOVAL & INSTALLATION

See Figure 10.

1. Before servicing the vehicle, refer to the precautions.
2. Remove front wheel.
3. Expand turning lock sufficiently to avoid damaging thread when releasing collar nut.
4. Remove collar nut; to do so, press brake pedal to floor.

Fig. 10 Press halfshaft with special tool 31 5 110

5. Remove reinforcement plate.
6. Remove tie rod end from ball joint.
7. On the right side only, remove guide joint from ball joint.
8. Remove control arm from ball joint.
9. Remove stabilizer link from spring strut.
10. Turn ball joint to one side.
11. Press halfshaft out of wheel hub and tie up.
12. Press halfshaft with special tool 31 5 110 out of front differential and remove.
13. Press halfshaft with special tool 31 5 110 out of bearing block and remove.

To install:

14. Replace shaft seal in front differential and coat sealing lips with front differential oil.
15. Replace shaft seal in bearing block and coat sealing lips with front differential oil.
16. Replace retaining ring and slide in halfshaft over resistance of retaining ring. Halfshaft must snap audibly into place.

⁂ WARNING

High installation forces indicate that the spline teeth on the halfshaft/rear differential side gear are damaged/deformed. Check spline teeth, replaced damaged parts.

17. Replace collar nut, oil collar nut/wheel bearing contact surface only and tighten to 311 ft. lbs. (420 Nm).

⁂ WARNING

Do not oil thread of shaft journal or collar nut.

18. Secure collar nut by positive peening on flat areas of halfshaft.
19. Install front wheel.
20. Check front differential oil level, correct if necessary

MANUAL TRANSMISSION FLUID

DRAIN & REFILL

⁂ WARNING

Aluminum-magnesium materials. On these transmissions, no steel bolts/bolts may be used due to the threat of electrochemical corrosion. A magnesium crankcase requires aluminum bolts/bolts exclusively.

Aluminum bolts/bolts must be replaced each time they are removed. The end faces of these bolts/bolts are painted blue for the purposes of reliable identification. Jointing torque and angle of rotation must be observed without fail (risk of damage).

1. Before servicing the vehicle, refer to the precautions.
2. Drive vehicle until gearbox is at normal operating temperature.
3. Raise and support vehicle.
4. Remove the oil drain plug and filler plug.
5. Allow oil to completely drain.
6. Clean oil drain plug and install. Tighten to specification below.
7. Fill transmission with fluid until overflowing.
8. Clean oil filler plug and install. Tighten to specification below.
9. Tighten bolts/nuts to specification as follows:
   - M18 x 1.5 hexagon socket: 26 ft. lbs. (35 Nm)
   - M12 x 1.5: 19 ft. lbs. (25 Nm)
   - M18 x 1.5 steel bolt without seal: 33 ft. lbs. (45 Nm)

PINION OIL SEAL

REMOVAL & INSTALLATION

See Figure 11.

1. Before servicing the vehicle, refer to the precautions.
2. Remove reinforcement plate.
3. Remove front propeller shaft.
4. Mark position of nut with respect to shaft with punch marks (arrow).
5. Pry out lock plate with a suitable tool.

⁂ WARNING

Do not place special tool on threaded holes of drive flange.

6. Secure drive flange with special tool 23 0 020 against turning and remove nut.
7. Mount special tool only with longer bolts (M10x30) on drive flange.
8. Pull drive flange off drive shaft with special tool 33 1 150.
9. Pry shaft seal out of front differential with a suitable screwdriver.

To install:

10. Drive in shaft seal with special tool 31 5 130 as far as it will go.
11. Coat sealing lips of new shaft seal with front differential oil.

⁂ WARNING

Do not tighten nut beyond punch marks. Otherwise the clamping sleeve will be damaged.

12. Clean drive flange and attach.
13. Tighten down nut until punch marks on nut and shaft are aligned.
14. Install new lock plate.
15. Install front propeller shaft.
16. Install reinforcement plate.
17. Check front differential oil level, correct if necessary

REAR AXLE HOUSING

REMOVAL & INSTALLATION

See Figure 12.

1. Before servicing the vehicle, refer to the precautions.
2. Remove propeller shaft from rear differential
3. Remove output shaft from rear differential at both ends and tie back

⁂ WARNING

Observe gap between special tool 33 4 420 and dust plates. To avoid grinding noises, make sure the dust plates are not bent.

4. Support rear differential with workshop jack and special tool 33 4 420.
5. Remove bolts.
6. Remove nut and remove screw towards rear.
7. Slowly lower workshop jack and remove rear differential towards rear.

To install:

⁂ WARNING

Adhere to the following installation sequence in order to prevent distortion of the rear differential during installation and thereby avoid potential complaints about noise.

8. Install rear differential with workshop jack and special tool 33 4 420.
9. Insert bolts but do not tighten down.
10. Insert screw from rear and replace nut but do not tighten down.
11. Lower workshop jack.
12. Tighten fasteners to specification.
    - Rear Differential-to-Carrier M12: 74 ft. lbs. (100 Nm)
    - Rear Differential-to-Carrier M14: 122 ft. lbs. (165 Nm)
    - Crankshaft damper M12: 74 ft. lbs. (100 Nm)
13. Check rear differential oil level, correct if necessary.

REAR DRIVESHAFT

REMOVAL & INSTALLATION

See Figures 13 and 14.

1. Before servicing the vehicle, refer to the precautions.
2. Remove underbody protection.
3. Remove complete exhaust system.
4. Remove heat shields.
5. Remove and discard the ZNS bolts and nuts at the front flange, rear flange and then the center bearing.
6. Using a screwdriver, pry constant velocity joint from drive shaft flange and remove driveshaft.

To install:

7. Inspect and lubricate the centering mount. If necessary, replace damaged mount.
8. Using new ZNS bolts and nuts, install the front flange, rear flange and center mount. Tighten to specification.

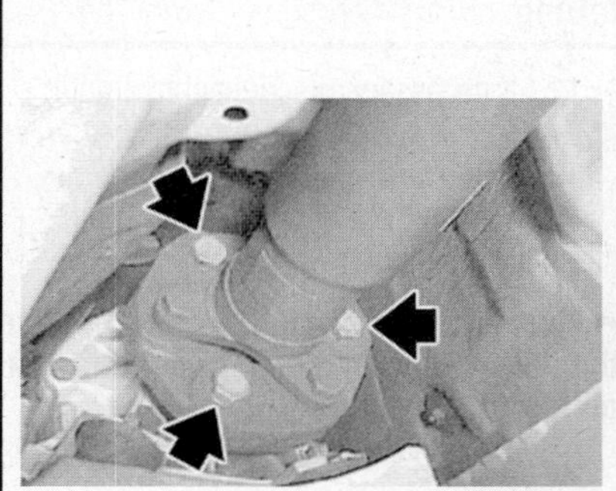

Fig. 13 Rear driveshaft connection with transmission

Fig. 11 Drive in shaft seal with special tool 31 5 130 as far as it will go

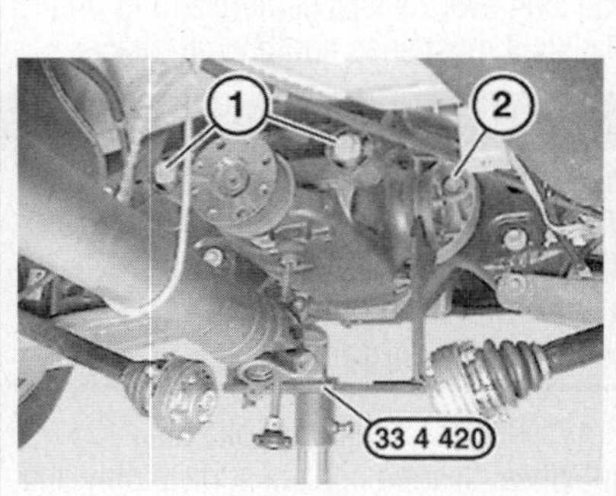

Fig. 12 Differential mounting bolt and nut

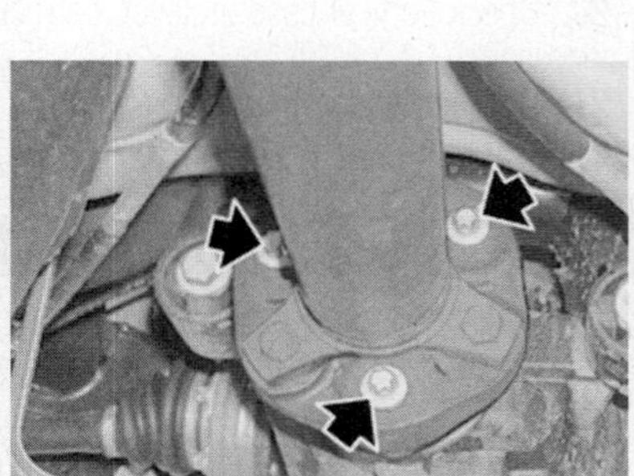

Fig. 14 Rear driveshaft connection with differential

- M10 x 10.9: 15 ft. lbs. (20 Nm) plus an additional 90°rotation
- M10 x 10.9 screw with ribbed teeth: 30 ft. lbs. (40 Nm) 45° rotation
- M12 x 10.9: 41 ft. lbs. (55 Nm) plus an additional 90° rotation

9. Install heat shields.
10. Install complete exhaust system.
11. Install underbody protection.

REAR HALFSHAFT

REMOVAL & INSTALLATION

See Figure 15.

1. Before servicing the vehicle, refer to the precautions.
2. Remove rear wheel.

⁂ WARNING

Expand turning lock sufficiently to avoid damaging thread when releasing collar nut.

3. Remove collar nut, activate handbrake for this purpose.
4. On the left side, remove strut if necessary.

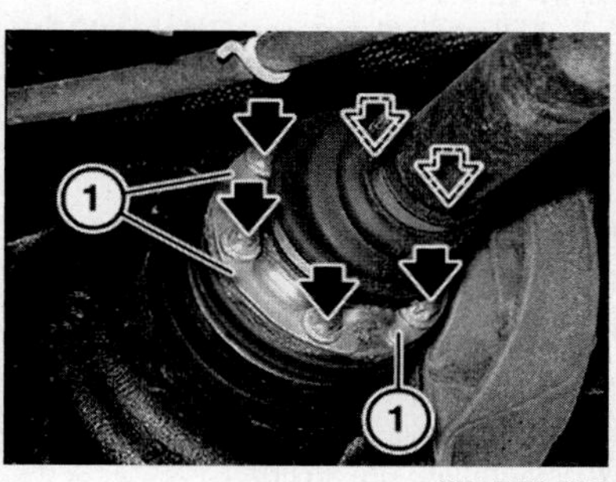

Fig. 15 Remove bolts and remove with washers

5. On the left side, lower exhaust system in rear area.
6. Remove bolts and remove with washers.
7. Press output shaft off drive flange using a suitable tool; if necessary, raise wheel carrier with workshop jack approximately 20 mm.

To install:

8. Before installing output shaft, make sure that drive flange is fully engaged in rear differential.
9. Replace bolts and washers and tighten to specification.
   - M8: 38 ft. lbs. (52 Nm)
   - M10 ZNS3: 52 ft. lbs. (70 Nm)
10. Replace collar nut, oil collar nut/wheel bearing contact surface only and tighten to specification.
   - M27: 311 ft. lbs. (420 Nm)
   - M24: 185 ft. lbs. (250 Nm)

⁂ WARNING

No oil permitted on thread of shaft journal or collar nut.

11. Secure collar nut by positive peening on flat areas of output shaft.
12. Check that output shaft is correctly seated in rear differential.
13. On the left side, raise exhaust system in rear area.
14. On the left side, install strut if necessary.
15. Install rear wheel.

ENGINE COOLING

ENGINE COOLANT

BLEEDING

M57 Engine

1. Fill the engine with coolant
   a. Switch ignition **ON**.
   b. Set heating to maximum temperature and fan to low speed (heating valves are opened and auxiliary coolant pump starts up).
   c. Slowly fill expansion tank with coolant.
   d. Close vent screw after bubble-free coolant emerges or after filling up to max. cold fill level.
2. On engines with auxiliary heater.
   a. Switch **OFF** engine and allow engine to cool to a temperature below 104°F (40°C).
   b. Open cap on expansion tank (AGB).
   c. Open vent screws on EGR cooler thermostat andcoolant return pipe.
   d. Switch ignition **ON**.
   e. Seat heating to maximum temperature and fan to low speed (heater valves are opened and auxiliary water pump starts up).
   f. Add coolant slowly.
   g. Close vent screws after coolant emerges or after filling up to max. cold fill level.
   h. Fill expansion tank to maximum cold fill level.
   i. Start engine and run at idle for 5 minutes (top up coolant to maximum cold fill level if required) .
   j. Close cap on expansion tank, press accelerator pedal several times to approximately 2500 rpm.
   k. Open cap on expansion tank, run engine at idle for a further 5 minutes (bubble-free coolant emerges at vent line in expansion tank).
   l. Fill to maximum cold fill level.
   m. Top up expansion tank with an additional 8.45 fl. oz (250 ml).
   n. Close expansion tank cap.
3. On vehicles with optional extra independent heating:
   a. Switch off engine.
   b. Run independent heating for approximately 2 minutes.
   c. Start engine and run briefly at idle.
   d. Press accelerator pedal twice up to approximately 2500 rpm.
   e. Open cap on expansion tank and add coolant up to max. cold fill level.
   f. Top up expansion tank with an additional 8.45 fl. oz (250 ml).
4. Check cooling system for leaks.

N20 and N26 Engines

⁂ WARNING

Never reuse used coolant.

⁂ WARNING

When replacing and removing components which rely on the corrosion protection effect of the coolant, it is essential to change the coolant. The cooling system must therefore be drained and refilled.

⁂ WARNING

In the case of other removal work involving the draining of part quantities of coolant, replace these quantities which have been drained with new coolant.

1. Fill cooling system using the vacuum filling device, after completing the filling procedure, remove the vacuum filling device.
2. Overfill expansion tank (to below the tank ventilation line).

3. Open the bleeder screw with the expansion tank open.
4. Open the bleeder screw on transmission oil cooler until coolant emerges without bubbles and then close it again.
5. Open the bleeder screw on radiator return hose until coolant emerges without bubbles and then close it again.
6. Close bleeder screw on expansion tank
7. Massage coolant hoses (supply and return radiator).
8. Connect battery charger.
9. Switch on ignition and low-beam headlight. Switch on the low-beam headlights to perform the bleeding procedure. If the low-beam headlights are not switched on, the ignition (Terminal 15) will switch off automatically after a certain period of time and interrupt the bleeding procedure.
10. FES (driving experience switch) must not be in ECO PRO.
11. Set heater to maximum temperature and turn blower down to lowest speed.
12. Press accelerator pedal for 10 seconds to floor. Engine must not be started.
13. The bleeding procedure is started when the accelerator pedal is pressed and takes approx. 12 minutes. (Electric coolant pump was activated and shuts down automatically after approx. 12 min).
14. Then adjust fluid level in coolant expansion tank to maximum level.
15. Check cooling system for water tightness.
16. Close coolant expansion tank.
17. After the bleeding procedure, let the engine run until it is warm and the electric fan starts running.
18. If venting has to be carried out again (e.g. if cooling system is leaking), allow DME to fall completely (leave ignition key removed for approx. 3 min), then repeat from Point 3.
19. Close the sealing cap until the arrows line up.

N52 and N54 Engines.

1. Before servicing the vehicle, refer to the precautions.

➡Do not open the coolant expansion tank cap during the venting procedure.

2. Connect battery charger.
3. Switch on ignition.
4. Set heater to maximum temperature and turn fan down to lowest speed.
5. Press accelerator pedal for 10 seconds to floor. Engine must not be started.
6. The venting procedure is started when the accelerator pedal is pressed and takes approximately 12 minutes.

➡Electric coolant pump activates and shuts down automatically after approximately 12 minutes.

7. Fill coolant expansion tank until the float rises 0.234 in. (6mm) above the expansion tank rim.
8. Check cooling system for leaks.

➡If venting has to be carried out again, leave ignition key removed for approximately 3 minutes.

9. Fill coolant expansion tank until the float rises 0.234 in. (6mm) above the expansion tank rim again.

WARNING

Fill the expansion tank in this manner only when bleeding the cooling system.

S65 Engine

1. Before servicing the vehicle, refer to the precautions.

➡Do not open the coolant expansion tank cap during the venting procedure.

2. Perform filling operation slowly.
3. Set heater to maximum temperature and turn fan down to lowest speed.
4. Start engine and run at idle speed.
5. Fill coolant expansion tank until the float rises 0.702 in. (18mm) above the expansion tank rim.
6. Run engine for 15 minutes, the cooling system vents itself.

➡Coolant level must drop to marking.

7. If necessary, correct coolant level.
8. Close cap on expansion tank.
9. Check cooling system for leaks.

DRAIN & REFILL

M57 Engine

1. Before servicing the vehicle, refer to the precautions.

CAUTION

Only work on the cooling system when the engine has cooled down.

WARNING

Some vehicles use a Lifetime coolant. If removing radiator, oil-coolant heat exchanger or transmission oil cooler, do not reuse drained coolant. Use only recommended coolant and observe mixture ratio (antifreeze/water).

2. Remove the intercooler.
3. Open cap on coolant expansion tank.
4. If fitted, release drain plugs on radiator at bottom. On coolant radiators which do not have a drain plug, remove coolant hose.
5. Drain, catch and dispose of coolant.
6. Replace sealing rings and tighten to 24 inch lbs. (3 Nm).

WARNING

Cover opening on turbocharger without fail.

7. Open drain plug on engine block.
8. Replace sealing rings and tighten to 19 ft. lbs. (25 Nm).
9. Open vent screw.
10. Drain, and recycle coolant.

To install:

11. Fill the engine with coolant
    a. Switch ignition **ON**.
    b. Set heating to maximum temperature and fan to low speed (heating valves are opened and auxiliary coolant pump starts up).
    c. Slowly fill expansion tank with coolant.
    d. Close vent screw after bubble-free coolant emerges or after filling up to max. cold fill level.
12. On engines with auxiliary heater.
    a. Switch **OFF** engine and allow engine to cool to a temperature below 104 °F (40°C).
    b. Open cap on expansion tank (AGB).
    c. Open vent screws on EGR cooler thermostat andcoolant return pipe.
    d. Switch ignition **ON**.
    e. Seat heating to maximum temperature and fan to low speed (heater valves are opened and auxiliary water pump starts up).
    f. Add coolant slowly.
    g. Close vent screws after coolant emerges or after filling up to max. cold fill level.
    h. Fill expansion tank to maximum cold fill level.
    i. Start engine and run at idle for 5 minutes (top up coolant to maximum cold fill level if required) .
    j. Close cap on expansion tank, press accelerator pedal several times to approximately 2500 rpm.
    k. Open cap on expansion tank, run engine at idle for a further 5 minutes (bubble-free coolant emerges at vent line in expansion tank).
    l. Fill to maximum cold fill level.
    m. Top up expansion tank with an additional 8.45 fl. oz (250 ml).
    n. Close expansion tank cap.

13. On vehicles with optional extra independent heating:
 a. Switch off engine.
 b. Run independent heating for approximately 2 minutes.
 c. Start engine and run briefly at idle.
 d. Press accelerator pedal twice up to approximately 2500 rpm.
 e. Open cap on expansion tank and add coolant up to max. cold fill level.
 f. Top up expansion tank with an additional 8.45 fl. oz (250 ml).
14. Check cooling system for leaks.

N20 and N26 Engines

CAUTION

Risk of scalding.

CAUTION

The repair work on the cooling system should only be carried out on an engine that has cooled down.

WARNING

Never reuse used coolant.

WARNING

When replacing and removing components which rely on the corrosion protection effect of the coolant, it is essential to change the coolant. The cooling system must therefore be drained and refilled.

WARNING

In the case of other removal work involving the draining of part quantities of coolant, replace these quantities which have been drained with new coolant.

WARNING

For dirt contamination of the cooling system (e.g. by engine oil), the cooling system must be rinsed with water until all dirt contamination is removed.

CAUTION

Risk of skidding due to coolant on the floor.

WARNING

Open cooling system only when it has cooled down.

WARNING

Opening the cooling system while hot can result in air entering the system. This can cause overheating with permanent damage to the engine.

WARNING

You must protect the alternator against dirt contamination before carrying out any repair work on the cooling circuit. Cover alternator with suitable materials. Failure to comply with this procedure may result in an alternator malfunction.

1. Remove intake silencer housing.
 a. Release connector on hot film air mass meter and disconnect.
 b. Release clamp.Tightening torque: 26 inch lbs. (3 Nm)
 c. Unclip Bowden cable from intake silencer housing.
 d. Pull off intake filter housing upward out of the rubber mounts and remove.
2. Remove front underbody protection.
3. Open sealing cap on coolant expansion tank. When installing, close sealing cap until the arrow marks line up.
4. Unlock and detach coolant hose from radiator.
5. Unlock coolant hose on coolant pump and detach.
6. Drain, catch and dispose of coolant.
7. Slowly fill coolant expansion tank up to lower edge of filler neck with recommended coolant.
8. Observe mixture ratio.
9. Bleed the cooling system.

WARNING

Have a cleaning cloth ready and mop up emerging coolant.

10. Perform the bleeding procedure.
11. Check cooling system for leaks.

N52 Engine

See Figures 16 and 17.

1. Before servicing the vehicle, refer to the precautions.

CAUTION

Only work on the cooling system when the engine has cooled down.

WARNING

Some vehicles use a Lifetime coolant. If removing radiator, oil-coolant heat exchanger or transmission oil cooler, do not reuse drained coolant. Use only recommended coolant and observe mixture ratio (antifreeze/water).

2. Remove front underbody protection
3. Open cap on coolant expansion tank.
4. Unlock lugs on front axle carrier and remove radiator cover in direction of arrow.
5. If fitted, release drain plugs on radiator at bottom. On coolant radiators which do not have a drain plug, remove coolant hose.
6. Drain, catch and dispose of coolant.
7. Replace sealing rings and tighten to 24 inch lbs. (3 Nm).
8. Unfasten and detach coolant hose from thermostat housing.
9. Drain, catch and recycle coolant.
10. Slowly fill the cooling system with the recommended coolant in the proper mixture ratio.
 a. Open vent screw.

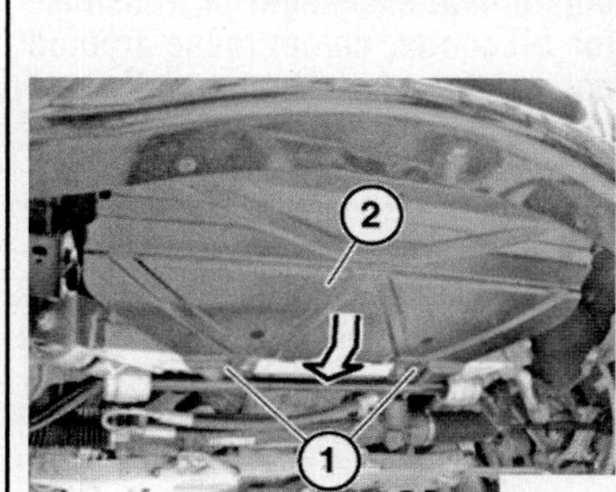

Fig. 16 Unlock lugs on front axle carrier and remove radiator cover in direction of arrow

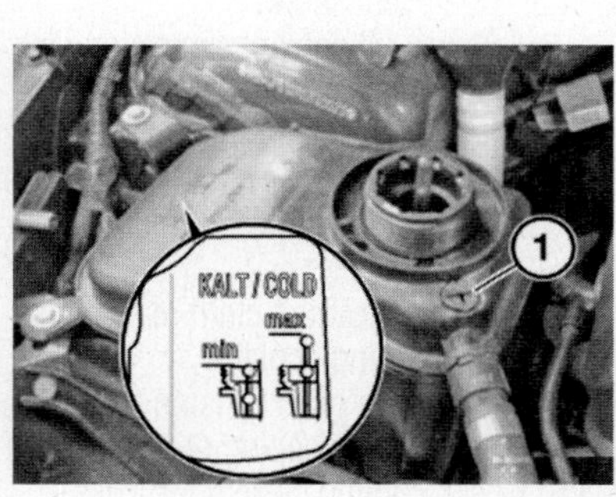

Fig. 17 Slowly fill the cooling system after opening vent screw

b. Slowly fill coolant expansion tank up to lower edge of filler neck with recommended coolant.

c. Observe mixture ratio.

d. Close vent screw until bubble-free coolant emerges.

e. Have a cleaning cloth ready and mop up emerging coolant.

f. Close cap on expansion tank.

11. Perform the bleeding procedure.
12. Check cooling system for leaks.

N54 Engine

1. Before servicing the vehicle, refer to the precautions.

⁂ CAUTION

Only work on the cooling system when the engine has cooled down.

⁂ WARNING

Some vehicles use a Lifetime coolant. If removing radiator, oil-coolant heat exchanger or transmission oil cooler, do not reuse drained coolant. Use only recommended coolant and observe mixture ratio (antifreeze/water).

2. Remove the intercooler.
3. Open cap on coolant expansion tank.
4. If fitted, release drain plugs on radiator at bottom. On coolant radiators which do not have a drain plug, remove coolant hose.
5. Drain, catch and dispose of coolant.
6. Replace sealing rings and tighten to 24 inch lbs. (3 Nm).
7. Unfasten and detach coolant hose from thermostat housing.
8. Drain, catch and recycle coolant.

To install:

9. Slowly fill the cooling system with the recommended coolant in the proper mixture ratio.

a. Open vent screw.

b. Slowly fill coolant expansion tank up to lower edge of filler neck with recommended coolant.

c. Observe mixture ratio.

d. Close vent screw until bubble-free coolant emerges.

e. Have a cleaning cloth ready and mop up emerging coolant.

f. Close cap on expansion tank.

10. Perform the bleeding procedure.
11. Check cooling system for leaks.

N55 Engine

1. Before servicing the vehicle, refer to the precautions.

⁂ CAUTION

Only work on the cooling system when the engine has cooled down.

⁂ WARNING

Some vehicles use a Lifetime coolant. If removing radiator, oil-coolant heat exchanger or transmission oil cooler, do not reuse drained coolant. Use only recommended coolant and observe mixture ratio (antifreeze/water).

2. Remove front underbody protection.
3. Open sealing capon coolant expansion tank. When installing, close sealing cap until the arrow marks line up.
4. Release screws.
5. Remove cover.
6. Release hose clamps and.
7. Pull off coolant hoses from coolant pump and drain coolant. Note installation hose clamps.
8. Slowly fill and bleed cooling system.
9. Observe mixture ratio.

⁂ WARNING

Have a cleaning cloth ready and mop up emerging coolant.

a. Close cap on expansion tank.

10. Check cooling system for leaks.

S65 Engine

1. Before servicing the vehicle, refer to the precautions.

⁂ CAUTION

Only work on the cooling system when the engine has cooled down.

⁂ WARNING

Some vehicles use a Lifetime coolant. If removing radiator, oil-coolant heat exchanger or transmission oil cooler, do not reuse drained coolant. Use only recommended coolant and observe mixture ratio (antifreeze/water).

2. Remove front underbody protection.

a. Release screws.

b. Release screws on both sides.

c. Remove tip of engine compartment shield on left/right.

d. Turn catch on cable through 90° and disengage in direction of arrow from bracket on both sides.

e. Pull underbody protection forwards under bumper trim and remove.

3. Open cap on coolant expansion tank.
4. If fitted, release drain plugs on radiator at bottom. On coolant radiators which do not have a drain plug, remove coolant hose.
5. Drain, catch and dispose of coolant.
6. Replace sealing rings and tighten to 24 inch lbs. (3 Nm).
7. Unfasten and detach coolant hose from thermostat housing.
8. Drain, catch and recycle coolant.
9. Slowly fill the cooling system with the recommended coolant in the proper mixture ratio.

a. Open vent screw.

b. Slowly fill coolant expansion tank up to lower edge of filler neck with recommended coolant.

c. Observe mixture ratio.

d. Close vent screw until bubble-free coolant emerges.

e. Have a cleaning cloth ready and mop up emerging coolant.

f. Close cap on expansion tank.

10. Perform the bleeding procedure.
11. Check cooling system for leaks.

FLUID RECOMMENDATIONS

Use only BMW approved coolant.

ELECTRIC ENGINE FAN

REMOVAL & INSTALLATION

M57 Engine

See Figures 18 and 19.

1. Before servicing the vehicle, refer to the precautions.
2. Remove the intake duct.

a. Unfasten screws.

b. Detach hose in direction of arrow.

c. Remove intake duct in direction of arrow.

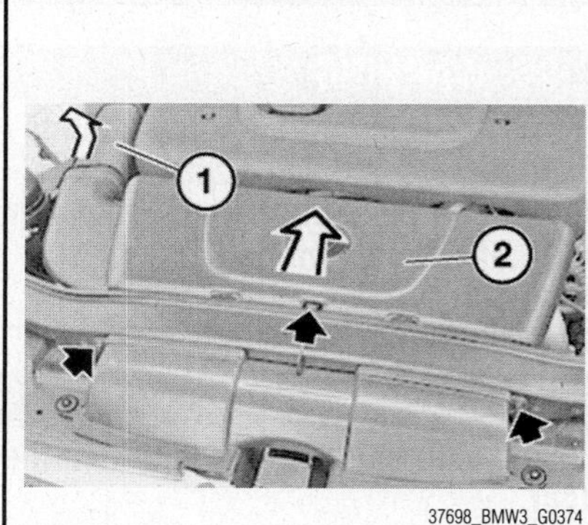

Fig. 18 Detach hose in direction of arrow. Remove intake duct in direction of arrow

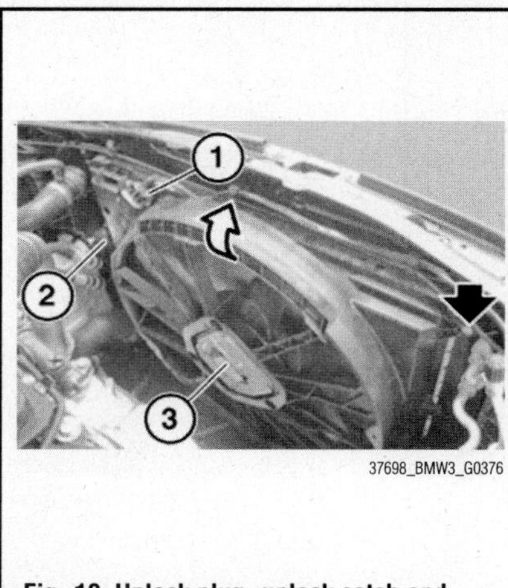

Fig. 19 Unlock plug, unlock catch and remove fan cowl towards top

3. Read out fault memory of DME control unit
4. On automatic transmission vehicles, remove front underbody protection.
   a. Release screws.
   b. Pull underbody protection forward under bumper trim.
5. On automatic transmission vehicles, release screw and unclip hose from fan cowl.
6. Unlock plug and remove.
7. Release screw.
8. Unlock catch and remove fan cowl towards top.

To install:

9. To install, reverse the removal procedure.
10. Check stored fault messages and clear the fault memory.

N20 and N26 Engines

See Figures 20 and 21.

1. Switch off ignition.
2. Remove intake silencer housing.

Automatic only:

3. Release screw. Tightening torque: 40 inch lbs. (4.5 Nm)
4. Pull off transmission oil cooler for automatic transmission in upward direction from fan cowl.

All:

5. Unlock and pull off connector and unclip cable from fan cowl.
6. Unlock catch.
7. Release screw. Tightening torque: 40 inch lbs. (4.5 Nm)
8. Feed out fan cowl upwards and remove.

To install:

To install, reverse the removal procedure noting the following.

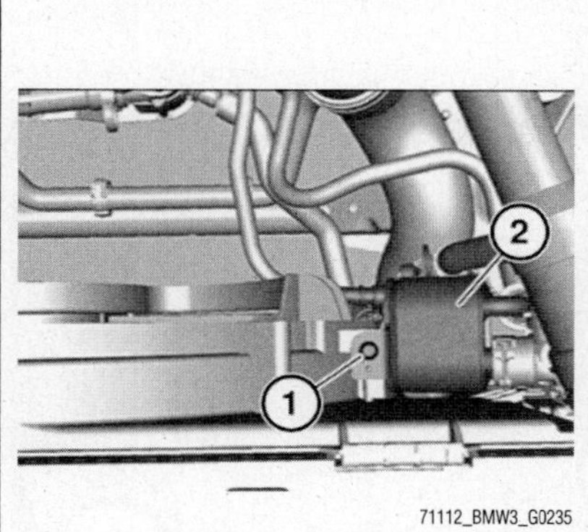

Fig. 20 Releasing screw and pulling off transmission oil cooler

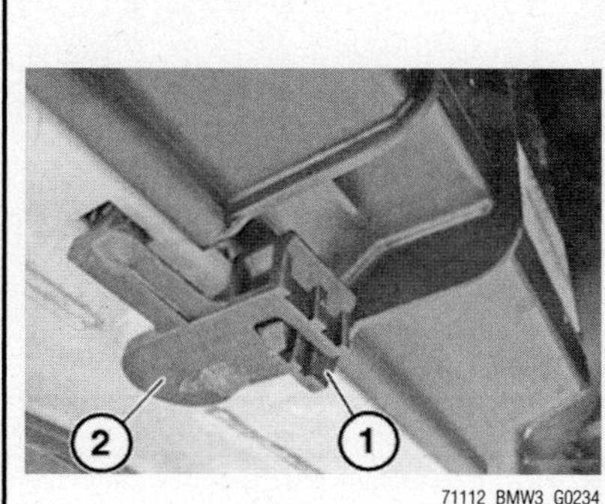

Fig. 21 Checking fan cowl and holder installation

9. Make sure fan cowl and holder are in correct installation position.

➡**Check stored fault messages.**

10. Delete fault memory.

N52 and N54 Engines

See Figure 22.

1. Before servicing the vehicle, refer to the precautions.
2. Read out fault memory of DME control unit.
3. Remove air cleaner housing and duct. Refer to engine mechanical, air cleaner housing, removal & installation.
4. On automatic transmission vehicles, remove front underbody protection and disconnect the cooler for automatic transmission from fan cowl.
5. Unlock plug and remove.
6. Disconnect line from fan cowl.
7. Disconnect cable strap from fan cowl.
8. Remove bolt.
9. Unlock catch.
10. Remove fan cowl towards top.

To install:

11. Install fan cowl.
12. Lock catch in the opposite direction of arrow.
13. Install bolt and tighten securely.
14. Connect cable strap to fan cowl.
15. Clip line to fan cowl.
16. Lock plug.
17. On automatic transmission vehicles, connect the cooler for automatic transmission to fan cowl.
18. Install front underbody protection.
19. Install intake duct.
20. Clear the fault memory.

N55 Engine

See Figures 23 and 24.

1. Switch off ignition.
2. Remove intake silencer housing.
3. Unlock and pull off connector and unclip cable from fan cowl.
4. Unlock catch.
5. Release screw. Tightening torque: 40 inch lbs. (4.5 Nm)
6. Feed out fan cowl upwards and remove.

To install:

To install, reverse the removal procedure noting the following.

7. Make sure fan cowl and holder are in correct installation position.

S65 Engine

See Figures 25 and 26.

1. Before servicing the vehicle, refer to the precautions.
2. Remove front underbody protection
   a. Release screws as shown.
   b. Release screws on both sides.
   c. Remove tip of engine compartment shield on left/right.
   d. Turn catch on cable through 90° and disengage in direction of arrow from bracket on both sides.
   e. Pull underbody protection forwards under bumper trim and remove.
3. Remove the intake duct.
   a. Remove expansion rivets.
   b. Release screws.
   c. Remove intake duct.
4. Unclip coolant lines from fan cowl.
5. Unlock connector and remove.

⁂ WARNING

When removing fan cowl, protect plug and housing against moisture; dry with compressed air if necessary.

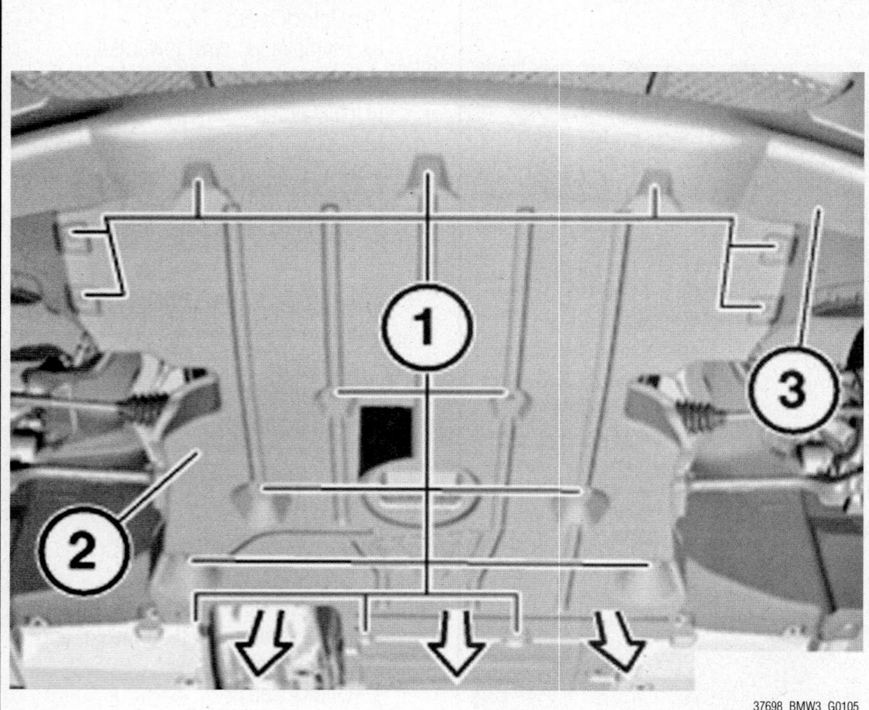

Fig. 22 Release screws and pull underbody protection forward under bumper trim

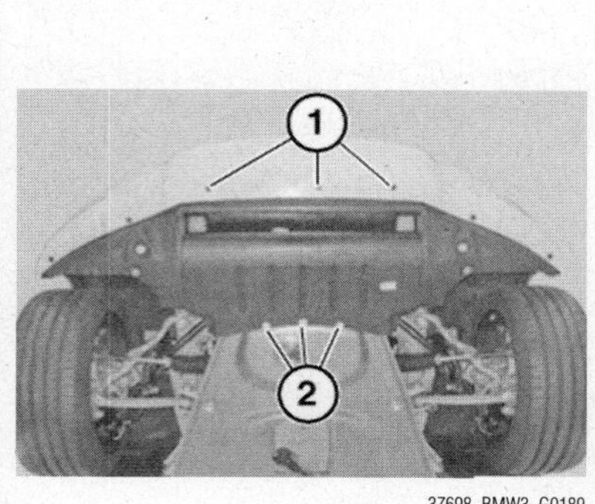

Fig. 25 Release screws as shown

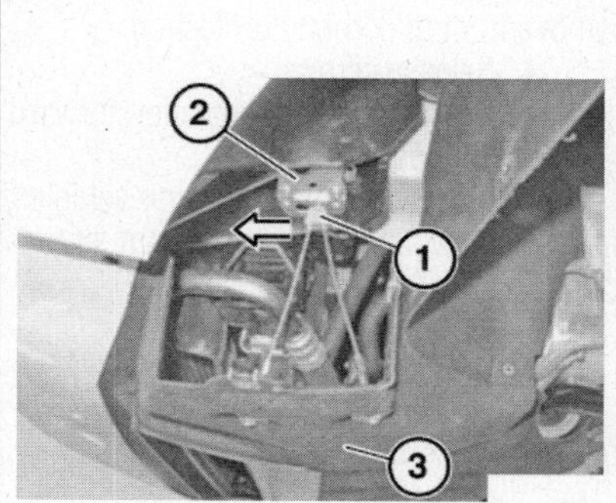

Fig. 26 Turn catch on cable through 90° and disengage in direction of arrow from bracket on both sides. Pull underbody protection forwards under bumper trim and remove

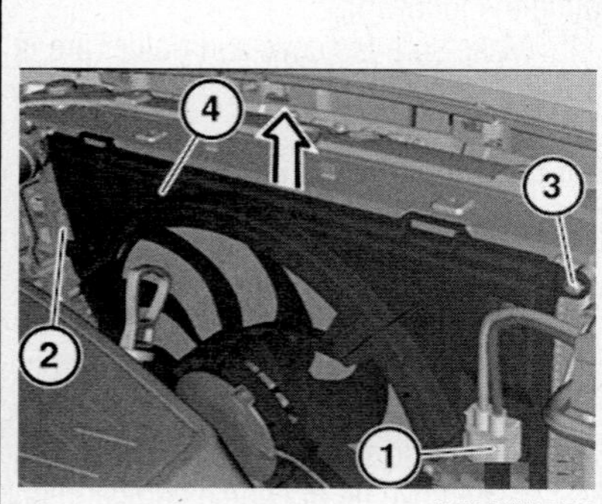

Fig. 23 Unlocking and pulling off connector, unlocking catch and releasing screw from fan cowl

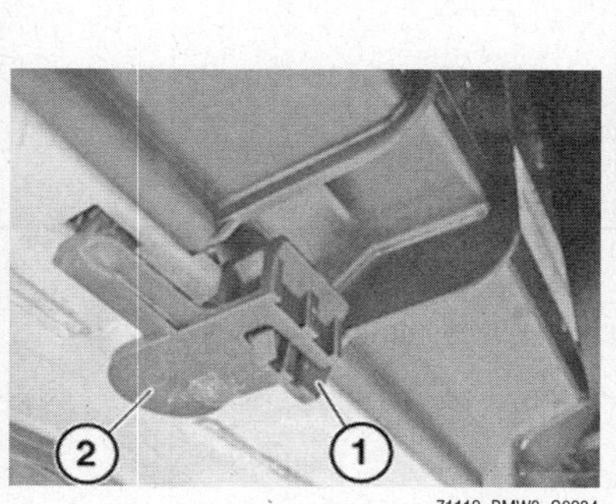

Fig. 24 Verifying fan cowl and holder positioning

6. Release retaining screw for fan cowl.
7. Unclip cable.
8. Unclip vent lines.
9. Turn lower hose holder through 90°.
10. Remove fan cowl towards top.

To install:

11. To install, reverse the removal procedure.
12. When installing fan cowl, make sure guide tabs are correctly positioned.
13. Clear DME fault memory.

RADIATOR

REMOVAL & INSTALLATION

M57 Engine

See Figure 27.

1. Before servicing the vehicle, refer to the precautions.

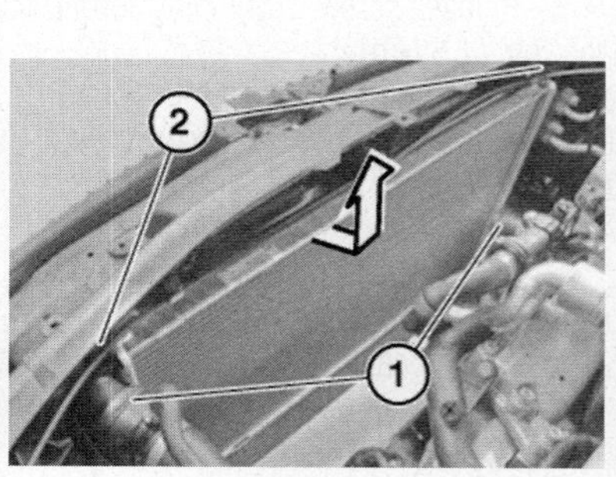

Fig. 27 Release and disconnect coolant hoses and unfasten screws

2. Remove engine fan. Refer to engine cooling, engine fan, removal & installation.
3. Drain and recycle coolant. Refer to engine cooling, engine coolant, removal & installation
4. Remove heat exchanger for automatic transmission fluid, if installed.
5. Release and disconnect coolant hoses.
6. Unfasten screws.
7. Remove radiator towards top.

To install:

8. To install, reverse the removal procedure.
9. Fill and vent cooling system and check for leaks.

N20, N26 and N55 Engines

See Figure 28.

1. Before servicing the vehicle, refer to the precautions.
2. Remove fan cowl.
3. Drain coolant.

Vehicles with automatic transmissions:

4. Unlock and detach coolant hose from transmission oil cooler on the radiator.

All:

5. Release and disconnect coolant hoses.
6. Unfasten screws. Tightening torque: 7 ft. lbs. (10 Nm)
7. Remove cover from the radiator.
8. Carefully feed out radiator towards top and remove.

To install:

To install, reverse the removal procedure noting the following.

9. Make sure the installation position of the cover on the left and right module carriers is correct.

Fig. 28 Removing cover and radiator

10. Reassemble the vehicle.
11. Check the cooling system for leaks.

N52 Engine

1. Before servicing the vehicle, refer to the precautions.
2. Drain and recycle the engine coolant.
3. Disconnect the negative battery cable.
4. Remove the intake filter housing.
5. Remove the fan cowl.
6. Remove the coolant hose from expansion tank/radiator.
7. Remove the coolant hose from expansion tank.
8. Remove the plug connection at level sensor.
9. On automatic transmission equipped vehicles, remove the A/T heat exchanger/oil cooler.
10. Remove the coolant hose from radiator.
11. Remove the radiator mounting bolts, lift radiator out of mountings.

To install:

12. Install the radiator and mounting bolts. Tighten to 2 ft. lbs. (3 Nm).
13. Install the coolant hose to radiator.
14. On automatic transmission equipped vehicles, install the A/T heat exchanger/oil cooler.
15. Install the plug connection at level sensor.
16. Install the coolant hose to expansion tank.
17. Install the coolant hose to expansion tank/radiator.
18. Install the fan cowl.
19. Install the intake filter housing.
20. Fill and vent cooling system and check for leaks.

N54 Engine

See Figure 29.

1. Before servicing the vehicle, refer to the precautions.
2. Drain and recycle the engine coolant.
3. Disconnect the negative battery cable.
4. Remove the fan cowl.
5. Drain and recycle the coolant.
6. Remove the coolant hoses from radiator.
7. Release clamp, detach charge-air duct and remove.
8. On automatic transmission equipped vehicles, release bolt and detach hose.
9. Remove the radiator mounting bolts, lift radiator out of mountings.

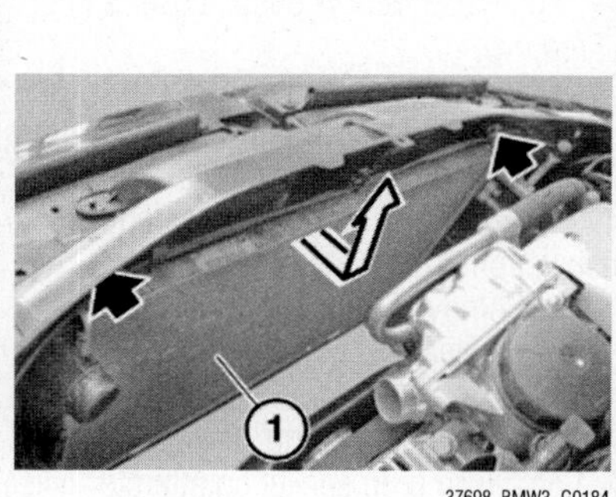

Fig. 29 Remove the radiator mounting bolts, lift radiator out of mountings as shown

To install:

10. To install, reverse the removal procedure.
11. Tighten radiator mounting bolts to 24 inch lbs. (3 Nm).
12. Fill and bleed cooling system and check for leaks.

S65 Engine

1. Before servicing the vehicle, refer to the precautions.
2. Drain and recycle the engine coolant.
3. Disconnect the negative battery cable.
4. Remove the air cleaner housing. Refer to engine mechanical, air cleaner housing, removal & installation.
5. Remove the fan cowl.
6. Drain and recycle the coolant.
7. Remove the coolant hoses from radiator.
8. On automatic transmission equipped vehicles, release bolt and detach hose.
9. Remove the radiator mounting bolts, lift radiator out of mountings.

To install:

10. To install, reverse the removal procedure.
11. Tighten radiator mounting bolts to 24 inch lbs. (3 Nm).
12. Fill and bleed cooling system and check for leaks.

THERMOSTAT

REMOVAL & INSTALLATION

M57 Engine

See Figures 30 through 32.

1. Before servicing the vehicle, refer to the precautions.
2. Remove the acoustic cover.

a. Release screws.
b. Raise front acoustic cover and remove.
3. Remove engine fan. Refer to engine cooling, engine fan, removal & installation.
4. Drain and recycle coolant. Refer to engine cooling, engine coolant, removal & installation
5. Remove EGR cooler.
a. Release clamp from exhaust gas recirculation cooler.
b. Disconnect plug.
c. Turn plug socket counterclockwise and remove in upward direction from holder.
d. Unlock and detach coolant hose.
6. Gently pull clip from electric changeover valve towards front and slide away to right side.
a. Release screws on EGR cooler/manifold.
b. Unfasten screw as shown.

Fig. 30 Release clamp and disconnect plug from exhaust gas temperature sensor

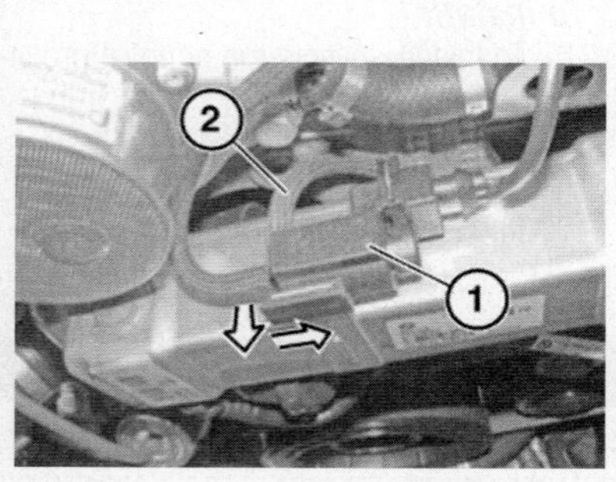

Fig. 31 Gently pull clip from electric changeover valve towards front and slide away to right side

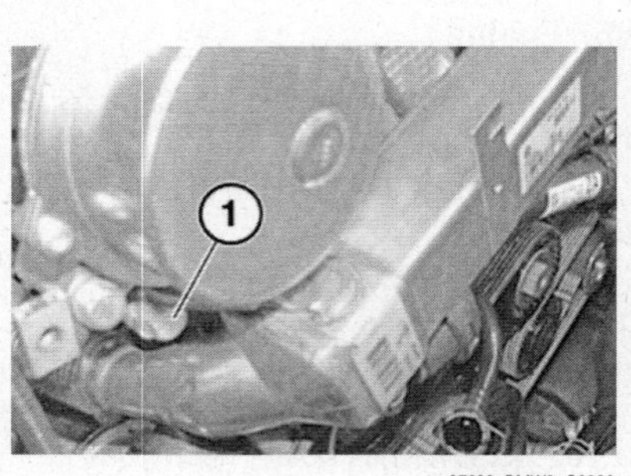

Fig. 32 Unfasten screw

c. Release bolt and remove exhaust gas recirculation cooler.
7. Lever out lock.
8. Lever out lock and detach coolant hose.
9. Release screws.
10. Carefully remove thermostat housing to one side.

WARNING

The coolant thermostat is integrated in the coolant thermostat housing and can only be replaced as a complete unit.

To install:

11. To install, reverse the removal procedure.
12. Clean sealing surfaces on coolant thermostat housing and replace seal.
13. Observe tightening sequence on the exhaust gas recirculation cooler.
a. Join bolts (3, 4 and 5).
b. Release bolts (3, 4 and 5) back by 90°.
c. Secure screws.
d. Secure profile clamp.
e. Tighten bolt.
f. Secure bolt on bracket.
g. Secure microencapsulated bolt.
14. Tighten bolts/nuts to specification as follows:
- Exhaust-gas recirculation cooler to exhaust manifold: 14 ft. lbs. (19 Nm)
- Exhaust-gas recirculation cooler to exhaust-gas recirculation valve: 44 inch lbs. (5 Nm)
- Exhaust-gas recirculation cooler to bracket (replace screw): 14 ft. lbs. (19 Nm)
- Exhaust-gas recirculation temperature sensor: 15 ft. lbs. (20 Nm)

N20 and N26 Engines

See Figure 33.

1. Before servicing the vehicle, refer to the precautions.
2. Remove top clean air pipe.
3. Remove engine ventilation line.
4. Disconnect plug connection.
5. Disconnect coolant hoses (2-4) on thermostat with clamping tongs.
6. Disconnect coolant hoses (2-4) from thermostat.
7. Release screws and remove thermostat. Tightening torque: 7 ft. lbs. (10 Nm)

To install:

To install, reverse the removal procedure noting the following.
8. Assemble engine.
9. Top off coolant.
10. Bleed cooling system.

N52 and N54 Engines

See Figures 34 and 35.

1. Before servicing the vehicle, refer to the precautions.
2. Remove the underbody protection.
3. Drain and recycle the coolant.
4. Remove hose clips.
5. Remove coolant hoses.
6. Unlock and detach coolant hoses.
7. Disconnect plug connection.
8. Remove bolts.
9. Remove coolant thermostat.

To install:

10. Install coolant thermostat.
11. Install bolts.
12. Connect plug connection.
13. Connect and lock coolant hoses.
14. Install coolant hoses.
15. Fasten hose clips.
16. Fill and vent cooling system and check for leaks.

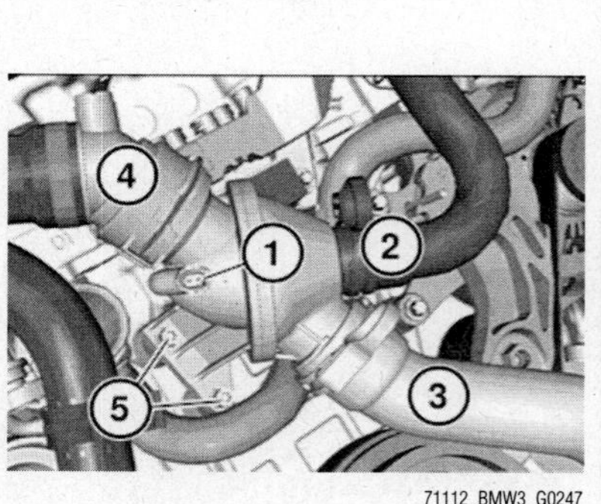

Fig. 33 Disconnecting plug connection and coolant hoses (2-4) and releasing screws

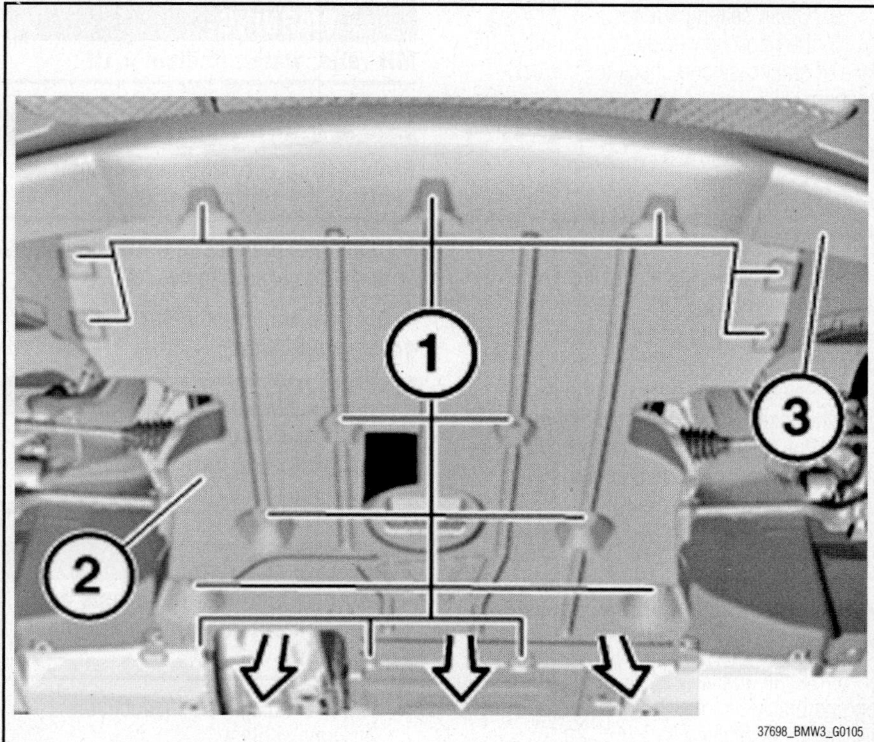

37698_BMW3_G0105

Fig. 34 Release screws and pull underbody protection forward under bumper trim

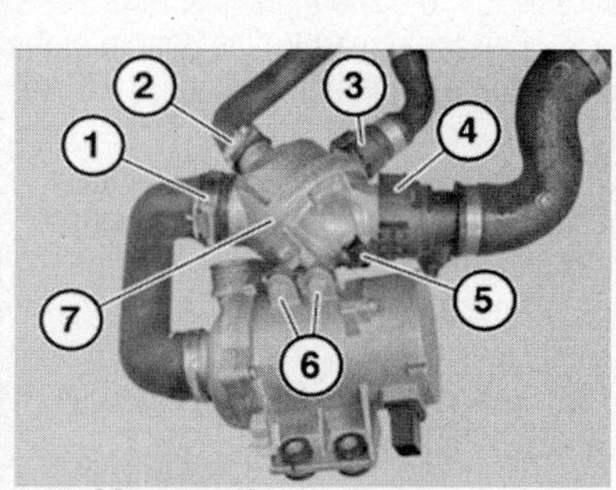

22205_BMWC_G0093

Fig. 35 Thermostat assembly

N55 Engine

See Figure 36.

1. Before servicing the vehicle, refer to the precautions.
2. Drain coolant.
3. Remove fan cowl.

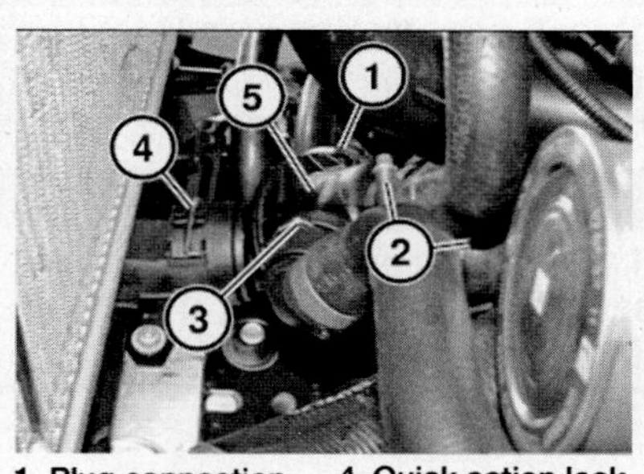

71112_BMW3_G0248

Fig. 36 Removing and installing thermostat

4. Remove front underbody protection.
5. Place collecting vessel for coolant under engine compartment.
6. Unscrew bolt and set expansion tank aside.
7. Unfasten plug connection.
8. Loosen hose clamps, detach coolant hoses from thermostat.
9. Unlock quick-action lock and detach coolant hose from thermostat.
10. Unlock quick-action lock and detach thermostat from radiator.
11. Remove thermostat toward the top.

To install:

To install, reverse the removal procedure noting the following.

12. Assemble engine.
13. Fill cooling system.
14. Observe capacities.

➡Check coolant hoses for cracks and damage. Replace coolant hoses as required.

➡On vehicles older than 5 years, renew coolant hoses.

15. Check function of cooling system.

S65 Engine

See Figures 37 and 38.

1. Before servicing the vehicle, refer to the precautions.
2. Remove intake air manifold. Refer to engine mechanical, intake manifold, removal & installation.
3. Drain and recycle the coolant.
4. Release unlocking element and detach vent line.
5. Disconnect fuel line from fuel rail.
6. Release screws and unlock wiring harness of fuel injectors.
7. Clip injection pipe out of holder.
8. Lay injection pipe, cylinders 5 to 8, to one side.
9. Disconnect plug connection on coolant temperature sensor and on solenoid valve.
10. Unlock coolant hoses and detach.
11. Release thermostat mounting screws.
12. Remove thermostat housing with thermostat forwards in direction of arrow.
13. Clean sealing surfaces.

37698_BMW3_G0204

Fig. 37 Release screws and unlock wiring harness of fuel injectors

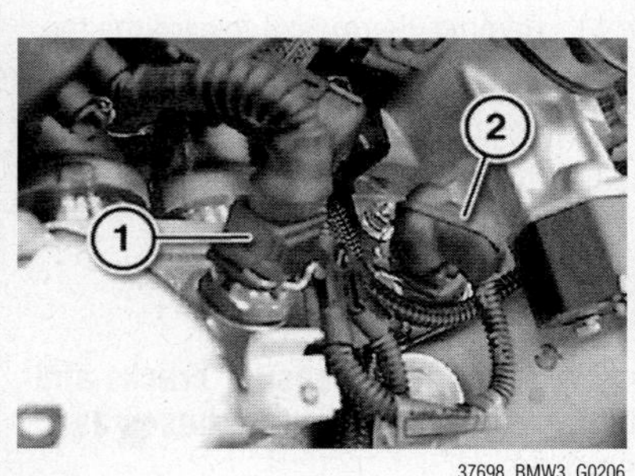

37698_BMW3_G0206

Fig. 38 Disconnect plug connection on coolant temperature sensor and on solenoid valve

14. Remove thermostat.
15. Check rubber section for damage and remove connecting pipes.

To install:

16. To install, reverse the removal procedure.
17. Replace sealing rings.
18. Replace all O-rings on connecting pipes.
19. Fill and bleed the cooling system and check for leaks.

WATER PUMP

REMOVAL & INSTALLATION

M57 Engine

Engine Driven Pump

1. Before servicing the vehicle, refer to the precautions.
2. Remove and install coolant thermostat.
3. Release screws.
4. Remove water pump.

⁂ WARNING

During the following work steps, the sealing face on the crankcase must not be damaged.

5. Cut connecting links on gasket accordingly.

⁂ WARNING

Do not damage sealing surface.

6. Cut through connecting links of gasket with a small cross-cut chisel.
7. Remove gasket.

To install:

8. To install, reverse the removal procedure.
9. Clean sealing surface.
10. Position new gasket on sealing face of crankcase and check for correct seating.
11. Fill and bleed cooling system and check for leaks.

Electric Auxiliary Pump

See Figure 39.

1. Before servicing the vehicle, refer to the precautions.
2. Unfasten plug connection and disconnect.
3. Release hose clamps and detach coolant hoses from auxiliary water pump.
4. Pull auxiliary water pump in direction of arrow out of front engine bracket.

To install:

5. To install, reverse the removal procedure.

➡Observe direction of flow of auxiliary water pump.

6. Install auxiliary water pump in front engine bracket so that rubber mounts slide exactly in associated locators.

N20 and N26 Engines

Coolant Pump

See Figures 40 through 42.

⁂ WARNING

Only perform this work after engine has cooled down.

⁂ WARNING

If a coolant pump that has already been operated is reused, it must be filled with coolant after removal.

1. Plug connection
2. Hose clamps
3. Coolant hoses
4. Auxiliary water pump
5. Front engine bracket

37698_BMW3_G0398

Fig. 39 Removing the electric auxiliary pump

⁂ WARNING

Mix ratio, water: Coolant = 1:1

⁂ WARNING

Protect plug connections against coolant and contamination.

➡Catch and dispose of drained coolant in suitable collecting vessel.

➡Observe country specific waste disposal regulations.

⁂ WARNING

All screws, nuts, bolts and hose clamps removed during the repair must be replaced.

⁂ WARNING

Retaining elements on chassis and suspension and steering parts must be replaced.

1. Follow diagnosis instruction.
2. Drain coolant.
3. Secure engine in installation position.
4. Release screws and remove cover (if installed).
5. Slightly raise engine to gain better accessibility to coolant pump screws.
6. Release screws on the bottom of the coolant pump. Tightening torque: 16 ft. lbs. (22 Nm)
7. Loosen hose clamps. Note the installation position of the hose clamps. Tightening torque: 26 inch lbs. (3 Nm)
8. Release coolant hoses and.
9. Unlock plug and remove.
10. Release screw. Tightening torque: 16 ft. lbs. (22 Nm)

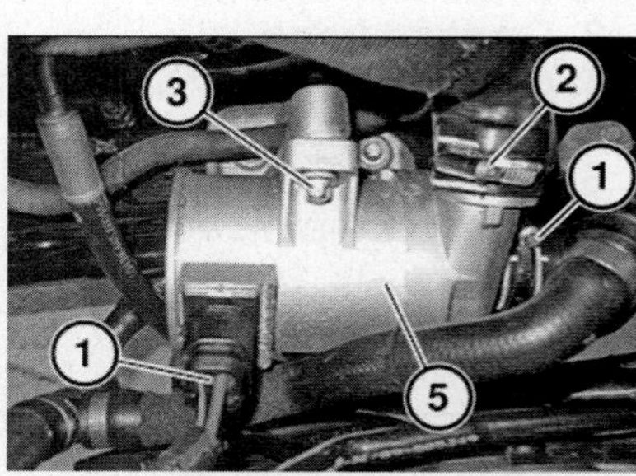

1. Coolant hose
2. Coolant hose
3. Screw
4. Plug
5. Coolant pump

71112_BMW3_G0252

Fig. 40 Removing and installing coolant pump

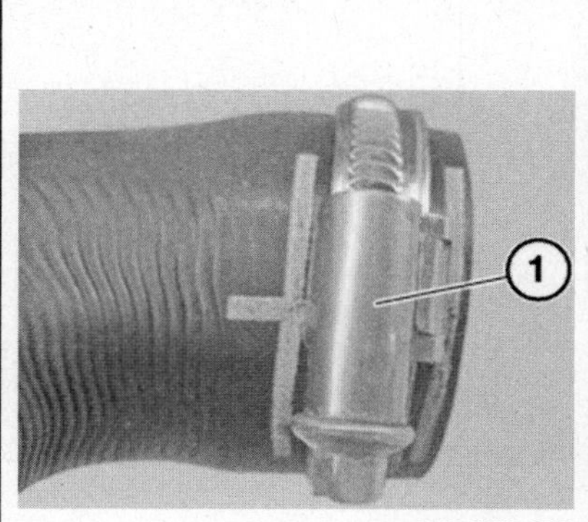

Fig. 41 Installing hose clamps

Fig. 42 Attaching coolant pump with screw and snapping connector into place

11. Remove coolant pump.

To install:

To install, reverse the removal procedure noting the following.

12. Hose clamps must be installed in the centre of the marked area.
13. Attach coolant pump with screw.
14. Connector must snap audibly into place.
15. If the electric coolant pump is reused, it must be rotated one turn due to the breakaway torque at the impeller.
16. Assemble engine.
17. Bleed the system.
18. Carry out wheel alignment check.

N52 and N54 Engines

See Figure 43.

✲✲ WARNING

Aluminum-magnesium material. No steel fasteners may be used due to the threat of electrochemical corrosion. A magnesium crankcase requires aluminum fasteners exclusively. Aluminum fasteners must be replaced each time they are removed. The end faces of aluminum fasteners are painted blue for purposes of identification. Torque specifications and torque angles must be observed for risk of damage.

✲✲ WARNING

If a water pump that has already been operated is reused, it must be filled with coolant immediately after removal.

1. Before servicing the vehicle, refer to the precautions.
2. Remove coolant thermostat.
3. Remove hose clamps.
4. Remove coolant hoses.
5. Disconnect plug connection.
6. Remove bolts and discard aluminum bolts.
7. Remove electric water pump.

To install:

✲✲ WARNING

If the electric water pump is reused, it must be rotated one turn due to the breakaway torque at the blade wheels.

8. Install electric water pump.
9. Install new bolts and tighten to 7 ft. lbs. (10 Nm) plus 90° additional rotation.
10. Connect plug connection.
11. Install coolant hoses.
12. Fasten hose clamps.
13. Install coolant thermostat.

1 2 5 3 4

1. Hose clamp
2. Hose clamp
4. Plug connection
3, 5. Bolts

22205_BMWC_G0094

Fig. 43 Water pump assembly

N55 Engine

Coolant Pump

See Figure 44.

✲✲ WARNING

Only perform this work after engine has cooled down.

✲✲ WARNING

If a coolant pump that has already been operated is reused, it must be filled with coolant after removal. Mixture ratio, water: coolant=1:1.

✲✲ WARNING

Protect plug connections against connections against coolant and contamination.

➡Catch and dispose of drained coolant in a suitable container.

➡Observe country-specific waste disposal regulations.

➡All screws, nuts, bolts and hose clamps removed during the repair must be replaced.

➡Retaining elements on chassis and suspension and steering parts must be replaced.

1. Follow diagnosis instructions.
2. Remove underbody protection.
3. Remove charge air cooler.
4. Drain coolant.
5. Release screws.
6. Remove cover.
7. Disconnect plug connection from coolant pump.

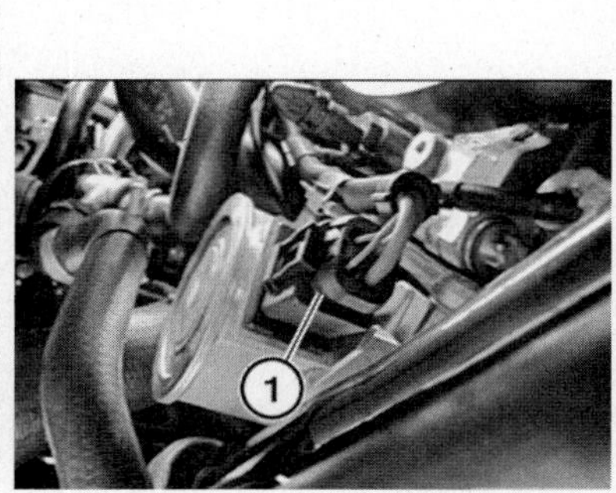

Fig. 44 Disconnecting plug connection from coolant pump

8. Release hose clamp. Note installation of hose clamps. Tightening torque: 26 inch lbs. (3 Nm)

9. Release screws. Tightening torque: 7 ft. lbs. (10 Nm) + 90°.

➡Replace aluminum screws.

10. Remove coolant pump.

To install:

To install, reverse the removal procedure noting the following.

11. If the electric coolant pump is reused, it must be rotated one turn due to the breakaway torque at the impellers.

12. Assemble engine.

➡Hose clamps must be installed in the centre of the marked area.

13. Bleed cooling system.

S65 Engine

Engine Driven Pump

See Figure 45.

1. Before servicing the vehicle, refer to the precautions.
2. Remove engine fan. Refer to engine cooling components, engine fan, removal & installation.
3. Remove radiator. Refer to engine cooling components, engine fan, removal & installation.
4. Remove A/C compressor drive belt. Refer to engine mechanical, accessory drive belts, removal & installation.
5. Remove upper idler pulley for A/C compressor.
6. Release screw.
7. Remove alternator drive belt.
8. Remove belt pulley.
9. Release screws.

➡To facilitate removal of the coolant pump, it is possible to insert M6 screws on left and right (see arrows).

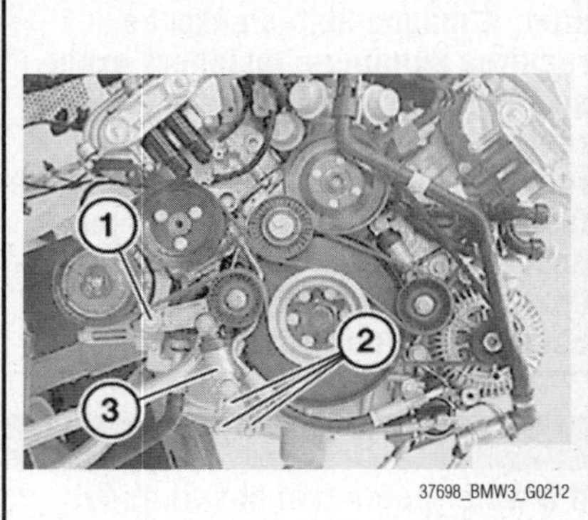

Fig. 45 Release screws (1 & 2) and remove belt tensioner with fixture

To install:

10. To install, reverse the removal procedure.

11. Replace all sealing rings.

12. Vent cooling system and check for leaks.

Electric Auxillary Pump

See Figures 46 and 47.

1. Before servicing the vehicle, refer to the precautions.
2. Remove the intake filter housing. Refer to engine mechanical, intake air filter, removal & installation.
3. Disconnect plug connection and remove auxiliary water pump towards top.

➡Mark position of water hoses prior to removal.

4. Disconnect water hoses and remove auxiliary water pump.

To install:

5. To install, reverse the removal procedure.

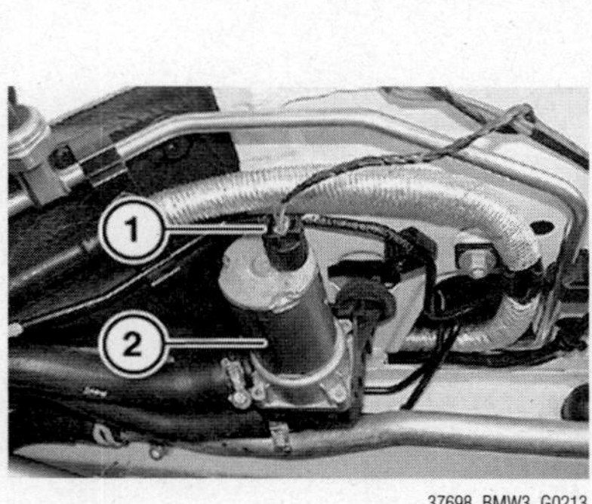

Fig. 46 Disconnect plug connection and remove auxiliary water pump towards top

Fig. 47 Install auxiliary water pump in front engine bracket so that rubber mounts slide exactly in associated locators

6. Observe direction of flow.
7. Install auxiliary water pump in front engine bracket so that rubber mounts slide exactly in associated locators.
8. Fill and vent cooling system and check for leaks.

BATTERY

REMOVAL & INSTALLATION

WARNING

If the ignition is not turned off when the battery is disconnected, fault memories may be set in some control units.

- There is a danger of mixing up battery leads: If the battery positive and negative leads are the same color and you are in doubt, follow the polarity to the battery, then mark and cover the leads.
- On vehicles with radio code: After disconnecting the battery, the radio code must be re-entered. Therefore obtain the radio code card from the customer beforehand. Note stored stations and restore them after connecting the battery.
- Stored settings of the on-board computer and clock will also be lost.
- All available central keys must be recoded for cars with first generation infrared transmitter locking systems.

WARNING

Do not under any circumstances use force to pull/lever off Intelligent Battery Sensor (IBS).

1. On sedan, convertible and coupe:
2. Open right luggage compartment trim panel.
   a. Turn fastener 90° to left.
   b. Open flap in luggage compartment trim and remove.
3. Loosen negative battery lead nut.
4. Disconnect battery negative lead and secure at side.
5. On wagon models:
6. Detach trim in direction of arrow from retainers.
7. Open flap at fastener to remove the luggage compartment trim.
8. Open right luggage compartment trim panel.
   a. Release clip and remove cover.
   b. Release clips and feed out panel.
9. Release clips and remove battery cover.
10. Loosen negative battery lead nut.
11. Disconnect battery negative lead and secure at side.
12. Remove the distribution box.
   a. Release screws and remove bracket.
   b. Disconnect plug connection.
   c. Unlock plug housing and release in direction of arrow.
   d. Fold up covers on nuts.
   e. Unscrew nuts.
   f. Disconnect plug connection.
   g. Disconnect plug connection of IBS cable.
   h. Press locking brackets downwards and unclip.
   i. If necessary, using a screwdriver, expand locking bracket at lower end and clip out.
   j. Remove power distributor towards top.
13. Unlock positive terminal cover and remove.
14. Detach vent in direction of arrow.
15. Release nut of safety battery terminal.
16. Detach safety battery terminal towards top, lay to one side and secure.
17. Release threaded pin and remove holder with battery crash element.
18. Fold back both bar fasteners and pull battery towards rear out of associated fixture.
19. Lift out battery.

To install:

20. To install, reverse the removal procedure.
21. Make sure battery is correctly seated in its fixture.
   - Distribution box: 11 ft. lbs. (15 Nm)
   - Rollover protection, battery (bar) to luggage compartment tray: 71 inch lbs. (8 Nm)
   - Battery positive lead, battery negative lead, safety battery terminal, IBS: 48 inch lbs. (5 Nm)
22. On vehicles with intelligent battery sensor (IBS), register battery replacement and read out fault memory, clear if necessary.

BATTERY RECONNECT/RELEARN PROCEDURE

After disconnecting/connecting battery some systems may be restricted and individual settings may be lost. Settings or activations must be carried out, depending on the equipment specification.

Active Front Steering

Adjustment of the active front steering must be carried out:

- After adjustment work on the front axle/steering
- After all mechanical work on the steering system
- After the battery has been disconnected or electrical plug connections on the steering column switch cluster have been disconnected

After replacement/programming or coding of the following components:

- Steering column switch cluster
- DSC control unit
- Active front steering control unit
- ARS control unit

Connect vehicle to BMW diagnosis system. Select and carry out initial operation/adjustment for active front steering under Service functions.

Sliding Sunroof

Initialization of the sliding sunroof comprises normalization and then learning of the characteristic curve. The mechanical end positions are recorded and stored during normalization. The characteristic curve is learnt immediately after normalization. When the characteristic curve is learned, the mechanical closing forces of the slide/tilt sunroof are recorded and stored for correct operation of the anti-trapping mechanism.

Carry out an initialization:

- If the slide/tilt sunroof has been mechanically moved by means of the emergency actuator
- In the event of malfunctions, e.g. no one-touch function, no opening or no comfort function possible
- After disengagement of the drive unit
- After work is carried out on the mechanism of the slide/tilt sunroof
- After the control unit has been replaced

WARNING

There is no anti-trapping protection during initialization.

Normalization

See Figure 48.

1. Press and hold the switch in the "Lift" direction.
2. In the event of delayed starting or sudden stopping of the slide/tilt sunroof, continue pressing the switch in the "Lift" direction
3. After reaching the lift end position, keep the switch pressed for approximately 15 seconds further.

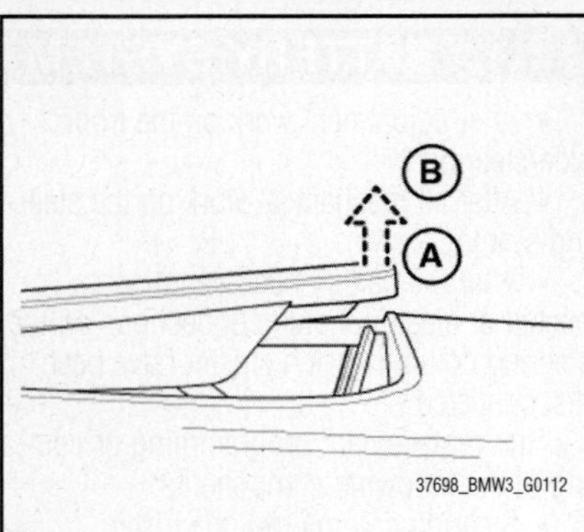

Fig. 48 Normalization is completed when the slide/tilt sunroof in lift end position (A) presses again briefly in the direction of position (B)

4. Normalization is completed when the slide/tilt sunroof in lift end position presses again briefly upward.

Learning Characteristic Curve

1. After normalization, keep switch pressed in "Lift" direction.
2. The slide/tilt sunroof stops for 5 seconds in the final raise position after normalization. It then moves into the "Closed" position (learning of the "Closing from raising" curve).
3. The slide/tilt sunroof then moves into the "Open" end position and immediately back into the "Closed" position (learning of the "Closing" curve) .
4. Release switch.

➡The entire operation lasts approximately 75 seconds. Learning of the curve is terminated when the switch is released. If the switch is released prematurely, the entire procedure must be repeated. Upon completion of successful initialization, the corresponding messages in the check control and the control display go out.

5. Carry out function check (tip function, anti-trapping protection and, if necessary, comfort function).

Power Windows

⁂ WARNING

There is no anti-trapping protection during initialization.

An initialization must be performed:

- In the event of malfunctions, e.g. no one-touch control function, no opening or if available no comfort function is possible
- After the power window drive has been replaced
- After work is carried out on the power window mechanism
- If necessary, after an open circuit, e.g. disconnection of the battery or disconnection of the power supply to the door
- After the door window glass has been removed and installed or replaced
- After adjustment work on the door window glass
- After adjustment work on the convertible top
- After replacement of seals

Initialization is performed on the power window switch of the relevant door.

- The ignition switch must be ON
- Doors and windows closed
- Sufficient battery voltage; connect charger if necessary

Initialization comprises erasure of the previous initialization and re-initialization.

Erasure of Initialization

1. Open door window glass fully
2. Actuate power window switch in "Open" position (second switch position) and hold down for between 15 and 20 seconds. This clears initialization of the power window. Anti-trapping protection and one-touch control (toll) function are inactive.
3. Check whether one-touch control (toll) function is inactive, otherwise repeat procedure.

Reinitialization

1. Close door window completely.
2. After upper end position is reached, interrupt actuation of power window switch and then hold switch again for approximately 1 second in "Close" position (second switch position).
3. Open door window glass fully.
4. After upper end position is reached, interrupt actuation of power window switch and then hold switch again for approximately 1 second in "Open" position (second switch position).
5. Close door window completely.
6. After upper end position is reached, interrupt actuation of power window switch and then hold switch again for approximately 1 second in "Close" position (second switch position).
7. Carry out function check (one-touch control function, anti-trapping protection and, if necessary, comfort function).

➡The power windows can also be initialized by connecting the vehicle to BMW diagnosis system.

Mirror with Compass

If may be necessary to calibrate the compass if:

- The vehicle battery has been disconnected for an extended period of time
- "C" appears in compass display
- There is no compass display

Setting Magnetic Deflection Zone

1. Switch ignition on.
2. Using a suitable tool, press pushbutton on mirror until a number appears in compass display.
3. Press pushbutton repeatedly until number of desired zone appears.
4. Wait until direction display appears.
5. Magnetic deflection zone is now set.

Calibrating Compass:

1. Switch ignition on.
2. Using a suitable tool, press pushbutton on mirror until "C" appears in compass display.
3. Drive vehicle 2–3 times in a circle at approximately 10 mph.
4. Calibration process is completed when direction display appears.

ALTERNATOR

REMOVAL & INSTALLATION

M57 Engine

See Figures 49 through 51.

1. Before servicing the vehicle, refer to the precautions.
2. Disconnect battery negative cable.
3. Remove fan cowl. Refer to engine cooling, engine fan, removal & installation.
4. Remove A/C compressor drive belt. Refer to engine mechanical, accessory drivebelt, removal & installation.
5. Remove alternator drive belt. Refer to engine mechanical, accessory drivebelt, removal & installation.
6. Remove front underbody protection.
   a. Release screws.

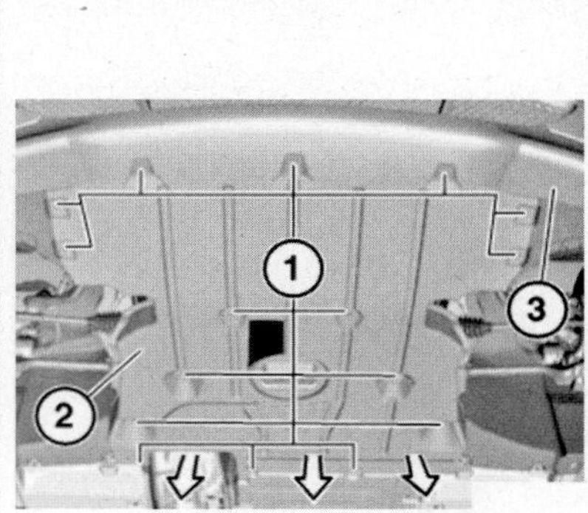

Fig. 49 Release screws and pull underbody protection forward under bumper trim

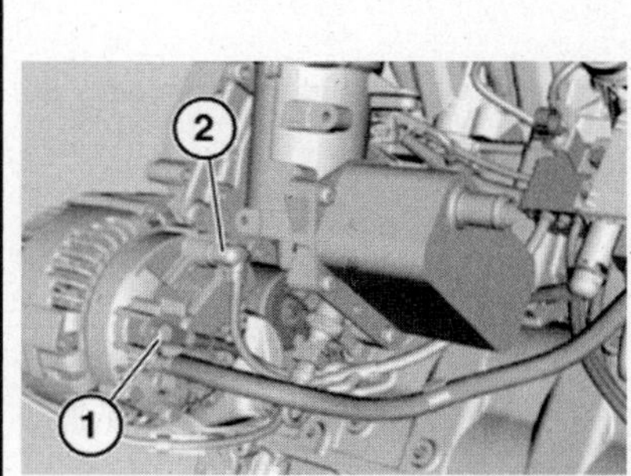

Fig. 50 Slacken nut and disconnect plug connection

Fig. 51 Removing the alternator

   b. Pull underbody protection forward under bumper trim.
7. Remove left turbocharger hose. Refer to engine mechanical, turbocharger, removal & installation.
8. Slacken nut.
9. Disconnect plug connection.
10. Remove cover.
11. Release screw underneath.
12. Remove deflecting element.
13. Release screw.
14. Remove idler pulley.
15. Release screws.
16. Remove alternator.

To install:

17. To install, reverse the removal procedure.
18. The positive power supply of the preheating control unit is also connected to terminal 30 of the alternator must be connected without fail, otherwise the preheating system will fail.
19. If the Dynamic Drive optional extra is fitted, the alternator must be removed towards the bottom.
20. Tighten bolts/nuts to specification as follows:
    - Wires to alternator (M8): 115 inch lbs. (13 Nm)
    - Alternator to crankcase (M10): 28 ft. lbs. (38 Nm)
21. Check function of DDE.

N20 and N26 Engines

See Figure 52.

Necessary preliminary tasks:

a. Switch off ignition
b. Disconnect battery earth lead and cover.
c. Remove intake silencer housing.

Fig. 52 Unlocking connector, releasing nut, disconnecting tank ventilation line and removing alternator

d. Remove clean air pipe, top.
e. Remove tensioning device for drive belt.

1. Release screws. Tightening torque: 28 ft. lbs. (38 Nm)
2. Unlock connector and remove.
3. Release nut and remove the positive battery cable. Tightening torque: 28 ft. lbs. (38 Nm)
4. Disconnect tank ventilation line and place to one side.
5. Feed out alternator to the left and remove.

To install:

To install, reverse the removal procedure.

N52 Engine

See Figure 53.

WARNING

Aluminum-magnesium materials. No steel bolts/bolts may be used due to the threat of electrochemical corrosion. A magnesium crankcase requires aluminum bolts/bolts exclusively. Aluminum bolts/bolts must be replaced each time they are Removed. The end faces of aluminum bolts/bolts are painted blue for the purposes of reliable identification. Jointing torque and angle of rotation must be observed without fail (risk of damage).

1. Before servicing the vehicle, refer to the precautions.
2. Disconnect the negative battery cable.
3. Remove intake filter housing.
4. Remove alternator drive belt.

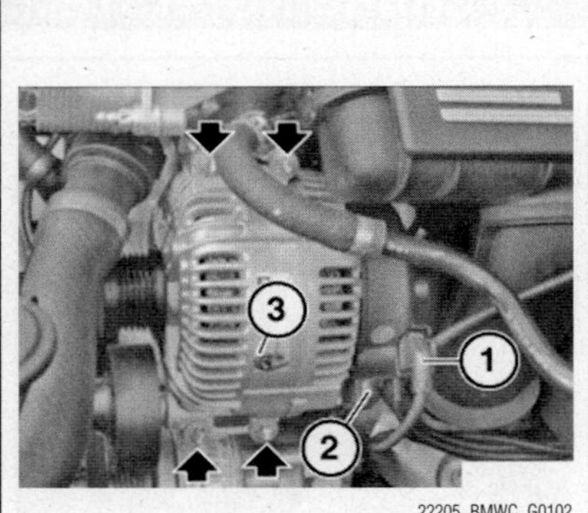

Fig. 53 Alternator, mounting bolts (arrows), B+ wire and plug

5. Unlock plug and remove.
6. Remove nut and disconnect B+ wire.
7. Remove aluminum bolts and discard
8. Remove alternator.

To install:

9. Install alternator.
10. Install new aluminum bolts tighten to
11. Connect B+ wire and tighten nut to 14 ft. lbs. (19 Nm).
12. Connect and lock plug.
13. Install alternator drive belt.
14. Install intake filter housing.
15. Connect the negative battery cable.

N54 Engine

See Figures 54 and 55.

1. Before servicing the vehicle, refer to the precautions.
2. Disconnect the negative battery cable.
3. Remove charge air duct.
4. Remove alternator drive belt
5. Remove the A/C compressor and place to one side.

➡Do not disconnect refrigerant lines from compressor.

6. Remove bolts a few turns until bracket is loose. Do not remove bracket.
7. Unlock plug and remove.
8. Remove protective cap and Remove nut underneath.
9. Disconnect B+ wire.
10. Remove bracket and alternator.

To install:

11. Install bracket and alternator.
12. Connect B+ wire.
13. Install protective cap and Remove nut underneath.
14. Install and lock plug.

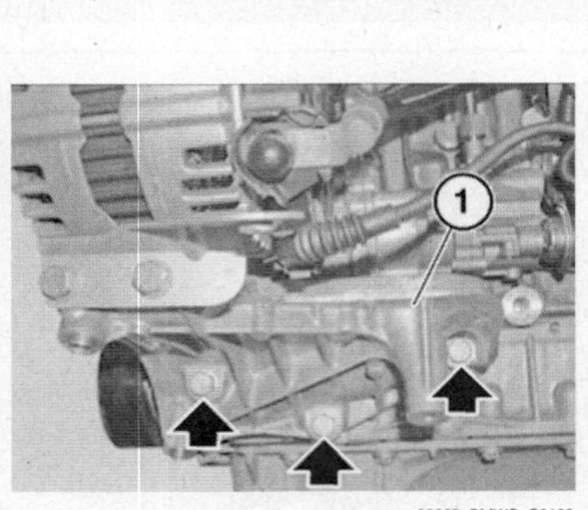

Fig. 54 Remove bolts a few turns until bracket is loose. Do not remove bracket

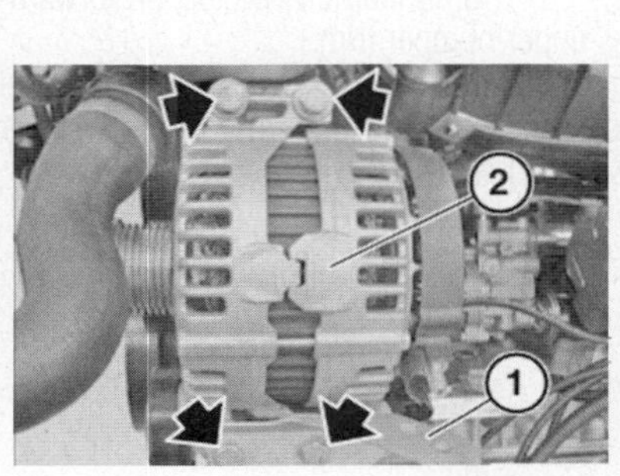

Fig. 55 Remove bracket and alternator

➡Do not disconnect refrigerant lines from compressor.

15. Install the A/C compressor.
16. Install alternator drive belt
17. Install charge air duct.
18. Connect the negative battery cable.

N55 Engine

See Figures 56 and 57.

Necessary preliminary tasks:

a. Switch off ignition.
b. Disconnect battery earth lead.
c. Remove left charge air duct.
d. Remove alternator drive belt.

➡In order to remove the alternator, it is necessary to remove the air conditioning compressor for the air cooling system.

➡In so doing:

e. Do not draw off A/C system refrigerant.
f. Do not detach refrigerant lines from A/C compressor.
g. Do not remove A/C compressor; instead, remove from bracket only and place to one side.

➡For purposes of improved clarity, illustrations and descriptions show A/C compressor removed.

1. Release bolts a few turns until bracket is loose. Do not remove bracket. Tightening torque: 14 ft. lbs. (19 Nm)
2. Unlock connector and remove.
3. Remove protective cap and release nut underneath. Tightening torque: 14 ft. lbs. (19 Nm)
Remove positive battery cable.
4. Release screws.
5. Remove bracket and alternator. Tightening torque: 14 ft. lbs. (19 Nm)

To install:

To install, reverse the removal procedure.

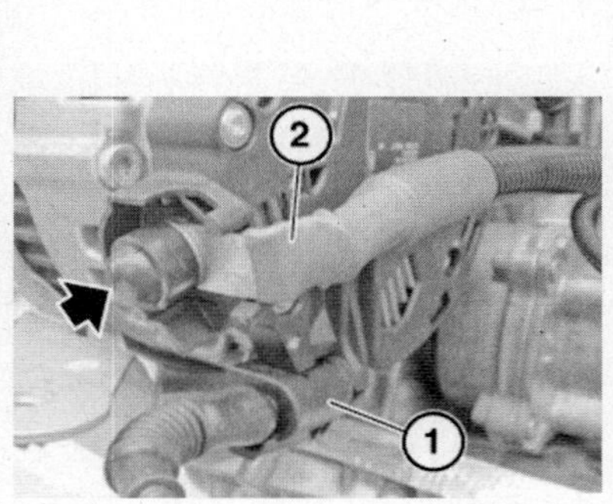

Fig. 56 Unlocking connector and removing positive battery cable

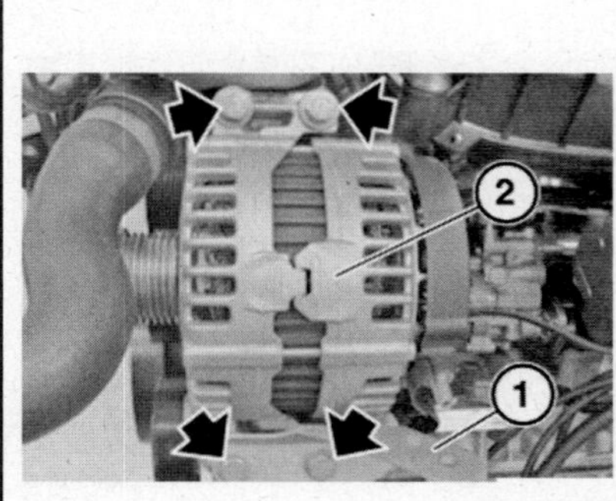

Fig. 57 Removing bracket and alternator

S65 Engine

See Figure 58.

1. Before servicing the vehicle, refer to the precautions.
2. Disconnect battery negative cable.
3. Remove air filter housing
4. Remove front underbody protection
   a. Release screws on both sides.
   b. Remove tip of engine compartment shield on left/right.
   c. Turn catch on cable through 90° and disengage in direction of arrow from bracket on both sides.
   d. Pull underbody protection forwards under bumper trim and remove.
5. Remove alternator drive belt. Refer to engine mechanical, accessory drivebelt, removal & installation.

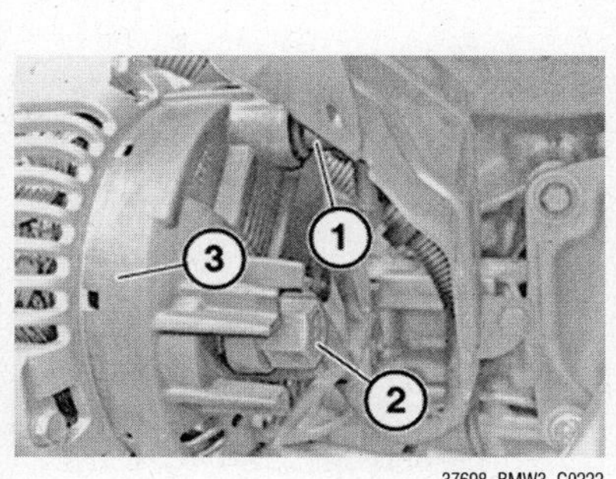

Fig. 58 Unlock plug and remove, release nut, remove battery positive lead from alternator and pull alternator upwards to remove

6. Release screws as shown.
7. Unclip hoses from hose holders on radiator.
8. Carefully press leads to one side.
9. Release screws.
10. Pull alternator forwards until connections are accessible.
11. Unlock plug and remove.
12. Release nut, remove battery positive lead from alternator.
13. Pull alternator upwards to remove.

To install:

14. To install, reverse the removal procedure.
15. Tighten the B+ lead to alternator to 14 ft. lbs. (19 Nm).
16. Read fault memory.

ENGINE ELECTRICAL

IGNITION SYSTEM

FIRING ORDER

See Figure 59.

IGNITION COIL

REMOVAL & INSTALLATION

N20 and N26 Engines

See Figures 60 and 61.

1. Read out the fault memory of the DME control unit.
2. Check stored fault messages and process procedure.
3. Switch off ignition.
4. Remove acoustic cover.

⁂ WARNING

Ignition coils must not be contaminated by fuel.

⁂ WARNING

The resistance of the silicone material is reduced significantly by contact with fuel, which may cause the ignition coil to fail. The silicone tube of the spark plug connector is coated with talc to reduce the pulling forces. The silicone tube must NOT be oiled or greased. This would greatly reduce the durability of the silicone material, which can lead to a malfunction of the ignition coil.

5. Unlock plug catch of ignition coil and disconnect plug.
6. Pull ignition coil up and out.

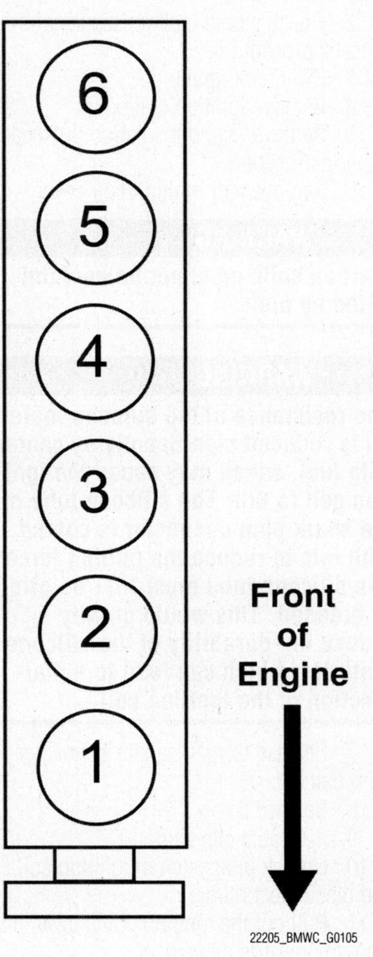

Fig. 59 3.0L I6 N52 engine Firing order: 1–5–3–6–2–4 Distributorless ignition system

➡There is a possibility that the silicone tube will tear and therefore be destroyed.

7. This procedure is applicable to all ignition coils.

To install:

8. Position the ignition coil and gently push it to the limit position, if necessary by twisting it back and forth slightly. Then check anti-twist lock.
9. The rubber cap must completely surround the sealing collar of the cylinder head cover.

➡If rubber parts are squashed, the ignition coil can slip out again during engine operation.

10. Push connector with connector catch open onto ignition coil.
11. Carefully close connector catch in direction of arrow.

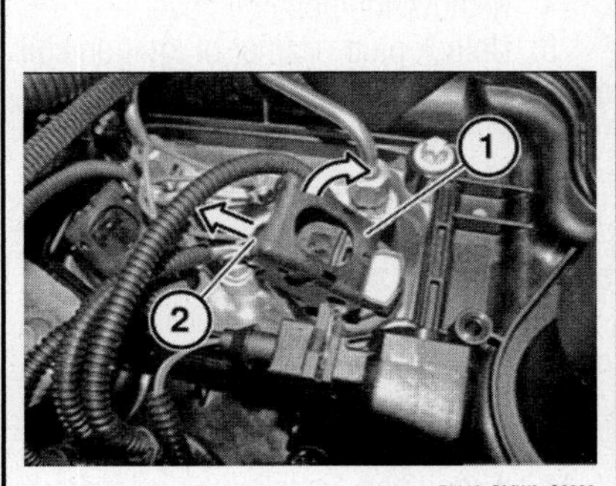

Fig. 60 Unlocking plug catch of ignition coil and removing

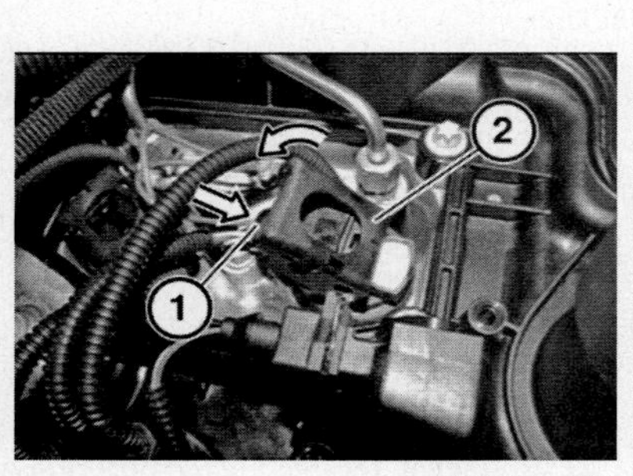

Fig. 61 Installing ignition coil

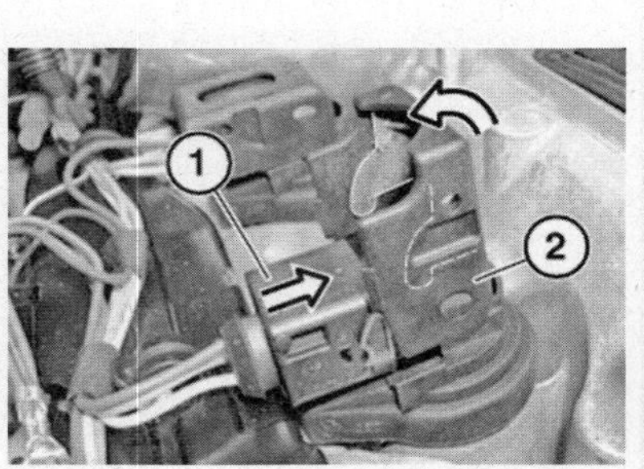

Fig. 62 Push plug with plug retainer open onto ignition coil

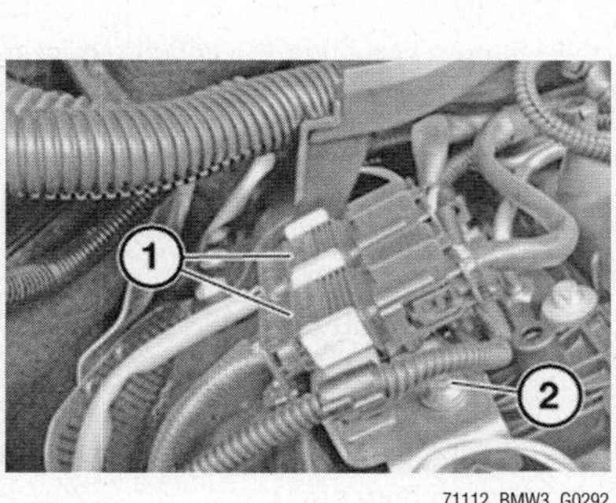

Fig. 63 Releasing oxygen sensor connector and screw

12. The connector must be positioned on the counter piece with hardly any gaps when the locking lever is being closed. In the process, the cheeks of the lever are positioned inside the counter piece.

➡The locking lever can become deformed if it is not installed correctly. This means that there is no longer a safety lock on the plug connection. As a result, the connector can slip out during engine operation (loose contact, misfiring).

13. The connector catch must snap into place without great effort.

➡Delete fault memory.

14. Assemble engine.

N52 and N54 Engines

See Figure 62.

1. Before servicing the vehicle, refer to the precautions.
2. Read out fault memory of DME control unit.
3. If equipped, remove engine cover.
4. Remove ignition coil cover.
5. Unlock plug retainer of ignition coil and disconnect plug.
6. Pull ignition coil up and out.

To install:

7. Check that rubber seal of ignition coil is correctly seated.
8. Push plug with plug retainer open onto ignition coil.
9. Carefully close plug retainer.
10. Install ignition coil cover.
11. If equipped, install engine cover.

➡The plug retainer must snap into place without great effort.

12. Clear the fault memory.

N55 Engine

See Figures 63 through 65.

1. Read out the fault memory of the DME control unit.
2. Check stored fault messages and process procedure.
3. Switch off ignition.
4. Remove ignition coil cover.
5. Remove sound insulation bulkhead upper part, centre.
6. Remove rear ignition coil cover.

WARNING

Ignition coils must not be contaminated by fuel.

WARNING

The resistance of the silicone material is reduced significantly by contact with fuel, which may cause the ignition coil to fail. The silicone tube of the spark plug connector is coated with talc to reduce the pulling forces. The silicone tube must NOT be oiled or greased. This would greatly reduce the durability of the silicone material, which can lead to a malfunction of the ignition coil.

7. Release oxygen sensor connector from bracket.
8. Release screw.
9. Put cable clip aside.
10. Unlock plug catch of ignition coil and disconnect plug.
11. Pull out the ignition coil slowly in a smooth upwards movement.

➡There is a possibility that the silicone tube will tear and therefore be destroyed.

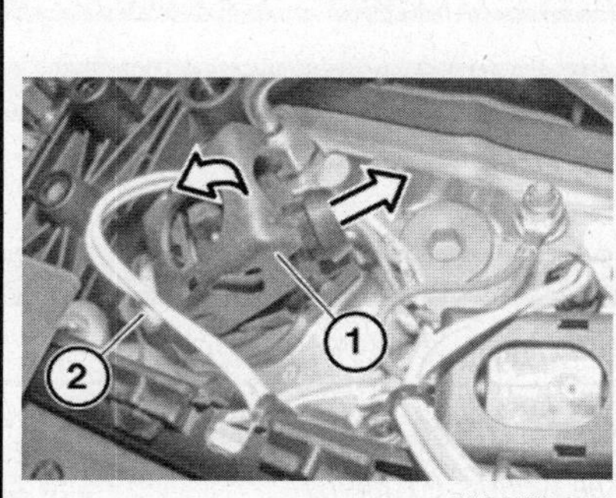

Fig. 64 Unlocking plug catch and removing coil

➡This procedure is applicable to all ignition coils.

To install:

12. Position the ignition coil and gently push it to the limit position, if necessary by twisting it back and forth slightly. Then check anti-twist lock.
13. The rubber cap must completely surround the sealing collar of the cylinder head cover.

➡If rubber parts are squashed, the ignition coil can slip out again during engine operation.

14. Push connector with connector catch open onto ignition coil.
15. Carefully close connector catch in direction of arrow.
16. The connector catch must snap into place without great effort.
17. The connector must be positioned on the counter piece with hardly any gaps when the locking lever is being closed. In

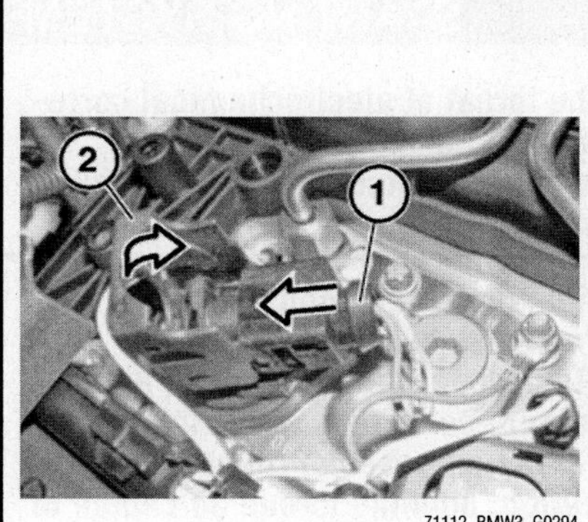

Fig. 65 Installing ignition coil, pushing connector with connector catch

the process, the cheeks of the lever are positioned inside the counter piece.

➡The locking lever can become deformed if it is not installed correctly. This means that there is no longer a safety lock on the plug connection. As a result, the connector can slip out during engine operation (loose contact, misfiring).

S65 Engine

See Figure 66.

1. Before servicing the vehicle, refer to the precautions.
2. Read out fault memory of DME control unit.
3. Switch ignition **OFF**.
4. Remove air filter housing.
5. Release and raise coolant expansion tank, do not kink hoses.
6. Remove ignition coil covers.
7. Pull off plug.
8. Pull out ignition coil in upward direction with aid of 11 9 980.

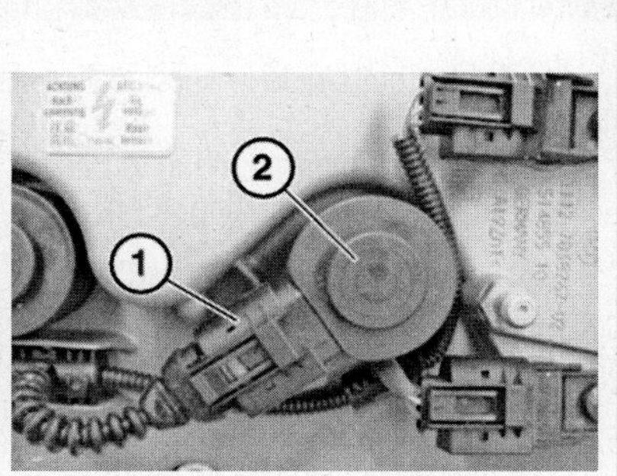

Fig. 66 Pull off plug and pull out ignition coil in upward direction with aid of 11 9 980

WARNING

Tool 11 9 980 is essential to ensure damage-free removal of the ignition coils.

To install:

9. To install, reverse the removal procedure.
10. Insert rubber seal on ignition coils between guides in valve cover.
11. Check stored fault messages and clear the fault memory.

IGNITION TIMING

INSPECTION & ADJUSTMENT

The ignition timing is controlled by the Digital Motor Electronics (DME). No adjustments are necessary.

SPARK PLUGS

REMOVAL & INSTALLATION

WARNING

Spark plugs must be replaced with the same type/number spark plug as the original. If another spark plug is substituted, damage may result.

➡Allow engine to cool completely prior to starting this procedure.

1. Before servicing the vehicle, refer to the precautions.
2. Disconnect the negative battery cable.
3. If equipped, removal engine cover.
4. Remove ignition coils.
5. Remove trailing links if equipped.
6. Unscrew spark plugs with special tool 12 1 171 (N52 and S65) or 12 1 220 (N54, N55, N20 and N26).

To install:

➡Special care should be taken when installing spark plugs into the cylinder head spark plug wells. Be sure the plugs do not drop into the plug wells as electrodes can be damaged.

7. Screw spark plugs in special tool.
8. Tighten spark plugs to 18 ft. lbs. (24 Nm).

WARNING

Always tighten spark plugs to the specified torque. Over tightening can cause distortion resulting in a change in the spark plug gap or a cracked porcelain insulator. Proper torque is especially important in the case of aluminum cylinder heads.

9. Install ignition coils.
10. If equipped, install engine cover.
11. Connect the negative battery cable.

STARTER

REMOVAL & INSTALLATION

M57 Engine

See Figures 67 and 68.

1. Before servicing the vehicle, refer to the precautions.
2. Disconnect battery negative cable.
3. Remove transmission underbody protection.
4. Slacken nuts.
5. Release screws as shown.
6. Press starter motor forwards and swivel past engine carrier.

To install:

7. To install, reverse the removal procedure.

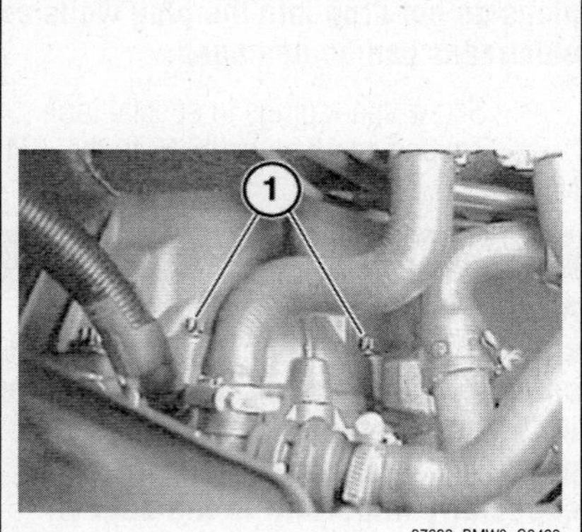

Fig. 67 Release screws

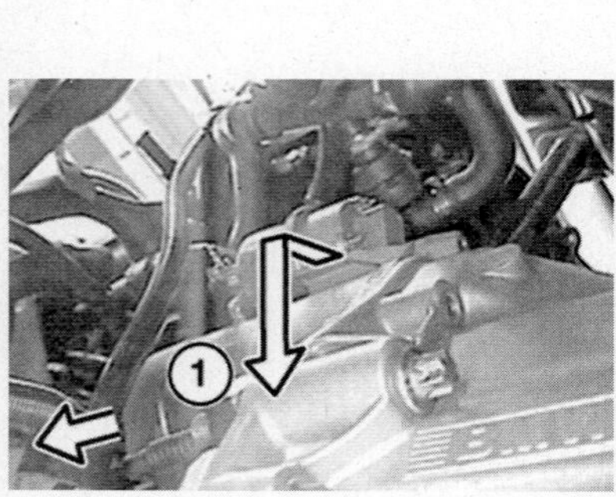

Fig. 68 Press starter motor forwards and swivel past engine carrier

8. Tighten bolts/nuts to specification as follows:
   - Starter motor mounting to transmission bell housing: 33 ft. lbs. (45 Nm)
   - Support to starter: 44 inch lbs. (5 Nm)
   - Electrical leads to starter (M5): 44 inch lbs. (5 Nm)
   - Electrical leads to starter (M6): 62 inch lbs. (7 Nm)
   - Electrical leads to starter (M8): 115 inch lbs. (13 Nm)

N20 and N26 Engines

See Figure 69.

1. Switch off ignition.
2. Disconnect battery negative lead.
3. Remove intake plenum.
4. Unlock connector and remove.
5. Release nuts and disconnect positive battery cables. Tightening torque: 10 ft. lbs. (13 Nm)
6. Release screws. Tightening torque: 14 ft. lbs. (19 Nm)
7. Feed out starter motor and remove.

To install:

To install, reverse the removal procedure.

➡Check starter pinion and ring gear for damage. Replace starter motor if necessary.

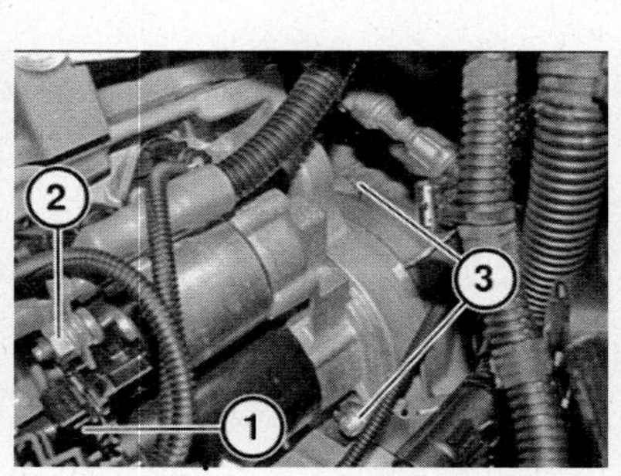

Fig. 69 Unlocking and removing connector, releasing nuts and screws and removing starter motor—N20 and N26 engines

N52 and N54 Engines

See Figure 70.

⁂ WARNING

Aluminum-magnesium materials. No steel bolts/bolts may be used due to the threat of electrochemical corrosion. A magnesium crankcase requires aluminum bolts/bolts exclusively.

Aluminum bolts/bolts must be replaced each time they are Removed. The end faces of aluminum bolts/bolts are painted blue for the purposes of reliable identification. Jointing torque and angle of rotation must be observed without fail (risk of damage).

1. Before servicing the vehicle, refer to the precautions.
2. Disconnect the negative battery cable.
3. Remove intake air manifold
4. Unlock plug and remove.
5. Remove the B+ cable from the starter.
6. Remove and discard the starter mounting bolts.
7. Remove starter motor.

To install:

8. Check starter pinion and ring gear for damage, replace damaged parts if necessary.
9. Install starter motor.
10. Install the starter mounting bolts and tighten to specification.
    - M10x85: 15 ft. lbs. (20 Nm) plus an additional 180° rotation
    - M10x30: 15 ft. lbs. (20 Nm) plus an additional 90° rotation
11. Install the B+ cable from the starter and tighten nut to 10 ft. lbs. (13 Nm).
12. Unlock plug and Install.
13. Install intake air manifold
14. Connect the negative battery cable.

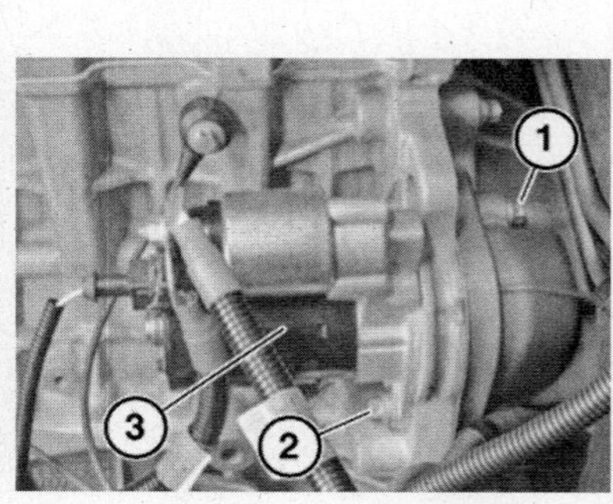

Fig. 70 Starter mounting bolt locations

S65 Engine

See Figure 71.

1. Before servicing the vehicle, refer to the precautions.
2. Switch ignition **OFF**.
3. Disconnect battery negative cable.
4. Remove intake air manifold. Refer to engine mechanical, intake manifold, removal & installation.
5. Remove the tank venting valve.
6. Remove idle actuator. Refer to gasoline fuel injection system, idle actuator, removal & installation.
7. Remove throttle valve actuating motor on left. Refer to components & systems, throttle actuator motor, removal & installation.
8. Remove idle actuator mounting.
9. Unlock plug and remove.

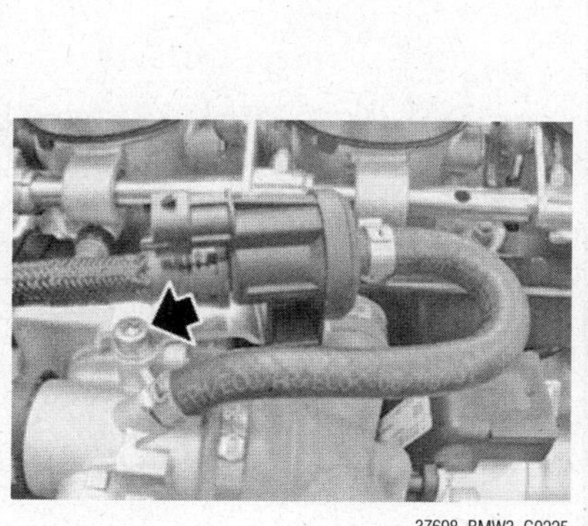

Fig. 71 Remove the tank venting valve

10. Unfasten nut.
11. Remove battery positive lead.
12. Release screw.
13. Release screws.
14. Pull starter motor out of transmission mount and remove.

To install:

15. To install, reverse the removal procedure.
16. Check starter pinion and ring gear for damage, replace damaged parts if necessary.
17. Tighten bolts/nuts to specification as follows:
   - B+ lead to starter terminal 30: 10 ft. lbs. (14 Nm)
   - Starter to transmission housing: 31 ft. lbs. (42 Nm)

ENGINE MECHANICAL

➡Disconnecting the negative battery cable may interfere with the functions of the on board computer systems and may require the computer to undergo a relearning process, once the negative battery cable is reconnected.

ACCESSORY DRIVE BELT SYSTEM

ADJUSTMENT

The belt tension is maintained by an automatic tensioner. No adjustment is possible.

BELT ROUTINGS

See Figures 72 through 78.

Fig. 72 Alternator belt routing—M57 engine. Press belt tensioner back in direction of arrow and remove drive belt

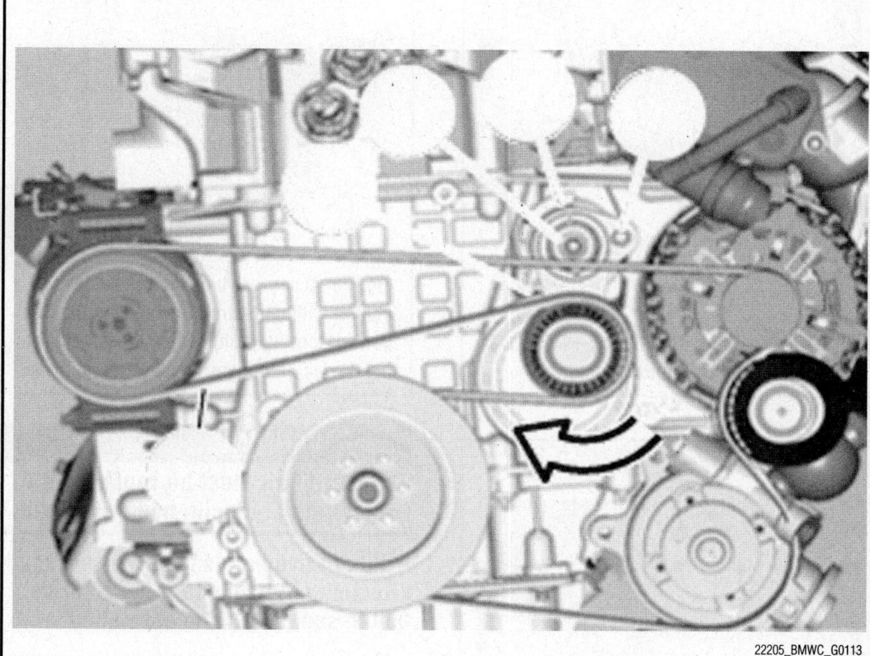

Fig. 73 Accessory belt routing—N52 engine

INSPECTION

Inspect the drive belt for signs of glazing or cracking. A glazed belt will be perfectly smooth from slippage, while a good belt will have a slight texture of fabric visible. Cracks will usually start at the inner edge of the belt and run outward. All worn or damaged drive belts should be replaced immediately.

REMOVAL & INSTALLATION

M57 Engine

Alternator Belt

See Figure 79.

1. Before servicing the vehicle, refer to the precautions.
2. Remove fan cowl. Refer to engine cooling, engine fan, removal & installation

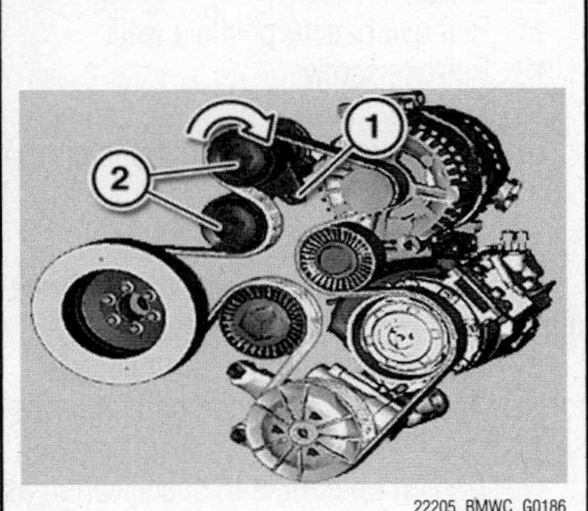

22205_BMWC_G0186

Fig. 74 Accessory belt routing—N54 engine

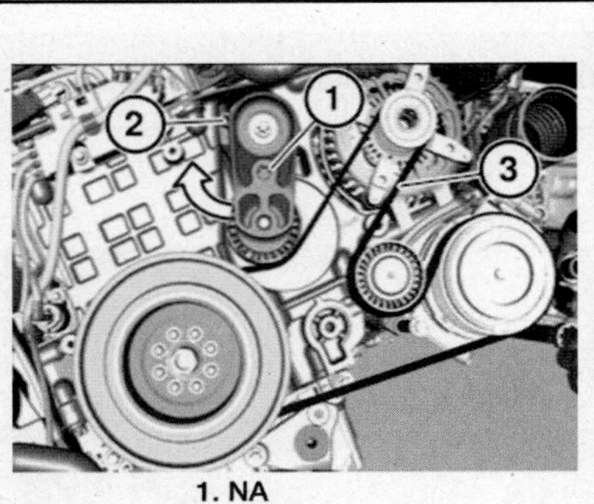

1. NA
2. Belt tensioner
3. Drive belt

71112_BMW3_G0297

Fig. 75 Accessory belt routing—N55 engine (without dynamic drive)

1. NA
2. Belt tensioner
3. Drive belt

71112_BMW3_G0298

Fig. 76 Accessory belt routing—N55 engine (with dynamic drive)

3. Remove A/C compressor drive belt
4. Check drive belt for coolant and oil residues, replace if necessary.

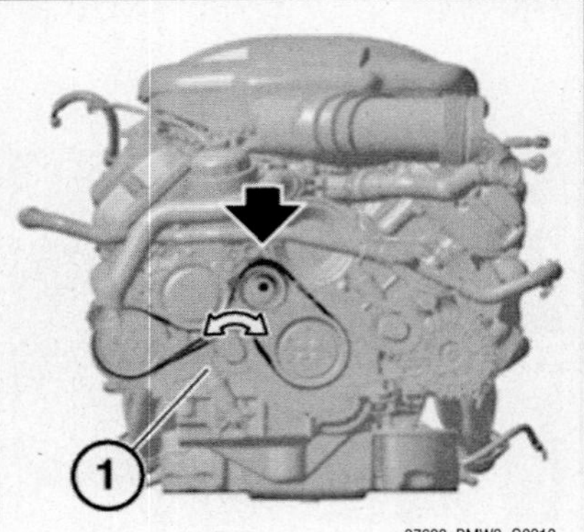

37698_BMW3_G0210

Fig. 77 Accessory belt routing—S65 engine with clockwise-rotating power steering pump. Press down tensioning device on damper in direction of arrow

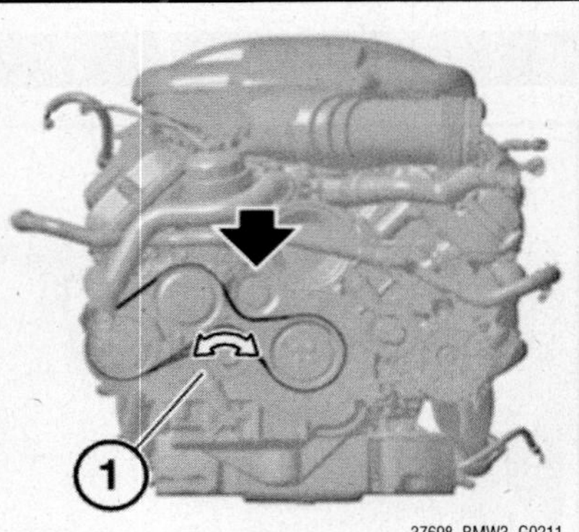

37698_BMW3_G0211

Fig. 78 Accessory belt routing—S65 engine with counterclockwise-rotating power steering pump. Press down tensioning device on damper in direction of arrow

WARNING

The drive belt must be replaced if it is contaminated with hydraulic fluid.

➡If the drive belt is to be reused, mark direction of travel and reinstall drive belt in same direction of rotation.

5. Press belt tensioner back in direction of arrow.
6. Remove drive belt.

To install:

7. To install, reverse the removal procedure.

A/C Compressor Belt

See Figure 80.

1. Before servicing the vehicle, refer to the precautions.
2. Remove front splash guard.
3. If necessary, release bracket on A/C compressor.

37698_BMW3_G0405

Fig. 79 Press belt tensioner back in direction of arrow and remove drive belt

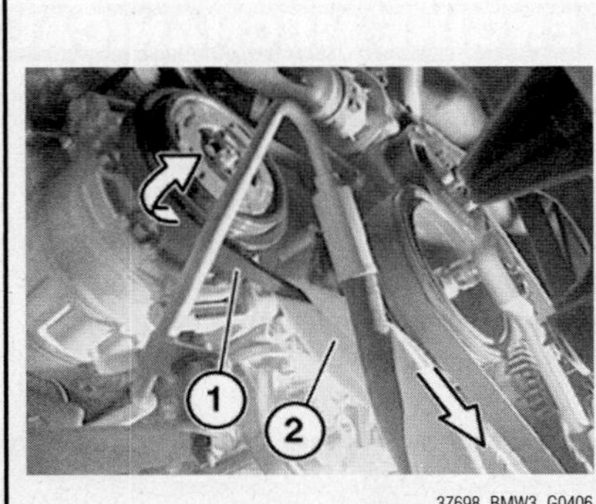

37698_BMW3_G0406

Fig. 80 At the same time, pull off drive belt towards front in direction of arrow using a clean cloth

4. Rotate engine with special tool 11 6 480 in direction of engine rotation.
5. At the same time, pull off drive belt towards front in direction of arrow using a clean cloth.
6. Remove drive belt towards front.

To install:

7. To install, reverse the removal procedure.
8. Fit drive belt on A/C compressor.
9. Mount drive belt with special tool 11 0 331 on belt pulley in direction of arrow.
10. Check installation position of drive belt.

N20 and N26 Engines

Air Conditioning Compressor and Alternatorbelt

See Figure 81.

1. Remove the clean air pipe to the exhaust turbocharger.

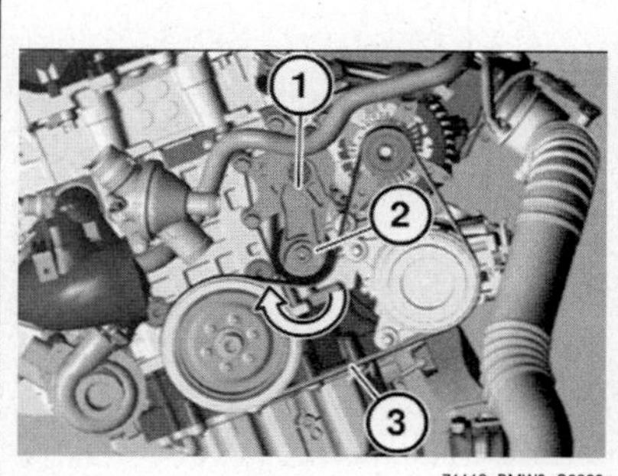

Fig. 81 Turning belt tensioner on the hexagon head and removing drive belt

Fig. 82 Secure belt tensioner with special tool 11 3 340

Fig. 83 Turn belt tensioner until bore is flush on housing

➡Mark the direction of travel of the drive belt if it is to be reused.

2. Turn belt tensioner on the hexagon head in direction of arrow until bore hole on the belt tensioner is flush with the dowel hole.
3. Keep the belt tensioner tensioned and position with a lock pin or special tool 11 0 390 , if applicable.
4. Remove drive belt.

To install:

To install, reverse the removal procedure noting the following.

5. Check drive belt for correct installation position and, if reusing, observe direction of travel.

N52 Engine

See Figure 82.

⁂ WARNING

Aluminum-magnesium materials. No steel bolts/bolts may be used due to the threat of electrochemical corrosion. A magnesium crankcase requires aluminum bolts/bolts exclusively.

Aluminum bolts/bolts must be replaced each time they are Removed. The end faces of aluminum bolts/bolts are painted blue for the purposes of reliable identification. Jointing torque and angle of rotation must be observed without fail (risk of damage).

1. Before servicing the vehicle, refer to the precautions.
2. Remove fan cowl with electric fan
3. Mark the direction of rotation of the drive belt if it is to be reused.
4. Turn belt tensioner clockwise until bore is flush on housing.
5. By holding belt tensioner under tension, the load is removed from tensioning pulley.
6. Secure belt tensioner with special tool 11 3 340.
7. Remove drive belt upwards.
8. Check drive belt for correct installation position and, if reusing, observe direction of rotation.

N54 Engine

See Figure 83.

➡Mark the direction of rotation of the drive belt if it is to be reused. Depending on the build date (version), the idler pulleys can be fitted with and without grooves.

1. Before servicing the vehicle, refer to the precautions.
2. Remove fan cowl.
3. Remove hose clip.
4. Remove quick-connect fastener 90°on boost pressure pipe.
5. Pull off air hose.
6. Disconnect line from holder.
7. Remove coolant hose from holder.
8. Remove screw.
9. Fold air duct down.

➡Do not remove air duct.

10. Turn belt tensioner until bore is flush on housing.
11. Secure belt tensioner in place with special tool 11 3 340.
12. Remove drive belt.

To install:

13. Install belt in the previously marked direction if reusing the old belt.
14. Pretension tensioning pulley.
15. Remove special tool 11 3 340.
16. On boost pressure pipe, bring lock back 90° into installation position.
17. Recirculated air hose must audibly snap into place.
18. Check that drive belt for is in correct installation position.

S65 Engine

A/C Compressor Belt

See Figures 84 and 85.

⁂ WARNING

Do not mix up the drive belts as this will result in failure of the power steering.

➡Mark the direction of rotation of the drive belt if it is to be reused. Replace the drive belt if it is fouled with coolant or engine oil.

⁂ WARNING

Different idler pulleys for counterclockwise and clockwise rotating power steering pumps.

1. Remove the engine fan. Refer to engine cooling components, engine fan, removal & instillation.
2. The belt routing of a clockwise-rotating power steering pump is as shown.
   a. Press down tensioning device on damper in direction of arrow and hold.
   b. Take off ribbed V-belt.
3. The belt routing of a counterclockwise-rotating power steering pump is as shown.
   a. The belt is a double-sided ribbed V-belt.
   b. Press down tensioning device on damper in direction of arrow and hold.

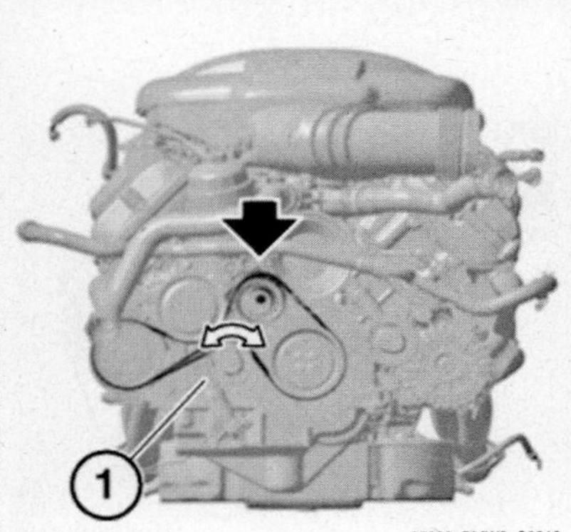

Fig. 84 The belt routing of a clockwise-rotating power steering pump is as shown. Press down tensioning device on damper in direction of arrow and hold

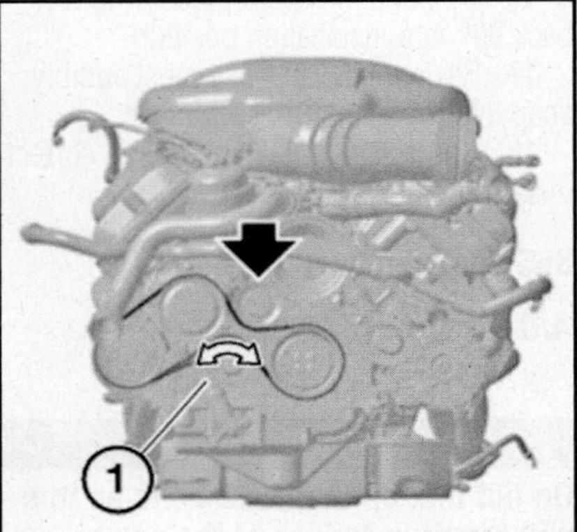

Fig. 85 The belt routing of a counterclockwise-rotating power steering pump is as shown. Press down tensioning device on damper in direction of arrow and hold

c. Take off ribbed V-belt.

To install:

4. To install, reverse the removal procedure.
5. Observe direction of rotation if reusing the drive belt.
6. Ensure drive belt is in correct installation position.

Alternator Belt

See Figure 86.

1. Before servicing the vehicle, refer to the precautions.

➡Mark the direction of rotation of the drive belt if it is to be reused.

⁂ WARNING

Replace the drive belt if it is fouled with coolant or engine oil.

Fig. 86 Press down tensioning device with standard tool in direction of arrow

2. Remove drive belt for A/C system.
3. Release cover with a screwdriver.
4. Press down tensioning device with standard tool in direction of arrow.
5. Remove drive belt.

To install:

6. To install, reverse the removal procedure.
7. Observe direction of rotation if reusing the drive belt.
8. Make sure drive belt is installed in correct position.

CRANKSHAFT FRONT SEAL

REMOVAL & INSTALLATION

M57 Engine

See Figures 87 through 91.

1. Before servicing the vehicle, refer to the precautions.
2. Removing vibration damper.
3. Fit special tool 11 1 212 to crankshaft.
4. Removing crankshaft seal:
5. Screw in special tool 11 1 210 until it has made firm contact with crankshaft seal.
6. Then remove crankshaft seal by turning screw.

To install:

7. To install, reverse the removal procedure.
8. Fit special tool 11 6 470 to crankshaft.
9. Lubricate special tool 11 6 470.

⁂ WARNING

Do not under any circumstances touch sealing lip of new crankshaft seal with your fingers.

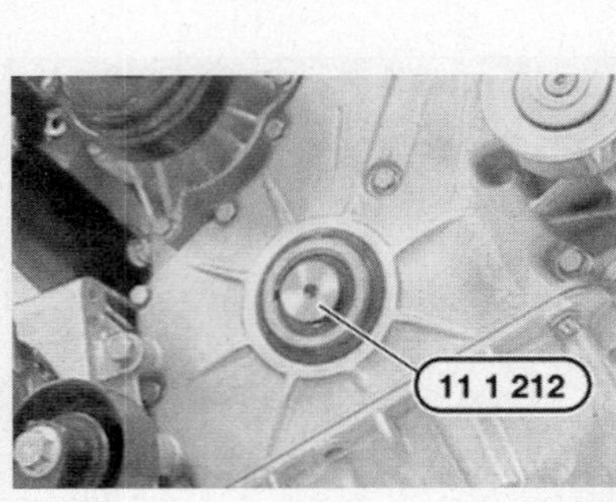

Fig. 87 Fit special tool 11 1 212 to crankshaft

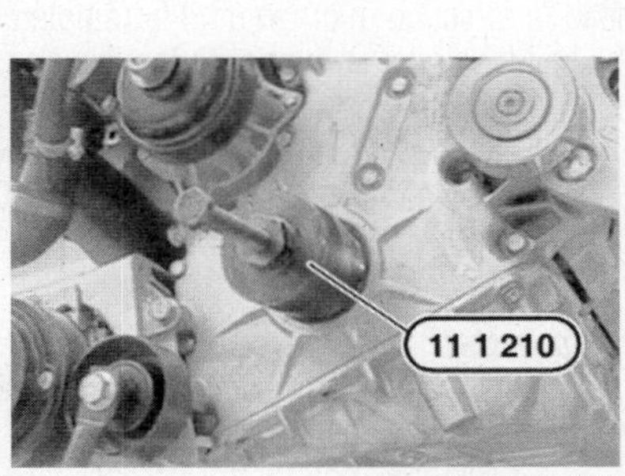

Fig. 88 Screw in special tool 11 1 210 until it has made firm contact with crankshaft seal

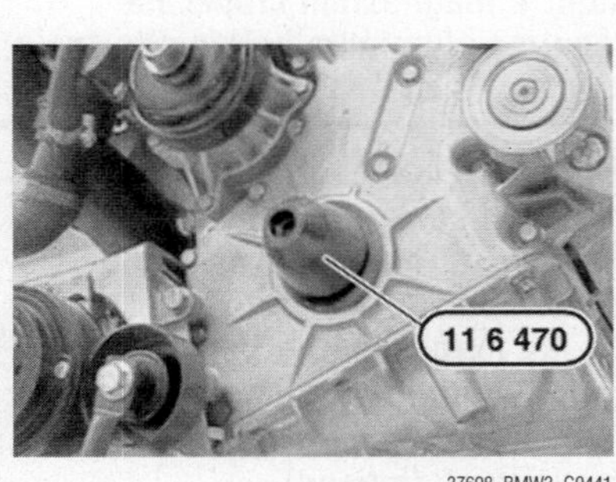

Fig. 89 Slide new crankshaft seal over special tool 11 6 470 until crankshaft seal rests against timing case cover

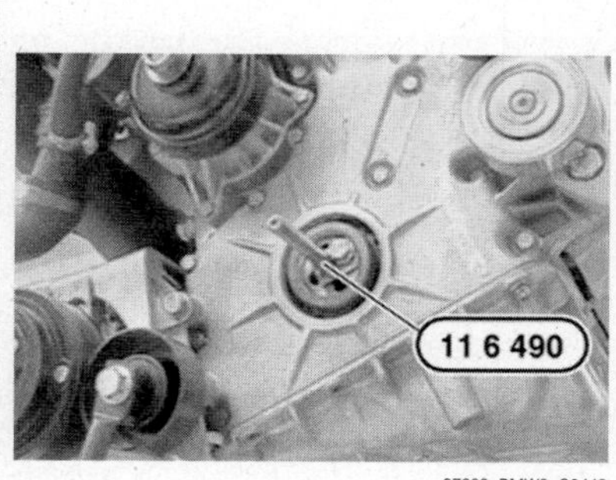

Fig. 90 Screw special tool 11 6 490 into crankshaft and tighten down

Fig. 91 With special tool 11 5 110 and central nut of special tool 11 6 490, insert crankshaft seal until it is flush with timing case cover

10. Slide new crankshaft seal over special tool 11 6 470 until crankshaft seal rests against timing case cover.
11. Remove special tool 11 6 470.
12. Screw special tool 11 6 490 into crankshaft and tighten down.
13. Fit special tool 11 5 110 to crankshaft.
14. With special tool 11 5 110 and central nut of special tool 11 6 490, insert crankshaft seal until it is flush with timing case cover.
15. Check engine for leaks.

N20 and N26 Engines

Front

See Figures 92 through 97.

1. Remove vibration damper.

Fig. 92 Screwing special tool 11 3 371 into crankshaft seal

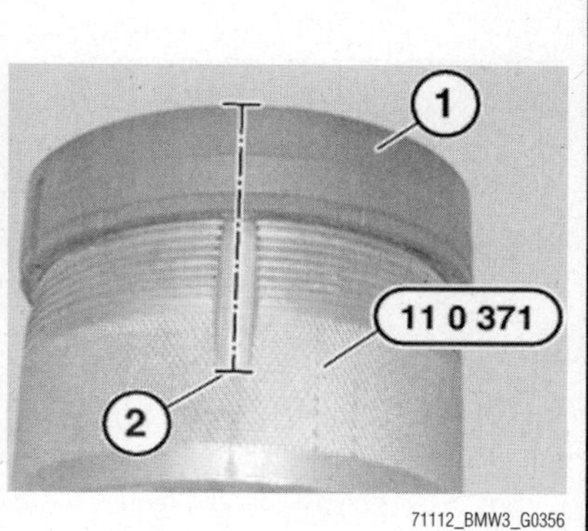

Fig. 93 Sawing crankshaft seal at cutting line

⁂ WARNING

Do not release central bolt. If the central bolt is released, the sprockets of the timing chain and the oil pump will no longer be non-positively connected to the crankshaft. Intake and exhaust camshafts can turn in relation to crankshaft. Risk of damage.

2. Screw special tool 11 0 371 to 37 ft. lbs. (50 Nm) into crankshaft seal.
3. Screw in spindle 11 0 372.
4. Release crankshaft seal from housing.
5. Repeat the operation several times if necessary.

➡Order number:83 30 0 496 275

6. Carefully saw open crankshaft seal at cutting line.

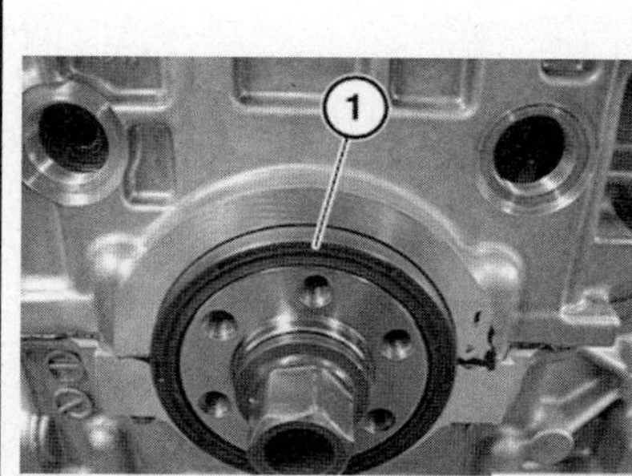

Fig. 94 Positioning radial shaft seal on crankshaft in direction of arrow

7. Remove crankshaft seal from special tool 11 0 371.

To install:

⁂ WARNING

The following text describes installation and sealing between the engine block and crankshaft seal.

⁂ WARNING

The engine block will not be leak proof at the outside of the crankshaft seal if you fail to comply with the individual work steps and the work sequence.

8. Carefully position radial shaft seal on crankshaft in direction of arrow.
9. Screw special tool onto crankshaft.

➡Order number: 83 30 2 212 822.

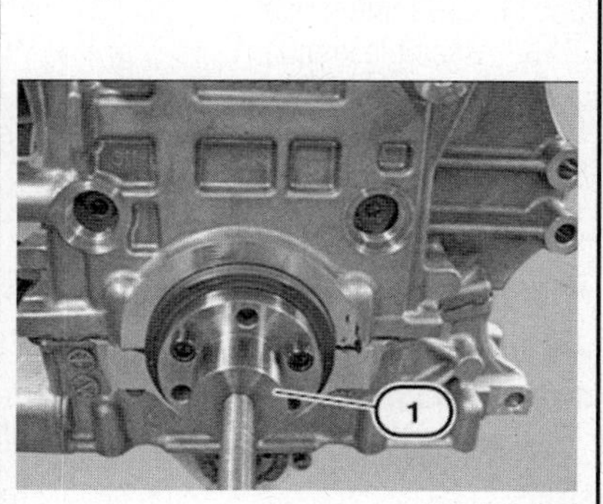

Fig. 95 Screwing special tool onto crankshaft

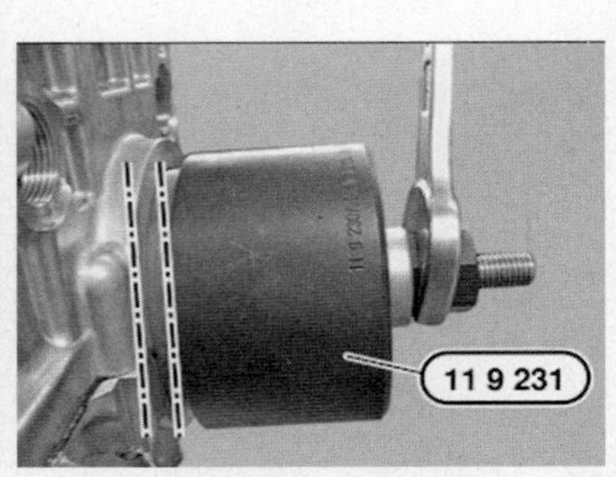

Fig. 96 Aligning radial shaft seal in parallel with special tool for housing separation

Fig. 98 Removing magnet wheel from crankshaft

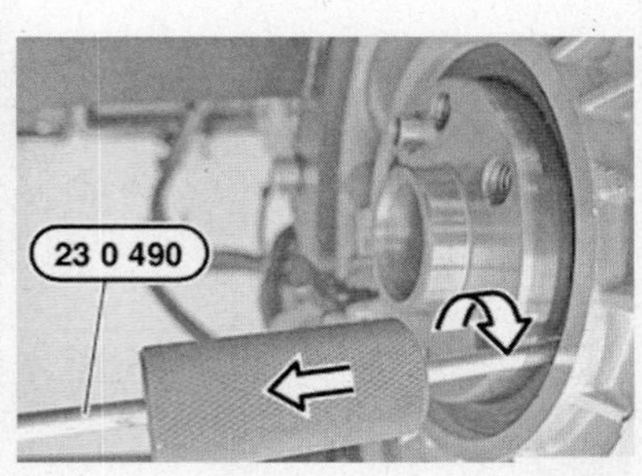

Fig. 100 Screwing in special tool in direction of arrow and driving out radial shaft seal with impact weight in direction of arrow

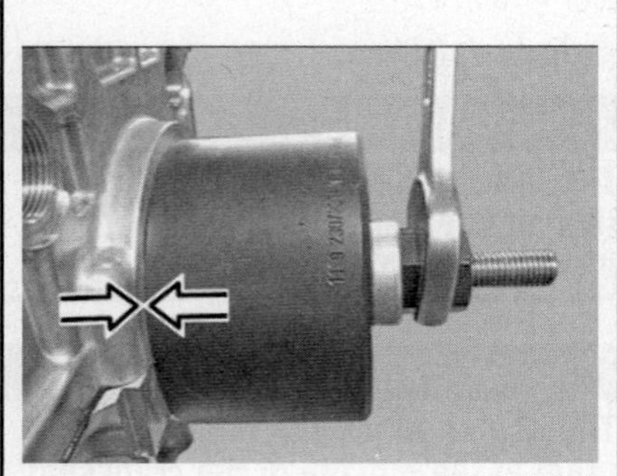

Fig. 97 Drawing in radial shaft seal with special tool 11 9 231 in conjunction with special tool 11 9 233 until flush

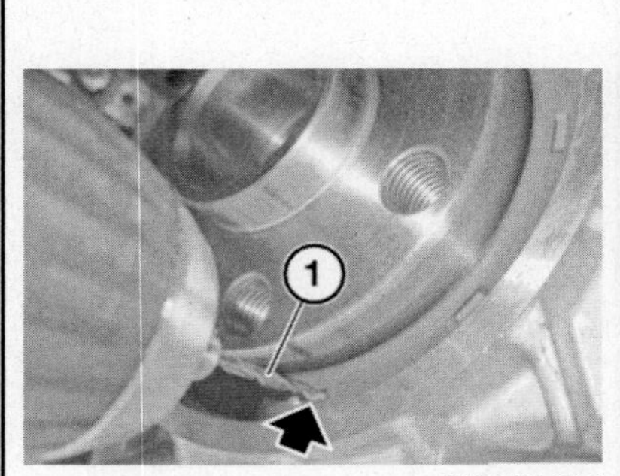

Fig. 99 Drilling hole with a drill in the radial shaft seal (see arrow)

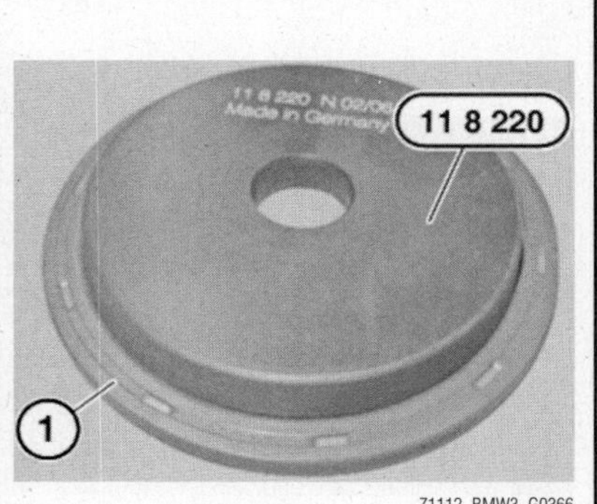

Fig. 101 Preparing radial shaft seal on special tool 11 8 220

10. Align radial shaft seal in parallel with special tool 11 9 231 for housing separation.
11. Order number:83 30 0 494 021
12. Draw in radial shaft seal with special tool 11 9 231 in conjunction with special tool 11 9 233 until flush.
13. Assemble engine.

Transmission Side

See Figures 98 through 103.

1. Remove flywheel.

➡Magnet wheel is magnetic.

➡Keep magnet wheel in a plastic bag away from swarf.

2. Remove magnet wheel from crankshaft.

➡When installing check the fitting sleeve for damage.

➡Note the installation position of the magnet wheel.

3. Release screw on pulse sensor.
4. Slide pulse sensor upwards.

➡Drill size maximum 2.5 mm. Remove swarf immediately.

5. Drill a hole with a drill in the radial shaft seal (see arrow).
6. Remove swarf from the radial shaft seal.

WARNING

Risk of damage at the crankcase and on the running surface of the crankshaft.

WARNING

Immediately carefully remove residual swarf.

7. Screw in special tool 23 0 490 in direction of arrow.
8. Drive out radial shaft seal with impact weight in direction of arrow.

To install:

9. Prepare radial shaft seal on special tool 11 8 220.
10. Position the radial shaft seal with special tool 11 8 220 on the crankshaft.
11. Brush radial shaft seal over the special tool 11 8 220.
12. Move radial shaft seal parallel up against the crankcase.
13. Fasten special tool 11 9 182 with special tool 11 9 184 on the crankshaft.

➡Prepare special tool11 9 181 for installation.

14. Connect special tool 2 212 827 onto special tool 11 9 181.
15. Pull on radial shaft seal with special tools 11 9 181 and 2 212 827 in combination with special tool 11 9 183.
16. Screw on radial shaft seal with special tool 11 9 183 to limit position.
17. Remove special tools.
18. Assemble engine.

Fig. 102 Pulling on radial shaft seal with special tools 11 9 181 and 2 212 827 in combination with special tool11 9 183

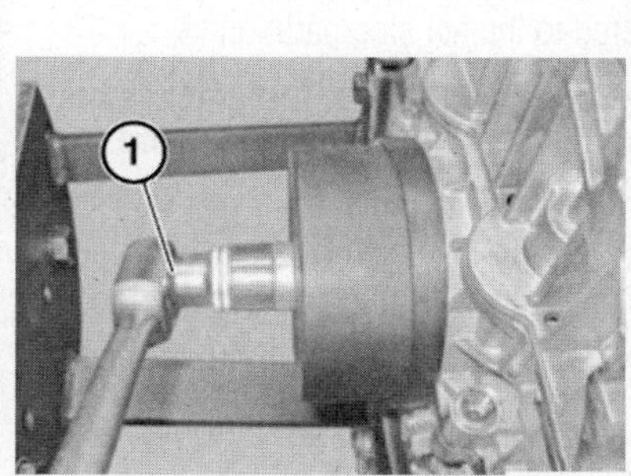

Fig. 103 Screwing on radial shaft seal with special tool 11 9 183 to limit position

N52 and N54 Engines

See Figures 104 through 107.

1. Before servicing the vehicle, refer to the precautions.
2. Remove crankshaft damper

WARNING

Do not Remove central bolt. If the central bolt is Removed, the sprocket wheels of the timing chain and the oil pump will no longer be non-positively connected to the crankshaft. Inlet and exhaust camshafts can turn in relation to crankshaft.

3. Turn back special tool 11 9 222.
4. Push special tool 11 9 221 onto crankshaft.

➡When bolts are tightened down (special tool 11 9 224), crankshaft seal is pressed inwards approximately 1 mm and thus slackened for subsequent removal.

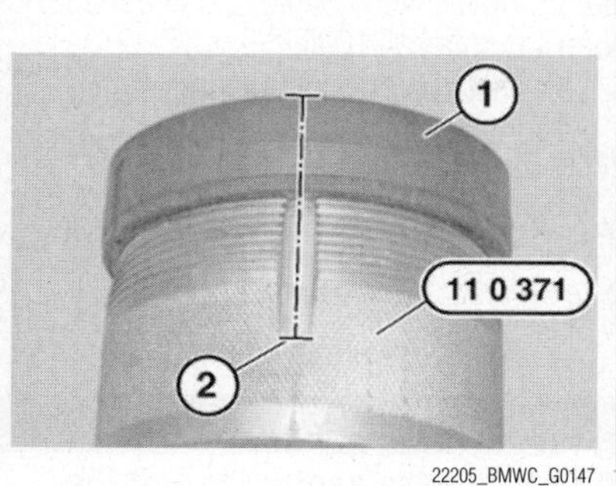

Fig. 104 Carefully saw open crankshaft seal at cutting line

5. Insert bolts (special tool 11 9 224) and tighten down to approximately 15 ft. lbs. (20 Nm).
6. Screw special tool 11 0 371 to 59 ft. lbs. (80 Nm) into crankshaft seal.
7. Screw in spindle 11 0 372.
8. Remove crankshaft seal from housing.

➡Repeat the operation several times if necessary.

9. Carefully saw open crankshaft seal at cutting line.
10. Remove crankshaft seal from special tool 11 0 371.

To install:

WARNING

The following text describes installation and sealing between the engine block and crankshaft seal.

The engine block will not be leak proof at the outside of the crankshaft seal if you fail to comply with the individual work steps and the work sequence.

11. Clean sealing surface and degrease thoroughly in area of housing partition.
12. Apply a light coat of oil to running surface of crankshaft seal.
13. Screw special tool 11 9 232 with bolts (special tool 11 9 234) to crankshaft.

➡Support sleeve is supplied with crankshaft seal.

14. When crankshaft seal is installed, only support sleeve may be used as a slip sleeve.
15. Crankshaft seal has a groove on both left and right sides.

WARNING

After installation, the grooves must be filled with sealing compound.

➡The required parts are available from the BMW Parts Service.

16. Remove screw caps from injector.
17. Screw on metering needle.
18. Insert piston for pressing out. Injector contains the sealing compound Loctite®, manufacturer's number 128357. Bottle contains the primer Loctite®, manufacturer's number 171000.
19. Push support sleeve with crankshaft seal onto special tool 11 9 232.

WARNING

Support sleeve remains on special tool 11 9 232, until crankshaft seal is drawn in.

20. Align groove centrally to housing partition.
21. Coat both grooves on crankshaft seal with Loctite® primer, manufacturer's number 171000, and expose to air for approximately one minute.
22. Draw in crankshaft seal with special tool 11 9 231 in conjunction with special tool 11 9 233 until flush.
23. Before filling with sealing compound, moisten brush with Loctite® primer, manufacturer's number 171000. Insert brush as far as possible into grooves on crankshaft seal in order to coat housing partition on engine block.
24. Using injector, fill both grooves flush with Loctite® sealing compound, manufacturer's number 128357.

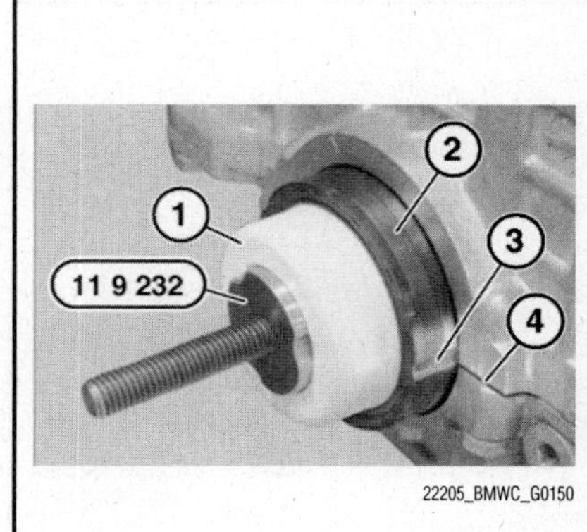

Fig. 105 Support sleeve, housing partition, grooves and crankshaft seal

➡Loctite® primer, manufacturer's number 171000, binds the Loctite® sealing compound, manufacturer's number 128357, and prevents leakage.

Fig. 106 Draw in crankshaft seal with special tool 11 9 231 in conjunction with special tool 11 9 233 until flush

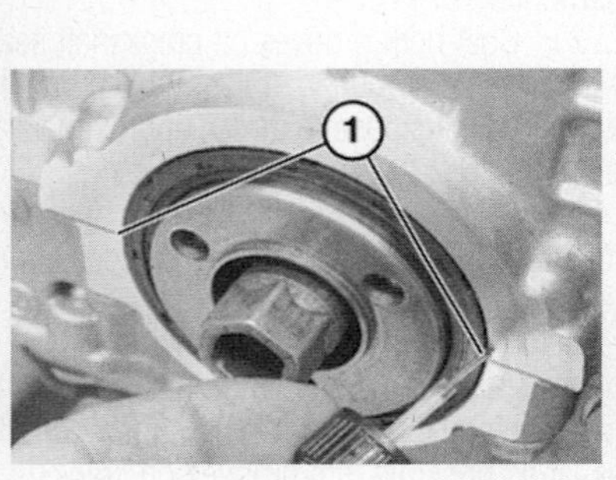

Fig. 107 Insert brush as far as possible into grooves on crankshaft seal in order to coat housing partition on engine block

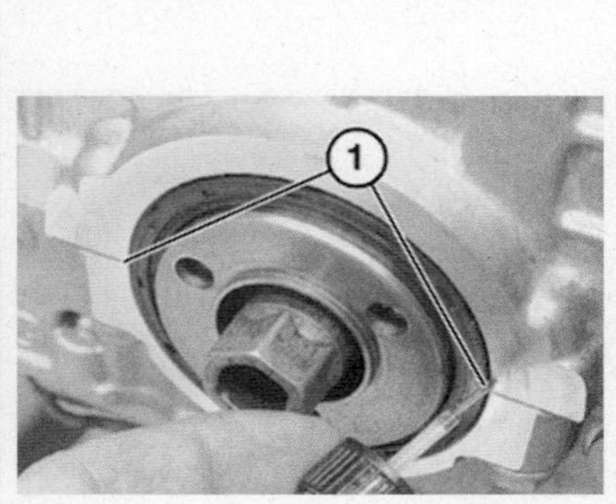

Fig. 108 Using injector, fill both grooves flush with Loctite® sealing compound, manufacturer's number 128357

25. Coat surface of sealing compound in both grooves with Loctite® primer, manufacturer's number 171000.
26. Install crankshaft damper.

N55 Engine

Front Seal

See Figures 109 through 111.

1. Remove vibration damper.

WARNING

Do not release central bolt. If the central bolt is released, the sprockets of the timing chain and the oil pump will no longer be non-positively connected to the crankshaft. Intake and exhaust camshafts can turn in relation to crankshaft. Risk of damage.

2. Screw special tool 11 0 371 with 59 ft. lbs. (80 Nm) into the crankshaft seal.
3. Screw in spindle 11 0 372.
4. Release crankshaft seal from housing.
5. Repeat the operation several times if necessary.
6. Carefully saw open crankshaft seal at cutting line.
7. Remove crankshaft seal from special tool 11 0 371.

To install:

WARNING

The following text describes installation and sealing between the engine block and crankshaft seal.

WARNING

The engine block will not be leak proof at the outside of the crankshaft seal if you fail to comply with the individual work steps and the work sequence.

8. Clean sealing surface and degrease thoroughly in area of housing partition.
9. Apply a light coat of oil to running surface of crankshaft seal.
10. Push radial shaft seal 11 9 235carefully in direction of arrow on the special tool.

WARNING

Special tool 11 9 235 can only be fastened with 2 opposite bolts. Determine hole pattern on special tool.

11. Screw special tool 11 9 235 with special tool 11 9 234 on crankshaft.
12. Align groove of radial shaft seal centered to the housing partition (3.

➡After installation, the grooves must be filled with sealing compound.

13. Draw in radial shaft seal with special tool 11 9 231 in conjunction with special tool 11 9 233 until flush.

➡Use primer 1.3 and liquid seal 1.4.

14. Prepare liquid sealing compound in special tool 11 4 370.
15. Remove sealing caps from injector.
16. Screw on metering needle.
17. Insert piston for pressing out.
18. Syringe contains the sealing compound Loctite®, manufacturer's number 128357.
19. Bottle contains the primer Loctite®, manufacturer's number 171000.
20. Before filling with sealing compound:

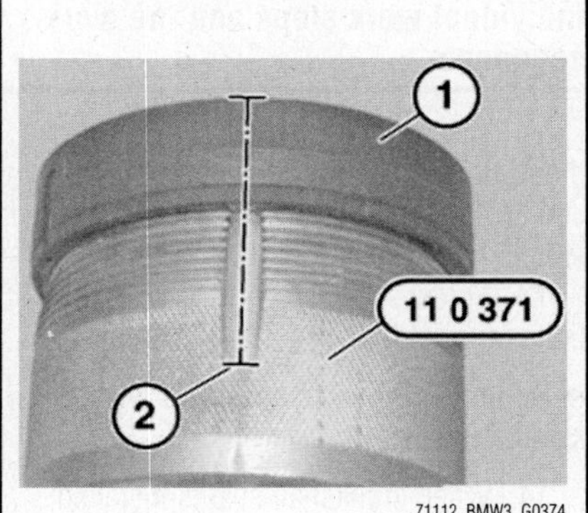

Fig. 109 Sawing crankshaft seal at cutting line

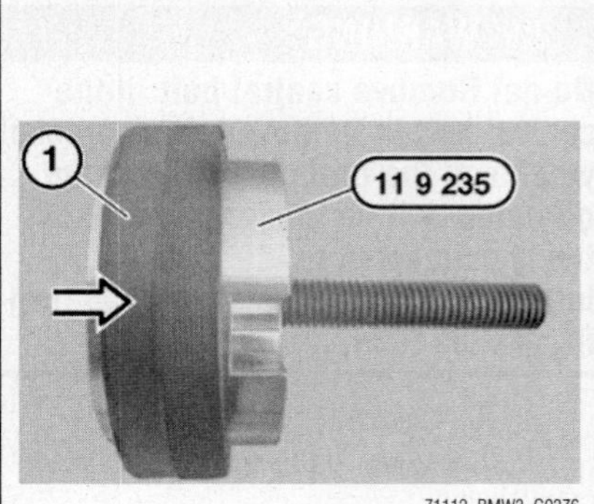

Fig. 110 Pushing radial shaft seal 11 9 235carefully in direction of arrow on the special tool

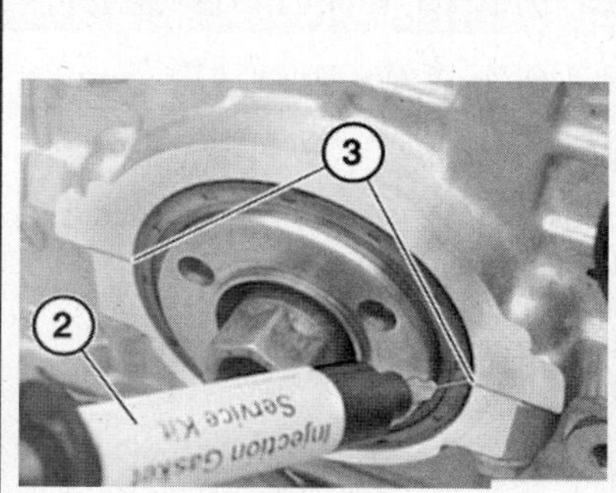

Fig. 111 Using syringe, fill both grooves flush with Loctite® sealing compound, manufacturer's number 128357

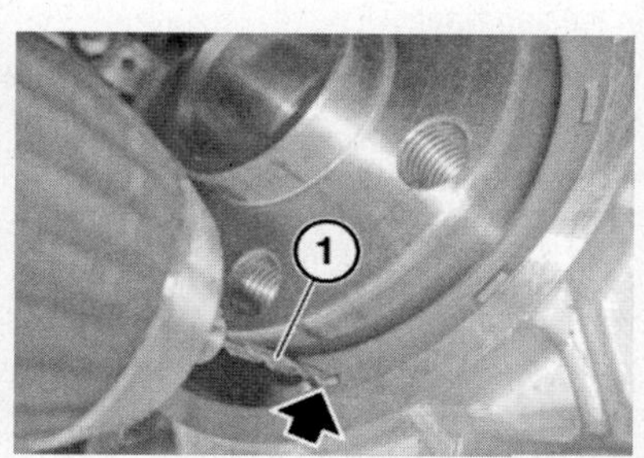

Fig. 112 Drilling hole with a drill in the radial shaft seal (see arrow)

a. Moisten brush with Loctite® primer, manufacturer's number 171000. Insert brush as far as possible into grooves on crankshaft seal in order to coat housing partition on engine block.

21. Using syringe, fill both grooves flush with Loctite® sealing compound, manufacturer's number 128357.

➡Loctite® primer, manufacturer's number 171000, binds the Loctite® sealing compound, manufacturer's number 128357, and prevents leakage.

22. Coat surface of sealing compound in both grooves with Loctite® primer, manufacturer's number 171000.

23. Assemble engine.

Transmission Side

See Figures 112 and 113.

1. Remove flywheel.

➡Magnet wheel is magnetic.

➡Keep magnet wheel in a plastic bag away from swarf.

2. Remove magnet wheel from crankshaft.

➡When installing check the fitting sleeve for damage.

➡Note the installation position of the magnet wheel.

3. Release screw on pulse sensor.
4. Slide pulse sensor upwards.

➡Drill size maximum 2.5 mm. Remove swarf immediately.

5. Drill a hole with a drill in the radial shaft seal (see arrow).
6. Remove swarf from the radial shaft seal.

⁂ WARNING

Risk of damage at the crankcase and on the running surface of the crankshaft.

⁂ WARNING

Immediately carefully remove residual swarf.

7. Screw in special tool 23 0 490 in direction of arrow.
8. Drive out radial shaft seal with impact weight in direction of arrow.

To install:

9. Prepare radial shaft seal on special tool 11 8 220.
10. Position the radial shaft seal with special tool 11 8 220 on the crankshaft.
11. Brush radial shaft seal over the special tool 11 8 220.

Fig. 113 Screwing in special tool in direction of arrow and driving out radial shaft seal with impact weight in direction of arrow

12. Move radial shaft seal parallel up against the crankcase.
13. Fasten special tool 11 9 182 with special tool 11 9 184 on the crankshaft.

➡Prepare special tool11 9 181 for installation.

14. Connect special tool 2 212 827 onto special tool 11 9 181.
15. Pull on radial shaft seal with special tools 11 9 181 and 2 212 827 in combination with special tool 11 9 183.
16. Screw on radial shaft seal with special tool 11 9 183 to limit position.
17. Remove special tools.
18. Assemble engine.

S65 Engine

See Figures 114 through 119.

1. Before servicing the vehicle, refer to the precautions.

Fig. 114 Lay special tool 11 2 386 on crankshaft

Fig. 115 Screw special tool 11 6 360 to 59 ft. lbs. (80 Nm) into radial seal

2. Remove engine fan. Refer to engine cooling components, engine fan, removal & installation.

3. Remove the crankshaft damper.Refer to engine mechanical, crankshaft damper, removal & installation.

4. Lay special tool 11 2 386 on crankshaft.

5. Screw special tool 11 6 360 to 59 ft. lbs. (80 Nm) into radial seal.

6. Release radial seal from housing.

7. Repeat the operation several times if necessary.

WARNING

Carefully saw open old radial shaft seal with an iron saw from special tool 11 6 360.

8. Remove remnants of sealant from sealant outlet on left and right.

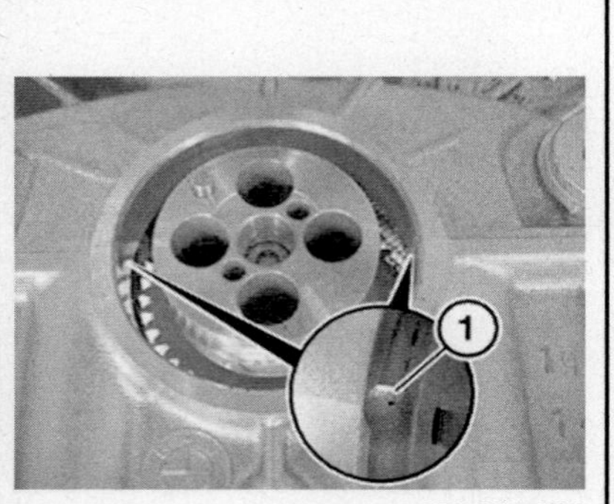

Fig. 116 Remove remnants of sealant from sealant outlet on left and right

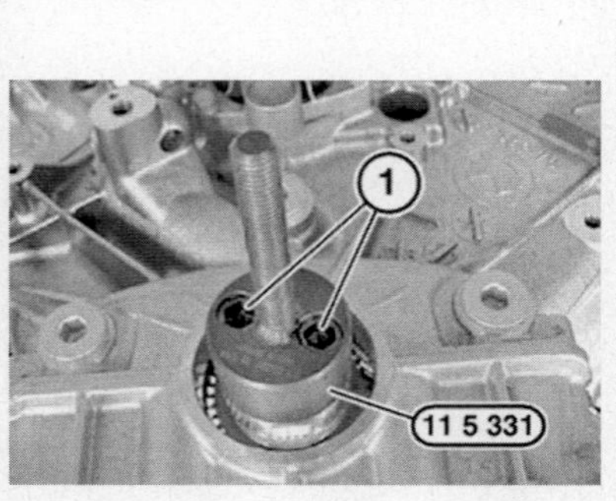

Fig. 117 Secure special tool 11 5 331 with bolts

To install:

9. Apply Drei Bond® sealant to outlet on left and right.

10. Secure special tool 11 5 331 with bolts.

➡Pay attention to dowel pin.

11. Push special tool 11 7 231 onto special tool 11 5 331 in direction of arrow.

12. Remove support ring from shaft seal.

13. Push shaft seal uniformly by way of fitting aid 11 7 231 onto special tool 11 5 331.

14. Position shaft seal approximately 0.195 in. (5 mm) before crankcase.

15. Remove special tool 11 7 231.

16. Press in shaft seal with special tools 11 5 332 and 11 5 333.

17. Setting time of shaft seal approximately 1 hour.

18. Correct engine oil level if necessary.

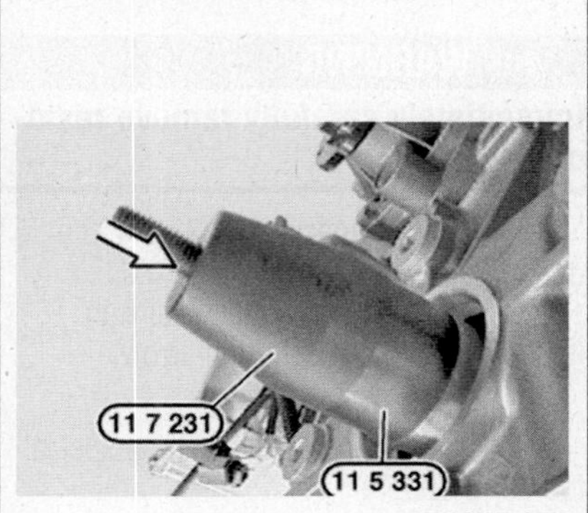

Fig. 118 Secure special tool 11 5 331 with bolts

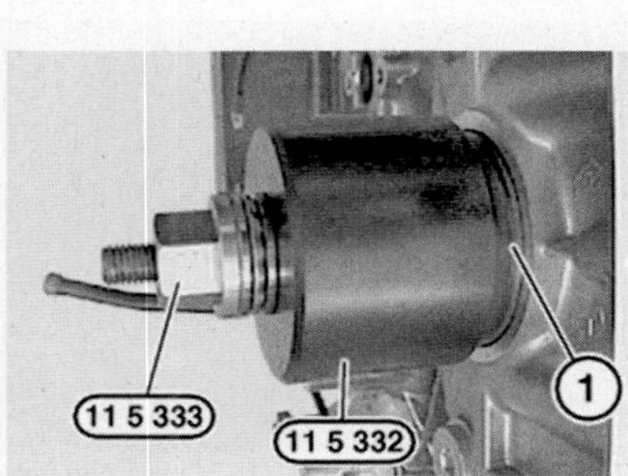

Fig. 119 Press in shaft seal with special tools 11 5 332 and 11 5 333

EXHAUST MANIFOLD

REMOVAL & INSTALLATION

M57 Engine

The M57 exhaust manifold is an integral part of the turbocharger assembly and is not serviced separately. Refer to engine mechanical, turbocharger, removal & installation.

N20 and N26

The N54 exhaust manifold is an integral part of the turbocharger assembly and is not serviced separately. Refer to engine mechanical, turbocharger, removal & installation.

N52 Engine

See Figure 120.

1. Before servicing the vehicle, refer to the precautions.

2. Remove the ignition coil cover.

3. Remove the coolant expansion tank.

4. Remove the underbody protection.

5. Remove the complete exhaust system.

6. On AWD vehicles, remove the reinforcement plate.

7. Remove the oxygen sensor plug from cylinders number 4 and 6 and remove the exhaust assembly.

8. Remove the manifold for cylinders number 1 and 3 downwards.

9. Remove the manifold for cylinders number 4 and 6 downwards.

To install:

10. Remove the old gasket from the cylinder head and exhaust manifold and replace the gasket. The gasket beads face the exhaust manifolds.

11. To install, reverse the removal procedure.

12. Coat screw connections with CRC copper paste.

13. Install new nuts and tighten the exhaust manifolds to 15 ft. lbs. (20 Nm).

N54 Engine

The N54 exhaust manifold is an integral part of the turbocharger assembly and is not serviced separately. Refer to engine mechanical, turbocharger, removal & installation.

N55 Engine

The N54 exhaust manifold is an integral part of the turbocharger assembly and is not serviced separately. Refer to engine mechanical, turbocharger, removal & installation.

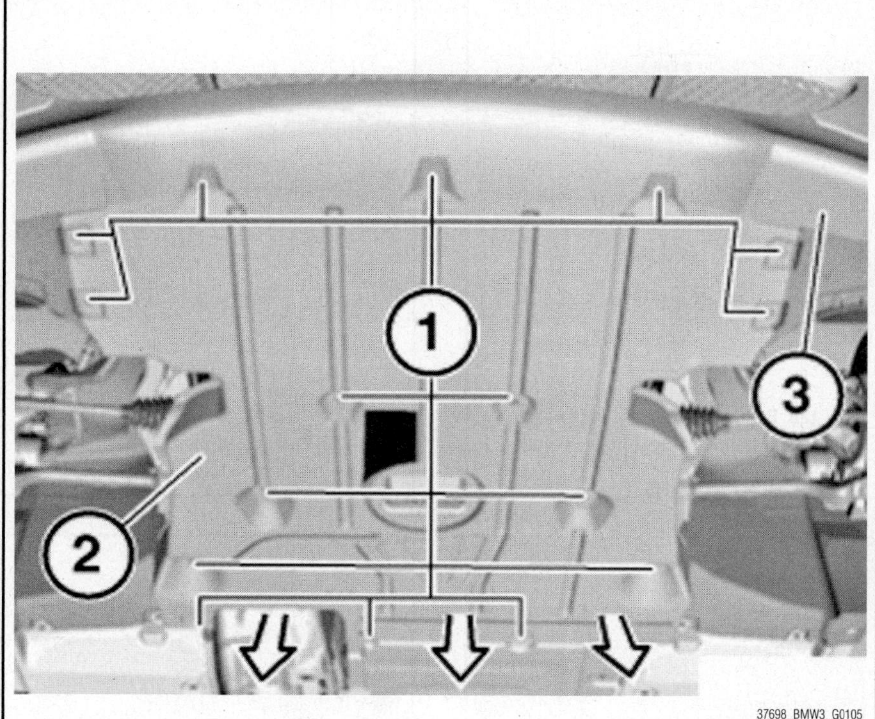

Fig. 120 Release screws and pull underbody protection forward under bumper trim

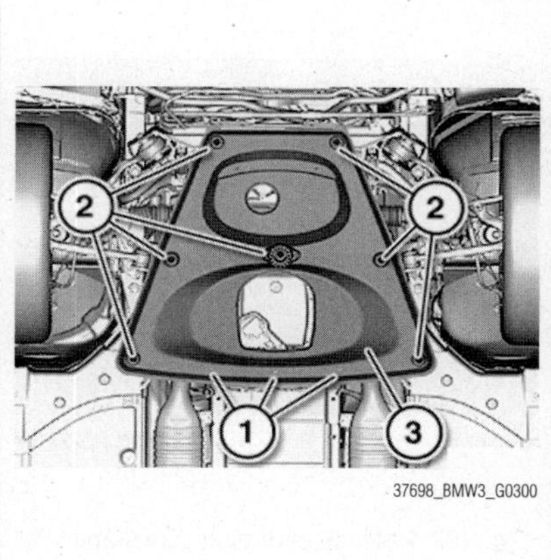

Fig. 123 Release screws, release screws and remove reinforcement plate

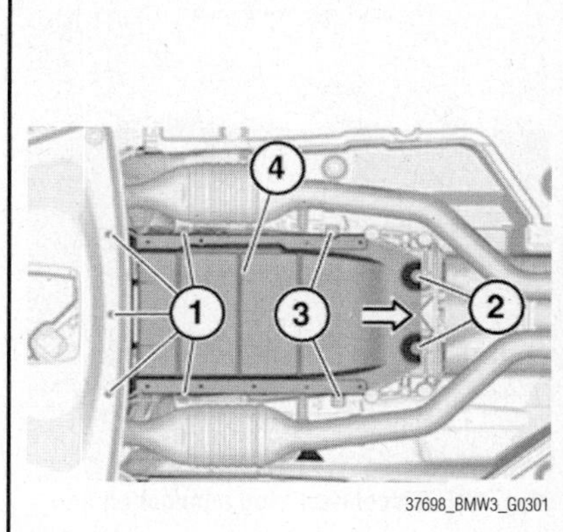

Fig. 124 Release screws (1 and 2), unscrew nuts and pull out underbody protection in direction of arrow towards bottom

S65 Engine

See Figures 121 through 132.

1. Before servicing the vehicle, refer to the precautions.
2. Remove alternator. Refer to engine electrical, alternator, removal & installation.
3. Remove complete exhaust system.
4. Secure engine in installation position with special tool.
5. Lower front axle carrier.
6. Remove reinforcement plate.
   a. Remove front underbody protection.
   b. Release screws and remove reinforcement plate.
7. Remove rear underbody protection.
8. Remove reinforcement cover on left and right.
9. Remove lower section of steering spindle from steering gear.

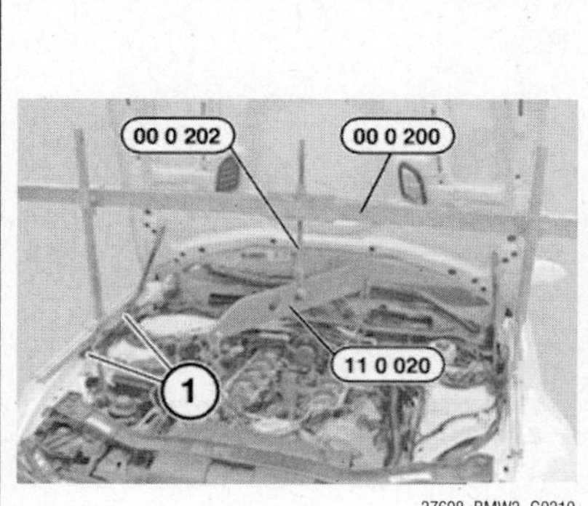

Fig. 121 Secure engine in installation position

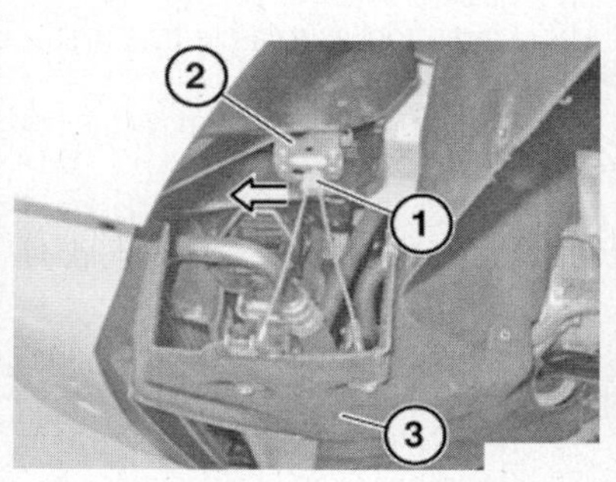

Fig. 122 Turn catch on cable through 90° and disengage in direction of arrow from bracket on both sides. Pull underbody protection forwards under bumper trim and remove

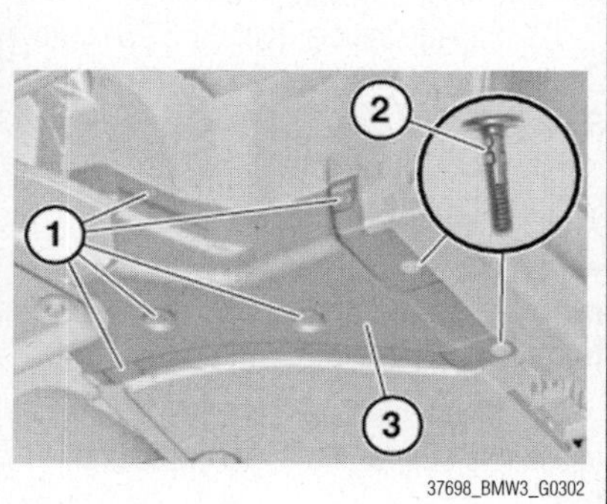

Fig. 125 Release screws (1 and 2) and remove reinforcement cover

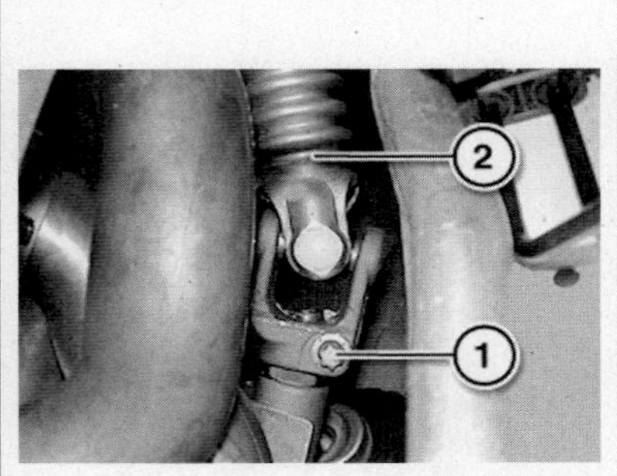

Fig. 126 Release clamping screw and detach steering spindle lower section from power steering gear

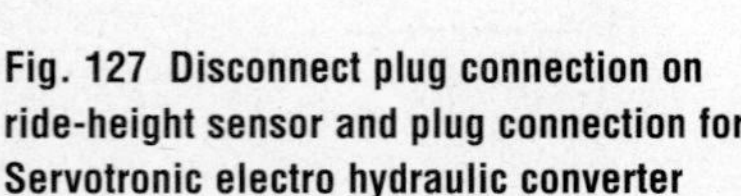

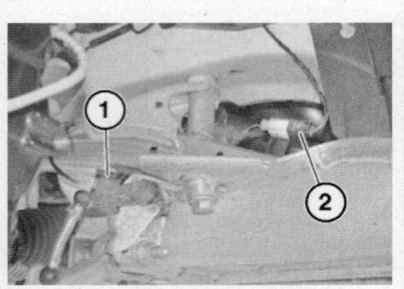

Fig. 127 Disconnect plug connection on ride-height sensor and plug connection for Servotronic electro hydraulic converter

a. Release clamping screw.

b. Detach steering spindle lower section from power steering gear.

10. Disconnect plug connection on ride-height sensor.

11. Disconnect plug connection for Servotronic electro hydraulic converter.

12. Engage special tool 31 5 251 with a 2nd person helping completely on workshop jack 00 2 030.

13. Insert special tools 31 5 253 in telescopic supports of a profile rail pair.

➡In a profile rail pair two profile rails are connected to each by teeth.

14. Insert special tools 31 5 256 in telescopic supports of other profile rail pair.

15. Align special tools 31 5 253 and 31 5 256 to front axle carrier.

16. Support front axle carrier by operating workshop jack 00 2 030.

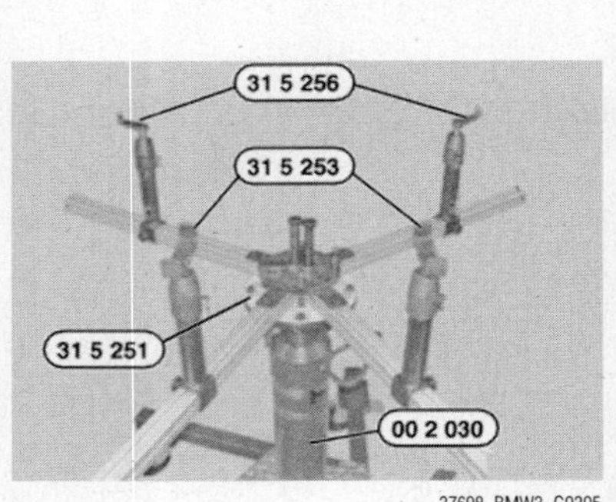

Fig. 128 Engage the special tool with a 2nd person helping completely on workshop jack

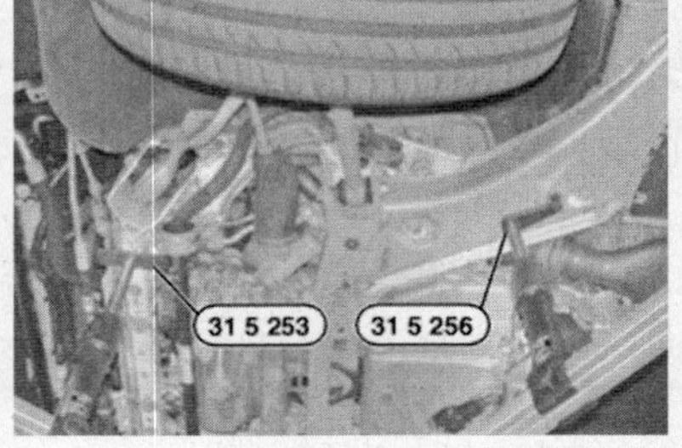

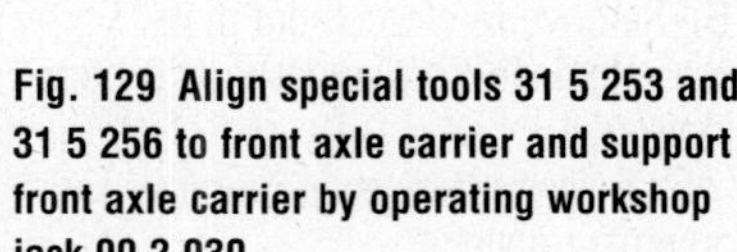

Fig. 129 Align special tools 31 5 253 and 31 5 256 to front axle carrier and support front axle carrier by operating workshop jack 00 2 030

⁂ WARNING

Pay attention to power steering hoses and lines when lowering and raising.

17. Release bolts (1–4).

18. Lower front axle carrier by a maximum of 4 inches (10 cm).

19. Release screws and remove the heat shield.

20. Release nuts of individual flange pairs and remove the exhaust manifold.

To install:

21. To install, reverse the removal procedure.

22. Replace exhaust manifold seals.

23. Replace nuts and tighten nuts on each flange to 19 ft. lbs. (25 Nm).

24. Raise the front axle carrier

a. Check threads for damage; if necessary, repair with Helicoil thread inserts.

b. Make sure screws are installed in correct positions.

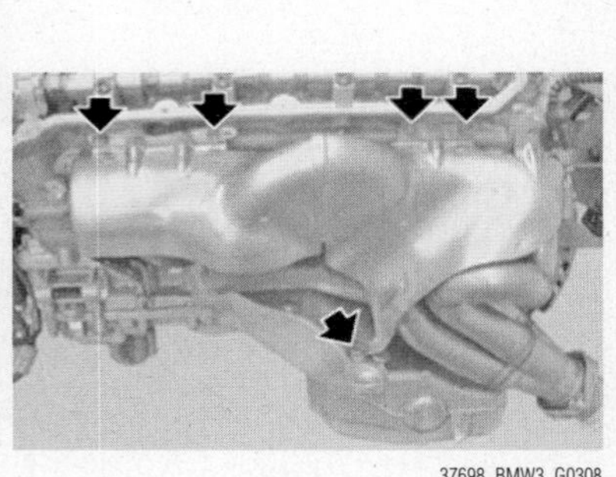

Fig. 130 Release screws (arrows) and remove the heat shield

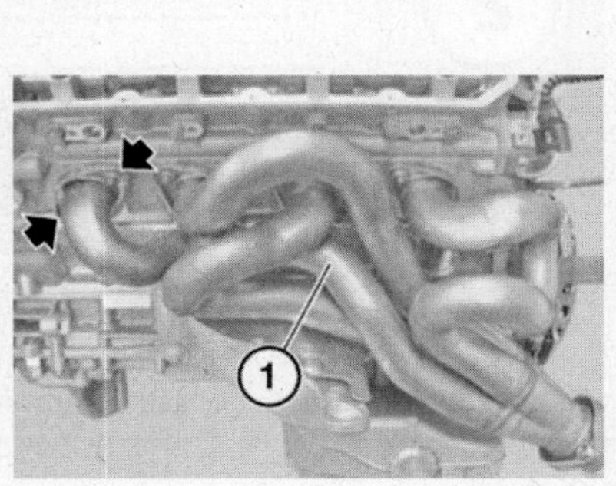

Fig. 131 Release nuts (arrows) of individual flange pairs and remove the exhaust manifold

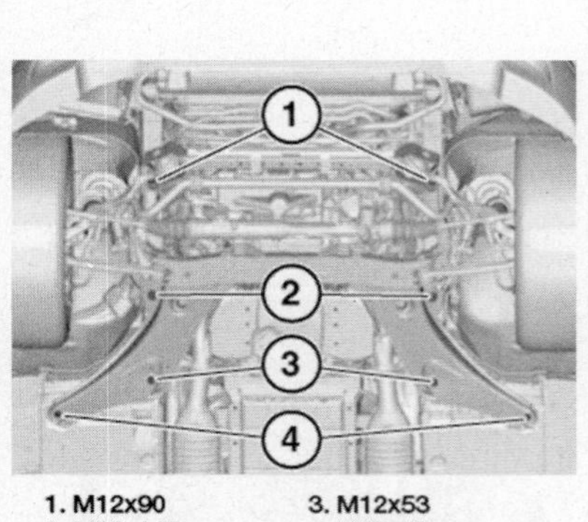

Fig. 132 Make sure screws are installed in correct positions.

c. Tighten down first screws and then screws (2, 3, 4), as follows:

- M12: 80 ft. lbs. (108 Nm)
- M10 x 42: 41 ft. lbs. (56 Nm) plus an additional 90° rotation

25. Connect steering spindle lower section to power steering gear.

a. Clean thread to remove all remnants of screw securing adhesive.

b. Lower section of steering spindle can only be attached in one position to the power steering gear.

c. Replace clamping screw.

d. Clamping screw must rest in groove of power steering gear.

e. Tighten to 16 ft. lbs. (21 Nm).

f. Turn steering wheel in both directions to full lock. The airbag warning lamp must not light up in the process.

26. Replace reinforcing plate screws and tighten to 41 ft. lbs. (56 Nm) plus an additional 90° rotation.

27. Carry out steering angle sensor adjustment.

OIL PAN

REMOVAL & INSTALLATION

M57 Engine

See Figures 133 through 135.

1. Before servicing the vehicle, refer to the precautions.
2. Secure engine in installation position.
3. Lower front axle. Refer to suspension, front axle, removal & installation.

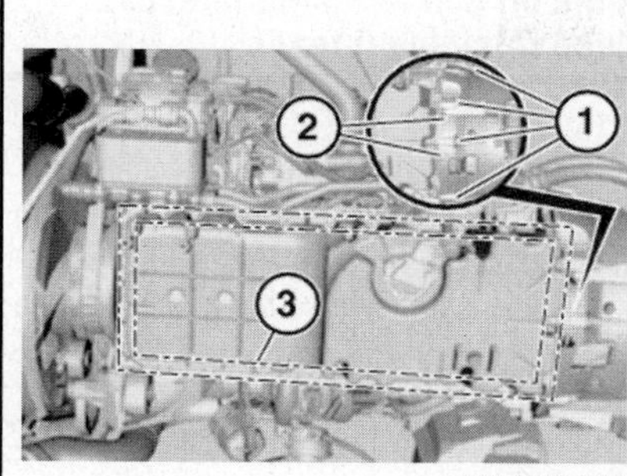

Fig. 134 Release bolts on transmission and bolts along line

4. Drain and recycle engine oil.
5. Release oil dipstick guide tube on oil sump.
6. Release bolts on transmission.
7. Release bolts along line.

To install:

8. To install, reverse the removal procedure.
9. Clean retaining threads and sealing faces.
10. Apply Drei Bond 1208 sealing compound in area of joints that are 0.117 in. (3 mm) high and 0.078 in. (2 mm) wide.

WARNING

There must be no adhesive residues in the lower crankcase retaining threads.

11. Replace all seals.
12. Replace aluminum screws.

WARNING

Bolts of oil sump have different lengths. Observe different tightening torques.

13. Tighten bolts/nuts to specification as follows:

- Oil sump to crankcase (M6): 71 inch lbs. (8 Nm)
- Oil sump to crankcase (M8x30): 14 ft. lbs. (19 Nm)
- Transmission to oil sump (M8x50): 14 ft. lbs. (19 Nm)
- Oil level sensor to oil sump: 71 inch lbs. (8 Nm)

14. Fill engine with oil and check for leaks.

N20 and N26 Engines

See Figure 136.

1. Drain engine oil.
2. Lower front axle.
3. Disconnect plug connection on oil level sensor.
4. Release bolts along line.
5. Tightening torque: 7 ft. lbs. (10 Nm)
6. Remove synthetic oil pan in downwards direction.

To install:

To install, reverse the removal procedure noting the following.

7. Add engine oil.

N52 and N54 Engines

See Figure 137.

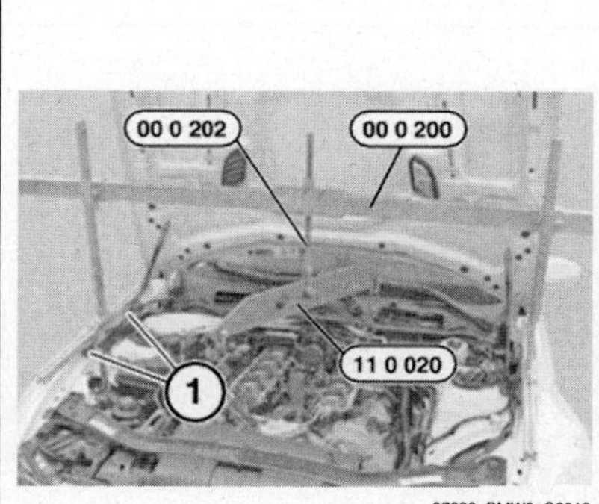

Fig. 133 Secure engine in installation position

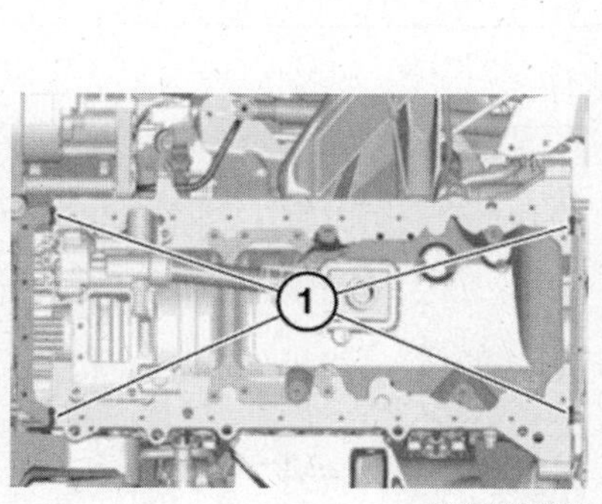

Fig. 135 Apply Drei Bond 1208 sealing compound in area of joints that are 0.117 in. (3 mm) high and 0.078 in. (2 mm) wide

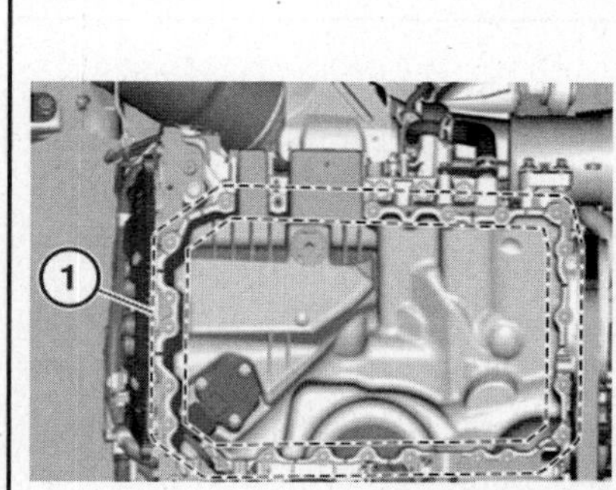

Fig. 136 Releasing bolts and removing oil pan

⁂ WARNING

Aluminum-magnesium material. No steel fasteners may be used due to the threat of electrochemical corrosion. A magnesium crankcase requires aluminum fasteners exclusively. Aluminum fasteners must be replaced each time they are removed. The end faces of aluminum fasteners are painted blue for purposes of identification. Torque specifications and torque angles must be observed for risk of damage.

1. Before servicing the vehicle, refer to the precautions.
2. Install engine support tool or equivalent.
3. Disconnect the negative battery cable.
4. Remove the lower front axle.
5. Remove the left drive shaft.
6. Remove the right drive shaft.
7. Remove the front axle differential.
8. Remove the engine oil.
9. On vehicles equipped with automatic transmission, oil lines must be detached from the engine oil pan.
10. If necessary, remove vane pump and set it aside.
11. Remove the two bolts securing oil pan to transmission.
12. Remove the oil return hose.
13. Remove oil pan bolts and remove the oil pan.
14. If necessary, remove oil level sensor bolts and oil level sensor.

To install

15. Clean the mounting surfaces and install a new gasket and all seals.

⁂ WARNING

There must be no adhesive residues in the oil pan retaining threads. Clean retaining threads.

16. Install oil pan.
17. Replace all aluminum fasteners and tighten 70 inch lbs (8 Nm) plus an additional 90° rotation
18. To install, reverse the removal procedure.
19. Fill the engine with oil.
20. Start the engine and check for leaks.

N55 Engine

See Figures 138 through 144.

⁂ WARNING

Aluminum screws/bolts are permitted with and without color coding (blue).

⁂ WARNING

Aluminum screws/bolts must be replaced each time they are released.

➡**For reliable identification:**

a. Aluminum screws/bolts are not magnetic.

⁂ WARNING

Jointing torque and angle of rotation must be observed without fail (risk of damage).

1. Lower front axle.
2. Drain engine oil.
3. Release bolts on transmission.

Tightening torque: 70 inch lbs. (8 Nm)

4. Disconnect plug connection on oil level sensor.
5. Release bolts along line.
6. If necessary, remove oil level sensor.

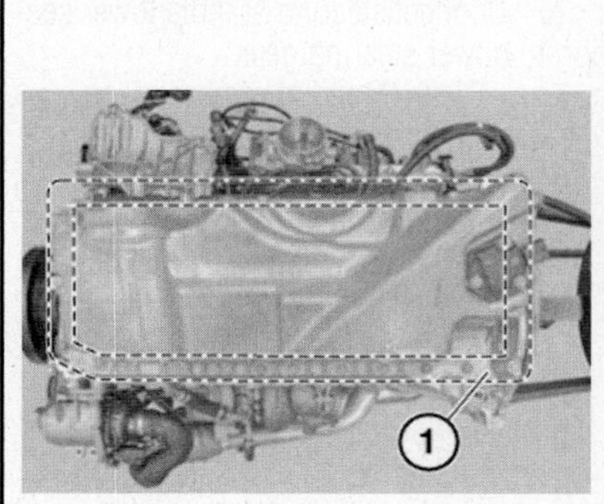

Fig. 139 Releasing bolts and removing oil pan

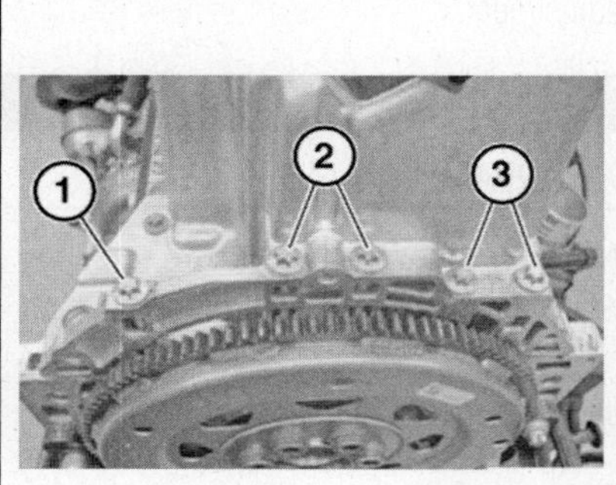

Fig. 140 Identifying screws M8x92 mm, M8x112 mm and M8x92 mm

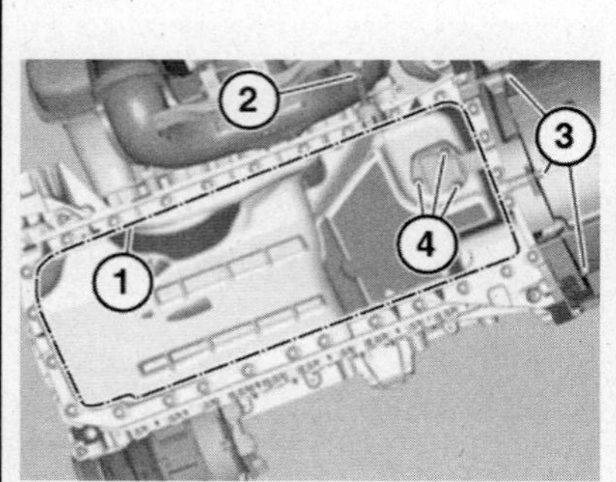

Fig. 137 Oil pan bolts, oil return hose, transmission bolts and oil level sensor

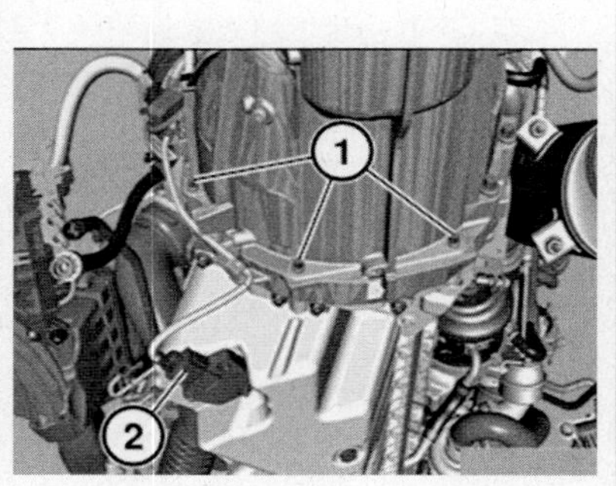

Fig. 138 Releasing bolts on transmission and disconnecting plug connection on oil level sensor

Fig. 141 Identifying screw M8x50 mm

To install:

To install, reverse the removal procedure noting the following.

7. Identifying screws before installing.
8. Replace all o-rings and seals.
9. Aluminum screws M8x92 mm and M8x112 mm. Tightening torque: 70 inch lbs. (8 Nm) + 180°
10. Aluminum screw M8x50 mm. Tightening torque: 70 inch lbs. (8 Nm) + 90°
11. Aluminum screws M8x26 mm. Tightening torque: 62 inch lbs.(4 Nm) + 90°

➡Special tool 11 8 780 is only required if gear is not installed as mechanical stop.

12. Secure special tool 11 8 780 with two bolts on crankcase.
13. If the engine is removed, position oil sump with no gaps until it contacts special tool11 8 780.
14. If the engine is installed, position the oil sump with no gaps until it contacts gearbox housing.
15. Bolt on oil sump.
16. Assemble engine.

S65 Engine

See Figures 145 through 158.

1. Before servicing the vehicle, refer to the precautions.
2. Drain and recycle engine oil.
3. Secure engine in installation position.
4. Lower front axle.
5. Remove reinforcement plate.
   a. Remove front underbody protection.
   b. Release screws and remove reinforcement plate.
6. Remove rear underbody protection.
7. Remove reinforcement cover on left and right.
8. Remove lower section of steering spindle from steering gear.
   a. Release clamping screw.

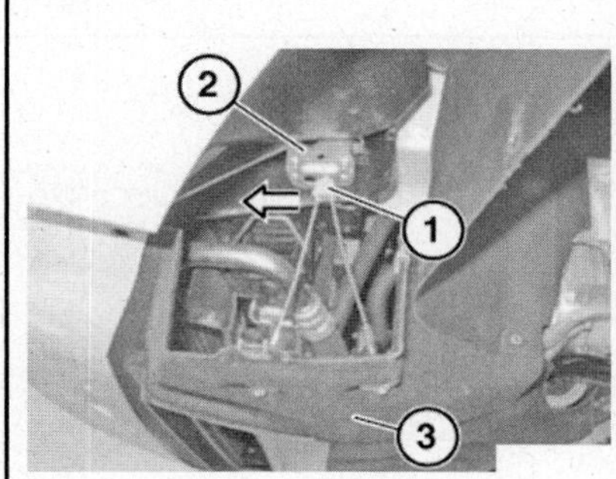

Fig. 146 Turn catch on cable through 90° and disengage in direction of arrow from bracket on both sides. Pull underbody protection forwards under bumper trim and remove

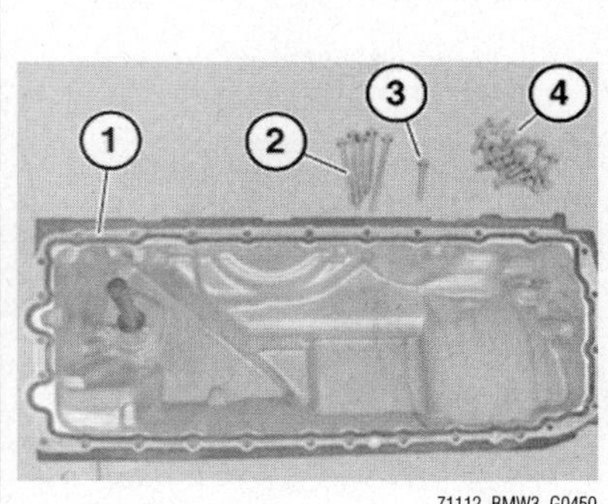

Fig. 142 Replacing o-rings and seals and identifying screw M8x92 mm and M8x112 mm, screw M8x50 mm and screw M8x26 mm

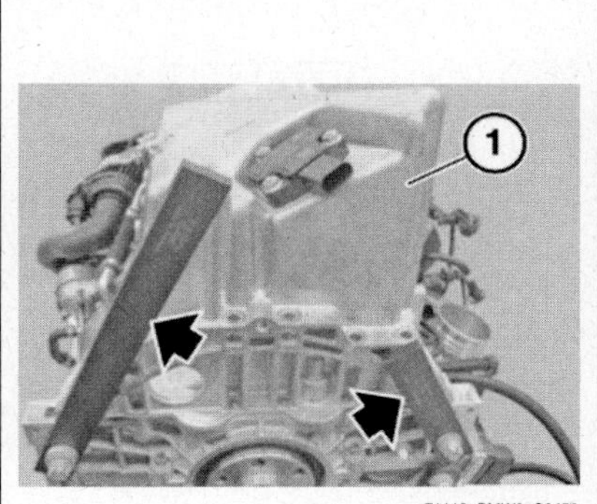

Fig. 144 Installing oil sump

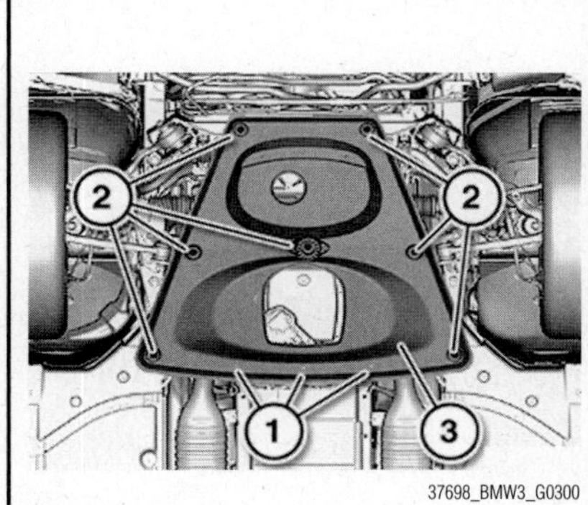

Fig. 147 Release screws, release screws and remove reinforcement plate

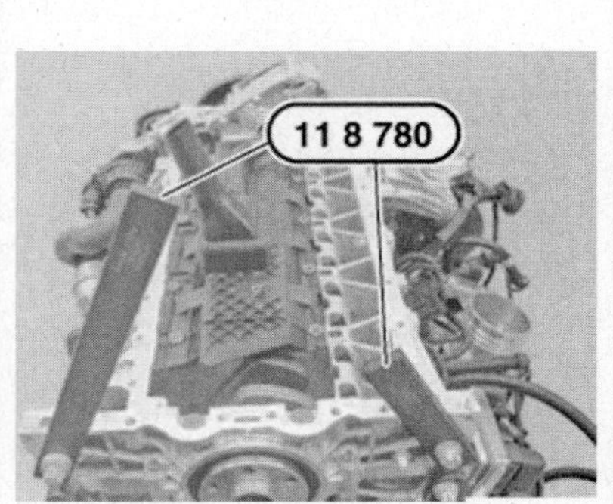

Fig. 143 Securing special tool 11 8 780 with two bolts on crankcase

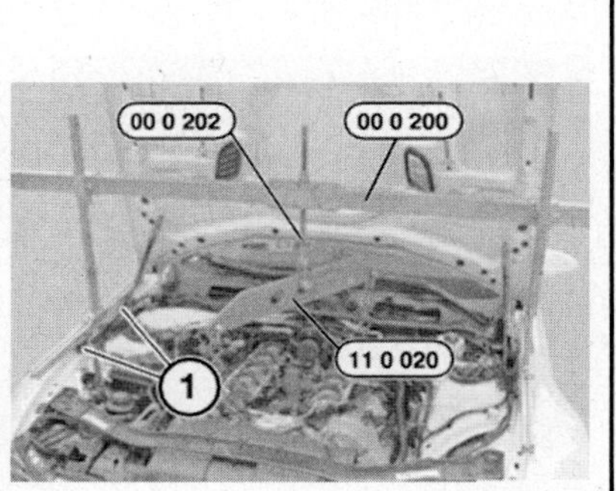

Fig. 145 Secure engine in installation position

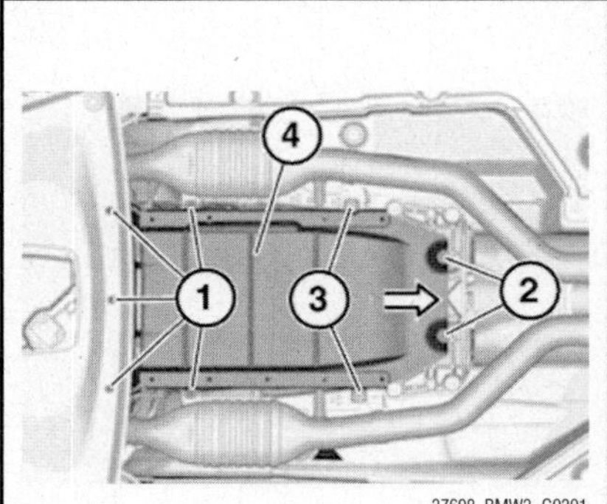

Fig. 148 Release screws (1 and 2), unscrew nuts and pull out underbody protection in direction of arrow towards bottom

b. Detach steering spindle lower section from power steering gear.

9. Disconnect plug connection on ride-height sensor.

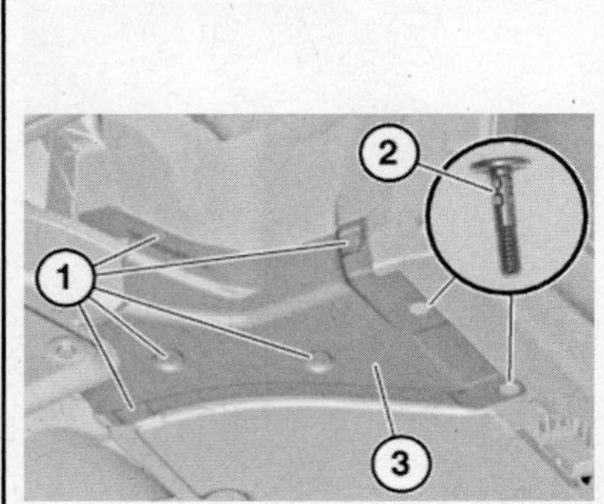

Fig. 149 Release screws (1 and 2) and remove reinforcement cover

10. Disconnect plug connection for Servotronic electro hydraulic converter.

11. Engage special tool 31 5 251 with a 2nd person helping completely on workshop jack 00 2 030.

12. Insert special tools 31 5 253 in telescopic supports of a profile rail pair.

➡In a profile rail pair two profile rails are connected to each by teeth.

13. Insert special tools 31 5 256 in telescopic supports of other profile rail pair.

14. Align special tools 31 5 253 and 31 5 256 to front axle carrier.

15. Support front axle carrier by operating workshop jack 00 2 030.

WARNING

Pay attention to power steering hoses and lines when lowering and raising.

16. Release bolts and lower front axle carrier by a maximum of 4 inches (10 cm).

17. Remove ribbed V-belt. Refer to engine mechanical, accessory drive belts, removal & installation.

18. Release 4x transmission bolts.

19. Release screws and take off holder.

20. Release the oil pan bolts and remove the oil pan.

To install:

21. To install, reverse the removal procedure.

22. Clean sealing faces with special tool 11 4 470.

23. Replace oil sump gasket.

24. Install and tighten oil pan bolts to 84 inch lbs. (10 Nm).

25. Raise the front axle carrier

a. Check threads for damage; if necessary, repair with Helicoil thread inserts.

b. Make sure screws are installed in correct positions.

c. Tighten down first screws and then screws (2, 3, 4), as follows:

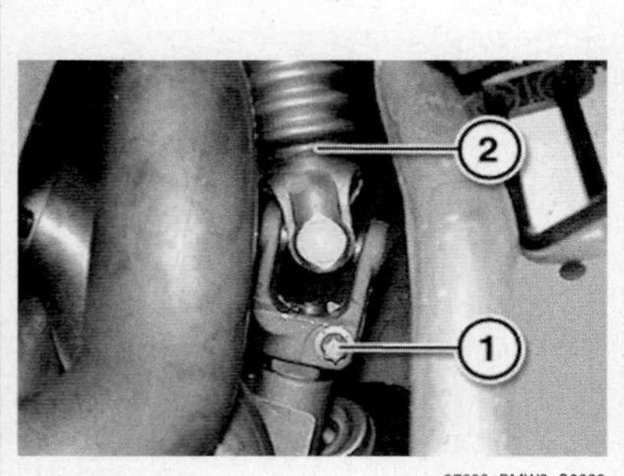

Fig. 150 Release clamping screw and detach steering spindle lower section from power steering gear

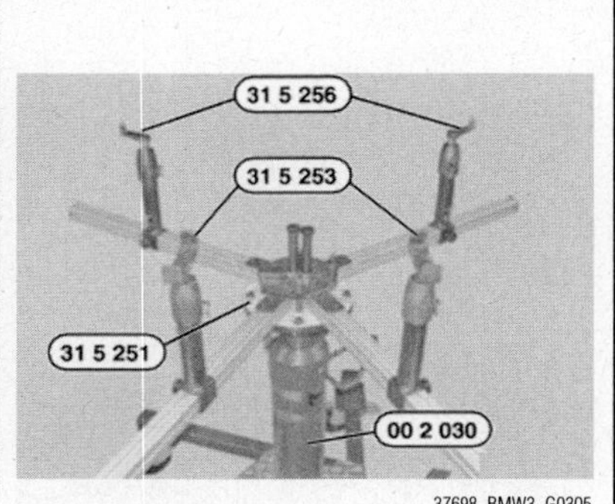

Fig. 152 Engage the special tool with a 2nd person helping completely on workshop jack

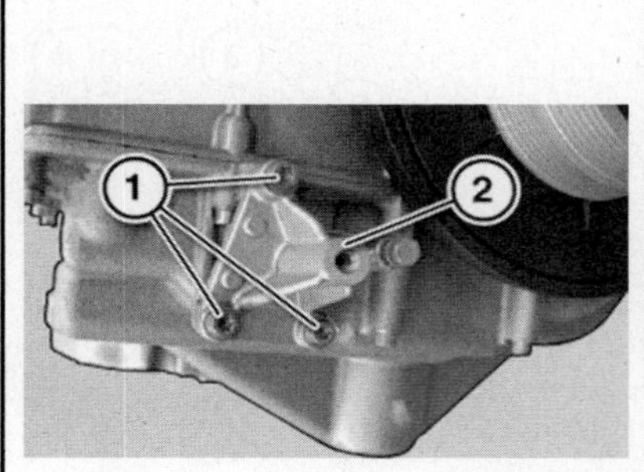

Fig. 154 Release screws and take off holder

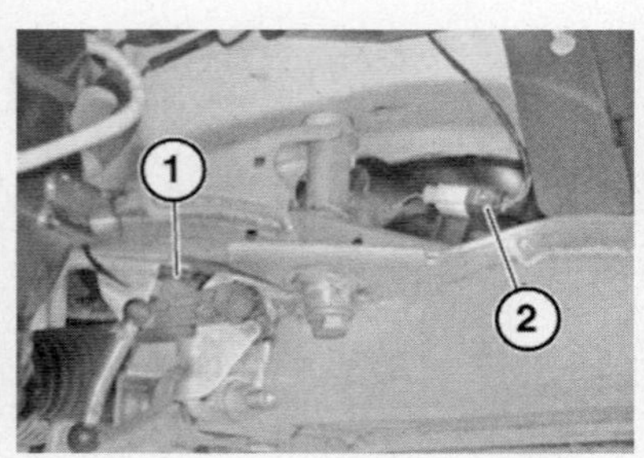

Fig. 151 Disconnect plug connection on ride-height sensor and plug connection for Servotronic electro hydraulic converter

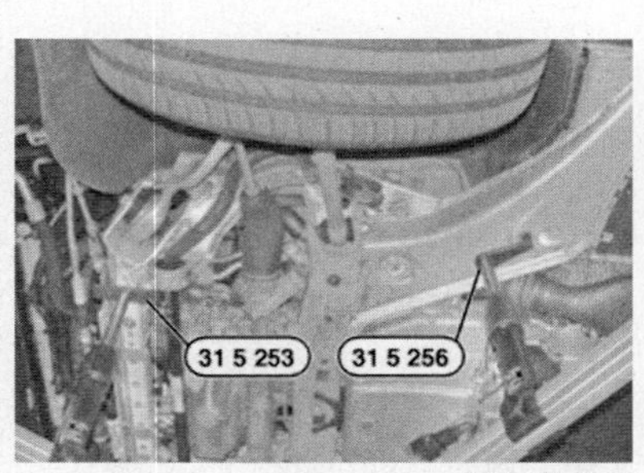

Fig. 153 Align special tools 31 5 253 and 31 5 256 to front axle carrier and support front axle carrier by operating workshop jack 00 2 030

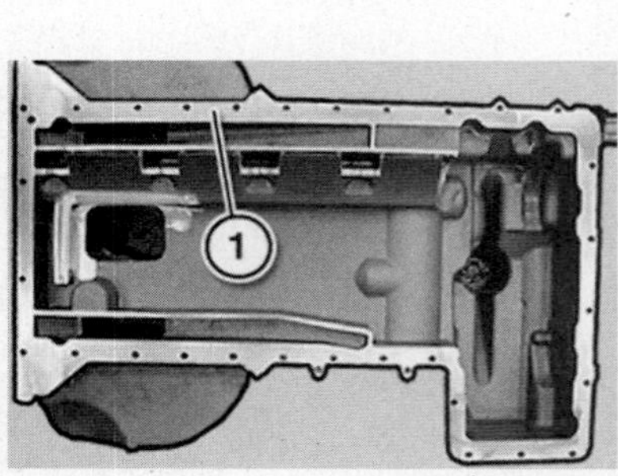

Fig. 155 Clean sealing faces with special tool 11 4 470

- M12: 80 ft. lbs. (108 Nm)
- M10 x 42: 41 ft. lbs. (56 Nm) plus an additional 90° rotation

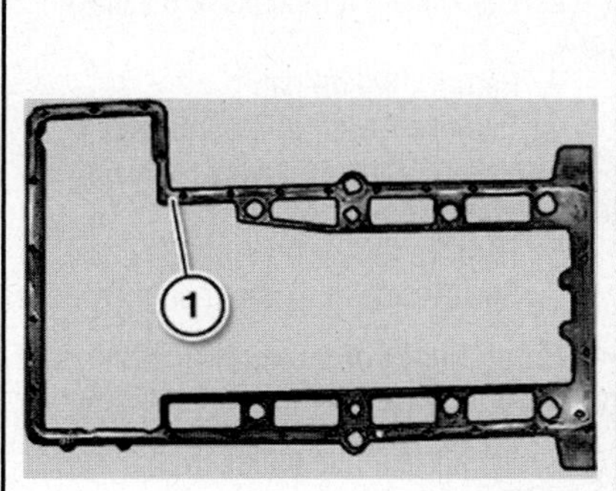

Fig. 156 Replace oil sump gasket

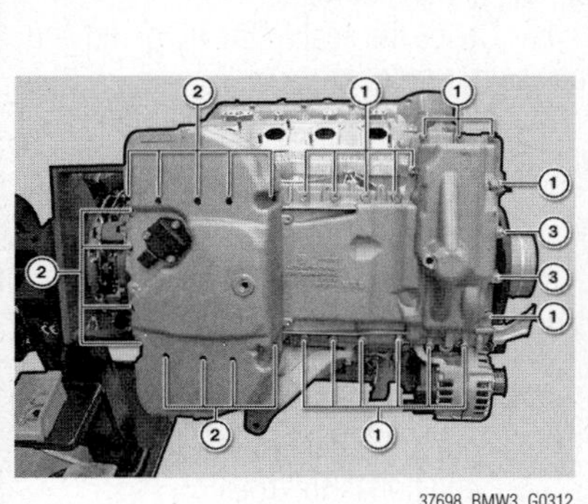

Fig. 157 Overview of oil sump screw/bolt connections M6x30, M6x50 and M6x75

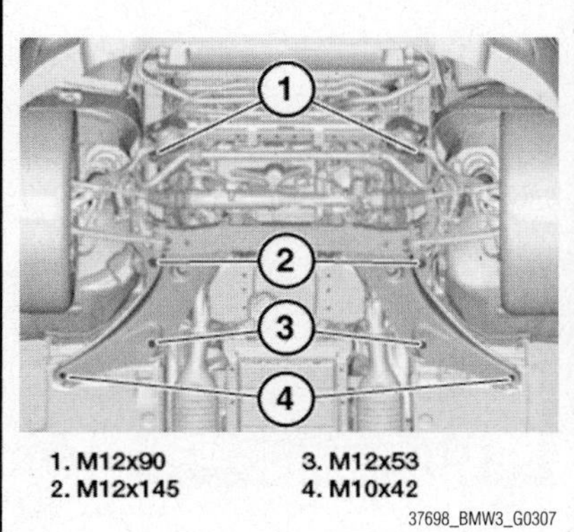

Fig. 158 Make sure screws are installed in correct positions.

26. Connect steering spindle lower section to power steering gear.
    a. Clean thread to remove all remnants of screw securing adhesive.
    b. Lower section of steering spindle can only be attached in one position to the power steering gear.
    c. Replace clamping screw.
    d. Clamping screw must rest in groove of power steering gear.
    e. Tighten to 16 ft. lbs. (21 Nm).
    f. Turn steering wheel in both directions to full lock. The airbag warning lamp must not light up in the process.
27. Replace reinforcing plate screws and tighten to 41 ft. lbs. (56 Nm) plus an additional 90° rotation.
28. Carry out steering angle sensor adjustment.

OIL PUMP

REMOVAL & INSTALLATION

M57 Engine

See Figure 159.

1. Before servicing the vehicle, refer to the precautions.
2. Remove oil pan. Refer to engine mechanical, oil pan, removal & installation
3. Release screw.
4. If necessary, detach oil intake pipe.
5. Release bolts and remove oil pump.

To install:

6. To install, reverse the removal procedure.
7. Replace sealing ring between oil pump and oil intake pipe.
8. Tighten bolts/nuts to specification as follows:

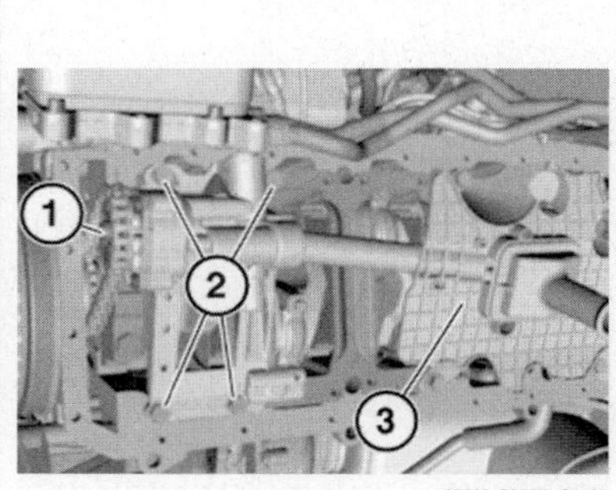

Fig. 159 Release screw, detach oil intake pipe and release bolts to remove oil pump

- Intake pipe to crankcase: 14 ft. lbs. (19 Nm)
- Oil pump to crankcase: 14 ft. lbs. (19 Nm)
- Sprocket to oil pump: 14 ft. lbs. (19 Nm)

N20 and N26 Engines

See Figures 160 through 165.

WARNING

The counterbalance shaft must be adjusted to the motor.

1. Remove the oil pan.

➡When installing, wet special tool2 219 548 with oil to simplify removal and installation.

➡Secure crankshaft with special tool 2 219 548 via the dowel hole.

2. Release screw.

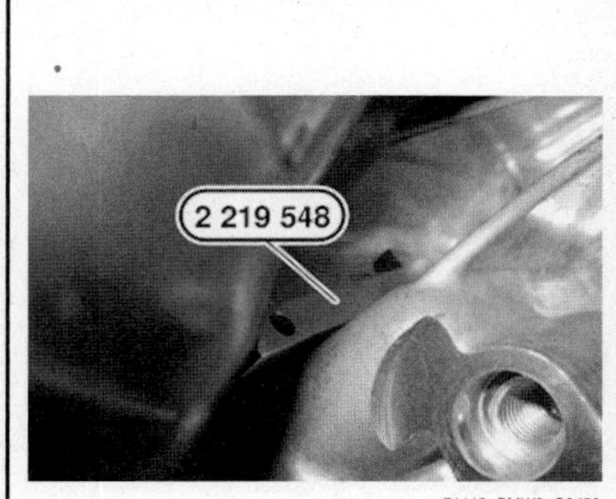

Fig. 160 Installing special tool 2 219 548

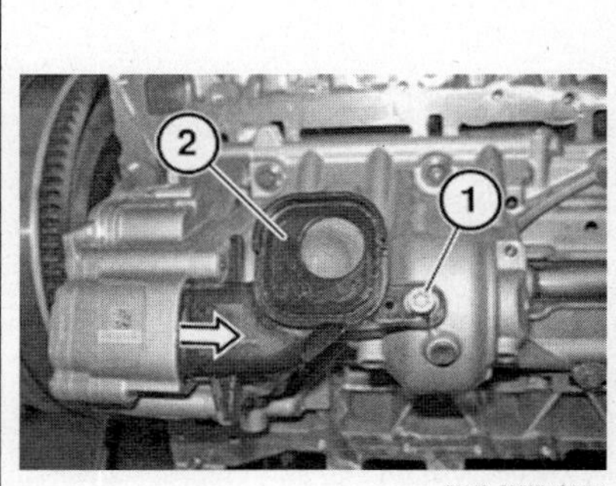

Fig. 161 Releasing screw and detaching intake snorkel in direction of arrow

3. Detach intake snorkel in direction of arrow.

4. Loosen sealing cap using a screwdriver.

➡When installing, position counterbalance shaft with special tool 2 212 825.

5. Secure special tool 2 212 825 on oil pump housing with screw.

6. If special tool 2 212 825 cannot be positioned, the timing must be readjusted.

7. Push back chain tensioner with tensioning rail and secure with special tool 11 4 120.

➡Sprocket must be blocked with special tool 2 318 117 in order to release central bolt.

8. Mount special tool 2 318 117 and secure with screws.

9. Release central bolt for oil pump drive shaft.

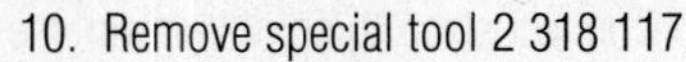

10. Remove special tool 2 318 117.

➡When installing, replace screw. Tightening torque: 70 ft. lbs. (95 Nm)

11. Release screws and pull off chain module off of oil pump drive shaft. Tightening torque: 88 inch lbs. (10 Nm).

WARNING

Observe different screw lengths.

12. Release screws.

13. Release screws, remove oil pump with counterbalance shaft. Tightening torque: 88 inch lbs. (10 Nm).

➡When installing, check spacer bushes for secure seating and damage; replace if necessary.

To install:

To install, reverse the removal procedure.

N52 and N54 Engines

See Figure 166.

1. Before servicing the vehicle, refer to the precautions.
2. Disconnect the negative battery cable.
3. Remove the oil pan.
4. Remove the oil pump intake pipe fasteners and oil pump intake pipe, pull towards transmission.
5. Remove the oil pump pulley bolt.
6. Remove the oil pump mounting bolts.

➡Timing chain of triangular drive is pressed upwards by chain tensioner.

7. Do not remove pulley from assembly.
8. Remove the oil pump pulley, pull towards front of engine bay.
9. Remove the oil pump.

To install:

10. Check the seals on the oil pipes and replace it if necessary. Lubricate the seals with oil and the oil pipes.
11. Check the seal in the oil pump and replace it if necessary.
12. Align twin surface on oil pump to sprocket wheel.
13. Replace all aluminum fasteners and tighten to specification.
    - Oil pump to bedplate: 25 ft. lbs. (34 Nm) plus an additional 180° rotation
    - Chain module to crankcase and oil pump 35 inch lbs. (4 Nm) plus an additional 45° rotation
    - Pulley to oil pump: 15 ft. lbs. (20 Nm) plus an additional 45° rotation
    - Intake pipe to bedplate: 35 inch lbs. (4 Nm) plus an additional 100°rotation

71112_BMW3_G0455

Fig. 162 Loosening sealing cap

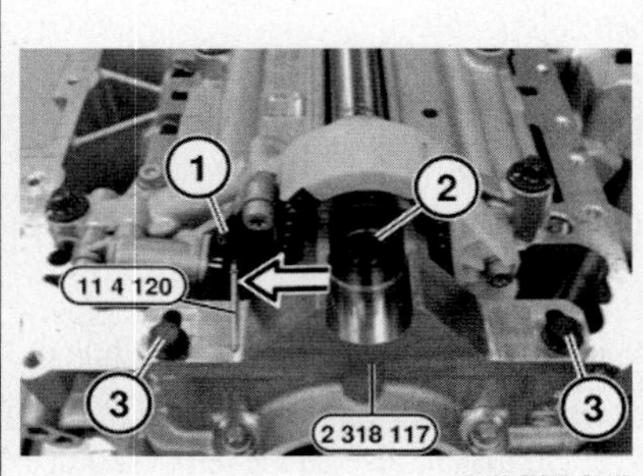

Fig. 164 Pushing back chain tensioner with tensioning rail, securing with special tool and screws and releasing central bolt

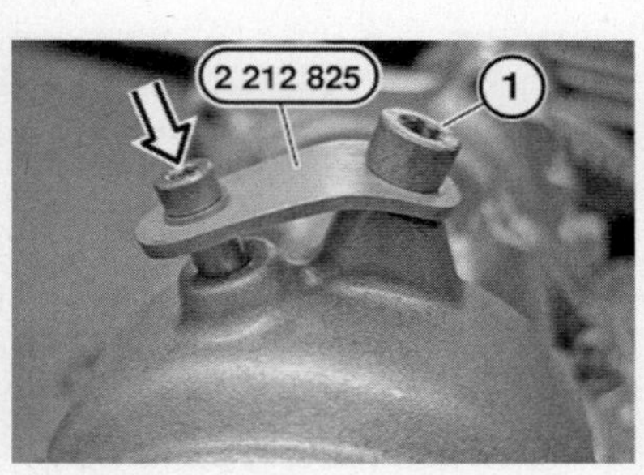

Fig. 163 Securing special tool 2 212 825 on oil pump housing with screw

Fig. 165 Releasing screws and pulling off chain module off of oil pump drive shaft

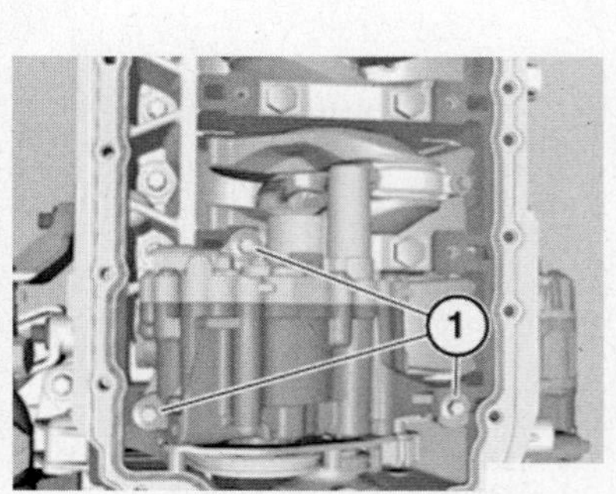

Fig. 166 Oil pump mounting bolts

14. To install, reverse the removal procedure.
15. Fill the engine with oil.
16. Start the engine and check for leaks.

S65 Engine

Oil Pump

See Figures 167 through 177.

1. Before servicing the vehicle, refer to the precautions.
2. Remove oil pan. Refer to engine mechanical, oil pan, removal & installation.
3. Release screws as shown.
4. Release screw, then detach oil pipes from oil pump.
5. Release screw, then detach oil pipes from oil pump.
6. Detach oil pipes from oil pump.
7. Slacken nut on sprocket.
8. Release screw, then fold sliding rail downwards.
9. Remove sprocket wheel from shaft.

WARNING

Chain tensioner piston may fall out.

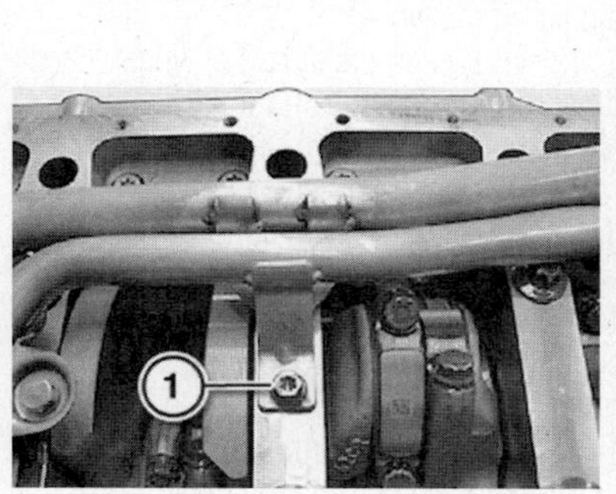

Fig. 169 Release screw, then detach oil pipes from oil pump

Fig. 172 Release screw (1 & 2), then fold sliding rail downwards

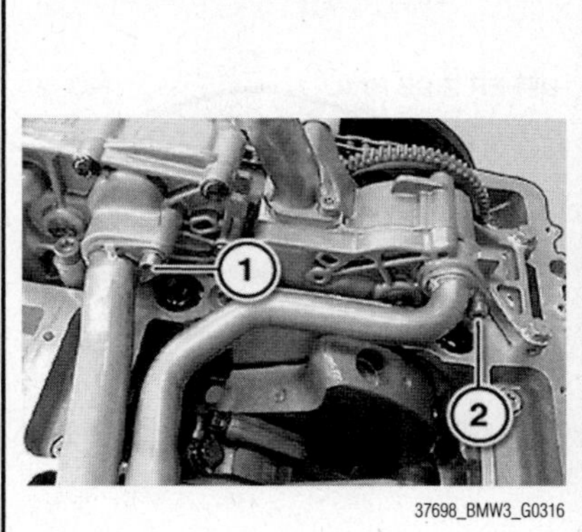

Fig. 167 Release screws (1 & 2)

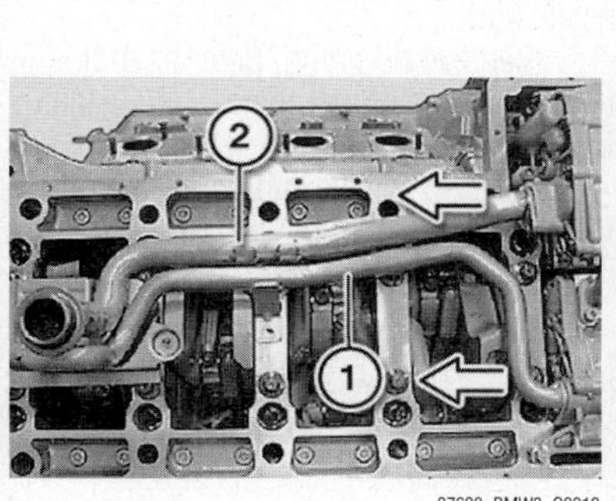

Fig. 170 Detach oil pipes (1 and 2) from oil pump

Fig. 173 Remove sprocket wheel from shaft

Fig. 168 Release screw (1 & 2), then detach oil pipes from oil pump

Fig. 171 Slacken nut on sprocket

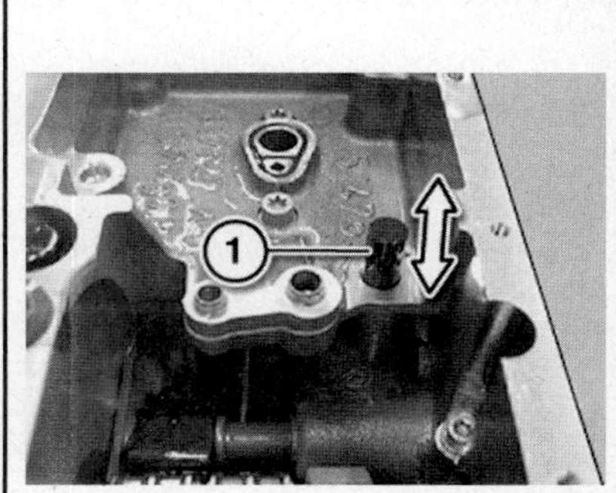

Fig. 174 Remove piston in direction of arrow

10. Remove piston in direction of arrow.
11. Release screws on oil pump.

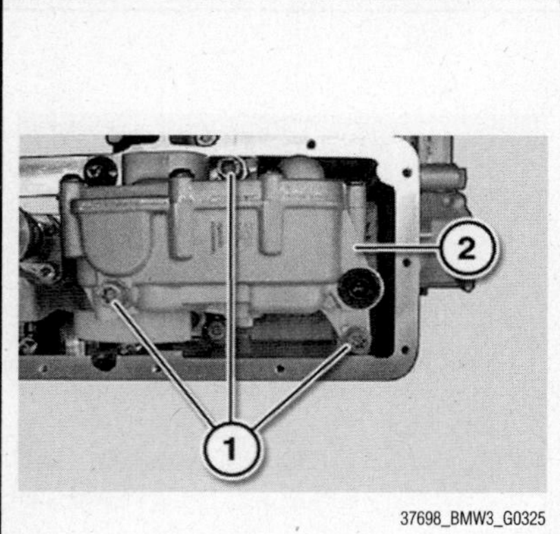

Fig. 175 Release screws on oil pump

Fig. 176 Replace sealing ring

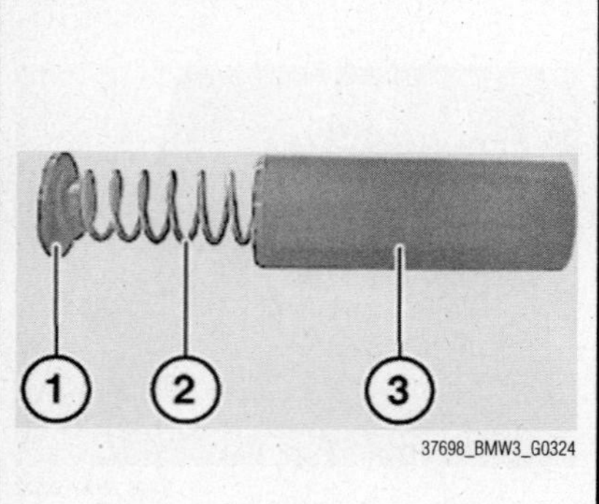

Fig. 177 Arrangement of the oil pump chain tensioner: base valve, spring and piston

To install:

12. To install, reverse the removal procedure.
13. Replace sealing ring.
14. Assemble the oil pump chain tensioner as shown
15. If reusing the sprocket wheel, check dihedron for damage and if necessary replace.
16. Replace microencapsulated nut and tighten to 19 ft. lbs. (25 Nm).
17. Replace oil pipe sealing rings. To facilitate fitting, apply a light coating of engine oil to sealing rings.
18. Clean all sealing surfaces.
19. Replace screws and clean threads before installation.

Oil Return Pump

See Figure 178.

1. Before servicing the vehicle, refer to the precautions.
2. Remove engine oil sump. Refer to engine mechanical, oil pan, removal & installation.
3. Remove oil pump. Refer to engine mechanical, oil pump, removal & installation.
4. Release screws and the return oil pump.

To install:

5. To install, reverse the removal procedure.
6. Tighten bolts to 84 inch lbs. (10 Nm).

PISTONS & RINGS

POSITIONING

See Figures 179 through 183.

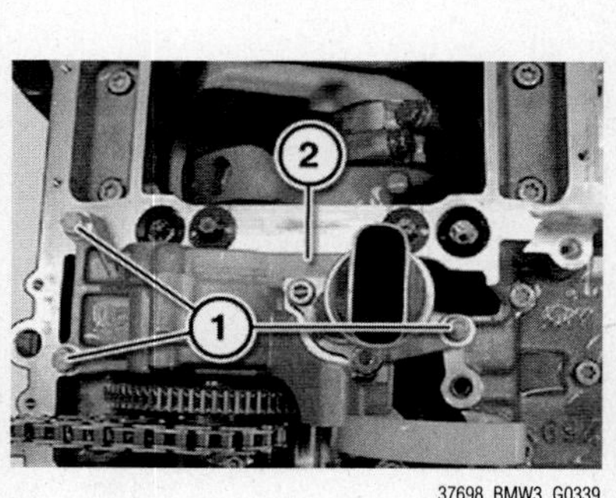

Fig. 178 Release screws and the return oil pump

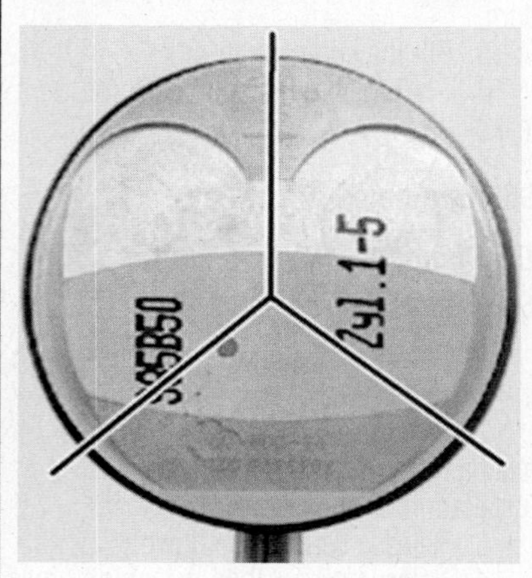

Fig. 179 Offset the contact points of the piston rings by approximately 120° to each other but do not position above the piston pin boss—M57 Engine

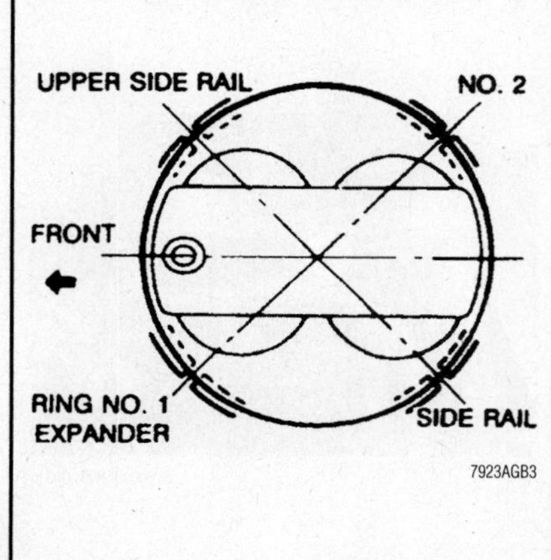

Fig. 180 Piston ring end-gap spacing—N52 and N54 Engines

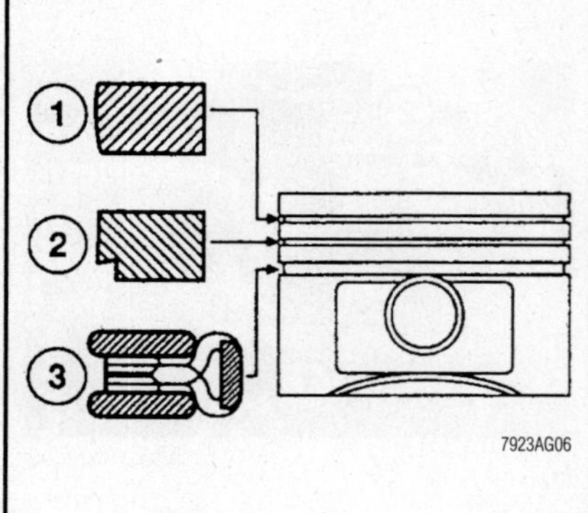

Fig. 181 Compression and oil control ring locations—N52 and N54 Engines

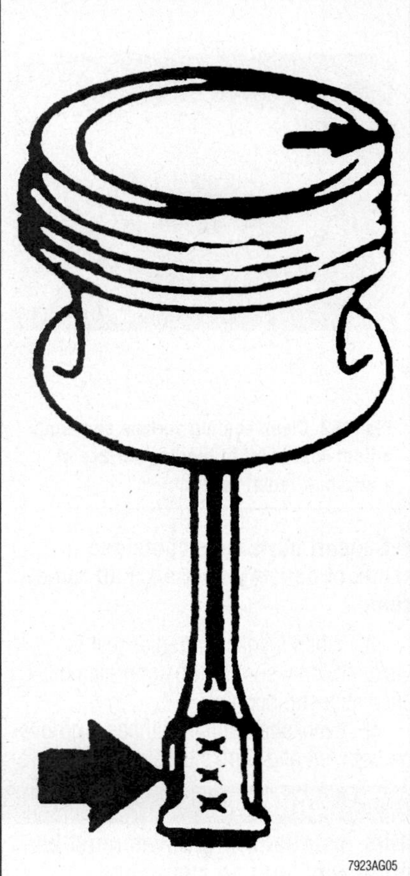

Fig. 182 Connecting rod-to-piston positioning—N52 and N54 Engines

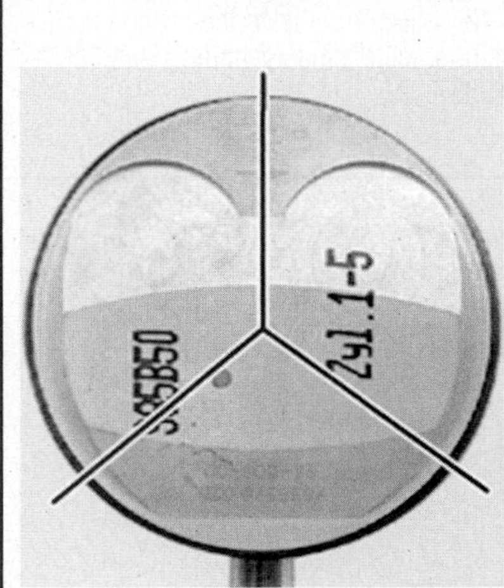

Fig. 183 Offset the contact points of the piston rings by approximately 120° to each other but do not position above the piston pin boss—S65 Engine

REAR MAIN SEAL

REMOVAL & INSTALLATION

M57 Engine

See Figures 184 through 188.

1. Before servicing the vehicle, refer to the precautions.
2. Drain and recycle engine oil.
3. Remove flywheel.
4. Unfasten oil sump screws on transmission end.
5. Loosen oil pan.
6. Release bolt and remove crankshaft sensor in direction of arrow.
7. Remove sensor gear.
8. Release bolts and remove end cover.

**** WARNING**

Check oil sump gasket for damage after removing end cover.

9. If necessary, remove oil sump and replace oil sump gasket.
10. Lubricate contact face of crankshaft.

**** WARNING**

When mounting the end cover with crankshaft seal on the crankshaft, only the "support bushing" may be used as an installation tool.

11. Push on end cover with support bushing straight and without tilting sideways.
12. Insert all screws and tighten down end cover.
13. The old and new crankshaft seal versions can be installed with the support bushing.
14. Make sure dowel sleeves are correctly seated.
15. Fit sensor gear.

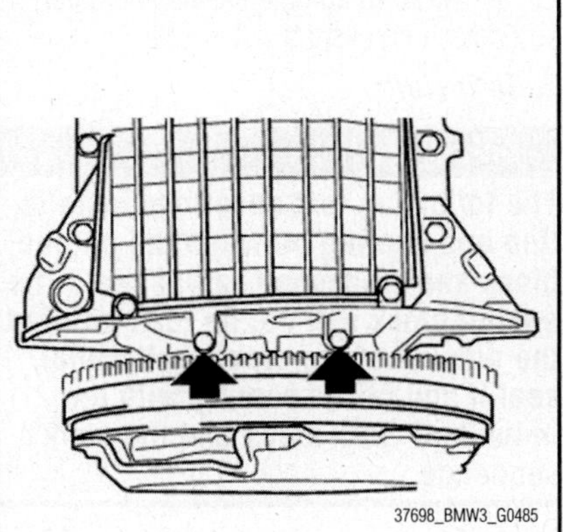

Fig. 184 Unfasten oil sump screws on transmission end

Fig. 186 Push on end cover with support bushing straight and without tilting sideways

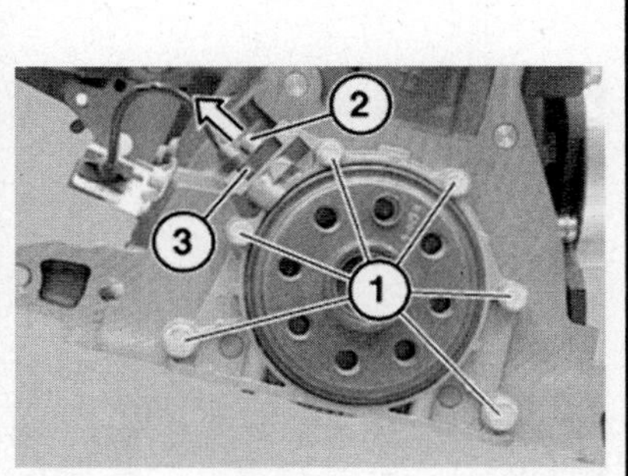

Fig. 185 Release bolt and remove crankshaft sensor in direction of arrow. Release bolts and remove end cover

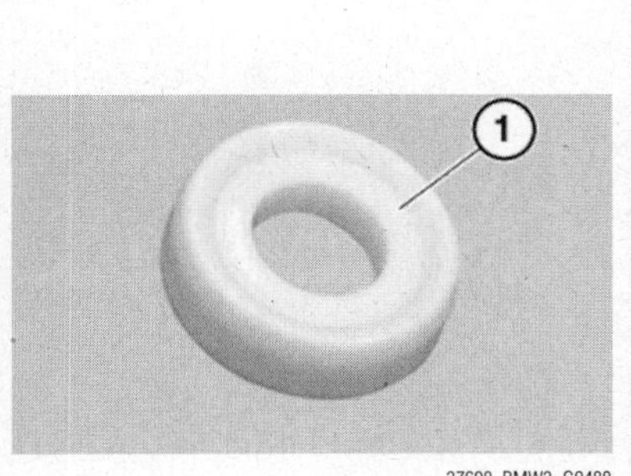

Fig. 187 The old and new crankshaft seal versions can be installed with the support bushing

Fig. 188 Make sure dowel sleeves are correctly seated

WARNING

The end cover is supplied in the set with a built-in radial shaft seal and a support bushing. The support bushing is fitted on the crankshaft seal (to provide protection during transportation and storage).

16. Check engine for leaks.

N52 and N54 Engines

See Figures 189 through 198.

1. Before servicing the vehicle, refer to the precautions.
2. Remove the transmission.
3. Remove the flywheel assembly.

➡Crankshaft radial seal has six removal openings for removal with special tool 11 9 200. If necessary, remove rubber coating on top side of crankshaft radial seal and expose a removal opening.

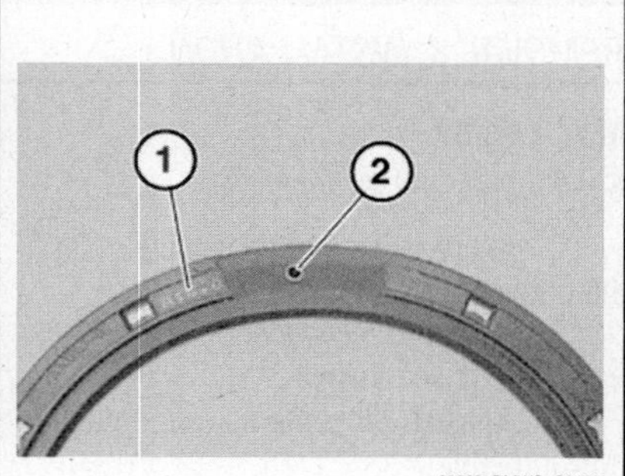

Fig. 190 If necessary, remove rubber coating on top side of crankshaft radial seal and expose a removal opening

4. Fit special tool 11 9 200. Insert sheet metal bolts into removal opening of crankshaft radial seal and fasten without play (do not overtighten sheet metal bolts).
5. Screw in spindle slowly and carefully and detach crankshaft radial seal.

To install:

WARNING

The following text describes installation and sealing between the engine block and crankshaft radial seal. The engine block will not be leak proof at the outside of the crankshaft radial seal if you fail to comply with the individual work steps and the work sequence.

6. Clean sealing surface and degrease thoroughly in area of housing partition.
7. Apply a light coat of oil to running surface of crankshaft radial seal.

Fig. 192 Clean sealing surface and apply a light coat of oil to running surface of crankshaft radial seal

➡Support bushing is contained in scope of delivery of crankshaft radial seal.

8. When crankshaft radial seal is installed, only support bushing may be used as a slip bushing.
9. Crankshaft radial seal has a groove on both left and right sides.

WARNING

After installation, grooves must be filled with sealing compound.

➡The required parts are available from the BMW Parts Service (ETK).

10. Remove screw caps from injector.
11. Screw on metering needle.
12. Insert piston for pressing out.
13. Injector contains the sealing compound Loctite®, manufacturer's number 128357.

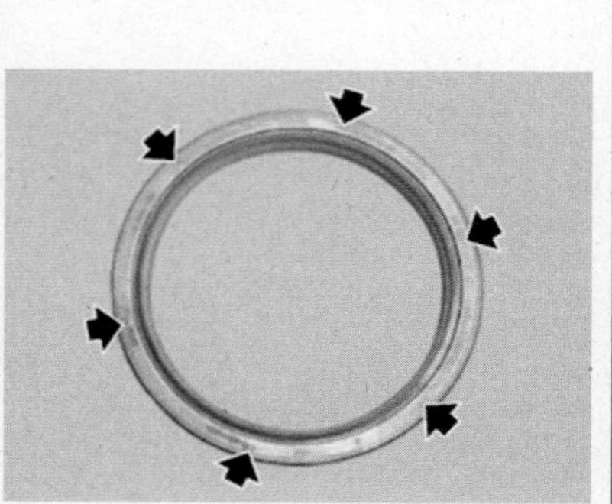

Fig. 189 Crankshaft radial seal has six removal openings for removal with special tool 11 9 200

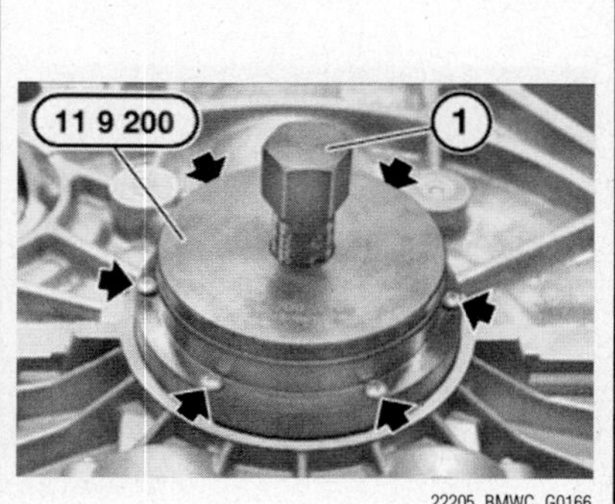

Fig. 191 Fit special tool 11 9 200. Screw in spindle slowly and carefully and detach crankshaft radial seal

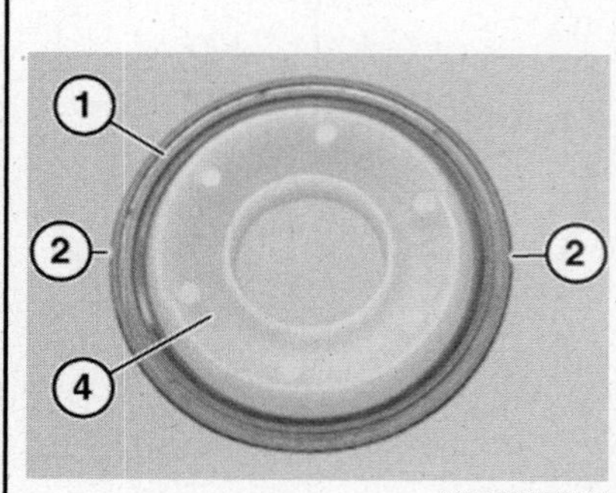

Fig. 193 Crankshaft radial seal, grooves and support bushing

14. Bottle contains the primer Loctite®, manufacturer's number 171000.
15. Fit support bushing with crankshaft radial seal on crankshaft.
16. Align groove centrally to housing partition.
17. Coat both grooves on crankshaft radial seal with Loctite® primer, manufacturer's number 171000, and expose to air for approximately one minute.
18. Push crankshaft radial seal by hand as far as possible onto running surface.
19. Carefully remove support sleeve.

➡Spacer ring is supplied with radial shaft seal.

20. Screw special tool 11 9 182 with bolts (special tool 11 9 184) to crankshaft.

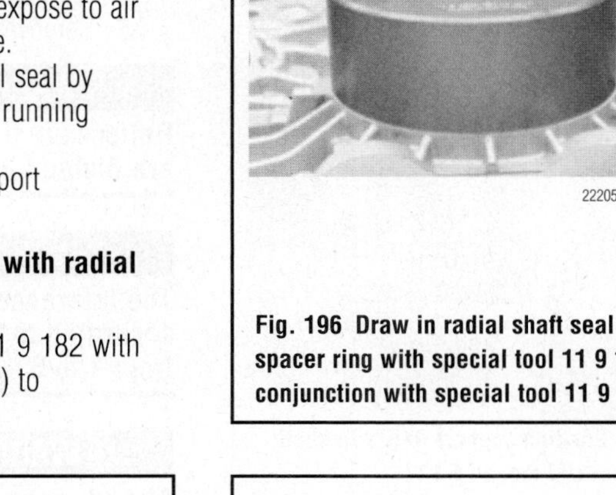

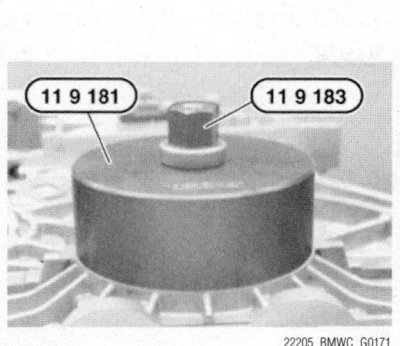

Fig. 196 Draw in radial shaft seal and spacer ring with special tool 11 9 181 in conjunction with special tool 11 9 183

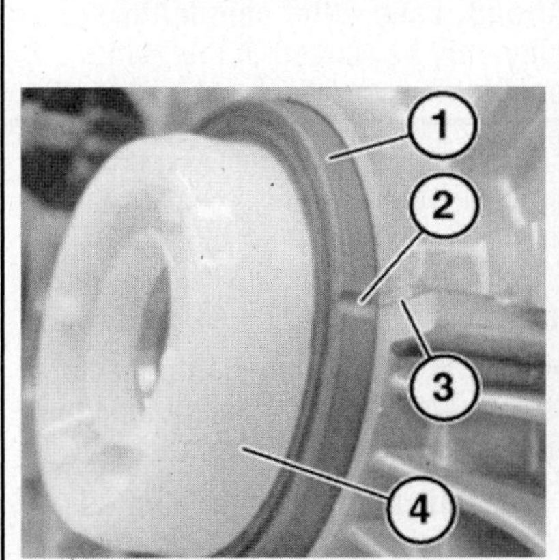

Fig. 194 Crankshaft radial seal, grooves housing partition and support bushing

Fig. 197 Insert brush as far as possible into grooves on crankshaft radial seal in order to coat housing partition on engine block

21. Fit spacer ring on preassembled radial shaft seal.
22. Draw in radial shaft seal and spacer ring with special tool 11 9 181 in conjunction with special tool 11 9 183.
23. Then remove spacer ring again.
24. Before filling with sealing compound, moisten brush with Loctite® primer, manufacturer's number 171000. Insert brush as far as possible into grooves on crankshaft radial seal in order to coat housing partition on engine block.
25. Using injector, fill both grooves flush with Loctite® sealing compound, manufacturer's number 128357.

➡Loctite® primer, manufacturer's number 171000, binds the Loctite® sealing compound, manufacturer's number 128357, and prevents leakage.

26. Coat surface of sealing compound in both grooves with Loctite® primer, manufacturer's number 171000.

S65 Engine

See Figures 199 through 204.

1. Before servicing the vehicle, refer to the precautions.
2. Remove transmission.
3. Remove clutch.
4. Remove flywheel.
5. Drill a 3 mm hole into shaft seal.

⁂ WARNING

Risk of damage. Remove chips/shavings immediately.

6. Screw in special tool 23 0 490 and drive out radial shaft seal with impact weight.
7. Remove remnants of sealant from sealant outlet on left and right.

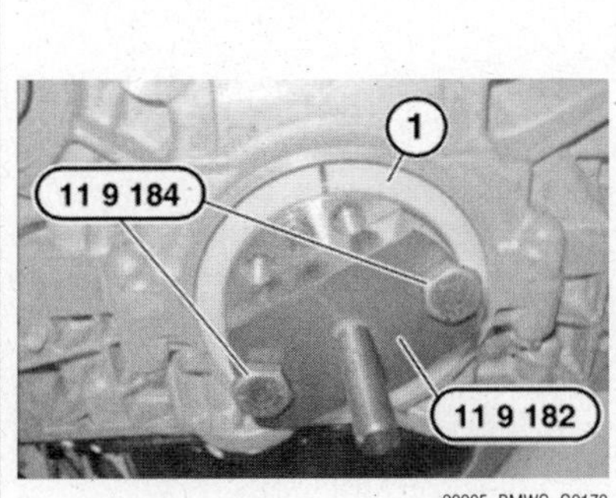

Fig. 195 Spacer ring is supplied with radial shaft seal. Screw special tool 11 9 182 with bolts (special tool 11 9 184) to crankshaft

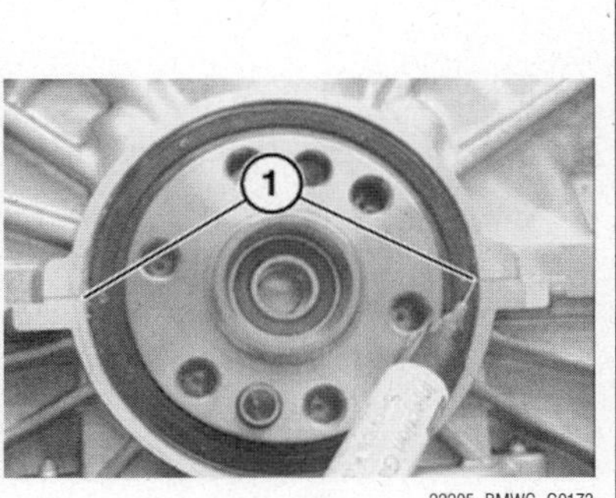

Fig. 198 Insert brush as far as possible into grooves on crankshaft radial seal in order to coat housing partition on engine block

Fig. 199 Screw in special tool 23 0 490 and drive out radial shaft seal with impact weight

To install:

8. Apply Drei Bond sealant 1209 to sealant outlet on left and right.

✲✲ WARNING

Special tool 11 5 311 must rest flat on crankshaft.

9. Mount special tool 11 5 311 with bolts.

10. Position support ring with shaft seal on special tool 11 5 311. Push shaft seal uniformly in direction of arrow over support ring onto special tool 11 5 311.

11. Position shaft seal approximately 0.195 in (5 mm) before crankcase.

12. Remove support ring.

➡Support ring is no longer needed.

13. Press in shaft seal with special tools 11 5 312 and 11 5 313.

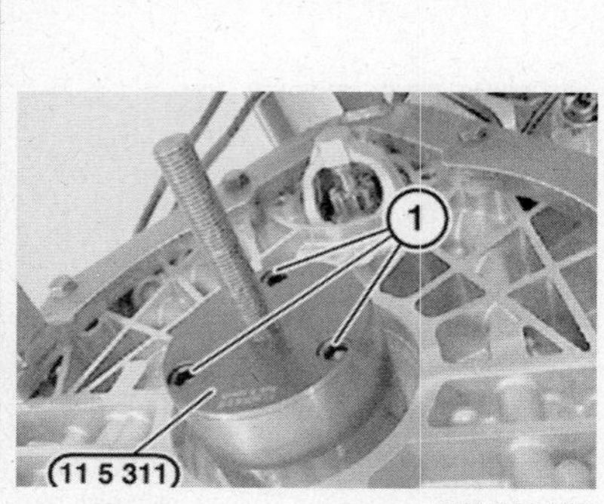

Fig. 200 Apply Drei Bond sealant 1209 to sealant outlet on left and right

Fig. 201 Mount special tool 11 5 311 with bolts

14. Settling time of radial shaft seal approximately 1 hour.

15. Correct engine oil level if necessary.

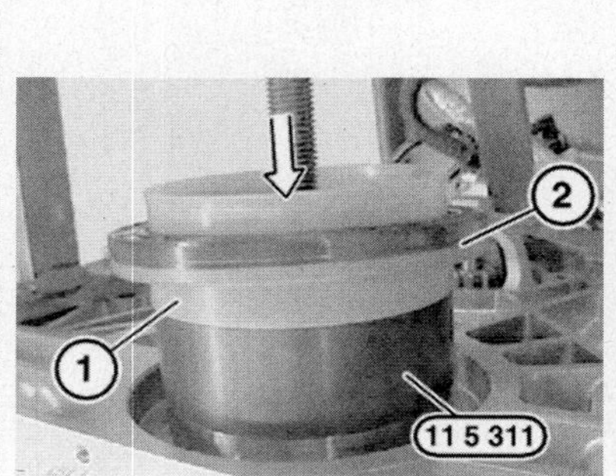

Fig. 202 Position support ring with shaft seal on special tool 11 5 311

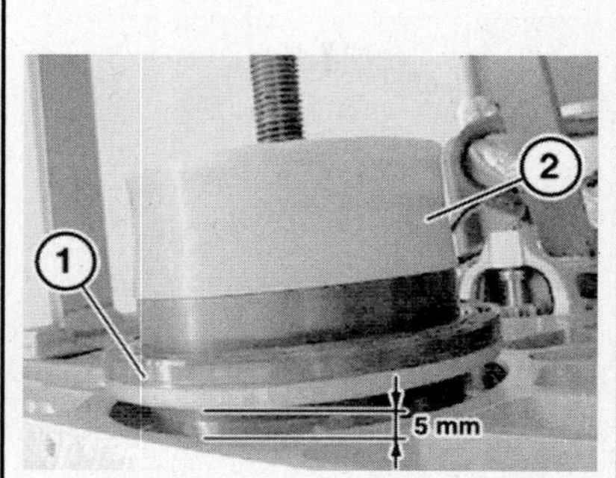

Fig. 203 Position shaft seal approximately 0.195 in (5 mm) before crankcase and remove support ring

Fig. 204 Press in shaft seal with special tools 11 5 312 and 11 5 313

ROCKER ARMS

REMOVAL & INSTALLATION

N20 and N26 Engines

See Figures 205 through 207.

1. Remove cylinder head cover.
2. Remove intermediate lever.
3. Remove exhaust camshaft.

✲✲ WARNING

Roller cam followers on intake side are divided into bearing classes.

✲✲ WARNING

The tolerance classes are marked according to the graphic in numbers from 1 to 5.

✲✲ WARNING

Already used roller cam followers may only be reused in the same position.

4. Detach roller cam followers from hydraulic valve clearance compensating element and remove.

5. Place all roller cam followers in neat order on special tool 11 4 481.

➡Prior to installation of intermediate levers, ensure proper installation position of roller cam followers.

Classification of roller cam follower intake:

a. Standard: Number 3. standard.
b. Number 2. slow idle.
c. Number 4. fast idle.

In case of repair: rough idling speed.

6. Repair: 1

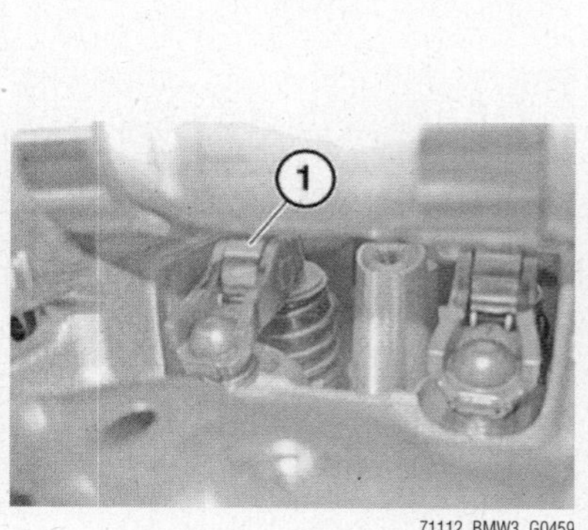

Fig. 205 Detaching roller cam followers

a. Number 1. lower engine speed in idle.

b. Number 5. higher engine speed in idle.

7. Detach roller cam follower on exhaust side from hydraulic valve clearance compensating element and remove.

8. Place all roller cam followers in neat order on special tool 11 4 482 .

➡Prior to installation of exhaust camshaft, ensure proper installation position of roller cam followers.

9. Remove hydraulic valve clearance compensating element on intake side in direction of arrow.

➡When installing, if hydraulic valve clearance compensating elements are reused, they must be placed together with rocker arms in neat order in special tool 11 4 481.

Fig. 206 Detaching roller cam follower on exhaust side from hydraulic valve clearance

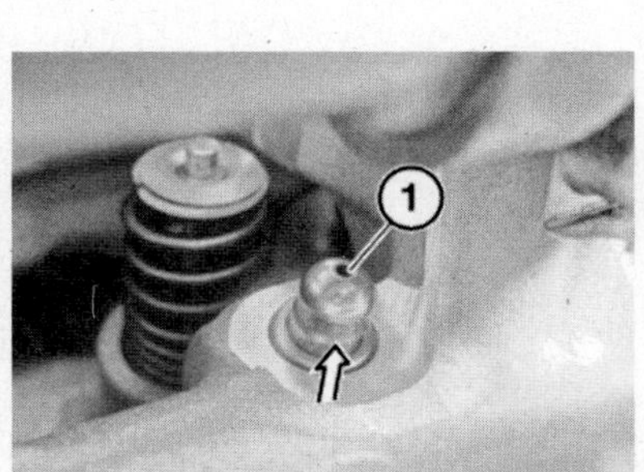

Fig. 207 Removing hydraulic valve clearance compensating element on intake side in direction of arrow

Fig. 208 Removing hydraulic valve clearance compensating element on exhaust side in direction of arrow

10. Remove hydraulic valve clearance compensating element on exhaust side in direction of arrow.

➡When installing, if hydraulic valve clearance compensating elements are reused, they must be placed together with rocker arms in neat order in special tool 11 4 482.

To install:

To install, reverse the removal procedure noting the following.

N55 Engine

See Figures 209 through 212.

1. Remove cylinder head cover.
2. Remove intermediate lever.
3. Remove exhaust camshaft.

WARNING

Roller cam followers on intake side are divided into bearing classes.

WARNING

The tolerance classes are marked according to the graphic in numbers from 1 to 5.

WARNING

Already used roller cam followers may only be reused in the same position.

4. Loosen and remove roller cam followers from hydraulic valve clearance compensating element.

5. Place all roller cam followers in neat order on special tool 11 4 481 .

➡Prior to installation of intermediate levers, ensure proper installation position of roller cam followers.

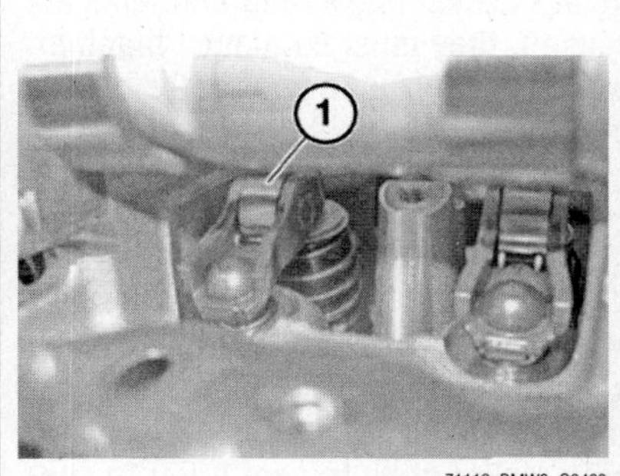

Fig. 209 Removing roller cam followers from hydraulic valve clearance compensating element

Classification of roller cam follower intake:

a. Standard: Number 3. standard.

b. Number 2. slow idle.

c. Number 4. fast idle.

In case of repair: rough idling speed:

a. Repair: 1

b. Number 1. slow speed in idle.

c. Number 5. high speed in idle.

6. Loosen and remove roller cam followers on exhaust side from hydraulic valve clearance compensating element.

7. Place all roller cam followers in neat order on special tool 11 4 482.

➡Prior to installation of exhaust camshaft, ensure proper installation position of roller cam followers.

8. Remove hydraulic valve clearance compensating element on intake side in direction of arrow.

Fig. 210 Removing roller cam followers on exhaust side from hydraulic valve clearance compensating element

➡**When installing, if hydraulic valve clearance compensating elements are reused, they must be placed together with rocker arms in neat order in special tool 11 4 481.**

9. Remove hydraulic valve clearance compensating element on exhaust side in direction of arrow.

➡**When installing, if hydraulic valve clearance compensating elements are reused, they must be placed together with rocker arms in neat order in special tool 11 4 482.**

To install:

To install, reverse the removal procedure noting the following.

10. Assemble engine.
11. Check function of DME; if necessary, readjust uniform mixture distribution.

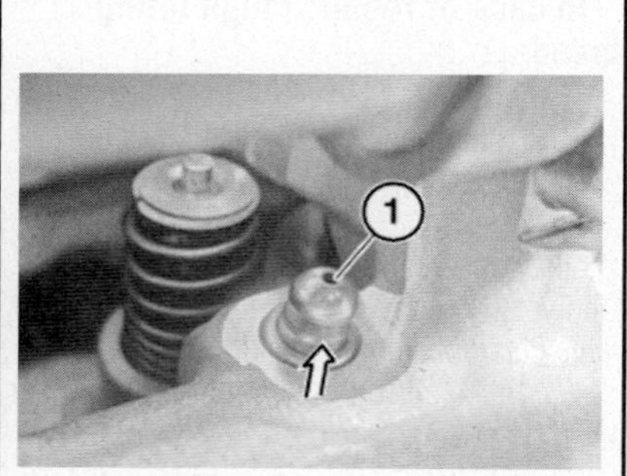

Fig. 211 Removing hydraulic valve clearance compensating element on intake side in direction of arrow

Fig. 212 Removing hydraulic valve clearance compensating element on exhaust side in direction of arrow

VALVE COVERS

REMOVAL & INSTALLATION

M57 Engine

See Figures 213 through 216.

1. Before servicing the vehicle, refer to the precautions.
2. Remove fan with fan cowl. Refer to engine cooling, engine fan, removal & installation
3. Remove air filter. Refer to engine mechanical, air cleaner, removal & installation.
4. Remove all injectors. Refer to diesel fuel system, injectors, removal & installation.

WARNING

Protect alternator against engine oil. Cover alternator with suitable apparatus.

5. Release screws as shown.
6. Remove suction pipe in direction of arrow.
7. Release all bolts (arrows).
8. Release bolts from outside to inside.
9. Remove cylinder head cover.
10. Release screws (arrows).
11. Replace profile gaskets.
12. Sealing faces clean and free of seal debris.
13. Remove gasket debris from sealing faces of cylinder head and clean.

To install:

14. To install, reverse the removal procedure.
15. Apply a bead of Drei Bond® 1209 sealing compound, approximately 0.117 in. (3 mm) wide and 0.078 in. (2 mm) high, in area of joints.

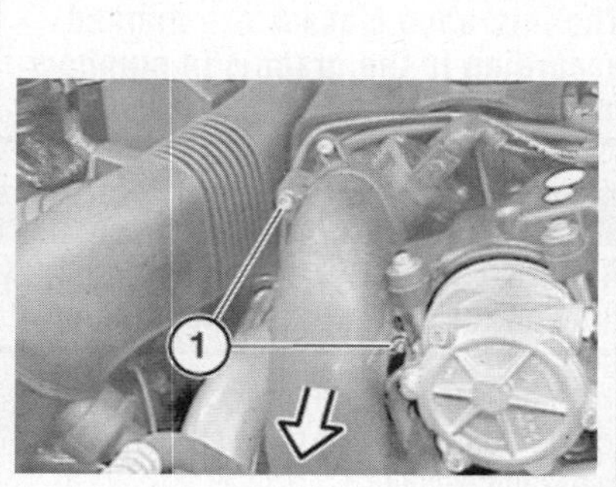

Fig. 213 Release screws

16. First tighten bolts from inside to outside.
17. Tighten down outer bolts diagonally and evenly.

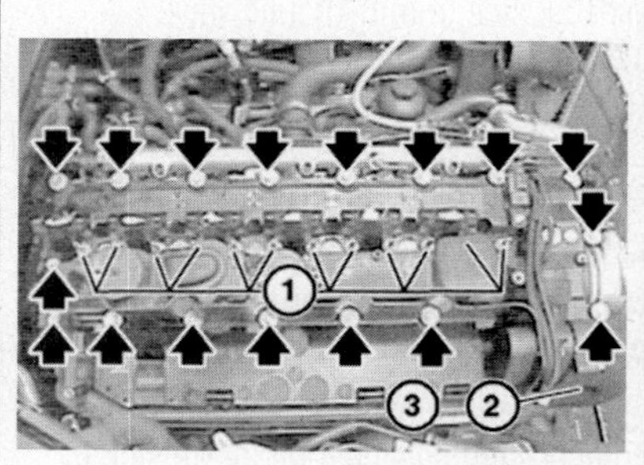

Fig. 214 Release all bolts (arrows), release bolts from outside to inside and remove cylinder head cover from cylinder head

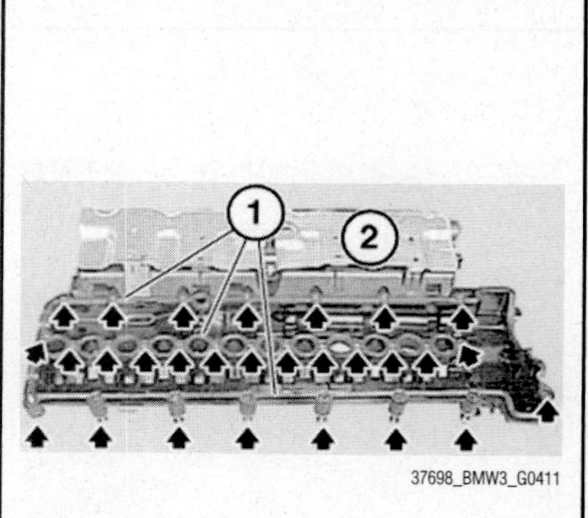

Fig. 215 Release screws (arrows), remover profile gaskets and debris from sealing faces

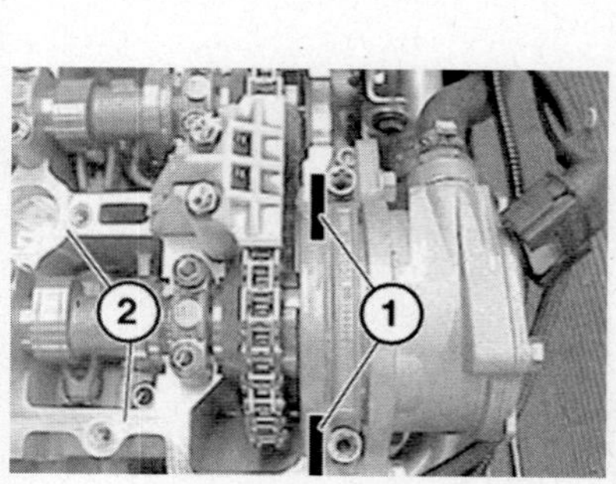

Fig. 216 Apply a bead of Drei Bond 1209 sealing compound, approximately 3 mm wide and 2 mm high, in area of joints

18. Fit charge air hoses dry and without grease.

N52 Engine

See Figure 217.

1. Before servicing the vehicle, refer to the precautions.
2. Remove ignition coils.
3. Remove ignition wiring harness in valve cover area.
4. Remove tension strut.
5. Unlock and detach vent hose.
6. If necessary, pull off metal bracket.
7. Remove screws on electric servomotor.

➡A further screw, which cannot be seen in the picture, must be Removed under the electric servomotor.

8. Remove screw on electric servomotor.
9. Remove servomotor.
10. If necessary, remove nuts.
11. If necessary, remove secondary air valve.

WARNING

Observe different screw lengths. Installation location of screws is specified by the different bushing shapes.

12. Remove screws in area.
13. Remove threaded pin.
14. Remove slotted sleeves.

To install:

15. To install, reverse the removal procedure.
16. Clean all sealing faces.

WARNING

Do not use any metal-cutting tools.

17. Replace gaskets.
18. Slotted sleeves for guiding ignition coils in valve cover must be replaced.
19. Replace aluminum screws.
20. Tighten bolts/nuts to specification as follows:
    - Electric servomotor to cylinder head and to valve cover: 8 ft. lbs. (10 Nm)
    - Secondary air valve to cylinder head: 6 ft. lbs. (8 Nm)
    - Valve cover to cylinder head: 7ft. lbs. (9 Nm)

N54 Engine

See Figure 218.

1. Before servicing the vehicle, refer to the precautions.
2. Disconnect negative battery lead.

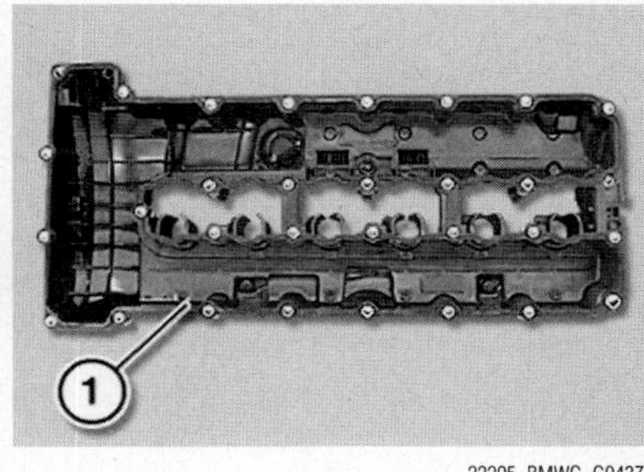

Fig. 218 Valve cover showing seal and mounting bolt locations

3. Remove acoustic cover.
4. Remove rod-type ignition coils.
5. Unclip wiring harness for injectors.
6. Remove injectors.
7. Remove tension strut.
8. Remove fresh air duct.
9. Disconnect vacuum lines and lay to one side.
10. Remove special screw with special tool 11 8 620.
11. Remove screws on valve cover.

To install:

12. To install, reverse the removal procedure.
13. Replace seal. Press gasket into valve cover.
14. Tighten valve cover to cylinder head bolts to 6 ft. lbs. (9 Nm).

S65 Engine

See Figures 219 through 221.

WARNING

Aluminum-magnesium material. No steel fasteners may be used due to the threat of electrochemical corrosion. A magnesium crankcase requires aluminum fasteners exclusively. Aluminum fasteners must be replaced each time they are removed. The end faces of aluminum fasteners are painted blue for purposes of identification. Torque specifications and torque angles must be observed for risk of damage.

1. Before servicing the vehicle, refer to the precautions.
2. Remove intake air manifold. Refer to engine mechanical, intake manifold, removal & installation.

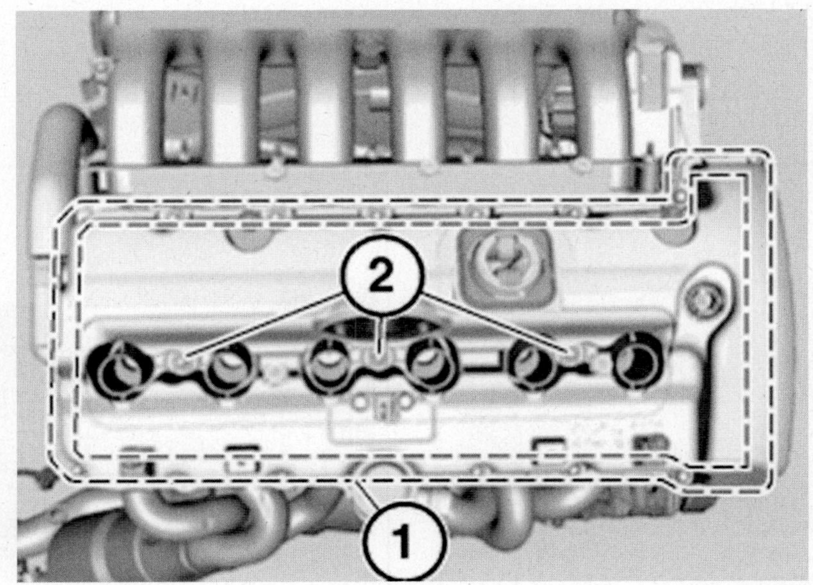

Fig. 217 Installation location of screws (1 and 2) is specified by the different bushing shapes

Fig. 219 Release bolts along line

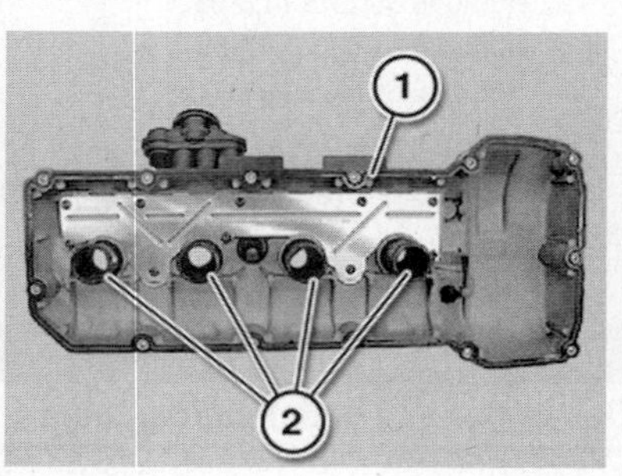

Fig. 220 Align gasket on valve cover groove and press in so that it is free from tension. Check rubber on spark plug tube for damage. Apply a light coating of engine oil prior to installation.

Fig. 221 Coat contact surfaces of joint with Drei Bond 1209.

3. Remove ignition coils.
4. Disconnect plug connection at camshaft sensors.
5. Release bolts along line, then release park plug tube.

To install:

6. To install, reverse the removal procedure.
7. Align new gasket on valve cover groove and press in so that it is free from tension.
8. Check rubber on spark plug tube for damage. Apply a light coating of engine oil prior to installation.
9. Coat contact surfaces of joint with Drei Bond® 1209.
10. Clean seal residue from sealing surfaces.
11. Check decoupling element for damage and replace if necessary.
12. Install valve cover.
13. Align spark plug tubes.
14. Tighten down all retaining elements diagonally from inside to outside.
15. Tighten decoupling adapter screw to valve cover to 48 inch lbs. (6 Nm).

VALVE LASH

ADJUSTMENT

All engines are equipped with hydraulic valve lash adjusters. No adjustments are possible.

ENGINE PERFORMANCE & EMISSION CONTROLS

CAMSHAFT POSITION (CMP) SENSOR

LOCATION

See Figures 222 through 225.

REMOVAL & INSTALLATION

M57 Engine

See Figure 226.

1. Before servicing the vehicle, refer to the precautions.
2. Read out fault memory of DDE control unit; if necessary, work through test schedules.
3. Switch **OFF** ignition.
4. Remove the acoustic cover.
   a. Release screws.

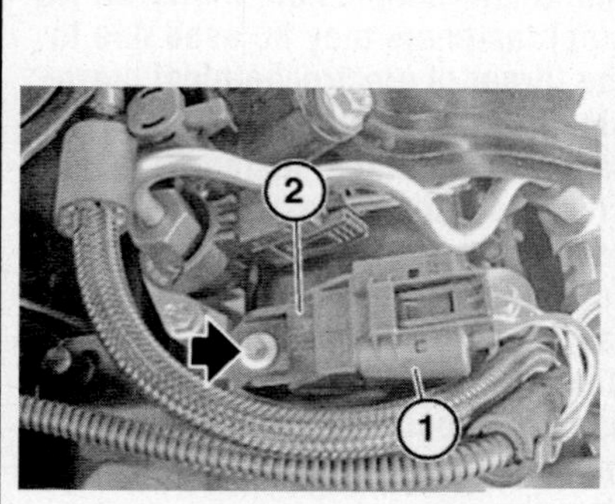

Fig. 222 CMP sensor and connector location—M57 Engine

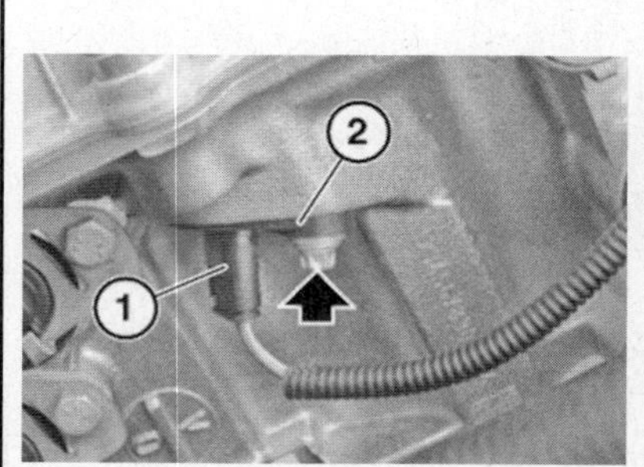

Fig. 223 Intake CMP sensor and connector location— N52 and N54 engines

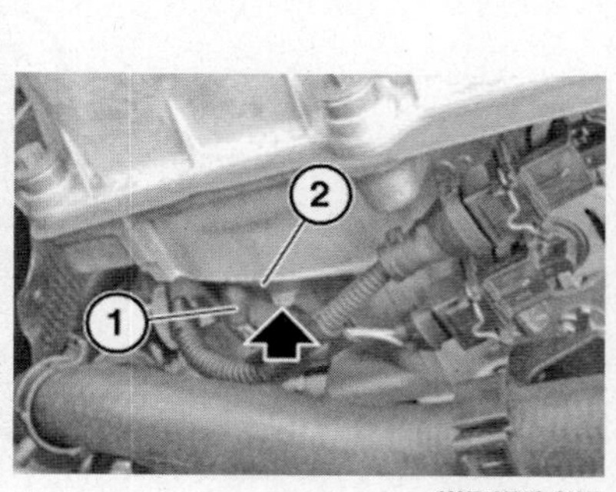

Fig. 224 Exhaust CMP sensor and connector location— N52 and N54 engines

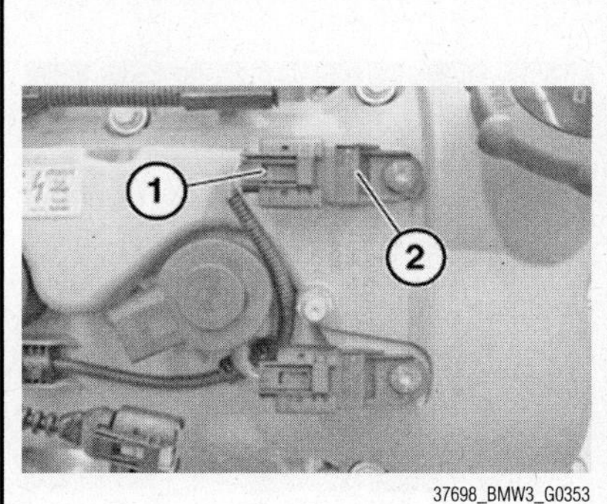

Fig. 225 CMP sensor and connector location—S65 Engine

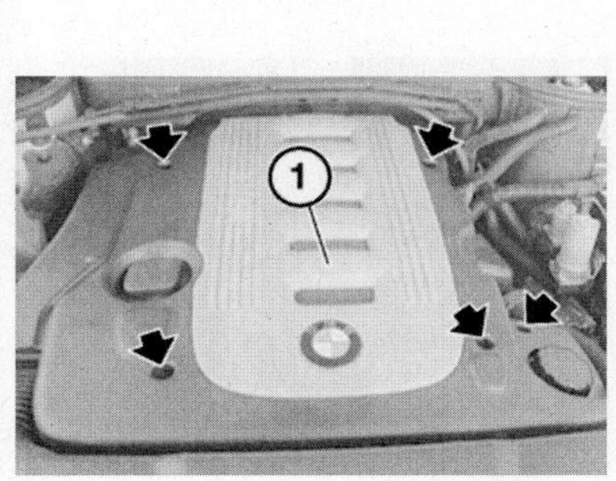

Fig. 226 Raise front acoustic cover and remove

b. Raise front acoustic cover and remove.
5. Unlock plug and remove.
6. Release screw.
7. Remove pulse generator.

To install:

8. To install, reverse the removal procedure.
9. Check sealing ring for damage and replace if necessary.
10. Tighten sensor to 40 inch lbs. (4.5 Nm).

N52 and N54 Engines

1. Before servicing the vehicle, refer to the precautions.
2. Read out fault memory of DME control unit; if necessary, work through test schedules
3. Switch ignition **OFF**.
4. Remove radiator cover.
5. Remove plug connector and pull off.
6. Remove screw.
7. Remove pulse generator.

To install:

8. To install, reverse the removal procedure.
9. If equipped, replace sealing ring and coat with anti-seize agent.
10. Tighten sensor to 7 ft. lbs. (9 Nm).
11. Check for stored fault messages, rectify faults and clear the fault memory.

S65 Engine

1. Before servicing the vehicle, refer to the precautions.
2. Read out fault memory of DME control unit; if necessary, work through test schedules .
3. Turn engine **OFF**.
4. On the left side, remove intake filter housing. Refer to engine mechanical, air filter housing, removal & installation.
5. On the right side, release and raise the coolant expansion tank.

➡Do not disconnect the hoses.

6. Remove ignition coil cover.
7. Release plug connector and pull off.
8. Release screw and remove pulse generator.

To install:

9. To install, reverse the removal procedure.
10. Replace sealing ring and coat with anti-seize agent.
11. Tighten camshaft sensor to 36 inch lbs. (4 Nm) plus an additional 45° rotation
12. Clear the fault memory.

CRANKSHAFT POSITION (CKP) SENSOR

LOCATION

See Figures 227 through 229.

REMOVAL & INSTALLATION

M57 Engine

1. Before servicing the vehicle, refer to the precautions.
2. Read fault memory of DDE control unit.
3. Remove starter motor. Refer to engine electrical, starter, removal & installation.
4. Pull plug off pulse generator.
5. Detach mating connector from holder.
6. Unscrew bolt.
7. Remove pulse generator.

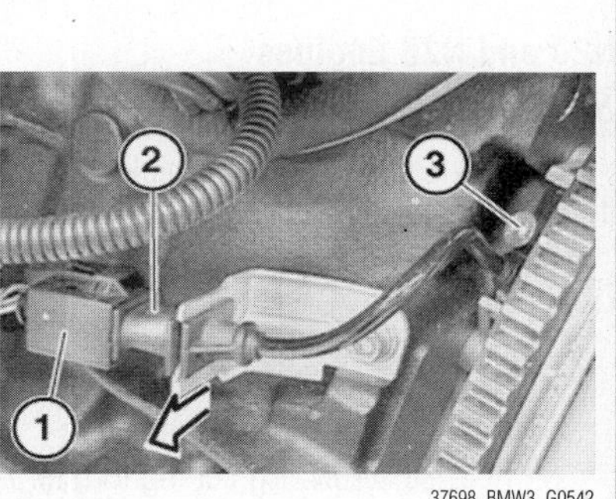

Fig. 227 CKP sensor plug, mating connector and sensor location—M57 Engine

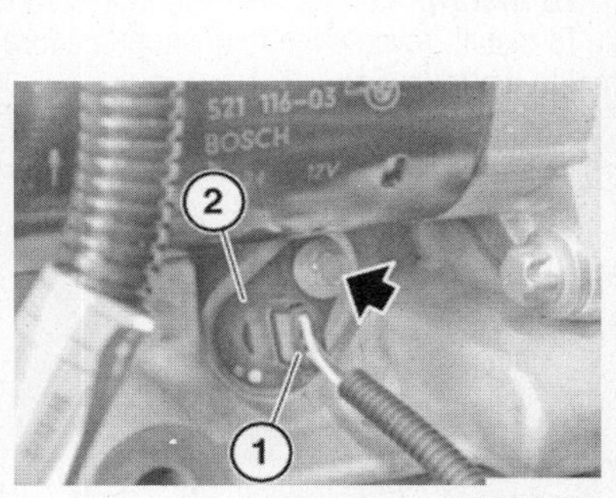

Fig. 228 CKP sensor and connector location— N52 and N54 engines

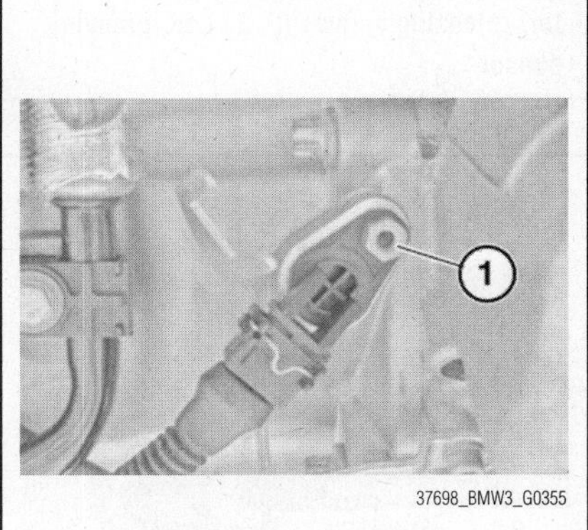

Fig. 229 CKP sensor location— S65 Engine

To install:

8. To install, reverse the removal procedure.

9. Clear DDE fault memory.

N20 and N26 Engines

See Figures 230 and 231.

1. Before servicing the vehicle, refer to the precautions.
2. Read out the fault memory of the DME control unit.
3. Switch off ignition.
4. Remove starter motor.
5. Unlock connector and remove.
6. Release screw. Tightening torque: 70 inch lbs. (8 Nm)
7. Remove connector housing from crankcase.
8. Release screw. Tightening torque: 70 inch lbs. (8 Nm)
9. Pull pulse sensor from crankcase and remove.

To install:

To install, reverse the removal procedure noting the following.

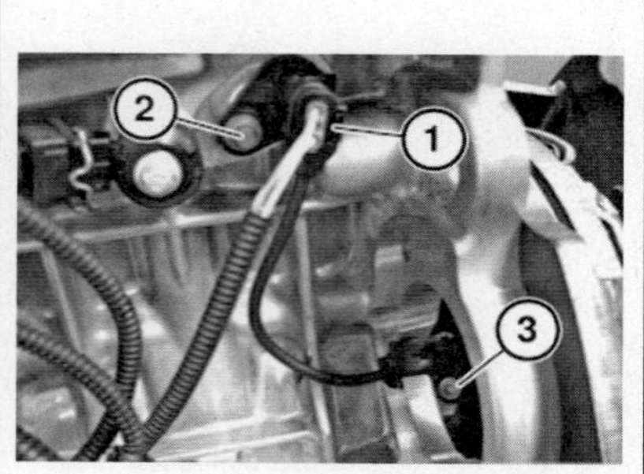

Fig. 230 Unlocking and removing connector, releasing screws (2, 3) and removing sensor

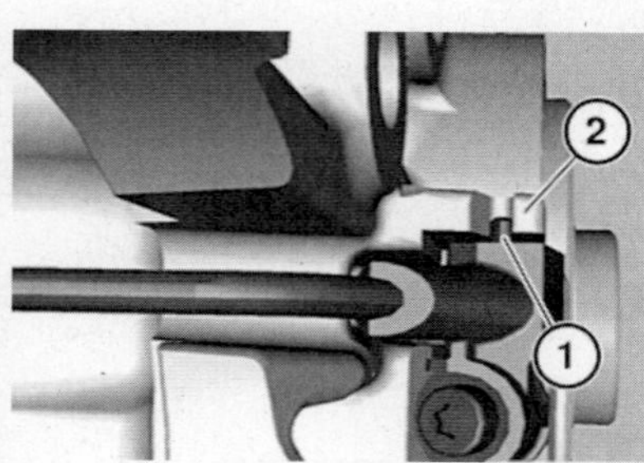

Fig. 231 Verifying guide pin of pulse sensor is inserted in guiding groove of crankcase

10. During installation of pulse sensor make sure that guide pin of pulse sensor is inserted in guiding groove of crankcase.
11. Assemble engine.
12. Check stored fault message.
13. Delete fault memory.

N52 and N54 Engines

WARNING

Aluminum-magnesium materials. No steel screws/bolts may be used due to the threat of electrochemical corrosion. A magnesium crankcase requires aluminum screws/bolts exclusively. Aluminum screws/bolts must be replaced each time they are Removed. The end faces of aluminum screws/bolts are painted blue for the purposes of reliable identification. Jointing torque and angle of rotation must be observed without fail (risk of damage).

1. Before servicing the vehicle, refer to the precautions.
2. Read out fault memory of DME control unit; if necessary, work through test schedules
3. Switch ignition **OFF**.
4. Remove intake air manifold. Refer to engine mechanical, intake manifold, removal & installation.
5. Disconnect plug
6. Disconnect the crankshaft pulse generator.
7. Remove and discard the aluminum bolts.
8. Remove pulse generator from crankcase.

To install:

9. Replace sealing ring.
10. Install pulse generator to crankcase.
11. Using new aluminum bolts, tighten to 2 ft. lbs (3 Nm) plus an additional 45° of rotation.
12. Connect the crankshaft pulse generator.
13. Install intake air manifold.

N55 Engine

See Figures 232 and 233.

1. Before servicing the vehicle, refer to the precautions.
2. Read out the fault memory of the DME control unit.
3. Switch off ignition.
4. Remove starter motor.
5. Unlock connector and remove.
6. Release screw. Tightening torque: 70 inch lbs. (8 Nm)

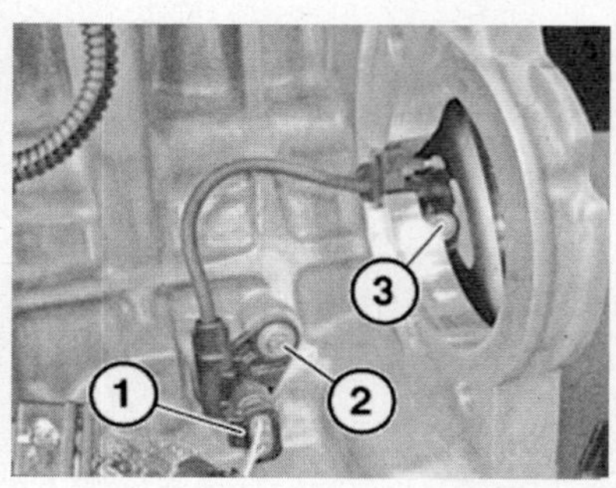

Fig. 232 Unlocking and removing connector, releasing screws (2, 3) and removing pulse sensor from crankcase

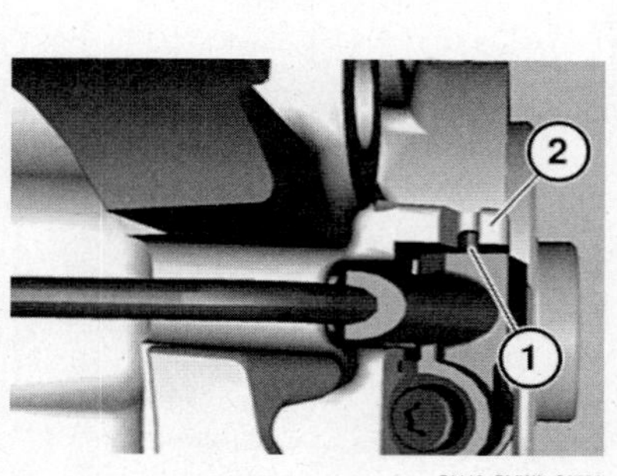

Fig. 233 Verifying pulse guide pin of pulse sensor is inserted in guiding groove of crankcase

7. Remove connector housing from crankcase.
8. Release screw. Tightening torque: 70 inch lbs. (8 Nm)
9. Pull pulse sensor from crankcase and remove.

To install:

To install, reverse the removal procedure noting the following.

10. During installation of pulse sensor make sure that guide pin of pulse sensor is inserted in guiding groove of crankcase.
11. Assemble engine.
12. Check stored fault message.
13. Delete fault memory.

S65 Engine

See Figure 234.

1. Before servicing the vehicle, refer to the precautions.
2. Read out fault memory of DME control unit; if necessary, work through test schedules

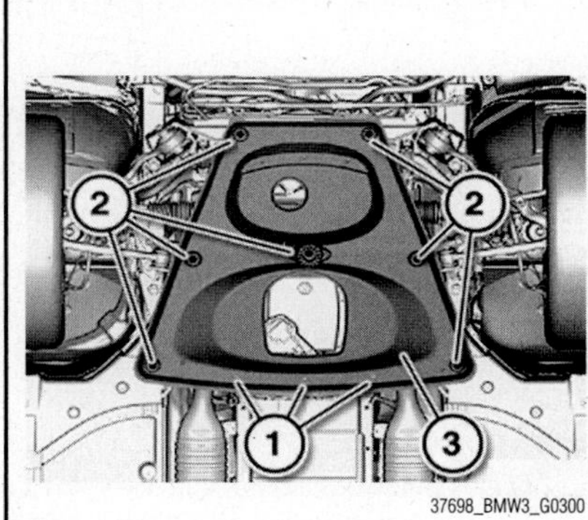

Fig. 234 Release screws, release screws and remove reinforcement plate

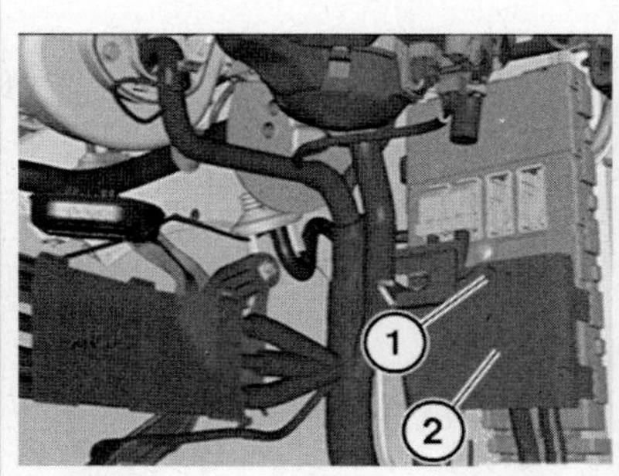

Fig. 235 Releasing screw and removing cover

3. Switch ignition **OFF**.
4. Remove reinforcement plate.
   a. Remove front underbody protection.
   b. Release screws and remove reinforcement plate.
5. Release screws and remove cover.
6. Unlock connector and remove.
7. Release screw and remove pulse generator.

To install:

8. To install, reverse the removal procedure.
9. Clear the fault memory.

ELECTRONIC CONTROL UNIT

REMOVAL & INSTALLATION

Front

See Figures 235 through 237.

1. Clamp off battery lead from negative connection point.
2. Remove side trim panel from footwell on right A-pillar.
3. Release screw and remove cover.

WARNING

Risk of damage to positive battery cable connector.

4. Unlock the positive battery cable connector:
   a. Loosen lock in direction of arrow.
   b. Unlock top positive battery cable connector in direction of arrow.
   c. Disconnect battery positive lead.
5. Unlock plug connections and disconnect.
6. Release bolt and remove control unit. Tightening torque: 15 inch lbs. (1.7 Nm)

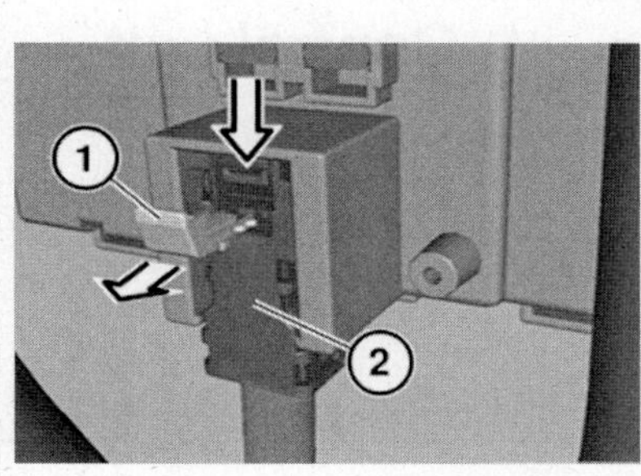

Fig. 236 Loosening lock and disconnecting positive lead

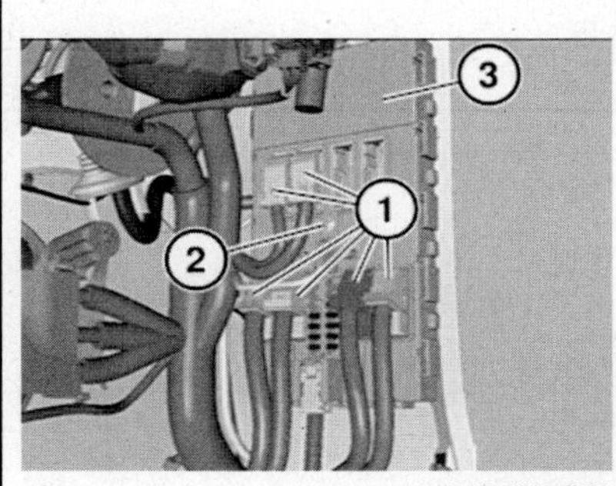

Fig. 237 Unlocking and disconnecting plug connections and releasing bolt and removing control unit

To install:

To install, reverse the removal procedure noting the following.

➡Make sure all plug connections are correctly latched.

7. Because the CAS is located in the FEM, it is absolutely essential after the FEM is replaced for all ID transmitters (ignition keys) to be re-initialized.

Rear

See Figure 238.

1. Disconnect the negative battery cable.
2. Unlock and disconnect all plug connections in area.
3. Unlock and disconnect positive battery cable. (Note removal instructions below)
4. Release screw. Tightening torque: 29 inch lbs. (3.3 Nm)
5. Remove control unit from guides in direction of arrow.

WARNING

Risk of damage to positive battery cable connector.

6. Unlock the positive battery cable connector:
   a. Loosen lock in direction of arrow.
   b. Unlock top positive battery cable connector in direction of arrow.
   c. Disconnect battery positive lead.

To install:

To install, reverse the removal procedure noting the following.

7. Make sure all plug connections are correctly latched.
8. Perform programming.

PROGRAMMING

In order to avoid incorrect programming procedures and fault messages, it is essential to always use the most current version when working with the ISTA/P programming system.

Battery voltage must not drop below 13.0 V during programming. Connect battery charger prior to programming.

WARNING

Use only BMW-recommended battery chargers.

Programming routine via ISTA/P:

1. Connect the battery charger to the vehicle.
2. Connect the programming system with the vehicle.
3. Determine the action plan and, if necessary, add complete car coding to the action plan.

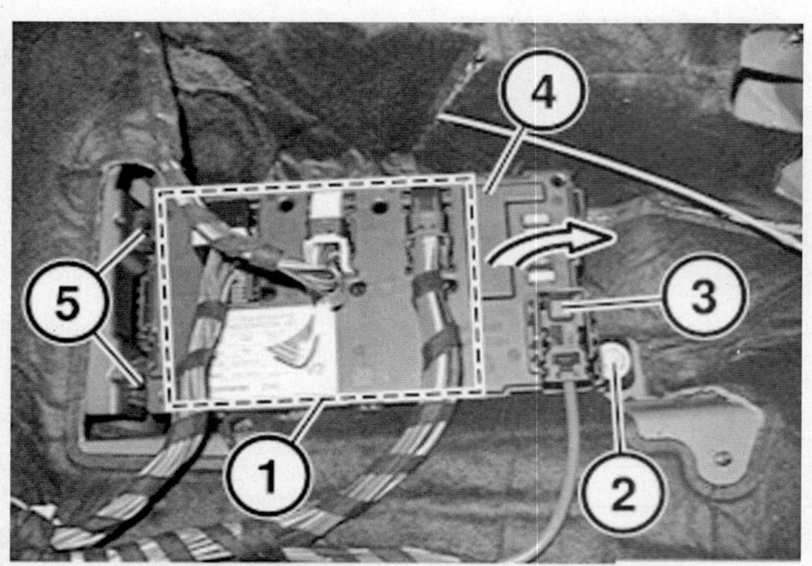

Fig. 238 Removing and installing the Rear Electronic Module (REM)

4. Accept action plan with the control units to be programmed/encoded and enabled, if necessary or work through.
5. Observe the reworking list.
6. Connect the workshop system to the vehicle.
7. Perform brief test and delete fault memory.

ENGINE COOLANT TEMPERATURE (ECT) SENSOR

LOCATION

See Figures 239 through 242.

REMOVAL & INSTALLATION

M57 Engine

1. Before servicing the vehicle, refer to the precautions.
2. Read out fault memory of DDE control unit; if necessary, work through test schedules.
3. Switch **OFF** ignition.
4. Remove intake air manifold. Refer to engine mechanical, intake manifold, removal & installation.

⁂ WARNING

Protect alternator against coolant. Cover alternator with suitable cover.

5. Unlock plug and remove.
6. Unfasten coolant temperature sensor.

To install:

7. To install, reverse the removal procedure.

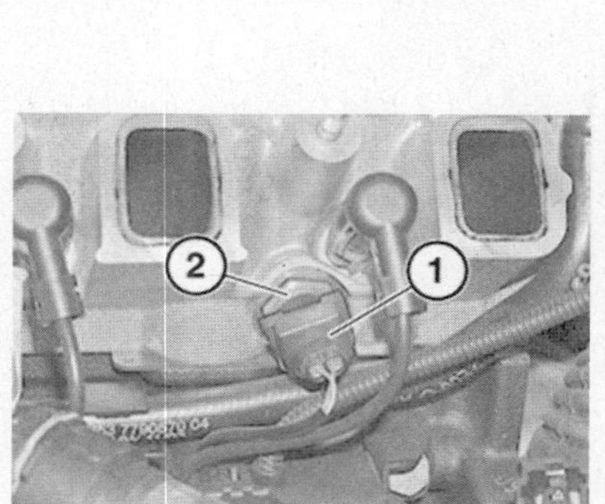

Fig. 239 ECT connector and sensor location—M57 engine

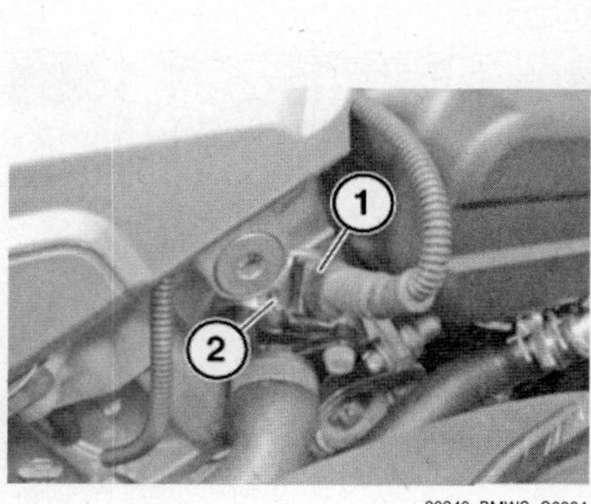

Fig. 240 ECT location—N52 engine

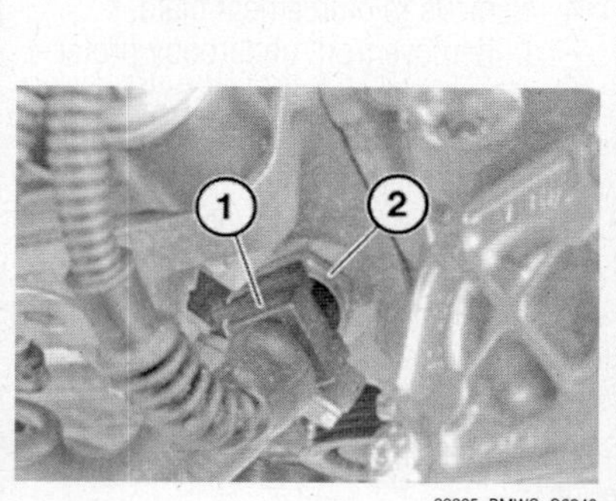

Fig. 241 ECT sensor and connector location—N54 engine

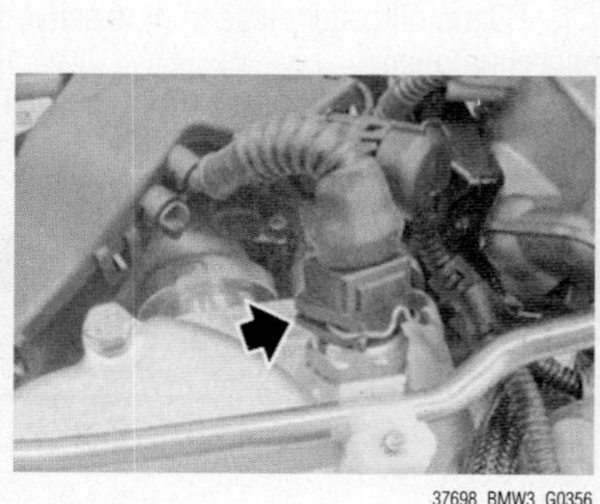

Fig. 242 ECT sensor location—S65 engine

8. Tighten sensor to 10 ft. lbs. (13 Nm)
9. Clear the fault memory.

N20 and N26 Engines

1. Before servicing the vehicle, refer to the precautions.
2. Read out the fault memory of the DME control unit.
3. Switch off ignition.

➡Coolant temperature sensor is mounted on the cylinder head at front.

4. Unlock connector and remove.
5. Unfasten coolant temperature sensor. Tightening torque: 9 ft. lbs. (13.5 Nm)

To install:

To install, reverse the removal procedure noting the following.

6. If necessary, top up coolant.
7. Check cooling system for leaks.
8. Check stored fault messages.
9. Delete fault memory.

N52 Engine

1. Before servicing the vehicle, refer to the precautions.
2. Read out fault memory of DME control unit; if necessary, work through test schedules
3. Switch ignition **OFF**.
4. Though you can avoid it, for easier access, remove the intake duct.
5. Unlock the plug on the sensor and remove it.
6. Remove the temperature sensor.

To install:

7. Reposition the sensor and lock the plug.
8. After returning the temperature sensor back to its position, make sure to vent the cooling system and check for leaks.
9. If necessary, top off the coolant in the reservoir.
10. Check for stored fault messages, rectify faults and clear the fault memory.

N54 Engine

See Figure 243.

1. Before servicing the vehicle, refer to the precautions.
2. Read out fault memory of DME control unit; if necessary, work through test schedules
3. Switch ignition **OFF**.
4. Remove the acoustic cover.
5. Remove the fan cowl.
6. Disconnect the oil line to gain access to the sensor.
7. Unlock the plug on the sensor and remove it.
8. Remove the temperature sensor.

Fig. 243 Disconnect the oil line to gain access to the sensor

To install:

9. Install the sensor and tighten to 10 ft. lbs. (14 Nm). Lock the plug.
10. Connect the oil line using new O-rings and tighten to 14 ft. lbs. (19 Nm).
11. Install the fan cowl.
12. Install the acoustic cover.
13. After returning the temperature sensor back to its position, make sure to vent the cooling system and check for leaks.
14. If necessary, top off the coolant in the reservoir.
15. Check for stored fault messages, rectify faults and clear the fault memory.

N55 Engine

1. Before servicing the vehicle, refer to the precautions.
2. Read out the fault memory of the DME control unit.
3. Switch off ignition.
4. Remove ignition coil cover.

➡Coolant temperature sensor is mounted on cylinder head at front.

5. Unlock connector and remove.
6. Unfasten coolant temperature sensor. Tightening torque: 9 ft. lbs. (13.5 Nm)

To install:

To install, reverse the removal procedure noting the following.

7. If necessary, top up coolant.
8. Check cooling system for leaks.
9. Check stored fault messages.
10. Delete fault memory.

S65 Engine

1. Before servicing the vehicle, refer to the precautions.
2. Read out fault memory of DME control unit; if necessary, work through test schedules
3. Switch ignition **OFF**.
4. Remove intake air manifold. Refer to engine mechanical, air filter housing, removal & installation.
5. Unlock plug and remove
6. Remove temperature sensor.

To install:

7. To install, reverse the removal procedure.
8. Tighten sensor to 10 ft. lbs. (14 Nm).
9. Clear the fault memory.

ENGINE OIL LEVEL AND TEMPERATURE SENSOR

LOCATION

See Figure 244.

REMOVAL & INSTALLATION

See Figure 245.

1. Before servicing the vehicle, refer to the precautions.

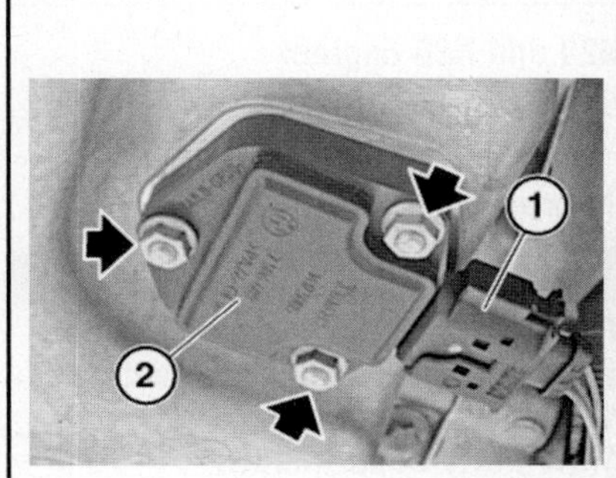

Fig. 244 Oil level and temperature sensor and plug

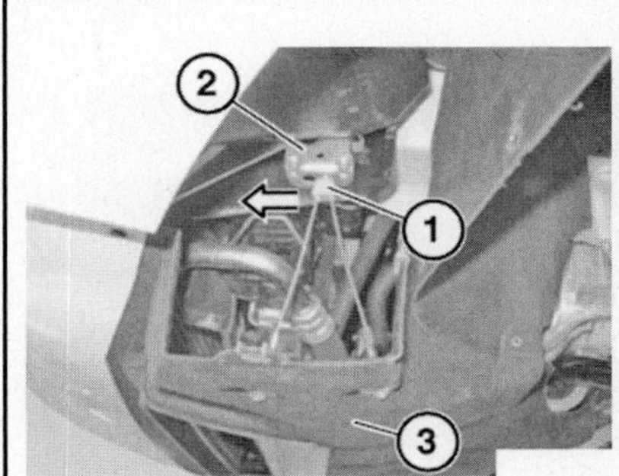

Fig. 245 Turn catch on cable through 90° and disengage in direction of arrow from bracket on both sides. Pull underbody protection forwards under bumper trim and remove—M3

2. Remove front underbody protection and as necessary reinforcement plate.
3. Drain and recycle the engine oil.
4. Unlock plug and remove the sensor.

To install:

5. Clean sealing face on oil sump.
6. Replace seal on oil level sensor.
7. Tighten the bolts to 72 inch lbs. (8 Nm).

⁂ WARNING

An excessively low torque value will result in oil leaks. An excessively high torque value will result in damage to the oil level sensor.

8. Refill engine with oil.

HEATED OXYGEN (HO2S) SENSOR

LOCATION

See Figures 246 through 249.

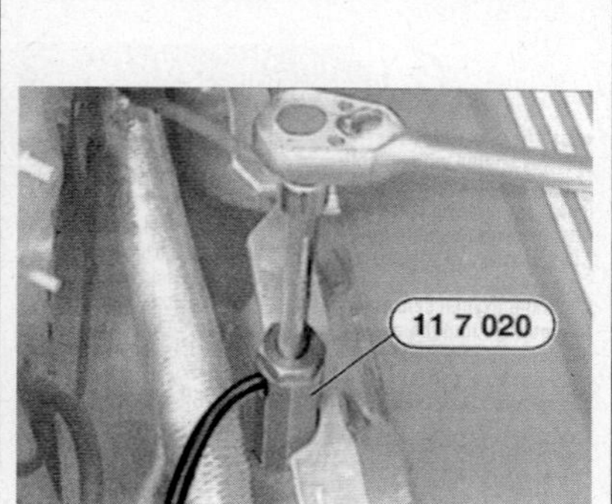

Fig. 246 HO2S sensor and special removal tool for cylinders 1–3 location — N52 and N54 engines

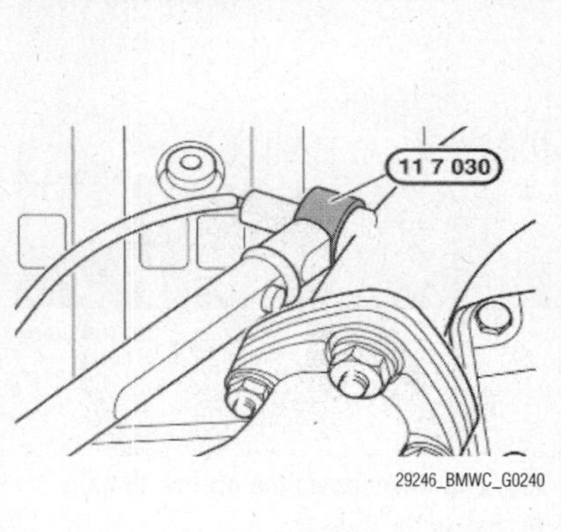

Fig. 247 HO2S sensor and special removal tool for cylinders 4–6 location — N52 and N54 engines

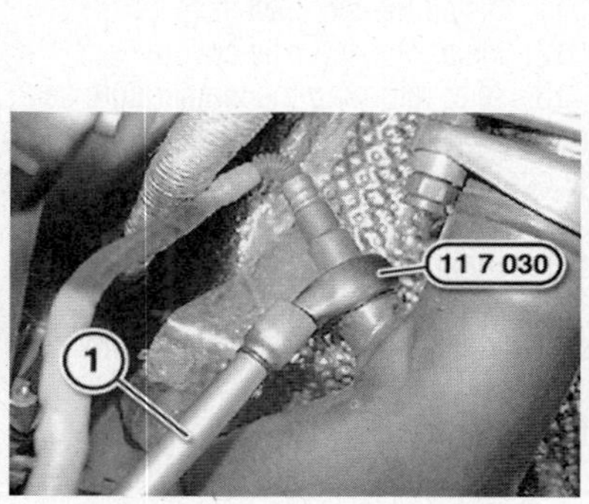

Fig. 248 HO2S sensor location—left side

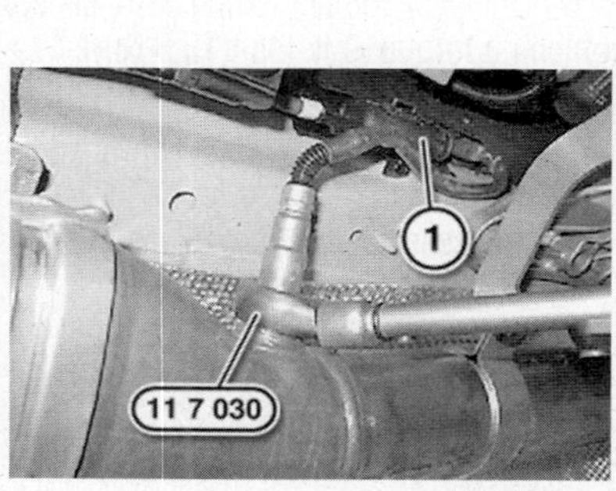

Fig. 249 HO2S sensor location—right side

REMOVAL & INSTALLATION

N20 and N26 Engines

See Figure 250.

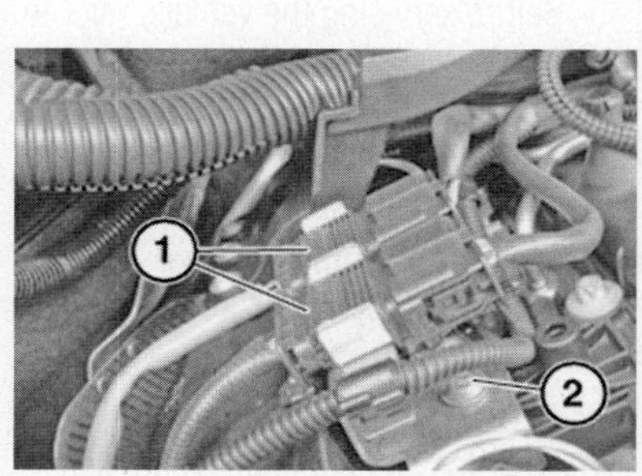

Fig. 250 Disconnecting plug connection on oxygen control sensor

1. Before servicing the vehicle, refer to the precautions.

⁂ WARNING

The threads of new oxygen control sensors are already coated with Never Seez Compound 4.3 (refer to BMW Parts Department).

⁂ WARNING

If an oxygen control sensor is to be reused, apply a thin and even coating of NEVER-SEEZ compound to the thread only.

⁂ WARNING

Sensor ceramics not cleaned and not coated with lubricant.

2. Remove acoustic cover.
3. Disconnect plug connection on oxygen control sensor.

➡Cable color of oxygen control sensor = black.

➡Cable color of oxygen monitoring sensor = grey.

⁂ WARNING

When using special tool 11 4 260, it is essential to reduce the prescribed tightly torque by 26 inch lbs. (3 Nm).

4. Release oxygen control sensor with special tool 11 4 260. Tightening torque: 37 ft. lbs. (50 Nm)

To install:

To install, reverse the removal procedure noting the following.

5. Reassemble the vehicle.
6. Check function of DME.

N52 and N54 Engines

See Figures 251 and 252.

1. Before servicing the vehicle, refer to the precautions.
2. Read out fault memory of DME control unit; if necessary, work through test schedules
3. Switch ignition **OFF**.
4. Remove the exhaust system.
5. Disconnect the plug connection from the sensors.
6. Disconnect the oxygen sensor from cylinders 4 to 6.

7. The oxygen sensor at cylinders 1 to 3 is accessible from above without the exhaust system having to be removed.

To install:

8. The threads of a new oxygen sensors are already coated with an anti-seize compound. If an oxygen sensor is to be used again, apply a thin and even coat of an anti-seize compound to the thread only.

**** WARNING**

Do not clean the oxygen sensor section which protrudes into the exhaust line and ensure that it avoids all contact with any lubricants.

➡Observe cable routing of the oxygen sensor so it doesn't interfere with any other system or the exhaust pipes.

9. Tighten sensor to 37 ft. lbs. (50 Nm).
10. Connect the oxygen sensors and their respective cables.

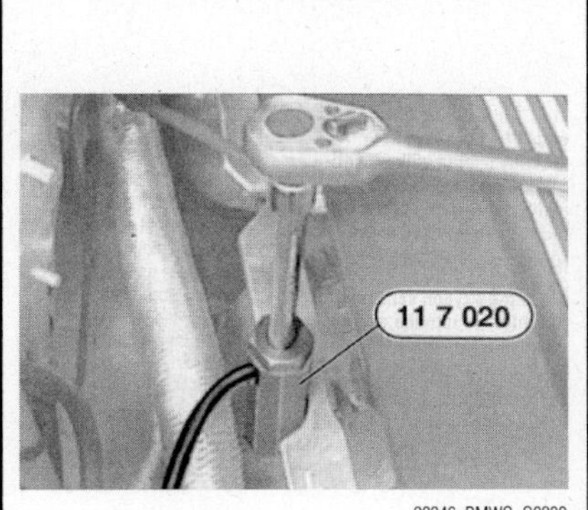

Fig. 251 HO2S sensor and special removal tool for cylinders 1–3 location — N52 engine

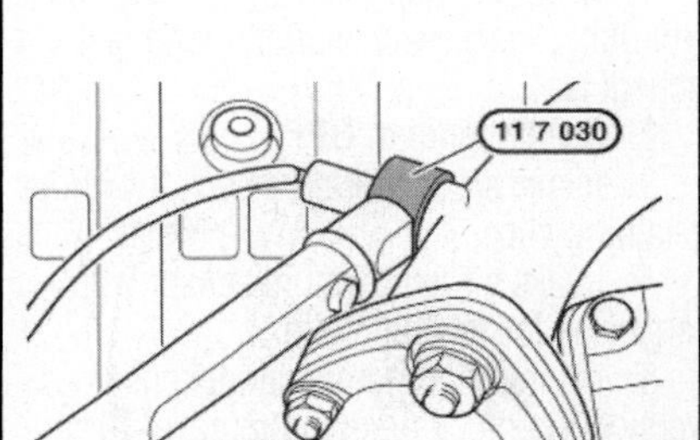

Fig. 252 HO2S sensor and special removal tool for cylinders 4–6 location — N52 engine

- The cable color for the sensor that leads to cylinders 1 to 3 is black.
- The cable color for the sensor that leads to cylinders 4 to 6 is gray.

11. Connect the plug connection to the sensors.
12. Check for stored fault messages, rectify faults and clear the fault memory.

N55 Engine

See Figures 253 and 254.

1. Before servicing the vehicle, refer to the precautions.

**** WARNING**

The threads of new oxygen control sensors are already coated with Never Seez Compound (refer to BMW Parts Department).

**** WARNING**

If a oxygen control sensor is to be reused, apply a thin and even coating of Never Seez compound to the thread only.

**** WARNING**

The part of the lambda control sensor which projects into the exhaust system branch (sensor ceramics) must not be cleaned and not coated with lubricant.

2. Remove rear ignition coil cover.
3. Disconnect plug connection on oxygen control sensor.

➡Cable color of oxygen control sensor = black.

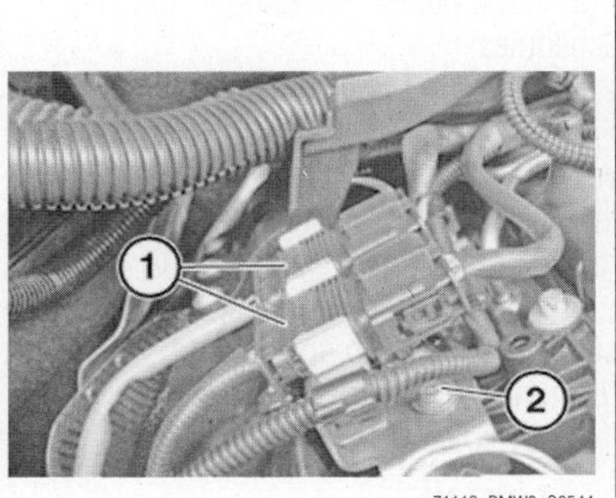

Fig. 253 Disconnecting plug connection on oxygen control sensor

➡Cable color of oxygen monitoring sensor = grey.

4. Unclip cable of control sensor out of holder.
5. Release oxygen sensor from above with special tool 11 4 260. Tightening torque: 36 ft. lbs. (50 Nm)

To install:

To install, reverse the removal procedure noting the following.

6. Check function of DME.

S65 Engine

See Figures 255 and 256.

1. Before servicing the vehicle, refer to the precautions.
2. Read out fault memory in Digital Motor Electronics (DME).
3. Remove transmission underbody protection.
4. Pull plug connection from holder.

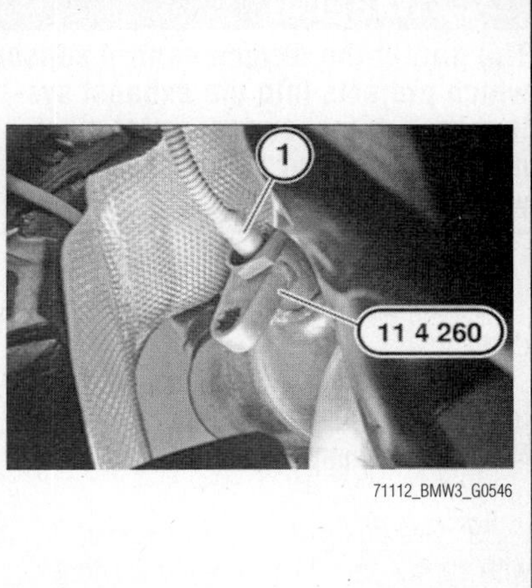

Fig. 254 Releasing oxygen sensor

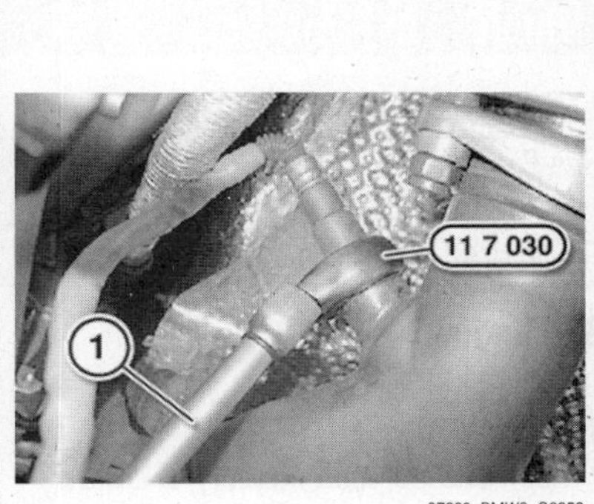

Fig. 255 Remove oxygen control sensor with special tool 11 7 030—left side

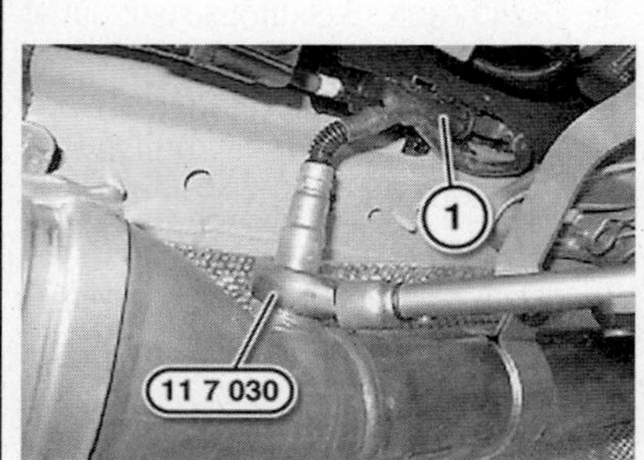

Fig. 256 Remove oxygen control sensor with special tool 11 7 030—right side

Fig. 257 IAC location. Air intake hose and idle air hose—S65 Engine

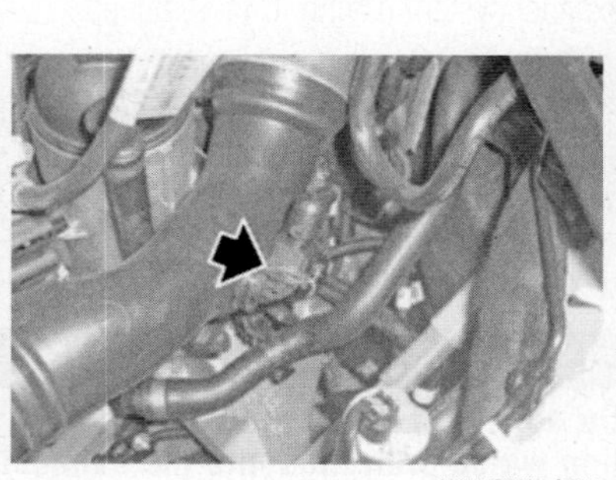

Fig. 258 IAT sensor location—M57 Engine version 1

5. Disconnect plug connection.
6. Remove oxygen control sensor with special tool 11 7 030.

WARNING

The part of the oxygen control sensor which projects into the exhaust system branch (sensor ceramic) must not be cleaned or come into contact with lubricant.

To install:

7. To install, reverse the removal procedure.
8. If the oxygen control sensor is reused, apply a thin and even coat of Never Seize Compound to the thread only.
9. Secure oxygen control sensor with special tool 11 7 030 and a torque wrench.
10. Tighten to 37 ft. lbs. (50 Nm)
11. Check function of DME.

IDLE AIR CONTROL (IAC) VALVE

LOCATION

See Figure 257.

REMOVAL & INSTALLATION

S65 Engine

1. Before servicing the vehicle, refer to the precautions.
2. Read out fault memory of DME control unit.
3. Switch ignition **OFF**.
4. Remove intake air manifold. Refer to engine mechanical, intake manifold, removal & installation.
5. Partially disconnect engine wiring harness, raise cable duct.
6. Remove the tank venting valve.
7. Release air intake hose.
8. Release idle air hose.
9. Replace clamps.
10. Unlock plug connection and disconnect.
11. Carefully lever idle actuator out of holder.

To install:

12. To install, reverse the removal procedure.
13. Clear the fault memory.

INTAKE AIR TEMPERATURE (IAT) SENSOR

REMOVAL & INSTALLATION

M57 Engine

See Figures 258 and 259.

1. Read out fault memory of DME control unit; if necessary, work through test schedules
2. Switch ignition **OFF**.
3. On intake air temperature sensor version 1, unlock plug and remove. Turn temperature sensor through 45° and remove.
4. On intake air temperature sensor version 2, unlock plug and remove. Pull off retaining clip, turn temperature sensor through 45° and remove.

To install:

5. To install, reverse the removal procedure.
6. Clear the fault memory.

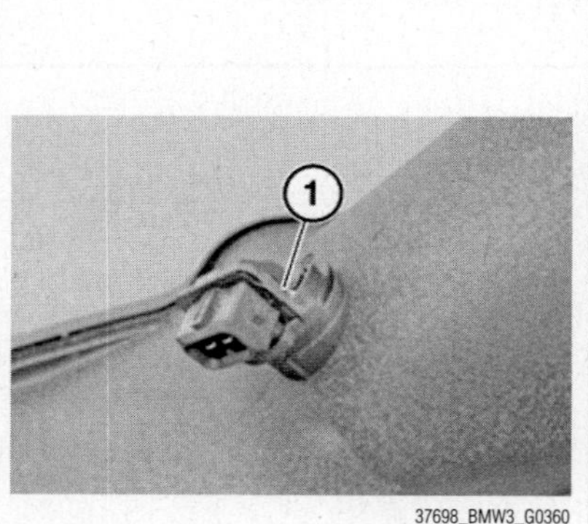

Fig. 259 IAT sensor location—M57 Engine version 2

S65 Engine

See Figures 260 and 261.

1. Read out fault memory of DME control unit; if necessary, work through test schedules
2. Switch ignition **OFF**.
3. Intake air temperature sensor without retaining clip.
4. Intake air temperature sensor with large ribs for retaining clip.
5. On intake air temperature sensor version 1, unlock plug and remove. Turn temperature sensor through 45° and remove.
6. On intake air temperature sensor version 2, unlock plug and remove. Pull off retaining clip, turn temperature sensor through 45° and remove.

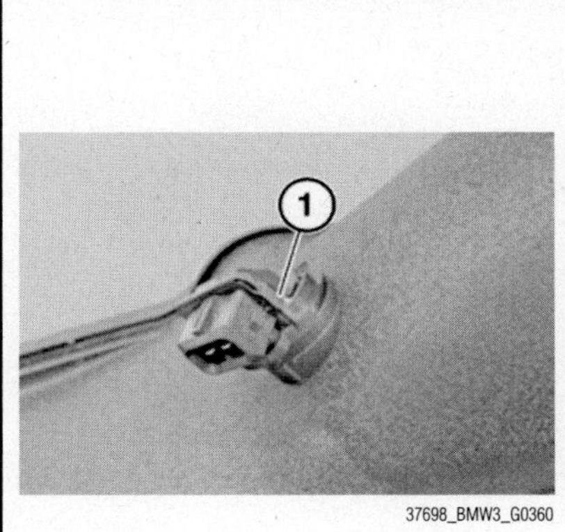

37698_BMW3_G0360

Fig. 260 IAT sensor location—version 1

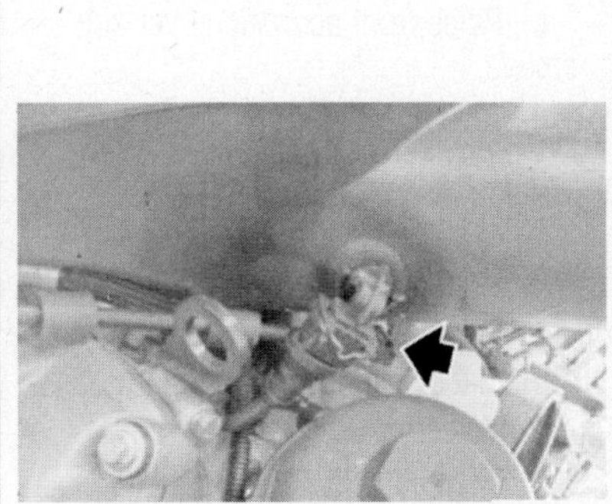
37698_BMW3_G0361

Fig. 261 IAT sensor location—version 2

To install:

7. To install, reverse the removal procedure.
8. Clear the fault memory.

KNOCK SENSOR (KS)

LOCATION

See Figure 262.

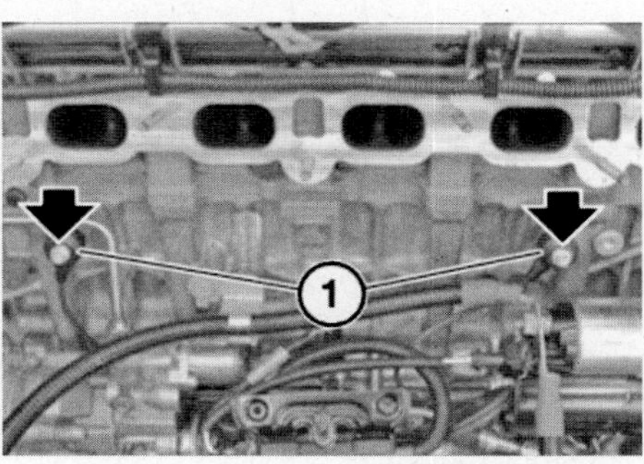

22205_BMWC_G0248

Fig. 262 KS sensor location— N52 and N54 engine

REMOVAL & INSTALLATION

N20 and N26 Engines

1st and 2nd Cylinder

1. Read out the fault memory of the DME control unit.
2. Switch off ignition.
3. Remove throttle valve assembly.
4. Unlock connector and remove.
5. Release bolt on knock sensor. Tightening torque: 15 ft. lbs. (21.5 Nm)
6. Remove knock sensor for 1st and 2nd cylinder.

To install:

To install, reverse the removal procedure noting the following.

7. Clean contact surface of knock sensors on engine block.
8. Reassemble the vehicle.
9. Check stored fault message.
10. Delete fault memory.

3rd and 4th Cylinder

1. Read out the fault memory of the DME control unit.
2. Switch off ignition.
3. Remove starter motor.
4. Unlock connector and remove.
5. Release bolt on knock sensor. Tightening torque: 15 ft. lbs. (21.5 Nm)
6. Remove knock sensor for 3rd and 4th cylinders.

To install:

To install, reverse the removal procedure noting the following.

7. Clean contact surface of knock sensors on engine block.
8. Reassemble the vehicle.
9. Check stored fault message.
10. Delete fault memory.

N52 and N54 Engines

See Figure 263.

WARNING

No steel bolts or bolts may be used due to the threat of electrochemical corrosion. A magnesium crankcase requires aluminum bolts and bolts exclusively. The end of the aluminum bolts and bolts are painted blue for the purposes of reliable identification.

1. Before servicing the vehicle, refer to the precautions.
2. Read out fault memory of DME control unit; if necessary, work through test schedules
3. Switch ignition **OFF**.
4. Disconnect the battery.
5. Remove the air intake manifold.
6. Unlock the plug connection and remove it.
7. Unscrew the bolts on both knock sensors and remove the sensors.

To install:

8. Clean the support face of the knock sensors on engine block.
9. Install the bolts on both knock sensors to replace the sensors.
10. Check for stored fault messages, rectify faults and clear the fault memory.

N55 Engine

See Figure 264.

WARNING

Aluminum screws/bolts must be replaced each time they are released.

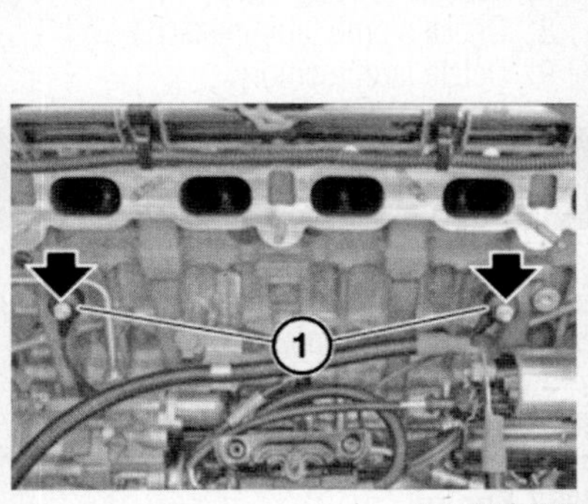

22205_BMWC_G0248

Fig. 263 Removing the KS sensor—N52 engine

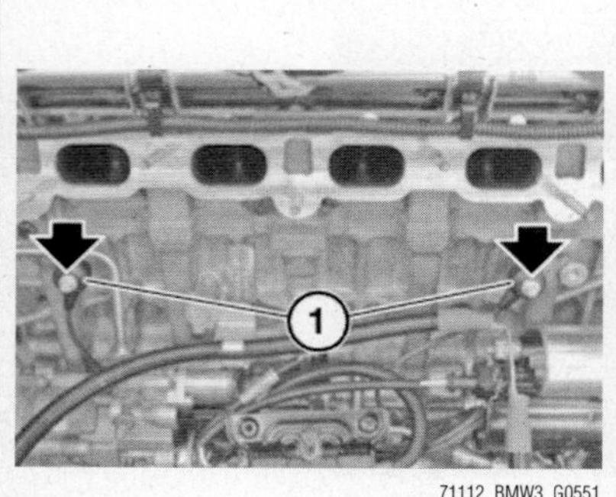

Fig. 264 Releasing screws and removing knock sensors

WARNING

Aluminum screws/bolts are permitted with and without color coding (blue).

WARNING

For reliable identification: Jointing torque and angle of rotation must be observed without fail (risk of damage).

1. Read out the fault memory of the DME control unit.
2. Switch off ignition.
3. Remove high pressure pump.
4. Unlock connector and remove.
5. Release screws on both knock sensors and remove knock sensors. Tightening torque: 15 ft. lbs. (21.5 Nm)

➡Replace aluminum screws.

To install:

To install, reverse the removal procedure noting the following.

6. Clean contact surface of knock sensors on engine block.
7. Reassemble the vehicle.
8. Check stored fault message.
9. Delete fault memory.

MANIFOLD ABSOLUTE PRESSURE (MAP) SENSOR

LOCATION

See Figures 265 through 267.

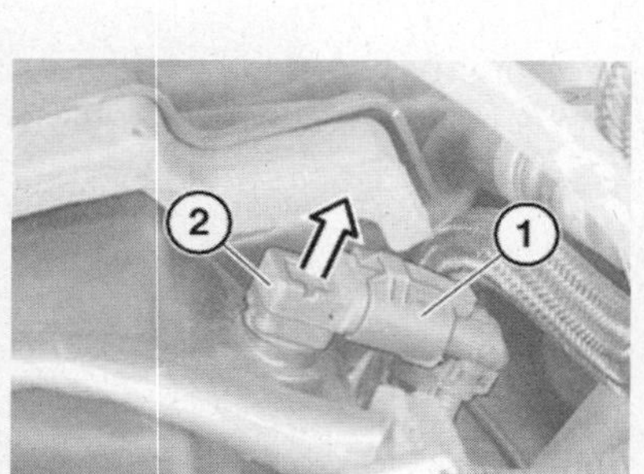

Fig. 265 Charge air pressure sensor location. Plug charge air pressure sensor—M57 Engine

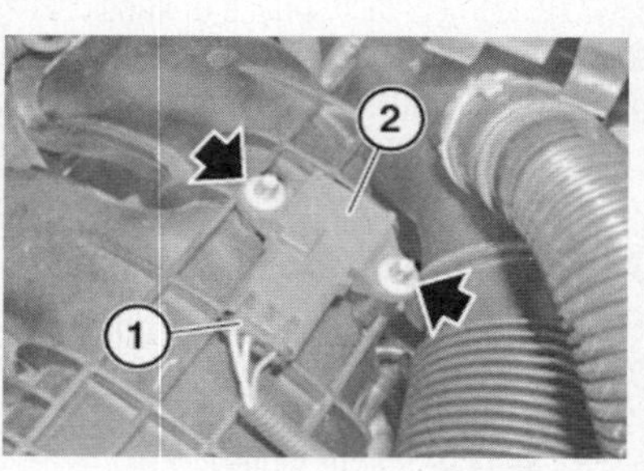

Fig. 266 MAP sensor location. Plug suction pressure sensor—N54 Engine

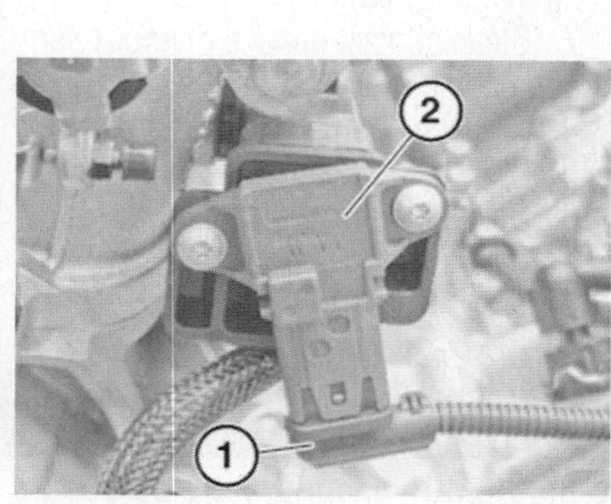

Fig. 267 MAP sensor location. Plug suction pressure sensor—S65 Engine

REMOVAL & INSTALLATION

M57 Engine

See Figure 268.

1. Before servicing the vehicle, refer to the precautions.
2. Read out fault memory of DDE control unit; if necessary, work through test schedules.
3. Switch **OFF** ignition.

Fig. 268 Charge air pressure sensor and plug

4. Remove the acoustic cover.
   a. Release screws.
   b. Raise front acoustic cover and remove.
5. Unlock plug and remove.
6. Remove charge-air pressure sensor in direction of arrow.

To install:

7. To install, reverse the removal procedure.
8. Replace sealing ring on charge-air pressure sensor.
9. Clear the fault memory.

N20 and N26 Engines

See Figure 269.

1. Read out the fault memory of the DME control unit.
2. Switch off ignition.
3. Partially undo the acoustic cover.
4. Unlock connector and remove.

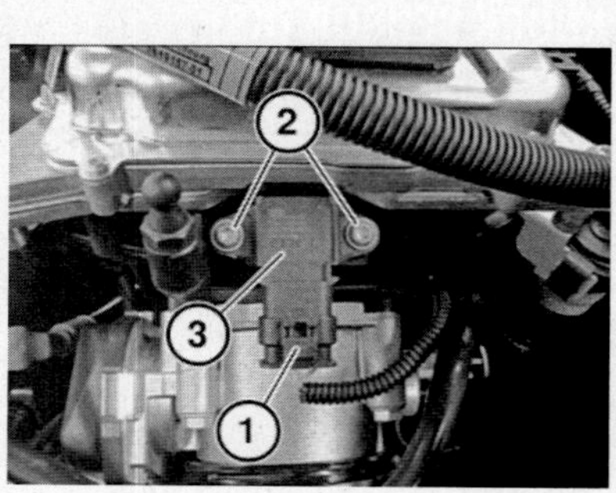

Fig. 269 Unlocking and removing connector and unfastening screws and removing vacuum pressure senor

5. Unfasten screws. Tightening torque: 33 inch lbs. (3.75 Nm)
6. Pull out the vacuum pressure sensor from the intake plenum.

To install:

To install, reverse the removal procedure noting the following.

7. Check sealing ring for damage. Replace damaged sealing ring.
8. When installing, coat sealing ring with suitable lubricant.
9. Reassemble the vehicle.
10. Check stored fault message.
11. Delete fault memory.

N54 Engine

See Figure 270.

1. Before servicing the vehicle, refer to the precautions.

➡The installation location of the suction pressure sensor is at the rear end of the intake air manifold.

2. Read out fault memory of DME control unit; if necessary, work through test schedules
3. Switch ignition **OFF**.
4. Remove air filter housing. Refer to engine mechanical, air filter housing, removal & installation.
5. Unlock plug and remove.
6. Release screws and pull suction pressure sensor out of intake air housing.

To install:

7. To install, reverse the removal procedure.
8. Check sealing ring for damage, replace if necessary.
9. When installing, coat sealing ring with suitable anti-seize agent.
10. Tighten screws to 36 inch lbs. (3.5 Nm).
11. Check stored fault messages and clear the fault memory.

S65 Engine

See Figure 271.

1. Before servicing the vehicle, refer to the precautions.

➡The installation location for the intake manifold pressure sensor is on the idle air duct at cylinder no. 8.

2. Before servicing the vehicle, refer to the precautions.
3. Read out fault memory of DME control unit; if necessary, work through test schedules
4. Switch ignition **OFF**.
5. Remove intake manifold. Refer to engine mechanical, intake manifold, removal & installation.
6. Remove secondary-air pump
7. Release cable duct for engine wiring harness.
8. Remove idle actuator suction hose.

Unlock plug, release screws and pull suction pressure sensor out of intake air housing.

To install:

9. To install, reverse the removal procedure.
10. To install, reverse the removal procedure.
11. Check sealing ring for damage, replace if necessary.
12. When installing, coat sealing ring with suitable anti-seize agent.
13. Tighten screws to 36 inch lbs. (3 Nm)
14. Check stored fault messages and clear the fault memory.

OUTPUT SHAFT SPEED (OSS) SENSOR

LOCATION

See Figures 272 and 273.

REMOVAL & INSTALLATION

GA6L45R Transmission

See Figures 274 through 276.

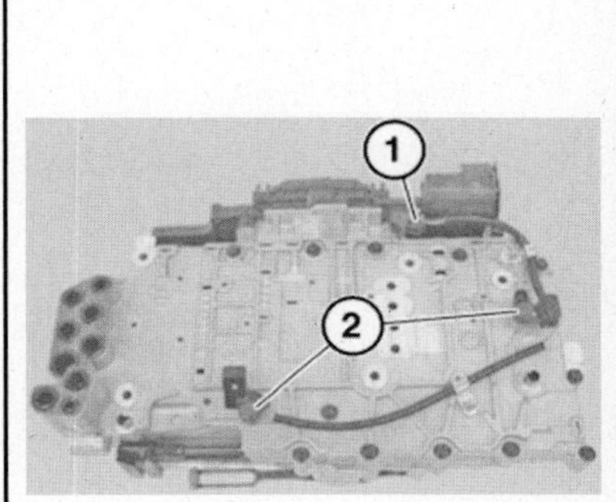

Fig. 272 Speed sensor location. Plug and attaching screws— GA6L45R Transmission

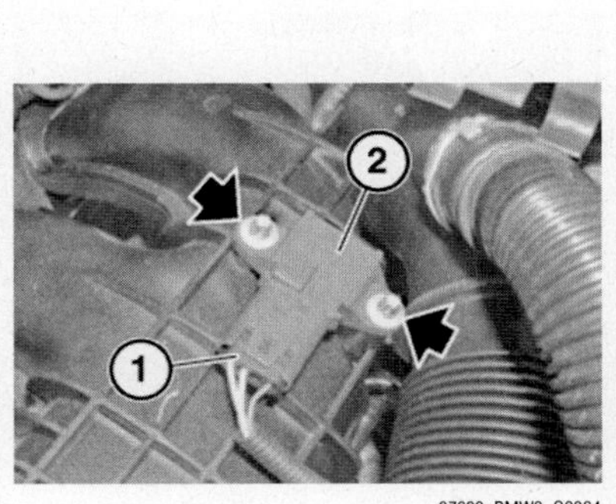

Fig. 270 Unlock plug, release screws and pull suction pressure sensor

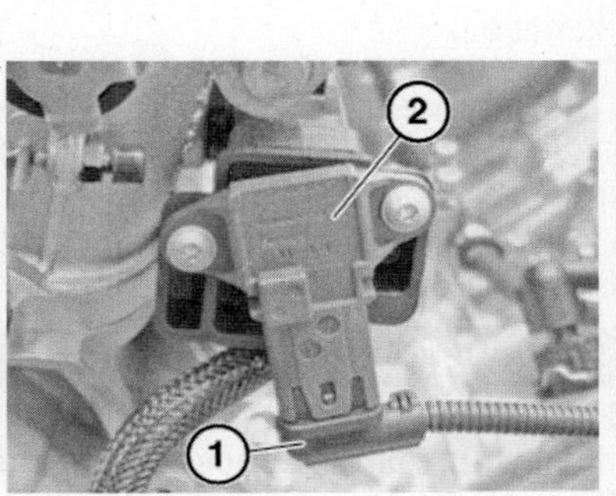

Fig. 271 Unlock plug, release screws and pull suction pressure sensor

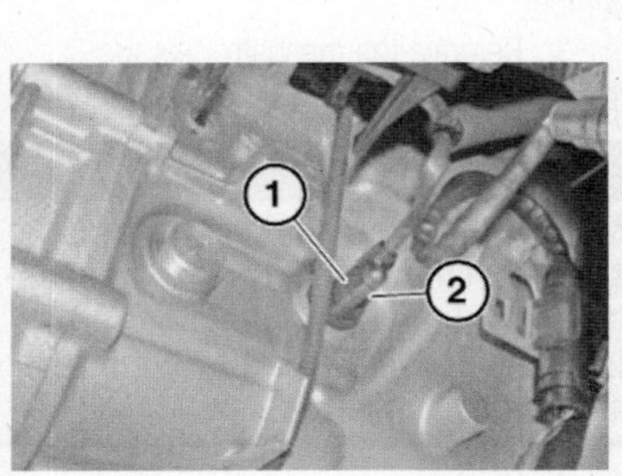

Fig. 273 Speed sensor location. Plug and attaching screws— GS6S53BZ Transmission

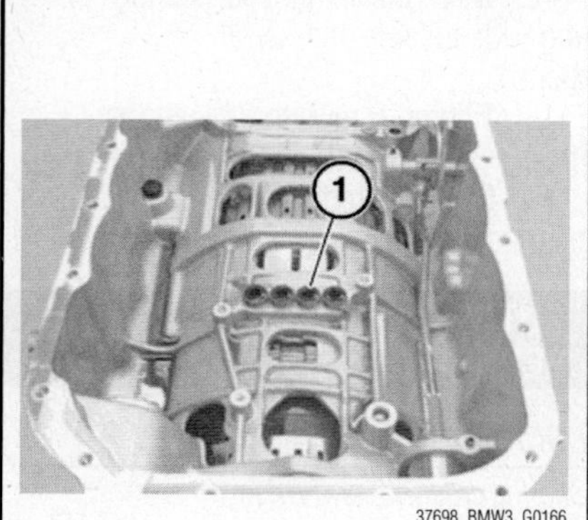

Fig. 274 Replace gaskets on transmission case

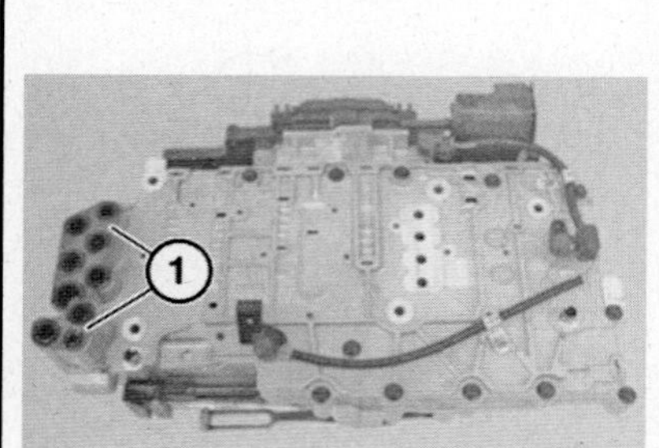

Fig. 275 Replace gaskets on mechatronics

1. Before servicing the vehicle, refer to the precautions.
2. Remove the transmission from the vehicle.
3. Remove the mechatronics as follows:

⁂ WARNING

Mechatronics can be destroyed by static discharges. Therefore the contacts inside the plug must not be touched. Insert special tool immediately after work step.

4. Unscrew plug and disconnect.
5. Insert special tool 24 2 390 in sealing sleeve.
6. Remove transmission oil sump.

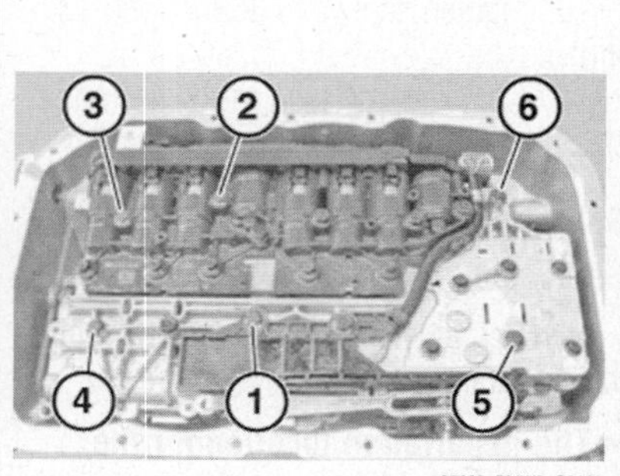

Fig. 276 Tighten down bolts in sequence (1 to 6) to 72 inch lbs. (8 Nm)

7. Unlock sealing sleeve with slide.
8. Note position of sealing sleeve and pull out.
9. Pull out sealing sleeve.
10. Release all bolts with special tool 24 4 350.
11. Remove mechatronics.
12. Unlock and disconnect plug.
13. Release screws.
14. Detach input and output speed sensor from mechatronics.

To install:

15. Install input and output speed sensor onmechatronics and tighten to 9 ft. lbs. (12 Nm).
16. Install mechatronics.
17. Screw in sealing sleeve partially (lug in upper area). Turn until lug engages in groove of transmission. 18. Slide in sealing sleeve.

⁂ WARNING

Lug on sealing sleeve must not be damaged.

19. Replace gasket.
20. Coat new seals with automatic transmission fluid and install.
21. Tighten down bolts in sequence (1 to 6) to 72 inch lbs. (8 Nm).

⁂ WARNING

Failure to comply with this requirement will result in serious damage to the automatic transmission.

22. Fill transmission with fluid.
23. Using a STAR DIAGNOSIS tool, load specific data version with DIS.

GS6S53BZ Transmission

1. Before servicing the vehicle, refer to the precautions.
2. Remove rear underbody protection.
3. Remove right heat shields.
4. Catch and dispose of gear oil with suitable equipment.
5. Unlock plug and remove.
6. Release screw.
7. Remove speed sensor.

To install:

8. To install, reverse the removal procedure.

THROTTLE POSITION SENSOR

LOCATION

See Figure 277.

REMOVAL & INSTALLATION

1. Before servicing the vehicle, refer to the precautions.
2. Read out fault memory of DME control unit; if necessary, work through test schedules
3. Switch ignition **OFF**.
4. Remove air intake hose.
5. Unlock plug and remove.
6. Remove throttle assembly.

To install:

7. Replace sealing ring of throttle assembly.
8. Install throttle assembly. Tighten bolts to 6 ft. lbs. (9 Nm).
9. Install air intake hose.
10. Check for stored fault messages, rectify faults and clear the fault memory.

Fig. 277 TPS sensor and connector location– N52 and N54 engines

FUEL SYSTEM SERVICE PRECAUTIONS

Safety is the most important factor when performing not only fuel system maintenance but any type of maintenance. Failure to conduct maintenance and repairs in a safe manner may result in serious personal injury or death. Maintenance and testing of the vehicle's fuel system components can be accomplished safely and effectively by adhering to the following rules and guidelines.

- To avoid the possibility of fire and personal injury, always disconnect the negative battery cable unless the repair or test procedure requires that battery voltage be applied.
- Always relieve the fuel system pressure prior to disconnecting any fuel system component (injector, fuel rail, pressure regulator, etc.), fitting or fuel line connection. Exercise extreme caution whenever relieving fuel system pressure to avoid exposing skin, face and eyes to fuel spray. Please be advised that fuel under pressure may penetrate the skin or any part of the body that it contacts.
- Always place a shop towel or cloth around the fitting or connection prior to loosening to absorb any excess fuel due to spillage. Ensure that all fuel spillage (should it occur) is quickly removed from engine surfaces. Ensure that all fuel soaked cloths or towels are deposited into a suitable waste container.
- Always keep a dry chemical (Class B) fire extinguisher near the work area.
- Do not allow fuel spray or fuel vapors to come into contact with a spark or open flame.
- Always use a back-up wrench when loosening and tightening fuel line connection fittings. This will prevent unnecessary stress and torsion to fuel line piping.
- Always replace worn fuel fitting O-rings with new. Do not substitute fuel hose or equivalent where fuel pipe is installed.

Before servicing the vehicle, make sure to also refer to the precautions in the beginning of this section as well.

RELIEVING FUEL SYSTEM PRESSURE

To relieve the pressure in the system, locate fuel pump relay located on the cowl. The relay can sometimes be distinguished by the orange color of the housing.

Unplug and remove the relay, and place it in a safe location. With the fuel pump relay removed, start the engine and operate it until it stalls. Crank the engine for 10 seconds after it stalls to remove any residual pressure.

FUEL FILTER

REMOVAL & INSTALLATION

M57 Engine

See Figures 278 through 280.

1. Before servicing the vehicle, refer to the precautions.
2. Switch **OFF** ignition.
3. Remove rear assembly underside protection:
4. Single-part underbody protection, except AWD.
   a. Release screws.
   b. Pull underbody protection in direction of arrow out of bracket.
5. Single-part underbody protection, AWD.
   a. Release screws.
   b. Remove underbody protection downwards.
6. Two-part underbody protection
   a. Release screws.
   b. Detach underbody protection from bracket and remove.
7. Release clamp.
8. Pull off hose.
9. Pull out retainer.
10. Detach fuel pre-heater in direction of arrow.
11. Release screw and remove fuel filter.

To install:

12. To install, reverse the removal procedure.
13. Check clamp, replacing if necessary.
14. Vent fuel system
15. Ensure correct seating of underbody protection.
16. Centre underbody protection and tighten down screws.

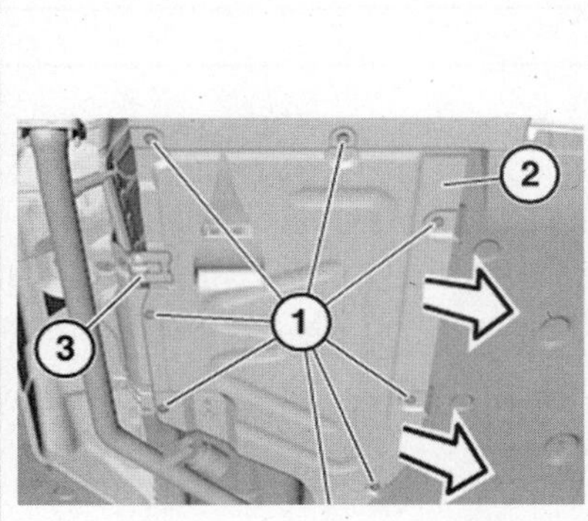

Fig. 278 Release screws, pull underbody protection in direction of arrow out of bracket

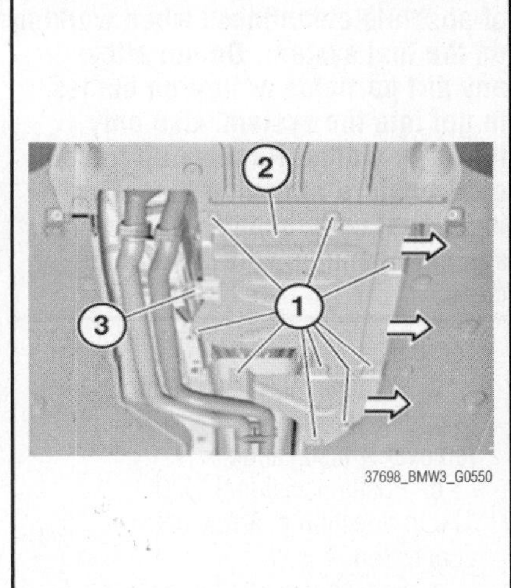

Fig. 279 Release screws, detach underbody protection from bracket and remove

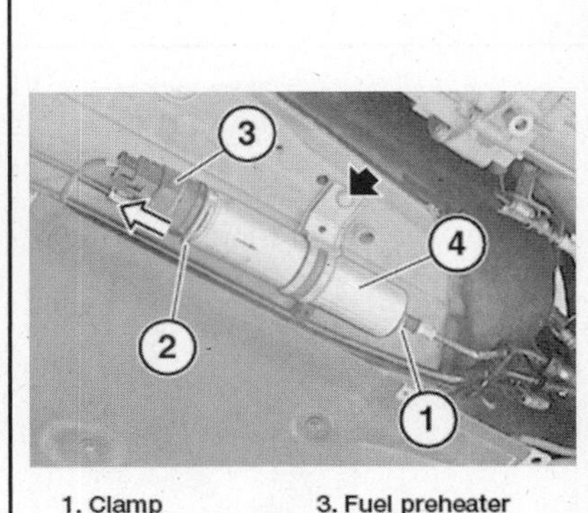

Fig. 280 Removing the fuel filter

FUEL INJECTORS

REMOVAL & INSTALLATION

M57 Engine

See Figures 281 through 284.

1. Before servicing the vehicle, refer to the precautions.
2. Read out fault memories of DDE control units.
3. Switch **OFF** ignition.
4. Remove the acoustic cover.
   a. Release screws.
   b. Raise front acoustic cover and remove.

⁂ WARNING

It is essential to adhere to conditions of absolute cleanliness when working on the fuel system. Do not allow any dirt particles or foreign bodies to get into the system. Use only fluff-free cloths. Remove all traces of dirt before removing pipes or individual components. Seal all fuel system openings with protective caps.

5. Detach leakage oil line.
   a. Remove intake air manifold. Refer to engine mechanical, intake manifold, removal & installation.
   b. Push special tool 13 0 170 in direction of arrow onto connection.
   c. Grip connection for leakage oil line.
   d. Release lock with special tool 13 0 170 in direction of arrow.
   e. Detach connection for leakage oil line in direction of arrow from injector.
   f. Release clamp.

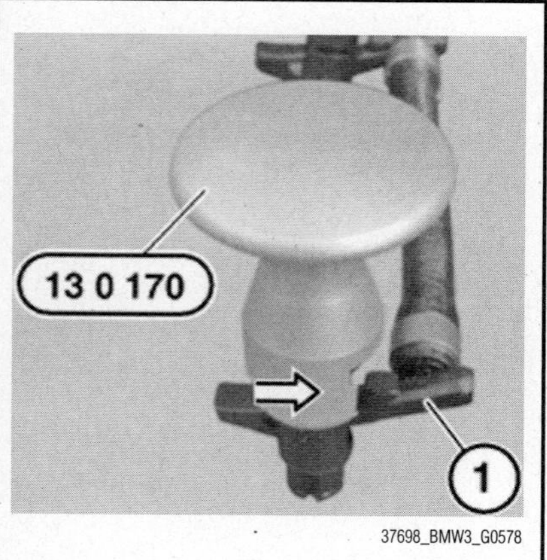

Fig. 281 Push special tool 13 0 170 in direction of arrow onto connection

   g. Carefully detach leakage oil line.
6. Remove all pressure lines. Refer to diesel fuel injection, injection lines, removal & installation.
7. Unlock plug and remove.
8. Unscrew nuts.
9. Remove injector.

To install:

10. To install, reverse the removal procedure.
11. Replace sealing rings and gasket.
12. Apply a light coating of highly temperature-resistant grease to injector stem.
13. Tighten injector to cylinder head to 78 inch lbs. (8.8 Nm)

⁂ WARNING

Danger of breakage of pressure line on injector. Observe tightening torque without fail.

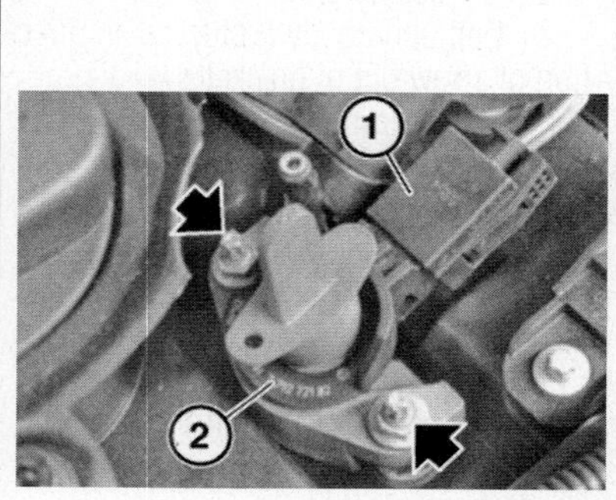

Fig. 282 Unlock plug and remove injector

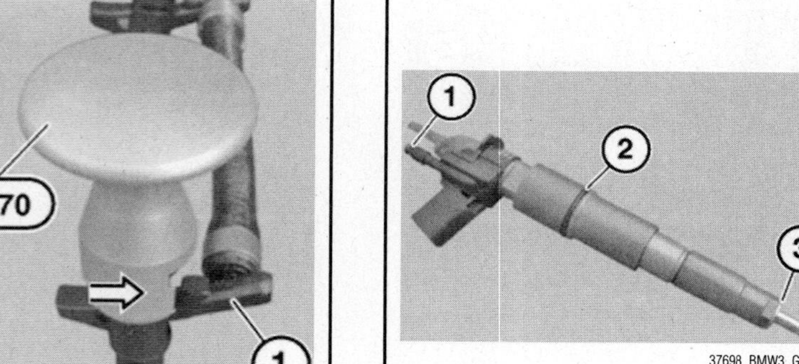

Fig. 283 Replace sealing rings (1 and 2) and replace gasket

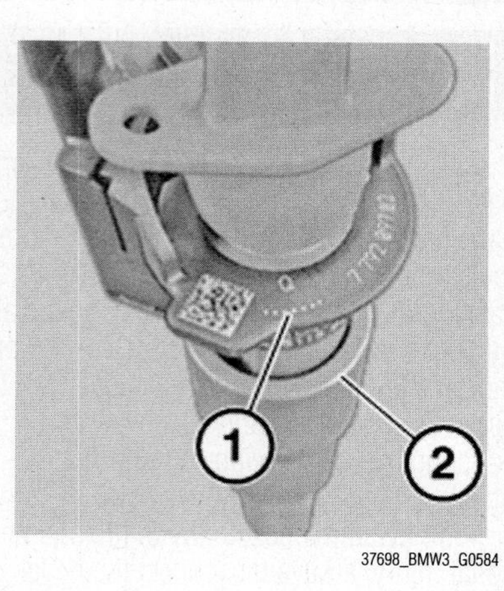

Fig. 284 Read off adjustment value on new injector

14. Install all pressure lines. Refer to diesel fuel injection, injection lines, removal & installation.
15. Replace sealing rings on leakage oil lines.

➡In the case of piezo injectors, the seven-digit adjustment value must be stored in the control unit after an injector has been replaced.

16. Read off adjustment value on new injector.
17. If injectors have been replaced, perform an "Injector map adjustment" using the STAR Diagnostic tool.
    a. Connect DIS Tester
    b. Identify car
18. Clear the fault memory.

FUEL SUPPLY PUMP

REMOVAL & INSTALLATION

M57 Engine

See Figures 285 through 287.

1. Before servicing the vehicle, refer to the precautions.
2. Drain the fuel tank. Refer to diesel fuel system, fuel tank, draining.
3. Remove rear seat bench.
   a. Unclip rear seat on left and right towards top.
   b. Lift out rear seat.
4. Release screws and remove cover from right side of fuel tank.
5. Disconnect plug connection.
6. If necessary, remove fuel line for independent heating.

7. Release screw cap with special tool 16 1 020 and remove service cap.
8. Pull out service cover.
9. Unlock and disconnect quick-release fastener of fuel feed line.
10. Disconnect line towards top
11. Unlock quick-release fastener and detach fuel return line.

WARNING

Do not use any tools to release the fuel feed line.

12. Draw off remaining fuel from surge chamber.
13. Carefully lift fuel pump with fuel level sensor out of fuel tank.

To install:

14. To install, reverse the removal procedure.
15. Clean sealing faces and install new rubber seal.
16. Locating rods must fit correctly in the hole of the delivery unit.
17. Make sure that the lever sensor moves freely before fitting the service cap.

WARNING

Service cap can only be installed in one position.

18. When installing, make sure lug of service cap engages in corresponding opening on fuel tank.

WARNING

Fit screw cap without using a tool and tighten hand-tight.

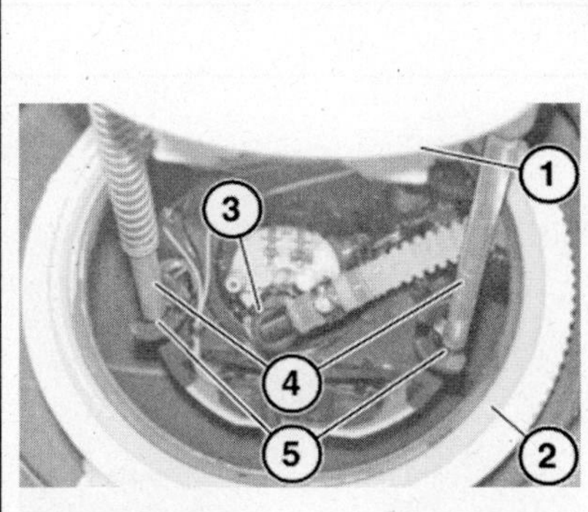

Fig. 285 Removing the pump module

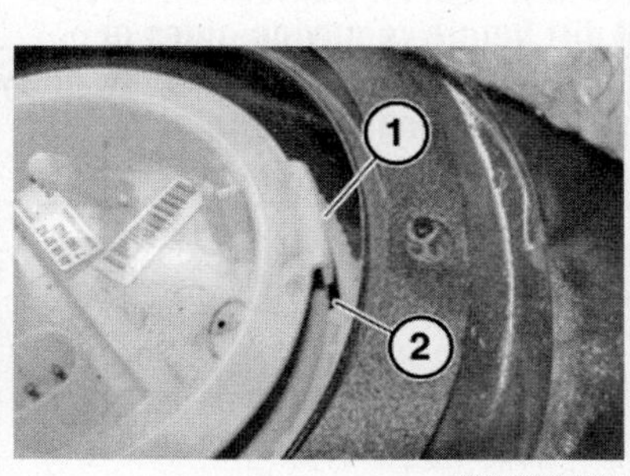

Fig. 286 When installing, make sure lug of service cap engages in corresponding opening on fuel tank.

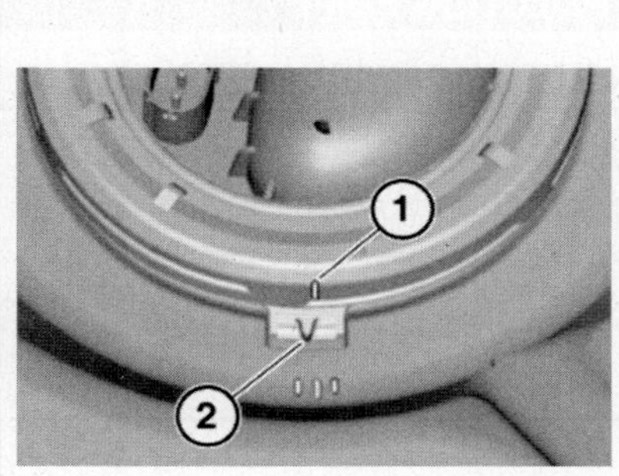

Fig. 287 Then tighten screw cap with special tool 16 1 020 until notch points to marking.

19. Then tighten screw cap with special tool 16 1 020 until notch points to marking.

WARNING

Before starting the engine for the first time, fill fuel tank with at least 1.3 gallons (5 liters) of fuel.

FUEL SYSTEM PURGING

BLEEDING

Turn on ignition and leave on for approximately 1 minute. In this period of time, the fuel pre-supply pump is activated and the fuel line to the high pressure pump vented.

GLOW PLUGS

REMOVAL & INSTALLATION

M57 Engine

See Figure 288.

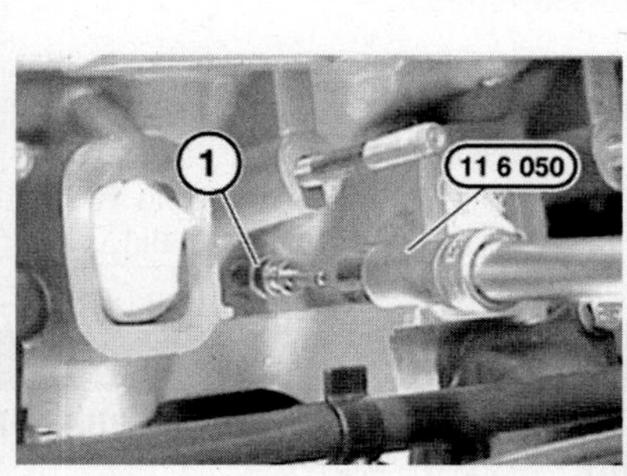

Fig. 288 Release glow plugs with special tool 11 6 050

1. Before servicing the vehicle, refer to the precautions.
2. Read out fault memory of DDE control unit.
3. Switch **OFF** ignition.

➡If malfunctions occur at the glow elements, it is absolutely essential to check the fuses behind the glove box.

4. Disconnect negative battery cable.
5. Remove intake air manifold. Refer to engine mechanical, intake manifold, removal & installation.
6. Unlock plug with special tool 12 2 300 and detach.
7. Release glow plugs with special tool 11 6 050.

➡If necessary, drill out special tool 11 6 050 with a 0.37 in. (9.5 mm) dia. twist drill bit approximately 0.78 in. (20 mm) deep.

To install:

8. To install, reverse the removal procedure.
9. Tighten bolts/nuts to specification as follows:
   - Glow plug: 19 ft. lbs. (25 Nm)
   - Glow plug (4 in.): 15 ft. lbs. (20 Nm)
10. Check stored fault messages and clear the fault memory.

INJECTION LINES

REMOVAL & INSTALLATION

M57 Engine

See Figure 289.

1. Before servicing the vehicle, refer to the precautions.

➡This procedure is applicable to all pressure lines.

2. Read fault memory of DDE control unit.
3. Switch **OFF** ignition.
4. Remove intake air manifold. Refer to engine mechanical, intake manifold, removal & installation.

⁂ WARNING

Cover intake ducts to prevent entry of dirt.

⁂ WARNING

When working on the oil, coolant or fuel circuit, you must protect the alternator against contamination. Cover alternator with suitable materials. Failure to comply with this procedure may result in an alternator malfunction.

⁂ WARNING

It is essential to adhere to conditions of absolute cleanliness when working on the fuel system. Do not allow any dirt particles or foreign bodies to get into the system. Use only fluff-free cloths. Remove all traces of dirt before removing pipes or individual components. Seal all fuel system openings with protective caps.

5. Release union nuts on pressure line with special tool 13 5 020.

To install:

6. To install, reverse the removal procedure.
7. Do not mix up pressure lines.
8. Hand-tighten all union nuts on pressure lines.
9. Tighten down union nuts on injectors to 17 ft. lbs. (23 Nm).
10. Check all components of common rail system for leaks.

INJECTION PUMP

REMOVAL & INSTALLATION

M57 Engine

See Figures 290 through 293

1. Before servicing the vehicle, refer to the precautions.

⁂ WARNING

Protect alternator against engine oil, coolant or fuel. Cover alternator with suitable cover.

2. Remove intake air manifold. Refer to engine mechanical, intake manifold, removal & installation.
3. Remove front splash guard.
4. Remove fan cowl. Refer to engine cooling, engine fan, removal & installation.
5. Remove alternator drive belt. Refer to engine mechanical, accessory drive belts, removal & installation.
6. Drain coolant from radiator. Refer to engine cooling, engine coolant, removal & installation.
7. Remove plastic return pipe.
8. Disconnect plug at high pressure pump.
9. Detach fuel feed line.
10. Detach fuel return line.

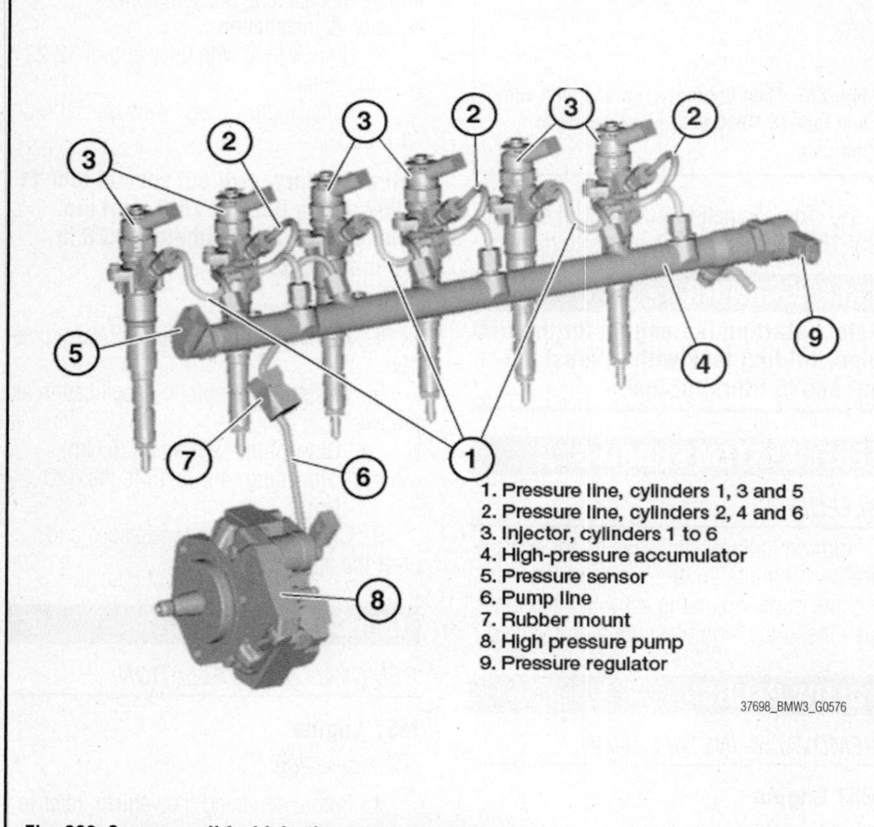

Fig. 289 Common rail fuel injection system components

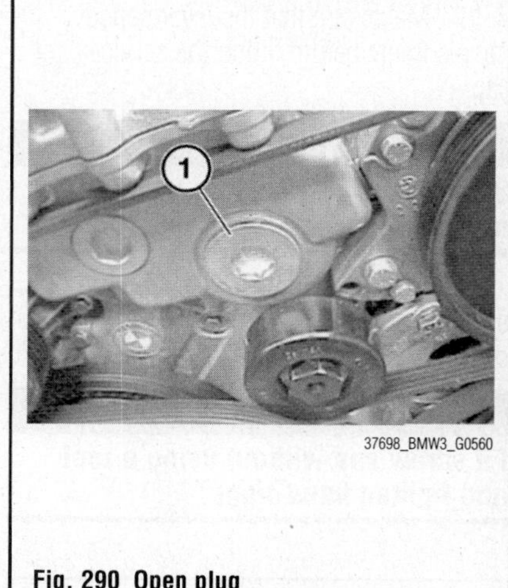

Fig. 290 Open plug

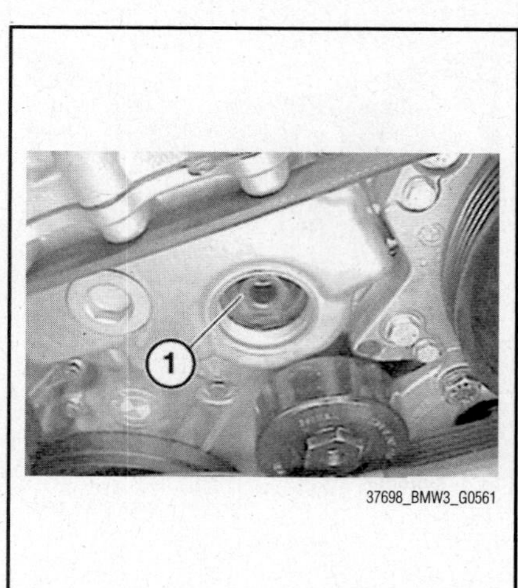

Fig. 291 Slacken nut

11. Release high-pressure line union nut with special tool 13 5 020.

12. Open plug as shown.

13. Slacken nut as shown.

14. Screw special tool 13 5 192 into timing case cover.

15. Firmly screw special tool 13 5 191 without jack screw into sprocket wheel by hand.

16. Screw in jack screw and pretension high pressure pump.

17. Unscrew nuts as shown.

18. Tighten jack screw until high-pressure pump is released from pump impeller.

WARNING

Special tools 13 5 191 and 13 5 192 must remain in timing case for securing purposes and must not be removed under any circumstances.

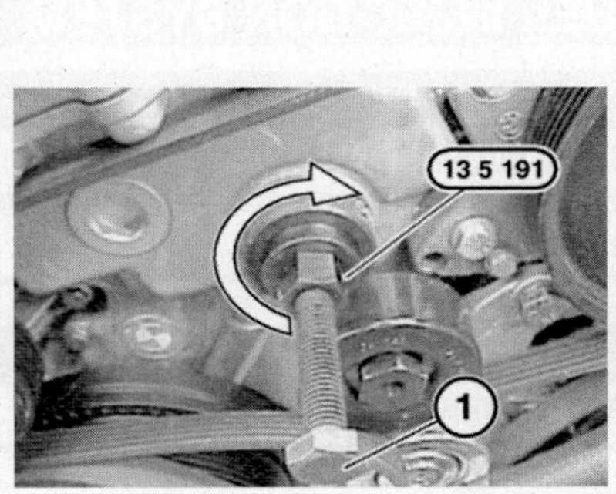

Fig. 292 Firmly screw special tool 13 5 191 without jack screw into sprocket wheel by hand. Screw in jack screwand pretension high pressure pump

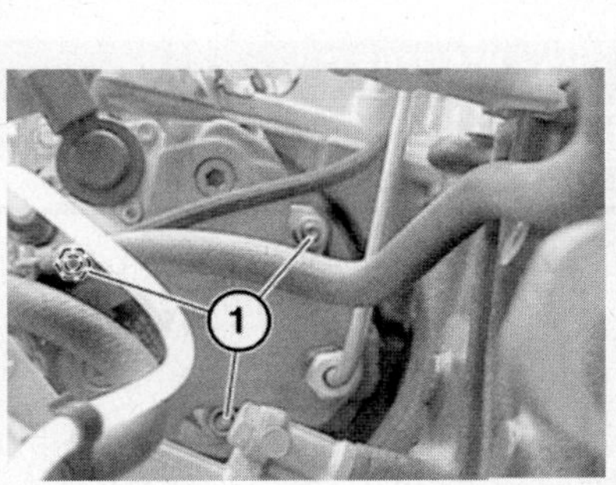

Fig. 293 Unscrew nuts

19. Remove jack screw to install high-pressure pump.

To install:

20. To install, reverse the removal procedure.

21. Replace high-pressure line.

22. Replace sealing ring on plug and apply light coat of oil to seal.

23. Replace high pressure pump gasket and position as previously noted.

WARNING

Sealing faces must be dry and grease-free.

24. Tighten bolts/nuts to specification as follows:

- Injector: 17 ft. lbs. (23 Nm)
- Pressure accumulator, fuel distributor or high-pressure pump: 17 ft. lbs. (23 Nm)
- Screw plug to timing case cover (M30x1): 52 ft. lbs. (70 Nm)
- Screw plug to timing case cover (M40x1.5): 22 ft. lbs. (30 Nm)
- Sprocket wheel to high pressure pump: 48 ft. lbs. (65 Nm)

25. To vent fuel system, turn on ignition for 1 minute.

OIL PRESSURE REGULATOR

REMOVAL & INSTALLATION

M57 Engine

See Figure 294.

1. Before servicing the vehicle, refer to the precautions.

2. Read fault memory of DDE control unit.

3. Switch **OFF** ignition.

4. Remove intake air manifold. Refer to engine mechanical, intake manifold, removal & installation.

WARNING

Cover intake ducts to prevent entry of dirt.

WARNING

Protect alternator against escaping fuel. Cover alternator with suitable material.

5. Disconnect connector.

➡Grip at hexagon head when removing pressure sensor.

6. Release hexagon screw connection on pressure accumulator.

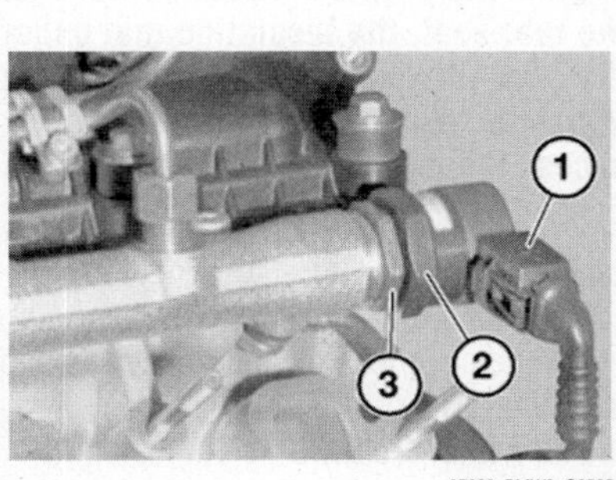

Fig. 294 Disconnect connector, grip at hexagon head when removing pressure sensor and release hexagon screw connection on pressure accumulator

To install:

7. To install, reverse the removal procedure.

➡Pressure regulator may only be used once. Note positioning before final tightening.

8. Secure position of pressure regulator and grip at hexagon fitting.

9. Tighten down hexagon screw connection.

10. Tighten rail pressure regulator to pressure accumulator as follows:

- Tighten to 45 ft. lbs. (60 Nm)
- Loosen by 90°
- Tighten to 63 ft. lbs. (85 Nm)

11. Clear the fault memory.

FUEL TANK

REMOVAL & INSTALLATION

1. Before servicing the vehicle, refer to the precautions.

2. Relive the fuel system pressure and disconnect the negative battery cable.

3. Drain the fuel, if filled beyond⅓of the capacity of the fuel tank. Drain the fuel tank enough to prevent spillage when removing the pump using an approved fuel removal device.

➡The fuel pump must be removed through the top of the fuel tank, thus the location of the fuel tank determines whether the fuel pump is accessed by removal of the rear seat, or removal of the trim panels in the trunk.

4. Remove the rear seat, or the trim panels in the trunk, depending on fuel tank location to access the top of the fuel tank

➡On models which require removal of the rear seat, the insulation mat under the seat must be cut in a "U" shape to allow the insulation to be folded up to access the top of the fuel tank.

5. Remove guide tube for handbrake cables.
6. Remove right wheel arch trim.
7. Remove rear left and right underbody paneling.
8. Remove left and right underbody cover.
9. Remove screws and remove cover from left and right sides of fuel tank.
10. Remove the fuel sending unit.
11. Remove hose clamp and detach fuel filler hose from fuel filler pipe.
12. Unlock quick-remove fastener and detach vent line.
13. Disconnect vent line from holder.
14. Support the fuel tank using a transmission jack.
15. Disconnect and discard the fuel tank-to-body self-locking nut.
16. Remove screws for tightening straps on left and right and remove tightening straps.
17. Carefully lower fuel tank.

⁂ WARNING

Carefully feed the vent line through the body when lowering the fuel tank.

To install:

➡Note rubber mount with spacer bush. Wide collar on spacer bush points to screw head.

18. Carefully raise fuel tank.

⁂ WARNING

Carefully feed the vent line through the body when raising the fuel tank.

19. Install tightening straps and tighten screws to 14 ft. lbs. (19 Nm).
20. Install a new fuel tank-to-body self-locking nut and tighten to 14 ft. lbs. (19 Nm).
21. Connect vent line to holder.
22. Connect vent line and lock quick-remove fastener.
23. Connect fuel filler hose to fuel filler pipe and secure hose clamp.
24. Install the fuel sending unit.
25. Install cover from left and right sides of fuel tank.
26. Install left and right underbody cover.
27. Install rear left and right underbody paneling.
28. Install right wheel arch trim.
29. Install guide tube for handbrake cables.
30. Install rear seat bench.

FUEL

GASOLINE FUEL INJECTION SYSTEM

FUEL SYSTEM SERVICE PRECAUTIONS

Safety is the most important factor when performing not only fuel system maintenance but any type of maintenance. Failure to conduct maintenance and repairs in a safe manner may result in serious personal injury or death. Maintenance and testing of the vehicle's fuel system components can be accomplished safely and effectively by adhering to the following rules and guidelines.

- To avoid the possibility of fire and personal injury, always disconnect the negative battery cable unless the repair or test procedure requires that battery voltage be applied.
- Always relieve the fuel system pressure prior to disconnecting any fuel system component (injector, fuel rail, pressure regulator, etc.), fitting or fuel line connection. Exercise extreme caution whenever relieving fuel system pressure to avoid exposing skin, face and eyes to fuel spray. Please be advised that fuel under pressure may penetrate the skin or any part of the body that it contacts.
- Always place a shop towel or cloth around the fitting or connection prior to loosening to absorb any excess fuel due to spillage. Ensure that all fuel spillage (should it occur) is quickly removed from engine surfaces. Ensure that all fuel soaked cloths or towels are deposited into a suitable waste container.
- Always keep a dry chemical (Class B) fire extinguisher near the work area.
- Do not allow fuel spray or fuel vapors to come into contact with a spark or open flame.
- Always use a back-up wrench when loosening and tightening fuel line connection fittings. This will prevent unnecessary stress and torsion to fuel line piping.
- Always replace worn fuel fitting O-rings with new Do not substitute fuel hose or equivalent where fuel pipe is installed.

Before servicing the vehicle, make sure to also refer to the precautions in the beginning of this section as well.

FUEL LINES & FITTINGS

REMOVAL & INSTALLATION

N20 and N26 Engines

Feed Line

See Figures 295 through 298.

⁂ WARNING

Disconnect negative battery terminal (risk of fire due to short circuit on removal).

⁂ WARNING

Electric fuel pump starts up automatically when door is opened.

⁂ WARNING

Carry out installation work on fuel system only with coolant temperature below 40 °C.

⁂ CAUTION

Wear safety goggles.

⁂ WARNING

Ignition coils must not be contaminated by fuel.

⁂ WARNING

The resistance of the silicone material is reduced significantly by contact with fuel, which may cause the ignition coil to fail.

⁂ WARNING

Cover ignition coil with suitable means.

1. Remove acoustic cover.
2. Remove middle bulkhead sound insulation.
3. Release screws.
4. Undo screw from cable clip at rear.
5. Lift out cable clip.
6. Detach the fuel line at the snap fastener.
7. Release bolt at rear of cylinder head. Tightening torque: 7-12 ft. lbs. (10-16 Nm)

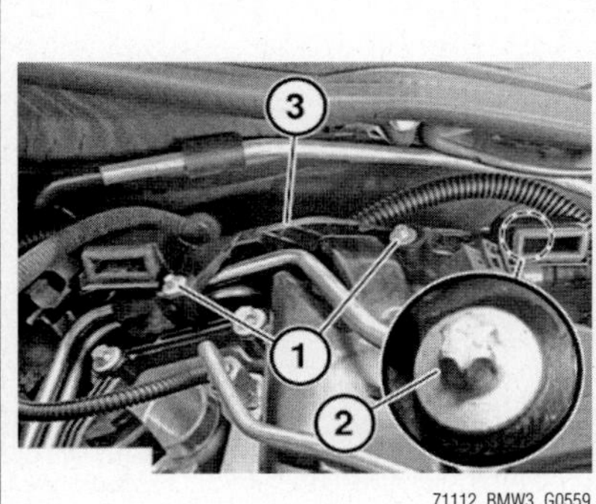

Fig. 295 Releasing screws, undoing screw from cable clip and removing

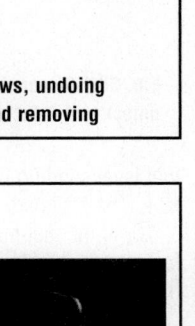

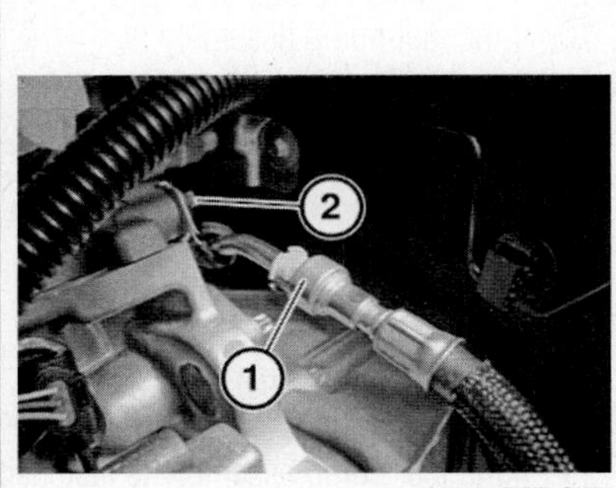

Fig. 296 Detaching fuel line at snap fastener and releasing bolt

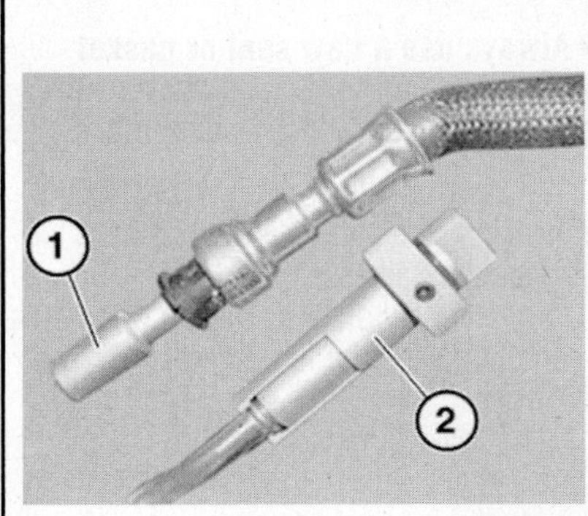

Fig. 297 Closing fuel lines with special tools (1 and 2)

8. Close fuel lines with special tools 13 5 161 and 13 5 162 from special tool set 13 5 160.

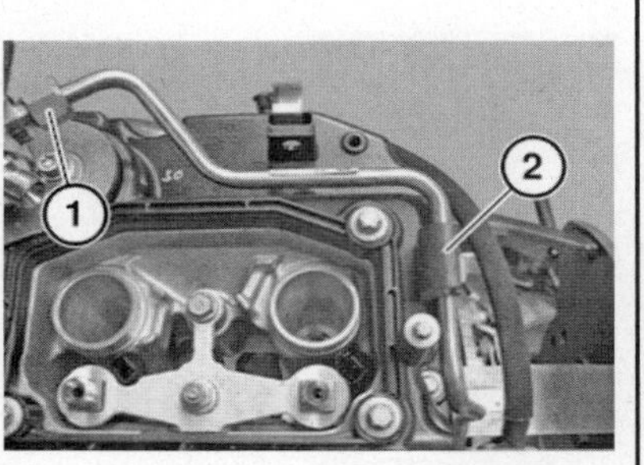

Fig. 298 Slackening nut and releasing feel line from clamp

9. Slacken nut. Tightening torque: 20-24 ft. lbs. (27-33 Nm)

10. Release the feed line from the clamp, thread out toward the top and remove.

To install:

To install, reverse the removal procedure noting the following.

11. Assemble engine.
12. Check fuel system for tightness.
13. Check function of DME.

N55 Engine

Feed Line

See Figures 299 through 301.

⁂ WARNING

Disconnect negative battery terminal (risk of fire due to short circuit on removal).

⁂ WARNING

Electric fuel pump starts up automatically when door is opened.

⁂ WARNING

Carry out installation work on fuel system only with coolant temperature below 40 °C.

⁂ CAUTION

Wear safety goggles.

⁂ WARNING

Ignition coils must not be contaminated by fuel.

⁂ WARNING

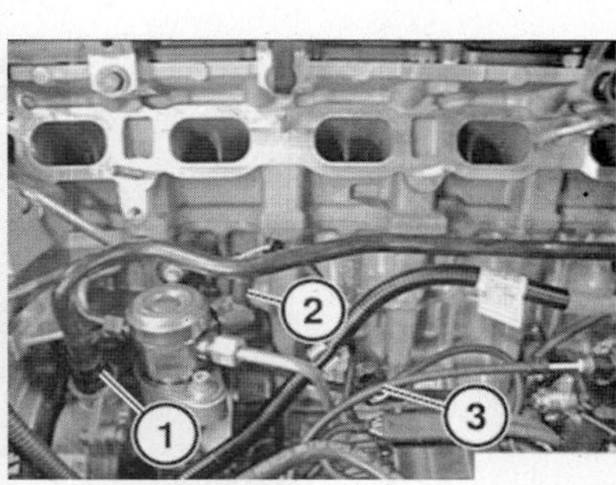

Fig. 299 Unlocking and detaching vacuum line and connector

The resistance of the silicone material is reduced significantly by contact with fuel, which may cause the ignition coil to fail.

⁂ WARNING

Cover ignition coil with suitable means.

1. Remove intake plenum.
2. Unlock and detach vacuum line from the vacuum pump.
3. Unlock and pull off connector from the high pressure pump and connector(3) from the oil temperature sensor.
4. Release screws below cable channel.
5. Replace aluminum screws.

➡Adhere to tightening/torque sequence.

6. Release fuel hose and seal with special tool 13 5 160.
7. Release nut on high pressure pump.
8. Remove feed line.
9. Close off feed line and high pressure pump with a matching plug from set of special tools 32 1 270.

To install:

To install, reverse the removal procedure noting the following.

➡When installing, adhere to tightening/torque sequence.

10. First, fit feed line on high pressure pump and engine block only hand-tight. Do not connect fuel hose to the feed line yet.
11. Tighten screws below the cable channel. Tightening torque: 44 inch lbs. (5 Nm) + 75-115°
12. Replace aluminum screws.
13. Tighten union nut with special tool

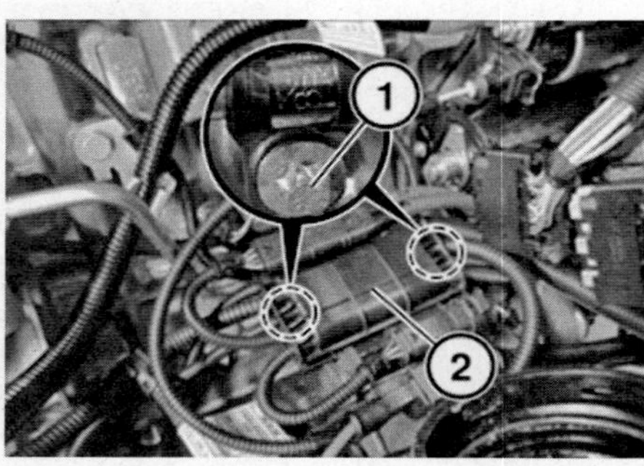

Fig. 300 Removing and installing screws below cable channel

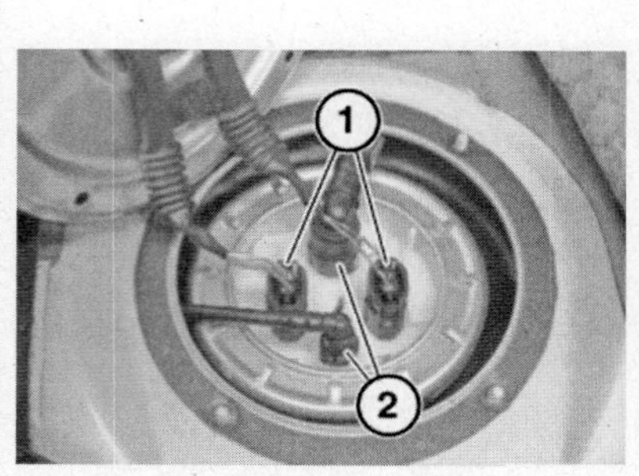

Fig. 302 Disconnect plug connection, unlock and detach vent lines

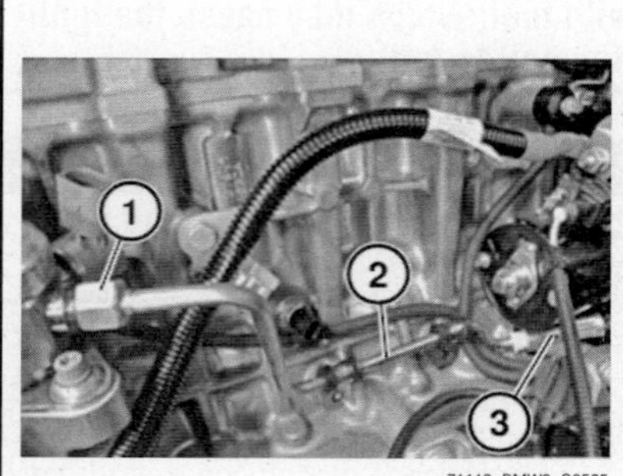

Fig. 301 Releasing fuel hose and seal with special tool and removing feed line

13 5 020. Tightening torque: 20-24 ft. lbs. (27-33 Nm)

14. Reconnect fuel hose to feed line.
15. Assemble engine.
16. Check fuel system for tightness.
17. Check function of DME.

FUEL FILTER

REMOVAL & INSTALLATION

The fuel filter is an integral component of the fuel level/fuel pump assembly in the fuel tank and is not normally serviced.

FUEL PUMP MODULE

REMOVAL & INSTALLATION

See Figure 302.

The fuel pump is mounted through the top of the fuel tank along with the fuel level sending unit. The fuel tank should not be filled more than ⅓ of the total fuel tank capacity to prevent fuel leakage during fuel pump removal. If the fuel tank is filled beyond this level, the fuel level must be reduced using an approved fuel removal device.

1. Before servicing the vehicle, refer to the precautions.
2. Relive the fuel system pressure and disconnect the negative battery cable.
3. Drain the fuel, if filled beyond⅓of the capacity of the fuel tank. Drain the fuel tank enough to prevent spillage when removing the pump using an approved fuel removal device.

➡The fuel pump must be removed through the top of the fuel tank, thus the location of the fuel tank determines whether the fuel pump is accessed by removal of the rear seat, or removal of the trim panels in the trunk.

4. Remove the rear seat, or the trim panels in the trunk, depending on fuel tank location to access the top of the fuel tank

➡On models which require removal of the rear seat, the insulation mat under the seat must be cut in a "U" shape to allow the insulation to be folded up to access the top of the fuel tank.

5. Remove the fasteners securing the metal cover located above the fuel tank, and remove the cover.
6. Remove the electrical connector at the top of the combination fuel pump and fuel level sending unit assembly.
7. Remove the fuel feed and return lines.
8. Match mark the combination fuel pump and fuel level sending unit assembly to the fuel tank to ensure proper installation during reassembly.
9. Remove the fasteners or fastener securing the combination fuel pump and fuel level sending unit assembly to the fuel tank. The fasteners are one of 2 types.
10. If the fuel pump assembly is fastened to the fuel tank with a series of 6 mm nuts:
    a. Loosen the nuts evenly using a crisscross sequence and carefully lift the cover and place aside.
    b. Compress the large plastic tongue to remove the fuel pump, and lift the pump along with the fuel sending unit out of the fuel tank.
11. If the fuel pump assembly is fastened to the fuel tank with a large sealing ring:
    a. Use tool No. 16-1-020 to loosen the sealing ring in a counterclockwise direction.
    b. With the seal ring removed, lift the fuel pump assembly out of the fuel tank.

To install:

➡Always use a new seal or gasket when installing the fuel pump or fuel level gauge sending unit assembly.

12. Install the fuel pump into the fuel tank taking care not to bend or damage the fuel sending unit assembly.
13. If the fuel pump is held in place by a plastic bracket in the fuel tank perform the following:
    a. Make sure the fuel pump is fully snapped in place.
    b. Install the fuel tank cover plate with a new gasket and torque the fasteners using a crisscross pattern to 57 inch lbs. (6.5 Nm).
14. If the fuel pump is held in place with a sealing ring perform the following:
    a. Ensure the pump is properly aligned with the fuel tank matchmarks made during disassembly.

b. Install a new seal and torque the sealing ring using tool No. 16-1-020 as follows:

- Metal sealing rings: 26 ft. lbs. (35 Nm)
- Plastic sealing rings: 41 ft. lbs. (55 Nm)

15. The balance of the assembly is in reverse order of disassembly.
16. Connect the negative battery cable.
17. Once the vehicle is started, check for leaks. If a strong fuel odor is present, or any fuel leakage is noted, stop the engine immediately and repair as necessary.

N54 Engine (High Pressure Pump)

See Figures 303 through 306.

1. Before servicing the vehicle, refer to the precautions.
2. Disconnect battery negative terminal.

⁂ WARNING

Electric fuel pump starts up automatically each time door is opened.

3. Remove intake air manifold. Refer to engine mechanical, intake manifold, removal & installation.
4. Unlock plug and remove.
5. Unlock and detach fuel line.
6. Catch and dispose of escaping fuel.
7. Seal fuel lines with special tools 13 5 281 and 13 5 282.
8. Remove nut, remove bolt and remove feed line.
9. Seal feed line with matching plug from special tool kit 32 1 270.

⁂ WARNING

Wear full face guard and protective gloves.

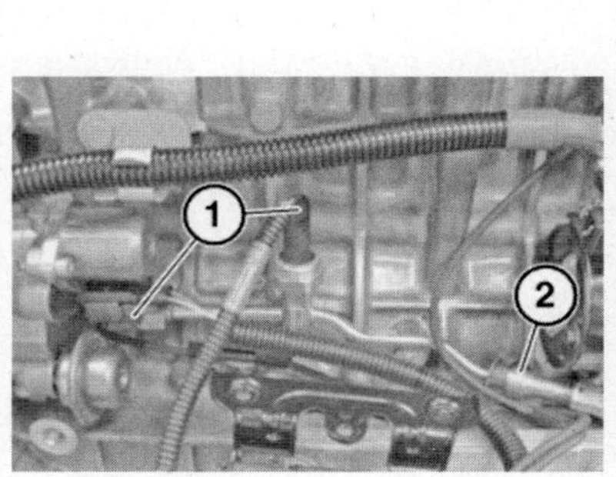

Fig. 303 Unlock plug and remove. Unlock and detach fuel line

10. Remove nut, slacken nut, unscrew bolt and disconnect high-pressure line.

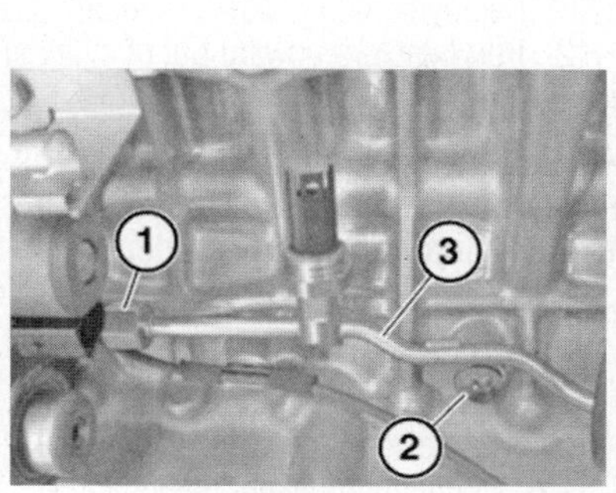

Fig. 304 Remove nut, remove bolt and remove feed line

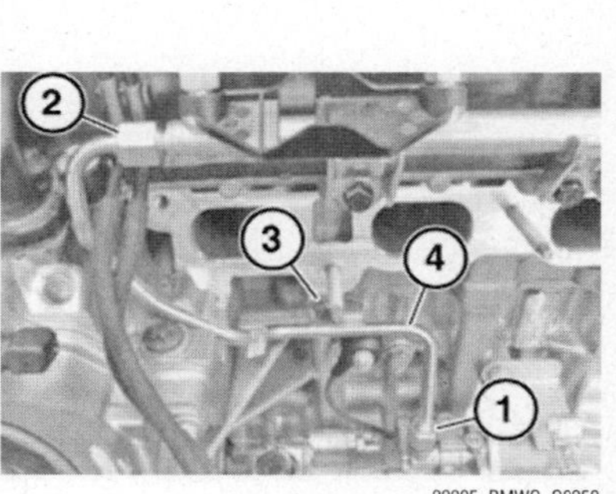

Fig. 305 Remove nut, slacken nut, unscrew bolt and disconnect high-pressure line

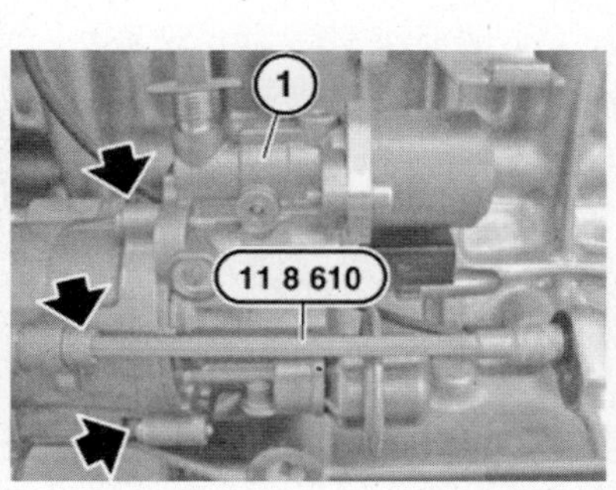

Fig. 306 Remove screws with special tool 11 8 610

11. Seal connections of high-pressure line with matching plugs from special tool kit 32 1 270.
12. Seal fuel line connections of high-pressure pump with matching plugs from special tool kit 32 1 270.
13. Remove screws with special tool 11 8 610.
14. Disconnect high-pressure pump and remove.

➡Engine oil can escape when pump is detached; have a cleaning cloth ready.

To install:

15. Replace sealing ring and clean contact faces.
16. When installing, turn high-pressure pump until bores for screws are flush.
17. Tighten screws of high-pressure pump with special tool 11 8 610 hand-tight only. It must still be possible to turn the high-pressure pump at the flange. This prevents twisting when high-pressure line is tightened.

➡Copper seals that may be fitted on the high-pressure line are no longer needed and must be removed. If reusing pressure line, lightly grease threads of pressure connections. Threads of new pressure lines are already coated.

18. Pre-install high-pressure line. Tighten screw connections hand-tight only. You must still be able to move the high-pressure line at the holder.
19. Only when high-pressure pump has if necessary turned into position and is thus pre-installed without twisting with high pressure-line should screws of high-pressure pump be tightened down with special tool 11 8 610. Tighten to 7 ft. lbs. (9 Nm).
20. Follow sequence of screw connections:
    - Coat with transmission oil. Tighten down nut with special tool 13 5 020 to 22 ft. lbs. (30 Nm).
    - Coat with transmission oil. Tighten nut to 22 ft. lbs. (30 Nm).
    - Tighten down screw for holder to 10 ft. lbs. (13 Nm).

➡Feed lines with soldered holder must be replaced by new version with Elastomeric clamp holder. Observe installation position of fuel low-pressure sensor. Lines for solenoid switches are laid behind fuel line.

21. Install feed line. In so doing, tighten screw connection hand-tight only
22. Follow sequence of screw connections:

- Coat with transmission oil and tighten down nut with special tool 13 5 020 to 22 ft. lbs. (30 Nm).
- Replace aluminum screw, coat with transmission oil and tighten to 8 ft. lbs. (10 Nm) plus an additional 90° of rotation.

23. Once the vehicle is started, check for leaks. If a strong fuel odor is present, or any fuel leakage is noted, stop the engine immediately and repair as necessary.

FUEL RAIL & INJECTORS

REMOVAL & INSTALLATION

N20 and N26 Engines

See Figures 307 through 324.

1. Before servicing the vehicle, refer to the precautions.
2. Remove ignition coils.
3. Release pressure line at high pressure pump and rail, do not remove.

WARNING

Observe screw fastening sequence without fail.

4. Unlock connector and remove.
5. Unscrew nuts.
6. Release screws a few threads until rail is loose.
7. Turn rail anticlockwise until injectors can be removed.

➡The following description applies to all injectors.

8. Unlock connector from injectors and detach.
9. Slacken nut. Tightening torque: 40 inch lbs. (4.5 Nm)
10. Remove ground cable.

WARNING

First, release screw. The, release screw. Otherwise, the hold-down device may tilt.

11. Remove holding-down element.
12. Pull injectors upward out of cylinder head and remove.

➡If several injectors are removed, ensure that each injector is reinstalled in its original location (cylinder).

13. Mark injectors.

In event of stuck injector

a. Use special tool 0 496 885 to remove injectors that are stuck.
b. Lightly oil pull-out thread and unscrew completely before using the special tool.

WARNING

Pull out thread is left hand thread.

14. Fit special tool 0 496 885 on injector slot. Join screws to injector slot by a few threads. Screw in pull-out thread until it is possible to screw the threaded sleeves onto the injectors. Screw threaded sleeves onto injectors and tighten down.

Tighten down screws. Tightening torque: 6 ft. lbs. (8 Nm)

WARNING

Set torque wrench to 5 Nm clockwise rotation. Together with special tool 0 496 885 this corresponds to a tensile force of max. 2000 N. The injector must be replaced if the torque wrench clicks when the injector is pulled out.

15. Fit torque wrench and special tool 00 9 170 on hexagon head of special tool 0 496 885.
16. Turn torque wrench in clockwise direction until the injector is pulled out.

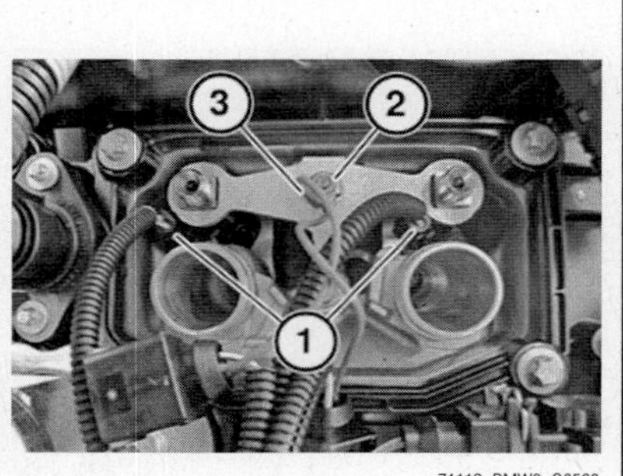

Fig. 308 Unlocking connector, slackening nut and removing ground cable

Fig. 310 Fitting special tool, joining screws, screwing on pull out thread until it is possible to screw the threaded sleeve onto the injectors

Fig. 307 Unlocking and removing connector, unscrewing nuts and releasing screws until rail is loose

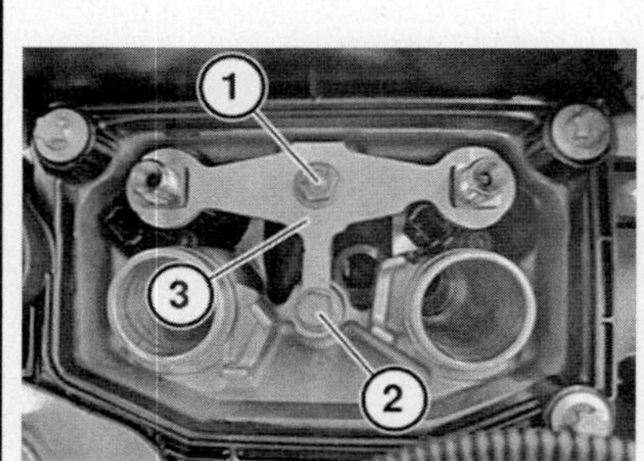

Fig. 309 Releasing screw, thenscrew and removing holding-down element

Fig. 311 Fitting torque wrench and special tool on hexagon head of special tool

17. After removing, fit protective caps (1 and 2) to injector tip and fuel line connection.

➡When installing a new injector, replace decoupling element.

➡When installing and reusing fuel injector, replace the decoupling element and Teflon ring.

➡A Teflon ring that has already been installed once in the cylinder head must be replaced before the injector is reinstalled.

➡Before replacing the Teflon ring, make sure your hands and the work surface are clean and free of oil.

WARNING

Avoid mechanical contact with injector tip.

18. Remove Teflon ring from injector with special tool 13 0 191 from set of special tools 13 0 190.

19. Use a fluff-free cloth only to remove combustion residues from cylindrical part of injector tip (do not use ultrasound or other tools/agents).

20. Do not clean injector tip.

21. Slide new Teflon ring onto installation cone13 0 283 from set of special tools 13 0 280.

22. Fit Teflon ring on injector tip with installation cone 13 0 283 from set of special tools 13 0 280.

WARNING

Do not use fingernails to slide Teflon ring on.

WARNING

Do not use any lubricating agents.

➡The sealing ring is expanded when slid on.

23. Use special tool 13 0 281 from set of special tools 13 0 280 to slide Teflon ring into groove on injector.

24. To bring the widened Teflon ring to the installation dimension, special tool 13 0 282 from set of special tools 13 0 280 must be slid up to limit position on injector.

WARNING

Do not use any lubricating agents.

25. Pull mounting tip of special tool 13 0 282 towards rear to release installation cone 13 0 281.

To install:

➡Before installing injector in engines that have been run:

WARNING

Injectors must not be twisted to 6 Nm.

WARNING

The injector must be replaced if this value is exceeded.

a. Check injector bore for dirt.

b. Clean only dirty injector bores.

WARNING

Important - do not damage injector.

Clean

c. injector bore: To do so, preferably slide injector without decoupling element but with new Teflon ring in and out of injector bores several times.

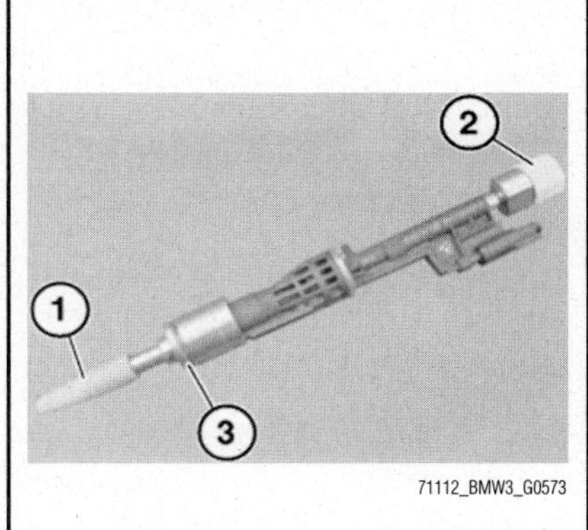

Fig. 312 Identifying protective caps (1 and 2) and decoupling elements

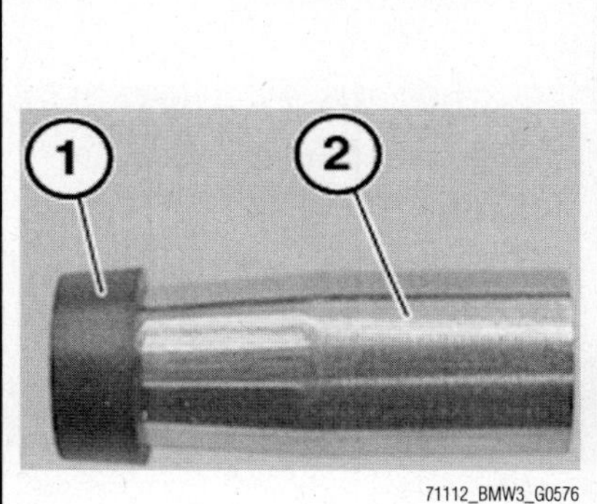

Fig. 314 Sliding new Teflon ring onto installation cone13 0 283 from set of special tools 13 0 280

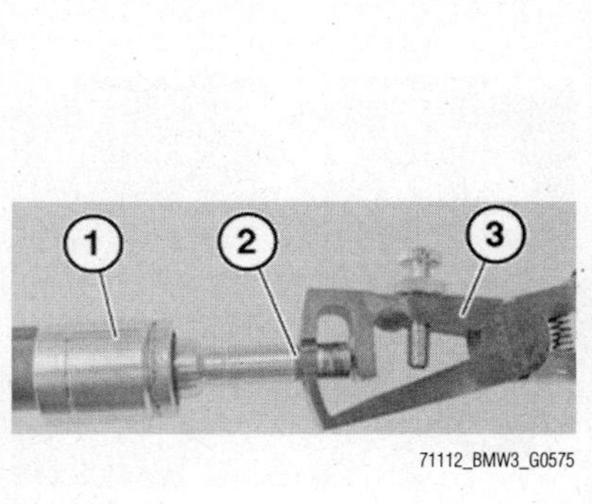

Fig. 313 Removing Teflon ring from injector with special tool

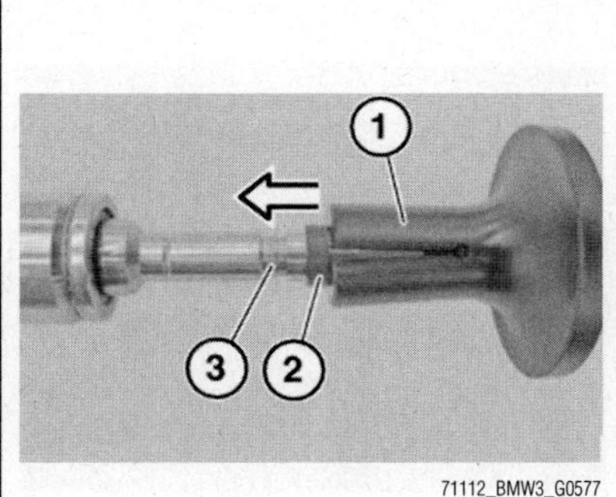

Fig. 315 Using special tool 13 0 281 from set of special tools 13 0 280 to slide Teflon ring into groove on injector

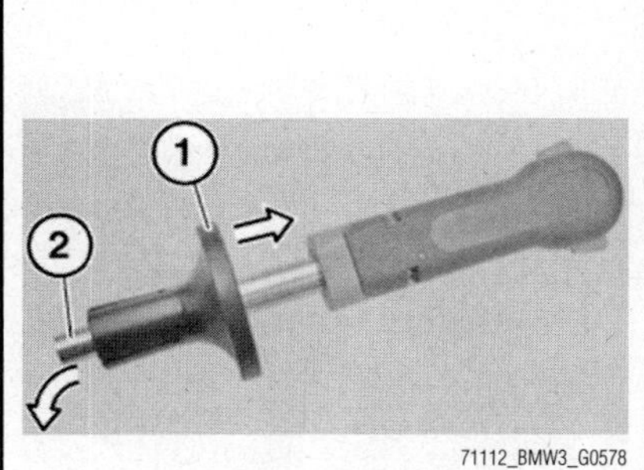

Fig. 316 Pulling mounting tip of special tool 13 0 282 towards rear to release installation cone 13 0 281

d. The Teflon ring must subsequently be replaced.

e. Clean contact surfaces of decoupling elements in cylinder head.

f. Replace decoupling element.

➡An injector quantity compensation must be carried out if an injector is replaced or changed on the cylinder side.

➡Injector quantity compensation is carried out with the aid of a so-called adjustment value.

➡The adjustment value is printed in three digits on the injector body.

➡The adjustment value must be read off before installation1

➡Enter the adjustment value according to the installation location (cylinder) of the injector.

➡If injector quantity compensation is not carried out, the engine may run roughly or fail to start.

26. Insert injectors in injector bores.

27. Fit special tool 0 496 885 on injector slot. Join screws to injector slot by a few threads. Screw in pull-out thread until it is possible to screw the threaded sleeves onto the injectors. Screw threaded sleeves onto injectors and tighten down.

28. Tighten down screws. Tightening torque: 6 ft lbs. (8 Nm)

➡Set torque wrench to 2 Nm counterclockwise rotation.

29. Fit torque wrench and special tool 00 9 170 on hexagon head of special tool 0 496 885.

30. Turn torque wrench in counterclockwise direction until 2 Nm are reached.

31. Install hold-down device with curvatures (black arrows) downward.

32. Fit hold-down device on injectors.

WARNING

Only hand-tighten screw. Screw the screw(2) in by only a few threads. Otherwise, the hold-down device may tilt.

33. Install rail, manually tightening nuts and bolts only.

➡Rail must still be displaceable on cylinder head.

➡Nuts must be able to be screwed on easily by hand.

34. Firstly tighten screw. Tightening torque: 8-11 ft. lbs. (11-15 Nm)

35. Then tighten down screw. Tightening torque: 8-11 ft. lbs. (11-15 Nm)

36. First tighten screws. Tightening torque: 4-6 ft. lbs. (6-8 Nm)

37. Then tighten nuts on the injectors. Tightening torque: 8-11 ft. lbs. (11-15 Nm)

38. Push on connector for high pressure fuel sensor.

39. Install pressure line.

40. Tighten nut manually only.

WARNING

Connect pressure line without tension only.

WARNING

To ensure distortion-free installation of the pressure line and to avoid damaging the thread, it must be possible for both nuts to be screwed on easily by hand.

Follow the correct screw connection sequence:

Fig. 318 Fitting torque wrench and special tool on hexagon head

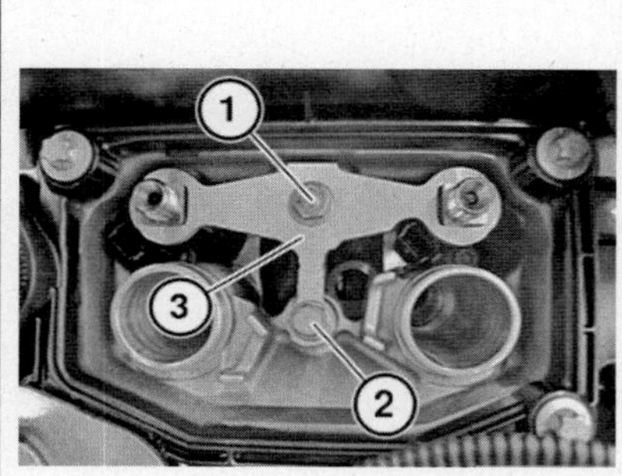

Fig. 320 Fitting hold down device on injectors, hand tightening screw and screwing the screw

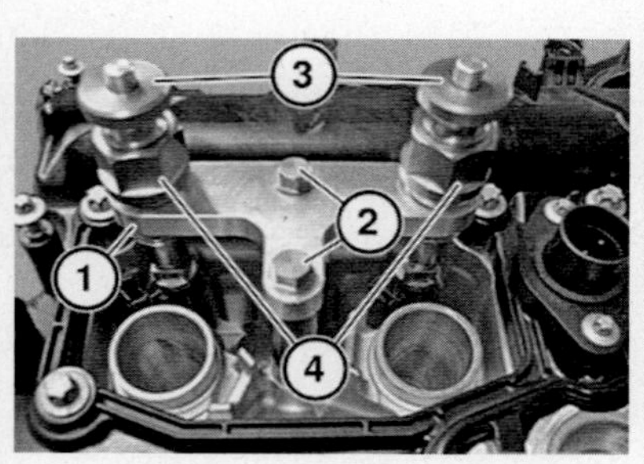

Fig. 317 Fitting special tool, joining screws, screwing threaded sleeves and pull out thread

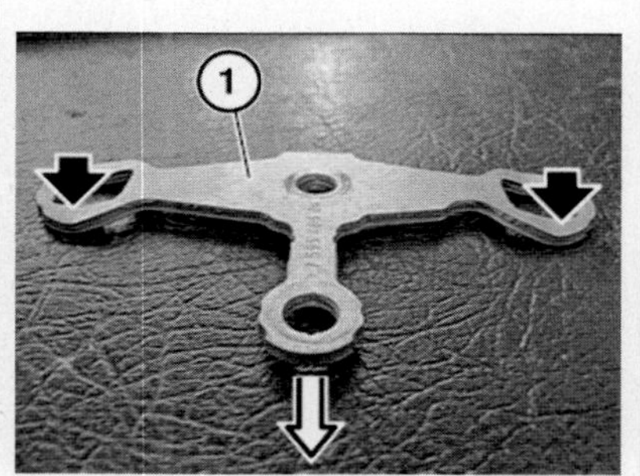

Fig. 319 Installing hold down device

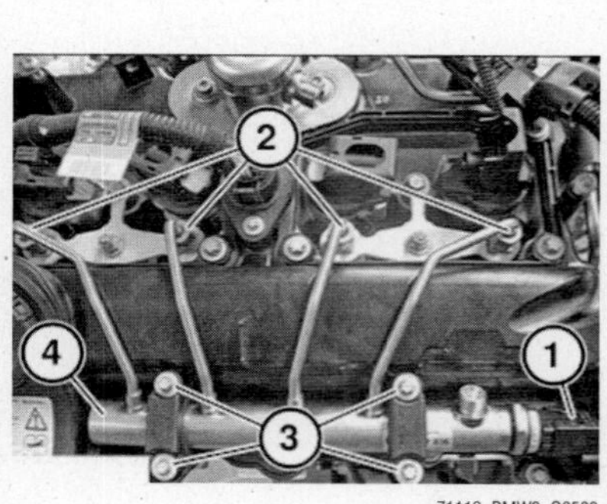

Fig. 321 Installing rail and manually tightening nuts and bolts

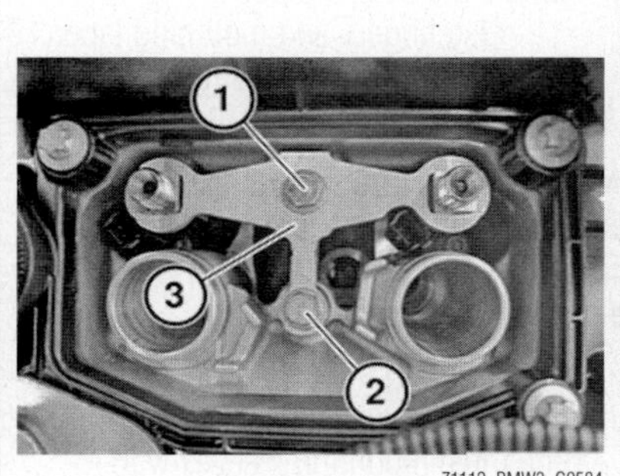

Fig. 322 Tightening screw then screw

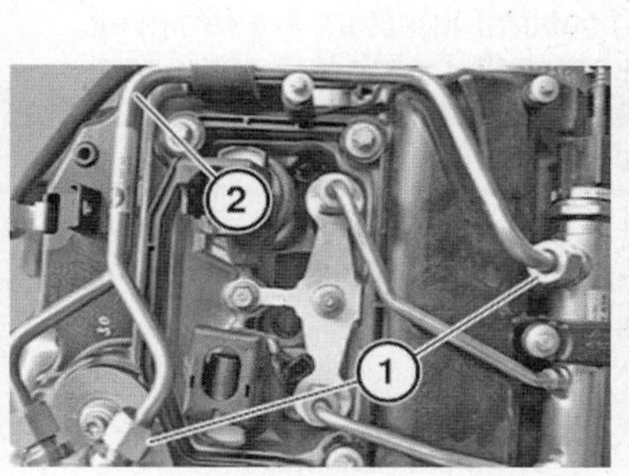

Fig. 324 Installing pressure line and tightening nut manually

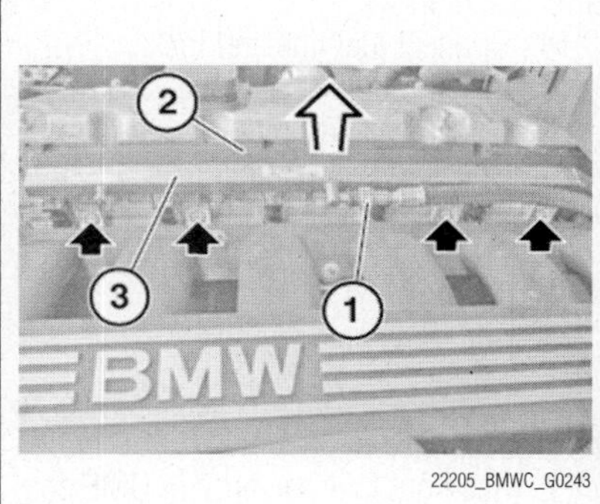

Fig. 326 Unlock and detach fuel line, detach connector strip, remove injection pipe.

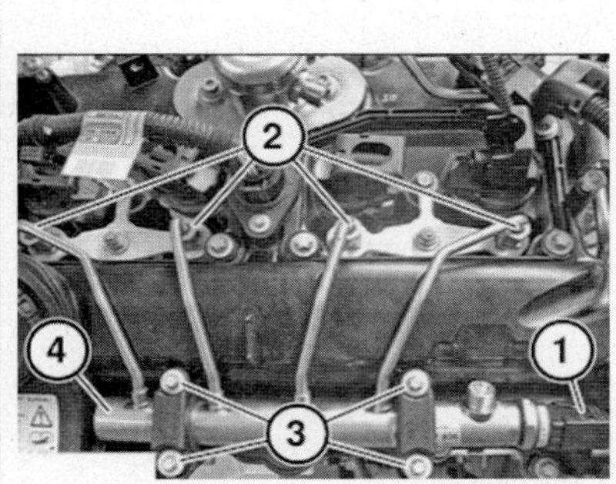

Fig. 323 Tightening screws, then nuts and pushing on connector

a. First tighten nut on high pressure pump. Tightening torque: 16-24 ft. lbs. (27-33 Nm)

b. Then tighten the nut on the rail. Tightening torque: 16-24 ft. lbs. (27-33 Nm)

41. Assemble the engine.
42. Check fuel system for tightness.
43. Check function of DME.
44. Perform an injection quantity compensation:

➡**The adjustment value is printed in three digits on the injector body.**

a. Connect BMW diagnosis system
b. Identify vehicle
c. Select "Function selection"
d. Select "Service functions"
e. Select "Engine electronics"
f. Select "Adjustment function"
g. Select "Adjust injectors"
h. Select "Test plan"
i. For each replaced injector, the adjustment value must be entered according to the installation location (cylinder).

45. Clean spark plug slot.
46. Assemble engine.
47. Check fuel system for tightness.
48. Check function of DME.

N52 Engine

See Figures 325 through 327.

1. Before servicing the vehicle, refer to the precautions.
2. Read out fault memory of DME control unit; if necessary, work through test schedules
3. Switch ignition **OFF**.
4. Remove clean air pipe.
5. Remove ignition coil cover.
6. If necessary, unclip plug connection from holder and disconnect. Unclip wiring harnesses from holder and connector strip. Disconnect holder from injection pipe.
7. Remove protective cap from compressed air valve. Connect compressed air line to compressed air valve. Blow fuel back into tank with a short blast of compressed air maximum of 43 PSI (3 bar).
8. Unlock and detach fuel line.
9. Disconnect connector strip.
10. Remove injection pipe.
11. Seal fuel hose with special tool 13 5 281.
12. Pry out retainers and pull fuel injectors out of injection pipe.

To install:

13. Replace sealing rings on fuel injectors and coat with anti-friction rubber coating.
14. Install injectors and capture with retainers.
15. Remove special tool 13 5 281.
16. Install injection pipe.

Fig. 325 Connect compressed air line to compressed air valve. Blow fuel back into tank with a short blast of compressed air maximum of 43 PSI (3 bar)

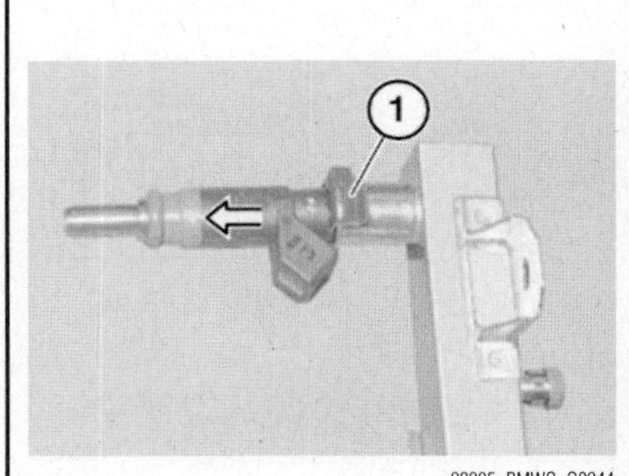

Fig. 327 Pry out retainers and pull fuel injectors out of injection pipe

17. Connect connector strip in reverse direction of arrow.
18. Connect fuel line and lock.
19. Install ignition coil cover.
20. Install clean air pipe.
21. Check for stored fault messages, rectify faults and clear the fault memory.

N54 Engine

See Figures 328 through 335.

1. Before servicing the vehicle, refer to the precautions.
2. Read out fault memory of DME control unit; if necessary, work through test schedules
3. Switch ignition **OFF**.
4. Remove the pressure line at the injector.
   a. Unlock plug and remove.
   b. Remove screw and remove holding-down element.
   c. Remove injector.

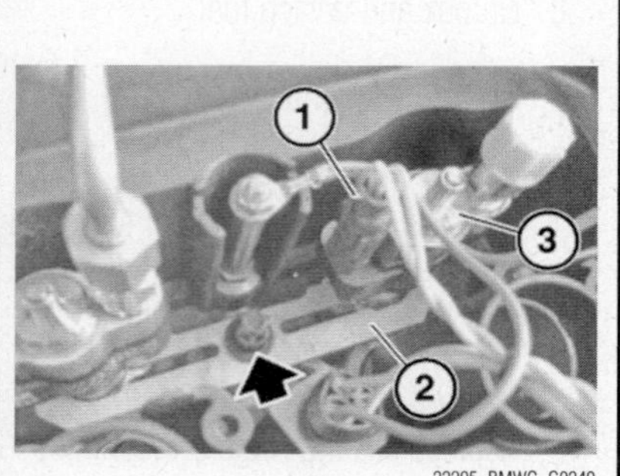

Fig. 328 Unlock plug, remove holding-down element and remove injector

⁂ WARNING

If several injectors are removed, ensure that each injector is reinstalled in its original location (cylinder). Mark injectors.

5. If the injector is stuck in its bore, perform the following procedure to free it:
   a. Mount special tool 13 0 180 on injector.
   b. Mount special tool 13 5 250.
   c. Carefully knock out injector with special tools 13 0 180 and 13 5 250.
   d. After removing, fit protective caps to injector tip and fuel line connection.

To install:

6. Installing a used fuel injector:
   a. Replace uncoupling element and the PTFE sealing ring.

⁂ WARNING

A PTFE seal which has been heated once by engine operation must be replaced before the fuel injector is reinstalled.

   b. Before replacing PTFE sealing ring, make sure hands and work surface are clean and free of oil.
   Avoid mechanical contact with injector tip.
   c. Remove PTFE sealing ring with special tool 13 0 191 from injector.
   d. Use a lint-free cloth only to remove combustion residues from cylindrical part of injector tip (do not use ultrasound or other tools/agents).

⁂ WARNING

Do not clean injector tip.

   e. Slide new PTFE sealing ring onto mounting taper 13 0 195.
   f. Use fingers and mounting taper 13 0 195 to slide PTFE sealing ring onto injector.

➡Do not use fingernails to slide PTFE sealing ring on. Do not use any lubricating agents. The sealing ring is expanded when slid on.

   g. To bring the expanded PTFE sealing ring to its installation dimension, slide three mounting sleeves with decreasing diameters onto the injector.
   h. Slide mounting sleeve with large opening first onto injector. Do not use any lubricating agents.
   i. First slide mounting sleeve 13 0 192 (large diameter) onto injector. Then slide mounting sleeve 13 0 193 (medium diameter) onto injector. Finally, press injector into mounting sleeve 13 0 194 (small diameter).

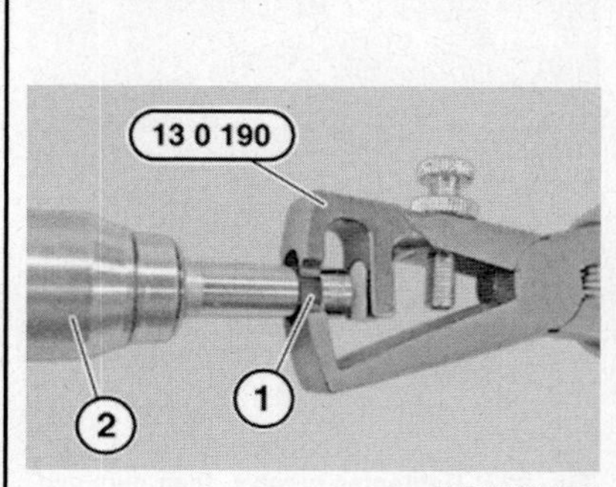

Fig. 331 Remove PTFE sealing ring with special tool 13 0 191 from injector

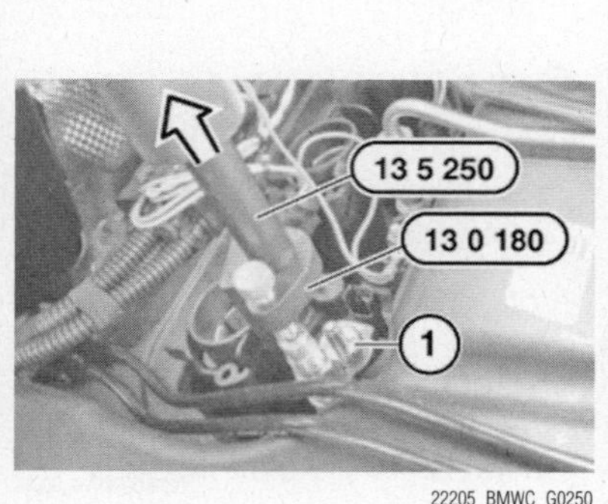

Fig. 329 Carefully knock out injector with special tools 13 0 180 and 13 5 250

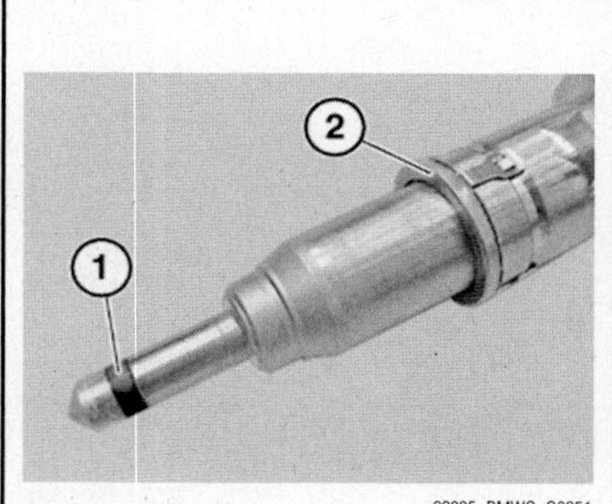

Fig. 330 Uncoupling element and the PTFE sealing ring

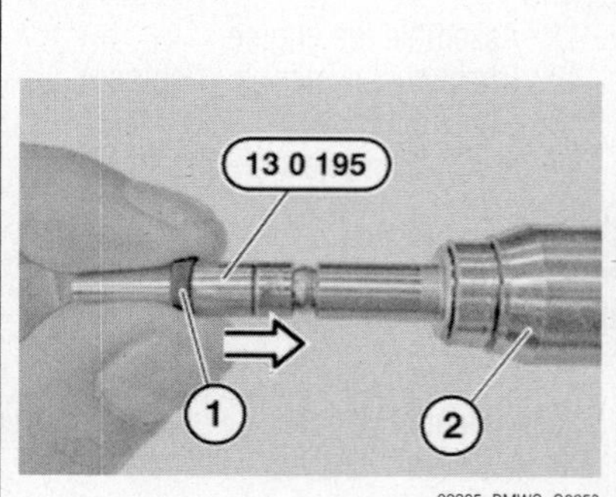

Fig. 332 Use fingers and mounting taper 13 0 195 to slide PTFE sealing ring onto injector

※ WARNING

Install injector within 10 minutes or slide on protective cap as the PTFE sealing ring swells up.

7. Installing a new injector:
   a. Use a new uncoupling element.
   b. Remove protective cap from injector tip max. 10 min. before installation (PTFE sealing ring swells up).
8. Before installing injector in engines that have been run:
   a. Clean contact surfaces of uncoupling elements in cylinder head.
   b. Clean injector bore: To do so, preferably slide injector without uncoupling element but with new PTFE sealing ring in and out of injector bores several times.
   c. The PTFE sealing ring must then be replaced.
   d. Replace uncoupling element.

※ WARNING

An injector adjustment must be carried out if an injector is replaced or changed on the cylinder side.

Injector adjustment is carried out with the aid of a so-called adjustment value. The adjustment value is printed in two blocks of three digits on the injector. The adjustment value must be read off before installation.

9. Enter the adjustment value according to the installation position (cylinder) of the injector.

※ WARNING

If injector adjustment is not carried out, the engine may run roughly or fail to start.

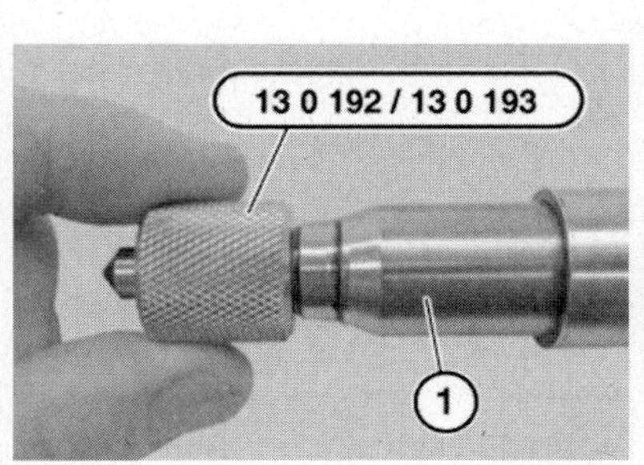

Fig. 333 To bring the expanded PTFE sealing ring to its installation dimension, slide three mounting sleeves with decreasing diameters onto the injector

Fig. 334 The adjustment value is printed in two blocks of three digits on the injector. The adjustment value must be read off before installation

Fig. 335 Make sure holding-down element is correctly seated

10. Install injector and holding-down element. Make sure holding-down element is correctly seated.

※ WARNING

Tighten screw hand-tight only so that holding-down element is slack and if necessary injector can still be turned.

11. Connect contact plug.

➡Copper seals that may be fitted on the pressure lines are no longer needed and must be removed.

12. Connect pressure line, tightening nuts hand-tight only in the process.

※ WARNING

Connect pressure line without tension only.

13. To ensure distortion-free installation of the pressure line and to avoid damaging the thread, it must be possible for both nuts to be screwed on easily by hand.
14. If the nuts cannot be screwed on easily by hand, the injector must if necessary be turned a little.
15. Turn injector if necessary until nuts on pressure line can be easily screwed on by hand.
16. Tighten nuts on pressure line hand-tight.
17. Then tighten down screw for holding-down element to 10 ft. lbs. (13 Nm).
18. Adhere to tightening sequence:
    - First tighten down nut on injector
    - Then tighten down nut on high-pressure rail
19. When tightening nut on injector, grip hexagon head of injector with wrench.
20. Coat screw connection with transmission oil. Tighten down nuts with special tool 37 1 151 to 19 ft. lbs. (25 Nm).
21. Using a BMW DIS Tester perform the injector adjustment:
22. Check fuel system for leaks.
23. Check for stored fault messages, rectify faults and clear the fault memory.

N55 Engine

See Figures 336 through 350.

1. Before servicing the vehicle, refer to the precautions.
2. Disconnect negative battery terminal (risk of fire due to short-circuiting on dismantling).
3. Remove ignition coil of corresponding cylinder.

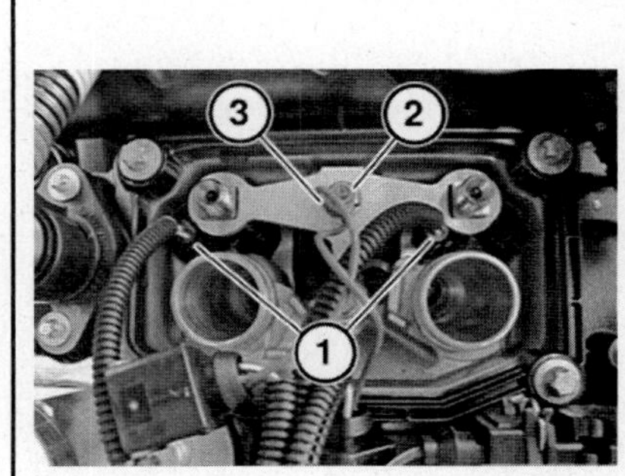

Fig. 336 Unlocking connector, slackening nut and removing ground cable

4. Disconnect pressure lines of corresponding cylinder.

➡The following description applies to all injectors in cylinders 1-6.

5. Unlock connector from injectors and detach.
6. Slacken nut. Tightening torque: 44 inch lbs. (5 Nm)
7. Remove ground cable.

⁂ WARNING

First, release screw. The, release screw. Otherwise, the hold-down device may tilt.

8. Remove holding-down element.
9. Pull injectors upward out of cylinder head and remove.

➡If several injectors are removed, ensure that each injector is reinstalled in its original location (cylinder).

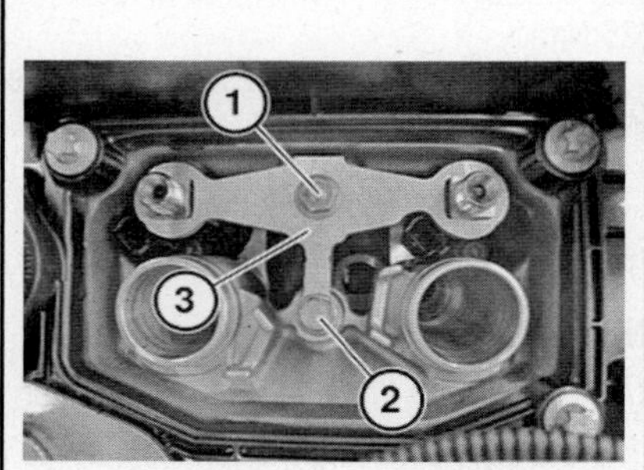

Fig. 337 Releasing screw then screw and removing holding down element

10. Mark injectors.

In event of stuck injector:

a. Use special tool 0 496 885 to remove injectors that are stuck.
b. Lightly oil pull out thread and unscrew completely before using the special tool.

⁂ WARNING

Pull out thread is a left hand thread.

11. Fit special tool 0 496 885 on injector slot. Join screws to injector slot by a few threads. Screw in pull-out thread until it is possible to screw the threaded sleeves onto the injectors. Screw threaded sleeves onto injectors and tighten down.
12. Tighten down screws. Tightening torque: 6 ft. lbs. (8.5 Nm)

⁂ WARNING

Set torque wrench to 5 Nm clockwise rotation. Together with special tool 0 496 885 this corresponds to a tensile force of max. 2000 N. The injector must be replaced if the torque wrench is activated when the injector is pulled out.

13. Fit torque wrench and special tool 00 9 170 on hexagon head of special tool 0 496 885.
14. Turn torque wrench in clockwise direction until the injector is pulled out.
15. After removing, fit protective caps (1 and 2) to injector tip and fuel line connection.

➡When installing a new injector, replace decoupling element.

➡When reusing fuel injector, replace decoupling element and Teflon ring.

⁂ WARNING

A Teflon ring that has already been installed once in the cylinder head must be replaced before the injector is reinstalled.

Replacing Teflon ring:

16. Before replacing the Teflon ring, make sure your hands and the work surface are clean and free of oil.
17. Avoid mechanical contact with injector tip.
18. Remove Teflon ring from injector with special tool 13 0 191 from set of special tools 13 0 190.
19. Use a fluff-free cloth only to remove combustion residues from cylindrical part of injector tip (do not use ultrasound or other tools/agents).

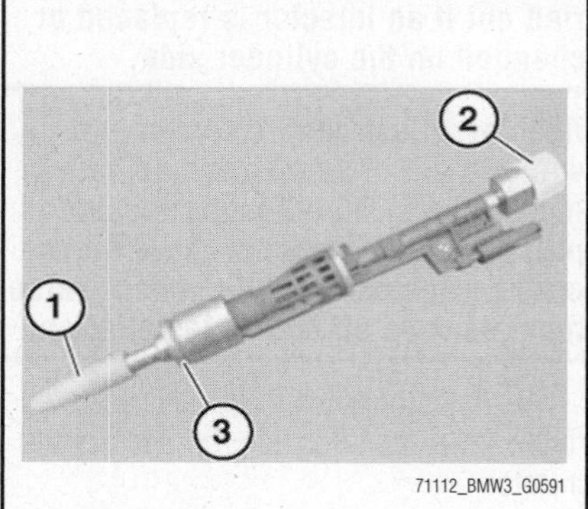

Fig. 340 Fitting protective caps (1, 2) and replacing decoupling element

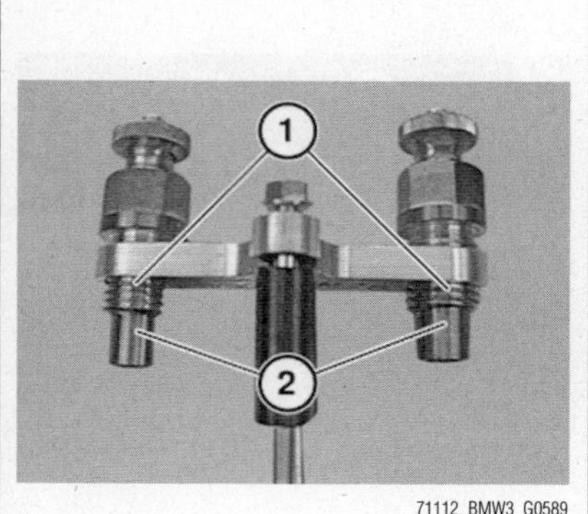

Fig. 338 Identifying pull out thread

Fig. 339 Fitting torque wrench and special tool on hexagon head of special tool

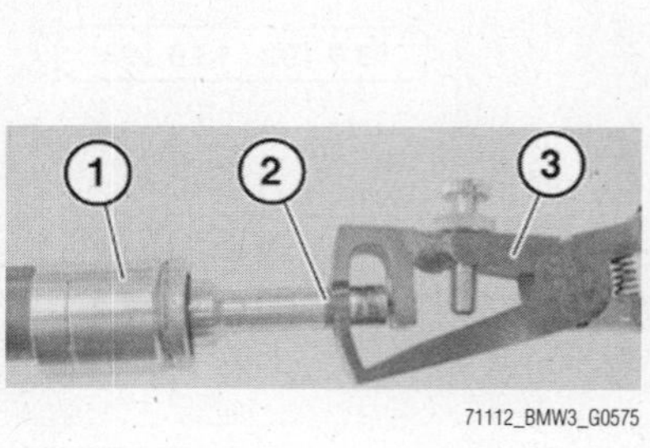

Fig. 341 Removing Teflon ring from injector with special tool

20. Do not clean injector tip.

21. Slide new Teflon ring onto installation cone13 0 283 from set of special tools 13 0 280.

22. Fit Teflon ring on injector tip with installation cone 13 0 283 from set of special tools 13 0 280.

WARNING

Do not use fingernails to slide Teflon ring on.

WARNING

Do not use any lubricating agents.

➡The sealing ring is expanded when slid on.

23. Use special tool 13 0 281 from set of special tools 13 0 280 to slide Teflon ring into groove on injector.

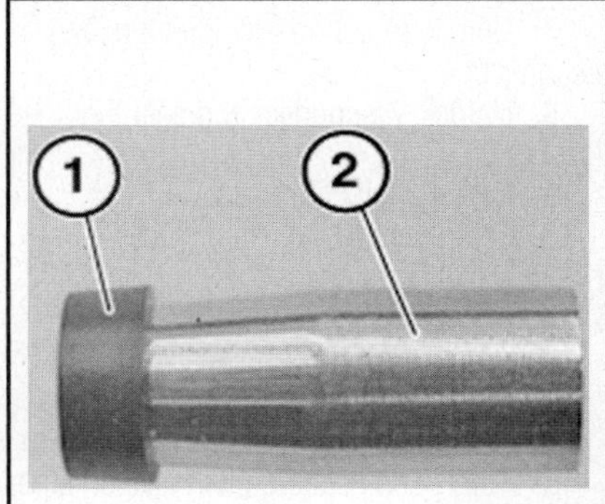

Fig. 342 Sliding new Teflon ring onto installation cone13 0 283 from set of special tools 13 0 280

24. To bring the widened Teflon ring to the installation dimension, special tool 13 0 282 from set of special tools 13 0 280 must be slid up to limit position on injector.

WARNING

Do not use any lubricating agents.

25. Pull mounting tip of special tool 13 0 282 towards rear to release installation cone 13 0 281.

To install:

WARNING

Before installing injector in engines that have been run:

a. Injectors must not be twisted to 6 Nm.

b. The injector must be replaced if this value is exceeded.

c. Check injector bore for dirt.

d. Clean only dirty injector bores.

e. Important - do not damage injector.

f. Clean injector bore: To do so, preferably slide injector without decoupling element but with new Teflon ring in and out of injector bores several times.

g. The Teflon ring must subsequently be replaced.

h. Clean contact surfaces of decoupling elements in cylinder head.

i. Replace decoupling element.

WARNING

An injector quantity compensation must be carried out if an injector is replaced or changed on the cylinder side.

WARNING

Injector quantity compensation is carried out with the aid of a so-called adjustment value.

➡The adjustment value is printed in three digits on the injector body.

WARNING

The adjustment value must be read off before installation.

26. Enter the adjustment value according to the installation location (cylinder) of the injector.

27. If injector quantity compensation is not carried out, the engine may run roughly or fail to start.

Injection quantity compensation:

The adjustment value is printed with three digits - depending on the version - on the injector body.

a. Connect BMW diagnosis system.

b. Identify vehicle.

c. Select "Function selection."

d. Select "Service functions."

e. Select "Engine electronics."

f. Select "Adjustment functions."

g. Select "Adjust injectors."

h. Select "Test plan"

i. For each replaced injector, the adjustment value must be entered according to the installation location (cylinder).

28. Insert injectors in injector bores.

29. Fit special tool 0 496 885 on injector slot. Join screws to injector slot by a few threads. Screw in the pull-out thread until the threaded sleeves can be screwed onto the injectors. Screw threaded sleeves onto injectors and tighten down.

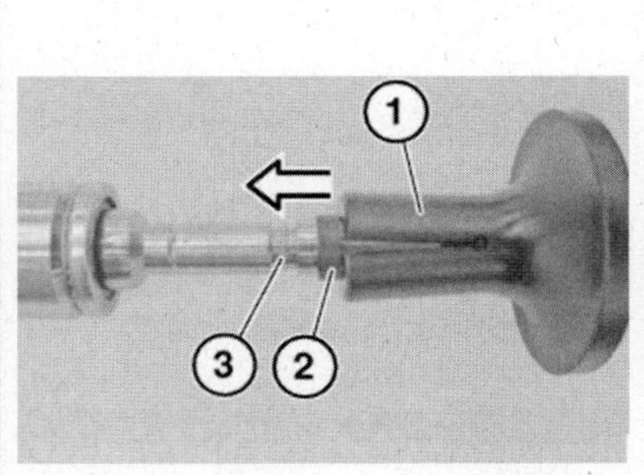

Fig. 343 Using special tool 13 0 281 from set of special tools 13 0 280 to slide Teflon ring into groove on injector

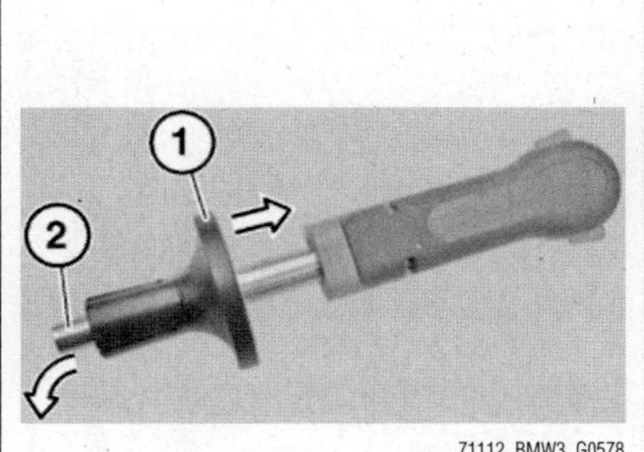

Fig. 344 Pulling mounting tip of special tool 13 0 282 towards rear to release installation cone 13 0 281

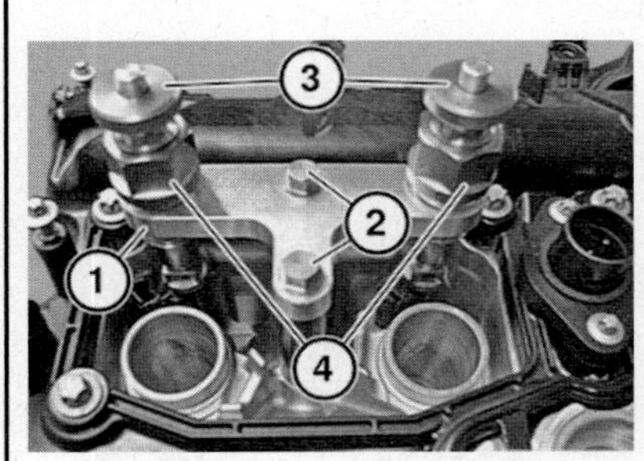

Fig. 345 Fitting special tool, joining screws, screwing in pull out thread until threaded sleeves can be screwed onto injectors

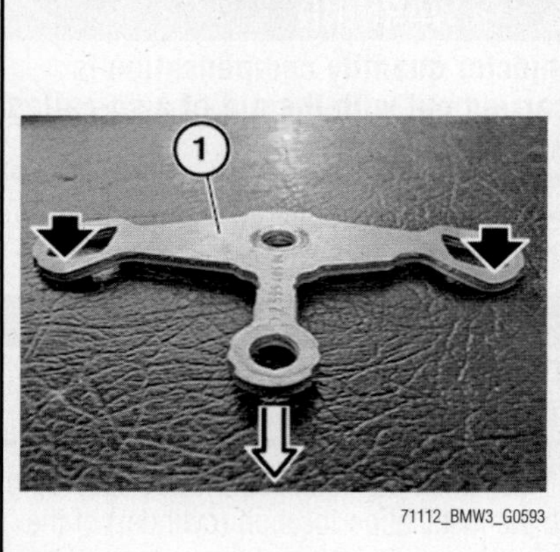

Fig. 346 Installing hold down device

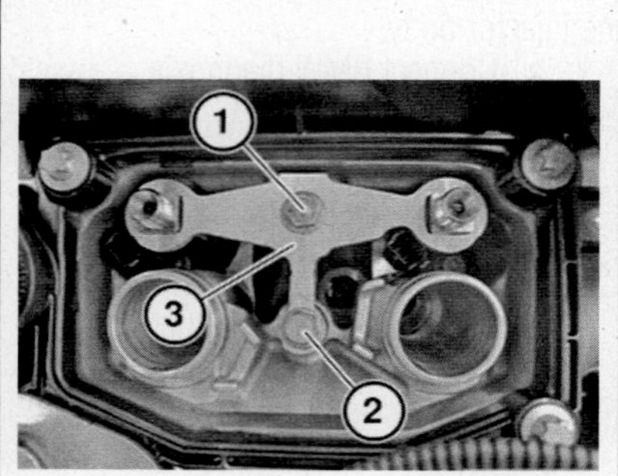

Fig. 347 Fitting hold down device and screws and loosely

30. Tighten down screws. Tightening torque: 6 ft. lbs. (8.5 Nm)
31. Set torque wrench to 2 Nm counter-clockwise rotation.

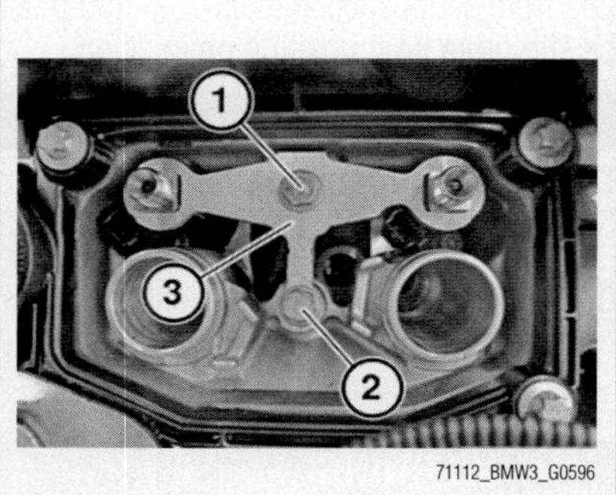

Fig. 349 Tightening screw and then screw

32. Fit torque wrench and special tool 00 9 170 on hexagon head of special tool 0 496 885.
33. Turn torque wrench in counterclockwise direction until 2 Nm are reached.
34. Install hold-down device with curvatures (black arrows) downward.
35. Fit hold-down device on injectors.
36. Fit screws hand-tight.
37. Only fit the screw loosely to prevent the hold-down device from tilting.
38. Fit pressure lines with rubber mount on injectors and rail. Tighten nuts and manually only.
39. Firstly tighten screw. Tightening torque: 8-10 ft. lbs. (12-14 Nm)
40. Then tighten down screw. Tightening torque: 8-10 ft. lbs. (12-14 Nm)
41. Tighten down pressure lines on injectors. Tightening torque: 15-19 ft. lbs. (20-26 Nm)
42. Then tighten down pressure lines on the rail. Tightening torque: 15-19 ft. lbs. (20-26 Nm)
43. Reinstall line damper.
44. Clean spark plug slot.
45. Assemble engine.
46. Check fuel system for tightness.
47. Check function of DME.

S65 Engine

See Figures 351 through 354.

1. Before servicing the vehicle, refer to the precautions.
2. Read out fault memory of DME control unit; if necessary, work through test schedules
3. Switch ignition **OFF**.
4. Remove intake air manifold. Refer to engine mechanical, intake manifold, removal & installation.

➡Fuel escapes when fuel line is detached. Catch and dispose of escaping fuel.

5. Release screws.
6. Unclip fuel line.
7. Unlock plugs on fuel injectors and disconnect.
8. Unlock, disconnect and seal fuel line.
9. Remove injection pipe.
10. Seal openings for fuel injectors in throttle valve housings with special tool 11 5 210.
11. Seal fuel hose with special tool 13 5 281.
12. Lever out retainers.
13. Pull fuel injectors out of injection pipe.

To install:

14. To install, reverse the removal procedure.
15. Replace sealing rings on fuel injectors and coat with anti-friction agent.

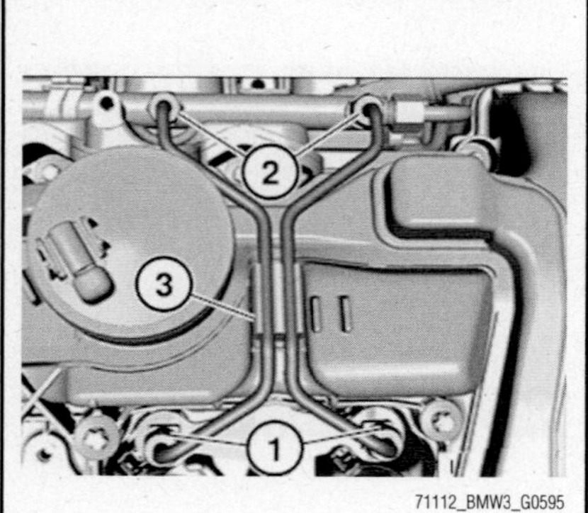

Fig. 348 Fitting pressure lines with rubber mount on injectors and rail and tightening nuts and manually

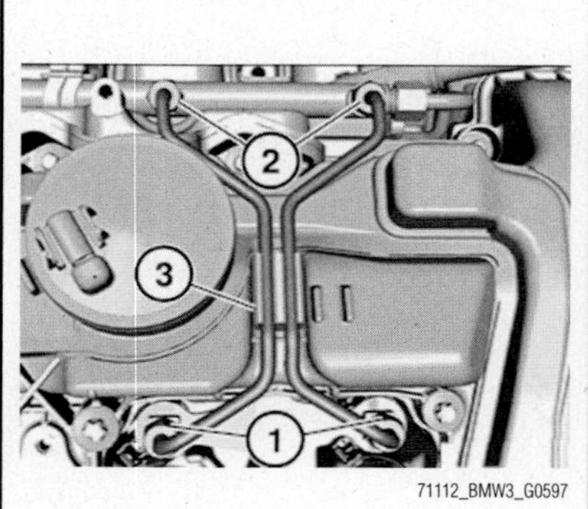

Fig. 350 Tightening pressure lines on injectors and rail and reinstalling damper

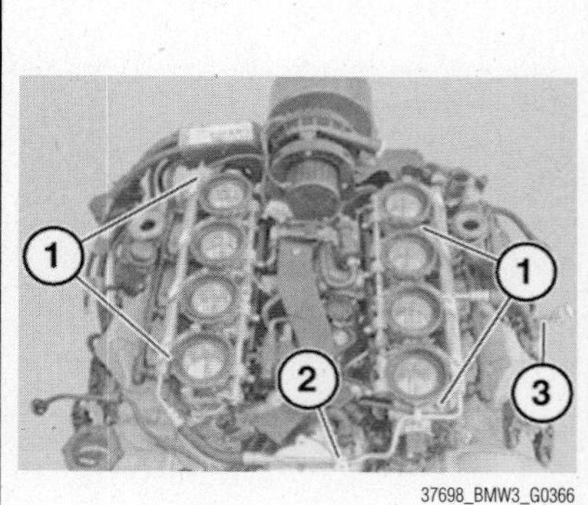

Fig. 351 Screws, fuel line and seal fuel line

16. Read out fault memory and clear the faults.

THROTTLE BODY

REMOVAL & INSTALLATION

N52 and N54 Engine

See Figures 352 through 353.

1. Before servicing the vehicle, refer to the precautions.
2. Read out fault memory of DME control unit; if necessary, work through test schedules
3. Switch ignition **OFF**.
4. Remove air intake hose.
5. Unlock plug and remove.
6. Remove throttle assembly.

To install:

7. Replace sealing ring of throttle assembly.
8. Install throttle assembly. Tighten bolts to 6 ft. lbs. (9 Nm).
9. Install air intake hose.
10. Check for stored fault messages, rectify faults and clear the fault memory.

N55

See Figures 354 and 355.

1. Before servicing the vehicle, refer to the precautions.
2. Switch off ignition.
3. Remove charge air duct.
4. Unlock connector and remove.
5. Release screws. Tightening torque: 62 inch lbs. (8 Nm)
6. Partially remove throttle body and unlock tank ventilation line and remove.
7. Remove throttle body.

To install:

To install, reverse the removal procedure noting the following.

8. Replace sealing ring of throttle body.
9. Check stored fault message.
10. Delete fault memory.

S65 Engine

See Figures 356 through 362.

1. Before servicing the vehicle, refer to the precautions.
2. Read out fault memory of DME control unit.
3. Switch ignition **OFF**.
4. Disconnect battery negative cable.
5. Remove intake air manifold. Refer to engine mechanical, intake manifold, removal & installation.
6. Remove all injectors. Refer to gasoline fuel injection system, fuel injectors, removal & installation.
7. Release and raise cable duct for engine wiring harness; to do so, partially remove engine wiring harness.
8. Disengage pull rods of throttle valve actuating motor.
9. Release all nuts of throttle valve flanges.
10. Release idle air hose connection.
11. Lift out throttle valve bank.
12. Release idle air duct on throttle valve bank.
13. Release all screw connections on shaft.

➡Grip screws, release nuts only. Replace screws and nuts.

To install:

14. To install, reverse the removal procedure.
15. Actuating lever of throttle valve actuating motor is offset by 180° to throttle valve actuating levers.
16. Clean sealing surfaces on cylinder head.
17. Replace O-rings on cylinder head.
18. Check adapter sleeves on throttle valves.

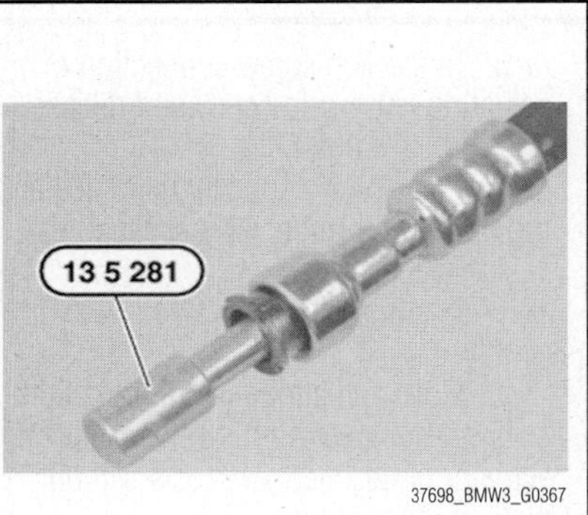

37698_BMW3_G0367

Fig. 352 Seal fuel hose with special tool 13 5 281

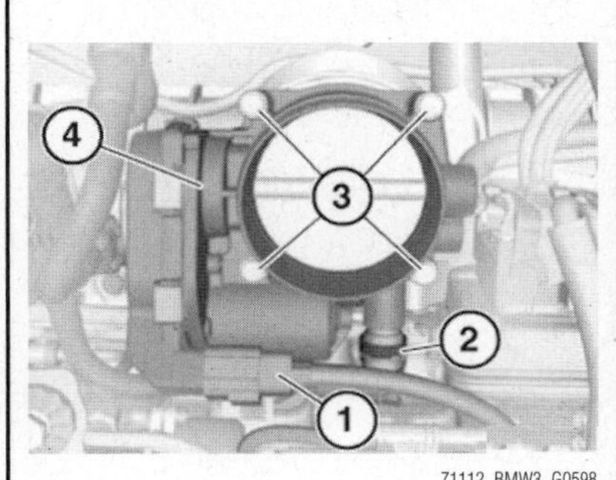

71112_BMW3_G0598

Fig. 354 Unlocking connector, releasing screws, unlocking tank ventilation line and removing throttle body

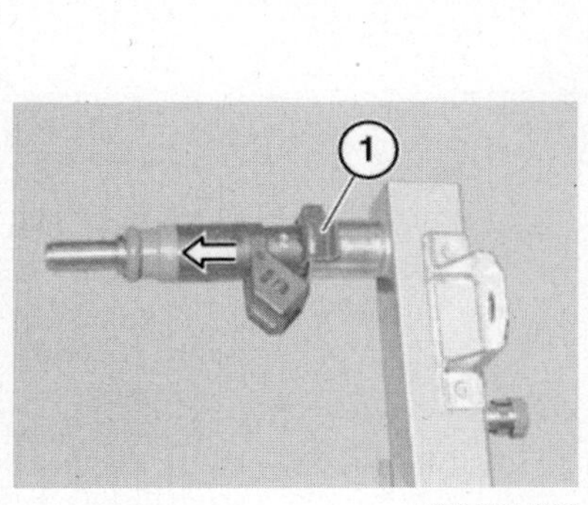

37698_BMW3_G0368

Fig. 353 Lever out retainers

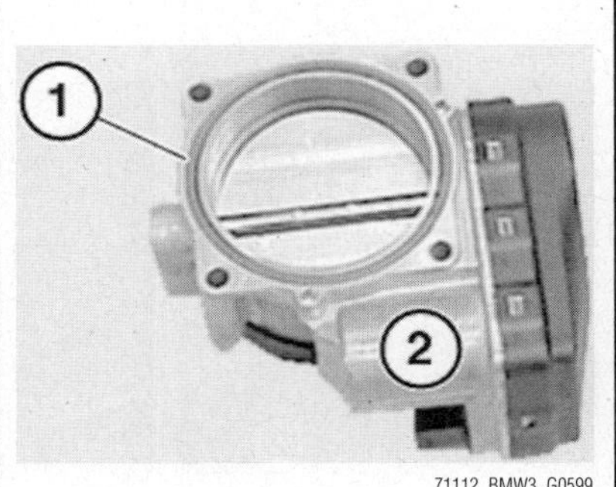

71112_BMW3_G0599

Fig. 355 Identifying sealing ring of throttle body

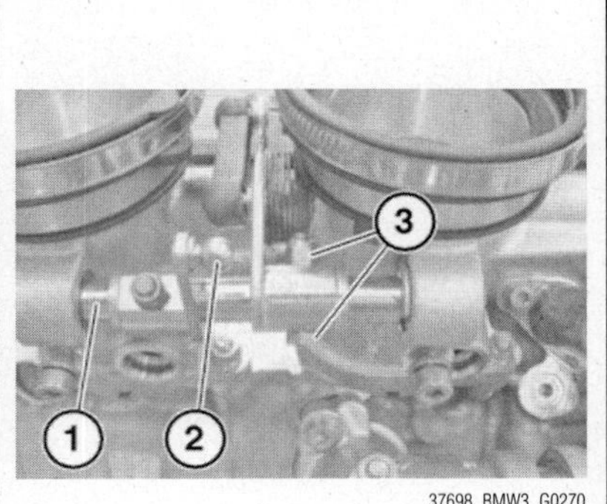

37698_BMW3_G0270

Fig. 356 Screw connections on shaft, actuating lever and screws and nuts

19. Perform basic throttle valve setting.

WARNING

Idle stops of throttle valve assemblies must not be altered. They have been set at the factory and secured against turning with locking paint. The throttle valve assembly must be replaced if the locking paint is damaged or the idle speed stop screw is twisted. Plastic caps on idle speed top screws must not be removed.

20. Checking throttle valve basic setting:
   a. Gap between stop screw and actuator of throttle valve must be less than 0.0019 in. (0.05 mm).
   b. To check gap, use a feeler gauge with a thickness of 0.0019 in. (0.05 mm).
   c. Pull rod of throttle valve actuator in opening direction of throttle valves.
   d. Slide feeler gauge between stop screw and actuator of throttle valve.
   e. Return throttle valves slowly to stops.
   f. When correctly adjusted, feeler gauge will jam between stop screw and actuator of throttle valve.
   g. Perform check on each throttle valve assembly.

21. Performing throttle valve basic setting:
   a. A basic setting must be performed if the gap is larger than 0.05 mm at one or more throttle valve assemblies.

WARNING

To perform correct throttle valve setting, it is necessary to slacken all the screw connections of the actuating lever with the actuating shaft. (Replace nuts). However, if increased play is ascertained, the corresponding cylinder bank must be reset. Do not slacken the screw connections of the actuating levers for the long pull rods. The long pull rods must not be disengaged from the actuating levers for the setting procedure.

   b. To slacken screw connection of actuating lever, grip screw and release nut. (Replace nuts).
   Release screw connections of actuating levers of throttle valve assemblies 1–4 and 5–8.

22. Adjusting a throttle valve assembly:
   a. Move actuating lever in direction of arrow, i.e. "close throttle valve", until actuator of throttle valve rests without play on stop screw.

WARNING

Do not exert any pressure.

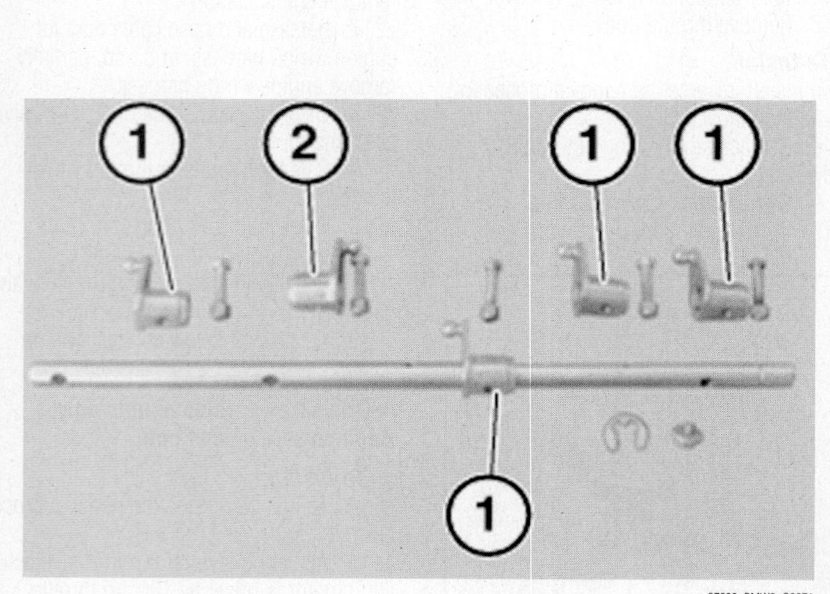

Fig. 357 Mounting sequence of actuating levers: Levers for throttle valves and Lever from actuator motor

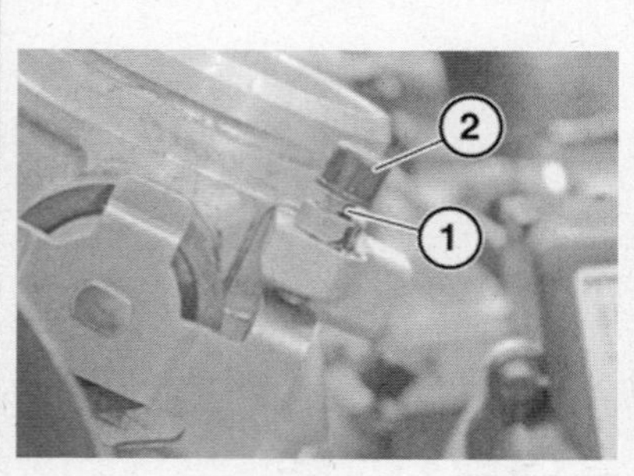

Fig. 358 The throttle valve assembly must be replaced if the locking paint is damaged or the idle speed stop screw is twisted. Plastic caps on idle speed top screws must not be removed.

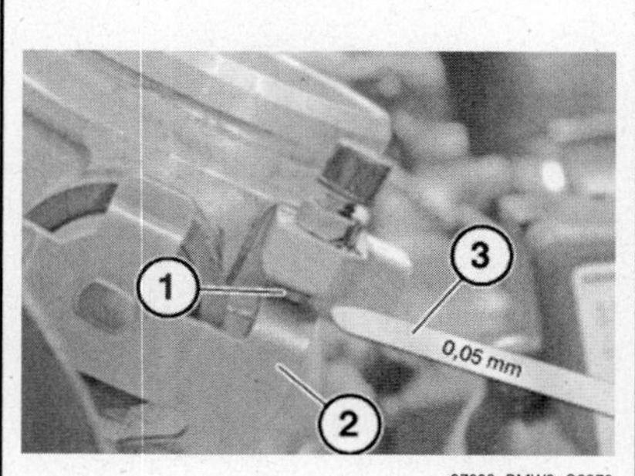

Fig. 359 Stop screw, actuator and feeler gauge

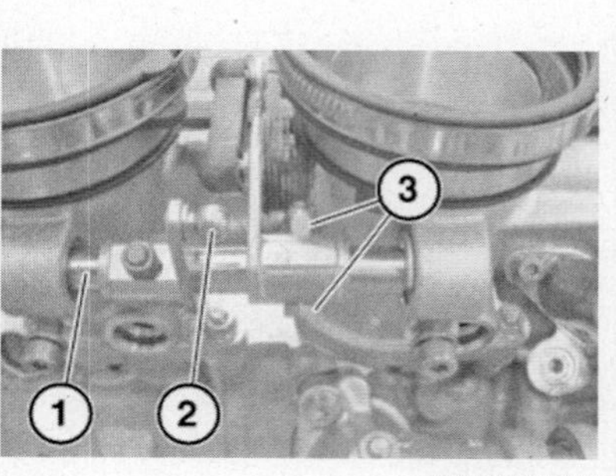

Fig. 360 Actuating shaft, actuating lever and screw connections

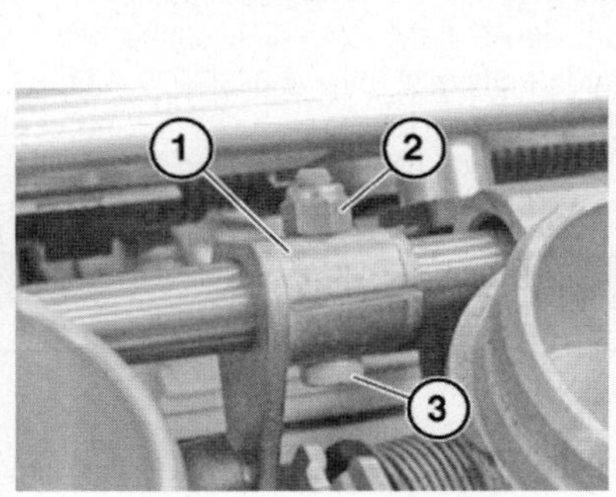

Fig. 361 Actuating lever, unit actuator and stop screw

b. Tighten down screw connection of actuating lever again to actuating shaft.

➡Observe the following instructions in tightening down screw connection of actuating lever

- Use nuts only once
- When pre-tightening screw connection (approximately 48 inch lbs. (5 Nm), hold actuating lever of throttle valve in direction of arrow at "close throttle valve"
- Only turn nut and grip screw.

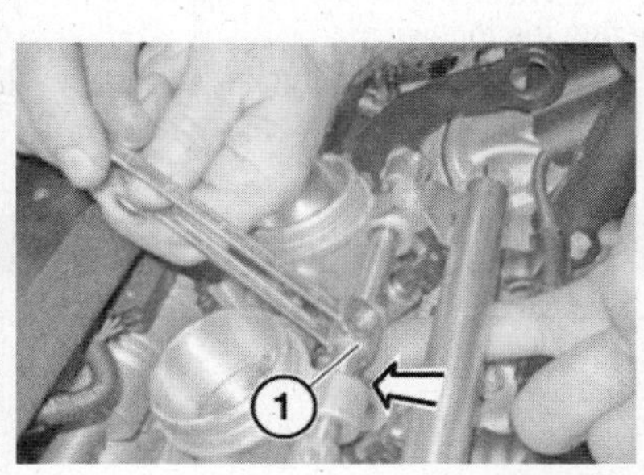

Fig. 362 Tighten down screw connection of actuating lever again to actuating shaft

- To screw down, use two open-end wrenches which are to be placed at right angles to actuating shaft.

In this way, no lever action is exerted on the throttle valve mechanism; such torque would impair the quality of adjustment.

- After pre-tightening actuating lever, actuate throttle valve several times at full load.

23. Adjusting throttle valve assemblies 1–4 and 5–8:

a. The previously described procedure applies to adjusting/setting throttle valve assemblies 1–4 and 5–8.

b. Adjust throttle valve assemblies 1–4 and 5–8 in sequence.

c. After successfully completing throttle valve basic setting and checking, tighten down all screw connections of throttle valve levers to 60 inch lbs. (7 Nm).

➡After completing adjustment, it is necessary to check the throttle valve basic setting. If during the checking of one or more throttle valve assemblies excessively large or small play is ascertained, it will be necessary to perform the throttle valve basic setting again.

⁂ WARNING

After performing work on the throttle valve system (throttle valve assembly, servomotor, Hall sensor), it is absolutely essential to carry out a throttle valve actuator system test with the BMW diagnosis system.

24. Check stored fault messages, then clear fault memory.

HEATING & AIR CONDITIONING SYSTEM

BLOWER MOTOR

REMOVAL & INSTALLATION

See Figure 363.

1. Before servicing the vehicle, refer to the precautions.

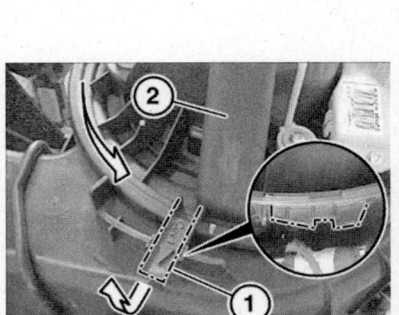

Fig. 363 Carefully raise lug and feed out housing by turning clockwise

2. Remove trim for instrument panel, bottom right
3. Partially Remove air duct at side
4. Disconnect plug connection.
5. Carefully raise lug and feed out housing by turning clockwise.

To install:

6. Install housing into vehicle.

➡Lug must not be damaged and must snap audibly into place.

7. Connect plug.
8. Connect air duct.
9. Install instrument panel trim.

HEATER CORE

REMOVAL & INSTALLATION

See Figure 364.

1. Before servicing the vehicle, refer to the precautions.

➡The heater case assembly must be removed to remove the heater core on all 3-Series vehicles.

2. Remove the heater unit.
3. Slide rubber grommet with foam seal forward slightly. Carefully feed pipe holder with pipes past rubber grommet.

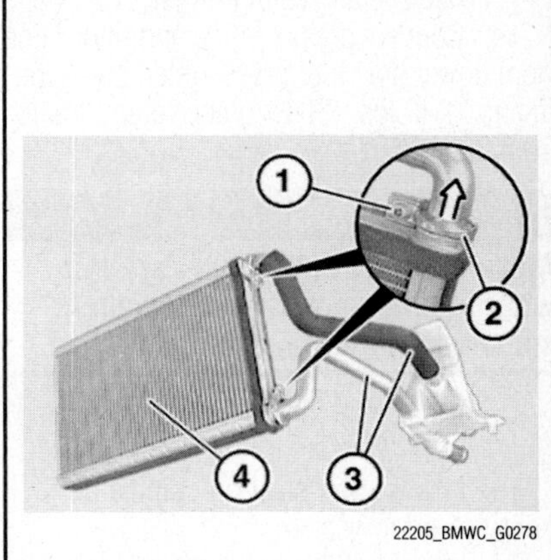

Fig. 364 Heater core assembly as removed from heater case

4. If necessary, remove coolant hose.
5. Remove heater core from heater/air conditioner.
6. Remove pipes from heater core.

To install:

7. Installation is the reverse of removal, noting the following:
8. When installing the heater core, make sure that the return-flow connection (larger opening) marked with a black dot is positioned at the top. Inflow connection accordingly may only be positioned at the bottom.
9. Fill and bleed the cooling system.

STEERING

POWER RACK & PINION STEERING GEAR

REMOVAL & INSTALLATION

See Figures 365 through 367.

1. Before servicing the vehicle, refer to the precautions.
2. Draw off and dispose of hydraulic fluid from fluid reservoir
3. Remove front underbody protection.
4. Remove both tie rod ends from ball joint.
5. Remove lower steering spindle from power steering gear
6. If necessary, remove heat shield from power steering gear.
7. Remove banjo bolts and disconnect pressure line and return line from power steering gear.
8. If necessary, remove hydraulic lines with bracket from power steering gear.
9. Remove nuts and remove screws towards bottom.
10. Remove power steering gear towards front.

To install:

11. Install power steering gear. Using new bolts and nuts, tighten to 41 ft. lbs. (56 Nm) plus 90° of additional rotation.
12. Install hydraulic lines with bracket to power steering gear.
13. Replace all sealing rings.
14. Connect pressure line and return line from power steering gear. Tighten pressure line to 22 ft. lbs. (30 Nm) and return line to 26 ft. lbs. (35 Nm).

⁂ WARNING

Make sure hydraulic lines are laid without tension and with sufficient spacing to adjoining components.

15. Install heat shield on power steering gear.
16. Install lower steering spindle on power steering gear
17. Install both tie rod ends on ball joint.
18. Install front underbody protection.
19. Fill and bleed hydraulic system.
20. Check pipe connections for leaks.
21. Perform chassis alignment check.

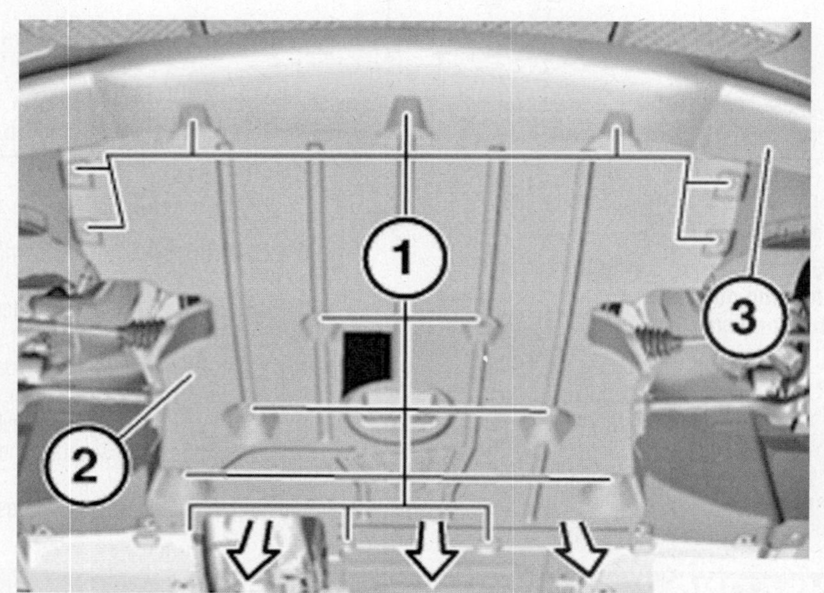

Fig. 365 Release screws and pull underbody protection forward under bumper trim

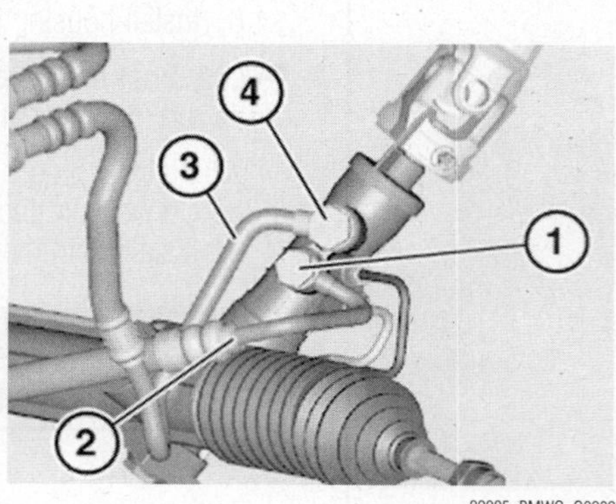

Fig. 366 Remove banjo bolts (1 and 4), then disconnect pressure line and return line from power steering gear

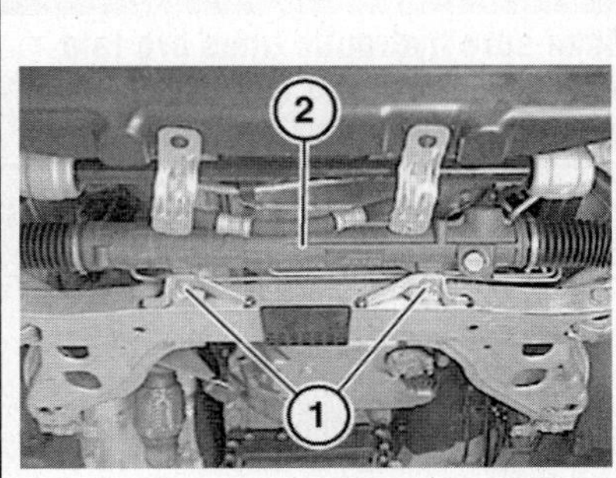

Fig. 367 Remove nuts and remove screws towards bottom, then remove power steering gear towards front

22. Carry out steering angle sensor adjustment.

POWER STEERING PUMP

BLEEDING

1. Before servicing the vehicle, refer to the precautions.

WARNING

Adhere to the utmost cleanliness. Do not allow any dirt to enter the hydraulic system. Using contaminated equipment to add fluid may introduce dirt particles into the fluid reservoir and significantly reduce the service life of the power steering system. Do not use any filler funnels or similar.

➡The fill level may only be checked or adjusted when the engine is stopped. The fluid temperature should be approximately 68°F (20°C) here. Ensure that the cap is fully screwed in prior to the fill level check.

2. Thoroughly clean fluid reservoir and its immediate surroundings
3. Check and correct fill level.

➡The fill level can come to rest above the MAX mark when the engine is at normal operating temperature. This is dictated by the design in that the marking on the dipstick is referred to a fluid temperature of 68°F (20°C). With the engine at normal operating temperature (approximately 122–140°F (50–60°C) fluid temperature adjust a fill height 0.39 in. (10 mm) above the MAX mark. Do not under any circumstances draw off the fluid to the MAX mark when the engine is at normal operating temperature.

4. Start engine.
5. Turn steering wheel left and right twice in each case up to full lock; if necessary, top up hydraulic fluid (e.g. if hydraulic system is completely drained).
6. Move steering wheel to straight-ahead position and turn off engine.
7. Check and correct fill level with engine stopped.
8. Check hydraulic system for leaks.

REMOVAL & INSTALLATION

M57 Engine

See Figure 368.

1. Before servicing the vehicle, refer to the precautions.
2. Evacuate and recycle the refrigerant.
3. Remove belt pulley.
   a. Slacken screws
   b. Relieve tension on drive belt and remove from belt pulley.
   c. Unscrew bolts and remove belt pulley.

WARNING

Cover alternator to prevent ingress of hydraulic fluid.

4. Release banjo bolt and disconnect pressure line.
5. Release hose clamp and detach suction line from vane pump.
6. Release screws and remove vane pump towards top.

To install:

7. To install, reverse the removal procedure.
8. Replace all sealing rings.

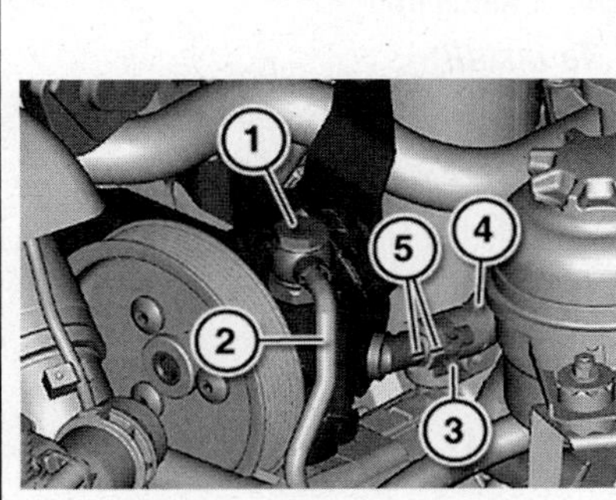

Fig. 368 Disconnecting the power steering fluid lines

WARNING

Make sure pressure line is laid without tension and with sufficient spacing to adjoining components.

9. Markings on suction line and vane pump connection must match up.
10. Make sure screws are installed in correct positions.
    a. Screw M8x80
    b. Screw M8x40
    c. Screw M6x85
11. Insert screws but do not tighten down.
12. Tighten down screws (1, 2), then tighten screw. See illustration for reference.
13. Tighten bolts/nuts to specification as follows:
    - Pressure line to power steering pump: 26 ft. lbs. (35 Nm)
    - Bracket of power steering pump to crankcase / oil sump: 14 ft. lbs. (19 Nm)
14. Fill and bleed hydraulic system.
15. Check pipe connections for leaks.
16. Lettering on belt pulley must point forwards.
17. Tighten belt pulley to power steering pump to 14 ft. lbs. (19 Nm)

N52 and N54 Engine

See Figure 369.

WARNING

Aluminum-magnesium materials. No steel screws/bolts may be used due to the threat of electrochemical corrosion. A magnesium crankcase requires aluminum screws/bolts exclusively.

Aluminum screws/bolts must be replaced each time they are Removed. The end faces of aluminum screws/bolts are painted blue for the purposes of reliable identification. Jointing torque and angle of rotation must be observed without fail (risk of damage).

1. Before servicing the vehicle, refer to the precautions.
2. Draw off and dispose of hydraulic fluid from fluid reservoir.
3. Remove intake filter housing.
4. Remove belt pulley.
5. Remove front underbody protection.
6. Remove radiator seal.
7. Remove hose clamp and detach suction line from vane pump.

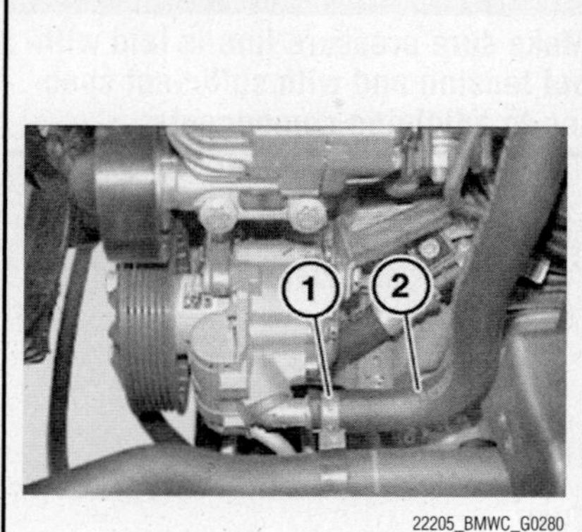

22205_BMWC_G0280

Fig. 369 Hose clamp and suction line

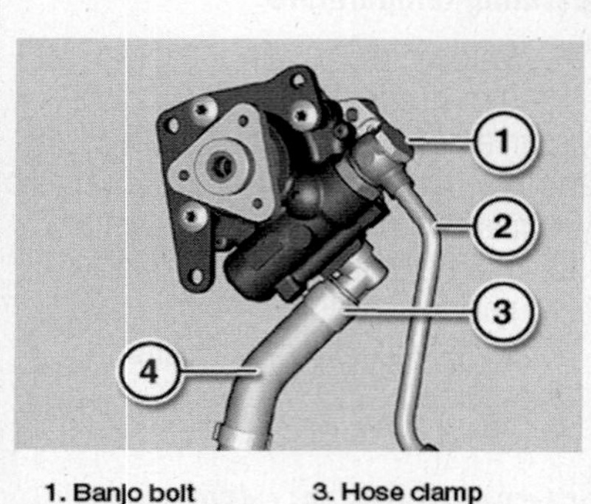

1. Banjo bolt
2. Pressure line
3. Hose clamp
4. Suction line

37698_BMW3_G0593

Fig. 370 Disconnecting pressure and suction lines from pump

8. Remove bolt and remove bracket with refrigerant line.
9. Remove screws.
10. Remove banjo bolt and disconnect pressure line.
11. Remove bolts and remove vane pump towards bottom.

To install:

12. Markings on suction line and vane pump connection must match up.
13. Replace aluminum screws.
14. Replace all sealing rings.
15. Make sure pressure line and return lines are laid without tension and with sufficient spacing to adjoining components. Tighten pressure line to 22 ft. lbs. (30 Nm) and return line to 26 ft. lbs. (35 Nm).
16. Tighten pump fasteners to specification as follows:
    - Secure vane pump with screws
    - Tighten side screws to 18 inch lbs. (2 Nm)
    - Tighten front screws to 18 inch lbs. (2 Nm)
    - Tighten down front screws to 15 ft. lbs. (20 Nm) plus an additional 90° rotation
    - Remove screws at side and check screw fastening points for gap freedom
    - Tighten down side screws to 15 ft. lbs. (20 Nm) plus an additional 90° rotation
17. Fill and bleed hydraulic system
18. Check pipe connections for leaks

S65 Engine

See Figure 370.

1. Before servicing the vehicle, refer to the precautions.
2. Draw off and dispose of hydraulic fluid from fluid reservoir
3. Remove belt pulley
4. Remove drive belt tensioner
5. Unclip cover, release screw behind and remove deflection pulley from oil filter housing.
6. Release banjo bolt and detach pressure line from vane pump.
7. Release hose clamp and detach suction line from vane pump.
8. Release screws and remove vane pump towards front.

To install:

9. To install, reverse the removal procedure.
10. Pin of deflection pulley must be correctly seated in oil filter housing.
11. Replace all sealing rings.

⁂ WARNING

Make sure hydraulic lines are laid without tension and with sufficient spacing to adjoining components.

12. Tighten bolts/nuts to specification as follows:
    - Tightening torque 32 41 8AZ.
    - Tightening torque 32 41 12AZ.
13. Fill and bleed hydraulic system.
14. Check pipe connections for leaks.

FLUID FILL PROCEDURE

⁂ WARNING

Adhere to the utmost cleanliness. Do not allow any dirt to enter the hydraulic system. Using contaminated equipment to add fluid may introduce dirt particles into the fluid reservoir and significantly reduce the service life of the power steering system. Do not use any filler funnels or similar.

➡The fill level may only be checked or adjusted when the engine is stopped. The fluid temperature should be approximately 68°F (20°C) here. Ensure that the cap is fully screwed in prior to the fill level check.

1. Thoroughly clean fluid reservoir and its immediate surroundings
2. Check and correct fill level.

➡The fill level can come to rest above the MAX mark when the engine is at normal operating temperature. This is dictated by the design in that the marking on the dipstick is referred to a fluid temperature of 68°F (20°C). With the engine at normal operating temperature (approximately 122–140°F (50–60°C) fluid temperature adjust a fill height 0.39 in. (10 mm) above the MAX mark. Do not under any circumstances draw off the fluid to the MAX mark when the engine is at normal operating temperature.

3. Bleed the system.

COIL SPRINGS

REMOVAL & INSTALLATION

See Figures 371 and 372.

※※ WARNING

Both coil springs on the relevant axle must be replaced only in the event of corrosion breakage.

※※ WARNING

Before servicing the vehicle, refer to the precautions.

※※ WARNING

All screws, nuts, bolts and hose clamps removed during the repair must be replaced.

※※ WARNING

Retaining elements on chassis and suspension and steering parts must be replaced.

1. Remove front spring strut.
2. Relieve tension on coil spring.

Loosen special tool 2 240 487 and remove the coil spring with protective tube and support bearing.

➡When installing, check support bearing and protective tube for damage, replace if necessary.

➡The flattened end of the spring is placed onto the support bearing.

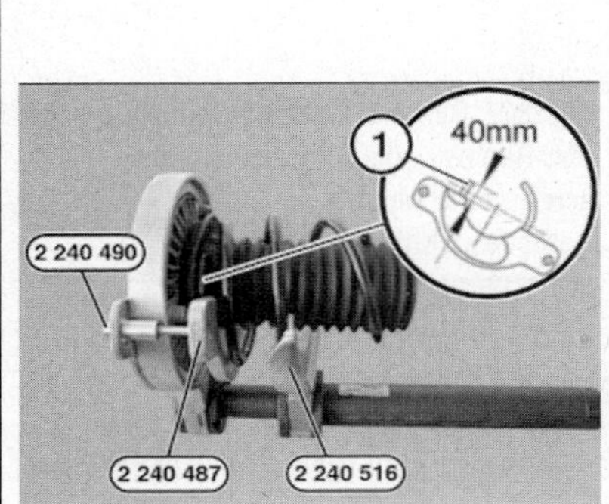

Fig. 371 Positioning spring so the end of the spring protrudes by 40 mm beyond pressure plate

※※ WARNING

Do not compress coil spring to full extent.

※※ WARNING

The gummed side of the pressure plate 2 240 487 is fitted against the top spring coil.

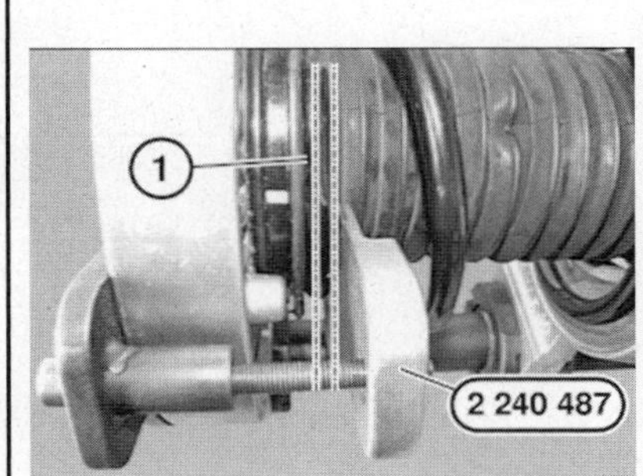

Fig. 372 Aligning the pressure plate with the top spring coil

To install:

Position the coil spring:

3. Insert the coil spring with protective tube and support bearing.
4. Assemble the pressure plate 2 240 487 with screws 2 240 490.
5. Position the spring so that the end of the spring protrudes by 40 mm beyond the pressure plate 2 240 487.
6. Tighten the screws 2 240 490 evenly at 62 inch lbs. (7 Nm).

※※ WARNING

The pressure plate 2 240 487 must be aligned parallel with the top spring coil.

7. Tension coil spring.

LOWER CONTROL ARMS

REMOVAL & INSTALLATION

1. Before servicing the vehicle, refer to the precautions.
2. Remove front wheel.
3. Remove front underbody protection.
4. If necessary, remove jointed rod of ride-height sensor from control arm.

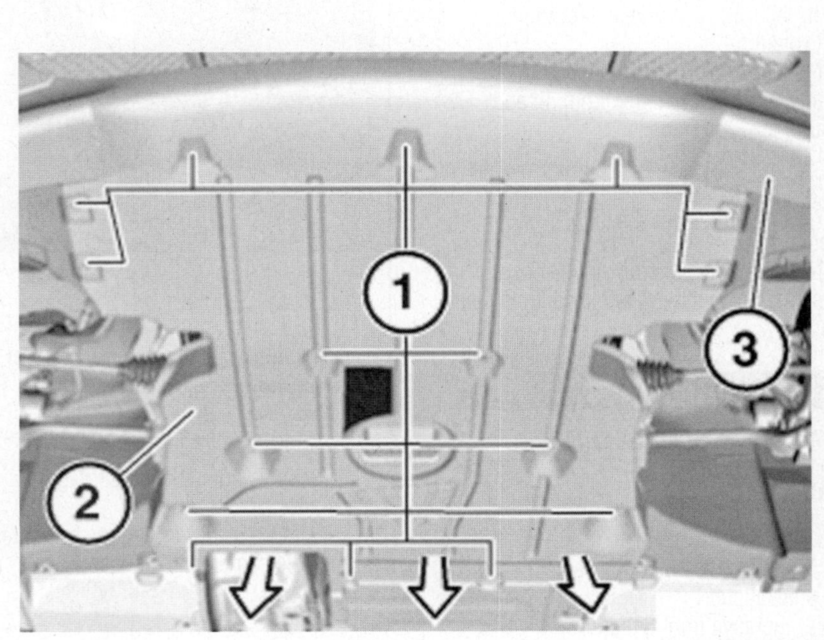

Fig. 373 Release screws and pull underbody protection forward under bumper trim

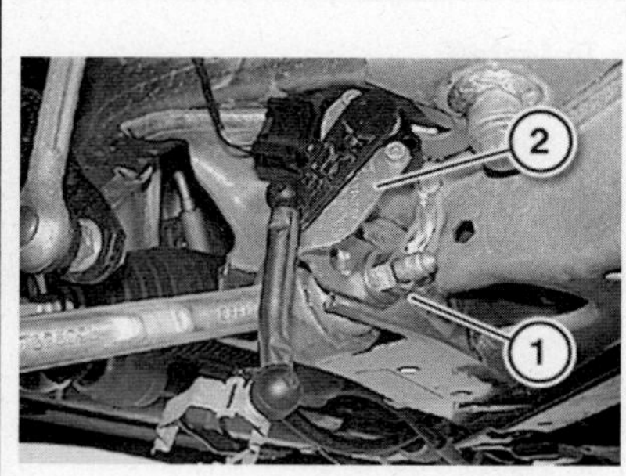

Fig. 374 Remove nut, then remove screw towards front. If necessary remove bracket with ride-height sensor

5. Remove lower ball joint nut; if necessary, grip at Torx® socket (T40).
6. Remove lower control arm nut. Remove screw towards front.
7. If necessary remove bracket with ride-height sensor.
8. Remove control arm.

To install:

9. Install control arm.

➡Screw head must point in direction of travel. Replace self-locking nut.

10. Temporarily tighten down bolt and nut. Once the vehicle is lowered to normal ride height, finish tightening to 50 ft. lbs. (68 Nm) plus an additional 90° rotation.
11. Keep control arm to ball joint connection clean and free from oil and grease.
12. Replace self-locking nut and tighten to 122 ft. lbs. (165 Nm).
13. Perform chassis alignment check.
14. Carry out steering angle sensor adjustment/adjustment for active front steering.

STABILIZER BAR & LINKS

REMOVAL & INSTALLATION

Stabilizer Bar

See Figures 375 through 377.

1. Before servicing the vehicle, refer to the precautions.
2. Remove front underbody protection.
3. Remove stabilizer link on both sides from stabilizer.
4. Remove bolts and remove brackets.

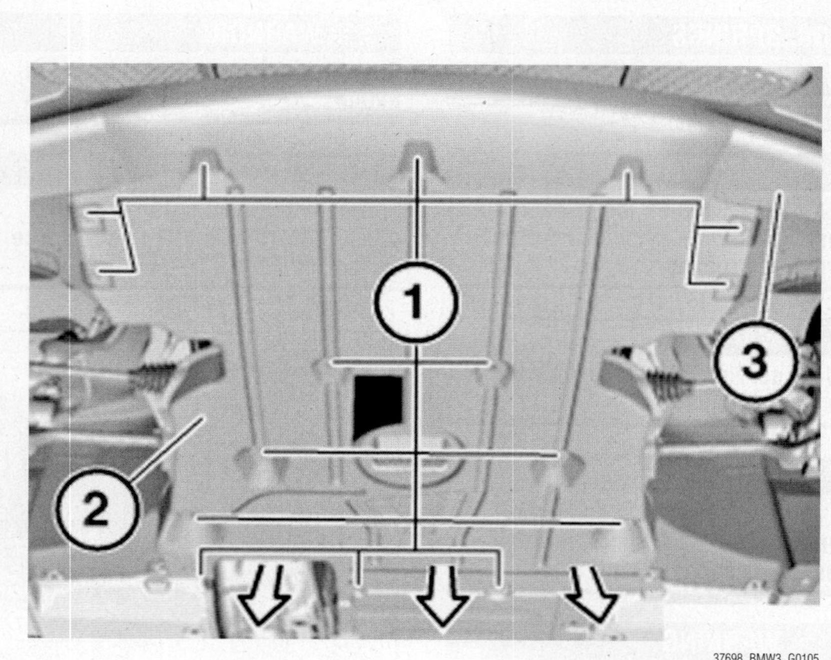

Fig. 375 Release screws and pull underbody protection forward under bumper trim

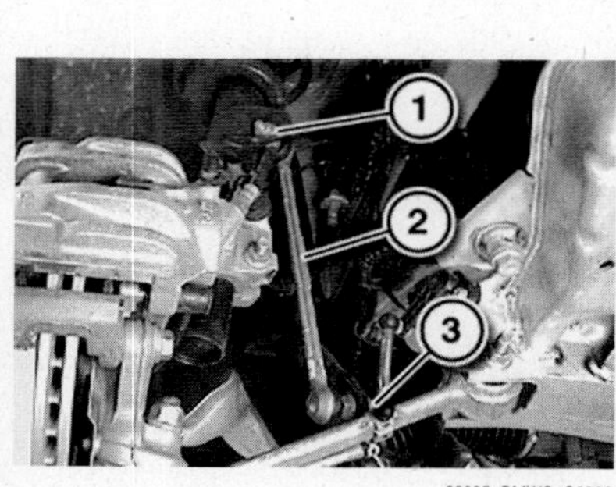

Fig. 376 Remove nut and remove bracket for brake hose. Remove nut and remove stabilizer link

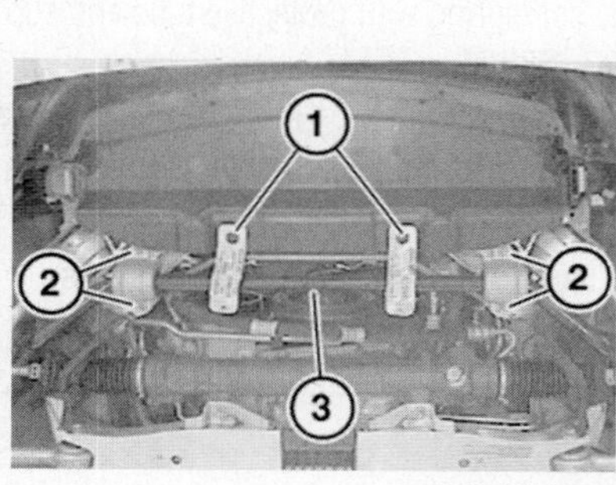

Fig. 377 Remove bolts and remove brackets. Remove nuts; if necessary, grip screws after repair. Remove stabilizer

5. Remove nuts; if necessary, grip screws after repair.
6. Remove stabilizer; if necessary, press off front axle carrier with a suitable tool.

To install:

7. If studs are damaged, repair as follows:
   a. Remove bolt.
   b. Raise locking nut in area of bore and detach from front axle carrier.
   c. Drive out studs in upwards direction and remove/feed out through an opening in front axle carrier.
   d. Insert new screws from above.
8. Check both rubber mounts for damage, replace if necessary.
9. Install stabilizer and secure with brackets.
10. Replace locking nut and tighten temporarily. Once vehicle is at normal ride height, tighten to 50 ft. lbs. (68 Nm) plus an additional 90° rotation.

WARNING

To avoid complaints being made by the customer about noise (e.g. grating), set the car on its wheels and tighten down the stabilizer mounting to specified torque.

11. Connect stabilizer link on both sides from stabilizer. Tighten nuts to 43 ft. lbs. (58 Nm).
12. Install front underbody protection.

STRUTS

REMOVAL & INSTALLATION

See Figure 378.

1. Before servicing the vehicle, refer to the precautions.
2. Remove front wheel.
3. Remove stabilizer link from spring strut.
4. Disconnect plug connection for pulse generator and expose line up to holder on spring strut.
5. Disconnect plug connection for brake pad sensor and expose line up to brake caliper.
6. Remove front brake disc.
7. If necessary, remove jointed rod of ride-height sensor from control arm.
8. Slacken control arm bolt connection on front axle carrier in order to prevent control arm rubber mount from being damaged.
9. Remove control arm from steering knuckle.
10. Remove tie rod end from steering knuckle.
11. Remove tension strut from steering knuckle.

WARNING

Secure spring strut against falling out.

12. Remove tension strut (on spring strut dome) and mark position of threaded pins to wheel arch.
13. Remove nuts and remove spring strut with steering knuckle towards bottom.

To install:

14. If necessary, replace faulty sealing washer.
15. Clean contact surface in spring strut dome.
16. Align spring strut using centering pin to bore in wheel arch or studs to wheel arch and push upwards.
17. Replace self-locking nuts and tighten to 25 ft. lbs. (34 Nm).
18. The remainder of the installation is the reverse of removal.
19. Perform chassis alignment check.
20. Carry out steering angle sensor adjustment/adjustment for active front steering.

OVERHAUL

See Figure 379 through 383.

This procedure details the removal of the coil spring from the MacPherson strut assembly.

CAUTION

This procedure calls for the spring to be compressed. A compressed spring has high potential energy and if removed suddenly can cause severe damage and personal injury.

1. Before servicing the vehicle, refer to the precautions.
2. Remove front spring strut.
3. Remove nut, remove holder and remove screw.
4. Expand ball joint with special tool 31 2 230 and detach from spring strut.
5. Clamp special tool 31 3 341 in vice.
6. Install insert 31 3 358 in special tool 31 3 354.
7. Position special tools 31 3 355 and 31 3 354 with insert 31 3 358 from above on special tool 31 3 341 until locking pins can be felt and heard to snap into place.
8. Check seating of special tools 31 3 355 and 31 3 354 with insert 31 3 358, correct if necessary.
9. Clean coil spring to remove coarse dirt and take up with special tools 31 3 355 and 31 3 354 with insert 31 3 358.
10. Twist spring strut until end of coil spring is flush with end of special tool 31 3 355.

WARNING

Special tool 31 3 354 and centering ring 31 3 358 must rest correctly on upper spring plate.

11. Lower coil of coil spring must rest completely in recess of special tool 31 3 355.
12. Compress coil spring until stress on piston rod is relieved.
13. Remove cap.
14. Remove nut with special tool 31 2 210 (grip piston rod in the process).
15. Remove support bearing, dust sleeve and supporting ring.
16. Remove shock absorber with auxiliary damper, gaiter and lower spring pad sideways from tensioned coil spring.
17. If necessary, remove auxiliary damper, gaiter and spring pad from shock absorber.

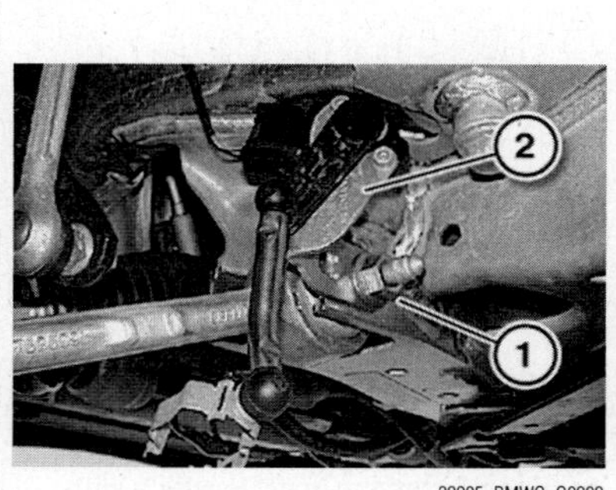

Fig. 378 Sealing washer and plate insert

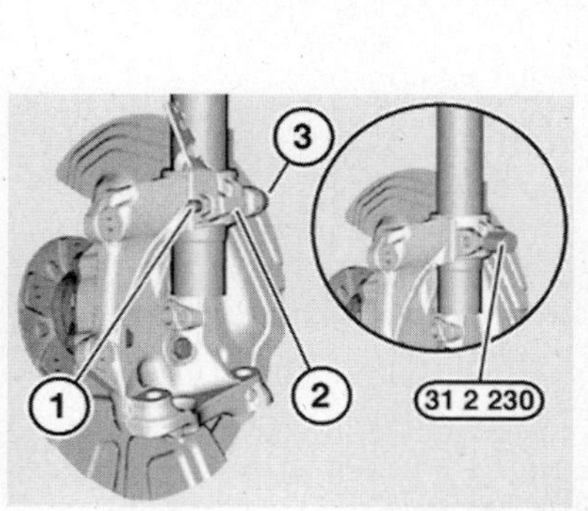

Fig. 379 Remove nut, remove holder and remove screw

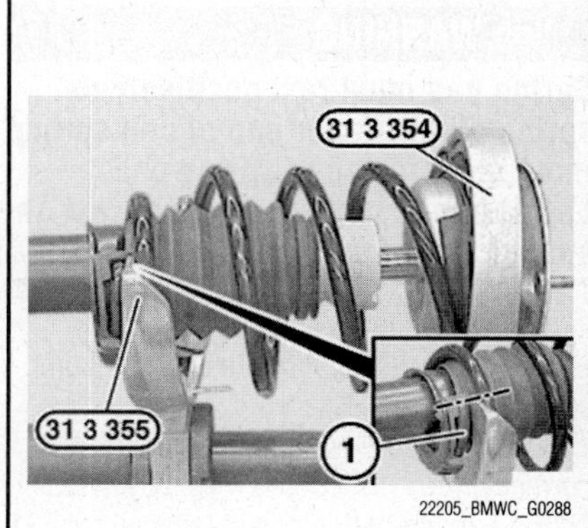

Fig. 380 Twist spring strut until end of coil spring

18. Relieve tension on coil spring.
19. Remove coil spring with spring plate from special tools 31 3 355, 31 3 358 and 31 3 354.

To install:

20. Check spring pad for damage, replace if necessary.

Connect spring plate with spring pad to coil spring.

➡End of coil spring must be positively aligned to spring pad.

21. Accommodate coil spring with spring plate with special tools 31 3 355, 31 3 358 and 31 3 354. Twist coil spring until lower end of coil spring is flush with end of special tool 31 3 355.

⁂ WARNING

Do not compress coil spring to full extent.

22. Special tool 31 3 354 and centering ring 31 3 358 must rest correctly on upper spring plate.
23. Lower coil of coil spring must rest completely in recess of special tool 31 3 355.
24. Tension coil spring.
25. Check auxiliary damper, gaiter and spring pad for damage, replace if necessary.

➡Make sure spring pad is correctly seated on shock absorber.

26. Insert shock absorber in tensioned coil spring.
27. Connect thrust washer to piston rod.
28. Check support bearing for damage, replace if necessary.
29. Connect dust sleeve and support bearing to piston rod.
30. Replace nut and tighten down with special tool 31 2 210 (grip piston rod in the process) to 47 ft. lbs. (64 Nm).
31. Fit cover cap.

⁂ WARNING

Spring pad must rest positively on spring plate. Upper end of coil spring must rest on stop of spring pad. Lower end of coil spring must rest on stop of spring pad.

32. Relieve tension on coil spring.
33. Check installation position of gaiter, correct fold if necessary.
34. Make sure ball joint contacts stop correctly.
35. Expand ball joint with special tool 31 2 230, align by way of gap to positioning pins on back of spring strut and press together up to stop.
36. Keep press fit of ball joint and spring strut in lower area clean and free from oil and grease. Screw head must point in direction of travel.
37. Replace self-locking nut and tighten to 60 ft. lbs. (81 Nm).
38. Perform chassis alignment check.
39. Carry out steering angle sensor adjustment/adjustment for active steering.

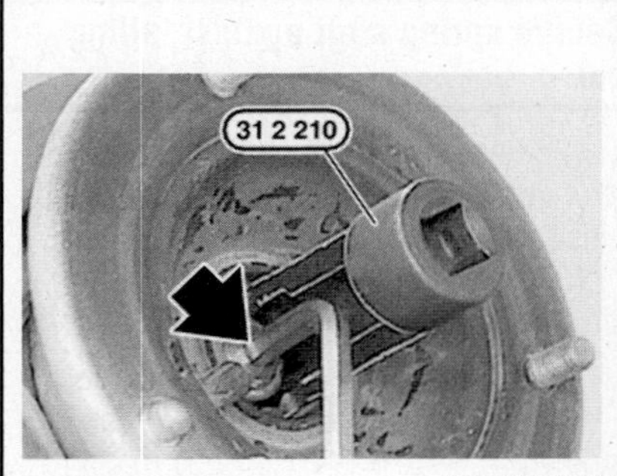

Fig. 381 Remove nut with special tool 31 2 210 (grip piston rod in the process)

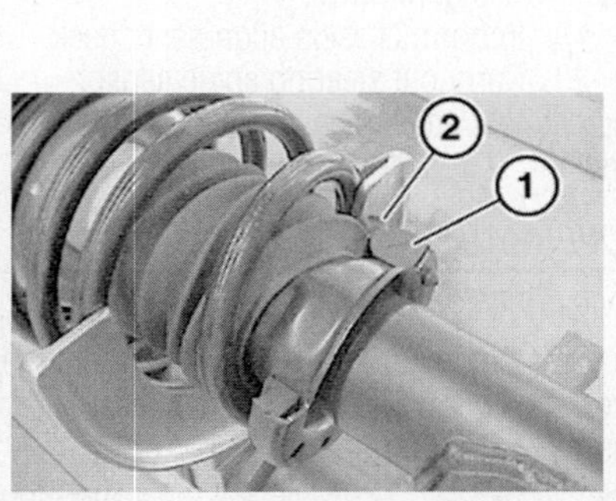

Fig. 382 Lower end of coil spring must rest on stop of spring pad

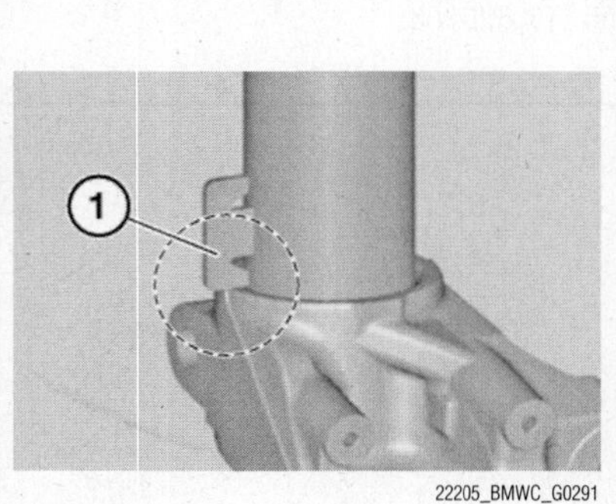

Fig. 383 Make sure ball joint contacts stop correctly

WHEEL HUBS & BEARINGS

ADJUSTMENT

Wheel bearings cannot be adjusted. The front wheel bearings are pressed into the hub and are not available separately. If a front wheel bearing is in need of replacement, it is replaces as a unit with the hub.

REMOVAL, PACKING, & INSTALLATION

See Figure 384.

1. Before servicing the vehicle, refer to the precautions.
2. Remove brake disk.
3. Remove bolts.
4. Press wheel bearing off steering knuckle with a suitable tool.

To install:

5. When reusing the wheel bearing, recut all the threads in the wheel bearing.
6. Keep contact surface of steering knuckle and wheel bearing clean and free from oil and grease.
7. Replace microencapsulated screws and tighten to 81 ft. lbs. (110 Nm).

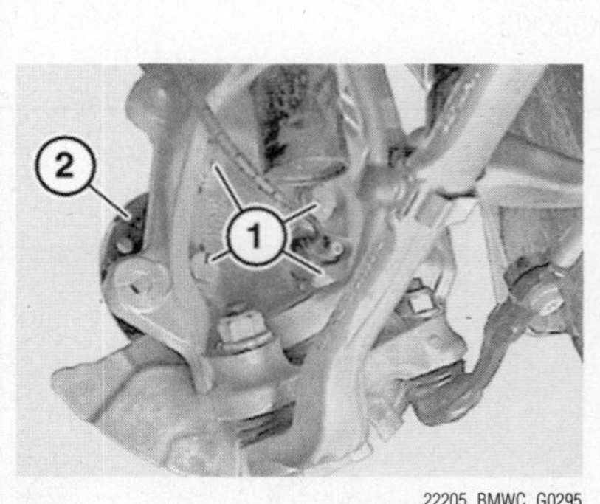

Fig. 384 Remove bolts and press wheel bearing off steering knuckle with a suitable tool

COIL SPRINGS

REMOVAL & INSTALLATION

See Figures 385 and 386.

1. Before servicing the vehicle, refer to the precautions.
2. Remove rear wheel.
3. Insert lower spring plate 33 5 012 centrally into coil spring and turn to lowest coil guide spindles 33 5 013, 33 5 014, 33 5 015 from below through camber arm and lower spring plate 33 5 012.
4. Insert upper spring plate 33 5 011 sideways into coil spring and turn to uppermost coil.

✲✲ WARNING

Make sure spindle (hexagon) is correctly seated in upper spring plate 33 5 011. pull spindle 33 5 013 downwards.

5. Align special tools 33 5 011, 33 5 012, 33 5 013, 33 5 014, 33 5 015 centrally to obtain the biggest possible contact surface on the coil spring.
6. Check installation position of special tools 33 5 011, 33 5 012 and 33 5 013, 33 5 014, 33 5 015, correct if necessary.
7. Tension coil spring using special tools 33 5 016 and 33 5 020, gripping spindle of spring tensioner with special tool 33 5 017 in the process.
8. Remove coil spring upwards.

To install:

9. Bottom end of coil spring must be flush with opening of spring plate 33 5 012.

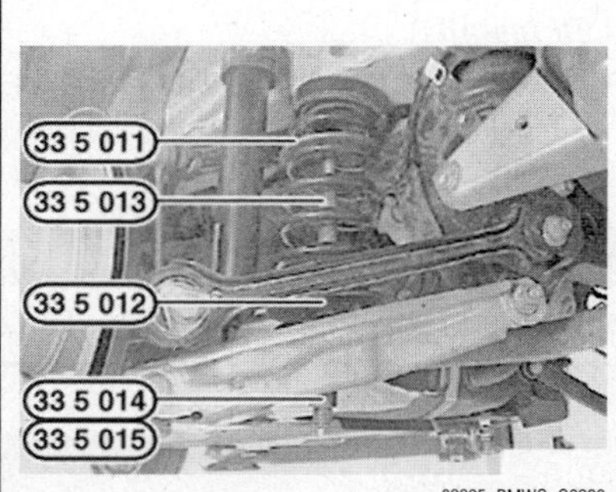

Fig. 385 Align special tools 33 5 011, 33 5 012, 33 5 013, 33 5 014, 33 5 015 centrally to obtain the biggest possible contact surface on the coil spring

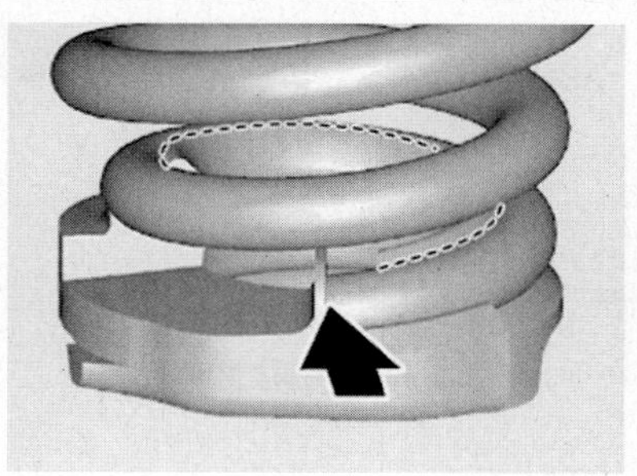

Fig. 386 Lower spring pad must be positively seated in the designated receptacle in the camber arm. The spring pad must come into contact with end of coil spring (arrow) and must rest flush on last coil (broken line)

10. Check spring mounts for damage, replace if necessary.
11. Remove spring plate and position with upper spring pad on coil spring.

➡Upper spring pad must come into contact with end of coil spring.

12. Lower spring pad must be positively seated in the designated receptacle in the camber arm
   a. Lower spring pad must come into contact with end of coil spring.
   b. Lower spring pad must rest flush on last coil.
13. Align coil spring by way of spring plate to opening in side member and relieve tension.
14. Remove special tools 33 5 011, 33 5 012 and 33 5 013, 33 5 014, 33 5 015.
15. Check headlight adjustment, correct if necessary.

CONTROL LINKS

REMOVAL & INSTALLATION

Trailing Arm

See Figure 387.

1. Before servicing the vehicle, refer to the precautions.
2. Remove rear wheel.
3. Remove nuts.
4. Unscrew bolts.
5. Remove trailing arm downwards.
6. Note insertion direction of bolts.
7. Replace self-locking nuts and tighten temporarily.
8. Lower vehicle to normal ride height and tighten bolts to 74 ft. lbs. (100 Nm).
9. Perform chassis alignment check.

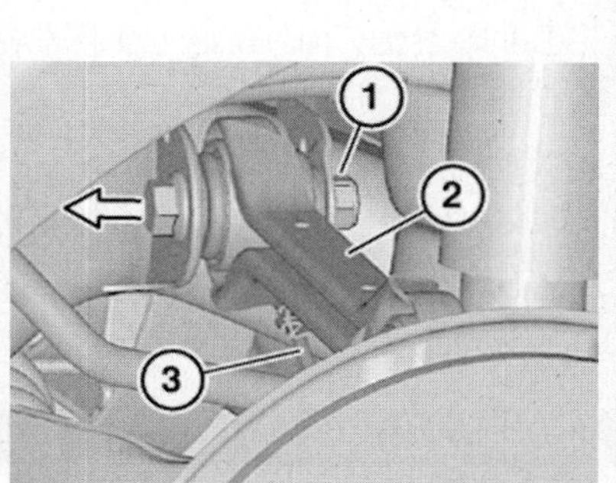

Fig. 387 Remove nut, remove control arm and line holder for pulse generator

Upper Control Arm

See Figure 389.

1. Before servicing the vehicle, refer to the precautions.
2. Remove rear wheel.
3. Remove bolt.
4. Remove nut and remove screw towards front.
5. Unclip line holder for pulse generator or brake pad sensor on control arm.
6. Remove control arm.

To install:

7. Install control arm.

✲✲ WARNING

Make sure during installation that in the connection area to the wheel carrier the tapered end of the bearing bushing (of the rubber mount) points in the direction of the wheel carrier.

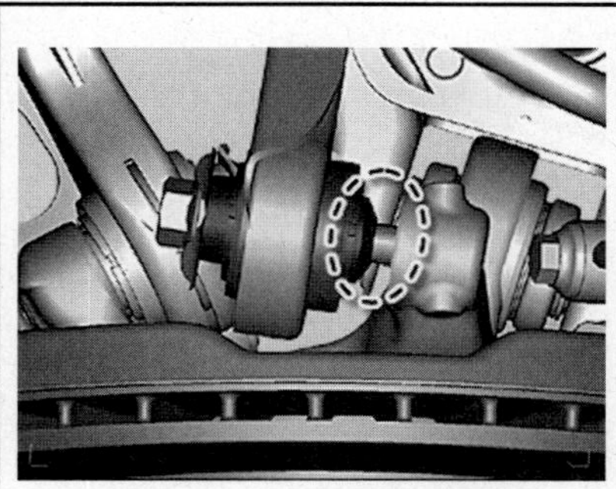

Fig. 388 Make sure during installation that in the connection area to the wheel carrier the tapered end of the bearing bushing (of the rubber mount) points in the direction of the wheel carrier

8. Install control arm to rear axle carrier bolt and point head in direction of travel.
9. Replace self-locking nut and tighten to 74 ft. lbs. (100 Nm).
10. If necessary, raise brake disk in drive flange area with workshop jack.
11. Replace control arm to wheel carrier bolt and tighten temporarily. Fully tighten the bolt once the vehicle is at ride height to 74 ft. lbs. (100 Nm) plus 90° additional rotation.
12. Perform chassis alignment check.

STABILIZER BAR & LINKS

REMOVAL & INSTALLATION

See Figures 389 and 390.

1. Before servicing the vehicle, refer to the precautions.
2. Remove both rear coil springs.
3. Remove left control arm on wheel carrier.
4. Remove both stabilizer links from stabilizer.
5. Lower rear axle carrier.
6. Remove bolts and remove both rubber mounts from stabilizer.
7. Turn stabilizer and remove sideways.

To install:

8. Check both rubber mounts for damage, replace if necessary.
9. Tightening fasteners to specification.
   - Retaining bracket, stabilizer bar to rear axle support: 16 ft. lbs. (21 Nm)
   - Stabilizer link to stabilizer: 43 ft. lbs. (58 Nm)
   - Stabilizer link to wheel carrier: 16 ft. lbs. (21 Nm)
10. Raise rear axle carrier.
11. Install both rear coil springs.

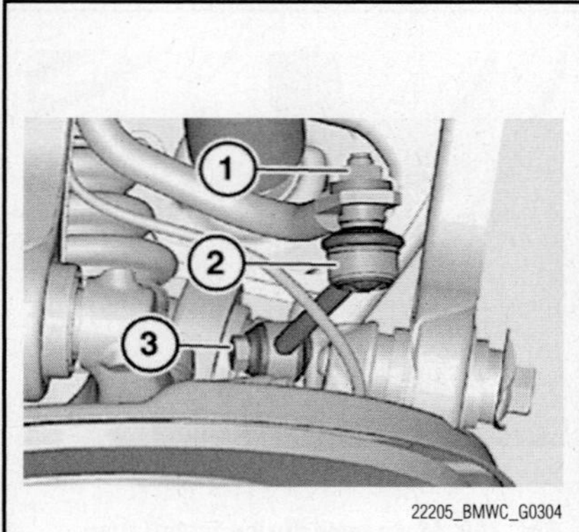

Fig. 389 Stabilizer link and mounting nut and bolt

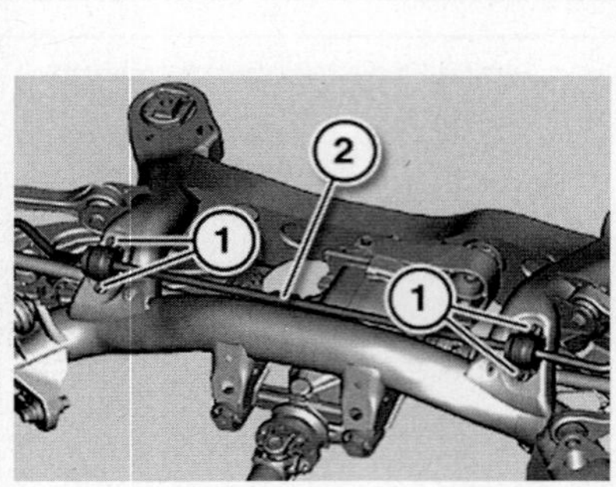

Fig. 390 Stabilizer bar and mounting bolts

12. Install left control arm on wheel carrier.
13. Bleed braking system.

STRUTS

REMOVAL & INSTALLATION

See Figure 391.

WARNING

All screws, nuts, bolts and hose clamps removed during the repair must be replaced.

WARNING

Retaining elements on chassis and suspension and steering parts must be replaced.

1. Remove front wheel.
2. Remove front brake disc.
3. Remove anti-roll bar link from spring strut.

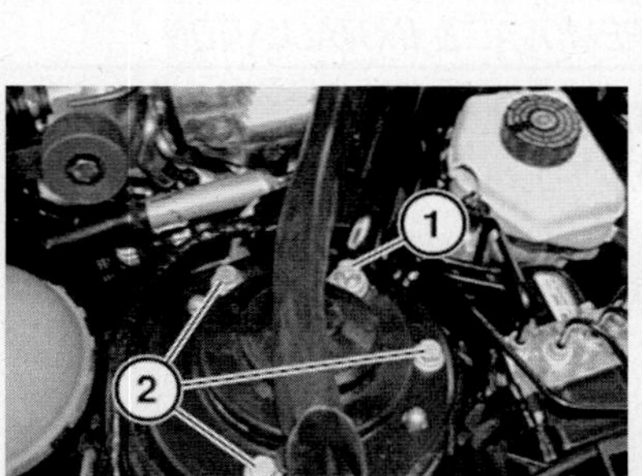

Fig. 391 Releasing screw on suspension cross brace and spring strut

4. Disconnect plug connection for pulse sensor and expose cable up to holder on spring strut.
5. Disconnect plug connection for brake pad wear sensor and expose cable up to brake caliper.

Only on ride height sensor at left:

6. Release link at wishbone.

All:

7. Slacken wishbone bolt connection on front axle support in order to prevent wishbone rubber mount from being damaged.
8. Remove wishbone from swivel bearing.
9. Remove track rod end from swivel bearing.
10. Remove trailing link from swivel bearing
11. Unlock closures. Press clamps together and lift.
12. Remove cover.

➡When installing, make sure closures are correctly locked.

WARNING

Secure spring strut against falling out.

13. Release screw on suspension crossbrace. Tightening torque: 41 ft. lbs. (56 Nm) + 90°

➡Replace screw.

14. Release screws and remove spring strut with swivel bearing towards bottom. Tightening torque: 41 ft. lbs. (56 Nm) + 90°

➡Clean inside contact surface at spring strut dome.

➡Align spring strut with boreholes on spring strut dome using centering pins and push up.

To install:

To install, reverse the removal procedure noting the following.

15. Carry out wheel alignment.

TRAILING ARMS

REMOVAL & INSTALLATION

See Figure 392.

WARNING

The trailing arm must be installed with the opening (U-section) facing downward.

1. Unscrew nuts. Tightening torque: 74 ft. lbs. (100 Nm)

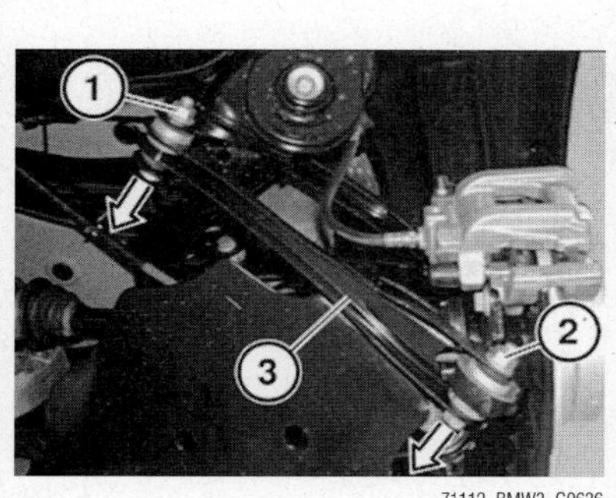

Fig. 392 Unscrewing nuts, slacken nut and removing trailing arm

2. Move screw toward the rear.

➡**Note direction of insertion of bolts.**

3. Replace nut.
4. Tighten down screw connection in normal position.
5. Slacken nut. Tightening torque: 74 ft. lbs. (100 Nm)
6. Move screws toward the rear.
7. Remove trailing arm downward.

➡**When installing, the trailing arm must be installed with the opening (U-section) facing downward.**

➡**Note direction of insertion of screw.**

8. Replace nut.
9. Tighten down screw connection in normal position.

To install:

To install, reverse the removal procedure.

UPPER BALL JOINTS

REMOVAL & INSTALLATION

See Figure 393.

WARNING

The ball joint may not be reused after it has been pressed out.

1. Remove rear wheel.
2. Remove camber arm cover.
3. Remove coil spring, rear.
4. Remove trailing arm.
5. Remove camber arm.
6. If applicable, remove jointed rod for ride height sensor from the camber arm bracket.
7. Pull out ball joint with special tool 33 3 010, 2 240 473 and 2 240 469.

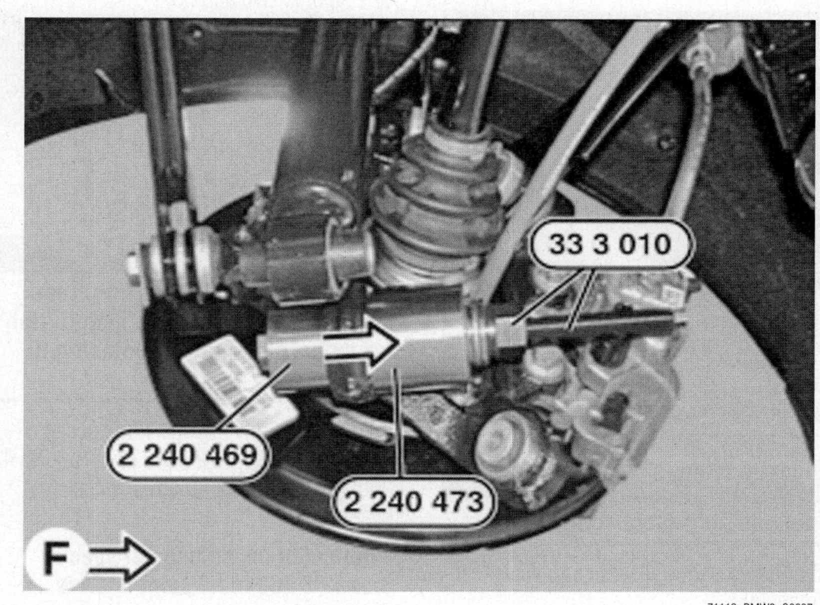

Fig. 393 Pulling out ball joint

To install:

8. Fit new ball joint with special tools 33 3 010, 2 240 473, and 2 240 476 until limit position.
9. To complete installation, reverse the removal procedure.
10. Carry out wheel alignment.

UPPER CONTROL ARMS

REMOVAL & INSTALLATION

See Figures 394 and 395.

1. Remove rear wheel.
2. Remove camber arm cover.
3. Release screw.

➡**When installing, observe installation sequence.**

4. Manually lift wheel carrier in region of brake caliper if necessary.
5. Replace screw.

WARNING

Make sure during installation that in the connection area to the wheel carrier the tapered end of the bearing bushing (of the rubber mount) points in the direction of the wheel carrier.

6. Slacken nut.

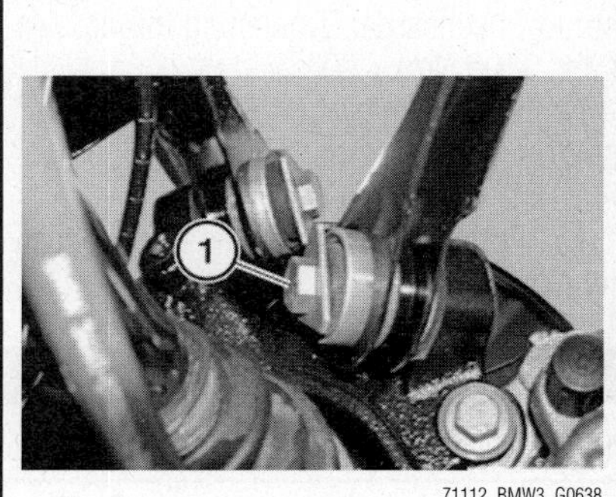

Fig. 394 Releasing screw

➡**When installing, observe installation sequence.**

7. Screw head faces away from direction of travel.
8. Replace self-locking nut.

To install:

WARNING

Failure to comply with these instructions may result in serious damage to the threads of the wheel carrier.

71112_BMW3_G0639

Fig. 395 Slackening nut

⁂ WARNING

Do not use an impact screwdriver.

9. Put on screw wishbone to wheel carrier manually.
10. Fit control arm to rear axle support, insert screw and screw on nut

⁂ WARNING

Tighten both screw connections in normal position only.

11. Tighten screw connection control arm to wheel carrier. Tightening torque: 74 ft. lbs. (100 Nm) + 90°
12. Tighten screw connection control arm to rear axle support. Tightening torque: 74 ft. lbs. (100 Nm)
13. Put on screw wishbone to wheel carrier manually.

WHEEL HUBS & BEARINGS

ADJUSTMENT

Wheel bearings cannot be adjusted. The rear bearings must be replaced as a unit and never be reused once removed.

REMOVAL, REPACKING, & INSTALLATION

See Figures 396 and 397.

1. Before servicing the vehicle, refer to the precautions.
2. Remove drive flange of rear axle shaft.
3. Remove output shaft.
4. Remove brake disk.
5. Remove pulse generator.

⁂ WARNING

Check sensor head and line from pulse generator prior to installation for external damage, replacing if necessary.

6. Force drive flange with special tools 33 2 116 / 33 2 201, 33 2 160, 33 4 200 and 5 wheel bolts out of wheel bearing.

➡Rounded inside edge of special tool 33 2 160 must point to drive flange.

7. Press retaining ring together using pliers and remove.
8. Pull out wheel bearing with special tools 33 4 041, 33 4 042, 33 4 031, 33 4 048 and 33 4 043.

To install:

9. Install retaining ring.
10. Check seating of retaining ring, correct if necessary.
11. Draw in new wheel bearing with special tools 33 4 041, 33 4 042, 33 4 049, 33 4 047 and 33 4 043.

⁂ WARNING

Do not reuse old wheel bearing. The wheel bearing is destroyed when the drive flange is removed and cannot be reused.

12. Replace wheel bearing.
13. Install output shaft.

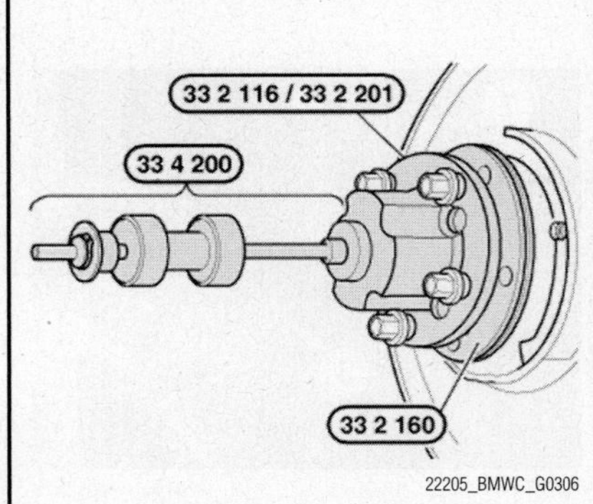

22205_BMWC_G0306

Fig. 396 Force drive flange with special tools 33 2 116 / 33 2 201, 33 2 160, 33 4 200 and 5 wheel bolts out of wheel bearing

22205_BMWC_G0305

Fig. 397 Pull out wheel bearing with special tools 33 4 041, 33 4 042, 33 4 031, 33 4 048 and 33 4 043

14. Oil drive flange lightly and attach to splines of output shaft.
15. Draw drive flange into wheel bearing.
16. Install brake disk.
17. Install pulse generator.
18. Adjust handbrake.

BMW

528I • 528XI • 535I • 535XI • 550I • 550IX

3

SPECIFICATIONS AND MAINTENANCE CHARTS

ENGINE AND VEHICLE IDENTIFICATION

Code	Liters (cc)	Cu. In.	Cyl.	Fuel Sys.	Engine Type	Eng. Mfg.
N20	2.0 (1997)	122	4	③	DOHC	BMW
N52	3.0 (2996)	183	6	②	DOHC	BMW
N55	3.0 (2979)	181	6	③	DOHC	BMW
N63	4.4 (4395)	268	8	③	DOHC	BMW

Model Year	
Code ①	Year
B	2011
C	2012

NA: Not Available

DOHC: Double Overhead Camshaft

SOHC: Single Overhead Camshaft

① 10th digit of the Vehicle Identification Number (VIN)

② Siemens MSV80 3-Series

③ Bosch

71112_BMW5_C0001

GENERAL ENGINE SPECIFICATIONS

Year	Model	Engine Displacement Liters (cc)	Engine ID/VIN	Fuel System Type	Net Horsepower @ rpm	Net Torque @ rpm (ft. lbs.)	Bore x Stroke (in.)	Com-pression Ratio	Oil Pressure @ rpm
2011	528i Sedan	3.0 (2996)	N52B30	①	230@6500	200@2750	3.35x3.46	10.7:1	7.3@idle
	528xi Sedan	3.0 (2996)	N52B30	①	230@6500	200@2750	3.35x3.46	10.7:1	7.3@idle
	535i Sedan	3.0 (2979)	N55B30	②	300@5800	300@1200	3.28x3.49	10.2:1	21.76@idle
	535xi Sedan	3.0 (2979)	N55B30	②	300@5800	300@1200	3.28x3.49	10.2:1	21.76@idle
	550iX Sedan	4.4 (4395)	N63B44	②	400@5500	450@1750	3.50x3.50	10.0:1	21.76@idle
	550i Sedan	4.4 (4395)	N63B44	②	400@5500	450@1750	3.50x3.50	10.0:1	21.76@idle
2012	528i Sedan	2.0 (1997)	N20B20	②	240@5000	260@1250	3.28x3.49	10.0:1	14.5@idle
	528xi Sedan	2.0 (1997)	N20B20	②	240@5000	260@1250	3.28x3.49	10.0:1	14.5@idle
	535i Sedan	3.0 (2979)	N55B30	②	300@5800	300@1200	3.28x3.49	10.2:1	21.76@idle
	535xi Sedan	3.0 (2979)	N55B30	②	300@5800	300@1200	3.31x3.53	10.2:1	21.76@idle
	550iX Sedan	4.4 (4395)	N63B44	②	③	④	3.31x3.53	10.5:1	14.5@idle
	550i Sedan	4.4 (4395)	N63B44	②	③	④	3.50x3.50	10.5:1	14.5@idle

① Siemens

② Bosch

③ 402@5500-6400

④ 400@1750-4500

71112_BMW5_C0002

ENGINE TUNE-UP SPECIFICATIONS

Year	Engine Displacement Liters	Engine ID/VIN	Spark Plug Gap (in.)	Ignition Timing (deg.) MT	Ignition Timing (deg.) AT	Fuel Pump (psi)	Idle Speed (rpm) MT	Idle Speed (rpm) AT	Valve Clearance In.	Valve Clearance Ex.
2011	3.0	N52B30	①	②	②	70-76	②	②	HYD	HYD
	3.0	N55B30	①	②	②	70-76	②	②	HYD	HYD
	4.4	N63B44	①	②	②	48-54	②	②	HYD	HYD
2012	2.0	N20B20	①	②	②	70-76	②	②	HYD	HYD
	3.0	N55B30	①	②	②	70-76	②	②	HYD	HYD
	4.4	N63B44	①	②	②	48-54	②	②	HYD	HYD

NOTE: The Vehicle Emission Control Information label reflects specification changes during production and must be used if they differ from this chart.

HYD: Hydraulic

① Three mass and four-mass electrodes cannot be adjusted

Dual mass electrodes: 0.035-0.039 inches

All others: 0.028-0.031 inches

② Controlled by the Engine Control Module (ECM) and cannot be adjusted

71112_BMW5_C0003

CAPACITIES

Year	Model	Engine Displacement Liters	Engine ID	Engine Oil with Filter (qts.)	Transmission (pts.) 6-Spd	Transmission (pts.) Auto.	Drive Axle Front (pts.)	Drive Axle Rear (pts.)	Fuel Tank (gal.)	Cooling System (qts.)
2011	528i Sedan	3.0	N52B30	6.9	①	②	1.3	2.5	18.5	③
	528xi Sedan	3.0	N52B30	6.9	①	②	1.3	2.5	18.5	③
	535i Sedan	3.0	N55B30	6.9	①	②	1.3	2.5	18.5	③
	535xi Sedan	3.0	N55B30	6.9	①	②	1.3	2.5	18.5	③
	550i Sedan	4.4	N63B44	9.0	①	②	1.3	2.5	23.3	③
	550i Sedan	4.4	N63B44	9.0	①	②	1.3	2.5	23.3	③
2012	528i Sedan	2.0	N20B20	④	①	②	1.3	2.5	18.5	③
	528xi Sedan	2.0	N20B20	④	①	②	1.3	2.5	18.5	③
	535i Sedan	3.0	N55B30	6.9	①	②	1.3	2.5	18.5	③
	535xi Sedan	3.0	N55B30	6.9	①	②	1.3	2.5	18.5	③
	550i Sedan	4.4	N63B44	9.0	①	②	1.3	2.5	23.3	③
	550iX Sedan	4.4	N63B44	9.0	①	②	1.3	2.5	23.3	③

NOTE: All capacities are approximate. Add fluid gradually and ensure a proper fluid level is obtained.

NOTE: Capacities given are service, not overhaul capacities

① GS6-37BZ/DZ / MECH Transmission: 3.18 pts.

E53 GS6-53DZ/BZ / MECH Transmission 3.18 pts.

GS6-17BG/DG / MECH Transmission 2.76 pts.

② GA6HP19Z Transmission: 19-21.2 pts.

GA6L45R Transmission: 19.0 pts.

③ M/T: 10.6 qts., A/T 11.2 qts.

④ 2WD: 5.28

AWD: 5.0

71112_BMW5_C0004

FLUID SPECIFICATIONS

Year	Model	Engine Displ. Liters	Engine Oil	Man. Trans.	Auto. Trans.	Rear Drive Axle	Power Steering Fluid	Brake Master Cylinder	Cooling System
2011	528i Sedan	3.0	5W-30	①	M-1375-4	②	Dexron® III	DOT 4	BMW Long Life Coolant
	528xi Sedan	3.0	5W-30	①	M-1375-4	②	Dexron® III	DOT 4	BMW Long Life Coolant
	535i Sedan	3.0	5W-30	①	M-1375-4	②	Dexron® III	DOT 4	BMW Long Life Coolant
	535xi Sedan	3.0	5W-30	①	M-1375-4	②	Dexron® III	DOT 4	BMW Long Life Coolant
	550i Sedan	4.4	5W-30	①	M-1375-4	②	Dexron® III	DOT 4	BMW Long Life Coolant
	550iX Sedan	4.4	5W-30	①	M-1375-4	②	Dexron® III	DOT 4	BMW Long Life Coolant
2012	528i Sedan	2.0	5W-30	①	M-1375-4	②	Dexron® III	DOT 4	BMW Long Life Coolant
	528xi Sedan	2.0	5W-30	①	M-1375-4	②	Dexron® III	DOT 4	BMW Long Life Coolant
	535i Sedan	3.0	5W-30	①	M-1375-4	②	Dexron® III	DOT 4	BMW Long Life Coolant
	535xi Sedan	3.0	5W-30	①	M-1375-4	②	Dexron® III	DOT 4	BMW Long Life Coolant
	550i Sedan	4.4	5W-30	①	M-1375-4	②	Dexron® III	DOT 4	BMW Long Life Coolant
	550iX Sedan	4.4	5W-30	①	M-1375-4	②	Dexron® III	DOT 4	BMW Long Life Coolant

NA: Not Available

DOT: Department Of Transpotation

① Orange Label: Dexron AFT

Green Label: Synthetic Mobil SCH630

Yellow Label: MTF-LT-1 or MTF-LT-2

6-Speed: MTF-LT-3

No label: MIL-L-2105

② Limited slip: SAF-XJ. Non-limited slip: SAF-XO

71112_BMW5_C0005

VALVE SPECIFICATIONS

Year	Engine Displacement Liters	Engine ID/VIN	Seat Angle (deg.)	Face Angle (deg.)	Spring Test Pressure (lbs. @ in.)	Spring Installed Height (in.)	Stem-to-Guide Clearance (in.)		Stem Diameter (in.)	
							Intake	Exhaust	Intake	Exhaust
2011	3.0	N52B30	①	45	NA	NA	② 0.0197	② 0.0197	0.0234-0.0235	0.0234-0.0235
	3.0	N55B30	①	45	NA	NA	② 0.0197	② 0.0197	0.0234-0.0235	0.0234-0.0235
	4.4	N63B44	④	45	NA	NA	② 0.0197	② 0.0197	0.0234-0.0235	0.0234-0.0235
2012	2.0	N52B30	③	45	NA	NA	② 0.0197	② 0.0197	0.0234-0.0235	0.0234-0.0235
	3.0	N55B30	①	45	NA	NA	② 0.0197	② 0.0197	0.0234-0.0235	0.0234-0.0235
	4.4	N63B44	④	45	NA	NA	② 0.0197	② 0.0197	0.0234-0.0235	0.0234-0.0235

NA: Not Available

① Valve seat angle: 45 degrees
Correction angle outside: 15 degrees
Correction angle inside: 60 degrees

② To measure: Insert a new valve into guide
with end of valve flush with end of guide.
Use a dial indicator to measure axial valve head movement.

③ Valve seat angle: 45 degrees
Correction angle outside : 35 degrees
Correction angle; inner exhaust valve: 60 degrees
Correction angle; outer exhaust valve: 65 degrees

④ Valve seat angle: 45 degrees
Correction angle outside: 15 degrees
Correction angle inside: 70 degrees

71112_BMW5_C0006

CAMSHAFT SPECIFICATIONS

All measurements in inches unless noted

Year	Engine Displacement Liters	Engine Code/ID	Journal Dia.	Brg. Oil Clearance	Shaft End-play	Circle Runout	Lobe Height	
							Intake	Exhaust
2011	3.0	N52B30	NA	NA	0.0007-0.0063	0.0021-0.0038	NA	NA
	3.0	N55B30	NA	NA	0.0007-0.0063	0.0021-0.0038	NA	NA
	4.8	N63B44	NA	NA	0.0025-0.0058	0.0001-0.0032	NA	NA
2012	2.0	N20B20	NA	NA	0.0007-0.0063	0.0015-0.0033	NA	NA
	3.0	N55B30	NA	NA	0.0007-0.0063	0.0021-0.0038	NA	NA
	4.4	N63B44	NA	NA	0.0025-0.0058	0.0001-0.0032	NA	NA

NA: Not Available

71112_BMW5_C0007

CRANKSHAFT AND CONNECTING ROD SPECIFICATIONS

All measurements are given in inches.

Year	Engine Disp. Liters	Engine ID/VIN	Crankshaft Main Brg. Journal Dia.	Crankshaft Main Brg. Oil Clearance	Crankshaft Shaft End-play	Crankshaft Thrust on No.	Connecting Rod Journal Diameter	Connecting Rod Oil Clearance	Connecting Rod Side Clearance
2011	3.0	N52B30	①	0.0007-0.0023	0.0031-0.0064	NA	1.7706-1.7712	0.0007-0.0022	NA
	3.0	N55B30	②	0.0007-0.0018	0.0058	NA	2.0904-2.0910	NA	NA
	4.4	N63B44	③	0.0008-0.0018	NA	NA	2.2464-2.2470	NA	NA
2012	2.0	N20B20	④	0.0007-0.0023	0.0058	NA	2.0904-2.0910	NA	NA
	3.0	N55B30	②	0.0007-0.0018	0.0058	NA	2.0904-2.0910	NA	NA
	4.4	N63B44	③	0.0008-0.0018	NA	NA	2.2464-2.2470	NA	NA

① Standard yellow 2.3615-2.3618 inches
Standard green: 2.3613-2.3615 inches
Standard white: 2.3611-2.3613 inches

② Designation S/1: 2.5347-2.5346 inches
Designation S/2: 2.5344-2.5346 inches
Designation S/3: 2.5342-2.5344 inches

③ S1:2.5339-2.5342
S2: 2.5341-2.5343
S3: 2.5338-2.5340

④ S/1: 1.9491-1.9493
S/2: 1.9489-1.9491
S/3: 1.9488-1.9492

71112_BMW5_C0008

PISTON AND RING SPECIFICATIONS

All measurements are given in inches

Year	Engine Disp. Liters	Engine ID/VIN	Piston Clearance	Ring Gap Top Compression	Ring Gap Bottom Compression	Ring Gap Oil Control	Ring Side Clearance Top Compression	Ring Side Clearance Bottom Compression	Ring Side Clearance Oil Control
2011	3.0	N52B30	0.0004-0.0016	0.0078-0.0157	0.0078-0.0157	0.0078-0.0177	0.0008-0.0024	0.0008-0.0024	0.0005-0.0023
	3.0	N55B30	①	0.0058 0.0117	0.0117-0.0195	0.0078-0.0351	0.00078-0.00234	0.00058-0.00234	NA
	4.4	N63B44	②	0.0058-0.0234	0.0117-0.0195	NA	.00078-0.00234	0.000585-0.00234	NA
2012	2.0	N20B20	③	0.0058 0.0117	0.0117 0.0195	0.0078-0.0351	0.0017-0.00312	0.00078-0.00234	NA
	3.0	N55B30	①	0.0058 0.0117	0.0117-0.0195	0.0078-0.0351	0.00078-0.00234	0.00058-0.00234	NA
	4.4	N63B44	②	0.0058-0.0234	0.0117-0.0195	NA	.00078-0.00234	0.000585-0.00234	NA

NA: Not Available

① New Piston: 0.0004-0.0012
Used Piston: 0.00078.0.0031

② New piston: 0.00-0.00117
Used piston: 0.00078-0.00195

③ New Piston: 0.00039-0.00117
Used piston: 0.00078-0.00195

71112_BMW5_C0009

TORQUE SPECIFICATIONS

All readings in ft. lbs.

Year	Engine Disp. Liters	Engine ID/VIN	Cylinder Head Bolts	Main Bearing Bolts	Rod Bearing Bolts	Crankshaft Damper Bolts	Flywheel Bolts	Manifold Intake	Manifold Exhaust	Spark Plugs	Oil Pan Drain Plug
2011	3.0	N52B30	①	②	③	27	89-93	11	15	18	18
	3.0	N55B30	④	⑤	⑥	27	77	15	13	18	18
	4.4	N63B44	①	⑦	③	30	77	15	7	18	18
2012	2.0	N20B20	⑧	⑨	⑥	27	⑩	11	13	18	18
	3.0	N55B30	④	⑤	⑥	27	77	15	13	18	18
	4.4	N63B44	①	⑧	③	30	77	15	7	18	18

① Cast iron block. Replace, wash and oil bolts
Step 1: 22 ft. lbs.
Step 2: 90 degrees
Step 3: 90 degrees
Step 3: 45 degrees

② Cast iron block. Replace, wash and oil bolts
Step 1: 14.8 ft. lbs.
Step 2: 50 degrees

③ Replace, wash and oil connecting rod bolts
Step 1: 14.8 ft. lbs.
Step 2: 70 degrees

④ Always use new bolts.
Step 1: Tighten bolts 1-10 (M11) to 22 ft. lbs.
Step 2: Tighten bolts 11-14 (M9) to 22 ft. lbs.
Step 3: Tighten bolts 1-14 90 degrees
Step 4: Tighten bolts 1-10 (M11) 90 degrees
Step 5: Tighten bolts 1-14 180 degrees

⑤ Always use new bolts.
Step 1: 14.8 ft. lbs.
Step 2: 70 degrees

⑥ Replace, wash and oil screws
Step 1: 14.75 ft. lbs.
Step 2: Tighten bolts 140 degrees

⑦ Always use new bolts. Do not remove coating
Step 1: 14.75 ft. lbs.
Step 2: 100 degrees

⑧ Step 1: Tighten bolts to 22 ft. lbs.
Step 2: Tighten bolts 90 degrees
Step 3: Tighten bolts 180 degrees

⑨ Always use new bolts.
Step 1: 14.75 ft. lbs.
Step 2: Tighten bolts 90 degrees

⑩ Always use new screws.
Step 1: 44 ft. lbs.
Step 2: Tighten screws 45 degrees

71112_BMW5_C0010

71112_BMW5_G0533

Fig. 1 Main bearing torque sequence—N20 Engine

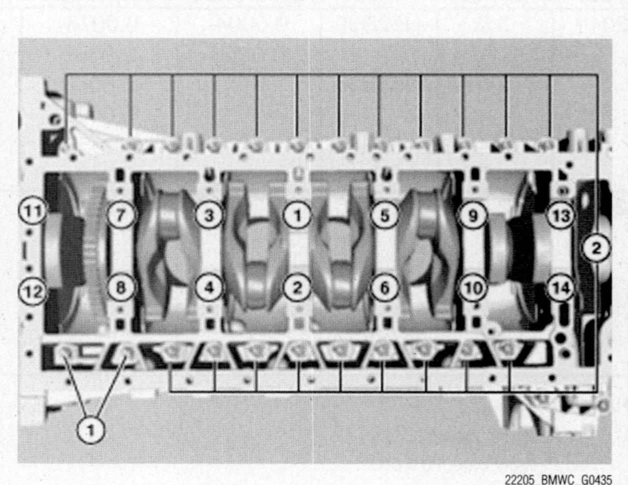

22205_BMWC_G0435

Fig. 2 Main bearing torque sequence—N52 Engines

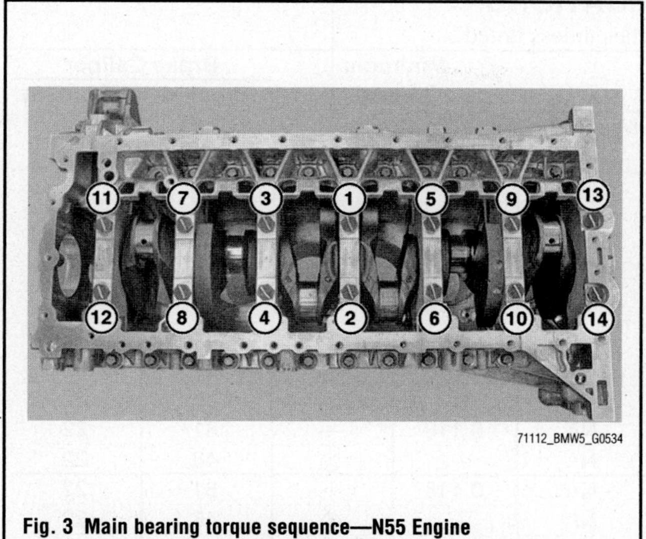

Fig. 3 Main bearing torque sequence—N55 Engine

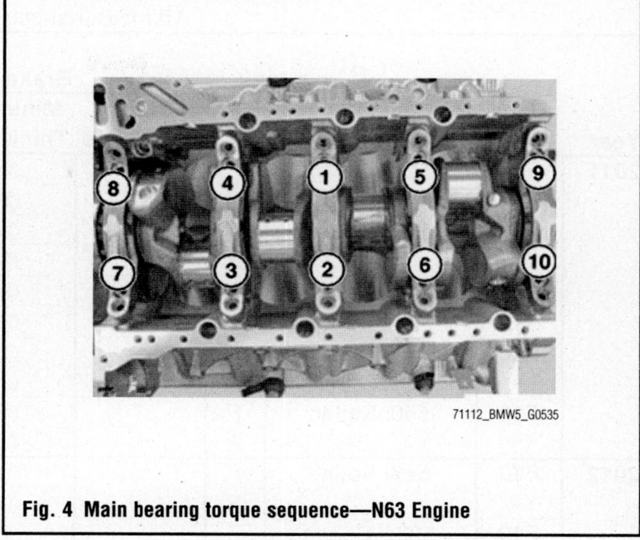

Fig. 4 Main bearing torque sequence—N63 Engine

WHEEL ALIGNMENT

			Caster		Camber			
				Preferred		Preferred		Steering
			Range	Setting	Range	Setting	Toe-in	Axis Inclination
Year	Model		(+/-Deg.)	(Deg.)	(+/-Deg.)	(Deg.)	(Deg.)	(Deg.)
2011	5 Series	F	0.15	0	20	-0.12	①	—
		R	—	—	0.20	-2	0.18+/- 0.10	—
2012	5 Series	F	0.15	0	20	-0.12	①	—
		R	—	—	0.20	-2	0.18+/- 0.10	—

NOTE: Load vehicle with 150 lbs. on the front seats, 150 lbs on the rear seats and 46 lbs in the trunk with a full fuel tank.

① 535xi Sport Wagon: 0.18+/- 0.10.
Except 535xi Sport Wagon: 0.08+/- 0.10.

71112_BMW5_C0011

TIRE, WHEEL AND BALL JOINT SPECIFICATIONS

		OEM Tires		Tire Pressures (psi)		Wheel	Ball Joint	Lug Nut Torque
Year	Model	Standard	Optional	Front	Rear	Size	Inspection	(ft. lbs.)
2011	5-Series	P225/50R17	①	②	②	NA	NA	89
2012	5-Series	P225/50R17	①	②	②	NA	NA	89

① P245/40R18, P245/35R19, P275/35R18, P275/30R19

② See door sticker.

71112_BMW5_C0012

BRAKE SPECIFICATIONS

All measurements in inches unless noted

Year	Body Type	Model		Brake Disc: Original Thickness	Brake Disc: Minimum Thickness	Brake Disc: Maximum Runout	Minimum Lining Thickness: Front	Minimum Lining Thickness: Rear	Brake Caliper: Bracket Bolts (ft. lbs.)	Brake Caliper: Mounting Bolts (ft. lbs.)
2011	F10	528i Sedan	F	①	②	NA	0.118	—	81	22
			R	③	②	NA	—	①	48	22
	F10	528xi Sedan	F	①	②	NA	0.118	—	81	22
			R	③	②	NA	—	①	48	22
	F10	535i Sedan	F	①	②	NA	0.118	—	81	22
			R	③	②	NA	—	①	48	22
	F10	535xi Sedan	F	①	②	NA	0.118	—	81	22
			R	③	②	NA	—	①	48	22
	F10	550i Sedan	F	①	②	NA	0.118	—	81	22
			R	③	②	NA	—	①	48	22
2012	F10	528i Sedan	F	①	②	NA	0.118	—	81	22
			R	③	②	NA	—	①	48	22
	F10	528xi Sedan	F	①	②	NA	0.118	—	81	22
			R	③	②	NA	—	①	48	22
	F10	535i Sedan	F	①	②	NA	0.118	—	81	22
			R	③	②	NA	—	①	48	22
	F10	535xi Sedan	F	①	②	NA	0.118	—	81	22
			R	③	②	NA	—	①	48	22
	F10	550i Sedan	F	①	②	NA	0.118	—	81	22
			R	③	②	NA	—	①	48	22

NA: Not Available

F: Front

R: Rear

① Depending on brake package: .945 in., 1.18 in. or 1.41in.

② Minimum thickness is stamped in the brake disk shell

Maximum machining limit per side: 0.315 inches

③ Depending on brake package: .787 in. or .945 in.

71112_BMW5_C0013

SCHEDULED MAINTENANCE INTERVALS
BMW—5 SERIES

TO BE SERVICED	TYPE OF SERVICE	SERVICE INTERVALS			
		INITIAL 1200 MILES	OIL SERVICE	INSPECTION I	INSPECTION II
Oil level	S/I	✓			
Engine oil	R				
Engine oil & filter	R		✓	✓	✓
Engine air cleaner element	R				✓
Spark plugs	R				✓
Fuel filter (California)	R				✓
Fuel, vapor lines & fuel cap	S/I	✓		✓	✓
Cooling system	S/I	✓		✓	✓
Exhaust pipe & muffler	S/I	✓		✓	✓
Catalytic converter & shielding	S/I	✓		✓	✓
Throttle linkage	S/I			✓	✓
Engine (check for leakage)	S/I	✓			
Engine drive belts	S/I				✓
Maintenance Indicators	RE		✓	✓	✓
Engine coolant	R	Every 2 years			
Oxygen sensor	R	Every 100,000 miles			
Intake air dust separators	S/I				✓
Brake & clutch fluids	S/I			✓	✓
Brake & clutch fluids	R	Every 2 years			
Brake pads & discs	S/I			✓	✓
Parking brake system	S/I			✓	✓
Power steering system	S/I			✓	✓
Rear axle fluid	S/I			✓	✓
Steering play, suspension track rods, front axle joints, steering linkage & joint disc	S/I			✓	✓
Transmission fluid/oil	S/I			✓	⑨
Wheel centering hubs	S/I			✓	✓
Rear axle fluid ⑩	R		✓		✓
OBD system for codes	S/I	✓		✓	✓

R: Replace S/I: Service or Inspect RE: Reset

Note: BMW does not rely solely on vehicle mileage to determine service intervals. An on-oboard diagnostic center, monitors engine operating conditions, along with mileage, to determine the most effective maintenance intervals. The information is then conveyed to the driver through the service indicator lights, located in the center of the instrument panel.

71112_BMW5_C0014

PRECAUTIONS

Before servicing any vehicle, please be sure to read all of the following precautions, which deal with personal safety, prevention of component damage, and important points to take into consideration when servicing a motor vehicle:

- Never open, service or drain the radiator or cooling system when the engine is hot; serious burns can occur from the steam and hot coolant.
- Observe all applicable safety precautions when working around fuel. Whenever servicing the fuel system, always work in a well-ventilated area. Do not allow fuel spray or vapors to come in contact with a spark, open flame, or excessive heat (a hot drop light, for example). Keep a dry chemical fire extinguisher near the work area. Always keep fuel in a container specifically designed for fuel storage; also, always properly seal fuel containers to avoid the possibility of fire or explosion. Refer to the additional fuel system precautions later in this section.
- Fuel injection systems often remain pressurized, even after the engine has been turned **OFF**. The fuel system pressure must be relieved before disconnecting any fuel lines. Failure to do so may result in fire and/or personal injury.
- Brake fluid often contains polyglycol ethers and polyglycols. Avoid contact with the eyes and wash your hands thoroughly after handling brake fluid. If you do get brake fluid in your eyes, flush your eyes with clean, running water for 15 minutes. If eye irritation persists, or if you have taken brake fluid internally, IMMEDIATELY seek medical assistance.
- The EPA warns that prolonged contact with used engine oil may cause a number of skin disorders, including cancer. You should make every effort to minimize your exposure to used engine oil. Protective gloves should be worn when changing oil. Wash your hands and any other exposed skin areas as soon as possible after exposure to used engine oil. Soap and water, or waterless hand cleaner should be used.
- All new vehicles are now equipped with an air bag system, often referred to as a Supplemental Restraint System (SRS) or Supplemental Inflatable Restraint (SIR) system. The system must be disabled before performing service on or around system components, steering column, instrument panel components, wiring and sensors. Failure to follow safety and disabling procedures could result in accidental air bag deployment, possible personal injury and unnecessary system repairs.
- Always wear safety goggles when working with, or around, the air bag system. When carrying a non-deployed air bag, be sure the bag and trim cover are pointed away from your body. When placing a non-deployed air bag on a work surface, always face the bag and trim cover upward, away from the surface. This will reduce the motion of the module if it is accidentally deployed. Refer to the additional air bag system precautions later in this section.
- Clean, high quality brake fluid from a sealed container is essential to the safe and proper operation of the brake system. You should always buy the correct type of brake fluid for your vehicle. If the brake fluid becomes contaminated, completely flush the system with new fluid. Never reuse any brake fluid. Any brake fluid that is removed from the system should be discarded. Also, do not allow any brake fluid to come in contact with a painted surface; it will damage the paint.
- Never operate the engine without the proper amount and type of engine oil; doing so WILL result in severe engine damage.
- Timing belt maintenance is extremely important. Many models utilize an interference-type, non-freewheeling engine. If the timing belt breaks, the valves in the cylinder head may strike the pistons, causing potentially serious (also time-consuming and expensive) engine damage. Refer to the maintenance interval charts for the recommended replacement interval for the timing belt, and to the timing belt section for belt replacement and inspection.
- Disconnecting the negative battery cable on some vehicles may interfere with the functions of the on-board computer system(s) and may require the computer to undergo a relearning process once the negative battery cable is reconnected.
- When servicing drum brakes, only disassemble and assemble one side at a time, leaving the remaining side intact for reference.
- Only an MVAC-trained, EPA-certified automotive technician should service the air conditioning system or its components.

BRAKES — ANTI-LOCK BRAKE SYSTEM (ABS)

GENERAL INFORMATION

PRECAUTIONS

- Certain components within the ABS system are not intended to be serviced or repaired individually.
- Do not use rubber hoses or other parts not specifically specified for and ABS system. When using repair kits, replace all parts included in the kit. Partial or incorrect repair may lead to functional problems and require the replacement of components.
- Lubricate rubber parts with clean, fresh brake fluid to ease assembly. Do not use shop air to clean parts; damage to rubber components may result.
- Use only DOT 3 brake fluid from an unopened container.
- If any hydraulic component or line is removed or replaced, it may be necessary to bleed the entire system.
- A clean repair area is essential. Always clean the reservoir and cap thoroughly before removing the cap. The slightest amount of dirt in the fluid may plug an orifice and impair the system function. Perform repairs after components have been thoroughly cleaned; use only denatured alcohol to clean components. Do not allow ABS components to come into contact with any substance containing mineral oil; this includes used shop rags.
- The Anti-Lock control unit is a microprocessor similar to other computer units in the vehicle. Ensure that the ignition switch is **OFF** before removing or installing controller harnesses. Avoid static electricity discharge at or near the controller.
- If any arc welding is to be done on the vehicle, the control unit should be unplugged before welding operations begin.

WHEEL SPEED SENSORS

REMOVAL & INSTALLATION

Front

See Figure 5.

1. Raise and safely support the vehicle securely on jackstands.
2. Remove the front wheel.
3. Open plug housing, pull plug connection out of bracket and disconnect.
4. Pull cable with rubber grommet out of bracket on spring strut.
5. Remove hexagon socket head cap

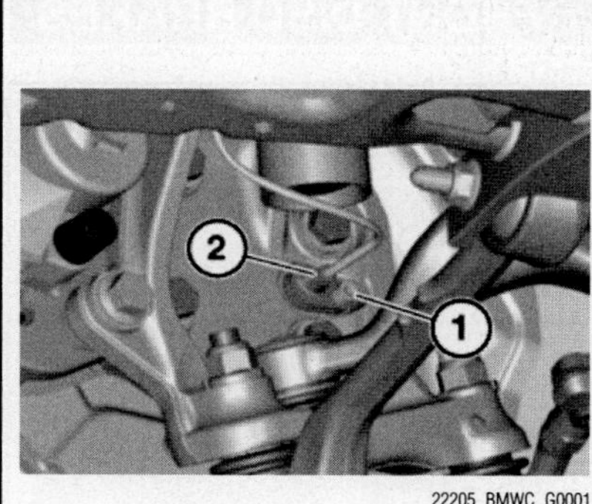

Fig. 5 Front speed sensor location

screw and pull wheel speed sensor out of bore.

To install:

6. Clean bore hole for speed sensor and grease with Staburags® NBU 12/K lubricating grease.
7. Install the sensor and tighten the cap screw to 6 ft. lbs. (8 Nm).
8. Install the front wheel if removed and lower the vehicle.
9. Check for proper ABS system function.

Rear

See Figure 6.

1. Raise and safely support the vehicle securely on jackstands.
2. Remove the rear wheel.
3. Open plug housing, pull plug connection out of bracket and disconnect.
4. Pull cable with rubber grommet out of bracket on spring strut.
5. Remove hexagon socket head cap screw and pull wheel speed sensor out of bore.

To install:

6. Clean bore hole for speed sensor and grease with Staburags® NBU 12/K lubricating grease.

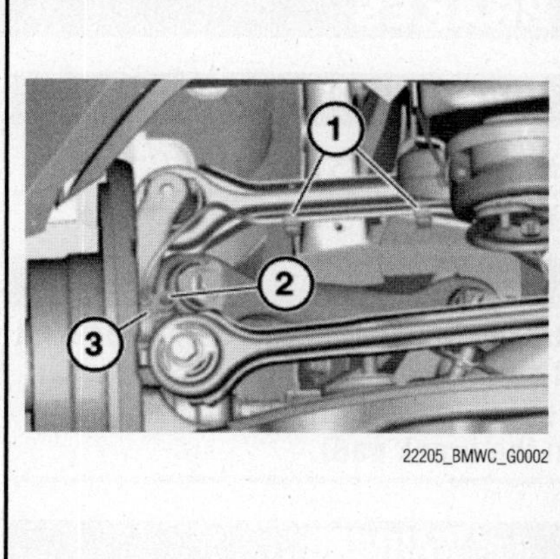

Fig. 6 Rear speed sensor location

7. Install the sensor and tighten the cap screw to 6 ft. lbs. (8 Nm).
8. Install the rear wheel if removed and lower the vehicle.
9. Check for proper ABS system function.

BRAKES — BLEEDING THE BRAKE SYSTEM

BLEEDING PROCEDURE

1. Before servicing the vehicle, refer to the precautions.
2. If necessary, remove lower section of micro filter housing. Refer to engine mechanical, air filter, removal & installation.
3. Connect a brake bleeding tool with a maximum 29 psi (2 Bar) filling pressure.

➡A second person is needed to help carry out this work.

4. Disconnect retaining tabs and remove the master cylinder cover.
5. Flushing brake system completely.
6. Connect bleeder hose with collecting tray to bleeder valve on rear right brake caliper.
   a. Open bleeder valve and purge until clear, bubble-free brake fluid emerges.
   b. Close bleed valve.
7. Follow same procedure on rear left, front right and front left wheel brake.
8. Bleeding rear-axle brake circuit.
   a. Connect bleeder hose with collecting tray to bleeder valve on rear right brake caliper.
   b. Bleed right brake caliper. After completing routine, press brake pedal 5 times to floor; clear and bubble-free brake fluid must flow out.
   c. Close bleed valve.
9. Repeat procedure at rear left.
10. Bleeding front-axle brake circuit.
   a. Connect bleeder hose with collecting tray to bleeder valve on front right brake caliper.
   b. Bleed right front brake caliper. After completing routine, press brake pedal 5 times to floor, clear and bubble-free brake fluid must flow out.
   c. Close bleed valve.
11. Repeat procedure at front left.
12. Disconnect the brake bleeding tool and remove from the master cylinder.
13. Check and adjust the brake fluid level.
14. Inspect the rubber seal in the brake fluid master cylinder cap. Replace as necessary.

BRAKE FLUID

FLUID RECOMMENDATIONS

The required characteristics are guaranteed by the DOT 4 brake fluids approved by BMW.

BRAKE CALIPER & PADS

REMOVAL & INSTALLATION

See Figures 7 through 11.

✻✻ WARNING

Brake pad wear sensor: after removal it must be replaced (brake pad wear sensor loses its retention capability in the break pad).

✻✻ WARNING

Retaining spring: for vehicles older than 48 months it is recommended to replace the retaining spring.

1. Remove wheels.
2. Remove brake pad wear sensor.
3. Drive out locking pins (1) in direction of arrow.

➡When inserting the retaining pin, the brake pad must be pressed against the spring force of the retaining spring.

4. Unscrew nuts.
5. Pull the brake caliper to the rear as far as the brake hose will allow.
6. Brake caliper stays on the stud bolts.
   a. Tightening torque: 70 ft. lbs. (95 Nm).
7. Feed the brake pads (2) out of the brake caliper (1).

✻✻ WARNING

Mark any worn brake pads.

✻✻ WARNING

In the event of one-sided brake pad wear, do not change brake pads round.

8. Observe minimum thickness of brake pads.

➡When installing, clean brake pads, brake caliper and guide pins.

9. Do not grease backs of brake pads sleeve.
10. Brake pads must be correctly seated on guide pins.
11. Check minimum brake disc thickness:
    a. Position special tool 34 1 280 at three measuring points in area (1) and measure.
    b. Compare measuring result and lowest value with set point value.

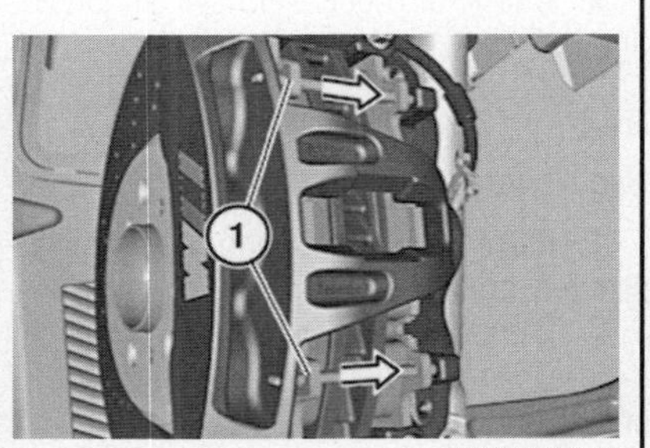

Fig. 7 Driving out locking pins (1) in direction of arrow

✻✻ WARNING

New brake pads may only be fitted if the brake disc thickness is greater than the minimum brake disc thickness (MIN TH).

✻✻ WARNING

Do not grease brake pads and guides with brake pad paste.

12. Clean contact surface (1) of brake pistons with brake cleaner.

✻✻ WARNING

Do not grease contact surfaces (1) with brake shoe paste.

13. Clean contact surface (1) of brake pistons with brake cleaner.

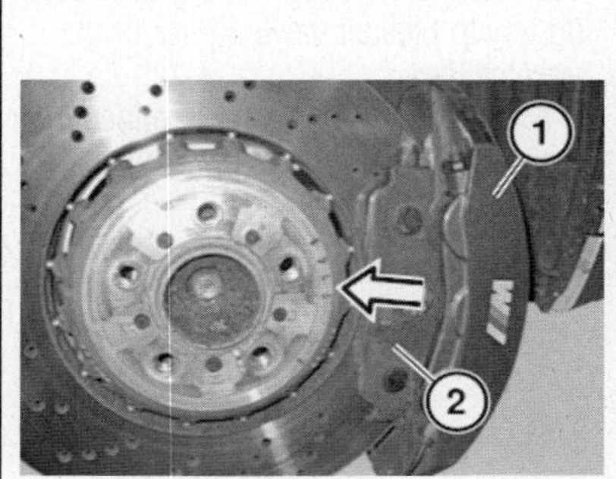

Fig. 8 Feeding brake pads (2) out of brake caliper (1)

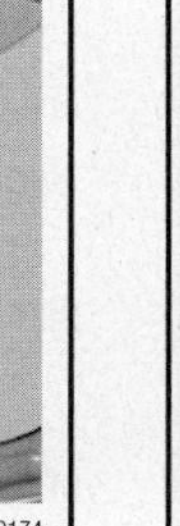

Fig. 9 Checking brake disc thickness at 3 measuring points (1)

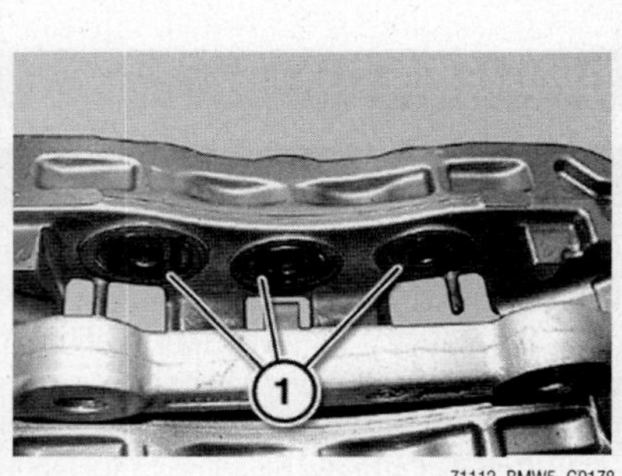

Fig. 10 Identifying brake piston contact surface (1)

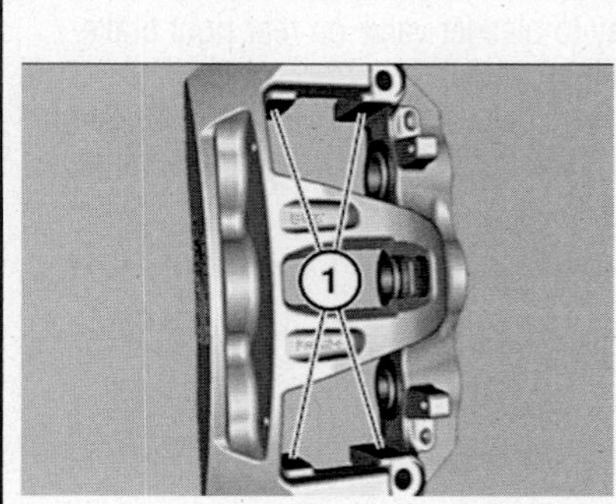

Fig. 11 Identifying brake piston contact surface (1)

To install:

14. To install, reverse the removal procedure noting the following.

15. When installing new brake pads at front and rear axles, brake fluid level must be brought up to "MAX" marking.

16. Fully depress brake pedal several times so that brake pads contact brake discs.

17. Read and comply with notes on braking in new brake discs / brake pads.

18. When replacing pads reset CBS display in accordance with factory specification.

BRAKES

REAR DISC BRAKES

BRAKE CALIPERS

REMOVAL & INSTALLATION

See Figure 12.

1. Before servicing the vehicle, refer to the precautions.
2. Remove wheels.
3. Press clutch pedal down to floor and secure with pedal support.

WARNING

The pedal support may only be removed when the brake lines are reconnected. This prevents brake fluid from emerging from the expansion tank and air from entering the system when the brake lines are opened.

4. On the right side, disconnect plug connection for wear indicator.
5. Remove brake hose on brake caliper.
6. Slacken connection for brake hose and brake line.
7. Remove screws and remove brake caliper.

To install:

8. Installation is the reverse of removal.
9. Move steering to straight-ahead position.
10. Screw brake hose to brake line, ensuring that brake hose is not twisted.
11. Tighten bolts/nuts to specification as follows:
    - Brake carrier on semi-trailing arm/wheel carrier: 81 ft. lbs. (110 Nm)
    - Brake hose to brake caliper, rear: 30 ft. lbs. (40 Nm)
    - Brake hose couplings: 18 ft. lbs. (24 Nm)
12. Bleed braking system.

BRAKE PADS

REMOVAL & INSTALLATION

See Figures 13 through 16.

1. Before servicing the vehicle, refer to the precautions.
2. Remove wheels.
3. Remove brake pad wear sensor.
4. Pry out retaining spring towards rear.
5. Remove plastic plugs.
6. On the left side, pull brake pad wear sensor towards rear out of pad.
7. Remove guide screws with special tool 34 1 080. Withdraw brake caliper backwards.
8. Press back brake pads and piston with special tool 34 6 320.

WARNING

Pay attention to brake fluid level in expansion tank; brake fluid that spills over will damage paintwork.

9. Press brake pads inwards and remove.

WARNING

The two brake pads are seated with a spring in the piston or in the brake caliper housing and must not be mixed up.

➡Do not apply grease to brake pad back plate.

10. Clean mounting faces and of brake pad hammer heads/brake caliper housing and coat with anti-squeak compound.
11. Grease contact surfaces on brake caliper at top and bottom.
12. Clean mounting face of brake caliper and apply a thin coating of anti-squeak compound.
13. Clean brake caliper holder at hammerhead guides and apply a thin coating of anti-squeak compound.

To install:

14. Installation is the reverse of removal.
15. Only clean guide screws; do not grease.

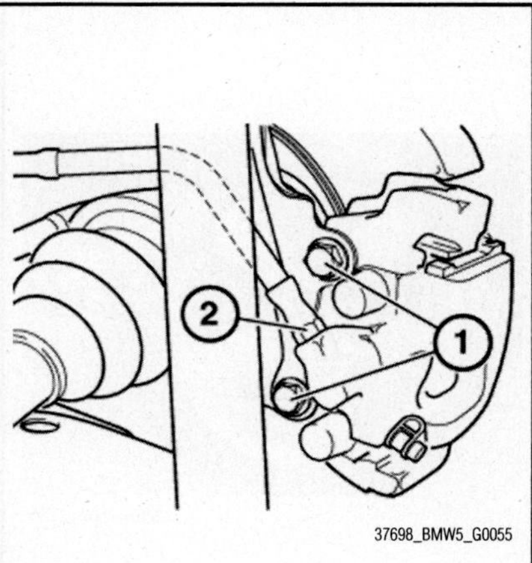

Fig. 12 Release screws (1) and disconnect brake hose (2)

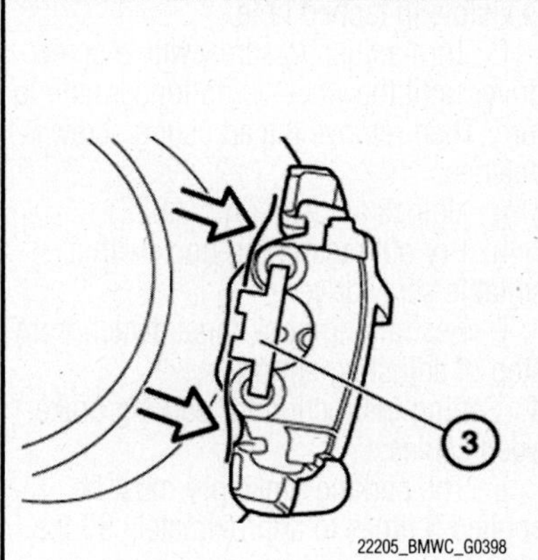

Fig. 13 Pry out retaining spring (3) towards rear

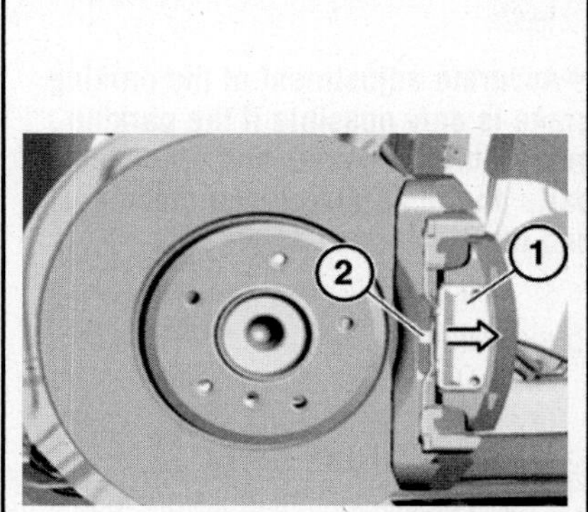

Fig. 14 Clean mounting faces (1) and (2) of brake pad hammer heads/brake caliper housing and coat with anti-squeak compound

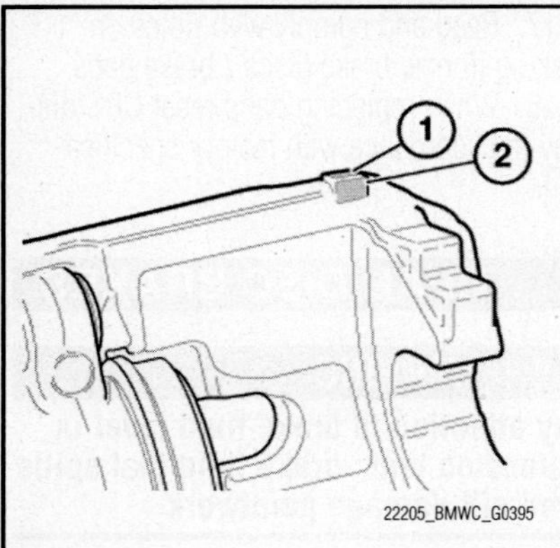

Fig. 15 Clean mounting face (3) of brake caliper and apply a thin coating of anti-squeak compound

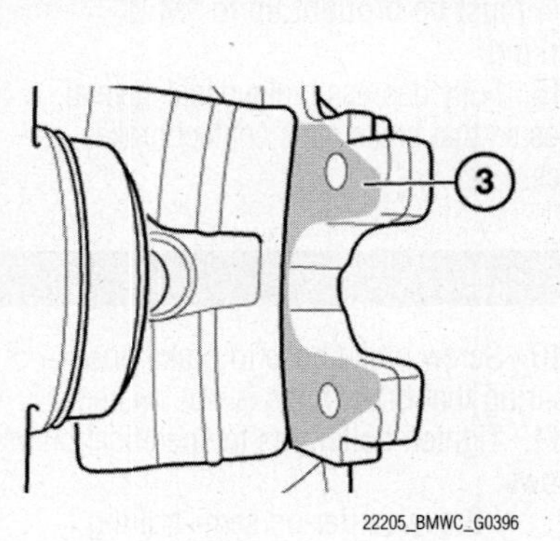

Fig. 16 Clean brake caliper holder at hammerhead guides and apply a thin coating of anti-squeak compound

16. Check threads.
17. Replace all guide screws which are not in perfect condition.
18. Tighten guide bolt to 22 ft. lbs. (30 Nm).
19. Attach retaining spring first at top and bottom and then allow retaining lug to engage in recess of brake caliper housing.
20. Fully depress brake pedal several times so that brake pads contact brake discs.
21. When installing new brake pads at front and rear axles, brake fluid level must be brought up to **MAX** marking.
22. When replacing pads reset CBS display in accordance with factory specification.

ADJUSTMENTS

CABLES

See Figures 17 and 18.

1. Before servicing the vehicle, refer to the precautions.
2. Perform inspection in the following manner:
   a. When 1st ratchet is engaged, no braking force should be exerted.
   b. The difference in wheel circumferential forces between the left and right wheels may deviate by max. 30% from the greater value (when measured on brake analyzer).
   c. Braking with locked wheels must be possible with the parking brake.
   d. The parking brake must be reset if the actuation stroke is greater than 10 teeth.

➡Accurate adjustment of the parking brake is only possible if the parking brake Bowden cables and all moving parts on the parking brake move easily and function correctly.

3. Setting instruction for brake shoes (basic setting):
   a. Disconnect gaiter for parking brake pry.
   b. Lock adjuster unit (ASZE).
   c. Actuate parking brake pry. Screw in special tool 32 1 030 partially. Press stop of adjusting spring back to such an extent that retaining hook engages in stop.
   d. Completely unscrew one wheel stud on each rear wheel.

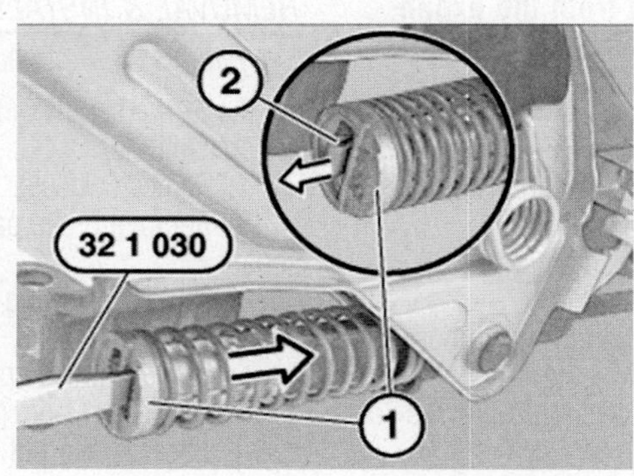

Fig. 17 Actuate parking brake pry. Screw in special tool 32 1 030 partially. Press stop (1) of adjusting spring back to such an extent that retaining hook (2) engages in stop (1)

   e. Turn wheel until adjustment screw is visible in tapped hole.
   f. Turn adjusting screw with a screwdriver until the wheel is no longer able to turn. Then remove the adjusting screw 8 notches.
   g. Unlock adjuster unit (ASZE).
   h. Pry out restraining hook with a suitable screwdriver.
   i. Restraining hook must detach from stop of adjusting spring.
4. Setting instruction for parking brake Bowden cables:
   a. The parking brake pry must be applied 5 times to approximately 90 lbs. (400 N) actuating force.
   b. With the parking brake removed and the transmission in **N** position, the brake force should have reached 34 lbs. (150 N) as measured on a brake analyzer.

Fig. 18 Turn wheel until adjustment screw is visible in tapped hole

c. With the parking brake on the 1st tooth, there should be no increase in braking force. However, the indicator lamp can be lit.

d. With the parking brake on the 2nd tooth, the indicator lamp must be lit.

e. With the parking brake on the 3rd tooth, there should be an increase in braking force.

f. With the parking brake on the 5th tooth, the brake force must have reached 90 lbs. (400 N).

5. If new pads are installed, perform the pad break in procedure:

a. At approximately 25 mph (40 km/h) apply parking brake pry until a braking effect can be felt.

b. Pull parking brake pry to next notch and drive on for approximately 1320 feet (quarter mile).

c. If necessary, repeat braking-in procedure.

d. Allow brake to cool down sufficiently.

PARKING BRAKE SHOES

REMOVAL & INSTALLATION

See Figures 17, 19 through 21.

1. Before servicing the vehicle, refer to the precautions.
2. Remove rear brake disc.
3. Actuate parking brake pry. Screw in special tool 32 1 030 partially. Press stop of adjusting spring back to such an extent that retaining hook engages in stop.
4. Disconnect return upper spring with brake spring pliers.
5. Disconnect return lower spring with brake spring pliers.

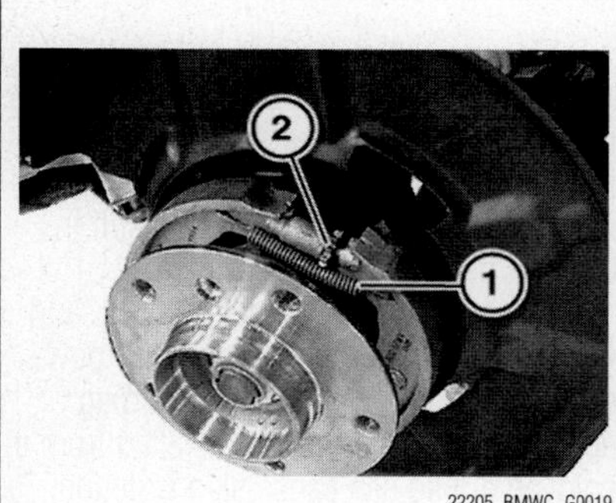

Fig. 19 Disconnect return upper spring (1) with brake spring pliers

Fig. 20 Disconnect return lower spring (1) with brake spring pliers

6. Turn clamping pins with special tool 34 4 000 through 90° and disconnect.

Fig. 21 Turn clamping pins (1) with special tool 34 4 000 through 90° and disconnect. Remove brake shoes (2)

7. Remove brake shoes.

To install:

8. Install brake shoes.
9. Turn clamping pins with special tool 34 4 000 through 90° to lock.
10. Check and if necessary replace return springs.
11. Connect return lower spring with brake spring pliers.
12. Connect return upper spring with brake spring pliers.

➡Pay attention to installation position of adjustment screw.

13. Apply a thin coat of grease to bush and screw threads.
14. Pry out restraining hook with a suitable screwdriver.
15. Restraining hook must detach from stop of adjusting spring.
16. Install rear brake disc.
17. Adjusting parking brake.

CHASSIS ELECTRICAL

AIR BAGS (SUPPLEMENTAL RESTRAINT SYSTEM)

PRECAUTIONS

⁂ CAUTION

These vehicles are equipped with an air bag system. The system must be disarmed before performing service on, or around, system components, the steering column, instrument panel components, wiring and sensors. Failure to follow the safety precautions and the disarming procedure could result in accidental air bag deployment, possible injury and unnecessary system repairs.

Disconnect and isolate the battery negative cable before beginning any airbag system component diagnosis, testing, removal, or installation procedures. Allow system capacitor to discharge for two minutes before beginning any component service. This will disable the airbag system. Failure to disable the airbag system may result in accidental airbag deployment, personal injury, or death.

Do not place an intact undeployed airbag face down on a solid surface. The airbag will propel into the air if accidentally deployed and may result in personal injury or death.

When carrying or handling an undeployed airbag, the trim side (face) of the airbag should be pointing towards the body to minimize possibility of injury if accidental deployment occurs. Failure to do this may result in personal injury or death.

Replace airbag system components with OEM replacement parts. Substitute parts may appear interchangeable, but internal differences may result in inferior occupant protection. Failure to do so may result in occupant personal injury or death.

Wear safety glasses, rubber gloves, and long sleeved clothing when cleaning powder residue from vehicle after an airbag deployment. Powder residue emitted from a deployed airbag can cause skin irritation. Flush affected area with cool water if irritation is experienced. If nasal or throat irritation is experienced, exit the vehicle for fresh air until the irritation ceases. If irritation continues, see a physician.

Do not use a replacement airbag that is not in the original packaging. This may result in improper deployment, personal injury, or death.

The factory installed fasteners, bolts and bolts used to fasten airbag components have a special coating and are specifically designed for the airbag system. Do not use substitute fasteners. Use only original equipment fasteners listed in the parts catalog when fastener replacement is required.

During, and following, any child restraint anchor service, due to impact event or vehicle repair, carefully inspect all mounting hardware, tether straps, and anchors for proper installation, operation, or damage. If a child restraint anchor is found damaged in any way, the anchor must be replaced. Failure to do this may result in personal injury or death.

Deployed and non-deployed airbags may or may not have live pyrotechnic material within the airbag inflator.

Do not dispose of driver/passenger/curtain airbags or seat belt tensioners unless you are sure of complete deployment. Refer to the Hazardous Substance Control System for proper disposal.

Dispose of deployed airbags and tensioners consistent with state, provincial, local, and federal regulations.

After any airbag component testing or service, do not connect the battery negative cable. Personal injury or death may result if the system test is not performed first.

DISARMING THE SYSTEM

1. Before servicing the vehicle, refer to the precautions.
2. Place the ignition switch in the **OFF**-position.
3. Disconnect the negative battery terminal and cover the battery terminal to prevent accidental contact.
4. Once the battery has been disconnected, wait for a period of approximately 10 minutes allowing the capacitor in the control unit to discharge.

ARMING THE SYSTEM

When repairs are completed, connect the negative battery cable.

DRIVE TRAIN

AUTOMATIC TRANSMISSION

DRAIN & REFILL

GA6HP19Z & GA6HP26Z Transmissions

See Figures 22 and 23.

1. Before servicing the vehicle, refer to the precautions.
2. Raise and support vehicle.
3. Undo filler plug.
4. Top up transmission fluid until it emerges from filling orifice.
5. Start engine.
6. Replenish transmission fluid until it emerges from filling orifice.
7. Replace sealing ring.
8. Screw in filler plug and tighten to 26 ft. lbs. (35 Nm).
9. Press brake pedal to floor and shift

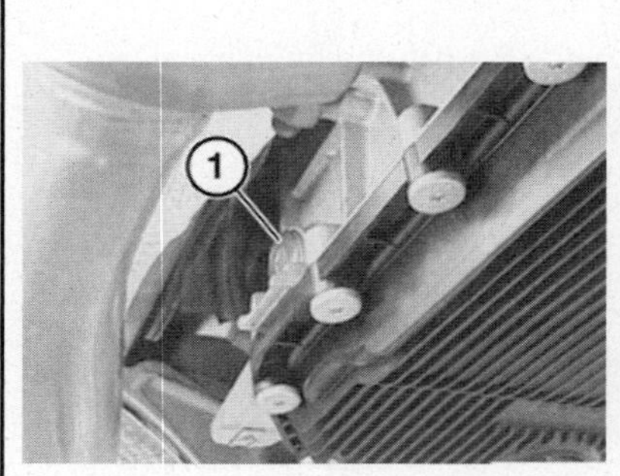

Fig. 22 Undo filler plug (1)

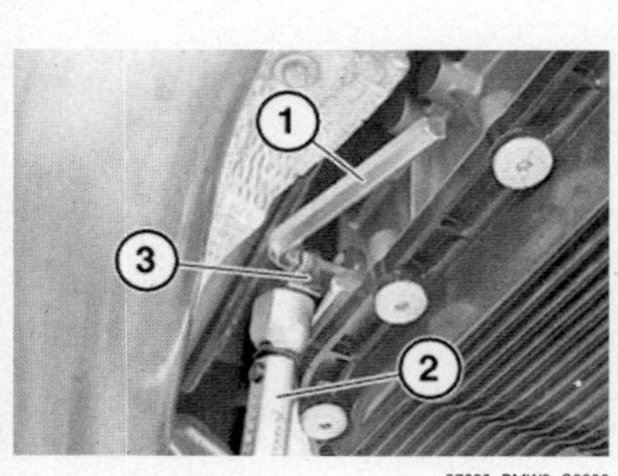

Fig. 23 Tightening filler plug using a hexagon wrench (1), torque wrench (2) and socket (3)

through all gears several times at idle speed. Then shift to "P" position (Park).

10. Check fluid level.
   a. Connect BMW Diagnosis and Information System (DIS) to vehicle.
   b. Call up Service functions (drive).
   c. Carry out fluid level check in accordance with instructions.

GA6L45R Transmission

See Figure 24.

1. Before servicing the vehicle, refer to the precautions.
2. Raise and support vehicle.
3. Remove exhaust system bracket.
4. Undo filler plug.
5. Top up transmission fluid until it emerges from filling orifice.
6. Start engine.
7. Replenish transmission fluid until it emerges from filling orifice.
8. Replace sealing ring.
9. Screw in filler plug and tighten to 14 ft. lbs. (19 Nm).
10. Press brake pedal to floor and shift through all gears several times at idle speed. Then shift to "P" position (Park).
11. Check fluid level.
   a. Connect BMW Diagnosis and Information System (DIS) to vehicle.
   b. Call up Service functions (drive).
   c. Carry out fluid level check in accordance with instructions.

FILTER REPLACEMENT

See Figures 25 through 30.

1. Before servicing the vehicle, refer to the precautions.
2. Raise and support the vehicle.
3. Remove rear underbody protection:

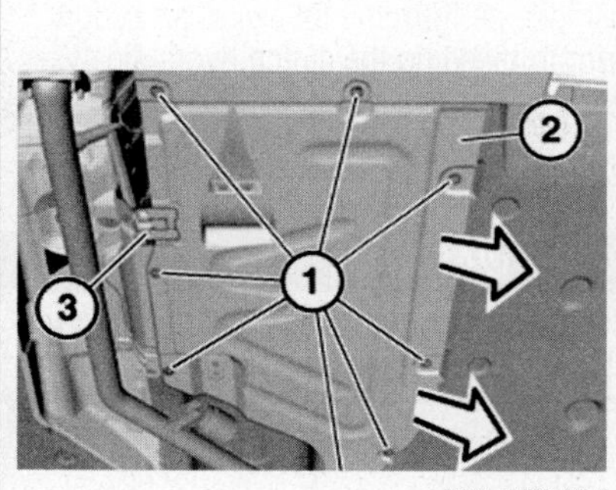

Fig. 25 Release screws (1), pull underbody protection (2) in direction of arrow out of bracket (3)

4. Single-part underbody protection, except AWD.
   a. Release screws.
   b. Pull underbody protection in direction of arrow out of bracket.
5. Single-part underbody protection, AWD.
   a. Release screws.
   b. Remove underbody protection downwards.
6. Two-part underbody protection
   a. Release screws.
   b. Detach underbody protection from bracket and remove.
7. Remove exhaust system bracket from transmission.
8. Remove oil drain plug.
9. Drain automatic transmission fluid.
10. Unscrew all bolts.
11. Remove transmission sump.
12. Remove gasket from transmission sump.

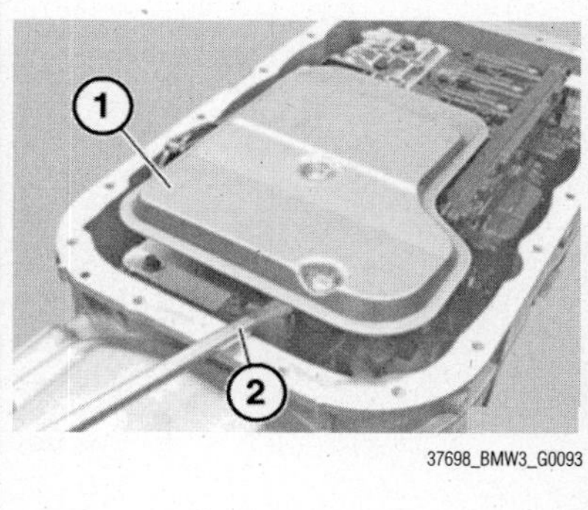

Fig. 27 Remove transmission oil filter (1) with a suitable tool (2)

13. Remove transmission oil filter with a suitable tool.
14. Pull transmission oil filter gasket out of housing with special tools 24 4 390 and 13 5 250.

To install:

15. Drive transmission filter gasket into housing with special tool 24 4 400.
16. Clean sealing faces and groove with a cloth.
17. Insert new gasket in transmission sump groove.

WARNING

Do not degrease transmission sump with cleaning agent.

18. Clean sump magnet and check for metal filings/borings.
19. The gasket is correctly installed when it is engaged in the locating openings of the transmission sump.

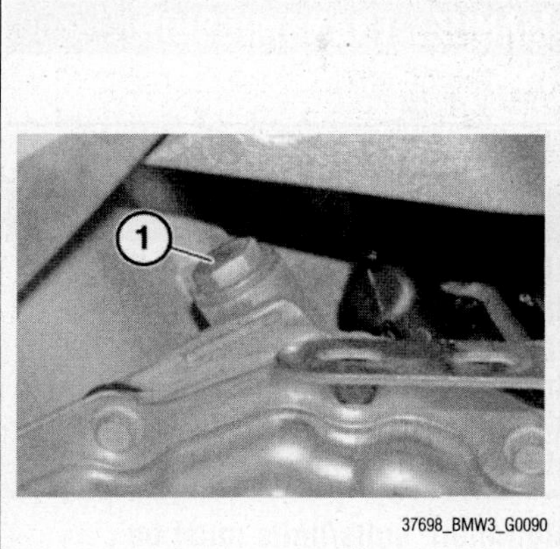

Fig. 24 Undo filler plug (1)

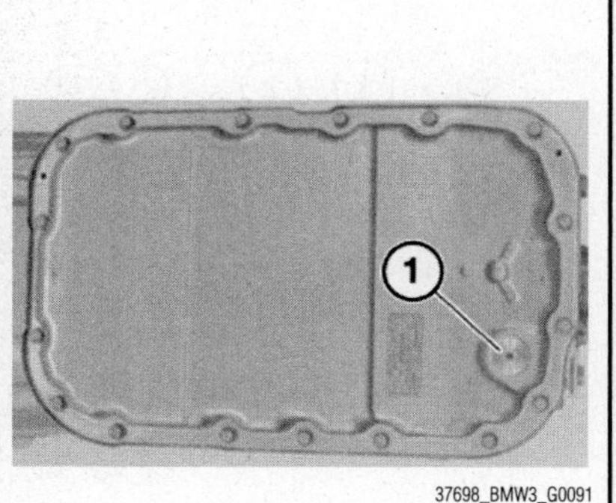

Fig. 26 Remove oil drain plug (1)

Fig. 28 Pull transmission oil filter gasket out of housing with special tools 24 4 390 and 13 5 250

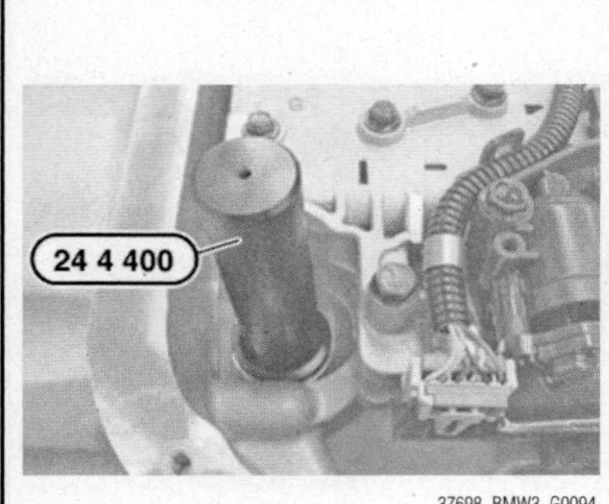

37698_BMW3_G0094

Fig. 29 Drive transmission filter gasket into housing with special tool 24 4 400

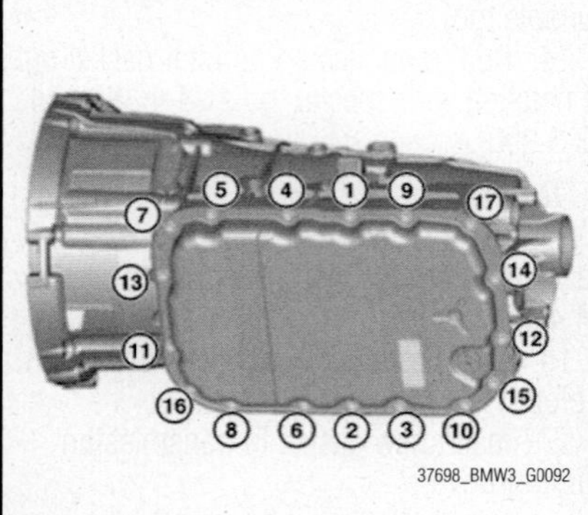

37698_BMW3_G0092

Fig. 30 Screw in bolts (1 to 17) in specified order until bolt heads make contact

20. Screw in bolts (1 to 17) in specified order until bolt heads make contact.
21. Tighten bolts/nuts to specification as follows:
    - Oil pan bolts: 96 inch lbs. (10 Nm).
    - Oil drain plug (replace) metal oil pan: 108 inch lbs. (12 Nm)
    - Oil drain plug (replace) metal oil pan: 96 inch lbs. (10 Nm)

CLUTCH HYDRAULIC SYSTEM BLEEDING

BLEEDING PROCEDURE

See Figures 31 and 32.

1. Before servicing the vehicle, refer to the precautions.
2. Remove underbody protection from transmission.
3. Remove micro filter housing as necessary.
4. If the vehicle uses a plastic slave cylinder, perform the following procedure prior to bleeding the clutch hydraulic system.
    a. Connect bleeder unit to brake fluid expansion tank.

WARNING

Charging pressure should not exceed 29 psi (2 bar).

    b. Connect bleeder hose to bleed valve.
    c. Open bleed valve and flush until clear brake fluid emerges without air bubbles.
    d. Close bleed valve.
    e. Switch off bleeder unit and remove from brake fluid expansion tank.
    f. Correct brake fluid level in expansion tank.
5. Remove nuts and remove clutch slave cylinder (pressure line remains connected).
6. Fit special tool 21 5 030 on clutch slave cylinder.
7. Press piston rod with aid of spindle completely into clutch slave cylinder.
8. Connect bleeder unit to brake fluid expansion tank.

WARNING

Charging pressure should not exceed 29 psi (2 bar).

9. Connect bleeder hose to bleed valve.
10. Hold clutch slave cylinder in illustrated position as shown with special tool 21 5 030.
11. Open bleeder valve.
12. If bubble-free brake fluid emerges, retract piston rod of clutch slave cylinder with aid of spindle a little and press in again.
13. If no air bubbles escape, close bleeder valve, otherwise repeat procedure.

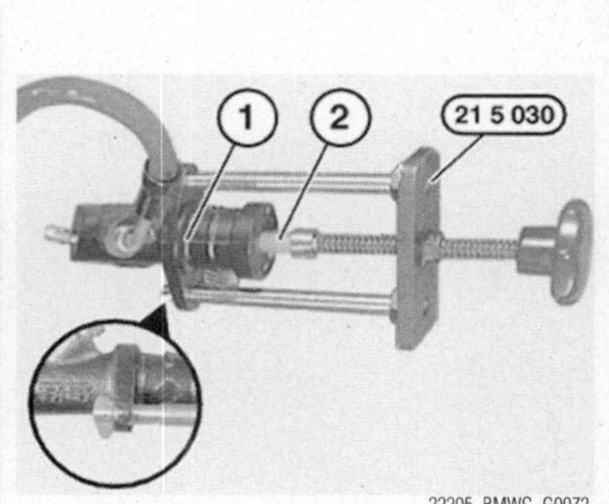

22205_BMWC_G0072

Fig. 31 Fit special tool 21 5 030 on clutch slave cylinder (1). Press piston rod (2) with aid of spindle completely into clutch slave cylinder.

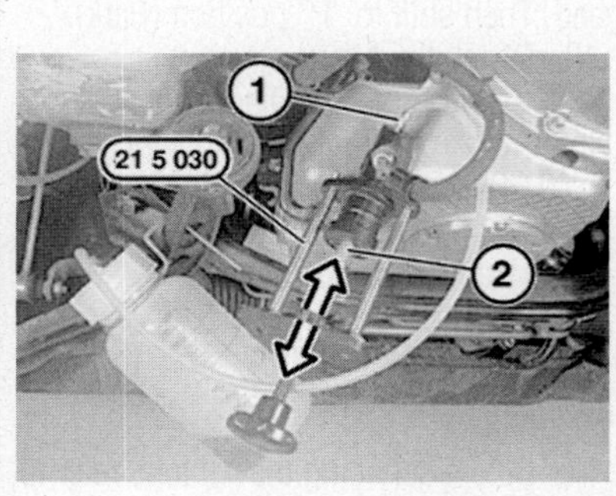

22205_BMWC_G0073

Fig. 32 Hold clutch slave cylinder in illustrated position as shown with special tool 21 5 030

WARNING

Do not under any circumstances remove special tool 21 5 030 from clutch slave cylinder when brake system is pressurized. Piston with push rod can jump out of clutch slave cylinder.

14. Switch off bleeder unit or remove from brake fluid expansion tank.
15. Slowly retract piston rod of clutch slave cylinder with special tool 21 5 030.
16. Remove special tool 21 5 030 from clutch slave cylinder.
17. Install clutch slave cylinder to transmission. Replace self-locking nuts and tighten to 16 ft. lbs. (22 Nm).
18. Correct brake fluid level in expansion tank.

MANUAL TRANSMISSION

DRAIN & REFILL

See Figure 33.

WARNING

Aluminum-magnesium materials. On these transmissions, no steel bolts/bolts may be used due to the threat of electrochemical corrosion. A magnesium crankcase requires aluminum bolts/bolts exclusively.

Aluminum bolts/bolts must be replaced each time they are removed. The end faces of these bolts/bolts are painted blue for the

purposes of reliable identification. Jointing torque and angle of rotation must be observed without fail (risk of damage).

1. Before servicing the vehicle, refer to the precautions.
2. Drive vehicle until gearbox is at normal operating temperature.
3. Raise and support vehicle.
4. Remove the oil drain plug and filler plug.
5. Allow oil to completely drain.
6. Clean oil drain plug and install. Tighten to specification below.
7. Fill transmission with fluid until overflowing.
8. Clean oil filler plug and install. Tighten to specification below.
9. Tighten bolts/nuts to specification as follows:
   - M18 x 1.5 hexagon socket: 26 ft. lbs. (35 Nm)
   - M12 x 1.5: 19 ft. lbs. (25 Nm)
   - M18 x 1.5 steel bolt without seal: 33 ft. lbs. (45 Nm)

TRANSFER CASE

DRAIN & REFILL

See Figures 34 and 35.

WARNING

Use only the approved transmission oil in the transfer box.

WARNING

Failure to comply with this requirement will result in serious damage to the transfer box.

➡Only change oil when transfer box is at normal operating temperature.

1. Remove transmission cross member.
2. Remove exhaust system holder from transmission.
3. Place oil collecting apparatus underneath.
4. Remove oil drain plug (1).
5. Drain and dispose of transmission oil.

➡Observe country-specific waste disposal regulations

6. Replace oil drain plug (1).
   a. Tightening torque: 44 ft. lbs. (60 Nm).
7. Undo oil filler plug (1).
8. Pour in transmission oil up to lower edge of opening for oil filler plug (1).

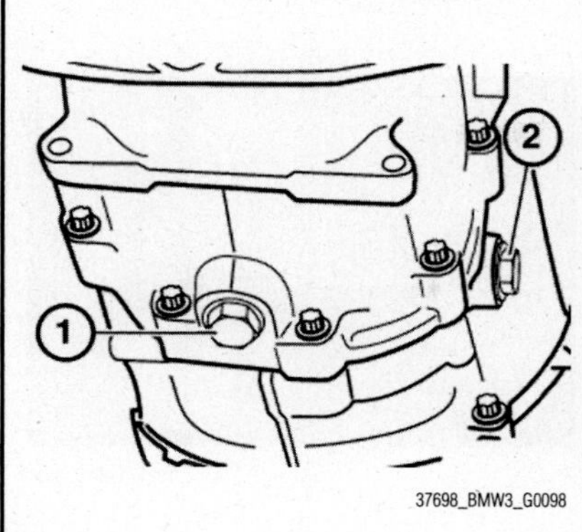

Fig. 33 Remove the oil drain plug (1) and filler plug (2)

   a. Tightening torque: 44 ft. lbs. (60 Nm).
9. Replace oil filler plug (1).

FLUID LEVEL CHECK

See Figure 37.

1. Undo oil filler plug (1).
2. Check transfer case oil level.
3. If necessary, pour in transmission oil up to lower edge of opening for oil filler plug (1).
   a. Tightening torque: 44 ft. lbs. (60 Nm).
4. Replace oil filler plug (1).

TRANSFER CASE

REMOVAL & INSTALLATION

See Figure 37.

1. Before servicing the vehicle, refer to the precautions.
2. Remove underbody protection.

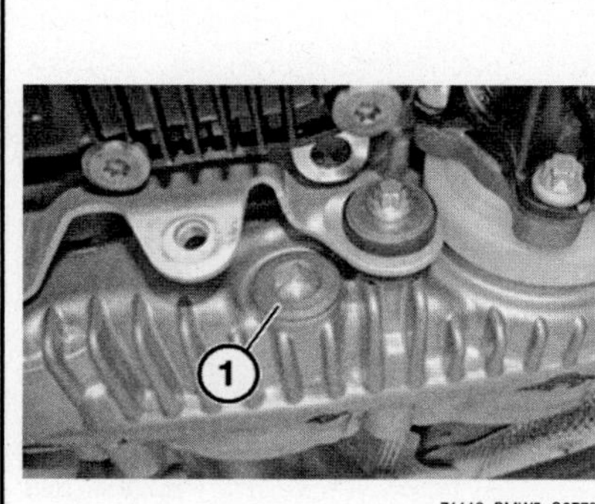

Fig. 34 Identifying drain plug (1)

Fig. 35 Identifying filler plug (1)

Fig. 36 Identifying oil filler plug (1)

3. Remove complete exhaust system.
4. Remove heat shields.
5. Remove front driveshaft at output flange of transfer case and tie to one side. Discard the bolts.
6. Remove driveshaft from transmission.
7. Remove center bearing.
8. Tie driveshaft to one side.
9. Support transmission with special tools 00 2 030 / 23 4 050.
10. Remove bolts and remove metal plate.
11. Disconnect plugs from servomotor.
12. Remove transmission cross-member.
13. Remove the transfer case bolts.
14. Remove transfer case.

To install:

15. Pay attention to dowel pin alignment. Grease dowel pin with Weicon Anti-Seize.
16. Install transfer case. Tighten bolts to specification.

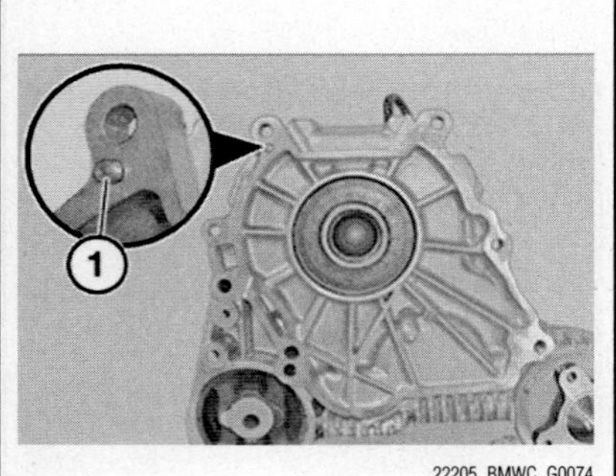

Fig. 37 Pay attention to dowel pin alignment. Grease dowel pin with Weicon Anti-Seize

WARNING

ZNS bolts and nuts have a shiny zinc coating and must be replaced each time they are removed. Torque and angle of rotation must be observed.

- M10 10.9 with ribbed teeth: 30 ft. lbs. (40 Nm) plus an additional 45° rotation.
- M10: 15 ft. lbs. (20 Nm) plus an additional 90° rotation.
- M12x55 10.9: 41 ft. lbs. (55 Nm) plus an additional 90° rotation.

17. Install cross-member. Tighten bolts to specification.
    - M10 bolts: 31 ft. lbs. (42 Nm)
    - M12 bolts: 53 ft. lbs. (72 Nm)
18. Connect plugs to servomotor.
19. Install metal plate.
20. Remove transmission support.
21. Install front driveshaft at output flange of transfer case and tighten new M10 bolt to 15 ft. lbs. (20 Nm) plus an additional 90° rotation.
22. Install heat shields.
23. Install complete exhaust system.
24. Install underbody protection.
25. Check gear oil level and top up if necessary.

DRIVESHAFT

REMOVAL & INSTALLATION

Front

See Figures 38 and 39.

1. Before servicing the vehicle, refer to the precautions.
2. Remove underbody protection.

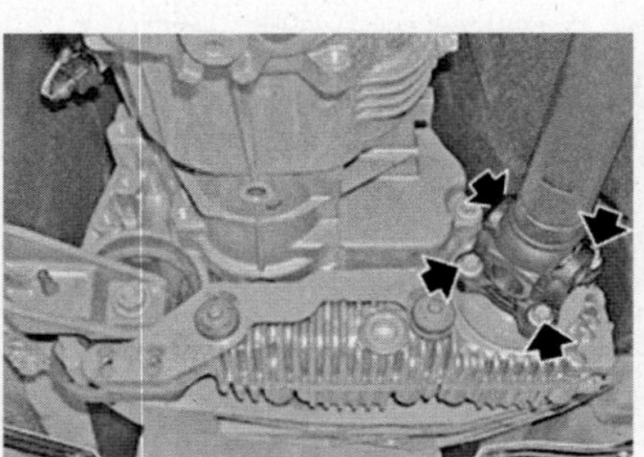

Fig. 38 Removing the driveshaft from the transfer case

3. Remove complete exhaust system.
4. Remove heat shields.
5. Remove and discard the ZNS bolts and nuts at the front flange and rear flange.
6. Using a screwdriver, pry constant velocity joint from drive shaft flange and remove driveshaft.

To install:

7. Inspect and lubricate the centering mount. If necessary, replace damaged mount.
8. Using new ZNS bolts and nuts, install the front flange and rear flange. Tighten to specification.
    - M10 10.9: 15 ft. lbs. (20 Nm) plus an additional 90° rotation
    - M10 10.9 screw with ribbed teeth: 30 ft. lbs. (40 Nm) 45° rotation
    - M12 10.9: 41 ft. lbs. (55 Nm) plus an additional 90° rotation

Fig. 39 Inspect and lubricate the centering mount

9. Install heat shields.
10. Install complete exhaust system.
11. Install underbody protection.

Rear

See Figures 39 through 41.

1. Before servicing the vehicle, refer to the precautions.
2. Remove underbody protection.
3. Remove complete exhaust system.
4. Remove heat shields.
5. Remove and discard the ZNS bolts and nuts at the front flange, rear flange and then the center bearing.
6. Using a screwdriver, pry constant velocity joint from drive shaft flange and remove driveshaft.

To install:

7. Inspect and lubricate the centering mount. If necessary, replace damaged mount.

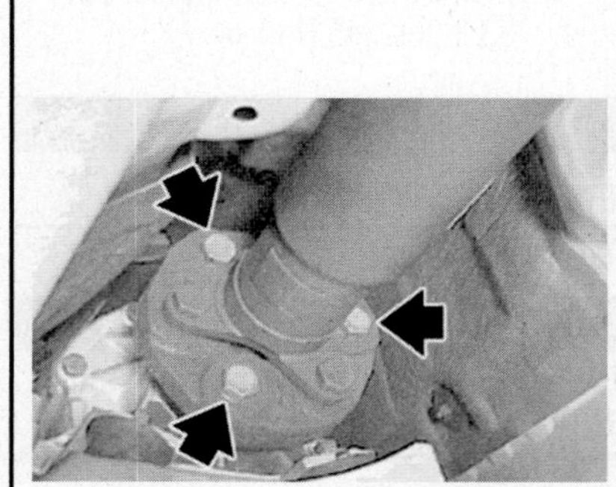

Fig. 40 Rear driveshaft connection with transmission

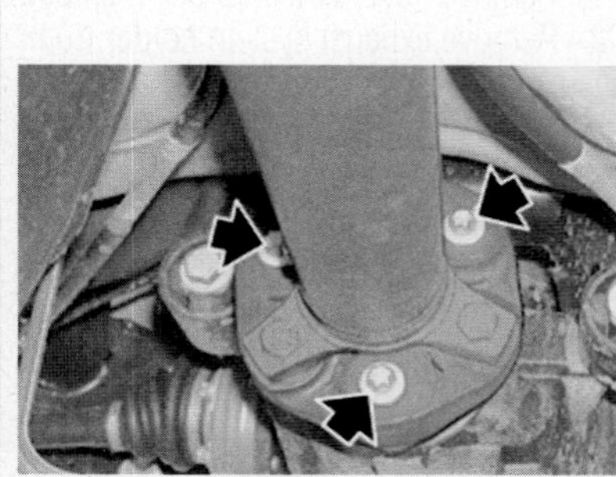

Fig. 41 Rear driveshaft connection with differential

8. Using new ZNS bolts and nuts, install the front flange, rear flange and center mount. Tighten to specification.
   - M10 10.9: 15 ft. lbs. (20 Nm) plus an additional 90° rotation
   - M10 10.9 screw with ribbed teeth: 30 ft. lbs. (40 Nm) 45° rotation
   - M12 10.9: 41 ft. lbs. (55 Nm) plus an additional 90° rotation
9. Install heat shields.
10. Install complete exhaust system.
11. Install underbody protection.

FRONT HALFSHAFT

REMOVAL & INSTALLATION

See Figure 42.

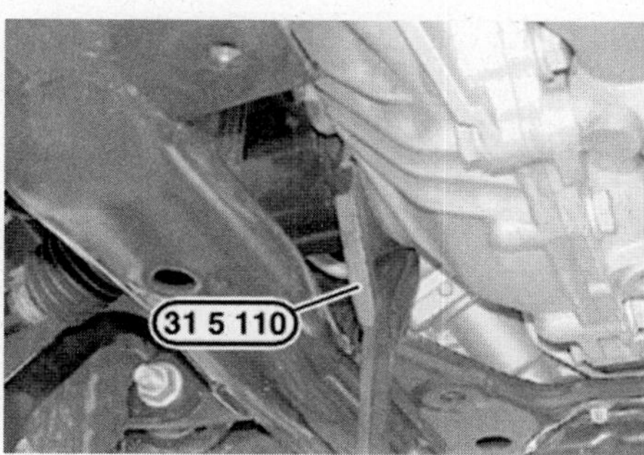

Fig. 42 Press halfshaft with special tool 31 5 110

1. Before servicing the vehicle, refer to the precautions.
2. Remove front wheel.
3. Expand turning lock sufficiently to avoid damaging thread when releasing collar nut.
4. Remove collar nut; to do so, press brake pedal to floor.
5. Remove reinforcement plate.
6. Remove tie rod end from ball joint.
7. On the right side only, remove guide joint from ball joint.
8. Remove control arm from ball joint.
9. Remove stabilizer link from spring strut.
10. Turn ball joint to one side.
11. Press halfshaft out of wheel hub and tie up.
12. Press halfshaft with special tool 31 5 110 out of front differential and remove.
13. Press halfshaft with special tool 31 5 110 out of bearing block and remove.

To install:

14. Replace shaft seal in front differential and coat sealing lips with front differential oil.
15. Replace shaft seal in bearing block and coat sealing lips with front differential oil.
16. Replace retaining ring and slide in halfshaft over resistance of retaining ring. Halfshaft must snap audibly into place.

⁂ WARNING

High installation forces indicate that the spline teeth on the halfshaft/rear differential side gear are damaged/deformed. Check spline teeth, replaced damaged parts.

17. Replace collar nut, oil collar nut/wheel bearing contact surface only and tighten to 311 ft. lbs. (420 Nm).

⁂ WARNING

Do not oil thread of shaft journal or collar nut.

18. Secure collar nut by positive peening on flat areas of halfshaft.
19. Install front wheel.
20. Check front differential oil level, correct if necessary.

REAR HALFSHAFT

REMOVAL & INSTALLATION

See Figure 43.

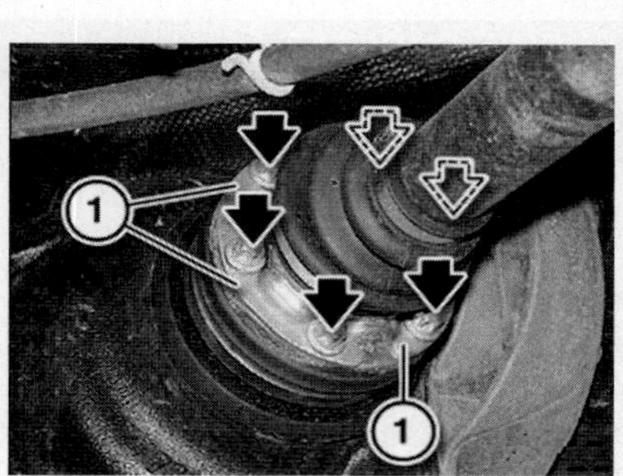

Fig. 43 Remove bolts and remove with washers (1)

1. Before servicing the vehicle, refer to the precautions.
2. Remove rear wheel.

⁂ WARNING

Expand turning lock sufficiently to avoid damaging thread when releasing collar nut.

3. Remove collar nut, activate handbrake for this purpose.
4. On the left side, remove strut if necessary.
5. On the left side, lower exhaust system in rear area.
6. Remove bolts and remove with washers.
7. Press output shaft off drive flange using a suitable tool; if necessary, raise wheel carrier with workshop jack approximately 20 mm.

To install:

8. Before installing output shaft, make sure that drive flange is fully engaged in rear differential.
9. Replace bolts and washers and tighten to specification.
   - M8: 38 ft. lbs. (52 Nm)
   - M10 ZNS3: 52 ft. lbs. (70 Nm)
10. Replace collar nut, oil collar nut/wheel bearing contact surface only and tighten to specification.
   - M27: 311 ft. lbs. (420 Nm)
   - M24: 185 ft. lbs. (250 Nm)

⁂ WARNING

No oil permitted on thread of shaft journal or collar nut.

11. Secure collar nut by positive peening on flat areas of output shaft.
12. Check that output shaft is correctly seated in rear differential.
13. On the left side, raise exhaust system in rear area.
14. On the left side, install strut if necessary.
15. Install rear wheel.

REAR DRIVE AXLE

DRAIN & REFILL

See Figure 44

1. Before servicing the vehicle, refer to the precautions.

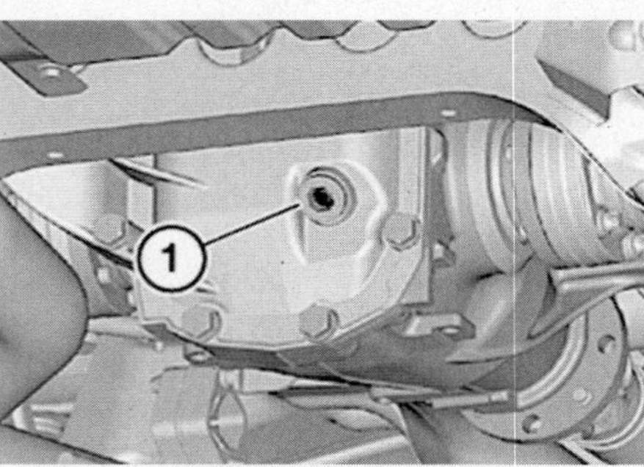

Fig. 44 Open plug (1).

➡The oil does not need to be changed in rear differentials carrying the "Life-Time-Oil" sticker.

2. Drive vehicle until rear differential is at normal operating temperature.
3. Raise and support vehicle.
4. Open plug.
5. Drain and dispose of differential oil.
6. Add differential oil up to lower edge of opening for screw plug.
7. Replace screw plug with a new one and tighten to 44 ft. lbs. (60 Nm).
8. Lower the vehicle.

ENGINE COOLING

ENGINE COOLANT

BLEEDING

1. Vent cooling system and check for leaks.

➡Before filling, turn ignition ON. Set blower to low level. Seat heating controller to maximum temperature. This ensures that the heater valves are fully opened and the auxiliary water pump starts up.

Important: The auxiliary water pump must deliver coolant in order to ensure fully venting.

a. Pour coolant into expansion tank up to **MAX** mark. Perform filling operation slowly.
b. Start engine and run at idle speed for approximately one minute (cap open). Then adjust coolant level to **MAX**.
c. Close cap and run engine up to operating temperature until main thermostat opens. Check cooling circuit and drain plug for leaks.

✲✲ WARNING

The engine must be cooled down before the coolant level is checked. Coolant temperature must not exceed 30°C. If ambient temperature is above 30°C, allow engine to cool down to ambient temperature at least.

d. Check coolant level and adjust to **MAX**.

➡Do not fill coolant expansion tank over MAX level as overfilling will cause the coolant to overflow.

DRAIN & REFILL

N20 Engine

✲✲ CAUTION

Before servicing the vehicle, refer to the precautions.

✲✲ CAUTION

Only carry out repair work on the cooling system after the engine has cooled down.

✲✲ WARNING

Never reuse used coolant.

➡When replacing and removing components which rely on the corrosion protection effect of the coolant, it is essential to change the coolant. The cooling system must therefore be drained and refilled.

➡In the case of other removal work involving the draining of part quantities of coolant, replace these quantities which have been drained with new coolant.

✲✲ WARNING

For dirt contamination of the cooling system (e.g. by engine oil), the cooling system must be rinsed with water until all dirt contamination is removed.

1. Catch and dispose of drained coolant in drip tray and if necessary special tool 00 2 030 (universal hydraulic lifting equipment).
2. Remove front underbody protection.
3. Open sealing cap on coolant expansion tank.

➡When installing, close the sealing cap until the arrows line up.

4. Unlock and pull off coolant hose at radiator and coolant thermostat.
5. Drain, catch and dispose of coolant.
6. Add coolant.
   a. Use only recommended coolant.
   b. Observe mixture ratio.
   c. Observe capacities.
   d. Fill and vent cooling system.
7. Observe bleeding instructions without fail.
8. Assemble engine.
9. Check cooling system for leaks.

N52 Engine

✲✲ CAUTION

Before servicing the vehicle, refer to the precautions.

✲✲ CAUTION

Only carry out repair work on the cooling system after the engine has cooled down.

✲✲ WARNING

Never reuse used coolant.

➡When replacing and removing components which rely on the corrosion protection effect of the coolant, it is essential to change the coolant. The cooling system must therefore be drained and refilled.

➡In the case of other removal work involving the draining of part quantities of coolant, replace these quantities which have been drained with new coolant.

⁂ WARNING

For dirt contamination of the cooling system (e.g. by engine oil), the cooling system must be rinsed with water until all dirt contamination is removed.

1. Catch and dispose of drained coolant in drip tray and if necessary special tool 00 2 030 (universal hydraulic lifting equipment).
2. Remove front underbody protection.
3. Open sealing cap on coolant expansion tank.

➡When installing, close the sealing cap until the arrows line up.

4. Unlock and pull off coolant hose (1) from radiator.
5. Drain, catch and dispose of coolant.
6. Add coolant.
    a. Use only recommended coolant.
    b. Observe mixture ratio.
    c. Observe capacities.
    d. Fill and vent cooling system.
7. Observe bleeding instructions without fail.
8. Assemble engine.
9. Check cooling system for leaks.

N55 and N63 Engines

⁂ CAUTION

Before servicing the vehicle, refer to the precautions.

⁂ CAUTION

Only carry out repair work on the cooling system after the engine has cooled down.

⁂ WARNING

Never reuse used coolant.

➡When replacing and removing components which rely on the corrosion protection effect of the coolant, it is essential to change the coolant. The cooling system must therefore be drained and refilled.

➡In the case of other removal work involving the draining of part quantities of coolant, replace these quantities which have been drained with new coolant.

⁂ WARNING

For dirt contamination of the cooling system (e.g. by engine oil), the cooling system must be rinsed with water until all dirt contamination is removed.

1. Catch and dispose of drained coolant in drip tray and if necessary special tool 00 2 030 (universal hydraulic lifting equipment).
2. Remove front underbody protection.
3. Remove fan cowl.
4. Open sealing cap on coolant expansion tank.

➡When installing, close the sealing cap until the arrows line up.

5. Unlock and pull off coolant hose from radiator.
6. Drain, catch and dispose of coolant.
7. Add coolant.
    a. Use only recommended coolant.
    b. Observe mixture ratio.
    c. Observe capacities.
    d. Fill and vent cooling system.
8. Observe bleeding instructions without fail.
9. Assemble engine.
10. Check cooling system for leaks.

FLUID RECOMMENDATIONS

⁂ WARNING

The use of antifreeze and corrosion inhibitors that contain nitrites and amines is no longer permissible.

LEVEL CHECK

1. Allow the engine to cool down.
2. Slowly turn the expansion tank sealing cap anticlockwise until the excess pressure is released.
3. Fully open the sealing cap.
4. The coolant level is correct when it lies between the minimum mark and the maximum mark in the coolant filler neck.
5. If required, slowly top up to the correct fluid level. Do not overfill.
6. Turn the sealing cap until a click is heard.
7. Have the cause of coolant loss rectified as soon as possible.

ELECTRIC ENGINE FAN

REMOVAL & INSTALLATION

N20 Engine

See Figures 45 and 46.

1. Read out the fault memory of the DME control unit.
2. Switch off ignition.
3. Remove cross connection.
4. Release coolant hose from fan cowl.

Vehicles with automatic transmission and four wheel drive:

5. Release screw (1).
    a. Tightening torque: 71 inch lbs. (8 Nm).
6. Pull off transmission oil cooler in upward direction from fan cowl.

All vehicles:

7. Release coolant hose from fan cowl.
8. Release screws (1).
9. Unlock and disconnect connectors (2) on fan cowl on right.
10. Release lock (3).
11. Feed out fan cowl upwards and remove.

To install:

12. To install, reverse the removal procedure noting the following.
13. Insert retaining tab at bottom of module carrier.
14. Check stored fault message.
15. Reassemble the vehicle.
16. Delete fault memory.

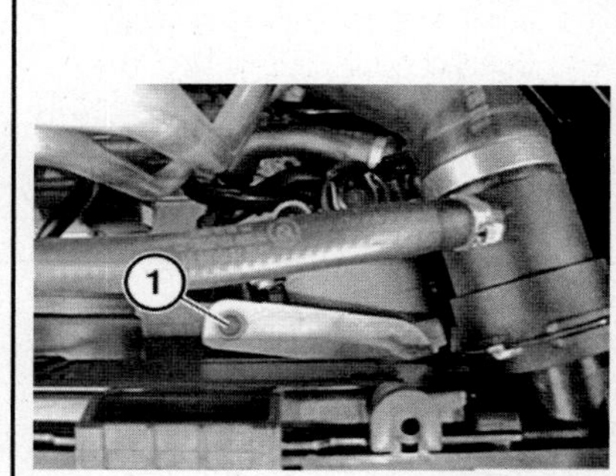

Fig. 45 Releasing screw (1)

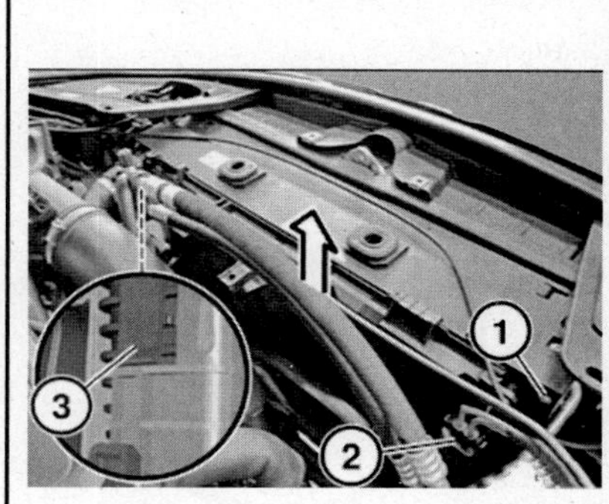

Fig. 46 Releasing screws (1), unlocking and disconnecting connectors (2) and releasing lock (3)

N52 Engine

See Figure 47.

1. Before servicing the vehicle, refer to the precautions.
2. Read out fault memory of DME control unit.
3. Remove intake duct. Refer to engine mechanical, air cleaner, removal & installation.
4. On automatic transmission vehicles, remove front underbody protection and disconnect the cooler for automatic transmission from fan cowl.
5. Unlock plug and remove.
6. Disconnect line from fan cowl.
7. Disconnect cable strap from fan cowl.
8. Remove bolt.
9. Unlock catch.
10. Remove fan cowl towards top.

To install:

11. Install fan cowl.
12. Lock catch in the opposite direction of arrow.
13. Install bolt and tighten securely.
14. Connect cable strap to fan cowl.
15. Clip line to fan cowl.
16. Lock plug.
17. On automatic transmission vehicles, connect the cooler for automatic transmission to fan cowl.
18. Install front underbody protection.
19. Install intake duct.
20. Clear the fault memory.

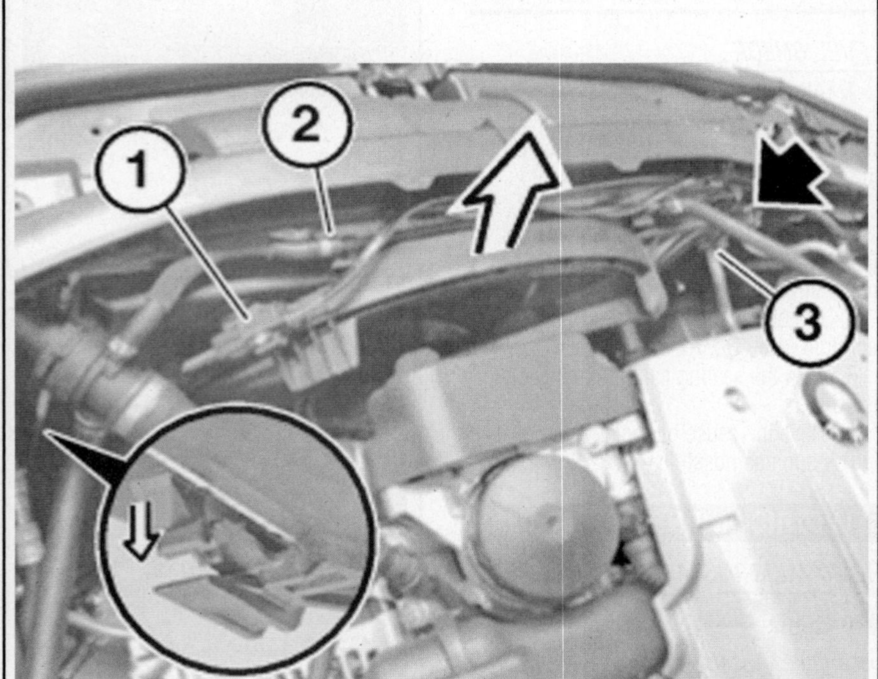

Fig. 47 Engine fan assembly showing plug (1), line (2) and cable strap (3)

N55 Engine

See Figure 48.

1. Turn off ignition.
2. Remove cross connection.
3. Release screw on fan cowl.
   a. Tightening torque: 44 inch lbs. (5 Nm).
4. Detach charge air duct from fan cowl.
5. Unlock and disconnect plug on fan cowl on right.
6. Unclip fan cowl (1) at clamps (2) on left and right, feed out in upward direction and remove.

To install:

7. To install, reverse the removal procedure noting the following.
8. Insert retaining tab at bottom of module carrier.
9. Check stored fault message.
10. Reassemble the vehicle.
11. Delete fault memory.

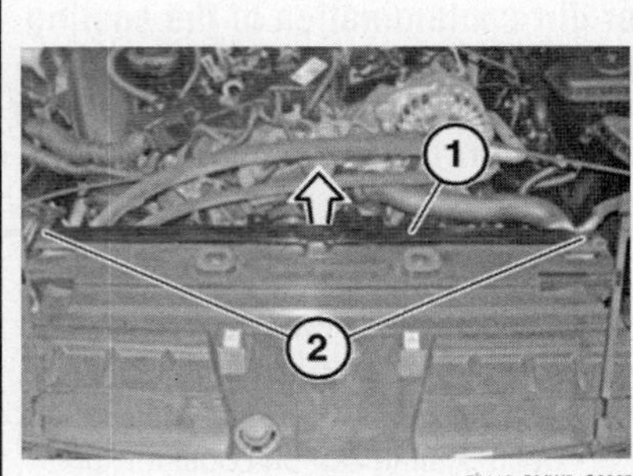

Fig. 48 Unclipping fan cowl (1) at clamps (2) on left and right, feeding out in upward direction and removing

N63 Engine

See Figures 49 through 51.

1. Switch off ignition.
2. Remove cross connection.
3. Remove intake manifolds on left and right.
4. Remove front underbody protection.
5. Detach coolant hose from fan cowl at retainer.
6. Unlock and disconnect plug (1) on fan cowl.
7. Release screw (2) on holder for coolant hoses.
   a. Tightening torque: 44 inch lbs. (5 Nm).
8. Detach coolant hoses with holder from fan cowl.
9. Release screw (1).
   a. Tightening torque: 44 inch lbs. (5 Nm).
10. Detach transmission oil cooler upwards from fan cowl.

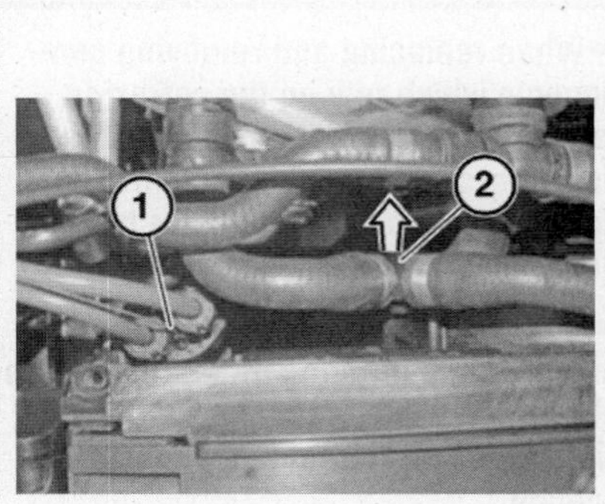

Fig. 49 Unlocking and disconnecting plug (1) and releasing screw (2)

Fig. 50 Releasing screw (1) and detaching transmission oil cooler (2)

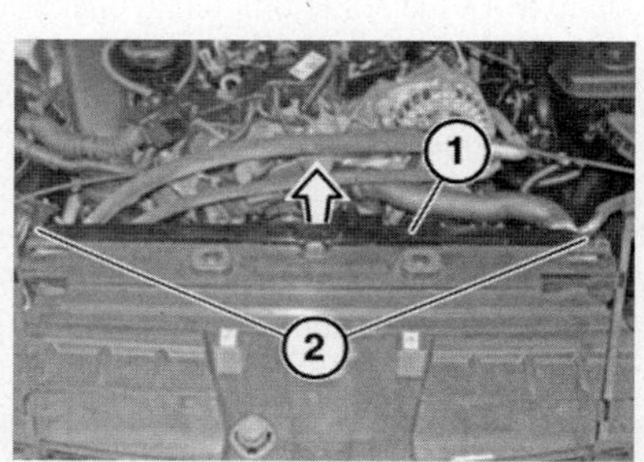

Fig. 51 Unclipping fan cowl (1) at clamps (2) on left and right, feeding out in upward direction and removing

11. Unclip fan cowl (1) at clamps (2) on left and right, feed out in upward direction and remove.

To install:

12. To install, reverse the removal procedure noting the following.
13. Insert retaining tab at bottom of module carrier.
14. Check stored fault message.
15. Reassemble the vehicle.
16. Delete fault memory.

RADIATOR

REMOVAL & INSTALLATION

N20 Engine

See Figures 52 and 53.

1. Before servicing the vehicle, refer to the precautions.
2. Remove fan cowl.
3. Drain and recycle the engine coolant.

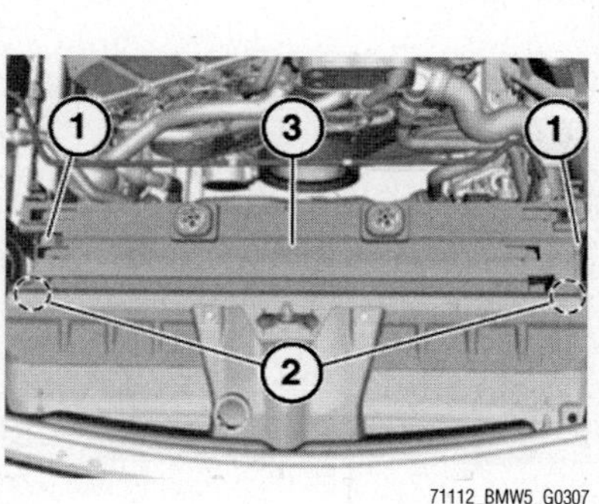

Fig. 52 Releasing screws (1) from cover (3) and behind sealing lip (2)

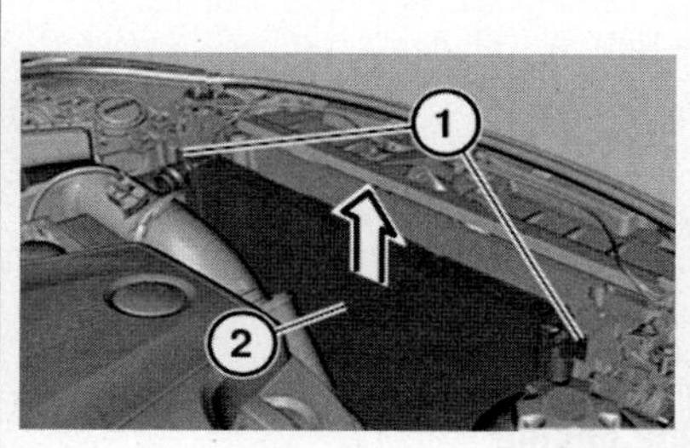

Fig. 53 Releasing screws (1) and removing radiator (2)

4. Unlock and detach coolant hoses on radiator.
5. Release screws (1) on left and right from cover (3).
   a. Tightening torque: 40 inch lbs. (4.5 Nm).
6. Release screws (2) behind sealing lip.
   a. Tightening torque: 40 inch lbs. (4.5 Nm).
7. Lift out cover (3).
8. Release screws (1).
   a. Tightening torque: 40 inch lbs. (4.5 Nm).
9. Remove radiator (2) towards top.

To install:

10. To install, reverse the removal procedure noting the following.
11. Check cooling system for leaks.

N52 Engine

1. Before servicing the vehicle, refer to the precautions.
2. Drain and recycle the engine coolant.
3. Disconnect the negative battery cable.
4. Remove intake duct. Refer to engine mechanical, air cleaner, removal & installation.
5. Remove the fan cowl.
6. Remove the coolant hose from expansion tank/radiator.
7. Remove the coolant hose from expansion tank.
8. Remove the plug connection at level sensor.
9. On automatic transmission equipped vehicles, remove the A/T heat exchanger/oil cooler.
10. Remove the coolant hose from radiator.
11. Remove the radiator mounting bolts, lift radiator out of mountings.

To install:

12. Install the radiator and mounting bolts. Tighten to 2 ft. lbs. (3 Nm).
13. Install the coolant hose to radiator.
14. On automatic transmission equipped vehicles, install the A/T heat exchanger/oil cooler.
15. Install the plug connection at level sensor.
16. Install the coolant hose to expansion tank.
17. Install the coolant hose to expansion tank/radiator.
18. Install the fan cowl.
19. Install the intake filter housing.
20. Vent cooling system and check for leaks.

N55 Engine

See Figure 54.

1. Before servicing the vehicle, refer to the precautions.
2. Remove fan cowl.
3. Drain coolant.
4. Unlock and detach coolant hoses from radiator.
5. Release screws (1) on left and right from cover (3).
   a. Tightening torque: 40 inch lbs. (4.5 Nm).
6. Release screws (2) behind sealing lip.
   a. Tightening torque: 40 inch lbs. (4.5 Nm).
7. Lift out cover (3).
8. Remove radiator towards top.

To install:

9. To install, reverse the removal procedure noting the following.
10. Check cooling system for leaks.

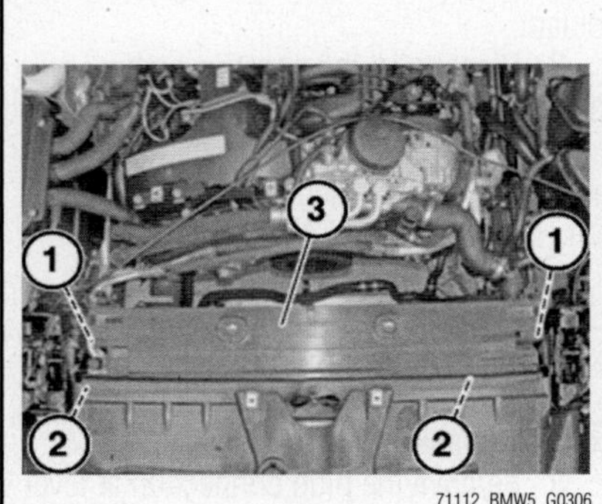

Fig. 54 Releasing screws (1) from cover (3) and from behind sealing lip

N63 Engine

See Figure 54

1. Before servicing the vehicle, refer to the precautions.
2. Remove fan cowl with electric fan.
3. Remove front splash guard.
4. Drain coolant.
5. Unlock and detach all coolant hoses on radiator.
6. Release screws (1) on left and right from cover (3).
    a. Tightening torque: 44 inch lbs. (5 Nm).
7. Release screws (2) behind sealing lip.
    a. Tightening torque: 44 inch lbs. (5 Nm).
8. Lift out cover (3).
9. Remove radiator towards top.

To install:

10. To install, reverse the removal procedure noting the following
11. Fill engine with coolant.
12. Check cooling system for leak tightness.

THERMOSTAT

REMOVAL & INSTALLATION

N20 Engine

See Figure 55.

1. Before servicing the vehicle, refer to the precautions.
2. Remove top clean air pipe.
3. Remove engine ventilation line.
4. Disconnect plug connection (1).
5. Disconnect coolant hoses (2-4) on thermostat with clamping tongs.
6. Disconnect coolant hoses (2-4) from thermostat.

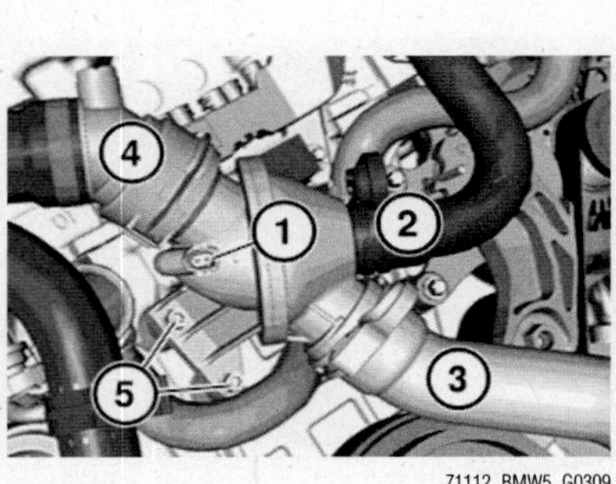

Fig. 55 Disconnecting plug connection (1) and hoses (2-4) and releasing screws (5)

7. Release screws (5) and remove thermostat.
    a. Tightening torque: 7 ft. lbs. (10 Nm).

To install:

8. To install, reverse the removal procedure noting the following.
9. Assemble engine.
10. Top up coolant.
11. Vent cooling system.

N52 Engine

See Figure 56.

1. Before servicing the vehicle, refer to the precautions.
2. Drain coolant.
3. Remove hose clips.
4. Remove coolant hoses.
5. Unlock and detach coolant hoses.
6. Disconnect plug connection.
7. Remove bolts.
8. Remove coolant thermostat.

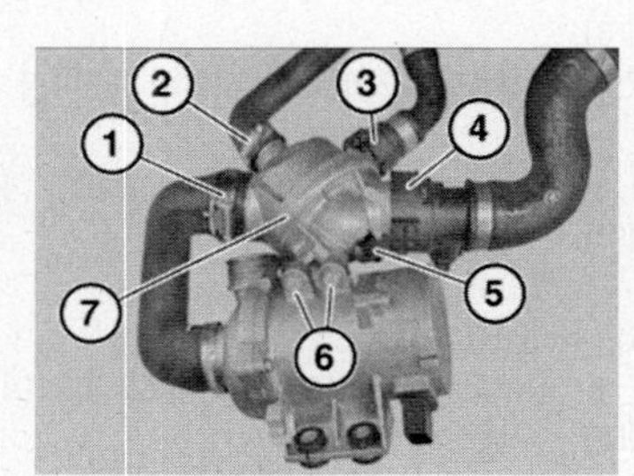

Fig. 56 Thermostat assembly

To install:

9. Install coolant thermostat.
10. Install bolts.
11. Connect plug connection.
12. Connect and lock coolant hoses.
13. Install coolant hoses.
14. Fasten hose clips.
15. Vent cooling system and check for leaks.

➡Before filling, turn ignitionON. Set blower to low level. Seat heating controller to maximum temperature. This ensures that the heater valves are fully opened and the auxiliary water pump starts up.

Important: The auxiliary water pump must deliver coolant in order to ensure fully venting.

a. Pour coolant into expansion tank up to **MAX** mark. Perform filling operation slowly.
b. Start engine and run at idle speed for approximately one minute (cap open). Then adjust coolant level to **MAX**.
c. Close cap and run engine up to operating temperature until main thermostat opens. Check cooling circuit and drain plug for leaks.

WARNING

The engine must be cooled down before the coolant level is checked. Coolant temperature must not exceed 30°C. If ambient temperature is above 30°C, allow engine to cool down to ambient temperature at least.

d. Check coolant level and adjust to **MAX**.

➡Do not fill coolant expansion tank over MAX level as overfilling will cause the coolant to overflow.

N55 Engine

See Figure 57.

1. Before servicing the vehicle, refer to the precautions.
2. Drain coolant at coolant pump.
3. Remove fan cowl with electronic motor.
4. Disconnect plug connection on coolant thermostat.
5. Unlock retaining clip in upward direction.
6. Detach coolant hose from coolant thermostat.
7. Lock hose clamp on coolant thermostat outlet with special tool 17 2 052.

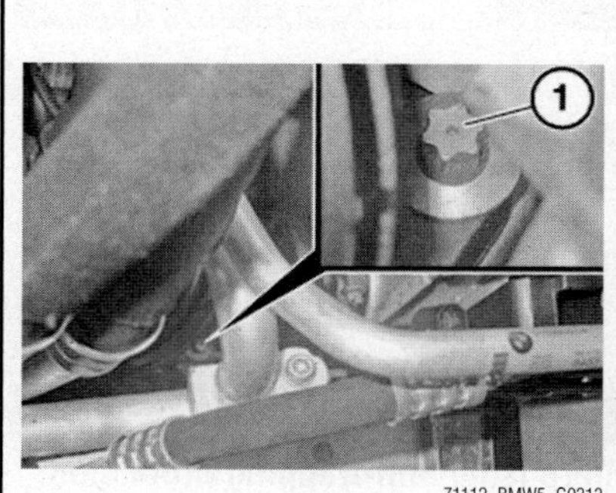

Fig. 57 Releasing screw (1) and removing thermostat

8. Detach coolant hose from thermostat.
9. Unfasten hose clamp on thermostat.
   a. Tightening torque: 26 inch lbs. (3 Nm).
10. Release screw (1) on holder.
   a. Tightening torque: 7 ft. lbs. (9 Nm).
11. Remove coolant thermostat.

⁂ WARNING

Only use special tool 17 2 050 to lock and release spring strap.

To install:

12. To install, reverse the removal procedure noting the following.
13. Fill and vent cooling system.

N63 Engine

See Figures 58 and 59.

1. Before servicing the vehicle, refer to the precautions.
2. Drain coolant.

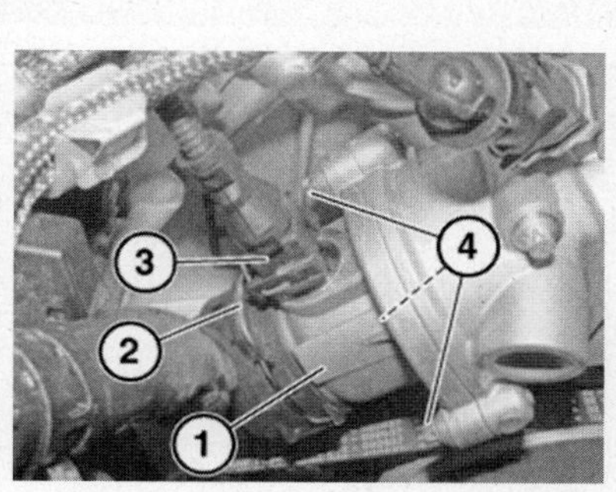

Fig. 58 Disconnecting plug connection (3), unlocking snap fastener and detaching coolant hose (2), releasing screws (4) and removing thermostat (1)

3. Remove fan cowl with electric fan.
4. Remove charge air cooler expansion tank.
5. Remove coolant pump.

⁂ WARNING

Coolant emerges when the coolant hoses are detached from the coolant thermostat.

⁂ WARNING

Cover surrounding components and plug connections with suitable apparatus.

➡For purposes of clarity, the graphic shows the auxiliary water pump removed.

6. Disconnect plug connection (3).

➡When installing, plug connection (3) must snap audibly into place.

7. Unlock snap fastener on coolant hose (2).

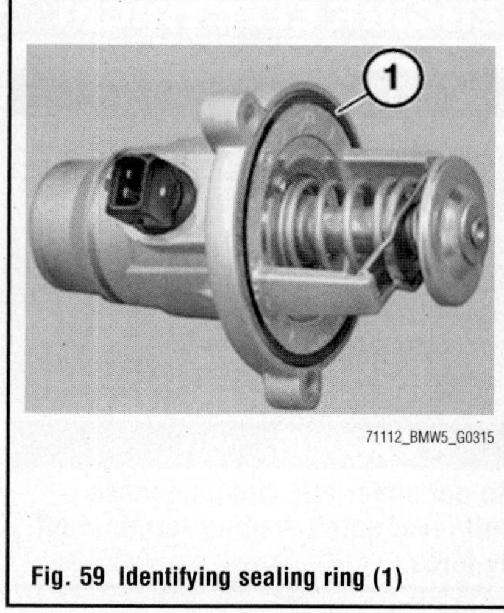

Fig. 59 Identifying sealing ring (1)

8. Detach coolant hose (2) and lay to one side.

➡One of the screws is not shown and is located at the rear under the coolant thermostat (1).

9. Release screws (4).
   a. Tightening torque: 7 ft. lbs. (10 Nm).
10. Lift out coolant thermostat (1).

➡The coolant thermostat is integrated in the housing cap. It can only be replaced as a complete unit.

11. Clean sealing surface.

➡When installing, replace sealing ring (1).

To install:

12. To install, reverse the removal procedure noting the following.
13. Assemble engine.
14. Top up coolant.
15. Bleeding instructions must be observed without fail.

ENGINE ELECTRICAL — BATTERY SYSTEM

BATTERY

REMOVAL & INSTALLATION

See Figures 60 and 61.

1. Disconnect battery negative lead
2. Disconnect plug connection of IBS cable.
3. Unscrew nut. Tightening torque 61 21 1AZ.

WARNING

Do not under any circumstances pull/lever safety battery terminal off by force.

4. Detach safety battery terminal towards top, lay to one side and secure.
5. Release nuts and remove rollover protection.
6. Release threaded pin and remove holder.
7. Detach vent in direction of arrow.
8. Fold both clips open.
9. Pull battery back from front fixture and remove towards top.

To install:

10. Make sure battery (5) is correctly seated in front fixture.
11. Read out fault memory, clear if necessary
12. Register battery replacement.

BATTERY RECONNECT/RELEARN PROCEDURE

After disconnecting/connecting battery some systems may be restricted and individual settings may be lost. Settings or activations must be carried out, depending on the equipment specification.

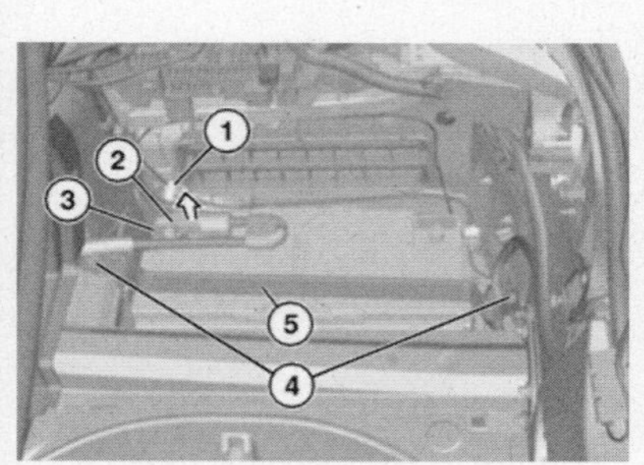

1. Plug connection
2. Battery terminal
3. Nut
4. Nuts
5. Rollover protection

37698_BMW5_G0091

Fig. 60 Removing battery cables and holder

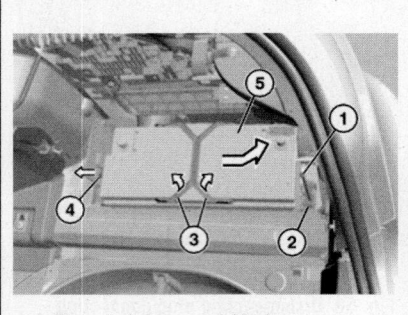

1. Threaded pin
2. Holder
3. Clips
4. Vent
5. Battery

37698_BMW5_G0092

Fig. 61 Removing battery from vehicle

Active Front Steering

Adjustment of the active front steering must be carried out:

- After adjustment work on the front axle/steering
- After all mechanical work on the steering system
- After the battery has been disconnected or electrical plug connections on the steering column switch cluster have been disconnected

After replacement/programming or coding of the following components:

- Steering column switch cluster
- DSC control unit
- Active front steering control unit
- ARS control unit

Connect vehicle to BMW diagnosis system. Select and carry out initial operation/adjustment for active front steering under Service functions.

Sliding Sunroof

Initialization of the sliding sunroof comprises normalization and then learning of the characteristic curve. The mechanical end positions are recorded and stored during normalization. The characteristic curve is learnt immediately after normalization. When the characteristic curve is learned, the mechanical closing forces of the slide/tilt sunroof are recorded and stored for correct operation of the anti-trapping mechanism.

Carry out an initialization:

- If the slide/tilt sunroof has been mechanically moved by means of the emergency actuator
- In the event of malfunctions, e.g. no one-touch function, no opening or no comfort function possible
- After disengagement of the drive unit
- After work is carried out on the mechanism of the slide/tilt sunroof
- After the control unit has been replaced

WARNING

There is no anti-trapping protection during initialization.

Normalization

See Figure 62.

1. Press and hold the switch in the "Lift" direction
2. In the event of delayed starting or sudden stopping of the slide/tilt sunroof, continue pressing the switch in the "Lift" direction
3. After reaching the lift end position, keep the switch pressed for approximately 15 seconds further.
4. Normalization is completed when the slide/tilt sunroof in lift end position presses again briefly upward.

Learning Characteristic Curve

1. After normalization, keep switch pressed in "Lift" direction.
2. The slide/tilt sunroof stops for 5 seconds in the final raise position after normalization. It then moves into the "Closed" position (learning of the "Closing from raising" curve).
3. The slide/tilt sunroof then moves into the "Open" end position and immediately back into the "Closed" position (learning of the "Closing" curve) .
4. Release switch.

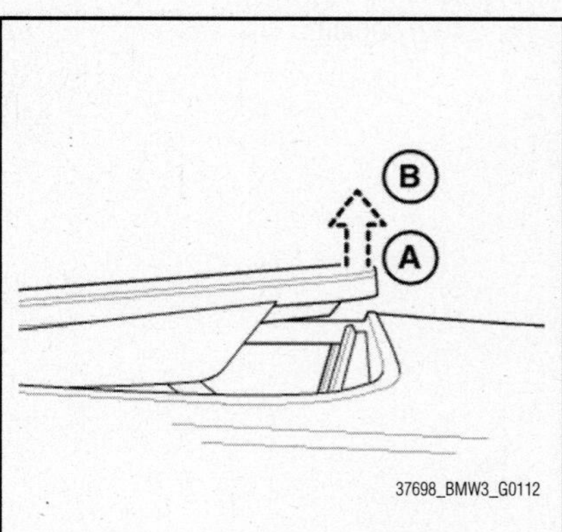

37698_BMW3_G0112

Fig. 62 Normalization is completed when the slide/tilt sunroof in lift end position (A) presses again briefly in the direction of position (B)

➡**The entire operation lasts approximately 75 seconds. Learning of the curve is terminated when the switch is released. If the switch is released prematurely, the entire procedure must be repeated. Upon completion of successful initialization, the corresponding messages in the check control and the control display go out.**

5. Carry out function check (tip function, anti-trapping protection and, if necessary, comfort function).

Power Windows

⁂ WARNING

There is no anti-trapping protection during initialization.

An initialization must be performed:

- In the event of malfunctions, e.g. no one-touch control function, no opening or if available no comfort function is possible
- After the power window drive has been replaced
- After work is carried out on the power window mechanism
- If necessary, after an open circuit, e.g. disconnection of the battery or disconnection of the power supply to the door
- After the door window glass has been removed and installed or replaced
- After adjustment work on the door window glass
- After adjustment work on the convertible top
- After replacement of seals

Initialization is performed on the power window switch of the relevant door.

- The ignition switch must be ON
- Doors and windows closed
- Sufficient battery voltage; connect charger if necessary

Initialization comprises erasure of the previous initialization and re-initialization.

Erasure of Initialization

1. Open door window glass fully
2. Actuate power window switch in "Open" position (second switch position) and hold down for between 15 and 20 seconds. This clears initialization of the power window. Anti-trapping protection and one-touch control (toll) function are inactive.
3. Check whether one-touch control (toll) function is inactive, otherwise repeat procedure.

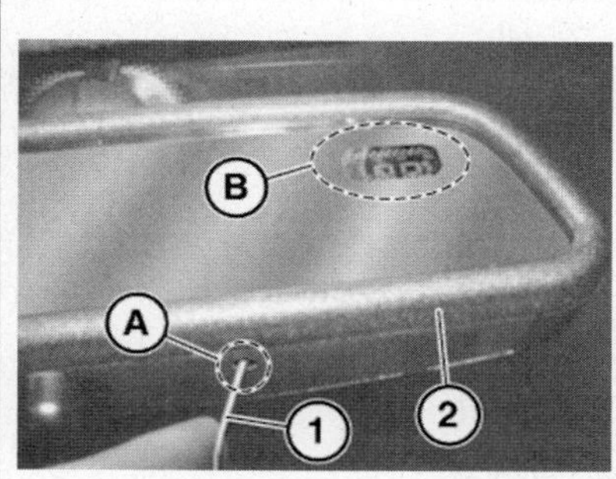

Fig. 63 Using a suitable tool (1), press pushbutton in area (A) of mirror (2) until a number appears in compass display (B)

Reinitialization

1. Close door window completely.
2. After upper end position is reached, interrupt actuation of power window switch and then hold switch again for approximately 1 second in "Close" position (second switch position).
3. Open door window glass fully.
4. After upper end position is reached, interrupt actuation of power window switch and then hold switch again for approximately 1 second in "Open" position (second switch position).
5. Close door window completely.
6. After upper end position is reached, interrupt actuation of power window switch and then hold switch again for approximately 1 second in "Close" position (second switch position).
7. Carry out function check (one-touch control function, anti-trapping protection and, if necessary, comfort function).

➡**The power windows can also be initialized by connecting the vehicle to BMW diagnosis system.**

Mirror with Compass

If may be necessary to calibrate the compass if:

- The vehicle battery has been disconnected for an extended period of time
- "C" appears in compass display
- There is no compass display

Setting Magnetic Deflection Zone

See Figure 63.

1. Switch ignition on.
2. Using a suitable tool, press pushbutton on mirror until a number appears in compass display.
3. Press pushbutton repeatedly until number of desired zone appears.
4. Wait until direction display appears.
5. Magnetic deflection zone is now set.

Calibrating Compass:

See Figure 64.

1. Switch ignition on.
2. Using a suitable tool, press pushbutton on mirror until "C" appears in compass display.
3. Drive vehicle 2–3 times in a circle at approximately 10 mph.
4. Calibration process is completed when direction display appears.

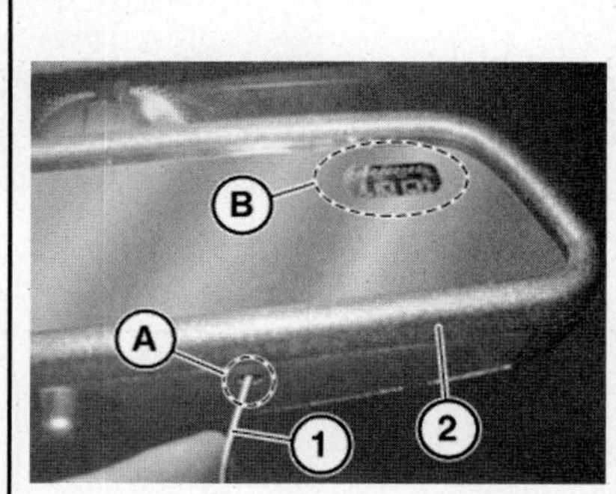

Fig. 64 Using a suitable tool (1), press pushbutton in area (A) of mirror (2) until "C" appears in compass display (B)

ALTERNATOR

REMOVAL & INSTALLATION

N20 Engine

See Figures 65 and 66.

1. Switch off ignition.
2. Disconnect battery earth lead and cover.
3. Remove intake silencer housing.
4. Remove clean air pipe, top.
5. Remove tensioning device for drive belt.
6. Release screws (1).
   a. Tightening torque: 28 ft. lbs. (38 Nm).
7. Unlock connector (1) and remove.
8. Release nut (2) and remove the positive battery cable.
   a. Tightening torque: 14 ft. lbs. (19 Nm).
9. Disconnect tank ventilation line (3) and place to one side.
10. Feed out alternator (4) to the left and remove.

To install:

11. To install, reverse the removal procedure.

N52 Engine

See Figure 67.

⁂ WARNING

Aluminum-magnesium materials. No steel bolts/bolts may be used due to the threat of electrochemical corrosion. A magnesium crankcase requires aluminum bolts/bolts exclusively. Aluminum bolts/bolts must be replaced each time they are removed. The end faces of aluminum bolts/bolts are painted blue for the purposes of reliable identification.

Jointing torque and angle of rotation must be observed without fail (risk of damage).

1. Before servicing the vehicle, refer to the precautions.
2. Disconnect the negative battery cable.
3. Remove intake filter housing.
4. Remove alternator drive belt.
5. Unlock plug and remove.
6. Remove nut and disconnect B+ wire.
7. Remove aluminum bolts and discard.
8. Remove alternator.

To install:

9. Install alternator.
10. Install new aluminum bolts tighten to
11. Connect B+ wire and tighten nut to 14 ft. lbs. (19 Nm).
12. Connect and lock plug.
13. Install alternator drive belt.
14. Install intake filter housing .
15. Connect the negative battery cable.

N55 Engine

See Figure 68.

1. Before servicing the vehicle, refer to the precautions.
2. Disconnect the negative battery cable.
3. Remove charge air duct.
4. Remove alternator drive belt
5. Remove the A/C compressor and place to one side.

➡Do not disconnect refrigerant lines from compressor.

Fig. 65 Releasing screws (1)

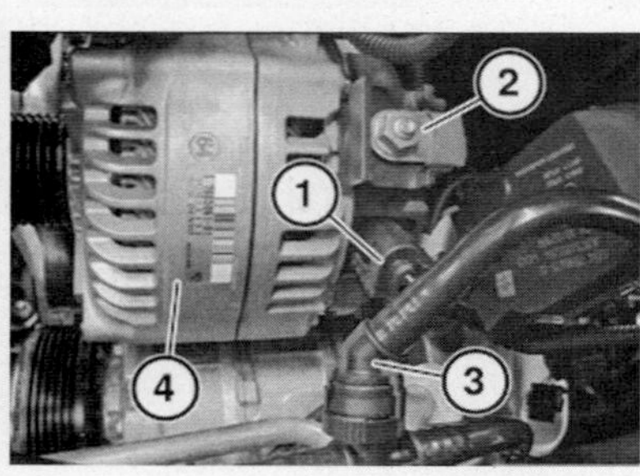

Fig. 66 Unlocking connector (1), releasing nut (2), disconnecting tank ventilation line (3) and removing alternator (4)

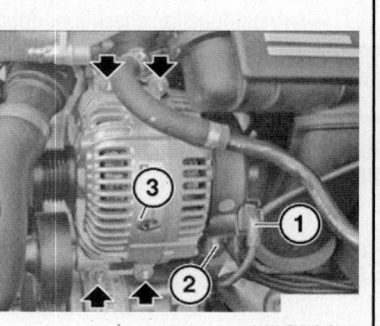

22205_BMWC_G0102

Fig. 67 Alternator (3), mounting bolts (arrows), B+ wire (1) and plug (2)

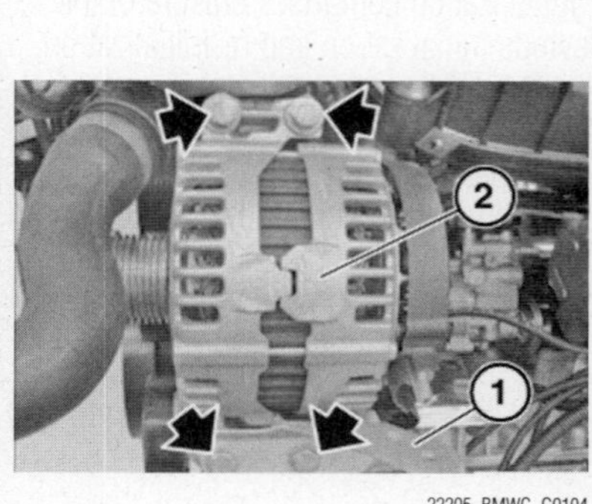

Fig. 68 Remove bracket (1) and alternator (2)

6. Remove bolts a few turns until bracket is loose. Do not remove bracket.
7. Unlock plug and remove.
8. Remove protective cap and remove nut underneath.
9. Disconnect B+ wire.
10. Remove bracket and alternator.

To install:

11. Install bracket and alternator.
12. Connect B+ wire.
13. Install protective cap and remove nut underneath.
14. Install and lock plug.

➡Do not disconnect refrigerant lines from compressor.

15. Install the A/C compressor.
16. Install alternator drive belt.
17. Install charge air duct.
18. Connect the negative battery cable.

N63 Engine

See Figures 69 through 71.

1. Switch off ignition.
2. Disconnect battery negative lead.

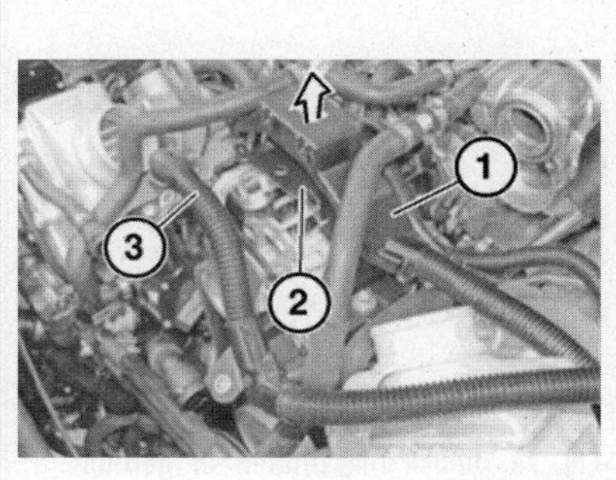

Fig. 69 Pulling off cable duct (1) from holder (2) and releasing cable (3)

Fig. 70 Pulling off plug (1), detaching cover (2) disconnecting positive lead (3) and removing fuel feed line (4)

3. Remove acoustic cover.
4. Remove left and right intake filter housings.
5. Remove alternator drive belt.
6. Remove intercooler expansion tank.
7. Remove fuel feed line.

WARNING

Cover radiator.

8. Release clamps.
   a. Tightening torque: 31 inch lbs. (3.5 Nm).
9. Release clamps.
10. Replace clamps.
11. Detach both charge-air ducts and remove.
12. Check gaskets on turbocharger, replacing if necessary.
13. Detach hoses from clean-air pipe.
14. Release screw.
   a. Tightening torque: 7 ft. lbs. (10 Nm).
15. Detach clean-air pipe in direction of travel from turbocharger.
16. Check seals on clean-air pipe, replacing if necessary.

Fig. 71 Removing alternator (1) with bracket (2)

17. Pull off cable duct (1) from cable holder (2) in upward direction.
18. Release cable (3) from holder.
19. Pull off plug (1).
20. Detach cover (2) and release nut underneath.
   a. Tightening torque: 14 ft. lbs. (19 Nm).

➡When installing, reinstall cover (2) without fail risk of short circuiting.

21. Disconnect battery positive lead (3) from alternator.
22. Remove fuel feed line (4).
23. Release screws on turbocharger coolant pump.
24. Place turbocharger coolant pump to one side. Do not remove turbocharger coolant pump.
25. Release screws.
   a. Tightening torque: 15 ft. lbs. (21 Nm).
26. Remove alternator (1) together with bracket (2) in direction of travel.

To install:

27. To install, reverse the removal procedure.

FIRING ORDERS

See Figure 72.

The N20 firing order is 1–3–4–2.

IGNITION COIL(S)

REMOVAL & INSTALLATION

N20 Engine

See Figure 73.

1. Read out the fault memory of the DME control unit.
2. Check stored fault messages and process procedure.
3. Switch off ignition.
4. Remove acoustic cover.
5. Ignition coils must not be contaminated by fuel.

WARNING

The resistance of the silicone material is reduced significantly by contact with fuel, which may cause the ignition coil to fail.

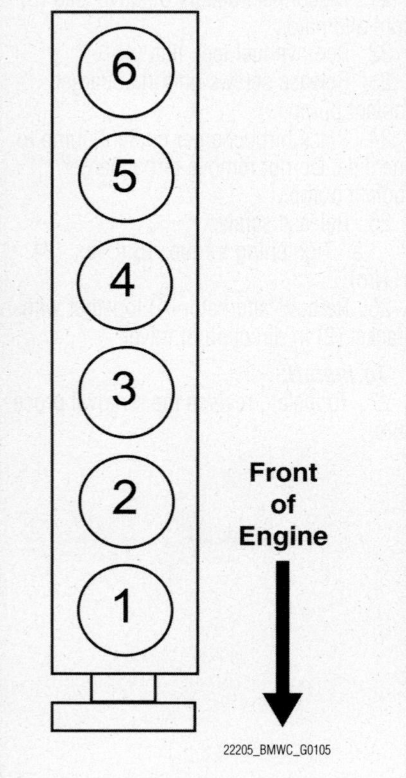

Fig. 72 3.0L I6 N52 and N55 engines Firing order: 1–5–3–6–2–4 Distributorless ignition system

WARNING

The silicone tube of the spark plug connector is coated with talc to reduce the pulling forces. The silicone tube must NOT be oiled or greased. This would greatly reduce the durability of the silicone material, which can lead to a malfunction of the ignition coil.

6. Unlock plug catch (1) of ignition coil (2) and disconnect plug.
7. Pull out the ignition coil (2) slowly in a smooth upwards movement.

➡There is a possibility that the silicone tube will tear and therefore be destroyed.

➡This procedure is applicable to all ignition coils.

To install:

8. Position the ignition coil and gently push it to the limit position, if necessary by twisting it back and forth slightly. Then check anti-twist lock.
9. The rubber cap must completely surround the sealing collar of the cylinder head cover.

➡If rubber parts are squashed, the ignition coil can slip out again during engine operation.

10. Push connector with connector catch open onto ignition coil.
11. Carefully close connector catch.
12. The connector must be positioned on the counter piece with hardly any gaps when the locking lever is being closed. In the process, the cheeks of the lever are positioned inside the counter piece.

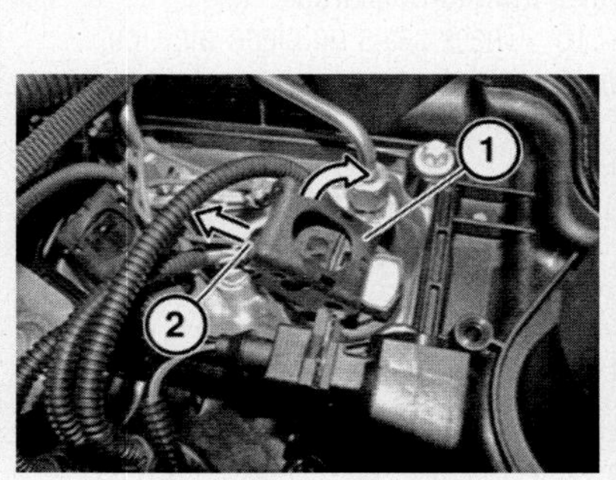

Fig. 73 Unlocking plug catch (1) of ignition coil (2)

➡The locking lever can become deformed if it is not installed correctly. This means that there is no longer a safety lock on the plug connection. As a result, the connector can slip out during engine operation (loose contact, misfiring).

13. The connector catch must snap into place without great effort.

➡Clear diagnostic fault entries from fault memory.

N52 Engine

See Figures 74 and 75.

1. Before servicing the vehicle, refer to the precautions.
2. Read out fault memory of DME control unit.
3. If equipped, remove engine cover.
4. Remove ignition coil cover.

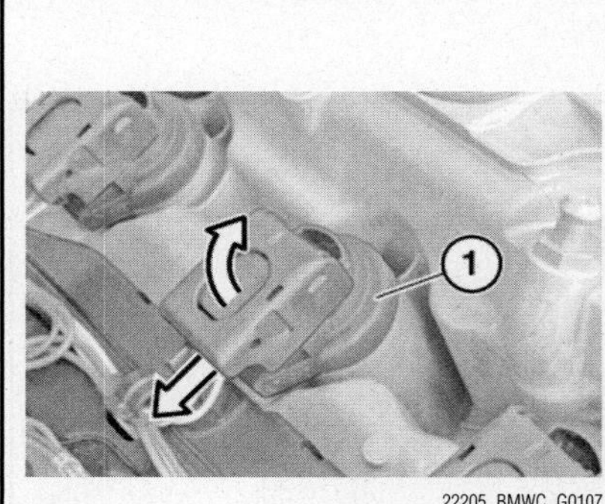

Fig. 74 Unlock plug retainer of ignition coil (1) and disconnect plug

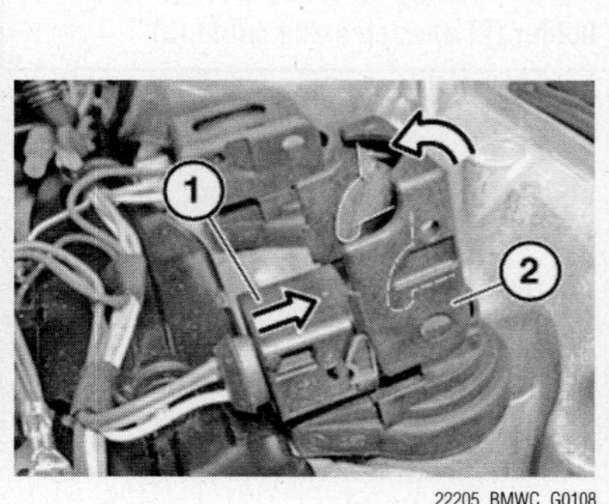

Fig. 75 Push plug (1) with plug retainer (2) open onto ignition coil

5. Unlock plug retainer of ignition coil and disconnect plug.
6. Pull ignition coil up and out.

To install:

7. Check that rubber seal of ignition coil is correctly seated.
8. Push plug with plug retainer open onto ignition coil.
9. Carefully close plug retainer.
10. Install ignition coil cover.
11. If equipped, install engine cover.

➡The plug retainer must snap into place without great effort.

12. Clear the fault memory.

N55 Engine

See Figure 76.

1. Read out fault code memory of the DME control unit.
2. Check stored fault messages and process procedure.
3. Switch off ignition.
4. Remove ignition coil cover.
5. Remove clean air pipe.

WARNING

Ignition coils must not be contaminated by fuel.

WARNING

The resistance of the silicone material is reduced significantly by contact with fuel, which may cause the ignition coil to fail.

WARNING

The silicone tube of the spark plug connector is coated with talc to reduce the pulling forces. The silicone tube must NOT be oiled or greased. This would greatly reduce the durability of the silicone material, which can lead to a malfunction of the ignition coil.

6. Release screws.
7. Slide cable channel to one side.
8. Release oxygen sensor connector from bracket.
9. Release screw.
10. Put cable clip aside.
11. Unlock plug catch (1) of ignition coil (2) and disconnect plug.
12. Pull out the ignition coil (2) slowly in a smooth upwards movement.

➡There is a possibility that the silicone tube will tear and therefore be destroyed.

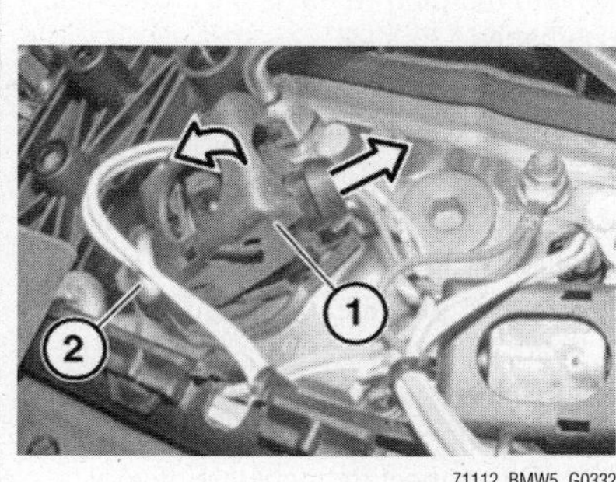

Fig. 76 Unlocking plug catch (1) of ignition coil (2) and disconnecting plug

➡This procedure is applicable to all ignition coils.

To install:

13. Position the ignition coil and gently push it to the limit position, if necessary by twisting it back and forth slightly. Then check anti-twist lock.
14. The rubber cap must completely surround the sealing collar of the cylinder head cover.

➡If rubber parts are squashed, the ignition coil can slip out again during engine operation.

15. Push connector with connector catch open onto ignition coil.
16. Carefully close connector catch.
17. The connector catch must snap into place without great effort.
18. The connector must be positioned on the counter piece with hardly any gaps when the locking lever is being closed. In the process, the cheeks of the lever are positioned inside the counter piece.

➡The locking lever can become deformed if it is not installed correctly. This means that there is no longer a safety lock on the plug connection. As a result, the connector can slip out during engine operation (loose contact, misfiring).

➡Delete fault memory.

19. Assemble engine.

N63 Engine

See Figures 77 and 88.

1. Before servicing the vehicle, refer to the precautions.
2. Read out fault memory of DME control unit.
3. Remove intake duct. Refer to engine mechanical, air cleaner, removal & installation.
4. Remove holder.
5. Pull ignition coil covers out of rubber grommets.
6. Unlock plug fastener of ignition coil.
7. Disconnect ignition coil connector.
8. Pull ignition coil up and out.

To install:

9. Check that rubber seal of ignition coil is correctly seated.
10. Connect ignition coil connector.
11. Lock plug fastener of ignition coil.
12. Push ignition coil covers into rubber grommets.
13. Install holder.
14. Install the intake filter housing.
15. Clear the fault memory.
16. Check for proper ignition system operation.

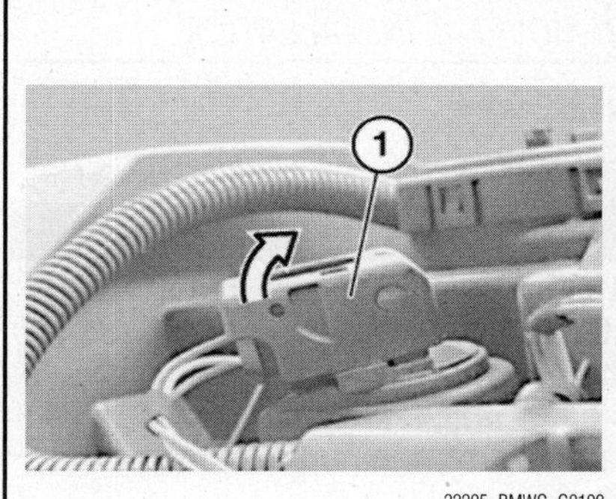

Fig. 77 Unlock plug fastener (1) of ignition coil

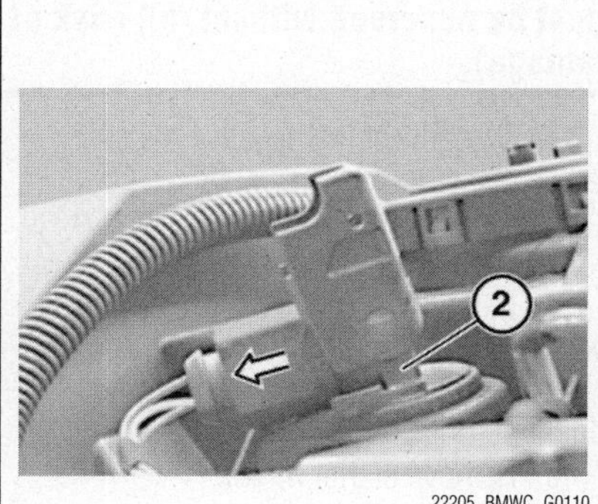

Fig. 78 Disconnect ignition coil (2) connector

IGNITION TIMING

INSPECTION & ADJUSTMENT

The ignition timing is controlled by the Digital Motor Electronics (DME). No adjustments are necessary.

SPARK PLUGS

REMOVAL & INSTALLATION

✲✲ WARNING

Spark plugs must be replaced with the same type/number spark plug as the original. If another spark plug is substituted, damage may result.

Special care should be taken when installing spark plugs into the cylinder head spark plug wells. Be sure the plugs do not drop into the plug wells as electrodes can be damaged.

Always tighten spark plugs to the specified torque. Over tightening can cause distortion resulting in a change in the spark plug gap or a cracked porcelain insulator. Proper torque is especially important in the case of aluminum cylinder heads.

1. Before servicing the vehicle, refer to the precautions.
2. Disconnect the negative battery cable.
3. If equipped, removal engine cover.
4. Remove ignition coils.
5. Unscrew spark plugs with special tool 12 1 171 (N52 and N62) or 12 1 220 (N54).

To install:

6. Screw spark plugs in special tool.
7. Tighten spark plugs to 18 ft. lbs. (24 Nm).
8. Install ignition coils.
9. If equipped, install engine cover.
10. Connect the negative battery cable.

SPARK PLUG WIRES

REMOVAL & INSTALLATION

When replacing the spark plug and ignition coil cables, route the cables correctly and secure them in the appropriate retainers. Failure to route the cables properly can cause the radio to reproduce ignition noise. It could cause cross ignition of the spark plugs or short circuit the cables to ground.

ENGINE ELECTRICAL — STARTING SYSTEM

STARTER

REMOVAL & INSTALLATION

N52 Engine

See Figure 79.

✲✲ WARNING

Aluminum-magnesium materials. No steel bolts/bolts may be used due to the threat of electrochemical corrosion. A magnesium crankcase requires aluminum bolts/bolts exclusively.

Aluminum bolts/bolts must be replaced each time they are removed. The end faces of aluminum bolts/bolts are painted blue for the purposes of reliable identification. Jointing torque and angle of rotation must be observed without fail (risk of damage).

1. Disconnect the negative battery cable.
2. Remove intake air manifold.
3. Unlock plug and remove.
4. Remove the B+ cable from the starter.
5. Remove and discard the starter mounting bolts.
6. Remove starter motor.

To install:

7. Check starter pinion and ring gear for damage, replace damaged parts if necessary.
8. Install starter motor.

Fig. 79 Starter mounting bolt locations

9. Install the starter mounting bolts and tighten to specification.
   - M10x85: 15 ft. lbs. (20 Nm) plus an additional 180° rotation
   - M10x30: 15 ft. lbs. (20 Nm) plus an additional 90° rotation
10. Install the B+ cable from the starter and tighten nut to 10 ft. lbs. (13 Nm).
11. Unlock plug and install.
12. Install intake air manifold.
13. Connect the negative battery cable.

N63 Engine

See Figure 80.

1. Before servicing the vehicle, refer to the precautions.
2. Disconnect the negative battery cable.
3. Remove reinforcement plate.
4. On E60 models, remove right exhaust manifold.
5. Remove heat shield.
6. Remove the B+ cable from the starter.
7. Unlock plug and remove.
8. Remove bolts and pull starter motor out of transmission mounting and remove.

To install:

9. Check starter pinion and ring gear for damage, replace damaged parts if necessary.
10. Install starter motor in transmission mounting and tighten bolts to 33 ft. lbs. (45 Nm).
11. Connect the B+ cable to the starter and tighten the nut.
12. Install and lock plug.
13. Install heat shield.
14. On E60 models, install right exhaust manifold.
15. Install reinforcement plate.
16. Connect the negative battery cable.

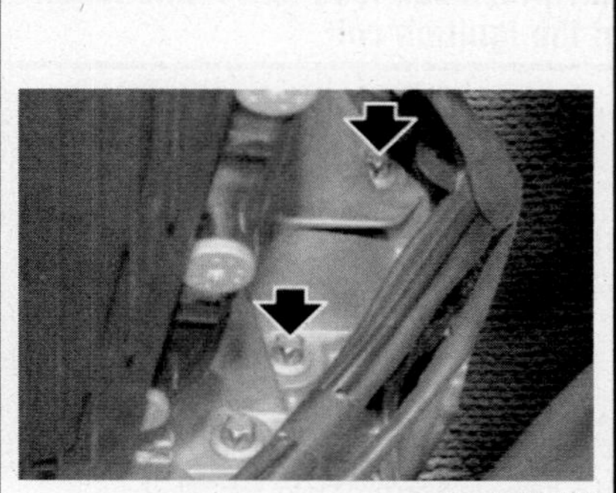

Fig. 80 Starter mounting bolt locations

ENGINE MECHANICAL

ACCESSORY DRIVE BELT SYSTEM

BELT ROUTINGS

See Figures 81 through 84.

INSPECTION

Inspect the drive belt for signs of glazing or cracking. A glazed belt will be perfectly smooth from slippage, while a good belt will have a slight texture of fabric visible. Cracks will usually start at the inner edge of the belt and run outward. All worn or damaged drive belts should be replaced immediately.

REMOVAL & INSTALLATION

Drive Belt

N20 Engine

See Figure 81

1. Remove the clean air pipe to the exhaust turbocharger.
2. Mark the direction of travel of the drive belt if it is to be reused.

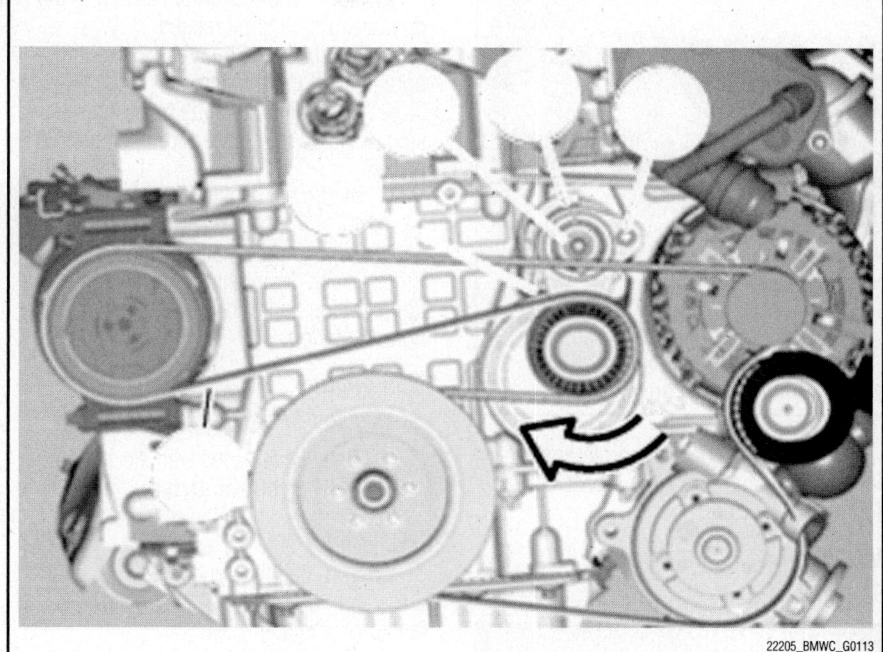

Fig. 82 Accessory belt routing—N52 engine

Fig. 81 Accessory belt routing—N20 engine

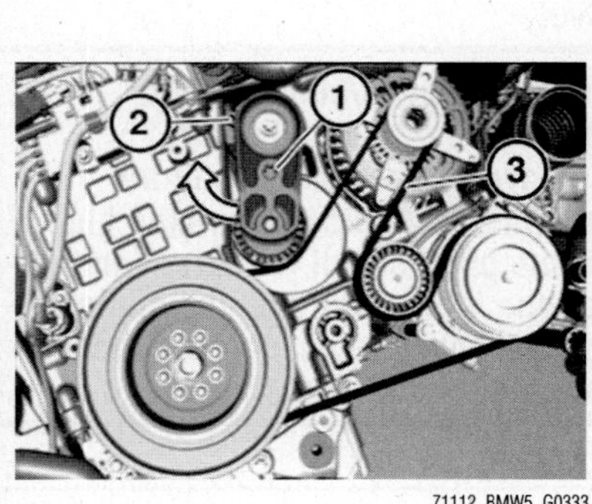

Fig. 83 Accessory belt routing—N55 engine (without Dynamic Drive)

3. Turn belt tensioner (1) on the hexagon head (2) in direction of arrow until bore hole on the belt tensioner is flush with the dowel hole.
4. Keep the belt tensioner (1) tensioned and position with a lock pin or special tool 11 0 390 , if applicable.
5. Remove drive belt (3).

To install:

6. To install, reverse the removal procedure noting the following.

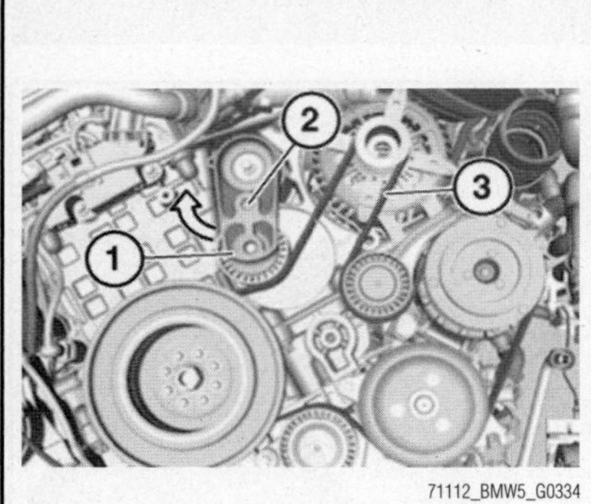

71112_BMW5_G0334

Fig. 84 Accessory belt routing—N55 engine (with Dynamic Drive)

7. Check drive belt for correct installation position and, if reusing, observe direction of travel.

N52 Engine

See Figure 85.

⁂ WARNING

Aluminum-magnesium materials. No steel bolts/bolts may be used due to the threat of electrochemical corrosion. A magnesium crankcase requires aluminum bolts/bolts exclusively.

Aluminum bolts/bolts must be replaced each time they are Removed. The end faces of aluminum bolts/bolts are painted blue for the purposes of reliable identification. Jointing torque and angle of rotation must be observed without fail (risk of damage).

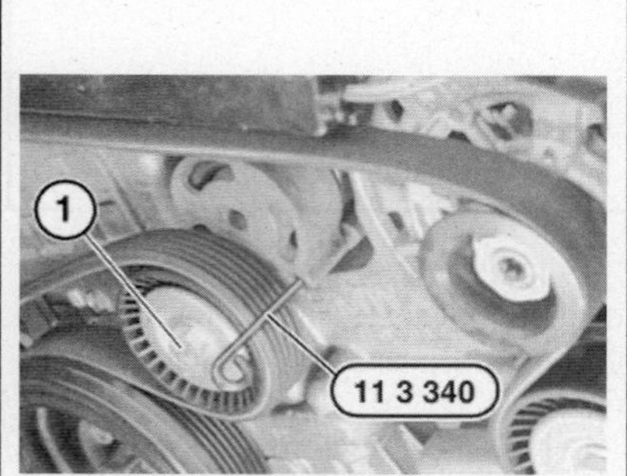

22205_BMWC_G0114

Fig. 85 Secure belt tensioner with special tool 11 3 340

1. Before servicing the vehicle, refer to the precautions.
2. Remove fan cowl with electric fan
3. Mark the direction of rotation of the drive belt if it is to be reused.
4. Turn belt tensioner clockwise until bore is flush on housing.
5. By holding belt tensioner under tension, the load is removed from tensioning pulley.
6. Secure belt tensioner with special tool 11 3 340.
7. Remove drive belt upwards.
8. Check drive belt for correct installation position and, if reusing, observe direction of rotation.

N55 Engine

See Figures 83 and 84

1. Remove fan cowl with electric fan.

Without Dynamic Drive:

2. Mark the direction of travel of the drive belt if it is to be reused.
3. Turn belt tensioner (1) in direction of arrow until bore hole (2) is aligned with belt tensioner and crankcase.
4. Hold belt tensioner (1) under tension.
5. Secure with special tool 11 0 390.
6. Remove drive belt (3).

With Dynamic Drive:

7. Mark the direction of travel of the drive belt if it is to be reuse.
8. Turn belt tensioner (2) in direction of arrow until bore hole is aligned with belt tensioner and crankcase.
9. Hold belt tensioner (2) under tension.
10. Secure with special tool 11 0 390.
11. Remove drive belt (3).

To install:

12. To install, reverse the removal procedure noting the following.
13. Check drive belt for correct installation position and, if reusing, observe direction of travel.

N63 Engine

See Figure 86.

⁂ WARNING

If contaminated with hydraulic fluid, replace drive belt.

⁂ WARNING

If the drive belt is to be reused, mark direction of travel and reinstall drive belt in same direction of rotation.

1. Remove fan cowl.
2. Release expansion tank for charge air cooler from mounting and press forwards.

⁂ WARNING

Coolant hoses do not need to be released.

⁂ CAUTION

Belt tensioner is under high initial spring preload.

3. Slowly and carefully pre-tension belt tensioner (1) in direction of arrow up to stop.
4. Secure special tool 11 3 340 in dowel hole (2).
5. Belt tensioner in installation position.
6. Remove drive belt.

➡On vehicles which do not have a power steering pump, a deflecting element (3) is fitted in place of the power steering pump.

To install:

⁂ CAUTION

Belt tensioner is under high initial spring preload.

7. Put on the drive belt.
8. Remove special tool 11 3 340 from dowel hole.
9. Slowly relieve tension on belt tensioner.

➡Make sure drive belt is in correct installation position.

10. Assemble engine.

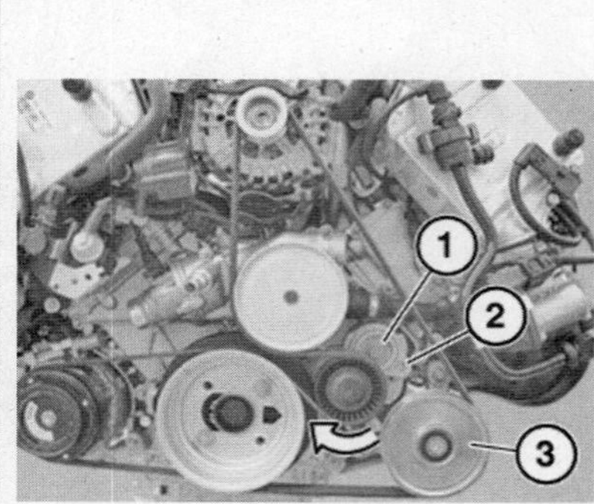

71112_BMW5_G0336

Fig. 86 Pre-tensioning belt tensioner (1), securing special tool in dowel hole (2), noting power steering pump or deflecting element (3) and removing drive belt

Drive Belt Tensioner

N20 Engine

See Figure 87.

1. Remove drive belt.
2. Remove special tool 11 0 390 to the belt tensioner (1), if applicable a lock pin (2).
3. Loosen screws (3) on the belt tensioner.
   a. Tightening torque: 14 ft. lbs. (19 Nm).

To install:

4. To install, reverse the removal procedure.

N52 Engine

See Figure 88.

⁂ WARNING

No steel screws/bolts may be used due to the threat of electrochemical corrosion.

⁂ WARNING

A magnesium crankcase requires aluminum screws/bolts exclusively.

⁂ WARNING

Aluminum screws/bolts must be replaced each time they are released.

⁂ WARNING

Aluminum screws/bolts are permitted with and without color coding (blue).

➡For reliable identification:

a. Aluminum screws/bolts are not magnetic.
b. Jointing torque and angle of rotation must be observed without fail (risk of damage).

1. Remove drive belt.
2. Remove special tool 11 3 340.
3. Release screw (3) on belt tensioner (4).
   a. Tightening torque 11 28 1AZ.

➡Replace aluminum screws.

4. Remove belt tensioner (4).

To install:

5. To install, reverse the removal procedure.

N63 Engine

See Figure 89.

1. Remove alternator drive belt.
2. If necessary, remove special tool 11 0 390 .

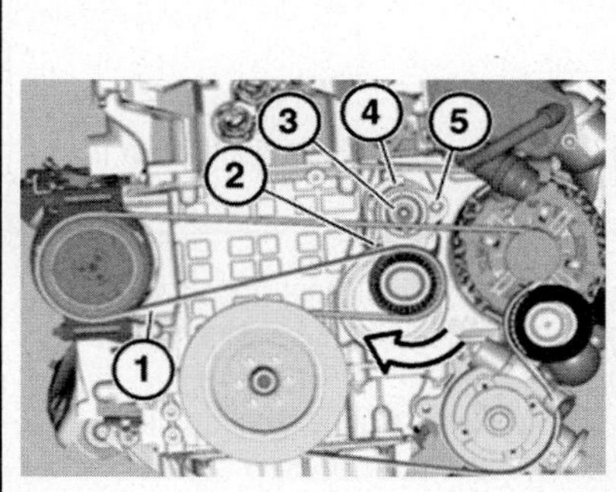

Fig. 88 Releasing screw (3) on belt tensioner (4) and removing tensioner

3. Release screw (1).
   a. Tightening torque 11 28 1AZ.
4. Remove belt tensioner with idler pulley (2).

To install:

5. To install, reverse the removal procedure.

AIR INTAKE SYSTEM

REMOVAL & INSTALLATION

Air Cleaner Assembly

N52 Engine

See Figures 90 through 92.

1. Before servicing the vehicle, refer to the precautions.
2. Remove fasteners from upper housing.
3. Remove upper section of air cleaner housing.
4. Release holder.
5. Release catches.
6. Remove right cover.
7. Remove the left cover in same way as right cover.
8. Release cable holder and remove hose from cover.
9. Press detent lugs.
10. Release cable strip in direction of arrow from lower section of air cleaner housing.
11. Release holder on both sides.
12. Release screw on both sides on lower section of air cleaner housing.
13. Feed out air cleaner housing lower section.
14. Unlock intake duct at side and detach from air cleaner housing.
15. Remove intake duct in direction of arrow.

Fig. 87 Removing special tool from belt tensioner (1), if applicable a lock pin (2), loosening screws (3) and removing tensioner

Fig. 89 Releasing screw (1) and removing belt tensioner with idler pulley (2)

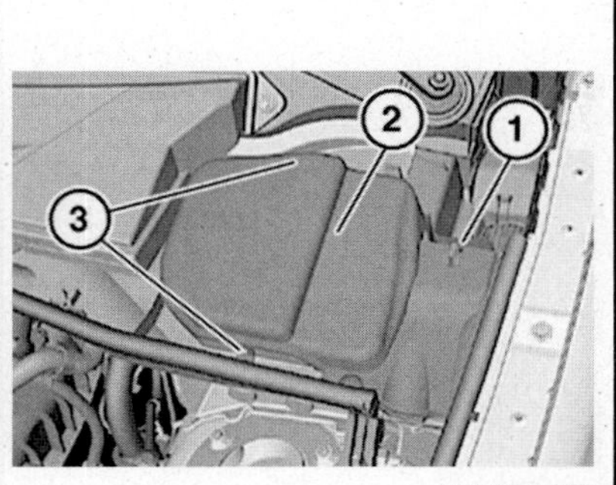

Fig. 90 Lower air cleaner housing right cover (2), holder (1) and catches (3)

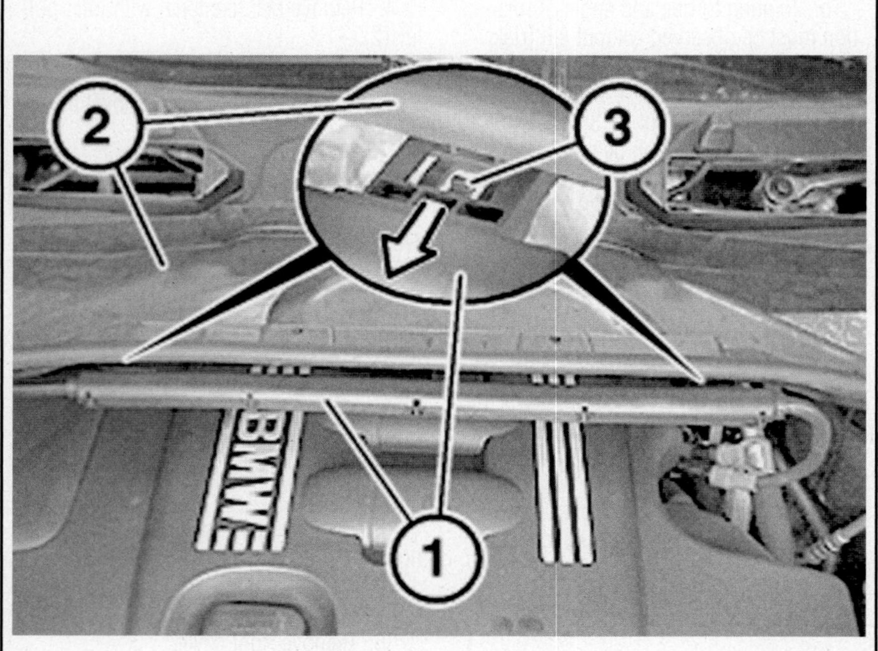

Fig. 91 Press detent lugs (3) and release cable strip (1) from lower section of air cleaner housing (2)

To install:

16. Installation is the reverse of removal.
17. Make sure cable strip is correctly seated.
18. Make sure right cover is correctly seated.
19. Retaining lugs must not be damaged or missing.
20. Make sure cable holder and hose are correctly seated in opening.
21. Make sure air cleaner housing lower section is correctly seated.

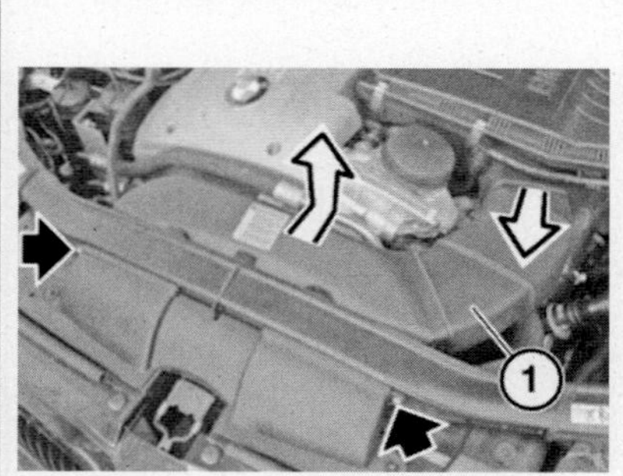

Fig. 92 Unlock intake duct (1) at side and detach from air cleaner housing

22. Seal of air cleaner housing lower section must not be damaged or missing.
23. Make sure upper section of air cleaner housing is correctly seated.

N63 Engine

See Figure 93.

1. Switch off ignition.
2. Remove acoustic cover.

➡Description for intake filter housing. Procedure on right side identical.

3. Release clamps (1).
    a. Tightening torque 13 62 9AZ.
4. Unfasten connector (2) on hot film air mass meter and disconnect.
5. Release clamp (3).
6. Unclip oxygen sensor cable from intake filter housing.
7. Detach intake air filter housing from intake port pull off upwards and remove.

To install:

8. To install, reverse the removal procedure.

Air Filter Element

N20 Engine

See Figure 94.

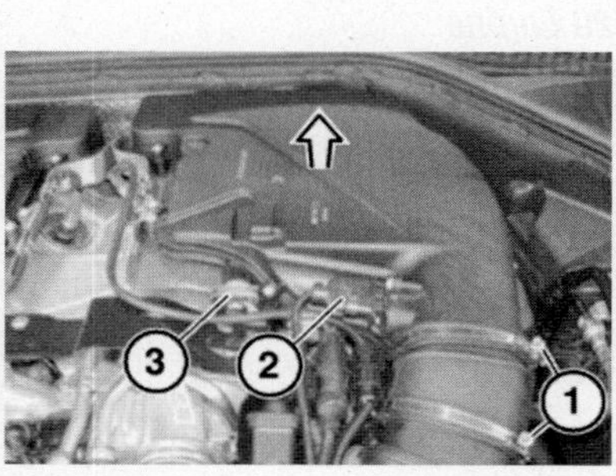

Fig. 93 Releasing clamps (1), unfastening connector (2), releasing clamp (3) and removing filter

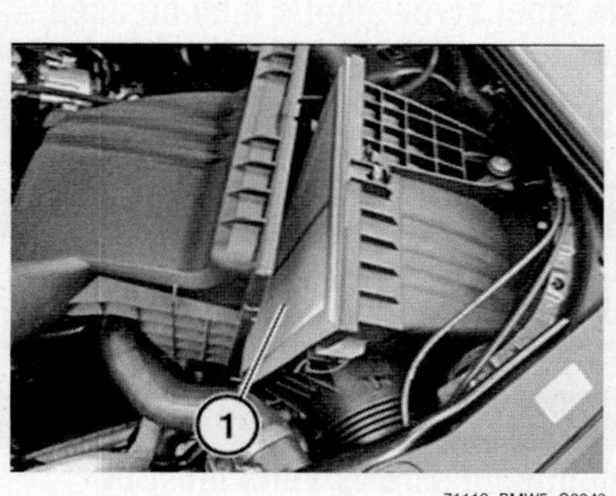

Fig. 94 Removing air filter element (1)

1. Remove left trailing link.
2. Release all clamps.
3. Release intake silencer housing lid.
4. Remove air filter element and replace.

➡When installing, clean intake filter housing from inside.

To install:

5. To install, reverse the removal procedure.

N52 Engines

See Figure 95.

1. Remove the upper portion of the air cleaner housing.
2. Release catches.
3. Release air cleaner in direction of arrow from upper section of housing.

To install:

4. Installation is the reverse of removal.
5. Make sure air cleaner is correctly seated.

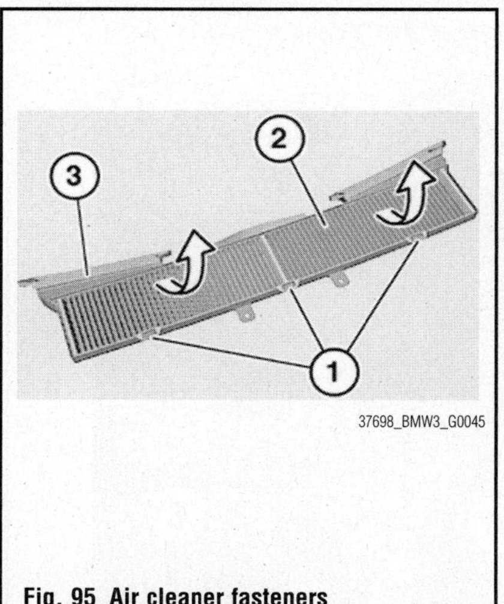

Fig. 95 Air cleaner fasteners

N55 Engine

See Figures 96 and 97.

1. Release clamp (1).
   a. Tightening torque: 27 inch lbs. (3 Nm).
2. Unfasten screws (2).
   a. Tightening torque: 22 inch lbs. (2.5 Nm).
3. Remove upper section of intake silencer housing.
4. Remove air cleaner element and replace.

➡**When installing, clean upper and lower sections of intake silencer housing from inside.**

To install:

5. To install, reverse the removal procedure.

N63 Engine

See Figures 98 and 99.

1. Switch off ignition.

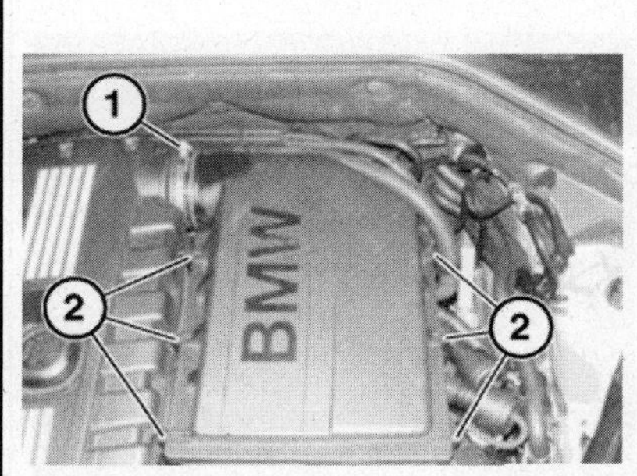

Fig. 96 Releasing clamp (1), unfastening screws (2) and removing upper section of intake silencer housing

Fig. 97 Removing air cleaner element (1)

2. Remove left and right intake filter housings.

➡**Description at left intake silencer housing. Procedure on right side identical.**

3. Release screws along line (1).
   a. Tightening torque: 29 inch lbs. (3.3 Nm).
4. Remove air filter cover (2).
5. Remove air filter insert.

➡**When installing, clean upper and lower sections of intake filter housing from inside.**

6. Replace air filter element.

To install:

7. To install, reverse the removal procedure.

CHARGE AIR COOLER SYSTEM

BLEEDING

See Figures 100 through 105.

✲✲ WARNING

Never reuse used coolant.

✲✲ WARNING

When replacing and removing components which rely on the corrosion protection effect of the coolant, it is essential to change the coolant. The cooling system must therefore be drained and refilled.

✲✲ WARNING

In the case of other removal work involving the draining of part quantities of coolant, replace these quantities which have been drained with new coolant.

✲✲ WARNING

You must protect the alternator against contamination by coolant when carrying out repair work on the cooling circuit.

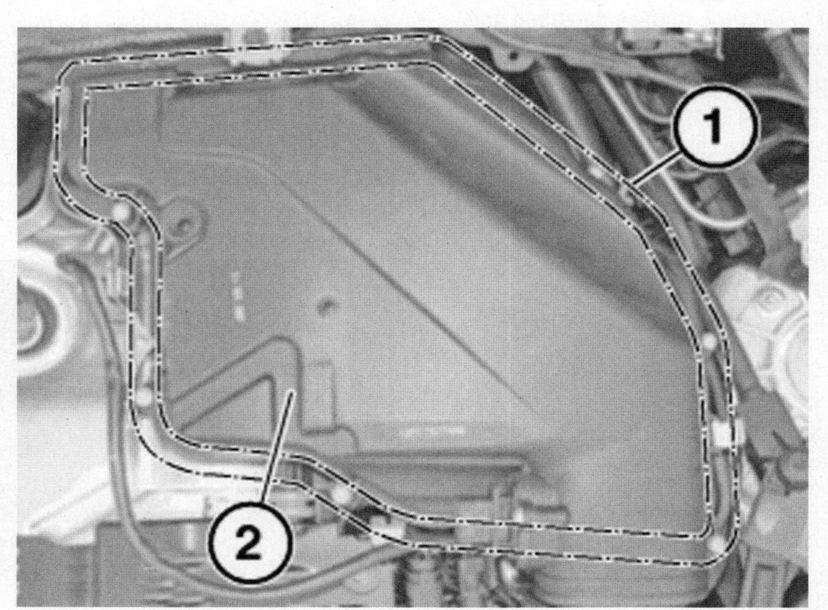

Fig. 98 Releasing screws (1) and removing air filter cover (2)

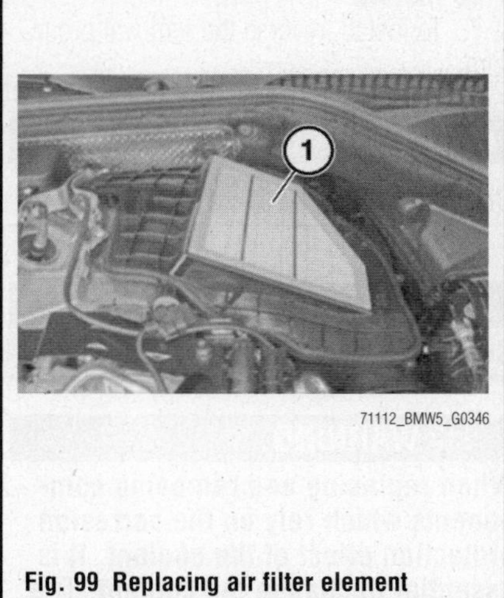

Fig. 99 Replacing air filter element

WARNING

Cover alternator with suitable materials.

WARNING

Failure to comply with this procedure may result in an alternator malfunction.

1. Catch and dispose of emerging coolant in drip tray (1) and if necessary special tool 00 2 030 (universal hydraulic lifting equipment).

➡Check all the coolant hoses before filling the cooling system with the vacuum filling unit.

➡If necessary, replace damaged and porous coolant hoses.

Preconditions:

2. The expansion tank of the cooling system for the charge air cooler must be empty.
3. There must be sufficiently premixed coolant in the filling unit container, 1 - 2 liters more than the vehicle filling capacity.
   a. Use only recommended coolant.
   b. Observe mixture ratio.
   c. Observe capacities.
4. Position the filling unit container at the same height as the coolant expansion tank.
5. Compressed-air connection with 6 bar pressure present.
6. Set heating to maximum temperature.

Application:

7. Connect filling unit (1) with a suitable adapter (2) from special tool set 17 0 100 to the charge air cooler expansion tank.

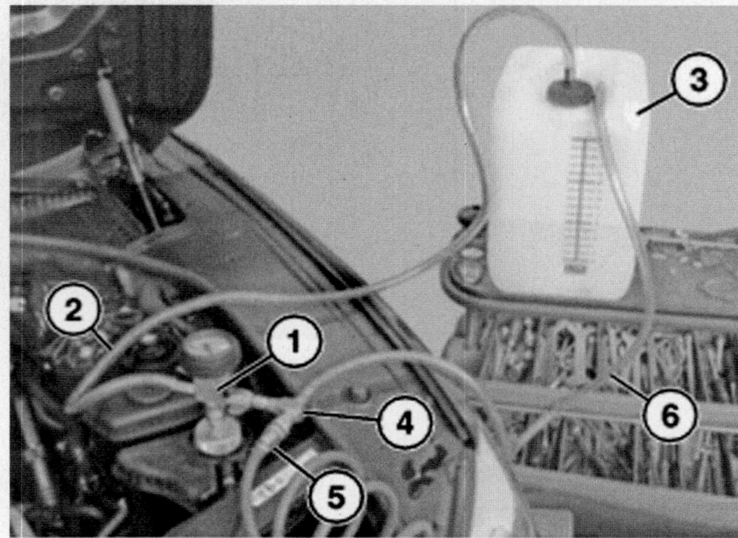

Fig. 100 Identifying vacuum filling unit

8. Shutoff valves (A) and (B) must be closed.
9. Connect venturi nozzle (1) to filling unit (2).
10. Connect compressed air (1) and open shutoff valve (B).

➡The venturi nozzle produces a flow noise.

11. Then open shutoff valve (A) until the filling hose (1) is free of bubbles. Close shutoff valve (A) again. The filling hose (1) is vented in this way.
12. Shutoff valve (B) remains open. Generate vacuum in cooling cycle for approx. 1 minute. The end vacuum is reached at a vacuum of -0.7 to -0.95 bar. Green scale on the vacuum meter.

➡The coolant hoses contract during vacuum build-up.

13. Then close shutoff valve (B) again.

Fig. 101 Connecting filling unit (1) with suitable adapter (2) and closing shutoff valves (A) and (B)

Fig. 102 Connecting venturi nozzle (1) to filling unit (2)

Fig. 103 Connecting compressed air (1) and opening shutoff valve (B)

14. Both shutoff valves (A) and (B) must be closed. Then seal Venturi nozzle.
15. The cooling system must hold the vacuum for 30 seconds. If the needle in the vacuum meter falls, this indicates a leak in the cooling system.
16. If the vacuum remains constant, proceed with filling.
17. In the event of a leak, check the cooling system for the charge air cooler for leaks.

WARNING

There must be sufficiently premixed coolant in the filling unit container, 1 - 2 liters more than the vehicle filling capacity.

WARNING

Position the filling unit container at the same height as the coolant expansion tank.

Fig. 104 Opening shutoff valve (A) until the filling hose (1) is free of bubbles and closing shutoff valve (A) again

Fig. 105 Shutting valve (B) and opening valve (A)

18. Shut-off valve (B) remains closed during the filling process.
19. To fill the cooling system, open shutoff valve (A) to filling unit container.
20. Coolant is now added.
21. The filling procedure is finished when the needle in the vacuum meter is at 0 bar or no longer falls.
22. If necessary, reduce remaining vacuum. Open shutoff valve (B) to do so.
23. Remove filling unit with adapter from expansion tank.
24. Perform venting cooling system for intercooler.
25. Close charge air cooler expansion tank.
26. Adjust coolant level to max.
27. Check cooling system for charge air cooler for leaks.

Venting Cooling System For Intercooler

See Figure 106.

WARNING

Open sealing cap only after engine has cooled down.

WARNING

Cooling system for intercooler has a separate cooling circuit.

WARNING

Coolant is added at intercooler expansion tank.

WARNING

Never reuse used coolant!

WARNING

When replacing and removing components which rely on the corrosion protection effect of the coolant, it is essential to change the coolant. The cooling system must therefore be drained and refilled.

WARNING

In the case of other removal work involving the draining of partial quantities of coolant, replace these quantities which have been drained with new coolant.

1. Catch and dispose of drained coolant in drip tray (1) and if necessary special tool 00 2 030 (universal hydraulic lifter).

WARNING

The following venting procedure is necessary when a part is replaced in the cooling system or when the cooling system is refilled.

Add Coolant:

2. Coolant is added at intercooler expansion tank.
3. Use only approved coolant.
4. Observe mixture ratio.

Venting Cooling System:

➡Do not leave the coolant expansion tank cap open during the venting procedure.

5. Add coolant up to top edge of expansion tank. Coolant must not drop any further! No drop in coolant for approx. 1 minute.
6. Connect battery charger.

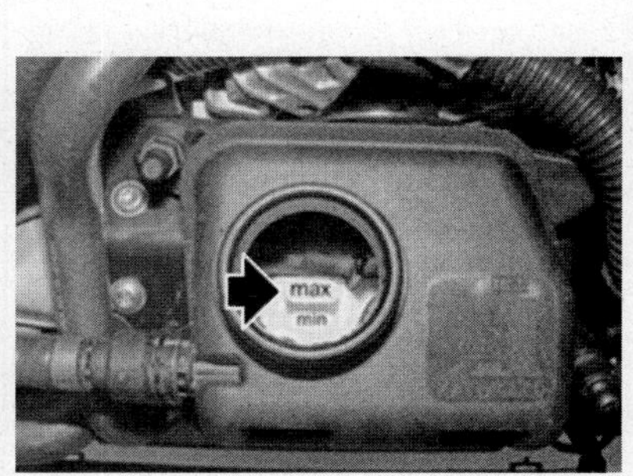

Fig. 106 Adding coolant

7. Switch on ignition.
8. Set heater to maximum temperature. Press "Automatic" button. Then reduce fan to lowest setting.
9. Press accelerator pedal for 15 seconds to floor. Engine must not be started.
10. The venting procedure is started when the accelerator pedal is pressed and takes approx. 12 minutes.
11. Refill expansion tank up to top edge immediately after drawing off until empty.
12. Adjust expansion tank to maximum level at end of venting process.
13. Check cooling system for leaks.
14. Close expansion tank.
15. If the venting procedure has to be carried out again, allow DME to drop completely (ignition key removed for approx. 3 minutes), then repeat from step 5.

REMOVAL & INSTALLATION

N55 Engine

See Figure 107.

1. Remove front underbody protection.
2. Coat sealing rings of snap fasteners with lubricant.
3. Pressure pipes cannot be fitted without lubricant.
4. Release screws.
   a. Tightening torque 17 10 2AZ.
5. Removing charge air cooler cover.
6. Unlock left charge air duct on charge air cooler and detach.
7. Unlock charge air cooler towards front from bracket.
8. Unlock right charge air duct (1) on charge air cooler and detach.
9. Unlock charge air cooler (2) towards front from bracket.
10. Unlock charge air cooler (1) towards front from brackets and remove towards bottom.

To install:

11. To install, reverse the removal procedure noting the following.

➡Charge air hoses must audibly snap into place.

12. Coat sealing rings of charge air hoses with lubricant.
13. Pressure pipes cannot be fitted without lubricant.
14. Check charge air system for leaks.
15. Assemble engine.

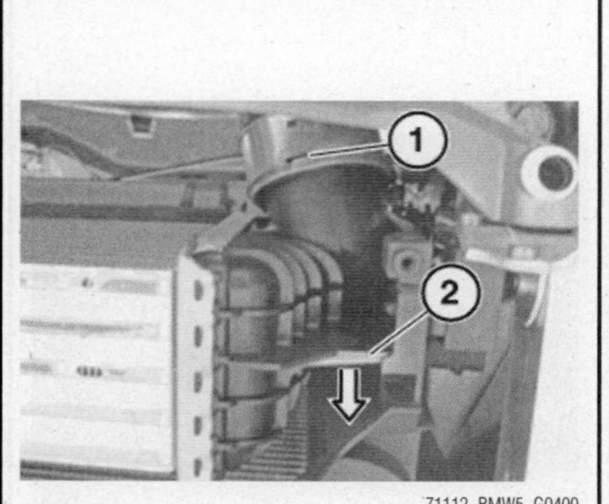

Fig. 107 Unlocking right charge air duct (1) and cooler (2)

N63 Engine

Left

See Figures 108 and 109.

***** WARNING**

Only perform this repair work after engine has cooled down.

1. Remove acoustic cover.
2. Remove front underbody protection.
3. Remove left intake port.
4. Drain coolant for charge air cooler.
5. Release clamp (1).
   a. Tightening torque: 31 inch lbs. (3.5 Nm).
6. Release clamp (2).
7. Replace clamp (2).
8. Remove left charge-air duct (3).

➡Check the gasket on the exhaust turbocharger. replacing if necessary.

***** WARNING**

When loosening the coolant hoses from the charge air cooler, make sure that the connector remains connected to the throttle body. Coolant may not penetrate the plug connection at the throttle body.

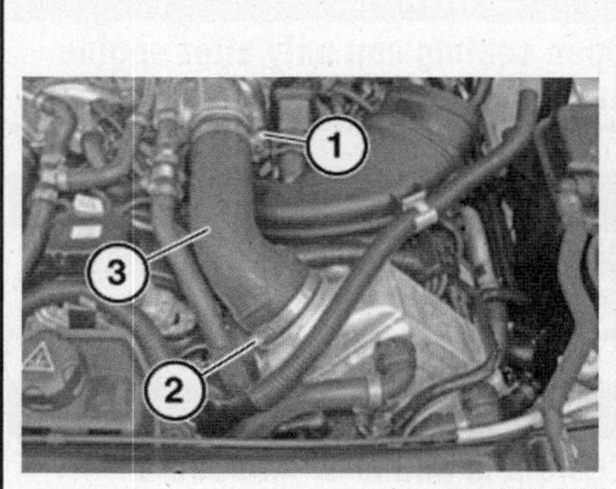

Fig. 108 Releasing clamp (1, 2) and removing left charge air duct

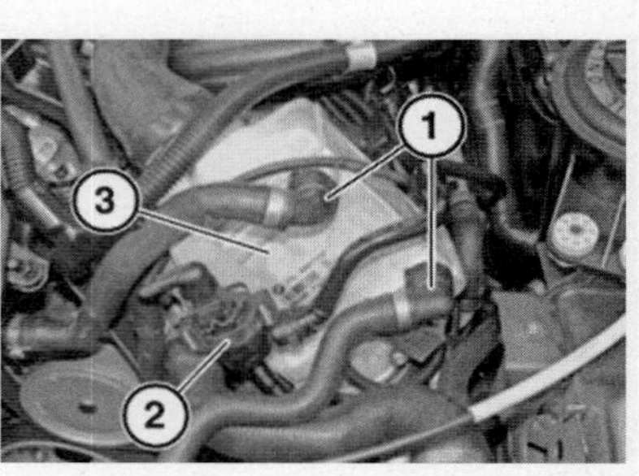

Fig. 109 Releasing and disconnecting coolant hoses (1) and removing tank vent valve (2) from charge air cooler (3)

9. Release and disconnect coolant hoses (1).
10. Remove tank vent valve (2) from charge air cooler (3).
11. Unlock connector (1) and remove.
12. Release screw (2).
    a. Tightening torque: 7 ft. lbs. (10 Nm).

➡Screw (2) is longer than screws (3)

13. Release screws (3).
    a. Tightening torque: 7 ft. lbs. (10 Nm).
14. Release clamp (4) on throttle valve unit.
    a. Tightening torque: 31 inch lbs. (3.5 Nm).
15. Lift out charge air cooler.

To install:

16. To install, reverse the removal procedure noting the following.
17. Replace faulty hose clamps.
18. After completion of work, top up and bleed coolant.

Right

See Figures 110 through 112.

***** WARNING**

Only perform this repair work after engine has cooled down.

1. Remove acoustic cover.
2. Remove front underbody protection.
3. Remove right intake duct.
4. Drain coolant for charge air cooler.
5. Release clamp (1).
   a. Tightening torque: 31 inch lbs. (3.5 Nm).
6. Release clamp (2).

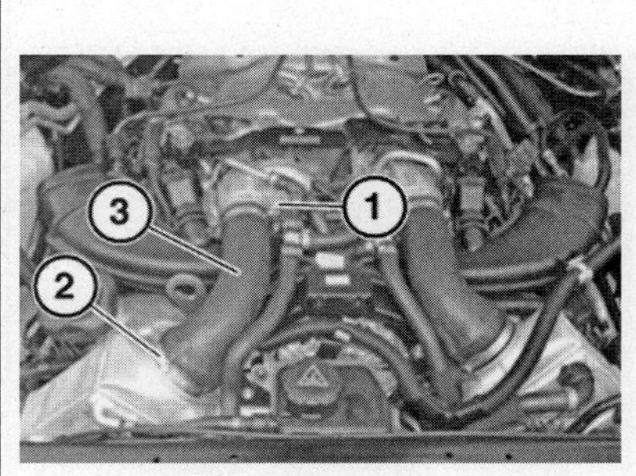

Fig. 110 Releasing clamps (1, 2) and removing right charge air duct (3)

7. Replace clamp (2).
8. Remove right charge-air duct (3).
9. Check the gasket on the exhaust turbocharger. replacing if necessary.

WARNING

When loosening the coolant hoses from the charge air cooler, make sure that the connector remains connected to the throttle body. Coolant may not penetrate the plug connection at the throttle body.

10. Release and disconnect coolant hoses (1).
11. Detach coolant hose (2) from charge air cooler.
12. Release connector (1) and remove.
13. Release screw (2).
    a. Tightening torque: 7 ft. lbs. (10 Nm).

➡**Screw (2) is longer than screws (3)**

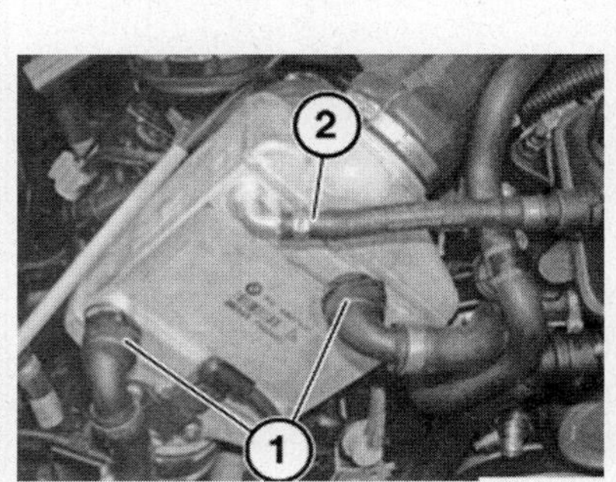

Fig. 111 Releasing and disconnecting coolant hoses (1) and detaching coolant hose (2) from charge air cooler

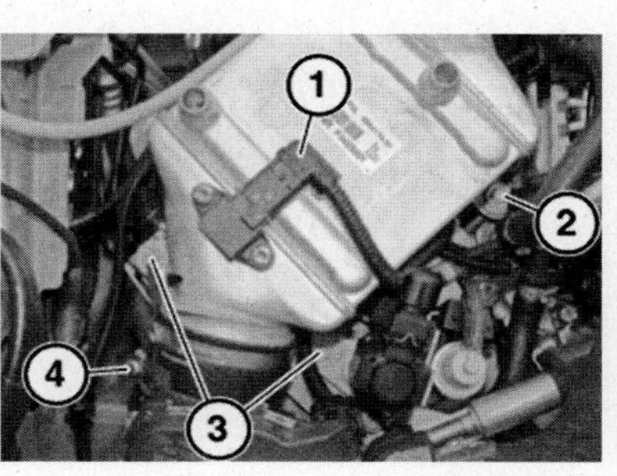

Fig. 112 Releasing connector (1) and screws (2, 3), releasing clamp (4) and removing charge air cooler

14. Release screws (3).
    a. Tightening torque: 7 ft. lbs. (10 Nm).
15. Release clamp (4) on throttle valve unit.
    a. Tightening torque: 31 inch lbs. (3.5 Nm).
16. Lift out charge air cooler.

To install:

17. To install, reverse the removal procedure noting the following.
18. Replace faulty hose clamps.
19. After completing all repair work, bleed the cooling system for the charge air cooler.

CRANKSHAFT DAMPER (BALANCER)

REMOVAL & INSTALLATION

N20 Engine

See Figures 113 through 116.

1. Remove drive belt.
2. Remove underbody protection at front and rear.
3. Block crankshaft with special tool 11 9 260.
4. Block crankshaft with special tool 11 8 180 .
5. Block crankshaft with special tool 22 2 742 .
6. Feed in special tool, slide screw forward and tighten.
7. Release screws (1).
8. Remove vibration damper.
    a. Tightening torque: 26 ft. lbs. (35 Nm).

To install:

9. To install, reverse the removal procedure.

Fig. 113 Blocking crankshaft with special tool (engine removed)

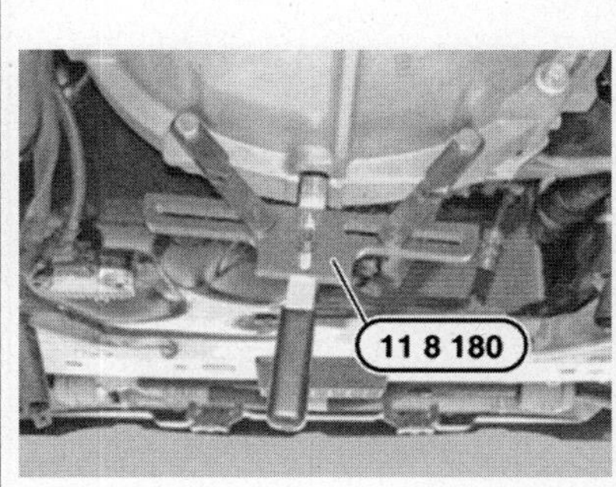

Fig. 114 Blocking crankshaft with special tool (engine installed with manual transmission)

Fig. 115 Blocking crankshaft with special tool (engine installed with automatic transmission)

N52 Engine

See Figure 117.

1. Before servicing the vehicle, refer to the precautions.

Fig. 116 Releasing screws (1) and removing vibration damper

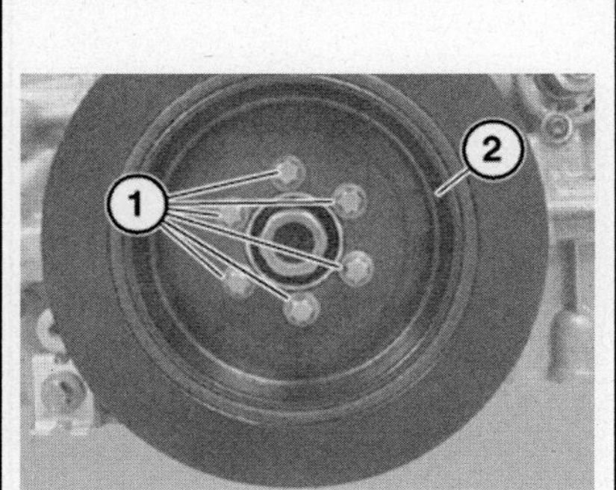

Fig. 117 Vibration damper (2) and fasteners (1)

2. Remove underbody protection.
3. Remove drive belt
4. Remove screws.
5. Remove vibration damper.

To install:

6. Installation is the reverse of removal.
7. Tighten vibration damper to hub to 26 ft. lbs. (35 Nm).

N55 Engine

See Figures 118 through 121.

1. Remove underbody protection.
2. Remove drive belt.
3. Block crankshaft with special tool 11 9 260.

➡Picture of flywheel removal.

4. Block crankshaft with special tool 11 8 180.
5. Block crankshaft with special tool 11 8 660.

Fig. 118 Blocking crankshaft with special tool (gearbox removed

⁂ WARNING

Do not release central bolt.

⁂ WARNING

If the central bolt is accidentally loosened, the timing must be readjusted.

6. Release screws (1 to 8).
7. Remove vibration damper (1).

Fig. 120 Block crankshaft with special tool (gearbox installed with automatic transmission)

8. Screws on vibration damper
   a. Tightening torque: 27 ft. lbs. (35 Nm).

N63 Engine

See Figures 122 through 124.

1. Remove fan cowl.
2. Remove A/C compressor drive belt.
3. Remove alternator drive belt.
4. Remove belt pulley for A/C system.

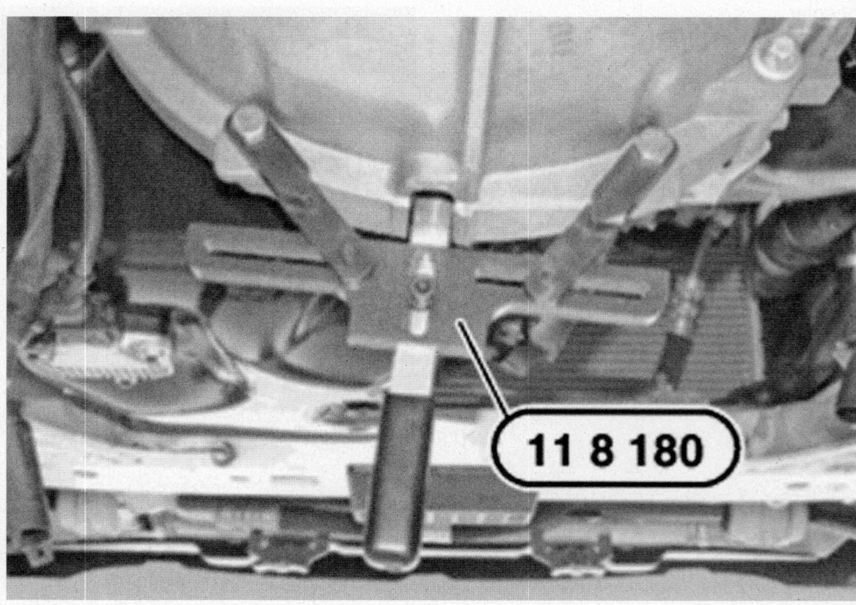

Fig. 119 Blocking crankshaft with special tool (gearbox installed with manual gearbox)

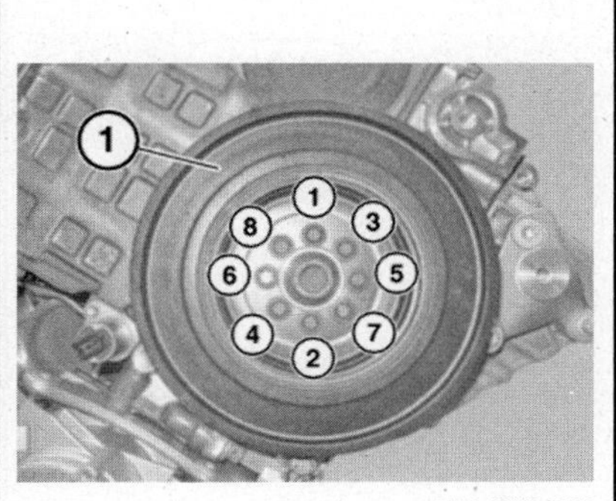

Fig. 121 Releasing screws 1 to 8 and removing vibration damper (1)

Fig. 122 Releasing screw (1) and removing belt tensioner with idler pulley (2)

5. Release screw (1).
   a. Tightening torque: 30 ft. lbs. (40 Nm).
6. Remove belt tensioner with idler pulley (2).
7. Secure special tool 11 8 090 with three screws (1) to vibration damper.
8. Secure special tool 11 8 090 with belt tensioner bolt (2) to timing case cover.
   a. Tightening torque: 30 ft. lbs. (40 Nm).

➡A 3/4 inch tool is needed to release the central bolt.

9. Release central bolt on vibration damper.
10. Secure central bolt with special tool 00 9 140 or 11 3 460 .
11. Position special tool 11 3 460 on special tool 11 8 090 .
12. Adjust special tool 11 9 453 on special tool 11 9 454 using clamping screw to 0° on scale.

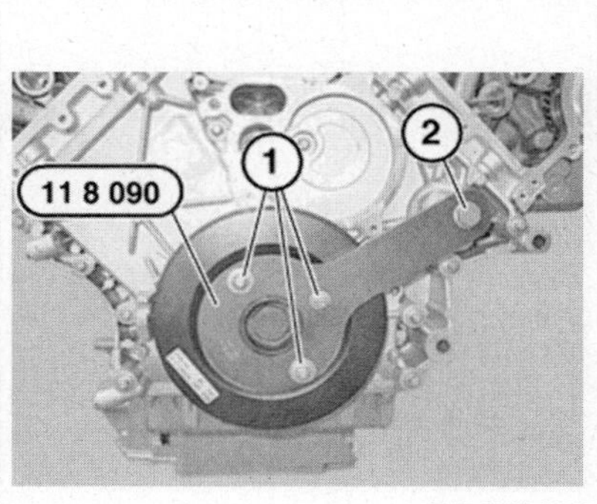

Fig. 123 Securing special tool with screws (1) to vibration damper and with belt tensioner bolt (2) to timing case cover

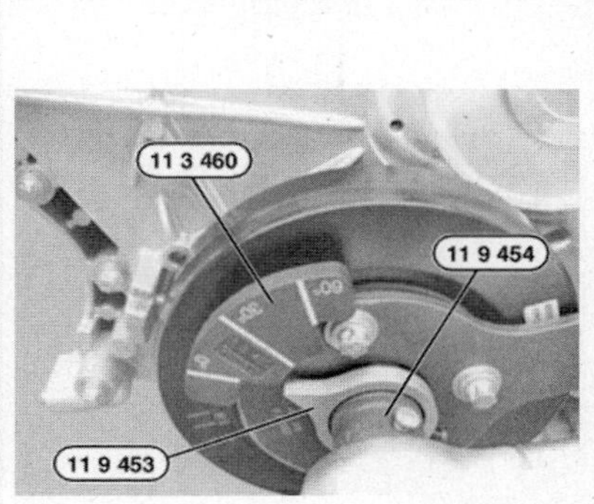

Fig. 124 Securing and positioning special tools

➡Replace screw.

   a. Tightening torque: 74 ft. lbs. (100 Nm) + 60° +60° + 60°.

To install:

13. To install, reverse the removal procedure.

CRANKSHAFT FRONT SEAL

REMOVAL & INSTALLATION

N20 Engine

See Figures 125 through 130.

1. Remove vibration damper.

WARNING

Do not release central bolt.

WARNING

If the central bolt is released, the sprockets of the timing chain and the oil pump will no longer be non-positively connected to the crankshaft. Intake and exhaust camshafts can turn in relation to crankshaft.

2. Screw special tool 11 0 371 to 37 ft. lbs. (50 Nm) into crankshaft seal.
3. Screw in spindle 11 0 372.
4. Release crankshaft seal from housing.
5. Repeat the operation several times if necessary.
6. Carefully saw open crankshaft seal (1) at cutting line (2).
7. Remove crankshaft seal (1) from special tool 11 0 371.

WARNING

The following text describes installation and sealing between the engine block and crankshaft seal.

Fig. 125 Installing special tools and releasing crankshaft seal from housing

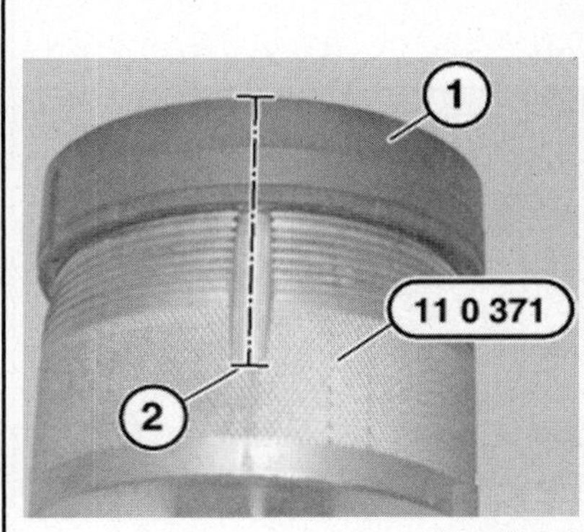

Fig. 126 Sawing open crankshaft seal (1) at cutting line (2)

WARNING

The engine block will not be leak proof at the outside of the crankshaft seal if you fail to comply with the individual work steps and the work sequence.

8. Carefully position radial shaft seal (1) on crankshaft in direction of arrow.
9. Screw special tool (1) onto crankshaft.
10. Align radial shaft seal in parallel with special tool 11 9 231 for housing separation.
11. Draw in radial shaft seal with special tool 11 9 231 in conjunction with special tool 11 9 233 until flush.

To install:

12. To install, reverse the removal procedure.

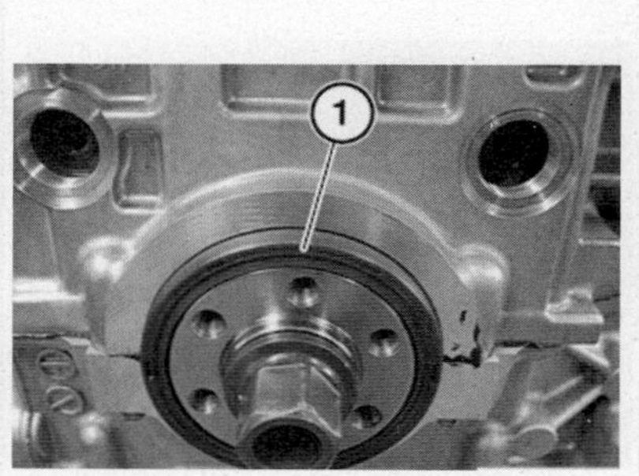

71112_BMW5_G0419

Fig. 127 Carefully positioning radial shaft seal (1) on crankshaft in direction of arrow

71112_BMW5_G0420

Fig. 128 Screwing special tool (1) onto crankshaft

71112_BMW5_G0421

Fig. 129 Aligning radial shaft seal in parallel with special tool for housing separation

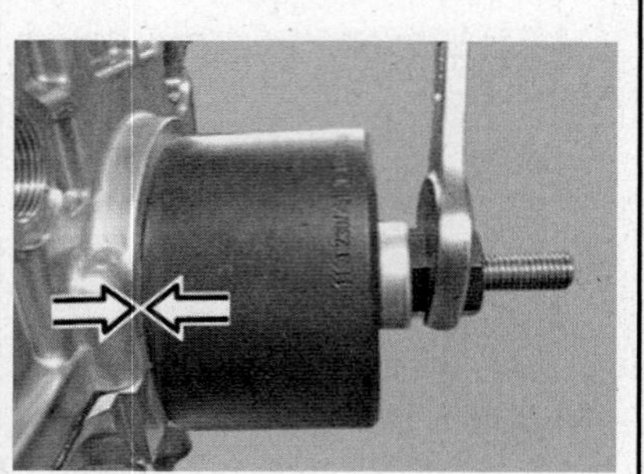
71112_BMW5_G0422

Fig. 130 Drawing in radial shaft seal with special tool 11 9 231 in conjunction with special tool 11 9 233 until flush

N52 Engine

See Figures 131 through 140.

1. Before servicing the vehicle, refer to the precautions.
2. Remove vibration damper

WARNING

Do not remove central bolt. If the central bolt is removed, the sprocket wheels of the timing chain and the oil pump will no longer be non-positively connected to the crankshaft. Inlet and exhaust camshafts can turn in relation to crankshaft.

3. Turn back special tool 11 9 222.
4. Push special tool 11 9 221 onto crankshaft.

➡When bolts are tightened down (special tool 11 9 224), crankshaft seal is pressed inwards approximately 1 mm and thus slackened for subsequent removal.

22205_BMWC_G0145

Fig. 131 Turn back special tool 11 9 222. Push special tool 11 9 221 onto crankshaft. When bolts are tightened down (special tool 11 9 224), crankshaft seal is pressed inwards

5. Insert bolts (special tool 11 9 224) and tighten down to approximately 15 ft. lbs. (20 Nm).
6. Screw special tool 11 0 371 to 59 ft. lbs. (80 Nm) into crankshaft seal.
7. Screw in spindle 11 0 372.
8. Remove crankshaft seal from housing.

➡Repeat the operation several times if necessary.

9. Carefully saw open crankshaft seal at cutting line.
10. Remove crankshaft seal from special tool 11 0 371.

To install:

WARNING

The following text describes installation and sealing between the engine block and crankshaft seal.

22205_BMWC_G0146

Fig. 132 Screw special tool 11 0 371 to 59 ft. lbs. (80 Nm) into crankshaft seal. Screw in spindle 11 0 372.

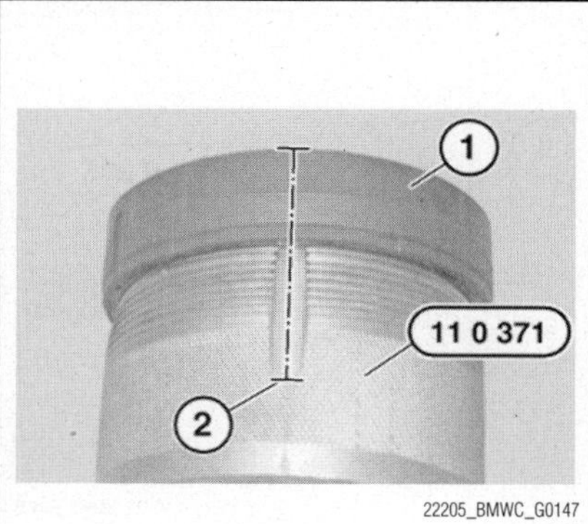

22205_BMWC_G0147

Fig. 133 Carefully saw open crankshaft seal (1) at cutting line (2)

The engine block will not be leak proof at the outside of the crankshaft seal if you fail to comply with the individual work steps and the work sequence.

11. Clean sealing surface and degrease thoroughly in area of housing partition.
12. Apply a light coat of oil to running surface of crankshaft seal.
13. Screw special tool 11 9 232 with bolts (special tool 11 9 234) to crankshaft.

➡Support sleeve is supplied with crankshaft seal.

14. When crankshaft seal is installed, only support sleeve may be used as a slip sleeve.
15. Crankshaft seal has a groove on both left and right sides.

WARNING

After installation, the grooves must be filled with sealing compound.

➡The required parts are available from the BMW Parts Service (Electronic Parts Catalogue ETK).

16. Remove screw caps from injector.
17. Screw on metering needle.
18. Insert piston for pressing out. Injector contains the sealing compound Loctite®, manufacturer's number 128357. Bottle contains the primer Loctite®, manufacturer's number 171000.
19. Push support sleeve with crankshaft seal onto special tool 11 9 232.

WARNING

Support sleeve remains on special tool 11 9 232, until crankshaft seal is drawn in.

20. Align groove centrally to housing partition.
21. Coat both grooves on crankshaft seal with Loctite® primer, manufacturer's number 171000, and expose to air for approximately one minute.
22. Draw in crankshaft seal with special tool 11 9 231 in conjunction with special tool 11 9 233 until flush.
23. Before filling with sealing compound, moisten brush with Loctite® primer, manufacturer's number 171000. Insert brush as far as possible into grooves on crankshaft seal in order to coat housing partition on engine block.
24. Using injector, fill both grooves flush with Loctite® sealing compound, manufacturer's number 128357.

➡Loctite® primer, manufacturer's number 171000, binds the Loctite® sealing compound, manufacturer's number 128357, and prevents leakage.

25. Coat surface of sealing compound in both grooves with Loctite® primer, manufacturer's number 171000.
26. Install vibration damper.

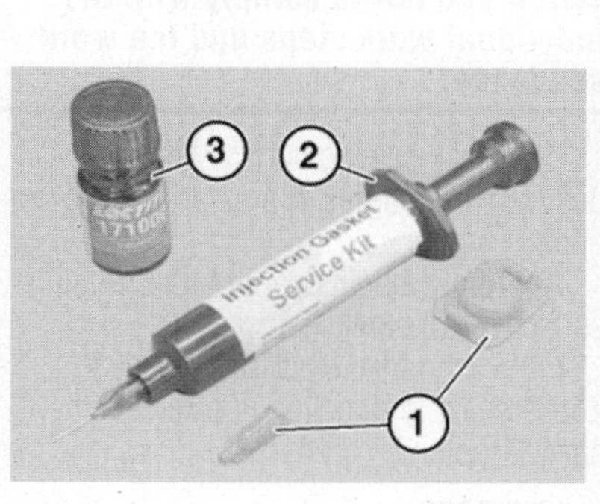

22205_BMWC_G0149

Fig. 135 Screw caps (1), injector (2) and Loctite® primer, manufacturer's number 171000 (3)

22205_BMWC_G0151

Fig. 137 Draw in crankshaft seal with special tool 11 9 231 in conjunction with special tool 11 9 233 until flush

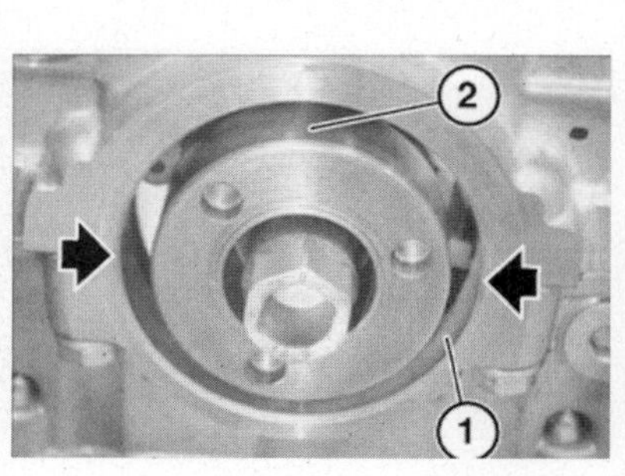

22205_BMWC_G0148

Fig. 134 Clean sealing surface (1) and apply a light coat of oil to running surface (2)

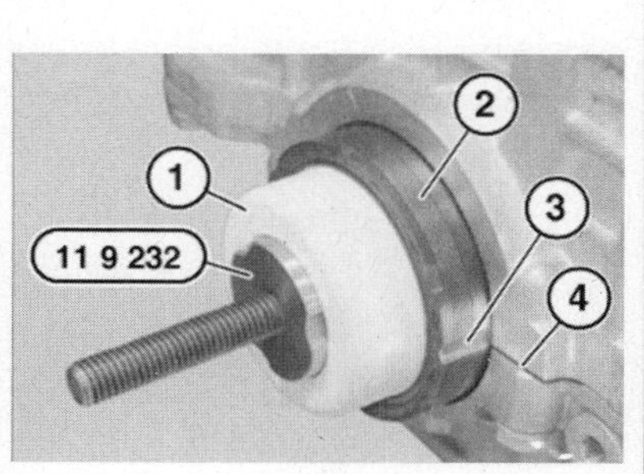

22205_BMWC_G0150

Fig. 136 Support sleeve (1), housing partition (4), grooves (3) and crankshaft seal (2)

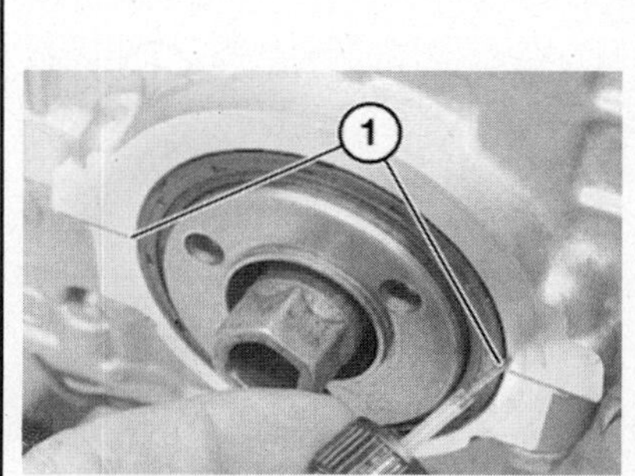

22205_BMWC_G0152

Fig. 138 Insert brush as far as possible into grooves (1) on crankshaft seal in order to coat housing partition on engine block

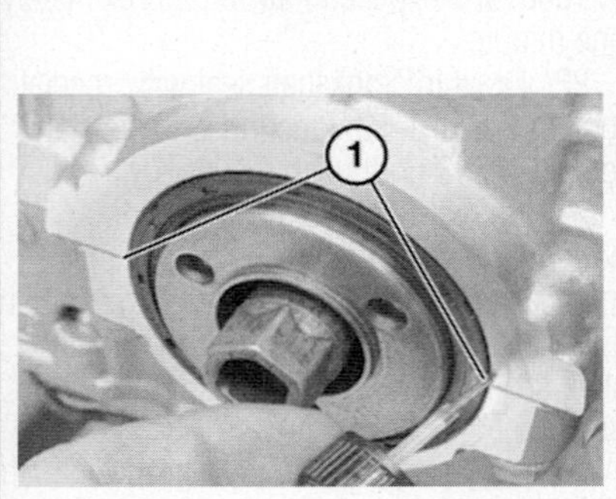

Fig. 139 Using injector (2), fill both grooves (3) flush with Loctite® sealing compound, manufacturer's number 128357

N55 Engine

See Figures 141 through 146.

1. Remove vibration absorber.
2. If the central bolt is released, the sprockets of the timing chain and the oil pump will no longer be non-positively connected to the crankshaft. Intake and exhaust camshafts can turn in relation to crankshaft.

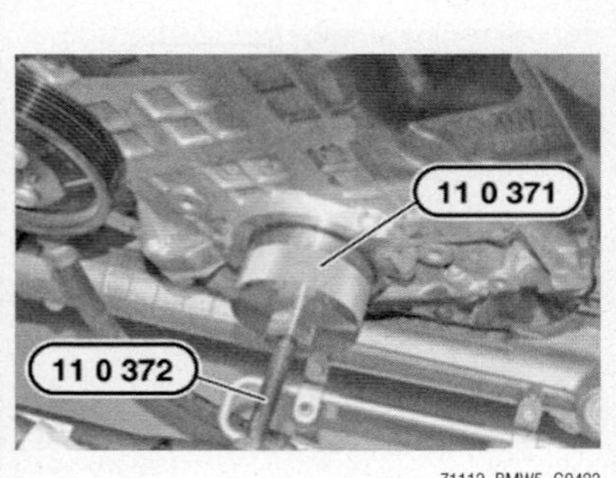

Fig. 140 Installing special tools and releasing crankshaft seal from housing

3. Screw special tool 11 0 371 to 59 ft. lbs. (80 Nm) into crankshaft seal.
4. Screw in spindle 11 0 372.
5. Release crankshaft seal from housing.
6. Repeat the operation several times if necessary.
7. Carefully saw open crankshaft seal (1) at cutting line (2).
8. Remove crankshaft seal (1) from special tool 11 0 371.

To install:

⁂ WARNING

The following text describes installation and sealing between the engine block and crankshaft seal.

⁂ WARNING

The engine block will not be leak proof at the outside of the crankshaft seal if you fail to comply with the individual work steps and the work sequence.

9. Clean sealing surface (1) and degrease thoroughly in area of housing partition.
10. Apply a light coat of oil to running surface (2) of crankshaft seal.
11. Push radial shaft seal (1) 11 9 235carefully in direction of arrow on the special tool.

➡11 9 235Special tool can only be fastened with 2 opposite bolts.

12. Determine hole pattern on special tool.

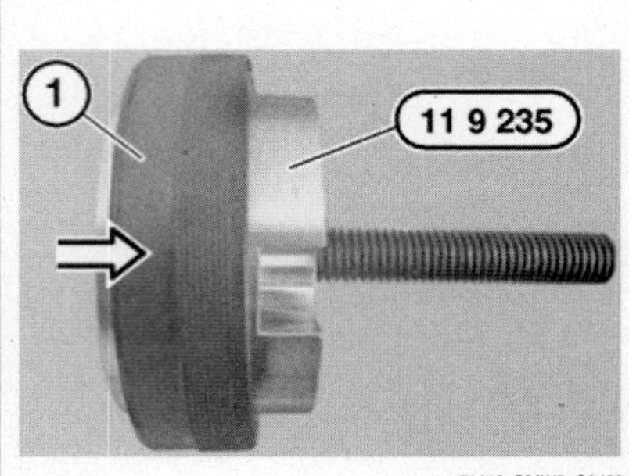

Fig. 143 Pushing radial shaft seal (1) 11 9 235carefully in direction of arrow on the special tool

13. Screw special tool 11 9 235 with special tool 11 9 234 on crankshaft.
14. Align groove (2) of radial shaft seal (1) centered to the housing partition (3).

⁂ WARNING

After installation, the grooves must be filled with sealing compound.

15. Draw in radial shaft seal with special tool 11 9 231 in conjunction with special tool 11 9 233 until flush.

➡Use primer 1.3 and liquid seal 1.4.

16. Prepare liquid sealing compound in special tool 11 4 370.
17. Remove sealing caps from injector.
18. Screw on metering needle.
19. Insert piston for pressing out.
20. Syringe contains the sealing compound Loctite®, manufacturer's number 128357.

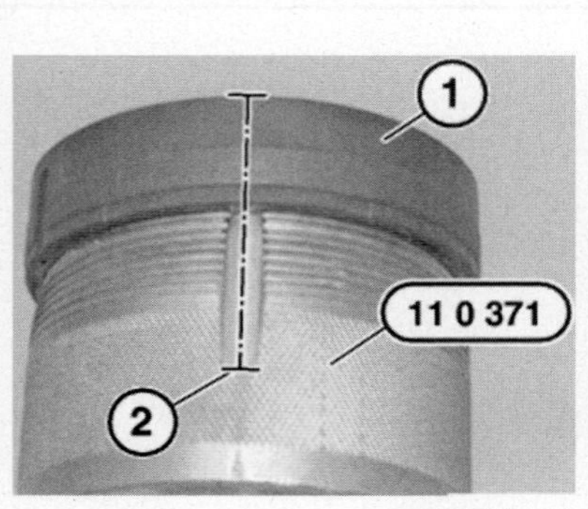

Fig. 141 Sawing open crankshaft seal (1) at cutting line (2)

Fig. 142 Cleaning sealing surface (1) and applying oil to running surface (2) of crankshaft seal

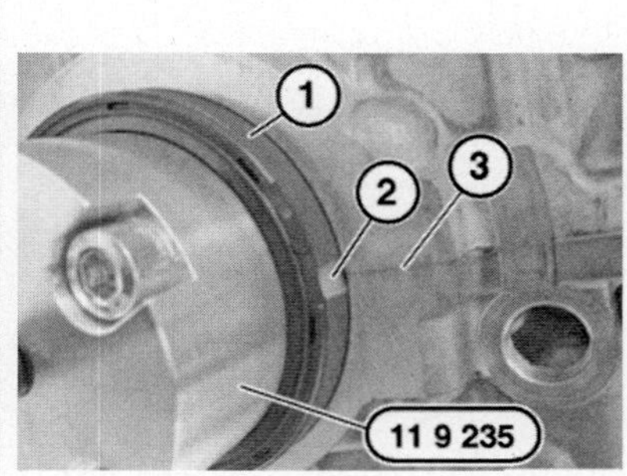

Fig. 144 Aligning groove (2) of radial shaft seal (1) centered to the housing partition (3)

21. Bottle contains the primer Loctite®, manufacturer's number 171000.

22. Before filling with sealing compound:

a. Moisten brush with Loctite® primer, manufacturer's number 171000. Insert brush as far as possible into grooves (1) on crankshaft seal in order to coat housing partition on engine block.

23. Using syringe (2), fill both grooves (3) flush with Loctite® sealing compound, manufacturer's number 128357.

➡Loctite® primer, manufacturer's number 171000, binds the Loctite® sealing compound, manufacturer's number 128357, and prevents leakage.

24. Coat surface of sealing compound in both grooves (1) with Loctite® primer, manufacturer's number 171000.

25. Assemble engine.

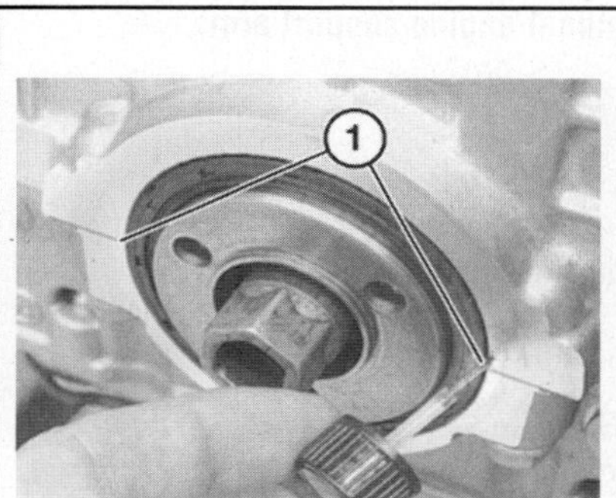

Fig. 145 Inserting brush into grooves (1) on crankshaft

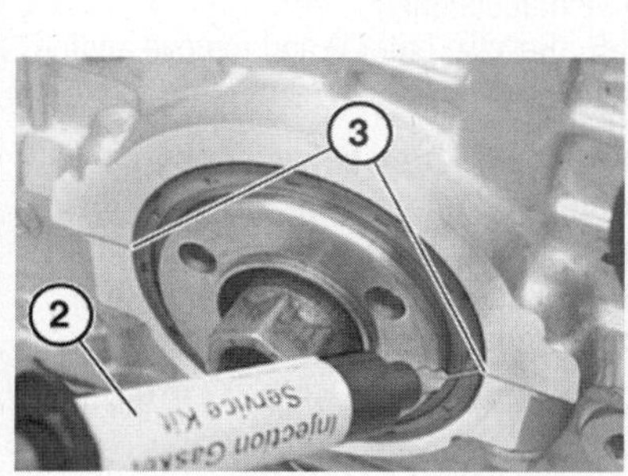

Fig. 146 Using syringe (2) to fill both grooves (3) with Loctite®

ENGINE COVER

REMOVAL & INSTALLATION

N63 Engine

See Figures 147 through 149.

1. Raise engine cover (1) at the four points (see arrows) and in upward direction.
2. Check lock (1) for damage.
3. Check lock (2) for damage.
4. Apply a light coating of anti-seize agent to take-ups (1).

To install:

5. To install, reverse the removal procedure.

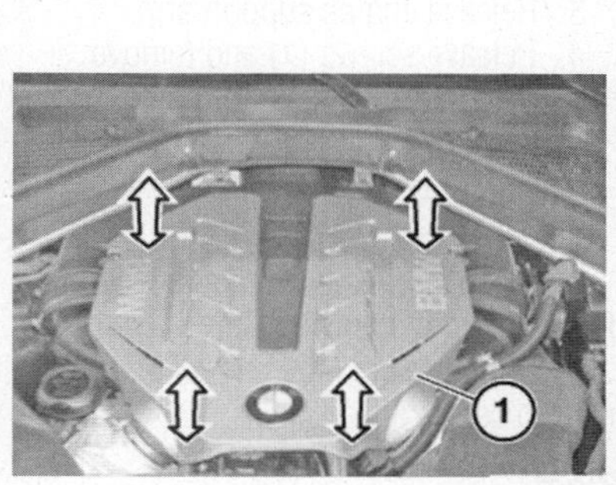

Fig. 147 Raising engine cover (1) at the four points (see arrows) and in upward direction

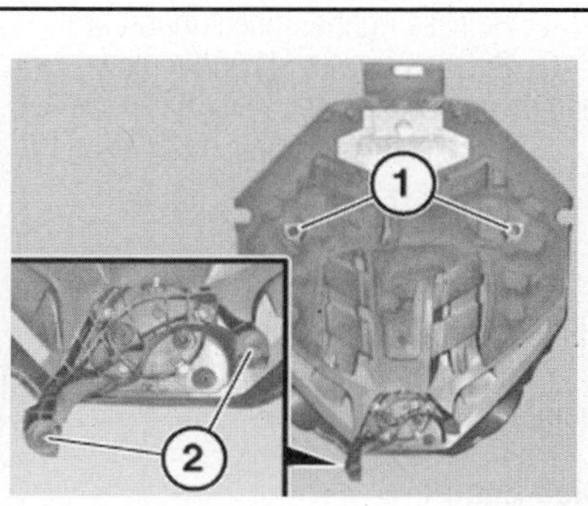

Fig. 148 Checking locks (1 and 2) for damage

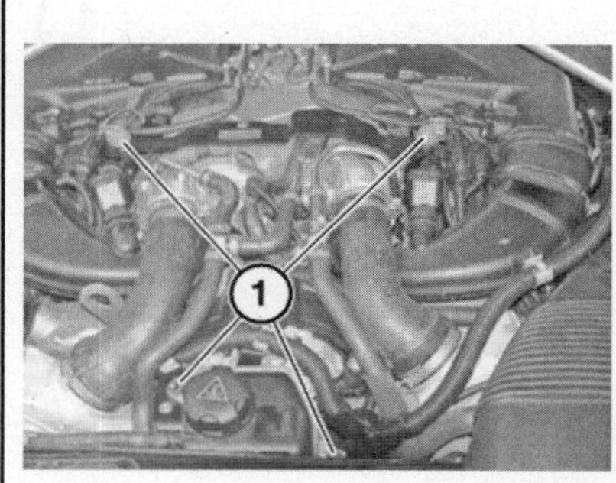

Fig. 149 Appling a light coating of anti-seize agent to take-ups (1)

ENGINE MOUNTS

REMOVAL & INSTALLATION

N20 Engine

Left

See Figures 150 and 151.

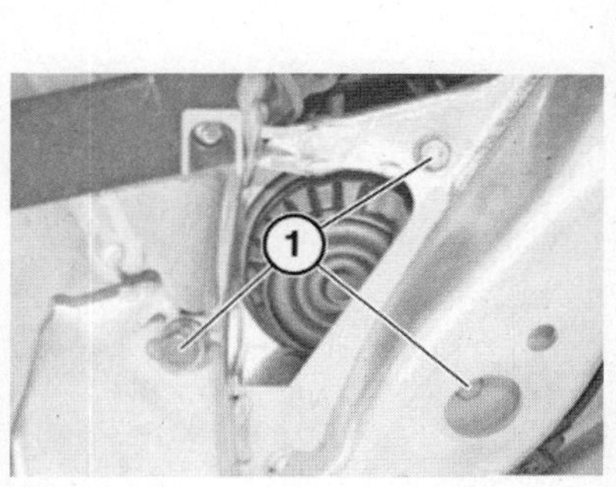

Fig. 150 Releasing screws (1) and removing engine mount—left

1. Secure engine in installation position.
2. Remove left charge air duct.
3. Remove rear underbody protection.
4. Release engine support arm.
5. Release screws (1) and remove engine mount.
   a. Tightening torque: 14 ft. lbs. (19 Nm).

To install:

6. To install, reverse the removal procedure noting the following.
7. Rubber part (1) of engine mount must point to center of vehicle.

Right

See Figures 151 through 152

1. Secure engine in installation position.
2. Partially release steering cover.
3. Remove rear underbody protection.
4. Release engine support arm.
5. Release screws (1) and remove engine mount.

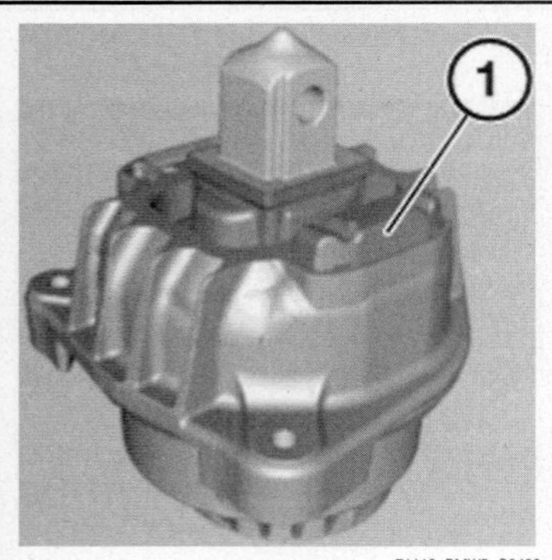

Fig. 151 Verifying rubber part (1) of engine mount is pointing to center of vehicle

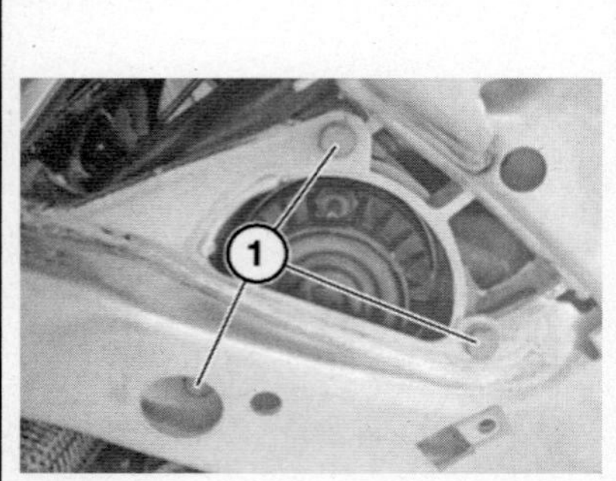

Fig. 152 Releasing screws (1) and removing engine mount—right

a. Tightening torque: 14 ft. lbs. (19 Nm).

To install:

6. To install, reverse the removal procedure noting the following.
7. Rubber part (1) of engine mount must point to center of vehicle.

N52 Engine

Left

See Figures 150 and 151.

1. Remove rear underbody protection.
2. Release engine support arm.
3. Release screws (1) and remove engine mount.
   a. Tightening torque: 14 ft. lbs. (19 Nm).

To install:

4. To install, reverse the removal procedure noting the following.
5. Rubber part (1) of engine mount must point to center of vehicle.

Right

See Figures 151 and 152.

1. Remove rear underbody protection.
2. Remove right cover.
3. Release right engine support arm.
4. Release screws (1) and remove engine mount.
   a. Tightening torque: 14 ft. lbs. (19 Nm).

To install:

5. To install, reverse the removal procedure noting the following.
6. Rubber part (1) of engine mount must point to center of vehicle.

N55 Engine

Left

See Figures 150 and 151.

1. Secure engine in installation position.
2. Remove rear underbody protection.
3. Release engine support arm.
4. Release screws (1) and remove engine mount.
   a. Tightening torque: 14 ft. lbs. (19 Nm).

To install:

5. To install, reverse the removal procedure noting the following.
6. Rubber part (1) of engine mount must point to center of vehicle.

Right

See Figures 151 and 152.

1. Secure engine in installation position.
2. Remove rear underbody protection.
3. Remove right cover.
4. Release right engine support arm.
5. Release screws (1) and remove engine mount.
   a. Tightening torque: 14 ft. lbs. (19 Nm).

To install:

6. To install, reverse the removal procedure noting the following.
7. Rubber part (1) of engine mount must point to center of vehicle.

N63 Engine

Left

See Figures 151 and 153.

1. Secure engine in installation position.
2. Lower front axle support.

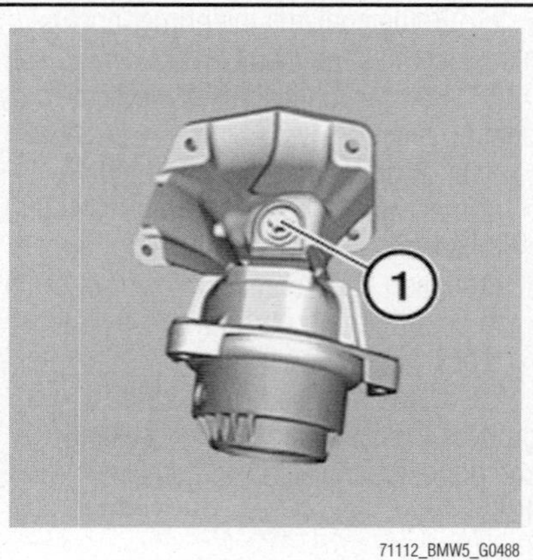

Fig. 153 Releasing bolt (1) and removing engine mount—left

3. Release bolt (1) and remove engine mount.

➡To ensure play between engine mount and engine support arm, lower the engine completely before tightening the screw connection (engine mount/engine support arm).

   a. Tightening torque: 74 ft. lbs. (100 Nm).

To install:

4. To install, reverse the removal procedure noting the following.
5. Rubber part (1) of engine mount must point to center of vehicle.

Right

See Figure 151.

1. Secure engine in installation position.
2. Remove rear underbody protection.
3. Release engine support arm (left-hand drive models only).
4. Lower front axle support (right-hand drive models only).
5. Release bolt (1) and remove engine mount.

➡To ensure play between engine mount and engine support arm, lower the engine completely before tightening the screw connection (engine mount/engine support arm).

   a. Tightening torque: 74 ft. lbs. (100 Nm).

To install:

6. To install, reverse the removal procedure noting the following.
7. Rubber part (1) of engine mount must point to center of vehicle.

ENGINE OIL & FILTER

OIL LEVEL CHECK

N20 Engine

1. Park vehicle on a horizontal surface.
2. Allow engine to run at operating temperature for three minutes with increased engine speed (approx. 1100 rpm).
3. Read off oil level in instrument cluster or on control display.
4. Top up engine oil if necessary.

N52 Engine

1. Before servicing the vehicle, refer to the precautions.
2. Park vehicle on a horizontal surface.
3. Start engine and run at idle until an engine oil temperature 158° F (70 ° C) is reached.
4. Pressing the BC button for more than 3 seconds results in the oil level been determined again.
5. If necessary, perform odometer reset.
6. Top up engine oil if necessary.

N55 Engine

1. Park vehicle on a horizontal surface.
2. Allow engine to run at operating temperature for three minutes with increased engine speed (approx. 1100 rpm).
3. Read off engine oil level in instrument panel or on Control Display.
4. Top up engine oil if necessary.

N63 Engine

1. Park vehicle on a horizontal surface.
2. Allow engine to run at operating temperature for three minutes with increased engine speed (approx. 1100 rpm).
3. Read off engine oil level in instrument panel or on Control Display.
4. Top up engine oil if necessary.

OIL & FILTER CHANGE

N20 Engine

See Figures 154 through 156.

WARNING

Carry out the engine oil service only when the engine is at operating temperature.

WARNING

Observe the exact engine oil filling capacity.

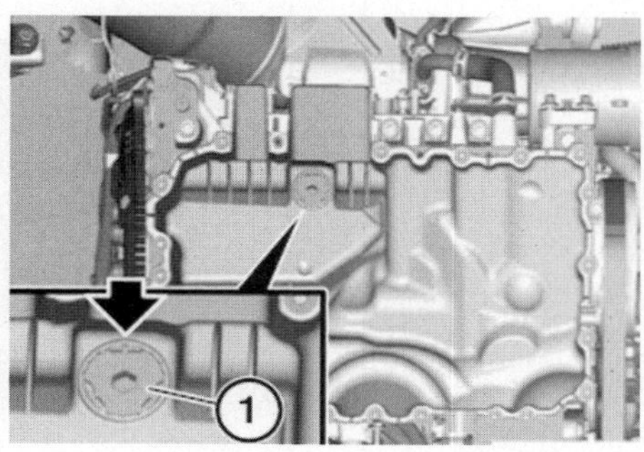

Fig. 154 Locating drain plug (1)

WARNING

Overfilling the engine with engine oil will result in engine damage.

WARNING

Checking and drip-off times (at least 10 minutes) must be observed.

WARNING

Protect belt drive against dirt.

WARNING

Cover with suitable materials.

1. Release oil filter cover with special tool 11 9 240.
   a. Tightening torque: 18 ft. lbs. (25 Nm).

➡Engine oil flows out of the oil filter housing and back into the oil sump.

Rear-wheel drive (plastic oil pan):

2. Open oil drain plug (1) on oil sump.
3. Drain engine oil.

➡Replace oil drain plug.

   a. Tightening torque: 71 inch lbs. (8 Nm).

4. If prescribed torque has been reached and oil drain plug (1) still does not latch, oil drain plug (1) must be positioned such that a latch mechanism is aligned (see arrow).
5. If applicable, oil drain plug (1) may need to be rotated back again (released).

Four-wheel drive (aluminum oil pan):

6. Open oil drain plug (1) of oil sump and drain engine oil.
7. Replace sealing ring.
   a. Tightening torque: 18 ft. lbs. (25 Nm).

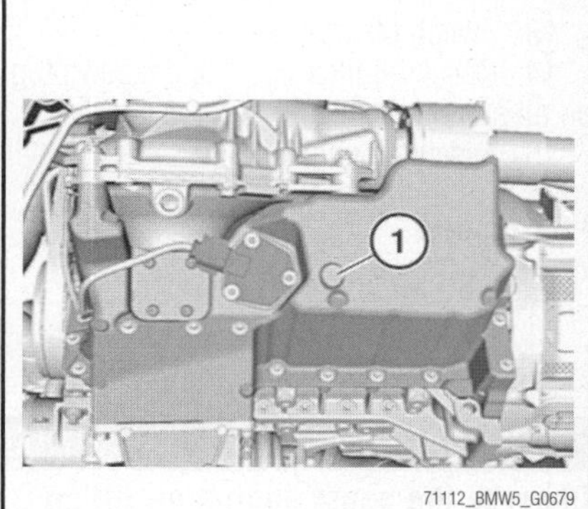

Fig. 155 Locating drain plug (1)

8. Remove and insert oil filter element (1) in direction of arrow.
9. Replace oil filter element (2) and sealing rings (1).

➡Moisten sealing rings (1) with engine oil.

10. Secure oil filter cover with special tool 11 9 240.
    a. Tightening torque: 18 ft. lbs. (25 Nm).

➡Pour in engine oil.

11. Start engine and run at idle speed.
12. Monitor control messages in instrument cluster or Check-Control messages.

WARNING

Check-Control message (red oil can) is only displayed if oil pressure drops below minimum permissible oil pressure for longer than approx. 8 seconds.

Fig. 156 Replacing oil filter element (2) and sealing rings (1)

13. Switch off engine
14. Check oil filter cover and screw plug on oil sump for leaks.
15. Assemble engine.

N52 Engine

See Figures 157 through 159.

1. Before servicing the vehicle, refer to the precautions.

⁂ WARNING

Observe the exact engine oil filling capacity. Overfilling the engine with engine oil will result in engine damage.

2. Drive the vehicle to bring the engine to normal operating temperature.
3. Release oil filter cap with special tool 11 9 240.

➡Engine oil flows out of the oil filter housing and back into the oil sump.

Fig. 157 Release oil filter cap with special tool 11 9 240

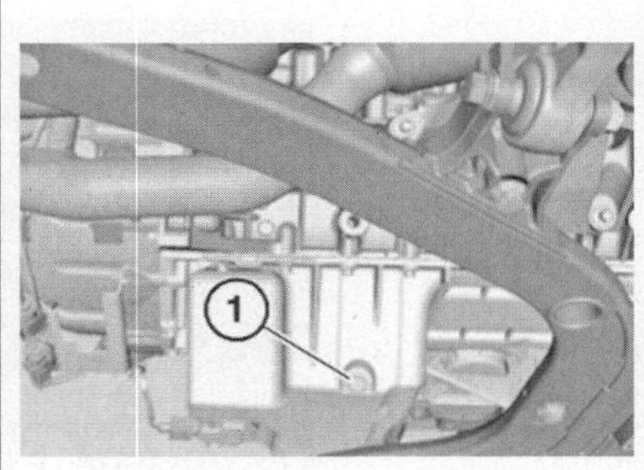

Fig. 158 Remove screw plug (1) from oil sump and drain engine oil

4. Raise and support the vehicle.
5. Unclip service opening on underbody protection.
6. Remove screw plug from oil sump and drain engine oil.
7. Replace screw plug using a new sealing ring and tighten to 19 ft. lbs. (25 Nm).
8. Remove oil filter element.

To install:

9. Replace oil filter element and sealing rings. Moisten sealing rings with engine oil.
10. Secure oil filter cap with special tool 11 9 240 and tighten to 19 ft. lbs. (25 Nm).
11. Pour in engine oil.
12. Start engine and run at idle until oil pressure warning lamp goes out.
13. Turn off engine.
14. Wait approximately 5 minutes and check engine oil level.
15. Top up engine oil if necessary.
16. Check oil filter cap and screw plug on oil sump for leaks.

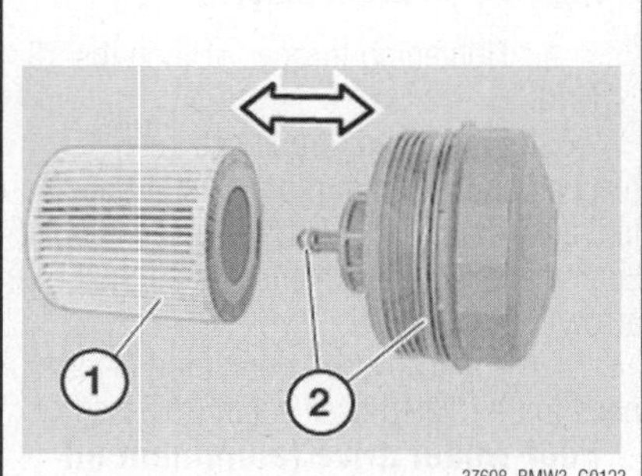

Fig. 159 Remove and insert oil filter element (1) in direction of arrow. Replace sealing rings (2) and moisten with engine oil

N55 Engine

See Figures 160 through 162.

⁂ WARNING

Carry out the engine oil service only when the engine is at operating temperature.

⁂ WARNING

Observe the exact engine oil filling capacity.

⁂ WARNING

Overfilling the engine with engine oil will result in engine damage.

⁂ WARNING

Checking and drip-off times (at least 10 minutes) must be observed.

1. Protect belt drive against dirt.
2. Cover with suitable materials.
3. Release oil filter cover with special tool 11 9 240.
   a. Tightening torque: 18 ft. lbs. (25 Nm).

➡Engine oil flows out of the oil filter housing and back into the oil sump.

Rear wheel drive:

4. Open oil drain plug (1) on oil sump.
5. Drain engine oil.

➡Replace sealing ring.

   a. Tightening torque: 18 ft. lbs. (25 Nm).

Four-wheel drive:

6. Open oil drain plug (1) of oil sump and drain engine oil.

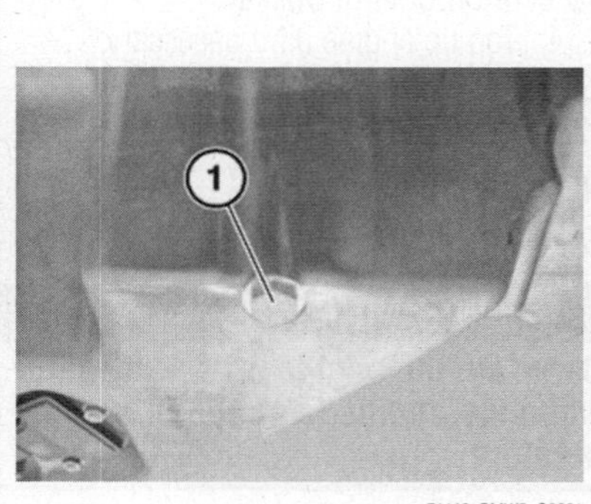

Fig. 160 Locating drain plug (1)

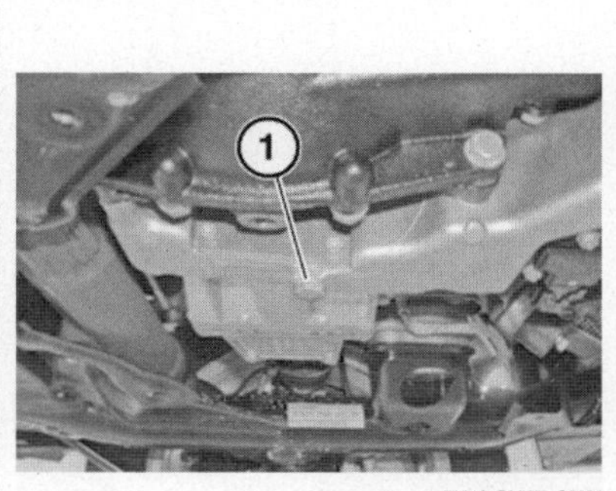

Fig. 161 Locating drain plug (1)

➡**Replace sealing ring.**

a. Tightening torque: 18 ft. lbs. (25 Nm).

7. Remove and insert oil filter element (1) in direction of arrow.

➡**Replace oil filter element (1) and sealing ring (2).**

8. Replace gasket (3) and renew if necessary.

➡**Coat sealing rings (2,3) with engine oil.**

9. Secure oil filter cover with special tool 11 9 240.

a. Tightening torque: 18 ft. lbs. (25 Nm).

➡**Pour in engine oil.**

10. Start engine and run at idle until oil pressure indicator light goes out.

11. Switch off engine

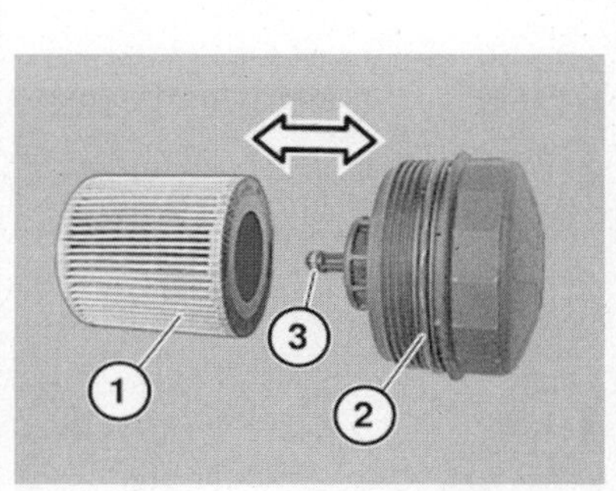

Fig. 162 Removing oil filter element (1) in direction of arrow and replacing filter element, sealing ring (2) and gasket (3)

12. Check oil filter cover and screw plug on oil sump for leaks.

13. Assemble engine.

N63 Engine

See Figures 163 through 166.

1. Release screw (4) on underbody paneling.

2. Expose sensor opening (2) for oil filter cover with aid of designated holes (3).

3. Release screw (5) on underbody paneling.

4. Expose sensor opening (1) for oil sump screw plug with aid of designated holes (3).

➡**For purposes of clarity, the graphic shows the underbody paneling and underbody protection removed.**

5. Release screw plug (1) of oil filter cover (2) with a suitable tool and drain engine oil.

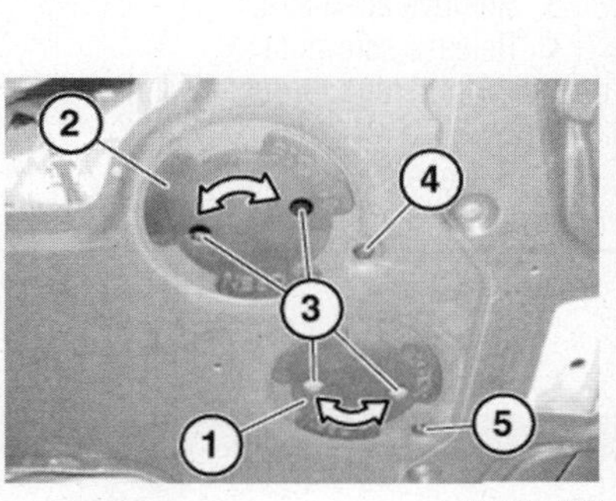

Fig. 163 Releasing screws (4, 5), exposing sensor opening (2) with aid of designated holes (3) and exposing sensor opening (1) for oil pan screw plug

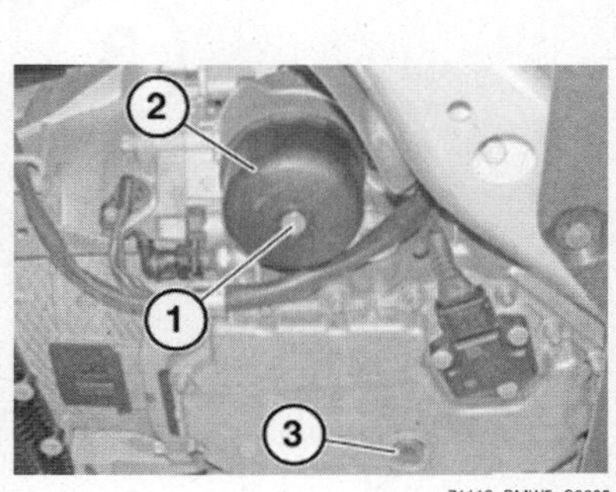

Fig. 164 Releasing screw plug (1) of oil filter cover (2) and removing screw plug (3) from oil pan

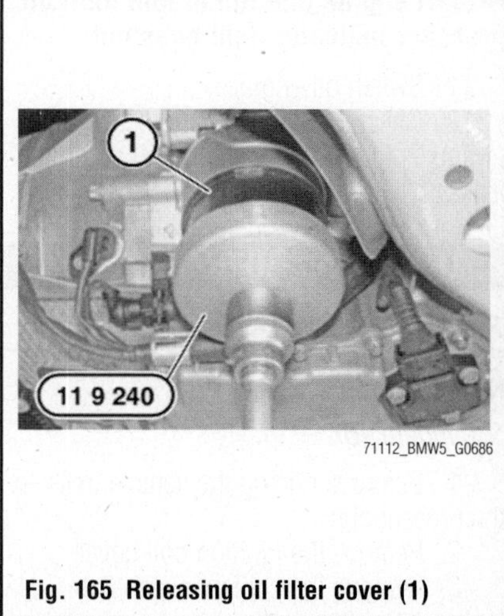

Fig. 165 Releasing oil filter cover (1)

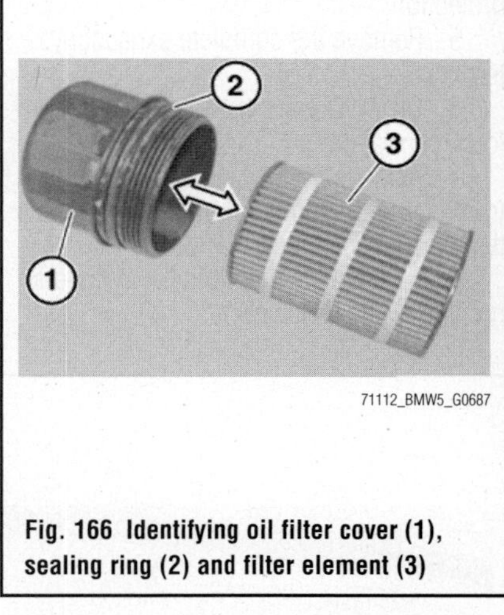

Fig. 166 Identifying oil filter cover (1), sealing ring (2) and filter element (3)

a. Tightening torque: 20 ft. lbs. (27 Nm).

6. Remove screw plug (3) from oil sump and drain engine oil.

a. Tightening torque: 30 ft. lbs. (40 Nm).

➡**Replace sealing rings.**

7. Release oil filter cover (1) with special tool 11 9 240.

a. Tightening torque: 22 ft. lbs. (30 Nm) - 180° + 30 ft. lbs. (40 Nm).

8. Remove and insert oil filter element (3) in direction of arrow.

➡**Oil filter element (3) must snap audibly into oil filter cover (1).**

➡**Replace oil filter element (3) and sealing ring (2).**

➡**Moisten sealing ring (2) with engine oil.**

9. Assemble engine.

10. Pour in engine oil.

➡**Start engine and run at idle until oil pressure indicator light goes out.**

11. Switch off engine
12. Check oil filter cap and screw plugs (1 and 2) for oil filter cap and oil sump for leaks.

EXHAUST MANIFOLD

REMOVAL & INSTALLATION

N52 Engine

See Figure 167.

1. Before servicing the vehicle, refer to the precautions.
2. Remove the ignition coil cover.
3. Remove the coolant expansion tank.
4. Remove the underbody protection.
5. Remove the complete exhaust system.
6. On AWD vehicles, remove the reinforcement plate.
7. Remove the oxygen sensor plug from cylinders number 4 and 6 and remove the exhaust assembly.
8. Remove the manifold for cylinders number 1 and 3 downwards.
9. Remove the manifold for cylinders number 4 and 6 downwards.

To install:

10. Remove the old gasket from the cylinder head and exhaust manifold and replace the gasket. The gasket beads face the exhaust manifolds.
11. Installation is the reverse of removal.
12. Coat screw connections with CRC copper paste.
13. Install new nuts and tighten the exhaust manifolds to 15 ft. lbs. (20 Nm).

N63 Engine

Left

See Figures 168 through 172.

⁂ CAUTION

Only perform this repair work on an engine that has cooled down.

1. Remove left turbocharger.
2. Remove right turbocharger.
3. Remove alternator.
4. Release screws (1).
   a. Tightening torque: 17 ft. lbs. (23 Nm).
5. Release screws (1).

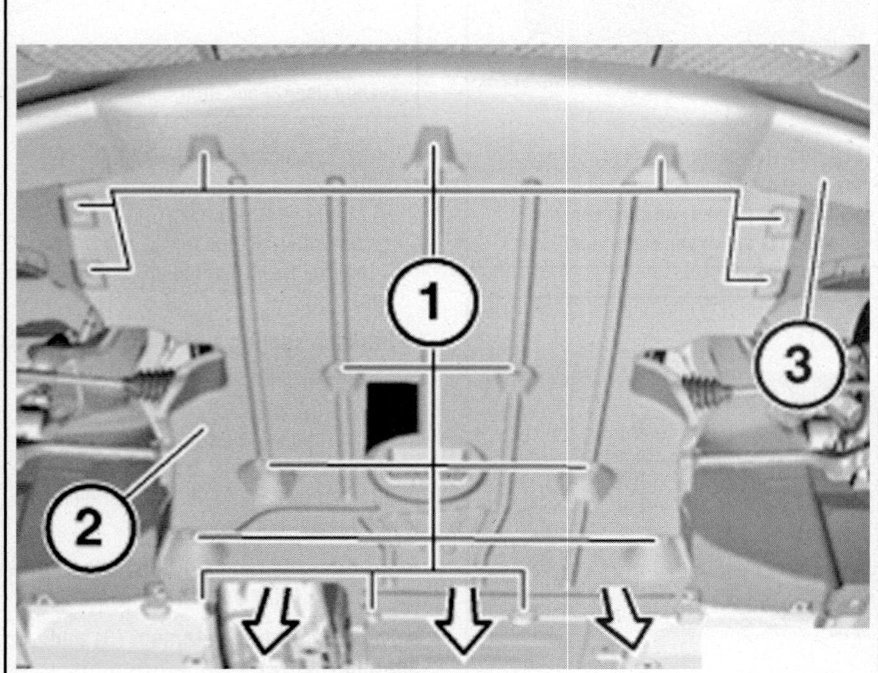

Fig. 167 Release screws (1) and pull underbody protection (2) forward under bumper trim (3)

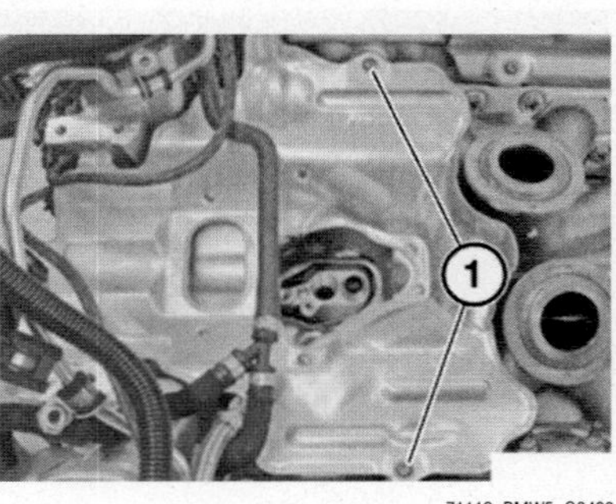

Fig. 168 Releasing screws (1)

   a. Tightening torque: 17 ft. lbs. (23 Nm).
6. Remove heat shield (2).
7. Release screws (1).
   a. Tightening torque: 17 ft. lbs. (23 Nm).
8. Remove heat shield (2) at rear left.
9. Unscrew nuts.
10. Replace nuts.
   a. Tightening torque: 7 ft. lbs. (10 Nm).
11. Remove exhaust manifold (1).

➡**When installing, replace gasket (2).**

12. Reinstall securing strip.

To install:

13. To install, reverse the removal procedure noting the following.
14. Replace gaskets (1).
15. Seal beads faces the exhaust manifold.
16. Coat threads with copper paste.

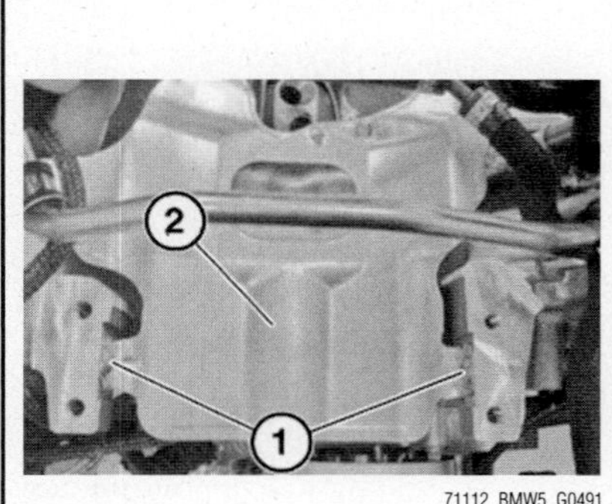

Fig. 169 Releasing screws (1) and removing heat shield (2)

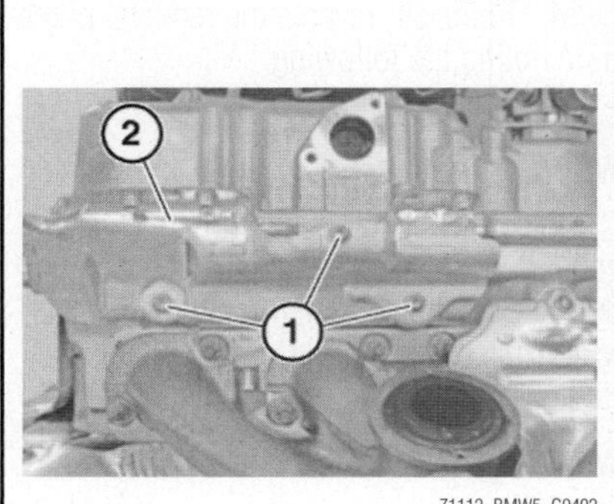

Fig. 170 Releasing screws (1) and removing heat shield (2) at rear left

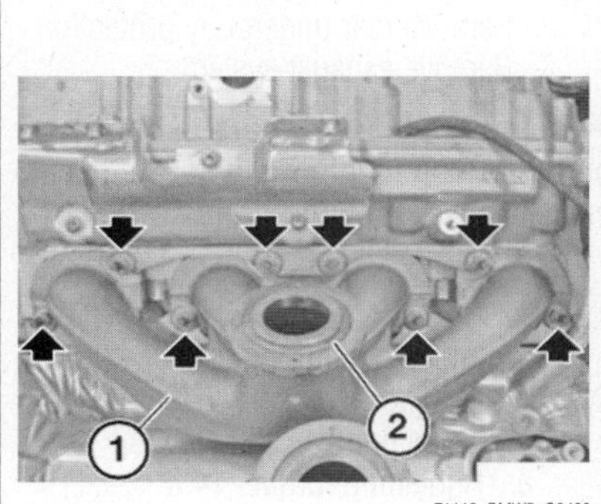

Fig. 171 Removing exhaust manifold (1) and replacing gasket (2)

17. Check exhaust system for leak tightness.

Right

See Figures 173 through 177.

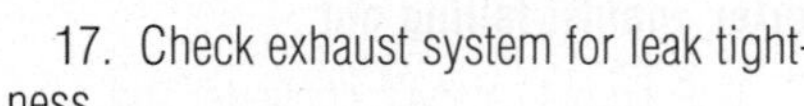

CAUTION

Only perform this repair work on an engine that has cooled down.

1. Remove left turbocharger.
2. Remove right turbocharger.
3. Remove alternator.
4. Release screws (1).
   a. Tightening torque: 17 ft. lbs. (23 Nm).
5. Release screws (1).
   a. Tightening torque: 17 ft. lbs. (23 Nm).
6. Remove heat shield (2).
7. Release screws (1).
   a. Tightening torque: 17 ft. lbs. (23 Nm).

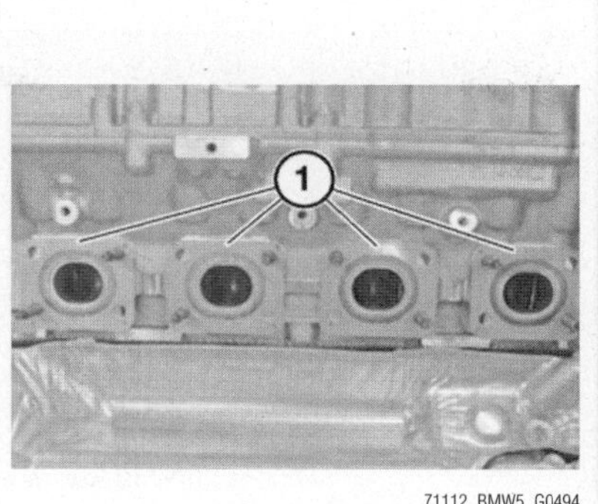

Fig. 172 Replacing gaskets (1)

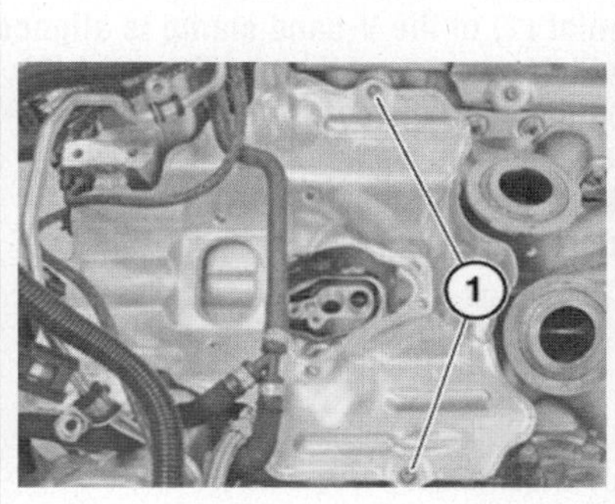

Fig. 173 Releasing screws (1)

8. Remove heat shield (2) at rear right.
9. Unscrew nuts.
10. Replace nuts.
    a. Tightening torque 18 31 3AZ.

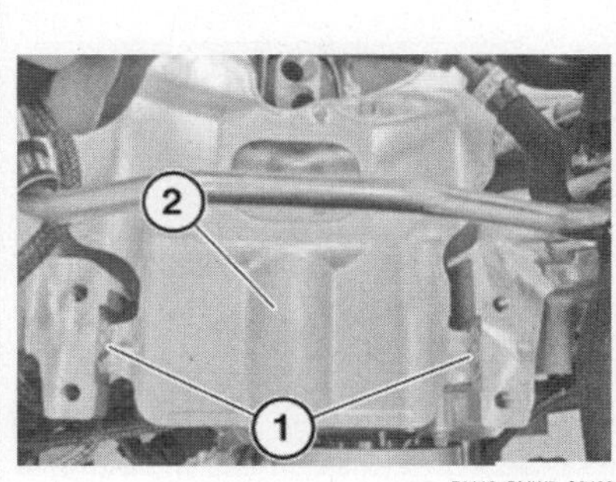

Fig. 174 Releasing screws (1) and removing heat shield (2)

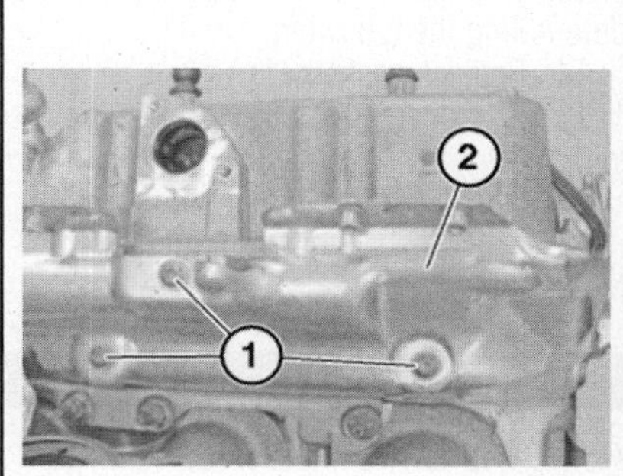

Fig. 175 Releasing screws (1) and removing heat shield (2) at rear right

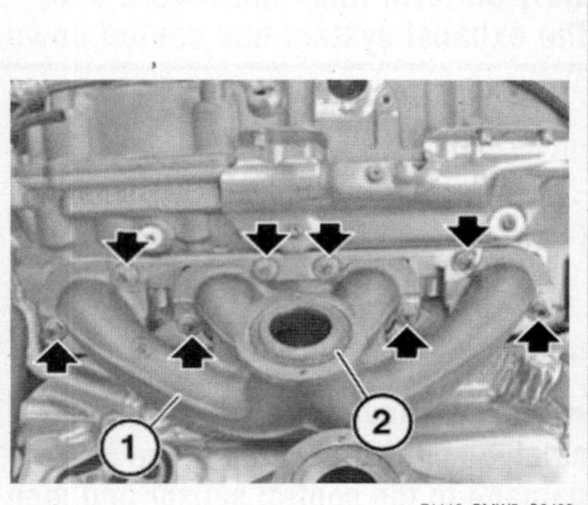

Fig. 176 Removing exhaust manifold (1) and replacing gasket (2)

11. Remove exhaust manifold (1).

➡**Replace gasket (2).**

12. Reinstall securing strip.

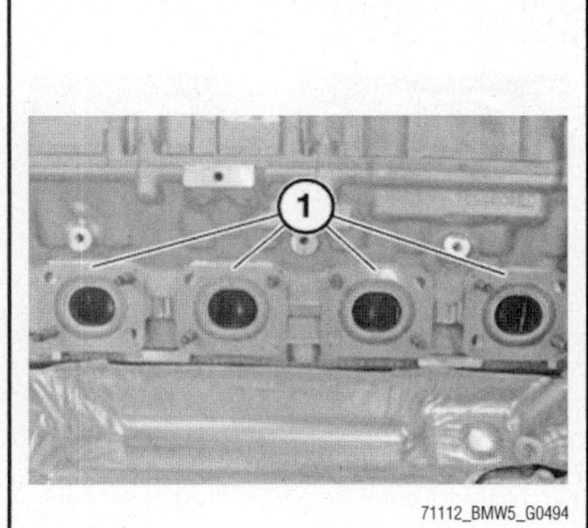

Fig. 177 Replacing gaskets (1)

To install:

13. To install, reverse the removal procedure noting the following.
14. Replace gaskets (1).
15. Seal beads faces the exhaust manifold.
16. Coat threads with copper paste.
17. Check exhaust system for leak tightness.

EXHAUST SYSTEM

REMOVAL & INSTALLATION

Catalytic Converter

N20 Engine

See Figures 178 through 180.

CAUTION

Only perform this repair work after the exhaust system has cooled down.

1. Remove front underbody protection.
2. Remove rear underbody protection.
3. Remove exhaust system.
4. Four-wheel drive vehicles only, remove stiffening plate

➡When removing and installing the catalytic converter there is the risk of damage to the control sensor and monitoring sensor.

5. Remove the control sensor.
6. Remove monitoring sensor.
7. Release clamp (1). The clamp must be renewed every time it is removed.
    a. Tightening torque 18 31 2AZ.

➡When installing, clean sealing surface. Renew clamp and seal.

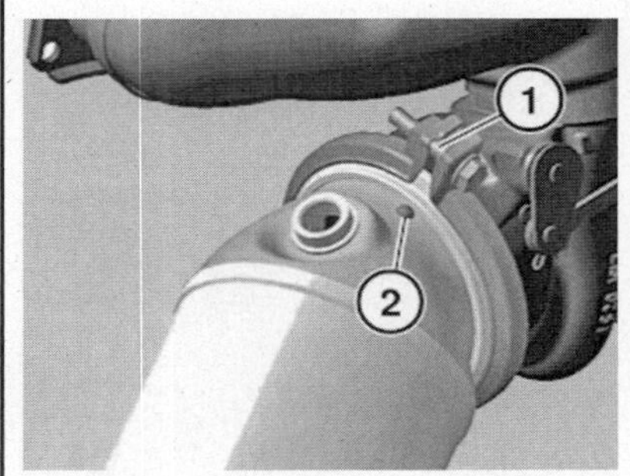

Fig. 179 Checking separation point (1) of V-band clamp is aligned with center of welding spot (2)

➡When installing the catalytic converter make sure that the separation point (1) of the V-band clamp is aligned with the center of the welding spot (2) on the catalytic converter. This guarantees that the wastegate valve lever does not collide with the V-band clamp.

8. Release nuts (1).
    a. Tightening torque: 21 ft. lbs. (28 Nm).
9. Pull off rubber mounts from the catalytic converter.
10. Unfasten screws (2).
    a. Tightening torque: 41 ft. lbs. (56 Nm).
11. Unscrew nuts (3).
    a. Tightening torque: 21 ft. lbs. (28 Nm).
12. Remove holder for catalytic converter.
13. Pull out catalytic converter towards the bottom and remove.

To install:

14. To install, reverse the removal procedure noting the following.
15. Check exhaust system for leaks.

N52 Engine

On the N52 engine the primary catalytic converters are an integral part of the exhaust manifolds. Refer to engine mechanical, exhaust manifold, removal & installation.

N55 Engine

See Figures 181 and 182.

CAUTION

Only perform this repair work after the exhaust system has cooled down.

1. Remove front underbody protection.
2. Remove rear underbody protection.
3. Remove exhaust system.

➡The oxygen sensors are in danger of being damaged when the catalytic converters are removed and installed.

4. Remove control sensor, cylinders 1 to 3.
5. Remove monitoring sensor from cylinders 1 to 3.
6. Release nuts (1) and (2).
    a. Tightening torque: 14 ft. lbs. (19 Nm).
7. Release clamp (1). The clamp must be renewed every time it is removed.
    a. Tightening torque 18 31 2AZ.

➡In so doing, secure catalytic converter against falling out.

8. Feed out catalytic converter and remove.

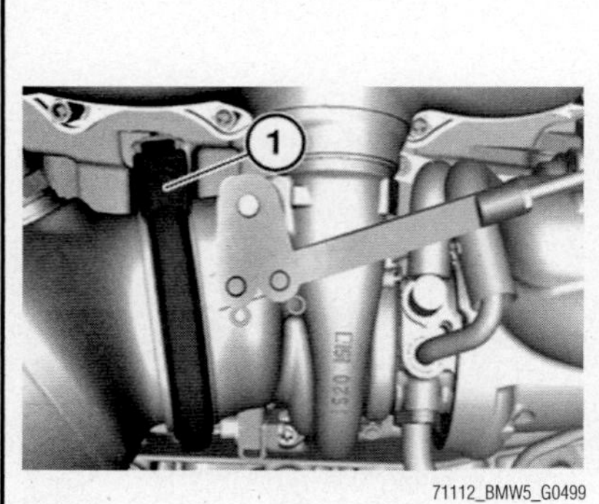

Fig. 178 Releasing clamp (1)

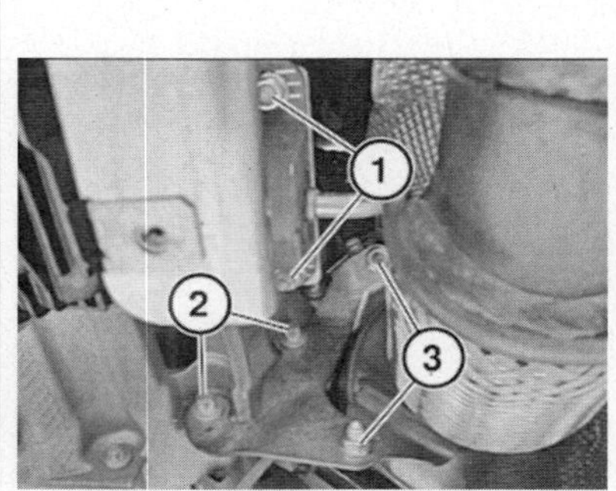

Fig. 180 Releasing nuts (1), unfastening screws (2) and unscrewing nuts (3)

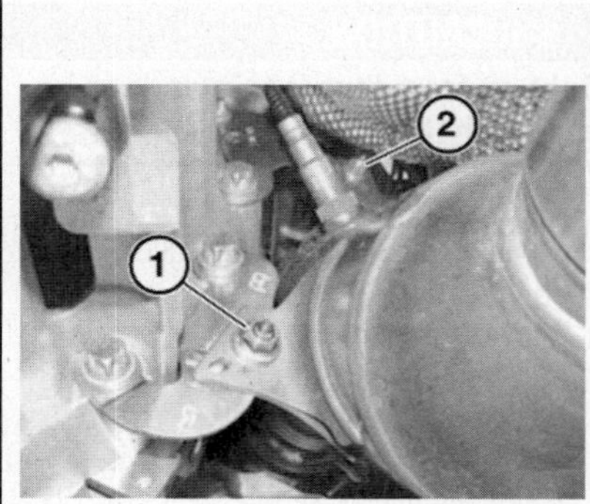

Fig. 181 Releasing nuts (1 and 2)

Fig. 182 Releasing clamp (1) and removing catalytic converter

➡When installing, clean sealing surface. Renew clamp and seal.

To install:

9. To install, reverse the removal procedure noting the following.
10. Check exhaust system for leaks.

N63 Engine

See Figures 183 through 195.

⁂ CAUTION

Only perform this repair work on an engine that has cooled down.

1. Remove acoustic cover.
2. Remove both intake silencer housings.
3. Remove exhaust system.
4. Remove both control sensors.
5. Remove both monitoring sensors.
6. Picture shows the left side, carry out the operation for the right side in an identical way.
7. Release screws (1).
8. Remove cable clips on left and right.
9. Remove rubber mounts (1) and release screws underneath.
   a. Tightening torque: 7 ft. lbs. (10 Nm).
10. Remove cable clip (2).
11. Remove the heat shield (3) at top.
12. Remove heat shield (1) at rear left and right.

➡This is described further below in the instructions.

13. Release screws (2) on catalytic converter.
   a. Tightening torque: 17 ft. lbs. (21 Nm).
14. Loosen the clamps (3) from the catalytic converter.
15. Replace clamps (3).

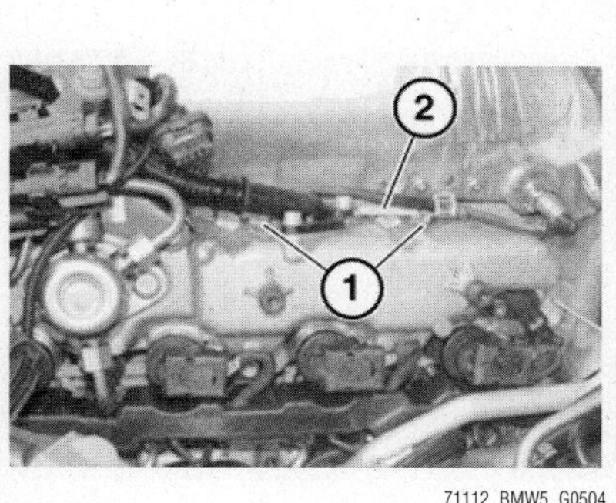

Fig. 183 Releasing screws (1)

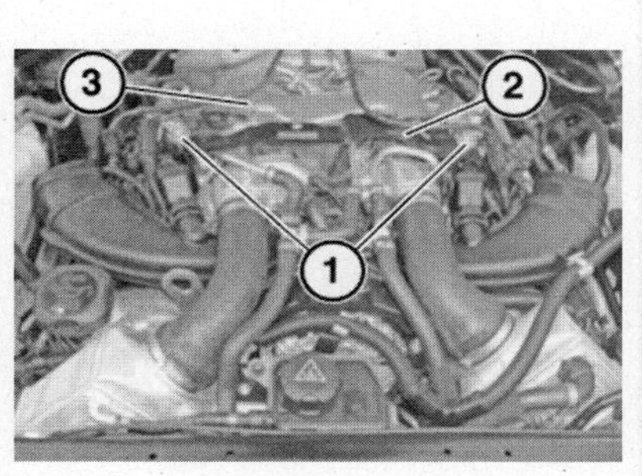

Fig. 184 Removing rubber mounts (1), cable clip (2) and heat shield (3)

a. Tightening torque: 14 ft. lbs. (19 Nm).

➡Clamps must be installed with the screws toward the inside (Figure). Otherwise, a top heat shield can no longer be installed.

➡The ends of the V-band clamps must rest parallel to each other.

b. Tightening torque: 14 ft. lbs. (19 Nm).

➡When installing, if you can see a gap between the ends of the V-band clamps, release and then repeat the screw connection.

c. Tightening torque: 14 ft. lbs. (19 Nm).

➡When installing, if the ends of the V-band clamps are positioned under each other, release and then repeat the screw connection.

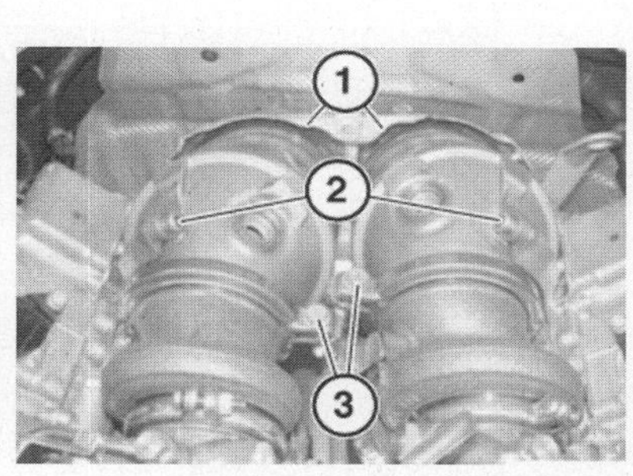

Fig. 185 Removing heat shield (1), releasing screws (2) and replacing clamps (3)

d. Tightening torque: 14 ft. lbs. (19 Nm).

16. Release screw (1) from heat shields (2) and (3).
17. Screw (1) is located between the catalytic converters.
18. Release screws (1) on left heat shield.
19. Unclip left heat shield and remove.
20. Release screw (1) on right heat shield.
21. Release screw (1) on heat shield at bottom right.
22. Unclip heat shield and remove.

➡Picture shows the left side, carry out the operation for the right side in an identical way.

23. Release screws (1).
24. Detach hose (2) from cylinder head cover.
25. Release screws (3) on holder.

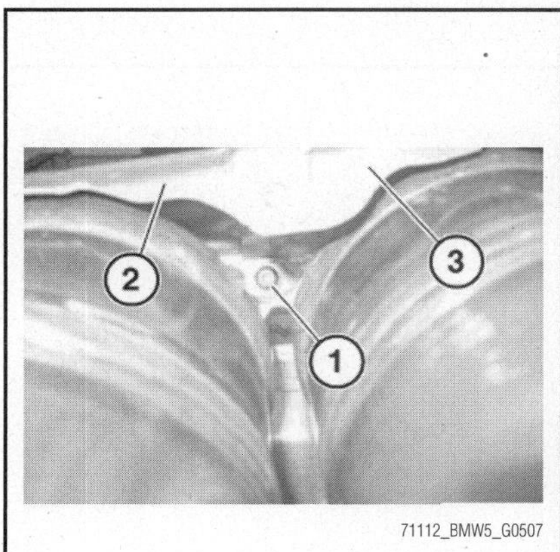

Fig. 186 Releasing screw (1) from heat shields (2 and 3)

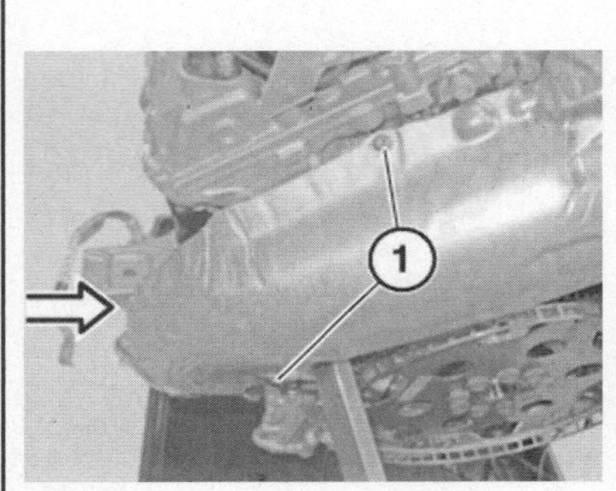

Fig. 187 Releasing screws (1) on left heat shield (shown with engine removed)

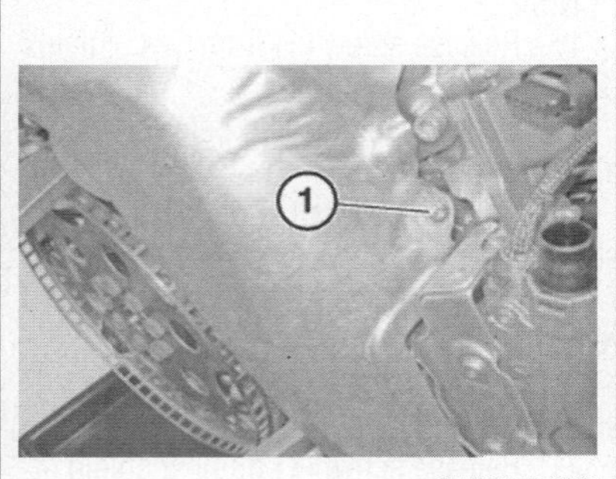

Fig. 188 Release screw (1) on right heat shield (shown with engine removed)

a. Tightening torque: 17 ft. lbs. (21 Nm).

26. Loosen screws (1) on the catalytic converter cylinders 1-4 on the back of the cylinder head.

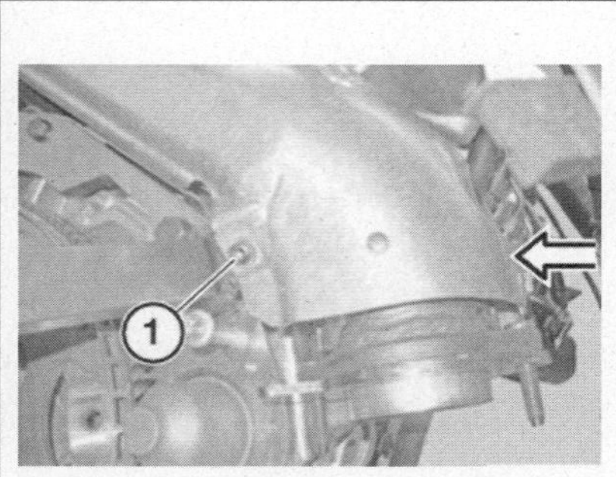

Fig. 189 Releasing screw (1) on heat shield at bottom right (shown with engine removed)

Fig. 190 Releasing screws (1), detaching hose (2) and releasing screws (3) from holder

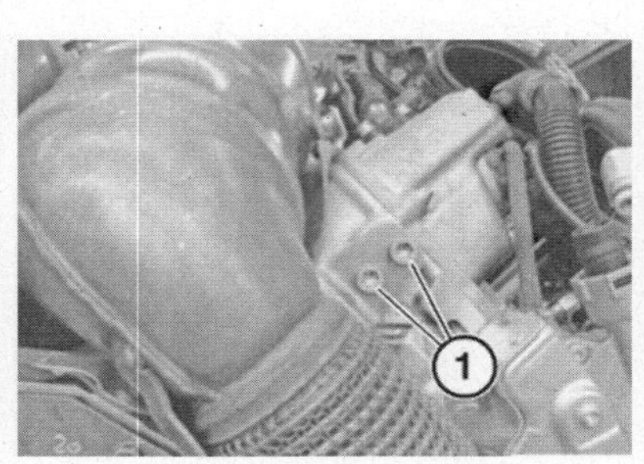

Fig. 191 Loosening screws (1) on catalytic converter cylinders 1-4 on back of cylinder head (shown with engine removed)

a. Tightening torque: 17 ft. lbs. (21 Nm).

27. Release screws (1) on catalytic converter, cylinders 5–8, rear, at cylinder head.

a. Tightening torque: 17 ft. lbs. (21 Nm).

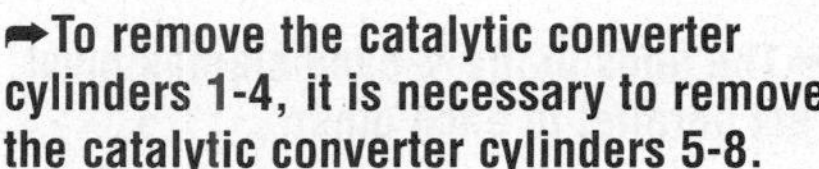

➡To remove the catalytic converter cylinders 1-4, it is necessary to remove the catalytic converter cylinders 5-8.

b. Remove catalytic converter for cylinders 5–8 (1).

c. Remove catalytic converter for cylinders 1–4 (2).

To install:

28. To install, reverse the removal procedure noting the following.

29. Replace seals (1) on the exhaust turbocharger.

30. Clean sealing surfaces.

31. Replace gasket (1).

32. Check exhaust system for leak tightness.

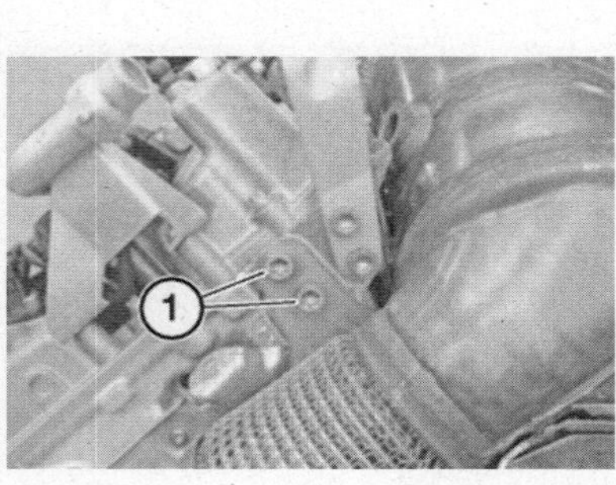

Fig. 192 Releasing screws (1) on catalytic converter, cylinders 5-8 rear, at cylinder head (shown with engine removed)

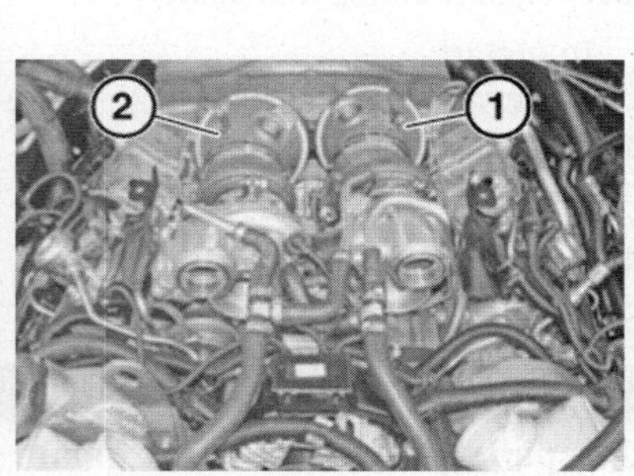

Fig. 193 Removing catalytic converter for cylinders 5-8 (1) and 1-4 (2)

Fig. 194 Replacing seals (1)

INTAKE MANIFOLD

REMOVAL & INSTALLATION

N52 Engine

See Figures 196 through 205.

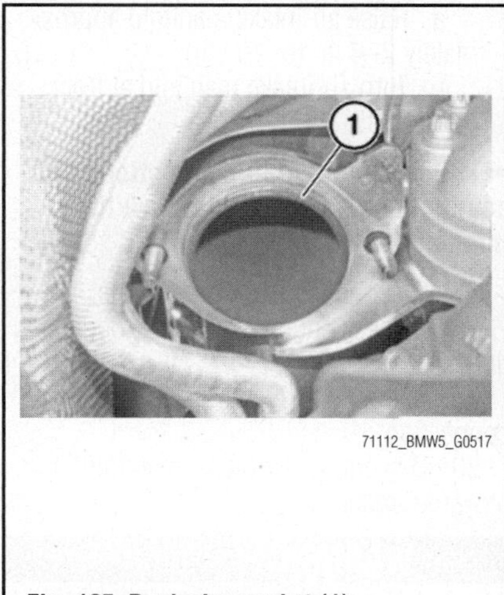

Fig. 195 Replacing gasket (1)

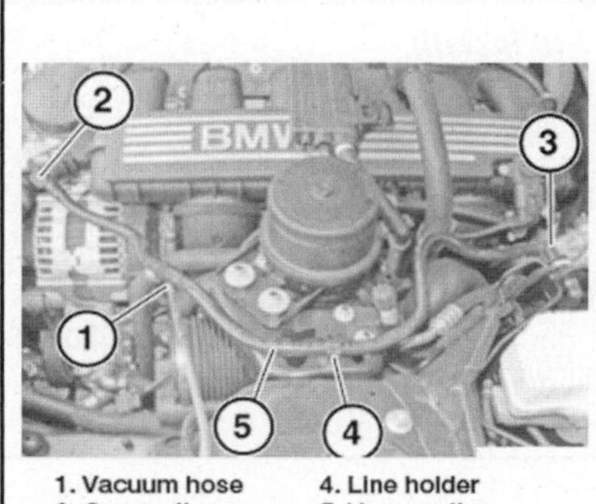

Fig. 196 Disconnecting the vacuum lines

1. Before servicing the vehicle, refer to the precautions.
2. Remove the tension strut.

⁂ WARNING

Driving without the tension strut is not permitted as otherwise the body may be damaged. Tension strut screws must be tightened to torque and then tightened down with special tool 00 9 120.

⁂ WARNING

Catch and seal of cover must not be damaged. Even a minimally damaged cover may result in water leaking in; if necessary, replace cover.

a. Remove cover (1) and release screw underneath.
b. Version 1: Turn cover (with notch) approximately 45° counterclockwise

Fig. 197 Unscrew nuts (1) and place oil reservoir (2) in direction of arrow to one side

c. Version 2: Snap out cover (without notch) in upward direction

⁂ WARNING

Grommet must not be pulled out of bulkhead because this eliminates the possibility of correct feeding in when installed.

d. Release screw.
e. Grip grommet and pull out tension strut in direction of arrow.

3. Remove intake filter housing. Refer to engine mechanical, air cleaner, removal & installation.
4. Remove ignition coil cover. Refer to engine electrical, ignition coil, removal & installation.
5. Disconnect vacuum lines as shown
6. Unscrew nuts.
7. Place oil reservoir in direction of arrow to one side.
8. Release rubber holders from guide.
9. Disconnect plug connection.
10. Unclip line from line holder.
11. Open cable duct.
12. Expose lines.
13. Lay cable duct (upper and lower sections) to one side.

➡The lines shown do not have to be detached in order to remove the air intake manifold.

14. Unfasten hose clip.
15. Detach clean-air gaiter at position in direction of arrow and remove.
16. Disconnect plug connection.

⁂ WARNING

Cover fitting with suitable apparatus to prevent objects getting into it.

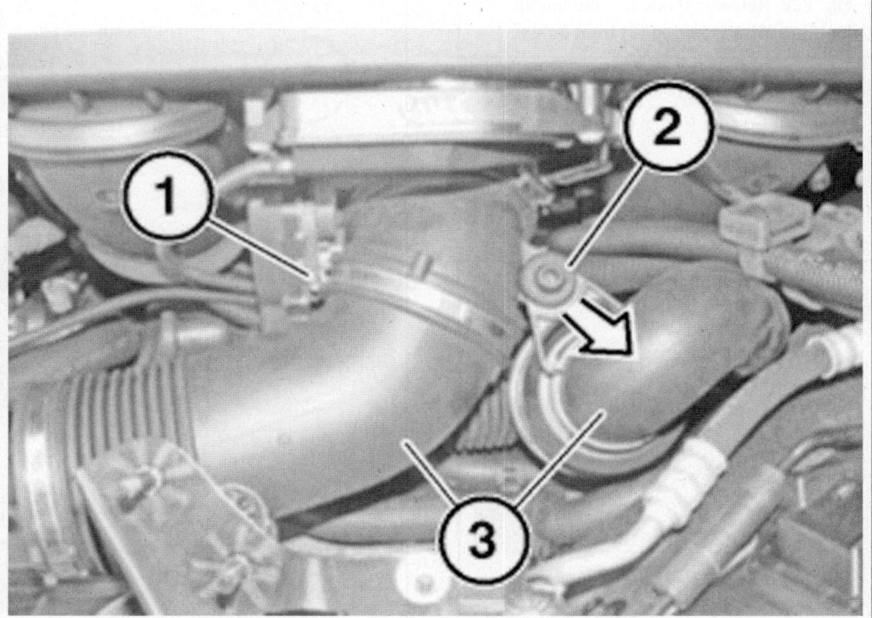

Fig. 198 Unfasten hose clip (1), detach clean-air gaiter (3) at position (2) in direction of arrow and remove

Fig. 199 Disconnect plug connection (1) and cover fitting (2) with suitable apparatus to prevent objects getting into it

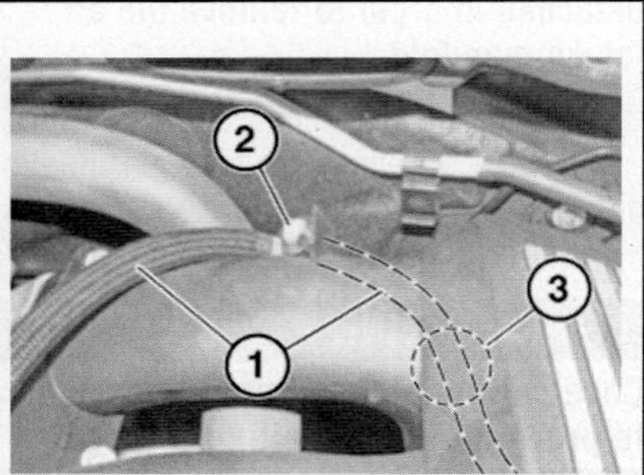

Fig. 200 Release screw (2) and unclip fuel line (1) at position (3) from holder.

17. Release screw.
18. Unclip fuel line at position from holder.
19. Disconnect plug connection and lay to one side.

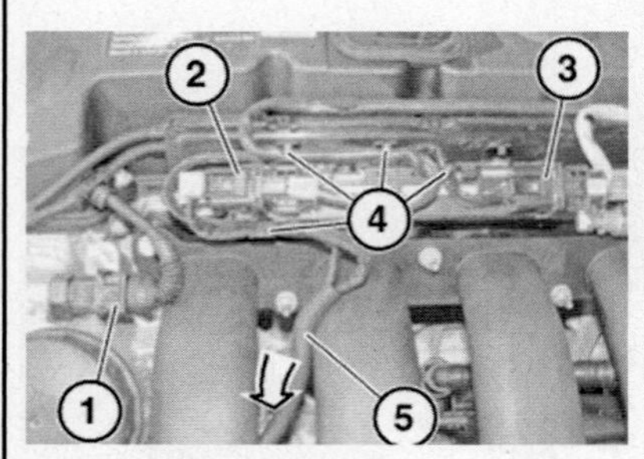

Fig. 201 Disconnect plug connection, unclip lines and lay both lines between intake ducts (direction of arrow) downwards

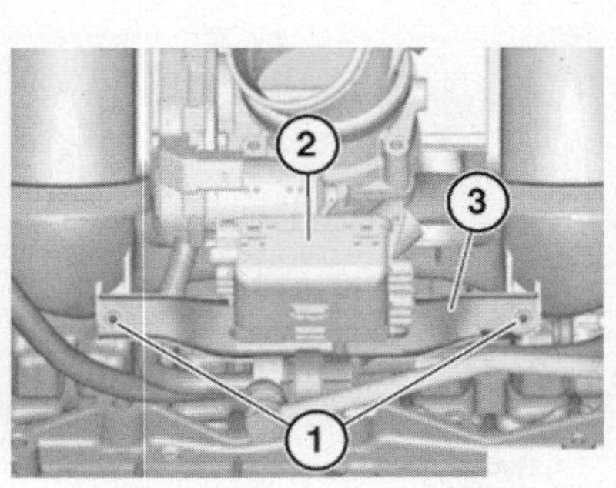

Fig. 202 Release screws (1) and lay cable duct (2) with bracket (3) and engine wiring harness to one side

20. Unclip lines at positions.
21. Remove plug connections.
22. Lay both lines between intake ducts (direction of arrow) downwards.
23. Release screws.
24. Lay cable duct with bracket and engine wiring harness to one side.
25. Unfasten intake manifold screws and nuts as shown.
26. Expose air intake manifold in following work steps, as shown:
   a. Raise air intake manifold approximately 2–4 In. (5–10 cm).
   b. Turn air intake manifold at front through 45°.

➡The following plug connections and connections are located below the intake ducts.

27. Disconnect plug connections.
28. Release engine ventilation connections.
29. Release tank venting connection.
30. Disconnect air intake manifold in upward direction.

WARNING

Cover intake entries with suitable apparatus to prevent objects getting into them.

To install:

31. Installation is the reverse of removal.
32. Replace self-locking nuts.
33. Replace all seals and gaskets.
34. Sealing faces must be free from oil and grease.
35. Tighten bolts/nuts to specification as follows:

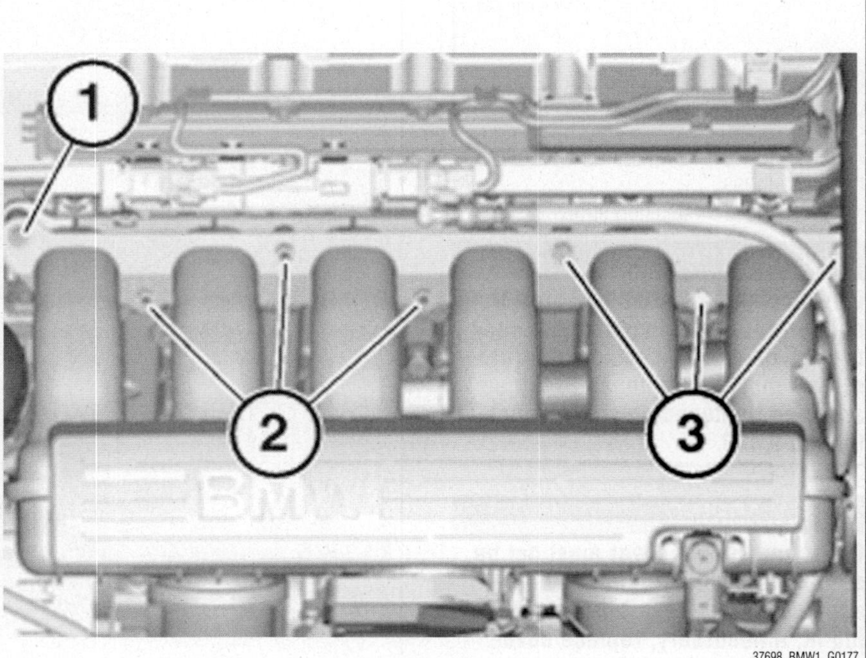

Fig. 203 Unfasten intake manifold screws (1 and 3) and nuts (2)

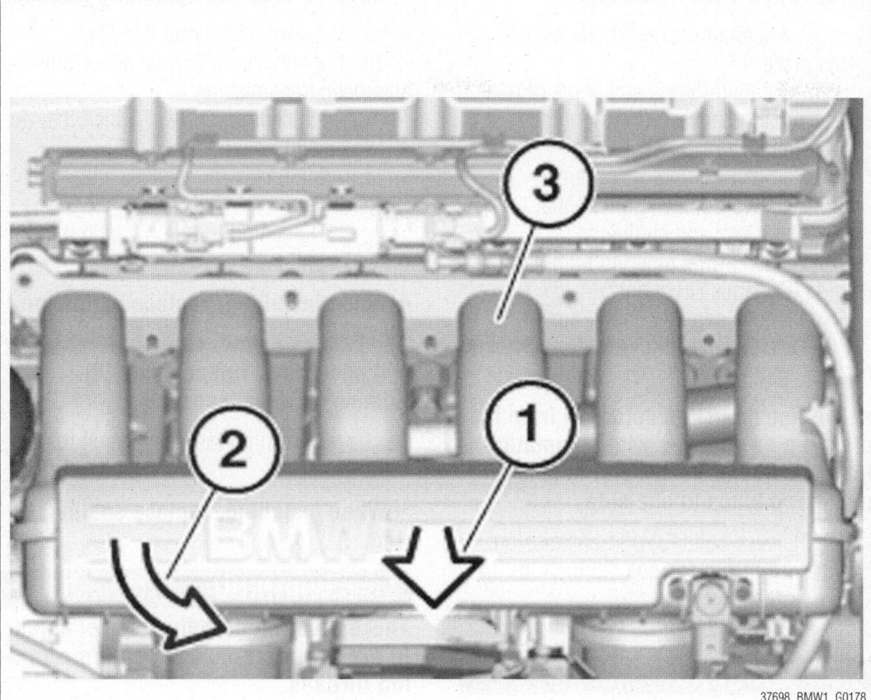

Fig. 204 Raise air intake manifold (3) approximately 2–4 In. (5–10 cm) (1) and turn air intake manifold at front through 45° (2)

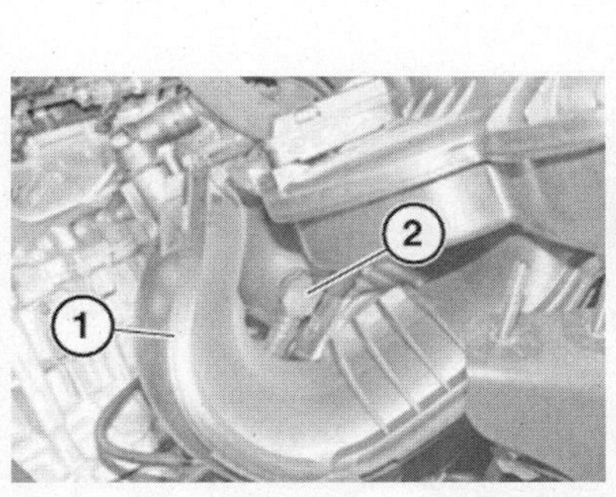

Fig. 205 Release tank venting connection (2) and disconnect air intake manifold (1) in upward direction

- Air intake manifold to cylinder head: 11 ft. lbs. (15 Nm)
- Clean-air gaiter to connection, throttle valve assembly: 27 inch lbs. (3 Nm)
- Fuel line to intake manifold: 53 inch lbs. (6 Nm)
- Holder, engine wiring harness, to intake manifold: 71 inch lbs. (8 Nm)
- Multipurpose holder to body / holder for oil reservoir: 45 inch lbs. (5 Nm)

36. Connections must snap audibly into place!
37. Check air intake system for leaks.

OIL PAN

REMOVAL & INSTALLATION

N20 Engine

See Figure 206.

1. Drain and add engine oil.
2. Remove front axle differential.
3. Remove engine support arm.
4. Disconnect plug connection on oil level sensor.
5. Release screws (1) and remove brackets for engine oil pipe.
6. Release bolts along line (2).
   a. Tightening torque: 7 ft. lbs. (10 Nm).
7. If applicable, remove or reposition oil level sensor.
   a. Tightening torque: 71 inch lbs. (8 Nm).
8. If applicable, remove or reposition bearing support.

➡When installing, replace O-ring.

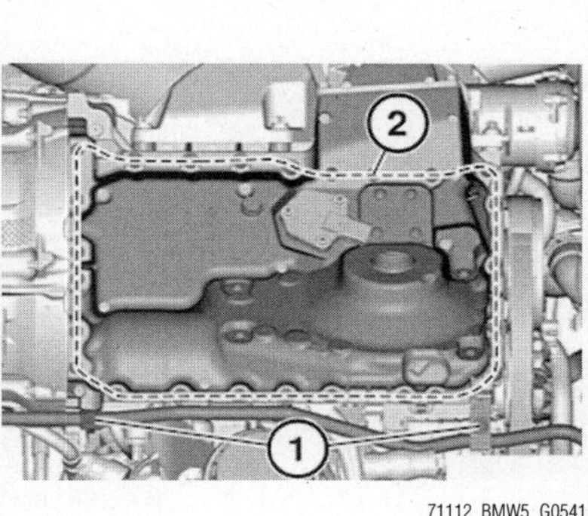

Fig. 206 Releasing screws (1) and bolts (2)

⁂ WARNING

There must be no adhesive residues in the lower crankcase section retaining threads.

⁂ WARNING

Clean retaining threads and sealing surfaces.

➡When installing, replace gasket.

To install:

9. To install, reverse the removal procedure.

N52 Engine

See Figure 207.

⁂ WARNING

Aluminum-magnesium material. No steel fasteners may be used due to the threat of electrochemical corrosion. A magnesium crankcase requires aluminum fasteners exclusively. Aluminum fasteners must be replaced each time they are removed. The end faces of aluminum fasteners are painted blue for purposes of identification. Torque specifications and torque angles must be observed for risk of damage.

1. Before servicing the vehicle, refer to the precautions.
2. Install engine support tool or equivalent.
3. Disconnect the negative battery cable.
4. Remove the lower front axle.
5. Remove the left drive shaft.
6. Remove the right drive shaft.
7. Remove the front axle differential.

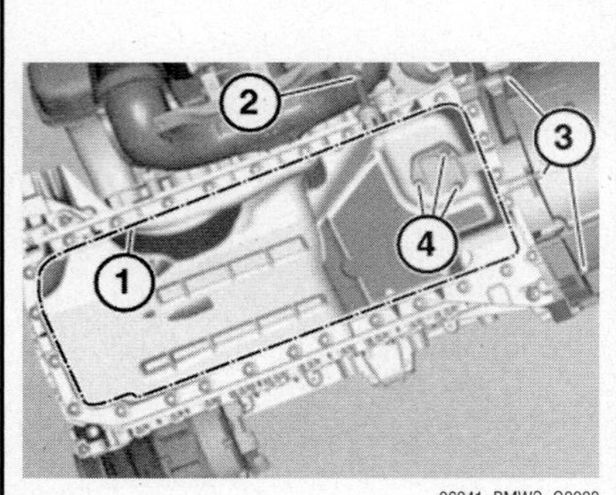

Fig. 207 Oil pan bolts (1), oil return hose (2), transmission bolts (3) and oil level sensor (4)

8. Remove the engine oil.
9. On vehicles equipped with automatic transmission, oil lines must be detached from the engine oil pan.
10. If necessary, remove vane pump and set it aside.
11. Remove the two bolts securing oil pan to transmission.
12. Remove the oil return hose.
13. Remove oil pan bolts and remove the oil pan.
14. If necessary, remove oil level sensor bolts and oil level sensor.

To install:

15. Clean the mounting surfaces and install a new gasket and all seals.

WARNING

There must be no adhesive residues in the oil pan retaining threads. Clean retaining threads.

16. Install oil pan.
17. Replace all aluminum fasteners and tighten 70 inch lbs (8 Nm) plus an additional 90° rotation
18. Installation is the reverse of removal.
19. Fill the engine with oil.
20. Start the engine and check for leaks.

N55 Engine

See Figure 208.

WARNING

Aluminum screws/bolts are permitted with and without color coding (blue).

WARNING

Aluminum screws/bolts must be replaced each time they are released.

➡For reliable identification:

a. Aluminum screws/bolts are not magnetic.

b. Jointing torque and angle of rotation must be observed without fail (risk of damage).

1. Remove left charge air duct.
2. Remove front axle differential.
3. Drain and add engine oil.
4. Detach power steering pump and set it aside (Dynamic Drive only).
5. Remove engine support arm.
6. Detach deflecting element and holder from oil sump.

➡The lines must be detached from the oil sump on vehicles with automatic transmission; if necessary, detach oil pump and place to one side.

7. Release bolts (3) on transmission.

a. Tightening torque: 35 inch lbs. (4 Nm) + 90°.

8. Detach return hose (2).

WARNING

For vehicles with four-wheel drive or automatic transmission, bolts of different lengths are installed for mounting the oil sump.

➡Observe different tightening torques.

9. Release bolts along line (1).
10. For vehicles with four-wheel drive or automatic transmission:

a. Tightening torque: 71 inch lbs. (8 Nm) + 180°.

11. Additionally for vehicles with four-wheel drive:

a. Tightening torque: 71 inch lbs. (8 Nm) + 90°.

➡When installing, replace aluminum screws.

➡If necessary, release nuts (4). Remove oil level sensor.

b. Tightening torque: 71 inch lbs. (8 Nm).

➡When installing, replace sealing ring.

WARNING

There must be no adhesive residues in the lower crankcase section retaining threads.

12. Clean retaining threads and sealing surfaces.

➡When installing, replace all gaskets.

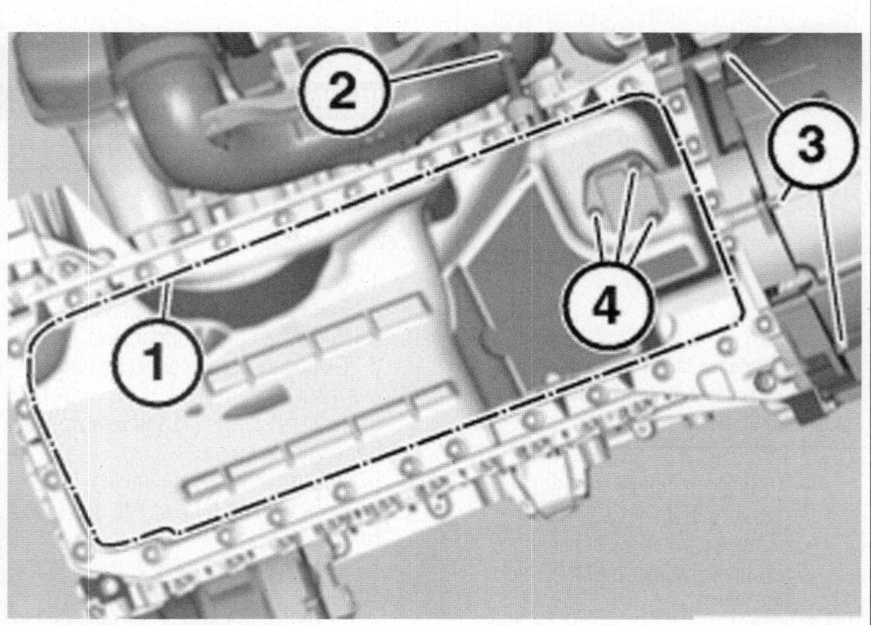

Fig. 208 Releasing bolts (3), detaching return hose (2), releasing bolts (1) and nuts (4)

To install:

13. To install, reverse the removal procedure.

N63 Engine

Lower

See Figure 209.

1. Remove underbody protection at front and rear.
2. Release oil drain plug and drain engine oil.
3. Unlock plug connection (1) on oil level sensor and disconnect.
4. Release screws (2) along line.
   a. Tightening torque: 20 ft. lbs. (27 Nm).
5. Remove lower oil sump section (3).

➡When installing, clean sealing surfaces.

6. Replace gasket.
7. Replace screws.

➡When replacing lower oil sump section:

   a. Convert oil level sensor.
   b. Replace sealing ring.

To install:

8. To install, reverse the removal procedure.

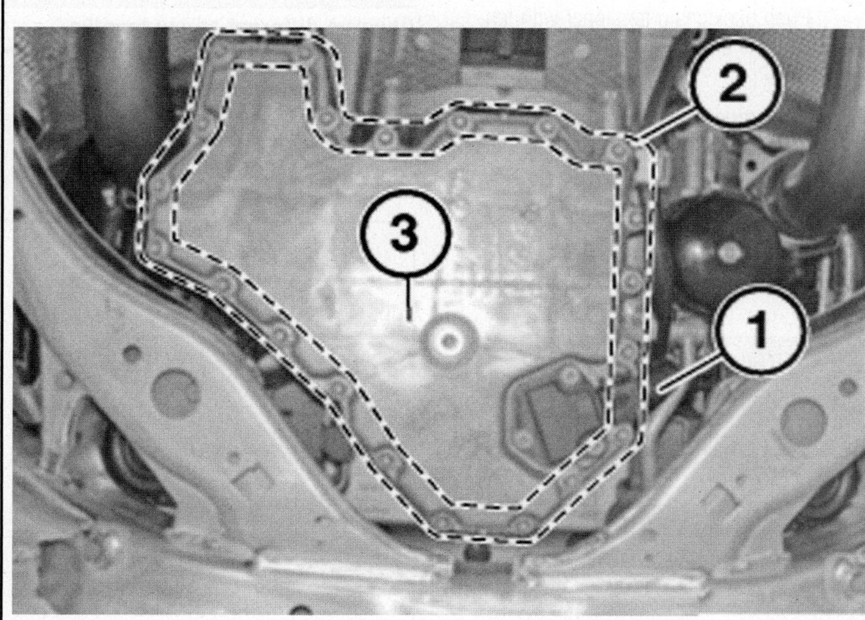

Fig. 209 Unlocking plug connection (1), releasing screws (2) and removing lower oil sump section (3)

Upper

See Figures 210 through 212.

1. Drain engine oil.
2. Secure engine in installation position.
3. Lower front axle.
4. Remove lower oil sump section.
5. Unclip wiring harness on oil sump.
6. Remove oil filter cover with oil filter (1) with special tool 11 9 240.
   a. Tightening torque: 22 inch lbs. (30 Nm) - 180° + 30 ft. lbs. (40 Nm).
7. Release bolt (1) and remove oil pipes (2) from oil filter housing.
8. Release holders of supply/return lines on oil sump.
9. Unfasten screws (2).
   a. Tightening torque: 7 ft. lbs. (10 Nm).
10. Release screws in area of line (1).
    a. Tightening torque 11 13 2AZ.
11. Release screws (2) on transmission end 24 00 1AZ.
12. Remove upper oil sump section (3).

➡When installing, free sealing surfaces of seal debris and clean.

13. Replace gasket.
14. Modify oil pressure switch if replacing oil sump.

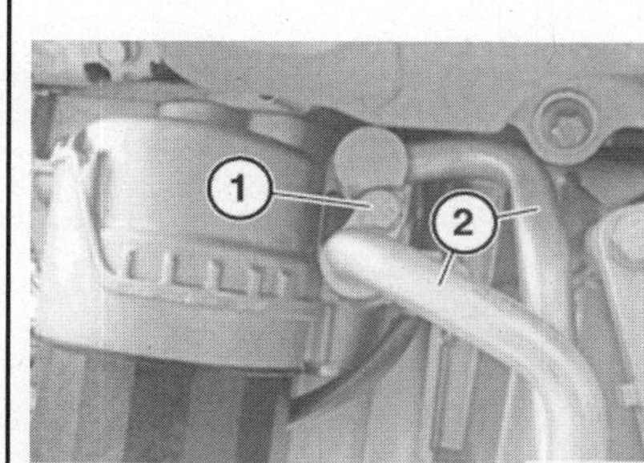

Fig. 210 Releasing bolt (1) and removing oil pipes (2)

Fig. 211 Unfastening screws (2)

To install:

15. To install, reverse the removal procedure.

OIL PUMP

REMOVAL & INSTALLATION

N20 Engine

See Figures 213 through 217.

⁂ WARNING

The counterbalance shaft must be adjusted to the motor.

1. Remove oil pan.

➡When installing, wet special tool 2 219 548 with oil to simplify dismantling and installation.

2. Secure crankshaft with special tool 2 219 548 via the dowel hole.
3. Release screw (1).

Fig. 212 Releasing screws (1 and 2) and removing upper oil sump section (3)

4. Detach intake snorkel (2) in direction of arrow.

5. Loosen sealing cap using a screwdriver.

➡When installing, position counterbalance shaft with special tool 2 212 825 .

6. Secure special tool 2 212 825 on oil pump housing with screw (1).

➡If special tool 2 212 825 cannot be positioned, the timing must be readjusted.

7. Push back chain tensioner with tensioning rail (1) and secure with special tool 11 4 120.

➡Sprocket must be blocked with special tool 2 318 117 in order to release central bolt (2).

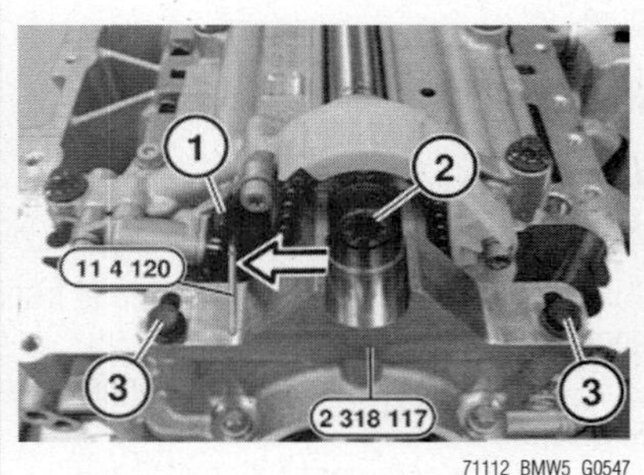

Fig. 215 Pushing back chain tensioner with tensioning rail (1), releasing central bolt (2) and mounting special tool with screws (3)

8. Mount special tool 2 318 117 and secure with screws (3).

9. Release central bolt (2) for oil pump drive shaft.

10. Remove special tool 2 318 117 .

➡When installing, replace screw.

a. Tightening torque: 70 ft. lbs. (95 Nm).

11. Release screws (1) and pull off chain module (2) off of oil pump drive shaft.

a. Tightening torque: 7 ft. lbs. (10 Nm).

WARNING

Observe different screw lengths.

12. Release screws (1).

13. Release screws, remove oil pump with counterbalance shaft.

a. Tightening torque 11 41 3AZ.

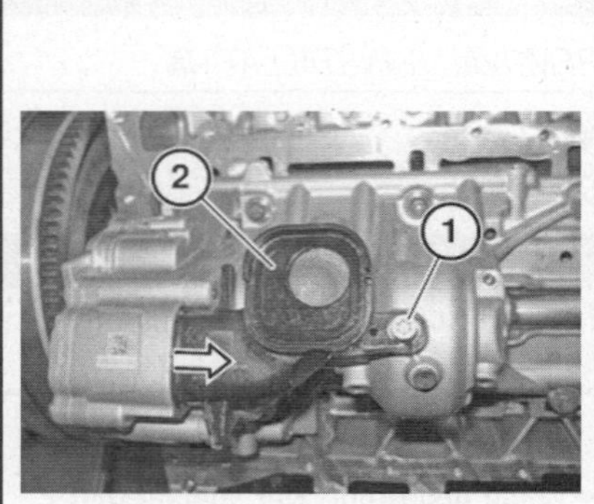

Fig. 213 Releasing screw (1) and detaching intake snorkel (2)

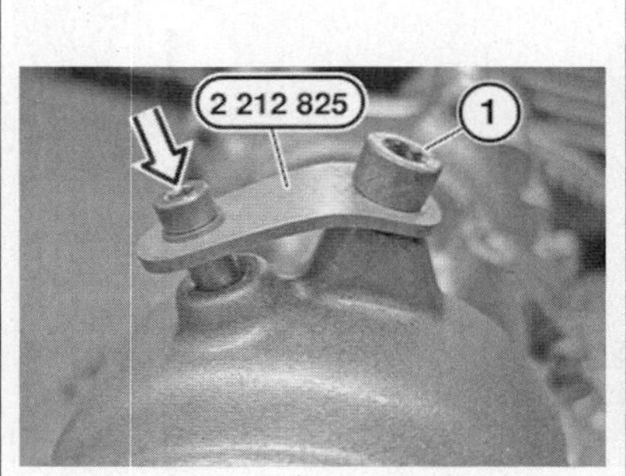

Fig. 214 Securing special tool on oil pump housing with screw (1)

Fig. 216 Releasing screws (1) and pulling off chain module (2) off of oil pump drive shaft

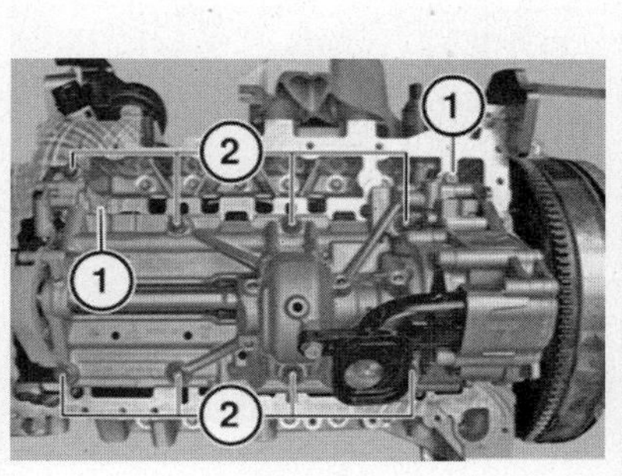

Fig. 217 Releasing screws (1) and removing oil pump with counterbalance shaft

➡When installing, check spacer bushes for secure seating and damage; replace if necessary.

To install:

14. To install, reverse the removal procedure.

N52 Engine

See Figure 218.

1. Before servicing the vehicle, refer to the precautions.
2. Disconnect the negative battery cable.
3. Remove the oil pan.
4. Remove the oil pump intake pipe fasteners and oil pump intake pipe, pull towards transmission.
5. Remove the oil pump pulley bolt.
6. Remove the oil pump mounting bolts.

➡Timing chain of triangular drive is pressed upwards by chain tensioner.

7. Do not remove pulley from assembly.
8. Remove the oil pump pulley, pull towards front of engine bay.
9. Remove the oil pump.

To install:

10. Check the seals on the oil pipes and replace it if necessary. Lubricate the seals with oil and the oil pipes.
11. Check the seal in the oil pump and replace it if necessary.
12. Align twin surface on oil pump to sprocket wheel.
13. Replace all aluminum fasteners and tighten to specification.
    - Oil pump to bedplate: 25 ft. lbs. (34 Nm) plus an additional 180° rotation
    - Chain module to crankcase and oil pump 35 inch lbs. (4 Nm) plus an additional 45° rotation
    - Pulley to oil pump: 15 ft. lbs. (20 Nm) plus an additional 45° rotation
    - Intake pipe to bedplate: 35 inch lbs. (4 Nm) plus an additional 100° rotation
14. Installation is the reverse of removal.
15. Fill the engine with oil.
16. Start the engine and check for leaks.

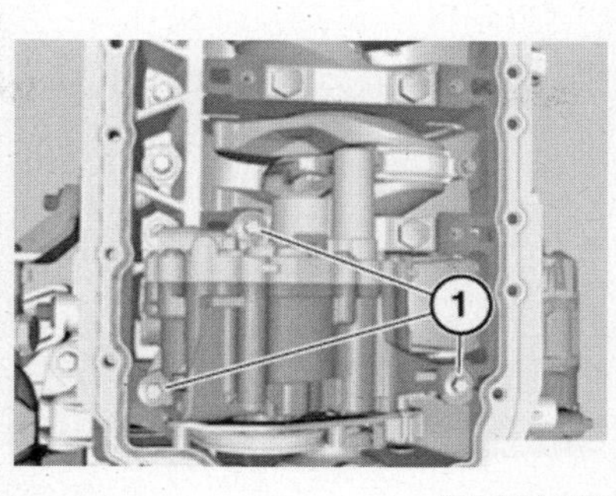

Fig. 218 Oil pump mounting bolts (1)

N55 Engine

See Figures 219 through 227.

⁂ WARNING

Aluminum screws/bolts must be replaced each time they are released.

⁂ WARNING

Aluminum screws/bolts are permitted with and without color coding (blue).

➡For reliable identification:

a. Aluminum screws/bolts are not magnetic.
b. Jointing torque and angle of rotation must be observed without fail (risk of damage).

1. Removing oil pan.
2. Remove sealing cap of vacuum pump.
3. Undo all the aluminum screws (1) along the line.

➡When installing, replace aluminum screws.

4. Remove intake pipe with oil deflector.

➡When installing, replace O-ring.

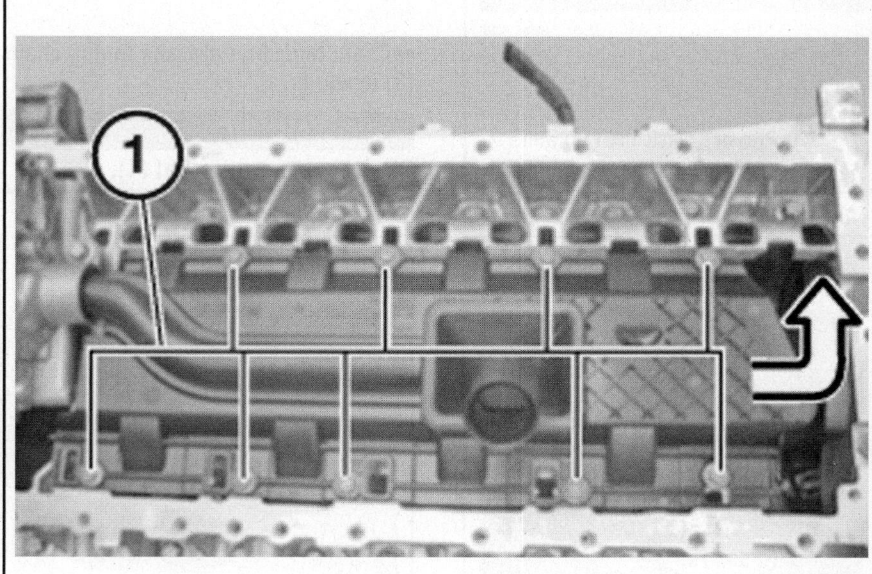

Fig. 219 Undoing aluminum screws (1) along line

WARNING

Before releasing the central bolt on the oil pump, the hydraulic chain tensioner must be drained.

5. Carefully press tensioning rail (1) with a suitable screwdriver (2) in direction of arrow.
6. As the oil pressure in the chain tensioner can only be drained pulsating, the tensioning rail (1) must be pressed several times.
7. Sprocket must be blocked in order to release central bolt (1).
8. Secure special tool 2 303 793 to crankcase.
9. Release oil pump central bolt (1).
   a. Tightening torque: 15 ft. lbs. (20 Nm) + 45°.
10. Release aluminum screws (1).
   a. Tightening torque: 35 inch lbs. (4 Nm) + 45°.

Fig. 220 Pressing tension rail (1) with screwdriver (2) in direction of arrow

Fig. 221 Identifying central bolt (1)

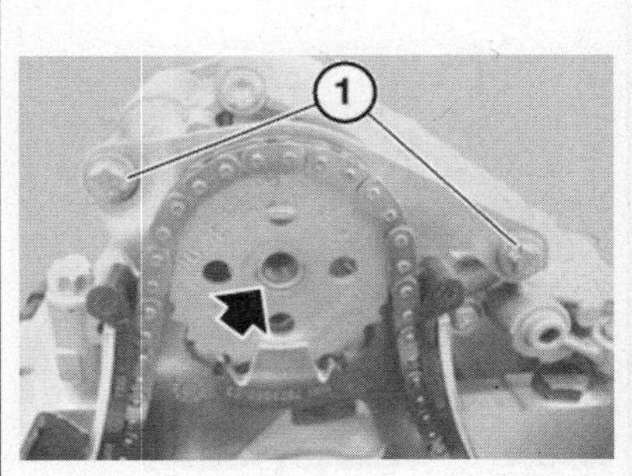

Fig. 222 Releasing screws (1)

➡When installing, replace aluminum screws.

11. Watch mounting flats on oil pump sprocket.

WARNING

Observe different screw lengths.

12. Release aluminum screws (1).
   a. Tightening torque (M8x123): 7 ft. lbs. (10 Nm) + 180°.
   b. Tightening torque (M8x31 and M8x37): 7 ft. lbs. (10 Nm) + 90°.

➡When installing, replace aluminum screws.

13. Detach sprocket (1) in direction of arrow.

➡Chain tensioner presses timing chain (3) upwards.

WARNING

Do not remove sprocket (1).

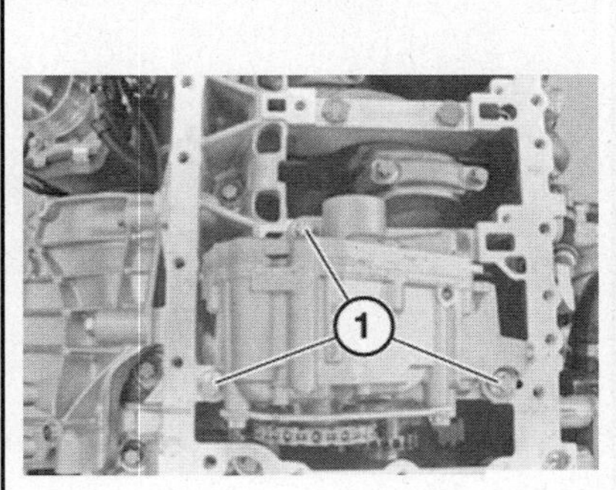

Fig. 223 Releasing aluminum screws (1)

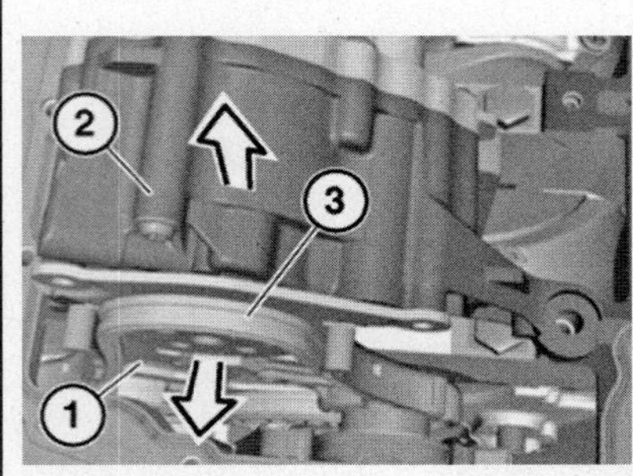

Fig. 224 Detaching sprocket (1), pressing timing chain (3) and removing oil pump (2) in direction of arrow

Fig. 225 Checking spacer bushes

14. Remove oil pump (2) in direction of arrow.

To install:

15. Check spacer bushes for secure seating and damage; replace if necessary.

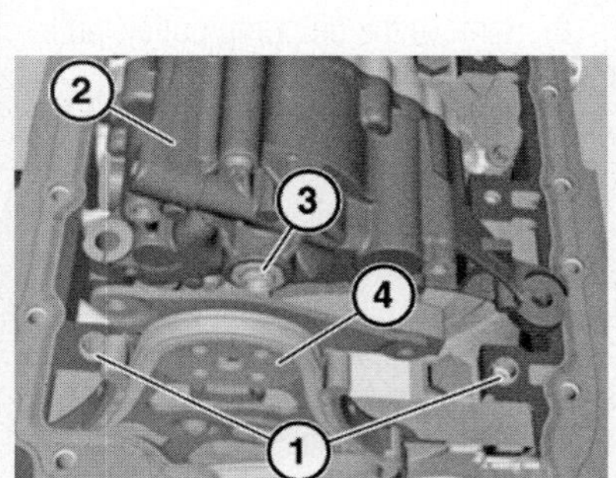

Fig. 226 Installing oil pump (2), aligning mounting flats (3) on oil pump to sprocket (4)

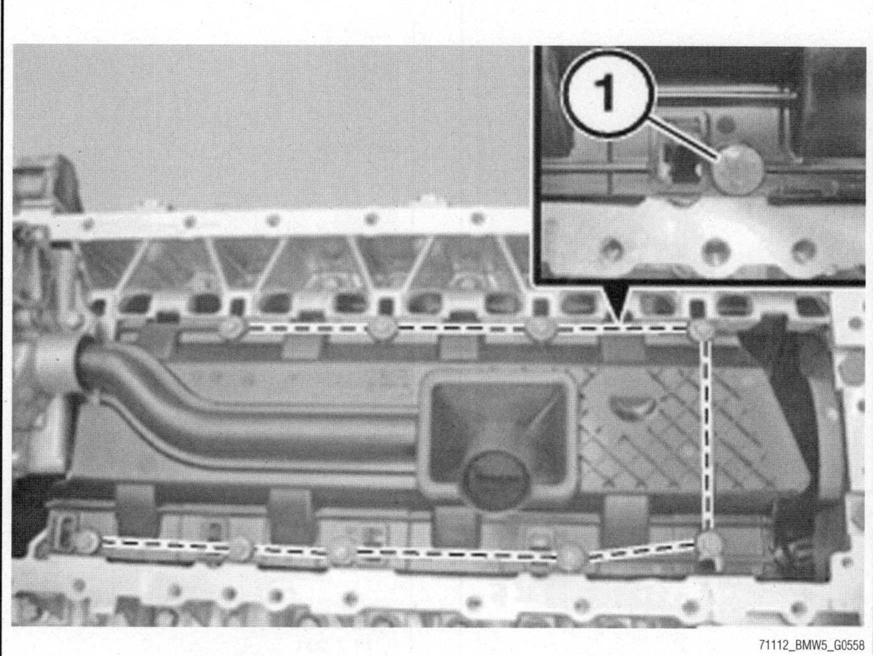

Fig. 227 Inserting aluminum screws (1) along line

16. Install oil pump (2).
17. Align mounting flats (3) on oil pump (2) to sprocket (4).
18. Install intake pipe with oil deflector.

➡When installing, replace O-ring.

19. Insert all the aluminum screws (1) along the line.

➡When installing, replace aluminum screws.

a. Tightening torque: 35 inch lbs. (4 Nm) + 90°.

20. Assemble engine.

N63 Engine

See Figures 228 through 245.

⁂ WARNING

All adjusting procedures on the chain drive must be observed.

⁂ WARNING

A timing chain which is tensioned too tautly can cause noises in the chain drive.

⁂ WARNING

A timing chain that is too slack can cause the timing chain to jump.

⁂ WARNING

Risk of damage in oil pump drive.

1. Drain engine oil.
2. Remove lower oil sump section.
3. Unscrew nuts.
   a. Tightening torque: 7 ft. lbs. (10 Nm).
4. Remove intake pipe.

➡When installing, replace O-ring.

5. Release all nuts (1) using special tool 11 7 201.
   a. Tightening torque: 7 ft. lbs. (10 Nm).
6. Remove oil pump drive gear.
7. Unscrew nuts (1).
8. Release screws, remove oil pump (1) with aid of a second person.

➡Replace screws.

a. Tightening torque: 18 ft. lbs. (24 Nm).

9. Detach oil lines (1) upwards in direction of arrow.

To install:

10. Replace sealing rings.
11. Lightly oil sealing ring 1.
12. Coat sealing ring with suitable lubricant.
13. Replace O-ring for oil feed line.

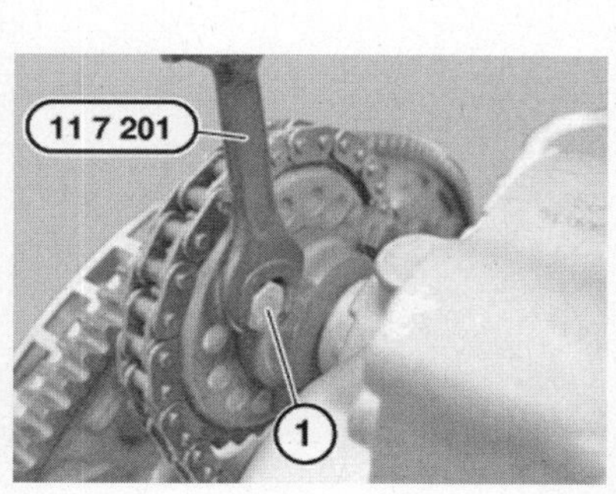

Fig. 228 Releasing all nuts (1) (shown with engine removed)

Fig. 229 Unscrewing nuts (1) and removing oil pump (shown without top oil pan)

14. Fit oil lines (1) in direction of arrow.

⁂ WARNING

Left-hand thread on oil pump screw connection.

Fig. 230 Detaching oil lines (1) upwards in direction of arrow (shown without top oil pan)

Fig. 231 Fitting oil lines (1) in direction of arrow

WARNING

Do not grip oil pump drive with a pair of pliers risk of damage.

WARNING

Nut (1) has left-hand thread.

15. Position special tool 11 8 920 on sprocket.
16. Slacken nut (1).
17. Check mounting flats on pump shaft (1) for damage.

WARNING

Nut (1) has left-hand thread.

18. Grip pump with assistance of a second person.
19. Secure nut (1) with special tool 00 9 120.
    a. Tightening torque: 15 ft. lbs. (20 Nm) + 40°.

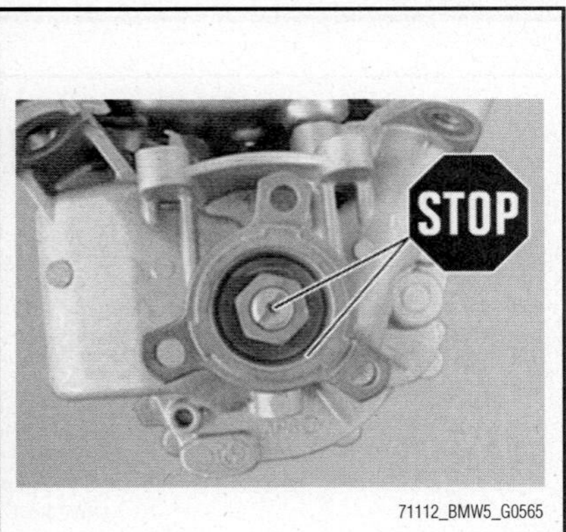

Fig. 232 Identifying left hand thread on oil pump screw connection

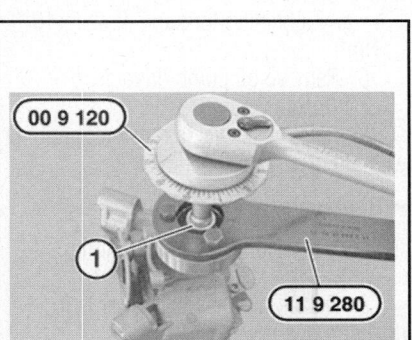

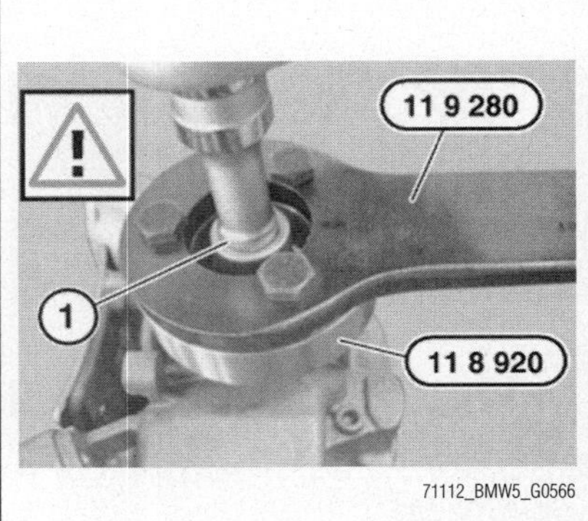

Fig. 233 Slackening nut (1)

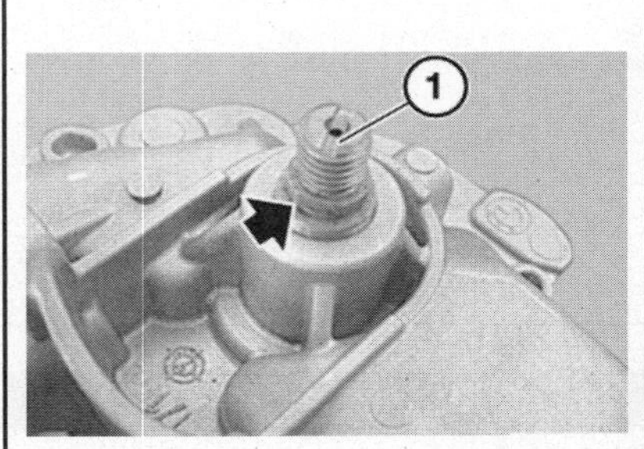

Fig. 234 Checking mounting flats on pump shaft (1)

20. Join and secure nuts (1).
    a. Tightening torque: 18 ft. lbs. (24 Nm).

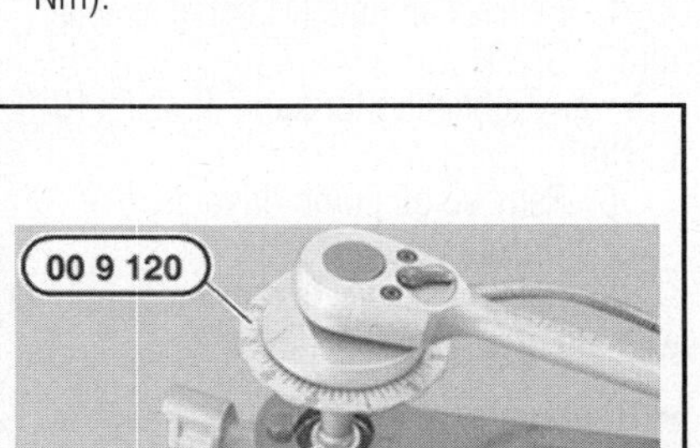

Fig. 235 Securing nut (1) with special tool

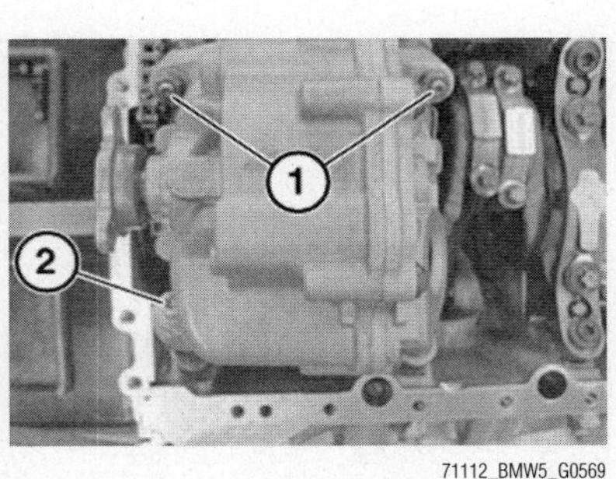

Fig. 236 Joining and securing nuts (1) (shown without top oil pan)

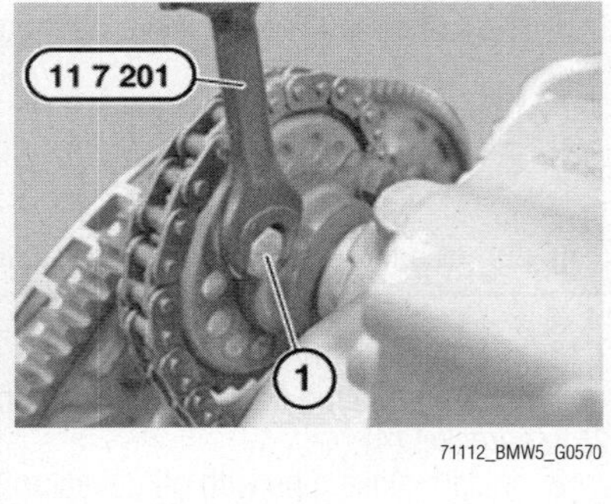

Fig. 237 Securing all nuts (1) with special tool

21. Install oil pump drive gear.
22. Secure all nuts (1) with special tool 11 7 201.
    a. Tightening torque: 7 ft. lbs. (10 Nm).
23. Adjust oil pump timing chain.
24. Pretension oil pump adjusting sleeve (1) with a hexagon socket wrench.
    a. Adjustment value 10 mm +2.

Procedure on removed engine: (Upper oil pan has been removed)

25. Minimally preload timing chain (1) with special tool 51 0 342.
26. Read off measured value A on special tool 51 0 342 and note down.

WARNING

Do not use force to preload timing chain (1).

27. Using a screwdriver (1), preload timing chain to minimal extent in direction of arrow.

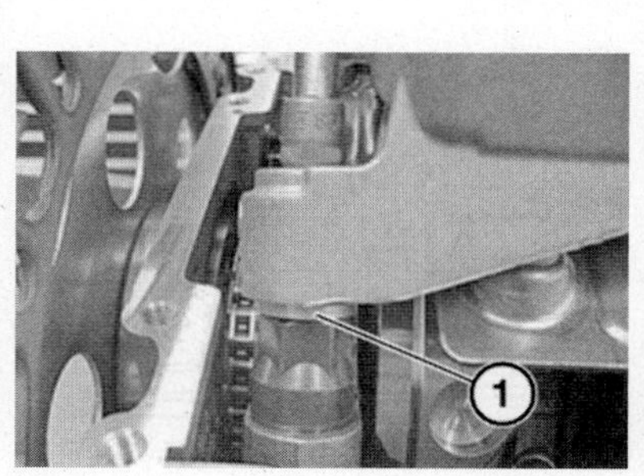

Fig. 238 Pretensioning oil pump adjusting sleeve (1) (shown without top oil pan)

28. Read off measured value B on special tool 51 0 342 and note down.

WARNING

Do not use force preload timing chain.

29. Measured value A minus measured value B results in the adjustment value.

a. Adjustment value 10 mm +2.

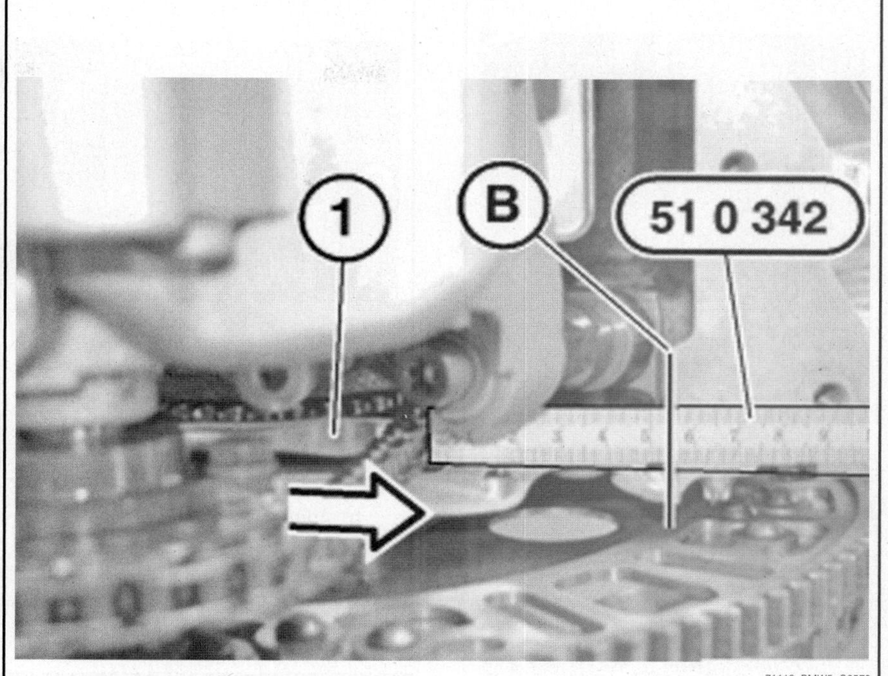

Fig. 240 Using a screwdriver (1), preload timing chain to minimal extent in direction of arrow

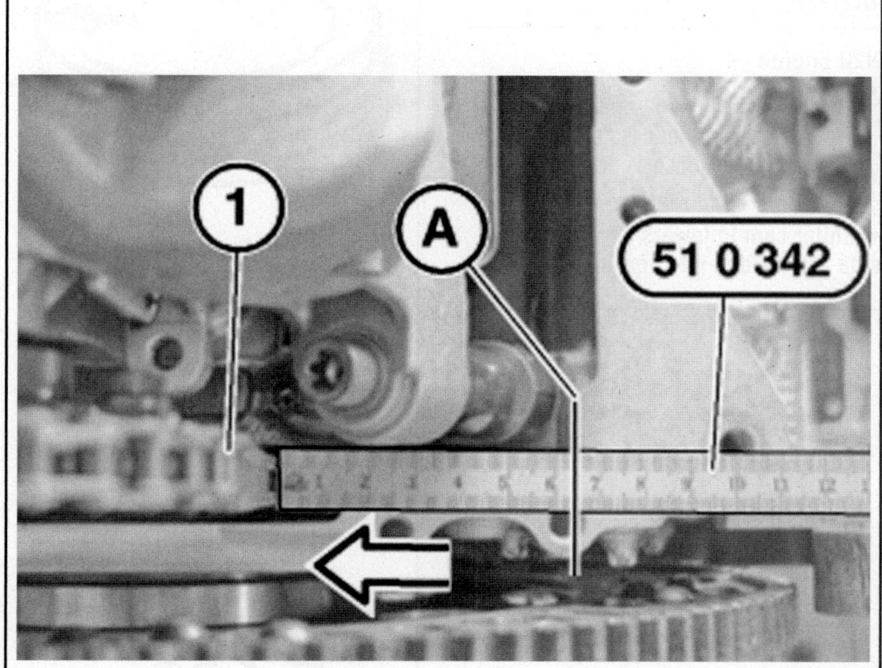

Fig. 239 Preloading timing chain (1) with special tool

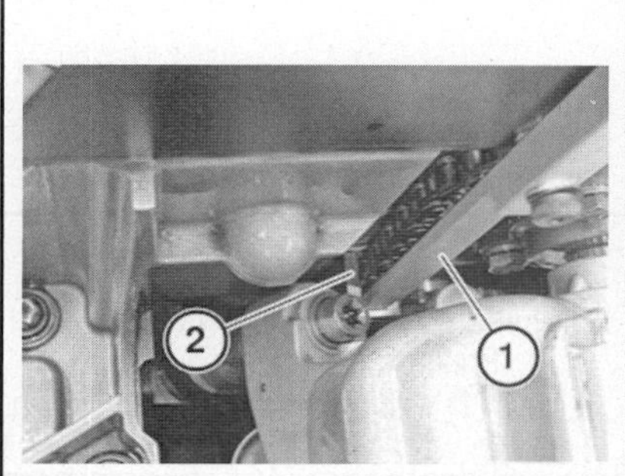

Fig. 241 Positioning drag pointer (1) of special tool 2 213 485 on oil pump chain

Procedure on installed engine: (Upper oil pan has been installed)

30. Position drag pointer (1) of special tool 2 213 485 on oil pump chain.

WARNING

Do not use force preload timing chain.

31. Push drag pointer (1) to the left and right until value has been determined.

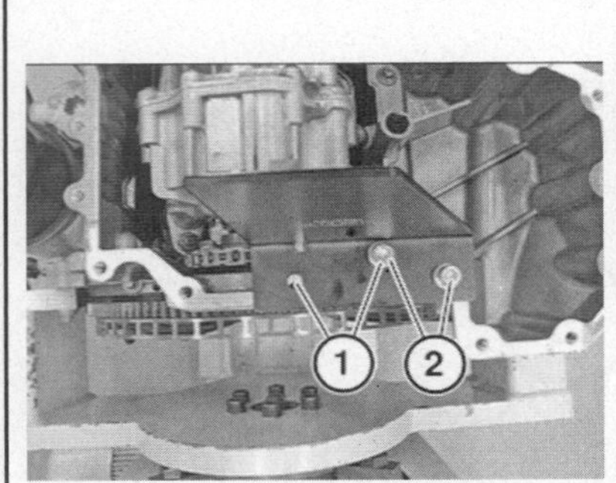

Fig. 242 Identifyiog attachment point (1)

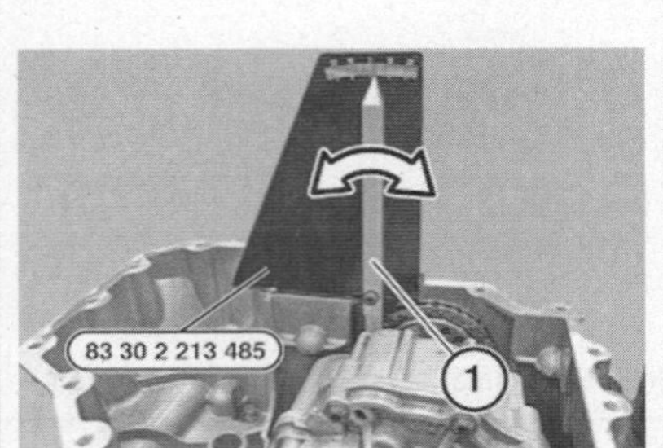

Fig. 243 Pushing drag pointer (1) to left and right until value has been determined

a. Adjustment value 10 mm +2.

32. Adjust oil pump timing chain.

a. Pretension oil pump adjusting sleeve (1) with a hexagon socket wrench.

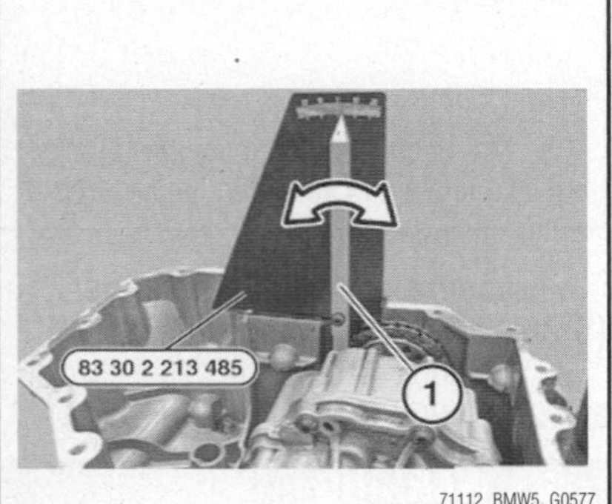

Fig. 244 Pretension oil pump adjusting sleeve (1) with a hexagon socket wrench

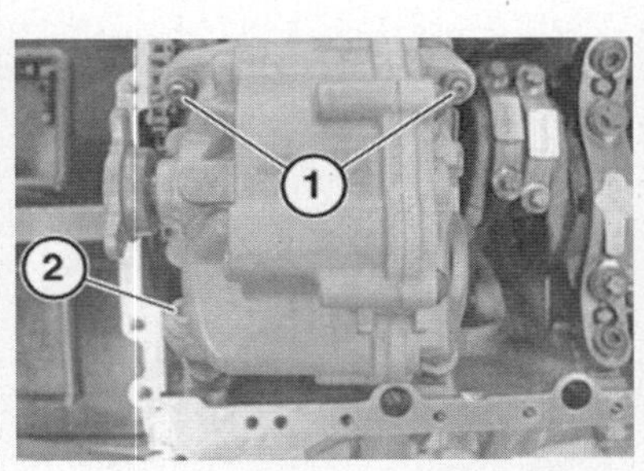

Fig. 245 Joining and securing screw (1) (shown without top oil pan)

b. Adjustment value 10 mm +2.

33. Join and secure screw (2).

a. Tightening torque: 18 ft. lbs. (24 Nm).

34. Assemble engine.

PISTONS & RINGS

POSITIONING

See Figures 246 through 248.

ROCKER ARMS

REMOVAL & INSTALLATION

N20 Engine

See Figures 249 through 253.

1. Remove cylinder head cover.
2. Remove intermediate lever.
3. Remove exhaust camshaft.

➡Roller cam followers (1) on intake side are divided into bearing classes.

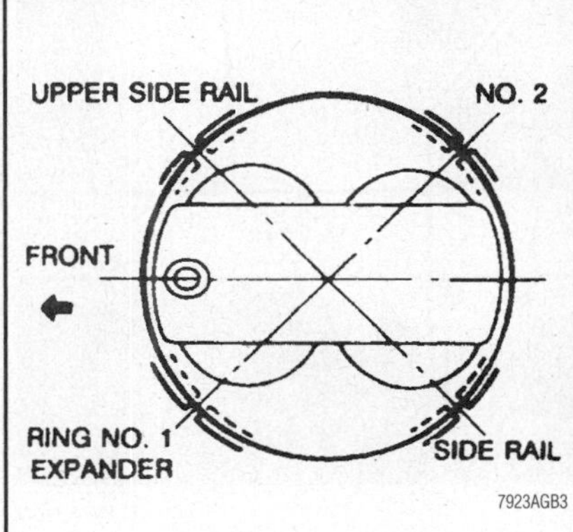

Fig. 246 Piston ring end-gap spacing—N52 Engine

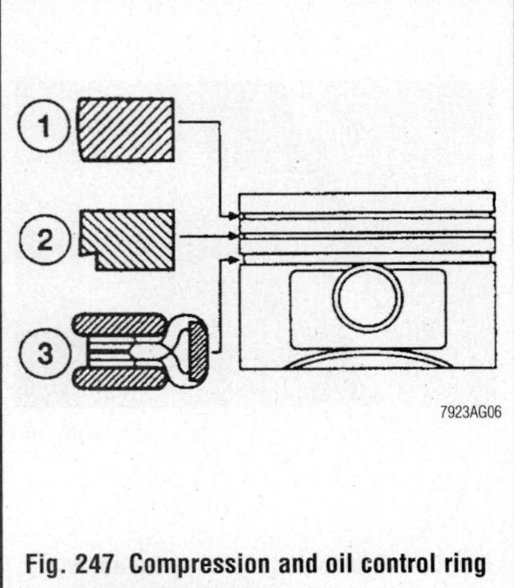

Fig. 247 Compression and oil control ring locations—N52 Engine

➡The tolerance classes are marked according to the graphic in numbers from 1 to 5.

➡Already used roller cam followers (1) may only be reused in the same position.

4. Detach roller cam followers (1) from hydraulic valve clearance compensating element and remove.

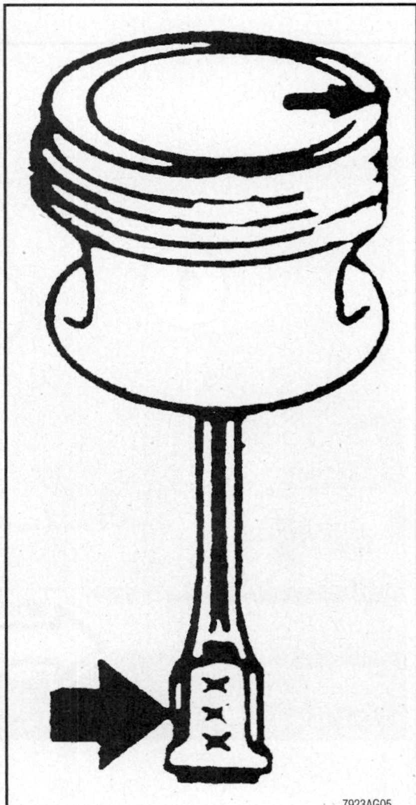

Fig. 248 Connecting rod-to-piston positioning—N52 Engine

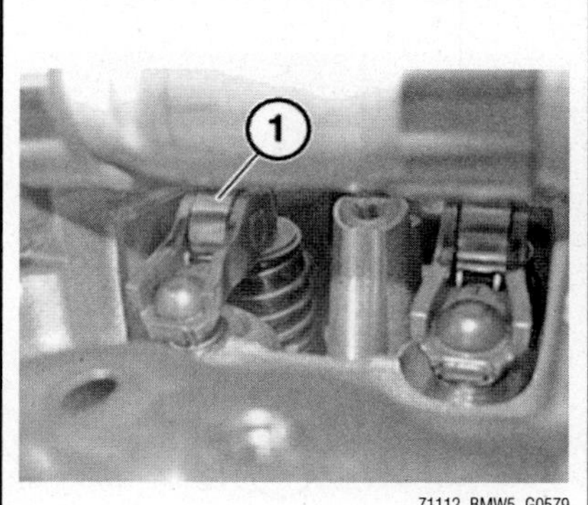

Fig. 249 Detaching roller cam followers (1)

5. Place all roller cam followers (1) in neat order on special tool 11 4 481 .

➡Prior to installation of intermediate levers, ensure proper installation position of roller cam followers (1).

6. Classification of roller cam follower intake.

a. Standard:

- Number 3. standard.
- Number 2. slow idle.
- Number 4. fast idle.

b. In case of repair: rough idling speed.

c. Repair: 1

- Number 1. lower engine speed in idle.
- Number 5. higher engine speed in idle.

7. Detach roller cam follower (1) on exhaust side from hydraulic valve clearance compensating element and remove.

Fig. 250 Identifying roller cam follower intake classification

Fig. 251 Detaching roller cam follower (1) on exhaust side

8. Place all roller cam followers (1) in neat order on special tool 11 4 482 .

➡Prior to installation of exhaust camshaft, ensure proper installation position of roller cam followers (1).

9. Remove hydraulic valve clearance compensating element (1) on intake side in direction of arrow.

➡When installing, if hydraulic valve clearance compensating elements (1) are reused, they must be placed together with rocker arms in neat order in special tool 11 4 481.

10. Remove hydraulic valve clearance compensating element (1) on exhaust side in direction of arrow.

➡When installing, if hydraulic valve clearance compensating elements (1) are reused, they must be placed together with rocker arms in neat order in special tool 11 4 482.

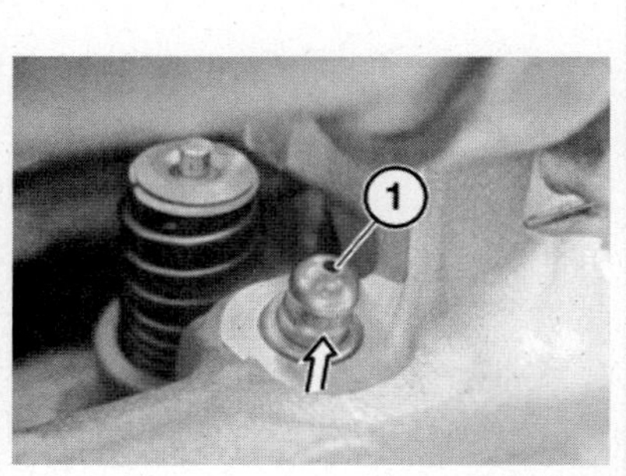

Fig. 252 Removing hydraulic valve clearance compensating element (1) on intake side

Fig. 253 Removing hydraulic valve clearance compensating element (1) on exhaust side

To install:

11. To install, reverse the removal procedure noting the following.

12. Check function of DME; if necessary, readjust uniform mixture distribution.

N52 Engine

See Figures 254 and 255.

1. Remove cylinder head cover.
2. Remove intermediate lever.
3. Remove exhaust camshaft.

➡Rocker arms (1) are divided into bearing categories.

➡The tolerance classes are marked according to the graphic in numbers from 1 to 5.

WARNING

Already used rocker arms (1) may only be reused in the same position.

4. Detach rocker arms (1) from HVCA element and remove.

5. Set down all rocker arms (1) in neat order in special tool 11 4 480.

➡Before installing exhaust camshaft or intermediate levers, make sure rocker arms (1) are correctly seated.

6. Remove HVC element (1) in direction of arrow.

➡If hydraulic valve clearance compensating elements (1) are reused, they must be placed together with rocker arms in neat order in special tool 11 4 480.

To install:

7. To install, reverse the removal procedure noting the following.

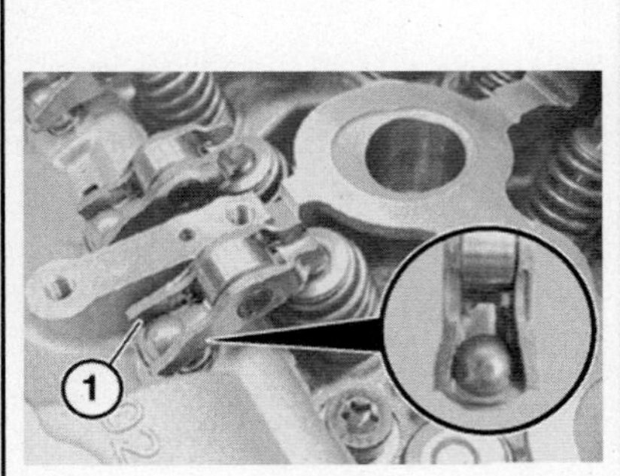

71112_BMW5_G0584

Fig. 254 Detaching rocker arms (1) from HVCA element and removing

8. Check function of DME; if necessary, readjust uniform mixture distribution.

N55 Engine

See Figures 257 through 261.

1. Remove cylinder head cover.
2. Remove intermediate lever.
3. Remove exhaust camshaft.

➡Roller cam followers (1) on intake side are divided into bearing classes.

➡The tolerance classes are marked according to the graphic in numbers from 1 to 5.

⁂ WARNING

Already used roller cam followers (1) may only be reused in the same position.

4. Detach roller cam followers (1) from hydraulic valve clearance compensating element and remove.

71112_BMW5_G0585

Fig. 255 Removing HVC element (1)

5. Place all roller cam followers (1) in neat order on special tool 11 4 481 .

➡Prior to installation of intermediate levers, ensure proper installation position of roller cam followers (1).

6. Classification of roller cam follower intake.
   a. Series:
      - Number 3. standard.
      - Number 2. slow idle.
      - Number 4. fast idle.
7. In case of repair: rough idle.
   a. Reparatur: 1
      - Number 1. slow speed in idle.
      - Number 5. high speed in idle.
8. Detach roller cam follower (1) on exhaust side from hydraulic valve clearance compensating element and remove.
9. Place all roller cam followers (1) in neat order on special tool 11 4 482.

➡Prior to installation of exhaust camshaft, ensure proper installation position of roller cam followers (1).

10. Remove hydraulic valve clearance compensating element (1) on intake side in direction of arrow.

➡If hydraulic valve clearance compensating elements (1) are reused, they must be placed together with rocker arms in neat order in special tool 11 4 481.

11. Remove hydraulic valve clearance compensating element (1) on exhaust side in direction of arrow.

➡If hydraulic valve clearance compensating elements (1) are reused, they must be placed together with rocker arms in neat order in special tool 11 4 482.

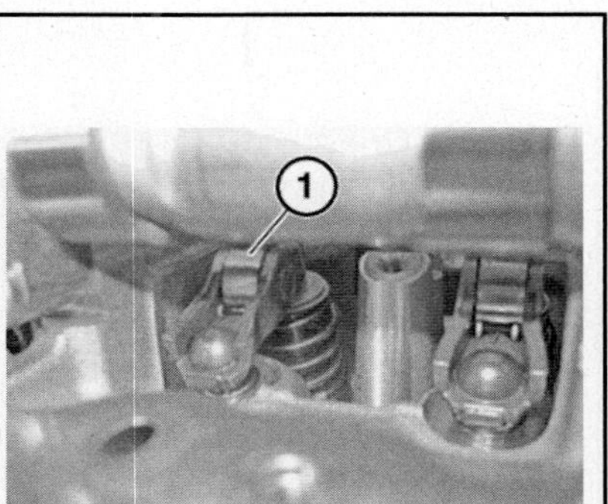

71112_BMW5_G0586

Fig. 256 Detaching roller cam followers (1) from hydraulic valve clearance compensating element and removing

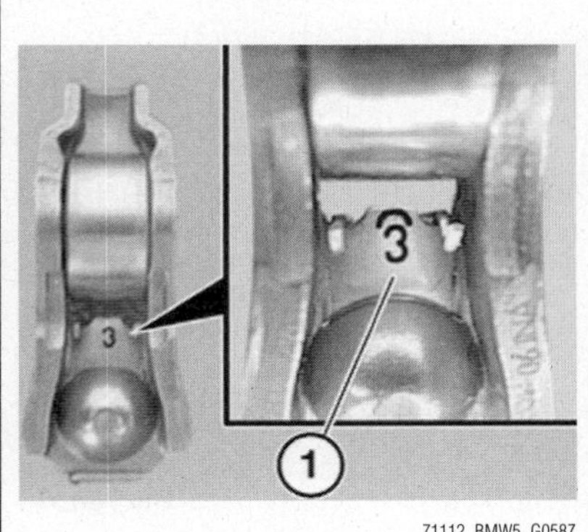

71112_BMW5_G0587

Fig. 257 Identifying roller cam follower intake classification

71112_BMW5_G0588

Fig. 258 Detaching roller cam follower (1) on exhaust side

To install:

12. To install, reverse the removal procedure noting the following.
13. Check function of DME; if necessary, readjust uniform mixture distribution.

N63 Engine

See Figure 262.

Cylinder bank 5-8:

1. Remove left inlet camshaft.
2. Remove left exhaust camshaft.

⁂ WARNING

Used rocker arms (1) may only be reused in the same position.

⁂ WARNING

Tolerance classes are not required.

3. Remove rocker arm (1) and set down in neat order in special tool 11 4 480.

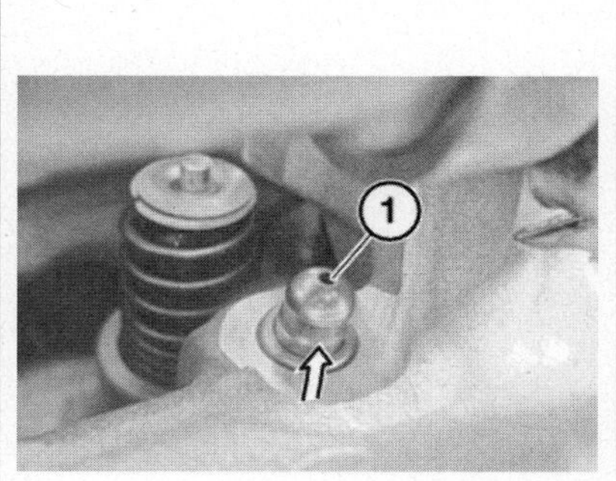

Fig. 259 Removing hydraulic valve clearance compensating element (1) on intake side

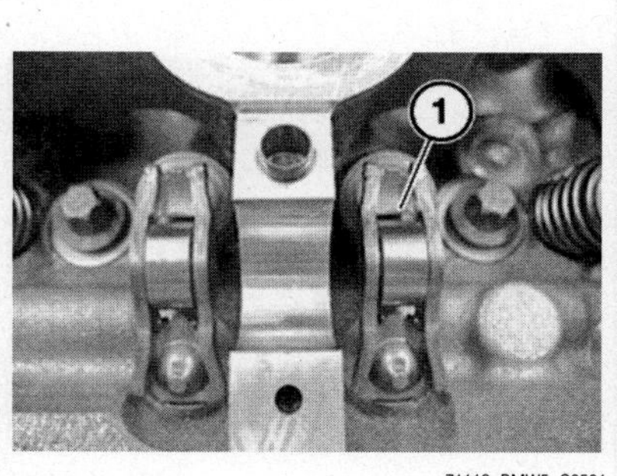

Fig. 261 Removing rocker arm (1)

Fig. 263 Screw special tool 11 0 371 to 59 ft. lbs. (80 Nm) into crankshaft seal. Screw in spindle 11 0 372.

Fig. 260 Removing hydraulic valve clearance compensating element (1) on exhaust side

Fig. 262 Turn back special tool 11 9 222. Push special tool 11 9 221 onto crankshaft. When bolts are tightened down (special tool 11 9 224), crankshaft seal is pressed inwards

4. Install rocker arm (1).
5. Align all rocker arms (1) straight.

To install:

6. To install, reverse the removal procedure.

TIMING CHAIN COVER SEAL

REMOVAL & INSTALLATION

N52 Engine

See Figures 262 through 270.

1. Before servicing the vehicle, refer to the precautions.
2. Remove crankshaft damper

WARNING

Do not remove central bolt. If the central bolt is Removed, the sprocket wheels of the timing chain and the oil pump will no longer be non-positively connected to the crankshaft.

Inlet and exhaust camshafts can turn in relation to crankshaft.

3. Turn back special tool 11 9 222.
4. Push special tool 11 9 221 onto crankshaft.

➡When bolts are tightened down (special tool 11 9 224), crankshaft seal is pressed inwards approximately 1 mm and thus slackened for subsequent removal.

5. Insert bolts (special tool 11 9 224) and tighten down to approximately 15 ft. lbs. (20 Nm).
6. Screw special tool 11 0 371 to 59 ft. lbs. (80 Nm) into crankshaft seal.
7. Screw in spindle 11 0 372.
8. Remove crankshaft seal from housing.

➡Repeat the operation several times if necessary.

9. Carefully saw open crankshaft seal at cutting line.
10. Remove crankshaft seal from special tool 11 0 371.

To install:

WARNING

The following text describes installation and sealing between the engine block and crankshaft seal.

The engine block will not be leak proof at the outside of the crankshaft seal if you fail to comply with the individual work steps and the work sequence.

11. Clean sealing surface and degrease thoroughly in area of housing partition.
12. Apply a light coat of oil to running surface of crankshaft seal.
13. Screw special tool 11 9 232 with bolts (special tool 11 9 234) to crankshaft.

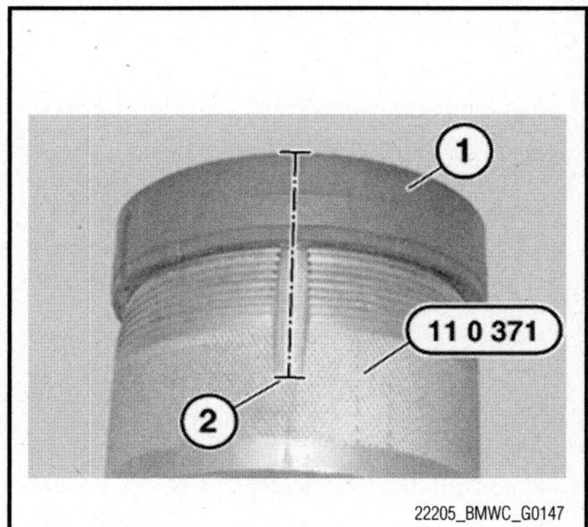

Fig. 264 Carefully saw open crankshaft seal (1) at cutting line (2)

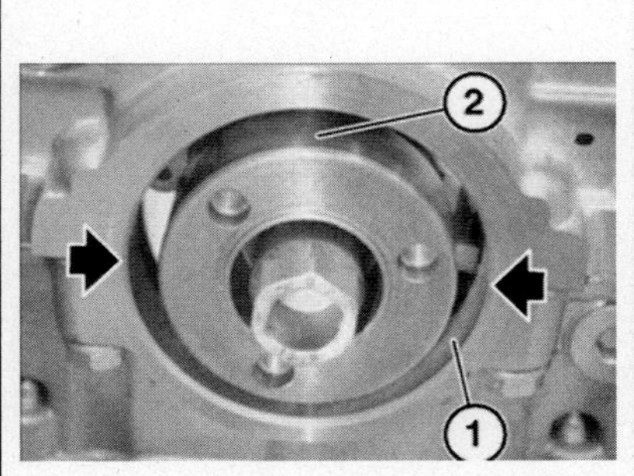

Fig. 265 Clean sealing surface (1) and apply a light coat of oil to running surface (2)

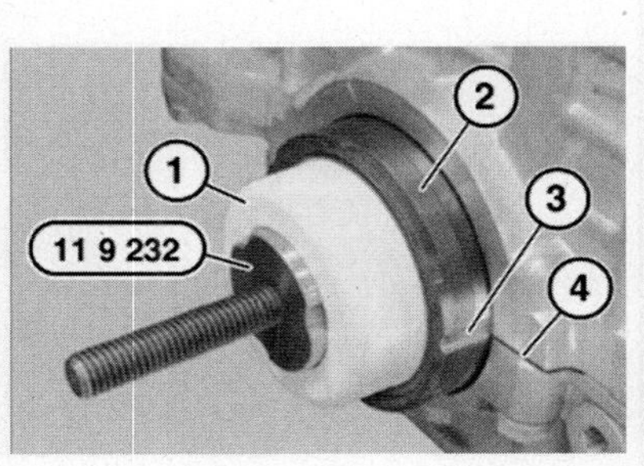

Fig. 267 Support sleeve (1), housing partition (4), grooves (3) and crankshaft seal (2)

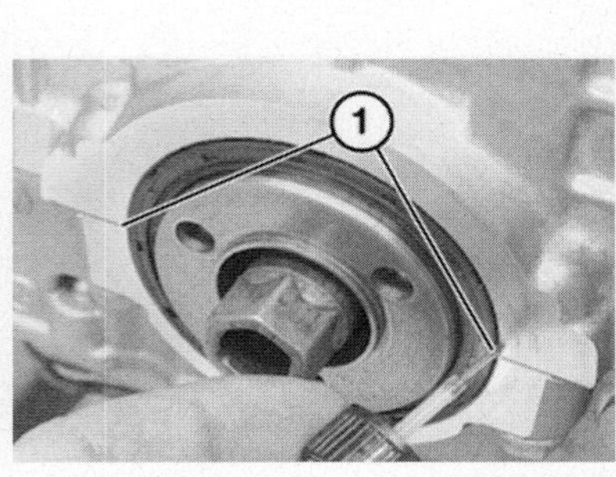

Fig. 269 Insert brush as far as possible into grooves (1) on crankshaft seal in order to coat housing partition on engine block

➡Support sleeve is supplied with crankshaft seal.

14. When crankshaft seal is installed, only support sleeve may be used as a slip sleeve.
15. Crankshaft seal has a groove on both left and right sides.

⁂ WARNING

After installation, the grooves must be filled with sealing compound.

➡The required parts are available from the BMW Parts Service (Electronic Parts Catalogue ETK).

16. Remove screw caps from injector.
17. Screw on metering needle.
18. Insert piston for pressing out. Injector contains the sealing compound Loctite, manufacturer's number 128357. Bottle contains the primer Loctite, manufacturer's number 171000.
19. Push support sleeve with crankshaft seal onto special tool 11 9 232.

⁂ WARNING

Support sleeve remains on special tool 11 9 232, until crankshaft seal is drawn in.

20. Align groove centrally to housing partition.
21. Coat both grooves on crankshaft seal with Loctite® primer, manufacturer's number 171000, and expose to air for approximately one minute.
22. Draw in crankshaft seal with special tool 11 9 231 in conjunction with special tool 11 9 233 until flush.
23. Before filling with sealing compound, moisten brush with Loctite® primer, manufacturer's number 171000. Insert brush as far as possible into grooves on crankshaft seal in order to coat housing partition on engine block.
24. Using injector, fill both grooves flush with Loctite® sealing compound, manufacturer's number 128357.

➡Loctite® primer, manufacturer's number 171000, binds the Loctite® sealing compound, manufacturer's number 128357, and prevents leakage.

25. Coat surface of sealing compound in both grooves with Loctite® primer, manufacturer's number 171000.
26. Install crankshaft damper.

TIMING CHAIN COVER, CHAIN, TENSIONER, & SPROCKETS

REMOVAL & INSTALLATION

N20 Engine

See Figures 271 through 286.

1. Remove cylinder head cover.
2. Remove all spark plugs.
3. Remove vibration damper.

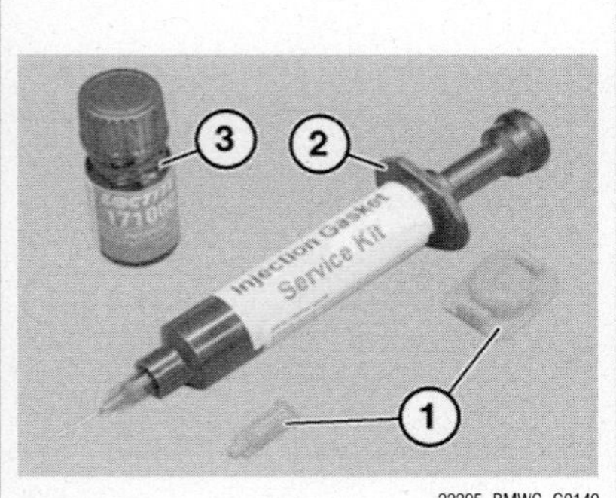

Fig. 266 Screw caps (1), injector (2) and Loctite® primer, manufacturer's number 171000 (3)

Fig. 268 Draw in crankshaft seal with special tool 11 9 231 in conjunction with special tool 11 9 233 until flush

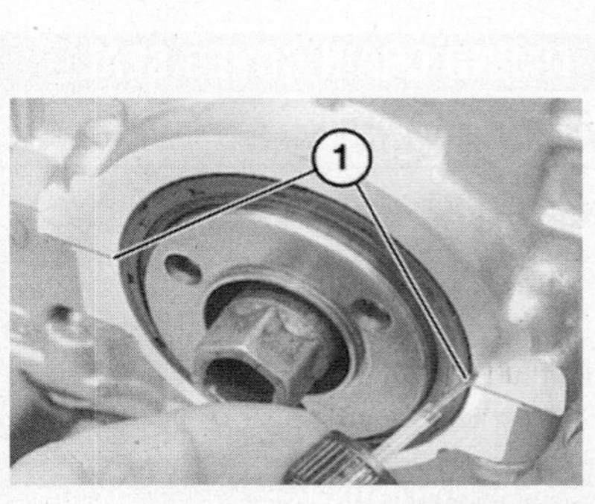

Fig. 270 Using injector (2), fill both grooves (3) flush with Loctite® sealing compound, manufacturer's number 128357

4. Remove crankshaft seal at front.
5. Check timing.
6. Removing oil pan.
7. Push back the chain tensioner with the tensioning rail (1).
8. Secure chain tensioner using special tool 11 4 120.
9. With engine removed, block crankshaft at flywheel with special tool 11 9 260.

WARNING

To release central bolt, remove special tool 11 0 300.

Vehicles with manual transmission:

10. Attach special tool 11 8 180 to manual transmission with existing transmission bolts (1).
11. Block crankshaft in direction of arrow with special tool.

Vehicles with automatic transmission:

12. Block crankshaft with special tool 11 8 660.
13. Feed in special tool, slide screw forward and tighten.

All vehicles:

WARNING

Breakaway torque of central bolt:> 600 Nm.

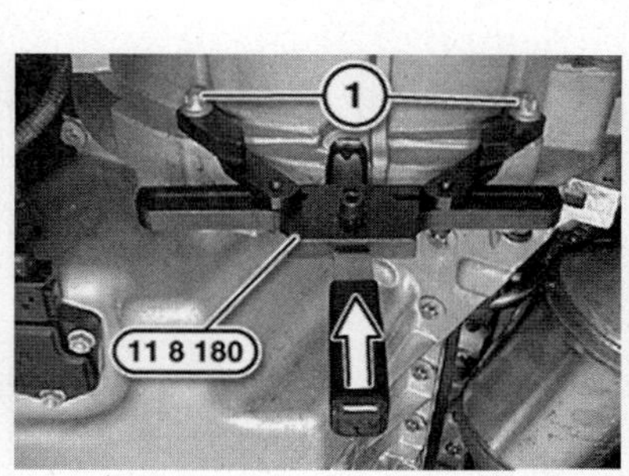

Fig. 272 Attaching special tool to manual transmission with existing transmission bolts (1)

WARNING

A 3/4 inch tool is needed to release the central bolt.

14. Release central bolt (1).
15. Tightening torque: 74 ft. lbs. (100 Nm) + 270°.
16. Remove special tool to release the central bolts on the intake and exhaust camshaft adjusters.
17. Remove intake and exhaust camshaft adjusters.
18. Remove chain tensioner.
    a. Release screws (1).
    b. Tightening torque: 16 ft. lbs. (22 Nm).
    c. Raise vacuum unit (1) slightly.
    d. Release chain tensioner (2).
    e. Tightening torque: 48 ft. lbs. (65 Nm).

➡**Have a cleaning cloth ready. A small quantity of engine oil will escape after the screw connection has been released.**

➡**Make sure no engine oil runs onto belt drive.**

➡**When installing, replace sealing ring.**

    f. If the chain tensioner is reused, its oil chamber must be drained.
    g. Place chain tensioner on a level support and slowly compress.
    h. Repeat process twice.

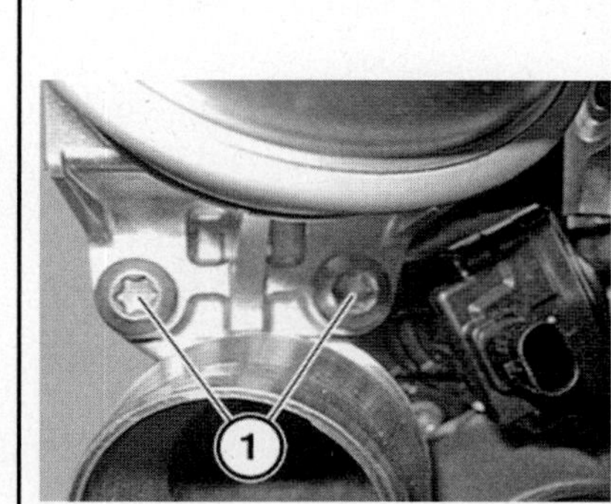

Fig. 273 Releasing screws (1)

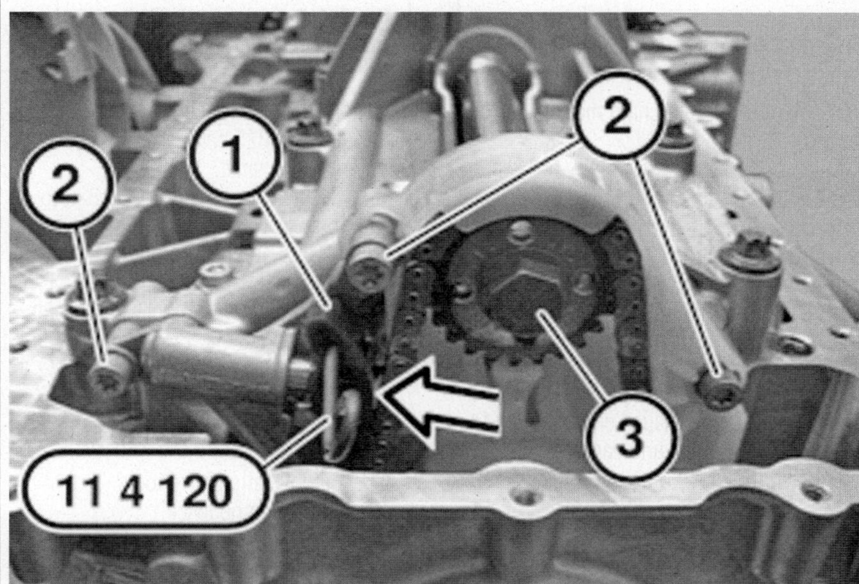

Fig. 271 Pushing back chain tensioner with tensioning rail (1)

Fig. 274 Raising vacuum unit (1) and releasing chain tensioner (2)

19. Screw in vibration absorber screws (1).

20. Pull out hub (2) on crankshaft forward in direction of arrow.

21. Open screw plug (1).

a. Tightening torque: 18 ft. lbs. (25 Nm).

22. Release bearing journal (1) from timing chain module on cylinder head.

a. Tightening torque: 10 ft. lbs. (14 Nm).

23. Release screw plugs (1 and 2).

24. Release bearing journal (1) on left and right of timing chain module for timing chain on crankcase.

a. Tightening torque: 15 ft. lbs. (20 Nm).

25. Release bolts (1) from timing chain module on cylinder head.

a. Tightening torque 11 31 4AZ.

26. Remove chain module with timing chain and camshaft sprocket upwards.

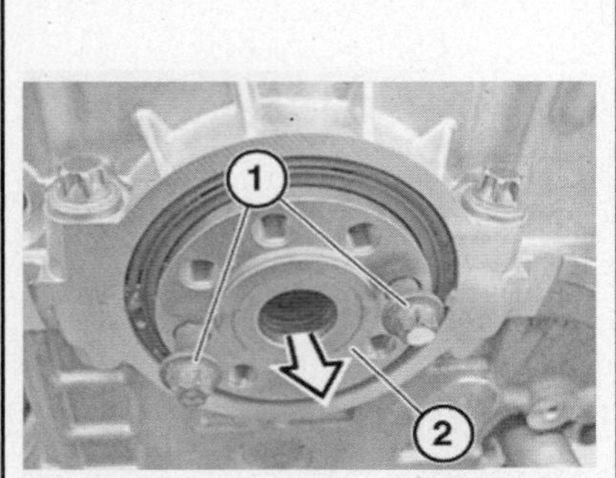

Fig. 275 Screwing in vibration absorber screws (1) and pulling out hub (2)

Fig. 276 Opening screw plug (1)

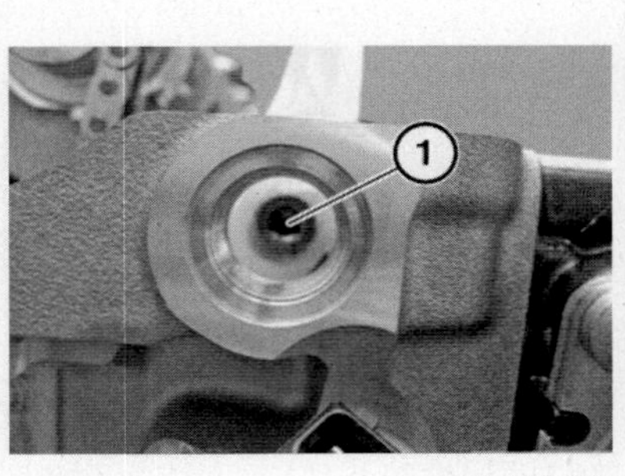

Fig. 277 Releasing bearing journal (1) from timing chain module

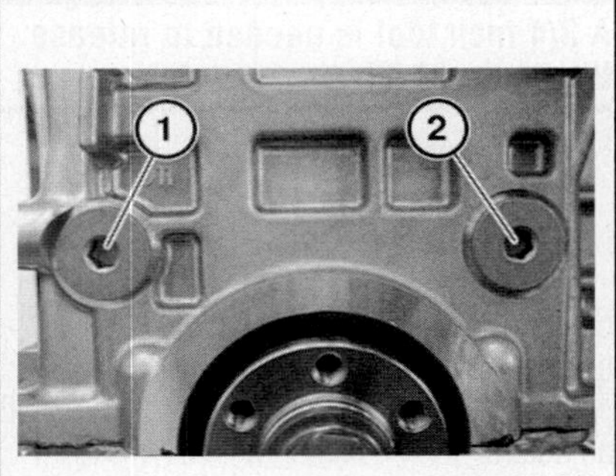

Fig. 278 Releasing screw plugs (1 and 2)

Fig. 279 Releasing bearing journal (1) on left and right of timing chain module

Fig. 280 Releasing bolts (1) from timing chain module on cylinder head

27. Remove timing chain module (1) upward.

WARNING

Note direction of installation of camshaft sprocket (2). Collar (see arrow) on sprocket (2) points to engine. Incorrect assembly will result in engine damage.

28. Pull timing chain upwards until camshaft sprocket engages chain guide (1). Install timing chain and camshaft sprocket in this position.

➡When installing, permanently hold timing chain under tension. Timing chain may jam on chain guide (1).

29. Loosen sealing cap using a screwdriver.

To install:

30. To install, reverse the removal procedure noting the following.

31. Turn engine at central bolt until special tool 2 212 825 can be positioned in counterbalance shaft.

32. Secure special tool 2 212 825 to oil pump housing with screw (1).

33. Fit hub and central bolt (1).

34. Remove special tool 11 4 120.

35. Insert central bolt (1) with hub for crankshaft.

36. Tighten down central bolt (1).

a. Tightening torque 11 21 1AZ.

37. Install intake and exhaust camshaft adjusters.

38. Remove all special tools.

39. Crank engine twice.

40. Check timing.

41. Replace front crankshaft seal.

42. Assemble engine.

N52 Engines

See Figures 287 through 303.

1. Before servicing the vehicle, refer to the precautions.

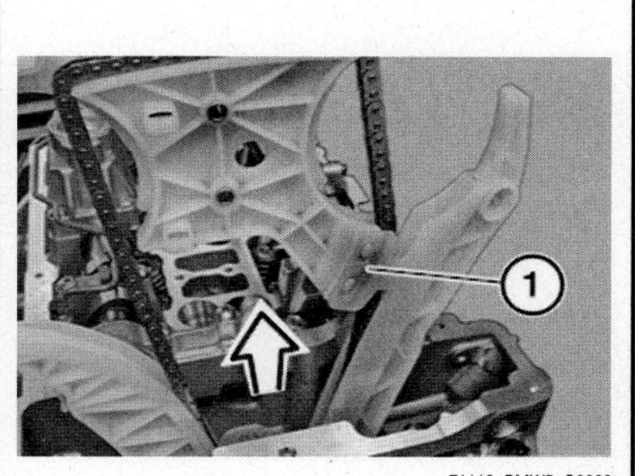

Fig. 281 Removing timing chain module (1) upward

Fig. 282 Identifying camshaft sprocket (2) and collar (arrow)

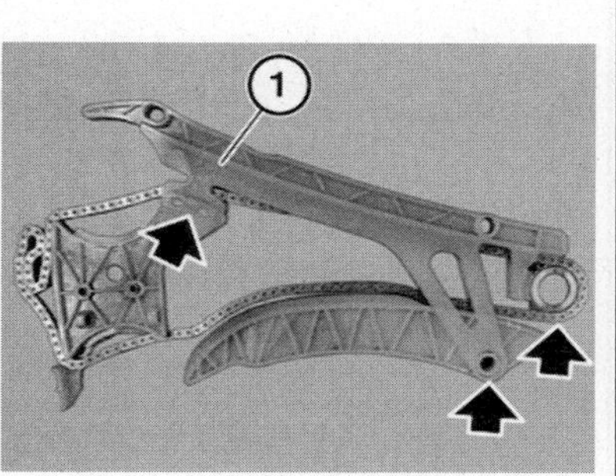

Fig. 283 Engaging chain on chain guide (1)

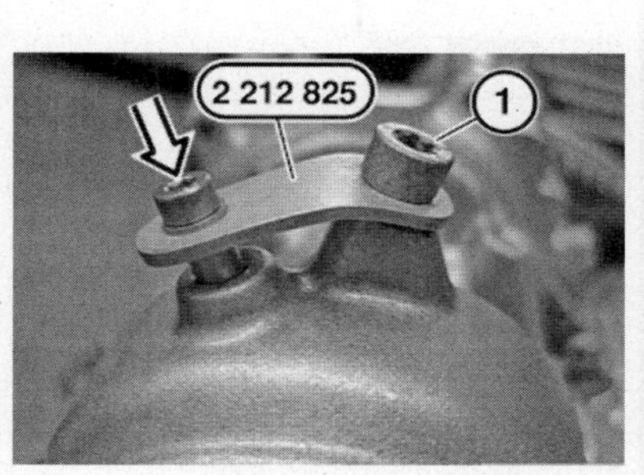

Fig. 284 Securing special tool to oil pump housing with a screw (1)

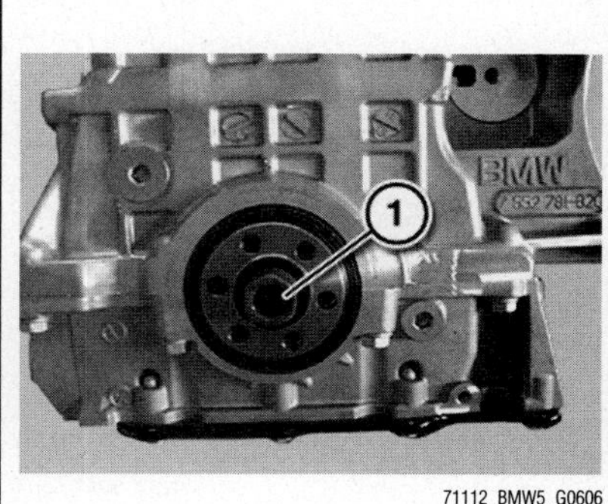

Fig. 285 Fitting hub and central bolt (1)

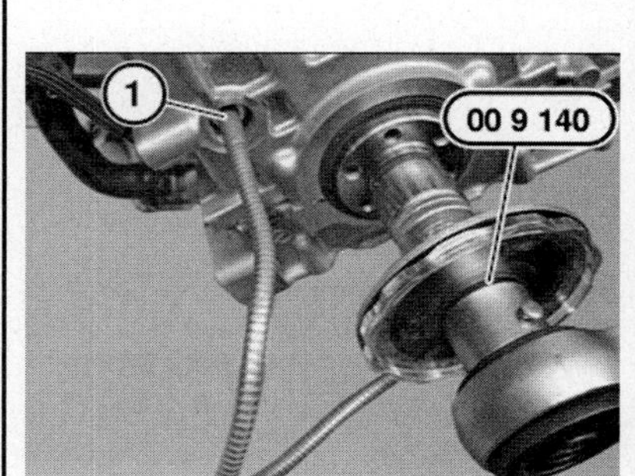

Fig. 286 Inserting central bolt (1) with hub for crankshaft

2. Remove valve cover.
3. Remove all spark plugs.
4. Remove chain tensioner.

➡Have a cleaning cloth ready. A small quantity of engine oil will emerge after the screw connection has been Removed.

WARNING

Make sure no engine oil runs onto belt drive.

5. Remove crankshaft front radial seal.
6. Remove accessory drive belt and tensioner.
7. Remove crankshaft damper.
8. Remove fastener.
9. Rotate crankshaft at central bolt into TDC position.
10. Slide special tool 11 0 300 into special tool bore and secure crankshaft.

WARNING

On vehicles with optional extra SA205 (automatic transmission), there is a large bore for the TDC position shortly before the special tool bore. This bore can be confused with the special tool bore.

If the flywheel is secured in the correct special tool bore with special tool 11 0 300, the engine can no longer be moved at the central bolt.

11. Do not remove special tool 11 0 300 to Remove central bolt. Employ a second person for gripping when releasing central bolt.
12. Screw special tool 11 9 280 onto hub of crankshaft damper.
13. Remove central bolt.
14. Remove hub towards front.
15. Open plug at top of cylinder head.
16. Open plug at lower left of engine block.
17. Remove bearing pin from timing chain module on cylinder head.
18. Remove bearing pin from timing chain module on crankcase.

WARNING

Install special tool 11 4 280 to Remove the central bolts on the inlet and exhaust adjustment units.

19. Secure special tool 11 4 283 to cylinder head with bolts.

➡Fit special tool 11 4 282 underneath on side of inlet camshaft.

20. Mount special tool 11 4 281 on inlet and exhaust camshafts.
21. Do not remove special tool 11 4 280.
22. Remove inlet and exhaust adjustment unit. Refer to "Engine Mechanical, Camshaft and Lifters, Removal & Installation."

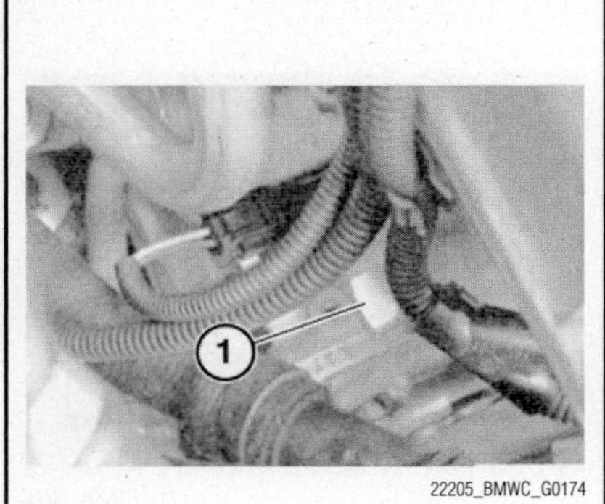

Fig. 287 Chain tensioner (1) location

Fig. 290 Do not remove special tool 11 0 300 to Remove central bolt (1). Screw special tool 11 9 280 onto hub of crankshaft damper

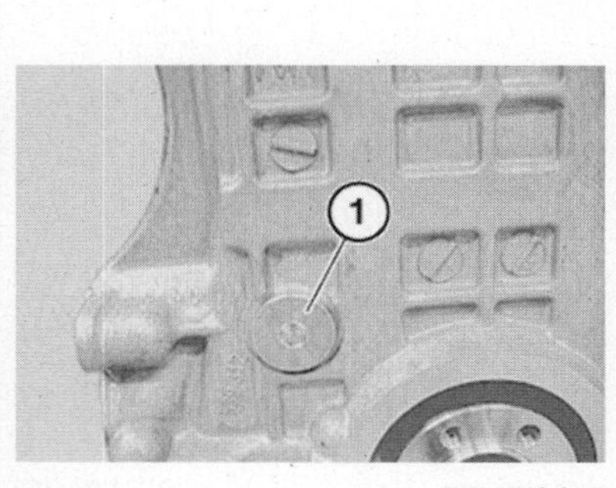

Fig. 292 Open plug at lower left of engine block

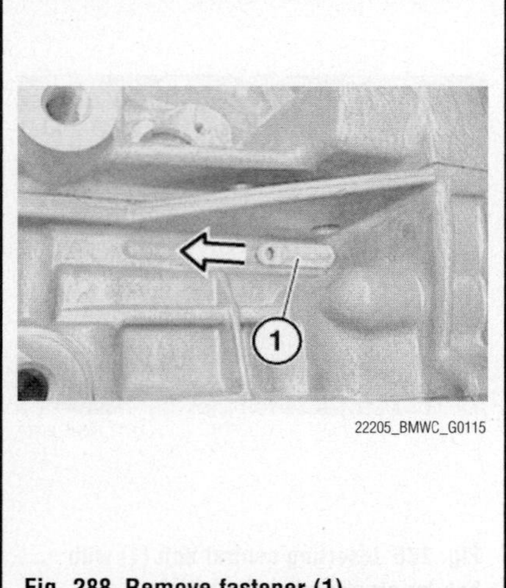

Fig. 288 Remove fastener (1)

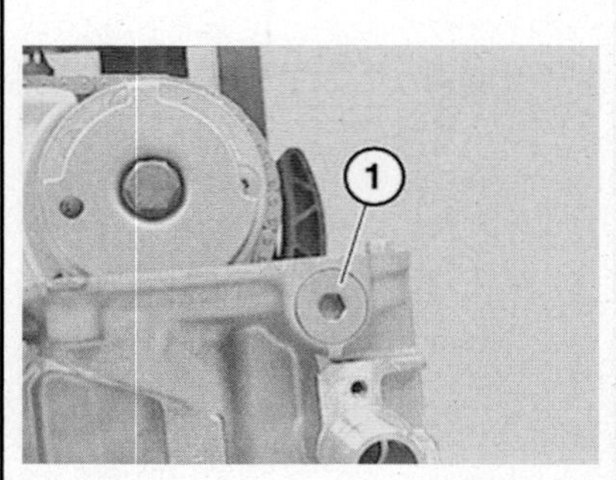

Fig. 291 Open plug at top of cylinder head

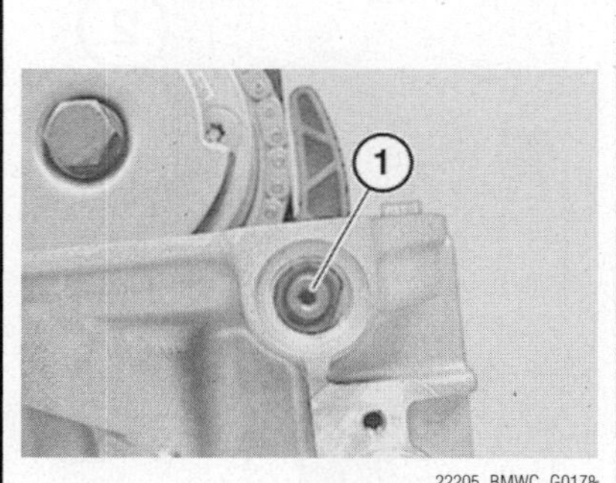

Fig. 293 Remove bearing pin (1) from timing chain module on cylinder head

23. Remove bolts (1) from timing chain module on cylinder head.
24. Remove chain module with timing chain and sprocket wheel upwards.

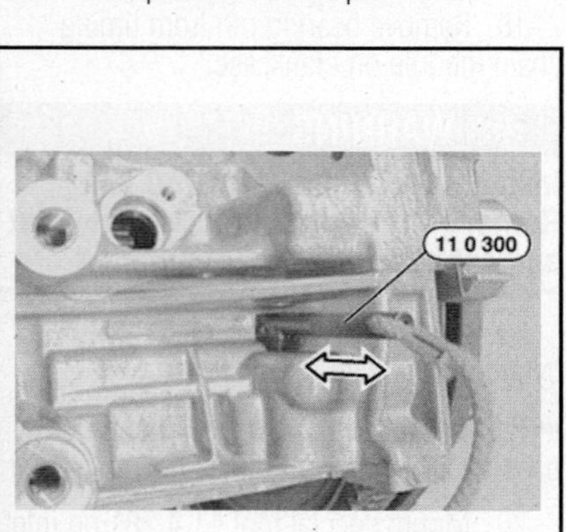

Fig. 289 Slide special tool 11 0 300 into special tool bore and secure crankshaft

To install:

WARNING

Note installation direction of sprocket wheel. Collar on sprocket wheel points to engine. Incorrect assembly will result in engine damage.

25. Pull timing chain upwards until sprocket wheel engages chain guide.
26. On N54 engines, special friction plates are required between the friction surfaces.

WARNING

The engine will incur damage if the plates are damaged or are not fitted.

a. Friction plates are clipped into place on sprocket wheel/oil pump module.
b. Make sure friction plate is in correct installation position.
c. Push on friction plate without retainers.
d. Insert chain module from above and secure with bolt.
e. Make sure gear wheels are in correct installation position.
f. Insert hub with friction plate.

27. Install timing chain and sprocket wheel in this position.

➡Always hold timing chain under tension. Timing chain may jam on chain guide.

28. Install hub with central bolt.
29. Tighten down special tool 11 5 200 with bolts to hub.
30. Install bolts from timing chain module on cylinder head and tighten to 7 ft. lbs. (9 Nm).
31. Install bearing pin from timing chain module on crankcase and tighten to 15 ft. lbs. (20 Nm).

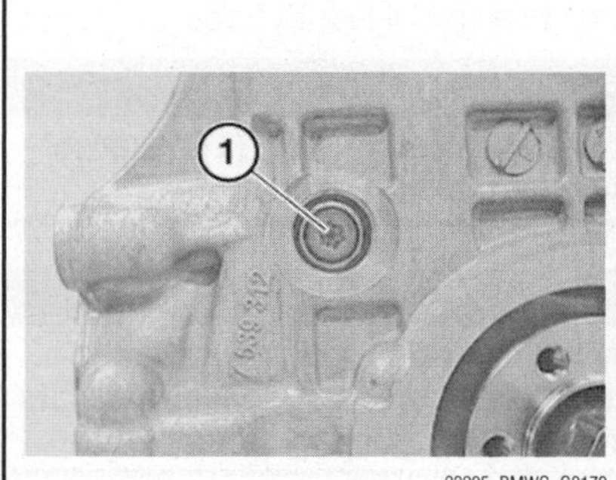

Fig. 294 Remove bearing pin (1) from timing chain module on crankcase

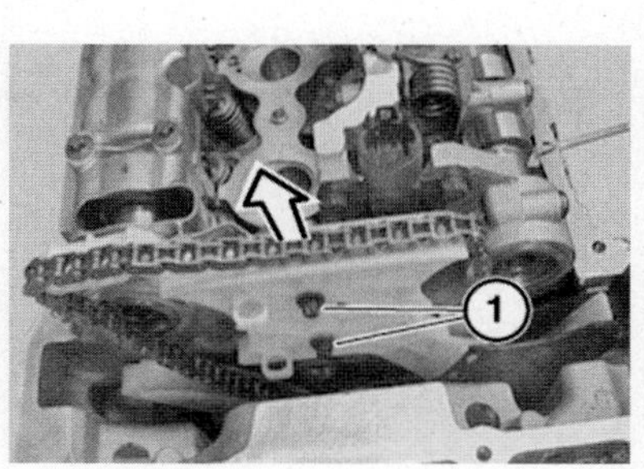

Fig. 296 Remove bolts (1) from timing chain module on cylinder head

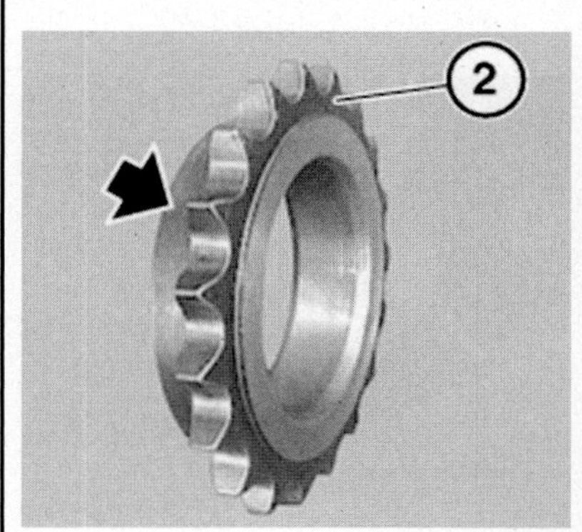

Fig. 297 Collar (see arrow) on sprocket wheel (2) points to engine

32. Install bearing pin from timing chain module on cylinder head and tighten to10 ft. lbs. (14 Nm).
33. Install plug and tighten to 19 ft. lbs. (25 Nm).
34. If not previously done, remove tensioner for drive belt.
35. Screw in special tool 11 4 362 from special tool kit 11 4 360.
36. Mount special tool 11 9 280 on 11 5 200.
37. Support special tool 11 9 280 on special tool 11 4 362.
38. Special tool 11 0 300 secures crankshaft.
39. Tighten central bolt to 74 ft. lbs. (100 Nm) plus an additional 360° of rotation.
40. Install inlet and exhaust adjustment units.
41. Install chain tensioner.
42. Crank engine twice.

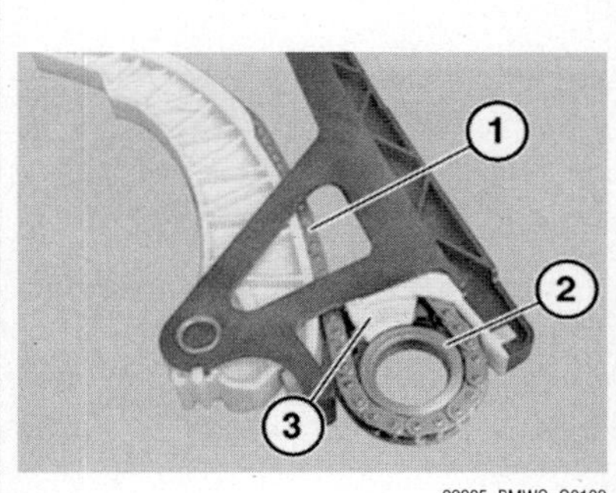

Fig. 298 Pull timing chain (1) upwards until sprocket wheel (2) engages chain guide (3)

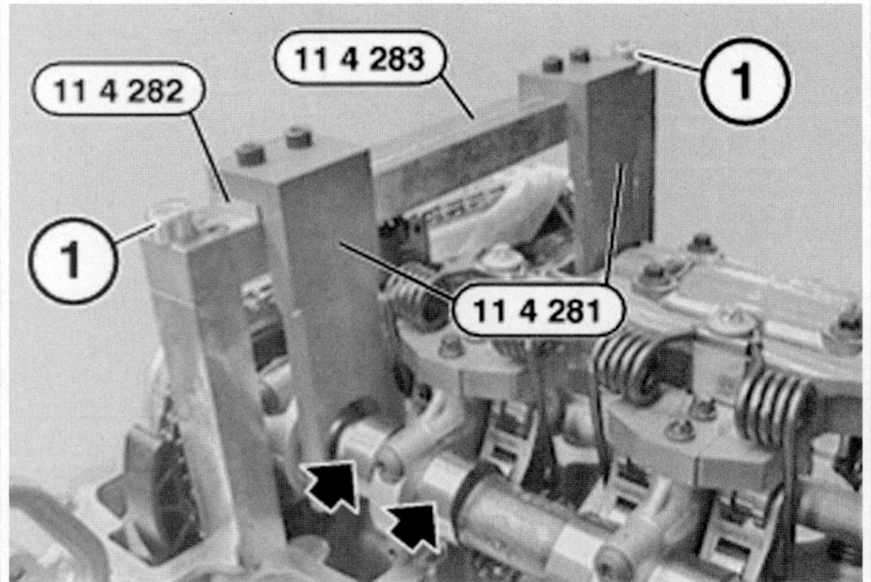

Fig. 295 Secure special tool 11 4 283 to cylinder head with bolts (1)

43. Check and if necessary adjust valve timing. Refer to "Engine Mechanical, Camshaft and Lifters, Removal & Installation."

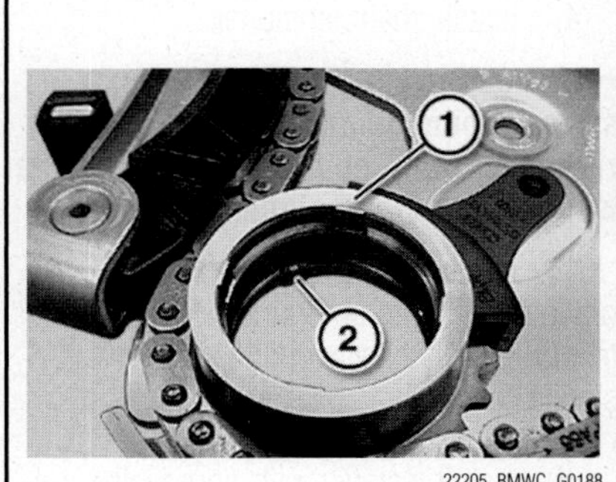

Fig. 299 On N54 engines, special friction plates (1 and 2) are required between the friction surfaces

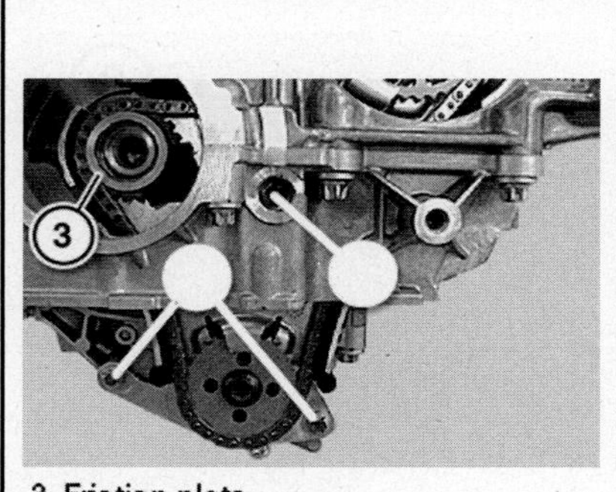

Fig. 300 Make sure friction plate (3) is in correct installation position

Fig. 301 Insert chain module from above and secure with bolt (1). Make sure gear wheels (2) are in correct installation position, then insert hub (3) with friction plate

44. Install crankshaft damper.
45. Install accessory drive belt and tensioner. Tighten tensioner mounting bolt to 19 ft. lbs. (25 Nm) plus an additional 90° rotation.
46. Install crankshaft front radial seal.
47. Install chain tensioner.

➡No sealing ring is fitted during series-production assembly. A sealing ring must be fitted by service personnel when the chain tensioner is fitted.

48. If the chain tensioner is reused, its oil chamber must be drained. Place chain tensioner on a level working surface and slowly compress.
49. Repeat procedure twice.
50. Install fastener with bore facing outwards.
51. Install tensioner and tighten to 41 ft. lbs. (55 Nm).
52. Install all spark plugs.
53. Install valve cover.

Fig. 302 Tighten down special tool 11 5 200 with bolts (1) to hub

N55 Engine

See Figures 304 through 316.

1. Remove cylinder head cover.
2. Remove all spark plugs.
3. Remove crankshaft radial seal at front.
4. Remove tensioning device for drive belt.
5. Remove vibration absorber.
6. Check timing.
7. With engine removed, block crankshaft with special tool 11 9 260.

⁂ WARNING

To release central bolt (1), remove special tool 11 0 300.

⁂ WARNING

When central bolt of crankshaft is released, there is no longer a secure connection to timing drive.

8. Mark position of crankshaft using a colored mark (1).

➡This will make future insertion of special tool 11 0 300 easier.

9. Vehicles with automatic transmission, block crankshaft with special tool 11 8 660.
10. Vehicles with manual gearbox, attach special tool 11 8 180 to manual gearbox with existing transmission bolts.
   a. Block crankshaft in direction of arrow with special tool.

⁂ WARNING

Breakaway torque of central bolt:> 443 ft. lbs. (600 Nm).

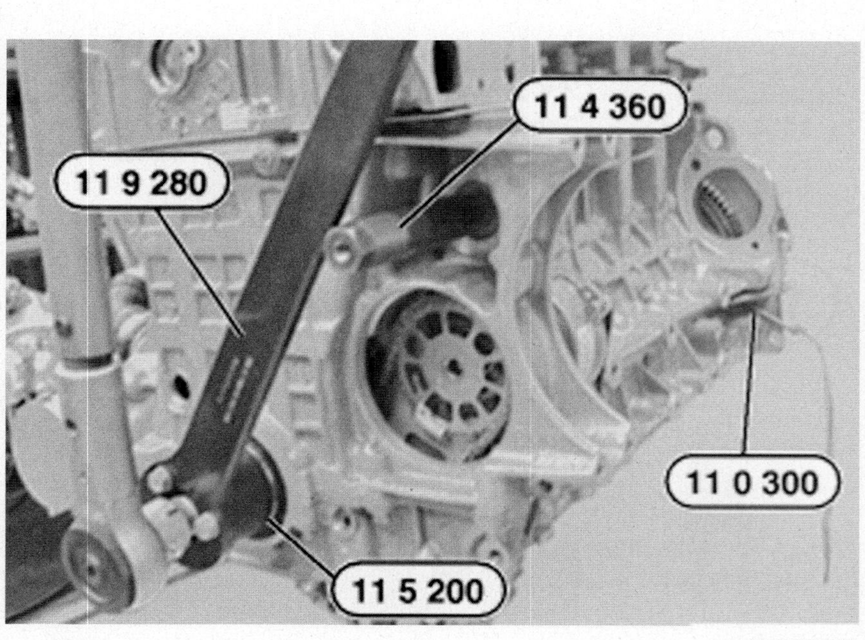

Fig. 303 Screw in special tool 11 4 362 from special tool kit 11 4 360

Fig. 304 Blocking crankshaft with special tool and removing central bolt (1)

Fig. 305 Marking crankshaft position (1)

⁂ WARNING

A 3/4-inch tool (large powered square) is required to release central bolt.

11. Release central bolt (1) with 3/4-inch tool (2).
    a. Tightening torque: 74 ft. lbs. (100 Nm) + 270°.
12. Remove chain tensioner.
    a. Remove air duct.
    b. Release chain tensioner (1).
    c. Tightening torque: 41 ft. lbs. (55 Nm).

⁂ WARNING

Have a cleaning cloth ready. A small quantity of engine oil will emerge after the screw connection has been released.

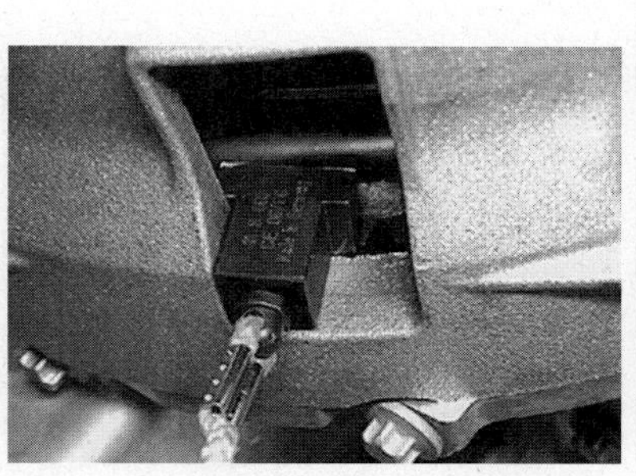

Fig. 306 Blocking crankshaft with special tool 11 8 660

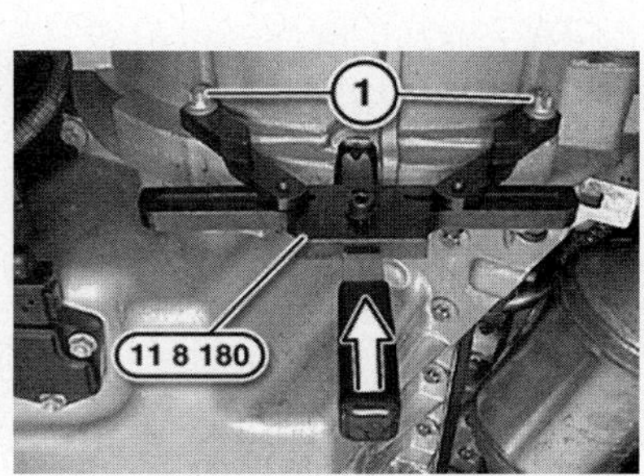

Fig. 307 Attaching special tool with existing transmission bolts (1) locking crankshaft with special tool

⁂ WARNING

Make sure no engine oil runs onto belt drive.

➡If the chain tensioner is reused, its oil chamber must be drained. Place chain tensioner on a level support and slowly compress.

    d. Repeat process twice.

➡When installing, replace sealing ring.

13. Screw in vibration absorber screws (1).
14. Move hub (2) on crankshaft forward in direction of arrow to remove.
15. Open screw plug (1).
    a. Tightening torque: 18 ft. lbs. (25 Nm).
16. Open screw plug (1).
    a. Tightening torque: 37 ft. lbs. (50 Nm).

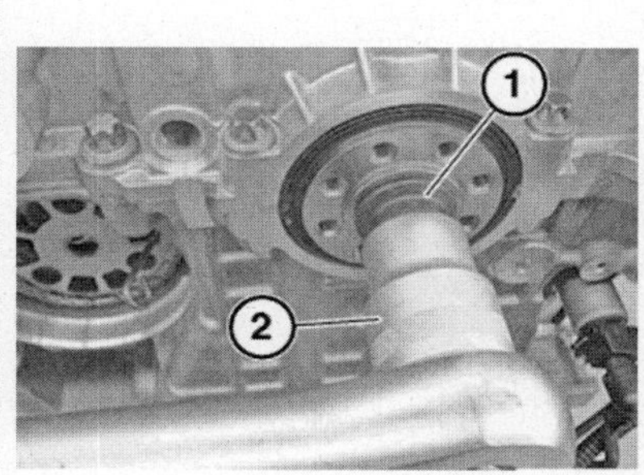

Fig. 308 Releasing central bolt (1) with ¾ inch tool (2)

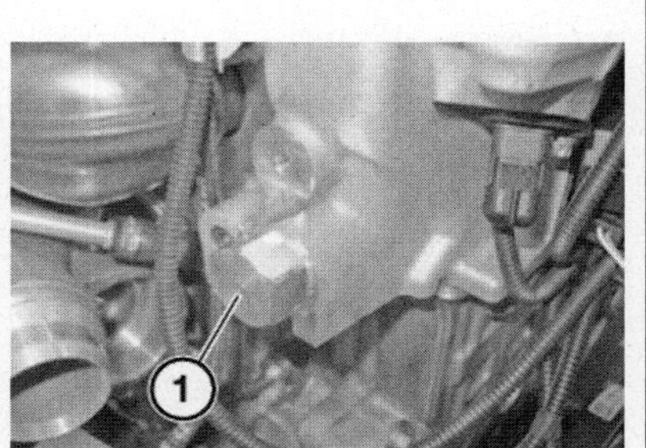

Fig. 309 Releasing chain tensioner (1)

➡When installing, replace aluminum screws.

17. Release bearing journal (1) from timing chain module on cylinder head.
    a. Tightening torque: 10 ft. lbs. (14 Nm).
18. Release bolts (1) from timing chain module on cylinder head.
    a. Tightening torque 11 31 4AZ.
19. Remove chain module with timing chain and camshaft sprocket upwards in direction of arrow.

⁂ WARNING

Note direction of installation of camshaft sprocket (2).

⁂ WARNING

Collar (see arrow) on camshaft sprocket (2) points to engine.

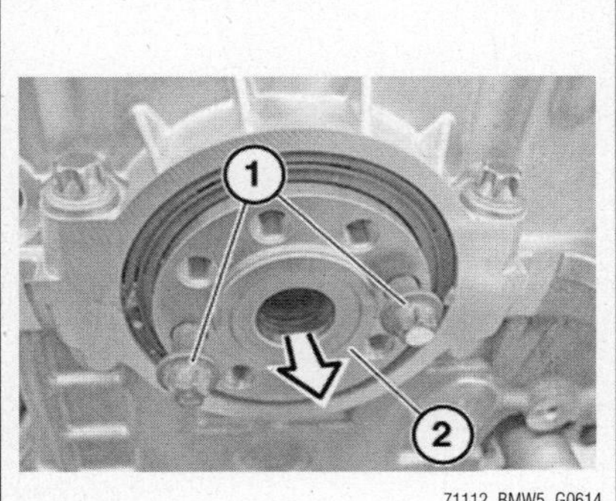

Fig. 310 Screwing in vibration absorber screws (1) and moving hub (2)

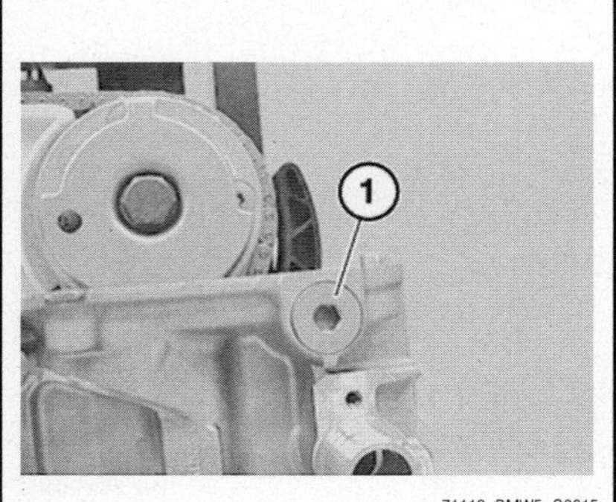

Fig. 311 Opening screw plug (1)

⁂ WARNING

Incorrect assembly will result in engine damage.

To install:

20. To install, reverse the removal procedure noting the following.
21. Pull timing chain (1) upwards until camshaft sprocket (2) engages chain guide (3).
22. Install timing chain (1) and camshaft sprocket (2) in this position.

➡When installing, always hold timing chain (1) under tension. Timing chain (1) may jam on chain guide (3).

23. Insert central bolt with hub for crankshaft.
24. Tighten down central bolt.
    a. Tightening torque: 74 ft. lbs. (100 Nm) + 270°.
25. Install intake and exhaust camshaft adjusters.

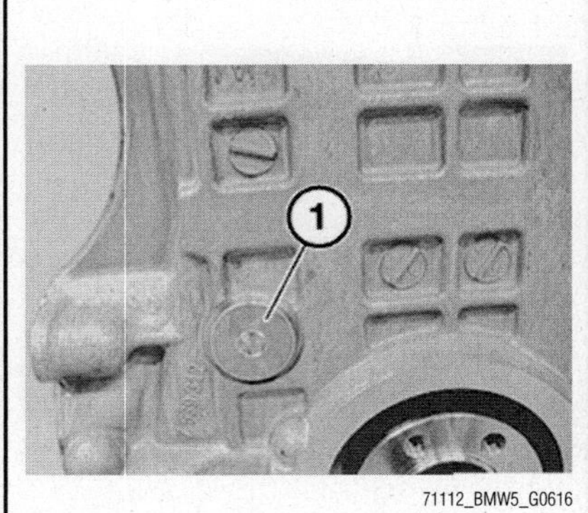

Fig. 312 Opening screw plug (1)

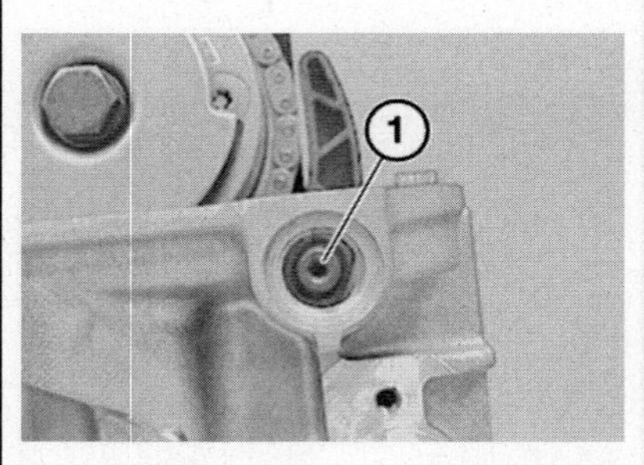

Fig. 313 Releasing bearing journal (1) from timing chain module

26. Install chain tensioner.
27. Crank engine twice.
28. Check timing.
29. If necessary, adjust valve timing.

Fig. 314 Releasing bolt (1) from timing chain module on cylinder head and removing chain module with timing chain and camshaft sprocket upwards in direction of arrow (N52 shown)

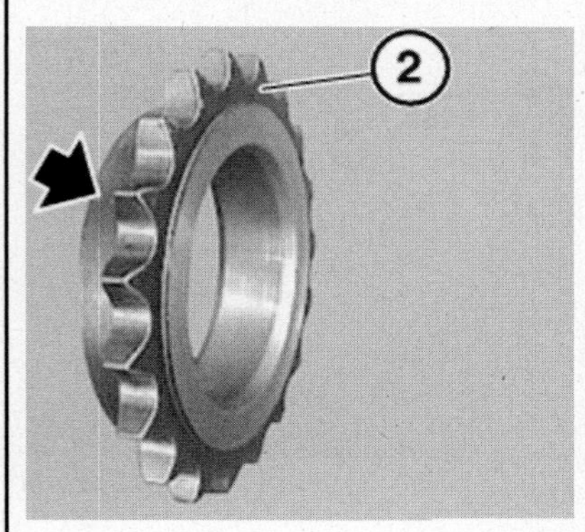

Fig. 315 Identifying camshaft sprocket (2) and collar (arrow)

30. Replace front crankshaft seal.
31. Assemble engine.

N63 Engine

See Figures 317 through 320.

1. Remove lower timing case cover
2. To facilitate removal and installation of timing chains, turn engine over with special tool 00 2 300.

Timing drive, cylinders 1 to 4

3. Remove guide rail (5) from bearing bolt.
4. Remove timing chain (3) with tensioning rail (4) from bearing bolt.

Timing drive, cylinders 5 to 8

5. Remove guide rail (1) from bearing bolt.
6. Remove timing chain (2) with tensioning rail (6) from bearing bolt.

Timing drive, cylinders 1 to 4:

7. Release bearing bolts (2) with a suitable tool.

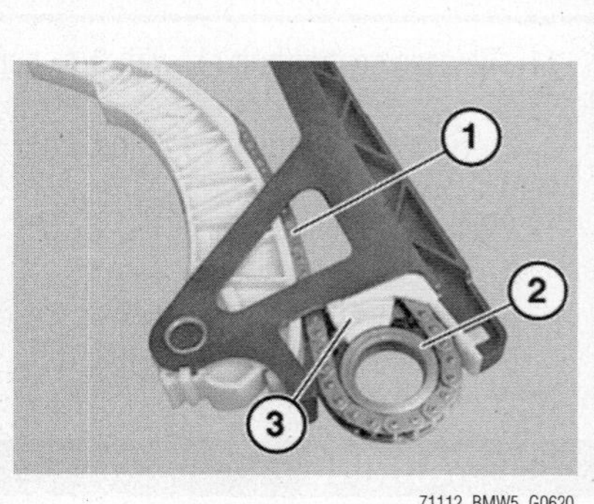

Fig. 316 Pulling timing chain (1) upwards until camshaft sprocket (2) engages chain guide (3)

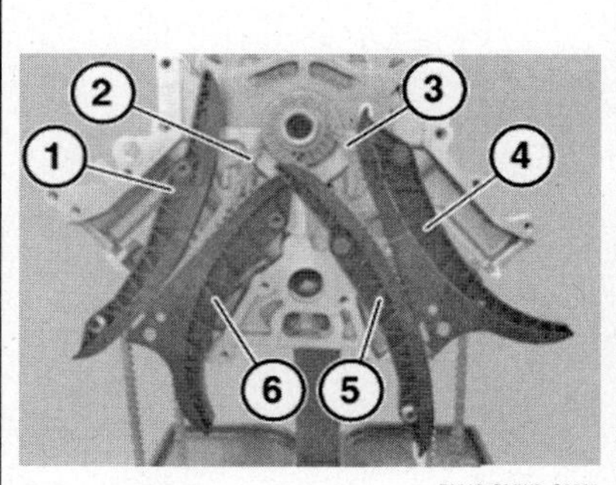

Fig. 317 Removing guide rail (5, 1) from bearing bolt, and timing chain (3, 2) with tensioning rail (4, 6) from bearing bolt

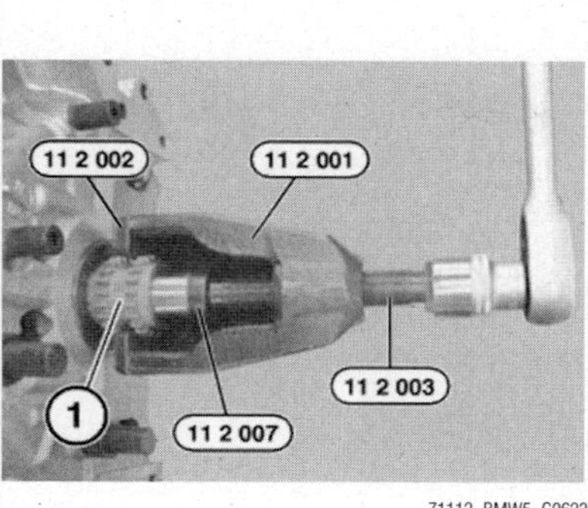

Fig. 319 Attaching special tools to the crankshaft

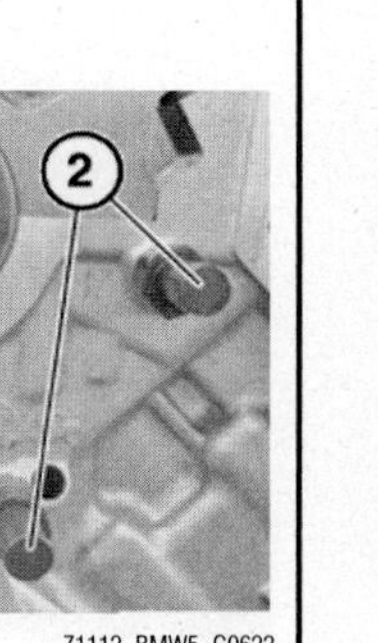

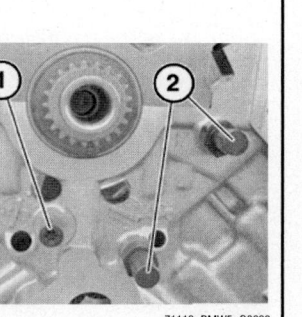

Fig. 318 Releasing bearing bolts (2, 1)

Fig. 320 Making sure Woodruff key (1) is installed correctly in crankshaft (2)

a. Tightening torque: 34 ft. lbs. (46 Nm).

Timing drive, cylinders 5 to 8:

8. Release bearing bolts (1).
   a. Tightening torque: 15 ft. lbs. (20 Nm).
9. Attach special tools 11 2 001 and 11 2 002 to the crankshaft.
10. Insert special tool 11 2 007 and remove sprocket wheel with special tool 11 2 003.

➡When installing, check sprocket wheels for wear, replace if necessary.

11. Heat sprocket wheel to 60° C.

⁂ CAUTION

Burning hazard. Wear gloves.

To install:

12. To install, reverse the removal procedure noting the following.
13. Make sure Woodruff key (1) is installed in correct position in crankshaft (2).
14. Maintain tension of timing chains when installing timing case cover.
15. Observe sparking protection on timing case cover.
16. Make sure timing chain is correctly installed when placing it in guide rail.
17. Assemble engine.

TURBOCHARGER

REMOVAL & INSTALLATION

N20 Engine

See Figures 322 through 333.

⁂ WARNING

The module consists of exhaust turbo charger and exhaust manifold.

1. Remove the catalytic converter.
2. Remove acoustic cover
3. Remove heat shield on side member.
4. Remove front right suspension cross-brace
5. Drain coolant.
6. Remove the right coolant hose.
7. Remove bottom clean air pipe.
8. Remove right charge-air duct.
9. Drain engine oil.
10. Unlock coolant hose from expansion tank and pull off.
11. Disconnect vacuum hose from vacuum line.
12. Disconnect plug connection on blow-off valve.
13. Unlock retaining clip with a suitable prytool in direction of arrow and hold.
14. Pull off retaining clip with suitable pliers in direction of arrow.
15. Pull off wastegate linkage from wastegate flap.
16. Release screws (1).
    a. Tightening torque: 16 ft. lbs. (22 Nm).

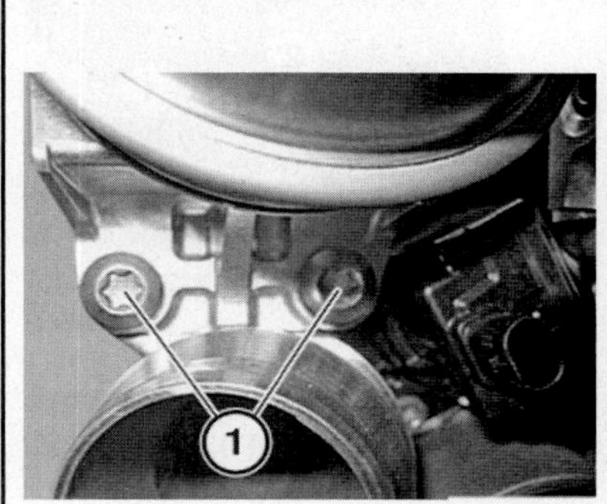

Fig. 321 Releasing screws (1) and removing vacuum unit

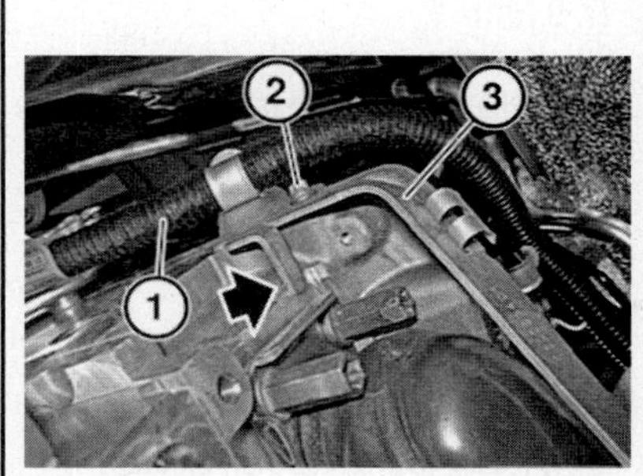

Fig. 322 Unclamping engine wiring harness (1), releasing screw (2) and removing holder (3)

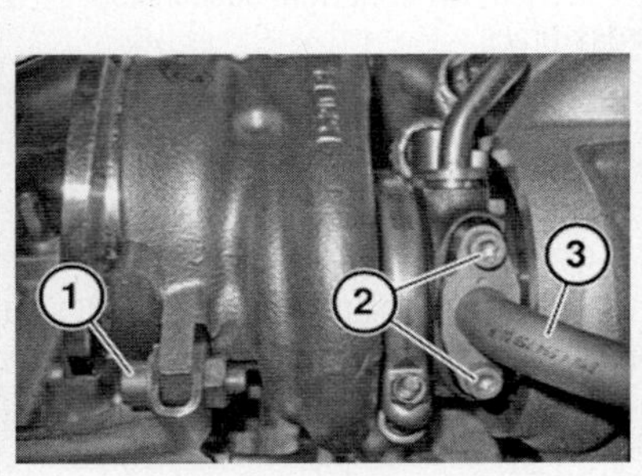

Fig. 343 Unfastening screws (1) and releasing oil return pipe (3)

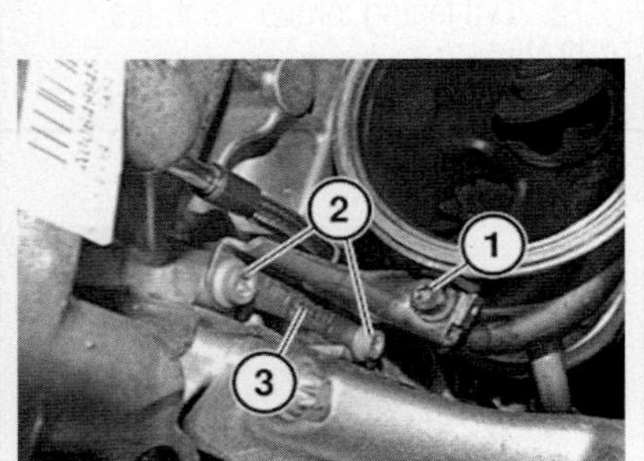

Fig. 324 Slackening bolt (1), releasing and removing screws (3) (holder (3) remains on exhaust turbocharger)

17. Remove vacuum unit.
18. Unclamp engine wiring harness (1) from bracket.
19. Release screw (2) and remove holder (3).
    a. Tightening torque: 53-80 inch lbs. (7-9 Nm).
20. Unfasten screws (2).
21. Release oil return pipe (3) and place to one side.
    a. Tightening torque: 7 ft. lbs. (10 Nm).

➡Replace gasket.

22. Slacken bolt (1).
23. Release and remove screws (2).
24. Holder (3) remains on exhaust turbocharger.
25. Release screw (1).
    a. Tightening torque: 7 ft. lbs. (10 Nm).
26. Remove oil return line (2).

Fig. 325 Releasing screw (1) and removing oil return line (2)

➡Replace O-ring.

27. Release screw (1).

➡If necessary, use appropriate tool to loosen coolant return line (3) and coolant flow line (2) at connection point.

➡Replace sealing rings.

28. Release screw (1).
    a. Tightening torque: 11 42 4AZ.
29. Release connection of oil feed line (2), if necessary with a suitable tool.

➡Replace sealing ring.

30. Pull off cable plug (2) of coolant pump.
31. Tape off engine support at front right with suitable auxiliary materials (risk of damage!).
32. Release nuts (1) to (10).
33. Feed out exhaust turbocharger towards top front and remove.

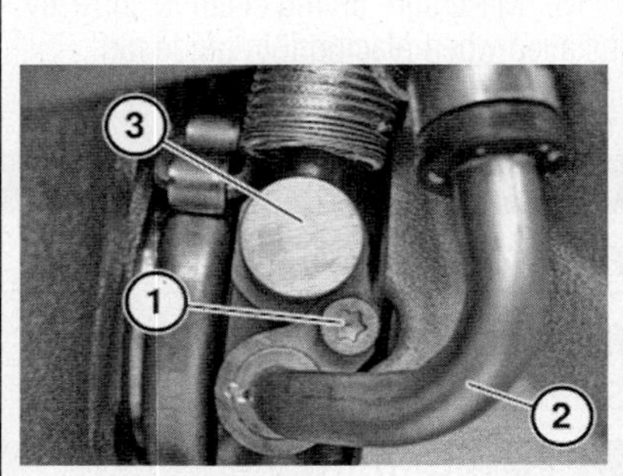

Fig. 326 Releasing screw (1) and using appropriate tool to loosen coolant return line (3) and coolant flow line (2)

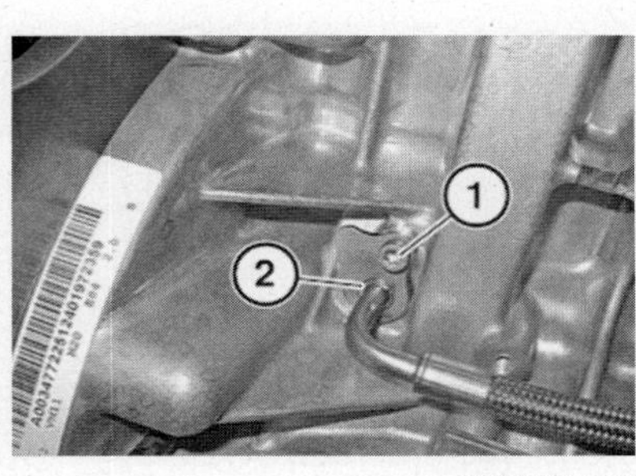

Fig. 327 Releasing screw (1) and connection of oil feed line (2)

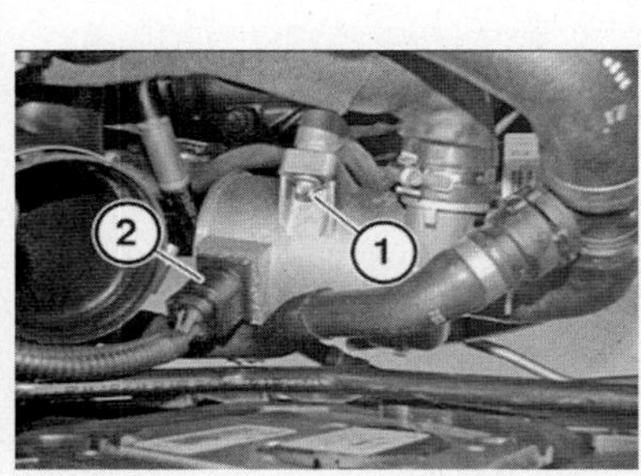

Fig. 328 Pulling off cable plug (2) of coolant pump

➡Oil supply line (2) can only be replaced after removal of the turbocharger.

34. Release screw (1).
    a. If necessary, use appropriate tool to loosen oil feeder lines at point of connection (2).

To install:

35. To install, reverse the removal procedure noting the following.
36. Replace all sealing rings (1).
37. Renew sealing rings of coolant return and feed lines.
38. Replace all graphite seals (1).

➡In order to be able to feed out the exhaust turbocharger more easily, twist holder (1) as far as possible in direction of arrow and lightly fasten with screw (2).

    a. Tightening torque: 10 ft. lbs. (13 Nm).

Fig. 329 Releasing nuts in order (1-10)

39. Position turbocharger on cylinder head and hold in place with two bolts.
    a. Join flange nuts to a torque of 8 Nm in sequence (1) to (10).
    b. Tighten flange nuts to a torque of 13 Nm in sequence (1) to (10).
40. Assemble engine.
41. Observe BMW Diagnostics System instruction.
42. Carry out BMW leak test for intake system.

Fig. 330 Releasing screw (1) and loosening oil feeder lines at point of connection (2)

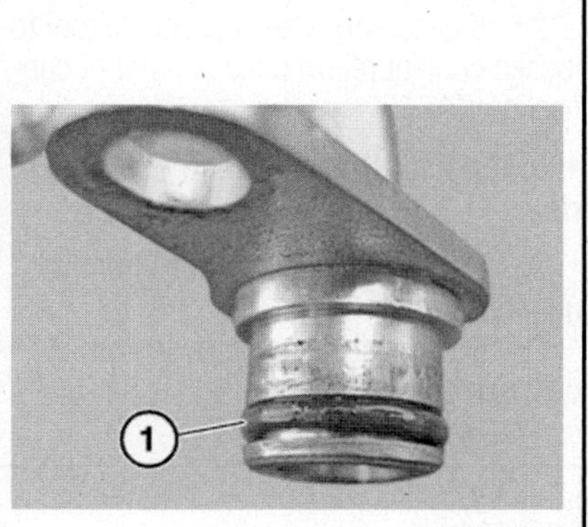

Fig. 331 Replacing sealing rings (1)

N55 Engine

See Figures 334 through 343.

⁂ WARNING

The module consists of exhaust turbo charger and exhaust manifold.

⁂ WARNING

The weight of the turbocharger is approx. 15 kg.

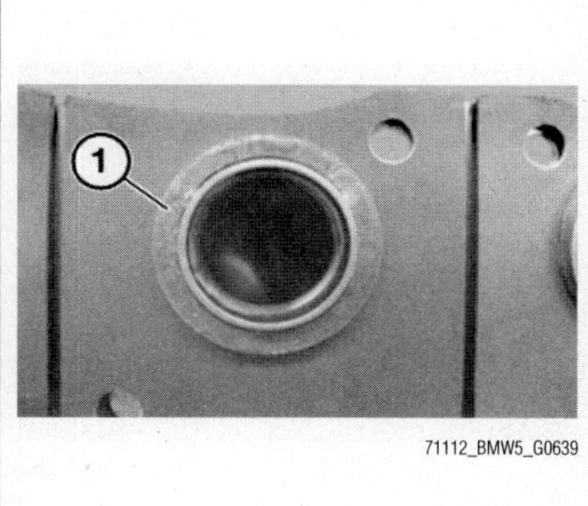

Fig. 332 Replacing all graphite seals (1)

1. Remove fan cowl with electric fan.
2. Drain coolant.
3. Remove front right wheel arch panel.
4. Remove coolant thermostat.

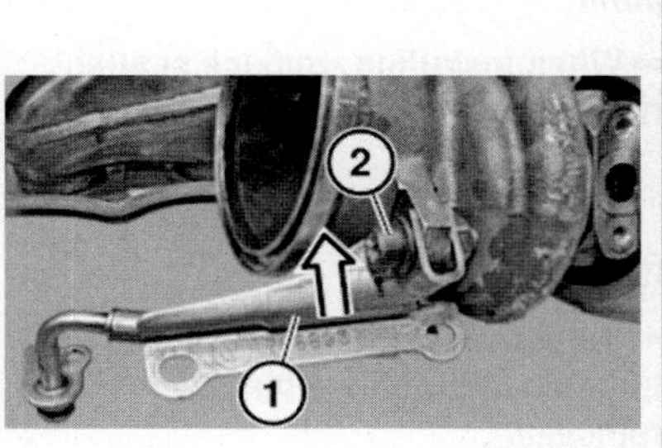

Fig. 333 Twisting holder (1) and fastening screw (2) and tightening nuts in sequence 1-10

5. Remove coolant pump.
6. Remove charge air cooler.
7. Remove the catalytic converter.
8. Remove right engine support arm.
9. Remove right engine mount.
10. Slacken nut.
11. Release screw.
12. Remove heat shield by lifting upwards.
13. Undo sheet metal nut.
14. Remove heat shield by maneuvering upwards.

➡When installing, check retaining clamps are properly seated.

15. Release screws (1).
    a. Tightening torque: 78 inch lbs. (8.5 Nm).

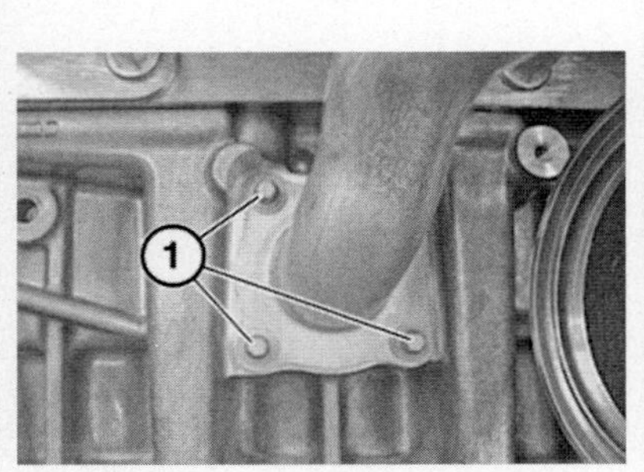

Fig. 334 Releasing screws (1)

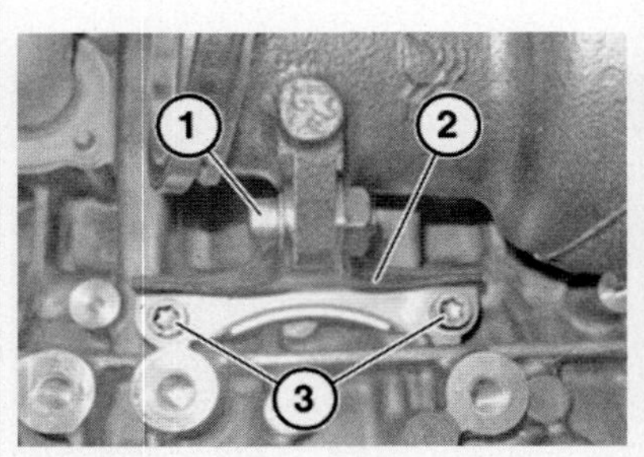

Fig. 336 Releasing screw (1), loosening screws (3) and identifying holder (2)

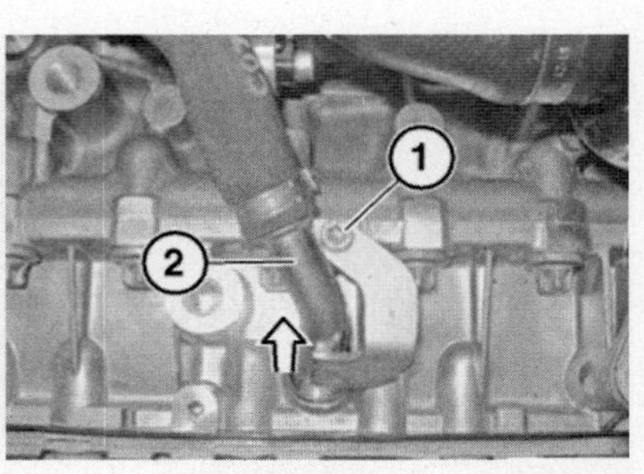

Fig. 338 Releasing screw (1) and loosening return lines (2)

16. Release screw (1).
    a. Tightening torque: 71 inch lbs. (8 Nm).

➡If necessary, use appropriate tool to loosen coolant return line (3) and coolant flow line (2) at connection point.

➡When installing, replace sealing rings.

17. Release screw (1).
18. Loosen screws (3) but do not remove.

➡Holder (2) can only be removed if turbocharger module has been removed.

19. Release screw (1).
    a. Tightening torque: 71 inch lbs. (8 Nm).
20. If necessary, use appropriate tool to loosen oil return lines at point of connection (2).

➡When installing, replace sealing ring.

21. Release screw (1).
    a. Tightening torque: 71 inch lbs. (8 Nm).
22. If necessary, use appropriate tool to loosen oil return lines (2).

➡When installing, replace sealing ring.

23. Release screw (1).
    a. Tightening torque: 80 inch lbs. (9 Nm).
24. If necessary, use appropriate tool to loosen coolant return lines at point of connection (2).

➡When installing, replace sealing ring.

25. Disconnect vacuum hose from vacuum line.
26. Disconnect vacuum hose from cylinder head cover.
27. Remove heat shield.
    a. Tightening torque: 71 inch lbs. (8 Nm).
28. Loosen all flange nuts (2) along the line.
29. Remove module by maneuvering downwards on gearbox side.

➡Overall weight of module is approximately 15 kg.

30. Remove both brackets from gearbox.
    a. Tightening torque M6: 7 ft. lbs. (9 Nm)
    b. Tightening torque M10: 28 ft. lbs. (38 Nm)
    c. Tightening torque M10x10.9: 41 ft. lbs. (56 Nm)
    d. Tightening torque M8: 14 ft. lbs. (19 Nm)
    e. Tightening torque M12: 49 ft. lbs. (66 Nm)

➡The following are aluminum screws:

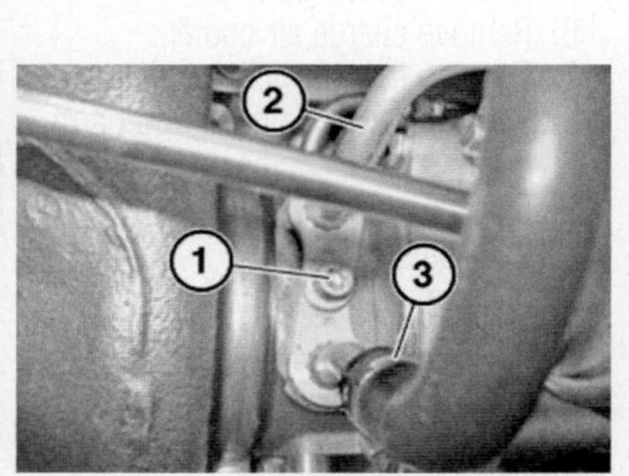

Fig. 335 Releasing screws (1) and loosening coolant return line (3) and flow line (2)

Fig. 337 Releasing screw (1) and loosening oil return lines at point of connection (2)

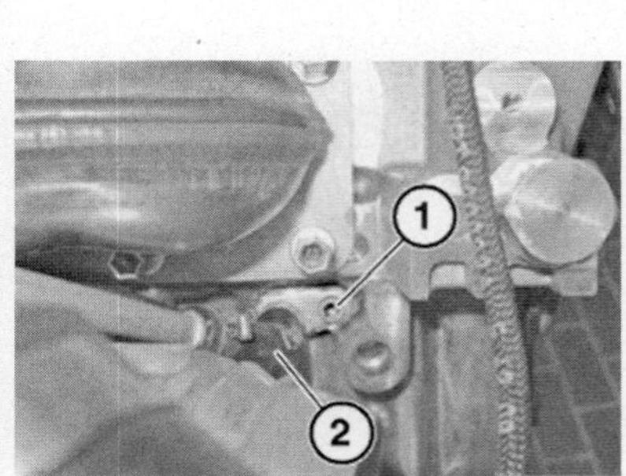

Fig. 339 Releasing screw (1) and loosening coolant return lines at point of connection (2)

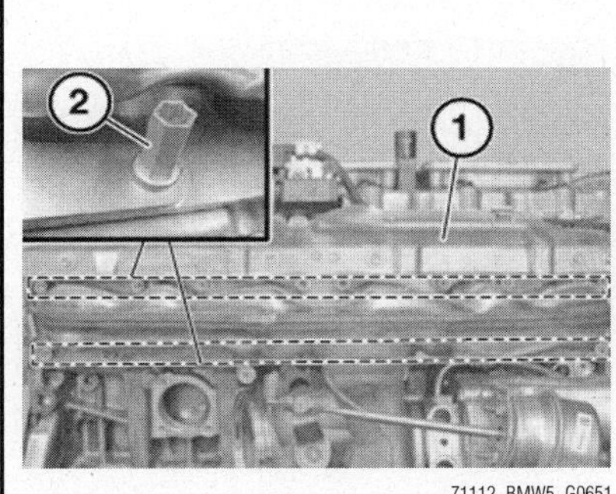

Fig. 340 Removing heat shield (1) and loosening flange nuts (2)

f. Tightening torque M10x30: 15 ft. lbs. (20 Nm) + 90-110°

g. Tightening torque M10x85: 15 ft. lbs. (20 Nm) + 180-200°

h. Tightening torque M12: 18 ft. lbs. (25 Nm) + 130°

➡Oil supply line (2) can only be replaced after removal of the turbocharger.

31. Release screw (1).

a. If necessary, use appropriate tool to loosen oil feeder lines at point of connection (2).

To install:

32. To install, reverse the removal procedure noting the following.
33. Replace all sealing rings.
34. Replace all graphite seals.
35. Position turbocharger on cylinder head and hold in place with two bolts.
36. Insert bolt (1) but do not tighten at this point.

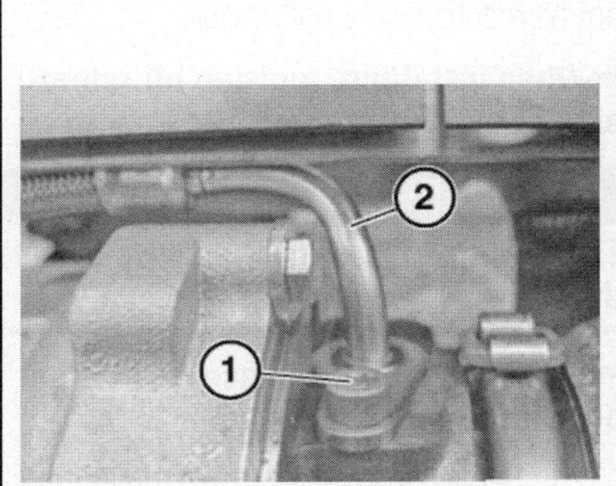

Fig. 341 Releasing screw (1) and loosening oil feeder lines at point of connection (2)

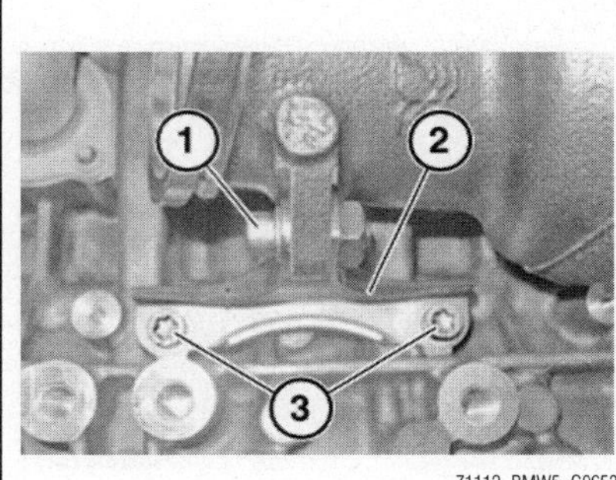

Fig. 342 Inserting bolt (1)

⁂ WARNING

The module consists of exhaust gas turbo loader and exhaust gas manifold and must be installed stress-free.

37. Torque and torque sequence must be observed without fail.
38. Tightening torque: 10 ft. lbs. (13 Nm).

a. Join all flange nuts in sequence 1 to 15 to 8 Nm.

b. Tighten all flange nuts to a torque of 13 Nm in sequence (1 to 15).

➡Flange nuts 1 to 5 are accessible from above.

➡Flange nuts 6 to 15 are accessible from below.

39. Secure screws (3).

a. Tightening torque: 15 ft. lbs. (20 Nm).

40. Tighten bolt (1).

a. Tightening torque: 15 ft. lbs. (20 Nm).

41. Assemble engine.
42. Observe BMW Diagnostics System instruction.
43. Carry out BMW leak test for intake system.

N63 Engine

Cylinders 5–8

See Figures 344 through 353.

⁂ WARNING

Risk of fire if oil lines are leaking.

⁂ WARNING

Risk of mixing up vacuum hoses.

1. Remove catalytic converter, cylinders 5–8.
2. Disconnect plug connection (1) on electric changeover valve (2).
3. Release screw (1).

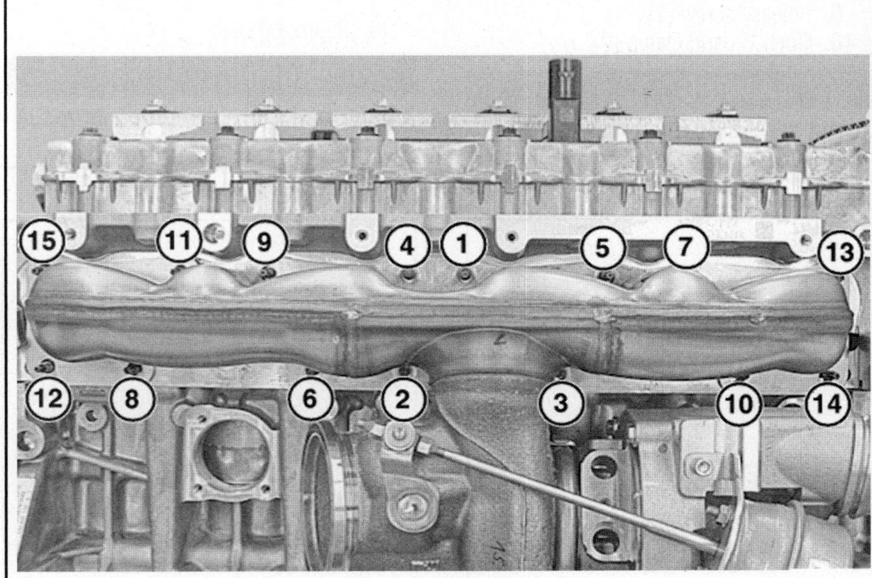

Fig. 343 Identifying bolt tightening sequence

Fig. 344 Disconnecting plug connection (1) on electric changeover valve (2)

a. Tightening torque 11 42 4AZ.
4. Unfasten banjo bolt (2).
a. Tightening torque 11 42 7AZ.
5. Lay oil line from turbocharger to side.

➡When installing, replace all sealing rings.

6. Open hose clamp.
7. Detach coolant feed line.

➡When installing, replace hose clamp.

8. Release screw (4) with a suitable tool.

➡Oil return pipe (3) can only be removed with turbocharger.

a. Tightening torque: 7 ft. lbs. (10 Nm).
9. Release screw (1).
10. Open V-band clamp (2).

⁂ WARNING

Do not mechanically deform oil return line.

Fig. 345 Releasing screw (1) and banjo bolt (2)

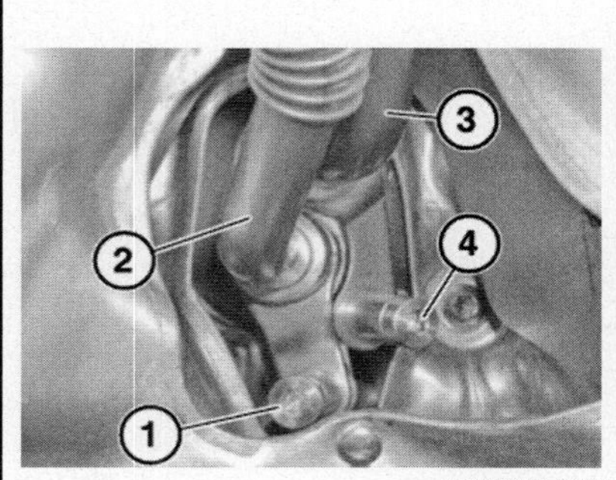

Fig. 346 Releasing screw (4) and identifying oil return pipe (3)

11. Remove turbocharger with oil return line in upward direction.

To install:

12. If necessary, convert coolant feed line to new turbocharger.
13. Release banjo bolt (1).
a. Tightening torque: 28 ft. lbs. (38 Nm).
14. Release screw (1).
a. Tightening torque: 7 ft. lbs. (10 Nm).
15. Modify coolant feed line (2).
16. Release screws (1).
a. Tightening torque: 7 ft. lbs. (10 Nm).
17. Remove oil return pipe (2).

➡When installing, a new oil return pipe must always be fitted.

18. Replace gasket.

⁂ WARNING

A deformed oil return pipe can result in leaks.

Fig. 347 Releasing screw (1) and opening V-band clamp (2)

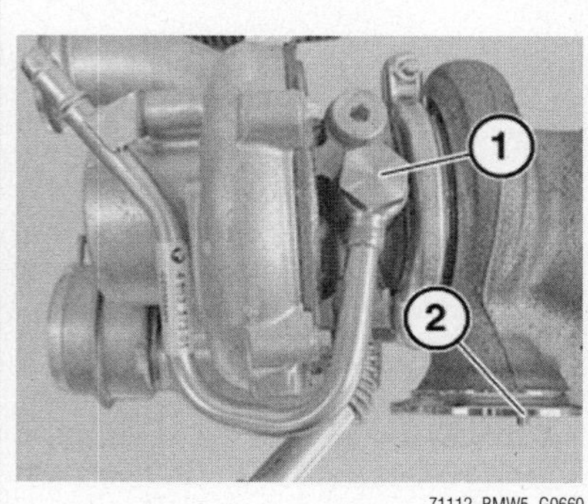

Fig. 348 Releasing banjo bolt (1)

Fig. 349 Releasing screw (1) and modifying coolant feed line (2)

⁂ WARNING

Risk of fire if oil line is leaking.

19. The thermal linear compensators (see arrows) on the oil return pipe (1) must not be mechanically deformed.

➡When installing, moisten oil return pipe at end with engine oil.

⁂ WARNING

The O-rings can easily fall into the oil duct.

➡When installing, replace O-rings on oil return cover (2).

20. Replace gasket on exhaust manifold.

➡Check locating apparatus on exhaust manifold.

21. Position turbocharger with oil return line on exhaust manifold.
22. Position V-band clamp (2).

Fig. 350 Releasing screws (1) and removing oil return pipe (2)

71112_BMW5_G0663

Fig. 351 Identifying thermal linear compensators (arrows) on the oil return pipe (1)

23. Insert screw (1).
    a. Tightening torque: 10 ft. lbs. (13 Nm).

➡The ends of the V-band clamp must rest parallel to each other.

    b. Tightening torque: 10 ft. lbs. (13 Nm).

➡The screw connection of V-band clamp is too loose if you can see a gap between the ends of the V-band clamps, release and then repeat the screw connection.

➡The screw connection of V-band clamp is too tight if the ends of the V-band clamp are positioned under each other, release and then repeat the screw connection.

24. Vacuum hose (1) for cylinders 5-8.
    a. Old version: black / blue.
    b. New version: black/yellow.
25. Assemble engine.

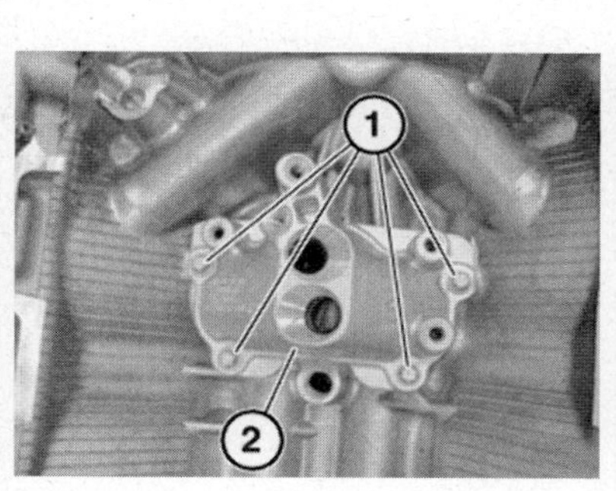

Fig. 352 Identifying O-rings on oil return cover (2)

Fig. 353 Positioning V-band clamp (2) and inserting screw (1)

26. Check vacuum connections.
27. Observe BMW diagnosis instructions.
    - Complete vehicle
    - Power train
    - Engine electrical system
    - Air supply
    - Charging pressure control

Cylinders 1–4

See Figures 354 through 360.

⁂ WARNING

Risk of fire if oil lines are leaking.

⁂ WARNING

Risk of mixing up vacuum hoses.

1. Remove catalytic converter for cylinders 1-4.
2. Disconnect plug connection (1) on electric changeover valve (2).

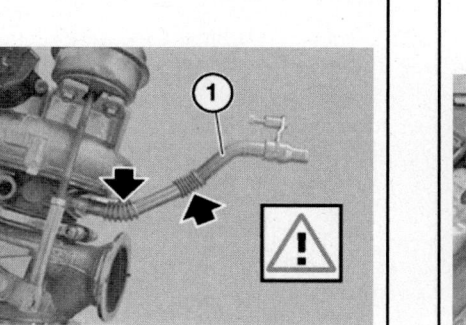

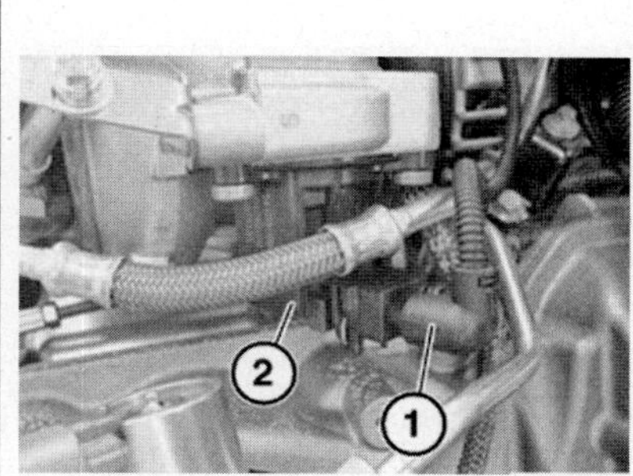

Fig. 354 Disconnecting plug connection (1) on electric changeover valve (2)

3. Release screw.
    a. Tightening torque: 7 ft. lbs. (10 Nm).
4. Unfasten banjo bolt.
    a. Tightening torque: 12 ft. lbs. (16 Nm).
5. Lay oil line from turbocharger to side.

➡When installing, replace all sealing rings.

6. Release screw.
    a. Tightening torque: 7 ft. lbs. (10 Nm).
7. Unfasten banjo bolt.
    a. Tightening torque: 28 ft. lbs. (38 Nm).
8. Lay coolant return line to one side.

➡When installing, replace all sealing rings.

9. Open hose clamp.
10. Detach coolant feed line.

➡When installing, replace hose clamp.

11. Release screw (1) with a suitable tool.

➡Oil return pipe (2) can only be removed with turbocharger.

    a. Tightening torque: 7 ft. lbs. (10 Nm).
12. Release screw (4).
13. Open V-band clamp (3).

⁂ WARNING

Do not mechanically deform oil return line.

14. Remove turbocharger with oil return line in upward direction.

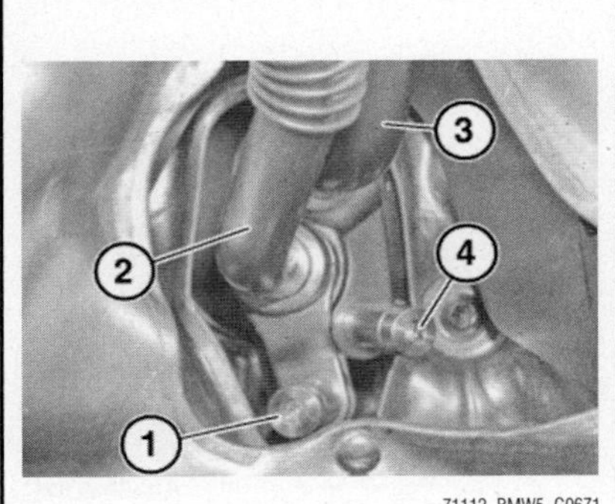

Fig. 355 Releasing screw (1) and identifying oil return pipe (2)

To install:

15. To install, reverse the removal procedure noting the following.

➡If necessary, convert coolant feed line to new turbocharger.

16. Release banjo bolt (1).
    a. Tightening torque: 28 ft. lbs. (38 Nm).
17. Release screw (1).
    a. Tightening torque: 7 ft. lbs. (10 Nm).
18. Modify coolant feed line (2).
19. Release screws (1).
    a. Tightening torque: 7 ft. lbs. (10 Nm).
20. Remove oil return pipe (2).

➡A new oil return pipe must always be fitted.

21. Replace gasket.

WARNING

A deformed oil return pipe can result in leaks.

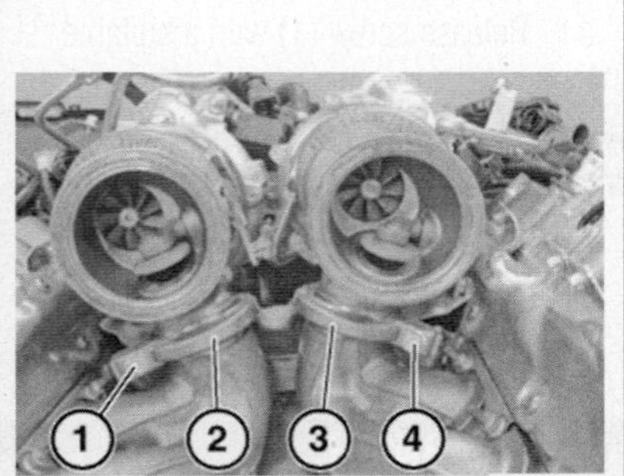

Fig. 356 Releasing screw (4), opening V-band clamp (3) and removing turbocharger

Fig. 357 Releasing screw (1) and modifying coolant feed line (2)

Fig. 358 Releasing screws (1) and removing oil return pipe (2)

WARNING

Risk of fire if oil line is leaking.

22. The thermal linear compensators (see arrows) on the oil return pipe (1) must not be mechanically deformed.

➡Moisten oil return pipe at end with engine oil.

WARNING

The O-rings can easily fall into the oil duct.

23. Replace O-rings on oil return cover.
24. Replace gasket on exhaust manifold.

➡Check locating apparatus on exhaust manifold.

25. Position turbocharger with oil return line on exhaust manifold.
26. Position V-band clamp (3).
27. Insert bolt (4).

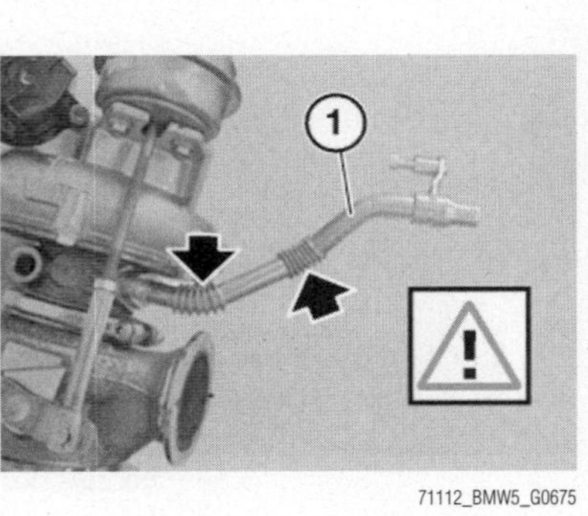

Fig. 359 Identifying thermal linear compensators (arrows) and oil return pipe (1)

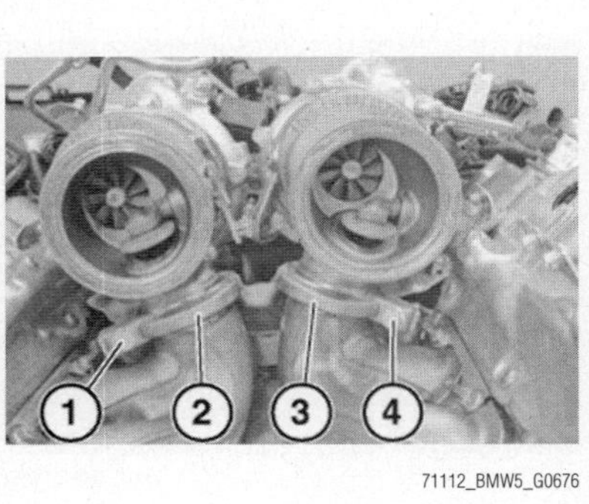

Fig. 360 Positioning V-band clamp (3) and inserting bolt (4)

a. Tightening torque: 10 ft. lbs. (13 Nm).

➡The ends of the V-band clamp must rest parallel to each other.

b. Tightening torque: 10 ft. lbs. (13 Nm).

➡The screw connection of V-band clamp is too loose, if you can see a gap between the ends of the V-band clamps, release and then repeat the screw connection.

➡The screw connection of V-band clamp is too tight, if the ends of the V-band clamp are positioned under each other, release and then repeat the screw connection.

➡Vacuum hose black/red for cylinders 1-4.

28. Assemble engine.
29. Check vacuum connections.

30. Observe BMW diagnosis instructions.
- Complete vehicle
- Powertrain
- Engine electrical system
- Air supply
- Charging pressure control

VALVE COVERS

REMOVAL & INSTALLATION

N52 Engine

See Figure 361.

1. Before servicing the vehicle, refer to the precautions.
2. Remove ignition coils.
3. Remove ignition wiring harness in valve cover area.
4. Remove tension strut.
5. Unlock and detach vent hose.
6. If necessary, pull off metal bracket.
7. Remove screws on electric servomotor.

➡A further screw, which cannot be seen in the picture, must be Removed under the electric servomotor.

8. Remove screw on electric servomotor.
9. Remove servomotor.
10. If necessary, remove nuts.
11. If necessary, remove secondary air valve.

⁂ WARNING

Observe different screw lengths. Installation location of screws is specified by the different bushing shapes.

12. Remove screws in area.
13. Remove threaded pin.

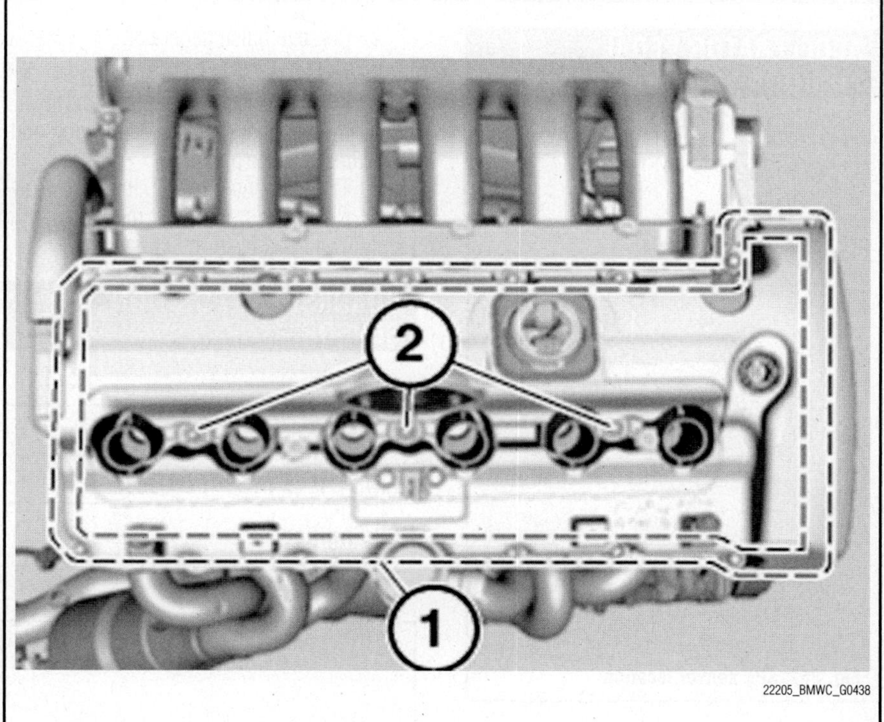

Fig. 361 Installation location of screws (1 and 2) is specified by the different bushing shapes

14. Remove slotted sleeves.

To install:

15. Installation is the reverse of removal.
16. Clean all sealing faces.

⁂ WARNING

Do not use any metal-cutting tools.

17. Replace gaskets.
18. Slotted sleeves for guiding ignition coils in valve cover must be replaced.
19. Replace aluminum screws.
20. Tighten bolts/nuts to specification as follows:
- Electric servomotor to cylinder head and to valve cover: 8 ft. lbs. (10 Nm)
- Secondary air valve to cylinder head: 6 ft. lbs. (8 Nm)
- Valve cover to cylinder head: 7ft. lbs. (9 Nm)

ENGINE PERFORMANCE & EMISSION CONTROLS

ACCELERATOR PEDAL POSITION SENSOR

LOCATION

See Figure 362.

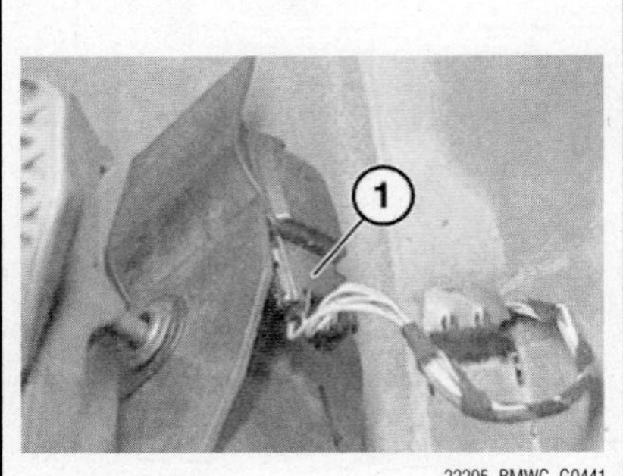

Fig. 362 APP sensor location

REMOVAL & INSTALLATION

See Figure 362.

1. Before servicing the vehicle, refer to the precautions.
2. Remove cap.
3. Remove screw.
4. Pull accelerator pedal module upwards out of fixture.
5. Pull off plug.
6. Remove accelerator pedal module.

To install:

7. Installation is the reverse of removal.
8. Tighten accelerator pedal module to body to 6 ft lbs. (8 Nm).

CAMSHAFT POSITION SENSOR

LOCATION

See Figures 363 and 364.

REMOVAL & INSTALLATION

N52 Engine

See Figures 363 through 364.

1. Before servicing the vehicle, refer to the precautions.
2. Read out fault memory of DME control unit; if necessary, work through test schedules
3. Switch ignition **OFF**.
4. Remove radiator cover.
5. Remove plug connector and pull off.
6. Remove screw.
7. Remove pulse generator.

To install:

8. Installation is the reverse of removal.
9. If equipped, replace sealing ring and coat with antiseize agent.
10. Tighten sensor to 7 ft. lbs. (9 Nm).
11. Check for stored fault messages, rectify faults and clear the fault memory.

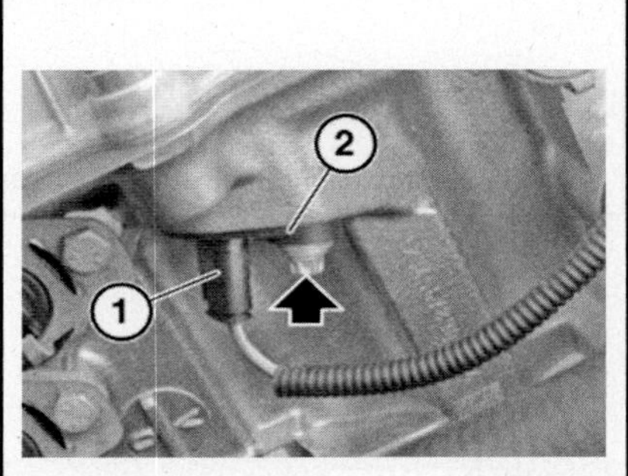

Fig. 363 Intake CMP sensor (2) and connector (1) location— N52 engine

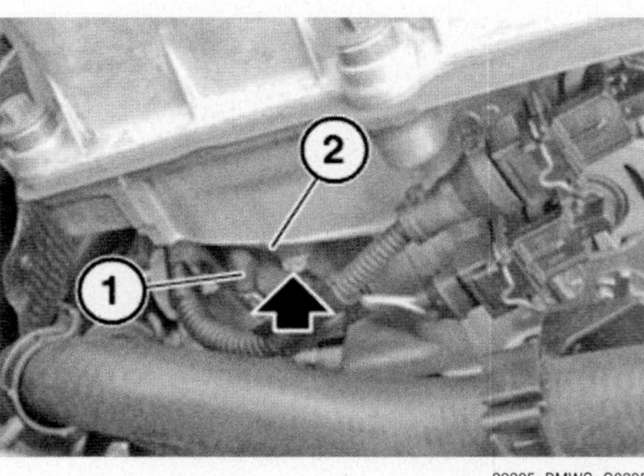

Fig. 364 Exhaust CMP sensor (2) and connector (1) location— N52 engine

CRANKSHAFT POSITION SENSOR

LOCATION

See Figures 365 and 366.

REMOVAL & INSTALLATION

N52 Engines

See Figure 365.

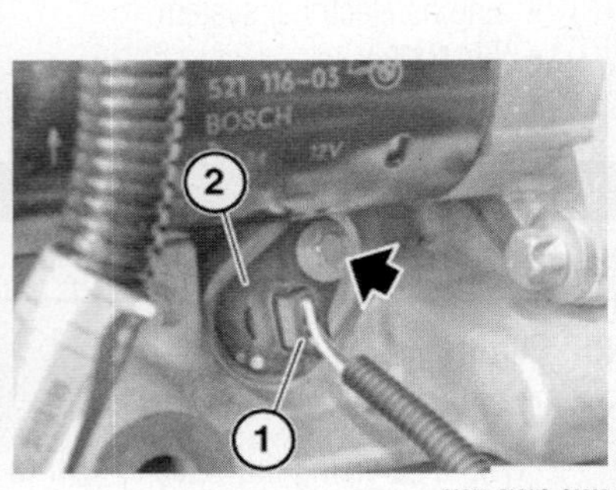

Fig. 365 CKP sensor (2) and connector (1) location—N52 and N54 engines

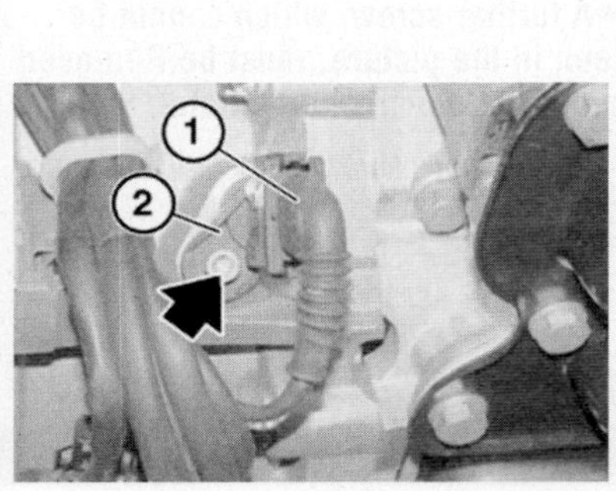

Fig. 366 CKP sensor (2) and connector (1) location—N62 engine

⁂ WARNING

Aluminum-magnesium materials. No steel screws/bolts may be used due to the threat of electrochemical corrosion. A magnesium crankcase requires aluminum screws/bolts exclusively. Aluminum screws/bolts must be replaced each time they are removed. The end faces of aluminum screws/bolts are painted blue for the purposes of reliable identification. Jointing torque and angle of rotation must be observed without fail (risk of damage).

1. Before servicing the vehicle, refer to the precautions.
2. Read out fault memory of DME control unit; if necessary, work through test schedules.
3. Switch ignition **OFF**.
4. Remove intake air manifold.
5. Disconnect plug.
6. Disconnect the crankshaft pulse generator.
7. Remove and discard the aluminum bolts.
8. Remove pulse generator from crankcase.

To install:

9. Replace sealing ring.
10. Install pulse generator to crankcase.
11. Using new aluminum bolts, tighten to 2 ft. lbs (3 Nm) plus an additional 45° of rotation.
12. Connect the crankshaft pulse generator.
13. Install intake air manifold.

ENGINE COOLANT TEMPERATURE SENSOR

LOCATION

See Figure 367.

REMOVAL & INSTALLATION

N52 Engine

See Figure 367.

1. Before servicing the vehicle, refer to the precautions.
2. Read out fault memory of DME control unit; if necessary, work through test schedules.
3. Switch ignition **OFF**.
4. Though you can avoid it, for easier access, remove the intake duct.
5. Unlock the plug on the sensor (1) and remove it.
6. Remove the temperature sensor (2).

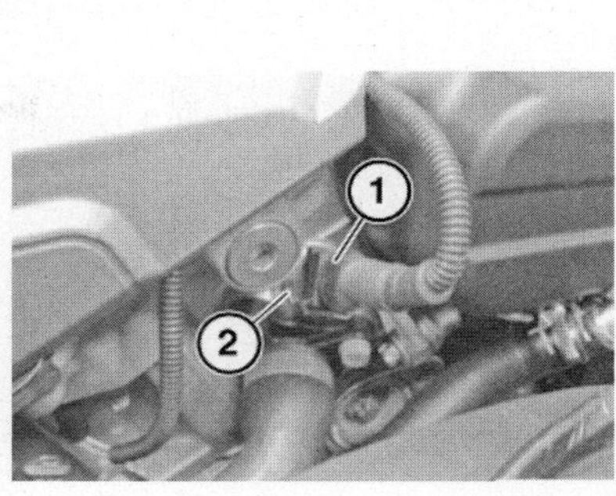

Fig. 367 ECT location, N52 engine. Unlock the plug on the sensor (1) and remove the temperature sensor (2)

To install:

7. Reposition the sensor and lock the plug.
8. After returning the temperature sensor back to its position, make sure to vent the cooling system and check for leaks.
9. If necessary, top off the coolant in the reservoir.
10. Check for stored fault messages, rectify faults and clear the fault memory.

ENGINE OIL TEMPERATURE SENSOR

LOCATION

See Figure 368.

REMOVAL & INSTALLATION

See Figure 368.

1. Before servicing the vehicle, refer to the precautions.
2. Remove reinforcement plate.
3. Drain and recycle the engine oil.
4. Release plug connector and pull off.
5. Unscrew nuts.
6. Remove level switch.

To install:

7. Clean sealing face on oil sump.
8. Replace seal on oil level sensor.
9. Tighten the bolts to 72 inch lbs. (8 Nm).

⁂ WARNING

An excessively low torque value will result in oil leaks. An excessively high torque value will result in damage to the oil level sensor.

10. Refill engine with oil.

EVAP CANISTER

LOCATION

See Figure 369.

REMOVAL & INSTALLATION

See Figure 369.

1. Before servicing the vehicle, refer to the precautions.
2. Remove the rear wheel arch.
   a. Remove rear wheel
   b. If necessary, disconnect and feed out plug connection on brake pad sensor
   c. Release screws.
   d. Unscrew nuts.
   e. Release expansion rivet.
   f. Carefully feed out rear wheel arch cover towards bottom.
3. Detach lines (1 and 2) from carbon canister.
4. Unfasten screws.
5. Remove carbon canister.

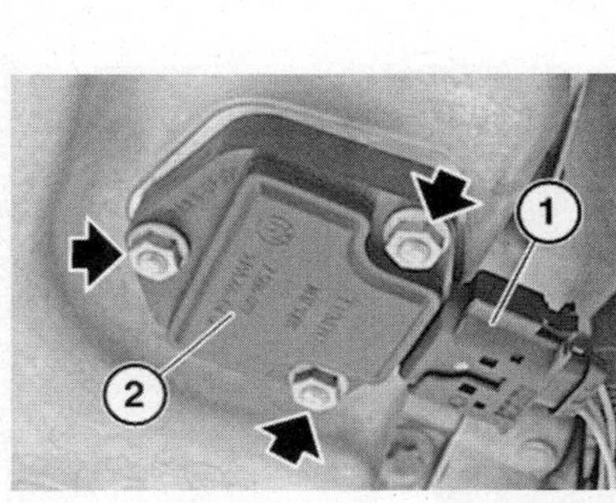

Fig. 368 Oil level and temperature sensor (2) and plug (1)

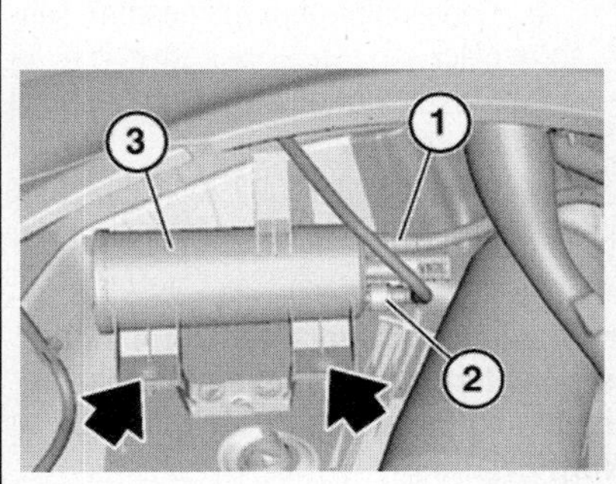

Fig. 369 EVAP location—Lines (1 and 2) and canister (3)

To install:

6. Installation is the reverse of removal.

7. Tighten carbon canister to body to 80 inch lbs. (9 Nm).

8. Make sure rear wheel arch cover is correctly seated.

HEATED OXYGEN SENSOR (HO2S)

REMOVAL & INSTALLATION

N20 Engine

See Figure 370.

CAUTION

Work should only be carried out on an exhaust system that has cooled down.

WARNING

The threads of new oxygen control sensors are already coated with Never Seez Compound 4.3 (refer to BMW Parts Department).

WARNING

If an oxygen control sensor is to be reused, apply a thin and even coating of NEVER-SEEZ compound to the thread only.

WARNING

Sensor ceramics not cleaned and not coated with lubricant.

1. Remove acoustic cover.

2. Disconnect plug connection on oxygen control sensor.

➡Installation note:

a. Cable color of oxygen control sensor = black.

b. Cable color of oxygen monitoring sensor = grey.

3. A suitable extension is needed for the screw connection of the oxygen control sensor.

➡When using special tool 11 4 260, it is essential to reduce the prescribed tightening torque by 27 inch lbs. (3 Nm).

4. Release oxygen control sensor (2) with special tool 11 4 260 with a suitable extension (1).

a. Tightening torque: 37 ft. lbs. (50 Nm).

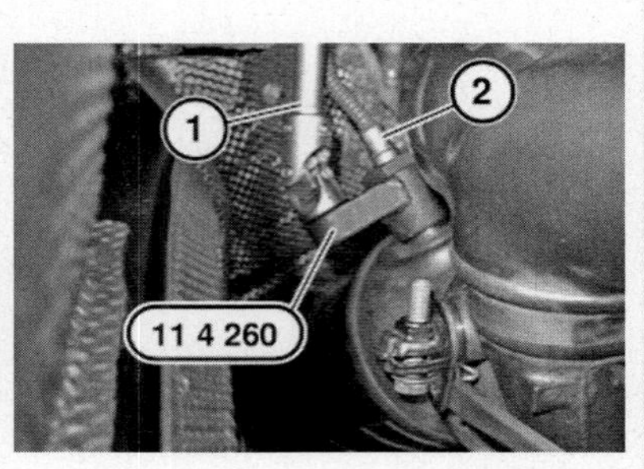

Fig. 370 Releasing oxygen control sensor (2) with special tool with suitable extension (1)

To install:

5. To install, reverse the removal procedure noting the following.

6. Reassemble the vehicle.

7. Check function of DME.

N52 Engine

See Figures 371 and 372.

1. Before servicing the vehicle, refer to the precautions.

2. Read out fault memory of DME control unit; if necessary, work through test schedules

3. Switch ignition **OFF**.

4. Remove the exhaust system.

5. Disconnect the plug connection from the sensors.

6. Disconnect the oxygen sensor from cylinders 4 to 6.

7. The oxygen sensor at cylinders 1 to 3 is accessible from above without the exhaust system having to be removed.

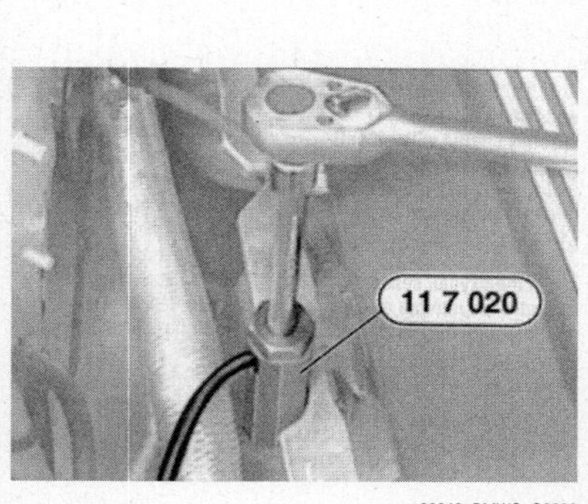

Fig. 371 HO2S sensor (1) and special removal tool for cylinders 1–3 location — N52 engine

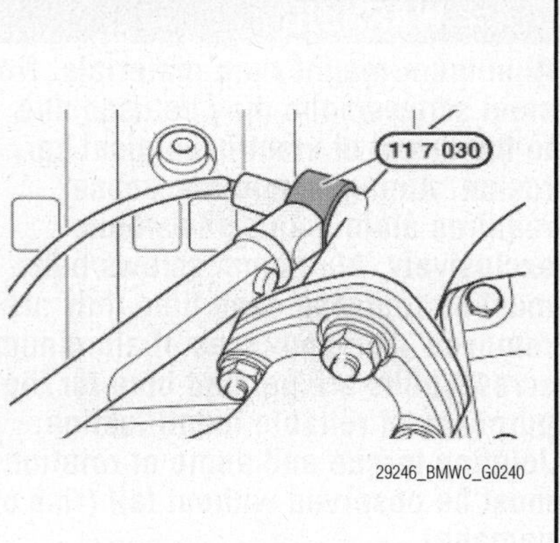

Fig. 372 HO2S sensor (1) and special removal tool (2) for cylinders 4–6 location —N52 engine

To install:

8. The threads of a new oxygen sensors are already coated with an anti-seize compound. If an oxygen sensor is to be used again, apply a thin and even coat of an anti-seize compound to the thread only.

WARNING

Do not clean the oxygen sensor section which protrudes into the exhaust line and ensure that it avoids all contact with any lubricants.

➡Observe cable routing of the oxygen sensor so it doesn't interfere with any other system or the exhaust pipes.

9. Tighten sensor to 37 ft. lbs. (50 Nm).

10. Connect the oxygen sensors and their respective cables.

- The cable color for the sensor that leads to cylinders 1 to 3 is black.
- The cable color for the sensor that leads to cylinders 4 to 6 is gray.

11. Connect the plug connection to the sensors.

12. Check for stored fault messages, rectify faults and clear the fault memory.

N55 Engine

See Figure 373.

CAUTION

Work should only be carried out on an exhaust system that has cooled down.

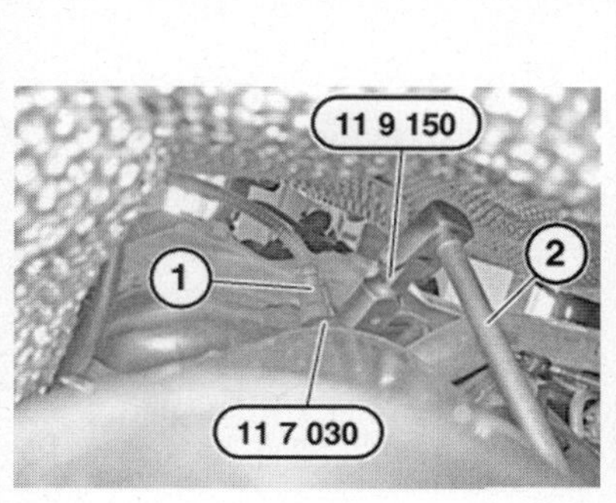

Fig. 373 Releasing oxygen control sensor (1) with special tools with a suitable extension (2)

✻✻ WARNING

The threads of new oxygen control sensors are already coated with NEVER-SEEZ compound (refer to BMW Parts Department).

✻✻ WARNING

If an oxygen control sensor is to be reused, apply a thin and even coating of NEVER-SEEZ compound to the thread only.

✻✻ WARNING

The part of the lambda control sensor which projects into the exhaust branch (sensor ceramics) must not be cleaned and not coated with lubricant.

1. Remove rear engine guard.
2. Remove air duct.
3. Disconnect plug connection on oxygen control sensor.

➡Installation note:

a. Cable color of oxygen control sensor = black.
b. Cable color of oxygen monitoring sensor = grey.

4. Release oxygen control sensor (1) with special tools 11 7 030 and 11 9 150 with a suitable extension (2).
   a. Tightening torque: 37 ft. lbs. (50 Nm).

✻✻ WARNING

When using special tool 11 7 030 in conjunction with special tool 11 9 150, it is essential to reduce the prescribed tightening torque by 27 inch lbs. (3 Nm).

To install:

5. To install, reverse the removal procedure.
6. Reassemble the vehicle.
7. Check function of DME.

KNOCK SENSOR (KS)

REMOVAL & INSTALLATION

N20 Engine

1st and 2nd Cylinder

See Figure 374.

1. Read out the fault memory of the DME control unit.
2. Switch off ignition.
3. Remove throttle body.
4. Unlock connector (1) and remove.
5. Release bolt (2) on knock sensor.
   a. Tightening torque: 16 ft. lbs. (21.5 Nm).
6. Remove knock sensor for 1st and 2nd cylinder.

To install:

7. To install, reverse the removal procedure noting the following.
8. Clean contact surface of knock sensors on engine block.
9. Reassemble the vehicle.
10. Check stored fault message.
11. Delete fault memory.

3rd and 4th Cylinder

See Figure 379.

1. Read out the fault memory of the DME control unit.
2. Switch off ignition.
3. Remove starter motor.
4. Unlock connector (1) and remove.

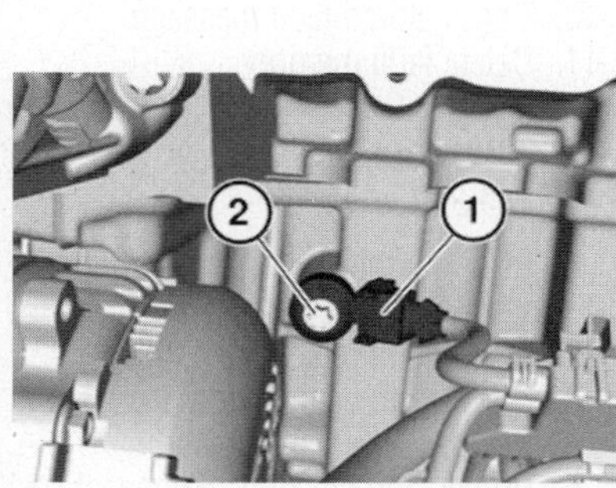

Fig. 374 Unlocking and removing connector (1) and releasing bolt (2) on knock sensor

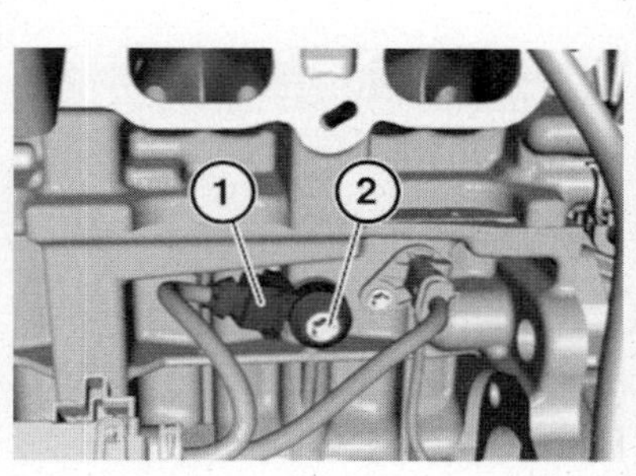

Fig. 375 Unlocking and removing connector (1) and releasing bolt (2) on knock sensor (2)

5. Release bolt (2) on knock sensor.
   a. Tightening torque: 16 ft. lbs. (21.5 Nm).
6. Remove knock sensor for 3rd and 4th cylinders.

To install:

7. To install, reverse the removal procedure noting the following.
8. Clean contact surface of knock sensor on engine block.
9. Reassemble the vehicle.
10. Check stored fault message.
11. Delete fault memory.

N52 Engine

See Figure 376.

✻✻ WARNING

No steel bolts or bolts may be used due to the threat of electrochemical corrosion. A magnesium crankcase requires aluminum bolts and bolts exclusively. The end of the aluminum bolts and bolts are painted blue for the purposes of reliable identification.

1. Before servicing the vehicle, refer to the precautions.
2. Read out fault memory of DME control unit; if necessary, work through test schedules
3. Switch ignition **OFF**.
4. Disconnect the battery.
5. Remove the air intake manifold.
6. Unlock the plug connection and remove it.
7. Unscrew the bolts on both knock sensors and remove the sensors.

To install:

8. Clean the support face of the knock sensors on engine block.

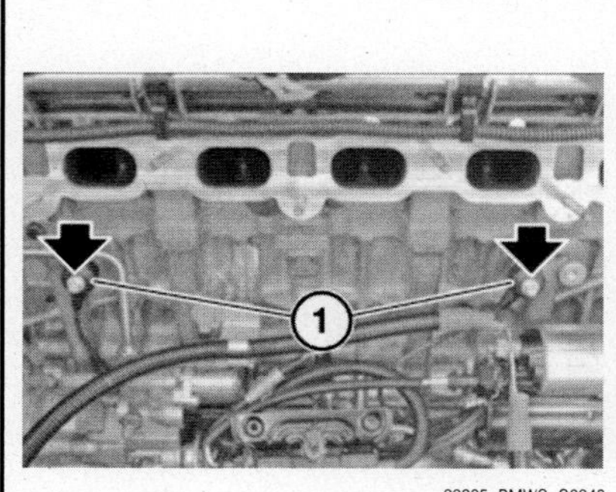

Fig. 376 Removing the KS sensor

Fig. 377 Unlocking and removing connector (1)

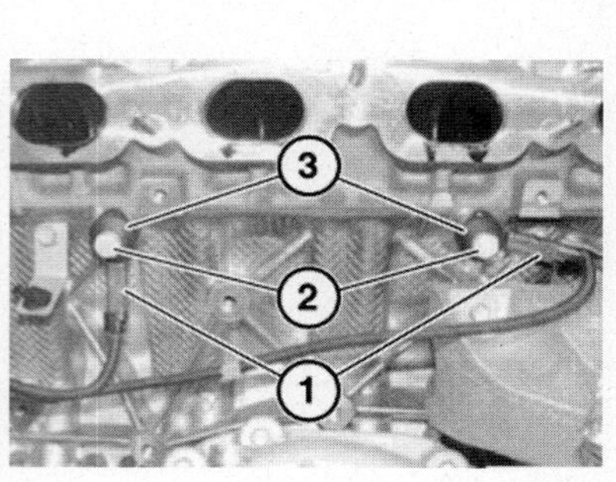

Fig. 379 Unlocking and disconnecting connector (1), releasing screws (2) and removing sensors (3)

9. Install the bolts on both knock sensors to replace the sensors.

10. Check for stored fault messages, rectify faults and clear the fault memory.

N55 Engine

See Figures 377 and 378.

WARNING

Aluminum screws/bolts must be replaced each time they are released.

WARNING

Aluminum screws/bolts are permitted with and without color coding (blue).

WARNING

For reliable identification:

a. Aluminum screws/bolts are not magnetic.

b. Jointing torque and angle of rotation must be observed without fail (risk of damage).

1. Read out the fault memory of the DME control unit.
2. Switch off ignition.
3. Remove intake plenum.
4. Unlock connector (1) and remove.
5. Feed out connector (1) behind feed line, remove feed line if necessary.
6. Release screws on both knock sensors (1) and remove knock sensors (1).

➡When installing, replace aluminum screws.

a. Tightening torque: 16 ft. lbs. (21.5 Nm).

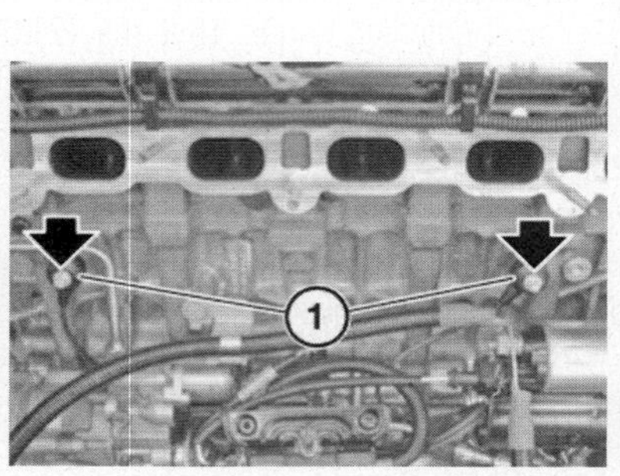

Fig. 378 Releasing screws on both knock sensors (1) and removing knock sensors

To install:

7. To install, reverse the removal procedure noting the following.
8. Clean contact surface of knock sensor on engine block.
9. Reassemble the vehicle.
10. Check stored fault message.
11. Delete fault memory.

N63 Engine

See Figure 379.

1. Read out the fault memory of the DME control unit.
2. Switch off ignition.
3. Disconnect battery earth lead.
4. Remove left intake plenum.
5. Unlock and disconnect connector (1) on both knock sensors.
6. Release screws on both knock sensors (2).

a. Tightening torque: 16 ft. lbs. (21.5 Nm).

7. Remove knock sensors (3).

To install:

8. To install, reverse the removal procedure noting the following.
9. Clean contact surface of knock sensor on engine block.
10. Reassemble the vehicle.
11. Check stored fault message.
12. Delete fault memory.

MALFUNCTION INDICATOR LIGHT

RESET PROCEDURE

1. Connect a STAR DIAGNOSTICS scan tool to the diagnostic connector.
2. Check whether any DTCs have been stored. Note them down if necessary.
3. Clear DTCs.
4. The MIL should turn off.

MASS AIR FLOW (MAF) SENSOR

REMOVAL & INSTALLATION

N52 Engine

See Figure 380.

1. Read out fault memory of DME control unit.
2. Turn off ignition.
3. Unlock plug (1) and remove.
4. Unfasten screws (2).

a. Tightening torque 13 62 8AZ.

5. Pull air-mass flow sensor (3) out of upper section of intake silencer housing.

To install:

6. To install, reverse the removal procedure noting the following.

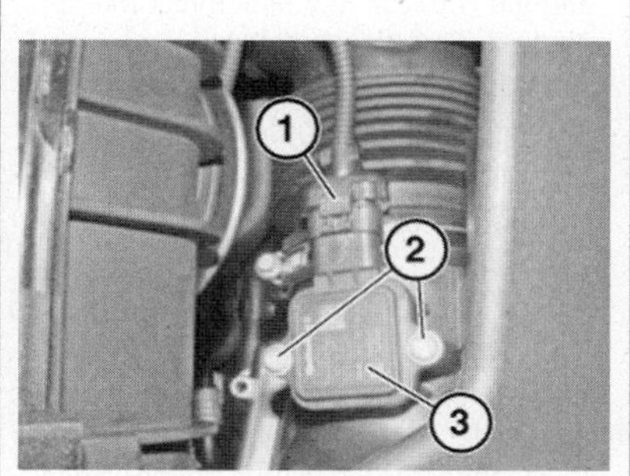

Fig. 380 Unlocking plug (1), unfastening screws (2) and removing air mass flow sensor (3)

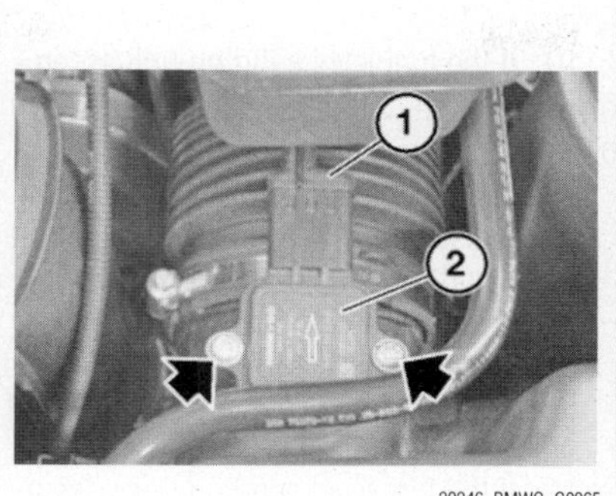

Fig. 381 Removing the MAF sensor

Fig. 382 Removing the TPS sensor (2) and connector (1)

7. Check stored fault message.
8. Delete fault memory.

MASS AIR FLOW/INTAKE AIR TEMPERATURE (MAF/IAT) SENSOR

REMOVAL & INSTALLATION

N52 Engine

See Figure 381.

1. Before servicing the vehicle, refer to the precautions.
2. Read out fault memory of DME control unit; if necessary, work through test schedules
3. Switch ignition **OFF**.
4. Remove the bolts that hold the sensor in place.
5. Unlock the plug and remove it.
6. Pull the mass airflow sensor out of the upper section of the intake filter housing.

To install:

7. Replace the sensor, screw it down and connect the plug-in connector.
8. Check stored fault messages.
9. Rectify faults.
10. Check for stored fault messages, rectify faults and clear the fault memory.

THROTTLE POSITION (TP) SENSOR

REMOVAL & INSTALLATION

See Figure 382.

1. Before servicing the vehicle, refer to the precautions.
2. Read out fault memory of DME control unit; if necessary, work through test schedules
3. Switch ignition **OFF**.
4. Remove air intake hose.
5. Unlock plug and remove.
6. Remove throttle assembly.

To install:

7. Replace sealing ring of throttle assembly.
8. Install throttle assembly. Tighten bolts to 6 ft. lbs. (9 Nm).
9. Install air intake hose.
10. Check for stored fault messages, rectify faults and clear the fault memory.

FUEL — GASOLINE FUEL INJECTION SYSTEM

FUEL SYSTEM SERVICE PRECAUTIONS

Safety is the most important factor when performing not only fuel system maintenance but any type of maintenance. Failure to conduct maintenance and repairs in a safe manner may result in serious personal injury or death. Maintenance and testing of the vehicle's fuel system components can be accomplished safely and effectively by adhering to the following rules and guidelines.

- To avoid the possibility of fire and personal injury, always disconnect the negative battery cable unless the repair or test procedure requires that battery voltage be applied.
- Always relieve the fuel system pressure prior to disconnecting any fuel system component (injector, fuel rail, pressure regulator, etc.), fitting or fuel line connection. Exercise extreme caution whenever relieving fuel system pressure to avoid exposing skin, face and eyes to fuel spray. Please be advised that fuel under pressure may penetrate the skin or any part of the body that it contacts.
- Always place a shop towel or cloth around the fitting or connection prior to loosening to absorb any excess fuel due to spillage. Ensure that all fuel spillage (should it occur) is quickly removed from engine surfaces. Ensure that all fuel soaked cloths or towels are deposited into a suitable waste container.
- Always keep a dry chemical (Class B) fire extinguisher near the work area.
- Do not allow fuel spray or fuel vapors to come into contact with a spark or open flame.
- Always use a back-up wrench when loosening and tightening fuel line connection fittings. This will prevent unnecessary stress and torsion to fuel line piping.
- Always replace worn fuel fitting O-rings with new Do not substitute fuel hose or equivalent where fuel pipe is installed.

Before servicing the vehicle, make sure to also refer to the precautions in the beginning of this section as well.

RELIEVING FUEL SYSTEM PRESSURE

➡BMW does not provide a specific pressure relieving procedure, but instructs that any fuel system disconnect will spill fuel, so be prepared to catch and clean up any spilled fuel.

To relieve the pressure in the system, locate fuel pump relay located on the cowl. The relay can sometimes be distinguished by the orange color of the housing. Unplug and remove the relay, and place it in a safe location. With the fuel pump relay removed, start the engine and operate it until it stalls. Crank the engine for 10 seconds after it stalls to remove any residual pressure.

FUEL LEVEL SENDING UNIT

REMOVAL & INSTALLATION

See Figure 383.

The fuel tank should not be filled more than ⅓ of the total fuel tank capacity to prevent fuel leakage during fuel level sending unit removal. If the fuel tank is filled beyond this level, the fuel level must be reduced using an approved fuel removal device.

1. Before servicing the vehicle, refer to the precautions.
2. Relive the fuel system pressure and disconnect the negative battery cable.
3. Drain the fuel, if filled beyond ⅓ of the capacity of the fuel tank. Drain the fuel tank enough to prevent spillage when removing the pump using an approved fuel removal device.

➡The fuel level sending unit must be removed through the top of the fuel tank, thus the location of the fuel tank determines whether the fuel level sending unit is accessed by removal of the rear seat, or removal of the trim panels in the trunk.

4. Remove the rear seat, or the trim panels in the trunk, depending on fuel tank location to access the top of the fuel tank

➡On models which require removal of the rear seat, the insulation mat under the seat must be cut in a "U" shape to allow the insulation to be folded up to access the top of the fuel tank.

5. Remove the fasteners securing the metal cover located above the fuel tank, and remove the cover.
6. Remove the electrical connector at the top of the combination fuel level sending unit and fuel level sending unit assembly.
7. Remove the fuel feed and return lines.
8. Match mark the combination fuel level sending unit and fuel level sending unit assembly to the fuel tank to ensure proper installation during reassembly.
9. Remove the fasteners or fastener securing the combination fuel level sending unit and fuel level sending unit assembly to the fuel tank. The fasteners are one of 2 types.
10. If the fuel level sending unit assembly is fastened to the fuel tank with a series of 6 mm nuts:
    a. Loosen the nuts evenly using a crisscross sequence and carefully lift the cover and place aside.
    b. Compress the large plastic tongue to remove the fuel level sending unit, and lift the pump along with the fuel sending unit out of the fuel tank.
11. If the fuel level sending unit assembly is fastened to the fuel tank with a large sealing ring:
    a. Use tool No. 16-1-020 to loosen the sealing ring in a counterclockwise direction.
    b. With the seal ring removed, lift the fuel level sending unit assembly out of the fuel tank.

To install:

➡Always use a new seal or gasket when installing the fuel level sending unit or fuel level gauge sending unit assembly.

12. Install the fuel level sending unit into the fuel tank taking care not to bend or damage the fuel sending unit assembly.
13. If the fuel level sending unit is held in place by a plastic bracket in the fuel tank perform the following:
    a. Make sure the fuel level sending unit is fully snapped in place.
    b. Install the fuel tank cover plate with a new gasket and torque the fasteners using a crisscross pattern to 57 inch lbs. (6.5 Nm).
14. If the fuel level sending unit is held in place with a sealing ring perform the following:
    a. Ensure the pump is properly aligned with the fuel tank matchmarks made during disassembly.
    b. Install a new seal and torque the sealing ring using tool No. 16-1-020 as follows:
        - Metal sealing rings: 26 ft. lbs. (35 Nm)
        - Plastic sealing rings: 41 ft. lbs. (55 Nm)
15. The balance of the assembly is in reverse order of disassembly.
16. Connect the negative battery cable.
17. Once the vehicle is started, check for leaks. If a strong fuel odor is present, or any fuel leakage is noted, stop the engine immediately and repair as necessary.

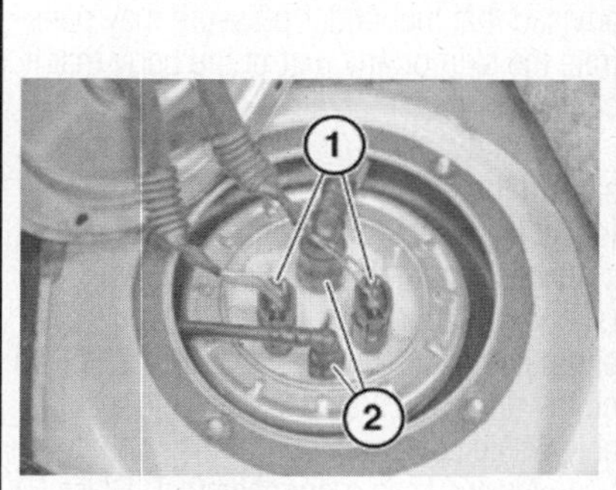

Fig. 383 Removing the fuel level sending unit

FUEL PUMP/ FUEL PUMP MODULE/FUEL TANK MODULE

REMOVAL & INSTALLATION

See Figure 384.

The fuel pump is mounted through the top of the fuel tank along with the fuel level sending unit. The fuel tank should not be filled more than ⅓ of the total fuel tank capacity to prevent fuel leakage during fuel pump removal. If the fuel tank is filled beyond this level, the fuel level must be reduced using an approved fuel removal device.

1. Before servicing the vehicle, refer to the precautions.
2. Relive the fuel system pressure and disconnect the negative battery cable.
3. Drain the fuel, if filled beyond⅓of the capacity of the fuel tank. Drain the fuel tank enough to prevent spillage when removing the pump using an approved fuel removal device.

➡The fuel pump must be removed through the top of the fuel tank, thus the location of the fuel tank determines whether the fuel pump is accessed by removal of the rear seat, or removal of the trim panels in the trunk.

4. Remove the rear seat, or the trim panels in the trunk, depending on fuel tank location to access the top of the fuel tank

➡On models which require removal of the rear seat, the insulation mat under the seat must be cut in a "U" shape to allow the insulation to be folded up to access the top of the fuel tank.

5. Remove the fasteners securing the metal cover located above the fuel tank, and remove the cover.
6. Remove the electrical connector at

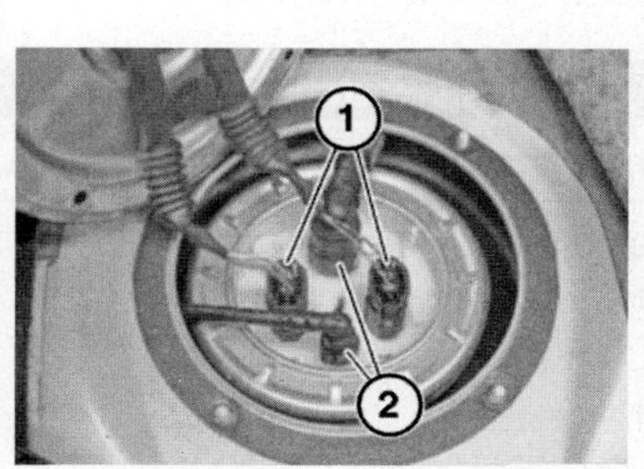

Fig. 384 Disconnect plug connection (1), unlock and detach vent lines (2)

the top of the combination fuel pump and fuel level sending unit assembly.

7. Remove the fuel feed and return lines.

8. Match mark the combination fuel pump and fuel level sending unit assembly to the fuel tank to ensure proper installation during reassembly.

9. Remove the fasteners or fastener securing the combination fuel pump and fuel level sending unit assembly to the fuel tank. The fasteners are one of 2 types.

10. If the fuel pump assembly is fastened to the fuel tank with a series of 6 mm nuts:

a. Loosen the nuts evenly using a crisscross sequence and carefully lift the cover and place aside.

b. Compress the large plastic tongue to remove the fuel pump, and lift the pump along with the fuel sending unit out of the fuel tank.

11. If the fuel pump assembly is fastened to the fuel tank with a large sealing ring:

a. Use tool No. 16-1-020 to loosen the sealing ring in a counterclockwise direction.

b. With the seal ring removed, lift the fuel pump assembly out of the fuel tank.

To install:

➡Always use a new seal or gasket when installing the fuel pump or fuel level gauge sending unit assembly.

12. Install the fuel pump into the fuel tank taking care not to bend or damage the fuel sending unit assembly.

13. If the fuel pump is held in place by a plastic bracket in the fuel tank perform the following:

a. Make sure the fuel pump is fully snapped in place.

b. Install the fuel tank cover plate with a new gasket and torque the fasteners using a crisscross pattern to 57 inch lbs. (6.5 Nm).

14. If the fuel pump is held in place with a sealing ring perform the following:

a. Ensure the pump is properly aligned with the fuel tank matchmarks made during disassembly.

b. Install a new seal and torque the sealing ring using tool No. 16-1-020 as follows:

- Metal sealing rings: 26 ft. lbs. (35 Nm)
- Plastic sealing rings: 41 ft. lbs. (55 Nm)

15. The balance of the assembly is in reverse order of disassembly.

16. Connect the negative battery cable.

17. Once the vehicle is started, check for leaks. If a strong fuel odor is present, or any fuel leakage is noted, stop the engine immediately and repair as necessary.

N63 High Pressure Fuel Pump

Left

See Figures 386 through 387.

WARNING

Observe warning on cylinder head cover.

WARNING

Disconnect battery negative terminal (risk of fire due to short-circuiting on removal).

WARNING

Electric fuel pump starts up automatically when door is opened!

WARNING

Carry out installation work on fuel system only with coolant temperature below 40°C.

CAUTION

Wear full face guard and protective gloves.

WARNING

Fuel can emerge spontaneously at high velocity when the high-pressure line is released.

WARNING

Adhere to conditions of absolute cleanliness when working on the high-pressure fuel system.

WARNING

Introduced contaminants can cause malfunctions in the system.

➡Do not allow any dirt particles or foreign bodies to get into the system.

➡Remove all traces of dirt before removing pipes or individual components.

➡Use only fluff-free cloths.

➡Seal all fuel system openings with protective caps or plugs.

1. Remove fuel feed line.

2. Remove high-pressure line from left high-pressure pump to rail.

WARNING

High-pressure pump can be pretensioned by camshaft cams.

3. Gently release screws (1) of high-pressure pump (2). If the high-pressure pump is pressed out, the engine must be rotated.

WARNING

Otherwise, it will not be possible to install the high-pressure pump.

4. Rotate engine at central bolt through 90° in direction of engine rotation.

5. Release screws (1).

6. Replace screws (1). Screws (1) are coated with sealant.

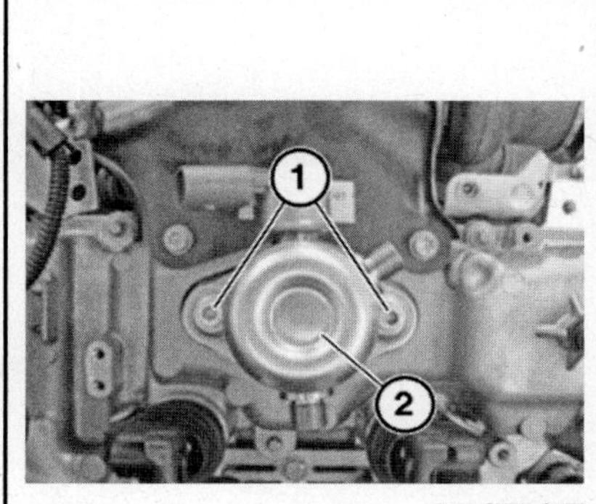

Fig. 385 Releasing screws (1) of high pressure pump (2)

⁂ WARNING

Pump plunger can fall out when high-pressure pump (2) is pulled out.

7. Detach high-pressure pump (2) and remove.
8. Engine oil can escape when pump is detached; have a cleaning cloth ready.

➡When installing, provisionally fasten screws (1) and tighten uniformly in 180° increments until final tightening.

a. Tightening torque: 9 ft. lbs. (12 Nm).

To install:

9. To install, reverse the removal procedure noting the following.
10. Replace sealing ring (1).
11. Clean contact surfaces.
12. Assemble engine.
13. Check fuel system for leaks.
14. Check function of DME.

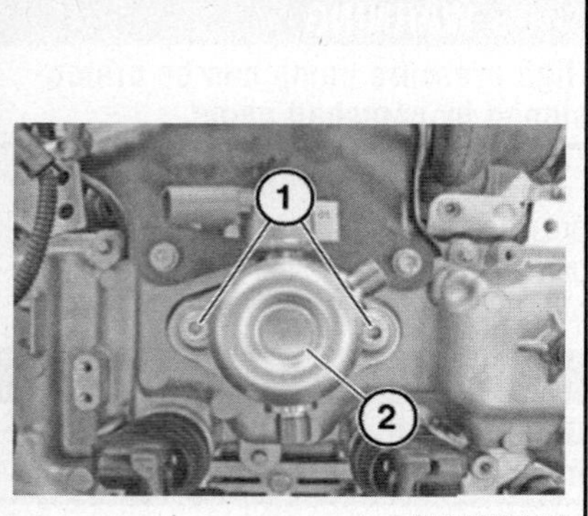

Fig. 386 Releasing screws (1) and detaching high pressure pump (2)

Fig. 387 Identifying sealing ring (1)

FUEL PRESSURE REGULATOR

REMOVAL & INSTALLATION

N52 Engine

See Figure 388.

1. Before servicing the vehicle, refer to the precautions.
2. Relive the fuel system pressure and disconnect the negative battery cable.
3. Drain the fuel, if filled beyond ⅓ of the capacity of the fuel tank. Drain the fuel tank enough to prevent spillage when removing the pump using an approved fuel removal device.

➡The fuel pump must be removed through the top of the fuel tank, thus the location of the fuel tank determines whether the fuel pump is accessed by removal of the rear seat, or removal of the trim panels in the trunk.

4. Remove fuel pump module from tank.
5. Remove fuel filter and hose pack with auxiliary cable to left.

To install:

➡Always use a new seal or gasket when installing the fuel pump or fuel level gauge sending unit assembly.

a. Install a new seal and torque the sealing ring using tool No. 16-1-020 as follows:
   - Metal sealing rings: 26 ft. lbs. (35 Nm)
   - Plastic sealing rings: 41 ft. lbs. (55 Nm)

6. The balance of the assembly is in reverse order of disassembly.
7. Connect the negative battery cable.
8. Once the vehicle is started, check for leaks. If a strong fuel odor is present, or any fuel leakage is noted, stop the engine immediately and repair as necessary.

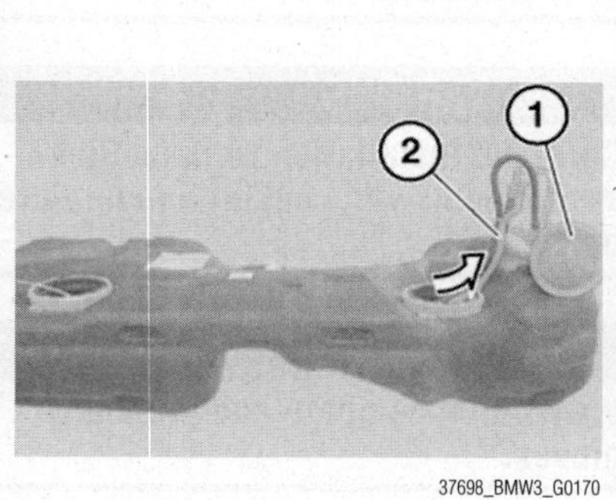

Fig. 388 Remove fuel filter (1) and hose pack (2) with auxiliary cable to left

FUEL RAIL & INJECTORS

REMOVAL & INSTALLATION

N52 Engine

See Figures 389 through 391.

1. Before servicing the vehicle, refer to the precautions.
2. Read out fault memory of DME control unit; if necessary, work through test schedules
3. Switch ignition **OFF**.
4. Remove clean air pipe.
5. Remove ignition coil cover.
6. If necessary, unclip plug connection from holder and disconnect. Unclip wiring harnesses from holder and connector strip. Disconnect holder from injection pipe.
7. Remove protective cap from compressed air valve. Connect compressed air line to compressed air valve. Blow fuel back into tank with a short blast of compressed air maximum of 43 PSI (3 bar).
8. Unlock and detach fuel line.
9. Disconnect connector strip.
10. Remove injection pipe.
11. Seal fuel hose with special tool 13 5 281.
12. Pry out retainers and pull fuel injectors out of injection pipe.

To install:

13. Replace sealing rings on fuel injectors and coat with anti-friction rubber coating.
14. Install injectors and capture with retainers.
15. Remove special tool 13 5 281.
16. Install injection pipe.

Fig. 389 Connect compressed air line to compressed air valve. Blow fuel back into tank with a short blast of compressed air maximum of 43 PSI (3 bar)

22205_BMWC_G0243

Fig. 390 Unlock and detach fuel line (1), detach connector strip (2), remove injection pipe (3).

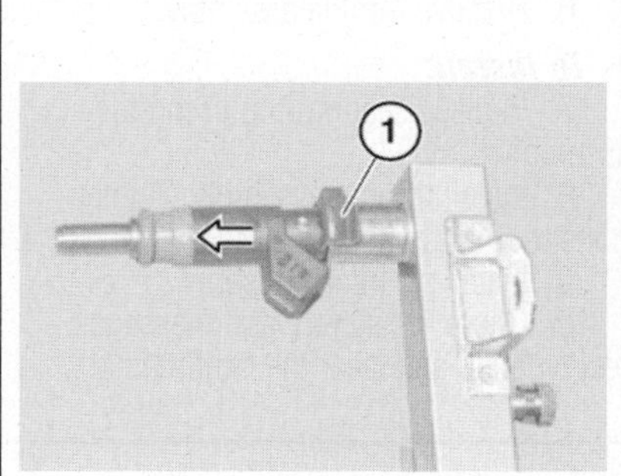

22205_BMWC_G0244

Fig. 391 Pry out retainers (1) and pull fuel injectors out of injection pipe

17. Connect connector strip in reverse direction of arrow.
18. Connect fuel line and lock.
19. Install ignition coil cover.
20. Install clean air pipe.
21. Check for stored fault messages, rectify faults and clear the fault memory.

FUEL TANK

DRAINING

Drawing Off Fuel

See Figures 392 and 393.

1. Start engine and allow to run.

➡The electric fuel pump runs. In this way, the fuel is re-pumped through the suction jet pump from the left to the right side of the fuel tank. Fuel can be drawn out of left and right sides of tank through filler neck, leaving only a small residue. The residual quantity is drawn off through the service opening (on right/left).

2. Insert special tool 16 1 080 into filler neck.

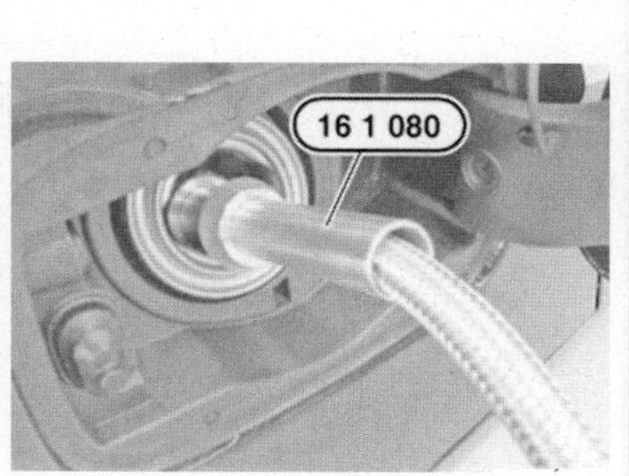

37698_BMW3_G0171

Fig. 392 Insert special tool 16 1 080 into filler neck

⁂ WARNING

Special tool 16 1 080 has two different diameters for petrol/gasoline and diesel vehicles.

3. Slide extraction hose of extractor unit, through special tool 16 1 080 into the fuel filler pipe, turning in the process if necessary. Insertion length approximately 47 in. (100 cm).
4. Draw off fuel as much as possible with extractor unit.

➡If the extraction hose meets resistance at an insertion length of approximately 47 in. (100 cm), a second person must press gently against the rubber hose of the filler pipe.

Drawing Off Fuel After Fault In Suction Jet Pump

1. Draw off right half of tank completely through fuel filler pipe.
2. Remove cap from left service opening.
3. Insert extraction hose through service opening in tank, fuel (also residual quantity) can be drawn off.

Fuel Filling

1. Insert special tool 16 1 080 into filler neck.
2. Slide extraction hose of extractor unit approximately 16 in. (40 cm) into fuel filler pipe.
3. Fill fuel from suction extractor unit.

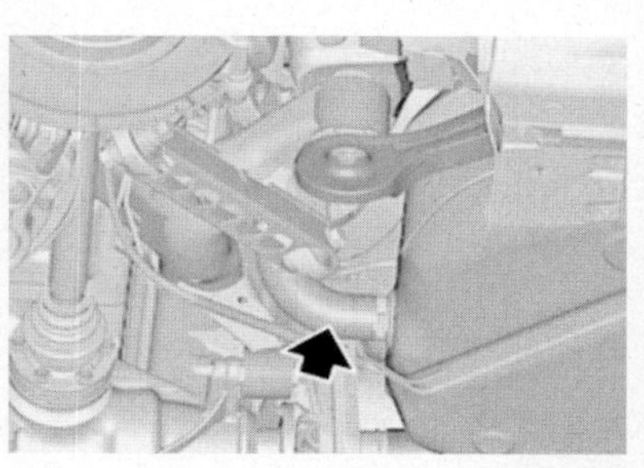
37698_BMW3_G0172

Fig. 393 If the extraction hose meets resistance at an insertion length of approximately 47 in. (100 cm), a second person must press gently against the rubber hose of the filler pipe

⁂ WARNING

Before starting the engine for the first time, if the tank has been run dry or drawn off, fill with diesel fuel and turn on ignition for approximately 1 minute. The fuel circuit is thus filled and vented, which results in the engine firing more quickly.

REMOVAL & INSTALLATION

See Figures 394 through 396.

1. Before servicing the vehicle, refer to the precautions.
2. Relive the fuel system pressure and disconnect the negative battery cable.
3. Drain the fuel tank enough to prevent spillage when removing the tank.
4. Remove rear right wheel arch trim.
5. Remove complete propeller shaft. Refer to drivetrain, driveshaft, removal & installation.
6. Remove handbrake Bowden cables from wheel carrier and unclip from fuel tank. Refer to parking brake, parking brake cables, removal & installation.
7. Remove right strut for rear axle. Refer to rear suspension, strut, removal & installation.
8. Disconnect hose clip.
9. Disconnect filler vent line from fuel filler pipe.
10. Disconnect service vent line from carbon canister.
11. Unclip both lines and remove retaining clip.
12. Unlock and disconnect plug connections of feed line.
13. If necessary, disconnect line for independent heating.
14. Remove screw as shown.

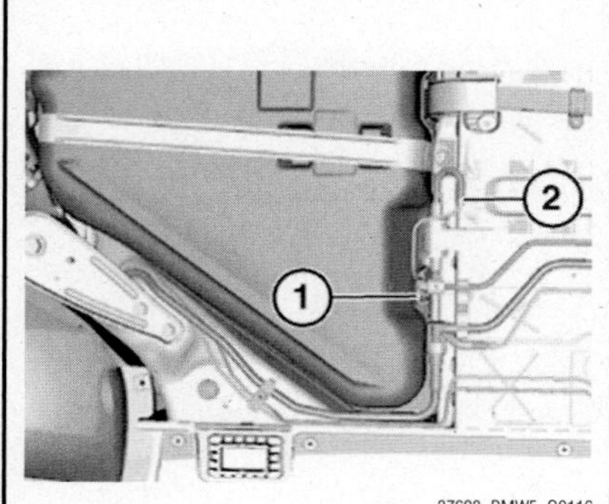

Fig. 394 Unlock and disconnect plug connections (1) of feed line and if necessary, disconnect line (2) for independent heating

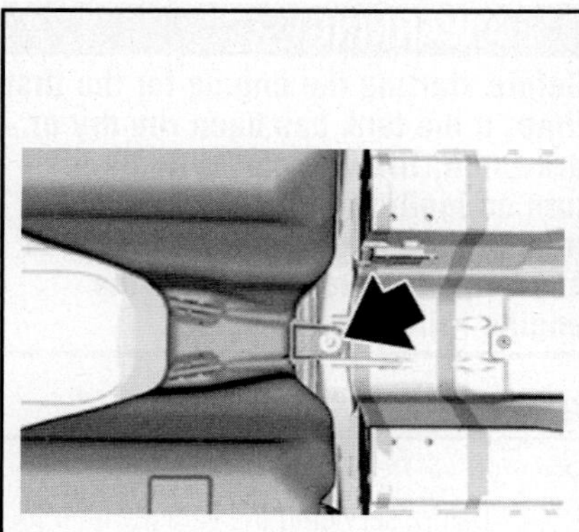

Fig. 395 Remove screw (1)

15. Support the fuel tank with a transmission jack.
16. Remove screws for tightening straps on left and right and remove tightening straps.
17. Lower tank until plug on top side of right tank half is accessible.
18. Unlock plug and detach from delivery unit.

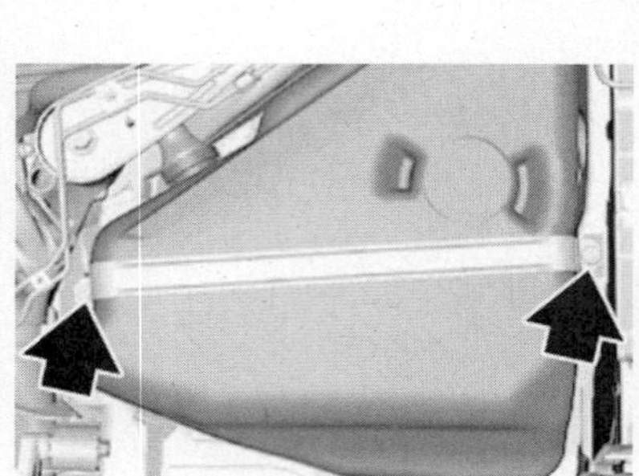

Fig. 396 Remove screws for tightening straps (arrows)

➡Get a second person to feed out vent lines to wheel arch while removing tank towards bottom.

19. Feed vent lines and through body.

⁂ WARNING

Do not kink lines.

To install:

20. Installation is the reverse of removal.

➡Note rubber mount with spacer bush. Wide collar on spacer bush points to screw head.

21. Carefully raise fuel tank.

⁂ WARNING

Carefully feed the vent line through the body when raising the fuel tank.

22. Tightening strap screws to 14 ft. lbs. (19 Nm).
23. Install a new fuel tank-to-body self-locking nut and tighten to 14 ft. lbs. (19 Nm).
24. Tighten the fuel filler-to-body nut to 2 ft. lbs. (3 Nm). Seal nut with under seal.

IDLE SPEED

ADJUSTMENTS

Idle speed is maintained by the by the Digital Motor Electronics (DME). No adjustment is necessary or possible.

THROTTLE BODY

REMOVAL & INSTALLATION

See Figure 397.

1. Before servicing the vehicle, refer to the precautions.
2. Read out fault memory of DME control unit; if necessary, work through test schedules
3. Switch ignition **OFF**.
4. Remove air intake hose.
5. Unlock plug and remove.
6. Remove throttle assembly.

To install:

7. Replace sealing ring of throttle assembly.
8. Install throttle assembly. Tighten bolts to 6 ft. lbs. (9 Nm).
9. Install air intake hose.
10. Check for stored fault messages, rectify faults and clear the fault memory.

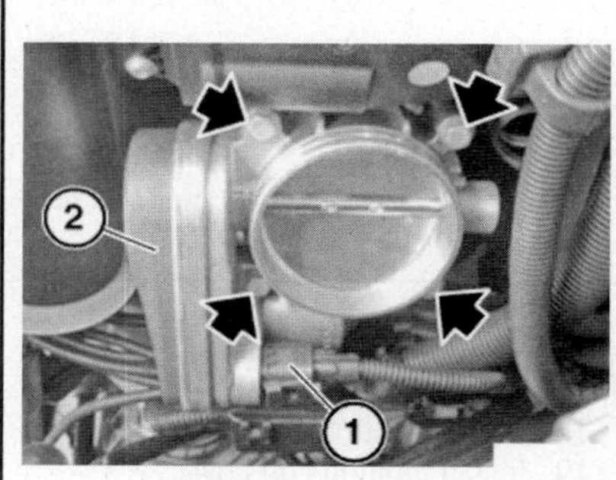

Fig. 397 TPS sensor (2) and connector (1) location

HEATING & AIR CONDITIONING SYSTM

BLOWER MOTOR

REMOVAL & INSTALLATION

See Figures 398 through 401.

1. Before servicing the vehicle, refer to the precautions.
2. Remove center console.
3. Remove audio system controller/Car Communication Computer.
4. Remove trim panel for pedal assembly.
5. Remove right glove box with housing.
6. Disconnect rear compartment air duct by moving it toward the rear of the vehicle.
7. Remove screws.
8. Remove middle function carrier.
9. If necessary, remove temperature sensor for cold-air distributor.
10. Disconnect plug connection.
11. Remove clips.
12. Disconnect plug connection.
13. Remove rear compartment air duct.
14. Disconnect air ducts.
15. Unlock plug and remove.
16. Remove screws.
17. Remove cover.
18. Remove screws.
19. Remove fan for heater-A/C unit.

To install:

20. Installation is the reverse of removal noting the following:
21. Make sure heater-A/C unit fan is correctly seated.

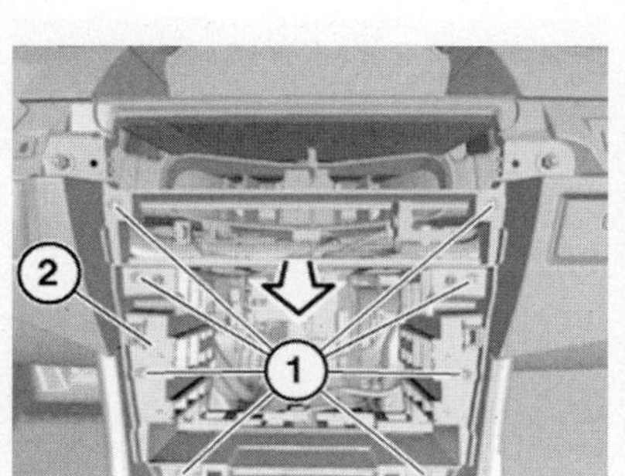

Fig. 398 Remove screws (1) and remove middle function carrier (2)

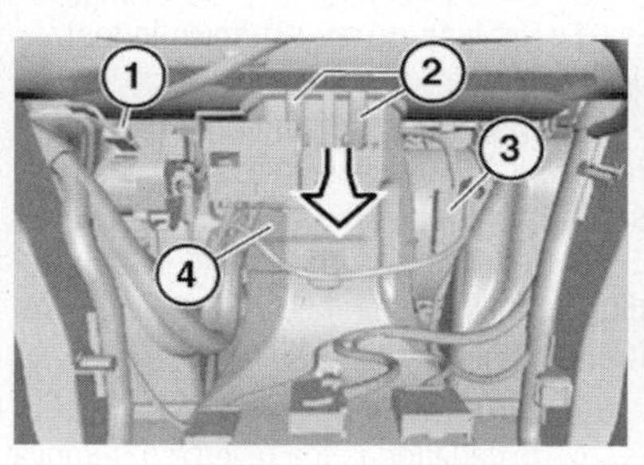

Fig. 399 Plug connection (1), clips (2), plug connection (3) and rear compartment air duct (4)

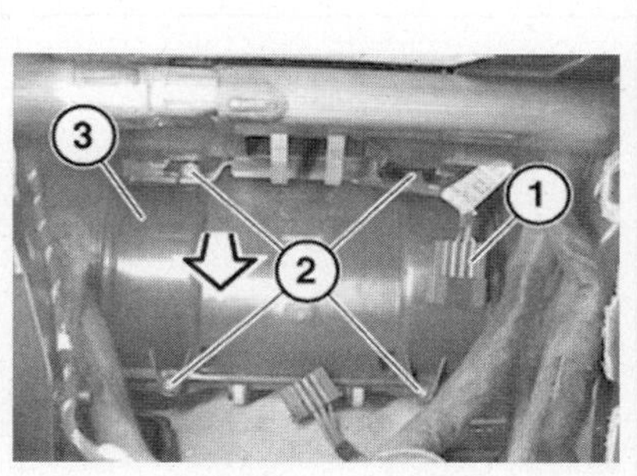

Fig. 400 Plug (1), screws (2) and cover (3)

22. Connect and lock the plug connections
23. Ensure correct cable routing.
24. Make sure seal is correctly seated in cover.
25. Install cover in reverse direction of arrow.
26. Connect air ducts in reverse direction of arrow.
27. Make sure right air duct is correctly seated.
28. Install rear compartment air duct in reverse direction of arrow.
29. Make sure rear compartment air duct is correctly seated.
30. Remove middle function carrier in reverse direction of arrow.
31. Make sure middle function carrier is correctly seated.
32. Ensure correct cable routing.

Fig. 401 Remove screws (1) and remove fan for heater-A/C unit (2)

HEATER CORE

REMOVAL & INSTALLATION

See Figures 402 through 406.

1. Before servicing the vehicle, refer to the precautions.

➡The heater case assembly must be removed to remove the heater core on all vehicles.

2. Disconnect the negative battery cable.
3. Drain the cooling system into a clean container for reuse.
4. Discharge and recover the air conditioning system refrigerant.
5. Remove fresh air duct.
6. Remove trim for instrument panel.

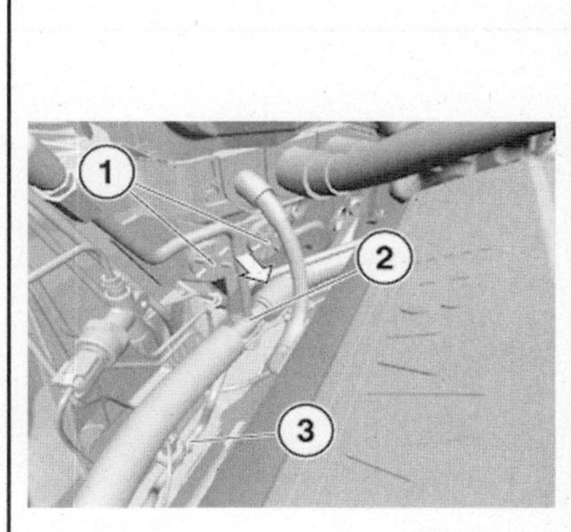

Fig. 402 Unscrew nuts (1), detach refrigerant line (2) and unclip refrigerant line (3)

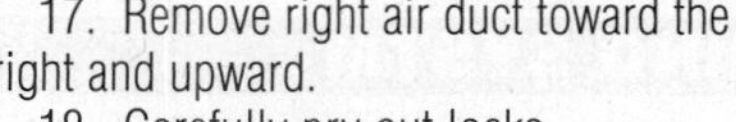

7. Remove temperature sensor for cold-air distributor.
8. Disconnect and unclip the refrigerant line.
9. Feed out rubber grommet.
10. Remove nut and detach refrigerant lines.
11. Remove nuts on right air duct.
12. Feed out rubber grommet.
13. Remove spring clamps and detach coolant hoses.

⁂ WARNING

Carefully blow through aluminum triple pipe to remove remaining coolant from heat exchanger for heating system.

14. Remove nuts on left air duct.
15. Disconnect rear compartment air duct toward rear of vehicle.
16. Remove left air duct toward the left of the vehicle.

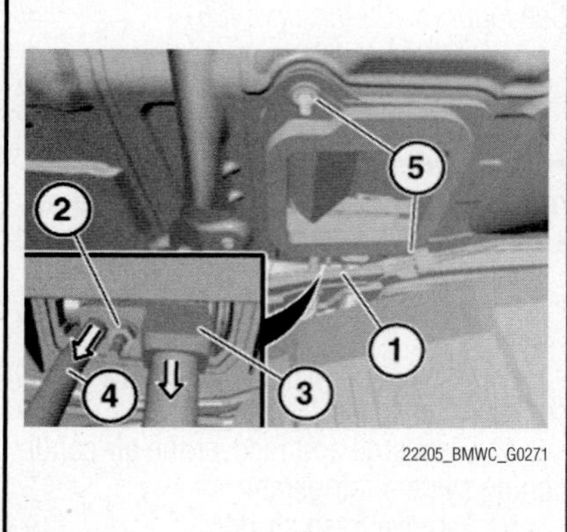

22205_BMWC_G0271

Fig. 403 Rubber grommet (1), nut (2), refrigerant lines (3) and (4) and nuts (5)

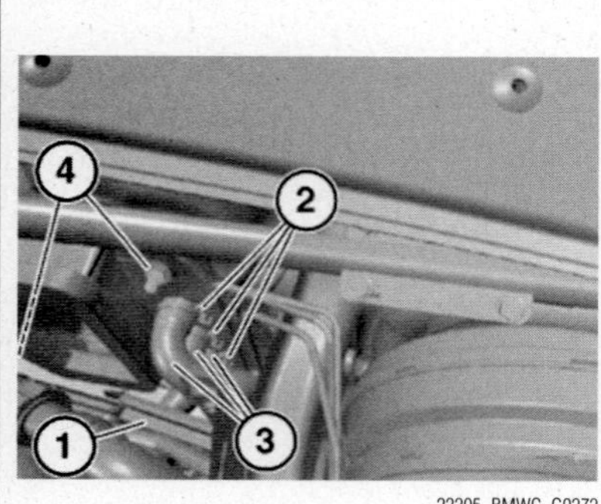

22205_BMWC_G0272

Fig. 404 Rubber grommet (1), spring clamps (2), coolant hoses (3) and nuts (4)

17. Remove right air duct toward the right and upward.
18. Carefully pry out locks.
19. Disconnect air distributor.
20. If necessary, remove CD changer.
21. Set fuse-carrier (3) down in foot well.
22. Disconnect support tube (2) and remove from vehicle with assistance of a second person.
23. If necessary, unlock and disconnect plug connections on heater. Remove heater toward the rear of the vehicle.

To install:

24. Installation is the reverse of removal, noting the following:
25. When installing heater, make sure left and right air ducts are correctly seated.
26. Check left and right air ducts for leaks.
27. If necessary, reseal left and right air ducts with butylene tape.

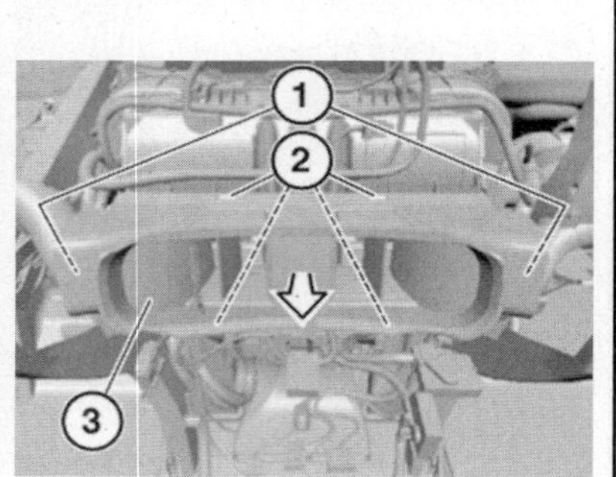

22205_BMWC_G0273

Fig. 405 Carefully pry out locks (1) and (2) and detach air distributor (3)

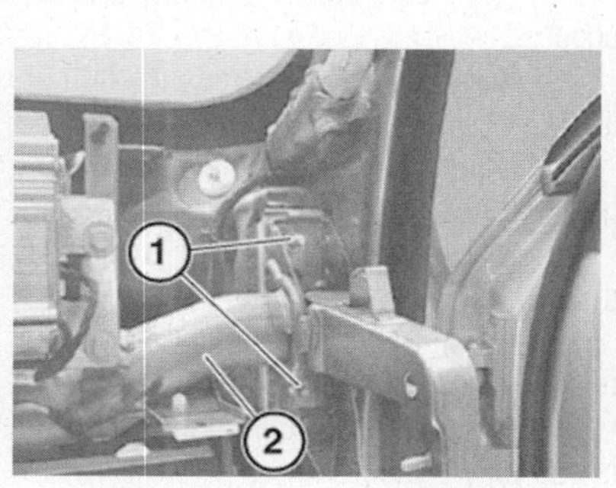

22205_BMWC_G0274

Fig. 406 Remove bolts (1) and detach support tube (2) and remove from vehicle

28. If left and right air ducts are resealed, make sure flaps can move freely.
29. Tighten fasteners to specification:
   - Support tube-to-body: 16 ft. lbs. (21 Nm)
   - Steering column-to-instrument panel / support tube: 16 ft. lbs. (21 Nm)
   - Air conditioner-to-bulkhead: 5 ft. lbs. (6 Nm)
   - Expansion valve-to-A/C heater: 5 ft. lbs. (6 Nm)
   - Refrigerant line-to-assembly compartment partition reinforcement: 6 ft. lbs. (8 Nm)

HEATER UNIT

REMOVAL & INSTALLATION

See Figures 408 through 422.

1. Before servicing the vehicle, refer to the precautions.
2. Draw off refrigerant from A/C system.
3. Remove fresh air duct.
4. Remove trim for instrument panel.
5. Remove temperature sensor for cold-air distributor.

⁂ WARNING

To avoid injury, cover holder on support tube.

6. Unscrew nuts.
7. Detach refrigerant line in direction of arrow.
8. Unclip refrigerant line.
9. Feed out rubber grommet.
10. Release nut and detach refrigerant lines and in direction of arrow.
11. Release nuts on right air duct.

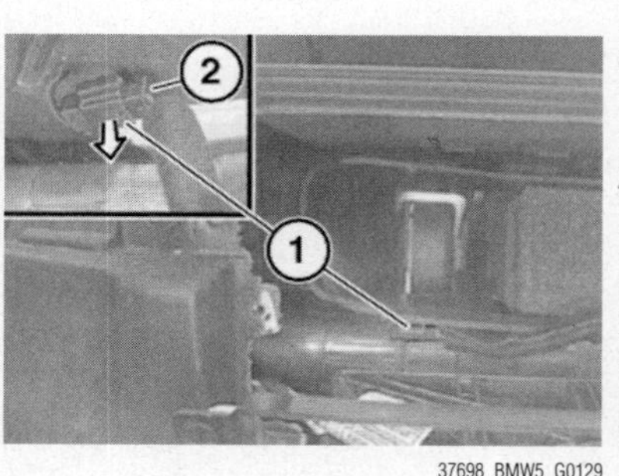

37698_BMW5_G0129

Fig. 407 Turn temperature sensor for cold-air distributor (1) through approximately 90° and pull out in direction of arrow. Unfasten plug connection (2) and disconnect

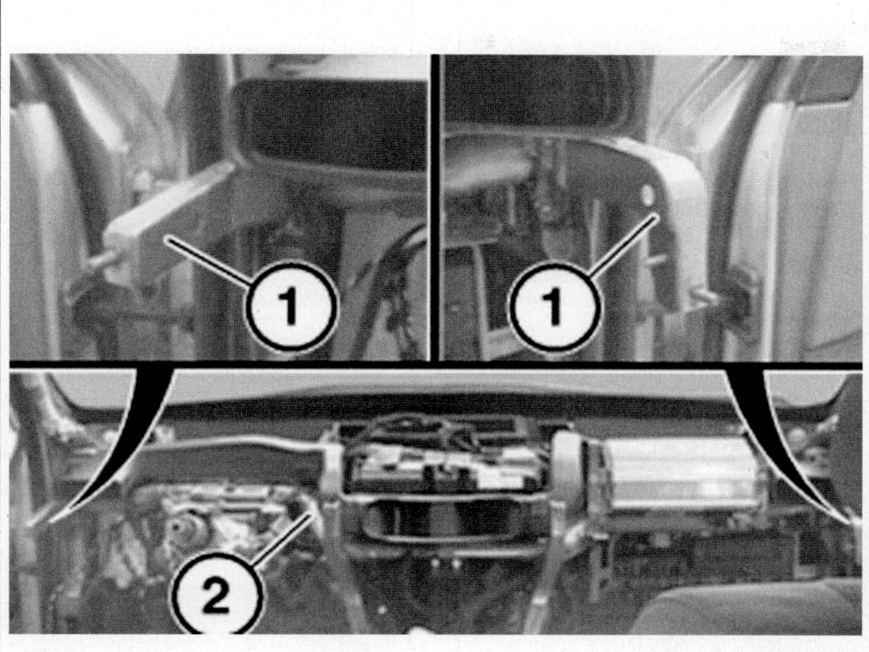

Fig. 408 To avoid injury, cover holder (1) on support tube (2)

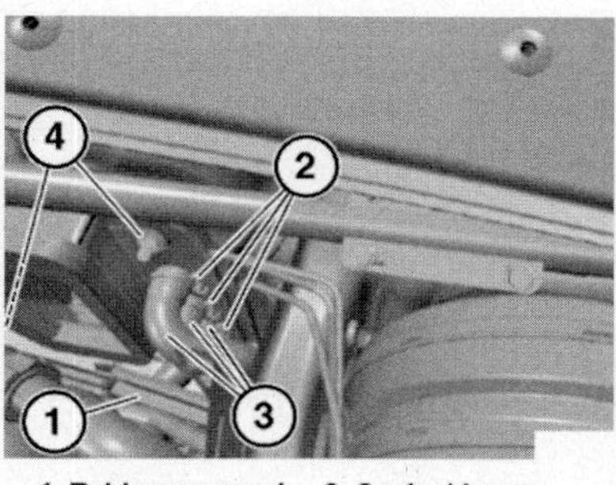

Fig. 411 Feed out rubber grommet, release spring clamps and detach coolant hoses. Release nuts on left air duct

12. Feed out rubber grommet.
13. Release spring clamps and detach coolant hoses.

WARNING

Carefully blow through aluminum triple pipe to remove remaining coolant from heat exchanger for heating system.

14. Release nuts on left air duct.
15. Disconnect rear compartment air duct in direction of arrow.
16. Release screws.
17. Remove left air duct in direction of arrow.
18. Release screws.
19. Remove right air duct in direction of arrow.
20. Carefully lever out locks and.

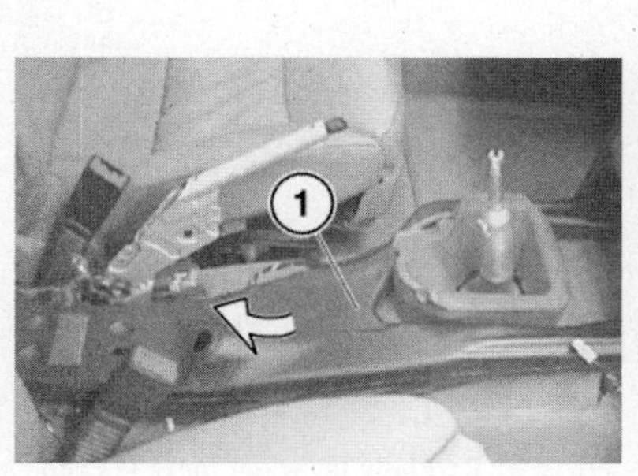

Fig. 412 Disconnect rear compartment air duct (1) in direction of arrow

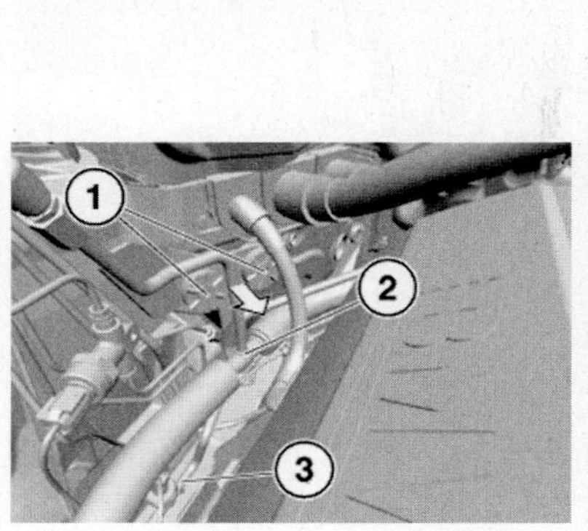

Fig. 409 Unscrew nuts (1), detach refrigerant line (2) in direction of arrow and unclip refrigerant line (3)

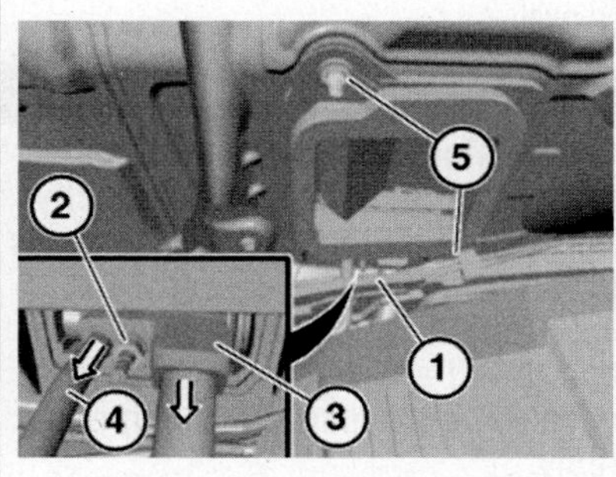

Fig. 410 Feed out rubber grommet, release nut and detach refrigerant lines in direction of arrow. Release nuts on right air duct

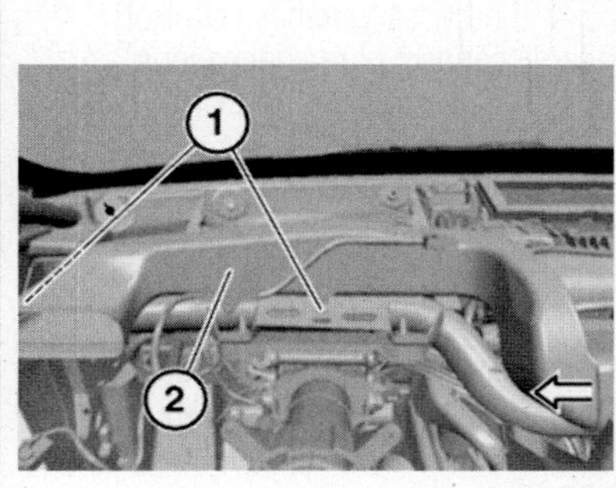

Fig. 413 Release screws (1) and remove left air duct (2) in direction of arrow

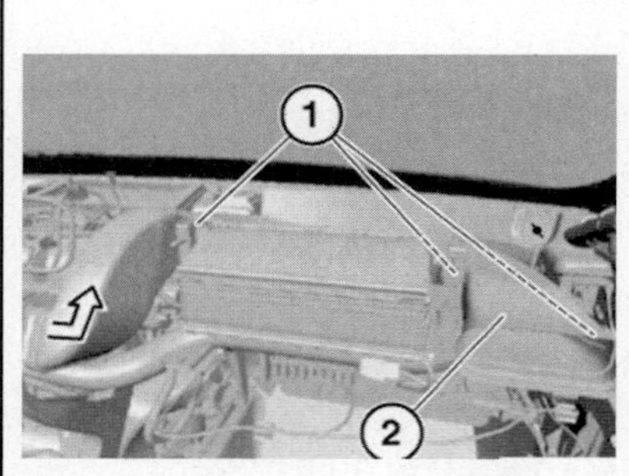

Fig. 414 Release screws (1) and remove right air duct (2) in direction of arrow

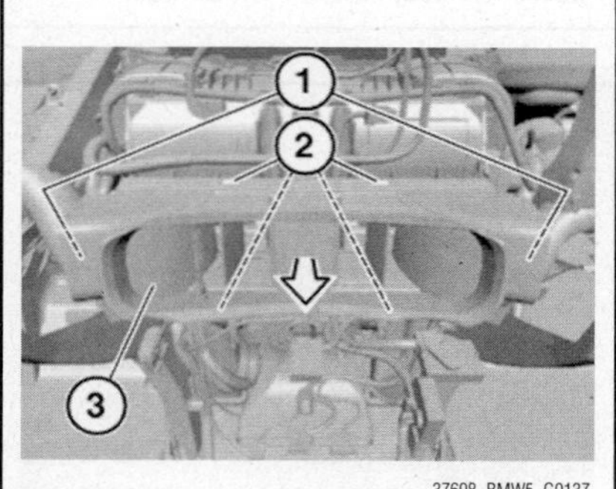

Fig. 415 Carefully lever out locks (1) and (2) and detach air distributor (3) in direction of arrow

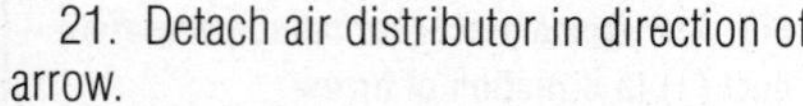

21. Detach air distributor in direction of arrow.
22. Disconnect all necessary cable ties on support tube.
23. Release wiring harnesses/cable ducts and lay to one side.
24. If necessary, remove control units/disconnect plug connections.
25. If necessary, remove CD changer.
26. Loosen screws.
27. Set fuse-carrier down in foot well.
28. Release screws as shown.
29. Release screws as shown.
30. Release screws as shown.
31. Unscrew nuts as shown.
32. Unscrew nuts as shown.
33. Detach support tube and remove from vehicle with assistance of a second person.
34. If necessary, unlock and disconnect plug connections on heater.

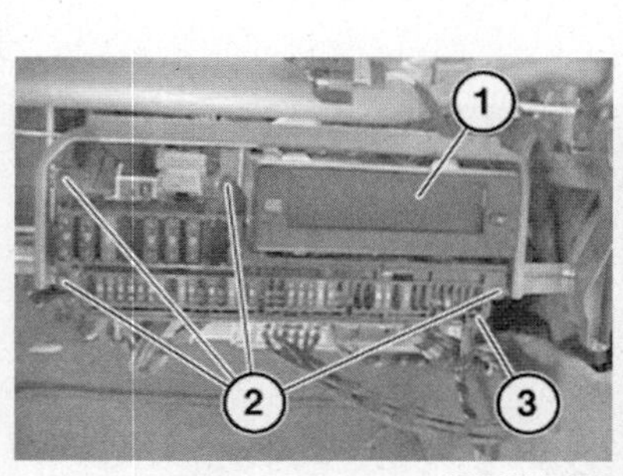

Fig. 416 Remove CD changer (1), loosen screws (2) and set fuse-carrier (3) down in foot well

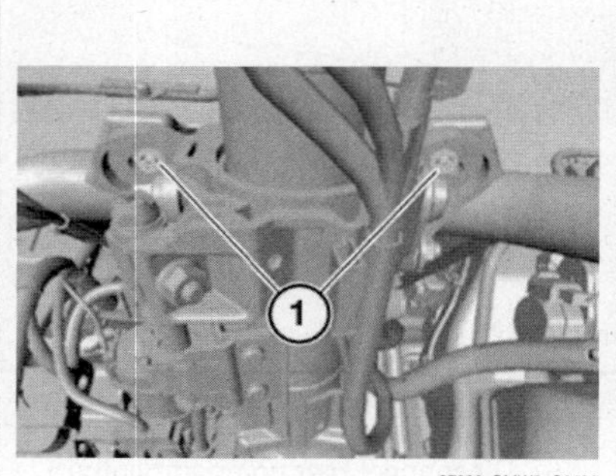

Fig. 417 Release screws (1)

35. Remove heater in direction of arrow.

To install:

36. Installation is the reverse of removal.

✲✲ WARNING

When installing heater, make sure left and right air ducts are correctly seated. Check left and right air ducts for leaks. If necessary, reseal left and right air ducts with butylene tape. If left and right air ducts are resealed, make sure flaps can move freely.

37. Replace sealing rings.
38. Make sure rubber grommet is correctly seated.
39. Make sure air distributor is correctly seated.
40. Vent cooling system and check for leaks.

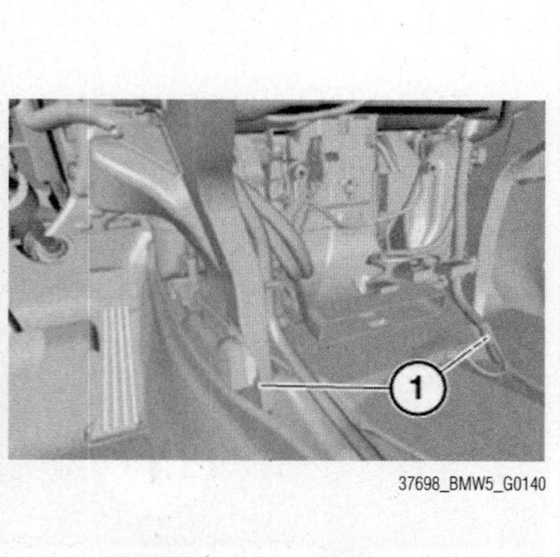

Fig. 418 Release screws (1)

Fig. 419 Release screws (1)

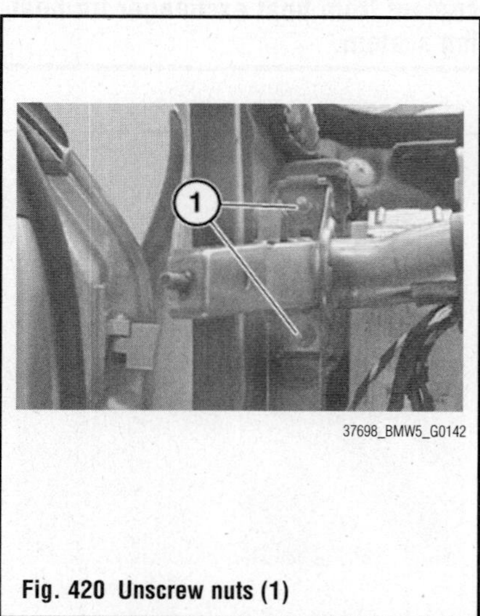

Fig. 420 Unscrew nuts (1)

41. Make sure rear compartment air duct is correctly seated.
42. Make sure wiring harnesses/cable ducts are correctly routed and secured.

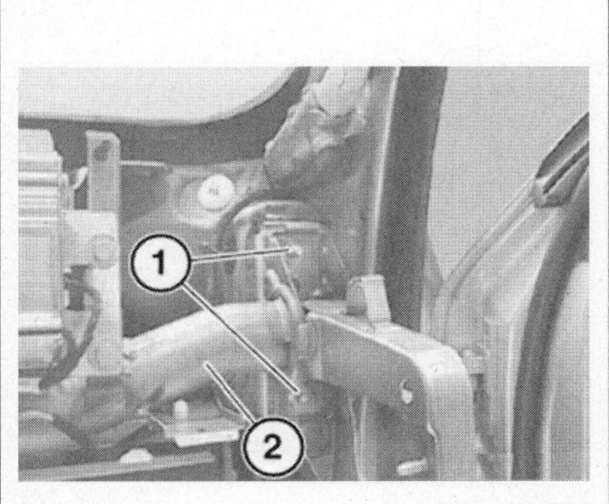

Fig. 421 Unscrew nuts (1) and detach support tube (2)

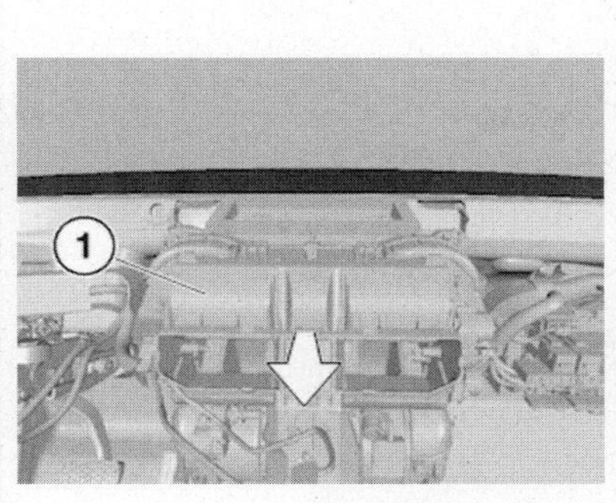

Fig. 422 Remove heater (1) in direction of arrow

43. Make sure heater is correctly seated.

44. Make sure condensate drain is correctly seated in grommet.

45. Tighten bolts/nuts to specification as follows:

- Refrigerant line to assembly compartment partition reinforcement: 67 inch lbs. (7.6 Nm)
- Refrigerant lines to expansion valve: 78 inch lbs. (8.8 Nm)
- Air conditioner to bulkhead: 53 inch lbs. (6 Nm)
- Steering column to instrument panel / support tube: 16 ft. lbs. (21 Nm)
- Support tube to body: 16 ft. lbs. (21 Nm)

STEERING

ELECTRONIC STEERING CONTROL UNIT

REMOVAL & INSTALLATION

See Figures 423 through 425.

1. Disconnect battery earth lead.
2. Release left front seat and tilt towards rear.
3. Remove front left door sill cover strip.
4. Remove footwell side trim panel on A-pillar.
5. Remove cover of bass speaker at left front.
6. Fold back front left carpet to one side.
7. Unscrew nuts (1).
   a. Tightening torque:71 inch lbs. (8 Nm).

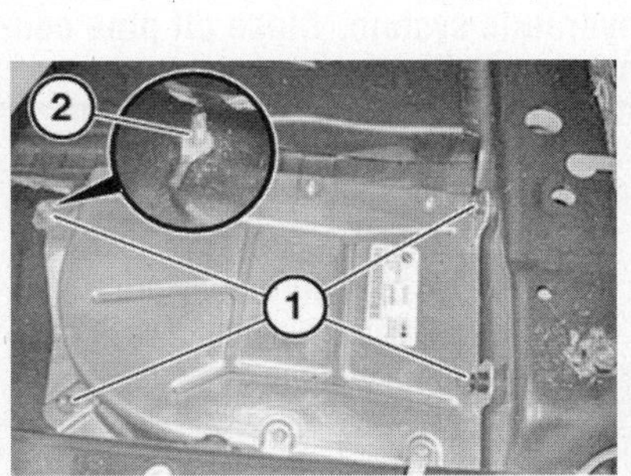

Fig. 423 Unscrewing nuts (1) and securing grounding strap (2)

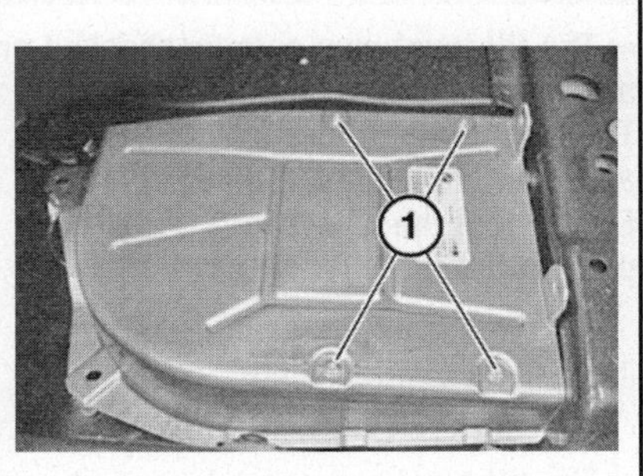

Fig. 424 Releasing screws (1)

➡When installing, secure grounding strap (2) to screw fastening point.

8. Release screws (1).
   a. Tightening torque: 35 inch lbs. (4 Nm).
9. Disconnect plug connections (1) and remove control unit.

To install:

10. To install, reverse the removal procedure.

POWER RACK & PINION STEERING GEAR

REMOVAL & INSTALLATION

See Figure 426.

1. Before servicing the vehicle, refer to the precautions.

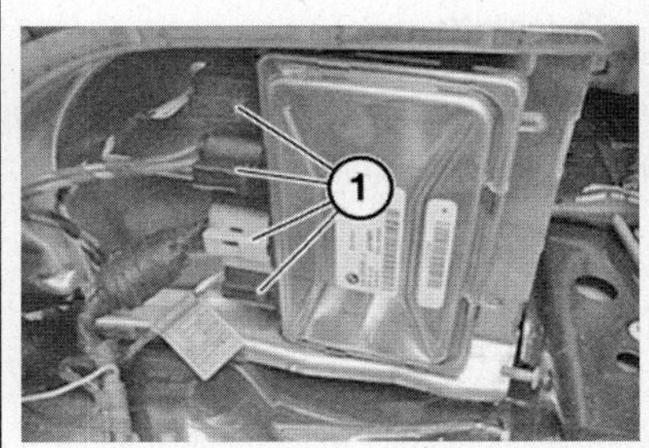

Fig. 425 Disconnecting plug connections (10 and removing control unit

2. Disconnect the negative battery cable.
3. Draw off and dispose of hydraulic fluid from fluid reservoir.
4. Secure engine in installation position.
5. Remove both tie rod ends from ball joint.
6. Lower front axle support.
7. Remove left mounting bracket or engine mount from front axle carrier.
8. If necessary, remove right engine mount from front axle carrier.
9. If necessary, remove heat shield from power steering gear.
10. Disconnect pressure line and return line from power steering gear.
11. Remove screw. Remove nuts and remove screws towards bottom.

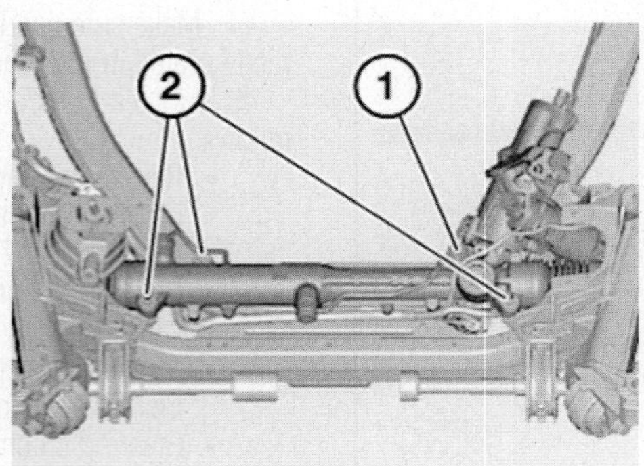

Fig. 426 Remove screw (1), remove nuts (2) and remove screws towards bottom

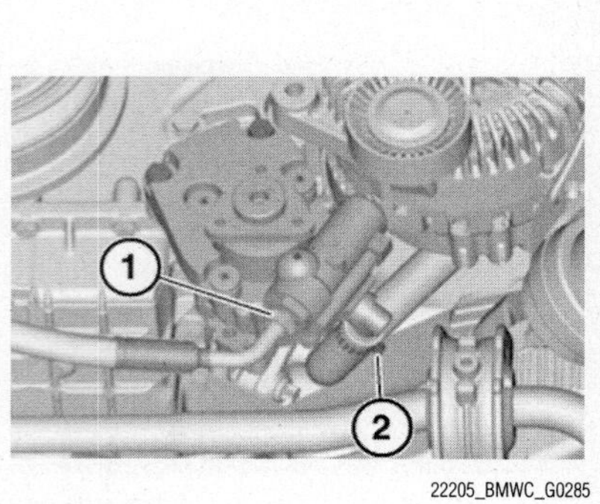

Fig. 427 Remove banjo bolt (1) and detach pressure line from vane pump. Remove hose clamp (2) and detach suction line from vane pump

12. On vehicles with active steering, disconnect plug connections.
13. Raise power steering gear and unclip wiring harness.
14. Move power steering gear to right and remove towards rear.

To install:

15. Install power steering gear.
16. Replace screws and self-locking nuts and tighten to specification.
    - 2WD: 42 ft. lbs. (56 Nm) plus an additional 90° rotation
    - AWD: 89 ft. lbs. (120 Nm)
17. Replace all sealing rings.
18. Make sure hydraulic lines are laid without tension and with sufficient spacing to adjoining components. Tighten to 26 ft. lbs. (35 Nm).

➡When replacing the power steering gear, the Banjo bolt for pressure line (expansion hose) must be replaced by a banjo bolt with non-return valve.

19. Fill and bleed hydraulic system.
20. Check pipe connections for leaks.
21. Perform chassis alignment check.
22. Carry out steering angle sensor adjustment/adjustment for active front steering.
23. If necessary, carry out initial Dynamic Drive operation.

POWER STEERING PUMP

BLEEDING

1. Before servicing the vehicle, refer to the precautions.

⁂ WARNING

Adhere to the utmost cleanliness. Do not allow any dirt to enter the hydraulic system. Using contaminated equipment to add fluid may introduce dirt particles into the fluid reservoir and significantly reduce the service life of the power steering system. Do not use any filler funnels or similar.

➡The fill level may only be checked or adjusted when the engine is stopped. The fluid temperature should be approximately 68° F (20° C) here. Ensure that the cap is fully screwed in prior to the fill level check.

2. Thoroughly clean fluid reservoir and its immediate surroundings
3. Check and correct fill level

➡The fill level can come to rest above the MAX mark when the engine is at normal operating temperature. This is dictated by the design in that the marking on the dipstick is referred to a fluid temperature of 68° F (20° C). With the engine at normal operating temperature (approximately 122–140° F (50–60° C) fluid temperature adjust a fill height .39 in. (10 mm) above the MAX mark. Do not under any circumstances draw off the fluid to the MAX mark when the engine is at normal operating temperature.

4. Start engine.
5. Turn steering wheel left and right twice in each case up to full lock; if necessary, top up hydraulic fluid (e.g. if hydraulic system is completely drained).
6. Move steering wheel to straight-ahead position and turn off engine.
7. Check and correct fill level with engine stopped.
8. Check hydraulic system for leaks.

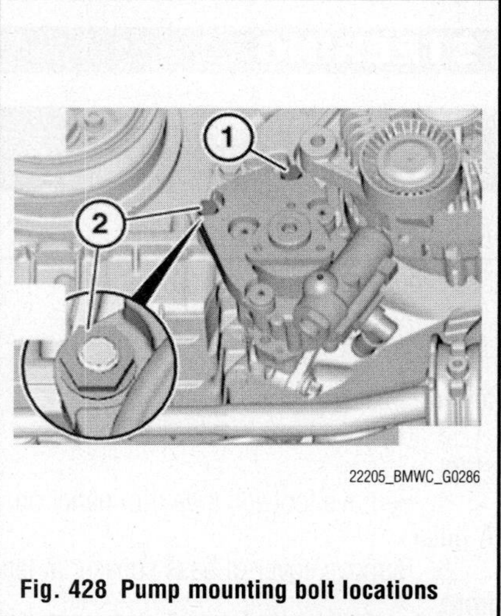

Fig. 428 Pump mounting bolt locations

REMOVAL & INSTALLATION

See Figures 427 and 428.

⁂ WARNING

Adhere to the utmost cleanliness. Do not allow any dirt to enter the hydraulic system. Close off pipe connections with plugs.

1. Draw off and dispose of hydraulic fluid from fluid reservoir.
2. Remove belt pulley.
3. Remove front underbody protection.
4. Remove banjo bolt and detach pressure line from vane pump.
5. Remove hose clamp and detach suction line from vane pump.
6. Remove bolt and nut.
7. Remove vane pump downwards.

To install:

8. Install vane pump and tighten bolt and nut to 16 ft. lbs. (21 Nm).

9. Connect suction line to vane pump and tighten hose clamp.

➡**Markings on suction line and vane pump connection must match up.**

10. Connect pressure line to vane pump. Replace all sealing rings and tighten banjo bolt to 24 ft. lbs. (33 Nm).

➡**Make sure pressure line is laid without tension and with sufficient spacing to adjoining components.**

11. Fill and bleed hydraulic system.
12. Check pipe connections for leaks.

POWER STEERING FLUID

FLUID RECOMMENDATIONS

ATF is the suggested steering fluid.

FLUID LEVEL CHECK

See Figure 430.

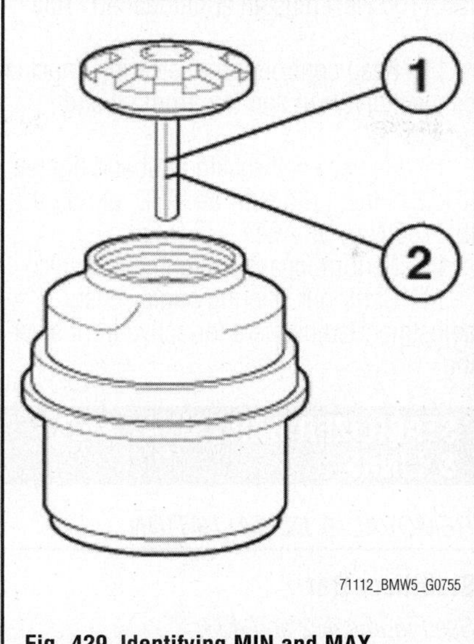

Fig. 429 Identifying MIN and MAX markings

1. Check fluid level with engine switched off at expansion tank of power steering/ride-height control system. The fluid temperature should be approx. 20°C here.
2. Ensure that the cap is fully screwed in prior to the fill level check.
3. If necessary, add hydraulic fluid (refer to Service Information Operating Fluids) up to Max. marking (1).

⁂ WARNING

If the fluid level has dropped to the Min. marking (2), you must check the power steering and ride-height control for leaks and issue a separate invoice for this work.

⁂ WARNING

It is not enough merely to top up the fluid.

SUSPENSION

FRONT SUSPENSION

COIL SPRINGS

REMOVAL & INSTALLATION

⁂ WARNING

Prior to each use, check the special tools for defects, modifications and operational reliability.

⁂ WARNING

Damaged/modified special tools must not be used.

⁂ WARNING

No changes or modifications may be made to the special tools.

⁂ WARNING

These special tools are intended solely for the purpose of tightening and relieving cylindrical and tapered suspension springs.

⁂ WARNING

Keep special tools dry, clean and (down to the spindle) free from grease.

⁂ WARNING

Impact screwdrivers are prohibited.

⁂ WARNING

Do not compress coil spring to full extent.

➡**All screws, nuts, bolts and hose clamps removed during the repair must be replaced.**

➡**Retaining elements on chassis and suspension and steering parts must be replaced.**

1. Remove front spring strut.
2. Relieve tension on coil spring and remove from special tools 83 30 2 318 833.

➡**To be able to align the support bearing to the spring-strut bore when assembling the spring strut, the spring in the spring tensioner must be positioned correctly.**

3. The spring coil with the largest diameter must be positioned against the support bearing.
4. The upper coil spring end must be in contact with the limit position of the spring pad.
5. Position spring with mounted support bearing and gauge 83 30 2 210 780 in spring tensioner so that marks (1) are positioned vertically towards top
6. Position the gauge on the support bearing:
   a. Right support bearing: Position mark "RIGHT B" on arrow at support bearing.
   b. Left support bearing: Position mark "LEFT" on arrow at support bearing.
7. Refer to repair instructions for spring strut.

⁂ WARNING

Do not compress coil spring to full extent.

⁂ WARNING

Coils of coil spring must be located completely in recesses of special tools 83 30 2 318 833.

8. Tension coil spring.

To install:

9. To install, reverse the removal procedure.
10. Refer to STRUT.

LOWER BALL JOINTS

REMOVAL & INSTALLATION

The lower ball joint is an integral part of the lower control arm and is not serviced separately.

LOWER CONTROL ARM BRACKET

REMOVAL & INSTALLATION

See Figures 430 and 431.

1. Before servicing the vehicle, refer to the precautions.

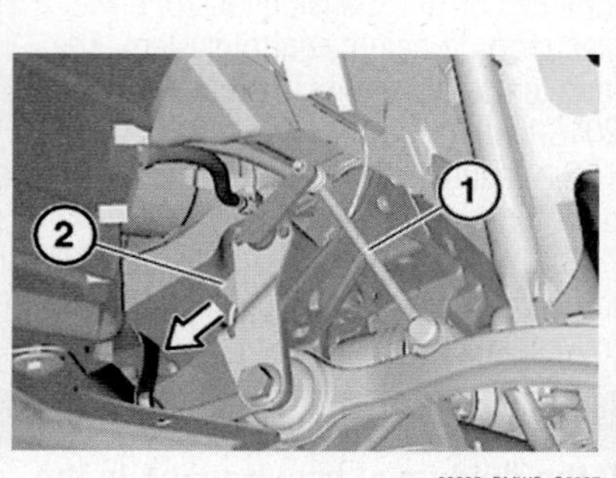

22205_BMWC_G0307

Fig. 430 Remove jointed rod (1) from control arm and disconnect plug connection (2) on ride-height sensor

2. If necessary, remove steering gear cover at side.
3. Right side only on version with xenon headlight:
   a. Remove nut that attaches the rod to control arm.
   b. Remove jointed rod from control arm.
   c. Disconnect plug connection on ride-height sensor.
4. Unscrew nut and remove screw towards rear.
5. Only on right side: If necessary, remove holder with ride-height sensor.
6. Remove nut; if necessary, grip at Torx® socket.
7. Remove control arm.

To install:

8. Install control arm.
9. Replace self-locking nut.
10. Temporarily tighten down bolt and nut. Once the vehicle is lowered to normal ride height, finish tightening to 74 ft. lbs. (100 Nm) plus an additional 90° rotation.
11. Keep control arm to steering knuckle connection clean and free from oil and grease.
12. Replace self-locking nut and tighten to122 ft. lbs. (165 Nm) on 2WD and 59 ft. lbs. (80 Nm) on AWD.
13. Perform chassis alignment check.
14. Carry out steering angle sensor adjustment/adjustment for active front steering.

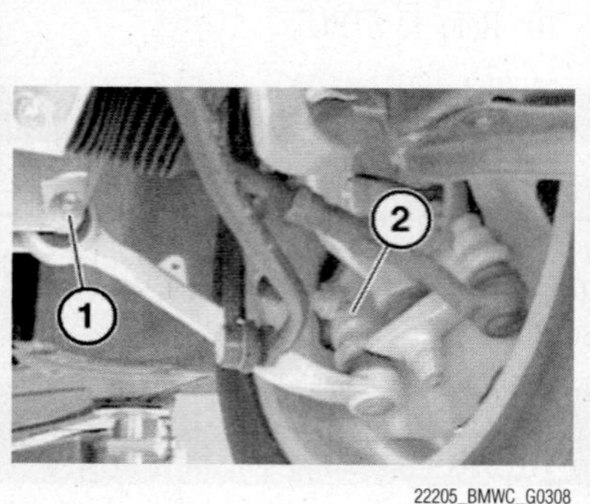

22205_BMWC_G0308

Fig. 431 Unscrew nut (1) and remove screw towards rear. Remove nut (2) and if necessary, grip at Torx® socket

STABILIZER BAR (SWAY BAR) & LINKS

REMOVAL & INSTALLATION

Stabilizer Bar

See Figures 432 and 433.

1. Before servicing the vehicle, refer to the precautions.
2. Remove front assembly underside protection.
3. If necessary, remove wheel suspension cover on both sides.
4. Remove stabilizer link on both sides from stabilizer.
5. If necessary, remove holder for hydraulic lines from retaining bracket.
6. Remove nut and screw at both ends.
7. Remove stabilizer from front axle carrier.

To install:

8. Installation is the reverse of removal.
9. Check both rubber mounts for damage, replace if necessary.
10. Replace self-locking nuts and tighten stabilizer bar mounts to 22 ft. lbs. (30 Nm).
11. Replace self-locking nuts and tighten stabilizer link to 48 ft. lbs. (65 Nm).

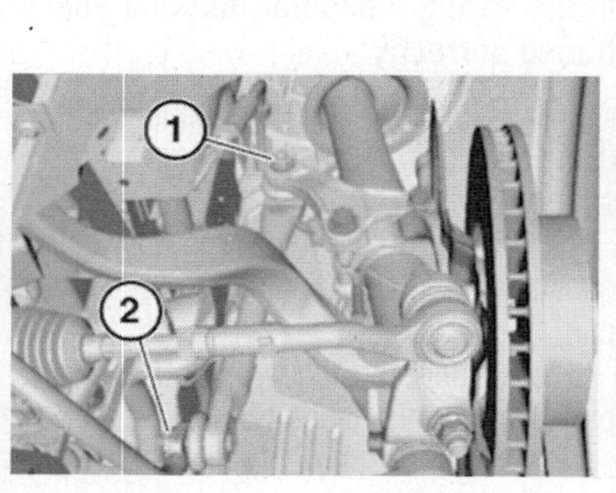

37698_BMW5_G0157

Fig. 432 Release nuts (1, 2); if necessary, grip at Torx socket

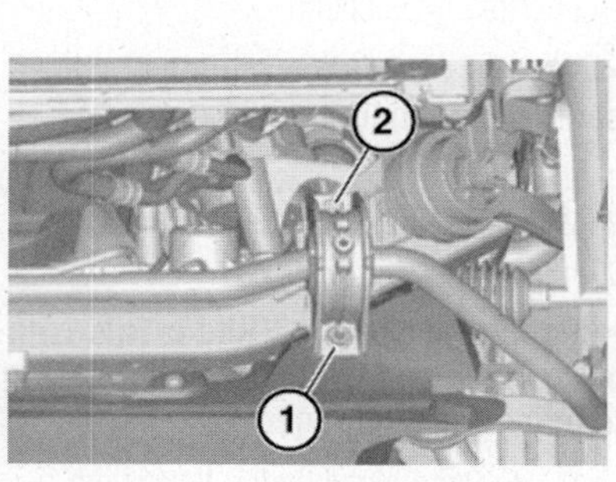

37698_BMW5_G0156

Fig. 433 Release nut (1) and screw (2) at both ends

12. If necessary, install wheel suspension cover on both sides.
13. Install front assembly underside protection.

STRUTS

REMOVAL & INSTALLATION

See Figures 434 and 435.

1. Before servicing the vehicle, refer to the precautions.
2. Remove steering knuckle. Refer to front suspension, steering knuckle, removal & installation.
3. If necessary, remove expander rivet.
4. If necessary, unclip spring strut dome cover from front cross-strut.
5. Make position of studs in relation to wheel arch.
6. Secure spring strut against falling out.
7. Unscrew nuts as shown.
8. Remove spring strut downwards out of wheel arch.

To install:

9. Align spring strut using centering pin to bore in wheel arch or studs to wheel arch and push upwards.
10. Replace self-locking nuts and tighten to 25 ft. lbs (34 Nm).
11. Carry out wheel alignment check if a spring strut with support bearing was or has been installed without centering pin.

OVERHAUL

See Figures 434 through 440.

This procedure details the removal of the coil spring from the MacPherson strut assembly.

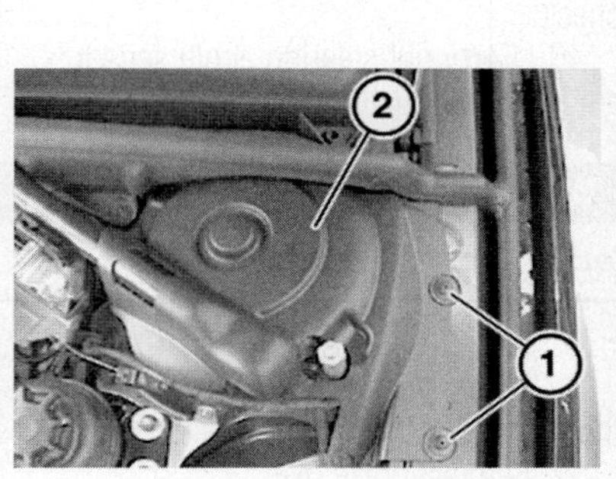

Fig. 434 Release expander rivet (1) and unclip spring strut dome cover (2) from front cross-strut

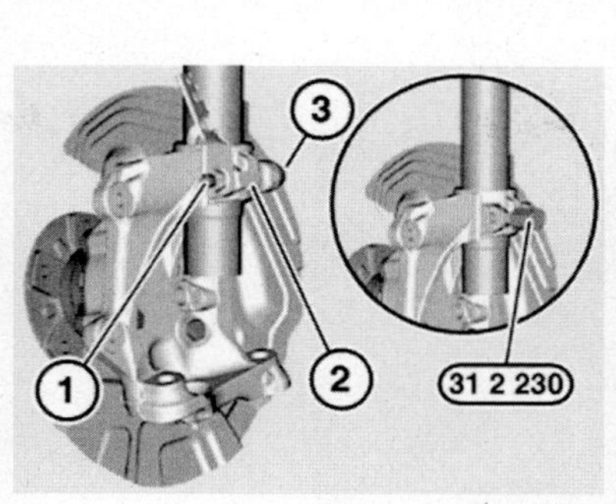

Fig. 436 Remove nut (1), remove holder (2) and remove screw (3)

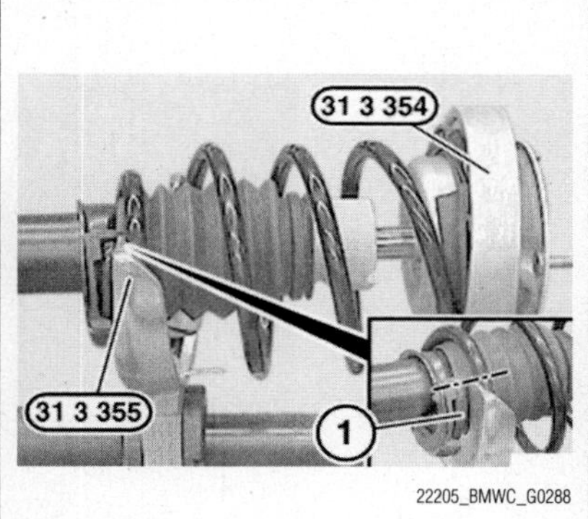

Fig. 437 Twist spring strut until end of coil spring (1)

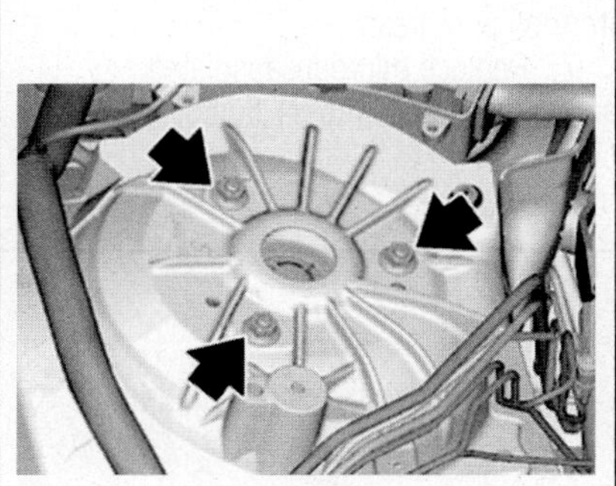

Fig. 435 Unscrew nuts (arrows)

CAUTION

This procedure calls for the spring to be compressed. A compressed spring has high potential energy and if removed suddenly can cause severe damage and personal injury.

1. Before servicing the vehicle, refer to the precautions.
2. Remove front spring strut.
3. Remove nut, remove holder and remove screw.
4. Expand ball joint with special tool 31 2 230 and detach from spring strut.
5. Clamp special tool 31 3 341 in vice.
6. Install insert 31 3 358 in special tool 31 3 354.
7. Position special tools 31 3 355 and 31 3 354 with insert 31 3 358 from above on special tool 31 3 341 until locking pins can be felt and heard to snap into place.
8. Check seating of special tools 31 3 355 and 31 3 354 with insert 31 3 358, correct if necessary.
9. Clean coil spring to remove coarse dirt and take up with special tools 31 3 355 and 31 3 354 with insert 31 3 358.
10. Twist spring strut until end of coil spring is flush with end of special tool 31 3 355.

WARNING

Special tool 31 3 354 and centering ring 31 3 358 must rest correctly on upper spring plate.

11. Lower coil of coil spring must rest completely in recess of special tool 31 3 355.
12. Compress coil spring until stress on piston rod is relieved.
13. Remove cap.
14. Remove nut with special tool 31 2 210 (grip piston rod in the process).
15. Remove support bearing, dust sleeve and supporting ring.
16. Remove shock absorber with auxiliary damper, gaiter and lower spring pad sideways from tensioned coil spring.
17. If necessary, remove auxiliary damper, gaiter and spring pad from shock absorber.
18. Relieve tension on coil spring.
19. Remove coil spring with spring plate from special tools 31 3 355, 31 3 358 and 31 3 354.

To install:

20. Check spring pad for damage, replace if necessary.
21. Connect spring plate with spring pad to coil spring.

➡End of coil spring must be positively aligned to spring pad.

Fig. 438 Remove nut with special tool 31 2 210 (grip piston rod in the process)

22. Accommodate coil spring with spring plate with special tools 31 3 355, 31 3 358 and 31 3 354. Twist coil spring until lower end of coil spring is flush with end of special tool 31 3 355.

WARNING

Do not compress coil spring to full extent.

23. Special tool 31 3 354 and centering ring 31 3 358 must rest correctly on upper spring plate.
24. Lower coil of coil spring must rest completely in recess of special tool 31 3 355.
25. Tension coil spring.
26. Check auxiliary damper, gaiter and spring pad for damage, replace if necessary.

➡Make sure spring pad is correctly seated on shock absorber.

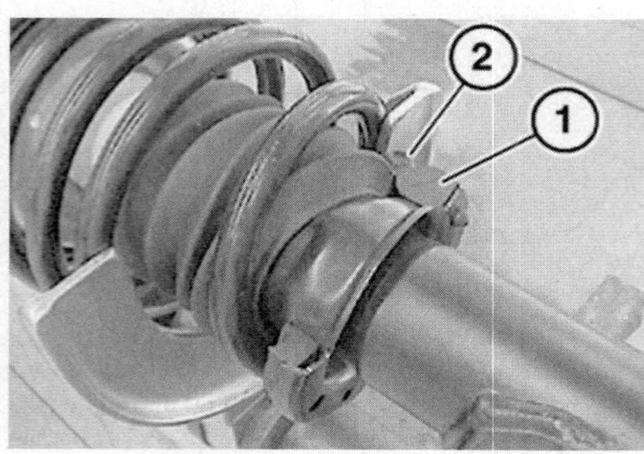

Fig. 439 Lower end of coil spring (2) must rest on stop of spring pad (1)

27. Insert shock absorber in tensioned coil spring.
28. Connect thrust washer to piston rod.
29. Check support bearing for damage, replace if necessary.
30. Connect dust sleeve and support bearing to piston rod.

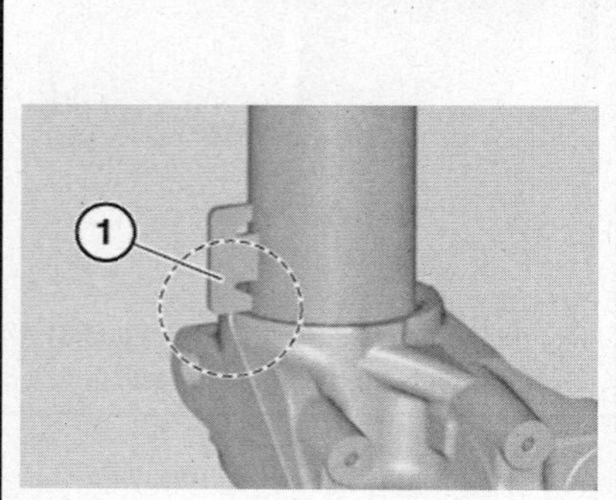

Fig. 440 Make sure ball joint contacts stop correctly

31. Replace nut and tighten down with special tool 31 2 210 (grip piston rod in the process) to 47 ft. lbs. (64 Nm).
32. Fit cover cap.

WARNING

Spring pad must rest positively on spring plate. Upper end of coil spring must rest on stop of spring pad. Lower end of coil spring must rest on stop of spring pad.

33. Relieve tension on coil spring.
34. Check installation position of gaiter, correct fold if necessary.
35. Make sure ball joint contacts stop correctly.
36. Expand ball joint with special tool 31 2 230, align by way of gap to positioning pins on back of spring strut and press together up to stop.
37. Keep press fit of ball joint and spring strut in lower area clean and free from oil and grease. Screw head must point in direction of travel.
38. Replace self-locking nut and tighten to 60 ft. lbs. (81 Nm).
39. Perform chassis alignment check.
40. Carry out steering angle sensor adjustment/adjustment for active steering.

WHEEL HUBS & BEARINGS

REMOVAL & INSTALLATION

See Figure 441.

1. Before servicing the vehicle, refer to the precautions.
2. Remove brake disc.
3. Remove bolts.
4. Press wheel bearing off steering knuckle with a suitable tool.

To install:

5. When reusing the wheel bearing, re-cut all the threads in the wheel bearing.
6. Keep contact surface of steering knuckle and wheel bearing clean and free from oil and grease.
7. Replace microencapsulated screws and tighten to 81 ft. lbs. (110 Nm).

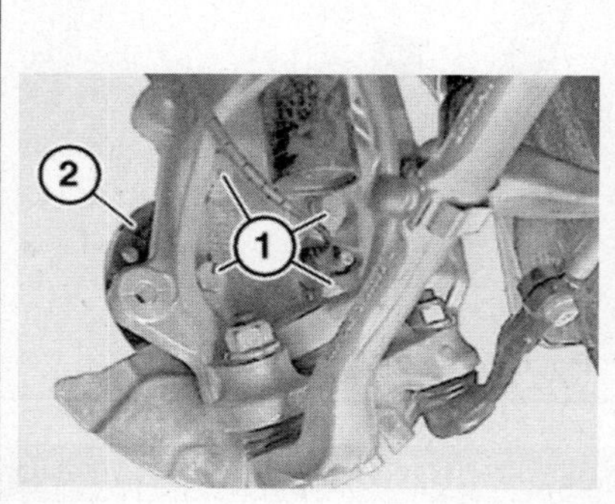

Fig. 441 Remove bolts (1) and press wheel bearing (2) off steering knuckle with a suitable tool

LOWER CONTROL ARMS

REMOVAL & INSTALLATION

See Figures 442 and 443.

1. Before servicing the vehicle, refer to the precautions.
2. Remove rear wheel.
3. On vehicles with Xenon headlights perform the following:
   a. Release nut (jointed rod on control arm).
   b. Remove jointed rod from control arm.
   c. Disconnect plug connection on ride-height sensor.
4. Remove stabilizer link from lower control arm.
5. Mark position of eccentric screw to rear axle carrier.
6. Support wheel carrier with workshop jack.
7. Remove nut and remove eccentric washer.
8. Remove eccentric screw towards front.
9. Remove nut and pull out bolt towards rear.
10. Disconnect nut.
11. Remove screw towards rear and remove lower control arm.

To install:

12. Install lower control arm.
13. Note insertion direction of eccentric screw. Align eccentric screw by means of marking to rear axle carrier. Refit eccentric washer.
14. Replace self-locking nuts. Temporarily tighten swinging arm to rear axle support nuts. Once vehicle is at normal ride height, tighten to 74 ft. lbs. (100 Nm).
15. Replace self-locking nuts. Temporarily tighten bolt connection, swinging arm, integral link, wheel carrier support nuts. Once vehicle is at normal ride height, tighten to 178 ft. lbs. (240 Nm).
16. Check that output shaft is correctly seated in rear differential.
17. Perform chassis alignment check.

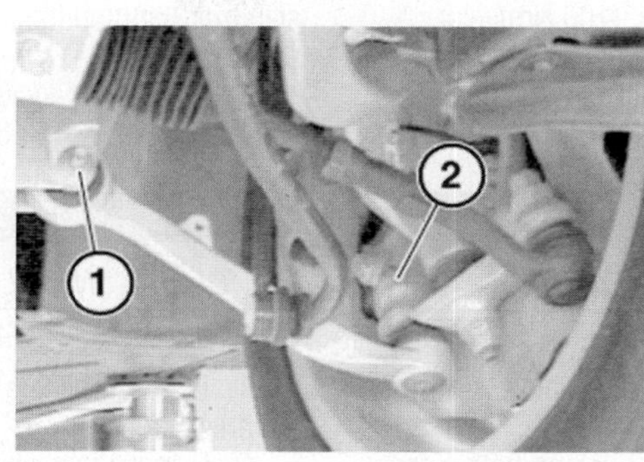

Fig. 443 Unscrew nut (1) and release nut (2); if necessary, grip at Torx socket.

PUSHROD/INTEGRAL LINK

REMOVAL & INSTALLATION

See Figure 444.

1. Before servicing the vehicle, refer to the precautions.

➡If the integral link is detached from the wheel carrier or swing arm, it is necessary after reinstallation to carry out a wheel/chassis alignment check.

2. Remove rear wheel.
3. Remove output shaft from rear differential.
4. Support wheel carrier with workshop jack.
5. Remove nut (1) and remove screw.
6. Remove screw (2), press swinging arm downward and remove integral link (3).

To install:

7. Installation is the reverse of removal.
8. Replace self-locking nut.
9. First install swinging arm and tighten bolt/nut hand-tight.
10. Lower vehicle to normal ride height.

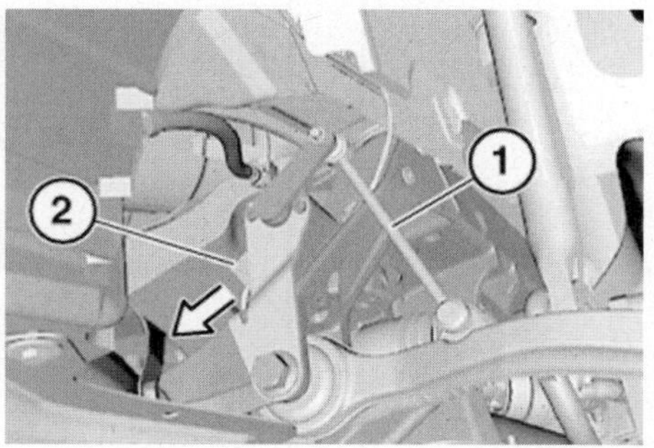

Fig. 442 Remove jointed rod (1) from control arm and disconnect plug connection (2) on ride-height sensor

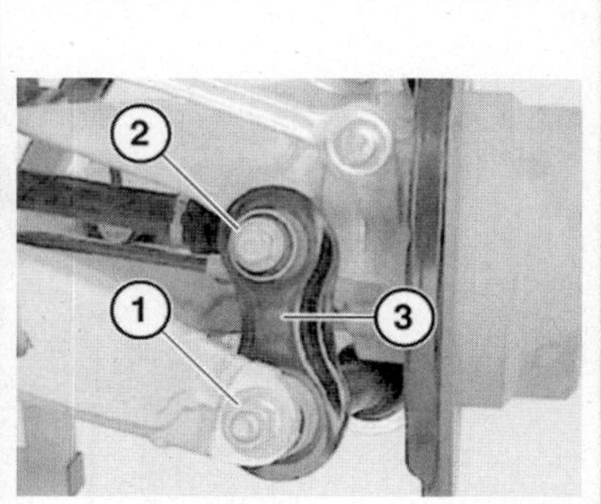

Fig. 444 Remove nut (1) and remove screw. Remove screw (2), press swinging arm downward and remove integral link (3)

11. Tighten screw connection, swinging arm, integral link, wheel carrier nut to 178 ft. lbs. (240 Nm).
12. Tighten integral link on front wheel carrier bolt to 74 ft. lbs. (100 Nm).
13. Check that output shaft is correctly seated in rear differential.
14. Perform chassis alignment check.

STABILIZER BAR

REMOVAL & INSTALLATION

See Figures 445 and 446.

1. Before servicing the vehicle, refer to the precautions.
2. Remove stabilizer link on both sides from stabilizer.
3. If necessary, remove vibration damper from right retaining bracket of stabilizer.
4. Remove nuts at both ends.
5. Remove stabilizer sideways.

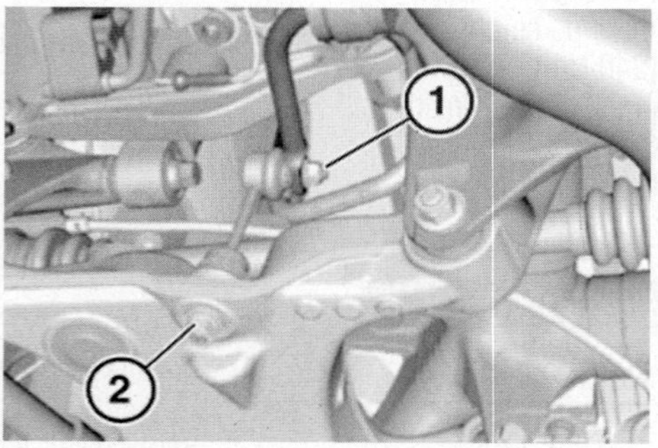

Fig. 445 Release nut (1); if necessary, grip at Torx socket. Release nut (2); if necessary, grip at Torx socket

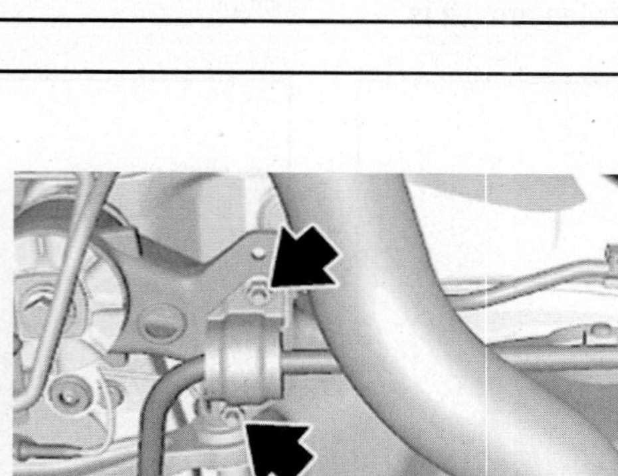

Fig. 446 Remove nuts at both ends (arrows)

To install:

6. Check rubber mount on both sides, replace if necessary.
7. Replace self-locking nuts and tighten stabilizer bar mounting bolts to 16 ft. lbs. (22 Nm).
8. Replace self-locking nuts and tighten stabilizer link nuts to 16 ft. lbs. (22 Nm).

STRUTS

REMOVAL & INSTALLATION

See Figures 447 and 448.

1. Before servicing the vehicle, refer to the precautions.
2. Remove rear wheel.
3. Remove rear wheel arch cover.
4. Remove stabilizer link on both sides from stabilizer.
5. Remove screw as shown.
6. Remove spring strut shock absorber from wheel carrier and tie up.

Fig. 447 Remove screw (arrow)

7. Remove trim panel for luggage compartment partition wall/luggage compartment wheel arch trim.
8. If necessary, remove sound insulation.
9. Unscrew nuts.
10. Press wheel carrier downwards, guide spring strut shock absorber downwards between guide arm and control arm and then remove in upwards direction.

To install:

➡Before tightening screw connection, check that spring strut shock absorber pin is correctly positioned in wheel carrier.

⁂ WARNING

Screw must not be used as an aid to installing the spring strut shock absorber.

11. Replace shock absorber to trailing

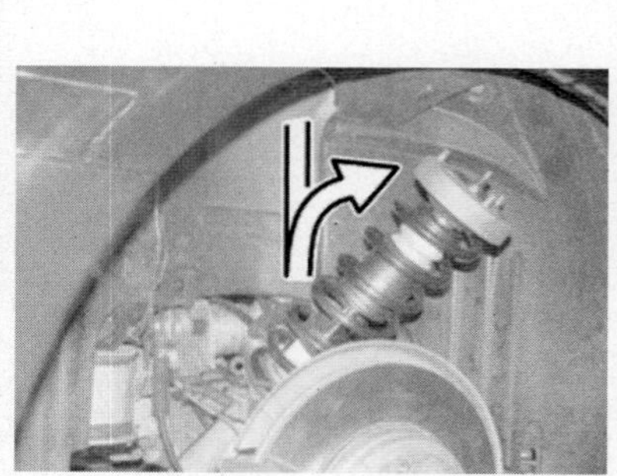

Fig. 448 Press wheel carrier downwards, guide spring strut shock absorber downwards between guide arm and control arm and then remove in upwards direction

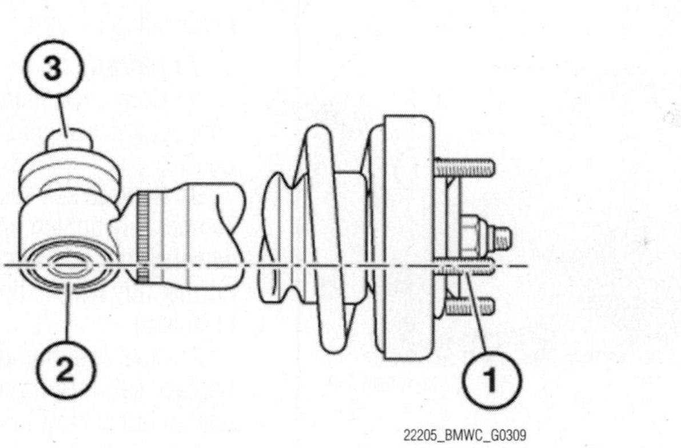

Fig. 449 One threaded pin on the thrust bearing must be on one plane with the bore in the rubber mount and the opposite side of the bush

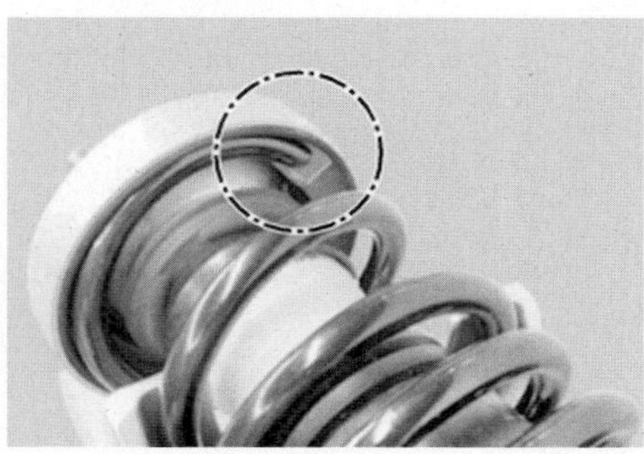

Fig. 450 Align support bearing by way of spring pad to end of coil spring

arm screw and temporarily tighten. After lowering vehicle to normal ride height, tighten to 122 ft. lbs. (165 Nm).

12. Replace support on body/rear axle carrier self-locking nuts and tighten to 21 ft. lbs. (28 Nm).

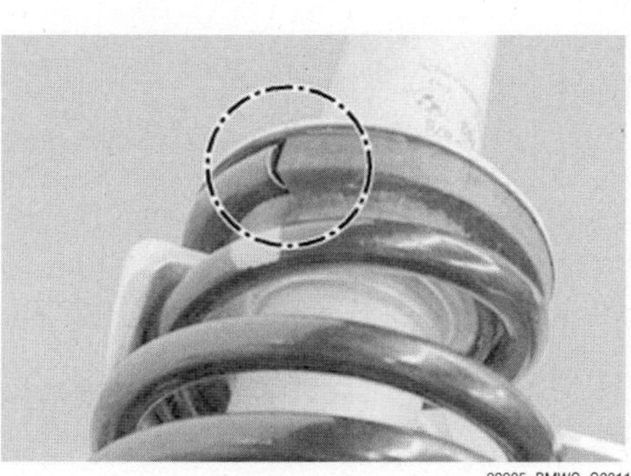

Fig. 451 Lower end of coil spring must rest on stop of spring pad

OVERHAUL

See Figures 450 through 452.

1. Before servicing the vehicle, refer to the precautions.
2. Remove rear wheel.
3. Remove rear spring strut shock absorber.
4. Clamp special tool 31 3 341 in vice.
5. Fit special tools 31 3 357 from above on special tool 31 3 341 until locking pins (1) can be felt and heard to snap into place.
6. Check seating of special tools 31 3 357, correct if necessary.
7. Clean coil spring to remove all coarse dirt and mount on special tools 31 3 357.

**** WARNING**

Coils of coil spring must be located completely in recesses of special tools 31 3 357.

8. Compress coil spring until stress on piston rod is relieved.
9. Remove nut (gripping piston rod in the process).
10. Remove plate and support bearing with spring pad.
11. Remove shock absorber with support pot, auxiliary damper, protective tube and spring pad sideways from tensioned coil spring.
12. If necessary, remove support pot, auxiliary damper (1) with protective tube and spring pad (2) from shock absorber.
13. Relieve tension on coil spring and remove from special tools 31 3 357.

To install:

14. Coils of coil spring must be located completely in recesses of special tools 31 3 357.
15. Tension coil spring.
16. Check auxiliary damper (1) with protective tube and spring pad (2) for damage, replace if necessary.
17. Connect support pot to piston rod.
18. Insert shock absorber in tensioned coil spring.
19. Check support bearing for damage, replace if necessary.
20. Connect support bearing and plate to piston rod.
21. Replace nut and tighten down (gripping piston rod in so doing) to 20 ft. lbs. (27 Nm).

**** WARNING**

One threaded pin on the thrust bearing must be on one plane with the bore in the rubber mount and the opposite side of the bush.

22. Align support bearing by way of spring pad to end of coil spring.
23. Lower end of coil spring must rest on stop of spring pad.
24. Relieve tension on coil spring.
25. Install rear spring strut shock absorber.

UPPER CONTROL ARMS

REMOVAL & INSTALLATION

See Figure 452.

1. Before servicing the vehicle, refer to the precautions.
2. Remove rear wheel.
3. Unscrew nut and remove control arm at top from wheel carrier.

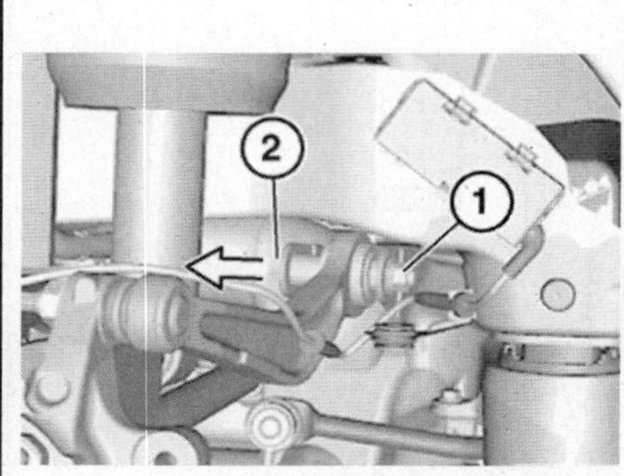

Fig. 452 Unscrew nut and remove control arm at top from wheel carrier. Unscrew nut and pull out bolt and remove control arm

4. Unscrew nut and pull out bolt and remove control arm.

To install:

5. Keep control arm to wheel carrier connection clean and free from oil and grease.
6. Replace self-locking nut. Temporarily tighten upper control arm to wheel carrier nut. After lowering vehicle to normal ride height, tighten to 130 ft. lbs. (175 Nm).
7. Note insertion direction of screw. Replace self-locking nut. Temporarily tighten upper control arm to rear axle carrier nut. When vehicle is at normal ride height, tighten to 74 ft. lbs. (100 Nm).
8. Perform chassis alignment check.

BMW

X3

4

SPECIFICATIONS AND MAINTENANCE CHARTS

ENGINE AND VEHICLE IDENTIFICATION

Engine							Model Year	
Code	Liters (cc)	Cu. In.	Cyl.	Fuel Sys.	Engine Type	Eng. Mfg.	Code ①	Year
N52	3.0 (2996)	183	6	②	DOHC	BMW	B	2011
N55	3.0 (2979)	181	6	③	DOHC	BMW	C	2012

NA: Not Available

DOHC: Double Overhead Camshaft

SOHC: Single Overhead Camshaft

① 10th digit of the Vehicle Identification Number (VIN)

② Siemens MSV80 3-Series

③ Bosch

71112_X1X3_C0001

GENERAL ENGINE SPECIFICATIONS

Year	Body Type	Model	Engine Displacement Liters (cc)	Engine ID	Fuel System Type	Net Horsepower @ rpm	Net Torque @ rpm (ft. lbs.)	Bore x Stroke (in.)	Compression Ratio	Oil Pressure @ rpm
2011	F25	X3 28i	3.0 (2996)	N52B30	①	230@6500	200@2750	3.35x3.46	10.7:1	7.3@idle
	F25	X3 35i	3.0 (2979)	N55B30	②	300@5800	300@1200	3.28x3.49	10.2:1	21.76@idle
2012	F25	X3 28i	3.0 (2996)	N52B30	①	230@6500	200@2750	3.35x3.46	10.7:1	7.3@idle
	F25	X3 35i	3.0 (2979)	N55B30	②	300@5800	300@1200	3.28x3.49	10.2:1	21.76@idle

① Siemens

② Bosch

71112_X1X3_C0002

ENGINE TUNE-UP SPECIFICATIONS

Year	Engine Displacement Liters	Engine ID	Spark Plug Gap (in.)	Ignition Timing (deg.)		Fuel Pump (psi)	Idle Speed (rpm)		Valve Clearance	
				MT	AT		MT	AT	In.	Ex.
2011	3.0	N52B30	①	②	②	70-76	②	②	HYD	HYD
	3.0	N55B30	①	②	②	70-76	②	②	HYD	HYD
2012	3.0	N52B30	①	②	②	70-76	②	②	HYD	HYD
	3.0	N55B30	①	②	②	70-76	②	②	HYD	HYD

NOTE: The Vehicle Emission Control Information label reflects specification changes during production and must be used if they differ from this chart.

HYD: Hydraulic

① Three mass and four-mass electrodes cannot be adjusted

Dual mass electrodes: 0.035-0.039 inches

All others: 0.028-0.031 inches

② Controlled by the Engine Control Module (ECM) and cannot be adjusted

71112_X1X3_C0003

CAPACITIES

Year	Body Type	Model	Engine Displacement Liters	Engine ID	Engine Oil with Filter (qts.)	Transmission (pts.) 6-Spd	Transmission (pts.) Auto.	Drive Axle Front (pts.)	Drive Axle Rear (pts.)	Fuel Tank (gal.)	Cooling System (qts.)
2011	F25	X3 28i	3.0	N52B30	6.9	NA	17.96	1.3	2.5	17.7	11.2
	F25	X3 35i	3.0	N55B30	6.9	NA	17.96	1.3	2.5	17.7	11.2
2012	F25	X3 28i	3.0	N52B30	6.9	NA	17.96	1.3	2.5	17.7	11.2
	F25	X3 35i	3.0	N55B30	6.9	NA	17.96	1.3	2.5	17.7	11.2

NOTE: All capacities are approximate. Add fluid gradually and ensure a proper fluid level is obtained.

NOTE: Capacities given are service, not overhaul capacities

71112_X1X3_C0004

FLUID SPECIFICATIONS

Year	Model	Engine Displ. Liters	Engine Oil	Auto. Trans.	Drive Axle Front	Drive Axle Rear	Power Steering Fluid	Brake Master Cylinder	Cooling System
2011	X3 28i	3.0	5W-30	M-1375-4	SAF-XO	NA	Dexron® III	DOT 4	BMW Long Life Coolant
	X3 35i	3.0	5W-30	M-1375-4	SAF-XO	NA	Dexron® III	DOT 4	BMW Long Life Coolant
2012	X3 28i	3.0	5W-30	M-1375-4	SAF-XO	NA	Dexron® III	DOT 4	BMW Long Life Coolant
	X3 35i	3.0	5W-30	M-1375-4	SAF-XO	NA	Dexron® III	DOT 4	BMW Long Life Coolant

NA: Not Available

DOT: Department Of Transpotation

71112_X1X3_C0005

VALVE SPECIFICATIONS

Year	Engine Displacement Liters	Engine ID/VIN	Seat Angle (deg.)	Face Angle (deg.)	Spring Test Pressure (lbs. @ in.)	Spring Installed Height (in.)	Stem-to-Guide Clearance (in.) Intake	Stem-to-Guide Clearance (in.) Exhaust	Stem Diameter (in.) Intake	Stem Diameter (in.) Exhaust
2011	3.0	N52B30	①	45	NA	NA	② 0.0197	② 0.0197	0.0234-0.0235	0.0234-0.0235
	3.0	N55B30	①	45	NA	NA	② 0.0197	② 0.0197	0.0234-0.0235	0.0234-0.0235
2012	3.0	N52B30	①	45	NA	NA	② 0.0197	② 0.0197	0.0234-0.0235	0.0234-0.0235
	3.0	N55B30	①	45	NA	NA	② 0.0197	② 0.0197	0.0234-0.0235	0.0234-0.0235

NA: Not Available

① Valve seat angle: 45 degrees
Correction angle outside: 15 degrees
Correction angle inside: 60 degrees

② To measure: Insert a new valve into guide with end of valve flush with end of guide.
Use a dial indicator to measure axial valve head movement.

71112_X1X3_C0006

CAMSHAFT SPECIFICATIONS

All measurements in inches unless noted

Year	Engine Displacement Liters	Engine Code/ID	Journal Dia.	Brg. Oil Clearance	Shaft End-play	Circle Runout	Lobe Height Intake	Lobe Height Exhaust
2011	3.0	N52B30	NA	NA	0.0007-0.0063	0.0021-0.0038	NA	NA
	3.0	N55B30	NA	NA	0.0007-0.0063	0.0021-0.0038	NA	NA
2012	3.0	N52B30	NA	NA	0.0007-0.0063	0.0021-0.0038	NA	NA
	3.0	N55B30	NA	NA	0.0007-0.0063	0.0021-0.0038	NA	NA

NA: Not Available

71112_X1X3_C0007

CRANKSHAFT AND CONNECTING ROD SPECIFICATIONS

All measurements are given in inches.

Year	Engine Displacement Liters	Engine ID/VIN	Crankshaft Main Brg. Journal Dia.	Crankshaft Main Brg. Oil Clearance	Crankshaft Shaft End-play	Crankshaft Thrust on No.	Connecting Rod Journal Diameter	Connecting Rod Oil Clearance	Connecting Rod Side Clearance
2011	3.0	N52B30	①	0.0007-0.0023	0.0031-0.0064	NA	1.7706-1.7712	0.0007-0.0022	NA
	3.0	N55B30	②	0.0007-0.0018	0.0058	NA	2.0904-2.0910	NA	NA
2012	3.0	N52B30	①	0.0007-0.0023	0.0031-0.0064	NA	1.7706-1.7712	0.0007-0.0022	NA
	3.0	N55B30	②	0.0007-0.0018	0.0058	NA	2.0904-2.0910	NA	NA

① Standard yellow 2.3615-2.3618 inches
Standard green: 2.3613-2.3615 inches
Standard white: 2.3611-2.3613 inches

② Designation S/1: 2.5347-2.5346 inches
Designation S/2: 2.5344-2.5346 inches
Designation S/3: 2.5342-2.5344 inches

71112_X1X3_C0008

PISTON AND RING SPECIFICATIONS

All measurements are given in inches

Year	Engine Disp. Liters	Engine ID	Piston Clearance	Ring Gap Top Compression	Ring Gap Bottom Compression	Ring Gap Oil Control	Ring Side Clearance Top Compression	Ring Side Clearance Bottom Compression	Ring Side Clearance Oil Control
2011	3.0	N52B30	0.0004-0.0016	0.0078-0.0157	0.0078-0.0157	0.0078-0.0177	0.0008-0.0024	0.0008-0.0024	0.0005-0.0023
	3.0	N55B30	①	0.0058 0.0117	0.0117-0.0195	0.0078-0.0351	0.00078-0.00234	0.00058-0.00234	NA
2012	3.0	N52B30	0.0004-0.0016	0.0078-0.0157	0.0078-0.0157	0.0078-0.0177	0.0008-0.0024	0.0008-0.0024	0.0005-0.0023
	3.0	N55B30	①	0.0058 0.0117	0.0117-0.0195	0.0078-0.0351	0.00078-0.00234	0.00058-0.00234	NA

NA: Not Available

① New Piston: 0.0004-0.0012
Used Piston: 0.00078.0.0031

71112_X1X3_C0009

TORQUE SPECIFICATIONS

All readings in ft. lbs.

Year	Engine Disp. Liters	Engine ID/VIN	Cylinder Head Bolts	Main Bearing Bolts	Rod Bearing Bolts	Crankshaft Damper Bolts	Flywheel Bolts	Manifold Intake	Manifold Exhaust	Spark Plugs	Oil Pan Drain Plug
2011	3.0	N52B30	①	②	③	④	⑤	⑥	⑦	⑧	18
	3.0	N55B30	⑨	⑩	⑪	④	⑫	15	13	⑧	18
2012	3.0	N52B30	①	②	③	④	⑤	⑥	⑦	⑧	18
	3.0	N55B30	⑨	⑩	⑪	④	⑫	15	13	⑧	18

① Cast iron block. Replace, wash and oil bolts
Step 1: 22 ft. lbs.
Step 2: 90 degrees
Step 3: 90 degrees

② Cast iron block. Replace, wash and oil bolts
Step 1: 14.8 ft. lbs.
Step 2: 50 degrees

③ Replace, wash and oil connecting rod bolts
Step 1: 14.8 ft. lbs.
Step 2: 70 degrees

④ Always use new bolts.
Step 1: 74 ft. lbs.
Step 2: Tighten bolts 270 degrees

⑤ New micro-encapsulated screws:
Automatic transmission: 88 ft. lbs.
Manual transmission: 77.4 ft. lbs.

⑥ All M6 fasteners: 88 inch lbs.
All M7 fasteners: 11 ft. lbs.
All M8 fasteners: 16 ft. lbs.

⑦ Coat with Molykkote HSC compound or equivalent
All M6 fasteners: 88 inch lbs.
All M7 fasteners: 14.8 ft. lbs.

⑧ M12x1.25:14.8-19.1 ft. lbs.
M14x1.25: 21.4-24.3 ft. lbs.

⑨ Always use new bolts.
Step 1: Tighten bolts 1-10 (M11) to 22 ft. lbs.
Step 2: Tighten bolts 11-14 (M9) to 22 ft. lbs.
Step 3: Tighten bolts 1-14 90 degrees
Step 4: Tighten bolts 1-10 (M11) 90 degrees
Step 5: Tighten bolts 1-14 180 degrees

⑩ Always use new bolts.
Step 1: 14.8 ft. lbs.
Step 2: 70 degrees

⑪ Replace, wash and oil screws
Step 1: 14.75 ft. lbs.
Step 2: Tighten bolts 140 degrees

⑫ Always use new screws.
Step 1: 44 ft. lbs.
Step 2: Tighten screws 45 degrees

71112_X1X3_C0010

WHEEL ALIGNMENT

Year	Model		Caster Range (+/-Deg.)	Caster Preferred Setting (Deg.)	Camber Range (+/-Deg.)	Camber Preferred Setting (Deg.)	Toe-in (Deg.)	Steering Axis Inclination (Deg.)
2011	X3	F	0.15	0	NS	+2	0	—
		R	—	—	NS	-2	0	—
2012	X3	F	0.15	0	NS	+2	0	—
		R	—	—	NS	-2	0	—

NOTE: Load vehicle with 150 lbs. on the front seats, 150 lbs on the rear seats and 46 lbs in the trunk with a full fuel tank.

71112_X1X3_C0011

TIRE, WHEEL AND BALL JOINT SPECIFICATIONS

Year	Model	OEM Tires Standard	OEM Tires Optional	Tire Pressures (psi) Front	Tire Pressures (psi) Rear	Ball Joint Inspection	Lugnut Torque (ft. lbs.)
2011	X3	235/55HR18	①	②	②	NS	80
2012	X3	235/55HR18	①	②	②	NS	80

① P245/40R18, P245/35R19, P275/35R18, P275/30R19

② See door sticker.

71112_X1X3_C0012

BRAKE SPECIFICATIONS

All measurements in inches unless noted

Year	Body Type	Model		Brake Disc Original Thickness	Brake Disc Minimum Thickness	Brake Disc Maximum Runout	Minimum Lining Thickness Front	Minimum Lining Thickness Rear	Brake Caliper Bracket Bolts (ft. lbs.)	Brake Caliper Mounting Bolts (ft. lbs.)
2011	F25	X3	F	①	②	NA	0.118	—	81	22
			R	③	②	NA	—	①	48	22
2012	F25	X3	F	①	②	NA	0.118	—	81	22
			R	③	②	NA	—	①	48	22

NA: Not Available

F: Front

R: Rear

① Depending on brake package: .945 in., 1.18 in. or 1.41in.

② Minimum thickness is stamped in the brake disk shell

Maximum machining limit per side: 0.315 inches

③ Depending on brake package: .787 in. or .945 in.

71112_X1X3_C0013

SCHEDULED MAINTENANCE INTERVALS

BMW—X3

TO BE SERVICED	TYPE OF SERVICE	SERVICE INTERVALS			
		INITIAL 1200 MILES	OIL SERVICE	INSPECTION I	INSPECTION II
Oil level	S/I	✓			
Engine oil	R				
Engine oil & filter	R		✓	✓	✓
Engine air cleaner element	R				✓
Spark plugs	R				✓
Fuel filter (California)	R				✓
Fuel, vapor lines & fuel cap	S/I	✓		✓	✓
Cooling system	S/I	✓		✓	✓
Exhaust pipe & muffler	S/I	✓		✓	✓
Catalytic converter & shielding	S/I	✓		✓	✓
Throttle linkage	S/I			✓	✓
Engine (check for leakage)	S/I	✓			
Engine drive belts	S/I				✓
Maintenance Indicators	RE		✓	✓	✓
Engine coolant	R	Every 2 years			
Oxygen sensor	R	Every 100,000 miles			
Intake air dust separators	S/I				✓
Brake & clutch fluids	S/I			✓	✓
Brake & clutch fluids	R	Every 2 years			
Brake pads & discs	S/I			✓	✓
Parking brake system	S/I			✓	✓
Power steering system	S/I			✓	✓
Rear axle fluid	S/I			✓	✓
Steering play, suspension track rods, front axle joints, steering linkage & joint disc	S/I			✓	✓
Transmission fluid/oil	S/I			✓	⑨
Wheel centering hubs	S/I			✓	✓
Rear axle fluid ⑩	R		✓		✓
OBD system for codes	S/I	✓		✓	✓

R: Replace S/I: Service or Inspect RE: Reset

Note: BMW does not rely solely on vehicle mileage to determine service intervals. An on-oboard diagnostic center, monitors engine operating conditions, along with mileage, to determine the most effective maintenance intervals. The information is then conveyed to the driver through the service indicator lights, located in the center of the instrument panel.

71112_X1X3_C0014

PRECAUTIONS

Before servicing any vehicle, please be sure to read all of the following precautions, which deal with personal safety, prevention of component damage, and important points to take into consideration when servicing a motor vehicle:

- Never open, service or drain the radiator or cooling system when the engine is hot; serious burns can occur from the steam and hot coolant.
- Observe all applicable safety precautions when working around fuel. Whenever servicing the fuel system, always work in a well-ventilated area. Do not allow fuel spray or vapors to come in contact with a spark, open flame, or excessive heat (a hot drop light, for example). Keep a dry chemical fire extinguisher near the work area. Always keep fuel in a container specifically designed for fuel storage; also, always properly seal fuel containers to avoid the possibility of fire or explosion. Refer to the additional fuel system precautions later in this section.
- Fuel injection systems often remain pressurized, even after the engine has been turned **OFF**. The fuel system pressure must be relieved before disconnecting any fuel lines. Failure to do so may result in fire and/or personal injury.
- Brake fluid often contains polyglycol ethers and polyglycols. Avoid contact with the eyes and wash your hands thoroughly after handling brake fluid. If you do get brake fluid in your eyes, flush your eyes with clean, running water for 15 minutes. If eye irritation persists, or if you have taken brake fluid internally, IMMEDIATELY seek medical assistance.
- The EPA warns that prolonged contact with used engine oil may cause a number of skin disorders, including cancer. You should make every effort to minimize your exposure to used engine oil. Protective gloves should be worn when changing oil. Wash your hands and any other exposed skin areas as soon as possible after exposure to used engine oil. Soap and water, or waterless hand cleaner should be used.
- All new vehicles are now equipped with an air bag system, often referred to as a Supplemental Restraint System (SRS) or Supplemental Inflatable Restraint (SIR) system. The system must be disabled before performing service on or around system components, steering column, instrument panel components, wiring and sensors. Failure to follow safety and disabling procedures could result in accidental air bag deployment, possible personal injury and unnecessary system repairs.
- Always wear safety goggles when working with, or around, the air bag system. When carrying a non-deployed air bag, be sure the bag and trim cover are pointed away from your body. When placing a non-deployed air bag on a work surface, always face the bag and trim cover upward, away from the surface. This will reduce the motion of the module if it is accidentally deployed. Refer to the additional air bag system precautions later in this section.
- Clean, high quality brake fluid from a sealed container is essential to the safe and proper operation of the brake system. You should always buy the correct type of brake fluid for your vehicle. If the brake fluid becomes contaminated, completely flush the system with new fluid. Never reuse any brake fluid. Any brake fluid that is removed from the system should be discarded. Also, do not allow any brake fluid to come in contact with a painted surface; it will damage the paint.
- Never operate the engine without the proper amount and type of engine oil; doing so WILL result in severe engine damage.
- Timing belt maintenance is extremely important. Many models utilize an interference-type, non-freewheeling engine. If the timing belt breaks, the valves in the cylinder head may strike the pistons, causing potentially serious (also time-consuming and expensive) engine damage. Refer to the maintenance interval charts for the recommended replacement interval for the timing belt, and to the timing belt section for belt replacement and inspection.
- Disconnecting the negative battery cable on some vehicles may interfere with the functions of the on-board computer system(s) and may require the computer to undergo a relearning process once the negative battery cable is reconnected.
- When servicing drum brakes, only disassemble and assemble one side at a time, leaving the remaining side intact for reference.
- Only an MVAC-trained, EPA-certified automotive technician should service the air conditioning system or its components.

BRAKES

ANTI-LOCK BRAKE SYSTEM (ABS)

GENERAL INFORMATION

PRECAUTIONS

- Certain components within the ABS system are not intended to be serviced or repaired individually.
- Do not use rubber hoses or other parts not specifically specified for and ABS system. When using repair kits, replace all parts included in the kit. Partial or incorrect repair may lead to functional problems and require the replacement of components.
- Lubricate rubber parts with clean, fresh brake fluid to ease assembly. Do not use shop air to clean parts; damage to rubber components may result.
- Use only DOT 3 brake fluid from an unopened container.
- If any hydraulic component or line is removed or replaced, it may be necessary to bleed the entire system.
- A clean repair area is essential. Always clean the reservoir and cap thoroughly before removing the cap. The slightest amount of dirt in the fluid may plug an orifice and impair the system function. Perform repairs after components have been thoroughly cleaned; use only denatured alcohol to clean components. Do not allow ABS components to come into contact with any substance containing mineral oil; this includes used shop rags.
- The Anti-Lock control unit is a microprocessor similar to other computer units in the vehicle. Ensure that the ignition switch is **OFF** before removing or installing controller harnesses. Avoid static electricity discharge at or near the controller.
- If any arc welding is to be done on the vehicle, the control unit should be unplugged before welding operations begin.

SPEED SENSORS

REMOVAL & INSTALLATION

Front

See Figure 1.

1. Disconnect the negative battery cable.
2. Raise and support the vehicle safely.
3. Remove the tire and wheel assembly.
4. Remove the wheel speed sensor mounting bolt.

➡Remove the rotor to gain access to the wheel sensor mounting bolt.

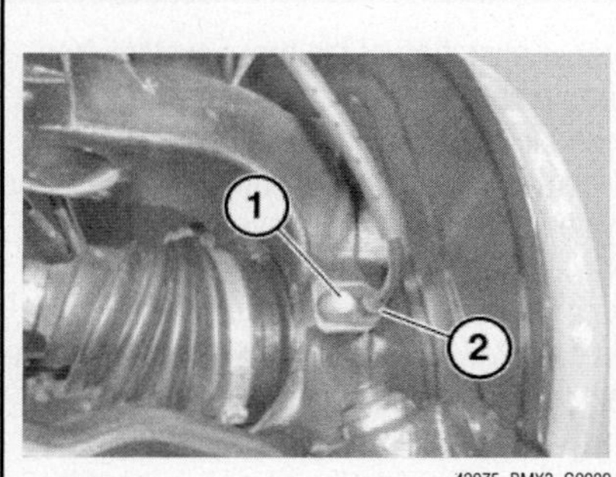

Fig. 1 Front speed sensor (2) and mounting bolt (1) location

5. Pull out the speed sensor, being careful to turn it as little as possible. Do not pull on the sensor harness.
6. Disconnect the wheel speed sensor electrical connector.
7. Remove the harness from its mount.

To install:

8. Before installing the sensor, be certain there are no foreign materials, like iron fragments adhering to:
- The pick-up part of the sensor
- The inside of the sensor mounting hole
- The rotor mounting surface.

9. Apply a thin coat of suitable grease (Staburags NBU 12/K) to the wheel sensor and mounting hole.
10. Tighten the sensor mounting bolt to 82 inch lbs. (8 Nm).
11. Continue the installation in the reverse order of the removal procedure.

Rear

See Figure 2.

1. Disconnect the negative battery cable.
2. Raise and support the vehicle safely.
3. Remove the tire and wheel assembly.
4. Remove the wheel speed sensor mounting bolt.
5. Pull out the sensor, being careful to turn it as little as possible. Do not pull on the sensor harness.
6. Disconnect the wheel speed sensor electrical connector.
7. Remove the harness from its mount.

To install:

8. Inspect the sensor O-ring, replace as required.
9. Before installing the sensor, be certain there are no foreign materials, like iron fragments adhering to:

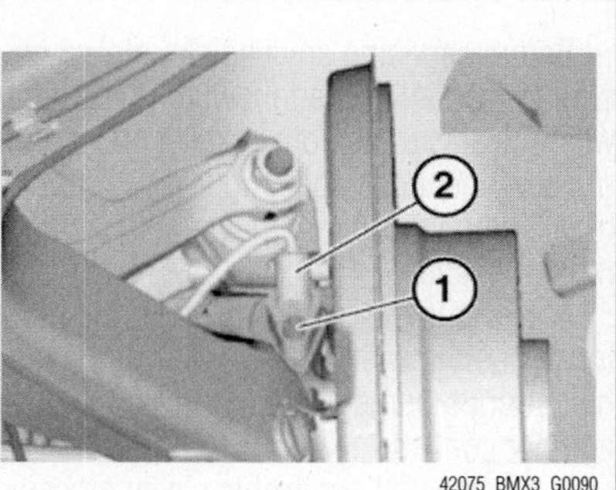

Fig. 2 Rear speed sensor (2) and mounting bolt (1) location

- The pick-up part of the sensor
- The inside of the sensor mounting hole
- The rotor mounting surface.

10. Apply a thin coat of suitable grease (Staburags NBU 12/K) to the wheel sensor and mounting hole.
11. Tighten the sensor mounting bolt to 72 inch lbs. (8 Nm).
12. Continue the installation in the reverse order of the removal procedure.

BRAKES — BLEEDING THE BRAKE SYSTEM

BLEEDING PROCEDURE

BLEEDING PROCEDURE

Front Axle Circuit

1. Disconnect retaining tabs and remove the master cylinder cover.
2. Connect a brake bleeding tool with a maximum 29 PSI (2 Bar) filling pressure.
3. Connect bleeder hose with collecting tray to bleeder valve on front right brake caliper.
4. Bleed right front brake caliper. After completing routine, press brake pedal 5 times to floor, clear and bubble-free brake fluid must flow out.
5. Close bleed valve.
6. Repeat procedure at front left.
7. Disconnect the brake bleeding tool and remove from the master cylinder.
8. Check and adjust the brake fluid level.
9. Inspect the rubber seal in the brake fluid master cylinder cap. Replace as necessary.

Rear Axle Circuit

1. Disconnect retaining tabs and remove the master cylinder cover.
2. Connect a brake bleeding tool with a maximum 29 PSI (2 Bar) filling pressure.
3. Connect bleeder hose with collecting tray to bleeder valve on rear right brake caliper.
4. Bleed right brake caliper. After completing routine, press brake pedal 5 times to floor; clear and bubble-free brake fluid must flow out.
5. Close bleed valve.
6. Repeat procedure at rear left.
7. Disconnect the brake bleeding tool and remove from the master cylinder.
8. Check and adjust the brake fluid level.
9. Inspect the rubber seal in the brake fluid master cylinder cap. Replace as necessary.

MASTER CYLINDER BLEEDING

See Figure 3.

1. Before servicing the vehicle, refer to the precautions section.
2. Remove transmission underbody protection if necessary.
3. Remove the microfilter housing if necessary.
4. Unfasten the nuts and remove the clutch slave cylinder (leave the pressure line connected).
5. Fit BMW special tool 21 5 030 on the clutch slave cylinder.

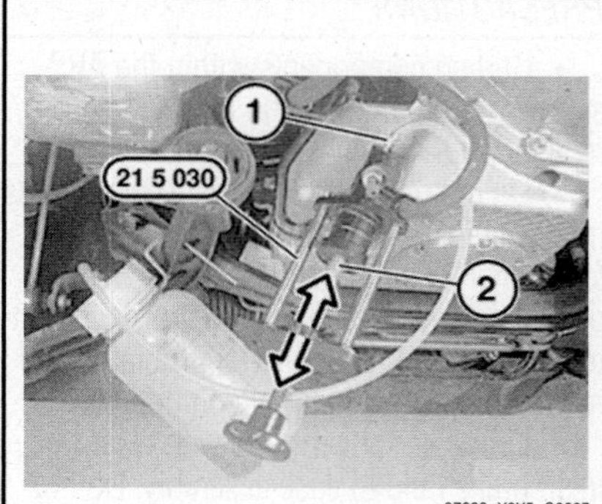

Fig. 3 Position the slave cylinder as shown

6. Press the piston rod completely into the clutch slave cylinder.

7. Connect a pressure bleeder unit to the brake fluid expansion tank. Charging pressure should not exceed 29 psi (2 bar).

8. Connect the bleeder hose to the bleed valve.

9. Hold the clutch slave cylinder in position as illustrated.

10. Open the bleeder valve.

11. If bubble free brake fluid emerges, retract the piston rod of the clutch slave cylinder a little and press in again.

12. If no air bubbles escape, close the bleeder valve, otherwise repeat the procedure.

CAUTION

Do not under any circumstances remove BMW special tool 21 5 030 from the clutch slave cylinder when the brake system is pressurized. The piston with the push rod can jump out of the clutch slave cylinder.

13. Switch off the pressure bleeder unit and remove from brake fluid expansion tank.

14. Slowly retract the piston rod of the clutch slave cylinder. Remove the special tool

15. Install the slave cylinder to the transmission.

16. Correct the brake fluid level in the expansion tank.

BLEEDING THE ABS SYSTEM

See Figure 4.

CAUTION

Brake fluid contains polyglycol ethers and polyglycols. Avoid contact with the eyes and wash your hands thoroughly after handling brake fluid. If you do get brake fluid in your eyes, flush your eyes with clean, running water for 15 minutes. If eye irritation persists, or if you have taken brake fluid internally, IMMEDIATELY seek medical assistance.

WARNING

Clean, high quality brake fluid is essential to the safe and proper operation of the brake system. You should always buy the highest quality brake fluid that is available. If the brake fluid becomes contaminated, drain and flush the system, then refill the master cylinder with new fluid. Never reuse any brake fluid. Any brake fluid that is removed from the system should be discarded. Also, do not allow any brake fluid to come in contact with a painted surface; it will damage the paint.

1. Remove the reservoir cap and fill the brake reservoir with brake fluid.

2. Connect a clear plastic tube to the wheel cylinder bleeder plug and insert the other end of the tube into a clear plastic bottle.

3. Activate pre-charging pump with Diagnosis and Information System (DIS).

4. Select and operate according to the instructions on the DIS screen:
   - Select: Service Functions
   - Select: Bleeding ABS/DSC3 Hydraulics

CAUTION

You must obey the maximum operating time of the ABS motor to prevent the motor pump from burning.

5. Connect bleeder unit to expansion tank and switch on.

6. Pump the brake pedal several times, and then loosen the bleeder screw until fluid starts to run out without bubbles. Then close the bleeder screw.

7. Bleed fluid from each wheel until there are no more bubbles exiting with the brake fluid. Run bleeding routine with DIS and bleeder valve open.

8. Press brake pedal 5 times to the floor clear and bubble-free brake fluid must flow out.

9. Close bleeder valve.

10. Repeat bleeding procedure on each wheel.

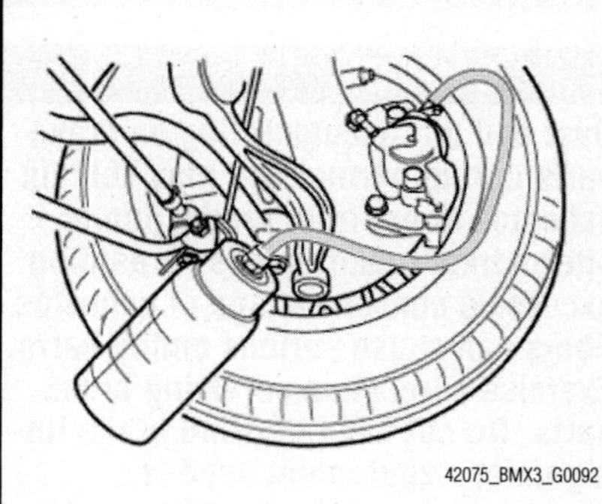

Fig. 4 Using a clear plastic tube and bottle at bleeder screw to observe fluid bubbles

11. After completion of the repair or correction of the problem, erase any stored fault codes.

12. Disconnect the DIS system.

13. Fill the brake reservoir with the proper amount of brake fluid.

14. Check for fluid leaks at all connections.

FLUID FILL PROCEDURE

➡A second person is needed to help carry out this work.

1. Disconnect the retaining tabs and remove the master cylinder cover.

2. Connect a brake bleeding tool with a maximum 29 PSI (2 Bar) filling pressure.

3. Flush the brake system completely.

4. Connect a bleeder hose with a collecting tray to the bleeder valve on the rear right brake caliper.

5. Open the bleeder valve and purge until clear, bubble-free brake fluid emerges.

6. Close the bleed valve.

7. Follow the same procedure on rear left, front right and front left wheel brake.

8. Disconnect the brake bleeding tool and remove from the master cylinder.

9. Check and adjust the brake fluid level.

10. Inspect the rubber seal in the brake fluid master cylinder cap. Replace as necessary.

BRAKES

FRONT DISC BRAKES

** CAUTION

Dust and dirt accumulating on brake parts during normal use may contain asbestos fibers from production or aftermarket brake linings. Breathing excessive concentrations of asbestos fibers can cause serious bodily harm. Exercise care when servicing brake parts. Do not sand or grind brake lining unless equipment used is designed to contain the dust residue. Do not clean brake parts with compressed air or by dry brushing. Cleaning should be done by dampening the brake components with a fine mist of water, then wiping the brake components clean with a dampened cloth. Dispose of cloth and all residue containing asbestos fibers in an impermeable container with the appropriate label. Follow practices prescribed by the Occupational Safety and Health Administration (OSHA) and the Environmental Protection Agency (EPA) for the handling, processing, and disposing of dust or debris that may contain asbestos fibers.

BRAKE CALIPER

REMOVAL & INSTALLATION

See Figure 5.

1. Before servicing the vehicle, refer to the precautions in the beginning of this section.
2. Remove or disconnect the following:
   - Negative battery cable
   - Wheel assembly
3. Apply the brake pedal slightly with a brake clamp.
   - Brake pipe from the connection with the brake hose
   - Connector for the wear indicator on the left side
   - Caliper guide bolts
   - Brake caliper

To install:

4. Install or connect the following:
   - Caliper and torque the guide bolts to 22 ft. lbs. (30 Nm)
   - Brake hose to the brake pipe to 13 ft. lbs. (18 Nm)
5. Set the wheel in a straight-ahead position.
6. Be sure brake hose is positively attached to the mounting fixture.
   - Wear indicator on the left side
   - Brake clamp
   - Front wheels
7. Fully depress brake pedal several times to set proper contact of pads with rotor.
8. Hold ignition key for at least 30 seconds in position "1" without starting engine. This clear any fault codes stored in system and prevent the wear indicator light from coming on.
9. Bleed brake system. If necessary.
10. Bleed the brakes.

DISC BRAKE PADS

REMOVAL & INSTALLATION

1. Before servicing the vehicle, refer to the precautions in the beginning of this section.
2. Remove the front wheels.
3. Remove the disk pad retaining spring from the caliper.
4. Remove the calipers from the disk.

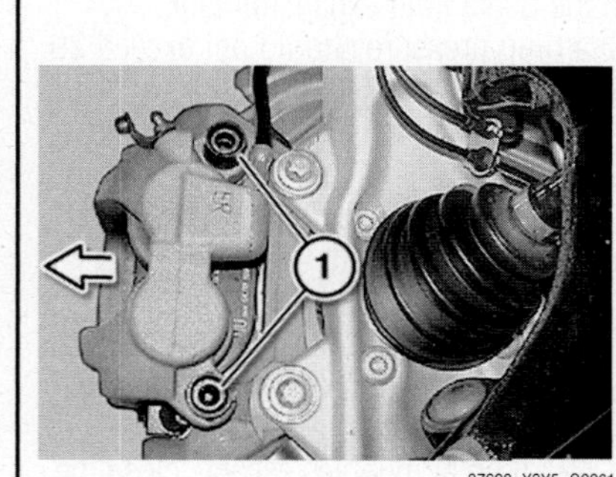

Fig. 5 Remove the caliper guide bolts

5. Use a special tool, 34–1–050, to force piston back into caliper.
6. Remove the outer brake pad (the inner pad is held in place with a spring in the piston).

To install:

7. Be sure the pads marked "L" and "R" are inserted properly on left and right sides, respectively.
8. Apply anti-squeak compound to all mounting surfaces.
9. Install the calipers.
10. Reposition the retaining spring.
11. Install the front wheels.
12. Fully depress brake pedal several times to set proper contact of pads with rotor.
13. Hold ignition key for at least 30 seconds in position "1" without starting engine. This clear any fault codes stored in system and prevent the wear indicator light from coming on.
14. Bleed brake system, if necessary.

BRAKES

REAR DISC BRAKES

** CAUTION

Dust and dirt accumulating on brake parts during normal use may contain asbestos fibers from production or aftermarket brake linings. Breathing excessive concentrations of asbestos fibers can cause serious bodily harm. Exercise care when servicing brake parts. Do not sand or grind brake lining unless equipment used is designed to contain the dust residue. Do not clean brake parts with compressed air or by dry brushing. Cleaning should be done by dampening the brake components with a fine mist of water, then wiping the brake components clean with a dampened cloth. Dispose of cloth and all residue containing asbestos fibers in an impermeable container with the appropriate label. Follow practices prescribed by the Occupational Safety and Health Administration (OSHA) and the Environmental Protection Agency (EPA) for the handling, processing, and disposing of dust or debris that may contain asbestos fibers.

BRAKE CALIPER

REMOVAL & INSTALLATION

See Figure 6.

1. Before servicing the vehicle, refer to the precautions in the beginning of this section.
2. Remove or disconnect the following:
   - Negative battery cable
   - Wheel assembly
3. Apply the brake pedal slightly with a brake clamp.
   - Slacken union nut

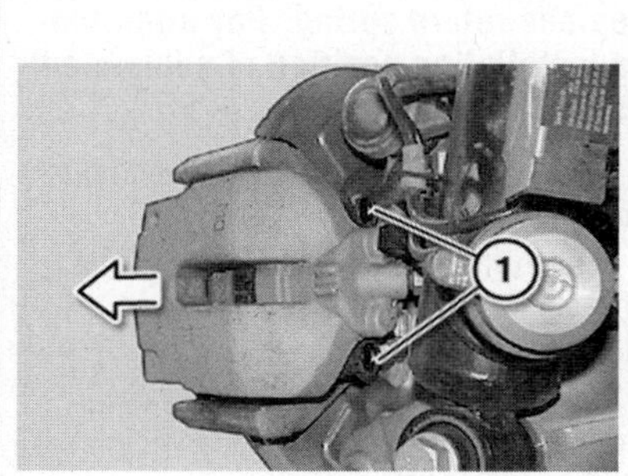

Fig. 6 Remove the caliper guide bolts

- Brake hose from the caliper fitting
- Connector for the wear indicator on the right side
- Caliper guide bolts and remove the brake caliper

To install:

4. Install or connect the following:
   - Caliper and torque the guide bolts to 21 ft. lbs. (28 Nm)
   - Brake hose to the brake pipe and torque to 14 ft. lbs. (19 Nm)
   - Wear indicator
5. Remove the brake clamp.
6. Install the rear wheels.
7. Bleed the brakes.

DISC BRAKE PADS

REMOVAL & INSTALLATION

1. Before servicing the vehicle, refer to the precautions in the beginning of this section.
2. Remove the rear wheels.
3. Remove the plastic plugs from the inside of the caliper.
4. Disconnect the plug connection for the wear indicator.
5. Remove the calipers from the disk.
6. Lift out the pad retaining spring from the caliper.
7. Use a special tool, 34–1–050, to force piston back into caliper.
8. Remove the outer brake pad (the inner pad is held in place with a spring in the piston).

To install:

9. Apply anti-squeak compound to all mounting surfaces.
10. Reposition retaining spring.
11. Install calipers.
12. Install rear wheels.
13. Fully depress brake pedal several times to set proper contact of pads with rotor.
14. Hold ignition key for at least 30 seconds in position "1" without starting engine. This clear any fault codes stored in system and prevent the wear indicator light from coming on.
15. Bleed brake system, if necessary.

BRAKES — PARKING BRAKE

PARKING BRAKE CABLES

ADJUSTMENT

See Figures 7 through 9.

Perform an inspection of the parking brake operation in the following manner: When 1st ratchet is engaged, no braking force should be exerted. The difference in wheel braking force between the left and right wheels may deviate by max. 30 percent. In event of larger deviations of wheel braking force, carry out readjustment. It must be possible to brake to the point of locked wheels with the handbrake. The handbrake must be readjusted whenever the actuation stroke is greater than 10 teeth.

➡The handbrake can only be adjusted correctly when the parking brake Bowden cables and all moving handbrake parts are free to move and fully operational.

1. Basic handbrake adjustment is necessary when:
   - Replacing parking brake shoes
   - Replacing rear brake disks
   - Actuation stroke exceeds 10 teeth
   - Replacing handbrake Bowden cables
2. Before servicing the vehicle, refer to the Precautions Section.
3. Lock adjuster unit:
   a. Press stop of adjusting spring back.
   b. Move retaining hook so that it engages in stop. Use special tool 32 1 030.
4. Remove one wheel stud on each rear wheel.
5. Turn wheel until adjustment screw is visible in tapped hole.
6. Turn adjusting screw with a screwdriver until the wheel is no longer able to turn.

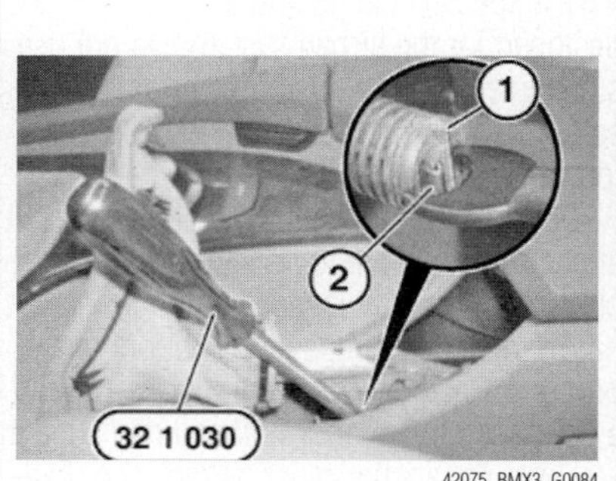

Fig. 7 Locking adjuster unit to retaining hook (2) using tool 32 1 030

Fig. 8 Location of adjustment screw access through rear wheel

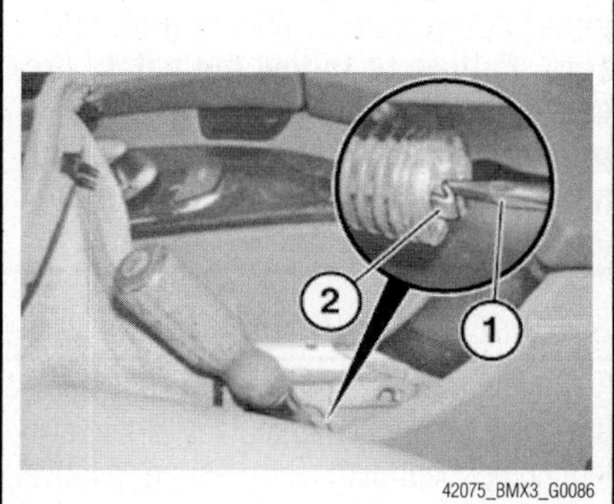

Fig. 9 Unlocking adjuster unit of parking brake

7. Turn adjusting screw 6 notches back toward brake release.
8. Unlock adjuster unit:
   a. Pry restraint hook outwards with a suitable screwdriver.
   b. Restraint hook must disengage from stop of adjusting spring.
9. Check parking brake operation.

PARKING BRAKE SHOES

REMOVAL & INSTALLATION

See Figures 10 through 12.

1. Before servicing the vehicle, refer to the Precautions Section.
2. Remove rear disc brake rotor.
3. Release parking brake lever.
4. Lock adjuster unit:
   a. Press stop of adjusting spring back.
   b. Move retaining hook so that it engages in stop. Use special tool 32 1 030.
5. Disconnect upper return spring with brake spring pliers.
6. Disconnect lower return spring with brake spring pliers.

➡Check and if necessary replace return spring. Pay attention to installation position of adjustment screw.

7. Apply a thin coat of grease to bushing and screw threads.
8. Turn clamping pins with special tool 34 4 000 through 90° and disconnect.
9. Remove brake shoes.

To install:

10. Installation is the reverse of the removal procedure.

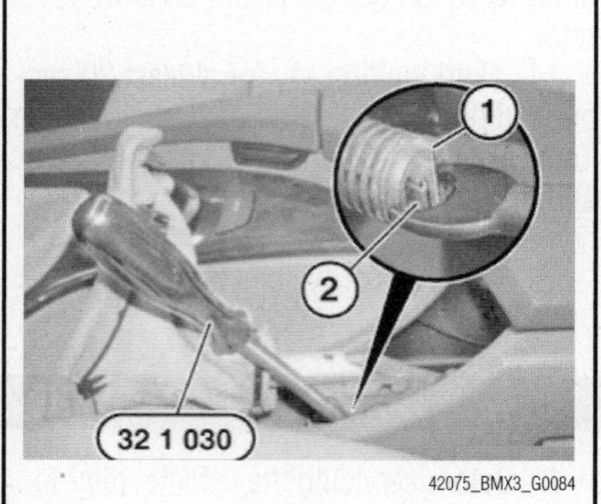

Fig. 10 Locking adjuster unit to retaining hook (2) using tool 32 1 030

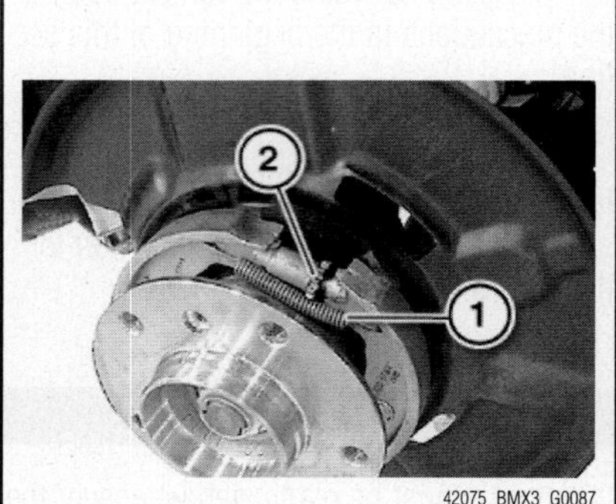

Fig. 11 Disconnecting return springs on parking brake

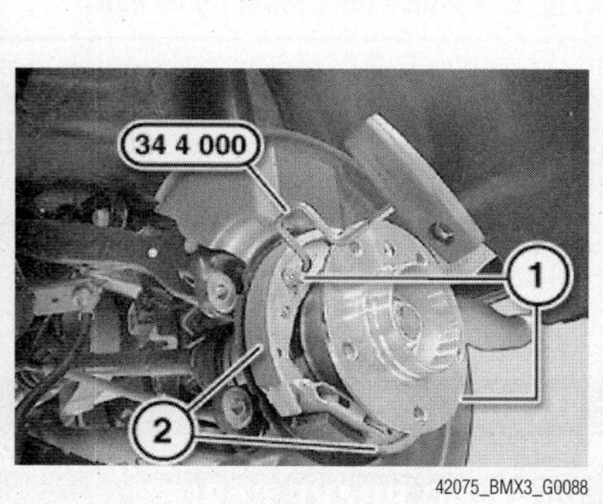

Fig. 12 Using special tool 34 4 000 to remove parking brake shoes

CHASSIS ELECTRICAL

AIR BAG (SUPPLEMENTAL RESTRAINT SYSTEM)

GENERAL INFORMATION

⁂ CAUTION

These vehicles are equipped with an air bag system. The system must be disarmed before performing service on, or around, system components, the steering column, instrument panel components, wiring and sensors. Failure to follow the safety precautions and the disarming procedure could result in accidental air bag deployment, possible injury and unnecessary system repairs.

SERVICE PRECAUTIONS

Disconnect and isolate the battery negative cable before beginning any airbag system component diagnosis, testing, removal, or installation procedures. Allow system capacitor to discharge for two minutes before beginning any component service. This will disable the airbag system. Failure to disable the airbag system may result in accidental airbag deployment, personal injury, or death.

Do not place an intact undeployed airbag face down on a solid surface. The airbag will propel into the air if accidentally deployed and may result in personal injury or death.

When carrying or handling an undeployed airbag, the trim side (face) of the airbag should be pointing away from the body to minimize possibility of injury if accidental deployment occurs. Failure to do this may result in personal injury or death.

Replace airbag system components with OEM replacement parts. Substitute parts may appear interchangeable, but internal differences may result in inferior occupant protection. Failure to do so may result in occupant personal injury or death.

Wear safety glasses, rubber gloves, and long sleeved clothing when cleaning powder residue from vehicle after an airbag deployment. Powder residue emitted from a deployed airbag can cause skin irritation. Flush affected area with cool water if irritation is experienced. If nasal or throat irritation is experienced, exit the vehicle for fresh air until the irritation ceases. If irritation continues, see a physician.

Do not use a replacement airbag that is not in the original packaging. This may result in improper deployment, personal injury, or death.

The factory installed fasteners, screws and bolts used to fasten airbag components have a special coating and are specifically designed for the airbag system. Do not use substitute fasteners. Use only original equipment fasteners listed in the parts catalog when fastener replacement is required.

During, and following, any child restraint anchor service, due to impact event or vehicle repair, carefully inspect all mounting hardware, tether straps, and anchors for proper installation, operation, or damage. If a child restraint anchor is found damaged in any way, the anchor must be replaced. Failure to do this may result in personal injury or death.

Deployed and non-deployed airbags may or may not have live pyrotechnic material within the airbag inflator.

Do not dispose of driver/passenger/curtain airbags or seat belt tensioners unless you are sure of complete deployment. Refer to the Hazardous Substance Control System for proper disposal.

Dispose of deployed airbags and tensioners consistent with state, provincial, local, and federal regulations.

After any airbag component testing or service, do not connect the battery negative cable. Personal injury or death may result if the system test is not performed first.

If the vehicle is equipped with the Occupant Classification System (OCS), do not connect the battery negative cable before performing the OCS Verification Test using the scan tool and the appropriate diagnostic information. Personal injury or death may result if the system test is not performed properly.

Never replace both the Occupant Restraint Controller (ORC) and the Occupant Classification Module (OCM) at the same time. If both require replacement, replace one, then perform the Airbag System test before replacing the other.

Both the ORC and the OCM store Occupant Classification System (OCS) calibration data, which they transfer to one another when one of them is replaced. If both are replaced at the same time, an irreversible fault will be set in both modules and the OCS may malfunction and cause personal injury or death.

If equipped with OCS, the Seat Weight Sensor is a sensitive, calibrated unit and must be handled carefully. Do not drop or handle roughly. If dropped or damaged, replace with another sensor. Failure to do so may result in occupant injury or death.

If equipped with OCS, the front passenger seat must be handled carefully as well. When removing the seat, be careful when setting on floor not to drop. If dropped, the sensor may be inoperative, could result in occupant injury, or possibly death.

If equipped with OCS, when the passenger front seat is on the floor, no one should sit in the front passenger seat. This uneven force may damage the sensing ability of the seat weight sensors. If sat on and damaged, the sensor may be inoperative, could result in occupant injury, or possibly death.

DISARMING THE SYSTEM

1. Before servicing the vehicle, refer to the precautions in the beginning of this section.
2. Place the ignition switch in the **OFF** position.
3. Disconnect the negative battery terminal and cover the battery terminal to prevent accidental contact.
4. Once the battery has been disconnected, wait for a period of approximately 3 minutes allowing the capacitor in the control unit to discharge. Once the capacitor is discharged, a trigger pulse cannot be generated inadvertently.

ARMING THE SYSTEM

1. Before servicing the vehicle, refer to the precautions in the beginning of this section.
2. Place the ignition switch in the **OFF** position.
3. Attach the sensors, the steering column connector and the seat belt tensioner connectors.
4. Connect the negative battery terminal.
5. Place the ignition switch in the **ON** position. Check that the SRS light illuminates for 6 seconds and then turns off. If it illuminates in any other pattern, check the components and their connections for proper operation and recheck operation of the warning light.

DRIVE TRAIN

AUTOMATIC TRANSMISSION FLUID

DRAIN AND REFILL

See Figure 13.

1. Before servicing the vehicle, refer to the precautions section.
2. Make sure the vehicle is on a level surface.
3. Loosen and remove the transmission pan drain plug.
4. Allow the transmission fluid to fully drain.
5. Install the plug. Tighten the plug on metal pans to 9 ft. lbs. (12 Nm). On plastic pans, tighten to 71 inch lbs. (8 Nm).
6. Loosen and remove the filler plug.
7. Fill with fluid until fluid emerges from the hole.
8. Start the engine.
9. Top off the fluid until fluid emerges from the hole again.
10. Install the filler plug. On M18 plugs, tighten to 26 ft. lbs. (35 Nm). On M30 plugs, tighten to 59 ft. lbs. (80 Nm).
11. Press brake pedal to floor and shift through all gears several times at idle speed. Then shift to "P" position (Park).
12. Call up the service functions using the BMW diagnosis system. Perform a fluid level check.

37698_X3X5_G0075

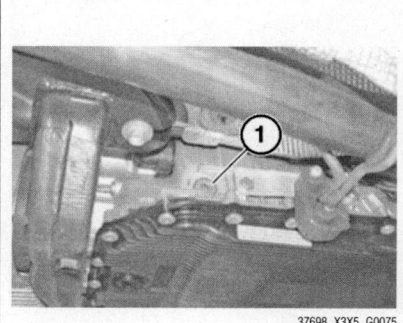

Fig. 13 Location of the transmission fill plug

TRANSFER CASE ASSEMBLY

REMOVAL & INSTALLATION

1. Before servicing the vehicle, refer to the precautions in the beginning of this section.
2. Remove or disconnect the following:
   - Negative battery cable
   - Exhaust system
   - Heat shield
   - Front propeller shaft set aside and secure
   - Propeller shaft nuts, bend shaft downward at center bearing
   - Propeller shaft from transmission and tie aside

➡Automatic transmissions: Use special tools 00-2-030, 24-5-301, 24-5-305. Manual transmission: Support with hydraulic lifter.

3. Support the transmission
   - Crossmember
   - Electrical connectors to servomotor
4. Support the transfer case. Remove the retaining bolts and remove the transfer case.

To install:

5. Check the condition of the dowel pins and replace if necessary.
6. Be sure the mating surfaces are clean.
7. Apply a thin coat of anti-seize grease to transfer case splines.

8. Replace the sealing ring of the driveshaft of the transfer case.

9. Install the transfer case and torque the retaining bolts to 32 ft. lbs. (43 Nm).

10. Reposition the propeller shaft in the center support bearing and to the flange. Torque the center support bearing nuts to 15 ft. lbs. (21 Nm) and the flange nuts to 24 ft. lbs. (32 Nm).

11. Install or connect the following:
- Cable to transfer case

12. Install the transmission crossmember. Torque the bolts as follows:
   a. To rubber mounts: 55 ft. lbs. (74 Nm).
   b. To body: 30 ft. lbs. (41 Nm).

13. Install or connect the following:
- Electrical connectors to servomotor
- Propeller shaft and center bearing
- Reinforcement plate
- Heat shields
- Exhaust system

14. Refill the transfer case.

FRONT DRIVESHAFT

REMOVAL & INSTALLATION

1. Before servicing the vehicle, refer to the precautions in the beginning of this section.
2. Remove or disconnect the following:
- Negative battery cable
- Bolts on rear flange (4)
- Bolts on front flange (4)
- Remove Shaft

To install:

3. Install or connect the following:
- Shaft
- Bolts on front flange (4)
- Bolts on rear flange (4)
- Negative battery cable

➡Torque shaft to specifications below:

- Compression nut M10-50 ft. lbs. (64 Nm)
- Torx® bolt universal joint M10-62 ft. lbs. (85 Nm)
- Torx® bolt constant velocity joint M10-52 ft. lbs. (70 Nm)
- Compression nut constant velocity joint M8-24 ft. lbs. (32 Nm)
- Finned nut M8-32 ft. lbs. (43 Nm)
- Finned nut M10-52 ft. lbs. (70 Nm)
- ZNS Screws and nuts, shiny zinc coating, all versions with universal or constant velocity joint

➡For ZNS hardware, replace bolts and nuts. Jointing torque and angle of rotation must be observed without fail.

- Universal or constant velocity joint M10-M 10.9 screws with ribbed teeth 29 ft. lbs. (40 Nm) plus 45°
- M10-M 10.9 joining torque 14.5 ft. lbs. (20 Nm) Plus 90°
- M12x55-M 10.9 replace screws and shims 52 ft. lbs. (70 Nm)
- Pivot to center propeller shaft (version without slide) 16 ft. lbs. (21 Nm)
- Center mount to body 16 ft. lbs. (21 Nm)
- Universal joint bolts M10-10.9 to 29 ft. lbs. (40 Nm) plus 45°

FRONT HALFSHAFT

REMOVAL & INSTALLATION

1. Before servicing the vehicle, refer to the precautions in the beginning of this section.
2. Remove or disconnect the following:
- Negative battery cable
- Front wheel
- Reinforcement plate
- Front splash guard
- ABS pulse generator
- Brake caliper from disc and tie out of the way with the hose still connected
- Steering gear tie rod from swivel bearing
- Tension strut, with guide joint, from swivel bearing
- Control arm from swivel bearing
- Collar nut on halfshaft, press halfshaft out of drive flange
- Halfshaft

To install:

3. Push in output shaft over the resistance of the retaining ring until it snaps in place.

➡Use a new snap ring on halfshaft spline

4. Install or connect the following:
- Collar nut
- Control arm to swivel bearing
- Tension strut to swivel bearing
- Tie rod to swivel bearing
- Brake caliper to disc
- ABS pulse generator
- Front wheel
- Splash guard
- Reinforcement plate

5. Check the front axle differential fluid level.

REAR AXLE FLUID

DRAIN & REFILL

See Figure 14.

1. Before servicing the vehicle, refer to the Precautions Section.
2. Raise and safely support the vehicle on a level surface.
3. Remove the drain/fill plug from the rear differential.
4. Using a suction device, remove all the fluid from the differential unit.

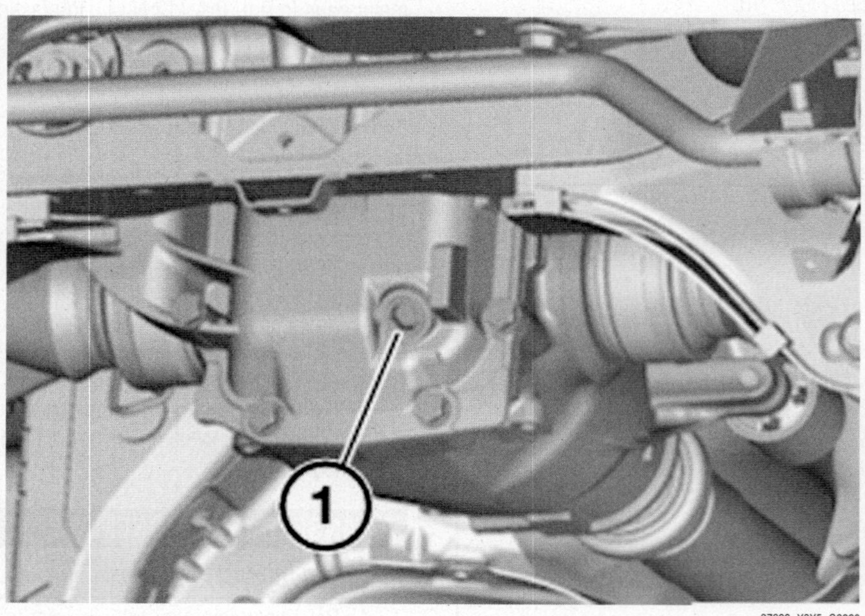

Fig. 14 Fill/drain plug location

5. Fill the differential unit with the proper amount and type of fluid. Fill up to the bottom of the opening.
6. Use a new sealing washer

REAR AXLE HOUSING

REMOVAL & INSTALLATION

See Figures 15 through 17.

1. Before servicing the vehicle, refer to the Precautions Section.
2. Remove or disconnect the following:
   - The exhaust system
   - The driveshaft from the rear differential

➡ **Match mark the shaft and flange**

   - Output shafts
   - Compression strut

➡**Support the rear differential with a jack.**

3. Remove release screws
4. Remove bolt in the center of the vehicle, if necessary, remove spacer.
5. Slowly lower the jack and tip the rear differential out toward the rear of the vehicle.

To install:

6. Install the rear differential the jack into the vehicle.
7. Insert the bolts, do not tighten.

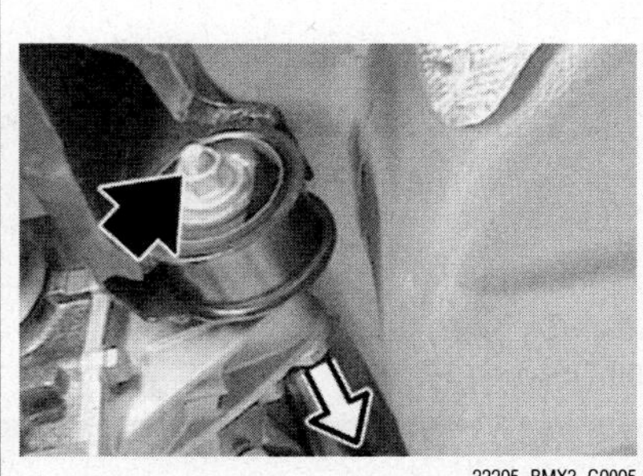

22205_BMX3_G0005

Fig. 16 Carrier bolt in center of vehicle

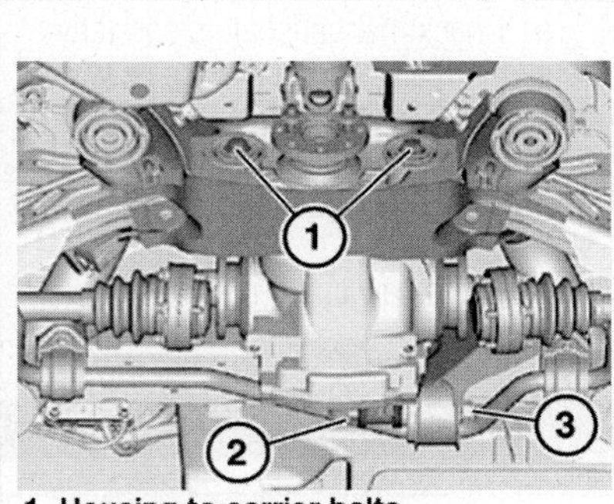

1. Housing to carrier bolts
2. Rear differential support bolt
3. Nut

22205_BMX3_G0006

Fig. 17 Housing bolts

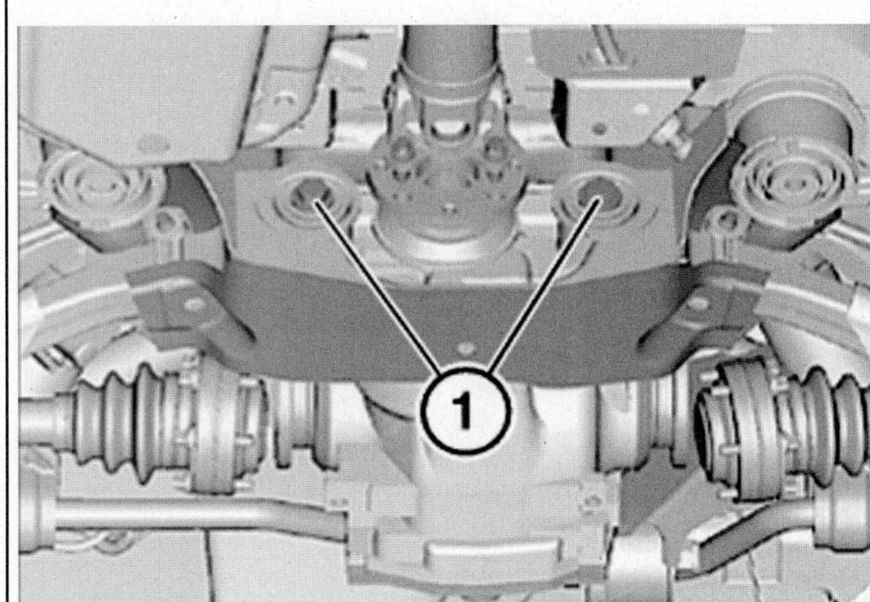

1. Release screws

22205_BMX3_G0004

Fig. 15 Release screw locations

8. Insert the bolts and nut, do not tighten.

➡**If necessary, fit spacer.**

9. Remove jack.
10. Install compression nut.
11. Tighten screws to 78 ft. lbs. (100 Nm).
12. Tighten nut to 120 ft. lbs. (165 Nm).

➡**Check differential oil**

13. Install the driveshaft to the rear differential using the match marks made at disassembly. output shafts
14. Install the exhaust system

REAR DRIVESHAFT

REMOVAL & INSTALLATION

1. Before servicing the vehicle, refer to the precautions in the beginning of this section.
2. Remove or disconnect the following:
   - Negative battery cable
   - Bolts on rear flange
   - Bolts on front flange
   - Remove shaft

To install:

3. Install or connect the following:
   - Shaft
   - Bolts on front flange
   - Bolts on rear flange
   - Negative battery cable

➡**Torque shaft to specifications below:**

   - Compression nut M10-50 ft. lbs. (64 Nm)
   - Torx® bolt universal joint M10-62 ft. lbs. (85 Nm)
   - Torx® bolt constant velocity joint M10-52 ft. lbs. (70 Nm)
   - Compression nut constant velocity joint M8-24 ft. lbs. (32 Nm)
   - Finned nut M8-32 ft. lbs. (43 Nm)
   - Finned nut M10-52 ft. lbs. (70 Nm)
   - ZNS Screws and nuts, shiny zinc coating, all versions with universal or constant velocity joint

➡**For ZNS hardware, replace bolts and nuts. Jointing torque and angle of rotation must be observed without fail.**

   - Universal or constant velocity joint M10-M 10.9 screws with ribbed teeth 29 ft. lbs. (40 Nm) plus 45°
   - M10-M 10.9 joining torque 14.5 ft. lbs. (20 Nm) Plus 90°
   - M12x55-M 10.9 replace screws and shims 52 ft. lbs. (70 Nm)

- Pivot to center propeller shaft (version without slide) 16 ft. lbs. (21 Nm)
- Center mount to body 16 ft. lbs. (21 Nm)
- Universal joint bolts M10-10.9 to 29 ft. lbs. (40 Nm) plus 45°

REAR HALFSHAFT

REMOVAL & INSTALLATION

See Figure 18.

1. Before servicing the vehicle, refer to the precautions section.
2. Remove the exhaust system.
3. Remove the rear wheel.

WARNING

Expand the tangs on the collar nut sufficiently to avoid damaging thread when releasing collar nut.

4. Remove the collar nut. Activate hand-brake to keep the wheel from turning.
5. Remove the stabilizer bar on the rear axle carrier.
6. Remove the bolts on the inner half-shaft flange and remove it with the washers.
7. Press the halfshaft off the drive flange using a suitable tool. If necessary, raise the trailing arm with a workshop jack. Remove it towards center of the vehicle.

WARNING

Do not drive halfshaft out of drive flange with an impact tool.

8. Installation is the reverse of removal. Note the following:
   a. Check that halfshaft is correctly seated in rear differential. Use new bolts and washers on the inner halfshaft flange. Tighten M8x40 bolts to 38 ft. lbs. (52 Nm) and M10 bolts to 59 ft. lbs. (80 Nm).
   b. Use a new collar nut. Oil the collar nut/wheel bearing contact surface lightly and tighten down to 221 ft. lbs. (300 Nm). Do not get oil on the nut or shaft threads. Peen the nut on the flat areas of the shaft threads.

Fig. 18 Peen the nut on the flat spots

ENGINE COOLING

ENGINE COOLANT

DRAIN & REFILL PROCEDURE

Draining

CAUTION

Do not open the coolant expansion tank until the engine has cooled down.

1. Before servicing the vehicle, refer to the Precautions Section.
2. Remove front underbody protection.
3. Open sealing cap on coolant expansion tank.
4. Release and detach coolant hoses at radiator.
5. Drain, catch and dispose of coolant.

Filling

See Figures 19 through 27.

WARNING

You must protect the alternator against contamination by coolant when carrying out repair work on the cooling circuit.

WARNING

Cover alternator with suitable materials.

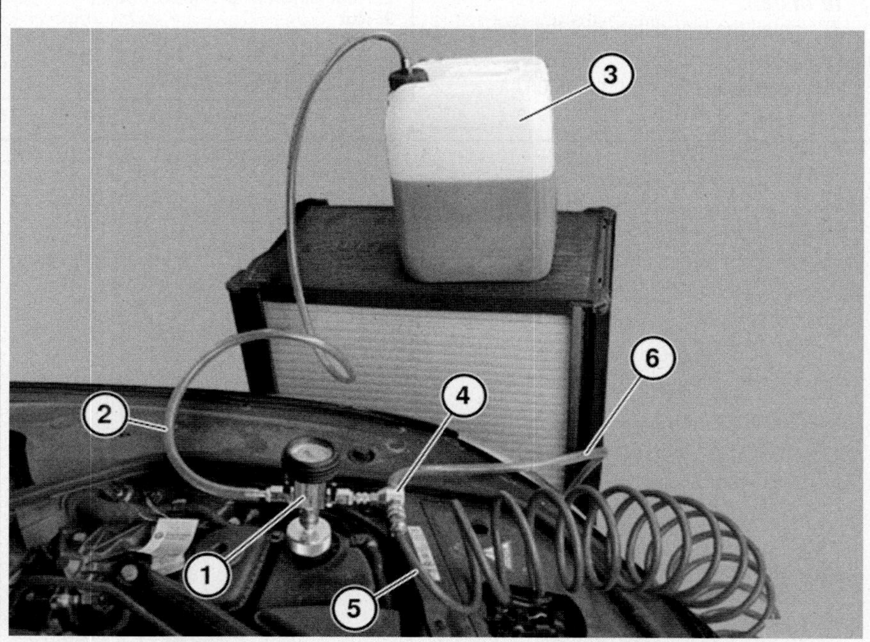

1. Filling unit with vacuum meter and shutoff valves
2. Filler hose
3. Coolant container
4. Venturi nozzle
5. Compressed air connection (max. 6 bar)
6. Outgoing-air hose (lead outgoing-air hose into a collecting container)

71112_X1X3_G0007

Fig. 19 Identifying vacuum filling unit

⁂ WARNING

Failure to comply with this procedure may result in an alternator malfunction.

➨Check all the coolant hoses before filling the cooling system with the vacuum filling unit.

➨If necessary, replace damaged and porous coolant hoses.

➨Cooling system expansion tank must be empty.

➨There must be sufficiently premixed coolant in the filling unit container, 1 - 2 liters more than the vehicle filling capacity.

⁂ WARNING

Use only recommended coolant.

⁂ WARNING

Observe mixture ratio.

⁂ WARNING

Observe capacities.

1. Position the filling unit container at the same height as the coolant expansion tank.

➨Compressed-air connection with 6 bar pressure present.

➨Set vehicle heater to maximum temperature.

2. Select adapter (Y) according to table and connect to coolant expansion tank.

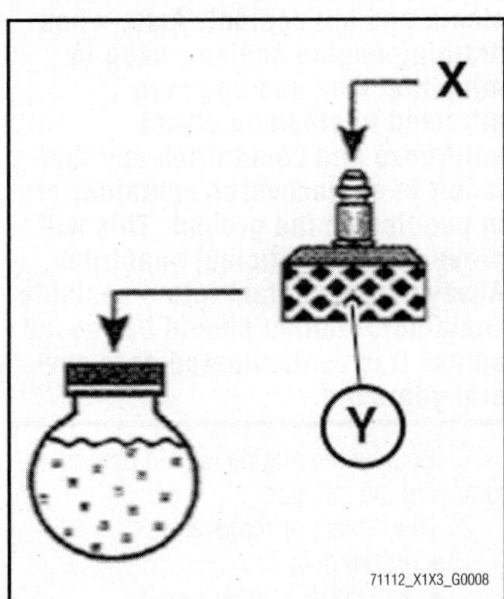

Fig. 20 Selecting adapter (Y) and connecting filler unit to adapter connection (X)

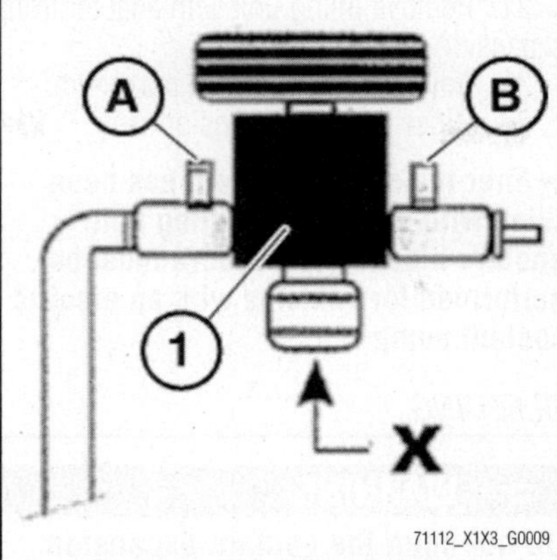

Fig. 21 Identifying shutoff valves (A and B) of filling unit (1) (X: expansion tank connection)

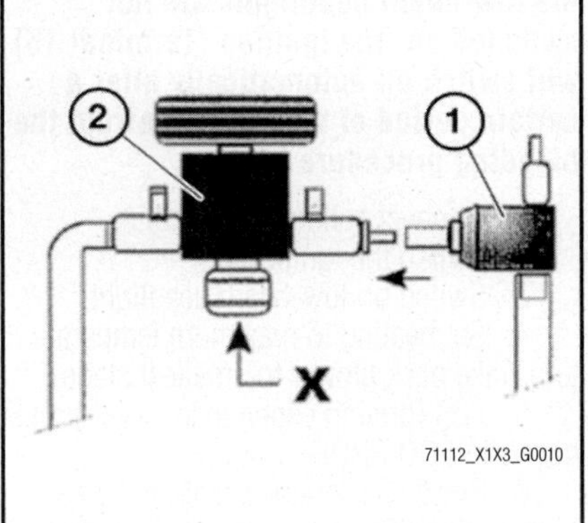

Fig. 22 Connecting venturi nozzle (1) to filling unit (2) (X: expansion tank connection)

3. Connect filler unit to adapter connection (X).

4. Shutoff valves (A) and (B) of the filling unit (1) must be closed.

5. Connect venturi nozzle (1) to filling unit (2).

6. Connect compressed air (1).

7. Open shutoff valve (B).

➨The venturi nozzle produces a flow noise.

8. Then open shutoff valve (A) until the filling hose (1) is free of bubbles.

9. Close shutoff valve (A) again. The filling hose (1) is vented in this way.

10. Shutoff valve (B) remains open. Generate vacuum in coolant system for approx. 2 minutes. The end vacuum is reached at a vacuum of -0.7 to -0.95 bar. Green scale on the vacuum meter.

➨The coolant hoses contract during vacuum build-up.

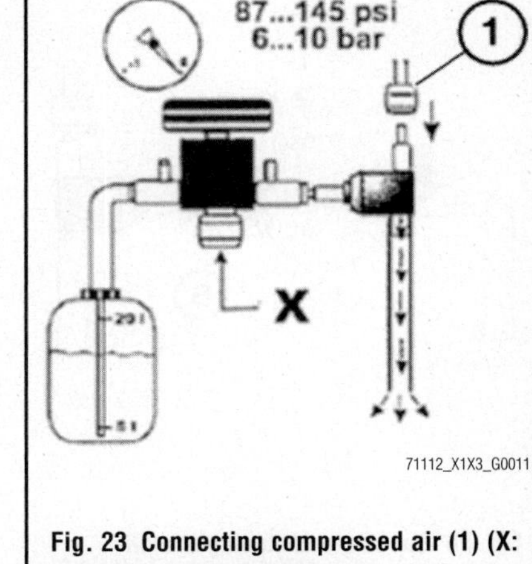

Fig. 23 Connecting compressed air (1) (X: expansion tank connection)

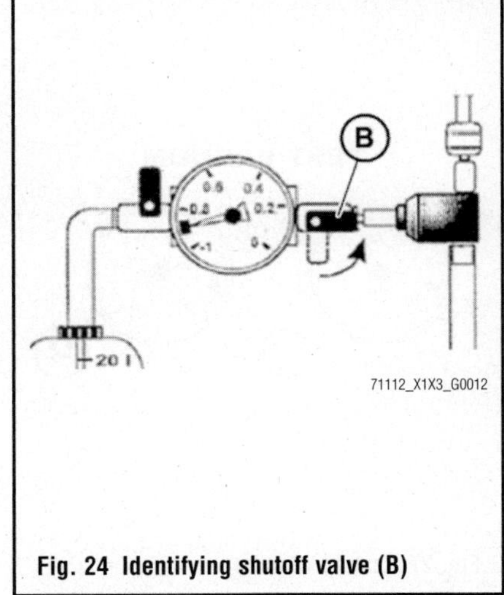

Fig. 24 Identifying shutoff valve (B)

11. Then close shutoff valve (B) again.

12. Both shutoff valves (A) and (B) must be closed. Then seal Venturi nozzle (1).

13. The cooling system must hold the vacuum for 30 s. If the needle in the vacuum meter falls, this indicates a leak in the cooling system.

14. If the vacuum remains constant, proceed with filling.

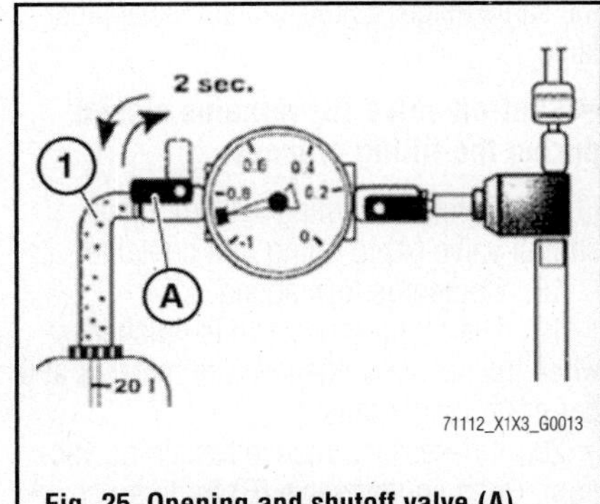

Fig. 25 Opening and shutoff valve (A)

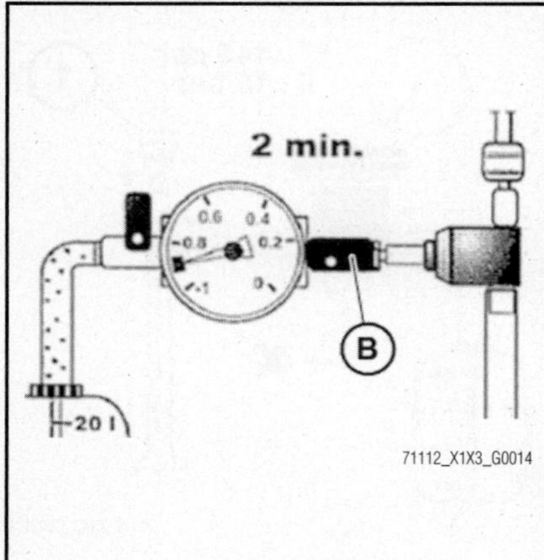

Fig. 26 Opening and closing shutoff valve (B)

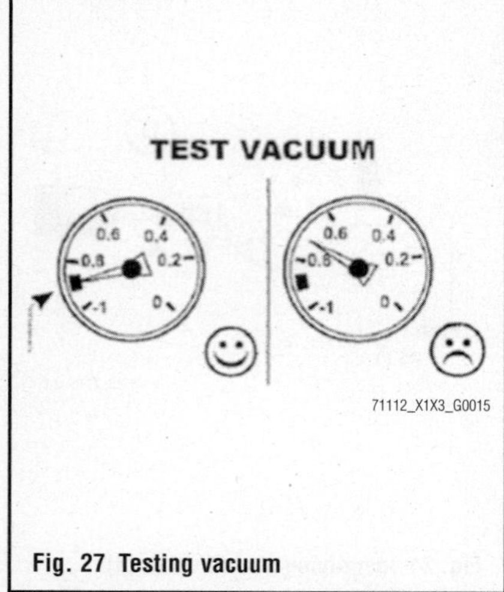

Fig. 27 Testing vacuum

15. In event of leaks, check cooling system for leaks.

⁂ WARNING

There must be sufficiently premixed coolant in the filling unit container: 1 -2 liters more than the vehicle filling capacity.

16. Position the filling unit container at the same height as the coolant expansion tank.

➡Shut-off valve (B) remains closed during the filling process.

17. To fill the cooling system, open shutoff valve (A) to filling unit container.
18. Coolant is now added.
19. The filling procedure is finished when the needle in the vacuum meter is at 0 bar or no longer falls.
20. If necessary, reduce remaining vacuum. Open shutoff valve (B) to do so.
21. Remove filling unit with adapter from expansion tank.
22. Adjust coolant level to maximum.
23. Close coolant expansion tank.

➡After the cooling system has been filled with the vacuum filling unit, another bleeding procedure must be performed for vehicles with an electric coolant pump.

BLEEDING

⁂ WARNING

Do not open the coolant expansion tank cap during the bleeding procedure.

➡Switch on the low-beam headlights to perform the bleeding procedure. If the low-beam headlights are not switched on, the ignition (Terminal 15) will switch off automatically after a certain period of time and interrupt the bleeding procedure.

1. Connect battery charger.
2. Switch the ignition on.
3. Switch on low-beam headlight.
4. Set heating to maximum temperature. Take back blower to smallest stage.
5. FES (driving experience switch) must not be in ECO PRO!
6. Press accelerator pedal for 10 seconds to floor. Engine must not be started.
7. The venting procedure is started when the accelerator pedal is pressed and takes approx. 12 minutes. (Electric coolant pump was activated and shuts down automatically after approx. 12 min).
8. Then adjust fluid level in the coolant expansion tank to maximum.
9. Check cooling system for leaks.
10. If the ventilation has to be performed again, deactivate DME completely (remove ignition key for approx. 3 minutes). Then repeat from point 3.
11. Check function of cooling system.
12. Check cooling system for tightness.

ENGINE FAN

REMOVAL & INSTALLATION

See Figure 28.

1. Before servicing the vehicle, refer to the Precautions Section.
2. Remove or disconnect the following:
   - Ground cable of battery
   - Intake duct
   - Electric connection to fan
   - Unlock 2 clips at top of fan cowl and remove

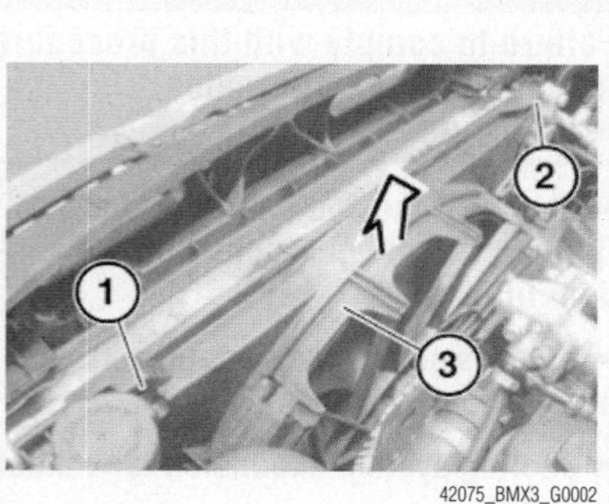

Fig. 28 Illustrated engine fan removal

   - Lift out expansion rivet
   - Release screw
   - Remove fan cowl towards top

To install:

3. Install or connect the following:
   - Engine fan cowl into place
   - Release screw. Tighten
   - Tighten 2 clips at top of fan cowl
   - Electric connection to engine fan
   - Intake duct
   - Ground cable battery

RADIATOR

REMOVAL & INSTALLATION

See Figure 29.

⁂ CAUTION

Never open, service or drain the radiator or cooling system when hot; serious burns can occur from the steam and hot coolant. Also, when draining engine coolant, keep in mind that cats and dogs are attracted to ethylene glycol antifreeze and could drink any that is left in an uncovered container or in puddles on the ground. This will prove fatal in sufficient quantities. Always drain coolant into a sealable container. Coolant should be reused unless it is contaminated or is several years old.

1. Be sure the engine is cold before removing the radiator.
2. Disconnect or remove:
   - Intake duct
   - Fan cowl
   - Drain coolant
   - Coolant hoses
   - If equipped with an automatic

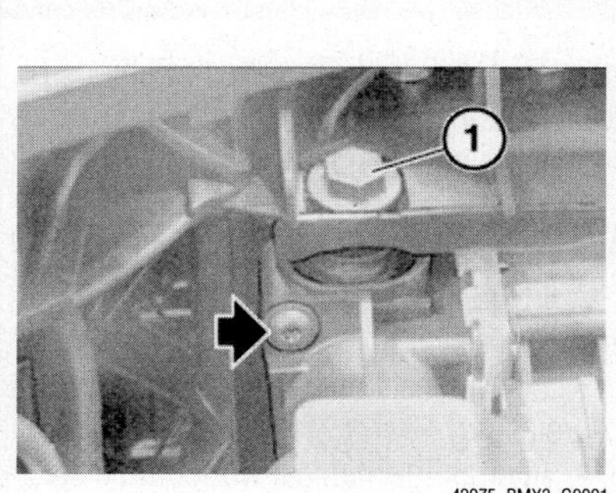

Fig. 29 Locking screw and bracket bolt location for radiator removal

transmission, remove tubing to heat exchanger core in radiator
- Locking screw (illustrated with an arrow)
- Bracket bolt (1) holding radiator
- Remove radiator up and out

To install:

3. Install or connect the following:
    - Radiator into position
    - Bracket bolt (1). Tighten to 24 inch lbs. (3 Nm)
    - If equipped with an automatic transmission, install tubing to heat exchanger core in radiator
    - Coolant hoses
    - Fan cowl. Tighten to 48 inch lbs. (5 Nm)
    - Intake duct
4. Be sure to refill the cooling system using the proper grade and type of engine coolant.
5. Start the engine and check for leaks.
6. Run engine and allow it to reach full operating temperature. Recheck the coolant level and transmission fluid level. Fill as required.

THERMOSTAT

REMOVAL & INSTALLATION

See Figure 30.

Fig. 30 Pull the locks (1) and detach the hoses from the thermostat housing

WARNING

Aluminum-magnesium materials. No steel bolts/bolts may be used due to the threat of electrochemical corrosion. A magnesium crankcase requires aluminum bolts/bolts exclusively. Aluminum bolts/bolts must be replaced each time they are removed. The end faces of these bolts/bolts are painted blue for the purposes of reliable identification. Torque and angle of rotation must be observed without fail (risk of damage).

1. Drain the cooling system.
2. Remove the engine fan.
3. Disconnect the coolant hoses from the thermostat housing.
4. Loosen the nut and mounting bolts on the thermostat housing.
5. Remove the thermostat assembly.

To install:

➡The thermostat is integrated into the housing and can only be replaced as a unit.

6. Clean the contact surfaces of any oil.
7. Replace the thermostat gasket before reinstalling.
8. The remainder of the installation is the reverse order of removal.
9. Refill the cooling system to the correct level.
10. Start the engine and check for leaks.

WATER PUMP

REMOVAL & INSTALLATION

See Figure 31.

1. Before servicing the vehicle, refer to the precautions in the beginning of this section.
2. Remove the alternator drive belt.
3. Drain the cooling system. Drain plug is located on exhaust side of block, next to cylinder number 2.
4. Remove the water pump pulley.
5. Remove the 4 water pump retaining bolts. Use 2 M6 bolts in holes next to mounting bolt holes and screw in until water pump releases from timing cover.

To install:

6. When installing, use a new O-ring.
7. Tighten mounting bolts as follows:
    a. M6 bolts: 88 inch lbs. (10 Nm).
    b. M7 bolts: 132 inch lbs. (15 Nm).
    c. M8 bolts: 16 ft. lbs. (22 Nm).
8. Install water pump pulley.
9. Refill cooling system.
10. Install the alternator drive belt.
11. Start the vehicle, check for leaks and repair as necessary.

Fig. 31 Showing water pump bolts—3.0L N52 engine

BATTERY

REMOVAL & INSTALLATION

See Figures 32 and 33.

WARNING

If the ignition is not turned off when the battery is disconnected, fault memories may be set in some control units.

- There is a danger of mixing up battery leads: If the battery positive and negative leads are the same color and you are in doubt, follow the polarity to the battery, then mark and cover the leads.
- On vehicles with radio code: After disconnecting the battery, the radio code must be re-entered. Therefore obtain the radio code card from the customer beforehand. Note stored stations and restore them after connecting the battery.
- Stored settings of the on-board computer and clock will also be lost.
- All available central keys must be recoded for cars with first generation infrared transmitter locking systems.

WARNING

Do not under any circumstances use force to pull/lever off Intelligent Battery Sensor (IBS).

1. Remove battery cover in the rear loading floor.
2. Loosen negative battery lead nut.

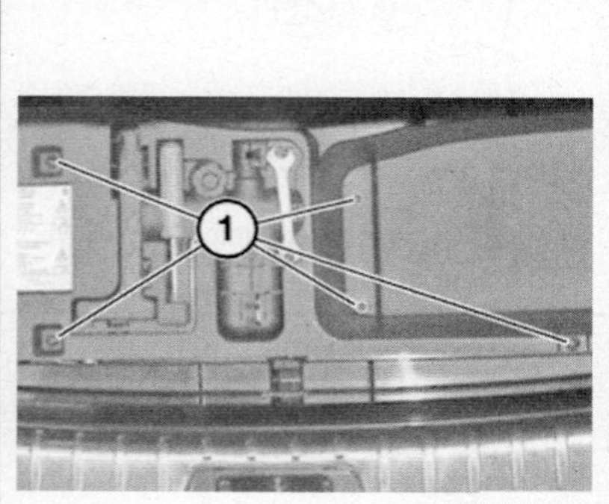

Fig. 32 Remove the bolts securing the battery cover

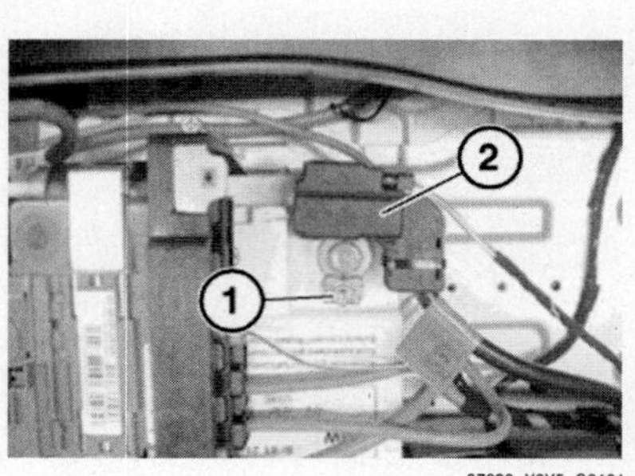

Fig. 33 Remove the nut (1) securing the negative battery lead. Be careful not to damage the IBS (2)

3. Disconnect battery negative lead and IBS then secure at side.
4. Remove the distribution box.
   a. Release screws and remove bracket.
   b. Disconnect plug connection.
   c. Unlock plug housing and release in direction of arrow.
   d. Fold up covers on nuts.
   e. Unscrew nuts.
   f. Disconnect plug connection.
   g. Press locking brackets downwards and unclip.
   h. If necessary, using a screwdriver, expand locking bracket at lower end and clip out.
   i. Remove power distributor towards top.
5. Unlock positive terminal cover and remove.
6. Detach vent to the left.
7. Release nut of safety battery terminal.
8. Detach safety battery terminal towards top, lay to one side and secure.
9. Lift out the battery.

To install:

10. Installation is the reverse of removal.
11. Make sure battery is correctly seated in its fixture.
    - Distribution box: 11 ft. lbs. (15 Nm)
    - Battery positive lead, battery negative lead, safety battery terminal, IBS: 48 inch lbs. (5 Nm)
12. On vehicles with intelligent battery sensor (IBS), register battery replacement and read out fault memory, clear if necessary.

BATTERY RECONNECT/RELEARN PROCEDURE

After disconnecting/connecting battery some systems may be restricted and individual settings may be lost. Settings or activations must be carried out, depending on the equipment specification.

Active Front Steering

Adjustment of the active front steering must be carried out:

- After adjustment work on the front axle/steering
- After all mechanical work on the steering system
- After the battery has been disconnected or electrical plug connections on the steering column switch cluster have been disconnected

After replacement/programming or coding of the following components:

- Steering column switch cluster
- DSC control unit
- Active front steering control unit
- ARS control unit

Connect vehicle to BMW diagnosis system. Select and carry out initial operation/adjustment for active front steering under Service functions.

Sliding Sunroof

Initialization of the sliding sunroof comprises normalization and then learning of the characteristic curve. The mechanical end positions are recorded and stored during normalization. The characteristic curve is learnt immediately after normalization. When the characteristic curve is learned, the mechanical closing forces of the slide/tilt sunroof are recorded and stored for correct operation of the anti-trapping mechanism.

Carry out an initialization:

- If the slide/tilt sunroof has been mechanically moved by means of the emergency actuator
- In the event of malfunctions, e.g. no one-touch function, no opening or no comfort function possible
- After disengagement of the drive unit
- After work is carried out on the mechanism of the slide/tilt sunroof
- After the control unit has been replaced

WARNING

There is no anti-trapping protection during initialization.

Normalization

1. Press and hold the switch in the Lift direction.

2. In the event of delayed starting or sudden stopping of the slide/tilt sunroof, continue pressing the switch in the Lift direction.

3. After reaching the lift end position, keep the switch pressed for approximately 15 seconds further.

4. Normalization is completed when the slide/tilt sunroof in lift end position presses again briefly upward.

Learning Characteristic Curve

1. After normalization, keep switch pressed in Lift direction.

2. The slide/tilt sunroof stops for 5 seconds in the final raise position after normalization. It then moves into the Closed position (learning of the "Closing from raising" curve).

3. The slide/tilt sunroof then moves into the Open end position and immediately back into the Closed position (learning of the "Closing" curve).

4. Release the switch.

➡The entire operation lasts approximately 75 seconds. Learning of the curve is terminated when the switch is released. If the switch is released prematurely, the entire procedure must be repeated. Upon completion of successful initialization, the corresponding messages in the check control and the control display go out.

5. Carry out function check (tip function, anti-trapping protection and, if necessary, comfort function).

Power Windows

WARNING

There is no anti-trapping protection during initialization.

An initialization must be performed:

- In the event of malfunctions, e.g. no one-touch control function, no opening or if available no comfort function is possible
- After the power window drive has been replaced
- After work is carried out on the power window mechanism
- If necessary, after an open circuit, e.g. disconnection of the battery or disconnection of the power supply to the door
- After the door window glass has been removed and installed or replaced
- After adjustment work on the door window glass
- After adjustment work on the convertible top
- After replacement of seals

Initialization is performed on the power window switch of the relevant door.

- The ignition switch must be ON
- Doors and windows closed
- Sufficient battery voltage; connect charger if necessary

Initialization comprises erasure of the previous initialization and re-initialization.

Erasure of Initialization

1. Open door window glass fully.

2. Actuate power window switch in Open position (second switch position) and hold down for between 15 and 20 seconds. This clears initialization of the power window. Anti-trapping protection and one-touch control function are inactive.

3. Check whether one-touch control function is inactive, otherwise repeat procedure.

Reinitialization

1. Close door window completely.

2. After upper end position is reached, interrupt actuation of power window switch and then hold switch again for approximately 1 second in Close position (second switch position).

3. Open door window glass fully.

4. After upper end position is reached, interrupt actuation of power window switch and then hold switch again for approximately 1 second in Open position (second switch position).

5. Close door window completely.

6. After upper end position is reached, interrupt actuation of power window switch and then hold switch again for approximately 1 second in Close position (second switch position).

7. Carry out function check (one-touch control function, anti-trapping protection and, if necessary, comfort function).

➡The power windows can also be initialized by connecting the vehicle to BMW diagnosis system.

Mirror with Compass

If may be necessary to calibrate the compass if:

- The vehicle battery has been disconnected for an extended period of time
- "C" appears in compass display
- There is no compass display

Setting Magnetic Deflection Zone

1. Switch ignition on.

2. Using a suitable tool, press pushbutton on mirror until a number appears in compass display.

3. Press pushbutton repeatedly until number of desired zone appears.

4. Wait until direction display appears.

5. Magnetic deflection zone is now set.

Calibrating Compass:

1. Switch ignition on.

2. Using a suitable tool, press pushbutton on mirror until "C" appears in compass display.

3. Drive the vehicle 2–3 times in a circle at approximately 10 mph.

4. Calibration process is completed when direction display appears.

ALTERNATOR

REMOVAL & INSTALLATION

N52 Engine

See Figure 34.

WARNING

Aluminum-magnesium materials. No steel bolts/bolts may be used due to the threat of electrochemical corrosion. A magnesium crankcase requires aluminum bolts/bolts exclusively. Aluminum bolts/bolts must be replaced each time they are removed. The end faces of aluminum bolts/bolts are painted blue for the purposes of reliable identification. Jointing torque and angle of rotation must be observed without fail (risk of damage).

1. Before servicing the vehicle, refer to the precautions.

Fig. 34 Alternator (3), mounting bolts (arrows), B+ wire (1) and plug (2)

2. Disconnect the negative battery cable.
3. Remove intake filter housing.
4. Remove alternator drive belt.
5. Unlock plug and remove.
6. Remove nut and disconnect B+ wire.
7. Remove aluminum bolts and discard.
8. Remove alternator.

To install:

9. Install alternator.
10. Install new aluminum bolts tighten to
11. Connect B+ wire and tighten nut to 14 ft. lbs. (19 Nm).
12. Connect and lock plug.
13. Install alternator drive belt.
14. Install intake filter housing .
15. Connect the negative battery cable.

N55 Engine

See Figures 35 and 36.

1. Before servicing the vehicle, refer to the precautions.
2. Disconnect the negative battery cable.
3. Remove charge air duct.

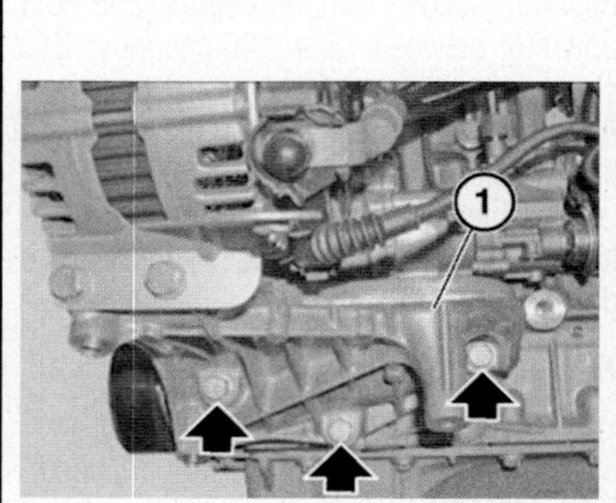

Fig. 35 Remove bolts a few turns until bracket (1) is loose. Do not remove bracket

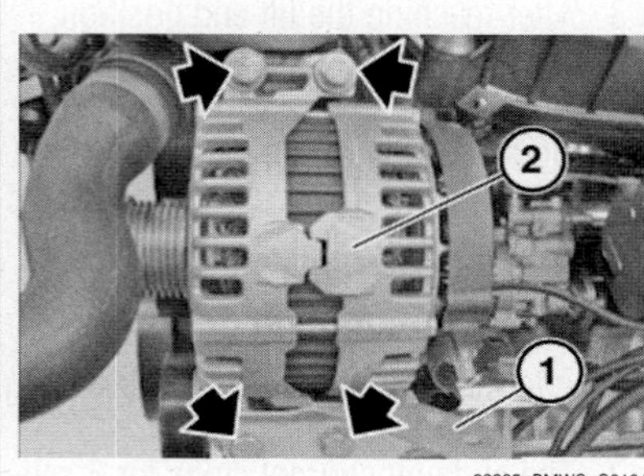

Fig. 36 Remove bracket (1) and alternator (2)

4. Remove alternator drive belt
5. Remove the A/C compressor and place to one side.

➡Do not disconnect refrigerant lines from compressor.

6. Remove bolts a few turns until bracket is loose. Do not remove bracket.
7. Unlock plug and remove.
8. Remove protective cap and remove nut underneath.
9. Disconnect B+ wire.
10. Remove bracket and alternator.

To install:

11. Install bracket and alternator.
12. Connect B+ wire.
13. Install protective cap and remove nut underneath.
14. Install and lock plug.

➡Do not disconnect refrigerant lines from compressor.

15. Install the A/C compressor.
16. Install alternator drive belt.
17. Install charge air duct.
18. Connect the negative battery cable.

FIRING ORDER

See Figure 37.

The N20 firing order is 1-3-4-2.

IGNITION COIL

REMOVAL & INSTALLATION

N52 Engine

See Figures 38 and 39.

1. Before servicing the vehicle, refer to the precautions.
2. Read out fault memory of DME control unit.
3. If equipped, remove engine cover.
4. Remove ignition coil cover.
5. Unlock plug retainer of ignition coil and disconnect plug.

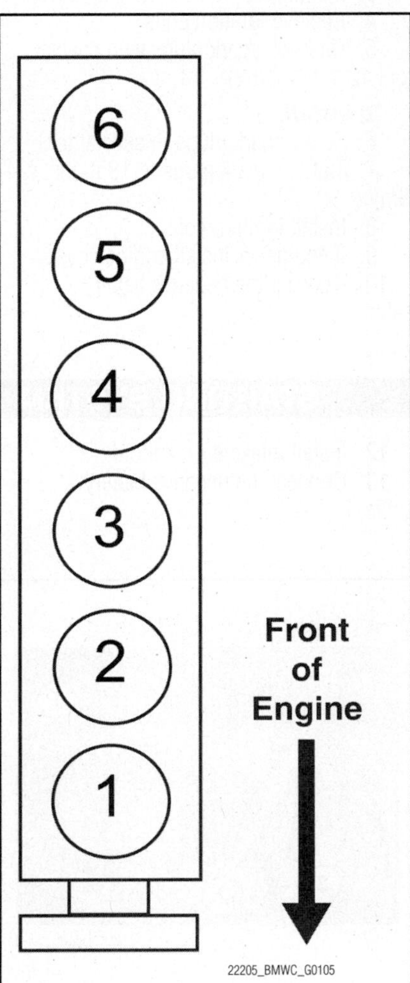

Fig. 37 3.0L I6 N52 and N55 engines Firing order: 1–5–3–6–2–4 Distributorless ignition system

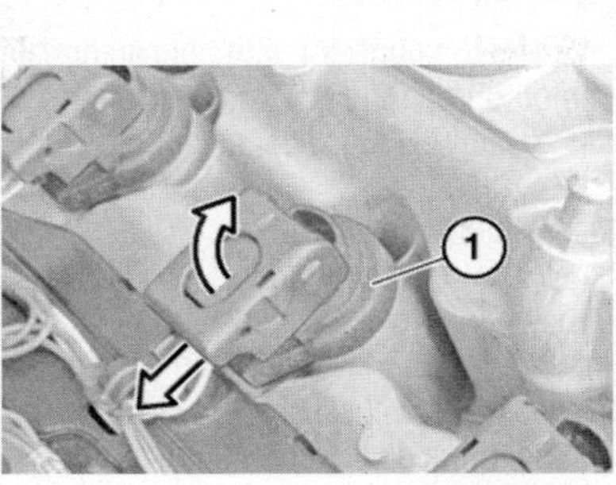

Fig. 38 Unlock plug retainer of ignition coil (1) and disconnect plug

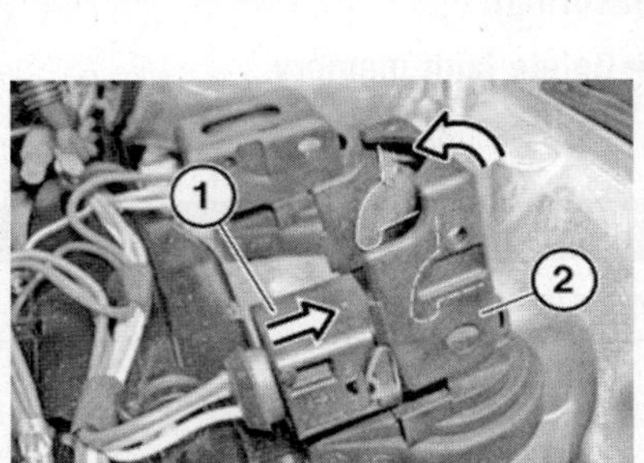

Fig. 39 Push plug (1) with plug retainer (2) open onto ignition coil

6. Pull ignition coil up and out.

To install:

7. Check that rubber seal of ignition coil is correctly seated.
8. Push plug with plug retainer open onto ignition coil.
9. Carefully close plug retainer.
10. Install ignition coil cover.
11. If equipped, install engine cover.

➡The plug retainer must snap into place without great effort.

12. Clear the fault memory.

N55 Engine

See Figures 40 through 42.

1. Read out fault code memory of the DME control unit.
2. Check stored fault messages and process procedure.
3. Switch off ignition.
4. Remove ignition coil cover.
5. Remove clean air pipe.

⁂ WARNING

Ignition coils must not be contaminated by fuel.

⁂ WARNING

The resistance of the silicone material is reduced significantly by contact with fuel, which may cause the ignition coil to fail.

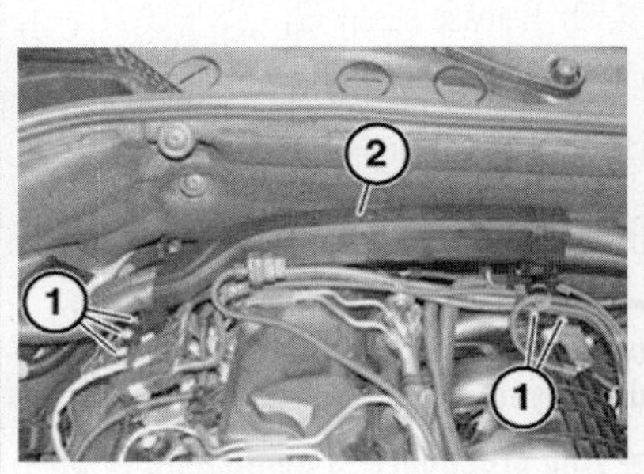

Fig. 40 Releasing screws (1) and sliding cable channel (2) to one side

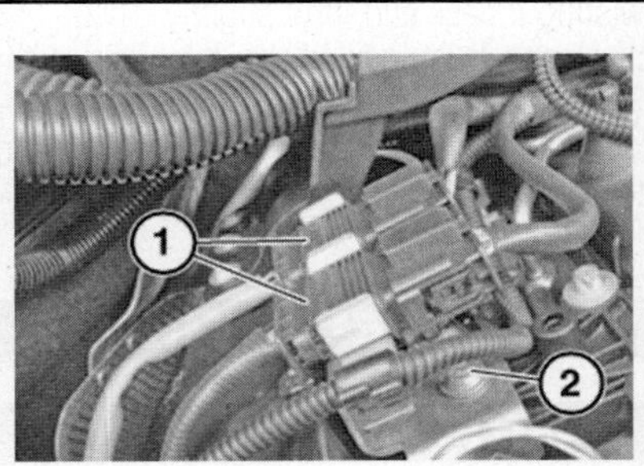

Fig. 41 Releasing oxygen sensor connector (1) from bracket and releasing screw (2)

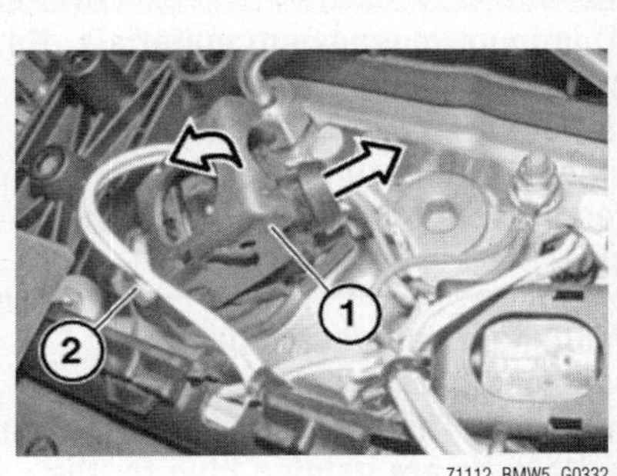

Fig. 42 Unlocking plug catch (1) of ignition coil (2) and disconnecting plug

⁂ WARNING

The silicone tube of the spark plug connector is coated with talc to reduce the pulling forces. The silicone tube must NOT be oiled or greased. This would greatly reduce the durability of the silicone material, which can lead to a malfunction of the ignition coil.

6. Release screws (1).
7. Slide cable channel (2) to one side.
8. Release oxygen sensor connector (1) from bracket.
9. Release screw (2).
10. Put cable clip aside.
11. Unlock plug catch (1) of ignition coil (2) and disconnect plug.
12. Pull out the ignition coil (2) slowly in a smooth upwards movement.

➡There is a possibility that the silicone tube will tear and therefore be destroyed.

➡This procedure is applicable to all ignition coils.

To install:

13. Position the ignition coil and gently push it to the limit position, if necessary by twisting it back and forth slightly. Then check anti-twist lock.
14. The rubber cap must completely surround the sealing collar of the cylinder head cover.

➡If rubber parts are squashed, the ignition coil can slip out again during engine operation.

15. Push connector with connector catch open onto ignition coil.
16. Carefully close connector catch.
17. The connector catch must snap into place without great effort.
18. The connector must be positioned on the counter piece with hardly any gaps when the locking lever is being closed. In the process, the cheeks of the lever are positioned inside the counter piece.

➡The locking lever can become deformed if it is not installed correctly. This means that there is no longer a safety lock on the plug connection. As a result, the connector can slip out during engine operation (loose contact, misfiring).

➡Delete fault memory.

19. Assemble engine.

IGNITION TIMING

ADJUSTMENT

The ignition timing is controlled by the Digital Motor Electronics (DME). No adjustments are necessary.

SPARK PLUGS

REMOVAL & INSTALLATION

⁂ WARNING

Spark plugs must be replaced with the same type/number spark plug as the original. If another spark plug is substituted, damage may result.

Special care should be taken when installing spark plugs into the cylinder head spark plug wells. Be sure the plugs do not drop into the plug wells as electrodes can be damaged.

Always tighten spark plugs to the specified torque. Over tightening can cause distortion resulting in a change in the spark plug gap or a cracked porcelain insulator. Proper torque is especially important in the case of aluminum cylinder heads.

1. Before servicing the vehicle, refer to the precautions.
2. Disconnect the negative battery cable.
3. If equipped, removal engine cover.
4. Remove ignition coils.
5. Unscrew spark plugs with special tool 12 1 171 (N52).

To install:

6. Screw spark plugs in special tool.
7. Tighten spark plugs to 18 ft. lbs. (24 Nm).
8. Install ignition coils.
9. If equipped, install engine cover.
10. Connect the negative battery cable.

ENGINE ELECTRICAL

STARTING SYSTEM

STARTER

REMOVAL & INSTALLATION

N52 Engine

See Figure 43.

⁂ WARNING

Aluminum-magnesium materials. No steel bolts/bolts may be used due to the threat of electrochemical corrosion. A magnesium crankcase requires aluminum bolts/bolts exclusively.

Aluminum bolts/bolts must be replaced each time they are removed. The end faces of aluminum bolts/bolts are painted blue for the purposes of reliable identification. Jointing torque and angle of rotation must be observed without fail (risk of damage).

1. Disconnect the negative battery cable.
2. Remove intake air manifold.
3. Unlock plug and remove.
4. Remove the B+ cable from the starter.
5. Remove and discard the starter mounting bolts.
6. Remove starter motor.

To install:

7. Check starter pinion and ring gear for damage, replace damaged parts if necessary.
8. Install starter motor.
9. Install the starter mounting bolts and tighten to specification.
   - M10x85: 15 ft. lbs. (20 Nm) plus an additional 180° rotation
   - M10x30: 15 ft. lbs. (20 Nm) plus an additional 90° rotation
10. Install the B+ cable from the starter and tighten nut to 10 ft. lbs. (13 Nm).
11. Unlock plug and install.
12. Install intake air manifold.
13. Connect the negative battery cable.

Fig. 43 Starter mounting bolt locations

ENGINE MECHANICAL

➡Disconnecting the negative battery cable may interfere with the functions of the on board computer systems and may require the computer to undergo a relearning process, once the negative battery cable is reconnected.

ACCESSORY DRIVE BELTS

ACCESSORY BELT ROUTING

See Figures 44 through 46.

INSPECTION

Inspect the drive belt for signs of glazing or cracking. A glazed belt will be perfectly smooth from slippage, while a good belt will have a slight texture of fabric visible. Cracks will usually start at the inner edge of the belt and run outward. All worn or damaged drive belts should be replaced immediately.

REMOVAL & INSTALLATION

N52 Engine

See Figure 47.

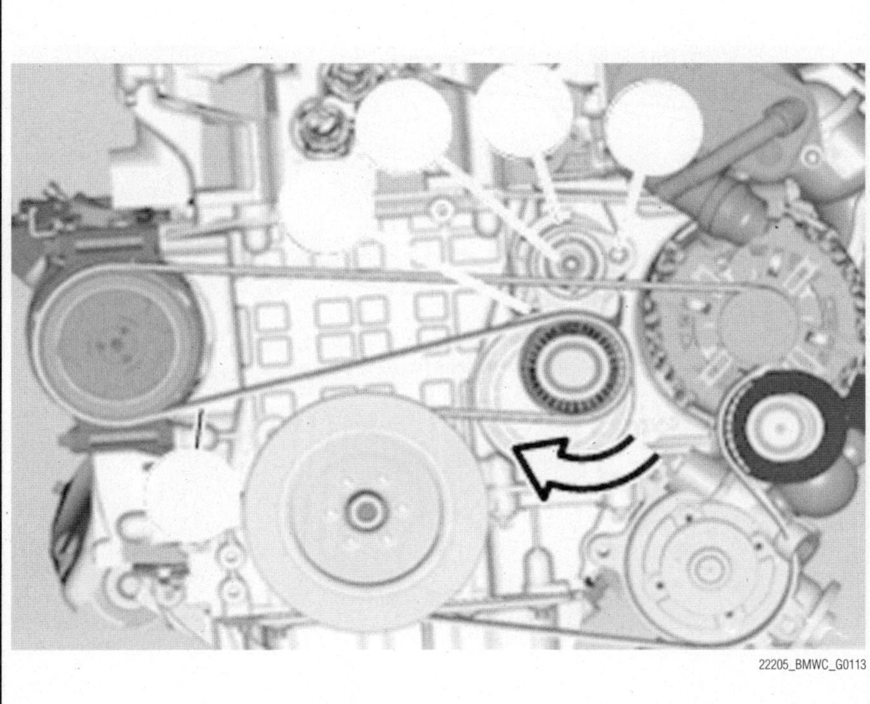

Fig. 44 Accessory belt routing—N52 engine

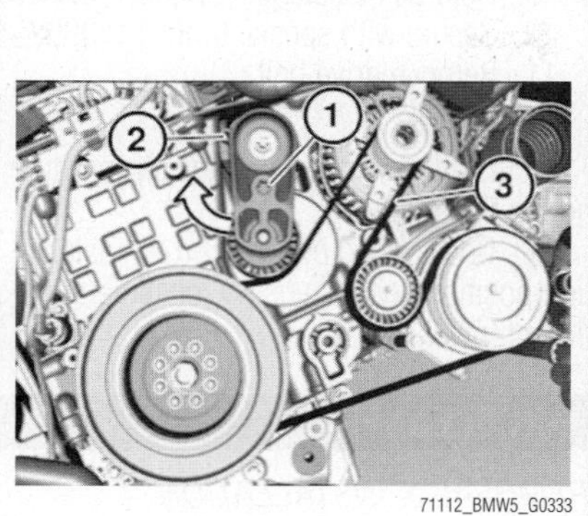

Fig. 45 Accessory belt routing—N55 engine (without Dynamic Drive)

⁂ WARNING

Aluminum-magnesium materials. No steel bolts/bolts may be used due to the threat of electrochemical corrosion. A magnesium crankcase requires aluminum bolts/bolts exclusively.

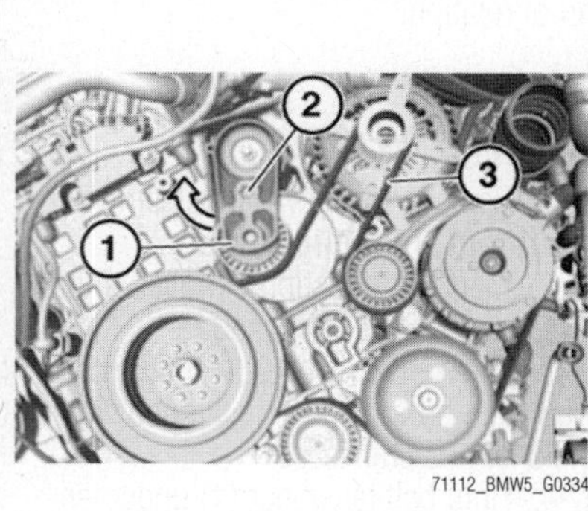

Fig. 46 Accessory belt routing—N55 engine (with Dynamic Drive)

Fig. 47 Secure belt tensioner with special tool 11 3 340

Aluminum bolts/bolts must be replaced each time they are Removed. The end faces of aluminum bolts/bolts are painted blue for the purposes of reliable identification. Jointing torque and angle of rotation must be observed without fail (risk of damage).

1. Before servicing the vehicle, refer to the precautions.
2. Remove fan cowl with electric fan
3. Mark the direction of rotation of the drive belt if it is to be reused.
4. Turn belt tensioner clockwise until bore is flush on housing.
5. By holding belt tensioner under tension, the load is removed from tensioning pulley.
6. Secure belt tensioner with special tool 11 3 340.

7. Remove drive belt upwards.

8. Check drive belt for correct installation position and, if reusing, observe direction of rotation.

N55 Engine

See Figures 48 and 49.

1. Remove fan cowl with electric fan.

Without Dynamic Drive:

2. Mark the direction of travel of the drive belt if it is to be reused.
3. Turn belt tensioner (1) in direction of arrow until bore hole (2) is aligned with belt tensioner and crankcase.
4. Hold belt tensioner (1) under tension.
5. Secure with special tool 11 0 390.
6. Remove drive belt (3).

With Dynamic Drive:

7. Mark the direction of travel of the drive belt if it is to be reuse.
8. Turn belt tensioner (2) in direction of arrow until bore hole is aligned with belt tensioner and crankcase.
9. Hold belt tensioner (2) under tension.
10. Secure with special tool 11 0 390.
11. Remove drive belt (3).

To install:

To install, reverse the removal procedure noting the following.

12. Check drive belt for correct installation position and, if reusing, observe direction of travel.

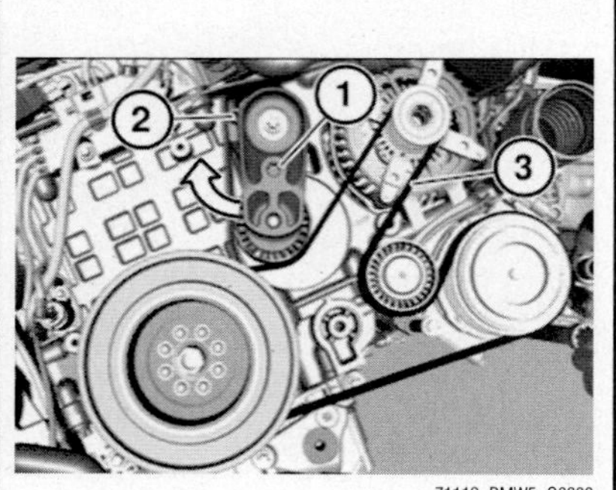

Fig. 48 Turning belt tensioner (1) until bore hole (2) is aligned with belt tensioner and crankcase and removing drive belt (3)

Fig. 49 Turning belt tensioner (1) until bore hole (2) is aligned with belt tensioner and crankcase and removing drive belt (3)

AIR CLEANER

REMOVAL & INSTALLATION

N52 Engine

See Figures 50 through 53.

1. Before servicing the vehicle, refer to the precautions.
2. Remove fasteners from upper housing.
3. Remove upper section of air cleaner housing.
4. Release holder.
5. Release catches.
6. Remove right cover.
7. Remove the left cover in same way as right cover.

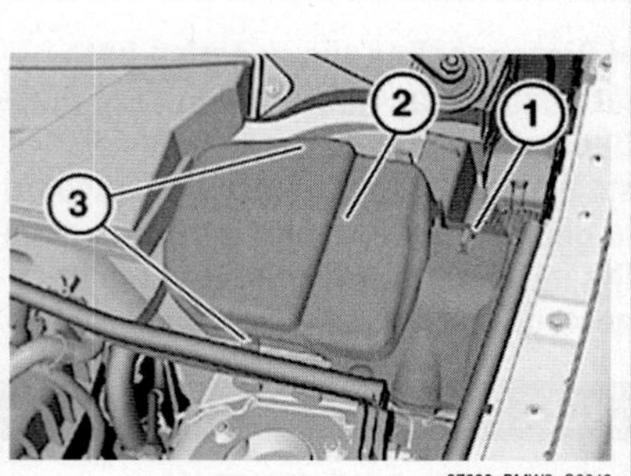

Fig. 50 Lower air cleaner housing right cover (2), holder (1) and catches (3)

8. Release cable holder and remove hose from cover.
9. Press detent lugs.
10. Release cable strip in direction of arrow from lower section of air cleaner housing.
11. Release holder on both sides.
12. Release screw on both sides on lower section of air cleaner housing.
13. Feed out air cleaner housing lower section.

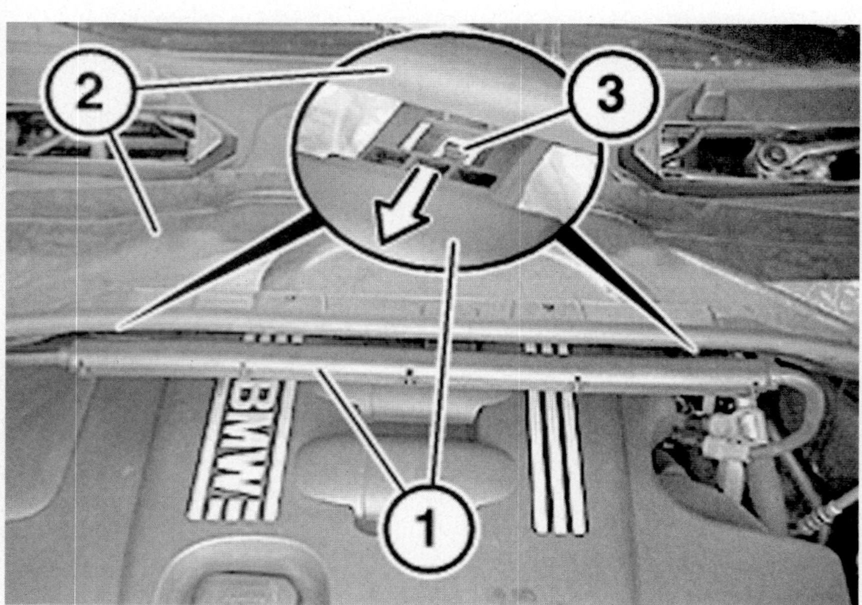

Fig. 51 Press detent lugs (3) and release cable strip (1) from lower section of air cleaner housing (2)

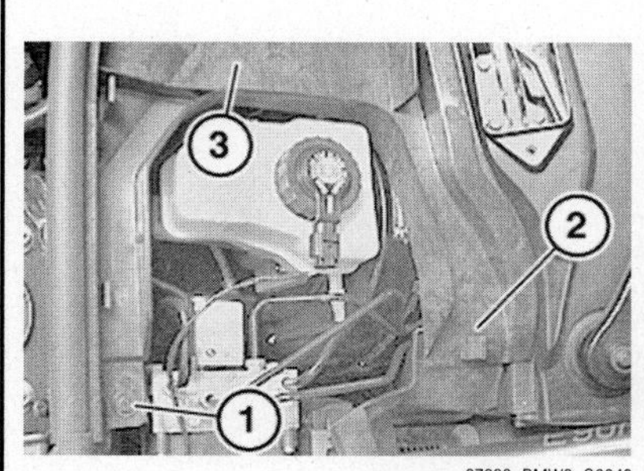

Fig. 52 Release holder (2) and screw (1) on both sides on lower section of air cleaner housing (3).

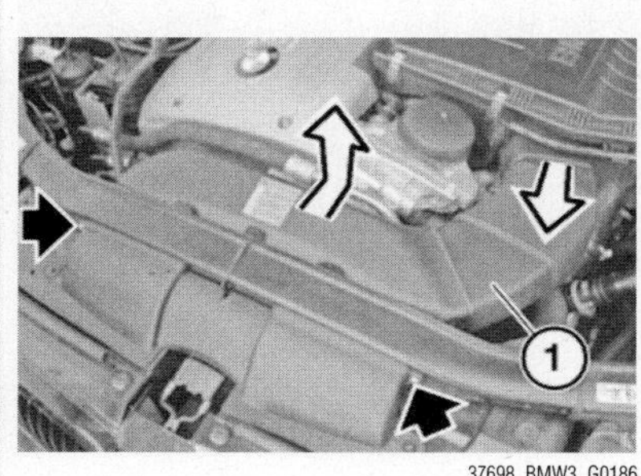

Fig. 53 Unlock intake duct (1) at side and detach from air cleaner housing

14. Unlock intake duct at side and detach from air cleaner housing.
15. Remove intake duct in direction of arrow.

To install:

16. Installation is the reverse of removal.
17. Make sure cable strip is correctly seated.
18. Make sure right cover is correctly seated.
19. Retaining lugs must not be damaged or missing.
20. Make sure cable holder and hose are correctly seated in opening.
21. Make sure air cleaner housing lower section is correctly seated.
22. Seal of air cleaner housing lower section must not be damaged or missing.
23. Make sure upper section of air cleaner housing is correctly seated.

FILTER/ELEMENT REPLACEMENT

N52 Engine

See Figure 54.

1. Remove the upper portion of the air cleaner housing.

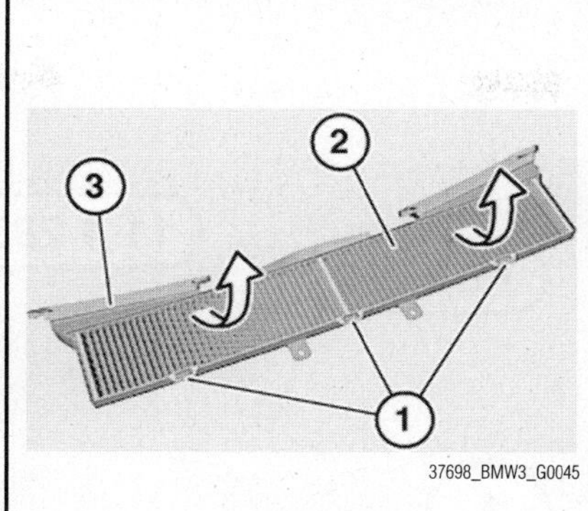

Fig. 54 Air cleaner fasteners

2. Release catches.
3. Release air cleaner in direction of arrow from upper section of housing.

To install:

4. Installation is the reverse of removal.
5. Make sure air cleaner is correctly seated.

N55 Engine

See Figure 55.

1. Release clamp (1).
   a. Tightening torque: 27 inch lbs. (3 Nm).
2. Unfasten screws (2).
   a. Tightening torque: 22 inch lbs. (2.5 Nm).
3. Remove upper section of intake silencer housing.
4. Remove air cleaner element and replace.

➡When installing, clean upper and lower sections of intake silencer housing from inside.

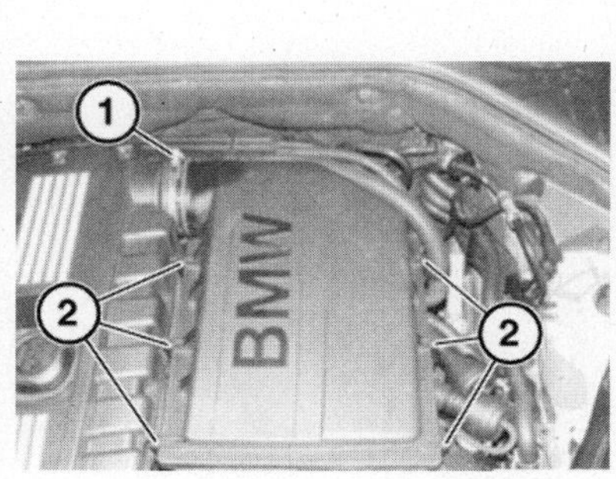

Fig. 55 Releasing clamp (1), unfastening screws (2) and removing upper section of intake silencer housing

To install:

5. To install, reverse the removal procedure.

CAMSHAFT AND VALVE LIFTERS

REMOVAL & INSTALLATION

N52 Engine

See Figures 56 through 84.

⁂ WARNING

Aluminum bolts/bolts must be replaced each time they are removed. The end faces of aluminum bolts/bolts are painted blue for the purposes of reliable identification. Jointing torque and angle of rotation must be observed without fail (risk of damage).

1. Before servicing the vehicle, refer to the precautions.

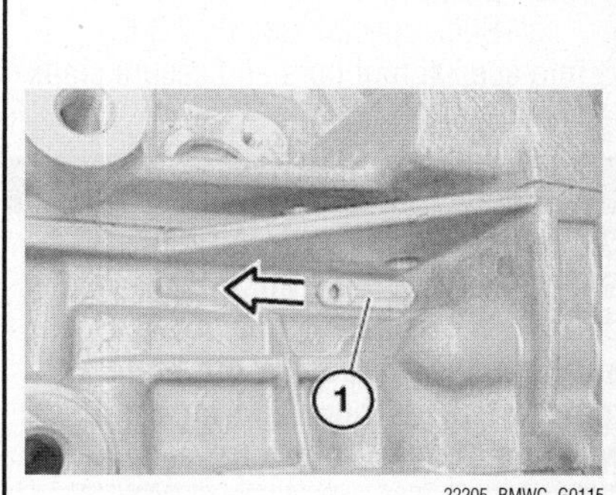

Fig. 56 Remove fastener (1)

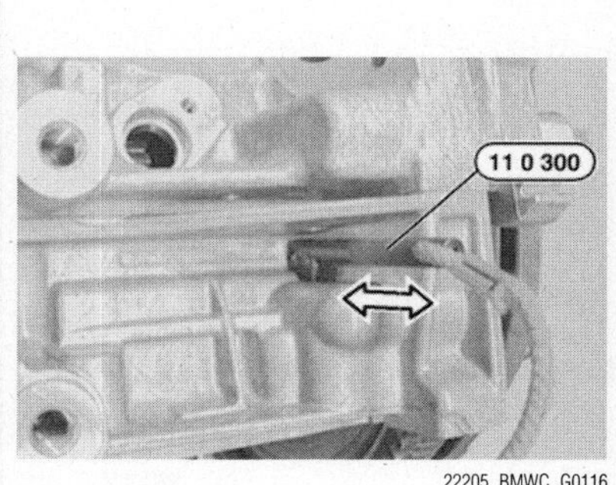

Fig. 57 Slide special tool 11 0 300 into special tool bore and secure crankshaft

Fig. 58 With 1st cylinder in firing TDC position, cams of inlet camshaft (1) at 1st cylinder point upwards at an angle

2. Remove cylinder head cover.
3. Remove the underbody protection.
4. Check the camshaft timing.
   a. Remove fastener.
   b. Rotate crankshaft at central bolt into TDC position.
   c. Slide special tool 11 0 300 into special tool bore and secure crankshaft.

WARNING

On vehicles with optional extra SA205 (automatic transmission), there is a large bore for the TDC position shortly before the special tool bore. This bore can be confused with the special tool bore.

   d. If the flywheel is secured in the correct special tool bore with special tool 11 0 300, the engine can no longer be moved at the central bolt.
   e. With 1st cylinder in firing TDC position, cams of inlet camshaft at 1st cylinder point upwards at an angle.
   f. The timings are correct when the part numbers on the inlet and exhaust camshafts point upwards.
   g. With 1st cylinder in firing TDC position, cams of exhaust camshaft at 6th cylinder point downwards at an angle.
   h. Cam follower (1) is not actuated.

➡When the engine is installed, the position of the exhaust camshaft (3) for the timing can only be checked with a mirror.

   i. Secure special tool 11 4 283 to cylinder head with bolts.

➡Fit special tool 11 4 282 underneath on side of inlet camshaft.

   j. Mount special tool 11 4 281 on inlet and exhaust camshafts.

5. Remove inlet and exhaust adjustment units.

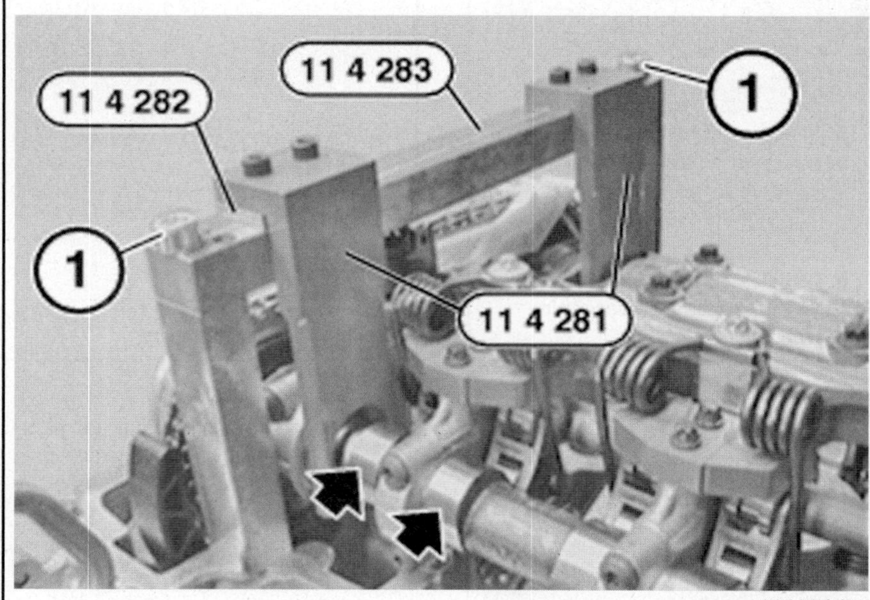

Fig. 60 Secure the special tools to cylinder head with bolts (1)

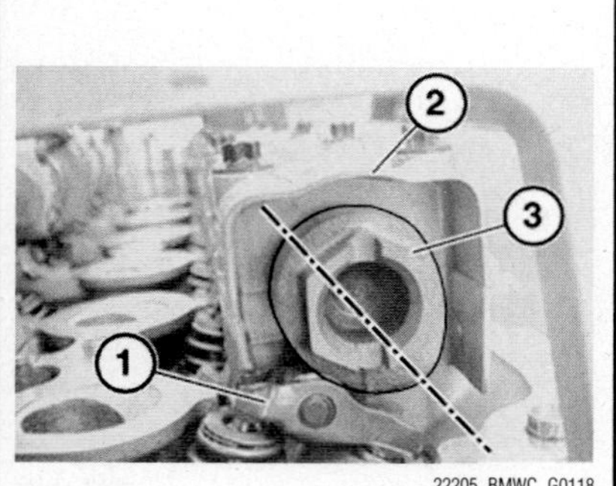

Fig. 59 With 1st cylinder in firing TDC position, cams of exhaust camshaft (3) at 6th cylinder point downwards at an angle

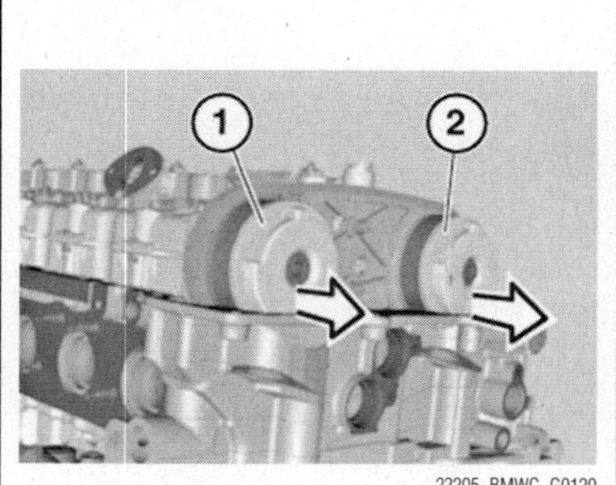

Fig. 61 Adjustment unit (1) from exhaust camshaft and (2) from inlet camshaft

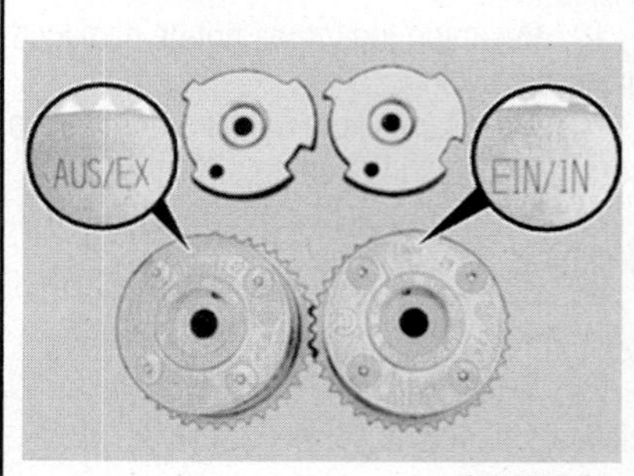

Fig. 62 Inlet and exhaust adjustment units are different. VANOS is marked with AUS/EX for the exhaust camshaft and EIN/IN for the inlet camshaft

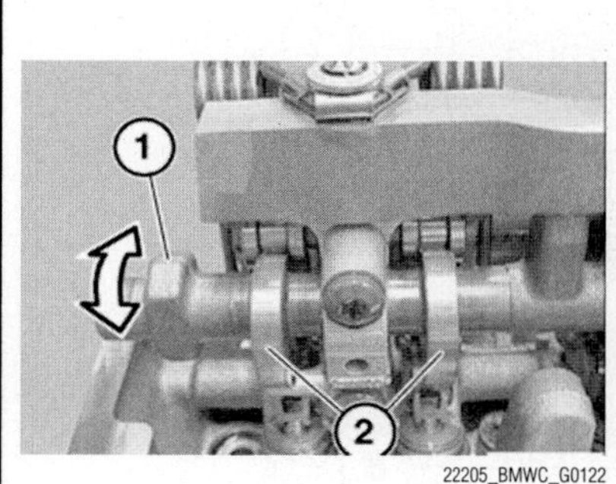

Fig. 63 If necessary, move eccentric shaft (1) on twin surface to minimum lift (2)

a. Remove chain tensioner.

b. Remove central bolts on inlet and exhaust adjustment units.

c. Remove exhaust adjustment unit from exhaust camshaft.

d. Remove inlet adjustment unit from inlet camshaft.

WARNING

Inlet and exhaust adjustment units are different. VANOS is marked with AUS/EX for the exhaust camshaft and EIN/IN for the inlet camshaft.

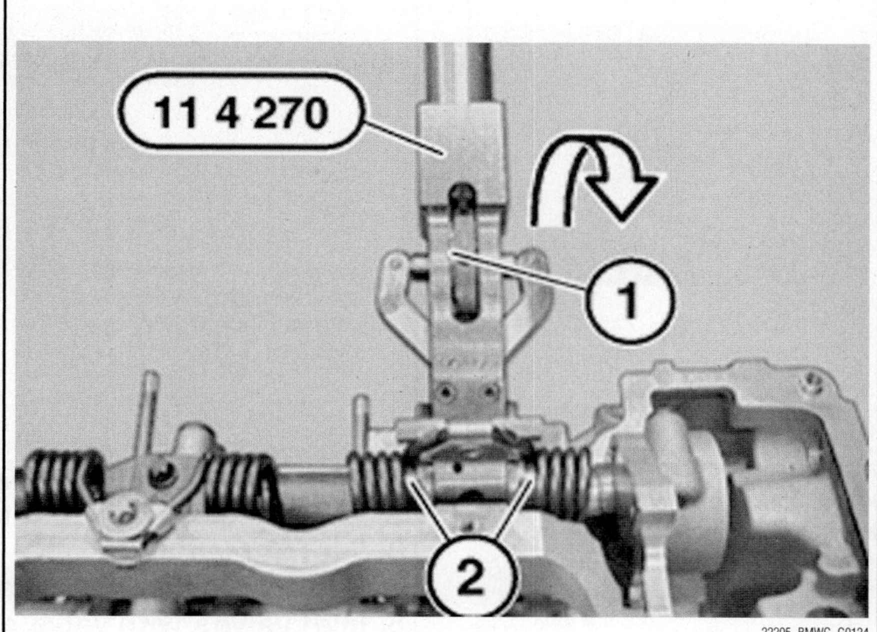

Fig. 65 Secure both bearing pins (2) in torsion springs with knurled screw (1) of special tool 11 4 270. Press special tool 11 4 270 as far as it will go

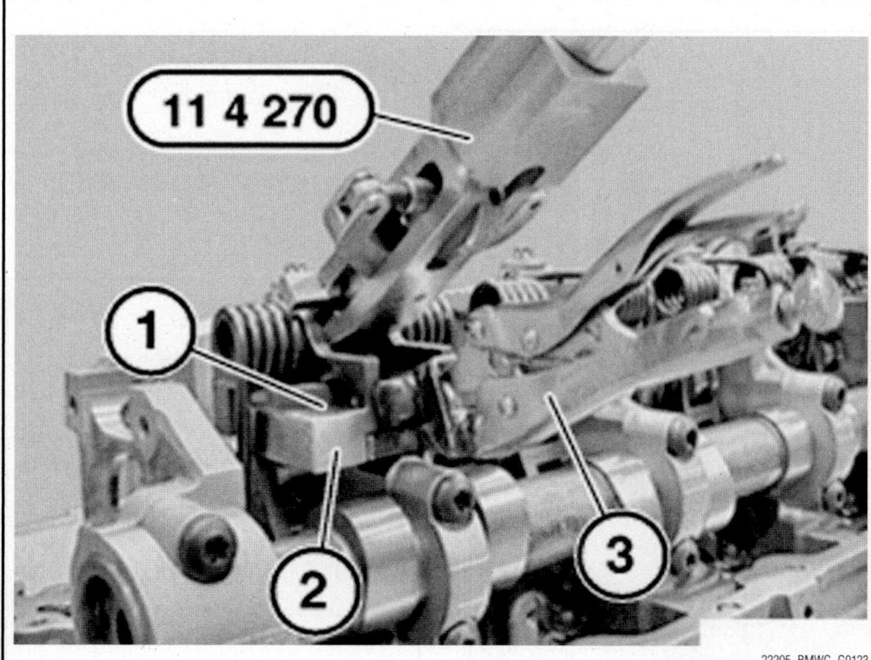

Fig. 64 Secure special tool 11 4 270 (1) with gripping pliers (3) to guide block (2)

e. If necessary, move eccentric shaft on twin surface to minimum lift.

➡Oil spray nozzle must be removed from 3rd cylinder. During removal make a note of installation position of oil spray nozzle.

f. Secure special tool 11 4 270 with gripping pliers to guide block.

WARNING

Special tool 11 4 270 is only secured to guide block (2). Adjusting the gripping pliers (3) on special tool 11 4 270 is not permitted.

g. Secure both bearing pins (2) in torsion springs with knurled screw (1) of special tool 11 4 270. Press special tool 11 4 270 as far as it will go.

h. Remove screw of torsion spring.

➡To avoid jamming of screw with torsion spring, it is necessary when releasing screw to relieve the pretension on special tool 11 4 270 uniformly.

i. Relieve tension on torsion spring with special tool 11 4 270.

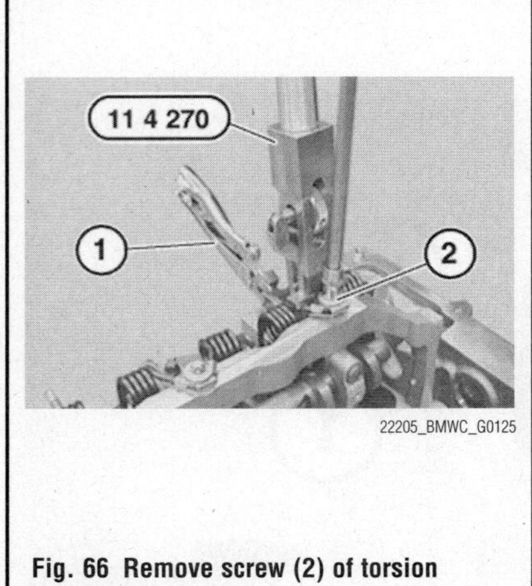

Fig. 66 Remove screw (2) of torsion spring

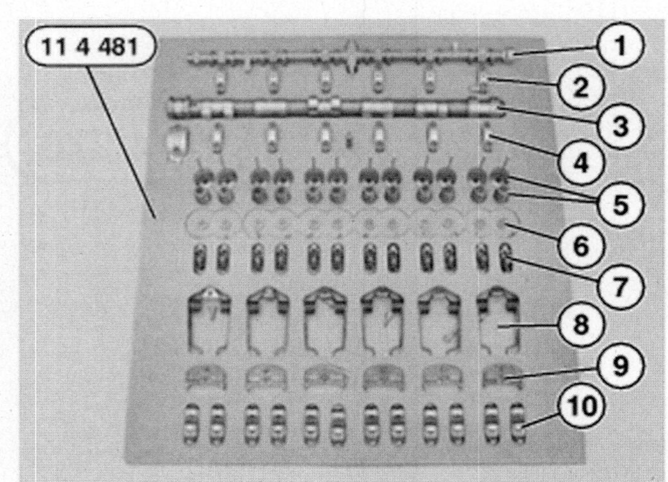

1. Eccentric shaft with bearing
2. Bearing caps of eccentric shaft (set out in order)
3. Inlet camshaft
4. Bearing caps of inlet camshaft (set out in order)
5. Inlet valves with valve springs
6. Valve plates and valve cotters
7. Cam followers with HVCA elements (set out in order)
8. Torsion springs
9. Guide blocks (set out in order)
10. Intermediate levers (set out in order)

22205_BMWC_G0127

Fig. 68 Place all components in clean and neat order in special tool 11 4 481

➡Metal lug cannot be disassembled and must not be removed.

j. Press torsion spring apart at positions. Remove torsion spring towards top.

k. Place all components in clean and neat order in special tool 11 4 481.

⁂ WARNING

All components must be reinstalled in the same positions in an engine which has already been in use.

l. Remove bolts on guide block.

m. Place all guide blocks in neat order in special tool 11 4 481.

n. Lift out intermediate rocker arms (2).

o. Place all intermediate rocker arms in neat order in special tool 11 4 481.

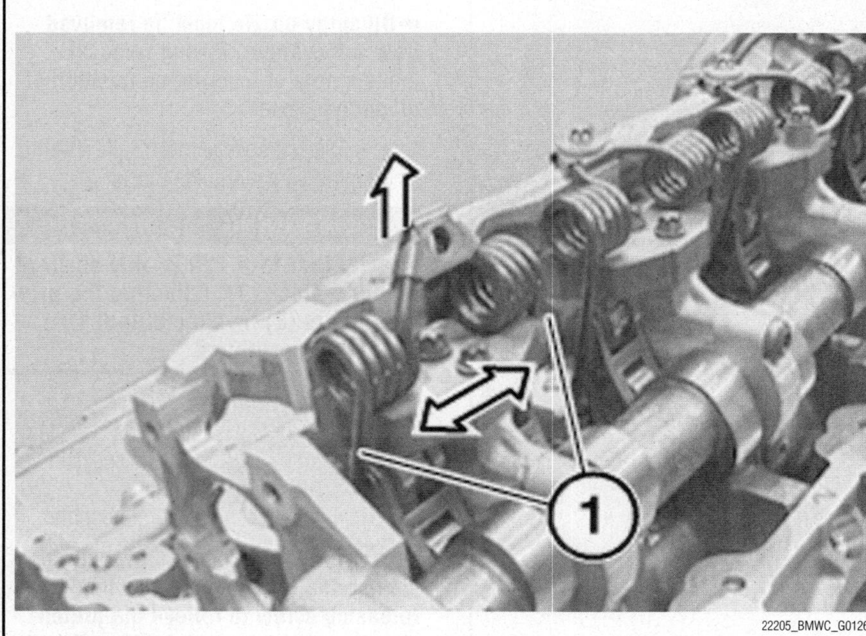

Fig. 67 Press torsion spring apart at positions (1)

Fig. 69 Remove bolts (1) on guide block (2)

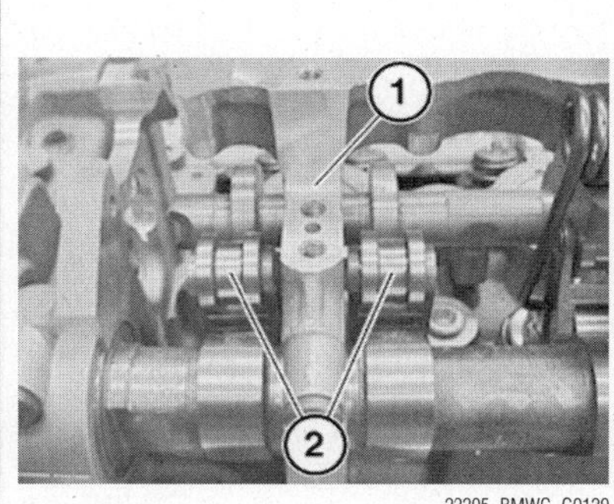

Fig. 70 Lift out intermediate rocker arms (2)

Fig. 71 All intermediate rocker arms are classified and must be reinstalled in the same positions in an engine which has already been in use

✲✲ WARNING

All intermediate rocker arms are classified and must be reinstalled in the same positions in an engine which has already been in use.

6. Remove inlet camshaft.

➡All bearing caps are marked with numbers from 1 to 6. Bearing cap is a thrust bearing.

a. Remove bolts on bearing caps 1 to 6.
b. Set all bearing caps down in special tool 11 4 481 in a tidy and orderly fashion.
c. Remove inlet camshaft towards top.

✲✲ WARNING

Markings of inlet and exhaust camshafts are different. Mixing up the inlet and exhaust camshaft will result in engine damage.

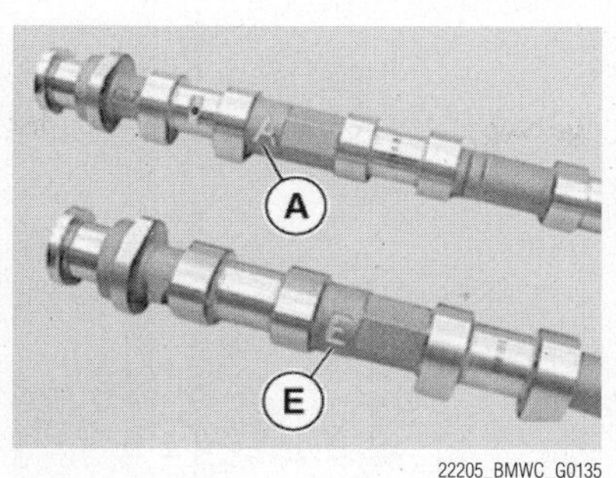

Fig. 72 Markings of inlet and exhaust camshafts are different. Mixing up the inlet (E) and exhaust (A) camshaft will result in engine damage

Fig. 73 Check plain compression rings (1) for damage and replace if necessary

7. Remove exhaust camshaft.
a. The screw connection of the bearing banks must be removed from the outside inwards.
b. Lift out upper and lower bearing banks with exhaust camshaft.
c. Remove upper bearing bank.
d. Remove exhaust camshaft from lower bearing bank.

To install:

8. Check plain compression rings for damage and replace if necessary.
a. Plain compression rings are engaged at joint.
b. Press plain compression rings apart upwards and downwards and removed towards front.

✲✲ WARNING

Plain compression rings can easily break.

9. Install exhaust camshaft.
a. Mounting bearing bank. Pre-install special tool 11 4 462 on cylinder No. 2.
b. Insert special tool 11 4 463 in screw connection of cylinder head cover.

➡Special tool 11 4 463 is a special screw.

c. Press down cam followers on cylinder no. 2 with spindle nut of special tool 11 4 462.
d. Before mounting the exhaust camshaft on the correct cam follower seat, pay attention to the hydraulic valve clearance adjustment element and the valve.

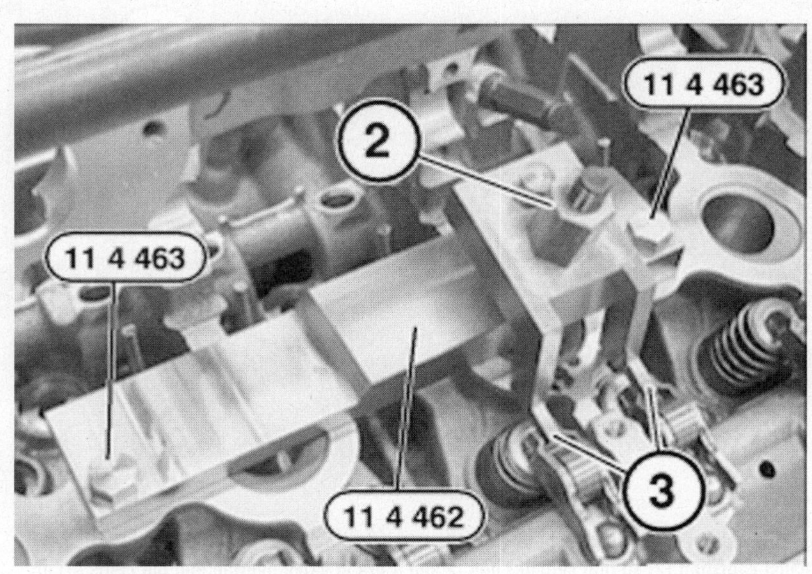

Fig. 74 Press down cam followers (3) on cylinder no. 2 with spindle nut (2) of special tool 11 4 462

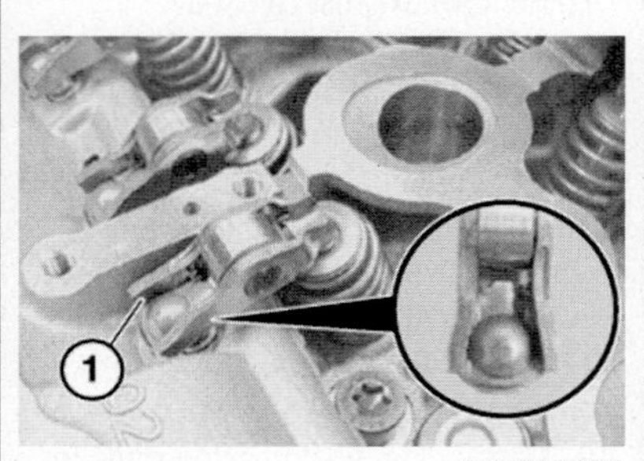

Fig. 75 Before mounting the exhaust camshaft on the correct cam follower seat (1), pay attention to the hydraulic valve clearance adjustment element and the valve

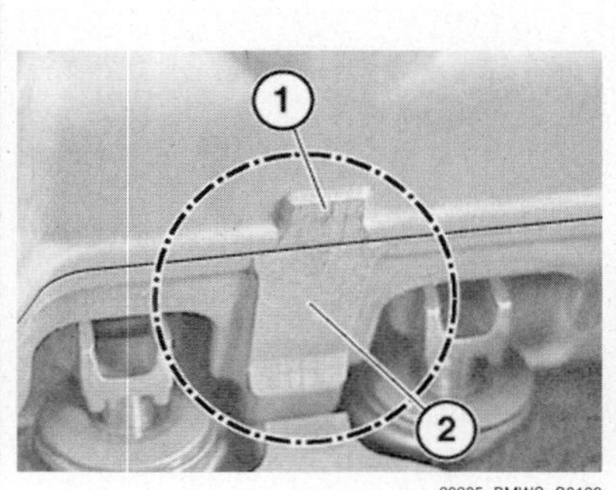

Fig. 77 Upper and lower bearing banks must be aligned to each other at ground surfaces (1) and (2)

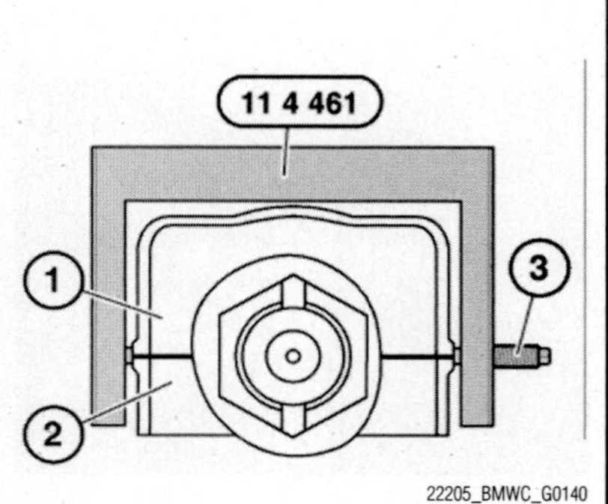

Fig. 78 Schematic depiction of special tool 11 4 461 at upper bearing bank (1) and lower bearing bank (2)

e. Position lower bearing bank with exhaust camshaft cam followers.

f. Align exhaust camshaft so that cylinder nos. 2 and 4 are at valve overlap and the cams on cylinder No. 1 point upwards at an angle. Part number on twin surface of exhaust camshaft points upwards.

WARNING

There must be no adhesive residues in the cylinder head tapped holes.

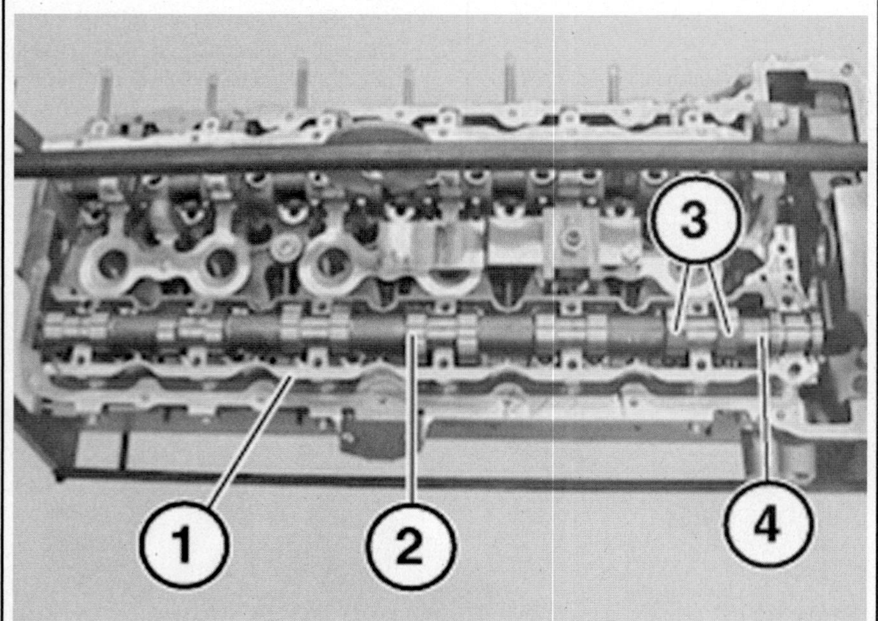

Fig. 76 Position lower bearing bank (1) with exhaust camshaft (2) cam followers. Align exhaust camshaft (2) so that cylinder nos. 2 and 4 are at valve overlap and the cams (3) on cylinder no. 1 point upwards at an angle. Part number (4) on twin surface of exhaust camshaft (2) points upwards

g. Clean tapped holes.

h. Fit upper bearing bank. Insert bolts dry and tension down upper bearing bank with exhaust camshaft at bearing points 3 and 5 through a ½ bolt turn.

i. Join exhaust camshaft to upper and lower bearing banks with torque wrench from inside outwards to 6 ft. lbs. (8 Nm).

j. Remove all bolts of upper bearing bank from outside inwards by 90°.

k. Upper and lower bearing banks must be aligned to each other at ground surfaces (1 and 2). Make sure that the thrust piece and the legs of special tools 11 4 461 rest on the milled surfaces.

➡Schematic depiction of special tool 11 4 461 at upper bearing bank and lower bearing bank.

Pretension all special tools 11 4 461 with special tool 11 4 350 only.

l. Tighten screw on thrust piece to 13 inch lbs. (2 Nm).

m. Position special tool 11 4 461 over screw connection of bearing banks.

n. Make sure that the legs rest exactly on the ground surfaces of the upper bearing bank and lower bearing bank.

o. Initially tighten screw of special tool 11 4 461 to ground surfaces of upper bearing bank and lower bearing bank.

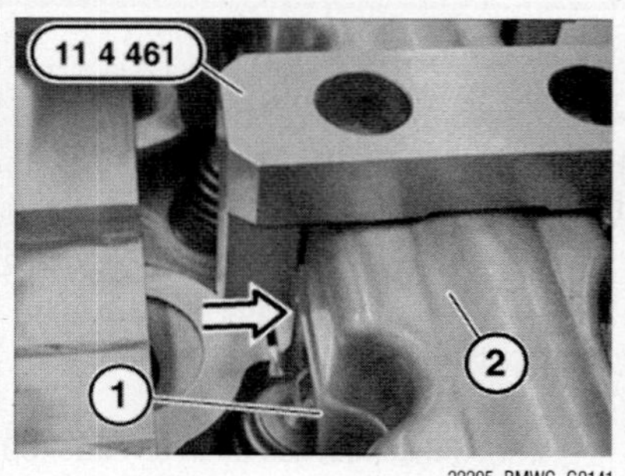

Fig. 79 Position special tool 11 4 461 over screw connection of bearing banks. Make sure that the legs rest exactly on the ground surfaces of the upper bearing bank (2) and lower bearing bank (1)

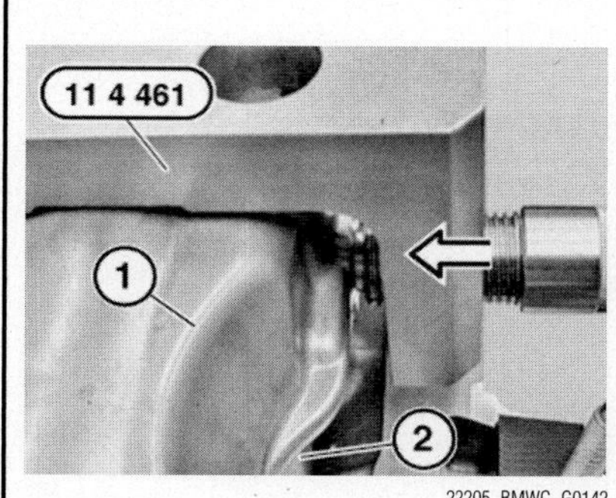

22205_BMWC_G0142

Fig. 80 Initially tighten screw of special tool 11 4 461 to ground surfaces of upper bearing bank (1) and lower bearing bank (2)

p. Tighten bolts on thrust piece to 13 inch lbs. (2 Nm).

WARNING

Set special tool 11 4 350 to 13 inch lbs. (2 Nm).

q. Pretension all special tools 11 4 461 with special tool 11 4 350 only.

r. Mount special tools 11 4 461 with screw to inside of cylinder head.

s. Mount special tool 11 4 461 with screw facing outwards on cylinder No. 2.

t. Position special tools 11 4 461 so that screw connections of bearing bank are easily accessible.

u. Insert bolts dry. Tighten upper and lower bearing banks bolts from inside outwards with special tool 00 9 120 to 6 ft. lbs. (8Nm) plus an additional 60° of rotation.

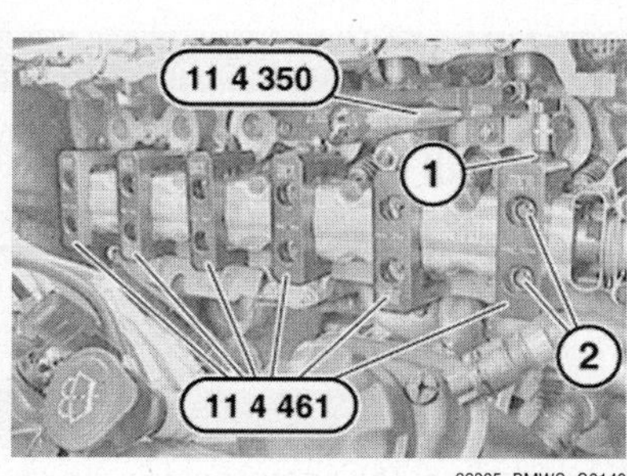

22205_BMWC_G0143

Fig. 81 Mount special tools 11 4 461 with screw (1) to inside of cylinder head. Position special tools 11 4 461 so that screw connections (2) of bearing bank are easily accessible

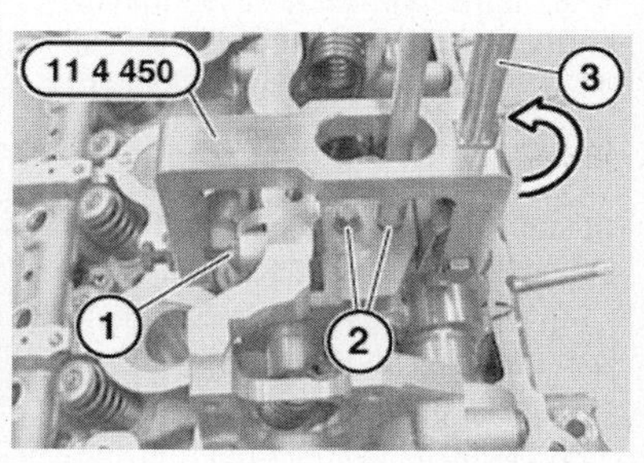

22205_BMWC_G0131

Fig. 82 Secure special tool 11 4 450 to bolt connection (1) of eccentric shaft. Turn eccentric pry (3) on special tool 11 4 450. Guide block is now pre-tensioned. Insert bolts (2) of guide blocks

WARNING

Remove special tool 11 4 461 only when exhaust camshaft screw connection is completed.

10. Install inlet camshaft.

a. Clean all bearing points and lubricate with oil.

b. Insert inlet camshaft so that part number on twin surface points upwards.

c. Position inlet camshaft so that cams point upwards at an angle.

d. Connect special tool 11 4 281 to twin surface.

e. Tighten bearing bolts to 7 ft. lbs. (9 Nm).

11. Install intermediate rocker arms.

a. Mixing up the guide blocks will cause the engine to suffer idle-speed fluctuations. This will result in maladjustment of uniform distribution.

b. All contact surfaces of guide block must be clean and free from oil and grease. If necessary, clean contact surfaces.

c. Mixing up the intermediate rocker arms will cause the engine to suffer idle-speed fluctuations.

d. All contact surfaces must be clean and free from oil and grease. If necessary, clean contact surfaces.

e. All intermediate rocker arms are classified and must be reinstalled in the same positions in an engine which has already been in use.

f. Before installing intermediate rocker arms, make sure cam followers are correctly positioned.

g. Install intermediate rocker arms.

h. Fit guide block cleanly into opening. Tighten bolts hand-tight.

i. Check that intermediate rocker arms are in correct installation position.

j. Remove bolts by a ¼ turn.

k. Secure special tool 11 4 450 to bolt connection of eccentric shaft.

l. Turn eccentric pry on special tool 11 4 450.

m. Guide block is now pre-tensioned. Insert bolts of guide blocks and tighten to 7 ft. lbs. (10 Nm).

n. At cylinder No. 3, the guide block can be pre-installed with one screw (internal) only.

o. Oil spray nozzle is fitted only after torsion spring has been installed.

p. Install torsion spring on guide block.

q. Insert torsion spring in intermediate pry.

r. Check that cam follower is in correct installation position.

s. Secure special tool 11 4 270 with gripping pliers to guide block.

➡Replace torsion spring if metal lug is faulty.

t. Secure both bearing pins in torsion springs with knurled screw of special tool 11 4 270.

u. Check torsion spring on intermediate pry to ensure correct installation position.

v. Press special tool 11 4 270 as far as it will go.

w. Insert screw of torsion spring and tighten to 7 ft. lbs. (10 Nm).

x. To avoid jamming of screw with torsion spring, it is necessary when inserting screw to increase pretension on special tool 11 4 270 uniformly.

y. Remove special tool 11 4 270.

z. At cylinder No. 3, adjust oil spray nozzle so that oil spray points precisely towards spline teeth.

22205_BMWC_G0132

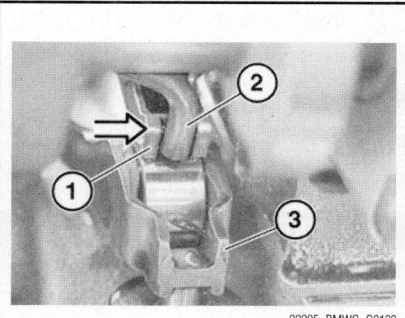

Fig. 83 Insert torsion spring (2) in intermediate pry (1) (arrow) and check that cam follower (3) is in correct installation position

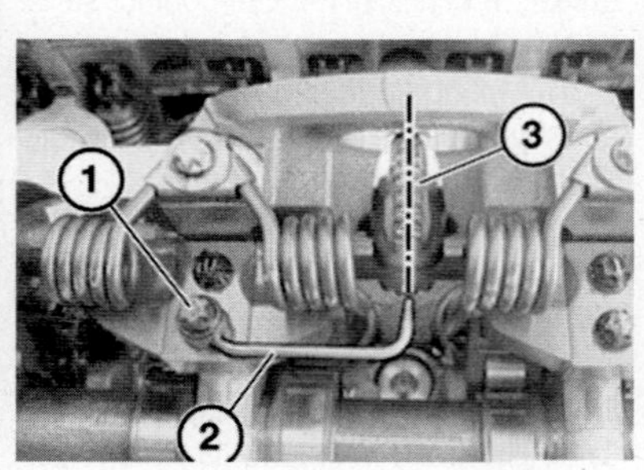

Fig. 84 At cylinder No. 3, adjust oil spray nozzle (2) so that oil spray points precisely towards spline teeth (3). Insert screw (1) with oil spray nozzle (2) (external)

aa. Insert screw with oil spray nozzle (external) and tighten to 7 ft. lbs. (10 Nm).

12. Install inlet and exhaust adjustment units.

a. To facilitate installation of the inlet and exhaust adjustment units, turn the sensor gears at the opening downwards.

WARNING

Do not mixing up the inlet and exhaust adjustment units. VANOS is marked with AUS/EX for the exhaust camshaft and EIN/IN for the inlet camshaft. Sensor gears can be fitted alternatively.

b. Position inlet and exhaust adjustment units on camshafts.

c. Insert new central bolts but do not tighten until after valve timing is checked. Grip inlet and exhaust camshafts at dihedron when tightening. Tighten bolts to 15 ft. lbs. (20 Nm) plus an additional 180° rotation.

13. Check valve timing.

a. Install special tool 11 4 280 to secure the central bolts on the inlet and exhaust adjustment units and camshafts.

b. Press clamping rail by hand against guide rail and make sure timing chain is guided in clamping rail.

c. Rotate crankshaft at central bolt into TDC position.

d. Slide special tool 11 0 300 into special tool bore and secure crankshaft.

WARNING

On vehicles with optional extra SA205 (automatic transmission), there is a large bore for the TDC position shortly before the special tool bore. This bore can be confused with the special tool bore.

e. If the flywheel is secured in the correct special tool bore with special tool 11 0 300, the engine can no longer be moved at the central bolt.

f. With 1st cylinder in firing TDC position, cams of inlet camshaft at 1st cylinder point upwards at an angle.

g. The timings are correct when the part numbers on the inlet and exhaust camshafts point upwards.

h. With 1st cylinder in firing TDC position, cams of exhaust camshaft at 6th cylinder point downwards at an angle.

i. Cam follower is not actuated.

➡When the engine is installed, the position of the exhaust camshaft for the timing can only be checked with a mirror.

j. Secure special tool 11 4 283 to cylinder head with bolts.

➡Fit special tool 11 4 282 underneath on side of inlet camshaft.

k. Mount special tool 11 4 281 on inlet and exhaust camshafts.

l. Make sure the chain tensioner is removed.

m. Turn sensor gears (2) until locating pins (1) on special tool 11 4 290 match up.

n. Slide on special tool 11 4 290.

o. Secure special tool 11 4 290 with bolts (1).

p. Screw special tool 11 9 340 into cylinder head.

q. Pretension timing chain with special tool 00 9 250 to 0.6 Nm.

r. Secure both central bolts of inlet and exhaust adjustment units with special tool 00 9 120 to inlet and exhaust camshafts. Tighten bolts to 15 ft. lbs. (20 Nm) plus an additional 180° rotation.

14. Install the chain tensioner.

15. Install fastener with bore facing outwards.

N55 Engine

Exhaust Camshafts

See Figures 85 through 96.

WARNING

It is absolutely essential to follow an exact procedure for removing and installing the exhaust camshaft.

WARNING

The upper and lower bearing strips must be preloaded with a total of six special tools 11 8 550.

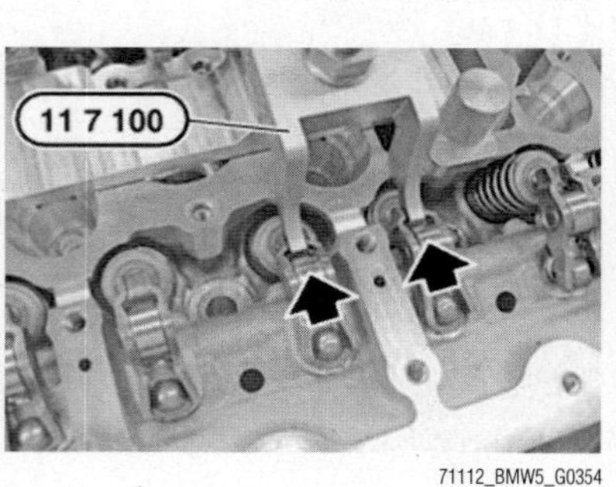

Fig. 85 Screwing in roller cam follower at 2nd cylinder using special tool

1. Remove cylinder head cover.
2. Remove all ignition coils and injector shafts.
3. Remove exhaust camshaft adjuster.
4. Adjust valve timing.
5. Position special tool 11 7 100 on cylinder 2.
6. Hand-tighten special tool 11 7 100 with special tool 11 8 552.
7. Screw in roller cam follower at 2nd cylinder using spindle nut of special tool 11 7 100 to end stop.
8. Release screw connection on bearing strip in sequence from 15 to 1.
9. Remove upper bearing strip (1).

➡The upper and lower bearing strips (1) can also be lifted out completely with exhaust camshaft.

10. Remove exhaust camshaft (1) from bearing strip in direction of arrow.
11. Set down exhaust camshaft (1) on special tool.

➡Marks of intake and exhaust camshafts are different.

WARNING

Mixing up the intake and exhaust camshaft will result in engine damage.

a. A = Exhaust camshaft.

b. E = Intake camshaft

WARNING

Plain rectangular compression rings (1) can easily break.

12. Plain rectangular compression rings (1) are engaged at joint.
13. Press plain rectangular compression rings (1) apart upwards and downwards and removed towards front.

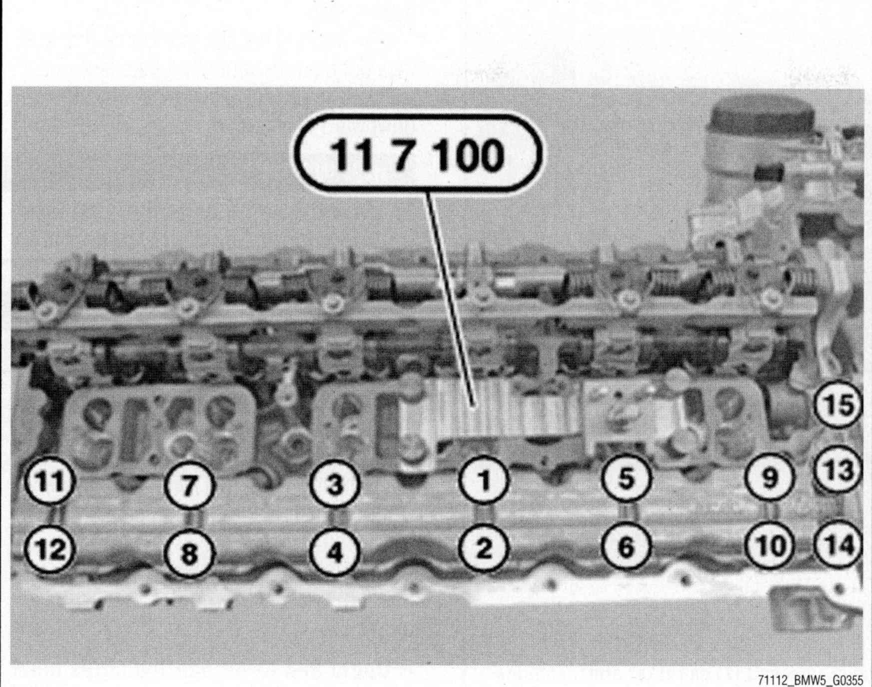

Fig. 86 Releasing screw connection on bearing strip in sequence from 15-1 and removing upper bearing strip (1)

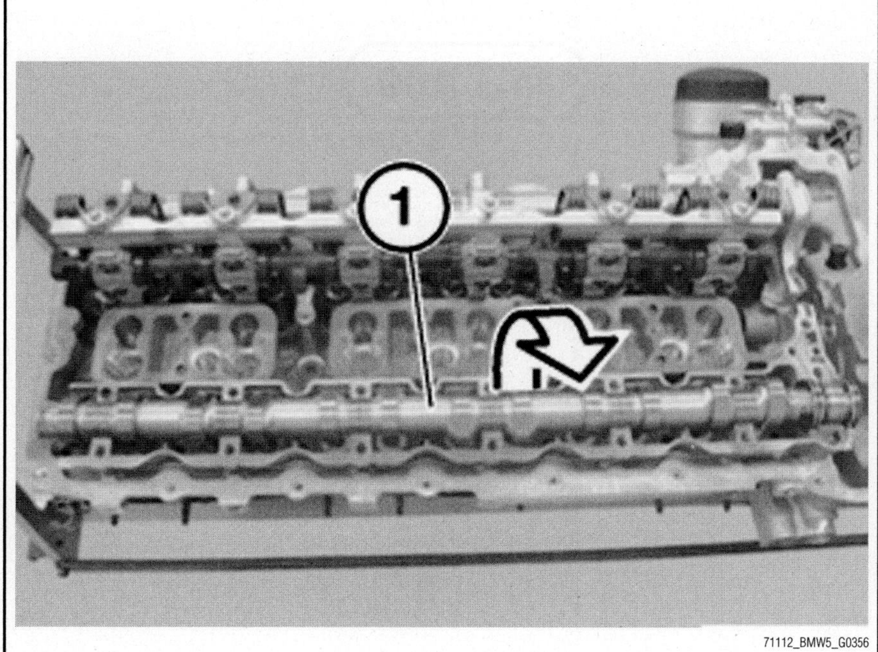

Fig. 87 Removing exhaust camshaft (1)

➡When installing, modify plain rectangular compression ring on new exhaust camshaft.

To install:

⁂ WARNING

Removal on engine: Set engine to ignition TDC at cylinder No. 1.

⁂ WARNING

Removed cylinder head: When using special tool 11 9 000, it will be necessary to remove the aluminum strip.

➡Before mounting the exhaust camshaft, make sure that the rocker arm (1) is well fitted and pay attention to the hydraulic valve clearance adjustment element and the valve.

14. Pre-install special tool 11 7 100 on cylinder no. 2.

➡Special tool 11 8 552 is a special screw.

15. Press down rocker arms on cylinder no. 2 with spindle nut of special tool 11 7 100 .
16. Position lower bearing strip (1) with exhaust camshaft (2) on rocker arms.
17. Align exhaust camshaft (2).
18. Cylinder nos. 2 and 4 are at valve overlap.
19. Cams (3) on cylinder no. 1 point upwards at an angle.
20. Part number (4) on mounting flats of exhaust camshaft (2) points upwards.
21. Insert exhaust camshaft so that none of the latching mechanisms for the plain rectangular compression rings (1) point to a bearing cap joint.
22. Centre latch mechanism of the plain

Fig. 88 Pressing plain rectangular compression rings (1) apart

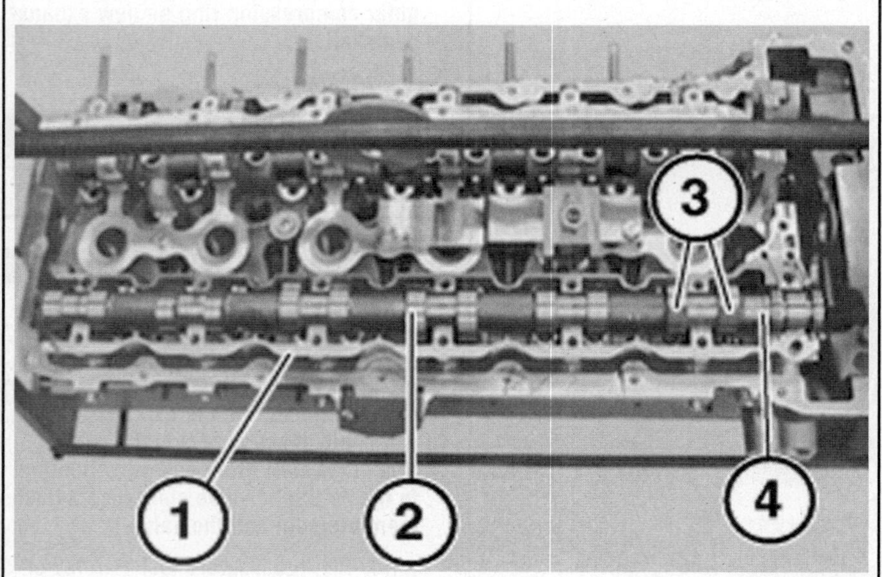

Fig. 89 Positioning lower bearing strip (1) with exhaust camshaft (2) on rocker arms, pointing cams (3) on cylinder No.1 upwards at an angle and part number (4) on mounting flats of exhaust camshaft (2) pointing upwards

rectangular compression rings with the bearing cap.

23. Insert exhaust camshaft so that the data code on the mounting flats faces up.

24. The cam (1) at cylinder 6 points downward at an angle.

⁂ WARNING

There must be no adhesive residues in the cylinder head threaded holes.

⁂ WARNING

Clean threaded holes.

25. Fit upper bearing strip (1).

26. Insert bolts dry.

27. Join exhaust camshaft to lower and upper bearing strips (1) with torque wrench (2) to 71 inch lbs. (8 Nm) in sequential order from 1 to 15.

28. Release all screws of upper bearing strip (1) from outside inwards by 90°.

➡Upper and lower bearing strips must be aligned to each other at ground surfaces (1 and 2).

Fig. 90 Inserting exhaust camshaft so that none of the latching mechanisms for the plain rectangular compression rings (1) point at bearing cap joint

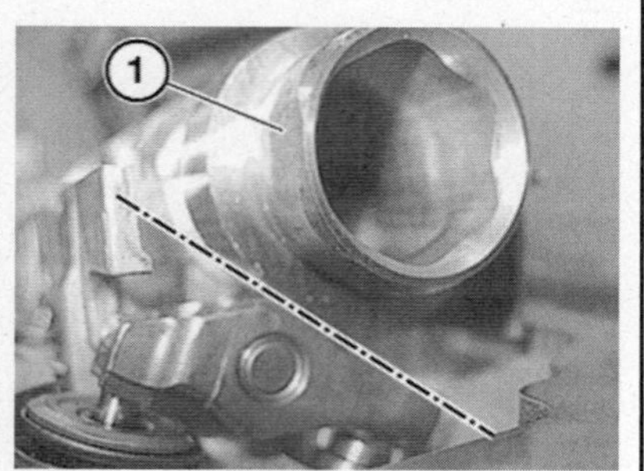

Fig. 91 Identifying cam (1) at cylinder 6 pointing downward at an angle

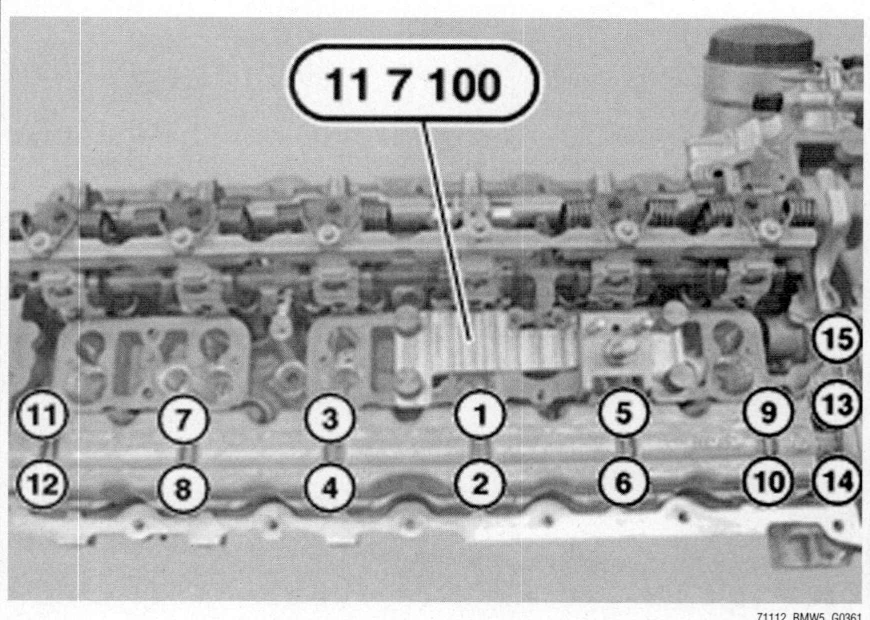

Fig. 92 Fitting upper bearing strip (1) with torque wrench (2)

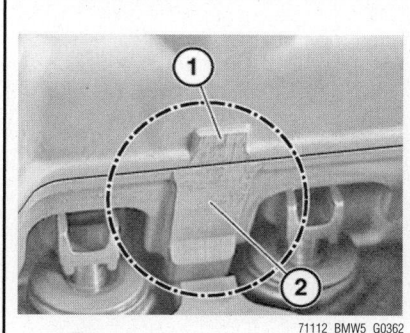

71112_BMW5_G0362

Fig. 93 Making sure the synchronizing key and shanks of special tools rest on milled surfaces

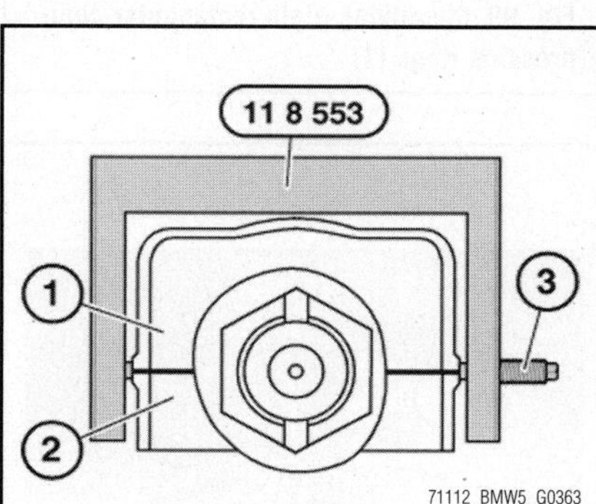

Fig. 94 Installing special tools on upper bearing strip (1) and lower bearing strip (2) and tightening screw (3)

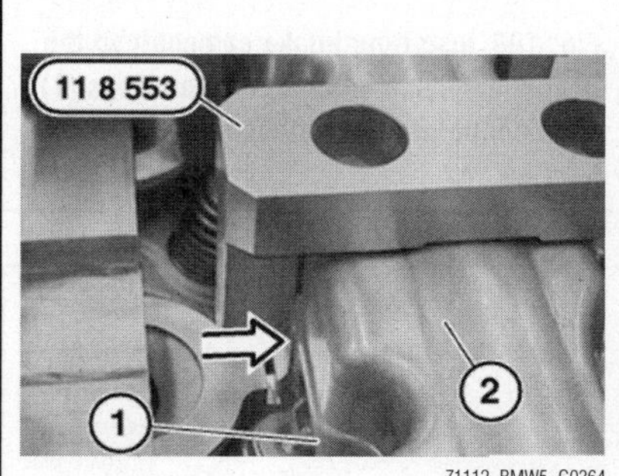

Fig. 95 Making sure the shanks rest exactly on ground surfaces of upper bearing strip (2) and lower bearing strip (1)

29. Make sure that the synchronizing key and the shanks of special tools 11 4 461 rest on the milled surfaces.

➡**Schematic diagram of special tool 11 8 553 at upper bearing strip (1) and lower bearing strip (2).**

Preload all special tools 11 8 553with special tool 11 4 350 only.

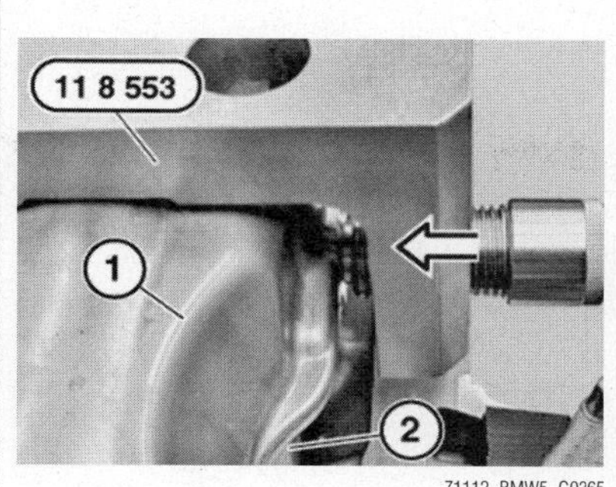

Fig. 96 Tightening screw of special tool to ground surfaces of upper bearing strip (1) and lower bearing strip (2)

⁂ WARNING

Tighten screw (3) on synchronizing key to 18 ft. lbs. (2 Nm.).

30. Position special tool 11 8 553 over screw connection of bearing strips.
31. Make sure that the shanks rest exactly on the ground surfaces of the upper bearing strip (2) and lower bearing strip (1).
32. Initially tighten screw of special tool 11 8 553 to ground surfaces of upper bearing strip (1) and lower bearing strip (2).

⁂ WARNING

Tighten screws on synchronizing key to 18 inch lbs. (2 Nm).

33. Set special tool 11 8 553 to 18 inch lbs. (2 Nm).
34. Preload all special tools 11 8 553with special tool 11 4 350 only.
35. Mount special tools 11 8 553 to inside of cylinder head with pressure bolt.
36. Mount special tool 11 8 553 on cylinder no. 2 with pressure bolt facing outward.
37. Position special tools 11 8 553 so that screw connections of bearing strip are easily accessible.
38. Tighten top and bottom bearing strip with special tool 00 9 120.
    a. Tightening torque: 71 ft. lbs. (8 Nm) + 60°.

⁂ WARNING

Remove special tool 11 8 553 only when exhaust camshaft screw connection is completed.

39. To complete installation, reverse remaining removal procedure.

Intake Camshafts

See Figures 97 through 102.

1. Remove cylinder head cover.
2. Remove intake adjuster.
3. Remove intermediate lever.
4. Adjust valve timing.

➡**All bearing caps are identified with numbers from 1 to 6.**

5. The front bearing cap is a thrust bearing and does not have an identification.
6. Release screws on thrust bearing cover.
7. Release screws on all bearing caps 1 to 6.
8. Set all bearing caps down in special tool 11 4 481 in a neat and orderly fashion.
9. Remove intake camshaft (2) towards top.

➡**When installing, clean all bearing positions and lubricate with oil.**

10. Check plain rectangular compression rings (1) for damage.

⁂ WARNING

Plain rectangular compression rings (1) can easily break.

11. Plain rectangular compression rings (1) are engaged at joint.
12. Press plain rectangular compression rings (1) apart upwards and downwards and removed towards front.

➡**Install plain rectangular compression ring on new intake camshaft.**

⁂ WARNING

Marks of intake and exhaust camshafts are different.

⁂ WARNING

Mixing up the intake and exhaust camshaft will result in engine damage.

    a. A= Exhaust camshaft.
    b. E= Intake camshaft

To install:

13. Install intake camshaft so that the latch mechanism of the plain rectangular compression rings (1) does not point to a contact point of the bearing cap
14. Centre latch mechanism of the plain rectangular compression rings with the bearing cap.
15. Insert intake camshaft so that data code (1) on mounting flats points upwards.
16. Position intake camshaft (1) so that cams point upwards at an angle and to the left.

➡**All bearing caps are identified with numbers from 1 to 6.**

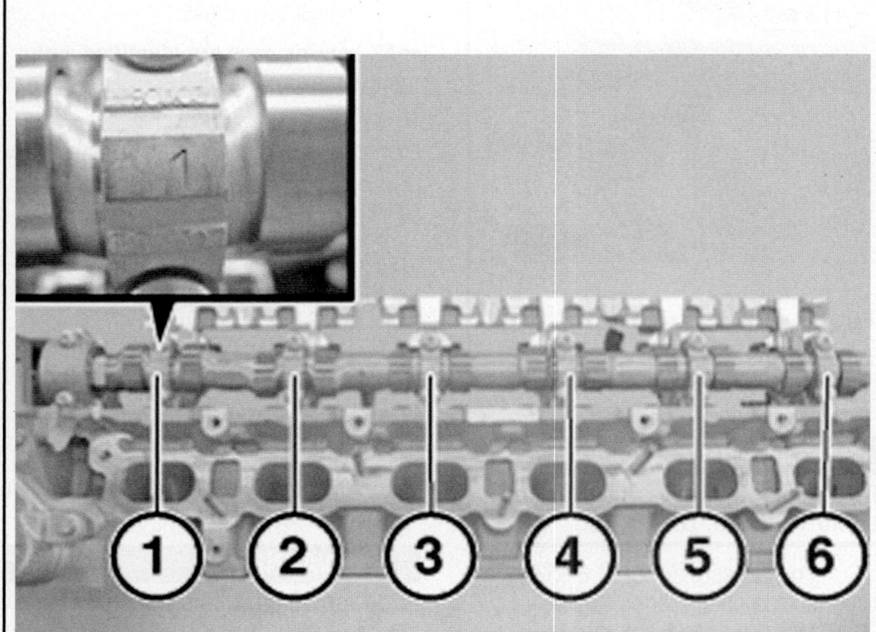

Fig. 97 Releasing screws on all bearing caps 1 to 6

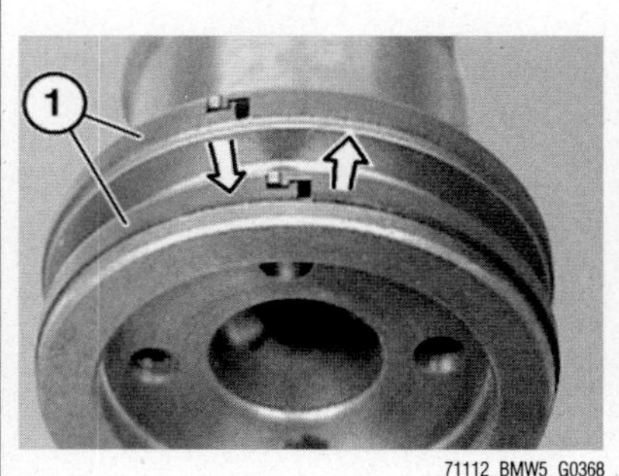

Fig. 99 Identifying plain rectangular compression rings (1)

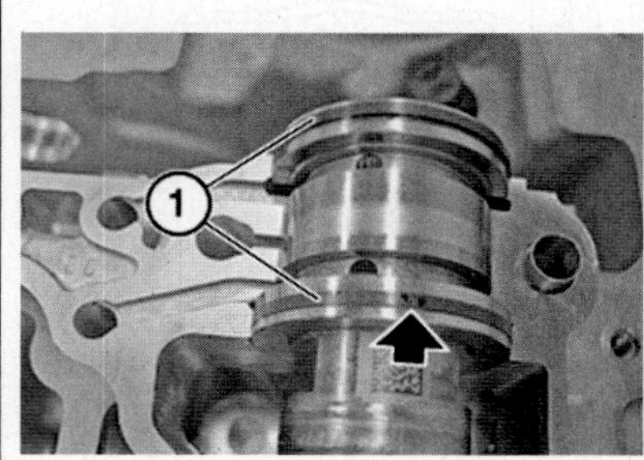

Fig. 100 Installing intake camshaft so the latch mechanism of compression rings (1) does not point to a contact point of bearing cap

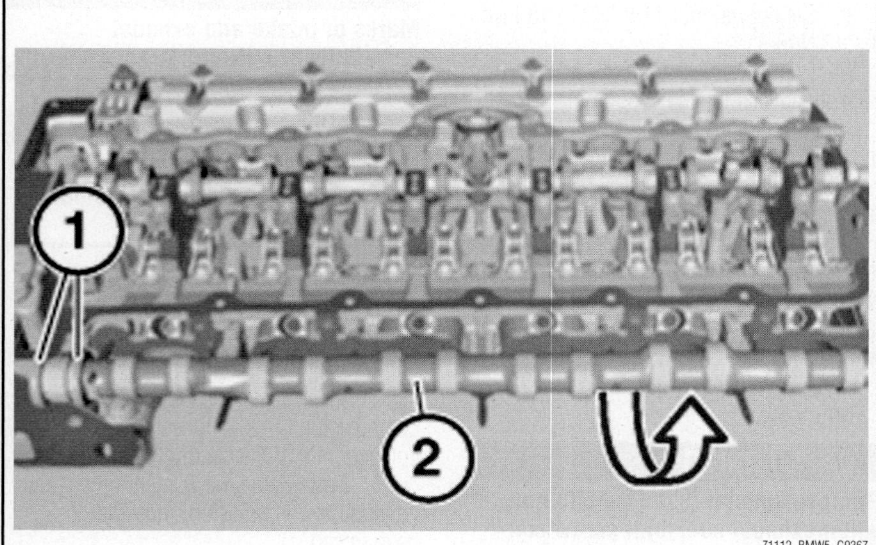

Fig. 98 Removing intake camshaft (2) and checking plain rectangular compression rings (1) for damage

Fig. 101 Inserting intake camshaft so that data code (1) on mounting flats points upwards

71112_BMW5_G0371

Fig. 102 Positioning intake camshaft (1) so that cams point upwards at an angle and to the left

17. The front bearing cap is a thrust bearing and does not have an identification.
18. Insert screws on all bearing caps 1 to 6.
19. Insert screws on thrust bearing cover.
    a. Tightening torque: 75 inch lbs. (8.5 Nm).
20. To complete installation, reverse remaining removal procedures.

CATALYTIC CONVERTER

REMOVAL & INSTALLATION

N52 Engine

On the N52 engine the primary catalytic converters are an integral part of the exhaust manifolds. Refer to engine mechanical, exhaust manifold, removal & installation.

N55 Engine

See Figures 103 and 104.

CAUTION

Only perform this repair work after the exhaust system has cooled down.

1. Remove front underbody protection.
2. Remove rear underbody protection.
3. Remove exhaust system.

➡The oxygen sensors are in danger of being damaged when the catalytic converters are removed and installed.

4. Remove control sensor, cylinders 1 to 3.
5. Remove monitoring sensor from cylinders 1 to 3.
6. Release nuts (1) and (2).
    a. Tightening torque: 14 ft. lbs. (19 Nm).

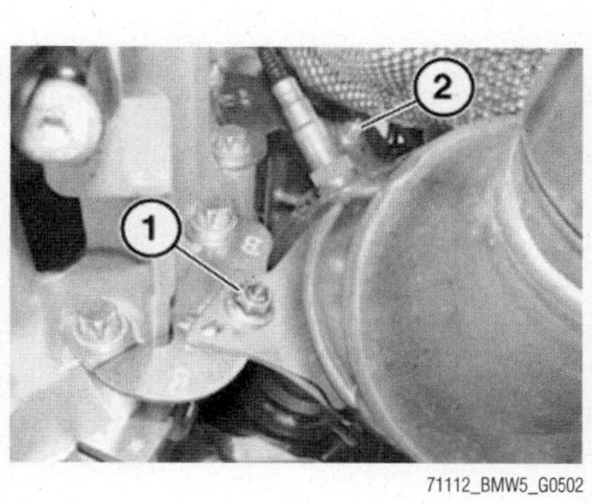

71112_BMW5_G0502

Fig. 103 Releasing nuts (1 and 2)

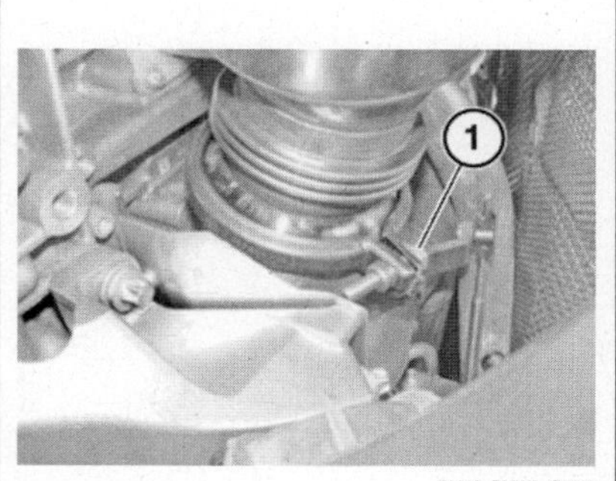

71112_BMW5_G0503

Fig. 104 Releasing clamp (1) and removing catalytic converter

7. Release clamp (1). The clamp must be renewed every time it is removed.

➡In so doing, secure catalytic converter against falling out.

8. Feed out catalytic converter and remove.

➡When installing, clean sealing surface. Renew clamp and seal.

To install:

To install, reverse the removal procedure noting the following.

9. Check exhaust system for leaks.

CRANKSHAFT FRONT SEAL

REMOVAL & INSTALLATION

N52 Engine

See Figures 105 through 113.

1. Before servicing the vehicle, refer to the precautions.

22205_BMWC_G0144

Fig. 105 Do not remove central bolt. If the central bolt is removed, the sprocket wheels of the timing chain and the oil pump will no longer be non-positively connected to the crankshaft. Inlet and exhaust camshafts can turn in relation to crankshaft

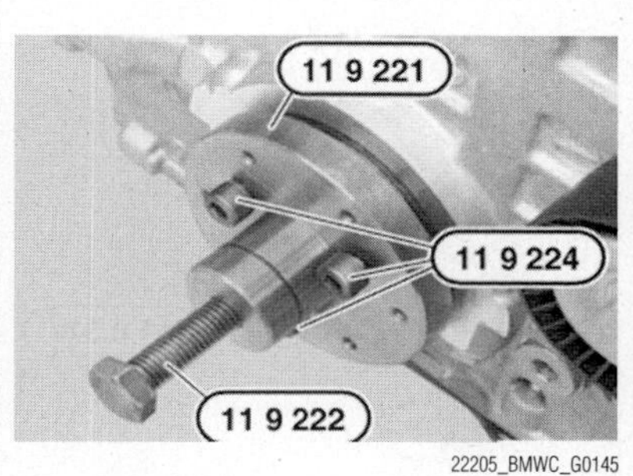

22205_BMWC_G0145

Fig. 106 Turn back special tool 11 9 222. Push special tool 11 9 221 onto crankshaft. When bolts are tightened down (special tool 11 9 224), crankshaft seal is pressed inwards

2. Remove vibration damper

WARNING

Do not remove central bolt. If the central bolt is removed, the sprocket wheels of the timing chain and the oil pump will no longer be non-positively connected to the crankshaft. Inlet and exhaust camshafts can turn in relation to crankshaft.

3. Turn back special tool 11 9 222.
4. Push special tool 11 9 221 onto crankshaft.

➡When bolts are tightened down (special tool 11 9 224), crankshaft seal is pressed inwards approximately 1 mm and thus slackened for subsequent removal.

5. Insert bolts (special tool 11 9 224) and tighten down to approximately 15 ft. lbs. (20 Nm).

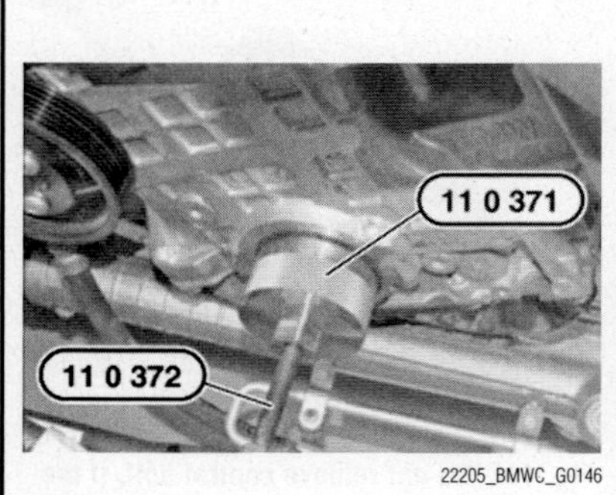

Fig. 107 Screw special tool 11 0 371 to 59 ft. lbs. (80 Nm) into crankshaft seal. Screw in spindle 11 0 372.

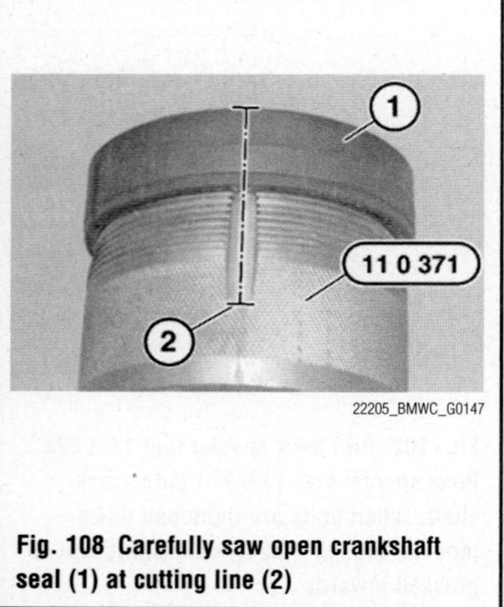

Fig. 108 Carefully saw open crankshaft seal (1) at cutting line (2)

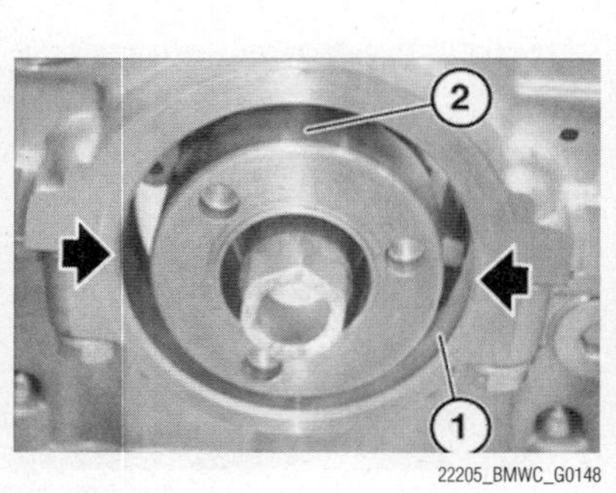

Fig. 109 Clean sealing surface (1) and apply a light coat of oil to running surface (2)

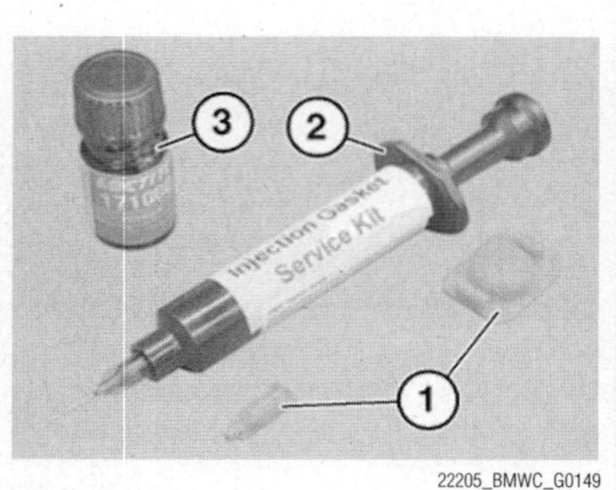

Fig. 110 Screw caps (1), injector (2) and Loctite® primer, manufacturer's number 171000 (3)

Fig. 111 Support sleeve (1), housing partition (4), grooves (3) and crankshaft seal (2)

Fig. 112 Draw in crankshaft seal with special tool 11 9 231 in conjunction with special tool 11 9 233 until flush

6. Screw special tool 11 0 371 to 59 ft. lbs. (80 Nm) into crankshaft seal.
7. Screw in spindle 11 0 372.
8. Remove crankshaft seal from housing.

➡Repeat the operation several times if necessary.

9. Carefully saw open crankshaft seal at cutting line.
10. Remove crankshaft seal from special tool 11 0 371.

To install:

WARNING

The following text describes installation and sealing between the engine block and crankshaft seal.

The engine block will not be leak proof at the outside of the crankshaft seal if you fail to comply with the individual work steps and the work sequence.

11. Clean sealing surface and degrease thoroughly in area of housing partition.
12. Apply a light coat of oil to running surface of crankshaft seal.
13. Screw special tool 11 9 232 with bolts (special tool 11 9 234) to crankshaft.

➡Support sleeve is supplied with crankshaft seal.

14. When crankshaft seal is installed, only support sleeve may be used as a slip sleeve.
15. Crankshaft seal has a groove on both left and right sides.

WARNING

After installation, the grooves must be filled with sealing compound.

➡The required parts are available from the BMW Parts Service (Electronic Parts Catalogue ETK).

16. Remove screw caps from injector.
17. Screw on metering needle.
18. Insert piston for pressing out. Injector contains the sealing compound Loctite®, manufacturer's number 128357. Bottle contains the primer Loctite®, manufacturer's number 171000.
19. Push support sleeve with crankshaft seal onto special tool 11 9 232.

WARNING

Support sleeve remains on special tool 11 9 232, until crankshaft seal is drawn in.

20. Align groove centrally to housing partition.
21. Coat both grooves on crankshaft seal with Loctite® primer, manufacturer's number 171000, and expose to air for approximately one minute.
22. Draw in crankshaft seal with special tool 11 9 231 in conjunction with special tool 11 9 233 until flush.

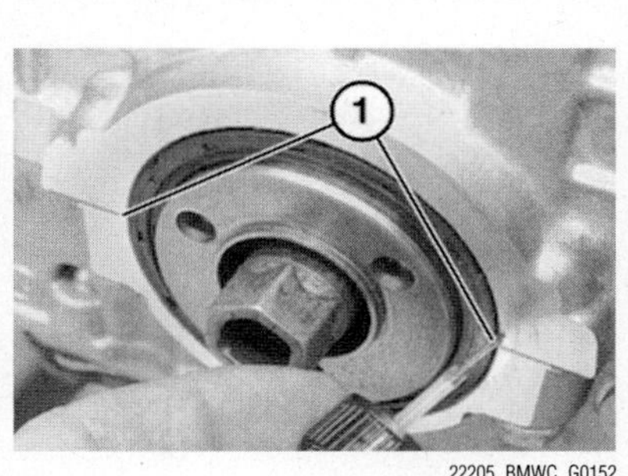

Fig. 113 Insert brush as far as possible into grooves (1) on crankshaft seal in order to coat housing partition on engine block

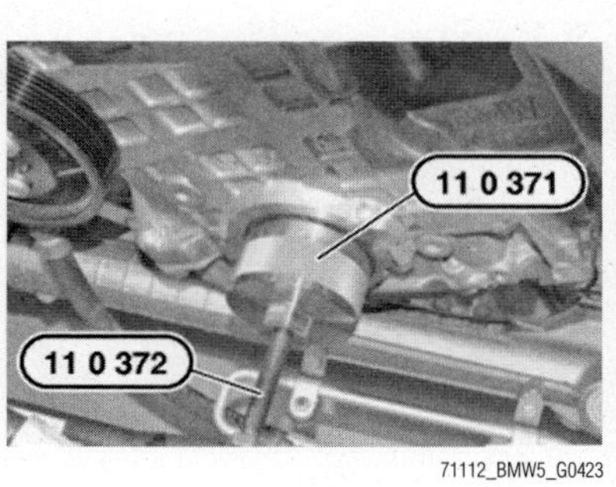

Fig. 115 Installing special tools and releasing crankshaft seal from housing

Fig. 117 Cleaning sealing surface (1) and applying oil to running surface (2) of crankshaft seal

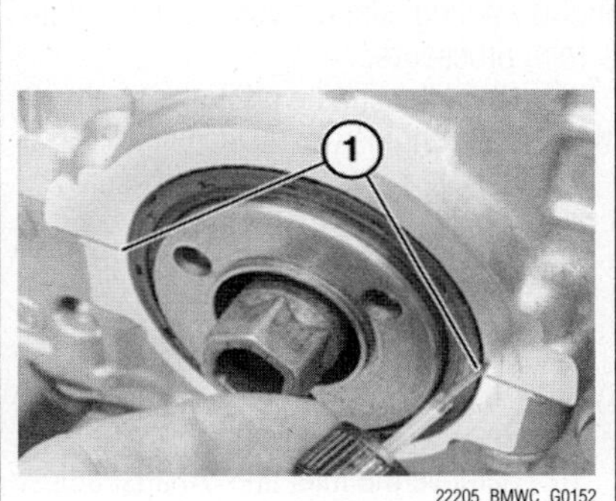

Fig. 114 Using injector (2), fill both grooves (3) flush with Loctite® sealing compound, manufacturer's number 128357

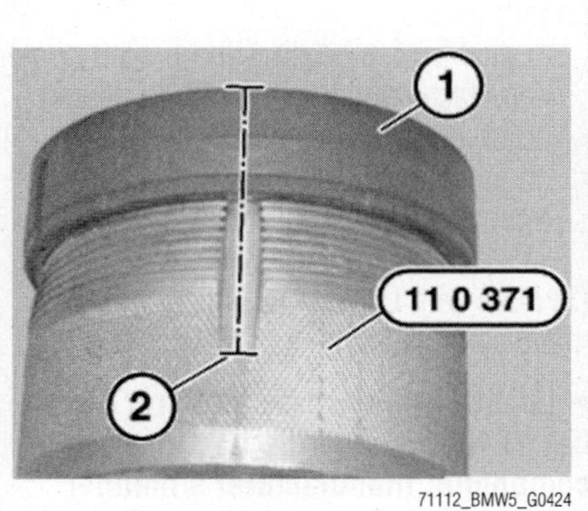

Fig. 116 Sawing open crankshaft seal (1) at cutting line (2)

Fig. 118 Pushing radial shaft seal (1) 11 9 235carefully in direction of arrow on the special tool

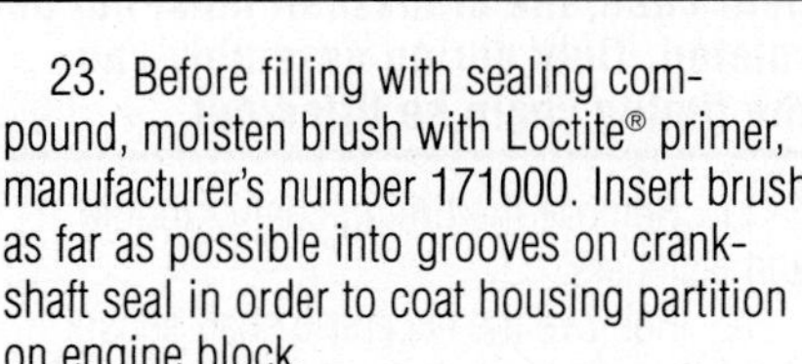

23. Before filling with sealing compound, moisten brush with Loctite® primer, manufacturer's number 171000. Insert brush as far as possible into grooves on crankshaft seal in order to coat housing partition on engine block.

24. Using injector, fill both grooves flush with Loctite® sealing compound, manufacturer's number 128357.

➡Loctite® primer, manufacturer's number 171000, binds the Loctite® sealing compound, manufacturer's number 128357, and prevents leakage.

25. Coat surface of sealing compound in both grooves with Loctite® primer, manufacturer's number 171000.

26. Install vibration damper.

N55 Engine

See Figures 115 through 121.

1. Remove vibration absorber.

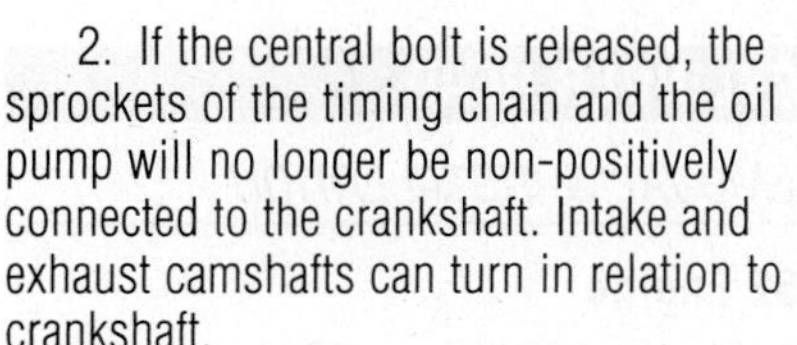

2. If the central bolt is released, the sprockets of the timing chain and the oil pump will no longer be non-positively connected to the crankshaft. Intake and exhaust camshafts can turn in relation to crankshaft.
3. Screw special tool 11 0 371 to 59 ft. lbs. (80 Nm) into crankshaft seal.
4. Screw in spindle 11 0 372.
5. Release crankshaft seal from housing.
6. Repeat the operation several times if necessary.
7. Carefully saw open crankshaft seal (1) at cutting line (2).
8. Remove crankshaft seal (1) from special tool 11 0 371.

To install:

⁂ WARNING

The following text describes installation and sealing between the engine block and crankshaft seal.

⁂ WARNING

The engine block will not be leak proof at the outside of the crankshaft seal if you fail to comply with the individual work steps and the work sequence.

9. Clean sealing surface (1) and degrease thoroughly in area of housing partition.
10. Apply a light coat of oil to running surface (2) of crankshaft seal.
11. Push radial shaft seal (1) 11 9 235carefully in direction of arrow on the special tool.

➡11 9 235Special tool can only be fastened with 2 opposite bolts.

12. Determine hole pattern on special tool.
13. Screw special tool 11 9 235 with special tool 11 9 234 on crankshaft.

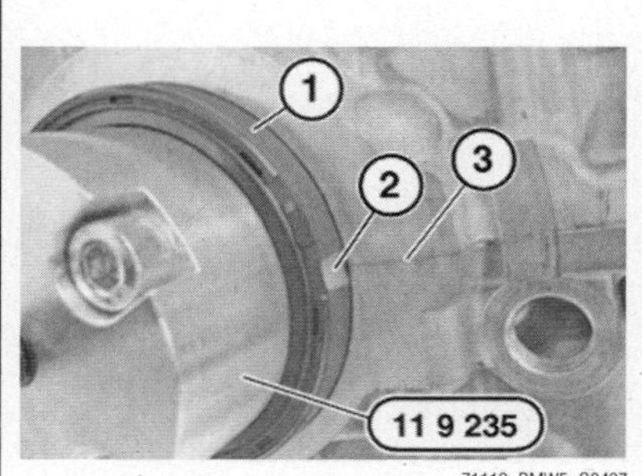

Fig. 119 Aligning groove (2) of radial shaft seal (1) centered to the housing partition (3)

14. Align groove (2) of radial shaft seal (1) centered to the housing partition (3).

⁂ WARNING

After installation, the grooves must be filled with sealing compound.

15. Draw in radial shaft seal with special tool 11 9 231 in conjunction with special tool 11 9 233 until flush.

➡Use primer 1.3 and liquid seal 1.4.

16. Prepare liquid sealing compound in special tool 11 4 370.
17. Remove sealing caps from injector.
18. Screw on metering needle.
19. Insert piston for pressing out.
20. Syringe contains the sealing compound Loctite®, manufacturer's number 128357.
21. Bottle contains the primer Loctite®, manufacturer's number 171000.

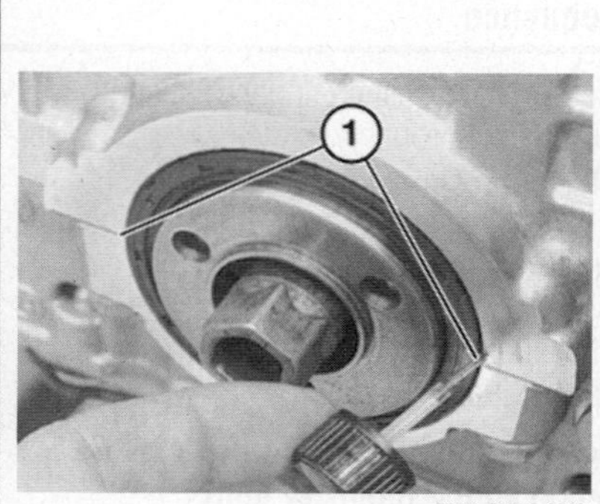

Fig. 120 Inserting brush into grooves (1) on crankshaft

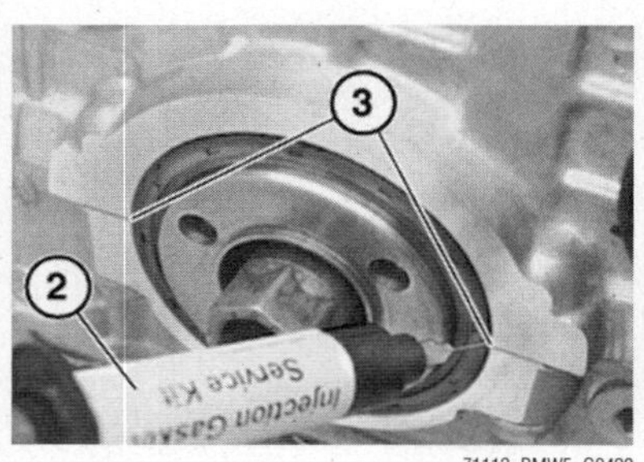

Fig. 121 Using syringe (2) to fill both grooves (3) with Loctite®

22. Before filling with sealing compound:
    a. Moisten brush with Loctite® primer, manufacturer's number 171000. Insert brush as far as possible into grooves (1) on crankshaft seal in order to coat housing partition on engine block.
23. Using syringe (2), fill both grooves (3) flush with Loctite® sealing compound, manufacturer's number 128357.

➡Loctite primer, manufacturer's number 171000, binds the Loctite sealing compound, manufacturer's number 128357, and prevents leakage.

24. Coat surface of sealing compound in both grooves (1) with Loctite® primer, manufacturer's number 171000.
25. Assemble engine.

CYLINDER HEAD

REMOVAL & INSTALLATION

N52 Engine

See Figures 122 through 131.

⁂ WARNING

Aluminum-magnesium material. No steel fasteners may be used due to the threat of electrochemical corrosion. A magnesium crankcase requires aluminum fasteners exclusively. Aluminum fasteners must be replaced each time they are removed. The end faces of aluminum fasteners are painted blue for purposes of identification. Torque specifications and torque angles must be observed for risk of damage.

1. Before servicing the vehicle, refer to the precautions.

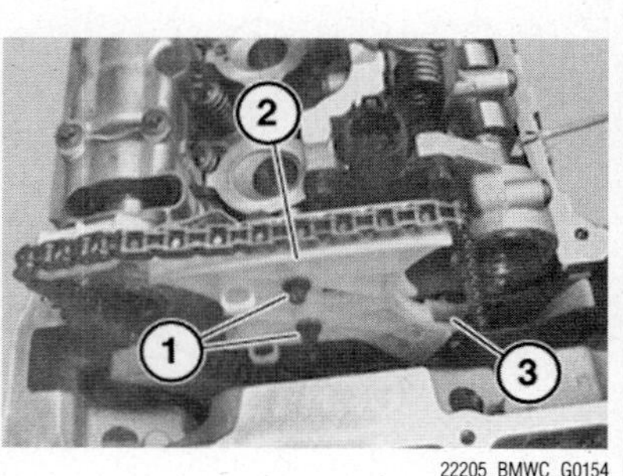

Fig. 122 Remove bolts (1), Disconnect timing chain module (2) at junction (3) and remove towards top

2. Drain the cooling system. Refer to engine cooling components, coolant, drain & refill procedure.
3. Drain the engine oil. Refer to engine mechanical, engine oil, replacement.
4. Relieve the fuel system pressure.
5. Remove the exhaust system.
6. Remove the exhaust manifolds.
7. Remove the intake manifold.
8. Remove the coolant hoses from cylinder head.
9. Remove the valve cover.
10. Remove the inlet and exhaust adjustment unit. Refer to engine mechanical, camshaft, removal & installation.

⁂ WARNING

If the timing chain is stored in the gear case, the crankshaft must not be rotated. Only during assembly can the timing chain be lifted out.

11. Remove the timing chain module and fasteners.
12. Remove the eccentric shaft sensor and fasteners towards front.
13. Remove the magnet wheel and fastener towards front.

⁂ WARNING

After removing, secure magnet wheel in a plastic bag. Magnet wheel must be protected against metal chips.

14. Pretension eccentric shaft upwards. Remove mini stop screw between first and second cylinders

⁂ WARNING

Secure bolt (2) with a gripper against falling down.

15. Remove and discard bolt (2).

Fig. 123 Remove bolts (2) for eccentric shaft sensor (1)

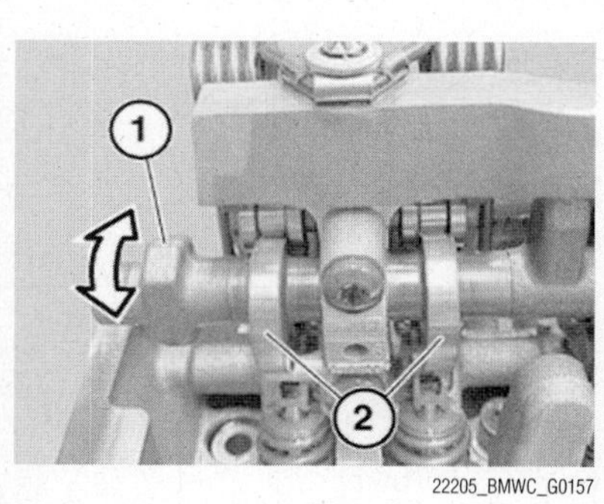

Fig. 125 Pretension eccentric shaft (1) upwards. Remove stop screw between 1st and 2nd cylinders (2)

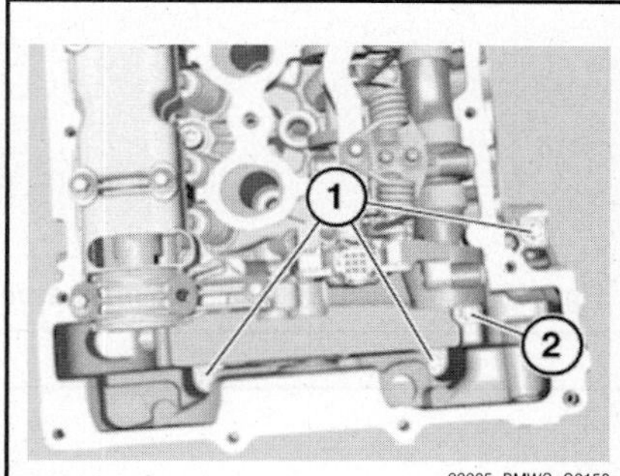

Fig. 126 Securing bolt (2) with a gripper against falling down and remove and discarding bolts (1) and (2)

➡Bolt (2) can only be Removed when the timing chain module is pressed forward slightly.

16. Remove and discard bolts (1).
17. Remove and discard M10 cylinder head bolts (1) with special tool 11 8 580.
18. Remove and discard M9 cylinder head bolts (2) with special tool 11 4 420.
19. Remove and discard M9 cylinder head bolts (1 and 3) with special tool 11 4 420.
20. Remove and discard M10 cylinder head bolts (2) with special tool 11 8 580 from outside inwards.

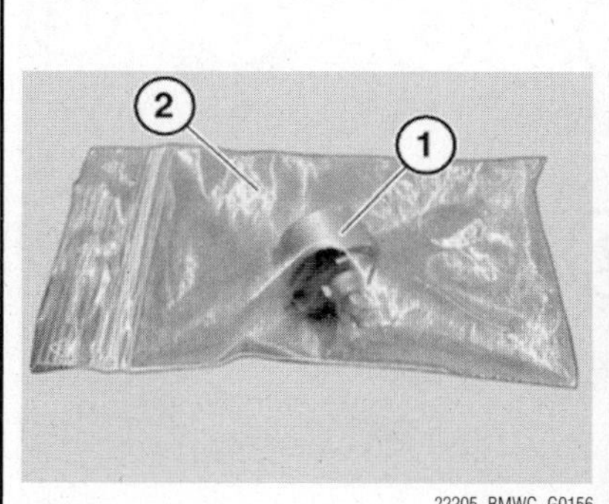

Fig. 124 Magnet wheel (1) is highly magnetic and must be protected against metal filings/borings in a plastic bag (2)

⁂ WARNING

All cylinder head bolts must be replaced.

21. Secure special tool 11 0 320 with

Fig. 127 Use the correct special tool for each bolt size M10 (1) and M9 (2)

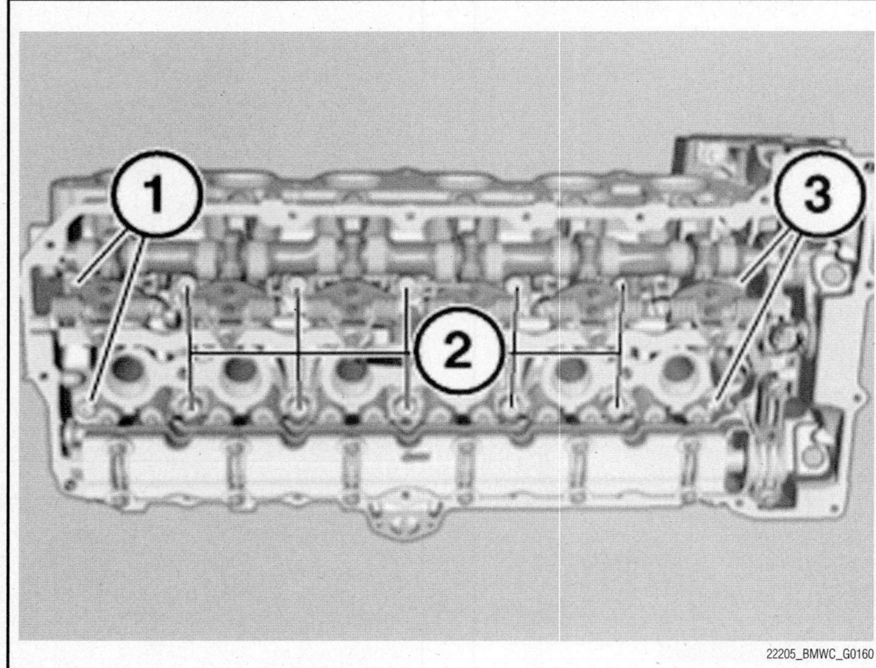

Fig. 128 Use the correct special tool for each bolt size M10 (2) and M9 (1) and (3)

Fig. 129 Secure special tool 11 0 320 with existing valve cover bolts (1)

existing valve cover bolts (1). Tighten to 7 ft. lbs. (9 Nm).

⁂ WARNING

Do not rest cylinder head on sealing surface.

22. Insert special tool 11 4 430 into bores.

To install:

Install bolts 1-10 with special tool No. 115190. Install bolts 11-14 with special tool No. 114420.

Torque following the tightening sequence as follows:

- Step 1: Tighten bolts 1-14 to 22 ft. lbs. (30 Nm)
- Step 2: Tighten bolts 1-14 an additional 90 degrees
- Step 3: Tighten bolts 1-10 an additional 90 degrees
- Step 4: Tighten bolts 1-14 an additional 45 degrees

23. The balance of installation is the reverse of the removal procedure.
24. Fill the cooling system.
25. Start the engine and check for leaks.

ENGINE OIL & FILTER

REPLACEMENT

N52 Engine

See Figures 132 through 134.

1. Before servicing the vehicle, refer to the precautions.

⁂ WARNING

Observe the exact engine oil filling capacity. Overfilling the engine with

Fig. 130 Insert special tool 11 4 430 into bores.

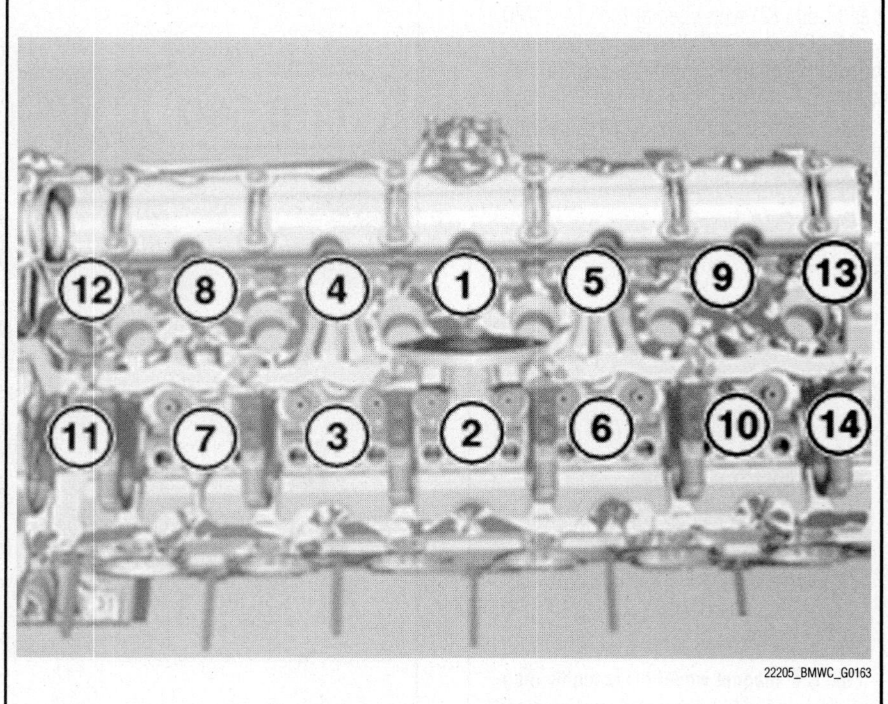

Fig. 131 Cylinder head bolt torque sequence

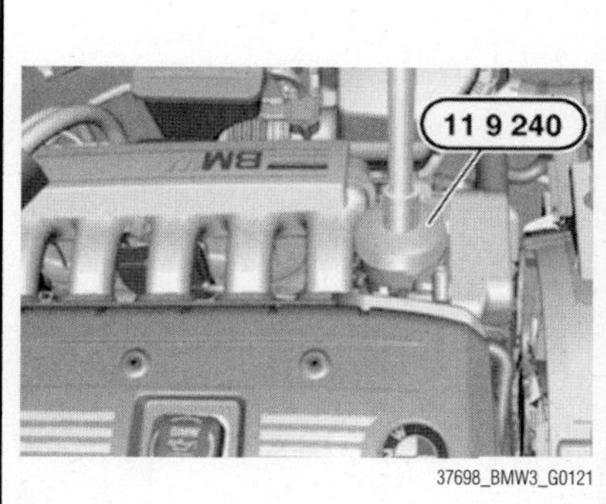

Fig. 132 Release oil filter cap with special tool 11 9 240

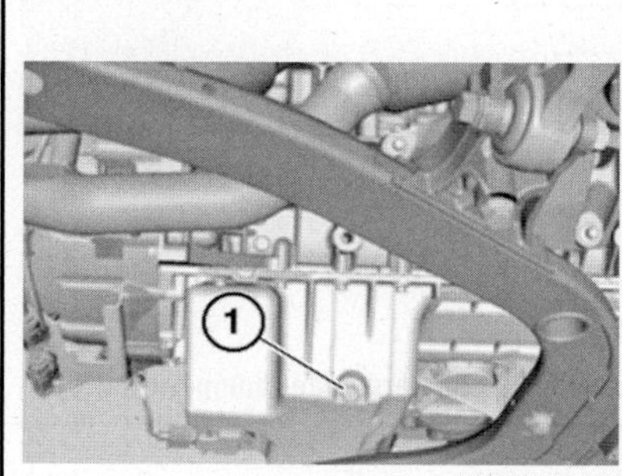

Fig. 133 Remove screw plug (1) from oil sump and drain engine oil

engine oil will result in engine damage.

2. Drive the vehicle to bring the engine to normal operating temperature.
3. Release oil filter cap with special tool 11 9 240.

➡Engine oil flows out of the oil filter housing and back into the oil sump.

4. Raise and support the vehicle.
5. Unclip service opening on underbody protection.
6. Remove screw plug from oil sump and drain engine oil.
7. Replace screw plug using a new sealing ring and tighten to 19 ft. lbs. (25 Nm).
8. Remove oil filter element.

To install:

9. Replace oil filter element and sealing rings. Moisten sealing rings with engine oil.

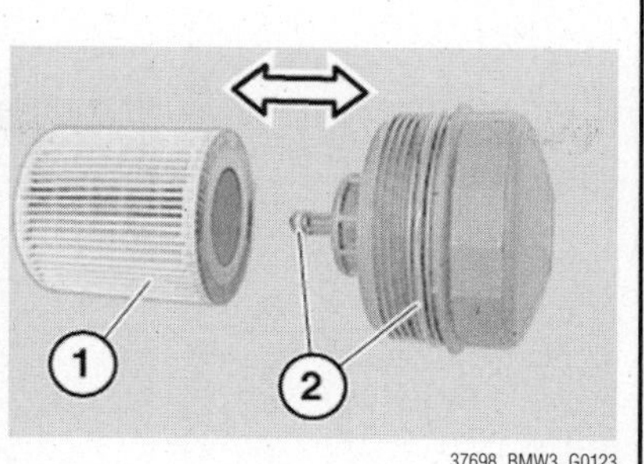

Fig. 134 Remove and insert oil filter element (1) in direction of arrow. Replace sealing rings (2) and moisten with engine oil

10. Secure oil filter cap with special tool 11 9 240 and tighten to 19 ft. lbs. (25 Nm).
11. Pour in engine oil.
12. Start engine and run at idle until oil pressure warning lamp goes out.
13. Turn off engine.
14. Wait approximately 5 minutes and check engine oil level.
15. Top up engine oil if necessary.
16. Check oil filter cap and screw plug on oil sump for leaks.

N55 Engine

See Figures 135 through 137.

⁂ WARNING

Carry out the engine oil service only when the engine is at operating temperature.

⁂ WARNING

Observe the exact engine oil filling capacity.

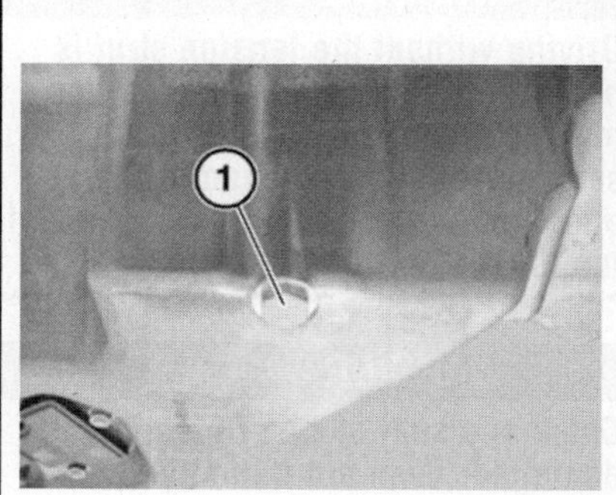

Fig. 135 Locating drain plug (1)

Fig. 136 Locating drain plug (1)

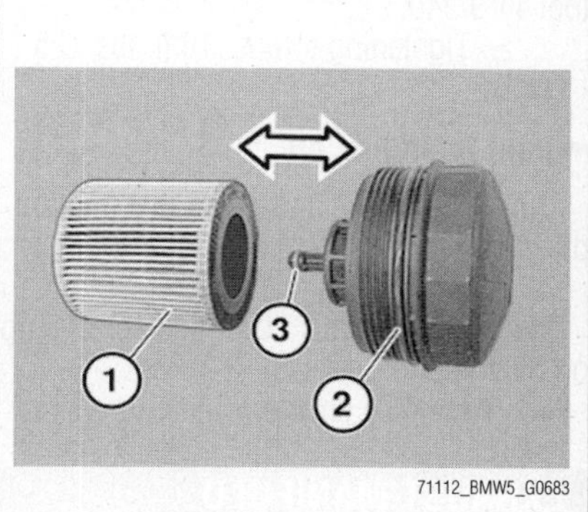

Fig. 137 Removing oil filter element (1) in direction of arrow and replacing filter element, sealing ring (2) and gasket (3)

⁂ WARNING

Overfilling the engine with engine oil will result in engine damage.

⁂ WARNING

Checking and drip-off times (at least 10 minutes) must be observed.

1. Protect belt drive against dirt.
2. Cover with suitable materials.
3. Release oil filter cover with special tool 11 9 240.
    a. Tightening torque: 18 ft. lbs. (25 Nm).

➡Engine oil flows out of the oil filter housing and back into the oil sump.

Rear wheel drive:

4. Open oil drain plug (1) on oil sump.
5. Drain engine oil.

➡Replace sealing ring.

a. Tightening torque: 18 ft. lbs. (25 Nm).

Four-wheel drive:

6. Open oil drain plug (1) of oil sump and drain engine oil.

➡Replace sealing ring.

a. Tightening torque: 18 ft. lbs. (25 Nm).

7. Remove and insert oil filter element (1) in direction of arrow.

➡Replace oil filter element (1) and sealing ring (2).

8. Replace gasket (3) and renew if necessary.

➡Coat sealing rings (2,3) with engine oil.

9. Secure oil filter cover with special tool 11 9 240.

a. Tightening torque: 18 ft. lbs. (25 Nm).

➡Pour in engine oil.

10. Start engine and run at idle until oil pressure indicator light goes out.
11. Switch off engine
12. Check oil filter cover and screw plug on oil sump for leaks.
13. Assemble engine.

EXHAUST MANIFOLD

REMOVAL & INSTALLATION

N52 Engine

See Figure 138.

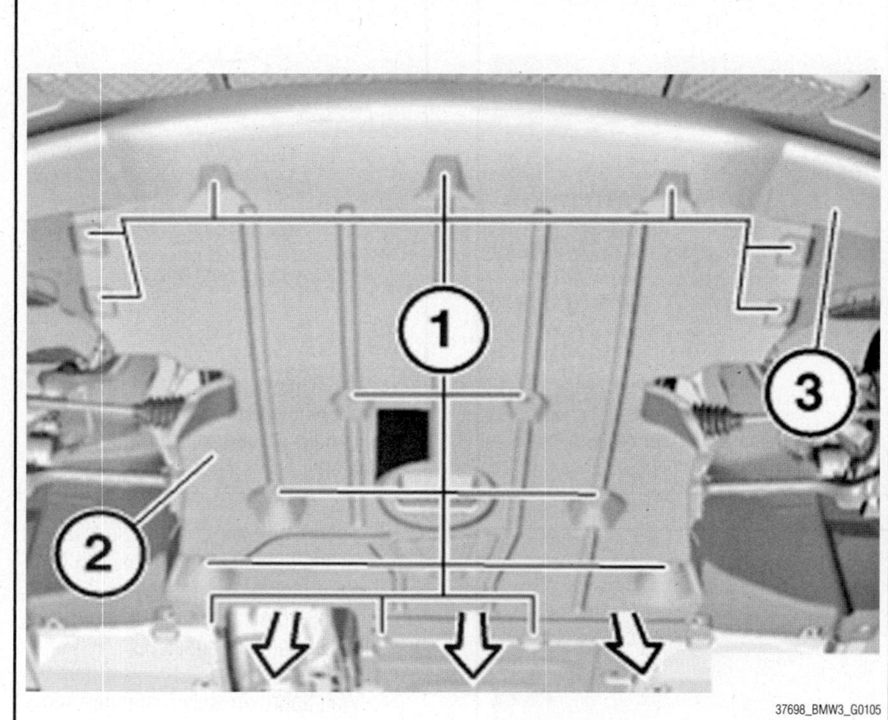

Fig. 138 Release screws (1) and pull underbody protection (2) forward under bumper trim (3)

1. Before servicing the vehicle, refer to the precautions.
2. Remove the ignition coil cover.
3. Remove the coolant expansion tank.
4. Remove the underbody protection.
5. Remove the complete exhaust system.
6. On AWD vehicles, remove the reinforcement plate.
7. Remove the oxygen sensor plug from cylinders number 4 and 6 and remove the exhaust assembly.
8. Remove the manifold for cylinders number 1 and 3 downwards.
9. Remove the manifold for cylinders number 4 and 6 downwards.

To install:

10. Remove the old gasket from the cylinder head and exhaust manifold and replace the gasket. The gasket beads face the exhaust manifolds.
11. Installation is the reverse of removal.
12. Coat screw connections with CRC copper paste.
13. Install new nuts and tighten the exhaust manifolds to 15 ft. lbs. (20 Nm).

INTAKE MANIFOLD

REMOVAL & INSTALLATION

N52 Engine

See Figures 139 through 151.

1. Before servicing the vehicle, refer to the precautions.
2. Remove the tension strut.

WARNING

Driving without the tension strut is not permitted as otherwise the body may be damaged. Tension strut screws must be tightened to torque and then tightened down with special tool 00 9 120.

WARNING

Catch and seal of cover must not be damaged. Even a minimally damaged cover may result in water leaking in; if necessary, replace cover.

a. Remove cover (1) and release screw underneath.

b. Version 1: Turn cover (with notch) approximately 45° counterclockwise.

c. Version 2: Snap out cover (without notch) in upward direction.

WARNING

Grommet must not be pulled out of bulkhead because this eliminates the possibility of correct feeding in when installed.

d. Release screw.

e. Grip grommet and pull out tension strut in direction of arrow.

3. Remove intake filter housing. Refer to engine mechanical, air cleaner, removal & installation.
4. Remove ignition coil cover. Refer to engine electrical, ignition coil, removal & installation.
5. Disconnect vacuum lines as shown.
6. Unscrew nuts.
7. Place oil reservoir in direction of arrow to one side.
8. Release rubber holders from guide.
9. Disconnect plug connection.
10. Unclip line from line holder.
11. Open cable duct.
12. Expose lines.

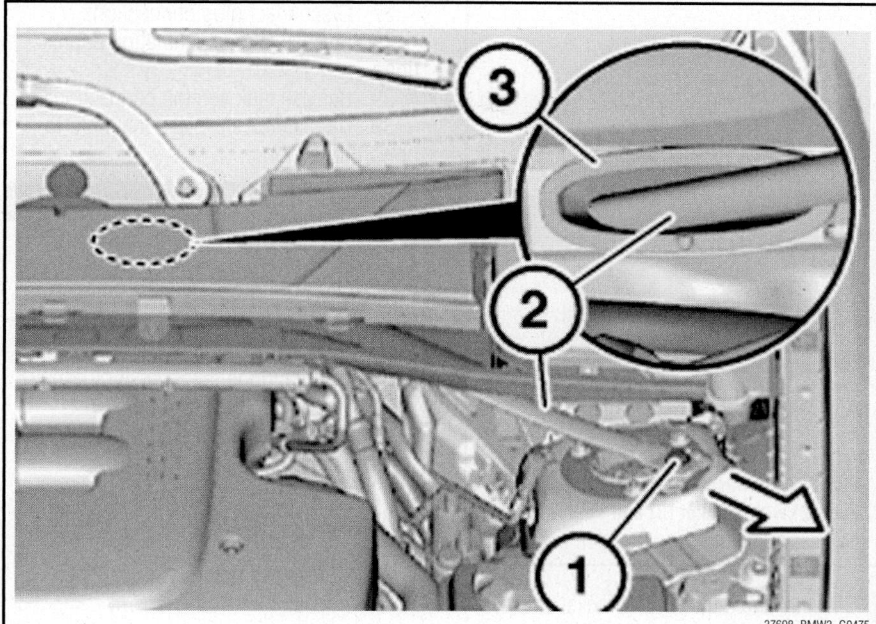

Fig. 139 Release screw (1), grip grommet (3) and pull out tension strut (2) in direction of arrow

Fig. 140 Unscrew nuts (1) and place oil reservoir (2) in direction of arrow to one side

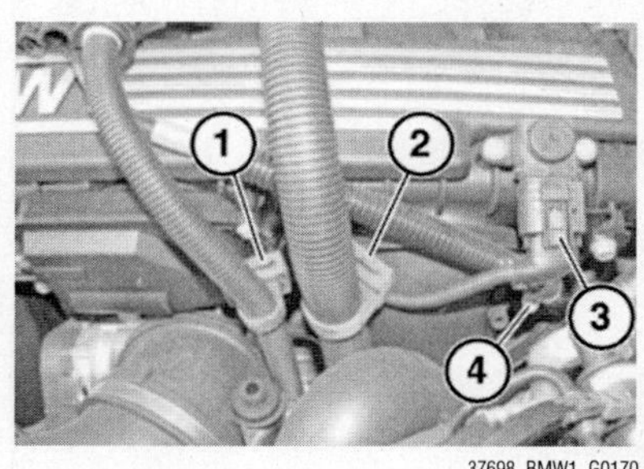

Fig. 141 Release rubber holders from guide, disconnect plug connection and unclip line from line holder

13. Lay cable duct (upper and lower sections) to one side.

➡The lines shown do not have to be detached in order to remove the air intake manifold.

14. Unfasten hose clip.
15. Detach clean-air gaiter at position in direction of arrow and remove.

Fig. 142 These lines do not have to be detached in order to remove the air intake manifold

16. Disconnect plug connection.

WARNING

Cover fitting with suitable apparatus to prevent objects getting into it.

17. Release screw.
18. Unclip fuel line at position from holder.
19. Disconnect plug connection and lay to one side.
20. Unclip lines at positions.
21. Remove plug connections.
22. Lay both lines between intake ducts (direction of arrow) downwards.
23. Release screws.

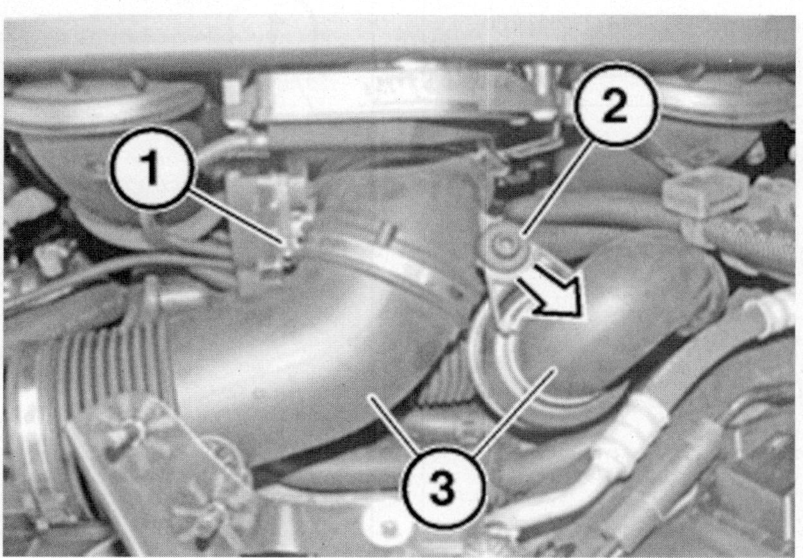

Fig. 143 Unfasten hose clip (1), detach clean-air gaiter (3) at position (2) in direction of arrow and remove

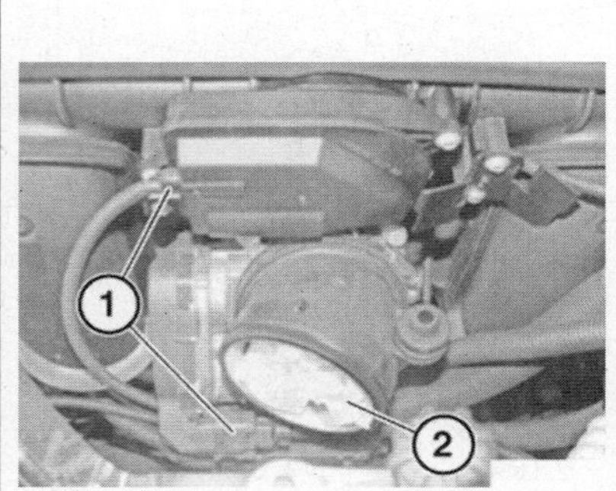

Fig. 144 Disconnect plug connection (1) and cover fitting (2) with suitable apparatus to prevent objects getting into it

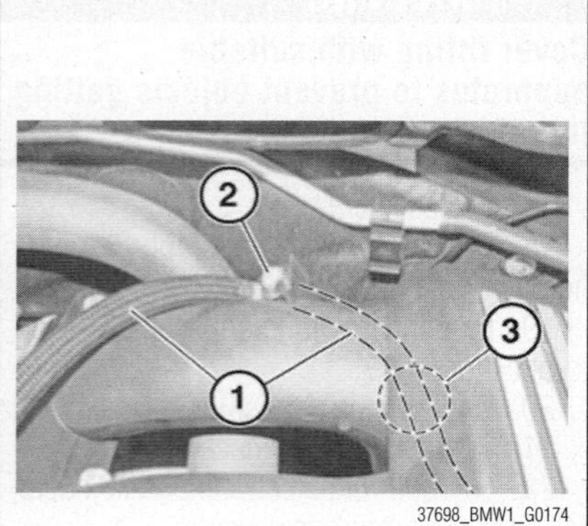

Fig. 145 Release screw (2) and unclip fuel line (1) at position (3) from holder

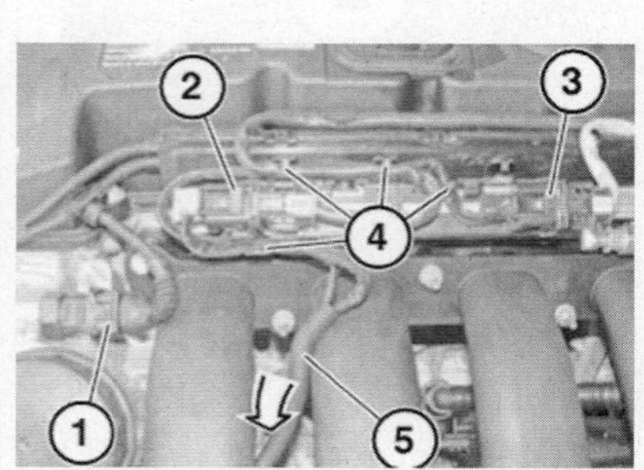

Fig. 146 Disconnect plug connection, unclip lines and lay both lines between intake ducts (direction of arrow) downwards

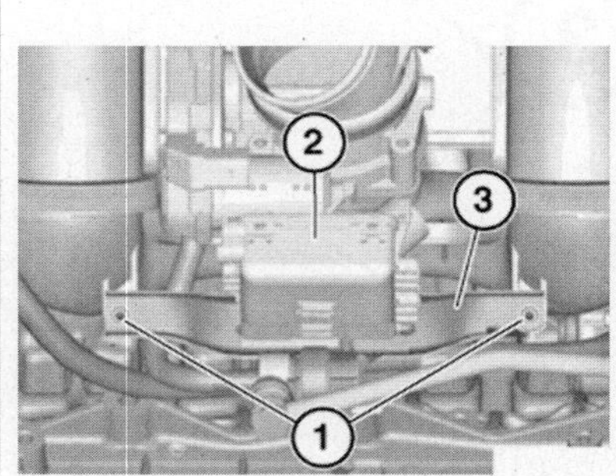

Fig. 147 Release screws (1) and lay cable duct (2) with bracket (3) and engine wiring harness to one side

24. Lay cable duct with bracket and engine wiring harness to one side.
25. Unfasten intake manifold screws and nuts as shown.
26. Expose air intake manifold in following work steps, as shown:
    a. Raise air intake manifold approximately 2–4 In. (5–10 cm).
    b. Turn air intake manifold at front through 45°.

➡**The following plug connections and connections are located below the intake ducts.**

27. Disconnect plug connections.
28. Release engine ventilation connections.
29. Release tank venting connection.
30. Disconnect air intake manifold in upward direction.

WARNING

Cover intake entries with suitable apparatus to prevent objects getting into them.

To install:

31. Installation is the reverse of removal.
32. Replace self-locking nuts.
33. Replace all seals and gaskets.
34. Sealing faces must be free from oil and grease.
35. Tighten bolts/nuts to specification as follows:
    - Air intake manifold to cylinder head: 11 ft. lbs. (15 Nm)
    - Clean-air gaiter to connection, throttle valve assembly: 27 inch lbs. (3 Nm)
    - Fuel line to intake manifold: 53 inch lbs. (6 Nm)
    - Holder, engine wiring harness, to intake manifold: 71 inch lbs. (8 Nm)
    - Multipurpose holder to body / holder for oil reservoir: 45 inch lbs. (5 Nm)
36. Connections must snap audibly into place!

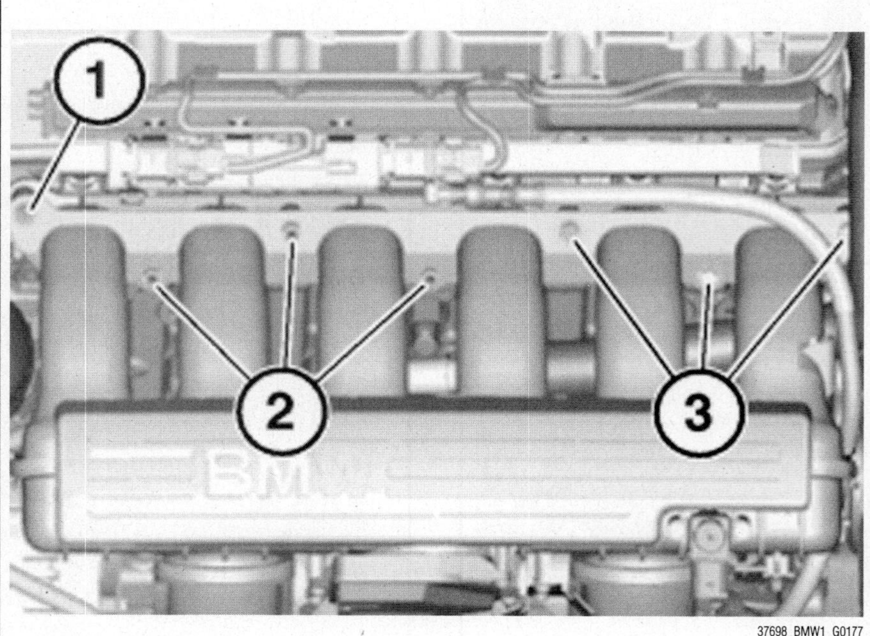

Fig. 148 Unfasten intake manifold screws (1 and 3) and nuts (2)

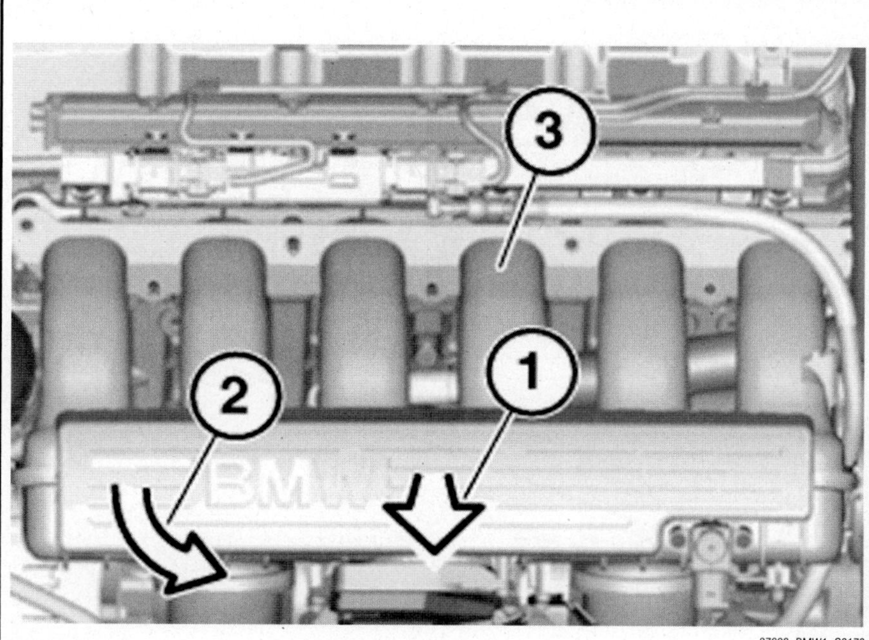

Fig. 149 Raise air intake manifold (3) approximately 2–4 In. (5–10 cm) (1) and turn air intake manifold at front through 45° (2)

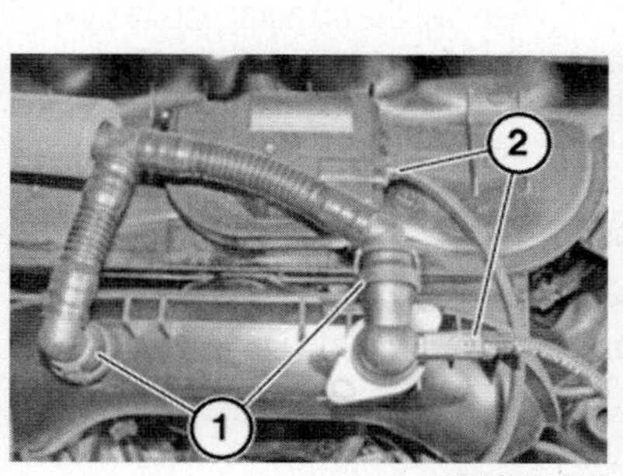

Fig. 150 Disconnect plug connections (2) and release engine ventilation connections (1)

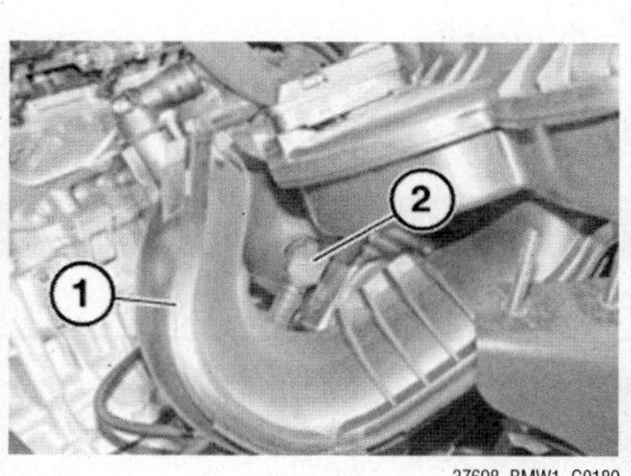

Fig. 151 Release tank venting connection (2) and disconnect air intake manifold (1) in upward direction

37. Check air intake system for leaks.

OIL PAN

REMOVAL & INSTALLATION

N52 Engine

See Figure 152.

WARNING

Aluminum-magnesium material. No steel fasteners may be used due to the threat of electrochemical corrosion. A magnesium crankcase requires aluminum fasteners exclusively. Aluminum fasteners must be replaced each time they are removed. The end faces of aluminum fasteners are painted blue for purposes of identification. Torque specifications and torque angles must be observed for risk of damage.

1. Before servicing the vehicle, refer to the precautions.
2. Install engine support tool or equivalent.
3. Disconnect the negative battery cable.
4. Remove the lower front axle.

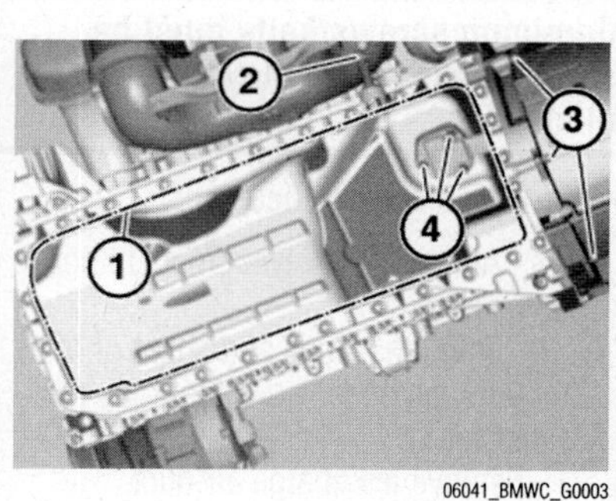

Fig. 152 Oil pan bolts (1), oil return hose (2), transmission bolts (3) and oil level sensor (4)

5. Remove the left drive shaft.
6. Remove the right drive shaft.
7. Remove the front axle differential.
8. Remove the engine oil.
9. On vehicles equipped with automatic transmission, oil lines must be detached from the engine oil pan.
10. If necessary, remove vane pump and set it aside.
11. Remove the two bolts securing oil pan to transmission.
12. Remove the oil return hose.
13. Remove oil pan bolts and remove the oil pan.
14. If necessary, remove oil level sensor bolts and oil level sensor.

To install

15. Clean the mounting surfaces and install a new gasket and all seals.

WARNING

There must be no adhesive residues in the oil pan retaining threads. Clean retaining threads.

16. Install oil pan.
17. Replace all aluminum fasteners and tighten 70 inch lbs. (8 Nm) plus an additional 90° rotation
18. Installation is the reverse of removal.
19. Fill the engine with oil.
20. Start the engine and check for leaks.

N55 Engine

See Figure 153.

WARNING

Aluminum screws/bolts are permitted with and without color coding (blue).

WARNING

Aluminum screws/bolts must be replaced each time they are released.

➡For reliable identification:

a. Aluminum screws/bolts are not magnetic.

b. Jointing torque and angle of rotation must be observed without fail (risk of damage).

1. Remove left charge air duct.
2. Remove front axle differential.
3. Drain and add engine oil.
4. Detach power steering pump and set it aside (Dynamic Drive only).
5. Remove engine support arm.
6. Detach deflecting element and holder from oil sump.

➡The lines must be detached from the oil sump on vehicles with automatic transmission; if necessary, detach oil pump and place to one side.

7. Release bolts (3) on transmission.

a. Tightening torque: 35 inch lbs. (4 Nm) + 90°.

8. Detach return hose (2).

WARNING

For vehicles with four-wheel drive or automatic transmission, bolts of different lengths are installed for mounting the oil sump.

➡Observe different tightening torques.

9. Release bolts along line (1).
10. For vehicles with four-wheel drive or automatic transmission:

a. Tightening torque: 71 inch lbs. (8 Nm) + 180°.

11. Additionally for vehicles with four-wheel drive:

a. Tightening torque: 71 inch lbs. (8 Nm) + 90°.

➡When installing, replace aluminum screws.

➡If necessary, release nuts (4). Remove oil level sensor.

b. Tightening torque: 71 inch lbs. (8 Nm).

➡When installing, replace sealing ring.

WARNING

There must be no adhesive residues in the lower crankcase section retaining threads.

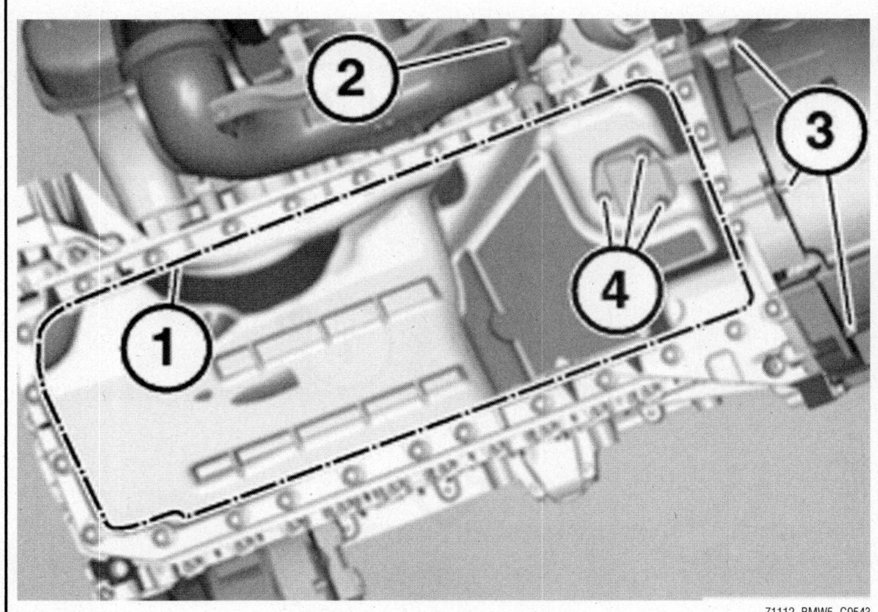

Fig. 153 Releasing bolts (3), detaching return hose (2), releasing bolts (1) and nuts (4)

12. Clean retaining threads and sealing surfaces.

➡When installing, replace all gaskets.

To install:

13. To install, reverse the removal procedure.

OIL PUMP

REMOVAL & INSTALLATION

N52 Engine

See Figure 154.

1. Before servicing the vehicle, refer to the precautions.

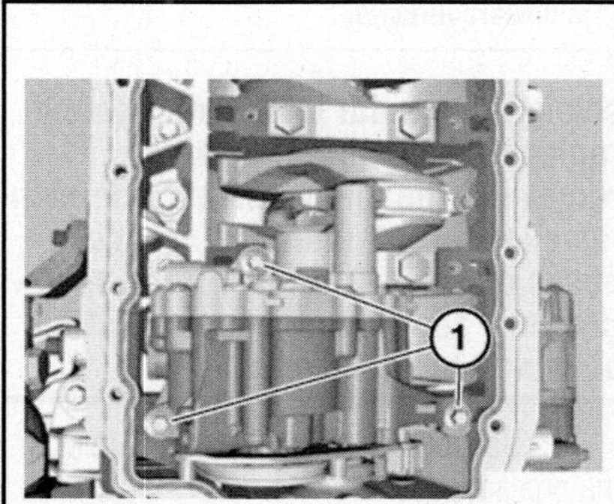

Fig. 154 Oil pump mounting bolts (1)

2. Disconnect the negative battery cable.
3. Remove the oil pan.
4. Remove the oil pump intake pipe fasteners and oil pump intake pipe, pull towards transmission.
5. Remove the oil pump pulley bolt.
6. Remove the oil pump mounting bolts.

➡Timing chain of triangular drive is pressed upwards by chain tensioner.

7. Do not remove pulley from assembly.
8. Remove the oil pump pulley, pull towards front of engine bay.
9. Remove the oil pump.

To install

10. Check the seals on the oil pipes and replace it if necessary. Lubricate the seals with oil and the oil pipes.
11. Check the seal in the oil pump and replace it if necessary.
12. Align twin surface on oil pump to sprocket wheel.
13. Replace all aluminum fasteners and tighten to specification.
    - Oil pump to bedplate: 25 ft. lbs. (34 Nm) plus an additional 180° rotation
    - Chain module to crankcase and oil pump 35 inch lbs. (4 Nm) plus an additional 45° rotation
    - Pulley to oil pump: 15 ft. lbs. (20 Nm) plus an additional 45° rotation

- Intake pipe to bedplate: 35 inch lbs. (4 Nm) plus an additional 100° rotation

14. Installation is the reverse of removal.
15. Fill the engine with oil.
16. Start the engine and check for leaks.

N55 Engine

See Figures 155 through 163.

WARNING

Aluminum screws/bolts must be replaced each time they are released.

WARNING

Aluminum screws/bolts are permitted with and without color coding (blue).

➡For reliable identification:

a. Aluminum screws/bolts are not magnetic.

b. Jointing torque and angle of rotation must be observed without fail (risk of damage).

1. Removing oil pan.
2. Remove sealing cap of vacuum pump.
3. Undo all the aluminum screws (1) along the line.

➡When installing, replace aluminum screws.

4. Remove intake pipe with oil deflector.

➡When installing, replace O-ring.

WARNING

Before releasing the central bolt on the oil pump, the hydraulic chain tensioner must be drained.

5. Carefully press tensioning rail (1) with a suitable screwdriver (2) in direction of arrow.
6. As the oil pressure in the chain tensioner can only be drained pulsating, the tensioning rail (1) must be pressed several times.
7. Sprocket must be blocked in order to release central bolt (1).
8. Secure special tool 2 303 793 to crankcase.
9. Release oil pump central bolt (1).

   a. Tightening torque: 15 ft. lbs. (20 Nm) + 45°.

10. Release aluminum screws (1).

    a. Tightening torque: 35 inch lbs. (4 Nm) + 45°.

➡When installing, replace aluminum screws.

11. Watch mounting flats on oil pump sprocket.

WARNING

Observe different screw lengths.

12. Release aluminum screws (1).

    a. Tightening torque (M8x123): 7 ft. lbs. (10 Nm) + 180°.

    b. Tightening torque (M8x31 and M8x37): 7 ft. lbs. (10 Nm) + 90°.

Fig. 156 Pressing tension rail (1) with screwdriver (2) in direction of arrow

Fig. 157 Identifying central bolt (1)

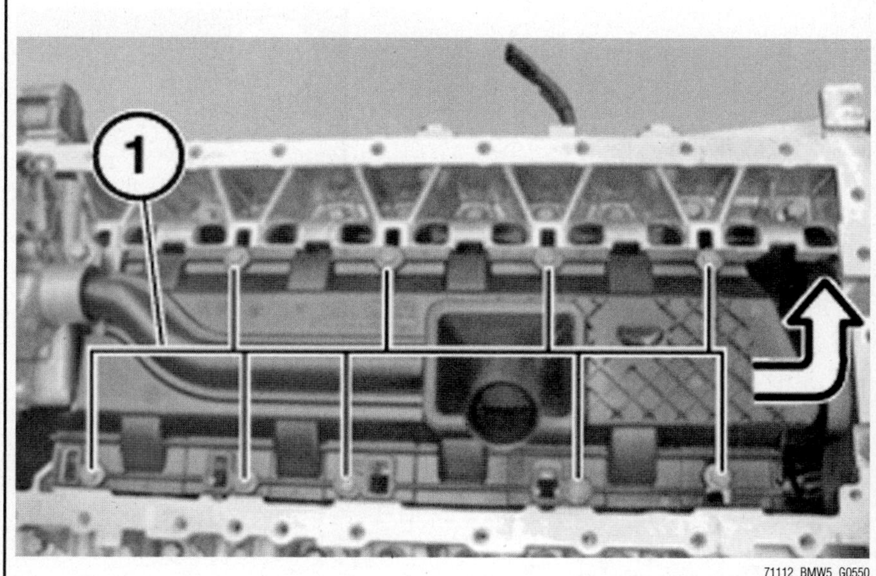

Fig. 155 Undoing aluminum screws (1) along line

Fig. 158 Releasing screws (1)

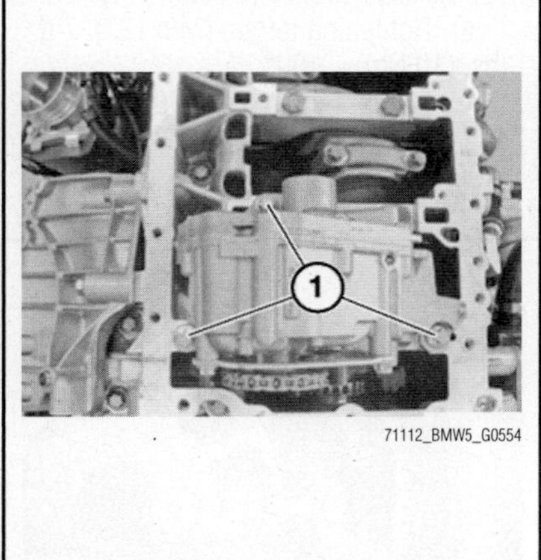

Fig. 159 Releasing aluminum screws (1)

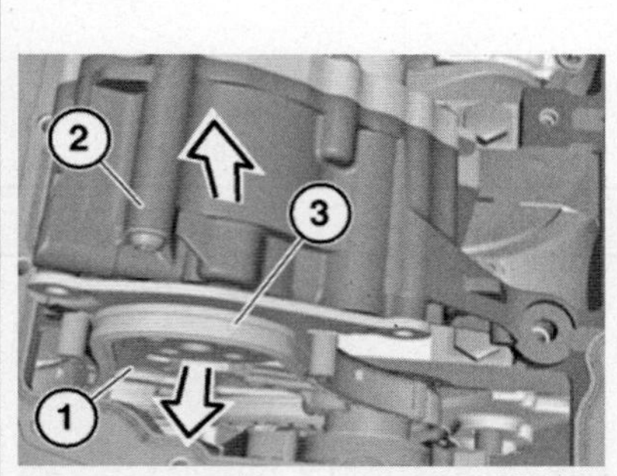

Fig. 160 Detaching sprocket (1), pressing timing chain (3) and removing oil pump (2) in direction of arrow

➡When installing, replace aluminum screws.

13. Detach sprocket (1) in direction of arrow.

➡Chain tensioner presses timing chain (3) upwards.

WARNING

Do not remove sprocket (1).

14. Remove oil pump (2) in direction of arrow.

To install:

15. Check spacer bushes for secure seating and damage; replace if necessary.
16. Install oil pump (2).
17. Align mounting flats (3) on oil pump (2) to sprocket (4).
18. Install intake pipe with oil deflector.

➡When installing, replace O-ring.

19. Insert all the aluminum screws (1) along the line.

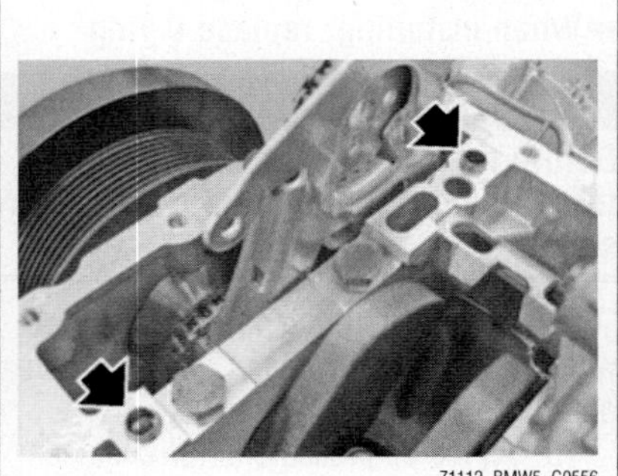

Fig. 161 Checking spacer bushes

➡When installing, replace aluminum screws.

a. Tightening torque: 35 inch lbs. (4 Nm) + 90°.

20. Assemble engine.

PISTON AND RING

POSITIONING

See Figures 164 through 166.

TIMING CHAIN FRONT COVER

REMOVAL & INSTALLATION

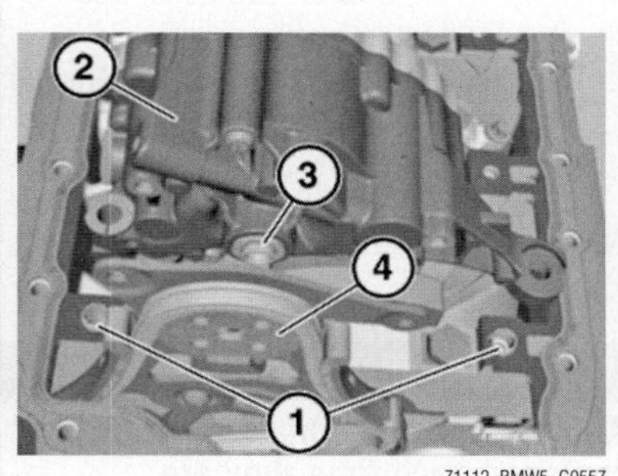

Fig. 162 Installing oil pump (2), aligning mounting flats (3) on oil pump to sprocket (4)

N52 Engine

See Figures 167 through 175.

1. Before servicing the vehicle, refer to the precautions.
2. Remove crankshaft damper

WARNING

Do not remove central bolt. If the central bolt is Removed, the sprocket wheels of the timing chain and the oil pump will no longer be non-positively connected to the crankshaft. Inlet and exhaust camshafts can turn in relation to crankshaft.

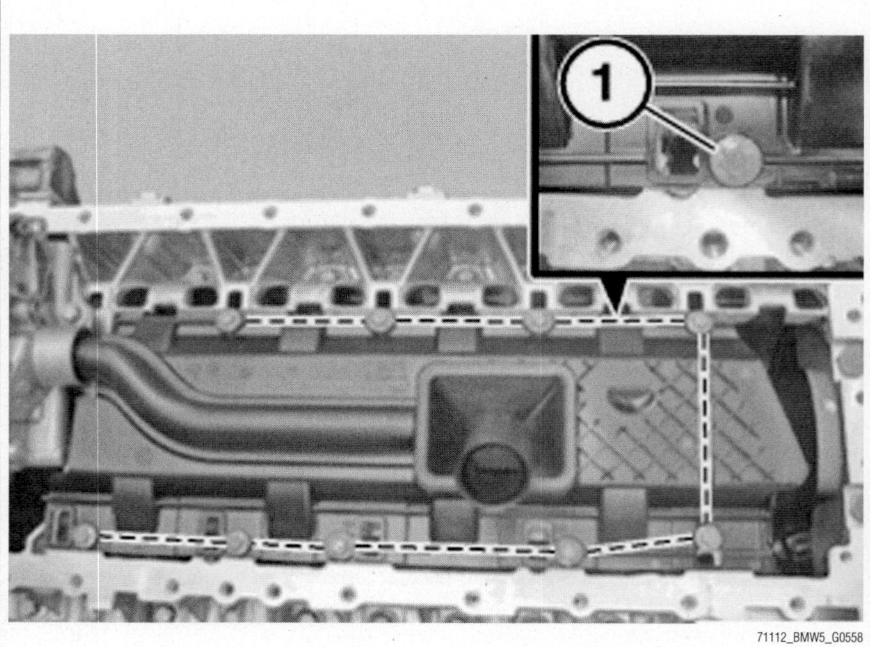

Fig. 163 Inserting aluminum screws (1) along line

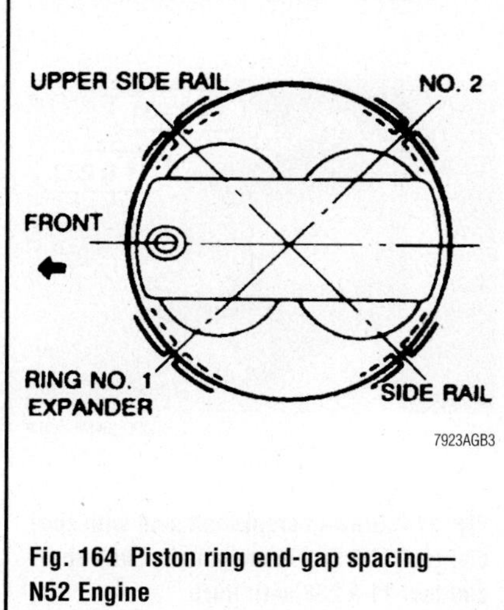

Fig. 164 Piston ring end-gap spacing—N52 Engine

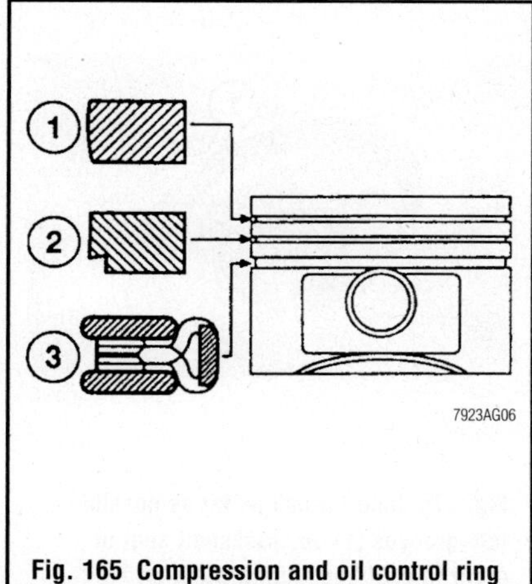

Fig. 165 Compression and oil control ring locations—N52 Engine

3. Turn back special tool 11 9 222.
4. Push special tool 11 9 221 onto crankshaft.

➡When bolts are tightened down (special tool 11 9 224), crankshaft seal is pressed inwards approximately 1 mm and thus slackened for subsequent removal.

5. Insert bolts (special tool 11 9 224) and tighten down to approximately 15 ft. lbs. (20 Nm).
6. Screw special tool 11 0 371 to 59 ft. lbs. (80 Nm) into crankshaft seal.
7. Screw in spindle 11 0 372.
8. Remove crankshaft seal from housing.

➡Repeat the operation several times if necessary.

9. Carefully saw open crankshaft seal at cutting line.
10. Remove crankshaft seal from special tool 11 0 371.

Fig. 166 Connecting rod-to-piston positioning—N52 Engine

To install:

⁂ WARNING

The following text describes installation and sealing between the engine block and crankshaft seal.

The engine block will not be leak proof at the outside of the crankshaft seal if you fail to comply with the individual work steps and the work sequence.

11. Clean sealing surface and degrease thoroughly in area of housing partition.
12. Apply a light coat of oil to running surface of crankshaft seal.
13. Screw special tool 11 9 232 with bolts (special tool 11 9 234) to crankshaft.

➡Support sleeve is supplied with crankshaft seal.

14. When crankshaft seal is installed, only support sleeve may be used as a slip sleeve.
15. Crankshaft seal has a groove on both left and right sides.

Fig. 167 Do not remove central bolt. If the central bolt is removed, the sprocket wheels of the timing chain and the oil pump will no longer be non-positively connected to the crankshaft. Inlet and exhaust camshafts can turn in relation to crankshaft

Fig. 168 Turn back special tool 11 9 222. Push special tool 11 9 221 onto crankshaft. When bolts are tightened down (special tool 11 9 224), crankshaft seal is pressed inwards

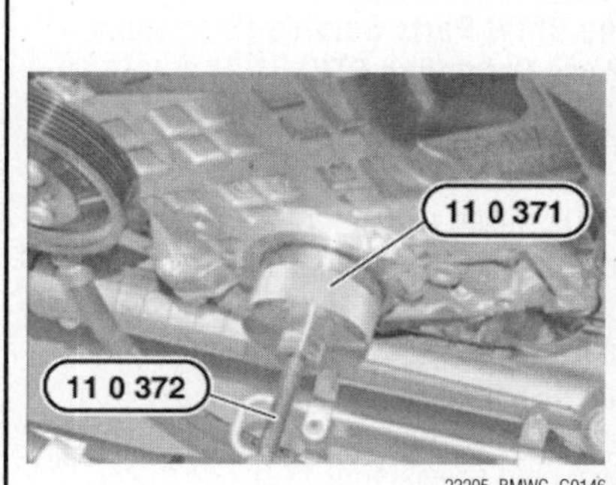

Fig. 169 Screw special tool 11 0 371 to 59 ft. lbs. (80 Nm) into crankshaft seal. Screw in spindle 11 0 372

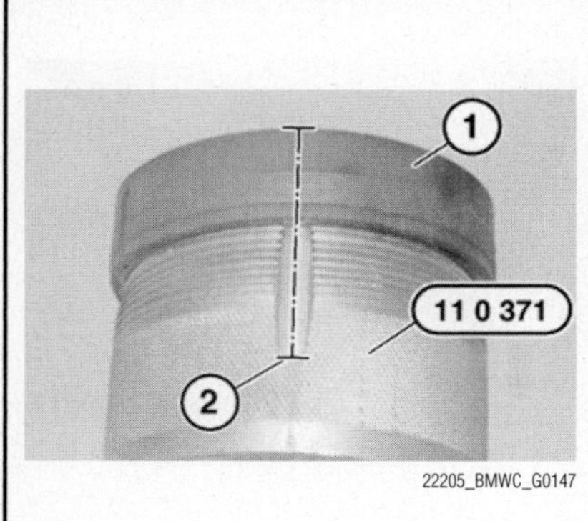

Fig. 170 Carefully saw open crankshaft seal (1) at cutting line (2)

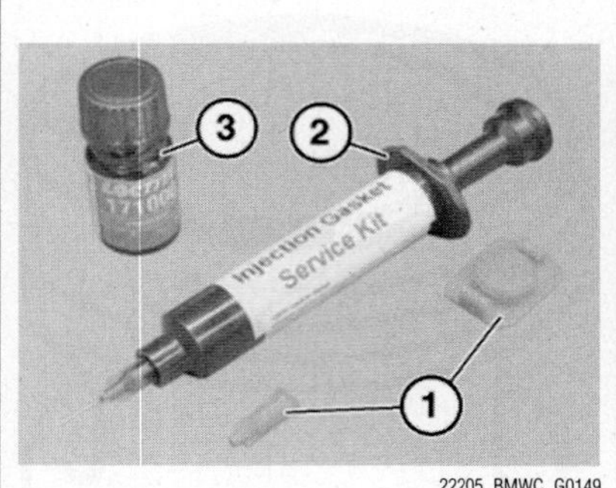

Fig. 172 Screw caps (1), injector (2) and Loctite primer, manufacturer's number 171000 (3)

Fig. 174 Draw in crankshaft seal with special tool 11 9 231 in conjunction with special tool 11 9 233 until flush

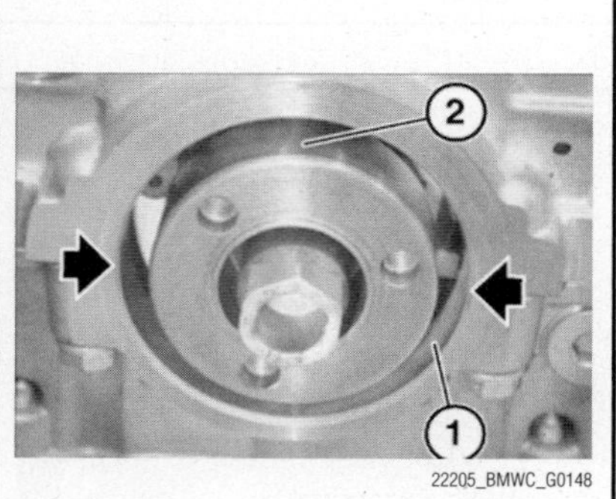

Fig. 171 Clean sealing surface (1) and apply a light coat of oil to running surface (2)

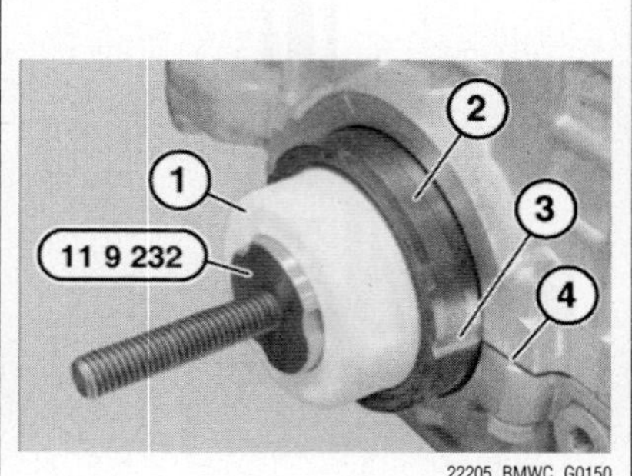

Fig. 173 Support sleeve (1), housing partition (4), grooves (3) and crankshaft seal (2)

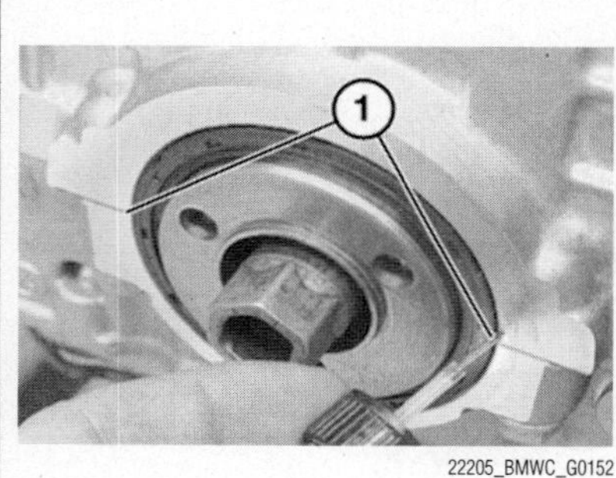

Fig. 175 Insert brush as far as possible into grooves (1) on crankshaft seal in order to coat housing partition on engine block

WARNING

After installation, the grooves must be filled with sealing compound.

➡The required parts are available from the BMW Parts Service (Electronic Parts Catalogue ETK).

16. Remove screw caps from injector.
17. Screw on metering needle.
18. Insert piston for pressing out. Injector contains the sealing compound Loctite®, manufacturer's number 128357. Bottle contains the primer Loctite®, manufacturer's number 171000.
19. Push support sleeve with crankshaft seal onto special tool 11 9 232.

WARNING

Support sleeve remains on special tool 11 9 232, until crankshaft seal is drawn in.

20. Align groove centrally to housing partition.
21. Coat both grooves on crankshaft seal with Loctite® primer, manufacturer's number 171000, and expose to air for approximately one minute.
22. Draw in crankshaft seal with special tool 11 9 231 in conjunction with special tool 11 9 233 until flush.
23. Before filling with sealing compound, moisten brush with Loctite® primer, manufacturer's number 171000. Insert brush as far as possible into grooves on crankshaft seal in order to coat housing partition on engine block.
24. Using injector, fill both grooves flush with Loctite® sealing compound, manufacturer's number 128357.

➡Loctite® primer, manufacturer's number 171000, binds the Loctite® sealing compound, manufacturer's number 128357, and prevents leakage.

25. Coat surface of sealing compound in both grooves with Loctite® primer, manufacturer's number 171000.
26. Install crankshaft damper.

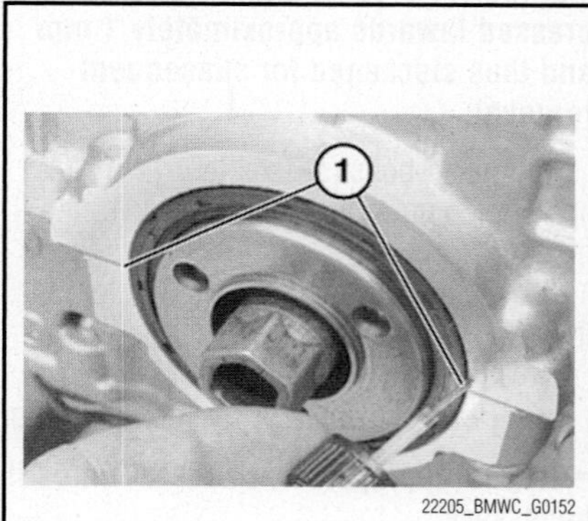

Fig. 176 Using injector (2), fill both grooves (3) flush with Loctite® sealing compound, manufacturer's number 128357

TIMING CHAIN & SPROCKETS

REMOVAL & INSTALLATION

N52 Engine

See Figures 177 through 192.

1. Before servicing the vehicle, refer to the precautions.
2. Remove valve cover.
3. Remove all spark plugs.
4. Remove chain tensioner.

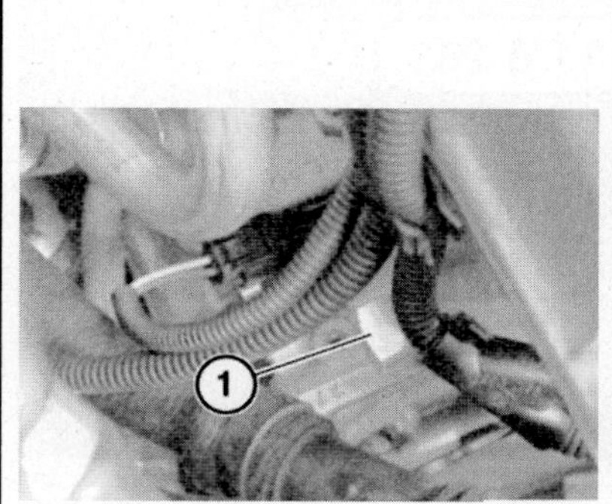

Fig. 177 Chain tensioner (1) location

➡Have a cleaning cloth ready. A small quantity of engine oil will emerge after the screw connection has been removed.

⁂ WARNING

Make sure no engine oil runs onto belt drive.

5. Remove crankshaft front radial seal.
6. Remove accessory drive belt and tensioner.
7. Remove crankshaft damper.
8. Remove fastener.
9. Rotate crankshaft at central bolt into TDC position.
10. Slide special tool 11 0 300 into special tool bore and secure crankshaft.

⁂ WARNING

On vehicles with optional extra SA205 (automatic transmission), there is a large bore for the TDC position shortly before the special tool bore. This bore can be confused with the special tool bore.

If the flywheel is secured in the correct special tool bore with special tool 11 0 300, the engine can no longer be moved at the central bolt.

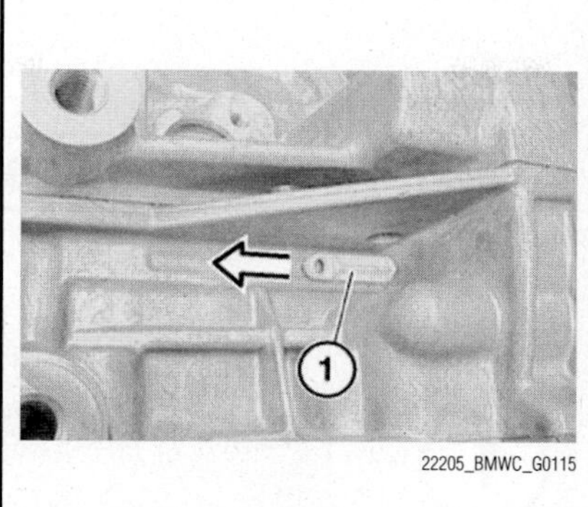

Fig. 178 Remove fastener (1)

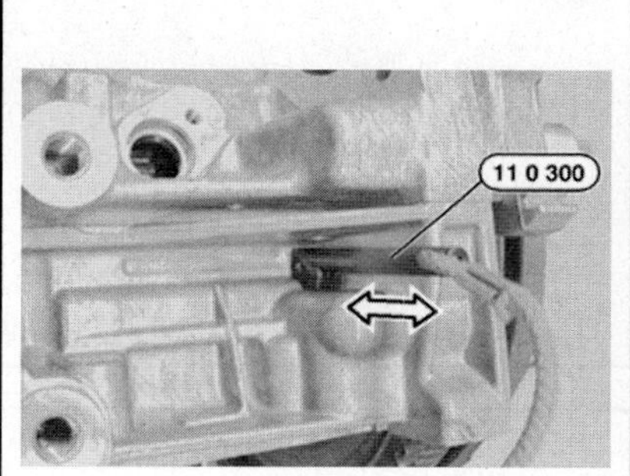

Fig. 179 Slide special tool 11 0 300 into special tool bore and secure crankshaft

11. Do not remove special tool 11 0 300 to Remove central bolt. Employ a second person for gripping when releasing central bolt.
12. Screw special tool 11 9 280 onto hub of crankshaft damper.
13. Remove central bolt.
14. Remove hub towards front.
15. Open plug at top of cylinder head.
16. Open plug at lower left of engine block.
17. Remove bearing pin from timing chain module on cylinder head.
18. Remove bearing pin from timing chain module on crankcase.

Fig. 180 Do not remove special tool 11 0 300 to Remove central bolt (1). Screw special tool 11 9 280 onto hub of crankshaft damper

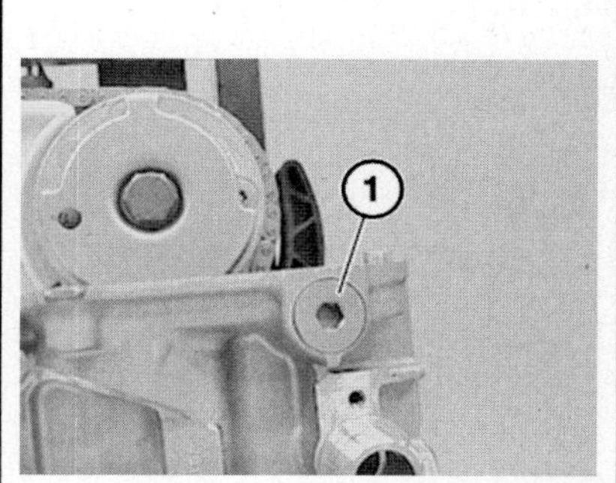

Fig. 181 Open plug at top of cylinder head

⁂ WARNING

Install special tool 11 4 280 to Remove the central bolts on the inlet and exhaust adjustment units.

19. Secure special tool 11 4 283 to cylinder head with bolts.

➡Fit special tool 11 4 282 underneath on side of inlet camshaft.

20. Mount special tool 11 4 281 on inlet and exhaust camshafts.
21. Do not remove special tool 11 4 280.
22. Remove inlet and exhaust adjustment unit. Refer to "Engine Mechanical, Camshaft and Lifters, Removal & Installation."
23. Remove bolts (1) from timing chain module on cylinder head.
24. Remove chain module with timing chain and sprocket wheel upwards.

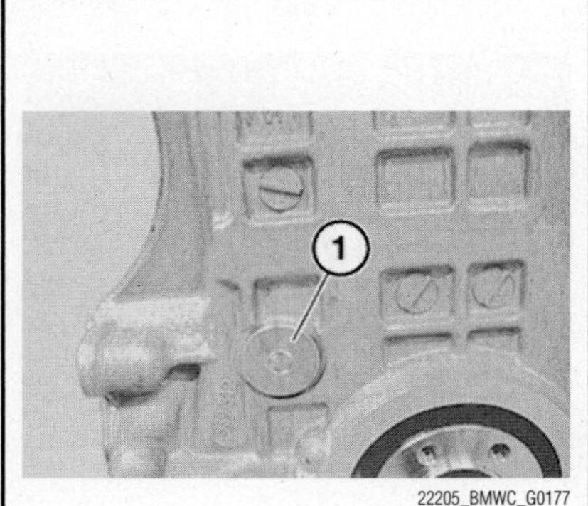

Fig. 182 Open plug at lower left of engine block

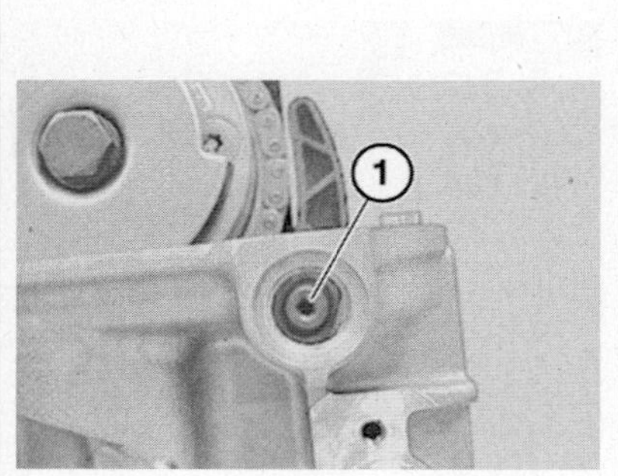

Fig. 183 Remove bearing pin (1) from timing chain module on cylinder head

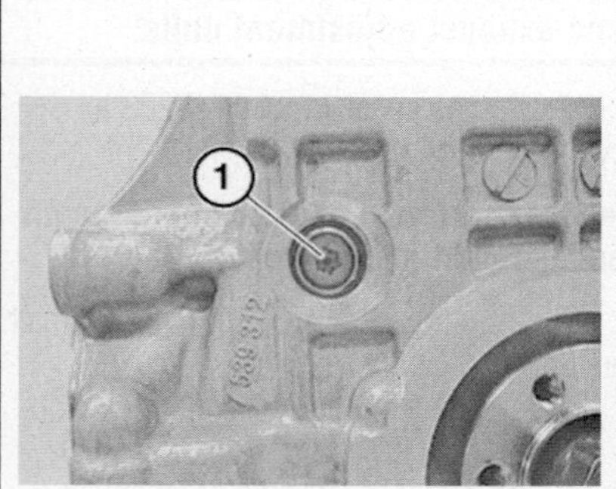

Fig. 184 Remove bearing pin (1) from timing chain module on crankcase

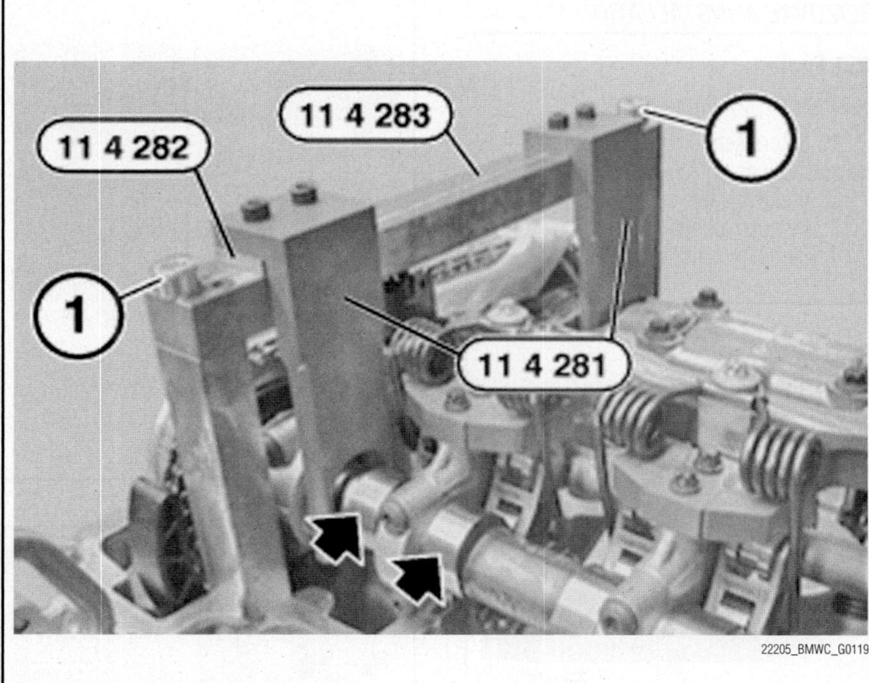

Fig. 185 Secure special tool 11 4 283 to cylinder head with bolts (1)

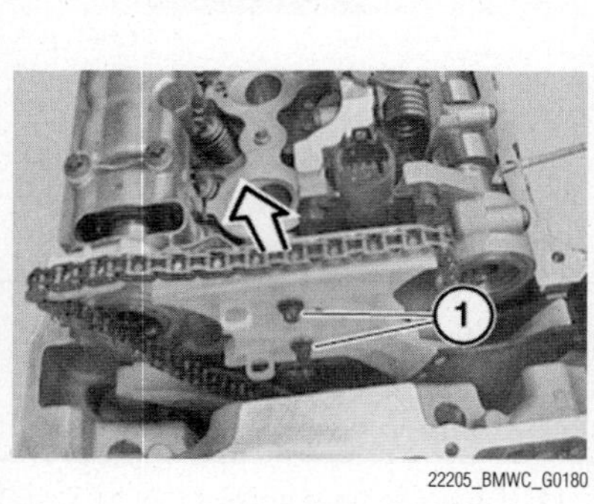

Fig. 186 Remove bolts (1) from timing chain module on cylinder head

Fig. 187 Collar (see arrow) on sprocket wheel (2) points to engine

To install:

WARNING

Note installation direction of sprocket wheel. Collar on sprocket wheel points to engine. Incorrect assembly will result in engine damage.

25. Pull timing chain upwards until sprocket wheel engages chain guide.
26. On some engines, special friction plates are required between the friction surfaces.

WARNING

The engine will incur damage if the plates are damaged or are not fitted.

a. Friction plates are clipped into place on sprocket wheel/oil pump module.
b. Make sure friction plate is in correct installation position.

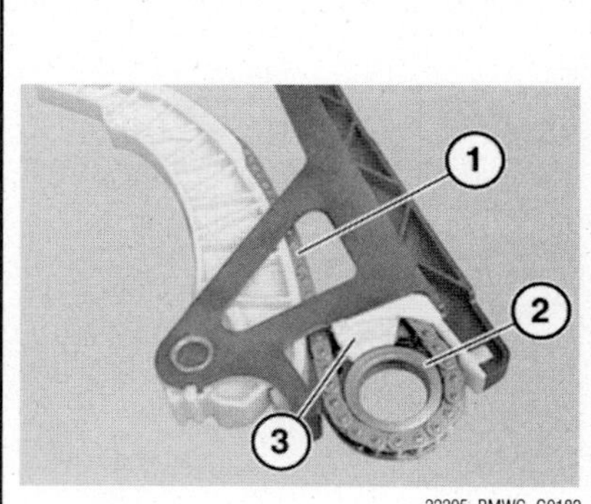

Fig. 188 Pull timing chain (1) upwards until sprocket wheel (2) engages chain guide (3)

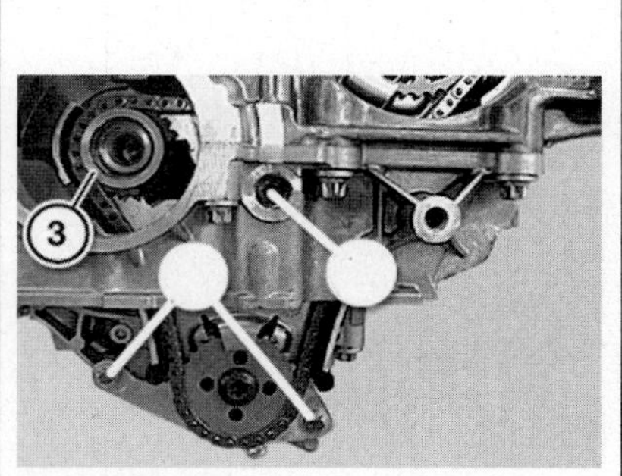

Fig. 189 Make sure friction plate (3) is in correct installation position

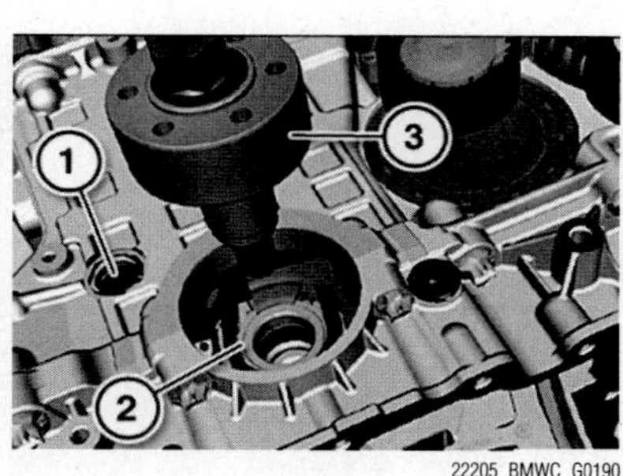

Fig. 190 Insert chain module from above and secure with bolt (1). Make sure gear wheels (2) are in correct installation position, then insert hub (3) with friction plate

Fig. 191 Tighten down special tool 11 5 200 with bolts (1) to hub

c. Push on friction plate without retainers.

d. Insert chain module from above and secure with bolt.

e. Make sure gear wheels are in correct installation position.

f. Insert hub with friction plate.

27. Install timing chain and sprocket wheel in this position.

➡Always hold timing chain under tension. Timing chain may jam on chain guide.

28. Install hub with central bolt.
29. Tighten down special tool 11 5 200 with bolts to hub.
30. Install bolts from timing chain module on cylinder head and tighten to 7 ft. lbs. (9 Nm).
31. Install bearing pin from timing chain module on crankcase and tighten to 15 ft. lbs. (20 Nm).
32. Install bearing pin from timing chain module on cylinder head and tighten to10 ft. lbs. (14 Nm).
33. Install plug and tighten to 19 ft. lbs. (25 Nm).
34. If not previously done, remove tensioner for drive belt.
35. Screw in special tool 11 4 362 from special tool kit 11 4 360.
36. Mount special tool 11 9 280 on 11 5 200.
37. Support special tool 11 9 280 on special tool 11 4 362.
38. Special tool 11 0 300 secures crankshaft.
39. Tighten central bolt to 74 ft. lbs. (100 Nm) plus an additional 360°of rotation.
40. Install inlet and exhaust adjustment units.
41. Install chain tensioner.
42. Crank engine twice.
43. Check and if necessary adjust valve timing. Refer to "Engine Mechanical, Camshaft and Lifters, Removal & Installation."
44. Install crankshaft damper.
45. Install accessory drive belt and tensioner. Tighten tensioner mounting bolt to 19 ft. lbs. (25 Nm) plus an additional 90° rotation.
46. Install crankshaft front radial seal.
47. Install chain tensioner.

➡No sealing ring is fitted during series-production assembly. A sealing ring must be fitted by service personnel when the chain tensioner is fitted.

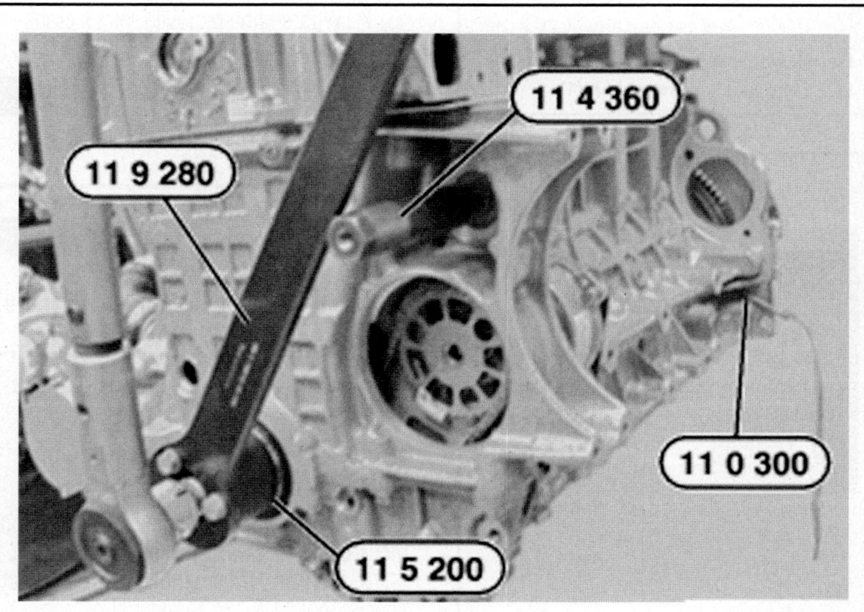

Fig. 192 Screw in special tool 11 4 362 from special tool kit 11 4 360

48. If the chain tensioner is reused, its oil chamber must be drained. Place chain tensioner on a level working surface and slowly compress.
49. Repeat procedure twice.
50. Install fastener with bore facing outwards.
51. Install tensioner and tighten to 41 ft. lbs. (55 Nm).
52. Install all spark plugs.
53. Install valve cover.

N55 Engine

See Figures 193 through 205.

1. Remove cylinder head cover.
2. Remove all spark plugs.
3. Remove crankshaft radial seal at front.
4. Remove tensioning device for drive belt.
5. Remove vibration absorber.
6. Check timing.

Fig. 193 Blocking crankshaft with special tool and removing central bolt (1)

Fig. 194 Marking crankshaft position (1)

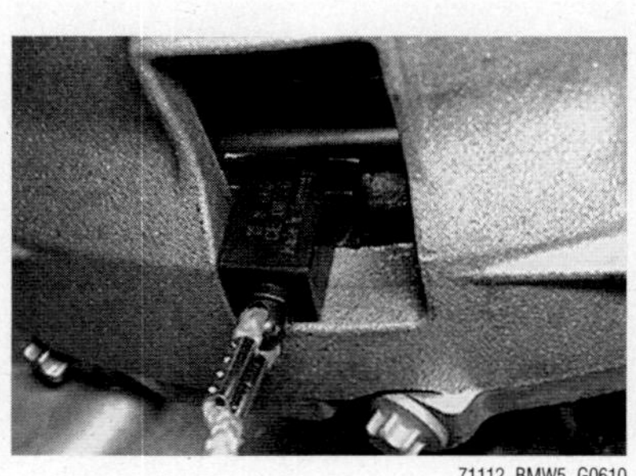

Fig. 195 Blocking crankshaft with special tool 11 8 660

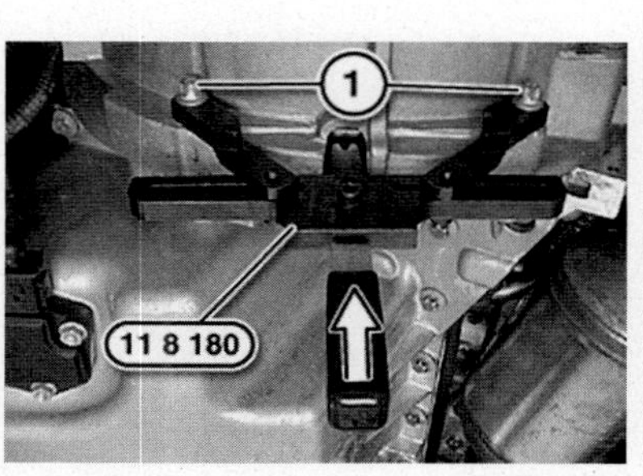

Fig. 196 Attaching special tool with existing transmission bolts (1) locking crankshaft with special tool

7. With engine removed, block crankshaft with special tool 11 9 260.

⁂ WARNING

To release central bolt (1), remove special tool 11 0 300.

⁂ WARNING

When central bolt of crankshaft is released, there is no longer a secure connection to timing drive.

8. Mark position of crankshaft using a colored mark (1).

➡This will make future insertion of special tool 11 0 300 easier.

9. Vehicles with automatic transmission, block crankshaft with special tool 11 8 660.
10. Vehicles with manual gearbox, attach special tool 11 8 180 to manual gearbox with existing transmission bolts.

Fig. 197 Releasing central bolt (1) with ¾ inch tool (2)

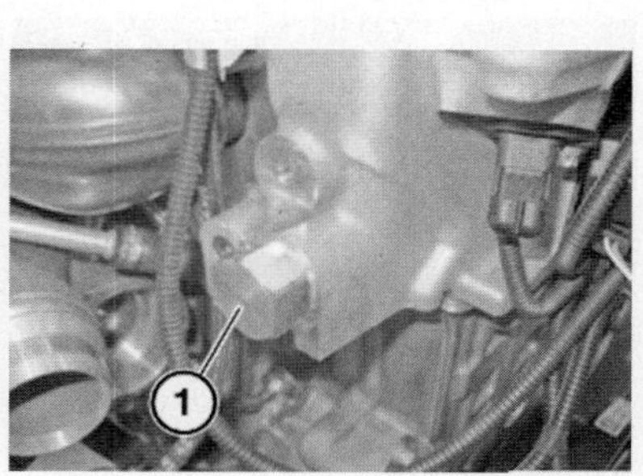

Fig. 198 Releasing chain tensioner (1)

a. Block crankshaft in direction of arrow with special tool.

⁂ WARNING

Breakaway torque of central bolt:> 443 ft. lbs. (600 Nm).

⁂ WARNING

A 3/4-inch tool (large powered square) is required to release central bolt.

11. Release central bolt (1) with 3/4-inch tool (2).
    a. Tightening torque: 74 ft. lbs. (100 Nm) + 270°.
12. Remove chain tensioner.
    a. Remove air duct.
    b. Release chain tensioner (1).
    c. Tightening torque: 41 ft. lbs. (55 Nm).

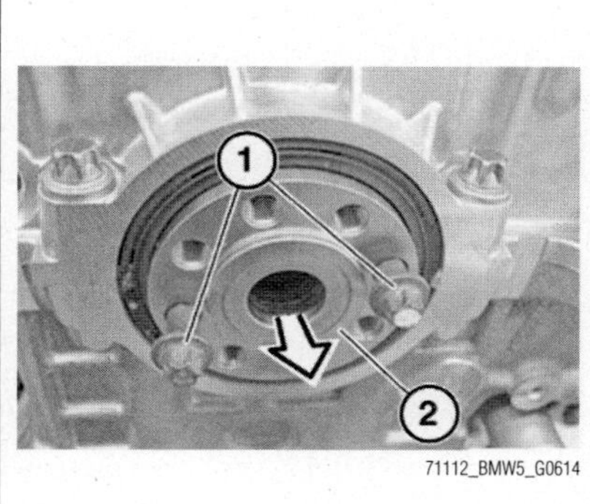

Fig. 199 Screwing in vibration absorber screws (1) and moving hub (2)

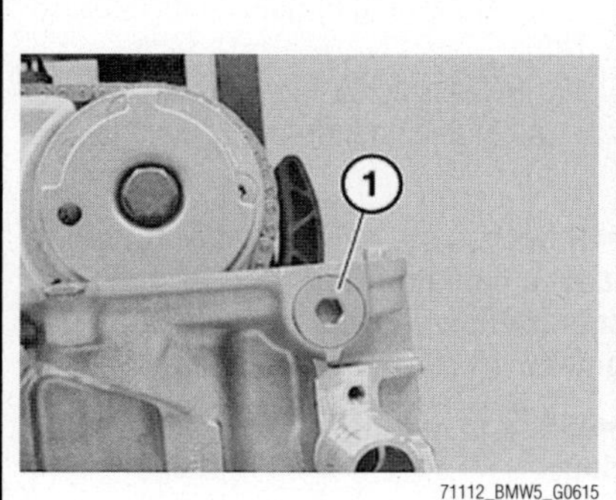

Fig. 200 Opening screw plug (1)

⁂ WARNING

Have a cleaning cloth ready. A small quantity of engine oil will emerge after the screw connection has been released.

⁂ WARNING

Make sure no engine oil runs onto belt drive.

➡If the chain tensioner is reused, its oil chamber must be drained. Place chain tensioner on a level support and slowly compress.

d. Repeat process twice.

➡When installing, replace sealing ring.

13. Screw in vibration absorber screws (1).

14. Move hub (2) on crankshaft forward in direction of arrow to remove.

Fig. 201 Opening screw plug (1)

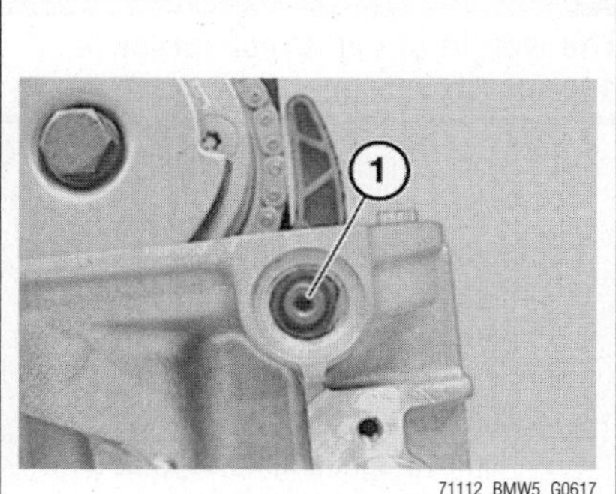

Fig. 202 Releasing bearing journal (1) from timing chain module

15. Open screw plug (1).
    a. Tightening torque: 18 ft. lbs. (25 Nm).
16. Open screw plug (1).
    a. Tightening torque: 37 ft. lbs. (50 Nm).

➡When installing, replace aluminum screws.

17. Release bearing journal (1) from timing chain module on cylinder head.
    a. Tightening torque: 10 ft. lbs. (14 Nm).
18. Release bolts (1) from timing chain module on cylinder head.
19. Remove chain module with timing chain and camshaft sprocket upwards in direction of arrow.

⁂ WARNING

Note direction of installation of camshaft sprocket (2).

Fig. 203 Releasing bolt (1) from timing chain module on cylinder head and removing chain module with timing chain and camshaft sprocket upwards in direction of arrow (N52 shown)

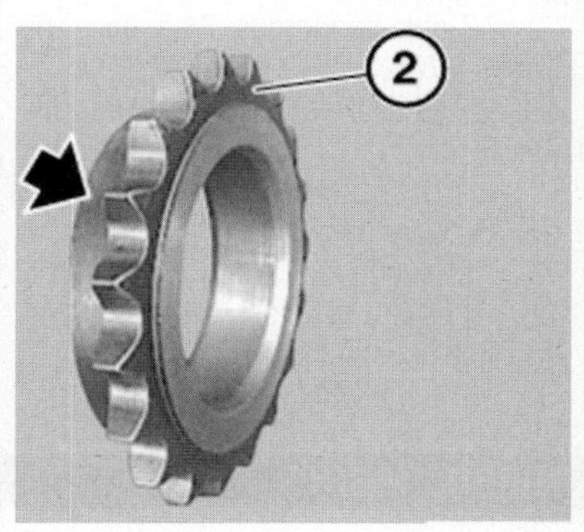

Fig. 204 Identifying camshaft sprocket (2) and collar (arrow)

⁂ WARNING

Collar (see arrow) on camshaft sprocket (2) points to engine.

⁂ WARNING

Incorrect assembly will result in engine damage.

To install:

To install, reverse the removal procedure noting the following.

20. Pull timing chain (1) upwards until camshaft sprocket (2) engages chain guide (3).

21. Install timing chain (1) and camshaft sprocket (2) in this position.

➡When installing, always hold timing chain (1) under tension. Timing chain (1) may jam on chain guide (3).

22. Insert central bolt with hub for crankshaft.

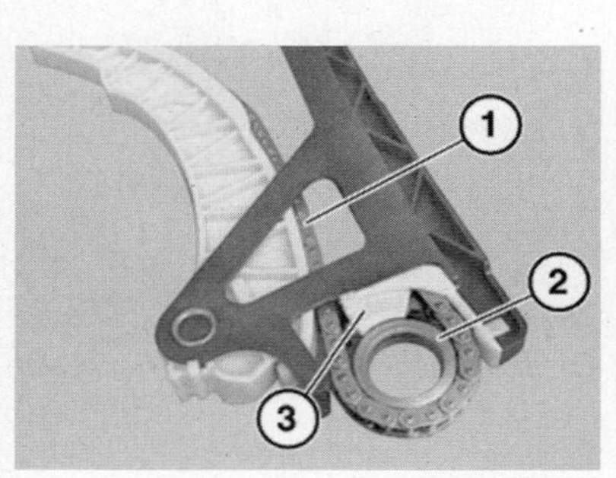

Fig. 205 Pulling timing chain (1) upwards until camshaft sprocket (2) engages chain guide (3)

23. Tighten down central bolt.
    a. Tightening torque: 74 ft. lbs. (100 Nm) + 270°.
24. Install intake and exhaust camshaft adjusters.
25. Install chain tensioner.
26. Crank engine twice.
27. Check timing.
28. If necessary, adjust valve timing.
29. Replace front crankshaft seal.
30. Assemble engine.

TURBOCHARGER

REMOVAL & INSTALLATION

N55 Engine

See Figures 206 through 219.

> **WARNING**
>
> **The module consists of exhaust turbo charger and exhaust manifold.**

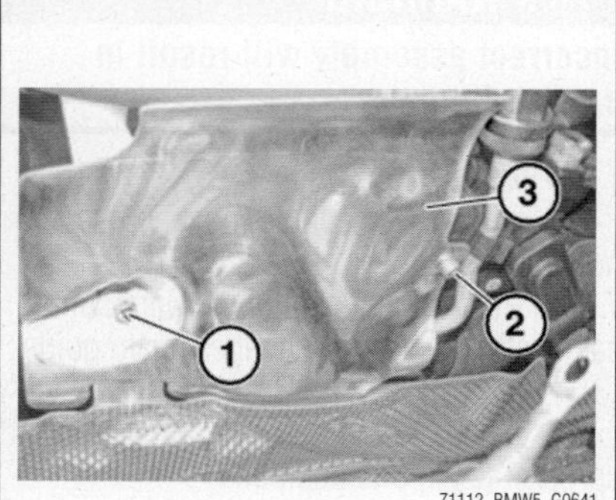

Fig. 206 Slackening nut (1), releasing screw (2) and removing heat shield (3)

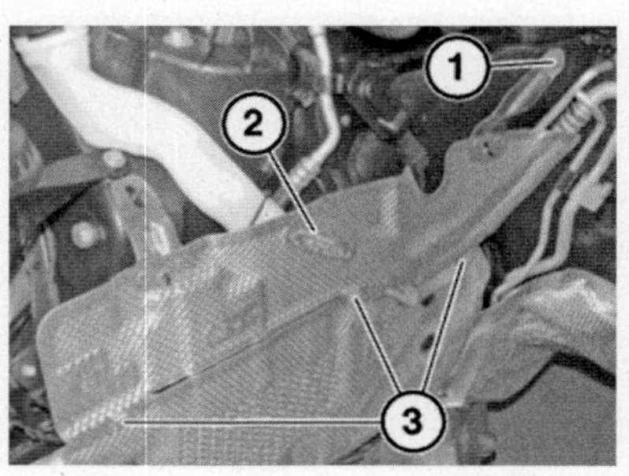

Fig. 207 Undoing sheet metal nut (1), removing heat shield (2) and checking retaining clamps (3)

> **WARNING**
>
> **The weight of the turbocharger is approx. 15 kg.**

1. Remove fan cowl with electric fan.
2. Drain coolant.
3. Remove front right wheel arch panel.
4. Remove coolant thermostat.
5. Remove coolant pump.
6. Remove charge air cooler.
7. Remove the catalytic converter.
8. Remove right engine support arm.
9. Remove right engine mount.
10. Slacken nut (1).
11. Release screw (2).
12. Remove heat shield (3) by lifting upwards.
13. Undo sheet metal nut (1).
14. Remove heat shield (2) by maneuvering upwards.

➡**When installing, check retaining clamps (3) are properly seated.**

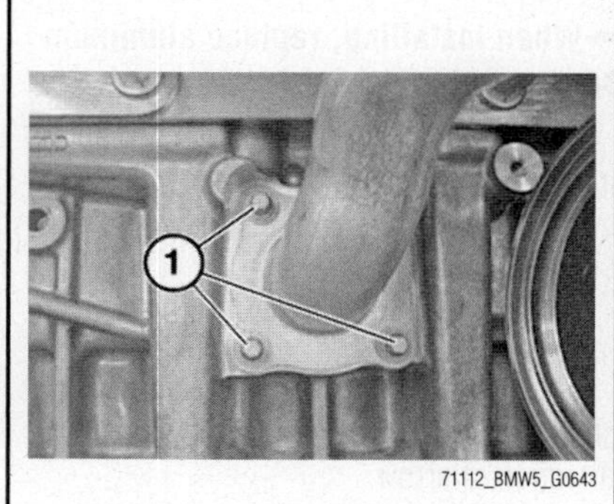

Fig. 208 Releasing screws (1)

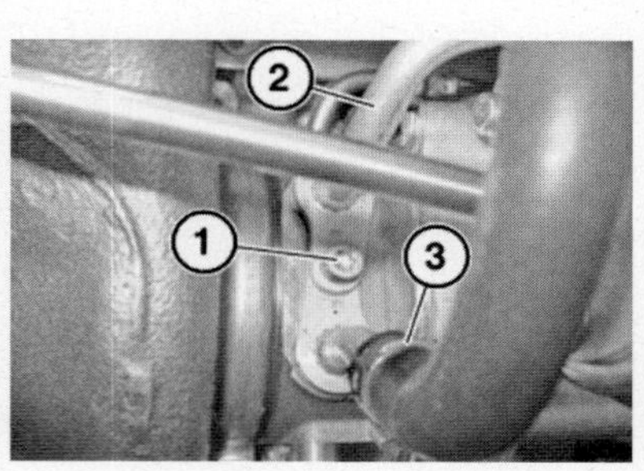

Fig. 209 Releasing screws (1) and loosening coolant return line (3) and flow line (2)

15. Release screws (1).
    a. Tightening torque: 78 inch lbs. (8.5 Nm).
16. Release screw (1).
    a. Tightening torque: 71 inch lbs. (8 Nm).

➡**If necessary, use appropriate tool to loosen coolant return line (3) and coolant flow line (2) at connection point.**

➡**When installing, replace sealing rings.**

17. Release screw (1).
18. Loosen screws (3) but Do not remove.

➡**Holder (2) can only be removed if turbocharger module has been removed.**

19. Release screw (1).
    a. Tightening torque: 71 inch lbs. (8 Nm).

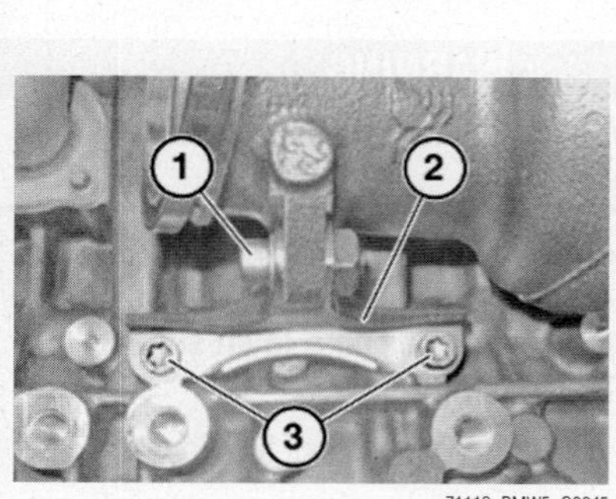

Fig. 210 Releasing screw (1), loosening screws (3) and identifying holder (2)

Fig. 211 Releasing screw (1) and loosening oil return lines at point of connection (2)

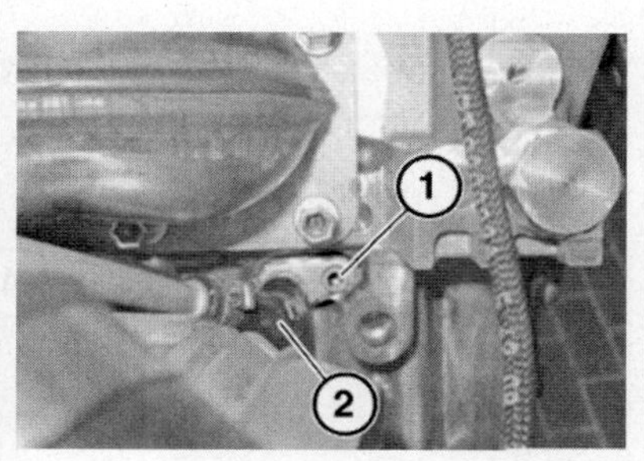

Fig. 213 Releasing screw (1) and loosening coolant return lines at point of connection (2)

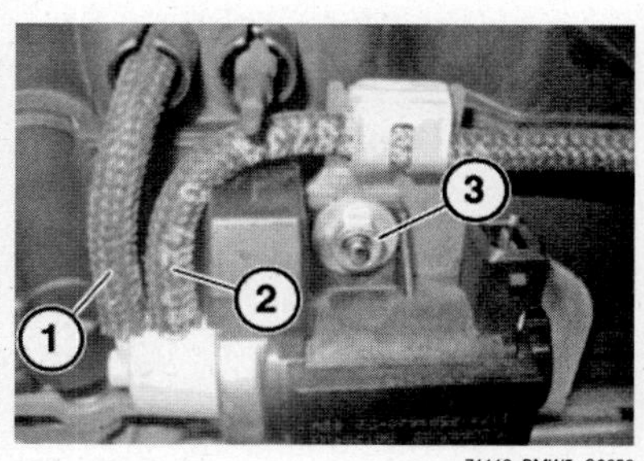

Fig. 215 Disconnecting vacuum hose (1) from cylinder head cover

20. If necessary, use appropriate tool to loosen oil return lines at point of connection (2).

➡When installing, replace sealing ring.

21. Release screw (1).
   a. Tightening torque: 71 inch lbs. (8 Nm).
22. If necessary, use appropriate tool to loosen oil return lines (2).

➡When installing, replace sealing ring.

23. Release screw (1).
   a. Tightening torque: 80 inch lbs. (9 Nm).
24. If necessary, use appropriate tool to loosen coolant return lines at point of connection (2).

➡When installing, replace sealing ring.

25. Disconnect vacuum hose (1) from vacuum line.
26. Disconnect vacuum hose (1) from cylinder head cover.
27. Remove heat shield (1).
   a. Tightening torque: 71 inch lbs. (8 Nm).
28. Loosen all flange nuts (2) along the line.
29. Remove module by maneuvering downwards on gearbox side.

➡Overall weight of module is approximately 15 kg.

30. Remove both brackets from gearbox.
   a. Tightening torque M6: 7 ft. lbs. (9 Nm)
   b. Tightening torque M10: 28 ft. lbs. (38 Nm)
   c. Tightening torque M10x10.9: 41 ft. lbs. (56 Nm)
   d. Tightening torque M8: 14 ft. lbs. (19 Nm)
   e. Tightening torque M12: 49 ft. lbs. (66 Nm)

➡The following are aluminum screws:

   f. Tightening torque M10x30: 15 ft. lbs. (20 Nm) + 90-110°
   g. Tightening torque M10x85: 15 ft. lbs. (20 Nm) + 180-200°
   h. Tightening torque M12: 18 ft. lbs. (25 Nm) + 130°

➡Oil supply line (2) can only be replaced after removal of the turbocharger.

31. Release screw (1).
   a. If necessary, use appropriate tool to loosen oil feeder lines at point of connection (2).

To install:

To install, reverse the removal procedure noting the following.

32. Replace all sealing rings.
33. Replace all graphite seals.

Fig. 212 Releasing screw (1) and loosening return lines (2)

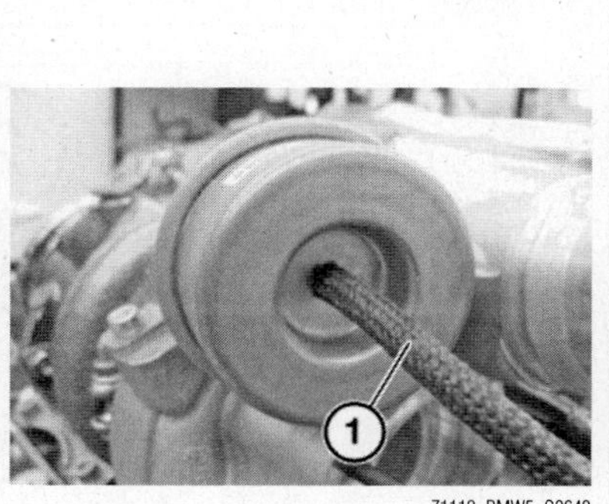

Fig. 214 Disconnecting vacuum hose (1) from vacuum line

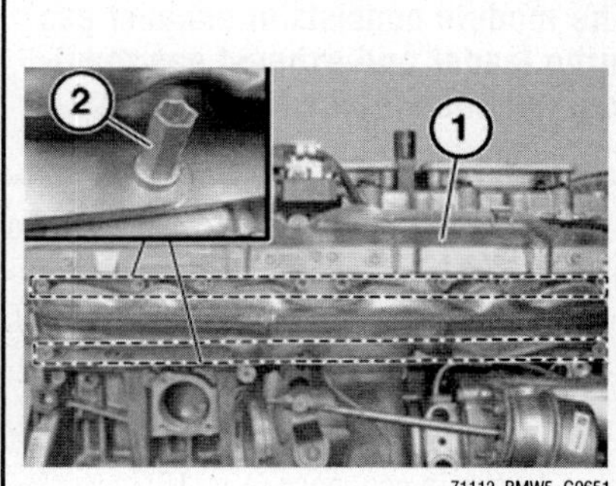

Fig. 216 Removing heat shield (1) and loosening flange nuts (2)

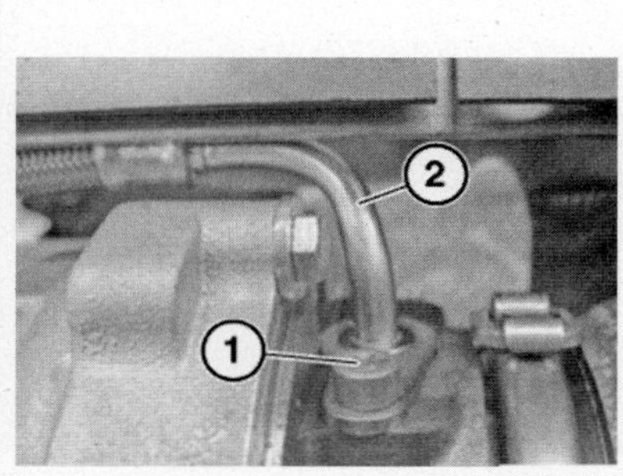

Fig. 217 Releasing screw (1) and loosening oil feeder lines at point of connection (2)

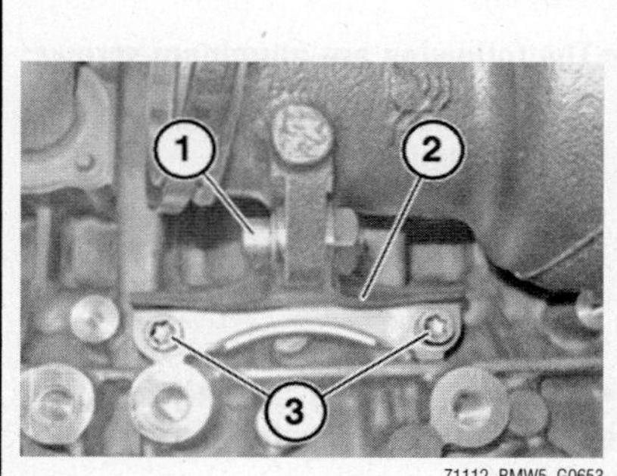

Fig. 218 Inserting bolt (1)

34. Position turbocharger on cylinder head and hold in place with two bolts.
35. Insert bolt (1) but do not tighten at this point.

⁂ WARNING

The module consists of exhaust gas turbo loader and exhaust gas manifold and must be installed stress-free.

36. Torque and torque sequence must be observed without fail.
37. Tightening torque: 10 ft. lbs. (13 Nm).
    a. Join all flange nuts in sequence 1 to 15 to 8 Nm.
    b. Tighten all flange nuts to a torque of 13 Nm in sequence (1 to 15).

➡Flange nuts 1 to 5 are accessible from above.

➡Flange nuts 6 to 15 are accessible from below.

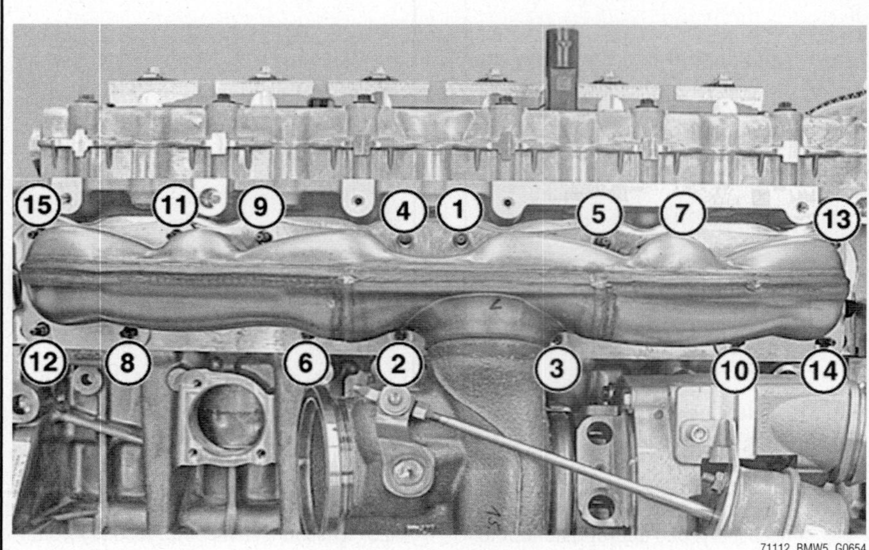

Fig. 219 Identifying bolt tightening sequence

38. Secure screws (3).
    a. Tightening torque: 15 ft. lbs. (20 Nm).
39. Tighten bolt (1).
    a. Tightening torque: 15 ft. lbs. (20 Nm).
40. Assemble engine.
41. Observe BMW Diagnostics System instruction.
42. Carry out BMW leak test for intake system.

VALVE COVERS

REMOVAL & INSTALLATION

N52 Engine

See Figure 220.

1. Before servicing the vehicle, refer to the precautions.
2. Remove ignition coils.
3. Remove ignition wiring harness in valve cover area.

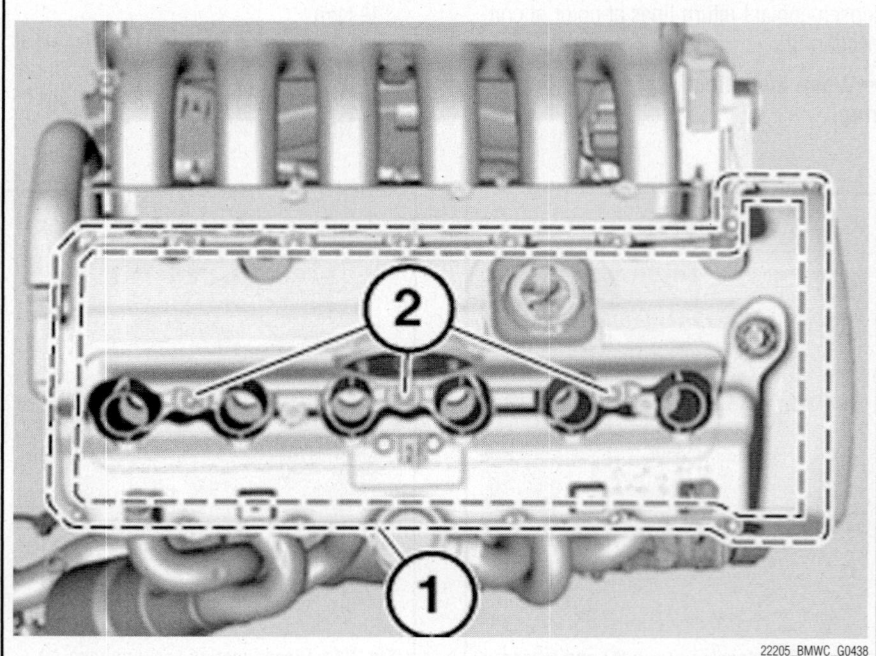

Fig. 220 Installation location of screws (1 and 2) is specified by the different bushing shapes

4. Remove tension strut.
5. Unlock and detach vent hose.
6. If necessary, pull off metal bracket.
7. Remove screws on electric servomotor.

➡A further screw, which cannot be seen in the picture, must be Removed under the electric servomotor.

8. Remove screw on electric servomotor.
9. Remove servomotor.
10. If necessary, remove nuts.
11. If necessary, remove secondary air valve.

⁂ WARNING

Observe different screw lengths. Installation location of screws is specified by the different bushing shapes.

12. Remove screws in area.
13. Remove threaded pin.
14. Remove slotted sleeves.

To install:

15. Installation is the reverse of removal.
16. Clean all sealing faces.

⁂ WARNING

Do not use any metal-cutting tools.

17. Replace gaskets.
18. Slotted sleeves for guiding ignition coils in valve cover must be replaced.
19. Replace aluminum screws.
20. Tighten bolts/nuts to specification as follows:
    - Electric servomotor to cylinder head and to valve cover: 8 ft. lbs. (10 Nm)
    - Secondary air valve to cylinder head: 6 ft. lbs. (8 Nm)
    - Valve cover to cylinder head: 7ft. lbs. (9 Nm)

ENGINE PERFORMANCE & EMISSION CONTROLS

CAMSHAFT POSITION (CMP) SENSOR

LOCATION

See Figures 221 and 222.

REMOVAL & INSTALLATION

N52 Engine

See Figures 221 through 222

1. Before servicing the vehicle, refer to the precautions.
2. Read out fault memory of DME control unit; if necessary, work through test schedules.
3. Switch ignition **OFF**.
4. Remove radiator cover.
5. Remove plug connector and pull off.
6. Remove screw.
7. Remove pulse generator.

To install:

8. Installation is the reverse of removal.

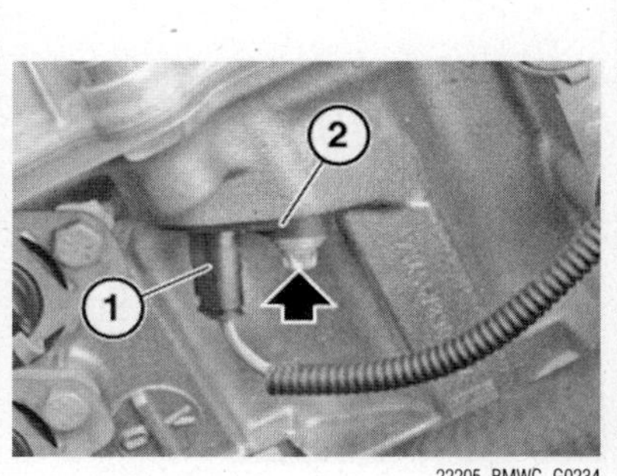

Fig. 221 Intake CMP sensor (2) and connector (1) location— N52 engine

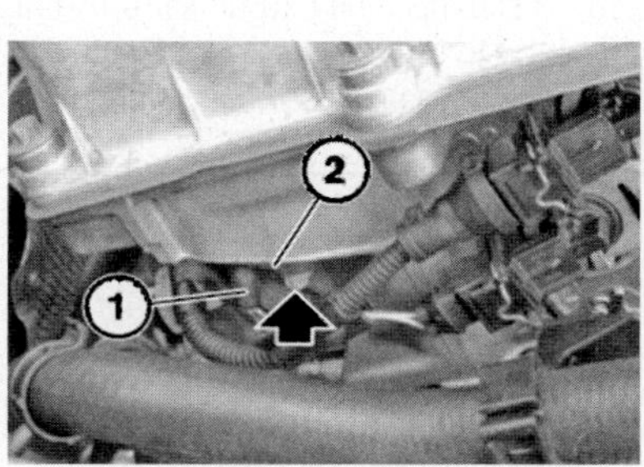

Fig. 222 Exhaust CMP sensor (2) and connector (1) location— N52 engine

9. If equipped, replace sealing ring and coat with antiseize agent.
10. Tighten sensor to 7 ft. lbs. (9 Nm).
11. Check for stored fault messages, rectify faults and clear the fault memory.

CRANKSHAFT POSITION (CKP) SENSOR

LOCATION

See Figure 223.

REMOVAL & INSTALLATION

N52 Engines

See Figure 223.

⁂ WARNING

Aluminum-magnesium materials. No steel screws/bolts may be used due to the threat of electrochemical corrosion. A magnesium crankcase requires aluminum screws/bolts exclusively. Aluminum screws/bolts must be replaced each time they are removed. The end faces of aluminum screws/bolts are painted blue for the purposes of reliable identification. Jointing torque and angle of rotation must be observed without fail (risk of damage).

1. Before servicing the vehicle, refer to the precautions.
2. Read out fault memory of DME control unit; if necessary, work through test schedules.
3. Switch ignition **OFF**.
4. Remove intake air manifold.
5. Disconnect plug.
6. Disconnect the crankshaft pulse generator.
7. Remove and discard the aluminum bolts.
8. Remove pulse generator from crankcase.

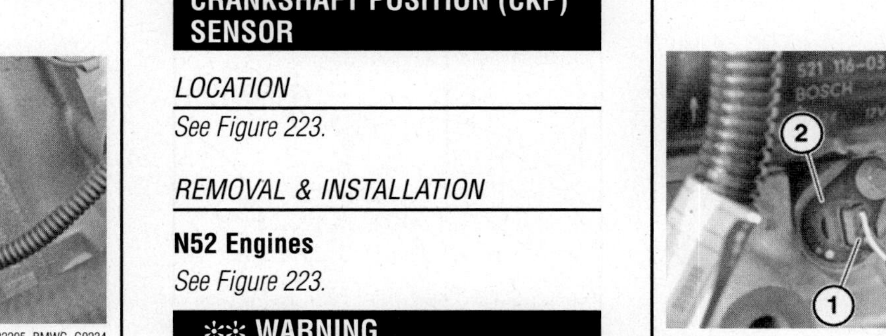

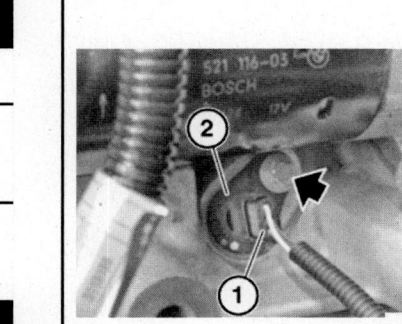

Fig. 223 CKP sensor (2) and connector (1) location—N52 engine

To install:

9. Replace sealing ring.
10. Install pulse generator to crankcase.
11. Using new aluminum bolts, tighten to 2 ft. lbs. (3 Nm) plus an additional 45° of rotation.
12. Connect the crankshaft pulse generator.
13. Install intake air manifold.

ENGINE COOLANT TEMPERATURE (ECT) SENSOR

LOCATION

See Figure 224.

REMOVAL & INSTALLATION

N52 Engine

See Figure 224.

1. Before servicing the vehicle, refer to the precautions.
2. Read out fault memory of DME control unit; if necessary, work through test schedules.
3. Switch ignition **OFF**.
4. Though you can avoid it, for easier access, remove the intake duct.
5. Unlock the plug on the sensor (1) and remove it.
6. Remove the temperature sensor (2).

To install:

7. Reposition the sensor and lock the plug.
8. After returning the temperature sensor back to its position, make sure to vent the cooling system and check for leaks.
9. If necessary, top off the coolant in the reservoir.
10. Check for stored fault messages, rectify faults and clear the fault memory.

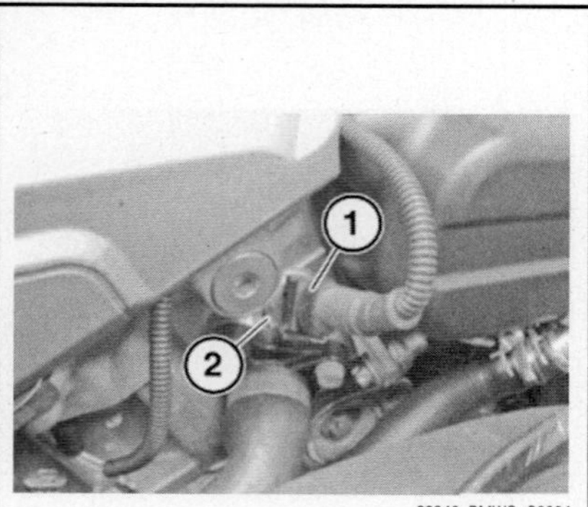

Fig. 224 ECT location—N52 engine

HEATED OXYGEN (HO2S) SENSOR

LOCATION

See Figures 225 and 226.

REMOVAL & INSTALLATION

N52 Engine

See Figures 225 through 226.

1. Before servicing the vehicle, refer to the precautions.
2. Read out fault memory of DME control unit; if necessary, work through test schedules
3. Switch ignition **OFF**.
4. Remove the exhaust system.
5. Disconnect the plug connection from the sensors.
6. Disconnect the oxygen sensor from cylinders 4 to 6.
7. The oxygen sensor at cylinders 1 to 3 is accessible from above without the exhaust system having to be removed.

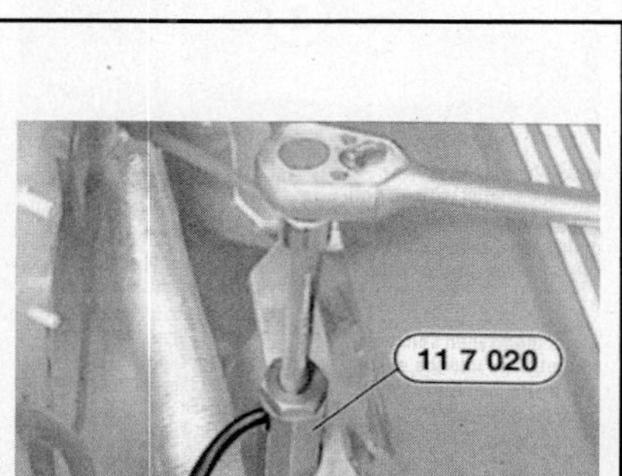

Fig. 225 HO2S sensor (1) and special removal tool for cylinders 1–3 location—N52 engine

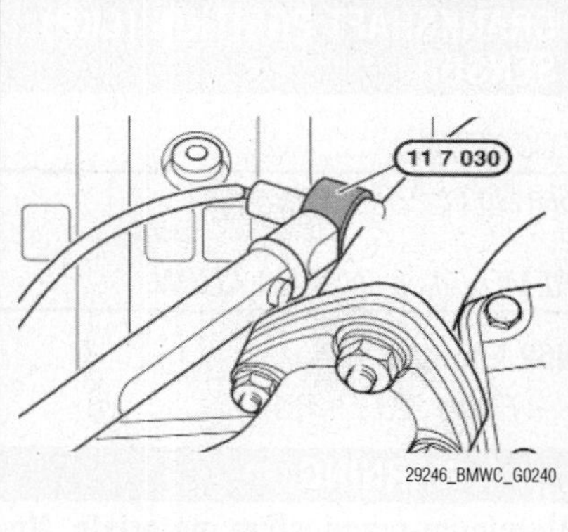

Fig. 226 HO2S sensor (1) and special removal tool (2) for cylinders 4–6 location—N52 engine

To install:

8. The threads of a new oxygen sensors are already coated with an anti-seize compound. If an oxygen sensor is to be used again, apply a thin and even coat of an anti-seize compound to the thread only.

**** WARNING**

Do not clean the oxygen sensor section which protrudes into the exhaust line and ensure that it avoids all contact with any lubricants.

➡Observe cable routing of the oxygen sensor so it doesn't interfere with any other system or the exhaust pipes.

9. Tighten sensor to 37 ft. lbs. (50 Nm).
10. Connect the oxygen sensors and their respective cables.
    - The cable color for the sensor that leads to cylinders 1 to 3 is black.
    - The cable color for the sensor that leads to cylinders 4 to 6 is gray.
11. Connect the plug connection to the sensors.
12. Check for stored fault messages, rectify faults and clear the fault memory.

N55 Engine

See Figures 227 and 228.

**** CAUTION**

Work should only be carried out on an exhaust system that has cooled down.

**** WARNING**

The threads of new oxygen control sensors are already coated with

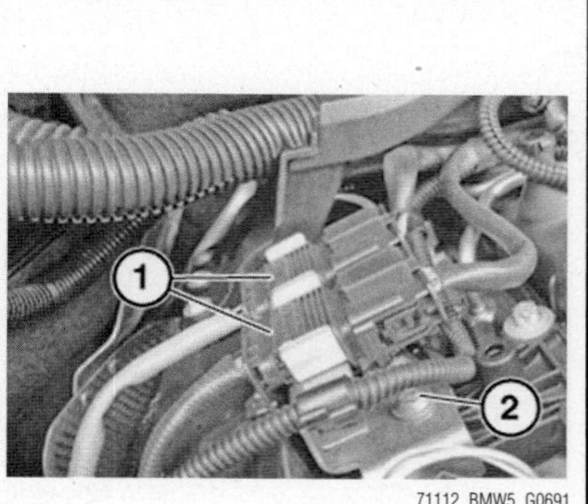

Fig. 227 Disconnecting plug connection on oxygen control sensor (1)

NEVER-SEEZ compound (refer to BMW Parts Department).

⁂ WARNING

If an oxygen control sensor is to be reused, apply a thin and even coating of NEVER-SEEZ compound to the thread only.

⁂ WARNING

The part of the lambda control sensor which projects into the exhaust branch (sensor ceramics) must not be cleaned and not coated with lubricant.

1. Remove rear engine guard.
2. Remove air duct.
3. Disconnect plug connection on oxygen control sensor (1).

➡Installation note:

a. Cable color of oxygen control sensor = black.
b. Cable color of oxygen monitoring sensor = grey.

4. Release oxygen control sensor (1) with special tools 11 7 030 and 11 9 150 with a suitable extension (2).

a. Tightening torque: 37 ft. lbs. (50 Nm).

⁂ WARNING

When using special tool 11 7 030 in conjunction with special tool 11 9 150, it is essential to reduce the prescribed tightening torque by 27 inch lbs. (3 Nm).

To install:

5. To install, reverse the removal procedure.
6. Reassemble the vehicle.
7. Check function of DME.

INTAKE AIR TEMPERATURE (IAT) SENSOR

LOCATION

The Intake Air Temperature (IAT) sensor is an integral part of the Mass Air Flow (MAF) sensor. Refer to components and systems, mass air flow (MAF) sensor.

KNOCK SENSOR (KS)

LOCATION

See Figure 229.

REMOVAL & INSTALLATION

N52 Engine

See Figure 229.

⁂ WARNING

No steel bolts or bolts may be used due to the threat of electrochemical corrosion. A magnesium crankcase requires aluminum bolts and bolts exclusively. The end of the aluminum bolts and bolts are painted blue for the purposes of reliable identification.

1. Before servicing the vehicle, refer to the precautions.
2. Read out fault memory of DME control unit; if necessary, work through test schedules.
3. Switch ignition **OFF**.
4. Disconnect the battery.
5. Remove the air intake manifold.
6. Unlock the plug connection and remove it.
7. Unscrew the bolts on both knock sensors and remove the sensors.

To install:

8. Clean the support face of the knock sensors on engine block.
9. Install the bolts on both knock sensors to replace the sensors.
10. Check for stored fault messages, rectify faults and clear the fault memory.

N55 Engine

See Figure 230.

⁂ WARNING

Aluminum screws/bolts must be replaced each time they are released.

⁂ WARNING

Aluminum screws/bolts are permitted with and without color coding (blue).

⁂ WARNING

For reliable identification:

a. Aluminum screws/bolts are not magnetic.
b. Jointing torque and angle of rotation must be observed without fail (risk of damage).

1. Read out the fault memory of the DME control unit.
2. Switch off ignition.
3. Remove intake plenum.
4. Unlock connector (1) and remove.
5. Feed out connector (1) behind feed line, remove feed line if necessary.
6. Release screws on both knock sensors (1) and remove knock sensors (1).

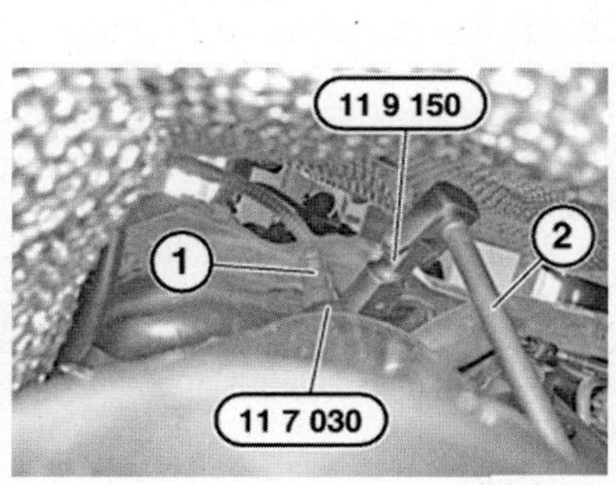

Fig. 228 Releasing oxygen control sensor (1) with special tools with a suitable extension (2)

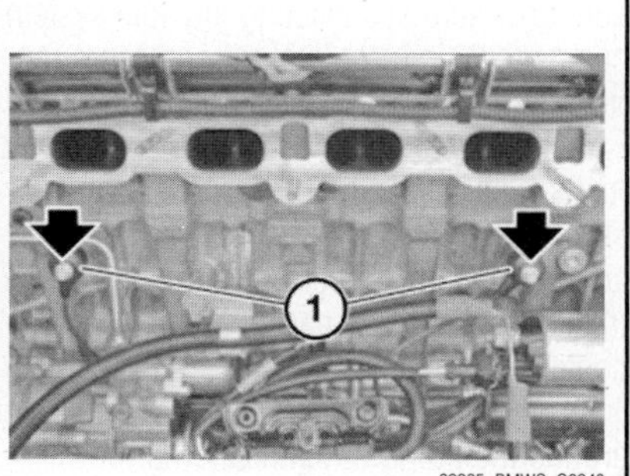

Fig. 229 Knock (KS) sensor location—N52 engine

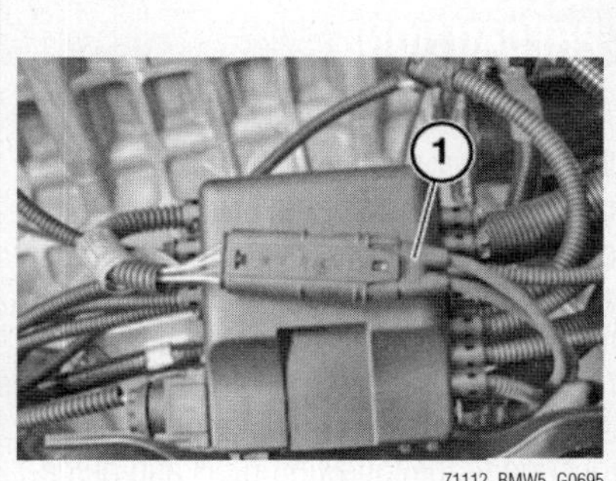

Fig. 230 Unlocking and removing connector (1)

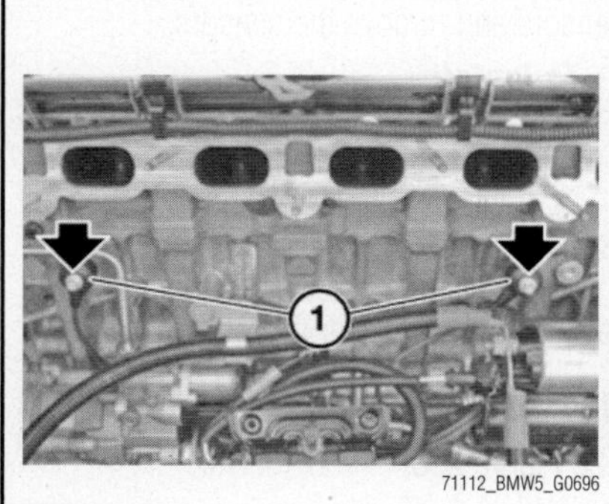

Fig. 231 Releasing screws on both knock sensors (1) and removing knock sensors

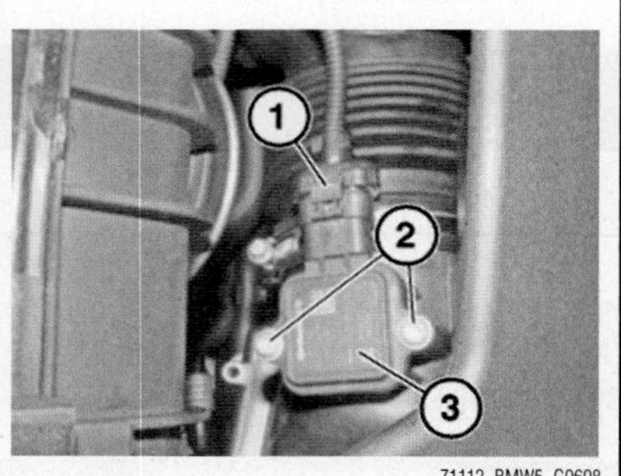

Fig. 232 Unlocking plug (1), unfastening screws (2) and removing air mass flow sensor (3)

Fig. 233 TPS sensor (2) and connector (1) location

➡When installing, replace aluminum screws.

a. Tightening torque: 16 ft. lbs. (21.5 Nm).

To install:

To install, reverse the removal procedure noting the following.

7. Clean contact surface of knock sensor on engine block.
8. Reassemble the vehicle.
9. Check stored fault message.
10. Delete fault memory.

MASS AIR FLOW (MAF) SENSOR

REMOVAL & INSTALLATION

N52 Engine

See Figure 232.

1. Read out fault memory of DME control unit.
2. Turn off ignition.
3. Unlock plug (1) and remove.
4. Unfasten screws (2).
5. Pull air-mass flow sensor (3) out of upper section of intake silencer housing.

To install:

To install, reverse the removal procedure noting the following.

6. Check stored fault message.
7. Delete fault memory.

THROTTLE POSITION SENSOR (TPS)

LOCATION

See Figure 233.

REMOVAL & INSTALLATION

See Figure 233.

1. Before servicing the vehicle, refer to the precautions.
2. Read out fault memory of DME control unit; if necessary, work through test schedules.
3. Switch ignition **OFF**.
4. Remove air intake hose.
5. Unlock plug and remove.
6. Remove throttle assembly.

To install:

7. Replace sealing ring of throttle assembly.
8. Install throttle assembly. Tighten bolts to 6 ft. lbs. (9 Nm).
9. Install air intake hose.
10. Check for stored fault messages, rectify faults and clear the fault memory.

FUEL — GASOLINE FUEL INJECTION SYSTEM

FUEL SYSTEM SERVICE PRECAUTIONS

Safety is the most important factor when performing not only fuel system maintenance but any type of maintenance. Failure to conduct maintenance and repairs in a safe manner may result in serious personal injury or death. Maintenance and testing of the vehicle's fuel system components can be accomplished safely and effectively by adhering to the following rules and guidelines.

- To avoid the possibility of fire and personal injury, always disconnect the negative battery cable unless the repair or test procedure requires that battery voltage be applied.
- Always relieve the fuel system pressure prior to disconnecting any fuel system component (injector, fuel rail, pressure regulator, etc.), fitting or fuel line connection. Exercise extreme caution whenever relieving fuel system pressure to avoid exposing skin, face and eyes to fuel spray. Please be advised that fuel under pressure may penetrate the skin or any part of the body that it contacts.
- Always place a shop towel or cloth around the fitting or connection prior to loosening to absorb any excess fuel due to spillage. Ensure that all fuel spillage (should it occur) is quickly removed from engine surfaces. Ensure that all fuel soaked cloths or towels are deposited into a suitable waste container.
- Always keep a dry chemical (Class B) fire extinguisher near the work area.
- Do not allow fuel spray or fuel vapors to come into contact with a spark or open flame.
- Always use a back-up wrench when loosening and tightening fuel line connection fittings. This will prevent unnecessary stress and torsion to fuel line piping.
- Always replace worn fuel fitting O-rings with new Do not substitute fuel hose or equivalent where fuel pipe is installed.

Before servicing the vehicle, make sure to also refer to the precautions in the beginning of this section as well.

RELIEVING FUEL SYSTEM PRESSURE

WARNING

The manufacturer does not provide a specific pressure relieving procedure, but instructs that any fuel system disconnect will spill fuel, so be prepared to catch and clean up any spilled fuel.

A safe way to relieve the pressure in the system is to locate the fuel pump relay located on the cowl. Unplug and remove the relay, and place it in a safe location. With the fuel pump relay removed, start the engine and operate it until it stalls. Crank the engine for 10 seconds after it stalls to remove any residual pressure.

FUEL FILTER

REMOVAL & INSTALLATION

See Figure 234.

1. Before servicing the vehicle, refer to the precautions in the beginning of this section.
2. Properly relieve the fuel system pressure.
3. Remove or disconnect the following:
   - Negative battery cable
   - Fuel pressure regulator and seal the fuel line before and after the filter
   - Clips and fuel line from the filter
   - Fuel filter

To install:

- New fuel filter
- New seal
- Fuel lines onto the correct fittings.

  Tighten the fuel line clamps until tight, but not to the point where the fuel lines become excessively pinched or damaged, then tighten the mounting bracket until snug.
- Negative battery cable and cycle the ignition **ON** and **OFF** several times to build fuel pressure

4. Start the vehicle and check for leaks, repair if necessary.

FUEL INJECTORS

REMOVAL & INSTALLATION

N52 Engine

➡This procedure involves removing the complete injection pipe with injectors.

1. Before servicing the vehicle, refer to the precautions section.
2. Properly relieve the fuel system pressure.
3. Mark the locations of each oxygen sensor connector for proper reinstallation.
4. Remove or disconnect the following:
   - Negative battery cable
   - Connectors from clips on injection pipe
   - Intake Air Temperature (IAT) sensor connector
   - Plug connection on solenoid valve for camshaft adjustment (VANOS) unit
   - Terminal strip for fuel injectors from injection pipe
5. Unclip the fuel line from its holder, then unlock the fuel line from the cylinder head at the rear (be prepared to catch any fuel).
6. Remove the retaining bolts and remove the injection pipe with the fuel injectors.

To install:

7. Coat the sealing rings of the injectors with anti-seize compound prior to fitting.
8. Install the fuel injectors and fuel pipe to the engine.
9. Install or connect the following:
   - Fuel line
   - Terminal strip to fuel injectors
   - Connectors as removed
   - Negative battery cable

FUEL PUMP

REMOVAL & INSTALLATION

See Figure 236.

1. Before servicing the vehicle, refer to the precautions in the beginning of this section.
2. Drain the fuel tank.
3. Properly relieve the fuel system pressure.
4. Remove or disconnect the following:
   - Negative battery cable
   - Rear seat bench
   - Rubber plug above the sender unit and fold the rubber mat back
   - Metal cover
   - Electrical connectors
   - Fuel lines and service vent line
   - Rotary connection with special tool 16–1–020
5. Raise the fuel level sensor and expose the spiral hose.
6. Remove the fuel level sensor and fuel pump from the tank.

To install:

➡Always use a new seal or gasket when installing the fuel pump or fuel level gauge sending unit assembly.

7. Install the fuel pump into the fuel

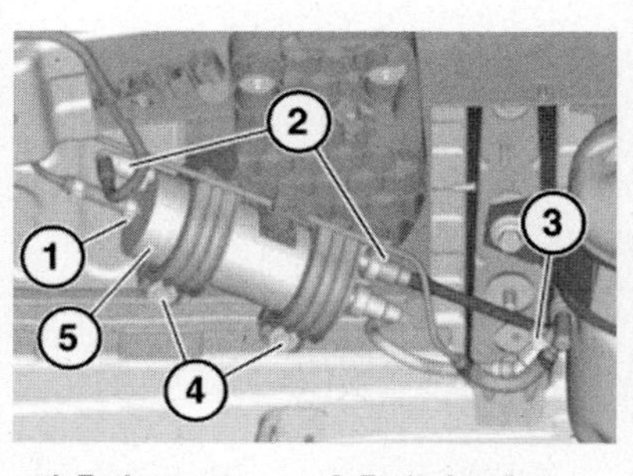

Fig. 234 Fuel filter mounting

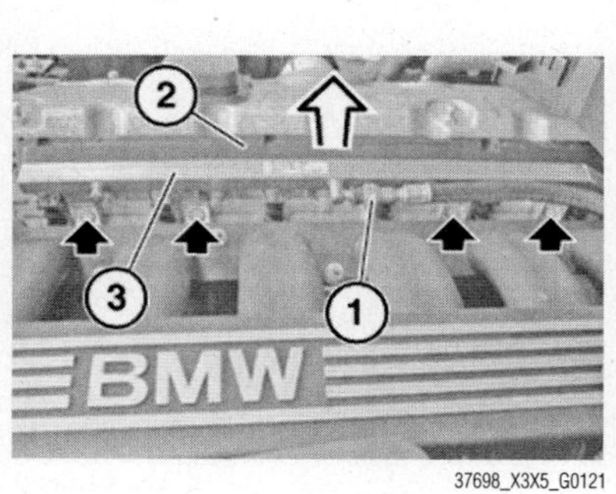

Fig. 235 Removing the fuel injection pipe—N52 engine

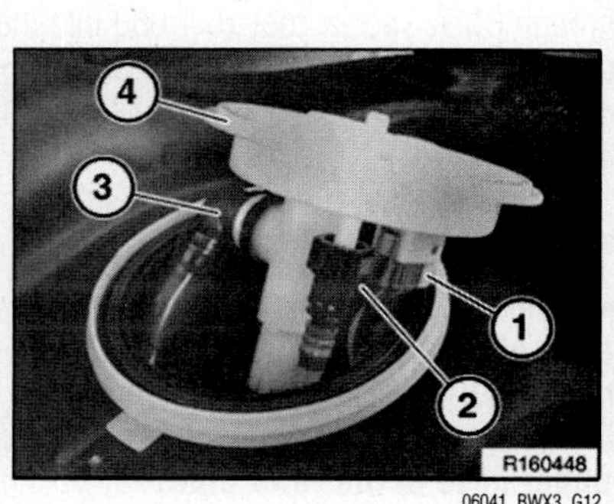

Fig. 236 Showing service cap, fuel line, vent line and electrical connector on fuel pump

tank, taking care not to bend or damage the fuel sending unit assembly.

8. Install a new seal and torque the sealing ring using tool No. 16-1-020 as follows:

a. Metal sealing rings: 26 ft. lbs. (35 Nm).

b. Plastic sealing rings: 41 ft. lbs. (55 Nm).

9. Install or connect the following:

- Fuel lines and service vent line
- Fuel gauge level sending unit electrical connector
- Metal cover
- Rubber plug above the sender unit
- Rear seat bench
- Negative battery cable

10. Start the vehicle and check for leaks, repair if necessary.

FUEL TANK

DRAINING

Suction Pump Functional:

1. Start engine and allow to run.

➡The electric fuel pump runs. In this way, the fuel is repumped through the suction jet pump from the left to the right side of the fuel tank. Fuel can be drawn out of left and right sides of tank through filler neck, leaving only a small residue. The residual quantity is drawn off through the service opening (on right/left).

2. Insert BMW special tool 16 1 080 into the filler neck.

WARNING

BMW special tool 16 1 080 has two different diameters for petrol/gasoline and diesel vehicles.

3. Slide extraction hose of extractor unit, through BMW special tool 16 1 080 into the fuel filler pipe, turning in the process if necessary. Insertion length approximately 47 in. (100 cm).

4. Draw off fuel as much as possible with extractor unit.

➡If the extraction hose meets resistance at an insertion length of approximately 47 in. (100 cm), a second person must press gently against the rubber hose of the filler pipe.

Suction Pump Non-Functional:

1. Draw off right half of tank completely through fuel filler pipe.

2. Remove cap from left service opening.

3. Insert extraction hose through service opening in tank, fuel (also residual quantity) can be drawn off.

REMOVAL & INSTALLATION

See Figures 237 through 239.

CAUTION

Observe all applicable safety precautions when working around fuel. Whenever servicing the fuel system, always work in a well-ventilated area. Do not allow fuel spray or vapors to come in contact with a spark or open flame. Keep a dry chemical fire extinguisher near the work area. Always keep fuel in a container specifically designed for fuel storage; also, always properly seal fuel containers to avoid the possibility of fire or explosion.

1. Before servicing the vehicle, refer to the Precautions Section.

2. Relieve the fuel system pressure.

3. Drain the fuel tank.

4. Remove or disconnect the following:

- Rear seat bench
- Underbody paneling
- Handbrake Bowden cables
- Complete driveshaft

5. Remove bolts and remove cover from right side of fuel tank.

6. Disconnect plug and service vent line from fuel pump assembly along with hose.

7. Remove hose clamps and detach fuel filler hose from fuel tank.

8. Unclip fuel vent line from clips on fuel tank.

9. Disconnect fuel feed line and fuel return line at the fittings joining the fuel lines to the front of the vehicle.

10. Remove bolt and unclip lines from fuel line holder.

➡Do not kink fuel lines when moving them aside. Seal the lines with special tools 13 5 281 and 13 5 282.

11. Support the fuel tank.

12. Remove bolts for fuel tank mounting strap on the left and right sides.

13. Lower fuel tank until line is accessible.

14. Unclip line (1) from the holders.

15. Move fuel tank downwards.

16. Feed out fuel line (2).

➡Do not kink fuel line.

17. Remove fuel tank.

To install:

18. Raise fuel tank to a height that will allow the installation of the vehicle's fuel line through the clips on the tank.

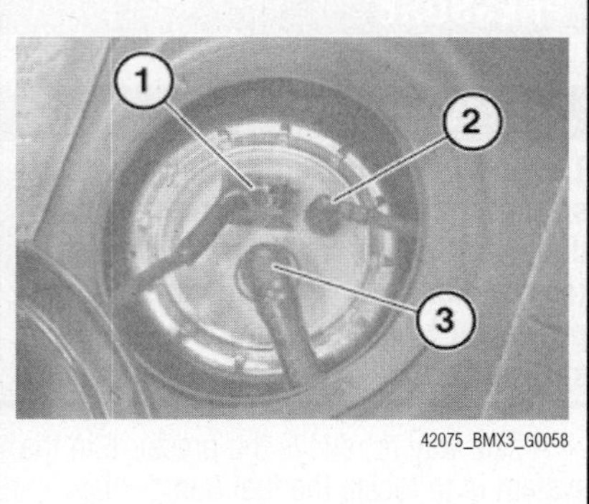

Fig. 238 Removing connections (1), (2), and (3) from the fuel pump assembly

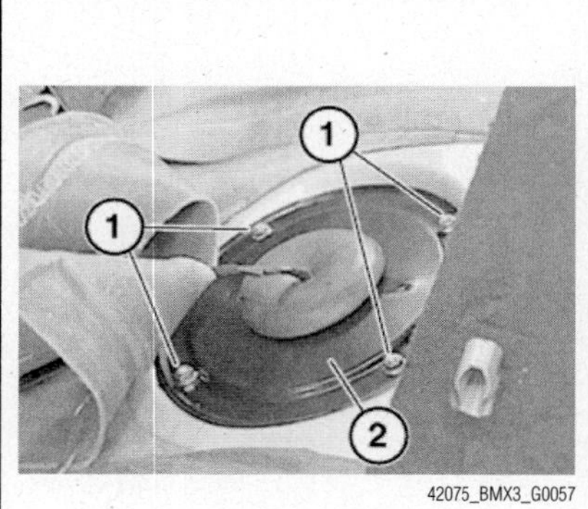

Fig. 237 Removing cover (2) and bolts (1) for fuel tank connection access

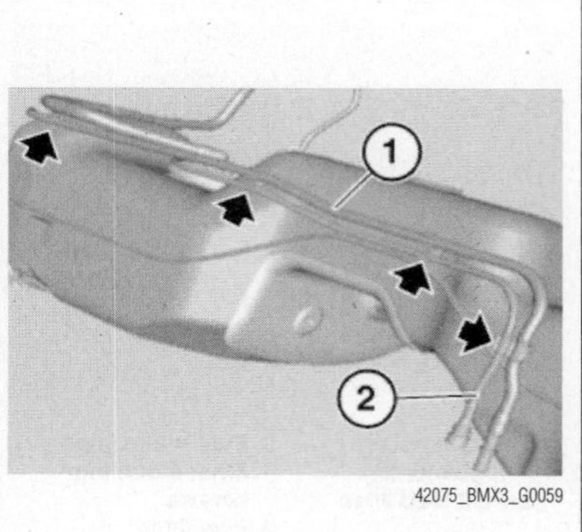

Fig. 239 Accessing fuel line (1) after lowering fuel tank

19. Clip the fuel lines to the tank.
20. Attach the fuel tank mounting straps around the fuel tank. Tighten the bolts in the straps to 14 ft. lbs. (19 Nm).
21. Install or connect the following:
   - The fuel lines beneath the vehicle
   - The fuel lines under the back seat area
   - The fuel fill hose and fuel fill vent hose
   - Clamps holding fuel supply and return lines
   - Electrical connection at fuel pump assembly
   - Driveshaft
   - Handbrake Bowden cables
   - Underbody paneling
   - Rear seat bench
22. Fill tank with at least 5 gallons of fuel and test function of fuel pump.
23. Check for fuel leakage in fuel delivery system.

IDLE SPEED

ADJUSTMENT

Idle speed is maintained by the Digital Motor Electronics control unit. No adjustment is necessary or possible.

THROTTLE BODY

REMOVAL & INSTALLATION

1. Before servicing the vehicle, refer to the Precautions Section.

Fig. 240 Location of resonance flap and idle-speed control valve

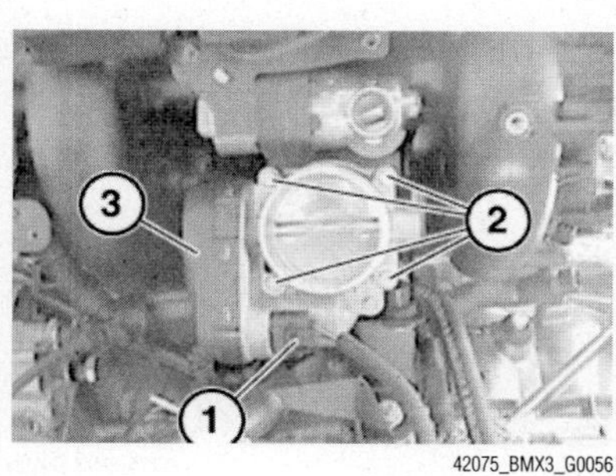

Fig. 241 Removing throttle body

2. Remove or disconnect the following:
   - The negative battery terminal
   - Intake filter housing
   - Intake hose (between intake filter housing and throttle body)
   - Disconnect the resonance flap
   - Disconnect the idle—speed control valve
   - Disconnect the oil pressure switch
   - Disconnect the oil temperature switch
   - Disconnect plug from tank venting valve
   - Remove screws on cable duct mounting
   - Remove screw and remove oil dipstick guide tube
   - Unlock plug and detach from throttle body
   - Remove screws and remove throttle body

To install:

3. Replace sealing ring between throttle body and intake manifold.

➡A faulty throttle adjusts the adaptation values stored in the DME control unit. These adaptation values must be reset after the throttle assembly has been replaced.

4. The installation continues in the reverse of the removal procedure.

HEATING & AIR CONDITIONING SYSTEM

BLOWER MOTOR

REMOVAL & INSTALLATION

See Figures 242 through 248.

1. Before servicing the vehicle, refer to the Precautions Section.
2. Remove the fuel injector cover:
   a. Unclip cover caps from bolts holding fuel injector cover.
   b. Remove bolts.
   c. Remove fuel injector cover.
3. Remove the ignition coil cover:
   a. Unclip cover caps from bolts holding ignition coil cover.
   b. Remove bolts.
   c. Remove sealing cap from cylinder head cover.
   d. Remove ignition coil cover.
   e. Replace cover cap on cylinder head to prevent foreign material entry.
4. Detach hose in direction of arrow from fitting.
5. Remove cover strip in direction of arrow from guide.
6. Pull lock in direction of arrow and feed out flap.
7. Unclip retainers.
8. Remove bolt.
9. Pull out fan cover.
10. Remove bolts.

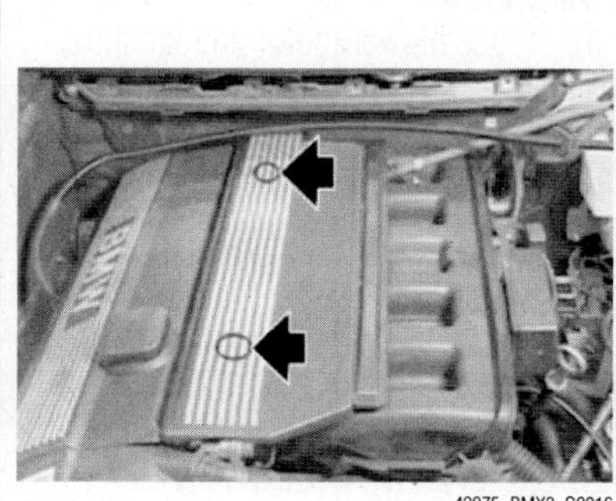

Fig. 242 Location of cover caps for removal of fuel injector cover

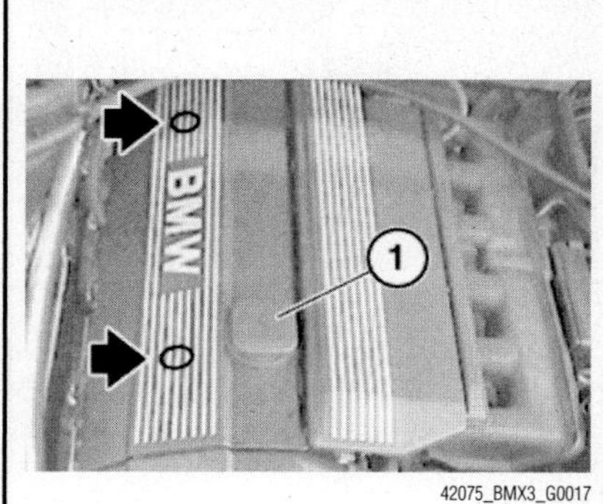

Fig. 243 Location of cylinder head cover cap and mounting cover caps for fuel injectors

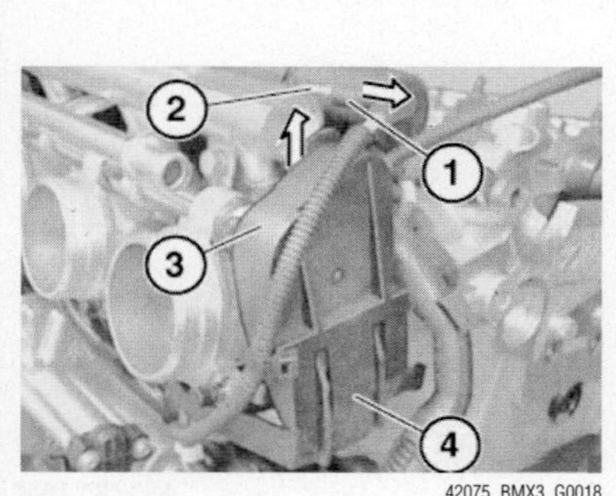

Fig. 244 Removing hose and fitting for blower motor access

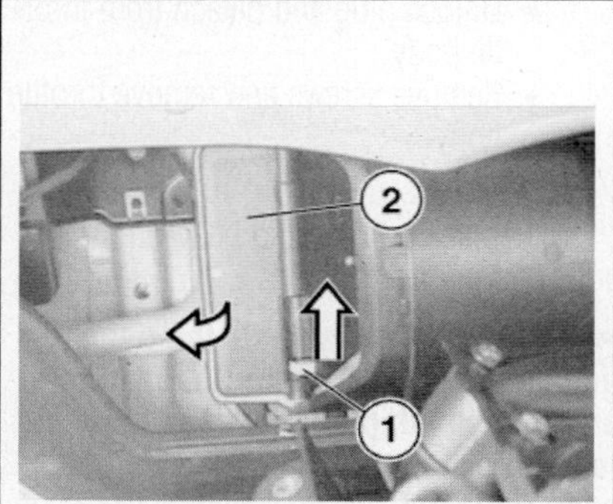

Fig. 245 Removing cover shroud of blower motor

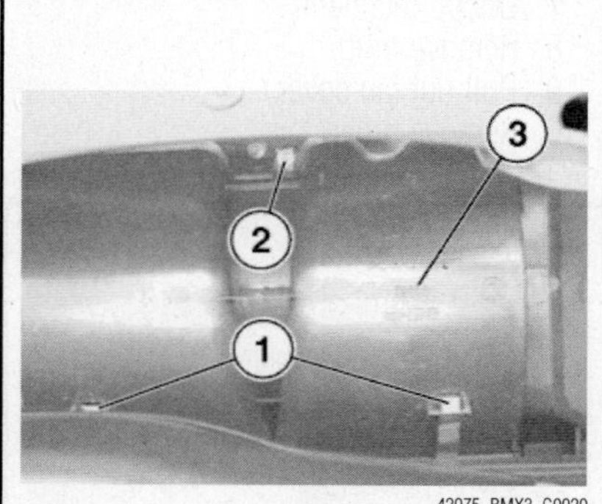

Fig. 246 Removing blower motor fan cover

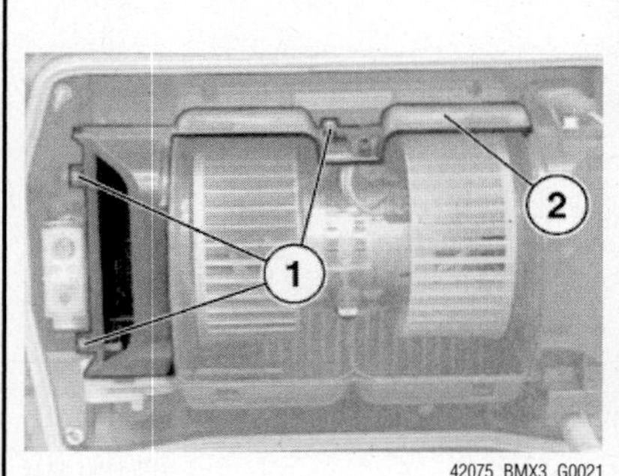

Fig. 247 Removing blower motor fan baffle

Fig. 248 Disconnecting the blower motor from retainer

11. Pull out fan baffle.
12. Disconnect the electrical connection to fan motor.
13. Release fan motor retainer with special tool 51 3 057.
14. Remove blower motor and squirrel fan.

To install:

15. Place blower motor and fan into position.
16. Make sure blower motor is seated correctly. Snap into retainer.
17. Connect electrical connections.
18. Installation continues in the reverse of the removal procedure.

HEATER CORE

REMOVAL & INSTALLATION

See Figure 249.

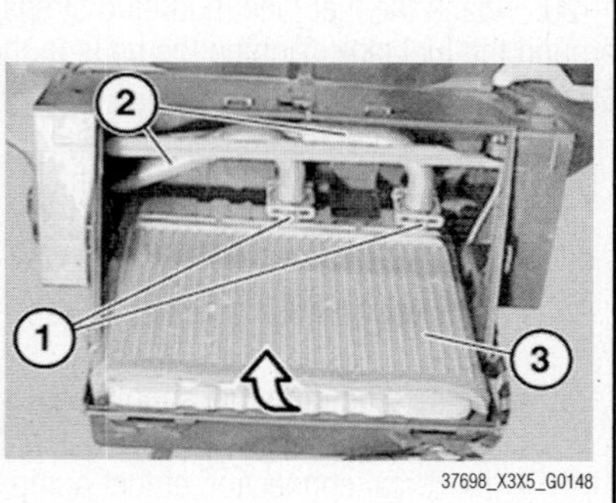

Fig. 249 Unclip the retainers (1) from the pipes (2) and lift it out housing (3)

1. Before servicing the vehicle, refer to the precautions in the beginning of this section.
2. Disconnect the negative battery cable.
3. Remove the heater bulkhead as follows:
    a. Pull off the weather strips on top of the bulkhead.
    b. Release the cowl retaining toggle clips.
    c. Lift out the cover.
    d. Remove the screws and remove the heater bulkhead.
4. Remove or disconnect the following:
    - Heater hoses from firewall connections
    - Air duct for left foot well from mountings
    - Left foot well vent
    - Heater pipes from under dash
    - Heater duct for right foot well
    - Air duct for rear foot well on right
    - Cover from heater housing
    - Evaporator temperature sensor (pull out to one side)
    - Heater core

To install:

5. Install or connect the following:
    - Heater core
    - Evaporator temperature sensor
    - Heater housing cover
    - Air ducts in foot wells
    - Heater pipes under dash
    - Heater hoses at firewall connections
    - Heater bulkhead
6. Reconnect the negative battery cable
7. Check coolant level

STEERING

POWER STEERING GEAR

REMOVAL & INSTALLATION

1. Before servicing the vehicle, refer to the precautions section.
2. Set the steering gear in the straight ahead position by aligning the marks on the steering gear and spindle.
3. Drain the power steering fluid.
4. Remove or disconnect the following:
    - Negative battery cable
    - Front wheels
    - Reinforcement plate
    - Nuts from the left and right engine support arms and raise the engine slightly
    - 2 bolts accessible through holes in frame
    - Lower clamping screw
    - Steering gear clamps (after locking wheels in straight-ahead position)
    - Tie rod by pressing it off with special tool 32-3-090
    - Self-locking nuts and brace the front axle support
    - Banjo bolts and slide the steering gear out through the left wheel opening

To install:

5. Install the steering gear through the left side wheel opening.
6. Install new sealing rings and banjo bolts. Torque the bolts as follows:
    a. M10: 7 ft. lbs. (12 Nm).
    b. M14: 25 ft. lbs. (35 Nm).
    c. M16: 29 ft. lbs. (40 Nm).
    d. M18: 34 ft. lbs. (45 Nm).
7. Install or connect the following:
    - Front axle support screws. Torque the screws to 74 ft. lbs. (100 Nm).
    - Self-locking nuts. Torque the nuts to 74 ft. lbs. (100 Nm).
    - Tie rod. Torque the castle nut to 58 ft. lbs. (80 Nm).
    - Steering gear to the spindle. Torque the fastener to 18 ft. lbs. (24 Nm).
    - Steering gear clamp
    - Engine support arm nuts. Torque the nuts to 60 ft. lbs. (85 Nm).
    - Reinforcement plate
    - Splash guard
    - Both front wheels
    - Negative battery cable
8. Fill and bleed the power steering system.
9. Start the vehicle and check for leaks, repair if necessary.

POWER STEERING PUMP

REMOVAL & INSTALLATION

See Figures 251 through 253.

1. Before servicing the vehicle, refer to the Precautions Section.

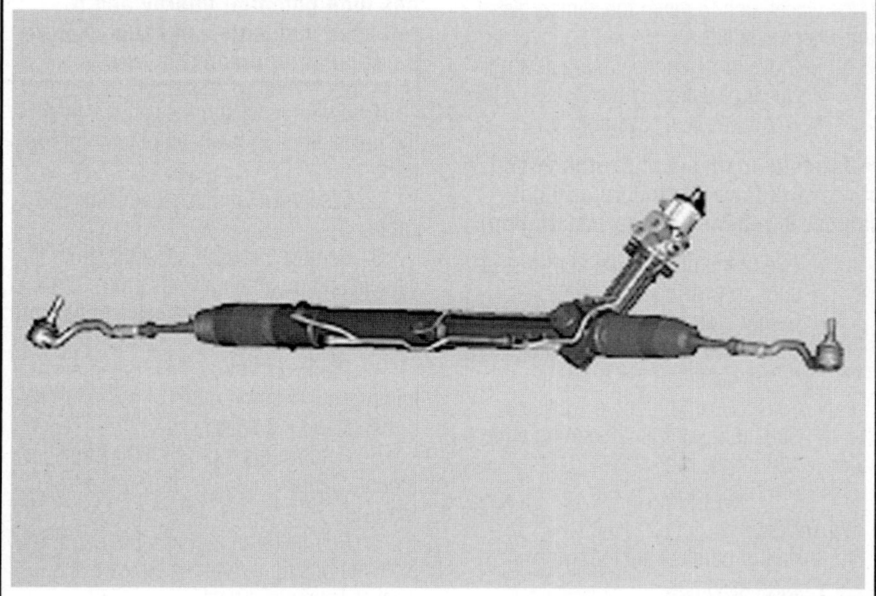

Fig. 250 Power steering rack

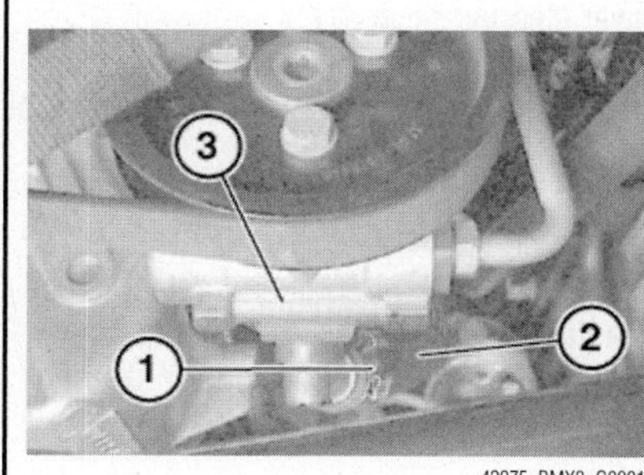

Fig. 251 Using tool 32 1 260 to detach suction line on power steering pump

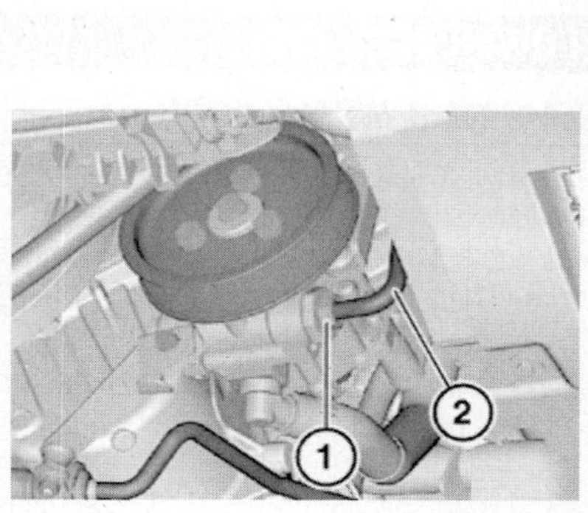

Fig. 252 Removing banjo blot (1) and pressure line (2) from power steering pump

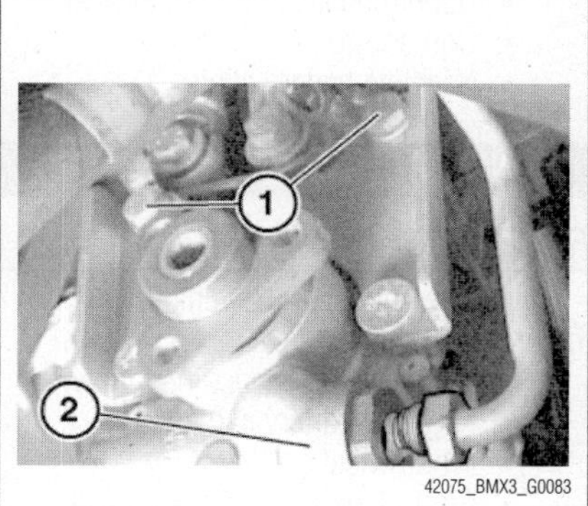

Fig. 253 Pulley and bolt (1) removal from power steering pump

2. Remove accessory drive belts. Refer to Accessory Drive Belts removal and installation.

3. Suction off hydraulic fluid from power steering reservoir.

4. Remove front underbody protection

5. Remove hose clamp with special tool 32 1 260.

6. Detach suction line from power steering pump.

7. Release banjo bolt and detach pressure line from power steering pump.

8. Remove pulley from power steering pump.

9. Remove power steering bracket bolts from engine crankcase.

10. Remove power steering pump with bracket through wheel arch.

To install:

11. Install or connect the following:

- Power steering pump. Tighten bracket bolts to 16 ft. lbs. (21 Nm)
- Pulley on power steering pump. Tighten bolts to 21 ft. lbs. (28 Nm)
- Replace sealing ring on pressure line. Tighten banjo bolt to 27 ft. lbs. (36 Nm)
- Suction line on power steering pump
- Hose clamp with special tool 32 1 260
- Front underbody protection

12. Fill power steering reservoir with hydraulic fluid.

13. Install accessory drive belts. Refer to Accessory Drive Belts removal and installation.

14. Bleed hydraulic system.

15. Check pipe connections for leaks.

SUSPENSION

FRONT SUSPENSION

COIL SPRING

REMOVAL & INSTALLATION

Refer to the Strut Overhaul procedure.

LOWER BALL JOINT

REMOVAL & INSTALLATION

1. Before servicing the vehicle, refer to the precautions in the beginning of this section.

2. Remove or disconnect the following:

- Negative battery cable
- Coil spring
- Upper control arm from trailing arm
- Shock absorber from the swinging arm

3. Using special tool 33–3–331/2/3 and pull the ball joint out of the steering knuckle.

To install:

4. Install or connect the following:

- Ball joint into the steering knuckle with special tools 33–3–332/3/4
- Shock absorber to the swinging arm
- Upper control arm to trailing arm
- Coil spring
- Negative battery cable

LOWER CONTROL ARM

REMOVAL & INSTALLATION

1. Before servicing the vehicle, refer to the precautions section.

2. Remove or disconnect the following:

- Negative battery cable
- Front wheel
- Control arm from the front axle support and loosen the nut from the control arm to swivel bearing
- Control arm from the swivel bearing by pressing it off with special tool 31-2-240

To install:

3. Install or connect the following:

- Lower control arm to the swivel bearing. Torque the nut to 58 ft. lbs. (80 Nm).
- Lower control arm to the front axle support. Torque the nut to 74 ft. lbs. (100 Nm) plus an additional 90 degrees.
- Front wheel
- Negative battery cable

4. Check and adjust the front end alignment as needed.

MACPHERSON STRUT

REMOVAL & INSTALLATION

1. Before servicing the vehicle, refer to the precautions in the beginning of this section.

2. Mark the position of the threaded pin to the wheel arch to retain the camber setting when installed.

3. Remove or disconnect the following:

- Negative battery cable
- Tire and wheel assembly

➡Carefully mark position of threaded pin to strut tower to ensure original camber is retained during installation.

- Two of the nuts on the spring strut support bearing
- Center strut bracket nut
- Speed sensor/brake wear cable and disconnect the plug housing
- Swivel bearing and tie it aside
- Remaining nut on the spring strut support bearing
- Strut assembly

To install:

4. Install or connect the following:

- Strut assembly
- One nut to the spring strut support bearing and hand tighten at this time
- Swivel bearing. Torque the new self-locking nut to 176 ft. lbs. (250 Nm).
- Speed sensor/brake wear cable and connect the housing plug
- Center strut bracket. Torque the nut to 74 ft. lbs. (100 Nm).

5. Align the three upper spring strut support bearing nuts and match the threaded pin with the mark made during the removal procedure. When aligned properly torque the nuts to 25 ft. lbs. (34 Nm).

6. Install the tire and wheel assembly.

7. Reconnect the negative battery cable.

OVERHAUL

⁂ CAUTION

This procedure calls for the spring to be compressed. A compressed spring has high potential energy and if released suddenly can cause severe damage and personal injury.

1. Before servicing the vehicle, refer to the precautions in the beginning of this section.

2. Disconnect the negative battery cable.

3. Remove the strut assembly from the vehicle and mount in a vise using a strut holder. This will prevent damage to the strut tube.

4. Using a proper spring compressor, compress the spring until the stress on the thrust bearing is released.

5. Remove the top nut of the strut mount. Counter hold the strut rod during removal.

6. Pull the strut mount off the strut rod. Note the positioning of the spacers and washer for replacement.

7. Pull the spring off the strut and place aside in a safe area.

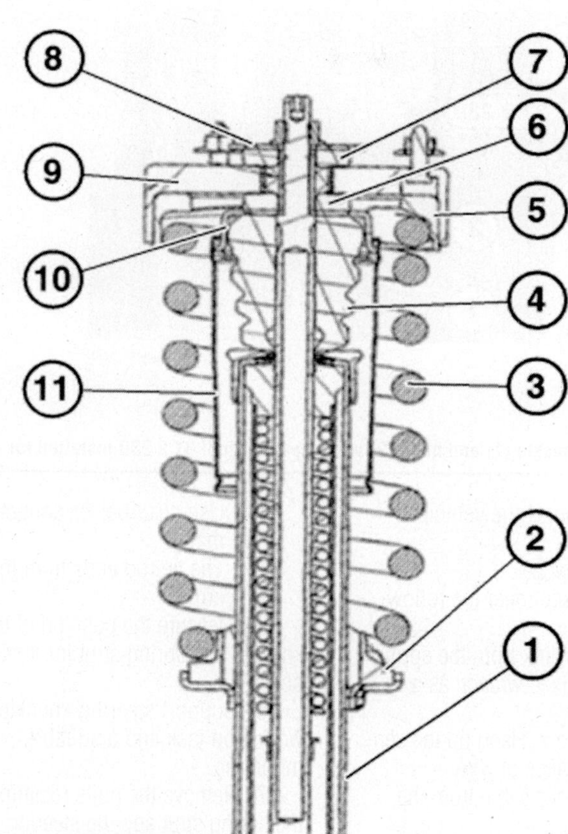

1. Spring strut shock absorber
2. Lower spring pad
3. Coil spring
4. Auxiliary damper
5. Upper spring pad
6. Support bearing lower section
7. Support bearing upper section
8. Joint seat
9. Support bearing flange
10. Support pot
11. Protective tube

37698_X3X5_G0157

Fig. 254 View of the strut components

8. Slowly release the compression of the spring.

To install:

9. Install or connect the following:
   - Spring in the compressor and compress
   - Spring and strut mount with all the spacers and washers in their original positions. Torque the new strut rod nut: 47 ft. lbs. (65 Nm).
10. Release the spring slowly and check that it seats in the spring holders. Install the strut in the vehicle.
11. Connect the negative battery cable.

STABILIZER BAR

REMOVAL & INSTALLATION

See Figures 255 through 257.

1. Before servicing the vehicle, refer to the Precautions Section.
2. Remove or disconnect the following:
   - Underside protection
   - Reinforcement plate
   - Partially detach front wheel arch trim on both sides toward rear of front fenders
   - Double pivot of lower steering spindle from power steering gear
   - Stabilizer links on both sides from stabilizer bar

WARNING

When supporting components, make sure that the vehicle can no longer be raised or lowered and that the vehicle does not lift off the locating plates on the lifting platform.

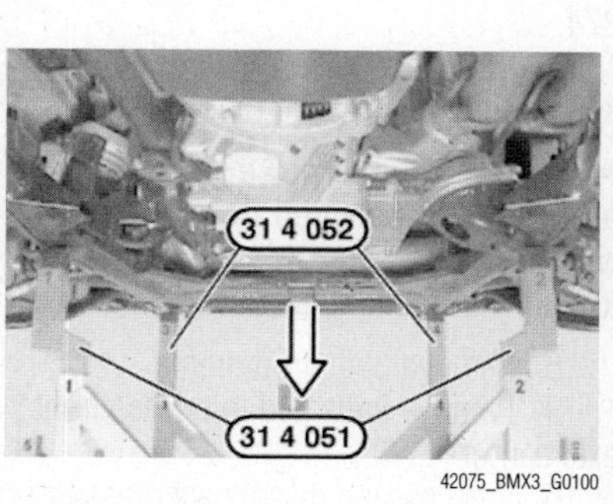

42075_BMX3_G0100

Fig. 255 Safely support the vehicle with special tools 31 4 051 and 31 4 052

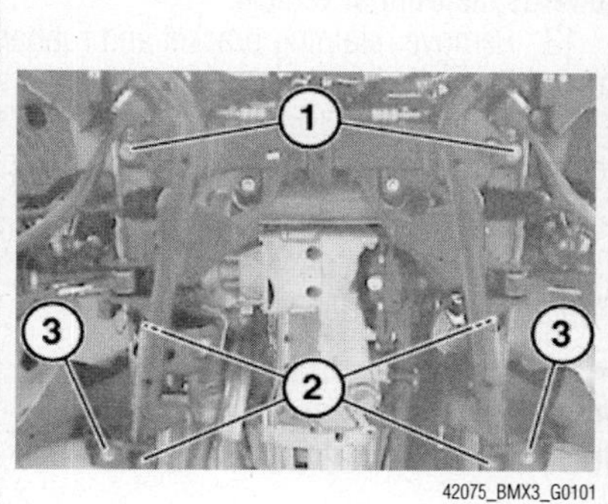

42075_BMX3_G0101

Fig. 256 Location of bolts (1), (2), and (3) to lower front axle carrier

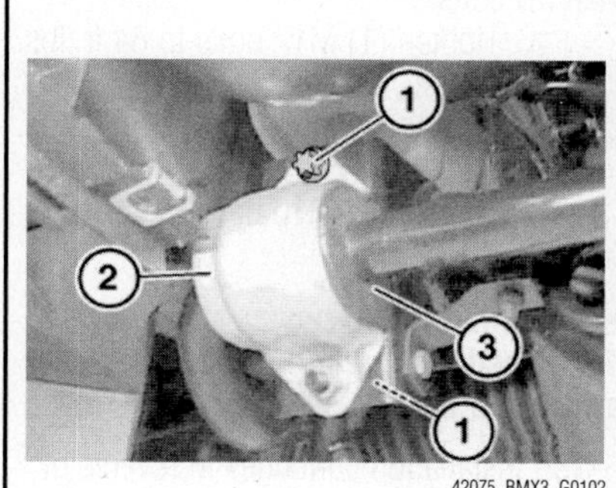

42075_BMX3_G0102

Fig. 257 Removing stabilizer bar bracket bolts (1), retaining bracket (2), and rubber mount (3)

3. If necessary, position special tool 00 2 040 with a 2nd person helping on a workshop jack.
4. Insert special tools 31 4 051 and 31 4 052 into corresponding mountings of special tool 00 2 040.
5. Align special tool 00 2 040 to front axle carrier.

6. If necessary, lower special tool 33 3 274.

7. Support front axle carrier by raising special tool 00 2 040.

➡Pay attention to power steering hoses and lines when lowering and raising. Hoses and lines must not be kinked, tensioned, or bent with force.

8. Remove bolts from frame.

9. Remove bolts and to release front axle carrier.

10. If necessary, disconnect pressure line for power steering from front axle carrier.

11. Carefully lower front axle carrier with workshop jack.

12. Release bolts and twist stabilizer bar towards the front of vehicle.

13. Remove retaining bracket and rubber mount on both sides.

14. Remove stabilizer bar sideways through wheel arch.

To install:

15. Check rubber mount on both sides. Replace if damaged.

➡Keep retaining bracket, rubber mount, and stabilizer bar clean and free from oil and grease.

16. Place stabilizer bar into position with rubber mountings and brackets.

17. Install stabilizer bar into place with new bolts. Tighten to 42 ft. lbs. (56 Nm).

18. Install front axle carrier into place with new bolts. Tighten in order (1), (2), then (3) bolts:

a. Tighten (1) M12 bolts to 84 ft. lbs. (113 Nm).

b. Tighten (2) M12 bolts to 74 ft. lbs. (100 Nm).

c. Tighten (3) M10 bolts to 37 ft. lbs. (50 Nm).

➡Pay attention to power steering hoses and lines when raising and lowering axle carrier.

19. Installation continues in reverse of the removal procedure.

20. Install stabilizer to stabilizer link. Tighten to 48 ft. lbs. (65 Nm).

21. Replace M10 bolts and install reinforcement plate to front axle support/engine carrier. Tighten to 55 ft. lbs. (74 Nm).

STEERING KNUCKLE

REMOVAL & INSTALLATION

See Figures 258 and 259.

1. Before servicing the vehicle, refer to the Precautions Section.

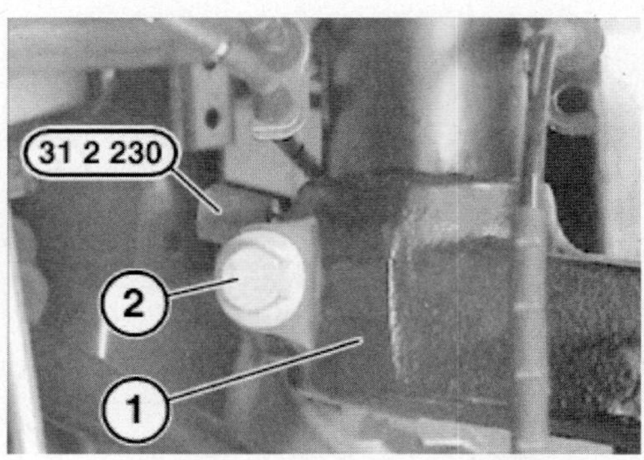

Fig. 258 Steering knuckle (1) and bolts (2) with expander tool 31 2 230 installed for removal

2. Raise and support the vehicle safely.

3. Remove front wheel.

4. Remove or disconnect the following:

- The stabilizer link from the spring strut. Use a fixed wrench as a counter hold
- The ABS sensor. Hang up the sensor using a piece of wire
- The ABS sensor cable from the spring strut
- The brake caliper mounting bolts. Hang the caliper up using a piece of wire
- The halfshaft bolt. Use a screwdriver as a counter hold on the brake disc
- The brake disc. Detach the end of the halfshaft in the hub by knocking the drive shaft into the hub approximately ⅓–½ inch (10–15mm). Use a rubber or copper mallet
- The tie rod ends from the steering arm

5. Measure the position of the steering knuckle and spring strut for installation purposes.

6. Support steering knuckle with workshop jack and a suitable mounting.

7. Remove the bolts retaining the spring strut and the steering knuckle.

8. Expand steering knuckle with special tool 31 2 230.

9. Lower workshop jack.

10. Suspend the drive shaft from a hook.

➡Take care not to damage the halfshaft boot.

11. Disconnect the ball joint pinion from the control arm.

12. Remove steering knuckle.

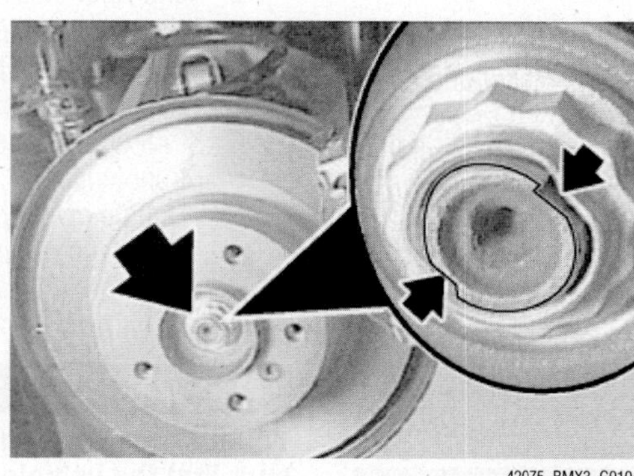

Fig. 259 Crimping halfshaft nut to axle during installation

To install:

13. Install the steering knuckle in approximately the same position from which it was removed.

14. Install a new nut on the ball joint. Tighten to 59 ft. lbs. (80° Nm).

➡Make sure that the mating surfaces on the ball joint and link are clean.

15. Clean the splines on the halfshaft.

16. Turn the steering knuckle and bring the halfshaft into the hub.

17. Install halfshaft bolt and finger-tighten. Lubricate the bolt.

18. Install bolts retaining the spring strut in the steering knuckle. Use new bolts and nuts. Tighten to 74 ft. lbs. (100 Nm).

19. Install or connect the following:
- The stabilizer link to the spring strut. Use a new nut. Counter hold using a wrench so that the boot is not damaged. Tighten to 48 ft. lbs. (65 Nm)
- The ABS sensor cable
- The ABS sensor onto the steering knuckle. Tighten the ABS sensor to 82 inch lbs. (8 Nm)

➡Ensure that the sensor seat in the steering knuckle is absolutely clean. Clean the ABS sensor with a soft brush.

- The tie rod end onto the steering knuckle. Use a new nut. Tighten to 59 ft. lbs. (80 Nm)
- The brake disc.

➡Ensure that the brake disc and wheel rim hub mating surfaces are clean.

20. Install new halfshaft nut. Tighten to 310 ft. lbs. (420 Nm). Crimp nut to axle.

21. Install the brake caliper. Use new bolts

22. Install the wheel. Tighten to 103 ft. lbs. (140 Nm).

UPPER CONTROL ARM

REMOVAL & INSTALLATION

1. Before servicing the vehicle, refer to the precautions in the beginning of this section.

2. Remove or disconnect the following:
- Negative battery cable
- Wheel assembly
- Coil spring
- Upper control arm from the stabilizer link from upper control arm
- If necessary, jointed rod of ride-height sensor from upper control arm

3. Support rear differential and release bearing bolts on rear differential. Halfshafts do not have to be removed.

4. Remove or disconnect the following:
- Upper control arm through bolts towards rear
- Upper control arm

To install:

5. Installation is reverse of removal.

6. Install and torque the following to correct torque specifications:
- Upper control arm. Torque the bolt to 78 ft. lbs. (106 Nm).
- Upper control arm to the steering knuckle. Torque the bolt to 74 ft. lbs. (100 Nm).
- Wheel assembly
- Negative battery cable

WHEEL BEARINGS

REMOVAL & INSTALLATION

➡The wheel bearings are only removed if they are worn. They cannot be removed without destroying them (due to side thrust created by the bearing puller). They cannot be disassembled, repacked or adjusted.

1. Before servicing the vehicle, refer to the precautions in the beginning of this section.

2. Remove or disconnect the following:
- Negative battery cable

CAUTION

To avoid damaging the dust sleeve, use special tool tools 33–2–160 to drive out and draw in the drive flange after removing the brake disk. Rounded inside edge of special tool must point to drive flange.

- Front brake disc
- Drive flange by installing special tools 33–2–116, 160 and 33–4–200
- Bearing inner race from the flange
- Swivel bearing
- Bearing by installing special tools 31–2–113, 33–4–266, 33–3–266 and 33–4–266/261

To install:

3. Install or connect the following:
- Wheel bearing with the wider chamfer facing the swivel bearing to the drive flange with special tools 31–2–113, 33–4–266, 33–3–266 and 33–4–266/261
- Snap ring and circlip
- Bearing inner race to the drive flange
- Drive flange to the swivel bearing by using special tool 33–2–116, 160 and 33–4–200
- Swivel bearing
- Front brake disc
- Negative battery cable

ADJUSTMENT

Wheel bearings cannot be adjusted and must be replaced as a unit and never be reused once removed.

COIL SPRING

REMOVAL & INSTALLATION

See Figure 260.

1. Before servicing the vehicle, refer to the Precautions Section.
2. Remove or disconnect the following:
   - Rear wheel
   - Output shaft from rear differential and tie back
   - Stabilizer link on both sides from stabilizer
   - Jointed rod from sensor lever of ride—height sensor, if necessary

➡Brake hose must not be exposed to tensile loads.

   - Bolt and bracket with brake hose
3. Support trailing arm with a workshop jack.
4. Remove lower bolt of shock absorber.
5. Lower workshop jack.
6. Press trailing arm downwards.
7. Pull out coil spring.

To install:

8. Position coil spring with upper spring pad and lower spring pad mounted in control arm and align to take-up locator/frame side member.
9. Raise trailing arm using a workshop jack.

➡Spring pads must be positively seated in the take-up locator/frame side member or control arm to prevent the coil spring from springing out of the centering mount.

10. Installation continues in the reverse of the removal procedure.
11. Tighten shock absorber to trailing arm to 74 ft. lbs. (100 Nm).
12. Tighten wheel bolts to 103 ft. lbs. (140 Nm).
13. Check headlight adjustment, correct if necessary

LOWER CONTROL ARM

REMOVAL & INSTALLATION

See Figures 261 through 263.

1. Before servicing the vehicle, refer to the Precautions Section.
2. Raise the vehicle.
3. Remove or disconnect the following:
   - The wheel
   - The stabilizer from rear axle carrier
   - The coil spring.
4. Support rear differential

➡To avoid damaging the output shaft, it will be necessary to support the trailing arm with the workshop jack.

5. Support trailing arm from underneath using a workshop jack.
6. Mark position of eccentric bolt to lower control arm with center marks.
7. Remove nut and eccentric washer.
8. Remove eccentric bolt towards front.
9. Remove bolt and remove thread plate downwards.
10. Press rear differential to side and remove bolt.
11. Remove lower control arm at side.

To install:

➡Tighten all joints and rubber bushings with the rear suspension in the

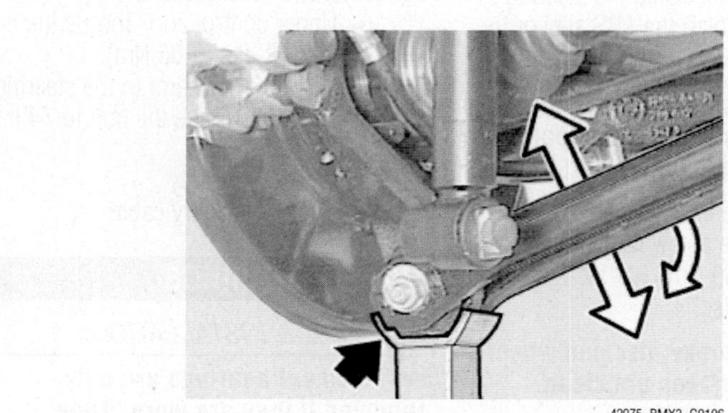

Fig. 261 Using workshop jack to support the trailing arm

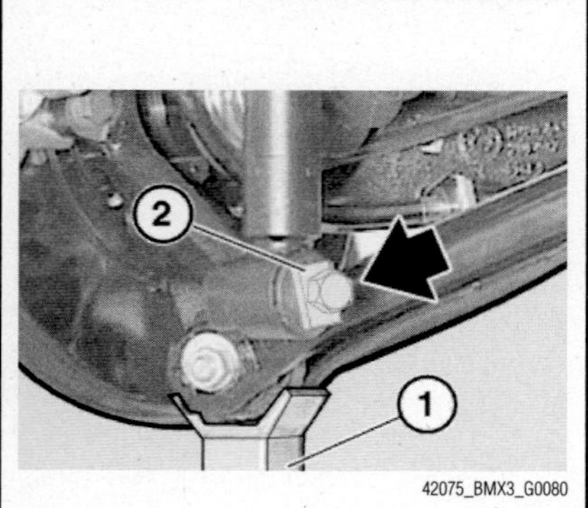

Fig. 260 Using workshop jack to support trailing arm in removal of rear coil spring

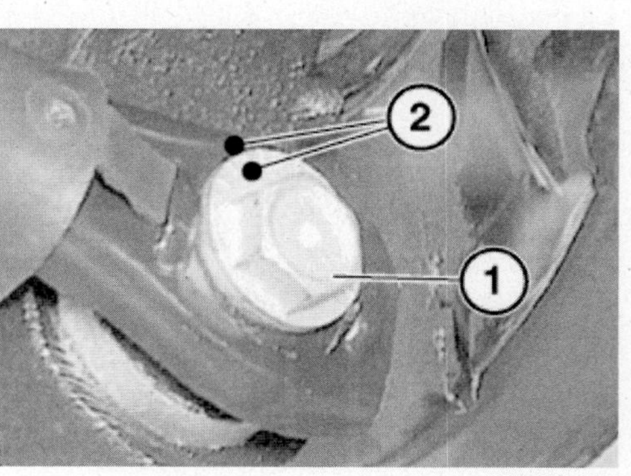

Fig. 262 Marking eccentric bolt (1) to lower control arm center marks (2)

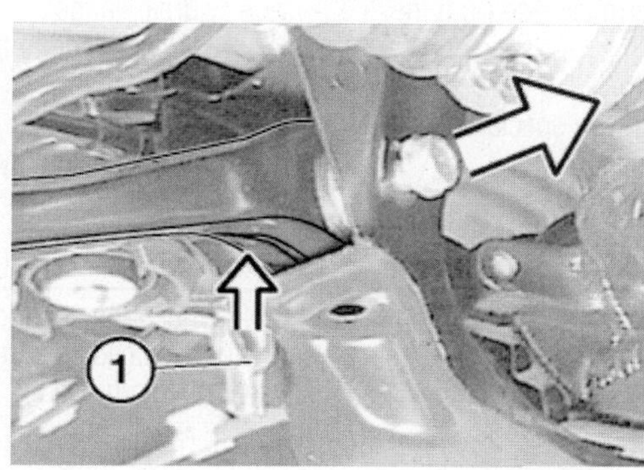

Fig. 263 Removing thread plate (1) to remove lower control arm

normal position. Weld seam of control arm must point upwards.

12. Install or connect the following:
    - Thread plate into opening in rear axle carrier. Tighten bolt to 57 ft. lbs. (77 Nm)
    - Eccentric bolt. Align by means of marking to lower control arm. Reinstall eccentric washer. Replace self-locking nut. Tighten bolt to 74 ft. lbs. (100 Nm)
    - The coil spring. Refer to Rear Suspension, Coil Spring removal and installation
    - The stabilizer to rear axle carrier
    - The wheel. Tighten bolts to 103 ft. lbs. (140 Nm).

STRUT & SPRING ASSEMBLY

REMOVAL & INSTALLATION

1. Before servicing the vehicle, refer to the precautions in the beginning of this section.
2. Remove or disconnect the following:
    - Negative battery cable
    - Wheel
    - Brake caliper
    - Stabilizer link from spring/strut
    - Tie rod end from swivel bearing
    - Line for pulse generator from spring/strut
    - If necessary, brake pad wear sensor
    - Swivel bearing from spring/strut, set aside and secure

➡ If the centering pin missing, mark the position of studs in relation to wheel arch.

3. Secure spring so that it doesn't fall out. Remove mounting nuts.

Remove shock absorber downwards out of wheel arch.

To install:

4. Installation is reverse of removal procedure.
5. Replace all bolts and self-locking nuts
6. Tighten all following fasteners to correct torque specifications:
    - Spring/strut support: 25 ft. lbs. (30 Nm)
    - Shock absorber piston rod on thrust bearing: 47 ft. lbs. (64 Nm)
    - Spring strut shock absorber to pivot mount: 73 ft. lbs. (100 Nm)

UPPER CONTROL ARM

REMOVAL & INSTALLATION

See Figure 264.

1. Before servicing the vehicle, refer to the Precautions Section.
2. Raise the vehicle.
3. Remove or disconnect the following:
    - The wheel.
    - The brake caliper. Hang the brake caliper on a hook in the sub-frame.
    - The coil spring.
    - The stabilizer link from upper control arm
4. Support rear differential.
5. Remove nut and bolt from control arm as illustrated.

➡Observe bolt insertion direction (F is direction of travel).

6. Remove or disconnect the following:
    - The bolt for the inner rear control arm mounting
    - The two bolts for the inner front control arm mounting
    - The control arm

To install:

7. Install or connect the following:
    - The bolts for the inner rear control arm mounting
    - The bolts for the front inner control arm mounting
    - The bolts for the outer control arm mounting

➡Replace self-locking nuts and bolts.

8. Tighten the M12 bolts for the inner rear control arm mounting to 57 ft. lbs. (77 Nm).
9. Tighten the M12 bolts for the front inner control arm mounting to 57 ft. lbs. (77 Nm).
10. Tighten the M12 bolts for the upper control arm to the trailing arm to 78 ft. lbs. (106 Nm).

➡Tighten the bolts when the rear suspension is in the normal position.

11. Install the wheel and tighten bolts to 103 ft. lbs. (140 Nm).

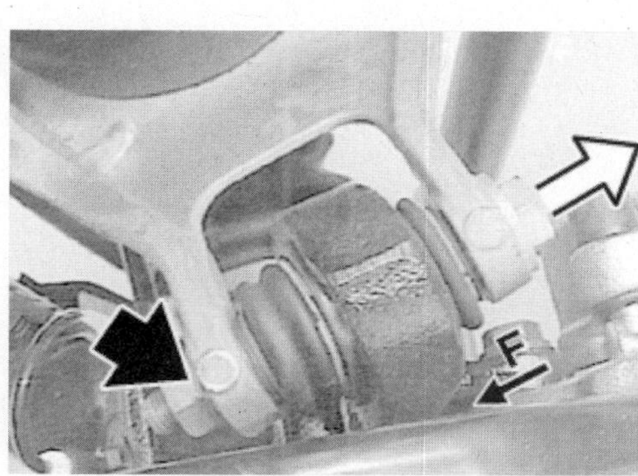

Fig. 264 Location of nut and bolt for removal of upper control arm

WHEEL BEARINGS

REMOVAL & INSTALLATION

1. Before servicing the vehicle, refer to the precautions in the beginning of this section.
2. Remove or disconnect the following:
   - Negative battery cable
   - Wheel assembly
   - Collar nut
   - Brake disc
   - Rear axle shaft drive flange
   - Wheel bearing inner race from the drive flange
   - Retaining ring
   - Wheel bearing with special tools 33–3–261/2/3

To install:

3. Install or connect the following:
   - New wheel bearing with special tools 33–3–261/4/5
   - Retaining ring
   - Wheel bearing inner race to the drive flange.
   - Drive flange to the axle shaft
   - Brake disc
   - Collar nut
   - Wheel assembly
   - Negative battery cable

ADJUSTMENT

Wheel bearings cannot be adjusted and must be replaced as a unit and never be reused once removed.

BMW

X5

5

SPECIFICATIONS AND MAINTENANCE CHARTS

ENGINE AND VEHICLE IDENTIFICATION

Engine							Model Year	
Code ①	Liters (cc)	Cu. In.	Cyl.	Fuel Sys.	Engine Type	Eng. Mfg.	Code ②	Year
N55	3.0 (2979)	183	6	Turbo	DOHC	BMW	B	2011
N63	4.4 (4400)	269	8	Twin Turbo	DOHC	BMW	C	2012

① 8th position of VIN

② 10th position of VIN

71112_X5X6_C0001

GENERAL ENGINE SPECIFICATIONS

All measurements are given in inches.

Year	Model	Engine Displacement Liters (cc)	Engine ID	Fuel System Type	Net Horsepower @ rpm	Net Torque @ rpm (ft. lbs.)	Bore x Stroke (in.)	Com-pression Ratio	Oil Pressure @ rpm
2011	X5 35iX	3.0 (2979)	N55	Turbo	300@5800	300@1300	3.30x3.53	10.2:1	22@idle
	X5 50iX	4.4 (4400)	N63	Turbo	400@5500	450@1750	3.50x3.48	10.0:1	22@idle
2012	X5 35iX	3.0 (2979)	N55	Turbo	300@5800	300@1300	3.30x3.53	10.2:1	22@idle
	X5 50iX	4.4 (4400)	N63	Turbo	400@5500	450@1750	3.50x3.48	10.0:1	22@idle

71112_X5X6_C0002

ENGINE TUNE-UP SPECIFICATIONS

Year	Engine Displacement Liters	Engine ID	Spark Plug Gap (in.)	Ignition Timing (deg.) MT	Ignition Timing (deg.) AT	Fuel Pump (psi)	Idle Speed (rpm) MT	Idle Speed (rpm) AT	Valve Clearance Intake	Valve Clearance Exhaust
2011	3.0	N55	0.024-0.028	NA	①	72	NA	750 ②	HYD	HYD
	4.4	N63	NA	NA	①	72	NA	750 ②	HYD	HYD
2012	3.0	N55	0.024-0.028	NA	①	72	NA	750 ②	HYD	HYD
	4.4	N63	NA	NA	①	72	NA	750 ②	HYD	HYD

NA: Not Available

HYD Engines use hydraulic lifters

① Ignition timing is controlled by the Engine Control Module (ECM). No adjustment is necessary or possible.

② Idle speed is controlled by the Powertrain Control Module (PCM). No adjustment is necessary or possible.

71112_X5X6_C0003

CAPACITIES

Year	Model	Engine Displacement Liters	Engine ID/VIN	Engine Oil with Filter	Transmission (pts.) Auto.	Transmission (pts.) Manual	Drive Axle (pts.) Front	Drive Axle (pts.) Rear	Transfer Case (pts.)	Fuel Tank (gal.)	Cooling System (qts.)
2011	X5 35iX	3.0	N55	5.7	19-21	NA	1.4	2.5	1.6	22.5	11.5
	X5 50iX	4.4	N63	9.0	19-21	NA	1.4	2.5	1.6	22.5	NA
2012	X5 35iX	3.0	N55	5.7	19-21	NA	1.4	2.5	1.6	22.5	11.5
	X5 50iX	4.4	N63	9.0	19-21	NA	1.4	2.5	1.6	22.5	NA

NOTE: All capacities are approximate. Add fluid gradually and ensure a proper fluid level is obtained.

NA: Not Available

71112_X5X6_C0004

FLUID SPECIFICATIONS

Year	Model	Engine Disp. Liters	Engine Oil	Manual Trans.	Auto. Trans.	Drive Axle Front	Drive Axle Rear	Transfer Case	Power Steering Fluid	Brake Master Cylinder	Cooling System
2011	X5 35iX	3.0	①	NA	Shell ATF	②	②	③	NA	DOT4	④
	X5 50iX	4.4	①	NA	Shell ATF	②	②	③	NA	DOT4	④
2012	X5 35iX	3.0	①	NA	Shell ATF	②	②	③	NA	DOT4	④
	X5 50iX	4.4	①	NA	Shell ATF	②	②	③	NA	DOT4	④

DOT: Department Of Transpotation

NA: Not Available

① BMW Longlife-04 engine oil 5W-30

② BMW differential oil SAF-XO/OSP

③ Transfer box oil TF 0870

④ BMW antifreeze

71112_X5X6_C0005

VALVE SPECIFICATIONS

Year	Engine Displacement Liters	Engine ID	Seat Angle (deg.)	Face Angle (deg.)	Spring Test Pressure (lbs. @ in.)	Spring Free-Length (in.)	Spring Installed Height (in.)	Stem-to-Guide Clearance (in.) Intake	Stem-to-Guide Clearance (in.) Exhaust	Stem Diameter (in.) Intake	Stem Diameter (in.) Exhaust
2011	3.0	N55	45	NS	NS	NS	NS	NS	NS	0.1953-0.1959	0.2344-0.2349
	4.4	N63	45	NS	NS	NS	NS	NS	NS	0.2362-0.2370	0.2362-0.2370
2012	3.0	N55	45	NS	NS	NS	NS	NS	NS	0.1953-0.1959	0.2344-0.2349
	4.4	N63	45	NS	NS	NS	NS	NS	NS	0.2362-0.2370	0.2362-0.2370

NA: Not Available

NS: Not Specified

71112_X5X6_C0006

CAMSHAFT SPECIFICATIONS

All measurements in inches unless noted

Year	Engine Displacement Liters	Engine Code	Journal Diameter	Brg. Oil Clearance	Shaft End-play	Runout	Journal Bore	Lobe Height Intake	Lobe Height Exhaust
2011	3.0	N55	0.7476-0.7484	NS	0.0031-0.0064	0.0021-0.0039	0.8618-0.8629	NS	NS
	4.4	N63	NS	NS	0.0009-0.0042	0.0039	NS	NS	NS
2012	3.0	N55	0.7476-0.7484	NS	0.0031-0.0064	0.0021-0.0039	0.8618-0.8629	NS	NS
	4.4	N63	NS	NS	0.0009-0.0042	0.0039	NS	NS	NS

NS: Not Specified

71112_X5X6_C0007

CRANKSHAFT AND CONNECTING ROD SPECIFICATIONS

All measurements are given in inches.

Year	Engine Displacement Liters	Engine ID	Crankshaft Main Brg. Journal Dia.	Crankshaft Main Brg. Oi Clearance	Crankshaft Shaft End-play	Crankshaft Thrust on No.	Connecting Rod Journal Diameter	Connecting Rod Oil Clearance	Connecting Rod Side Clearance
2011	3.0	N55	①	0.0008-0.0018	NS	NS	1.9674-1.9682	0.0010-0.0028	0.0024-0.0098
	4.4	N63	2.5558-2.5580	0.0008-0.0018	NS	NS	2.2671-2.2683	0.0011-0.0028	NS
2012	3.0	N55	①	0.0008-0.0018	NS	NS	1.9674-1.9682	0.0010-0.0028	0.0024-0.0098
	4.4	N63	2.5558-2.5580	0.0008-0.0018	NS	NS	2.2671-2.2683	0.0011-0.0028	NS

NS Not Specified

① Journal No. 1: 2.2035-2.2043 inches
Journal Nos. 2-6: 2.2039-2.2047 inches
Journal No. 7: 2.5582-2.5590 inches

71112_X5X6_C0008

PISTON AND RING SPECIFICATIONS

All measurements are given in inches.

Year	Engine Displacement Liters	Engine ID/VIN	Piston Clearance	Ring Gap Top Compression	Ring Gap Bottom Compression	Ring Gap Oil Control	Ring Side Clearance Top Compression	Ring Side Clearance Bottom Compression	Ring Side Clearance Oil Control
2011	3.0	N55	0.0004-0.0012	0.0059-0.0118	0.0118-0.0197	0.0079-0.0354	①	①	①
	4.4	N63	0.0000-0.0012	0.0059-0.0118	0.0118-0.0197	①	NS	NS	NS
2012	3.0	N55	0.0004-0.0012	0.0059-0.0118	0.0118-0.0197	0.0079-0.0354	①	①	①
	4.4	N63	0.0000-0.0012	0.0059-0.0118	0.0118-0.0197	①	NS	NS	NS

NS: Not Specified

① Cannot be measured

71112_X5X6_C0009

TORQUE SPECIFICATIONS

All readings in ft. lbs.

Year	Engine Disp. Liters	Engine ID/VIN	Cylinder Head Bolts	Main Bearing Bolts	Rod Bearing Bolts	Crankshaft Damper Bolts	Flywheel Bolts	Manifold Intake	Manifold Exhaust	Spark Plugs	Oil Pan Drain Plug
2011	3.0	N55	①	②	③	221	④	11	17	17	18
	4.4	N63	⑤	⑥	⑦	221	77	⑧	⑧	17	30
2012	3.0	N55	①	②	③	221	④	11	17	17	18
	4.4	N63	⑤	⑥	⑦	221	77	⑧	⑧	17	30

① Step 1: 22 ft. lbs.
Step 2: Additional 90 degrees
Step 3: Additional 180 degrees
② Step 1: 15 ft. lbs.
Step 2: Additional 70 degrees
③ Step 1: 15 ft. lbs.
Step 2: Additional 140 degrees
④ Step 1: 44 ft. lbs.
Step 2: Additional 45 degrees
⑤ Step 1: 22 ft. lbs.
Step 2: Additional 90 degrees
Step 3: Additional 90 degrees
⑥ Step 1: 15 ft. lbs.
Step 2: Additional 100 degrees
⑦ Step 1: 4 ft. lbs.
Step 2: 15 ft. lbs.
Step 3: Additional 70 degrees
⑧ M8 thread: 16 ft. lbs.
M7 thread: 11 ft. lbs.
M6 thread: 7 ft. lbs.

71112_X5X6_C0010

WHEEL ALIGNMENT

Year	Model		Caster Range (+/-Deg.)	Caster Preferred Setting (Deg.)	Camber Range (+/-Deg.)	Camber Preferred Setting (Deg.)	Toe-in (in.)
2011	X5 35iX	F	0.15	0.0	0.25	-0.20	0.10+/-0.04
		R			0.05	-1.30	0.10+/-0.04
	X5 50iX	F	0.15	0.0	0.25	-0.20	0.10+/-0.04
		R			0.05	-1.30	0.10+/-0.04
2012	X5 35iX	F	0.15	0.0	0.25	-0.20	0.10+/-0.04
		R			0.05	-1.30	0.10+/-0.04
	X5 50iX	F	0.15	0.0	0.25	-0.20	0.10+/-0.04
		R			0.05	-1.30	0.10+/-0.04

71112_X5X6_C0011

TIRE, WHEEL AND BALL JOINT SPECIFICATIONS

Year	Model	OEM Tires Standard	OEM Tires Optional	Tire Pressures (psi) Front	Tire Pressures (psi) Rear	Wheel Size	Ball Joint Inspection	Lug Nut (ft. lbs.)
2011	X5 35iX	255/55R18	NA	32	32	18x8.5	NA	103
	X5 50iX	255/55R18	NA	32	32	18x8.5	NA	103
2012	X5 35iX	255/55R18	NA	32	32	18x8.5	NA	103
	X5 50iX	255/55R18	NA	32	32	18x8.5	NA	103

OEM: Original Equipment Manufacturer

PSI: Pounds Per Square Inch

NA: Information not available

71112_X5X6_C0012

BRAKE SPECIFICATIONS

All measurements in inches unless noted

Year	Model		Brake Disc Original Thickness	Brake Disc Minimum Thickness	Brake Disc Max. Runout	Minimum Pad/Lining Thickness Front	Minimum Pad/Lining Thickness Rear	Brake Caliper Bracket Bolts (ft. lbs.)	Brake Caliper Mounting Bolts (ft. lbs.)
2011	X5 35iX	F	1.417	1.354	0.0004	0.146	—	81	41
		R	0.945	0.787	0.0004	—	0.146	81	22
	X5 50iX	F	1.417	1.354	0.0004	0.146	—	81	41
		R	0.945	0.787	0.0004	—	0.146	81	22
2012	X5 35iX	F	1.417	1.354	0.0004	0.146	—	81	41
		R	0.945	0.787	0.0004	—	0.146	81	22
	X5 50iX	F	1.417	1.354	0.0004	0.146	—	81	41
		R	0.945	0.787	0.0004	—	0.146	81	22

F: Front

R: Rear

NA: Information not available

71112_X5X6_C0013

SCHEDULED MAINTENANCE INTERVALS

BMW—X5

TO BE SERVICED	TYPE OF SERVICE	SERVICE INTERVALS			
		INITIAL 1200 MILES	OIL SERVICE	INSPECTION I	INSPECTION II
Oil level	S/I	✓			
Engine oil	R				
Engine oil & filter	R		✓	✓	✓
Engine air cleaner element	R				✓
Spark plugs	R				✓
Fuel filter (California)	R				✓
Fuel, vapor lines & fuel cap	S/I	✓		✓	✓
Cooling system	S/I	✓		✓	✓
Exhaust pipe & muffler	S/I	✓		✓	✓
Catalytic converter & shielding	S/I	✓		✓	✓
Throttle linkage	S/I			✓	✓
Engine (check for leakage)	S/I	✓			
Engine drive belts	S/I				✓
Maintenance Indicators	RE		✓	✓	✓
Engine coolant	R	Every 2 years			
Oxygen sensor	R	Every 100,000 miles			
Intake air dust separators	S/I				✓
Brake & clutch fluids	S/I			✓	✓
Brake & clutch fluids	R	Every 2 years			
Brake pads & discs	S/I			✓	✓
Parking brake system	S/I			✓	✓
Power steering system	S/I			✓	✓
Rear axle fluid	S/I			✓	✓
Steering play, suspension track rods, front axle joints, steering linkage & joint disc	S/I			✓	✓
Transmission fluid/oil	S/I			✓	⑨
Wheel centering hubs	S/I			✓	✓
Rear axle fluid ⑩	R		✓		✓
OBD system for codes	S/I	✓		✓	✓

R: Replace S/I: Service or Inspect RE: Reset

Note: BMW does not rely solely on vehicle mileage to determine service intervals. An on-oboard diagnostic center, monitors engine operating conditions, along with mileage, to determine the most effective maintenance intervals. The information is then conveyed to the driver through the service indicator lights, located in the center of the instrument panel.

71112_X5X6_C0014

PRECAUTIONS

Before servicing any vehicle, please be sure to read all of the following precautions, which deal with personal safety, prevention of component damage, and important points to take into consideration when servicing a motor vehicle:

- Never open, service or drain the radiator or cooling system when the engine is hot; serious burns can occur from the steam and hot coolant.
- Observe all applicable safety precautions when working around fuel. Whenever servicing the fuel system, always work in a well-ventilated area. Do not allow fuel spray or vapors to come in contact with a spark, open flame, or excessive heat (a hot drop light, for example). Keep a dry chemical fire extinguisher near the work area. Always keep fuel in a container specifically designed for fuel storage; also, always properly seal fuel containers to avoid the possibility of fire or explosion. Refer to the additional fuel system precautions later in this section.
- Fuel injection systems often remain pressurized, even after the engine has been turned **OFF**. The fuel system pressure must be relieved before disconnecting any fuel lines. Failure to do so may result in fire and/or personal injury.
- Brake fluid often contains polyglycol ethers and polyglycols. Avoid contact with the eyes and wash your hands thoroughly after handling brake fluid. If you do get brake fluid in your eyes, flush your eyes with clean, running water for 15 minutes. If eye irritation persists, or if you have taken brake fluid internally, IMMEDIATELY seek medical assistance.
- The EPA warns that prolonged contact with used engine oil may cause a number of skin disorders, including cancer. You should make every effort to minimize your exposure to used engine oil. Protective gloves should be worn when changing oil. Wash your hands and any other exposed skin areas as soon as possible after exposure to used engine oil. Soap and water, or waterless hand cleaner should be used.
- All new vehicles are now equipped with an air bag system, often referred to as a Supplemental Restraint System (SRS) or Supplemental Inflatable Restraint (SIR) system. The system must be disabled before performing service on or around system components, steering column, instrument panel components, wiring and sensors. Failure to follow safety and disabling procedures could result in accidental air bag deployment, possible personal injury and unnecessary system repairs.
- Always wear safety goggles when working with, or around, the air bag system. When carrying a non-deployed air bag, be sure the bag and trim cover are pointed away from your body. When placing a non-deployed air bag on a work surface, always face the bag and trim cover upward, away from the surface. This will reduce the motion of the module if it is accidentally deployed. Refer to the additional air bag system precautions later in this section.
- Clean, high quality brake fluid from a sealed container is essential to the safe and proper operation of the brake system. You should always buy the correct type of brake fluid for your vehicle. If the brake fluid becomes contaminated, completely flush the system with new fluid. Never reuse any brake fluid. Any brake fluid that is removed from the system should be discarded. Also, do not allow any brake fluid to come in contact with a painted surface; it will damage the paint.
- Never operate the engine without the proper amount and type of engine oil; doing so WILL result in severe engine damage.
- Timing belt maintenance is extremely important. Many models utilize an interference-type, non-freewheeling engine. If the timing belt breaks, the valves in the cylinder head may strike the pistons, causing potentially serious (also time-consuming and expensive) engine damage. Refer to the maintenance interval charts for the recommended replacement interval for the timing belt, and to the timing belt section for belt replacement and inspection.
- Disconnecting the negative battery cable on some vehicles may interfere with the functions of the on-board computer system(s) and may require the computer to undergo a relearning process once the negative battery cable is reconnected.
- When servicing drum brakes, only disassemble and assemble one side at a time, leaving the remaining side intact for reference.
- Only an MVAC-trained, EPA-certified automotive technician should service the air conditioning system or its components.

BRAKES

ANTI-LOCK BRAKE SYSTEM (ABS)

GENERAL INFORMATION

PRECAUTIONS

- Certain components within the ABS system are not intended to be serviced or repaired individually.
- Do not use rubber hoses or other parts not specifically specified for and ABS system. When using repair kits, replace all parts included in the kit. Partial or incorrect repair may lead to functional problems and require the replacement of components.
- Lubricate rubber parts with clean, fresh brake fluid to ease assembly. Do not use shop air to clean parts; damage to rubber components may result.
- Use only DOT 3 brake fluid from an unopened container.
- If any hydraulic component or line is removed or replaced, it may be necessary to bleed the entire system.
- A clean repair area is essential. Always clean the reservoir and cap thoroughly before removing the cap. The slightest amount of dirt in the fluid may plug an orifice and impair the system function. Perform repairs after components have been thoroughly cleaned; use only denatured alcohol to clean components. Do not allow ABS components to come into contact with any substance containing mineral oil; this includes used shop rags.
- The Anti-Lock control unit is a microprocessor similar to other computer units in the vehicle. Ensure that the ignition switch is **OFF** before removing or installing controller harnesses. Avoid static electricity discharge at or near the controller.
- If any arc welding is to be done on the vehicle, the control unit should be unplugged before welding operations begin.

WHEEL SPEED SENSORS (PULSE SENSOR)

REMOVAL & INSTALLATION

Front

See Figure 1.

1. Disengage cable guides.
2. Open connector housing, pull plug connection out of holder and disconnect.
3. Pull cable with rubber grommet out of holders.
4. Disengage cable guides.
5. Release Torx® socket screw and pull pulse sensor out of bore.

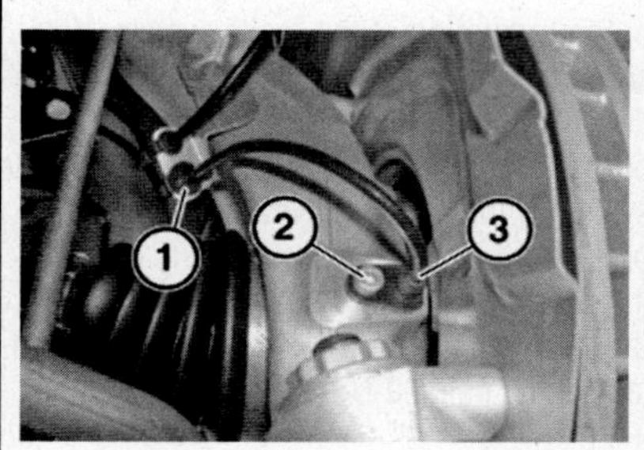

Fig. 1 Disengage cable guides (1), then release Torx® socket screw (2) and pull pulse sensor (3) out of bore

To install:

6. Installation is the reverse order of removal.

➡Check sensor head prior to installation for external damage, replacing if necessary.

7. Clean bore for pulse sensor and lubricate with Staburags NBU 12/K lubricating grease.
8. Ensure proper locking of plug connector and proper seating of rubber grommets.

Fig. 2 Disengage cable (1) along marked lines from holders

Rear

See Figures 2 and 3.

1. Partially detach rear wheel arch trim.
2. Open housing cover.
3. Disconnect plug connection.
4. Disengage cable along marked lines from holders.
5. Release Torx® socket screw.
6. Withdraw wheel speed sensor from bore hole.

To install:

7. Installation is the reverse order of removal.

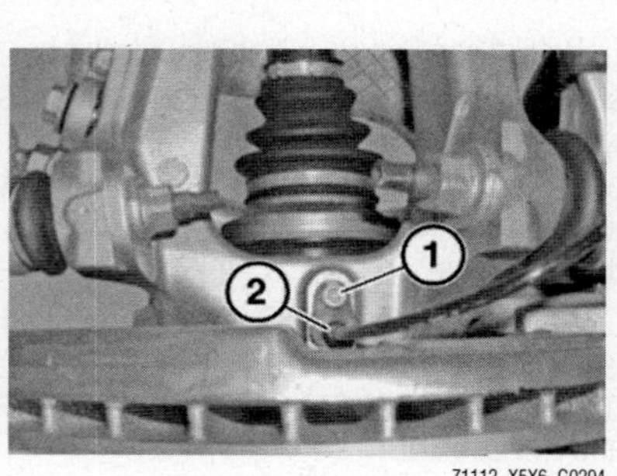

Fig. 3 Release Torx® socket screw (1), then withdraw wheel speed sensor (2) from bore hole

8. Ensure proper locking of the holders and proper seating of the cable in the holders.
9. Ensure proper locking of the plug connector and proper seating of the cable in the brackets.
10. Clean bore for pulse generator and lubricate with Staburags NBU 12/K lubricating grease.

➡Check sensor head prior to installation for external damage, replacing if necessary.

BRAKES — BLEEDING THE BRAKE SYSTEM

BLEEDING PROCEDURE

See Figure 4.

CAUTION

Brake fluid contains polyglycol ethers and polyglycols. Avoid contact with the eyes and wash your hands thoroughly after handling brake fluid. If you do get brake fluid in your eyes, flush your eyes with clean, running water for 15 minutes. If eye irritation persists, or if you have taken brake fluid internally, IMMEDIATELY seek medical assistance.

WARNING

Clean, high quality brake fluid is essential to the safe and proper operation of the brake system. You should always buy the highest quality brake fluid that is available. If the brake fluid becomes contaminated, drain and flush the system, then refill the master cylinder with new fluid. Never reuse any brake fluid. Any brake fluid that is removed from the system should be discarded. Also, do not allow any brake fluid to come in contact with a painted surface; it will damage the paint.

1. Remove the reservoir cap and fill the brake reservoir with brake fluid.
2. Connect a clear plastic tube to the wheel cylinder bleeder plug and insert the other end of the tube into a clear plastic bottle.
3. Activate pre-charging pump with Diagnosis and Information System (DIS).
4. Select and operate according to the instructions on the DIS screen:
   - Select: Service Functions
   - Select: Bleeding ABS/DSC3 Hydraulics

CAUTION

You must obey the maximum operating time of the ABS motor to prevent the motor pump from burning.

5. Connect bleeder unit to expansion tank and switch on.
6. Pump the brake pedal several times, and then loosen the bleeder screw until fluid starts to run out without bubbles. Then close the bleeder screw.

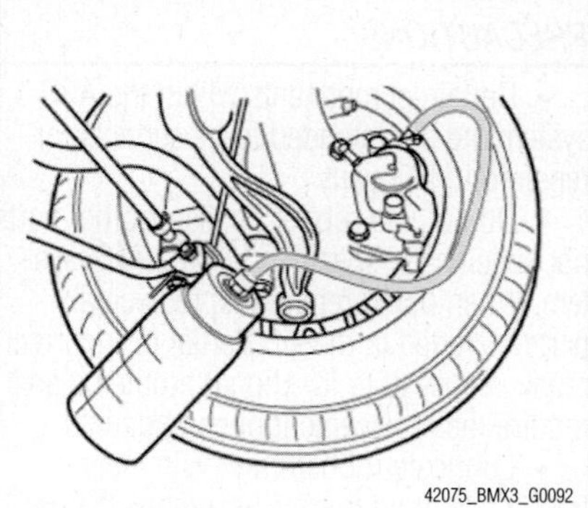

Fig. 4 Using a clear plastic tube and bottle at bleeder screw to observe fluid bubbles

7. Bleed fluid from each wheel until there are no more bubbles exiting with the brake fluid. Run bleeding routine with DIS and bleeder valve open.

8. Press brake pedal 5 times to the floor clear and bubble-free brake fluid must flow out.

9. Close bleeder valve.

10. Repeat bleeding procedure on each wheel.

11. After completion of the repair or correction of the problem, erase any stored fault codes.

12. Disconnect the DIS system.

13. Fill the brake reservoir with the proper amount of brake fluid.

14. Check for fluid leaks at all connections.

FLUID FILL PROCEDURE

➡A second person is needed to help carry out this work.

1. Disconnect the retaining tabs and remove the master cylinder cover.
2. Connect a brake bleeding tool with a maximum 29 PSI (2 Bar) filling pressure.
3. Flush the brake system completely.
4. Connect a bleeder hose with a collecting tray to the bleeder valve on the rear right brake caliper.
5. Open the bleeder valve and purge until clear, bubble-free brake fluid emerges.
6. Close the bleed valve.
7. Follow the same procedure on rear left, front right and front left wheel brake.
8. Disconnect the brake bleeding tool and remove from the master cylinder.
9. Check and adjust the brake fluid level.
10. Inspect the rubber seal in the brake fluid master cylinder cap. Replace as necessary.

BRAKE FLUID

FLUID RECOMMENDATIONS

Use only BMW brake fluid DOT 4 with low viscosity.

All vehicles with DSC without a precharge pump must be filled with new brake fluid DOT 4 with low viscosity.

All other vehicles can be filled with the new brake fluid DOT 4 with low viscosity; it is possible to mix DOT 4 and DOT 4 with low viscosity.

BRAKES

FRONT DISC BRAKES

BRAKE CALIPERS

REMOVAL & INSTALLATION

See Figures 6 through 9.

1. Remove wheel.
2. Remove brake pad wear sensor.
    a. Disengage cable guides.
    b. Open cover on plug housing.
    c. Disconnect plug connection.
    d. Disengage cable from cable guide.
    e. Pull brake pad sensor in direction of arrow out of brake pad.
    f. Disengage cable of brake pad sensor from holders.
3. Detach retainer from bracket on spring strut in upward direction.

➡Grip brake hose at square head so that connecting piece cannot rotate in retaining bracket.

4. Disconnect brake hose from brake line.
5. Detach brake hose from brake caliper.
6. Release screws.
7. Detach brake caliper in direction of arrow from swivel bearing.

Fig. 5 Pull brake pad sensor (1) in direction of arrow out of brake pad, then disengage cable of brake pad sensor from holders (2)

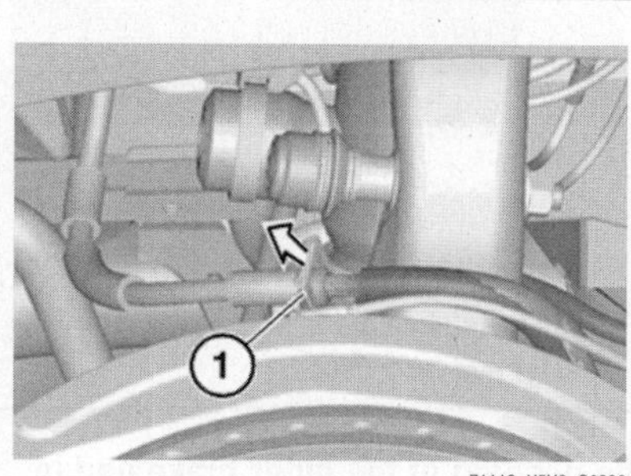

Fig. 6 Detach retainer (1) from bracket on spring strut in upward direction

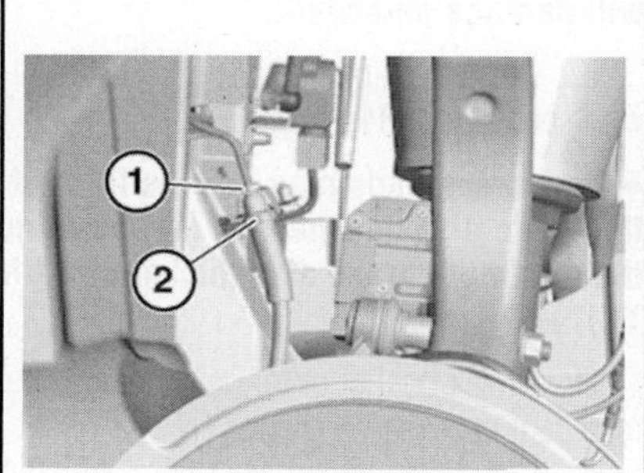

Fig. 7 Disconnect brake hose from brake line (1); square head (2)

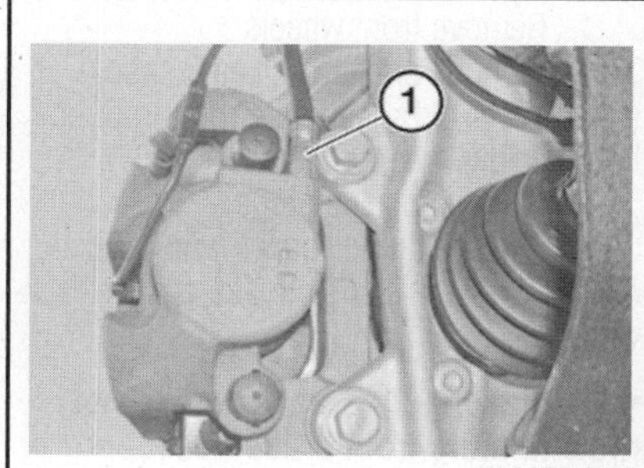

Fig. 8 Detach brake hose from brake caliper (1)

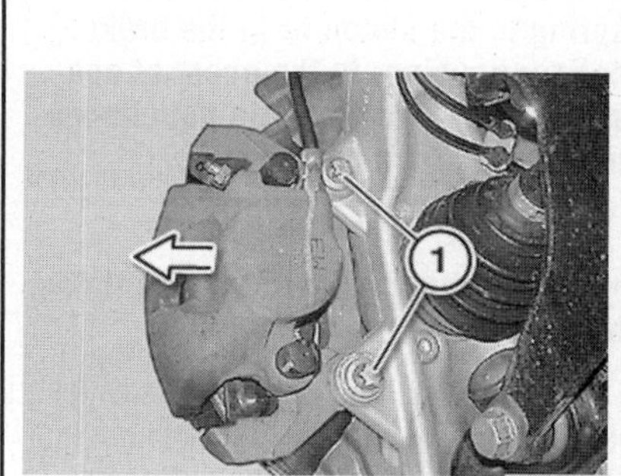

Fig. 9 Release screws (1)

To install:

8. Installation is the reverse order of removal.

➡First tighten brake hose on brake caliper.

9. Move wheels into straight-ahead position.
10. Insert brake hose in bracket and screw onto brake pipe.

➡Never twist brake hose when installing it and avoid all contact with parts attached rigidly to the body.

11. Caliper mounting screws tightening torque 81 ft. lbs. (110 Nm).
12. Brake hose to brake caliper tightening torque 18 ft. lbs. (24 Nm).
13. Retainer must be felt and heard to snap into place. Ensure correct seating in guide.
14. After completing work, bleed braking system

BRAKE PADS

REMOVAL & INSTALLATION

See Figures 10 through 14.

1. Remove front wheels
2. Remove brake pad wear sensor
3. Lever out retaining spring in direction of arrow towards rear.
4. Remove plastic plugs.
5. Release guide screws with special tool 34 1 080. Withdraw brake caliper backwards.

➡Tie brake caliper back and do not allow to hang from brake hose.

6. Remove outer brake pad in direction of arrow.
7. Force inner brake pad in direction of arrow off piston and remove.

To install:

➡The inner brake pad is seated with a spring in the piston or in the brake caliper housing. In the event of one-sided brake pad wear, do not change brake pads round.

8. Clean brake pads.

➡Do not apply grease to brake lining backplate.

9. When putting on the brake caliper, it is absolutely necessary to make sure that the brake pad T-head of the outer brake pad is seated correctly on the contact surface.

➡With brake pads that are already partially worn, pay particular attention that the position of the outer brake pad in relation to the contact surface is ensured.

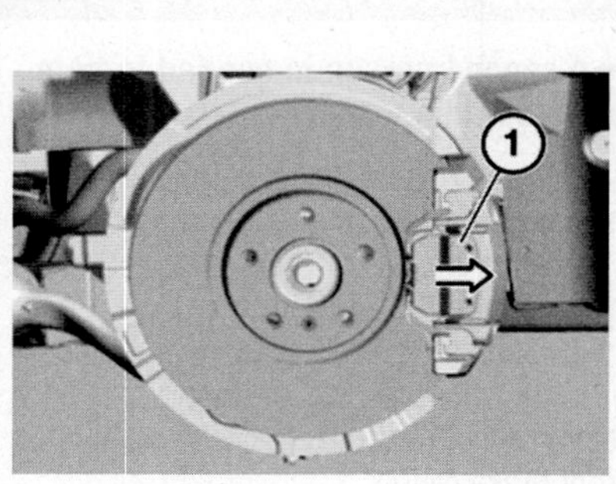

Fig. 10 Lever out retaining spring (1) in direction of arrow towards rear

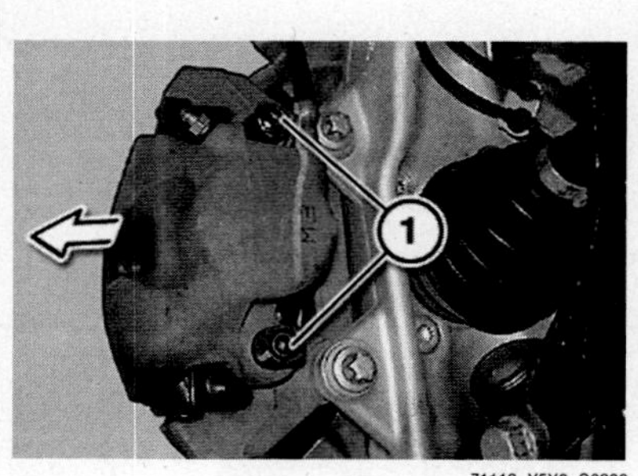

Fig. 11 Release guide screws (1) with special tool 34 1 080

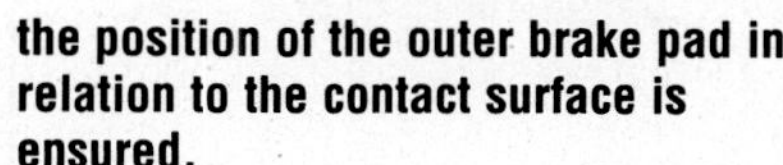

➡When pressing piston back: Pay attention to brake fluid level in expansion tank; brake fluid that spills over will damage paintwork.

10. Press back brake pads and piston with special tool 34 1 050.

➡New brake pads may only be fitted if the brake disc thickness is greater than the minimum brake disc thickness (MIN TH).

11. Check dust boot for damage and replace if necessary.
12. Clean contact surface of brake piston with brake cleaner and apply a thin coating of brake pad paste.

➡Dust boot must not come into contact with brake pad paste as this may cause the dust boot to swell.

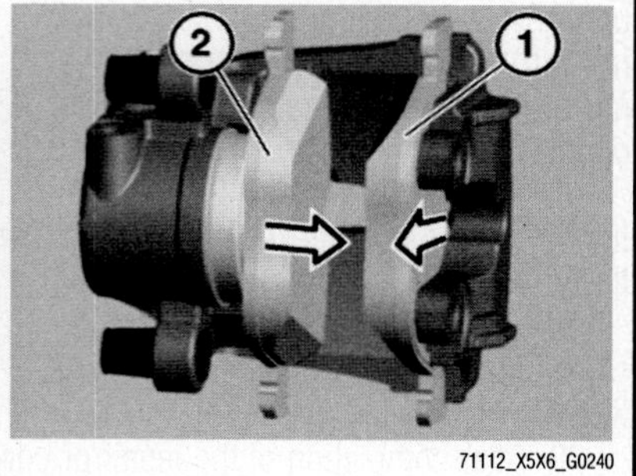

Fig. 12 Remove outer brake pad (1) in direction of arrow; Force inner brake pad (2) in direction of arrow off piston and remove

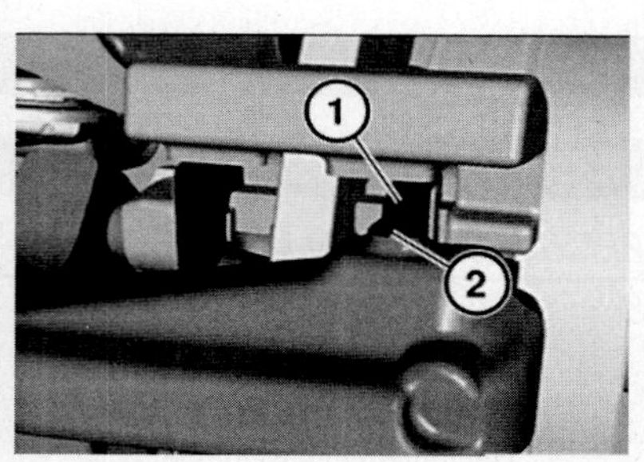

Fig. 13 When putting on the brake caliper, it is absolutely necessary to make sure that the brake pad T-head (1) of the outer brake pad is seated correctly on the contact surface (2)

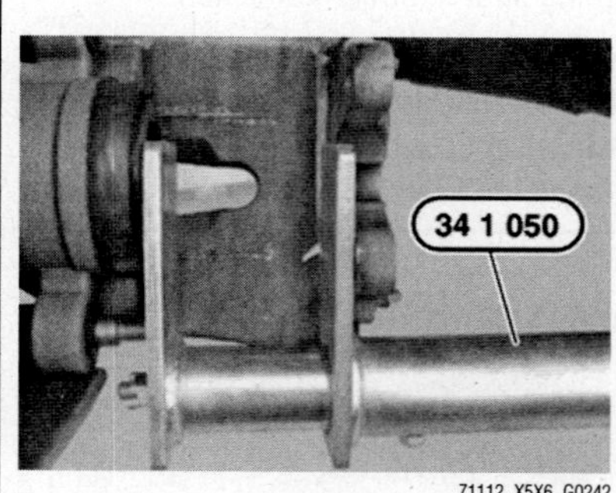

Fig. 14 Press back brake pads and piston with special tool 34 1 050

13. Clean contact surfaces with brake cleaner and apply a thin coating of brake pad paste.

➡Grease contact surfaces on brake caliper at top and bottom.

➡So as not to damage the surface coating, if possible do not mechanically clean the guide surfaces for the brake pads on the brake caliper mounting bracket. Instead, clean with brake cleaner and apply a thin coating of brake pad paste.

14. Clean contact surface of brake caliper with brake cleaner and apply a thin coating of brake pad paste.

➡So as not to damage the surface coating, if possible do not mechanically clean pad guides (1). Instead, clean with brake cleaner and apply a thin coating of brake pad paste.

15. After completing repair work:

a. Fully depress brake pedal several times so that brake pads contact brake discs.

b. When installing new brake pads at front and rear axles, brake fluid level must be brought up to "MAX" marking.

c. When replacing pads, reset CBS display in accordance with factory specification.

16. Attach retaining spring first at top and bottom on brake caliper and then allow to engage in recesses of brake caliper housing.

BRAKES

REAR DISC BRAKES

BRAKE CALIPERS

REMOVAL & INSTALLATION

See Figures 15 and 16.

1. Remove wheel.
2. Detach retaining clip in direction of arrow.

➡Grip brake hose at square head to prevent connecting piece from turning in retaining bracket.

3. Disconnect brake hose from brake line.
4. Detach brake hose from brake caliper.
5. Remove brake pads.
6. Release screws.
7. Remove brake anchor plate in direction of arrow.

To install:

8. Brake anchor plate-to-wheel carrier; Tightening torque 81 ft. lbs. (110 Nm).
9. Brake hose to brake caliper: Tightening torque 18 ft. lbs. (24 Nm).
10. Insert brake hose in bracket and screw onto brake pipe.

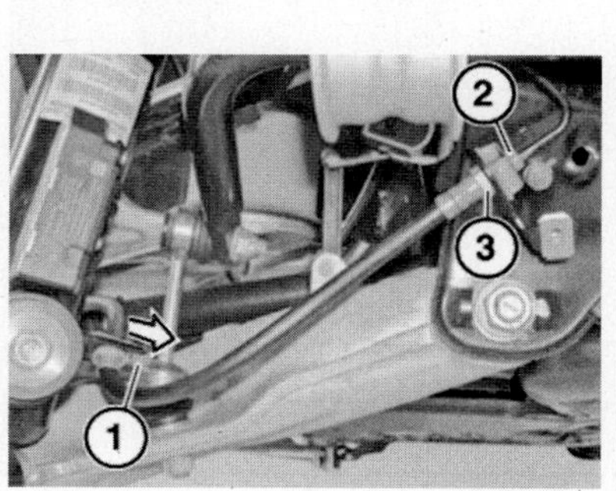

Fig. 15 Detach retaining clip (1) in direction of arrow, disconnect brake hose from brake line (2); square head (3)

Fig. 16 Release screws (1)

➡First tighten brake hose on brake caliper.

➡Never twist brake hose when installing it and avoid all contact with parts attached rigidly to the body.

➡Retaining clip must be felt and heard to snap into place.

11. After completing work: Bleed braking system

BRAKE PADS

REMOVAL & INSTALLATION

See Figures 17 through 19.

1. Remove wheels.
2. Remove brake pad wear sensor.
3. Lift out retaining spring.
4. Remove cover plugs.
5. Unscrew guide bolts.
6. Withdraw brake caliper backwards.

➡Tie brake caliper back and do not allow to hang from brake hose.

7. Mark any worn brake pads.

➡In the event of one-sided brake pad wear, do not change brake pads round.

Fig. 17 Lift out retaining spring (1)

8. Remove outer brake pad.
9. Inner brake pad is located with its spring in the piston.

To install:

10. Clean brake pads.

➡Do not grease backs of brake pads sleeve.

11. Check dust boot for damage and replace if necessary.

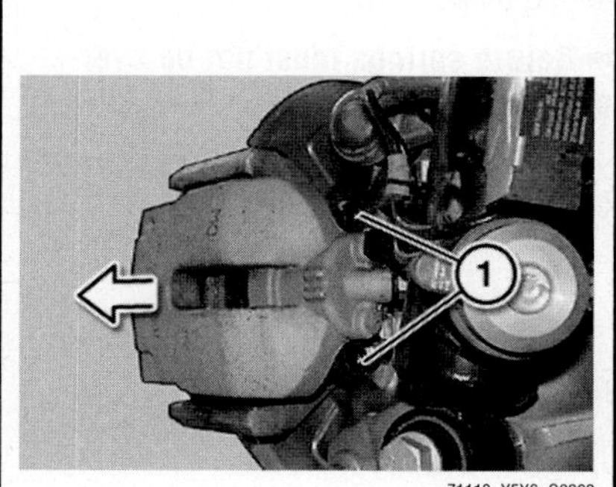

Fig. 18 Unscrew guide bolts (1)

⁂ WARNING

Dust boot must not come into contact with brake pad paste as this may cause the dust boot to swell.

12. When pressing down piston, note brake fluid level in expansion tank. Overflowing brake fluid will damage the paintwork.
13. Turn piston back fully with special tool 34 1 050.
14. Clean contact surface of brake piston with brake cleaner and apply a thin coating of brake pad paste.
15. Clean contact surfaces of brake pad tee heads/brake caliper housing with brake cleaner and apply a thin coating of brake pad paste.
16. Clean contact surface of brake caliper with brake cleaner and apply a thin coating of brake pad paste.

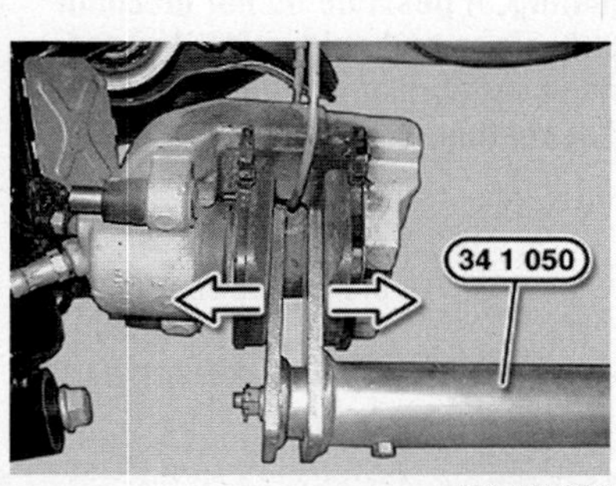

Fig. 19 Turn piston back fully with special tool 34 1 050

➡So as not to damage the surface coating, if possible do not mechanically clean the guide surfaces for the brake pads on the brake caliper mounting bracket. Instead, clean with brake cleaner and apply a thin coating of brake pad paste.

17. Replace guide bolts: Tightening torque 22 ft. lbs. (30 Nm).
    a. Clean guide bolts only; do not grease.
    b. Check threads.
    c. Replace all guide bolts which are not in perfect condition.
18. After completing work:
    a. Fully depress brake pedal several times so that brake pads contact brake discs.
    b. When installing new brake pads at front and rear axles, brake fluid level must be brought up to "MAX" marking.
    c. If necessary, when replacing pads, reset CBS display in accordance with factory specification.

ADJUSTMENTS

1. Raise and safely support the vehicle.
2. Completely unscrew one wheel stud on each rear wheel. Turn the wheel until the tapped hole is located at the bottom.
3. Turn adjusting screw with a screwdriver until the wheel is no longer able to turn. Then back off the adjusting screw 10 notches.
4. Reinstall the wheel studs.

PARKING BRAKE SHOES

REMOVAL & INSTALLATION

See Figures 20 and 21.

1. Remove rear brake disc.
2. Release electromechanical parking brake (EMF).
3. Disconnect return springs with brake spring pliers.

➡Return springs must not be overelongated.

4. Twist roll pins 90 degrees with special tool 34 4 000 and detach.
5. Remove brake pads.

To install:

6. Installation is the reverse order of removal.
7. Check return springs and replace if necessary.

➡Return springs must not be mixed up.

➡Note the installation position of adjusting screw.

8. Apply a thin coat of grease to bush and screw threads.

➡During replacement of the hand brake coverings, the following components must also be renewed:

- Brake shoe expander
- Adjusting screw
- Spring set

9. After completing repair work, adjust parking brake.

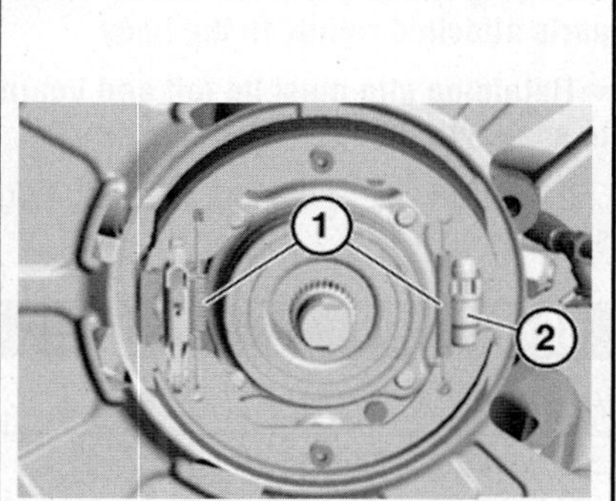

Fig. 20 Disconnect return springs (1) with brake spring pliers; adjusting screw (2)

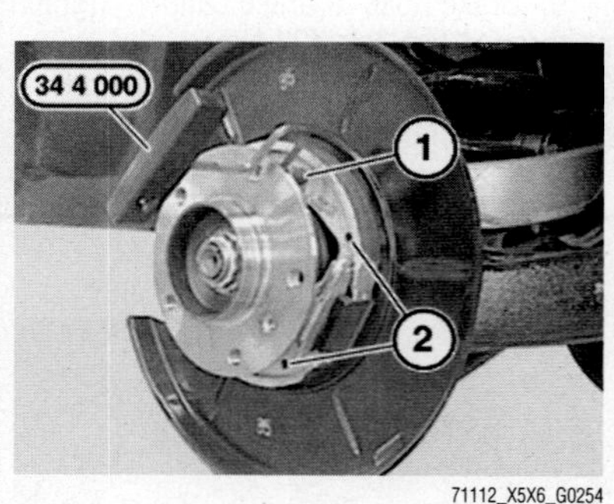

Fig. 21 Twist roll pins (1) 90 degrees with special tool 34 4 000 and detach, then remove brake pads (2)

PRECAUTIONS

Before servicing any vehicle, please be sure to read all of the following precautions, which deal with personal safety, prevention of component damage, and important points to take into consideration when servicing a motor vehicle:

- Never open, service or drain the radiator or cooling system when the engine is hot; serious burns can occur from the steam and hot coolant.
- Observe all applicable safety precautions when working around fuel. Whenever servicing the fuel system, always work in a well-ventilated area. Do not allow fuel spray or vapors to come in contact with a spark, open flame, or excessive heat (a hot drop light, for example). Keep a dry chemical fire extinguisher near the work area. Always keep fuel in a container specifically designed for fuel storage; also, always properly seal fuel containers to avoid the possibility of fire or explosion. Refer to the additional fuel system precautions later in this section.
- Fuel injection systems often remain pressurized, even after the engine has been turned **OFF**. The fuel system pressure must be relieved before disconnecting any fuel lines. Failure to do so may result in fire and/or personal injury.
- Brake fluid often contains polyglycol ethers and polyglycols. Avoid contact with the eyes and wash your hands thoroughly after handling brake fluid. If you do get brake fluid in your eyes, flush your eyes with clean, running water for 15 minutes. If eye irritation persists, or if you have taken brake fluid internally, **IMMEDIATELY** seek medical assistance.
- The EPA warns that prolonged contact with used engine oil may cause a number of skin disorders, including cancer. You should make every effort to minimize your exposure to used engine oil. Protective gloves should be worn when changing oil. Wash your hands and any other exposed skin areas as soon as possible after exposure to used engine oil. Soap and water, or waterless hand cleaner should be used.
- All new vehicles are now equipped with an air bag system, often referred to as a Supplemental Restraint System (SRS) or Supplemental Inflatable Restraint (SIR) system. The system must be disabled before performing service on or around system components, steering column, instrument panel components, wiring and sensors. Failure to follow safety and disabling procedures could result in accidental air bag deployment, possible personal injury and unnecessary system repairs.
- Always wear safety goggles when working with, or around, the air bag system. When carrying a non-deployed air bag, be sure the bag and trim cover are pointed away from your body. When placing a non-deployed air bag on a work surface, always face the bag and trim cover upward, away from the surface. This will reduce the motion of the module if it is accidentally deployed. Refer to the additional air bag system precautions later in this section.
- Clean, high quality brake fluid from a sealed container is essential to the safe and proper operation of the brake system. You should always buy the correct type of brake fluid for your vehicle. If the brake fluid becomes contaminated, completely flush the system with new fluid. Never reuse any brake fluid. Any brake fluid that is removed from the system should be discarded. Also, do not allow any brake fluid to come in contact with a painted surface; it will damage the paint.
- Never operate the engine without the proper amount and type of engine oil; doing so WILL result in severe engine damage.
- Timing belt maintenance is extremely important. Many models utilize an interference-type, non-freewheeling engine. If the timing belt breaks, the valves in the cylinder head may strike the pistons, causing potentially serious (also time-consuming and expensive) engine damage. Refer to the maintenance interval charts for the recommended replacement interval for the timing belt, and to the timing belt section for belt replacement and inspection.
- Disconnecting the negative battery cable on some vehicles may interfere with the functions of the on-board computer system(s) and may require the computer to undergo a relearning process once the negative battery cable is reconnected.
- When servicing drum brakes, only disassemble and assemble one side at a time, leaving the remaining side intact for reference.
- Only an MVAC-trained, EPA-certified automotive technician should service the air conditioning system or its components.

DISARMING THE SYSTEM

1. Before servicing the vehicle, refer to the precautions in the beginning of this section.
2. Place the ignition switch in the **OFF** position.
3. Disconnect the negative battery terminal and cover the battery terminal to prevent accidental contact.
4. Once the battery has been disconnected, wait for a period of approximately 3 minutes allowing the capacitor in the control unit to discharge. Once the capacitor is discharged, a trigger pulse cannot be generated inadvertently.

ARMING THE SYSTEM

1. Before servicing the vehicle, refer to the precautions in the beginning of this section.
2. Place the ignition switch in the **OFF** position.
3. Attach the sensors, the steering column connector and the seat belt tensioner connectors.
4. Connect the negative battery terminal.
5. Place the ignition switch in the **ON** position. Check that the SRS light illuminates for 6 seconds and then turns off. If it illuminates in any other pattern, check the components and their connections for proper operation and recheck operation of the warning light.

DRIVETRAIN

DRIVESHAFT

REMOVAL & INSTALLATION

Front

See Figures 22 through 24.

1. Remove underbody protection. Release screws and remove underbody protection.
2. Remove reinforcement plate
   a. Release bolts for assembly underside protection at front.
   b. Unfasten screws.
   c. Remove reinforcement plate.
3. Release screws.
4. Slide propeller shaft towards rear and remove flexible disc with centering flange.

To install:

5. Slide propeller shaft fully towards rear.

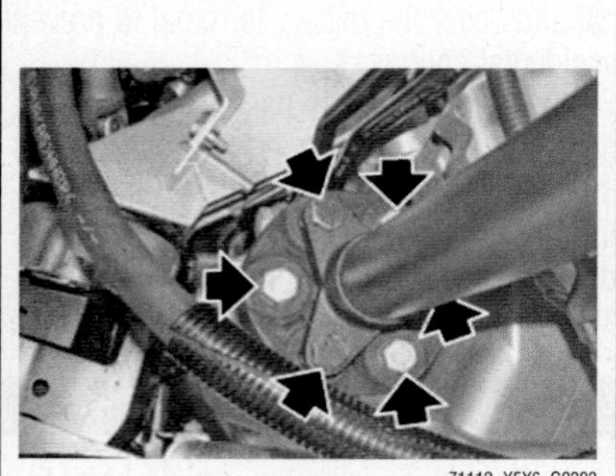

Fig. 22 Release screws

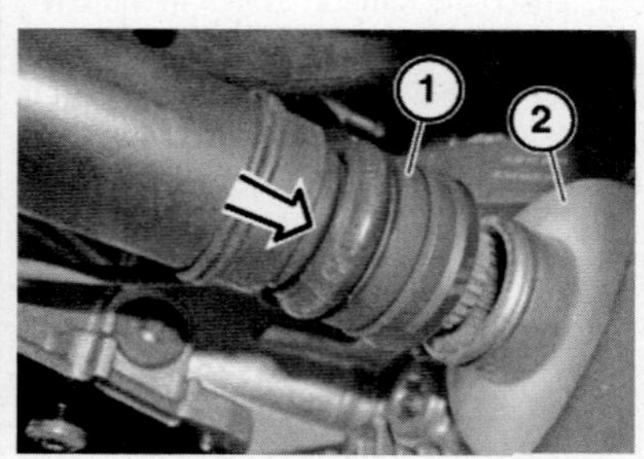

Fig. 23 Sealing cup (1) must snap audibly into place and rest entirely on dust guard (2)

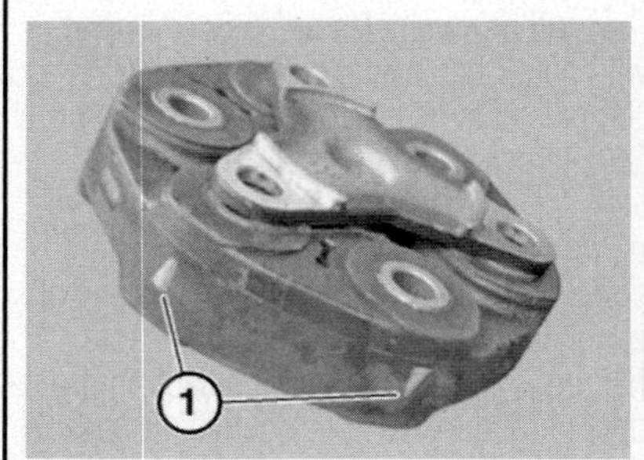

Fig. 24 During installation arrows (1) on circumference of flexible disc must point to flange arms

6. Sealing cup must snap audibly into place and rest entirely on dust guard.
7. Replace screws and nuts.
   a. M8 threads: tighten to 15 ft. lbs. (20 Nm).
   b. M10 threads: tighten to 7 ft. lbs. (10 Nm).

➡During installation arrows on circumference of flexible disc must point to flange arms.

Rear

See Figures 25 through 32.

1. Remove complete exhaust system
2. Remove underbody protection with holders
3. Remove heat shields

➡To avoid buzzing sound after refitting the propeller shaft:

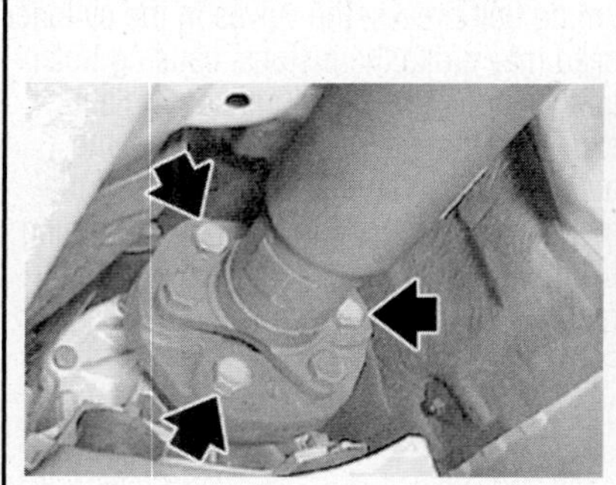

Fig. 25 Release screws

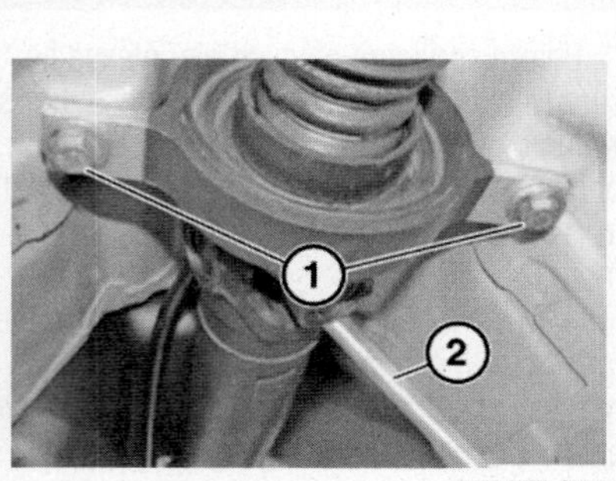

Fig. 26 Loosen screws (1); Using a suitable tool (2), secure propeller shaft at centre universal joint against turning

   a. The flexible disc connection on the front at the propeller shaft must be marked in one plane with the flexible disc and the three-bolt flange before removal.
   b. During installation the three-bolt flange must be forced back together again with the flexible disc in the same position.
4. Release screws.
5. Loosen screws.
6. Using a suitable tool, secure propeller shaft at centre universal joint against turning.
7. Remove screws of centre mount fully only after opening insert nut.

➡The bi-hexagonal flange nut must not be used for bracing. Failure to comply with this instruction may result in serious damage to the rear axle final drive.

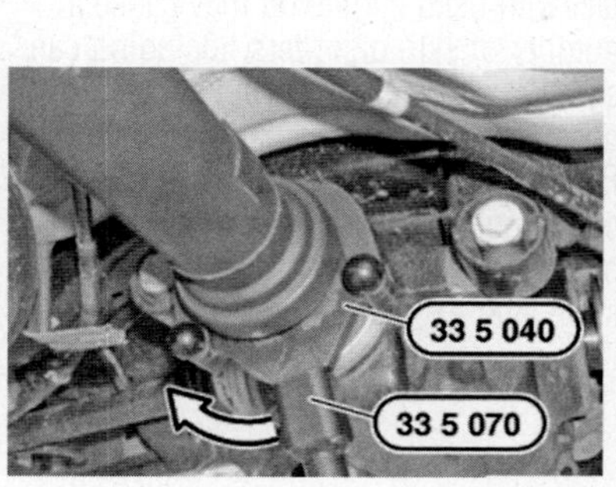

Fig. 27 Release insert nut against direction of travel in clockwise direction with special tools 33 5 040 and 33 5 070

Fig. 28 Clean insert collar (1) on flange nut and gearing on bevel pinion (2)

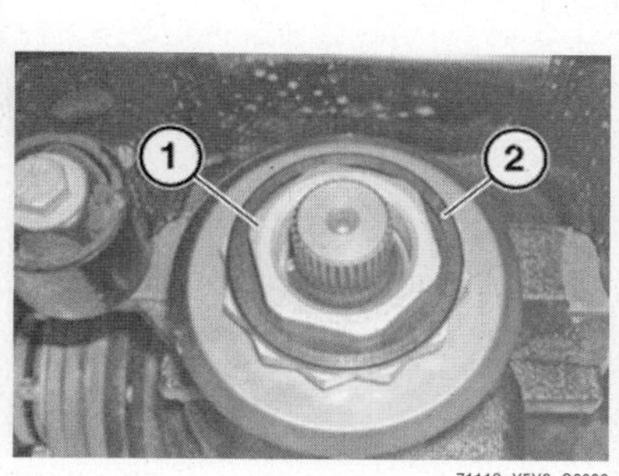

Fig. 30 Place flange nut (1) with gasket in insert collar of flange nut, and install retaining clip (2)

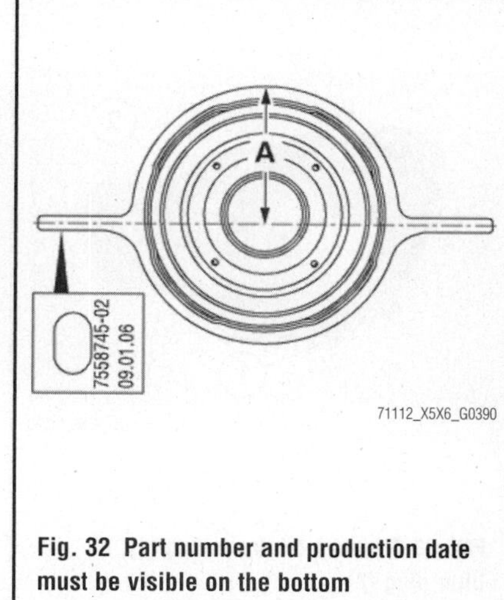

Fig. 32 Part number and production date must be visible on the bottom

Fig. 29 Clean thread (1) of joint hub to remove adhesive residues, and clean hub teeth (2), then coat with grease

Fig. 31 Slide propeller shaft (1) to the limit position onto insert nut and secure; bi-hexagonal flange nut (2)

8. Release insert nut against direction of travel in clockwise direction with special tools 33 5 040 and 33 5 070.
9. Remove retaining clip and gasket.
10. Remove insert nut.

To install:

➡Adhere without fail to installation and screw-fastening sequence.

11. Installation sequence:
    a. Join propeller shaft to transmission
    b. Join propeller shaft to rear axle final drive
    c. Join centre mount
12. Screw-fastening sequence:
    a. Insert nut

➡Insert nut must be replaced.

    b. Flexible disc to transmission
    c. Centre mount
13. Before installing propeller shaft:
    a. Clean insert collar on flange nut and gearing on bevel pinion.
    b. Fill insert collar with grease.
    c. Clean thread of joint hub to remove adhesive residues.
    d. Clean hub teeth, then coat with grease.

➡Thread of joint hub must not be fouled with grease.

14. Retaining clip and gasket must be replaced. Tightening torque 16 ft. lbs. (21 Nm).
15. Place flange nut (1) with gasket in insert collar of flange nut.
16. Install retaining clip.

➡The bi-hexagonal flange nut must not be used for bracing. Failure to comply with this instruction may result in serious damage to the rear axle final drive.

17. Insert nut must be screwed into place within 5 minutes.
18. Slide propeller shaft (1) to the limit position onto insert nut and secure.
19. Secure propeller shaft at centre universal joint against turning with a mounting lever. Tightening torque 63 ft. lbs. (85 Nm).

➡Check installation position. Part number and production date must be visible on the bottom.

➡The bolting points of the centre mount are not in the centre position. Component A of the propeller shaft centre bearing must be installed upwards into the transmission tunnel.

20. Centre mount tightening torque 16 ft. lbs. (21 Nm).

FRONT DRIVE AXLE

FLUID RECOMMENDATIONS

Use BMW differential oil SAF-XO/OSP

LEVEL CHECK

1. Undo oil filler plug.
2. Check front differential oil level.
3. If necessary, pour in front differential oil up to lower edge of opening for oil filler plug.
4. Replace oil filler plug. Tighten to 44 ft. lbs. (60 Nm).

DRAIN & REFILL

See Figure 33.

➡Only change oil when front differential is at normal operating temperature.

1. Remove reinforcement plate
2. Remove steering gear cover at top left
3. Place oil collecting apparatus underneath.
4. Remove oil drain plug.
5. Drain front differential oil.
6. Replace oil drain plug. Tighten to 44 ft. lbs. (60 Nm).

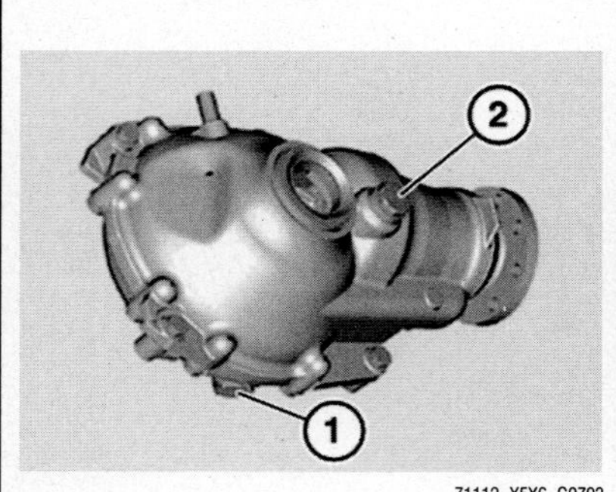

Fig. 33 Remove oil drain plug (1), oil filler plug (2)

Fig. 35 Pull drive flange off drive flange with special tool 33 1 150

Fig. 37 Drive in shaft seal with special tool31 5 130 up to limit position

7. Undo oil filler plug.
8. Pour in front differential oil up to lower edge of opening for oil filler plug (2).
9. Replace oil filler plug. Tighten to 44 ft. lbs. (60 Nm).

FRONT PINION OIL SEAL

REMOVAL & INSTALLATION

See Figures 34 through 37.

1. Remove reinforcement plate.
   a. Release bolts for assembly underside protection at front.
   b. Unfasten screws.
   c. Remove reinforcement plate.
2. Remove front propeller shaft.
3. Mark position of nut with respect to shaft with punch marks.
4. Lever out lockplate with a suitable tool.

➡Do not place special tool on threaded holes of drive flange.

5. Secure drive flange with special tool 23 0 020 against turning and release nut.

➡Mount special tool only with longer screws (M10x30) on drive flange.

6. Pull drive flange off drive flange with special tool 33 1 150.
7. Lever shaft seal out of front axle differential with a suitable screwdriver (2).

To install:

8. Drive in shaft seal with special tool 31 5 130 up to limit position.

➡Coat sealing lips of new shaft seal with front axle differential oil.

WARNING

Do not tighten nut beyond the punch marks or else the clamping sleeve will be damaged.

9. Clean drive flange and attach.
10. Tighten down nut until punch marks on nut and shaft are aligned.
11. Install new lockplate.
12. Check front axle gearbox oil level, correct if necessary.

HALFSHAFTS (OUTPUT SHAFTS)

REMOVAL & INSTALLATION

Left Output Shaft

See Figures 38 through 42.

1. Remove front wheel.

➡Expand anti-twist lock sufficiently to avoid damaging thread when releasing collar nut.

2. Release collar nut, press brake pedal to floor for this purpose.
3. Remove left microfilter housing cover.
   a. Detach mucket in working area.
   b. Unlock rotary catches and remove microfilter housing cover.

Fig. 34 Secure drive flange with special tool 23 0 020 against turning and release nut (1)

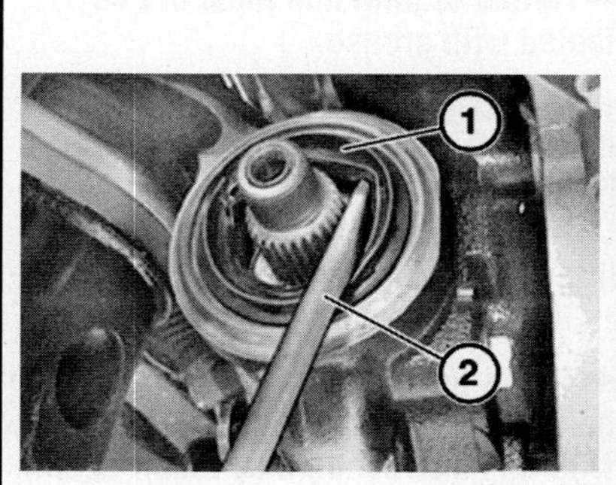

Fig. 36 Lever shaft seal (1) out of front axle differential with a suitable screwdriver (2)

Fig. 38 Detach mucket (1) in working area, unlock rotary catches (2) and remove microfilter housing cover

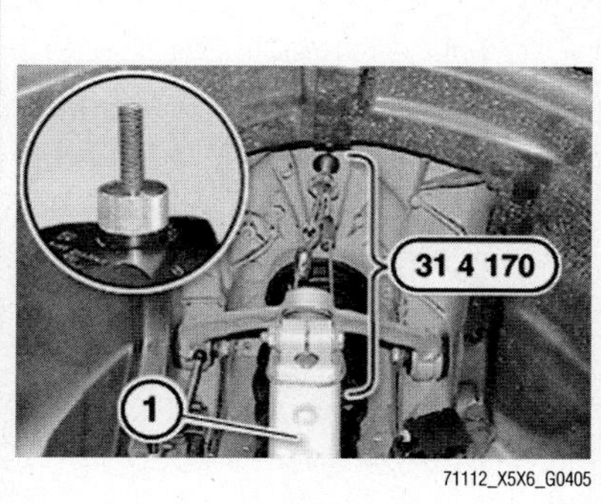

Fig. 39 Secure swivel bearing (1) with special tool 31 4 170

WARNING

Use special tool to avoid preliminary damage to ball joint in upper control arm.

4. Press plugs out of spring strut dome.
5. Secure swivel bearing (1) with special tool 31 4 170 in installation position.
6. Remove reinforcement plate.
   a. Release bolts for assembly underside protection at front.
   b. Unfasten screws.
   c. Remove reinforcement plate.
7. Remove steering gear cover at top and bottom.
8. Remove lower control arm front spring strut holder and front axle support.
9. Press output shaft out of drive flange.

➡**Tape off output shaft and secure against falling off.**

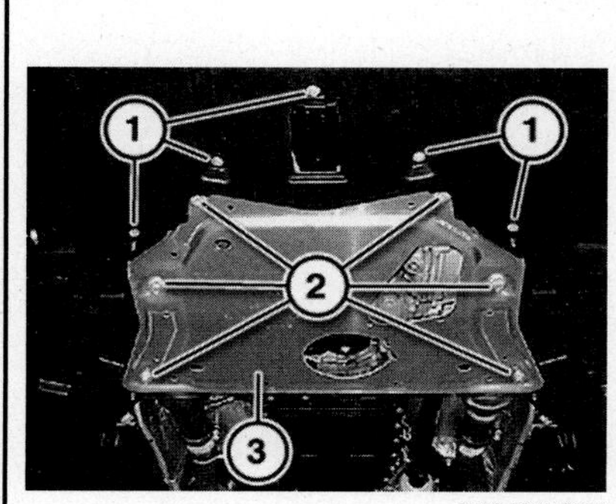

Fig. 40 Release bolts (1), unfasten screws (2), and remove reinforcement plate (3)

10. When removing output shaft, make sure that tripod does not fall into gaiter.
11. Turn steering wheel to right.
12. Press swivel bearing slightly to one side and remove output shaft from wheel bearing.
13. Use two tire levers on both sides to push the drive shaft out of the front axle differential. Remove drive shaft from between suspension strut mounting and control arm

To install:

14. Replace shaft seal in front differential.
15. Check front axle gearbox oil level, correct if necessary.

WARNING

High installation forces indicate that the output shaft spline teeth are damaged or deformed.

16. Check splines and replaced parts if damaged.
17. Install retaining ring.
18. Coat highlighted contact surface of output shaft with approved front axle gearbox oil.

➡**When installing output shaft, make sure that tripod does not fall into gaiter.**

19. Press swivel bearing slightly to one side and insert output shaft into front differential.
20. Pull out assembly protection ring at lug until one of the two predetermined breaking points gives.
21. Slide output shaft to the limit position into front axle differential. Output shaft must snap audibly into place.
22. Press swivel bearing slightly to one side and insert output shaft into wheel bearing.
23. Move steering to straight-ahead position.
24. Draw output shaft into drive flange.
25. Install lower control arm.
26. Install steering gear cover at top and bottom.
27. Install reinforcement plate.
28. Remove special tool 31 4 170 for swivel bearing.
29. Use plugs from spring strut dome.
30. Install left microfilter housing cover.
31. Replace collar nut, oil collar nut/wheel bearing contact surface only and tighten down. Tightening torque 310 ft. lbs. (420 Nm).

➡**No oil permitted on thread of shaft journal or collar nut.**

32. Secure collar nut by positive peening on flat areas of output shaft.

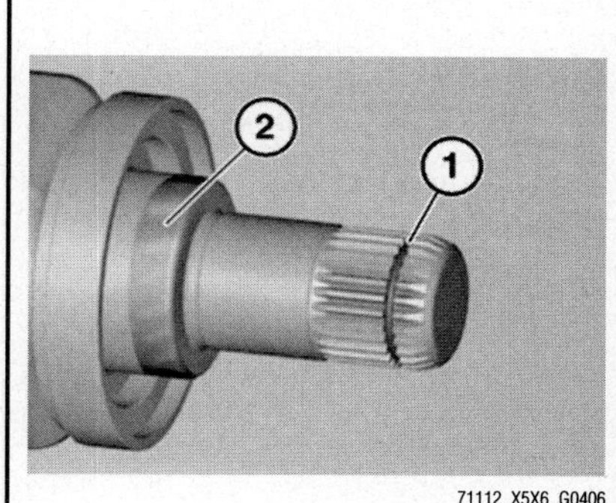

Fig. 41 Install retaining ring (1), coat highlighted contact surface (2) of output shaft with approved front axle gearbox oil

Fig. 42 Pull out assembly protection ring at lug (1) until one of the two predetermined breaking points gives

33. Install front wheel.
34. Perform chassis alignment check

Right Output Shaft

1. Remove right spring strut
2. Further procedure is identical to remove and install/replace left output shaft.

REAR DRIVE AXLE

FLUID RECOMMENDATIONS

Use BMW differential oil SAF-XO / OSP

LEVEL CHECK

See Figure 43.

1. Undo oil filler plug.
2. Check oil level.
3. If necessary, pour in rear differential oil up to lower edge of opening for oil filler plug.
4. Replace oil filler plug with O-ring. Tighten to 44 ft. lbs. (60 Nm).

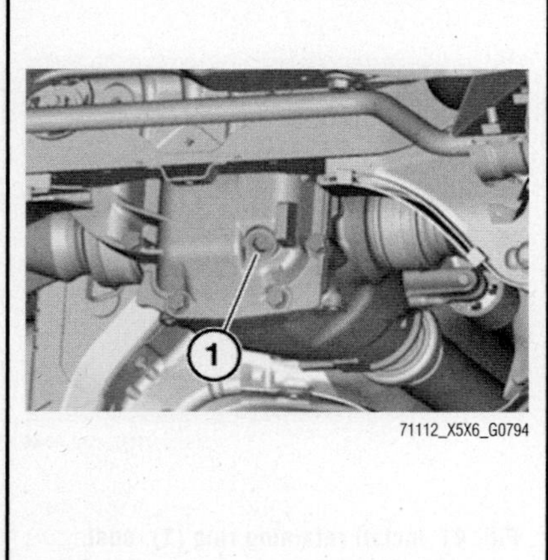

Fig. 43 Undo oil filler plug (1)

DRAIN & REFILL

➡The oil does not need to be changed in rear differentials carrying the "Life-Time-Oil" sticker.

CAUTION

Only change oil when rear differential is at normal operating temperature.

1. Open plug.
2. Drain and dispose of differential oil.
3. Add differential oil up to lower edge of opening for screw plug.
4. Replace screw plug. Tighten to 44 ft. lbs. (60 Nm).

DIFFERENTIAL HOUSING COVER

REMOVAL & INSTALLATION

See Figures 44 and 45.

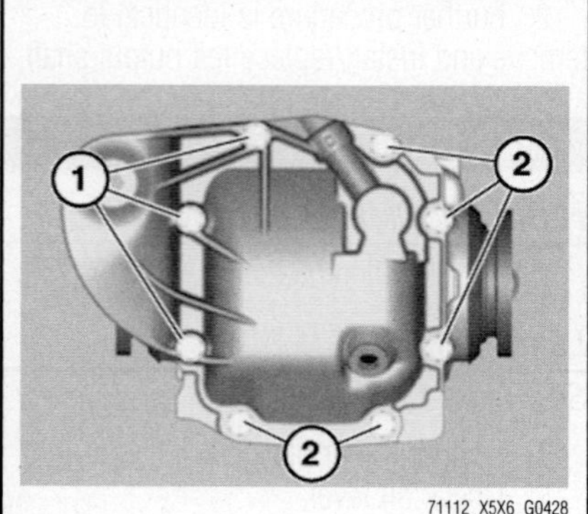

Fig. 44 Release screws (1, 2) (188L/188LW Final Drive)

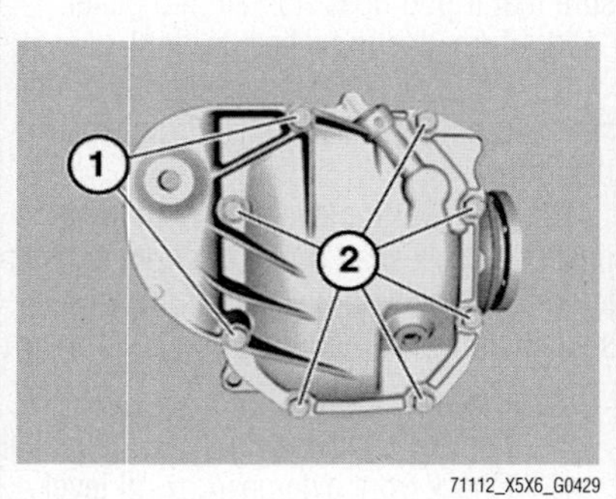

Fig. 45 Release screws (1, 2) (215L/215LW Final Drive)

1. Release screws.
2. Remove cover.

To install:

3. If necessary, remove remnants of liquid sealing compound with scraper.
4. Clean sealing face on cover and rear differential.
5. If a paper gasket was fitted, a paper gasket or liquid sealing compound can be used.
6. Tightening torque for all screws 41 ft. lbs. (55 Nm).

REAR HALFSHAFTS (OUTPUT SHAFTS)

REMOVAL & INSTALLATION

See Figures 46 through 48.

1. Remove rear wheel.

➡Expand anti-twist lock sufficiently to avoid damaging thread when releasing collar nut.

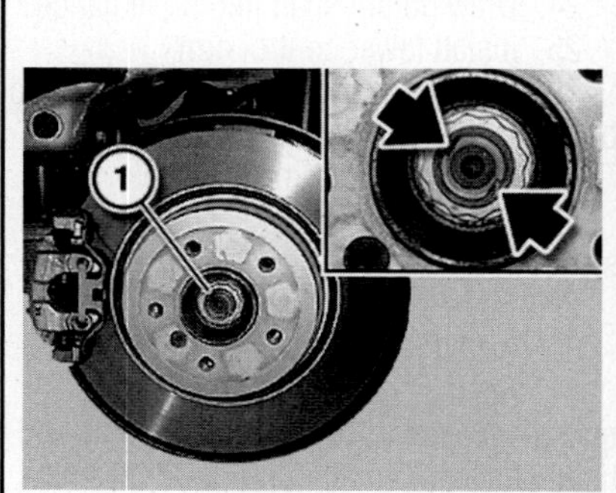

Fig. 46 Release collar nut (1), activate parking brake for this purpose

Fig. 47 Do not damage dust plates (1, 2) when setting down output shaft

2. Release collar nut, activate parking brake for this purpose.
3. Secure output shaft against falling out.
4. Do not damage dust plates when setting down output shaft.
5. Press output shaft out of drive flange and remove towards centre of vehicle.

To install:

➡High installation forces indicate that the output shaft gearing is damaged or deformed.

6. Check gearing, replaced damaged parts if necessary.
7. Check dust plate for damage, renew if necessary.
8. Replace circlip.
9. Coat contact surface of output shaft with approved rear axle final drive oil.
10. Replace collar nut, oil collar nut/wheel bearing contact surface only and tighten down. Tightening torque: 310 ft. lbs. (420 Nm).

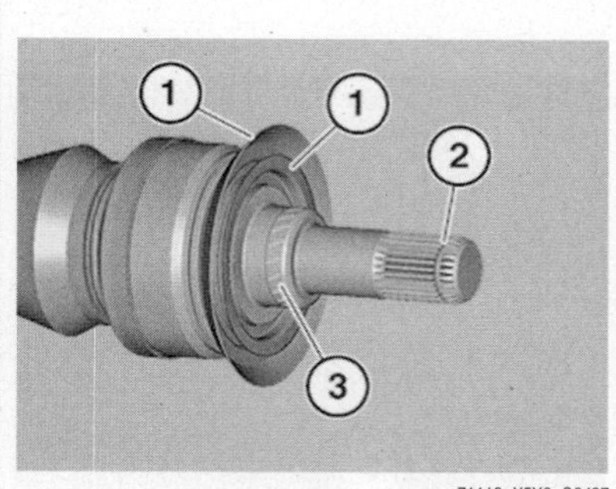

Fig. 48 Check dust plate (1), replace circlip (2), and coat contact surface (3) of output shaft with approved rear axle final drive oil

➡**No oil permitted on thread of shaft journal or collar nut.**

11. Secure collar nut by positive peening on flat areas of output shaft.
12. Check final drive oil level, correct if necessary

PINION OIL SEAL

REMOVAL & INSTALLATION

See Figures 49 and 50.

1. Remove rear axle final drive
2. Use special tools 00 5 010 and 32 1 060 / 33 1 308 to remove radial shaft seal.

➡**The installation protective ring serves to protect the sealing lips on shaft seal when the output shaft is being installed.**

➡**Installation protective ring must not slip out of shaft seal.**

3. Coat housing plate flange of shaft seal with approved final drive oil.

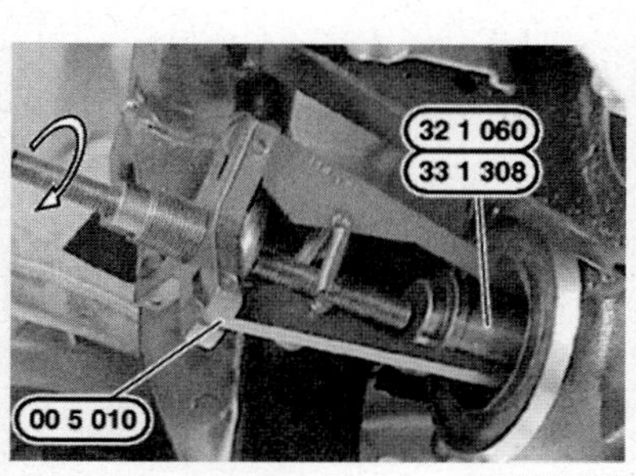

Fig. 49 Use special tools 00 5 010 and 32 1 060 / 33 1 308 to remove radial shaft seal

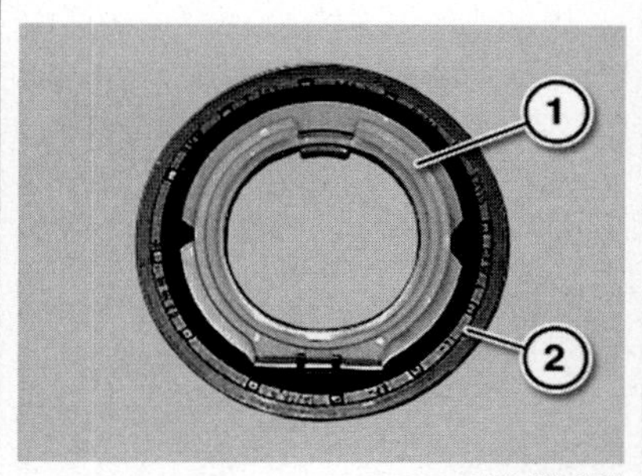

Fig. 50 The installation protective ring (1) serves to protect the sealing lips on shaft seal (2) when the output shaft is being installed

4. Drive in shaft seal as far as it will go with following special tool(s) (depending on rear differential /outside diameter).
5. Carefully remove special tool.
6. Open installation protective ring.
7. Check final drive oil level, correct if necessary

ENGINE COOLING

ENGINE COOLANT

BLEEDING

➡**Do not leave the coolant expansion tank cap open during the venting procedure.**

1. Open vent plugs on coolant feed lines to turbocharger.
2. Add coolant up to top edge of expansion tank. Coolant level must not drop further. No drop in coolant for approximately 1 minute. Close vent plugs on turbocharger when coolant emerges.
3. Set heater to maximum temperature. Press Automatic button. Then turn blower down to lowest stage for a minimum period of 5 minutes.
4. After switching off heater pump, add further coolant up to top edge of expansion tank.
5. Check cooling system for leaks.
6. Close expansion tank.
7. Start engine. Allow engine to idle for approximately 1 minute. During this period, press accelerator pedal 3 times (each time lasting 5 seconds) to approximately 3000 rpm.
8. Warm up engine and activate map thermostat via BMW diagnosis system.
9. When engine has cooled down, check coolant level and adjust to max.
10. Close coolant expansion tank.
11. Close cap on expansion tank until arrow markings are flush.

DRAIN & REFILL

CAUTION

Only carry out repair work on the cooling system after the engine has cooled down.

➡**Note the following instructions regarding the cooling system and the coolant:**

- Never reuse used coolant.
- When replacing and removing components which rely on the corrosion protection effect of the coolant, it is essential to change the coolant. The cooling system must therefore be drained and refilled.
- In the case of other removal work involving the draining of part quantities of coolant, replace these quantities which have been drained with new coolant.
- Open cooling system only when it has cooled down. Opening the cooling system while hot can result in air entering the system.
- Protect the alternator against dirt contamination before carrying out any repair work on the cooling circuit. Cover alternator with suitable materials. Failure to comply with this procedure may result in an alternator malfunction.
- Do not fill coolant expansion tank over MAX level as overfilling will cause the coolant to overflow. This may give rise to traces of coolant on the expansion tank or in the engine compartment and wrongly suggest possible leaks.

3.0L Engine

See Figure 51.

1. Remove underbody protection
2. Remove intake port.
   a. Release intake port at front of air duct.
   b. Loosen clamps. Release and remove intake port from air filter housing.
3. Unclip Bowden cable for engine compartment lid operation from transverse reinforcement (1).
4. Detach A/C line from bracket.
5. Release screws on left and right sides.
6. Remove transverse reinforcement.

Draining Coolant:

See Figure 52.

1. Open sealing cap on coolant expansion tank.
2. Unfasten and detach coolant hose from thermostat housing.
3. Drain, catch and dispose of coolant.

Fig. 51 Transverse reinforcement (1)

Fig. 52 Open coupling (1) on coolant hose below charge air cooler

4. With supplementary radiator:
   a. Open coupling on coolant hose below charge air cooler.
   b. Drain, catch and dispose of coolant.
5. Close sealing cap until the arrow marks line up.

Adding Coolant:

1. Use only recommended coolant.
2. Observe mixture ratio.
3. Observe capacities.

➡Observe bleeding instructions without fail.

4. Fill and bleed cooling system.
5. Visual inspection of cooling system for tightness.

4.4L Engine

1. Remove underbody protection.

Draining Coolant:

See Figure 53.

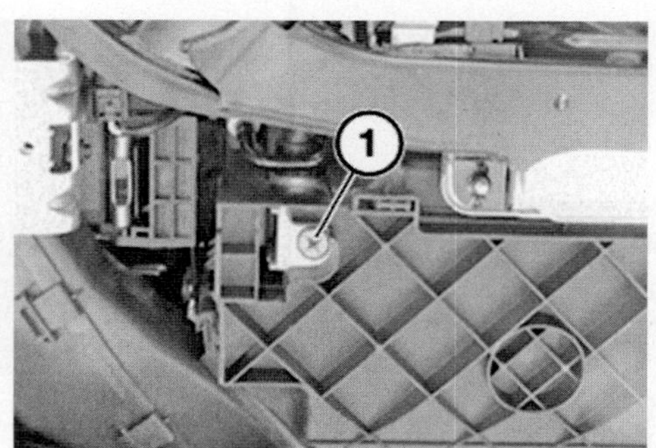

Fig. 53 If fitted, release coolant drain plug (1) on radiator

1. Open sealing cap on coolant expansion tank.
2. If fitted, release coolant drain plug on radiator. For radiators without coolant drain plug, unlock and pull off coolant hose.
3. Drain, catch and dispose of coolant.
4. Replace drain plug sealing ring.
5. Close sealing cap until the arrow marks line up.

Adding Coolant:

1. Use only recommended coolant.
2. Observe mixture ratio.

➡Observe bleeding instructions without fail.

3. Fill and vent cooling system
4. Visual inspection of cooling system for tightness.

FLUID RECOMMENDATIONS

With the protection of the environment in mind, BMW has been filling all of its vehicles with nitrite- and amino-free antifreeze and corrosion inhibitors since mid-1986 as standard practice.

The use of antifreeze and corrosion inhibitors that contain nitrites and amines is no longer permissible.

The following list of approved antifreezes for use in BMW engines:

- BMW antifreeze
- Castrol Anti-Freeze NF
- GlycoShell
- Havoline AFC (BD04)

LEVEL CHECK

Coolant level should be up to the "MAX" line on expansion tank when engine is cool.

ELECTRIC ENGINE FAN

REMOVAL & INSTALLATION

3.0L Engine

See Figures 53, 54 through 57.

1. Switch off ignition.
2. Remove the underbody protection.
3. Remove intake manifold.
4. Unclip Bowden cable for engine bonnet/hood actuator from transverse reinforcement.
5. Detach A/C line from holder.
6. Release screws on left and right sides.
7. Remove cross-brace.
8. Release coolant hose from fan cowl.
9. Unlock plug and remove.
10. Pull pressure pipe out of bracket.
11. Press lock.
12. Raise fan cowl until holder can be folded into centre of vehicle.

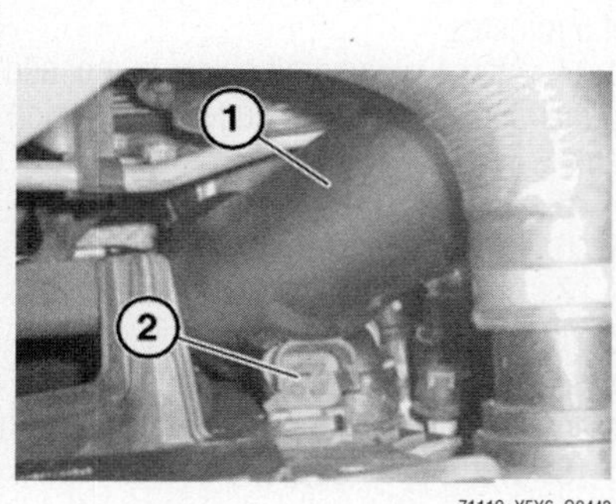

Fig. 54 Pull pressure pipe (1) out of bracket (2)

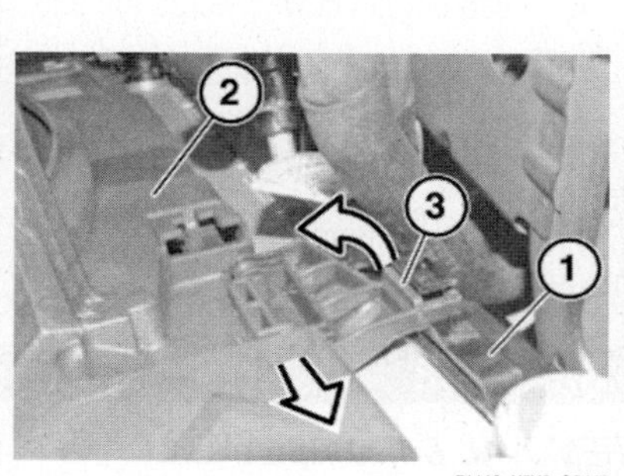

Fig. 55 Press lock (1), raise fan cowl (2) until holder (3) can be folded into centre of vehicle

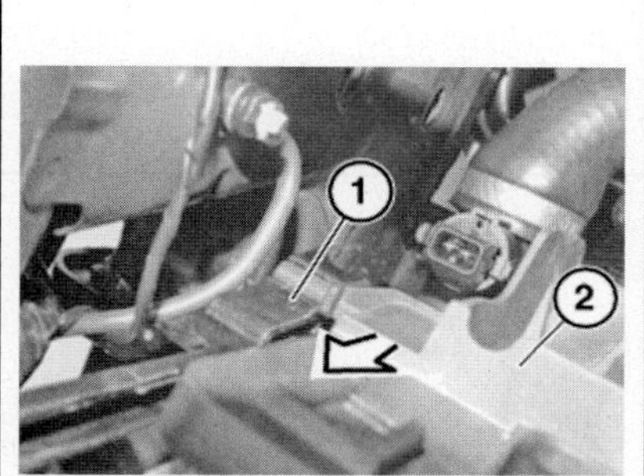

Fig. 56 Press lock (1), and feed out fan cowl (2) towards top and remove

➡For reasons of clarity, illustration and text show coolant hose removed. Do not raise fan cowl by fan impeller.

13. Press lock.
14. Feed out fan cowl towards top and remove.

To install:

15. Installation is the reverse order of removal.
16. Insert retaining tab at bottom on module carrier.

4.4L Engine

See Figures 51, 55 through 57.

1. Switch off ignition.
2. Remove intake manifold.
3. Unclip Bowden cable for engine bonnet/hood actuator from transverse reinforcement.
4. Detach A/C line from holder.
5. Release screws on left and right sides.

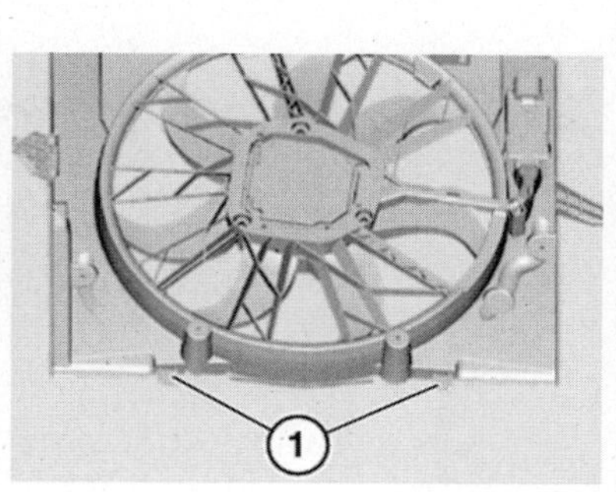

Fig. 57 Insert retaining tab (1) at bottom on module carrier

6. Remove cross-brace.
7. Release coolant hose from fan cowl.
8. Unlock plug and remove.
9. Press lock.
10. Raise fan cowl until holder can be folded into centre of vehicle.

➡For reasons of clarity, illustration and text show coolant hose removed. Do not raise fan cowl by fan impeller.

11. Press lock.
12. Feed out fan cowl towards top and remove.

To install:

13. Installation is the reverse order of removal.
14. Insert retaining tab at bottom on module carrier.

ELECTRIC WATER PUMP

REMOVAL & INSTALLATION

3.0L Engine

See Figures 58 through 60.

1. Remove engine splash guard.
2. Remove charge air cooler.
3. Drain coolant.
4. Remove thermostat.
5. Remove reinforcement plate.
6. Disconnect plug connection.
7. Release coolant hose.
8. Release coolant hose.
9. Release aluminum screws.
10. Unclip cable from bracket.
11. Release screw.

To install:

12. Installation is the reverse order of removal.

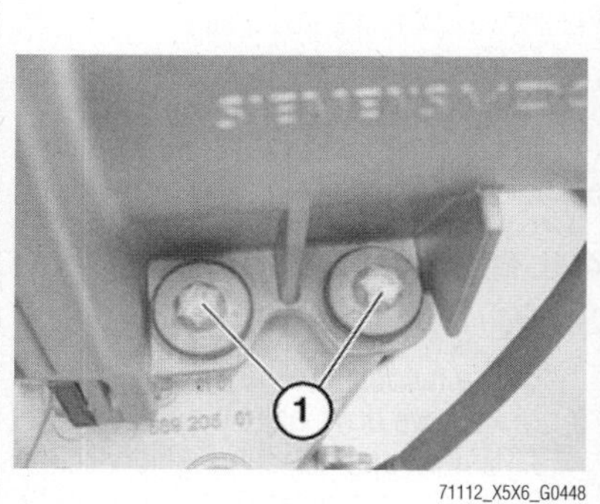

Fig. 58 Release aluminum screws (1)

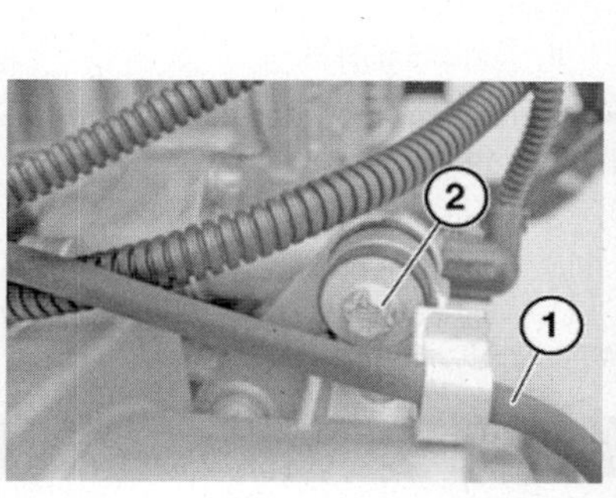

Fig. 59 Unclip cable (1) from bracket, release screw (2)

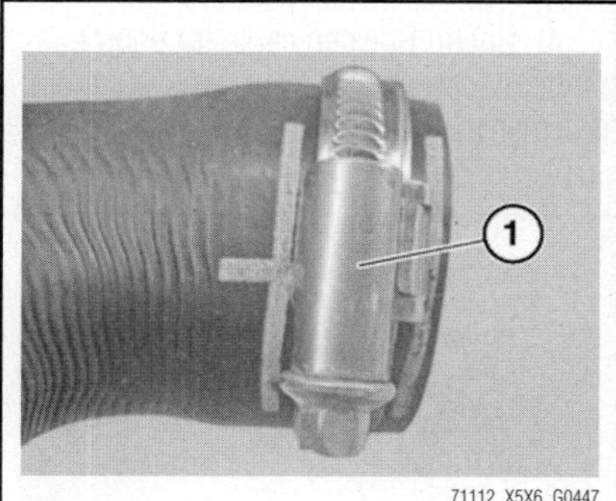

Fig. 60 Hose clamps (1) must be installed in the centre of the marked area

⁂ WARNING

If the electric coolant pump is reused, it must be rotated one turn due to the breakaway torque at the impellers.

13. Hose clamps (1) must be installed in the centre of the marked area.
14. Replace aluminum screws.
15. Assemble engine.
16. Bleeding instructions must be observed without fail.

4.4L Engine

See Figure 61.

1. Drain coolant
2. Remove drive belt
3. Unlock and detach plug connections.
4. Unlock and detach all coolant hoses on coolant pump.
5. Unfasten screws.
6. Lift out coolant pump with a swiveling movement.

To install:

7. Installation is the reverse order of removal.
8. Replace gasket.

➡Remove coolant thermostat from faulty coolant pump.

9. Replace sealing ring.
10. Assemble engine.
11. Vent cooling system and check for water leaks.

FAN SHROUD

REMOVAL & INSTALLATION

3.0L Engine

See Figures 51, 54 through 56 and 62.

1. Switch off ignition.
2. Remove the underbody protection.
3. Remove intake manifold.
4. Unclip Bowden cable for engine bonnet/hood actuator from transverse reinforcement.

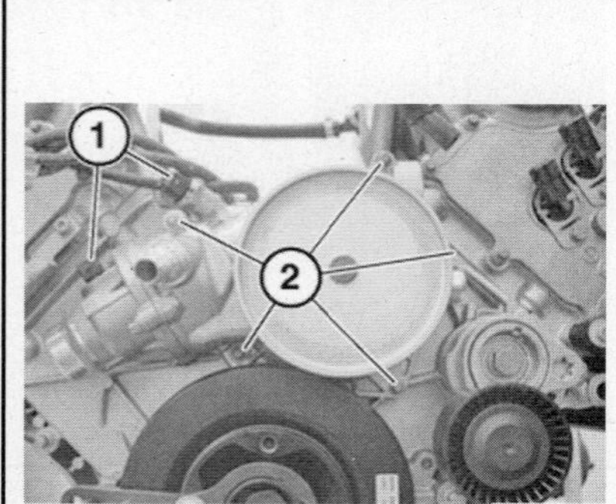

Fig. 61 Unlock and detach plug connections (1), unfasten screws (2)

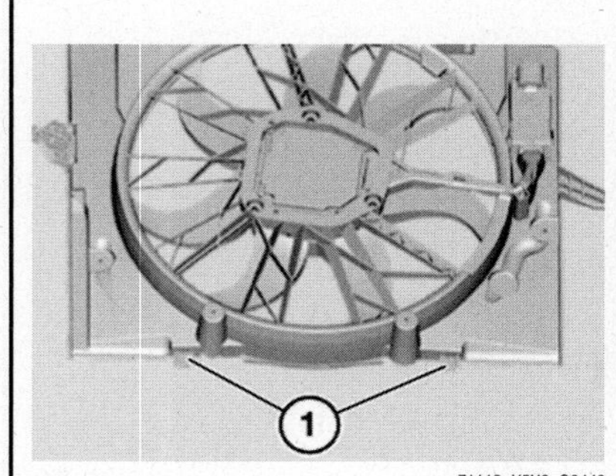

Fig. 62 Insert retaining tab (1) at bottom on module carrier

5. Detach A/C line from holder.
6. Release screws on left and right sides.
7. Remove cross-brace.
8. Release coolant hose from fan cowl.
9. Unlock plug and remove.
10. Pull pressure pipe out of bracket.
11. Press lock.
12. Raise fan cowl until holder can be folded into centre of vehicle.

➡For reasons of clarity, illustration and text show coolant hose removed. Do not raise fan cowl by fan impeller.

13. Press lock.
14. Feed out fan cowl towards top and remove.

To install:

15. Installation is the reverse order of removal.
16. Insert retaining tab at bottom on module carrier.

4.4L Engine

See Figures 51 and 55 through 57.

1. Switch off ignition.
2. Remove intake manifold.
3. Unclip Bowden cable for engine bonnet/hood actuator from transverse reinforcement.
4. Detach A/C line from holder.
5. Release screws on left and right sides.
6. Remove cross-brace.
7. Release coolant hose from fan cowl.
8. Unlock plug and remove.
9. Press lock.
10. Raise fan cowl until holder can be folded into centre of vehicle.

➡For reasons of clarity, illustration and text show coolant hose removed. Do not raise fan cowl by fan impeller.

11. Press lock.
12. Feed out fan cowl towards top and remove.

To install:

13. Installation is the reverse order of removal.
14. Insert retaining tab at bottom on module carrier.

RADIATOR

REMOVAL & INSTALLATION

3.0L Engine

See Figures 63 and 64.

1. Remove fan cowl.
2. Drain coolant.
3. Unlock coolant hoses and detach.
4. Release screws.
5. Remove cover.
6. Remove radiator towards top.

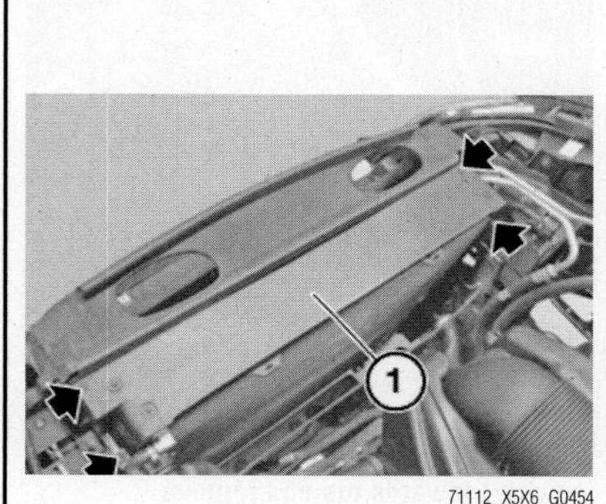

Fig. 63 Remove cover (1)

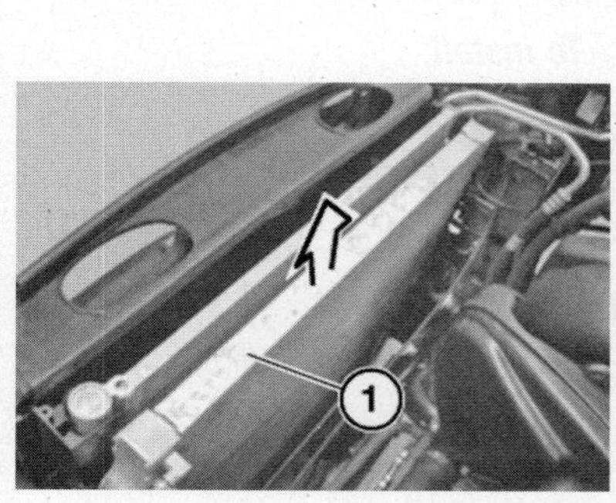

Fig. 64 Remove radiator (1) towards top

To install:

7. Installation is the reverse order of removal.
8. Reassemble the vehicle.

4.4L Engine

See Figures 63 and 64.

1. Remove underbody protection
2. Remove fan cowl
3. Drain coolant
4. Unlock and detach coolant hoses on radiator
5. Release radiator air duct. Do not remove air duct.
6. Release screws.
7. Remove cover.
8. Remove radiator towards top.

To install:

9. Installation is the reverse order of removal.
10. Reassemble the vehicle.

THERMOSTAT

REMOVAL & INSTALLATION

3.0L Engine

See Figure 65.

1. Remove front underbody protection.
2. Drain coolant.
3. Release hose clamp and detach coolant hoses.
4. Unlock and detach coolant hoses.
5. Disconnect plug connection.
6. Release screws.
7. Remove coolant thermostat.

To install:

8. Installation is the reverse order of removal.
9. Assemble engine.

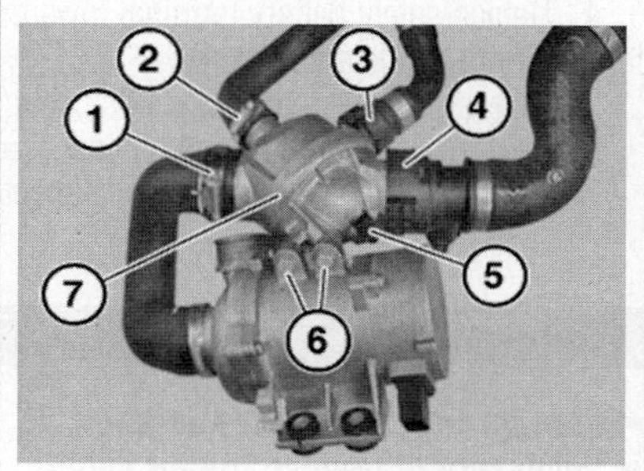

1. Hose clamp
2. Hose clamp
3. Coolant hose
4. Coolant hose
5. Plug connection
6. Screws
7. Thermostat

71112_X5X6_G0458

Fig. 65 Release hose clamp and detach coolant hoses

4.4L Engine

See Figures 66 and 67.

1. Drain coolant.
2. Remove fan cowl with electric fan.
3. Remove charge air cooler expansion tank.
4. Remove electric coolant pump.
5. Unlock plug connection and pull off.
6. Unlock and detach coolant hose.
7. Unfasten nut.
8. Release screws.
9. Remove coolant thermostat.

To install:

10. Installation is the reverse order of removal.

➡The coolant thermostat is integrated into the housing cover and can only be replaced as a complete unit.

11. Clean sealing surfaces.
12. Replace sealing ring.
13. Assemble engine.

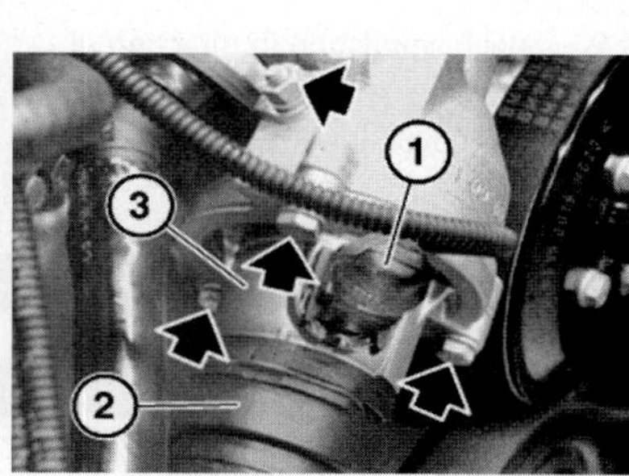

71112_X5X6_G0456

Fig. 66 Unlock plug connection (1) and pull off, Unlock and detach coolant hose (2), and Remove coolant thermostat (3)

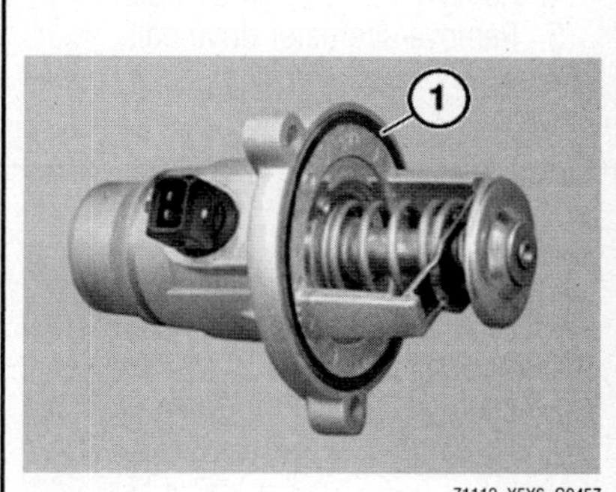

71112_X5X6_G0457

Fig. 67 Replace sealing ring (1)

14. Top up coolant.
15. Vent cooling system and check for water leaks.

ENGINE ELECTRICAL

BATTERY SYSTEM

BATTERY

REMOVAL & INSTALLATION

See Figures 68 and 69.

1. Remove distribution box.
   a. Disconnect battery negative cable.
   b. Disconnect Security positive battery cable.
   c. Disconnect plug connection.
   d. Open cover, release nut underneath and disconnect positive battery cable.
   e. Open cover and release nut.
   f. Using a suitable tool, expand locking bracket at lower end and clip out.

1. Plug connection
2. Distribution box
3. Nut
4. Nut
5. Cover
6. Locking bracket

71112_X5X6_G0459

Fig. 68 Remove distribution box

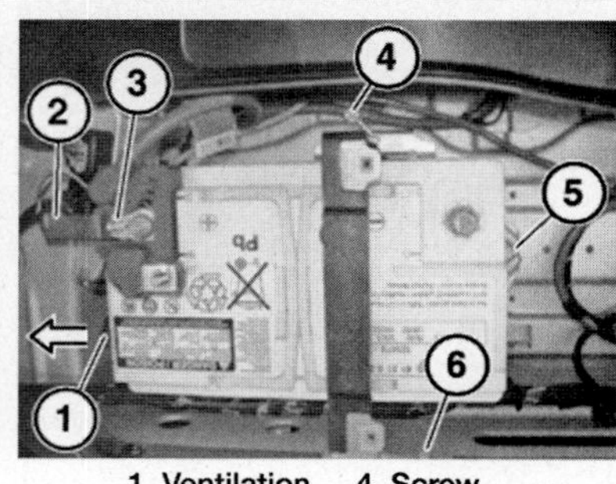

1. Ventilation
2. Cover
3. Nut
4. Screw
5. Screw
6. Screw

71112_X5X6_G0460

Fig. 69 Detach ventilation in direction of arrow

g. Lift power distribution box out of battery.

2. Detach ventilation in direction of arrow.

3. Open cover and release nut.

4. Detach safety battery terminal towards top, lay to one side and secure.

5. Release screws and remove brackets.

6. Release screw and remove holder.

7. Lift battery out of luggage compartment.

To install:

8. Installation is the reverse order of removal.

9. Make sure battery is correctly seated in associated fixture.

ENGINE ELECTRICAL

CHARGING SYSTEM

ALTERNATOR

REMOVAL & INSTALLATION

3.0L Engine

See Figures 70 through 72.

1. Switch off ignition

2. Disconnect battery negative cable and cover.

3. Remove front charge-air duct.

4. Remove rear charge-air duct.

5. Remove alternator drive belt.

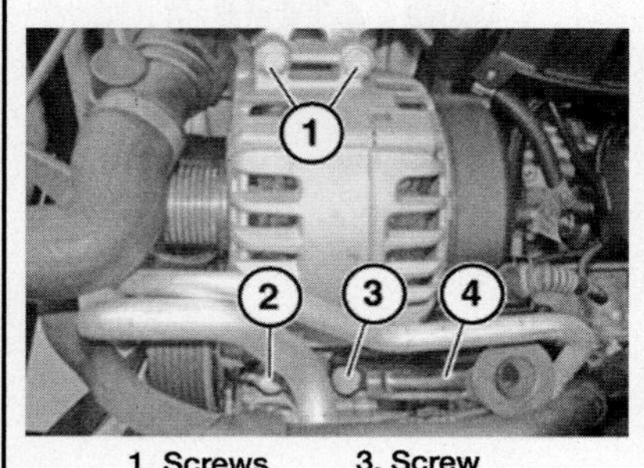

Fig. 70 Release screws

➡In order to remove the alternator, it is necessary to remove the air conditioning compressor.

a. Do not draw off A/C system refrigerant.

b. Do not detach refrigerant lines from A/C compressor.

c. Do not remove air conditioning compressor; instead, release from holder only and place to one side.

6. Release screws.

7. Release screw and remove with holder.

8. Unlock connector and remove.

9. Remove protective cap and release nut underneath.

10. Remove positive battery cable.

➡For purposes of improved clarity, illustrations and description show A/C compressor removed.

11. Release screws a few turns until holder is loose. Do not remove holder.

12. Feed out alternator and remove.

13. Installation is the reverse order of removal.

4.4L Engine

See Figures 73 through 75.

1. Turn off ignition.

2. Disconnect battery negative lead.

3. Remove acoustic cover.

4. Remove intake filter housing.

➡Description relates to the left intake filter housing. Procedure for the right side is identical.

a. Release clamps.

b. Disconnect plug on air-mass sensor.

c. Release clip.

d. Remove intake filter housing by pulling upwards.

5. Remove fan cowl with electric fan.

6. Remove alternator drive belt.

7. Remove intercooler expansion tank.

8. Remove fuel feed line.

➡Cover radiator to prevent damage.

9. Release clamps.

10. Detach both charge-air ducts and remove.

11. Check gaskets on turbocharger, replacing if necessary.

➡Left side, the procedure for the right side is identical.

12. Detach hoses from clean-air pipe.

13. Release screw.

14. Detach clean-air pipe in direction of travel from turbocharger.

15. Check seals on clean-air pipe, replacing if necessary.

16. Pull off cable duct from cable holder in upward direction.

17. Release cable from holder.

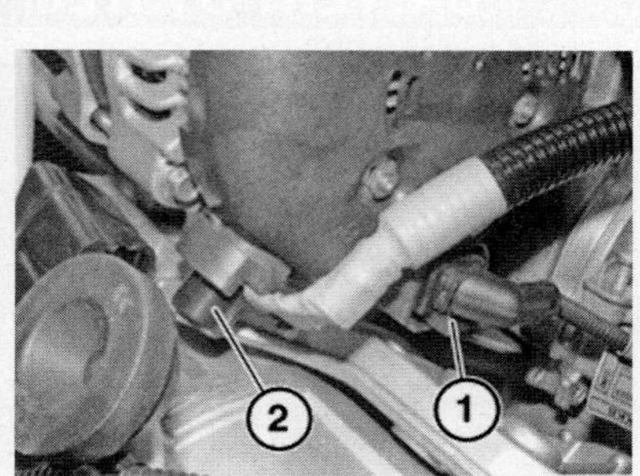

Fig. 71 Unlock connector (1) and remove, Remove protective cap (2) and release nut underneath, then Remove positive battery cable (3)

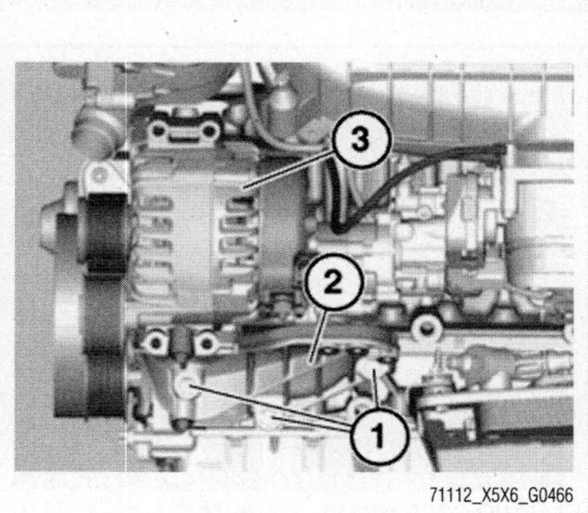

Fig. 72 Release screws (1) a few turns until holder (2) is loose, feed out alternator (3) and remove

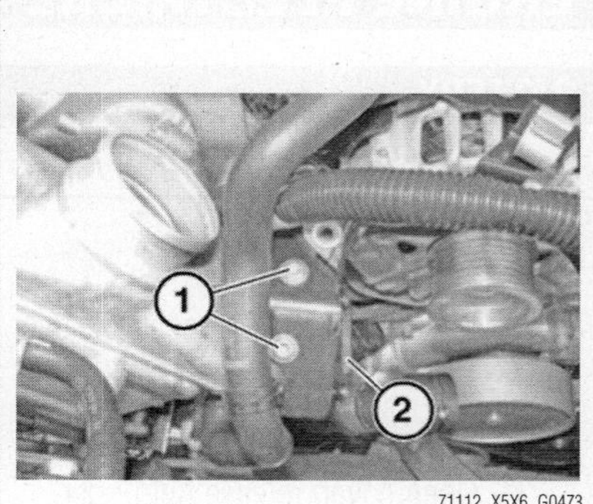

Fig. 73 Release screws (1) on turbocharger coolant pump (2)

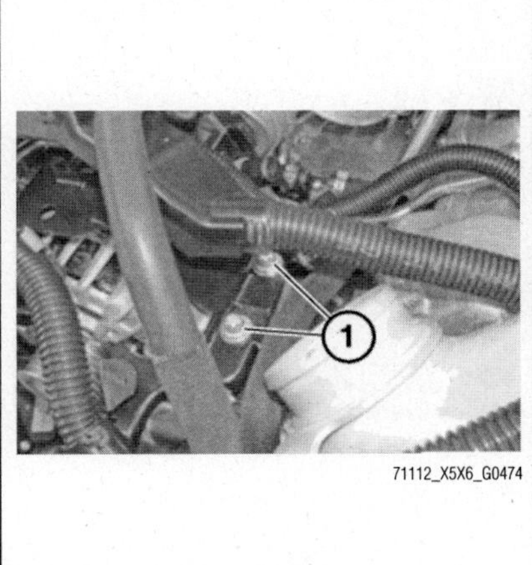

Fig. 74 Release screws (1)

Fig. 75 Remove alternator (1) together with bracket (2)

18. Pull off plug.
19. Detach cover and release nut underneath.

➡Reinstall cover to prevent risk of short circuiting.

20. Disconnect battery positive lead from alternator.
21. Remove fuel feed line.
22. Release screws on turbocharger coolant pump.
23. Release screws.
24. Remove alternator together with bracket in direction of travel.
25. Installation is the reverse order of removal.
26. Alternator mounting bolts tighten to 16 ft. lbs. (21 Nm).

ENGINE ELECTRICAL — DISTRIBUTORLESS IGNITION SYSTEM

IGNITION COIL(S)

REMOVAL & INSTALLATION

3.0L Engine

See Figures 76 and 77.

1. Switch off ignition.
2. Remove ignition coil cover.
3. Remove clean air pipe.
4. Remove rear ignition coil cover.

➡Ignition coils must not be contaminated by fuel. The resistance of the silicone material is reduced significantly by contact with fuel, which may cause the ignition coil to fail. The silicone tube of the spark plug connector is coated with talc to reduce the pulling forces. The silicone tube must NOT be oiled or greased. This would greatly reduce the durability of the silicone material, which can lead to a malfunction of the ignition coil.

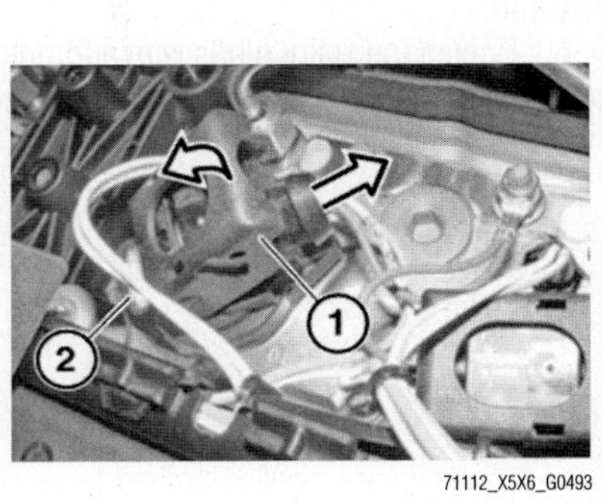

Fig. 76 Unlock plug catch (1) of ignition coil (2) and disconnect plug

5. Release screws.
6. Slide cable channel to one side.
7. Release oxygen sensor connector from bracket.
8. Release screw.
9. Put cable clip aside.
10. Unlock plug catch of ignition coil and disconnect plug.
11. Pull out the ignition coil slowly in a smooth upwards movement.

WARNING

There is a possibility that the silicone tube will tear and therefore be destroyed.

➡This procedure is applicable to all ignition coils.

To install:

12. Position the ignition coil and gently push it to the limit position, if necessary by twisting it back and forth slightly. Then check anti-twist lock.
13. The rubber cap must completely surround the sealing collar of the cylinder head cover.

➡If rubber parts are squashed, the ignition coil can slip out again during engine operation.

14. Push connector with connector catch open onto ignition coil.
15. Carefully close connector catch in direction of arrow.
16. The connector catch must snap into place without great effort.

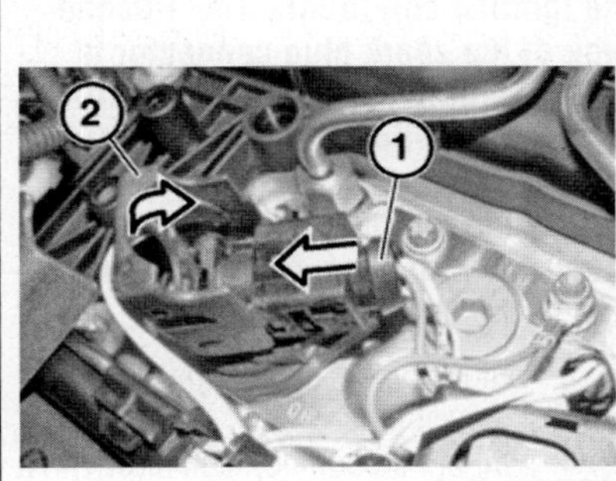

Fig. 77 Push connector (1) with connector catch (2) open onto ignition coil

17. The connector must be positioned on the counter piece with hardly any gaps when the locking lever is being closed. In the process, the cheeks of the lever are positioned inside the counter piece.

➡The locking lever can become deformed if it is not installed correctly. This means that there is no longer a safety lock on the plug connection. As a result, the connector can slip out during engine operation (loose contact, misfiring).

4.4L Engine

See Figures 78 through 80.

1. Switch off ignition.
2. Remove left and right intake filter housings.

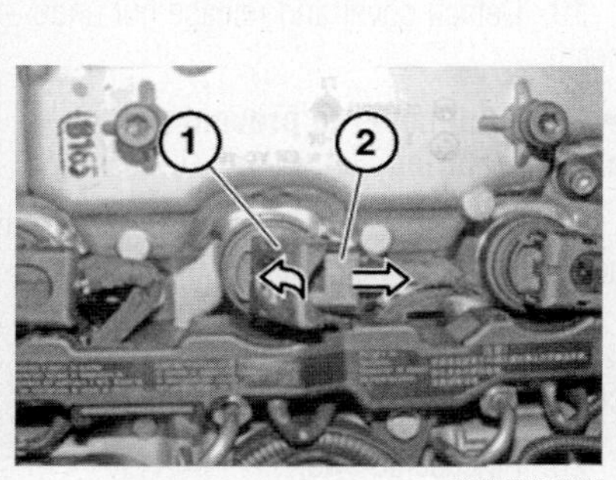

Fig. 78 Unlock plug catch (1) of ignition coil (2) and disconnect plug

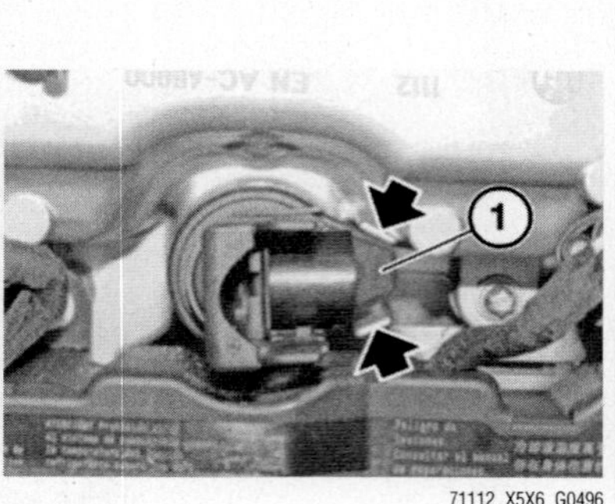

Fig. 79 Position the ignition coil (1) and gently push it to the limit position

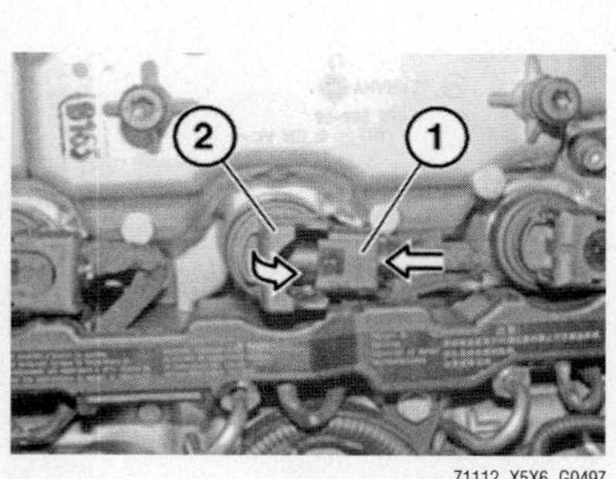

Fig. 80 Push connector (1) with connector catch (2) open onto ignition coil

➡Ignition coils must not be contaminated by fuel. The resistance of the silicone material is reduced significantly by contact with fuel, which may cause the ignition coil to fail. The silicone tube of the spark plug connector is coated with talc to reduce the pulling forces. The silicone tube must NOT be oiled or greased. This would greatly reduce the durability of the silicone material, which can lead to a malfunction of the ignition coil.

3. Unlock plug catch of ignition coil and disconnect plug.
4. Pull out the ignition coil slowly in a smooth upwards movement.

WARNING

There is a possibility that the silicone tube will tear and therefore be destroyed.

➡This procedure is applicable to all ignition coils.

To install:

5. Position the ignition coil and gently push it to the limit position, if necessary by twisting it back and forth slightly. Then check anti-twist lock.
6. The rubber cap must completely surround the sealing collar of the cylinder head cover.

➡If rubber parts are squashed, the ignition coil can slip out again during engine operation.

7. Push connector with connector catch open onto ignition coil.
8. Carefully close connector catch in direction of arrow.
9. The connector catch must snap into place without great effort.
10. The connector must be positioned on the counter piece with hardly any gaps when the locking lever is being closed. In the process, the cheeks of the lever are positioned inside the counter piece.

➡The locking lever can become deformed if it is not installed correctly. This means that there is no longer a safety lock on the plug connection. As a result, the connector can slip out during engine operation (loose contact, misfiring).

IGNITION TIMING

INSPECTION & ADJUSTMENT

Ignition timing is controlled by the Engine Control Module (ECM). No adjustment is necessary or possible.

SPARK PLUGS

REMOVAL & INSTALLATION

1. Switch off ignition.
2. Remove ignition coils.
3. Unscrew spark plugs with special tool 12 1 220 and an extension with min. 8° kink.

WARNING

Flexible ratchet extensions must always be used. If rigid mounting tools are used, there is a risk of insulator breakages. Also do not use a variable plug connection with locking capability as this also poses a risk of insulator breakages.

To install:

4. Attach new spark plug (1) to special tool 12 1 230.

WARNING

Do not let spark plugs fall into the spark plug shaft. This can lead to a reduction of the electrode gap and so impair the smooth running of the engine, especially in idle mode.

5. Screw the spark plug hand-tight with special tool 12 1 230 into the cylinder head plug thread to the limit position.
6. Tighten the spark plugs with a torque wrench, special tool 12 1 220 and an extension with a minimum kink of 8°.
7. Observe tightening torque.
   a. Tightening torque:
      - M12x1.25 thread: 17 ft. lbs. (23 Nm)
      - M14x1.25 thread: 22 ft. lbs. (30 Nm)

STARTER

REMOVAL & INSTALLATION

3.0L Engine

See Figure 81.

1. Switch off ignition.
2. Disconnect battery negative lead.
3. Remove intake plenum.
4. Unlock connector and remove.
5. Release nuts and disconnect positive battery cables.
6. Release screws.
7. Remove starter motor.

To install:

8. Installation is the reverse order of removal.
9. Replace aluminum screws.
10. Pay attention to the different screw lengths. Tighten to 28 ft. lbs. (38 Nm).
11. Check starter pinion and ring gear for damage. Replace starter motor if necessary.

4.4L Engine

See Figures 82 and 83.

1. Turn off ignition.
2. Disconnect battery negative lead.
3. Remove right engine support arm.
4. Unlock plug and remove.
5. Loosen nut.
6. Detach starter positive cable.
7. Release screws.
8. Disengage cable from holder.
9. Pull out starter in direction of travel, feed out and remove.

To install:

10. Installation is the reverse order of removal.
11. Check starter pinion and ring gear for damage. Replace damaged parts if necessary.
12. Reassemble the vehicle.

Fig. 81 Unlock connector and remove

Fig. 82 Unlock plug (1) and remove, loosen nut (2)

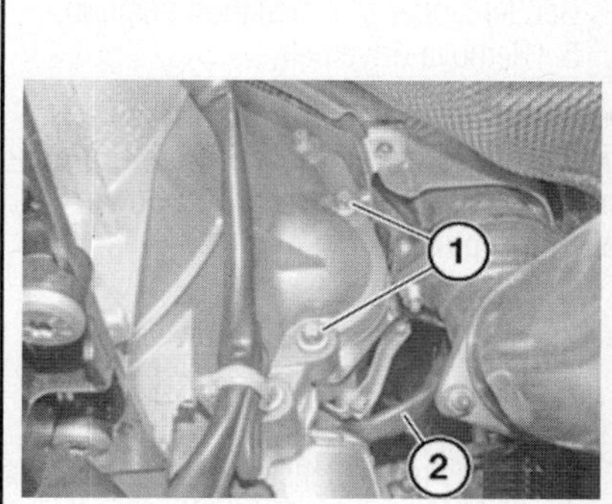

Fig. 83 Release screws (1), disengage cable (2) from holder

ENGINE MECHANICAL

➡Disconnecting the negative battery cable may interfere with the functions of the on board computer systems and may require the computer to undergo a relearning process, once the negative battery cable is reconnected.

ACCESSORY DRIVE BELTS

ACCESSORY BELT ROUTING

Refer to the graphics in the Removal and Installation section for drive belt routing.

ADJUSTMENT

Tension for the serpentine accessory drive belt is maintained by the belt tensioner. No adjustment is necessary.

REMOVAL & INSTALLATION

3.0L Engine

See Figure 84.

1. Remove fan cowl with electric fan

➡Mark the direction of travel of the drive belt if it is to be reused.

2. Turn belt tensioner in direction of arrow until belt tensioner bore hole is flush on crankcase.
3. Hold belt tensioner under tension.
4. Secure special tool 11 0 390.
5. Remove drive belt.

To install:

6. Installation is the reverse order of removal.
7. Check drive belt for correct installation position and, if reusing, observe direction of travel.

Fig. 84 Turn belt tensioner (2) in direction of arrow, Secure special tool 11 0 390 (1), remove drive belt (3)

4.4L Engine

Drive Belt for Alternator

See Figure 85.

1. Remove fan cowl.
2. Release expansion tank for charge air cooler from bracket and press forwards.

➡Coolant hoses do not need to be released.

CAUTION

Belt tensioner is under high initial spring preload.

3. Slowly and carefully pretension belt tensioner in direction of arrow up to stop.
4. Secure special tool 11 3 340 in dowel hole.
   Belt tensioner in installation position.
5. Remove drive belt.

➡On vehicles which do not have a power steering pump, a deflecting element is fitted in place of the power steering pump.

To install:

6. Put on the drive belt.
7. Remove special tool 11 3 340 from dowel hole.
8. Slowly relieve tension on belt tensioner.
9. Make sure drive belt is in correct installation position.

Drive Belt for A/C Compressor

See Figures 86 and 87.

1. Remove drive belt for alternator.

➡Observe direction of engine rotation.

2. Crank engine at central bolt until marking (see arrow) is reached on vibration absorber.

Fig. 85 pretension belt tensioner (1) in direction of arrow up to stop, Secure special tool 11 3 340 in dowel hole (2); deflecting element (3)

Fig. 86 Release screws (1)

Fig. 87 Remove Elasto-Belt (1)

3. Release screws.

CAUTION

Belt pulley is pre-tensioned. Belt pulley tension is relieved abruptly during the cranking process.

4. Remove Elasto-Belt.

To install:

5. Installation is the reverse order of removal.
6. Belt pulley screws tightening torque: 30 ft. lbs. (40 Nm).

AIR CLEANER

FILTER/ELEMENT REPLACEMENT

3.0L Engine

See Figures 88 and 89.

1. Release clamp.
2. Unfasten screws.

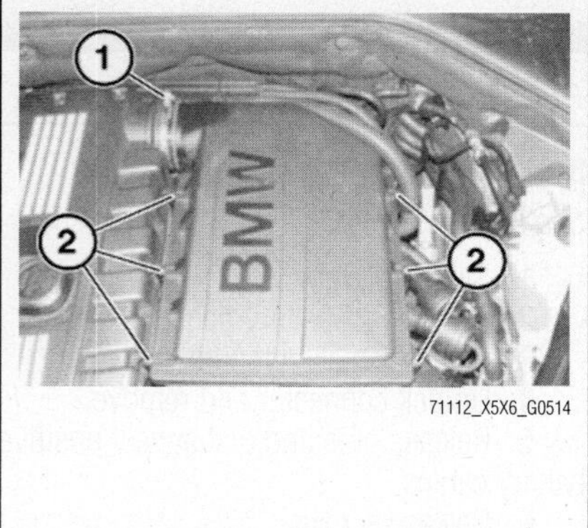

Fig. 88 Release clamp (1), unfasten screws (2)

Fig. 89 Remove air filter element (1) and replace

3. Remove upper section of intake silencer housing
4. Remove air filter element and replace.

To install:

5. Installation is the reverse order of removal.
6. Clean upper part and lower section of intake silencer housing from inside.
7. Reassemble the vehicle.

4.4L Engine

See Figures 90 and 91.

1. Turn off ignition
2. Remove tension struts on left and right
3. Remove acoustic cover

➡Description relates to the left intake filter housing. Procedure for the right side is identical.

4. Release clamp.
5. Disconnect plug on air-mass sensor.

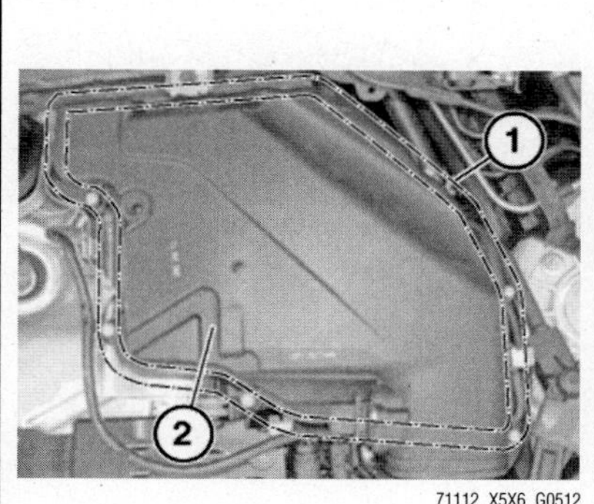

Fig. 90 Release screws along line (1), remove air filter cover (2)

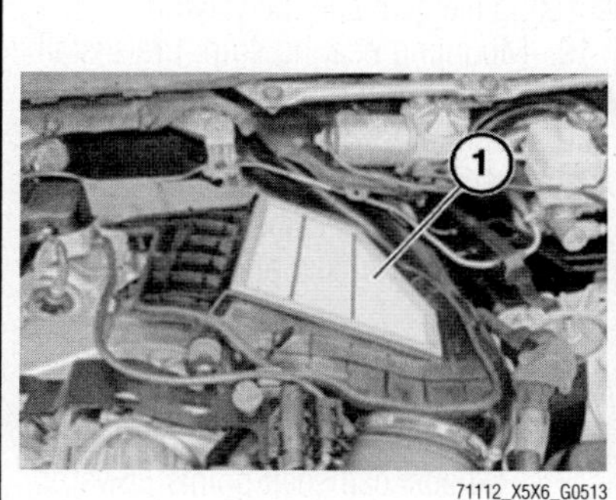

Fig. 91 Remove air filter insert (1)

6. Release screws along line.
7. Remove air filter cover.
8. Remove air filter insert.

To install:

9. Installation is the reverse order of removal.
10. Clean upper and lower sections of intake filter housing from inside.
11. Replace air filter elements.

CAMSHAFT AND VALVE LIFTERS

REMOVAL & INSTALLATION

3.0L Engine

Exhaust Camshaft

See Figures 92 through 105.

1. Remove cylinder head cover.
2. Remove all ignition coils and injector shafts.
3. Remove exhaust camshaft adjuster

Fig. 92 Position special tool 11 7 100 on cylinder 2

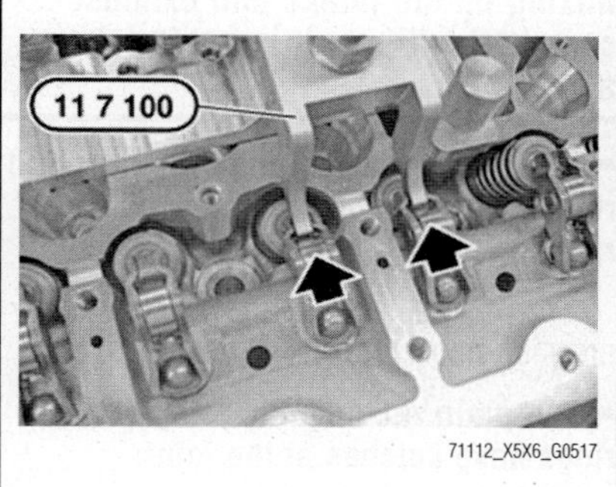

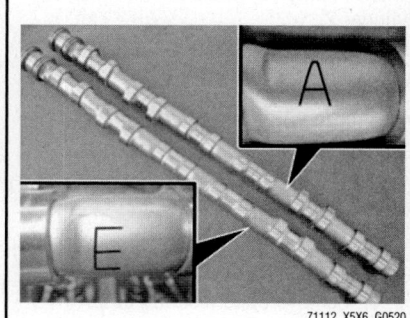

Fig. 93 Screw in roller cam follower at 2nd cylinder using spindle nut of special tool 11 7 100 to end stop

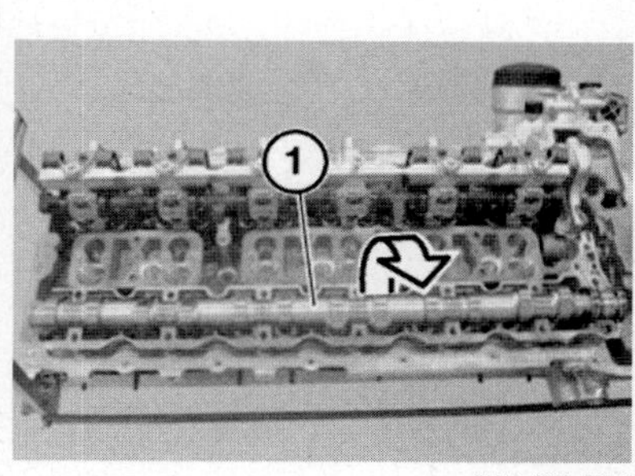

Fig. 95 Remove exhaust camshaft from bearing strip in direction of arrow

Fig. 96 Marks of intake and exhaust camshafts are different. A =Exhaust camshaft; E =Intake camshaft

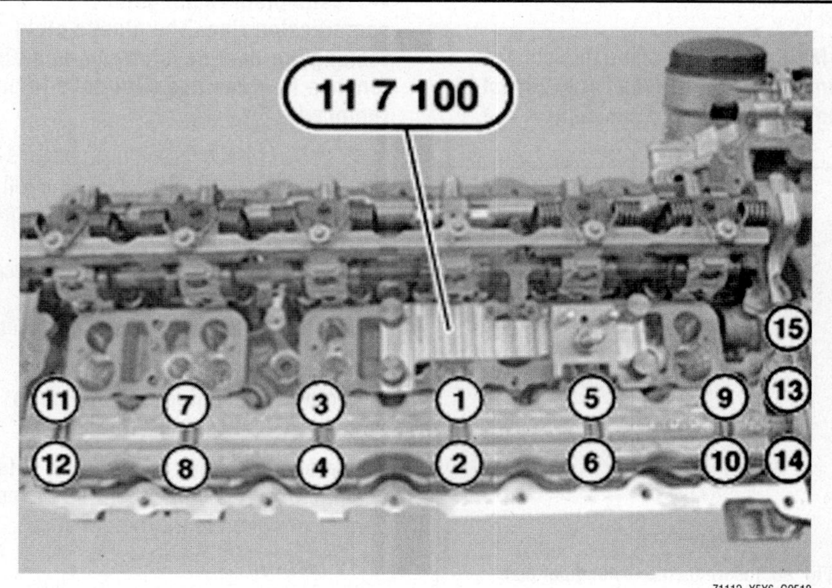

Fig. 94 Release screw connection on bearing strip in sequence from 15 to 1

Fig. 97 Plain rectangular compression rings (1) can easily break

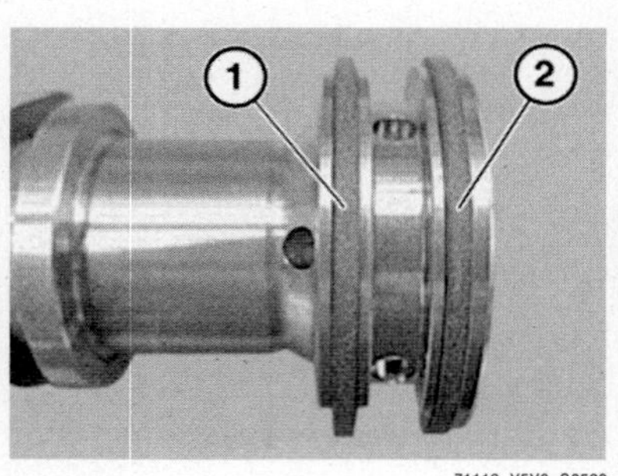

Fig. 99 Check plastic plain rectangular compression ring (1 and 2) for freedom of movement

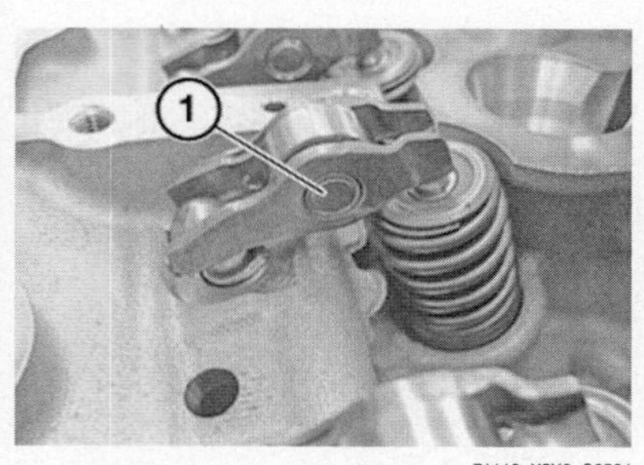

Fig. 100 Before mounting the exhaust camshaft, ensure the correct fit of the rocker arm (1) on the hydraulic valve clearance compensating element and the valve

4. Adjust valve timing.
5. Position special tool 11 7 100 on cylinder 2.
6. Hand-tighten special tool 11 7 100 with special tool 11 8 552.

➡Graphic without bearing strip.

7. Screw in roller cam follower at 2nd cylinder using spindle nut of special tool 11 7 100 to end stop.
8. Release screw connection on bearing strip in sequence from 15 to 1.
9. Remove upper bearing strip.

➡The upper and lower bearing strips can also be lifted out completely with exhaust camshaft.

10. Remove exhaust camshaft from bearing strip in direction of arrow.
11. Set down exhaust camshaft on special tool.

➡Marks of intake and exhaust camshafts are different. A =Exhaust camshaft; E =Intake camshaft

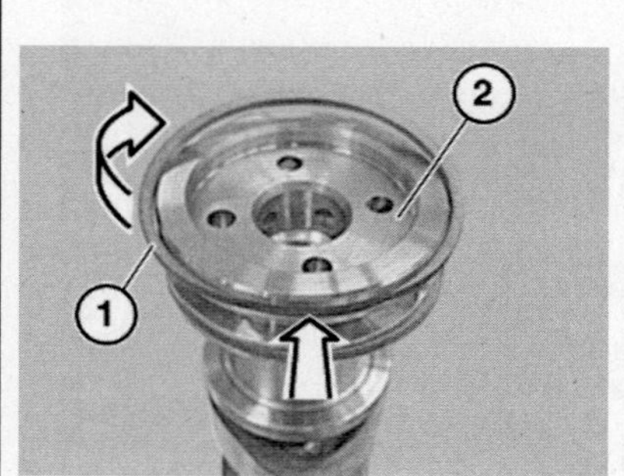

Fig. 98 Insert plastic rectangular compression ring (1) into groove of exhaust camshaft (2) (see arrow)

WARNING

Mixing up the intake and exhaust camshaft will result in engine damage.

➡Metal plain rectangular compression ring: Plain rectangular compression rings can easily break.

12. Only replace plain rectangular compression rings when they are broken.

➡The plain rectangular compression rings have catches at the joint.

13. Press plain rectangular compression rings apart upwards and downwards and removed towards front.
14. Make sure plain rectangular compression rings can move freely.

➡Plastic plain rectangular compression ring: The plastic plain rectangular compression ring is maintenance free and does not have to be replaced.

15. Insert plastic rectangular compression ring into groove of exhaust camshaft.
16. Lightly oil plastic rectangular compression ring and rotate in direction of arrow until compression ring is positioned on the exhaust camshaft.
17. Check plastic plain rectangular compression ring for freedom of movement.

➡Removal on engine: Set engine to ignition TDC at cylinder No. 1.

➡Removed cylinder head: When using special tool 11 9 000, it will be necessary to remove the aluminum strip.

To install:

18. Before mounting the exhaust camshaft, ensure the correct fit of the rocker arm on the hydraulic valve clearance compensating element and the valve.
19. Mounting bearing strip: Pre-install special tool 11 7 100 on cylinder no. 2.
20. Position lower bearing strip with exhaust camshaft on rocker arms.
21. Align exhaust camshaft.
    - Cylinder nos. 2 and 4 are at valve overlap.
    - Cams on cylinder no. 1 point upwards at an angle.
    - Part number on mounting flats of exhaust camshaft points upwards.
22. Insert exhaust camshaft so that none of the latching mechanisms for the plain rectangular compression rings point to a bearing cap joint.
23. Centre latch mechanism of the plain rectangular compression rings with the bearing cap.
24. Insert exhaust camshaft so that the data code on the mounting flats faces up.
25. The cam at cylinder 6 points downward at an angle.

➡There must be no oil residues in the cylinder head threaded holes. Clean threaded holes.

26. Fit upper bearing strip.
27. Insert bolts dry.
28. Join exhaust camshaft to lower and upper bearing strips with torque wrench to 6 ft. lbs. (8 Nm) in sequential order from 1 to 15.
29. Loosen all screws of upper bearing strip from outside inwards by 90°.

➡Upper and lower bearing strips must be aligned to each other at ground surfaces.

30. Make sure that the synchronizing key and the shanks of special tools 11 4 461 rest on the milled surfaces.

Fig. 101 Position lower bearing strip with exhaust camshaft on rocker arms

31. Position special tool 11 8 553 over screw connection of bearing strips.
32. Make sure that the shanks rest exactly on the ground surfaces of the upper bearing strip and lower bearing strip.
33. Initially tighten screw of special tool 11 8 553 to ground surfaces of upper bearing strip and lower bearing strip.
34. Tighten screws on synchronizing key to 2 Nm.
35. Mount special tools 11 8 553 to inside of cylinder head with pressure bolt.
36. Mount special tool 11 8 553 on cylinder no. 2 with pressure bolt facing outward.
37. Position special tools 11 8 553 so that screw connections of bearing strip are easily accessible.
38. Tighten top and bottom bearing strip with special tool 00 9 120.

Fig. 102 Insert exhaust camshaft so that the data code (1) on the mounting flats faces up

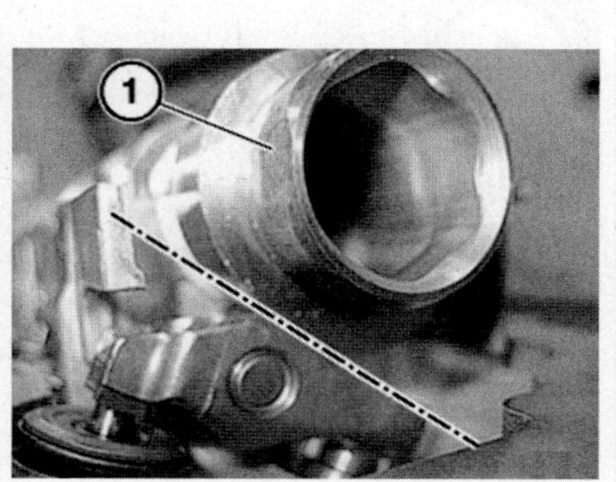

Fig. 103 The cam (1) at cylinder 6 points downward at an angle

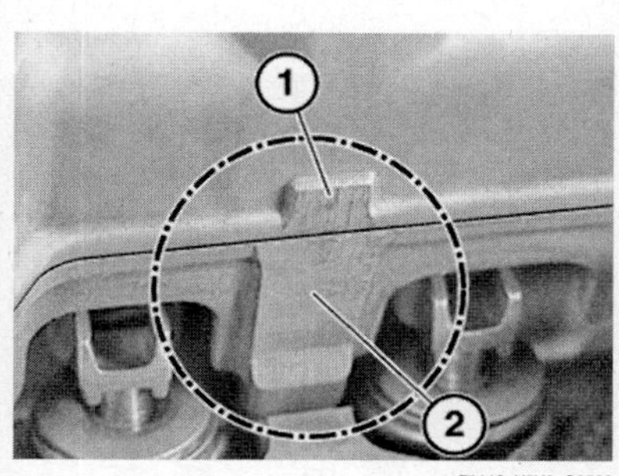

Fig. 104 Upper and lower bearing strips must be aligned to each other at ground surfaces (1 and 2)

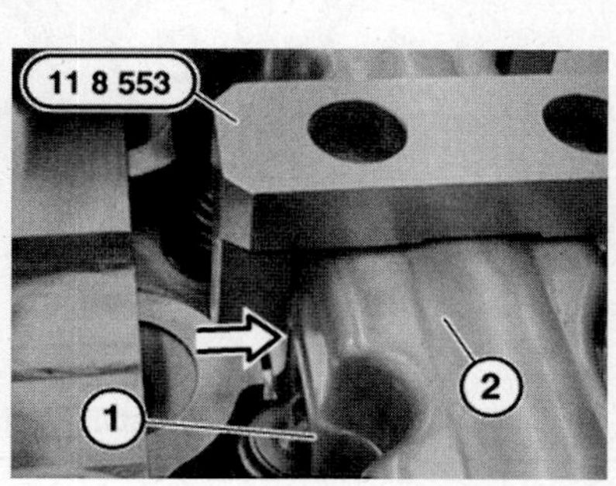

Fig. 105 Position special tool 11 8 553 over screw connection of bearing strips; upper bearing strip (1) and lower bearing strip (2)

➡Remove special tool 11 8 553 only when exhaust camshaft screw connection is completed.

39. Assemble engine.

Intake Camshaft

See Figures 106 through 112.

1. Remove cylinder head cover.
2. Remove intake adjuster.
3. Remove intermediate lever.
4. Adjust valve timing.

➡All bearing caps are identified with numbers from 1 to 6. The front bearing cap is a thrust bearing and does not have an identification.

5. Release screws on thrust bearing cover.
6. Release screws on all bearing caps 1 to 6.
7. Set all bearing caps down in special tool 11 4 481 in a neat and orderly fashion.

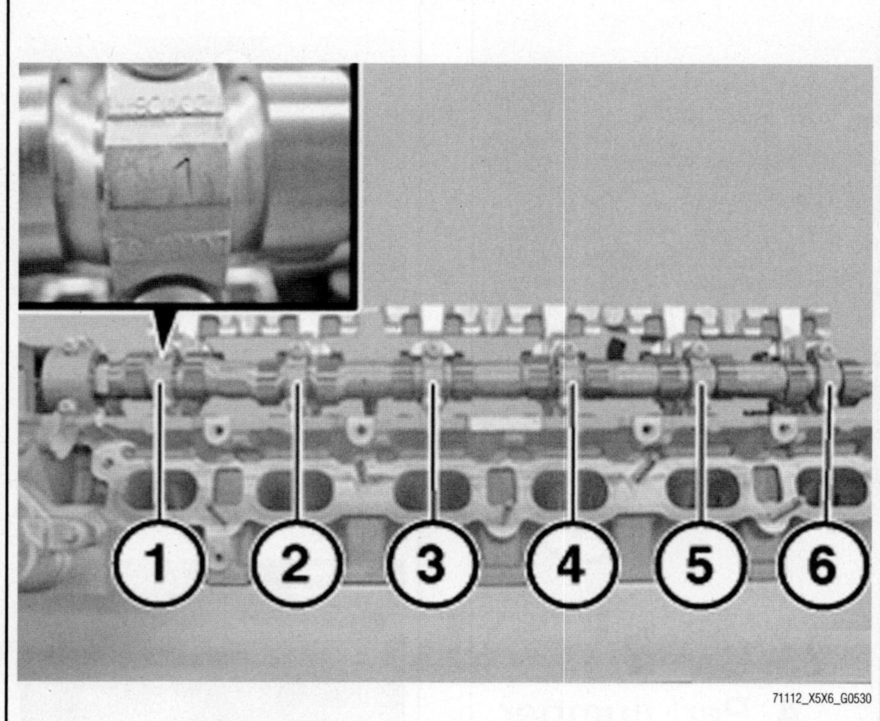

Fig. 106 All bearing caps are identified with numbers from 1 to 6

8. Remove intake camshaft towards top.

To install:

9. Clean all bearing positions and lubricate with oil.

10. Check plain rectangular compression rings for damage.

11. Metal plain rectangular compression ring:

a. Plain rectangular compression rings can easily break.

b. Only replace plain rectangular compression rings when they are broken.

c. The plain rectangular compression rings have catches at the joint.

d. Press plain rectangular compression rings apart upwards and downwards and removed towards front.

e. Make sure plain rectangular compression rings can move freely.

f. When intake camshafts are inserted, no joint must point to a separating joint.

12. Plastic plain rectangular compression ring:

a. The plastic plain rectangular compression ring is maintenance free and does not have to be replaced.

b. Insert plastic plain rectangular compression ring into groove of intake camshaft.

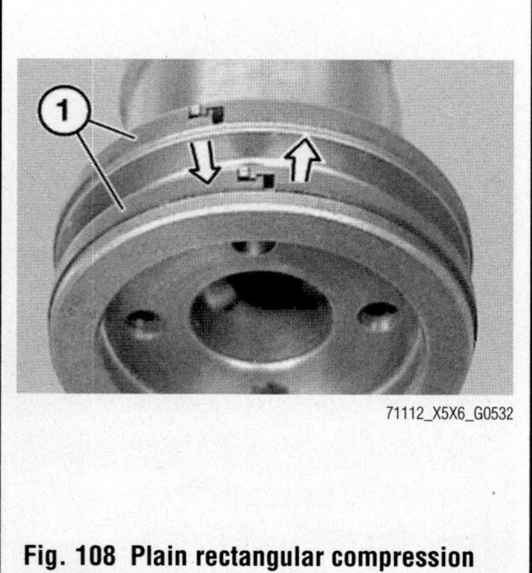

Fig. 108 Plain rectangular compression rings (1) can easily break

c. Lightly oil plastic plain rectangular compression ring and rotate in direction of arrow until plastic plain rectangular compression ring is positioned on the intake camshaft.

d. Check plastic plain rectangular compression ring for freedom of movement.

➡Marks of intake and exhaust camshafts are different. A=Exhaust camshaft, E=Intake camshaft

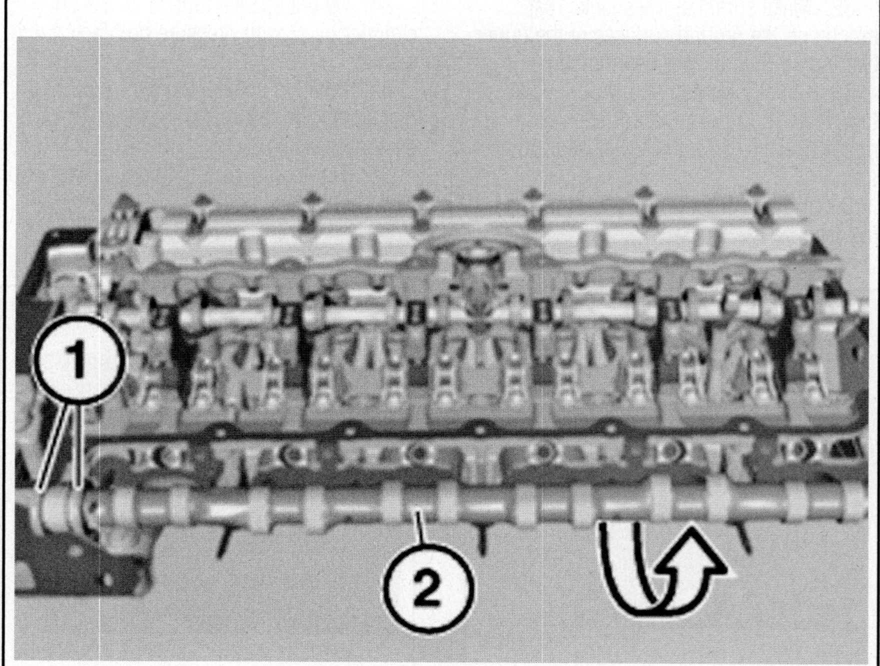

Fig. 107 Remove intake camshaft (2) towards top; compression rings (1)

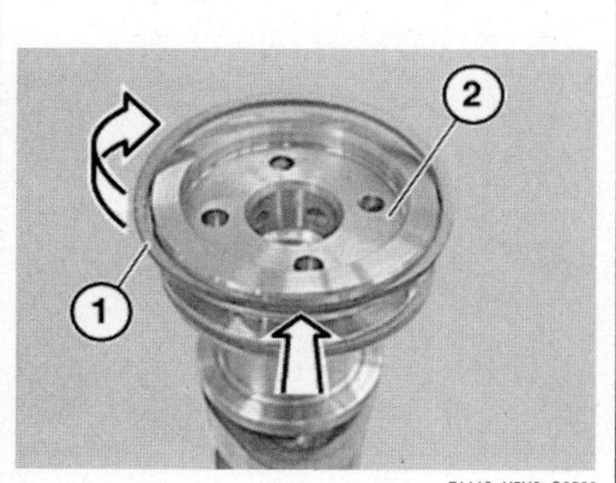

Fig. 109 Insert plastic plain rectangular compression ring (1) into groove of intake camshaft (2) (see arrow)

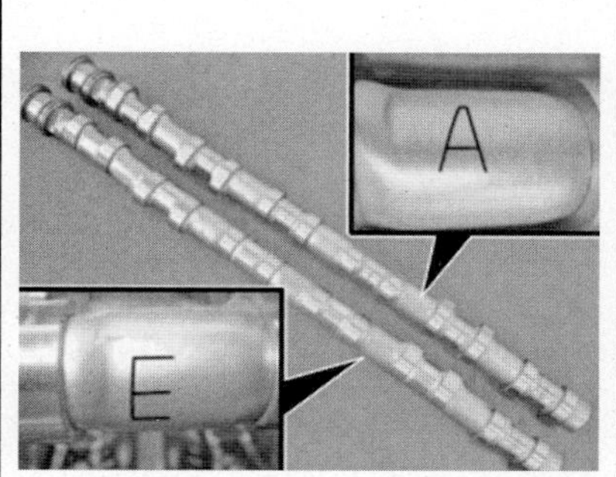

Fig. 110 Marks of intake and exhaust camshafts are different. A =Exhaust camshaft; E =Intake camshaft

Fig. 111 Insert intake camshaft so that data code (1) on mounting flats points upwards

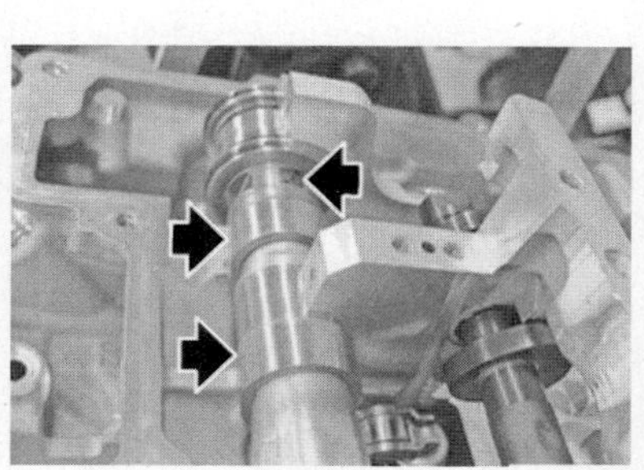

Fig. 112 Position intake camshaft (1) so that cams point upwards at an angle and to the left

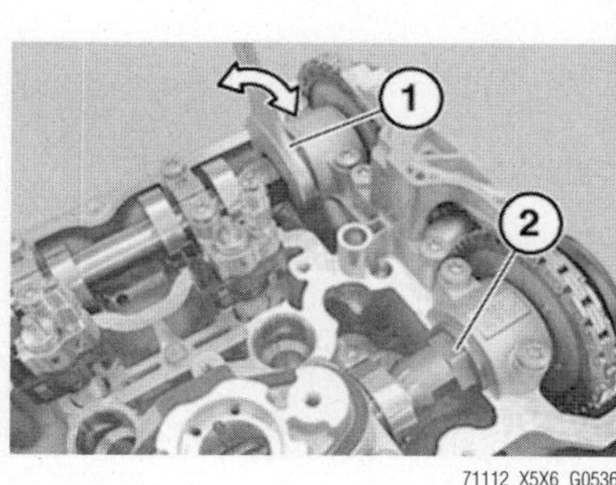

Fig. 113 Rotate exhaust camshaft (2) at dihedron with a fork wrench (1) into a suitable position

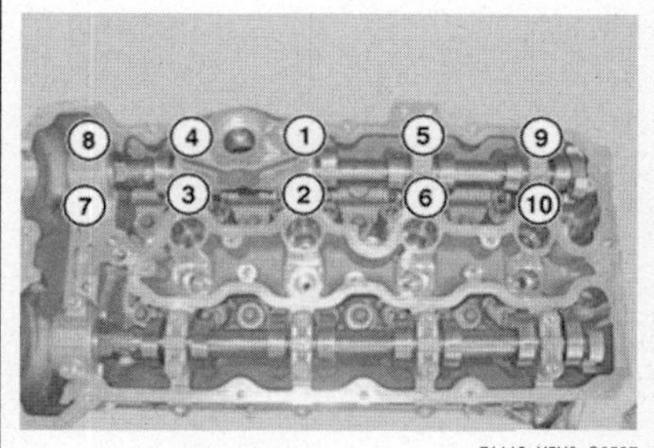

Fig. 114 Release bolts of camshaft bearings in sequence (10 to 1) in ½ turns

WARNING

Mixing up the intake and exhaust camshaft will result in engine damage.

13. Install intake camshaft so that the latch mechanism of the plain rectangular compression rings does not point to a contact point of the bearing cap
14. Centre latch mechanism of the plain rectangular compression rings with the bearing cap.
15. Insert intake camshaft so that data code on mounting flats points upwards.
16. Position intake camshaft so that cams point upwards at an angle and to the left.
17. Insert screws on all bearing caps 1 to 6.
18. Insert screws on thrust bearing cover.
19. Assemble engine.

4.4L Engine

Exhaust Camshaft (Left)

See Figures 113 through 118.

1. Remove left cylinder head cover.
2. Check timing.
3. Remove left inlet adjustment unit.

➡No cam on the exhaust camshaft is permitted to press directly onto a roller cam follower.

➡With cylinder no. 1 at 150° before firing TDC there is no piston in the TDC position.

4. Rotate exhaust camshaft at dihedron with a fork wrench into a suitable position.
5. Release bolts of camshaft bearings in sequence (10 to 1) in ½ turns.
6. Set down all bearing caps in a tidy and orderly fashion on special tool 11 4 480.
7. Remove roller tappet from bearing caps 2 and 3 of high pressure pump and set down on special tool 11 4 480.
8. Remove left exhaust camshaft and set down on special tool 11 4 480.

➡Used rocker arms may only be reused in the same position.

➡Rocker arms are freely accessible after exhaust camshaft has been removed.

WARNING

Do not remove rocker arms on exhaust side.

To install:

➡Plain compression rings can easily break.

9. If necessary, replace plain compression rings.
10. Press compression ring on one side into groove, pull up on other side and remove catch.
11. Carefully pull compression ring apart and remove towards front.

Fig. 115 If necessary, replace plain compression rings

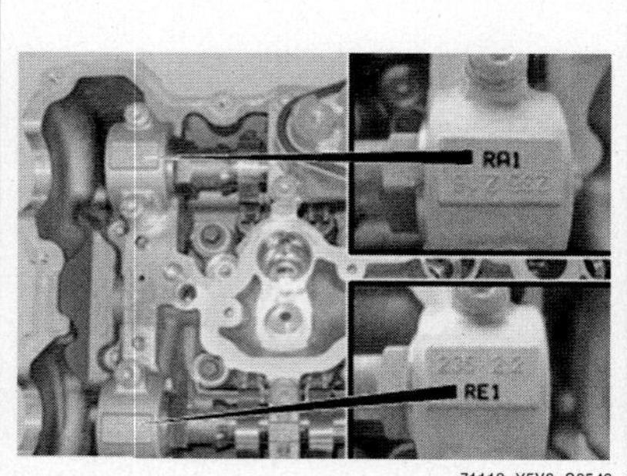

Fig. 117 All bearing caps are marked

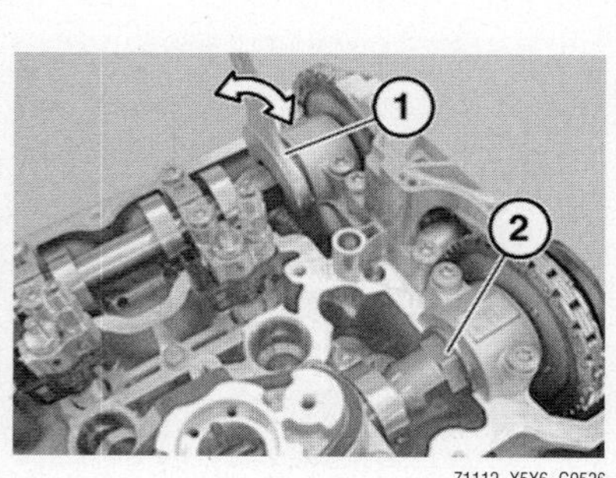

Fig. 119 Rotate exhaust camshaft (2) at dihedron with a fork wrench (1) into a suitable position

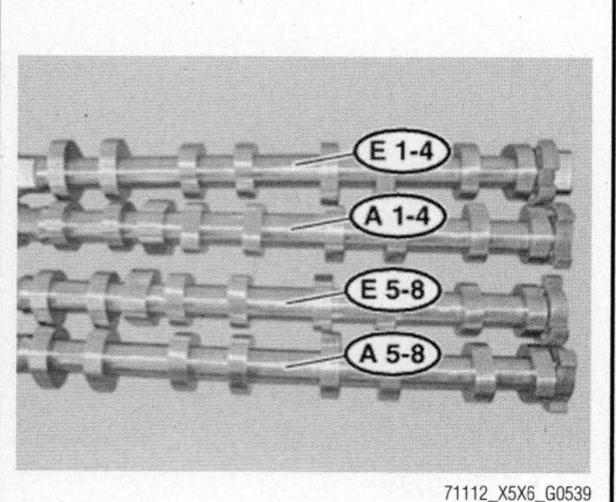

Fig. 116 Exhaust camshaft of cylinder bank 1 to 4 is marked with "A 1–4"

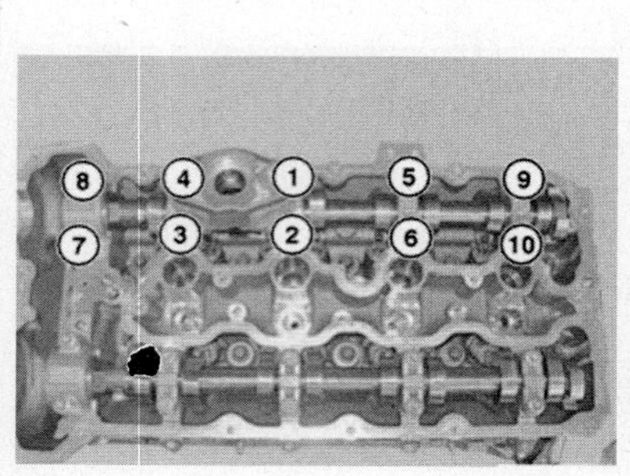

Fig. 118 Tighten bolts in sequence (1 to 10) in ½ turns

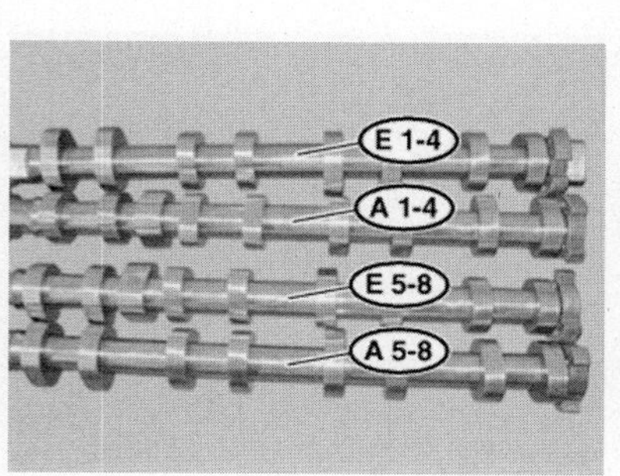

Fig. 120 Exhaust camshaft of cylinder bank 5 to 8 is marked with "A 5–8"

12. Ends of compression rings point upwards.
13. Make sure compression rings are engaged at ends.

➡Exhaust camshaft of cylinder bank 1 to 4 is marked with "A 1–4".

➡Rocker arms slip slightly when exhaust camshaft is fitted.

14. Make sure rocker arms are secured on hydraulic valve clearance compensating elements and on valves.
15. Align all rocker arms straight.
16. Coat all bearing positions with engine oil.
17. Install exhaust camshaft.
18. Insert exhaust camshaft so that cams point to side at cylinder 5.

➡Do not mix up the bearing caps of cylinders 1 to 4 and 5 to 8.

19. All bearing caps are coded and can only be installed in one position.
20. All bearing caps are marked:
    a. L=Cylinders 1–4.
    b. R=Cylinders 5–8.
    c. E=Intake side
    d. A=Exhaust side
    e. 1=designation from 1 to 5
21. Insert all bolts.
22. Tighten down bolts in sequence (1 to 10) in ½ turns.
23. Tightening torque: 11 ft. lbs. (15 Nm).
24. Insert tappets for high-pressure pump.
25. Install inlet adjustment units.
26. Adjust valve timing.
27. Assemble engine.

Exhaust Camshaft (Right)

See Figures 119 through 122.

1. Remove right high-pressure pump
2. Remove right cylinder head cover
3. Remove right exhaust camshaft adjuster

➡No cam on the exhaust camshaft is permitted to press directly onto a roller cam follower.

4. With cylinder no. 1 at 150° before TDC firing position there is no piston in the TDC position.
5. Rotate exhaust camshaft at dihedron with a fork wrench into a suitable position.

➡The exhaust camshaft of cylinder bank 5–8 is marked "A 5–8".

6. Release bolts of camshaft bearings in sequence (10 to 1) in ½ turns.
7. Set all bearing caps down in special tool 11 4 480 in a neat and orderly fashion.
8. Remove roller tappet from bearing caps (2 and 3) of high pressure pump and lay down in special tool 11 4 480.
9. Remove left exhaust camshaft and lay down in special tool 11 4 480.

Fig. 121 Release bolts of camshaft bearings in sequence (10 to 1) in ½ turns

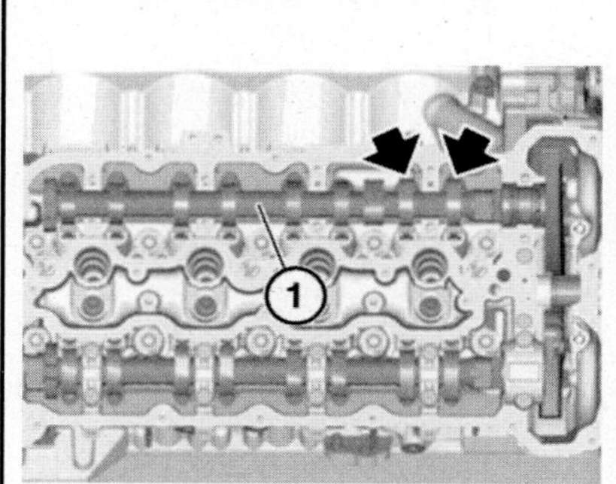

Fig. 122 Turn exhaust camshaft (1) until cams point to side at cylinder no. 1

To install:

➡**Rocker arms of can slip slightly when inlet camshaft is fitted.**

10. Make sure rocker arms are secured on hydraulic valve clearance compensating elements and on valves.
11. Align all rocker arms straight.

➡**Plain compression rings can easily break.**

12. If necessary, replace plain compression rings.
13. Press compression ring on one side into groove, pull up on other side and remove latch mechanism.
14. Carefully pull compression ring apart and remove towards front.
15. Ends of compression rings point upwards.
16. Make sure compression rings are engaged at ends.
17. Coat all bearing positions with engine oil.
18. Install exhaust camshaft.
19. Turn exhaust camshaft until cams point to side at cylinder no. 1.

➡**Bearing caps of cylinders 1–4 and cylinders 5–8 must not be interchanged.**

20. All bearing caps are coded and can only be installed in one position.
21. All bearing caps are marked with letters and numbers:
    a. L=Cylinder bank 1–4.
    b. R=Cylinder bank 5–8.
    c. E=Intake side
    d. A=Exhaust side
    e. 1=Marking, bearing point, from 1 to 5
22. Insert all bolts.
23. Tighten down bolts in sequence (1 to 10) in ½ turns. Tightening torque 11ft. lbs. (15 Nm).
24. Install right inlet and exhaust camshaft adjusters.
25. Adjust valve timing.
26. Assemble engine.

Intake Camshaft (Left)

See Figures 123 through 125.

1. Remove left cylinder head cover.
2. Check timing.
3. Remove left inlet adjustment unit.

➡**No cam on the inlet camshaft is permitted to press directly onto a roller cam follower. With cylinder no. 1 at 150° before firing TDC there is no piston in the TDC position.**

4. Rotate left inlet camshaft at dihedron with a fork wrench into a suitable position.
5. Release bolts of camshaft bearings in sequence (10 to 1) in ½ turns.
6. Set down all bearing caps in a tidy and orderly fashion on special tool 11 4 480.

To install:

➡**Used rocker arms may only be reused in the same position.**

➡**Rocker arms are freely accessible after inlet camshaft has been removed. Do not remove rocker arm (1) on intake side.**

➡**Plain compression rings can easily break.**

7. If necessary, replace plain compression rings.
8. Press compression ring on one side into groove, pull up on other side and remove catch.
9. Carefully pull compression ring apart and remove towards front.

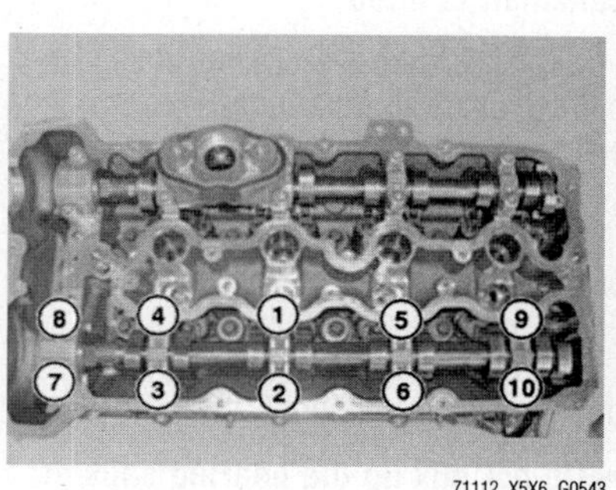

Fig. 123 Release bolts of camshaft bearings in sequence (10 to 1) in ½ turns

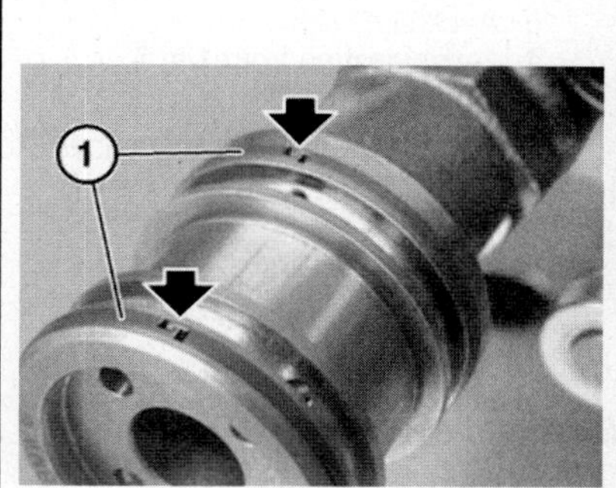

Fig. 124 If necessary, replace plain compression rings (1)

10. Ends of compression rings point upwards.
11. Make sure compression rings are engaged at ends.

➡**The intake camshaft of cylinder bank 5 to 8 is marked with "E 5–8".**

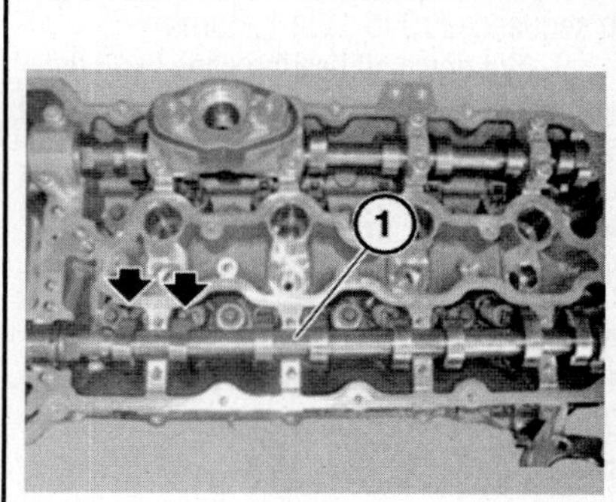

Fig. 125 Insert inlet camshaft (1) so that cams point to side at cylinder 5

➡Rocker arms slip slightly when inlet camshaft is fitted.

12. Make sure rocker arms are secured on hydraulic valve clearance compensating elements and on valves.
13. Align all rocker arms straight.
14. Coat all bearing positions with engine oil.
15. Insert intake camshaft.
16. Insert inlet camshaft so that cams point to side at cylinder 5.

➡Do not mix up the bearing caps of cylinders 1 to 4 and 5 to 8.

17. All bearing caps are coded and can only be installed in one position.
18. All bearing caps are marked:
    a. L=Cylinders 1–4.
    b. R=Cylinders 5–8.
    c. E=Intake side
    d. A=Exhaust side
    e. 1=designation from 1 to 5
19. Insert all bolts.
20. Tighten down bolts in sequence (1 to 10) in ½ turns. Tightening torque: 11 ft. lbs. (15 Nm).
21. Install inlet adjustment units.
22. Adjust valve timing.
23. Assemble engine.

Intake Camshaft (Right)

See Figures 126 through 130.

1. Remove right cylinder head cover.
2. Check timing.
3. Remove right inlet adjustment unit.

➡No cam on the inlet camshaft is permitted to press directly onto a roller cam follower. With cylinder no. 1 at 150° before firing TDC there is no piston in the TDC position.

4. Rotate right inlet camshaft at dihedron with a fork wrench into a suitable position.
5. Release bolts of camshaft bearings in sequence (10 to 1) in ½ turns.
6. Set down all bearing caps in a tidy and orderly fashion on special tool 11 4 480.

To install:

➡Used rocker arms may only be reused in the same position.

➡Rocker arms are freely accessible after inlet camshaft has been removed. Do not remove rocker arm on intake side.

➡Plain compression rings can easily break.

7. If necessary, replace plain compression rings.

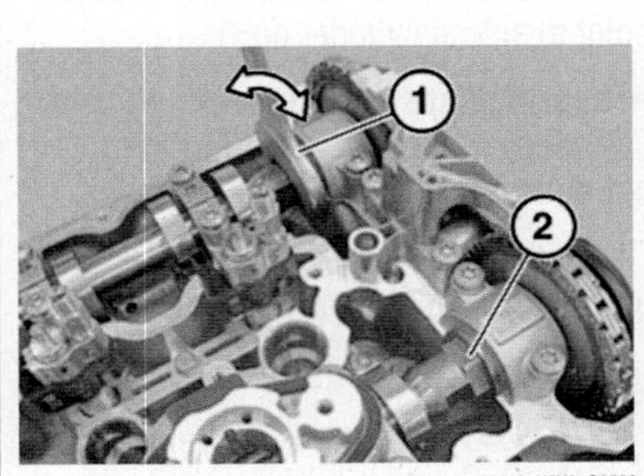

Fig. 126 Rotate exhaust camshaft (2) at dihedron with a fork wrench (1) into a suitable position

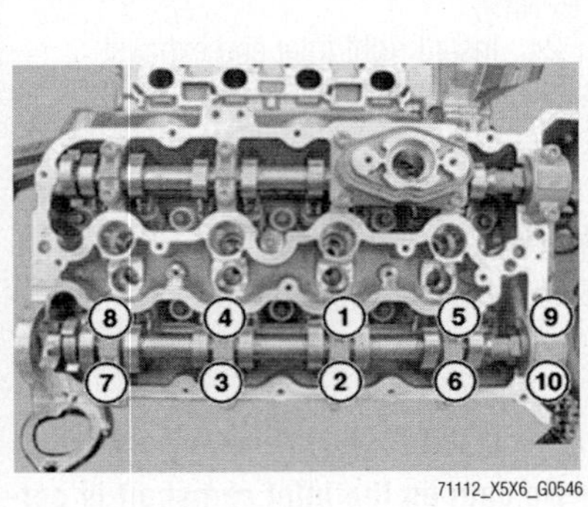

Fig. 127 Release bolts of camshaft bearings in sequence (10 to 1) in ½ turns

8. Press compression ring on one side into groove, pull up on other side and remove catch.
9. Carefully pull compression ring apart and remove towards front.
10. Ends of compression rings point upwards.
11. Make sure compression rings are engaged at ends.

➡The intake camshaft of cylinder bank 5 to 8 is marked with "E 5-8".

➡Rocker arms slip slightly when inlet camshaft is fitted.

12. Make sure rocker arms are secured on hydraulic valve clearance compensating elements and on valves.
13. Align all rocker arms straight.
14. Coat all bearing positions with engine oil.
15. Insert intake camshaft.
16. Insert inlet camshaft (1) so that cams point to side at cylinder 1.

Fig. 128 If necessary, replace plain compression rings (1)

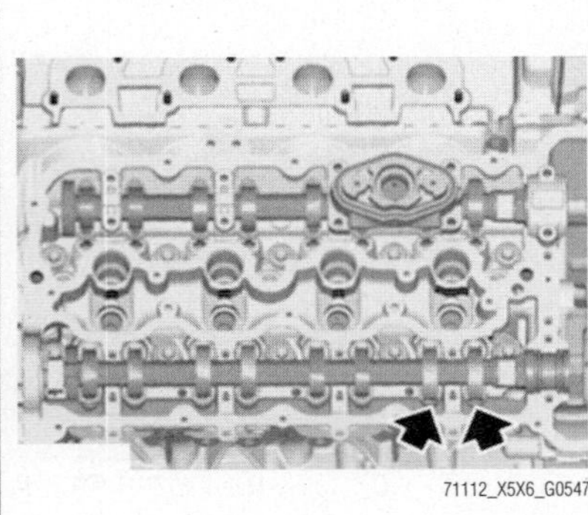

Fig. 129 Insert inlet camshaft (1) so that cams point to side at cylinder 1

➡Do not mix up the bearing caps of cylinders 1 to 4 and 5 to 8.

17. All bearing caps are coded and can only be installed in one position.
18. All bearing caps are marked with letters and numbers:
    a. L=Cylinder bank 1-4.

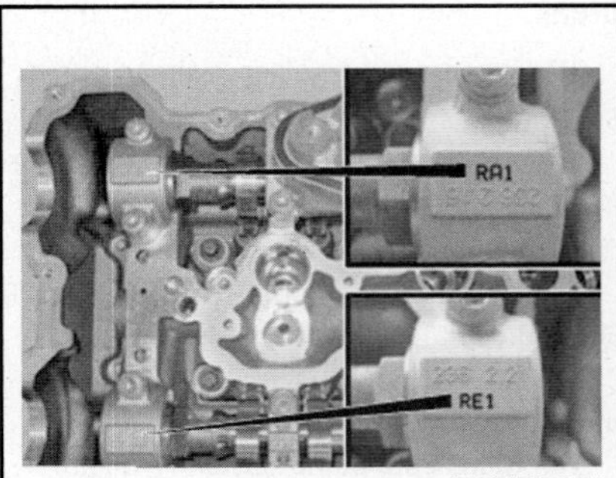

Fig. 130 All bearing caps are marked

b. R=Cylinder bank 5-8.
c. E=Intake side
d. A=Exhaust side
e. 1=designation, bearing point, from 1 to 5

19. Insert all bolts.
20. Tighten down bolts in sequence (1 to 10) in 1/2 turns. Tightening torque: 11 ft. lbs. (15 Nm).
21. Install inlet adjustment units.
22. Adjust valve timing.
23. Assemble engine.

CATALYTIC CONVERTER

REMOVAL & INSTALLATION

3.0L Engine

See Figures 131 and 132.

1. Remove right engine support arm.
2. Remove exhaust system.

➡The oxygen sensors are in danger of being damaged when the catalytic converters are removed and installed.

3. Remove control sensor, cylinders 1 to 3.
4. Remove monitoring sensor from cylinders 1 to 3.
5. Release nuts.
6. Release clamp. The clamp must be replaced every time it is removed.

➡Secure catalytic converter against falling out.

7. Feed out catalytic converter and remove.

To install:

8. Clean sealing surface. Renew clamp and seal.
9. Clamp Tightening torque 33 ft. lbs. (45 Nm).

Fig. 132 Release clamp (1)

10. Catalytic converter to holder Tightening torque 14 ft. lbs. (19 Nm).
11. Reassemble the vehicle.
12. Check exhaust system for leaks.

4.4L Engine

See Figures 133 through 135.

1. Remove acoustic cover
2. Remove both intake filter housings
3. Remove exhaust system
4. Remove both connecting pipes
5. Remove both control sensors
6. Remove both monitor sensors

➡Picture shows the left side, carry out the operation for the right side in an identical way.

7. Release screws.
8. Remove cable holders on left and right.
9. Remove rubber mounts and release screws underneath.
10. Remove cable holder.

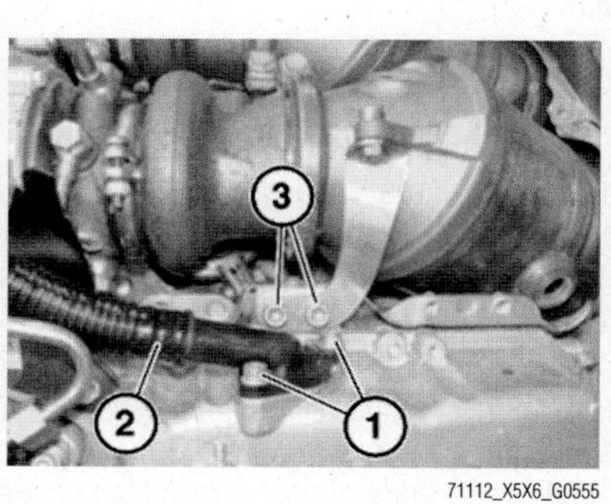

Fig. 134 Release screws (1), detach hose (2) from cylinder head cover, release screws (3) on holder

11. Remove heat shield at top.
12. Remove heat shield at rear left and right.

a. Release screw on catalytic converter.
b. Release clamp on catalytic converter.
c. Replace clamp.
d. Release screw from heat shields.

➡Screw is located between catalytic exhaust-gas converters.

e. Release screws on left heat shield.
f. Unclip left heat shield and remove.
g. Release screw on right heat shield.
h. Release screw on heat shield at bottom right.
i. Unclip heat shield and remove.

13. Release screws.
14. Detach hose from cylinder head cover.
15. Release screws on holder.
16. Release screws on catalytic converter, cylinders 5–8, rear, at cylinder head.

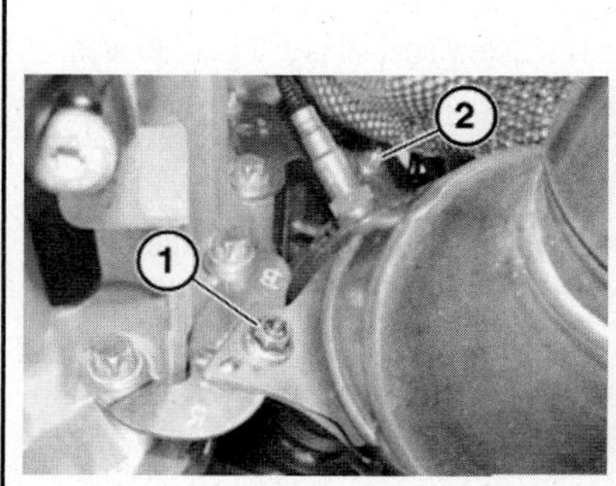

Fig. 131 Release nuts (1) and (2)

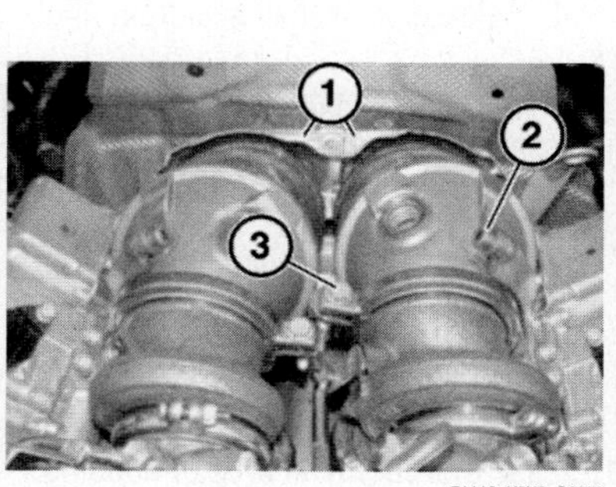

Fig. 133 Remove heat shield (1) at rear left and right, release screw (2) on catalytic converter, release clamp (3)

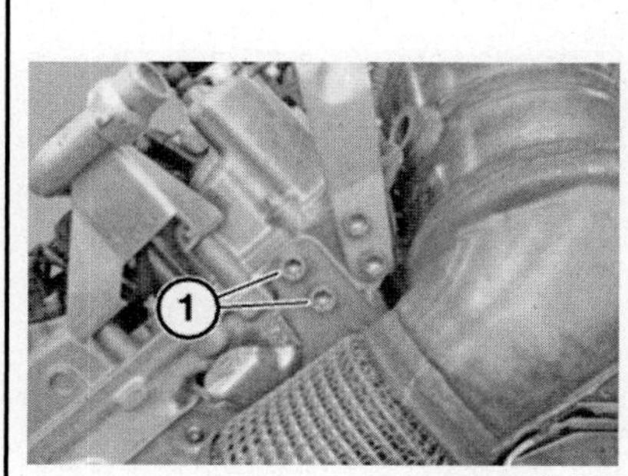

Fig. 135 Release screws (1) on catalytic converter, cylinders 5–8, rear, at cylinder head

17. Remove catalytic converter for cylinders 5–8.

To install:

18. Replace gasket on left turbocharger.
19. Clamp must be fitted with the screw pointing inwards. Otherwise it will not be possible to install the heat shield at the top.
20. The ends of the V-band clamps must rest parallel to each other.
21. If you can see a gap between the ends of the V-band clamps, release and then repeat the screw connection.
22. If the ends of the V-band clamps are positioned under each other, release and then repeat the screw connection.
23. Catalytic exhaust-gas converter to cylinder head Tightening torque 16 ft. lbs. (21 Nm).
24. Catalytic exhaust-gas converter, holder, inlet funnel, to cylinder head Tightening torque 16 ft. lbs. (21 Nm).
25. Catalytic exhaust-gas converter to bracket Tightening torque 16 ft. lbs. (21 Nm).
26. Assemble engine.
27. Check exhaust system for leaks.

CRANKSHAFT FRONT SEAL

REMOVAL & INSTALLATION

3.0L Engine

See Figures 136 through 143.

1. Remove vibration damper

WARNING

Do not release central bolt. If the central bolt is released, the sprockets of the timing chain and the oil pump will no longer be non-positively connected to the crankshaft.

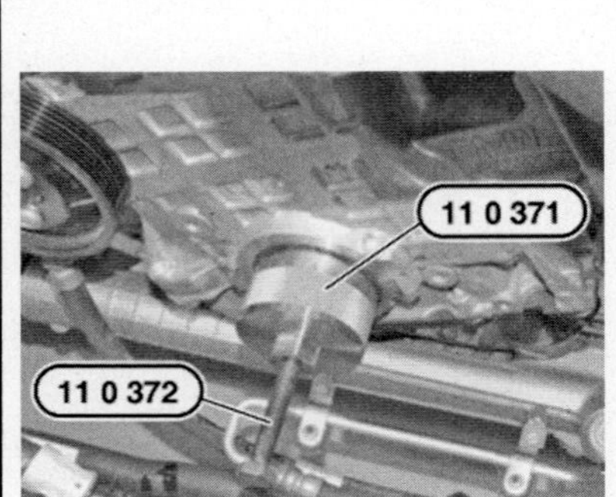

Fig. 136 Screw special tool 11 0 371 with 59 ft. lbs. (80 Nm) into the crankshaft seal

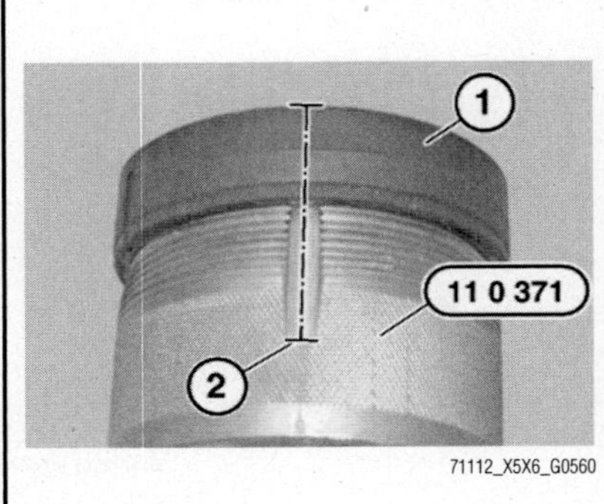

Fig. 137 Carefully saw open crankshaft seal (1) at cutting line (2)

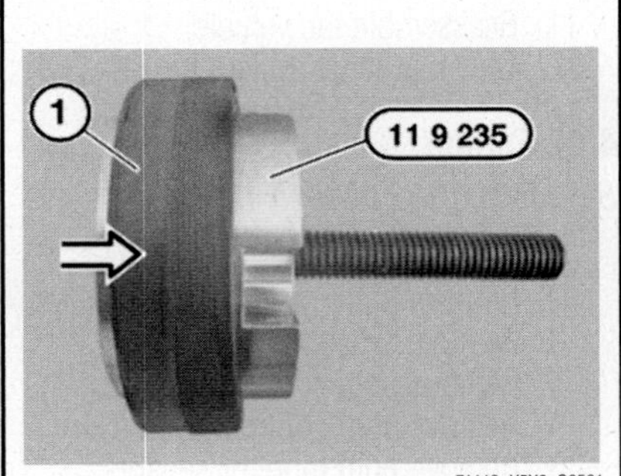

Fig. 138 Push radial shaft seal (1) 11 9 235 carefully in direction of arrow on the special tool

Intake and exhaust camshafts can turn in relation to crankshaft.

2. Screw special tool 11 0 371 with 59 ft. lbs. (80 Nm) into the crankshaft seal.
3. Screw in spindle 11 0 372.
4. Release crankshaft seal from housing.
5. Repeat the operation several times if necessary.
6. Carefully saw open crankshaft seal at cutting line.
7. Remove crankshaft seal from special tool 11 0 371.

To install:

8. Clean sealing surface and degrease thoroughly in area of housing partition.
9. Apply a light coat of oil to running surface of crankshaft seal.
10. Push radial shaft seal 11 9 235 carefully in direction of arrow on the special tool.

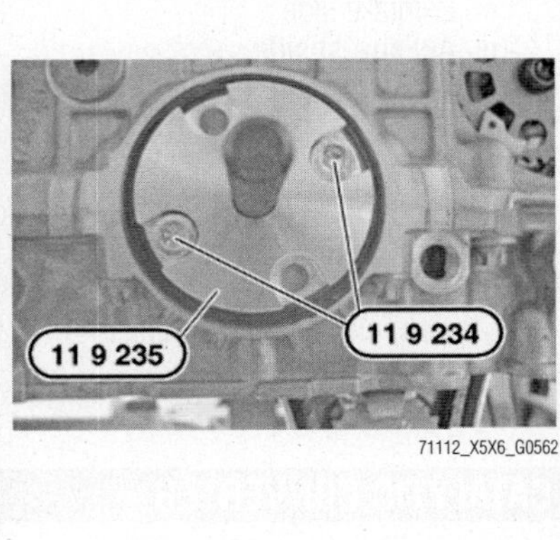

Fig. 139 Screw special tool 11 9 235 with special tool 11 9 234 on crankshaft

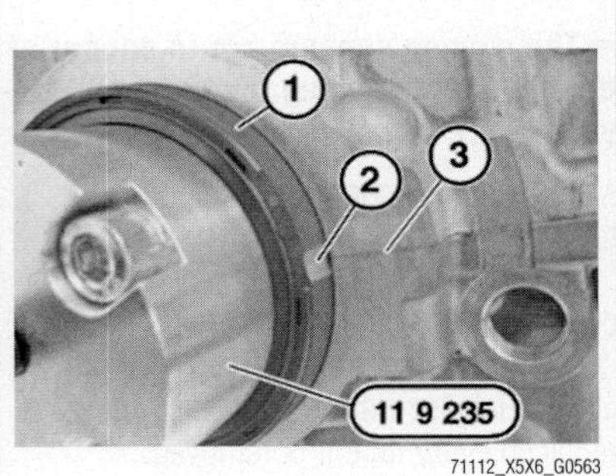

Fig. 140 Align groove (2) of radial shaft seal (1) centered to the housing partition (3)

➡11 9 235Special tool can only be fastened with

2 opposite bolts.

11. Determine hole pattern on special tool.
12. Screw special tool 11 9 235 with special tool 11 9 234 on crankshaft.
13. Align groove of radial shaft seal centered to the housing partition.

➡After installation, the grooves must be filled with sealing compound.

14. Draw in radial shaft seal with special tool 11 9 231 in conjunction with special tool 11 9 233 until flush.

➡Use primer 1.3 and liquid seal 1.4.

15. Prepare liquid sealing compound in special tool 11 4 370.
    a. Remove sealing caps from syringe.
    b. Screw on metering needle.
    c. Insert piston for pressing out.

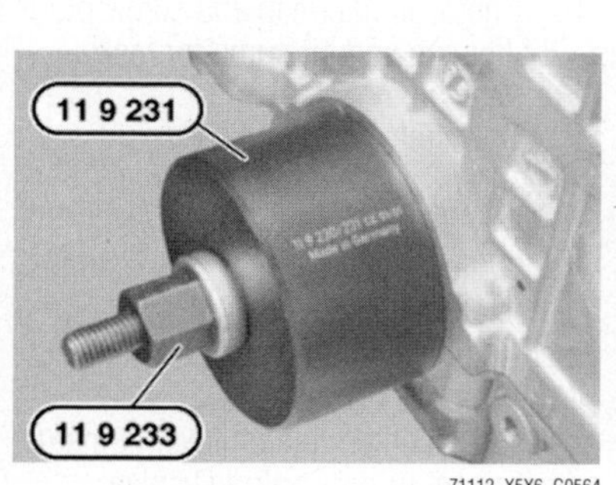

Fig. 141 Draw in radial shaft seal with special tool 11 9 231 in conjunction with special tool 11 9 233 until flush

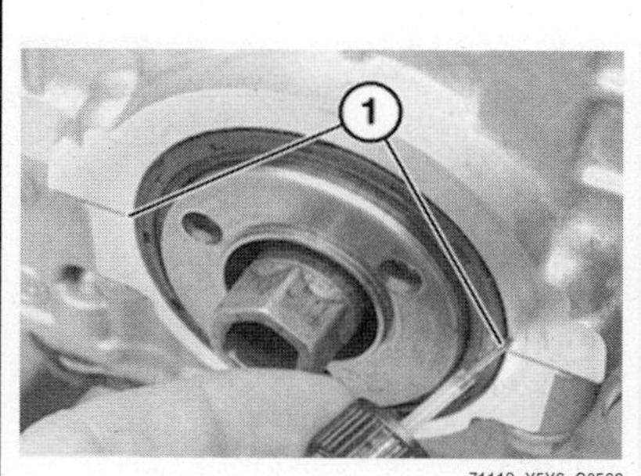

Fig. 143 Insert brush as far as possible into grooves (1) on crankshaft seal

Fig. 145 Open oil drain plug (1) on oil sump

d. Syringe contains the sealing compound Loctite®, manufacturer's number 128357.

e. Bottle contains the primer Loctite®, manufacturer's number 171000.

16. Before filling with sealing compound: Moisten brush with Loctite® primer, manufacturer's number 171000.

17. Insert brush as far as possible into grooves on crankshaft seal in order to coat housing partition on engine block.

18. Using syringe, fill both grooves flush with Loctite® sealing compound, manufacturer's number 128357.

➡Loctite® primer, manufacturer's number 171000, binds the Loctite® sealing compound, manufacturer's number 128357, and prevents leakage.

19. Coat surface of sealing compound in both grooves with Loctite® primer, manufacturer's number 171000.

20. Assemble engine.

ENGINE OIL & FILTER

REPLACEMENT

3.0L Engine

See Figures 144 through 147.

Note the following:

- Carry out the engine oil service only when the engine is at operating temperature.
- Observe the exact engine oil filling capacity.
- Overfilling the engine with engine oil will result in engine damage.
- Checking and drip-off times (at least 10 minutes) must be observed.

1. Release oil filter cover with special tool 11 9 240.

➡Engine oil flows out of the oil filter housing and back into the oil sump.

2. Rear wheel drive: Open oil drain plug on oil sump.
3. Drain engine oil.
4. Replace sealing ring and install oil drain plug. Tighten to 18 ft. lbs. (25 Nm).
5. Four-wheel drive: Open oil drain plug of oil sump and drain engine oil.
6. Replace sealing ring and install oil drain plug. Tighten to 18 ft. lbs. (25 Nm).
7. Remove and insert oil filter element in direction of arrow.
8. Replace gasket and renew if necessary.

➡Coat sealing ring and gasket with engine oil.

9. Secure oil filter cover with special tool 11 9 240. Tightening torque 18 ft. lbs. (25 Nm).
10. Pour in engine oil.
11. Start engine and run at idle until oil pressure indicator light goes out.
12. Switch off engine
13. Check oil filter cover and screw plug on oil sump for leaks.
14. Assemble engine.

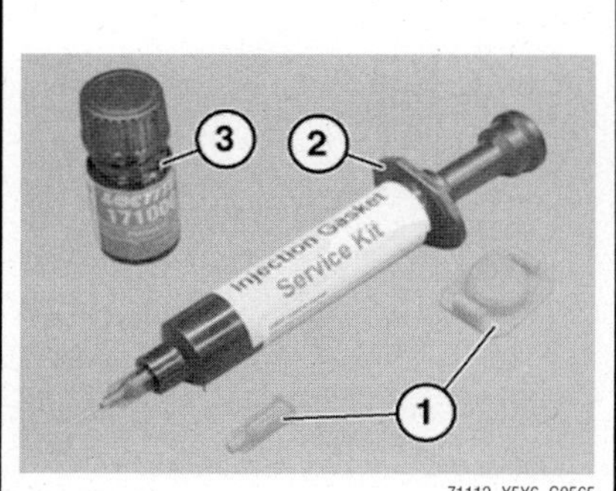

Fig. 142 Prepare liquid sealing compound; sealing caps (1), syringe (2), bottle (3)

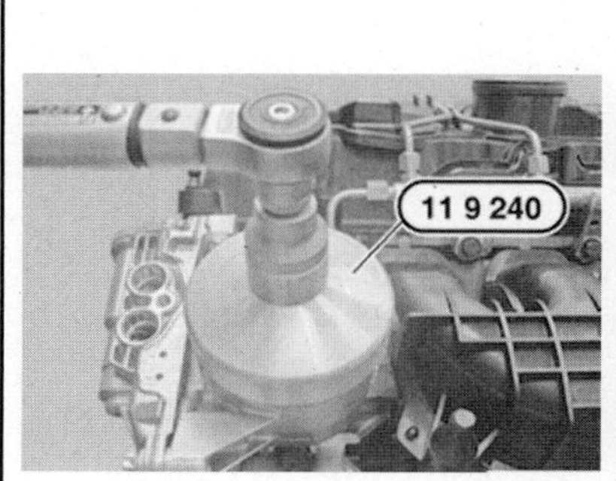

Fig. 144 Release oil filter cover with special tool 11 9 240

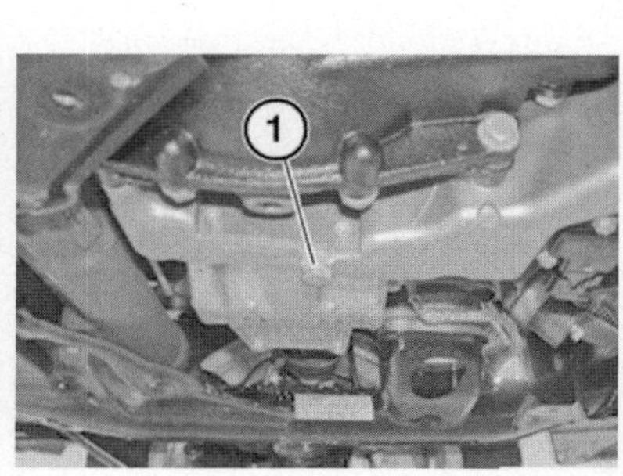

Fig. 146 Open oil drain plug (1) of oil sump and drain engine oil

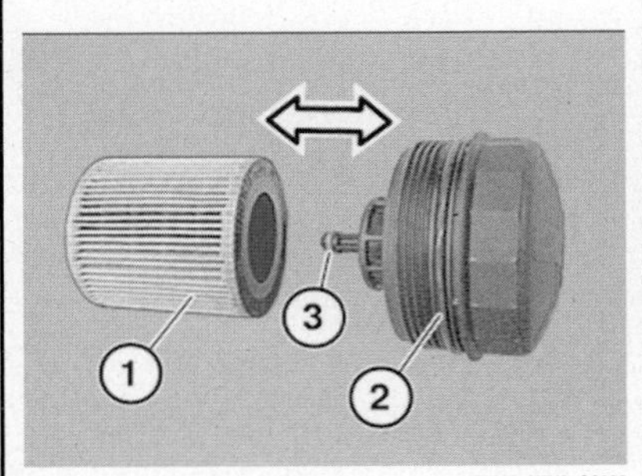

Fig. 147 Remove and insert oil filter element (1) in direction of arrow; sealing ring (2), gasket (3)

15. Checking engine oil level:
    a. Park vehicle on a horizontal surface
    b. Allow engine to run at operating temperature for three minutes with increased engine speed (approximately 1100 rpm)
    c. Read off engine oil level in instrument panel or on Control Display
    d. Top up engine oil if necessary

4.4L Engine

See Figures 148 through 150.

Note the following:

- Carry out the engine oil service only when the engine is at operating temperature.
- Observe the exact engine oil filling capacity.
- Overfilling the engine with engine oil will result in engine damage.
- Checking and drip-off times (at least 10 minutes) must be observed.

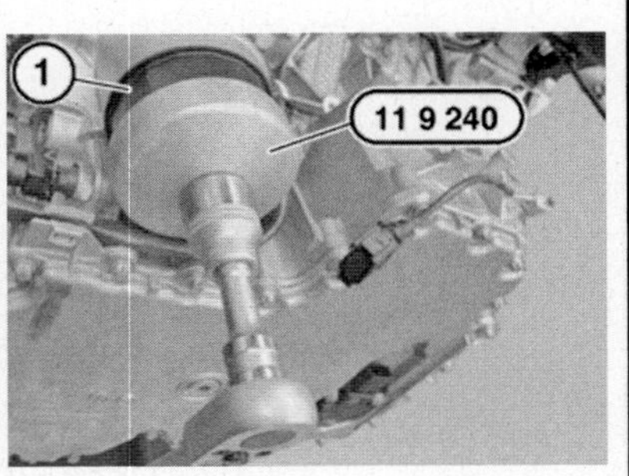

Fig. 149 Release oil filter cover (1) with special tool 11 9 240

1. Release screw plug on oil filter cap.
2. Remove screw plug from oil sump and drain engine oil.
3. Release oil filter cover with special tool 11 9 240.
4. Insert oil filter element into oil filter cover.
    a. Renew sealing ring and wet with oil.
    b. Check sealing ring and renew, if installed.
    c. Renew oil filter element and slide into the oil filter cover.
    d. Oil filter element must snap audibly into place.
5. Insert screw plug for oil sump and tighten to 30 ft. lbs. (40 Nm).
6. Insert screw plug (1) for oil filter cap and tighten 7 ft. lbs. (10 Nm).
7. Pour in engine oil.
8. Start engine and run at idle until oil pressure indicator light goes out.
9. Switch off engine
10. Check oil filter cap and screw plugs for oil filter cap and oil sump for leaks.
11. Assemble engine.
12. Checking engine oil level:
    a. Park vehicle on a horizontal surface
    b. Allow engine to run at operating temperature for three minutes with increased engine speed (approximately 1100 rpm)
    c. Read off engine oil level in instrument panel or on Control Display
    d. Top up engine oil if necessary

EXHAUST MANIFOLD

REMOVAL & INSTALLATION

3.0L Engine

Exhaust manifold is an integral part of the turbocharger. Refer to Turbocharger Removal and Installation.

4.4L Engine

See Figures 151 and 152.

1. Remove left turbocharger.
2. Remove right turbocharger.
3. Remove alternator
4. Release screws from heat shield.
5. Release screws.
6. Remove heat shield.
7. Release screws.
8. Remove heat shield at rear right.
9. Unscrew nuts.
10. Remove exhaust manifold.

To install:

11. Replace gaskets.
12. Replace seal.

➡Seal beads faces the exhaust manifold.

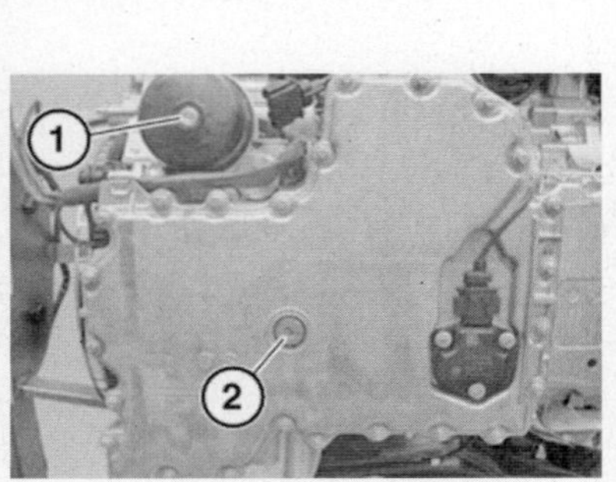

Fig. 148 Release screw plug (1) on oil filter cap, remove screw plug (2) from oil sump and drain engine oil

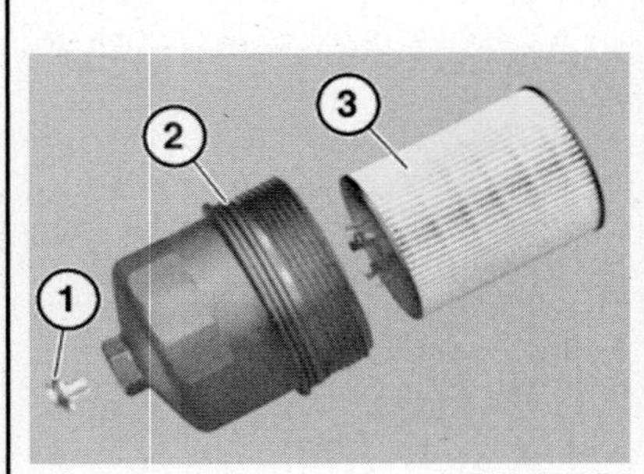

Fig. 150 Sealing ring (1, 2), and oil filter element (3)

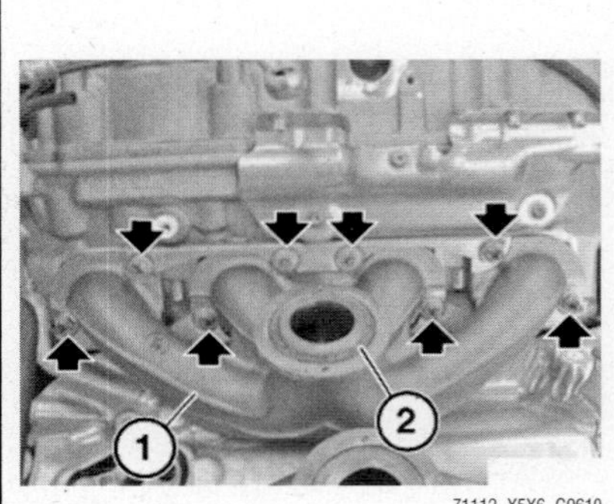

Fig. 151 Unscrew nuts, remove exhaust manifold (1); seal (2)

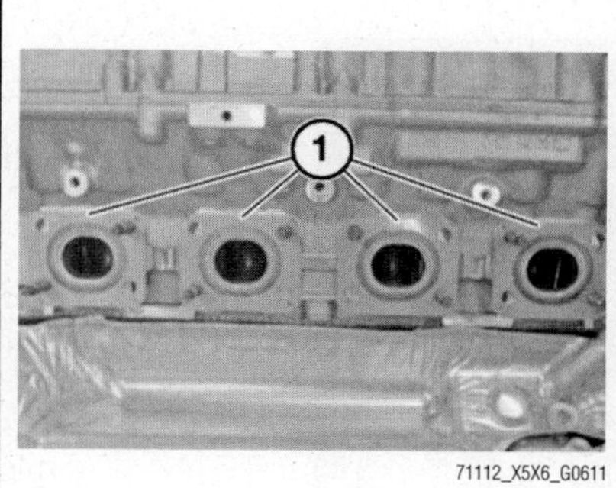

Fig. 152 Replace gaskets (1)

13. Coat threads with copper paste.
14. Replace nuts. Tightening torque 11 ft. lbs. (15 Nm).
15. Assemble engine.
16. Check exhaust system for leaks.

INTAKE MANIFOLD

REMOVAL & INSTALLATION

3.0L Engine

See Figures 153 through 159.

1. Disconnect battery negative lead.
2. Remove intake filter housing.
3. Remove left charge air duct
4. Remove ignition coil cover.
5. Disconnect all plug connections on engine control unit.
6. Open retaining clip.
7. Release wiring harness section from retaining clip.

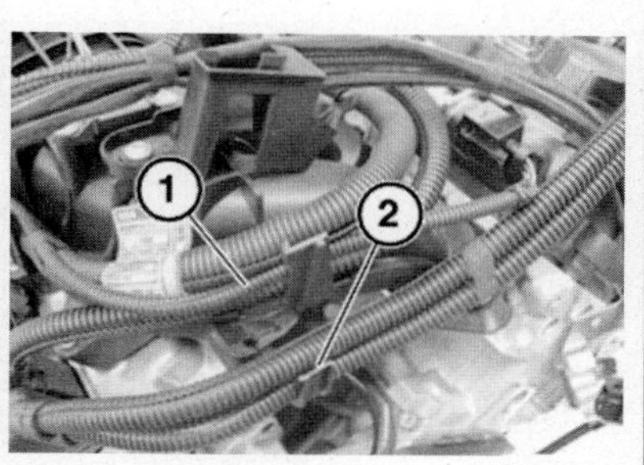

Fig. 154 Release all wiring harness sections from holders (1 and 2)

8. Release all wiring harness sections from holder.
9. Disconnect plug connection at charging pressure sensor.
10. Release all wiring harness sections from holders.
11. Disconnect plug connection on tank vent valve.
12. Press and hold down the unlocking device on the vacuum line (1) on the vacuum reservoir (cylinder head cover).
13. Detach vacuum line in upward direction.
14. Detach vacuum line in upward direction.
15. Disconnect plug connection on throttle valve drive.
16. Release screw.
17. Unscrew nuts.
18. Remove intake plenum.

To install:

19. Installation is the reverse order of removal.

Fig. 156 Press and hold down the unlocking device on the vacuum line (1) on the vacuum reservoir (cylinder head cover) in direction of arrow

20. Replace all gaskets.
21. Tighten screw and nuts on intake plenum to 11 ft. lbs. (15 Nm).
22. Assemble engine.

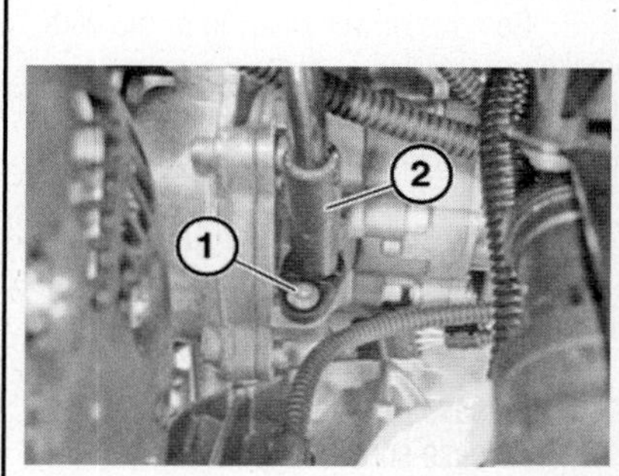

Fig. 157 Detach vacuum line (2) in upward direction; screw (1)

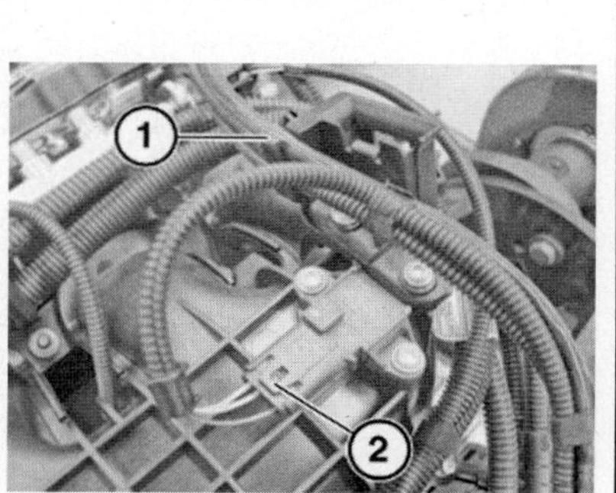

Fig. 153 Release all wiring harness sections from holder (1), disconnect plug connection (2) at charging pressure sensor

Fig. 155 Disconnect plug connection (1) on tank vent valve

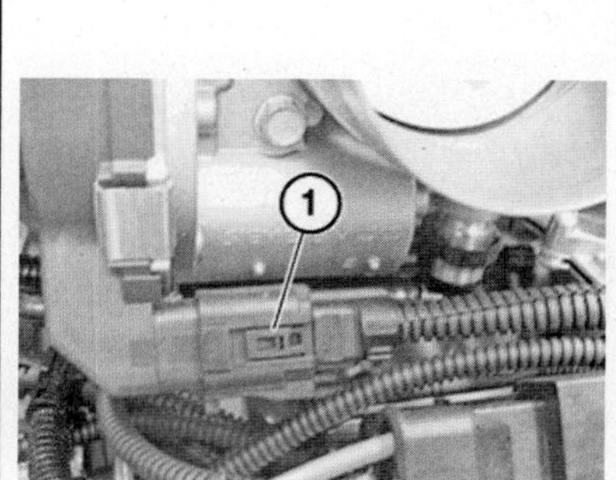

Fig. 158 Disconnect plug connection (1) on throttle valve drive

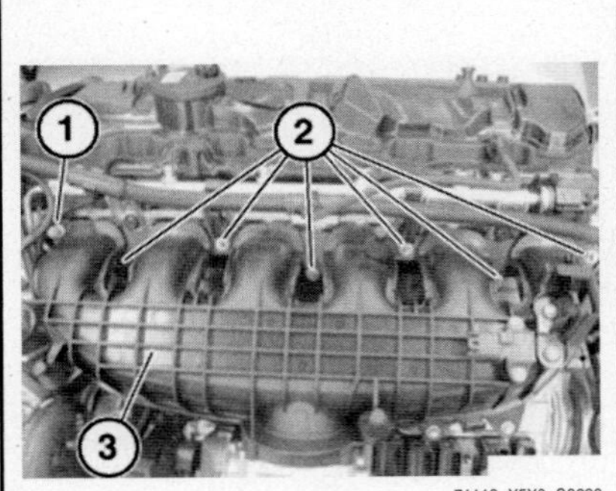

Fig. 159 Release screw (1), unscrew nuts (2), remove intake plenum (3)

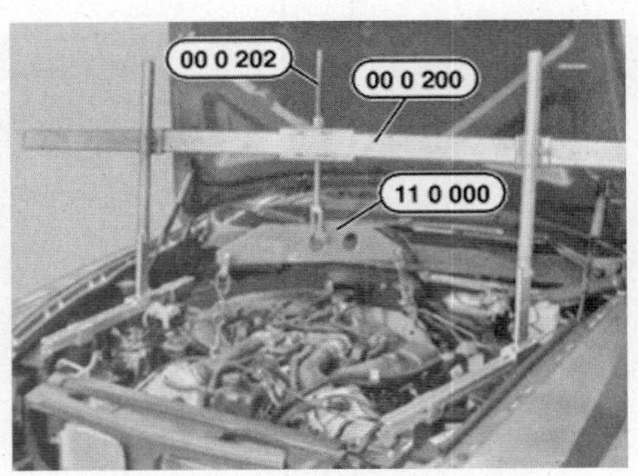

Fig. 161 Fit special tool 00 0 200

4.4L Engine

Left Side

See Figures 160 through 163.

1. Remove complete front panel.
2. Remove complete cooling core with condenser.
3. Remove power steering pump with bracket.
4. Remove left injection pipe.
5. Detach engine ventilation hose.
6. Unscrew nuts.
7. Fit special tool 00 0 200.
8. Release nuts on left and right engine support arms.
9. Raise engine.
10. Release throttle valve.
11. Release screw.

To install:

12. Installation is the reverse order of removal.
13. Replace all profile seals.

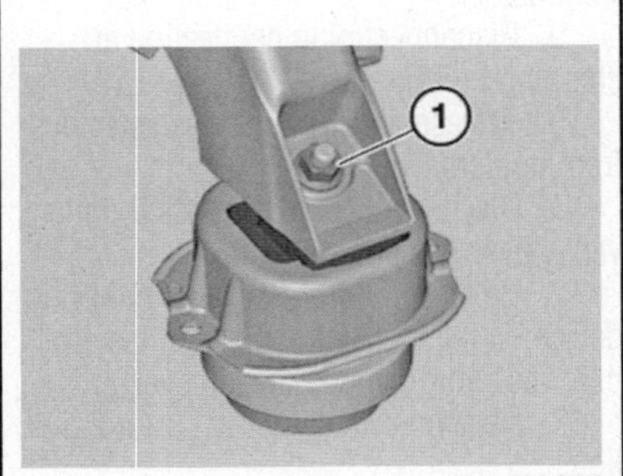

Fig. 162 Release nuts (1) on engine mount on left and right

14. Assemble engine and vehicle.
15. Check intake system for leaks.

Right Side

See Figures 164 through 165.

1. Remove complete front panel.
2. Remove complete cooling core with condenser.
3. Remove power steering pump with bracket.
4. Remove right injection pipe.
5. Detach engine ventilation hose.
6. Unscrew nuts.
7. Fit special tool 00 0 200.
8. Release nuts on left and right engine support arms.
9. Raise engine.
10. Remove throttle valve.
11. Release screw.

To install:

12. Installation is the reverse order of removal.
13. Replace all profile seals.
14. Assemble engine and vehicle.
15. Check intake system for leaks.

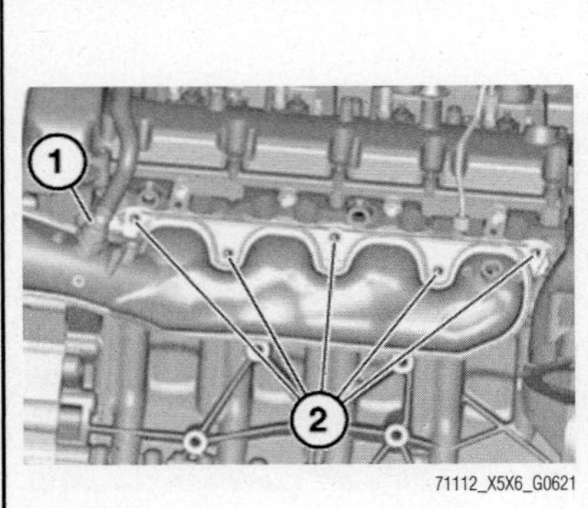

Fig. 160 Detach engine ventilation hose (1), unscrew nuts (2)

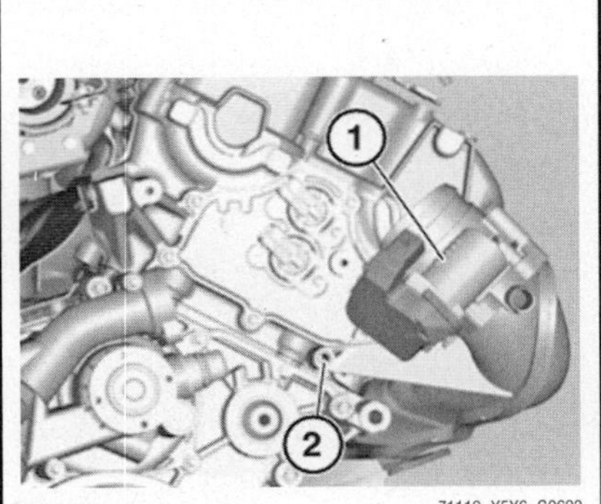

Fig. 163 Release throttle valve (1), Release screw (2)

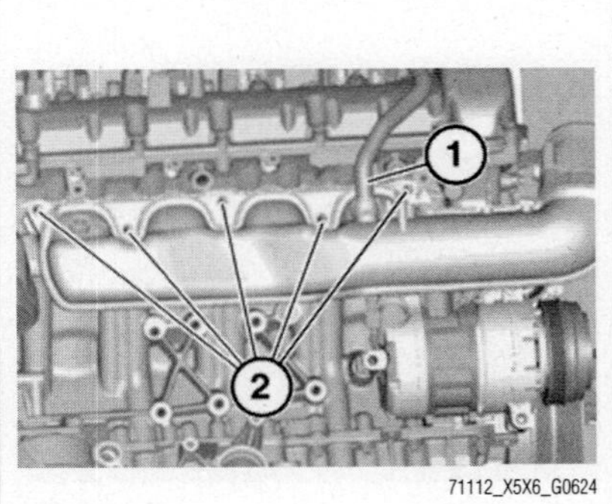

Fig. 164 Detach engine ventilation hose (1), unscrew nuts (2)

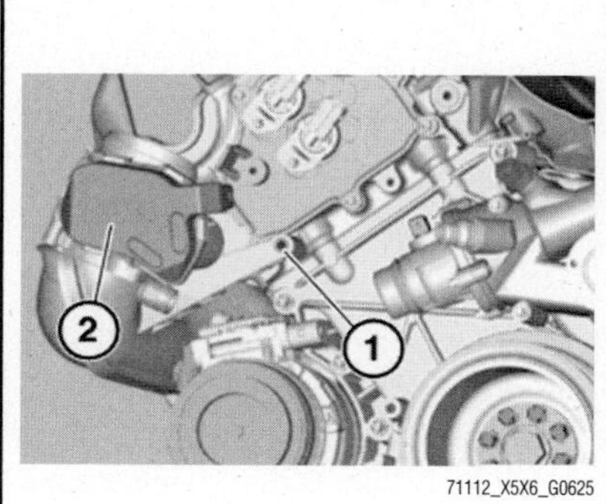

Fig. 165 Remove throttle valve (2), Release screw (1)

OIL PAN

REMOVAL & INSTALLATION

3.0L Engine

See Figure 166.

1. Remove front axle differential.
2. Drain and add engine oil.

➡The lines must be detached from the oil sump on vehicles with automatic transmission; if necessary, detach oil pump and place to one side.

3. Release bolts on transmission.
4. Detach return hose.

➡Different screw lengths for securing the oil sump are fitted in vehicles with all-wheel drive or with or without automatic transmission.

5. Release bolts along line.
6. If necessary, release nuts. Remove oil level sensor.

To install:

7. Installation is the reverse order of removal.
8. Replace aluminum screws.
9. Replace sealing ring.

➡There must be no adhesive residues in the lower crankcase section retaining threads.

10. Clean retaining threads and sealing surfaces.
11. Replace all gaskets.
12. Assemble engine.

4.4L Engine

Lower Section

See Figure 167.

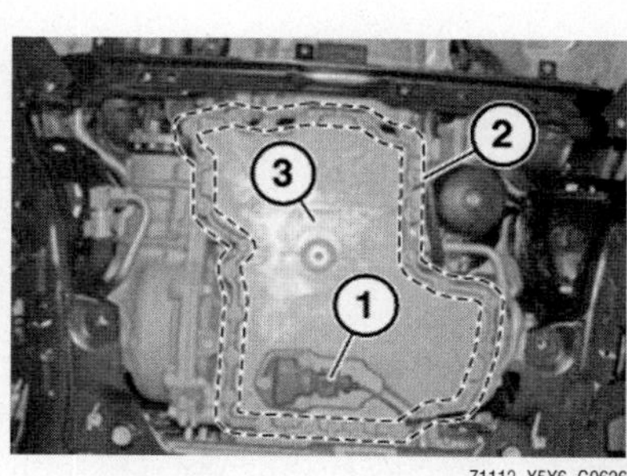

Fig. 167 Unlock plug connection (1) on oil level sensor and disconnect, release screws (2), remove lower sump section (3)

1. Remove reinforcement plate
2. Remove oil drain plug and drain engine oil.
3. Unlock plug connection on oil level sensor and disconnect.
4. Release screws along line.
5. Remove lower oil sump section.

To install:

6. Installation is the reverse order of removal.
7. Clean sealing surfaces.
8. Replace gasket.
9. When replacing oil sump bottom section:
    a. Convert oil level sensor.
    b. Replace sealing ring.
10. Replace screws. Tighten to 20 ft. lbs. (27 Nm).

Upper Section

See Figures 168 through 170.

1. Drain off engine oil

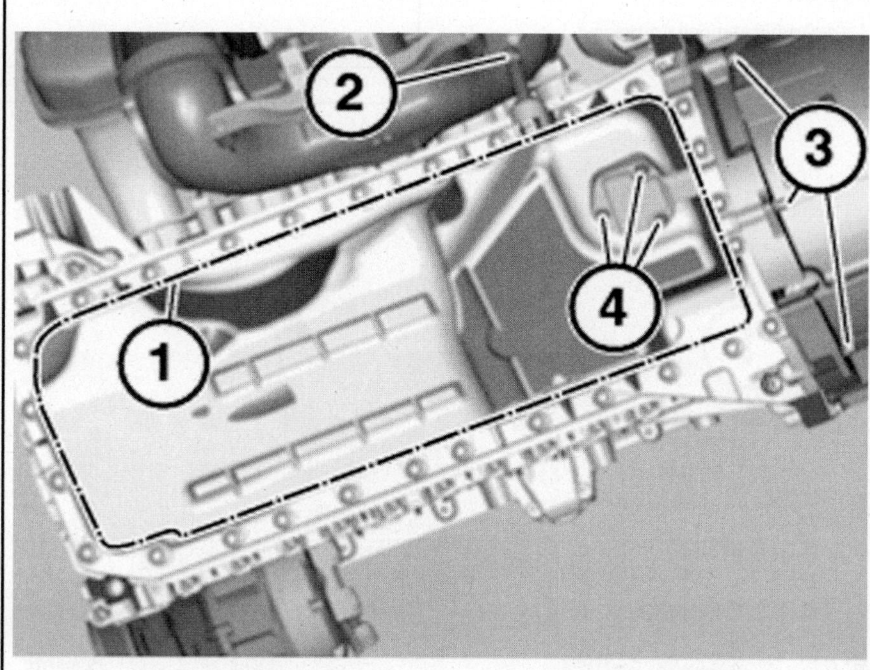

Fig. 166 Release bolts on transmission

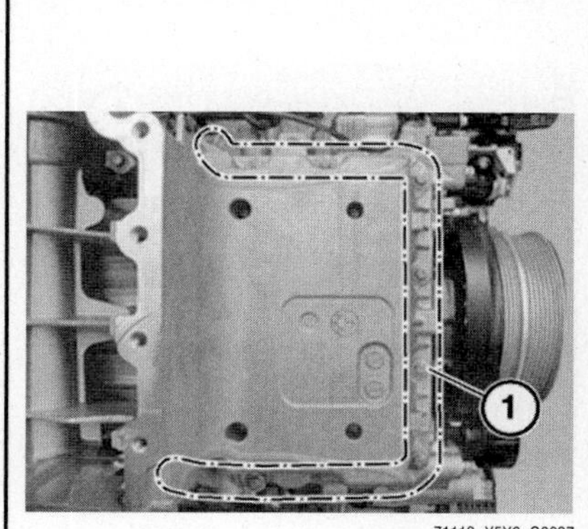

Fig. 168 Release bolts in area of line (1)

Fig. 169 Release bolts in area of line (1)

2. Secure engine in installation position
3. Lower front axle
4. Remove front axle differential
5. Remove lower oil sump section
6. Remove oil pump.
7. Release supply/return lines on oil filter
8. Release holders of supply/return lines on oil sump
9. Detach plug from oil pressure switch
10. Unclip wiring harness on oil sump
11. Remove oil filter cover with oil filter.
12. Release bolts in area of line.
13. Release bolts in area of line.
14. Release bolts in area of line.
15. Release 4 bolts on transmission side.
16. Remove upper oil sump section.

To install:

17. Installation is the reverse order of removal.
18. Free sealing surfaces of seal debris and clean.

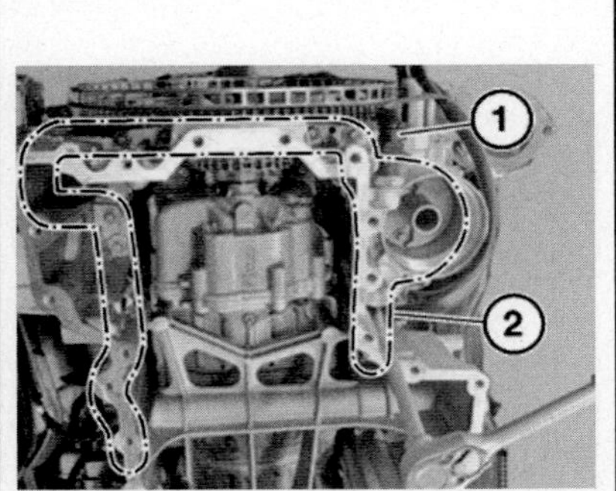

Fig. 170 Release bolts in area of line (2), upper oil sump section (1)

19. Replace gasket.
20. Modify oil pressure switch if replacing oil sump.
21. Assemble engine.

OIL PUMP

REMOVAL & INSTALLATION

3.0L Engine

See Figures 171 through 176.

1. Remove oil sump.
2. Undo all the aluminum screws along the line.
3. Remove intake pipe with oil deflector.

➡Sprocket must be blocked in order to release central bolt.

4. Insert pin between sprocket and housing of oil pump.
5. Release oil pump central bolt.
6. Release aluminum screws.

➡Watch mounting flats on oil pump sprocket.

➡Observe different screw lengths.

7. Release aluminum screws.
8. Detach sprocket in direction of arrow.

➡Chain tensioner presses timing chain upwards.

9. Do not remove sprocket.

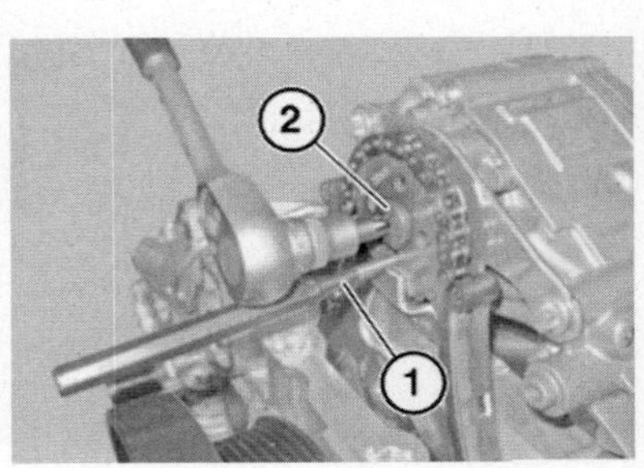

Fig. 172 Insert pin (1) between sprocket and housing of oil pump; release oil pump central bolt (2)

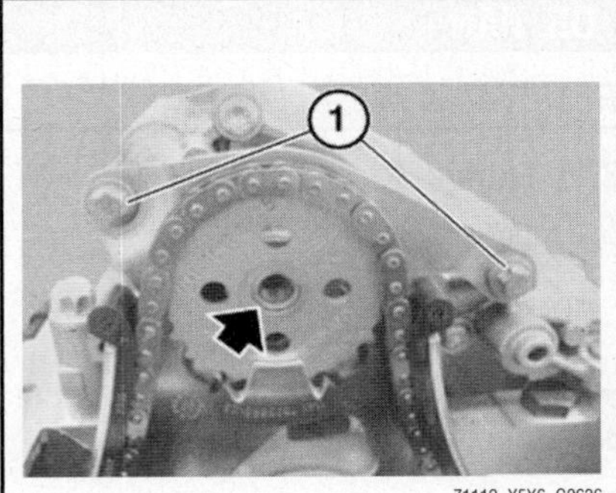

Fig. 173 Release aluminum screws (1)

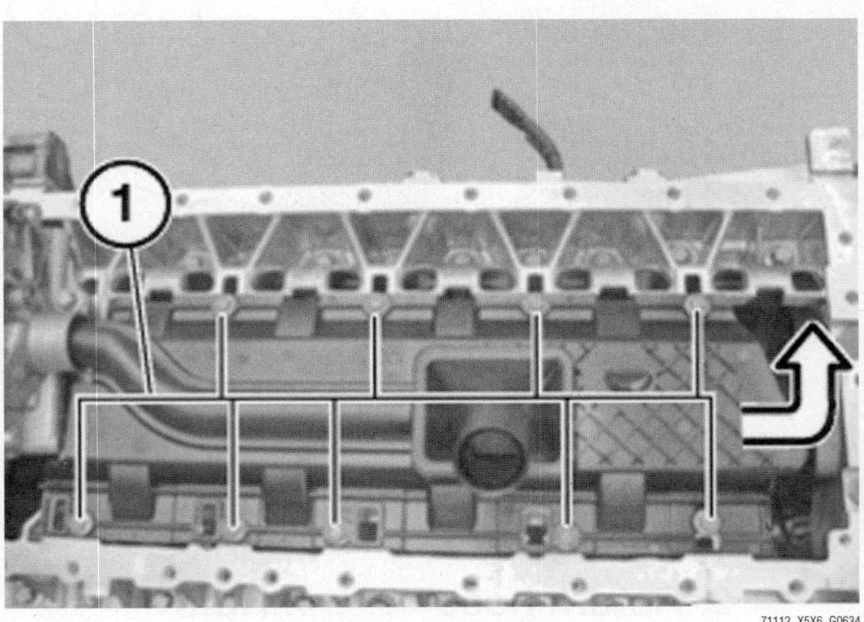

Fig. 171 Undo all the aluminum screws (1) along the line

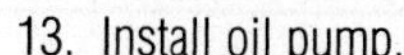

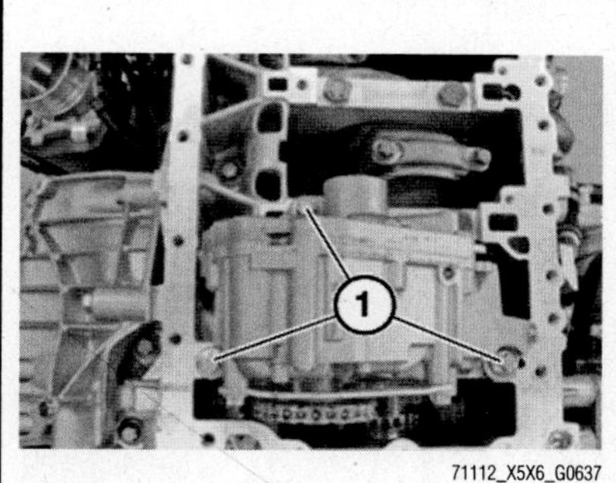

Fig. 174 Release aluminum screws (1)

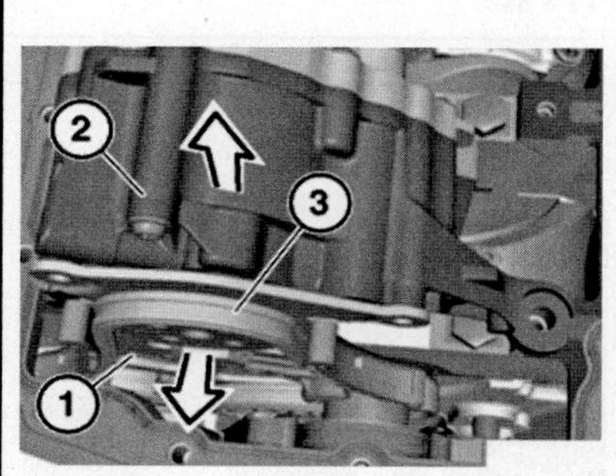

Fig. 175 Detach sprocket (1) in direction of arrow, remove oil pump (2); timing chain (3)

10. Remove oil pump in direction of arrow.

To install:

11. Installation is the reverse order of removal.
12. Check spacer bushes for secure seating and damage; replace if necessary.

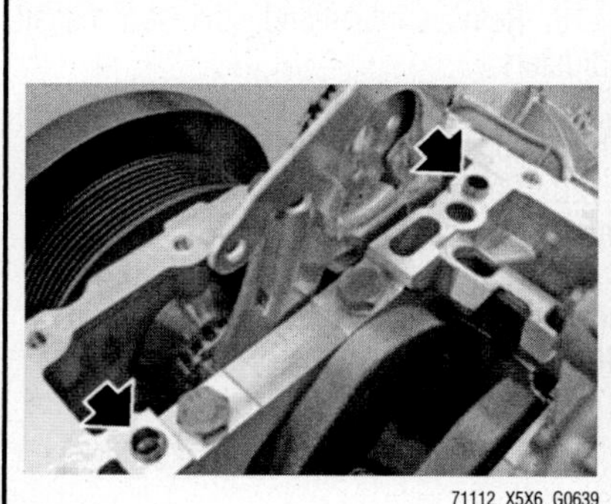

Fig. 176 Check spacer bushes for secure seating and damage; replace if necessary

13. Install oil pump.
14. Align mounting flats on oil pump to sprocket.
15. Tighten sprocket bolt to 15 ft. lbs. (20 Nm) plus an additional 45°.
16. Install intake pipe with oil deflector.
17. Replace aluminum screws.
18. Replace O-ring.
19. Insert all the aluminum screws along the line.
20. Assemble engine.

4.4L Engine

See Figures 177 through 179.

1. Drain engine oil.
2. Remove lower oil sump section.
3. Unscrew nuts.
4. Remove intake pipe.
5. Release all nuts using special tool 11 7 201.
6. Remove oil pump drive gear.

➡Graphic shows engine removed

7. Unscrew nuts.

Fig. 177 Unscrew nuts (2), remove intake pipe (1)

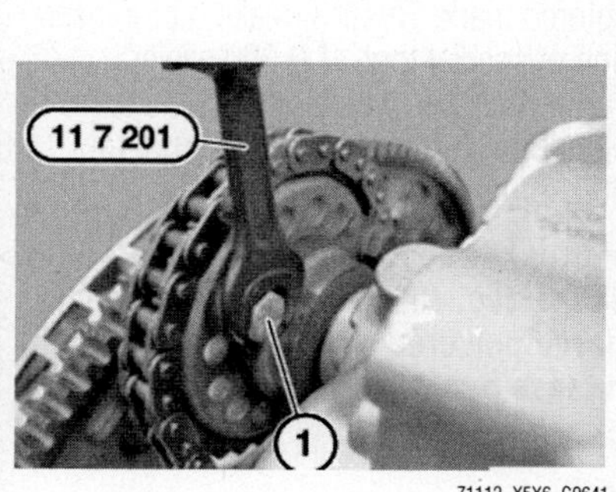

Fig. 178 Release all nuts (1) using special tool 11 7 201

Fig. 179 Unscrew nuts (1), release screw (2), remove oil pump

8. Release screw, remove oil pump with aid of a second person.

➡Graphic without top oil sump

9. Detach oil lines upwards.

To install:

10. Installation is the reverse order of removal.
11. Replace sealing rings.
12. Coat sealing ring with suitable lubricant.
13. Replace O-ring for oil feed line.
14. Install oil pump and secure nuts.
15. Install oil pump drive gear.
16. Secure all nuts with special tool 11 7 201.
17. Replace screws.
18. Assemble engine.

PISTON AND RING

POSITIONING

See Figures 180 through 182.

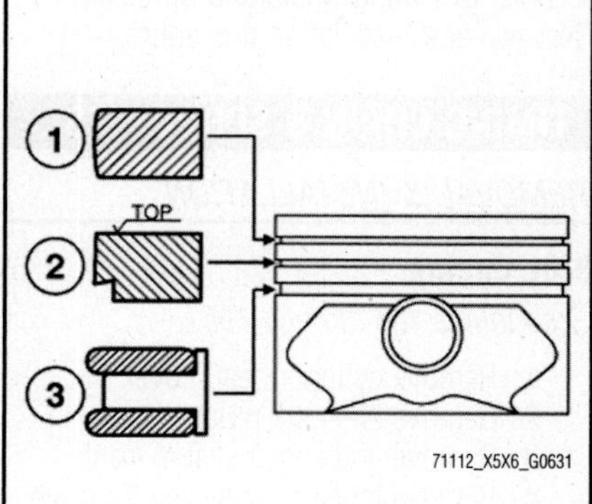

Fig. 180 Plain rectangular compression ring (1), piston ring (2), steel band with M-flex ring (3)

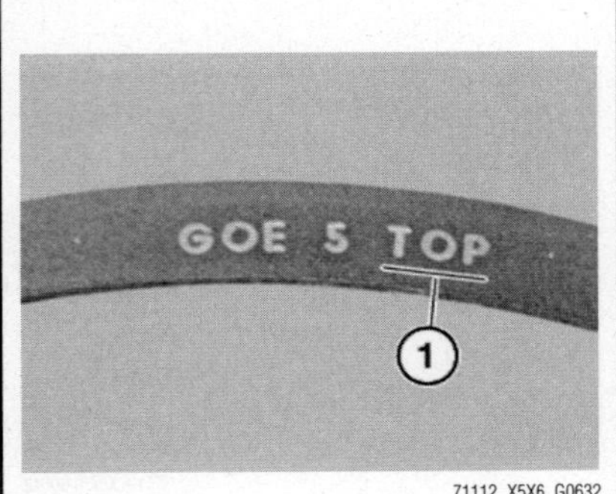

Fig. 181 Piston rings with "TOP" identification (1) must point to piston crown.

Fig. 183 If engine is removed, block crankshaft with special tool 11 9 260

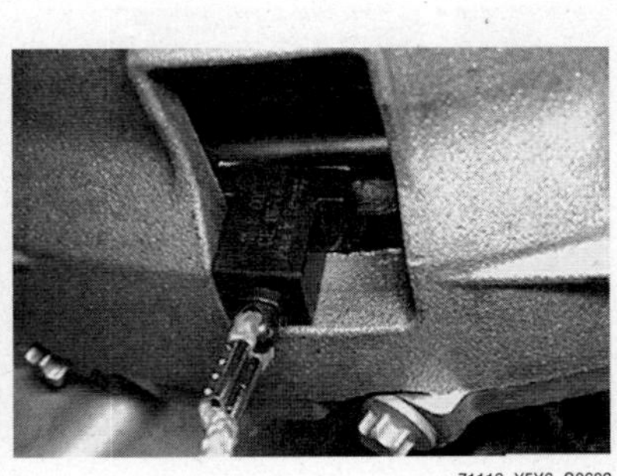

Fig. 185 Vehicles with automatic transmission: Block crankshaft with special tool 11 8 660

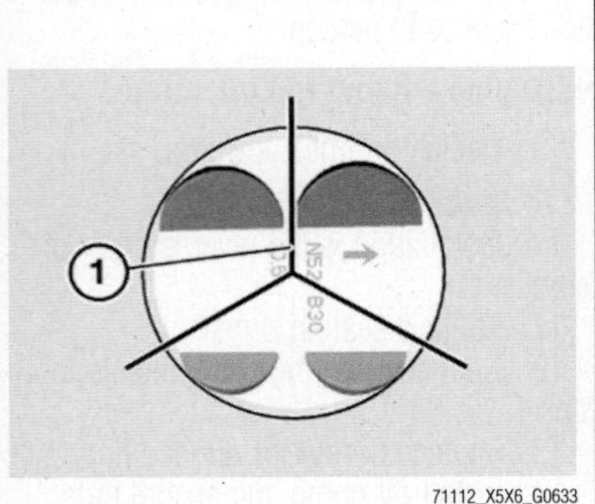

Fig. 182 The ring gaps (1) of the piston rings must be arranged offset by approximately 120°

Fig. 184 Mark position of crankshaft using a colored mark (1)

Fig. 186 Release central bolt (1) with ¾ inch tool (2)

TIMING CHAIN FRONT COVER

REMOVAL & INSTALLATION

3.0L Engine

Refer to Timing Chain and Sprockets Removal and Installation procedure.

TIMING CHAIN & SPROCKETS

REMOVAL & INSTALLATION

3.0L Engine

See Figures 183 through 195.

1. Remove cylinder head cover.
2. Remove all spark plugs.
3. Remove crankshaft seal at front
4. Remove tensioning device for drive belt.
5. Remove vibration absorber.
6. Check timing.
7. If engine is removed, block crankshaft with special tool 11 9 260.

➡To release central bolt (1), remove special tool 11 0 300. When central bolt of crankshaft is released, there is no longer a secure connection to timing drive.

8. Mark position of crankshaft using a colored mark. This will make future insertion of special tool 11 0 300 easier.
9. Vehicles with automatic transmission: Block crankshaft with special tool 11 8 660.

➡Breakaway torque of the central bolt> 443 ft. lbs. (600 Nm). A ¾ inch tool (large powered square) is required to release central bolt.

10. Release central bolt with ¾ inch tool.
11. Remove chain tensioner.
12. Screw in vibration absorber screws.
13. Move hub on crankshaft forward to remove.
14. Open screw plug.
15. Open screw plug.
16. Release bearing journal from timing chain module on cylinder head.
17. Install special tool 11 4 280 to release the central bolts on the intake and exhaust camshaft adjusters.
18. Remove intake and exhaust camshaft adjusters.
19. Release bearing journal from timing chain module on crankcase.
20. Release bolts from timing chain module on cylinder head.
21. Remove chain module with timing chain and camshaft sprocket upwards in direction of arrow.

To install:

22. Installation is the reverse order of removal.
23. Pull timing chain upwards until camshaft sprocket engages chain guide.
24. Install timing chain and sprocket in this position.

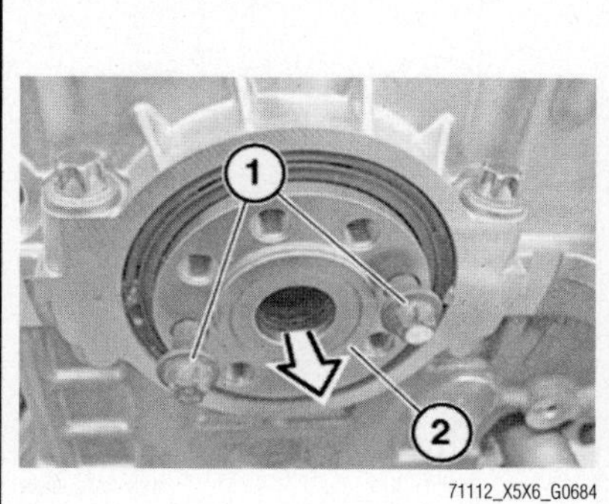

Fig. 187 Screw in vibration absorber screws (1), move hub (2) on crankshaft forward in direction of arrow to remove

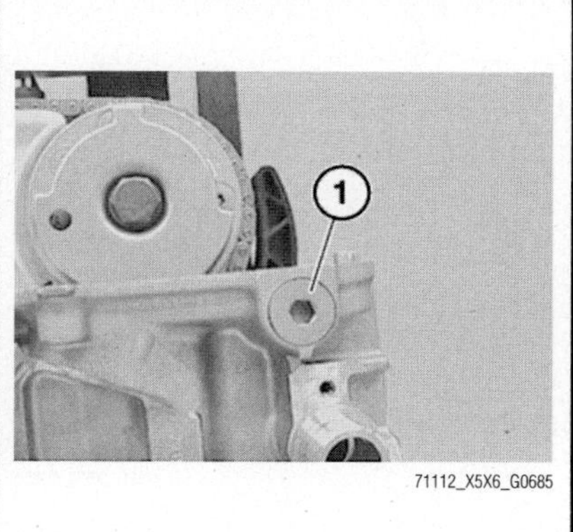

Fig. 188 Open screw plug (1)

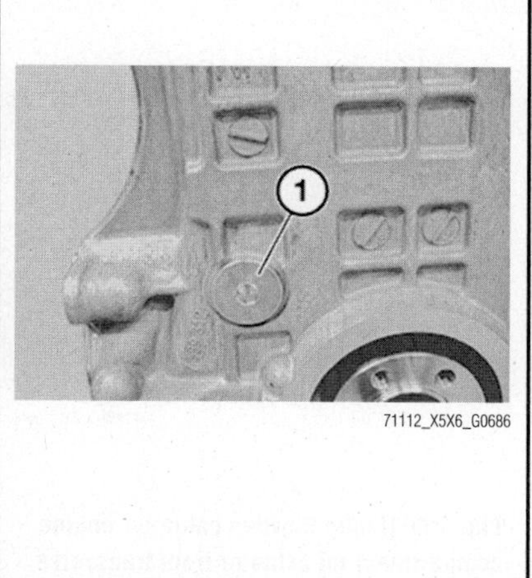

Fig. 189 Open screw plug (1)

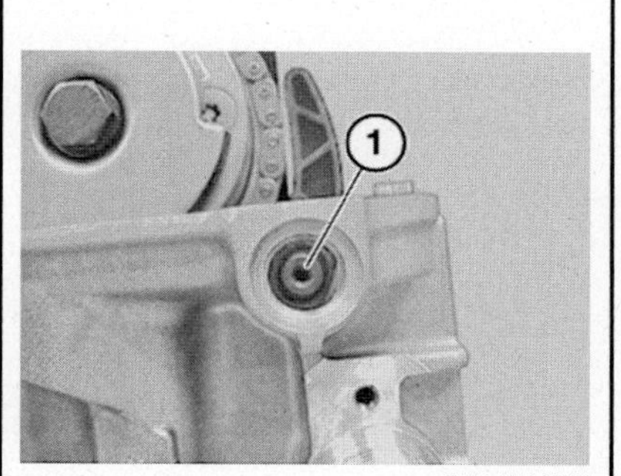

Fig. 190 Release bearing journal (1) from timing chain module on cylinder head

Fig. 192 Release bearing journal (1) from timing chain module on crankcase

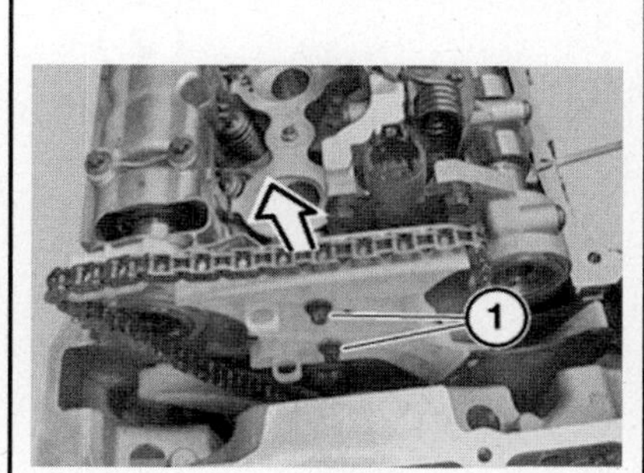

Fig. 193 Release bolts (1) from timing chain module on cylinder head

➡Always hold timing chain under tension. Timing chain may jam on chain guide.

➡Note direction of installation of camshaft sprocket. Collar on sprocket points to engine.

WARNING

Incorrect assembly will result in engine damage.

25. Insert central bolt with hub for crankshaft.
26. Tighten down central bolt. Tightening torque 74 ft. lbs. (100 Nm) plus 270°.
27. Install intake and exhaust camshaft adjusters.
28. Install chain tensioner.
29. Tighten guide rail to crankcase to 15 ft. lbs. (20 Nm).
30. Tighten guide rail to cylinder head to 10 ft. lbs. (14 Nm).

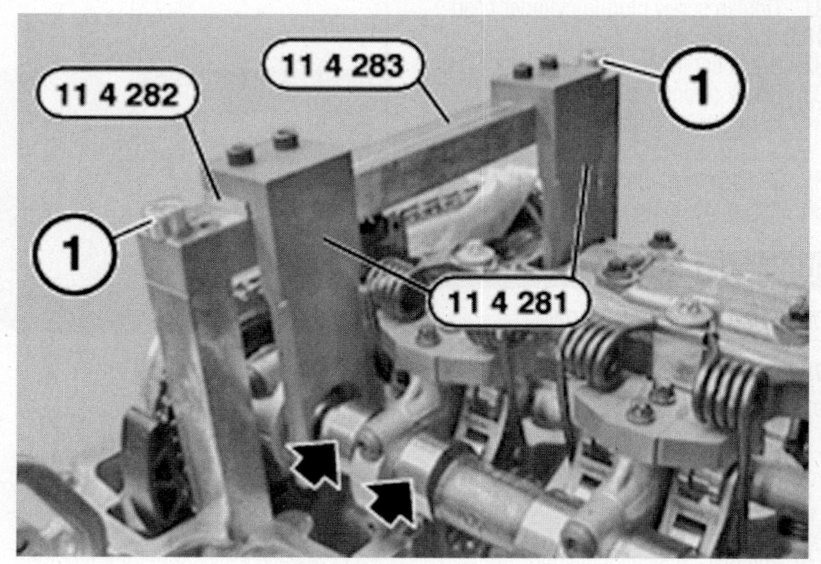

Fig. 191 Install special tool 11 4 280 to release the central bolts on the intake and exhaust camshaft adjusters

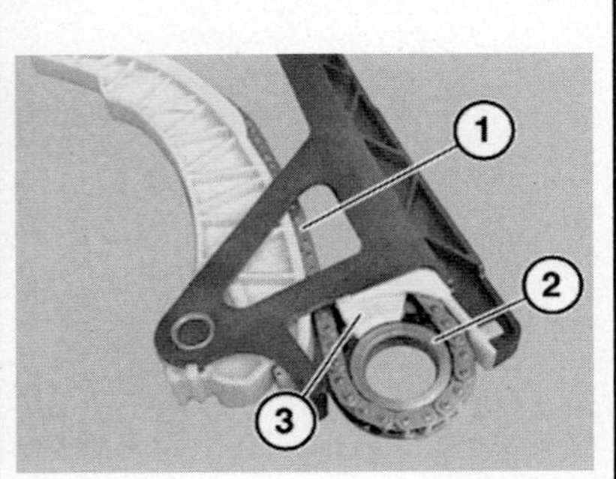

Fig. 194 Pull timing chain (1) upwards until camshaft sprocket (2) engages chain guide (3)

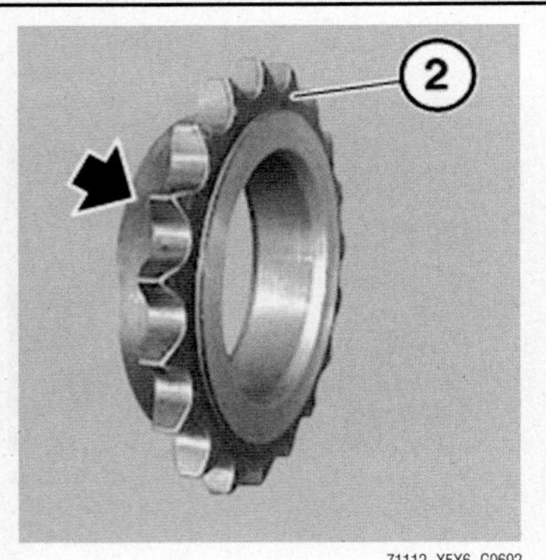

Fig. 195 Collar (see arrow) on sprocket (2) points to engine

31. Tighten screw plug in cylinder head to 18 ft. lbs. (25 Nm).
32. Crank engine twice.
33. Check timing.
34. If necessary, adjust valve timing.
35. Replace front crankshaft seal.
36. Assemble engine.

TURBOCHARGER

REMOVAL & INSTALLATION

3.0L Engine

See Figures 196 through 208.

1. Drain coolant.
2. Remove coolant thermostat.
3. Remove coolant pump.
4. Remove charge air cooler.
5. Remove catalytic converters
6. Unclip Bowden cable for engine compartment lid actuator from transverse reinforcement.

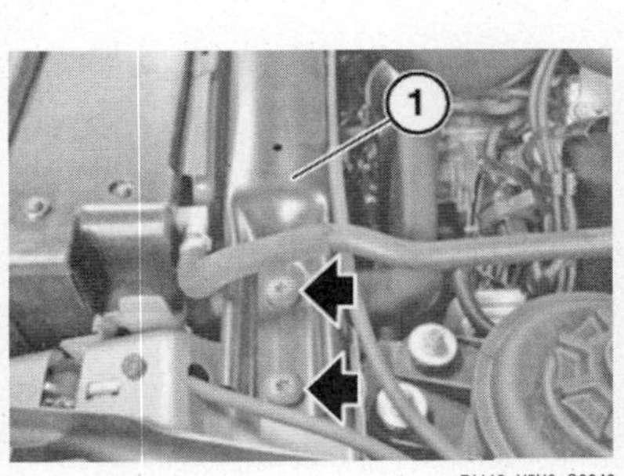

Fig. 196 Unclip Bowden cable for engine compartment lid actuator from transverse reinforcement (1)

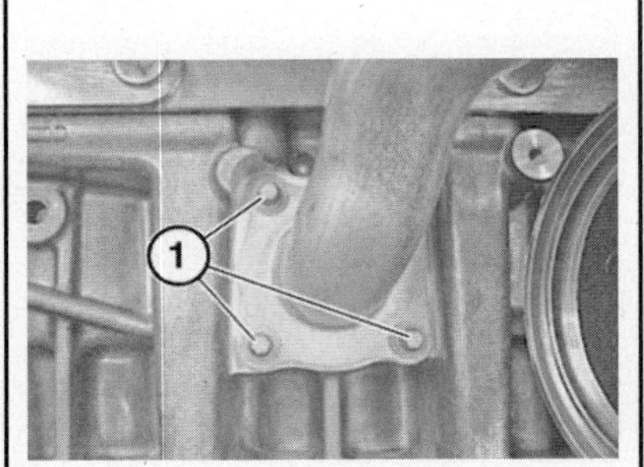
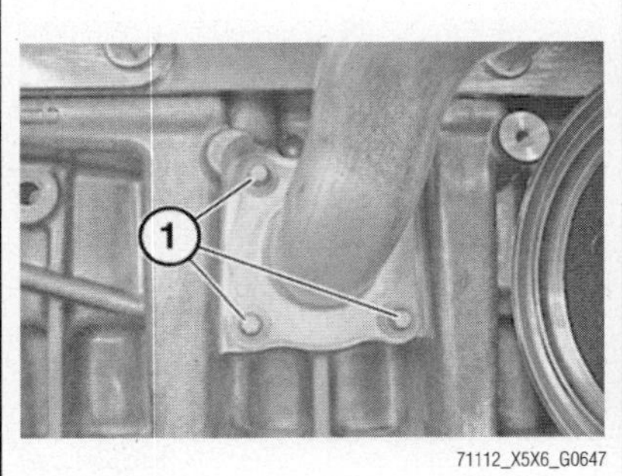

Fig. 197 Release screws (1)

Fig. 198 Release screw (1), loosen coolant return line (3) and coolant flow line (2)

7. Detach air conditioning line from bracket.
8. Release screws on left and right sides.

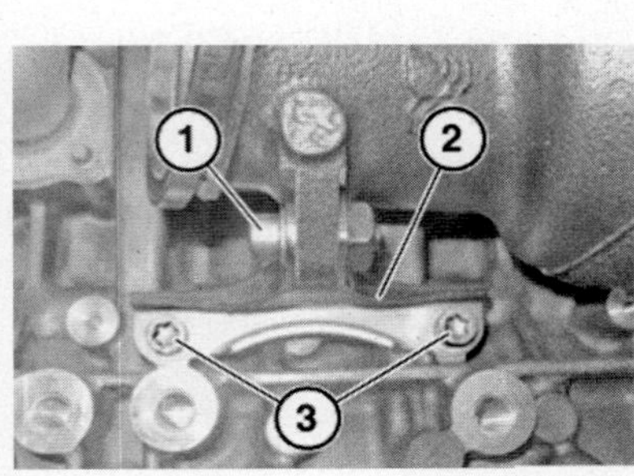

Fig. 199 Release screw (1), loosen screws (3) but do not remove

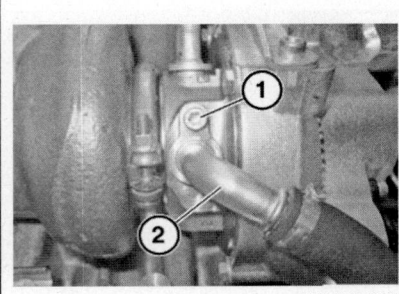

Fig. 200 Release screw (1), loosen connection of oil return lines (2)

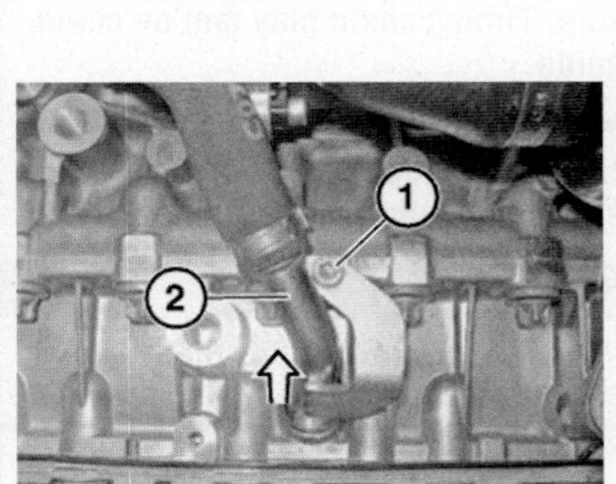

Fig. 201 Release screw (1), loosen connection of oil return lines (2)

9. Remove transverse reinforcement.
10. Release screws.
11. Release screw.
12. If necessary, use appropriate tool to

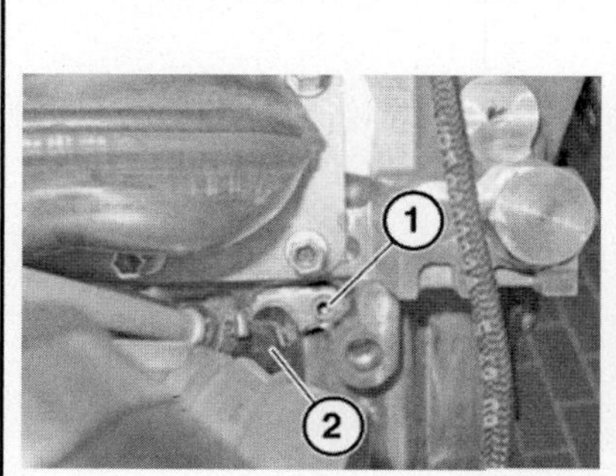

71112_X5X6_G0652

Fig. 202 Release screw (1), loosen coolant return lines (2) at connection point

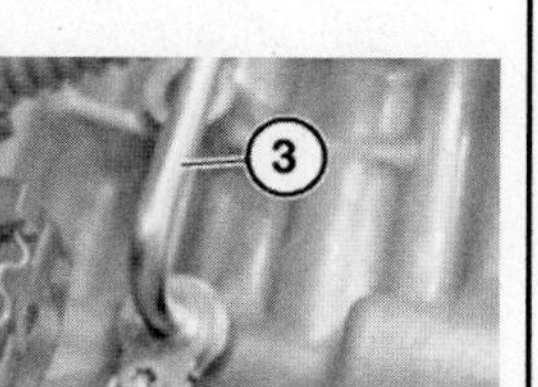

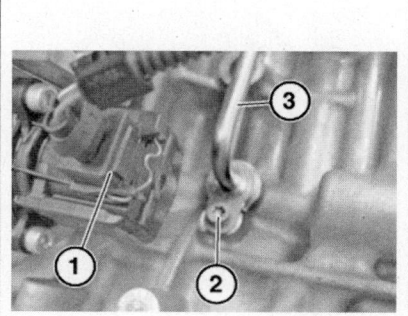

71112_X5X6_G0653

Fig. 203 Loosen plug connection (1) at blow-off valve, Release screw (2), loosen oil feeder lines at point of connection (3)

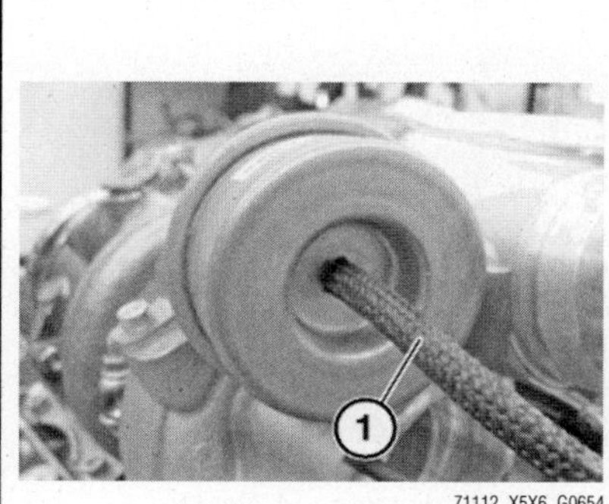

71112_X5X6_G0654

Fig. 204 Disconnect vacuum line (1) from vacuum unit

loosen coolant return line and coolant flow line at connection point.

13. Release screw.
14. Loosen screws but do not remove.

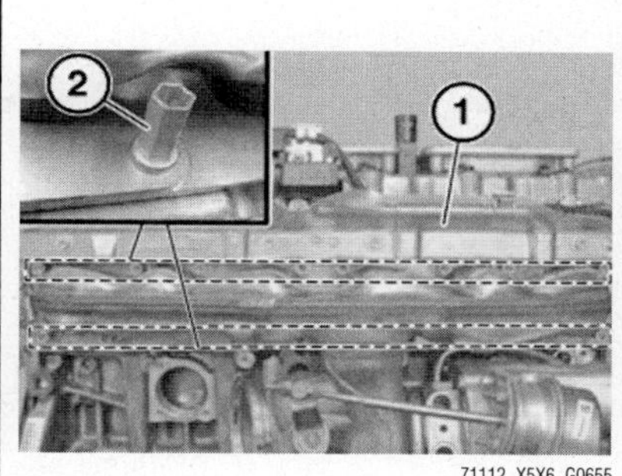

71112_X5X6_G0655

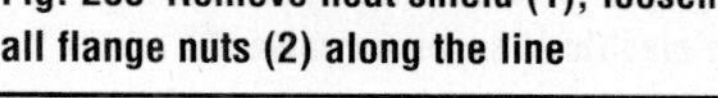

Fig. 205 Remove heat shield (1), loosen all flange nuts (2) along the line

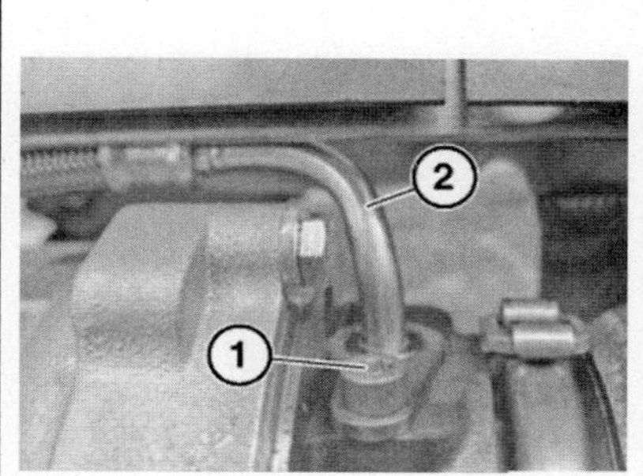

71112_X5X6_G0656

Fig. 206 Release screw (1), loosen oil feeder lines at point of connection (2)

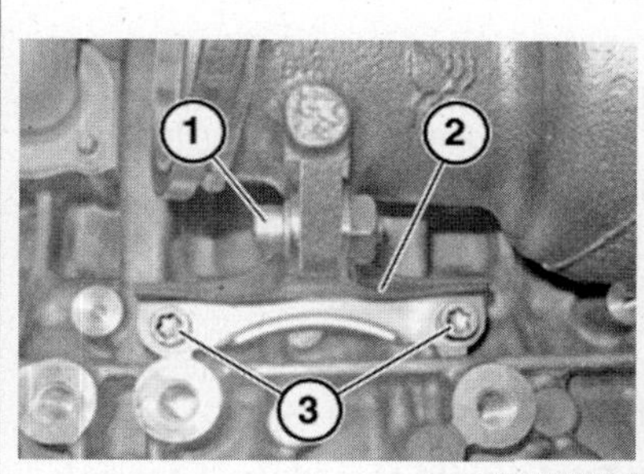

71112_X5X6_G0649

Fig. 208 Install turbocharger holder (2) to cylinder crankcase screw (3) and holder to turbocharger bolts (1)

15. Release screw.
16. If necessary, use appropriate tool to loosen connection of oil return lines.
17. Release screw.
18. If necessary, use appropriate tool to loosen connection of oil return lines.

➡Possibility of oil escaping when oil return line is disconnected.

19. Release screw (1).
20. If necessary, use appropriate tool to loosen coolant return lines (2) at connection point.
21. Loosen plug connection at blow-off valve.
22. Release screw.
23. If necessary, use appropriate tool to loosen oil feeder lines at point of connection.

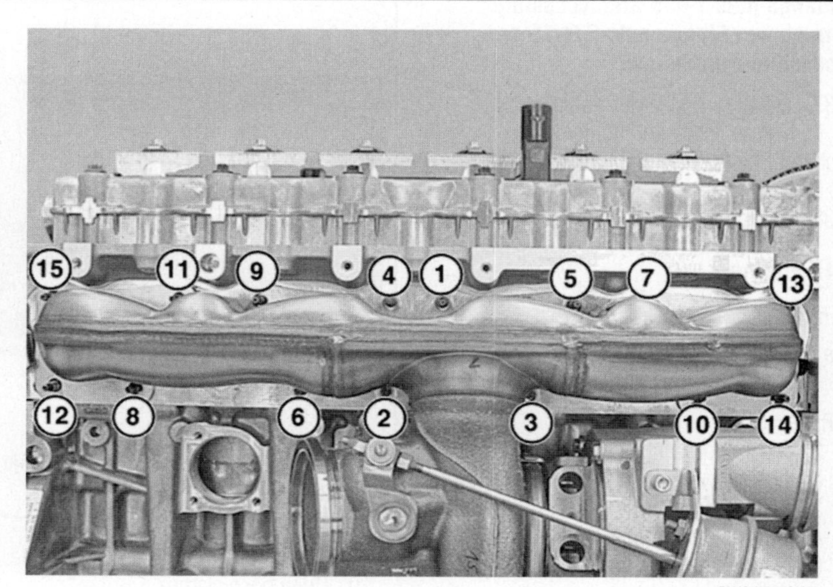

71112_X5X6_G0657

Fig. 207 Flange nut tightening sequence

➡**Possibility of oil escaping when oil return line is disconnected.**

24. Disconnect vacuum line from vacuum unit.
25. Disconnect vacuum line from cylinder head cover.
26. Remove heat shield.
27. Loosen all flange nuts along the line.
28. Remove module by maneuvering downwards on gearbox side.

➡**Total weight of module is approximately 15 kg.**

➡**Oil supply line can only be replaced after removal of the turbocharger.**

29. Release screw.
30. If necessary, use appropriate tool to loosen oil feeder lines at point of connection.

To install:

31. Replace all sealing rings.
32. Replace all graphite seals.
33. Position turbocharger on cylinder head and hold in place with two bolts.
34. Insert bolt but do not tighten at this point.

➡**The module consists of exhaust turbocharger and exhaust manifold and must be installed stress-free. Torque and tightening sequence must be observed without fail.**

35. Tighten all flange nuts in sequence 1 to 15 to 6 ft. lbs. (8 Nm).
36. Tighten all flange nuts to a torque of 10 ft. lbs. (13 Nm) in sequence (1 to 15).

➡**Flange nuts 1 to 5 are accessible from above. Flange nuts 6 to 15 are accessible from below.**

37. Install turbocharger holder to cylinder crankcase screw and holder to turbocharger bolts. Tighten bolts to 15 ft. lbs. (20 Nm).
38. Assemble engine.

4.4L Engine

Left Side

See Figures 209 through 218.

1. Remove catalytic converter, cylinders 5–8.
2. Disconnect plug connection on electric changeover valve.
3. Release screw.
4. Unfasten banjo bolt.
5. Lay oil line from turbocharger to side.
6. Release screw.
7. Release banjo bolt.

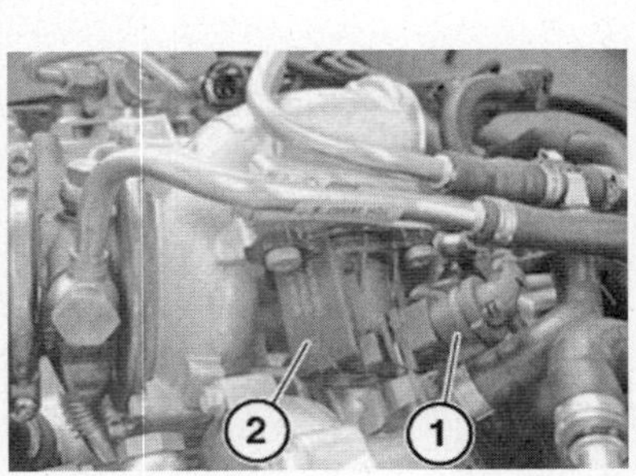

Fig. 209 Disconnect plug connection (1) on electric changeover valve (2)

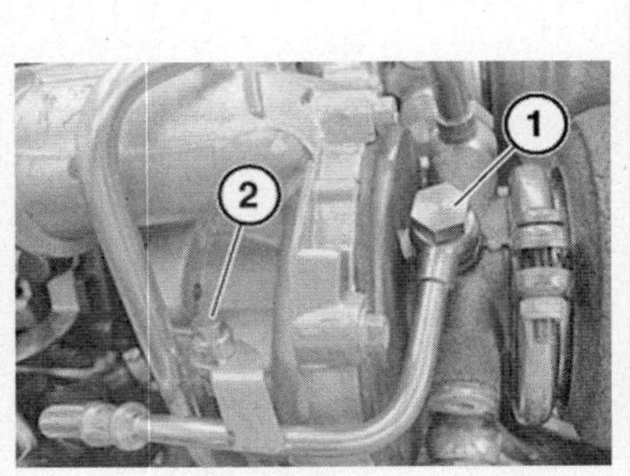

Fig. 210 Release screw (1), unfasten banjo bolt (2)

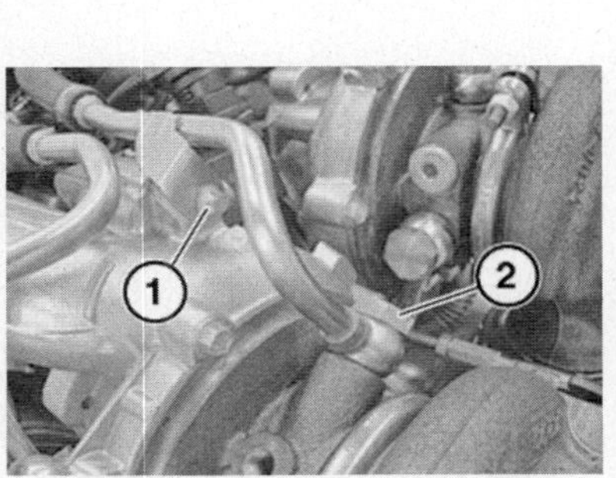

Fig. 211 Release screw (1), release banjo bolt (2)

8. Lay coolant return line to one side.
9. Open hose clamp.
10. Detach coolant feed line.
11. Release screw with a suitable tool.

Fig. 212 Open hose clamp (1), detach coolant feed line (2)

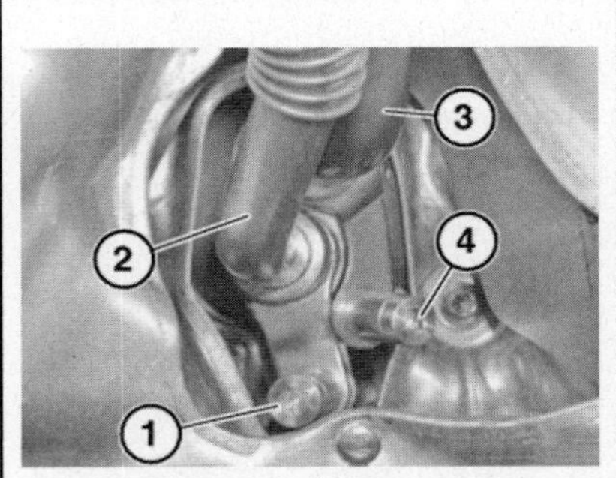

Fig. 213 Release screw with a suitable tool

Fig. 214 Release screw, open V-band clamp

➡**Oil return pipe can only be removed with turbocharger.**

12. Release screw.
13. Open V-band clamp.

⁂ WARNING

Do not mechanically deform oil return line.

14. Remove turbocharger with oil return line in upward direction.
15. Release screw.
16. Move coolant feed line.
17. Release screws.
18. Remove oil return pipe.

⁂ WARNING

A deformed oil return pipe can result in leaks. Risk of fire if oil line is leaking. The thermal linear compensators on the oil return pipe (1) must not be mechanically deformed.

To install:

19. Moisten oil return pipe at end with engine oil.

➡The O-rings can easily fall into the oil duct.

20. Replace O-rings on oil return cover.

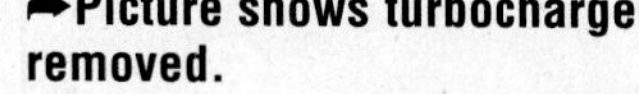

➡Picture shows turbocharger removed.

21. Replace gasket on exhaust manifold.
22. Check locating apparatus on exhaust manifold.
23. Position turbocharger with oil return line on exhaust manifold.
24. Position V-band clamp.
25. Insert screw.

➡The ends of the V-band clamp must rest parallel to each other. Screw connection of V-band clamp is too loose: If you can see a gap between the ends of the V-band clamps, release and then repeat the screw connection.

➡Screw connection of V-band clamp is too tight: If the ends of the V-band clamp are positioned under each other, release and then repeat the screw connection.

⁂ WARNING

Risk of mixing up vacuum hoses. Vacuum hose for cylinders 5–8:

- Old version: black / blue
- New version: black/yellow

26. Assemble engine.
27. Check vacuum connections.

Right Side

See Figures 219 through 228.

1. Remove catalytic converter for cylinders 1–4.
2. Disconnect plug connection on electric changeover valve.
3. Release screw.
4. Unfasten banjo bolt.
5. Lay oil line from turbocharger to side.
6. Release screw.
7. Unfasten banjo bolt.
8. Lay coolant return line to one side.
9. Open hose clamp.

71112_X5X6_G0664

Fig. 215 Release screw (1), Move coolant feed line (2)

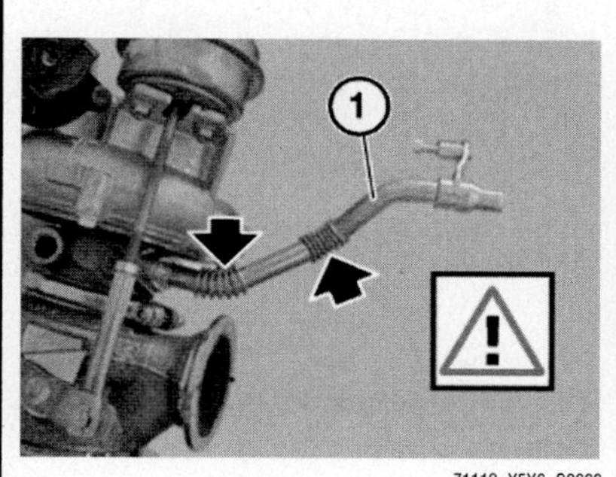

71112_X5X6_G0666

Fig. 217 The thermal linear compensators (see arrows) on the oil return pipe (1) must not be mechanically deformed

71112_X5X6_G0668

Fig. 219 Disconnect plug connection (1) on electric changeover valve (2)

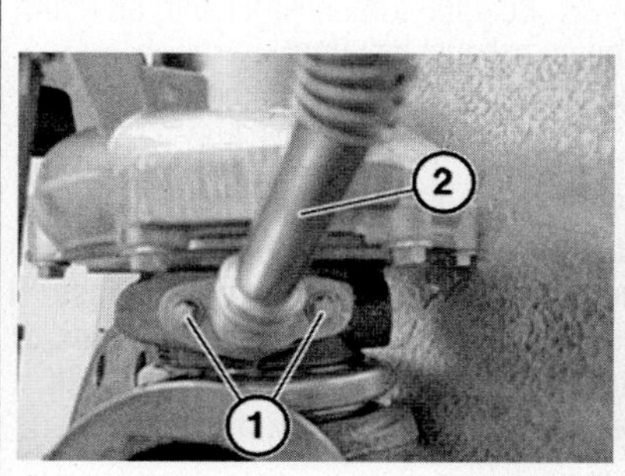

71112_X5X6_G0665

Fig. 216 Release screws (1), remove oil return pipe (2)

71112_X5X6_G0667

Fig. 218 Vacuum hose (1) for cylinders 5–8

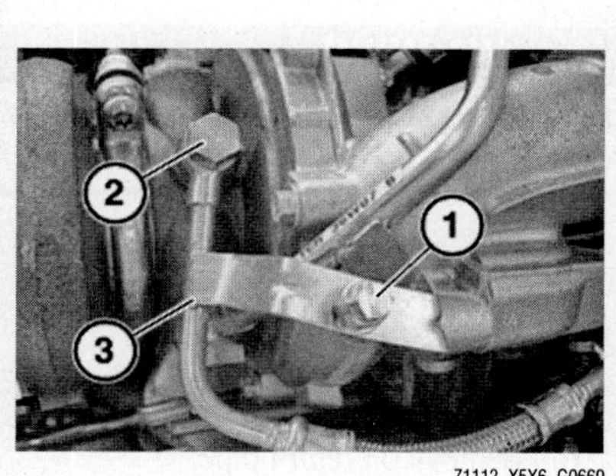

71112_X5X6_G0669

Fig. 220 Release screw (1), unfasten banjo bolt (2), lay oil line (3) from turbocharger to side

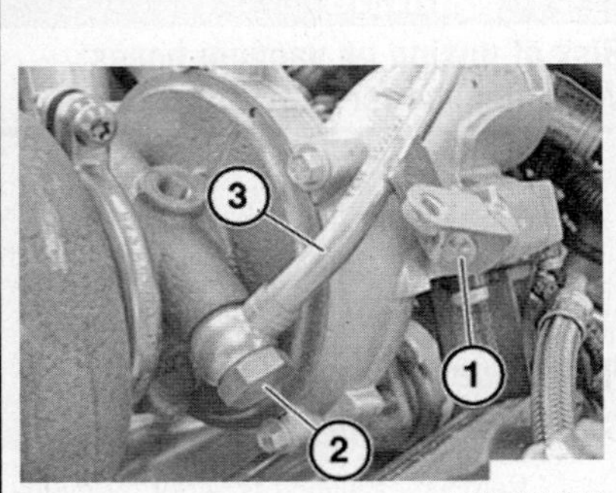

Fig. 221 Release screw (1), unfasten banjo bolt (2), lay coolant return line (3) to one side

Fig. 222 Open hose clamp (1), detach coolant feed line (2)

10. Detach coolant feed line.
11. Release screw with a suitable tool.

➡**Oil return pipe can only be removed with turbocharger.**

12. Release screw.
13. Open V-band clamp.

WARNING

Do not mechanically deform oil return line.

14. Remove turbocharger with oil return line in upward direction.
15. Release screw.
16. Move coolant feed line.
17. Release screws.
18. Remove oil return pipe.

WARNING

A deformed oil return pipe can result in leaks. Risk of fire if oil line is leaking. The thermal linear compensators on the oil return pipe must not be mechanically deformed.

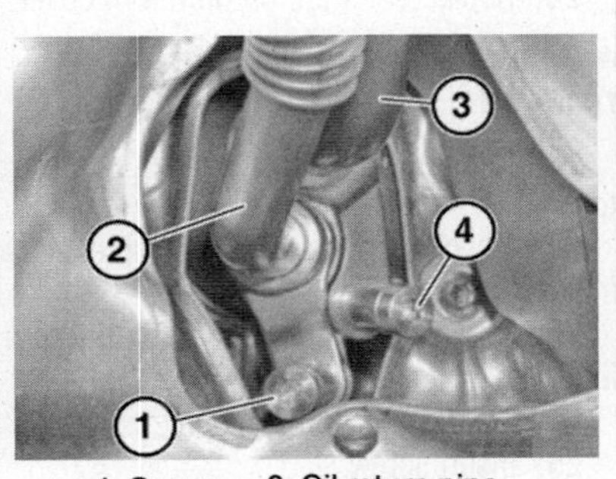

Fig. 223 Release screw with a suitable tool

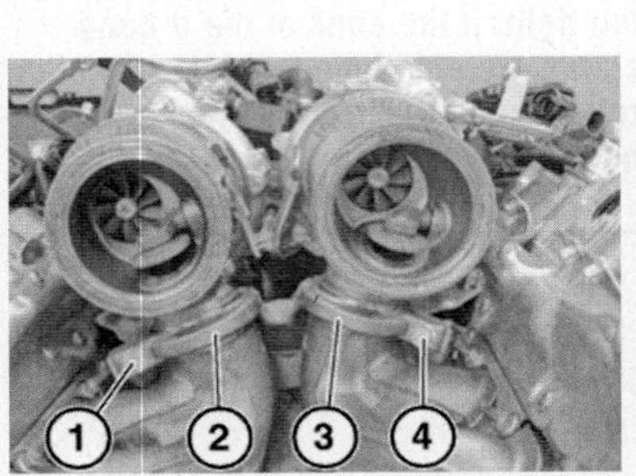

Fig. 224 Release screw, open V-band clamp

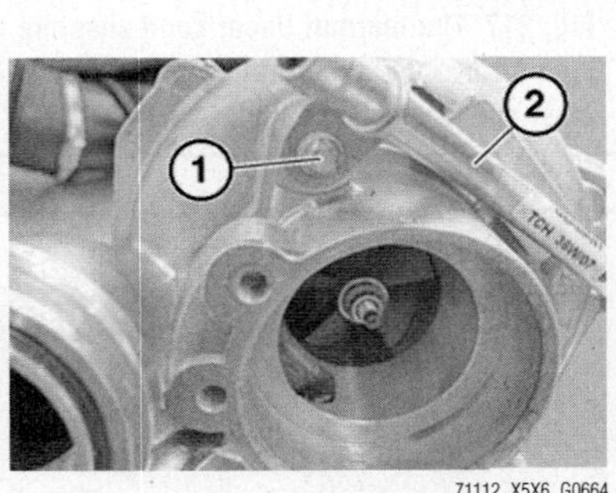

Fig. 225 Release screw (1), Move coolant feed line (2)

To install:

19. Moisten oil return pipe at end with engine oil.

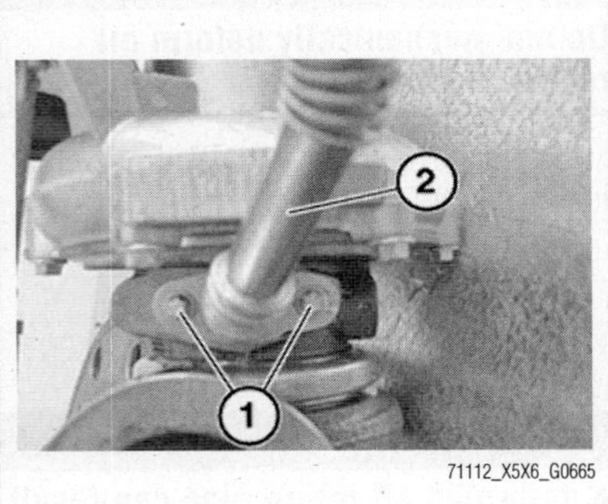

Fig. 226 Release screws (1), remove oil return pipe (2)

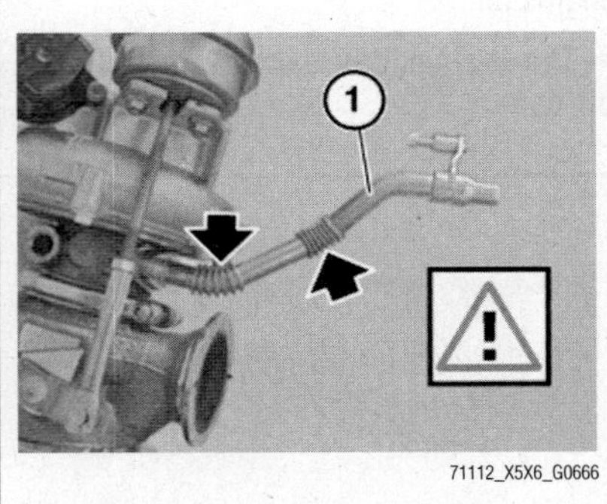

Fig. 227 The thermal linear compensators (see arrows) on the oil return pipe (1) must not be mechanically deformed

➡**The O-rings can easily fall into the oil duct.**

20. Replace O-rings on oil return cover.
21. Replace gasket on exhaust manifold.
22. Check locating apparatus on exhaust manifold.
23. Position turbocharger with oil return line on exhaust manifold.
24. Position V-band clamp.
25. Insert bolt.

➡**The ends of the V-band clamp must rest parallel to each other. Screw connection of V-band clamp is too loose: If you can see a gap between the ends of the V-band clamps, release and then repeat the screw connection.**

➡**Screw connection of V-band clamp is too tight: If the ends of the V-band clamp are positioned under each other, release and then repeat the screw connection.**

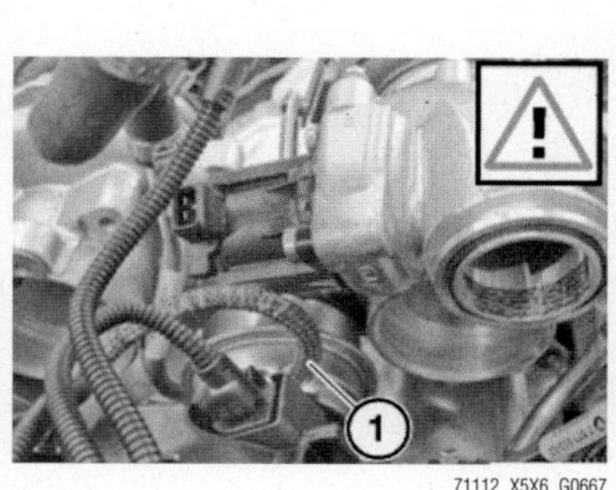

Fig. 228 Vacuum hose (1) for cylinders 1–4

⁂ WARNING

Risk of mixing up vacuum hoses.

26. Vacuum hose (1) black/red for cylinders 1–4.
27. Assemble engine.
28. Check vacuum connections.

VALVE COVERS

REMOVAL & INSTALLATION

3.0L Engine

See Figures 229 through 231.

1. Remove right trailing link.
2. Release engine wire harness in the area of the cylinder head cover.
3. Disconnect pressure lines.
4. Remove clean air pipe.
5. Release screws.
6. Remove flange.
7. Press and hold down the unlocking device on the vacuum line (1) on the vacuum reservoir (cylinder head cover).
8. Detach vacuum line in upward direction.

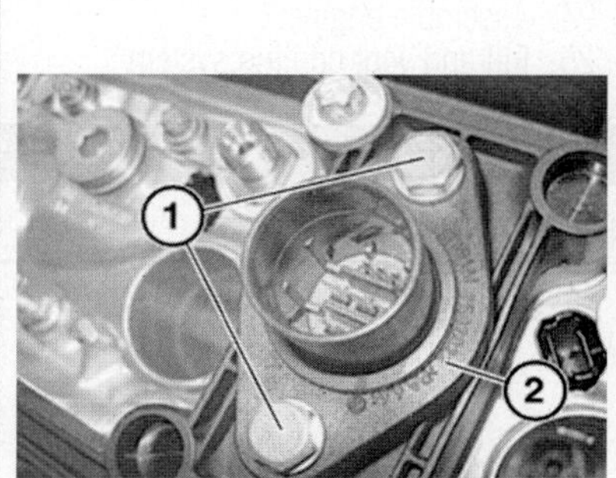

Fig. 229 Release screws (1), remove flange (2)

Fig. 230 Press and hold down the unlocking device on the vacuum line (1) on the vacuum reservoir (cylinder head cover) in the direction of the arrow

➡Do not loosen the engine vent line on the cylinder head cover. To dismantle the engine vent line, loosen the screws on the air intake system.

➡When changing a faulty engine vent line, the clutch on the coupling on the cylinder head cover may be broken open.

9. Release screws of cylinder head cover in sequence (24 to 1) in ½ turns.
10. Remove cylinder head cover.

To install:

11. Installation is the reverse order of removal.
12. Replace all gaskets.
13. Fit cylinder head cover.
14. Insert screws of the cylinder head cover.
15. Tighten fit screws to 6 ft. lbs. (8.5 Nm).
16. Tighten positional screw to 6 ft. lbs. (8.5 Nm).
17. Tighten remaining screws of cylinder head cover in sequence 3 to 24 by ½ turns. Tightening torque: 6 ft. lbs. (8.5 Nm).

4.4L Engine

Left Side

See Figures 232 and 233.

1. Remove acoustic cover.
2. Disconnect negative battery terminal.
3. Remove left charge air cooler.
4. Remove intake filter housing.
5. Remove expansion tank.
6. Remove coolant valve for heater feed line.
7. Disconnect fuel feed line.
8. Detach wiring harness for injectors and lay to one side.
9. Remove ignition coils, cylinders 5–8.
10. Remove injectors, cylinders 5–8.

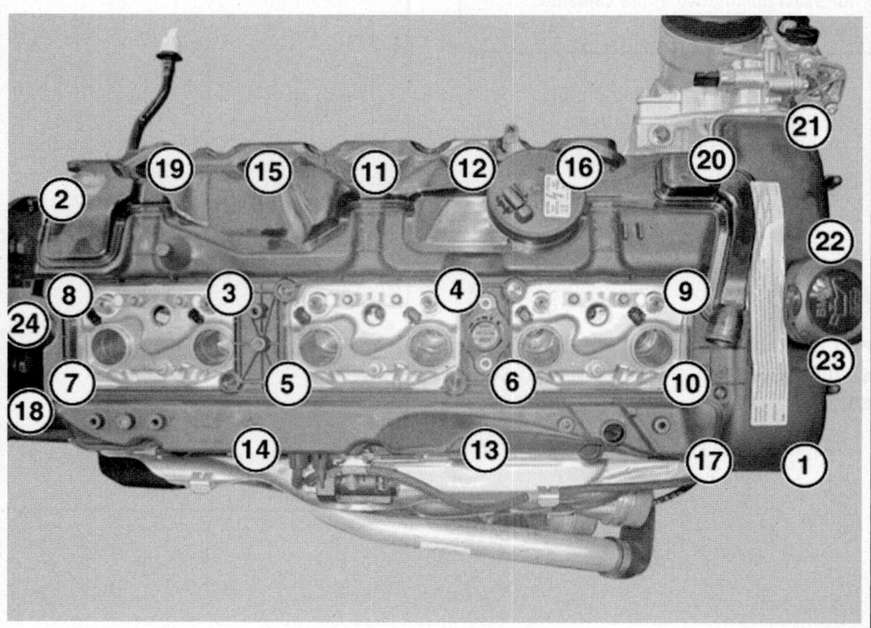

Fig. 231 Tighten fit screws (1), and positional screw (2), then tighten remaining screws of cylinder head cover in sequence (3 to 24) by ½ turns

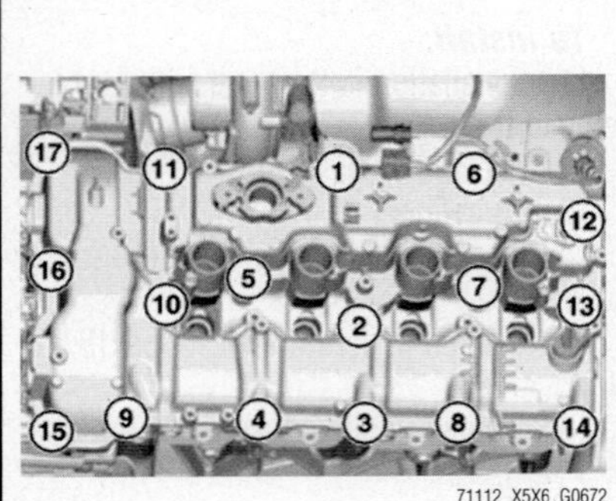

71112_X5X6_G0672

Fig. 232 Release bolts in sequence (17 to 1)

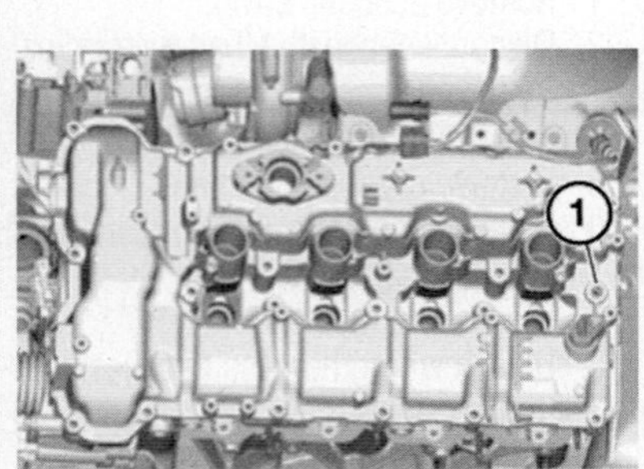

71112_X5X6_G0673

Fig. 233 It is important to join screw(1) for exact positioning of the camshaft sensors

11. Remove high-pressure pump.
12. Release bolts in sequence (17 to 1).
13. Remove cylinder head cover.

To install:

14. Installation is the reverse order of removal.
15. Clean sealing surface with special tool 11 4 470 .

➡It is important to join screw for exact positioning of the camshaft sensors.

16. Fit cylinder head cover.
17. Position screw.
18. Release screw by 90°.
19. Secure cylinder head cover in sequence (1 to 17) in two work steps.
20. Assemble engine.

Right Side

See Figures 234 through 236.

1. Remove acoustic cover.
2. Disconnect negative battery terminal.
3. Release battery positive terminal.
4. Drain coolant.
5. Remove right intercooler.
6. Remove intake filter housing.
7. Disconnect fuel delivery line
8. Detach wiring harness for injectors and lay to one side.
9. Remove ignition coils, cylinders 1–4.
10. Remove injectors, cylinders 1–4
11. Remove high pressure pump.
12. Release screws.
13. Remove oil filler neck.
14. Release bolts in sequence (17 to 1).
15. Remove cylinder head cover.

To install:

16. Installation is the reverse order of removal.
17. Clean sealing surface with special tool 11 4 470 .
18. Replace gaskets.
19. Renew profile seal of cylinder head cover.

➡It is important to join screw for exact positioning of the camshaft sensors.

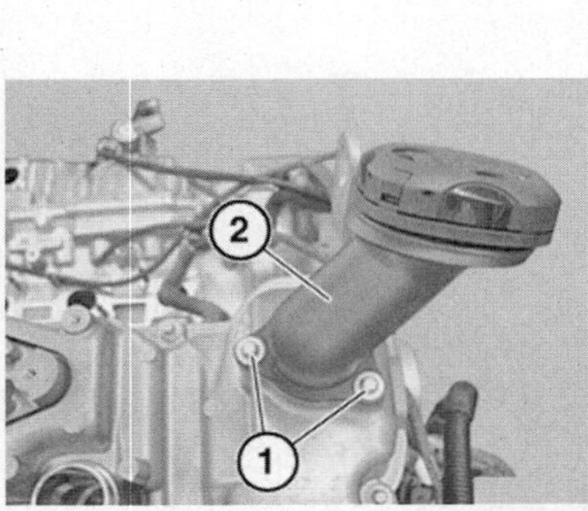

71112_X5X6_G0674

Fig. 234 Release screws (1), remove oil filler neck (2)

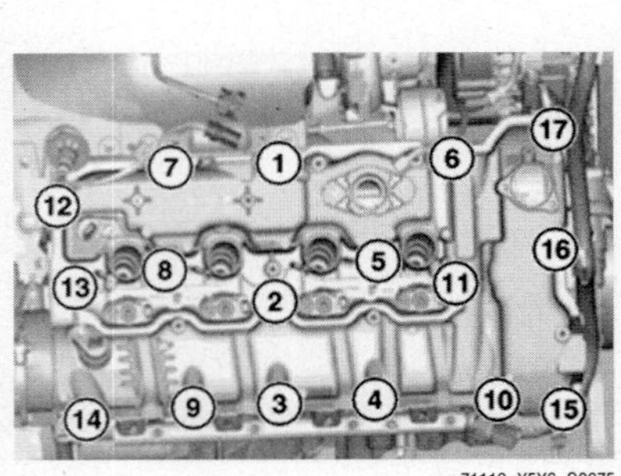

71112_X5X6_G0675

Fig. 235 Release bolts in sequence (17 to 1)

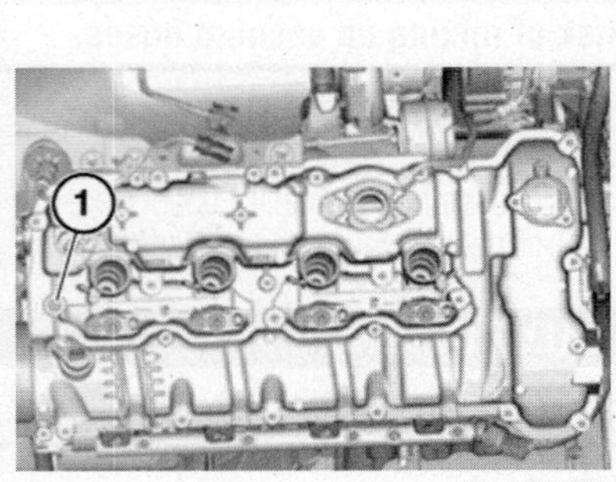

71112_X5X6_G0676

Fig. 236 It is important to join screw (1) for exact positioning of the camshaft sensors

20. Fit cylinder head cover.
21. Position screw.
22. Release screw by 90°.
23. Secure cylinder head cover in sequence (1 to 17) in two work steps.
24. Assemble engine.
25. Fill and vent cooling system

VALVE LASH

ADJUSTMENT

Engines use hydraulic valve lifters.

ENGINE PERFORMANCE & EMISSION CONTROLS

CAMSHAFT POSITION (CMP) SENSOR

REMOVAL & INSTALLATION

1. Read out fault memory of DME control unit; if necessary, work through test schedules.
2. Switch ignition **OFF**.
3. Remove acoustic cover.
4. Remove left ignition coil cover.
5. Remove plug connector and pull off.
6. Remove screw.
7. Remove pulse generator.

To install:

8. Installation is the reverse of removal.
9. Replace sealing ring and coat with anti-seize agent.
10. Check for stored fault messages, rectify faults and clear the fault memory.

CRANKSHAFT POSITION (CKP) SENSOR

REMOVAL & INSTALLATION

1. Read out fault memory of DME control unit; if necessary, work through test schedules.
2. Switch ignition **OFF**.
3. If necessary, remove underbody protection.
4. Unlock plug and remove.
5. Remove screw.
6. Withdraw pulse generator from transmission housing.

To install:

7. Replace sealing ring.
8. Install pulse generator to transmission housing.
9. Replace screw.
10. Check for stored fault messages, rectify faults and clear the fault memory.

HEATED OXYGEN SENSOR (HO2S)

REMOVAL & INSTALLATION

3.0L Engine

See Figures 237 through 239.

1. Remove rear ignition coil cover.
2. Remove microfilter housing.
3. Lever out expanding rivet.
4. Remove gasket.
5. Unfasten screws.
6. Feed out partition wall and remove.
7. Disconnect plug connection on oxygen control sensor.

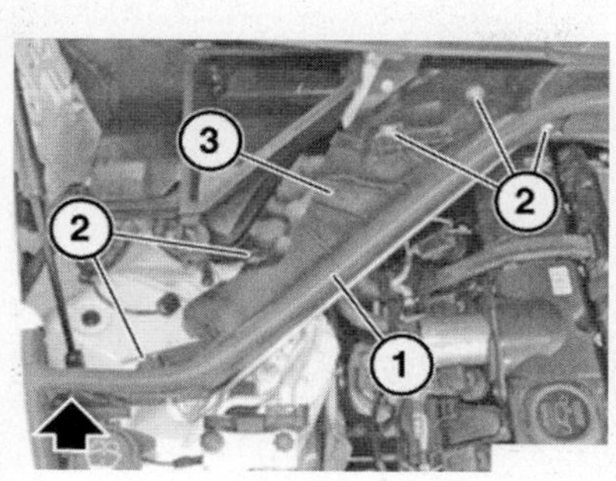

Fig. 237 Remove gasket (1), unfasten screws (2), feed out partition wall (3) and remove

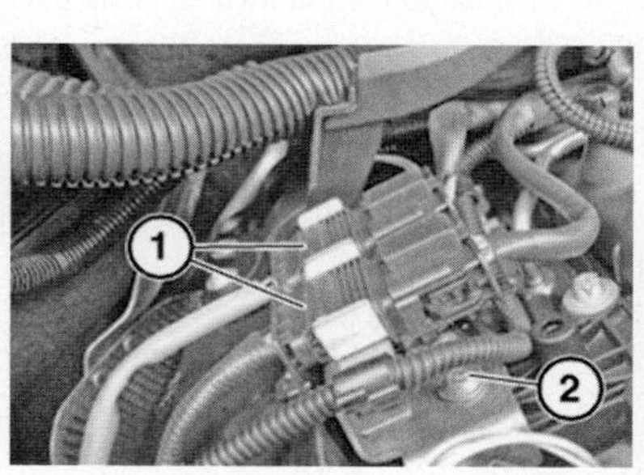

Fig. 238 Disconnect plug connection on oxygen control sensor (1); screw (2)

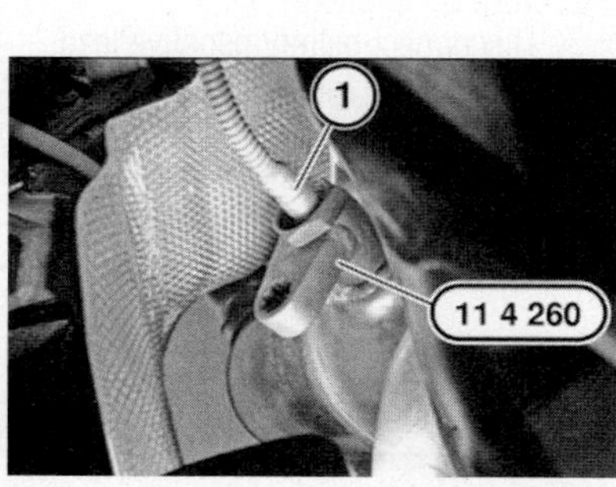

Fig. 239 Release oxygen sensor (1) from above with special tool 11 4 260

8. Release oxygen sensor from above with special tool 11 4 260.

To install:

9. Installation is the reverse order of removal.
   a. Cable color of oxygen control sensor is black.
   b. Cable color of oxygen monitoring sensor is grey.
10. Tightening torque 37 ft. lbs. (50 Nm).
11. Reassemble the vehicle.
12. Check function of DME.

4.4L Engine

Left Side

See Figures 240 and 241.

1. Check function of DME control unit
2. Switch off ignition
3. Remove air filter housing
4. Release retaining clip.
5. Remove heat shield wire ring over oxygen sensor.
6. Detach oxygen sensor cable from retaining clips.
7. Release monitoring sensor (1) with special tool 11 7 020.

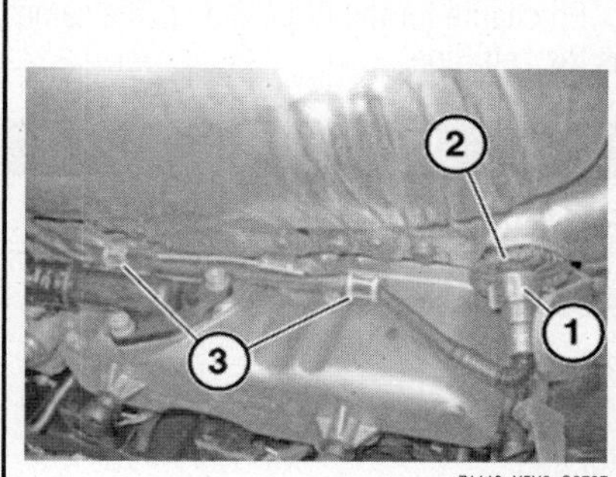

Fig. 240 Release retaining clip (1), remove heat shield wire ring (2) over oxygen sensor, detach oxygen sensor cable from retaining clips (3)

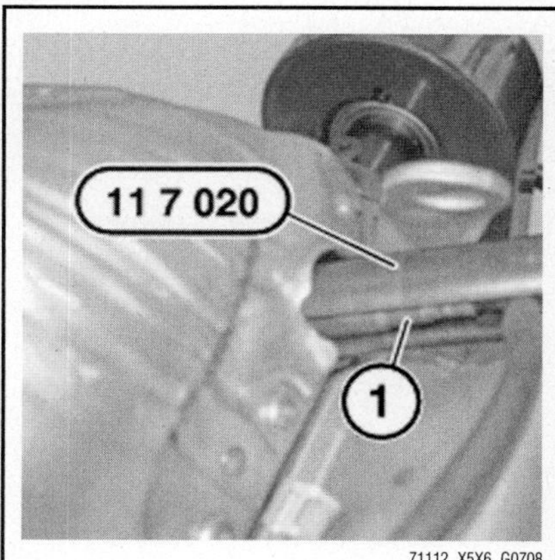

Fig. 241 Release monitoring sensor (1) with special tool 11 7 020

To install:

8. Installation is the reverse order of removal.
    - The threads of new lambda control/monitoring sensors are already coated with Never Seez Compound.
    - If a lambda control/monitoring sensor is to be reused, apply a thin and even coating of Never Seez Compound to the thread only.
    - The part of the lambda control/monitoring sensor which projects into the exhaust branch (sensor ceramics) must not be cleaned and not coated with lubricant.
9. Fasten monitoring sensor (1) with special tool 11 7 020.
10. Tightening torque 37 ft. lbs. (50 Nm).
11. Check function of DME control unit.
12. Pay attention to cable routing of monitor sensor.

Right Side

Procedure for the Right Side is the same as the Left Side.

KNOCK SENSOR (KS)

REMOVAL & INSTALLATION

3.0L Engine

See Figures 242 and 243.

1. Read out fault memory of DME control unit.
2. Switch off ignition.
3. Remove intake plenum.
4. Unlock connector and remove.
5. Feed out connector behind feed line, remove feed line if necessary.
6. Release screws on both knock sensors and remove knock sensors.

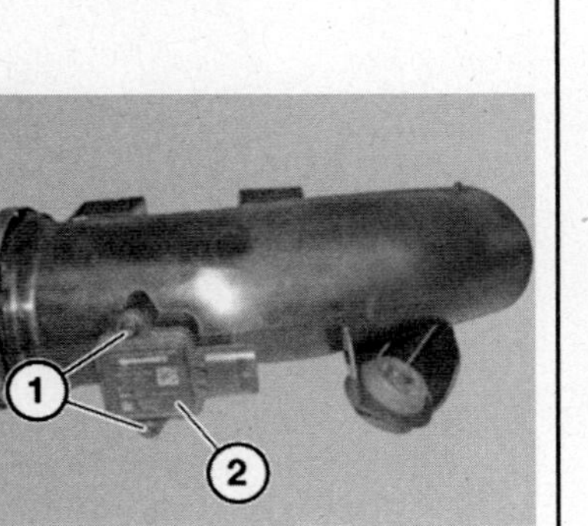

Fig. 242 Unlock connector (1) and remove

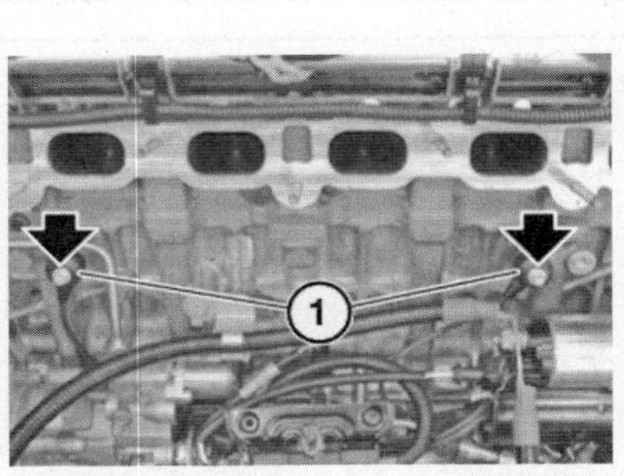

Fig. 249 Release screws on both knock sensors (1) and remove knock sensors

To install:

7. Installation is the reverse order of removal.
8. Clean contact surface of knock sensors on engine block.
9. Replace aluminum screws.
10. Knock sensor tightening torque 16 ft. lbs. (21 Nm).
11. Reassemble the vehicle.
12. Check stored fault message.
13. Delete fault memory.

4.4L Engine

Left Side

See Figure 250.

1. Read out fault memory of DME control unit.
2. Turn off ignition.
3. Disconnect battery negative lead.
4. Remove left intake manifold.
5. Unlock and disconnect plugs on both knock sensors.

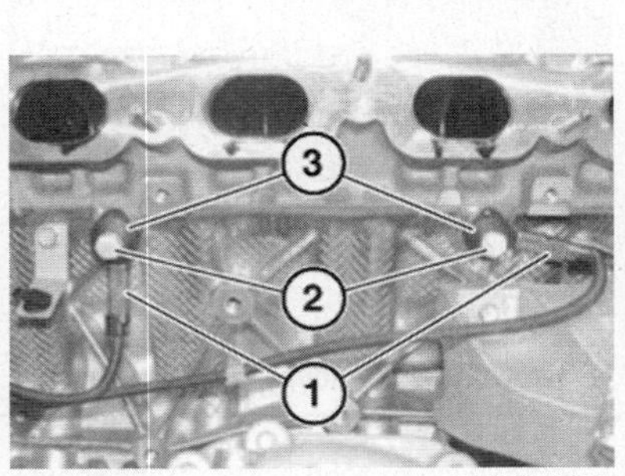

Fig. 244 Unlock and disconnect plugs (1) on both knock sensors, Release screws on both knock sensors (2), Remove knock sensors (3)

6. Release screws on both knock sensors.
7. Remove knock sensors.

To install:

8. Installation is the reverse order of removal.
9. Clean support face of knock sensors on engine block.
10. Tightening torque 16 ft. lbs. (21 Nm).
11. Check stored fault message.
12. Delete fault memory.

Right Side

Procedure for the Right Side is the same as the Left Side.

MASS AIR FLOW (MAF) SENSOR

REMOVAL & INSTALLATION

3.0L Engine

See Figures 245 and 246.

1. Read out fault memory of DME control unit.

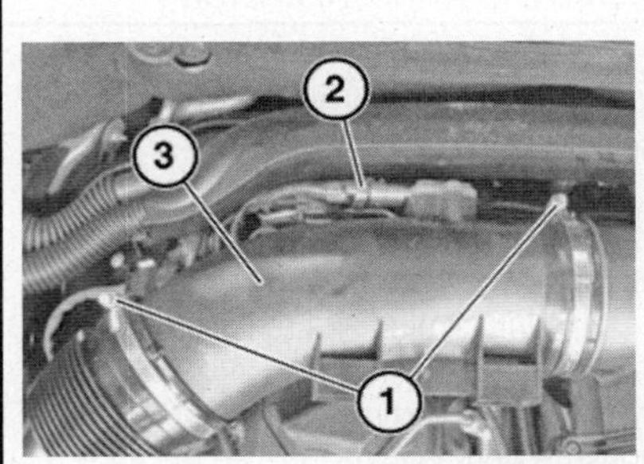

Fig. 245 Release clamps (1), unlock connector (2), disconnect clean air pipe (3)

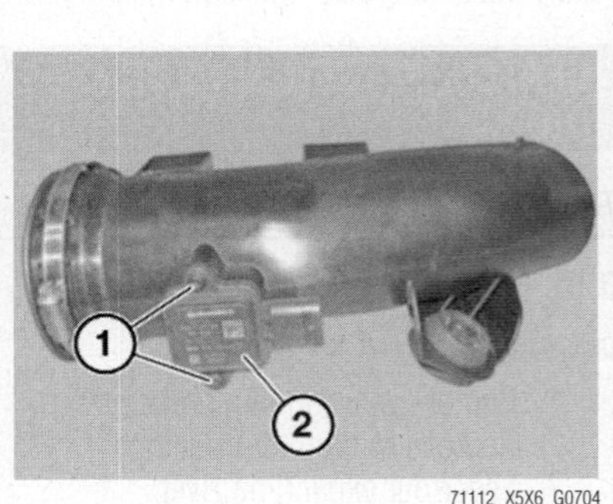

Fig. 246 Release screws (1), pull hot film air mass meter (2)

2. Switch off ignition.
3. Remove ignition coil cover.
4. Release clamps.
5. Unlock connector on hot film air mass meter and disconnect.
6. Disconnect clean air pipe from rubber mount at top and remove.
7. Release screws.
8. Pull hot film air mass meter out of upper section of intake silencer housing.

To install:

9. Installation is the reverse order of removal.
10. Check stored fault message.
11. Delete fault memory.

4.4L Engine

See Figure 247.

Fig. 247 Unlock plug (1), release screws (2), pull air-mass flow sensor (3)

1. Read out fault memory of DME control unit
2. Switch off ignition
3. Remove acoustic cover

➡Picture shows the left side, the procedure for the right side is identical.

4. Unlock plug and remove.
5. Release screws.
6. Pull air-mass flow sensor out of upper section of intake filter housing.

To install:

7. Installation is the reverse order of removal.
8. Replace gasket on air-mass flow sensor.
9. Check stored fault message.
10. Now clear the fault memory.

FUEL — GASOLINE FUEL INJECTION SYSTEM

FUEL SYSTEM SERVICE PRECAUTIONS

Safety is the most important factor when performing not only fuel system maintenance but any type of maintenance. Failure to conduct maintenance and repairs in a safe manner may result in serious personal injury or death. Maintenance and testing of the vehicle's fuel system components can be accomplished safely and effectively by adhering to the following rules and guidelines.

- To avoid the possibility of fire and personal injury, always disconnect the negative battery cable unless the repair or test procedure requires that battery voltage be applied.
- Always relieve the fuel system pressure prior to disconnecting any fuel system component (injector, fuel rail, pressure regulator, etc.), fitting or fuel line connection. Exercise extreme caution whenever relieving fuel system pressure to avoid exposing skin, face and eyes to fuel spray. Please be advised that fuel under pressure may penetrate the skin or any part of the body that it contacts.
- Always place a shop towel or cloth around the fitting or connection prior to loosening to absorb any excess fuel due to spillage. Ensure that all fuel spillage (should it occur) is quickly removed from engine surfaces. Ensure that all fuel soaked cloths or towels are deposited into a suitable waste container.
- Always keep a dry chemical (Class B) fire extinguisher near the work area.
- Do not allow fuel spray or fuel vapors to come into contact with a spark or open flame.
- Always use a back-up wrench when loosening and tightening fuel line connection fittings. This will prevent unnecessary stress and torsion to fuel line piping.
- Always replace worn fuel fitting O-rings with new Do not substitute fuel hose or equivalent where fuel pipe is installed.

Before servicing the vehicle, make sure to also refer to the precautions in the beginning of this section as well.

RELIEVING FUEL SYSTEM PRESSURE

WARNING

The manufacturer does not provide a specific pressure relieving procedure, but instructs that any fuel system disconnect will spill fuel, so be prepared to catch and clean up any spilled fuel.

A safe way to relieve the pressure in the system is to locate the fuel pump relay located on the cowl. Unplug and remove the relay, and place it in a safe location. With the fuel pump relay removed, start the engine and operate it until it stalls. Crank the engine for 10 seconds after it stalls to remove any residual pressure.

FUEL FILTER

REMOVAL & INSTALLATION

See Figure 248.

1. Remove side left underbody paneling.
2. Remove tank under ride protection on left.

CAUTION

Fuel in fuel lines is under pressure. Fuel escapes when fuel lines are disconnected.

3. Catch and dispose of escaping fuel.
4. Release single-ear clip and detach pressure reference line.
5. Detach fuel feed lines.
6. Detach fuel return line.
7. Release screws and remove bracket.
8. Remove fuel filter.

To install:

9. Installation is the reverse order of removal.
10. Replace single-ear clip.
11. After completing tasks, check fuel system for leaks.

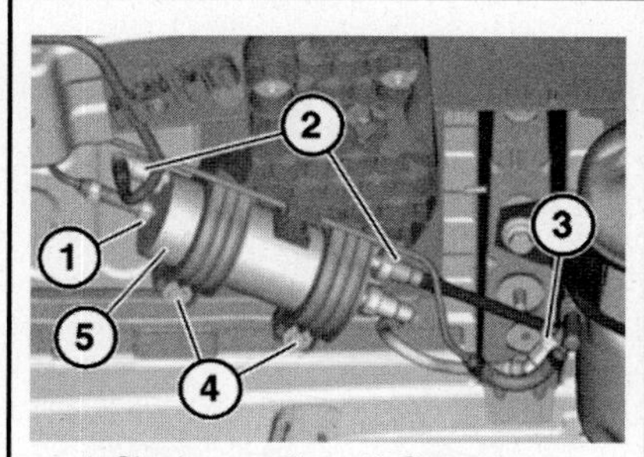

Fig. 248 Release single-ear clip and detach pressure reference line

FUEL INJECTORS

REMOVAL & INSTALLATION

3.0L Engine

➡There are two different injector versions and hold-down device versions for the 3.0L engine. A mixed installation of the components (hold-down device, spark plug shafts, injectors, cylinder heads and screws) between the two hold-down device versions is not possible/permitted. Removal and installation of the various injectors are described separately according to the hold-down device version. The hold-down device version must be identified beforehand in order to select the correct repair instructions.

Bottom Hold-Down Device Version

See Figures 249 through 259.

1. Remove acoustic cover.
2. The bottom hold-down device version can be found on the electromagnetic compatibility panel installed above the injectors.
3. Removing and installing injector up to engine number 02167648.
4. Disconnect negative battery terminal.
5. Remove ignition coil of corresponding cylinder.
6. Disconnect pressure lines of corresponding cylinder.

➡The following description applies to all injectors cylinder 1–6.

7. Loosen nut.
8. Remove ground cable.
9. Unlock connector from injectors and detach.
10. Release screw plug and remove.
11. Release screws.
12. Remove clamping plate and counter support bridge.

➡Clamping plate is a disposable part and must be replaced following removal.

13. Remove EMC plate.
14. Release screw.
15. Feed out hold-down device and remove.
16. Lift injectors out of cylinder head and remove.

➡If several injectors are removed, ensure that each injector is reinstalled in its original location (cylinder). Mark injectors.

➡Procedure in event of stuck injector:

17. Use special tool 13 0 270 to remove injectors that are stuck.
18. Lightly oil pull-out thread and unscrew completely before using the special tool.

➡Pull-out thread is a left-hand thread.

1. Screws 2. Clamping plate 3. Counter support bridge 4. EMC plate

71112_X5X6_G0713

Fig. 249 Release screws

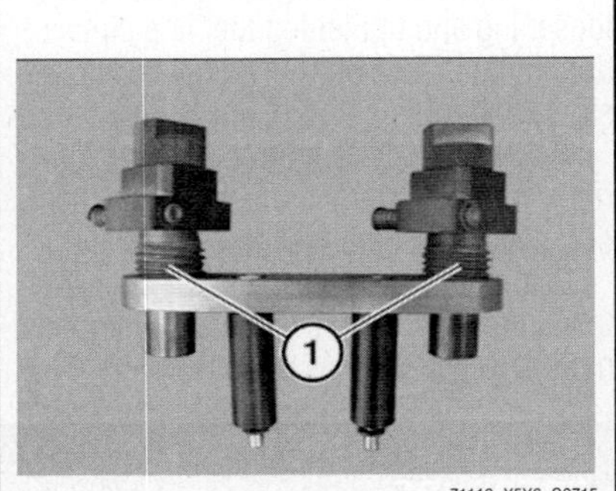

71112_X5X6_G0715

Fig. 251 Lightly oil pull-out thread (1) and unscrew completely before using the special tool

1. Torque wrench 2. Special tool 00 9 170 3. Square head 4. Retaining pin

71112_X5X6_G0717

Fig. 253 Fit torque wrench and special tool 00 9 170 on square head of special tool 13 0 270

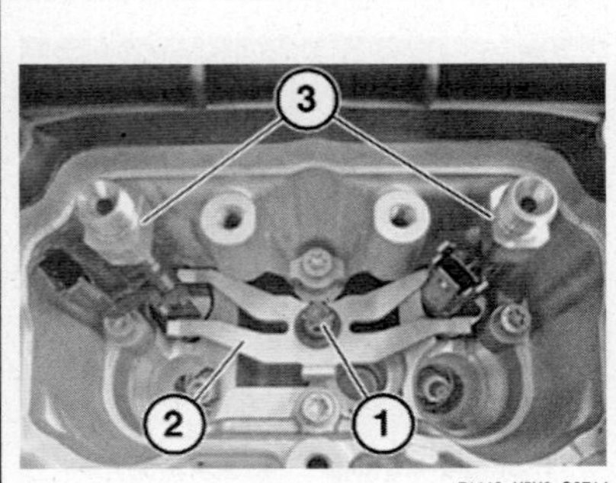

71112_X5X6_G0714

Fig. 250 Release screw (1), feed out hold-down device (2), lift injectors (3) out of cylinder head

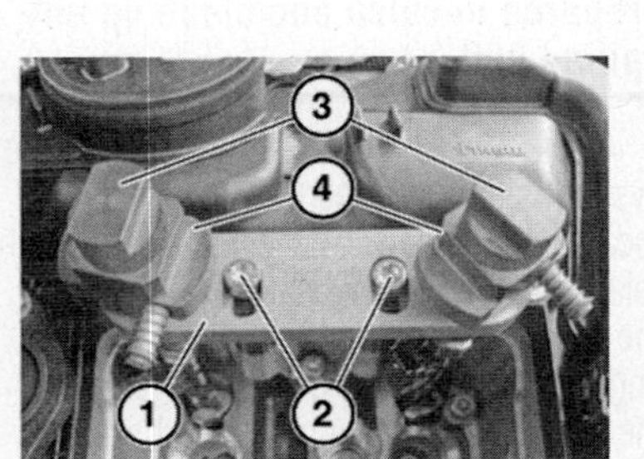

1. Special tool 13 0 270 2. Screws 3. Threaded sleeves 4. Pull-out thread

71112_X5X6_G0716

Fig. 252 Fit special tool 13 0 270 on injector slot

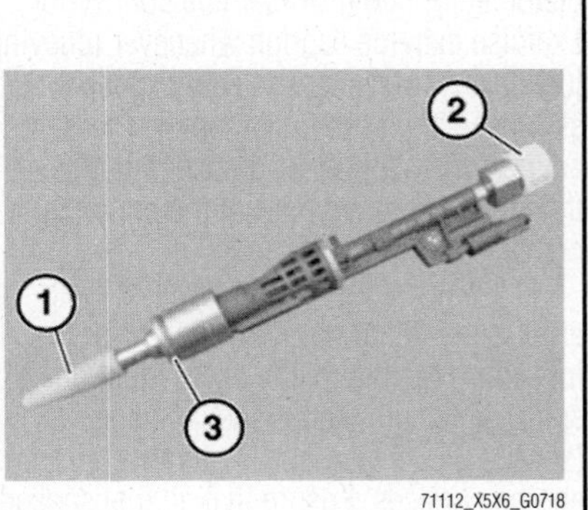

71112_X5X6_G0718

Fig. 254 After removing, fit protective caps (1 and 2) to injector tip and fuel line connection; decoupling element (3)

19. Fit special tool 13 0 270 on injector slot.

a. Join screws to injector slot by a few threads.

b. Screw in pull-out thread until it is possible to screw the threaded sleeves onto the injectors.

c. Screw threaded sleeves onto injectors and tighten down.

d. Tighten down screws.

➡Set torque wrench to 44 inch lbs. (5 Nm) clockwise rotation. Together with special tool 13 0 270 this corresponds to a tensile force of max. 450 lbs. (2000 N). The injector must be replaced if the torque wrench is activated when the injector is pulled out.

20. Fit torque wrench and special tool 00 9 170 on square head of special tool 13 0 270.

21. Turn torque wrench in clockwise direction until the injector is pulled out.

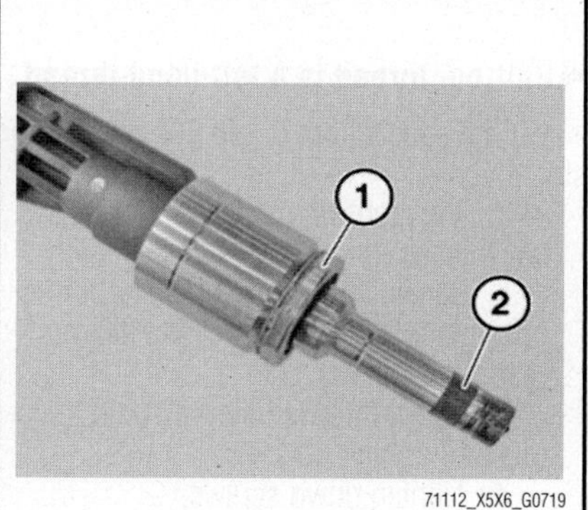

Fig. 255 When reusing fuel injector: Replace decoupling element (1), replace PTFE sealing ring (2)

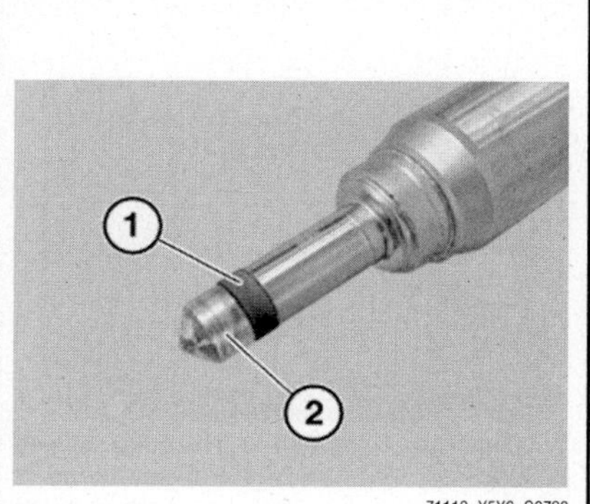

Fig. 256 PTFE seal (1), injector tip (2)

22. Make sure that retaining pin does not touch the cylinder head cover; if necessary, press the retaining pin back.

23. After removing, fit protective caps to injector tip and fuel line connection.

24. When installing a new injector: Replace decoupling element.

25. When reusing fuel injector: Replace decoupling element.

26. Replace PTFE sealing ring.

➡A PTFE sealing ring which has been installed in the cylinder head must be renewed before the injector is reinstalled.

➡Renew the PTFE sealing ring:

27. Before replacing PTFE seal, make sure hands and work surface are clean and free of oil.

28. Avoid mechanical contact with injector tip.

29. Remove PTFE sealing ring with special tool (3) 13 0 191 from injector.

30. Use a fluff-free cloth only to remove combustion residues from cylindrical part of injector tip (do not use ultrasound or other tools/agents).

31. Do not clean injector tip.

32. Slide new PTFE sealing ring onto mounting taper 13 0 283.

33. Mount PTFE sealing ring with mounting taper 13 0 283 onto injector tip.

➡Do not use fingernails to slide PTFE sealing ring on. Do not use any lubricating agents. The sealing ring is expanded when slid on.

34. Using special tool 13 0 281 push PTFE sealing ring into injector groove.

35. To bring the widened PTFE sealing ring to installation size, push special tool 13 0 282 as far as it will go onto injector.

➡Pull mounting tip) of special tool 13 0 282 towards rear to release mounting taper 13 0 281.

➡Installation of injector is described separately from removal.

➡Before installing injector in engines that have been run:

WARNING

Injectors must not be twisted to 53 inch lbs. (6 Nm). The injector must be replaced if this value is exceeded.

36. Check injector bore for dirt. Clean only dirty injector bores.

37. Clean injector bore: To do so, preferably slide injector without decoupling element but with new PTFE sealing ring in and out of injector bores several times. The PTFE sealing ring must then be replaced.

38. Clean contact surfaces of decoupling elements in cylinder head.

39. Replace decoupling element.

➡Injection Quantity Compensation

➡An injector quantity compensation must be carried out if an injector is replaced or changed on the cylinder side.

Injector quantity compensation is carried out with the aid of an adjustment value.

The adjustment value is printed with three digits, depending on the version, on the injector body.

The adjustment value must be read off before installation. Enter the adjustment value according to the installation location (cylinder) of the injector.

If injector quantity compensation is not carried out, the engine may run roughly or fail to start.

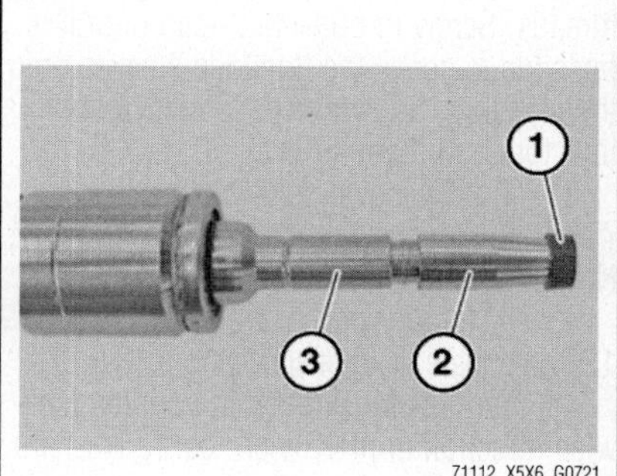

Fig. 257 Mount PTFE sealing ring (1) with mounting taper (2) 13 0 283 onto injector tip (3)

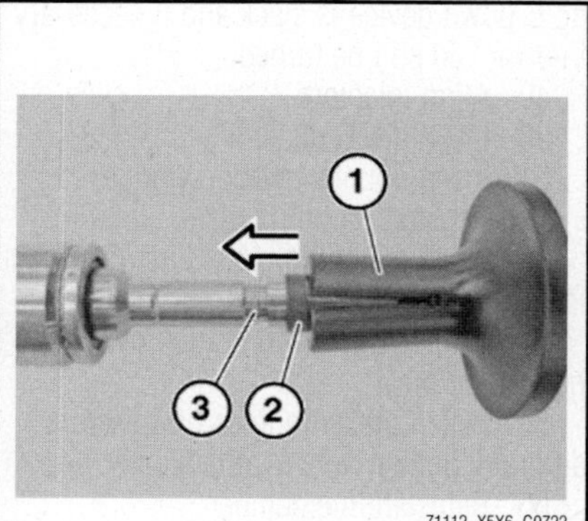

Fig. 258 Using special tool (1) 13 0 281 push PTFE sealing ring (2) into injector groove (3)

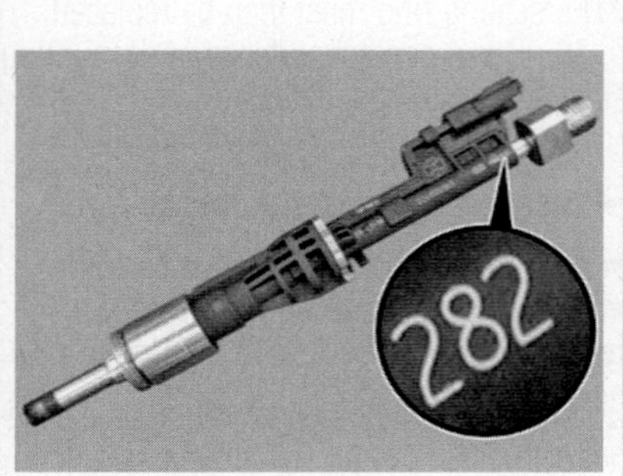

71112_X5X6_G0723

Fig. 259 The adjustment value is printed with three digits—depending on the version—on the injector body

➡Injection quantity compensation is described at the end of these instructions.

To install:

40. Fit special tool 13 0 270 on injector slot. Join screws to injector slot by a few threads. Screw in pull-out thread until it is possible to screw the threaded sleeves onto the injectors. Screw threaded sleeves onto injectors and tighten down.
41. Tighten down screws.
42. Set torque wrench to 18 inch lbs. (2 Nm) counterclockwise rotation.
43. Fit torque wrench and special tool 00 9 170 on square head of special tool 13 0 270.
44. Turn torque wrench in counterclockwise direction until 18 inch lbs. (2 Nm) are reached.
45. Make sure that retaining pin does not touch the cylinder head cover; if necessary, press the retaining pin back.
46. Install injectors.
47. Install hold-down device.
48. Tighten screw hand-tight only so that hold-down device is slack and if necessary injector can still be turned.
49. Align injectors.
50. Install EMC plate.
51. Insert counter support bridge.
52. Replace clamping plate.
53. Insert clamping plate. Ensure correct installation position.
54. Insert screws and tighten down hand-tight only.
55. Install pressure lines on injectors and rail. Tighten nuts manually only.
56. Reinstall line damper.
57. Tighten down hold-down screw through EMC plate. Tightening torque 10 ft. lbs. (13 Nm).
58. Tighten down screws of EMC plate uniformly.
59. Tighten down screw plug on EMC plate. Tightening torque 18 ft. lbs. (25 Nm).
60. Tighten down pressure lines on injectors. Tightening torque 17 ft. lbs. (23 Nm).
61. Then tighten down pressure lines on the rail. Tightening torque 17 ft. lbs. (23 Nm).
62. Reinstall line damper.

➡Perform an injection quantity compensation:

The adjustment value is printed with three digits—depending on the version—on the injector body.

63. Connect BMW diagnosis system.
64. Identify vehicle.
65. Select "Function selection."
66. Select "Service functions."
67. Select "Engine electronics."
68. Select "Adjustment functions."
69. Select "Adjust injectors."
70. Select "Test schedule"
71. For each replaced injector, the adjustment value must be entered according to the installation location (cylinder).
72. Clean spark plug slot.
73. Assemble engine.
74. Check fuel system for tightness.
75. Check function of DME.

Top Hold-Down Device Version

See Figures 260 through 265.

The top hold-down device version can be found on the hold-down device installed on top. Removing and installing injector from engine number 02167649.

1. Disconnect negative battery terminal (risk of fire due to short-circuiting on dismantling).
2. Remove ignition coil of corresponding cylinder.
3. Disconnect pressure lines of corresponding cylinder.

➡The following description applies to all injectors cylinder 1–6.

4. Unlock connector from injectors and detach.
5. Loosen nut.
6. Remove ground cable.
7. First, release screw #2, then release screw #1. Otherwise, the hold-down device may tilt.
8. Remove hold-down element.
9. Pull injectors upward out of cylinder head and remove.

➡If several injectors are removed, ensure that each injector is reinstalled in its original location (cylinder).

10. Mark injectors.

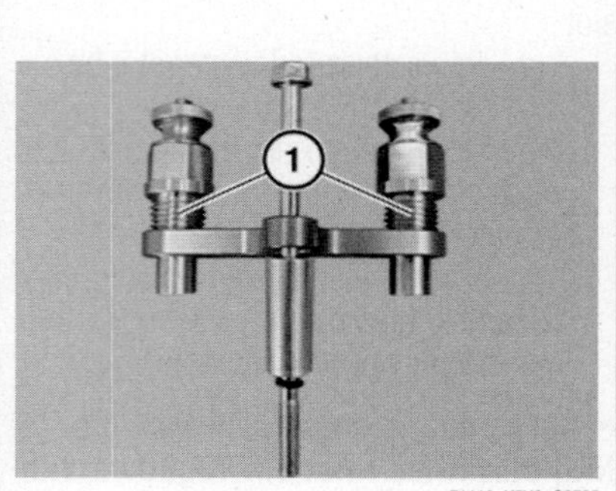

71112_X5X6_G0725

Fig. 260 Lightly oil pull-out thread (1) and unscrew completely before using the special tool

➡Procedure in event of stuck injector:

11. Use special tool 0 496 885 to remove injectors that are stuck.
12. Lightly oil pull-out thread and unscrew completely before using the special tool.

➡Pull-out thread is a left-hand thread.

13. Fit special tool 0 496 885 on injector slot.
    a. Join screws to injector slot by a few threads.
    b. Screw in pull-out thread until it is possible to screw the threaded sleeves onto the injectors.
    c. Screw threaded sleeves onto injectors and tighten down.
    d. Tighten down screws.

➡Set torque wrench to 44 inch lbs. (5 Nm) clockwise rotation. Together with special tool 0 496 885 this corresponds to a tensile force of max. 2000 N. The

1. Special tool 0 496 885 3. Threaded sleeves
2. Screws 4. Pull-out thread
71112_X5X6_G0726

Fig. 261 Fit special tool 0 496 885 on injector slot

Fig. 262 Fit torque wrench (1) and special tool (2) 00 9 170 on hexagon head (3) of special tool 0 496 885

injector must be replaced if the torque wrench clicks when the injector is pulled out

14. Fit torque wrench and special tool 00 9 170 on hexagon head of special tool 0 496 885.

15. Turn torque wrench in clockwise direction until the injector is pulled out.

16. After removing, fit protective caps (1 and 2) to injector tip and fuel line connection.

17. When installing a new injector: Replace decoupling element.

18. When reusing fuel injector: Replace decoupling element.

19. Replace PTFE sealing ring.

➡A PTFE sealing ring which has been installed in the cylinder head must be renewed before the injector is reinstalled.

➡Renew the PTFE sealing ring:

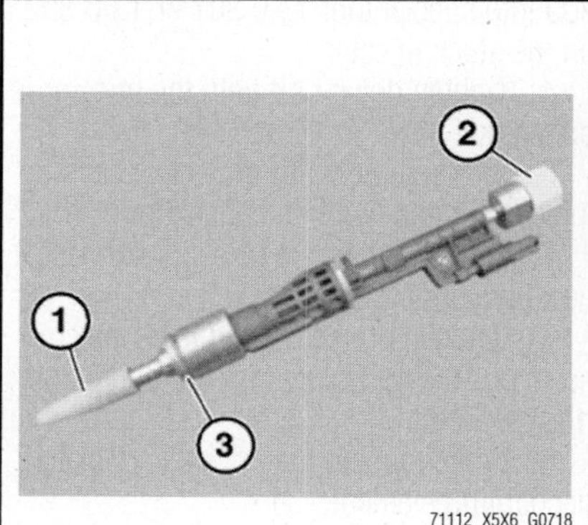

Fig. 263 After removing, fit protective caps (1 and 2) to injector tip and fuel line connection; decoupling element (3)

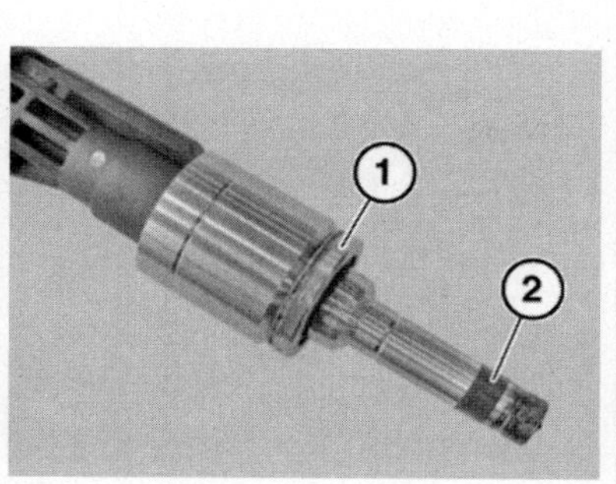

Fig. 264 When reusing fuel injector: Replace decoupling element (1), replace PTFE sealing ring (2)

20. Before replacing PTFE seal, make sure hands and work surface are clean and free of oil.

21. Avoid mechanical contact with injector tip.

22. Remove PTFE sealing ring with special tool 13 0 191 from injector.

23. Use a fluff-free cloth only to remove combustion residues from cylindrical part of injector tip (do not use ultrasound or other tools/agents).

24. Do not clean injector tip.

25. Slide new PTFE sealing ring onto mounting taper 13 0 283.

26. Mount PTFE sealing ring with mounting taper 13 0 283 onto injector tip.

➡Do not use fingernails to slide PTFE sealing ring on. Do not use any lubricating agents. The sealing ring is expanded when slid on.

27. Using special tool 13 0 281 push PTFE sealing ring into injector groove.

Fig. 265 The adjustment value is printed in three digits on the injector body

28. To bring the widened PTFE sealing ring to installation size, push special tool 13 0 282 as far as it will go onto injector.

➡Pull mounting tip of special tool 13 0 282 towards rear to release mounting taper 13 0 281.

To install:

➡Before installing injector in engines that have been run.

WARNING

Injectors must not be twisted to 53 inch lbs. (6 Nm). The injector must be replaced if this value is exceeded.

29. Check injector bore for dirt.

30. Clean only dirty injector bores.

31. Clean injector bore: To do so, preferably slide injector without decoupling element but with new PTFE sealing ring in and out of injector bores several times.

32. The PTFE sealing ring must then be replaced.

33. Clean contact surfaces of decoupling elements in cylinder head.

34. Replace decoupling element.

➡An injector quantity compensation must be carried out if an injector is replaced or changed on the cylinder side. Injector quantity compensation is carried out with the aid of a so-called adjustment value. The adjustment value is printed in three digits on the injector body. The adjustment value must be read off before installation.

35. Enter the adjustment value according to the installation location (cylinder) of the injector. If injector quantity compensation is not carried out, the engine may run roughly or fail to start. Injection quantity compensation is described at the end of these instructions.

36. Insert injectors in injector bores.

37. Fit special tool 0 496 885 on injector slot. Join screws to injector slot by a few threads. Screw in pull-out thread until it is possible to screw the threaded sleeves onto the injectors. Screw threaded sleeves onto injectors and tighten down.

38. Tighten down screws.

➡Set torque wrench to 18 inch lbs. (2 Nm) counterclockwise rotation.

39. Fit torque wrench and special tool 00 9 170 on hexagon head of special tool 0 496 885.

40. Turn torque wrench in counterclockwise direction until 18 inch lbs. (2 Nm) are reached.

41. Install hold-down device with curvatures downward.
42. Fit hold-down device on injectors.
43. Only hand-tighten screw. Screw the screw in by only a few threads. The screw head may not touch; otherwise, the hold-down device may tilt.
44. Install pressure lines on injectors and rail. Tighten nuts manually only.
45. Reinstall line damper.
46. First tighten screw #1. Tightening torque 10 ft. lbs. (13 Nm).
47. Then tighten down screw #2. Tightening torque 10 ft. lbs. (13 Nm).
48. Tighten down pressure lines on injectors. Tightening torque 17 ft. lbs. (23 Nm).
49. Then tighten down pressure lines on the rail. Tightening torque 17 ft. lbs. (23 Nm).
50. Reinstall line damper.

➡Perform an injection quantity compensation:

The adjustment value is printed with three digits—depending on the version—on the injector body.

51. Connect BMW diagnosis system.
52. Identify vehicle.
53. Select "Function selection."
54. Select "Service functions."
55. Select "Engine electronics."
56. Select "Adjustment functions."
57. Select "Adjust injectors."
58. Select "Test schedule"
59. For each replaced injector, the adjustment value must be entered according to the installation location (cylinder).
60. Clean spark plug slot.
61. Assemble engine.
62. Check fuel system for tightness.
63. Check function of DME.

4.4L Engine

See Figures 266 and 267.

1. Remove ignition coils

➡Ignition coils must not be fouled by fuel.

➡The resistance of the silicone material is reduced significantly by contact with fuel, which may cause the ignition coil to fail. It is therefore essential to protect the spark plug slot against ingress of fuel with a cloth.

2. Before installing ignition coils, clean spark plug slots with compressed air.
3. Make sure the spark plug slot is absolutely clean.
4. Remove pressure lines on injectors.

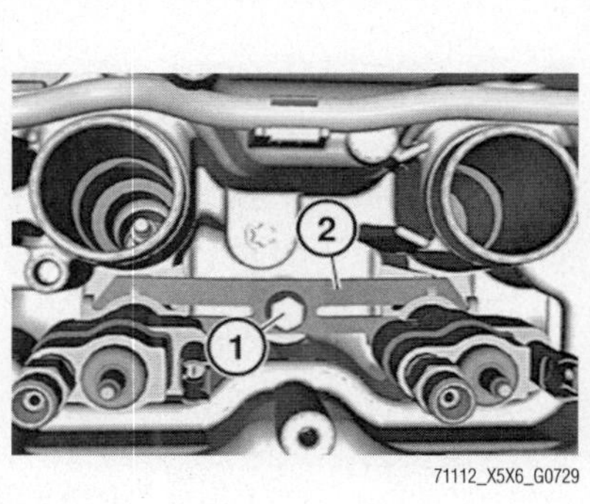

Fig. 266 Release bolt (1) and remove hold-down element (2)

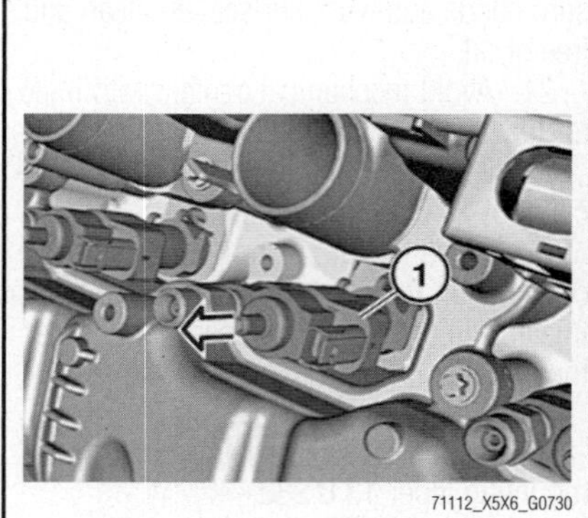

Fig. 267 Remove injector (1)

➡The following description applies to all injectors.

5. Release bolt and remove hold-down element.
6. Remove injector.

➡If several injectors are removed, ensure that each injector is reinstalled in its original location (cylinder).

7. Mark injectors.

Procedure in Event of Stuck Injectors

See Figures 268 through 271.

1. Mount special tool 13 0 301 or 13 0 302 (from set of special tools 13 0 300) on the stuck injector. In so doing, attach the special tool at the bottom to the injector and secure at the top with the knurled screw to the injector feed.
2. Mount special tool 13 0 300 over the stuck injector with special tool 13 0 301 or 13 0 302. In so doing, insert screws (1) in the designated holes and screw down. Tightening torque 7 ft. lbs. (10 Nm).
3. Twist bolt through special tool 13 0 300 into special tool 13 0 301 or 13 0 302 on the stuck injector.
4. Tighten down bolt until the injector is pulled out.
5. After removing, fit protective caps to injector tip and fuel line connection.
6. When installing a new injector: Use a new uncoupling element.
7. Remove protective cap from injector tip max. 10 min. before installation (Teflon ring swells up)
8. When reusing fuel injector: Replace decoupling element.
9. Replace Teflon ring.

➡A Teflon ring which has been heated once by engine operation must be replaced before the injector is reinstalled.

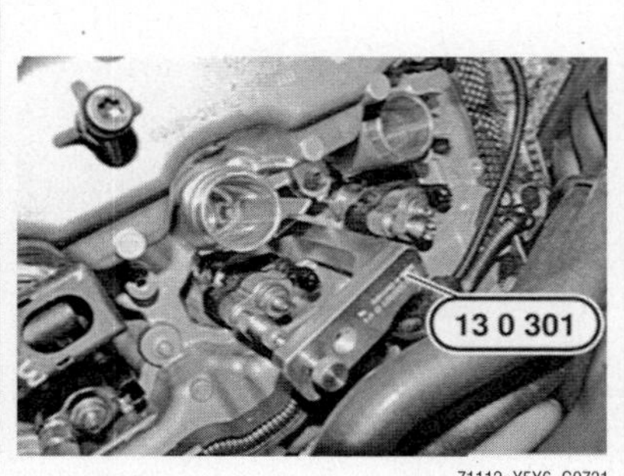

Fig. 268 Mount special tool 13 0 301 or 13 0 302 (from set of special tools 13 0 300) on the stuck injector

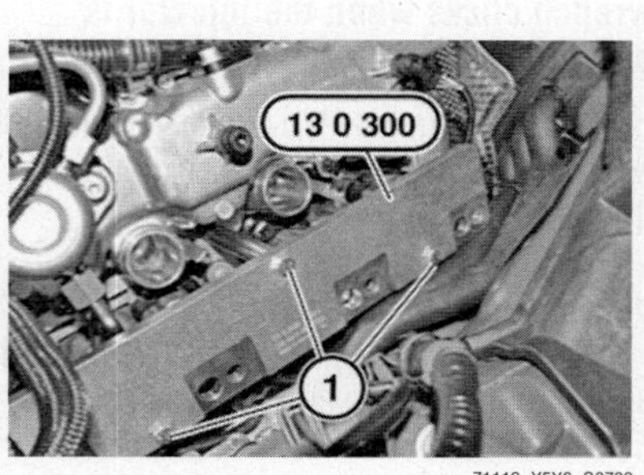

Fig. 269 Mount special tool 13 0 300 over the stuck injector with special tool 13 0 301 or 13 0 302, insert screws (1) in the designated holes and screw down

Fig. 270 Twist bolt (1) through special tool 13 0 300 into special tool 13 0 301 or 13 0 302 on the stuck injector

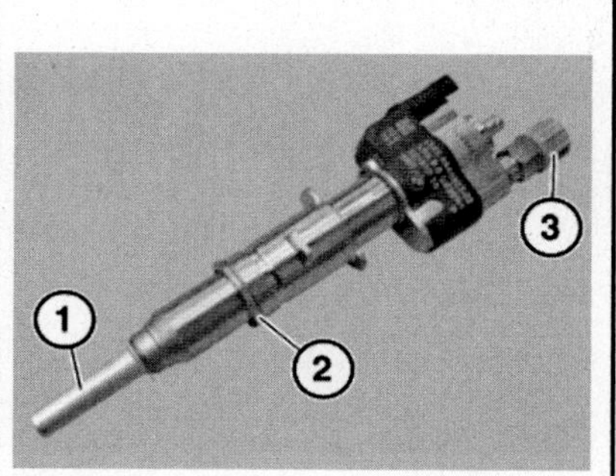

Fig. 271 After removing, fit protective caps (1 and 3) to injector tip and fuel line connection; uncoupling element (2)

Replace Teflon Ring

See Figure 272.

1. Before replacing the Teflon ring, make sure your hands and the work surface are clean and free of oil.
2. Avoid mechanical contact with injector tip.
3. Remove Teflon ring with special tool 13 0 191 from injector.
4. Use a fluff-free cloth only to remove combustion residues from cylindrical part of injector tip (do not use ultrasound or other tools/agents).
5. Do not clean injector tip.
6. Push new Teflon ring onto the installation cone 13 0 195.
7. Push Teflon ring with fingers assisted by the installation cone 13 0 195 onto the injector.

➡Do not use fingernails to slide Teflon ring on. Do not use any lubricating agents. The sealing ring is expanded when slid on.

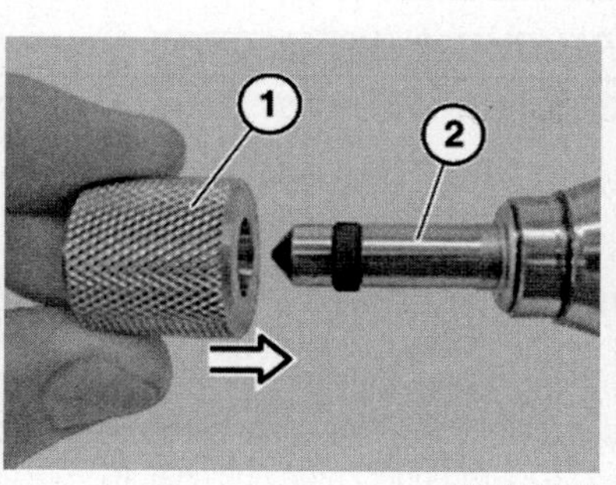

Fig. 272 Slide assembly sleeve (1) with large opening first onto injector (2)

8. To bring the expanded Teflon ring to its installation dimension, slide three assembly sleeves with decreasing diameters onto the injector.
9. Slide assembly sleeve with large opening first onto injector.
10. First slide assembly sleeve 13 0 192 (large diameter) onto injector.
11. Then slide assembly sleeve 13 0 193 (medium diameter) onto injector.
12. Finally, press injector into assembly sleeve 13 0 194 (small diameter).

➡Install injector within 10 minutes or slide on protective cap Teflon ring swells up.

To install:

➡Installation of injector is described separately from removal.

13. Before installing injector in engines that have been run:
    a. Check injector bore for dirt.
    b. Clean only dirty injector bores.
    c. Clean injector bore: To do so, preferably slide injector without decoupling element but with new Teflon ring in and out of injector bore several times.
    d. The Teflon ring must subsequently be replaced.
    e. Clean contact surfaces of uncoupling elements in cylinder head.
    f. Replace decoupling element.

Injection Quantity Compensation

See Figures 273 and 274.

An injector quantity compensation must be carried out if an injector is replaced or changed on the cylinder side.

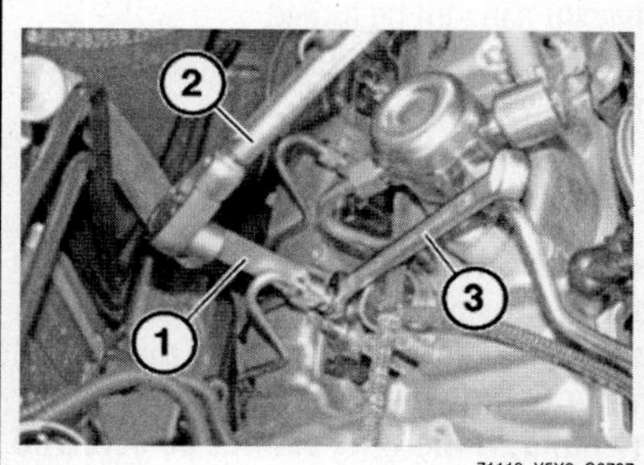

Fig. 273 Tighten nut on the injector using special tool (1) 13 0 161 (from the set of special tools 13 0 160) and torque wrench (2), grip hexagon head of injector with wrench (3)

Injector quantity compensation is carried out with the aid of a so-called adjustment value.

The adjustment value is printed in two blocks of three digits on the injector.

The adjustment value must be read off before installation.

1. Enter the adjustment value according to the installation location (cylinder) of the injector.
2. If injector quantity compensation is not carried out, the engine may run roughly or fail to start.

➡Description of injector quantity compensation at end of instructions.

3. Install hold-down device with curvature facing upwards.
4. Install injector.
5. Install hold-down device.

➡Make sure hold-down device is correctly seated.

6. Tighten bolt hand-tight only so that

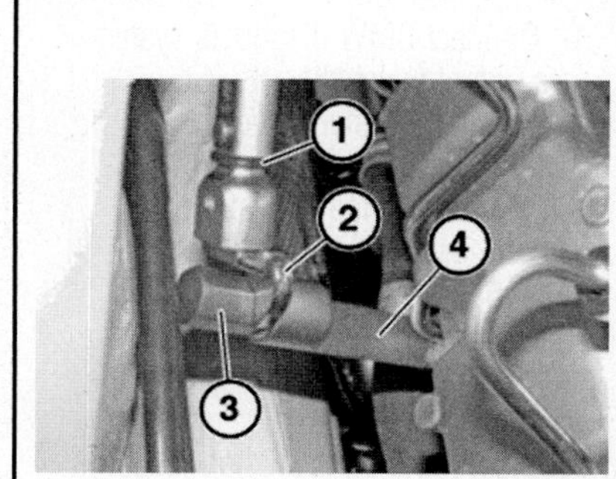

Fig. 274 Tighten pressure line on rail with torque wrench and special tools 00 1 440, 13 0 162 and 13 0 161 (from the set of special tools13 0 160).

hold-down element is slack and if necessary injector can still be turned.

7. Install pressure line. Tighten nuts manually only.

8. Connect pressure line without tension only.

➡To ensure distortion-free installation of the pressure line and to avoid damaging the thread, it must be possible for both nuts to be screwed on easily by hand. If the nuts cannot be screwed on easily by hand, the injector must if necessary be turned a little.

9. Turn injector if necessary until nuts on pressure line can be easily screwed on by hand.

10. Tighten nut of pressure line hand-tight.

11. Then tighten down bolt for hold-down device. Tightening torque 10 ft. lbs. (14 Nm).

12. Adhere to tightening sequence:

a. First tighten down pressure line on injector.

b. Tighten nut on the injector using special tool 13 0 161 (from the set of special tools 13 0 160) and torque wrench. In so doing, grip hexagon head of injector with wrench. Tighten initial torque to 7 ft. lbs. (10 Nm), then to final torque of 17 ft. lbs. (23 Nm). Retorque twice.

c. After this, tighten pressure line on rail.

d. Tighten pressure line on rail with torque wrench and special tools 00 1 440, 13 0 162 and 13 0 161 (from the set of special tools13 0 160). Tighten initial torque to 7 ft. lbs. (10 Nm), then to final torque of 17 ft. lbs. (23 Nm). Retorque twice.

Perform an Injection Quantity Compensation:

1. Connect BMW diagnosis system

a. Identify vehicle

b. Select "Function selection"

c. Select "Service functions"

d. Select "Engine electronics"

e. Select "Adjustment function"

f. Select "Adjust injectors"

g. Change "Test schedule"

h. For each replaced injector, the adjustment value must be entered according to the installation location (cylinder).

2. Assemble engine.

3. Bleed fuel system with BMW diagnosis system.

4. Check fuel system for tightness.

5. Check function of DME.

FUEL PUMP

REMOVAL & INSTALLATION

See Figures 275 through 280.

1. Draw off fuel from fuel tank

2. Remove rear seat bench

3. If necessary, disconnect plug connection.

4. Remove cover.

5. Release nuts and remove cover for service opening from right side of fuel tank.

6. Disconnect plug connection.

7. Unlock quick-release fastener and detach vent line.

8. If necessary, unlock quick-release fastener for fuel feed line of independent heating and detach.

9. If necessary, disconnect plug connection for independent heating fuel pump.

10. Measure gap dimension A at clamping ring.

11. Release hose clamp and remove from clamping ring.

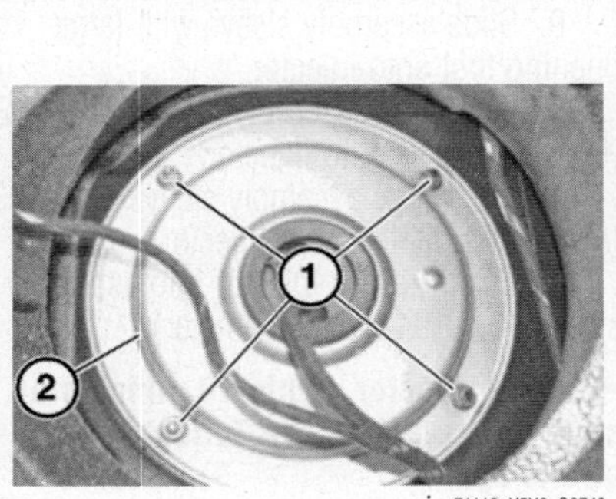

Fig. 275 Release nuts (1) and remove cover for service opening (2) from right side of fuel tank

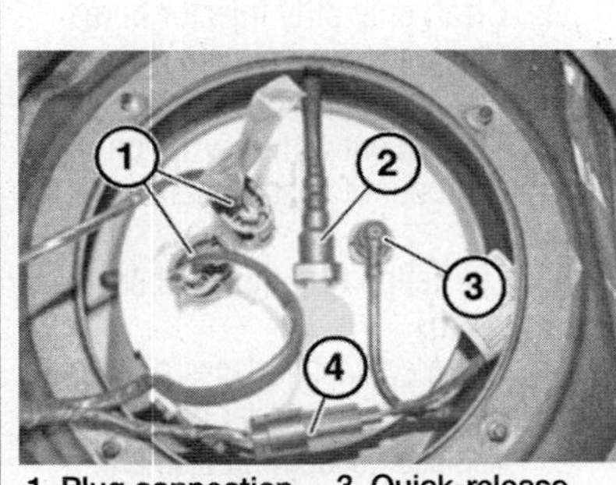

Fig. 276 Disconnect plug connection

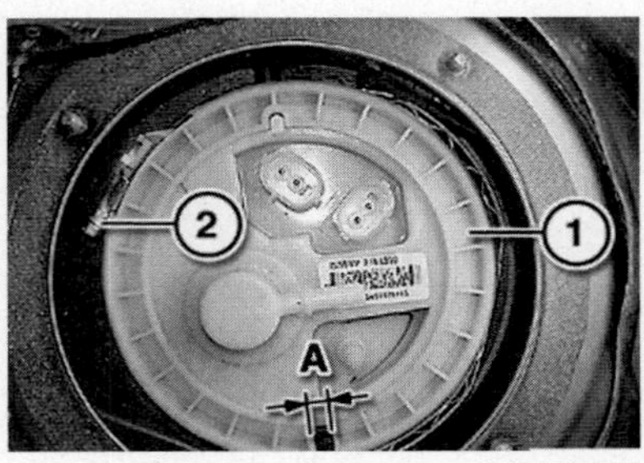

Fig. 277 Measure gap dimension A at clamping ring (1), release hose clamp (2)

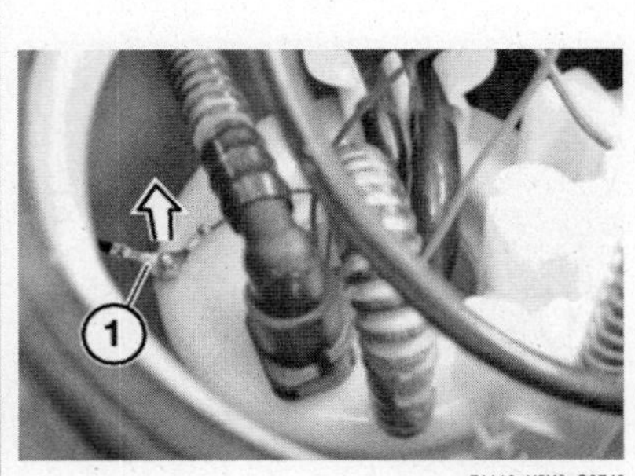

Fig. 278 Disconnect grounding cable (1) towards top

12. Press clamping ring apart at open end and remove.

13. Disconnect grounding cable towards top.

14. Carefully raise service cover.

15. Unclip plastic tube.

16. Unlock and disconnect quick-connect coupling.

17. Remove fuel pump.

➡Catch escaping fuel in suitable container. No fuel is permitted to get into the interior.

18. With fuel pump removed, disconnect plug connection and replace grounding cable.

To install:

19. Installation is the reverse order of removal.

20. Make sure that service cover is installed in correct position.

21. Indentation on clamping ring must line up with raised section of tank.

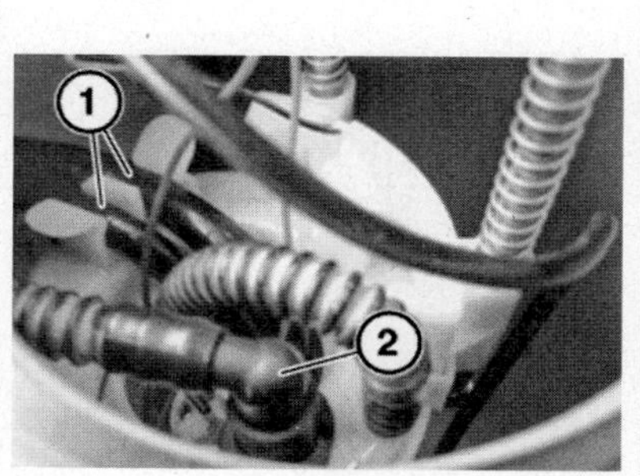

Fig. 279 Unclip plastic tube (1), unlock and disconnect quick-connect coupling (2)

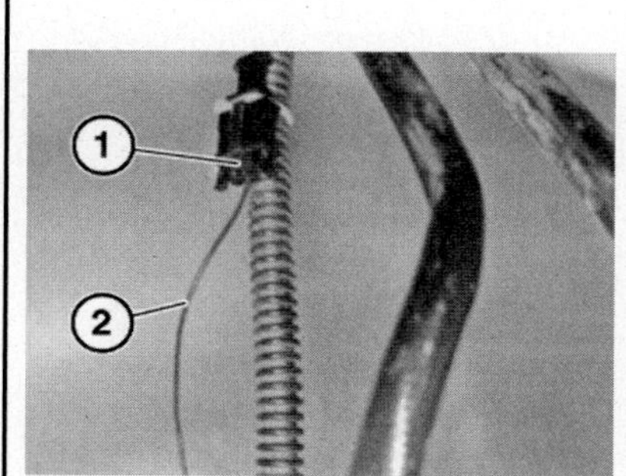

Fig. 280 With fuel pump removed, disconnect plug connection (1) and replace grounding cable (2)

22. Pin on service cover must line up with indentation on clamping ring.
23. Hose clamp must always be replaced (pay attention to correct position).
24. Tighten hose clamp until clamping ring gap dimension is obtained.
25. Seal must always be replaced.

➡Grounding cable must be replaced if it has been detached once.

FUEL TANK

DRAINING

1. Start engine and allow to run. The electric fuel pump runs. In this way, the fuel is re-pumped through the suction jet pump from the left to the right side of the fuel tank.

➡Fuel can be drawn out of left and right sides of tank through filler neck, leaving only a small residue. The residual quantity is drawn off through the service opening (on right/left).

2. Insert special tool 16 1 080 into filler neck.

➡Special tool 16 1 080 has two different diameters for petrol/gasoline and diesel vehicles.

3. Slide extraction hose of extractor unit, through special tool 16 1 080 into the fuel filler pipe, turning in the process if necessary. Insertion length approximately 67 inches (170 cm).
4. Draw off fuel with suction unit as far as possible.

➡Follow drawing off of fuel on fuel gauge in instrument cluster.

5. Draw off residual fuel amount is not included in this operation.
   a. Ensure car interior is adequately ventilated.
   b. Catch dripping fuel in a suitable container.
   c. Remove left sensor unit.
   d. Remove right sensor unit.
   e. Draw off residual fuel quantity through service openings.

REMOVAL & INSTALLATION

See Figures 281 through 286.

1. Draw off fuel from fuel tank.
2. Remove propeller shaft.
3. Remove underbody paneling on left and right.
4. Remove rear right wheel arch panel.
5. Release nuts and remove holder.

➡There may be residual amounts of fuel in the fuel tank.

6. Catch escaping fuel in a suitable collecting vessel.
7. Release hose clamp and detach fuel filling hose.

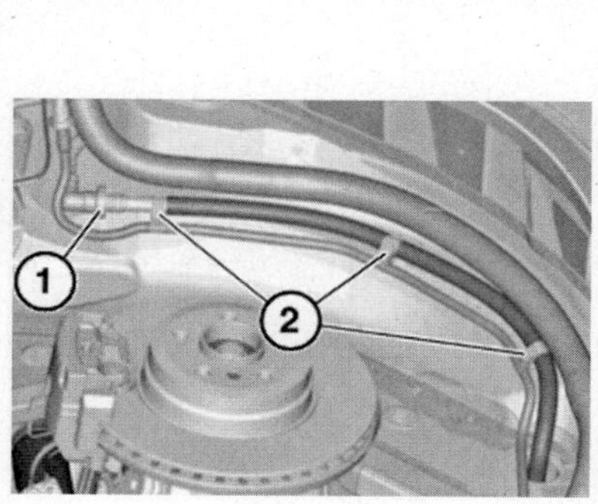

Fig. 281 Unlock the snap fastener (1) and pull off the tank ventilation line, Detach tank ventilation line from holders (2)

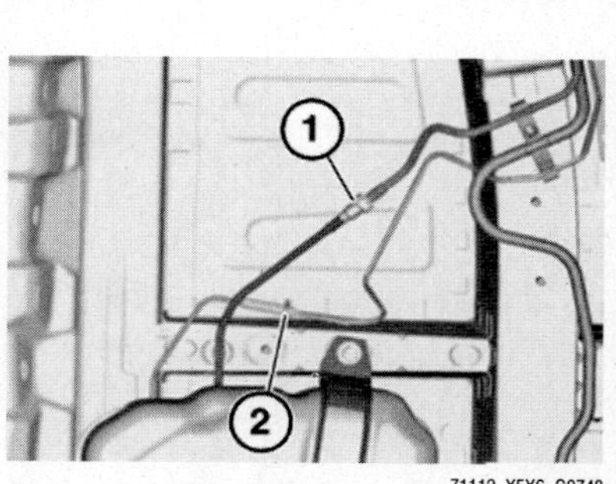

Fig. 282 Unlock fuel delivery line at quick-release fastener (1) and disconnect, with auxiliary heater: release single_ear clip (2) and detach pressure line

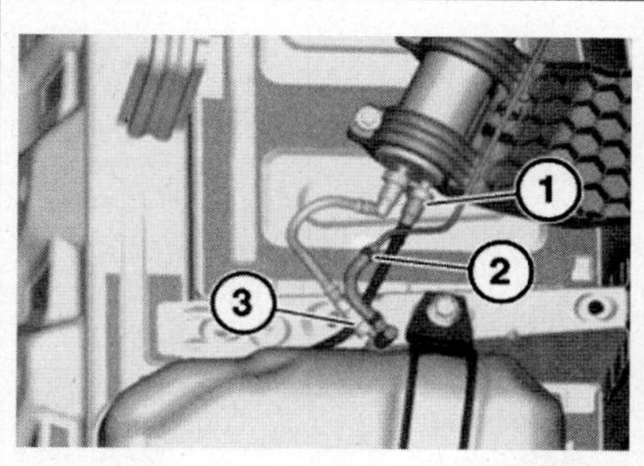

Fig. 283 With outer fuel filter: Unlock fuel delivery line at quick-release fastener (1) and disconnect, Release single_ear clip (2) and detach pressure reference line, Release snap fastener (3) and pull off return line

8. Unlock the snap fastener and pull off the tank ventilation line.
9. Detach tank ventilation line from holders.
10. Unlock fuel delivery line at quick-release fastener and disconnect.
11. With auxiliary heater: Release single_ear clip and detach pressure line.
12. With outer fuel filter: Unlock fuel delivery line at quick-release fastener and disconnect.
13. Release single-ear clip and detach pressure reference line.
14. Release snap fastener and pull off return line.

CAUTION

Secure fuel tank against slipping and falling out.

15. Safely support the fuel tank.
16. Release screws on clamping bands on left and right.

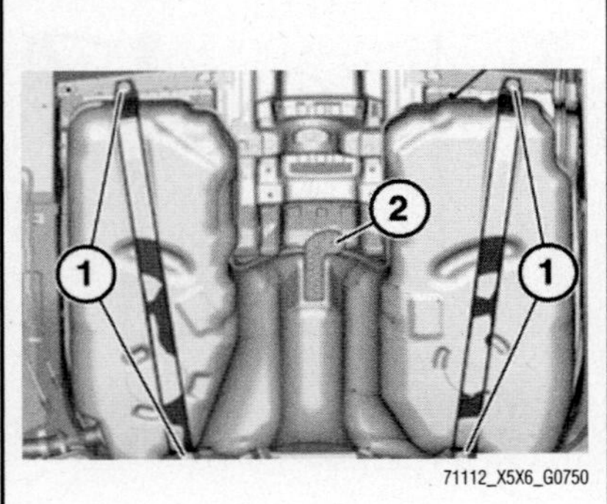

Fig. 284 Release screws (1) on clamping bands on left and right, remove nut (2)

Fig. 285 Disconnect plug connection (1)

17. Remove nut.

➡**When lowering the component, also pass the fuel tank ventilation line through the opening in the body.**

18. Lower the fuel tank slightly to be able to reach the sensor units.
19. Disconnect plug connection.
20. Disconnect plug connection.
21. Lower fuel tank.

To install:

22. Installation is the reverse order of removal.
23. Tighten the fuel tank to body nut to 14 ft. lbs. (9 Nm).
24. Tighten the Tank strap to body screws to 14 ft. lbs. (9 Nm)

➡**The following components must be modified when the fuel tank is replaced:**

- Right sensor unit
- Left sensor unit

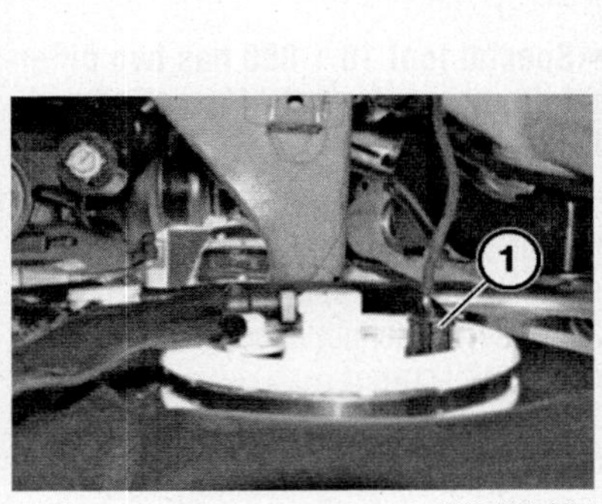

Fig. 286 Disconnect plug connection (1)

- Fuel delivery line
- Fuel return line, if applicable
- Lines for auxiliary heater, if applicable

IDLE SPEED

ADJUSTMENT

Idle speed is maintained by the Digital Motor Electronics control unit. No adjustment is necessary or possible.

THROTTLE BODY

REMOVAL & INSTALLATION

3.0L Engine

See Figures 287 through 289.

1. Switch off ignition.
2. Remove rear charge-air duct.
3. Unlock connector and remove.
4. Unlock and disconnect hoses.

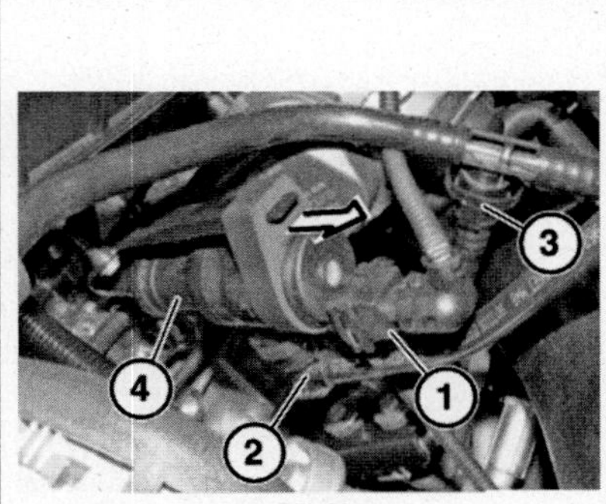

Fig. 287 Unlock connector and remove

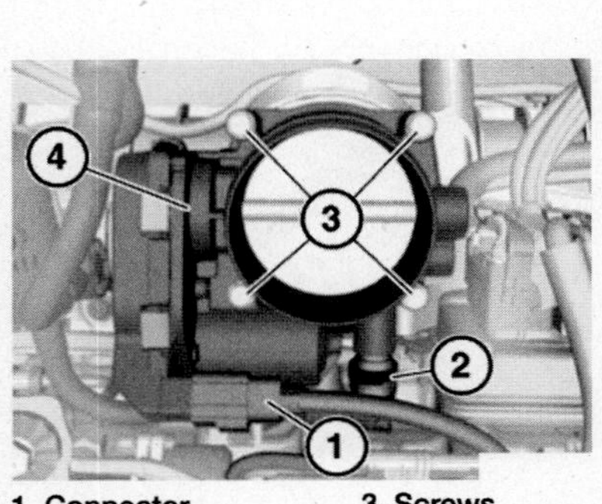

Fig. 288 Unlock connector and remove

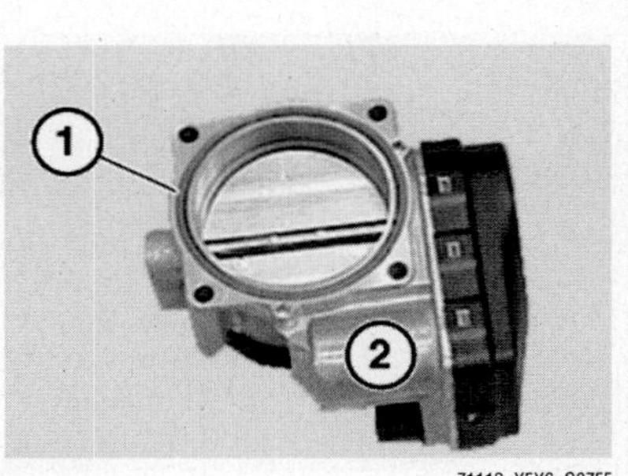

Fig. 289 Replace sealing ring (1) of throttle body (2)

5. Remove tank vent valve from holder and place aside.
6. Unlock connector and remove.
7. Release screws.
8. Partially remove throttle body and unlock tank ventilation line and remove.
9. Remove throttle body.

To install:

10. Installation is the reverse order of removal.
11. Replace sealing ring of throttle body.
12. Check stored fault message.
13. Delete fault memory.

4.4L Engine

See Figure 290.

1. Turn off ignition
2. Remove right intercooler

➡**Procedure is the left throttle valve assembly, the procedure for the right side is identical.**

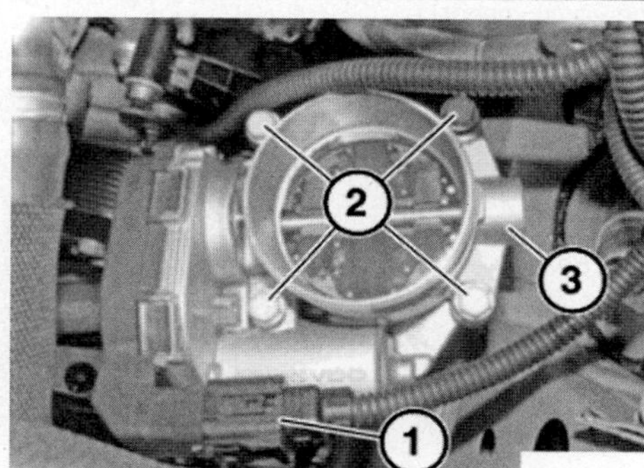

Fig. 290 Unlock plug (1), unfasten screws (2), remove throttle valve assembly (3)

3. Unlock plug and remove.
4. Unfasten screws.
5. Remove throttle valve assembly.

To install:

6. Installation is the reverse order of removal.
7. Check plug connection for coolant remnants. Clean soiled plug connection with compressed air.
8. Replace sealing ring of throttle assembly.
9. Check stored fault message.
10. Delete fault memory.

STEERING

POWER STEERING GEAR

REMOVAL & INSTALLATION

See Figure 291.

1. Disconnect battery negative lead
2. Remove front left wheel arch cover (rear section)
3. Release nut and disconnect ground cable.
4. Disconnect plug connections.
5. Unclip cable holder.
6. Release nuts.
7. Remove active front steering control unit.

To install:

8. Installation is the reverse order of removal.
9. Replacement only: Carry out programming/coding.
10. Carry out adjustment for active front steering.

ADJUSTMENT

1. Adjustment of the active front steering must be carried out:
   a. after adjustment work on the front axle/steering
   b. after all mechanical work on the steering system
   c. after replacement/programming or coding of the following components:
      - Steering column switch cluster
      - DSC control unit
      - Active front steering control unit
      - ARS control unit
2. Connect vehicle to BMW diagnosis system.
3. Select and carry out initial operation/adjustment for active front steering under Service functions.

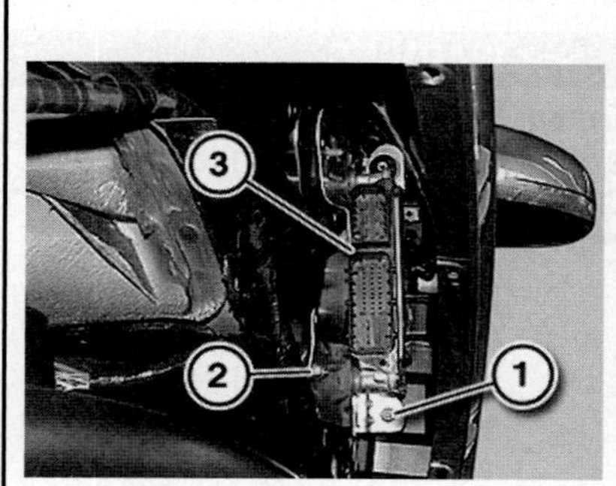

Fig. 291 Release nuts (1, 2), Remove active front steering control unit (3)

SUSPENSION

FRONT SUSPENSION

LOWER CONTROL ARM

REMOVAL & INSTALLATION

See Figures 292 through 294.

➡If the lower control arm is detached from the front axle carrier, it is necessary after reinstallation to carry out a wheel/chassis alignment check.

1. Remove front wheel
2. Remove steering gear cover at side bottom
3. Secure special tool 31 5 220 with wheel studs to drive flange.
4. Support swivel bearing with special tool 31 5 220 and workshop jack.
5. Release nut and remove screw.
6. Loosen nut.

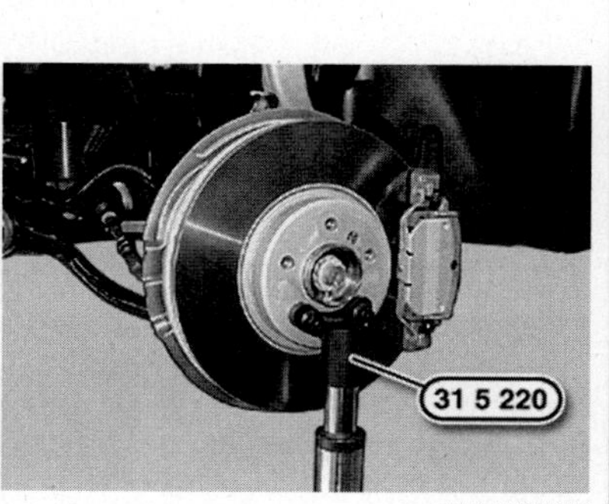

Fig. 292 Secure special tool 31 5 220 with wheel studs to drive flange

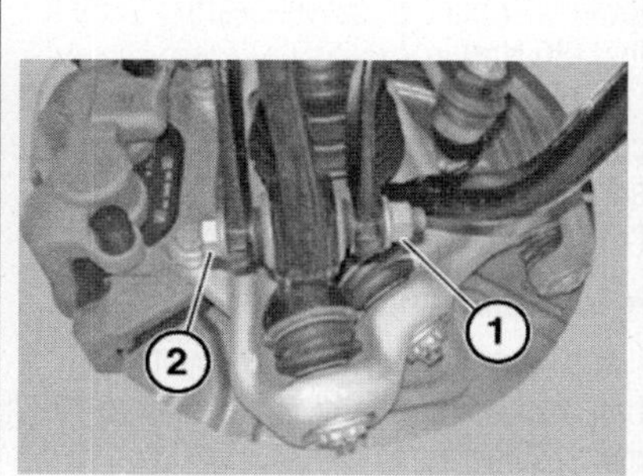

Fig. 293 Release nut (1) and remove screw (2)

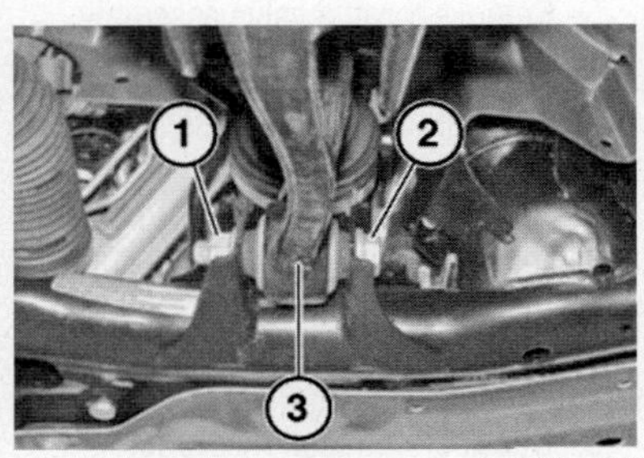

Fig. 294 Loosen nut (1), remove screw (2) and remove control arm (3) from front axle carrier

7. Remove screw and remove control arm from front axle carrier.

WARNING

Do not release control arm from swivel bearing with impact tool.

➡Note the following:

- Make sure special tool rests correctly on steel bushing of swivel bearing. The swivel bearing must be removed if the steel bushing moves.
- Rubber gaiter of control arm must not be damaged.
- Do not pull stainless steel ring off journal.

To install:

8. Installation is the reverse order of removal.

➡Keep control arm to swivel bearing connection clean and free from oil and grease.

9. Replace self-locking nut. Tighten lower wishbone to swivel bearing to 59 ft. lbs. (80 Nm).
10. Replace screw and nut. Tighten bolt connection for lower wishbone to front axle support in normal position to 122 ft. lbs. (165 Nm).

➡Note insertion direction of screw.

11. Replace self-locking nut. Tighten bolt connection in normal position to 122 ft. lbs. (165 Nm).

➡Note insertion direction of screw.

12. Perform chassis alignment check adjustment for active steering.
13. Teach in software stop for electrical steering box.
14. Carry out steering angle sensor adjustment.

STABILIZER BAR

REMOVAL & INSTALLATION

See Figures 295 through 298.

1. Remove front wheels.
2. Remove front underbody protection.
3. Remove front right wheel arch cover (front section).
4. Remove radiator air duct.
5. Remove both brake air ducts with holder.
6. Remove fan cowl.
7. Remove heat exchanger from front axle support and tie up.
8. Remove both anti-roll bar links from anti-roll bar.
9. Remove radiator box from engine support, extend out, press upwards and support with workshop jack.
10. Mark installation position of control lines to swivel motor.
11. Release banjo nuts and remove control lines from swivel motor.
12. Seal control lines and connections of swivel motor with clean seal plugs.
13. Release screws.
14. Remove both control lines from upper retaining brackets and tie up.
15. Remove upper retaining brackets.
16. Remove anti-roll bar with rubber mounts from lower retaining brackets.
17. Remove both rubber mounts from anti-roll bar.

To install:

18. Installation is the reverse order of removal.

➡Rubber lips must be situated between retaining brackets.

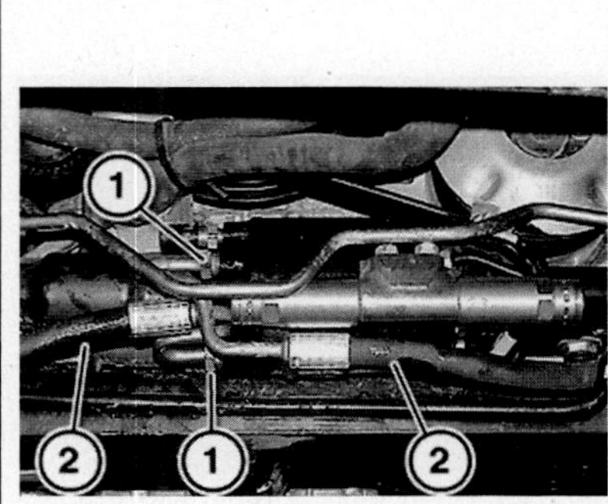

Fig. 295 Release banjo nuts (1) and remove control lines (2) from swivel motor

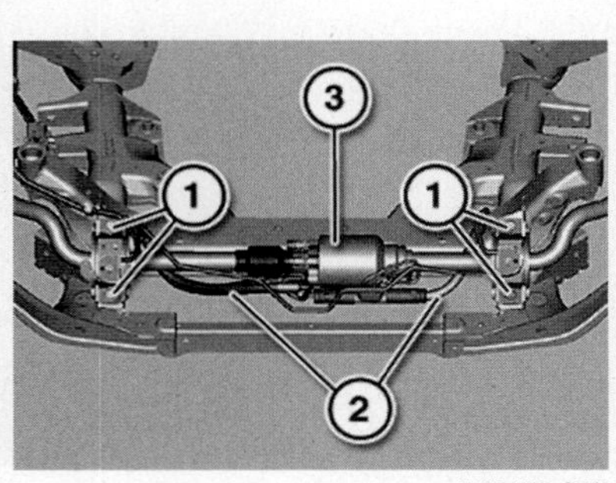

Fig. 296 Release screws (1), remove both control lines (2), remove anti-roll bar (3)

19. Check rubber mount of radiator box for correct fit.
    a. First adjust minimum distance A = 0.12 inches (3 mm) between control line and swivel motor.
    b. Then adjust control line with minimum distance B = 0.32 inches (8 mm) to control line.
    c. Check roller bearing for damage, replace anti-roll bar if necessary (slight discharge of grease OK).
20. Keep facing for rubber mount on a roller bearing clean and free from oil and grease.
21. Check rubber mount for damage, replace if necessary.

➡To remove the risk of mixing up after removal of the control lines at the holders, observe the following:

- Holder in direction of travel, left: Stud bolt arranged virtually centrally on the holder.

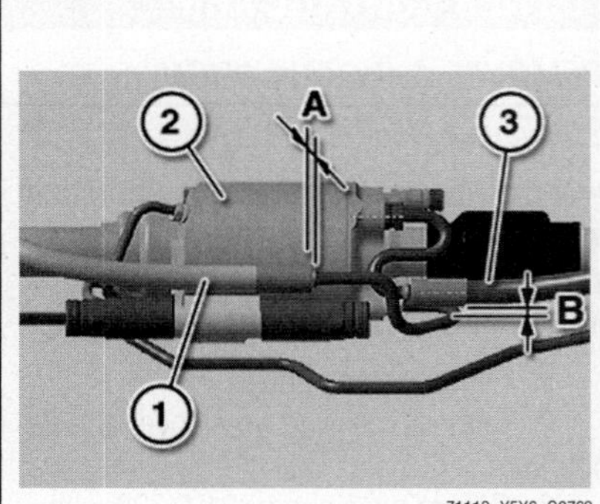

Fig. 297 Control line (1), swivel motor (2), control line (3)

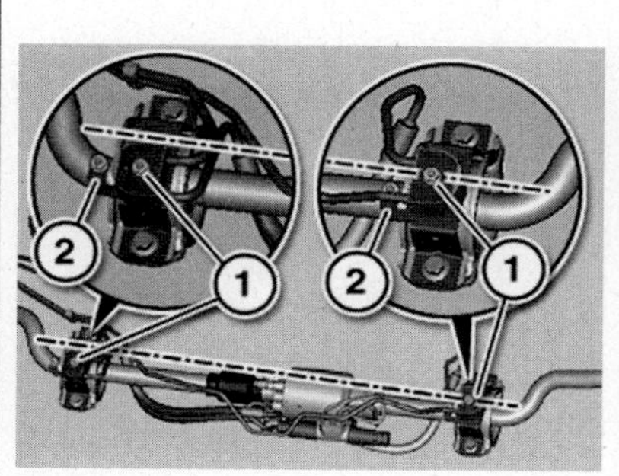

Fig. 298 Stud bolt (1) arranged virtually centrally on the holder, Align holders by way of additional tabs (2)

- Holder in direction of travel, right: Stud bolt arranged off-center to the front of the holder.
- Align holders by way of additional tabs; both tabs point in direction of travel to right.

22. Tighten screws for retaining bar to front axle carrier to 41 ft. lbs. (56 Nm).
23. Tighten control lines to oscillating motor to 22 ft. lbs. (30 Nm).

STRUT & SPRING ASSEMBLY

REMOVAL & INSTALLATION

See Figures 299 through 302.

1. Remove partition wall of units compartment sideways.
   a. Release expansion rivet.
   b. Release screws.
   c. Left only: Unclip connecting line.
   d. Remove partition wall.
2. Remove spring strut holder.

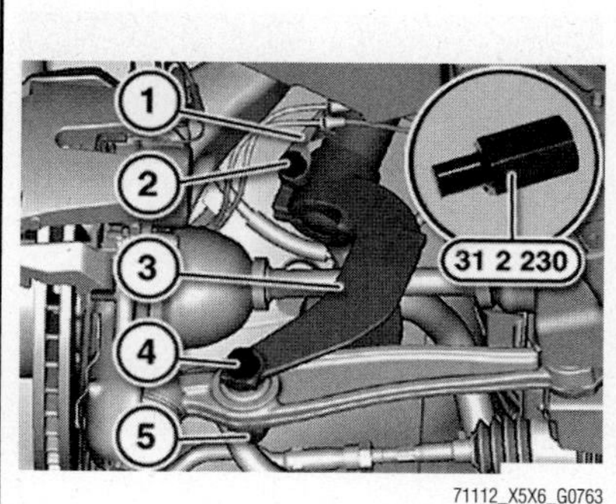

Fig. 300 Remove spring strut holder

   a. Release bolt and remove with holder.
   b. Expand spring strut holder with special tool 31 2 230.
   c. Release nut and remove screw.
   d. Lower swivel bearing until spring strut holder is below spring strut.
   e. Remove spring strut holder, taking care not to damage the output shaft.

➡Secure spring strut against falling out.

3. Unscrew nuts.
4. Vehicles with Vertical Dynamics Management: Disconnect both plug connections.
   a. Disconnect plug connection on pulse sensor.
   b. Disconnect plug connection from brake lining sensor.
5. Remove spring strut downwards out of wheel arch.

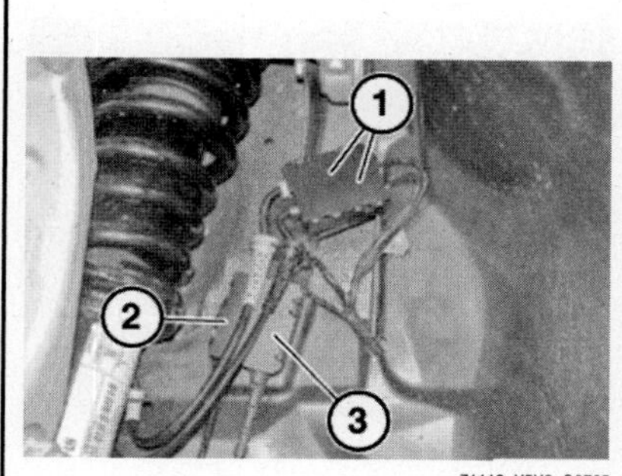

Fig. 302 Plug connections (1, 2, 3)

To install:

6. Installation is the reverse order of removal.
7. Clean contact surface in spring strut dome.
8. Replace self-locking nuts. Tightening torque 21 ft. lbs. (28 Nm).
9. Tighten spring strut holder to spring strut shock absorber to 60 ft. lbs. (81 Nm).
10. Tighten Spring strut holder to lower control arm to 122 ft. lbs. (165 Nm).

UPPER CONTROL ARM

REMOVAL & INSTALLATION

See Figures 303 through 307.

1. Remove left partition wall for units compartment
   a. Release expansion rivet.
   b. Release screws.
   c. Left only: Unclip connecting line.
   d. Remove partition wall.

Fig. 299 Remove left partition wall for units compartment

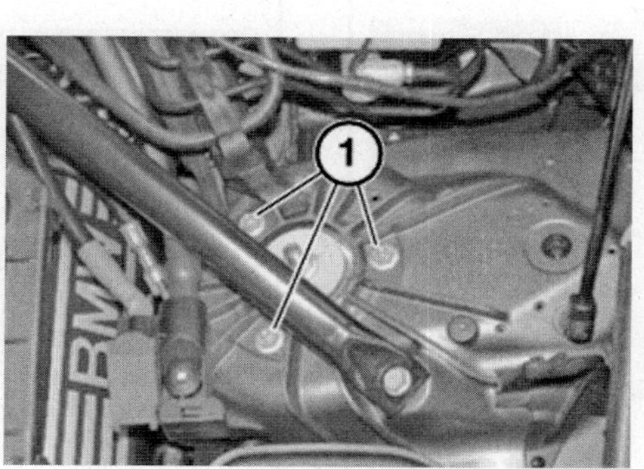

Fig. 301 Unscrew nuts (1)

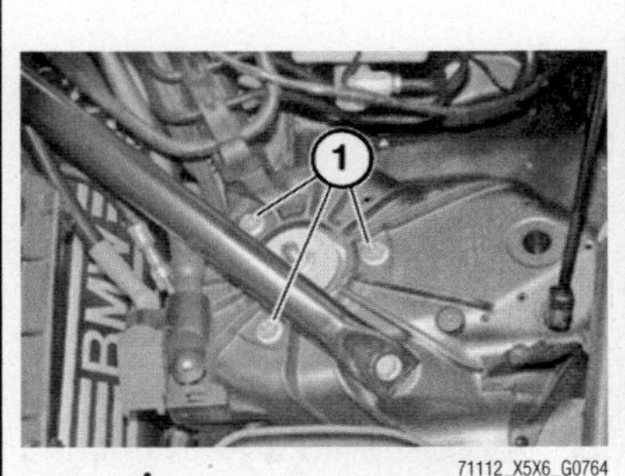

Fig. 303 Unscrew nuts (1)

Fig. 305 Secure special tool 31 5 220 with wheel studs to drive flange

Fig. 307 Release nuts of screws (1), remove wishbone (2) from swivel bearing

2. Detach coolant expansion tank and place to one side

➡Level switch can slip out of the coolant expansion tank in the process.

3. Remove front wheel
4. Unscrew nuts.
5. Loosen nut.
6. Remove jointed rod from upper wishbone.
7. Secure special tool 31 5 220 with wheel studs to drive flange.
8. Support swivel bearing with special tool 31 5 220 and workshop jack.
9. Unfasten nut and remove screw.
10. Release nuts of screws.
11. Remove screws; if necessary, lower/raise swivel bearing and spring strut using workshop jack.
12. Remove wishbone from swivel bearing.

To install:

13. Installation is the reverse order of removal.
14. Keep wishbone to swivel bearing connection clean and free from oil and grease.
15. Note direction of insertion of screw. Screw must rest correctly in groove of ball stud.
16. Replace self-locking nut for upper wishbone to swivel bearing. Tightening torque 41 ft. lbs. (56 Nm).
17. Replace screws and nuts.
18. Set ride height at front left (right) to normal position and tighten screw/bolt connection. Tightening torque 28 ft. lbs. (38 Nm) plus additional 90 degrees.
19. Replace self-locking nuts for support bearing flange to body. Tightening torque 21 ft. lbs. (28 Nm).
20. Replace self-locking nut for jointed rod to upper wishbone.
21. Carry out ride height adjustment

RIDE HEIGHT ADJUSTMENT

Ride-height-calibration must be carried out after the following work:

- Removal/replacement of ride-height sensor or its control rod
- Replacement of wiring harness
- Replacement of air supply unit control unit
- Replacement of Vertical Dynamics Management control unit

1. Connect BMW diagnosis system.
2. Switch the ignition on.
3. Carry out ride-height-calibration (menu item: "Service function").
4. Vehicles with Run Flat Indicator: initialize Run Flat Indicator
5. Vehicles with Tire Pressure Control: carry out resetting

WHEEL BEARINGS

REMOVAL & INSTALLATION

See Figures 308 through 311.

➡Bearing cannot be dismantled. Do not wash out bearing.

1. Remove front wheel.

➡Expand anti-twist lock sufficiently to avoid damaging thread when releasing collar nut.

2. Release collar nut, press brake pedal to floor for this purpose.
3. Remove brake disc.
4. Release screw and pull pulse sensor out of bore.
5. Release screws and remove holder from swivel bearing.
6. Release bolts and remove wheel bearing.
7. Screw on special tools 33 2 203, 33 2 207 and 33 2 201 with three wheel bolts to drive flange.
8. Pull wheel bearing off output shaft, gripping basic body 33 2 201 with special tools 33 2 202 and 33 5 070.

Fig. 304 Loosen nut (1), remove jointed rod (2) from upper wishbone (3)

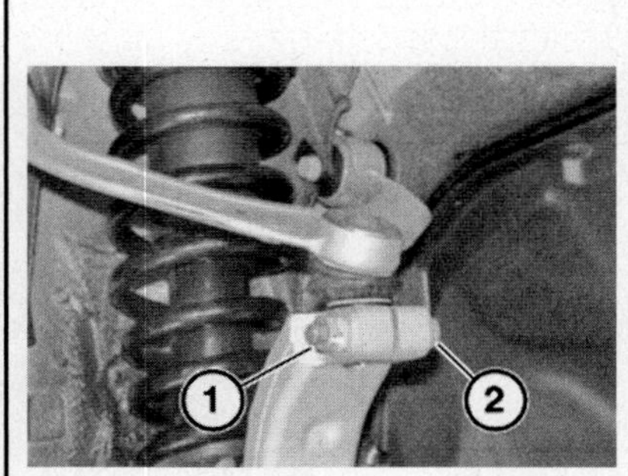

Fig. 306 Unfasten nut (1) and remove screw (2)

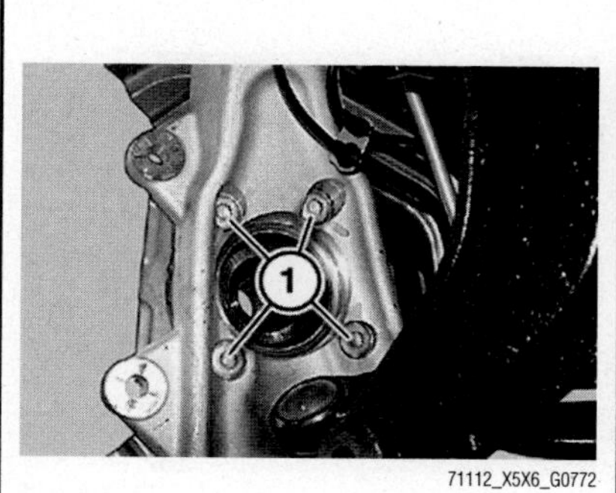

71112_X5X6_G0772

Fig. 308 Release bolts (1) and remove wheel bearing

71112_X5X6_G0774

Fig. 310 Screw special tool 33 2 118 onto output shaft

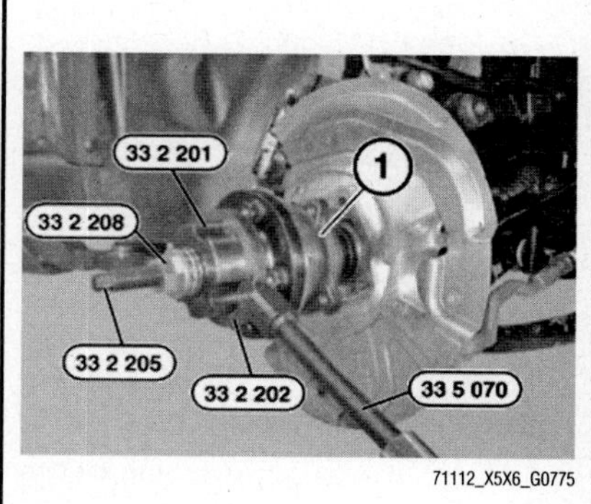

71112_X5X6_G0775

Fig. 311 Draw in wheel bearing (1) with special tool 33 2 208 up to stop

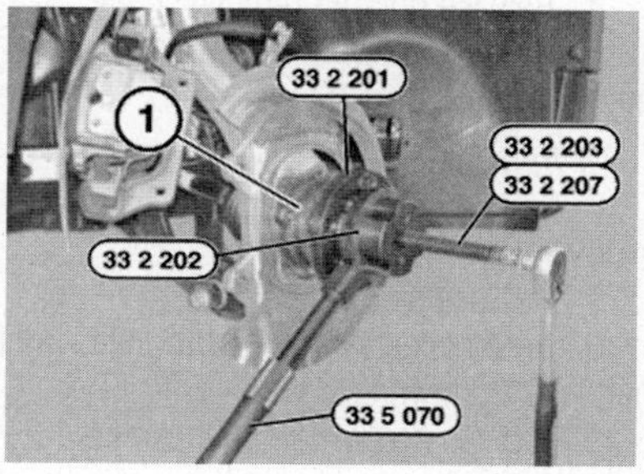

71112_X5X6_G0773

Fig. 309 Pull wheel bearing (1) off output shaft

To install:

9. Installation is the reverse order of removal.

⁂ WARNING

Do not damage inner race of wheel bearing.

➡No oil permitted on shaft journal thread.

10. Lightly oil spline teeth of output shaft.
11. Screw special tool 33 2 118 onto output shaft.
12. Mount special tool 33 2 201 with three wheel bolts to drive flange.
13. Draw in wheel bearing with special tool 33 2 208 up to stop, gripping basic body 33 2 201 with special tools 33 2 202 and 33 5 070.
14. Replace collar nut, oil collar nut/wheel bearing contact surface only and tighten down.

➡No oil permitted on thread of shaft journal or collar nut.

15. Secure collar nut by positive peening on flat areas of output shaft.
16. Clean bore for pulse sensor and lubricate with Staburags NBU 12/K lubricating grease.
17. Replace screws.
18. Keep contact surface of swivel bearing and wheel bearing clean and free from oil and grease.

SUSPENSION — REAR SUSPENSION

COIL SPRING

REMOVAL & INSTALLATION

See Figures 312 through 316.

➡Use spring tensioner 33 5 100 to remove and install the coil spring in order to avoid over-elongating the rubber mounts (wishbone, control arm, swinging arm).

1. Remove rear wheel.
2. Remove anti-roll bar link from swinging arm.
3. Remove rear shock absorber from swinging arm (remove brake hose).
4. Lower workshop jack and place to one side.
5. Lever conical cover (1) with a suitable tool out of lower spring pad.
6. Feed spindle 33 5 103 into coil

71112_X5X6_G0787

Fig. 312 Lever conical cover (1) with a suitable tool out of lower spring pad

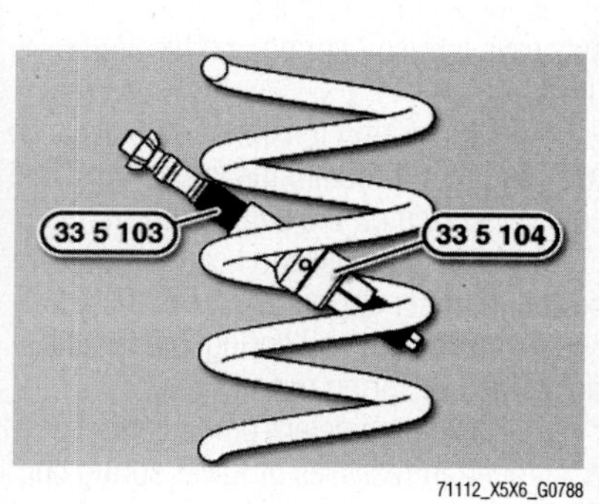

71112_X5X6_G0788

Fig. 313 Feed spindle 33 5 103 into coil spring and turn synchronizing key 33 5 104 downwards

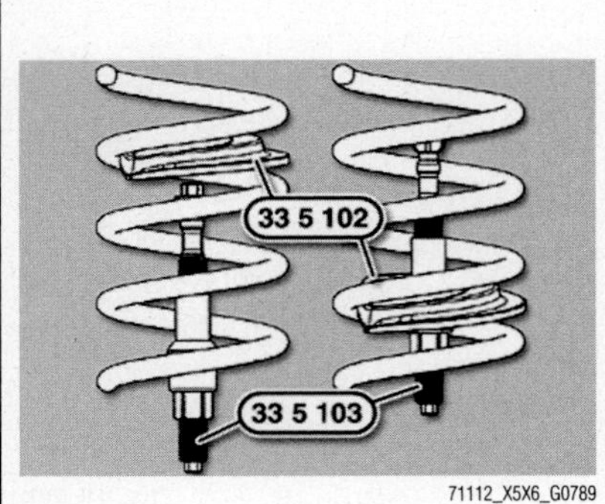

Fig. 314 Insert lower spring cup 33 5 102 into coil spring and turn downwards over spindle 33 5 103

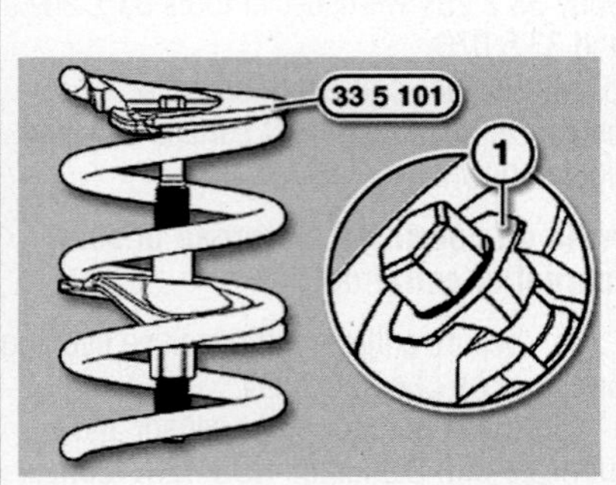

Fig. 315 Make sure hexagon cap (1) is correctly seated in upper spring cup 33 5 101

spring and turn synchronizing key 33 5 104 downwards.

7. Insert lower spring cup 33 5 102 into coil spring and turn downwards over spindle 33 5 103.
8. Insert upper spring cup 33 5 101 sideways into coil spring and turn fully upwards.
9. Align spring tensioner 33 5 100 centrally in order to obtain the largest possible contact surface on the coil spring.
10. Make sure hexagon cap is correctly seated in upper spring cup 33 5 101.
11. Make sure coil spring is correctly positioned in spring cups.
12. Make sure detent pin is correctly positioned in recesses of lower spring cup 33 5 102.
13. Check installation position of spring tensioner 33 5 100, correcting if necessary.
14. Make sure there is sufficient clearance between spindle 33 5 103 and lower spring pad.

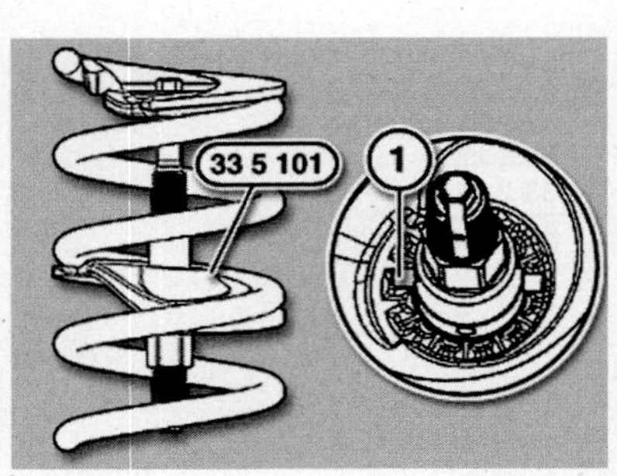

Fig. 316 Make sure detent pin (1) is correctly positioned in recesses of lower spring cup 33 5 102

15. Tension coil spring using special tool 33 5 105; if necessary, grip coil spring.
16. Turn coil spring through 30° in clockwise direction.
17. Press wheel carrier downwards a little and remove coil spring sideways.
18. Remove upper spring pad from coil spring, check for damage and replace if necessary.
19. If necessary, relieve tension on coil spring.

To install:

20. Check lower spring pad for damage.
21. Make sure spring pad is correctly installed in order to prevent the coil spring from jumping out.
22. If necessary, lever out upper part with a suitable tool and replace spring pad with upper part.
23. Make sure spring pad is correctly installed in order to prevent the coil spring from jumping out.
24. Install upper spring pad in locator or frame side member and turn clockwise as far as it will go.
25. Make sure coil spring is correctly seated in spring pads.
26. Insert coil spring with spring tensioner 33 5 100 between upper and lower spring pads and relieve tension.
27. Relieve tension on spring tensioner 33 5 100 and remove.
28. Check headlight adjustment, correct if necessary.

INTEGRAL LINK

REMOVAL & INSTALLATION

See Figure 317.

1. Remove rear wheel.
2. Tension coil spring using special tool 33 5 100 (and leave on vehicle).

Fig. 317 Release nut (1) and remove screw, release screw (2) and remove integral link (3)

3. Vehicles with ride-height control: Deactivate and empty air spring system.
4. Release nut and remove screw.
5. Release screw and remove integral link.

To install:

6. Installation is the reverse order of removal.
7. Replace self-locking nut.
8. First install swinging arm hand-tight, then tighten down screw.
9. Tighten screw/bolt connections in normal position.
10. Tightening torque (nut) 96 ft. lbs. (130 Nm) plus additional 180 degrees.
11. Tightening torque (bolt) 74 ft. lbs. (100 Nm).
12. Activate and fill air spring system
13. Perform chassis alignment check

SWINGING ARM

REMOVAL & INSTALLATION

1. Remove rear wheel.
2. Deactivate and empty air spring system.

Deactivating Air Suspension System:

1. Fold down power distribution box in passenger compartment.
2. Pull out fuse for air supply system.

Draining Air Spring System:

See Figures 318 through 322.

1. Connect BMW diagnosis system.
2. Switch on the ignition.
3. Drain air springs with aid of BMW diagnosis system (control unit functions, "Brake bleeding procedure" menu item).

➡Depending on the output pressure in the air spring, it may be necessary to repeat the brake bleeding procedure.

4. Raise vehicle until wheels are freely suspended.
5. Remove ignition key.
6. Remove anti-roll bar link from swinging arm
7. Release expanding rivets.
8. Remove cover from rear axle carrier.
9. Mark position of eccentric screw to rear axle carrier.
10. Loosen nut.
11. Remove jointed rod from swinging arm.
12. Support wheel carrier with workshop jack.
13. Release nuts and remove screw.
14. Remove rear shock absorber from swinging arm.
15. Loosen nut.
16. Remove bolt towards rear.
17. Release nut, remove eccentric washer and pull out eccentric screw towards front.
18. Release screw and remove locking nut.

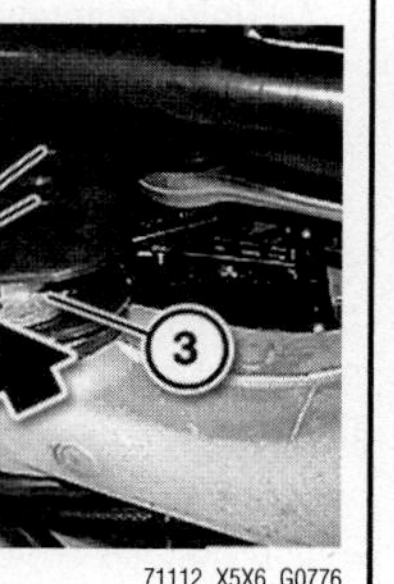

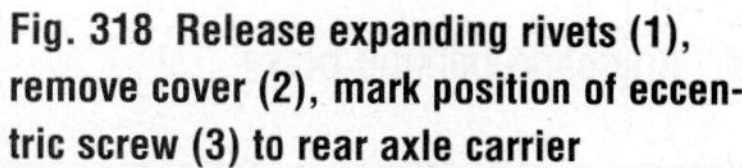

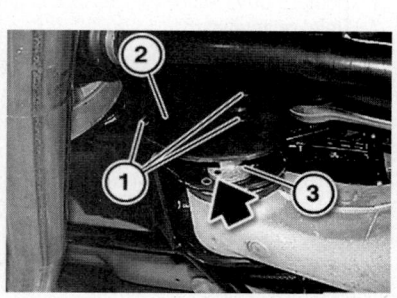

Fig. 318 Release expanding rivets (1), remove cover (2), mark position of eccentric screw (3) to rear axle carrier

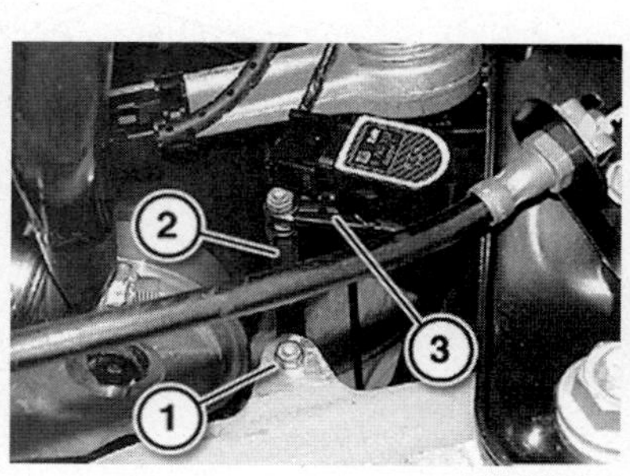

Fig. 319 Loosen nut (1), remove jointed rod (2) from swinging arm; sensor lever (3)

To install:

19. Installation is the reverse order of removal.

➡Note insertion direction of eccentric screw.

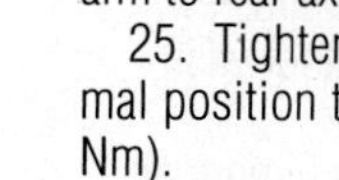

20. Align eccentric bolt to rear axle support by means of marking.
21. Refit eccentric washer.
22. Replace locking nut for swinging arm to rear axle carrier (front).
23. Tighten bolt connection in normal position to 74 ft. lbs. (100 Nm) plus additional 90 degrees.
24. Replace locking nut for swinging arm to rear axle carrier (rear).
25. Tighten bolt connection in normal position to 184 ft. lbs. (250 Nm).
26. Replace self-locking nut for swing arm to wheel carrier/integral link. Tighten to 96 ft. lbs. (130 Nm) plus additional 90 degrees

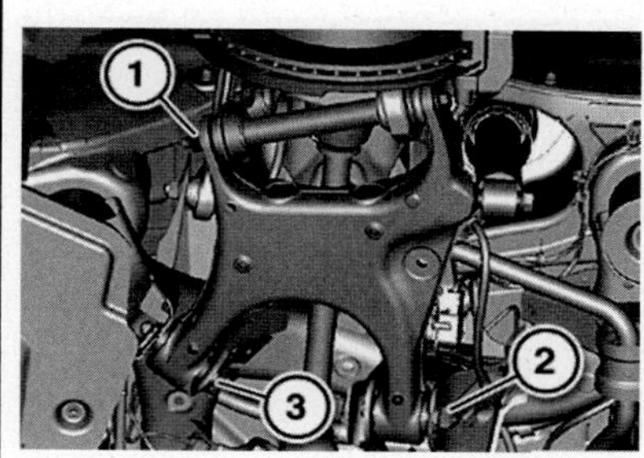

Fig. 320 Release nuts (1, 2) and remove screw (3)

Fig. 321 Loosen nut (1), remove bolt (2) towards rear

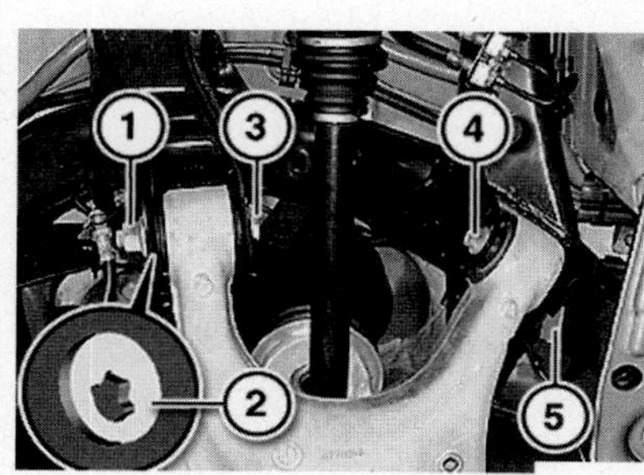

Fig. 322 Release nut, remove eccentric washer and pull out eccentric screw towards front

➡Sensor lever must point from ride-height sensor to respective rear wheel.

27. Replace self-locking nut for jointed rod to swinging arm.
28. Replace faulty expander rivets.
29. Make sure cover is correctly positioned.
30. Check that output shaft is correctly seated in rear differential.
31. Activate and fill air suspension system
32. Carry out ride-height calibration
33. Perform chassis alignment check

TRACTION STRUT

REMOVAL & INSTALLATION

1. Remove rear wheel
2. Deactivate and empty air spring system

Deactivating Air Suspension System:

1. Fold down power distribution box in passenger compartment.
2. Pull out fuse for air supply system.

Draining Air Spring System:

See Figures 323 and 324.

1. Connect BMW diagnosis system.
2. Switch on the ignition.
3. Drain air springs with aid of BMW diagnosis system (control unit functions, "Brake bleeding procedure" menu item).

➡Depending on the output pressure in the air spring, it may be necessary to repeat the brake bleeding procedure.

4. Raise vehicle until wheels are freely suspended.
5. Remove ignition key.
6. Loosen nut.

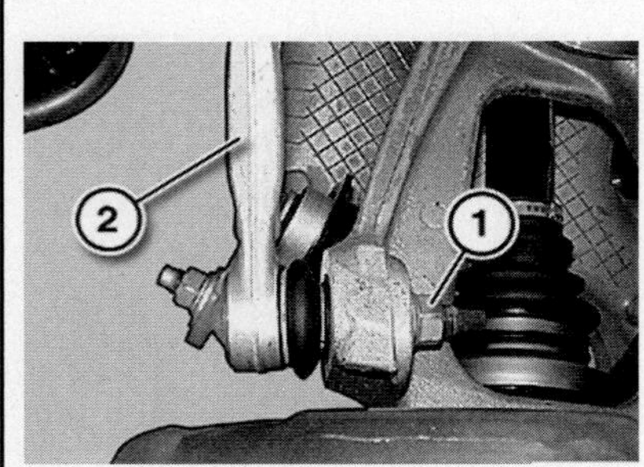

Fig. 323 Loosen nut (1), remove guide arm (2) from wheel carrier

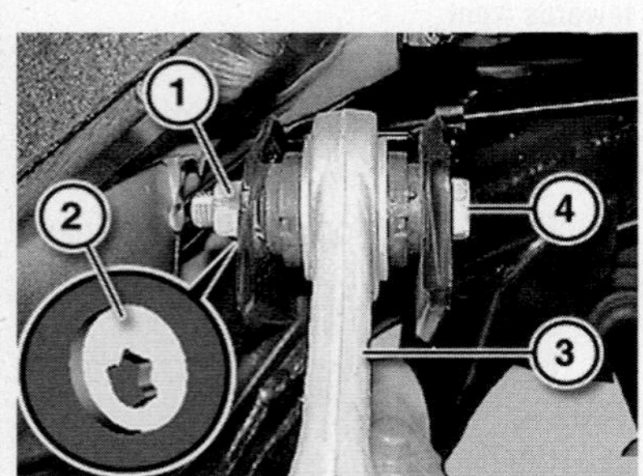

Fig. 324 Mark position of eccentric screw to rear axle carrier

7. Remove guide arm from wheel carrier.
8. Mark position of eccentric screw to rear axle carrier.
9. Release nut and remove eccentric washer.
10. Pull out eccentric screw and remove guide arm.

To install:

11. Installation is the reverse order of removal.
12. Refit eccentric washer.
13. Replace self-locking nut.
14. Align eccentric bolt to rear axle support by means of marking.
15. Tighten bolt connection in normal position to 74 ft. lbs. (100 Nm).
16. Keep guide arm to wheel carrier connection clean and free from oil and grease.
17. Replace self-locking nut for guide arm to wheel carrier. Tighten to 74 ft. lbs. (100 Nm).
18. Perform chassis alignment check

UPPER CONTROL ARM

REMOVAL & INSTALLATION

See Figures 325 through 327.

1. Remove rear wheel.
2. Deactivate and empty air spring system.
3. Remove holders (1) from control arm.
4. Loosen nut.
5. Remove control arm from wheel carrier.
6. Loosen nut.
7. Release bolt and remove control arm.

To install:

8. Installation is the reverse order of removal.
9. Note insertion direction of screw.
10. Replace self-locking nut for wishbone to rear axle support.
11. Tighten bolt connection in normal position to 74 ft. lbs. (100 Nm) plus additional 90 degrees.
12. Keep control arm to wheel carrier connection clean and free from oil and grease.

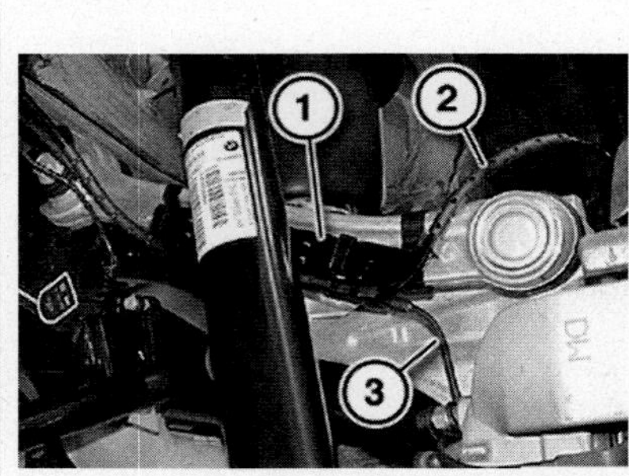

Fig. 325 Remove holders (1) from control arm, lead for pulse generator (2), only on right side: lead for brake pad sensor (3)

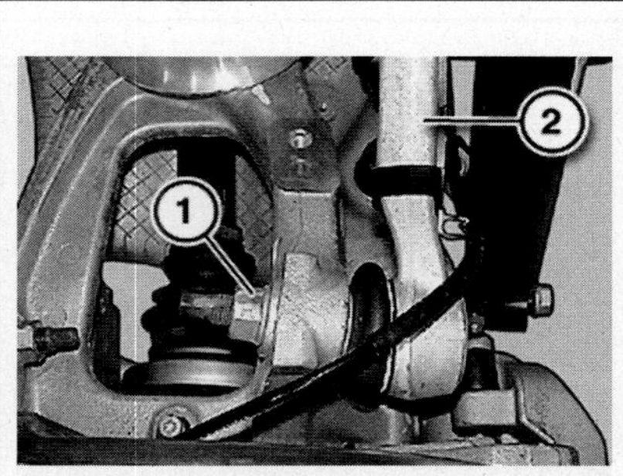

Fig. 326 Loosen nut (1), Remove control arm (2) from wheel carrier

Fig. 327 Loosen nut (1), release bolt (2) and remove control arm (3)

13. Replace self-locking nut for wishbone to wheel carrier. Tighten to 122 ft. lbs. (165 Nm)
14. Perform chassis alignment check

WHEEL BEARINGS

REMOVAL & INSTALLATION

See Figure 328.

1. Remove drive flange for rear axle shaft.
2. Release screws.
3. Remove wheel bearing.

To install:

4. Installation is the reverse order of removal.
5. Keep contact surface of wheel bearing/wheel carrier clean and free from oil and grease.
6. Except when replacing: Recondition tapped holes.
7. Install new wheel bearing.
8. Replace screws. Tighten to 74 ft. lbs. (100 Nm).
9. Adjusting parking brake

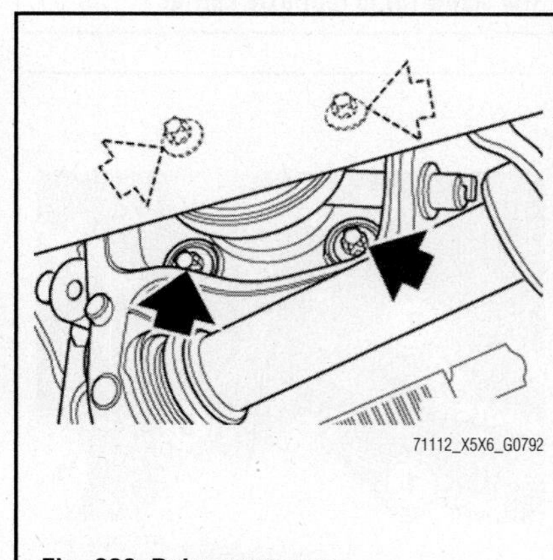

Fig. 328 Release screws

BMW

Diagnostic Trouble Codes

DIAGNOSTIC TROUBLE CODES

OBD II VEHICLE APPLICATIONS

BMW

128i, 135i
2011–2012
- 3.0L ....Engine Code: N52B30
- 3.0L ....Engine Code: N54B30
- 3.0L ....Engine Code: N55B30

328Ci, 328i, 328xi
2011–2012
- 2.0L ....Engine Code: N20B20
- 3.0L ....Engine Code: N52B30

335Ci, 335d, 335i, 335xi
2011–2012
- 3.0L ....Engine Code: N54B30
- 3.0L .... Engine Code: M57D30

M3
2011–2012
- 4.0L ....Engine Code: S65B40

528i, 528xi, 535i, 550i, 550iX
2011–2012
- 3.0L ....Engine Code: N52B30
- 3.0L ....Engine Code: N55B30
- 4.4L ....Engine Code: N63B44
- 2.0L ....Engine Code: N20B20

X1, X3, X5
2011–2012
- 3.0L ....Engine Code: N52B30
- 3.0L ....Engine Code: N55B30
- 4.4L ....Engine Code: N63B44

OBD II Trouble Code List (P0XXX Codes)

DTC	Trouble Code Title and Conditions
DTC: P0010 **1T DME, MIL: Yes** **Year:** 2011, 2012 **Model:** 1 Series M, 128i, 135i, 323i, 328i, 328i xDrive, 335is, 528i, 535i, X1, X3, X5 **Engine:** 2.5L L6, 3.0L L6, 4.4L V8	**"A" Camshaft Position Actuator Circuit (Bank 1):** Key on or engine running; and the DME detected an unexpected high voltage or low voltage condition on the camshaft position sensor. The relative position between the camshaft and crankshaft needs to be optimal so the engine has better torque, fuel economy and emissions. **Note: The camshaft adjustment is load and RPM-dependant. The electrical camshaft adjustment valve 1 switches oil pressure onto camshaft adjuster (mechanical adjustment mechanism), which adjusts the camshaft.**
DTC: P0011 **1T DME, MIL: Yes** **Year:** 2011, 2012 **Model:** 1 Series M, 128i, 135i, 323i, 328i, 328i xDrive, 335is, 528i, 535i, X1, X3, X5 **Engine:** 2.5L L6, 3.0L L6, 4.4L V8	**"A" Camshaft Position Timing Over-Advanced (Bank 1):** Engine started and driven at an engine speed of more than 400rpm; and the DME detected the camshaft timing exceeded the maximum calibrated advance value, or the camshaft remained in an advanced position during the CCM test. The valve timing did not change from the current valve timing or it remained fixed during the testing. **Note: The camshaft adjustment is load and RPM-dependant. The electrical camshaft adjustment valve 1 switches oil pressure onto camshaft adjuster (mechanical adjustment mechanism), which adjusts the camshaft.**
DTC: P0012 **1T DME, MIL: Yes** **Year:** 2011, 2012 **Model:** 1 Series M, 128i, 135i, 323i, 328i, 328i xDrive, 335is, 528i, 535i, X1, X3, X5 **Engine:** 2.5L L6, 3.0L L6, 4.4L V8	**"A" Camshaft Position Over-Retarded (Bank 1):** Engine started and driven at an engine speed of more than 400rpm; and the DME detected the camshaft timing exceeded the minimum calibrated retarded value, or the camshaft remained in an retarded position during the CCM test. The valve timing did not change from the current valve timing or it remained fixed during the testing. **Note: The camshaft adjustment is load- and RPM dependant. The electrical camshaft adjustment valve 1 switches oil pressure onto camshaft adjuster (mechanical adjustment mechanism), which adjusts the camshaft.**
DTC: P0013 **1T DME, MIL: Yes** **Year:** 2011, 2012 **Model:** 1 Series M, 128i, 135i, 323i, 328i, 328i xDrive, 335is, 528i, 535i, X1, X3, X5 **Engine:** 2.5L L6, 3.0L L6, 4.4L V8	**"B" Camshaft Position Actuator Circuit (Bank 1):** Key on or engine running; and the DME detected an unexpected high voltage or low voltage condition on the camshaft position sensor. The relative position between the camshaft and crankshaft needs to be optimal so the engine has better torque, fuel economy and emissions. **Note: The camshaft adjustment is load- and RPM dependant. The electrical camshaft adjustment valve 1 switches oil pressure onto camshaft adjuster (mechanical adjustment mechanism), which adjusts the camshaft.**
DTC: P0014 **1T DME, MIL: Yes** **Year:** 2011, 2012 **Model:** 1 Series M, 128i, 135i, 323i, 328i, 328i xDrive, 335is, 528i, 535i, X1, X3, X5 **Engine:** 2.5L L6, 3.0L L6, 4.4L V8	**"B" Camshaft Position Timing Over-Advanced (Bank 1):** Engine started and driven at an engine speed of more than 400rpm; and the DME detected the camshaft timing exceeded the maximum calibrated advance value, or the camshaft remained in an advanced position during the CCM test. The valve timing did not change from the current valve timing or it remained fixed during the testing. The VANOS is in the end position. **Note: The camshaft adjustment is load- and RPM dependant. The electrical camshaft adjustment valve 1 switches oil pressure onto camshaft adjuster (mechanical adjustment mechanism), which adjusts the camshaft.**
DTC: P0015 **1T DME, MIL: Yes** **Year:** 2011, 2012 **Model:** 1 Series M, 128i, 135i, 323i, 328i, 328i xDrive, 335is, 528i, 535i, X1, X3, X5 **Engine:** 2.5L L6, 3.0L L6, 4.4L V8	**"B" Camshaft Position Over-Retarded (Bank 1):** Engine started and driven at an engine speed of more than 400rpm; and the DME detected the camshaft timing exceeded the minimum calibrated retarded value, or the camshaft remained in an retarded position during the CCM test. The valve timing did not change from the current valve timing or it remained fixed during the testing. **Note: The camshaft adjustment is load- and RPM dependant. The electrical camshaft adjustment valve 1 switches oil pressure onto camshaft adjuster (mechanical adjustment mechanism), which adjusts the camshaft.**
DTC: P0017 **1T DME, MIL: Yes** **Year:** 2011, 2012 **Model:** 1 Series M, 128i, 135i, 328i, 328i xDrive, 335is, 528i, 535i, X1, X3, X5 **Engine:** 3.0L L6	**Crankshaft Position - Camshaft Position Correlation Bank 1 Sensor B:** Engine started, engine running, and the DME detected a deviation between the crankshaft position sensor signal and the camshaft position sensor. A rationality error has been detected for camshaft position out of phase with crankshaft.
DTC: P0020 **1T DME, MIL: Yes** **Year:** 2011, 2012 **Model:** 1 Series M, 128i, 135i, 328i, 328i xDrive, 335is, 528i, 535i, X1, X3, X5 **Engine:** 3.0L L6, 4.4L V8	**"A" Camshaft Position Timing Over-Advanced (Bank 2):** Engine started and driven at an engine speed of more than 400rpm; and the DME detected the camshaft timing exceeded the maximum calibrated advance value, or the camshaft remained in an advanced position during the CCM test. The valve timing did not change from the current valve timing or it remained fixed during the testing.

DTC	Trouble Code Title and Conditions
DTC: P0021 **1T DME, MIL: Yes** **Year:** 2011, 2012 **Model:** 1 Series M, 128i, 135i, 323i, 328i, 328i xDrive, 335is, 528i, 535i, X1, X3, X5 **Engine:** 2.5L L6, 3.0L L6, 4.4L V8	**"A" Camshaft Position Actuator Circuit (Bank 2):** Key on or engine running; and the DME detected an unexpected high voltage or low voltage condition on the camshaft position sensor. The relative position between the camshaft and crankshaft needs to be optimal so the engine has better torque, fuel economy and emissions.
DTC: P0022 **1T DME, MIL: Yes** **Year:** 2011, 2012 **Model:** 1 Series M, 128i, 135i, 323i, 328i, 328i xDrive, 335is, 528i, 535i, X1, X3, X5 **Engine:** 2.5L L6, 3.0L L6, 4.4L V8	**"A" Camshaft Position Over-Retarded (Bank 2):** Engine started and driven at an engine speed of more than 400rpm; and the DME detected the camshaft timing exceeded the minimum calibrated retarded value, or the camshaft remained in an retarded position during the CCM test. The valve timing did not change from the current valve timing or it remained fixed during the testing.
DTC: P0024 **1T DME, MIL: Yes** **Year:** 2011, 2012 **Model:** 1 Series M, 128i, 135i, 323i, 328i, 328i xDrive, 335is, 528i, 535i, X1, X3, X5 **Engine:** 2.5L L6, 3.0L L6, 4.4L V8	**"B" Camshaft Position Timing Over-Advanced (Bank 2):** Engine started and driven at an engine speed of more than 400rpm; and the DME detected the camshaft timing exceeded the maximum calibrated advance value, or the camshaft remained in an advanced position during the CCM test. The valve timing did not change from the current valve timing or it remained fixed during the testing. The engine speed should be more than 500rpm and the VANOS is in the end position.
DTC: P0025 **1T DME, MIL: Yes** **Year:** 2011, 2012 **Model:** 1 Series M, 128i, 135i, 323i, 328i, 328i xDrive, 335is, 528i, 535i, X1, X3, X5 **Engine:** 2.5L L6, 3.0L L6, 4.4L V8	**"B" Camshaft Position Over-Retarded (Bank 2):** Engine started and driven at an engine speed of more than 600rpm; and the DME detected the camshaft timing exceeded the minimum calibrated retarded value, or the camshaft remained in an retarded position during the CCM test. The valve timing did not change from the current valve timing or it remained fixed during the testing.
DTC: P0031 **1T DME, MIL: Yes** **Year:** 2011, 2012 **Model:** 1 Series M, 128i, 135i, 328i, 328i xDrive, 335is, 528i, 535i, X1, X3, X5 **Engine:** 3.0L L6, 4.4L V8	**HO2S Heater (Bank 1 Sensor 1) Circuit Low Input:** Engine started, battery voltage must be at least 11.5v, all electrical components must be off, the ground between the engine and the chassis must be well connected, the exhaust system must be properly sealed between the catalytic converter and the cylinder head, the coolant temperature must be 80 degrees Celsius, and the oxygen sensor heater for oxygen sensor before the catalytic converter must be properly functioning. The DME detected the HO2S signal was in a negative voltage range referred to as "character shift downward". This code sets when the HO2S signal remains in a low state. In effect, it does not switch properly in the closed loop operation. The HO2S (before the three-way catalytic converter) has a short circuit to ground that has lasted longer than 200 seconds.
DTC: P0032 **1T DME, MIL: Yes** **Year:** 2011, 2012 **Model:** 1 Series M, 128i, 135i, 328i, 328i xDrive, 335is, 528i, 535i, X1, X3, X5 **Engine:** 3.0L L6, 4.4L V8	**HO2S Heater (Bank 1 Sensor 1) Circuit High Input:** Engine started, battery voltage must be at least 11.5v, all electrical components must be off, the ground between the engine and the chassis must be well connected, the exhaust system must be properly sealed between the catalytic converter and the cylinder head, the coolant temperature must be 80 degrees Celsius, and the oxygen sensor heater for oxygen sensor before the catalytic converter must be properly functioning. The DME detected the HO2S signal remained in a high state. **Note: The HO2S signal circuit may be shorted to the heater power circuit due to tracking inside of the HO2S connector. Remove the connector and visually inspect the connector for signs of oil or water.**
DTC: P0036 **1T DME, MIL: Yes** **Year:** 2011, 2012 **Model:** 1 Series M, 128i, 135i, 323i, 328i, 328i xDrive, 335is, 528i, 535i, X1, X3, X5 **Engine:** 2.5L L6, 3.0L L6, 4.4L V8	**HO2S Heater (Bank 1 Sensor 2) Control Circuit Malfunction:** Engine started, battery voltage must be at least 11.5v, all electrical components must be off, the ground between the engine and the chassis must be well connected, the exhaust system must be properly sealed between the catalytic converter and the cylinder head, the coolant temperature must be 80 degrees Celsius, and the oxygen sensor heater for oxygen sensor before the catalytic converter must be properly functioning. The DME detected the HO2S signal was in a negative voltage range referred to as "character shift downward". This code sets when the HO2S signal remains in a low state.
DTC: P0037 **1T DME, MIL: Yes** **Year:** 2011, 2012 **Model:** 1 Series M, 128i, 135i, 328i, 328i xDrive, 335is, 528i, 535i, X1, X3, X5 **Engine:** 3.0L L6, 4.4L V8	**HO2S Heater (Bank 1 Sensor 2) Circuit Low Input:** Engine started, battery voltage must be at least 11.5v, all electrical components must be off, the ground between the engine and the chassis must be well connected, the exhaust system must be properly sealed between the catalytic converter and the cylinder head, the coolant temperature must be 80 degrees Celsius, and the oxygen sensor heater for oxygen sensor before the catalytic converter must be properly functioning. The DME detected the HO2S signal was in a negative voltage range referred to as "character shift downward". This code sets when the HO2S signal remains in a low state. In effect, it does not switch properly in the closed loop operation. The HO2S (before the three-way catalytic converter) has a short circuit to ground that has lasted longer than 200 seconds.

DTC	Trouble Code Title and Conditions
DTC: P0038 **1T DME, MIL: Yes** **Year:** 2011, 2012 **Model:** 1 Series M, 128i, 135i, 328i, 328i xDrive, 335is, 528i, 535i, X1, X3, X5 **Engine:** 3.0L L6, 4.4L V8	**HO2S Heater (Bank 1 Sensor 2) Circuit High Input:** Engine started, battery voltage must be at least 11.5v, all electrical components must be off, the ground between the engine and the chassis must be well connected, the exhaust system must be properly sealed between the catalytic converter and the cylinder head, the coolant temperature must be 80 degrees Celsius, and the oxygen sensor heater for oxygen sensor before the catalytic converter must be properly functioning. The DME detected the HO2S signal remained in a high state. **Note: The HO2S signal circuit may be shorted to the heater power circuit due to tracking inside of the HO2S connector. Remove the connector and visually inspect the connector for signs of oil or water.**
DTC: P0050 **1T DME, MIL: Yes** **Year:** 2011, 2012 **Model:** 1 Series M, 128i, 135i, 323i, 328i, 328i xDrive, 335is, 528i, 535i, X1, X3, X5 **Engine:** 2.5L L6, 3.0L L6, 4.4L V8	**HO2S Heater (Bank 2 Sensor 1) Control Circuit Malfunction:** Engine started, battery voltage must be at least 11.5v, all electrical components must be off, the ground between the engine and the chassis must be well connected, the exhaust system must be properly sealed between the catalytic converter and the cylinder head, and the coolant temperature must be 80 degrees Celsius. The DME detected the HO2S signal was in a negative voltage range referred to as "character shift downward".
DTC: P0051 **1T DME, MIL: Yes** **Year:** 2011, 2012 **Model:** 1 Series M, 128i, 135i, 323i, 328i, 328i xDrive, 335is, 528i, 535i, X1, X3, X5 **Engine:** 2.5L L6, 3.0L L6, 4.4L V8	**HO2S Heater (Bank 2 Sensor 1) Circuit Low Input:** Engine started, battery voltage must be at least 11.5v, all electrical components must be off, the ground between the engine and the chassis must be well connected, the exhaust system must be properly sealed between the catalytic converter and the cylinder head, and the coolant temperature must be 80 degrees Celsius. The DME detected the HO2S signal was in a negative voltage range referred to as "character shift downward". This code sets when the HO2S signal remains in a low state. In effect, it does not switch properly in the closed loop operation. The HO2S (before the three-way catalytic converter) has a short circuit to ground that has lasted longer than a specified time.
DTC: P0052 **1T DME, MIL: Yes** **Year:** 2011, 2012 **Model:** 1 Series M, 128i, 135i, 323i, 328i, 328i xDrive, 335is, 528i, 535i, X1, X3, X5 **Engine:** 2.5L L6, 3.0L L6, 4.4L V8	**HO2S Heater (Bank 2 Sensor 1) Circuit High Input:** Engine started, battery voltage must be at least 11.5v, all electrical components must be off, the ground between the engine and the chassis must be well connected, the exhaust system must be properly sealed between the catalytic converter and the cylinder head, and the coolant temperature must be 80 degrees Celsius. The DME detected the HO2S signal was in a negative voltage range referred to as "character shift downward". This code sets when the HO2S signal remains in a low state. In effect, it does not switch properly in the closed loop operation. The HO2S (before the three-way catalytic converter) has a short circuit to ground that has lasted longer than a specified time.
DTC: P0056 **1T DME, MIL: Yes** **Year:** 2011, 2012 **Model:** 1 Series M, 128i, 135i, 323i, 328i, 328i xDrive, 335is, 528i, 535i, X1, X3, X5 **Engine:** 2.5L L6, 3.0L L6, 4.4L V8	**HO2S Heater (Bank 2 Sensor 2) Circuit High Input:** Engine started, battery voltage must be at least 11.5v, all electrical components must be off, the ground between the engine and the chassis must be well connected, the exhaust system must be properly sealed between the catalytic converter and the cylinder head, and the coolant temperature must be 80 degrees Celsius. The DME detected the HO2S signal remained in a high state. **Note: The HO2S signal circuit may be shorted to the heater power circuit due to tracking inside of the HO2S connector. Remove the connector and visually inspect the connector for signs of oil or water.**
DTC: P0057 **1T DME, MIL: Yes** **Year:** 2011, 2012 **Model:** 1 Series M, 128i, 135i, 323i, 328i, 328i xDrive, 335is, 528i, 535i, X1, X3, X5 **Engine:** 2.5L L6, 3.0L L6, 4.4L V8	**HO2S Heater (Bank 2 Sensor 2) Control Circuit Malfunction:** Engine started, battery voltage must be at least 11.5v, all electrical components must be off, the ground between the engine and the chassis must be well connected, the exhaust system must be properly sealed between the catalytic converter and the cylinder head, and the coolant temperature must be 80 degrees Celsius. The DME detected the HO2S signal was in a negative voltage range referred to as "character shift downward".
DTC: P0058 **1T DME, MIL: Yes** **Year:** 2011, 2012 **Model:** 1 Series M, 128i, 135i, 323i, 328i, 328i xDrive, 335is, 528i, 535i, X1, X3, X5 **Engine:** 2.5L L6, 3.0L L6, 4.4L V8	**HO2S Heater (Bank 2 Sensor 2) Circuit Low Input:** Engine started, battery voltage must be at least 11.5v, all electrical components must be off, the ground between the engine and the chassis must be well connected, the exhaust system must be properly sealed between the catalytic converter and the cylinder head, and the coolant temperature must be 80 degrees Celsius. The DME detected the HO2S signal was in a negative voltage range referred to as "character shift downward". This code sets when the HO2S signal remains in a low state. In effect, it does not switch properly in the closed loop operation. The HO2S (before the three-way catalytic converter) has a short circuit to ground that has lasted longer than a specified time. The difference between the outside and coolant temperature is greater than 3 degrees Celsius.
DTC: P0070 **1T DME, MIL: Yes** **Year:** 2011 **Model:** 323i **Engine:** 2.5L L6	**Ambient Air Temperature Sensor Malfunction:** Key on or engine running (at over 800rpm), the vehicle velocity is over 25mph for 26 seconds, the ambient temperature is 20 degrees above or below the model figure for four seconds. This is a thermistor-type sensor with a variable resistance that changes when exposed to different temperatures. This means: the higher the temperature, the lower the resistance value.

DTC	Trouble Code Title and Conditions
DTC: P0100 **1T DME, MIL: Yes** **Year:** 2011, 2012 **Model:** 1 Series M, 128i, 135i, 328i, 328i xDrive, 335is, 528i, 535i, X1, X3, X5 **Engine:** 3.0L L6	**Mass or Volume Air Flow Circuit "A" Conditions:** Engine running, with the system voltage more than 11.0v, and the temperature must be at least 185-degrees (F) and all electrical equipment (A/C, lights, etc) must be off. The DME has detected that the MAF signal was out of a calculated range with the engine (or undetectable) for a certain period of time. The engine speed is greater than 200rpm.
DTC: P0101 **1T DME, MIL: Yes** **Year:** 2011, 2012 **Model:** 1 Series M, 128i, 135i, 323i, 328i, 328i xDrive, 335is, 528i, 535i, X1, X3, X5 **Engine:** 2.5L L6, 3.0L L6, 4.4L V8	**Mass or Volume Air Flow Circuit Range/Performance Conditions:** Engine running, with the system voltage more than 11.0v, and the temperature must be at least 185-degrees (F) and all electrical equipment (A/C, lights, etc) must be off. The DME has detected that the MAF signal was out of a calculated range with the engine (or undetectable) for a certain period of time.
DTC: P0102 **1T DME, MIL: Yes** **Year:** 2011, 2012 **Model:** 323i, X5 **Engine:** 2.5L L6, 4.4L V8	**MAF Sensor Circuit Low Input:** Key on, engine started, and the DME detected the MAF sensor signal was less than the minimum calibrated value. The engine temperature must beat least 185-degrees (F) and all electrical equipment (A/C, lights, etc) must be off. The DME has detected that the MAF signal was less than the required minimum. The engine speed is greater than 150rpm and the battery voltage is greater than 6 volts.
DTC: P0103 **1T DME, MIL: Yes** **Year:** 2011, 2012 **Model:** 323i, X5 **Engine:** 2.5L L6, 4.4L V8	**MAF Sensor Circuit High Input:** Key on, engine started, and the DME detected the MAF sensor signal was more than the minimum calibrated value. The engine temperature must beat least 185-degrees (F) and all electrical equipment (A/C, lights, etc) must be off. The DME has detected that the MAF signal was more than the required minimum. The engine speed is greater than 150rpm and the battery voltage is greater than 6 volts.
DTC: P0111 **1T DME, MIL: Yes** **Year:** 2011, 2012 **Model:** 1 Series M, 128i, 135i, 323i, 328i, 328i xDrive, 335is, 528i, 535i, X1, X3, X5 **Engine:** 2.5L L6, 3.0L L6, 4.4L V8	**Intake Air Temperature Sensor Circuit Low Input:** Key on or engine running, the temperature must beat least 185-degrees (F) and all electrical equipment (A/C, lights, etc) must be off; and the DME detected the IAT sensor signal was less than the self-test minimum. This is a thermistor-type sensor with a variable resistance that changes when exposed to different temperatures. This means: the higher the temperature, the lower the resistance value.
DTC: P0112 **1T DME, MIL: Yes** **Year:** 2011, 2012 **Model:** 323i, X5 **Engine:** 2.5L L6, 4.4L V8	**Intake Air Temperature Sensor Circuit Low Input:** Key on or Engine running, the temperature must beat least 185-degrees (F) and all electrical equipment (A/C, lights, etc) must be off; and the DME detected the IAT sensor signal was less than the self-test minimum. This is a thermistor-type sensor with a variable resistance that changes when exposed to different temperatures. This means: the higher the temperature, the lower the resistance value.
DTC: P0113 **1T DME, MIL: Yes** **Year:** 2011, 2012 **Model:** 1 Series M, 128i, 135i, 323i, 328i, 328i xDrive, 335is, 528i, 535i, X1, X3, X5 **Engine:** 2.5L L6, 3.0L L6, 4.4L V8	**Intake Air Temperature Sensor Circuit High Input:** Key on or engine running, the temperature must beat least 185-degrees (F) and all electrical equipment (A/C, lights, etc) must be off; and the DME detected the IAT sensor signal was more than the self-test maximum. This is a thermistor-type sensor with a variable resistance that changes when exposed to different temperatures. This means: the higher the temperature, the lower the resistance value.
DTC: P0116 **1T DME, MIL: Yes** **Year:** 2011, 2012 **Model:** 1 Series M, 128i, 135i, 323i, 328i, 328i xDrive, 335is, 528i, 535i, X1, X3, X5 **Engine:** 2.5L L6, 3.0L L6, 4.4L V8	**ECT Sensor Signal Range/Performance:** Engine started (cold), battery voltage must be 11.5, and all equipment must be off. The DME detected the ECT sensor exceeded the required calibrated value, or the engine is at idle and doesn't reach operating temperature quickly enough; the Catalyst, Fuel System, HO2S and Misfire Monitor did not complete, or the timer expired. Testing completion of procedure, the engine's temperature must rise uniformly during idle.
DTC: P0117 **1T DME, MIL: Yes** **Year:** 2011, 2012 **Model:** 1 Series M, 128i, 135i, 323i, 328i, 328i xDrive, 335is, 528i, 535i, X1, X3, X5 **Engine:** 2.5L L6, 3.0L L6, 4.4L V8	**ECT Sensor Circuit Low Input:** Engine started (cold) for 10 seconds, battery voltage must be 11.5, and all equipment must be off. The DME detected the ECT sensor signal was less than the self-test minimum. This is a thermistor-type sensor with a variable resistance that changes when exposed to different temperatures

DTC	Trouble Code Title and Conditions
DTC: P0118 **1T DME, MIL: Yes** **Year:** 2011, 2012 **Model:** 1 Series M, 128i, 135i, 323i, 328i, 328i xDrive, 335is, 528i, 535i, X1, X3, X5 **Engine:** 2.5L L6, 3.0L L6, 4.4L V8	**ECT Sensor Circuit High Input:** Engine started (cold) for 10 seconds, battery voltage must be 11.5, and all equipment must be off. The DME detected the ECT sensor signal was more than the self-test maximum. This is a thermistor-type sensor with a variable resistance that changes when exposed to different temperatures
DTC: P0120 **1T DME, MIL: Yes** **Year:** 2011, 2012 **Model:** 323i, X5 **Engine:** 2.5L L6, 4.4L V8	**Throttle/Pedal Position Sensor (A) Circuit Malfunction:** Engine started, at idle (to 1320rpm), the temperature must be 80 degrees Celsius. The throttle position sensor supplies implausible signal to the DME. The throttle valve activation occurs via an electric motor (throttle drive) in the throttle valve control module. It is activated by the Engine Control Module (DME) according to specifications of the two sensors, Throttle Position (TP) Sensor and Accelerator Pedal Position Sensor 2.
DTC: P0121 **1T DME, MIL: Yes** **Year:** 2011, 2012 **Model:** 323i, X5 **Engine:** 2.5L L6, 4.4L V8	**Throttle/Pedal Position Sensor Signal Range/Performance:** Engine started; then immediately following a condition where the engine was running under at off-idle, the DME detected the TP sensor signal indicated the throttle did not return to its previous closed position during the Rationality test. The engine speed is greater than 1320rpm.
DTC: P0122 **1T DME, MIL: Yes** **Year:** 2011, 2012 **Model:** 323i, X5 **Engine:** 2.5L L6, 4.4L V8	**Throttle/Pedal Position Sensor Circuit Low Input:** Engine started, at idle, the temperature must be at least 80 degrees Celsius. The throttle position sensor supplies implausible signal to the DME.
DTC: P0123 **1T DME, MIL: Yes** **Year:** 2011, 2012 **Model:** 323i, X5 **Engine:** 2.5L L6, 4.4L V8	**TP Sensor Circuit High Input:** Engine started, at idle, the temperature must be at least 80 degrees Celsius. The DME detected the TP sensor signal was more than the self-test maximum during testing.
DTC: P0125 **1T DME, MIL: Yes** **Year:** 2011, 2012 **Model:** 323i, X5 **Engine:** 2.5L L6, 4.4L V8	**ECT Sensor Insufficient for Closed Loop Fuel Control:** Engine started (cold), battery voltage must be 11.5, and all equipment must be off. The DME detected the ECT sensor exceeded the required calibrated value, or the engine is at idle and doesn't reach operating temperature quickly enough; the Catalyst, Fuel System, HO2S and Misfire Monitor did not complete, or the timer expired. Testing completion of procedure, the engine's temperature must rise uniformly during idle.
DTC: P0128 **1T DME, MIL: Yes** **Year:** 2011, 2012 **Model:** 323i, X5 **Engine:** 2.5L L6, 4.4L V8	**Coolant Thermostat (Coolant Temperature Below Thermostat Regulating Temperature):** The engine's warm up performance is monitored by comparing measured coolant temperature with the modeled coolant temperature to detect a defective coolant thermostat. The engine temperature must be less than 65 degrees Celsius, engine speed greater than 800rpm (with the vehicle speed greater than 10 but less than 90km/h) and the ambient temperature greater than -8 degrees Celsius. The thermostat should be wide open when cold, but is in error if it opens below desired control temperature.
DTC: P0130 **1T DME, MIL: Yes** **Year:** 2011, 2012 **Model:** 323i, X5 **Engine:** 2.5L L6, 4.4L V8	**O2 Sensor Circuit Bank 1 Sensor 1:** Engine running, battery voltage 11.5, all electrical components off, ground between engine and chassis well connected and the exhaust system must be properly sealed between catalytic converter and the cylinder head. The DME detected the HO2S signal was implausible or not detected. The response rate for the sensor signal period is greater than 3.8/second. The engine speed is 1280 to 2400rpm, the catalyst temperature is greater than 300 degrees Celsius and the heater has been on for less than 90 seconds.
DTC: P0131 **1T DME, MIL: Yes** **Year:** 2011, 2012 **Model:** 323i, X5 **Engine:** 2.5L L6, 4.4L V8	**HO2S (Bank 1 Sensor 1) Circuit Low Input:** Engine running, battery voltage 11.5, all electrical components off, ground between engine and chassis well connected and the exhaust system must be properly sealed between catalytic converter and the cylinder head. The DME detected the HO2S signal was in a negative voltage range referred to as "character shift downward". This code sets when the HO2S signal remains in a low state for a measured period of time. In effect, it does not switch properly in the closed loop operation.
DTC: P0132 **1T DME, MIL: Yes** **Year:** 2011, 2012 **Model:** 323i, X5 **Engine:** 2.5L L6, 4.4L V8	**HO2S (Bank 1 Sensor 1) Circuit High Input:** Engine running, battery voltage 11.5, all electrical components off, ground between engine and chassis well connected and the exhaust system must be properly sealed between catalytic converter and the cylinder head. The DME detected the HO2S signal was in a high state. This code sets when the HO2S signal remains in a high state for a measured period of time. In effect, it does not switch properly in the closed loop operation. **Note: The HO2S signal circuit may be shorted to the heater power circuit due to tracking inside of the HO2S connector. Remove the connector and visually inspect the connector for signs of oil or water.**

DTC	Trouble Code Title and Conditions
DTC: P0133 **1T DME, MIL: Yes** **Year:** 2011, 2012 **Model:** 323i, X5 **Engine:** 2.5L L6, 4.4L V8	**HO2S (Bank 1 Sensor 1) Circuit Slow Response:** Engine running, battery voltage 11.5, all electrical components off, ground between engine and chassis well connected and the exhaust system must be properly sealed between catalytic converter and the cylinder head. The DME detected the HO2S amplitude and frequency were out of the normal range (e.g., the HO2S rich to lean switch) during the HO2S Monitor test. The response rate for the sensor signal period is greater than 3.8/second. The engine speed is 1280 to 2400rpm, the catalyst temperature is greater than 300 degrees Celsius and the heater has been on for less than 90 seconds. For the 1999 M62: The idle speed variation is between 1400 and 2600rpm, the engine load variation is between 20 and 54 while the catalyst temperature should be greater than 360 degrees Celsius.
DTC: P0134 **1T DME, MIL: Yes** **Year:** 2011, 2012 **Model:** 323i, X5 **Engine:** 2.5L L6, 4.4L V8	**HO2S (Bank 1 Sensor 1) Circuit No Activity:** Engine running, battery voltage 11.5, all electrical components off, ground between engine and chassis well connected and the exhaust system must be properly sealed between catalytic converter and the cylinder head. The DME detected the HO2S signal failed to meet the maximum or minimum voltage levels (i.e., it failed the voltage range check).
DTC: P0135 **1T DME, MIL: Yes** **Year:** 2011, 2012 **Model:** 323i, X5 **Engine:** 2.5L L6, 4.4L V8	**HO2S (Bank 1 Sensor 1) Heater Circuit Malfunction:** Engine running, battery voltage 11.5, all electrical components off, ground between engine and chassis well connected and the exhaust system must be properly sealed between catalytic converter and the cylinder head. The DME detected an unexpected voltage condition, or it detected excessive current draw in the heater circuit during the CCM test. The response rate for the sensor signal period is greater than 3.8/second. The engine speed is 1280 to 2400rpm, the catalyst temperature is greater than 300 degrees Celsius and the heater has been on for less than 90 seconds.
DTC: P0136 **1T DME, MIL: Yes** **Year:** 2011, 2012 **Model:** 323i, X5 **Engine:** 2.5L L6, 4.4L V8	**HO2S (Bank 1 Sensor 2) Circuit Malfunction:** Engine running, battery voltage 11.5, all electrical components off, ground between engine and chassis well connected and the exhaust system must be properly sealed between catalytic converter and the cylinder head. The DME detected the HO2S signal failed to meet the maximum or minimum voltage levels (i.e., it failed the voltage range check). The heater has been on for less than 90 seconds, the fuel system status is in fuel cut-off, the output voltage is between 400mV and 500mV and it is 120 seconds after engine start up.
DTC: P0137 **1T DME, MIL: Yes** **Year:** 2011, 2012 **Model:** 323i, X5 **Engine:** 2.5L L6, 4.4L V8	**HO2S (Bank 1 Sensor 2) Circuit Low Input:** Engine running, battery voltage 11.5, all electrical components off, ground between engine and chassis well connected and the exhaust system must be properly sealed between catalytic converter and the cylinder head. The DME detected the HO2S signal remained in a high state. **Note: The HO2S signal circuit may be shorted to the heater power circuit due to "tracking inside of the HO2S connector. Remove the connector and visually inspect the connector for signs of oil or water.**
DTC: P0138 **1T DME, MIL: Yes** **Year:** 2011, 2012 **Model:** 323i, X5 **Engine:** 2.5L L6, 4.4L V8	**HO2S (Bank 1 Sensor 2) Circuit High Input:** Engine running, battery voltage 11.5, all electrical components off, ground between engine and chassis well connected and the exhaust system must be properly sealed between catalytic converter and the cylinder head. The DME detected the HO2S signal remained in a high state. **Note: The HO2S signal circuit may be shorted to the heater power circuit due to "tracking inside of the HO2S connector. Remove the connector and visually inspect the connector for signs of oil or water.**
DTC: P0139 **1T DME, MIL: Yes** **Year:** 2011, 2012 **Model:** 323i, X5 **Engine:** 2.5L L6, 4.4L V8	**HO2S (Bank 1 Sensor 2) Slow Response:** Engine running, battery voltage 11.5, all electrical components off, ground between engine and chassis well connected and the exhaust system must be properly sealed between catalytic converter and the cylinder head. The DME detected the HO2S amplitude and frequency were out of the normal range during the HO2S Monitor test. The heater has been on for less than 90 seconds, the fuel system status is in fuel cut-off, the output voltage is between 400mV and 500mV and it is 120 seconds after engine start up.
DTC: P0140 **1T DME, MIL: Yes** **Year:** 2011, 2012 **Model:** 323i, X5 **Engine:** 2.5L L6, 4.4L V8	**HO2S (Bank 1 Sensor 2) No Activity:** Engine running, battery voltage 11.5, all electrical components off, ground between engine and chassis well connected and the exhaust system must be properly sealed between catalytic converter and the cylinder head. The DME detected the HO2S signal failed to meet the maximum or minimum voltage levels (i.e., it failed the voltage range check).
DTC: P0141 **1T DME, MIL: Yes** **Year:** 2011, 2012 **Model:** 323i, X5 **Engine:** 2.5L L6, 4.4L V8	**HO2S (Bank 1 Sensor 2) Malfunction:** Engine running, battery voltage 11.5, all electrical components off, ground between engine and chassis well connected and the exhaust system must be properly sealed between catalytic converter and the cylinder head. The DME detected the HO2S signal failed to meet the maximum or minimum voltage levels (i.e., it failed the voltage range check). The engine speed is greater than 40rpm, the battery voltage must be between 10.7 and 15.5 volts, and the fault occurs 200 seconds after engine start up.
DTC: P0150 **1T DME, MIL: Yes** **Year:** 2011, 2012 **Model:** 323i, X5 **Engine:** 2.5L L6, 4.4L V8	**HO2S (Bank 2 Sensor 1) Circuit Malfunction:** Engine running, battery voltage 11.5, all electrical components off, ground between engine and chassis well connected and the exhaust system must be properly sealed between catalytic converter and the cylinder head. The DME detected the HO2S signal failed to meet the maximum or minimum voltage levels (i.e., it failed the voltage range check). The response rate for the sensor signal period is greater than 3.8/second. The engine speed is 1280 to 2400rpm, the catalyst temperature is greater than 300 degrees Celsius and the heater has been on for less than 90 seconds.

DTC	Trouble Code Title and Conditions
DTC: P0151 **1T DME, MIL: Yes** **Year:** 2011, 2012 **Model:** 323i, X5 **Engine:** 2.5L L6, 4.4L V8	**HO2S (Bank 2 Sensor 1) Low Input:** Engine running, battery voltage 11.5, all electrical components off, ground between engine and chassis well connected and the exhaust system must be properly sealed between catalytic converter and the cylinder head. The DME detected the HO2S signal remained in a high state. **Note: The HO2S signal circuit may be shorted to the heater power circuit due to "tracking inside of the HO2S connector. Remove the connector and visually inspect the connector for signs of oil or water.**
DTC: P0152 **1T DME, MIL: Yes** **Year:** 2011, 2012 **Model:** 323i, X5 **Engine:** 2.5L L6, 4.4L V8	**HO2S (Bank 2 Sensor 1) Circuit High Input:** Engine running, battery voltage 11.5, all electrical components off, ground between engine and chassis well connected and the exhaust system must be properly sealed between catalytic converter and the cylinder head. The DME detected the HO2S signal remained in a high state (more than 1.5v). **Note: The HO2S signal circuit may be shorted to the heater power circuit due to "tracking inside of the HO2S connector. Remove the connector and visually inspect the connector for signs of oil or water.**
DTC: P0153 **1T DME, MIL: Yes** **Year:** 2011, 2012 **Model:** 323i, X5 **Engine:** 2.5L L6, 4.4L V8	**HO2S (Bank 2 Sensor 1) Circuit Slow Response:** Engine running, battery voltage 11.5, all electrical components off, ground between engine and chassis well connected and the exhaust system must be properly sealed between catalytic converter and the cylinder head. The DME detected the HO2S amplitude and frequency were out of the normal range during the HO2S Monitor test. For the 1999 M62: The idle speed variation is between 1400 and 2600rpm, the engine load variation is between 20 and 54 while the catalyst temperature should be greater than 360 degrees Celsius.
DTC: P0154 **1T DME, MIL: Yes** **Year:** 2011, 2012 **Model:** 323i, X5 **Engine:** 2.5L L6, 4.4L V8	**HO2S (Bank 2 Sensor 1) Circuit No Activity:** Engine running, battery voltage 11.5, all electrical components off, ground between engine and chassis well connected and the exhaust system must be properly sealed between catalytic converter and the cylinder head. The DME detected the HO2S signal failed to meet the maximum or minimum voltage (i.e., it failed the voltage check).
DTC: P0155 **1T DME, MIL: Yes** **Year:** 2011, 2012 **Model:** 1 Series M, 128i, 135i, 323i, 328i, 328i xDrive, 335is, 528i, 535i, X1, X3, X5 **Engine:** 2.5L L6, 3.0L L6, 4.4L V8	**HO2S (Bank 2 Sensor 1) Heater Circuit Malfunction:** Engine running, battery voltage 11.5, all electrical components off, ground between engine and chassis well connected and the exhaust system must be properly sealed between catalytic converter and the cylinder head. The DME detected an open or shorted condition, or excessive current draw in the heater circuit. The response rate for the sensor signal period is greater than 3.8/second. The engine speed is 1280 to 2400rpm, the catalyst temperature is greater than 300 degrees Celsius and the heater has been on for less than 90 seconds.
DTC: P0156 **1T DME, MIL: Yes** **Year:** 2011, 2012 **Model:** X5 **Engine:** 4.4L V8	**HO2S (Bank 2 Sensor 2) Circuit No Activity:** Engine running, battery voltage 11.5, all electrical components off, ground between engine and chassis well connected and the exhaust system must be properly sealed between catalytic converter and the cylinder head. The DME detected the HO2S signal failed to meet the maximum or minimum voltage (i.e., it failed the voltage check). The heater has been on for less than 90 seconds, the fuel system status is in fuel cut-off, the output voltage is between 400mV and 500mV and it is 120 seconds after engine start up.
DTC: P0157 **1T DME, MIL: Yes** **Year:** 2011, 2012 **Model:** 323i, X5 **Engine:** 2.5L L6, 4.4L V8	**HO2S (Bank 2 Sensor 2) Circuit Low Voltage:** Engine running, battery voltage 11.5, all electrical components off, ground between engine and chassis well connected and the exhaust system must be properly sealed between catalytic converter and the cylinder head. The DME detected the HO2S signal remained in a high state. **Note: The HO2S signal circuit may be shorted to the heater power circuit due to "tracking inside of the HO2S connector. Remove the connector and visually inspect the connector for signs of oil or water.**
DTC: P0158 **1T DME, MIL: Yes** **Year:** 2011, 2012 **Model:** 1 Series M, 128i, 135i, 323i, 328i, 328i xDrive, 335is, 528i, 535i, X1, X3, X5 **Engine:** 2.5L L6, 3.0L L6, 4.4L V8	**HO2S (Bank 2 Sensor 2) Circuit High Input:** Engine running, battery voltage 11.5, all electrical components off, ground between engine and chassis well connected and the exhaust system must be properly sealed between catalytic converter and the cylinder head. The DME detected the HO2S signal remained in a high state (i.e., more than 1.5v). **Note: The HO2S signal circuit may be shorted to the heater power circuit due to "tracking inside of the HO2S connector. Remove the connector and visually inspect the connector for signs of oil or water.**
DTC: P0159 **1T DME, MIL: Yes** **Year:** 2011, 2012 **Model:** 323i, X5 **Engine:** 2.5L L6, 4.4L V8	**HO2S (Bank 2 Sensor 2) Circuit Slow Response:** Engine running, battery voltage 11.5, all electrical components off, ground between engine and chassis well connected and the exhaust system must be properly sealed between catalytic converter and the cylinder head. The DME detected the HO2S amplitude and frequency were out of the normal range during the HO2S Monitor test. The heater has been on for less than 90 seconds, the fuel system status is in fuel cut-off, the output voltage is between 400mV and 500mV and it is 120 seconds after engine start up.
DTC: P0160 **1T DME, MIL: Yes** **Year:** 2011, 2012 **Model:** 323i, X5 **Engine:** 2.5L L6, 4.4L V8	**HO2S (Bank 2 Sensor 2) Circuit No Activity Detected:** Engine running, battery voltage 11.5, all electrical components off, ground between engine and chassis well connected and the exhaust system must be properly sealed between catalytic converter and the cylinder head. The DME detected the HO2S signal failed to meet the maximum or minimum voltage (i.e., it failed the voltage check).

DTC	Trouble Code Title and Conditions
DTC: P0161 **1T DME, MIL: Yes** **Year:** 2011, 2012 **Model:** 1 Series M, 128i, 135i, 323i, 328i, 328i xDrive, 335is, 528i, 535i, X1, X3, X5 **Engine:** 2.5L L6, 3.0L L6, 4.4L V8	**HO2S (Bank 2 Sensor 2) Heater Circuit Malfunction:** Engine running, battery voltage 11.5, all electrical components off, ground between engine and chassis well connected and the exhaust system must be properly sealed between catalytic converter and the cylinder head. The DME detected an open or shorted condition, or excessive current draw in the heater circuit. The engine speed is greater than 40rpm, the battery voltage must be between 10.7 and 15.5 volts, and the fault occurs 200 seconds after engine start up.
DTC: P0171 **1T DME, MIL: Yes** **Year:** 2011, 2012 **Model:** 323i, X5 **Engine:** 2.5L L6, 4.4L V8	**Fuel System Too Lean (Cylinder Bank 1):** Key on or engine running, all electrical components off and coolant temperature at least 80 degrees Celsius; and the DME detected the Bank 1 Adaptive Fuel Control System reached its rich correction limit (a lean A/F condition). The fuel status is in a closed loop pattern, the coolant temperature is between 69 and 100 degrees Celsius, and the engine speed is between 800 and 6000rpm.
DTC: P0172 **1T DME, MIL: Yes** **Year:** 2011, 2012 **Model:** 323i, X5 **Engine:** 2.5L L6, 4.4L V8	**Fuel System Too Rich (Cylinder Bank 1):** Key on or engine running, all electrical components off and coolant temperature at least 80 degrees Celsius; and the DME detected the Bank 1 Adaptive Fuel Control System reached its rich correction limit (a rich A/F condition). The fuel status is in a closed loop pattern, the coolant temperature is between 69 and 100 degrees Celsius, and the engine speed is between 800 and 6000rpm.
DTC: P0174 **1T DME, MIL: Yes** **Year:** 2011, 2012 **Model:** 323i, X5 **Engine:** 2.5L L6, 4.4L V8	**Fuel System Too Lean (Cylinder Bank 2):** Key on or engine running, all electrical components off and coolant temperature at least 80 degrees Celsius; and the DME detected the Bank 2 Fuel Control System reached its lean correction limit. The fuel status is in a closed loop pattern, the coolant temperature is between 69 and 100 degrees Celsius, and the engine speed is between 800 and 6000rpm.
DTC: P0175 **1T DME, MIL: Yes** **Year:** 2011 **Model:** 323i **Engine:** 2.5L L6	**Fuel System Too Rich (Cylinder Bank 2):** Key on or engine running, all electrical components off and coolant temperature at least 80 degrees Celsius; and the DME detected the Bank 2 Adaptive Fuel Control System reached its rich correction limit (a rich A/F condition). The fuel status is in a closed loop pattern, the coolant temperature is between 69 and 100 degrees Celsius, and the engine speed is between 800 and 6000rpm.
DTC: P0201 **1T DME, MIL: Yes** **Year:** 2011, 2012 **Model:** 1 Series M, 128i, 135i, 323i, 328i, 328i xDrive, 335is, 528i, 535i, X1, X3, X5 **Engine:** 2.5L L6, 3.0L L6, 4.4L V8	**Cylinder 1 Injector Circuit Malfunction:** Engine started, and the DME detected the fuel injector "1" control circuit was in a high state when it should have been low, or in a low state when it should have been high (wiring harness & injector okay). The battery voltage should be between 9.5 and 17 volts while the engine speed is less than 40rpm.
DTC: P0202 **1T DME, MIL: Yes** **Year:** 2011, 2012 **Model:** 1 Series M, 128i, 135i, 323i, 328i, 328i xDrive, 335is, 528i, 535i, X1, X3, X5 **Engine:** 2.5L L6, 3.0L L6, 4.4L V8	**Cylinder 2 Injector Circuit Malfunction:** Engine started, and the DME detected the fuel injector "2" control circuit was in a high state when it should have been low, or in a low state when it should have been high (wiring harness & injector okay). The battery voltage should be between 9.5 and 17 volts while the engine speed is less than 40rpm.
DTC: P0203 **1T DME, MIL: Yes** **Year:** 2011, 2012 **Model:** 1 Series M, 128i, 135i, 323i, 328i, 328i xDrive, 335is, 528i, 535i, X1, X3, X5 **Engine:** 2.5L L6, 3.0L L6, 4.4L V8	**Cylinder 3 Injector Circuit Malfunction:** Engine started, and the DME detected the fuel injector "3" control circuit was in a high state when it should have been low, or in a low state when it should have been high (wiring harness & injector okay). The battery voltage should be between 9.5 and 17 volts while the engine speed is less than 40rpm.
DTC: P0204 **1T DME, MIL: Yes** **Year:** 2011, 2012 **Model:** 1 Series M, 128i, 135i, 323i, 328i, 328i xDrive, 335is, 528i, 535i, X1, X3, X5 **Engine:** 2.5L L6, 3.0L L6, 4.4L V8	**Cylinder 4 Injector Circuit Malfunction:** Engine started, and the DME detected the fuel injector "4" control circuit was in a high state when it should have been low, or in a low state when it should have been high (wiring harness & injector okay). The battery voltage should be between 9.5 and 17 volts while the engine speed is less than 40rpm.

DTC	Trouble Code Title and Conditions
DTC: P0205 **1T DME, MIL: Yes** **Year:** 2011, 2012 **Model:** 1 Series M, 128i, 135i, 323i, 328i, 328i xDrive, 335is, 528i, 535i, X1, X3, X5 **Engine:** 2.5L L6, 3.0L L6, 4.4L V8	**Cylinder 5 Injector Circuit Malfunction:** Engine started, and the DME detected the fuel injector "5" control circuit was in a high state when it should have been low, or in a low state when it should have been high (wiring harness & injector okay). The battery voltage should be between 9.5 and 17 volts while the engine speed is less than 40rpm.
DTC: P0206 **1T DME, MIL: Yes** **Year:** 2011, 2012 **Model:** 1 Series M, 128i, 135i, 323i, 328i, 328i xDrive, 335is, 528i, 535i, X1, X3, X5 **Engine:** 2.5L L6, 3.0L L6, 4.4L V8	**Cylinder 6 Injector Circuit Malfunction:** Engine started, and the DME detected the fuel injector "6" control circuit was in a high state when it should have been low, or in a low state when it should have been high (wiring harness & injector okay). The battery voltage should be between 9.5 and 17 volts while the engine speed is less than 40rpm.
DTC: P0207 **1T DME, MIL: Yes** **Year:** 2011, 2012 **Model:** 1 Series M, 128i, 135i, 323i, 328i, 328i xDrive, 335is, 528i, 535i, X1, X3, X5 **Engine:** 2.5L L6, 3.0L L6, 4.4L V8	**Cylinder 7 Injector Circuit Malfunction:** Engine started, and the DME detected the fuel injector "7" control circuit was in a high state when it should have been low, or in a low state when it should have been high (wiring harness & injector okay). The battery voltage should be between 9.5 and 17 volts while the engine speed is less than 40rpm. **Note: Monitor the INJIF PID Fault "flags" with the Scan Tool. The appropriate INJF PID "flag" will read Yes when this code is set.**
DTC: P0208 **1T DME, MIL: Yes** **Year:** 2011, 2012 **Model:** X5 **Engine:** 4.4L V8	**Cylinder 8 Injector Circuit Malfunction:** Engine started, and the DME detected the fuel injector "8" control circuit was in a high state when it should have been low, or in a low state when it should have been high (wiring harness & injector okay). The battery voltage should be between 9.5 and 17 volts while the engine speed is less than 40rpm. **Note: Monitor the INJIF PID Fault "flags" with the Scan Tool. The appropriate INJF PID "flag" will read Yes when this code is set.**
DTC: P0221 **1T DME, MIL: Yes** **Year:** 2011, 2012 **Model:** 1 Series M, 128i, 135i, 323i, 328i, 328i xDrive, 335is, 528i, 535i, X1, X3, X5 **Engine:** 2.5L L6, 3.0L L6, 4.4L V8	**Throttle Position Sensor 'B' Signal Performance:** Engine started, battery voltage at least 11.5v, all electrical components off, ground connections between engine and chassis well connected, coolant temperature at least 80-degrees Celsius and the throttle valve must not be damaged or dirty; and the DME detected the TP Sensor 'B' circuit was out of its normal operating range during a condition with the throttle wide open, or with it completely closed. The throttle valve activation occurs via an electric motor (throttle drive) in the throttle valve control module. It is activated by the DME according to specifications of the two sensors, Throttle Position Sensor and Accelerator Pedal Position Sensor 2. Slowly depress accelerator pedal up to Wide Open Throttle (WOT) stop while observing the percentage display on the PID data function of the scan tool. The percentage display must increase uniformly. The engine speed is greater than 1320rpm.
DTC: P0222 **1T DME, MIL: Yes** **Year:** 2011, 2012 **Model:** 1 Series M, 128i, 135i, 323i, 328i, 328i xDrive, 335is, 528i, 535i, X1, X3, X5 **Engine:** 2.5L L6, 3.0L L6, 4.4L V8	**Throttle Position Sensor 'B' Circuit Low Input:** Engine started, battery voltage at least 11.5v, all electrical components off, ground connections between engine and chassis well connected, coolant temperature at least 80-degrees Celsius and the throttle valve must not be damaged or dirty; and the DME detected the TP Sensor 'B' circuit was out of its normal operating range during a condition with the throttle wide open, or with it completely closed. The throttle valve activation occurs via an electric motor (throttle drive) in the throttle valve control module. It is activated by the DME according to specifications of the two sensors, Throttle Position Sensor and Accelerator Pedal Position Sensor 2. Slowly depress accelerator pedal up to Wide Open Throttle (WOT) stop while observing the percentage display on the PID data function of the scan tool. The percentage display must increase uniformly.
DTC: P0223 **1T DME, MIL: Yes** **Year:** 2011, 2012 **Model:** 1 Series M, 128i, 135i, 323i, 328i, 328i xDrive, 335is, 528i, 535i, X1, X3, X5 **Engine:** 2.5L L6, 3.0L L6, 4.4L V8	**Throttle Position Sensor 'B' Circuit High Input:** Engine started, battery voltage at least 11.5v, all electrical components off, ground connections between engine and chassis well connected, coolant temperature at least 80-degrees Celsius and the throttle valve must not be damaged or dirty; and the DME detected the TP Sensor 'B' circuit was out of its normal operating range during a condition with the throttle wide open, or with it completely closed. The throttle valve activation occurs via an electric motor (throttle drive) in the throttle valve control module. It is activated by the DME according to specifications of the two sensors, Throttle Position Sensor and Accelerator Pedal Position Sensor 2. Slowly depress accelerator pedal up to Wide Open Throttle (WOT) stop while observing the percentage display on the PID data function of the scan tool. The percentage display must increase uniformly.
DTC: P0261 **2T DME, MIL: Yes** **Year:** 2011, 2012 **Model:** 1 Series M, 128i, 135i, 323i, 328i, 328i xDrive, 335is, 528i, 535i, X1, X3, X5 **Engine:** 2.5L L6, 3.0L L6, 4.4L V8	**Cylinder 1 Injector Circuit Low Input/Short to Ground:** Key on or engine running, fuses in the instrument panel and the E-box in the engine compartment must be functioning, and the ground connections between the engine ad the chassis must be well connected; and the DME detected an unexpected voltage condition on the injector circuit.

DTC	Trouble Code Title and Conditions
DTC: P0262 **2T DME, MIL: Yes** **Year:** 2011, 2012 **Model:** 1 Series M, 128i, 135i, 323i, 328i, 328i xDrive, 335is, 528i, 535i, X1, X3, X5 **Engine:** 2.5L L6, 3.0L L6, 4.4L V8	**Cylinder 1 Injector Circuit Low Input/Short to B+:** Key on or engine running, fuses in the instrument panel and the E-box in the engine compartment must be functioning, and the ground connections between the engine ad the chassis must be well connected; and the DME detected an unexpected voltage condition on the injector circuit.
DTC: P0264 **2T DME, MIL: Yes** **Year:** 2011, 2012 **Model:** 1 Series M, 128i, 135i, 323i, 328i, 328i xDrive, 335is, 528i, 535i, X1, X3, X5 **Engine:** 2.5L L6, 3.0L L6, 4.4L V8	**Cylinder 2 Injector Circuit Low Input/Short to Ground:** Key on or engine running, fuses in the instrument panel and the E-box in the engine compartment must be functioning, and the ground connections between the engine and the chassis must be well connected; and the DME detected an unexpected voltage condition on the injector circuit.
DTC: P0265 **2T DME, MIL: Yes** **Year:** 2011, 2012 **Model:** 1 Series M, 128i, 135i, 323i, 328i, 328i xDrive, 335is, 528i, 535i, X1, X3, X5 **Engine:** 2.5L L6, 3.0L L6, 4.4L V8	**Cylinder 2 Injector Circuit Low Input/Short to B+:** Key on or engine running, fuses in the instrument panel and the E-box in the engine compartment must be functioning, and the ground connections between the engine and the chassis must be well connected; and the DME detected an unexpected voltage condition on the injector circuit.
DTC: P0267 **2T DME, MIL: Yes** **Year:** 2011, 2012 **Model:** 1 Series M, 128i, 135i, 323i, 328i, 328i xDrive, 335is, 528i, 535i, X1, X3, X5 **Engine:** 2.5L L6, 3.0L L6, 4.4L V8	**Cylinder 3 Injector Circuit Low Input/Short to Ground:** Key on or engine running, fuses in the instrument panel and the E-box in the engine compartment must be functioning, and the ground connections between the engine ad the chassis must be well connected; and the DME detected an unexpected voltage condition on the injector circuit.
DTC: P0268 **2T DME, MIL: Yes** **Year:** 2011, 2012 **Model:** 1 Series M, 128i, 135i, 323i, 328i, 328i xDrive, 335is, 528i, 535i, X1, X3, X5 **Engine:** 2.5L L6, 3.0L L6, 4.4L V8	**Cylinder 3 Injector Circuit Low Input/Short to B+:** Key on or engine running, fuses in the instrument panel and the E-box in the engine compartment must be functioning, and the ground connections between the engine ad the chassis must be well connected; and the DME detected an unexpected voltage condition on the injector circuit.
DTC: P0270 **2T DME, MIL: Yes** **Year:** 2011, 2012 **Model:** 1 Series M, 128i, 135i, 323i, 328i, 328i xDrive, 335is, 528i, 535i, X1, X3, X5 **Engine:** 2.5L L6, 3.0L L6, 4.4L V8	**Cylinder 4 Injector Circuit Low Input/Short to Ground:** Key on or engine running, fuses in the instrument panel and the E-box in the engine compartment must be functioning, and the ground connections between the engine ad the chassis must be well connected; and the DME detected an unexpected voltage condition on the injector circuit.
DTC: P0271 **2T DME, MIL: Yes** **Year:** 2011, 2012 **Model:** 1 Series M, 128i, 135i, 323i, 328i, 328i xDrive, 335is, 528i, 535i, X1, X3, X5 **Engine:** 2.5L L6, 3.0L L6, 4.4L V8	**Cylinder 4 Injector Circuit Low Input/Short to B+:** Key on or engine running, fuses in the instrument panel and the E-box in the engine compartment must be functioning, and the ground connections between the engine ad the chassis must be well connected; and the DME detected an unexpected voltage condition on the injector circuit.
DTC: P0273 **2T DME, MIL: Yes** **Year:** 2011, 2012 **Model:** 1 Series M, 128i, 135i, 323i, 328i, 328i xDrive, 335is, 528i, 535i, X1, X3, X5 **Engine:** 2.5L L6, 3.0L L6, 4.4L V8	**Cylinder 5 Injector Circuit Low Input/Short to Ground:** Key on or engine running, fuses in the instrument panel and the E-box in the engine compartment must be functioning, and the ground connections between the engine ad the chassis must be well connected; and the DME detected an unexpected voltage condition on the injector circuit.

DTC	Trouble Code Title and Conditions
DTC: P0274 **2T DME, MIL: Yes** **Year:** 2011, 2012 **Model:** 323i, X5 **Engine:** 2.5L L6, 4.4L V8	**Cylinder 5 Injector Circuit Low Input/Short to B+:** Key on or engine running, fuses in the instrument panel and the E-box in the engine compartment must be functioning, and the ground connections between the engine ad the chassis must be well connected; and the DME detected an unexpected voltage condition on the injector circuit.
DTC: P0276 **2T DME, MIL: Yes** **Year:** 2011, 2012 **Model:** 1 Series M, 128i, 135i, 323i, 328i, 328i xDrive, 335is, 528i, 535i, X1, X3, X5 **Engine:** 2.5L L6, 3.0L L6, 4.4L V8	**Cylinder 6 Injector Circuit Low Input/Short to Ground:** Key on or engine running, fuses in the instrument panel and the E-box in the engine compartment must be functioning, and the ground connections between the engine ad the chassis must be well connected; and the DME detected an unexpected voltage condition on the injector circuit.
DTC: P0277 **2T DME, MIL: Yes** **Year:** 2011, 2012 **Model:** 1 Series M, 128i, 135i, 323i, 328i, 328i xDrive, 335is, 528i, 535i, X1, X3, X5 **Engine:** 2.5L L6, 3.0L L6, 4.4L V8	**Cylinder 6 Injector Circuit Low Input/Short to B+:** Key on or engine running, fuses in the instrument panel and the E-box in the engine compartment must be functioning, and the ground connections between the engine ad the chassis must be well connected; and the DME detected an unexpected voltage condition on the injector circuit.
DTC: P0279 **2T DME, MIL: Yes** **Year:** 2011, 2012 **Model:** 1 Series M, 128i, 135i, 328i, 328i xDrive, 335is, 528i, 535i, X1, X3, X5 **Engine:** 3.0L L6, 4.4L V8	**Cylinder 7 Injector Circuit Low Input/Short to Ground:** Key on or engine running, fuses in the instrument panel and the E-box in the engine compartment must be functioning, and the ground connections between the engine ad the chassis must be well connected; and the DME detected an unexpected voltage condition on the injector circuit.
DTC: P0280 **2T DME, MIL: Yes** **Year:** 2011, 2012 **Model:** 1 Series M, 128i, 135i, 328i, 328i xDrive, 335is, 528i, 535i, X1, X3, X5 **Engine:** 4.4L V8	**Cylinder 7 Injector Circuit Low Input/Short to B+:** Key on or engine running, fuses in the instrument panel and the E-box in the engine compartment must be functioning, and the ground connections between the engine ad the chassis must be well connected; and the DME detected an unexpected voltage condition on the injector circuit.
DTC: P0282 **2T DME, MIL: Yes** **Year:** 2011, 2012 **Model:** 1 Series M, 128i, 135i, 328i, 328i xDrive, 335is, 528i, 535i, X1, X3, X5 **Engine:** 4.4L V8	**Cylinder 8 Injector Circuit Low Input/Short to Ground:** Key on or engine running, fuses in the instrument panel and the E-box in the engine compartment must be functioning, and the ground connections between the engine ad the chassis must be well connected; and the DME detected an unexpected voltage condition on the injector circuit.
DTC: P0283 **2T DME, MIL: Yes** **Year:** 2011, 2012 **Model:** 1 Series M, 128i, 135i, 328i, 328i xDrive, 335is, 528i, 535i, X1, X3, X5 **Engine:** 4.4L V8	**Cylinder 8 Injector Circuit Low Input/Short to B+:** Key on or engine running, fuses in the instrument panel and the E-box in the engine compartment must be functioning, and the ground connections between the engine ad the chassis must be well connected; and the DME detected an unexpected voltage condition on the injector circuit.
DTC: P0298 **1T DME, MIL: Yes** **Year:** 2011, 2012 **Model:** 1 Series M, 128i, 135i, 328i, 328i xDrive, 335is, 528i, 535i, X1, X3, X5 **Engine:** 3.0L L6	**Engine Oil Over Temperature:** The oil temperature difference of greater than 100 degrees within one second. The ignition must be on. The DME detected an error in the Engine Oil Temperature sensor. This occurs during attempted start value calibration.

DTC	Trouble Code Title and Conditions
DTC: P0300 **1T DME, MIL: Yes** **Year:** 2011, 2012 **Model:** 1 Series M, 128i, 135i, 323i, 328i, 328i xDrive, 335is, 528i, 535i, X1, X3, X5 **Engine:** 2.5L L6, 3.0L L6, 4.4L V8	**Random/Multiple Misfire Detected:** Engine running at an RPM greater than 400 but less than 6400 the DME detected a misfire or uneven engine running in two or more cylinders within 200 crankshaft rotations. Engine speed is between 480 and 4500rpm, load change is 0.4ms at ignition with a speed change of 2800rpms and the ASC is not active. **Note: If the misfire is severe, the MIL will flash on/off on the first trip!**
DTC: P0301 **1T DME, MIL: Yes** **Year:** 2011, 2012 **Model:** 1 Series M, 128i, 135i, 323i, 328i, 328i xDrive, 335is, 528i, 535i, X1, X3, X5 **Engine:** 2.5L L6, 3.0L L6, 4.4L V8	**Cylinder Number 1 Misfire Detected:** Engine running at an RPM greater than 400 but less than 6400 the DME detected a misfire or uneven engine running in two or more cylinders within 200 crankshaft rotations. Engine speed is between 480 and 4500rpm, load change is 0.4ms at ignition with a speed change of 2800rpms and the ASC is not active. **Note: If the misfire is severe, the MIL will flash on/off on the first trip!**
DTC: P0302 **1T DME, MIL: Yes** **Year:** 2011, 2012 **Model:** 1 Series M, 128i, 135i, 323i, 328i, 328i xDrive, 335is, 528i, 535i, X1, X3, X5 **Engine:** 2.5L L6, 3.0L L6, 4.4L V8	**Cylinder Number 2 Misfire Detected:** Engine running at an RPM greater than 400 but less than 6400 the DME detected a misfire or uneven engine running in two or more cylinders within 200 crankshaft rotations. Engine speed is between 480 and 4500rpm, load change is 0.4ms at ignition with a speed change of 2800rpms and the ASC is not active. **Note: If the misfire is severe, the MIL will flash on/off on the 1st trip!**
DTC: P0303 **1T DME, MIL: Yes** **Year:** 2011, 2012 **Model:** 1 Series M, 128i, 135i, 323i, 328i, 328i xDrive, 335is, 528i, 535i, X1, X3, X5 **Engine:** 2.5L L6, 3.0L L6, 4.4L V8	**Cylinder Number 3 Misfire Detected:** Engine running at an RPM greater than 400 but less than 6400 the DME detected a misfire or uneven engine running in two or more cylinders within 200 crankshaft rotations. Engine speed is between 480 and 4500rpm, load change is 0.4ms at ignition with a speed change of 2800rpms and the ASC is not active. **Note: If the misfire is severe, the MIL will flash on/off on the 1st trip!**
DTC: P0304 **1T DME, MIL: Yes** **Year:** 2011, 2012 **Model:** 1 Series M, 128i, 135i, 323i, 328i, 328i xDrive, 335is, 528i, 535i, X1, X3, X5 **Engine:** 2.5L L6, 3.0L L6, 4.4L V8	**Cylinder Number 4 Misfire Detected:** Engine running at an RPM greater than 400 but less than 6400 the DME detected a misfire or uneven engine running in two or more cylinders within 200 crankshaft rotations. Engine speed is between 480 and 4500rpm, load change is 0.4ms at ignition with a speed change of 2800rpms and the ASC is not active. **Note: If the misfire is severe, the MIL will flash on/off on the 1st trip!**
DTC: P0305 **1T DME, MIL: Yes** **Year:** 2011, 2012 **Model:** 1 Series M, 128i, 135i, 323i, 328i, 328i xDrive, 335is, 528i, 535i, X1, X3, X5 **Engine:** 2.5L L6, 3.0L L6, 4.4L V8	**Cylinder Number 5 Misfire Detected:** Engine running under positive torque conditions, and the DME detected a misfire or uneven engine function. Engine speed is between 480 and 4500rpm, load change is 0.4ms at ignition with a speed change of 2800rpms and the ASC is not active. **Note: If the misfire is severe, the MIL will flash on/off on the 1st trip!**
DTC: P0306 **1T DME, MIL: Yes** **Year:** 2011, 2012 **Model:** 1 Series M, 128i, 135i, 323i, 328i, 328i xDrive, 335is, 528i, 535i, X1, X3, X5 **Engine:** 2.5L L6, 3.0L L6, 4.4L V8	**Cylinder Number 6 Misfire Detected:** Engine running under positive torque conditions, and the DME detected a misfire or uneven engine function. Engine speed is between 480 and 4500rpm, load change is 0.4ms at ignition with a speed change of 2800rpms and the ASC is not active. **Note: If the misfire is severe, the MIL will flash on/off on the 1st trip!**
DTC: P0307 **1T DME, MIL: Yes** **Year:** 2011, 2012 **Model:** X5 **Engine:** 4.4L V8	**Cylinder Number 7 Misfire Detected:** Engine running under positive torque conditions, and the DME detected a misfire or uneven engine function. Engine speed is between 480 and 4500rpm, load change is 0.4ms at ignition with a speed change of 2800rpms and the ASC is not active. **Note: If the misfire is severe, the MIL will flash on/off on the 1st trip!**
DTC: P0308 **1T DME, MIL: Yes** **Year:** 2011, 2012 **Model:** X5 **Engine:** 4.4L V8	**Cylinder Number 8 Misfire Detected:** Engine running under positive torque conditions, and the DME detected a misfire or uneven engine function. Engine speed is between 480 and 4500rpm, load change is 0.4ms at ignition with a speed change of 2800rpms and the ASC is not active. **Note: If the misfire is severe, the MIL will flash on/off on the 1st trip!**

DTC	Trouble Code Title and Conditions
DTC: P0313 **1T DME, MIL: Yes** **Year:** 2011, 2012 **Model:** 1 Series M, 128i, 135i, 323i, 328i, 328i xDrive, 335is, 528i, 535i, X1, X3, X5 **Engine:** 2.5L L6, 3.0L L6	**Misfire Detected with Low Fuel:** Engine running under positive torque conditions, and the DME detected a misfire or uneven engine function. **Note: If the misfire is severe, the MIL will flash on/off on the 1st trip!**
DTC: P0325 **1T DME, MIL: Yes** **Year:** 2011, 2012 **Model:** 1 Series M, 128i, 135i, 323i, 328i, 328i xDrive, 335is, 528i, 535i, X1, X3, X5 **Engine:** 2.5L L6, 3.0L L6, 4.4L V8	**Knock Sensor 1 Circuit Malfunction:** Engine started, vehicle driven at 1520rpm for 3 seconds or to a temperature of 40 degrees Celsius, and the DME detected the Knock Sensor 1 (KS1) signal was not recognized. The engine speed is greater than 2080rpm but less than 6000rpm and the coolant temperature is greater than 40.5 degrees Celsius.
DTC: P0327 **1T DME, MIL: Yes** **Year:** 2011, 2012 **Model:** 1 Series M, 128i, 135i, 323i, 328i, 328i xDrive, 335is, 528i, 535i, X1, X3, X5 **Engine:** 2.5L L6, 3.0L L6, 4.4L V8	**Knock Sensor 1 Signal Low Input:** Engine started, vehicle driven at 2000rpm for 3 seconds or to a temperature of 40 degrees Celsius, and the DME detected the Knock Sensor 1 (KS1) signal was too low or not recognized by the DME
DTC: P0328 **1T DME, MIL: Yes** **Year:** 2011, 2012 **Model:** 1 Series M, 128i, 135i, 323i, 328i, 328i xDrive, 335is, 528i, 535i, X1, X3, X5 **Engine:** 2.5L L6, 3.0L L6, 4.4L V8	**Knock Sensor 1 Signal High Input:** Engine started, vehicle driven at 1600rpm for 3 seconds or to a temperature of 40 degrees Celsius, and the DME detected the Knock Sensor 1 (KS1) signal was too high
DTC: P0330 **1T DME, MIL: Yes** **Year:** 2011, 2012 **Model:** 1 Series M, 128i, 135i, 323i, 328i, 328i xDrive, 335is, 528i, 535i, X1, X3, X5 **Engine:** 2.5L L6, 3.0L L6, 4.4L V8	**Knock Sensor 1 Circuit Malfunction:** Engine started, vehicle driven at 1520rpm for 3 seconds or to a temperature of 40 degrees Celsius, and the DME detected the Knock Sensor 1 (KS1) signal was not recognized. The engine speed is greater than 2080rpm but less than 6000rpm and the coolant temperature is greater than 40.5 degrees Celsius.
DTC: P0332 **1T DME, MIL: Yes** **Year:** 2011, 2012 **Model:** 1 Series M, 128i, 135i, 323i, 328i, 328i xDrive, 335is, 528i, 535i, X1, X3, X5 **Engine:** 2.5L L6, 3.0L L6, 4.4L V8	**Knock Sensor 2 Signal Low Input:** Engine started, vehicle driven, and the DME detected the Knock Sensor 1 (KS1) signal was too low or not recognized by the DME
DTC: P0333 **1T DME, MIL: Yes** **Year:** 2011, 2012 **Model:** X5 **Engine:** 4.4L V8	**Knock Sensor 2 Signal High Input:** Engine started, vehicle driven, and the DME detected the Knock Sensor 1 (KS1) signal was too high
DTC: P0335 **1T DME, MIL: Yes** **Year:** 2011, 2012 **Model:** 1 Series M, 128i, 135i, 323i, 328i, 328i xDrive, 335is, 528i, 535i, X1, X3, X5 **Engine:** 2.5L L6, 3.0L L6, 4.4L V8	**Camshaft Position Sensor "A" Circ Malfunction:** Engine started, battery voltage must be at least 11.5v, all electrical components must be off, parking brake must be engaged (to keep daytime driving lights off), automatic transmission selector must be in park and the ground between the engine and the chassis must be well connected. The DME detected the CMP sensor signal was implausible. Engine speed is greater than 500rpm, and the fault is tolerable as long as there are no misfired occurring at the same time.

DTC	Trouble Code Title and Conditions
DTC: P0336 **1T DME, MIL: Yes** **Year:** 2011, 2012 **Model:** 1 Series M, 128i, 135i, 328i, 328i xDrive, 335is, 528i, 535i, X1, X3, X5 **Engine:** 3.0L L6	**Camshaft Position Sensor "A" Circ Range/Performance:** Engine started (and engine speed is less than 25rpm), battery voltage must be at least 11.5v, all electrical components must be off, parking brake must be engaged (to keep daytime driving lights off), automatic transmission selector must be in park and the ground between the engine and the chassis must be well connected. The DME detected the CMP sensor signal was implausible.
DTC: P0339 **1T DME, MIL: Yes** **Year:** 2011 **Model:** 323i **Engine:** 2.5L L6	**Camshaft Position Sensor Circuit Malfunction:** Engine started, battery voltage must be at least 11.5v, all electrical components must be off, parking brake must be engaged (to keep daytime driving lights off), automatic transmission selector must be in park and the ground between the engine and the chassis must be well connected. The DME detected the CMP sensor signal was missing or it was erratic. There is no signal or an invalid one, and the engine speed is greater than 200rpm for two cycles.
DTC: P0340 **1T DME, MIL: Yes** **Year:** 2011, 2012 **Model:** 1 Series M, 128i, 135i, 323i, 328i, 328i xDrive, 335is, 528i, 535i, X1, X3, X5 **Engine:** 2.5L L6, 3.0L L6, 4.4L V8	**Camshaft Position Sensor Circuit Malfunction:** Engine started, battery voltage must be at least 11.5v, all electrical components must be off, parking brake must be engaged (to keep daytime driving lights off), automatic transmission selector must be in park and the ground between the engine and the chassis must be well connected. The DME detected the CMP sensor signal was missing or it was erratic. There is no signal or an invalid one, and the engine speed is greater than 200rpm for two cycles.
DTC: P0341 **1T DME, MIL: Yes** **Year:** 2011, 2012 **Model:** 1 Series M, 128i, 135i, 328i, 328i xDrive, 335is, 528i, 535i, X1, X3, X5 **Engine:** 3.0L L6	**Camshaft Position Sensor Circ Range/Performance:** Engine started, battery voltage must be at least 11.5v, all electrical components must be off, parking brake must be engaged (to keep daytime driving lights off), automatic transmission selector must be in park and the ground between the engine and the chassis must be well connected. The DME detected the CMP sensor signal was implausible.
DTC: P0342 **1T DME, MIL: Yes** **Year:** 2011, 2012 **Model:** 1 Series M, 128i, 135i, 328i, 328i xDrive, 335is, 528i, 535i, X1, X3, X5 **Engine:** 3.0L L6	**Camshaft Position Sensor "A" Circuit (Bank 1 or Single Sensor) Low Input:** Engine started, battery voltage must be at least 11.5v, all electrical components must be off, parking brake must be engaged (to keep daytime driving lights off), automatic transmission selector must be in park and the ground between the engine and the chassis must be well connected. The DME detected the CMP sensor signal exceeded the bounds of the specified maximum limit.
DTC: P0343 **1T DME, MIL: Yes** **Year:** 2011, 2012 **Model:** 1 Series M, 128i, 135i, 328i, 328i xDrive, 335is, 528i, 535i, X1, X3, X5 **Engine:** 3.0L L6	**Camshaft Position Sensor "A" Circuit (Bank 1 or Single Sensor) High Input:** Engine started, battery voltage must be at least 11.5v, all electrical components must be off, parking brake must be engaged (to keep daytime driving lights off), automatic transmission selector must be in park and the ground between the engine and the chassis must be well connected. The DME detected the CMP sensor signal did not reach the specified minimum limit.
DTC: P0345 **1T DME, MIL: Yes** **Year:** 2011, 2012 **Model:** X5 **Engine:** 4.4L V8	**Camshaft Position Sensor "A" Circuit (Bank 2):** Engine started, battery voltage must be at least 11.5v, all electrical components must be off, parking brake must be engaged (to keep daytime driving lights off), automatic transmission selector must be in park and the ground between the engine and the chassis must be well connected. The DME detected the CMP sensor signal was missing or it was erratic.
DTC: P0346 **1T DME, MIL: Yes** **Year:** 2011, 2012 **Model:** 1 Series M, 128i, 135i, 328i, 328i xDrive, 335is, 528i, 535i, X1, X3, X5 **Engine:** 3.0L L6	**Camshaft Position Sensor "A" Circuit (Bank 2) Range/Performance:** Engine started, battery voltage must be at least 11.5v, all electrical components must be off, parking brake must be engaged (to keep daytime driving lights off), automatic transmission selector must be in park and the ground between the engine and the chassis must be well connected. The DME detected the CMP sensor signal was implausible.
DTC: P0347 **1T DME, MIL: Yes** **Year:** 2011, 2012 **Model:** 1 Series M, 128i, 135i, 328i, 328i xDrive, 335is, 528i, 535i, X1, X3, X5 **Engine:** 3.0L L6	**Camshaft Position Sensor "A" Circuit (Bank 2) Low Input:** Engine started, battery voltage must be at least 11.5v, all electrical components must be off, parking brake must be engaged (to keep daytime driving lights off), automatic transmission selector must be in park and the ground between the engine and the chassis must be well connected. The DME detected the CMP sensor signal exceeded the bounds of the specified maximum limit.

DTC	Trouble Code Title and Conditions
DTC: P0348 **1T DME, MIL: Yes** **Year:** 2011, 2012 **Model:** 1 Series M, 128i, 135i, 328i, 328i xDrive, 335is, 528i, 535i, X1, X3, X5 **Engine:** 3.0L L6	**Camshaft Position Sensor "A" Circuit (Bank 2) High Input:** Engine started, battery voltage must be at least 11.5v, all electrical components must be off, parking brake must be engaged (to keep daytime driving lights off), automatic transmission selector must be in park and the ground between the engine and the chassis must be well connected. The DME detected the CMP sensor signal did not reach the specified minimum limit.
DTC: P0351 **1T DME, MIL: Yes** **Year:** 2011, 2012 **Model:** 1 Series M, 128i, 135i, 328i, 328i xDrive, 335is, 528i, 535i, X1, X3, X5 **Engine:** 3.0L L6	**Ignition Coilpack A Primary/Secondary Circuit Malfunction:** Engine started, battery voltage must be at least 11.5v, all electrical components must be off, parking brake must be engaged (to keep daytime driving lights off), automatic transmission selector must be in park and the ground between the engine and the chassis must be well connected. The DME did not receive any valid pulses from the ignition module for the Ignition Coilpack A primary circuit. **Note: Ignition coils and power output stages are one component and cannot be replaced individually.**
DTC: P0353 **1T DME, MIL: Yes** **Year:** 2011, 2012 **Model:** 1 Series M, 128i, 135i, 328i, 328i xDrive, 335is, 528i, 535i, X1, X3, X5 **Engine:** 3.0L L6	**Ignition Coilpack C Primary/Secondary Circuit Malfunction:** Engine started, battery voltage must be between 9 and 17 volts. The DME did not receive any valid pulses from the ignition module for the Ignition Coilpack C primary circuit. Voltage supplied and ground must be connected for ignition system spark plugs and coils. Check wiring harness, ground connection and plug-in contacts. Visual inspection of spark plug, ignition coil (replace if damaged). After excluding all of these faults, replace the control module. The injection is deactivated with a combustion miss and supplementary recognition of a rough running diagnosis. **Note: Ignition coils and power output stages are one component and cannot be replaced individually.**
DTC: P0354 **1T DME, MIL: Yes** **Year:** 2011, 2012 **Model:** 1 Series M, 128i, 135i, 328i, 328i xDrive, 335is, 528i, 535i, X1, X3, X5 **Engine:** 3.0L L6	**Ignition Coilpack D Primary/Secondary Circuit Malfunction:** Engine started, battery voltage must be between 9 and 17 volts. The DME did not receive any valid pulses from the ignition module for the Ignition Coilpack C primary circuit. Voltage supplied and ground must be connected for ignition system spark plugs and coils. Check wiring harness, ground connection and plug-in contacts. Visual inspection of spark plug, ignition coil (replace if damaged). After excluding all of these faults, replace the control module. The injection is deactivated with a combustion miss and supplementary recognition of a rough running diagnosis. **Note: Ignition coils and power output stages are one component and cannot be replaced individually.**
DTC: P0355 **1T DME, MIL: Yes** **Year:** 2011, 2012 **Model:** 1 Series M, 128i, 135i, 328i, 328i xDrive, 335is, 528i, 535i, X1, X3, X5 **Engine:** 3.0L L6	**Ignition Coilpack E Primary/Secondary Circuit Malfunction:** Engine started, battery voltage must be between 9 and 17 volts. The DME did not receive any valid pulses from the ignition module for the Ignition Coilpack C primary circuit. Voltage supplied and ground must be connected for ignition system spark plugs and coils. Check wiring harness, ground connection and plug-in contacts. Visual inspection of spark plug, ignition coil (replace if damaged). After excluding all of these faults, replace the control module. The injection is deactivated with a combustion miss and supplementary recognition of a rough running diagnosis. **Note: Ignition coils and power output stages are one component and cannot be replaced individually.**
DTC: P0356 **1T DME, MIL: Yes** **Year:** 2011, 2012 **Model:** 1 Series M, 128i, 135i, 328i, 328i xDrive, 335is, 528i, 535i, X1, X3, X5 **Engine:** 3.0L L6	**Ignition Coilpack F Primary/Secondary Circuit Malfunction:** Engine started, battery voltage must be between 9 and 17 volts. The DME did not receive any valid pulses from the ignition module for the Ignition Coilpack C primary circuit. Voltage supplied and ground must be connected for ignition system spark plugs and coils. Check wiring harness, ground connection and plug-in contacts. Visual inspection of spark plug, ignition coil (replace if damaged). After excluding all of these faults, replace the control module. The injection is deactivated with a combustion miss and supplementary recognition of a rough running diagnosis. **Note: Ignition coils and power output stages are one component and cannot be replaced individually.**
DTC: P0357 **1T DME, MIL: Yes** **Year:** 2011, 2012 **Model:** 1 Series M, 128i, 135i, 328i, 328i xDrive, 335is, 528i, 535i, X1, X3, X5 **Engine:** 3.0L L6	**Ignition Coilpack G Primary/Secondary Circuit Malfunction:** Engine started, battery voltage must be between 9 and 17 volts. The DME did not receive any valid pulses from the ignition module for the Ignition Coilpack C primary circuit. Voltage supplied and ground must be connected for ignition system spark plugs and coils. Check wiring harness, ground connection and plug-in contacts. Visual inspection of spark plug, ignition coil (replace if damaged). After excluding all of these faults, replace the control module. The injection is deactivated with a combustion miss and supplementary recognition of a rough running diagnosis. **Note: Ignition coils and power output stages are one component and cannot be replaced individually.**
DTC: P0358 **1T DME, MIL: Yes** **Year:** 2011, 2012 **Model:** 1 Series M, 128i, 135i, 328i, 328i xDrive, 335is, 528i, 535i, X1, X3, X5 **Engine:** 3.0L L6	**Ignition Coilpack H Primary/Secondary Circuit Malfunction:** Engine started, battery voltage must be between 9 and 17 volts. The DME did not receive any valid pulses from the ignition module for the Ignition Coilpack C primary circuit. Voltage supplied and ground must be connected for ignition system spark plugs and coils. Check wiring harness, ground connection and plug-in contacts. Visual inspection of spark plug, ignition coil (replace if damaged). After excluding all of these faults, replace the control module. The injection is deactivated with a combustion miss and supplementary recognition of a rough running diagnosis. **Note: Ignition coils and power output stages are one component and cannot be replaced individually.**

DTC	Trouble Code Title and Conditions
DTC: P0365 **1T DME, MIL: Yes** **Year:** 2011, 2012 **Model:** 1 Series M, 128i, 135i, 323i, 328i, 328i xDrive, 335is, 528i, 535i, X1, X3, X5 **Engine:** 2.5L L6, 3.0L L6, 4.4L V8	**Camshaft Position Sensor "B" Circuit (Bank 1):** Engine started, battery voltage must be at least 11.5v, all electrical components must be off, parking brake must be engaged (to keep daytime driving lights off), automatic transmission selector must be in park and the ground between the engine and the chassis must be well connected. The DME detected the CMP sensor signal exceeded the bounds of the specified maximum limit. Flank number within three camshaft revolutions not 0, 1, 11, 12, 13. The number of phase flanks per cycle is implausible.
DTC: P0366 **1T DME, MIL: Yes** **Year:** 2011, 2012 **Model:** 1 Series M, 128i, 135i, 328i, 328i xDrive, 335is, 528i, 535i, X1, X3, X5 **Engine:** 3.0L L6	**Camshaft Position Sensor "B" Circuit (Bank 1) Range/Performance:** Engine started, battery voltage must be at least 11.5v, all electrical components must be off, parking brake must be engaged (to keep daytime driving lights off), automatic transmission selector must be in park and the ground between the engine and the chassis must be well connected. The DME detected the CMP sensor signal exceeded the bounds of the specified maximum limit.
DTC: P0367 **1T DME, MIL: Yes** **Year:** 2011, 2012 **Model:** 1 Series M, 128i, 135i, 328i, 328i xDrive, 335is, 528i, 535i, X1, X3, X5 **Engine:** 3.0L L6	**Camshaft Position Sensor "B" Circuit (Bank 1) Low Input:** Engine started, battery voltage must be at least 11.5v, all electrical components must be off, parking brake must be engaged (to keep daytime driving lights off), automatic transmission selector must be in park and the ground between the engine and the chassis must be well connected. The DME detected the CMP sensor signal exceeded the bounds of the specified maximum limit.
DTC: P0368 **1T DME, MIL: Yes** **Year:** 2011, 2012 **Model:** 1 Series M, 128i, 135i, 328i, 328i xDrive, 335is, 528i, 535i, X1, X3, X5 **Engine:** 3.0L L6	**Camshaft Position Sensor "B" Circuit (Bank 1) High Input:** Engine turning over for at least nine faults, battery voltage must be at least 11.5v, there must be multiple reference points lost, signal faults or intermittent contact on KWG signal wire. VVT emergency default mode (max stroke) active, VANOS emergency default mode (spec. 120 degrees) active, RPM sensor emergency default mode active.
DTC: P0369 **1T DME, MIL: Yes** **Year:** 2011, 2012 **Model:** 1 Series M, 128i, 135i, 323i, 328i, 328i xDrive, 335is, 528i, 535i, X1, X3, X5 **Engine:** 2.5L L6, 3.0L L6	**Crankshaft Position Sensor Rationality Check:** Engine started, battery voltage must be at least 11.5v, all electrical components must be off, parking brake must be engaged (to keep daytime driving lights off), automatic transmission selector must be in park and the ground between the engine and the chassis must be well connected. The DME detected the CMP sensor signal did not reach the specified minimum or maximum limit, or the difference between the actual and target position was incorrectly reported. This fault occurs 120 seconds after start up.
DTC: P0370 **1T DME, MIL: Yes** **Year:** 2011, 2012 **Model:** 1 Series M, 128i, 135i, 328i, 328i xDrive, 335is, 528i, 535i, X1, X3, X5 **Engine:** 3.0L L6, 4.4L V8	**Crankshaft Position Sensor Timing Reference High:** Engine started, battery voltage must be at least 11.5v, all electrical components must be off, parking brake must be engaged (to keep daytime driving lights off), automatic transmission selector must be in park and the ground between the engine and the chassis must be well connected. The DME detected the CMP sensor signal did not reach the specified minimum limit.
DTC: P0372 **1T DME, MIL: Yes** **Year:** 2011, 2012 **Model:** 1 Series M, 128i, 135i, 328i, 328i xDrive, 335is, 528i, 535i, X1, X3, X5 **Engine:** 3.0L L6	**Crankshaft Position Sensor Timing Reference High Resolution Signal "A" Too Few Pulses:** Engine started, battery voltage must be at least 11.5v, all electrical components must be off, parking brake must be engaged (to keep daytime driving lights off), automatic transmission selector must be in park and the ground between the engine and the chassis must be well connected. The DME detected the CMP sensor signal did not reach the specified minimum limit.
DTC: P0373 **1T DME, MIL: Yes** **Year:** 2011, 2012 **Model:** 1 Series M, 128i, 135i, 328i, 328i xDrive, 335is, 528i, 535i, X1, X3, X5 **Engine:** 3.0L L6	**Crankshaft Position Sensor Timing Reference High Resolution Signal "A" Intermittent/Erratic Pulses:** Engine started, battery voltage must be at least 11.5v, all electrical components must be off, parking brake must be engaged (to keep daytime driving lights off), automatic transmission selector must be in park and the ground between the engine and the chassis must be well connected. The DME detected the CMP sensor signal did not reach the specified minimum limit.

DTC	Trouble Code Title and Conditions
DTC: P0390 **1T DME, MIL: Yes** **Year:** 2011, 2012 **Model:** 1 Series M, 128i, 135i, 328i, 328i xDrive, 335is, 528i, 535i, X1, X3, X5 **Engine:** 3.0L L6	**Camshaft Position Sensor "B" Circuit (Bank 2):** Engine started, battery voltage must be at least 11.5v, all electrical components must be off, parking brake must be engaged (to keep daytime driving lights off), automatic transmission selector must be in park and the ground between the engine and the chassis must be well connected. The DME detected the CMP sensor signal was missing or it was erratic.
DTC: P0391 **1T DME, MIL: Yes** **Year:** 2011, 2012 **Model:** 1 Series M, 128i, 135i, 328i, 328i xDrive, 335is, 528i, 535i, X1, X3, X5 **Engine:** 3.0L L6	**Camshaft Position Sensor "B" Circuit (Bank 2) Range/Performance:** Engine started, battery voltage must be at least 11.5v, all electrical components must be off, parking brake must be engaged (to keep daytime driving lights off), automatic transmission selector must be in park and the ground between the engine and the chassis must be well connected. The DME detected the CMP sensor signal exceeded the bounds of the specified maximum limit.
DTC: P0392 **1T DME, MIL: Yes** **Year:** 2011, 2012 **Model:** 1 Series M, 128i, 135i, 328i, 328i xDrive, 335is, 528i, 535i, X1, X3, X5 **Engine:** 3.0L L6	**Camshaft Position Sensor "B" Circuit (Bank 2) Low Input:** Engine started, battery voltage must be at least 11.5v, all electrical components must be off, parking brake must be engaged (to keep daytime driving lights off), automatic transmission selector must be in park and the ground between the engine and the chassis must be well connected. The DME detected the CMP sensor signal exceeded the bounds of the specified maximum limit.
DTC: P0393 **1T DME, MIL: Yes** **Year:** 2011, 2012 **Model:** 1 Series M, 128i, 135i, 328i, 328i xDrive, 335is, 528i, 535i, X1, X3, X5 **Engine:** 3.0L L6	**Camshaft Position Sensor "B" Circuit (Bank 2) High Input:** Engine started, battery voltage must be at least 11.5v, all electrical components must be off, parking brake must be engaged (to keep daytime driving lights off), automatic transmission selector must be in park and the ground between the engine and the chassis must be well connected. The DME detected the CMP sensor signal did not reach the specified minimum limit.
DTC: P0411 **1T DME, MIL: Yes** **Year:** 2011, 2012 **Model:** 1 Series M, 128i, 135i, 323i, 328i, 328i xDrive, 335is, 528i, 535i, X1, X3, X5 **Engine:** 2.5L L6, 3.0L L6, 4.4L V8	**Secondary Air Injection System Upstream Flow Detected:** Engine started, battery voltage must be at least 11.5v, all electrical components must be off, parking brake must be engaged (to keep daytime driving lights off), automatic transmission selector must be in park and the ground between the engine and the chassis must be well connected. The DME detected the Secondary AIR pump airflow was not diverted correctly when requested during the self-test. The pump is functioning but the quantity of air is recognized as insufficient by HO2S. **Note: The solenoid valve is closed when no voltage is present.**
DTC: P0412 **1T DME, MIL: Yes** **Year:** 2011, 2012 **Model:** 323i, X5 **Engine:** 2.5L L6, 4.4L V8	**Secondary Air Injection Solenoid Circuit Malfunction:** Engine started, battery voltage must be at least 11.5v, all electrical components must be off, parking brake must be engaged (to keep daytime driving lights off), automatic transmission selector must be in park and the ground between the engine and the chassis must be well connected. The DME detected an unexpected low or high voltage condition on the AIR solenoid control circuit during testing.
DTC: P0413 **1T DME, MIL: Yes** **Year:** 2011, 2012 **Model:** 323i, X5 **Engine:** 2.5L L6, 4.4L V8	**Secondary Air Injection Solenoid Circuit Open:** Engine started, battery voltage must be at least 11.5v, all electrical components must be off, parking brake must be engaged (to keep daytime driving lights off), automatic transmission selector must be in park and the ground between the engine and the chassis must be well connected. The DME detected an unexpected low or high voltage condition on the AIR solenoid control circuit during testing.
DTC: P0414 **1T DME, MIL: Yes** **Year:** 2011, 2012 **Model:** 323i, X5 **Engine:** 2.5L L6, 4.4L V8	**Secondary Air Injection Solenoid Circuit Short:** Engine started, battery voltage must be at least 11.5v, all electrical components must be off, parking brake must be engaged (to keep daytime driving lights off), automatic transmission selector must be in park and the ground between the engine and the chassis must be well connected. The DME detected an unexpected low or high voltage condition on the AIR solenoid control circuit during testing.
DTC: P0418 **1T DME, MIL: Yes** **Year:** 2011, 2012 **Model:** 1 Series M, 128i, 135i, 323i, 328i, 328i xDrive, 335is, 528i, 535i, X1, X3, X5 **Engine:** 2.5L L6, 3.0L L6, 4.4L V8	**Secondary Air Injection Relay (A) Circuit Malfunction:** Engine started, battery voltage must be at least 11.5v, all electrical components must be off, parking brake must be engaged (to keep daytime driving lights off), automatic transmission selector must be in park and the ground between the engine and the chassis must be well connected. The DME detected an unexpected low or high voltage condition on the AIR solenoid control circuit during testing. The fuel status is in a closed loop pattern, the coolant temperature is between 69 and 100 degrees Celsius, and the engine speed is between 800 and 6000rpm. 2001: 3.2L-S54 (M3, M-Coupe/Roadster);

DTC	Trouble Code Title and Conditions
DTC: P0420 **1T DME, MIL: Yes** **Year:** 2011, 2012 **Model:** 1 Series M, 128i, 135i, 323i, 328i, 328i xDrive, 335is, 528i, 535i, X1, X3, X5 **Engine:** 2.5L L6, 3.0L L6, 4.4L V8	**Catalyst System Efficiency (Bank 1) Below Threshold:** Engine started, battery voltage must be at least 11.5v, all electrical components must be off, parking brake must be engaged (to keep daytime driving lights off), automatic transmission selector must be in park, the exhaust system must be properly sealed between the catalytic converter and the cylinder head, coolant temperature must be at least 80 degrees Celsius and oxygen sensor heaters for oxygen sensors before the catalytic converter must be functioning properly and the ground between the engine and the chassis must be well connected. The DME detected the switch rate of the rear HO2S-12 was close to the switch rate of front HO2S (it should be much slower). The exhaust-gas mass airflow is less than 22g/sec. The engine speed is between 980 and 1920rpm, the catalyst temperature is greater than 300 degrees Celsius, the fuel system status is in a closed loop and the purge vapor factor is less than 3.5.
DTC: P0430 **1T DME, MIL: Yes** **Year:** 2011, 2012 **Model:** 1 Series M, 128i, 135i, 323i, 328i, 328i xDrive, 335is, 528i, 535i, X1, X3, X5 **Engine:** 2.5L L6, 3.0L L6, 4.4L V8	**Catalyst System Efficiency (Bank 2) Below Threshold:** Engine started, battery voltage must be at least 11.5v, all electrical components must be off, parking brake must be engaged (to keep daytime driving lights off), automatic transmission selector must be in park, the exhaust system must be properly sealed between the catalytic converter and the cylinder head, coolant temperature must be at least 80 degrees Celsius and oxygen sensor heaters for oxygen sensors before the catalytic converter must be functioning properly and the ground between the engine and the chassis must be well connected. The DME detected the switch rate of the rear HO2S-12 was close to the switch rate of front HO2S (it should be much slower). The engine speed is between 980 and 1920rpm, the catalyst temperature is greater than 300 degrees Celsius, the fuel system status is in a closed loop and the purge vapor factor is less than 3.5.
DTC: P0440 **1T DME, MIL: Yes** **Year:** 2011, 2012 **Model:** 1 Series M, 128i, 135i, 323i, 328i, 328i xDrive, 335is, 528i, 535i, X1, X3, X5 **Engine:** 2.5L L6, 3.0L L6, 4.4L V8	**EVAP System Malfunction:** ECT sensor is cold during startup, engine started, battery voltage must be at least 11.5v, all electrical components must be off, parking brake must be engaged (to keep daytime driving lights off), automatic transmission selector must be in park, the exhaust system must be properly sealed between the catalytic converter and the cylinder head, coolant temperature must be at least 80 degrees Celsius and oxygen sensor heaters for oxygen sensors before the catalytic converter must be functioning properly and the ground between the engine and the chassis must be well connected. The DME detected the switch rate of the rear HO2S-12 was close to the switch rate of front HO2S (it should be much slower). DME detected a problem in the EVAP system during the EVAP System Monitor test. The fuel system adaptation has finished, the coolant temperature is greater than 60 degrees Celsius, normal purge is on, vehicle speed is zero, and engine is at idle.
DTC: P0441 **1T DME, MIL: Yes** **Year:** 2011, 2012 **Model:** 323i, X5 **Engine:** 2.5L L6, 4.4L V8	**EVAP Control System Incorrect Purge Flow:** ECT sensor is cold during startup, engine started, battery voltage must be at least 11.5v, all electrical components must be off, parking brake must be engaged (to keep daytime driving lights off), automatic transmission selector must be in park, the exhaust system must be properly sealed between the catalytic converter and the cylinder head, coolant temperature must be at least 80 degrees Celsius and oxygen sensor heaters for oxygen sensors before the catalytic converter must be functioning properly and the ground between the engine and the chassis must be well connected. The DME detected the switch rate of the rear HO2S-12 was close to the switch rate of front HO2S (it should be much slower). DME detected a problem in the EVAP system during the EVAP System Monitor test.
DTC: P0442 **1T DME, MIL: Yes** **Year:** 2011, 2012 **Model:** 1 Series M, 128i, 135i, 323i, 328i, 328i xDrive, 335is, 528i, 535i, X1, X3, X5 **Engine:** 2.5L L6, 3.0L L6, 4.4L V8	**EVAP Control System Small Leak Detected:** Engine started, battery voltage must be at least 11.5v, all electrical components must be off, parking brake must be engaged (to keep daytime driving lights off), automatic transmission selector must be in park, the exhaust system must be properly sealed between the catalytic converter and the cylinder head, coolant temperature must be at least 80 degrees Celsius and oxygen sensor heaters for oxygen sensors before the catalytic converter must be functioning properly and the ground between the engine and the chassis must be well connected. The DME detected a leak in the EVAP system as small as 0.040 inches during the EVAP Monitor Test. The fuel system adaptation has finished, the coolant temperature is greater than 60 degrees Celsius, normal purge is on, vehicle speed is zero, and engine is at idle. Engine start temperature must be greater than 2 degrees Celsius and the last driving cycle greater than 20 minutes.
DTC: P0443 **1T DME, MIL: Yes** **Year:** 2011, 2012 **Model:** 1 Series M, 128i, 135i, 323i, 328i, 328i xDrive, 335is, 528i, 535i, X1, X3, X5 **Engine:** 2.5L L6, 3.0L L6, 4.4L V8	**EVAP Vapor Management Valve Circuit Malfunction:** Engine started, battery voltage must be at least 11.5v, all electrical components must be off, parking brake must be engaged (to keep daytime driving lights off), automatic transmission selector must be in park, the exhaust system must be properly sealed between the catalytic converter and the cylinder head, coolant temperature must be at least 80 degrees Celsius and oxygen sensor heaters for oxygen sensors before the catalytic converter must be functioning properly and the ground between the engine and the chassis must be well connected. The DME detected an unexpected high or low voltage condition on the Vapor Management Valve (VMV) circuit when the device was cycled On/Off during testing.
DTC: P0444 **1T DME, MIL: Yes** **Year:** 2011, 2012 **Model:** 323i, X5 **Engine:** 2.5L L6, 4.4L V8	**Evaporative Emission System Purge Control Valve Circuit Open:** Engine started, battery voltage must be at least 11.5v, all electrical components must be off, parking brake must be engaged (to keep daytime driving lights off), automatic transmission selector must be in park, the exhaust system must be properly sealed between the catalytic converter and the cylinder head, coolant temperature must be at least 80 degrees Celsius and oxygen sensor heaters for oxygen sensors before the catalytic converter must be functioning properly and the ground between the engine and the chassis must be well connected. The DME detected an unexpected voltage condition on the EVAP circuit when the device was cycled On/Off during testing.

DTC	Trouble Code Title and Conditions
DTC: P0445 **1T DME, MIL: Yes** **Year:** 2011, 2012 **Model:** 323i, X5 **Engine:** 2.5L L6, 4.4L V8	**Evaporative Emission System Purge Control Valve Circuit Shorted:** Engine started, battery voltage must be at least 11.5v, all electrical components must be off, parking brake must be engaged (to keep daytime driving lights off), automatic transmission selector must be in park, the exhaust system must be properly sealed between the catalytic converter and the cylinder head, coolant temperature must be at least 80 degrees Celsius and oxygen sensor heaters for oxygen sensors before the catalytic converter must be functioning properly and the ground between the engine and the chassis must be well connected. The DME detected an unexpected voltage condition on the EVAP circuit when the device was cycled On/Off during testing.
DTC: P0455 **1T DME, MIL: Yes** **Year:** 2011, 2012 **Model:** 1 Series M, 128i, 135i, 323i, 328i, 328i xDrive, 335is, 528i, 535i, X1, X3, X5 **Engine:** 2.5L L6, 3.0L L6, 4.4L V8	**EVAP Control System Large Leak Detected:** Engine started, battery voltage must be at least 11.5v, all electrical components must be off, parking brake must be engaged (to keep daytime driving lights off), automatic transmission selector must be in park, the exhaust system must be properly sealed between the catalytic converter and the cylinder head, coolant temperature must be at least 80 degrees Celsius and oxygen sensor heaters for oxygen sensors before the catalytic converter must be functioning properly and the ground between the engine and the chassis must be well connected. The DME detected multiple small fuel vapor leaks; or it detected a large leak in the system during the leak test.
DTC: P0456 **1T DME, MIL: Yes** **Year:** 2011, 2012 **Model:** 323i, X5 **Engine:** 2.5L L6, 4.4L V8	**EVAP Control System Small Leak Detected:** Engine started, battery voltage must be at least 11.5v, all electrical components must be off, parking brake must be engaged (to keep daytime driving lights off), automatic transmission selector must be in park, the exhaust system must be properly sealed between the catalytic converter and the cylinder head, coolant temperature must be at least 80 degrees Celsius and oxygen sensor heaters for oxygen sensors before the catalytic converter must be functioning properly and the ground between the engine and the chassis must be well connected. The DME detected multiple small fuel vapor leaks; or it detected a large leak in the system during the leak test.
DTC: P0458 **1T DME, MIL: Yes** **Year:** 2011, 2012 **Model:** 1 Series M, 128i, 135i, 328i, 328i xDrive, 335is, 528i, 535i, X1, X3, X5 **Engine:** 3.0L L6	**Evaporative Emission System Purge Control Valve Circuit Low:** Engine started, battery voltage must be at least 11.5v, all electrical components must be off, parking brake must be engaged (to keep daytime driving lights off), automatic transmission selector must be in park, the exhaust system must be properly sealed between the catalytic converter and the cylinder head, coolant temperature must be at least 80 degrees Celsius and oxygen sensor heaters for oxygen sensors before the catalytic converter must be functioning properly and the ground between the engine and the chassis must be well connected. The DME detected an unexpected voltage condition on the EVAP circuit when the device was cycled On/Off during testing.
DTC: P0459 **1T DME, MIL: Yes** **Year:** 2011, 2012 **Model:** 1 Series M, 128i, 135i, 328i, 328i xDrive, 335is, 528i, 535i, X1, X3, X5 **Engine:** 3.0L L6	**Evaporative Emission System Purge Control Valve Circuit High:** Engine started, battery voltage must be at least 11.5v, all electrical components must be off, parking brake must be engaged (to keep daytime driving lights off), automatic transmission selector must be in park, the exhaust system must be properly sealed between the catalytic converter and the cylinder head, coolant temperature must be at least 80 degrees Celsius and oxygen sensor heaters for oxygen sensors before the catalytic converter must be functioning properly and the ground between the engine and the chassis must be well connected. The DME detected an unexpected voltage condition on the EVAP circuit when the device was cycled On/Off during testing.
DTC: P0460 **1T DME, MIL: Yes** **Year:** 2011, 2012 **Model:** 1 Series M, 128i, 135i, 328i, 328i xDrive, 335is, 528i, 535i, X1, X3, X5 **Engine:** 3.0L L6	**Fuel Level Sensor "A" Circuit Malfunction:** KOEO or KOER Self-Test enabled, and the DME detected a lack of power (VPWR) to the Fuel Pressure Regulator Control (FPRC) solenoid circuit. Cluster received incorrect fuel level from CAN or no message at all, calculated consumption does not correspond to transmitted fuel quantity.
DTC: P0461 **1T DME, MIL: Yes** **Year:** 2011, 2012 **Model:** 1 Series M, 128i, 135i, 328i, 328i xDrive, 335is, 528i, 535i, X1, X3, X5 **Engine:** 3.0L L6	**Fuel Level Sensor "A" Circuit Range/Performance:** KOEO or KOER Self-Test enabled, and the DME detected a lack of power (VPWR) to the Fuel Pressure Regulator Control (FPRC) solenoid circuit. Cluster received incorrect fuel level from CAN, calculated consumption does not correspond to transmitted fuel quantity. There is a stuck fuel level sensor, and the fault is recorded after driving roughly 50 miles (or 2.6 gallons of gas).
DTC: P0477 **2T DME, MIL: Yes** **Year:** 2011, 2012 **Model:** 1 Series M, 128i, 135i, 328i, 328i xDrive, 335is, 528i, 535i, X1, X3, X5 **Engine:** 3.0L L6	**Exhaust Pressure Control Valve Low:** Engine started, battery voltage must be at least 11.5v, all electrical components must be off, parking brake must be engaged (to keep daytime driving lights off), automatic transmission selector must be in park, the exhaust system must be properly sealed between the catalytic converter and the cylinder head, coolant temperature must be at least 80 degrees Celsius and oxygen sensor heaters for oxygen sensors before the catalytic converter must be functioning properly and the ground between the engine and the chassis must be well connected. The DME detected an unexpected voltage condition on the EVAP circuit when the device was cycled On/Off during testing. The driver circuit has detected a short to ground.

DTC	Trouble Code Title and Conditions
DTC: P0478 **2T DME, MIL: Yes** **Year:** 2011, 2012 **Model:** 1 Series M, 128i, 135i, 328i, 328i xDrive, 335is, 528i, 535i, X1, X3, X5 **Engine:** 3.0L L6	**Exhaust Pressure Control Valve High:** Engine started, battery voltage must be at least 11.5v, all electrical components must be off, parking brake must be engaged (to keep daytime driving lights off), automatic transmission selector must be in park, the exhaust system must be properly sealed between the catalytic converter and the cylinder head, coolant temperature must be at least 80 degrees Celsius and oxygen sensor heaters for oxygen sensors before the catalytic converter must be functioning properly and the ground between the engine and the chassis must be well connected. The DME detected an unexpected voltage condition on the EVAP circuit when the device was cycled On/Off during testing. The driver circuit has detected a short to battery voltage
DTC: P0479 **2T DME, MIL: Yes** **Year:** 2011, 2012 **Model:** 1 Series M, 128i, 135i, 328i, 328i xDrive, 335is, 528i, 535i, X1, X3, X5 **Engine:** 3.0L L6	**Exhaust Pressure Control Valve Intermittent:** Engine started, battery voltage must be at least 11.5v, all electrical components must be off, parking brake must be engaged (to keep daytime driving lights off), automatic transmission selector must be in park, the exhaust system must be properly sealed between the catalytic converter and the cylinder head, coolant temperature must be at least 80 degrees Celsius and oxygen sensor heaters for oxygen sensors before the catalytic converter must be functioning properly and the ground between the engine and the chassis must be well connected. The DME detected an unexpected voltage condition on the EVAP circuit when the device was cycled On/Off during testing. The driver circuit has detected a implausible signal.
DTC: P0491 **2T DME, MIL: Yes** **Year:** 2011, 2012 **Model:** 1 Series M, 128i, 135i, 323i, 328i, 328i xDrive, 335is, 528i, 535i, X1, X3, X5 **Engine:** 2.5L L6, 3.0L L6, 4.4L V8	**Secondary Air Injection System Insufficient Flow (Bank 1):** Engine started, battery voltage must be at least 11.5v, all electrical components must be off, parking brake must be engaged (to keep daytime driving lights off), automatic transmission selector must be in park and the ground between the engine and the chassis must be well connected. The DME detected the Secondary AIR pump airflow was not diverted correctly when requested during the self-test. The pump is functioning but the quantity of air is recognized as insufficient by HO2S. The secondary air pump is on, the oxygen sensor is heated up the cold start enrichment is activated and the coolant temperature is between negative 12 and 30 degrees Celsius.
DTC: P0492 **2T DME, MIL: Yes** **Year:** 2011, 2012 **Model:** 1 Series M, 128i, 135i, 323i, 328i, 328i xDrive, 335is, 528i, 535i, X1, X3, X5 **Engine:** 2.5L L6, 3.0L L6, 4.4L V8	**Secondary Air Injection System Insufficient Flow (Bank 2):** Engine started, battery voltage must be at least 11.5v, all electrical components must be off, parking brake must be engaged (to keep daytime driving lights off), automatic transmission selector must be in park and the ground between the engine and the chassis must be well connected. The DME detected the Secondary AIR pump airflow was not diverted correctly when requested during the self-test. The pump is functioning but the quantity of air is recognized as insufficient by HO2S. The secondary air pump is on, the oxygen sensor is heated up the cold start enrichment is activated and the coolant temperature is between negative 12 and 30 degrees Celsius.
DTC: P0500 **1T DME, MIL: Yes** **Year:** 2011, 2012 **Model:** 1 Series M, 128i, 135i, 323i, 328i, 328i xDrive, 335is, 528i, 535i, X1, X3, X5 **Engine:** 2.5L L6, 3.0L L6, 4.4L V8	**Vehicle Speed Sensor "A" Malfunction:** Engine started; engine speed above the TCC stall speed, and the DME detected a loss of the VSS signal over a period of time or the signal is not usable. **Note: The DME receives vehicle speed data from the VSS, TCSS, ABS module, CTM or GEM controller, depending up the application. Speed Signal from DSC too high because of possible tampering. Check DSC and wires. The engine speed is greater than 2000rpm, engine load greater than 3.5msec/rev., and the vehicle speed is more than 55mph. The fuel system status is in fuel cut-off mode.**
DTC: P0501 **1T DME, MIL: Yes** **Year:** 2011, 2012 **Model:** 1 Series M, 128i, 135i, 323i, 328i, 328i xDrive, 335is, 528i, 535i, X1, X3, X5 **Engine:** 2.5L L6, 3.0L L6, 4.4L V8	**Vehicle Speed Sensor or PSOM Range/Performance:** Engine started; engine speed above the TCC stall speed, and the DME detected a loss of the VSS signal over a period of time or the signal is not usable. **Note: The DME receives vehicle speed data from the VSS, TCSS, ABS module, CTM or GEM controller, depending up the application. The engine speed is between 1000 and 1320rpm. The fuel system status is in the fuel cut-off mode. The coolant temperature is greater than 60 degrees Celsius. The vehicle speed is zero.**
DTC: P0503 **1T DME, MIL: Yes** **Year:** 2011, 2012 **Model:** 1 Series M, 128i, 135i, 328i, 328i xDrive, 335is, 528i, 535i, X1, X3, X5 **Engine:** 3.0L L6	**Vehicle Speed Sensor "A" Intermittent/Erratic/High:** Engine started; engine speed above the TCC stall speed, and the DME detected a loss of the VSS signal over a period of time or the signal is not usable. **Note: The DME receives vehicle speed data from the VSS, TCSS, ABS module, CTM or GEM controller, depending up the application. Speed Signal from DSC too high because of possible tampering. Check DSC and wires**
DTC: P0505 **1T DME, MIL: Yes** **Year:** 2011, 2012 **Model:** 1 Series M, 128i, 135i, 323i, 328i, 328i xDrive, 335is, 528i, 535i, X1, X3, X5 **Engine:** 2.5L L6, 3.0L L6, 4.4L V8	**Idle Air Control Valve Malfunction:** Engine started, battery voltage at least 11.5v, all electrical components off, ground connections between engine and chassis well connected, coolant temperature at least 80-degrees Celsius. The DME detected deviation from the normal operating parameters of the Idle Air Control Valve. The vehicle speed can be zero mph and the engine load must be less than 1.5ms.

DTC	Trouble Code Title and Conditions
DTC: P0506 **1T DME, MIL: Yes** **Year:** 2011, 2012 **Model:** 1 Series M, 128i, 135i, 323i, 328i, 328i xDrive, 335is, 528i, 535i, X1, X3, X5 **Engine:** 2.5L L6, 3.0L L6, 4.4L V8	**Idle Air Control System RPM Lower Than Expected:** Engine started, battery voltage must be at least 11.5v, all electrical components must be off, parking brake must be engaged (to keep daytime driving lights off), automatic transmission selector must be in park, the exhaust system must be properly sealed between the catalytic converter and the cylinder head, coolant temperature must be at least 80 degrees Celsius and oxygen sensor heaters for oxygen sensors before the catalytic converter must be functioning properly and the ground between the engine and the chassis must be well connected. The DME detected it could not control the idle speed correctly, as it is constantly more than 100 rpm less than specification.
DTC: P0507 **1T DME, MIL: Yes** **Year:** 2011, 2012 **Model:** 1 Series M, 128i, 135i, 323i, 328i, 328i xDrive, 335is, 528i, 535i, X1, X3, X5 **Engine:** 2.5L L6, 3.0L L6, 4.4L V8	**Idle Air Control System RPM Higher Than Expected:** Engine started, battery voltage must be at least 11.5v, all electrical components must be off, parking brake must be engaged (to keep daytime driving lights off), automatic transmission selector must be in park, the exhaust system must be properly sealed between the catalytic converter and the cylinder head, coolant temperature must be at least 80 degrees Celsius and oxygen sensor heaters for oxygen sensors before the catalytic converter must be functioning properly and the ground between the engine and the chassis must be well connected. The DME detected it could not control the idle speed correctly, as it is constantly more than 200 rpm more than specification.
DTC: P0512 **1T DME, MIL: Yes** **Year:** 2011, 2012 **Model:** 1 Series M, 128i, 135i, 328i, 328i xDrive, 335is, 528i, 535i, X1, X3, X5 **Engine:** 3.0L L6	**Starter Request Circuit Malfunction:** The engine is on for more than one second and the injection and ignition have not yet released. Engine rpm present before DME triggers the starter, or the starter relay sticks in IVM, crankshaft sensor intermittent contact, the starter is grounded.
DTC: P0520 **1T DME, MIL: Yes** **Year:** 2011, 2012 **Model:** 1 Series M, 128i, 135i, 328i, 328i xDrive, 335is, 528i, 535i, X1, X3, X5 **Engine:** 3.0L L6	**Engine Oil Pressure Sensor/Switch Circuit Malfunction:** The ignition must be on. The DME detected an error in the Engine Oil Pressure sensor. There is a short to ground. The plug has fallen off of the oil pressure switch. There is an open circuit in the harness. The pressure switch is defective.
DTC: P0530 **1T DME, MIL: Yes** **Year:** 2011, 2012 **Model:** 1 Series M, 128i, 135i, 328i, 328i xDrive, 335is, 528i, 535i, X1, X3, X5 **Engine:** 3.0L L6	**A/C Refrigerant Pressure Sensor "A" Circuit Malfunction:** The DME detected an implausible condition on the sensor.
DTC: P0532 **1T DME, MIL: Yes** **Year:** 2011, 2012 **Model:** 1 Series M, 128i, 135i, 328i, 328i xDrive, 335is, 528i, 535i, X1, X3, X5 **Engine:** 3.0L L6	**A/C Refrigerant Pressure Sensor "A" Circuit Low:** The DME detected a low condition on the sensor.
DTC: P0533 **1T DME, MIL: Yes** **Year:** 2011, 2012 **Model:** 1 Series M, 128i, 135i, 328i, 328i xDrive, 335is, 528i, 535i, X1, X3, X5 **Engine:** 3.0L L6	**A/C Refrigerant Pressure Sensor "A" Circuit High:** The DME detected a high condition on the sensor.
DTC: P0560 **1T DME, MIL: Yes** **Year:** 2011, 2012 **Model:** 1 Series M, 128i, 135i, 328i, 328i xDrive, 335is, 528i, 535i, X1, X3, X5 **Engine:** 3.0L L6	**System Voltage Malfunction:** Engine started, battery voltage must be at least 11.5v, all electrical components must be off, parking brake must be engaged (to keep daytime driving lights off), automatic transmission selector must be in park, and the ground between the engine and the chassis must be well connected. The DME has detected a voltage value that is implausible or erratic. Engine speed must be greater than 1400rpm.

DTC	Trouble Code Title and Conditions
DTC: P0561 **1T DME, MIL: Yes** **Year:** 2011, 2012 **Model:** 1 Series M, 128i, 135i, 328i, 328i xDrive, 335is, 528i, 535i, X1, X3, X5 **Engine:** 3.0L L6	**System Voltage Unstable:** Engine started, battery voltage must be at least 11.5v, all electrical components must be off, parking brake must be engaged (to keep daytime driving lights off), automatic transmission selector must be in park, and the ground between the engine and the chassis must be well connected. The DME has detected a voltage value that is too erratic for the system to function properly.
DTC: P0562 **1T DME, MIL: Yes** **Year:** 2011, 2012 **Model:** 128i, 328i, 328i xDrive, 528i, 535i, X1, X3, X5 **Engine:** 3.0L L6	**System Voltage Low:** Engine started, battery voltage must be at least 11.5v, all electrical components must be off, parking brake must be engaged (to keep daytime driving lights off), automatic transmission selector must be in park, and the ground between the engine and the chassis must be well connected. The DME has detected a voltage value that is below the specified minimum limit for the system to function properly.
DTC: P0563 **1T DME, MIL: Yes** **Year:** 2011, 2012 **Model:** 128i, 328i, 328i xDrive, 528i, 535i, X1, X3, X5 **Engine:** 3.0L L6	**System Voltage High:** Engine started for 18 seconds, battery voltage must be at least 11.5v, all electrical components must be off, parking brake must be engaged (to keep daytime driving lights off), automatic transmission selector must be in park, and the ground between the engine and the chassis must be well connected. The DME has detected a voltage value that has exceeded the specified maximum limit for the system to function properly. The vehicle was connected to 24 volts for too long after a jump start. ADC in ECU is defective. Delete stored fault codes from log. If fault reoccurs replace the ECU.
DTC: P0571 **1T DME, MIL: Yes** **Year:** 2011, 2012 **Model:** 128i, 328i, 328i xDrive, 528i, 535i, X1, X3, X5 **Engine:** 3.0L L6	**Cruise/Brake Switch (A) Circuit Malfunction:** Engine started, battery voltage must be at least 11.5v, all electrical components must be off, parking brake must be engaged (to keep daytime driving lights off), automatic transmission selector must be in park, and the ground between the engine and the chassis must be well connected. The DME has detected a voltage value that is implausible or erratic.
DTC: P0597 **1T DME, MIL: Yes** **Year:** 2011, 2012 **Model:** 1 Series M, 128i, 135i, 328i, 328i xDrive, 335is, 528i, 535i, X1, X3, X5 **Engine:** 3.0L L6	**Thermostat Heater Control Circuit Open:** The engine's warm up performance is monitored by comparing measured coolant temperature with the modeled coolant temperature to detect a defective coolant thermostat that is reading false. The engine temperature must be less than 65 degrees Celsius, engine speed greater than 800rpm (with the vehicle speed greater than 10 but less than 90km/h) and the ambient temperature greater than -8 degrees Celsius. The thermostat should be wide open when cold, but is in error if it opens below desired control temperature
DTC: P0598 **1T DME, MIL: Yes** **Year:** 2011, 2012 **Model:** 1 Series M, 128i, 135i, 328i, 328i xDrive, 335is, 528i, 535i, X1, X3, X5 **Engine:** 3.0L L6	**Thermostat Heater Control Circuit Low:** The engine's warm up performance is monitored by comparing measured coolant temperature with the modeled coolant temperature to detect a defective coolant thermostat that is reading false. The engine temperature must be less than 65 degrees Celsius, engine speed greater than 800rpm (with the vehicle speed greater than 10 but less than 90km/h) and the ambient temperature greater than -8 degrees Celsius. The thermostat should be wide open when cold, but is in error if it opens below desired control temperature.
DTC: P0599 **1T DME, MIL: Yes** **Year:** 2011, 2012 **Model:** 1 Series M, 128i, 135i, 328i, 328i xDrive, 335is, 528i, 535i, X1, X3, X5 **Engine:** 3.0L L6	**Thermostat Heater Control Circuit High:** The engine's warm up performance is monitored by comparing measured coolant temperature with the modeled coolant temperature to detect a defective coolant thermostat that is reading false. The engine temperature must be less than 65 degrees Celsius, engine speed greater than 800rpm (with the vehicle speed greater than 10 but less than 90km/h) and the ambient temperature greater than -8 degrees Celsius. The thermostat should be wide open when cold, but is in error if it opens below desired control temperature.
DTC: P0600 **1T DME, MIL: Yes** **Year:** 2011, 2012 **Model:** 1 Series M, 128i, 135i, 323i, 328i, 328i xDrive, 335is, 528i, 535i, X1, X3, X5 **Engine:** 2.5L L6, 3.0L L6, 4.4L V8	**Serial Communication Link (Data BUS) Message Missing:** The Engine Control Module (DME) communicates with all databus-capable control modules via a CAN databus. These databus-capable control modules are connected via two data bus wires which are twisted together (CAN_High and CAN_Low), and exchange information (messages). Missing information on the databus is recognized as a malfunction and stored. Trouble-free operation of the CAN-Bus requires that it have a terminal resistance. This central terminal resistor is located in the Engine Control Module (DME).
DTC: P0601 **1T DME, MIL: Yes** **Year:** 2011, 2012 **Model:** 1 Series M, 128i, 135i, 323i, 328i, 328i xDrive, 335is, 528i, 535i, X1, X3, X5 **Engine:** 2.5L L6, 3.0L L6, 4.4L V8	**Internal Control Module Memory Check Sum Error:** Key on, the DME has detected a programming error. The RAM and ROM check displays an invalid check-sum at power up/down.

DTC	Trouble Code Title and Conditions
DTC: P0604 **1T DME, MIL: Yes** **Year:** 2011, 2012 **Model:** 1 Series M, 128i, 135i, 323i, 328i, 328i xDrive, 335is, 528i, 535i, X1, X3, X5 **Engine:** 2.5L L6, 3.0L L6, 4.4L V8	**Internal Control Module Random Access Memory (RAM) Error:** Key on, and the DME detected an internal memory fault. This code will set if KAPWR to the DME is interrupted (at the initial key on). Watchdog on.
DTC: P0605 **1T DME, MIL: Yes** **Year:** 2011, 2012 **Model:** 323i, X5 **Engine:** 2.5L L6, 4.4L V8	**DME Read Only Memory (ROM) Test Error:** Key on, and the DME detected a ROM test error (ROM inside DME is corrupted). The DME is normally replaced if this code has set.
DTC: P0606 **1T DME, MIL: Yes** **Year:** 2011, 2012 **Model:** 323i, X5 **Engine:** 2.5L L6, 4.4L V8	**DME Internal Communication Error:** Key on, and the DME detected an internal communications register read back error during the initial key on check period.
DTC: P0620 **1T DME, MIL: Yes** **Year:** 2011, 2012 **Model:** 1 Series M, 128i, 135i, 328i, 328i xDrive, 335is, 528i, 535i, X1, X3, X5 **Engine:** 3.0L L6	**Generator Control Circuit Error:** The engine is running for at least 25 seconds, and there is no communication faults at the BSD Interface.
DTC: P0704 **1T DME, MIL: Yes** **Year:** 2011, 2012 **Model:** 128i, 328i, 328i xDrive, 528i, 535i, X1, X3, X5 **Engine:** 3.0L L6	**Clutch Switch Input Circuit Malfunction:** Engine started, battery voltage must be at least 11.5v, all electrical components must be off, parking brake must be engaged (to keep daytime driving lights off), automatic transmission selector must be in park, and the ground between the engine and the chassis must be well connected. The DME detected a voltage outside the normal performance range to allow the system to properly function.
DTC: P0705 **1T DME, MIL: Yes** **Year:** 2011, 2012 **Model:** 128i, 323i, 328i, 328i xDrive, 528i, 535i, X1, X3, X5 **Engine:** 2.5L L6, 3.0L L6, 4.4L V8	**TR Sensor Circuit Malfunction:** Engine started, battery voltage must be at least 11.5v, all electrical components must be off, parking brake must be engaged (to keep daytime driving lights off), automatic transmission selector must be in park, and the ground between the engine and the chassis must be well connected. The DME detected a voltage or signal outside the normal performance range to allow the system to properly function. The engine speed is between 200 and 440rpm.
DTC: P0710 **1T DME, MIL: Yes** **Year:** 2011, 2012 **Model:** 128i, 323i, 328i, 328i xDrive, 528i, 535i, X1, X3, X5 **Engine:** 2.5L L6, 3.0L L6	**Transmission Fluid Temperature Sensor Circuit Malfunction:** Engine started, battery voltage must be at least 11.5v, all electrical components must be off, parking brake must be engaged (to keep daytime driving lights off), automatic transmission selector must be in park, and the ground between the engine and the chassis must be well connected. The DME detected the Transmission fluid temperature sensor circuit was outside the normal range in the test to allow proper function.
DTC: P0711 **1T DME, MIL: Yes** **Year:** 2011, 2012 **Model:** 128i, 323i, 328i, 328i xDrive, 528i, 535i, X1, X3, X5 **Engine:** 2.5L L6, 3.0L L6	**Transmission Fluid Temperature Sensor Signal Range/Performance:** Engine started, battery voltage must be at least 11.5v, all electrical components must be off, parking brake must be engaged (to keep daytime driving lights off), automatic transmission selector must be in park, and the ground between the engine and the chassis must be well connected. The DME detected the Transmission Fluid Temperature (TFT) sensor value was not close its normal operating temperature.
DTC: P0712 **1T DME, MIL: Yes** **Year:** 2011, 2012 **Model:** 128i, 323i, 328i, 328i xDrive, 528i, 535i, X1, X3, X5 **Engine:** 2.5L L6, 3.0L L6	**Transmission Fluid Temperature Sensor Circuit Low Input:** Engine started, battery voltage must be at least 11.5v, all electrical components must be off, parking brake must be engaged (to keep daytime driving lights off), automatic transmission selector must be in park, and the ground between the engine and the chassis must be well connected. The DME detected the Transmission Fluid Temperature (TFT) sensor was less than its minimum self-test range in the test.

DTC	Trouble Code Title and Conditions
DTC: P0713 **1T DME, MIL: Yes** **Year:** 2011, 2012 **Model:** 128i, 323i, 328i, 328i xDrive, 528i, 535i, X1, X3, X5 **Engine:** 2.5L L6, 3.0L L6	**Transmission Fluid Temperature Sensor Circuit High Input:** Engine started, battery voltage must be at least 11.5v, all electrical components must be off, parking brake must be engaged (to keep daytime driving lights off), automatic transmission selector must be in park, and the ground between the engine and the chassis must be well connected. The DME detected the Transmission Fluid Temperature (TFT) sensor was more than its maximum self-test range in the test.
DTC: P0714 **1T DME, MIL: Yes** **Year:** 2011, 2012 **Model:** 128i, 323i, 328i, 328i xDrive, 528i, 535i, X1, X3, X5 **Engine:** 2.5L L6, 3.0L L6	**Transmission Fluid Temperature Sensor Circuit Intermittent:** Engine started, battery voltage must be at least 11.5v, all electrical components must be off, parking brake must be engaged (to keep daytime driving lights off), automatic transmission selector must be in park, and the ground between the engine and the chassis must be well connected. The DME detected the Transmission Fluid Temperature (TFT) sensor was giving a false reading or was not reading at all.
DTC: P0715 **1T DME, MIL: Yes** **Year:** 2011, 2012 **Model:** 128i, 323i, 328i, 328i xDrive, 528i, 535i, X1, X3, X5 **Engine:** 2.5L L6, 3.0L L6, 4.4L V8	**Input/Turbine Speed Sensor Circuit Malfunction:** Engine started, vehicle driven with the vehicle speed sensor indicating more than 1 mph, and the DME detected the Transmission Vehicle Speed Sensor signals were erratic, or that they were missing for a period of time. The engine speed is greater than 600rpm. Any gear can be selected, output speed must be greater than 600rpm, and wheel speed greater than 400rpm.
DTC: P0716 **1T DME, MIL: Yes** **Year:** 2011, 2012 **Model:** X5 **Engine:** 4.4L V8	**Input Turbine/Speed Sensor Circuit Range/Performance:** Engine started, vehicle driven with the vehicle speed sensor indicating more than 1 mph, and the DME detected the Transmission Vehicle Speed Sensor signals were erratic, or that they were missing for a period of time.
DTC: P0717 **1T DME, MIL: Yes** **Year:** 2011, 2012 **Model:** X5 **Engine:** 4.4L V8	**Transmission Speed Shaft Sensor Signal Intermittent:** Engine started, vehicle speed sensor indicating over 1 mph, and the DME detected an intermittent loss of TSS signals (i.e., the TSS signals were erratic, irregular or missing).
DTC: P0720 **1T DME, MIL: Yes** **Year:** 2011, 2012 **Model:** 128i, 323i, 328i, 328i xDrive, 528i, 535i, X1, X3, X5 **Engine:** 2.5L L6, 3.0L L6, 4.4L V8	**Output/Turbine Speed Sensor Circuit Malfunction:** Engine started, vehicle driven with the vehicle speed sensor indicating more than 1 mph, and the DME detected the Transmission Vehicle Speed Sensor signals were erratic, or that they were missing for a period of time. The engine speed is greater than 600rpm. Any gear can be selected, output speed must be greater than 600rpm, and wheel speed greater than 400rpm.
DTC: P0721 **1T DME, MIL: Yes** **Year:** 2011, 2012 **Model:** X5 **Engine:** 4.4L V8	**A/T Output Shaft Speed Sensor Noise Interference:** Engine started, VSS signal more than 1 mph, and the DME detected "noise" interference on the Output Shaft Speed (OSS) sensor circuit.
DTC: P0722 **1T DME, MIL: Yes** **Year:** 2011, 2012 **Model:** X5 **Engine:** 4.4L V8	**A/T Output Speed Sensor No Signal:** Engine started, and the DME did not detect any Vehicle Speed Sensor (VSS) sensor signals upon initial vehicle movement.
DTC: P0731 **1T DME, MIL: Yes** **Year:** 2011, 2012 **Model:** 128i, 323i, 328i, 328i xDrive, 528i, 535i, X1, X3, X5 **Engine:** 2.5L L6, 3.0L L6, 4.4L V8	**Incorrect First Gear Ratio:** Engine started, vehicle operating with 1st gear commanded "on", and the DME detected an incorrect 1st gear ratio during the test.
DTC: P0732 **1T DME, MIL: Yes** **Year:** 2011, 2012 **Model:** 128i, 323i, 328i, 328i xDrive, 528i, 535i, X1, X3, X5 **Engine:** 2.5L L6, 3.0L L6, 4.4L V8	**Incorrect Second Gear Ratio:** Engine started, vehicle operating with 2nd Gear commanded "on", and the DME detected an incorrect 2nd gear ratio during the test. Input speed must be greater than 400rpm, and output speed must be greater than 250rpm for 10ms of continuous time.

DTC	Trouble Code Title and Conditions
DTC: P0733 **1T DME, MIL: Yes** **Year:** 2011, 2012 **Model:** 128i, 323i, 328i, 328i xDrive, 528i, 535i, X1, X3, X5 **Engine:** 2.5L L6, 3.0L L6, 4.4L V8	**Incorrect Third Gear Ratio:** Engine started, vehicle operating with 3rd Gear commanded "on", and the DME detected an incorrect 3rd gear ratio during the test. Input speed must be greater than 400rpm, and output speed must be greater than 250rpm for 10ms of continuous time.
DTC: P0734 **1T DME, MIL: Yes** **Year:** 2011, 2012 **Model:** 128i, 323i, 328i, 328i xDrive, 528i, 535i, X1, X3, X5 **Engine:** 2.5L L6, 3.0L L6, 4.4L V8	**Incorrect Fourth Gear Ratio:** Engine started, vehicle operating with 4th Gear commanded "on", and the DME detected an incorrect 4th gear ratio during the test. Input speed must be greater than 400rpm, and output speed must be greater than 250rpm for 10ms of continuous time.
DTC: P0735 **1T DME, MIL: Yes** **Year:** 2011, 2012 **Model:** 128i, 323i, 328i, 328i xDrive, 528i, 535i, X1, X3, X5 **Engine:** 2.5L L6, 3.0L L6, 4.4L V8	**Incorrect Fifth Gear Ratio:** Engine started, vehicle operating with 5th Gear commanded "on", and the DME detected an incorrect 5th gear ratio during the test. Input speed must be greater than 400rpm, and output speed must be greater than 250rpm for 10ms of continuous time.
DTC: P0741 **1T DME, MIL: Yes** **Year:** 2011, 2012 **Model:** X5 **Engine:** 4.4L V8	**TCC Mechanical System Range/Performance:** Engine started, vehicle driven in gear with VSS signals received, and the DME detected excessive slippage while in normal operation. The TCC is stuck off.
DTC: P0743 **1T DME, MIL: Yes** **Year:** 2011, 2012 **Model:** 128i, 323i, 328i, 328i xDrive, 528i, 535i, X1, X3, X5 **Engine:** 2.5L L6, 3.0L L6, 4.4L V8	**TCC Solenoid Circuit Malfunction:** Engine started, KOER Self-Test enabled, vehicle driven at cruise speed, and the DME did not detect any voltage drop across the TCC solenoid circuit during the test period.
DTC: P0745 **1T DME, MIL: Yes** **Year:** 2011, 2012 **Model:** X5 **Engine:** 4.4L V8	**Pressure Regulator Valve 1 Plausibility:** The current to/from the pressure regulator valve is either higher or lower than the threshold value.
DTC: P0748 **1T DME, MIL: Yes** **Year:** 2011, 2012 **Model:** 128i, 323i, 328i, 328i xDrive, 528i, 535i, X1, X3, X5 **Engine:** 2.5L L6, 3.0L L6, 4.4L V8	**Pressure Regulator Valve 2 Upper Threshold:** The signal to/from the pressure regulator valve has been interrupted.
DTC: P0750 **1T DME, MIL: Yes** **Year:** 2011, 2012 **Model:** X5 **Engine:** 4.4L V8	**Shift Solenoid "A" Circuit Continuity Short to Battery:** Engine started, vehicle driven with the solenoid applied, and the DME detected an unexpected voltage condition on the SS1/A solenoid circuit was incorrect during the test.
DTC: P0751 **1T DME, MIL: Yes** **Year:** 2011, 2012 **Model:** X5 **Engine:** 4.4L V8	**Solenoid Valve 1 Plausibility:** The signal to/from the pressure regulator valve is interrupted or does not exist.
DTC: P0752 **1T DME, MIL: Yes** **Year:** 2011, 2012 **Model:** X5 **Engine:** 4.4L V8	**A/T Shift Solenoid 1/A Function Range/Performance:** Engine started, vehicle driven with the solenoid applied, and the DME detected a mechanical failure while operating the Shift Solenoid 1/A during the CCM test period.

DTC	Trouble Code Title and Conditions
DTC: P0753 **1T DME, MIL: Yes** **Year:** 2011, 2012 **Model:** 128i, 323i, 328i, 328i xDrive, 528i, 535i, X1, X3, X5 **Engine:** 2.5L L6, 3.0L L6, 4.4L V8	**Solenoid Valve 1 Upper Threshold:** The signal to/from the pressure regulator valve is interrupted or short circuited to supply.
DTC: P0755 **1T DME, MIL: Yes** **Year:** 2011, 2012 **Model:** X5 **Engine:** 4.4L V8	**Shift Solenoid "B" Circuit Continuity Short to Battery:** Engine started, vehicle driven with the solenoid applied, and the DME detected an unexpected voltage condition on the SS1/B solenoid circuit was incorrect during the test.
DTC: P0756 **1T DME, MIL: Yes** **Year:** 2011, 2012 **Model:** X5 **Engine:** 4.4L V8	**Solenoid Valve 2 Plausibility:** The signal to/from the pressure regulator valve is interrupted or does not exist.
DTC: P0757 **1T DME, MIL: Yes** **Year:** 2011, 2012 **Model:** X5 **Engine:** 4.4L V8	**A/T Shift Solenoid 2/B Function Range/Performance:** Engine started, vehicle driven with the solenoid applied, and the DME detected a mechanical failure while operating the Shift Solenoid 2/B during the CCM test period.
DTC: P0758 **1T DME, MIL: Yes** **Year:** 2011, 2012 **Model:** 128i, 323i, 328i, 328i xDrive, 528i, 535i, X1, X3, X5 **Engine:** 2.5L L6, 3.0L L6, 4.4L V8	**Solenoid Valve 2 Upper Threshold:** The signal to/from the pressure regulator valve is interrupted or short circuited to supply.
DTC: P0760 **1T DME, MIL: Yes** **Year:** 2011, 2012 **Model:** X5 **Engine:** 4.4L V8	**Shift Solenoid "C" Circuit Continuity Short to Battery:** Engine started, vehicle driven with the solenoid applied, and the DME detected an unexpected voltage condition on the SS1/C solenoid circuit was incorrect during the test.
DTC: P0761 **1T DME, MIL: Yes** **Year:** 2011, 2012 **Model:** X5 **Engine:** 4.4L V8	**Solenoid Valve 3 Plausibility:** The signal to/from the pressure regulator valve is interrupted or does not exist.
DTC: P0762 **1T DME, MIL: Yes** **Year:** 2011, 2012 **Model:** X5 **Engine:** 4.4L V8	**A/T Shift Solenoid 3/C Function Range/Performance:** Engine started, vehicle driven with Shift Solenoid 3/C applied, and the DME detected a mechanical failure occurred (stuck "on") while operating Shift Solenoid 3/C during the test.
DTC: P0763 **1T DME, MIL: Yes** **Year:** 2011, 2012 **Model:** 323i, X5 **Engine:** 2.5L L6, 4.4L V8	**Solenoid Valve 3 Upper Threshold:** The signal to/from the pressure regulator valve is interrupted or short circuited to supply.
DTC: P0775 **1T DME, MIL: Yes** **Year:** 2011, 2012 **Model:** X5 **Engine:** 4.4L V8	**Pressure Regulator Valve 2 Plausibility:** The current to/from the pressure regulator valve is either higher or lower than the threshold value.
DTC: P0778 **1T DME, MIL: Yes** **Year:** 2011, 2012 **Model:** 128i, 323i, 328i, 328i xDrive, 528i, 535i, X1, X3, X5 **Engine:** 2.5L L6, 3.0L L6, 4.4L V8	**Pressure Control Solenoid "B" Electrical:** Engine started, vehicle driven with the solenoid applied, and the DME detected an unexpected voltage condition on the SS3/C solenoid circuit was incorrect during the test.

DTC	Trouble Code Title and Conditions
DTC: P0781 **1T DME, MIL: Yes** **Year:** 2011, 2012 **Model:** 128i, 323i, 328i, 328i xDrive, 528i, 535i, X1, X3, X5 **Engine:** 2.5L L6, 3.0L L6	**1-2 Shift Range Monitoring:** Engine running and vehicle driven, the DME detected a mechanical malfunction within the transmission. The output speed is greater than 300rpm, the transmission oil temperature is greater than 0 degrees Celsius, the engine speed is greater or equal to 600rpm and the range position is P, R, or N.
DTC: P0782 **1T DME, MIL: Yes** **Year:** 2011, 2012 **Model:** X5 **Engine:** 4.4L V8	**2-3 Shift Range Monitoring:** Engine running and vehicle driven, the DME detected a mechanical malfunction within the transmission. The output speed is greater than 300rpm, the transmission oil temperature is greater than 0 degrees Celsius, the engine speed is greater or equal to 600rpm and the range position is P, R, or N.
DTC: P0783 **1T DME, MIL: Yes** **Year:** 2011, 2012 **Model:** X5 **Engine:** 4.4L V8	**3-4 Shift Range Monitoring:** Engine running and vehicle driven, the DME detected a mechanical malfunction within the transmission. The output speed is greater than 300rpm, the transmission oil temperature is greater than 0 degrees Celsius, the engine speed is greater or equal to 600rpm and the range position is P, R, or N.
DTC: P0784 **1T DME, MIL: Yes** **Year:** 2011, 2012 **Model:** 128i, 323i, 328i, 328i xDrive, 528i, 535i, X1, X3, X5 **Engine:** 2.5L L6, 3.0L L6	**4-5 Shift Range Monitoring:** Engine running and vehicle driven, the DME detected a mechanical malfunction within the transmission. The output speed is greater than 300rpm, the transmission oil temperature is greater than 0 degrees Celsius, the engine speed is greater or equal to 600rpm and the range position is P, R, or N.
DTC: P0795 **1T DME, MIL: Yes** **Year:** 2011, 2012 **Model:** X5 **Engine:** 4.4L V8	**Pressure Regulator Valve 3 Plausibility:** The current to/from the pressure regulator valve is either higher or lower than the threshold value.
DTC: P0798 **2T DME, MIL: Yes** **Year:** 2011, 2012 **Model:** 128i, 323i, 328i, 328i xDrive, 528i, 535i, X1, X3, X5 **Engine:** 2.5L L6, 3.0L L6	**Pressure Regulator Valve 2 Upper Threshold:** The signal to/from the pressure regulator valve has been interrupted.
DTC: P0962 **2T DME, MIL: Yes** **Year:** 2011, 2012 **Model:** X5 **Engine:** 4.4L V8	**Pressure Regulator Valve 1 Lower Threshold:** The signal to/from the pressure regulator valve is interrupted or short circuited to ground.
DTC: P0963 **2T DME, MIL: Yes** **Year:** 2011, 2012 **Model:** X5 **Engine:** 4.4L V8	**Pressure Regulator Valve 1 Upper Threshold:** The signal to/from the pressure regulator valve is interrupted or short circuited to supply.
DTC: P0966 **2T DME, MIL: Yes** **Year:** 2011, 2012 **Model:** X5 **Engine:** 4.4L V8	**Pressure Regulator Valve 2 Lower Threshold:** The signal to/from the pressure regulator valve is interrupted or short circuited to ground.
DTC: P0967 **2T DME, MIL: Yes** **Year:** 2011, 2012 **Model:** X5 **Engine:** 4.4L V8	**Pressure Regulator Valve 2 Upper Threshold:** The signal to/from the pressure regulator valve is interrupted or short circuited to supply.
DTC: P0970 **2T DME, MIL: Yes** **Year:** 2011, 2012 **Model:** X5 **Engine:** 4.4L V8	**Pressure Regulator Valve 3 Lower Threshold:** The signal to/from the pressure regulator valve is interrupted or short circuited to ground.

DTC	Trouble Code Title and Conditions
DTC: P0971 **2T DME, MIL: Yes** **Year:** 2011, 2012 **Model:** X5 **Engine:** 4.4L V8	**Pressure Regulator Valve 3 Upper Threshold:** The signal to/from the pressure regulator valve is interrupted or short circuited to supply.
DTC: P0973 **2T DME, MIL: Yes** **Year:** 2011, 2012 **Model:** X5 **Engine:** 4.4L V8	**Solenoid Valve 1 Lower Threshold:** The signal to/from the pressure regulator valve is interrupted or short circuited to ground.
DTC: P0979 **2T DME, MIL: Yes** **Year:** 2011, 2012 **Model:** X5 **Engine:** 4.4L V8	**Solenoid Valve 3 Lower Threshold:** The signal to/from the pressure regulator valve is interrupted or short circuited to ground.

OBD II Trouble Code List (P1XXX Codes)

DTC	Trouble Code Title and Conditions
DTC: P1001 **1T DME, MIL:** **Year:** 2011, 2012 **Model:** 128i, 328i, 328i xDrive, 528i, 535i, X1, X3, X5 **Engine:** 3.0L L6	**Valvetronic (VVT) Limp Home Request High Input:** After 500ms the there is detected a short to battery voltage. If there are simultaneous CAN faults detected, Terminal 15 is probably open at VVT-SG, otherwise check Kb-B.
DTC: P1002 **1T DME, MIL:** **Year:** 2011, 2012 **Model:** 128i, 328i, 328i xDrive, 528i, 535i, X1, X3, X5 **Engine:** 3.0L L6	**Valvetronic (VVT) Limp Home Request Low Input:** After 500ms the there is detected a short to ground. If there are simultaneous CAN faults detected, Terminal 15 is probably open at VVT-SG, otherwise check Kb-B.
DTC: P1003 **1T DME, MIL:** **Year:** 2011, 2012 **Model:** 128i, 328i, 328i xDrive, 528i, 535i, X1, X3, X5 **Engine:** 3.0L L6	**Valvetronic (VVT) Limp Home Request Open Circuit:** After 500ms the there is detected a short. If there are simultaneous CAN faults detected, Terminal 15 is probably open at VVT-SG, otherwise check Kb-B.
DTC: P1004 **1T DME, MIL: Yes** **Year:** 2011, 2012 **Model:** 128i, 328i, 328i xDrive, 528i, 535i, X1, X3, X5 **Engine:** 3.0L L6	**Valvetronic (VVT) Guiding Sensor Solenoid Loss (Bank 1):** After 3ms and the DME and VVT are active, it is detected that the sensor is missing a magnet.
DTC: P1005 **1T DME, MIL: Yes** **Year:** 2011, 2012 **Model:** 128i, 328i, 328i xDrive, 528i, 535i, X1, X3, X5 **Engine:** 3.0L L6	**Valvetronic (VVT) Guiding Sensor Reset Error (Bank 1):** After 1.5ms and the DME and VVT are active, it is detected that the sensor is not properly resetting.
DTC: P1006 **1T DME, MIL: Yes** **Year:** 2011, 2012 **Model:** 128i, 328i, 328i xDrive, 528i, 535i, X1, X3, X5 **Engine:** 3.0L L6	**Valvetronic (VVT) Guiding Sensor Parity Error (Bank 1):** After 12ms and the DME and VVT are active, it is detected that the sensor is not properly communicating. The plug is defective on the sensor or there is an open circuit

DTC	Trouble Code Title and Conditions
DTC: P1007 **1T DME, MIL: Yes** **Year:** 2011, 2012 **Model:** 128i, 328i, 328i xDrive, 528i, 535i, X1, X3, X5 **Engine:** 3.0L L6	**Valvetronic (VVT) Guiding Sensor Gradient Error (Bank 1):** After 9ms and the DME and VVT are active, it is detected that the sensor has a gradient violation/identity, causing a reading of implausible sensor data. The plug is defective on the sensor or there is an open circuit
DTC: P1008 **1T DME, MIL: Yes** **Year:** 2011, 2012 **Model:** 128i, 328i, 328i xDrive, 528i, 535i, X1, X3, X5 **Engine:** 3.0L L6	**Valvetronic (VVT) Guiding Sensor Solenoid Loss (Bank 2):** After 3ms and the DME and VVT are active, it is detected that the sensor is missing a magnet.
DTC: P1009 **1T DME, MIL: Yes** **Year:** 2011, 2012 **Model:** 128i, 328i, 328i xDrive, 528i, 535i, X1, X3, X5 **Engine:** 3.0L L6	**Valvetronic (VVT) Guiding Sensor Reset Error (Bank 2):** After 1.5ms and the DME and VVT are active, it is detected that the sensor is not properly resetting.
DTC: P1010 **1T DME, MIL: Yes** **Year:** 2011, 2012 **Model:** 128i, 328i, 328i xDrive, 528i, 535i, X1, X3, X5 **Engine:** 3.0L L6	**Valvetronic (VVT) Guiding Sensor Parity Error (Bank 2):** After 12ms and the DME and VVT are active, it is detected that the sensor is not properly communicating. The plug is defective on the sensor or there is an open circuit
DTC: P1011 **1T DME, MIL: Yes** **Year:** 2011, 2012 **Model:** 128i, 328i, 328i xDrive, 528i, 535i, X1, X3, X5 **Engine:** 3.0L L6	**Valvetronic (VVT) Guiding Sensor Gradient Error (Bank 2):** After 9ms and the DME and VVT are active, it is detected that the sensor has a gradient violation/identity, causing a reading of implausible sensor data. The plug is defective on the sensor or there is an open circuit
DTC: P1012 **1T DME, MIL: Yes** **Year:** 2011, 2012 **Model:** 128i, 328i, 328i xDrive, 528i, 535i, X1, X3, X5 **Engine:** 3.0L L6	**Valvetronic (VVT) Reference Sensor Solenoid Loss (Bank 1):** After 3ms and the DME and VVT are active, it is detected that the sensor is missing a magnet.
DTC: P1013 **1T DME, MIL: Yes** **Year:** 2011, 2012 **Model:** 128i, 328i, 328i xDrive, 528i, 535i, X1, X3, X5 **Engine:** 3.0L L6	**Valvetronic (VVT) Reference Sensor Reset Error (Bank 1):** After 1.5ms and the DME and VVT are active, it is detected that the sensor is not properly resetting.
DTC: P1014 **1T DME, MIL: Yes** **Year:** 2011, 2012 **Model:** 128i, 328i, 328i xDrive, 528i, 535i, X1, X3, X5 **Engine:** 3.0L L6	**Valvetronic (VVT) Reference Sensor Parity Error (Bank 1):** After 12ms and the DME and VVT are active, it is detected that the sensor is not properly communicating. The plug is defective on the sensor or there is an open circuit
DTC: P1015 **1T DME, MIL: Yes** **Year:** 2011, 2012 **Model:** 128i, 328i, 328i xDrive, 528i, 535i, X1, X3, X5 **Engine:** 3.0L L6	**Valvetronic (VVT) Reference Sensor Gradient Error (Bank 1):** After 9ms and the DME and VVT are active, it is detected that the sensor has a gradient violation/identity, causing a reading of implausible sensor data. The plug is defective on the sensor or there is an open circuit.

DTC	Trouble Code Title and Conditions
DTC: P1022 **1T DME, MIL: Yes** **Year:** 2011, 2012 **Model:** 128i, 328i, 328i xDrive, 528i, 535i, X1, X3, X5 **Engine:** 3.0L L6	**Valvetronic (VVT), Eccentric Shaft Sensor 2 Circuit Low Input:** With the engine running, the fault is a low voltage supply to the sensor after 3ms. The DME, VVT are active at 4.5 to 5.5 volts.
DTC: P1023 **1T DME, MIL: Yes** **Year:** 2011, 2012 **Model:** 128i, 328i, 328i xDrive, 528i, 535i, X1, X3, X5 **Engine:** 3.0L L6	**Valvetronic (VVT) Self-Learning Function Faulty Adjustment Range (Bank 1):** With the engine running, the fault is an out of range adjustment for the self-learning function of the VVT. Check the balance spring installation and the mechanical components for wear.
DTC: P1024 **1T DME, MIL: Yes** **Year:** 2011, 2012 **Model:** 128i, 328i, 328i xDrive, 528i, 535i, X1, X3, X5 **Engine:** 2.0L L4, 3.0L L6	**Valvetronic (VVT) Self-Learning Function Faulty Lower Learning Range (Bank 1):** With the engine running, the fault is an out of range adjustment for the self-learning function of the VVT at the lower range. Check the installation and the mechanical components for wear.
DTC: P1025 **1T DME, MIL: Yes** **Year:** 2011, 2012 **Model:** 128i, 328i, 328i xDrive, 528i, 535i, X1, X3, X5 **Engine:** 3.0L L6	**Valvetronic (VVT) Self-Learning Function No Positions Stored (Bank 1):** With the engine running, no travel limit has been initialized. Check the installation and the mechanical components for wear. This fault is because the system is operated for the first time with a new VVT-SG as there is no automatic limit initialization.
DTC: P1026 **1T DME, MIL: Yes** **Year:** 2011, 2012 **Model:** 128i, 328i, 328i xDrive, 528i, 535i, X1, X3, X5 **Engine:** 3.0L L6	**Valvetronic (VVT) Self-Learning Function Faulty Adjustment Range (Bank 2):** With the engine running, the fault is an out of range adjustment for the self-learning function of the VVT. Check the balance spring installation and the mechanical components for wear.
DTC: P1027 **1T DME, MIL: Yes** **Year:** 2011, 2012 **Model:** 128i, 328i, 328i xDrive, 528i, 535i, X1, X3, X5 **Engine:** 3.0L L6	**Valvetronic (VVT) Self-Learning Function Faulty Lower Learning Range (Bank 2):** With the engine running, the fault is an out of range adjustment for the self-learning function of the VVT at the lower range. Check the installation and the mechanical components for wear.
DTC: P1028 **1T DME, MIL: Yes** **Year:** 2011, 2012 **Model:** 128i, 328i, 328i xDrive, 528i, 535i, X1, X3, X5 **Engine:** 3.0L L6	**Valvetronic (VVT) Self-Learning Function No Positions Stored (Bank 2):** With the engine running, no travel limit has been initialized. Check the sensor installation and the mechanical components for wear. This fault is because the system is operated for the first time with a new VVT-SG as there is no automatic limit initialization.
DTC: P1030 **1T DME, MIL: Yes** **Year:** 2011, 2012 **Model:** 128i, 328i, 328i xDrive, 528i, 535i, X1, X3, X5 **Engine:** 3.0L L6	**Valvetronic (VVT) Actuator Monitoring Position Control, Control Deviation (Bank 1):** The engine is on and running for 45ms at 9.6 to 15.5 volts and a sluggish monitoring movement, direction or rotation was detected. This function monitors the VVT system for resistance to motion and is always active when the driver circuits are released for operation, there's no control with pulse-duty factor, no relay/enable fault, no under voltage, the travel limits are initialized, and there is no reference sensor faults after sensor switching. Check the wiring harness for shorts, the sensor installation, and for wear and mechanical sticking.
DTC: P1031 **1T DME, MIL: Yes** **Year:** 2011, 2012 **Model:** 128i, 328i, 328i xDrive, 528i, 535i, X1, X3, X5 **Engine:** 3.0L L6	**Valvetronic (VVT) Actuator Monitoring Recognition of Direction of Rotation Plausibility (Bank 1):** The engine is on and running for 63 to 498ms at 9.6 to 15.5 volts. Check to determine whether adjustment can be approved. Check VVT system once before each power application within one driving cycle for correct servo motor polarity and sticking in the system.

DTC	Trouble Code Title and Conditions
DTC: P1033 **1T DME, MIL: Yes** **Year:** 2011, 2012 **Model:** 128i, 328i, 328i xDrive, 528i, 535i, X1, X3, X5 **Engine:** 3.0L L6	**Valvetronic (VVT) Actuator Monitoring Position Control, Control Deviation (Bank 2):** The engine is on and running for 45ms at 9.6 to 15.5 volts and a sluggish monitoring movement, direction or rotation was detected. This function monitors the VVT system for resistance to motion and is always active when the driver circuits are released for operation, there's no control with pulse-duty factor, no relay/enable fault, no under voltage, the travel limits are initialized, and there is no reference sensor faults after sensor switching. Check the wiring harness for shorts, the sensor installation, and for wear and mechanical sticking.
DTC: P1034 **1T DME, MIL: Yes** **Year:** 2011, 2012 **Model:** 128i, 328i, 328i xDrive, 528i, 535i, X1, X3, X5 **Engine:** 3.0L L6	**Valvetronic (VVT) Actuator Monitoring Recognition of Direction of Rotation Plausibility (Bank 1):** The engine is on and running for 63 to 498ms at 9.6 to 15.5 volts. Check to determine whether adjustment can be approved. Check VVT system once before each power application within one driving cycle for correct servo motor polarity and sticking in the system.
DTC: P1035 **1T DME, MIL: Yes** **Year:** 2011, 2012 **Model:** 128i, 328i, 328i xDrive, 528i, 535i, X1, X3, X5 **Engine:** 3.0L L6	**Valvetronic (VVT) CAN Message Monitoring Faulty Desired Message (Bank 1):** After the DME is active or the engine running for 500ms, with a voltage of 7 on Terminal 87, the monitoring system displayed a faulty message.
DTC: P1036 **1T DME, MIL: Yes** **Year:** 2011, 2012 **Model:** 128i, 328i, 328i xDrive, 528i, 535i, X1, X3, X5 **Engine:** 3.0L L6	**Valvetronic (VVT) CAN Timeout VVT-Desired Message (Bank 1):** After the key has been on for 800ms (within two messages) or the engine running for 400ms, with a battery voltage at 10 volts, the difference between the deactivation and the starting positions exceeds specification. No suspension of BUS activity.
DTC: P1037 **1T DME, MIL: Yes** **Year:** 2011, 2012 **Model:** 128i, 328i, 328i xDrive, 528i, 535i, X1, X3, X5 **Engine:** 3.0L L6	**Valvetronic (VVT) CAN Timeout Message (Bank 1):** After the key has been on for 800ms (within two messages) or the engine running for 400ms, with a battery voltage at 10 volts, the difference between the deactivation and the starting positions exceeds specification. No suspension of BUS activity.
DTC: P1038 **1T DME, MIL: Yes** **Year:** 2011, 2012 **Model:** 128i, 328i, 328i xDrive, 528i, 535i, X1, X3, X5 **Engine:** 3.0L L6	**Valvetronic (VVT) CAN Message Monitoring Faulty Desired Message (Bank 2):** After the DME is active or the engine running for 500ms, with a voltage of 7 on Terminal 87, the monitoring system displayed a faulty message.
DTC: P1039 **1T DME, MIL: Yes** **Year:** 2011, 2012 **Model:** 128i, 328i, 328i xDrive, 528i, 535i, X1, X3, X5 **Engine:** 3.0L L6	**Valvetronic (VVT) CAN Timeout VVT-Desired Message (Bank 2):** After the key has been on for 800ms (within two messages) or the engine running for 400ms, with a battery voltage at 10 volts, the difference between the deactivation and the starting positions exceeds specification. No suspension of BUS activity.
DTC: P1040 **1T DME, MIL: Yes** **Year:** 2011, 2012 **Model:** 128i, 328i, 328i xDrive, 528i, 535i, X1, X3, X5 **Engine:** 3.0L L6	**Valvetronic (VVT) CAN Timeout Message (Bank 2):** After the key has been on for 800ms (within two messages) or the engine running for 400ms, with a battery voltage at 10 volts, the difference between the deactivation and the starting positions exceeds specification. No suspension of BUS activity.
DTC: P1041 **1T DME, MIL: Yes** **Year:** 2011, 2012 **Model:** 128i, 328i, 328i xDrive, 528i, 535i, X1, X3, X5 **Engine:** 3.0L L6	**Valvetronic (VVT) Actuator Control Module EEPROM Error (Bank 1):** Ignition on for 50ms, the DME detected a control module malfunction (software). To achieve optimal anti-theft protection for the vehicle, an anti-theft immobilizer is installed. The anti-theft immobilizer is a system for enabling and locking the Engine Control Module (DME). So that this system cannot be circumvented, it is necessary to perform adaptation of the anti-theft immobilizer using the Vehicle Diagnostic and Information System VAS 5052 in the On Board Diagnostic (OBD) function. The great availability of equipment options makes it necessary to adapt the Engine Control Module (DME) to the vehicle (e.g. throttle valve control module or cruise control system). This "writing" function is not possible with the generic scan tool.

DTC	Trouble Code Title and Conditions
DTC: P1042 **1T DME, MIL: Yes** **Year:** 2011, 2012 **Model:** 128i, 328i, 328i xDrive, 528i, 535i, X1, X3, X5 **Engine:** 3.0L L6	**Valvetronic (VVT) Actuator Control Module Random Access Memory Error (Bank 1):** Key on for 50ms, and the DME detected an internal memory fault. This code will set if KAPWR to the DME is interrupted (at the initial key on).
DTC: P1043 **1T DME, MIL: Yes** **Year:** 2011, 2012 **Model:** 128i, 328i, 328i xDrive, 528i, 535i, X1, X3, X5 **Engine:** 3.0L L6	**Valvetronic (VVT) Actuator Control Module Read Only Memory Error (Bank 1):** Key on for 50ms, and the DME detected an internal memory fault. This code will set if KAPWR to the DME is interrupted (at the initial key on).
DTC: P1044 **1T DME, MIL: Yes** **Year:** 2011, 2012 **Model:** 128i, 328i, 328i xDrive, 528i, 535i, X1, X3, X5 **Engine:** 3.0L L6	**Valvetronic (VVT) Actuator Control Module EEPROM Error (Bank 2):** Ignition on for 50ms, the DME detected a control module malfunction (software). To achieve optimal anti-theft protection for the vehicle, an anti-theft immobilizer is installed. The anti-theft immobilizer is a system for enabling and locking the Engine Control Module (DME). So that this system cannot be circumvented, it is necessary to perform adaptation of the anti-theft immobilizer using the Vehicle Diagnostic and Information System VAS 5052 in the On Board Diagnostic (OBD) function. The great availability of equipment options makes it necessary to adapt the Engine Control Module (DME) to the vehicle (e.g. throttle valve control module or cruise control system). This "writing" function is not possible with the generic scan tool.
DTC: P1045 **1T DME, MIL: Yes** **Year:** 2011, 2012 **Model:** 128i, 328i, 328i xDrive, 528i, 535i, X1, X3, X5 **Engine:** 3.0L L6	**Valvetronic (VVT) Actuator Control Module Random Access Memory Error (Bank 2):** Key on for 50ms, and the DME detected an internal memory fault. This code will set if KAPWR to the DME is interrupted (at the initial key on).
DTC: P1046 **1T DME, MIL: Yes** **Year:** 2011, 2012 **Model:** 128i, 328i, 328i xDrive, 528i, 535i, X1, X3, X5 **Engine:** 3.0L L6	**Valvetronic (VVT) Actuator Control Module Read Only Memory Error (Bank 2):** Key on for 50ms, and the DME detected an internal memory fault. This code will set if KAPWR to the DME is interrupted (at the initial key on).
DTC: P1047 **1T DME, MIL: Yes** **Year:** 2011, 2012 **Model:** 128i, 328i, 328i xDrive, 528i, 535i, X1, X3, X5 **Engine:** 3.0L L6	**Valvetronic (VVT) Actuator Control Circuit High Input (Bank 1):** Key on for 3ms, and the DME detected a short to positive.
DTC: P1048 **1T DME, MIL: Yes** **Year:** 2011, 2012 **Model:** 128i, 328i, 328i xDrive, 528i, 535i, X1, X3, X5 **Engine:** 3.0L L6	**Valvetronic (VVT) Actuator Control Circuit Low Input (Bank 1):** Key on for 3ms, and the DME detected a short to ground.
DTC: P1050 **1T DME, MIL: Yes** **Year:** 2011, 2012 **Model:** 128i, 328i, 328i xDrive, 528i, 535i, X1, X3, X5 **Engine:** 3.0L L6	**Valvetronic (VVT) Control Circuit (Bank 1):** Key on for 3ms, and the DME detected that the Control Circuit triggered a general fault.
DTC: P1051 **1T DME, MIL: Yes** **Year:** 2011, 2012 **Model:** 128i, 328i, 328i xDrive, 528i, 535i, X1, X3, X5 **Engine:** 3.0L L6	**Valvetronic (VVT) Control Circuit High Input (Bank 1):** Key on for 3ms, and the DME detected a short to positive. Check wiring harness or otherwise replace the servo.

DTC	Trouble Code Title and Conditions
DTC: P1052 **1T DME, MIL: Yes** **Year:** 2011, 2012 **Model:** 128i, 328i, 328i xDrive, 528i, 535i, X1, X3, X5 **Engine:** 3.0L L6	**Valvetronic (VVT) Control Circuit Low Input (Bank 1):** Key on for 3ms, and the DME detected a short to ground. Check wiring harness or otherwise replace the servo.
DTC: P1054 **1T DME, MIL: Yes** **Year:** 2011, 2012 **Model:** 128i, 328i, 328i xDrive, 528i, 535i, X1, X3, X5 **Engine:** 3.0L L6	**Valvetronic (VVT) Control Circuit (Bank 2):** Key on for 3ms, and the DME detected that the Control Circuit triggered a general fault.
DTC: P1055 **1T DME, MIL: Yes** **Year:** 2011, 2012 **Model:** 128i, 328i, 328i xDrive, 528i, 535i, X1, X3, X5 **Engine:** 3.0L L6	**Valvetronic (VVT) Supply Voltage Control Motor High Input (Bank 1):** Key on for 200ms, the DME detected that the supply voltage was too high (more than 17 volts). This is a jump-start detection that throws a fault if there is 24 volts of power for longer than 21 seconds.
DTC: P1056 **1T DME, MIL: Yes** **Year:** 2011, 2012 **Model:** 128i, 328i, 328i xDrive, 528i, 535i, X1, X3, X5 **Engine:** 3.0L L6	**Valvetronic (VVT) Supply Voltage Control Motor Low Input (Bank 1):** Key on for 200ms, the DME detected that the supply voltage was too low (less than 5 volts).
DTC: P1057 **1T DME, MIL: Yes** **Year:** 2011, 2012 **Model:** 128i, 328i, 328i xDrive, 528i, 535i, X1, X3, X5 **Engine:** 3.0L L6	**Valvetronic (VVT) Supply Voltage Control Motor Electrical (Bank 1):** Key on for 50ms, the DME detected that the supply voltage was irregular.
DTC: P1058 **1T DME, MIL: Yes** **Year:** 2011, 2012 **Model:** 128i, 328i, 328i xDrive, 528i, 535i, X1, X3, X5 **Engine:** 3.0L L6	**Valvetronic (VVT) Supply Voltage Control Motor High Input (Bank 2):** Key on for 200ms, the DME detected that the supply voltage was too high (more than 17 volts). This is a jump-start detection that throws a fault if there is 24 volts of power for longer than 21 seconds.
DTC: P1059 **1T DME, MIL: Yes** **Year:** 2011, 2012 **Model:** 128i, 328i, 328i xDrive, 528i, 535i, X1, X3, X5 **Engine:** 3.0L L6	**Valvetronic (VVT) Supply Voltage Control Motor Low Input (Bank 2):** Key on for 200ms, the DME detected that the supply voltage was too low (less than 5 volts).
DTC: P1060 **1T DME, MIL: Yes** **Year:** 2011, 2012 **Model:** 128i, 328i, 328i xDrive, 528i, 535i, X1, X3, X5 **Engine:** 3.0L L6	**Valvetronic (VVT) Supply Voltage Control Motor Electrical (Bank 2):** Key on for 50ms, the DME detected that the supply voltage was irregular.
DTC: P1061 **1T DME, MIL: Yes** **Year:** 2011, 2012 **Model:** 128i, 328i, 328i xDrive, 528i, 535i, X1, X3, X5 **Engine:** 3.0L L6	**Valvetronic (VVT) Limp Home Request RPM and Charge Limitation (Bank 1):** After 3000ms the charge difference between the two banks (caused by other VVT faults) lead to an rpm charge limit.

DTC	Trouble Code Title and Conditions
DTC: P1062 **1T DME, MIL: Yes** **Year:** 2011, 2012 **Model:** 128i, 328i, 328i xDrive, 528i, 535i, X1, X3, X5 **Engine:** 3.0L L6	**Valvetronic (VVT) Limp Home Request Full Stroke Position Not Reached (Bank 1):** After 3000ms the eccentric angle fails to close at the full stroke position. Other VVT fault issues maximum stroke command but the position is not reached.
DTC: P1063 **1T DME, MIL: Yes** **Year:** 2011, 2012 **Model:** 128i, 328i, 328i xDrive, 528i, 535i, X1, X3, X5 **Engine:** 3.0L L6	**Valvetronic (VVT) Limp Home Request Air Mass Plausibility (Bank 1):** After 4000ms the eccentric overload angle detected a fault with the mass airflow plausibility. Other VVT fault issues maximum stroke command but the position is not reached.
DTC: P1064 **1T DME, MIL: Yes** **Year:** 2011, 2012 **Model:** 128i, 328i, 328i xDrive, 528i, 535i, X1, X3, X5 **Engine:** 3.0L L6	**Valvetronic (VVT) Value Comparison Starting Position/Parking Position Plausibility (Bank 1):** After 500ms the difference between the deactivation and the starting positions exceeds specification. Usually occurs after repairs.
DTC: P1065 **1T DME, MIL: Yes** **Year:** 2011, 2012 **Model:** 128i, 328i, 328i xDrive, 528i, 535i, X1, X3, X5 **Engine:** 3.0L L6	**Valvetronic (VVT) CAN Timeout No Signal:** After the key has been on for 800ms (within two messages) or the engine running for 400ms, with a battery voltage at 10 volts, the difference between the deactivation and the starting positions exceeds specification. No suspension of BUS activity. CAN signal is missing, therefore considered in a time out.
DTC: P1066 **1T DME, MIL: Yes** **Year:** 2011, 2012 **Model:** 128i, 328i, 328i xDrive, 528i, 535i, X1, X3, X5 **Engine:** 3.0L L6	**Valvetronic (VVT) CAN Message Monitoring Faulty Actual Message:** After the DME is active or the engine running for 500ms, with a voltage of 7 on Terminal 87, the monitoring system displayed a faulty message.
DTC: P1067 **1T DME, MIL: Yes** **Year:** 2011, 2012 **Model:** 128i, 328i, 328i xDrive, 528i, 535i, X1, X3, X5 **Engine:** 3.0L L6	**Valvetronic (VVT) Reference Sensor Solenoid Loss (Bank 2):** After 3ms and the DME and VVT are active, it is detected that the sensor is missing a magnet.
DTC: P1068 **1T DME, MIL: Yes** **Year:** 2011, 2012 **Model:** 128i, 328i, 328i xDrive, 528i, 535i, X1, X3, X5 **Engine:** 3.0L L6	**Valvetronic (VVT) Reference Sensor Reset Error (Bank 2):** After 1.5ms and the DME and VVT are active, it is detected that the sensor is not properly resetting.
DTC: P1069 **1T DME, MIL: Yes** **Year:** 2011, 2012 **Model:** 128i, 328i, 328i xDrive, 528i, 535i, X1, X3, X5 **Engine:** 3.0L L6	**Valvetronic (VVT) Reference Sensor Parity Error (Bank 2):** After 12ms and the DME and VVT are active, it is detected that the sensor is not properly communicating. The plug is defective on the sensor or there is an open circuit.
DTC: P1070 **1T DME, MIL: Yes** **Year:** 2011, 2012 **Model:** 128i, 328i, 328i xDrive, 528i, 535i, X1, X3, X5 **Engine:** 3.0L L6	**Valvetronic (VVT) Reference Sensor Gradient Error (Bank 2):** After 9ms and the DME and VVT are active, it is detected that the sensor has a gradient violation/identity, causing a reading of implausible sensor data. The plug is defective on the sensor or there is an open circuit.

DTC	Trouble Code Title and Conditions
DTC: P1071 **1T DME, MIL: Yes** **Year:** 2011, 2012 **Model:** 128i, 328i, 328i xDrive, 528i, 535i, X1, X3, X5 **Engine:** 3.0L L6	**Valvetronic (VVT) Control Module Watchdog or Temperature Sensor Error (Bank 1):** Key on for 10ms, and the DME detected an internal fault relating to an internal temperature sensor. Ignore single isolated appearances and only respond to repeated occurrences by replacing the VVT-SG.
DTC: P1072 **1T DME, MIL: Yes** **Year:** 2011, 2012 **Model:** 128i, 328i, 328i xDrive, 528i, 535i, X1, X3, X5 **Engine:** 3.0L L6	**Valvetronic (VVT) Control Module Watchdog or Temperature Sensor Error (Bank 2):** Key on for 10ms, and the DME detected an internal fault relating to an internal temperature sensor. Ignore single isolated appearances and only respond to repeated occurrences by replacing the VVT-SG.
DTC: P1075 **1T DME, MIL: Yes** **Year:** 2011, 2012 **Model:** 128i, 328i, 328i xDrive, 528i, 535i, X1, X3, X5 **Engine:** 3.0L L6	**Valvetronic (VVT) Overload Protection (Bank 1):** After the ignition is on for 45ms, the temperature was recorded as too high.
DTC: P1076 **1T DME, MIL: Yes** **Year:** 2011, 2012 **Model:** 128i, 328i, 328i xDrive, 528i, 535i, X1, X3, X5 **Engine:** 3.0L L6	**Valvetronic (VVT) Overload Protection ECU Temperature High Input (Bank 1):** After the ignition is on for 45ms, the ECU temperature was recorded as too high.
DTC: P1077 **1T DME, MIL: Yes** **Year:** 2011, 2012 **Model:** 128i, 328i, 328i xDrive, 528i, 535i, X1, X3, X5 **Engine:** 3.0L L6	**Valvetronic (VVT) Overload Protection Control Motor Temperature High Input (Bank 1):** After the ignition is on for 45ms, the E motor temperature was recorded as too high.
DTC: P1078 **1T DME, MIL: Yes** **Year:** 2011, 2012 **Model:** 128i, 328i, 328i xDrive, 528i, 535i, X1, X3, X5 **Engine:** 3.0L L6	**Valvetronic (VVT) Overload Protection Control Motor Current High Input (Bank 1):** After the ignition is on for 45ms, the E motor activation current is too high.
DTC: P1079 **1T DME, MIL: Yes** **Year:** 2011, 2012 **Model:** 128i, 328i, 328i xDrive, 528i, 535i, X1, X3, X5 **Engine:** 3.0L L6	**Valvetronic (VVT) Overload Protection (Bank 1):** After the ignition is on for 45ms, the temperature was recorded as too high.
DTC: P1080 **1T DME, MIL: Yes** **Year:** 2011, 2012 **Model:** 128i, 328i, 328i xDrive, 528i, 535i, X1, X3, X5 **Engine:** 3.0L L6	**Valvetronic (VVT) Overload Protection ECU Temperature High Input (Bank 2):** After the ignition is on for 45ms, the ECU temperature was recorded as too high.
DTC: P1081 **1T DME, MIL: Yes** **Year:** 2011, 2012 **Model:** 128i, 328i, 328i xDrive, 528i, 535i, X1, X3, X5 **Engine:** 3.0L L6	**Valvetronic (VVT) Overload Protection Control Motor Temperature High Input (Bank 2):** After the ignition is on for 45ms, the E motor temperature was recorded as too high.

DTC	Trouble Code Title and Conditions
DTC: P1082 **1T DME, MIL: Yes** **Year:** 2011, 2012 **Model:** 128i, 328i, 328i xDrive, 528i, 535i, X1, X3, X5 **Engine:** 3.0L L6	**Valvetronic (VVT) Overload Protection Control Motor Current High Input (Bank 2):** After the ignition is on for 45ms, the E motor activation current is too high.
DTC: P1084 **2T DME, MIL: Yes** **Year:** 2011, 2012 **Model:** 128i, 328i, 328i xDrive, 528i, 535i, X1, X3, X5 **Engine:** 3.0L L6	**Fuel System Too Lean:** Key on or engine running, all electrical components off and coolant temperature at least 80 degrees Celsius; and the DME detected the Bank 1 Adaptive Fuel Control System reached its rich correction limit (a lean A/F condition). The fuel status is in a closed loop pattern, the coolant temperature is between 69 and 100 degrees Celsius, and the engine speed is between 800 and 6000rpm.
DTC: P1085 **2T DME, MIL: Yes** **Year:** 2011, 2012 **Model:** 128i, 328i, 328i xDrive, 528i, 535i, X1, X3, X5 **Engine:** 3.0L L6	**Fuel System Too Rich:** Key on or engine running, all electrical components off and coolant temperature at least 80 degrees Celsius; and the DME detected the Bank 2 Adaptive Fuel Control System reached its rich correction limit (a rich A/F condition). The fuel status is in a closed loop pattern, the coolant temperature is between 69 and 100 degrees Celsius, and the engine speed is between 800 and 6000rpm.
DTC: P1086 **2T DME, MIL: Yes** **Year:** 2011, 2012 **Model:** 128i, 328i, 328i xDrive, 528i, 535i, X1, X3, X5 **Engine:** 3.0L L6	**Fuel System Too Lean:** Key on or engine running, all electrical components off and coolant temperature at least 80 degrees Celsius; and the DME detected the Bank 2 Fuel Control System reached its lean correction limit. The fuel status is in a closed loop pattern, the coolant temperature is between 69 and 100 degrees Celsius, and the engine speed is between 800 and 6000rpm.
DTC: P1104 **1T DME, MIL: Yes** **Year:** 2011, 2012 **Model:** 128i, 328i, 328i xDrive, 528i, 535i, X1, X3, X5 **Engine:** 3.0L L6	**Differential Pressure Sensor Intake Manifold Pressure Too Low (Bank 1):** Engine started, battery voltage must be at least 11v, and the differential pressure sensor detected a control deviation at the minimum limit. The closed loop control of the differential pressure in the intake manifold is suspended and replaced by a direct specification.
DTC: P1105 **1T DME, MIL: Yes** **Year:** 2011, 2012 **Model:** 128i, 328i, 328i xDrive, 528i, 535i, X1, X3, X5 **Engine:** 3.0L L6	**Differential Pressure Sensor Intake Manifold Pressure Too High (Bank 1):** Engine started, battery voltage must be at least 11v, and the differential pressure sensor detected a control deviation at the maximum limit. The closed loop control of the differential pressure in the intake manifold is suspended and replaced by a direct specification.
DTC: P1129 **1T DME, MIL: Yes** **Year:** 2011, 2012 **Model:** 128i, 328i, 328i xDrive, 528i, 535i, X1, X3, X5 **Engine:** 3.0L L6	**Engine Oil Level Sensor Signal Oil Level Too Low:** Engine started, and the oil sensor has detected that the level is too low.
DTC: P1130 **1T DME, MIL: Yes** **Year:** 2011, 2012 **Model:** 128i, 328i, 328i xDrive, 528i, 535i, X1, X3, X5 **Engine:** 3.0L L6	**Long Term Fuel Trim at Lean Limit:** Engine started, battery voltage must be at least 11.5v, all electrical components must be off, the ground between the engine and the chassis must be well connected, the exhaust system must be properly sealed between the catalytic converter and the cylinder head, and the oxygen sensor heater for oxygen sensor before the catalytic converter must be properly functioning. The DME detected the HO2S circuit was too lean, or that it could no longer change Fuel Trim because it was at its lean limit.
DTC: P1197 **1T DME, MIL: Yes** **Year:** 2011, 2012 **Model:** 1 Series M, 128i, 135i, 328i, 328i xDrive, 335is, 528i, 535i, X1, X3, X5 **Engine:** 3.0L L6	**Differential Pressure Sensor Intake Manifold High Input (Bank 1):** Engine started, battery voltage must be at least 11v, and the differential pressure sensor wiring shorted to battery voltage. The closed loop control of the differential pressure in the intake manifold is suspended and replaced by a direct specification.

DTC	Trouble Code Title and Conditions
DTC: P1198 **1T DME, MIL: Yes** **Year:** 2011, 2012 **Model:** 1 Series M, 128i, 135i, 328i, 328i xDrive, 335is, 528i, 535i, X1, X3, X5 **Engine:** 3.0L L6	**Differential Pressure Sensor Intake Manifold Low Input (Bank 1):** Engine started, battery voltage must be at least 11v, and the differential pressure sensor wiring shorted to ground. The closed loop control of the differential pressure in the intake manifold is suspended and replaced by a direct specification.
DTC: P1199 **1T DME, MIL: Yes** **Year:** 2011, 2012 **Model:** 1 Series M, 128i, 135i, 328i, 328i xDrive, 335is, 528i, 535i, X1, X3, X5 **Engine:** 3.0L L6	**Differential Pressure Sensor Intake Manifold Pressure Plausibility (Bank 1):** Engine started, battery voltage must be at least 11v, and the differential pressure sensor signal is malfunction or is not present. The closed loop control of the differential pressure in the intake manifold is suspended and replaced by a direct specification.
DTC: P1327 **1T DME, MIL: Yes** **Year:** 2011, 2012 **Model:** 1 Series M, 128i, 135i, 328i, 328i xDrive, 335is, 528i, 535i, X1, X3, X5 **Engine:** 3.0L L6	**Knock Sensor 2 Signal Low Input:** Engine started, vehicle driven at 2000rpm for 3 seconds or to a temperature of 40 degrees Celsius, and the DME detected the Knock Sensor 1 (KS1) signal was too low or not recognized by the DME.
DTC: P1328 **1T DME, MIL: Yes** **Year:** 2011, 2012 **Model:** 1 Series M, 128i, 135i, 328i, 328i xDrive, 335is, 528i, 535i, X1, X3, X5 **Engine:** 3.0L L6, 4.4L V8	**Knock Sensor 2 Signal High Input:** Engine started, vehicle driven at 1600rpm for 3 seconds or to a temperature of 40 degrees Celsius, and the DME detected the Knock Sensor 1 (KS1) signal was too high.
DTC: P1329 **1T DME, MIL: Yes** **Year:** 2011, 2012 **Model:** 1 Series M, 128i, 135i, 328i, 328i xDrive, 335is, 528i, 535i, X1, X3, X5 **Engine:** 3.0L L6	**Knock Sensor 3 Signal Low Input:** Engine started, vehicle driven at 2000rpm for 3 seconds or to a temperature of 40 degrees Celsius, and the DME detected the Knock Sensor 1 (KS1) signal was too low or not recognized by the DME.
DTC: P1330 **1T DME, MIL: Yes** **Year:** 2011, 2012 **Model:** 1 Series M, 128i, 135i, 328i, 328i xDrive, 335is, 528i, 535i, X1, X3, X5 **Engine:** 3.0L L6	**Knock Sensor 3 Signal High Input:** Engine started, vehicle driven at 1600rpm for 3 seconds or to a temperature of 40 degrees Celsius, and the DME detected the Knock Sensor 1 (KS1) signal was too high.
DTC: P1332 **1T DME, MIL: Yes** **Year:** 2011, 2012 **Model:** 1 Series M, 128i, 135i, 328i, 328i xDrive, 335is, 528i, 535i, X1, X3, X5 **Engine:** 3.0L L6, 4.4L V8	**Knock Sensor 4 Signal Low Input:** Engine started, vehicle driven at 2000rpm for 3 seconds or to a temperature of 40 degrees Celsius, and the DME detected the Knock Sensor 1 (KS1) signal was too low or not recognized by the DME.
DTC: P1333 **1T DME, MIL: Yes** **Year:** 2011, 2012 **Model:** 1 Series M, 128i, 135i, 328i, 328i xDrive, 335is, 528i, 535i, X1, X3, X5 **Engine:** 3.0L L6, 4.4L V8	**Knock Sensor 4 Signal High Input:** Engine started, vehicle driven at 1600rpm for 3 seconds or to a temperature of 40 degrees Celsius, and the DME detected the Knock Sensor 1 (KS1) signal was too high.

DTC	Trouble Code Title and Conditions
DTC: P1342 **1T DME, MIL: Yes** **Year:** 2011, 2012 **Model:** 1 Series M, 128i, 135i, 328i, 328i xDrive, 335is, 528i, 535i, X1, X3, X5 **Engine:** 3.0L L6, 4.4L V8	**Random/Multiple Misfire Detected:** Engine running at an RPM greater than 400 but less than 6400 the DME detected a misfire or uneven engine running in two or more cylinders within 200 crankshaft rotations. Engine speed is between 480 and 4500rpm, load change is 0.4ms at ignition with a speed change of 2800rpms and the ASC is not active. **Note: If the misfire is severe, the MIL will flash on/off on the first trip!**
DTC: P1344 **1T DME, MIL: Yes** **Year:** 2011, 2012 **Model:** 1 Series M, 128i, 135i, 328i, 328i xDrive, 335is, 528i, 535i, X1, X3, X5 **Engine:** 3.0L L6, 4.4L V8	**Random/Multiple Misfire Detected:** Engine running at an RPM greater than 400 but less than 6400 the DME detected a misfire or uneven engine running in two or more cylinders within 200 crankshaft rotations. Engine speed is between 480 and 4500rpm, load change is 0.4ms at ignition with a speed change of 2800rpms and the ASC is not active. **Note: If the misfire is severe, the MIL will flash on/off on the first trip!**
DTC: P1346 **1T DME, MIL: Yes** **Year:** 2011, 2012 **Model:** 1 Series M, 128i, 135i, 328i, 328i xDrive, 335is, 528i, 535i, X1, X3, X5 **Engine:** 3.0L L6, 4.4L V8	**Random/Multiple Misfire Detected:** Engine running at an RPM greater than 400 but less than 6400 the DME detected a misfire or uneven engine running in two or more cylinders within 200 crankshaft rotations. Engine speed is between 480 and 4500rpm, load change is 0.4ms at ignition with a speed change of 2800rpms and the ASC is not active. **Note: If the misfire is severe, the MIL will flash on/off on the first trip!**
DTC: P1348 **1T DME, MIL: Yes** **Year:** 2011, 2012 **Model:** 1 Series M, 128i, 135i, 328i, 328i xDrive, 335is, 528i, 535i, X1, X3, X5 **Engine:** 3.0L L6, 4.4L V8	**Random/Multiple Misfire Detected:** Engine running at an RPM greater than 400 but less than 6400 the DME detected a misfire or uneven engine running in two or more cylinders within 200 crankshaft rotations. Engine speed is between 480 and 4500rpm, load change is 0.4ms at ignition with a speed change of 2800rpms and the ASC is not active. **Note: If the misfire is severe, the MIL will flash on/off on the first trip!**
DTC: P1350 **1T DME, MIL: Yes** **Year:** 2011, 2012 **Model:** 1 Series M, 128i, 135i, 328i, 328i xDrive, 335is, 528i, 535i, X1, X3, X5 **Engine:** 3.0L L6, 4.4L V8	**Random/Multiple Misfire Detected:** Engine running at an RPM greater than 400 but less than 6400 the DME detected a misfire or uneven engine running in two or more cylinders within 200 crankshaft rotations. Engine speed is between 480 and 4500rpm, load change is 0.4ms at ignition with a speed change of 2800rpms and the ASC is not active. **Note: If the misfire is severe, the MIL will flash on/off on the first trip!**
DTC: P1352 **1T DME, MIL: Yes** **Year:** 2011, 2012 **Model:** X5 **Engine:** 4.4L V8	**Random/Multiple Misfire Detected:** Engine running at an RPM greater than 400 but less than 6400 the DME detected a misfire or uneven engine running in two or more cylinders within 200 crankshaft rotations. Engine speed is between 480 and 4500rpm, load change is 0.4ms at ignition with a speed change of 2800rpms and the ASC is not active. **Note: If the misfire is severe, the MIL will flash on/off on the first trip!**
DTC: P1354 **1T DME, MIL: Yes** **Year:** 2011, 2012 **Model:** X5 **Engine:** 4.4L V8	**Random/Multiple Misfire Detected:** Engine running at an RPM greater than 400 but less than 6400 the DME detected a misfire or uneven engine running in two or more cylinders within 200 crankshaft rotations. Engine speed is between 480 and 4500rpm, load change is 0.4ms at ignition with a speed change of 2800rpms and the ASC is not active. **Note: If the misfire is severe, the MIL will flash on/off on the first trip!**
DTC: P1355 **1T DME, MIL: Yes** **Year:** 2011, 2012 **Model:** X5 **Engine:** 4.4L V8	**Random/Multiple Misfire Detected:** Engine running at an RPM greater than 400 but less than 6400 the DME detected a misfire or uneven engine running in two or more cylinders within 200 crankshaft rotations. Engine speed is between 480 and 4500rpm, load change is 0.4ms at ignition with a speed change of 2800rpms and the ASC is not active. **Note: If the misfire is severe, the MIL will flash on/off on the first trip!**
DTC: P1356 **1T DME, MIL: Yes** **Year:** 2011, 2012 **Model:** X5 **Engine:** 4.4L V8	**Random/Multiple Misfire Detected:** Engine running at an RPM greater than 400 but less than 6400 the DME detected a misfire or uneven engine running in two or more cylinders within 200 crankshaft rotations. Engine speed is between 480 and 4500rpm, load change is 0.4ms at ignition with a speed change of 2800rpms and the ASC is not active. **Note: If the misfire is severe, the MIL will flash on/off on the first trip!**

DTC	Trouble Code Title and Conditions
DTC: P1357 **1T DME, MIL: Yes** **Year:** 2011, 2012 **Model:** X5 **Engine:** 4.4L V8	**Random/Multiple Misfire Detected:** Engine running at an RPM greater than 400 but less than 6400 the DME detected a misfire or uneven engine running in two or more cylinders within 200 crankshaft rotations. Engine speed is between 480 and 4500rpm, load change is 0.4ms at ignition with a speed change of 2800rpms and the ASC is not active. **Note: If the misfire is severe, the MIL will flash on/off on the first trip!**
DTC: P1377 **1T DME, MIL: Yes** **Year:** 2011, 2012 **Model:** 1 Series M, 128i, 135i, 328i, 328i xDrive, 335is, 528i, 535i, X1, X3, X5 **Engine:** 3.0L L6	**Camshaft Position Sensor Master Camshaft Not Defined:** Engine started, battery voltage must be at least 11.5v, after five camshaft revolutions, the DME detected the CMP sensor signal was implausible. Perhaps a defect in the power supply. Reduced power occurs and once the engine is turned off, it is impossible to restart it.
DTC: P1381 **1T DME, MIL: Yes** **Year:** 2011, 2012 **Model:** 1 Series M, 128i, 135i, 328i, 328i xDrive, 335is, 528i, 535i, X1, X3, X5 **Engine:** 3.0L L6, 4.4L V8	**Control Module Self-Test, Knock Control Offset (Bank 1):** Engine started, vehicle driven at 1520rpm for 10 seconds or to a temperature of 40 degrees Celsius, and the DME detected the Knock chip is defective.
DTC: P1382 **1T DME, MIL: Yes** **Year:** 2011, 2012 **Model:** 1 Series M, 128i, 135i, 328i, 328i xDrive, 335is, 528i, 535i, X1, X3, X5 **Engine:** 3.0L L6, 4.4L V8	**Control Module Self-Test, Knock Control Test Pulse (Bank 1):** Engine started, vehicle driven at 1520rpm for 10 seconds or to a temperature of 40 degrees Celsius, and the DME detected the Knock chip is defective.
DTC: P1384 **1T DME, MIL: Yes** **Year:** 2011, 2012 **Model:** 1 Series M, 128i, 135i, 328i, 328i xDrive, 335is, 528i, 535i, X1, X3, X5 **Engine:** 3.0L L6	**Knock Sensor 3 Circuit Malfunction:** Engine started, vehicle driven at 1520rpm for 3 seconds or to a temperature of 40 degrees Celsius, and the DME detected the Knock Sensor 1 (KS1) signal was not recognized. The engine speed is greater than 2080rpm but less than 6000rpm and the coolant temperature is greater than 40.5 degrees Celsius.
DTC: P1385 **1T DME, MIL: Yes** **Year:** 2011, 2012 **Model:** 1 Series M, 128i, 135i, 328i, 328i xDrive, 335is, 528i, 535i, X1, X3, X5 **Engine:** 3.0L L6	**Knock Sensor 4 Circuit Malfunction:** Engine started, vehicle driven at 1520rpm for 3 seconds or to a temperature of 40 degrees Celsius, and the DME detected the Knock Sensor 1 (KS1) signal was not recognized. The engine speed is greater than 2080rpm but less than 6000rpm and the coolant temperature is greater than 40.5 degrees Celsius.
DTC: P1386 **1T DME, MIL: Yes** **Year:** 2011, 2012 **Model:** 1 Series M, 128i, 135i, 328i, 328i xDrive, 335is, 528i, 535i, X1, X3, X5 **Engine:** 3.0L L6, 4.4L V8	**Control Module Self-Test, Knock Control Circuit Baseline Test (Bank 1):** Engine started, vehicle driven at 1520rpm for 10 seconds or to a temperature of 40 degrees Celsius, and the DME detected the Knock chip is defective. The engine speed is greater than 2080rpm but less than 6000rpm and the coolant temperature is greater than 40.5 degrees Celsius.
DTC: P1396 **1T DME, MIL: Yes** **Year:** 2011, 2012 **Model:** 1 Series M, 128i, 135i, 323i, 328i, 328i xDrive, 335is, 528i, 535i, X1, X3, X5 **Engine:** 2.5L L6, 3.0L L6, 4.4L V8	**Camshaft Position Sensor "A" Circ Malfunction:** Engine started, battery voltage must be at least 11.5v, all electrical components must be off, parking brake must be engaged (to keep daytime driving lights off), automatic transmission selector must be in park and the ground between the engine and the chassis must be well connected. The DME detected the CMP sensor signal was implausible. Engine speed is greater than 500rpm, and the fault is tolerable as long as there are no misfired occurring at the same time.

DTC	Trouble Code Title and Conditions
DTC: P1413 **1T DME, MIL: Yes** **Year:** 2011, 2012 **Model:** 1 Series M, 128i, 135i, 328i, 328i xDrive, 335is, 528i, 535i, X1, X3, X5 **Engine:** 3.0L L6	**Secondary Air Injector Pump Relay Control Circuit Signal Low:** The Engine Control Module detects a short circuit when activating the secondary air injection solenoid valve. **Note: Solenoid valve is closed when no voltage is present.**
DTC: P1414 **1T DME, MIL: Yes** **Year:** 2011, 2012 **Model:** 1 Series M, 128i, 135i, 328i, 328i xDrive, 335is, 528i, 535i, X1, X3, X5 **Engine:** 3.0L L6	**Secondary Air Injector Pump Relay Control Circuit Signal High:** The Engine Control Module detects a short circuit when activating the secondary air injection solenoid valve. **Note: Solenoid valve is closed when no voltage is present.**
DTC: P1500 **1T DME, MIL: Yes** **Year:** 2011, 2012 **Model:** X5 **Engine:** 4.4L V8	**Idle Air Control Valve Malfunction:** Engine started, battery voltage at least 11.5v, all electrical components off, ground connections between engine and chassis well connected, coolant temperature at least 80-degrees Celsius. The DME detected deviation from the normal operating parameters of the Idle Air Control Valve. The vehicle speed can be zero mph and the engine load must be less than 1.5ms.
DTC: P1501 **1T DME, MIL: Yes** **Year:** 2011, 2012 **Model:** X5 **Engine:** 4.4L V8	**Idle Air Control Valve Malfunction:** Engine started, battery voltage at least 11.5v, all electrical components off, ground connections between engine and chassis well connected, coolant temperature at least 80-degrees Celsius. The DME detected deviation from the normal operating parameters of the Idle Air Control Valve. The vehicle speed can be zero mph and the engine load must be less than 1.5ms.
DTC: P1502 **1T DME, MIL: Yes** **Year:** 2011, 2012 **Model:** X5 **Engine:** 4.4L V8	**Idle Air Control Valve Circuit Short to B+:** Engine running the DME detected that the idle air control valve was intermittent.
DTC: P1503 **1T DME, MIL: Yes** **Year:** 2011, 2012 **Model:** X5 **Engine:** 4.4L V8	**Idle Air Control Valve Circuit Short to Ground:** Engine running the DME detected that the idle air control valve was intermittent.
DTC: P1504 **1T DME, MIL: Yes** **Year:** 2011, 2012 **Model:** X5 **Engine:** 4.4L V8	**Idle Air Control Valve Circuit Continuity-Open Load:** Engine running the DME detected that the idle air control valve signal was intermittent.
DTC: P1506 **1T DME, MIL: Yes** **Year:** 2011, 2012 **Model:** X5 **Engine:** 4.4L V8	**Idle Air Control Valve Circuit Short to B+:** Engine running the DME detected that the idle air control valve signal was intermittent.
DTC: P1507 **1T DME, MIL: Yes** **Year:** 2011, 2012 **Model:** X5 **Engine:** 4.4L V8	**Idle Air Control Valve Circuit Short to Ground:** Engine running the DME detected that the idle air control valve signal was intermittent.
DTC: P1508 **1T DME, MIL: Yes** **Year:** 2011, 2012 **Model:** X5 **Engine:** 4.4L V8	**Idle Air Control Valve Circuit Continuity-Open Load:** Engine running the DME detected that the idle air control valve signal was intermittent.

DTC	Trouble Code Title and Conditions
DTC: P1512 **1T DME, MIL: Yes** **Year:** 2011, 2012 **Model:** 1 Series M, 128i, 135i, 328i, 328i xDrive, 335is, 528i, 535i, X1, X3, X5 **Engine:** 3.0L L6	**Differentiated Intake Manifold Control Circuit Signal Low:** Engine started, and the DME detected the changeover valve circuit was shorting to negative during the continuous self test.
DTC: P1513 **1T DME, MIL: Yes** **Year:** 2011, 2012 **Model:** 1 Series M, 128i, 135i, 328i, 328i xDrive, 335is, 528i, 535i, X1, X3, X5 **Engine:** 3.0L L6	**Differentiated Intake Manifold Control Circuit Signal High:** Engine started, and the DME detected the changeover valve circuit was shorting to positive during the continuous self test.
DTC: P1515 **1T DME, MIL: Yes** **Year:** 2011, 2012 **Model:** 1 Series M, 128i, 135i, 328i, 328i xDrive, 335is, 528i, 535i, X1, X3, X5 **Engine:** 3.0L L6	**Engine Off Timer Plausibility:** The DME detected an implausible instrument cluster and/or power module signal. CAN signal failure while the DME was operating at a range between 6 and 16 volts. CAN Bus lost communications. The system time (time pulse) is implausible relative to the DME's internal counter.
DTC: P1517 **1T DME, MIL: Yes** **Year:** 2011, 2012 **Model:** 1 Series M, 128i, 135i, 328i, 328i xDrive, 335is, 528i, 535i, X1, X3, X5 **Engine:** 3.0L L6	**Rough Road Detection, No Wheel Speed Signal:** The DME detected an electrical malfunction on the main relay circuit
DTC: P1518 **1T DME, MIL: Yes** **Year:** 2011, 2012 **Model:** 1 Series M, 128i, 135i, 328i, 328i xDrive, 335is, 528i, 535i, X1, X3, X5 **Engine:** 3.0L L6	**Rough Road Detection, Wheel Speed Too High:** The DME detected an electrical malfunction on the main relay circuit
DTC: P1520 **1T DME, MIL: Yes** **Year:** 2011, 2012 **Model:** 1 Series M, 128i, 135i, 328i, 328i xDrive, 335is, 528i, 535i, X1, X3, X5 **Engine:** 3.0L L6	**Engine Oil Quality Sensor Level Measurement Error:** After 60 seconds with the ignition on, a miscommunication between the oil sensor and the DME was detected.
DTC: P1521 **1T DME, MIL: Yes** **Year:** 2011, 2012 **Model:** 1 Series M, 128i, 135i, 328i, 328i xDrive, 335is, 528i, 535i, X1, X3, X5 **Engine:** 3.0L L6	**Engine Oil Quality Sensor Communication Error:** After 60 seconds with the ignition on, a miscommunication between the oil sensor and the DME was detected.
DTC: P1526 **1T DME, MIL: Yes** **Year:** 2011, 2012 **Model:** X5 **Engine:** 4.4L V8	**Camshaft Control Circuit Ground:** Engine started and driven at an engine speed of more than 400rpm; and the DME detected the camshaft timing exceeded the calibrated levels. The valve timing did not change from the current valve timing or it remained fixed during the testing. **Note: The camshaft adjustment is load- and RPM dependant. The electrical camshaft adjustment valve 1 switches oil pressure onto camshaft adjuster (mechanical adjustment mechanism), which adjusts the camshaft.**

DTC	Trouble Code Title and Conditions
DTC: P1535 **1T DME, MIL: Yes** **Year:** 2011, 2012 **Model:** 1 Series M, 128i, 135i, 328i, 328i xDrive, 335is, 528i, 535i, X1, X3, X5 **Engine:** 3.0L L6	**Differentiated Intake Manifold Coil Temperature Limit Value Exceeded:** This fault stems from the 4.8L-N62 equipped with an infinitely adjustable control of induction system. The temperature of the coil has exceeded the predetermined limits.
DTC: P1536 **1T DME, MIL: Yes** **Year:** 2011, 2012 **Model:** 1 Series M, 128i, 135i, 328i, 328i xDrive, 335is, 528i, 535i, X1, X3, X5 **Engine:** 3.0L L6	**Differentiated Intake Manifold Controller Monitoring, Control Deviation:** This fault stems from the 4.8L-N62 equipped with an infinitely adjustable control of induction system.
DTC: P1537 **1T DME, MIL: Yes** **Year:** 2011, 2012 **Model:** 1 Series M, 128i, 135i, 328i, 328i xDrive, 335is, 528i, 535i, X1, X3, X5 **Engine:** 3.0L L6	**Differentiated Intake Manifold Potentiometer Voltage in Lower Diagnosis Range:** This fault stems from the 4.8L-N62 equipped with an infinitely adjustable control of induction system.
DTC: P1538 **1T DME, MIL: Yes** **Year:** 2011, 2012 **Model:** 1 Series M, 128i, 135i, 328i, 328i xDrive, 335is, 528i, 535i, X1, X3, X5 **Engine:** 3.0L L6	**Differentiated Intake Manifold Potentiometer Voltage in Upper Diagnosis Range:** This fault stems from the 4.8L-N62 equipped with an infinitely adjustable control of induction system.
DTC: P1539 **1T DME, MIL: Yes** **Year:** 2011, 2012 **Model:** 1 Series M, 128i, 135i, 328i, 328i xDrive, 335is, 528i, 535i, X1, X3, X5 **Engine:** 3.0L L6	**Differentiated Intake Manifold Coil Temperature Threshold Exceeded:** This fault stems from the 4.8L-N62 equipped with an infinitely adjustable control of induction system. The temperature of the coil has exceeded the predetermined limits.
DTC: P1550 **1T DME, MIL: Yes** **Year:** 2011, 2012 **Model:** X5 **Engine:** 4.4L V8	**Idle Air Control Valve:** Engine started, battery voltage at least 11.5v, all electrical components off, ground connections between engine and chassis well connected, coolant temperature at least 80-degrees Celsius. The DME detected deviation from the normal operating parameters of the charge pressure sensor.
DTC: P1551 **2T DME, MIL: Yes** **Year:** 2011, 2012 **Model:** 1 Series M, 128i, 135i, 328i, 328i xDrive, 335is, 528i, 535i, X1, X3, X5 **Engine:** 3.0L L6	**Engine Off Timer Timeout:** The DME detected a CAN signal failure while the DME was operating at a range between 6 and 16 volts. CAN Bus lost communications.
DTC: P1561 **2T DME, MIL: Yes** **Year:** 2011, 2012 **Model:** 1 Series M, 328i, 328i xDrive **Engine:** 2.0L L4, 3.0L L6	**MOTOR COMMUNICATION SENSOR B CIRCUIT LOW INPUT:** **Note: This fault code is a GERENRIC fault code, some cars may change the meaning of this fault code.**
DTC: P1604 **2T DME, MIL: Yes** **Year:** 2011 **Model:** 323i **Engine:** 2.5L L6	**Internal Control Module Driver Error:** Ignition on, the DME detected a control module malfunction. To achieve optimal anti-theft protection for the vehicle, an anti-theft immobilizer is installed. The anti-theft immobilizer is a system for enabling and locking the Engine Control Module (DME). So that this system cannot be circumvented, it is necessary to perform adaptation of the anti-theft immobilizer using the Vehicle Diagnostic and Information System VAS 5052 in the On Board Diagnostic (OBD) function. The great availability of equipment options makes it necessary to adapt the Engine Control Module (DME) to the vehicle (e.g. throttle valve control module or cruise control system). This "writing" function is not possible with the generic scan tool.

DTC	Trouble Code Title and Conditions
DTC: P1614 **2T DME, MIL: Yes** **Year:** 2011, 2012 **Model:** 1 Series M, 128i, 135i, 328i, 328i xDrive, 335is, 528i, 535i, X1, X3, X5 **Engine:** 3.0L L6	**Serial Communication Link ACC Malfunction:** Key on after 800ms or engine running for 100ms, the DME detected an electrical malfunction regarding the Adaptive Cruise Control circuit. Check the ACC fuse, the ECU or CAN for fault, measure the resistance on the BUS, check the wiring harness. If this fault occurs when the ACC is not installed, the DME has been incorrectly initialized for the ACC version.
DTC: P1628 **1T DME, MIL: Yes** **Year:** 2011, 2012 **Model:** 1 Series M, 128i, 135i, 328i, 328i xDrive, 335is, 528i, 535i, X1, X3, X5 **Engine:** 3.0L L6	**Throttle Valve Adaptation Spring Test Malfunction During Opening (Bank 1):** Engine started, and the battery voltage is greater than 7 volts, this fault is only diagnosed during the throttle valve's adaptation phase. DVE fails to close from emergency air position. Vehicle speed is zero, throttle pedal is less than 14.9 percent, coolant temperature is between 5.3 and 100.5 degrees Celsius and the intake air temperature is 5.3 degrees Celsius.
DTC: P1629 **1T DME, MIL: Yes** **Year:** 2011, 2012 **Model:** 1 Series M, 128i, 135i, 328i, 328i xDrive, 335is, 528i, 535i, X1, X3, X5 **Engine:** 3.0L L6	**Throttle Valve Adaptation Spring Test Stop, Spring Does Not Open (Bank 1):** Engine started, and the battery voltage is greater than 7 volts, this fault is only diagnosed during the throttle valve's adaptation phase. Emergency air position not achieved from closed valve. Vehicle speed is zero, throttle pedal is less than 14.9 percent, coolant temperature is between 5.3 and 100.5 degrees Celsius and the intake air temperature is 5.3 degrees Celsius.
DTC: P1631 **1T DME, MIL: Yes** **Year:** 2011, 2012 **Model:** 1 Series M, 128i, 135i, 328i, 328i xDrive, 335is, 528i, 535i, X1, X3, X5 **Engine:** 3.0L L6	**Throttle Valve Adaptation Spring Test (Bank 1):** Engine started, and the battery voltage is greater than 7 volts, this fault is only diagnosed during the throttle valve's adaptation phase. It is not possible to move DVE from emergency air position. Vehicle speed is zero, throttle pedal is less than 14.9 percent, coolant temperature is between 5.3 and 100.5 degrees Celsius and the intake air temperature is 5.3 degrees Celsius.
DTC: P1633 **1T DME, MIL: Yes** **Year:** 2011, 2012 **Model:** 1 Series M, 128i, 135i, 328i, 328i xDrive, 335is, 528i, 535i, X1, X3, X5 **Engine:** 3.0L L6	**Throttle Valve Adaptation Limp-Home Position Unknown:** Engine started, and the battery voltage is greater than 7 volts, this fault is only diagnosed during the throttle valve's adaptation phase. Check on throttle valve's emergency default position as determined during throttle valve adaptation. There is a failure to reach emergency air position with DVE switched off. Vehicle speed is zero, throttle pedal is less than 14.9 percent, coolant temperature is between 5.3 and 100.5 degrees Celsius and the intake air temperature is 5.3 degrees Celsius.
DTC: P1634 **1T DME, MIL: Yes** **Year:** 2011, 2012 **Model:** 1 Series M, 128i, 135i, 328i, 328i xDrive, 335is, 528i, 535i, X1, X3, X5 **Engine:** 3.0L L6	**Throttle Valve Adaptation Spring Test Failed (Bank 1):** Engine started, and the battery voltage is greater than 7 volts, this fault is only diagnosed during the throttle valve's adaptation phase. Vehicle speed is zero, throttle pedal is less than 14.9 percent, coolant temperature is between 5.3 and 100.5 degrees Celsius and the intake air temperature is 5.3 degrees Celsius.
DTC: P1635 **1T DME, MIL: Yes** **Year:** 2011, 2012 **Model:** 1 Series M, 128i, 135i, 328i, 328i xDrive, 335is, 528i, 535i, X1, X3, X5 **Engine:** 3.0L L6	**Throttle Valve Adaptation Lower Mechanical Stop Not Adapted (Bank 1):** Engine started, and the battery voltage is greater than 7 volts, there was no throttle valve adaptation conducted yet and the fuel-supply safety was shutdown until adaptation is successful. There was a failure to reach the lower mechanical travel limit
DTC: P1636 **1T DME, MIL: Yes** **Year:** 2011, 2012 **Model:** 1 Series M, 128i, 135i, 328i, 328i xDrive, 335is, 528i, 535i, X1, X3, X5 **Engine:** 3.0L L6	**Throttle Valve Position Control, Range Check (Bank 1):** Engine started, and the battery voltage is greater than 7 volts, and the comparison of the throttle valve's actual angle to its specified angle is great than 0.2 seconds and less than 0.5 seconds greater than a valve calculated from rpm and temperature readings. The throttle valve activation occurs via an electric motor (throttle drive) in the throttle valve control module. It is activated by the Engine Control Module (DME) according to specifications of the two sensors, Throttle Position (TP) Sensor and Accelerator Pedal Position Sensor 2.

DTC	Trouble Code Title and Conditions
DTC: P1637 **1T DME, MIL: Yes** **Year:** 2011, 2012 **Model:** 1 Series M, 128i, 135i, 328i, 328i xDrive, 335is, 528i, 535i, X1, X3, X5 **Engine:** 3.0L L6	**Throttle Valve Position Control, Control Deviation (Bank 1):** Engine started, and the battery voltage is greater than 7 volts, and the comparison of the throttle valve's actual angle to its specified angle is great than 0.2 seconds and less than 0.5 seconds greater than a valve calculated from rpm and temperature readings. The throttle valve activation occurs via an electric motor (throttle drive) in the throttle valve control module. It is activated by the Engine Control Module (DME) according to specifications of the two sensors, Throttle Position (TP) Sensor and Accelerator Pedal Position Sensor 2.
DTC: P1638 **1T DME, MIL: Yes** **Year:** 2011, 2012 **Model:** 1 Series M, 128i, 135i, 328i, 328i xDrive, 335is, 528i, 535i, X1, X3, X5 **Engine:** 3.0L L6	**Throttle Valve Position Control Throttle Stuck Temporarily (Bank 1):** Engine started, and the battery voltage is greater than 7 volts, and despite control signal to throttle valve, no position change was detected in 0.6 seconds. The throttle valve activation occurs via an electric motor (throttle drive) in the throttle valve control module. It is activated by the Engine Control Module (DME) according to specifications of the two sensors, Throttle Position (TP) Sensor and Accelerator Pedal Position Sensor 2.
DTC: P1639 **1T DME, MIL: Yes** **Year:** 2011, 2012 **Model:** 1 Series M, 128i, 135i, 328i, 328i xDrive, 335is, 528i, 535i, X1, X3, X5 **Engine:** 3.0L L6	**Accelerator Pedal Position Sensor 1+2 Range/Performance:** Engine started, battery voltage at least 11.5v, all electrical components off, ground connections between engine and chassis well connected, the DME detected that the accelerator pedal position sensor signal was too high. **Note: Both the Throttle Position (TP) Sensor and Accelerator Pedal Position Sensor 2 are located at the accelerator pedal module and communicate the driver's intentions to the DME completely independently of each other. Both sensors are stored in one housing.**
DTC: P1641 **1T DME, MIL: Yes** **Year:** 2011, 2012 **Model:** 1 Series M, 128i, 135i, 328i, 328i xDrive, 335is, 528i, 535i, X1, X3, X5 **Engine:** 3.0L L6	**Throttle Valve Adaptation Stop Due to Environmental Conditions:** Engine started, and the battery voltage is greater than 7 volts, this fault is only diagnosed during the throttle valve's adaptation phase. Environmental conditions for throttle valve adaptation were not present and adaptation aborted and failed to satisfy conditions. If the previous adaptation was valid, the fault code entry is for information only.
DTC: P1642 **1T DME, MIL: Yes** **Year:** 2011, 2012 **Model:** 1 Series M, 128i, 135i, 328i, 328i xDrive, 335is, 528i, 535i, X1, X3, X5 **Engine:** 3.0L L6	**Throttle Valve Adaptation Stop Due to Environmental Values:** Engine started, and the battery voltage is greater than 7 volts, this fault is only diagnosed during the throttle valve's adaptation phase. Environmental conditions for throttle valve adaptation were not present and adaptation aborted and failed to satisfy conditions. If the previous adaptation was valid, the fault code entry is for information only.
DTC: P1643 **1T DME, MIL: Yes** **Year:** 2011, 2012 **Model:** 1 Series M, 128i, 135i, 328i, 328i xDrive, 335is, 528i, 535i, X1, X3, X5 **Engine:** 3.0L L6	**Throttle Valve Actuator Start Test Amplifier Balancing Plausibility:** Engine started, and the battery voltage is greater than 7 volts, this fault is only diagnosed during the throttle valve's adaptation phase. The fault during amplifier calibration leads to operation with unamplified signal from potentiometer 1. The throttle valve activation occurs via an electric motor (throttle drive) in the throttle valve control module. It is activated by the Engine Control Module (DME) according to specifications of the two sensors, Throttle Position (TP) Sensor and Accelerator Pedal Position Sensor 2.
DTC: P1644 **1T DME, MIL: Yes** **Year:** 2011, 2012 **Model:** 1 Series M, 128i, 135i, 328i, 328i xDrive, 335is, 528i, 535i, X1, X3, X5 **Engine:** 3.0L L6	**Throttle Valve Adaptation Stop Relearning Lower Mechanical Stop:** Engine started, and the battery voltage is greater than 7 volts, this fault is only diagnosed during the throttle valve's adaptation phase. There was no throttle valve adaptation conducted yet and the fuel-supply safety was shutdown until adaptation is successful. The fault was triggered during an attempt to repeat the initialization and there was a failure to reach the lower mechanical travel limit.
DTC: P1645 **1T DME, MIL: Yes** **Year:** 2011, 2012 **Model:** 1 Series M, 128i, 135i, 328i, 328i xDrive, 335is, 528i, 535i, X1, X3, X5 **Engine:** 3.0L L6	**Internal Control Module Random Access Memory (RAM) Reading Error:** Key on, and the DME detected an internal memory fault. This code will set if KAPWR to the DME is interrupted (at the initial key on).

DTC	Trouble Code Title and Conditions
DTC: P1649 **1T DME, MIL: Yes** **Year:** 2011, 2012 **Model:** 1 Series M, 128i, 135i, 328i, 328i xDrive, 335is, 528i, 535i, X1, X3, X5 **Engine:** 3.0L L6	**Internal Control Module Random Access Memory (RAM) Writing Error:** Key on, and the DME detected an internal memory fault. This code will set if KAPWR to the DME is interrupted (at the initial key on).
DTC: P1650 **1T DME, MIL: Yes** **Year:** 2011, 2012 **Model:** 1 Series M, 128i, 135i, 328i, 328i xDrive, 335is, 528i, 535i, X1, X3, X5 **Engine:** 3.0L L6	**Start While Engine is Running:** Engine speed must be at least 1200rpm, the starter is engaged with the engine running and the DME detected an internal memory fault. This code will set if KAPWR to the DME is interrupted (at the initial key on). Check the starter and the starter relay and inspect CAS-SG.
DTC: P1660 **1T DME, MIL: Yes** **Year:** 2011, 2012 **Model:** 1 Series M, 128i, 135i, 328i, 328i xDrive, 335is, 528i, 535i, X1, X3, X5 **Engine:** 3.0L L6	**EWS (Electronic Immobilizer) Telegram Error:** Key on the DME detected an electrical malfunction regarding the EWS. Check the EWS fuse, the ECU or CAN for fault, turn the ignition off and then on to repeat start calibration.
DTC: P1661 **1T DME, MIL: Yes** **Year:** 2011, 2012 **Model:** 128i, 328i, 328i xDrive, 528i, 535i, X1, X3, X5 **Engine:** 3.0L L6	**Timeout EWS (Electronic Immobilizer) Telegram:** Key on the DME detected an electrical malfunction regarding the EWS. Check the EWS fuse, the ECU or CAN for fault, turn the ignition off and then on to repeat start calibration.
DTC: P1662 **1T DME, MIL: Yes** **Year:** 2011, 2012 **Model:** 1 Series M, 128i, 135i, 328i, 328i xDrive, 335is, 528i, 535i, X1, X3, X5 **Engine:** 3.0L L6	**EWS (Electronic Immobilizer) Telegram Parity Error:** Key on the DME detected an electrical malfunction regarding the EWS. Check the EWS fuse, the ECU or CAN for fault, turn the ignition off and then on to repeat start calibration.
DTC: P1663 **1T DME, MIL: Yes** **Year:** 2011, 2012 **Model:** 1 Series M, 128i, 135i, 328i, 328i xDrive, 335is, 528i, 535i, X1, X3, X5 **Engine:** 3.0L L6	**EWS (Electronic Immobilizer) Rolling Code Faulty Storage in EEPROM:** Key on the DME detected an electrical malfunction regarding the EWS. Check the EWS fuse, the ECU or CAN for fault, turn the ignition off and then on to repeat start calibration.
DTC: P1664 **1T DME, MIL: Yes** **Year:** 2011, 2012 **Model:** 1 Series M, 128i, 135i, 328i, 328i xDrive, 335is, 528i, 535i, X1, X3, X5 **Engine:** 3.0L L6	**EWS (Electronic Immobilizer) Writing/Reading Error in EEPROM:** Key on the DME detected an electrical malfunction regarding the EWS. Check the EWS fuse, the ECU or CAN for fault, turn the ignition off and then on to repeat start calibration.
DTC: P1665 **1T DME, MIL: Yes** **Year:** 2011, 2012 **Model:** 1 Series M, 128i, 135i, 328i, 328i xDrive, 335is, 528i, 535i, X1, X3, X5 **Engine:** 3.0L L6	**EWS (Electronic Immobilizer) Tampering Via Rolling Code:** Key on the DME detected an electrical malfunction regarding the EWS. Check the EWS fuse, the ECU or CAN for fault, turn the ignition off and then on to repeat start calibration.

DTC	Trouble Code Title and Conditions
DTC: P1666 **1T DME, MIL: Yes** **Year:** 2011, 2012 **Model:** 1 Series M, 128i, 135i, 328i, 328i xDrive, 335is, 528i, 535i, X1, X3, X5 **Engine:** 3.0L L6	**EWS (Electronic Immobilizer) Tampering/Start Value Not Yet Programmed:** Key on the DME detected an electrical malfunction regarding the EWS. Check the EWS fuse, the ECU or CAN for fault, turn the ignition off and then on to repeat start calibration.
DTC: P1667 **1T DME, MIL: Yes** **Year:** 2011, 2012 **Model:** 1 Series M, 128i, 135i, 328i, 328i xDrive, 335is, 528i, 535i, X1, X3, X5 **Engine:** 3.0L L6	**EWS (Electronic Immobilizer) Start Value Not Yet Programmed:** Key on the DME detected an electrical malfunction regarding the EWS. Check the EWS fuse, the ECU or CAN for fault, turn the ignition off and then on to repeat start calibration.
DTC: P1668 **1T DME, MIL: Yes** **Year:** 2011, 2012 **Model:** 1 Series M, 128i, 135i, 328i, 328i xDrive, 335is, 528i, 535i, X1, X3, X5 **Engine:** 3.0L L6	**EWS (Electronic Immobilizer) Start Value Destroyed:** Key on the DME detected an electrical malfunction regarding the EWS. Check the EWS fuse, the ECU or CAN for fault, turn the ignition off and then on to repeat start calibration.
DTC: P1677 **1T DME, MIL: Yes** **Year:** 2011, 2012 **Model:** 1 Series M, 128i, 135i, 328i, 328i xDrive, 335is, 528i, 535i, X1, X3, X5 **Engine:** 3.0L L6	**Adaptive Cruise Control No Activity Detected:** Key on after 800ms or engine running for 100ms, the DME detected an electrical malfunction regarding the Adaptive Cruise Control circuit. Check the ACC fuse, the ECU or CAN for fault, measure the resistance on the BUS, check the wiring harness. If this fault occurs when the ACC is not installed, the DME has been incorrectly initialized for the ACC version.
DTC: P1680 **1T DME, MIL: Yes** **Year:** 2011, 2012 **Model:** 1 Series M, 128i, 135i, 328i, 328i xDrive, 335is, 528i, 535i, X1, X3, X5 **Engine:** 3.0L L6	**Electronic Throttle Control Monitor Level 2/3 ADC Processor Fault:** Key on, engine running to at least 1200rpm, the DME has detected an internal fault in the computer or internal fault in the control modules. The Torque monitoring feature compares the torque demand (from accelerator pedal, FGR, electrical equipment, transmission) with the torque provided (calculated from HFM, injector valves, ignition angle, throttle valve angle, differential pressure, lambda). Deviations trigger fuel-supply safety shutdown to prevent vehicle from autonomous acceleration. Internal fault in computer or in electronic control modules (check whether all ADC channels have been converted). If additional fault codes are entered in the DME, resolve these issues. If fault remains, replace the DME.
DTC: P1743 **1T DME, MIL: Yes** **Year:** 2011, 2012 **Model:** X5 **Engine:** 4.4L V8	**Pressure Regulator Valve 5 Upper Threshold:** The signal to/from the pressure regulator valve has been interrupted.
DTC: P1763 **1T DME, MIL: Yes** **Year:** 2011, 2012 **Model:** X5 **Engine:** 4.4L V8	**Shift Solenoid C Short to Ground:** The shift solenoid valve is shorting to ground after 50ms of operation.

OBD II Trouble Code List (P2XXX Codes)

DTC	Trouble Code Title and Conditions
DTC: P2089 **1T DME, MIL: Yes** **Year:** 2011, 2012 **Model:** 323i, X5 **Engine:** 2.5L L6, 4.4L V8	**Inlet "A" Camshaft Position Control Circuit High Bank 1:** Key on or engine running; and the DME detected an unexpected voltage condition on the Camshaft Position Control circuit during the CCM test period. The relative position between the camshaft and crankshaft needs to be optimal so the engine has better torque, fuel economy and emissions. **Note: camshaft adjustment is load- and RPM dependant. The electrical camshaft adjustment valve 1 switches oil pressure onto camshaft adjuster (mechanical adjustment mechanism), which adjusts the camshaft.**

DTC	Trouble Code Title and Conditions
DTC: P2090 **1T DME, MIL: Yes** **Year:** 2011, 2012 **Model:** 323i, X5 **Engine:** 2.5L L6, 4.4L V8	**Outlet "B" Camshaft Position Control Circuit Low Bank 1:** Key on or engine running; and the DME detected an unexpected voltage condition on the Camshaft Position Control circuit during the CCM test period. The relative position between the camshaft and crankshaft needs to be optimal so the engine has better torque, fuel economy and emissions. **Note: camshaft adjustment is load- and RPM dependant. The electrical camshaft adjustment valve 1 switches oil pressure onto camshaft adjuster (mechanical adjustment mechanism), which adjusts the camshaft.**
DTC: P2091 **1T DME, MIL: Yes** **Year:** 2011, 2012 **Model:** 323i, X5 **Engine:** 2.5L L6, 4.4L V8	**Outlet "B" Camshaft Position Control Circuit High Bank 1:** Key on or engine running; and the DME detected an unexpected voltage condition on the Camshaft Position Control circuit during the CCM test period. The relative position between the camshaft and crankshaft needs to be optimal so the engine has better torque, fuel economy and emissions. **Note: camshaft adjustment is load- and RPM dependant. The electrical camshaft adjustment valve 1 switches oil pressure onto camshaft adjuster (mechanical adjustment mechanism), which adjusts the camshaft.**
DTC: P2092 **1T DME, MIL: Yes** **Year:** 2011, 2012 **Model:** 323i, X5 **Engine:** 2.5L L6, 4.4L V8	**Inlet "A" Camshaft Position Control Circuit Low Bank 1:** Key on or engine running; and the DME detected an unexpected voltage condition on the Camshaft Position Control circuit during the CCM test period. The relative position between the camshaft and crankshaft needs to be optimal so the engine has better torque, fuel economy and emissions. **Note: camshaft adjustment is load- and RPM dependant. The electrical camshaft adjustment valve 1 switches oil pressure onto camshaft adjuster (mechanical adjustment mechanism), which adjusts the camshaft.**
DTC: P2093 **1T DME, MIL: Yes** **Year:** 2011, 2012 **Model:** X5 **Engine:** 4.4L V8	**Inlet "A" Camshaft Position Control Circuit Low Bank 2:** Key on or engine running; and the DME detected an unexpected voltage condition on the Camshaft Position Control circuit during the CCM test period. The relative position between the camshaft and crankshaft needs to be optimal so the engine has better torque, fuel economy and emissions. **Note: camshaft adjustment is load- and RPM dependant. The electrical camshaft adjustment valve 1 switches oil pressure onto camshaft adjuster (mechanical adjustment mechanism), which adjusts the camshaft.**
DTC: P2094 **1T DME, MIL: Yes** **Year:** 2011, 2012 **Model:** X5 **Engine:** 4.4L V8	**Outlet "B" Camshaft Position Control Circuit Low Bank 2:** Key on or engine running; and the DME detected an unexpected voltage condition on the Camshaft Position Control circuit during the CCM test period. The relative position between the camshaft and crankshaft needs to be optimal so the engine has better torque, fuel economy and emissions. **Note: camshaft adjustment is load- and RPM dependant. The electrical camshaft adjustment valve 1 switches oil pressure onto camshaft adjuster (mechanical adjustment mechanism), which adjusts the camshaft.**
DTC: P2095 **1T DME, MIL: Yes** **Year:** 2011, 2012 **Model:** X5 **Engine:** 4.4L V8	**Outlet "B" Camshaft Position Control Circuit High Bank 2:** Key on or engine running; and the DME detected an unexpected voltage condition on the Camshaft Position Control circuit during the CCM test period. The relative position between the camshaft and crankshaft needs to be optimal so the engine has better torque, fuel economy and emissions. **Note: camshaft adjustment is load- and RPM dependant. The electrical camshaft adjustment valve 1 switches oil pressure onto camshaft adjuster (mechanical adjustment mechanism), which adjusts the camshaft.**
DTC: P2096 **1T DME, MIL: Yes** **Year:** 2011, 2012 **Model:** 1 Series M, 128i, 135i, 323i, 328i, 328i xDrive, 335is, 528i, 535i, X1, X3, X5 **Engine:** 2.5L L6, 3.0L L6	**Post Catalyst Fuel Trim System Too Lean (Bank 1):** Engine started, battery voltage must be at least 11.5v, all electrical components must be off, the ground between the engine and the chassis must be well connected, the exhaust system must be properly sealed between the catalytic converter and the cylinder head, and the oxygen sensor heater for oxygen sensor before the catalytic converter must be properly functioning. The DME detected a problem with the fuel mixture. Trim control 1 segment (precision controller with oxygen sensor behind cat.) below delta lambda threshold of less than -0.03. Fault monitoring criterion must remain present for over one second. The engine speed must be between 1060 and 3000 rpm and the catalytic converter temperature must be 280 degrees Celsius. **Note: For resistance testing of sensor heating, oxygen sensor should be cooled to ambient temperature. High temperatures at oxygen sensor may lead to inaccurate measurements.**
DTC: P2097 **1T DME, MIL: Yes** **Year:** 2011, 2012 **Model:** 1 Series M, 128i, 135i, 323i, 328i, 328i xDrive, 335is, 528i, 535i, X1, X3, X5 **Engine:** 2.5L L6, 3.0L L6	**Post Catalyst Fuel Trim System Too Rich (Bank 1):** Engine started, battery voltage must be at least 11.5v, all electrical components must be off, the ground between the engine and the chassis must be well connected, the exhaust system must be properly sealed between the catalytic converter and the cylinder head, and the oxygen sensor heater for oxygen sensor before the catalytic converter must be properly functioning. The DME detected a problem with the fuel mixture. Trim control 1 segment (precision controller with oxygen sensor behind cat.) below delta lambda threshold of less than -0.03. Fault monitoring criterion must remain present for over one second. The engine speed must be between 1060 and 3000 rpm and the catalytic converter temperature must be 280 degrees Celsius. **Note: For resistance testing of sensor heating, oxygen sensor should be cooled to ambient temperature. High temperatures at oxygen sensor may lead to inaccurate measurements.**

DTC	Trouble Code Title and Conditions
DTC: P2098 **1T DME, MIL: Yes** **Year:** 2011, 2012 **Model:** 1 Series M, 128i, 135i, 323i, 328i, 328i xDrive, 335is, 528i, 535i, X1, X3, X5 **Engine:** 2.5L L6, 3.0L L6	**Post Catalyst Fuel Trim System Too Lean (Bank 2):** Engine started, battery voltage must be at least 11.5v, all electrical components must be off, the ground between the engine and the chassis must be well connected, the exhaust system must be properly sealed between the catalytic converter and the cylinder head, and the oxygen sensor heater for oxygen sensor before the catalytic converter must be properly functioning. The DME detected a problem with the fuel mixture. Trim control 1 segment (precision controller with oxygen sensor behind cat.) below delta lambda threshold of less than -0.03. Fault monitoring criterion must remain present for over one second. The engine speed must be between 1060 and 3000 rpm and the catalytic converter temperature must be 280 degrees Celsius. **Note: For resistance testing of sensor heating, oxygen sensor should be cooled to ambient temperature. High temperatures at oxygen sensor may lead to inaccurate measurements.**
DTC: P2099 **1T DME, MIL: Yes** **Year:** 2011, 2012 **Model:** 1 Series M, 128i, 135i, 328i, 328i xDrive, 335is, 528i, 535i, X1, X3, X5 **Engine:** 3.0L L6	**Post Catalyst Fuel Trim System Too Rich (Bank 2):** Engine started, battery voltage must be at least 11.5v, all electrical components must be off, the ground between the engine and the chassis must be well connected, the exhaust system must be properly sealed between the catalytic converter and the cylinder head, and the oxygen sensor heater for oxygen sensor before the catalytic converter must be properly functioning. The DME detected a problem with the fuel mixture. Trim control 1 segment (precision controller with oxygen sensor behind cat.) below delta lambda threshold of less than -0.03. Fault monitoring criterion must remain present for over one second. The engine speed must be between 1060 and 3000 rpm and the catalytic converter temperature must be 400 degrees Celsius. **Note: For resistance testing of sensor heating, oxygen sensor should be cooled to ambient temperature. High temperatures at oxygen sensor may lead to inaccurate measurements.**
DTC: P2100 **1T DME, MIL: Yes** **Year:** 2011, 2012 **Model:** 1 Series M, 128i, 135i, 328i, 328i xDrive, 335is, 528i, 535i, X1, X3, X5 **Engine:** 3.0L L6	**Throttle Actuator "A" Control Motor Circuit Open:** Engine started, battery voltage must be at least 7v, coolant temperature must be at least 80 degrees Celsius. The DME detected an unexpected low or high voltage condition on the Throttle Actuator Control Motor (TACM) circuit during the CCM test. **Note: The throttle valve activation occurs via an electric motor (throttle drive) in the throttle valve control module. It is activated by the Engine Control Module (DME) according to specifications of the two sensors, Throttle Position (TP) Sensor and Sender 2 for accelerator pedal position.**
DTC: P2102 **1T DME, MIL: Yes** **Year:** 2011, 2012 **Model:** 1 Series M, 128i, 135i, 328i, 328i xDrive, 335is, 528i, 535i, X1, X3, X5 **Engine:** 3.0L L6	**Throttle Actuator "A" Control Motor Circuit Low:** Engine started, battery voltage must be at least 7v, coolant temperature must be at least 80 degrees Celsius. The DME detected an unexpected low or high voltage condition on the Throttle Actuator Control Motor (TACM) circuit during the CCM test. **Note: The throttle valve activation occurs via an electric motor (throttle drive) in the throttle valve control module. It is activated by the Engine Control Module (DME) according to specifications of the two sensors, Throttle Position (TP) Sensor and Sender 2 for accelerator pedal position.**
DTC: P2103 **1T DME, MIL: Yes** **Year:** 2011, 2012 **Model:** 1 Series M, 128i, 135i, 328i, 328i xDrive, 335is, 528i, 535i, X1, X3, X5 **Engine:** 3.0L L6	**Throttle Actuator "A" Control Motor Circuit High:** Engine started, battery voltage must be at least 7v, coolant temperature must be at least 80 degrees Celsius. The DME detected an unexpected low or high voltage condition on the Throttle Actuator Control Motor (TACM) circuit during the CCM test. **Note: The throttle valve activation occurs via an electric motor (throttle drive) in the throttle valve control module. It is activated by the Engine Control Module (DME) according to specifications of the two sensors, Throttle Position (TP) Sensor and Sender 2 for accelerator pedal position.**
DTC: P2122 **1T DME, MIL: Yes** **Year:** 2011, 2012 **Model:** 1 Series M, 128i, 135i, 323i, 328i, 328i xDrive, 335is, 528i, 535i, X1, X3, X5 **Engine:** 2.5L L6, 3.0L L6	**Accelerator Pedal Position Sensor 'D' Circuit Low Input:** Engine started, battery voltage at least 11.5v, all electrical components off, ground connections between engine and chassis well connected, the DME detected that the accelerator pedal position sensor signal was outside the parameters to function normally. **Note: Both the Throttle Position (TP) Sensor and Accelerator Pedal Position Sensor are located at the accelerator pedal module and communicate the driver's intentions to the DME completely independently of each other. Both sensors are stored in one housing.**
DTC: P2123 **1T DME, MIL: Yes** **Year:** 2011, 2012 **Model:** 1 Series M, 128i, 135i, 323i, 328i, 328i xDrive, 335is, 528i, 535i, X1, X3, X5 **Engine:** 2.5L L6, 3.0L L6	**Accelerator Pedal Position Sensor 'D' Circuit High Input:** Engine started, battery voltage at least 11.5v, all electrical components off, ground connections between engine and chassis well connected, the DME detected that the accelerator pedal position sensor signal was outside the parameters to function normally. **Note: Both the Throttle Position (TP) Sensor and Accelerator Pedal Position Sensor are located at the accelerator pedal module and communicate the driver's intentions to the DME completely independently of each other. Both sensors are stored in one housing.**
DTC: P2127 **1T DME, MIL: Yes** **Year:** 2011, 2012 **Model:** 1 Series M, 128i, 135i, 323i, 328i, 328i xDrive, 335is, 528i, 535i, X1, X3, X5 **Engine:** 2.5L L6, 3.0L L6	**Accelerator Pedal Position Sensor 'E' Circuit Low Input:** Engine started, battery voltage at least 11.5v, all electrical components off, ground connections between engine and chassis well connected, the DME detected that the accelerator pedal position sensor signal was outside the parameters to function normally. **Note: Both the Throttle Position (TP) Sensor and Accelerator Pedal Position Sensor are located at the accelerator pedal module and communicate the driver's intentions to the DME completely independently of each other. Both sensors are stored in one housing.**

DTC	Trouble Code Title and Conditions
DTC: P2128 **1T DME, MIL: Yes** **Year:** 2011, 2012 **Model:** 1 Series M, 128i, 135i, 323i, 328i, 328i xDrive, 335is, 528i, 535i, X1, X3, X5 **Engine:** 2.5L L6, 3.0L L6	**Accelerator Pedal Position Sensor 'E' Circuit High Input:** Engine started, battery voltage at least 11.5v, all electrical components off, ground connections between engine and chassis well connected, the DME detected that the accelerator pedal position sensor signal was outside the parameters to function normally. **Note: Both the Throttle Position (TP) Sensor and Accelerator Pedal Position Sensor are located at the accelerator pedal module and communicate the driver's intentions to the DME completely independently of each other. Both sensors are stored in one housing.**
DTC: P2138 **1T DME, MIL: Yes** **Year:** 2011, 2012 **Model:** 1 Series M, 128i, 135i, 323i, 328i, 328i xDrive, 335is, 528i, 535i, X1, X3, X5 **Engine:** 2.5L L6, 3.0L L6	**Throttle Position Sensor D/E Voltage Correlation:** Engine started, battery voltage must be at least 11.5v, all electrical components must be off, parking brake must be engaged (to keep daytime driving lights off), automatic transmission selector must be in park; and the DME detected the Throttle Position 'D' (TPD) and Throttle Position 'B' (TPE) sensors disagreed, or that the TPD sensor should not be in its detected position, or that the TPE sensor should not be in its detected position during testing. **Note: Both the Throttle Position (TP) Sensor and Accelerator Pedal Position Sensor are located at the accelerator pedal module and communicate the driver's intentions to the DME completely independently of each other. Both sensors are stored in one housing.**
DTC: P2177 **2T DME, MIL: Yes** **Year:** 2011, 2012 **Model:** 1 Series M, 128i, 135i, 328i, 328i xDrive, 335is, 528i, 535i, X1, X3, X5 **Engine:** 3.0L L6, 4.4L V8	**System Too Lean Off Idle Bank 1:** Engine started, battery voltage must be at least 11.5v, all electrical components must be off, the ground between the engine and the chassis must be well connected, the exhaust system must be properly sealed between the catalytic converter and the cylinder head, and the oxygen sensor heater for oxygen sensor before the catalytic converter must be properly functioning. The DME detected the system indicated a lean signal, or it could no longer control bank 1 because it was at its lean limit.
DTC: P2178 **2T DME, MIL: Yes** **Year:** 2011, 2012 **Model:** 1 Series M, 128i, 135i, 328i, 328i xDrive, 335is, 528i, 535i, X1, X3, X5 **Engine:** 3.0L L6, 4.4L V8	**System Too Rich Off Idle Bank 1:** Engine started, battery voltage must be at least 11.5v, all electrical components must be off, the ground between the engine and the chassis must be well connected, the exhaust system must be properly sealed between the catalytic converter and the cylinder head, and the oxygen sensor heater for oxygen sensor before the catalytic converter must be properly functioning. The DME detected the system indicated a rich signal, or it could no longer control bank 1 because it was at its rich limit.
DTC: P2179 **2T DME, MIL: Yes** **Year:** 2011, 2012 **Model:** 1 Series M, 128i, 135i, 328i, 328i xDrive, 335is, 528i, 535i, X1, X3, X5 **Engine:** 3.0L L6, 4.4L V8	**System Too Lean Off Idle Bank 2:** Engine started, battery voltage must be at least 11.5v, all electrical components must be off, the ground between the engine and the chassis must be well connected, the exhaust system must be properly sealed between the catalytic converter and the cylinder head, and the oxygen sensor heater for oxygen sensor before the catalytic converter must be properly functioning. The DME detected the system indicated a lean signal, or it could no longer control bank 2 because it was at its lean limit.
DTC: P2180 **2T DME, MIL: Yes** **Year:** 2011, 2012 **Model:** 1 Series M, 128i, 135i, 328i, 328i xDrive, 335is, 528i, 535i, X1, X3, X5 **Engine:** 3.0L L6, 4.4L V8	**System Too Rich Off Idle Bank 2:** Engine started, battery voltage must be at least 11.5v, all electrical components must be off, the ground between the engine and the chassis must be well connected, the exhaust system must be properly sealed between the catalytic converter and the cylinder head, and the oxygen sensor heater for oxygen sensor before the catalytic converter must be properly functioning. The DME detected the system indicated a rich signal, or it could no longer control bank 2 because it was at its rich limit.
DTC: P2183 **1T DME, MIL: Yes** **Year:** 2011, 2012 **Model:** 1 Series M, 128i, 135i, 328i, 328i xDrive, 335is, 528i, 535i, X1, X3, X5 **Engine:** 3.0L L6	**ECT Sensor Signal Range/Performance Rationality:** Engine started (cold), battery voltage must be 11.5, and all equipment must be off. The DME detected the ECT sensor exceeded the required calibrated value, or the engine is at idle and doesn't reach operating temperature quickly enough; the Catalyst, Fuel System, HO2S and Misfire Monitor did not complete, or the timer expired. Testing completion of procedure, the engine's temperature must rise uniformly during idle. The ECT is greater than 101.3 degrees Celsius for more than 60 seconds. The engine speed is greater than 1100rpm. The ambient temperature is greater than negative 7 degrees Celsius. The vehicle speed less than 62.5mph.
DTC: P2184 **1T DME, MIL: Yes** **Year:** 2011, 2012 **Model:** 1 Series M, 128i, 135i, 328i, 328i xDrive, 335is, 528i, 535i, X1, X3, X5 **Engine:** 3.0L L6	**ECT Sensor 2 Circuit Range Check (Minimum):** Engine started (cold) for 10 seconds, battery voltage must be 11.5, and all equipment must be off. The DME detected the ECT sensor signal was less than the self-test minimum. This is a thermistor-type sensor with a variable resistance that changes when exposed to different temperatures

DTC	Trouble Code Title and Conditions
DTC: P2185 **1T DME, MIL: Yes** **Year:** 2011, 2012 **Model:** 1 Series M, 128i, 135i, 328i, 328i xDrive, 335is, 528i, 535i, X1, X3, X5 **Engine:** 3.0L L6	**ECT Sensor 2 Circuit Range Check (Maximum):** Engine started (cold) for 10 seconds, battery voltage must be 11.5, and all equipment must be off. The DME detected the ECT sensor signal was less than the self-test minimum. This is a thermistor-type sensor with a variable resistance that changes when exposed to different temperatures.
DTC: P2186 **1T DME, MIL: Yes** **Year:** 2011, 2012 **Model:** 1 Series M, 128i, 135i, 328i, 328i xDrive, 335is, 528i, 535i, X1, X3, X5 **Engine:** 3.0L L6	**ECT Sensor 2 Circuit High Input:** Engine started (cold) for 10 seconds, battery voltage must be 11.5, and all equipment must be off. The DME detected the ECT sensor signal was more than the self-test maximum. This is a thermistor-type sensor with a variable resistance that changes when exposed to different temperatures.
DTC: P2187 **2T DME, MIL: Yes** **Year:** 2011, 2012 **Model:** 1 Series M, 128i, 135i, 328i, 328i xDrive, 335is, 528i, 535i, X1, X3, X5 **Engine:** 3.0L L6, 4.4L V8	**System Too Lean at Idle Bank 1:** Engine started, battery voltage must be at least 11v, all electrical components must be off, the ground between the engine and the chassis must be well connected, the exhaust system must be properly sealed between the catalytic converter and the cylinder head, and the oxygen sensor heater for oxygen sensor before the catalytic converter must be properly functioning. The engine temperature must be greater than 63 degrees Celsius for approximately 10 to 20 minutes. The air intake temperature must be less than or equal to 80 degrees Celsius, and the engine speed must be less than or equal to 800rpm.
DTC: P2188 **2T DME, MIL: Yes** **Year:** 2011, 2012 **Model:** 1 Series M, 128i, 135i, 328i, 328i xDrive, 335is, 528i, 535i, X1, X3, X5 **Engine:** 3.0L L6, 4.4L V8	**System Too Rich at Idle Bank 1:** Engine started, battery voltage must be at least 11v, all electrical components must be off, the ground between the engine and the chassis must be well connected, the exhaust system must be properly sealed between the catalytic converter and the cylinder head, and the oxygen sensor heater for oxygen sensor before the catalytic converter must be properly functioning. he engine temperature must be greater than 63 degrees Celsius for approximately 10 to 20 minutes. The air intake temperature must be less than or equal to 80 degrees Celsius, and the engine speed must be less than or equal to 800rpm.
DTC: P2189 **2T DME, MIL: Yes** **Year:** 2011, 2012 **Model:** 1 Series M, 128i, 135i, 328i, 328i xDrive, 335is, 528i, 535i, X1, X3, X5 **Engine:** 3.0L L6, 4.4L V8	**System Too Lean at Idle Bank 2:** Engine started, battery voltage must be at least 11v, all electrical components must be off, the ground between the engine and the chassis must be well connected, the exhaust system must be properly sealed between the catalytic converter and the cylinder head, and the oxygen sensor heater for oxygen sensor before the catalytic converter must be properly functioning. he engine temperature must be greater than 63 degrees Celsius for approximately 10 to 20 minutes. The air intake temperature must be less than or equal to 80 degrees Celsius, and the engine speed must be less than or equal to 800rpm.
DTC: P2190 **2T DME, MIL: Yes** **Year:** 2011, 2012 **Model:** 1 Series M, 128i, 135i, 328i, 328i xDrive, 335is, 528i, 535i, X1, X3, X5 **Engine:** 3.0L L6, 4.4L V8	**System Too Rich at Idle Bank 2:** Engine started, battery voltage must be at least 11v, all electrical components must be off, the ground between the engine and the chassis must be well connected, the exhaust system must be properly sealed between the catalytic converter and the cylinder head, and the oxygen sensor heater for oxygen sensor before the catalytic converter must be properly functioning. he engine temperature must be greater than 63 degrees Celsius for approximately 10 to 20 minutes. The air intake temperature must be less than or equal to 80 degrees Celsius, and the engine speed must be less than or equal to 800rpm.
DTC: P2191 **2T DME, MIL: Yes** **Year:** 2011, 2012 **Model:** 1 Series M, 128i, 135i, 328i, 328i xDrive, 335is, 528i, 535i, X1, X3, X5 **Engine:** 3.0L L6, 4.4L V8	**System Too Lean at Higher Load Bank 1:** Engine started, battery voltage must be at least 11v, all electrical components must be off, the ground between the engine and the chassis must be well connected, the exhaust system must be properly sealed between the catalytic converter and the cylinder head, and the oxygen sensor heater for oxygen sensor before the catalytic converter must be properly functioning. The engine temperature must be greater than 63 degrees Celsius for approximately 10 to 20 minutes. The air intake temperature must be less than or equal to 80 degrees Celsius.
DTC: P2192 **2T DME, MIL: Yes** **Year:** 2011, 2012 **Model:** 1 Series M, 128i, 135i, 328i, 328i xDrive, 335is, 528i, 535i, X1, X3, X5 **Engine:** 3.0L L6, 4.4L V8	**System Too Rich at Higher Load Bank 1:** Engine started, battery voltage must be at least 11v, all electrical components must be off, the ground between the engine and the chassis must be well connected, the exhaust system must be properly sealed between the catalytic converter and the cylinder head, and the oxygen sensor heater for oxygen sensor before the catalytic converter must be properly functioning. The engine temperature must be greater than 63 degrees Celsius for approximately 10 to 20 minutes. The air intake temperature must be less than or equal to 80 degrees Celsius.

DTC	Trouble Code Title and Conditions
DTC: P2193 **2T DME, MIL: Yes** **Year:** 2011, 2012 **Model:** 1 Series M, 128i, 135i, 328i, 328i xDrive, 335is, 528i, 535i, X1, X3, X5 **Engine:** 3.0L L6, 4.4L V8	**System Too Lean at Higher Load Bank 2:** Engine started, battery voltage must be at least 11.5v, all electrical components must be off, the ground between the engine and the chassis must be well connected, the exhaust system must be properly sealed between the catalytic converter and the cylinder head, and the oxygen sensor heater for oxygen sensor before the catalytic converter must be properly functioning. DME detected the system indicated a lean signal, or it could no longer control bank 2 because it was at its lean limit. The engine temperature must be greater than 63 degrees Celsius for approximately 10 to 20 minutes. The air intake temperature must be less than or equal to 80 degrees Celsius.
DTC: P2194 **2T DME, MIL: Yes** **Year:** 2011, 2012 **Model:** 1 Series M, 128i, 135i, 328i, 328i xDrive, 335is, 528i, 535i, X1, X3, X5 **Engine:** 3.0L L6, 4.4L V8	**System Too Rich at Higher Load Bank 2:** Engine started, battery voltage must be at least 11v, all electrical components must be off, the ground between the engine and the chassis must be well connected, the exhaust system must be properly sealed between the catalytic converter and the cylinder head, and the oxygen sensor heater for oxygen sensor before the catalytic converter must be properly functioning. The engine temperature must be greater than 63 degrees Celsius for approximately 10 to 20 minutes. The air intake temperature must be less than or equal to 80 degrees Celsius.
DTC: P2195 **1T DME, MIL: Yes** **Year:** 2011, 2012 **Model:** 1 Series M, 128i, 135i, 328i, 328i xDrive, 335is, 528i, 535i, X1, X3, X5 **Engine:** 3.0L L6	**O2 Sensor Signal Stuck Lean Bank 1 Sensor 1:** Engine running in closed loop, and the DME detected the O2S indicated a lean signal, or it could no longer control Fuel Trim because it was at lean limit.
DTC: P2196 **1T DME, MIL: Yes** **Year:** 2011, 2012 **Model:** 1 Series M, 128i, 135i, 328i, 328i xDrive, 335is, 528i, 535i, X1, X3, X5 **Engine:** 3.0L L6	**O2 Sensor Signal Stuck Rich Bank 1 Sensor 1:** Engine running in closed loop, and the DME detected the O2S indicated a rich signal, or it could no longer control Fuel Trim because it was at its rich limit. The sensor temperature is heated up. The relative engine load change is less than or equal to 3 percent per camshaft revolution.
DTC: P2197 **1T DME, MIL: Yes** **Year:** 2011, 2012 **Model:** 1 Series M, 128i, 135i, 328i, 328i xDrive, 335is, 528i, 535i, X1, X3, X5 **Engine:** 3.0L L6	**O2 Sensor Signal Stuck Lean Bank 2 Sensor 1:** Engine running in closed loop, and the DME detected the O2S indicated a lean signal, or it could no longer control Fuel Trim because it was at lean limit. The sensor temperature is heated up. The relative engine load change is less than or equal to 3 percent per camshaft revolution.
DTC: P2198 **1T DME, MIL: Yes** **Year:** 2011, 2012 **Model:** 1 Series M, 128i, 135i, 328i, 328i xDrive, 335is, 528i, 535i, X1, X3, X5 **Engine:** 3.0L L6	**O2 Sensor Signal Stuck Rich Bank 2 Sensor 1:** Engine running in closed loop, and the DME detected the O2S indicated a rich signal, or it could no longer control Fuel Trim because it was at its rich limit. The sensor temperature is heated up. The relative engine load change is less than or equal to 3 percent per camshaft revolution.
DTC: P2228 **1T DME, MIL: Yes** **Year:** 2011, 2012 **Model:** 1 Series M, 128i, 135i, 328i, 328i xDrive, 335is, 528i, 535i, X1, X3, X5 **Engine:** 3.0L L6	**Barometric Circuit Low:** Engine started, the temperature must beat least 185-degrees (F) and all electrical equipment (A/C, lights, etc) must be off. The DME detected the BARO sensor was out of range during the CCM test. The BARO sensor signal should be in 4.5v. The BARO sensor is a variable capacitance unit used to detect altitude. There is a short to ground and the internal voltage measurement in ambient pressure sensor is greater than 4.7998 and the ambient pressure is greater than 1150 hPa.
DTC: P2229 **1T DME, MIL: Yes** **Year:** 2011, 2012 **Model:** 1 Series M, 128i, 135i, 328i, 328i xDrive, 335is, 528i, 535i, X1, X3, X5 **Engine:** 3.0L L6	**Barometric Circuit High:** Engine started, the temperature must beat least 185-degrees (F) and all electrical equipment (A/C, lights, etc) must be off. The DME detected the BARO sensor was out of range during the CCM test. The BARO sensor signal should be in 4.5v. The BARO sensor is a variable capacitance unit used to detect altitude. There is a short to battery voltage and the internal voltage measurement in ambient pressure sensor is greater than 4.7998 and the ambient pressure is greater than 1150 hPa.

DTC	Trouble Code Title and Conditions
DTC: P2231 **2T DME, MIL: Yes** **Year:** 2011, 2012 **Model:** 1 Series M, 128i, 135i, 328i, 328i xDrive, 335is, 528i, 535i, X1, X3, X5 **Engine:** 3.0L L6	**O2 Sensor Signal Circuit Shorted to Heater Circuit Bank 1 Sensor 1:** Engine started, battery voltage must be at least 11.5v, all electrical components must be off, parking brake must be engaged (to keep daytime driving lights off), automatic transmission selector must be in park. The DME detected an unexpected voltage condition, or it detected an unexpected current draw in the sensor circuit during the CCM test.
DTC: P2234 **2T DME, MIL: Yes** **Year:** 2011, 2012 **Model:** 1 Series M, 128i, 135i, 328i, 328i xDrive, 335is, 528i, 535i, X1, X3, X5 **Engine:** 3.0L L6	**O2 Sensor Signal Circuit Shorted to Heater Circuit (Bank 2 Sensor 1):** Engine started, battery voltage must be at least 11.5v, all electrical components must be off, parking brake must be engaged (to keep daytime driving lights off), automatic transmission selector must be in park. The DME detected an unexpected voltage condition, or it detected an unexpected current draw in the sensor circuit during the CCM test.
DTC: P2237 **2T DME, MIL: Yes** **Year:** 2011, 2012 **Model:** 1 Series M, 128i, 135i, 328i, 328i xDrive, 335is, 528i, 535i, X1, X3, X5 **Engine:** 3.0L L6	**O2S Sensor Positive Current Control Circuit/Open Circuit (Bank 1 Sensor 1):** Engine started, the fault criterion must remain present for over 2 seconds, the Lambda specification is outside three percent relative to Lambda = 1, and the closed loop lambda control is active.
DTC: P2240 **2T DME, MIL: Yes** **Year:** 2011, 2012 **Model:** 1 Series M, 128i, 135i, 328i, 328i xDrive, 335is, 528i, 535i, X1, X3, X5 **Engine:** 3.0L L6	**O2S Sensor Positive Current Control Circuit/Open Circuit (Bank 2 Sensor 1):** Engine started, the fault criterion must remain present for over 2 seconds, the Lambda specification is outside three percent relative to Lambda = 1, and the closed loop lambda control is active.
DTC: P2243 **2T DME, MIL: Yes** **Year:** 2011, 2012 **Model:** 1 Series M, 128i, 135i, 328i, 328i xDrive, 335is, 528i, 535i, X1, X3, X5 **Engine:** 3.0L L6	**O2 Sensor Reference Voltage Circuit/Open Bank 1 Sensor 1:** Engine started, battery voltage must be at least 11.5v, all electrical components must be off, parking brake must be engaged (to keep daytime driving lights off), automatic transmission selector must be in park. The DME detected an unexpected voltage condition, or it detected an unexpected current draw in the sensor circuit during the CCM test. The voltage is out of range. The sensor temperature is heated up and the battery voltage is between 11 and 16 volts. **Note: Vehicle must be raised before connector for oxygen sensors is accessible.**
DTC: P2247 **T** **Year:** 2011, 2012 **Model:** 1 Series M, 128i, 135i, 328i, 328i xDrive, 335is, 528i, 535i, X1, X3, X5 **Engine:** 3.0L L6	**O2 Sensor Reference Voltage Circuit/Open Bank 2 Sensor 1:** Engine started, battery voltage must be at least 11.5v, all electrical components must be off, parking brake must be engaged (to keep daytime driving lights off), automatic transmission selector must be in park. The DME detected an unexpected voltage condition, or it detected an unexpected current draw in the sensor circuit during the CCM test. The voltage is out of range. The sensor temperature is heated up and the battery voltage is between 11 and 16 volts.
DTC: P2251 **2T DME, MIL: Yes** **Year:** 2011, 2012 **Model:** 1 Series M, 128i, 135i, 328i, 328i xDrive, 335is, 528i, 535i, X1, X3, X5 **Engine:** 3.0L L6	**O2 Sensor Negative Voltage Circuit/Open Bank 1 Sensor 1:** Engine started, battery voltage must be at least 11.5v, all electrical components must be off, parking brake must be engaged (to keep daytime driving lights off), automatic transmission selector must be in park. The DME detected an unexpected voltage condition, or it detected an unexpected current draw in the sensor circuit during the CCM test. Fault monitoring criterion must remain present for over five seconds. The voltage is within critical range. The sensor temperature is heated up and the battery voltage is between 11 and 16 volts.
DTC: P2254 **2T DME, MIL: Yes** **Year:** 2011, 2012 **Model:** 1 Series M, 128i, 135i, 328i, 328i xDrive, 335is, 528i, 535i, X1, X3, X5 **Engine:** 3.0L L6	**O2 Sensor Negative Voltage Circuit/Open Bank 2 Sensor 1:** Engine started, battery voltage must be at least 11.5v, all electrical components must be off, parking brake must be engaged (to keep daytime driving lights off), automatic transmission selector must be in park. The DME detected an unexpected voltage condition, or it detected an unexpected current draw in the sensor circuit during the CCM test. Fault monitoring criterion must remain present for over five seconds. The voltage is within critical range. The sensor temperature is heated up and the battery voltage is between 11 and 16 volts. **Note: Vehicle must be raised before connector for oxygen sensors is accessible.**

DTC	Trouble Code Title and Conditions
DTC: P2270 **2T DME, MIL: Yes** **Year:** 2011, 2012 **Model:** 1 Series M, 128i, 135i, 328i, 328i xDrive, 335is, 528i, 535i, X1, X3, X5 **Engine:** 3.0L L6, 4.4L V8	**O2 Sensor Signal Stuck Lean Bank 1 Sensor 2:** Engine started, battery voltage must be at least 11.5v, all electrical components must be off, parking brake must be engaged (to keep daytime driving lights off), automatic transmission selector must be in park. The DME detected an unexpected voltage condition, or it detected an unexpected current draw in the heater circuit during the CCM test.
DTC: P2271 **2T DME, MIL: Yes** **Year:** 2011, 2012 **Model:** 1 Series M, 128i, 135i, 328i, 328i xDrive, 335is, 528i, 535i, X1, X3, X5 **Engine:** 3.0L L6, 4.4L V8	**O2 Sensor Signal Stuck Rich Bank 1 Sensor 2:** Engine started, battery voltage must be at least 11.5v, all electrical components must be off, parking brake must be engaged (to keep daytime driving lights off), automatic transmission selector must be in park. The DME detected an unexpected voltage condition, or it detected an unexpected current draw in the heater circuit during the CCM test.
DTC: P2272 **2T DME, MIL: Yes** **Year:** 2011, 2012 **Model:** 1 Series M, 128i, 135i, 328i, 328i xDrive, 335is, 528i, 535i, X1, X3, X5 **Engine:** 3.0L L6, 4.4L V8	**O2 Sensor Signal Stuck Lean Bank 2 Sensor 2:** Engine started, battery voltage must be at least 11.5v, all electrical components must be off, parking brake must be engaged (to keep daytime driving lights off), automatic transmission selector must be in park. The DME detected an unexpected voltage condition, or it detected an unexpected current draw in the heater circuit during the CCM test. **Note: Vehicle must be raised before connector for oxygen sensors is accessible.**
DTC: P2273 **2T DME, MIL: Yes** **Year:** 2011, 2012 **Model:** 1 Series M, 128i, 135i, 328i, 328i xDrive, 335is, 528i, 535i, X1, X3, X5 **Engine:** 3.0L L6, 4.4L V8	**O2 Sensor Signal Stuck Rich Bank 2 Sensor 2:** Engine started, battery voltage must be at least 11.5v, all electrical components must be off, parking brake must be engaged (to keep daytime driving lights off), automatic transmission selector must be in park. The DME detected an unexpected voltage condition, or it detected an unexpected current draw in the heater circuit during the CCM test. **Note: Vehicle must be raised before connector for oxygen sensors is accessible.**
DTC: P2400 **1T DME, MIL: Yes** **Year:** 2011, 2012 **Model:** 1 Series M, 128i, 135i, 328i, 328i xDrive, 335is, 528i, 535i, X1, X3, X5 **Engine:** 3.0L L6	**EVAP Leak Detection Pump (LDP) Control Circuit Open:** Engine started, battery voltage must be at least 11.5v, all electrical components must be off, parking brake must be engaged (to keep daytime driving lights off), automatic transmission selector must be in park, the exhaust system must be properly sealed between the catalytic converter and the cylinder head, coolant temperature must be at least 80 degrees Celsius and oxygen sensor heaters for oxygen sensors before the catalytic converter must be functioning properly and the ground between the engine and the chassis must be well connected. The DME detected voltage irregularity in the leak detection pump control circuit.
DTC: P2401 **1T DME, MIL: Yes** **Year:** 2011, 2012 **Model:** 1 Series M, 128i, 135i, 328i, 328i xDrive, 335is, 528i, 535i, X1, X3, X5 **Engine:** 3.0L L6	**EVAP Leak Detection Pump Control Circuit Low:** Engine started, battery voltage must be at least 11.5v, all electrical components must be off, parking brake must be engaged (to keep daytime driving lights off), automatic transmission selector must be in park, the exhaust system must be properly sealed between the catalytic converter and the cylinder head, coolant temperature must be at least 80 degrees Celsius and oxygen sensor heaters for oxygen sensors before the catalytic converter must be functioning properly and the ground between the engine and the chassis must be well connected. The DME detected voltage irregularity in the leak detection pump control circuit.
DTC: P2402 **1T DME, MIL: Yes** **Year:** 2011, 2012 **Model:** 1 Series M, 128i, 135i, 328i, 328i xDrive, 335is, 528i, 535i, X1, X3, X5 **Engine:** 3.0L L6	**EVAP Leak Detection Pump Control Circuit High:** Engine started, battery voltage must be at least 11.5v, all electrical components must be off, parking brake must be engaged (to keep daytime driving lights off), automatic transmission selector must be in park, the exhaust system must be properly sealed between the catalytic converter and the cylinder head, coolant temperature must be at least 80 degrees Celsius and oxygen sensor heaters for oxygen sensors before the catalytic converter must be functioning properly and the ground between the engine and the chassis must be well connected. The DME detected voltage irregularity in the leak detection pump control circuit.
DTC: P2414 **1T DME, MIL: Yes** **Year:** 2011, 2012 **Model:** 1 Series M, 128i, 135i, 328i, 328i xDrive, 335is, 528i, 535i, X1, X3, X5 **Engine:** 3.0L L6	**O2 Sensor Exhaust Sample Error Bank 1 Sensor 1:** Engine running (ground connections between the engine and the chassis must be well connected), and the DME detected an error on the OS Sensor. **Note: Intake Flap Motor and Intake Manifold Runner Position Sensor are one component and cannot be replaced individually.** **Note: Vacuum in the intake system sucks in the leak detection spray with false air. Leak detection spray decreases ignition quality of the fuel mixture. This causes a drop in engine speed and changes the value produced by the Heated Oxygen Sensor (HO2S). The voltage is out of range. The sensor temperature is heated up and the battery voltage is between 11 and 16 volts.**

DTC	Trouble Code Title and Conditions
DTC: P2415 **1T DME, MIL: Yes** **Year:** 2011, 2012 **Model:** 1 Series M, 128i, 135i, 328i, 328i xDrive, 335is, 528i, 535i, X1, X3, X5 **Engine:** 3.0L L6	**O2 Sensor Exhaust Sample Error Bank 2 Sensor 1:** Engine running (ground connections between the engine and the chassis must be well connected), and the DME detected an error on the OS Sensor. **Note: Intake Flap Motor and Intake Manifold Runner Position Sensor are one component and cannot be replaced individually. The voltage is out of range. The sensor temperature is heated up and the battery voltage is between 11 and 16 volts.** **Note: Vacuum in the intake system sucks in the leak detection spray with false air. Leak detection spray decreases ignition quality of the fuel mixture. This causes a drop in engine speed and changes the value produced by the Heated Oxygen Sensor (HO2S).**
DTC: P2418 **1T DME, MIL: Yes** **Year:** 2011, 2012 **Model:** 1 Series M, 128i, 135i, 323i, 328i, 328i xDrive, 335is, 528i, 535i, X1, X3, X5 **Engine:** 2.5L L6, 3.0L L6	**Evaporative Emission System Switching Valve Control Circuit Open:** Engine started, battery voltage must be at least 11.5v, all electrical components must be off, parking brake must be engaged (to keep daytime driving lights off), automatic transmission selector must be in park, the exhaust system must be properly sealed between the catalytic converter and the cylinder head, coolant temperature must be at least 80 degrees Celsius and oxygen sensor heaters for oxygen sensors before the catalytic converter must be functioning properly and the ground between the engine and the chassis must be well connected. The DME detected an unexpected EVAP malfunction. **Note: Solenoid valve is closed when no voltage is present.**
DTC: P2419 **1T DME, MIL: Yes** **Year:** 2011, 2012 **Model:** 1 Series M, 128i, 135i, 323i, 328i, 328i xDrive, 335is, 528i, 535i, X1, X3, X5 **Engine:** 2.5L L6, 3.0L L6	**Evaporative Emission System Switching Valve Control Circuit Low:** Engine started, battery voltage must be at least 11.5v, all electrical components must be off, parking brake must be engaged (to keep daytime driving lights off), automatic transmission selector must be in park, the exhaust system must be properly sealed between the catalytic converter and the cylinder head, coolant temperature must be at least 80 degrees Celsius and oxygen sensor heaters for oxygen sensors before the catalytic converter must be functioning properly and the ground between the engine and the chassis must be well connected. The DME detected an unexpected EVAP malfunction. **Note: Solenoid valve is closed when no voltage is present.**
DTC: P2420 **1T DME, MIL: Yes** **Year:** 2011, 2012 **Model:** 1 Series M, 128i, 135i, 323i, 328i, 328i xDrive, 335is, 528i, 535i, X1, X3, X5 **Engine:** 2.5L L6, 3.0L L6	**Evaporative Emission System Switching Valve Control Circuit High:** Engine started, battery voltage must be at least 11.5v, all electrical components must be off, parking brake must be engaged (to keep daytime driving lights off), automatic transmission selector must be in park, the exhaust system must be properly sealed between the catalytic converter and the cylinder head, coolant temperature must be at least 80 degrees Celsius and oxygen sensor heaters for oxygen sensors before the catalytic converter must be functioning properly and the ground between the engine and the chassis must be well connected. The DME detected an unexpected EVAP malfunction. **Note: Solenoid valve is closed when no voltage is present.**
DTC: P2430 **1T DME, MIL: Yes** **Year:** 2011 **Model:** 323i **Engine:** 2.5L L6	**Secondary Air Mass Flow Sensor Rationality Check:** Engine started, battery voltage must be at least 11.5v, all electrical components must be off, parking brake must be engaged (to keep daytime driving lights off), automatic transmission selector must be in park, the exhaust system must be properly sealed between the catalytic converter and the cylinder head, coolant temperature must be at least 80 degrees Celsius and oxygen sensor heaters for oxygen sensors before the catalytic converter must be functioning properly and the ground between the engine and the chassis must be well connected. The DME detected an unexpected secondary air system malfunction. It is disconnected or stuck. **Note: Solenoid valve is closed when no voltage is present.**
DTC: P2540 **1T DME, MIL: Yes** **Year:** 2011 **Model:** 323i **Engine:** 2.5L L6	**Secondary Air System Vent Valve Stuck Closed:** Engine started, battery voltage must be at least 11.5v, all electrical components must be off, parking brake must be engaged (to keep daytime driving lights off), automatic transmission selector must be in park, the exhaust system must be properly sealed between the catalytic converter and the cylinder head, coolant temperature must be at least 80 degrees Celsius and oxygen sensor heaters for oxygen sensors before the catalytic converter must be functioning properly and the ground between the engine and the chassis must be well connected. The DME detected an unexpected secondary air system malfunction. **Note: Solenoid valve is closed when no voltage is present.**
DTC: P2626 **1T DME, MIL: Yes** **Year:** 2011, 2012 **Model:** 1 Series M, 128i, 135i, 323i, 328i, 328i xDrive, 335is, 528i, 535i, X1, X3, X5 **Engine:** 2.5L L6, 3.0L L6	**O2 Sensor Pumping Current Trim Circuit/Open Bank 1 Sensor 1:** Engine started and the fault entry trips after the criterion remains present for 1 second, battery voltage must be at least 11v, the trailing throttle overrun abort is present for at least two seconds, the O2 sensor is heated to an adequate temperature and the exhaust gas temperature before the catalytic converter is less than 750 degrees Celsius.
DTC: P2629 **1T DME, MIL: Yes** **Year:** 2011, 2012 **Model:** 1 Series M, 128i, 135i, 323i, 328i, 328i xDrive, 335is, 528i, 535i, X1, X3, X5 **Engine:** 2.5L L6, 3.0L L6	**O2 Sensor Pumping Current Trim Circuit/Open Bank 2 Sensor 1:** Engine started, battery voltage must be at least 11.5v, all electrical components must be off, parking brake must be engaged (to keep daytime driving lights off), automatic transmission selector must be in park, the exhaust system must be properly sealed between the catalytic converter and the cylinder head, coolant temperature must be at least 80 degrees Celsius and oxygen sensor heaters for oxygen sensors before the catalytic converter must be functioning properly and the ground between the engine and the chassis must be well connected. The DME detected a voltage value that doesn't fall within the desired parameters for a properly functioning O2 system.

DTC	Trouble Code Title and Conditions
DTC: P2729 **1T DME, MIL: Yes** **Year:** 2011, 2012 **Model:** X5 **Engine:** 4.4L V8	**Pressure Regulator Valve 5 Lower Threshold:** The signal to/from the pressure regulator valve is interrupted or short circuited to ground.
DTC: P2730 **1T DME, MIL: Yes** **Year:** 2011, 2012 **Model:** X5 **Engine:** 4.4L V8	**Pressure Regulator Valve 5 Upper Threshold:** The signal to/from the pressure regulator valve is interrupted or short circuited to supply.
DTC: P2761 **1T DME, MIL: Yes** **Year:** 2011, 2012 **Model:** X5 **Engine:** 4.4L V8	**Pressure Regulator Valve 4 Plausibility:** The current to/from the pressure regulator valve is either higher or lower than the threshold value.
DTC: P2763 **1T DME, MIL: Yes** **Year:** 2011, 2012 **Model:** X5 **Engine:** 4.4L V8	**Pressure Regulator Valve 4 Upper Threshold:** The signal to/from the pressure regulator valve is interrupted or short circuited to power.
DTC: P2764 **1T DME, MIL: Yes** **Year:** 2011, 2012 **Model:** X5 **Engine:** 4.4L V8	**Pressure Regulator Valve 4 Lower Threshold:** The signal to/from the pressure regulator valve is interrupted or short circuited to ground.

MERCEDES BENZ

CL • CLS

6

SPECIFICATIONS AND MAINTENANCE CHARTS

ENGINE AND VEHICLE IDENTIFICATION CHART

Engine						
Code ①	Liters (cc)	Cu. In.	Cyl.	Fuel Sys.	Type	Eng. Mfg.
271.860	1.8L (1796)	110	I4	SEFI	DOHC	MB
272.947	3.0L (2996)	183	V6	SEFI	DOHC	MB
272.948	3.0L (2996)	183	V6	SEFI	DOHC	MB
272.961	3.5L (3498)	268	V6	SEFI	DOHC	MB
276.957	3.5L (3498)	268	V6	SEFI	DOHC	MB
278.922	4.7L (4663)	285	V8	SEFI	DOHC	MB
273.960	5.5L (5461)	333	V8	SEFI	DOHC	MB
157.981	5.5L (5461)	333	V8	SEFI	DOHC	MB
156.985	6.2L (6208)	379	V8	SEFI	DOHC	MB

Model Year	
Code ②	Year
B	2011
C	2012

SEFI: Sequential Electronic Fuel Injection

DOHC: Double overhead camshafts

① Stamped into the crankcase

② 10th digit of the VIN

71112_MBCL_C0001

GENERAL ENGINE SPECIFICATIONS

Year	Engine Displacement Liters	Engine ID/VIN	Net Horsepower @ rpm	Net Torque@rpm (ft. lbs.)	Bore x Stroke (in.)	Com-pression Ratio	Oil Pressure @ rpm
2011	3.0	272.947	228@6000	221@2700	3.46x3.23	11.3:1	NA
	3.0	272.948	228@6000	221@2700	3.46x3.23	11.3:1	NA
	3.5	272.961	268@6000	258@2400	3.66x3.39	10.7:1	NA
	5.5	273.960	382@6000	391@2800	3.86x3.56	10.7:1	NA
	6.2	156.983	507@6800	465@5200	4.02x3.72	11.3:1	NA
	6.2	156.985	451@6800	443@5000	4.02x3.72	11.3:1	NA
2012	1.8	271.860	201@5500	229@2200	3.23x3.35	9.3:1	NA
	3.0	272.948	228@6000	221@2700	3.46x3.23	11.3:1	NA
	3.5	276.957	302@6500	273@3500	3.66x3.39	12.0:1	NA
	4.7	278.922	402@5000	443@1800	3.66x3.39	10.5:1	NA
	5.5	157.981	518@5250	516@1700	3.86x3.56	10.0:1	NA
	6.2	156.985	451@6500	443@5000	4.02x3.72	11.3:1	NA

NA: Not Available

71112_MBCL_C0002

GASOLINE ENGINE TUNE-UP SPECIFICATIONS

Year	Engine Displacement Liters	Engine ID/VIN	Spark Plug Gap (in.)	Ignition Timing (deg.) MT	Ignition Timing (deg.) AT	Fuel Pump (psi)	Idle Speed (rpm) MT	Idle Speed (rpm) AT	Valve Clearance In.	Valve Clearance Ex.
2011	3.0	272.947	①	②	②	NS	②	②	HYD	HYD
	3.0	272.948	①	NA	②	NS	NA	②	HYD	HYD
	3.5	272.961	①	NA	②	NS	NA	②	HYD	HYD
	5.5	273.960	0.039	NA	②	NS	NA	②	HYD	HYD
	6.2	156.983	0.039	NA	②	NS	NA	②	HYD	HYD
	6.2	156.985	0.039	NA	②	NS	NA	②	HYD	HYD
2012	1.8	271.860	①	NA	②	NS	NA	②	HYD	HYD
	3.0	272.948	①	NA	②	NS	NA	②	HYD	HYD
	3.5	276.957	①	NA	②	NS	NA	②	HYD	HYD
	4.7	278.922	①	NA	②	NS	NA	②	HYD	HYD
	5.5	157.981	①	NA	②	NS	NA	②	HYD	HYD
	6.2	156.985	①	NA	②	NS	NA	②	HYD	HYD

NOTE: The Vehicle Emission Control Information label often reflects specification changes changes made during production.

NA: Not Applicable

NS: Not Specified

HYD: Hydraulic

① Spark plugs using Iridium or other precious metals should not be gapped.
Other park plugs should be gapped at 0.031 in.

② Ignition timing and idle speed are controlled by the ME engine controller. No adjustment is possible.

71112_MBCL_C0003

CAPACITIES

Year	Model	Engine Displacemen Liters	Engine ID/VIN	Engine Oil with Filter (qts.)	Transmission (pts.) Man.	Transmission (pts.) Auto.	Drive Axle Front (pts.)	Drive Axle Rear (pts.)	Fuel Tank (gal.)	Cooling System (qts.)
2011	C300	3.0	272.947	8.5	3.2	19.0	1.3	①	17.4	8.9
	C300 4MATIC	3.0	272.948	7.4	—	19.0	1.3	①	17.4	8.9
	C350	3.5	272.961	8.5	—	19.0	1.3	①	17.4	8.9
	C63 AMG	6.2	156.985	9.0	—	15.0	1.3	2.5	17.4	12.4
	CLS550	5.5	273.960	9.0	—	19.4	1.3	2.6	21.1	11.9
	CLS63 AMG	6.2	156.983	9.3	—	18.6	1.3	2.6	21.1	12.5
2012	C250	1.8	271.860	5.8	—	15.9	1.3	①	15.6	7.6
	C300 4MATIC	3.0	272.948	7.4	—	19.0	1.3	①	17.4	8.9
	C350	3.5	276.957	6.9	—	19.0	1.3	①	17.4	NA
	C63 AMG	6.2	156.985	9.0	—	②	1.3	2.5	17.4	12.4
	CLS550	4.7	278.922	9.0	—	19.0	1.3	③	21.1	13.4
	CLS63 AMG	5.5	157.981	8.5	—	15.0	1.3	③	21.1	④

NOTE: All capacities are approximate. Add fluid gradually and check to be sure a proper fluid level is obtained.

NA: Not Available

① 187 mm Diameter Rear Differential: 2.0 pts.
200 mm Diameter Rear Differential: 2.3 pts.
215 mm Diameter Rear Differential: 2.5 pts.

② Without auxiliary radiator: 13.6 qt
With auxiliary radiator: 14.8 qt

③ 200 mm Diameter Rear Differential: 2.3 pts
215 mm Diameter Rear Differential: 2.5 pts

④ Sedan: 19.0 pts
Coupe: 15.0 pts

71112_MBCL_C0004

FLUID SPECIFICATIONS

Year	Model	Engine Displacement Liters	Engine ID/VIN	Engine Oil	Man. Trans.	Auto. Trans.	Drive Axle Front	Drive Axle Rear	Transfer Case	Power Steering Fluid	Brake Master Cylinder	Cooling System
2011	C300	3.0	272.947	①	MB317	ATF 134	75W-85	75W-85	—	CHF11S	DOT4	②
	C300 4MATIC	3.0	272.948	①	—	ATF 134	75W-85	75W-85	—	CHF11S	DOT4	②
	C350	3.5	272.961	①	—	ATF 134	75W-85	75W-85	—	CHF11S	DOT4	②
	C63 AMG	6.2	156.985	①	—	ATF 134	75W-85	75W-85	—	CHF11S	DOT4	②
	CLS550	5.5	273.960	①	—	ATF 134	75W-85	75W-85	—	CHF11S	DOT4	②
	CLS63 AMG	6.2	156.983	①	—	ATF 134	75W-85	75W-85	—	CHF11S	DOT4	②
2012	C250	1.8	271.860	①	—	ATF 134	75W-85	75W-85	—	CHF11S	DOT4	②
	C300 4MATIC	3.0	272.948	①	—	ATF 134	75W-85	75W-85	—	CHF11S	DOT4	②
	C350	3.5	276.957	①	—	ATF 134	75W-85	75W-85	—	CHF11S	DOT4	②
	C63 AMG	6.2	156.985	①	—	ATF 134	75W-85	75W-85	—	CHF11S	DOT4	②
	CLS550	4.7	278.922	①	—	ATF 134	75W-85	75W-85	—	CHF11S	DOT4	②
	CLS63 AMG	5.5	157.981	①	—	ATF 134	75W-85	75W-85	—	CHF11S	DOT4	②

DOT: Department Of Transpotation

① In cold climate: 5W-40 (Semi-Synthetic)

In moderate climate: 10w-30 (Semi-Synthetic)

In hot climate: 20w-40 (Semi-Synthetic)

② 50/50 mix of coolant with a corrosion inhibitor and water

71112_MBCL_C0005

VALVE SPECIFICATIONS

Year	Engine VIN	Engine Displacement Liters	Seat Angle (deg.)	Face Angle (deg.)	Spring Test Pressure (lbs. @ in.)	Spring Installed Height (in.)	Stem-to-Guide Clearance (in.) Intake	Stem-to-Guide Clearance (in.) Exhaust	Stem Diameter (in.) Intake	Stem Diameter (in.) Exhaust
2011	272.947	3.0	45	NA	NA	NA	NA	NA	0.2346-0.2352	0.2344-0.2350
	272.948	3.0	45	NA	NA	NA	NA	NA	0.2346-0.2352	0.2344-0.2350
	272.961	3.5	45.5	NA	NA	NA	NA	NA	0.2346-0.2352	0.2344-0.2350
	273.960	5.5	45	NA	NA	NA	NA	NA	0.2346-0.2352	0.2344-0.2350
	156.983	6.2	45	NA	NA	NA	NA	NA	0.2348-0.2354	0.2344-0.2350
	156.985	6.2	45	NA	NA	NA	NA	NA	0.2348-0.2354	0.2344-0.2350
2012	271.860	1.8	NA	NA	NA	NA	NA	NA	NA	NA
	272.948	3.0	45	NA	NA	NA	NA	NA	0.2344-0.2350	0.2344-0.2350
	276.957	3.5	NA	NA	NA	NA	NA	NA	NA	NA
	278.922	4.7	NA	NA	NA	NA	NA	NA	NA	NA
	157.981	5.5	NA	NA	NA	NA	NA	NA	NA	NA
	156.985	6.2	45	NA	NA	NA	NA	NA	0.2348-0.2354	0.2344-0.2350

NA: Not Available

71112_MBCL_C0006

CRANKSHAFT AND CONNECTING ROD SPECIFICATIONS

All measurements are given in inches.

Year	Engine Displacement Liters	Engine ID/VIN	Main Brg. Oil Clearance	Shaft End-play	Thrust on No.	Connecting Rod Journal Diameter	Connecting Rod Oil Clearance	Connecting Rod Side Clearance
2011	3.0	272.947	0.0008-0.0018	0.0039-0.0104	NA	NA	0.0008-0.0026	NA
	3.0	272.948	0.0008-0.0018	0.0039-0.0104	NA	NA	0.0008-0.0026	NA
	3.5	272.961	0.0008-0.0018	0.0039-0.0104	NA	NA	0.0008-0.0026	NA
	5.5	273.960	0.0008-0.0018	0.0039-0.0104	NA	NA	0.0008-0.0026	NA
	6.2	156.983	0.0008-0.0016	0.0059-0.0124	NA	NA	0.0011-0.0024	NA
	6.2	156.985	0.0008-0.0016	0.0059-0.0124	NA	NA	0.0011-0.0024	NA
2012	1.8	271.860	0.0008-0.0018	0.0039-0.0118	3	NA	NA	NA
	3.0	272.948	0.0008-0.0018	0.0039-0.0104	NA	NA	0.0008-0.0026	NA
	3.5	276.957	0.0008-0.0018	0.0039-0.0104	3	NA	0.0008-0.0026	NA
	4.7	278.922	NA	NA	NA	NA	NA	NA
	5.5	157.981	NA	NA	NA	NA	NA	NA
	6.2	156.985	0.0008-0.0016	0.0059-0.0124	NA	NA	0.0011-0.0024	NA

NA: Not Available

71112_MBCL_C0008

PISTON AND RING SPECIFICATIONS

All measurements are given in inches.

Year	Engine Disp. Liters	Engine ID/VIN	Piston Clearance	Ring Gap Top Compression	Ring Gap Bottom Compression	Ring Gap Oil Control	Ring Side Clearance Top Compression	Ring Side Clearance Bottom Compression	Ring Side Clearance Oil Control
2011	3.0	272.947	0.0002-0.0016	0.0078-0.0138	0.0118-0.0197	0.0078-0.0354	0.0012-0.0031	0.0008-0.0024	NA
	3.0	272.948	0.0002-0.0016	0.0078-0.0138	0.0118-0.0197	0.00178-0.0354	0.0012-0.0031	0.0008-0.0024	NA
	3.5	272.961	0.0002-0.0016	0.0078-0.0138	0.0118-0.0197	0.00178-0.0354	0.0008-0.0024	0.0006-0.0020	NA
	5.5	273.960	0.0002-0.0016	0.0078-0.0138	0.0118-0.0197	0.00178-0.0354	0.0008-0.0028	0.0008-0.0024	NA
	6.2	156.983	NA	NA	NA	NA	NA	NA	NA
	6.2	156.985	NA	NA	NA	NA	NA	NA	NA
2012	1.8	271.860	NA	NA	NA	NA	NA	NA	NA
	3.0	272.948	0.0002-0.0016	0.0078-0.0138	0.0118-0.0197	0.00178-0.0354	0.0012-0.0031	0.0008-0.0024	NA
	3.5	276.957	NA	0.0078-0.0138	0.0118-0.0197	0.00178-0.0354	0.0012-0.0031	0.0006-0.0024	NA
	4.7	278.922	NA	0.0006-0.0118	0.0157-0.0236	0.0078-0.0276	0.0010-0.0030	0.0006-0.0022	NA
	5.5	157.981	NA	0.0006-0.0118	0.0157-0.0236	0.0010-0.0197	0.0020-0.0031	0.0006-0.0020	NA
	6.2	156.985	NA	NA	NA	NA	NA	NA	NA

NA: Not Available

71112_MBCL_C0009

TORQUE SPECIFICATIONS

All readings in ft. lbs.

Year	Engine Displacement Liters	Engine ID/VIN	Cylinder Head Bolts	Main Bearing Bolts	Rod Bearing Bolts	Crankshaft Damper Bolts	Flywheel Bolts	Manifold Intake	Manifold Exhaust	Spark Plugs	Lug Nut
2011	3.0	272.947	①	②	③	④	⑤	7	12	17	96
	3.0	272.948	①	②	③	④	⑤	7	12	17	96
	3.5	272.961	①	②	③	④	⑤	7	12	17	96
	5.5	273.960	①	②	③	④	⑤	7	12	17	96
	6.2	156.983	⑥	⑦	⑧	⑨	⑩	⑪	16	16	96
	6.2	156.985	⑥	⑦	⑧	⑨	⑩	⑪	16	16	96
2012	1.8	271.860	⑫	⑬	⑭	④	⑤	10	15	17	96
	3.0	272.948	①	②	③	④	⑤	7	12	17	96
	3.5	276.957	①	②	③	④	⑮	7	12	17	96
	4.7	278.922	⑯	②	⑰	⑱	⑮	7	18	17	96
	5.5	157.981	⑯	②	⑰	⑱	⑮	7	18	17	96
	6.2	156.985	⑥	⑦	⑧	⑨	⑩	⑪	16	16	96

① M8 Cylinder head to timing case
Step 1: 11 ft. lbs.
M11 Cylinder head to crankcase
Step 1: 15 ft. lbs.
Step 2: 30 ft. lbs.
Step 3: plus 90 degrees
Step 4: plus 90 degrees

② M8 Side crankshaft bearing cap
Step 1: 22 ft. lbs.
Step 2: plus 90 degrees
M8 Crankshaft bearing cap
Step 1: 15 ft. lbs.
Step 2: plus 90 degrees
M10 Cranksahft bearing cap
Step 1: 4 ft. lbs.
Step 2: 22 ft. lbs.
Step 3: plus 90 degrees

③ Step 1: 4 ft. lbs.
Step 2: 15 ft. lbs.
Step 3: plus 90 degrees

④ Step 1: 148 ft. lbs.
Step 2: 90 degrees

⑤ Step 1: 33 ft. lbs.
Step 2: plus 90 degrees

⑥ Step 1: 7 ft. lbs.
Step 2: 37 ft. lbs.
Step 3: plus 90 degrees
Step 4: plus 90 degrees
Step 5: plus 90 degrees
All M8 bolts: 15 ft lbs.

⑦ M9 bearing bolts:
Step 1: 15 ft. lbs.
Step 2: M9- 24 ft. lbs. M10- 30 ft. lt
Step 3: plus 90 degrees
Step 4: plus 90 degrees
Step 5: Release all tension
Step 6: 15 ft. lbs.
Step 7: M9- 24 ft. lbs. M10- 30 ft. lt
Step 8: plus 90 degrees
Step 9: plus 90 degrees
M6 bearing bolts: 6 ft. lbs.
M8 bearing bolts: 15 ft. lbs.

⑧ Step 1: 7 ft. lbs.
Step 2: 30 ft. lbs.
Step 3: plus 120 degrees
Step 4: Release all tension
Step 5: plus 10 degrees
Step 6: 30 ft. lbs.
Step 7: plus 90 degrees

⑨ Step 1: 184 ft. lbs.
Step 2: Release all tension
Step 3: 148 ft. lbs.
Step 4: plus 180 degrees

⑩ Step 1: 35 inch lbs.
Step 2: 22 ft. lbs.
Step 3: plus 90 degrees

⑪ Step 1: 88 inch lbs.
Step 2: plus 90 degrees
Step 3: plus 10 degrees

⑫ Step 1: 33 ft. lbs.
Step 2: plus 90 degrees
Step 3: plus 90 degrees

⑬ Step 1: 22 ft. lbs.
Step 2: plus 90 degrees

⑭ Step 1: 44 inch lbs.
Step 2: 11 ft. lbs.
Step 3: plus 90 degrees

⑮ Step 1: 15 ft. lbs.
Step 2: 33 ft. lbs.
Step 3: plus 90 degrees

⑯ M7 Cylinder head to timing ca
Step 1: 10 ft. lbs.
M11 Cylinder head to crankc
Step 1: 15 ft. lbs.
Step 2: 30 ft. lbs.
Step 3: plus 90 degrees
Step 4: plus 90 degrees
Step 5: plus 90 degrees

⑰ Step 1: 44 inch lbs.
Step 2: 18 ft. lbs.
Step 3: plus 90 degrees

⑱ Step 1: 148 ft. lbs.
Step 2: 180 degrees

71112_MBCL_C0010

TIRE, WHEEL AND BALL JOINT SPECIFICATIONS

Year	Model	OEM Tires		Tire Pressures (psi)		Wheel	Ball Joint
		Standard	Optional	Front	Rear	Size	Inspection
2011	C300	225/45R17	None	①	①	7.5J	NA
	C300 4MATIC	225/45R17	None	①	①	7.5J	NA
	C350	F: 225/45R17 R: 245/40R17	None	①	①	7.5J 8.5J	NA NA
	C63 AMG	F: 235/40ZR18 R: 235/40ZR18	None	①	①	8.0J 9.0J	NA
	CLS550	F: 245/40R18 R: 275/35R18	F: 245/40ZR18 R: 285/35ZR18	①	①	8.5J 9.5J	NA
	CLS63 AMG	F: 255/35ZR19 R: 285/30ZR19	None	①	①	7.5J 8.5J	NA
2012	C250	F: 225/45R17 R: 245/40R17	F: 225/40R18 R: 255/35R18	①	①	7.5J 8.5J	NA
	C300 4MATIC	F: 225/45R17 R: 245/50R17	F: 225/40R18 R: 255/35R18	①	①	7.5J 8.5J	NA
	C350	F: 225/45ZR17 R: 245/40ZR17	F: 225/40R18 R: 255/35R18	①	①	7.5J 8.5J	NA
	C63 AMG	F: 235/40R18 R: 255/35R18	F: 235/35R19 R: 255/30R19	①	①	8.0J 9.0J	NA
	CLS550	F: 255/40R18 R: 285/35R18	F: 255/35R19 R: 285/30R19	①	①	8.5J 9.5J	NA
	CLS550 4MATIC	F: 255/40R18 R: 285/35R18	F: 255/35R19 R: 285/30R19	①	①	8.5J 9.5J	NA
	CLS63 AMG	F: 255/35R19 R: 285/30R19	None	①	①	9.0J 10.0J	NA

Note: Always follow the specifications provided on the vehicle sticker.

OEM: Original Equipment Manufacturer

PSI: Pounds Per Square Inch

F: Front

R: Rear

NA: Not Available

① Refer to recommended pressure on driver's door B-pillar

71112_MBCL_C0011

BRAKE SPECIFICATIONS

All measurements in inches unless noted

		Front Brake Disc			Rear Brake Disc			Minimum Lining Thickness		Brake Caliper	
Year	Model	Original Thickness	Minimum Thickness	Max. Runout	Original Thickness	Minimum Thickness	Max. Runout	Front	Rear	Bracket Bolts (ft. lbs.)	Mounting Bolts (ft. lbs.)
2011	C300	1.102	1.024	NA	0.394	0.327	NA	0.079	0.079	25	85
	C300 4MATIC	1.102	1.024	NA	0.394	0.327	NA	0.079	0.079	25	85
	C350	1.102	1.024	NA	0.866	0.764	NA	0.079	0.079	25	85
	C63 AMG	1.417	1.315	NA	1.024	0.945	NA	0.079	0.079	25	①
	CLS550	1.260	1.181	NA	0.944	0.843	NA	0.079	0.079	22	132
	CLS63 AMG	1.417	1.299	NA	1.024	0.945	NA	0.099	0.079	22	132
2012	C250	1.102	1.024	NA	0.394	0.327	NA	0.079	0.079	25	85
	C300 4MATIC	1.102	1.024	NA	0.394	0.327	NA	0.079	0.079	25	85
	C350	1.260	1.181	NA	0.866	0.764	NA	0.079	0.079	25	①
	C63 AMG	1.417	1.315	NA	1.024	0.945	NA	0.079	0.079	25	①
	CLS550	1.260	1.181	NA	0.944	0.843	NA	0.079	0.079	22	132
	CLS550 4MATIC	1.260	1.181	NA	0.944	0.843	NA	0.079	0.079	22	132
	CLS63 AMG	1.417	1.299	NA	1.024	0.945	NA	0.099	0.079	22	132

NA: Not Available

① Front 85 ft. lbs.
Rear 81 ft. lbs.

71112_MBCL_C0012

SCHEDULED MAINTENANCE INTERVALS

2011-12 Mercedes C-Class

TO BE SERVICED	TYPE OF SERVICE	VEHICLE MILEAGE INTERVAL (x1000)												
		10	20	30	40	50	60	70	80	90	100	110	120	130
Engine oil & filter	R	✓	✓	✓	✓	✓	✓	✓	✓	✓	✓	✓	✓	✓
Tires	Rotate	Every 5,000 miles												
Tire pressure, tread depth and TPMS	I	✓	✓	✓	✓	✓	✓	✓	✓	✓	✓	✓	✓	✓
Engine hood and catches	I	✓	✓	✓	✓	✓	✓	✓	✓	✓	✓	✓	✓	✓
Water drain in air duct	S&I	✓	✓	✓	✓	✓	✓	✓	✓	✓	✓	✓	✓	✓
Brake pads and rotors	I	✓	✓	✓	✓	✓	✓	✓	✓	✓	✓	✓	✓	✓
Engine coolant	S&I	✓	✓	✓	✓	✓	✓	✓	✓	✓	✓	✓	✓	✓
Brake fluid	S&I	✓		✓		✓		✓		✓		✓		✓
Brake fluid	R		✓		✓		✓		✓		✓		✓	
Power steering fluid	S&I	✓	✓	✓	✓	✓	✓	✓	✓	✓	✓	✓	✓	✓
Wiper blades	S&I	✓	✓	✓	✓	✓	✓	✓	✓	✓	✓	✓	✓	✓
Lighting system components	I	✓	✓	✓	✓	✓	✓	✓	✓	✓	✓	✓	✓	✓
Battery & Starter	I	✓	✓	✓	✓	✓	✓	✓	✓	✓	✓	✓	✓	✓
Brake system components & hoses	I	✓	✓	✓	✓	✓	✓	✓	✓	✓	✓	✓	✓	✓
Accessory drive belts	I		✓		✓		✓		✓		✓		✓	
Cabin air filter	R		✓		✓		✓		✓		✓		✓	
Ball joints and rubber boots	I		✓		✓		✓		✓		✓		✓	
Halfshafts	I		✓		✓		✓		✓		✓		✓	
Steering components & boots	I		✓		✓		✓		✓		✓		✓	
Parking brake	I		✓		✓		✓		✓		✓		✓	
Sunroof or convertible mechanism	L		✓		✓		✓		✓		✓		✓	
Windshield & headlamp washer system	I	✓	✓	✓	✓	✓	✓	✓	✓	✓	✓	✓	✓	✓
Chassis & load bearing body components	I		✓		✓		✓		✓		✓		✓	
Spark plugs	R						✓						✓	
Auto. Trans. oil & filter	R				✓				✓					
Fuel filter	R	every 150,000 miles												
Engine air filter	R				✓				✓					
Rear axle diff. fluid (AMG only)	R	At 2,000 miles, then at 80,000 miles												

R: Replace S: Service I: Inspect L: Lubricate

Special Operating Condition Requirements

When operating under severe operating conditions, the following items may need to be replaced more frequently:

Interior filters (Cabin dust filter, air filter, activated charcoal filter, etc.)

Spark plugs

Engine coolant

71112_MBCL_C0013

SCHEDULED MAINTENANCE INTERVALS

2011-12 Mercedes CLS-Class

		VEHICLE MILEAGE INTERVAL (x1000)												
TO BE SERVICED	**TYPE OF SERVICE**	**10**	**20**	**30**	**40**	**50**	**60**	**70**	**80**	**90**	**100**	**110**	**120**	**130**
Engine oil & filter	R	✓	✓	✓	✓	✓	✓	✓	✓	✓	✓	✓	✓	✓
Tires	Rotate	Every 5,000 miles												
Tire pressure, tread depth and TPMS	I	✓	✓	✓	✓	✓	✓	✓	✓	✓	✓	✓	✓	✓
Engine hood and catches	I	✓	✓	✓	✓	✓	✓	✓	✓	✓	✓	✓	✓	✓
Brake pads and rotors	I	✓	✓	✓	✓	✓	✓	✓	✓	✓	✓	✓	✓	✓
Engine coolant	S&I	✓	✓	✓	✓	✓	✓	✓	✓	✓	✓	✓	✓	✓
Brake fluid	S&I	✓		✓		✓		✓		✓		✓		✓
Brake fluid	R		✓		✓		✓		✓		✓		✓	
Power steering fluid	S&I	✓	✓	✓	✓	✓	✓	✓	✓	✓	✓	✓	✓	✓
Wiper blades	S&I	✓	✓	✓	✓	✓	✓	✓	✓	✓	✓	✓	✓	✓
Lighting system components	I	✓	✓	✓	✓	✓	✓	✓	✓	✓	✓	✓	✓	✓
Battery & Starter	I	✓	✓	✓	✓	✓	✓	✓	✓	✓	✓	✓	✓	✓
Brake system components & hoses	I	✓	✓	✓	✓	✓	✓	✓	✓	✓	✓	✓	✓	✓
Accessory drive belts	I		✓		✓		✓		✓		✓		✓	
Cabin air filter	R		✓		✓		✓		✓		✓		✓	
Ball joints and rubber boots	I		✓		✓		✓		✓		✓		✓	
Halfshafts	I		✓		✓		✓		✓		✓		✓	
Steering components & boots	I		✓		✓		✓		✓		✓		✓	
Parking brake	I		✓		✓		✓		✓		✓		✓	
Windshield & headlamp washer system	I	✓	✓	✓	✓	✓	✓	✓	✓	✓	✓	✓	✓	✓
Chassis & load bearing body components	I		✓		✓		✓		✓		✓		✓	
Spark plugs	R						✓						✓	
Auto. Trans. oil & filter	R				✓				✓					
Fuel filter	R	every 150,000 miles												
Engine air filter	R				✓				✓					
Rear axle diff. fluid (AMG only)	R	At 2,000 miles, 40,000 miles, then every 40,000 miles												

R: Replace S: Service I: Inspect L: Lubricate

Special Operating Condition Requirements

When operating under severe operating conditions, the following items may need to be replaced more frequently:

Interior filters (Cabin dust filter, air filter, activated charcoal filter, etc.)

Spark plugs

Engine coolant

71112_MBCL_C0014

PRECAUTIONS

Before servicing any vehicle, please be sure to read all of the following precautions, which deal with personal safety, prevention of component damage, and important points to take into consideration when servicing a motor vehicle:

- Never open, service or drain the radiator or cooling system when the engine is hot; serious burns can occur from the steam and hot coolant.
- Observe all applicable safety precautions when working around fuel. Whenever servicing the fuel system, always work in a well-ventilated area. Do not allow fuel spray or vapors to come in contact with a spark, open flame, or excessive heat (a hot drop light, for example). Keep a dry chemical fire extinguisher near the work area. Always keep fuel in a container specifically designed for fuel storage; also, always properly seal fuel containers to avoid the possibility of fire or explosion. Refer to the additional fuel system precautions later in this section.
- Fuel injection systems often remain pressurized, even after the engine has been turned **OFF**. The fuel system pressure must be relieved before disconnecting any fuel lines. Failure to do so may result in fire and/or personal injury.
- Brake fluid often contains polyglycol ethers and polyglycols. Avoid contact with the eyes and wash your hands thoroughly after handling brake fluid. If you do get brake fluid in your eyes, flush your eyes with clean, running water for 15 minutes. If eye irritation persists, or if you have taken brake fluid internally, IMMEDIATELY seek medical assistance.
- The EPA warns that prolonged contact with used engine oil may cause a number of skin disorders, including cancer. You should make every effort to minimize your exposure to used engine oil. Protective gloves should be worn when changing oil. Wash your hands and any other exposed skin areas as soon as possible after exposure to used engine oil. Soap and water, or waterless hand cleaner should be used.
- All new vehicles are now equipped with an air bag system, often referred to as a Supplemental Restraint System (SRS) or Supplemental Inflatable Restraint (SIR) system. The system must be disabled before performing service on or around system components, steering column, instrument panel components, wiring and sensors. Failure to follow safety and disabling procedures could result in accidental air bag deployment, possible personal injury and unnecessary system repairs.
- Always wear safety goggles when working with, or around, the air bag system. When carrying a non-deployed air bag, be sure the bag and trim cover are pointed away from your body. When placing a non-deployed air bag on a work surface, always face the bag and trim cover upward, away from the surface. This will reduce the motion of the module if it is accidentally deployed. Refer to the additional air bag system precautions later in this section.
- Clean, high quality brake fluid from a sealed container is essential to the safe and proper operation of the brake system. You should always buy the correct type of brake fluid for your vehicle. If the brake fluid becomes contaminated, completely flush the system with new fluid. Never reuse any brake fluid. Any brake fluid that is removed from the system should be discarded. Also, do not allow any brake fluid to come in contact with a painted surface; it will damage the paint.
- Never operate the engine without the proper amount and type of engine oil; doing so WILL result in severe engine damage.
- Timing belt maintenance is extremely important. Many models utilize an interference-type, non-freewheeling engine. If the timing belt breaks, the valves in the cylinder head may strike the pistons, causing potentially serious (also time-consuming and expensive) engine damage. Refer to the maintenance interval charts for the recommended replacement interval for the timing belt, and to the timing belt section for belt replacement and inspection.
- Disconnecting the negative battery cable on some vehicles may interfere with the functions of the on-board computer system(s) and may require the computer to undergo a relearning process once the negative battery cable is reconnected.
- When servicing drum brakes, only disassemble and assemble one side at a time, leaving the remaining side intact for reference.
- Only an MVAC-trained, EPA-certified automotive technician should service the air conditioning system or its components.

BRAKES — ANTI-LOCK BRAKE SYSTEM (ABS)

GENERAL INFORMATION

PRECAUTIONS

- Certain components within the ABS system are not intended to be serviced or repaired individually.
- Do not use rubber hoses or other parts not specifically specified for and ABS system. When using repair kits, replace all parts included in the kit. Partial or incorrect repair may lead to functional problems and require the replacement of components.
- Lubricate rubber parts with clean, fresh brake fluid to ease assembly. Do not use shop air to clean parts; damage to rubber components may result.
- Use only DOT 3 brake fluid from an unopened container.
- If any hydraulic component or line is removed or replaced, it may be necessary to bleed the entire system.
- A clean repair area is essential. Always clean the reservoir and cap thoroughly before removing the cap. The slightest amount of dirt in the fluid may plug an orifice and impair the system function. Perform repairs after components have been thoroughly cleaned; use only denatured alcohol to clean components. Do not allow ABS components to come into contact with any substance containing mineral oil; this includes used shop rags.
- The Anti-Lock control unit is a microprocessor similar to other computer units in the vehicle. Ensure that the ignition switch is **OFF** before removing or installing controller harnesses. Avoid static electricity discharge at or near the controller.
- If any arc welding is to be done on the vehicle, the control unit should be unplugged before welding operations begin.

SPEED SENSORS

REMOVAL & INSTALLATION

Front

C-Class Models

See Figure 1.

1. Raise and safely support the vehicle.
2. Disconnect the negative battery cable.
3. Remove the front wheel.

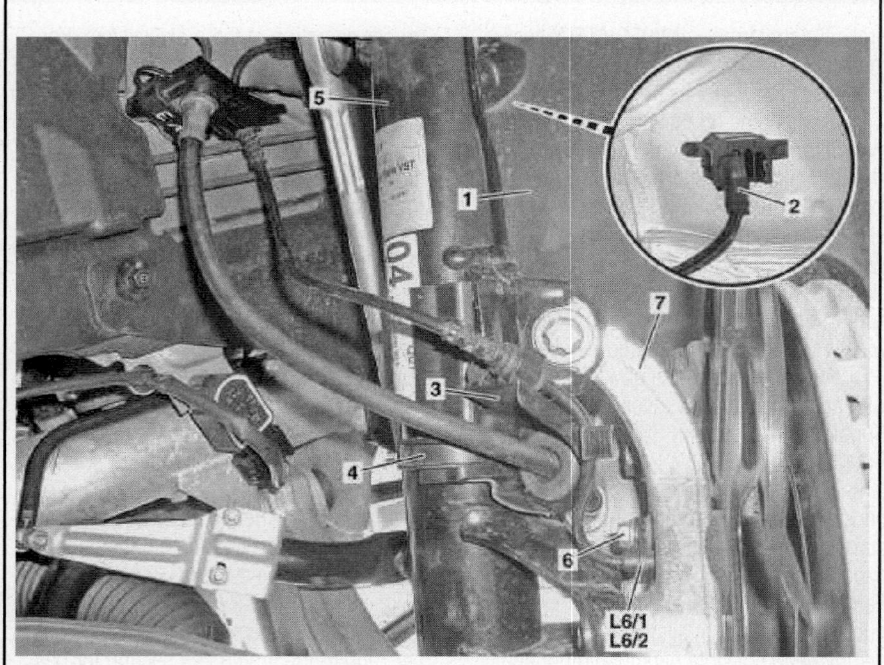

Fig. 1 Location of the speed sensor related components—C-Class models

4. Remove the rear section of the fender liner.
5. Disconnect the electrical connector on the front axle electrical distributor.
6. Unclip the electrical line of the speed sensor from the line bracket.
7. Remove the cable tie, if equipped, from the suspension strut.
8. Remove the mounting bolt and pull the speed sensor out of the steering knuckle.
9. Installation is the reverse order of removal.

CLS-Class Models

1. Remove the front section of the lower engine compartment paneling.
2. Using a screwdriver, push the detent upwards and pull the wheel speed sensor connector out of the bracket.
3. Unplug the wheel speed sensor connector.
4. Unclip the electric lead from the retaining clamp.
5. Remove the mounting bolt and discard.
6. Remove the wheel speed sensor out of the wheel knuckle.
7. Installation is the reverse order of removal. Tighten the new mounting bolt to 18 ft. lbs. (25 Nm).

BRAKES — BLEEDING THE BRAKE SYSTEM

BLEEDING PROCEDURE

BLEEDING PROCEDURE (PRESSURE)

1. Connect a battery charger.
2. Connect an electric brake fluid change/bleeder unit.
   - Following the manufacturer's instructions.
3. Connect the STAR Diagnosis system.
4. Raise and safely support the vehicle.
5. Remove the any wheels necessary to access bleed screws.
6. Carry out the bleeding operation using the STAR Diagnosis system.

BLEEDING THE ABS SYSTEM

See Figure 2.

1. Before servicing the vehicle, refer to the precautions.
2. Attach a pressure bleeding unit and adjust the pressure to 29 PSI (2.0 bar).
3. Remove dust caps of bleed screws (1, 2, 3, 4, 5, 6) on the brake calipers.
4. Open bleed screw and allow approx. 80 cm 3 of brake fluid bleed.

➡New brake fluid must flow out free of bubbles.

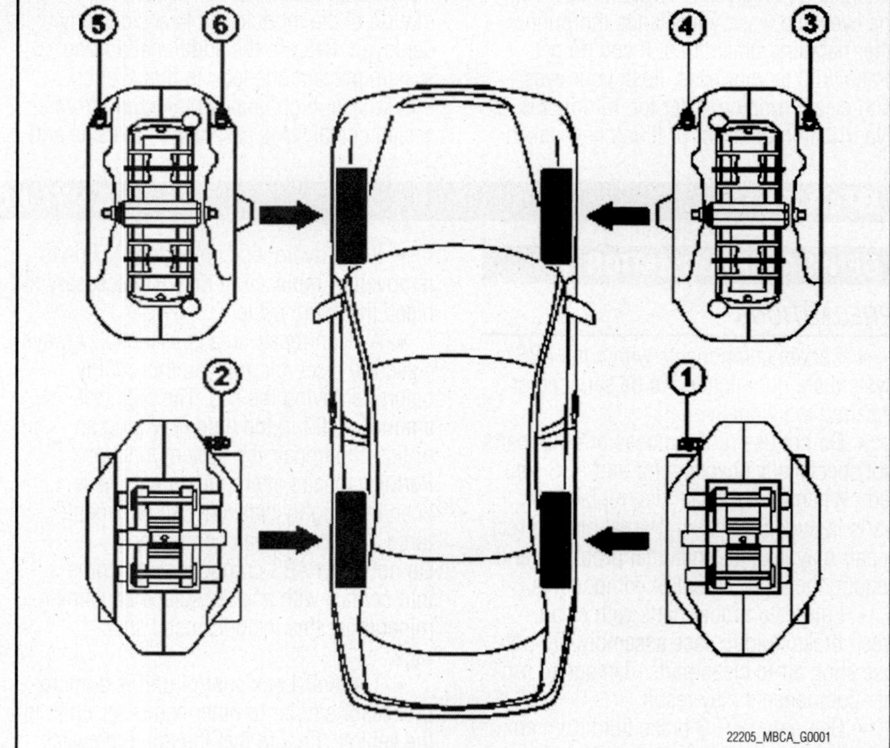

Fig. 2 The numbering of the bleed screws (1, 2, 3, 4, 5, 6) represents the opening sequence

5. Close bleed screw and pull off bleed hose.

6. Repeat process at the bleed screws (2, 3, 4, 5, 6).

➡The numbering of the bleed screws (1, 2, 3, 4, 5, 6) represents the opening sequence.

7. On Vehicles with manual transmission, remove cover from bell housing and repeat process at bleed screw of the central clutch release bearing.

8. Attach dust caps of bleed screws (1, 2, 3, 4, 5, 6) and cover to bell housing.

9. Tighten the bleeding screws to 60 inch lbs. (7 Nm).

10. Refill the fluid level in the master cylinder and check the system for leaks.

FLUID FILL PROCEDURE

Check the fluid level in the expansion reservoir. The fluid level must be between the "MIN" and "MAX" markings stamped on the reservoir. If the fluid is too low, fluid should be added. If fluid is too high, the fluid should be extracted down to the "MAX" level.

BRAKES

FRONT DISC BRAKES

⁂ CAUTION

Dust and dirt accumulating on brake parts during normal use may contain asbestos fibers from production or aftermarket brake linings. Breathing excessive concentrations of asbestos fibers can cause serious bodily harm. Exercise care when servicing brake parts. Do not sand or grind brake lining unless equipment used is designed to contain the dust residue. Do not clean brake parts with compressed air or by dry brushing. Cleaning should be done by dampening the brake components with a fine mist of water, then wiping the brake components clean with a dampened cloth. Dispose of cloth and all residue containing asbestos fibers in an impermeable container with the appropriate label. Follow practices prescribed by the Occupational Safety and Health Administration (OSHA) and the Environmental Protection Agency (EPA) for the handling, processing, and disposing of dust or debris that may contain asbestos fibers.

BRAKE CALIPER

REMOVAL & INSTALLATION

C-Class Models

See Figure 3.

1. Siphon off some of the brake fluid from the reservoir.

2. Raise and safely support the vehicle.

3. Remove the wheel.

4. Detach the spring from the brake caliper.

5. If removing the right side caliper, disconnect the brake wear sensor wiring harness.

6. Remove the caliper mounting bolts and remove the caliper from the rotor. Support the caliper assembly so it does not hang from the brake hose.

7. Remove the brake pads from the caliper.

8. Remove the screw that secures the electrical connector to the caliper. Remove the electrical connector.

9. Disconnect the brake hose from the caliper.

10. Installation is the reverse order of removal. Tighten the caliper guide pin bolts to 25 ft. lbs. (34 Nm).

CLS-Class Models

1. Deactivate the Sensotronic Brake Control (SBC) system using the STAR Diagnosis tool.

2. Raise and safely support the vehicle.

3. Remove the wheel.

4. Disconnect the brake hose.

5. Remove the brake pads.

6. Disconnect the brake pad sensor connector, if equipped.

7. Remove the piston mounting bolts.

8. Installation is the reverse order of removal. Tighten the mounting bolts to 133 ft. lbs. (180 Nm).

9. Bleed the brake system.

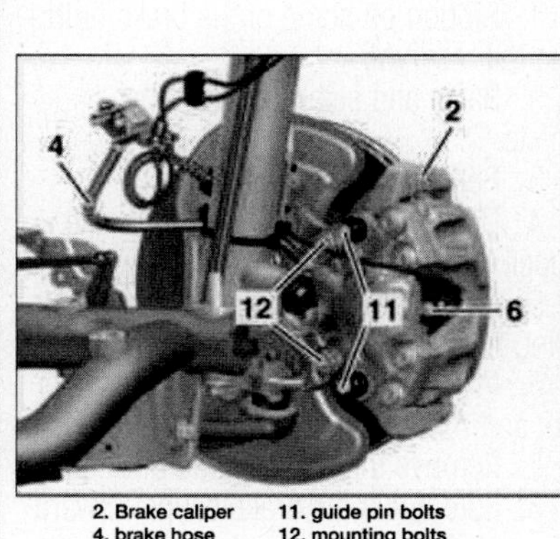

Fig. 3 Brake caliper components—C-Class models

BRAKE PADS

REMOVAL & INSTALLATION

C-Class Models

See Figure 4.

1. Siphon off some of the brake fluid from the reservoir.

2. Raise and safely support the vehicle.

3. Remove the wheel.

4. Detach the spring from the brake caliper.

5. If removing the right side caliper, disconnect the brake wear sensor wiring harness.

6. Remove the caliper mounting bolts and remove the caliper from the rotor. Support the caliper assembly so it does not hang from the brake hose.

7. Remove the brake pads from the caliper.

To install:

8. Using a suitable brake pusher tool, depress the brake piston.

9. Insert the inner brake pad with the spring into the brake piston.

10. Detach the protective foil form the outer brake pad and glue into the brake caliper.

11. The remainder of the installation is the reverse order of removal.

CLS-Class Models

1. Siphon off some of the brake fluid from the reservoir.

2. Deactive the Sensotronic Brake Control (SBC) system using the STAR Diagnosis tool.

3. Raise and safely support the vehicle.

4. Remove the wheel.

5. Disconnect the brake pad sensor connector, if equipped.

6. Drive out the retaining pins using a punch and remove the retaining springs.

Fig. 4 Using a suitable brake pusher tool (1) to depress the brake piston (8) before installing new brake pads

7. Pull the brake pads out of the caliper.

To install:

8. Install the brake pads. The marking on the brake pad must point in the direction of the rotation of the wheel.
9. Seat the retaining springs correctly and knock the retaining pins all the way in.
10. The remainder of the installation is the reverse order of removal.

CAUTION

Dust and dirt accumulating on brake parts during normal use may contain asbestos fibers from production or aftermarket brake linings. Breathing excessive concentrations of asbestos fibers can cause serious bodily harm. Exercise care when servicing brake parts. Do not sand or grind brake lining unless equipment used is designed to contain the dust residue. Do not clean brake parts with compressed air or by dry brushing. Cleaning should be done by dampening the brake components with a fine mist of water, then wiping the brake components clean with a dampened cloth. Dispose of cloth and all residue containing asbestos fibers in an impermeable container with the appropriate label. Follow practices prescribed by the Occupational Safety and Health Administration (OSHA) and the Environmental Protection Agency (EPA) for the handling, processing, and disposing of dust or debris that may contain asbestos fibers.

BRAKE CALIPER

REMOVAL & INSTALLATION

C-Class Models

1. Siphon off some of the brake fluid from the reservoir.
2. Raise and safely support the vehicle.
3. Remove the wheel.
4. Detach the spring from the brake caliper.
5. Disconnect the brake wear sensor wiring harness, if equipped.
6. Pry the protective cap off the upper boot and remove.
7. Remove the upper guide pin.
8. Fold down the brake caliper toward the rear of the vehicle.
9. Remove the brake caliper from the lower guide pin.
10. Remove the brake pads from the calipers.
11. Remove the screw and remove the electrical connector from the caliper if equipped with a wear sensor.
12. Disconnect the brake hose from the caliper.
13. Installation is the reverse order of removal. Tighten the caliper guide pins to 18 ft. lbs. (25 Nm).

CLS-Class Models

See Figure 5.

1. Deactivate the Sensotronic Brake Control (SBC) system using the STAR Diagnosis tool.
2. Disconnect the brake hose.
3. Disconnect the brake pad sensor connector, if equipped.
4. Remove the brake pads.
5. Remove the bolts of the brake caliper from the wheel carrier.
6. Remove the brake caliper.
7. Installation is the reverse order of removal. Tighten the mounting bolts as follows:
   - Floating caliper: 85 ft. lbs. (115 Nm)
   - Fixed caliper: 133 ft. lbs. (180 Nm)

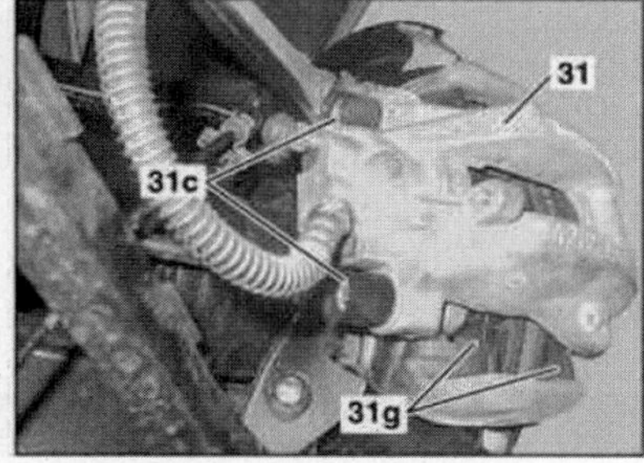

31. Brake caliper
31c. Bolts
31g. Brake pads
S10. Brake pad sensor

71112_MBCL_G0155

Fig. 5 Rear brake calipers—CLS-Class models shown

BRAKE PADS

REMOVAL & INSTALLATION

1. Siphon off some of the brake fluid from the reservoir.
2. Raise and safely support the vehicle.
3. Remove the wheel.
4. Detach the spring from the brake caliper.
5. Disconnect the brake wear sensor wiring harness, if equipped.
6. Pry the protective cap off the upper boot and remove.
7. Remove the upper guide pin.
8. Fold down the brake caliper toward the rear of the vehicle.
9. Remove the brake caliper from the lower guide pin.
10. Safely support the brake caliper assembly and do not let it hang by the brake hose.
11. Remove the brake pads from the calipers.

To install:

12. Using a suitable caliper spreader tool, push in the brake piston.
13. Insert the inner brake pad, then insert the outer pad into the caliper.
14. The remainder of the installation is the reverse order of removal. Tighten the caliper guide pins to 18 ft. lbs. (25 Nm).
15. Adjust the parking brake as necessary.

BRAKES — PARKING BRAKE

PARKING BRAKE CABLES

ADJUSTMENT

See Figure 6.

1. Raise and safely support the vehicle.
2. Release the parking brake.
3. Remove the rear wheels.
4. Using a screwdriver, turn the right and left adjustment wheels until the brake shoes abut the drums.
5. Confirm the brake rotor do not turn by hand.
6. Release the left and right adjusting wheels. Be sure to release both wheels the same number of teeth.
7. Confirm the brake rotor can be turned by hand.
8. Operate the parking brake.
9. Confirm the brake rotors do not turn by hand.
10. Release the parking brake.
11. Confirm the brake rotor can be turned by hand.
12. Install the rear wheels.

71112_MBCL_G0154

Fig. 6 Parking brake components—CLS-Class shown

PARKING BRAKE SHOES

REMOVAL & INSTALLATION

C-Class Models

See Figure 7.

1. Remove the brake rotor.
2. Unhook the retracting spring using a suitable brake tool.
3. Compress the retaining springs and turn 90° to remove.
4. Remove the brake shoes with the adjusting mechanism and retracting spring.
5. Remove the retracting spring and adjusting mechanism.
6. Fold up the expansion lock and press the bolt out of the lock and rear brake cable.

To install:

7. Inspect the brake cables for chafing and replace any cables for necessary.

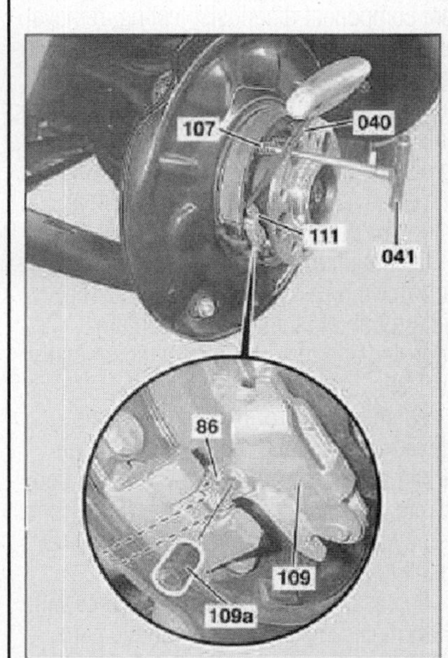

40. Brake removal tool
41. Brake installation tool
86. Rear brake cable
107. Retaining springs
109. Expansion lock
109a. Pin
111. Return spring

71112_MBCL_G0038

Fig. 7 Removing the parking brake shoe assembly—C-Class models

8. Grease the bolt and the bearing and sliding surfaces of the expansion lock lightly with suitable brake grease.

9. Install the expansion lock.

10. Apply a light coating of brake grease to the thread of the thrust piece and inner cylinder of the adjusting mechanism and mount so the thrust piece contact the upper brake shoe.

11. The remainder of the installation is the reverse order of removal.

CLS-Class Models

1. Deactive the Sensotronic Brake Control (SBC) system using the STAR Diagnosis tool.

2. Remove the rear brake rotors. For additional information, refer to the following section, "Brake Disc, Removal & Installation."

3. Remove the front and rear retracting springs using a suitable brake tool.

4. Compress the upper retaining spring and turn 90° to the right or left to remove.

5. Take off the top brake shoe.

6. Remove the adjusting mechanism.

7. Remove the lower retaining spring using a suitable brake tool and remove the lower brake shoes.

8. Fold open the expansion lock and press the pin out of the lock and rear brake cable.

9. Installation is the reverse order of removal.

CHASSIS ELECTRICAL

AIR BAG (SUPPLEMENTAL RESTRAINT SYSTEM)

GENERAL INFORMATION

⁂ CAUTION

These vehicles are equipped with an air bag system. The system must be disarmed before performing service on, or around, system components, the steering column, instrument panel components, wiring and sensors. Failure to follow the safety precautions and the disarming procedure could result in accidental air bag deployment, possible injury and unnecessary system repairs.

SERVICE PRECAUTIONS

Disconnect and isolate the battery negative cable before beginning any airbag system component diagnosis, testing, removal, or installation procedures. Allow system capacitor to discharge for two minutes before beginning any component service. This will disable the airbag system. Failure to disable the airbag system may result in accidental airbag deployment, personal injury, or death.

Do not place an intact undeployed airbag face down on a solid surface. The airbag will propel into the air if accidentally deployed and may result in personal injury or death.

When carrying or handling an undeployed airbag, the trim side (face) of the airbag should be pointing towards the body to minimize possibility of injury if accidental deployment occurs. Failure to do this may result in personal injury or death.

Replace airbag system components with OEM replacement parts. Substitute parts may appear interchangeable, but internal differences may result in inferior occupant protection. Failure to do so may result in occupant personal injury or death.

Wear safety glasses, rubber gloves, and long sleeved clothing when cleaning powder residue from vehicle after an airbag deployment. Powder residue emitted from a deployed airbag can cause skin irritation. Flush affected area with cool water if irritation is experienced. If nasal or throat irritation is experienced, exit the vehicle for fresh air until the irritation ceases. If irritation continues, see a physician.

Do not use a replacement airbag that is not in the original packaging. This may result in improper deployment, personal injury, or death.

The factory installed fasteners, screws and bolts used to fasten airbag components have a special coating and are specifically designed for the airbag system. Do not use substitute fasteners. Use only original equipment fasteners listed in the parts catalog when fastener replacement is required.

During, and following, any child restraint anchor service, due to impact event or vehicle repair, carefully inspect all mounting hardware, tether straps, and anchors for proper installation, operation, or damage. If a child restraint anchor is found damaged in any way, the anchor must be replaced. Failure to do this may result in personal injury or death.

Deployed and non-deployed airbags may or may not have live pyrotechnic material within the airbag inflator.

Do not dispose of driver/passenger/curtain airbags or seat belt tensioners unless you are sure of complete deployment. Refer to the Hazardous Substance Control System for proper disposal.

Dispose of deployed airbags and tensioners consistent with state, provincial, local, and federal regulations.

After any airbag component testing or service, do not connect the battery negative cable. Personal injury or death may result if the system test is not performed first.

If the vehicle is equipped with the Occupant Classification System (OCS), do not connect the battery negative cable before performing the OCS Verification Test using the scan tool and the appropriate diagnostic information. Personal injury or death may result if the system test is not performed properly.

Never replace both the Occupant Restraint Controller (ORC) and the Occupant Classification Module (OCM) at the same time. If both require replacement, replace one, then perform the Airbag System test before replacing the other.

Both the ORC and the OCM store Occupant Classification System (OCS) calibration data, which they transfer to one another when one of them is replaced. If both are replaced at the same time, an irreversible fault will be set in both modules and the OCS may malfunction and cause personal injury or death.

If equipped with OCS, the Seat Weight Sensor is a sensitive, calibrated unit and must be handled carefully. Do not drop or handle roughly. If dropped or damaged, replace with another sensor. Failure to do so may result in occupant injury or death.

If equipped with OCS, the front passenger seat must be handled carefully as well. When removing the seat, be careful when setting on floor not to drop. If dropped, the sensor may be inoperative, could result in occupant injury, or possibly death.

If equipped with OCS, when the passenger front seat is on the floor, no one should sit in the front passenger seat. This uneven force may damage the sensing ability of the seat weight sensors. If sat on and damaged, the sensor may be inoperative, could result in occupant injury, or possibly death.

DISARMING THE SYSTEM

To avoid injury when working on vehicles equipped with an air bag, the negative battery cable must be disconnected and insulated before working on the system. Failure to do so may result in accidental deployment of the air bag.

ARMING THE SYSTEM

To rearm the air bag system, reattach the battery cable(s).

DRIVE TRAIN

DRIVESHAFT

REMOVAL & INSTALLATION

CLS-Class Models

1. Remove the exhaust system.
2. Remove the underfloor panels.
3. Remove the heat shield.
4. Disconnect the crossmember.
5. Matchmark the driveshaft to mark the position relative to the transmission, rear axle center assembly and center bearing so the factory installation position can be restored when installing.
6. Loosen the bolts of the drive shaft intermediate bearing.
7. Disconnect the front and rear flexible coupling from the transmission and rear axle center assembly.
8. Undo the fitting sleeves of the front and rear flexible coupling.
9. Remove the bolts of the driveshaft center bearing and remove the driveshaft.
10. Installation is the reverse order of removal.

FRONT AXLE HOUSING

REMOVAL & INSTALLATION

C-Class Models

1. Deactivate the easy entry/exit function , if equipped with memory package.
2. Extend the adjustable steering column fully out.
3. Ensure the front wheels are in the straight ahead position.

➡If the steering wheel is turned when the steering coupling is detached, the clock spring will be destroyed.

4. Raise and safely support the vehicle.
5. Remove the suspensions struts. For additional information, refer to the following section, "Struts, Removal & Installation."
6. Insert one bolt each from the underside in the suspension strut towers and faster with nuts in order to secure the engine lifting device.
7. Remove the air intake assembly.
8. Fasten the radiator on the left and right radiator crossmember with cable ties.
9. Siphon any oil from the power steering expansion reservoir.
10. Mount a suitable engine lifting device.
11. If equipped with 4MATIC, remove the front axle shafts.
12. Loosen the wheel house linings in the area of the diagonal struts.
13. Detach the front door sill panels.
14. Remove any engine compartment paneling.
15. Remove the lower bottom sections of soundproofing.
16. Disconnect all electrical connectors of the front axle in the wheel wells.
17. Separate the steering coupling
18. Unscrew the brake line on the left and right from the brake hoses and seal the openings.
19. Separate the electrical connector on the speed- sensitive power steering solenoid valve and unclip retaining clip from front axle carrier.
20. Remove the bolt from the bracket of hydraulic line on the front axle carrier.
21. If equipped with 4MATIC, remove the bolt from the bracket of hydraulic lines to housing of rack-and-pinion steering.
22. Remove the retaining bolt and disconnect the hydraulic lines on the rack-and-pinion steering. Plug the lines and discard the sealing rings.
23. Unscrew the nut of the bracket from the wheelhouse oil cooler and detach the oil line, AMG models only.
24. Remove the diagonal struts.
25. Remove the bolts by the engine mounts.
26. Install protective washers to protect the brake disc dust shields.
27. Lift the engine slightly with the engine lifting device.
28. Support the front axle assembly with a suitable transmission jack.
29. Detach the support strut on the vehicle underbody and detach the front axle carrier, AMG models only.
30. Remove the bolts from the longitudinal members and discard,
31. Lower the front axle.
32. Installation is the reverse order of removal.
33. Bleed the brake system.
34. Refill and bleed the power steering pump.
35. Perform a wheel alignment check.

REAR AXLE HOUSING

REMOVAL & INSTALLATION

C-Class Models

See Figure 8.

1. Shift the transmission into position "N" or into idle position.
2. Switch off the ignition.
3. Raise and safely support the vehicle.

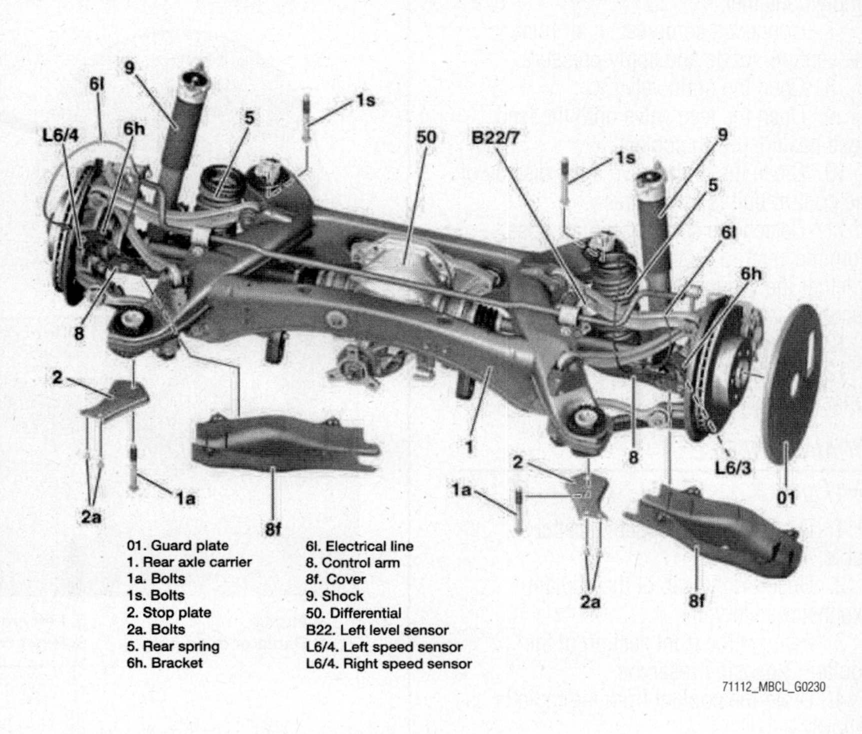

Fig. 8 Exploded view of the rear axle assembly

4. Remove the rear wheels.
5. Remove the left and right underfloor paneling.
6. Detach the exhaust system at connecting point of catalytic converter/ center muffler and remove.
7. Disconnect the driveshaft from the differential.
8. Remove the rear heat shield above driveshaft.
9. Separate the brake cable at separation point and unclip brake cables from brackets.
10. Detach the covers from the control arms.
11. Remove rear springs.
12. Disconnect the shock absorbers from the control arms.
13. Detach the wheel speed sensors from the wheel carriers.
14. Unscrew electrical connector from right rear brake caliper and unclip electrical line of the right rear brake wear sensor from brackets wear sensor on right wheel carrier.
15. Disconnect any remaining electrical connectors from their brackets.
16. Remove the rear brake calipers.
17. Disconnect the rear brake hoses from the brake lines and seal the openings.
18. Support the center differential with a suitable transmission jack and strap the differential to the transmission support plate.
19. Remove the mounting bolts and lower the axle assembly.
20. Installation is the reverse order of removal. Tighten mounting bolts as follows:
- Step 1: 59 ft. lbs. (80 Nm)
- Step 2: Release all tension
- Step 3: 59 ft. lbs. (80 Nm)
- Step 4: Plus 90°

ENGINE COOLING

ENGINE COOLANT

BLEEDING

1. Unscrew the cooling system cap and screw on a test cap at the coolant expansion reservoir.
2. Attach the control unit to the test cap.
3. Attach a venture nozzle to the control unit.
4. Close the drain valve and feed valve.
5. Attach the feed hose of coolant to the coolant container.
6. Guide the waste air hose into the an empty container.
7. Connect a compressed air hose to the venture nozzle and apply pressure.
8. Open the drain valve.
9. Open the feed valve until the feed hose has filled with coolant.
10. Close the drain valve if the display of the control unit is in the green.
11. Detach the compressed air hose from the venture nozzle and monitor whether the vacuum remains stable for 30 seconds.
12. Open the feed valve.
13. Open the drain valve if there is no longer suction.

DRAIN & REFILL

See Figure 9.

1. Disconnect the negative battery cable.
2. Unscrew the cap of the coolant expansion reservoir.
3. Remove the front section of the coolant expansion reservoir.
4. Drain the coolant from the radiator as follows:
   a. Slide a siphon hose onto the left fitting at the radiator.
   b. Open the drain plug and drain the coolant from the radiator.
   c. Tighten the drain plug and remove the siphon hose.
5. Drain the coolant from the crankcase as follows:
   a. Loosen left crankcase drain plug and right crankcase drain plug at crankcase until they can be turned by hand.
   b. Loosen left or right crankcase drain plug and slide siphon hose onto right crankcase drain plug.
   c. Continue to manually loosen left crankcase Follow regulations for the disposal of drain plug and right crankcase drain plug coolant and drain off coolant.
   d. Detach drain hose and tighten drain plug on left crankcase or drain plug on right crankcase.

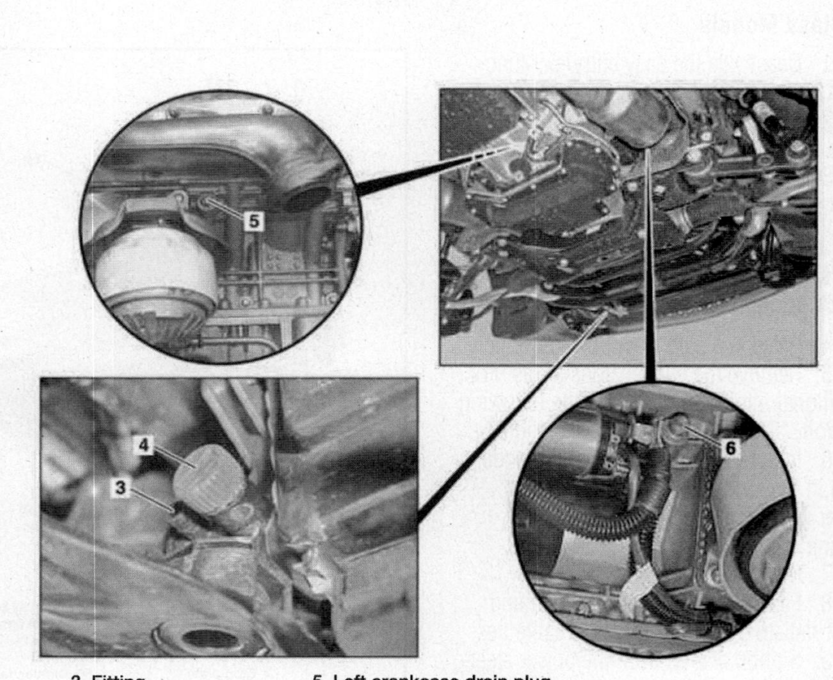

Fig. 9 Radiator and crankcase coolant drain plugs

6. Refill with coolant and bleed the system.

ELECTRIC ENGINE FAN

REMOVAL & INSTALLATION

C-Class Models

See Figures 10 and 11.

1. Remove the engine air intake assembly.
2. If equipped with 1.8L engine, remove the air guide between the air filter housing and turbocharger.
3. Remove the front engine cover and engine intake air ducts upstream of the air intake housing.
4. Remove the cold air intake assembly.
5. Remove the radiator grille.
6. Remove the radiator supports.
7. Remove the middle radiator reinforcements.
8. Unclip the retaining lug for the upper air ducting from the fan unit.
9. Remove the engine compartment paneling, AMG models only.
10. Disconnect the electrical connector from the fan unit.
11. Press the unlocking lugs apart and unclip the lower air ducts on the left and right from the fan unit.
12. Remove the hold down bolt for transmission oil cooling lines to the fan unit, if equipped.
13. Unhook the fan unit from the radiator mount and pull out upwards.
14. Installation is the reverse order of removal.

RADIATOR

REMOVAL & INSTALLATION

Engine ID 272

See Figure 12.

1. Remove the cold air intake assembly.
2. Remove the middle reinforcement at the front.
3. Remove the fan assembly. For additional information, refer to the following section, "Electric Engine Fan, Removal & Installation."
4. Remove engine compartment paneling.
5. Properly drain the cooling system.
6. Lift the radiator assembly upwards and lower in the direction of the engine.
7. Disconnect the electrical connectors and unclip the lines from the clamps.
8. Disconnect the coolant hoses from the radiator.
9. Disconnect the oil cooling lines from the radiator and pull out.
10. Unclip the condenser from the radiator the left and right.
11. Remove the radiator.

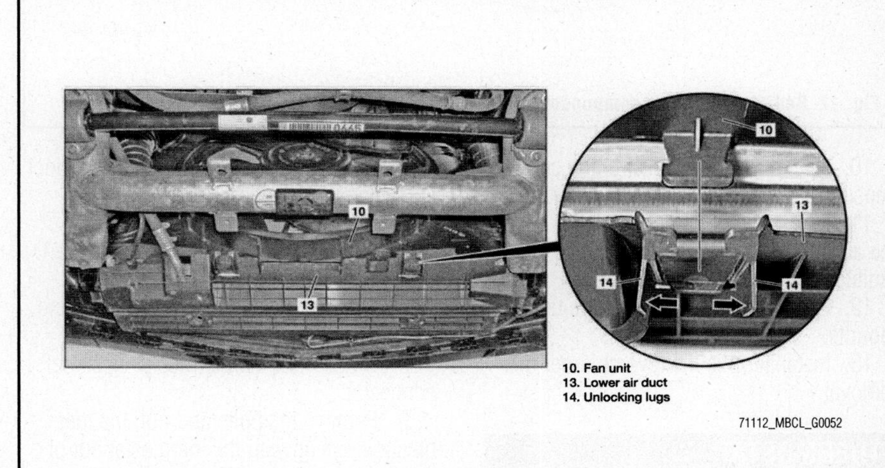

Fig. 11 Removing the fan unit—C-Class models

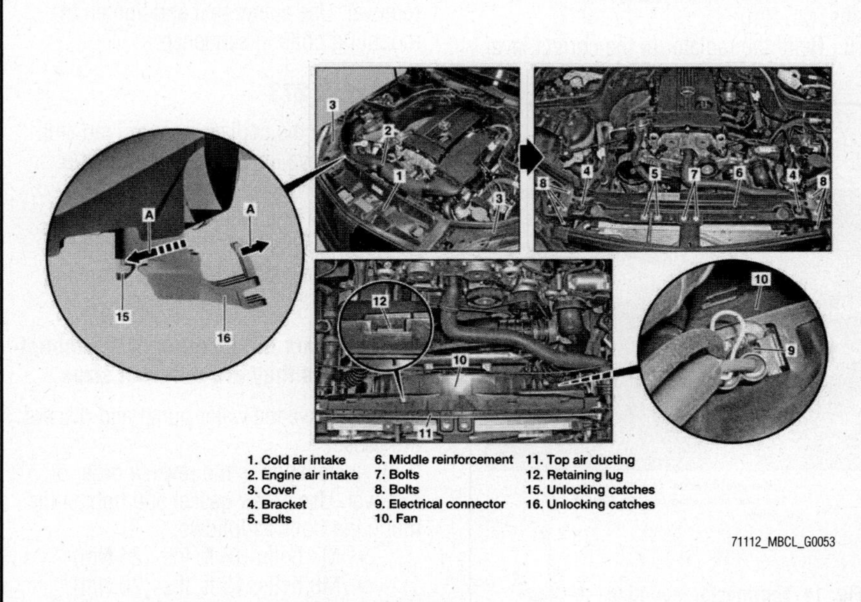

Fig. 10 Engine fan components—C-Class models

12. Installation is the reverse order of removal.
13. Refill the cooling system to the correct level.
14. Start the engine and check for leaks.

Engine ID 273

1. Pull out the front engine cover from the mounts.
2. Remove the left and right air intake ducts.
3. Remove the fan shroud.
4. Remove the front and center sections of the lower engine compartment paneling.
5. Drain the coolant from the radiator.
6. Remove the upper radiator cross-member.
7. Disconnect the coolant hoses from the radiator.
8. Remove the oil lines from the top of the radiator.
9. Unclip the power steering cooler from the mount.

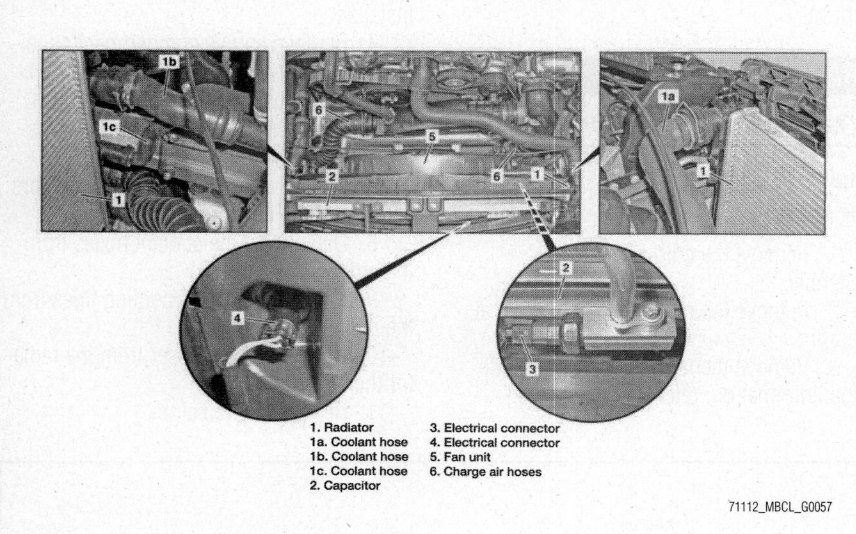

Fig. 12 Radiator mounting components—3.0L & 3.5L engines

10. Unclip the top bracket of the condenser from the mount at the radiator.
11. Unclip the bottom bracket for the air ducts from the mounts on the radiator.
12. Lift out the radiator from the bottom mounts.
13. Installation is the reverse order of removal.

THERMOSTAT

REMOVAL & INSTALLATION

C-Class Models

See Figures 13 and 14.

1. Drain the coolant from the radiator.
2. Remove the left engine air intake duct and front engine cover.
3. Remove the upper coolant hose from the thermostat housing. Discard the O-ring.
4. Remove the accessory drive belt and guide pulley.
5. Disconnect the thermostat electrical connector.
6. Remove the bolts and pull the thermostat housing with the thermostat out of the timing case cover. Discard the gasket and O-ring.
7. Installation is the reverse order of removal, using new gaskets and O-rings. Tighten the thermostat mounting bolt to 18 ft. lbs. (25 Nm).
8. Refill the radiator to the correct level.

Fig. 13 Thermostat mounting location—C-Class models

Fig. 14 Thermostat mounting—C-Class models

CLS-Class Models

1. Drain the coolant from the radiator.
2. Remove the left engine air intake duct and pull the front engine cover upwards and out of the mounts.
3. Loosen the coolant pipe from the thermostat and front cover at the left cylinder head and move aside.
4. Remove the idler pulley.
5. Disconnect the thermostat wiring harness.
6. Remove the mounting bolts and pull out the thermostat housing with the thermostat.

To install:

7. Replace the thermostat gasket.
8. Install the thermostat housing with the thermostat and tighten the mounting bolts to 18 ft. lbs. (25 Nm).
9. The remainder of the installation is the reverse order of removal.
10. Refill the cooling system to the correct level.

WATER PUMP

REMOVAL & INSTALLATION

Engine ID 272

See Figures 15 and 16.

1. Properly drain the cooling system.
2. Remove the accessory drive belt and guide pulley.
3. Disconnect the coolant hose from the water pump.
4. Remove mounting bolts and remove the water pump. Discard the seal.
5. Installation is the reverse order of removal. Use a new seal and tighten the mounting bolts in sequence.

Engine ID 273

1. Drain the coolant from the radiator.
2. Remove the guide pulleys of the accessory drive belt.
3. Pry off the retaining clamp of the electrical connector from the water pump.
4. Remove the water pump mounting bolts.

➡Matchmark the location of the mounting bolts as they are different sizes.

5. Remove the water pump and discard the gasket.
6. Installation is the reverse order of removal. Use a new gasket and tighten the mounting bolts as follows:
   - M7 bolts: 18 ft. lbs. (25 Nm)
   - M8 bolts: 15 ft. lbs. (20 Nm)
7. Refill the cooling system to the correct level.

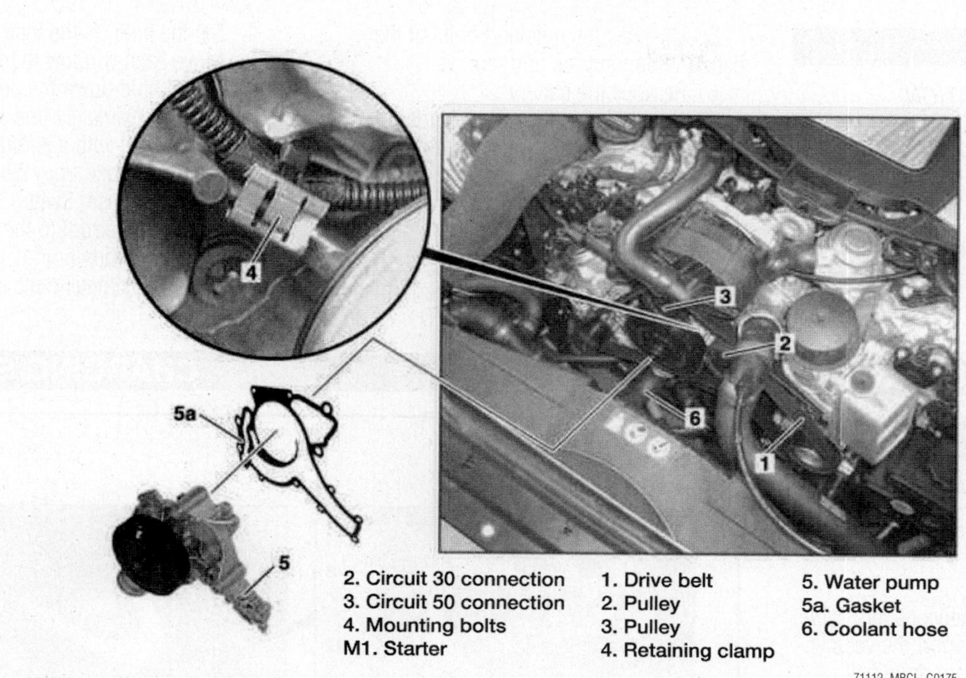

Fig. 15 Water pump mounting

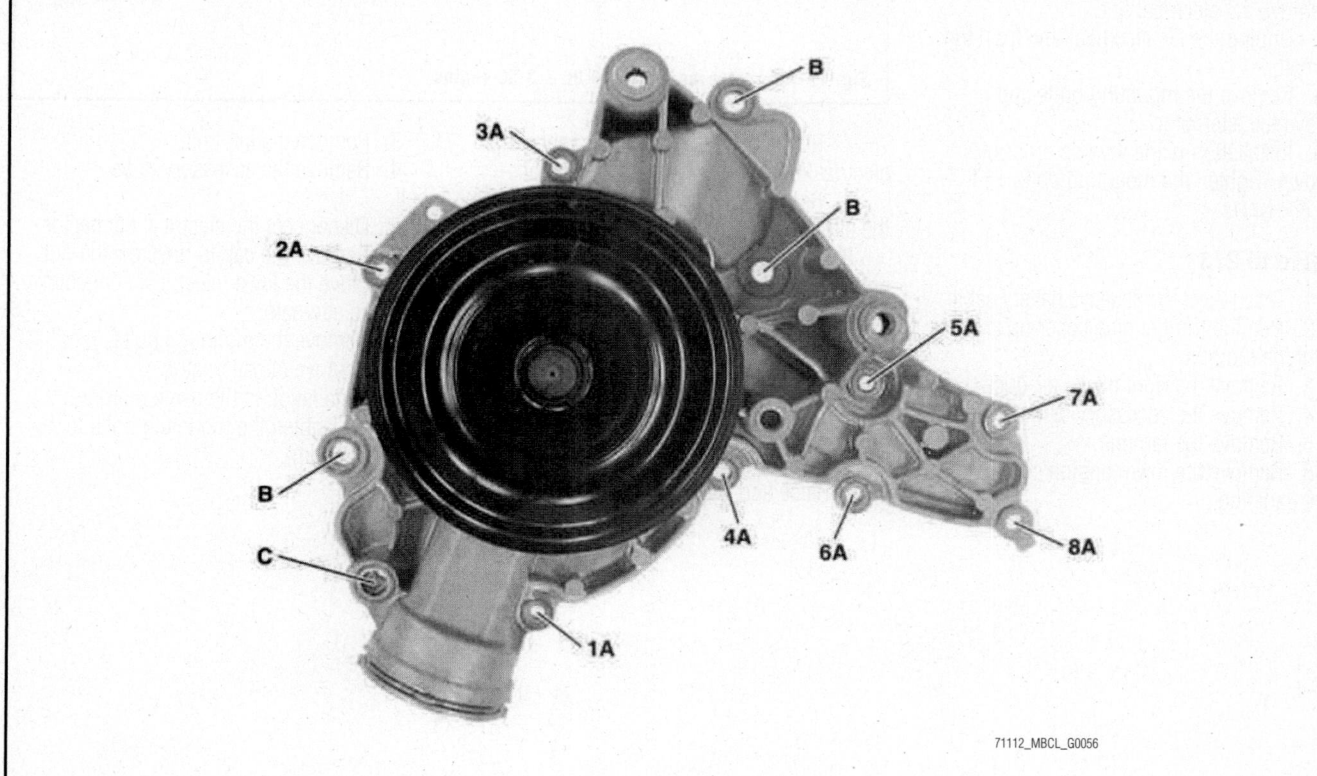

Fig. 16 Water pump mounting bolt tightening sequence—3.0L & 3.5L Engines

ENGINE ELECTRICAL — BATTERY SYSTEM

BATTERY

REMOVAL & INSTALLATION

1. Remove the air duct to access the battery compartment.
2. Disconnect the negative battery cable.
3. Remove the cover and disconnect the positive battery cable.
4. Disconnect the vent hose.
5. Unscrew the nuts and bolts of the battery mounting rail and remove.
6. Remove the battery.
7. Installation is the reverse order of removal. Ensure the positive battery cable is firmly seated before replacing the cover.

BATTERY RECONNECT/RELEARN PROCEDURE

Basic programming must be performed after the battery is reconnected.

1. Set the time on the instrument cluster.
2. Move each window to the top stop position and hold down the power window switch for approximately one second.
3. If equipped with a sliding/tilting glass roof, remove the fuse from the fuse box and then reinsert the fuse. Switch on the ignition and move the slide roof to the front and rear stops then down then hold down the roof switch for approximately one second.

ENGINE ELECTRICAL — CHARGING SYSTEM

ALTERNATOR

REMOVAL & INSTALLATION

Engine ID 272

See Figure 17.

1. Disconnect the negative battery cable.
2. Raise and safely support the vehicle.
3. Remove the accessory drive belt.
4. Remove the lower engine compartment panelings.
5. Remove the bolt for the power steering pressure line from the holder on the alternator.
6. Detach the cap and unscrew the nut to remove the electrical line.
7. Unplug the D+ electrical line from the alternator.
8. Remove the mounting bolts and remove the alternator.
9. Installation is the reverse order of removal. Tighten the mounting bolts 15 ft. lbs. (20 Nm).

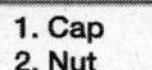

Fig. 17 Alternator mounting—3.0L & 3.5L engine

Engine ID 273

1. Disconnect the negative battery cable.
2. Pull the front engine cover up and out of the mounts.
3. Remove the right intake air duct.
4. Remove the accessory drive belt.
5. Remove the fan unit.
6. Remove the lower engine compartment paneling.
7. Remove the CAP and disconnect the electrical connectors from the alternator.
8. Remove the lower mounting bolts of the alternator.
9. Remove the upper mounting bolts and remove the alternator.
10. Installation is the reverse order of removal. Tighten the mounting bolts to 15 ft. lbs. (20 Nm).

Engine ID 278 & 157

1. Disconnect the negative battery cable.
2. Raise and safely support the vehicle.
3. Remove the fan unit.
4. Remove the accessory drive belt.
5. Disconnect the electrical connector.
6. Remove the cap to unscrew the nut and remove the lower electrical connector from the alternator.
7. Remove the mounting bolts.
8. Remove the alternator.
9. Installation is the reverse order of removal. Tighten the mounting bolts to 15 ft. lbs. (20 Nm).

ENGINE ELECTRICAL — IGNITION SYSTEM

IGNITION COIL

REMOVAL & INSTALLATION

Engine ID 272 & 273

1. Remove the air intake assembly.
2. Disconnect the electrical connectors from the ignition coils.
3. Remove the ignition coil mounting bolts.
4. Pull the ignition coils with the spark plug connectors upwards.
5. Detach the ignition line from the ignition coils.
6. Installation is the reverse order of removal.

Engine ID 157 & 278

1. Remove the upper engine covers.
2. Remove the air intake assembly.
3. Disconnect the ignition coil electrical connectors.
4. Remove the ignition coil mounting bolts.
5. Pull the ignition coils with the spark plug connectors upwards and out.
6. Installation is the reverse order of removal.

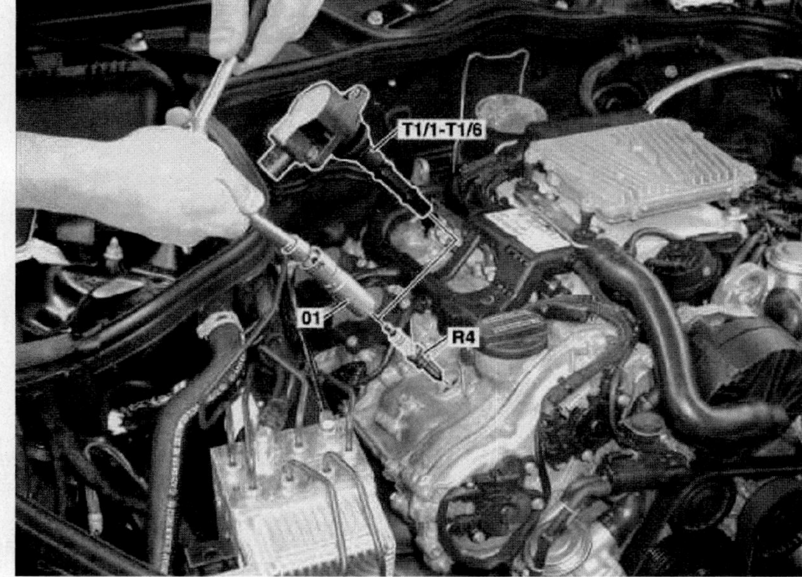

Fig. 18 Removing the spark plugs from the cylinder head—3.0L Engine shown

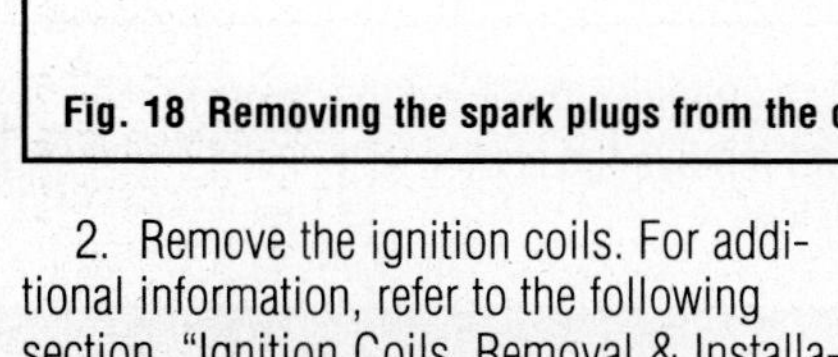

SPARK PLUGS

REMOVAL & INSTALLATION

See Figure 18.

1. Turn the ignition to the **OFF** position.
2. Remove the ignition coils. For additional information, refer to the following section, "Ignition Coils, Removal & Installation."
3. Remove the spark plugs from the cylinder using a suitable spark plug socket.
4. Installation is the reverse order of removal. Tighten the spark plug to 17 ft. lbs. (23 Nm).

ENGINE ELECTRICAL — STARTING SYSTEM

STARTER

REMOVAL & INSTALLATION

Engine ID 272

1. Disconnect the negative battery cable.
2. Remove the lower engine compartment paneling.
3. Detach the protective cap and remove the electrical lines to the electrical connections.
4. Remove the mounting bolts and remove the starter from the bottom of the engine compartment.
5. Installation is the reverse order of removal. Tighten the mounting bolt to 30 ft. lbs. (40 Nm).

Engine ID 156

1. Disconnect the negative battery cable.
2. Raise and safely support the vehicle.
3. Remove the engine compartment paneling.
4. Loosen the engine mounts from below.
5. Attaching a suitable engine lift and raise the engine slightly.
6. Place the right engine mount to one side.
7. Unclip the electrical line and hang to one side.
8. Detach the protective cap and remove the electrical lines to the electrical connections.
9. Remove the mounting bolts and remove the starter from the bottom of the engine compartment.
10. Installation is the reverse order of removal. Tighten the mounting bolt to 30 ft. lbs. (40 Nm).

Engine ID 273

See Figure 19.

1. Disconnect the negative battery cable.
2. Disconnect the terminal 50 electrical connector from the starter.
3. Remove the starter mounting bolts and pull the starter forward.
4. Pull off the protective cap and disconnect the circuit 30 electrical connection.
5. Remove the from the starter from the front at the bottom, between the steering and front axle carrier.
6. Installation is the reverse order of

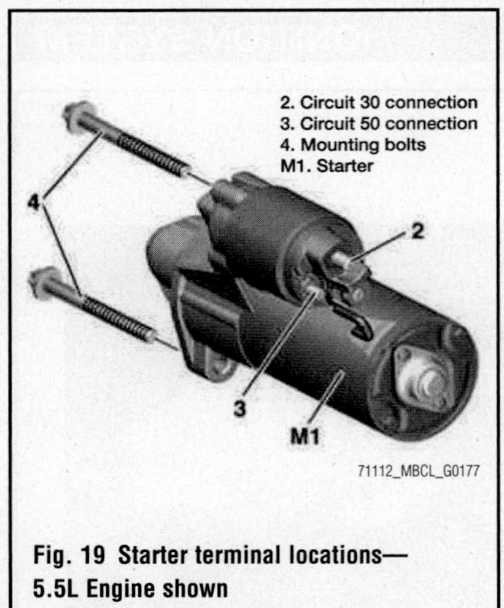

Fig. 19 Starter terminal locations—5.5L Engine shown

removal. Tighten the mounting bolts to 30 ft. lbs. (40 Nm).

Engine ID 157 & 278

See Figure 20.

1. Ensure the wheels are in the straight-ahead position and secure the steering wheel.
2. Disconnect the negative battery cable.
3. Remove the bottom engine compartment paneling.
4. Remove the steering coupling, if equipped with 4MATIC.
5. Remove the starter shield.
6. Disconnect the starter electrical connections.

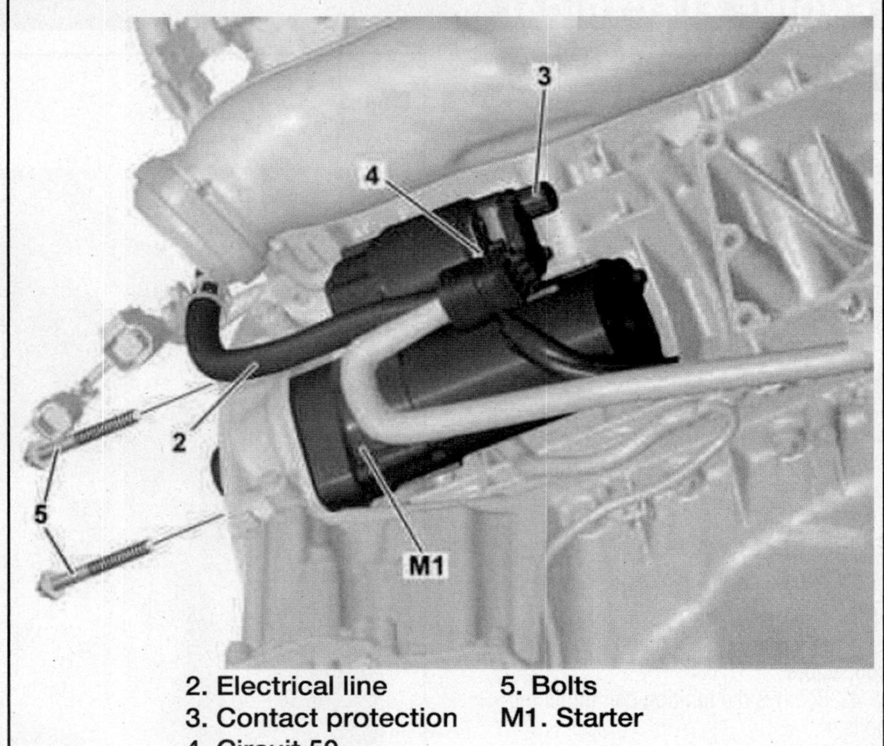

Fig. 20 Starter mounting location—Engine ID 157 & 278

7. Remove the mounting bolts and remove the starter from below.
8. Installation is the reverse order of removal. Tighten the mounting bolts to 30 ft. lbs. (40 Nm).

ENGINE MECHANICAL

➡Disconnecting the negative battery cable may interfere with the functions of the on board computer systems and may require the computer to undergo a relearning process, once the negative battery cable is reconnected.

ACCESSORY DRIVE BELTS

ADJUSTMENT

The accessory drive belt tension is maintained by an automatic belt tensioner. Manual adjustment is not possible.

BELT ROUTINGS

See Figures 21 and 22.

INSPECTION

V-Ribbed Serpentine Belt With Chunks of Rib Missing

See Figure 23.

There should be no chunks missing from the belt ribs. If the belt shows any evidence of this, install a new accessory drive belt.

V- Ribbed Serpentine Belt With Piling

See Figure 24.

➡Piling is an excessive buildup in the V-grooves of the belt.

The condition of the V-ribbed drive belt should be compared against the illustration and appropriate action taken.

1. Small scattered deposits of rubber material. This is not a concern, therefore, installation of a new belt is not required.
2. Longer deposit areas building up to 50 percent of the rib height. This is not considered a concern but it can result in excessive noise. If noise is apparent, install a new belt.
3. Heavy deposits building up along the grooves resulting in a possible noise and belt stability concern. If heavy deposits are apparent, install a new belt.

Visual Inspection

See Figure 25.

⁂ WARNING

Under no circumstances should the accessory drive belt, tensioner or pulleys be lubricated as potential damage to the belt material and tensioner damping mechanism will occur. Do not apply any fluids or belt dressing to the accessory drive belt or pulleys.

The water pump drive belt is on back of engine. It is driven off the rear cam pulley and does not have any adjustments.

Visually inspect the belt for obvious signs of mechanical damage:

- Drive belt cracking/chunking/wear
- Belt/pulley contamination
- Incorrectly routed belt
- Pulley misalignment or excessive pulley runout
- Loose or mislocated hardware

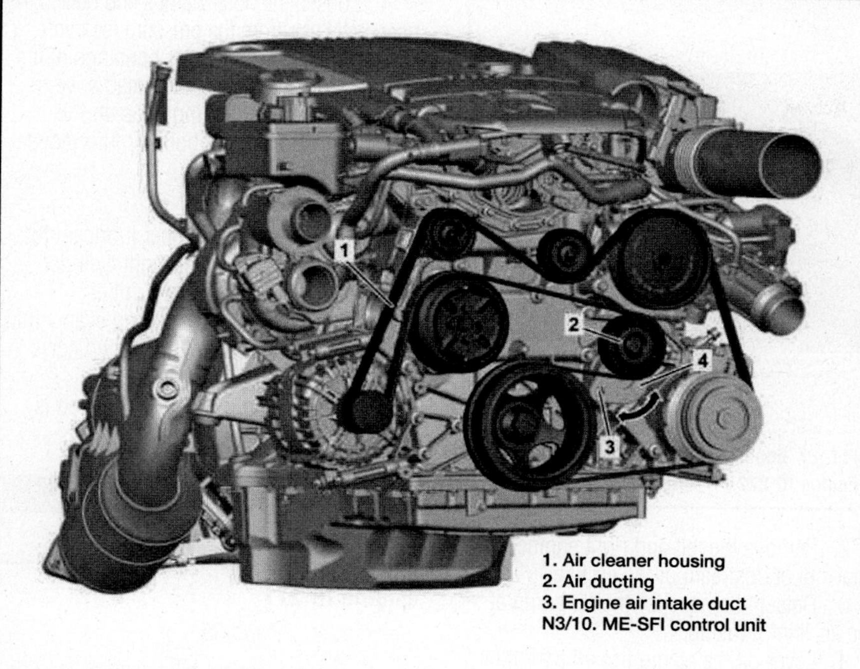

Fig. 21 1.8L Engine drive belt routing

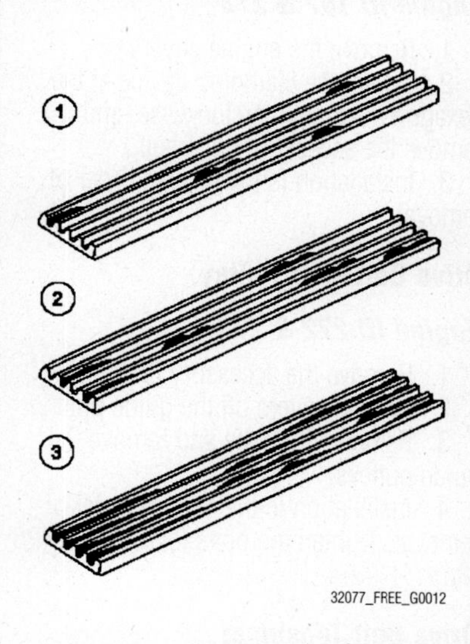

Fig. 24 Compare the condition of the belt with the accompanying text

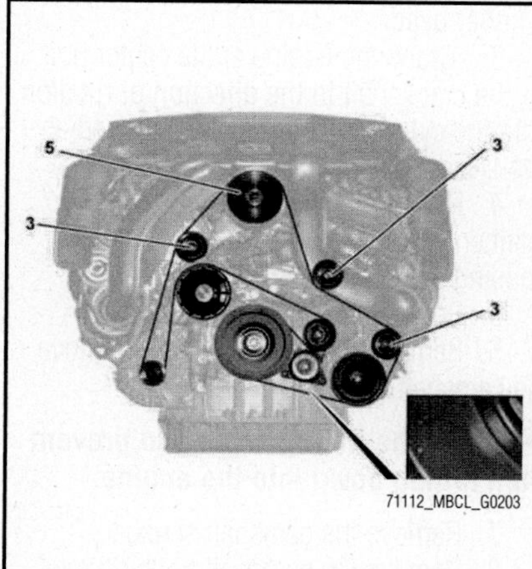

Fig. 22 Engine drive belt routing—4.7L engine shown

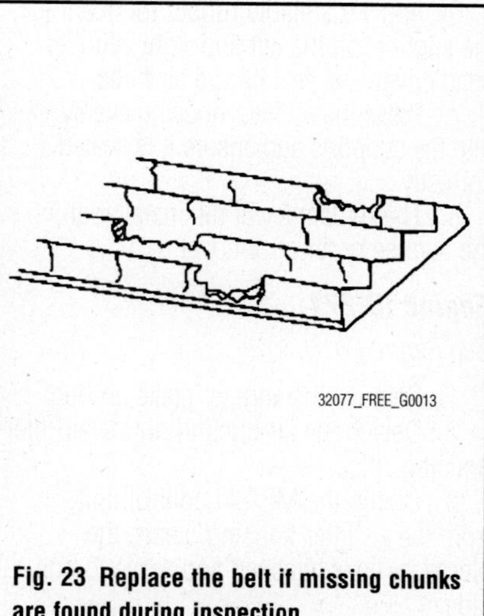

Fig. 23 Replace the belt if missing chunks are found during inspection

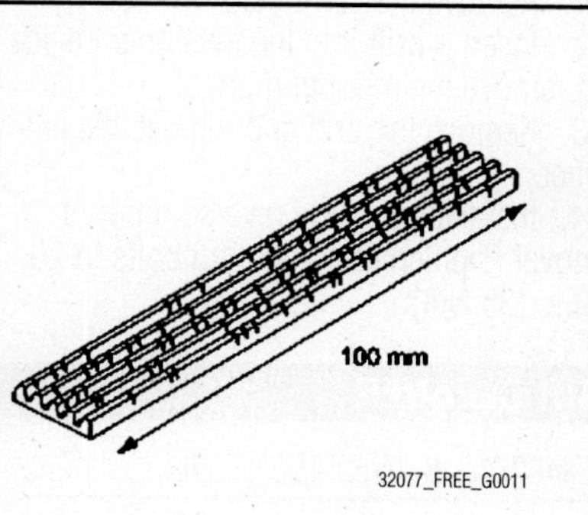

Fig. 25 Up to 15 cracks in a rib over a distance of 4 inches can be considered acceptable. If cracks exceed this standard, install a new belt

• Incorrectly routed power steering tubes (rubbing)

➡Up to 15 cracks in a rib over a distance of 4 inches can be considered acceptable. If damage exceeds the acceptable limit or any chunks are found to be missing from the ribs, a new belt must be installed.

1. Check the belt for cracks. Up to 15 cracks in a rib over a distance of 4 inches can be considered acceptable. If cracks exceed this standard, install a new belt.

REMOVAL & INSTALLATION

Drive Belt

Engine ID 271

1. Remove the engine appearance cover.
2. Loosen the nut under the tensioner pulley and slacken the accessory drive belt.
3. Remove the accessory drive belt.
4. Installation is the reverse order of removal.

Engine ID 272 & 273

1. Using the Torx® recess under the tensioner pulley, reduce the tension on the accessory drive belt.
2. Remove the accessory drive belt.
3. Installation is the reverse order of removal.

Engine ID 156

1. Remove the engine intake air duct and front engine cover.
2. Remove the bottom engine compartment paneling.
3. Loosen the nut under the tensioner pulley and lock the tensioning device with a drift pin.
4. Remove the accessory drive belt.
5. Installation is the reverse order of removal.

Engine ID 157 & 278

1. Remove the engine covers.
2. Swivel the clamping device at the hexagon head counterclockwise, and remove the accessory drive belt.
3. Installation is the reverse order of removal.

Drive Belt Idler Pulley

Engine ID 272 & 273

1. Remove the accessory drive belt.
2. Pry the covers off the guide pulleys.
3. Remove the bolts and remove the guide pulleys.
4. Installation is the reverse order of removal. Tighten the bolts to 18 ft. lbs. (25 Nm).

Drive Belt Tensioner

Engine ID 272 & 273

See Figure 26.

1. Remove the drive belt.
2. Insert a drift into the tensioner device and remove the mounting bolts.
3. Remove the drift and remove the tensioner.
4. Installation is the reverse order of removal. Tighten the mounting bolts to 26 ft. lbs. (35 Nm).

AIR CLEANER

REMOVAL & INSTALLATION

Air Cleaner Assembly

Engine ID 272 & 273

See Figure 27.

1. Pull off the front engine cover.

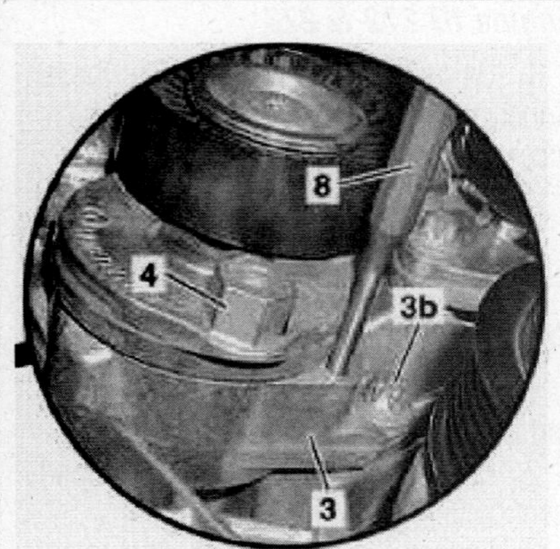

71112_MBCL_G0064

Fig. 26 Insert a drift (8) in the tensioner to remove the mounting bolts (3b)—3.0L engine

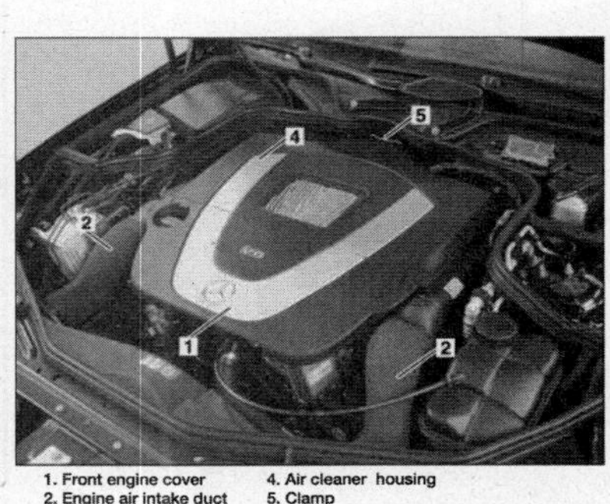

1. Front engine cover
2. Engine air intake duct
4. Air cleaner housing
5. Clamp

71112_MBCL_G0070

Fig. 27 Engine air cleaner housing—Engine ID 272

2. Remove the left and right engine air intake duct upstream of the air filter.
3. Detach the hose for the air pump at the air filter housing.
4. Lever off the clamp from the air filter housing, if necessary.
5. Remove the air filter housing upwards from the mounts.

To install:

6. Apply a suitable rubber lubricant to the support on the left and right cylinder head cover and seal on the air filter.
7. Press the air filter housing evenly into the supports and ensure it is seated correctly.
8. The remainder of the installation is the reverse order of removal.

Engine ID 271

See Figure 28.

1. Remove the engine intake air duct.
2. Detach the air ducting on the air filter housing.
3. Unclip the ME-SFI control unit from the air filter housing. Leave the electrical lines attached and move to one side.
4. Unclip the electrical line from the support on the air filter housing.
5. Unlock the electrical line to the air filter housing.
6. Remove the air filter housing upwards out of the supports.
7. Installation is the reverse order of removal.

Engine ID 156

1. Remove the front engine cover.
2. Remove the covers.
3. Release and disconnect electrical connectors at left and right hot film mass air flow sensors.
4. Loosen the hose clamps and detach the pneumatic line from the pressure reservoir.
5. Loosen both air filter housings of the intake manifold and cylinder head covers.
6. Unlock the retaining clips on the intake port and remove both air filter housings with the intake port.

To install:

7. Apply a suitable rubber lubricant to the support on the left and right cylinder head cover and seal on the air filter.
8. Press the air filter housing evenly into the supports and ensure it is seated correctly.
9. The remainder of the installation is the reverse order of removal.

CAMSHAFT & BEARINGS

REMOVAL & INSTALLATION

Engine ID 271

See Figures 29 and 30.

1. Remove the cylinder head cover. For additional information, refer to the following section, "Cylinder Head Cover, Removal & Installation."
2. Remove the front cover from the cylinder head.
3. Crank the engine at the center bolt for the crankshaft in the direction of rotation until the cylinder 1 piston is positioned at Top Dead Center (TDC).
4. Mount the special tool camshaft retainer over the cutouts in the camshaft housing top section.
5. Remove the chain tensioner.
6. Remove the center bolt and remove the camshaft adjusters.

➡Secure the timing chain and prevent from falling down into the engine.

7. Remove the camshaft sensor.
8. Remove the camshaft housing top section.
9. Take out the intake camshaft.
10. Remove the exhaust camshaft.
11. Installation is the reverse order of removal.

Engine ID 272

1. Remove the air filter housing.
2. Remove the timing chain tensioner. For additional information, refer to the following section, "Timing Chain Cover, Chain, Tensioner, & Sprockets, Removal & Installation."
3. Remove the camshaft adjuster as follows:
   a. Remove the cap.
   b. Detach the center valve.

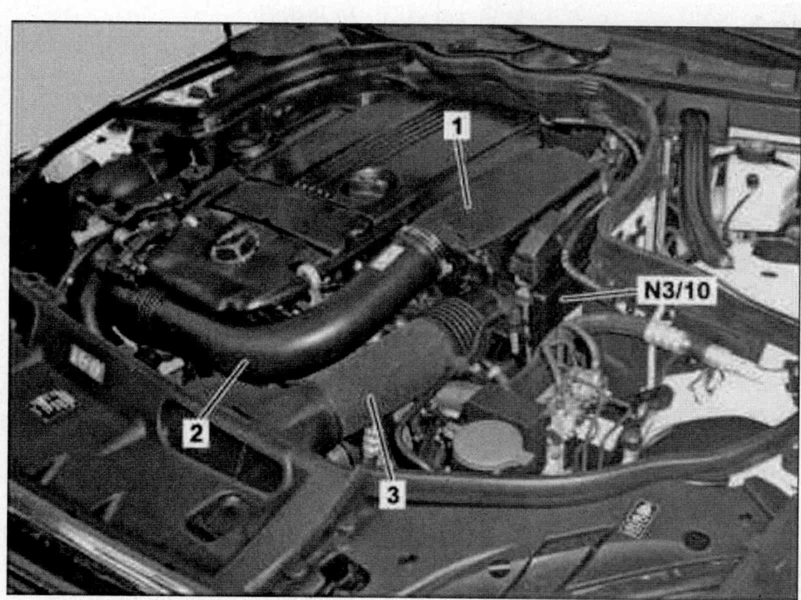

Fig. 28 Engine air cleaner housing—Engine ID 271

Fig. 29 Camshaft locations—Engine ID 272

c. Remove the cylinder head cover. For additional information, refer to the following section, "Cylinder Head Cover, Removal & Installation."

d. Rotate the engine in the direction of rotation so that it is at 40° After Top Dead Center of cylinder 1.

e. Matchmark the timing chain to the camshaft adjuster.

f. Remove the tensioning rail.

g. Remove the center valve and pulse wheel.

4. Lift the timing chain and pull off the camshaft adjuster from the intake camshaft.
5. Remove the auxiliary bearing cap.
6. Remove the intake camshaft.
7. Installation is the reverse order of removal.

Engine ID 273

1. Remove the air filter housing.
2. Remove the engine front cover.
3. Detach the crankcase ventilation hose at the centrifuge cover.
4. Remove the hold down bolts and remove the centrifuge cover.
5. Remove the mounting bolt and remove the centrifuge.
6. Rotate the engine in the direction of rotation so that it is at 40° After Top Dead Center (TDC) of cylinder 1.
7. Lock the gear backlash compensation for the camshaft adjusters at the exhaust adjusters.
8. Loosen the center valves.
9. Remove the cylinder head cover. For additional information, refer to the following section, "Cylinder Head Cover, Removal & Installation."
10. Remove the center valves on the exhaust camshafts and take out the pulse wheels.
11. Counterhold the exhaust camshafts at the rear using a suitable tool and detach the camshaft adjuster to the front from the exhaust camshafts.
12. Remove the auxiliary bearing cap on the exhaust camshafts and take out the exhaust camshafts.
13. With the engine positioned at 40° after TD, mark the timing chain relative to the camshaft adjust of the intake camshafts using color codes.
14. Remove the chain tensioner.
15. Remove the tensioning rail bolt.
16. Pull the tensioning rail upward and out of engine.
17. Remove the center valves on the intake camshafts and remove the pulse wheels.

Fig. 30 Removing the camshaft adjusters—1.8L Engines

18. Pull out the camshaft adjuster from the intake camshafts towards the front.

19. Remove the auxiliary bearing cap on the intake camshafts and take out the intake camshafts.

20. Installation is the reverse order of removal. Tighten the bolt for the center valves to 107 ft. lbs. (145 Nm) and auxiliary bearing cap to 71 inch lbs. (8 Nm).

Engine ID 156

See Figures 31 and 32.

1. Remove the air filter housing.
2. Remove the spark plugs.
3. Rotate the engine in the direction of rotation so that it is at 40° after Top Dead Center of cylinder 1.
4. Remove the cylinder head covers. For additional information, refer to the following section, "Cylinder Head Cover, Removal & Installation."
5. Remove the camshaft adjusters as follows:
    a. Loosen the oil dipstick guide tubes on the cylinder head and turn to the side, right side only.
    b. Remove the cylinder head covers. For additional information, refer to the following section, "Cylinder Head Cover, Removal & Installation."
    c. Disconnect the electrical connectors on the left camshaft intake solenoid and left exhaust solenoid.
    d. Remove the bolt from the ground strap.
    e. Insert safety screws in the bores on the rear of the camshaft adjusters in order to lock the gear backlash adjustment.
    f. Remove the bolts and remove the camshaft adjuster.
6. Remove the bolts for the camshaft bearing caps.

➡Matchmark the bearing caps if they have no identification markings.

7. Remove the camshafts.

➡Matchmark the intake and exhaust side camshafts if they have no identification markings.

To install:

8. Oil the bearing surfaces and install the camshafts.
9. Install the camshaft bearing caps and tighten in sequence to 89 inch lbs. (10 Nm).
10. Turn the camshafts into the basic position.
11. The remainder of the installation is the reverse order of removal.

Engine ID 157 & 278

See Figure 33.

1. Rotate the engine in the direction of rotation so that it is at 40° after Top Dead Center of cylinder 1.
2. Remove the cylinder head cover.
3. Mount the hold-down device on the camshafts.
4. Remove the oil filter housing.
5. Remove the mounting bolts from the chain tensioner.
6. Remove the chain tensioner.
7. Hold the camshaft and loosen the central valve and remove.
8. Remove the camshaft adjuster from the camshaft.
9. Remove the auxiliary bearing cap on the camshaft.
10. Remove the camshafts.
11. Installation is the reverse order of removal. Tighten the camshaft bearing cap to 71 inch lbs. (8 Nm) plus 90°.

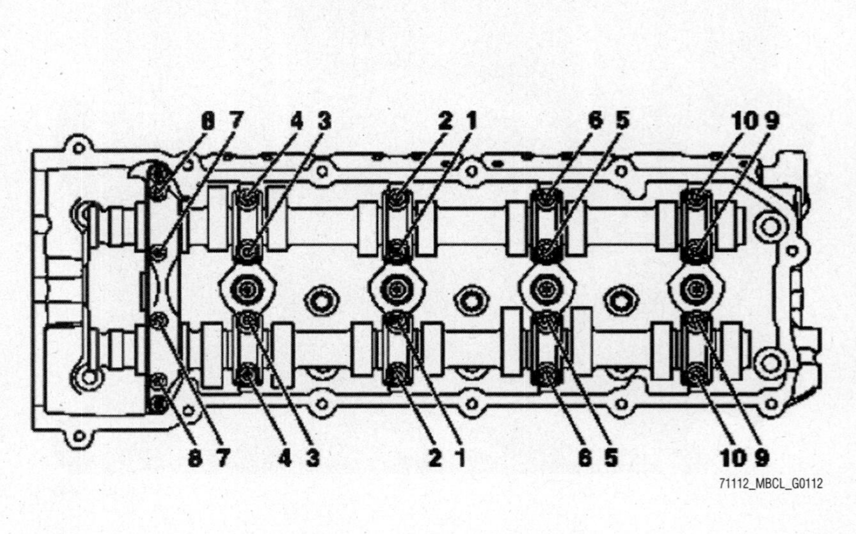

Fig. 31 Left side camshaft bearing cap tightening sequence—6.2L Engine

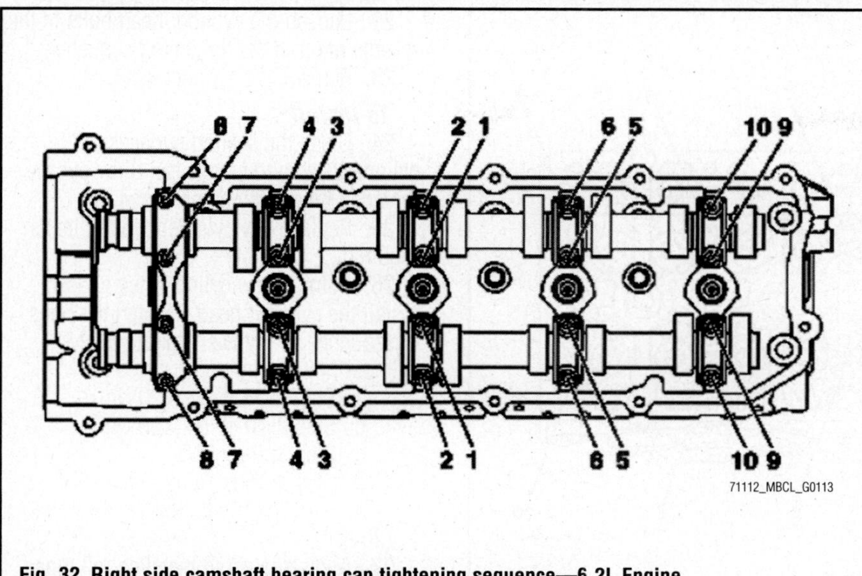

Fig. 32 Right side camshaft bearing cap tightening sequence—6.2L Engine

5. Detach boost pressure control hose (5) on pressure transducer
6. Remove charge air manifold (9) on the turbocharger
7. Remove shield (4) and support brace from the turbocharger
8. Remove the power steering expansion reservoir with the lines connected move to one side.
9. Remove the combination valve.
10. Remove the bracket on the cylinder head.

Remove the oil return line of the turbocharger.

11. Remove the coolant feed pipe for the turbocharger.
12. Remove the crankcase ventilation system pipe and coolant pipe.
13. Remove the cylinder head cover.
14. Remove the oil dipstick guide tube.
15. Remove the vacuum pump.

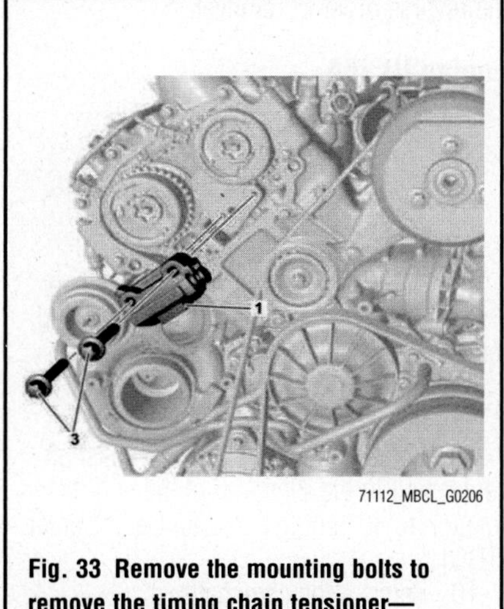

Fig. 33 Remove the mounting bolts to remove the timing chain tensioner—Engine ID 157 & 278

CRANKSHAFT FRONT SEAL

REMOVAL & INSTALLATION

See Figure 34.

1. Remove the crankshaft damper. For additional information, refer to the following section, "Crankshaft Damper, Removal & Installation".
2. Using a screwdriver, carefully pry out the front seal.

To install:

3. Using a suitable seal install sleeve, install the front crankshaft seal.
4. The reminder of the installation is the reverse order of removal.
5. Refill the engine oil to the correct level.

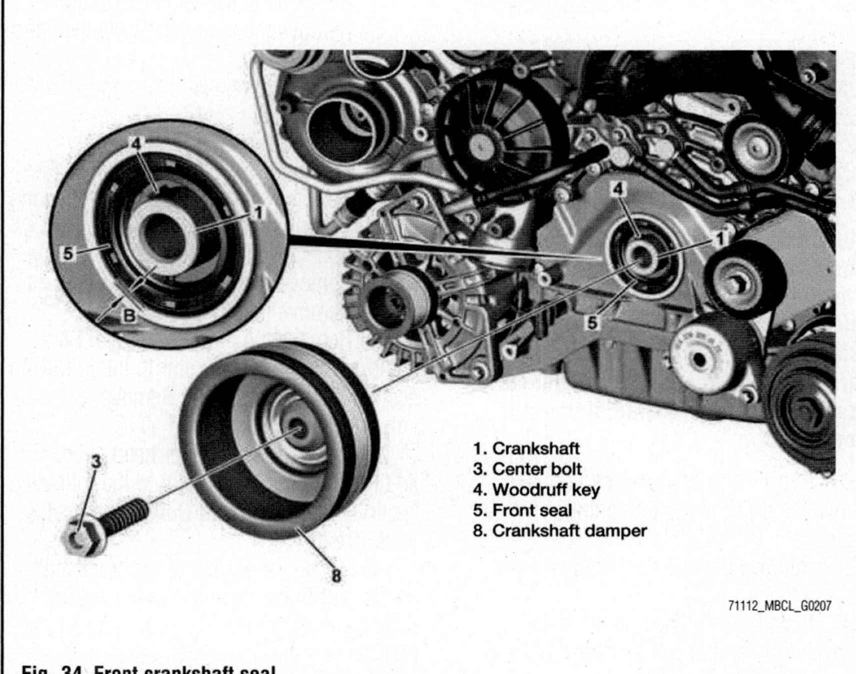

Fig. 34 Front crankshaft seal

CYLINDER HEAD

REMOVAL & INSTALLATION

Engine ID 271

See Figure 35.

1. Disconnect the negative battery cable.
2. Properly drain the cooling system.
3. Remove the vacuum hose from radiator shutters adjuster.
4. Remove air ducting (2) on turbocharger
16. Remove the intake manifold.
17. Disconnect the connector for electrical line on rail pressure sensor
18. Disconnect the connector for electrical line for fuel injectors to rail
19. Remove the high-pressure pump.
20. Remove the coolant connection to cylinder head at the rear
21. Remove the front cover at cylinder head.
22. Remove the chain tensioner.

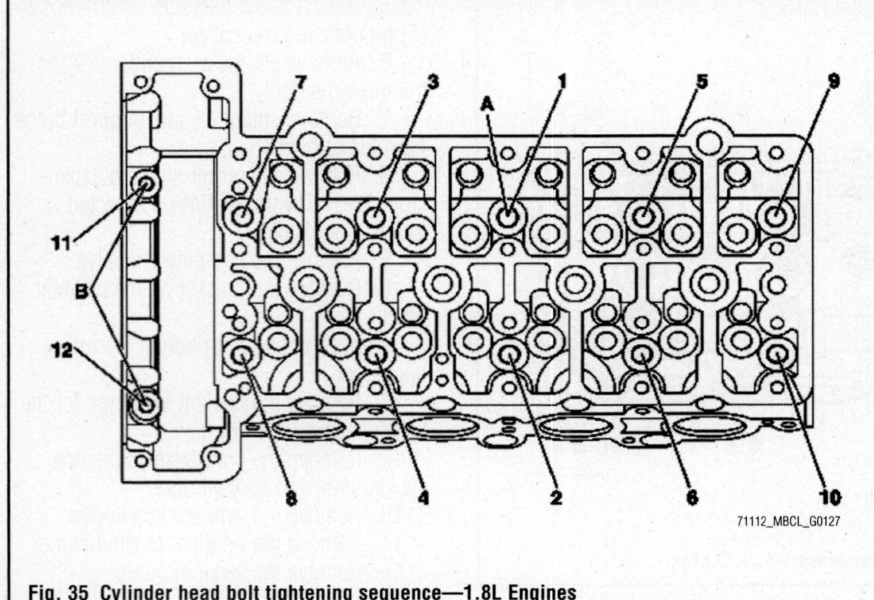

Fig. 35 Cylinder head bolt tightening sequence—1.8L Engines

23. Pull the guide rail pins out of cylinder head.
24. Remove the camshaft adjuster for the exhaust camshafts.
25. Remove the tensioning rail.
26. Remove the camshaft housing.
27. Remove the roller type cam following with the compensation elements.

➡When removing more than one compensation elements, ensure that cam followers and compensation elements which were not replaced are re-installed at their previous location. Mark cam follower relative to the corresponding compensation element if necessary.

28. Loosen the cylinder head bolts in the reverse order of the tightening sequence.
29. Remove the cylinder head and gasket.
30. Installation is the reverse order of removal. Tighten the cylinder head bolts in sequence as follows:
    - Step 1: 33 ft. lbs. (45 Nm)
    - Step 2: Plus 90°
    - Step 3: Plus an additional 90°

Engine ID 272 & 273

See Figure 36.

1. Disconnect the negative battery cable.
2. Properly drain the cooling system.
3. Remove the exhaust line and disconnect the catalytic converter from the exhaust manifold.
4. Remove the air filter housing.
5. Remove the ME-SFI control unit.
6. Remove the accessory drive belt and drive belt tensioner.
7. Remove the power steering expansion reservoir.
8. Remove the oil filter housing.
9. Remove the engine front cover. For additional information, refer to the following section, "Engine Front Cover, Removal & Installation."
10. Remove the ignition oils.
11. Remove the oil separator.
12. Remove the intake manifold. For additional information, refer to the following section, "Intake Manifold, Removal & Installation."
13. Remove the cylinder head cover. For additional information, refer to the following section, "Cylinder Head Cover, Removal & Installation."
14. Rotate the engine at the crankshaft center bolt in the direction of the engine rotation to 40° angle after Top Dead Center (TDC).
15. Remove the timing chain tensioner.
16. Remove the camshaft adjusters from the intake and exhaust camshafts. For additional information, refer to the following section, "Camshafts, Removal & Installation".
17. Remove the air shutoff valve.
18. Remove the intermediate flange of the air shutoff valve.
19. Detach the coolant hose from the heater valve.
20. Disconnect the coolant temperature sensor electrical connector.
21. Remove the slide rail pins.
22. Loosen the cylinder head bolts in the reverse order of the tightening sequence.
23. Remove the cylinder head.

To install:

24. Clean the sealing surfaces of the cylinder head and crankcase. Blow out the threaded holes with compressed air.
25. Replace any cylinder head bolts as required.
26. Using a new cylinder head gasket, install the cylinder head. Tighten the bolts in sequence as follows: Tighten the M11 cylinder bolts as follows:
    a. Step 1: 15 ft. lbs. (20 Nm)
    b. Step 2: 37 ft. lbs. (50 Nm)
    c. Step 3: Plus 90°
    d. Step 4: Plus an additional 90°
    e. Tighten the M8 bolts to 15 ft. lbs. (20 Nm).
27. Apply sealant to the slide rail pins, then install the pins.
28. The remainder of the installation is the reverse order of removal.

Engine ID 156

1. Disconnect the negative battery cable.
2. Properly drain the cooling system.
3. Remove the cooling fan.
4. Remove the alternator.
5. Remove the timing chain tensioner.
6. Remove the catalytic converter from the exhaust manifold.
7. Remove the intake manifold.
8. Remove the spark plugs.
9. Rotate the engine at the crankshaft center bolt in the direction of the engine rotation to 40° angle after Top Dead Center (TDC).
10. Remove the camshafts.
11. Remove air shutoff valve and air line on the cylinder head.

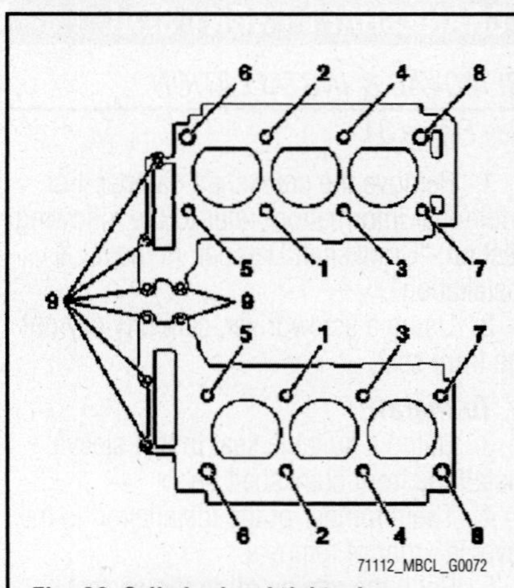

Fig. 36 Cylinder head tightening sequence—Engine ID 272 & 273

12. Remove oil filter housing, left cylinder head only.
13. Remove the guide pulley, right cylinder head only.
14. Pull out guide rail pins.
15. Loosen cylinder head bolts in stages in reverse order of tightening procedure and remove them.
16. Remove cylinder head from crankcase.

To install:

17. Clean the sealing surfaces of the cylinder head and crankcase. Blow out the threaded holes with compressed air.
18. Replace any cylinder head bolts as required.
19. Using a new cylinder head gasket, install the cylinder head. Tighten the bolts in sequence as follows: Tighten the M11 cylinder bolts as follows:
    a. Step 1: 89 inch lbs. (10 Nm)
    b. Step 2: 37 ft. lbs. (50 Nm)
    c. Step 3: Plus 90°
    d. Step 4: Plus an additional 90°
    e. Step 5: An additional 90°
    f. Tighten the M8 bolts to 15 ft. lbs. (20 Nm).

Engine ID 157 & 278

See Figure 37.

1. Remove the engine assembly with the front axle carrier.
2. Remove the cylinder head cover. For additional information, refer to the following section, "Cylinder Head Covers, Removal & Installation."
3. Remove the intake manifold. For additional information, refer to the following section, "Intake Manifold, Removal & Installation."
4. Remove the chain tensioner.
5. Remove the bearing cap for the camshafts.
6. Lift the camshafts at the rear and remove the timing chain from the camshaft adjusters.
7. Remove the camshafts.
8. Pull the sliding rail bolts out of the cylinder head.
9. Disconnect the turbocharger with the exhaust manifold from the cylinder head.
10. Loosen the cylinder head bolts in the reverse order of the tightening sequence in several stages.
11. Remove the cylinder head and discard the gasket.

To install:

12. Install the cylinder using a new gasket.

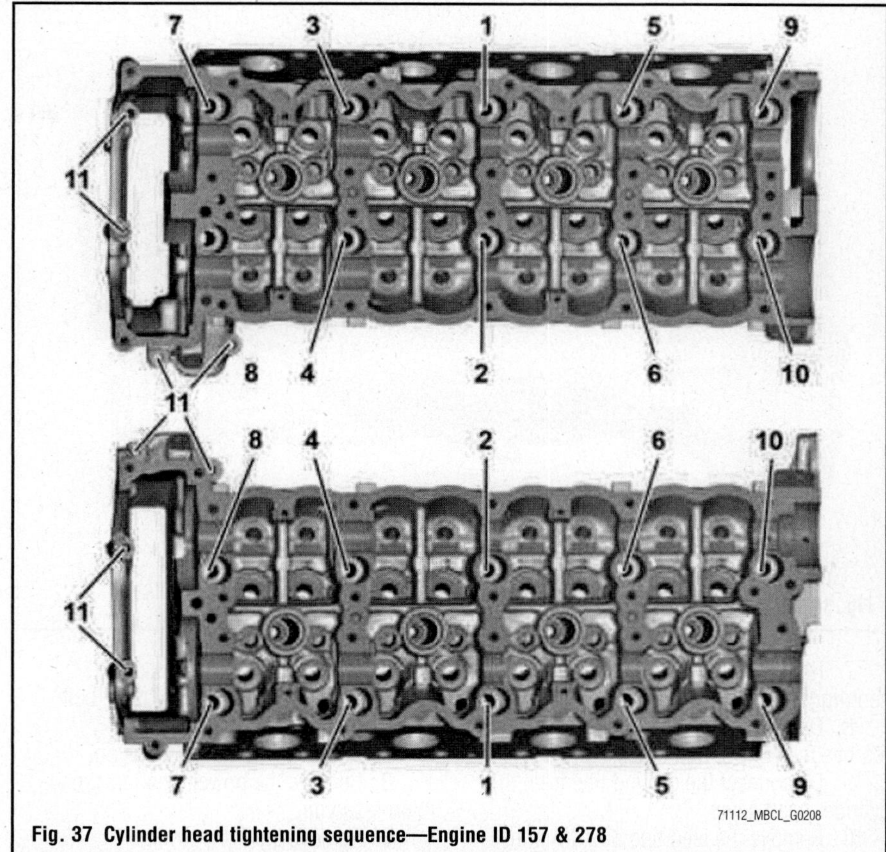

Fig. 37 Cylinder head tightening sequence—Engine ID 157 & 278

13. Using new bolts, tighten the cylinder head bolts in sequence as follows:
    a. Bolts 1–10 to 15 ft. lbs. (20 Nm)
    b. Bolts 1–10 to 30 ft. lbs. (40 Nm)
    c. Bolts 1–10 plus 90°
    d. Bolts 1–10 plus an additional 90°
    e. Bolts 1–10 plus an additional 90°
    f. Bolt 11 to 97 inch lbs. (11 Nm)
14. The remainder of the installation is the reverse order of removal. Apply sealant to the slide rail pins before inserting them.

CYLINDER HEAD COVERS

REMOVAL & INSTALLATION

Engine ID 271

1. Remove the engine appearance cover.
2. Remove the ignition coils. For additional information, refer to the following section, "Ignition coils, Removal & Installation."
3. Remove the secondary air system pipework from the combination valve and cylinder, the remove the bracket.
4. Detach the engine wiring harness.
5. Remove the crankcase ventilation system pipe from the cylinder head and cylinder head cover.
6. Disconnect the vacuum line from the air pump switchover valve.
7. Unhook the air pump switchover valve from the bracket.
8. Remove the oil dipstick guide tube from the cylinder head cover.
9. Remove the mounting bolts and take off the cylinder head cover.

To install:

10. Replace the cylinder head cover gaskets.
11. Install the cylinder head cover and tighten the mounting bolts in sequence to 71 inch lbs. (8 Nm).
12. The remainder of the installation is the reverse order of removal.

Engine ID 272 & 273

Right Side

See Figure 38.

1. Turn the ignition key to the **OFF** position.
2. Remove the air filter housing.
3. Remove the switchover valve by removing the bracket from the front engine cover.
4. Remove the air shutoff valve.
5. Remove the front cover.
6. Remove the ignition coils on the right cylinder head.

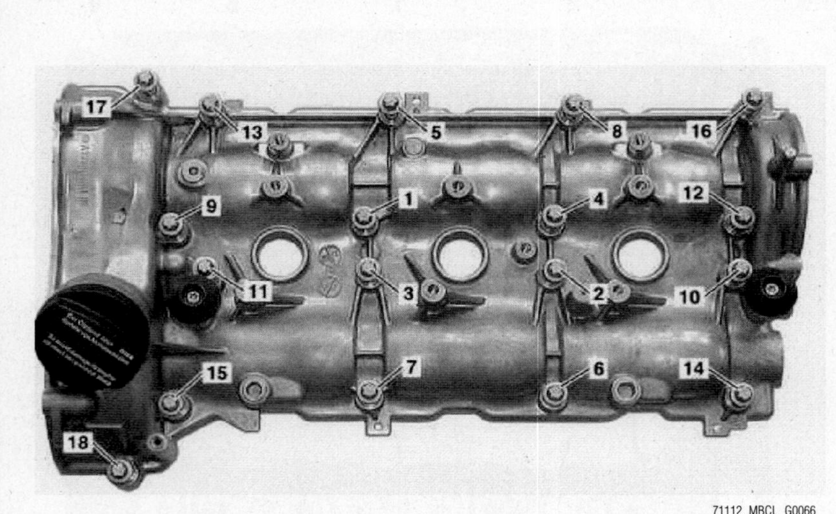

Fig. 38 Right cylinder head cover torque sequence—Engine ID 272

7. Remove the cover on the centrifuge.
8. Detach the ME-SFI control unit and remove the control unit bracket.
9. Disconnect the ground line from the cylinder head cover.
10. Remove the feed line duct from the intake manifold, cylinder head cover and right engine suspension lug and place aside.
11. Loosen the bolts for the cylinder head cover in the reverse order of the tightening sequence.
12. Carefully pry off the cylinder head cover from the cylinder head.

WARNING

Ensure the sealing surfaces are not damaged with the pry tool.

13. Installation is the reverse order of removal.
14. Clean the sealing surfaces of the cylinder head and cylinder head cover.
15. Apply new sealant to the sealing surfaces of the cylinder head cover.
16. Tighten the mounting bolts in sequence to 106 inch lbs. (12 Nm) plus 90°.

Left Side

See Figure 39.

1. Turn the ignition key to the **OFF** position.
2. Remove the bottom engine compartment paneling.
3. Properly drain the cooling system.
4. Remove the air filter housing.
5. Remove the accessory drive belt.
6. Remove the thermostat.
7. Remove the oil filter housing.
8. Remove the power steering expansion reservoir.
9. Remove the front cover.
10. Detach the purge line at the separation point, unclip it from the brackets on the oil separator and feed line duct and place it aside.
11. Properly relieve the fuel system pressure.
12. Detach the fuel line at the fuel distributor.
13. Remove the ignition coils on the left cylinder head.
14. Disconnect the ground line from the cylinder head cover.
15. Remove the rear engine suspension lug.
16. Remove the feed line duct from the cylinder head cover.
17. Remove the heat shield.
18. Loosen the cylinder head mounting bolts in the reverse order of the tightening procedure and remove.
19. Carefully pry off the cylinder head cover from the cylinder head.

WARNING

Ensure the sealing surfaces are not damaged with the pry tool.

20. Installation is the reverse order of removal.
21. Clean the sealing surfaces of the cylinder head and cylinder head cover.
22. Apply new sealant to the sealing surfaces of the cylinder head cover.
23. Tighten the mounting bolts in sequence to 106 inch lbs. (12 Nm) plus 90°.

Engine ID 156

1. Remove the air filter housing assembly.
2. Remove the foam cover from the fuel distributor.
3. Remove the ignition coils.
4. Disconnect the purge line from the purge valve and move the purge line to one side, left cylinder head cover only.

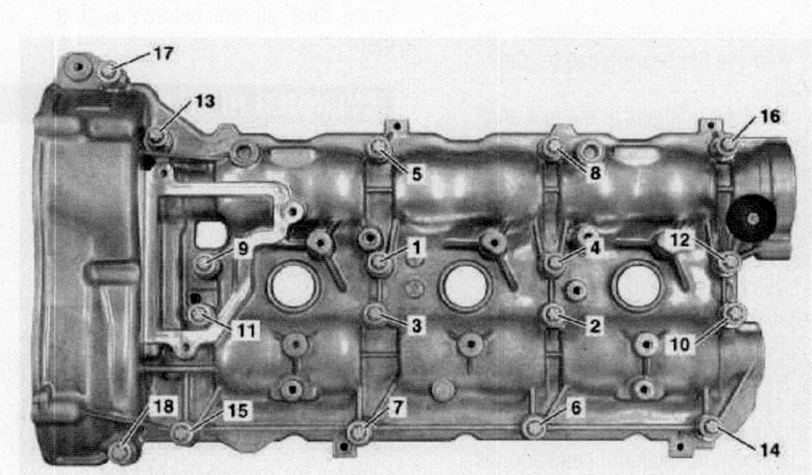

Fig. 39 Left cylinder head cover torque sequence—Engine ID 272

5. Remove the wiring harness bracket and any retaining clamps.
6. Remove the cylinder head cover.

⁂ WARNING

Do not insert any tools between to pry off the cylinder head cover to avoid damage to the cylinder head cover.

7. Installation is the reverse order of removal.

Engine ID 157 & 278

See Figures 40 and 41.

1. Remove the fuel rail.
2. Remove the ignition coils.
3. Disconnect the engine wiring harness on the cylinder head cover.
4. Disconnect the oil lines for the turbocharger on the cylinder head cover and move to one side.
5. Remove the partial load crankcase ventilation on the cylinder head cover.
6. Remove the bracket and lifting eye on the cylinder head cover.
7. Remove the left charge air ducts.
8. Remove the oil filter housing, Engine ID 157 only.
9. Disconnect the electrical connections and lines on the cylinder head front cover.
10. Remove the front cover mounting bolts and discard.
11. Remove the cylinder head front cover.
12. Loosen the cylinder head cover bolts in the reverse order of the tightening sequence and discard.
13. Carefully pry the cylinder head cover and remove.

To install:

14. Apply sealant to the clean sealing surfaces of cylinder head cover and install.
15. Tighten the mounting bolts in sequence as follows:
    - Step 1: 106 inch lbs. (12 Nm)
    - Step 2: Plus 90°

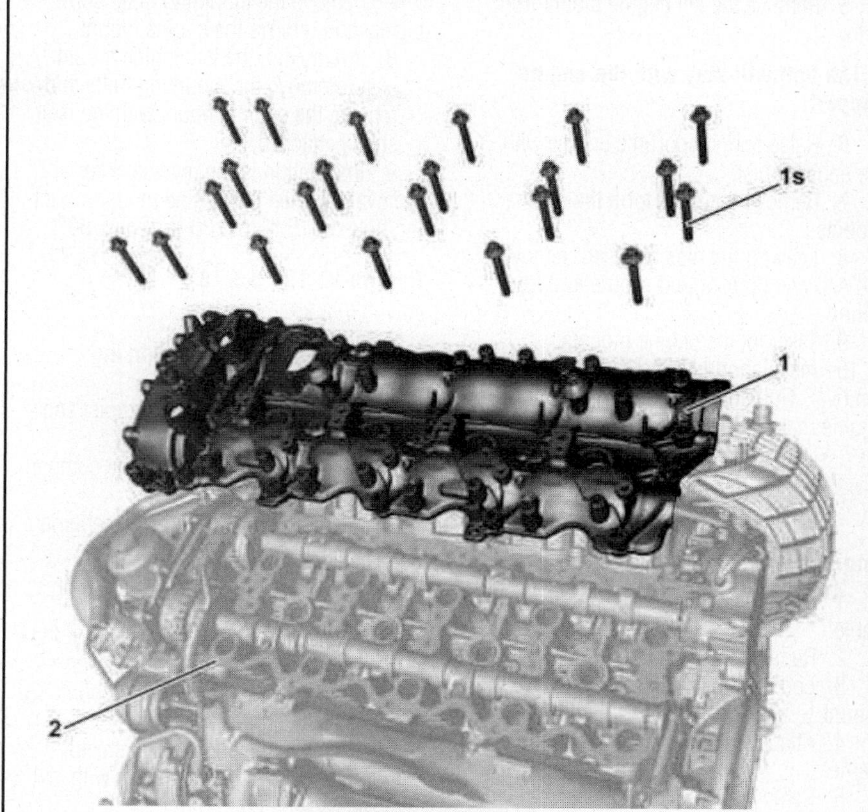

Fig. 40 Cylinder head cover mounting—Engine ID 157 & 278

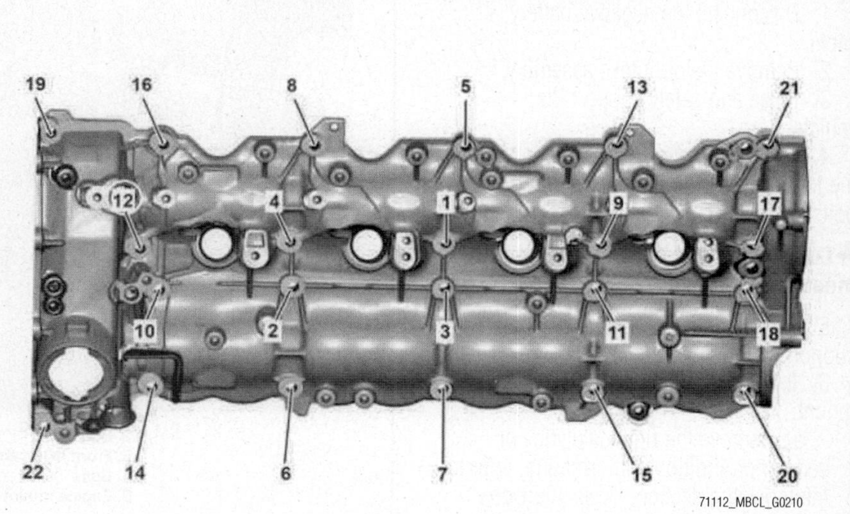

Fig. 41 Cylinder head cover bolt tightening sequence—Engine ID 157 & 278

ENGINE MOUNTS

REMOVAL & INSTALLATION

Engine ID 271

1. Remove the engine air duct from the cold air duct.
2. Remove the bolt on the right engine mount from above.
3. Install a suitable engine hoist.
4. Remove the engine compartment paneling.

5. Remove the left engine mount from below.

➡**The bolt will stay with the engine support.**

6. Raise and support the engine with the engine hoist.
7. Remove the bolts form the engine mounts.
8. Leaving the pips attached, remove the A/C compressor and secure to it from falling.
9. Take out the engine mounts.
10. Installation is the reverse order of removal. Tighten the mounting bolts for the engine mounts as follows:
    - M10 bolts: 37 ft. lbs. (50 Nm)
    - M12 bolts: 63 ft. lbs. (85 Nm) plus 90°

Engine ID 273

1. Disconnect the negative battery cable.
2. Remove the air filter housing.
3. Loosen the bolts on the engine mount.
4. Attach a suitable engine support frame.
5. Remove the bottom engine compartment paneling.
6. Remove the lower mounting bolt.
7. Raise the engine slightly.
8. Remove the upper mounting bolts and heat shields.
9. Remove the engine mount.
10. Installation is the reverse order of removal. Tighten the mounting bolts to 26 ft. lbs. (35 Nm).

Engine ID 156

1. Disconnect the negative battery cable.
2. Remove the air intake assembly.
3. Raise and safely support the vehicle.
4. Loosen the engine mountings from the front axle carrier by unscrewing the bolts.

➡**Loosen the bolt on the right engine mount from above.**

5. Install a suitable engine hoist and support the engine assembly.
6. If removing the right engine mount:
    a. Remove the right catalytic converter. For additional information, refer to the following section, "Catalytic Converter, Removal & Installation."
    b. Disconnect the electrical circuit at the starter.
7. Remove the mounting bolts completely and remove the engine mount.
8. If removing the left engine mount:
    a. Remove the mounting bolts and remove the engine mount with the heat shield attached.
9. Installation is the reverse order of removal. Tighten the engine mount mounting bolts to 15 ft. lbs (20 Nm) plus 90°.

Engine ID 157 & 278

See Figure 42.

1. Raise and safely support the vehicle.
2. Install a suitable engine hoist and raise the engine slightly.
3. Remove the bottom engine compartment paneling.
4. Remove center bolt for the engine mounts on the engine support.
5. Remove the front axle carrier, if equipped with 4MATIC.
6. Remove the mounting bolts for the engine mount on the front axle carrier.
7. If removing the left hand mount, remove the steering coupling.
8. Remove the engine heat shield.
9. Raise the engine to assist with removal.
10. Remove the engine mount towards the rear.
11. Installation is the reverse order of removal. Tighten the bolts for the engine mount to the front axle carrier to 21 ft. lbs. (28 Nm).

EXHAUST MANIFOLD

REMOVAL & INSTALLATION

Engine ID 272

See Figure 43.

1. Remove the air filter housing.
2. Remove the left and right upper bolt on heat shield for engine mount from engine support
3. Remove the rear and middle section of engine compartment paneling
4. If removing right exhaust manifold:
    a. Remove right catalytic converter
    b. Detach electrical wiring harness for alternator, starter on cylinder head at front and middle
    c. Unscrew the nuts from above
    d. Remove the left and right upper bolt on heat shield for engine mount from engine support and remove heat shield.

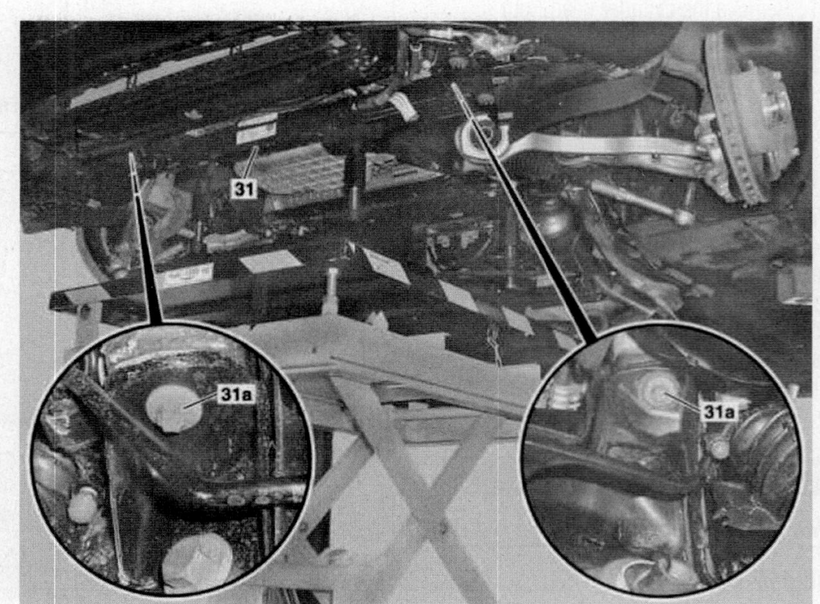

2. Bolt
3. Front axle carrier
4. Bolts
5. Engine mount
6. Heat shield
7. Retaining clamp
8. Engine support

71112_MBCL_G0211

Fig. 42 Front engine mount components—CLS Models

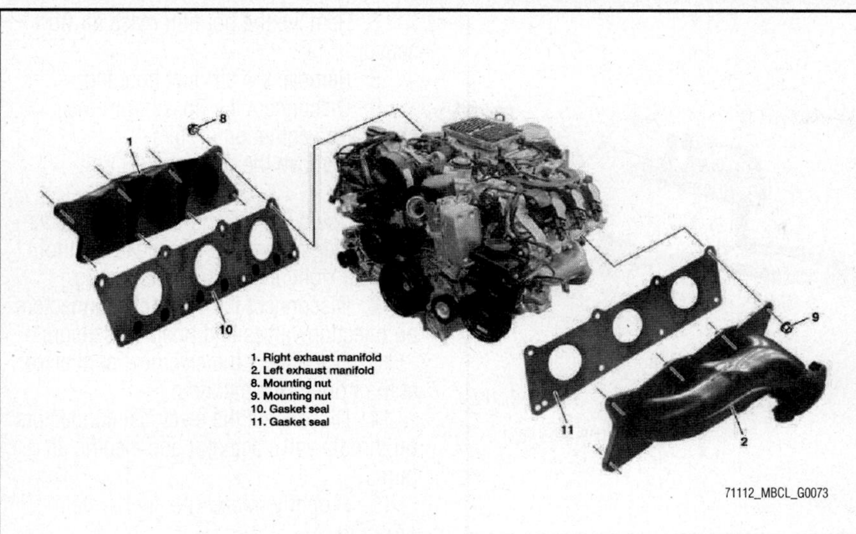

Fig. 43 Exhaust manifold mounting—Engine ID 272

e. Unscrew the nuts from below and remove. Discard the mounting nuts and seal.

5. If removing the left exhaust manifold:

a. Disconnect the negative battery cable.

b. Remove the left catalytic converter.

c. Unscrew the nuts from above.

d. Remove left and right upper bolt on heat shield for engine mount from engine support and remove heat shield.

e. Remove the lower mounting nuts and remove the exhaust manifold. Discard the mounting nuts and seal.

6. Installation is the reverse order of removal. Tighten the mounting nuts to 12 ft. lbs. (16 Nm).

Engine ID 273

1. Disconnect the negative battery cable.
2. Remove the air filter housing.
3. Remove any accessible mounting nuts before the vehicle is raised.
4. Raise and safely support the vehicle.
5. Remove the bottom engine compartment paneling.
6. Remove the applicable catalytic convert.
7. Remove the exhaust system.
8. Remove the heat shield.
9. Remove the remaining mounting nuts.
10. Remove the exhaust manifold and gasket.
11. Installation is the reverse order of removal. Tighten the mounting nuts to 12 ft. lbs. (16 Nm).

Engine ID 156

Right Side

1. Remove the right side engine mount. For additional information, refer to the following section, "Engine Mounts, Removal & Installation."
2. Carefully push the engine to the left side to access the mounting nuts of the exhaust manifold.
3. Remove the mounting nuts of the exhaust manifold and discard.
4. Remove the exhaust manifold from the bottom of the engine and discard the gasket.

To install:

5. Install the exhaust manifold with a new gasket. Tighten the mounting nuts to 16 ft. lbs. (22 Nm).
6. The remainder of the installation is the reverse order of removal.

Left Side

1. Remove the left side engine mount. For additional information, refer to the following section, "Engine Mounts, Removal & Installation."
2. Carefully push the engine to the right side to access the mounting nuts of the exhaust manifold.
3. Remove the mounting nuts of the exhaust manifold and discard.
4. Remove the exhaust manifold from the bottom of the engine and discard the gasket.

To install:

5. Install the exhaust manifold with a new gasket. Tighten the mounting nuts to 16 ft. lbs. (22 Nm).
6. The remainder of the installation is the reverse order of removal.

Engine ID 157 & 278

The exhaust manifold is remove with the turbocharger as an assembly. For additional information, refer to the following section, "Turbocharger, Removal & Installation."

CATALYTIC CONVERTER

REMOVAL & INSTALLATION

C-Class Models

See Figure 44.

1. Raise and safely support the vehicle.
2. Remove any engine compartment paneling as necessary.
3. Disconnect the wiring harness for the O2 sensors.
4. Remove the mounting bolts from the catalytic converters to the exhaust manifold.
5. Remove the mounting bolt from the catalytic converter holder to the catalytic converter.
6. Remove any exhaust support components in order to facilitate removal of the catalytic converter.
7. Installation is the reverse order of removal. Tighten the catalytic convert mounting bolts to 15 ft. lbs. (20 Nm).

CLS-Class Models

See Figures 45 and 46.

1. Raise and safely support the vehicle.
2. Remove any engine compartment paneling as necessary.
3. Remove the crossmember.
4. Disconnect the wiring harness for the O2 sensors.
5. Remove the catalytic converter from the bracket.
6. Support the exhaust system with a suitable transmission jack.
7. Remove the catalytic converter from the center muffler by removing the bolts.
8. Installation is the reverse order of removal. Tighten the catalytic convert mounting bolts to 15 ft. lbs. (20 Nm).

INTAKE MANIFOLD

REMOVAL & INSTALLATION

Engine ID 271

See Figure 47.

1. Remove the engine appearance cover.
2. Remove the air filter housing.

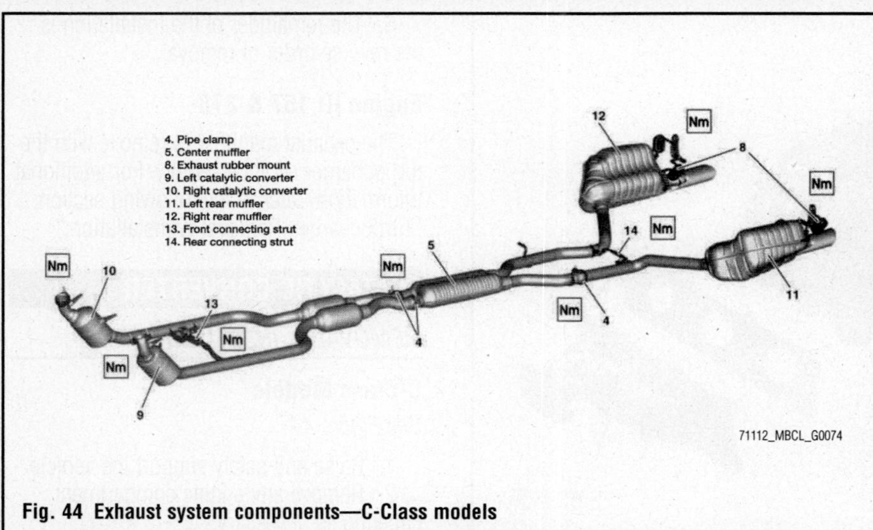

Fig. 44 Exhaust system components—C-Class models

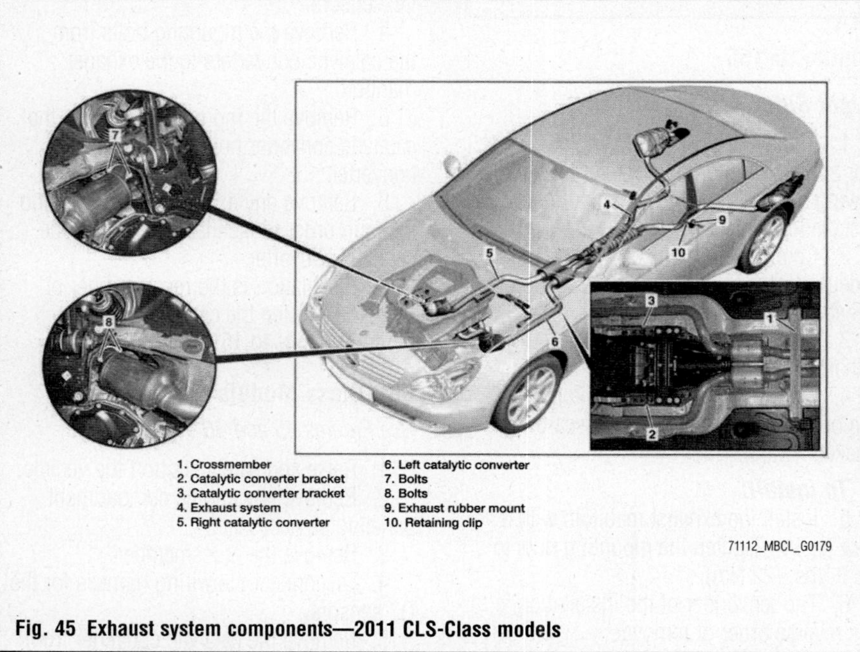

Fig. 45 Exhaust system components—2011 CLS-Class models

3. Disconnect the connectors for electrical lines to the throttle valve actuator, actuator motor, pressure sensor, and temperature sensor.
4. Unclip the electrical wiring harness on intake manifold.
5. Detach the charge air hose on the throttle valve actuator.
6. Remove the line from the intake manifold.
7. Detach the hose form the sound generator on the intake manifold at the front.
8. Remove the hose from the combination valve.
9. Remove the intake manifold mounting bolts.
10. Detach the purge line from the vent cable on the underside of the intake pipe.
11. Remove the intake manifold.
12. Installation is the reverse order of removal. Tighten the mounting bolts to 10 ft. lbs. (14 Nm).

Engine ID 272

See Figure 48.

1. Remove the air filter housing.
2. Disconnect the right connector at ME-SFI control unit.
3. Disconnect the electrical connectors.
4. Remove the jack for electrical connector on the fuel distributor.
5. Remove the electrical feed line from left the control unit bracket.
6. Pull the ME-SFI control unit out of the brackets and place aside.
7. Remove the hot film mass air flow sensor.
8. Remove the air duct housing.
9. Disconnect the hoses from the crankcase ventilation system.
10. Remove the right control unit bracket.
11. the supply ducts from the cylinder head cover, resonance the intake manifold and rear right engine suspension lug.
12. Disconnect the electrical connectors on injection valves and position sensors.
13. Disconnect the electrical connector at the front of the manifold.
14. Disconnect the electrical connectors on throttle valve actuator and electric air pump.
15. Properly release the fuel system pressure.
16. Disconnect fuel line from the fuel distributor and seal the openings.
17. Remove the manifold mounting bolts.
18. Lift out the intake manifold and disconnect the pneumatic lines. Discard the gaskets.

To install:

19. Install the intake manifold using new gaskets and tighten the mounting bolts to 80 inch lbs. (9 Nm).
20. The remainder of the installation is the reverse order of removal.

Engine ID 273

1. Remove the air filter housing.
2. Disconnect the right connector at ME-SFI control unit.
3. Disconnect the electrical connectors.
4. Remove the jack for the electrical connector on fuel distributor.
5. Remove the electrical feed line from the left control unit bracket.
6. Detach the ME-SFI control unit from the left control unit bracket and control unit bracket and lay to one side.
7. Detach the brake booster vacuum hose from the intake manifold.
8. Remove the mass air flow sensor.
9. Remove the air duct housing.
10. Disconnect the hose for the crankcase ventilation system.
11. Remove the right control unit bracket.
12. Remove the feed duct from cylinder head cover and resonance intake manifold
13. Remove the feed duct from resonance intake manifold
14. Remove the left rear engine lifting eye

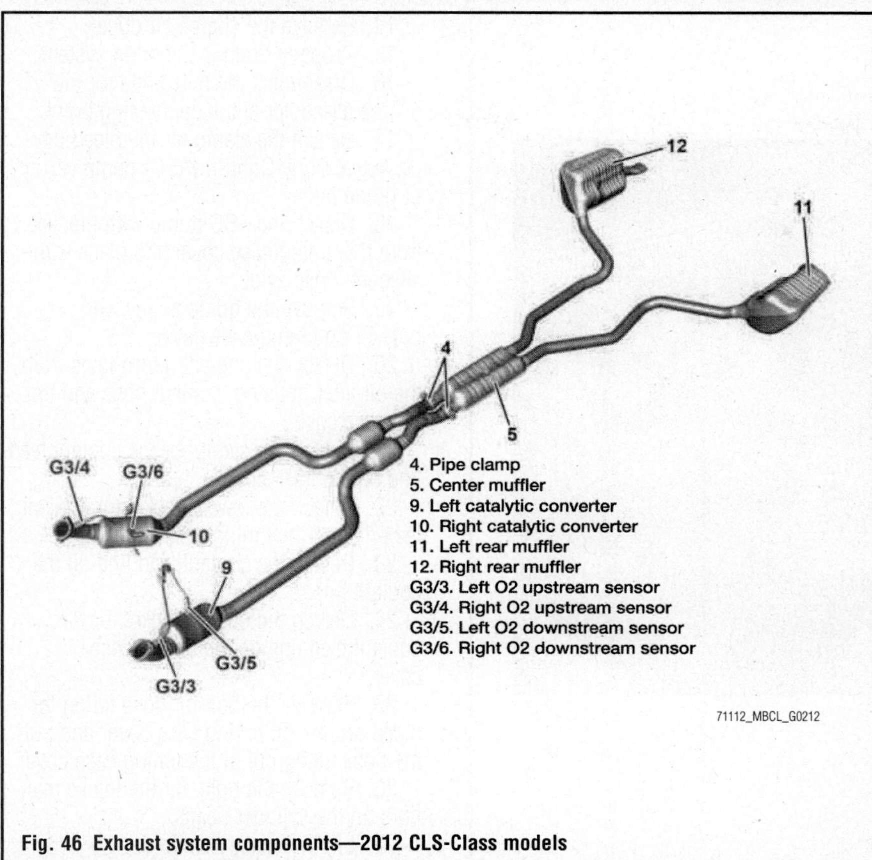

Fig. 46 Exhaust system components—2012 CLS-Class models

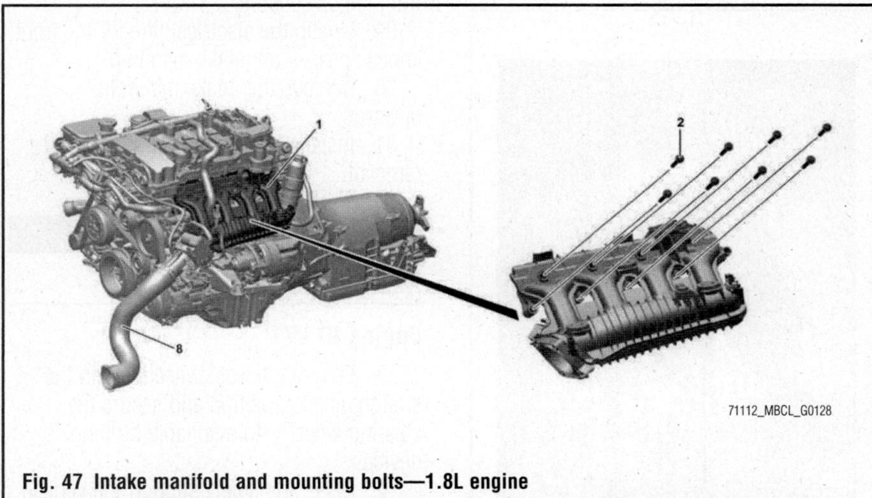

Fig. 47 Intake manifold and mounting bolts—1.8L engine

15. Remove the feed duct from cylinder head cover
16. Release and disconnect the electrical connectors at the fuel injection valves.
17. Release and disconnect the electrical connectors on the left intake manifold tumble flap position sensor and right intake manifold tumble flap position sensor.
18. Disconnect the electrical connector
19. Release and disconnect the electrical connector at the throttle valve actuator
20. Disconnect the electrical connector from electrical air pump
21. Properly relieve the fuel system pressure at the service valve.
22. Disconnect the fuel line from the fuel rail.
23. Remove the mounting bolts.
24. Lift the intake manifold to the front and disconnect the pneumatic lines from the connection fittings at the intake manifold.
25. Remove the intake manifold and gasket.

To install:

26. Install the intake manifold using new gaskets and tighten the mounting bolts to 80 inch lbs. (9 Nm).
27. The remainder of the installation is the reverse order of removal.

Engine ID 156

See Figure 49.

1. Remove the air intake assembly.
2. Remove the air filter housing.
3. Properly relieve the fuel system pressure.
4. Disconnect the fuel line from the fuel distributor and discard the sealing rings.
5. Disconnect the electrical connectors from the front of the intake manifold.
6. Remove the vacuum line from the intake manifold and disconnect from the brake booster.
7. Remove the foam plastic cover from the fuel distributor.
8. Disconnect the injector wiring harnesses.
9. Remove the hold down bolt and remove the purge line from the intake manifold.
10. Disconnect the vacuum hose from the intake manifold and remove.
11. Disconnect the remaining wiring harnesses.
12. Remove the mounting bolts from the intake manifold and lift off in the upward direction.
13. Installation is the reverse order of removal. Tighten the manifold mounting bolts as follows:
    - Step 1: 89 inch lbs. (10 Nm)
    - Step 2: Plus 90°
    - Step 3: Plus 10°

Engine ID 157 & 278

See Figures 50 and 51.

1. Remove the ME-SFI control unit.
2. Remove both air filter housings.
3. Remove the insulation between the air filter housings and cylinder head cover.
4. Remove the center section of the bulkhead.
5. Remove the crash plate on high-pressure pumps and remove insulation from high-pressure pumps.
6. Detach the vacuum line for brake booster on vacuum pump and intake manifold.
7. Detach the vacuum line for centrifuge on the intake manifold.

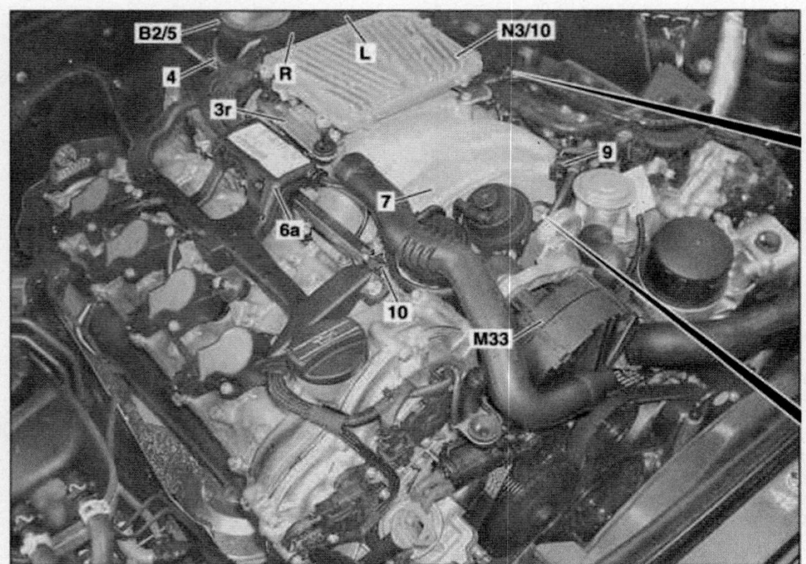

Fig. 48 Intake manifold engine view—Engine ID 272

Fig. 49 Location of the intake manifold mounting bolts—6.2L Engines

8. Disconnect the engine wiring harness on the intake manifold and cylinder head cover and lay down towards the rear.
9. Remove the high-pressure lines.
10. Disconnect the electrical line on the intake manifold.
11. Detach the purge line on the intake manifold.
12. Detach the vacuum line for boost pressure control pressure transducer on vacuum pump.

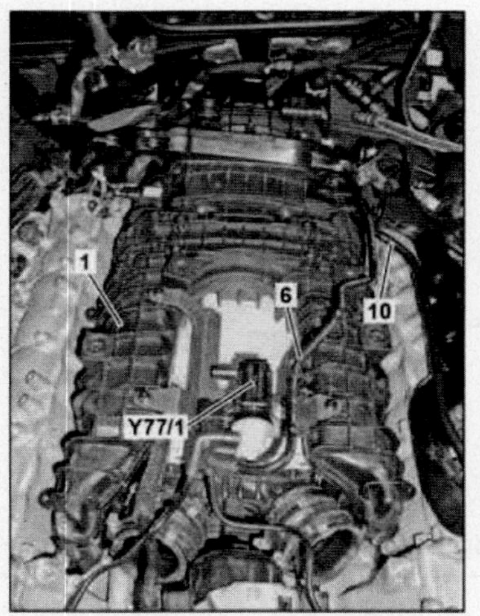

Fig. 50 Intake manifold mounting shown with all components removed—CLS Class models

13. Detach the boost pressure control pressure transducer with bracket on intake manifold and lay down to the front.
14. Remove the charge air ducts.
15. Properly drain the cooling system.
16. Disconnect the bleed line for the charge air cooler at the connecting point.
17. Detach the clamp for the bleed line on Active Body Control (ABC) pump carrier or guide pulley.
18. Detach the ABC pump with bracket from the timing case cover and place with attached lines aside.
19. Remove the guide pulley with bracket on timing case cover.
20. Detach the coolant return lines from the oil filter housing, coolant hose and timing case cover.
21. Detach the clamp for the coolant feed line on the front cover.
22. Detach the lower bracket for coolant feed line on the timing case cover.
23. Detach the coolant feed line on the coolant hose.
24. Detach the upper bracket for the coolant feed line on the timing case cover.
25. Remove the bolt for hose fitting for bleed on line on timing case cover and pull the hose fitting out of the timing case cover.
26. Remove the bolts for the intake manifold on the cylinder heads.
27. Lift the intake manifold.
28. Disconnect the electrical line on the front knock sensors.
29. Unclip the electrical line for the front knock sensors on intake manifold.
30. Remove the intake manifold upwards.
31. Installation is the reverse order of removal.

OIL PAN

REMOVAL & INSTALLATION

Engine ID 271

1. Ensure the front wheels are in the straight ahead position and secure the steering wheel with a suitable holding device.
2. Raise and safely support the vehicle.
3. Drain the engine oil.
4. Detach both engine mounts from the front axle carrier.
5. Remove the engine appearance cover.
6. Remove the vacuum line from the vacuum pump.
7. Attach a suitable engine lifting device and raise the engine slightly.
8. Lower the front axle carrier.
9. Remove the oil cooling lines from the transmission and oil pan.

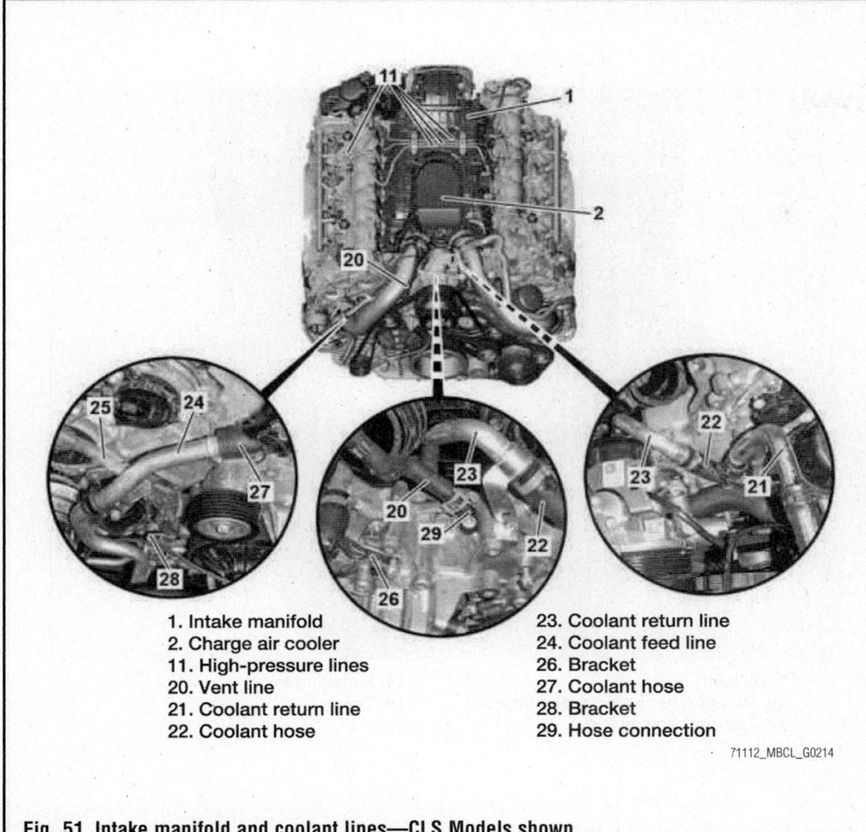

Fig. 51 Intake manifold and coolant lines—CLS Models shown

10. Remove the retaining clamp from the oil pan.
11. Disconnect the oxygen sensor electrical connectors and unclip the wiring from the brackets.
12. Remove the oil pan mounting bolts.

➡Matchmark the bolts as they are different lengths and diameters.

13. Carefully pry off the oil pan from the crankcase without damaging the sealing surfaces.
14. Installation is the reverse order of removal. Tighten the mounting bolts as follows:
    - M6x30 bolts: 80 inch lbs. (9 Nm)
    - M6x90 bolts: 80 inch lbs. (9 Nm)
    - M8x35 bolts: 15 ft. lbs. (20 Nm)

Engine ID 272

1. Drain the engine oil.
2. Attach an engine support frame and lift the engine slightly.
3. Remove the lower engine compartment paneling.
4. Remove the oil pan bottom section.
5. Disconnect the engine mount from the front axle carrier.
6. Detach the catalytic converters from exhaust manifolds and remove both holders.
7. Disconnect the electrical connectors of oxygen sensors and detach the holder from the transmission.
8. Detach the pressure line from holder.
9. Detach the A/C compressor from the timing case over and engine support.
10. Remove the oil cooling lines to the automatic transmission and oil pan.
11. Remove the oil dipstick guide tube.
12. Remove hot film mass air flow sensor.
13. Remove air duct housing.
14. Remove the cover panel.
15. Remove the centrifuge cover.
16. Raise the engine slightly.
17. Disconnect the oil level check switch electrical connector.
18. Remove the oil pan mounting bolts. Matchmark the bolts as they are different sizes.
19. Remove the oil pan from the engine block.

⁂ WARNING

Do not pry the oil pan from the block on the sealing surfaces will be damaged. Use a heat gun to loosen the sealant if necessary.

20. Installation is the reverse order of removal.
21. Clean the sealing surfaces before applying more Loctite®.
22. Tighten the oil pan mounting bolts as follows:
    - M8x30 bolts: 15 ft. lbs. (20 Nm).
    - Remaining bolts: 80 inch lbs. (9 Nm).

Engine ID 273

1. Remove air filter housing.
2. Remove hot film mass air flow sensor.
3. Remove air duct housing.
4. Detach lower engine compartment paneling.
5. Drain the engine oil.
6. Drain the coolant at the radiator.
7. Remove the oil dipstick guide tube.
8. Detach both catalytic converters from the exhaust manifolds.
9. Detach catalytic converter bracket from the transmission and catalytic converters and secure the exhaust system from falling down.
10. Unclip the electrical lines for O2 sensors from the brackets.
11. Disconnect both engine mounts from the front axle carrier by unscrewing bolts.
12. Detach pressure line for power steering from oil pan by unscrewing the bolt.
13. Remove the coolant line from heater system shutoff valve.
14. Disconnect coolant hose from coolant pipe to thermostat housing.
15. Attach a suitable engine hoist and raise the engine slightly.

➡Make sure when lifting out engine that no cables and lines are damaged and that engine does not hit against partition wall.

16. Detach the oil lines for the automatic transmission from the oil pan by detaching the retaining clamps.
17. Detach the electrical connector from oil sensor.
18. Remove the oil pan bottom section.
19. Detach the oil pan by unscrewing bolts

➡Observe the different bolt lengths and bolt diameters.

20. Loosen the oil pan from cylinder crankcase and remove it towards the rear of the engine.
21. Clean all sealing surfaces on oil pan and on the cylinder crankcase before reinstalling.
22. Installation is the reverse order of removal.

Engine ID 156

See Figure 52.

1. Disconnect the negative battery cable.
2. Ensure the front wheels are in the straight-ahead and secure the steering wheel with a holding device.
3. Remove the air filter housing.
4. Drain the power steering fluid from the power steering reservoir.
5. Remove the accessory drive belt.
6. Remove the mounting bolts for the dipstick guide tube bracket.
7. Install a suitable engine hoist to the engine and raise slightly.
8. Remove the cold air intake.
9. Secure radiator assembly with ties.
10. Disconnect the oil lines of the automatic transmission at the oil pan.
11. Remove the oil pan bottom section.
12. Loosen engine mounts on front axle carrier.
13. Detach the steering coupling from steering shaft.
14. Disconnect the electrical connector at the speed sensitive power steering solenoid valve of the rack-and-pinion steering and unclip at front axle carrier.
15. Disconnect the electrical connector at oil level check switch.
16. Detach bracket of the connecting linkage of the headlamp range adjustment/level sensor at the stabilizer bar
17. Disconnect and seal power steering hydraulic line at the separation point at the front axle carrier.
18. Loosen the nut of the wheel arch oil cooler bracket at the front axle carrier.
19. Disconnect the lower engine oil line on the connecting flange.
20. Detach the diagonal strut at the front axle carrier and underfloor.
21. Detach the support strut at the underfloor and front axle carrier.
22. Loosen and lower the front axle carrier. Support the front axle carrier.
23. Disconnect the A/C compressor wiring harness.
24. Remove the A/C compressor from the crankcase but leave the lines attached.
25. Remove the support for the power steering pump.
26. Disconnect and the power steering lines and cap the lines.
27. Remove the engine oil lines from the cylinder crankcase and seal the openings.
28. Insert a bolt and using a suitable wedge to loosen and pry off the front cover from the oil pan.
29. Remove the oil pan mounting bolts.
30. Pry off the oil pan by turning a bolt on the crankcase and loosen with a suitable wedge.

Fig. 52 Oil pan mounting—6.2L Engine shown

To install:

31. Clean the sealing surfaces of the oil pan and crankcase.
32. Apply a new bead of sealant to the sealant area and install the oil pan. Tighten the oil pan mounting bolts to 74 inch lbs. (8.4 Nm).
33. The remainder of the installation is the reverse order of removal.

Engine ID 157 & 278

See Figure 53.

1. If equipped with air suspension, completely discharge the front struts using the STAR Diagnosis tool.
2. Ensure the front wheels are in the straight-ahead and secure the steering wheel with a holding device.
3. Disconnect the negative battery cable.
4. Install an engine hoist and raise the engine slightly.
5. Raise and safely support the vehicle.
6. Remove the bottom engine compartment paneling.
7. Drain the engine oil.
8. Remove the alternator.
9. Remove the oil line for transmission cooling.
10. Disconnect the oil dipstick guide tube from the oil and pan and cylinder head cover and place aside.
11. Remove the steering coupling.
12. Remove the oil lines for the turbocharger at the oil pan and place aside.
13. Separate and unclip the electrical connector for the oil level check switch.
14. Detach the bracket for the level sensors from the control arm.
15. If equipped with 4MATIC, remove the front axle gear and support brace.
16. Without 4MATIC, loosen and slightly lower the front axle carrier.
17. Remove the oil pan bottom section.
18. Remove the oil pan mounting bolts.

➡The bolts are different lengths, keep the bolts in the correct order.

19. Remove the oil pan from the crankcase.

To install:

20. Clean the sealing surfaces of the oil pan and crankcase.
21. Apply a new bead of sealant to the sealant area and install the oil pan. Tighten the oil pan mounting bolts to 80 inch lbs. (9 Nm).

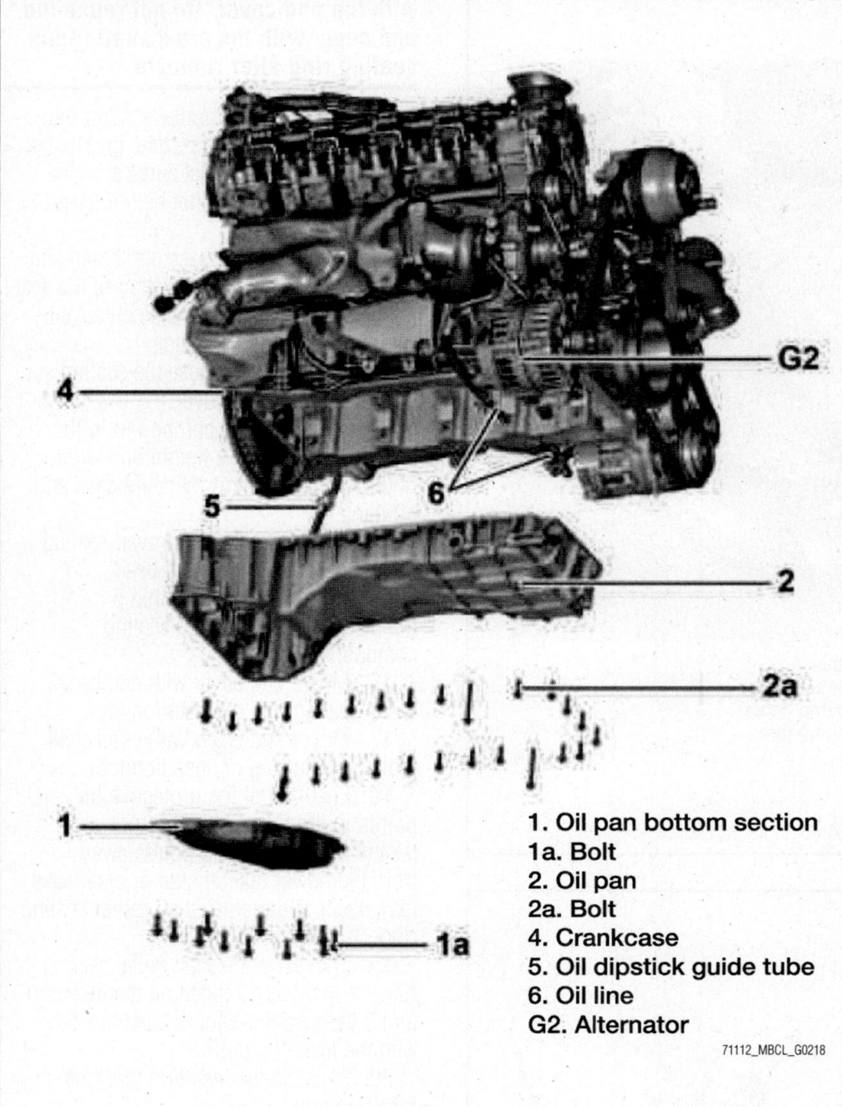

Fig. 53 Oil pan mounting—Engine 278 shown

22. The remainder of the installation is the reverse order of removal.

OIL PUMP

REMOVAL & INSTALLATION

Engine ID 272 & 156 & 273

See Figure 54.

1. Remove the oil pan. For additional information, refer to the following section, "Oil Pan, Removal & Installation."
2. Remove the mounting bolts and remove the oil suction pipe. Discard the sealing ring.
3. Remove the mounting bolts.
4. Press back the chain tensioner, remove the oil pump chain from the oil pump gear.
5. Remove the oil pump.

To install:

6. Fill the oil pump with clean engine oil before installation.
7. Install the oil pump and tighten the mounting bolts as follows:
   a. Step 1: 44 inch lbs.
   b. Step 2: 15 ft. lbs. (20 Nm).
8. The remainder of the installation is the reverse order of removal.

Engine ID 271

1. Remove the oil pan. For additional information, refer to the following section, "Oil Pan, Removal & Installation."
2. Remove the mounting bolts and remove the cover from the oil pump.
3. Remove the drive wheel center bolt while counter holding the balance shaft with a wrench and remove the drive wheel.
4. Remove the mounting bolts and remove the oil pump.

To install:

5. Clean the oil pump sealing surfaces.
6. Coat the oil pump with clean engine oil before installing.
7. Install the oil pump and tighten the mounting bolts to 80 inch lbs. (9 Nm).
8. Install the drive gear and tighten the center bolt to 15 ft. lbs. (20 Nm).
9. The remainder of the installation is the reverse order of removal.

Engine ID 157 & 278

See Figure 55.

1. Remove the oil pan. For additional information, refer to the following section, "Oil Pan, Removal & Installation."
2. Detach the oil baffle with intake manifold from the oil pump and crankcase.
3. Remove the oil pump by removing the mounting bolts.
4. Disconnect the electrical connector.

To install:

5. Fill the oil pump with clean engine oil before installation.
6. Install the oil pump and tighten the mounting bolts as follows:
   a. Step 1: 44 inch lbs.
   b. Step 2: 15 ft. lbs. (20 Nm).
7. The remainder of the installation is the reverse order of removal.

PISTONS & RINGS

POSITIONING

Install piston rings with identical ring width. Observe the installation position, with "TOP" or other manufacturer designation pointing toward the piston crown.

REAR MAIN SEAL

REMOVAL & INSTALLATION

Engine ID 272

See Figures 56 through 61.

1. Before servicing the vehicle, refer to the precautions.
2. Remove the transmission.
3. Remove the flywheel/drive plate.
4. Drain the engine oil.

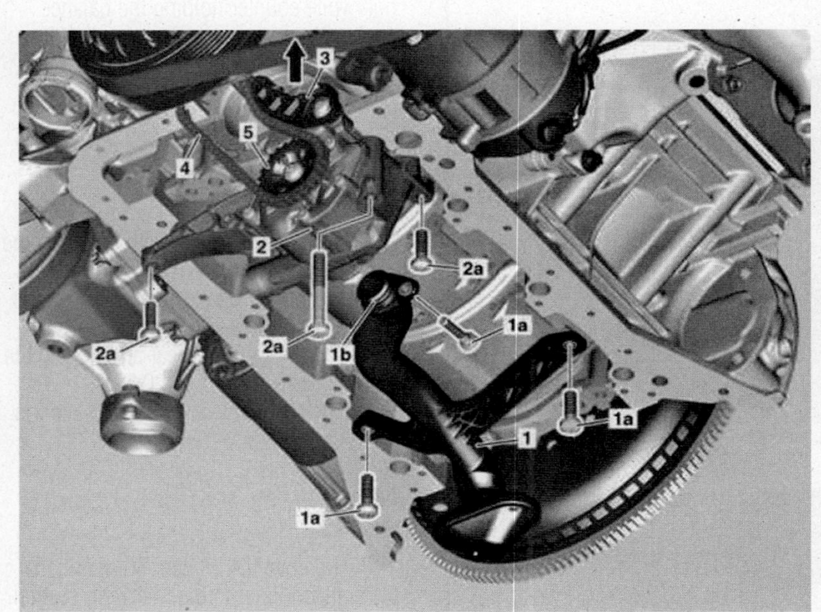

Fig. 54 Oil pump mounting components—Engine ID 272

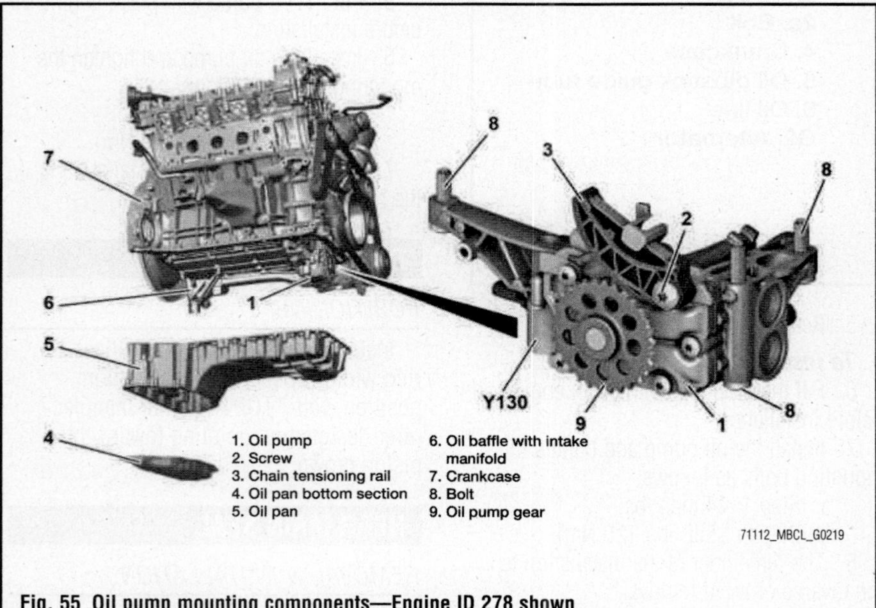

Fig. 55 Oil pump mounting components—Engine ID 278 shown

5. Remove the oil pan bottom section.
6. Clean crankcase and oil pan in area of end cover.
7. Remove the end cover mounting bolts.
8. Pry off the end cover with crankshaft radial sealing ring from crankcase.
9. Remove the end cover.

To install:

⁂ WARNING

The crankshaft radial sealing ring is vulcanized in the end cover and it can therefore only be replaced together with the end cover. Do not reuse the end cover with the crankshaft radial sealing ring after removal.

10. The crankshaft radial sealing ring has both a lip and a protective lip. The lip, protective lip and contact surface on the crankshaft flange must not be lubricated for assembly purposes!
11. Clean and degrease crankcase and oil pan in the area of application of the sealing compound as well as the contact surface on the crankshaft flange.
12. Clean and degrease the sealing surface on the new end cover.
13. Apply sealing compound in the form of a bead with a height and width of 0.078 in. (2.0 mm) the crankcase and oil pan.
14. Use exclusively approved sealing compounds. Do not spread bead.
15. Mount end cover within 5 minutes after applying the sealing compound.
16. Mount end cover with crankshaft radial sealing ring on insertion tool.
17. Mount end cover with crankshaft radial sealing ring on insertion tool.
18. Ensure that the protective lip points in the direction of the power takeoff side and the lip points away from the power takeoff side or else leaks may occur at the crankshaft radial sealing ring.
19. The rear crankshaft radial sealing ring can only be mounted on the insertion tool if the insertion tool is fitted together with the insertion tool.
20. Separate the insertion tool from insertion tool.
21. Mount the end cover with the crankshaft radial shaft sealing ring and insertion tool on the contact surface on the crankshaft flange.
22. The contact surface must not be removed with an emery cloth, as this can destroy the surface of the crankshaft and render the crankshaft unusable.
23. Tighten the horizontal bolts stepwise diagonally and then tighten the vertical bolts. Tighten to 6 ft. lbs.
24. Detach the insertion tool from the crankshaft flange
25. Lift protective lip carefully and check for correct installation position of the lip.

⁂ WARNING

A wrong installation position leads to leakage.

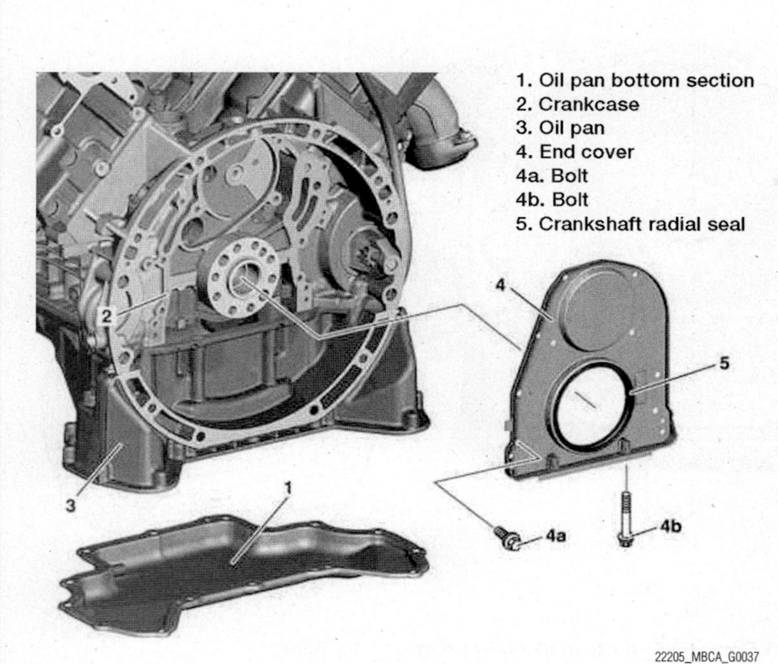

Fig. 56 The crankshaft radial sealing ring is vulcanized in the end cover and it can therefore only be replaced together with the end cover. Do not reuse the end cover with the crankshaft radial sealing ring after removal

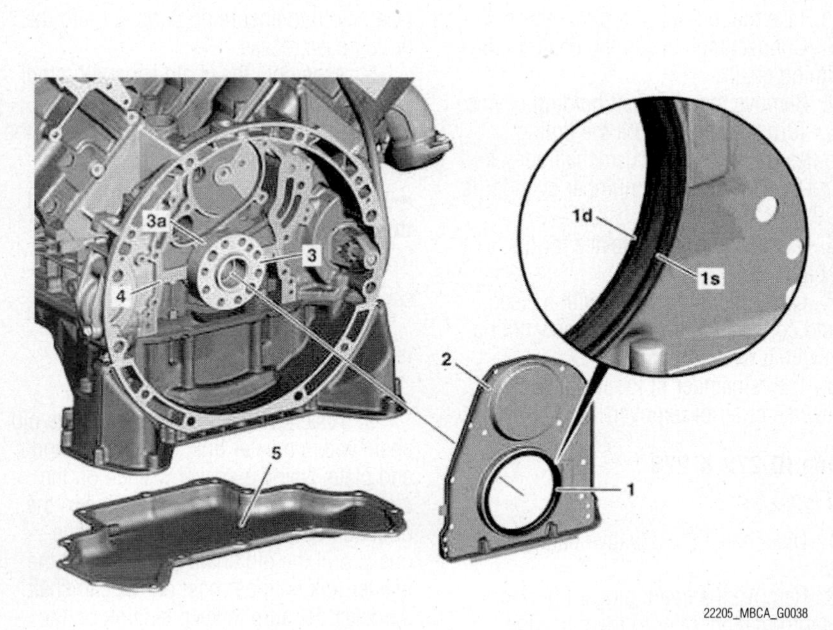

Fig. 57 Rear main seal and crankshaft end cover

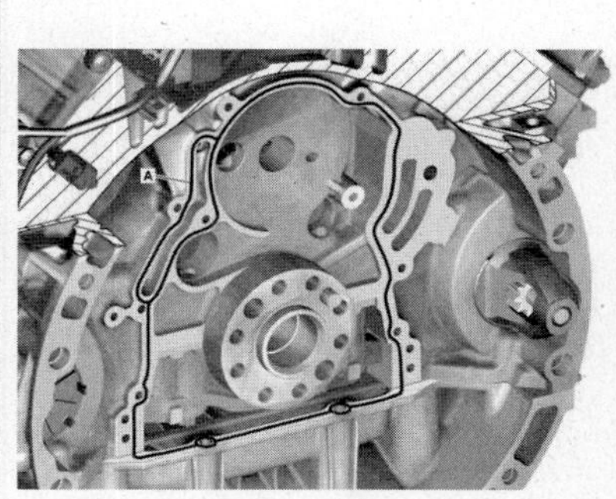

Fig. 58 Apply sealing compound in the form of a bead with a height and width of 0.078 in. (2.0 mm) the crankcase and oil pan

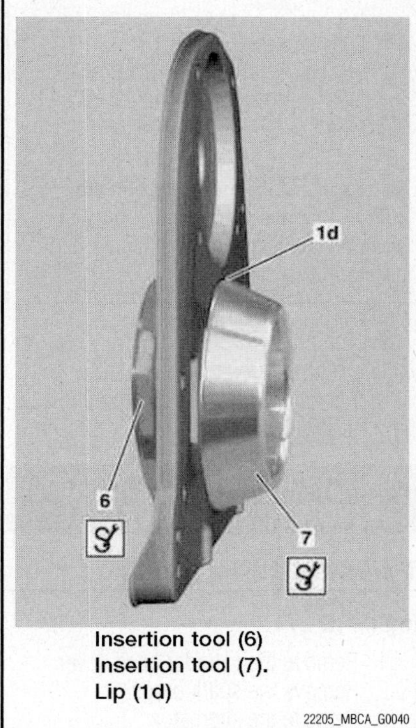

Fig. 59 Insertion tool is fitted together with the insertion tool. Ensure that the lip points away from the transmission side

26. The lip must point over it whole extent towards the crankcase.

27. Check for correct installation position of the protective lip

WARNING

An incorrect installation position leads to premature wear of the crankshaft radial sealing ring.

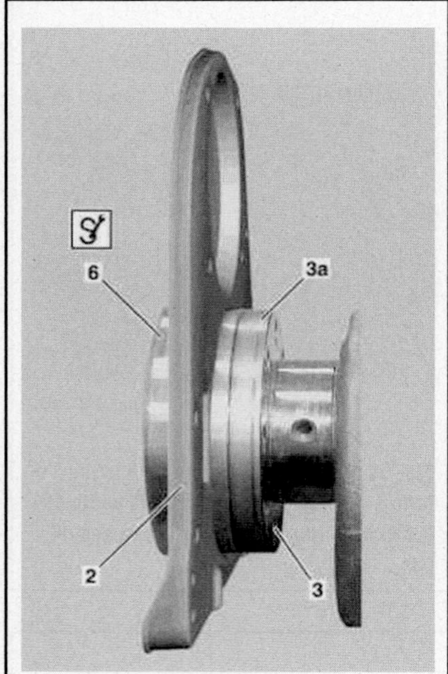

Fig. 60 Mount the end cover with the crankshaft radial shaft sealing ring and insertion tool on the contact surface on the crankshaft flange

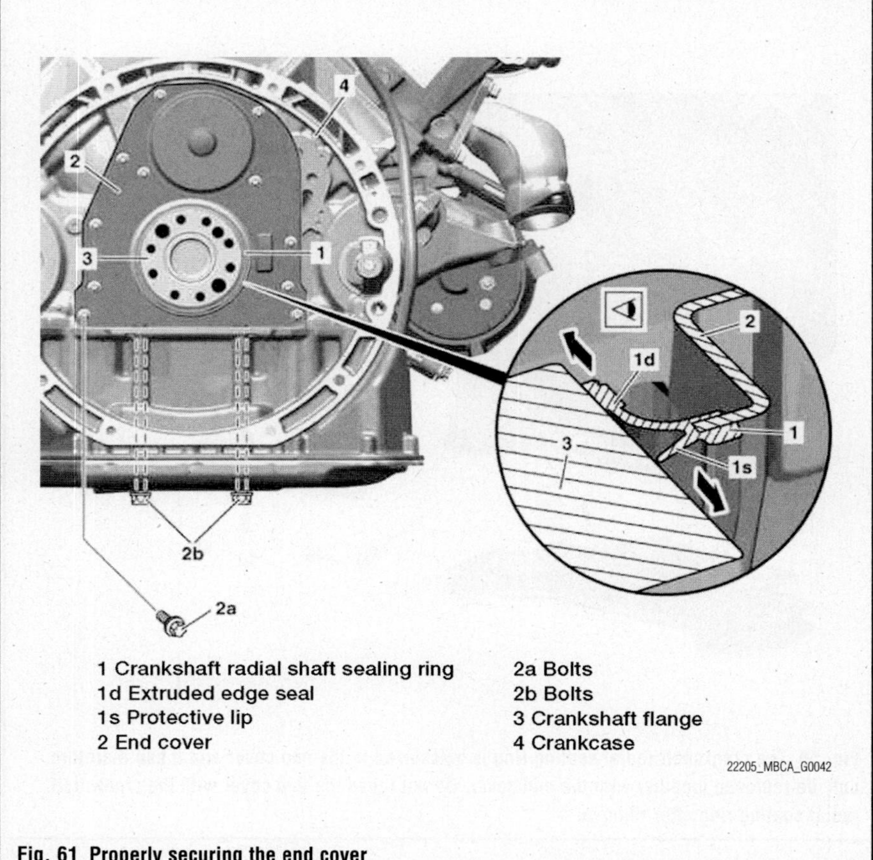

Fig. 61 Properly securing the end cover

28. The protective lip must point over it whole extent towards the crankcase.
29. Fill engine with oil, start engine and check for leak.

TIMING CHAIN COVER, CHAIN, TENSIONER, & SPROCKETS

REMOVAL & INSTALLATION

Engine ID 271

1. Remove the cylinder head cover.
2. Remove the spark plugs.
3. Remove the alternator.
4. Remove the chain tensioner.
5. Remove the slide rail.
6. Remove the guides for the timing chain.
7. Mount the retainer tool onto the cylinder.
8. Turn the engine at the crankshaft until the number 1 cylinder is at Top Dead Center (TDC).
9. Install the holding device for the camshafts.
10. Cover the timing case recess and cylinder head with a clean rag.
11. Using a chain separator tool, disconnect the old timing chain.

To install:

12. Take the rag out of timing recess.
13. Connect the new timing chain to the old timing chain.
14. Remove the camshaft holding device.
15. Turn the engine until the timing chain lies on the exhaust camshaft sprockets and the piston for the number cylinder is at TDC.
16. Install the holding device for the camshaft.
17. Cover the timing case with a clean rag and connect the ends of the new timing chain with a riveted link.
18. The remainder of the installation is the reverse order of removal.

Engine ID 272 & 273

See Figure 62.

1. Disconnect the negative battery cable.
2. Remove the spark plugs. For additional information, refer to the following section, "Spark Plugs, Removal & Installation."
3. Remove the camshafts. For additional information, refer to the following section, "Camshafts, Removal & Installation."
4. Cover the timing case recess with a clean cloth to ensure no parts fall into the timing case recess.
5. Assembly the chain separating tool and pressure screw together.
6. Fit the chain separating tool onto the timing chain.

➡Ensure that the pressure pin lies at the pin of the timing chain link.

7. Screw in the pressure screw and separate the timing chain.
8. Remove the pressure screw and remove the chain separating tool.

To install:

9. Attach a new timing chain to the old chain with a master link, center plate and end plate. Using a socket wrench on the crankshaft, slowly rotate the engine in the direction of normal rotation. Simultaneously, pull the old chain through until the master link is uppermost on the camshaft sprocket. Be sure to keep tension on the chain throughout this procedure.
10. Disconnect the old timing chain and connect the ends of the new chain with the master link. Insert the new connecting link from the rear so the lockwashers can be seen from the front.

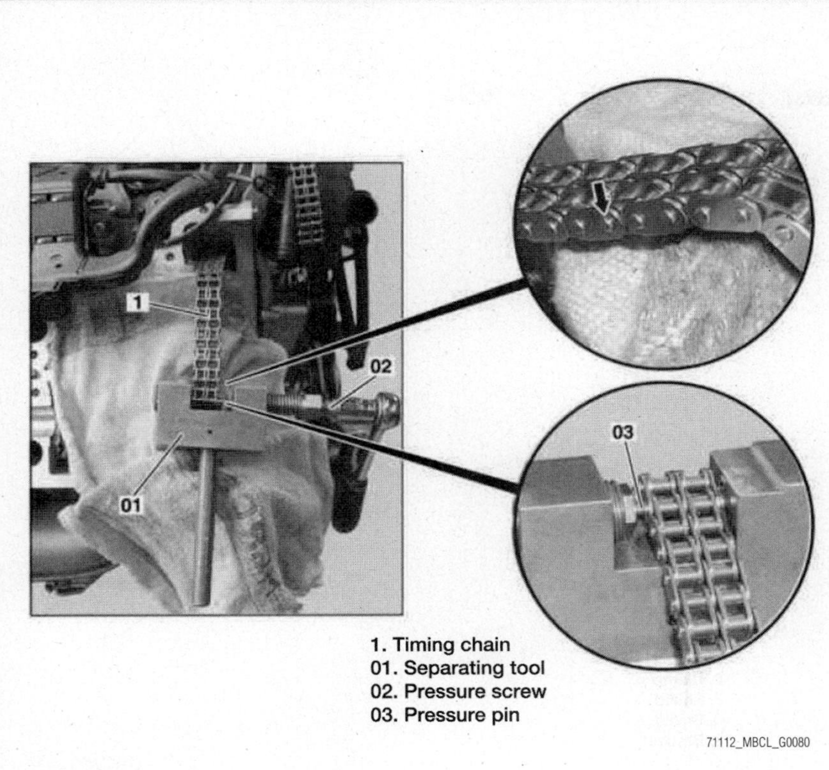

Fig. 62 Attaching the timing chain separating tool to break the timing chain.

11. Rotate the engine in the direction of rotation until the timing marks align at 55° Before Top Dead Center.

12. The markings on the pulse wheels of the intake and exhaust camshafts at the left cylinder head must be located centrally in the bores of the camshaft sensors. If not, rotate the engine another revolution.

13. Rotate the engine in the direction of rotation 95° so that it is at 40° After Top Dead Center of cylinder 1.

14. The remainder of the installation is the reverse order of removal.

Engine ID 157 & 278

See Figure 63.

1. Disconnect the negative battery cable.
2. Remove the cylinder head cover.
3. Rotate the engine at the crankshaft center bolt in the direction of engine rotation to 40° After Top Dead Center (TDC) of cylinder 1.
4. Remove the oil filter housing, if removing left side.
5. Remove the mounting bolt and remove the timing chain tensioner.
6. Remove the camshaft bearing cap.
7. Remove the camshaft with the adjusters as an assembly.
8. Cover the timing case recess and cylinder head with a clean rag.
9. Using a chain separator tool, disconnect the old timing chain.

To install:

10. Attach a new timing chain to the old chain with an assembly link. Using a socket wrench on the crankshaft, slowly rotate the engine in the direction of normal rotation. Simultaneously, pull the old chain through until the master link is uppermost on the camshaft sprocket. Be sure to keep tension on the chain throughout this procedure.
11. Remove the assembly link and separate the old timing chain from the new timing chain.
12. Insert a riveted link with both middle plates in the ends of the timing chain.
13. Place an assembly insert in the rivet press tool and fix in place with the mounting screw.
14. Place the assembly insert in the rivet press tool.
15. Insert outer plate into the assembly insert.
16. Screw in the pressure screw on the rivet press tool until there is firm resistance.
17. The remainder of the installation is the reverse order of removal.

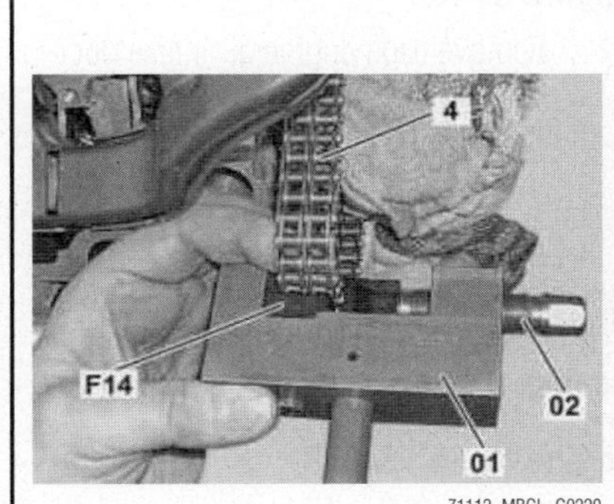

Fig. 63 Using the riveting tool to install a riveted link on a new timing chain

TURBOCHARGER

REMOVAL & INSTALLATION

Engine ID 271

1. Disconnect the negative battery cable.
2. Remove the engine compartment paneling.
3. Remove the three-way catalytic converter.
4. Remove the combination valve.
5. Remove the power steering expansion reservoir, leaving the lines attached and move to one side.
6. Remove the combination valve bracket.
7. Remove the secondary air system pipework.
8. Remove the turbocharger shield.
9. Properly drain the coolant from the radiator.
10. Disconnect the coolant hose from the turbocharger.
11. Remove the coolant lines for the turbocharger.
12. Remove the turbocharger oil line.
13. Disconnect the connector for electrical line to bypass air switchover valve.
14. Disconnect the boost pressure control hose from the boost pressure control pressure transducer and unclip from the right engine lifting eye
15. Remove the mounting nuts and lift the turbocharger upwards to remove.
16. Installation is the reverse order of removal.
17. Refill the engine with coolant to the correct level.
18. Check the engine oil level.

Engine ID 157 & 278

See Figure 64.

1. Drain the engine oil.
2. Remove the engine with the front axle carrier.
3. Detach the clamp on the shield, if removing the right side.
4. Remove the refrigerant line on the A/C compressor, if removing the left side.
5. Remove the shield on the cylinder head.
6. Detach the vacuum hose for boost pressure control valve on turbocharger with exhaust manifold.
7. Remove the charge air ducts and seal the openings.
8. Detach the coolant line for charge air cooler on the timing case cover, if removing the right side.
9. Remove any coolant lines necessary.
10. Detach the upper oil line on turbocharger with exhaust manifold.
11. Detach the lower oil line on oil pan.
12. Remove the bracket between the exhaust pipe and cylinder head.
13. Remove the exhaust pipe.
14. Remove the lock washer on the turbocharger.
15. Unscrew the mounting nuts.
16. Remove the turbocharger with the exhaust manifold from the cylinder head.

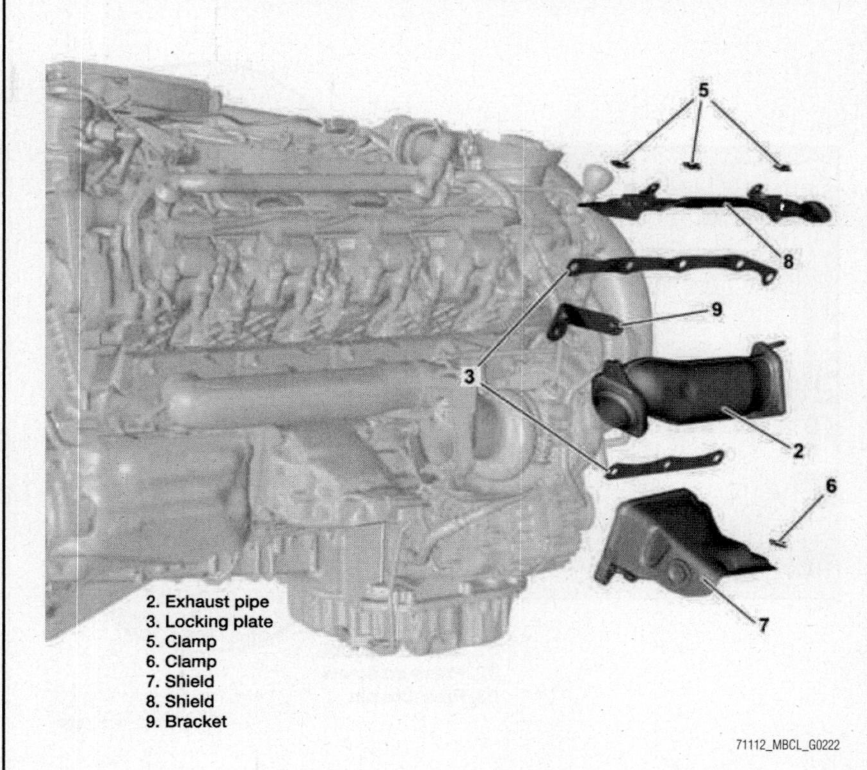

Fig. 64 Exploded view of the turbocharger/exhaust manifold assembly—Engine ID 278 shown

17. Installation is the reverse order of removal. Tighten the mounting nuts as follows:
    - M7: 11 ft. lbs. (15 Nm)
    - M8: 15 ft. lbs. (20 Nm)

VALVE LASH

ADJUSTMENT

Mercedes-Benz engines use hydraulic valve lifters. There is no provision for valve clearance adjustments.

ENGINE PERFORMANCE & EMISSION CONTROLS

CAMSHAFT POSITION (CMP) SENSOR

LOCATION

Engine ID 272

See Figure 65.

Engine ID 157 & 278

See Figure 66.

REMOVAL & INSTALLATION

Engine ID 272

1. Remove the left engine intake air duct and front appearance cover.
2. Disconnect the sensor electrical connector.
3. Remove the mounting bolts and remove the sensor. Discard the sealing ring.
4. Installation is the reverse order of removal. Use a new sealing ring.

Engine ID 156

1. Remove each engine air intake duct.
2. Unclip the hydraulic lines and hose from the bracket, left side only.
3. Disconnect the sensor electrical connector.
4. Remove the mounting bolts and remove the sensor. Discard the sealing ring.
5. Installation is the reverse order of removal. Use a new sealing ring.

Engine ID 157 & 278

1. Remove the front engine cover.
2. Remove the air intake assembly upstream of the air filter.
3. Remove the purge line from the cylinder head cover.
4. Disconnect the sensor electrical connector.
5. Remove the mounting bolt and pull the sensor from the cylinder head cover.
6. Installation is the reverse order of removal.

CRANKSHAFT POSITION (CKP) SENSOR

LOCATION

See Figures 67 and 68.

REMOVAL & INSTALLATION

Engine ID 272

See Figure 69.

1. Remove air filter housing.
2. Remove hot film mass air flow sensor.
3. Remove air duct housing.

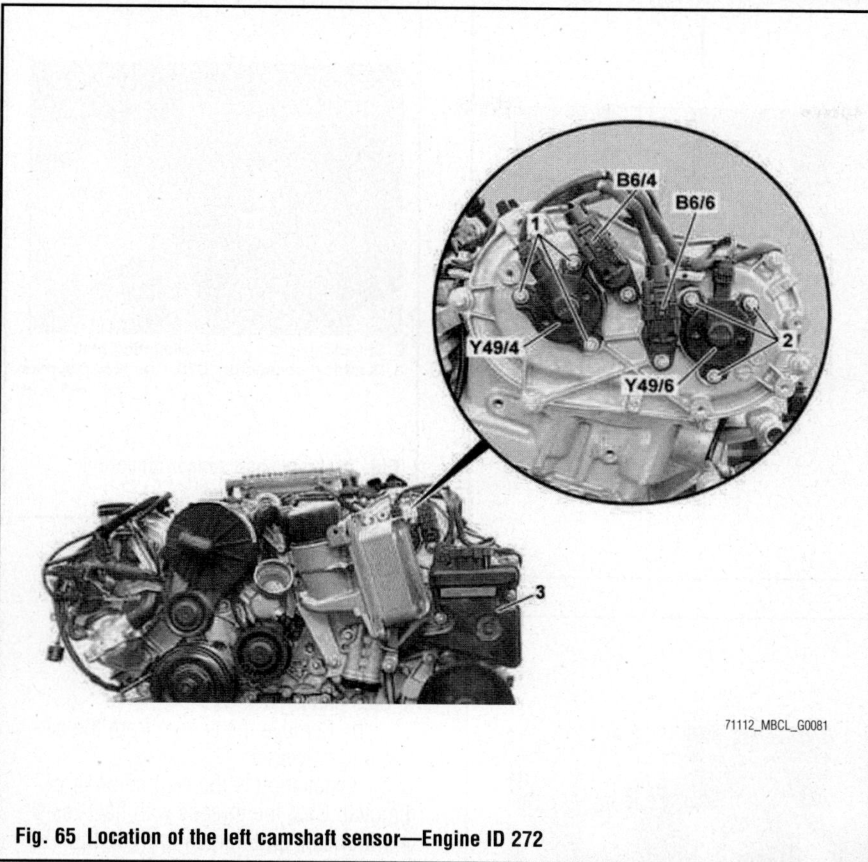

Fig. 65 Location of the left camshaft sensor—Engine ID 272

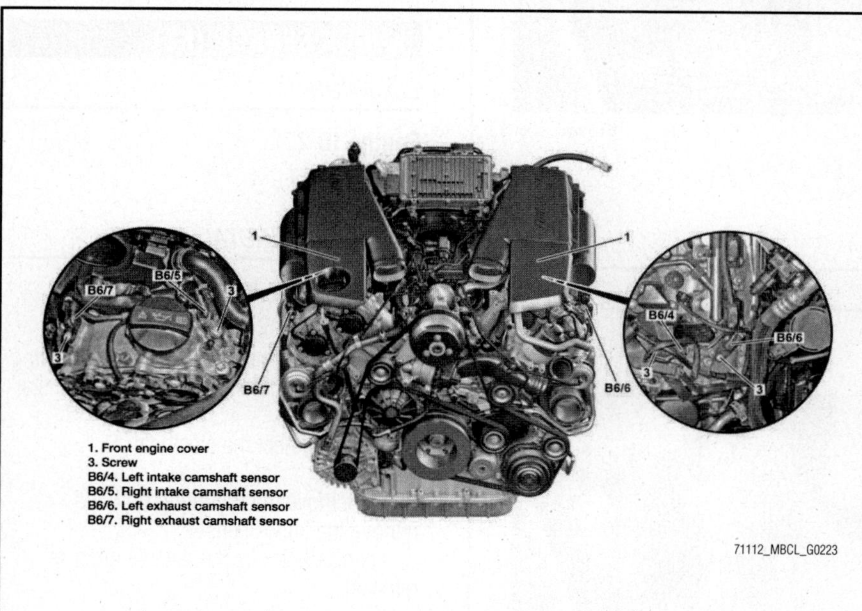

Fig. 66 Camshaft sensor locations—Engine ID 157 & 278

4. Release and disconnect electrical connector at crankshaft Hall sensor.
5. Remove bolt.
6. Pull the crankshaft Hall sensor out of crankcase.

To install:

7. Installation is the reverse of removal.
8. Tighten the crankshaft Hall sensor to crankcase bolt to 6 ft. lbs (8 Nm).

9. Carry out the initialization and then sensor rotor adaptation using STAR DIAGNOSIS tool.

Engine ID 273

1. Remove the air intake assembly.
2. Disconnect the crankshaft position (CKP) sensor wiring harness.
3. Remove the mounting bolt and remove the CKP sensor.
4. Installation is the reverse order of removal.

Engine ID 156

See Figure 70.

1. Remove the front engine cover.
2. Remove the air filter housing.
3. Properly drain the cooling system.
4. Remove the engine mount from the front axle carrier. For additional information, refer to the following section, "Engine Mount, Removal & Installation."
5. Disconnect the exhaust system at separation point of the catalytic converter/center muffler.
6. Raise the transmission slightly with a suitable jack.
7. Remove the firewall edge stripping in the area around the wiring harness. Push out the wiring harness upwards from the firewall.
8. Disconnect the coolant hose at the firewall.
9. Disconnect the crankshaft sensor electrical connector.
10. Remove the mounting bolt and remove the crankshaft sensor.
11. Installation is the reverse order of removal.

HEATED OXYGEN (HO2S) SENSOR

LOCATION

Engine ID 157 & 278

See Figures 71 and 72.

REMOVAL & INSTALLATION

Engine ID 157 & 278

1. Raise and safely support the vehicle.
2. Remove the engine compartment paneling.
3. Removing the left sensor:
   a. Detach the rear engine crossmember from the vehicle underbody and lower the transmission.
   b. Disconnect the catalytic converter from the exhaust manifold and transmission and secure to prevent from falling.

Fig. 67 CKP sensor location—C-Class engine shown

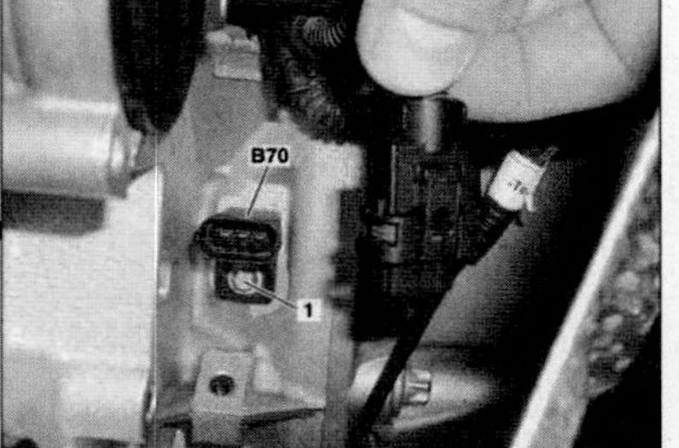

Fig. 68 CKP sensor location—Engine ID 273 shown

Fig. 69 Removing the CKP sensor

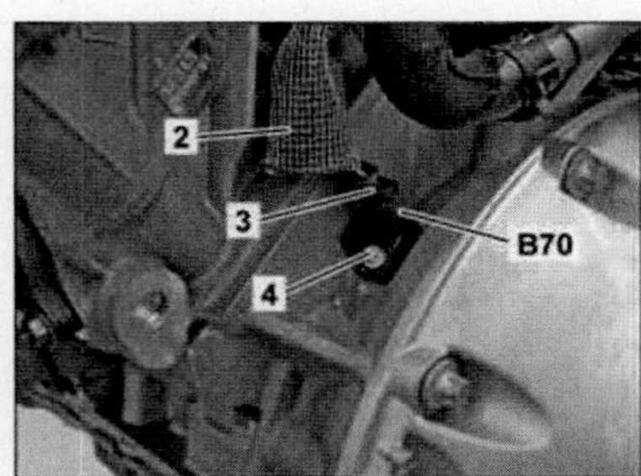

Fig. 70 Crankshaft sensor mounting location—6.2L Engine

c. Unclip the electrical connector from the O2 sensor from the bracket.

d. Remove the oxygen sensor.

4. Removing the right sensor:

a. Disconnect the electrical connector.

b. Remove the sensor from the catalytic converter.

5. Installation is the reverse order of removal. Coat the threads with heat-resistant lubricant and tighten to 37 ft. lbs. (50 Nm).

KNOCK SENSOR (KS)

LOCATION

Engine ID 272

See Figure 73.

REMOVAL & INSTALLATION

Engine ID 272 & 273

1. Remove the intake manifold. For additional information, refer to the following section, "Intake Manifold, Removal & Installation."

2. Disconnect the electrical connector.

3. Remove the mounting bolt and remove the knock sensor.

4. Installation is the reverse order of removal.

MASS AIR FLOW (MAF) SENSOR

LOCATION

Engine ID 272 & 273

See Figure 74.

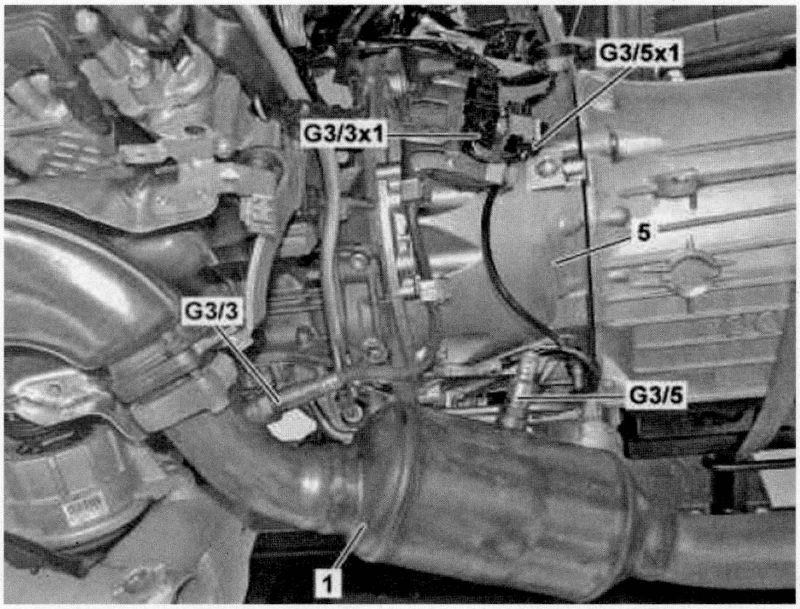

71112_MBCL_G0224

Fig. 71 Location of left O2 sensor (G3/3 & (G3/5)—CLS Class

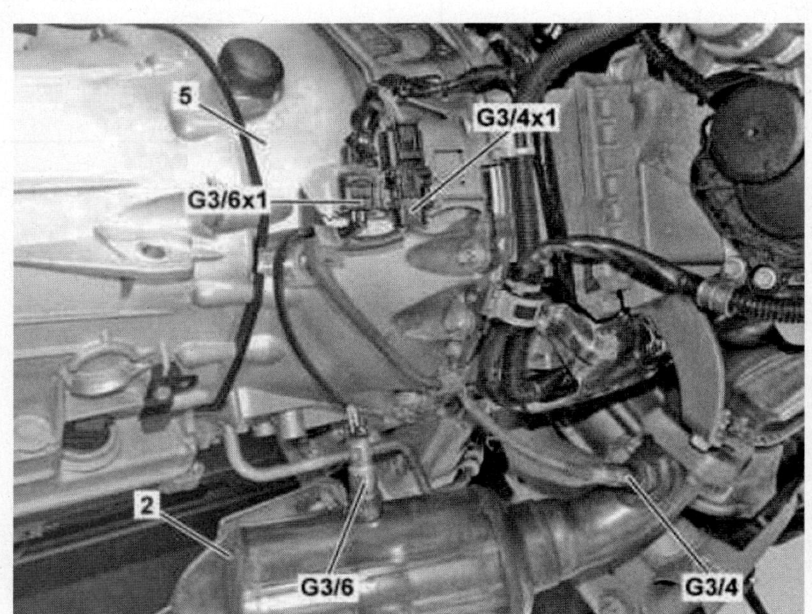

Fig. 72 Location of right O2 sensor (G3/4 & (G3/6)—CLS Class

REMOVAL & INSTALLATION

Engine ID 272 & 273

1. Before servicing the vehicle, refer to the precautions.
2. Remove air filter housing.
3. Remove the electrical connector at the hot film mass air flow sensor.
4. Disengage the right notch of the hot film mass air flow sensor at the resonance intake manifold.
5. Unlatch left notch for hot film MAF sensor on resonance intake manifold and tip hot film MAF sensor somewhat to the rear.
6. Disengage the spring steel sheet and remove the hot film mass air flow sensor from the air duct housing.
7. Check seal between air duct housing and hot film MAF sensor for damage; replace if necessary.
8. Check right notch, left notch and spring steel sheet for damage; replace if necessary.

To install:

9. Installation is the reverse of removal.
10. Connect STAR DIAGNOSIS or equivalent scan tool and read out fault memory.

THROTTLE CONTROL ACTUATOR

LOCATION

Engine ID 272

See Figure 75.

Engine ID 157 & 278

See Figure 76.

REMOVAL & INSTALLATION

Engine ID 272

See Figure 77.

1. Before servicing the vehicle, refer to the precautions.
2. Remove air filter housing.
3. Remove mass air flow sensor.
4. Remove air guide tube.
5. Release and disconnect electrical connector at throttle valve actuator.
6. Pull bleed house out of throttle valve actuator.
7. Remove bolts.
8. Remove throttle valve actuator.
9. Remove gasket.

To install:

10. Installation is the reverse of removal.
11. Tighten bolt connecting throttle valve actuator to resonance intake manifold: 80 inch lbs. (9 Nm)

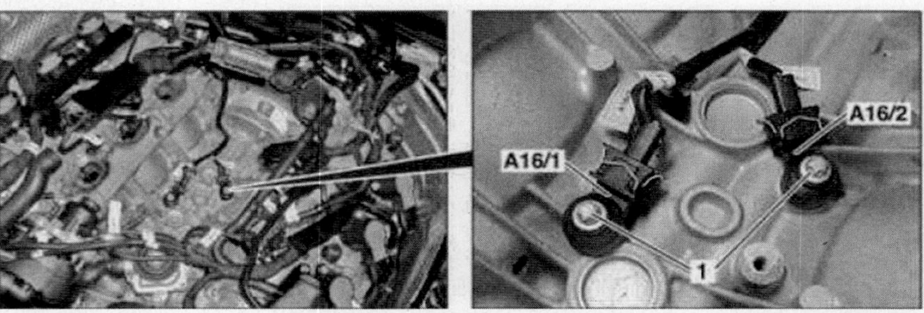

Fig. 73 Knock sensor location—Engine ID 272 & 273

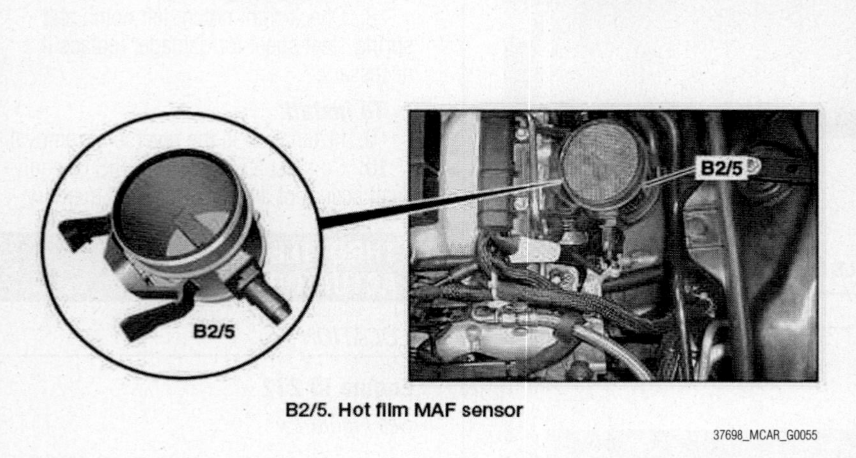

Fig. 74 MAF sensor location

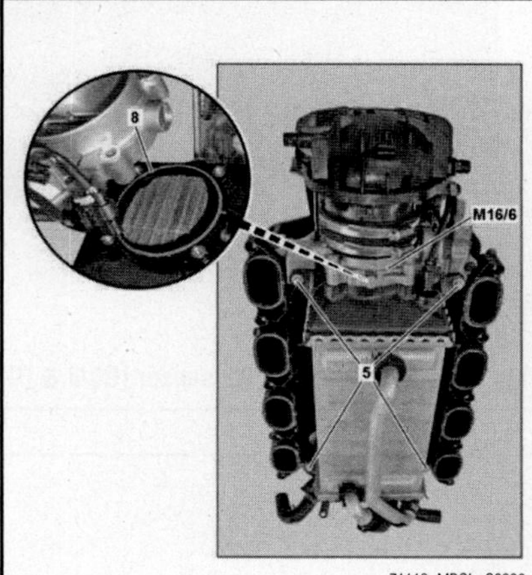

Fig. 76 Throttle valve actuator on the intake manifold

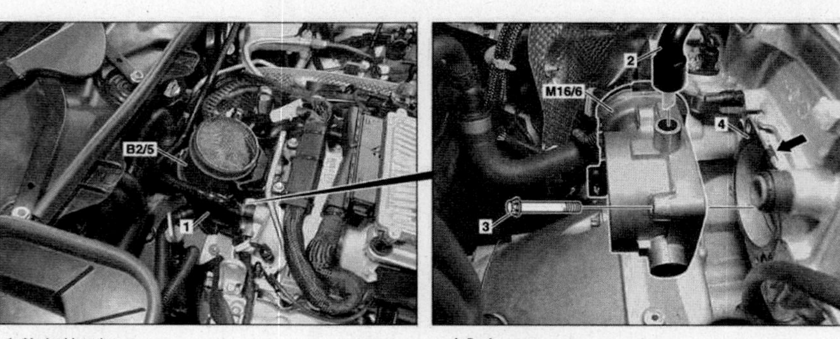

Fig. 75 Throttle control actuator location

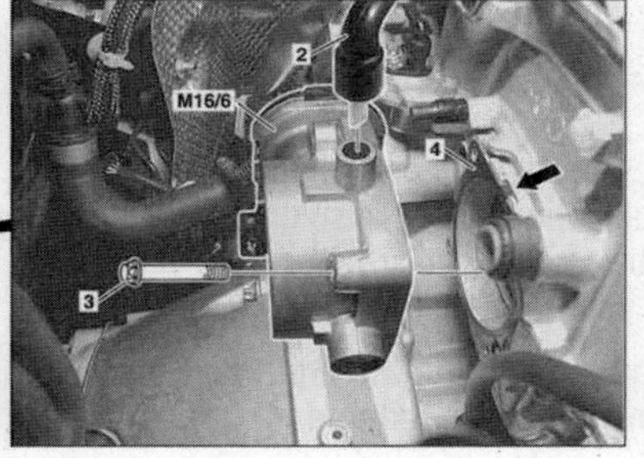

37698_MERC_G0058

Fig. 77 Removing throttle control actuator

Engine ID 157 & 278

1. Remove the intake manifold. For additional information, refer to the following section, "Intake Manifold, Removal & Installation."
2. Disconnect the electrical connectors on intake air temperature sensor and pressure sensor downstream of throttle valve.
3. Disconnect electrical plug connector on throttle valve actuator.
4. Unclip the electrical line on the throttle valve actuator.
5. Unscrew the bolts for the charge air cooler on intake manifold.
6. Loosen the clamp for intake manifold on throttle valve actuator.
7. Detach the charge air cooler and the throttle valve actuator on the intake manifold.
8. Unclip the electrical line on the throttle valve actuator.
9. Remove the bolts on the throttle valve actuator.
10. Detach the throttle valve actuator from the charge air cooler.
11. Remove the seal for the throttle valve actuator on the charge air cooler.
12. Installation is the reverse order of removal.

FUEL

GASOLINE FUEL INJECTION SYSTEM

FUEL SYSTEM SERVICE PRECAUTIONS

Safety is the most important factor when performing not only fuel system maintenance but any type of maintenance. Failure to conduct maintenance and repairs in a safe manner may result in serious personal injury or death. Maintenance and testing of the vehicle's fuel system components can be accomplished safely and effectively by adhering to the following rules and guidelines.

- To avoid the possibility of fire and personal injury, always disconnect the negative battery cable unless the repair or test procedure requires that battery voltage be applied.
- Always relieve the fuel system pressure prior to disconnecting any fuel system component (injector, fuel rail, pressure regulator, etc.), fitting or fuel line connection. Exercise extreme caution whenever relieving fuel system pressure to avoid exposing skin, face and eyes to fuel spray. Please be advised that fuel under pressure may penetrate the skin or any part of the body that it contacts.
- Always place a shop towel or cloth around the fitting or connection prior to loosening to absorb any excess fuel due to spillage. Ensure that all fuel spillage (should it occur) is quickly removed from engine surfaces. Ensure that all fuel soaked cloths or towels are deposited into a suitable waste container.
- Always keep a dry chemical (Class B) fire extinguisher near the work area.
- Do not allow fuel spray or fuel vapors to come into contact with a spark or open flame.
- Always use a back-up wrench when loosening and tightening fuel line connection fittings. This will prevent unnecessary stress and torsion to fuel line piping.
- Always replace worn fuel fitting O-rings with new Do not substitute fuel hose or equivalent where fuel pipe is installed.

Before servicing the vehicle, make sure to also refer to the precautions in the beginning of this section as well.

RELIEVING FUEL SYSTEM PRESSURE

1. Before servicing the vehicle, refer to the precautions.
2. Disconnect the negative battery cable.
3. Connect a fuel pressure gauge with a pressure release valve to the service port on the fuel supply rail.
4. Place the fuel release tube into a container and open the valve.
5. Remove the fuel pressure gauge from the service port on the fuel supply rail.

FUEL FILTER

REMOVAL & INSTALLATION

C-Class Models

See Figure 78.

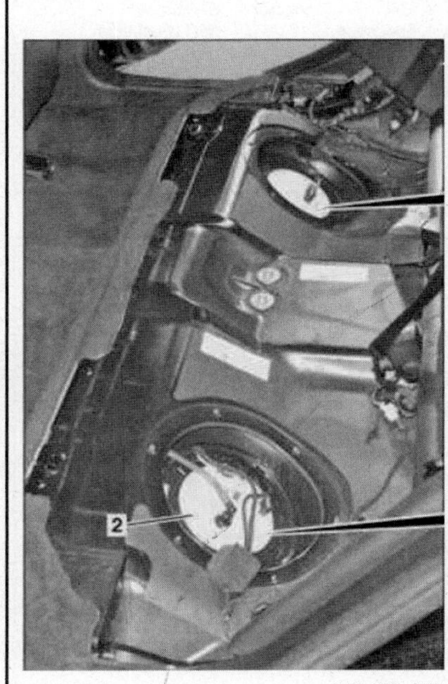

71112_MBCL_G0083

Fig. 78 Location of the fuel filter (2) in the left fuel chamber—C-Class models

1. Disconnect the fuel lines from the fuel pump.
2. Remove the cap of the left service opening.
3. Using a suitable fuel pump wrench, remove the left locking ring.
4. Remove the fuel filter assembly from the left chamber of the fuel tank.
5. Disconnect the left fuel level indicator sensor from the fuel filter.
6. Disconnect the fuel pressure sensor from the fuel filter, if equipped with Engine ID 272.
7. Installation is the reverse order of removal.

CLS-Class Models

See Figures 79 and 80.

1. Remove the fuel pump assembly from the fuel tank.
2. Detach the fuel hose from the fuel filter.

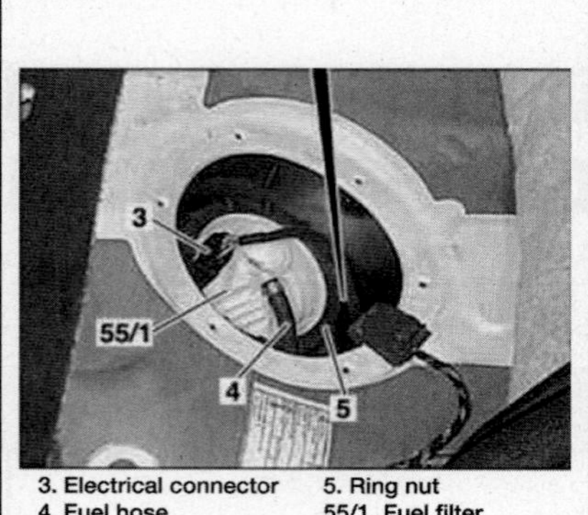

3. Electrical connector
4. Fuel hose
5. Ring nut
55/1. Fuel filter

71112_MBCL_G0182

Fig. 79 Uses a claw-type wrench to remove the ring nut—CLS-Class models

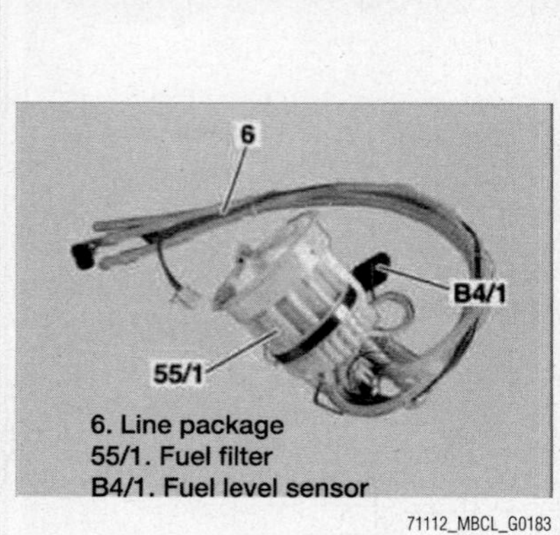

6. Line package
55/1. Fuel filter
B4/1. Fuel level sensor

71112_MBCL_G0183

Fig. 80 Remove the fuel filter assembly from the fuel tank—CLS-Class models

3. Using a suitable claw-type wrench to unscrew the ring nut.
4. Remove the fuel filter along with the line package from the fuel tank.
5. Discard the fuel filter gasket.

To install:

6. Replace the fuel filter gasket.
7. Tie up the ends of the lines in the line package with a cable tie so the line package can be easily installed between the chambers of the fuel tank.

➡The marking on the fuel filter must align with the marking on the fuel tank.

8. The remainder of the installation is the reverse order of removal.

FUEL PUMP

REMOVAL & INSTALLATION

C-Class Models

1. Properly drain the fuel tank.

⁂ WARNING

The fuel tank must be less than ¼ full or fuel will leak out.

2. Remove the rear seat cushion.
3. Remove the cover for the right service opening.
4. Remove the right locking ring using a suitable fuel pump wrench.
5. Unlock and disconnect the any electrical connectors from the locating cover and remove.
6. Remove the locking ring on the left fuel tank chamber using a suitable fuel pump wrench, AMG models only.
7. Disconnect the fuel lines from the fuel pump assembly.
8. AMG models only, release the locks and detach the connector upwards from the swirl pot. Pry apart the swirl pots carefully using a screwdriver.
9. Remove the swirl pots with the pump out of the right chamber of the fuel pump.

➡Handle the fuel lever sensor carefully to avoid deforming the float linkage.

10. Installation is the reverse order of removal. If the fuel pump is being replaced, the fuel lever sensor must be transferred.

CLS-Class Models

See Figure 81.

1. Properly drain the fuel tank.

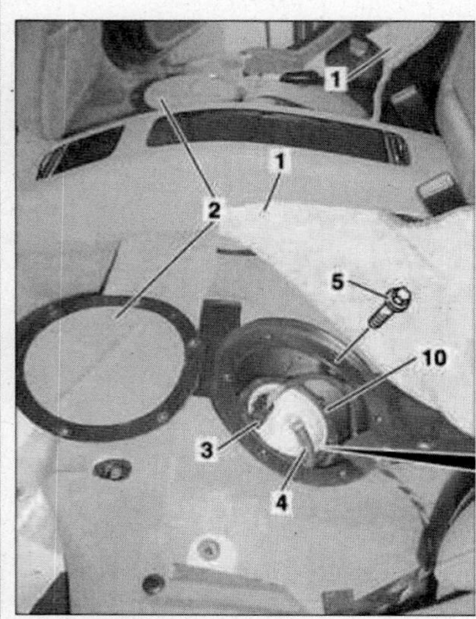

1. Sound deadening mat
2. Cap
3. Electrical connector
4. Fuel hose
5. Bolts
10. Ring nut

71112_MBCL_G0184

Fig. 81 The fuel pump is accessible through the service openings—CLS-Class models

⁂ WARNING

The fuel tank must be less than ¼ full or fuel will leak out.

2. Remove the rear seat cushions.
3. Push back the sound deadening mats.
4. Remove the hold down bolts and detach the service opening caps.
5. Disconnect the electrical connector at the fuel level sensor.
6. Remove the fuel hose from the fitting on the fuel level sensor.
7. Unscrew the ring nuts on the fuel tank using a suitable claw-type wrench.
8. Remove the position holder from the right chamber of the fuel tank.
9. Remove the sealing ring.
10. Release and disconnect the electrical connector from the fuel pump.
11. Take the fuel lines out of the brackets at the fuel pump.
12. Remove the fuel pump from the right chamber of the fuel tank.
13. Remove the fuel level sensor from the left tank half of the fuel tank.
14. Installation is the reverse order of removal.

FUEL RAIL & INJECTORS

REMOVAL & INSTALLATION

Engine ID 272 & 273

See Figures 82 and 83.

1. Ensure the ignition is in the **OFF** position.
2. Properly relieve the fuel system pressure.
3. Remove the air filter housing.
4. Disconnect the fuel rail wiring harnesses.
5. Remove the jack for the wiring harnesses.
6. Disconnect the right-side electrical connector for the fuel injection control unit.
7. Remove the control unit from the mounting bracket and set aside.
8. Remove the right control unit bracket.
9. Disconnect the supply ducts from the cylinder head cover, intake manifold and suspension lug.
10. Remove the rear left engine lifting eye from the cylinder head.
11. Disconnect the hoses from the crankcase ventilation (CCV) system.
12. Disconnect fuel injector electrical connectors.

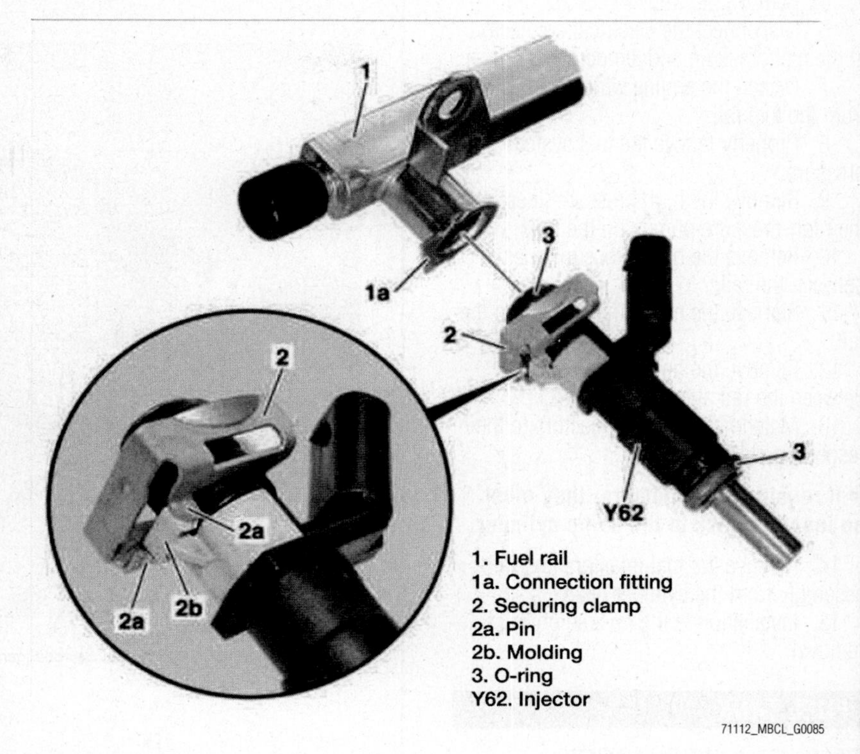

Fig. 83 Fuel injector components—Engine ID 272 & 273

2a. Service port
3a. Right control unit bracket
3b. Left control unit bracket
4a. Feed duct
4b. Feed duct
4c. Feed duct
N3/10. ME-SFE control unit
R. Right connector
L. Left connector

71112_MBCL_G0084

Fig. 82 Fuel rail mounting components—Engine ID 272

13. Disconnect the fuel line from the fuel rail. Immediately plug the line.
14. Remove the mounting bolts and remove the fuel rail with the injectors attached.
15. Pull out each injection valve from the fuel rail.

To install:

16. Replace the O-rings of the fuel injectors.
17. Slide the securing clamps onto the injectors. Push on so that the cone on the safety clips encloses the moldings on the fuel injectors.
18. Apply a suitable liquid lubricant paste to the O-rings.
19. Insert each injector into the correct position on the fuel rail. The shape of the clips and fittings determines the correct position of the injectors.
20. The remainder of the installation is the reverse order of removal. Tighten the fuel rail mounting bolts to 80 inch lbs. (9 Nm).

Engine ID 157 & 278

1. Disconnect the negative battery cable.
2. Remove the engine covers.
3. Remove the air filter housings.

4. Remove the fuel rail insulation.
5. Remove the ME-SFI control unit.
6. Disconnect the electrical connector at the fuel pressure and temperature sensor.
7. Detach the engine wiring harness from the fuel rail.
8. Properly relieve the fuel system pressure.
9. Remove the high pressure lines from the high-pressure pumps on the rails.
10. Remove the high-pressure lines between the rails.
11. Remove the mounting bolts from the rail.
12. Remove the hold-down device between the rail and fuel injectors.
13. Matchmark the fuel injectors to their respective cylinders.

➡If reusing fuel injectors, they must be inserted back to the same cylinder.

14. Remove the fuel injectors and rail assembly from the cylinder head.
15. Installation is the reverse order of removal.

FUEL TANK

REMOVAL & INSTALLATION

C-Class Models

See Figures 84 and 85.

1. Properly drain the fuel tank.
2. Remove the rear seat cushion.
3. Unlock and disconnect the fuel pump harness and tank electrical connector.
4. Unlock and disconnect the fuel pressure sensor electrical connector, except AMG models.
5. Raise and safely support the vehicle.
6. Remove the rear axle assembly. For additional information, refer to the following section, "Rear Axle, Removal & Installation."
7. Remove the fender liner from the right rear fender.
8. Remove the filler neck connection at the filler pipe.
9. Detach the hose on the activated charcoal canister.
10. Disconnect the drain hose from the filler neck depression.
11. Pull the boot from the rear fender.
12. Disconnect the fuel line from the frame floor assembly.
13. Remove the heat shield.
14. Support the fuel tank with a suitable jack.
15. Remove the mounting bolts and nuts.
16. Pull the filler pipe out of the boot and lower the fuel tank.

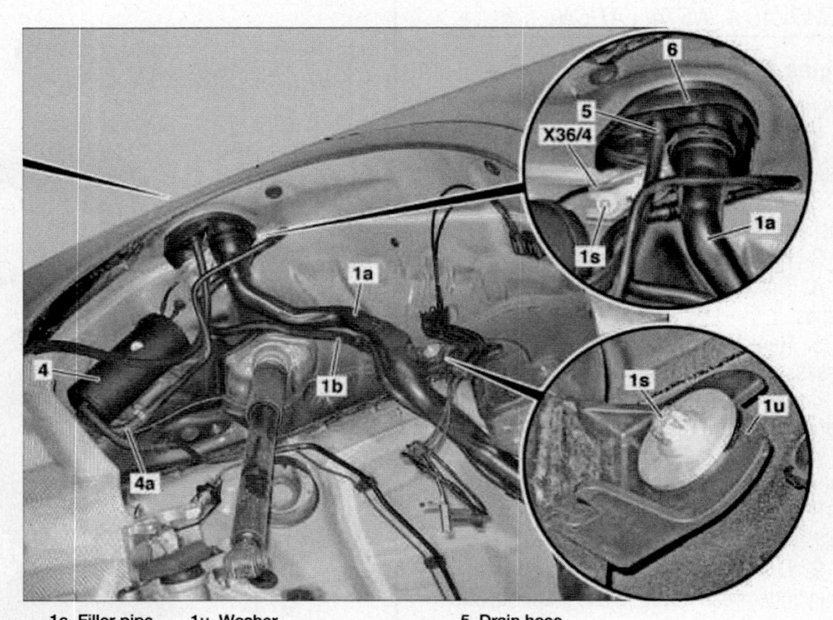

Fig. 84 Fuel tank mounting from the right fender—C-Class models

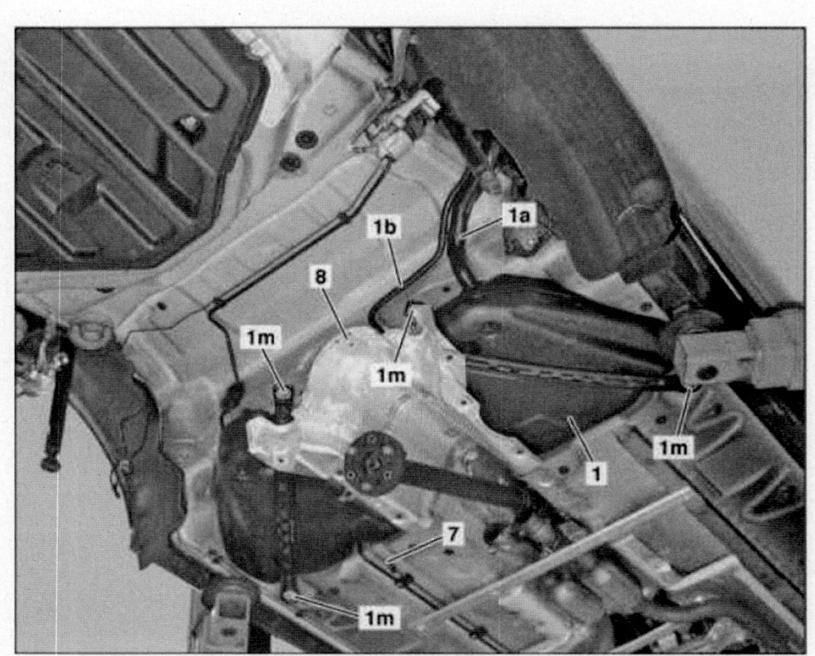

Fig. 85 Fuel tank mounting—C-Class models

⁂ WARNING

Never handle the fuel tank at the filler pipe or vent line to avoid damage. These parts cannot be replaced separately and if damaged, the entire fuel tank must be replaced.

To install:

17. Spread a suitable lubricating paste onto the boot and insert the filler pipe into the boot.
18. Raise the fuel tank into place.
19. Align the filler pipe so the boot surrounds and seals the filler neck over its whole circumference.
20. Tighten the fuel tank mounting fasteners to 15 ft. lbs. (20 Nm).
21. The remainder of the installation is the reverse order of removal.

CLS-Class Models

1. Properly drain the fuel tank.
2. Remove both rear seat cushions.
3. Fold back the insulation mat.
4. Remove the left service access cap.
5. Disconnect the wiring harness.
6. Remove the rear stowage compartment.
7. Unscrew the nut from the grub screw of the fuel tank.
8. Remove the crossmember.
9. Remove the both rear sections of the underfloor paneling.
10. Remove the exhaust system from the flange connection.
11. Remove the heat shields.
12. Disconnect the driveshaft form the rear axle center assembly.
13. Remove the bolts from the center support bearing and remove the rear part of the driveshaft.
14. Remove the heat shield.
15. Unhook the rear brake cables from the automatic slack adjuster on the parking brake.
16. Disconnect the filler hose at the fuel tank.
17. Disconnect the connector hose from the fuel feed and return lines.
18. Support the fuel tank with a suitable jack.
19. Disconnect the retaining straps on the underfloor and lower the fuel tank slightly.
20. Detach the connector hoses from the vent lines.
21. Lower the fuel tank and remove.
22. Installation is the reverse order of removal.

DRAINING

1. Open the fuel filler cap to release fuel tank pressure.
2. Properly relieve the fuel system pressure.
3. Remove the valve and attach a pressure hose to pump off the fuel at the service valve into a suitable container.
4. Connect the STAR DIAGNOSIS tool and activate the fuel pump.
5. After the fuel is drained, remove the pressure hose and reinstall the valve element.
6. Install the protective cap onto the service.

THROTTLE BODY

REMOVAL & INSTALLATION

Engine ID 272 & 273

See Figure 86.

1. Before servicing the vehicle, refer to the precautions.
2. Remove air filter housing.
3. Remove mass air flow sensor.
4. Remove air guide tube.
5. Release and disconnect electrical connector at throttle valve actuator.
6. Pull bleed house out of throttle valve actuator.
7. Remove bolts.
8. Remove throttle valve actuator.
9. Remove gasket.

To install:

10. Installation is the reverse of removal.
11. Tighten bolt connecting throttle valve actuator to resonance intake manifold: 80 inch lbs. (9 Nm)
12. Connect STAR DIAGNOSIS tool, read out and clear fault memory.

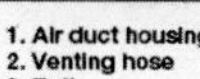

1. Air duct housing
2. Venting hose
3. Bolt

4. Seal
B2/5. Hot film mass air flow sensor
M16/6. Throttle valve actuator

37698_MERC_G0058

Fig. 86 Removing throttle control actuator

HEATING & AIR CONDITIONING SYSTEM

BLOWER MOTOR

REMOVAL & INSTALLATION

C-Class Models

FRONT

See Figure 87.

1. Remove the cover below instrument panel.
2. Disconnect the coupling from electronic blower control unit.
3. Unclip the electrical connector from blower motor.
4. Detach the cable tie from electrical line
5. Unhook the electrical line from retaining tab (arrow) of blower motor.
6. Release the shackle.
7. Twist the blower motor assembly until the markings line up. This unlocks the bayonet connection and the blower motor can be removed.
8. Installation is the reverse order of removal.

REAR

See Figures 88 and 89.

1. Remove the center console.
2. Disconnect the rear blower motor electrical connector.
3. Release the catch hook (arrow A) and remove plug of rear blower motor electrical connector from bracket at center console.
4. Disconnect the Audio/COMAND control panel electrical connector.
5. Remove the white plug of the Audio/COMAND control panel electrical connector from plug of the rear blower motor electrical connector.
6. Free the wiring harnesses from lugs. There are 5 lugs, each to the right and left at the rear blower motor .
7. Loosen the retaining clamp.
8. Disconnect the electrical connector at rear When replacing the rear blower motor footwell vent air outlet temperature sensor, remove the rear footwell vent air outlet temperature sensor.
9. Remove the screws/bolts and remove the rear blower motor.
10. Installation is the reverse order of removal.

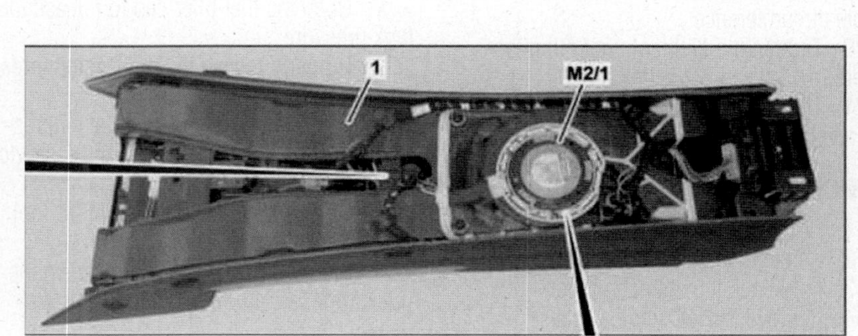

Fig. 88 The rear blower motor (M2/1) is mounted in the center console (1)—C-Class models

Fig. 87 Front blower motor mounting—C-Class models

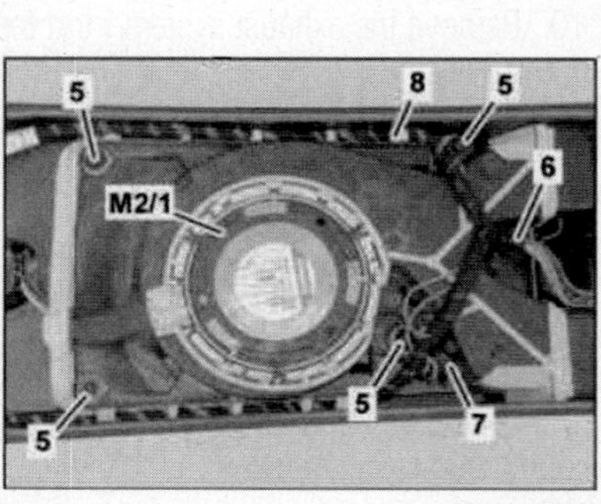

Fig. 89 Rear blower motor mounting—C-Class models

CLS-Class Models

1. Remove the cover below the instrument panel.
2. Disconnect the electrical connector.
3. Remove the mounting bolts and remove the blower base.
4. Remove the mounting bolts and remove the blower motor with the regulator as an assembly.
5. Installation is the reverse order of removal.

HEATER CORE

REMOVAL & INSTALLATION

C-Class Models

See Figure 90.

1. Remove the air conditioner housing.
2. Detach the left blend air flap actuator motor and right blend air flap actuator motor.
3. Expose electrical lines of left blend air flap actuator motor and right blend air flap actuator motor and place left blend air flap actuator motor and right blend air flap actuator motor to one side with electrical lines still connected.
4. Detach the seals, electrical connectors, and mounting bolts and remove the diffuser fitting and move to the side.
5. Unhook the relay lever and remove the actuator motors carrier.
6. Remove the mounting bolt and remove the heater core bracket.
7. Moisten the seal in the area of the line bracket with rubber lubricant and guide over the line bracket.

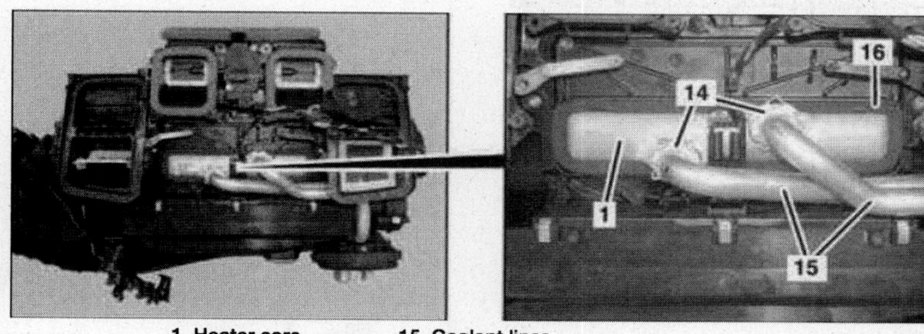

1. Heater core
14. Retaining clips
15. Coolant lines
16. Gasket

71112_MBCL_G0096

Fig. 90 Heater core mounting—C-Class models

8. Remove the bolts and remove the line bracket.
9. Unclip an y retaining clamps from the coolant lines.
10. Pull the coolant lines out of the heater core.
11. Pull the heater core out of the air conditioner housing.
12. Installation is the reverse order of removal. Ensure the correct seating of the gaskets and sealing rings.
13. Properly charge the system with refrigerant.
14. Start the engine and check for leaks.

CLS-Class Models

1. Remove the air conditioner housing.
2. Separate the self-adhesive dampening from the A/C housing.
3. Separate the electrical connector, remove the mounting screws and remove the actuator motors.
4. Detach the seals and remove the covers.
5. Open the bracket of the clamping bracket and remove the bracket upwards.
6. Unclip the brackets all the way around, remove the air distributor.
7. Remove the heater core from the evaporator housing.
8. Installation is the reverse order of removal. Ensure the correct seating of the gaskets and sealing rings.
9. Properly charge the system with refrigerant.

STEERING

POWER RACK & PINION STEERING GEAR

REMOVAL & INSTALLATION

C-Class Models

1. Remove the front engine cover.
2. Remove the left engine intake air duct.
3. Using a suitable pump, remove the power steering fluid from the expansion reservoir.
4. Raise and safely support the vehicle.
5. Ensure the steering wheel is centered and the wheels are in the straight-ahead position. Fix the steering wheel in this position in this retaining device.
6. Remove the front wheels.
7. Remove any engine compartment paneling necessary.
8. Disconnect the tie rods from the steering knuckles.
9. Detach the steering coupling from the rack-and-pinion gear. Discard the self-locking nut.
10. Disconnect the electrical connector from the solenoid valve, if equipped.
11. Remove the mounting bolts and remove the rack and pinion steering gear. Discard the bolts.
12. Installation is the reverse order of removal.
13. Tighten the steering gear mounting bolts to 52 ft. lbs. (70 Nm) plus 90°.

CLS-Class Models

See Figure 91.

1. Extend out the adjusting steering column fully.
2. Ensure the steering wheel is centered and the wheels are in the straight-ahead position. Fix the steering wheel in this position in this retaining device.
3. Remove the front engine cover.
4. Using a suitable pump, remove the power steering fluid from the expansion reservoir.
5. Raise and safely support the vehicle.
6. Remove the front wheels.
7. Remove any engine compartment paneling necessary.
8. Press the tie rod joints off of the steering knuckles.
9. Detach the head shield from the front axle carrier.
10. Disconnect the steering coupling from the lower steering shaft and removing the bolt.

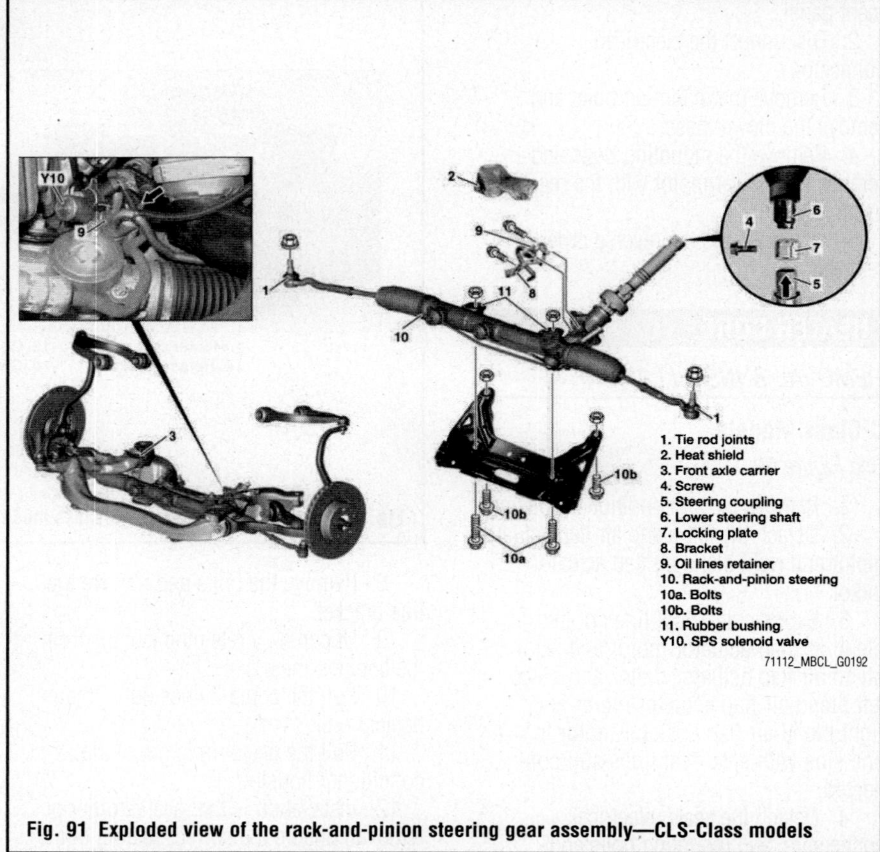

Fig. 91 Exploded view of the rack-and-pinion steering gear assembly—CLS-Class models

11. Pull the lower steering shaft upward to extract it from the steering coupling.
12. Cut the cable tie and disconnect the plug from the SPS solenoid valve.
13. Dismantle the bracket from the rack-and-pinion steering.
14. Remove the oil line retaining plate from the steering gear and pull out the oil lines. Discard the O-rings.
15. Support the steering gear with a suitable jack.
16. Remove the steering gear from the front axle carrier by removing the mounting bolts.
17. Carefully lower and remove the steering gear assembly.
18. Installation is the reverse order of removal. Tighten the steering gear mounting bolts to 52 ft. lbs. (70 Nm) plus 90°.

POWER STEERING PUMP

BLEEDING

1. Raise and safely support the vehicle.
2. Remove the left engine intake duct.
3. Remove the front engine cover.
4. Remove the cap from the power steering reservoir.
5. Fill the power steering reservoir to 0.4 inches (10 mm) from the upper edge of the reservoir with suitable power steering fluid.
6. Without the engine running, turn the steering wheel slowly from lock to lock. Repeat this process until no bubbles are visible in the power steering reservoir.
7. Start the engine and allow the engine to run for approximately 1 minute at idle speed.

➡The level of the power steering fluid must be monitored and adding fluid should be added if necessary.

8. Slowly turn the steering wheel from lock to lock several times until no bubbles are visible in the reservoir and the fluid level stays constant.
9. Installation is the reverse order of removal.

REMOVAL & INSTALLATION

Engine ID 272

1. Remove the power steering expansion reservoir.

2. Remove the accessory drive belt. For additional information, refer to the following section, "Accessory Drive Belt, Removal & Installation."

3. Remove the front and center sections of the lower engine compartment paneling.

4. Disconnect the high pressure expansion hose form the power steering pump.

5. Disconnect the ground line from the power steering pump.

6. Remove the mounting bolts and remove the power steering pump.

7. Installation is the reverse order of removal. Tighten the mounting bolts to 15 ft. lbs. (20 Nm).

Engine ID 273

1. Remove the accessory drive belt. For additional information, refer to the following section, "Accessory Drive Belt, Removal & Installation."

2. Remove the front engine cover.

3. Remove the left engine intake air duct, upstream of the air filter.

4. Using a suitable pump, remove the power steering fluid from the expansion reservoir.

5. Disconnect the return line from the reservoir.

6. Remove the mounting screws and clip, and remove the power steering reservoir.

7. Undo the banjo bolt to detach the pressure line of the power steering from the pump.

8. Disconnect the plug from the power steering pump pressure regulator valve.

9. Remove the mounting bolts for the power steering pump.

10. Disconnect the ground line for the steering pump and remove the pump upwards out of the vehicle.

11. Installation is the reverse order of removal. Tighten the mounting bolts as follows:

- M8x30 bolts: 15 ft. lbs. (20 Nm)
- M8x34 bolts: 26 ft. lbs. (35 Nm)

12. Properly bleed the powers steering pump.

SUSPENSION

KNUCKLE & SPINDLE

REMOVAL & INSTALLATION

See Figure 92.

C-Class Models

1. Raise and safely support the vehicle.

2. Remove the front wheel.

3. Remove the front wheel hub. For additional information, refer to the following section, "Wheel Hubs & Bearings, Removal & Installation."

4. Remove the caliper dust shield.

5. Remove the strut from the steering knuckle.

6. Disconnect the wheel speed sensor from the steering knuckle.

7. Disconnect the tie rod from the steering knuckle.

8. Remove the torque strut from the steering knuckle.

9. Remove the steering knuckle.

10. Installation is the reverse order of removal.

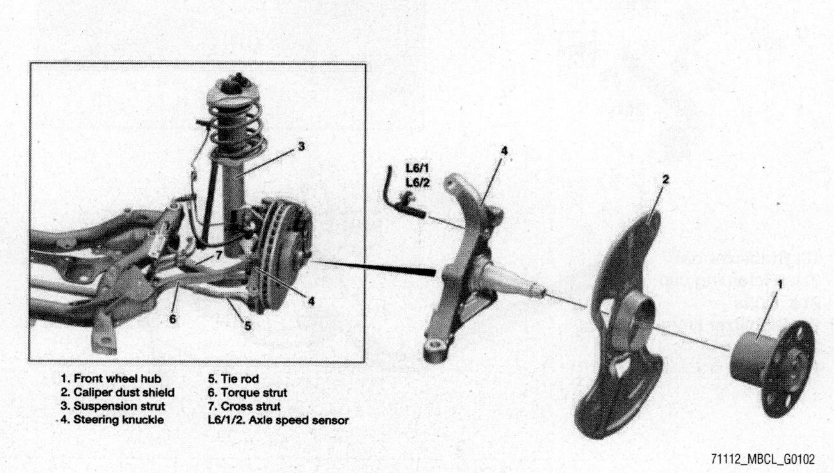

Fig. 92 Steering knuckle components—C-Class models

STABILIZER BAR & LINKS

REMOVAL & INSTALLATION

Stabilizer Links

C-Class Models

See Figure 93.

1. Raise and safely support the vehicle.

2. Remove any engine compartment paneling as needed.

3. Remove the lower bottom sections of sound proofing.

4. Remove the mounting nuts and press the link rods out of the stabilizer bar.

5. Installation is the reverse order of removal. Tighten the mounting nuts to 72 ft. lbs. (98 Nm).

CLS-Class Models

See Figure 94.

1. Evacuate the front air suspension struts, if equipped with AIRmatic suspension.

2. Remove the air filter housing with the air ducts.

3. Lower the front axle assembly.

4. Remove the clamp on the front axle carrier.

5. Remove the bracket and mounting bolts and remove the retaining bracket.

6. Remove the mounting nuts and remove the link rods from the stabilizer bar.

7. Installation is the reverse order of removal. Tighten the mounting nuts to 96 ft. lbs. (130 Nm).

Stabilizer Bar

C-Class Models

1. Raise and safely support the vehicle.

2. Remove any engine compartment paneling as needed.

3. Remove the lower bottom sections of sound proofing.

4. Remove the mounting nuts and press the link rods out of the stabilizer bar.

5. Remove the bracket form the stabilizer bar, if equipped.

6. Secure the rack-and-pinion steering gear to prevent it from falling, AMG models only.

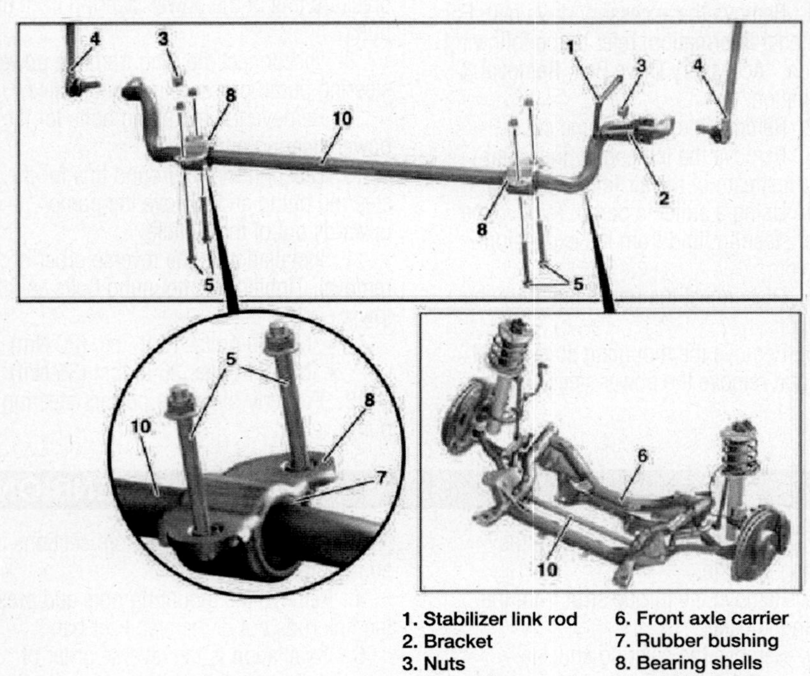

Fig. 93 Stabilizer bar components—C-Class models

7. Remove the mounting plate on the front axle carrier, AMG models only.
8. Remove the mounting bolts and remove the stabilizer bar.
9. Installation is the reverse order of removal. Tighten the mounting bolts to 22 ft. lbs. (30 Nm).

CLS-Class Models

1. Evacuate the front air suspension struts, if equipped with AIRmatic suspension.
2. Remove the air filter housing with the air ducts.
3. Lower the front axle assembly.
4. Remove the clamp on the front axle carrier.
5. Remove the bracket and mounting bolts and remove the retaining bracket.
6. Remove the mounting nuts and remove the link rods from the stabilizer bar.
7. Remove the expansion rivets and remove the fender liner in the right front fender.
8. Remove the stabilizer bar towards the front.
9. Installation is the reverse order of removal. Tighten the mounting nuts to 96 ft. lbs. (130 Nm).
10. Inflate the front air suspension struts, if equipped.

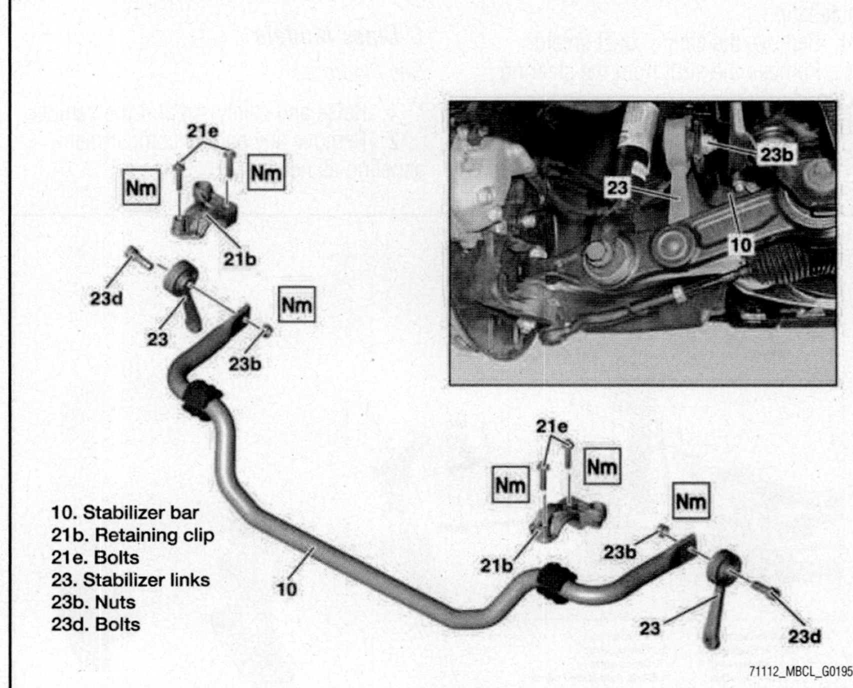

Fig. 94 Exploded view front stabilizer bar components—CLS-Class Models

STRUTS

REMOVAL & INSTALLATION

C-Class Models

See Figure 95.

1. Open the hood to the vertical position.
2. Raise and safely support the vehicle.
3. Remove the front wheel.
4. Remove the mounting nut and press the link stabilizer link rod out of the suspension strut.
5. Unclip the electrical line from the line bracket.
6. Remove the cable tie from the suspension strut.
7. Unclip the line holder from the suspension strut and move aside.
8. Remove the lower mounting bolts from the steering knuckle.
9. Remove the mounting nut and pull out the upper mounting bolt.
10. Press the suspension strut out of the steering knuckle.
11. Remove the mounting bolts from the top of the strut tower.
12. Press the retaining clamps of the cap together and remove the suspension strut from the vehicle.

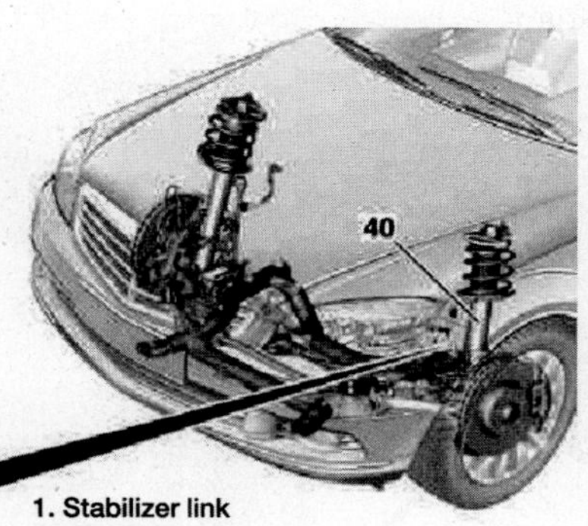

1. Stabilizer link
1a. Nut
2. electrical line
3. Line bracket
4. Cable tie
5. Bolts
6. Steering knuckle
7. Nut
8. Screw
9. Bolts
10. Cap
40. Suspension strut

71112_MBCL_G0101

Fig. 95 Suspension strut components—C-Class models

13. Installation is the reverse order of removal.
14. Tighten the mounting bolts as follows:
    - Upper steering knuckle bolts: 74 ft. lbs. (100 Nm) plus 90°
    - Lower steering knuckle bolts: 52 ft. lbs. (70 Nm), release all tension then tighten to 74 ft. lbs. (100 Nm)
    - Strut tower bolts: 24 ft. lbs. (33 Nm)

CLS-Class Models

1. Raise and safely support the vehicle.
2. Ensure the front wheels are in the straight-ahead position.
3. Remove the front wheel.
4. Remove the mounting nuts.
5. Disconnect the strut from the control arm.
6. Press the control arm downwards and remove the strut assembly towards the rear.
7. Installation is the reverse order of removal. Tighten the mounting nuts to 18 ft. lbs. (25 Nm) and control arm bolt to 122 ft. lbs. (165 Nm).

OVERHAUL

1. Remove the strut from the vehicle.
2. Clamp the tensioning device securely in a vise, and insert clamping plates and place tension on the front spring.
3. Remove the nut from the piston rod.
4. Remove the shock absorber from the tensioning device.
5. Remove the dust boot, stop buffer, cap and rubber insert.
6. Release the tension from the front spring.
7. Remove the front spring.
8. Remove the spring cup from the front spring.
9. Installation is the reverse order of removal. Tighten the piston rod nut to 74 ft. lbs. (100 Nm).

UPPER CONTROL ARMS

REMOVAL & INSTALLATION

CLS-Class Models

Left Side

See Figure 96.

1. Discharge the front air suspension strut using the STAR Diagnosis tool, if equipped.
2. Raise and safely support the vehicle.
3. Remove the front wheel.
4. Press the follower joint out of the steering knuckle. Secure the steering knuckle so the brake hose and electrical cables are not stretched.
5. Remove the left front suspension strut.
6. Remove the left front fuse box and relay box in the engine compartment.
7. Undo the expansion reservoir for the coolant and place aside.
8. Detach the upper control arm from the front end.
9. Installation is the reverse order of removal.
10. Perform a wheel alignment.

Right Side

1. Discharge the front air suspension strut using the STAR Diagnosis tool, if equipped.
2. Raise and safely support the vehicle.
3. Remove the front wheel.
4. Press the follower joint out of the steering knuckle. Secure the steering knuckle so the brake hose and electrical cables are not stretched.
5. Remove the right front suspension strut.
6. Remove the cabin air filter housing.
7. Remove the auxiliary battery.
8. Dismantle the lever control of the xenon headlamp from the control arm, if equipped.
9. Detach the upper control arm from the front end.
10. Installation is the reverse order of removal.
11. Perform a wheel alignment.

WHEEL HUBS & BEARINGS

ADJUSTMENT

See Figure 97.

1. Raise and safely support the vehicle.
2. Remove the front wheel.
3. Insert a wheel bolt opposite the safety screw far enough to fix the brake disc into place.
4. Press the brake pads back into the brake caliper.
5. Pull off the hub cap.
6. Loosen hexagon socket head screw and tighten the clamp nut while turning the front wheel hub lightly to set up the wheel bearing.
7. Loosen the clamping nut slightly until a small amount of play is noticeable.
8. Mount the dial indicator holder to the brake rotor.

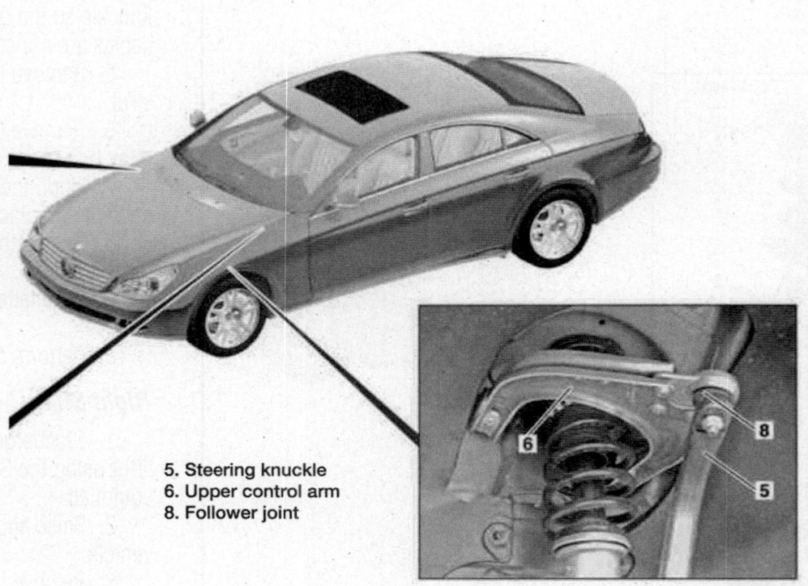

Fig. 96 Upper control arm location—CLS-Class models

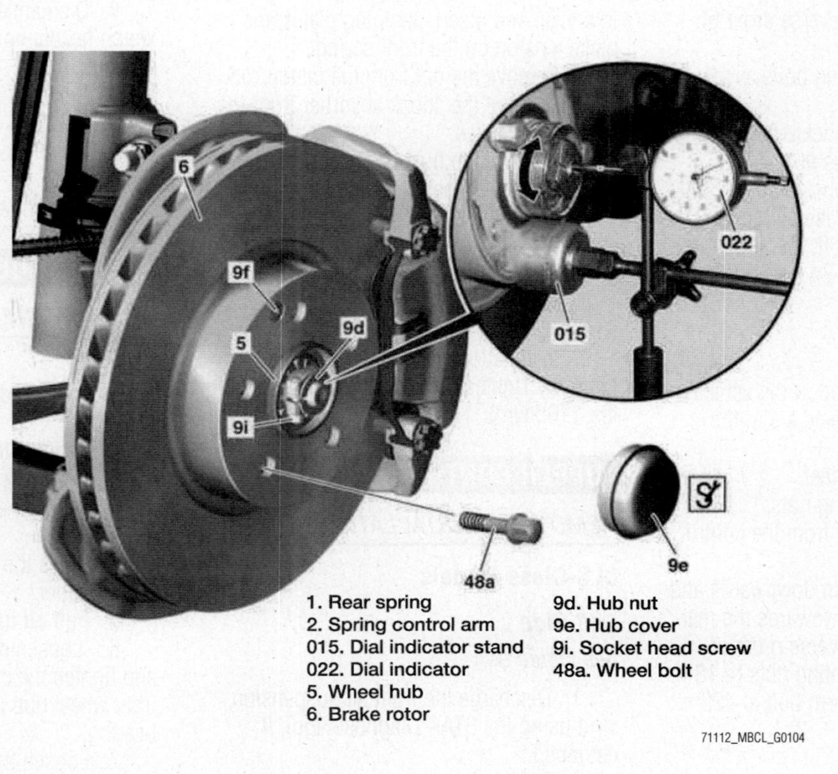

Fig. 97 Measuring for front axial play—C-Class models shown

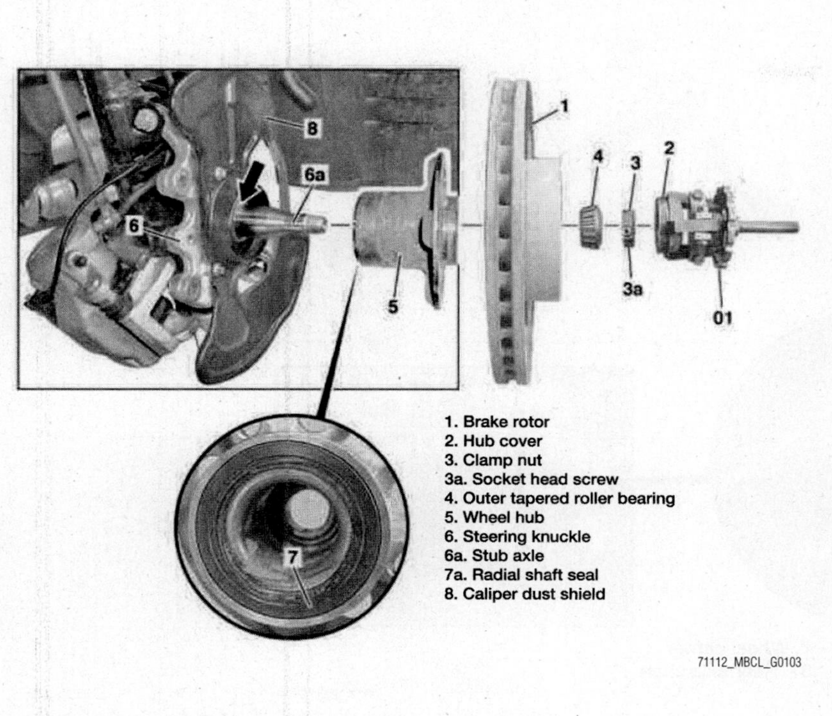

Fig. 98 Front wheel hub components—C-Class models shown

9. Adjust the wheel bearing play by turning the clamping nut in stages and pushing and pulling the rotor firmly back and forth.
10. Tighten the socket head screw and check the wheel bearing play again. If the wheel bearing play is within 0.0004–0.0008 inches (0.01–0.02 mm), remove the dial gauge and stand.
11. Fill the hub cap with a high temperature bearing grease.
12. The remainder of the installation is the reverse order of removal.

REMOVAL & INSTALLATION

See Figure 98.

1. Raise and safely support the vehicle.
2. Remove the brake rotor.
3. Pull off the hub cap.
4. Loosen the socket head screw and remove the clamping nut.
5. Remove the outer tapered roller bearing.
6. Remove the front wheel hub from the steering knuckle.
7. Installation is the reverse order of removal.

SUSPENSION

REAR SUSPENSION

COIL SPRINGS

REMOVAL & INSTALLATION

C-Class Models

See Figure 99.

1. Raise and safely support the vehicle.
2. Remove the rear wheel.
3. Remove the cover of the rear control arm.
4. Install a spring compressor to the rear spring and apply tension to the rear spring to compress it.
5. Remove the rear spring from the control arm.
6. Installation is the reverse order of removal.

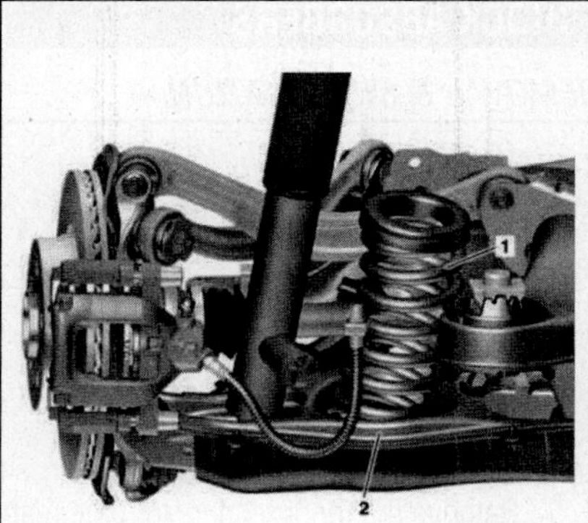

Fig. 99 Rear spring location—C-Class models

CLS-Class Models

See Figure 100.

1. Raise and safely support the vehicle.
2. Remove the rear wheel.
3. Remove the cover of the control arm.
4. Remove pilot stud.
5. Install a suitable spring compressor onto the coil spring and tension the spring enough to remove it.
6. Installation is the reverse order of removal.

LOWER CONTROL ARMS

REMOVAL & INSTALLATION

CLS-Class Models

1. Raise and safely support the vehicle.
2. Completely empty the air springs using the STAR Diagnosis tool, if equipped.
3. Remove the rear wheel.
4. Remove the control arm cover.
5. Remove the rear spring. For additional information, refer to the following section, "Coil Spring, Removal & Installation."
6. Disconnect the shock from the control arm.
7. Using a suitable jack, raise the wheel carrier until the rear axle shaft is horizontal.

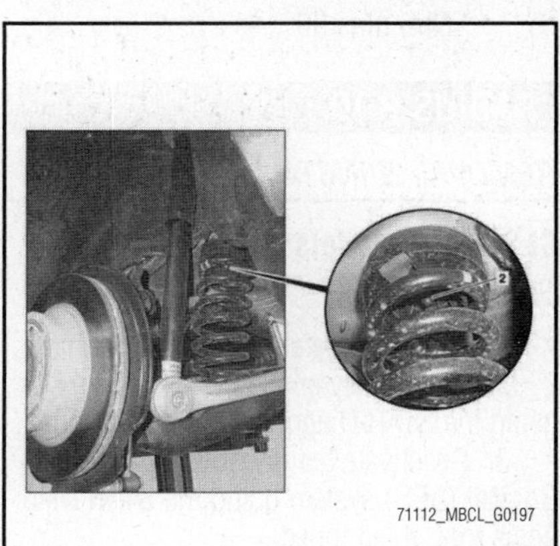

Fig. 100 Rear spring location—CLS-Class models

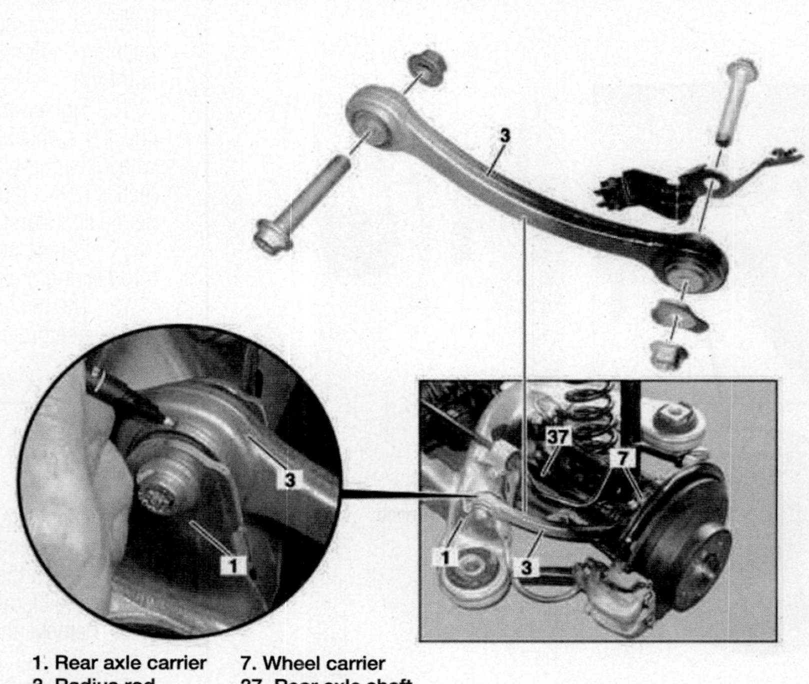

Fig. 101 Radius rod mounting—CLS-Class models

8. Disconnect the tie rod from the wheel carrier and swing upwards out of the way.
9. Remove the brake caliper from the rear axle carrier.
10. Disconnect the control arm from the rear axle carrier.
11. Disconnect the control arm from the wheel carrier and remove.
12. Installation is the reverse order of removal. Tighten the bolts as follows:
   - Bolt to rear axle carrier: 37 ft. lbs. (50 Nm) plus 90°
   - Bolt to wheel carrier: 59 ft. lbs. (80 Nm) plus 90°

RADIUS ROD

REMOVAL & INSTALLATION

CLS-Class Models

See Figure 101.

1. Raise and safely support the vehicle.
2. Completely empty the air springs using the STAR Diagnosis tool, if equipped.
3. Deactivate the Sensotronic Brake Control (SBS) system using the STAR Diagnosis tool, if equipped.
4. Remove the exhaust system at the flange connection.
5. Remove the rear section components on the underfloor paneling.
6. Unhook the rear brake cables from the parking brake automatic slack adjuster.
7. Disconnect the driveshaft from the rear axle differential.
8. Detach the fitting sleeves of the flexible coupling on the flange of the rear differential.
9. Remove the driveshaft mounting bolts to the center bearing and remove the rear half of the driveshaft.
10. Remove the rear wheel.
11. Remove the brake calipers and securely hang the caliper to prevent damaging the brake hoses.
12. Remove the fender liners from the rear fender, if equipped with air suspension.
13. Unclip the electrical feed lines from their retaining clamps.
14. Remove the left and right rear springs.
15. Disconnect the left and right shock absorbers from the control arms.
16. Raise the wheel carrier using a suitable jack until the rear axle shaft is horizontal.
17. Disconnect the radius rod from the wheel carrier.
18. Properly drain the fuel tank.
19. Matchmark the installation position of the radius rod on the rear axle carrier and radius rod.

⁂ WARNING

Do not scratch or notch the components, this could reduce their service life.

20. Disconnect the radius rod from the rear axle carrier and remove.
21. Installation is the reverse order of removal. Tighten bolts as follows:
   - M12 bolts: 37 ft. lbs. (50 Nm) plus 90°
   - M14 bolts: 59 ft. lbs. (80 Nm) plus 90°

SHOCK ABSORBERS

REMOVAL & INSTALLATION

C-Class Models

1. Raise and safely support the vehicle.
2. Remove the rear wheel.
3. Remove the cover on the spring control arm.
4. Disconnect the electrical connector from the shock absorber, if equipped.
5. Remove the inner fender from the rear fender.
6. Remove lower mounting nut from the shock absorber and remove the mounting bolt.

7. Remove the side paneling in the trunk.
8. Remove the upper mounting nut and remove the shock by compressing the damper and moving it out backwards over the brake hose.
9. Installation is the reverse order of removal.

CLS-Class Models

1. Remove the left or right panel in the luggage compartment.
2. Counterhold the piston rod using an open end wrench and remove the top piston nut.
3. Remove the washer and upper rubber mount.
4. Raise and safely support the vehicle.
5. Remove the rear wheel.
6. Remove the cover of the spring control arm.
7. Remove the mounting nut and bolt, then remove the shock absorber from the control arm.
8. Slide the shock absorber together and remove.
9. Installation is the reverse order of removal. Tighten the lower nut to 41 ft. lbs. (55 Nm) and upper nut to 15 ft. lbs. (20 Nm).

STABILIZER BAR & LINKS

REMOVAL & INSTALLATION

C-Class Models

1. Lower the rear axle carrier assembly.
2. Disconnect the stabilizer links from the stabilizer bar.
3. Disconnect the stabilizer bar from the rear axle carrier and remove.
4. Installation is the reverse order of removal. Tighten the stabilizer mounting to 59 ft. lbs. (80 Nm).

CLS-Class Models

1. Deactivate the Sensotronic Brake Control (SBC) system using the STAR Diagnosis tool, if equipped.
2. Raise and safely support the vehicle.
3. Completely empty the air springs using the STAR Diagnosis tool, if equipped.
4. Remove the rear wheels.
5. Remove the crossmember.
6. Remove the exhaust system at the flange connection.
7. Remove the rear section components on the underfloor paneling.
8. Remove the heat shields.
9. Disconnect the driveshaft from the flange on the rear axle center assembly.
10. Unhook the brake cables from the brackets on the rear axle.
11. Remove the rear brake pads and suspend the caliper to prevent damage to the brake hose.
12. Unclip the electrical lines from the wheel speed sensors, brake wear sensor and rear axle level sensor.
13. Properly drain the fuel tank.
14. Remove the filler hose from the fuel tank.
15. Support the rear axle at the center assembly with a suitable jack.
16. Unclip the linkage of the rear axle level sensor on the stabilizer bar.
17. Disconnect the stabilizer bar from the left and right stabilizer links.
18. Disconnect the left and right bearing of the stabilizer bar from the rear axle.
19. Remove the stabilizer bar out of the right side of the vehicle.
20. Installation is the reverse order of removal. Tighten the stabilizer link nuts to 30 ft. lbs. (40 Nm) and mounting bolts to 52 ft. lbs. (70 Nm).

TIE RODS

REMOVAL & INSTALLATION

CLS-Class Models

See Figure 102.

1. Raise and safely support the vehicle.

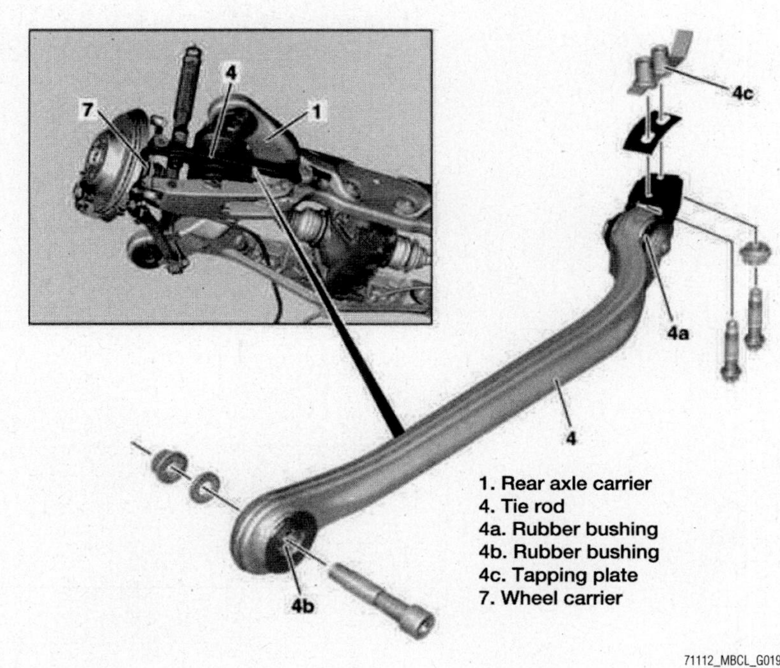

Fig. 102 Tie rod mounting—CLS-Class models

2. If equipped, empty the rear air springs with the STAR Diagnosis tool.
3. Remove the rear wheel.
4. Lift the wheel carrier using a suitable jack until the rear axle shaft is horizontal.
5. Disconnect the tie rod from the wheel carrier.
6. Disconnect the tie rod from the rear axle carrier.
7. Installation is the reverse order of removal. Tighten the bolts as follows:

- Nut at the wheel carrier: 30 ft. lbs. (40 Nm) plus 90°.
- Nut at the rear axle carrier: 52 ft. lbs. (70 Nm).

MERCEDES BENZ

7

E-Class • SLK

SPECIFICATIONS AND MAINTENANCE CHARTS

ENGINE AND VEHICLE IDENTIFICATION CHART

Engine						
Code ①	Liters (cc)	Cu. In.	Cyl.	Fuel Sys.	Type	Eng. Mfg.
271.861	1.8 (1796)	110	I4	SEFI	DOHC	MB
642.850	3.0 (2987)	182	V6	Diesel/EFI	DOHC	MB
272.942	3.0 (2996)	182	V6	SEFI	DOHC	MB
272.969	3.5 (3498)	214	V6	SEFI	DOHC	MB
272.977	3.5 (3498)	213	V6	SEFI	DOHC	MB
272.980	3.5 (3498)	213	V6	SEFI	DOHC	MB
276.952	3.5 (3498)	213	V6	SEFI	DOHC	MB
276.956	3.5 (3498)	213	V6	SEFI	DOHC	MB
278.922	4.7 (4664)	285	V8	SEFI	DOHC	MB
152.980	5.5 (5461)	333	V8	SEFI	DOHC	MB
157.981	5.5 (5461)	333	V8	SEFI	DOHC	MB
273.970	5.5 (5461)	333	V8	SEFI	DOHC	MB
273.971	5.5 (5461)	333	V8	SEFI	DOHC	MB
156.985	6.2 (6208)	379	V8	SEFI	DOHC	MB

Model Year	
Code ②	Year
B	2011
C	2012

SEFI: Sequential Electronic Fuel Injection

DOHC: Double overhead camshafts

① Stamped into the crankcase

② 10th digit of the VIN

71112_MBES_C0001

GENERAL ENGINE SPECIFICATIONS

Year	Engine Displacement Liters	Engine ID/VIN	Net Horsepower @ rpm	Net Torque@rpm (ft. lbs.)	Bore x Stroke (in.)	Com-pression Ratio	Oil Pressure @ rpm
2011	3.0	642.850	210@3800	400@1600	3.27x3.62	16.5:1	NA
	3.0	272.942	228@6000	221@2500	3.47x3.24	11.3:1	NA
	3.5	272.980	260@6000	258@2400	3.66x3.39	10.7:1	NA
	3.5	272.977	260@6000	258@2400	3.66x3.39	10.7:1	NA
	3.5	272.969	300@6500	265@4900	3.66x3.39	11.7:1	NA
	5.5	273.970	382@6000	391@2800	3.86x3.56	10.7:1	NA
	5.5	273.971	382@6000	391@2800	3.86x3.56	10.7:1	NA
	6.2	156.985	518@6800	465@5200	4.02x3.72	11.3:1	NA
2012	1.8	172.447	201@5500	229@2000	3.23x3.35	9.3:1	NA
	3.0	642.850	210@3800	400@1600	3.27x3.62	16.5:1	NA
	3.5	276.952	302@6500	272@3500	3.66x3.39	12.0:1	NA
	3.5	276.956	302@6500	272@3500	3.66x3.39	12.0:1	NA
	4.7	278.922	402@5000	443@1600	3.66x3.39	10.5:1	NA
	5.5	152.980	415@6800	398@4500	3.86x3.56	12.6:1	NA
	6.2	157.981	518@5250	516@1750	3.86x3.56	10.0:1	NA

NA: Not Available

71112_MBES_C0002

GASOLINE ENGINE TUNE-UP SPECIFICATIONS

Year	Engine Displacement Liters	Engine ID/VIN	Spark Plug Gap (in.)	Ignition Timing (deg.) MT	Ignition Timing (deg.) AT	Fuel Pump (psi)	Idle Speed (rpm) MT	Idle Speed (rpm) AT	Valve Clearance In.	Valve Clearance Ex.
2011	3.0	272.942	①	②	②	NS	②	②	HYD	HYD
	3.5	272.980	0.031	②	②	NS	NA	②	HYD	HYD
	3.5	272.977	0.031	②	②	NS	NA	②	HYD	HYD
	3.5	272.969	0.031	②	②	NS	②	②	HYD	HYD
	5.5	273.970	①	②	②	NS	NA	②	HYD	HYD
	5.5	273.971	①	②	②	NS	NA	②	HYD	HYD
	6.2	156.985	①	②	②	NS	NA	②	HYD	HYD
2012	1.8	271.861	①	②	②	NS	②	②	HYD	HYD
	3.5	276.952	①	②	②	NS	NA	②	HYD	HYD
	3.5	276.956	①	②	②	NS	NA	②	HYD	HYD
	4.7	278.922	①	②	②	NS	NA	②	HYD	HYD
	5.5	152.980	①	②	②	NS	NA	②	HYD	HYD
	6.2	157.981	①	②	②	NS	NA	②	HYD	HYD

NOTE: The Vehicle Emission Control Information label often reflects specification changes changes made during production.

NA: Not Applicable

NS: Not Specified

HYD: Hydraulic

① Spark plugs using Iridium or other precious metals should not be gapped.

② Ignition timing and idle speed are controlled by the ME engine controller. No adjustment is possible.

71112_MBES_C0003

DIESEL ENGINE TUNE-UP SPECIFICATIONS

Year	Engine Displ. Liters	Engine VIN	Valve Clearance Intake (in.)	Valve Clearance Exhaust (in.)	Injection Pump Setting (deg.)	Injection Nozzle Pressure (psi) New	Injection Nozzle Pressure (psi) Used	Idle Speed (rpm)	Cranking Compression Pressure (psi)
2011	3.0	642.850	HYD	HYD	NA	NA	NA	NA	NA
2012	3.0	642.850	HYD	HYD	NA	NA	NA	NA	NA

NOTE: The Vehicle Emission Control Information label often reflects specification changes made during production. The label figures must be used if they differ from those in this chart

NA: Not Available

① PCM controlled

② Pump output pressure: 450-4,000 psi

③ See underhood emission label

71112_MBES_C0015

CAPACITIES

Year	Model	Engine Displacement Liters	Engine ID/VIN	Engine Oil with Filter (qts.)	Transmission (pts.) Man.	Transmission (pts.) Auto.	Drive Axle Front (pts.)	Drive Axle Rear (pts.)	Fuel Tank (gal.)	Cooling System (qts.)
2011	E350 Bluetec	3.0	642.850	8.5	3.8	19.0	1.3	①	21.1	12.2
	E350	3.5	272.980	8.5	-	19.0	1.3	①	21.1	8.9
	E350 4MATIC	3.5	272.977	7.4	-	19.0	1.3	①	21.1	8.9
	E550	5.5	273.971	9.0	-	20.5	1.3	①	21.1	10.9
	E550 4MATIC	5.5	273.970	9.0	-	20.5	1.3	①	21.1	10.9
	E63 AMG	6.2	156.985	9.3	-	19.0	1.3	2.5	21.1	11.6
	SLK300	3.0	272.942	8.5	3.2	19.6	-	2.2	18.5	10.4
	SLK350	3.5	272.969	8.5	3.2	19.6	-	2.4	18.5	10.4
2012	E350 Bluetec	3.0	642.850	8.5	3.8	19.0	1.3	①	21.1	13.0
	E350	3.5	276.952	6.9	-	19.0	1.3	①	21.1	10.1
	E550	4.7	278.922	8.5	-	19.0	1.3	①	21.1	13.4
	E63 AMG	6.2	157.981	9.0	-	19.0	1.3	2.5	21.1	13.6
	SLK250	1.8	271.861	5.8	3.6	19.0	-	①	18.5	10.1
	SLK350	3.5	276.956	6.9	-	19.0	-	①	18.5	11.0
	SLK55	5.5	152.980	10.0	-	19.0	-	2.5	18.5	10.0

NOTE: All capacities are approximate. Add fluid gradually and check to be sure a proper fluid level is obtained.

① 187 mm Diameter Rear Differential: 2.0 pts.
200 mm Diameter Rear Differential: 2.3 pts.
215 mm Diameter Rear Differential: 2.5 pts.

71112_MBES_C0004

FLUID SPECIFICATIONS

Year	Model	Engine Disp. Liters	Engine ID/VIN	Engine Oil	Man. Trans.	Auto. Trans.	Drive Axle Front	Drive Axle Rear	Power Steering Fluid	Brake Master Cylinder	Cooling System
2011	E350 Bluetec	3.0	642.850	①	MB317	ATF 134	75W-85	75W-85	CHF11S	DOT4	④
	E350	3.5	272.980	②	—	ATF 134	75W-85	75W-85	CHF11S	DOT4	④
	E350 4MATIC	3.5	272.977	②	—	ATF 134	75W-85	75W-85	CHF11S	DOT4	④
	E550	5.5	273.971	②	—	ATF 134	75W-85	75W-85	CHF11S	DOT4	④
	E550 4MATIC	5.5	273.970	②	—	ATF 134	75W-85	75W-85	CHF11S	DOT4	④
	E63 AMG	6.2	156.985	③	—	ATF 134	75W-85	75W-85	CHF11S	DOT4	④
	SLK300	3.0	272.942	②	MB317	ATF 134	75W-85	75W-85	CHF11S	DOT4	④
	SLK350	3.5	272.969	②	MB317	ATF 134	75W-85	75W-85	CHF11S	DOT4	④
2012	E350 Bluetec	3.0	642.850	①	MB317	ATF 134	75W-85	75W-85	CHF11S	DOT4	④
	E350	3.5	276.952	②	—	ATF 134	75W-85	75W-85	CHF11S	DOT4	④
	E550	4.7	278.922	②	—	ATF 134	75W-85	75W-85	CHF11S	DOT4	④
	E63 AMG	6.2	157.981	③	—	ATF 134	75W-85	75W-85	CHF11S	DOT4	④
	SLK250	1.8	271.861	②	MB317	ATF 134	75W-85	75W-85	CHF11S	DOT4	④
	SLK350	3.5	276.956	②	—	ATF 134	75W-85	75W-85	CHF11S	DOT4	④
	SLK55	5.5	152.980	②	—	ATF 134	75W-85	75W-85	CHF11S	DOT4	④

DOT: Department Of Transpotation

① Oil meeting the MB Specification 229.51

② Oil meeting the MB Specification 229.5

③ Only 0W-40 & 5W-40 Oil meeting the MB Specification 229.5

④ 50/50 mix of coolant with a corrosion inhibitor and water

71112_MBES_C0005

VALVE SPECIFICATIONS

Year	Engine VIN	Engine Displacement Liters	Seat Angle (deg.)	Face Angle (deg.)	Spring Test Pressure (lbs. @ in.)	Spring Installed Height (in.)	Stem-to-Guide Clearance (in.)		Stem Diameter (in.)	
							Intake	Exhaust	Intake	Exhaust
2011	642.850	3.0	45	45	NA	NA	NA	NA	0.2340-0.2352	0.2346-0.2352
	272.980	3.5	45	45	NA	NA	NA	NA	0.2346-0.2352	0.2344-0.2350
	272.977	3.5	45	45	NA	NA	NA	NA	0.2346-0.2352	0.2344-0.2350
	273.971	5.5	44.75-45.25	44.75-45.25	NA	NA	NA	NA	0.2346-0.2352	0.2344-0.2350
	273.970	5.5	44.75-45.25	44.75-45.25	NA	NA	NA	NA	0.2346-0.2352	0.2344-0.2350
	156.985	6.2	45	45	NA	NA	NA	NA	0.2348-0.2360	0.2344-0.2356
	272.942	3.0	44.75-45.25	44.75-45.25	NA	NA	NA	NA	0.2348-0.2354	0.2344-0.2350
	272.969	3.5	44.75-45.25	44.75-45.25	NA	NA	NA	NA	0.2348-0.2354	0.2344-0.2350
2012	642.850	3.0	45	45	NA	NA	NA	NA	0.2340-0.2352	0.2346-0.2352
	276.952	3.5	44.75-45.25	44.75-45.25	NA	NA	NA	NA	0.2346-0.2352	0.2344-0.2350
	278.922	4.7	44.75-45.25	44.75-45.25	NA	NA	NA	NA	0.2346-0.2352	0.2344-0.2350
	157.981	6.2	44.75-45.25	44.75-45.25	NA	NA	NA	NA	0.2346-0.2352	0.2344-0.2350
	271.861	1.8	NA	NA	NA	NA	NA	NA	NA	NA
	276.956	3.5	44.75-45.25	44.75-45.25	NA	NA	NA	NA	0.2346-0.2352	0.2344-0.2350
	152.980	5.5	NA	NA	NA	NA	NA	NA	NA	NA

NA: Not Available

71112_MBES_C0006

CRANKSHAFT AND CONNECTING ROD SPECIFICATIONS

All measurements are given in inches.

	Engine		Crankshaft				Connecting Rod	
Year	Displacement Liters	Engine ID/VIN	Main Brg. Oil Clearance	Shaft End-play	Thrust on No.	Journal Diameter	Oil Clearance	Side Clearance
2011	3.0	642.850	0.0011-0.0022	0.0039-0.0097	NA	NA	NA	NA
	3.5	272.980	0.0008-0.0016	0.0059-0.0124	NA	NA	0.0011-0.0025	NA
	3.5	272.977	0.0008-0.0016	0.0059-0.0124	NA	NA	0.0011-0.0025	NA
	5.5	273.971	0.0008-0.0016	0.0059-0.0124	NA	NA	0.0011-0.0025	NA
	5.5	273.970	0.0008-0.0016	0.0059-0.0124	NA	NA	0.0011-0.0025	NA
	6.2	156.985	0.0008-0.0016	0.0059-0.0124	NA	NA	0.0011-0.0025	NA
	3.0	272.942	0.0008-0.0018	0.0039-0.0105	NA	NA	0.0008-0.0026	NA
	3.5	272.969	0.0008-0.0018	0.0039-0.0105	NA	NA	0.0008-0.0026	NA
2012	3.0	642.850	0.0011-0.0022	0.0039-0.0097	NA	NA	NA	NA
	3.5	276.952	NA	NA	NA	NA	NA	NA
	4.7	278.922	NA	NA	NA	NA	NA	NA
	6.2	157.981	NA	NA	NA	NA	NA	NA
	1.8	271.861	0.0008-0.0018	0.0039-0.0118	NA	NA	0.0008-0.0026	NA
	3.5	276.956	NA	NA	NA	NA	NA	NA
	5.5	152.980	NA	NA	NA	NA	NA	NA

NA: Not Available

71112_MBES_C0008

PISTON AND RING SPECIFICATIONS

All measurements are given in inches.

Year	Engine Displacement Liters	Engine ID/VIN	Piston Clearance	Ring Gap Top Compression	Ring Gap Bottom Compression	Ring Gap Oil Control	Ring Side Clearance Top Compression	Ring Side Clearance Bottom Compression	Ring Side Clearance Oil Control
2011	3.0	642.850	NA	0.0157-0.0216	0.0098-0.0197	0.0079-0.0157	0.0047-0.0063	0.0026-0.0043	0.0012-0.0028
	3.5	272.980	0.0001-0.0020	0.0079-0.0138	0.0118-0.0197	0.0079-0.0354	0.0079-0.0276	0.0006-0.0020	NA
	3.5	272.977	0.0001-0.0020	0.0079-0.0138	0.0118-0.0197	0.0079-0.0354	0.0079-0.0276	0.0006-0.0020	NA
	5.5	273.971	0.0003-0.0017	0.0079-0.0138	0.0118-0.0197	0.0079-0.0354	0.0008-0.0028	0.0008-0.0024	NA
	5.5	273.970	0.0003-0.0017	0.0079-0.0138	0.0118-0.0197	0.0079-0.0354	0.0008-0.0028	0.0008-0.0024	NA
	6.2	156.985	NA	NA	NA	NA	NA	NA	NA
	3.0	272.942	0.0001-0.0017	0.0079-0.0138	0.0118-0.0197	0.0079-0.0138	0.0012-0.0031	0.0008-0.0024	NA
	3.5	272.969	0.0001-0.0020	0.0079-0.0138	0.0118-0.0197	0.0079-0.0138	0.0008-0.0028	0.0006-0.0020	NA
2012	3.0	642.850	NA	0.0157-0.0216	0.0098-0.0197	0.0079-0.0157	0.0047-0.0063	0.0026-0.0043	0.0012-0.0028
	3.5	276.952	NA	0.0079-0.0118	0.0157-0.0236	0.0079-0.0276	0.0012-0.0031	0.0006-0.0024	NA
	4.7	278.922	NA	0.0059-0.0118	0.0157-0.0236	0.0079 0.0276	0.0010-0.0030	0.0006-0.0022	NA
	6.2	157.981	NA	0.0059-0.0118	0.0157-0.0236	0.0098-0.0197	0.0020-0.0031	0.0006-0.0020	NA
	1.8	271.861	NA	0.0079-0.0138	0.0118-0.0197	0.0079-0.0276	0.0012-0.0026	0.0006-0.0026	0.0004-0.0007
	3.5	276.956	NA	0.0079-0.0118	0.0157-0.0236	0.0079-0.0276	0.0012-0.0031	0.0006-0.0024	NA
	5.5	152.980	NA	NA	NA	NA	NA	NA	NA

NA: Not Available

71112_MBES_C0009

TORQUE SPECIFICATIONS

All readings in ft. lbs.

Year	Engine Displacement Liters	Engine ID/VIN	Cylinder Head Bolts	Main Bearing Bolts	Rod Bearing Bolts	Crankshaft Damper Bolts	Flywheel Bolts	Manifold Intake	Manifold Exhaust	Spark Plugs	Lug Nut
2011	3.0	642.850	①	②	③	④	⑤	-	18	-	96
	3.5	272.980	⑦	⑧	⑨	⑩	⑤	7	12	17	96
	3.5	272.977	⑦	⑧	⑨	⑩	⑤	7	12	17	96
	5.5	273.971	⑦	⑧	⑨	⑩	⑤	7	12	17	96
	5.5	273.970	⑦	⑧	⑨	⑩	⑤	7	12	17	96
	6.2	156.985	⑪	⑫	⑬	⑭	⑮	⑯	16	16	96
	3.0	272.942	⑦	⑧	⑨	⑩	⑤	7	12	17	96
	3.5	272.969	⑦	⑧	⑨	⑩	⑤	7	12	17	96
2012	3.0	642.850	①	②	③	④	⑤	-	18	-	96
	3.5	276.952	⑰	⑧	⑱	⑲	⑮	7	12	17	96
	4.7	278.922	⑳	⑧	⑱	⑲	⑮	7	-	17	96
	6.2	157.981	⑳	⑧	⑱	⑧	⑮	7	9	17	96
	1.8	271.861	㉑	⑤	⑨	⑩	⑤	10	15	17	96
	3.5	276.956	⑰	⑧	⑱	⑲	⑮	7	12	17	96
	5.5	152.980	⑳	⑧	㉒	⑧	⑲	7	9	17	96

① M8 Cylinder head to crankcase
Step 1: 15 ft. lbs.
M12 Cylinder head to crankcase
Step 1: 7 ft. lbs.
Step 2: 44 ft. lbs.
Step 3: plus 90 degrees
Step 4: plus 90 degrees
Step 5: plus 90 degrees

② M10 Bearing Cap Bolt
Step 1: 4 ft. lbs.
Step 2: 26 ft. lbs.
Step 3: plus 95 degrees
Step 4: plus 95 degrees
M10 Lateral bolt
Step 1: 39 ft. lbs.
Step 2: plus 95 degrees

③ Step 1: Short arm 11 ft. lbs.
Step 2: Long arm 15 ft. lbs.
Step 3: Short arm 22 ft. lbs.
Step 4: Long arm 30 ft. lbs.
Step 5: Short arm 30 ft. lbs.
Step 6: Short arm plus 90 degrees
Step 7: Long arm plus 90 degrees
Step 8: Short arm plus 90 degrees
Step 9: Long arm plus 90 degrees

④ Step 1: 148 ft. lbs.
Step 2: plus 90 degrees
Step 3: plus 90 degrees

⑤ Step 1: 33 ft. lbs.
Step 2: plus 90 degrees

⑦ M8 Cylinder head to crankcase
Step 1: 15 ft. lbs.
M11 Cylinder head to crankcase
Step 1: 15 ft. lbs.
Step 2: 37 ft. lbs.
Step 3: plus 90 degrees
Step 4: plus 90 degrees

⑧ M8 bearing bolts:
Step 1: 15 ft. lbs.
Step 2: Plus 90 degrees
M10 bearing bolts
Step 1: 4 ft. lbs.
Step 2: 22 ft. lbs.
Step 3: Plus 90 degrees

⑨ Step 1: 44 inch lbs.
Step 2: 15 ft. lbs.
Step 3: Plus 90 degrees

⑩ Step 1: 148 ft. lbs.
Step 2: plus 90 degrees

⑪ Step 1: 89 inch lbs.
Step 2: 37 ft. lbs.
Step 3: Plus 90 degrees
Step 4: Plus 90 degrees
Step 5: Plus 90 degrees

⑫ M9 bearing bolts:
Step 1: 15 ft. lbs.
Step 2: M9- 24 ft. lbs. M10- 30 ft. lbs.
Step 3: plus 90 degrees
Step 4: plus 90 degrees
Step 5: Release all tension
Step 6: 15 ft. lbs.
Step 7: M9- 24 ft. lbs. M10- 30 ft. lbs.
Step 8: plus 90 degrees
Step 9: plus 90 degrees
M6 bearing bolts: 6 ft. lbs.
M8 bearing bolts: 15 ft. lbs.

⑬ Step 1: 89 inch lbs.
Step 2: 37 ft. lbs.
Step 3: Plus 90 degrees

⑭ Step 1: 184 ft. lbs.
Step 2: Release all tension
Step 3: 148 ft. lbs.
Step 4: plus 180 degrees

⑮ Step 1: 15 ft. lbs.
Step 2: 33 ft. lbs.
Step 3: plus 90 degrees

⑯ Step 1: 89 inch lbs.
Step 2: Plus 90 degrees
Step 3: plus 10 degrees

⑰ M7 Cyl. head to timing case
Step 1: 10 ft. lbs.
M11 Cyl head to crankcase
Step 1: 15 ft. lbs.
Step 2: 30 ft. lbs.
Step 3: plus 90 degrees
Step 4: plus 90 degrees

⑱ Step 1: 44 inch lbs.
Step 2: 18 ft. lbs.
Step 3: plus 90 degrees

⑲ Step 1: 148 ft. lbs.
Step 2: 180 degrees

⑳ Step 1: 15 ft. lbs.
Step 2: 30 ft. lbs.
Step 3: Plus 90 degrees
Step 4: Plus 90 degrees
Step 5: Plus 90 degrees

㉑ Step 1: 33 ft. lbs.
Step 2: plus 90 degrees
Step 3: plus 90 degrees

㉒ Step 1: 30 ft. lbs.
Step 2: plus 90 degrees

71112_MBES_C0010

TIRE, WHEEL AND BALL JOINT SPECIFICATIONS

		OEM Tires		Tire Pressures (psi)		Wheel	Ball Joint
Year	Model	Standard	Optional	Front	Rear	Size	Inspection
2011	E350 Bluetec	245/45R17	None	①	①	8.0J	NA
	E350	235/45R17	245/45R17	①	①	8.0J	NA
	E550	235/40R18	245/40R18	①	①	8.0J	NA
	E63 AMG	255/40R18	None	①	①	9.0J	NA
	SLK300	225/45R17	None	①	①	NA	NA
	SLK350	225/40R18	None	①	①	NA	NA
2010	E350 Bluetec	245/45R17	None	①	①	NA	NA
	E350	245/45R17	245/45R17	①	①	NA	NA
	E550	235/40R18	245/40R18	①	①	NA	NA
	E63 AMG	255/35R19	None	①	①	NA	NA
	SLK250	225/45R17	None	①	①	NA	NA
	SLK350	225/40R18	None	①	①	NA	NA
	SLK55	235/40R18	None	①	①	NA	NA

Note: Always follow the specifications provided on the vehicle sticker.

OEM: Original Equipment Manufacturer

PSI: Pounds Per Square Inch

F: Front

R: Rear

NA: Not Available

① Refer to recommended pressure on driver's door B-pillar

71112_MBES_C0011

BRAKE SPECIFICATIONS

All measurements in inches unless noted

		Front Brake Disc		Rear Brake Disc		Minimum Lining Thickness		Brake Caliper	
Year	Model	Original Thickness	Minimum Thickness	Original Thickness	Minimum Thickness	Front	Rear	Bracket Bolts (ft. lbs.)	Mounting Bolts (ft. lbs.)
2011	E350 Bluetec	1.260	1.181	0.866	0.764	0.079	0.079	85	25
	E350	1.260	1.157	0.866	0.764	0.079	0.079	85	25
	E550	1.260	1.157	0.945	0.843	0.079	0.079	85	25
	E63 AMG	1.417	1.299	1.024	0.945	0.079	0.079	133	22
	SLK300	1.102	1.000	0.394	0.327	0.079	0.079	85	25
	SLK350	1.102	1.024	0.394	0.327	0.079	0.079	85	25
2012	E350 Bluetec	1.260	1.181	0.866	0.764	0.079	0.079	85	25
	E350	1.260	1.157	0.866	0.764	0.079	0.079	85	25
	E550	1.417	1.339	0.945	0.843	0.079	0.079	85	25
	E63 AMG	1.417	1.299	1.024	0.945	0.079	0.079	133	22
	SLK250	1.260	1.181	0.394	0.327	0.079	0.079	85	25
	SLK350	1.260	1.181	0.394	0.327	0.079	0.079	85	25
	SLK55	NA	NA	NA	NA	0.079	0.079	85	25

71112_MBES_C0012

SCHEDULED MAINTENANCE INTERVALS

2011-12 Mercedes E-Class

TO BE SERVICED	TYPE OF SERVICE	VEHICLE MILEAGE INTERVAL (x1000)												
		10	20	30	40	50	60	70	80	90	100	110	120	130
Engine oil & filter	R	✓	✓	✓	✓	✓	✓	✓	✓	✓	✓	✓	✓	✓
Tires	Rotate	Every 5,000 miles												
Tire pressure, tread depth and TPMS	I	✓	✓	✓	✓	✓	✓	✓	✓	✓	✓	✓	✓	✓
Diesel exhaust fluid	S&I	✓		✓		✓		✓		✓		✓		✓
Diesel exhaust fluid	R		✓		✓		✓		✓		✓		✓	
Engine hood and catches	I	✓	✓	✓	✓	✓	✓	✓	✓	✓	✓	✓	✓	✓
Water drain in air duct	S&I	✓	✓	✓	✓	✓	✓	✓	✓	✓	✓	✓	✓	✓
Brake pads and rotors	I	✓	✓	✓	✓	✓	✓	✓	✓	✓	✓	✓	✓	✓
Engine coolant	S&I	✓	✓	✓	✓	✓	✓	✓	✓	✓	✓	✓	✓	✓
Brake fluid	S&I	✓		✓		✓		✓		✓		✓		✓
Brake fluid	R		✓		✓		✓		✓		✓		✓	
Power steering fluid	S&I	✓	✓	✓	✓	✓	✓	✓	✓	✓	✓	✓	✓	✓
Wiper blades	R	✓	✓	✓	✓	✓	✓	✓	✓	✓	✓	✓	✓	✓
Lighting system components	I	✓	✓	✓	✓	✓	✓	✓	✓	✓	✓	✓	✓	✓
Battery & Starter	I	✓	✓	✓	✓	✓	✓	✓	✓	✓	✓	✓	✓	✓
Brake system components & hoses	I	✓	✓	✓	✓	✓	✓	✓	✓	✓	✓	✓	✓	✓
Accessory drive belts	I		✓		✓		✓		✓		✓		✓	
Cabin air filter	R		✓		✓		✓		✓		✓		✓	
Ball joints and rubber boots	I		✓		✓		✓		✓		✓		✓	
Halfshafts	I		✓		✓		✓		✓		✓		✓	
Steering components & boots	I		✓		✓		✓		✓		✓		✓	
Parking brake	I		✓		✓		✓		✓		✓		✓	
Sunroof or convertible mechanism	L		✓		✓		✓		✓		✓		✓	
Windshield & headlamp washer system	I	✓	✓	✓	✓	✓	✓	✓	✓	✓	✓	✓	✓	✓
Chassis & load bearing body components	I		✓		✓		✓		✓		✓		✓	
Spark plugs	R						✓						✓	
Auto. Trans. oil & filter	R				✓				✓					
Fuel filter (gas engines)	R	every 150,000 miles												
Fuel filter (diesel engines)	R		✓		✓		✓		✓		✓		✓	
Engine air filter	R				✓				✓					
Rear axle diff. fluid (AMG only)	R	At 2,000 miles, then at 80,000 miles												

R: Replace S: Service I: Inspect L: Lubricate

Special Operating Condition Requirements

When operating under severe operating conditions, the following items may need to be replaced more frequently:

Interior filters (Cabin dust filter, air filter, activated charcoal filter, etc.)

Spark plugs

Engine coolant

71112_MBES_C0013

SCHEDULED MAINTENANCE INTERVALS

2011-12 Mercedes SLK-Class

TO BE SERVICED	TYPE OF SERVICE	VEHICLE MILEAGE INTERVAL (x1000)												
		10	20	30	40	50	60	70	80	90	100	110	120	130
Engine oil & filter	R	✓	✓	✓	✓	✓	✓	✓	✓	✓	✓	✓	✓	✓
Tires	Rotate	Every 5,000 miles												
Tire pressure, tread depth and TPMS	I	✓	✓	✓	✓	✓	✓	✓	✓	✓	✓	✓	✓	✓
Engine hood and catches	I	✓	✓	✓	✓	✓	✓	✓	✓	✓	✓	✓	✓	✓
Brake pads and rotors	I	✓	✓	✓	✓	✓	✓	✓	✓	✓	✓	✓	✓	✓
Engine coolant	S&I	✓	✓	✓	✓	✓	✓	✓	✓	✓	✓	✓	✓	✓
Brake fluid	S&I	✓		✓		✓		✓		✓		✓		✓
Brake fluid	R		✓		✓		✓		✓		✓		✓	
Power steering fluid	S&I	✓	✓	✓	✓	✓	✓	✓	✓	✓	✓	✓	✓	✓
Wiper blades	S&I	✓	✓	✓	✓	✓	✓	✓	✓	✓	✓	✓	✓	✓
Lighting system components	I	✓	✓	✓	✓	✓	✓	✓	✓	✓	✓	✓	✓	✓
Battery & Starter	I	✓	✓	✓	✓	✓	✓	✓	✓	✓	✓	✓	✓	✓
Brake system components & hoses	I	✓	✓	✓	✓	✓	✓	✓	✓	✓	✓	✓	✓	✓
Accessory drive belts	I		✓		✓		✓		✓		✓		✓	
Cabin air filter	R		✓		✓		✓		✓		✓		✓	
Ball joints and rubber boots	I		✓		✓		✓		✓		✓		✓	
Halfshafts	I		✓		✓		✓		✓		✓		✓	
Steering components & boots	I		✓		✓		✓		✓		✓		✓	
Parking brake	I		✓		✓		✓		✓		✓		✓	
Windshield & headlamp washer system	I	✓	✓	✓	✓	✓	✓	✓	✓	✓	✓	✓	✓	✓
Chassis & load bearing body components	I		✓		✓		✓		✓		✓		✓	
Spark plugs	R						✓						✓	
Auto. Trans. oil & filter	R				✓				✓					
Fuel filter	R	every 150,000 miles												
Engine air filter	R				✓				✓					
Rear axle diff. fluid (AMG only)	R	At 2,000 miles, 40,000 miles, then every 40,000 miles												

R: Replace S: Service I: Inspect L: Lubricate

Special Operating Condition Requirements

When operating under severe operating conditions, the following items may need to be replaced more frequently:

Interior filters (Cabin dust filter, air filter, activated charcoal filter, etc.)

Spark plugs

Engine coolant

71112_MBES_C0014

PRECAUTIONS

Before servicing any vehicle, please be sure to read all of the following precautions, which deal with personal safety, prevention of component damage, and important points to take into consideration when servicing a motor vehicle:

- Never open, service or drain the radiator or cooling system when the engine is hot; serious burns can occur from the steam and hot coolant.
- Observe all applicable safety precautions when working around fuel. Whenever servicing the fuel system, always work in a well-ventilated area. Do not allow fuel spray or vapors to come in contact with a spark, open flame, or excessive heat (a hot drop light, for example). Keep a dry chemical fire extinguisher near the work area. Always keep fuel in a container specifically designed for fuel storage; also, always properly seal fuel containers to avoid the possibility of fire or explosion. Refer to the additional fuel system precautions later in this section.
- Fuel injection systems often remain pressurized, even after the engine has been turned **OFF**. The fuel system pressure must be relieved before disconnecting any fuel lines. Failure to do so may result in fire and/or personal injury.
- Brake fluid often contains polyglycol ethers and polyglycols. Avoid contact with the eyes and wash your hands thoroughly after handling brake fluid. If you do get brake fluid in your eyes, flush your eyes with clean, running water for 15 minutes. If eye irritation persists, or if you have taken brake fluid internally, IMMEDIATELY seek medical assistance.
- The EPA warns that prolonged contact with used engine oil may cause a number of skin disorders, including cancer. You should make every effort to minimize your exposure to used engine oil. Protective gloves should be worn when changing oil. Wash your hands and any other exposed skin areas as soon as possible after exposure to used engine oil. Soap and water, or waterless hand cleaner should be used.
- All new vehicles are now equipped with an air bag system, often referred to as a Supplemental Restraint System (SRS) or Supplemental Inflatable Restraint (SIR) system. The system must be disabled before performing service on or around system components, steering column, instrument panel components, wiring and sensors. Failure to follow safety and disabling procedures could result in accidental air bag deployment, possible personal injury and unnecessary system repairs.
- Always wear safety goggles when working with, or around, the air bag system. When carrying a non-deployed air bag, be sure the bag and trim cover are pointed away from your body. When placing a non-deployed air bag on a work surface, always face the bag and trim cover upward, away from the surface. This will reduce the motion of the module if it is accidentally deployed. Refer to the additional air bag system precautions later in this section.
- Clean, high quality brake fluid from a sealed container is essential to the safe and proper operation of the brake system. You should always buy the correct type of brake fluid for your vehicle. If the brake fluid becomes contaminated, completely flush the system with new fluid. Never reuse any brake fluid. Any brake fluid that is removed from the system should be discarded. Also, do not allow any brake fluid to come in contact with a painted surface; it will damage the paint.
- Never operate the engine without the proper amount and type of engine oil; doing so WILL result in severe engine damage.
- Timing belt maintenance is extremely important. Many models utilize an interference-type, non-freewheeling engine. If the timing belt breaks, the valves in the cylinder head may strike the pistons, causing potentially serious (also time-consuming and expensive) engine damage. Refer to the maintenance interval charts for the recommended replacement interval for the timing belt, and to the timing belt section for belt replacement and inspection.
- Disconnecting the negative battery cable on some vehicles may interfere with the functions of the on-board computer system(s) and may require the computer to undergo a relearning process once the negative battery cable is reconnected.
- When servicing drum brakes, only disassemble and assemble one side at a time, leaving the remaining side intact for reference.
- Only an MVAC-trained, EPA-certified automotive technician should service the air conditioning system or its components.

BRAKES — ANTI-LOCK BRAKE SYSTEM (ABS)

GENERAL INFORMATION

PRECAUTIONS

- Certain components within the ABS system are not intended to be serviced or repaired individually.
- Do not use rubber hoses or other parts not specifically specified for and ABS system. When using repair kits, replace all parts included in the kit. Partial or incorrect repair may lead to functional problems and require the replacement of components.
- Lubricate rubber parts with clean, fresh brake fluid to ease assembly. Do not use shop air to clean parts; damage to rubber components may result.
- Use only DOT 3 brake fluid from an unopened container.
- If any hydraulic component or line is removed or replaced, it may be necessary to bleed the entire system.
- A clean repair area is essential. Always clean the reservoir and cap thoroughly before removing the cap. The slightest amount of dirt in the fluid may plug an orifice and impair the system function. Perform repairs after components have been thoroughly cleaned; use only denatured alcohol to clean components. Do not allow ABS components to come into contact with any substance containing mineral oil; this includes used shop rags.
- The Anti-Lock control unit is a microprocessor similar to other computer units in the vehicle. Ensure that the ignition switch is **OFF** before removing or installing controller harnesses. Avoid static electricity discharge at or near the controller.
- If any arc welding is to be done on the vehicle, the control unit should be unplugged before welding operations begin.

SPEED SENSORS

REMOVAL & INSTALLATION

Front

See Figure 1.

1. Raise and safely support the vehicle.
2. Remove the rear wheel.
3. Remove the fender liner of the front fender.
4. Disconnect the wheel speed sensor electrical connector from the front axle electrical distributor.
5. Unclip the wiring from the line bracket.

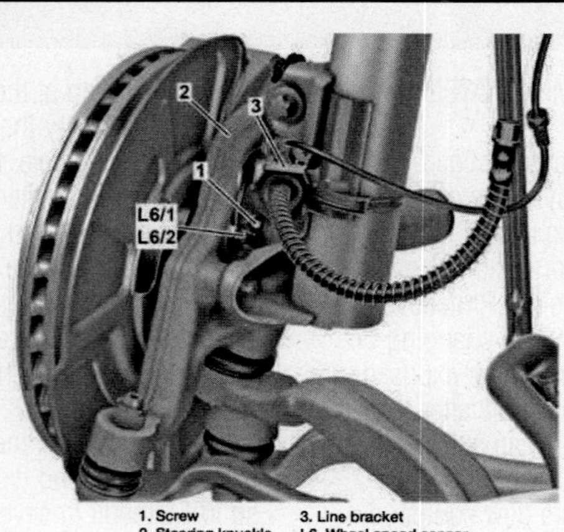

Fig. 1 Wheel speed sensor mounting—E-Class models

6. Remove the mounting bolt and pull the wheel speed sensor out of the steering knuckle.
7. Installation is the reverse order of removal.

Rear

1. Raise and safely support the vehicle.
2. Remove the rear wheel.
3. Disconnect the wheel speed sensor electrical connector from the rear axle electrical distributor.
4. Unclip the electrical line of the wheel speed sensor from the bracket.
5. Remove bolt, 2011 SLK Models only.
6. Pull the wheel speed sensor out of the wheel carrier.
7. Installation is the reverse order of removal.

BRAKES — BLEEDING THE BRAKE SYSTEM

BLEEDING PROCEDURE

BLEEDING PROCEDURE (PRESSURE)

1. Connect a battery charger.
2. Connect an electric brake fluid change/bleeder unit.
   - Following the manufacturer's instructions.
3. Connect the STAR Diagnosis system.
4. Raise and safely support the vehicle.
5. Remove the any wheels necessary to access bleed screws.
6. Carry out the bleeding operation using the STAR Diagnosis system.

BLEEDING THE ABS SYSTEM

See Figure 2.

1. Before servicing the vehicle, refer to the precautions.
2. Attach a pressure bleeding unit and adjust the pressure to 29 PSI (2.0 bar).
3. Remove dust caps of bleed screws (1, 2, 3, 4, 5, 6) on the brake calipers.
4. Open bleed screw and allow approx. 80 cm 3 of brake fluid bleed.

➡New brake fluid must flow out free of bubbles.

5. Close bleed screw and pull off bleed hose.
6. Repeat process at the bleed screws (2, 3, 4, 5, 6).

➡The numbering of the bleed screws (1, 2, 3, 4, 5, 6) represents the opening sequence.

7. On Vehicles with manual transmission, remove cover from bell housing and repeat process at bleed screw of the central clutch release bearing.
8. Attach dust caps of bleed screws (1, 2, 3, 4, 5, 6) and cover to bell housing.
9. Tighten the bleeding screws to 60 inch lbs. (7 Nm).
10. Refill the fluid level in the master cylinder and check the system for leaks.

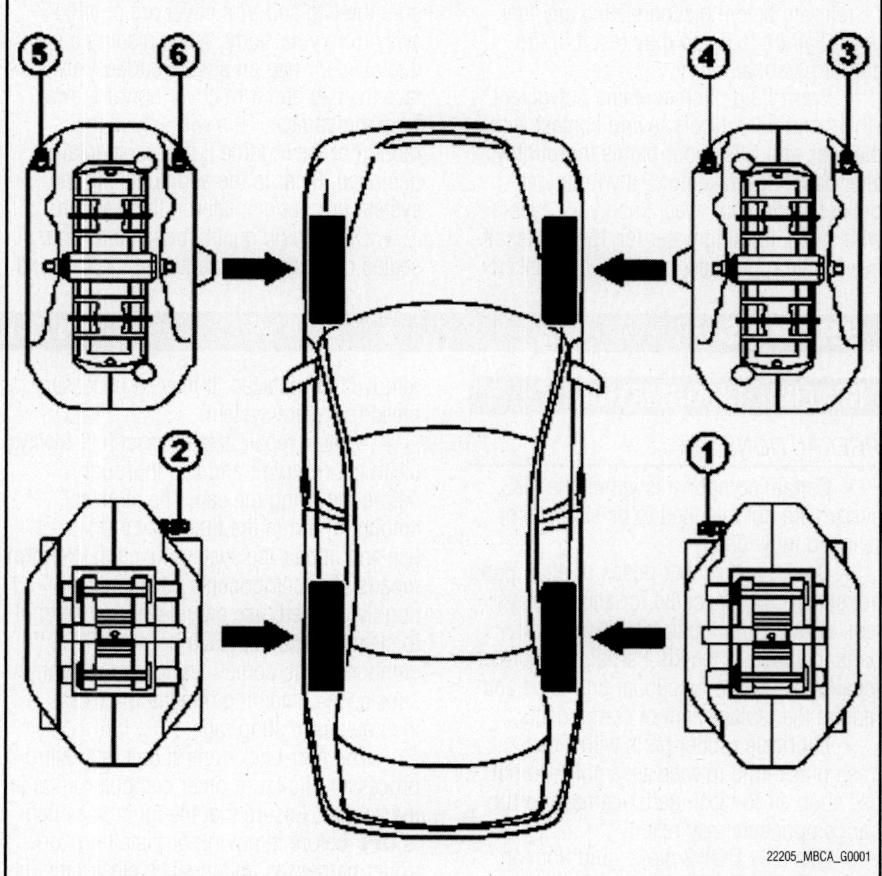

Fig. 2 The numbering of the bleed screws (1, 2, 3, 4, 5, 6) represents the opening sequence

FLUID FILL PROCEDURE

1. Open the engine hood.
2. If equipped, remove the cover above the brake fluid reservoir.
3. The fluid level must be between the "MIN" and "MAX" markings on the brake fluid reservoir.
4. Remove the cap and add fluid as necessary.
5. Replace the cap.

BRAKES

FRONT DISC BRAKES

⁂ CAUTION

Dust and dirt accumulating on brake parts during normal use may contain asbestos fibers from production or aftermarket brake linings. Breathing excessive concentrations of asbestos fibers can cause serious bodily harm. Exercise care when servicing brake parts. Do not sand or grind brake lining unless equipment used is designed to contain the dust residue. Do not clean brake parts with compressed air or by dry brushing. Cleaning should be done by dampening the brake components with a fine mist of water, then wiping the brake components clean with a dampened cloth. Dispose of cloth and all residue containing asbestos fibers in an impermeable container with the appropriate label. Follow practices prescribed by the Occupational Safety and Health Administration (OSHA) and the Environmental Protection Agency (EPA) for the handling, processing, and disposing of dust or debris that may contain asbestos fibers.

BRAKE CALIPER

REMOVAL & INSTALLATION

E-Class Models

See Figure 3.

1. Siphon off some of the brake fluid from the reservoir.
2. Raise and safely support the vehicle.
3. Remove the wheel.
4. Separate the brake wear sensor from the electrical connector, right side only.
5. Drive out the retaining pins using a punch and remove the retaining spring.
6. Pull the brake pads from the brake pads.
7. Detach the brake hose from the brake caliper.
8. Remove the mounting bolt for the electrical connector, right side only.
9. Remove the mounting bolts from the steering knuckle and remove the caliper and discard the bolts.
10. Installation is the reverse order of removal. Tighten the new caliper mounting bolts to 85 ft. lbs. (115 Nm).

2011 SLK-Class Models

1. Raise and safely support the vehicle.
2. Remove the front wheel.
3. Unscrew brake line from brake hose and seal the openings.
4. Unclip the brake hose from the bracket on the damper.
5. Unscrew the brake hose from the brake caliper and seal with a stop plug.
6. Disconnect connector from right front brake pad contact sensor, if removing right side.
7. Remove screw of right front brake pad contact sensor from the brake caliper, if removing right side.
8. Remove bolts of brake caliper from the brake caliper support and remove the brake caliper. Discard the bolts.
9. Installation is the reverse order of removal. Tighten the new self-locking bolts to 85 ft. lbs. (115 Nm).

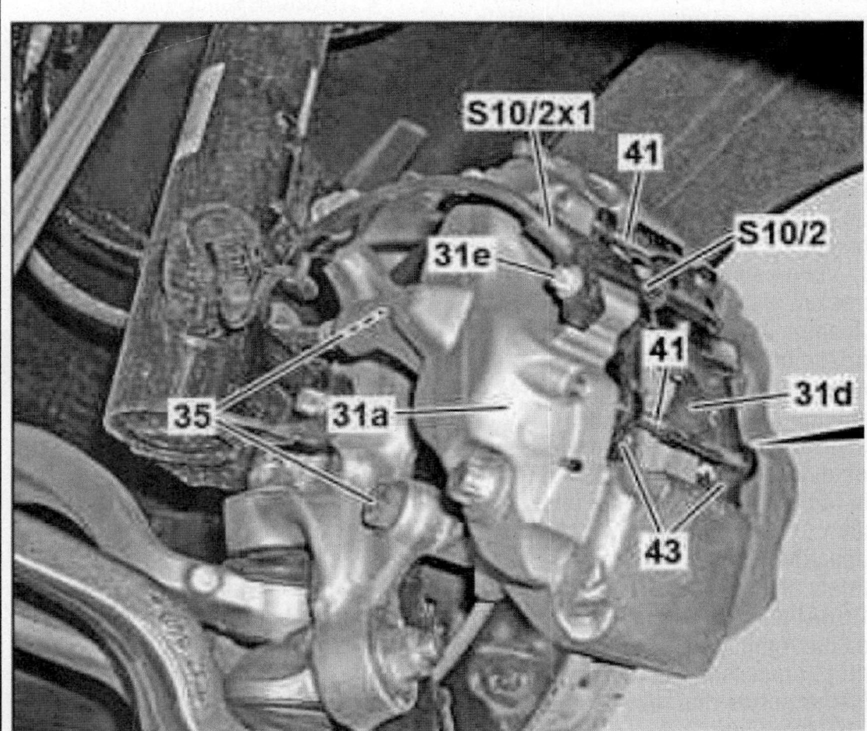

31a. Brake caliper
31d. Retaining spring
31e. Screw
35. Bolts
41. Retaining pin
43. Brake pads
S10. Brake wear sensor
S10x1. Brake wear sensor electrical connector

71112_MBES_G0033

Fig. 3 Brake caliper components—E-Class models

2012 SLK-Class Models

1. Remove the brake pads. For additional information, refer to the following section, "Brake Pads, Removal & Installation."
2. Remove the bolt and disconnect the electrical connector for the right front brake wear sensor from the brake caliper, if removing right side.
3. Disconnect the brake hose and seal with stop plugs only if the brake caliper is being replaced.
4. Remove bolts of brake caliper from the brake caliper support and remove the brake caliper. Discard the bolts.
5. Installation is the reverse order of removal. Tighten the new self-locking bolts to 85 ft. lbs. (115 Nm).

BRAKE PADS

REMOVAL & INSTALLATION

E-Class Models

1. Siphon off some of the brake fluid from the reservoir.
2. Raise and safely support the vehicle.
3. Remove the wheel.
4. Separate the brake wear sensor from the electrical connector, right side only.
5. Drive out the retaining pins using a punch and remove the retaining spring.
6. Pull the brake pads from the brake pads.
7. Installation is the reverse order of removal.
8. Refill the brake fluid reservoir to the correct level.

SLK-Class Models

1. Siphon off some of the brake fluid from the reservoir.
2. Raise and safely support the vehicle.
3. Remove the wheel.
4. Remove the spring from the brake caliper.
5. Disconnect the brake wear sensor, if removing right side.
6. Remove the bolts from the brake caliper support.
7. Remove the brake caliper from the brake caliper support.
8. Remove the brake pads from the brake caliper support.
9. Installation is the reverse order of removal.
10. Refill the brake fluid reservoir to the correct level.

BRAKES — REAR DISC BRAKES

⁂ CAUTION

Dust and dirt accumulating on brake parts during normal use may contain asbestos fibers from production or aftermarket brake linings. Breathing excessive concentrations of asbestos fibers can cause serious bodily harm. Exercise care when servicing brake parts. Do not sand or grind brake lining unless equipment used is designed to contain the dust residue. Do not clean brake parts with compressed air or by dry brushing. Cleaning should be done by dampening the brake components with a fine mist of water, then wiping the brake components clean with a dampened cloth. Dispose of cloth and all residue containing asbestos fibers in an impermeable container with the appropriate label. Follow practices prescribed by the Occupational Safety and Health Administration (OSHA) and the Environmental Protection Agency (EPA) for the handling, processing, and disposing of dust or debris that may contain asbestos fibers.

BRAKE CALIPER

REMOVAL & INSTALLATION

E-Class Models

See Figure 4.

1. Siphon off some of the brake fluid from the reservoir.
2. Raise and safely support the vehicle.
3. Remove the wheel.
4. Detach the spring from the brake caliper.
5. Disconnect the brake wear sensor electrical connector, right side only.
6. Pry off and remove the protective caps from the boots.
7. Remove both guide pins.
8. Remove the brake caliper from the brake caliper from the brake caliper support.

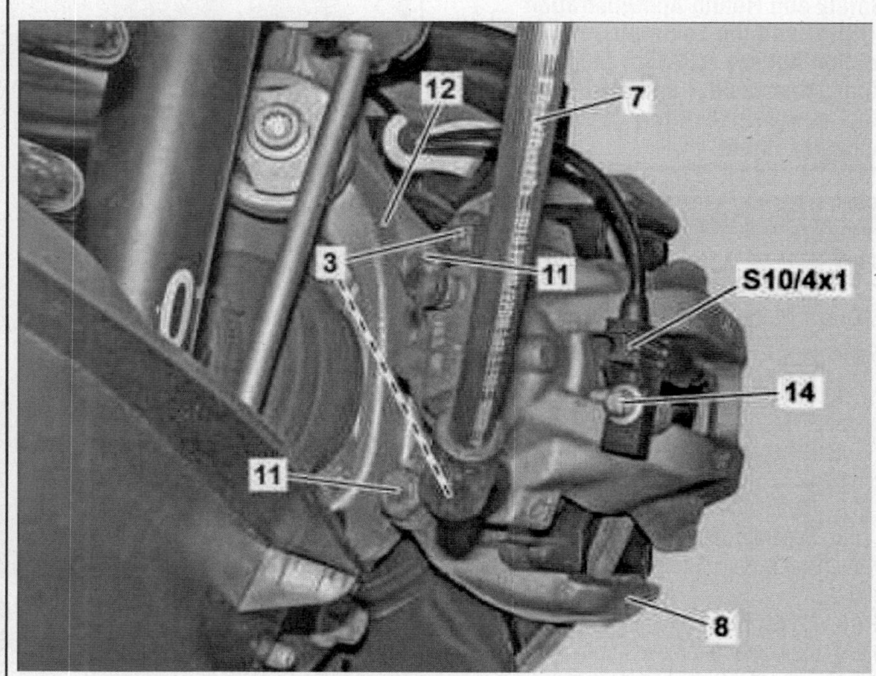

3. Protective caps
7. Brake hose
8. Caliper support
11. Bolts
12. Wheel carrier
14. Screw
S10. Wear sensor

71112_MBES_G0045

Fig. 4 Rear brake caliper components—E-Class models

9. Detach the brake hose from the brake caliper and seal the connection.

10. Installation is the reverse order of removal. Tighten the caliper support bolts to 85 ft. lbs. (115 Nm).

2011 SLK-Class Models

See Figure 5.

1. Raise and safely support the vehicle.
2. Remove the rear wheel.
3. Remove the brake pads.
4. Disconnect the brake wear sensor electrical connector, right side only.
5. Detach the brake hose from the brake caliper and seal the connection.
6. Remove the bolts and remove the brake caliper.
7. Installation is the reverse order of removal. Tighten the mounting bolts to 40 ft. lbs. (55 Nm).

2012 SLK-Class Models

1. Move the brake pads into the assembly position via the workshop menu in the instrument cluster.
2. Siphon off some of the brake fluid from the reservoir.
3. Raise and safely support the vehicle.
4. Remove the rear wheel.
5. Disconnect the brake wear sensor, right side only.
6. Remove the mounting bolt and remove the brake wear sensor, right side only.
7. Unclip the electrical line on the retaining frame, if replacing the caliper.
8. Disconnect electrical connector from the electric parking brake actuator motor.
9. Remove the bolts from the guide pin.
10. Disconnect the brake hose from the brake caliper and plug the connections.
11. Remove the brake caliper from the caliper support. Tighten the guide pings to 21 ft. lbs. (28 Nm).
12. Installation is the reverse order of removal.

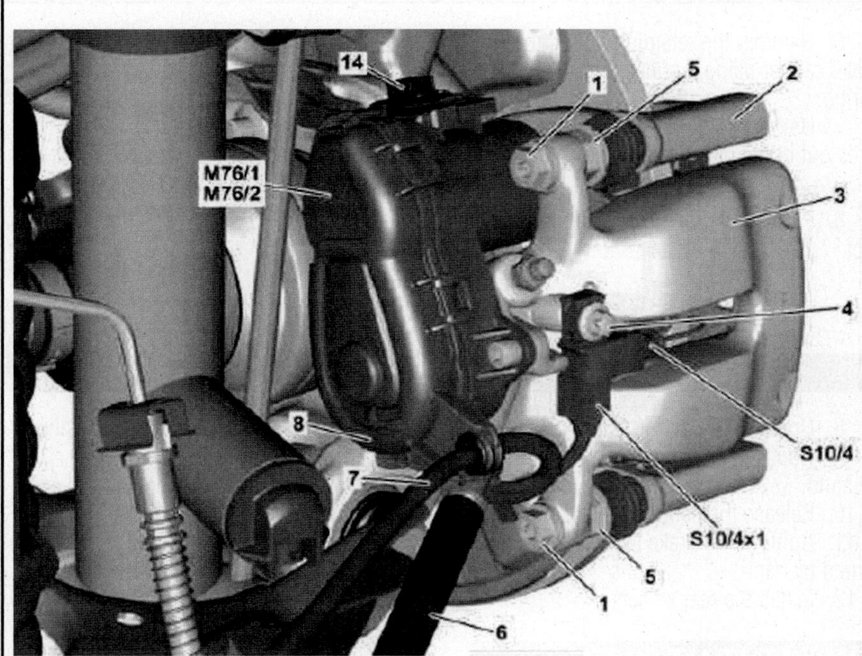

Fig. 5 Rear brake caliper components—2012 SLK-Class models

BRAKE PADS

REMOVAL & INSTALLATION

E-Class Models

See Figure 6.

1. Siphon off some of the brake fluid from the reservoir.
2. Raise and safely support the vehicle.
3. Remove the wheel.
4. Detach the spring from the brake caliper.
5. Disconnect the brake wear sensor electrical connector, right side only.
6. Pry off and remove the protective caps from the boots.
7. Remove both guide pins.
8. Remove the brake caliper from the brake caliper from the brake caliper support.
9. Take out the brake pads.

To install:

10. Insert the inner brake pad with the riveted-on spring into the brake piston.
11. Insert the outer brake pad into the brake caliper support and mount the brake caliper.
12. Press back the piston using a pusher tool.
13. The remainder of the installation is the reverse order of removal.

2012 SLK-Class Models

1. Move the brake pads into the assembly position via the workshop menu in the instrument cluster.
2. Siphon off some of the brake fluid from the reservoir.
3. Raise and safely support the vehicle.
4. Remove the rear wheel.
5. Disconnect the brake wear sensor, right side only.
6. Remove the mounting bolt and remove the brake wear sensor, right side only.
7. Unclip the electrical line on the retaining frame.
8. Remove the bolt on the lower guide pin.
9. Swivel the brake caliper upwards.
10. Remove the brake pads from the brake caliper support.
11. Pull out the wear sensor if replacing the right side.

To install:

12. Press back the piston using a pusher tool.
13. The remainder of the installation is the reverse order of removal.
14. Depress brake pedal several times until the brake pads rest against the brake disc.
15. Refill the brake fluid reservoir to the correct level.

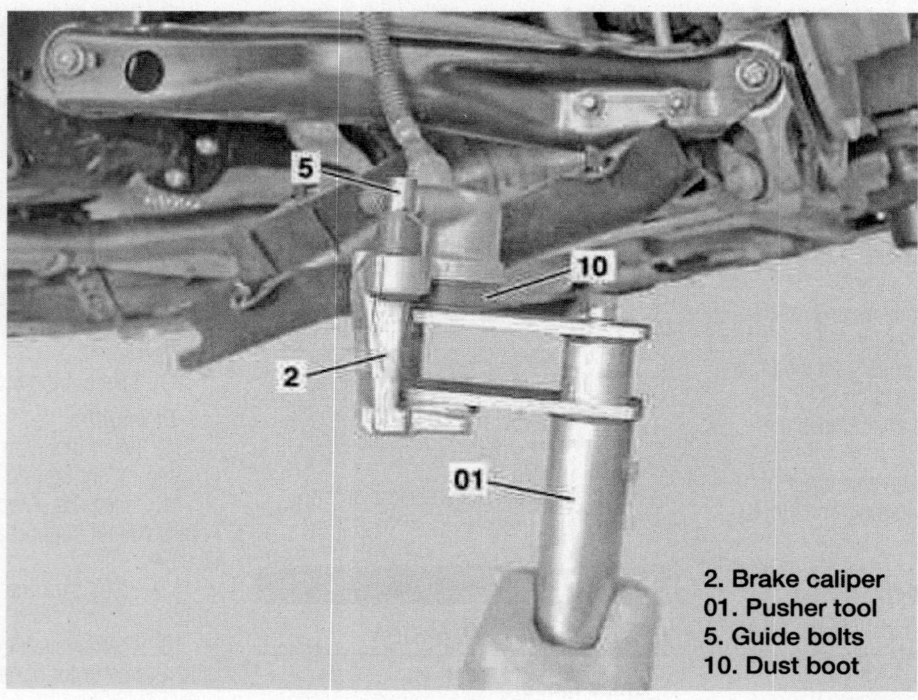

Fig. 6 Press back the piston using a pusher tool—E-Series models

2011 SLK-Class Models

1. Siphon off some of the brake fluid from the reservoir.
2. Raise and safely support the vehicle.
3. Remove the rear wheel.
4. Disconnect the brake wear sensor, right side only.
5. Remove the mounting bolt and remove the brake wear sensor, right side only.
6. Hammer the retaining pin out of the brake caliper using a punch and remove the spring.
7. Using a suitable lever, pry the brake pads out of the brake caliper.

To install:

8. Press back the piston using a pusher tool.
9. Install the brake pads to the caliper.
10. Hammer the retaining pin as far as the stop in the brake caliper.
11. The remainder of the installation is the reverse order of removal.
12. Refill the brake fluid reservoir to the correct level.

BRAKES — PARKING BRAKE

PARKING BRAKE CABLES

ADJUSTMENT

1. Raise and safely support the vehicle.
2. Release the parking brake.
3. Remove the rear wheels.
4. Using a screwdriver, turn the right and left adjustment wheels until the brake shoes abut the drums.
5. Confirm the brake rotor do not turn by hand.
6. Release the left and right adjusting wheels. Be sure to release both wheels the same number of teeth.
7. Confirm the brake rotor can be turned by hand.
8. Operate the parking brake.
9. Confirm the brake rotors do not turn by hand.
10. Release the parking brake.
11. Confirm the brake rotor can be turned by hand.
12. Install the rear wheels.

PARKING BRAKE SHOES

REMOVAL & INSTALLATION

2011 SLK-Class Models & E-Class Models

See Figures 7 and 8.

1. Remove the rear brake disc.
2. Unhook the retracting spring using a suitable brake tool.
3. Compress the retaining springs and turn 90° to remove.
4. Remove the brake shoes with the adjusting mechanism and retracting spring.
5. Remove the retracting spring and adjusting mechanism from the brake shoe.
6. Fold up the expansion lock and press the bolt out of the expansion lock and rear brake cable.

To install:

7. Apply a light coating of grease to the threads on the thrust piece and inner cylinder of the adjusting mechanism. Turn back the

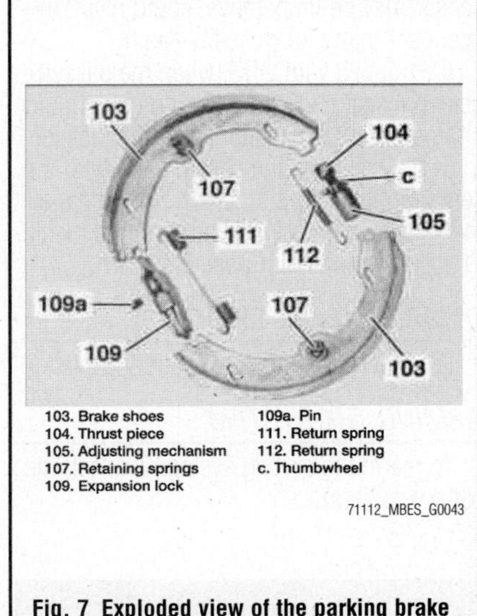

Fig. 7 Exploded view of the parking brake shoe assembly—E-Series models

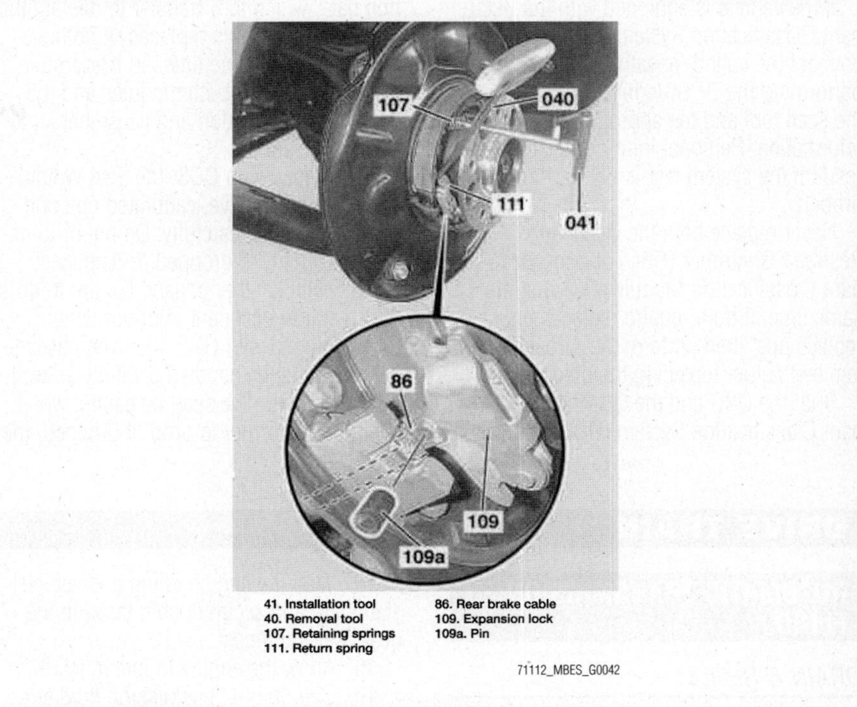

Fig. 8 Using the special tools to remove the retaining springs and expansion lock—E-Class models shown

adjusting mechanism and mount so that the thrust piece contacts the upper brake shoe.

8. The remainder of the installation is the reverse order of removal.
9. Adjust the parking brake.

CHASSIS ELECTRICAL

AIR BAG (SUPPLEMENTAL RESTRAINT SYSTEM)

GENERAL INFORMATION

** CAUTION

These vehicles are equipped with an air bag system. The system must be disarmed before performing service on, or around, system components, the steering column, instrument panel components, wiring and sensors. Failure to follow the safety precautions and the disarming procedure could result in accidental air bag deployment, possible injury and unnecessary system repairs.

SERVICE PRECAUTIONS

Disconnect and isolate the battery negative cable before beginning any airbag system component diagnosis, testing, removal, or installation procedures. Allow system capacitor to discharge for two minutes before beginning any component service. This will disable the airbag system. Failure to disable the airbag system may result in accidental airbag deployment, personal injury, or death.

Do not place an intact undeployed airbag face down on a solid surface. The airbag will propel into the air if accidentally deployed and may result in personal injury or death.

When carrying or handling an undeployed airbag, the trim side (face) of the airbag should be pointing towards the body to minimize possibility of injury if accidental deployment occurs. Failure to do this may result in personal injury or death.

Replace airbag system components with OEM replacement parts. Substitute parts may appear interchangeable, but internal differences may result in inferior occupant protection. Failure to do so may result in occupant personal injury or death.

Wear safety glasses, rubber gloves, and long sleeved clothing when cleaning powder residue from vehicle after an airbag deployment. Powder residue emitted from a deployed airbag can cause skin irritation. Flush affected area with cool water if irritation is experienced. If nasal or throat irritation is experienced, exit the vehicle for fresh air until the irritation ceases. If irritation continues, see a physician.

Do not use a replacement airbag that is not in the original packaging. This may result in improper deployment, personal injury, or death.

The factory installed fasteners, screws and bolts used to fasten airbag components have a special coating and are specifically designed for the airbag system. Do not use substitute fasteners. Use only original equipment fasteners listed in the parts catalog when fastener replacement is required.

During, and following, any child restraint anchor service, due to impact event or vehicle repair, carefully inspect all mounting hardware, tether straps, and anchors for proper installation, operation, or damage. If a child restraint anchor is found damaged in any way, the anchor must be replaced. Failure to do this may result in personal injury or death.

Deployed and non-deployed airbags may or may not have live pyrotechnic material within the airbag inflator.

Do not dispose of driver/passenger/curtain airbags or seat belt tensioners unless you are sure of complete deployment. Refer to the Hazardous Substance Control System for proper disposal.

Dispose of deployed airbags and tensioners consistent with state, provincial, local, and federal regulations.

After any airbag component testing or service, do not connect the battery negative cable. Personal injury or death may result if the system test is not performed first.

If the vehicle is equipped with the Occupant Classification System (OCS), do not connect the battery negative cable before performing the OCS Verification Test using the scan tool and the appropriate diagnostic information. Personal injury or death may result if the system test is not performed properly.

Never replace both the Occupant Restraint Controller (ORC) and the Occupant Classification Module (OCM) at the same time. If both require replacement, replace one, then perform the Airbag System test before replacing the other.

Both the ORC and the OCM store Occupant Classification System (OCS) calibration data, which they transfer to one another when one of them is replaced. If both are replaced at the same time, an irreversible fault will be set in both modules and the OCS may malfunction and cause personal injury or death.

If equipped with OCS, the Seat Weight Sensor is a sensitive, calibrated unit and must be handled carefully. Do not drop or handle roughly. If dropped or damaged, replace with another sensor. Failure to do so may result in occupant injury or death.

If equipped with OCS, the front passenger seat must be handled carefully as well. When removing the seat, be careful when setting on floor not to drop. If dropped, the sensor may be inoperative, could result in occupant injury, or possibly death.

If equipped with OCS, when the passenger front seat is on the floor, no one should sit in the front passenger seat. This uneven force may damage the sensing ability of the seat weight sensors. If sat on and damaged, the sensor may be inoperative, could result in occupant injury, or possibly death.

DISARMING THE SYSTEM

Disconnect the negative battery cable.

ARMING THE SYSTEM

To rearm the air bag system, reattach the battery cable(s).

DRIVE TRAIN

AUTOMATIC TRANSMISSION FLUID

DRAIN & REFILL

E-Class Models

1. Move the automatic transmission into the neutral position and switch the ignition to the **OFF** position.
2. Raise and safely support the vehicle.
3. Remove the drain plug and collect the automatic transmission fluid in a suitable container.
4. Pry the overflow pipe off the base using a suitable drift. Collect any remaining automatic transmission fluid in a suitable container.
5. Remove the drain plug from the torque converter and collect the automatic transmission fluid in a suitable container.
6. Reinstall the torque converter drain plug and tighten to 89 inch lbs. (10 Nm).
7. Reinstall the drain plug and tighten to 16 ft. lbs. (22 Nm).
8. Pump 6 liters of transmission oil into the transmission.
9. Start the engine.
10. Connect the STAR Diagnosis tool and call up the transmission fluid temperature.
11. Bring the transmission temperature up to 95°F (113°C) if there is no transmission cooler or 194°F (90°C) if equipped with a transmission cooler.
12. Switch the engine off and allow the transmission to cool.
13. Start the engine and allow it to run with the transmission in PARK.
14. Pump in the remaining 4 liters of transmission oil.
15. With the engine idling and vehicle stationary and secured, shift through the gears several times.
16. Allow the engine to idle in PARK.
17. Call up the transmission fluid temperature using the STAR diagnosis tool. Ensure the transmission temperature up to 95°F (113°C) if there is no transmission cooler or 194°F (90°C) if equipped with a transmission cooler.
18. Remove the drain plug from the overflow pipe and drain off the constant oil flow until only drops come out.
19. Replace the sealing ring and screw in the drain plug.
20. Turn off the engine and lower the vehicle.

FILTER REPLACEMENT

E-Class Models

1. Move the automatic transmission into the neutral position and switch the ignition to the **OFF** position.
2. Raise and safely support the vehicle.
3. Remove the drain plug and collect the automatic transmission fluid in a suitable container.
4. Pry the overflow pipe off the base using a suitable drift. Collect any remaining automatic transmission fluid in a suitable container.
5. Remove the drain plug from the torque converter and collect the automatic transmission fluid in a suitable container.
6. Remove the oil pan mounting bolts and sprag and remove the oil pan.
7. Remove the overflow pipe from the oil pan.
8. Clean the magnet and check for damage. Replace if necessary.
9. Thoroughly clean the sealing surfaces of the oil pan until they are free of any oil and grease.
10. Install a new filter with a new o-ring.
11. Press a new overflow pipe firmly onto the base in the oil pan.
12. Install the oil pan with a new gasket.
13. Pump 6 liters of transmission oil into the transmission.
14. Start the engine.
15. Connect the STAR Diagnosis tool and call up the transmission fluid temperature.
16. Bring the transmission temperature up to 95°F (113°C) if there is no transmission cooler or 194°F (90°C) if equipped with a transmission cooler.
17. Switch the engine off and allow the transmission to cool.
18. Start the engine and allow it to run with the transmission in PARK.
19. Pump in the remaining 4 liters of transmission oil.
20. With the engine idling and vehicle stationary and secured, shift through the gears several times.
21. Allow the engine to idle in PARK.
22. Call up the transmission fluid temperature using the STAR diagnosis tool. Ensure the transmission temperature up to 95°F (113°C) if there is no transmission cooler or 194°F (90°C) if equipped with a transmission cooler.
23. Remove the drain plug from the overflow pipe and drain off the constant oil flow until only drops come out.
24. Replace the sealing ring and screw in the drain plug.
25. Turn off the engine and lower the vehicle.

DRIVESHAFT

REMOVAL & INSTALLATION

Front

SLK-Class Models

See Figure 9.

1. Raise and safely support the vehicle.
2. Remove the rear engine compartment panel.
3. Remove the exhaust system from the flange connection rearward, Engine ID 171.
4. Remove exhaust system starting from flange connection between exhaust manifold with catalytic converter and under floor catalytic converter, Engine ID 172.
5. Remove the bolts of the left and right under floor paneling.
6. Remove the heat shield.
7. Detach the front stiffening bridge.
8. Detach the rear stiffening bridge.
9. Apply colored dots to mark the propeller shaft position relative to the transmission, the rear axle differential and the propeller shaft intermediate bearing so that the factory installation position can be restored when installing.
10. Undo the bolts at propeller shaft intermediate bearing by a few turns, but do not unscrew fully.
11. Detach the front flexible coupling from the transmission.
12. Detach the rear flex disk from differential.
13. Unscrew the bolts from driveshaft intermediate bearing and remove the driveshaft downward.
14. Installation is the reverse order of removal. Tighten the flex disk locking nuts to 50 ft. lbs. (68 Nm) and center support bearing mounting nuts to 15 ft. lbs. (20 Nm).

Rear

E-Class Models

See Figure 10.

1. Shift the transmission into neutral.
2. Remove the rear engine compartment paneling, if equipped with gas engine.
3. Remove the bottom part of the rear soundproofing.
4. Detach the underfloor paneling in the rear of the heat shields at the clips.
5. Remove the rear engine crossmember.
6. Detach the heat shields and remove.
7. Matchmark the position of the driveshaft relative to the flanges on the transmission and differential.
8. Detach the front flex disk from the transmission.
9. Detach the rear flex disk from the differential.
10. Remove the exhaust system from the flange connection of the catalytic converter/diesel particulate filter.
11. Matchmark the position of the driveshaft center support bearing relative to the vehicle underbody.
12. Remove the mounting bolts of the driveshaft center support bearing.
13. Remove the driveshaft down and out.
14. Installation is the reverse order of removal. Tighten the flex disk locking nuts to 50 ft. lbs. (68 Nm) and center support bearing mounting nuts to 15 ft. lbs. (20 Nm).

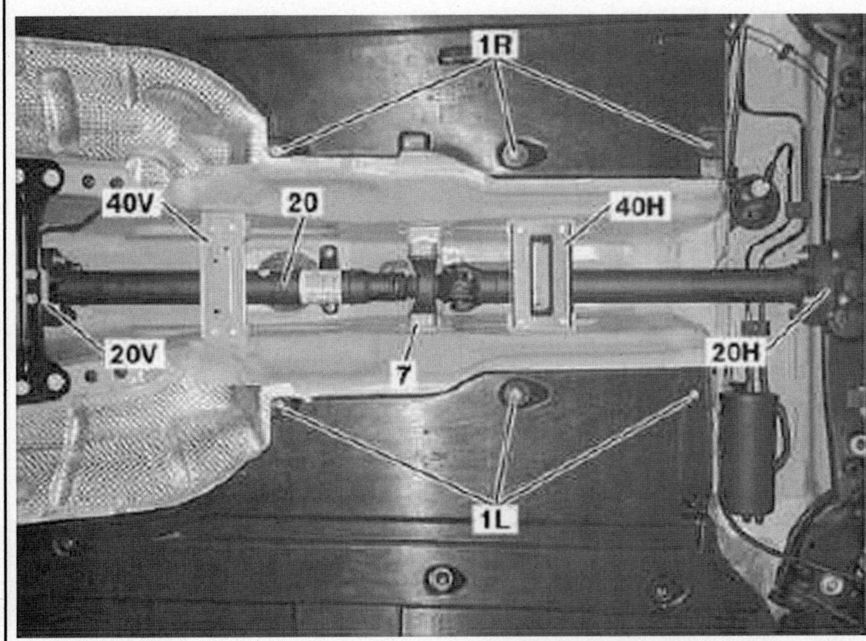

1L. Bolts
1R. Bolts
7. Center support bearing
20. Driveshaft
20H. Rear flex disk
20V. Front flex disk
40H. Rear stiffening bridge
40V. Front stiffening bridge

71112_MBES_G0245

Fig. 9 Driveshaft components—SLK-Class models

FRONT AXLE HOUSING

REMOVAL & INSTALLATION

E-Class Models

See Figures 11 through 13.

1. Deactivate the easy entry/exit function, if equipped with memory package.
2. Extend out fully the adjustable steering column.
3. Move the front wheels to the straight-ahead position and secure the steering wheel.
4. Open the hood and raise to the vertical position.
5. Remove the air filter housing, engine IDs 272 and 272 only.
6. Remove the cold air intake crossmember, diesel engines only.
7. Fasten the radiator on the left and right to the radiator crossmember using cable ties.
8. Suction off fluid from the power steering reservoir using a hand pump.
9. Raise and safely support the vehicle.
10. Remove the front wheels.
11. Detaching the engine compartment paneling, gas engines only.
12. Remove the bottom section of soundproofing, diesel engines only.
13. Remove the front halfshafts.
14. Remove the rear sections of fender liners in the front fenders.
15. Unscrew the brake line at the left and right from the brake hose and seal the connections.
16. Remove the suspension struts.
17. Insert one M8 bolt each from the underside into the suspension strut towers and fasten with nuts.

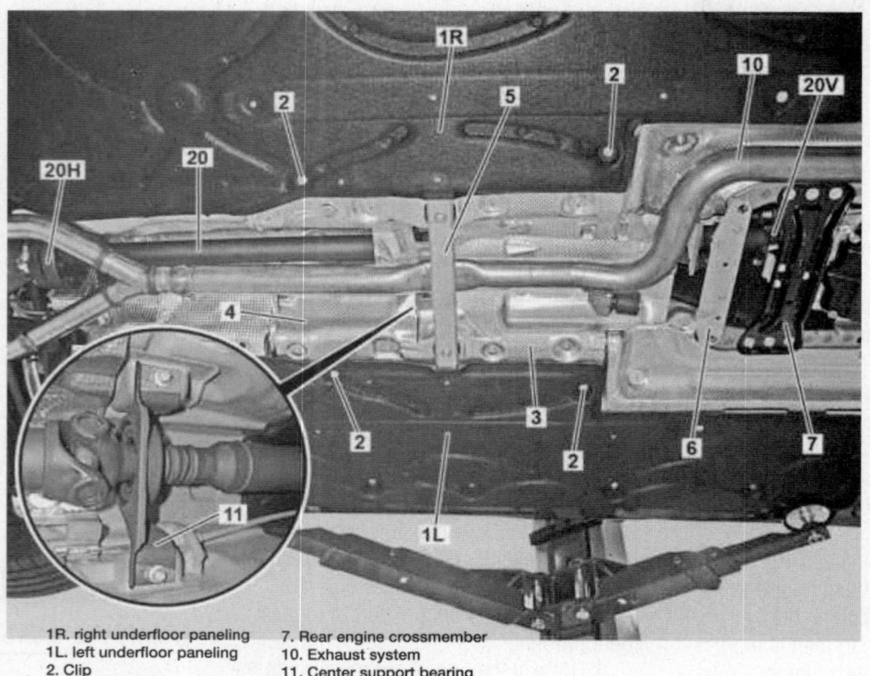

1R. right underfloor paneling
1L. left underfloor paneling
2. Clip
3. Heat shield
4. Heat shield
5. Cross strut
6. Front exhaust bracket
7. Rear engine crossmember
10. Exhaust system
11. Center support bearing
20. Driveshaft
20H. Rear flex disk
20V. Front flex disk

71112_MBES_G0083

Fig. 10 Driveshaft components—E-Class models

8. Link rod
11. Cross strut
12. Torque strut
14. Bracket
30. Front axle shaft
33. Stabilizer bar

71112_MBES_G0084

Fig. 11 Detach the bracket of the link rod of the front level sensor from the cross strut—E-Class models

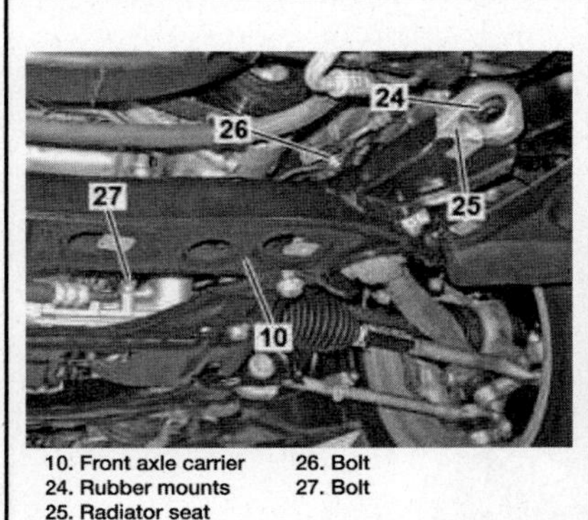

Fig. 12 Remove the bolts from the hydraulic line bracket to front axle carrier—E-Class models

18. Attach a suitable engine hoist.
19. Separate the electrical connectors of the front axle in the wheel wells.
20. Detach the bracket of the link rod of the front level sensor from the cross strut, if equipped with AIRmatric suspension.
21. Detach the steering coupling from the steering gear.
22. Separate the electrical connector on speed-sensitive power steering solenoid valve and unclip the retaining clip from the front axle carrier, if equipped.
23. Remove the bolt from the bracket of the hydraulic line to the front axle carrier, without 4MATIC.
24. Remove the bolt from the hydraulic line bracket to the front axle carrier and rack-and-pinion steering.
25. Detach the front door seals.
26. Remove the diagonal struts.
27. Remove the bolts from the engine mounts.
28. If not equipped with 4MATIC, install protective washers to protect the brake disc dust shields.
29. Lift the engine assembly slightly.
30. Prop up the front axle assembly using a lifting platform and strap it down using suitable straps.
31. Detach the support strut on the vehicle underbody and detach the front axle carrier, AMG models only.
32. Remove the bolts on the front axle carrier.
33. Lower the front axle assembly to remove.

Fig. 13 Remove the diagonal struts—E-Class models

34. Installation is the reverse order of removal.
35. Properly bleed the brake system.
36. Refill the power steering system to the correct level and bleed as necessary.
37. Perform a wheel alignment check.

REAR AXLE HOUSING

REMOVAL & INSTALLATION

E-Class Models

See Figure 14.

1. Move the transmission into neutral or idle position and release the parking brake.
2. Raise and safely support the vehicle.
3. If equipped with AIRmatic, deflate the air springs with the STAR Diagnosis tool.
4. Turn the ignition to the **OFF** position.
5. Remove the rear wheel.s
6. Release the left and right underfloor paneling in the area of the threaded axle connection.
7. Remove the exhaust system from the flange connection back.
8. Detach the exhaust system at the connecting point of the catalytic converter/center muffler and remove, AMG models only.
9. Undo the threaded connections of driveshaft center support bearing to frame floor assembly by 3 to 4 turns.
10. Disconnect the driveshaft from the differential. For additional information, refer to the following section, "Driveshaft, Removal & Installation."
11. Remove the center brake cable.
12. Detach the right rear brake wear sensor from the electrical connector on the brake caliper.
13. Detach the electrical connector of the right rear brake wear sensor from the brake caliper.
14. If equipped with AIRmatic suspension:
    a. Detach the electrical connector from the left rear level sensor and unclip from the bracket.
    b. Detach the electrical connector from the right rear elvel sensor and unclip from the holder.
    c. Detach the electrical lines of the damping valve units on the left and right rear axle from the shock absorbers and unclip from the brackets on the wheel carrier.

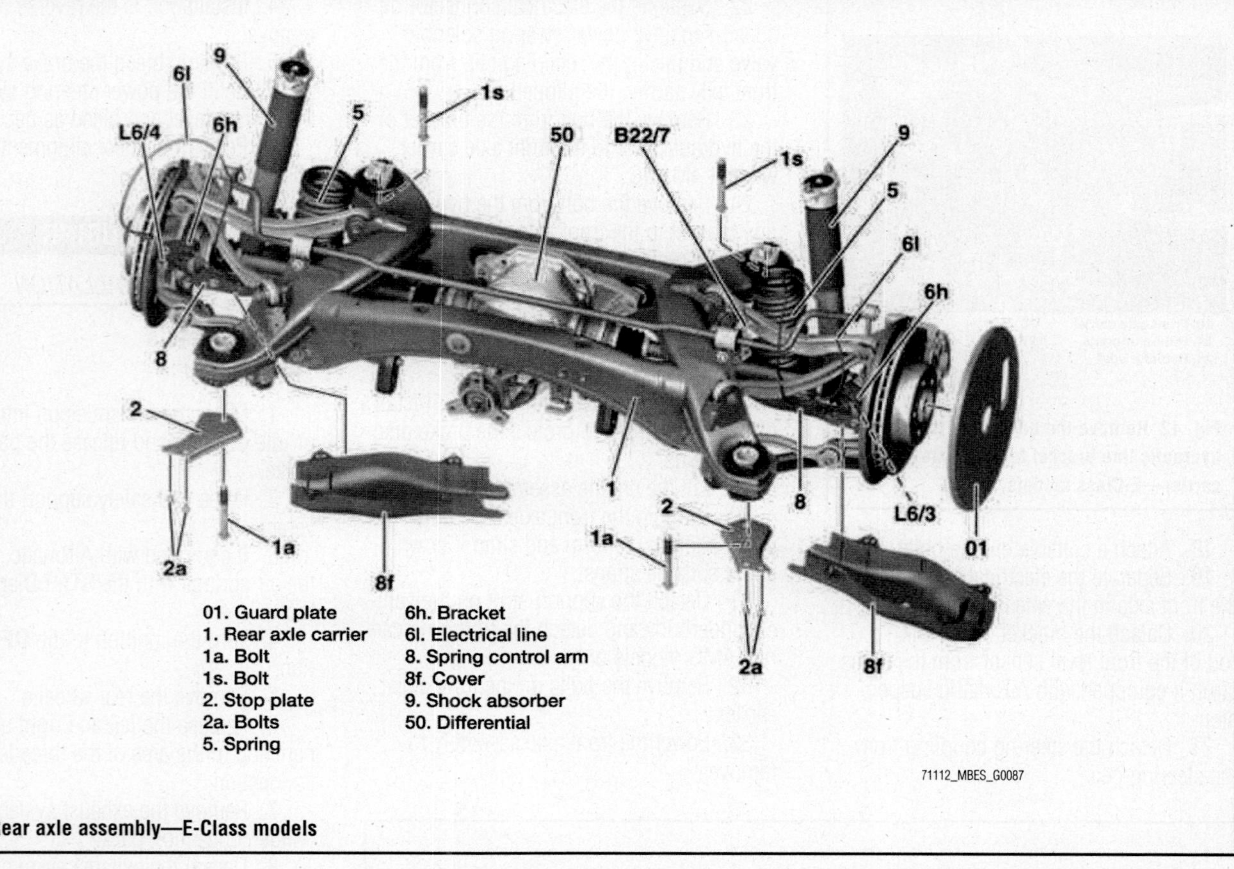

Fig. 14 Rear axle assembly—E-Class models

15. Remove the left and right rear wheel speed sensors from the wheel carrier.
16. Detach the covers from the spring control arms.
17. Detach the left and right rear brake hoses from the brake lines.
18. Remove the rear springs.
19. Detach the shock absorber at the top from the body.
20. Detach the left and right rear brake caliper from the brake caliper support.
21. If equipped with AIRmatric, unclip the air springs from the spring control arms.
22. Detach the shock absorbers from the spring control arms.
23. Support the differential with a suitable jack and secure using suitable straps.
24. Install guard plates.
25. Remove the mounting bolts and remove the stop plates.
26. Lower the rear axle assembly.
27. Installation is the reverse order of removal.

SLK-Class Models

See Figure 15.

1. Detach the shock absorber at the top from the vehicle.
2. Raise and safely support the vehicle.
3. Disconnect the driveshaft from the rear axle differential.

➡The flexible coupling stays on the driveshaft.

4. Unhook the parking brake cables from the cable slack adjuster and unclip from the support, 2011 SLK only.
5. Detach electrical connection (7) from the left electric parking brake actuator motor

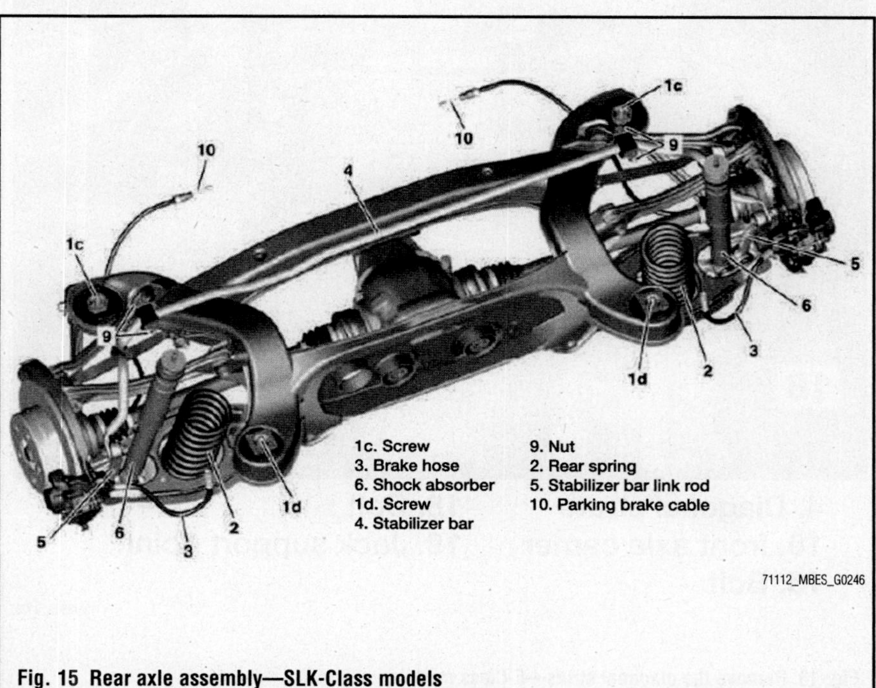

Fig. 15 Rear axle assembly—SLK-Class models

and right electric parking brake actuator motor (M76/2) and remove left and right electrical line (8) from rear axle carrier, 2012 SLK only.

6. Detach electrical connection of rear axle wheel speed sensors from the electrical connection for rear-axle distributor (X62/8) and detach relevant electrical lines from frame floor assembly.

7. Detach electrical connector (11) from the rear level sensor and detach relevant electrical lines (12) from rear axle carrier, 2012 SLK only.

8. Unscrew nuts (9) and remove stabilizer bar from the frame floor assembly.

9. Remove the rear springs.

10. Unscrew the rear brake hoses from the brake lines. Plug the openings with stop plugs.

11. Mount protective washers for brake cover plate .

12. Support the rear axle assembly using a suitable transmission jack and assembly fixture.

13. Remove the mounting bolts from the left and right attachment points of the rear axle assembly.

14. Lower the rear axle assembly.

15. Installation is the reverse order of removal. Tighten the rear axle assembly mounting bolts as follows:

- 2011 SLK-Class: 44 ft. lbs. (60 Nm) plus 90°
- 2012 SLK-Class: 59 ft. lbs. (80 Nm), release all torque and then tighten to 44 ft. lbs. (60 Nm) plus 90°

REAR AXLE SHAFT, BEARING & SEAL

REMOVAL & INSTALLATION

SLK-Class Models

See Figure 16.

1. Raise and safely support the vehicle.

2. Remove the wheel.

3. Remove the drain plug and drain the oil from the differential.

4. Remove twelve-point collar nut from the rear axle shaft.

5. Detach the wheel speed sensor from the wheel carrier and unclip the holder for the electrical line of the wheel speed sensor from the wheel carrier.

6. Unhook the electrical line for the parking brake actuator motor, 2012 SLK only.

7. Detach the camber strut from the wheel carrier.

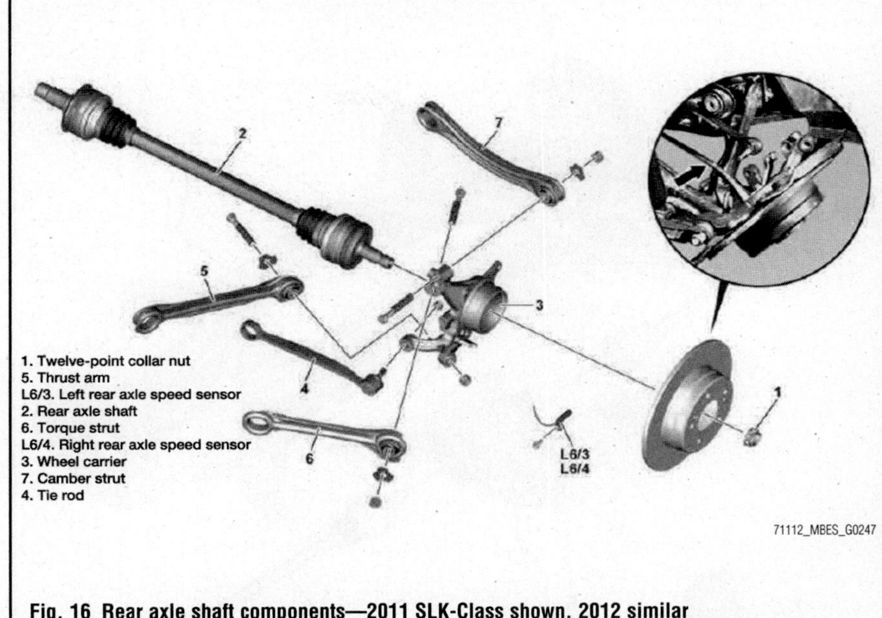

Fig. 16 Rear axle shaft components—2011 SLK-Class shown, 2012 similar

8. Remove the thrust arm from the wheel carrier.

9. Disconnect the tie rod from the wheel carrier.

10. Fold wheel carrier (3) outwards and simultaneously press the rear axle shaft out of the rear axle shaft flange.

11. Use a suitable tool to pry the rear axle shaft on the joint ring far enough out of the differential until the rear axle shaft is disengaged.

12. Pull the rear axle shaft out of the rear axle center assembly.

13. Using a suitable screwdriver, press the radial sealing ring out of the rear axle center assembly.

To install:

14. Coat the sealing lip of the new sealing ring with gear oil.

15. Press the seal ring into the rear axle center assembly using a suitable drift.

16. Press the rear axle shaft into rear axle differential until the retaining ring noticeably engages.

➡Position joint ring horizontally so that the splined profile is not tilted when inserted. When pressing the rear axle shaft into the rear axle center assembly, do not damage the radial sealing ring. The joint ring must close flush with the rear axle housing.

17. The remainder of the installation is the reverse order of removal.

18. Check the differential oil level and refill if necessary. The oil level should reach the bottom edge of the oil filler threaded hole.

REAR DIFFERENTIAL CARRIER

REMOVAL & INSTALLATION

E-Class Models

See Figure 17.

1. Raise and safely support the vehicle.

2. Remove the left rear axle shaft.

3. Remove the exhaust system from the flange connection back.

4. Disconnect the driveshaft from the joint flange on the differential.

5. Loosen the fitting sleeves of the flex disc on the joint flange of the differential.

6. Tie down the differential on the rear axle carrier with a suitable strap.

7. Remove the mounting bolts of the rear differential mount.

8. Support the differential assembly with a transmission jack and support plate and lash down securely.

9. Loosen the lashing of the rear axle differential to the rear axle carrier.

10. Remove the bolt of the front differential mount.

11. Lower the differential slightly.

12. Secure the right-hand rear axle shaft to prevent it from falling.

13. Pry the right-hand rear axle shaft out of the differential.

14. Lower the differential assembly.

15. Installation is the reverse order of removal.

16. Check the differential oil level and refill if necessary. The oil level should reach the bottom edge of the oil filler threaded hole.

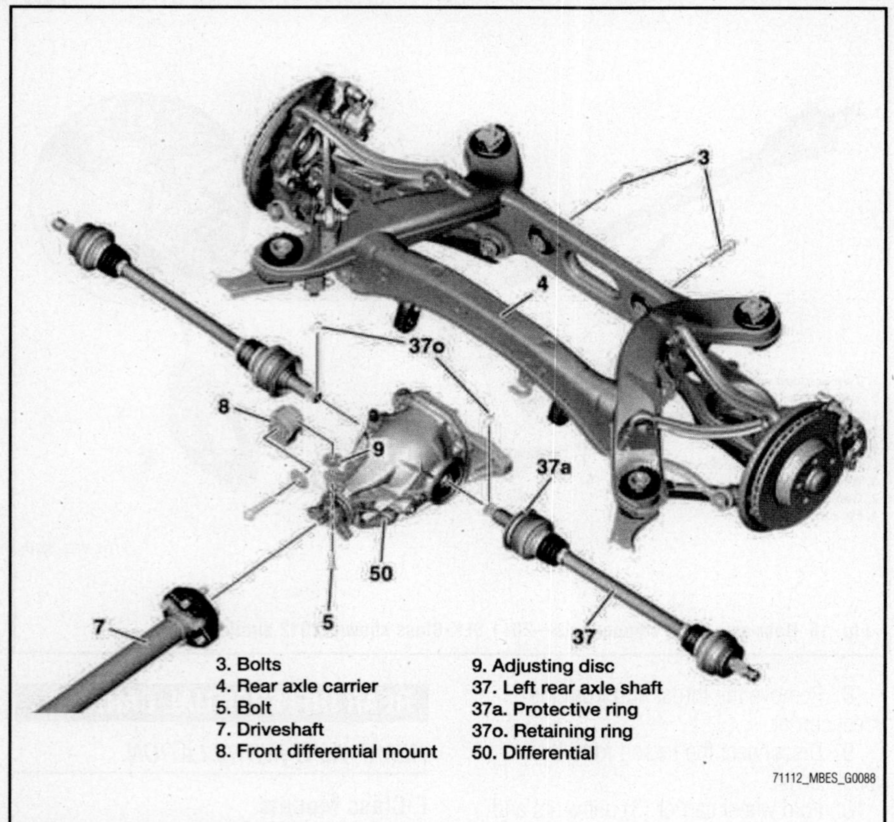

Fig. 17 Rear differential assembly—E-Class models

SLK-Class Models

See Figure 18.

1. Raise and safely support the vehicle.
2. Disconnect the driveshaft from the rear axle differential.

➡**The flexible coupling stays on the driveshaft.**

3. Undo the fitting sleeves of flexible coupling on the joint flange.
4. Remove the left rear axle shaft.
5. Disconnect the heat sink from the rear axle differential, 2012 SLK AMG models only.
6. Support the rear axle differential using a suitable transmission jack and assembly attachment and secure in place using suitable straps.
7. Remove the mounting bolt for the front mounting of the differential.
8. Open the trunk and remove covering for spare wheel well.
9. Remove the bolts of the rear mounting of the rear axle center assembly.
10. Lower and remove the differential.
11. Installation is the reverse order of removal.
12. Check the differential oil level and refill if necessary. The oil level should reach the bottom edge of the oil filler threaded hole.

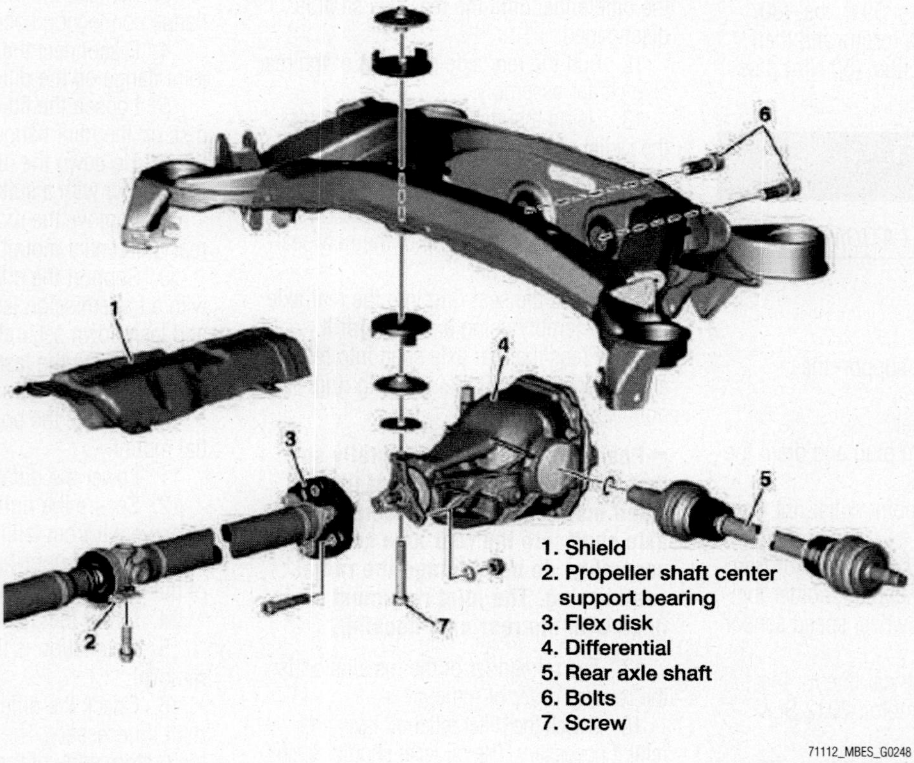

1. Shield
2. Propeller shaft center support bearing
3. Flex disk
4. Differential
5. Rear axle shaft
6. Bolts
7. Screw

71112_MBES_G0248

Fig. 18 Rear differential assembly—SLK-Class models

ENGINE COOLING

ENGINE COOLANT

BLEEDING

See Figure 19.

1. Unscrew the cooling system closure cap and screw on test cap at coolant expansion reservoir.
2. Attach the control unit to the test cap.
3. Attach a venturi nozzle to the control unit.
4. Close the drain valve and feed valve.
5. Attach a feed hose of coolant to coolant container.

➡To avoid suctioning in of air, put at least 2 liters more coolant in the coolant reservoir than the maxium capacity of the cooling system.

6. Guide the waste air hose into an empty container.
7. Connect a compressed-air hose to the venture nozzle and apply pressure.
8. Open the drain valve.
9. Open the feed valve until the feed hose has filled with coolant.
10. Close the drain valve if the display of the control unit is in the green area.
11. Detach the compressed air hose from the venture nozzle and monitor whether the vacuum remains stable for 30 seconds.
12. Open the feed valve.
13. Open the drain valve if the coolant is no longer suctioned.
14. Remove the control unit along with all connections and test cap.
15. Fill the coolant up to the bottom edge of the filler neck of the coolant expansion reservoir.
16. Replace the coolant expansion cap.

DRAIN & REFILL

Engine IDs 272 & 273

See Figure 20.

1. Disconnect the negative battery cable, if draining coolant from the right cylinder crankcase.
2. Unscrew the cap on the coolant reservoir.
3. Remove the front section of lower engine compartment paneling.
4. Drain coolant from the radiator as follows:
   a. Slide a drain hose on to the left fitting at the radiator.
   b. Slacken the siphon hose at the radiator and drain the coolant.
   c. Tighten the drain screw of the radiator and detach the drain hose.
5. Drain the coolant from the crankcase as follows:
   a. Loosen the left or right drain screw of the crankcase so it can be turned by hand.
   b. Slide a drain hose onto the left or right drain screw.
   c. Loosen the drain screw by hand and drain the coolant.
   d. Detach the drain hose and tighten the drain screw of the crankcase.
6. Refill the cooling system to the correct level specified.
7. Bleed the cooling system as necessary.

2012 E-Class Models

See Figure 21.

1. Unscrew the cap on the coolant reservoir.
2. Remove the front section of lower engine compartment paneling.
3. Drain the coolant from the radiator as follows:
   a. Push the drain hose onto the left fitting on the radiator.
   b. Open the drain plug at the radiator and drain the coolant.
4. Drain the coolant from the water pump as follows:
   a. Loosen the drain screw.
   b. Push the drain hose onto the drain screw.
   c. Open the drain screw on the water pump and drain the coolant.
5. Tighten the drain plug on the cooler and detach the drain hose from the fitting.
6. Tighten the drain plug at the water pump and detach the siphon hose from the fitting.
7. Refill the system with coolant and bleed the system as necessary.
8. After the coolant is added, turn the ignition key for about 5 seconds in ignition lock in position 1 and then turn key again into position 0.

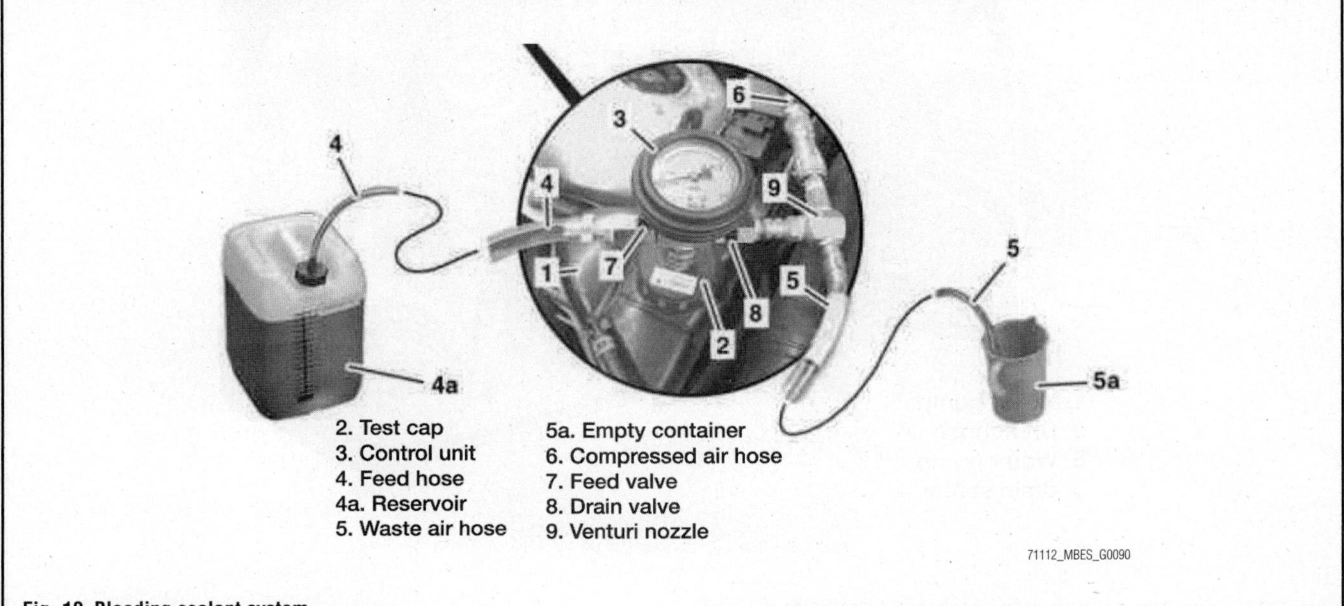

Fig. 19 Bleeding coolant system

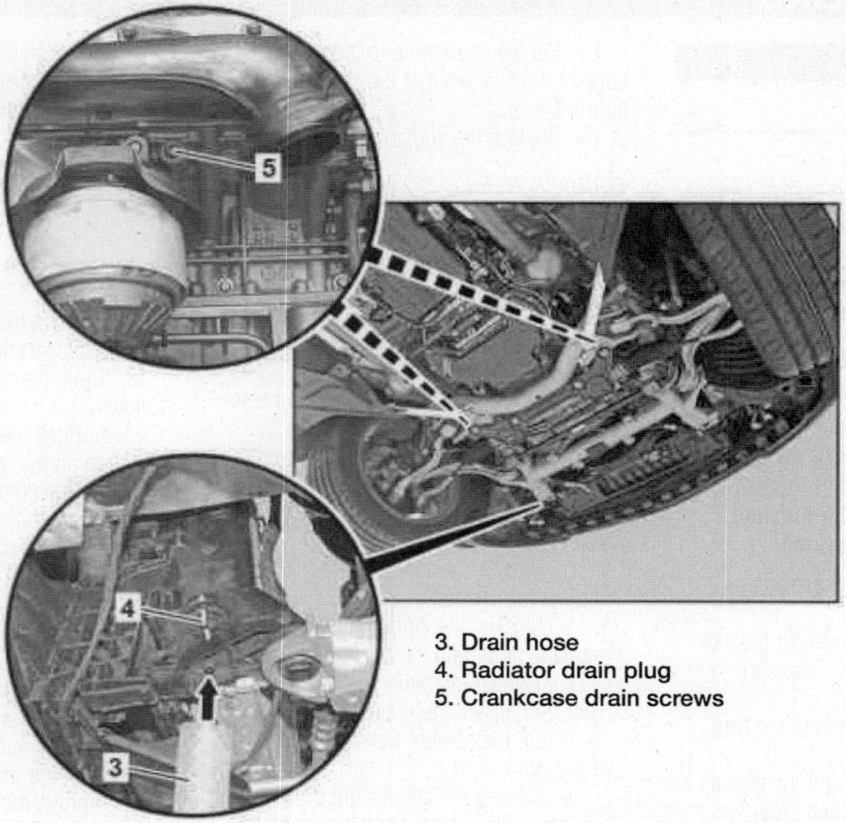

5
4
3
3. Drain hose
4. Radiator drain plug
5. Crankcase drain screws
71112_MBES_G0089

Fig. 20 Drain plugs for the coolant—3.5L Engines

1
5
3
1. Water pump
3. Drain hose
5. Water pump
drain screw
71112_MBES_G0099

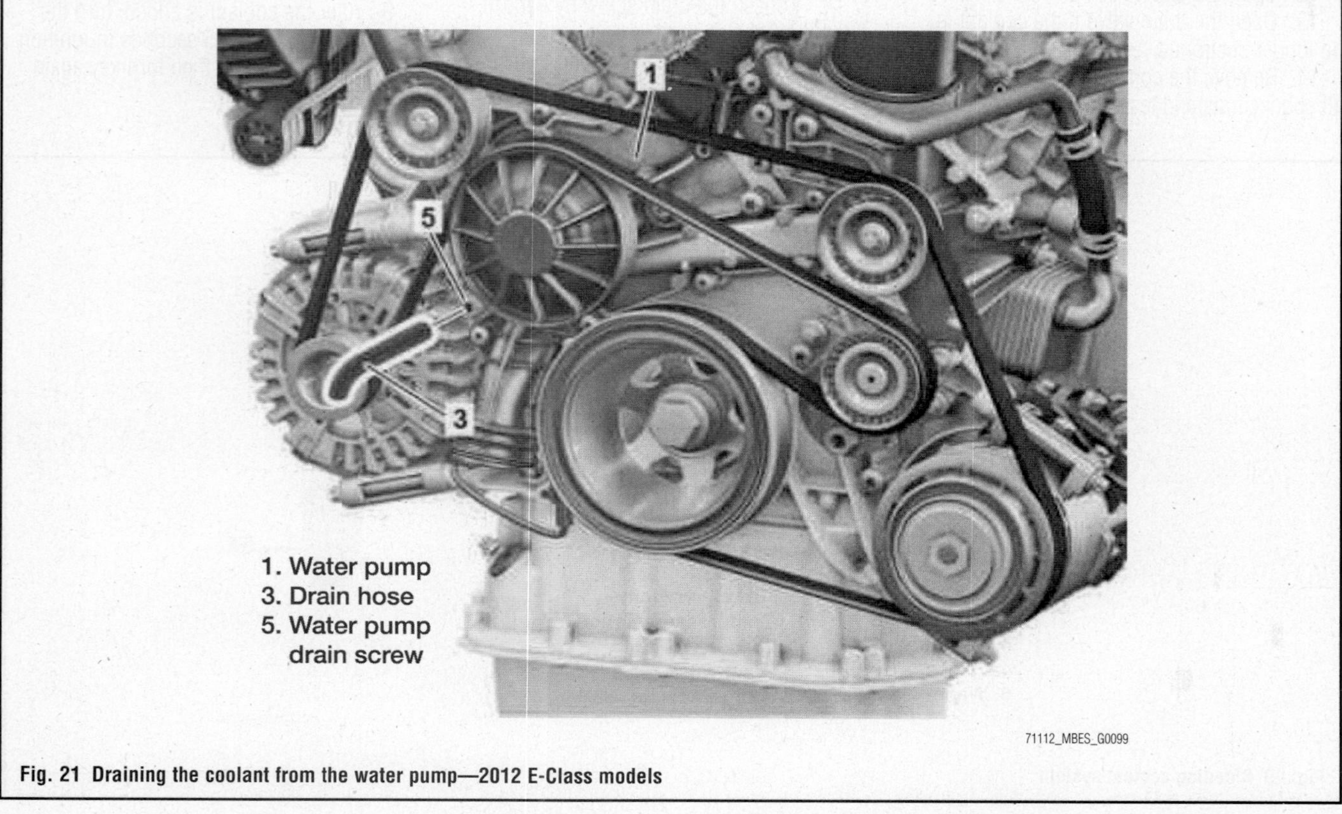

Fig. 21 Draining the coolant from the water pump—2012 E-Class models

9. Repeat the process after waiting about 30 seconds in order to charge and bleed the low-temperature water circuit.

2011 AMG Models

See Figure 22.

Engine ID 271

1. Disconnect the negative battery cable.
2. Unscrew the cap of the coolant expansion reservoir.
3. Remove the front and center engine compartment panelings.
4. Drain the coolant from the radiator as follows:
    a. Slide a siphon hose onto the left fitting at the radiator.
    b. Open the drain plug and drain the coolant from the radiator.
    c. Tighten the drain plug and remove the siphon hose.
5. Refill with coolant and bleed the system.

FLUID RECOMMENDATIONS

The coolant used should be a 50/50 mix of antifreeze and water.

LEVEL CHECK

1. Unscrew the cap the coolant reservoir.
2. When the engine is cold, the coolant level must be level with the marking in the coolant reservoir.
3. If the engine is warm, it must be approximately 1 cm above this mark.

ELECTRIC ENGINE FAN

REMOVAL & INSTALLATION

E-Class Models

See Figures 23 and 24.

1. Remove the front engine cover and both engine air intake ducts upstream of the air filter.
2. Remove the middle reinforcement at the front.
3. Remove the front part of the engine compartment paneling or bottom sections of soundproofing.
4. Remove the bolt for the automatic transmission oil lines on the fan unit.
5. Press the unlocking fishplates apart (arrows) and unclip the lower air ducting on the left and right from the fan unit.
6. Detach the electrical connector and unclip the wiring harness from the fan unit.
7. Detach the vacuum hose from the radiator shutters adjuster.
8. Disconnect the electrical connector.
9. Unclip the air ducting from the fan unit.
10. Close off the vacuum line from the vacuum pump, unhook the vacuum reservoir and place aside.
11. Unhook the fan unit from the radiator mount and pull out upwards.
12. Installation is the reverse order of removal.

2011 SLK-Class Models

1. Raise and safely support the vehicle.
2. Unclip front engine cover.
3. Remove left and right engine intake air duct.
4. Drain the coolant at the radiator, if equipped with automatic transmission.
5. Unclip retaining clamp from coolant hose at the oil filter housing.
6. Detach coolant hose from radiator and place it on the engine, if equipped with automatic transmission.
7. Pull off the connector of fan shroud.
8. Unlatch the upper mounts at the radiator and take out the fan shroud from the upper and lower mounts at the cooler.

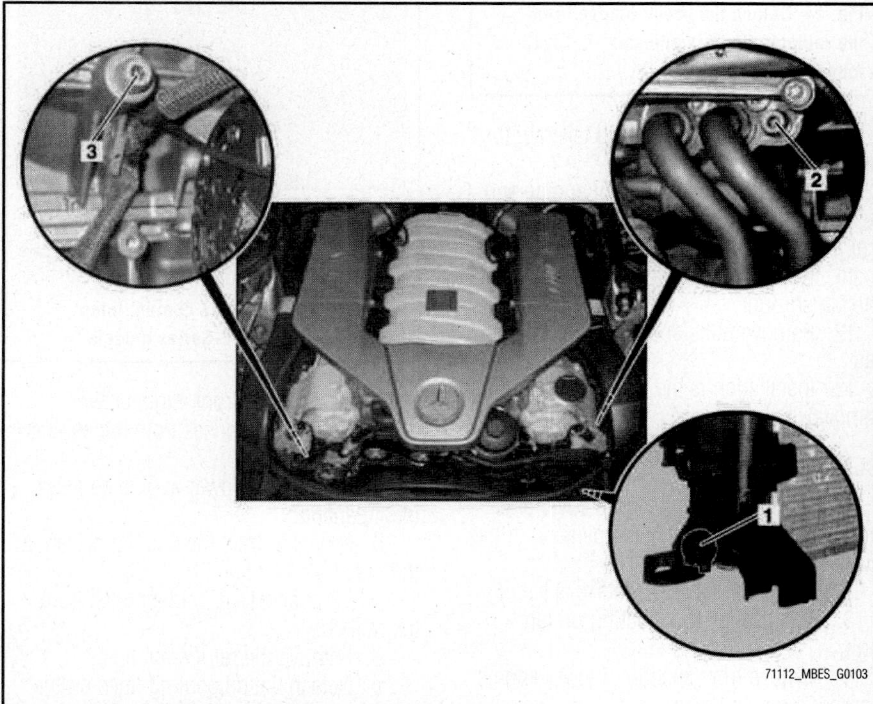

Fig. 22 Location of the draincocks—6.2L Engine

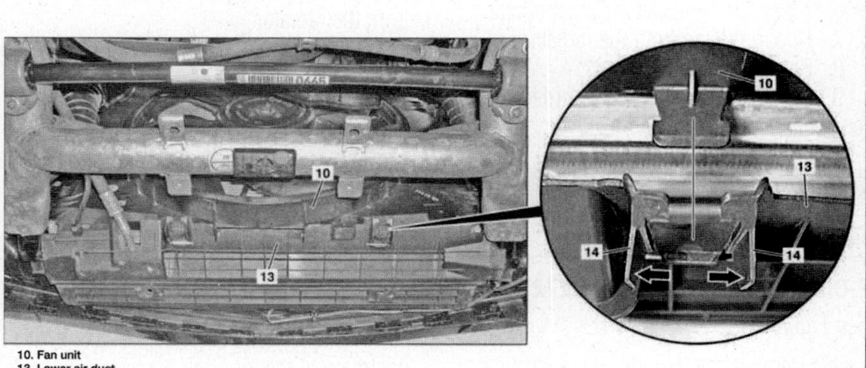

Fig. 23 Press the unlocking fishplates apart (arrows) and unclip the lower air ducting on the left and right from the fan unit—E-Class models

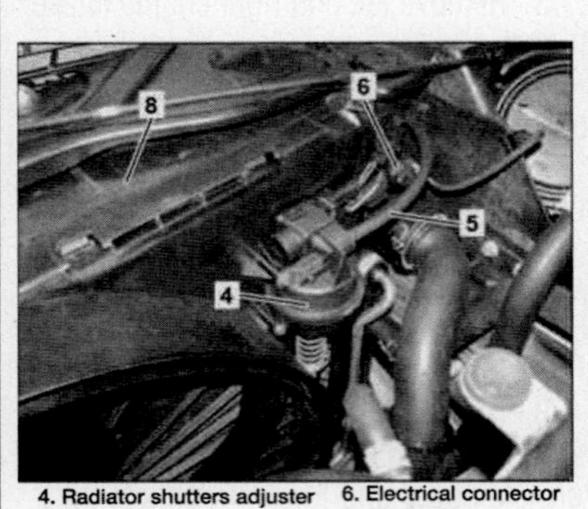

4. Radiator shutters adjuster
5. Vacuum hose
6. Electrical connector
8. Air ducting

71112_MBES_G0093

Fig. 24 Detach the vacuum hose from the radiator shutters adjuster—E-Class models

9. Remove the screws and take out the fan wheel.
10. Loosen electrical line of engine and AC electric suction fan with integrated control from fan shroud.
11. Unclip the electrical connector from the fan shroud.
12. Remove bolts and remove engine fan.
13. Installation is the reverse order of removal.

SLK-Class Models

1. Remove the front engine cover and both engine air intake ducts upstream of the air filter.
2. Remove the cold air intake assembly.
3. Unclip upper air ducting on fan unit.
4. Remove front section of lower engine compartment paneling
5. Press the unlocking fishplates apart and unclip the lower air ducting on the left and right from the fan unit.
6. Disconnect the electrical connector.
7. Unclip the fan from the radiator.
8. Remove the fan upwards.
9. Installation is the reverse order of removal.

RADIATOR

REMOVAL & INSTALLATION

E-Class Models Engine IDs 272 & 273

See Figure 25.

1. Remove the fan unit. For additional information, refer to the following section, "Electric Engine Fan, Removal & Installation."
2. Remove the middle reinforcement at the front.

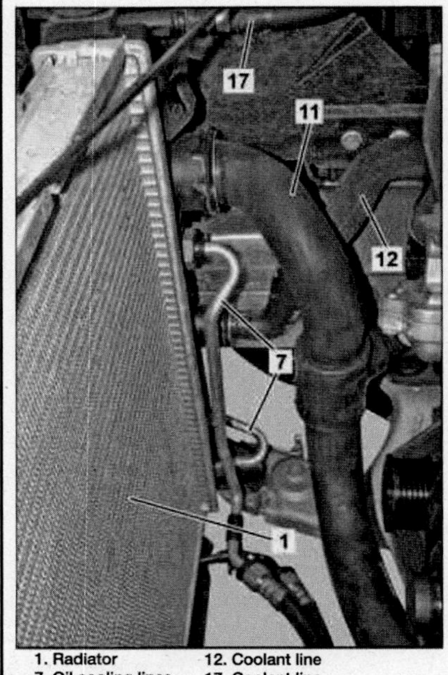

1. Radiator
7. Oil cooling lines
11. Coolant line
12. Coolant line
17. Coolant line

71112_MBES_G0096

Fig. 25 Disconnect the coolant lines from the radiator—E-Series models

3. Remove the front engine cover.
4. Remove the hoses from the engine air intake duct.
5. Remove the lower engine compartment paneling.
6. Properly drain the cooling system at the radiator.
7. Disconnect the coolant lines from the radiator.
8. Remove the refrigerant line.
9. Detach the oil cooling lines on the cooler.
10. Unclip the lower air ducting from the radiator.
11. Unclip the low-temperature cooler from the radiator.
12. Unclip the condenser and cooler for the power steering.
13. Take out the radiator in the upward direction.
14. Installation is the reverse order of removal.
15. Refill the cooling system to the correct level.

2012 E350 Models

1. Remove the engine air intake duct upstream of the air filter.
2. Remove the cold air intake and central reinforcement.
3. Remove the fan unit.
4. Remove the lower engine compartment paneling.
5. Disconnect the coolant lines from the radiator.
6. Detach the oil cooling lines on the cooler.
7. Unclip the lower air ducting from the radiator.
8. Take out the radiator in the upward direction.
9. Installation is the reverse order of removal.
10. Refill the cooling system to the correct level.

2011 SLK-Class Models

See Figure 26.

1. Properly drain the engine coolant.
2. Remove the fan shroud. For additional information, refer to the following section, "Fan Shroud, Removal & Installation."
3. Push back clamps (3) using a screwdriver until the clamps (3) engage.
4. Unplug the coolant hoses at the radiator and discard the sealing rings.
5. Disengage upper radiator supports (5) on the left and right using a screwdriver and detach upwards.

9 Push together catch hook (arrows) on the right and left and pinch off cooler (2) from condenser.

6. Lift the radiator out of its mounts, swivel right to the rear and remove upwards.
7. Installation is the reverse order of removal.
8. Refill the cooling system to the correct level.

Engine ID 271

1. Remove the cold air intake assembly.
2. Remove the middle reinforcement at the front.
3. Remove the fan assembly. For additional information, refer to the following section, "Electric Engine Fan, Removal & Installation."
4. Remove engine compartment paneling.
5. Properly drain the cooling system.
6. Lift the radiator assembly upwards and lower in the direction of the engine.
7. Disconnect the electrical connectors and unclip the lines from the clamps.
8. Disconnect the coolant hoses from the radiator.
9. Disconnect the oil cooling lines from the radiator and pull out.
10. Unclip the condenser from the radiator the left and right.
11. Remove the radiator.
12. Installation is the reverse order of removal.

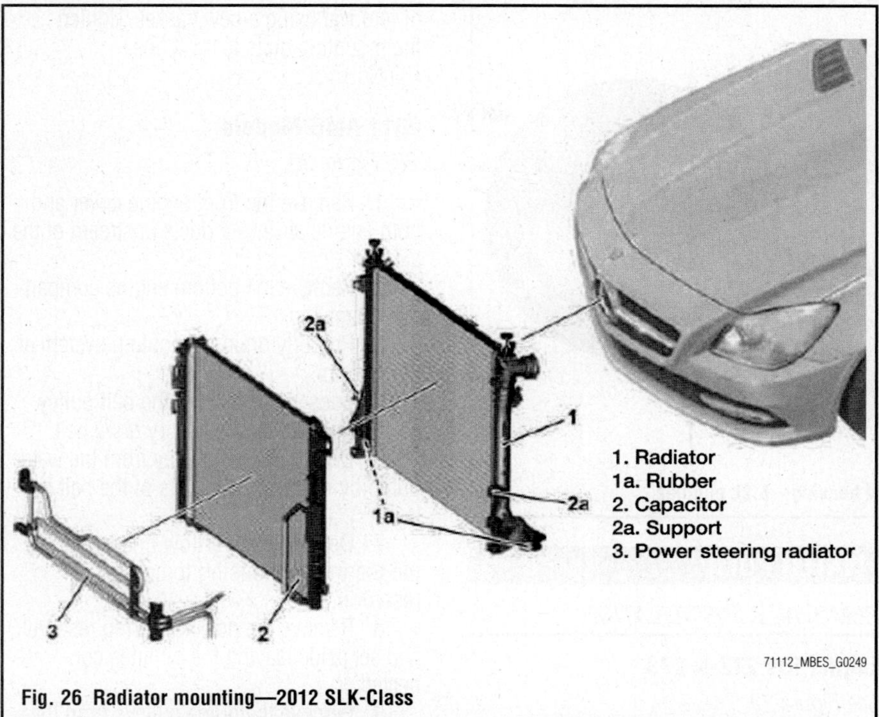

Fig. 26 Radiator mounting—2012 SLK-Class

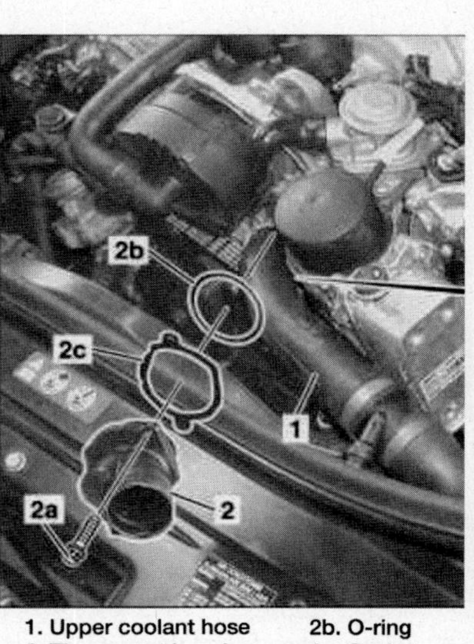

Fig. 27 The thermostat is mounted in the thermostat housing—3.5L engines

13. Refill the cooling system to the correct level.
14. Start the engine and check for leaks.

Engine IDs 276 & 152

1. Properly drain the cooling system.
2. Detach the coolant hose on the thermostat housing and on cooler and place to one side.
3. Detach the coolant hose on cooler, Engine ID 276
4. Detach the coolant hoses at the right on cooler, Engine ID 152.
5. Remove the coolant line at radiator.
6. Detach the coolant hose on water pump.
7. Unclip the upper air ducting on cooler.
8. Disconnect the electrical connection on outside temperature sensor.
9. Detach the electrical line on lower air ducting.
10. Remove the lower air ducting.
11. Detach the hydraulic lines for power steering on the oil pan, front axle carrier and longitudinal member, Engine ID 152.
12. Remove the retaining clamps from condenser on cooler.
13. Unclip the cooler on condenser.
14. Remove the upper air ducting with air ducting on the side, Engine ID 152.
15. Secure the condenser to prevent it from falling down
16. Remove the radiator.
17. Installation is the reverse order of removal.
18. Refill the cooling system to the correct level.
19. Start the engine and check for leaks.

THERMOSTAT

REMOVAL & INSTALLATION

Engine IDs 272 & 273

See Figure 27.

1. Properly drain the cooling system at the radiator.
2. Remove the left engine intake air duct and front engine cover.
3. Remove the upper coolant hose form the thermostat housing.
4. Remove the accessory drive belt and guide pulley.
5. Release and disconnect the electrical connector on the thermostat.
6. Remove the mounting bolts and pull the thermostat housing out of the timing case cover.
7. Remove the thermostat from the housing.
8. Installation is the reverse order of removal using a new gasket. Tighten the mounting bolts to 18 ft. lbs. (25 Nm).

2011 AMG Models

See Figure 28.

1. Remove the switchover valve.
2. Remove the expansion reservoir of the power steering and set it aside, leaving the lines connected.
3. Remove the bottom engine compartment paneling.
4. Properly drain the cooling system at the radiator.
5. Disconnect the coolant hose from the thermostat housing.
6. Remove overflow hose from coolant thermostat housing to coolant expansion reservoir and place to one side.
7. Release and disconnect electrical connector on coolant thermostat.
8. Unscrew the bolt and pull out the thermostat housing with the thermostat from the timing case cover.
9. Installation is the reverse order of removal using new O-ring.
10. Properly refill the cooling system to the correct level.

Engine IDs 276 & 278

1. Properly drain the cooling system at the radiator.
2. Remove the intake manifold.
3. Disconnect the electrical connector on the coolant thermostat heating element.
4. Detach the coolant hose from the coolant thermostat housing.
5. Detach the coolant line for the oil cooler on the coolant thermostat housing.

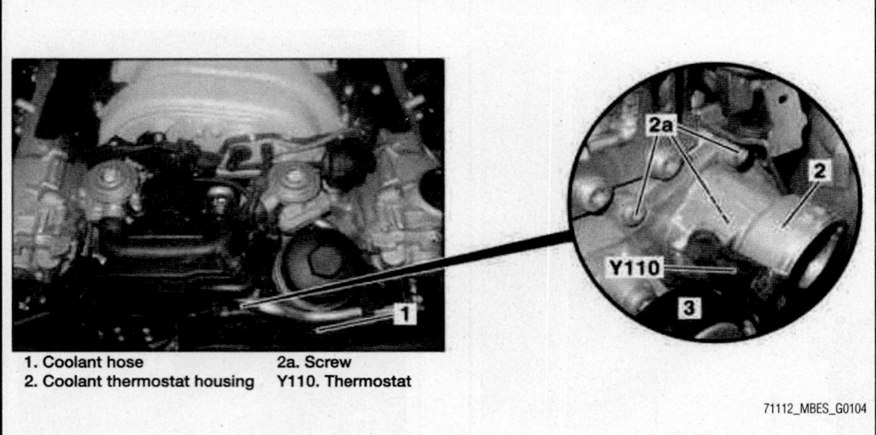

Fig. 28 The thermostat is mounted in the thermostat housing—6.2L engines

6. Remove the coolant thermostat housing on the timing case cover and cylinder heads.
7. Installation is the reverse order of removal using new gaskets and seals.

Engine ID 271

1. Drain the coolant from the radiator.
2. Remove the air guide between the air filter housing and turbocharger.
3. Remove the heating system shutoff valve.
4. Remove the expansion reservoir for the power steering system.
5. Disconnect the coolant hose from the thermostat housing.
6. Remove the mounting bolts and remove the thermostat housing.
7. Remove the thermostat from the thermostat housing.
8. Installation is the reverse order of removal, using new gaskets and O-rings.
9. Refill the radiator to the correct level.

WATER PUMP

REMOVAL & INSTALLATION

Engine IDs 272 & 273

See Figure 29.

1. Properly drain the cooling system at the radiator.
2. Disconnect the coolant hose from the water pump.
3. Remove the accessory drive belt.
4. Remove the right engine intake air duct and front engine cover.
5. Detach the electric air pump with bracket attached and place to the rear.
6. Remove the guide pulleys.
7. Remove the mounting bolts and water pump from the timing case cover.
8. Installation is the reverse order of removal using a new gasket. Tighten the mounting bolts to 15 ft. lbs. (20 Nm).

2011 AMG Models

See Figure 30.

1. Remove the front engine cover and both engine air intake ducts upstream of the air filter.
2. Remove the bottom engine compartment paneling.
3. Properly drain the cooling system at the radiator.
4. Loosen the bolts of the belt pulley.
5. Remove the accessory drive belt.
6. Detach the belt pulley from the water pump by removing the bolts of the belt pulley.
7. Detach the overflow line from the thermostat housing to coolant reservoir.
8. Remove the power steering reservoir and set aside leaving the oil lines connected.
9. Remove the guide pulleys from the water pump.
10. Disconnect the coolant hose from the thermostat housing to the radiator and place it aside.
11. Remove the guide pulley from the timing case cover.
12. Detach the coolant hose on the water pump.
13. Remove the mounting bolts and remove the water pump from the timing case cover.
14. Installation is the reverse order of removal using new gaskets.

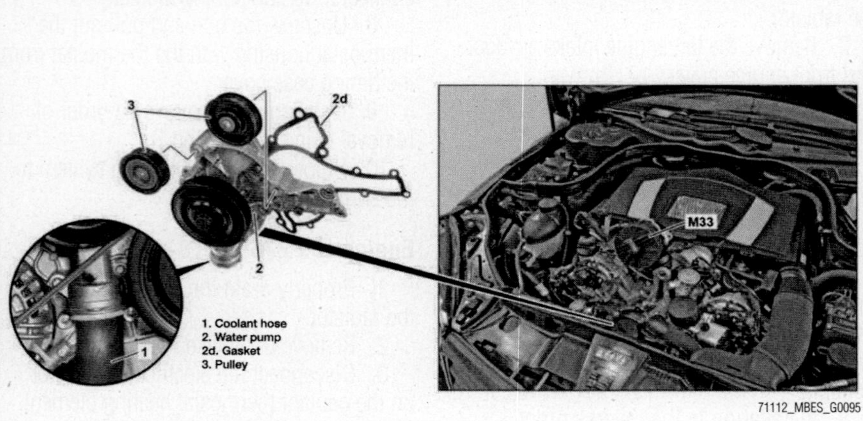

Fig. 29 Water pump mounting—3.5L Engines

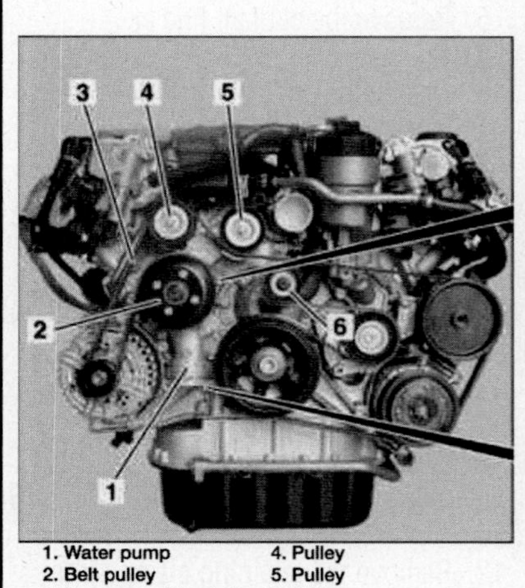

Fig. 30 Water pump mounting—6.2L Engines

2012 E350 Models

See Figure 31.

1. Remove the thermostat. For additional information, refer to the following section, "Thermostat, Removal & Installation."
2. Remove the accessory drive belt.
3. Detach the coolant hose on the water pump.
4. Remove the mounting bolts on the water pump.
5. Remove the water pump from the timing case cover.
6. Remove the water pump cover from the water pump.

➡If the water pump is being replaced, the pulley should be transferred to the new pump.

7. Installation is the reverse order of removal using a new gasket.
8. Refill the cooling system to the correct level.

Engine ID 271

1. Properly drain the cooling system at the radiator.
2. Loosen the mounting bolts for belt pulley on the water pump.
3. Remove the accessory drive belt.
4. Remove the belt pulley for the water pump.
5. Remove the mounting bolts and remove the water pump.
6. Installation is the reverse order of removal using a new gasket.

Fig. 31 Water pump mounting—2012 3.5L Engines

7. Refill the cooling system to the correct level.

Engine ID 276

1. Properly drain the cooling system at the radiator.
2. Remove the thermostat. For additional information, refer to the following section, "Thermostat, Removal & Installation."
3. Remove the accessory drive belt.
4. Remove the guide pulley bracket.
5. Detach the coolant hose on the water pump.
6. Remove the guide pulley from the water pump, only if replacing the water pump.
7. Remove the water pump mounting bolts.
8. Remove the water pump and discard the water pump cover.

➡The gasket is integrated into the water pump cover so the cover must be replaced.

9. Installation is the reverse order of removal.
10. Refill the cooling system to the correct level.
11. Start the engine and check for leaks.

Engine ID 152

1. Properly drain the cooling system.
2. Detach the lower coolant hose on the water pump.
3. Remove the oil lines for the engine oil cooling from the oil filter housing and remove the bracket and set aside.
4. Detach the power steering pump with the power steering reservoir from the engine and move aside, leaving the lines connected.
5. Remove the thermostat. For additional information, refer to the following section, "Thermostat, Removal & Installation."
6. Remove the guide pulley from the water pump.
7. Remove the water pump mounting bolts.
8. Remove the water pump.
9. Installation is the reverse order of removal using a new gasket.

ENGINE ELECTRICAL

BATTERY

BATTERY FLUID

In each cell, the fluid must reach the web let into the filler opening. Use only distilled water for refilling.

1. Remove the battery cover.
2. Unscrew the nut and remove the retaining clip.
3. Unscrew the plugs of the battery cells from the battery.
4. Check the fluid level in the cells of the battery.
5. Installation is the reverse order of removal.

CHARGING

CAUTION

The chemical reaction which takes place in all batteries generates explosive hydrogen gas. A spark can cause the battery to explode and splash acid. To avoid personal injury, be sure there is proper ventilation and take appropriate fire safety precautions when working with or near a battery.

A battery should be charged at a slow rate to keep the plates inside from getting too hot. However, if some maintenance-free batteries are allowed to discharge until they are almost "dead," they may have to be charged at a high rate to bring them back to "life." Always follow the charger manufacturer's instructions on charging the battery.

REMOVAL & INSTALLATION

See Figure 32.

1. Disconnect the negative battery cable from the battery.
2. Remove the cover.
3. Disconnect the positive cable from the battery.
4. Disconnect the vent hose.
5. Remove the bolt and remove the mounting rail.
6. Remove the battery.
7. Installation is the reverse order of removal. Tighten the mounting rail bolt to 15 ft. lbs. (20 Nm).

BATTERY RECONNECT/RELEARN PROCEDURE

Basic programming must be performed after the battery is reconnected.

1. Set the time on the instrument cluster.
2. Move each window to the top stop position and hold down the power window switch for approximately one second.
3. If equipped with a sliding/tilting glass roof, remove the fuse from the fuse box and then reinsert the fuse. Switch on the ignition and move the slide roof to the front and rear stops then down then hold down the roof switch for approximately one second.

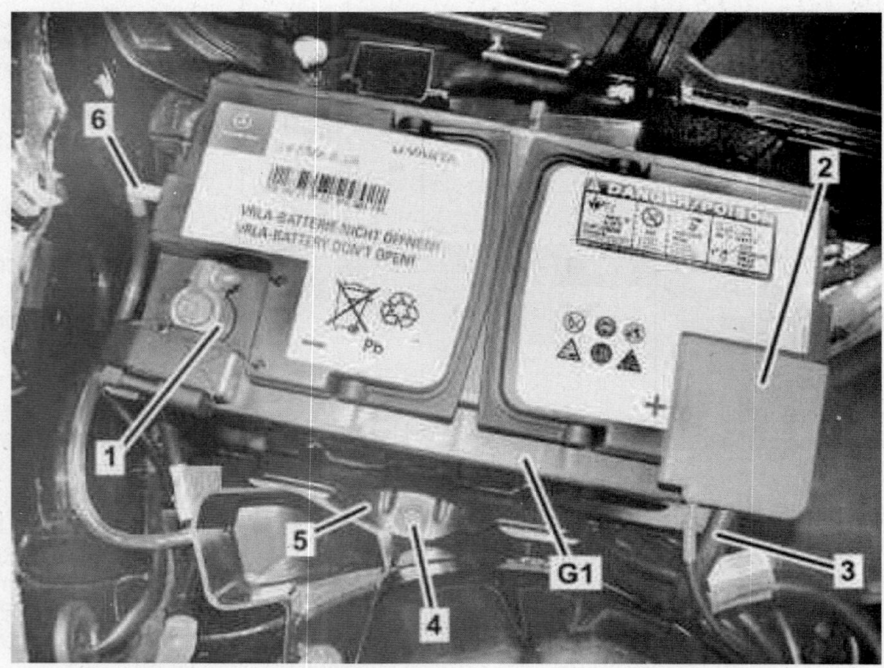

1. Ground terminal
2. Cover
3. Positive line
4. Screw
5. Mounting rail
6. Vent hose
G1. Battery

71112_MBES_G0106

Fig. 32 Battery mounting—E-Class models

ENGINE ELECTRICAL

CHARGING SYSTEM

ALTERNATOR

REMOVAL & INSTALLATION

Engine IDs 272 & 273

See Figure 33.

1. Disconnect the negative battery cable.
2. Remove the engine fan assembly.
3. Remove the accessory drive belt.
4. Detach the front and middle part of the engine compartment paneling.
5. Remove the bolt for the power steering pressure line from the holder on the alternator.
6. Remove the mounting bolts from the alternator.
7. Detach the cap, unscrew the nut and remove the electrical line from the alternator.
8. Remove the plug from the alternator.
9. Remove the alternator down and out of the vehicle.
10. Installation is the reverse order of removal. Tighten the alternator mounting bolts to 15 ft. lbs. (20 Nm).

2011 E-Class AMG Models

1. Disconnect the negative battery cable.
2. Remove the engine intake air duct and front engine cover.
3. Remove the engine fan assembly.
4. Attach a guard plate for the radiator/condenser assembly.

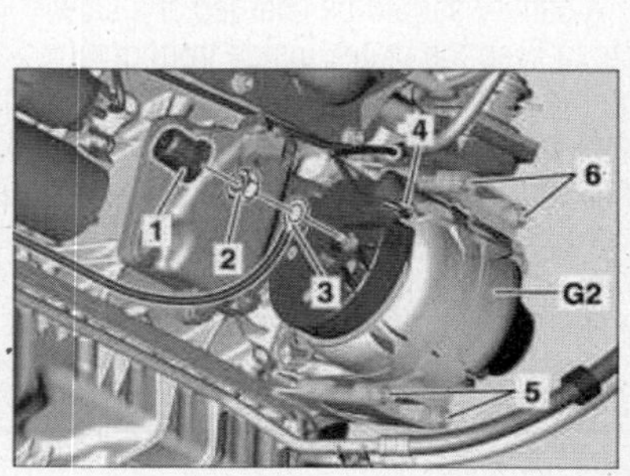

71112_MBES_G0107

Fig. 33 Detach the cap and unscrew the nut to remove the electrical line from the alternator—Engine IDs 272 & 273

5. Remove the bottom engine compartment paneling.
6. Remove the accessory drive belt.
7. Unscrew the cap and unscrew the nut to disconnect the B+ cable from the alternator.
8. Remove the D+ line plug from the alternator.
9. Undo the clip from the cable harness at the alternator.
10. Remove the mounting bolts and remove the alternator down and out of the vehicle.
11. Installation is the reverse order of removal.

2011 SLK-Class Models

1. Raise and safely support the vehicle.
2. Remove the engine compartment paneling.
3. Properly drain the coolant from the radiator, if equipped with automatic transmission.
4. Unscrew cap and disconnect terminal 30 electrical line from alternator by unscrewing nut.

5. Unplug connector of circuit 61 electrical line from generator.
6. Remove lower bolts for alternator.
7. Lower vehicle with vehicle lift
8. Remove fan shroud
9. Mount guard plate for radiator.
10. Remove the accessory drive belt.
11. Remove the upper mounting bolts for the alternator.
12. Remove the alternator from below.
13. Installation is the reverse order of removal. Tighten the alternator mounting bolts to 15 ft. lbs. (20 Nm).
14. Refill the cooling system to the correct level.

Engine ID 271

1. Disconnect the negative battery cable.
2. Remove the accessory drive belt.
3. Unlock and detach connector on electrical connection circuit 61 (D+).
4. Detach cap, unscrew nuts and remove the electrical line from electrical connector circuit 30 (B+).
5. Remove the mounting bolts and pull alternator upwards and out.
6. Installation is the reverse order of removal. Tighten the alternator mounting bolts to 15 ft. lbs. (20 Nm).

Engine ID 276

1. Disconnect the negative battery cable.
2. Remove the front engine cover.
3. Remove the air intake assembly.
4. Remove the accessory drive belt.
5. Detach cap, unscrew nut and remove the electrical line (4) from alternator.
6. Remove the alternator mounting bolts.
7. Move the alternator aside and disconnect the final electrical connector.
8. Remove the alternator from below.
9. Installation is the reverse order of removal. Tighten the alternator mounting bolts to 15 ft. lbs. (20 Nm).

Engine ID 152

1. Disconnect the negative battery cable.
2. Remove the accessory drive belt.
3. Remove the engine compartment paneling.
4. Remove the front diagonal braces.
5. Detach hydraulic lines on the RH engine support, on oil pan and on front axle carrier.
6. Detach the rack-and-pinion steering from the front axle carrier.

➡Fold down rack-and-pinion steering downwards with attached hydraulic lines. The tie rod ball joints must not be pried off on steering knuckle.

7. Remove cap, unscrew nut and remove the electrical line from alternator.
8. Unplug the electrical connector at the alternator.
9. Remove screw/bolts and pull alternator downwards and out.
10. Installation is the reverse order of removal. Tighten the alternator mounting bolts to 15 ft. lbs. (20 Nm).

ENGINE ELECTRICAL

IGNITION SYSTEM

IGNITION COILS

REMOVAL & INSTALLATION

See Figure 34

2011 Models

1. Ensure the ignition is in the **OFF** position.
2. Remove the air filter housing.
3. Remove the mounting bolts for the ignition coils.
4. Disconnect the electrical connectors from the ignition coils.
5. Remove the ignition coils upwards to remove.
6. Installation is the reverse order of removal.

2012 E-Class Models

See Figure 35.

1. Ensure the ignition is in the **OFF** position.
2. Remove the intake manifold, 3.5L engine only. For additional information, refer to the following section, "Intake Manifold, Removal & Installation."
3. Remove the upper engine cover, 4.7L engine only.
4. Remove the engine air intake ducts upstream of the air filter housing, 4.7L engine only.
5. Remove the air filter housing, 3.5L engine only.
6. Remove any insulation on the rail.
7. Remove the mounting bolts of the ignition coils.
8. Pull the ignition coils with the spark plug connectors upwards to remove.

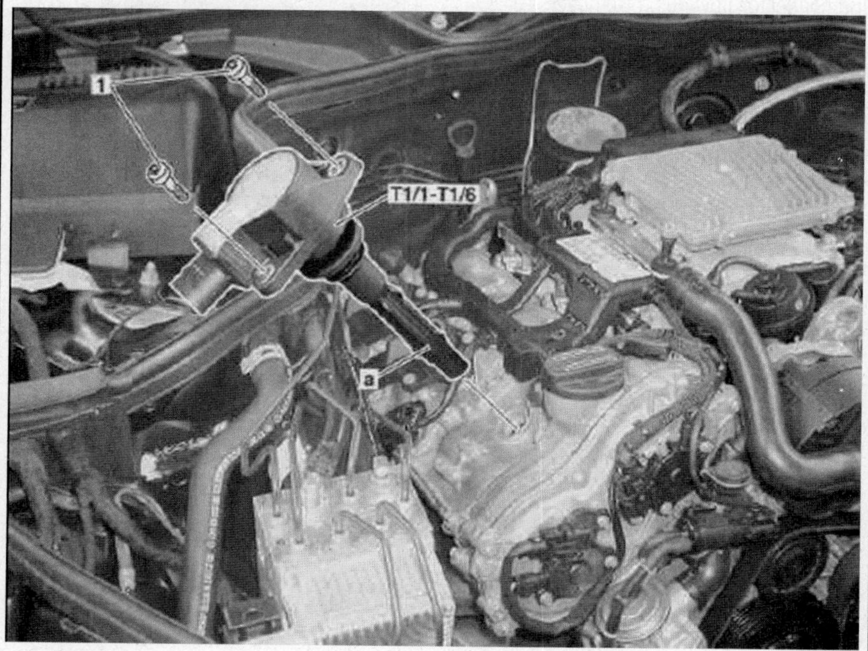

1. Bolts
T1/(1-6). Ignition coil

71112_MBES_G0110

Fig. 34 Remove the mounting bolts to remove the ignition coils—2011 E-Series models shown

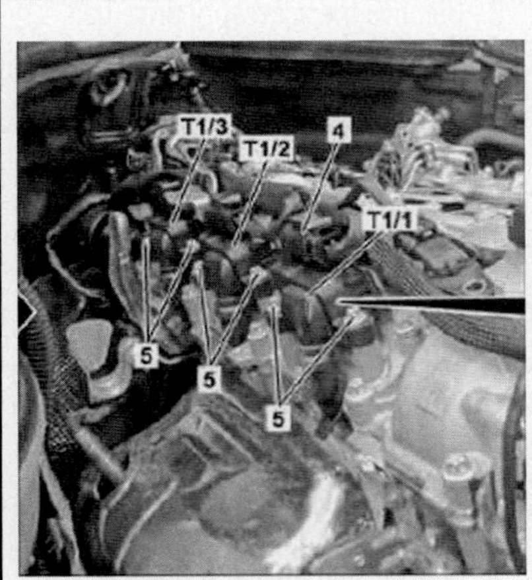

4. Spark plug connector
5. Bolts
T1/1-3. Ignition coil

71112_MBES_G0109

Fig. 35 Remove the mounting bolts to remove the ignition coils—2012 E-Series models

9. Installation is the reverse order of removal.

Engine ID 271

1. Remove the engine trim panel.
2. Disconnect the connector from the ignition coils.
3. Remove the ignition coil mounting bolts.
4. Pull the ignition coils with the spark plug connector upwards to remove.
5. Installation is the reverse order of removal.

Engine ID 152

1. Engine the ignition is in the **OFF** position.
2. Remove the air filter housing.
3. Remove the soundproofing on the cylinder head covers.
4. Disconnect the electrical connector from the ignition coils.
5. Remove the ignition coil mounting bolts.
6. Pull the ignition coils with the spark plug connector upwards to remove.
7. Installation is the reverse order of removal.

SPARK PLUGS

REMOVAL & INSTALLATION

See Figure 36.

1. Turn the ignition to the **OFF** position.
2. Remove the ignition coils. For additional information, refer to the following section, "Ignition Coils, Removal & Installation."
3. Remove the spark plugs from the cylinder using a suitable spark plug socket.
4. Installation is the reverse order of removal. Tighten the spark plug to 17 ft. lbs. (23 Nm).

1. Spark plug connector
3. Ignition coil connector
4. Ignition cable
01. Spark plug socket
R4. Spark plug

71112_MBES_G0111

Fig. 36 Removing the spark plug—3.5L engine shown

STARTER

REMOVAL & INSTALLATION

Engine ID 276 & 152

See Figure 37.

1. Disconnect the negative battery cable.
2. Raise and safely support the vehicle.
3. Remove the bottom engine compartment paneling.
4. Remove the starter shield.
5. Pull off the protective cap and disconnect the circuit 30 electrical connection.
6. Disconnect the wiring harnesses from the starter.
7. Remove the starter from the engine.
8. Remove the starter from below the engine.
9. Installation is the reverse order of removal.

Engine IDs 272 & 273

See Figure 38.

1. Disconnect the negative battery cable.
2. Raise and safely support the vehicle.
3. Remove the rear and middle section of the engine compartment paneling.
4. Remove the left catalytic converter. For additional information, refer to the following section, "Catalytic Converter, Removal & Installation."
5. Detach the protective cap and disconnect the electrical connections from the starter.
6. Remove the mounting bolts and remove the starter from the bottom of the engine.
7. Installation is the reverse order of removal. Tighten the mounting bolts to 30 ft. lbs. (40 Nm).

Engine ID 156

See Figure 39.

1. Disconnect the negative battery cable.
2. Remove the engine intake air duct and engine cove.r
3. Remove the engine compartment paneling.
4. Remove the heat shield and loosen the right engine mount.
5. Unclip the electrical line in front of the starter and move aside.
6. Detach the protective caps and disconnect the electrical connections from the starter.
7. Remove the mounting bolts and lower the starter down and out.
8. Installation is the reverse order of removal. Tighten the mounting bolts to 30 ft. lbs. (40 Nm).

71112_MBES_G0112

Fig. 37 Location of the starter on the engine—2012 3.5L Engines

71112_MBES_G0113

Fig. 38 Location of the starter on the engine—2011 3.5L & 5.5LEngines

Engine IDs 157 & 278

See Figure 40.

1. Turn the wheels to the straight-ahead position and secure the steering with a suitable holding device.
2. Disconnect the negative battery cable.
3. Remove the bottom engine compartment paneling.
4. Remove the steering coupling, if equipped with 4MATIC.

WARNING

If the steering wheel is turned with the steering coupling detached, the clock spring will be destroyed.

5. Remove the shield over the starter.

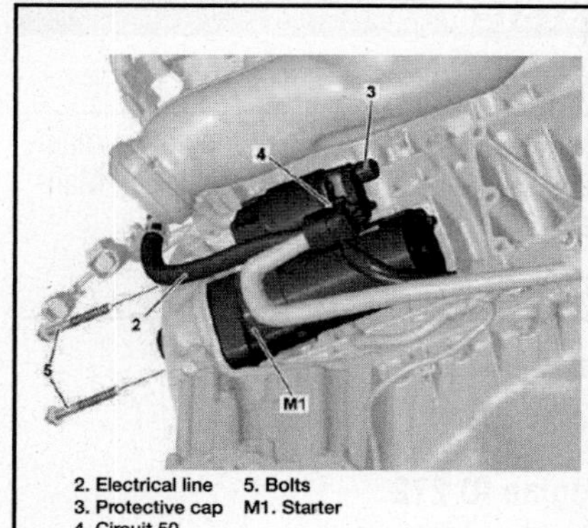

71112_MBES_G0115

Fig. 40 Location of the starter on the engine—2012 5.5L & 6.2L Engines

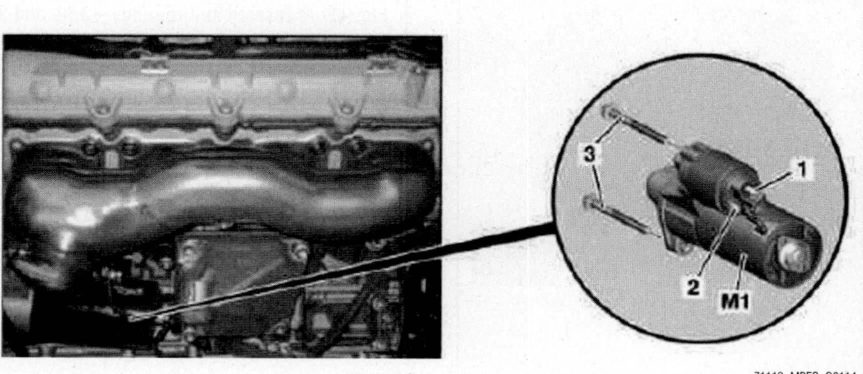

71112_MBES_G0114

Fig. 39 Location of the starter on the engine—2011 6.2L Engines

6. Remove the protective caps and disconnect the electrical connections from the starter.
7. Remove the mounting bolts and lower the starter down and out.
8. Installation is the reverse order of removal. Tighten the mounting bolts to 30 ft. lbs. (40 Nm).

Engine ID 642

1. Disconnect the negative battery cable.
2. Remove the bottom sections of soundproofing.
3. Remove the protective caps and disconnect the electrical connections from the starter.
4. Remove the mounting bolts and lower the starter down and out.
5. Installation is the reverse order of removal. Tighten the mounting bolts to 30 ft. lbs. (40 Nm).

Engine ID 271

1. Disconnect the negative battery cable.
2. Remove the bottom engine compartment paneling.
3. Remove the bolt from the bracket on the oil pan.
4. Remove the steering coupling.
5. Detach the air hose form the electrical air pump.
6. Remove the electrical lines from the starter terminal connections.
7. Remove the mounting bolts and remove the starter from below.
8. Installation is the reverse order of removal. Tighten the mounting bolts to 30 ft. lbs. (40 Nm).

ENGINE MECHANICAL

➡Disconnecting the negative battery cable may interfere with the functions of the on board computer systems and may require the computer to undergo a relearning process, once the negative battery cable is reconnected.

ACCESSORY DRIVE BELT SYSTEM

ADJUSTMENT

The accessory drive belt tension is maintained by an automatic belt tensioner. Manual adjustment is not possible.

BELT ROUTINGS

Engine IDs 157 & 278

See Figure 41.

Engine ID 272

See Figure 42.

Engine ID 271

See Figure 43.

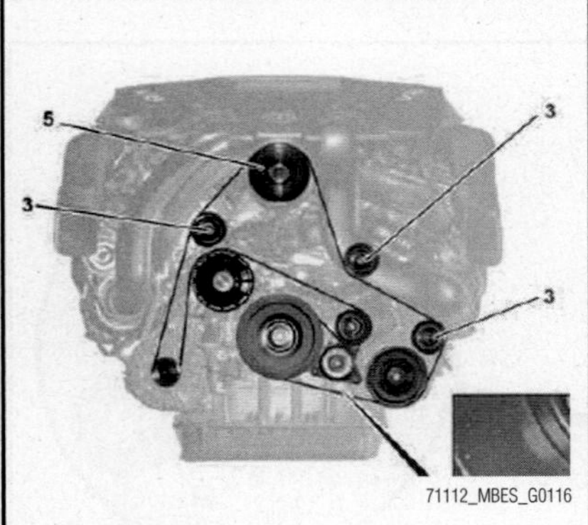

Fig. 41 Accessory belt routings—2012 5.5L and 6.2L engines

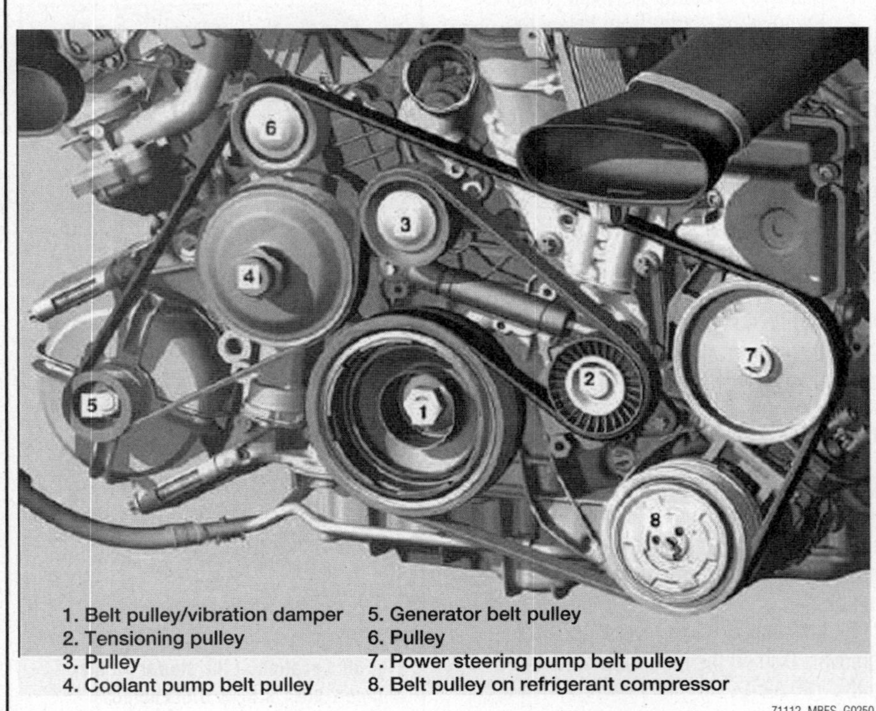

Fig. 42 Accessory belt routings—3.0L and 3.5L engines

INSPECTION

V-Ribbed Serpentine Belt With Chunks of Rib Missing

See Figure 44.

There should be no chunks missing from the belt ribs. If the belt shows any evidence of this, install a new accessory drive belt.

V- Ribbed Serpentine Belt With Piling

See Figure 45.

➡Piling is an excessive buildup in the V-grooves of the belt.

The condition of the V-ribbed drive belt should be compared against the illustration and appropriate action taken.

1. Small scattered deposits of rubber material. This is not a concern, therefore, installation of a new belt is not required.
2. Longer deposit areas building up to 50 percent of the rib height. This is not considered a concern but it can result in excessive noise. If noise is apparent, install a new belt.
3. Heavy deposits building up along the grooves resulting in a possible noise and belt stability concern. If heavy deposits are apparent, install a new belt.

Fig. 43 Accessory belt routings—1.8L engines

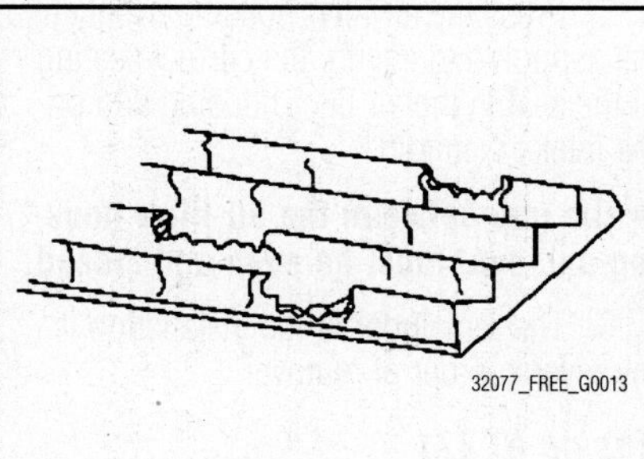

Fig. 44 Replace the belt if missing chunks are found during inspection

Visual Inspection

See Figure 46.

⁂ WARNING

Under no circumstances should the accessory drive belt, tensioner or pulleys be lubricated as potential damage to the belt material and tensioner damping mechanism will occur. Do not apply any fluids or belt dressing to the accessory drive belt or pulleys.

The water pump drive belt is on back of engine. It is driven off the rear cam pulley and does not have any adjustments.

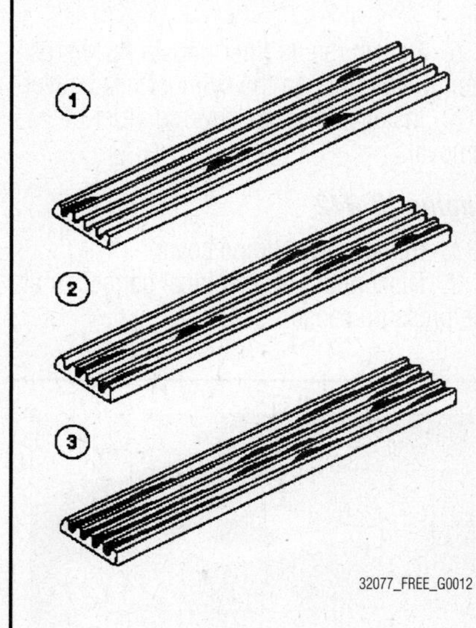

Fig. 45 Compare the condition of the belt with the accompanying text

Visually inspect the belt for obvious signs of mechanical damage:

- Drive belt cracking/chunking/wear
- Belt/pulley contamination
- Incorrectly routed belt

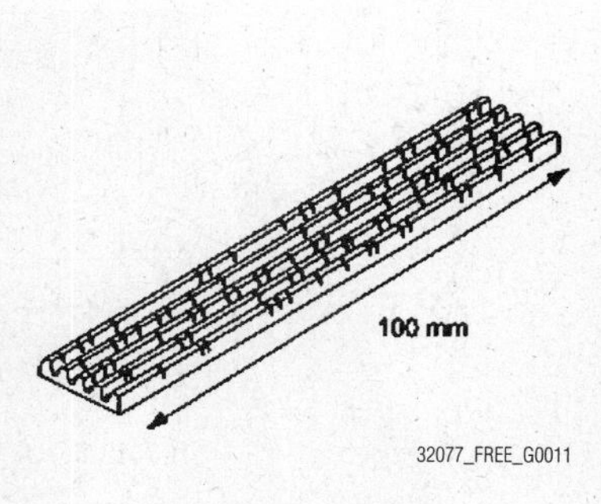

Fig. 46 Up to 15 cracks in a rib over a distance of 4 inches can be considered acceptable. If cracks exceed this standard, install a new belt

- Pulley misalignment or excessive pulley runout
- Loose or mislocated hardware
- Incorrectly routed power steering tubes (rubbing)

➡Up to 15 cracks in a rib over a distance of 4 inches can be considered acceptable. If damage exceeds the acceptable limit or any chunks are found to be missing from the ribs, a new belt must be installed.

1. Check the belt for cracks. Up to 15 cracks in a rib over a distance of 4 inches can be considered acceptable. If cracks exceed this standard, install a new belt.

REMOVAL & INSTALLATION

Drive Belt

1. Remove the engine covers.
2. Slacken the accessory drive belt by swiveling the clamping device counterclockwise.
3. Remove the accessory drive belt.
4. Installation is the reverse order of removal.

AIR CLEANER

REMOVAL & INSTALLATION

Air Cleaner Assembly

Engine IDS 276, 276 & 157

See Figure 47.

1. Ensure the ignition is in the **OFF** position.
2. Remove the bolts and remove the air filter housings.
3. Detach the intake air duct from the air ducting.

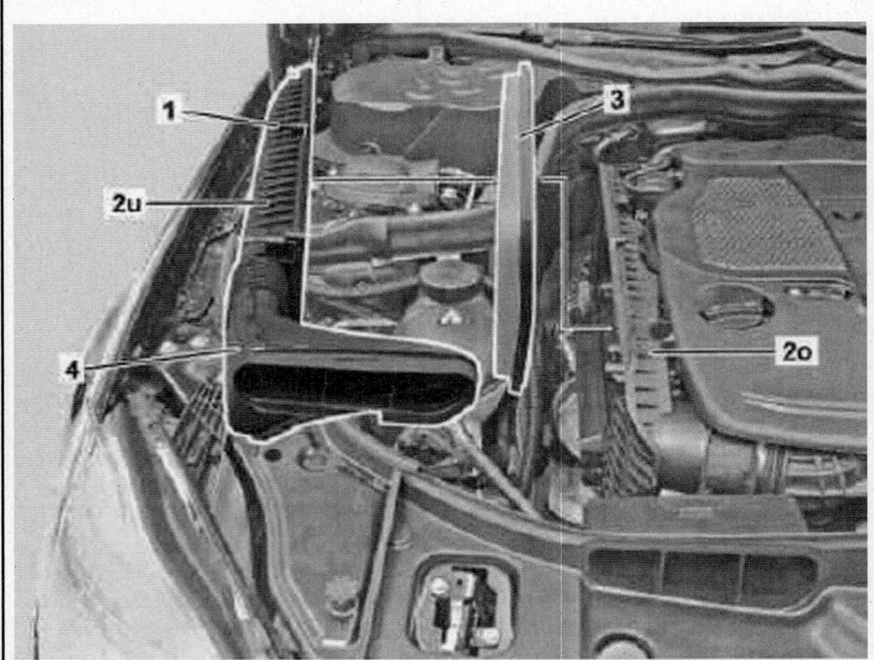

Fig. 47 Air filter housing—2012 E-Class models

4. Installation is the reverse order of removal.

Engine IDS 272 & 273

See Figure 48.

1. Pull off the front engine cover from above.
2. Remove the left and right engine air intake duct upstream of the air filter.
3. Detach the hose for the air pump at the air filter housing.
4. Pry the clamp off the air filter housing.
5. Detach the air filter housing upwards from the mounts on the cylinder head cover.
6. Installation is the reverse order of removal.

Engine ID 642

1. Remove the engine cover.
2. Disconnect the electrical connector at the pressure sensor.
3. Remove the left and right engine air intake duct (upstream of the air filter).
4. Loosen the engine air intake duct downstream of the air filter by loosening the clamps.
5. Remove the mounting bolts and detach the air filter housing on the engine intake air duct downstream of the air filter.
6. Pull the air filter housing up and out to remove.
7. Installation is the reverse order of removal. Tighten the mounting bolts to 80 inch lbs. (9 Nm).

Engine ID 152

See Figure 50.

1. Pull the off the front engine cover from above.
2. Remove the left and right engine air intake duct upstream of the air filter.
3. Detach the air filter housing upwards from the mounts on the left and right cylinder head cover.

➡The air filter housing must be lain on a padded base to prevent damage.

To install:

4. Apply lubricant to the support on the left and right cylinder head cover and the seal on the air filter housing using a suitable tool.
5. Press the air filter housing evenly into the support and ensure the correct seating of the seal in the air filter housing and on the intake manifold.

➡The gap between the air filter housing and seal must be even and closed.

6. The remainder of the installation is the reverse order of removal.

Engine ID 271

1. Remove the engine intake air duct.
2. Detach the air ducting on the air filter housing.
3. Unclip the ME-SFI control unit from the air filter housing. Leave the electrical lines attached and move to one side.
4. Unclip the electrical line from the support on the air filter housing.
5. Unlock the electrical line to the air filter housing.
6. Remove the air filter housing upwards out of the supports.
7. Installation is the reverse order of removal.

Air Filter Element

Engine IDS 276, 278 & 157

1. Ensure the ignition is in the **OFF** position.

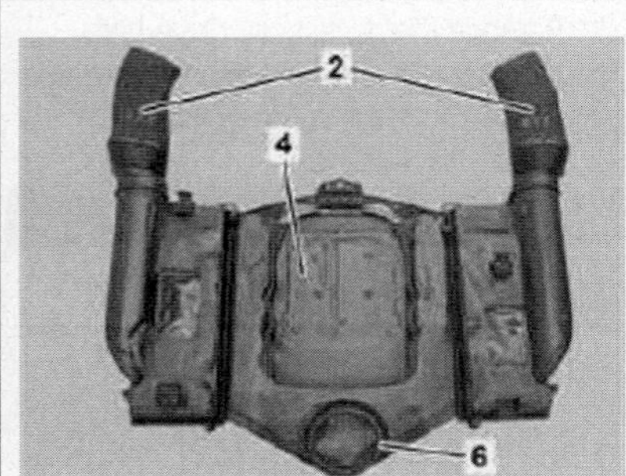

Fig. 48 Air filter housing—Engine IDs 272 & 273

Fig. 49 Remove the front engine cover to access the air intake assembly—Engine IDs 272 & 273

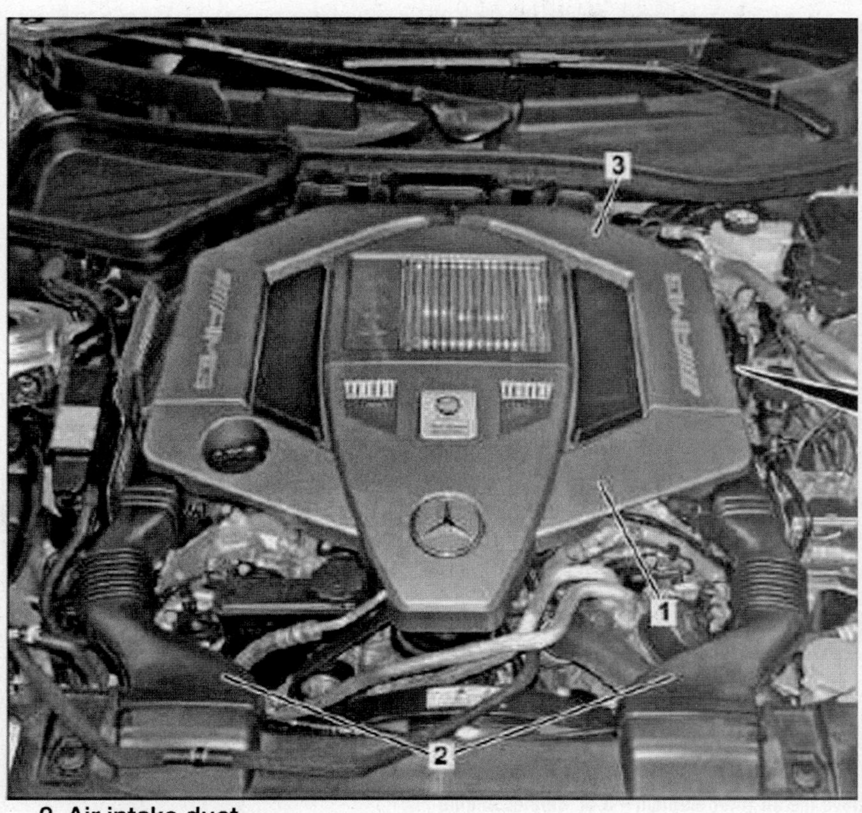

Fig. 50 Air filter housing—Engine ID 152

2. Remove the bolts and remove the air filter housings.
3. Detach the intake air duct from the air ducting.
4. Loosen the bolts and remove the housing cover and remove the air filter element.

➡The bolts remain in the housing cover.

5. Installation is the reverse order of removal.

Engine IDS 272 & 273

1. Pull off the front engine cover from above.
2. Remove the left and right engine air intake duct upstream of the air filter.
3. Detach the hose for the air pump at the air filter housing.
4. Pry the clamp off the air filter housing.
5. Detach the air filter housing upwards from the mounts on the cylinder head cover.
6. Slacken the bolts.

➡The bolts remain in the lower sections of the housing.

7. Remove the lower sections from the air filter housing.
8. Remove the air filter elements.
9. Installation is the reverse order of removal.

Engine ID 642

1. Remove the upper engine cover.
2. Remove the pressure sensor downstream of the air filter.
3. Remove the mounting bolts.
4. Open and unhook the clamps.
5. Pry the left and right air filter housing upper part off the engine air intake duct.
6. Remove the air filter.
7. Installation is the reverse order of removal.

Engine ID 152

1. Remove the engine cover and air filter housing with the air intake assembly.
2. Remove the left and right housing cover.
3. Remove the air filter inserts.
4. Installation is the reverse order of removal.

Engine ID 271

1. Remove the air filter housing cover.
2. Take out the air filter element.

➡Never clean, always replace the air filter element.

3. Installation is the reverse order of removal.

CAMSHAFT & BEARINGS

REMOVAL & INSTALLATION

Engine IDs 272 & 273

See Figures 54 55

1. Disconnect the negative battery cable.
2. Remove the air intake assembly.
3. Remove the timing chain tensioner.

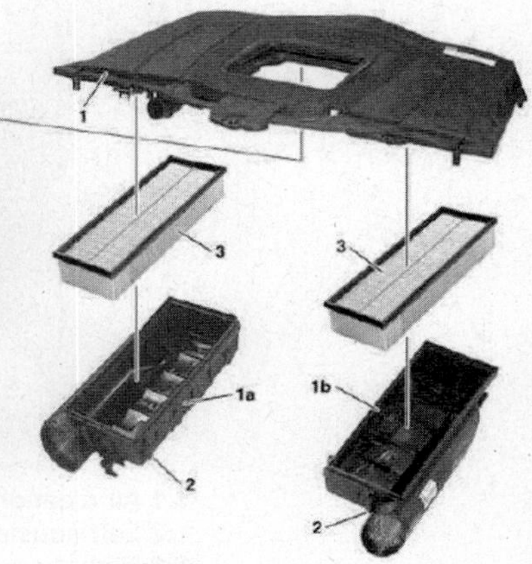

Fig. 51 Removing the air filter elements—Engine IDs 272 & 273

1k. Clamp
1s. Bolt
B28/5. Sensor
3. Air intake duct

71112_MBES_G0121

Fig. 52 Remove the clamps, bolts and sensor to remove the air filter element—3.0L Bluetec engine

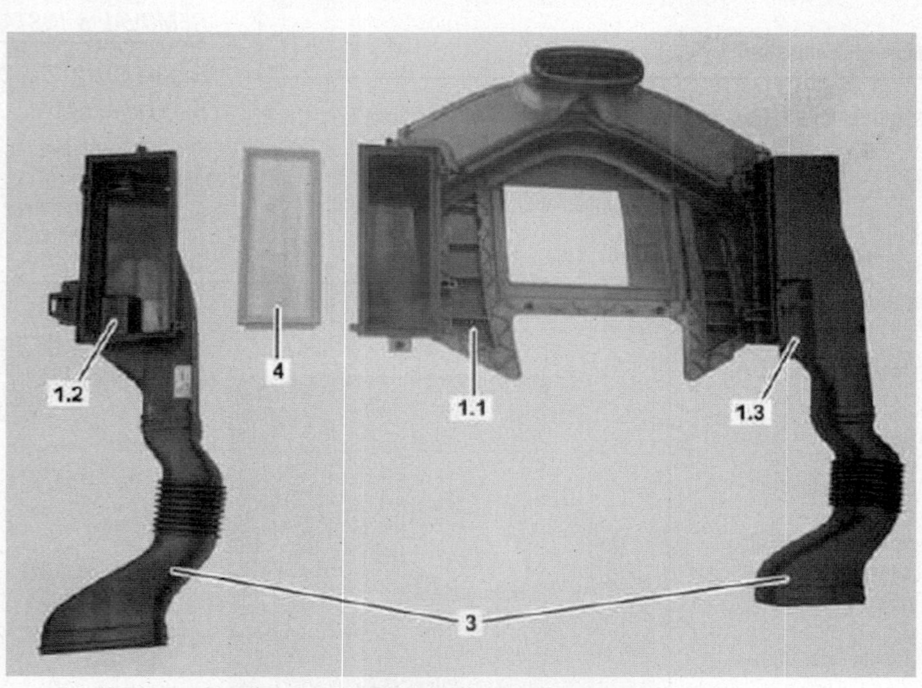

1.1 Air cleaner housing
1.2 Left housing cover
1.3 Right housing cover
3. Intake air ducts
4. Air filter element

71112_MBES_G0253

Fig. 53 Remove the air filter housing to access the air filter elements—Engine ID 152

1. Camshaft adjuster
2. Intake auxiliary bearing cap
3. Intake camshaft
4. Exhaust auxiliary bearing cap
5. Exhaust camshaft

71112_MBES_G0123

Fig. 54 Camshaft mounting—Engine IDs 272 & 273

For additional information, refer to the following section, "Timing Chain Cover, Chain, Tensioner, & Sprockets, Removal & Installation."

4. Remove the front cover at the necessary cylinder head.
5. Remove the centrifuge by detaching the hose on the cover and removing the mounting bolts.
6. Remove the cap.
7. Rotate the engine in the direction of rotation so that it is at 40° After Top Dead Center (TDC) of cylinder 1.
8. Lock the gear backlash compensation for the respective camshaft adjuster.
9. Detach the center valve.
10. Remove the cylinder head cover.
11. Matchmark the timing chain relative to the camshaft adjuster.
12. Remove the tensioning rail.
13. Remove the center value and pulse wheel.
14. Lift the timing chain and pull of the camshaft adjuster from the intake camshaft.
15. Remove the auxiliary bearing cap and remove the intake camshaft.

2d. Bolt
3. Centrifuge
3a. Bolt

71112_MBES_G0124

Fig. 55 Remove the mounting bolts to remove the centrifuge—Engine IDs 272 & 273

To install:

16. Install the camshaft. Tighten the auxiliary bearing cap to 71 inch lbs. (8 Nm).
17. Lubricate the contact surfaces to the intake camshaft and camshaft adjuster before the mounting camshaft adjuster.
18. Align the matchmarks on the camshaft adjuster and timing chain with each other. Align the dowel pin in camshaft adjuster with fitted bore in intake camshaft.
19. The remainder of the installation is the reverse order of removal. Tighten the center valve to 107 ft. lbs. (145 Nm).

Engine ID 642

See Figure 56.

1. Remove the cylinder head cover. For additional information, refer to the following section, "Cylinder Head Cover, Removal & Installation."
2. Attach a set of hold-down devices to the cylinder head.
3. Set the piston on cylinder 1 to Top Dead Center (TDC).
4. Matchmark the position of the timing chain relative to the camshaft sprocket.
5. Loosen the bolt by turning the engine on the vibration damper until the bolt is accessible.
6. Position the piston of cylinder 1 to TDC again.
7. Loosen the camshaft sprocket bolts, but do not remove.
8. Remove the chain tensioner.
9. Remove the hold-down device.
10. Remove the camshaft holder.
11. Affix a cable tie to the timing chain.
12. Remove camshafts with the camshaft sprockets attached.
13. Remove the camshaft sprocket from the camshafts by removing the bolts.
14. Installation is the reverse order of removal. Tighten the bolts as follows:
    - Camshaft sprocket mounting bolts: 13 ft. lbs. (18 Nm)
    - Camshaft retainer bracket bolts: 71 inch lbs. (8 Nm)

Engine IDs 276, 278 & 157

1. Rotate the engine in the direction of rotation so that it is at 40° after Top Dead Center of cylinder 1.
2. Remove the cylinder head cover.
3. Mount the hold-down device on the camshafts.

71112_MBES_G0125

Fig. 56 Install a set of hold-down devices to the cylinder—Engine ID 642

4. Remove the oil filter housing.
5. Remove the mounting bolts from the chain tensioner.
6. Remove the chain tensioner.
7. Hold the camshaft and loosen the central valve and remove.
8. Remove the camshaft adjuster from the camshaft.
9. Remove the auxiliary bearing cap on the camshaft.
10. Remove the camshafts.
11. Installation is the reverse order of removal. Tighten the camshaft bearing cap to 71 inch lbs. (8 Nm) plus 90°.

Engine ID 156

See Figures 57 and 58.

1. Remove the air filter housing.
2. Remove the spark plugs.
3. Rotate the engine in the direction of rotation so that it is at 40° after Top Dead Center of cylinder 1.
4. Remove the cylinder head covers. For additional information, refer to the following section, "Cylinder Head Cover, Removal & Installation."
5. Remove the camshaft adjusters as follows:
   a. Loosen the oil dipstick guide tubes on the cylinder head and turn to the side, right side only.
   b. Remove the cylinder head covers. For additional information, refer to the following section, "Cylinder Head Cover, Removal & Installation."
   c. Disconnect the electrical connectors on the left camshaft intake solenoid and left exhaust solenoid.
   d. Remove the bolt from the ground strap.

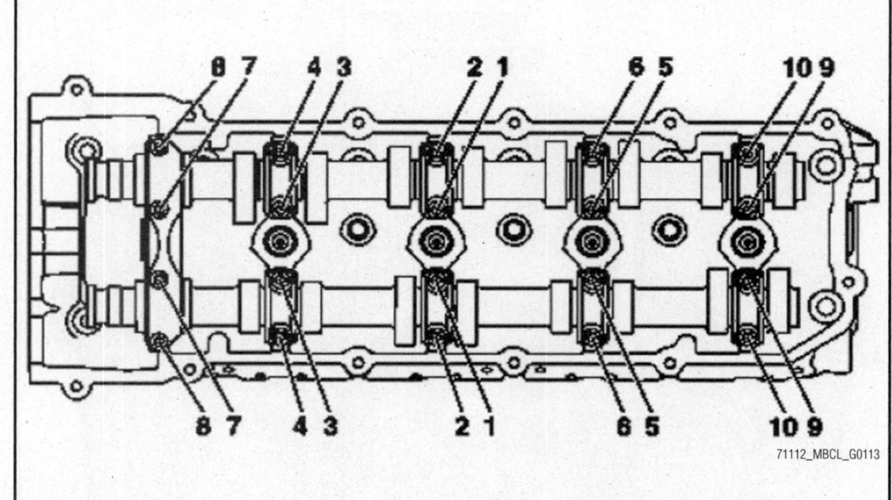

Fig. 58 Right side camshaft bearing cap tightening sequence—6.2L Engine

   e. Insert safety screws in the bores on the rear of the camshaft adjusters in order to lock the gear backlash adjustment.
   f. Remove the bolts and remove the camshaft adjuster.
6. Remove the bolts for the camshaft bearing caps.

➡Matchmark the bearing caps if they have no identification markings.

7. Remove the camshafts.

➡Matchmark the intake and exhaust side camshafts if they have no identification markings.

To install:

8. Oil the bearing surfaces and install the camshafts.
9. Install the camshaft bearing caps and tighten in sequence to 89 inch lbs. (10 Nm).
10. Turn the camshafts into the basic position.
11. The remainder of the installation is the reverse order of removal.

Engine ID 152

1. Remove the respective chain tensioner.
2. Remove the engine fan unit.
3. Rotate the engine at the crankshaft center bolt in the direction of rotation of the engine to a 40° crankshaft angle after top dead center (TDC) on cylinder 1.
4. Remove the oil filter housing, if removing left side.
5. Remove the cylinder head front cover.
6. Remove the mounting bolts from the chain tensioner.
7. Remove the respective chain tensioner.
8. Remove the cylinder head cover. For additional information, refer to the following section, "Cylinder Head Cover, Removal & Installation."
9. Remove camshaft hold-down device.
10. Remove the exhaust camshaft.
11. Remove the intake camshaft.

To install:

12. Oil the compensation elements and camshaft bearing points.

➡The cams on the intake camshaft must be pointing upright at an angle after inserting intake camshaft on cylinder 1. There is a risk of breakage otherwise.

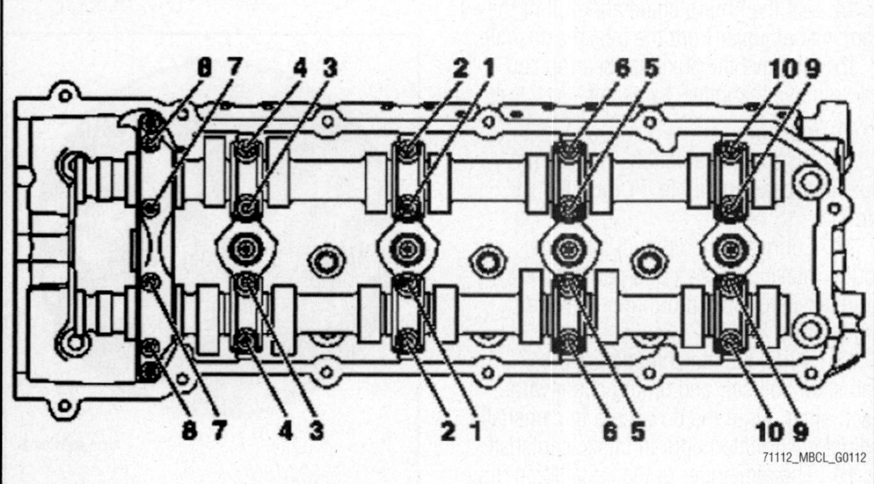

Fig. 57 Left side camshaft bearing cap tightening sequence—6.2L Engine

13. The remainder of the installation is the reverse order of removal.

Engine ID 271

See Figure 59.

1. Remove the cylinder head cover. For additional information, refer to the following section, "Cylinder Head Cover, Removal & Installation."
2. Remove the high-pressure pump.
3. Remove the front cover from the cylinder head. For additional information, refer to the following section, "Cylinder Head, Removal & Installation."
4. Crank the engine at the center bolt for the crankshaft in the direction of rotation until the cylinder 1 piston is positioned at Top Dead Center (TDC).
5. Remove the camshaft adjust for the exhaust camshaft.
6. Remove the exhaust camshaft sensor.
7. Remove the camshaft housing top section by removing the bolts in the reverse order of the tightening sequence.
8. Remove the intake camshaft.
9. Remove the exhaust camshaft.

To install:

10. Oil the compensation elements and camshaft bearing points.

➡The cams on the intake camshaft must be pointing upright at an angle after inserting intake camshaft on cylinder 1. There is a risk of breakage otherwise.

11. Install the camshafts into the bottom housing.
12. Install the camshaft top housing and tighten the bolts in sequence as follows:
    - Step 1: 88 inch lbs. (10 Nm)
    - Step 2: Plus 90°
13. The remainder of the installation is the reverse order of removal.

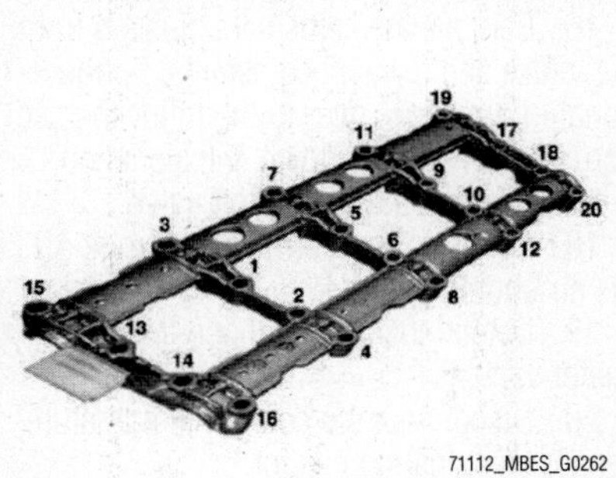

Fig. 59 Camshaft housing bolt tightening sequence—Engine ID 271

CRANKSHAFT DAMPER

REMOVAL & INSTALLATION

Engine ID 152, 157, 272, 273, 276, 278 & 642

1. Remove the air filter housing, except 3.0L engine.
2. Remove bottom sections of soundproofing, 3.0L engine only.
3. Remove the accessory drive belt.
4. Install a retaining lock for the crankshaft/starter ring gear.
5. Remove the damper center bolt and discard.
6. Remove the crankshaft damper from the crankshaft.

To install:

7. Inspect the contact surface of the sealing ring at the hub of the damper. Replace the damper if necessary.
8. Place the crankshaft damper on the crankshaft and rotate to ensure that the groove of the damper is engage in the feather key of the crankshaft.
9. Tighten the damper bolt to 148 ft. lbs. (200 Nm) plus 180°.
10. The remainder of the installation is the reverse order of removal.

Engine ID 156

1. Remove the front engine cover and both engine air intake ducts.
2. Remove the fan shroud.
3. Remove the accessory drive belt.
4. Remove the damper bolt and discard.
5. Remove the crankshaft damper.

To install:

6. Inspect the contact surface of the sealing ring at the hub of the damper. Replace the damper if necessary.
7. Place the crankshaft damper on the crankshaft and rotate to ensure that the groove of the damper is engage in the feather key of the crankshaft.
8. Tighten the damper bolt as follows:
    - Step 1: Tighten to 184 ft. lbs. (250 Nm)
    - Step 2: Release all tension
    - Step 3: Tighten to 148 ft. lbs. (200 Nm)
    - Step 4: Plus 180°
9. The remainder of the installation is the reverse order of removal.

Engine ID 271

See Figure 60.

1. Remove the accessory drive belt. For additional information, refer to the following section, "Accessory Drive Belt, Removal & Installation."

Fig. 60 Using the counterholder tool to remove the crankshaft damper—1.8L Engine

2. Remove the engine compartment paneling.
3. Insert the counterholder tool into the crankshaft damper and unscrew the center bolt.
4. Pull off the crankshaft damper.

➡A suitable puller can be used if it does not come off by hand.

CRANKSHAFT FRONT SEAL

REMOVAL & INSTALLATION

See Figure 61.

1. Remove the crankshaft damper. For additional information, refer to the following section, "Crankshaft Damper, Removal & Installation".
2. Using a screwdriver, carefully pry out the front seal.

To install:

3. Using a suitable seal install sleeve, install the front crankshaft seal.
4. The reminder of the installation is the reverse order of removal.
5. Refill the engine oil to the correct level.

CYLINDER HEAD

REMOVAL & INSTALLATION

Engine ID 642

See Figure 62.

1. Disconnect the negative battery cable.
2. Remove the bottom section of soundproofing.
3. Drain the engine oil.
4. Properly drain the cooling system.

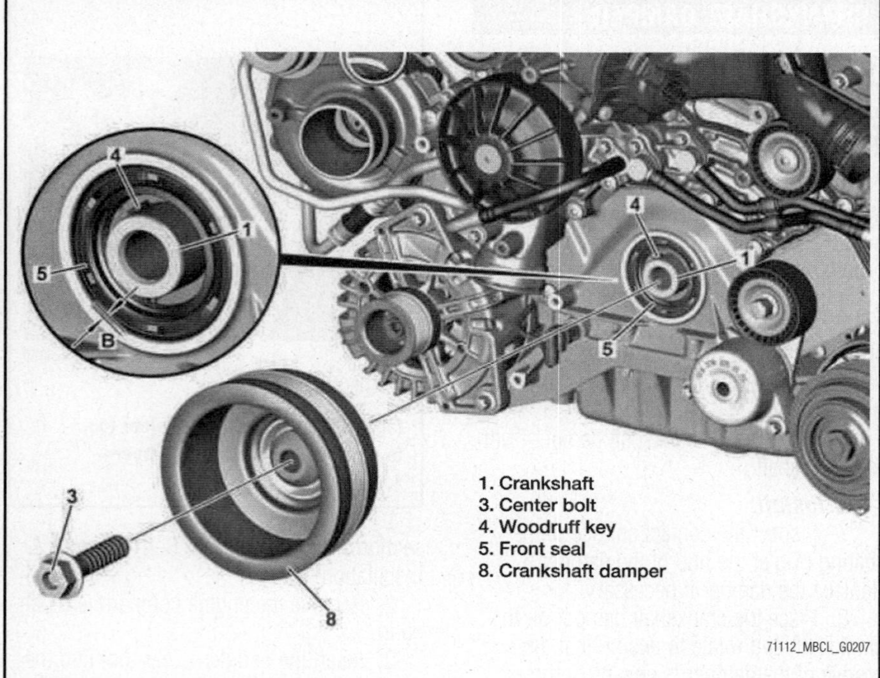

Fig. 61 Front crankshaft seal

5. Remove the charge air manifold
6. Remove the particulate filter
7. Remove the cylinder head covers. For additional information, refer to the following section, "Cylinder Head Covers, Removal & Installation."
8. Remove the glow plugs.
9. Remove the oil filter housing.
10. Remove the camshafts and camshaft sprockets. For additional information, refer to the following section, "Camshafts, Removal & Installation."

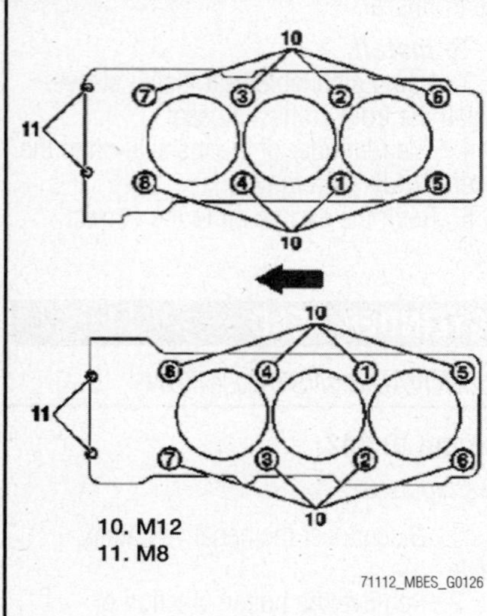

Fig. 62 Cylinder head bolt tightening sequence—Engine ID 642

11. Remove the heat shields above exhaust manifolds
12. Remove the high-pressure pump
13. Remove the slide rail pins.
14. Loosen the cylinder head bolts in stages and remove.
15. Remove the cylinder heads and gaskets.

To install:

16. Clean the threaded holes and sealing surfaces of any gasket material.
17. Check the cylinder head bolts and replace if their maximum length exceeds 8.14 inches (207 mm).
18. Install the cylinder head.
19. Tighten the bolts in the correct sequence using the follow procedure:
    - Step 1: Tighten the M12 bolts to 89 inch lbs. (10 Nm)
    - Step 2: Tighten the M8 bolts to 15 ft. lbs. (20 Nm)
    - Step 3: Tighten the M12 bolts to 44 ft. lbs. (60 Nm)
    - Step 4: Retighten the M8 bolts to 15 ft. lbs. (20 Nm)
    - Step 5: Tighten the M12 bolts an additional 90°
    - Step 6: Retighten the M8 bolts to 15 ft. lbs. (20 Nm)
    - Step 7: Tighten the M12 bolts an additional 90°
    - Step 8: Retighten the M8 bolts to 15 ft. lbs. (20 Nm)
    - Step 9: Tighten the M12 bolts an additional 90°
    - Step 10: Retighten the M8 bolts to 15 ft. lbs. (20 Nm)
20. The remainder of the installation is the reverse order of removal.
21. Refill the cooling system to the correct level.
22. Refill the engine with oil to the correct level.
23. Start the engine and check for leaks.

Engine IDs 272 & 273

See Figure 63.

1. Disconnect the negative battery cable.
2. Properly drain the cooling system.
3. Remove the exhaust line and disconnect the catalytic converter from the exhaust manifold.
4. Remove the air filter housing.
5. Remove the ME-SFI control unit.
6. Remove the accessory drive belt and drive belt tensioner.
7. Remove the power steering expansion reservoir.
8. Remove the oil filter housing.
9. Remove the engine front cover. For additional information, refer to the following section, "Engine Front Cover, Removal & Installation."
10. Remove the ignition oils.
11. Remove the oil separator.
12. Remove the intake manifold. For additional information, refer to the following section, "Intake Manifold, Removal & Installation."
13. Remove the cylinder head cover. For additional information, refer to the following section, "Cylinder Head Cover, Removal & Installation."
14. Rotate the engine at the crankshaft center bolt in the direction of the engine rotation to 40° angle after Top Dead Center (TDC).
15. Remove the timing chain tensioner.
16. Remove the camshaft adjusters from the intake and exhaust camshafts. For additional information, refer to the following section, "Camshafts, Removal & Installation".
17. Remove the air shutoff valve.
18. Remove the intermediate flange of the air shutoff valve.
19. Detach the coolant hose from the heater valve.
20. Disconnect the coolant temperature sensor electrical connector.
21. Remove the slide rail pins.
22. Loosen the cylinder head bolts in the reverse order of the tightening sequence.
23. Remove the cylinder head.

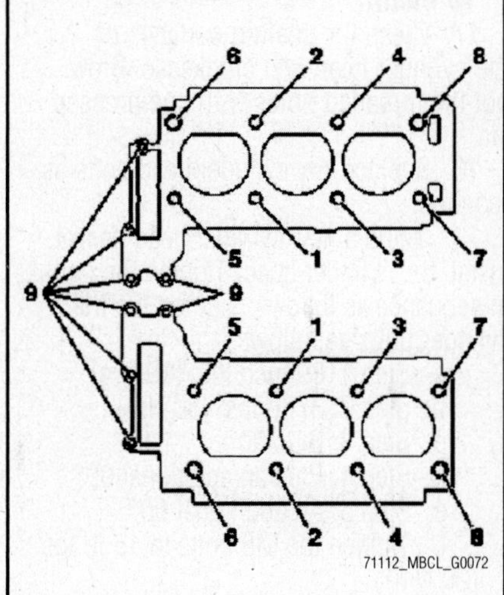

Fig. 63 Cylinder head tightening sequence—Engine ID 272 & 273

To install:

24. Clean the sealing surfaces of the cylinder head and crankcase. Blow out the threaded holes with compressed air.
25. Replace any cylinder head bolts as required.
26. Using a new cylinder head gasket, install the cylinder head. Tighten the bolts in sequence as follows: Tighten the M11 cylinder bolts as follows:
    a. Step 1: 15 ft. lbs. (20 Nm)
    b. Step 2: 37 ft. lbs. (50 Nm)
    c. Step 3: Plus 90°
    d. Step 4: Plus an additional 90°
    e. Tighten the M8 bolts to 15 ft. lbs. (20 Nm).
27. Apply sealant to the slide rail pins, then install the pins.
28. The remainder of the installation is the reverse order of removal.

Engine ID 276

See Figures 64 and 65.

1. Remove the center section of the bulkhead.
2. Remove the oil dipstick guide tube.
3. Remove the cylinder head cover. For additional information, refer to the following section, "Cylinder Head Cover, Removal & Installation."
4. Remove the coolant thermostat.
5. Remove the coolant pipe.
6. Unclip the electrical line for the knock sensors on the heating system shutoff valve.
7. Detach the coolant hose for the exhaust gas recirculation positioner and coolant hose to the heater cooler at heating system shutoff valve.

Fig. 64 Remove the coolant pipe to remove the cylinder head—Engine ID 276

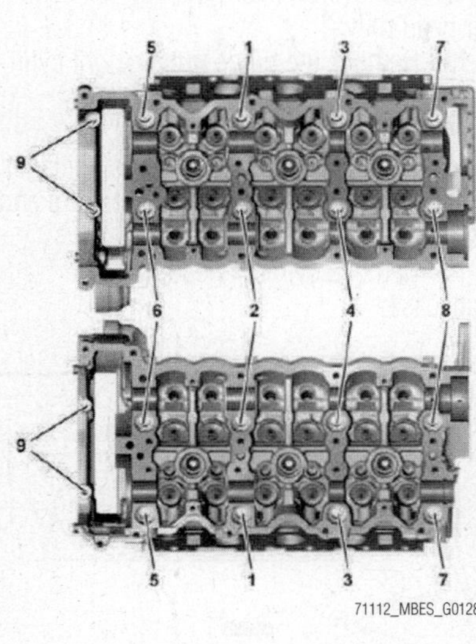

Fig. 65 Cylinder head bolt tightening sequence—Engine ID 276

8. Remove the heating system shutoff valve. Discard the seal.
9. Pull the coolant temperature sensor out of the cylinder head.
10. Remove the chain tensioner.
11. Pull the slide rail bolts out of the cylinder head.
12. Remove the auxiliary bearing cap for the camshafts.
13. Lift the camshaft at the rear and remove the timing chain from the camshaft adjuster.
14. Remove the camshafts.
15. Loosen the cylinder head bolts in the stages in the reverse order of the tightening procedure and remove them.
16. Remove the cylinder head.

To install:

17. Clean the sealing surfaces of the cylinder head and crankcase. Blow out the threaded holes with compressed air.
18. Replace any cylinder head bolts as required.
19. Using a new cylinder head gasket, install the cylinder head. Tighten the bolts in sequence as follows: Tighten the M11 cylinder bolts as follows:
    a. Step 1: 15 ft. lbs. (20 Nm)
    b. Step 2: 30 ft. lbs. (40 Nm)
    c. Step 3: Plus 90°
    d. Step 4: Plus an additional 90°
    e. Tighten the M7 bolts to 15 ft. lbs. (20 Nm).
20. The remainder of the installation is the reverse order of removal.

Engine IDs 152, 157 & 278

See Figures 66 and 67.

1. Remove the engine assembly.
2. Remove the cylinder head cover. For additional information, refer to the following section, "Cylinder Head Cover, Removal & Installation."
3. Remove the intake manifold. For additional information, refer to the following section, "Intake Manifold, Removal & Installation."
4. Remove the timing chain tensioner. For additional information, refer to the following section, "Timing Chain Cover, Chain, Tensioner, & Sprockets, Removal & Installation."
5. Remove the camshaft bearing caps.
6. Lift the camshafts from the rear and remove the timing chain from the camshaft adjuster.
7. Remove the camshaft assembly.
8. Pull out the slide rail bolts out of the cylinder head.
9. Detach the turbocharger, with the exhaust manifold attached, from the cylinder head.
10. Loosen the cylinder head bolts in the

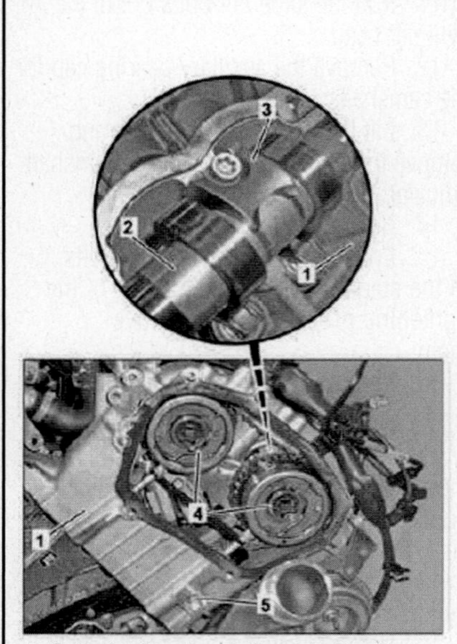

Fig. 66 Pull the slide rail pins from the cylinder head—Engine ID 278 shown

reverse order of the tightening sequence and remove.

11. Remove the cylinder head and gasket.

To install:

12. Clean the sealing surfaces of the cylinder head and crankcase. Blow out the threaded holes with compressed air.
13. Replace any cylinder head bolts as required.
14. Using a new cylinder head gasket, install the cylinder head. Tighten the bolts in sequence as follows: Tighten the M11 cylinder bolts as follows:
    a. Step 1: 15 ft. lbs. (20 Nm)
    b. Step 2: 30 ft. lbs. (40 Nm)
    c. Step 3: Plus 90°
    d. Step 4: Plus an additional 90°
    e. Step 5: Plus an additional 90°
    f. Tighten the M7 bolts to 10 ft. lbs. (14 Nm).
15. The remainder of the installation is the reverse order of removal.
16. Change the engine oil.

Engine ID 156

See Figure 68.

1. Disconnect the negative battery cable.
2. Properly drain the cooling system.
3. Remove the cooling fan.
4. Remove the alternator.
5. Remove the timing chain tensioner.

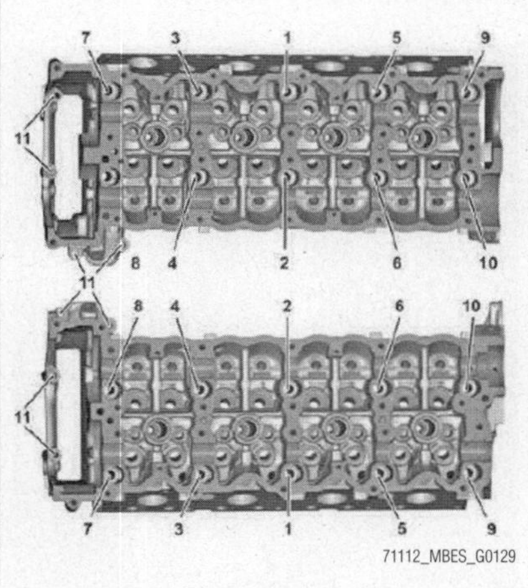

Fig. 67 Cylinder head bolt tightening sequence—Engine IDs 157 & 276

6. Remove the catalytic converter from the exhaust manifold.
7. Remove the intake manifold.
8. Remove the spark plugs.
9. Rotate the engine at the crankshaft center bolt in the direction of the engine rotation to 40° angle after Top Dead Center (TDC).
10. Remove the camshafts.
11. Remove air shutoff valve and air line on the cylinder head.
12. Remove oil filter housing, left cylinder head only.
13. Remove the guide pulley, right cylinder head only.
14. Pull out guide rail pins.
15. Loosen cylinder head bolts in stages in reverse order of tightening procedure and remove them.
16. Remove cylinder head from crankcase.

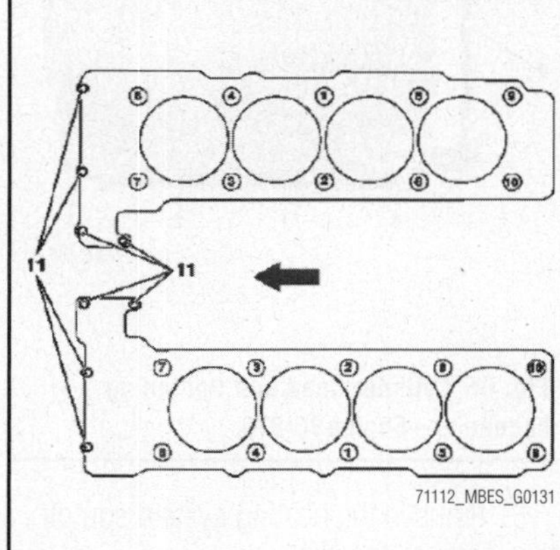

Fig. 68 Cylinder head bolt tightening sequence—Engine IDs 156

To install:

17. Clean the sealing surfaces of the cylinder head and crankcase. Blow out the threaded holes with compressed air.
18. Replace any cylinder head bolts as required.
19. Using a new cylinder head gasket, install the cylinder head. Tighten the bolts in sequence as follows: Tighten the M11 cylinder bolts as follows:
    a. Step 1: 89 inch lbs. (10 Nm)
    b. Step 2: 37 ft. lbs. (50 Nm)
    c. Step 3: Plus 90°
    d. Step 4: Plus an additional 90°
    e. Step 5: An additional 90°
    f. Tighten the M8 bolts to 15 ft. lbs. (20 Nm).

Engine ID 271

See Figure 69.

1. Disconnect the negative battery cable.
2. Remove the catalytic converter. For additional information, refer to the following section, "Catalytic Converter, Removal & Installation."
3. Properly drain the cooling system.
4. Remove the vacuum hose from radiator shutters adjuster.
5. Remove air ducting on turbocharger.
6. Detach boost pressure control hose on pressure transducer.
7. Remove charge air manifold on the turbocharger.
8. Remove shield and support brace from the turbocharger.
9. Remove the power steering expansion reservoir with the lines connected move to one side.
10. Remove the combination valve.
11. Remove the bracket on the cylinder head.
12. Remove the oil return line of the turbocharger.
13. Remove the coolant feed pipe for the turbocharger.
14. Remove the crankcase ventilation system pipe and coolant pipe.
15. Remove the cylinder head cover.
16. Remove the oil dipstick guide tube.
17. Remove the vacuum pump.
18. Remove the intake manifold.
19. Disconnect the connector for electrical line on rail pressure sensor
20. Disconnect the connector for electrical line for fuel injectors to rail
21. Remove the high-pressure pump.
22. Remove the coolant connection to cylinder head at the rear
23. Remove the front cover at cylinder head.

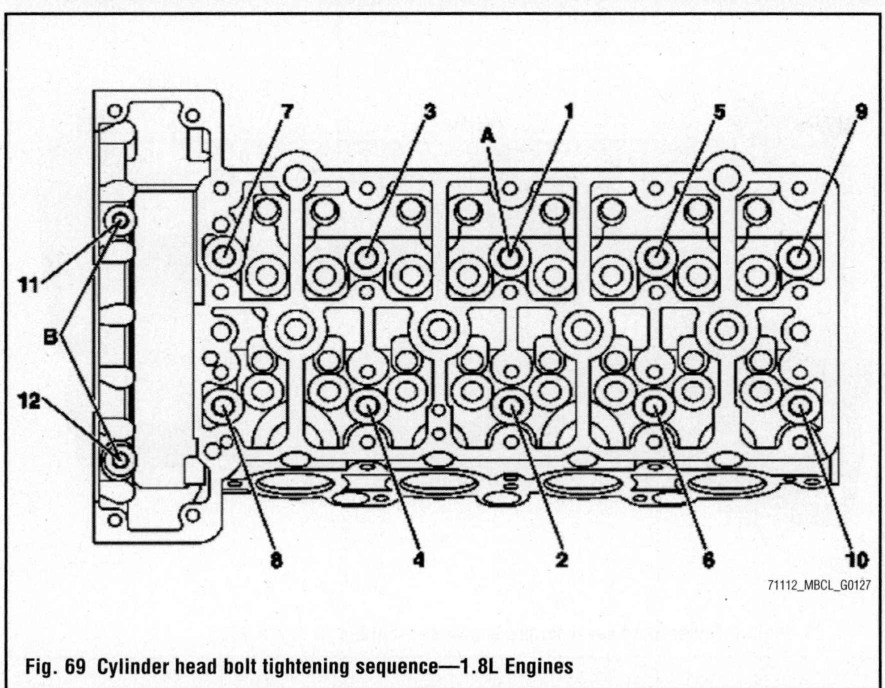

Fig. 69 Cylinder head bolt tightening sequence—1.8L Engines

24. Remove the chain tensioner.
25. Pull the guide rail pins out of cylinder head.
26. Remove the camshaft adjuster for the exhaust camshafts.
27. Remove the tensioning rail.
28. Remove the camshaft housing.
29. Remove the roller type cam following with the compensation elements.

➡When removing more than one compensation elements, ensure that cam followers and compensation elements which were not replaced are re-installed at their previous location. Mark cam follower relative to the corresponding compensation element if necessary.

30. Loosen the cylinder head bolts in the reverse order of the tightening sequence.
31. Remove the cylinder head and gasket.
32. Installation is the reverse order of removal. Tighten the cylinder head bolts in sequence as follows:
- Step 1: 33 ft. lbs. (45 Nm)
- Step 2: Plus 90°
- Step 3: Plus an additional 90°

CYLINDER HEAD COVERS

REMOVAL & INSTALLATION

Engine IDs 272 & 273

Left Side

See Figure 70.

1. Turn the ignition key to the **OFF** position.
2. Remove the bottom engine compartment paneling.
3. Properly drain the cooling system.
4. Remove the air filter housing.
5. Remove the accessory drive belt.
6. Remove the thermostat.
7. Remove the oil filter housing.
8. Remove the power steering expansion reservoir.
9. Remove the front cover. For additional information, refer to the following section, "Engine Cover, Removal & Installation."
10. Detach the purge line at the separation point, unclip it from the brackets on the oil separator and feed line duct and place it aside.
11. Properly relieve the fuel system pressure.
12. Detach the fuel line at the fuel distributor.
13. Remove the ignition coils on the left cylinder head.
14. Disconnect the ground line from the cylinder head cover.
15. Remove the rear engine suspension lug.
16. Remove the feed line duct from the cylinder head cover.
17. Remove the heat shield.
18. Remove the vacuum pump, Engine ID 272 only.
19. Loosen the cylinder head mounting bolts in the reverse order of the tightening procedure and remove.
20. Carefully pry off the cylinder head cover from the cylinder head.

⁂ WARNING

Ensure the sealing surfaces are not damaged with the pry tool.

To install:

21. Clean the sealing surfaces of the cylinder head and cylinder head cover.
22. Apply new sealant to the sealing surfaces of the cylinder head cover.
23. Tighten the mounting bolts in sequence to 106 inch lbs. (12 Nm) plus 90°.
24. The remainder of the installation is the reverse order of removal.

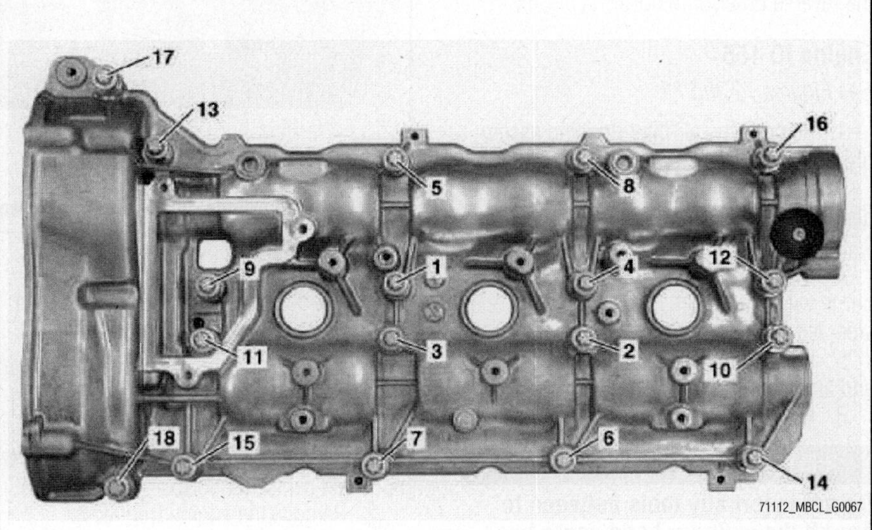

Fig. 70 Left cylinder head cover torque sequence—Engine ID 272 & 273

Right Side

See Figure 71.

1. Turn the ignition key to the **OFF** position.
2. Remove the air filter housing.
3. Remove the switchover valve by removing the bracket from the front engine cover.
4. Remove the air shutoff valve.
5. Remove the front cover.
6. Remove the ignition coils on the right cylinder head.
7. Remove the cover on the centrifuge.
8. Detach the ME-SFI control unit and remove the control unit bracket.
9. Disconnect the ground line from the cylinder head cover.
10. Remove the feed line duct from the intake manifold, cylinder head cover and right engine suspension lug and place aside.
11. Loosen the bolts for the cylinder head cover in the reverse order of the tightening sequence.
12. Carefully pry off the cylinder head cover from the cylinder head.

⁂ WARNING

Ensure the sealing surfaces are not damaged with the pry tool.

To install:

13. Clean the sealing surfaces of the cylinder head and cylinder head cover.
14. Apply new sealant to the sealing surfaces of the cylinder head cover.
15. Tighten the mounting bolts in sequence to 106 inch lbs. (12 Nm) plus 90°.
16. The remainder of the installation is the reverse order of removal.

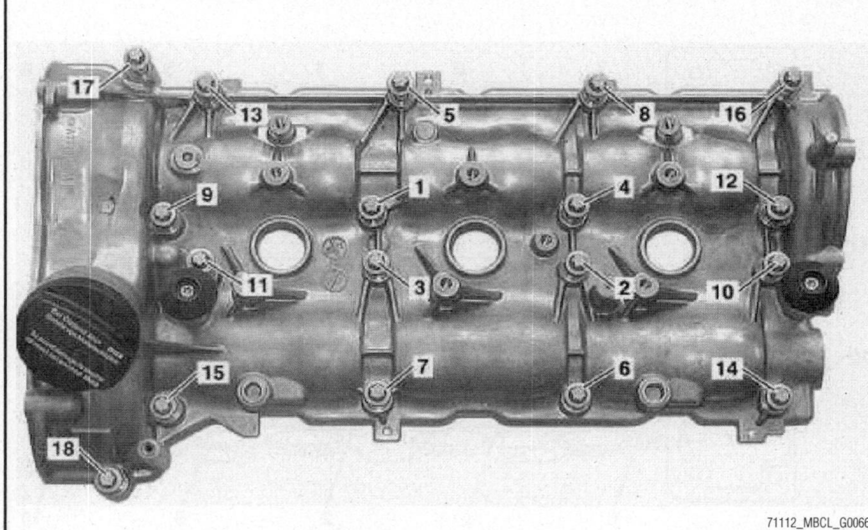

Fig. 71 Right cylinder head cover torque sequence—Engine ID 272 & 273

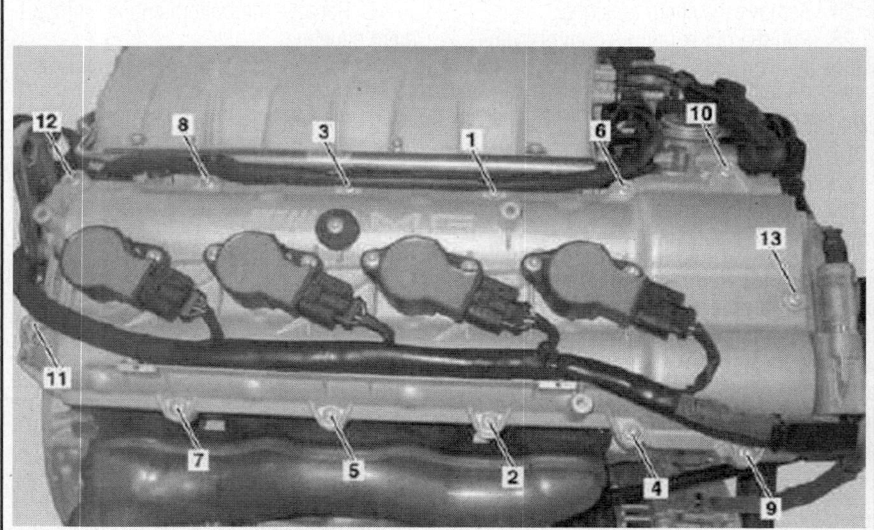

Fig. 72 Right cylinder head cover torque sequence—Engine ID 156

Engine ID 156

See Figures 72 and 73.

1. Remove the air filter housing assembly.
2. Remove the foam cover from the fuel distributor.
3. Remove the ignition coils.
4. Disconnect the purge line from the purge valve and move the purge line to one side, left cylinder head cover only.
5. Remove the wiring harness bracket and any retaining clamps.
6. Remove the cylinder head cover.

⁂ WARNING

Do not insert any tools between to pry off the cylinder head cover to avoid damage to the cylinder head cover.

7. Installation is the reverse order of removal. Tighten the cylinder head bolts in sequence to 75 inch lbs. (8.5 Nm).

Engine ID 276

See Figures 74 through 76.

1. Remove the engine appearance cover (bulkhead center section).
2. Remove the engine front cover.
3. Detach the oil dipstick tube from the cylinder head cover and move aside.
4. Remove the fuel rail. For additional information, refer to the following section, "Fuel Rail, Removal & Installation."
5. Detach engine wiring harness on the cylinder head cover.
6. Remove the ignition coils.
7. Remove the bolt for heating system shutoff valve on the cylinder head cover.
8. Remove the vacuum reservoir for the vacuum pump.
9. Remove the bracket for ME-SFI [ME] control unit.
10. Loosen the bolts for the cylinder

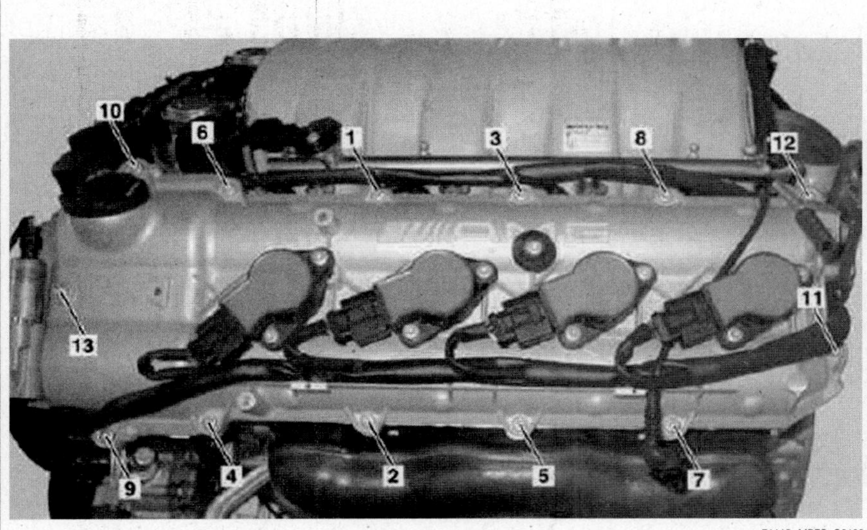

Fig. 73 Left cylinder head cover torque sequence—Engine ID 156

head cover in the reverse order of the tightening sequence.

11. Carefully pry off the cylinder head cover from the cylinder head.

WARNING

Ensure the sealing surfaces are not damaged with the pry tool.

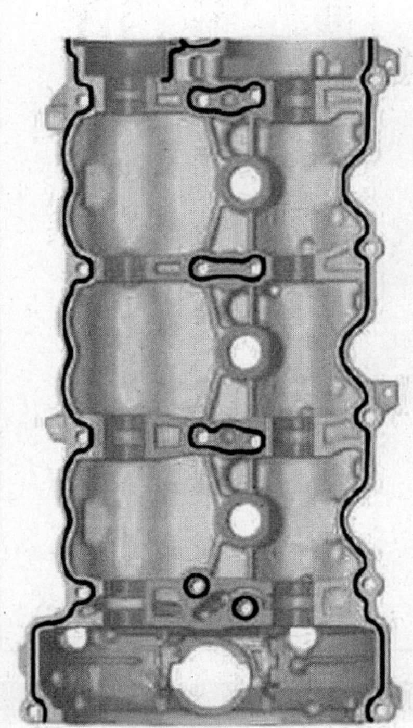

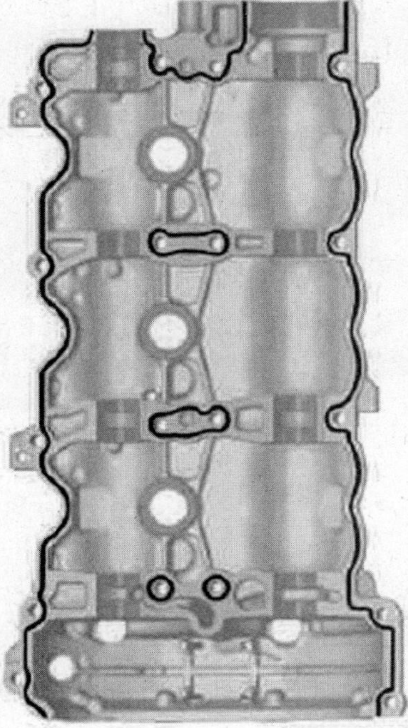

Fig. 74 Sealant location for the cylinder head cover—Engine ID 276

To install:

12. Apply suitable sealant to the mounting surfaces for the cylinder head cover.

➡Check for the correct seating of the cap of the exhaust camshaft between the cylinder head cover and the cylinder head.

13. Install the cylinder head cover.
14. Tighten the cylinder head bolts in sequence to 106 inch lbs. (12 Nm) plus 90°
15. The remainder of the installation is the reverse order of removal.

Engine ID 157 & 278

See Figures 77 through 79.

1. Remove the fuel rail.
2. Remove the ignition coils.
3. Disconnect the engine wiring harness on the cylinder head cover.
4. Disconnect the oil lines for the turbocharger on the cylinder head cover and move to one side.
5. Remove the partial load crankcase ventilation on the cylinder head cover.
6. Remove the bracket and lifting eye on the cylinder head cover.
7. Remove the left charge air ducts.
8. Remove the oil filter housing, Engine ID 157 only.
9. Disconnect the electrical connections and lines on the cylinder head front cover.
10. Remove the front cover mounting bolts and discard.
11. Remove the cylinder head front cover.
12. Loosen the cylinder head cover bolts in the reverse order of the tightening sequence and discard.
13. Carefully pry the cylinder head cover and remove.

To install:

14. Apply sealant to the clean sealing surfaces of cylinder head cover and install.
15. Tighten the mounting bolts in sequence as follows:
    - Step 1: 106 inch lbs. (12 Nm)
    - Step 2: Plus 90°

Engine ID 642

Left Side

See Figures 80 through 82.

1. Remove the engine air intake duct downstream of the air filter.
2. Remove the charge air duct from the turbocharger.
3. Remove the exhaust gas recirculation positioned.
4. Remove the fuel injectors.
5. Remove the fuel rail.

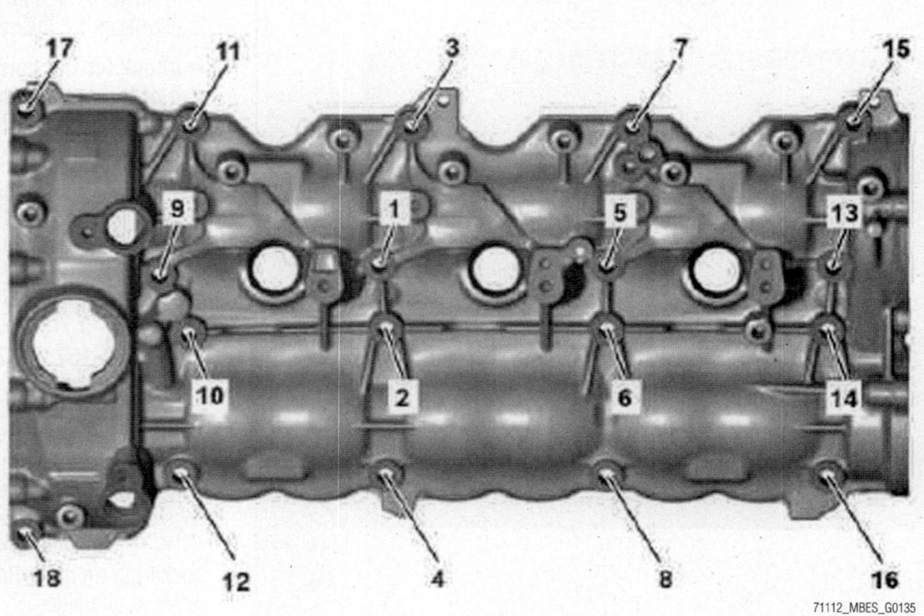

Fig. 75 Right cylinder head cover torque sequence—Engine ID 276

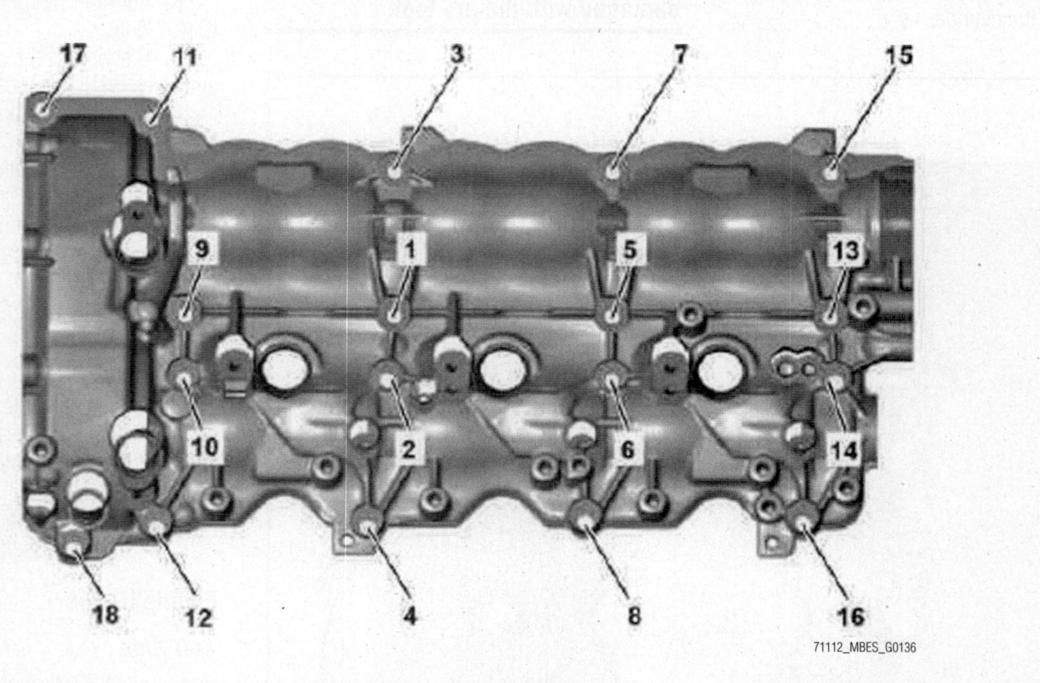

Fig. 76 Left cylinder head cover torque sequence—Engine ID 276

6. Detach the container for the power steering pump on the cylinder head cover.

7. Unscrew the fuel line on the cylinder head cover and remove it with the flexible feed and return hose.

8. Loosen the dipstick guide tube above and below.

9. Loosen the cylinder head cover bolts in the reverse order of the tightening sequence.

10. Carefully pry off the cylinder head cover from the cylinder head.

✲✲ WARNING

Ensure the sealing surfaces are not damaged with the pry tool.

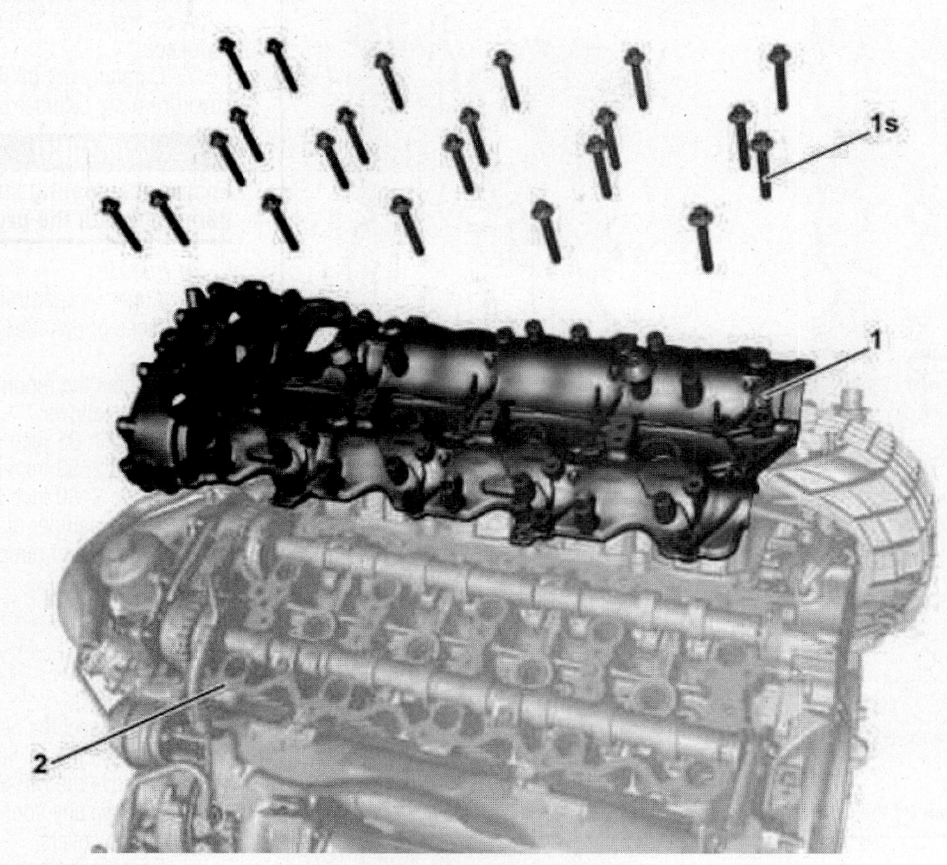

Fig. 77 Cylinder head cover mounting—Engine ID 157 & 278

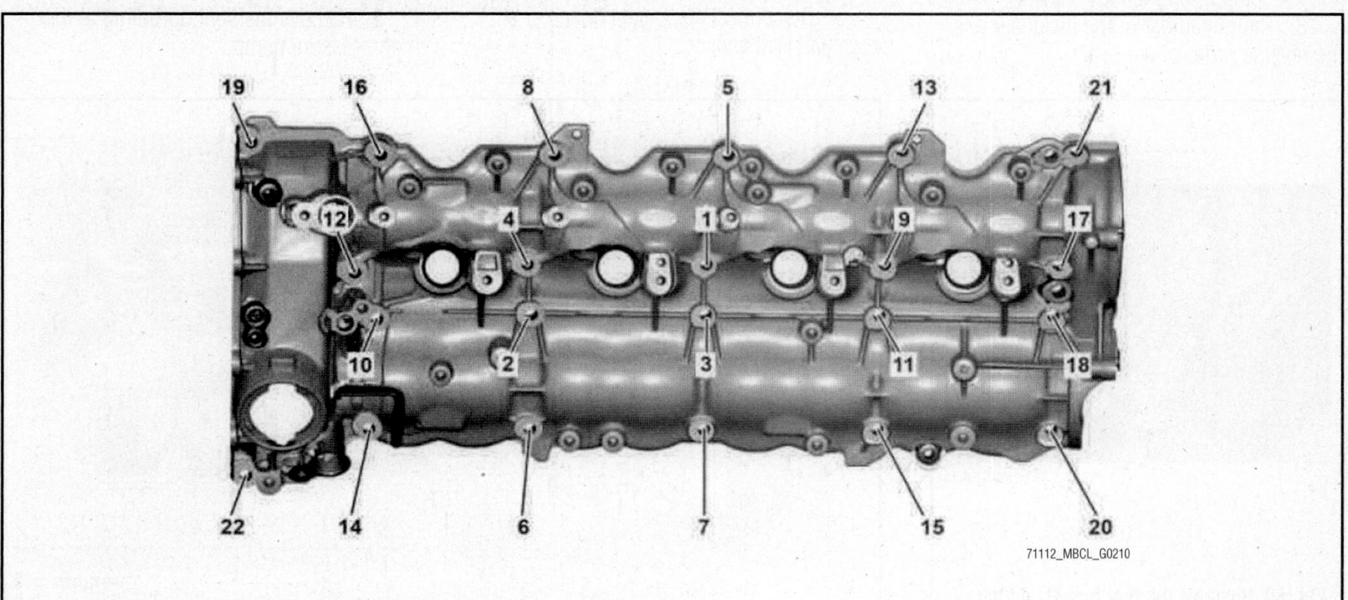

Fig. 78 Cylinder head cover bolt tightening sequence—Engine ID 157 & 278

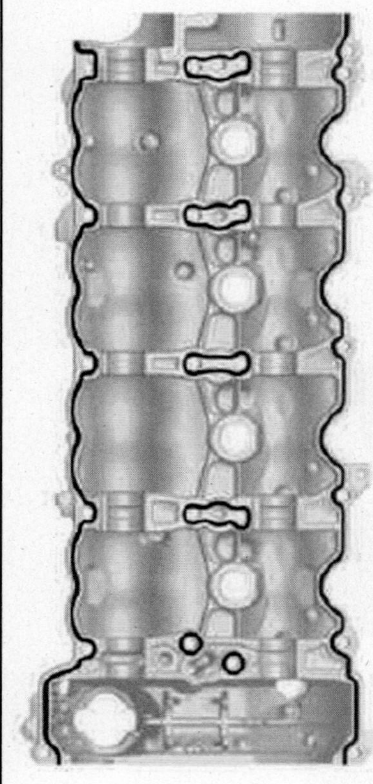
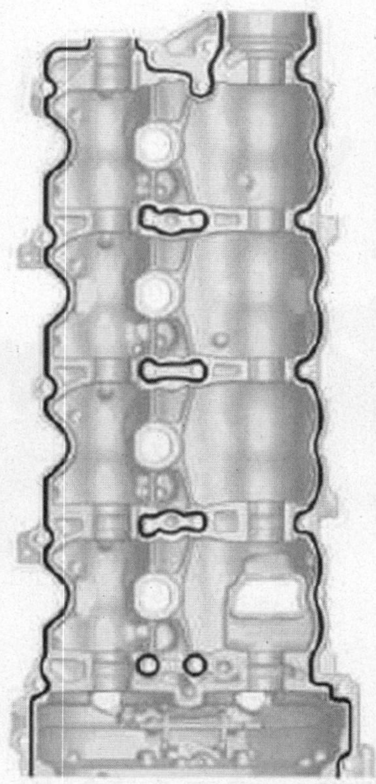

Fig. 79 Sealant location for the cylinder head cover—Engine ID 157 & 278

To install:

11. Apply sealant to the clean sealing surfaces of cylinder head cover and install.
12. Tighten the mounting bolts in sequence as follows:
    - Step 1: 35 inch lbs. (4 Nm)
    - Step 2: 53 inch lbs. (6 Nm)
    - Step 3: 80 inch lbs. (9 Nm)
13. The remainder of the installation is the reverse order of removal.

Right Side

See Figures 83 and 84.

1. Remove the fuel injectors.
2. Remove the fuel rail.
3. Remove the oil separator.
4. Remove the connection fitting for the oil separator and discard the sealing rings.
5. Disconnect electrical connector at camshaft Hall sensor.
6. Loosen the cylinder head cover bolts in the reverse order of the tightening sequence.
7. Carefully pry off the cylinder head cover from the cylinder head.

⁂ WARNING

Ensure the sealing surfaces are not damaged with the pry tool.

To install:

8. Apply sealant to the clean sealing surfaces of cylinder head cover and install.
9. Tighten the mounting bolts in sequence as follows:
    - Step 1: 35 inch lbs. (4 Nm)
    - Step 2: 53 inch lbs. (6 Nm)
    - Step 3: 80 inch lbs. (9 Nm)
10. The remainder of the installation is the reverse order of removal.

Engine ID 152

Right Side

See Figure 85.

1. Disconnect the negative battery cable.
2. Remove the air filter housing.
3. Remove the ME-SFI control unit.
4. Remove any soundproofing from the cylinder head covers.
5. Remove the bottom engine compartment paneling.
6. Remove the engine fan unit.
7. Turn the engine at central bolt of the crankshaft in direction of engine rotation to a 40° crank angle on cylinder 1.
8. Properly relieve the fuel system pressure.
9. Remove the soundproofing at the high pressure pump.

Fig. 80 Unscrew the fuel line (1) on the cylinder head cover—Engine ID 642

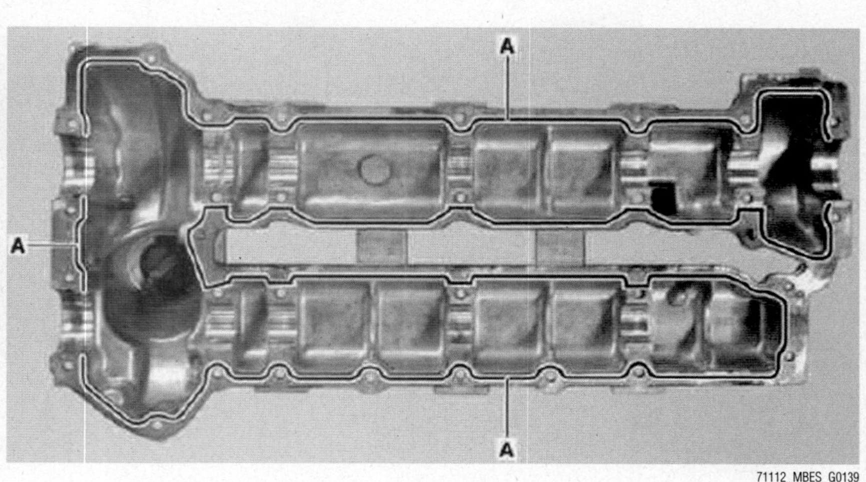

Fig. 81 Sealant location for the cylinder head cover—Engine ID 642

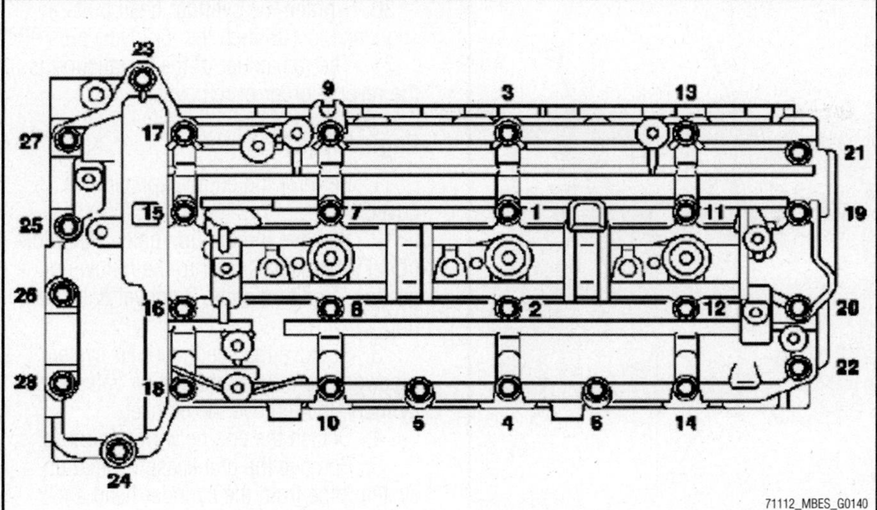

Fig. 82 Left cylinder head cover bolt tightening sequence—Engine ID 642

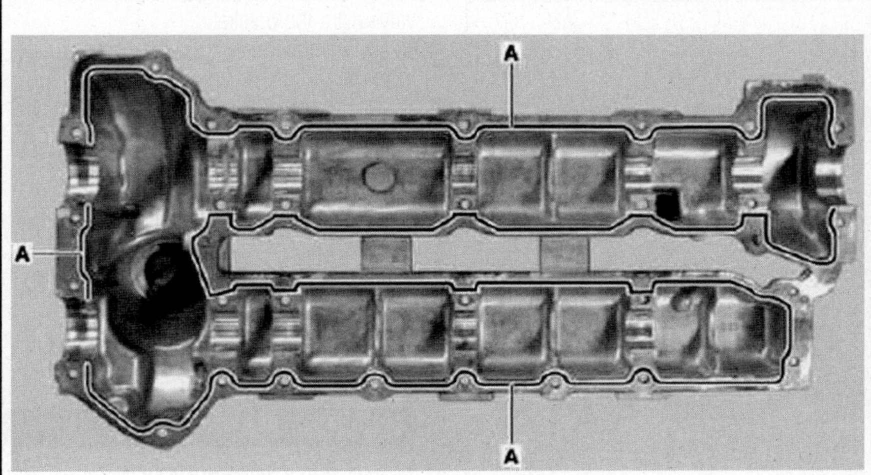

Fig. 83 Sealant location for the cylinder head cover—Engine ID 642

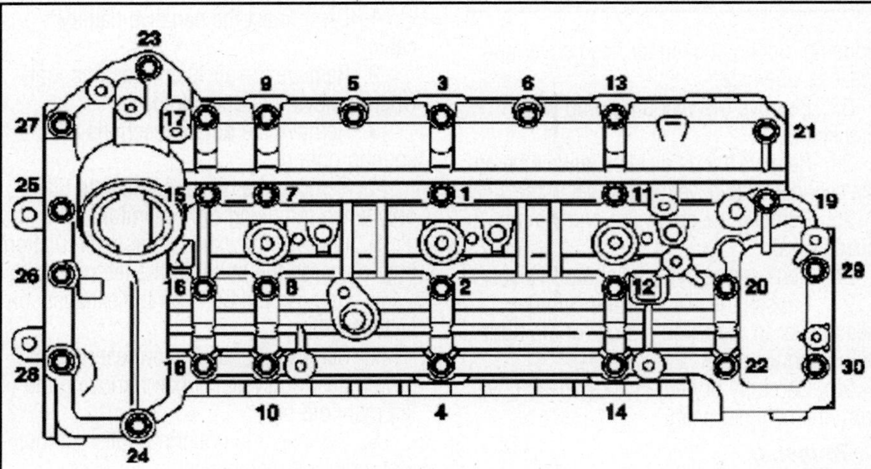

Fig. 84 Right cylinder head cover bolt tightening sequence—Engine ID 642

10. Disconnect electrical connector from quantity control valve at the high-pressure pump.
11. Remove high-pressure lines which are mounted on the high-pressure pump.
12. Remove the pump mounting bolts and discard the bolts.
13. Remove the high-pressure pump.
14. Remove the high-pressure lines.
15. Remove the fuel rail.
16. Remove the ignition coils. For additional information, refer to the following section, "Ignition Coils, Removal & Installation."
17. Detach engine wiring harness on cylinder head cover.
18. Remove the front cover.
19. Remove the centrifuge cover.
20. Remove the oil pump for cylinder shutoff.
21. Remove the cylinder shutoff valves.
22. Loosen the bolts for the cylinder head cover in the reverse order of the tightening sequence.
23. Carefully pry the cylinder head cover from the cylinder head.

To install:

24. Apply sealant to the clean sealing surfaces of cylinder head cover and install.
25. Tighten the cylinder head bolts in sequence to 106 inch lbs. (12 Nm) plus 90°
26. The remainder of the installation is the reverse order of removal.

Left Side

See Figures 86 and 00.

1. Disconnect the negative battery cable.
2. Remove the air filter housing.
3. Remove the ME-SFI control unit.
4. Remove any soundproofing from the cylinder head covers.
5. Remove the bottom engine compartment paneling.
6. Remove the engine fan unit.
7. Turn the engine at central bolt of the crankshaft in direction of engine rotation to a 40° crank angle on cylinder 1.
8. Properly relieve the fuel system pressure.
9. Remove the soundproofing at the high pressure pump.
10. Disconnect electrical connector from quantity control valve at the high-pressure pump.
11. Remove high-pressure lines which are mounted on the high-pressure pump.
12. Remove the pump mounting bolts and discard the bolts.
13. Remove the high-pressure pump.
14. Remove the high-pressure lines.

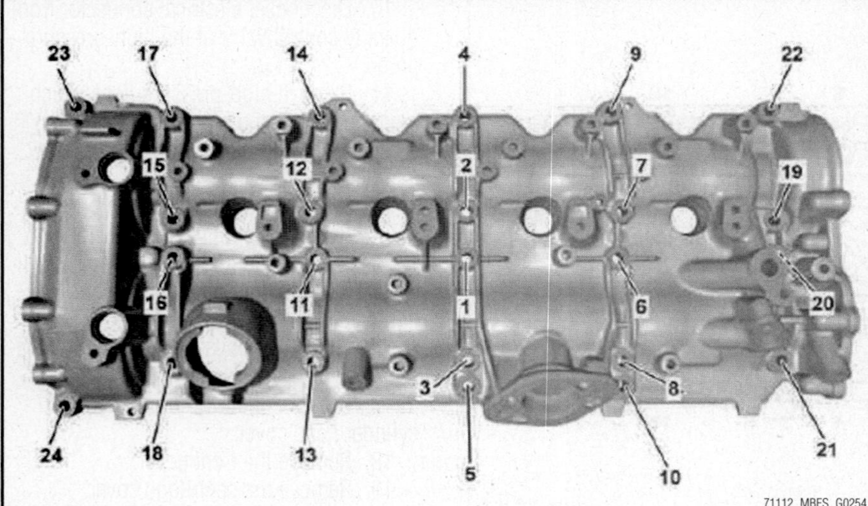

Fig. 85 Right cylinder head cover bolt tightening sequence—Engine ID 152

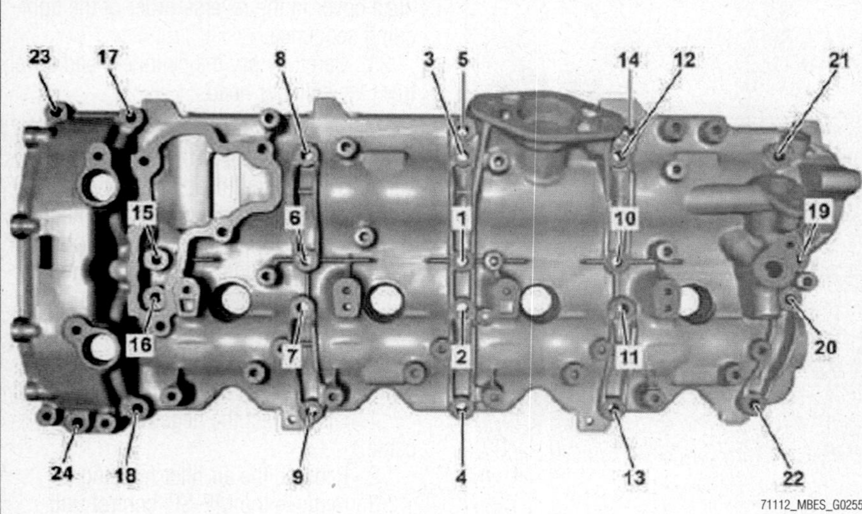

Fig. 86 Left cylinder head cover bolt tightening sequence—Engine ID 152

15. Remove the fuel rail.
16. Remove the ignition coils. For additional information, refer to the following section, "Ignition Coils, Removal & Installation."
17. Detach engine wiring harness on cylinder head cover.
18. Detach vehicle wiring harness on intake manifold, cylinder head and engine suspension lug and place to one side.
19. Remove the front cover.
20. Detach the vacuum line on vacuum pump and intake manifold and place to one side.
21. Detach the oil separator on cylinder head cover, unclip on intake manifold and place with attached line to one side.
22. Detach the purge line at air duct housing, unclip at cylinder head cover and place to one side.
23. Remove the vacuum pump with bracket.
24. Remove the oil dipstick guide tube on the cylinder head cover and swivel to the side.
25. Remove the stop plug on cylinder head cover.
26. Remove the cylinder shutoff valves
27. Loosen the bolts for the cylinder head cover in the reverse order of the tightening sequence.
28. Carefully pry the cylinder head cover from the cylinder head.

To install:

29. Apply sealant to the clean sealing surfaces of cylinder head cover and install.
30. Tighten the cylinder head bolts in sequence to 106 inch lbs. (12 Nm) plus 90°
31. The remainder of the installation is the reverse order of removal.

Engine ID 271

1. Remove the engine appearance cover.
2. Remove the ignition coils. For additional information, refer to the following section, "Ignition coils, Removal & Installation."
3. Remove the secondary air system pipework from the combination valve and cylinder, the remove the bracket.
4. Detach the engine wiring harness.
5. Remove the crankcase ventilation system pipe from the cylinder head and cylinder head cover.
6. Disconnect the vacuum line from the air pump switchover valve.
7. Unhook the air pump switchover valve from the bracket.
8. Remove the oil dipstick guide tube from the cylinder head cover.
9. Remove the mounting bolts and take off the cylinder head cover.

To install:

10. Replace the cylinder head cover gaskets.
11. Install the cylinder head cover and tighten the mounting bolts in sequence to 71 inch lbs. (8 Nm).
12. The remainder of the installation is the reverse order of removal.

EXHAUST MANIFOLD

REMOVAL & INSTALLATION

Engine ID 642

See Figure 87.

1. Disconnect the negative battery cable.
2. Remove the air filter housings, only when removing left manifold.
3. Remove the bottom sections of soundproofing.
4. Remove the diesel particulate filter, only when removing right manifold.
5. Remove the exhaust gas recirculation line to access the bolts for the left manifold.
6. Remove the bolts on the exhaust collector pipe.
7. Remove the expansion reservoir of power steering system when removing the left manifold only.
8. Remove the mounting bolts and nut and remove the heat shield.
9. Remove the exhaust manifold.
10. Installation is the reverse order of

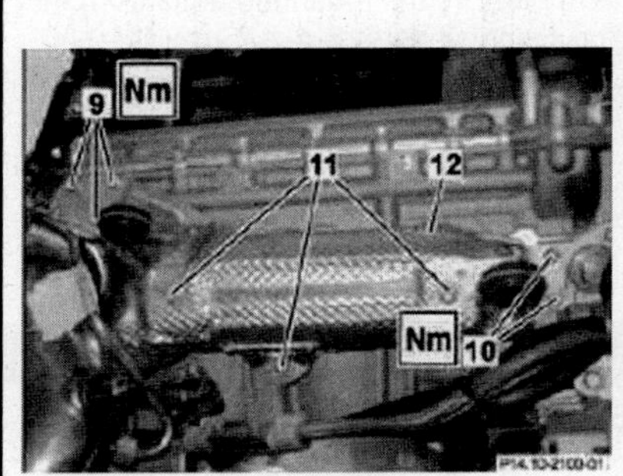

9. Bolts 11. Nuts
10. Bolts 12. Heat shield

71112_MBES_G0150

Fig. 87 Remove the heat shield for the exhaust manifold—Engine ID 642

removal. Tighten the mounting bolts to 15 ft. lbs. (20 Nm) plus 90°.

Engine IDs 272 & 273

See Figure 88.

Right Side

1. Remove the air intake assembly.
2. Remove the lower engine compartment paneling.
3. Disconnect the negative battery cable.
4. Disconnect the flange connection for the catalytic converter on the exhaust manifold.
5. Remove the nuts and remove the exhaust manifold and gasket upwards. Discard the gasket.
6. Installation is the reverse order of removal. Using a new gasket, tighten the mounting nuts to 11 ft. lbs. (16 Nm).

Left Side

1. Remove the air intake assembly.
2. Remove the lower engine compartment paneling.
3. Remove all accessible mounting nuts from above.
4. Remove the catalytic converter.
5. Remove the remaining mounting nuts from below.
6. Remove the exhaust manifold and gasket downward. Discard the gasket.
7. Installation is the reverse order of removal. Using a new gasket, tighten the mounting nuts to 11 ft. lbs. (16 Nm).

Engine ID 276

See Figures 89 and 90.

1. Remove the bottom engine compartment paneling.
2. Detach the exhaust manifold with catalytic converter attached from the bracket on the transmission.
3. Remove the EGR line from the exhaust manifold and discard the gasket.
4. Remove the mounting bolts for the NOx storage catalytic converter clamp on the exhaust manifold.
5. If removing the left side manifold:
   a. Remove the front engine cover.
   b. Remove the ME-SFI control unit.
   c. Disconnect the electrical connector from the engine wiring harness.
   d. Unclip the engine wiring harness from the vacuum reservoir.
   e. Remove the vacuum reservoir.
   f. Unclip the electrical connectors for the oxygen sensors from the holder and disconnect.
   g. Unclip the engine wiring harness from the shield.

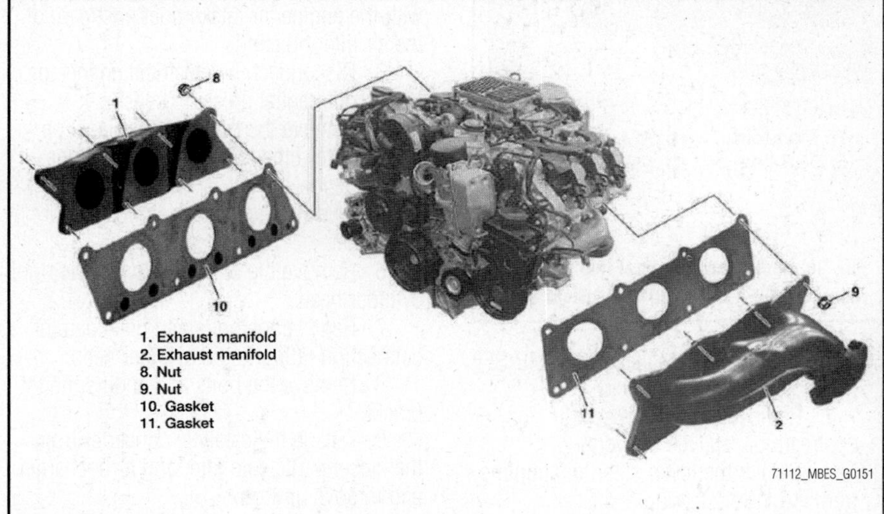

1. Exhaust manifold
2. Exhaust manifold
8. Nut
9. Nut
10. Gasket
11. Gasket

71112_MBES_G0151

Fig. 88 Exhaust manifold mounting—Engine IDs 272 & 273

1I. Exhaust manifold
2. Engine wiring harness
4. Crankcase breather line
6. Electrical connector
7. Vacuum reservoir
10. Shield
11. Bracket
G3/3. Oxygen sensor

71112_MBES_G0152

Fig. 89 Disconnect the electrical connector from the engine wiring harness—Engine ID 276 - Left Side

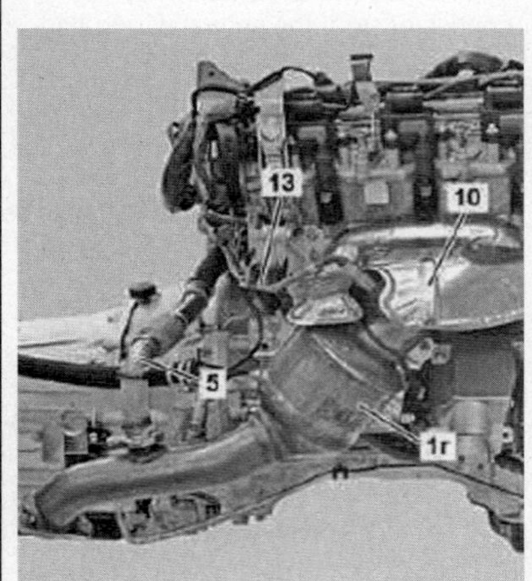

Fig. 90 Unclip the electrical line at the mount shield—Engine ID 276 - Right Side

h. Remove the bracket for the ME-SFI [ME] control unit.

i. Remove the oxygen sensor upstream of catalytic converter.

j. Detach the lower steering coupling from the lower steering shaft.

6. If removing the right side manifold:

a. Remove the air intake assembly.

b. Unclip the electrical connectors for the oxygen sensor from the holder and disconnect.

c. Unclip the electrical line at the mount shield.

7. Remove the shield on the exhaust manifold.

8. Unscrew the mounting nuts for the exhaust manifold.

9. Remove the exhaust manifold upwards with the catalytic converter attached.

10. Installation is the reverse order of removal. Tighten the mounting nuts to 11 ft. lbs. (16 Nm).

Engine ID 152

1. Remove the bottom engine compartment paneling.
2. Remove the catalytic converter.
3. Remove the air filter housing.
4. Remove the soundproofing on cylinder head cover.
5. Remove the heat shield over the exhaust manifold.
6. Detach the locking plate on nuts for the exhaust manifold.
7. Unscrew the nuts and discard.
8. Remove the exhaust manifold gasket from below.
9. Installation is the reverse order of removal. Use and new gasket and tighten the new mounting nuts to 9 ft. lbs. (12 Nm).

CATALYTIC CONVERTER

REMOVAL & INSTALLATION

Engine ID 642

See Figure 91.

1. Remove the engine cover.
2. Remove the right air filter housing with the engine air intake duct upstream of the air filter housing.
3. Disconnect the electrical connector for the differential pressure sensor.
4. Remove the bolt and set diesel particulate filter differential pressure sensor and set aside.
5. Remove the heat shield for the turbocharger.
6. Remove the oil separator on the right cylinder head.
7. Remove the bolts and oil separator connection fitting to the cylinder head.
8. Remove the bolts and engine mount bracket.
9. Detach the catalytic converter from the diesel particulate filter and turbocharger and remove upwards.
10. Installation is the reverse order of removal.

Engine ID 271

1. Raise and safely support the vehicle.
2. Unscrew the nuts from the catalytic converter on the turbocharger.
3. Remove any engine compartment paneling as necessary.
4. Disconnect the wiring harness for the O2 sensors.
5. Remove the mounting bolts from the catalytic converters.
6. Remove the catalytic converter downwards.
7. Installation is the reverse order of removal. Tighten the catalytic convert mounting bolts to 15 ft. lbs. (20 Nm).

INTAKE MANIFOLD

REMOVAL & INSTALLATION

Engine IDs 272 & 273

See Figure 92.

1. Remove the air filter housing.
2. Disconnect the right connector at ME-SFI control unit.
3. Disconnect the electrical connectors.
4. Remove the jack for electrical connector on the fuel distributor.
5. Remove the electrical feed line from left the control unit bracket.
6. Pull the ME-SFI control unit out of the brackets and place aside.
7. Remove the hot film mass air flow sensor.
8. Remove the air duct housing.
9. Disconnect the hoses from the crankcase ventilation system.
10. Remove the right control unit bracket.
11. Detach the supply ducts from the cylinder head cover, resonance the intake manifold and rear right engine suspension lug.
12. Disconnect the electrical connectors on injection valves and position sensors.
13. Disconnect the electrical connector at the front of the manifold.
14. Disconnect the electrical connectors on throttle valve actuator and electric air pump.

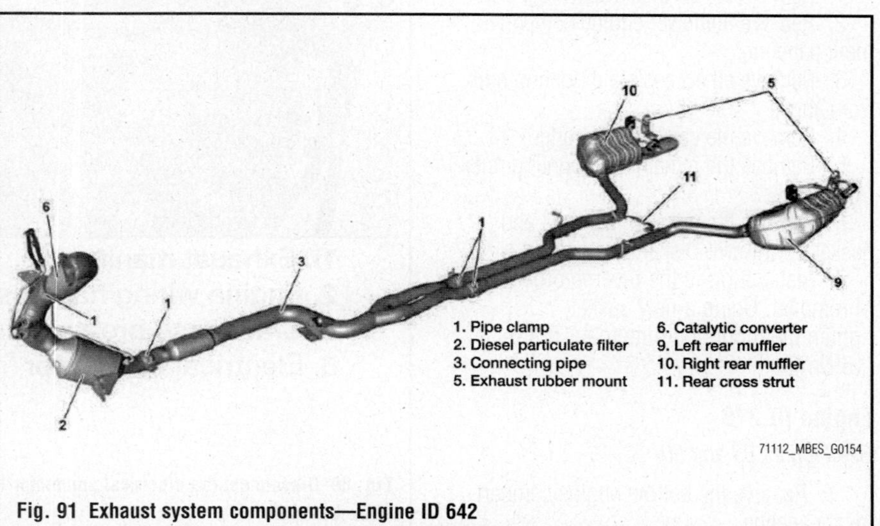

Fig. 91 Exhaust system components—Engine ID 642

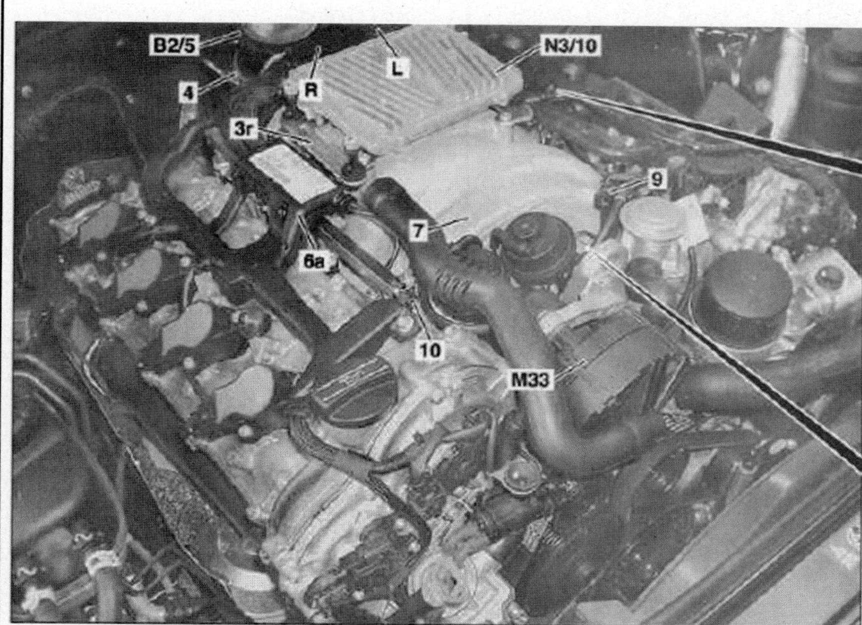

Fig. 92 Intake manifold mounting and components—Engine IDs 272 & 273

15. Properly release the fuel system pressure.
16. Disconnect fuel line from the fuel distributor and seal the openings.
17. Remove the manifold mounting bolts.
18. Lift out the intake manifold and disconnect the pneumatic lines. Discard the gaskets.

To install:

19. Install the intake manifold using new gaskets and tighten the mounting bolts to 80 inch lbs. (9 Nm).
20. The remainder of the installation is the reverse order of removal.

Engine ID 156

See Figure 93.

1. Remove the air intake assembly.
2. Remove the air filter housing.
3. Properly relieve the fuel system pressure.
4. Disconnect the fuel line from the fuel distributor and discard the sealing rings.
5. Disconnect the electrical connectors from the front of the intake manifold.
6. Remove the vacuum line from the intake manifold and disconnect from the brake booster.
7. Remove the foam plastic cover from the fuel distributor.
8. Disconnect the injector wiring harnesses.
9. Remove the hold down bolt and remove the purge line from the intake manifold.
10. Disconnect the vacuum hose from the intake manifold and remove.
11. Disconnect the remaining wiring harnesses.

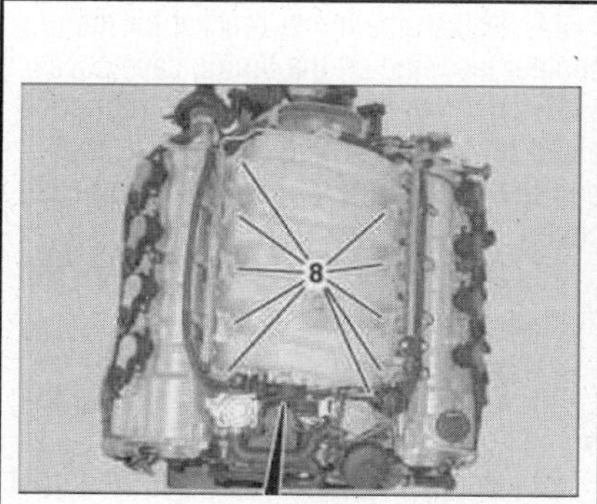

Fig. 94 Location of the intake manifold mounting bolts—6.2L Engines

12. Remove the mounting bolts from the intake manifold and lift off in the upward direction.
13. Installation is the reverse order of removal. Tighten the manifold mounting bolts as follows:
    - Step 1: 89 inch lbs. (10 Nm)
    - Step 2: Plus 90°
    - Step 3: Plus 10°

Engine ID 276

1. Remove the engine appearance cover.
2. Remove the air filter housing.
3. Loosen the clamp for the intake hose on the hot film MAF sensor.
4. Pull off the purge line from the intake manifold.
5. Detach the crankcase breather line on the intake hose and unclip on the intake manifold.
6. Detach the crankcase breather line on the intake manifold.
7. Disconnect the electrical connector at the pressure sensor downstream of throttle valve.
8. Disconnect the electrical plug connector on the throttle valve actuator.
9. Unclip the electrical line on throttle valve actuator.
10. Remove the vacuum line for the brake booster to vacuum line.
11. Remove the vacuum line to the vacuum pump.
12. Unclip the vacuum hose on the intake manifold.
13. Detach the vacuum hose on the vacuum line.
14. Disconnect the electrical connection on the intake manifold intake air temperature sensor.
15. Disconnect the electrical connection on the selector drum switchover valve and intake manifold resonance flap switchover valve.
16. Remove the intake manifold cover.
17. Remove the intake manifold mounting bolts.
18. Remove the intake manifold.
19. Installation is the reverse order of removal. Tighten the intake manifold bolts to 80 inch lbs. (9 Nm).

Engine ID 157 & 278

See Figure 94.

1. Remove the ME-SFI control unit.
2. Remove both air filter housings.
3. Remove the insulation between the air filter housings and cylinder head cover.
4. Remove the center section of the bulkhead.

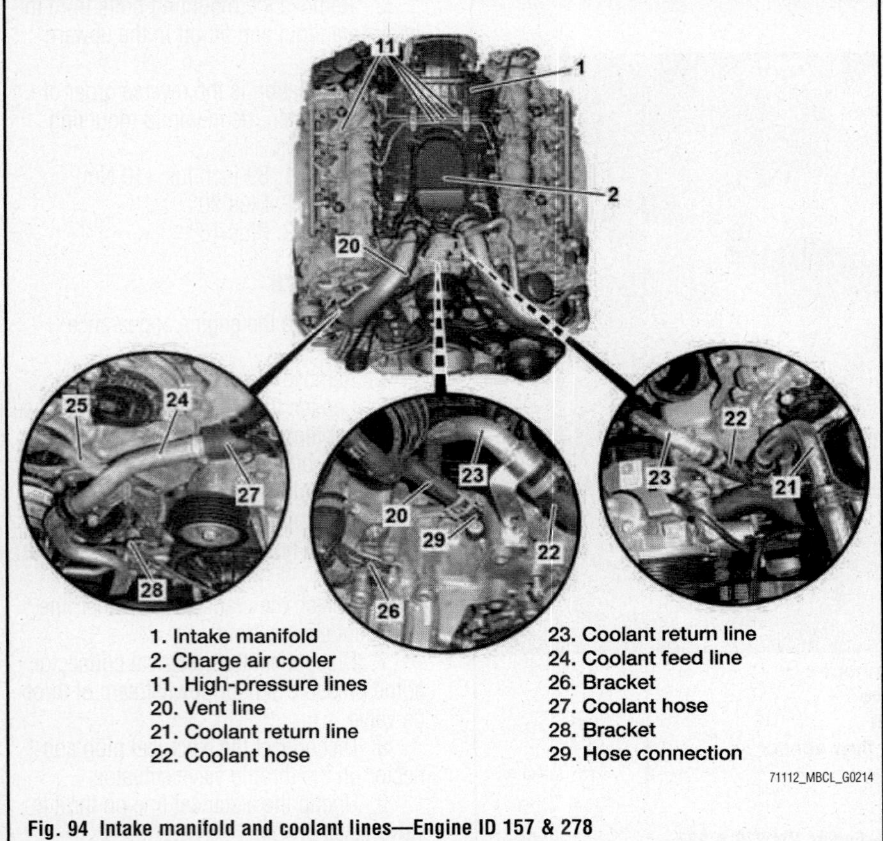

Fig. 94 Intake manifold and coolant lines—Engine ID 157 & 278

5. Remove the crash plate on high-pressure pumps and remove insulation from high-pressure pumps.
6. Detach the vacuum line for brake booster on vacuum pump and intake manifold.
7. Detach the vacuum line for centrifuge on the intake manifold.
8. Disconnect the engine wiring harness on the intake manifold and cylinder head cover and lay down towards the rear.
9. Remove the high-pressure lines.
10. Disconnect the electrical line on the intake manifold.
11. Detach the purge line on the intake manifold.
12. Detach the vacuum line for boost pressure control pressure transducer on vacuum pump.
13. Detach the boost pressure control pressure transducer with bracket on intake manifold and lay down to the front.
14. Remove the charge air ducts.
15. Properly drain the cooling system.
16. Disconnect the bleed line for the charge air cooler at the connecting point.
17. Detach the clamp for the bleed line on Active Body Control (ABC) pump carrier or guide pulley.
18. Detach the ABC pump with bracket from the timing case cover and place with attached lines aside.
19. Remove the guide pulley with bracket on timing case cover.
20. Detach the coolant return lines from the oil filter housing, coolant hose and timing case cover.
21. Detach the clamp for the coolant feed line on the front cover.
22. Detach the lower bracket for coolant feed line on the timing case cover.
23. Detach the coolant feed line on the coolant hose.
24. Detach the upper bracket for the coolant feed line on the timing case cover.
25. Remove the bolt for hose fitting for bleed on line on timing case cover and pull the hose fitting out of the timing case cover.
26. Remove the bolts for the intake manifold on the cylinder heads.
27. Lift the intake manifold.
28. Disconnect the electrical line on the front knock sensors.
29. Unclip the electrical line for the front knock sensors on intake manifold.
30. Remove the intake manifold upwards.
31. Installation is the reverse order of removal.

Engine ID 152

See Figure 95.

1. Disconnect the negative battery cable.
2. Remove the ME-SFI control unit.
3. Disconnect electrical connector for vehicle wiring harness
4. Unclip bracket of the vehicle wiring harness on bracket of the ME-SFI [ME] control unit and engine suspension lug and place vehicle wiring harness to one side.
5. Remove both soundproofing on high pressure pumps and on cylinder head cover.
6. Disconnect electrical connection on A/C compressor and unclip associated wiring harness on engine.
7. Disconnect electrical connection on coolant thermostat and unclip associated wiring harness on engine.
8. Disconnect electrical connector on power steering pump.
9. Detach engine wiring harness on LH front cover.
10. Detach brackets for engine wiring harness on the RH cylinder head cover.
11. Unclip starter wiring harness on intake manifold (1) and cylinder head and place to one side.
12 Detach engine wiring harness on LH cylinder head cover and on intake manifold (1) and place to one side.
12. Properly relieve the fuel system pressure.
13. Unclip bleed line (5) at the front on intake manifold.
15 Remove intake air temperature sensor.
16 Detach hose (7) for centrifuge on air duct housing.
14. Unclip air duct housing (8) on throttle body and place to one side with the bleed line attached.
15. Detach vacuum line from brake booster on intake manifold (1) and vacuum pump and place to one side
19 Detach purge line (9) on throttle valve actuator and on cylinder head cover
20 Disconnect electrical connection on throttle valve actuator and unclip electrical line
16. Remove the high and low pressure lines.
17. Unclip the oil line for the cylinder deactivation auxiliary oil pump on the intake manifold.
18. Raise the intake manifold slightly and unclip the electrical connectors for the knock sensors.
19. Remove the intake manifold.
20. Installation is the reverse order of removal. Tighten the mounting bolts in sequence to 106 inch lbs. (9 Nm).

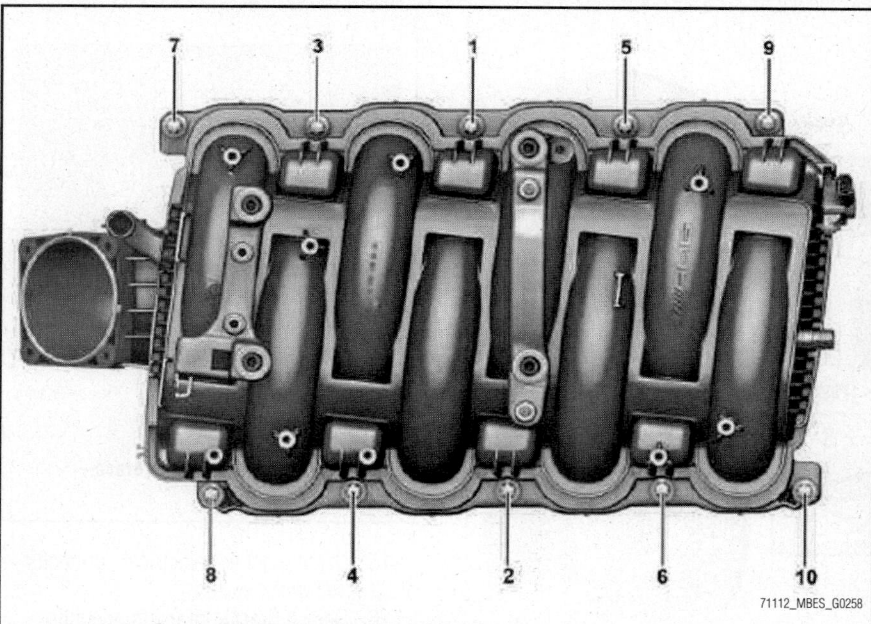

Fig. 95 Intake manifold tightening sequence—Engine ID 152

Engine ID 271

1. Remove the engine appearance cover.
2. Remove the air filter housing.
3. Disconnect the connectors for electrical lines to the throttle valve actuator, actuator motor, pressure sensor, and temperature sensor.
4. Unclip the electrical wiring harness on intake manifold.
5. Detach the charge air hose on the throttle valve actuator.
6. Remove the line from the intake manifold.
7. Detach the hose form the sound generator on the intake manifold at the front.
8. Remove the accessory drive belt, if necessary.
9. Remove the hose from the combination valve.
10. Remove the intake manifold mounting bolts.
11. Detach the purge line from the vent cable on the underside of the intake pipe.
12. Remove the intake manifold.
13. Installation is the reverse order of removal. Tighten the mounting bolts to 10 ft. lbs. (14 Nm).

OIL PAN

REMOVAL & INSTALLATION

Engine ID 642

See Figures 96 and 97.

1. Remove the engine appearance cover.
2. Remove the mounting bolt for the dipstick guide tube.
3. Attach a suitable engine lifting device and raise the engine slightly.
4. Remove the bottom sections of the sound proofing.
5. Remove the transmission assembly.
6. Remove the end cover.
7. Remove the engine mounting bolts.
8. Drain the engine oil.
9. Unscrew the oil line bracket on the oil pan.
10. Unscrew the bolt for the guide tube at the oil pan.
11. Remove the screw/bolts from high pressure expansion hose bracket.
12. Remove the oil pan bottom section.

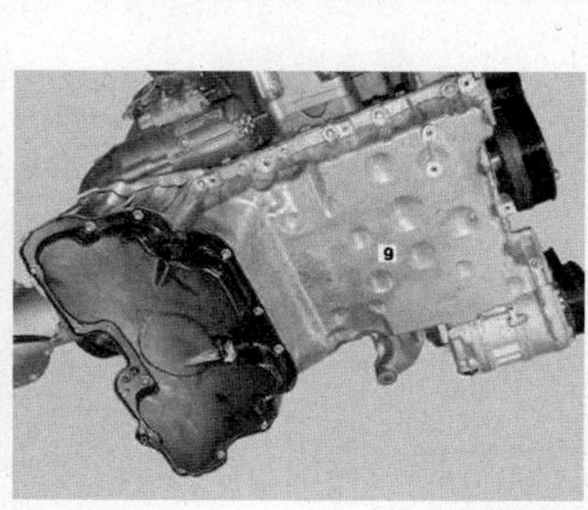

Fig. 96 The oil pan is made up of two sections—Engine ID 642

13. Disconnect the oil level sensor connector.
14. Remove the refrigerant compressor bolt at the oil pan top section.
15. Remove the insulation mat for the oil pan top section.
16. Remove the oil pan.
17. Installation is the reverse order of removal.
18. Clean the sealing surfaces before applying more Loctite®.
19. Tighten the oil pan mounting bolts as follows:
    - M6 bolts: 10 ft. lbs. (14 Nm)
    - M8 bolts: 15 ft. lbs. (20 Nm)

Engine IDs 272 & 273

See Figures 98 and 99.

1. Remove the transmission assembly.
2. Remove the oil pan bottom section.
3. Remove the oil suction pipe.
4. Remove the support brace by removing the bolts and retaining clamps.
5. Remove the oil dipstick guide from the oil pan.

➡Remove the oil pan only, the dipstick guide remains in the engine compartment.

6. Disconnect the electrical connector on oil level sensor.
7. Remove the retaining clamps and push the automatic oil lines to the side.
8. Loosen high-pressure line of power steering at the alternator.
9. Remove the plugs.
10. Remove the oil pan mounting bolts.

➡Observe the different bolt lengths and bolt diameters.

11. Remove the oil pan.
12. Clean all sealing surfaces on oil pan and on the cylinder crankcase before reinstalling.
13. Installation is the reverse order of removal. Tighten the oil pan mounting bolts to 15 ft. lbs. (20 Nm).

Engine ID 156

See Figure 100.

1. Disconnect the negative battery cable.
2. Ensure the front wheels are in the straight-ahead and secure the steering wheel with a holding device.
3. Remove the air filter housing.
4. Drain the power steering fluid from the power steering reservoir.

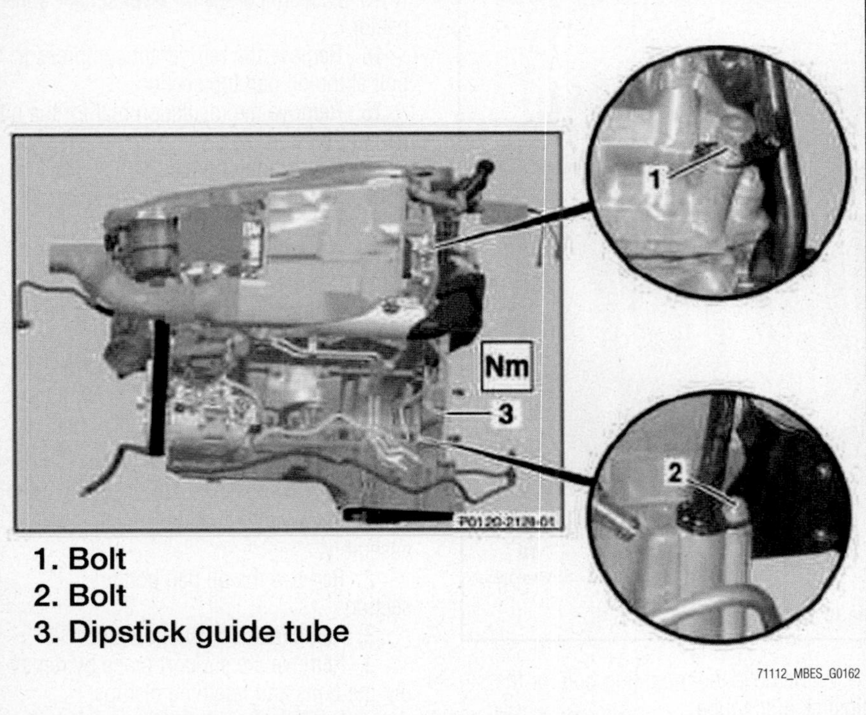

1. Bolt
2. Bolt
3. Dipstick guide tube

71112_MBES_G0162

Fig. 97 Oil dipstick guide tube mounting bolts—Engine ID 642

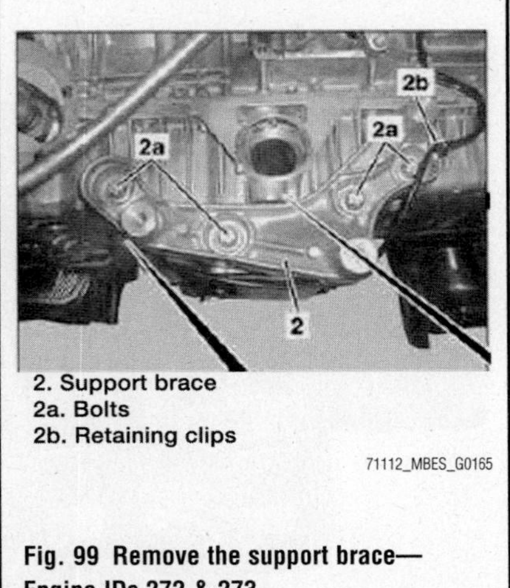

2. Support brace
2a. Bolts
2b. Retaining clips

71112_MBES_G0165

Fig. 99 Remove the support brace—Engine IDs 272 & 273

5. Remove the accessory drive belt.
6. Remove the mounting bolts for the dipstick guide tube bracket.
7. Install a suitable engine hoist to the engine and raise slightly.
8. Remove the cold air intake.
9. Secure radiator assembly with ties.
10. Disconnect the oil lines of the automatic transmission at the oil pan.
11. Remove the oil pan bottom section.
12. Loosen engine mounts on front axle carrier.
13. Detach the steering coupling from steering shaft.
14. Disconnect the electrical connector at the speed sensitive power steering solenoid valve of the rack-and-pinion steering and unclip at front axle carrier.
15. Disconnect the electrical connector at oil level check switch.
16. Detach bracket of the connecting linkage of the headlamp range adjustment/level sensor at the stabilizer bar
17. Disconnect and seal power steering hydraulic line at the separation point at the front axle carrier.
18. Loosen the nut of the wheel arch oil cooler bracket at the front axle carrier.
19. Disconnect the lower engine oil line on the connecting flange.
20. Detach the diagonal strut at the front axle carrier and underfloor.

71112_MBES_G0164

Fig. 98 Remove the oil suction pipe by removing the mounting bolts—Engine IDs 272 & 273

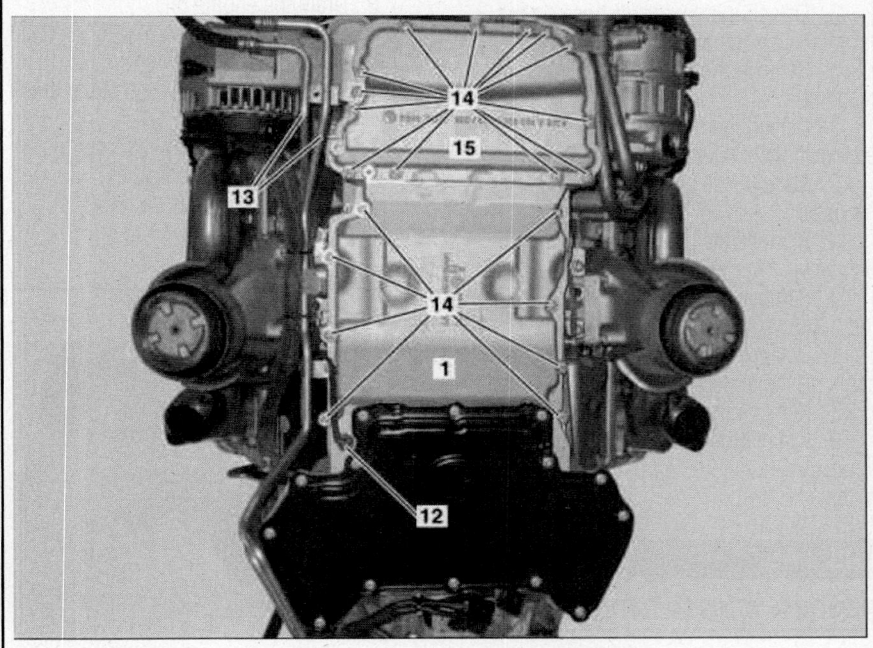

1. Oil pan
12. Oil level check electrical connector
13. Transmission oil lines
14. Mounting bolts
15. Cover

71112_MBCL_G0115

Fig. 100 Oil pan mounting—6.2L Engine shown

21. Detach the support strut at the underfloor and front axle carrier.
22. Loosen and lower the front axle carrier. Support the front axle carrier.
23. Disconnect the A/C compressor wiring harness.
24. Remove the A/C compressor from the crankcase but leave the lines attached.
25. Remove the support for the power steering pump.
26. Disconnect and the power steering lines and cap the lines.
27. Remove the engine oil lines from the cylinder crankcase and seal the openings.
28. Insert a bolt and using a suitable wedge to loosen and pry off the front cover from the oil pan.
29. Remove the oil pan mounting bolts.
30. Pry off the oil pan by turning a bolt on the crankcase and loosen with a suitable wedge.

To install:

31. Clean the sealing surfaces of the oil pan and crankcase.
32. Apply a new bead of sealant to the sealant area and install the oil pan. Tighten the oil pan mounting bolts to 74 inch lbs. (8.4 Nm).
33. The remainder of the installation is the reverse order of removal.

Engine ID 276

See Figures 101 and 102.

1. Remove the front engine cover.
2. Remove the air filter housing with engine air intake upstream of the air filter.
3. Remove the intake manifold. For additional information, refer to the following section, "Intake Manifold, Removal & Installation."
4. Raise and safely support the vehicle.
5. Remove the bottom engine compartment paneling.
6. Drain the engine oil.
7. Properly drain the cooling system.
8. Remove the NOx catalytic coverters at the CATs.
9. Disconnect electrical connector for the oil level sensor.
10. Remove the ME-SFI control unit.
11. Remove the center section of the bulkhead.
12. Remove the accessory drive belt.
13. Disconnect the electrical connector for the A/C compressor.
14. Remove the A/C compressor from the timing case cover and engine support, leaving the lines attached and lay aside.
15. Disconnect the coolant hose at the thermostat housing.
16. Remove the oil dipstick guide tube.
17. Remove the transmission assembly.
18. Mount a suitable engine hoist and raise the engine slightly so the engine mounts are no longer under tension.
19. Remove the heat shield for the engine mount and bolts for the engine mount.
20. Raise the engine with the hoist.

⁂ WARNING

Make sure when lifting out the engine that no cables and lines are damaged and that the engine does not hit against the partition wall.

21. Detach the guard plate for the rack-and-pinion steering from the front axle carrier and remove the bolts for the rack-and-pinion steering on the front axle carrier.
22. Remove the electrical transmission oil pump.
23. Detach clamps and bracket for the transmission fluid lines from the oil pan and transmission and set aside.
24. Remove the oil pan bottom section.
25. Remove the oil pan mounting bolts and remove the oil pan.

⁂ WARNING

When detaching it, do not insert any tools between the cylinder crankcase and the oil pan, otherwise the sealing surfaces may be damaged.

To install:

26. Clean the sealing surfaces of the oil pan and crankcase.
27. Apply a new bead of sealant to the sealant area and install the oil pan.
28. Tighten the oil pan mounting bolts as follows:
    - M6 bolts: 80 inch lbs. (9 Nm)
    - M8 bolts: 15 ft. lbs. (20 Nm)
    - Bottom oil pan bolts: 10 ft. lbs. (14 Nm)
29. The remainder of the installation is the reverse order of removal.

Engine ID 157 & 278

See Figure 103.

1. If equipped with air suspension, completely discharge the front struts using the STAR Diagnosis tool.
2. Ensure the front wheels are in the straight-ahead and secure the steering wheel with a holding device.
3. Disconnect the negative battery cable.
4. Install an engine hoist and raise the engine slightly.

71112_MBES_G0166

Fig. 101 Remove the center section of the bulkhead—Engine ID 276

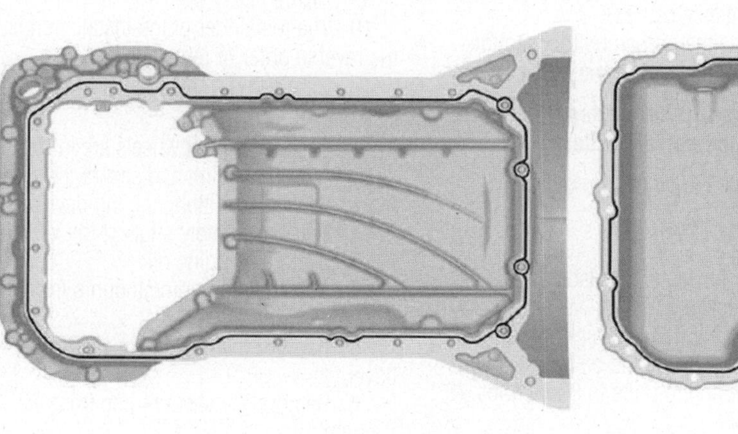

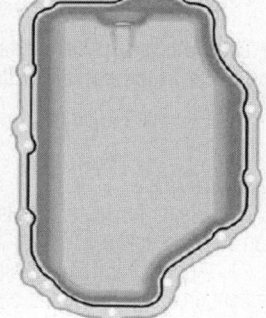

71112_MBES_G0167

Fig. 102 Sealant path for installing the oil pan—Engine ID 276

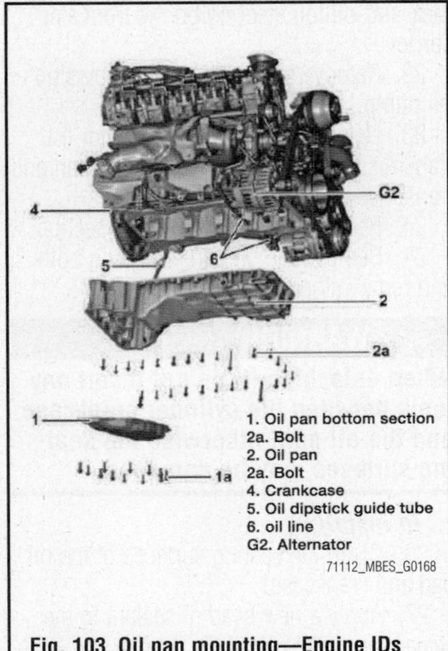

Fig. 103 Oil pan mounting—Engine IDs 157 & 278

5. Raise and safely support the vehicle.
6. Remove the bottom engine compartment paneling.
7. Drain the engine oil.
8. Remove the alternator.
9. Remove the oil line for transmission cooling.
10. Disconnect the oil dipstick guide tube from the oil and pan and cylinder head cover and place aside.
11. Remove the steering coupling.
12. Remove the oil lines for the turbocharger at the oil pan and place aside.
13. Separate and unclip the electrical connector for the oil level check switch.
14. Detach the bracket for the level sensors from the control arm.
15. If equipped with 4MATIC, remove the front axle gear and support brace.
16. Without 4MATIC, loosen and slightly lower the front axle carrier.
17. Remove the oil pan bottom section.
18. Remove the oil pan mounting bolts.

➡The bolts are different lengths, keep the bolts in the correct order.

19. Remove the oil pan from the crankcase.

To install:

20. Clean the sealing surfaces of the oil pan and crankcase.
21. Apply a new bead of sealant to the sealant area and install the oil pan. Tighten the oil pan mounting bolts to 80 inch lbs. (9 Nm).
22. The remainder of the installation is the reverse order of removal.

Engine ID 152

1. Remove the air intake assembly.
2. Raise and safely support the vehicle.
3. Remove bottom engine compartment paneling.
4. Properly drain the engine oil.
5. Remove dipstick guide tube.
6. Remove the front wheels.
7. Lower the front axle assembly.
8. Remove the alternator. For additional information, refer to the following section, "Alternator, Removal & Installation."
9. Detach clamps and bracket for transmission fluid lines from oil pan and transmission and set aside.
10. Detach hydraulic oil lines for oil lines on the power steering to oil pan.
11. Unclip the electrical lines and connectors for a heated O2 sensor from brackets on transmission.
12. Disconnect the electrical connector on oil level sensor and place electrical line to one side.
13. Remove screw/bolts on oil pan bottom section (1) and loosen oil pan bottom section from the oil pan and remove.
14. Remove the mounting bolts from the oil pan.

➡The bolts are different lengths, keep the bolts in the correct order.

15. Detach the oil pan from the crankcase and remove towards the rear.

To install:

16. Clean the sealing surfaces of the oil pan and crankcase.
17. Apply a new bead of sealant to the sealant area and install the oil pan.
18. Tighten the oil pan mounting bolts as follows:
    - M6 bolts: 8 ft. lbs. (11 Nm)
    - M8 bolts: 15 ft. lbs. (20 Nm)
    - Bottom oil pan bolts: 10 ft. lbs. (14 Nm)
19. The remainder of the installation is the reverse order of removal.

Engine ID 271

1. Ensure the front wheels are in the straight ahead position and secure the steering wheel with a suitable holding device.
2. Raise and safely support the vehicle.
3. Drain the engine oil.
4. Detach both engine mounts from the front axle carrier.
5. Remove the engine appearance cover.
6. Remove the vacuum line from the vacuum pump.
7. Attach a suitable engine lifting device and raise the engine slightly.
8. Lower the front axle carrier.
9. Remove the oil cooling lines from the transmission and oil pan.
10. Remove the retaining clamp from the oil pan.
11. Disconnect the oxygen sensor electrical connectors and unclip the wiring from the brackets.
12. Remove the oil pan mounting bolts.

➡Matchmark the bolts as they are different lengths and diameters.

13. Carefully pry off the oil pan from the crankcase without damaging the sealing surfaces.
14. Installation is the reverse order of removal. Tighten the mounting bolts as follows:
    - M6x30 bolts: 80 inch lbs. (9 Nm)
    - M6x90 bolts: 80 inch lbs. (9 Nm)
    - M8x35 bolts: 15 ft. lbs. (20 Nm)

OIL PUMP

REMOVAL & INSTALLATION

Engine ID 642

See Figure 104.

1. Remove the oil pan. For additional information, refer to the following section, "Oil Pan, Removal & Installation."
2. Remove the oil pump cover with the oil pipe.
3. Remove the oil pump mounting bolts.
4. Remove the oil pump. Press tensioning rail away from oil pump chain, unhook oil pump out of oil pump chain.
5. Installation is the reverse order of removal.

➡If the oil pump is dry, fill it with engine oil so that oil is delivered when the engine is started.

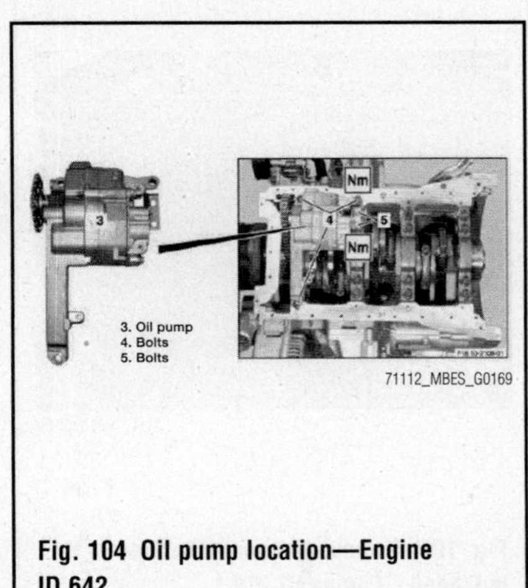

Fig. 104 Oil pump location—Engine ID 642

Engine IDs 156, 272 & 273

See Figures 105 and 106.

1. Remove the oil pan. For additional information, refer to the following section, "Oil Pan, Removal & Installation."
2. Remove the assembly mounting bolts.
3. Press the chain tensioner to the back, remove the oil pump chain from the oil pump gear. Take out the oil pump together with the oil suction pipe.
4. Remove the bolt and disconnect the oil suction pipe from the oil pump. Discard the O-ring.
5. Installation is the reverse order of removal. Clean the oil strainer before installation.

Engine ID 157, 276 & 278

See Figure 107.

1. Remove the oil pan. For additional information, refer to the following section, "Oil Pan, Removal & Installation."
2. Detach the oil baffle with intake manifold from the oil pump and crankcase.
3. Remove the mounting bolts and oil filter housing from the crankcase.
4. Disconnect the electrical connector on the oil pump valve.
5. Push back the chain tensioning rail and take the oil pump chain off the oil pump gear.
6. Remove the oil pump.
7. Installation is the reverse order of removal.

➡If the oil pump is dry, fill it with engine oil so that oil is delivered when the engine is started.

Engine ID 152

1. Remove the oil pan. For additional information, refer to the following section, "Oil Pan, Removal & Installation."
2. Detach the oil baffle with intake manifold from the oil pump and crankcase.
3. Remove the oil pump from the crankcase by removing the mounting bolts.
4. Disconnect the electrical connector on the oil pump valve.
5. Push back the chain tensioning rail, take the oil pump chain off of the oil pump gear and remove the oil pump.

To install:

6. Fill the oil pump with clean engine oil before installing.

➡So the pump delivers oil immediately when the engine is first started.

7. Installation is the reverse order of removal. Tighten the oil pump mounting bolts first to 44 inch lbs. then 15 ft. lbs. (20 Nm).

Engine ID 271

1. Remove the oil pan. For additional information, refer to the following section, "Oil Pan, Removal & Installation."
2. Remove the mounting bolts and remove the cover from the oil pump.
3. Remove the drive wheel center bolt while counter holding the balance shaft with a wrench and remove the drive wheel.
4. Remove the mounting bolts and remove the oil pump.

To install:

5. Clean the oil pump sealing surfaces.
6. Coat the oil pump with clean engine oil before installing.
7. Install the oil pump and tighten the mounting bolts to 80 inch lbs. (9 Nm).
8. Install the drive gear and tighten the center bolt to 15 ft. lbs. (20 Nm).
9. The remainder of the installation is the reverse order of removal.

PISTONS & RINGS

POSITIONING

Install piston rings with identical ring width. Observe the installation position,

Fig. 105 Oil pump assembly—Engine IDs 272 & 273

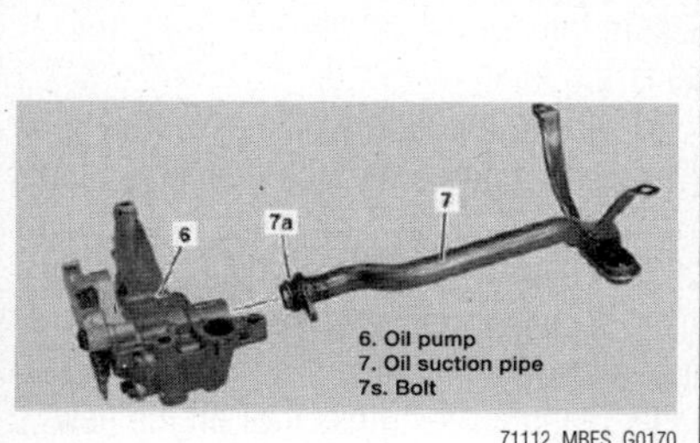

Fig. 106 Remove the oil suction pipe from the oil pipe—Engine IDs 272 & 273

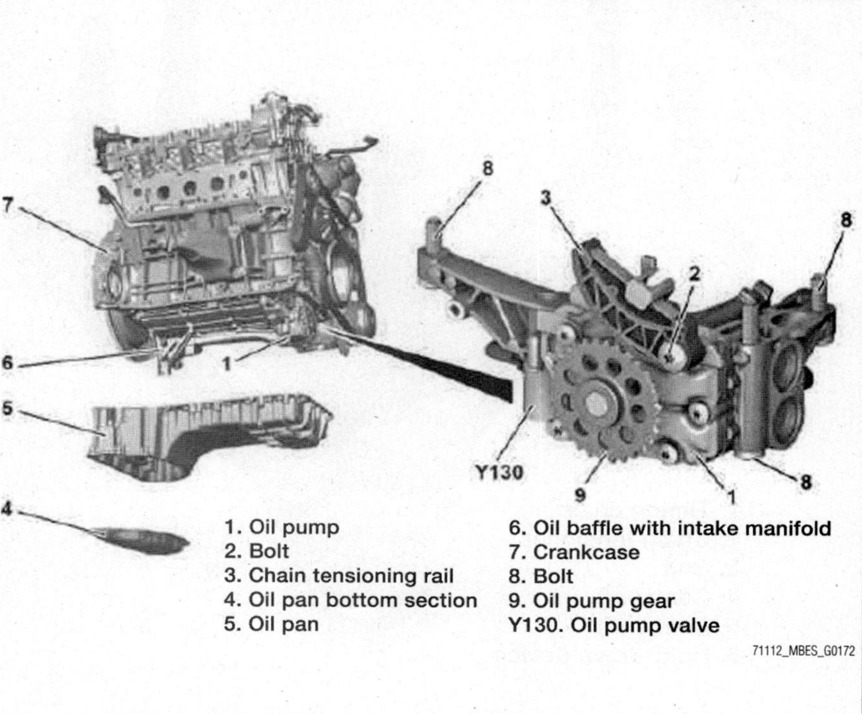

Fig. 107 Oil pump assembly—Engine IDs 157, 276 & 278

with "TOP" or other manufacturer designation pointing toward the piston crown.

TIMING CHAIN COVER, CHAIN, TENSIONER, & SPROCKETS

REMOVAL & INSTALLATION

Engine ID 642

See Figures 108 through 110.

1. Remove the engine appearance cover.
2. Remove the mounting bolts and bracket cover the glow output stage.
3. Unplug the electrical connector at the glow output stage.
4. Remove the glow output stage.
5. Remove the right cylinder head cover.
6. Attach a hold-down device to the center bearing points of the camshafts.
7. Remove the timing chain tensioner.
8. Disconnect the timing chain using a suitable separator tool as follows:
   a. Insert the pressure pin in the pressure screw and tighten the union nut.
   b. Screw the pressure pin into the guide sleeve.

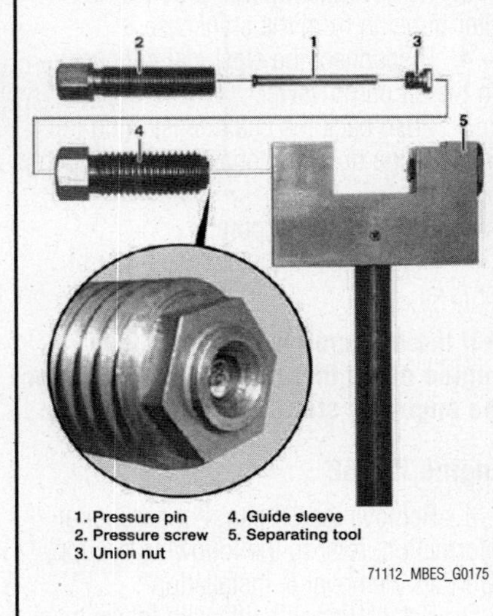

Fig. 109 Timing chain separator tool

   c. Screw the guide sleeve into the chain separating tool.
   d. Cover the timing case recess and cylinder head with shop towels to avoid damage to the engine.
   e. Fit the chain separating tool onto the timing chain.
   f. Screw the guide sleeve into the chain separating tool until the openings on the guide sleeve and the guide surround the timing chain bolt.
   g. Screw the pressure pin into the guide sleeve and press out the timing chain bolts.
   h. Remove the timing chain bolt from the guide.
   i. Remove the pressure pin from the guide sleeve and remove the chain separating tool.

To install:

9. Draw in a new timing chain as follows:
   a. Ensure the timing case recess and cylinder head is still covered with a clean rag.
   b. Connect the new timing chain and old timing chain with the assembly connecting link, the outer assembly plate and the assembly locking element.

➡The bores of the new timing chain must point outwards.

   c. Remove the rag from timing case recess and cylinder head.

➡This prevents the rag from being drawn into the timing case recess when cranking the engine.

   d. Slowly turn the engine at the center bolt of the crankshaft in the direction of engine rotation until the ends of the new control chain can be connected.
   e. Cover timing case recess and cylinder head with clean rag.
   f. Remove the assembly locking element, outer assembly plate, assembly connecting link and old timing chain.
10. Insert a new riveted link and new middle plate together with centering fork into the ends of the new timing chain. Secure the new center shackle using the centering fork.
11. Insert and tighten the assembly insert with digit F5 into the rivet press tool.
12. Insert the assembly insert with digit D9 into the rivet press tool. The assembly insert is able to move on pressure screw and is loosely mounted.
13. Mount rivet press tool on the new timing chain such that the assembly insert touches the new riveted link and the centering fork can be pressed out.
14. Screw in thrust spindle and press in new riveted link up to the stop. Remove the

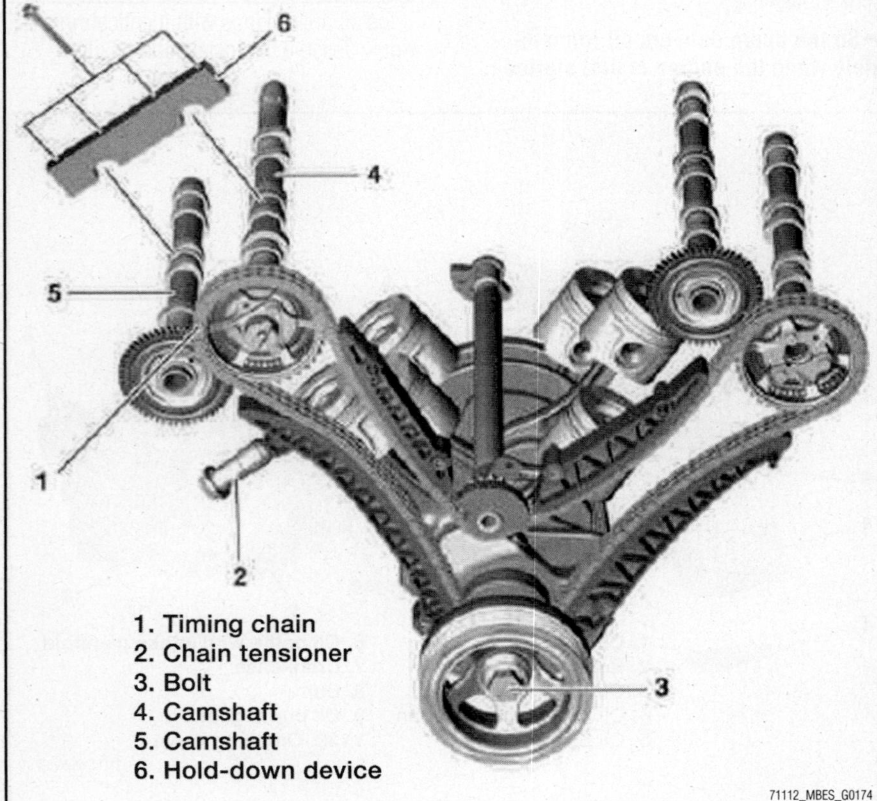

Fig. 108 Attach a hold-down device to the center bearing points of the camshafts—Engine ID 642

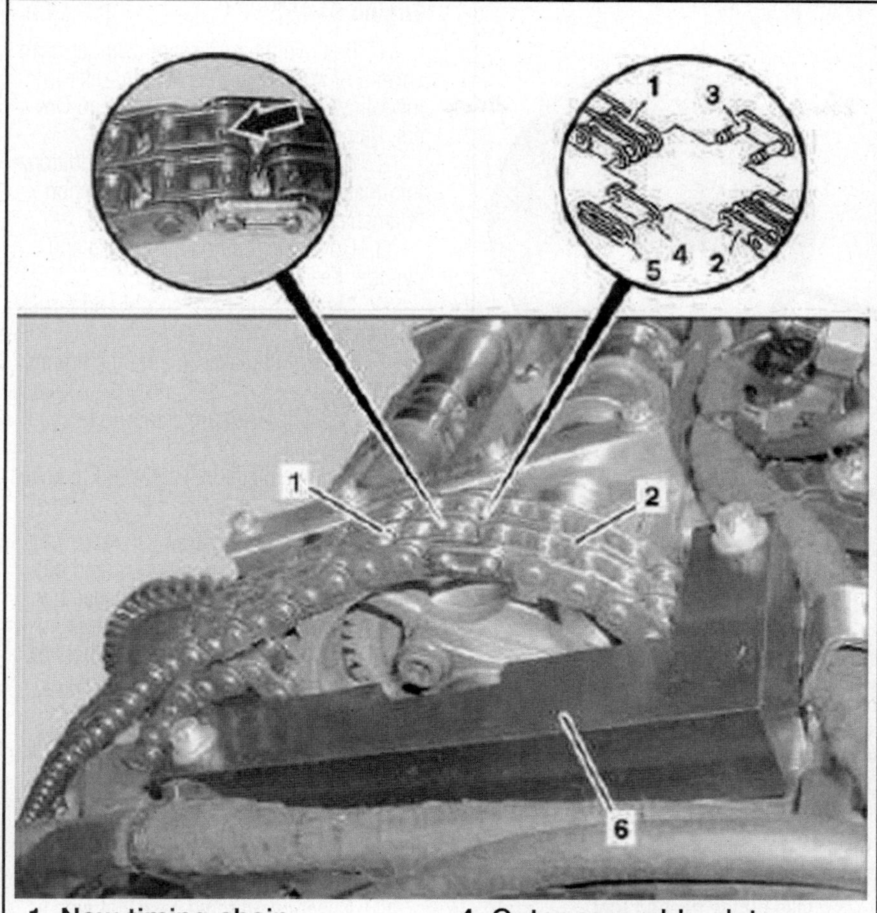

Fig. 110 Installing a new timing chain—Engine ID 642

centering fork are aligned. Do not allow the centering fork which is pressed out to drop into the timing case recess.

15. Remove pressure screw and rivet press tool from rivet press tool with digit F1 into the rivet press tool with digit D8 into the riveting tool.

16. Insert new outer plate into the thrust piece is held firmly by the magnetic thrust piece such that the spacer bushing of the assembly insert makes contact with the timing chain rolls on rivet press tool until there is firm resistance. While pressing on ensure that the bolt of the new rivet link in the bores break in the new outer plate.

17. Remove pressure screw and rivet press tool.

18. Install the timing chain tensioner.

19. Remove the hold-down device.

20. The remainder of the installation is the reverse order of removal.

Engine IDs 272 & 273

See Figure 111.

1. Disconnect the negative battery cable.

2. Remove the spark plugs. For additional information, refer to the following section, "Spark Plugs, Removal & Installation."

3. Remove the camshafts. For additional information, refer to the following section, "Camshafts, Removal & Installation."

4. Cover the timing case recess with a clean cloth to ensure no parts fall into the timing case recess.

5. Assemble the chain separating tool and pressure screw together.

6. Fit the chain separating tool onto the timing chain.

➡Ensure that the pressure pin lies at the pin of the timing chain link.

7. Screw in the pressure screw and separate the timing chain.

8. Remove the pressure screw and remove the chain separating tool.

To install:

9. Attach a new timing chain to the old chain with a master link, center plate and end plate. Using a socket wrench on the crankshaft, slowly rotate the engine in the direction of normal rotation. Simultaneously, pull the old chain through until the master link is uppermost on the camshaft sprocket. Be sure to keep tension on the chain throughout this procedure.

10. Disconnect the old timing chain and connect the ends of the new chain with the master link. Insert the new connecting link from the rear so the lockwashers can be seen from the front.

11. Rotate the engine in the direction of rotation until the timing marks align at 55° Before Top Dead Center.

12. The markings on the pulse wheels of the intake and exhaust camshafts at the left cylinder head must be located centrally in the bores of the camshaft sensors. If not, rotate the engine another revolution.

13. Rotate the engine in the direction of rotation 95° so that it is at 40° After Top Dead Center of cylinder 1.

14. The remainder of the installation is the reverse order of removal.

Engine ID 157, 276 & 278

See Figure 112.

1. Disconnect the negative battery cable.

2. Remove the cylinder head cover.

3. Rotate the engine at the crankshaft center bolt in the direction of engine rotation to 40° After Top Dead Center (TDC) of cylinder 1.

4. Remove the oil filter housing, if removing left side.

5. Remove the mounting bolt and remove the timing chain tensioner.

6. Remove the camshaft bearing cap.

7. Remove the camshaft with the adjusters as an assembly.

8. Cover the timing case recess and cylinder head with a clean rag.

9. Mount chain breaker tool and thrust spindle.

10. Fit chain breaker tool on the timing chain.

11. Screw in pressure screw and separate timing chain.

12. Remove pressure screw and remove chain separating tool.

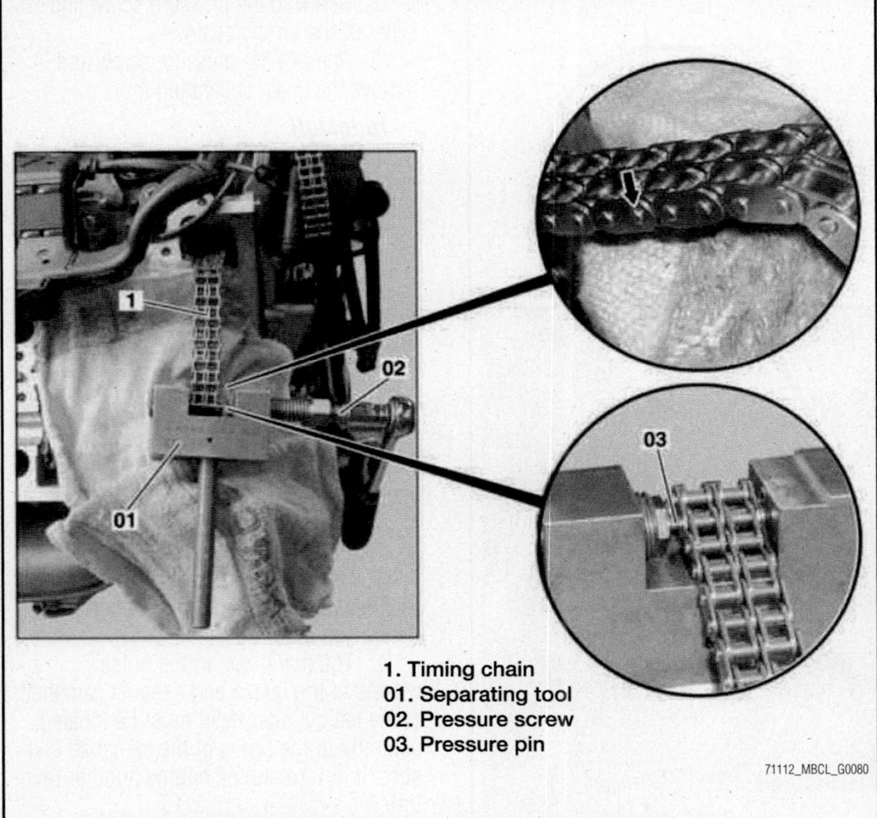

Fig. 111 Attaching the timing chain separating tool to break the timing chain.

To install:

13. Connect new timing chain and old timing chain together using the assembly link in the direction opposite to that in which the timing chain is drawn; otherwise it could get jammed on the slide rails and come off when the timing chain is drawn.

14. Remove rags from the timing case recess.

15. Turn crankshaft slowly in the engine's direction of rotation and draw in the new timing chain until the ends of the new timing chain can be connected.

16. Cover over timing case slot with a clean cloth.

17. Detach the assembly link from the new timing chain.

18. Insert the riveted link with both middle plates in the ends of the timing chain.

19. Place the assembly insert in the rivet press tool and fix in place with the mounting screw.

20. Place the assembly insert in the rivet press tool into the assembly insert.

21. Place the rivet press tool in such a way that the spacer bushing of the assembly insert lies on the timing chain.

22. Screw in the pressure screw on rivet press tool until there is firm resistance.

23. Take off the riveting tool.

24. Turn over the assembly insert to the riveting section.

25. Place the rivet press tool in the middle on a rivet link bolt.

26. Tighten the thrust spindle on rivet press tool.

27. Take off the riveting tool.

28. The remainder of the installation is the reverse order of removal.

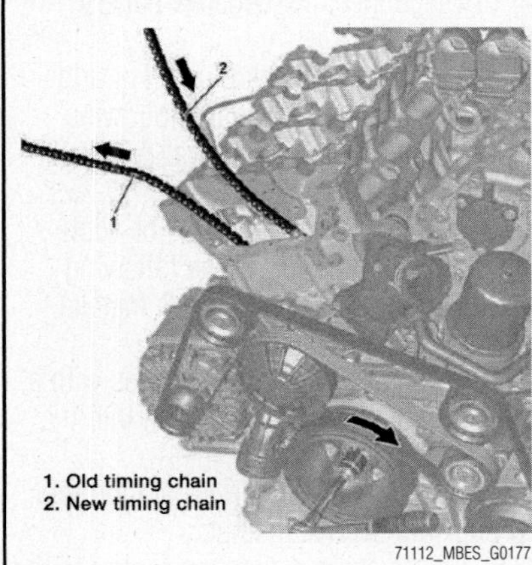

Fig. 112 Turn crankshaft slowly in the engine's direction of rotation and draw in the new timing chain.

Engine ID 152

1. Remove the necessary cylinder head cover. For additional information, refer to the following section, "Cylinder Head Covers, Removal & Installation."

2. Remove the camshafts. For additional information, refer to the following section, "Camshafts, Removal & Installation."

3. Cover the timing case recess and cylinder head with a clean rag.

4. Mount chain breaker tool and thrust spindle.

5. Fit chain breaker tool on the timing chain.

6. Screw in pressure screw and separate timing chain.

7. Remove pressure screw and remove chain separating tool.

To install:

8. Connect new timing chain and old timing chain together using the assembly link in the direction opposite to that in which the timing chain is drawn; otherwise it could get jammed on the slide rails and come off when the timing chain is drawn.

9. Remove rags from the timing case recess.

10. Turn crankshaft slowly in the engine's direction of rotation and draw in the new timing chain until the ends of the new timing chain can be connected.

11. Cover over timing case slot with a clean cloth.

12. Detach the assembly link from the new timing chain.

13. Insert the riveted link with both middle plates in the ends of the timing chain.

14. Place the assembly insert in the rivet press tool and fix in place with the mounting screw.

15. Place the assembly insert in the rivet press tool into the assembly insert.

16. Place the rivet press tool in such a way that the spacer bushing of the assembly insert lies on the timing chain.

17. Screw in the pressure screw on rivet press tool until there is firm resistance.

18. Take off the riveting tool.

19. Turn over the assembly insert to the riveting section.

20. Place the rivet press tool in the middle on a rivet link bolt.

21. Tighten the thrust spindle on rivet press tool.

22. Take off the riveting tool.

23. The remainder of the installation is the reverse order of removal.

Engine ID 271

1. Remove the cylinder head cover.
2. Remove the spark plugs.

3. Remove the alternator.
4. Remove the chain tensioner.
5. Remove the slide rail.
6. Remove the guides for the timing chain.
7. Mount the retainer tool onto the cylinder.
8. Turn the engine at the crankshaft until the number 1 cylinder is at Top Dead Center (TDC).
9. Install the holding device for the camshafts.
10. Cover the timing case recess and cylinder head with a clean rag.
11. Using a chain separator tool, disconnect the old timing chain.

To install:

12. Connect new timing chain and old timing chain together using the assembly link in the direction opposite to that in which the timing chain is drawn; otherwise it could get jammed on the slide rails and come off when the timing chain is drawn.
13. Remove rags from the timing case recess.
14. Turn crankshaft slowly in the engine's direction of rotation and draw in the new timing chain until the ends of the new timing chain can be connected.
15. Cover over timing case slot with a clean cloth.
16. Detach the assembly link from the new timing chain.
17. Insert the riveted link with both middle plates in the ends of the timing chain.
18. Place the assembly insert in the rivet press tool and fix in place with the mounting screw.
19. Place the assembly insert in the rivet press tool into the assembly insert.
20. Place the rivet press tool in such a way that the spacer bushing of the assembly insert lies on the timing chain.
21. Screw in the pressure screw on rivet press tool until there is firm resistance.
22. Take off the riveting tool.
23. Turn over the assembly insert to the riveting section.
24. Place the rivet press tool in the middle on a rivet link bolt.
25. Tighten the thrust spindle on rivet press tool.
26. Take off the riveting tool.
27. Remove the camshaft holding device.
28. Turn the engine until the timing chain lies on the exhaust camshaft sprockets and the piston for the number cylinder is at TDC.
29. Install the holding device for the camshaft.
30. Cover the timing case with a clean rag and connect the ends of the new timing chain with a riveted link.
31. The remainder of the installation is the reverse order of removal.

TURBOCHARGER

REMOVAL & INSTALLATION

Engine ID 642

See Figures 113 through 115.

1. Remove the engine appearance cover.
2. Remove the air intake assembly downstream of the air filter.
3. Disconnect the electrical connector on the exhaust back pressure sensor.
4. Remove the heat shield.
5. Remove the bracket.
6. Remove the catalytic converter.
7. Remove the exhaust gas recirculation pipe and discard the gaskets.
8. Unscrew the mounting bolts on the exhaust collector pipe.
9. Remove the bolts on the exhaust collector pipe support brace.
10. Properly drain the cooling system.
11. Remove the mounting bolt for the coolant line.
12. Remove the bolts on the oil supply connection fittings.
13. Disconnect the electrical connector on the temperature sensor.
14. Disconnect electrical connector from charge pressure positioned.
15. Remove the turbocharger and discard the gasket.
16. Installation is the reverse order of removal. Tighten the mounting bolts to 15 ft. lbs. (20 Nm) plus 90°.

Engine ID 157 & 278

See Figure 116.

1. Remove the engine assembly with the front axle carrier.
2. Detach the clamp on the shield, right side only.
3. Remove the refrigerant line on the A/C compressor, left side only.
4. Remove the shield on the engine support.
5. Remove the shield on the cylinder head.
6. Detach the vacuum hose for the boost pressure control valve on the turbocharger with exhaust manifold.
7. Remove the charge air ducts.
8. Detach the coolant line for the charge air cooler on the timing case cover, right side only.

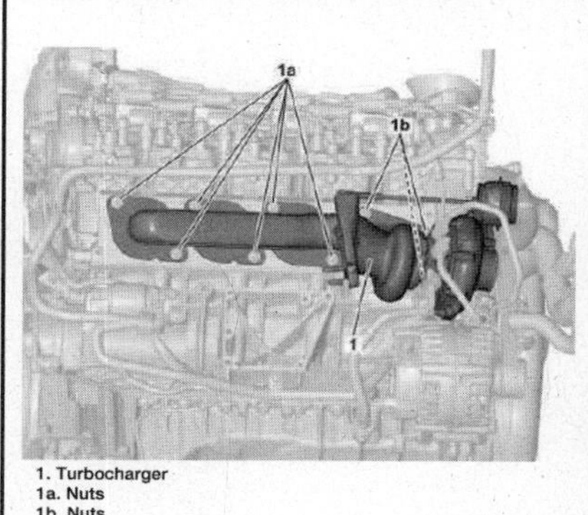

Fig. 113 Turbocharger mounted on the engine assembly—Engine ID 157 & 278

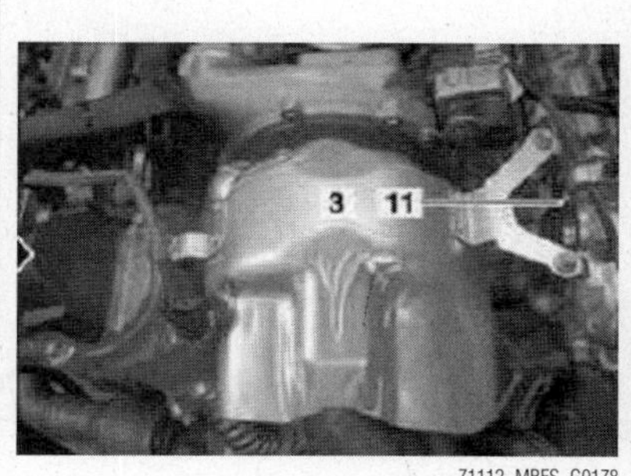

Fig. 114 Remove the heat shield and bracket—Engine ID 642

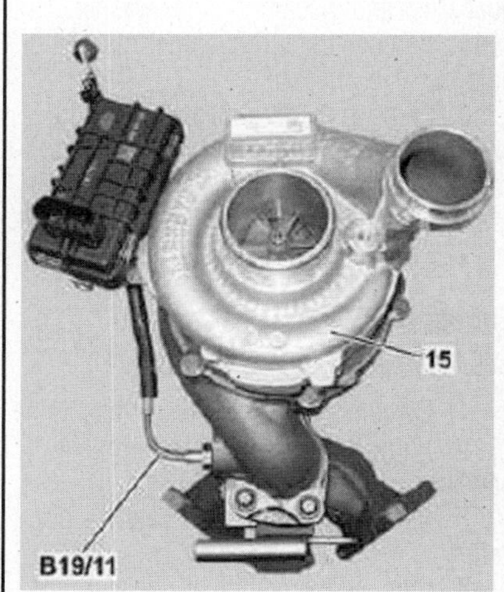

Fig. 115 Location of the temperature sensor upstream of the turbocharger—Engine ID 642

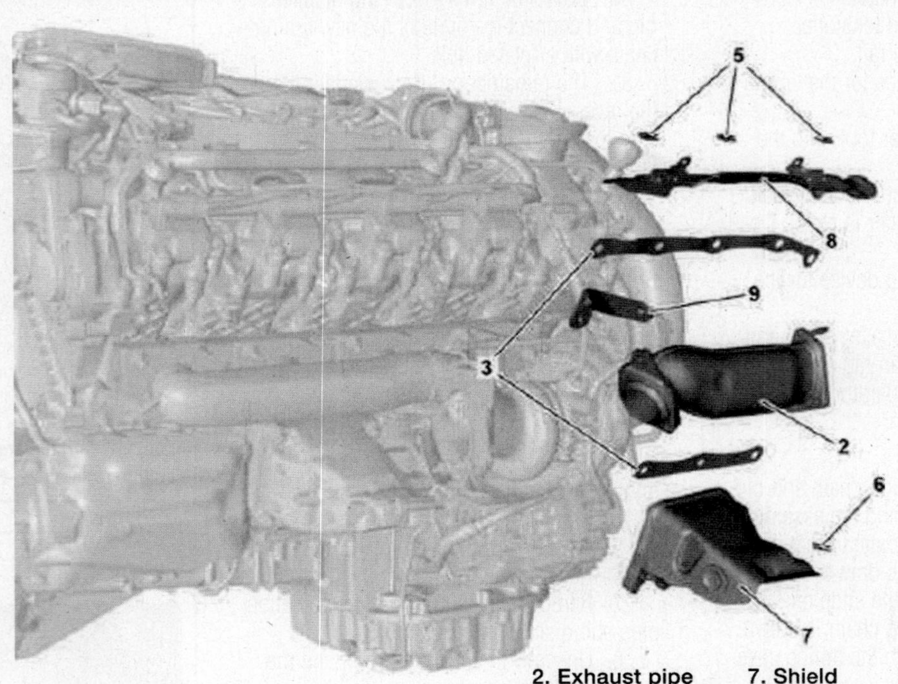

Fig. 116 Components to remove to access the turbocharger—Engine IDs 157 & 278

9. Remove the coolant lines.
10. Detach the upper oil line on the turbocharger with the exhaust manifold.
11. Detach the lower oil line on the oil pan.
12. Remove the bracket between the exhaust pipe and cylinder head.
13. Remove the exhaust pipe.
14. Remove the lock washer on the turbocharger and discard the lock washer.
15. Remove the turbocharger mounting nuts.
16. Remove the turbocharger with the exhaust manifold from the cylinder head.
17. Installation is the reverse order of removal. Tighten the mounting nuts to 18 ft. lbs. (25 Nm).

Engine ID 271

See Figures 117 and 118.

1. Disconnect the negative battery cable.
2. Remove the engine compartment paneling.
3. Remove the three-way catalytic converter.
4. Remove the combination valve.
5. Remove the power steering expansion reservoir, leaving the lines attached and move to one side.
6. Remove the combination valve bracket.

Fig. 117 Turbo charger engine mounting—1.8L Engine

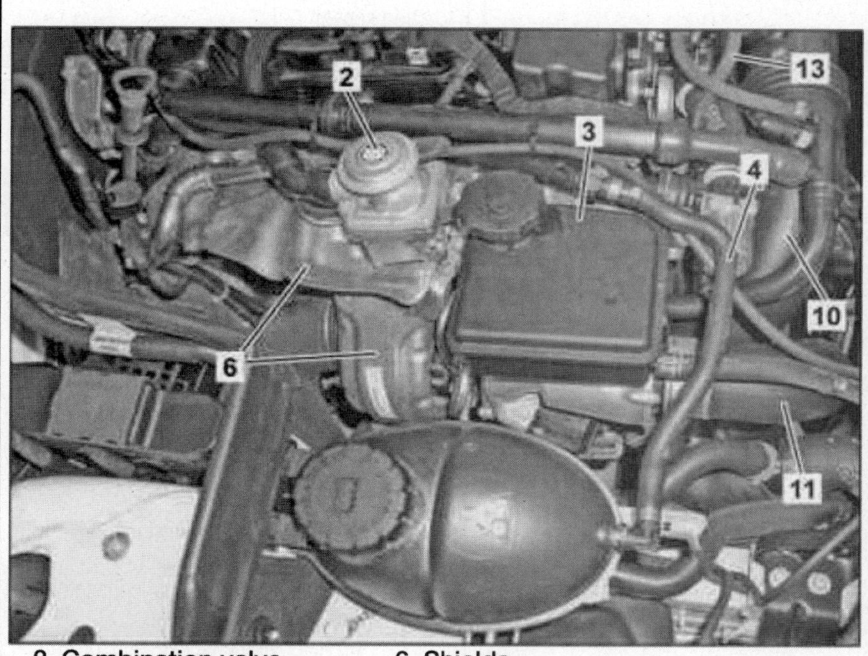

2. Combination valve
3. Expansion reservoir
4. Coolant return flow hose
6. Shields
10. Air ducting
11. Charge air ducting

71112_MBCL_G0120

Fig. 118 Turbocharger components—1.8L Engine

7. Remove the secondary air system pipework.
8. Remove the turbocharger shield.
9. Properly drain the coolant from the radiator.
10. Disconnect the coolant hose from the turbocharger.
11. Remove the coolant lines for the turbocharger.
12. Remove the turbocharger oil line.
13. Disconnect the connector for electrical line to bypass air switchover valve.
14. Disconnect the boost pressure control hose from the boost pressure control pressure transducer and unclip from the right engine lifting eye
15. Remove the mounting nuts and lift the turbocharger upwards to remove.
16. Installation is the reverse order of removal.
17. Refill the engine with coolant to the correct level.
18. Check the engine oil level.

VALVE LASH

ADJUSTMENT

Mercedes-Benz engines use hydraulic valve lifters. There is no provision for valve clearance adjustments.

ENGINE PERFORMANCE & EMISSION CONTROLS

CAMSHAFT POSITION (CMP) SENSOR

REMOVAL & INSTALLATION

Engine ID 156

1. Remove each engine air intake duct.
2. Unclip the hydraulic lines and hose from the bracket, left side only.
3. Disconnect the sensor electrical connector.
4. Remove the mounting bolts and remove the sensor. Discard the sealing ring.
5. Installation is the reverse order of removal. Use a new sealing ring.

CRANKSHAFT POSITION (CKP) SENSOR

LOCATION

Engine IDs 272 & 273

See Figure 119.

REMOVAL & INSTALLATION

Engine IDs 272 & 273

1. Remove air filter housing.
2. Remove hot film mass air flow sensor.
3. Remove air duct housing.
4. Release and disconnect electrical connector at crankshaft Hall sensor.
5. Remove bolt.
6. Pull the crankshaft Hall sensor out of crankcase.

To install:

7. Installation is the reverse of removal.
8. Tighten the crankshaft Hall sensor to crankcase bolt to 6 ft. lbs.
9. Carry out the initialization and then sensor rotor adaptation using STAR DIAGNOSIS tool.

Engine ID 156

See Figure 120.

1. Remove the left-side catalytic converter. For additional information, refer to the following section, "Catalytic Converter, Removal & Installation."

71112_MBES_G0182

Fig. 119 Location of the crankshaft position sensor—Engine IDs 272 & 273

Fig. 120 Mounting components for the crankshaft position sensor—Engine ID 156

2. Disconnect the electrical connector at the crankshaft position (CKP) sensor.
3. Remove the mounting bolt for the sensor and remove the CKP sensor.
4. Installation is the reverse order of removal.

Engine ID 276

See Figure 121.

1. Remove the front engine cover.
2. Remove the intake manifold. For additional information, refer to the following section, "Intake Manifold, Removal & Installation."
3. Remove the ME-SFI control unit and support bracket for the control unit.
4. Remove the mounting bolts for the shield for the crankshaft position (CKP) sensor.
5. Disconnect the electrical connector for the CKP sensor.
6. Remove the mounting bolt for the CKP sensor and remove the CKP sensor.
7. Installation is the reverse order of removal.

Engine ID 271

1. Remove rear part section of engine compartment paneling.

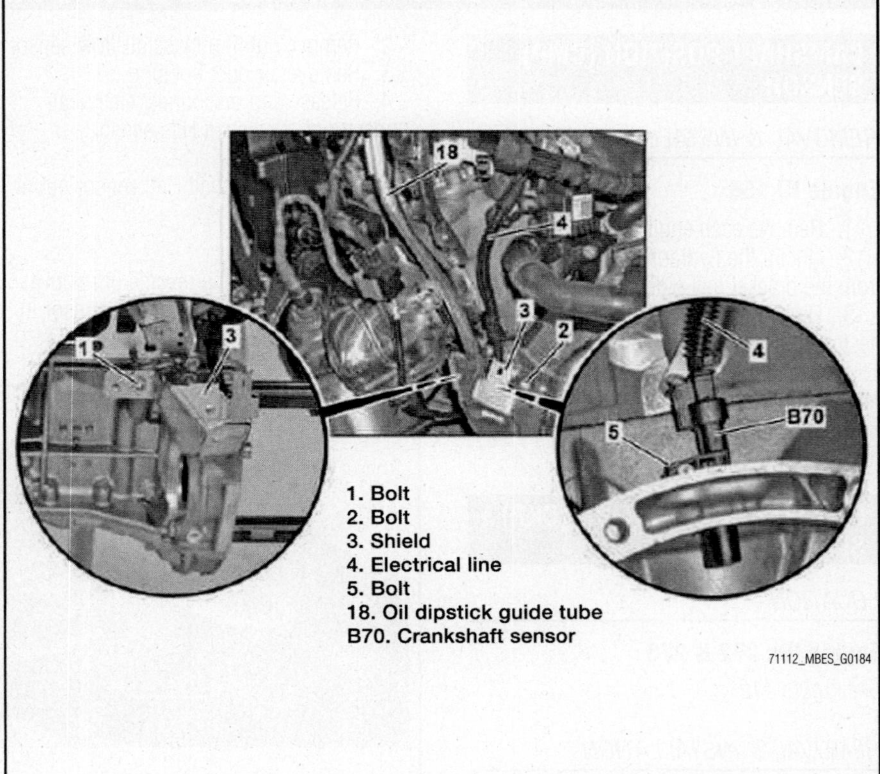

Fig. 121 Mounting components for the crankshaft position sensor—Engine ID 276

2. Unplug the plug on crankshaft position sensor.
3. Remove the bolt and crankshaft position sensor.
4. Installation is the reverse order of removal.

HEATED OXYGEN SENSOR (HO2S)

REMOVAL & INSTALLATION

Engine ID 276

1. Remove the air intake assembly, if removing right side sensors.
2. To remove the oxygen sensor downstream of the catalytic converter:
   a. Remove the engine compartment paneling.
   b. Unclip the electrical feed line from the heat shield and bracket.
   c. Unclip the electrical connector at the bracket and disconnect.
   d. Remove the oxygen sensor from the catalytic converter.
3. To remove the oxygen sensor upstream of the catalytic converter:
   a. Remove the ME-SFI control unit.
   b. Unclip the electrical fee d line for

oxygen sensor from the heat shield and bracket.

c. Unclip the electrical connector at the bracket and disconnect.

4. Remove the oxygen sensor from the catalytic converter.

5. Installation is the reverse order of removal. Coat the threads of the oxygen sensor with heat-resistant lubricant and tighten to 37 ft. lbs. (50 Nm).

Engine ID 157 & 278

See Figures 122 and 123.

1. Raise and safely support the vehicle.
2. Remove the engine compartment paneling.
3. Remove the left side sensors as follows:

a. Detach the rear engine crossmember from the underbody and lower transmission.

b. Detach the catalytic converter from the exhaust manifold and transmission and secure from falling.

c. Unclip the electrical connection for the oxygen sensor from bracket on the transmission.

d. Remove the oxygen sensors from the catalytic converter.

4. Remove the right side sensors as follows:

a. Unclip the electrical connection for the oxygen sensor from bracket on the transmission.

b. Remove the oxygen sensors from the catalytic converter.

5. Installation is the reverse order of removal. . Coat the threads of the oxygen sensor with heat-resistant lubricant and tighten to 37 ft. lbs. (50 Nm).

1. Left catalytic converter
5. Transmission
G3/3. Upstream oxygen sensor
G3/5. Downstream oxygen sensor
G3/3x1. Electrical connector
G3/5x1. Electrical connector

71112_MBES_G0185

Fig. 122 Left side oxygen sensors—Engine IDs 157 & 278

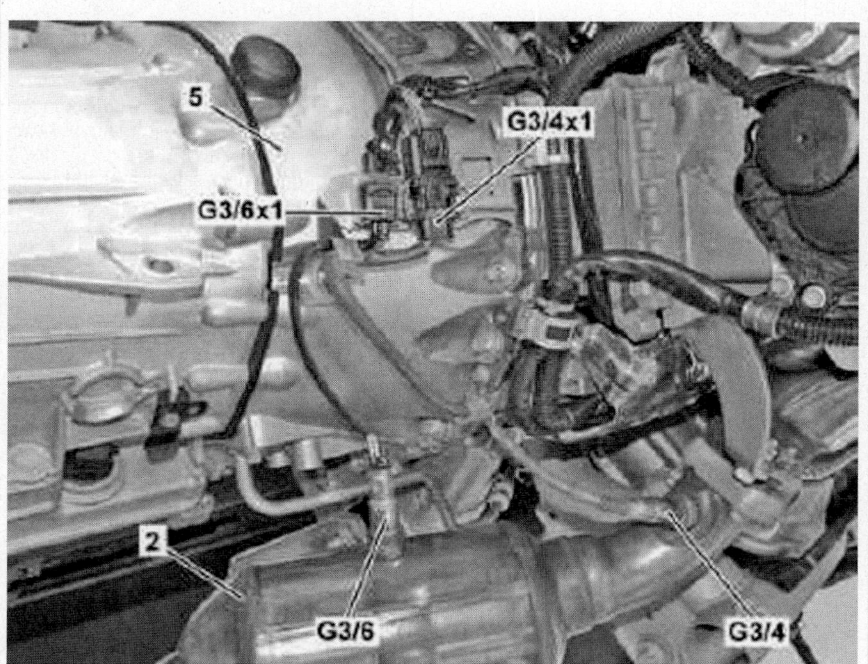

2. Right catalytic converter
5. Transmission
G3/4. Upstream oxygen sensor
G3/6. Downstream oxygen sensor
G3/4x1. Electrical connector
G3/6x1. Electrical connector

71112_MBES_G0186

Fig. 123 Right side oxygen sensors—Engine IDs 157 & 278

KNOCK SENSOR (KS)

LOCATION

Engine ID 271

See Figure 124.

REMOVAL & INSTALLATION

Engine IDs 272 & 273

1. Remove the intake manifold. For additional information, refer to the following section, "Intake Manifold, Removal & Installation."
2. Disconnect the electrical connector.
3. Remove the mounting bolt and remove the knock sensor.
4. Installation is the reverse order of removal.

Engine ID 156

See Figures 125 and 126.

1. Remove the left knock sensor as follows:
   a. Remove the heat shield by removing the mounting bolt.
   b. Release and disconnect the knock sensor electrical connector.
   c. Remove the knock sensor.
2. Remove the right knock sensor as follows:
   a. Disconnect the negative battery cable.
   b. Remove the front engine cover and the air intake assembly from both sides.
   c. Remove the bottom engine compartment paneling.
   d. Remove the bolts of the front engine mounts on the front axle carrier.
   e. Mount a suitable engine hoist and raise the engine.
   f. Unscrew the loosened bolt from the right engine mount at the engine support from the bottom and place the engine mount along with the heat shield to one side.
   g. Remove the protection against accidental contact for circuit 30 electrical line from the starter.
   h. Remove the electrical line terminal 30 and electrical line clamping device 50 on the starter and place aside.
   i. Remove the bolt and remove the heat shield.
   j. Release and disconnect the electrical connector on the knock sensor.
   k. Remove the knock sensor.
3. Installation is the reverse order of removal.

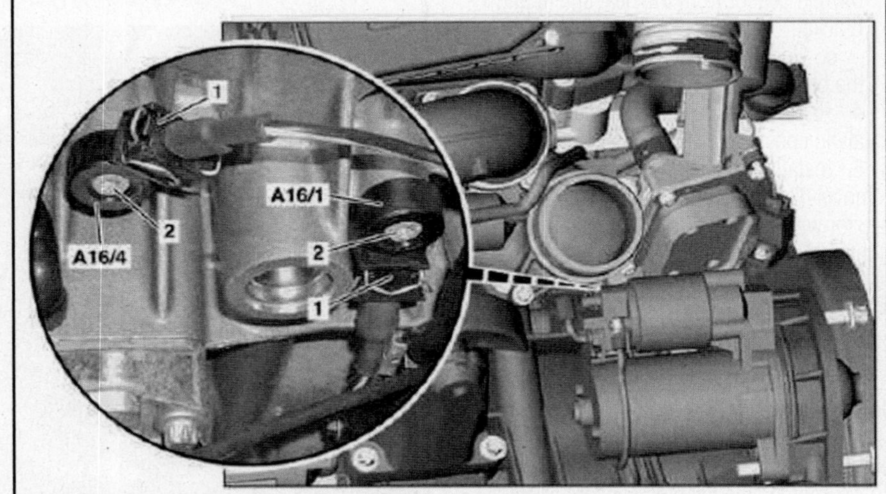

Electrical connector A16/1. Rear knock sensor
2. Bolt A16/4. Front knock sensor

71112_MBES_G0264

Fig. 124 Location of the front and rear knock sensor—Engine ID 271

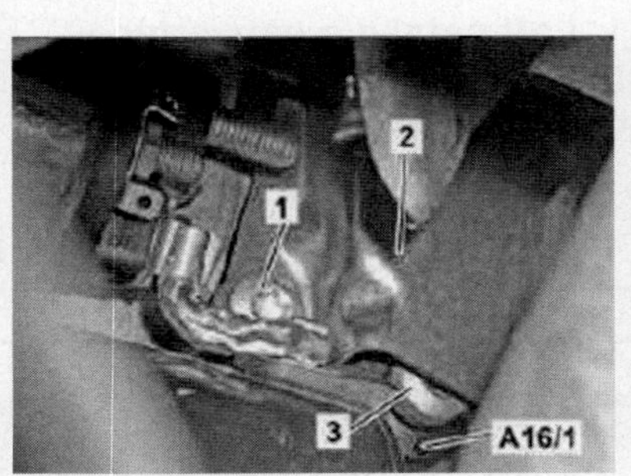

1. Bolt 3. Bolt
2. Heat shield A16/1. Right knock sensor

71112_MBES_G0187

Fig. 125 Right knock sensor assembly—Engine ID 156

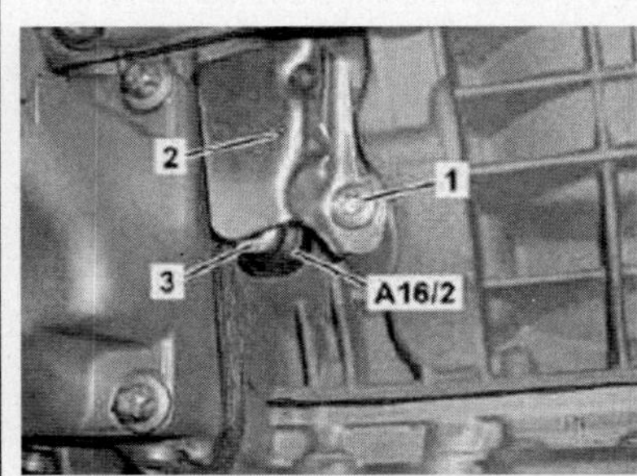

1. Bolt 3. Bolt
2. Heat shield A16/2. Left knock sensor

71112_MBES_G0188

Fig. 126 Left knock sensor assembly—Engine ID 156

Engine ID 271

1. Remove the air pump.
2. Disconnect the electrical connector on the knock sensor (front or rear).
3. Remove the mounting bolt to remove the knock sensor (front or rear).
4. Installation is the reverse order of removal.

FUEL SYSTEM SERVICE PRECAUTIONS

Safety is the most important factor when performing not only fuel system maintenance but any type of maintenance. Failure to conduct maintenance and repairs in a safe manner may result in serious personal injury or death. Maintenance and testing of the vehicle's fuel system components can be accomplished safely and effectively by adhering to the following rules and guidelines.

- To avoid the possibility of fire and personal injury, always disconnect the negative battery cable unless the repair or test procedure requires that battery voltage be applied.
- Always relieve the fuel system pressure prior to disconnecting any fuel system component (injector, fuel rail, pressure regulator, etc.), fitting or fuel line connection. Exercise extreme caution whenever relieving fuel system pressure to avoid exposing skin, face and eyes to fuel spray. Please be advised that fuel under pressure may penetrate the skin or any part of the body that it contacts.
- Always place a shop towel or cloth around the fitting or connection prior to loosening to absorb any excess fuel due to spillage. Ensure that all fuel spillage (should it occur) is quickly removed from engine surfaces. Ensure that all fuel soaked cloths or towels are deposited into a suitable waste container.
- Always keep a dry chemical (Class B) fire extinguisher near the work area.
- Do not allow fuel spray or fuel vapors to come into contact with a spark or open flame.
- Always use a back-up wrench when loosening and tightening fuel line connection fittings. This will prevent unnecessary stress and torsion to fuel line piping.
- Always replace worn fuel fitting O-rings with new. Do not substitute fuel hose or equivalent where fuel pipe is installed.

Before servicing the vehicle, make sure to also refer to the precautions in the beginning of this section as well.

FUEL FILTER

REMOVAL & INSTALLATION

See Figure 127.

1. Remove the upper engine cover.
2. Remove the air intake assembly downstream of the air filter.
3. Remove the charge air duct.
4. Unlock and disconnect the electrical connector on the heating element of fuel preheating system or condensation sensor of fuel filter with heating element.
5. Detach the fuel hoses from the fuel filter and discard the clamps.
6. Remove the screw and lift out the fuel filter.

To install:

7. Install the fuel filter.
   - Press down the fuel filter up to the end stop in the bracket, otherwise the engine air intake duct (1) cannot be installed.
8. Transfer the heating element of the fuel preheating system to the new fuel filter.
9. The remainder of the installation is the reverse order of removal.

FUEL INJECTION LINES

REMOVAL & INSTALLATION

1. Remove the air intake assembly.
2. Remove the engine air intake duct downstream of the air filter.
3. Take off the acoustic insulation.
4. Unclip the leak oil line and the injectors. Pull the fuse upwards and remove the line.
5. Unscrew the bracket of the engine wiring harness.
6. Undo the union nuts of the injector lines.
7. Remove the injection lines and immediately seal the openings.
8. Installation is the reverse order of removal.

FUEL RAIL & INJECTORS

REMOVAL & INSTALLATION

1. Remove the injection lines. For additional information, refer to the following section, "Fuel Injection Lines, Removal & Installation."
2. Disconnect electrical connector on rail pressure sensor.

3 Disconnect electrical connector on pressure regulator valve.

4 Disconnect return line.

3. Unscrew the union nuts on the pressure lines.
4. Remove the pressure lines.
5. Remove the bolt and remove the fuel rail.

Fig. 127 Fuel filter—E-Class diesel models

6. Installation is the reverse order of removal.

FUEL SUPPLY PUMP

REMOVAL & INSTALLATION

See Figure 128.

- The fuel tank cannot be filled to more than 25% of capacity or fuel may leak out during this process. For additional information, refer to the following section, "Fuel Tank, Draining"

1. Open the fuel filler flap and open the filler cap to relieve any pressure in fuel tank.
2. Remove the rear seat cushion.
3. Remove the cover for the service openings.
4. Remove the locking rings using a suitable claw wrench as follows:
   a. Unlock, detach and set aside the electrical connections on the fixture cover and fuel filter.
   b. Unlock, detach and set aside the fuel lines on the fuel filter.
   c. Insert the claw wrench in the opening openings on the outside on the locking ring.
   d. Insert the long locking handle into the claw wrench and turn the locking ring counterclockwise.
   e. Remove the locking handle with the claw wrench and locking ring.
5. Pull the transfer unit out of the left chamber of the fuel tank.
   - Handle the transfer unit and fuel tank level indicator fill level sensor carefully to avoid deforming the float linkage.
6. Remove the fuel lines at the transfer unit.
7. Remove the swirl pot, fuel pump and fuel lines out of the right chamber of the fuel tank.
8. Installation is the reverse order of removal.
9. If replacing the fuel pump, mount the fuel level indicator fill level sensor on the new swirl pot.
10. Close the locking ring as follows:
    a. Clean the contact surface of the sealing ring on fuel tank and locking ring.
    b. Replace the sealing ring and lay in groove on fuel tank.
    c. Hold by the locking ring and insert locating cover or fuel filter through the opening on the fuel tank in such a way that the recess points in the direction of travel.
    d. Press locating cover or fuel filter on its seat in the fuel tank and lay the locking ring in place.
    e. Turn the locking ring clockwise until the catch tab lies on the left on the fastening claws.
    f. Carefully insert the claw wrench with locking handle into the openings on the outside on the locking ring clockwise until the catch tab lies on the left on the recesses in the fastening claw
    g. Turn the locking ring clockwise until the catch tabs between the recesses on the fastening claws engage.
    h. Check for correct engagement of the locking ring and locking handle.

1. Insulation mat
2. Cover
2a. Bolts

71112_MBES_G0191

Fig. 128 Remove the cover for the service openings—E-Class models

⁂ WARNING

An incorrectly engaged locking ring can loosen which can lead to fuel tank leakage.

GLOW PLUGS

REMOVAL & INSTALLATION

See Figure 129.

1. Remove the engine trim panel.
2. Remove the engine air intake assembly downstream of the air filter.
3. Unscrew the distributor leak oil line.
4. Remove the engine wiring harness from the rail and discard the cable ties.
5. Disconnect the electrical connectors at the glow plugs.
6. Unscrew the glow plugs.

➡If it requires more than 18 ft. lbs. (25 Nm) of force to release the glow plugs, it is recommended to bring the engine up to operating temperature in order to avoid breaking off the glow plugs.

7. Installation is the reverse order of removal.

FUEL TANK

DRAINING

1. Open the fuel filler flap and filler cap.
2. Push the end of an extraction hose through filler neck.
3. Pump off the fuel using a suitable fuel transfer unit.

REMOVAL & INSTALLATION

E-Class Models

See Figure 130.

1. Drain the fuel tank, if necessary.
2. Remove the rear seat cushion.

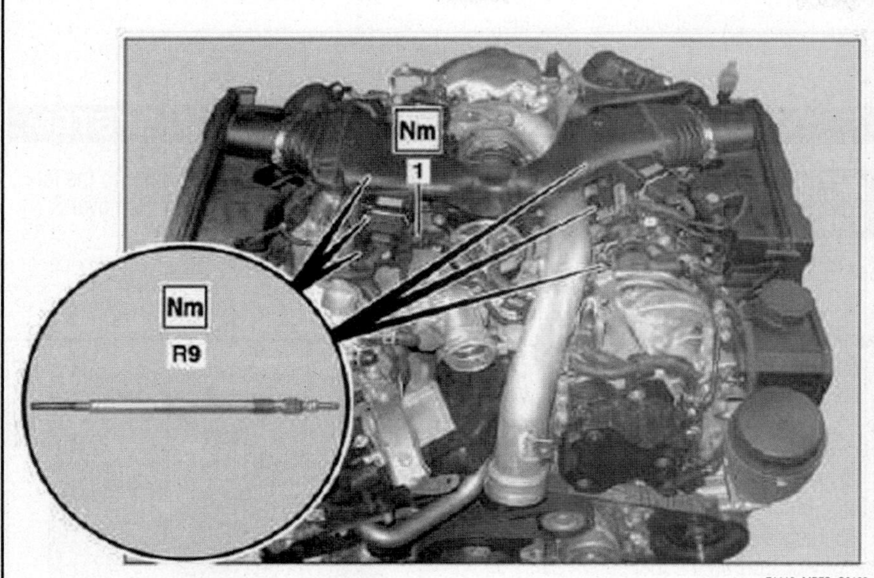

Fig. 129 Location of the glow plugs—Engine ID 642

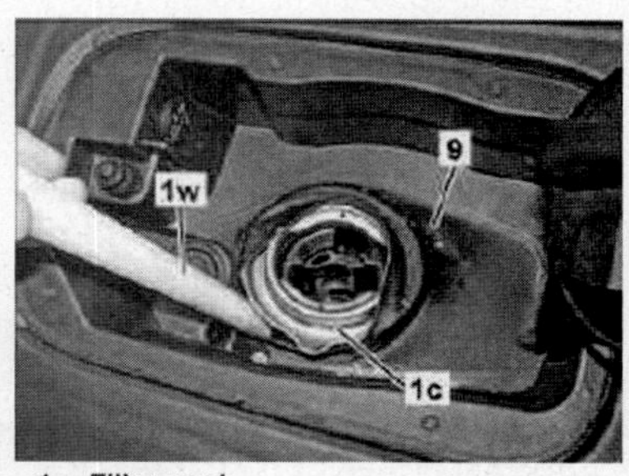

Fig. 130 Loosen the trim ring with a long wedge from the filler neck

3. Remove the cover for the service openings.
4. Unlock the fuel pump harness electrical connector and fuel tank electrical connector, disconnect and set aside.
5. Unlock the electrical connectors on the fuel pressure sensor, disconnect and set aside.
6. Remove the rear axle. For additional information, refer to the following section, "Rear Axle, Removal & Installation.
7. Remove the right and left hand underfloor paneling.
8. Remove the fender liner in the right rear fender.
9. Remove the filler neck/ground screw connection at the filler pipe.
10. Detach the drain hose from the filler neck depression.
11. Pull the boot out of the rear fender.
12. Unlock and detach the fuel line on frame floor assembly.
13. Remove the mounting bolts for the filler pipe.
14. Loosen the trim ring with a long wedge from the filler neck.
15. Remove the heat shield.
16. Remove the mounting nuts and lower the fuel tank.
17. Installation is the reverse order of removal. Tighten the mounting nuts to 15 ft. lbs. (20 Nm).

SLK-Class Models

See Figure 131.

1. Drain the fuel tank, if necessary.
2. Properly relieve the fuel system pressure.
3. Remove the upper tank cover as follows:
   a. Close the roof completely.
   b. Position the trunk lid to the assembly position.
   c. Open the retractable trunk partition.
   d. Remove the retractable trunk partition.
   e. Remove the spare tire paneling.
   f. Remove the center trunk paneling.
   g. Detach the equipment bridges and move toward the rear.
   h. Loosen bolts on tank cover and unscrew
   i. Loosen nuts on tank cover and unscrew
   j. Remove the tank cover.
4. Detach tank vent hose located at the top right of the tank.
5. Dismount the fuel hose and plug the connection.
6. Slacken boot from the circular groove and press into the vehicle interior.

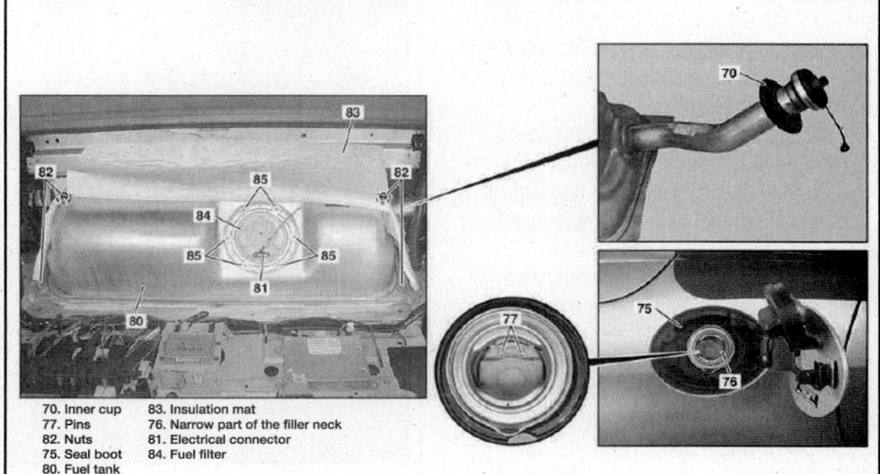

Fig. 131 Fuel tank and related components—2011 SLK-Class shown

7. Turn around the insulation mat towards the top.

8. Disconnect the electrical connector at fuel filter and loosen cable from fuel tank.

9. Unscrew the nuts.

10. Pull back the inner boot into the vehicle interior

11. Lift the fuel tank and pull it a little to the left.

12. Detach the seal boot from the filler neck.

13. Swivel the bottom side of the fuel tank to the rear and remove the fuel tank.

14. Installation is the reverse order of removal.

FUEL — GASOLINE FUEL INJECTION SYSTEM

FUEL SYSTEM SERVICE PRECAUTIONS

Safety is the most important factor when performing not only fuel system maintenance but any type of maintenance. Failure to conduct maintenance and repairs in a safe manner may result in serious personal injury or death. Maintenance and testing of the vehicle's fuel system components can be accomplished safely and effectively by adhering to the following rules and guidelines.

- To avoid the possibility of fire and personal injury, always disconnect the negative battery cable unless the repair or test procedure requires that battery voltage be applied.
- Always relieve the fuel system pressure prior to disconnecting any fuel system component (injector, fuel rail, pressure regulator, etc.), fitting or fuel line connection. Exercise extreme caution whenever relieving fuel system pressure to avoid exposing skin, face and eyes to fuel spray. Please be advised that fuel under pressure may penetrate the skin or any part of the body that it contacts.
- Always place a shop towel or cloth around the fitting or connection prior to loosening to absorb any excess fuel due to spillage. Ensure that all fuel spillage (should it occur) is quickly removed from engine surfaces. Ensure that all fuel soaked cloths or towels are deposited into a suitable waste container.
- Always keep a dry chemical (Class B) fire extinguisher near the work area.
- Do not allow fuel spray or fuel vapors to come into contact with a spark or open flame.
- Always use a back-up wrench when loosening and tightening fuel line connection fittings. This will prevent unnecessary stress and torsion to fuel line piping.
- Always replace worn fuel fitting O-rings with new Do not substitute fuel hose or equivalent where fuel pipe is installed.

Before servicing the vehicle, make sure to also refer to the precautions in the beginning of this section as well.

RELIEVING FUEL SYSTEM PRESSURE

See Figure 132.

1. Before servicing the vehicle, refer to the precautions.
2. Disconnect the negative battery cable.
3. Connect a fuel pressure gauge with a pressure release valve to the service port on the fuel supply rail.
4. Place the fuel release tube into a container and open the valve.
5. Remove the fuel pressure gauge from the service port on the fuel supply rail.

FUEL FILTER

REMOVAL & INSTALLATION

E-Class Models

See Figure 133.

1. Remove the fuel pump and detach the fuel lines from the fuel pump and swirl pot. For additional information, refer to the following section, "Fuel Pump, Removal & Installation."
2. Remove the cap of the left service opening.

2. Fuel filter B4/1. Fuel level indicator sensor
3. Float linkage B4/7. Fuel pressure sensor

71112_MBES_G0194

Fig. 133 Remove fuel filter with the fuel level sensor and fuel lines out of the left-hand chamber of the fuel tank—E-Class models

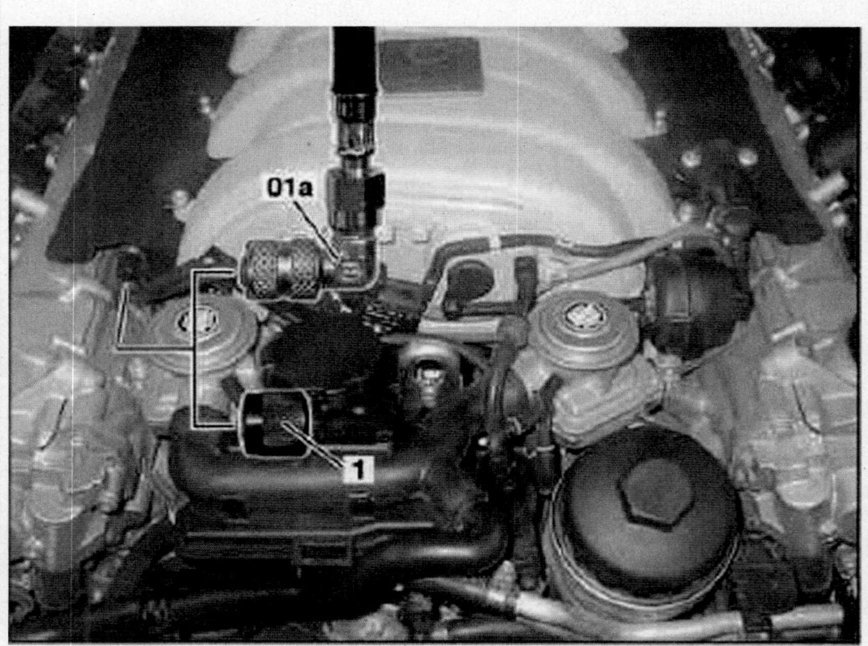

71112_MBES_G0195

Fig. 132 Connect a fuel pressure gauge with a pressure release valve to the service port on the fuel supply rail—E-Class Models

3. Remove the left locking ring.
4. Remove fuel filter with the fuel level sensor and fuel lines out of the left-hand chamber of the fuel tank.
5. Remove the fuel level sensor from the fuel filter.
6. Remove the pressure sensor from the fuel filter.
7. Installation is the reverse order of removal.

2011 SLK-Class Models

See Figure 134.

1. Close the roof.
2. Ensure the ignition is in the **OFF** position.
3. Drain the fuel tank.
4. Open the fuel filler flap and open filler cap and reseal to reduce fuel tank pressure.
5. Remove the upper tank cover. For additional information, refer to the following section, "Fuel Tank, Removal & Installation."
6. Remove the mounting nuts.
7. Remove the ring.
8. Remove the fuel filter from the fuel tank.
9. Release and detach the electrical connector.
10. Remove the clamp and disconnect the fuel lines from the fuel filter.
11. Replace the fuel filter.

2012 SLK-Class Models

See Figure 135.

1. Close the roof.
2. Ensure the ignition is in the **OFF** position.
3. Drain the fuel tank.
4. Open the fuel filler flap and open filler cap and reseal to reduce fuel tank pressure.
5. Place the fuel pump control module with connected lines to one side. For additional information, refer to the following section, "Fuel Pump Control Module, Removal & Installation."
6. Release and disconnect electrical connection on outside of fuel filter and on fuel pressure sensor.
7. Unscrew the nuts and remove the locking ring.
8. Lift the fuel filter out of the fuel tank.
9. Unlock and disconnect electrical connector (arrow) on inside of fuel filter.
10. Unlock fuel lines and detach from the fitting on the fuel filter.
11. Installation is the reverse order of removal. Using a new sealing ring on the tank opening.

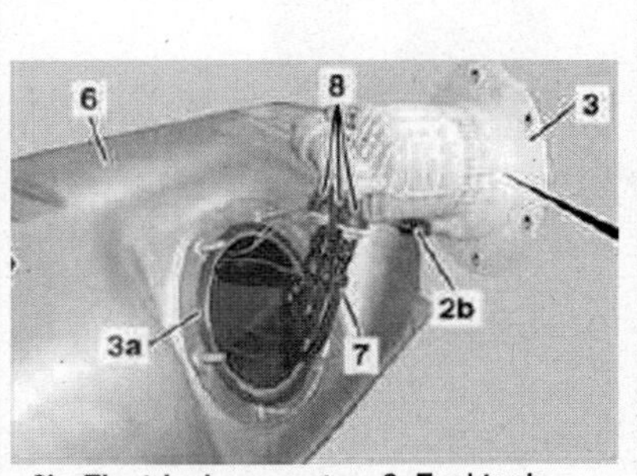

2b. Electrical connector 6. Fuel tank
3. Fuel filter 7. Clamp
3a. Sealing ring 8. Fuel lines

71112_MBES_G0269

Fig. 134 Disconnect the electrical connector and fuel lines from the fuel filter—2011 SLK-Class

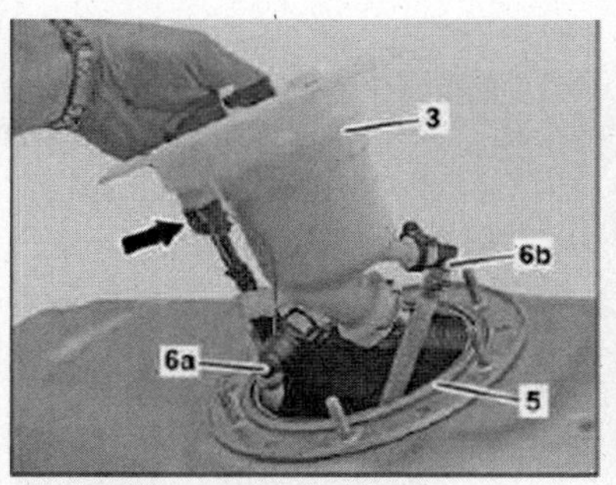

3. Fuel filter 6a. Fuel line
5. Sealing ring 6b. Fuel line

71112_MBES_G0267

Fig. 135 Disconnect the fuel lines from the fuel filter—2012 SLK-Class

FUEL PUMP

REMOVAL & INSTALLATION

E-Class Models

- The fuel tank cannot be filled to more than 25% of capacity or fuel may leak out during this process. For additional information, refer to the following section, "Fuel Tank, Draining"

1. Open the fuel filler flap and open filler cap and reseal.
2. Remove the rear seat cushion.
3. Remove the cover for the right service opening.
4. Remove the right locking ring.
5. Unlock and disconnect the electrical connectors on the locating cover and remove the locating cover.
6. Unlock and detach the fuel lines to the fuel pump and upper cover of the swirl pot.
7. Remove the swirl pot and fuel pump out of the right chamber of the fuel tank.
8. If the fuel pump is being replaced, the fill sensor must be transferred to the new swirl pot.
9. Installation is the reverse order of removal. Take care not to kink any of the electrical or fuel lines during installation.

SLK-Class Models

See Figure 136.

1. Remove the fuel filter. For additional information, refer to the following section, "Fuel Filter, Removal & Installation."
2. Press the catch spring together and detach the fuel level indicator sensor upwards.
3. Disconnect the electrical connector at the fuel pump.
4. Unclip the return adapter from the fuel pump.
5. Turn the rotary valve in the direction of the arrow and remove the fuel pump upwards.
6. Installation is the reverse order of removal.

FUEL RAIL & INJECTORS

REMOVAL & INSTALLATION

Engine IDs 272 & 273

See Figures 137 and 138.

1. Ensure the ignition is in the **OFF** position.
2. Properly relieve the fuel system pressure.
3. Remove the air filter housing.

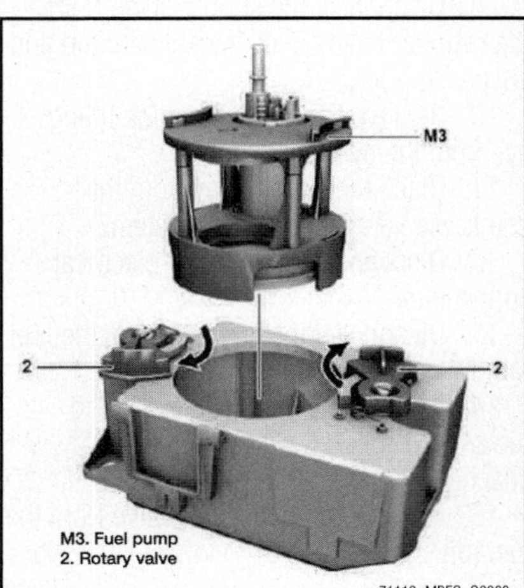

M3. Fuel pump
2. Rotary valve

71112_MBES_G0268

Fig. 136 Turn the rotary valve in the direction of the arrow and remove the fuel pump upwards—2012 SLK-Class shown

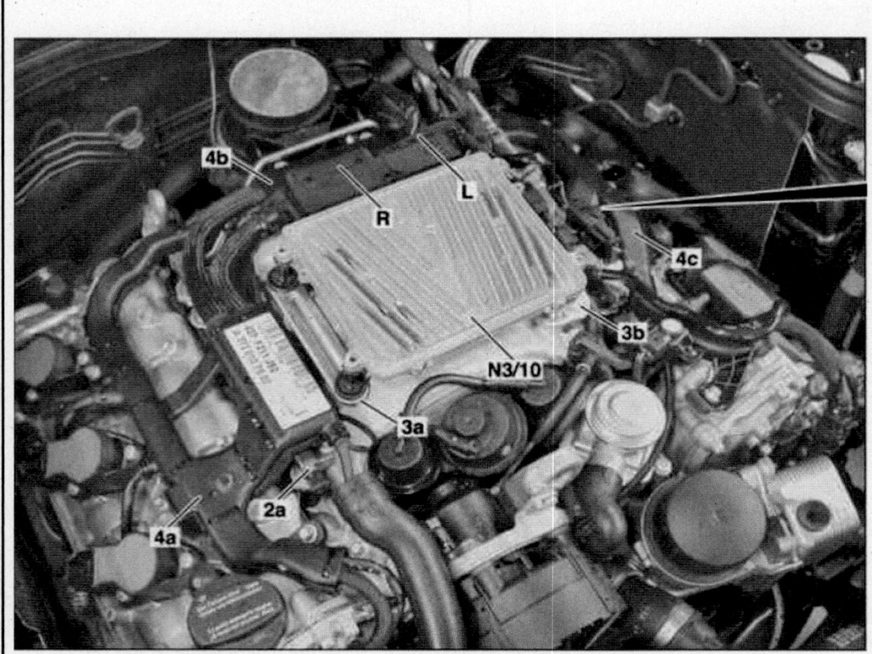

Fig. 137 Fuel rail mounting components—Engine ID 272 & 273

4. Disconnect the fuel rail wiring harnesses.
5. Remove the jack for the wiring harnesses.
6. Disconnect the right-side electrical connector for the fuel injection control unit.
7. Remove the control unit from the mounting bracket and set aside.
8. Remove the right control unit bracket.
9. Disconnect the supply ducts from the cylinder head cover, intake manifold and suspension lug.
10. Remove the rear left engine lifting eye from the cylinder head.
11. Disconnect the hoses from the crankcase ventilation (CCV) system.
12. Disconnect fuel injector electrical connectors.
13. Disconnect the fuel line from the fuel rail. Immediately plug the line.
14. Remove the mounting bolts and remove the fuel rail with the injectors attached.
15. Pull out each injection valve from the fuel rail.

To install:

16. Replace the O-rings of the fuel injectors.
17. Slide the securing clamps onto the injectors. Push on so that the cone on the safety clips encloses the moldings on the fuel injectors.
18. Apply a suitable liquid lubricant paste to the O-rings.
19. Insert each injector into the correct position on the fuel rail. The shape of the clips and fittings determines the correct position of the injectors.
20. The remainder of the installation is the reverse order of removal. Tighten the fuel rail mounting bolts to 80 inch lbs. (9 Nm).
21. Connect STAR DIAGNOSIS tool, read out and clear fault memory.

Engine ID 156

1. Ensure the ignition is in the **OFF** position.
2. Properly relieve the fuel system pressure.
3. Remove the air filter housing.
4. Detach the fuel line from the fuel rail.

➡Collect any fuel in a suitable container.

5. Disconnect the electrical connectors at the injectors.
6. Detach the electrical connectors on fuel rail.

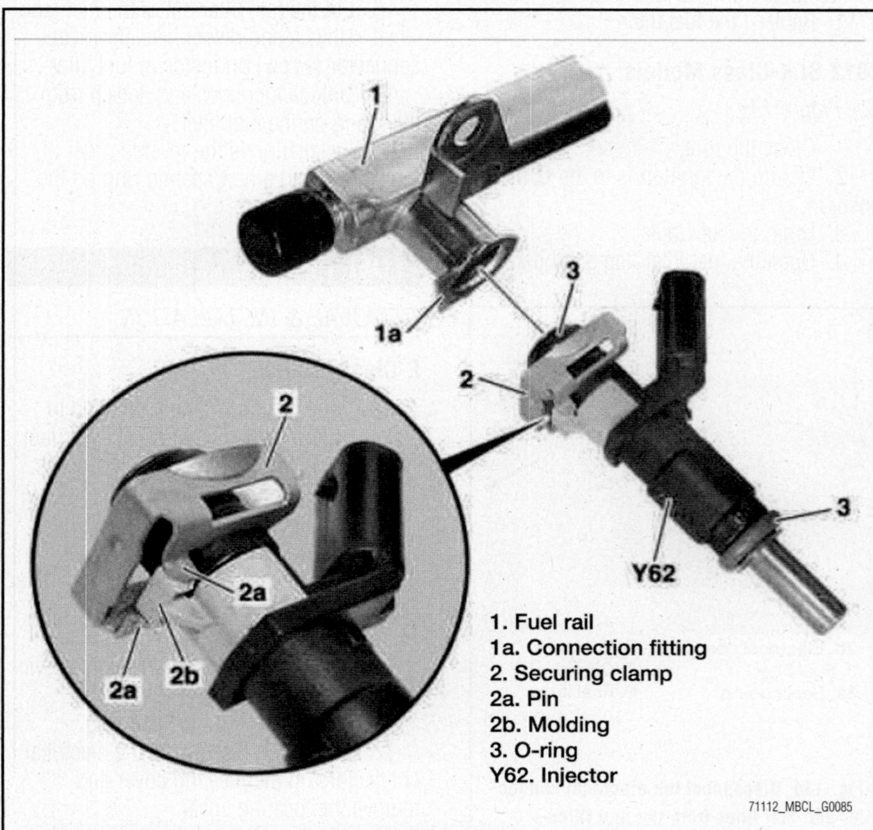

Fig. 138 Fuel injector components—Engine ID 272 & 273

7. Remove the mounting bolts and remove the fuel rail with the injectors attached.

8. Pull out each injection valve from the fuel rail.

To install:

9. Check and replace any fuel injector seal rings as necessary.

10. Moisten the seal rings with a suitable lubricant paste before inserting the injectors into the fuel rail.

11. The remainder of the installation is the reverse order of removal. Tighten the fuel rail mounting bolts to 80 inch lbs. (9 Nm).

12. Connect STAR DIAGNOSIS tool, read out and clear fault memory.

Engine ID 276

See Figure 139.

1. Disconnect the negative battery cable.

2. Remove the center section of the engine bulkhead.

3. Remove the air filter housing.

4. Remove the intermediate flange for the intake manifold.

5. Remove the crash plate and insulation on the high pressure pump.

6. Properly relieve the fuel system pressure.

7. Loose the high-pressure line and low-pressure line on the fuel rail and high-pressure pump.

8. Disconnect the electrical connector on the right-hand exhaust camshaft sensor, if removing right side rail.

9. Disconnect the electrical connector on fuel pressure and temperature sensor, if removing left side rail.

10. Detach the engine wiring harness on the fuel rail.

11. Remove the support for the intake manifold.

12. Remove the fuel rail mounting bolts.

⁂ CAUTION

The mounting bolts must be removed by turning each one half of a revolution starting from the middle outwards, otherwise the fuel rail will be damaged.

13. Remove the hold-down clip between the fuel rail and injectors.

14. Remove the fuel rail.

15. Remove the fuel injectors using a suitable extractor tool as follows:

a. Place the extractor tool over the injector.

01. Extractor tool
2. Support guide
Y76. Injector

71112_MBES_G0196

Fig. 139 Remove the fuel injectors using a suitable extractor tool—Engine ID 276

b. Turn the injector nozzle back and forth using the tool to loosen the injector from the cylinder head.

c. Pull out the injector using the tool.

To install:

➡If reusing fuel injectors, they must be inserted back to the same cylinder.

16. Replace the sealing rings and seals on the fuel injectors.

17. Install the injectors into the fuel rail.

18. Install the fuel rail assembly to the cylinder head.

⁂ CAUTION

The mounting bolts must be tightened by turning each one half of a revolution starting from the middle outwards, otherwise the fuel rail will be damaged.

19. The remainder of the installation is the reverse order of removal.

20. Connect STAR DIAGNOSIS tool, read out and clear fault memory.

Engine ID 157 & 278

1. Disconnect the negative battery cable.

2. Remove the engine covers.

3. Remove the air filter housings.

4. Remove the fuel rail insulation.

5. Remove the ME-SFI control unit.

6. Disconnect the electrical connector at the fuel pressure and temperature sensor.

7. Detach the engine wiring harness from the fuel rail.

8. Properly relieve the fuel system pressure.

9. Remove the high pressure lines from the high-pressure pumps on the rails.

10. Remove the high-pressure lines between the rails.

11. Remove the mounting bolts from the rail.

12. Remove the hold-down clip between the rail and fuel injectors.

13. Matchmark the fuel injectors to their respective cylinders.

➡If reusing fuel injectors, they must be inserted back to the same cylinder.

14. Remove the fuel injectors and rail assembly from the cylinder head.

15. Installation is the reverse order of removal.

16. Connect STAR DIAGNOSIS tool, read out and clear fault memory.

THROTTLE BODY

REMOVAL & INSTALLATION

Engine IDs 272 & 273

See Figure 140.

1. Before servicing the vehicle, refer to the precautions.
2. Remove the air filter housing.
3. Remove the mass air flow sensor.
4. Remove the air guide tube.
5. Release and disconnect the electrical connector at throttle valve actuator.
6. Pull the bleed hose out of throttle valve actuator.
7. Remove the bolts.
8. Remove the throttle valve actuator.
9. Remove the gasket.

To install:

10. Installation is the reverse of removal.
11. Tighten bolt connecting throttle valve actuator to resonance intake manifold: 80 inch lbs. (9 Nm)
12. Connect STAR DIAGNOSIS tool, read out and clear fault memory.

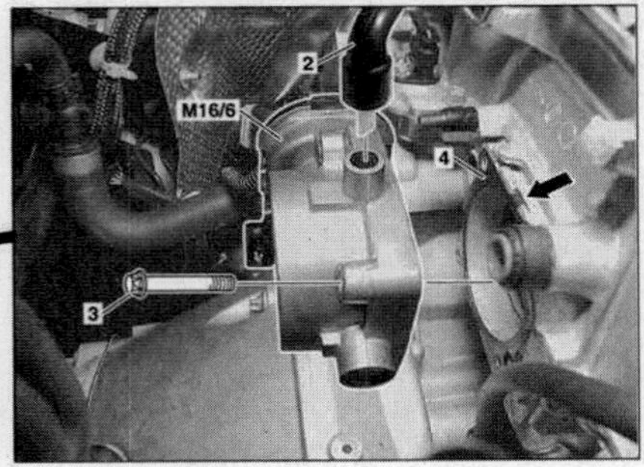

1. Air duct housing
2. Venting hose
3. Bolt
4. Seal
B2/5. Hot film mass air flow sensor
M16/6. Throttle valve actuator

37698_MERC_G0058

Fig. 140 Removing throttle control actuator

Engine ID 157 & 278

1. Remove the intake manifold. For additional information, refer to the following section, "Intake Manifold, Removal & Installation."
2. Disconnect the electrical connectors on intake air temperature sensor and pressure sensor downstream of throttle valve.
3. Disconnect the electrical plug connector on throttle valve.
4. Unclip the electrical line on the throttle body.
5. Unscrew the bolts for the charge air cooler on intake manifold.
6. Loosen the clamp for the intake manifold on the throttle valve.
7. Detach the charge air cooler and throttle valve on the intake manifold.
8. Unclip the electrical line on the throttle valve.
9. Remove the bolts on the throttle valve actuator.
10. Remove the throttle body from the charge air cooler.
11. Remove the seal for the throttle body on the charge air cooler and discard.
12. Installation is the reverse order of removal.

Engine ID 156

1. Remove the air intake assembly.
2. Remove the intake manifold.
3. Push the rubber grommet out of the collector.
4. Unscrew the collector from the intake manifold.
5. Unclip the clamping ring and electrical line at the throttle body.
6. Disconnect the electrical connector.
7. Remove the throttle body mounting bolts and remove the throttle body.
8. Installation is the reverse order of removal. Tighten the throttle body mounting bolts to 80 inch lbs. (9 Nm).

HEATING & AIR CONDITIONING SYSTEM

BLOWER MOTOR

REMOVAL & INSTALLATION

E-Class Models

See Figure 141.

1. Remove the cover on the right under the dashboard.
2. Disconnect the electrical connector from the blower motor.
3. Detach the cable tie from the electrical line.
4. Unhook the electrical line from the retaining tab of the blower motor.
5. Release the shackle by pressing lightly downwards.
6. Twist the blower motor until the markings match to unlock the bayonet connection.
7. Remove the blower motor.
8. Installation is the reverse order of removal.

2011 SLK-Class Models

1. Remove the cover on the right under the dashboard.
2. Move sliding piece and sliding piece direction of arrow, remove cover downwards and move the sliding piece back to the locking position.
3. Disconnect the electrical plug.
4. Remove the mounting bolts for the blower motor and remove downwards.
5. Turn blower motor around, release locking lug on plug, slide plug downwards and remove.
6. Remove the blower motor.
7. Installation is the reverse order of removal.

2012 SLK-Class Models

See Figure 142.

1. Remove the cover on the right under the dashboard.
2. Disconnect the electrical connectors.
3. Turn the blower motor in the direction of the arrow until the lug rests against the end stop.
4. Remove the blower motor.
5. Installation is the reverse order of removal.

HEATER CORE

REMOVAL & INSTALLATION

E-Class Models

1. Remove the air conditioner housing.
2. Detach the left blend air flap actuator motor and right blend air flap actuator motor.
3. Expose electrical lines of left blend air flap actuator motor and right blend air flap actuator motor and place left blend air

2. Electrical connector
3. Markings
4. Cable tie
5. Electrical connector
A32. AC Housing
A32m1. Blower motor

71112_MBES_G0197

Fig. 141 Blower motor assembly—E-Class models

flap actuator motor and right blend air flap actuator motor to one side with electrical lines still connected.

4. Detach the seals, electrical connectors, and mounting bolts and remove the diffuser fitting and move to the side.
5. Unhook the relay lever and remove the actuator motors carrier.
6. Remove the mounting bolt and remove the heater core bracket.
7. Moisten the seal in the area of the line bracket with rubber lubricant and guide over the line bracket.
8. Remove the bolts and remove the line bracket.
9. Unclip any retaining clamps from the coolant lines.
10. Pull the coolant lines out of the heater core.
11. Pull the heater core out of the air conditioner housing.
12. Installation is the reverse order of removal. Ensure the correct seating of the gaskets and sealing rings.
13. Properly charge the system with refrigerant.
14. Start the engine and check for leaks.

2011 SLK-Class Models

1. Remove the air conditioner housing.
2. Detach the electrical connector on left and right defroster flaps actuator motor.
3. Detach the electrical connector on fresh air flaps actuator motor.
4. Remove the AC bus wiring harness from fixtures and put aside.

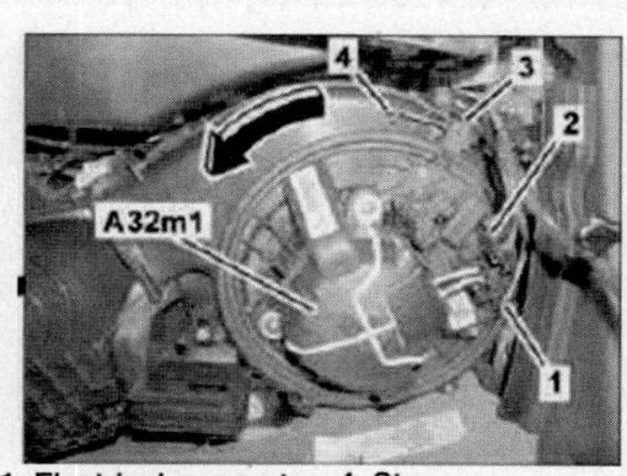

1. Electrical connector 4. Stop
2. Electrical connector A32m1. Blower motor
3. Lug

71112_MBES_G0272

Fig. 142 Turn the blower motor assembly to remove—2012 SLK-Class

5. Remove the mounting bolts and remove the left heat exchanger temperature sensor and right heat exchanger temperature sensor from upper part of housing.
6. Release the retaining clamps and remove the top section of the housing.
7. Undo the screws and remove pipeline holder.
8. Remove the sealing from connecting pipe.
9. Raise the air ducting and remove the heater core.
10. Installation is the reverse order of removal.

2012 SLK-Class Models

1. Remove the air conditioner housing.
2. Unscrew the bolts and remove the blend air flap actuator motor from the A/C housing and hang to the side with the lines connected.
3. Unscrew the bolt and open the line bracket.
4. Remove the mounting bolts, release the catch hooks and pull the heater core out of the A/C housing.
5. Installation is the reverse order of removal. Replace any damaged spring clips.

STEERING

POWER RACK & PINION STEERING GEAR

REMOVAL & INSTALLATION

E-Class Models

See Figure 143.

1. Ensure the steering wheel is centered and the wheels are in the straight-ahead position. Fix the steering wheel in this position with a retaining device.
2. Open the hood.
3. Remove the left engine air intake assembly, Engine ID 272 & 273 only.
4. Remove the upper engine cover, Engine ID 642 only.
5. Remove the front engine cover, Engine ID 156 only.
6. Using a suitable pump, remove the power steering fluid from the expansion reservoir.
7. Raise and safely support the vehicle.
8. Remove the front wheels.
9. Remove the center and rear section of the lower engine compartment paneling or soundproofing.
10. Remove the tie rods from the steering knuckles.
11. Detach the steering coupling from the rack and pinion steering and discard the self-locking nut.
12. Remove the bolt from the rack and pinion steering.
13. Pry the clamping plate off the rack and pinion steering gear and pull out the power steering oil lines. Seal the openings and discard the O-rings.
14. Support the rack and pinion steering gear with a suitable jack to prevent it from falling.
15. Take out the retaining plate with the rack-and-pinion steering gear.
16. Installation is the reverse order of removal.
17. Properly bleed the power system system.

SLK-Class Models

1. Open the hood and move to the vertical position.
2. Remove the left engine air intake duct upstream of the air filter, 2011 SLK-Class
3. Remove the front engine cover, 2012 SLK-Class
4. Using a suitable pump, remove the power steering fluid from the expansion reservoir.
5. Raise and safely support the vehicle.

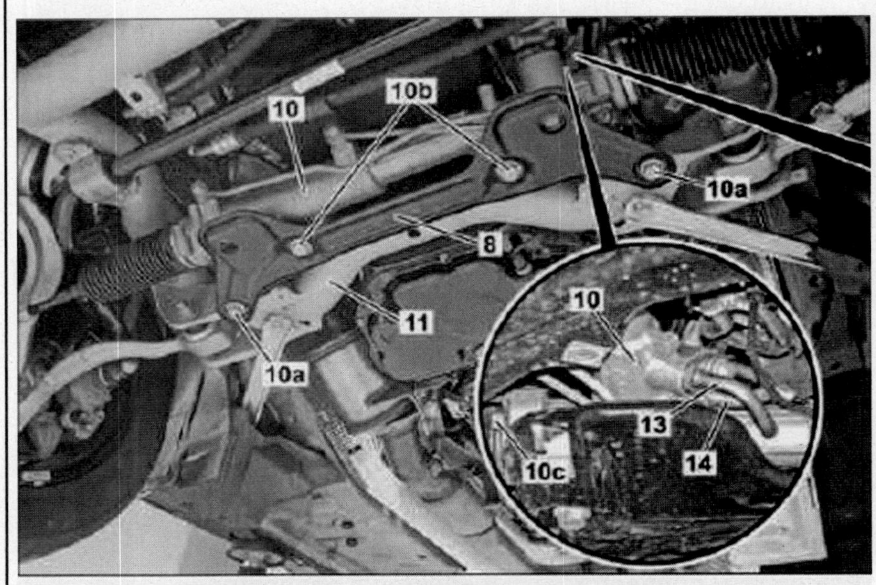

8. Retaining plate
9. Clamping plate
10. Rack and pinion gear
10a. Bolts
10b. Bolts
11. Front axle carrier
13. Power steering oil line
14. Power steering oil line

71112_MBES_G0203

Fig. 143 Rack-and-pinion steering gear assembly—E-Class Models

6. Disconnect the steering coupling from the lower steering shaft.
7. Remove the front wheels.
8. Remove the front diagonal braces.
9. Disconnect the electrical connection from the solenoid valve, if equipped with speed sensitive steering.
10. Remove the bolt of the retaining plate for the oil lines.
11. Remove the retaining plate of the oil lines from the steering gear, pull the high pressure expansion hose and hydraulic line out of the rack-and-pinion steering and seal line connections using stop plugs.
12. Remove the bolts and disconnect the high-pressure expansion hose and hydraulic line of the steering gear, 2011 SLK-Class.
13. Open the left and right paneling at the separation point, 2012 SLK-Class only.
14. Press the tie rod joints off the steering knuckles.
15. Support the rack-and-pinion assembly with a suitable jack.
16. Unscrew the bolts of retaining plate as well as the bolts of the steering assembly and remove the retaining plate.
17. Carefully lower the steering gear assembly.
18. Installation is the reverse order of removal.
19. Properly bleed the power system system.

POWER STEERING PUMP

REMOVAL & INSTALLATION

Engine IDs 272 & 273

1. Open engine hood and raise to the vertical position.
2. Remove the front engine cover.
3. Remove the left air intake assembly.
4. Remove the coolant hose from the bracket on the oil-water heat exchanger.
5. Remove the power steering fluid reservoir.
6. Remove the accessory drive belt.
7. Remove the front and center section of the engine compartment paneling.
8. Detach the A/C compressor from the engine, leaving the lines connected.
9. Disconnect the electrical connector on the power steering pump.
10. Detach the pressure line from the power steering pump.

11. Remove the mounting bolts and remove the power steering pump.
12. Installation is the reverse order of removal.
13. Refill and bleed the power steering system.

Engine ID 276

1. Raise and safely support the vehicle.
2. Remove the front and center lower engine compartment paneling.
3. Remove the accessory drive belt.
4. Remove the tensioner pulley.
5. Open the cable ties.
6. Disconnect the engine compartment electrical connector.
7. Remove the ME-SFI control unit upward out of the bracket and set asides with the lines connected.
8. Using a suitable pump, remove the power steering fluid from the expansion reservoir.
9. Remove the return line from the expansion reservoir.
10. Remove the bolt and remove the pressure line from the power steering pump.
11. Unhook the vacuum line from the expansion reservoir.
12. Remove the mounting bolts and remove the power steering pump with the expansion reservoir from the control housing.
13. Installation is the reverse order of removal. Tighten mounting bolts to 15 ft. lbs. (20 Nm).

FLUID FILL PROCEDURE

1. Raise and safely support the vehicle.
2. Open the hood.
3. Remove the air intake assembly.
4. Remove the upper engine cover.
5. Remove the cap from the power steering reservoir.
6. Fill the reservoir with recommended fluid to 10 mm below the upper edge of the reservoir.
7. Turn the steering wheel from steering stop to steering stop until bubbles are no longer visible in the reservoir.

➡Refill the reservoir with steering fluid continuously until the fluid level remains constant.

8. Start the engine.
9. Turn the steering wheel from steering stop to steering stop until bubbles are no longer visible in the reservoir.

➡Refill the reservoir with steering fluid continuously until the fluid level remains constant.

SUSPENSION

FRONT SUSPENSION

KNUCKLE & SPINDLE

REMOVAL & INSTALLATION

E-Class Models

See Figures 144 and 145.

1. Raise and safely support the vehicle.
2. Remove the front wheel.
3. Remove the front wheel hub. For additional information, refer to the following section, "Wheel Hubs & Bearings, Removal & Installation."
4. Remove the caliper dust shield.
5. Remove the strut from the steering knuckle.
6. Disconnect the wheel speed sensor from the steering knuckle.
7. Disconnect the tie rod from the steering knuckle.
8. Remove the torque strut from the steering knuckle.
9. Remove the steering knuckle.
10. Installation is the reverse order of removal.

2011 SLK-Class Models

1. Raise and safely support the vehicle.
2. Remove the front wheel.
3. Remove the front wheel hub. For additional information, refer to the following section, "Wheel Hubs & Bearings, Removal & Installation."
4. Remove the caliper dust shield.
5. Press the tie rod joint from the steering knuckle.
6. Unscrew the nut and pull out the bolt.
7. Remove the wheel speed sensor from the steering knuckle.
8. Pry the cross strut off the steering knuckle.
9. Pry the torque strut off the steering knuckle.
10. Remove the steering knuckle.
11. Installation is the reverse order of removal. Tighten the self-locking nut to 37 ft. lbs. (50 Nm) plus 60°.

2012 SLK-Class Models

1. Raise and safely support the vehicle.
2. Remove the front wheel.
3. Remove the front wheel hub. For additional information, refer to the following section, "Wheel Hubs & Bearings, Removal & Installation."
4. Remove the caliper dust shield.
5. Remove the strut from the steering knuckle.
6. Disconnect the wheel speed sensor from the steering knuckle.
7. Disconnect the tie rod from the steering knuckle.
8. Remove the torque strut from the steering knuckle.
9. Remove the steering knuckle.
10. Installation is the reverse order of

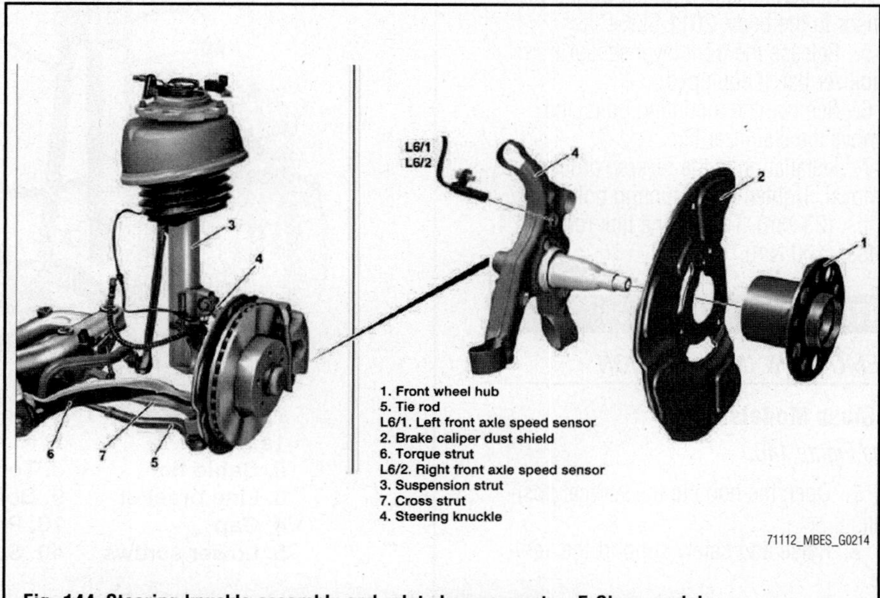

Fig. 144 Steering knuckle assembly and related components—E-Class models

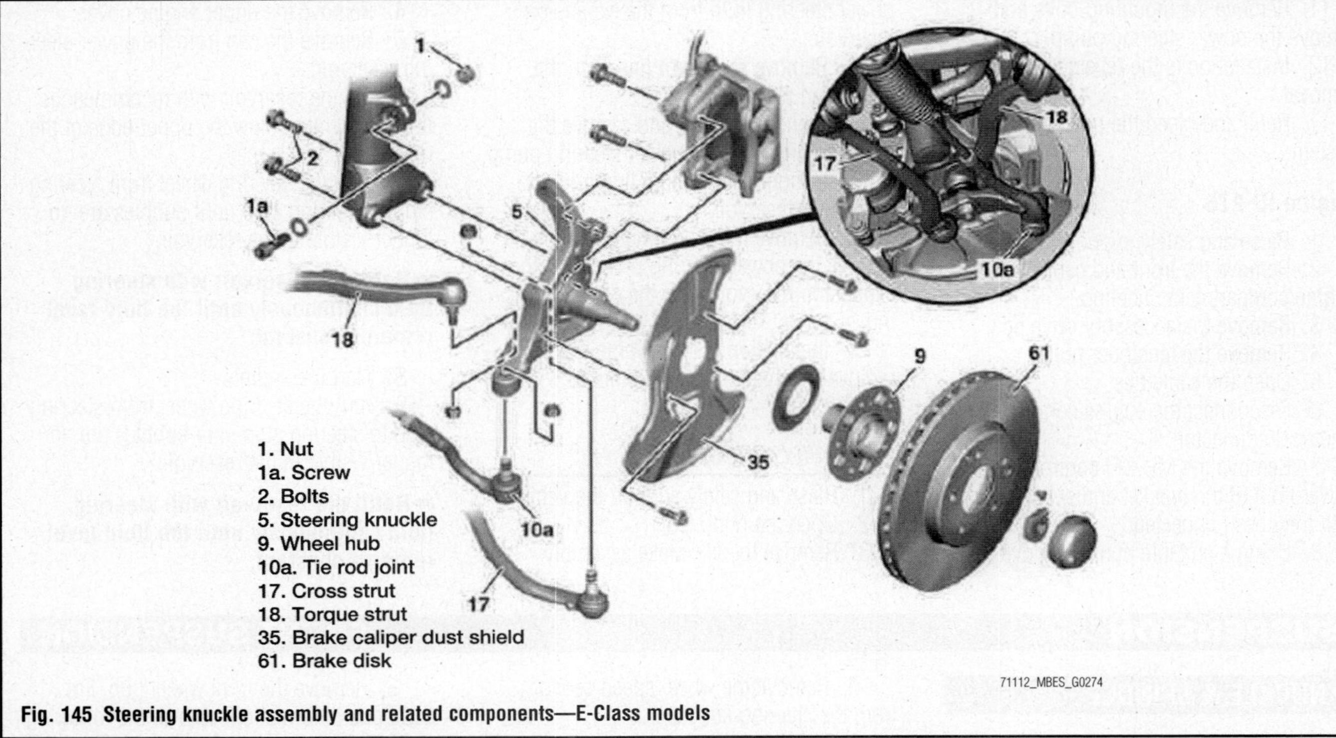

Fig. 145 Steering knuckle assembly and related components—E-Class models

removal. Tighten the self-locking nut to 37 ft. lbs. (50 Nm) plus 60°.

STABILIZER BAR & LINKS

REMOVAL & INSTALLATION

SLK-Class Models

1. Lower the front axle assembly.
2. Remove the front wheels.
3. Detach the link rods from the stabilizer bar.
4. Detach linkage from left front level sensor to the body, 2011 SLK-Class.
5. Release the front level sensor from stabilizer bar, if equipped.
6. Remove the mounting bolts and remove the stabilizer bar.
7. Installation is the reverse order of removal. Tighten the mounting bolts to 17 ft. lbs. (23 Nm). Tighten the link rods to 74 ft. lbs. (100 Nm).

STRUTS

REMOVAL & INSTALLATION

E-Class Models

See Figure 146.

1. Open the hood to the vertical position.
2. Raise and safely support the vehicle.
3. Remove the front wheel.

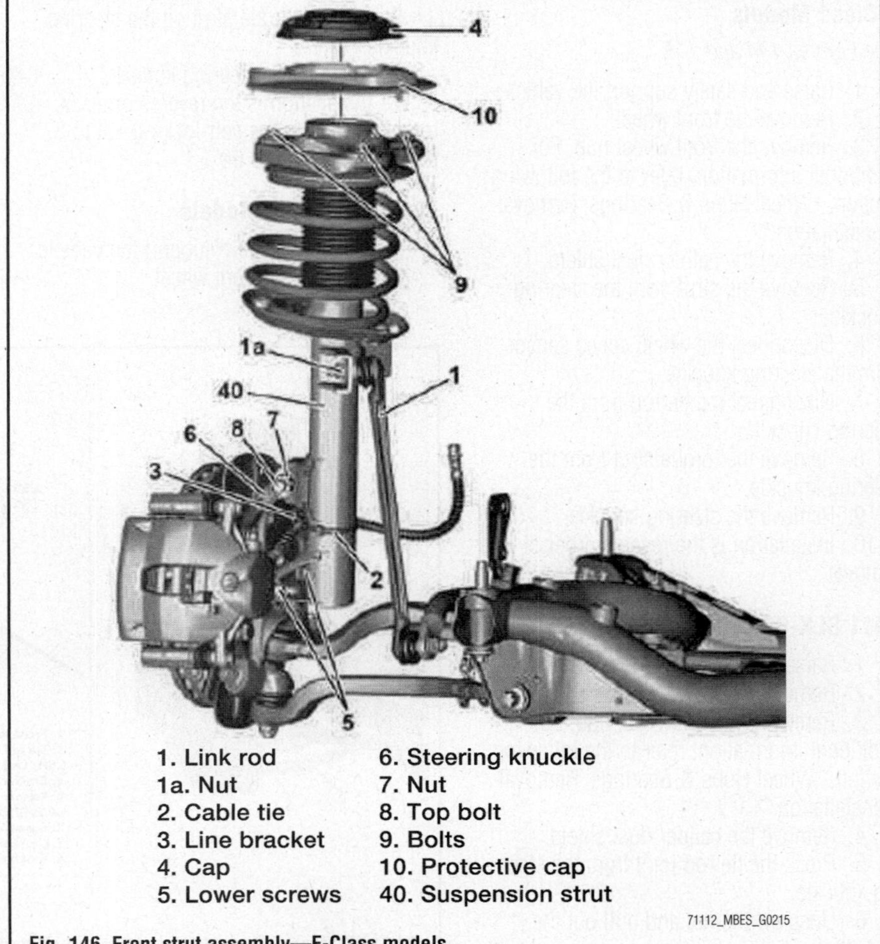

Fig. 146 Front strut assembly—E-Class models

4. Remove the mounting nut and press the link stabilizer link rod out of the suspension strut.

5. Unclip the electrical line from the line bracket.

6. Remove the cable tie from the suspension strut.

7. Unclip the line holder from the suspension strut and move aside.

8. Remove the lower mounting bolts from the steering knuckle.

9. Secure the steering knuckle to prevent it from tilting away.

10. Remove the mounting nut and pull out the upper mounting bolt.

11. Remove the lower bolts from the steering knuckle.

12. Remove the cap and remove the bolts from the suspension strut tower.

13. Remove the suspension strut.

14. Installation is the reverse order of removal.

15. Tighten the mounting bolts as follows:

- Upper steering knuckle bolts: 74 ft. lbs. (100 Nm) plus 90°
- Lower steering knuckle bolts: 52 ft. lbs. (70 Nm), release all tension then tighten to 74 ft. lbs. (100 Nm)
- Strut tower bolts: 24 ft. lbs. (33 Nm)

2011 SLK-Class Models

1. Open the hood to the vertical position.

2. Raise and safely support the vehicle.

3. Remove the front wheel.

4. Remove cable ties by pushing the bracket along the brake hose as far as possible upwards and fasten.

5. Detach the stabilizer bar links from the strut assembly.

6. Unscrew the nut of the suspension strut on the top of the upright and pull out the bolt.

7. Detach the suspension strut from the bottom of the upright.

8. Unscrew the nuts on the suspension strut support.

9. Remove the strut assembly.

10. Installation is the reverse order of removal.

11. Tighten the mounting bolts as follows:

- Upper steering knuckle bolts: 74 ft. lbs. (100 Nm) plus 90°
- Lower steering knuckle bolts: 81 ft. lbs. (110 Nm).
- Strut tower bolts: 26 ft. lbs. (35 Nm)

2012 SLK-Class Models

1. Open the hood to the vertical position.

2. Raise and safely support the vehicle.

3. Remove the front wheel.

4. Remove the mounting nut and press the link stabilizer link rod out of the suspension strut.

5. Unclip the electrical line from the line bracket.

6. Remove the cable tie from the suspension strut.

7. Unclip the line holder from the suspension strut and move aside.

8. Remove the lower mounting bolts from the steering knuckle.

9. Remove the mounting nut and pull out the upper mounting bolt.

10. Press the suspension strut out of the steering knuckle.

11. Remove the mounting bolts from the top of the strut tower.

12. Press the retaining clamps of the cap together and remove the suspension strut from the vehicle.

13. Installation is the reverse order of removal.

14. Tighten the mounting bolts as follows:

- Upper steering knuckle bolts: 74 ft. lbs. (100 Nm) plus 90°
- Lower steering knuckle bolts: 52 ft. lbs. (70 Nm), release all tension then tighten to 74 ft. lbs. (100 Nm)
- Strut tower bolts: 24 ft. lbs. (33 Nm)

OVERHAUL

1. Remove the strut from the vehicle.

2. Clamp the tensioning device securely in a vise, and insert clamping plates and place tension on the front spring.

3. Remove the nut from the piston rod.

4. Remove the shock absorber from the tensioning device.

5. Remove the dust boot, stop buffer, cap and rubber insert.

6. Release the tension from the front spring.

7. Remove the front spring.

8. Remove the spring cup from the front spring.

9. Installation is the reverse order of removal. Tighten the piston rod nut to 74 ft. lbs. (100 Nm).

WHEEL HUBS & BEARINGS

ADJUSTMENT

1. Raise and safely support the vehicle.

2. Remove the front wheel.

3. Insert a wheel bolt opposite the safety screw far enough to fix the brake disc into place.

4. Press the brake pads back into the brake caliper.

5. Pull off the hub cap.

6. Loosen hexagon socket head screw and tighten the clamp nut while turning the front wheel hub lightly to set up the wheel bearing.

7. Loosen the clamping nut slightly until a small amount of play is noticeable.

8. Mount the dial indicator holder to the brake rotor.

9. Adjust the wheel bearing play by turning the clamping nut in stages and pushing and pulling the rotor firmly back and forth.

10. Tighten the socket head screw and check the wheel bearing play again. If the wheel bearing play is within 0.0004–0.0008 inches (0.01–0.02 mm), remove the dial gauge and stand.

11. Fill the hub cap with a high temperature bearing grease.

12. The remainder of the installation is the reverse order of removal.

REMOVAL & INSTALLATION

See Figures 147 and 148.

1. Raise and safely support the vehicle.

2. Remove the brake rotor.

3. Pull off the hub cap.

4. Loosen the socket head screw and remove the clamping nut.

5. Remove the outer tapered roller bearing.

6. Remove the front wheel hub from the steering knuckle.

7. Installation is the reverse order of removal.

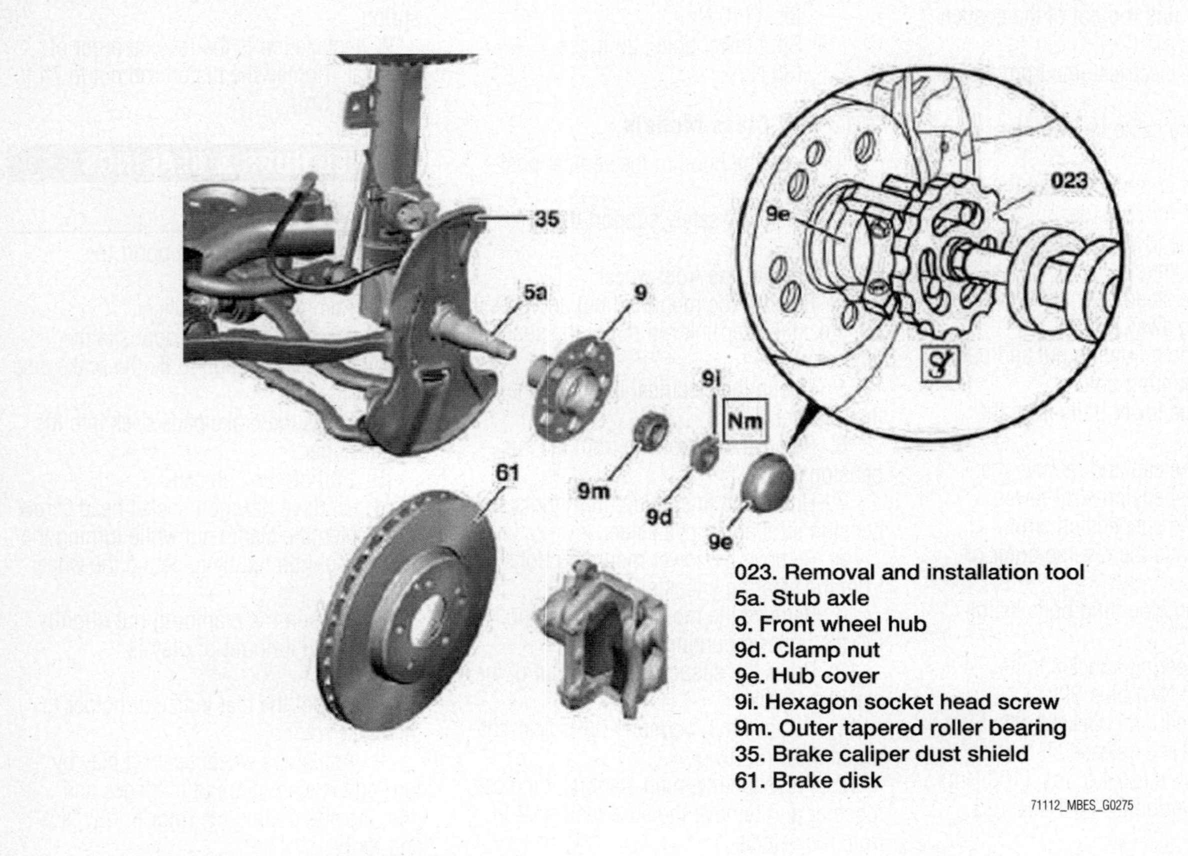

Fig. 147 Wheel hub assembly and related components—2011 SLK-Class models

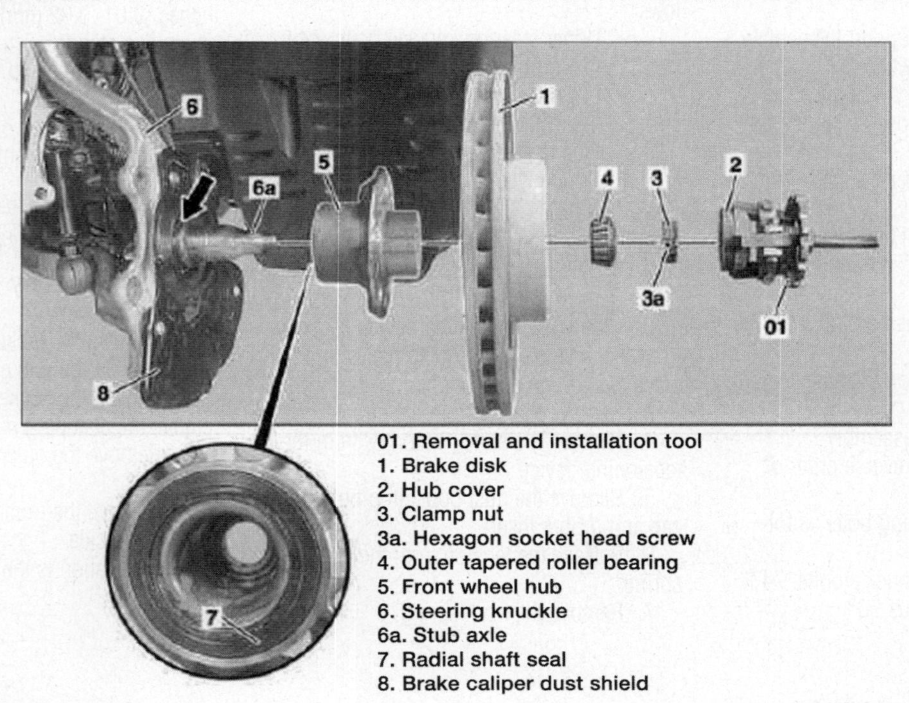

Fig. 148 Wheel hub assembly and related components—E-Class models

COIL SPRINGS

REMOVAL & INSTALLATION

SLK-Class Models

See Figure 149.

1. Raise and safely support the vehicle.
2. Remove the covering on the spring control arm.
3. Using a suitable spring compressor, tension the coil spring.
4. Unscrew the nut, pull out the bolt and detach the spring control arm from the rear axle arrier.
5. Remove the rear spring.
6. Installation is the reverse order of removal. Tighten the self-locking nut to 37 ft. lbs. (50 Nm) plus 45°.

RADIUS ROD

REMOVAL & INSTALLATION

E-Class Models

1. Raise and safely support the vehicle.
2. Completely empty the air springs using the STAR Diagnosis tool, if equipped.
3. Remove the rear wheels.
4. Release left and right underfloor paneling (1) in area of threaded axle connection
5. Remove the left and rear diagonal strut, wagon model only.
6. Loosen the left heat shield.
7. Remove the exhaust tips, engine ID 273 only.
8. Unhook exhaust system from rubber exhaust bushings on differential and detach rubber exhaust mounts.
9. Secure exhaust system at rear muffler (6)
10. Unhook rear muffler (6) from rubber exhaust bushings
11. Undo the threaded connections of driveshaft center support bearing to the frame floor assembly by 3 or 4 turns.
12. Disconnect the driveshaft from the differential.
13. Support rear axle carrier (4) at differential using transmission jack and transmission plate and lash down securely.
14. Unclip electrical lines of left rear axle rpm sensor (L6/3) and right rear axle rpm sensor (L6/4) from brackets (8) on wheel carriers.
15. Unclip the electrical lines of the wear sensors from the brackets.
16. Unclip rubber mount (12) of rear brake cable from bracket.
17. Remove bolts (2s, 3s) and remove stop plates.
18. Lower the rear axle carrier.
19. Remove the radius rod from the rear axle carrier.
20. Installation is the reverse order of removal. Tighten bolts as follows:
    - M12 bolts: 37 ft. lbs. (50 Nm) plus 90°
    - M14 bolts: 59 ft. lbs. (80 Nm) plus 90°

SHOCK ABSORBERS

REMOVAL & INSTALLATION

E-Class Models

1. Raise and safely support the vehicle.
2. Remove the rear wheel.
3. Remove the inner fender from the rear fender.
4. Remove the cover on the spring control arm.
5. Remove lower mounting nut from the shock absorber and remove the mounting bolt.
6. Remove the side paneling in the trunk.
7. Remove the upper mounting nut and remove the shock by compressing the damper and moving it out backwards over the brake hose.
8. Installation is the reverse order of removal.

SLK-Class Models

See Figure 150.

1. Raise and safely support the vehicle.
2. Cut hole in left or right side luggage compartment lining.
3. Detach the upper shock absorber mounting.
4. Remove the rear wheel.
5. Remove the control arm shield.
6. Detach the shock absorber from the control arm.
7. Installation is the reverse order of removal. Tighten the self-locking nut to 30 ft. lbs. (40 Nm) plus 90°.

STABILIZER BAR & LINKS

REMOVAL & INSTALLATION

SLK-Class Models

See Figure 151.

1. Lower the rear axle assembly.
2. Remove the rear springs.
3. Detach the stabilizer bar links form the stabilizer bar.
4. Unscrew the nuts and remove the stabilizer bar from the frame floor assembly.
5. Installation is the reverse order of removal. Tighten the self-locking nut to 17 ft. lbs. (23 Nm).

THRUST ARM

REMOVAL & INSTALLATION

SLK-Class Models

1. Raise and safely support the vehicle.
2. Remove the wheel.

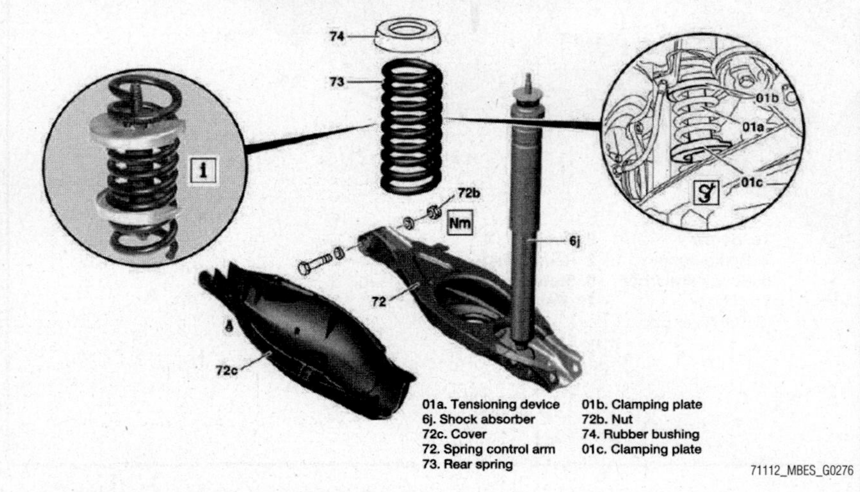

01a. Tensioning device
6j. Shock absorber
72c. Cover
72. Spring control arm
73. Rear spring
01b. Clamping plate
72b. Nut
74. Rubber bushing
01c. Clamping plate

71112_MBES_G0276

Fig. 149 Rear spring assembly—SLK-Class models

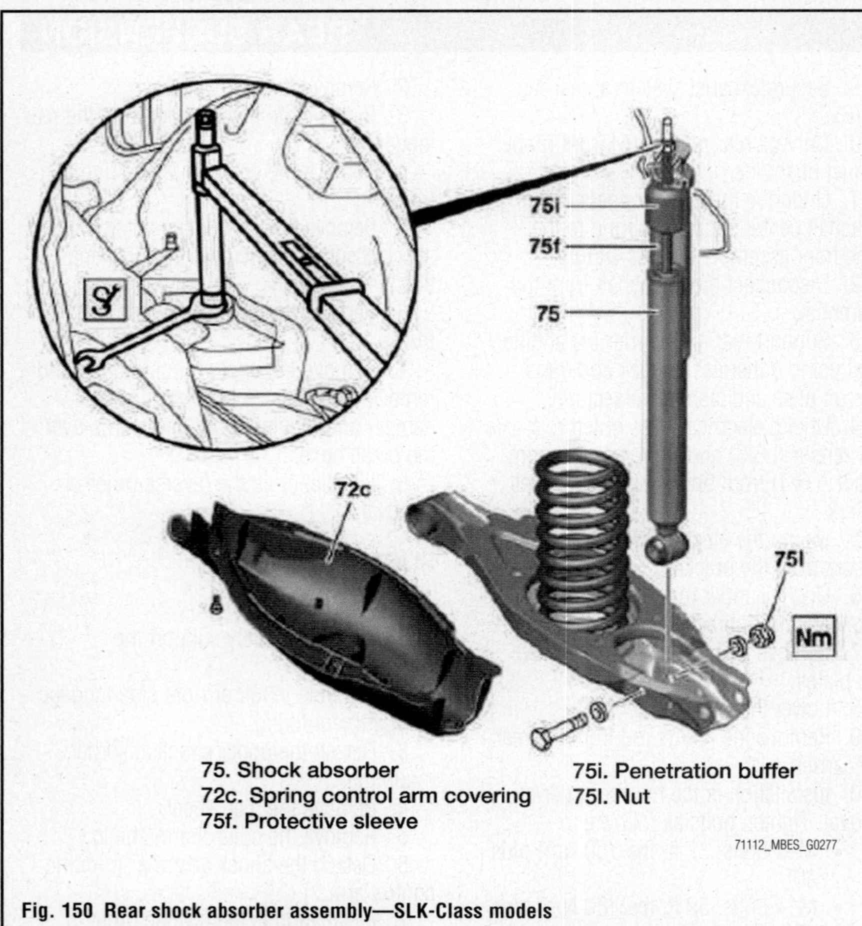

Fig. 150 Rear shock absorber assembly—SLK-Class models

3. Disconnect the thrust arm from the wheel carrier.
4. Disconnect the thrust arm from the rear axle carrier.
5. Installation is the reverse order of removal. Tighten the new self-locking nuts to 37 ft. lbs. (50 Nm) plus 45°.

TRACK ROD

REMOVAL & INSTALLATION

2012 SLK-Class Models

1. Raise and safely support the vehicle.
2. Remove the wheel.
3. Unclip the lever of the rear level sensor, if equipped.
4. Detach the tie rod from the wheel carrier.
5. Matchmark the eccentric disk of the tie rod relative to the rear axle carrier.
6. Detach the tie rod from the rear axle carrier.
7. Installation is the reverse order of removal. Tighten the track bolts as follows:
   - Self-locking nut, tie rod at wheel carrier: 22 ft. lbs. (30 Nm) plus 90°.
   - Self-locking nut, track rod to rear axle carrier: 52 ft. lbs. (70 Nm).

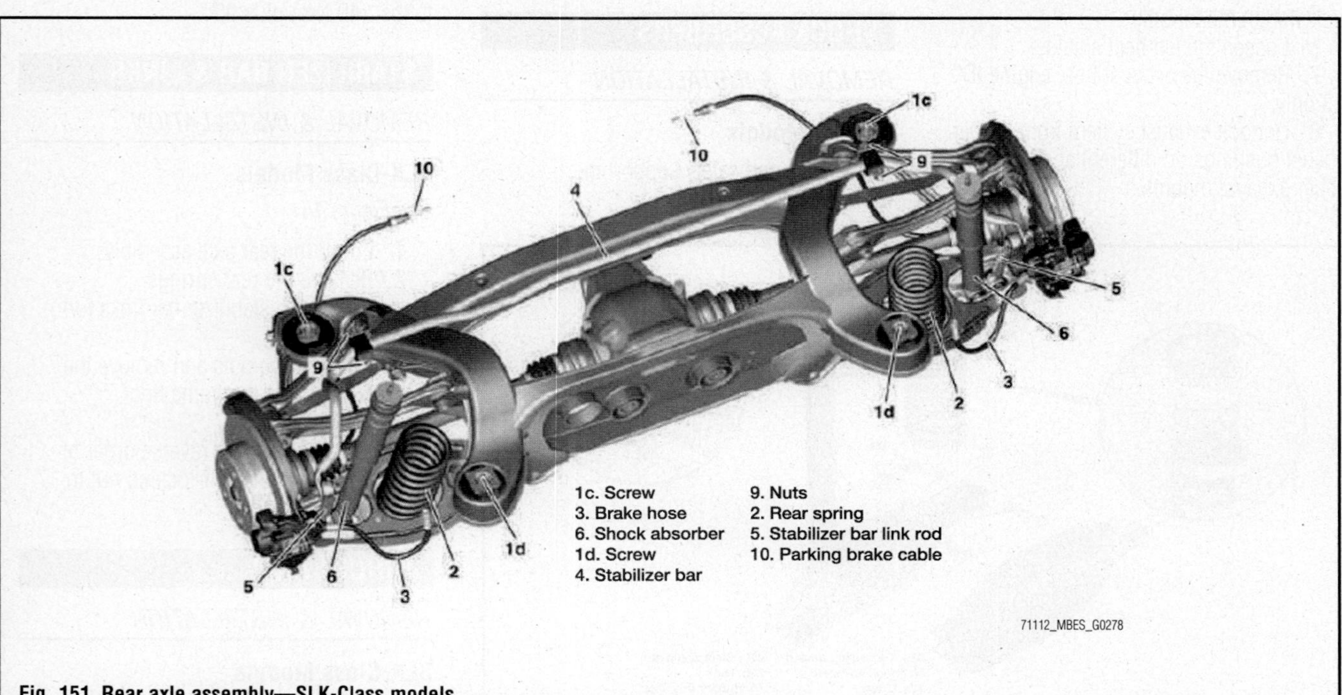

Fig. 151 Rear axle assembly—SLK-Class models

MERCEDES BENZ

8

ML450 Hybrid

SPECIFICATIONS AND MAINTENANCE CHARTS

ENGINE AND VEHICLE IDENTIFICATION CHART

Engine							Model Year	
Code ①	Liters (cc)	Cu. In.	Cyl.	Fuel Sys.	Type	Eng. Mfg.	Code ②	Year
M272.973	3.5 (3498)	213	V6	ME9.7 MFI	DOHC	MB	B	2011

MFI: Multiport Fuel Injection

DOHC: Double overhead camshafts

① Stamped on engine block

② 11th digit of the VIN

71112_ML45_C0001

GENERAL ENGINE SPECIFICATIONS

Year	Engine Displacement Liters	Engine ID/VIN	Net Horsepower @ rpm	Net Torque@rpm (ft. lbs.)	Bore x Stroke (in.)	Com-pression Ratio	Oil Pressure @ rpm
2011	3.5	M272.973	268@6000	258@2400	3.54x3.31	10.7:1	NS

NS - Not Specified

71112_ML45_C0002

GASOLINE ENGINE TUNE-UP SPECIFICATIONS

Year	Engine Displacement Liters	Engine ID/VIN	Spark Plug Gap (in.)	Ignition Timing (deg.)		Fuel Pump (psi)	Idle Speed (rpm)		Valve Clearance	
				MT	AT		MT	AT	In.	Ex.
2011	3.5	M272.973	①	NA	②	NS	NA	②	HYD.	HYD.

NA: Not Applicable

NS: Not Specified

HYD: Hydraulic

① Spark plugs using Iridium or other precious metals should not be gapped.
Other park plugs should be gapped at 0.031 in.

② Ignition timing and idle speed are controlled by the ME engine controller and not adjustable.

71112_ML45_C0003

CAPACITIES

Year	Model	Engine Displacement Liters	Engine ID/VIN	Engine Oil with Filter (qts.)	Transmission (pts.) Man.	Transmission (pts.) Auto.	Drive Axle Front (pts.)	Drive Axle Rear (pts.)	Fuel Tank (gal.)	Cooling System (qts.)
2011	ML450 Hybrid	3.5	M272.973	8.5	NA	19.2	2.4	2.4	25.1	6.89

NOTE: All capacities are approximate. Add fluid gradually and check to be sure a proper fluid level is obtained.

NA - Not Applicable

71112_ML45_C0004

FLUID SPECIFICATIONS

Year	Model	Engine Displacement Liters	Engine ID/VIN	Engine Oil	Auto. Trans.	Drive Axle Front	Drive Axle Rear	Power Steering Fluid	Brake Master Cylinder	Cooling System
2011	ML450 Hybrid	3.5	M272.973	5W-40	①	85W-90	85W-90	ATF	DOT-4	LLC

DOT: Department Of Transpotation

LLC: Long Life Coolant

① Dexron® VI

71112_ML45_C0005

CRANKSHAFT AND CONNECTING ROD SPECIFICATIONS

All measurements are given in inches.

Year	Engine Displacement Liters	Engine ID/VIN	Main Brg. Oil Clearance	Shaft End-play	Thrust on No.	Connecting Rod Journal Diameter	Connecting Rod Oil Clearance	Connecting Rod Side Clearance
2011	3.5	M272.973	0.0008-0.0018	0.0039-0.0104	3	NS	0.0008-0.0018	NS

NS - Not Specified

71112_ML45_C0006

PISTON AND RING SPECIFICATIONS

All measurements are given in inches.

Year	Engine Disp. Liters	Engine ID/VIN	Piston Clearance	Ring Gap Top Compression	Ring Gap Bottom Compression	Ring Gap Oil Control	Ring Side Clearance Top Compression	Ring Side Clearance Bottom Compression	Ring Side Clearance Oil Control
2011	3.5	M272.973	0.0001-0.0020	0.0078-0.0136	0.0117-0.0195	0.0078-0.0351	0.0008-0.0027	0.0006-0.0019	NA

NA: Not Available

71112_ML45_C0007

TORQUE SPECIFICATIONS

All readings in ft. lbs.

Year	Engine Displacement Liters	Engine ID/VIN	Cylinder Head Bolts	Main Bearing Bolts	Rod Bearing Bolts	Crank Damper Bolts	Flywheel Bolts	Manifold Intake	Manifold Exhaust	Spark Plugs
2011	3.5	M272.973	①	②	③	④	⑤	7	12	17

NA - Not Applicable

① M8 Cylinder head to timing case
Step 1: 11 ft. lbs.
Step 2: plus 90 degrees
M11 Cylinder head to crankcase
Step 1: 15 ft. lbs.
Step 2: 30 ft. lbs.
Step 3: plus 90 degrees
Step 4: plus 90 degrees

② M8 Side crankshaft bearing cap
Step 1: 22 ft. lbs.
M8 Crankshaft bearing cap
Step 1: 15 ft. lbs.
Step 2: plus 90 degrees
M10 Cranksahft bearing cap
Step 1: 4 ft. lbs.
Step 2: 22 ft. lbs.
Step 3: plus 90 degrees

③ Step 1: 4 ft. lbs.
Step 2: 15 ft. lbs.
Step 3: plus 90 degrees

④ Step 1: 148 ft. lbs.
Step 2: 95 degrees

⑤ Step 1: 33 ft. lbs.
Step 2: 90 degrees

71112_ML45_C0008

TIRE, WHEEL AND BALL JOINT SPECIFICATIONS

Year	Model	OEM Tires Standard	OEM Tires Optional	Tire Pressures (psi) Front	Tire Pressures (psi) Rear	Wheel Size	Lug Nut (ft. lbs.)
2011	ML450 Hybrid	P235/65R-17	NA	①	①	8.0J	111

NA: Not Applicable

NS: Not Specified

① Refer to pressure on door sticker.

71112_ML45_C0009

BRAKE SPECIFICATIONS

All measurements in inches unless noted

Year	Model	Front Brake Disc Original Thickness	Front Brake Disc Minimum Thickness	Rear Brake Disc Original Thickness	Rear Brake Disc Minimum Thickness	Minimum Lining Thickness Front	Minimum Lining Thickness Rear	Brake Caliper Bracket Bolts (ft. lbs.)	Brake Caliper Mounting Bolts (ft. lbs.)
2011	ML450 Hybrid	1.248	1.326	0.858	0.780	0.226	0.195	NA	①

NA: Not applicable

① Front Caliper to knuckle: 59 ft. lbs. plus an additional 45 deg. rotation
Front Guide Pin: 41 ft. lbs.
Rear Caliper to knuckle: 44 ft. lbs. plus an additional 45 deg. rotation
Rear Guide Pin: 19 ft. lbs.

71112_ML45_C0010

SCHEDULED MAINTENANCE INTERVALS

MERCEDES ML450 Hybrid

Mercedes-Benz vehicles follow a maintenance schedule as programmed into the vehicle called the ASSYST/ASSYST PLUS system. Calculation of oil changes is determined by the ASSYST system and the remainder of maintenance services are determined by the ASSYST PLUS system. Mileage based maintenance intervals are not used. The only exceptions are brake fluid 2-years and coolant 15-years or 15,500 miles.

71112_ML45_C0011

PRECAUTIONS

Before servicing any vehicle, please be sure to read all of the following precautions, which deal with personal safety, prevention of component damage, and important points to take into consideration when servicing a motor vehicle:

- Never open, service or drain the radiator or cooling system when the engine is hot; serious burns can occur from the steam and hot coolant.
- Observe all applicable safety precautions when working around fuel. Whenever servicing the fuel system, always work in a well-ventilated area. Do not allow fuel spray or vapors to come in contact with a spark, open flame, or excessive heat (a hot drop light, for example). Keep a dry chemical fire extinguisher near the work area. Always keep fuel in a container specifically designed for fuel storage; also, always properly seal fuel containers to avoid the possibility of fire or explosion. Refer to the additional fuel system precautions later in this section.
- Fuel injection systems often remain pressurized, even after the engine has been turned **OFF**. The fuel system pressure must be relieved before disconnecting any fuel lines. Failure to do so may result in fire and/or personal injury.
- Brake fluid often contains polyglycol ethers and polyglycols. Avoid contact with the eyes and wash your hands thoroughly after handling brake fluid. If you do get brake fluid in your eyes, flush your eyes with clean, running water for 15 minutes. If eye irritation persists, or if you have taken brake fluid internally, IMMEDIATELY seek medical assistance.
- The EPA warns that prolonged contact with used engine oil may cause a number of skin disorders, including cancer. You should make every effort to minimize your exposure to used engine oil. Protective gloves should be worn when changing oil. Wash your hands and any other exposed skin areas as soon as possible after exposure to used engine oil. Soap and water, or waterless hand cleaner should be used.
- All new vehicles are now equipped with an air bag system, often referred to as a Supplemental Restraint System (SRS) or Supplemental Inflatable Restraint (SIR) system. The system must be disabled before performing service on or around system components, steering column, instrument panel components, wiring and sensors. Failure to follow safety and disabling procedures could result in accidental air bag deployment, possible personal injury and unnecessary system repairs.
- Always wear safety goggles when working with, or around, the air bag system. When carrying a non-deployed air bag, be sure the bag and trim cover are pointed away from your body. When placing a non-deployed air bag on a work surface, always face the bag and trim cover upward, away from the surface. This will reduce the motion of the module if it is accidentally deployed. Refer to the additional air bag system precautions later in this section.
- Clean, high quality brake fluid from a sealed container is essential to the safe and proper operation of the brake system. You should always buy the correct type of brake fluid for your vehicle. If the brake fluid becomes contaminated, completely flush the system with new fluid. Never reuse any brake fluid. Any brake fluid that is removed from the system should be discarded. Also, do not allow any brake fluid to come in contact with a painted surface; it will damage the paint.
- Never operate the engine without the proper amount and type of engine oil; doing so WILL result in severe engine damage.
- Timing belt maintenance is extremely important. Many models utilize an interference-type, non-freewheeling engine. If the timing belt breaks, the valves in the cylinder head may strike the pistons, causing potentially serious (also time-consuming and expensive) engine damage. Refer to the maintenance interval charts for the recommended replacement interval for the timing belt, and to the timing belt section for belt replacement and inspection.
- Disconnecting the negative battery cable on some vehicles may interfere with the functions of the on-board computer system(s) and may require the computer to undergo a relearning process once the negative battery cable is reconnected.
- When servicing drum brakes, only disassemble and assemble one side at a time, leaving the remaining side intact for reference.
- Only an MVAC-trained, EPA-certified automotive technician should service the air conditioning system or its components.

BRAKES — ANTI-LOCK BRAKE SYSTEM (ABS)

GENERAL INFORMATION

PRECAUTIONS

- Certain components within the ABS system are not intended to be serviced or repaired individually.
- Do not use rubber hoses or other parts not specifically specified for and ABS system. When using repair kits, replace all parts included in the kit. Partial or incorrect repair may lead to functional problems and require the replacement of components.
- Lubricate rubber parts with clean, fresh brake fluid to ease assembly. Do not use shop air to clean parts; damage to rubber components may result.
- Use only DOT 3 brake fluid from an unopened container.
- If any hydraulic component or line is removed or replaced, it may be necessary to bleed the entire system.
- A clean repair area is essential. Always clean the reservoir and cap thoroughly before removing the cap. The slightest amount of dirt in the fluid may plug an orifice and impair the system function. Perform repairs after components have been thoroughly cleaned; use only denatured alcohol to clean components. Do not allow ABS components to come into contact with any substance containing mineral oil; this includes used shop rags.
- The Anti-Lock control unit is a microprocessor similar to other computer units in the vehicle. Ensure that the ignition switch is **OFF** before removing or installing controller harnesses. Avoid static electricity discharge at or near the controller.
- If any arc welding is to be done on the vehicle, the control unit should be unplugged before welding operations begin.

WHEEL SPEED SENSORS

REMOVAL & INSTALLATION

Front

See Figure 1.

1. Before servicing the vehicle, refer to the precautions.
2. Turn steering wheel to side being serviced.
3. Turn ignition switch **OFF**.
4. Raise vehicle.

5. Remove inner fender liner.
6. Remove bolt and sensor from knuckle.
7. Disconnect sensor harness at body socket.
8. Remove harness from bracket and sensor from vehicle.

To install:

9. Feed sensor harness through bracket.
10. Connect sensor harness at body socket.
11. Install sensor and bolt at knuckle. Tighten to 6 foot lbs. (8 Nm).
12. Install inner fender liner.
13. Lower vehicle.

Rear

See Figure 1.

1. Before servicing the vehicle, refer to the precautions.
2. Turn ignition switch **OFF**.
3. Raise vehicle. Remove rear wheel.
4. Remove bolt and sensor from wheel carrier.
5. Remove harness from bracket.
6. Disconnect sensor harness at body socket and remove sensor from vehicle.

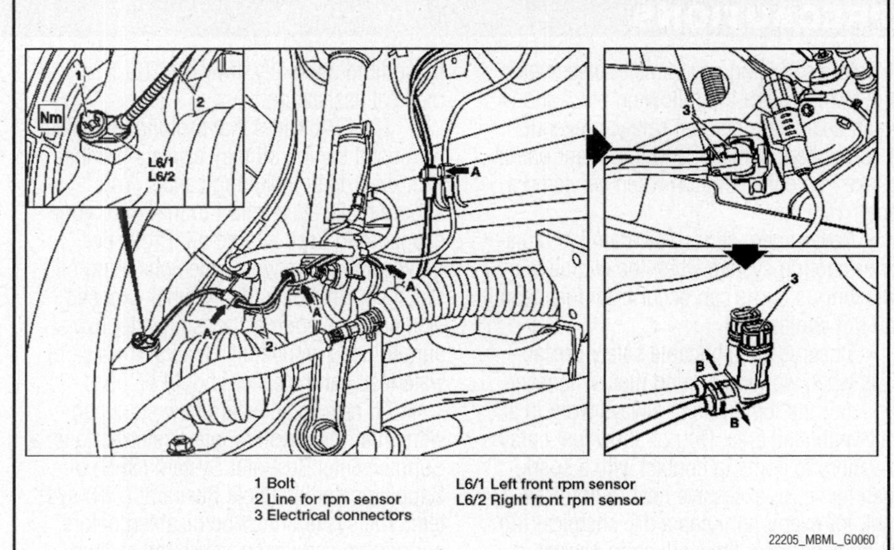

Fig. 1 Wheel speed sensor

To install:

7. Feed sensor harness through bracket.
8. Connect sensor harness at body socket.
9. Install sensor and bolt at knuckle. Tighten to 6 foot lbs. (8 Nm).
10. Install wheel.
11. Lower vehicle.
12. Connect STAR DIAGNOSIS and check fault memory.

BRAKES — BLEEDING THE BRAKE SYSTEM

BLEEDING PROCEDURE

BLEEDING PROCEDURE

See Figure 2.

1. Before servicing the vehicle, refer to the precautions.
2. Attach a pressure bleeding unit and adjust the pressure to 29 PSI (2.0 bar).

Fig. 2 Bleed screw locations

3. Remove dust caps of bleed screws on the brake calipers.

4. Open bleed screw and allow brake fluid to bleed.

➡New brake fluid must flow out free of bubbles.

5. Close bleed screw and pull off bleed hose.

6. Repeat process at the bleed screws.

➡Bleed screw calipers on right rear axle, left rear axle, right front axle and left front axle in that order.

7. On Vehicles with manual transmission, remove cover from bell housing and repeat process at bleed screw of the central clutch release bearing.

8. Attach dust caps of bleed screws.

9. Tighten bleeding screws to 5 ft. lbs. (7 Nm).

10. Refill the fluid level in the master cylinder and check the system for leaks.

BRAKES

FRONT DISC BRAKES

BRAKE CALIPER

REMOVAL & INSTALLATION

See Figure 3.

CAUTION

Dust and dirt accumulating on brake parts during normal use may contain asbestos fibers from production or aftermarket brake linings. Breathing excessive concentrations of asbestos fibers can cause serious bodily harm. Exercise care when servicing brake parts. Do not sand or grind brake lining unless equipment used is designed to contain the dust residue. Do not clean brake parts with compressed air or by dry brushing. Cleaning should be done by dampening the brake components with a fine mist of water, then wiping the brake components clean with a dampened cloth. Dispose of cloth and all residue containing asbestos fibers in an impermeable container with the appropriate label. Follow practices prescribed by the Occupational Safety and Health Administration (OSHA) and the Environmental Protection Agency (EPA) for the handling, processing, and disposing of dust or debris that may contain asbestos fibers.

1. Before servicing the vehicle, refer to the precautions.
2. Remove wheels, rotate if necessary.
3. Remove brake pads from floating brake caliper.
4. Detach brake hose from floating brake caliper.
5. Seal brake hose immediately with stop plugs. The brake fluid expansion reservoir must not run empty otherwise air gets into the brake system
6. Detach electrical feed line of front brake pad contact sensor from floating brake caliper.
7. Remove floating brake caliper.
8. Unscrew bolts and remove floating caliper carrier(s).

To install:

9. Install in the reverse order.
10. Replace bolts.
11. Tighten bolts/nuts to specification as follows:
    - Brake line to floating brake caliper: 16 ft. lbs. (22 Nm)
    - Self-locking bolt, caliper support to steering knuckle: 59 ft. lbs. (80 Nm) plus an additional 45° rotation.
12. Fill and bleed the brake system.

DISC BRAKE PADS

REMOVAL AND INSTALLATION

See Figure 4.

1. Before servicing the vehicle, refer to the precautions.
2. Remove wheels, rotate if necessary.
3. Disconnect electrical connector of the brake pad contact sensor.
4. Pry off spring steel sheet and remove.
5. Remove protective caps and unscrew bolts of guide pins.
6. Remove floating brake caliper with brake pads.
7. Remove brake pads from floating brake caliper.
8. Check brake pad thickness and brake disks.
9. Check brake lining thickness.
10. Inspect condition of brake disks.
11. Pull brake pad contact sensor out of the pad backing plate of the brake pad and check.
12. Check guide pins and boots.
13. Check floating brake caliper.
14. Press back brake piston using pusher tool.
15. Check fall of the dust boot.
16. Clean the contact surfaces of brake pads on floating brake caliper and floating caliper carrier with a rag.
17. In the process do not damage the dust boot and boots. Do not use any sharp-edged or pointed tools, otherwise the floating brake caliper or floating caliper carrier will be damaged.

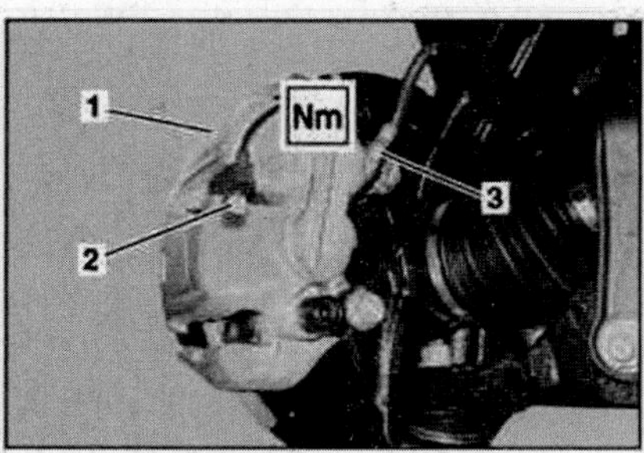

1. Floating caliper
2. Front brake pad contact sensor
3. Brake hose

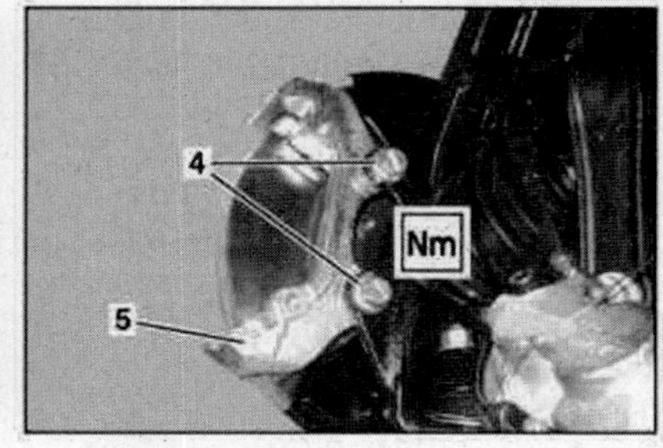

4. Bolts
5. Floating caliper support

37698_MSUV_G0004

Fig. 3 Front brake floating caliper

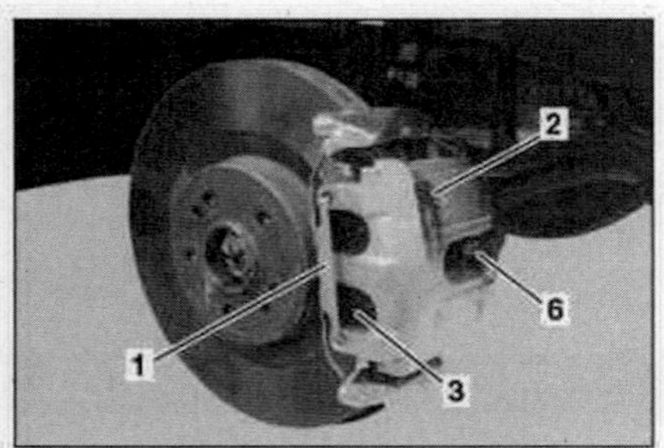

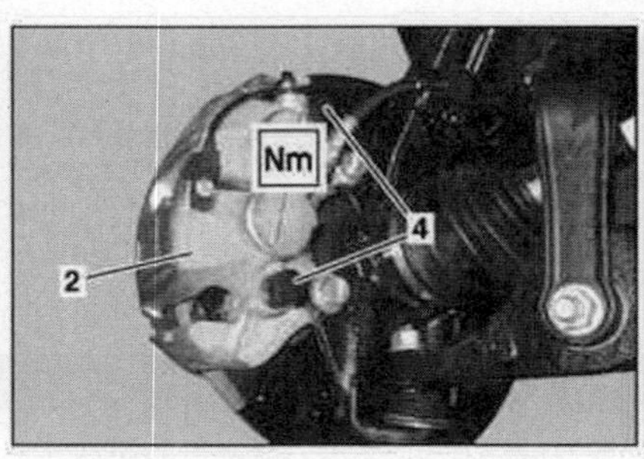

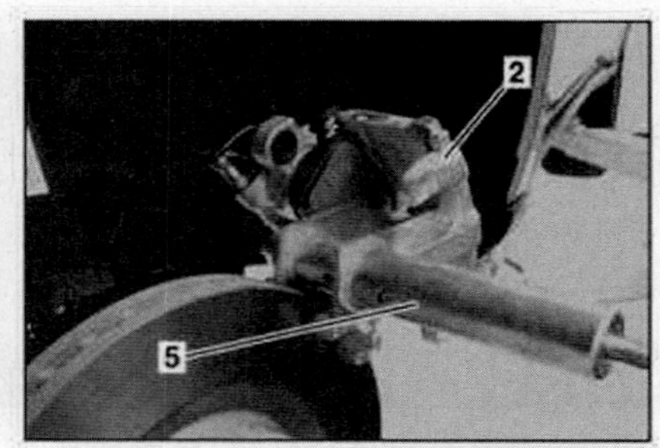

1. Spring steel sheet
2. Floating caliper
3. Brake pad
4. Protective cap
5. Pusher tool

37698_MSUV_G0006

Fig. 4 Floating caliper brake pads

18. Apply brake paste.

To install:

19. Install in the reverse order.
20. Install new bolts.
21. Check the correct routing of the brake hose.
22. Tighten guide pin on caliper support to 19 ft. lbs. (25 Nm).

BRAKES

REAR DISC BRAKES

BRAKE CALIPER

REMOVAL & INSTALLATION

See Figure 5.

⁂ CAUTION

Dust and dirt accumulating on brake parts during normal use may contain asbestos fibers from production or aftermarket brake linings. Breathing excessive concentrations of asbestos fibers can cause serious bodily harm. Exercise care when servicing brake parts. Do not sand or grind brake lining unless equipment used is designed to contain the dust residue. Do not clean brake parts with compressed air or by dry brushing. Cleaning should be done by dampening the brake components with a fine mist of water, then wiping the brake components clean with a dampened cloth. Dispose of cloth and all residue containing asbestos fibers in an impermeable container with the appropriate label. Follow practices prescribed by the Occupational Safety and Health Administration (OSHA) and the Environmental Protection Agency (EPA) for the handling, processing, and disposing of dust or debris that may contain asbestos fibers.

1. Before servicing the vehicle, refer to the precautions.
2. Remove wheels, rotate if necessary.
3. Remove brake pads from floating brake caliper.
4. Detach brake hose from floating brake caliper.
5. Seal brake hose immediately with stop plugs. The brake fluid expansion reservoir must not run empty otherwise air gets into the brake system.
6. Remove floating brake caliper.
7. Unscrew bolts and remove floating caliper carrier.

To install:

8. Install in the reverse order.
9. Tighten bolts/nuts to specification as follows:
   - Brake line to floating brake caliper: 16 ft. lbs. (22 Nm).
   - Self-locking bolt, brake caliper to steering knuckle: 44 ft. lbs. (60 Nm) plus an additional 45° rotation.
10. Replace the bolts.
11. Fill and bleed brake system.

DISC BRAKE PADS

REMOVAL & INSTALLATION

See Figure 6.

1. Before servicing the vehicle, refer to the precautions.
2. Remove wheels, rotate if necessary.

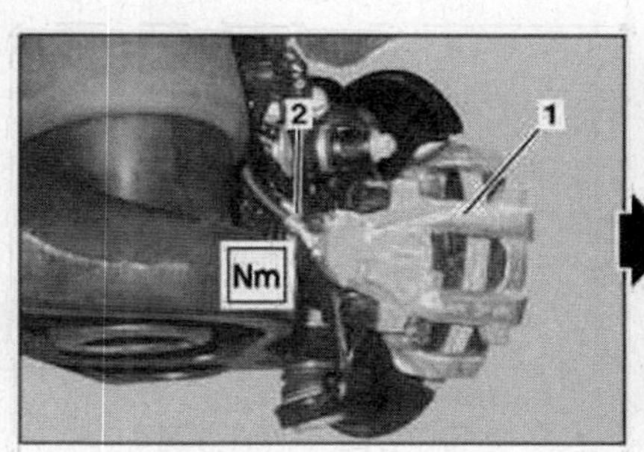

1. Floating caliper
2. Brake hose
3. Bolts
4. Floating caliper support

37698_MSUV_G0007

Fig. 5 Rear axle brake caliper

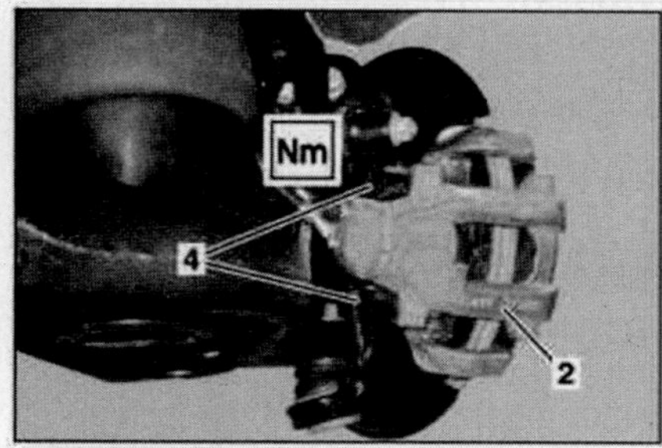

1. Spring steel sheet
2. Floating caliper
3. Brake pad
4. Protective cap
5. Pusher tool

37698_MSUV_G0008

Fig. 6 Floating caliper brake pads

3. Disconnect electrical connector of the brake pad contact sensor.
4. Pry off spring steel sheet and remove.
5. Remove protective caps and unscrew bolts of guide pins.
6. Remove floating brake caliper with brake pads.
7. Remove brake pads from floating brake caliper.
8. Check brake pad thickness and brake disks.
9. Check brake lining thickness.
10. Inspect condition of brake disks.
11. Pull brake pad contact sensor out of the pad backing plate of the brake pad and check.
12. Check guide pins and boots.
13. Check floating brake caliper.
14. Press back brake piston using pusher tool.
15. Check fall of the dust boot.
16. Clean the contact surfaces of brake pads on floating brake caliper and floating caliper carrier with a rag.
17. In the process do not damage the dust boot and boots. Do not use any sharp-edged or pointed tools, otherwise the floating brake caliper or floating caliper carrier will be damaged.
18. Apply brake paste.

To install:

19. Install in the reverse order.
20. Install new bolts.
21. Check the correct routing of the brake hose.
22. Tighten guide pin on caliper support to 19 ft. lbs. (25 Nm).

BRAKES — PARKING BRAKE

PARKING BRAKE CABLES

ADJUSTMENT

See Figure 7.

1. Before servicing the vehicle, refer to the precautions.
2. Remove wheels, rotate if necessary.
3. Remove rubber insert.
4. Bring brake shoes into contact with parking brake drum.
5. Turn the adjusting wheel by means of a screw driver until the brake shoes contact the brake drum and the brake disk cannot be turned by hand anymore.
6. Turn both adjustment wheels from above downwards.
7. Detach adjustment wheel.
8. Loosen left and right adjustment wheel by the same number of teeth. It must be possible to rotate the rear wheel or brake disk completely freely by hand.

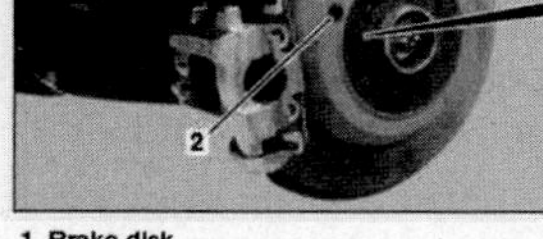

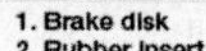

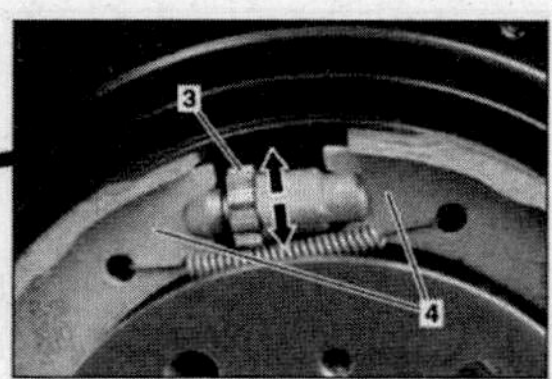

1. Brake disk
2. Rubber insert
3. Thumbwheel
4. Brake shoes

37698_MSUV_G0009

Fig. 7 Adjusting parking brake cable

9. Operate the parking brake lever several times and check the travel of the parking brake lever.
10. Number of notches at which the parking brake must be adjusted if up to that point there is insufficient braking effect is 7.
11. Release parking brake and check unobstructed movement of rear wheels or brake disks.

CHASSIS ELECTRICAL

AIR BAG (SUPPLEMENTAL RESTRAINT SYSTEM)

GENERAL INFORMATION

CAUTION

These vehicles are equipped with an air bag system. The system must be disarmed before performing service on, or around, system components, the steering column, instrument panel components, wiring and sensors. Failure to follow the safety precautions and the disarming procedure could result in accidental air bag deployment, possible injury and unnecessary system repairs.

SERVICE PRECAUTIONS

CAUTION

Disconnect and isolate the battery negative cable before beginning any airbag system component diagnosis, testing, removal, or installation procedures. Wait at least 90 seconds after the ignition switch is turned off and the negative (-) terminal cable is disconnected from the battery before starting the operation. The SRS is equipped with a backup power source, so if work is started within 90 seconds after disconnecting the negative (-) terminal cable from the battery, the SRS may be deployed. Failure to disable the airbag system may result in accidental airbag deployment, personal injury, or death.

DISARMING THE SYSTEM

CAUTION

Mercedes-Benz vehicles are equipped with an air bag system. The system must be disabled before performing service on or around system components, steering column, instrument panel components, wiring and sensors. Failure to follow safety and disabling procedures could result in accidental air bag deployment, possible personal injury and unnecessary system repairs.

To avoid personal injury when working on vehicles equipped with an air bag, the negative battery cable must be disconnected and insulated before working on the system. Failure to do so may result in accidental deployment of the air bag.

ARMING THE SYSTEM

To rearm the air bag system, reattach the battery cable(s).

CLOCKSPRING CENTERING

See Figure 8.

1. Before servicing the vehicle, refer to the precautions.

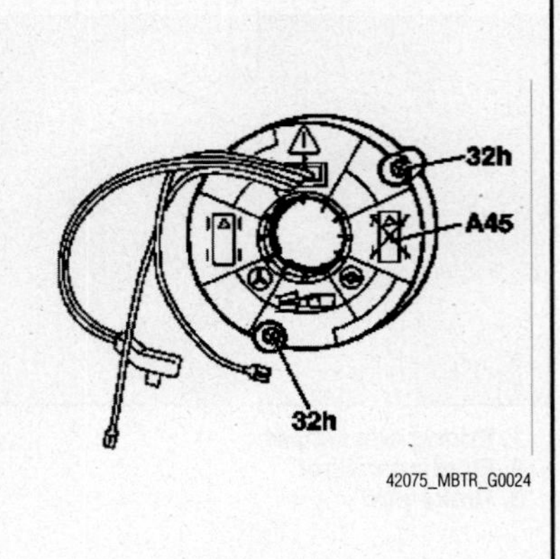

Fig. 8 Clockspring securing screws (32h) and contact (A45)

2. Tighten the mounting screws completely into the horn and airbag clockspring contact.
3. Rotate the clockspring contact counterclockwise until a slight resistance is noticeable (clockspring contact is rolled up completely).
4. Rotate the clockspring contact approximately 3–3.5 revolutions clockwise, until the mounting screws can be unscrewed again through the openings and fix the clockspring contact in position.

➡The entire rotation range of the clockspring contact is approximately 6 to 7 revolutions.

DRIVE TRAIN

TRANSFER CASE ASSEMBLY

REMOVAL & INSTALLATION

See Figure 9.

1. Before servicing the vehicle, refer to the precautions.
2. Raise and safely support vehicle.
3. Remove bottom part of rear soundproofing.
4. Disconnect exhaust system to flange connection between catalytic converter and center muffler.
5. Separate exhaust system at hose clamp between diesel particulate filter and pipeline.
6. Separate exhaust system at hose clamp and at flange connection between diesel particulate filter and pipeline.
7. Detach heat shield from transfer case.
8. Detach transfer case actuator motor connector, detach transfer case absolute sensor connector and transfer case switchover valve connector.
9. Mark position of propeller shaft relative to flange of transfer case.
10. Undo rear propeller shaft at output flange to rear axle on transfer case.
11. Remove bolts and nuts, remove bracket.
12. Detach bracket from pressure measuring hoses and pressure sensors.
13. Remove bolts, remove cross strut.
14. Disconnect diagonal strut from transmission suspension and frame floor assembly.
15. Mark position of front propeller shaft relative to flange of transfer case.
16. Detach front propeller shaft on output flange to front axle.
17. Use support brace to prop up transfer case on housing.
18. Remove bolts and remove transmission suspension.
19. Remove lower four bolts on transfer case.
20. Remove support brace from housing of transfer case and attach to rubber mount, support transfer case with transmission jack and transmission platform.
21. Slowly lower drivetrain slightly until the upper bolts on the transfer case are accessible.
22. Remove upper four bolts on transfer case.
23. Slide transfer case rearwards until transfer case is separated completely from the transmission, lower transfer case.

To install:

24. Install in the reverse order.

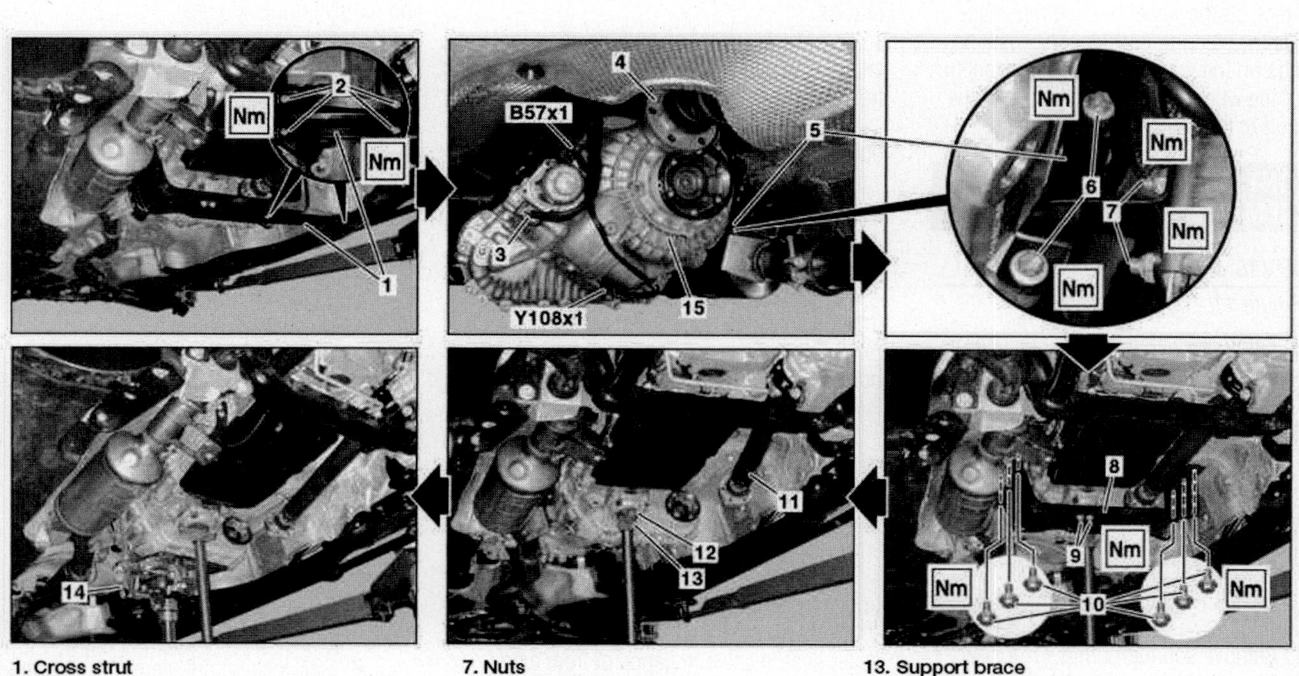

Fig. 9 Removing transfer case

25. Slightly grease teeth of transfer case input shaft.

26. Observe tightening procedure for rear propeller shaft to transfer case.

27. Tighten bolts/nuts to specification as follows:

- Bolt, rear engine crossmember to body: 41 ft. lbs. (55 Nm)
- Bolt for cross strut on engine crossmember: 33 ft. lbs. (45 Nm)
- Bolt for diagonal strut on engine crossmember: 33 ft. lbs. (45 Nm)
- Bolt for cross strut on body: 33 ft. lbs. (45 Nm)
- Bolt for diagonal strut on body: 33 ft. lbs. (45 Nm)
- Screw plug to transfer case: 19 ft. lbs. (25 Nm)
- Bolt, transfer case to automatic transmission: 33 ft. lbs. (45 Nm)
- Self-locking bolt of propeller shaft to transfer case (to rear axle): 30 ft. lbs. (40 Nm) plus an additional 90° rotation
- Self-locking bolt, propeller shaft to transfer case (to front axle) : 30 ft. lbs. (40 Nm) plus an additional 90° rotation
- Self-locking nut, diesel particulate filter to transfer case bracket: 15 ft. lbs. (20 Nm)
- Bolt, transfer case bracket to transfer case: 25 ft. lbs. (34 Nm)

28. Check oil quantity in transfer case and correct if necessary.

29. Perform calibration using STAR DIAGNOSIS, read out fault memory and erase if necessary.

FRONT AXLE BEARING & SEAL

REMOVAL & INSTALLATION

See Figure 10.

1. Before servicing the vehicle, refer to the precautions.
2. Remove steering knuckle.
3. Press out front axle shaft flange.
4. Detach circlip.
5. Press wheel bearing out of steering knuckle.

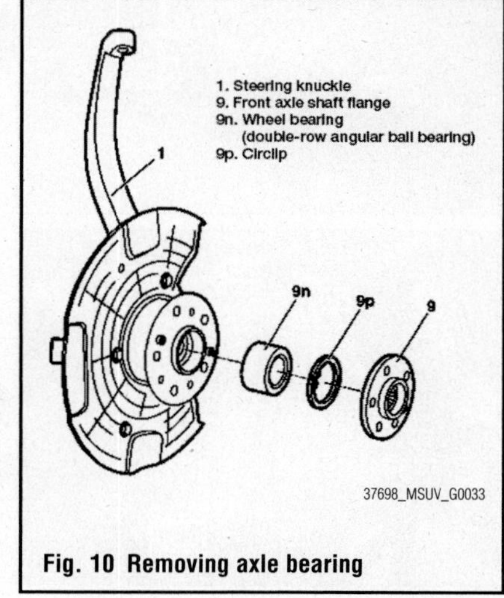

Fig. 10 Removing axle bearing

To install:

6. Install in the reverse order.
7. Generally, the front axle shaft flange and wheel bearing should be replaced.
8. Check circlip is correctly seated in steering knuckle.

9. Installation position must be knuckle observed. The dots, the line or the black inner race on the wheel bearing must face towards the steering knuckle. The marking depends on the manufacturer. The magnetic side of the wheel bearing must point in the direction of the steering knuckle.

FRONT DIFFERENTIAL ASSEMBLY

REMOVAL & INSTALLATION

See Figure 11.

1. Before servicing the vehicle, refer to the precautions.
2. Remove transmitter key or Keyless-Go start and stop button.
3. Raise and safely support vehicle .
4. Remove wheels, rotate if necessary.
5. Unscrew right collar nut on front axle shaft.
6. Raise and safely support vehicle.
7. Detach lower engine compartment paneling.
8. Remove soundproofing.
9. Lower vehicle on two-post lift.
10. Remove electrical lines from brackets.
11. Cut off cable ties.
12. Remove brake hose from brake hose bracket.
13. Attach extraction and insertion tool and detach right front axle shaft from right front axle shaft flange.
14. Unscrew nut and press right tie rod out of right steering knuckle.
15. Unscrew nut and press right steering knuckle out of transverse control arm.
16. Swivel right steering knuckle out of working area.
17. Withdraw right front axle shaft from front axle gear (arrow A) and remove.
18. Remove brake hose from brake hose bracket.
19. Cut off cable ties.
20. Unscrew nut and press left tie rod out of left steering knuckle.
21. Unscrew nut and remove left steering knuckle from upper left transverse control arm.
22. Withdraw left front axle shaft from front axle gear (arrow B).
23. Mark position of front axle gear propeller shaft relative to flange of front axle gear.
24. Remove bolts and detach front axle gear propeller shaft from front axle gear.
25. Detach hose.
26. Remove collar bolt and collar bolt and remove front axle gear.
27. Install in the reverse order.

To install:

28. Install in the reverse order.
29. Tighten bolts/nuts to specification as follows:
    - Self-locking nut, upper wishbone follower joint to steering knuckle: 15 ft. lbs. (20 Nm) plus an additional 90° rotation
    - Collar nut, front axle shaft to front axle shaft flange: 19 ft. lbs. (250 Nm) plus an additional 45° rotation
    - Collar bolt, front axle gear to left front axle carrier: 69 ft. lbs. (93 Nm)
    - Collar bolt, front axle gear to right front axle carrier: 37 ft. lbs. (50 Nm)
    - Self-locking bolt, propeller shaft to front axle gear: 30 ft. lbs. (40 Nm) plus an additional 90° rotation
    - Self-locking nut, tie rod to steering knuckle: 33 ft. lbs. (45 Nm) plus an additional 90° rotation

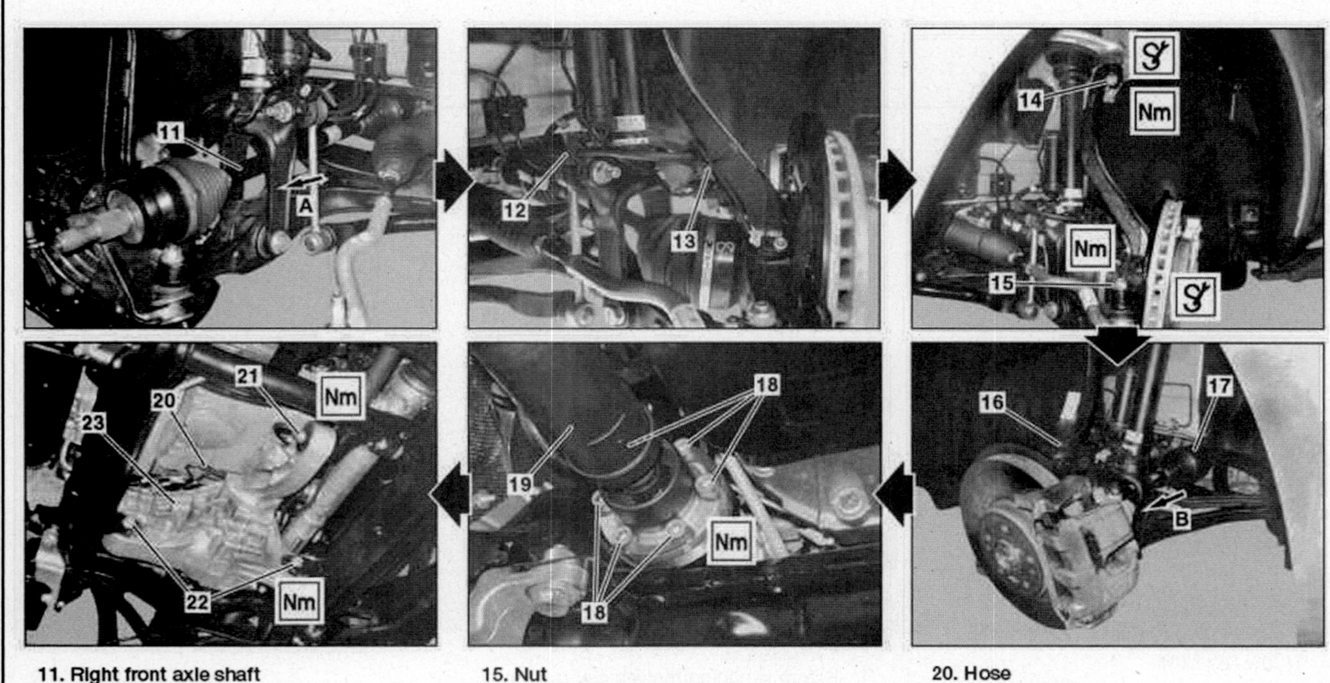

11. Right front axle shaft
12. Brake hose bracket
13. Cable tie
14. Nut
15. Nut
16. Left steering knuckle
17. Left front axle shaft
18. Bolts
19. Front axle gear propeller shaft
20. Hose
21. Collar bolt
22. Collar bolts
23. Front axle gear

37698_MSUV_G0148

Fig. 11 Removing differential assembly

- Oil filler screw, front axle gear: 26 ft. lbs. (35 Nm)
- Bolt, exhaust pipe bracket to transmission: 15 ft. lbs. (20 Nm)
- Bolt, exhaust pipe bracket to exhaust pipe: 15 ft. lbs. (20 Nm)
- Bolt, exhaust system to main floor panel: 15 ft. lbs. (20 Nm)
- Bolt, exhaust system to main floor panel: 37 ft. lbs. (50 Nm)
- Nut, suspension ring to connecting pipe: 15 ft. lbs. (20 Nm)
- Bolt, torque converter to drive plate connection (Straight threaded): 31 ft. lbs. (42 Nm)
- Bolt, torque converter to drive plate connection (Angled threaded connection): 35 inch lbs. (4 Nm), then 22 ft. lbs. (30 Nm) plus an additional 90° rotation

30. Check oil level in front axle gear and top up if necessary.

FRONT DRIVESHAFT

REMOVAL & INSTALLATION

See Figure 12.

1. Before servicing the vehicle, refer to the precautions.
2. Remove plastic connecting piece between rear section of under ride guard and engine crossmember.
3. Remove diagonal strut from right-hand side of rear engine crossmember.
4. Remove cross strut from left-hand side of rear engine crossmember.
5. Support rear of engine crossmember and detach from underfloor.
6. Lower transfer case slightly.
7. Mark position of propeller shaft relative to flange of front axle gear and relative to flange of transfer case.
8. Remove bolts from transfer case.
9. Remove bolts from front axle gear.
10. Remove propeller shaft downward.
11. Check constant velocity joint and double cardan U-joint for wear and damage.

To install:

12. Install in the reverse order.
13. It is absolutely essential to observe tightening procedure otherwise noise can develop and vibrations can occur.
14. Pay attention to cleanliness of the contact surfaces, if necessary clean the contact surfaces of the bolts.
15. Tighten bolts/nuts to specification as follows:
    - Self-locking bolt, propeller shaft to transfer case (to front axle): 30 ft. lbs. (40 Nm) plus an additional 90° rotation.
    - Self-locking bolt, propeller shaft to front axle gear: 30 ft. lbs. (40 Nm) plus an additional 90° rotation.
    - Bolt, rear engine crossmember to body: 41 ft. lbs. (55 Nm).
    - Bolt for cross strut on engine crossmember: 33 ft. lbs. (45 Nm).
    - Bolt for diagonal strut on engine crossmember: 33 ft. lbs. (45 Nm).
    - Bolt for cross strut on body: 33 ft. lbs. (45 Nm).
    - Bolt for diagonal strut on body: 33 ft. lbs. (45 Nm).

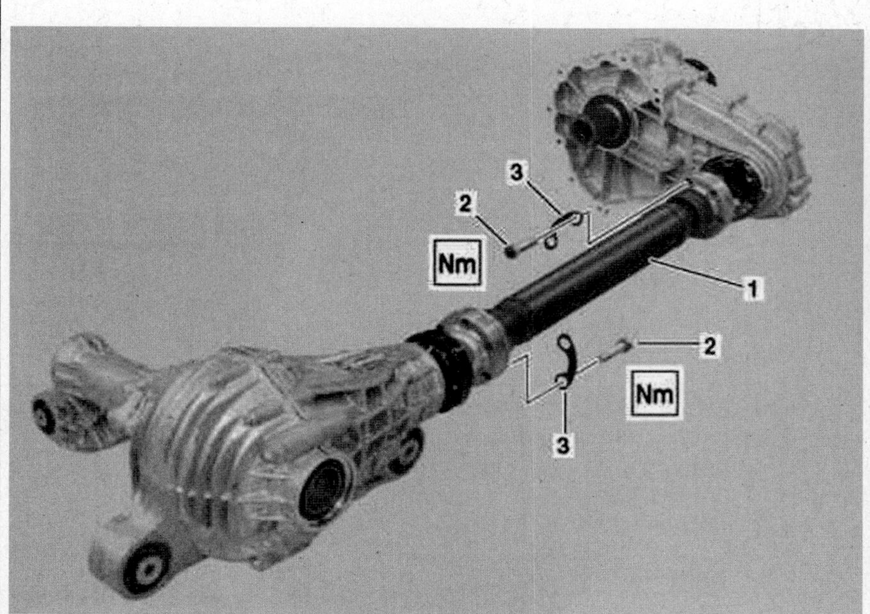

Fig. 12 Removing front driveshaft

FRONT HALFSHAFTS

REMOVAL & INSTALLATION

See Figure 13.

1. Before servicing the vehicle, refer to the precautions.
2. Remove transmitter key or Keyless-Go start and stop button.
3. Raise and securely support vehicle.
4. Connect STAR DIAGNOSIS and read out fault memory.
5. Remove wheels, rotate if necessary.
6. Undo collar nut on front axle shaft.
7. Raise and safely support vehicle.
8. Detach lower engine compartment paneling.
9. Remove sound proofing.
10. Remove under ride guard.
11. Lower vehicle.
12. Remove electrical lines from bracket and bracket.
13. Cut off cable ties.
14. Remove brake hose from brake hose bracket.
15. Undo nut and remove tie rod from steering knuckle.
16. Undo nut and remove steering knuckle from upper transverse control arm.
17. Mount extraction and insertion tool and undo front axle shaft from front axle shaft flange.
18. Swivel steering knuckle out of working area.
19. Unscrew nut from front shock absorber, pull out bolt and detach front shock absorber from transverse control arm.
20. Withdraw front axle shaft from front axle gear (arrow A) and remove.

To install:

21. Install in the reverse order.
22. Tighten bolts/nuts to specification as follows:
    - Self-locking nut, shock absorber to wishbone: 196 ft. lbs. (265 Nm).
    - Self-locking nut, upper wishbone follower joint to steering knuckle:

Fig. 13 Halfshaft extraction and insertion tool

15 ft. lbs. (20 Nm) plus an additional 90° rotation.

- Collar nut, front axle shaft to front axle shaft flange: 185 ft. lbs. (250 Nm).
- Self-locking nut, tie rod to steering knuckle: 33 ft. lbs. (45 Nm).

CV-BOOTS INSPECTION

1. Raise and safely support the vehicle securely on jackstands.
2. Turn the steering wheel to full right lock.
3. Inspecting from behind the halfshaft, examine the driver's side CV boot while slowly turning the wheel.
4. Inspect the valleys between the folds. If cracks are apparent, replace the boot.
5. Also inspect the circumference where the boot covers the edge of the hub, as cracks can appear there too. If large cracks (large enough to fit a finger nail in) are apparent, replace the boot.
6. Repeat for the inner boot.
7. Turn the steering wheel to full left lock and examine the passenger side boots in the same manner.

FRONT PINION SEAL

REMOVAL & INSTALLATION

See Figure 14.

1. Before servicing the vehicle, refer to the precautions.
2. Remove tires, rotate if necessary.
3. Raise and safely support vehicle.
4. Detach lower engine compartment paneling.
5. Remove soundproofing.
6. Remove front axle brake caliper.
7. Mark position of front axle gear propeller shaft relative to flange of front axle gear and to flange of transfer case.
8. Remove front axle gear propeller shaft.
9. Remove bolts, swivel front axle gear propeller shaft out of working area and secure in place.
10. Measure and note down total friction torque of drive pinion.
11. Mark position of flange relative to input shaft and front axle gear housing.
12. Dismantle hexagon collar nut on flange.
13. Remove flange.
14. Use suitable tool to pry radial sealing ring off front axle gear.

To install:

15. Install in the reverse order.
16. Check oil level in front axle gear; correct if necessary.
17. Oil filler screw, front axle gear: 26 ft. lbs. (35 Nm).
18. Self-locking bolt, propeller shaft to front axle gear: 30 ft. lbs. (40 Nm) plus an additional 90° rotation.
19. It is essential to observe the tightening instructions. Failure to do so can result in noises and vibrations.
20. Replace hexagon collar nut.
21. Tighten hexagon collar nut gradually, until the measured and noted total friction torque is reached.
22. Coat lip of radial sealing ring with universal hypoid gear oil.
23. Press radial seal using drift into front axle gear.

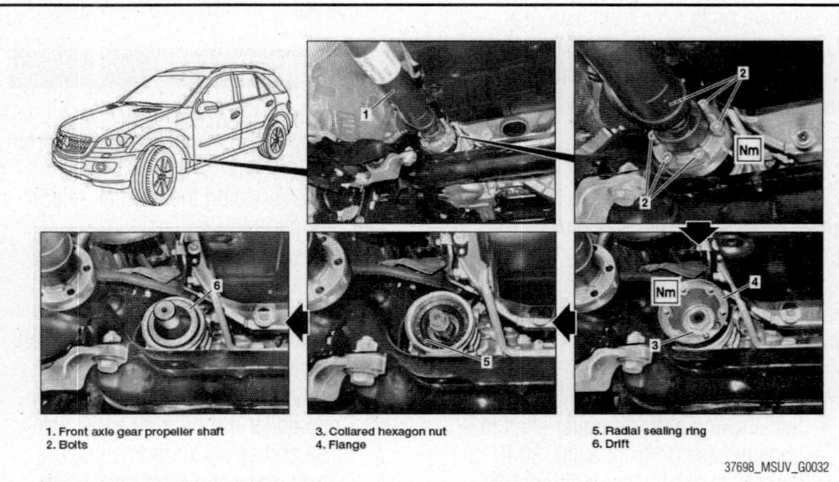

Fig. 14 Removing pinion seal

REAR DIFFERENTIAL ASSEMBLY

REMOVAL & INSTALLATION

See Figure 15.

1. Before servicing the vehicle, refer to the precautions.
2. Raise and safely support vehicle.
3. Remove wheels, rotate if necessary.
4. Remove rear part of underfloor paneling.
5. Remove left rear muffler.
6. Remove left rear axle shaft and right rear axle shaft.
7. Detach propeller shaft from flange on rear axle center assembly.
8. Disconnect connectors for differential actuator motor (M70x1, M70x2).
9. Support rear axle center assembly using transmission jack and transmission platform and secure on transmission platform.
10. Undo rear axle center assembly at front fastening shackle.
11. Undo rear axle center assembly on both rear fastening shackles.
12. Lower the rear axle center assembly slightly.
13. Lower front rear axle center assembly, in doing so push the propeller shaft forward, until the rear axle center assembly separates from the propeller shaft. Slide rear axle center assembly(10) forward, until the hexagon bolt of the differential lock is free.
14. Unscrew bleed screw on rear axle center assembly.
15. Lower rear axle differential.

To install:

16. Install in the reverse order.
17. Tighten bolts/nuts to specification as follows:
    - Oil filler screw, rear axle differential: 22 ft. lbs. (30 Nm).
    - Self-locking nut of rear axle center assembly suspension to rear axle carrier: 81 ft. lbs. (110 Nm).
    - Self-locking nut of front axle center assembly suspension to rear axle carrier: 81 ft. lbs. (110 Nm).
18. Check oil level in the rear axle differential and correct if necessary.
19. Perform function test with STAR DIAGNOSIS, read out fault memory, clear.

REAR AXLE SHAFT BEARING & SEAL

REMOVAL & INSTALLATION

See Figure 16.

1. Before servicing the vehicle, refer to the precautions.
2. Remove wheel carrier.
3. Pull out rear axle shaft flange.
4. Remove retaining ring.
5. Pull wheel bearing out of wheel carrier.

To install:

6. Install in the reverse order.
7. In general the rear axle shaft flange and wheel bearing should be replaced.
8. Pay attention to correct seat of circlip in wheel carrier.

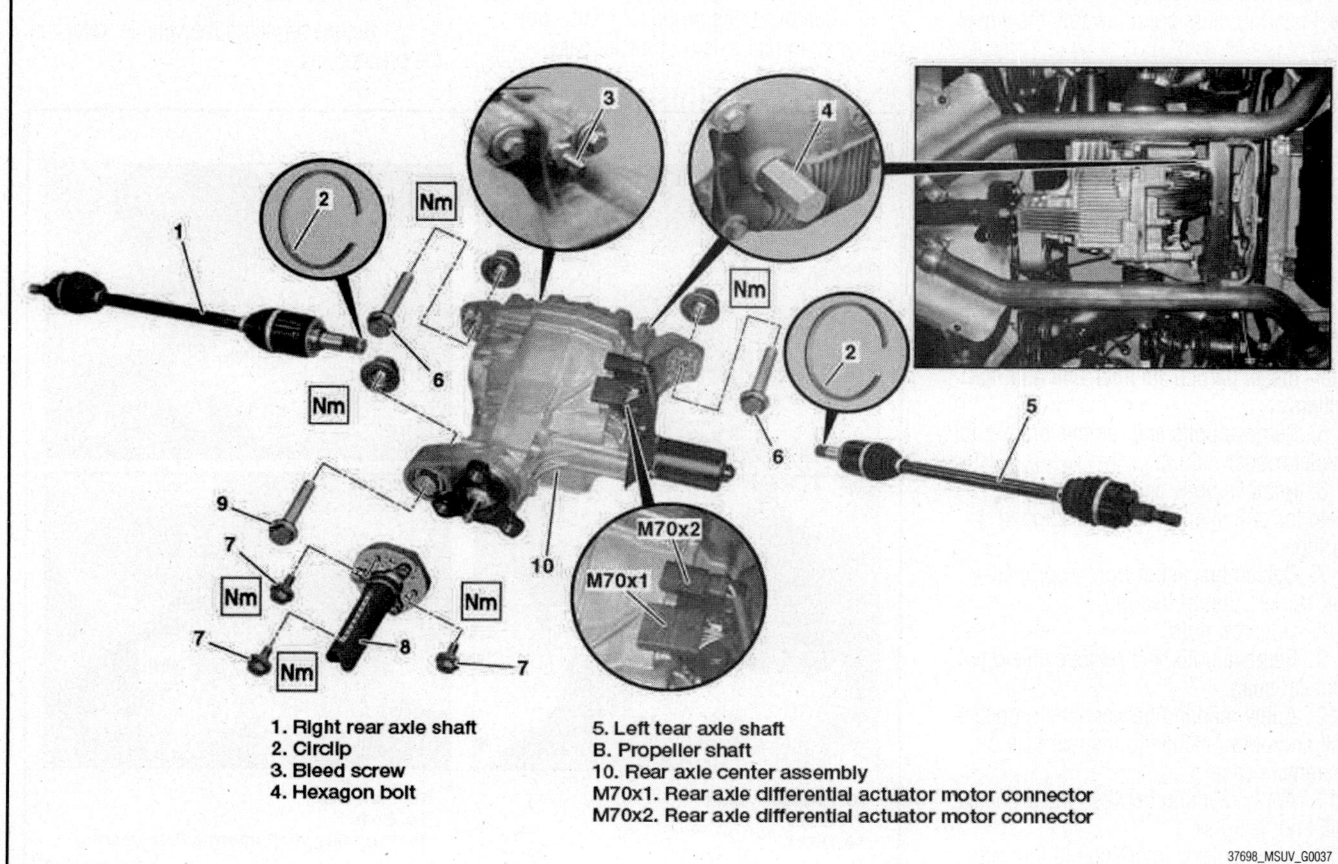

Fig. 15 Rear axle differential assembly

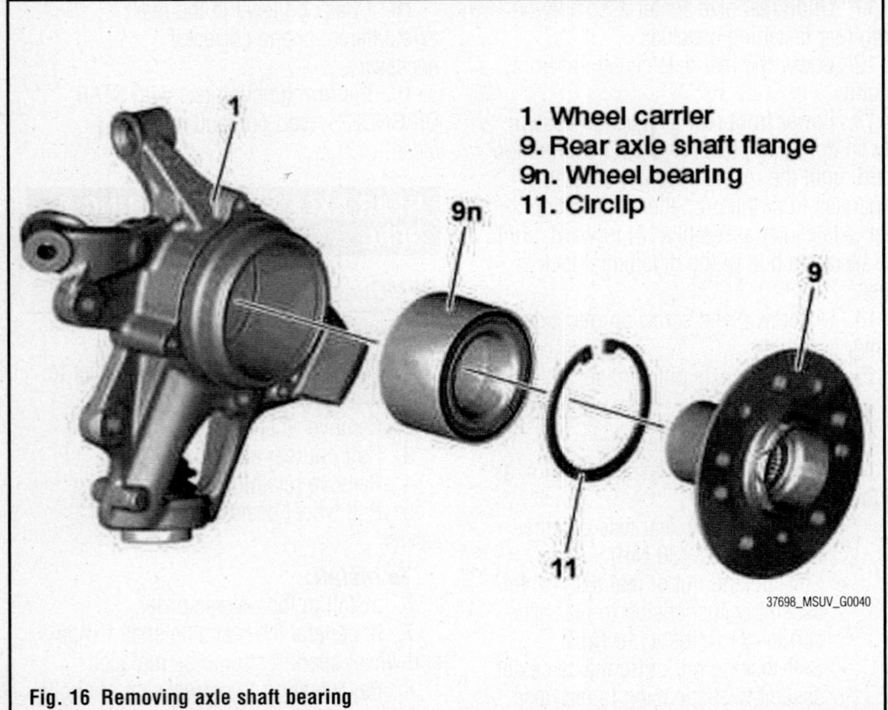

Fig. 16 Removing axle shaft bearing

9. Installation position must be observed. The points or the line on the wheel bearing must point towards the wheel carrier.

REAR DRIVESHAFT

REMOVAL & INSTALLATION

See Figure 17.

1. Before servicing the vehicle, refer to the precautions.
2. Raise and safely support vehicle.
3. Remove center muffler.
4. Center pipe between catalytic converter- diesel particulate filter-unit and rear mufflers.
5. Remove bolts and remove bracket for exhaust rubber mount.
6. Remove bolts and remove shield for propeller shaft center support bearing.
7. Detach bracket in front of propeller shaft center support bearing.
8. Unscrew nuts.
9. Remove bolts and remove shield for propeller shaft.
10. Apply marking between the propeller shaft and output flange to the rear axle on the transfer case.
11. Apply marking between the propeller shaft and flex disk.
12. Make colored markings to indicate position of propeller shaft relative to transfer case so that ex-factory installation position can be reproduced on reinstallation, otherwise drive train vibrations can occur.
13. Remove bolts propeller shaft - output flange to rear axle on transfer case.
14. Loosen bolts propeller shaft - rear axle center assembly.
15. Remove bolts from propeller shaft center support bearing and remove propeller shaft downwards.
16. Check flexible coupling of propeller shaft for wear and replace if necessary.

To install:

17. Install in the reverse order.
18. Observe tightening procedure for rear propeller shaft to transfer case.
19. Tighten bolts/nuts to specification as follows:
    - Self-locking bolt of propeller shaft to transfer case (to rear axle): 30 ft. lbs. (40 Nm) plus an additional 90° rotation.
    - Self-locking bolt on rear propeller shaft/rear axle center assembly: 47 ft. lbs. (64 Nm).
    - Bolt, propeller shaft intermediate bearing to frame floor assembly: 30 ft. lbs. (40 Nm).

REAR HALFSHAFTS

REMOVAL & INSTALLATION

See Figures 18 through 20.

1. Before servicing the vehicle, refer to the precautions.

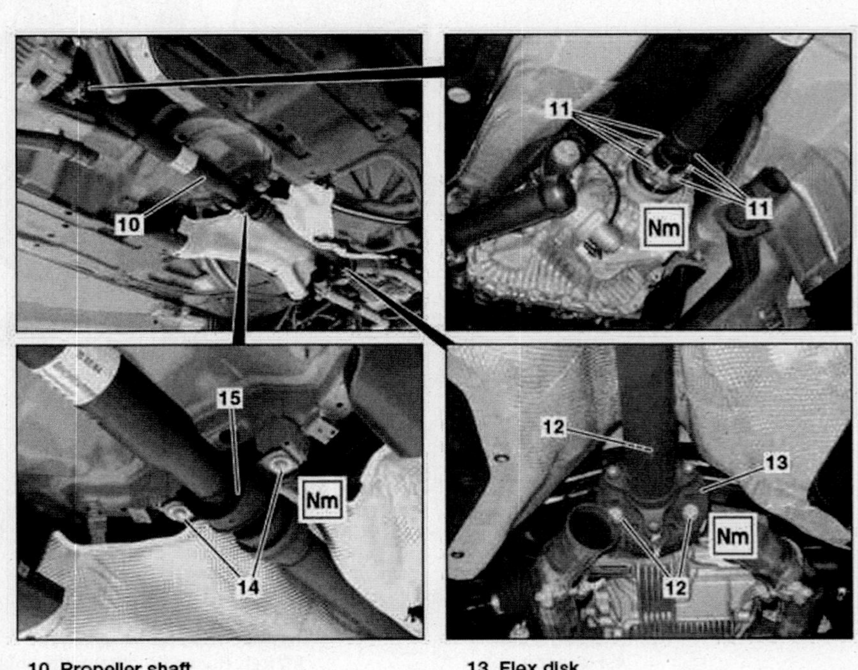

Fig. 17 Removing driveshaft

2. Raise vehicle with vehicle lift.
3. Connect STAR DIAGNOSIS and read out fault memory.
4. Switch off ignition and remove the transmitter key from the EIS [EZS] control unit.
5. Remove wheels, rotate if necessary.
6. Remove lock and cut brake cable in center.
7. Unclip brake cable from bracket of rear axle carrier.
8. Remove hexagon collar nut on rear axle shaft.
9. Undo bolt of tie rod from wheel carrier.
10. Unclip cable set bracket to camber strut and unhook to front (arrow A).
11. Undo nut of camber strut on wheel carrier.
12. Undo nut of torque strut on wheel carrier.
13. Press rear axle shaft out of the rear axle shaft flange.
14. Compress rear axle shaft as far as the stop in the direction of the rear axle center assembly. Swing wheel carrier out towards the front.
15. Do not damage the rubber boot on the rear axle shaft.
16. Support spring control arm using transmission jack and transmission platform.

37698_MSUV_G0036

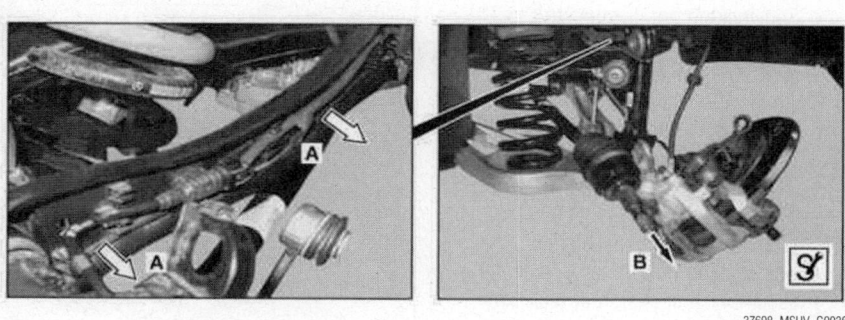

Fig. 19 Unclip cable set bracket to camber strut and unhook to front (arrow A)

17. Detach rear shock absorbers on spring control arm.
18. Support rear axle center assembly with transmission jack and transmission platform.
19. Detach rear rear-axle differential suspension.
20. Lower rear axle differential slightly.
21. Pull rear axle shaft out of rear axle center assembly.
22. Check insertion direction of bolt for rear rear-axle differential suspension.
23. Change insertion direction of bolt for rear rear-axle differential suspension.

To install:

24. Install in the reverse order.
25. Tighten bolts/nuts to specification as follows:
    - Self-locking nut, tie rod at wheel carrier: 81 ft. lbs. (110 Nm)

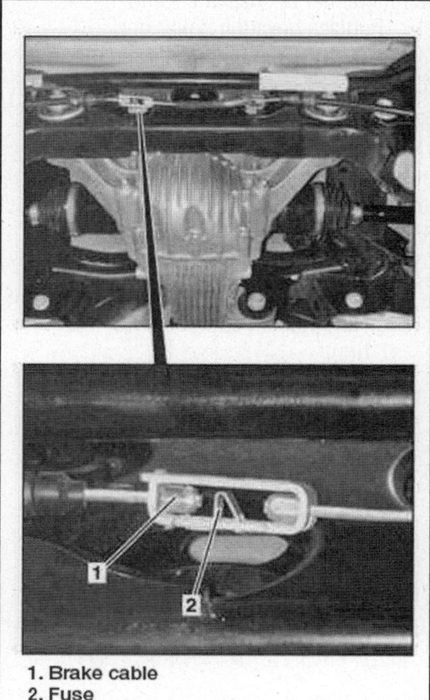

1. Brake cable
2. Fuse

37698_MSUV_G0034

Fig. 18 Brake cable

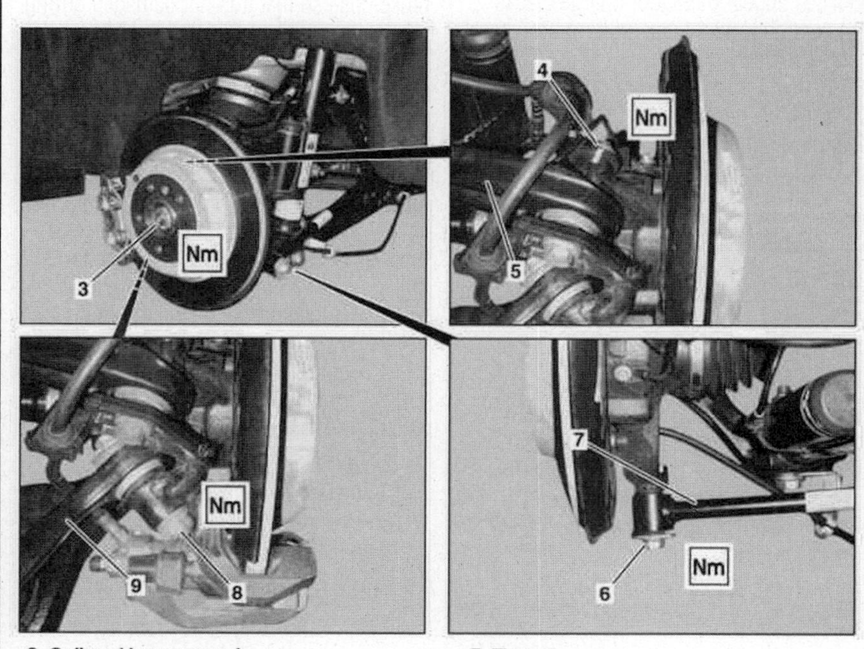

3. Collared hexagon nut
4. Nut
5. Camber strut
6. Screw
7. Tie rod
8. Nut
9. Torque strut

37698_MSUV_G0035

Fig. 20 Knuckle assembly

- Self-locking nut, camber strut to wheel carrier: 41 ft. lbs. (55 Nm) plus 90° additional rotation
- Self-locking nut, torque strut to wheel carrier: 37 ft. lbs. (50 Nm) plus 90° additional rotation
- Collar nut, rear axle shaft to rear axle shaft flange: 185 ft. lbs. (250 Nm) plus 45° additional rotation
- Self-locking nut, damper to spring control arm: 74 ft. lbs. (100 Nm) plus 120° additional rotation
- Self-locking nut of rear axle center assembly suspension to rear axle carrier: 81 ft. lbs. (110 Nm)

26. Replace self-locking hexagon collar nut.
27. Locate dog bone washers between the brake hose clip and camber strut.

CV-BOOT INSPECTION

1. Raise and safely support the vehicle securely on jackstands.
2. Turn the steering wheel to full right lock.
3. Inspecting from behind the halfshaft, examine the driver's side CV boot while slowly turning the wheel.
4. Inspect the valleys between the folds. If cracks are apparent, replace the boot.
5. Also inspect the circumference where the boot covers the edge of the hub, as cracks can appear there too. If large cracks (large enough to fit a finger nail in) are apparent, replace the boot.
6. Repeat for the inner boot.
7. Turn the steering wheel to full left lock and examine the passenger side boots in the same manner.

REAR PINION SEAL

REMOVAL & INSTALLATION

See Figure 21.

Fig. 21 Removing pinion seal

1. Before servicing the vehicle, refer to the precautions.
2. Remove wheels, rotate if necessary.
3. Remove exhaust at flange connection.
4. Remove rear axle brake caliper. Do not disconnect the brake hose. Attach brake caliper to vehicle without tension to relieve brake hose so that it is not damaged during repair.
5. Mark position of propeller shaft relative to flange on transfer case and flange on rear axle differential.
6. Remove propeller shaft.
7. Measure and note down total friction torque of drive pinion.
8. Mark position of flange relative to input shaft and rear axle differential housing.
9. Remove hexagon collar nut on flange.
10. Remove flange.
11. Pry radial sealing ring out of rear axle differential using a suitable tool.

To install:

12. Install in the reverse order.
13. Replace radial sealing ring.
14. Coat sealing lip of radial sealing ring with Universal hypoid gear oil.
15. Press radial sealing ring into the rear axle differential by means of drift.
16. Replace hexagon collar nut.
17. Gradually tighten hexagon collar nut until the measured and noted total friction torque is reached.
18. If the required torque is not reached, replace differential.
19. Tighten bolts/nuts to specification as follows:
    - Collar nut, rear axle shaft to rear axle shaft flange: 185 ft. lbs. (250 Nm) plus an additional 45° rotation.
    - Oil filler screw, rear axle differential: 22 ft. lbs. (30 Nm).
20. Check oil level in rear axle differential and correct if necessary.

ENGINE COOLING

ENGINE FAN

REMOVAL & INSTALLATION

See Figure 22.

1. Before servicing the vehicle, refer to the precautions.
2. Remove left and right engine intake air duct.
3. Remove upper radiator crossmember.
4. Unplug electrical connection on fan shroud.
5. Unscrew bolts at fan shroud.
6. Remove fan shroud from lower mounts on radiator.
7. When removing fan shroud observe that none of attached lines are damaged on radiator.

To install:

8. Install in the reverse order.
9. Connect STAR DIAGNOSIS and read fault memory and clear.

RADIATOR

REMOVAL & INSTALLATION

See Figure 23.

1. Before servicing the vehicle, refer to the precautions.
2. Remove front engine cover.
3. Remove left and right engine intake air ducts.
4. Remove upper radiator crossmember.
5. Remove electrician.
6. Remove engine compartment paneling.
7. Drain coolant at radiator.
8. Detach coolant hose at radiator.
9. Detach coolant hoses from connection fitting on radiator and place to one side.
10. Detach automatic transmission oil lines from connections on radiator.
11. Detach power steering oil lines from connections on radiator.
12. Seal the connections using stop plugs to prevent dirt from entering.
13. Remove bolts to air ducting from radiator.
14. Remove front section of fender liner in left front fender.
15. Partially remove left bumper.
16. Remove bolt of refrigerant line mounting on radiator.
17. Lift radiator with condenser of air conditioning system upwards out of rubber mounts, push towards engine and put down.
18. Remove bolts from air ducting.
19. Remove air ducting.
20. Unclip condenser of air conditioning from upper supports on radiator and pull condenser upwards and out of lower supports.
21. Take out radiator in an upward direction.

To install:

22. Install in the reverse order.
23. Install engine compartment paneling only after engine test run.
24. Check condition of coolant hose and replace if necessary. Ensure coolant hose is fitted correctly on radiator.
25. Check condition of coolant hoses; replace if necessary. Ensure that coolant hoses are correctly fitted to radiator.
26. Replace sealing rings. .
27. Make sure that automatic transmission oil lines are correctly fitted to radiator .

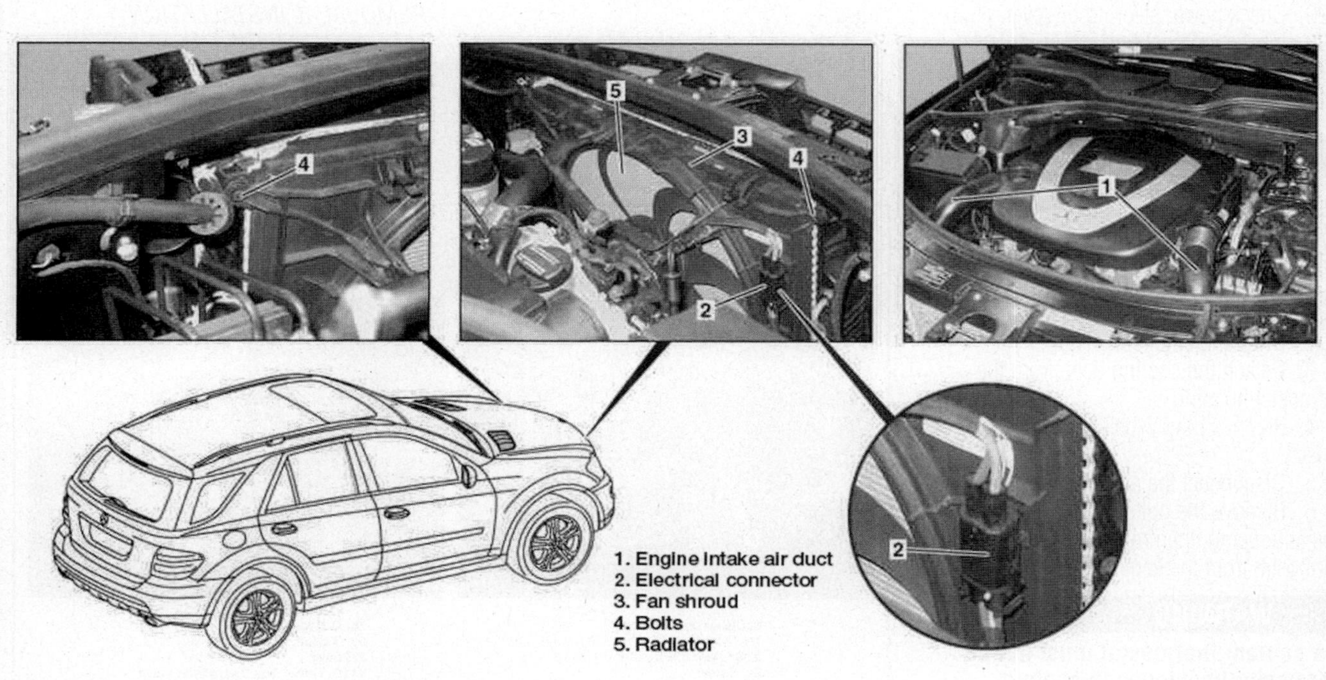

Fig. 22 Fan and shroud assembly

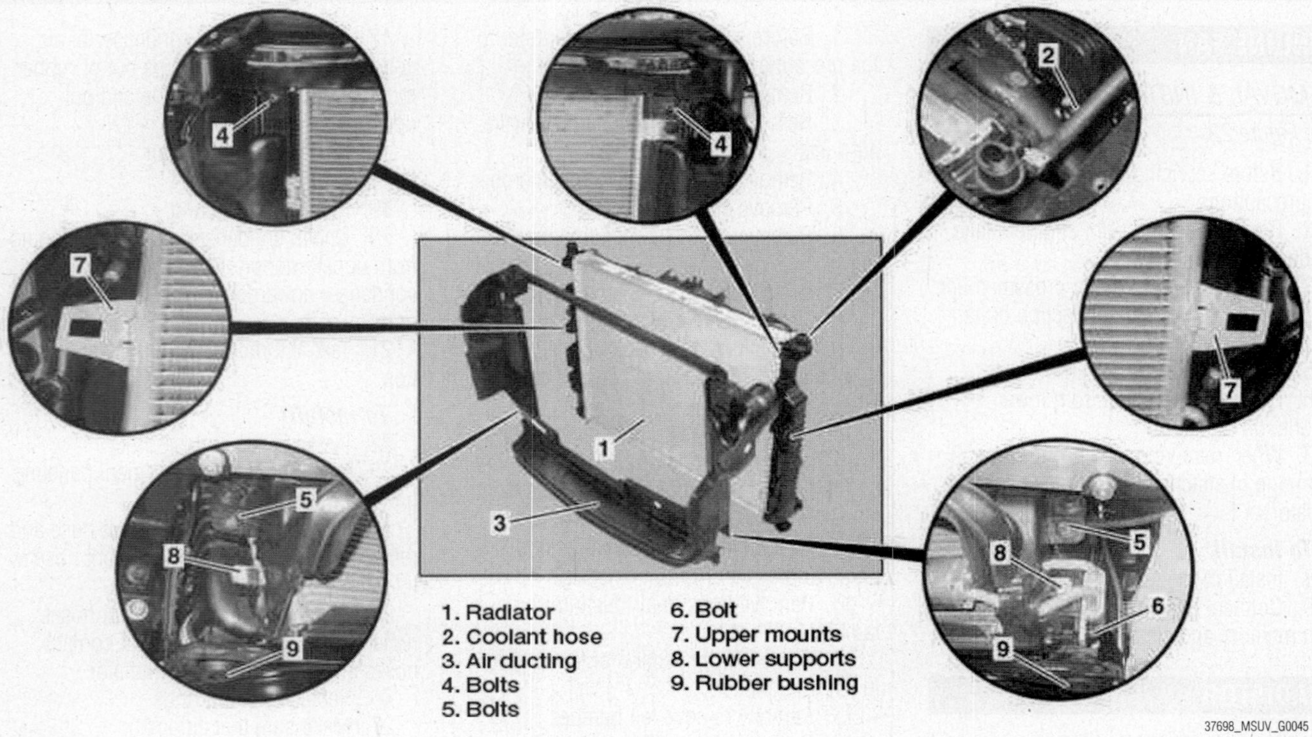

1. Radiator
2. Coolant hose
3. Air ducting
4. Bolts
5. Bolts
6. Bolt
7. Upper mounts
8. Lower supports
9. Rubber bushing

37698_MSUV_G0045

Fig. 23 Radiator mounting

28. Check transmission oil level and correct if necessary.
29. Check power steering oil level.
30. Inspecting cooling system for leaks.
31. Connect STAR DIAGNOSIS and read fault memory.

THERMOSTAT

REMOVAL & INSTALLATION

See Figure 24.

1. Before servicing the vehicle, refer to the precautions.
2. Drain the engine coolant.
3. Detach the cooling hose from the thermostat housing.
4. Remove poly V-belt and guide pulley.
5. Disconnect the electrical connector
6. Remove the bolts securing the thermostat housing, then remove it and the thermostat from the engine.

⁂ WARNING

The coolant thermostat must not be thermostat housing with coolant removed from the housing. If this is done it thermostat will be destroyed. Re-installation is not possible.

To install:

7. Installation is the reverse of removal.
8. Install new gasket and O-rings.
9. Tighten the thermostat housing bolts to 18 ft. lbs. (25 Nm)
10. Fill the engine with coolant and bleed the system as necessary.

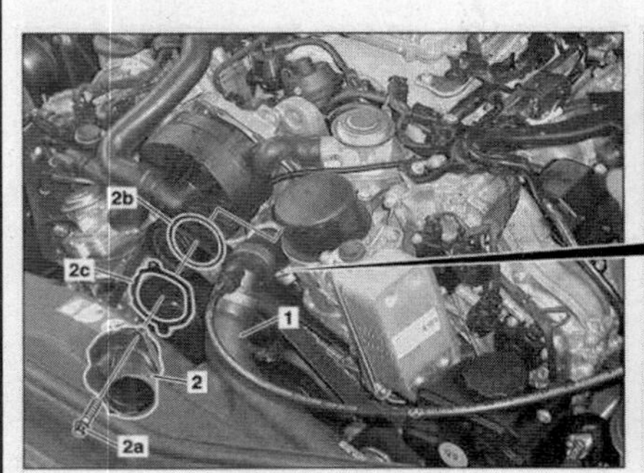

1. Upper coolant hose
1a. O-ring
2. Coolant thermostat housing
2a. Screw
2b. O-ring
2c. Gasket
3. Pulley
Y110. Three-disk thermostat valve

22205_MBML_G0075

Fig. 24 Coolant thermostat and housing

WATER PUMP

REMOVAL & INSTALLATION

See Figure 25.

1. Before servicing the vehicle, refer to the precautions.
2. Remove cooling fan.

3. Drain the engine coolant.
4. Remove engine cover.
5. Lock the automatic belt tensioner by rotating the tensioner counterclockwise until a 5mm drift or pin fits through the tensioner.
6. Remove serpentine belt.
7. Remove pry off wiring retaining clamp from water pump.
8. Remove coolant hoses from the water pump.
9. Remove belt pulley.
10. Remove water pump mounting bolts.
11. Remove water pump.
12. Clean and dry the gasket mating surface for the water pump.

To install:

13. Installation is the reverse of removal.
14. Install new gasket and O-rings.
15. Tighten bolts/nuts to specification as follows:
    - Self-tapping bolt to timing case cover: 18 ft. lbs. (25 Nm)
    - Pump to crankcase bolts: 15 ft. lbs. (20 Nm).
16. Fill the engine with coolant and bleed the system.
17. Start the vehicle and check for leaks.

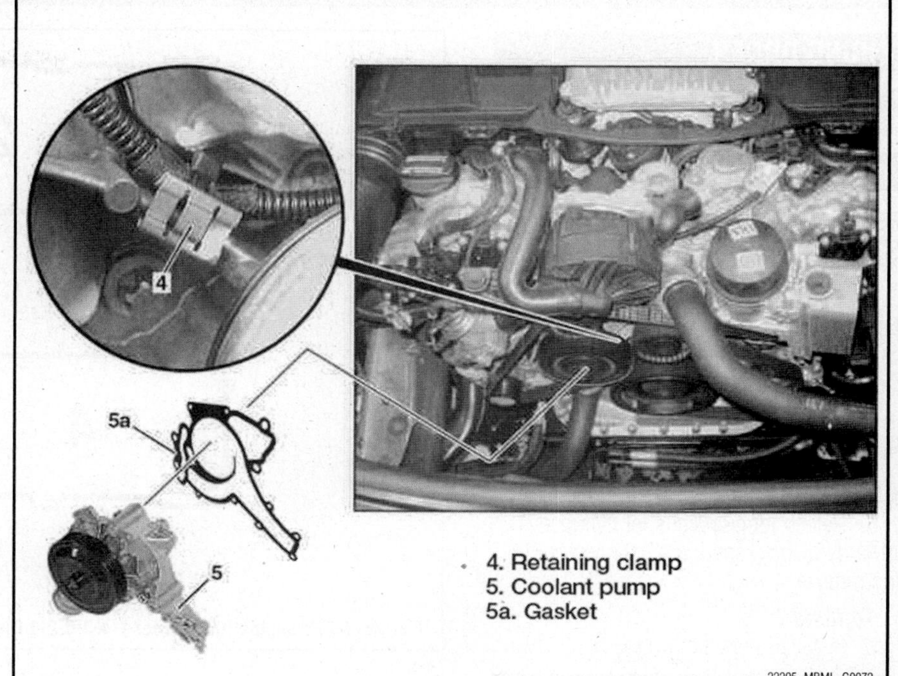

Fig. 25 Removing water pump

ENGINE ELECTRICAL

CHARGING SYSTEM

ALTERNATOR

REMOVAL & INSTALLATION

See Figure 26.

1. Before servicing the vehicle, refer to the precautions.
2. Disconnect the negative battery cable.
3. Remove the front engine cover.
4. Remove the left and right engine intake air ducts.
5. Remove the accessory drive belt.
6. Remove the alternator electrical wires.
7. Remove the alternator bolts.
8. Remove the alternator.

To install:

9. Install the alternator assembly. Torque the mounting bolts to 15 ft. lbs. (20 Nm).
10. Install the alternator electrical wires.
11. Install the right inner fender liner.
12. Install the accessory drive belt.
13. Connect the negative battery cable.
14. Start the engine and check for proper operation.

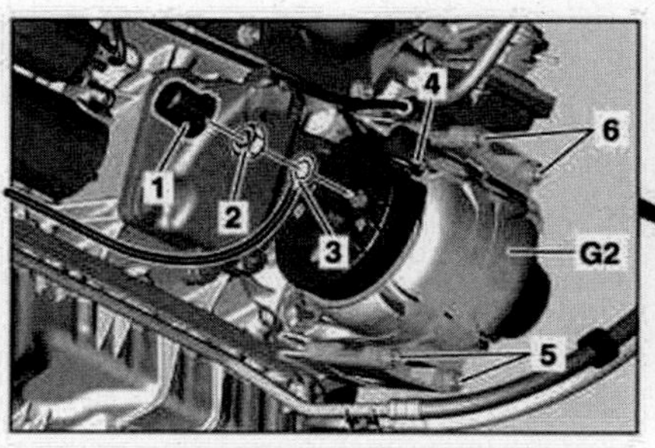

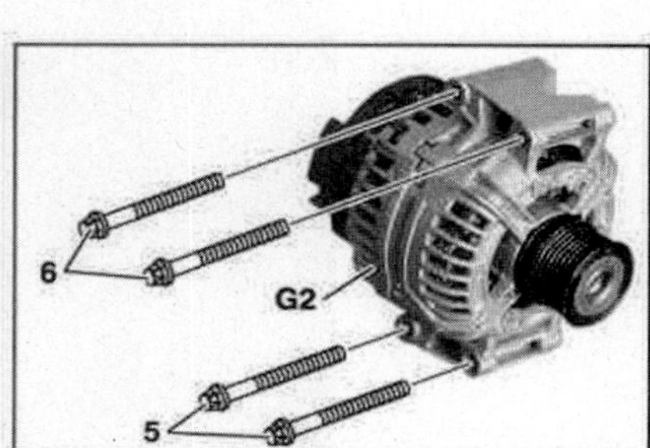

Fig. 26 Removing the alternator

FIRING ORDER

See Figure 27.

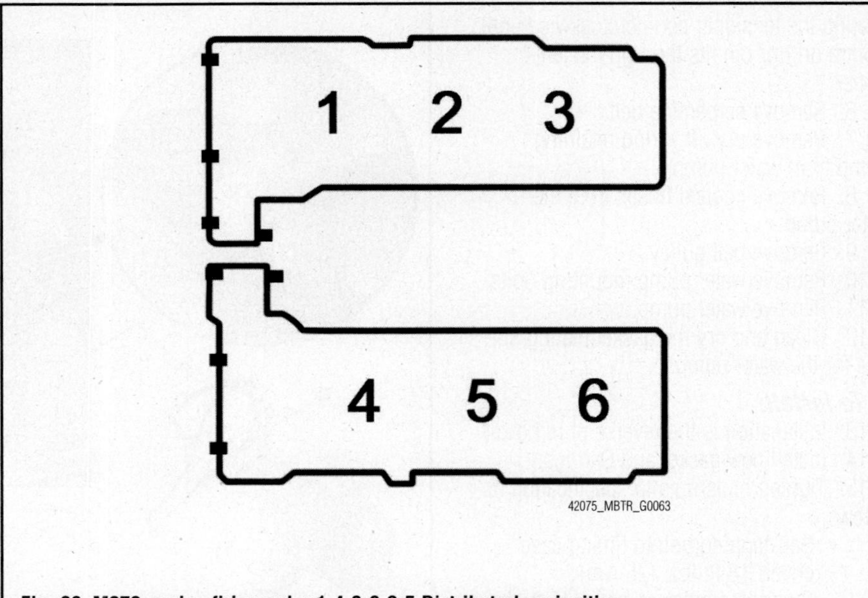

Fig. 28 M272 engine firing order 1-4-3-6-2-5 Distributorless ignition

IGNITION COIL MODULE

REMOVAL & INSTALLATION

See Figure 28.

1. Before servicing the vehicle, refer to the precautions.
2. Turn key in ignition switch **OFF**.
3. Remove air filter housing
4. Disconnect electrical connectors on ignition coils
5. Unscrew bolts (1) for ignition coils
6. Detach ignition coils for cylinders upwards using a spark plug connector (a) and remove

To install:

7. Installation is the reverse of removal.

***** WARNING**

Replace all self-locking, micro-encapsulated and aluminum bolts and nuts. Chase threads to remove micro-encapsulated residue from old bolts/nuts.

8. Tighten ignition coil to cylinder head cover to 7 ft. lbs. (9 Nm).
9. Connect STAR DIAGNOSIS or equivalent scan tool and read out fault memory.

1 Bolts
T1/1 Cylinder 1 ignition coil
T1/2 Cylinder 2 ignition coil
T1/3 Cylinder 3 ignition coil
T1/4 Cylinder 4 ignition coil
T1/5 Cylinder 5 ignition coil
T1/6 Cylinder 6 ignition coil
a Spark plug connector

22205_MBCA_G0022

Fig. 28 Ignition coil—M272 engine

ENGINE ELECTRICAL

STARTER

REMOVAL & INSTALLATION

See Figure 29.

1. Before servicing the vehicle, refer to the precautions.
2. Raise and safely support the vehicle securely on jackstands.
3. Dismount lower engine compartment paneling.
4. Detach the right catalytic converter from exhaust manifold and the catalytic converter. bracket.
5. Remove complete exhaust system.
6. Remove exhaust shielding plate on the right for front axle gear propeller shaft.
7. Pull out protective cap and dismantle electrical connection circuit 30 at starter.
8. Dismount cable holder from starter).
9. Dismount electrical connection terminal 50 at starter.
10. Remove bolts and starter from the bottom.
11. Crank engine at center bolt of crankshaft in the direction of rotation of the engine and check the ring gear at the flywheel/drive plate for wear and damage.

To install:

12. Installation is the reverse of removal.

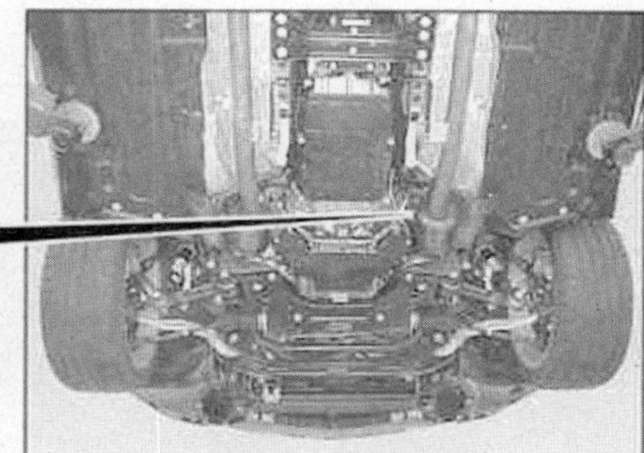

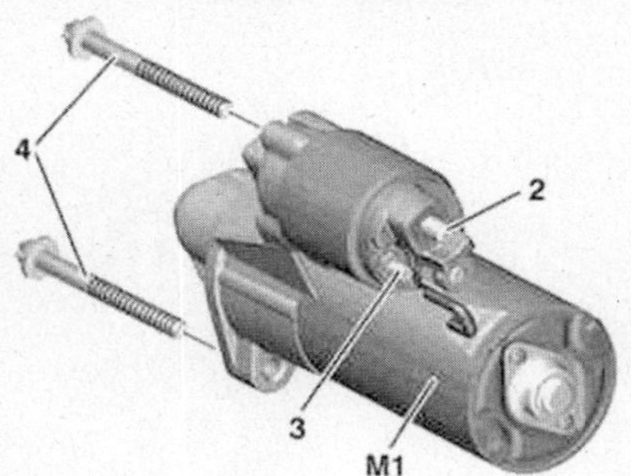

1 Protective cap
1a Cable holder
2 Electrical connection circuit 30
3 Electrical connection circuit 50
4 Bolts
M1 Starter

22205_MBCA_G0025

Fig. 29 Exploded view of starter assembly

⁂ WARNING

Replace all self-locking, micro-encapsulated and aluminum bolts and nuts. Chase threads to remove micro-encapsulated residue from old bolts/nuts.

13. Tighten bolts/nuts to specification as follows:

- Nut for connection of circuit 30: 11 ft. lbs. (15 Nm)
- Nut for connection of circuit 50: 6 ft. lbs. (8 Nm)
- Bolt connecting starter to crankcase: 30 ft. lbs. (40 Nm)

ENGINE MECHANICAL

➡Disconnecting the negative battery cable may interfere with the functions of the on board computer systems and may require the computer to undergo a relearning process, once the negative battery cable is reconnected.

ACCESSORY DRIVE BELTS

ACCESSORY BELT ROUTING

See Figure 30.

INSPECTION

V-Ribbed Serpentine Belt With Chunks of Rib Missing

See Figure 31.

There should be no chunks missig from the belt ribs. If the belt shows any evidence of this, install a new accessory drive belt.

V- Ribbed Serpentine Belt With Piling

See Figure 32.

➡Piling is an excessive buildup in the V-grooves of the belt.

The condition of the V-ribbed drive belt should be compared against the illustration and appropriate action taken.

1. Small scattered deposits of rubber material. This is not a concern, therefore, installation of a new belt is not required.
2. Longer deposit areas building up to 50 percent of the rib height. This is not considered a concern but it can result in excessive noise. If noise is apparent, install a new belt.
3. Heavy deposits building up along the grooves resulting in a possible noise and belt stability concern. If heavy deposits are apparent, install a new belt.

Visual Inspection

See Figure 33.

⁂ WARNING

Under no circumstances should the accessory drive belt, tensioner or pulleys be lubricated as potential damage to the belt material and tensioner damping mechanism will occur. Do not apply any fluids or belt dressing to the accessory drive belt or pulleys.

1. Belt pulley/vibration damper
2. Tensioning pulley
3. Pulley
4. Coolant pump belt pulley
5. Generator belt pulley
6. Pulley
7. Power steering pump belt pulley
8. Belt pulley on refrigerant compressor

42075_MBCA_G0009

Fig. 30 Accessory drive belt routing

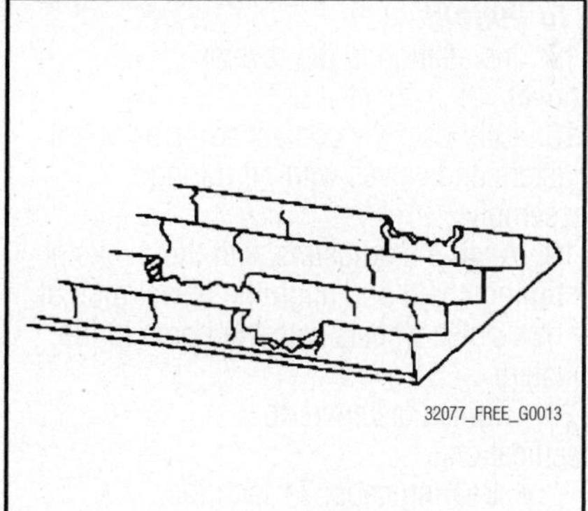

Fig. 31 Replace the belt if missing chunks are found during inspection

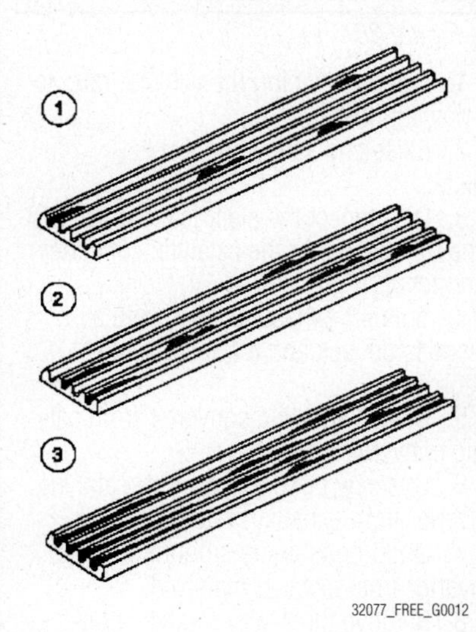

Fig. 32 Compare the condition of the belt with the accompanying text

The water pump drive belt is on back of engine. It is driven off the rear cam pulley and does not have any adjustments.

Visually inspect the belt for obvious signs of mechanical damage:

- Drive belt cracking/chunking/wear
- Belt/pulley contamination
- Incorrectly routed belt
- Pulley misalignment or excessive pulley runout
- Loose hardware
- Incorrectly routed power steering tubes (rubbing)

➡Up to 15 cracks in a rib over a distance of 4 inches (100mm) can be considered acceptable. If damage exceeds the acceptable limit or any chunks are found to be missing from the ribs, a new belt must be installed.

1. Check the belt for cracks. Up to 15 cracks in a rib over a distance of 4 inches (100mm) can be considered acceptable. If cracks exceed this standard, install a new belt.

ADJUSTMENT

The belt is tensioned automatically. If the belt is slipping, either the belt has stretched beyond its serviceable limit or the tensioner is faulty.

REMOVAL & INSTALLATION

See Figure 30

1. Before servicing the vehicle, refer to the precautions.
2. If additional access is needed, remove the cooling fan and fan shroud.
3. Using a breaker bar and appropriate sized Torx socket (or appropriate drive belt removal tool), relieve the belt tension by rotating the tensioner.
4. Remove the belt from the pulleys.

To install:

5. Installation is the reverse of removal.
6. Be sure to follow the belt routing diagram.

CAMSHAFT AND VALVE LIFTERS

INSPECTION

1. Before servicing the vehicle, refer to the precautions.
2. Remove the camshaft from the engine.
3. Check the camshaft bearing journals for damage and binding.
4. If the journals are binding, check the cylinder head for damage.
5. Check the cylinder head for clogged oil holes.
6. Check the camshaft surface for abnormal wear and damage. Replace the camshaft, as required.

REMOVAL & INSTALLATION

See Figures 34 through 37.

1. Before servicing the vehicle, refer to the precautions.
2. Remove the air filter housing assembly.
3. Remove the covers from the front of the cylinder heads.
4. Detach the crankcase ventilation hose from the centrifuge housing. Remove the bolts securing the housing, then remove the bolt securing the centrifuge on the end of the camshaft.
5. Rotate the engine in the direction of rotation so that it is at 40° After Top Dead Center (ATDC) of cylinder 1.
6. Lock the gear backlash compensators using a drift pin (refer to the illustration). This must be done to avoid damaging the camshaft adjusters.
7. Loosen, but do not remove, the center valves in the direction of the arrows (refer to the illustration). Use a Torx wrench on the rears of the camshafts to counterhold them.
8. Remove the cylinder head covers.
9. Remove the center valves on the exhaust camshafts and remove the pulse wheels. Discard the pulse wheels as they must be replaced with new ones during installation.

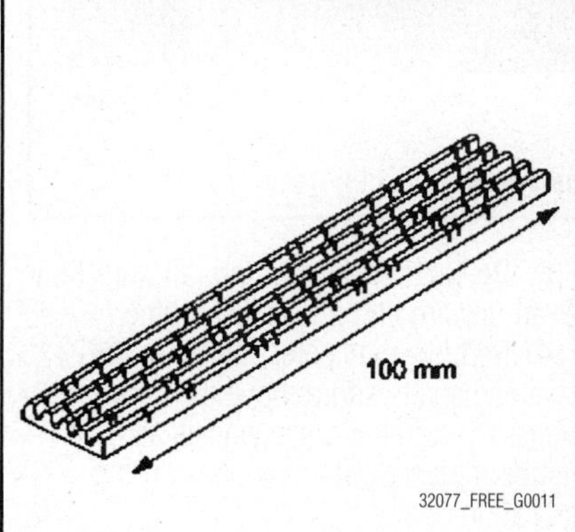

Fig. 33 Up to 15 cracks in a rib over a distance of 4 inches (100mm) can be considered acceptable. If cracks exceed this standard, install a new belt

Fig. 34 Lock the compensators as shown

42075_MBCA_G0026

Fig. 35 Loosen the center valves in the direction of the arrows

➡When removing the pulse wheels, check if the dowel pin is still intact. If not, remove the pin from the adjusters.

10. Counterhold the exhaust camshafts and pull the camshaft adjuster forward off of the exhaust camshafts.
11. Remove the bearing caps on the exhaust camshaft, then remove the camshaft.
12. Make sure the marks on the timing chain still align, then remove the chain tensioner.
13. Remove the tensioning rail bolt. Pull the rail upward and out of the engine.
14. Remove the center valves on the intake camshafts and remove the pulse wheels. Discard the pulse wheels as they must be replaced with new ones during installation.
15. Counterhold the intake camshafts and pull the camshaft adjuster forward off of the camshafts.
16. Remove the bearing caps on the intake camshaft, then remove the camshaft.

To install:

17. Installation is the reverse of removal.
18. Lubricate the contact surfaces of the adjusters and valves with oil during reassembly.
19. Align the adjusters with the marks on the timing chain and align the dowel pins of the new pulse wheels with the bores in the adjusters.
20. Tighten fasteners to specification:
    - Bearing caps: 71 inch lbs. (8 Nm)
    - Center valves: 107 ft. lbs. (145 Nm)

CATALYTIC CONVERTER

REMOVAL & INSTALLATION

See Figure 38.

1. Before servicing the vehicle, refer to the precautions.
2. Raise and safely support vehicle.
3. Disconnect the electrical connectors of the 02 sensors of the catalytic converter for removal.
4. Support exhaust system with a transmission jack and a transmission platform.
5. Detach catalytic converter from catalytic converter bracket.
6. Unscrew bolts and remove catalytic converter from exhaust system.
7. Undo bolts and dismount catalytic convertor from exhaust manifold.
8. Remove three-way catalytic converter.
9. Remove 02 sensors from respective catalytic converter.

To install:

10. Install in the reverse order.
11. Tighten bolts/nuts to specification as follows:
    - Bolt connecting crossmember to body: 19 ft. lbs. (25 Nm)
    - Bolt connecting catalytic converter to exhaust manifold: 15 ft. lbs. (20 Nm)
    - Bolt connecting catalytic converter to center muffler: 15 ft. lbs. (20 Nm)
    - Nut connecting catalytic converter bracket to catalytic converter: 15 ft. lbs. (20 Nm)
    - 02 sensor to catalytic converter: 37 ft. lbs. (50 Nm)
12. Inspect installation position and clearance of exhaust system.
13. Clean connecting points of combus-

14. Bore in camshaft adjuster
15. Dowel pin in pulse wheel

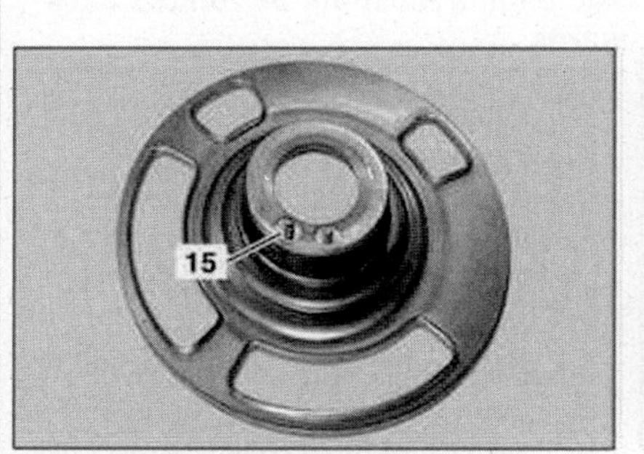

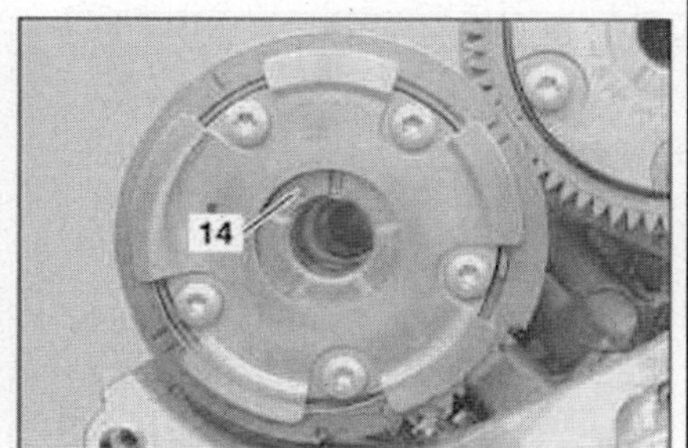

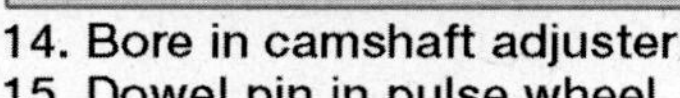

22205_MBCA_G0027

Fig. 36 Camshaft adjuster as shown on exhaust camshaft

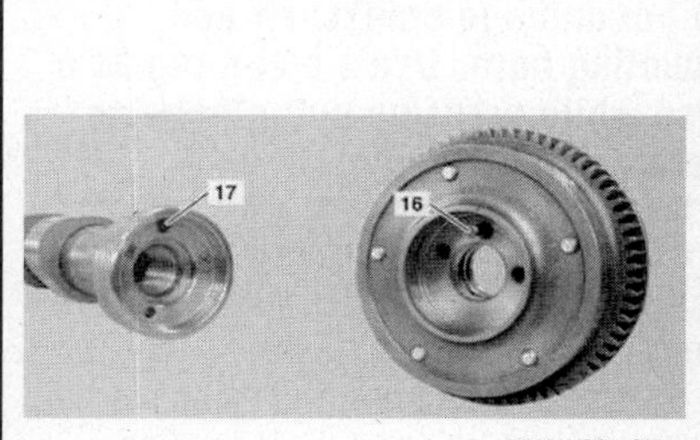

22205_MBCA_G0028

Fig. 37 Camshaft adjuster as it fits into the exhaust camshaft

tion and corrosion residues. Install new seals and bolts.

14. Apply heat-resistant lubricant to thread of 02 sensors.
15. The exhaust system must be installed free of stress. Realign exhaust system if necessary.
16. Conduct engine test run and inspect exhaust system for leaks.

CRANKSHAFT FRONT SEAL

REMOVAL & INSTALLATION

See Figure 39.

1. Before servicing the vehicle, refer to the precautions.
2. Remove front engine cover.
3. Remove intake air ducts from air filter.
4. Remove poly-V-belt.
5. Install retaining lock for crankshaft/starter ring gear.
6. Remove belt pulley / vibration damper.
7. Press out crankshaft radial sealing ring from mounting bore with a screwdriver.

1. Catalytic converter
2. Exhaust bracket
3. Center muffler
4. Exhaust rubber mount in the middle
5. Rear muffler reinforcement
6. Rear muffler
7. Inner exhaust rubber mount
8. Outer exhaust rubber bearing

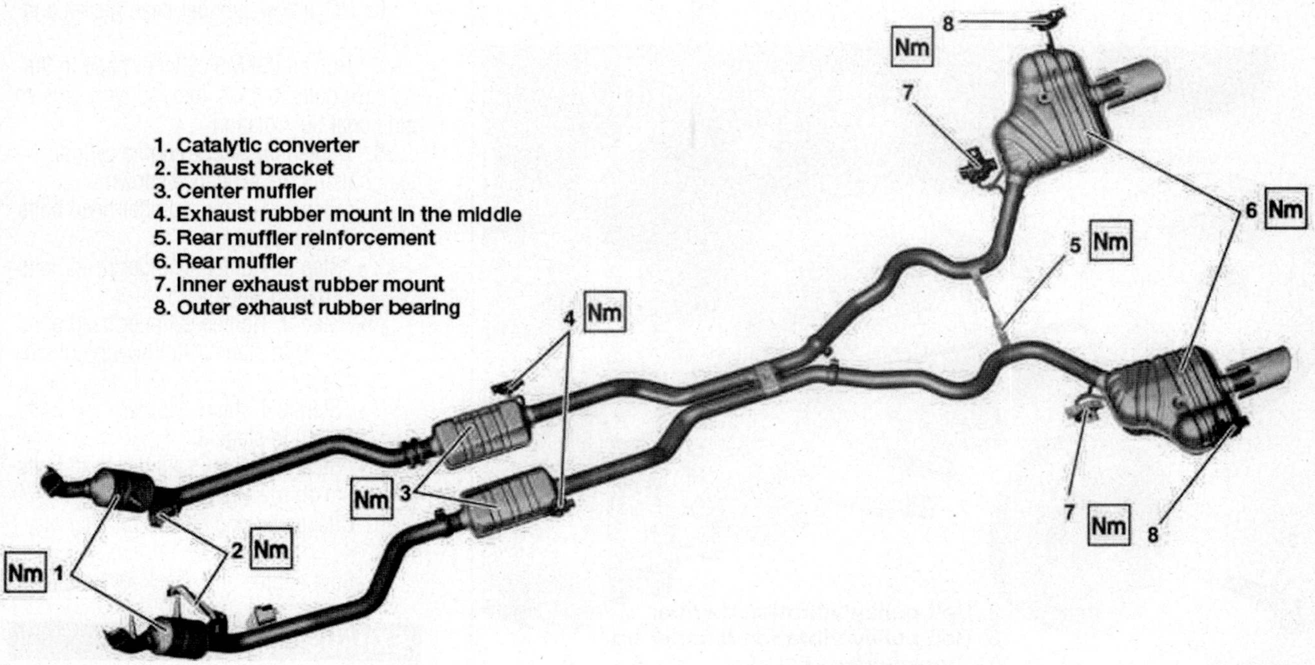

37698_MSUV_G0053

Fig. 38 Exhaust system components

⁂ WARNING

Do not damage crankshaft and mounting bore. Use a clean rag as a base while pressing out; otherwise there can be leakage.

8. Check tread of crankshaft radial sealing ring at hub of belt pulley/vibration damper.
9. Check for scoring and galling, if necessary, replace belt pulley/vibration damper.

To install:

10. Installation is the reverse of removal.

⁂ WARNING

Replace all self-locking, micro-encapsulated and aluminum bolts and nuts. Chase threads to remove micro-encapsulated residue from old bolts/nuts.

11. Tighten bolts to specification as follows:
    - Step 1: Tighten bolt to 148 ft. lbs. (200 Nm)
    - Step 2: Tighten bolt an additional 90° rotation
12. Start engine and check for leaks.

Fig. 39 Exploded view of the crankshaft damper and seal

CYLINDER HEAD

REMOVAL & INSTALLATION

See Figures 40 through 42.

1. Before servicing the vehicle, refer to the precautions.
2. Disconnect the negative battery cable.
3. Remove the engine cover.
4. Drain the engine coolant.
5. Remove the exhaust pipes from exhaust manifolds.
6. Remove the air cleaner housing.
7. Remove the ME control unit.
8. Remove the resonance intake manifold.
9. Remove the air shutoff valve.
10. Remove the front cover.
11. Remove the ignition coils.
12. Remove the cylinder head cover.
13. Remove the accessory drive belt.
14. Remove the top guide pulley.
15. Remove the alternator.
16. Rotate the engine clockwise to position the crankshaft 40° After Top Dead Center (ATDC).

⁂ WARNING

The engine must not be rotated backwards.

17. Remove the timing chain tensioner.
18. Remove the camshaft adjusters.
19. Remove the guide rail pin on the right cylinder head.
20. Remove the air pump and aspirator valve.
21. Remove the oil dipstick guide tube bolt.
22. Remove the guide bolts for slide rail on the left cylinder head.
23. Remove the cylinder head bolts in the reverse order of the tightening sequence shown.

⁂ CAUTION

Never use a prybar between the head and block.

➡The rear left bolt on the right cylinder head cannot be removed until the head is removed from the engine. Pull the bolt up slightly and use a cable tie to keep it from sliding back down.

24. Remove the cylinder head and clean all gasket material from the sealing surfaces.

To install:

25. Installation is the reverse of removal.
26. Use a new cylinder head gasket and bolts.
27. Tighten the M8 cylinder head to timing case bolts to 11 ft. lbs. (15 Nm) plus an additional 90° rotation.
28. Tighten the M272 engine cylinder head bolts in the sequence shown.
    - Step 1: Tighten cylinder head bolts (1-8) to stage 1
    - Step 2: Tighten cylinder head bolts (1-8) to stage 2
    - Step 3: Tighten cylinder head bolts (1-8) to stage 2 (follow-up tightening)
    - Step 4: Tighten cylinder head bolts (1-8) to stage 3
    - Step 5: Tighten cylinder head bolts (1-8) to stage 4
29. Change engine oil and oil filter element.
30. Start engine and check for leaks.

EXHAUST MANIFOLD

REMOVAL & INSTALLATION

See Figures 43 and 44.

1. Before servicing the vehicle, refer to the precautions.

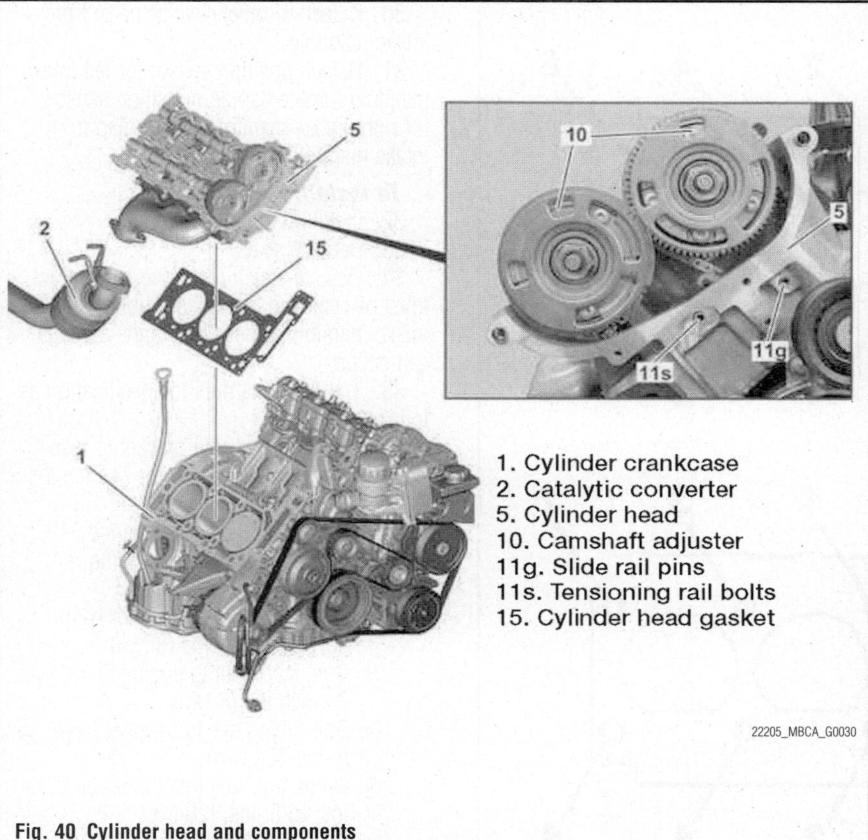

Fig. 40 Cylinder head and components

2. Properly relieve the fuel system pressure.
3. Disconnect the negative battery cable.
4. Remove the engine undercover.
5. Remove the air filter housing assembly.
6. Remove the catalytic converter and exhaust pipe.
7. Remove the exhaust manifold from the bottom.

To install:

8. Installation is the reverse of removal.
9. Clean sealing surfaces at exhaust manifold and at cylinder head
10. Use new gaskets.

⁂ WARNING

Replace all self-locking, micro-encapsulated and aluminum bolts and nuts. Chase threads to remove micro-encapsulated residue from old bolts/nuts.

11. Tighten bolts/nuts to specification as follows:
   - Nut on exhaust manifold: 12 ft. lbs. (16 Nm)
   - Nut, exhaust manifold to cylinder head: 16 ft. lbs. (22 Nm)

INTAKE MANIFOLD

REMOVAL & INSTALLATION

See Figures 45 and 46.

1. Before servicing the vehicle, refer to the precautions.
2. Remove air filter housing.
3. Remove power electronics with power distributor.
4. Disconnect right connector at ME-SFI [ME] control unit.
5. Disconnect electrical connectors.
6. Detach jack of electrical connector on fuel distributor.
7. Detach electrical feed line from left control unit bracket.
8. Pull ME-SFI [ME] control unit out of left control unit bracket and place to one side. Do not disconnect left connector at ME-SFI [ME] control unit.
9. Remove hot film mass air flow sensor.
10. Remove air duct housing.
11. Disconnect hoses from crankcase ventilation system.
12. Remove right control unit holder.
13. Detach feed duct from cylinder head cover and intake manifold.

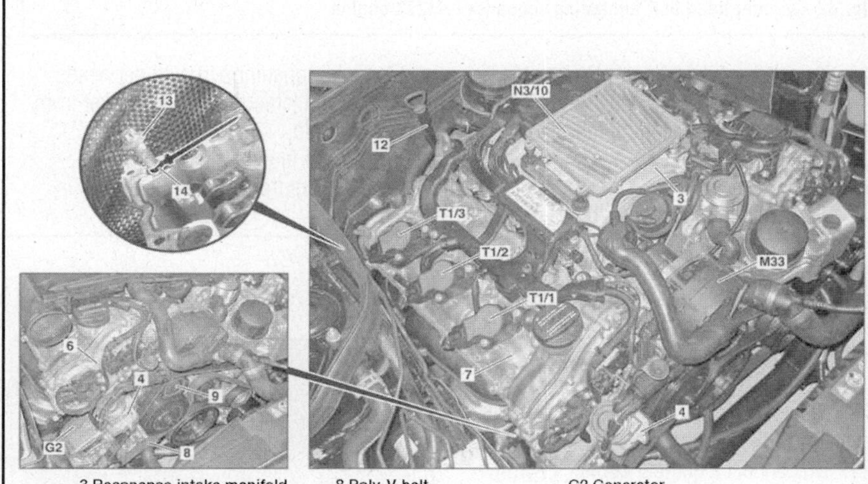

Fig. 41 Removing components necessary to access cylinder head

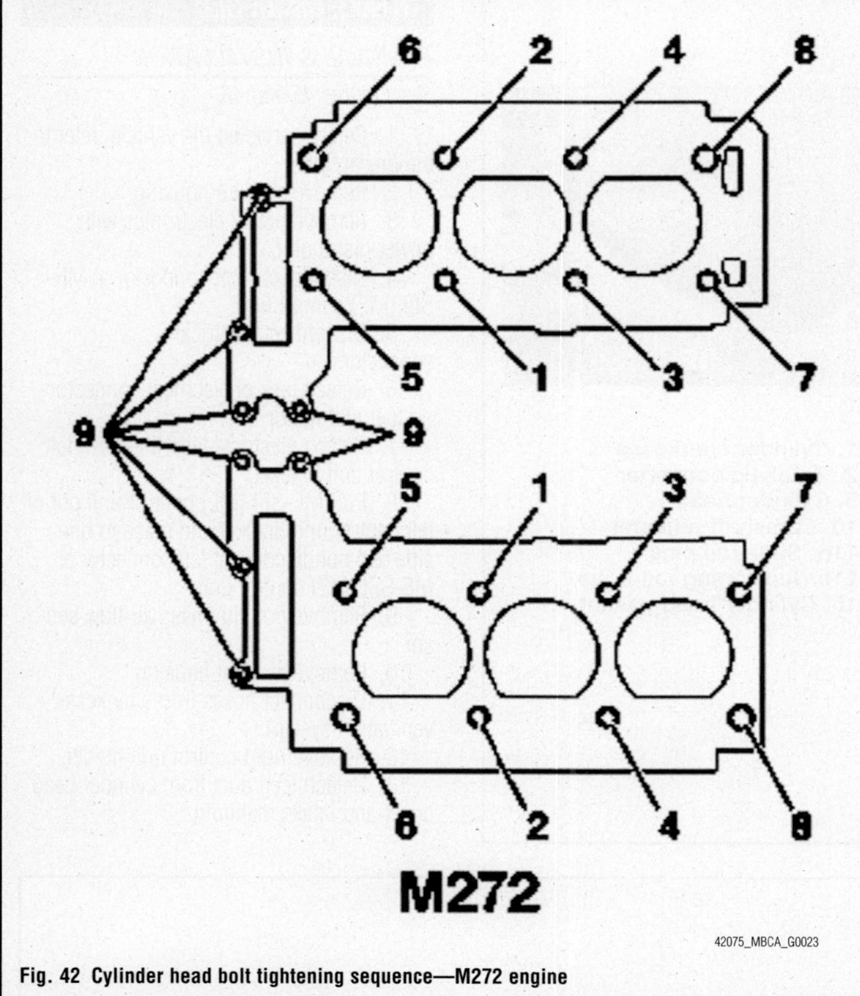

Fig. 42 Cylinder head bolt tightening sequence—M272 engine

14. Detach feed duct from intake manifold.
15. Remove left rear engine lifting eye.
16. Remove feed duct from cylinder head cover.
17. Release and disconnect the electrical connectors on fuel injection valves.
18. Unlock electrical connectors on position sensor for left intake manifold tumble flap and position sensor for right intake manifold tumble flap and disconnect.
19. Disconnect electrical connector.
20. Release and disconnect the electrical connector at the throttle valve actuator.
21. Disconnect electrical connector from electrical air pump.
22. Reduce fuel pressure with the pressure hose via the service valve.
23. Disconnect fuel line from fuel distributor.
24. Remove bolts.
25. Raise intake manifold at front and detach pneumatic lines from the connection fittings on intake manifold.
26. Take out intake manifold.
27. Cover openings in cylinder heads.
28. Detach left control unit bracket from intake manifold.
29. Detach fuel distributor with fuel injection valves from intake manifold.
30. Detach throttle valve actuator from intake manifold.
31. Detach position sensor for left intake manifold tumble flap and position sensor for right intake manifold tumble flap from intake manifold.

To install:

32. Install in the reverse order.
33. Replace seals.
34. Objects which reach the intake tract must be removed before assembling the intake manifold, otherwise engine damage can occur.
35. Tighten bolts/nuts to specification as follows:
    - Bolt, control unit bracket to resonance intake manifold: 71 inch lbs (8 Nm)
    - Bolt, feed duct to resonance intake manifold: 71 inch lbs (8 Nm)
    - Bolt, feed duct to cylinder head cover: 71 inch lbs (8 Nm)
    - Bolt, feed duct to engine lifting eye: 71 inch lbs (8 Nm)
    - Bolt, lifting eye to cylinder head: 15 ft. lbs. (20 Nm)
    - Union nut, fuel line to fuel distributor: 15 ft. lbs. (20 Nm)
    - Bolt, fuel distributor to resonance intake manifold: 80 inch lbs. (9 Nm)
    - Protective cap on service valve Plastic: 18 inch lbs. (2 Nm)
    - Protective cap on service valve Metal: 11 ft. lbs. (15 Nm)
    - Bolt, resonance intake manifold to cylinder head: 80 inch lbs. (9 Nm)
    - Bolt, tumble flap position sensor to resonance intake manifold: 53 inch lbs. (6 Nm)

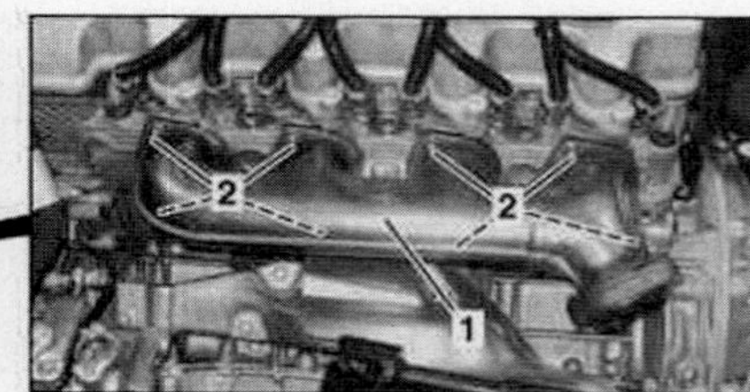

1. Exhaust manifold
2. Bolts

37698_MSUV_G0064

Fig. 43 Exhaust manifold components—left

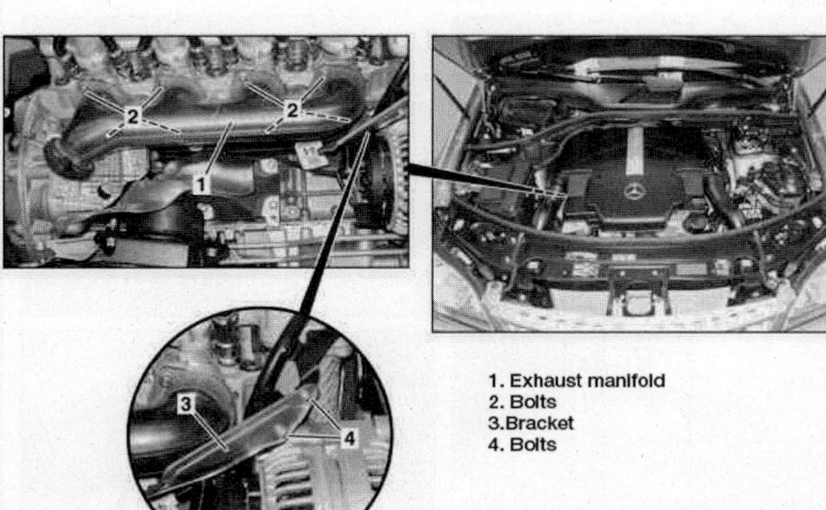

Fig. 44 Exhaust manifold components—right

- Bolt, throttle valve actuator to resonance intake manifold: 80 inch lbs. (9 Nm)

OIL PAN

REMOVAL & INSTALLATION

See Figures 47 through 49.

1. Before servicing the vehicle, refer to the precautions.
2. Disconnect the negative battery cable.
3. Remove the engine under cover.
4. Remove the engine oil.
5. Remove the bolts from the oil pan.

➡It may be necessary to tap on the oil pan with a rubber mallet to dislodge it from the engine block.

6. Remove the oil pan.

To install:

7. Installation is the reverse of removal.
8. Clean all gasket material from the sealing surfaces using solvent, do not scrape the surface.
9. Apply sealant A 003 989 98 20 or equivalent sealant to the oil pan as shown.

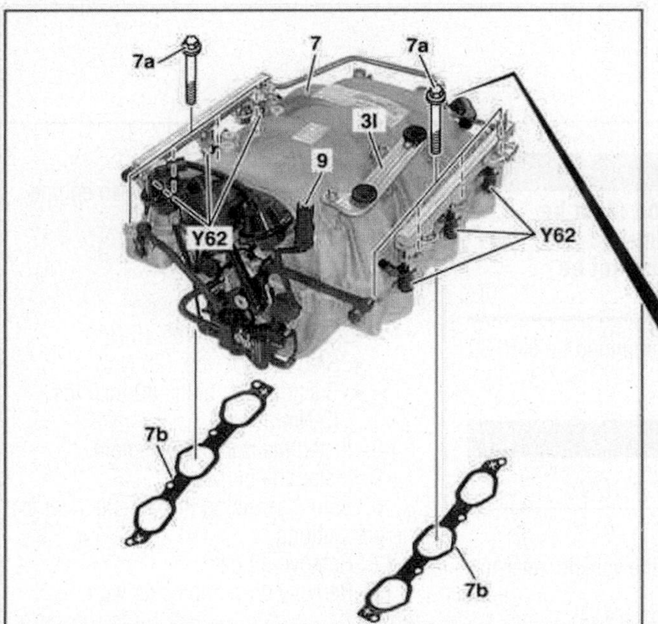

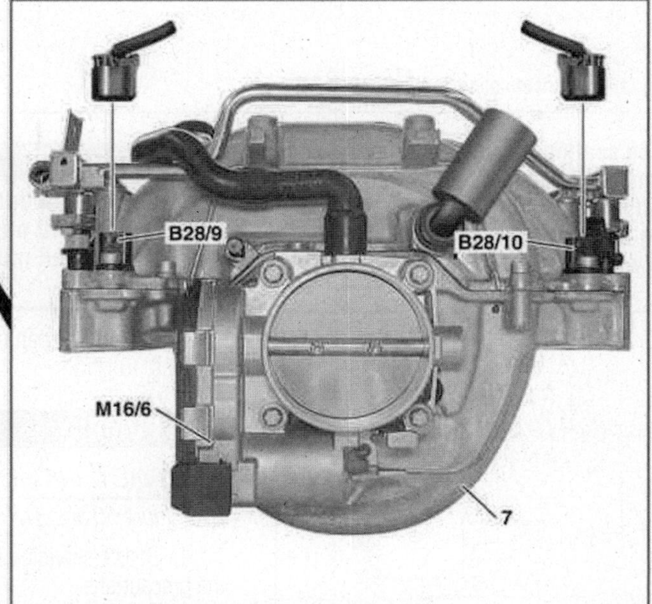

3l. Left control unit bracket
7. Intake manifold
7a. Bolt
7b. Gasket
9. Electrical connector

B28/9. Left intake manifold tumble flap position sensor
B28/10. Right intake manifold tumble flap position sensor
M16/6. Throttle valve actuator
Y62. Fuel injection valves

37698_MSUV_G0066

Fig. 45 Intake manifolds

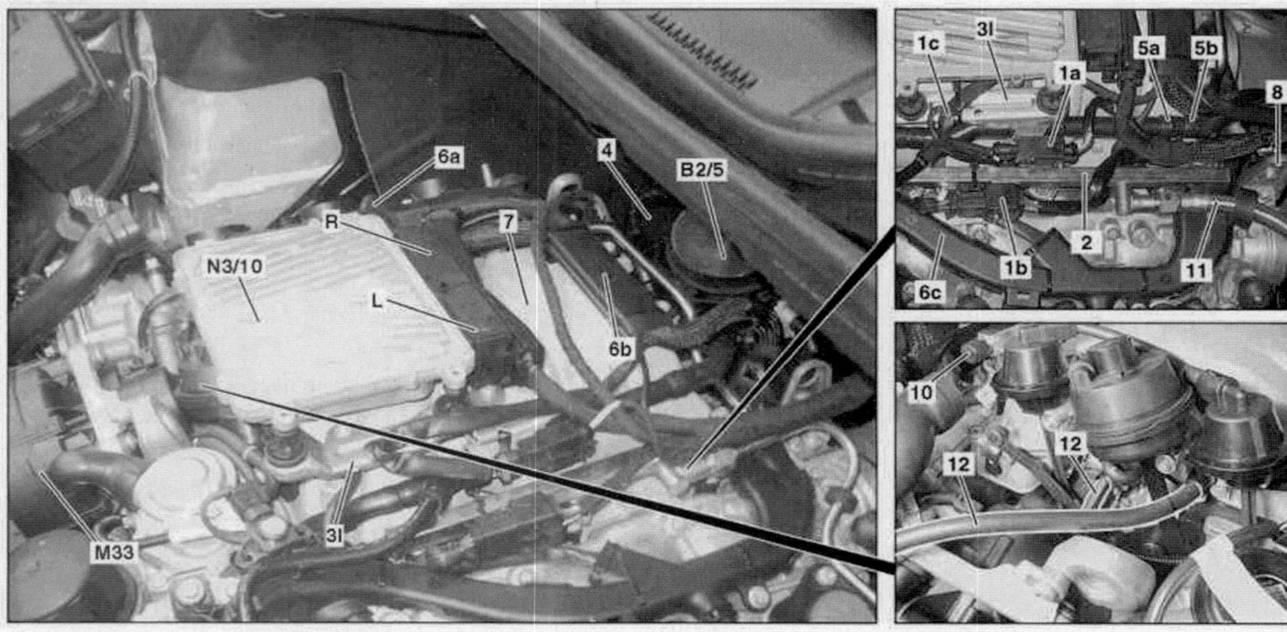

Fig. 46 Electrical connectors

➡The sealing surface must be cleaned. The sealant must only be applied to the specified surface in the form of a bead and a height of 2.0 mm and width of 0.5 mm.

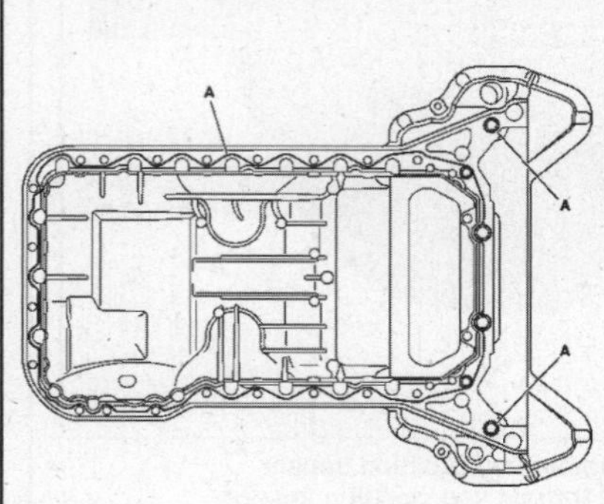

Fig. 47 Application of sealant (A) to oil pan bottom section for engine with rear sump

⁂ WARNING

The sealing compound must be applied within 10 minutes.
The sealant bead must not be spread.

10. Tighten the pan mounting bolts to 80 inch lbs. (9 Nm).

OIL PUMP

REMOVAL & INSTALLATION

See Figure 50 and 51.

1. Before servicing the vehicle, refer to the precautions.
2. Remove the lower oil pan.
3. Remove the bolts from the oil suction tube.
4. Push the chain tensioner back and remove the pump drive chain.
5. Unbolt and remove the oil pump together with the suction tube.

To install:

6. Fill the oil pump with clean engine oil and install it to the engine.
7. Tighten the fasteners to specification
   - Oil pump to crankcase:
   - Step 1: 44 inch lbs. (5 Nm)
   - Step 2: 15 ft. lbs. (20 Nm)
   - Suction tube bolts: 80 inch lbs. (9 Nm)
8. Install the pump drive chain.
9. Install the oil pan.
10. Before servicing the vehicle, refer to the precautions.
11. Remove oil pan.
12. Remove oil pump cover with oil pipe.
13. Disconnect the oil pump from the crankcase.
14. Remove oil pump. Press tensioning rail away from oil pump chain, unhook oil pump out of oil pump chain.

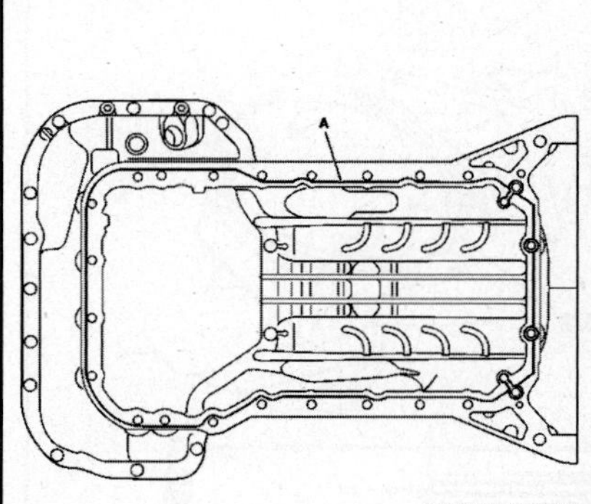

Fig. 48 Application of sealant (A) to oil pan bottom section for engine with front sump

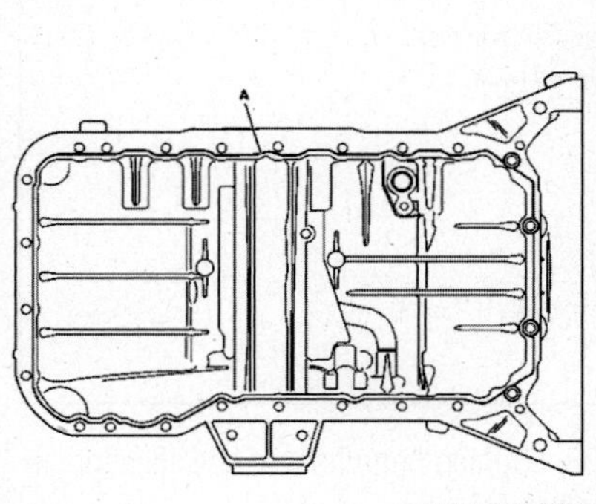

Fig. 49 Application of sealant (A) to oil pan bottom section for engine with middle sump

To install:

15. Install in reverse order.
16. Tighten bolts/nuts to specification as follows:
    - Bolt for oil pump: 14 ft. lbs. (19 Nm)
    - Bolt for oil pump cover with oil pipe to oil pump: 106 inch lbs. (12 Nm)
    - Oil pump bracket: 80 inch lbs. (9 Nm)
17. Clean strainer on oil pump and renew sealing ring. If oil pump is dry, fill it with engine oil so that oil is deliver rod when first starting engine.

PISTON AND RING

POSITIONING

See Figures 52 and 53.

1 Oil suction pipe
2 Bolt 4 Bolt
3 Oil pump
5 Bolt
6 Chain tensioner
7 Oil pump chain
8 Oil pump gear

22205_MBCA_G0036

Fig. 50 Oil pump and chain

TIMING CHAIN FRONT COVER

REMOVAL & INSTALLATION

See Figure 54.

1. Before servicing the vehicle, refer to the precautions.
2. Remove air filter housing.
3. Remove lower engine compartment paneling.
4. Drain coolant at radiator.
5. Remove electric fan.
6. Attach guard plate for radiator/ condenser Guard plate for radiator/ condenser.
7. Remove poly-V belt.

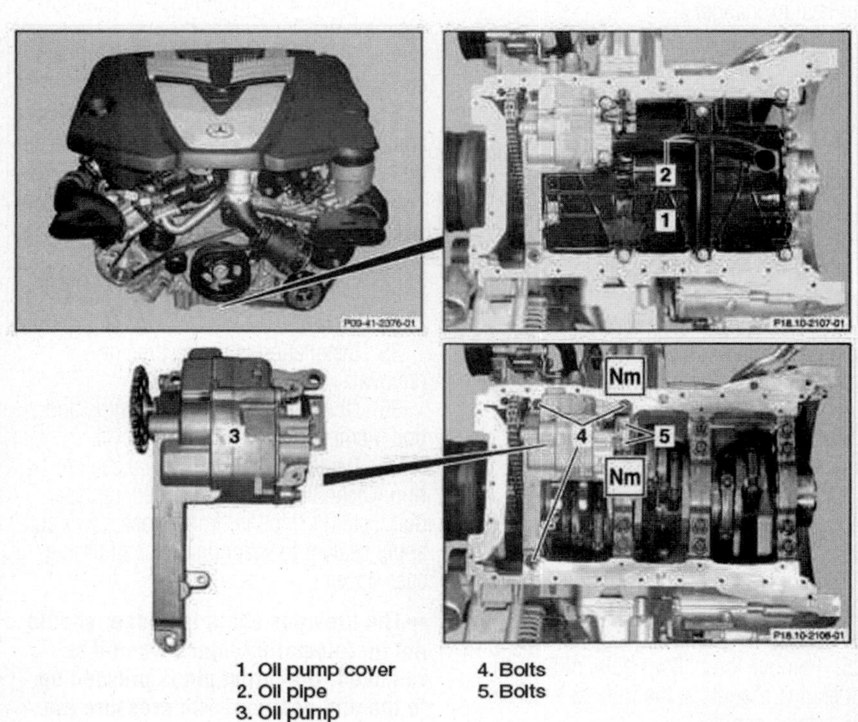

Fig. 51 Removing oil pump

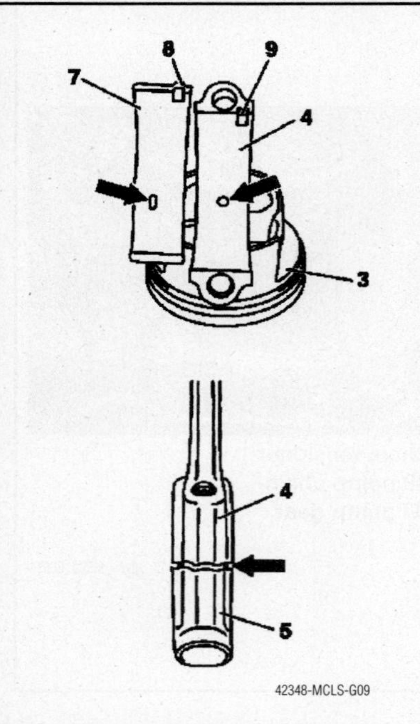

Fig. 52 Install pistons so the code next to the piston pin and group number are pointing in the direction of travel, and the anti-twist lock (8) and the groove (9) are matched

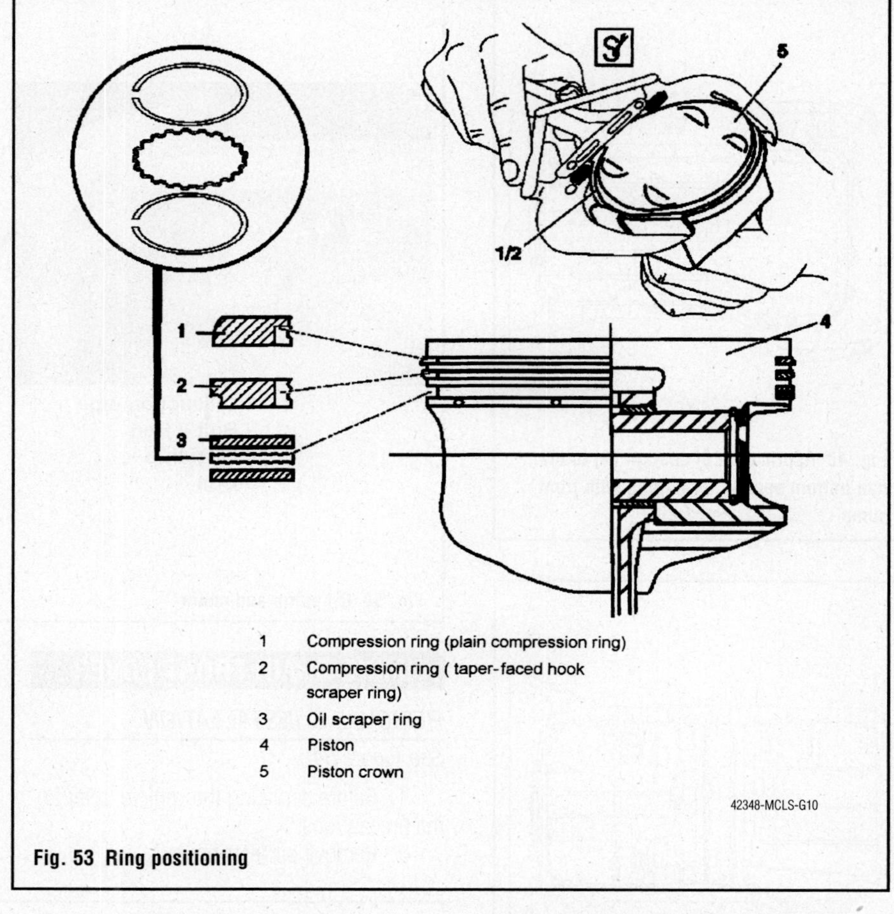

Fig. 53 Ring positioning

8. Remove poly-V-belt tensioning device.
9. Remove oil filter housing with oil-water heat exchanger.
10. Remove power steering expansion reservoir.
11. Remove front cover at left cylinder head.
12. Remove front cover at the right cylinder head.
13. Remove air pump.
14. Remove left air shutoff valve.
15. Remove flange for aspirator shutoff valve.
16. Detach power steering pump from timing case cover and put it to one side with connected lines.
17. Detach refrigerant compressor and put it on the side with connected lines.
18. Remove alternator.
19. Remove chain tensioner.
20. Remove belt pulley/vibration damper.
21. Detach guide pulley.
22. Remove the oil dipstick guide tube.
23. Remove complete exhaust system.
24. Mount engine hoist.
25. Remove the bottom bolts of both the front engine mounts at the front axle carrier.
26. Raise engine.
27. Remove oil pan bottom section.
28. Remove oil pan.
29. Lower engine and disconnect from engine hoist.
30. Detach the coolant hose of the coolant pump.
31. Remove segmental disks of camshaft adjuster and again tighten central valves finger-tight.
32. Remove bolts with a flex head socket wrench.
33. Remove bolt.
34. Detach timing case cover.

To install:

35. Installation is the reverse of removal.
36. Observe different bolt lengths and bolt diameters on timing case cover.
37. Replace crankshaft radial sealing ring. Clean the sealing surfaces, replace both sealing rings in timing case cover and apply sealant to sealing surface of timing case cover.

➡The previous chain tensioner should not be reinstalled, since when it is removed, the thrust pin is pressed up to the end position. The pressure pin latch prevents this return stroke. This would overstretch the timing chain on reinstalling.

38. Tighten bolts/nuts to specification as follows:
   - Bolt, left air shutoff valve intermediate flange to cylinder head: 10 ft. lbs. (14 Nm)
   - Bolt, poly-V-belt guide pulley to coolant pump: 26 ft. lbs. (35 Nm)
   - Cylinder head bolt on timing case M8: 11 ft. lbs. (15 Nm) plus an additional 90° rotation
   - Bolt, timing case cover to cylinder crankcase M8: 15 ft. lbs. (20 Nm)
   - Bolt, refrigerant compressor to timing case cover or engine support: 15 ft. lbs. (20 Nm)
39. Check engine oil level, correct if necessary.

TIMING CHAIN & SPROCKETS

REMOVAL & INSTALLATION

See Figures 55 and 56.

➡An endless timing chain is used on production engines, but a split chain with a connecting link is used for service. The endless chain can be separated with a "chain breaker". Only 1

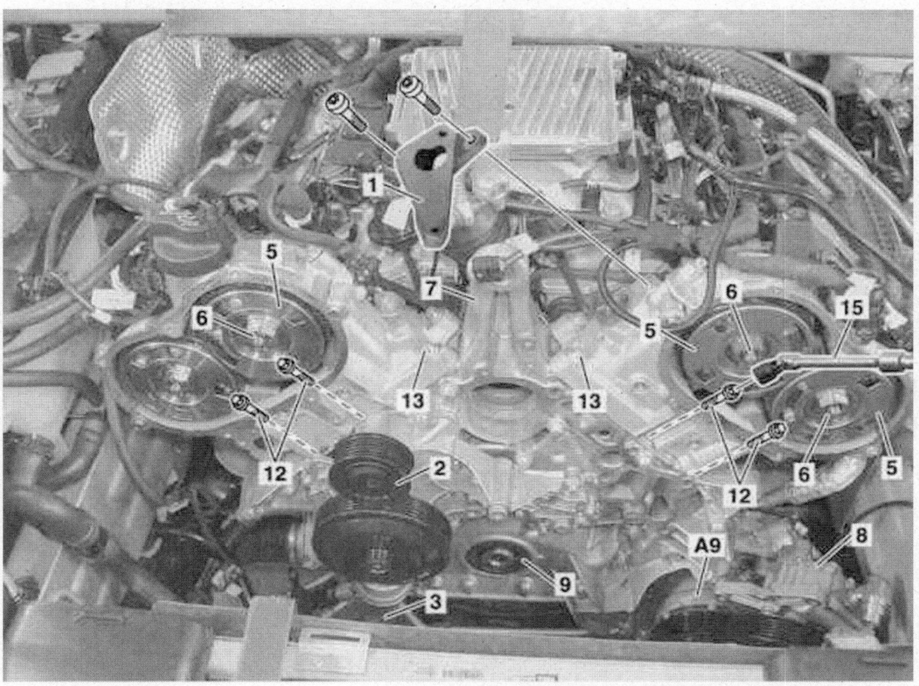

1. Flange
2. Pulley
3. Coolant hose
5. Segmental disks
6. Central valves
7. Timing case cover
8. Power steering pump
9. Crankshaft radial sealing ring
12. Bolts
13. Bolts
15. Flex head socket wrench
A9. Refrigerant compressor

22205_MBCA_G0212

Fig. 54 Timing cover removal

master link (connecting link) should be used on a chain.

1. Before servicing the vehicle, refer to the precautions.
2. Disconnect the negative battery cable.
3. Remove the spark plugs.
4. Remove the camshafts.
5. Clamp the chain to the camshaft gear and cover the opening of the timing chain case.
6. Separate the chain with a chain breaker.

To install:

7. Attach a new timing chain to the old chain with a master link, center plate and end plate. Using a socket wrench on the crankshaft, slowly rotate the engine in the direction of normal rotation. Simultaneously, pull the old chain through until the master link is uppermost on the camshaft sprocket. Be sure to keep tension on the chain throughout this procedure.

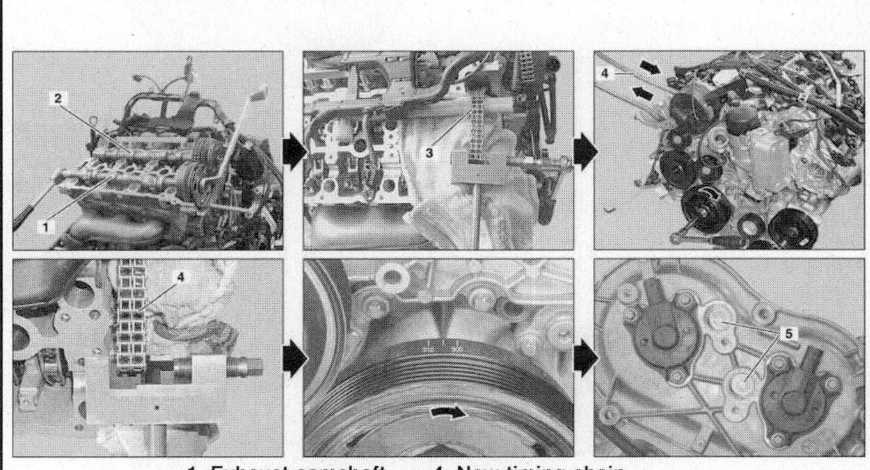

1. Exhaust camshaft
2. Intake camshaft
3. Old timing chain
4. New timing chain
5. Markings on pulse wheels

22205_MBCA_G0043

Fig. 55 Illustrating the timing chain removal procedure

6. Markings on camshaft adjuster
7. Markings on camshaft adjuster

22205_MBCA_G0044

Fig. 57 Markings on the crankshaft damper and camshaft adjusters

8. Disconnect the old timing chain and connect the ends of the new chain with the master link. Insert the new connecting link from the rear so the lockwashers can be seen from the front.
9. Rotate the engine in the direction of rotation until the timing marks align at 55° Before Top Dead Center (BTDC).
10. The markings on the pulse wheels of the intake and exhaust camshafts at the left cylinder head must be located centrally in the bores of the camshaft sensors. If not, rotate the engine another revolution.
11. Rotate the engine in the direction of rotation 95° so that it is at 40° After Top Dead Center (ATDC) of cylinder 1.
12. Install the camshafts on the right cylinder head. The marks should point upwards and match with the markings on the cylinder head covers.
13. Rotate the engine in the direction of rotation until the timing marks align at 55° BTDC again. The markings on the pulse wheels of the intake and exhaust camshafts at the left cylinder head must be located centrally in the bores of the camshaft sensors.
14. Install the spark plugs.
15. Connect the negative battery cable.
16. Start the engine and check operation.

ENGINE PERFORMANCE & EMISSION CONTROLS

CAMSHAFT POSITION (CMP) SENSOR

LOCATION

See Figure 57.

REMOVAL & INSTALLATION

1. Before servicing the vehicle, refer to the precautions.
2. Remove engine trim panel.
3. Detach the electrical connector at the intake camshaft Hall sensor.
4. Remove bolt.
5. Remove intake camshaft Hall sensor.

To install:

6. Installation is the reverse of removal.
7. Replace sealing rings.
8. Tighten camshaft position sensor to 6 ft. lbs.

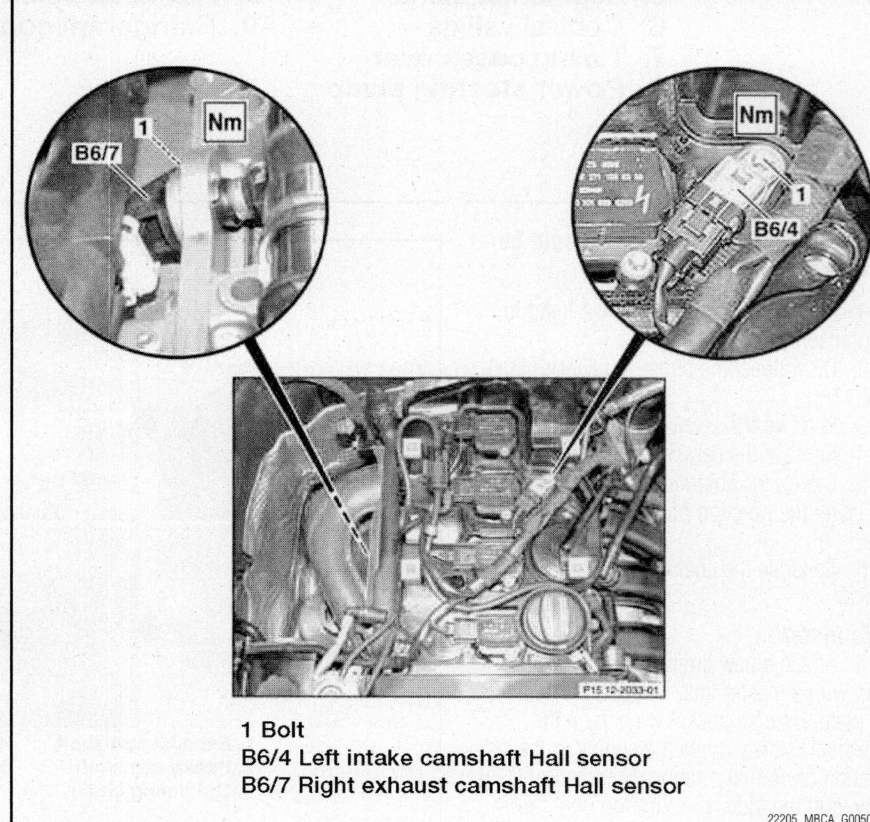

1 Bolt
B6/4 Left intake camshaft Hall sensor
B6/7 Right exhaust camshaft Hall sensor

22205_MBCA_G0050

Fig. 57 CMP sensor location

CRANKSHAFT POSITION (CKP) SENSOR

LOCATION

See Figure 58.

REMOVAL & INSTALLATION

1. Before servicing the vehicle, refer to the precautions.
2. Remove air filter housing.

1. Crankshaft position sensor
B70 electrical connector

22205_MBCA_G0045

Fig. 58 CKP sensor location

N3/10. Control unit T1/2. Ignition coil
T1/3. Ignition coil T1/1. Ignition coil

37698_MERC_G0057

Fig. 59 ECM location

3. Remove hot film mass air flow sensor.
4. Remove air duct housing.
5. Release and disconnect electrical connector at crankshaft Hall sensor.
6. Remove bolt.
7. Pull crankshaft Hall sensor out of crankcase.

To install:

8. Installation is the reverse of removal.
9. Tighten crankshaft Hall sensor to crankcase bolt to 6 ft. lbs.
10. Carry out first initialization and then sensor rotor adaptation using STAR DIAGNOSIS tool.

ELECTRONIC CONTROL MODULE (ECM)

LOCATION

See Figure 59.

REMOVAL & INSTALLATION

1. Before servicing the vehicle, refer to the precautions.
2. Remove air filter housing.
3. Move shift interlocks for electrical connectors on control unit outward and remove electrical connectors from ME control unit.
4. Pull out control unit upwards out of right control unit bracket and left control unit bracket.
5. Detach ball-type support braces from control unit.
6. Detach right control unit bracket and left control unit bracket as required from resonance intake manifold.

To install:

7. Installation is the reverse of removal.
8. Tighten control unit holder to resonance intake manifold bolt to 6 ft. lbs.
9. Tighten ball head support to control unit to 3 ft. lbs.
10. When replacing the control unit, perform the following using STAR DIAGNOSIS or equivalent scan tool.
    - Sensor rotor adaptation
    - Release the transport protection on control unit
    - Personalize and activate the control unit

ENGINE COOLANT TEMPERATURE (ECT) SENSOR

LOCATION

See Figure 60.

REMOVAL & INSTALLATION

1. Before servicing the vehicle, refer to the precautions.
2. Remove rear section of lower engine compartment paneling.
3. Open engine hood and raise to vertical position.
4. Reduce pressure in cooling system, to do this, slowly open the cap at expansion reservoir and reclose.
5. Remove air filter housing.

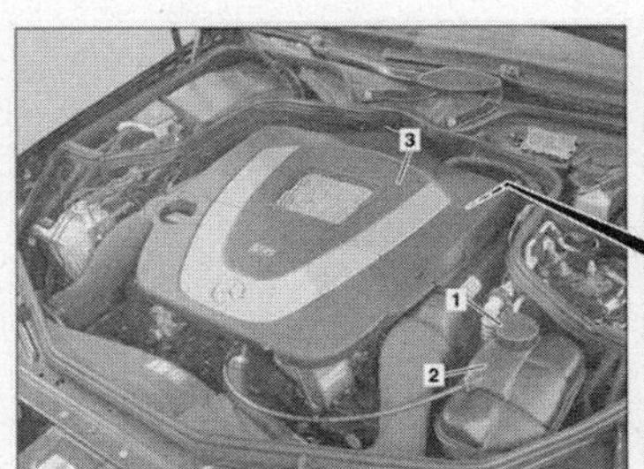

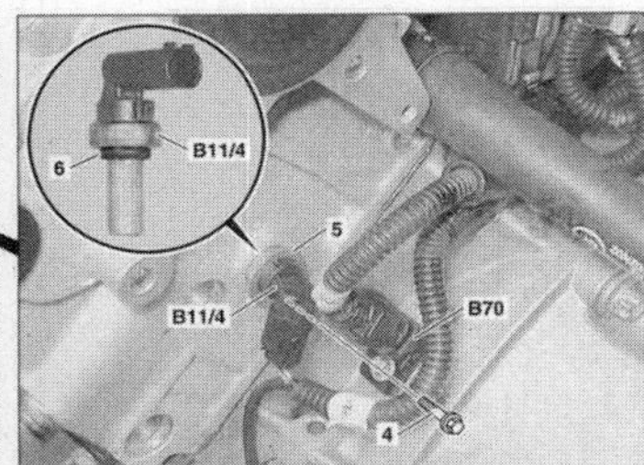

1. Cap
2. Coolant expansion reservoir
3. Air filter housing
4. Bolt
5. Clamping plate
6. O-ring
B11/4. Coolant temperature sensor
B70. Crankshaft Hall sensor

22205_MBCA_G0048

Fig. 60 ECT sensor location

6. Release and disconnect electrical connector at crankshaft Hall sensor.
7. Unlatch the electrical connector at the coolant temperature sensor and disconnect.
8. Unscrew bolt and remove clamping plate.
9. Fit new O-ring to new coolant temperature sensor.
10. Pull coolant temperature sensor out of cylinder head and immediately insert new coolant temperature sensor.

To install:

11. Installation is the reverse of removal.
12. Tighten clamping plate for coolant temperature sensor to cylinder head to 6 ft. lbs.
13. Pour in coolant and bleed cooling system.
14. Read out fault memory and erase if required.

HEATED OXYGEN SENSOR (HO2S)

LOCATION

See Figure 61.

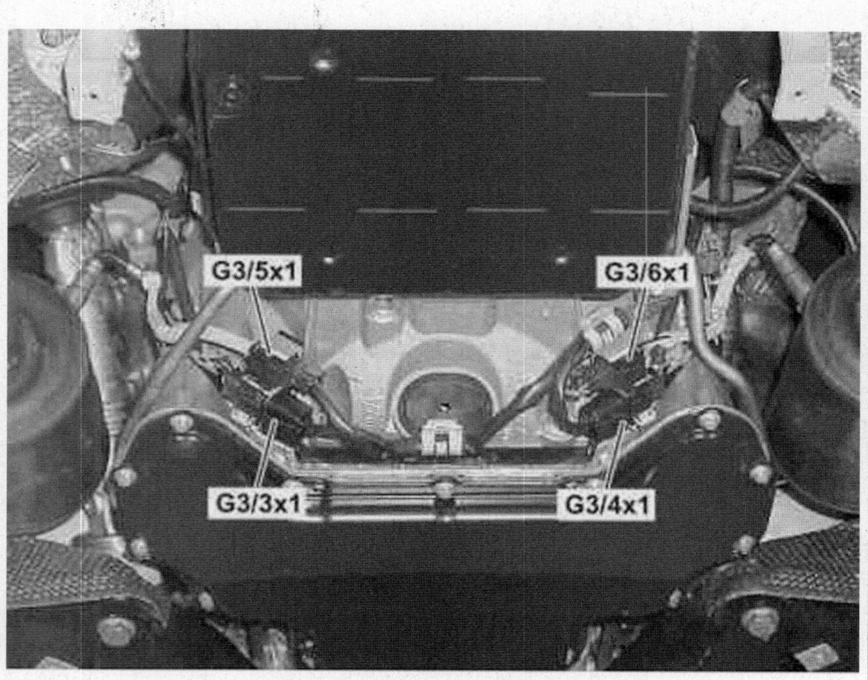

Fig. 61 Oxygen sensor connector locations

REMOVAL & INSTALLATION

1. Before servicing the vehicle, refer to the precautions.
2. Raise and safely support vehicle.
3. Detach the rear section of the lower engine compartment paneling.
4. Unclip the electrical connectors and electrical lines of the 02 sensors of the catalytic converter for removal from the retaining clamps.
5. Disconnect the electrical connectors of the 02 sensors of the catalytic converter for removal.
6. Remove 02 sensors from respective catalytic converter.

To install:

7. Install in the reverse order.
8. Apply heat-resistant lubricant to thread of 02 sensors.
9. Tighten 02 sensor to 37 ft. lbs. (50 Nm).
10. Conduct engine test run and inspect exhaust system for leaks.

KNOCK SENSOR (KS)

LOCATION

See Figure 62.

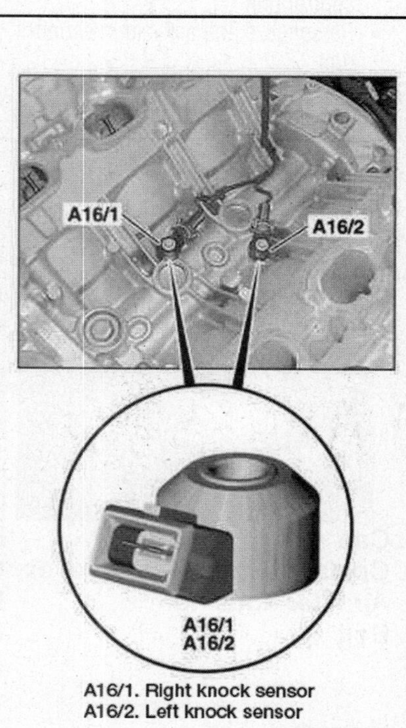

Fig. 62 KS sensor location

REMOVAL & INSTALLATION

1. Before servicing the vehicle, refer to the precautions.
2. Remove air filter housing.
3. Remove resonance intake manifold.
4. Disconnect electrical connector at right knock sensor or left knock sensor.
5. Remove bolt and take out right knock sensor or left knock sensor.

To install:

6. Installation is the reverse of removal.
7. Tighten knock sensor to crankcase bolt to 15 ft. lbs. (20 Nm).
8. Connect STAR DIAGNOSIS or equivalent scan tool and read out fault memory.

MASS AIR FLOW (MAF) SENSOR

LOCATION

See Figure 63.

REMOVAL & INSTALLATION

1. Before servicing the vehicle, refer to the precautions.
2. Remove air filter housing.
3. Remove the electrical connector at the hot film mass air flow sensor.
4. Disengage the right notch of the hot

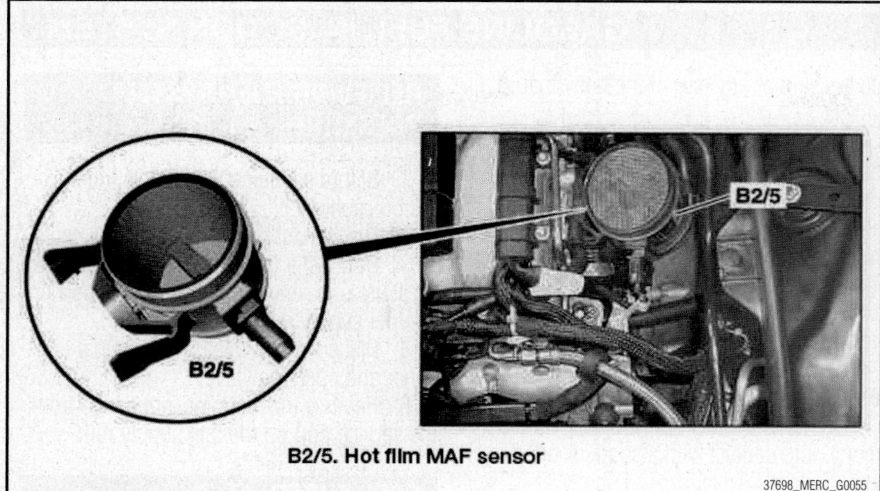

Fig. 63 MAF sensor location

film mass air flow sensor at the resonance intake manifold.

5. Unlatch left notch for hot film MAF sensor on resonance intake manifold and tip hot film MAF sensor somewhat to the rear.
6. Disengage the spring steel sheet and remove the hot film mass air flow sensor from the air duct housing.
7. Check seal between air duct housing and hot film MAF sensor for damage; replace if necessary.
8. Check right notch, left notch and spring steel sheet for damage; replace if necessary.

To install:

9. Installation is the reverse of removal.
10. Connect STAR DIAGNOSIS or equivalent scan tool and read out fault memory.

THROTTLE CONTROL ACTUATOR (TAC)

LOCATION

See Figure 64.

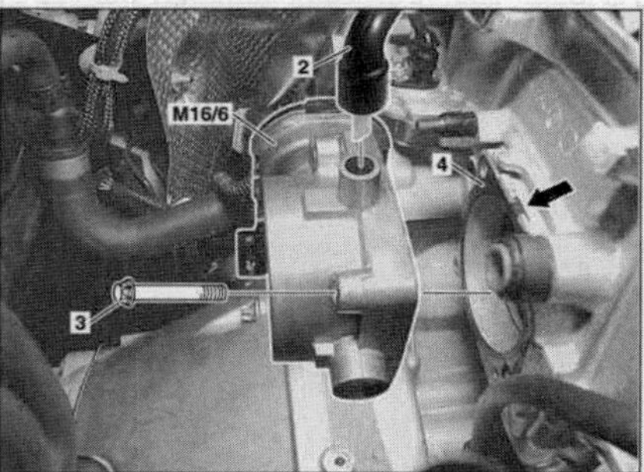

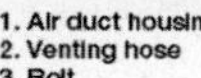

4. Seal
B2/5. Hot film mass air flow sensor
M16/6. Throttle valve actuator

37698_MERC_G0058

Fig. 64 Throttle control actuator location

REMOVAL & INSTALLATION

1. Before servicing the vehicle, refer to the precautions.
2. Remove air filter housing.
3. Remove mass air flow sensor.
4. Remove air guide tube.
5. Release and disconnect electrical connector at throttle valve actuator.
6. Pull bleed house out of throttle valve actuator.
7. Remove bolts.
8. Remove throttle valve actuator.
9. Remove gasket.

To install:

10. Installation is the reverse of removal.
11. Tighten bolt connecting throttle valve actuator to resonance intake manifold: 80 inch lbs. (9 Nm)
12. Connect STAR DIAGNOSIS tool, read out and clear fault memory.

FUEL SYSTEM SERVICE PRECAUTIONS

Safety is the most important factor when performing not only fuel system maintenance but any type of maintenance. Failure to conduct maintenance and repairs in a safe manner may result in serious personal injury or death. Maintenance and testing of the vehicle's fuel system components can be accomplished safely and effectively by adhering to the following rules and guidelines.

- To avoid the possibility of fire and personal injury, always disconnect the negative battery cable unless the repair or test procedure requires that battery voltage be applied.
- Always relieve the fuel system pressure prior to disconnecting any fuel system component (injector, fuel rail, pressure regulator, etc.), fitting or fuel line connection. Exercise extreme caution whenever relieving fuel system pressure to avoid exposing skin, face and eyes to fuel spray. Please be advised that fuel under pressure may penetrate the skin or any part of the body that it contacts.
- Always place a shop towel or cloth around the fitting or connection prior to loosening to absorb any excess fuel due to spillage. Ensure that all fuel spillage (should it occur) is quickly removed from engine surfaces. Ensure that all fuel soaked cloths or towels are deposited into a suitable waste container.
- Always keep a dry chemical (Class B) fire extinguisher near the work area.
- Do not allow fuel spray or fuel vapors to come into contact with a spark or open flame.
- Always use a back-up wrench when loosening and tightening fuel line connection fittings. This will prevent unnecessary stress and torsion to fuel line piping.
- Always replace worn fuel fitting O-rings with new Do not substitute fuel hose or equivalent where fuel pipe is installed.

Before servicing the vehicle, make sure to also refer to the precautions in the beginning of this section as well.

RELIEVING FUEL SYSTEM PRESSURE

1. Before servicing the vehicle, refer to the precautions.
2. Disconnect the negative battery cable.
3. Connect a fuel pressure gauge with a pressure release valve to the service port on the fuel supply rail.
4. Place the fuel release tube into a container and open the valve.
5. Remove the fuel pressure gauge from the service port on the fuel supply rail.

FUEL FILTER

REMOVAL & INSTALLATION

See Figure 65.

1. Before servicing the vehicle, refer to the precautions.
2. Drain fuel tank.
3. Disconnect ground lead from battery.
4. Loosen fuel lines on the fuel pump.
5. Remove/install fuel pump and fuel level sensor.

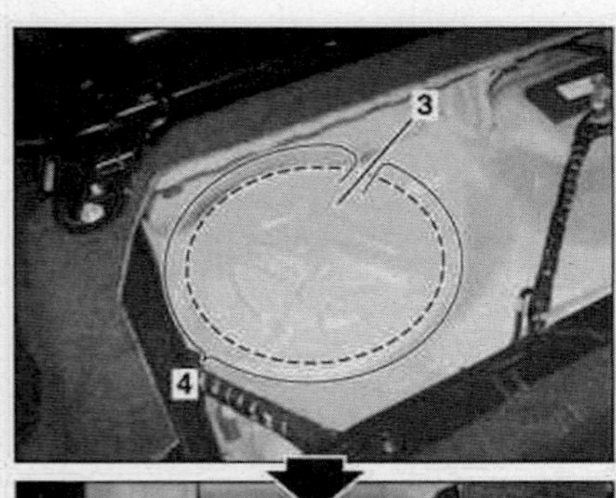

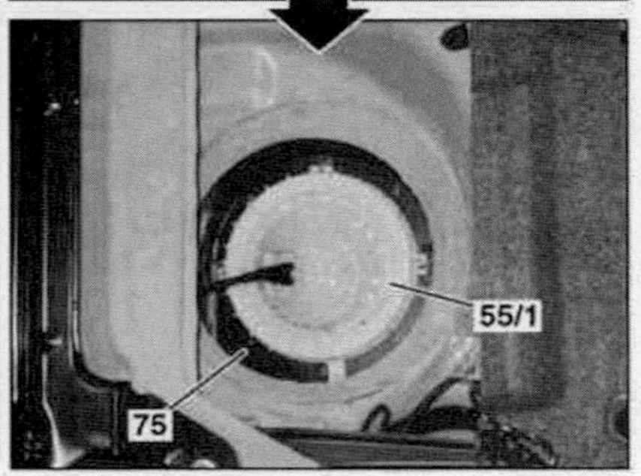

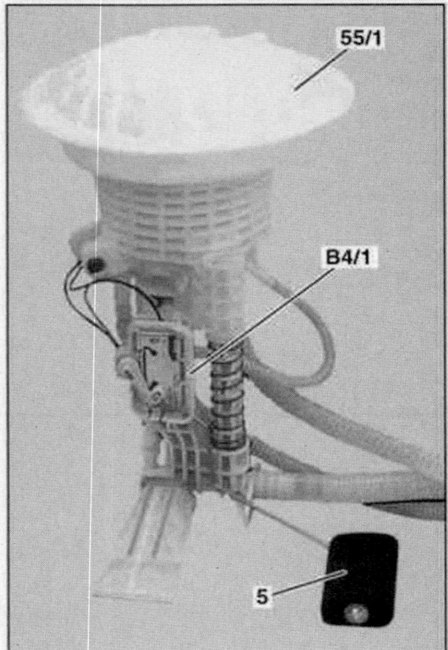

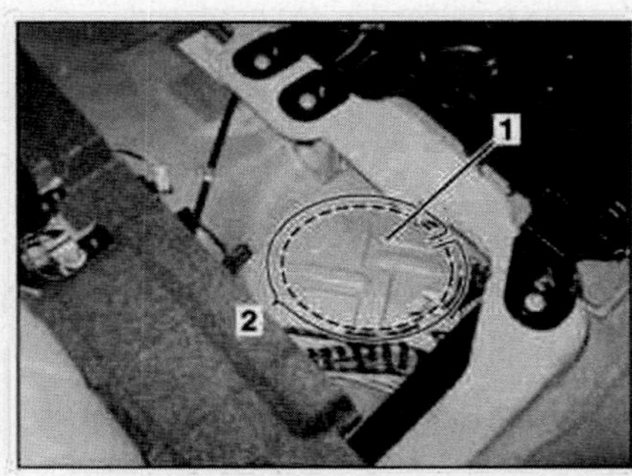

55/1. Fuel filter
75. Fuel tank
B4/1. Left fuel level sensor

37698_MSUV_G0077

Fig. 65 Removing fuel filter

6. Remove fuel filter from the left chamber of the fuel tank.

➡The fuel filter and fuel level sensor, left tank half form a unit. The fuel filter cannot be replaced separately.

To install:

7. Install in the reverse order.

FUEL PUMP/ FUEL PUMP MODULE/FUEL TANK MODULE

REMOVAL & INSTALLATION

See Figure 66.

1. Before servicing the vehicle, refer to the precautions.
2. Fold forward rear seat cushion.
3. Raise sound deadening mat and place to one side out of working area.
4. Remove support for step protection.
5. Disconnect cap on the right at the marked separation point and remove.

➡The right cap is glued in with body sealer. Heat with hot air blower to make it easier to remove.

6. Disconnect electrical connector.
7. Use pronged wrench to unscrew on ring nut.
8. Disconnect electrical connector and remove locating cover.
9. Disconnect fuel feed line, fuel return line and level line from fuel pump with fuel level sensor.
10. Remove swirl pot and fuel pump with fuel level sensor.

To install:

11. Install in the reverse order.
12. The parts kit with ring nut, sealing ring and threaded ring must be replaced.
13. Replace cap on the right and insert with new sealing mass.
14. Tighten fuel tank ring nut to 81 ft. lbs. (110 Nm).

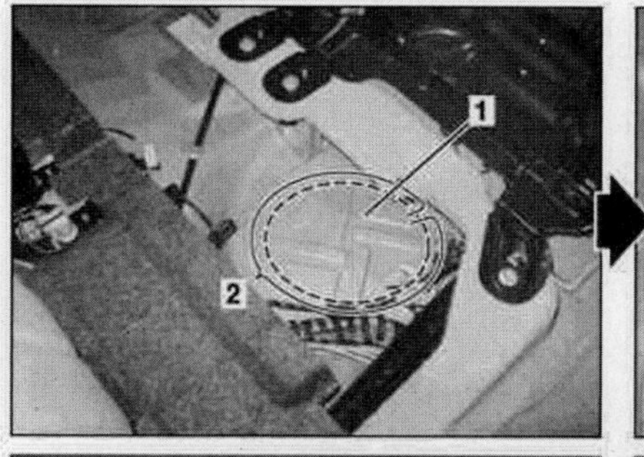

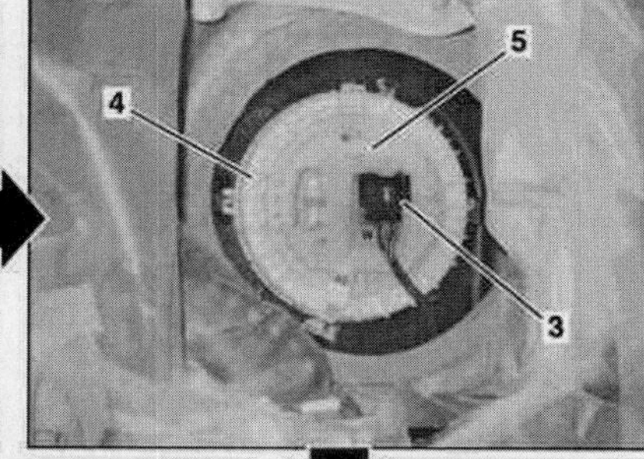

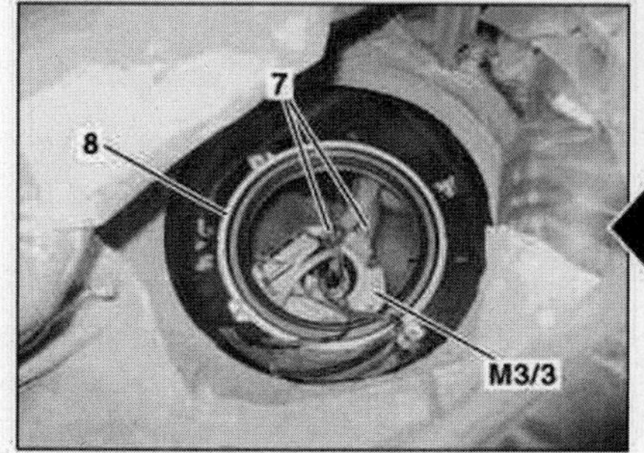

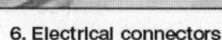

1. Right cap
2. Separation point
3. Electrical connector
4. Ring nut
5. Locating cover
6. Electrical connectors
7. Fuel feed line, fuel return line and level line
8. Threaded ring

M3/3. Fuel pump with fuel level sensor

37698_MSUV_G0078

Fig. 66 Removing fuel pump

FUEL RAIL AND INJECTOR

REMOVAL & INSTALLATION

See Figure 67.

1. Before servicing the vehicle, refer to the precautions.
2. Remove air filter housing.
3. Remove power electronics with power distributor.
4. Disconnect electrical connector and electrical connector.
5. Detach jack of electrical connector on fuel distributor.
6. Disconnect right connector on ME-SFI [ME] control unit.
7. Remove ME-SFI [ME] control unit.
8. Remove right control unit bracket and left control unit bracket.
9. Detach feed duct from cylinder head cover, intake manifold and rear right engine suspension lug.
10. Detach feed duct from intake manifold.
11. Detach feed duct from cylinder head cover.
12. Detach rear left engine suspension lug from cylinder head.
13. Disconnect hose and hose for crankcase ventilation system.
14. Remove the electrical connectors at the fuel injection valves.
15. Relieve fuel overpressure with pressure hose via service valve.
16. Detach fuel line from fuel distributor.
17. Remove bolts and take off fuel distributor with fuel injection valves.

To install:

18. Install in the reverse order.
19. Tighten bolts/nuts to specification as follows:

- Bolt, control unit bracket to resonance intake manifold: 71 inch lbs. (8 Nm).
- Bolt, feed duct to resonance intake manifold: 71 inch lbs. (8 Nm).
- Bolt, feed duct to cylinder head cover: 71 inch lbs. (8 Nm).
- Bolt, feed duct to engine lifting eye: 71 inch lbs. (8 Nm).
- Bolt, lifting eye to cylinder head: 15 ft. lbs. (20 Nm).
- Union nut, fuel line to fuel distributor: 15 ft. lbs. (20 Nm).
- Bolt, fuel distributor to resonance intake manifold: 80 inch lbs. (9 Nm)

FUEL TANK

REMOVAL & INSTALLATION

See Figures 68 and 69.

1. Before servicing the vehicle, refer to the precautions.
2. Drain fuel tank.
3. Detach underfloor paneling on fuel tank.
4. Remove exhaust system at flange.
5. connection.
6. Remove propeller shaft.
7. Detach filler neck from fuel tank.
8. Disconnect connection of feed line.
9. Disconnect connection of feed line and return line.
10. Support fuel tank with a transmission jack and a transmission plate.

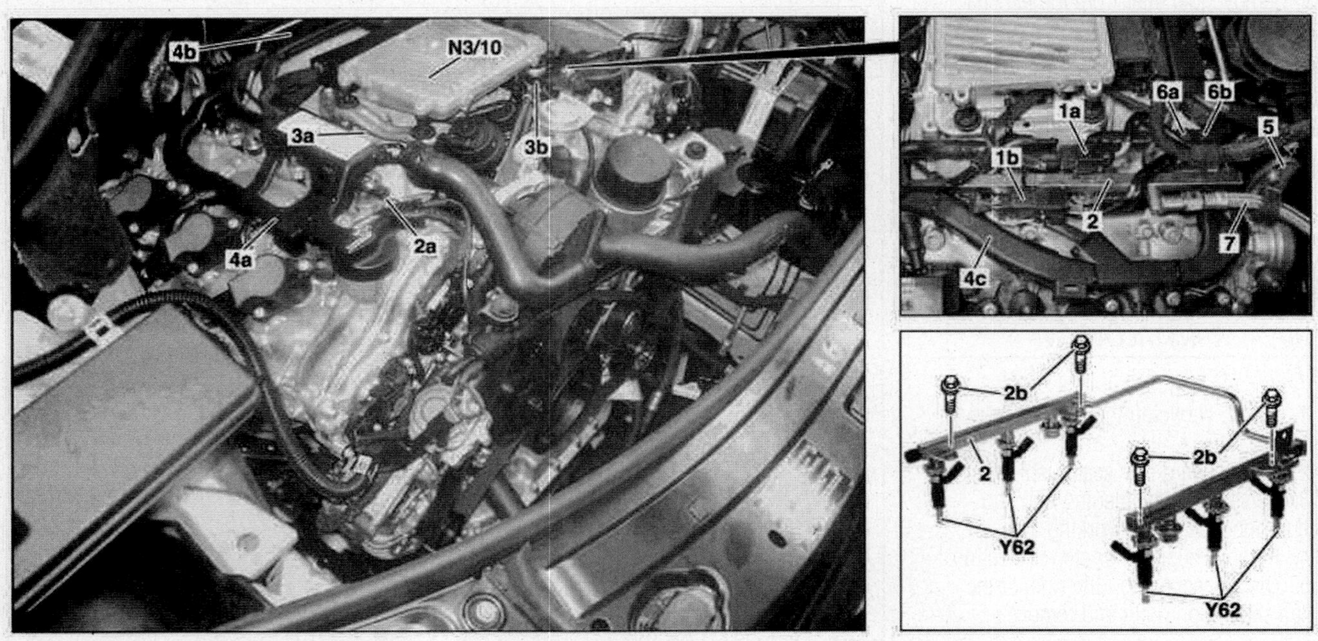

1a. Electrical connector
1b. Electrical connector
2. Fuel distributor
2a. Service valve
2b. Bolts
3a. Right control unit bracket
3b. Left control unit bracket
4a. Feed duct
4b. Feed duct
4c. Feed duct
5. Engine lifting eye
6a. Hose
6b. Hose
7. Fuel pipe
N3/10. ME-SFI [ME] control unit
Y62. Fuel injection valves

37698_MSUV_G0081

Fig. 67 Removing fuel rail and injectors

11. Remove bolts from retaining strap mounts.
12. Remove bolts from mounts.
13. Remove nut from mount.
14. Lower fuel tank slightly.
15. Disconnect electrical connectors.
16. Remove vent line.
17. Remove fuel tank.

To install:

18. Install in the reverse order.
19. Tighten bolts/nuts to specification as follows:
    - Self-locking nut, fuel tank to undercarriage: 17 ft. lbs. (23 Nm).
    - Bolt, fuel tank to undercarriage: 17 ft. lbs. (23 Nm)
    - Bolt, fuel tank retaining strap to undercarriage: 17 ft. lbs. (23 Nm)
20. Perform basic programming.

THROTTLE BODY

REMOVAL & INSTALLATION

See Figure 70.

1. Before servicing the vehicle, refer to the precautions.
2. Remove air filter housing.
3. Remove mass air flow sensor.

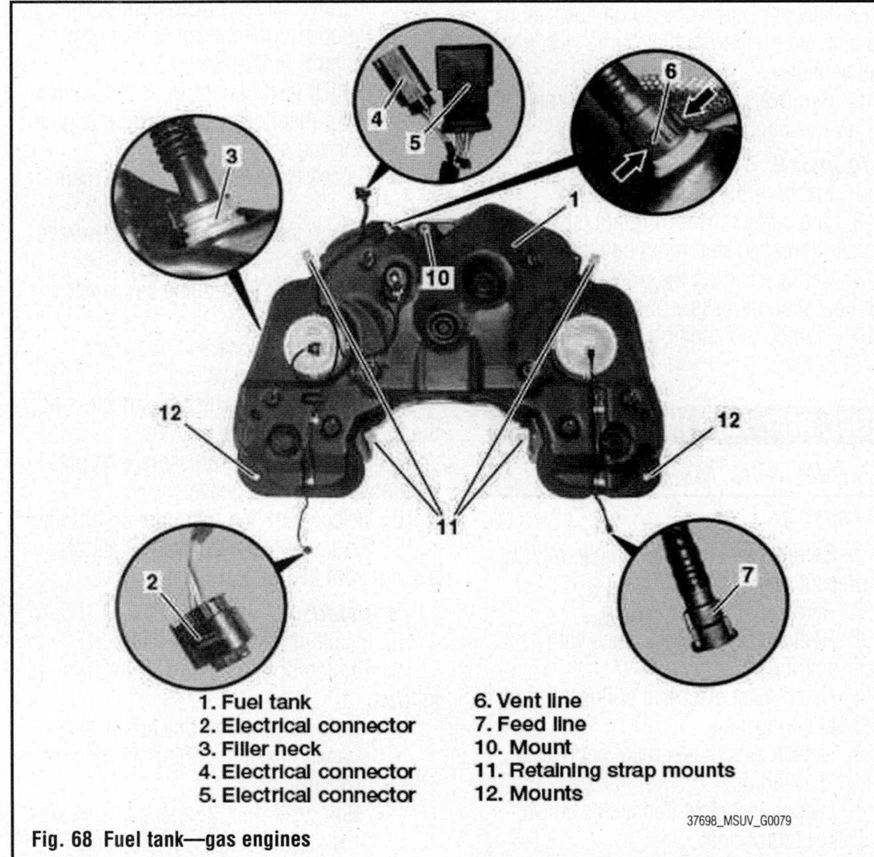

1. Fuel tank
2. Electrical connector
3. Filler neck
4. Electrical connector
5. Electrical connector
6. Vent line
7. Feed line
10. Mount
11. Retaining strap mounts
12. Mounts

37698_MSUV_G0079

Fig. 68 Fuel tank—gas engines

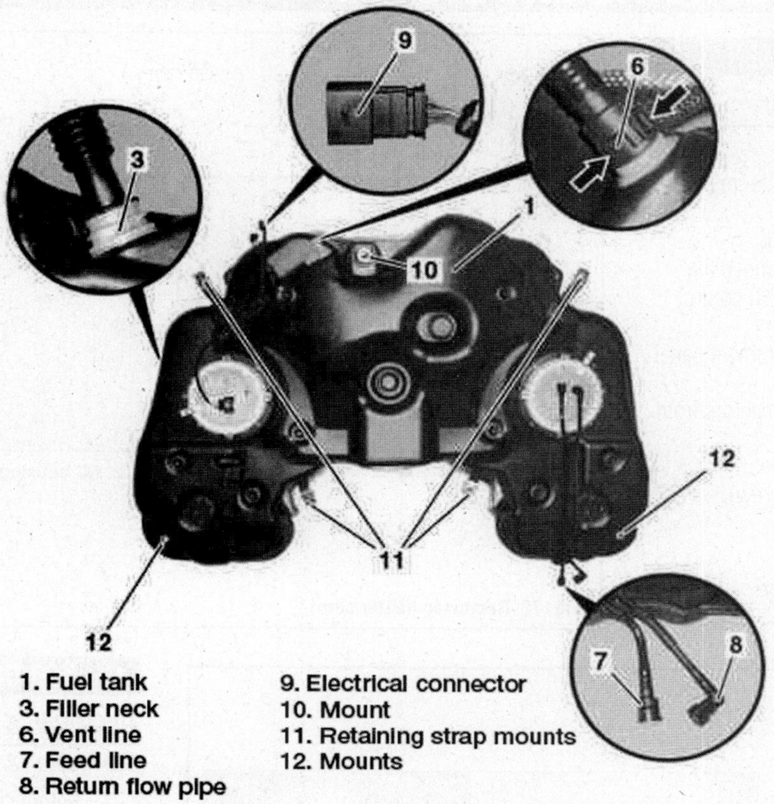

9
6
3
1
10
12
11
12
7
8
1. Fuel tank
3. Filler neck
6. Vent line
7. Feed line
8. Return flow pipe
9. Electrical connector
10. Mount
11. Retaining strap mounts
12. Mounts

37698_MSUV_G0080

Fig. 69 Fuel tank—diesel engine

B2/5
1
M16/6
2
4
3

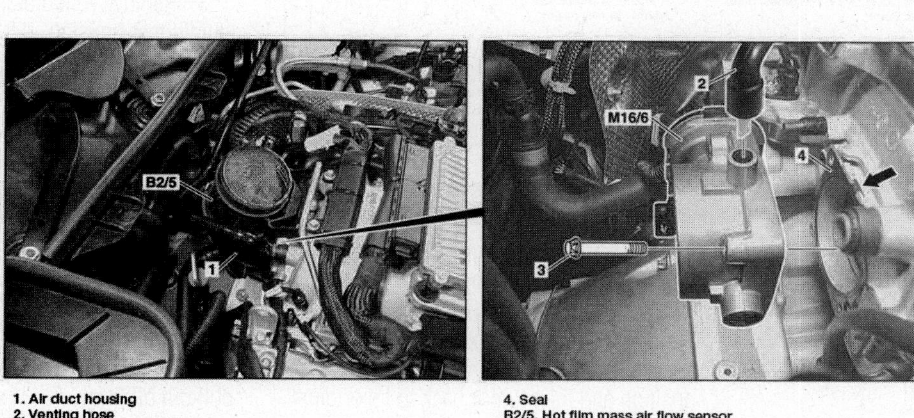

1. Air duct housing
2. Venting hose
3. Bolt
4. Seal
B2/5. Hot film mass air flow sensor
M16/6. Throttle valve actuator

37698_MERC_G0058

Fig. 70 Removing throttle control actuator

4. Remove air guide tube.
5. Release and disconnect electrical connector at throttle valve actuator.
6. Pull bleed house out of throttle valve actuator.
7. Remove bolts.
8. Remove throttle valve actuator.
9. Remove gasket.

To install:

10. Installation is the reverse of removal.
11. Tighten bolt connecting throttle valve actuator to resonance intake manifold: 80 inch lbs. (9 Nm)
12. Connect STAR DIAGNOSIS tool, read out and clear fault memory.

HEATING & AIR CONDITIONING SYSTEM

BLOWER MOTOR

REMOVAL & INSTALLATION

See Figure 71.

1. Before servicing the vehicle, refer to the precautions.
2. Move passenger seat back.
3. Switch off ignition and remove the transmitter key from the EIS [EZS] control unit.
4. Remove cover under instrument panel on right side.
5. Disconnect electrical connectors from blower motor.
6. Unscrew bolt.
7. Unclip wiring harness (arrow).
8. Remove blower motor.

To install:

9. Install in the reverse order.

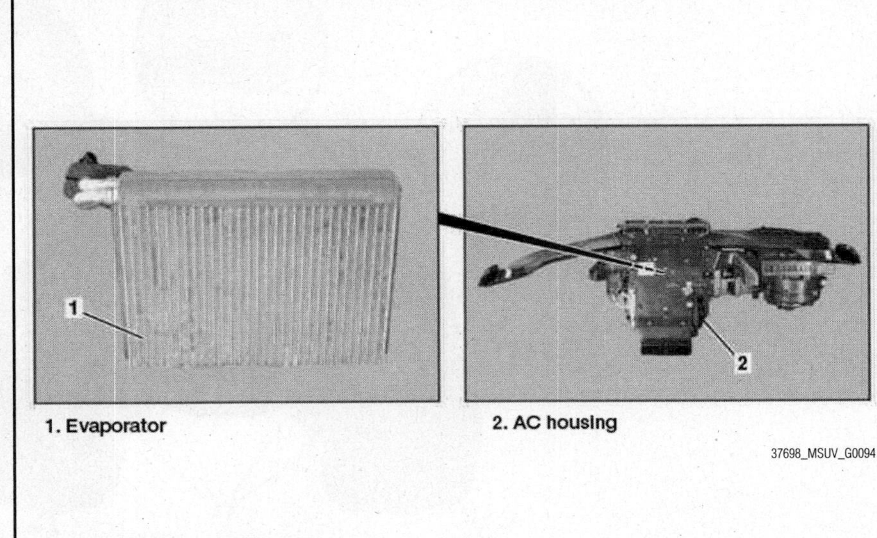

Fig. 72 Removing heater core

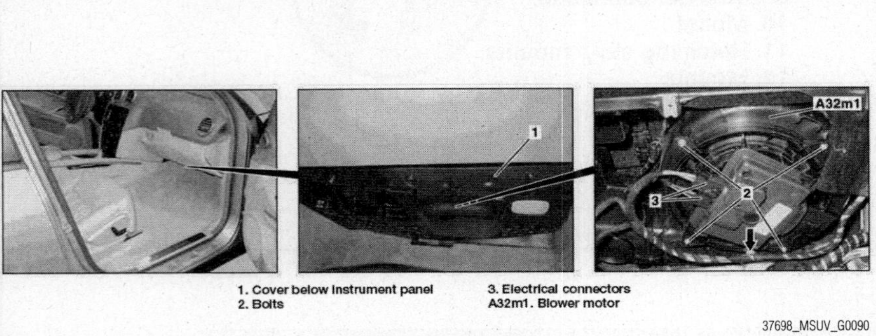

Fig. 71 Removing blower motor

HEATER CORE

REMOVAL & INSTALLATION

See Figure 72.

1. Before servicing the vehicle, refer to the precautions.
2. Remove and disassemble AC housing.

➡Blower motor does not need not be electrically disconnected and removed.

3. Remove evaporator upwards out of air conditioner housing .

To install:

4. Install in the reverse order.

STEERING

POWER RACK & PINION STEERING GEAR

REMOVAL & INSTALLATION

See Figure 73.

1. Before servicing the vehicle, refer to the precautions.
2. Remove engine trim panel.
3. Extract fluid out of the power steering pump's fluid reservoir using a hand pump.
4. Detach lower engine compartment paneling.
5. Remove bottom section of soundproofing.
6. Loosen outer tie rod.
7. Unplug electrical connector from control valve of rack-and-pinion steering.
8. Remove lower bolt of steering coupling from rack-and-pinion steering. To do so, turn steering coupling to appropriate position and then turn it back to its original position.
9. Turn steering wheel to central position (front wheels in straight ahead position) and secure with the retaining device. The steering wheel must not be turned when the steering coupling is detached, otherwise the clock spring contact will be destroyed.
10. Remove catalytic converter diesel particulate filter unit.
11. Push steering coupling together and carefully pull it out of rack-and-pinion steering.
12. Remove bolt securing retaining plate for oil lines.
13. from rack-and-pinion steering and pull out oil lines.
14. Remove front axle gear.
15. Detach retaining plate of rack-and-pinion steering and retaining plate from front axle carrier; to do so, remove bolts.
16. Guide the rack-and-pinion steering as far as possible to the right, then swivel to the lower left out of the front axle carrier.
17. Check rubber mounts of rack-and-pinion steering mounting for damage.

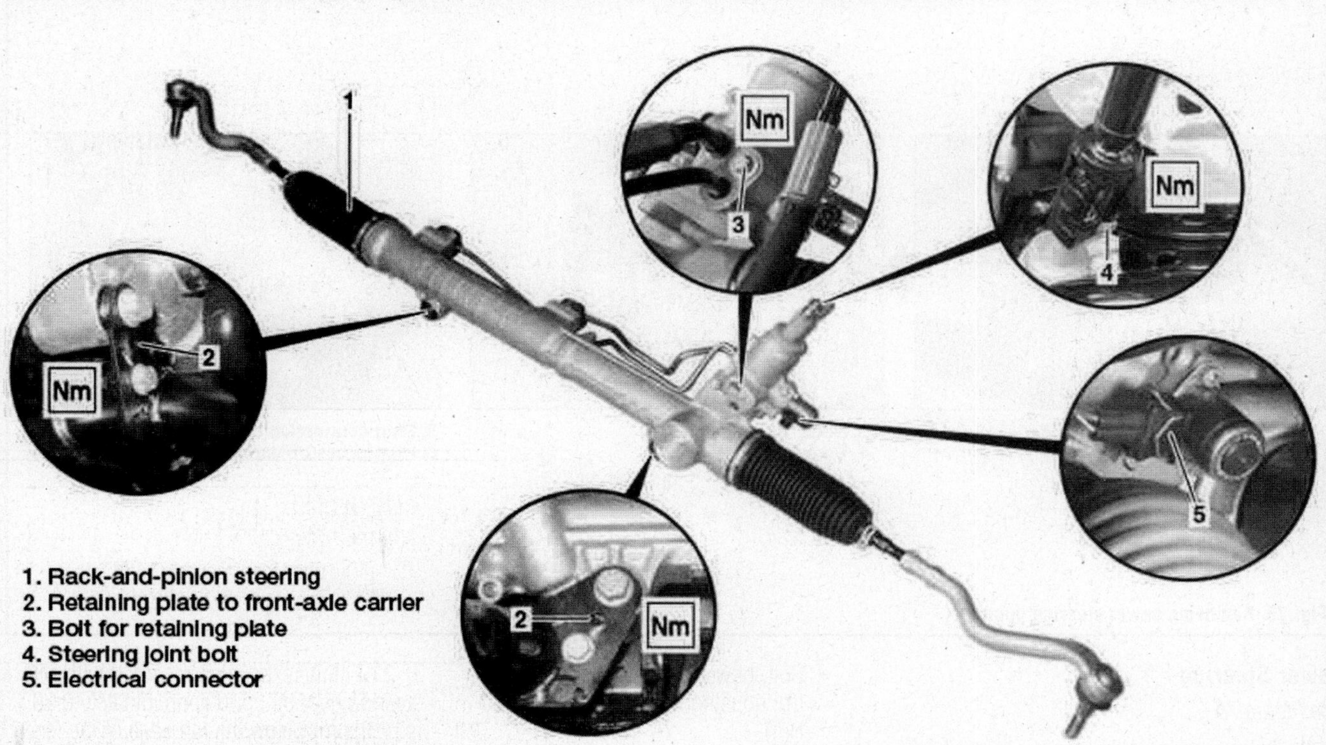

1. Rack-and-pinion steering
2. Retaining plate to front-axle carrier
3. Bolt for retaining plate
4. Steering joint bolt
5. Electrical connector

37698_MSUV_G0101

Fig. 73 Removing rack and pinion steering gear

To install:

18. Install in the reverse order.
19. Turn rack-and-pinion steering to center position and mount steering coupling.
20. Replace 0-rings.
21. The bolts, nuts and contact surfaces of the retaining plate and front axle carrier must be free of oil, grease and preservative. Heating causes the lubricants to melt and spread, which may cause the bolted connections to work loose.
22. Tighten bolts/nuts to specification as follows:
    - Self-locking nut, tie rod to steering knuckle: 33 ft. lbs. (45 Nm) plus an additional 90° rotation
    - Bolt, steering coupling to rack-and-pinion steering: 24 ft. lbs. (33 Nm)
    - Bolt, oil line retaining plate to rack-and-pinion steering: 13 ft. lbs. (18 Nm)
    - Bolted connection, rack-and-pinion steering to front axle carrier: 37 ft. lbs. (50 Nm), Loosen 180°, 37 ft. lbs. (50 Nm) plus an additional 90 ° rotation
    - Bolted connection, supporting plate to front axle carrier: 24 ft. lbs. (32 Nm)
23. Fill power steering pump.
24. Check steering for function and leaks.
25. Perform a wheel alignment check.

POWER STEERING PUMP

REMOVAL & INSTALLATION

Electrohydraulic Power Steering

See Figure 74.

1. Before servicing the vehicle, refer to the precautions.
2. Extract oil from expansion reservoir of electrohydraulic power steering.
3. Remove fender liner front section in front fender.
4. Unclip the wiring harness from the electrohydraulic power steering.
5. Clamp off hose of expansion reservoir of electrohydraulic power steering and detach.
6. Remove bolt at connection of high-pressure expansion hose of electrohydraulic power steering.
7. Seal openings using stop plugs.
8. Unscrew bolts or nuts.
9. Remove electrohydraulic power steering with bracket.

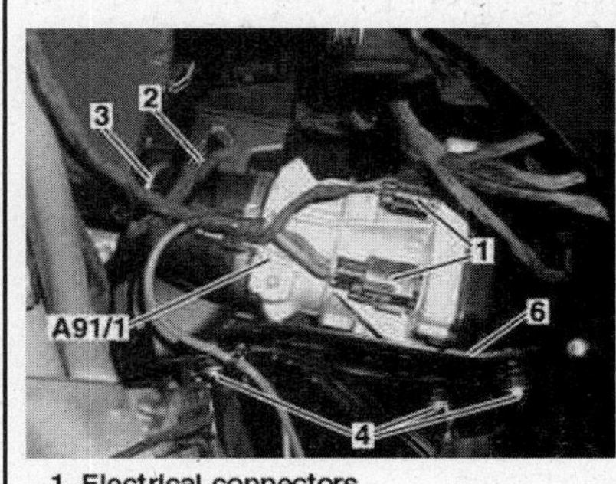

1. Electrical connectors
2. Hose
3. High-pressure expansion hose
4. Screws
6. Bracket
A91/1. Electrohydraulic power steering

37698_MSUV_G0102

Fig. 74 Removing power steering pump

To install:

10. Install in the reverse order.
11. Fill and bleed electrohydraulic power steering using PENTOSIN power steering fluid.
12. Replace sealing rings.
13. Banjo bolt, power steering pressure line to power steering pump: 33 ft. lbs. (45 Nm).

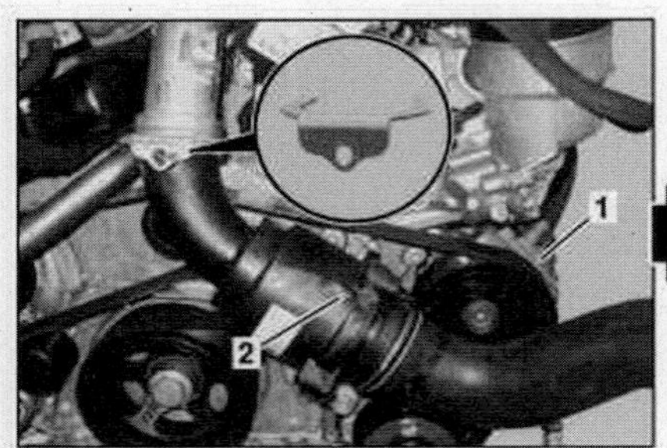

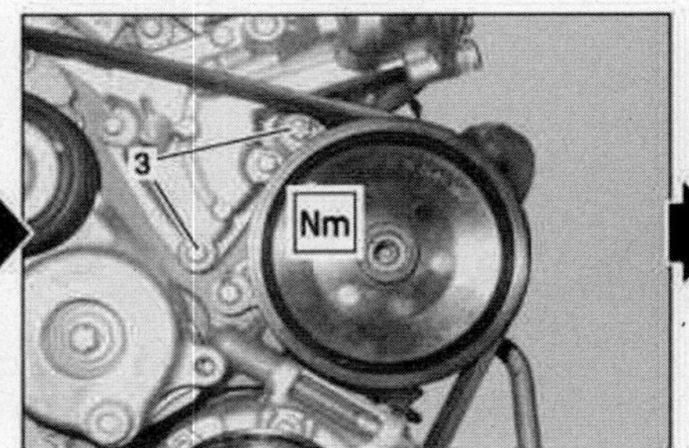

1. Power steering pump
2. Charge-air duct hose
3. Bolts
4. Screw
5. Plug connection of pressure regulator valve
6. High-pressure expansion hose connection

37698_MSUV_G0103

Fig. 75 Removing power steering pump

Power Steering

See Figure 75.

1. Before servicing the vehicle, refer to the precautions.
2. Remove engine trim panel, on diesel engine.
3. Remove charge-air duct hose, on diesel engine.
4. Extract oil from expansion reservoir of power steering pump.
5. Remove expansion reservoir of power steering pump.
6. Disconnect hose of expansion reservoir at power steering pump.
7. Remove poly-V belt from power steering pump.
8. Remove banjo bolt from high-pressure expansion hose connection of power steering pump.
9. Disconnect pressure regulator valve connector from power steering pump, on diesel engine.
10. Remove bolts and bolt of power steering pump from timing case cover, on diesel engine.
11. Remove power steering pump.

To install:

12. Install in the reverse order.
13. Tighten bolts/nuts to specification as follows:
    - Bolt, power steering pump to control housing M8x20: 15 ft. lbs. (20 Nm)
    - Bolt, power steering pump to control housing M8x30: 15 ft. lbs. (20 Nm)
    - Bolt, power steering pump to control housing M8x34: 26 ft. lbs. (35 Nm)
    - Bolt, power steering pump to control housing M8x44: 26 ft. lbs. (35 Nm)
    - Banjo bolt, high pressure expansion hose to power steering pump: 33 ft. lbs. (45 Nm)
14. Replace sealing rings.
15. Fill and bleed power steering pump.
16. Check the steering system for leaks when the engine is running.

BLEEDING

1. Before servicing the vehicle, refer to the precautions.

⁂ WARNING

Do not start the engine! If the engine is started there is a risk of air entering the hydraulic steering system, which is then extremely difficult to remove.

2. Fill the expansion reservoir with MB steering gear oil up to approximately 0.39 in. (10 mm) below the top edge of the reservoir. Add MB steering gear oil continuously, until the fluid level remains constant.
3. Slowly turn steering wheel from steering stop to steering stop until no more bubbles are ascertained in the expansion reservoir. Repeat turning the steering from stop to stop several times (up to 30 times). During this process MB steering gear oil must be added to the expansion reservoir by an assistant.
4. Start the engine and allow engine to run for approximately 1 min at idle speed. During this process an assistant must observe the steering gear oil level in the expansion reservoir and add MB steering gear oil if necessary.
5. When the engine is running, turn the steering wheel slowly several times from steering stop to steering stop, in the meantime refilling the expansion reservoir with MB steering gear oil.
6. Repeat process until the steering gear oil level remains constant in the expansion reservoir and there are no more bubbles.
7. Check oil level in expansion reservoir and fill to maximum fill level.
8. Check steering system for leaks.

LOWER CONTROL ARM

REMOVAL & INSTALLATION

See Figure 76.

1. Before servicing the vehicle, refer to the precautions.
2. Remove transmitter key or Keyless-Go start and stop button.
3. Raise and safely support vehicle.
4. Remove wheels, rotate if necessary.
5. Detach lower engine compartment paneling.
6. Remove soundproofing.
7. Remove bolts and carefully swivel stabilizer bar downward.
8. Mark the installation position of the rear bearing bracket of the lower transverse control arm relative to the front axle carrier.
9. Remove bolts.
10. Remove screw.
11. Unscrew nut and detach lower transverse control arm from steering knuckle.
12. Remove lower transverse control arm.
13. Install in the reverse order.

To install:

14. Install in the reverse order.
15. Only tighten nuts and bolts of chassis components when vehicle is at normal ride height.
16. Tighten bolts/nuts to specification as follows:
    - Self-locking nut, shock absorber to wishbone: 211 ft. lbs. (285 Nm)
    - Bolt, stabilizer bar bracket to axle/engine subframe: 37 ft. lbs. (50 Nm)
    - Self-locking nut, lower transverse control arm to steering knuckle: 170 ft. lbs. (230 Nm)
    - Self-locking nut, lower front transverse control arm to front axle carrier: 200 ft. lbs. (270 Nm)
    - Bolt, lower transverse control arm at inside rear to front axle carrier: 163 ft. lbs. (220 Nm)
    - Bolt, lower transverse control arm at outside rear to front axle carrier: 133 ft. lbs. (180 Nm)
17. Perform a wheel alignment check.

STEERING KNUCKLE

REMOVAL & INSTALLATION

See Figure 77.

1. Before servicing the vehicle, refer to the precautions.
2. Remove transmitter key or Keyless-Go start and stop button.
3. Raise vehicle with vehicle lift.
4. Remove wheels, rotate if necessary.
5. Remove front brake disk.
6. Notes on installing brake hoses.
7. Detach left front rpm sensor and right front rpm sensor from steering knuckle and place to one side.
8. Detach bracket from steering knuckle and place to one side. Note installation position of bracket from steering knuckle and observed it during installation.
9. Detach tie rod from steering knuckle.
10. Detach collar nut from front axle shaft.
11. Pressing front axle shaft out of front axle shaft flange.
12. Unscrew self-locking nut from follower joint.

Fig. 76 Removing lower control arm

13. Push follower joint out of upper transverse control arm.

14. Undo self-locking nut securing lower transverse control arm to steering knuckle.

To install:

15. Install in the reverse order.

16. Tighten bolts/nuts to specification as follows:

- Self-locking bolt, front axle rpm sensor to steering knuckle: 71 inch lbs. (8 Nm)
- Self-locking nut, tie rod to steering knuckle: 33 ft. lbs. (45 Nm) plus an additional 90° rotation
- Collar nut, front axle shaft to front axle shaft flange: 185 ft. lbs. (250 Nm) plus an additional 45° rotation
- Self-locking nut, upper wishbone follower joint to steering knuckle: 15 ft. lbs. (20 Nm) plus an additional 90° rotation
- Self-locking nut, lower transverse control arm to steering knuckle: 170 ft. lbs. (230 Nm)

STRUT

REMOVAL & INSTALLATION

See Figure 78.

1. Before servicing the vehicle, refer to the precautions.

2. Open engine hood and raise to vertical position.

3. Remove strut lower brace.

4. Remove 3 nuts on threaded connections for the strut mounting stay, front suspension brace and loosen one nut on the threaded connection.

5. Lift strut mounting stay, front suspension brace and place on holder.

6. Raise vehicle until the wheels are clear of the ground.

7. Unscrew nuts on front end.

8. Remove front wheel.

9. Remove fender liner front section in front fender.

10. Remove brake hose from brake hose bracket.

11. Detach left front axle damping valve unit connector front axle damping valve unit connector.

12. Undo nut and remove tie rod from steering knuckle.

13. Undo nut of link rod and remove link rod from front shock absorber.

14. Undo nut and remove steering knuckle from upper transverse control arm.

15. Push front axle shaft out of front axle shaft flange, remove front axle shaft.

16. Undo nut from front shock absorber and remove front shock absorber from transverse control arm.

17. Press transverse control arm downwards and remove front suspension strut.

To install:

18. Install in the reverse order.

19. Installation position must be observed.

20. Use new cable ties.

21. Tighten bolts/nuts to specification as follows:

- Nut, link rod to front shock: 74 ft. lbs. (100 Nm), loosen 180°, 148 ft. lbs. (200 Nm)
- Air suspension pressure line to front air suspension: 44 inch lbs. (5 Nm)

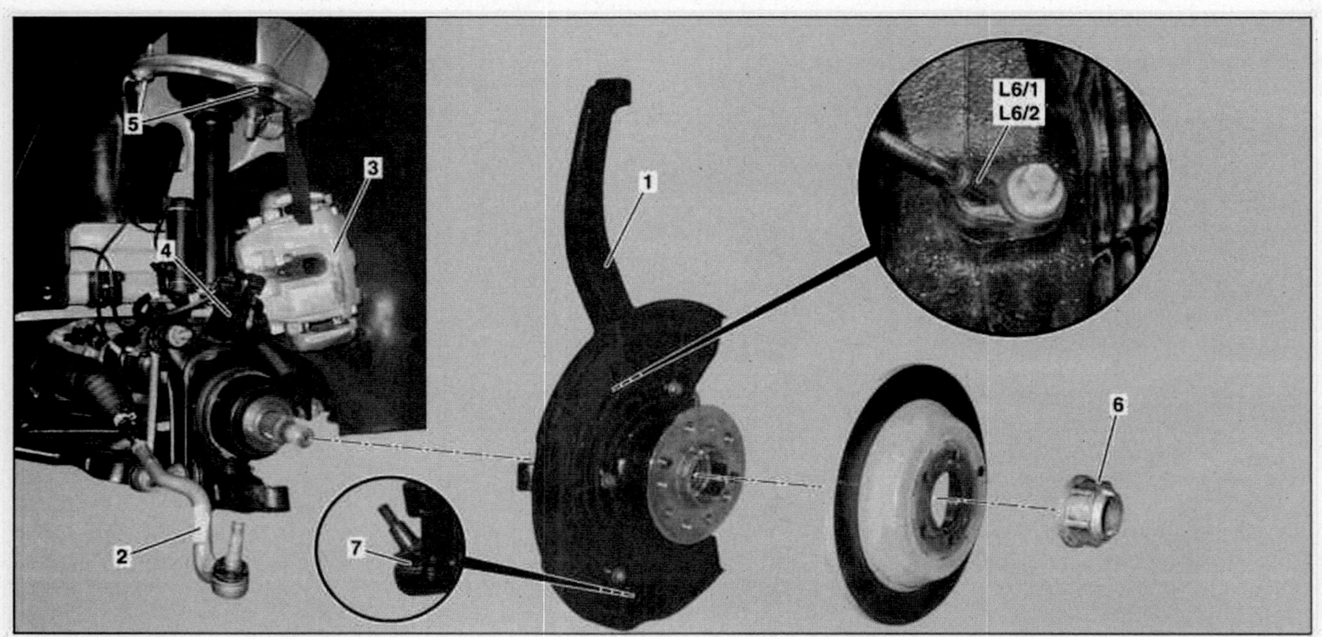

1. Steering knuckle
2. Tie rod
3. Brake caliper
4. Bracket
5. Follower joint
6. Collar nut
7. Support joint
L6/1. Left front rpm sensor
L6/2. Right front rpm sensor

37698_MSUV_G0111

Fig. 77 Removing steering knuckle

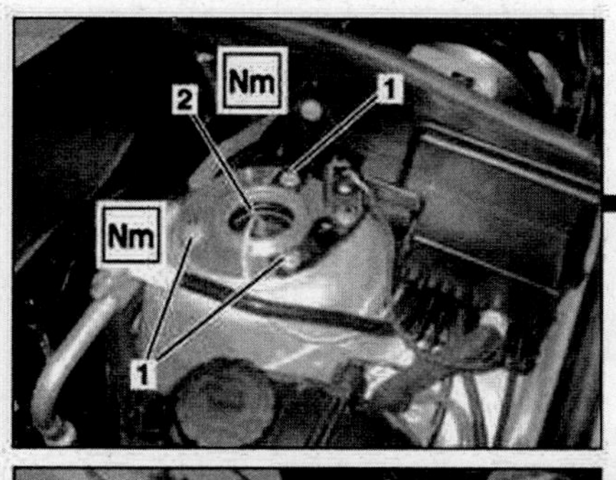

1. Nuts
2. Pressure line connection
3. Front suspension strut
4. Cable tie
5. Brake hose bracket
6. Brake hose
7. Cable tie
8. ADS line connector
9. Nut
10. Nut connector
11. Nut
Y51x1. Left front axle damping valve unit
Y52x1. Right front axle damping valve unit

37698_MSUV_G0106

Fig. 78 Removing front strut

- Nut for shock absorber on front end: 22 ft. lbs. (30 Nm), loosen 180°, 20 ft. lbs. (27 Nm)
- Self-locking nut, shock absorber to wishbone: 196 ft. lbs. (265 Nm)
- Self-locking nut, upper wishbone follower joint to steering knuckle: 15 ft. lbs. (20 Nm) plus an additional 90° rotation

22. Perform a wheel alignment check.

OVERHAUL

See Figure 79.

1. Before servicing the vehicle, refer to the precautions.
2. Remove front suspension strut.
3. Clamp tensioning device in vise and insert clamping plate.
4. Insert suspension strut into tensioning device.
5. Clamp spring until the upper spring cup is relieved of load.
6. Remove cap.
7. Undo fastening nut and remove shock absorber.
8. Remove bellows and stop damper.
9. Release tensioning device and remove spring with upper spring cup and spring seat.
10. Inspect shock absorber.
11. Check bellows, stop damper(s) and spring seat for signs of wear.

To install:

12. Assemble in the reverse order.
13. Tighten piston rod nut to 22 ft. lbs. (30 Nm).
14. Install front suspension strut.

STABILIZER BAR

REMOVAL & INSTALLATION

See Figure 80.

1. Before servicing the vehicle, refer to the precautions.
2. Raise and safely support vehicle.
3. Detach lower engine compartment paneling Vehicles with gasoline engine.
4. Remove noise encapsulation Vehicles with diesel engine .
5. Mark positioning of torsion bar retaining clamps and retaining clamps for torsion bushings on torsion bar.
6. Remove nuts of link rods and detach link rods from stabilizer bar. Only if link rods are obviously undamaged.
7. Remove nuts of link rods and detach link rods from front shock absorbers.
8. Remove bolts of stabilizer bar retaining clamps and detach both stabilizer bar retaining clamps.
9. Remove stabilizer bar from front axle carrier.
10. Unscrew bolts of torsion bushing retaining clamps and detach torsion bushings from torsion bar.
11. Detach link rods from stabilizer bar.
12. Check link rods and torsion bushings for damage.
13. Attach link rods to stabilizer bar.
14. Attach torsion bearings to torsion bar and preassemble bolts with nuts to torsion bushing retaining clamps.
15. Position stabilizer bar on front axle carrier, mount stabilizer bar retaining clamps and insert bolts.
16. Mount link rods onto front shock absorbers and screw on nuts.
17. Mount link rods onto stabilizer bar and screw on nuts.
18. Make sure that stabilizer bar, torsion bushing retaining clamps and stabilizer bar retaining clamps are positioned correctly.

To install:

19. Install in the reverse order.
20. Only tighten nuts and bolts of chassis components when vehicle is at normal ride height.

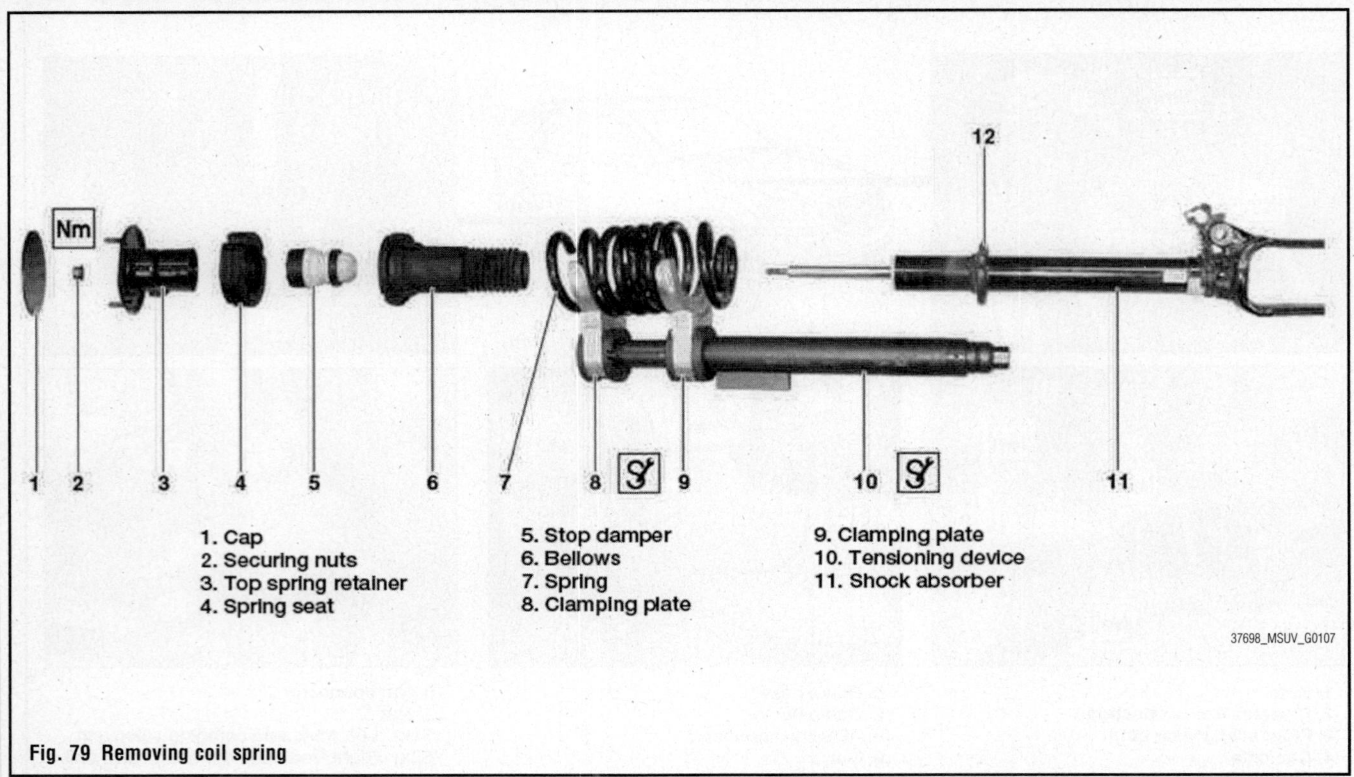

Fig. 79 Removing coil spring

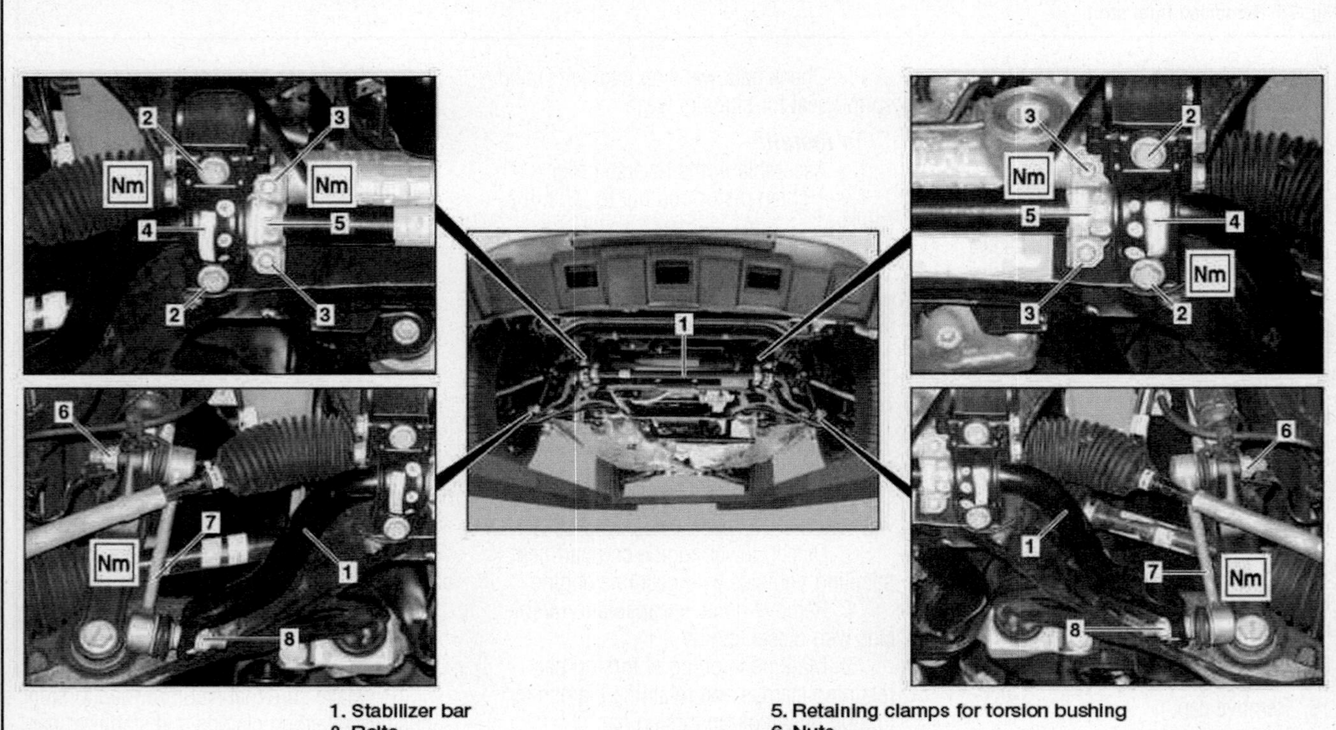

Fig. 80 Removing stabilizer bar

21. Tighten bolts/nuts to specification as follows:

- Bolt, stabilizer bar retaining clamp to bearing bracket: 133 ft. lbs. (180 Nm)
- Bolt, torsion bushing retaining clamp: 30 ft. lbs. (40 Nm)
- Nut, link rod to front shock: 74 ft. lbs. (100 Nm), loosen 180°, 148 ft. lbs. (200 Nm)
- Nut, link rod to stabilizer bar: 74 ft. lbs. (100 Nm), loosen 180°, 33 ft. lbs. (45 Nm) plus an additional 60° rotation

22. Install lower engine compartment paneling.
23. Install noise encapsulation.
24. Laser vehicle using drive-on lifting platform.

UPPER CONTROL ARM

REMOVAL & INSTALLATION

See Figure 81.

1. Before servicing the vehicle, refer to the precautions.
2. Open engine hood and raise to vertical position.
3. Remove air plenum chamber.
4. Raise vehicle until the wheels are clear of the ground.
5. Remove wheels, rotate if necessary.
6. Unscrew nut and detach steering knuckle from the upper transverse control arm.
7. Unscrew bolt and detach the bracket of the right front level sensor from the upper suspension .
8. Unscrew nuts from front end.
9. Pull out bolts.
10. Detach upper wishbone from front end.
11. Check follower joint. If the follower joint is defective, replace upper transverse control arm. .

To install:

12. Install in the reverse order.
13. Tighten nuts and bolts of chassis components only when vehicle is at normal ride height.
14. Tighten bolts/nuts to specification as follows:

- Self-locking nut, upper wishbone follower joint to steering knuckle: 15 ft. lbs. (20 Nm) plus an additional 90° rotation
- Self-locking nut of upper wishbone on front end: 45 ft. lbs. (61 Nm)

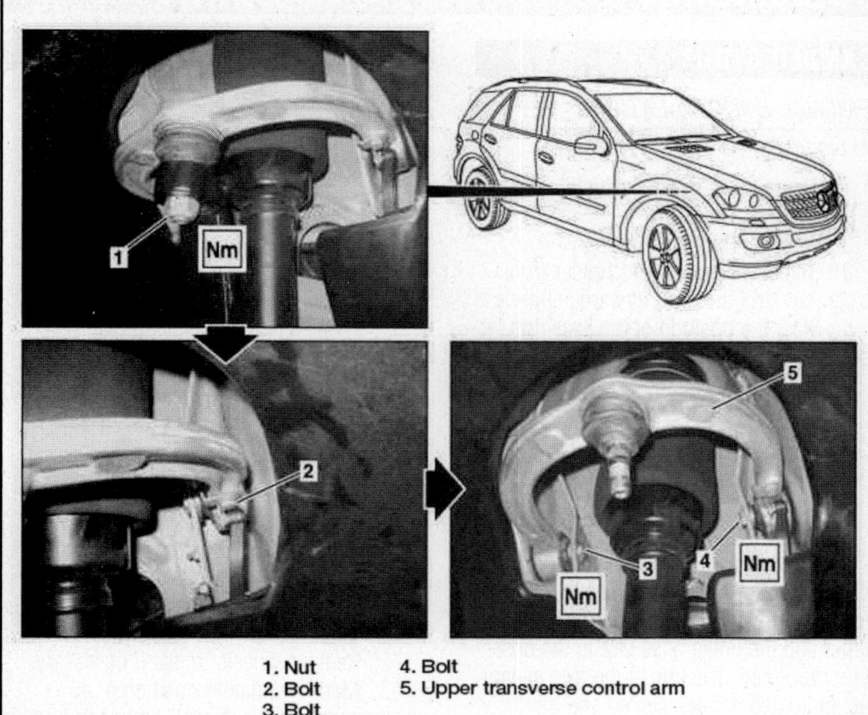

Fig. 81 Removing upper control arm

WHEEL HUB & BEARING

REMOVAL & INSTALLATION

See Figure 82.

1. Before servicing the vehicle, refer to the precautions.
2. Remove steering knuckle.
3. Press out front axle shaft flange.
4. Detach circlip.
5. Press wheel bearing out of steering knuckle.

To install:

6. Install in the reverse order.
7. Installation position must be observed. The dots, the line or the black inner race on the wheel bearing must face towards the steering knuckle. The marking depends on the manufacturer. The magnetic side of the wheel bearing must point in the direction of the steering knuckle.
8. Check circlip is correctly seated in steering knuckle.
9. Generally, the front axle shaft flange and wheel bearing should be replaced.

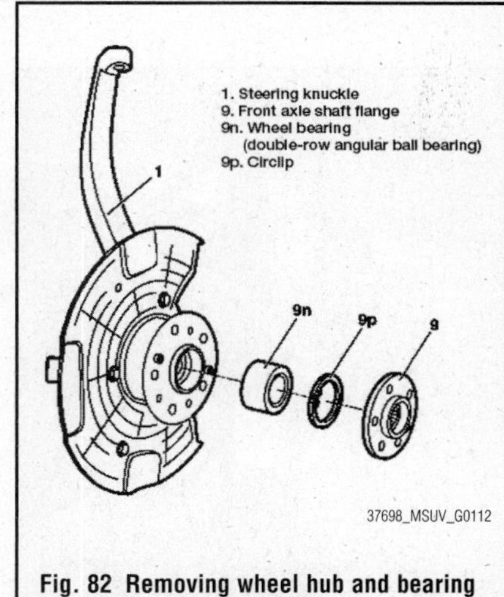

Fig. 82 Removing wheel hub and bearing

CAMBER STRUT

REMOVAL & INSTALLATION

See Figure 83.

1. Before servicing the vehicle, refer to the precautions.
2. Remove, rotate if necessary
3. Unclip wiring harness holder from the camber strut and pull forwards slightly.
4. Mark the position of the eccentric disk using a colored pencil.
5. Remove screws.
6. Remove camber strut.
7. Check rubber mounts of camber strut for signs of damage.

To install:

8. Install in the reverse order.
9. Insert bolt and screw on a new self-locking nut. The screw head points the direction of travel. Arrange the dog bone washer and the brake hose clip in the position represented. The line of the rpm sensor must be routed as represented and be clipped into the bracket.
10. Lift the suspension using the telescoping plate, transmission jack and transmission platform under the supporting joint until the suspension is deflected to the driving level.
11. Tighten bolts/nuts to specification as follows:
    - Self-locking nut, camber strut to rear axle carrier: 69 ft. lbs. (93 Nm)
    - Self-locking nut, camber strut to wheel carrier: 41 ft. lbs. (55 Nm) plus an additional 90° rotation
12. Lower wheel suspension using telescoping transmission jack, then remove telescoping transmission jack.
13. Perform a wheel alignment check.

COIL SPRING

REMOVAL & INSTALLATION

See Figure 84.

1. Before servicing the vehicle, refer to the precautions.
2. Remove wheels, rotate if necessary.
3. Mark installation position of all spring parts relative to each other and body and to lower transverse control arm.
4. Break out bars on left or right lower spring cup, closed and smooth broken edges so that the tensioning device can be slid through.
5. Compress and remove left or right rear spring.
6. Make sure that the tabs on the upper end of the tensioning device engage into the recesses on the top clamping plate.
7. The tensioning device must not be tensioned or released using an electrically or pneumatically powered tool.
8. Insert the top clamping plate and lower clamping plate as far apart to each other into the spring coils.
9. Release left or right rear spring and clamp in new rear spring.
10. Remove lower spring cup, closed or lower spring cup, punched.
11. Remove top spring cup and rubber insert.
12. Detach rubber boot and plastic ring from top spring cup, add spacer washer to raise vehicle level or remove to reduce vehicle level.
13. Remove spreader clip on frame floor.
14. Check vehicle level, adjust if necessary.

To install:

15. Install in the reverse order.

LOWER CONTROL ARMS

REMOVAL & INSTALLATION

See Figure 85.

1. Before servicing the vehicle, refer to the precautions.
2. Remove wheels, rotate if necessary.
3. Raise and safely support vehicle.
4. Remove rear spring.
5. Remove bolts lower exhaust system and support.
6. Remove bolt and remove bracket.
7. Unscrew nut and detach link rod from spring control arm.
8. Remove bolt.
9. Remove bolts at front of rear axle carrier.
10. Remove bolts and remove propeller shaft together with flexible coupling from flange of rear axle center assembly.
11. Lower rear axle carrier in front area.
12. Remove bolts and remove spring control arm downwards from rear axle carrier (arrow E).
13. Unscrew nut and detach spring control arm from supporting joint.

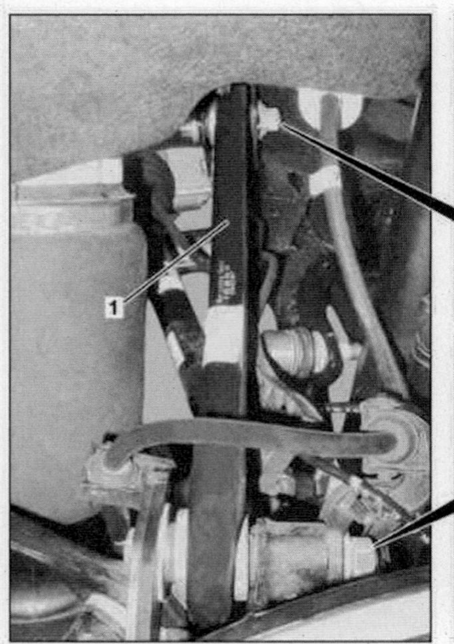

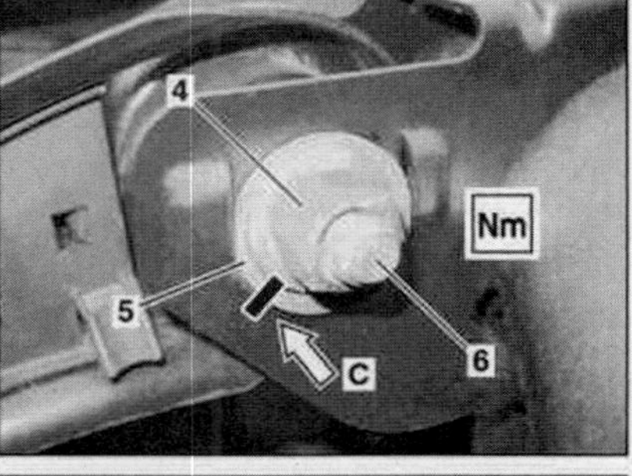

1. Camber strut
4. Self-locking nut
5. Eccentric disk
6. Screw
7. Dog bone washer
8. Brake hose clip
9. Self-locking nut
10. Screw

37698_MSUV_G0120

Fig. 83 Removing camber strut

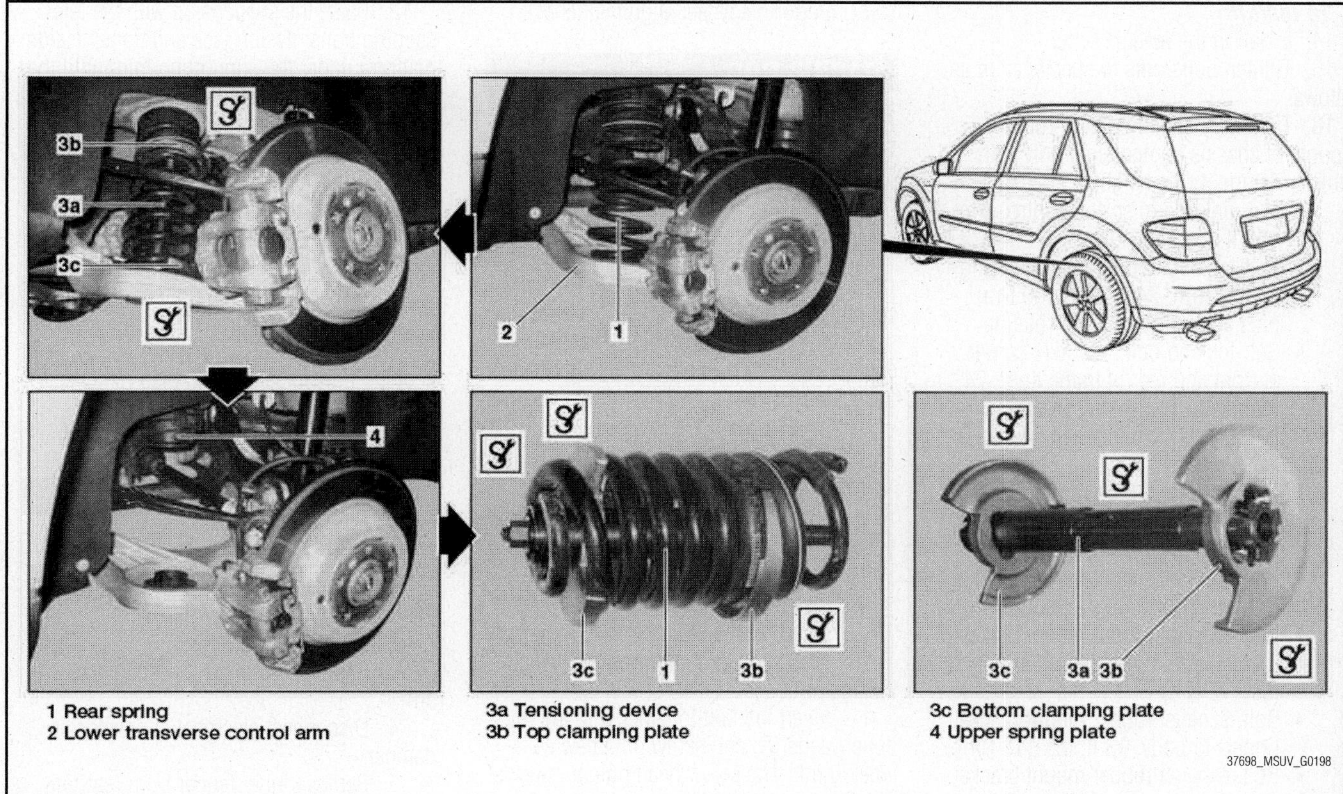

1 Rear spring
2 Lower transverse control arm
3a Tensioning device
3b Top clamping plate
3c Bottom clamping plate
4 Upper spring plate

37698_MSUV_G0198

Fig. 84 Removing rear spring

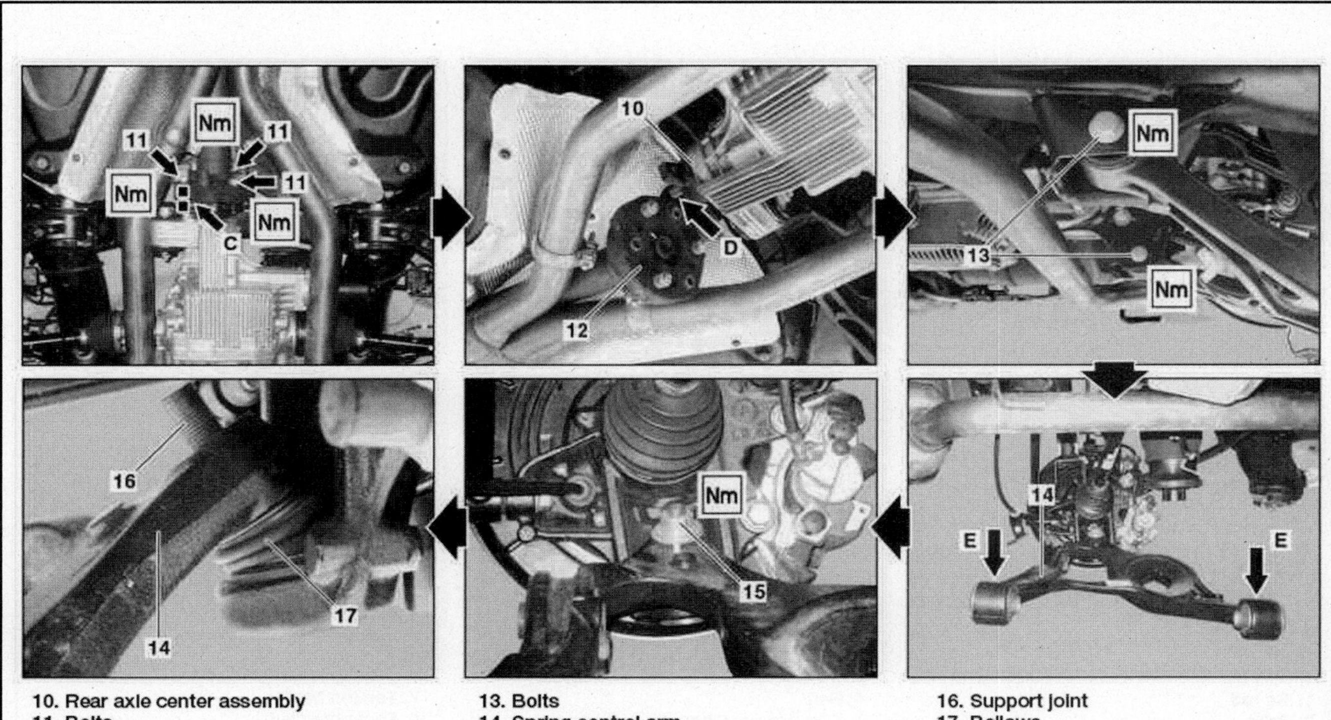

10. Rear axle center assembly
11. Bolts
12. Flex disk
13. Bolts
14. Spring control arm
15. Nut
16. Support joint
17. Bellows

37698_MSUV_G0119

Fig. 85 Removing lower control arm

To install:

14. Install in the reverse order.
15. Tighten bolts/nuts to specification as follows:
16. Tighten nuts and bolts of rubber mounts of chassis components only with vehicle at normal ride height.
    - Nut, link rod to spring control arm: 133 ft. lbs. (180 Nm)
    - Self-locking nut, damper to spring control arm: 74 ft. lbs. (100 Nm) plus an additional 120° rotation
    - Self-locking bolt, rear axle carrier at front and rear of frame floor: 74 ft. lbs. (100 Nm), loosen 180°, 74 ft. lbs. (100 Nm) plus an additional 120° rotation
    - Self-locking bolt on rear propeller shaft/rear axle center assembly: 47 ft. lbs. (64 Nm)
    - Bolt, exhaust rubber mount bracket (inner) to body: 15 ft. lbs. (20 Nm)
    - Bolt, exhaust rubber mount bracket (outer) to bumper bracket: 106 inch lbs. (12 Nm)
    - Bolt, exhaust rubber mount bracket (inner) to body: 13 ft. lbs. (18 Nm)
    - Bolt, exhaust rubber mount bracket (outer) to bumper bracket: 13 ft. lbs. (18 Nm)
17. Perform a wheel alignment check

RADIUS ROD

REMOVAL & INSTALLATION

See Figure 86.

1. Before servicing the vehicle, refer to the precautions.
2. Remove wheels, rotate if necessary.
3. Raise the suspension with the telescoping transmission jack and transmission platform under the supporting joint far enough until the suspension is slightly deflected.
4. Unscrew bolt.
5. Remove screw.
6. Remove torque strut.
7. Check torque strut rubber mounts for damage.

To install:

8. Install in the reverse order.
9. Insert torque strut.
10. Insert bolt and screw on a new self-locking nut.
11. Insert the bolt together with the dog bone washer(S) and screw on a new self-locking nut. The screw head points towards the direction of travel. Arrange the dog bone washer in the position represented.
12. Raise the suspension with the telescoping transmission jack and transmission platform under the supporting joint until the suspension is deflected to the vehicle level.
13. Tighten bolts/nuts to specification as follows:
    - Self-locking nut, tension arm to rear axle carrier: 81 inch lbs. (110 Nm)
    - Self-locking nut, torque strut to wheel carrier: 37 ft. lbs. (50 Nm) plus an additional 90° rotation
14. Lower wheel suspension using telescoping transmission jack, then remove telescoping transmission jack .
15. Perform a wheel alignment check.

SHOCK ABSORBER

REMOVAL & INSTALLATION

1. Before servicing the vehicle, refer to the precautions.
2. Remove wheels.
3. Remove cover on spring control arm.
4. Disconnect electrical connector on damper.
5. Remove inner tender from rear tender.
6. Clamping rear spring.

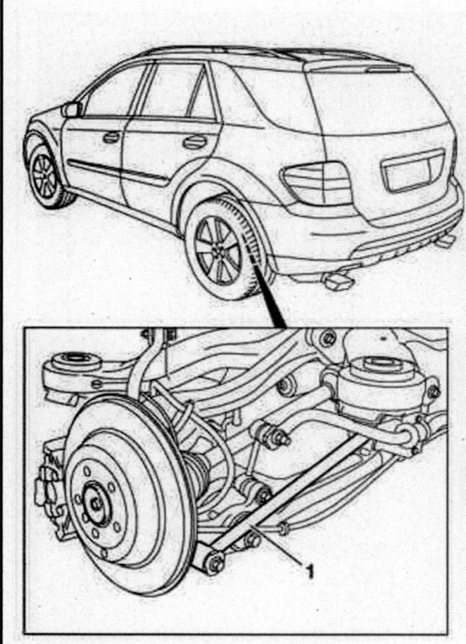

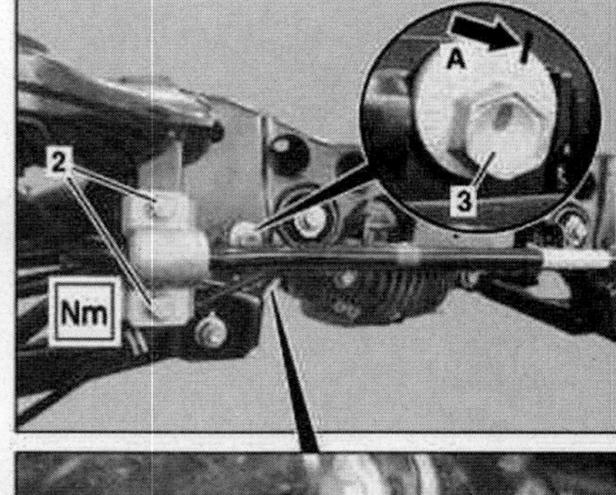

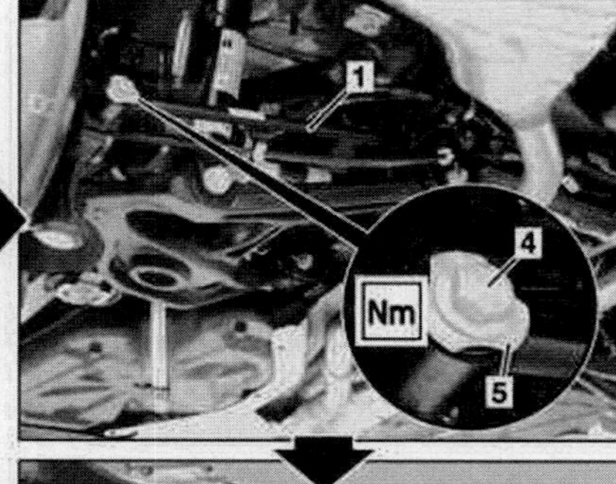

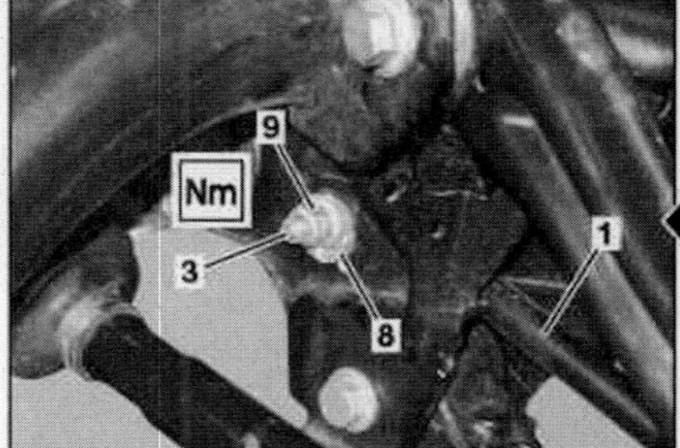

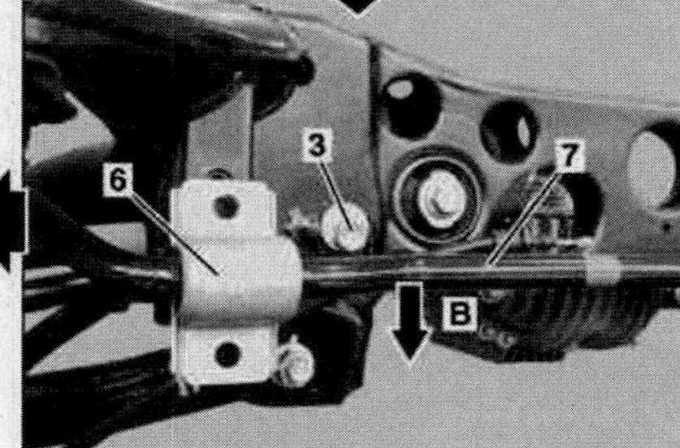

1. Tie rod
2. Bolts
3. Bolt
4. Bolt
5. Dog bone washer
6. Torsion bar clip
7. Torsion bar
8. Eccentric disk
9. Self-locking nut

37698_MSUV_G0114

Fig. 86 Removing radius rod

7. Loosen spring control arm on rear axle carrier and lower.
8. Remove rear spring.
9. Unscrew nut.
10. Remove bolt from spring control arm.
11. Remove side paneling in trunk.
12. Remove interior lining on side of cargo area.
13. Remove guide rail for load compartment cover.
14. Unscrew nuts from support bushing.
15. Remove shock absorber.
16. Check shock absorber.
17. Check support bushing for damage.
18. Unscrew nut from piston rod.
19. Remove support bushing.
20. Remove stop buffer with protective cap.
21. Install in the reverse order.

To install:

22. Install in the reverse order.
23. Tighten bolts/nuts to specification as follows:
- Self-locking nut, damper to spring control arm: 41 ft. lbs. (55 Nm) plus an additional 60° rotation
- Self-locking nut, damper to body: first 11 ft. lbs. (15 Nm), then 26 ft. lbs. (35 nm)
- Self-locking nut, damper to piston rod: 21 ft. lbs. (28 Nm)

STABILIZER BAR

REMOVAL & INSTALLATION

See Figure 88.

1. Before servicing the vehicle, refer to the precautions.
2. Raise and safely support vehicle.
3. Undo nuts of link rods and remove link rods from stabilizer bar.
4. Undo bolts of retaining clamps for stabilizer bar and remove stabilizer bar.
5. Undo nuts of link rods and remove link rods from spring control arms.
6. Check rubber mount of stabilizer bar for signs of damage.
7. Position stabilizer bar on rear axle carrier and insert bolts.
8. Mount link rods onto spring control arm and screw on nuts.
9. Mount link rods onto stabilizer bar and screw on nuts.
10. Check stabilizer bar is correctly positioned.

To install:

11. Install in the reverse order.
12. Tighten nuts and bolts of chassis components only when vehicle is at normal ride height.
13. Tighten bolts/nuts to specification as follows:
- Bolt, stabilizer bar retaining clamp to rear axle carrier: 81 ft. lbs. (110 Nm)
- Nut, link rod to spring control arm: 133 ft. lbs. (180 Nm)
- Nut, link rod to stabilizer bar: 133 ft. lbs. (180 Nm)

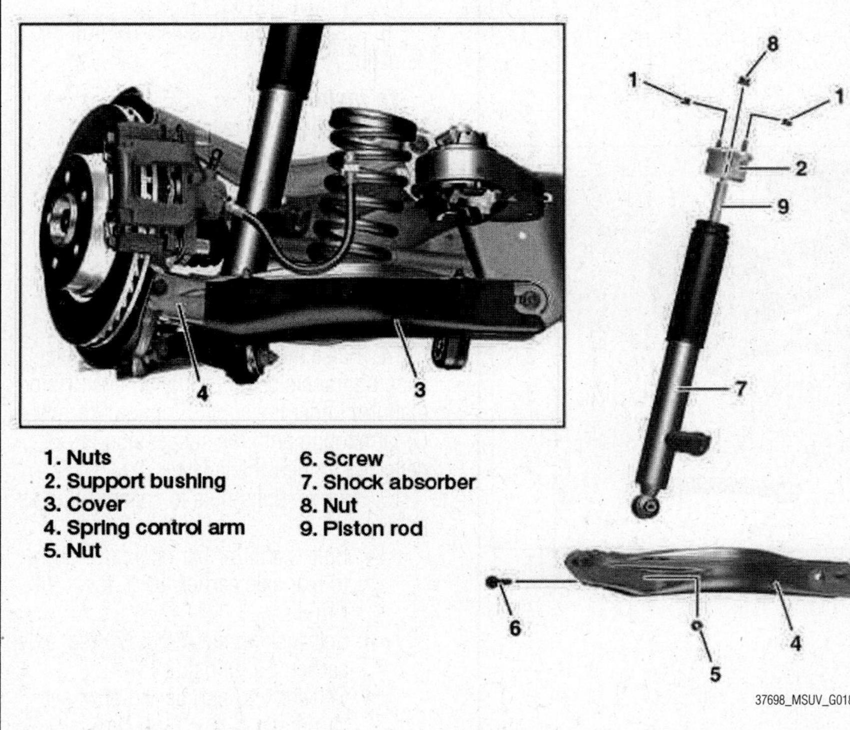

Fig. 87 Removing shock absorber

THRUST ARM

REMOVAL & INSTALLATION

See Figure 89.

1. Before servicing the vehicle, refer to the precautions.
2. Remove wheels.
3. Support rear axle carrier with transmission jack and transmission platform.
4. Loosen underfloor paneling at rear, to do this unscrew nut.
5. Remove bolts and remove stop plate.
6. Remove thrust arm from rear axle carrier and wheel carrier.
7. Remove panel from thrust arm.
8. Check rubber mounts in wheel carder.

To install:

9. Install in the reverse order.
- Self-locking bolt, front rear axle carrier rubber mount to frame floor: 59 ft. lbs. (80 Nm), fully release, 59 ft. lbs. (80 Nm) plus an additional 90° rotation
- Bolt, stop plate to body: 21 ft. lbs. (28 Nm)
- Self-locking nut, torque strut to rear axle carrier: 37 ft. lbs. (50 Nm) plus an additional 90° rotation
- Self-locking nut, thrust arm to wheel carrier: 37 ft. lbs. (50 Nm) plus an additional 90° rotation

TRACK ROD

REMOVAL & INSTALLATION

See Figure 90.

1. Before servicing the vehicle, refer to the precautions.
2. Remove wheels, rotate if necessary.
3. Unscrew bolt.
4. Using a colored pencil mark the position at the cam of the bolt (arrow A). The mark at the cam is used for approximately positioning the tie rod (original position) when assembling.
5. Remove screw.

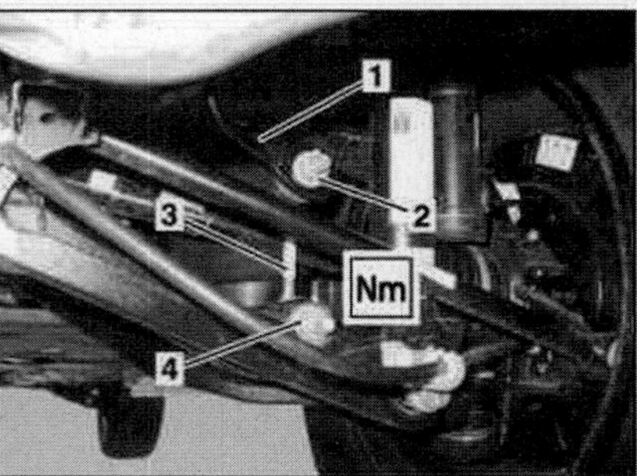

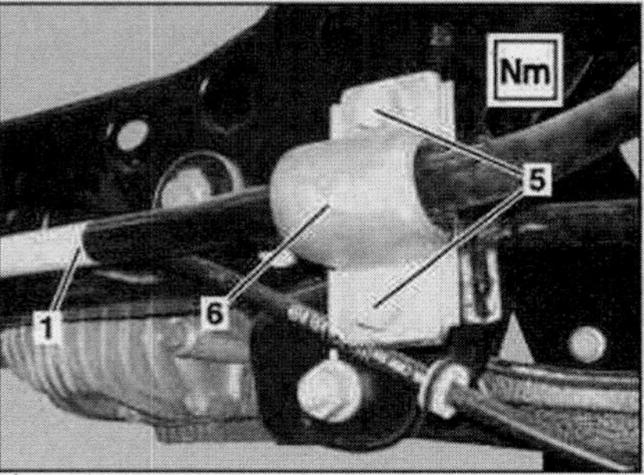

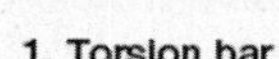

Fig. 88 Removing stabilizer bar

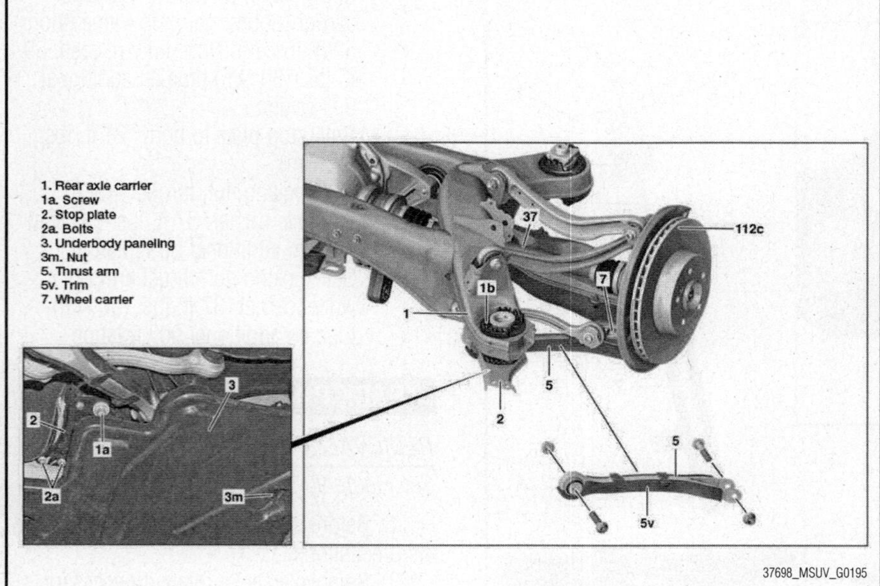

Fig. 89 Removing thrust arm

6. Lower torsion bar downwards slightly (arrow B) and remove bolt.
7. Remove tie rod.
8. Check rubber mounts of tie rod for damage.

To install:

9. Install in the reverse order.
10. Insert tie rod.
11. Insert bolt, position eccentric disk and screw on a new self-locking nut.
12. Insert bolt with dog bone washer(s) and screw on a new self-locking nut.
13. Position torsion bar clip and insert bolts.
14. Raise the suspension with the telescoping transmission jack and transmission platform under the supporting joint (arrow C) far enough until the suspension is deflected to the vehicle level.
15. Tighten bolts/nuts to specification as follows:
    - Bolt, stabilizer bar retaining clamp to rear axle carrier: 81 ft. lbs. (100 Nm)
    - Self-locking nut, tie rod to rear axle carrier: 69 ft. lbs. (93 Nm)
    - Self-locking nut, tie rod at wheel carrier: 81 ft. lbs. (100 Nm)
16. Perform chassis alignment.

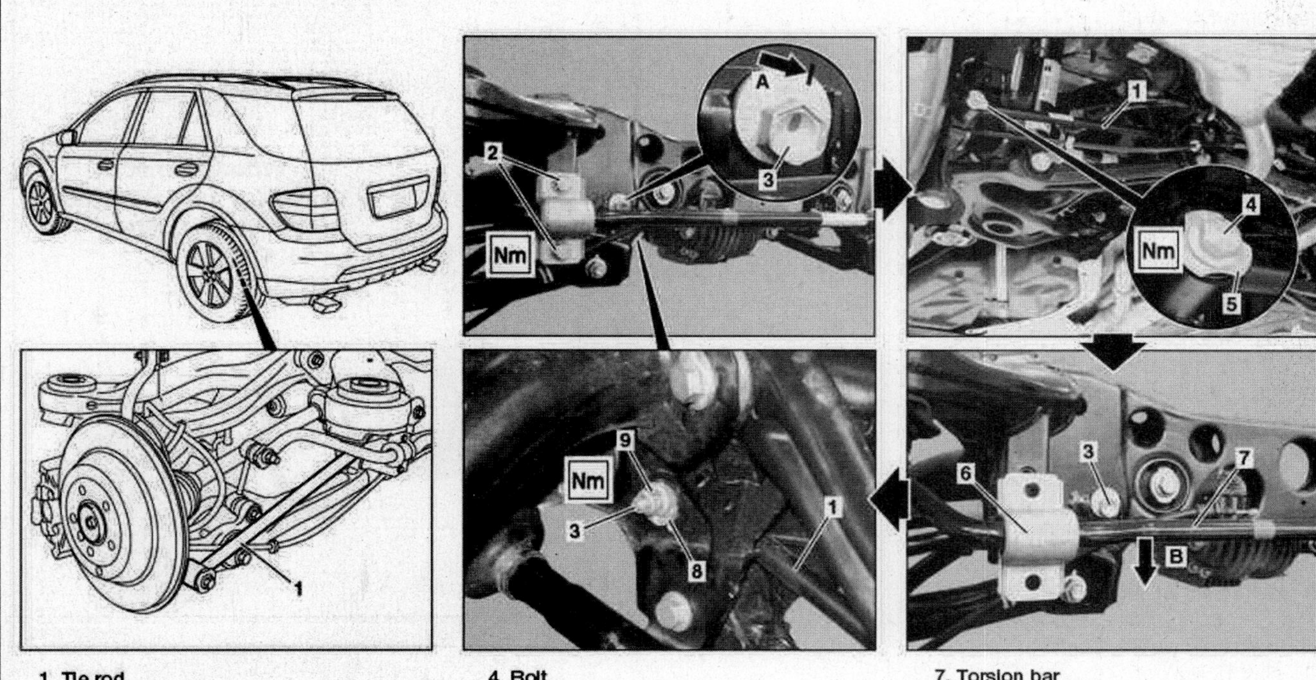

Fig. 90 Removing track rod

WHEEL CARRIER

REMOVAL & INSTALLATION

See Figures 91 and 92.

1. Before servicing the vehicle, refer to the precautions.
2. Remove wheels, rotate if necessary.
3. Remove hexagon collar nut on rear axle shaft.
4. Remove brake disc.
5. Detach brake cover plate.
6. Remove lock and cut brake cable in center.
7. Remove parking brake shoes.
8. Remove brake cable from wheel carder.
9. Detach left rear rpm sensor or right rear rpm sensor from wheel carrier.
10. Raise wheel carder using transmission jack and transmission platform until rear axle shaft is roughly horizontal.
11. Detach bolt of tie rod from wheel carrier.
12. Detach nut of camber strut from wheel carrier.
13. Detach nut of torque strut from wheel carrier.
14. Lower transmission jack.
15. Press rear axle shaft out of the rear axle shaft flange.

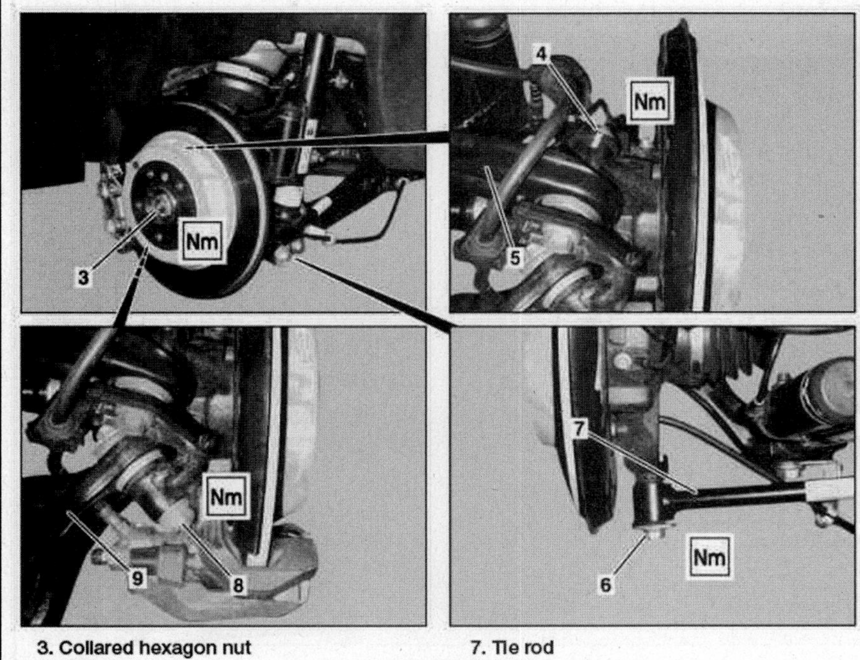

Fig. 91 Removing wheel carrier

16. Unscrew self-locking nut of supporting joint on wheel carrier.
17. Remove wheel carrier with supporting joint.

To install:

18. Install in the reverse order.
19. Install in the reverse order.
20. Replace hexagon collar nut.
21. Bolt on tie rod loosely.
22. Align the dog bone washer between the brake hose clip and camber strut.
23. Bolt on camber strut loosely.
24. Bolt on torque strut loosely.
25. Lift the wheel carrier using the transmission jack and transmission platform until the rear axle shaft is approximately horizontal.
26. Tighten bolts/nuts to specification as follows:
    - Collar nut, rear axle shaft to rear axle shaft flange: 185 ft. lbs. (250 Nm) plus an additional 45° rotation
    - Self-locking bolt of rear axle rpm sensor to wheel carrier: 71 inch lbs. (8 Nm)
    - Self-locking bolt, brake caliper to steering knuckle: 44 ft. lbs. (60 Nm) plus an additional 45° rotation
    - Self-locking nut, tie rod at wheel carrier: 81 ft. lbs. (110 Nm)
    - Self-locking nut, camber strut to wheel carrier: 41 ft. lbs. (55 Nm) plus an additional 90° rotation
    - Self-locking nut, torque strut to wheel carrier: 37 ft. lbs. (50 Nm) plus an additional 90° rotation
    - Self-locking nut of supporting joint of spring control arm to wheel carrier: 152 ft. lbs. (205 Nm)
27. Adjust parking brake.

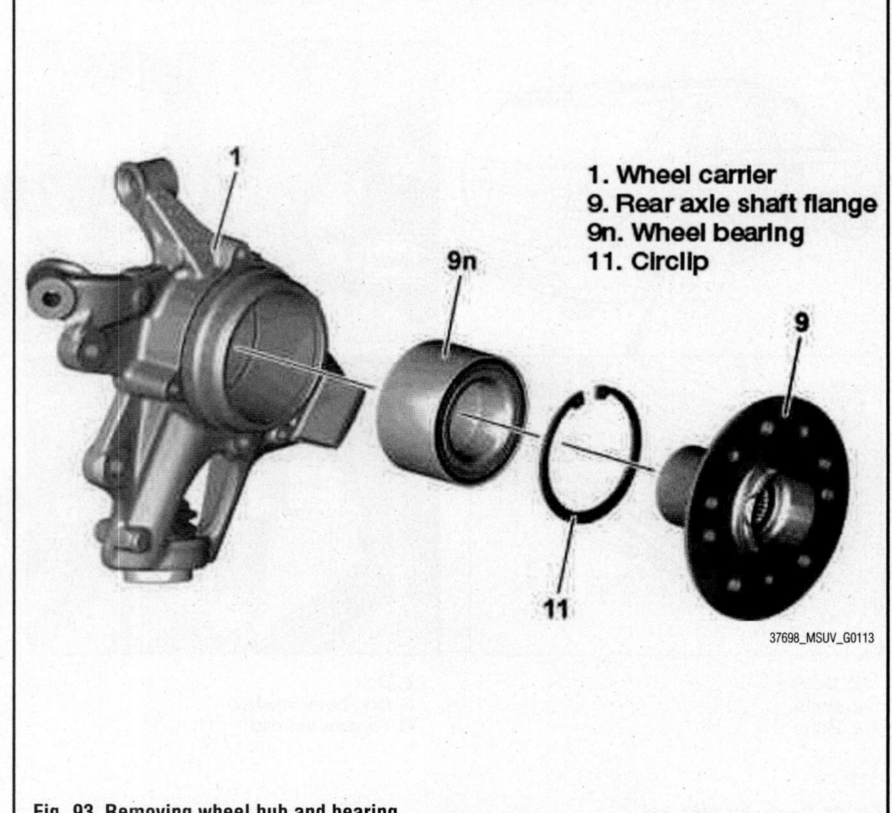

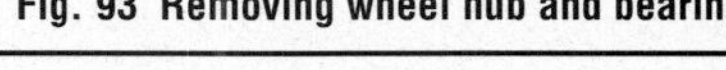
Fig. 93 Removing wheel hub and bearing

Fig. 92 Pressing rear axle shaft out of the rear axle shaft flange

WHEEL HUB & BEARING

REMOVAL & INSTALLATION

See Figure 93.

1. Before servicing the vehicle, refer to the precautions.
2. Remove wheel carrier.
3. Pull out rear axle shaft flange.
4. Remove retaining ring.
5. Pull wheel bearing out of wheel carrier.

To install:

6. Install in the reverse order.
7. Installation position must be observed. The points or the line on the wheel bearing must point towards the wheel carrier.
8. Pay attention to correct seat of circlip in wheel carrier.
9. In general the rear axle shaft flange and wheel bearing should be replaced.

MERCEDES BENZ

Sprinter

9

SPECIFICATIONS

ENGINE & MODEL YEAR IDENTIFICATION

Engine						
Code/VIN ①	Liters (cc)	Cu. In.	Cyl.	Fuel Sys.	Engine Type	Eng. Mfg.
642898/C	3.0 (2987)	182.2	6	CDI	DOHC	Mercedes-Benz

Model Year	
Code ②	Year
A	2010
B	2011
C	2012

CDI: Common rail Diesel Injection

DOHC: Dual Overhead Camshafts

① 642898 is the MB engine code; C is the 8th position of VIN

② 10th position of the VIN

71112_MBSV_C0001

GENERAL ENGINE SPECIFICATIONS

Year	Engine Displacement Liters (cc)	Engine ID/VIN	Fuel System Type	Net Horsepower @ rpm	Net Torque @ rpm (ft. lbs.)	Bore x Stroke (in.)	Compression Pressure (psi)	Oil Pressure psi @ rpm
2010	3.0 (2987)	642898/C	Diesel	188@1400	325@2400	3.27x3.62	392-464	43.5 @ 3000
2011	3.0 (2987)	642898/C	Diesel	188@1400	325@2400	3.27x3.62	392-464	43.5 @ 3000
2012	3.0 (2987)	642898/C	Diesel	188@1400	325@2400	3.27x3.62	392-464	43.5 @ 3000

71112_MBSV_C0002

DIESEL ENGINE TUNE-UP SPECIFICATIONS

Year	Engine Displacement Liters (cc)	Engine ID/VIN	Injection Pressure (psi)	Fuel Pressure (psi)	Idle Speed (rpm)	Valve Clearance (in.)	
						Intake	Exhaust
2010	3.0 (2987)	642898/C	NA	NA	650	HYD	HYD
2011	3.0 (2987)	642898/C	NA	NA	650	HYD	HYD
2012	3.0 (2987)	642898/C	NA	NA	650	HYD	HYD

NA: Information Not Available

71112_MBSV_C0003

CAPACITIES

Year	Engine ID/VIN	Engine Oil with Filter (qts.)	Automatic Transmission (pts.) *	Rear Drive Axle (pts.)	Fuel Tank (gal.)	Cooling System (qts.)	Air Conditioning System	
							R-134a (lbs.)	Oil (oz.)
2010	642898/C	13.2	①	②	26.4	10.5	③	④
2011	642898/C	13.2	①	②	26.4	10.5	③	④
2012	642898/C	13.2	①	②	26.4	10.5	③	④

* Figure given is the approximate refill capacity for a drain & refill without converter drain unless otherwise specified

NOTE: All capacities are approximate. Add fluid gradually and ensure a proper fluid level is obtained.

① Transmission 722.500/501/502/503/504/505/506/507/508/509/510: 13.1 pts.
Transmission 722.649: 13.7 pts.
Transmission 722.7: 6.97 pts.
Transmission 722.33/37: 16.69 pts.
Transmission 722.681 with torque converter: 14.79 pts.
Transmission 722.681 without torque converter: 10.56 pts.
Transmission 722.683/684/685/686 with torque converter: 15.0 pts.
Transmission 722.9 with torque converter: 14.79 pts.
Transmission 722.683/684/685/686 without torque converter: 11.6 pts.
Transmission 722.9 without torque converter: 11.6 pts.

② Axles 741.13 & 741.408/409: 3.8 pts.
Axle 741.407: 3.17 pts.

③ With code H08: 2.2
With code HH7: 2.62
With code HH9: 1.76
With code HK4: 3.86

④ With code H08 or HK4: 5.41
With code HH7 or HH9: 6.42

71112_MBSV_C0004

FLUID SPECIFICATIONS

Year	Engine ID/VIN	Engine Oil	Automatic Transmission	Rear Drive Axle	Power Steering Fluid	Brake Master Cylinder	Cooling System
2010	642898/C	①	②	75W-90	③	DOT 4	④
2011	642898/C	①	②	75W-90	③	DOT 4	④
2012	642898/C	①	②	75W-90	③	DOT 4	④

DOT: Department Of Transpotation

① Engine oil meeting MB229.51 specification, available at Mercedes-Benz dealers

② ATF meeting MB specification, available at Mercedes-Benz dealers

③ PS fluid meeting MB specification, available at Mercedes-Benz dealers

④ Coolant meeting MB approval 325.0

71112_MBSV_C0005

VALVE SPECIFICATIONS

Year	Engine ID/VIN	Valve Seat (deg.)	Valve Stem Diameter (in.) Intake	Valve Stem Diameter (in.) Exhaust	Valve Stem-to-Base of Camshaft Bearing (in.) Intake	Valve Stem-to-Base of Camshaft Bearing (in.) Exhaust	Valve Setback (in.) Intake	Valve Setback (in.) Exhaust
2010	642898/C	①	0.2346-0.2352	0.2340-0.2352	0.854-0.886	0.858-0.889	0.0394-0.0551	0.0275-0.4330
2011	642898/C	①	0.2346-0.2352	0.2340-0.2352	0.854-0.886	0.858-0.889	0.0394-0.0551	0.0275-0.4330
2012	642898/C	①	0.2346-0.2352	0.2340-0.2352	0.854-0.886	0.858-0.889	0.0394-0.0551	0.0275-0.4330

① Compound angle. Intake & exhaust vales, two cuts: 45 degrees & 30 degrees

71112_MBSV_C0006

CRANKSHAFT & CONNECTING ROD SPECIFICATIONS

All measurements are given in inches.

Year	Engine ID/VIN	Crankshaft Main Brg. Journal Dia.	Crankshaft Main Brg. Journal Width	Crankshaft Main Brg. Oil Clearance	Connecting Rod Journal Diameter	Connecting Rod Oil Clearance	Connecting Rod Bearing Radial Play
2010	642898/C	①	②	③	2.51732-2.5183	0.0008-0.0024	0.0006-0.0023
2011	642898/C	①	②	③	2.51732-2.5183	0.0008-0.0024	0.0006-0.0023
2012	642898/C	①	②	③	2.51732-2.5183	0.0008-0.0024	0.0006-0.0023

NA: Information Not Available

① Stage 1 (blue): 2.9906-2.9907 in.
Stage 2 (yellow): 2.9904-2.9906 in.
Stage 3 (red): 2.9902-2.9904 in.
Stage 4 (white): 2.9899-2.9902 in.
Stage 5 (violet): 2.9898-2.9899 in.

② N (colorless): 1.1614-1.1627 in.
N1 (red): 1.1654-1.1667 in.

③ Radial measurement (new): 0.0011-0.0020 in.; wear limit: 0.0031 in.
Axial measurement (new): 0.0039-0.0100 in.; wear limit: 0.0118 in.

71112_MBSV_C0008

PISTON & RING SPECIFICATIONS

All measurements are given in inches.

Year	Engine ID/VIN	Piston Diameter	Ring Gap Top Compression	Ring Gap Bottom Compression	Ring Gap Oil Control	Ring Side Clearance Top Compression	Ring Side Clearance Bottom Compression	Ring Side Clearance Oil Control
2010	642898/C	①	0.0079-0.0157	0.0157-0.0236	0.0079-0.0157	0.0071-0.0094	0.0019-0.0039	0.0012-0.0028
2011	642898/C	①	0.0079-0.0157	0.0157-0.0236	0.0079-0.0157	0.0071-0.0094	0.0019-0.0039	0.0012-0.0028
2012	642898/C	①	0.0079-0.0157	0.0157-0.0236	0.0079-0.0157	0.0071-0.0094	0.0019-0.0039	0.0012-0.0028

① Group A: 3.2611-3.2614 in.
Group B: 3.2616-3.2619 in.
Group X: 3.2613-3.2617 in,

71112_MBSV_C0009

TORQUE SPECIFICATIONS

All readings in ft. lbs. unless otherwise noted

Year	Engine ID/VIN	Cylinder Head Bolts	Main Bearing Bolts	Rod Bearing Bolts	Crankshaft Damper Bolts	Flexplate Bolts	Charge Air Manifold	Exhaust Manifold	Oil Pan Drain Plug
2010	642898/C	①	②	③	④	⑤	16	18	22
2011	642898/C	①	②	③	④	⑤	16	18	22
2012	642898/C	①	②	③	④	⑤	16	18	22

① Step 1: 84 inch lbs.
Step 2: 44 ft. lbs.
Step 3: +90 deg.
Step 4: +90 deg.
Step 5: +90 deg.

② Bearing cap bolts
Step 1: 26 ft. lbs.
Step 2: +95 deg.
Step 3: +95 deg.
Lateral bolts: 39 ft. lbs. +95 deg.
Cap bolts: 37 ft. lbs. +95 deg.

③ Step 1: Short arm: 11 ft. lbs.
Step 2: long arm 14 ft. lbs.
Step 3: Short arm 22 ft. lbs.
Step 4: long arm 28 ft. lbs.
Step 5: Short arm 28 ft. lbs.
Step 6: long arm +90 deg.
Step 7: short arm +90 deg.

④ 155 ft. lbs. +180 deg.

⑤ 45 ft. lbs. +90 degrees

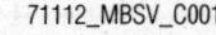

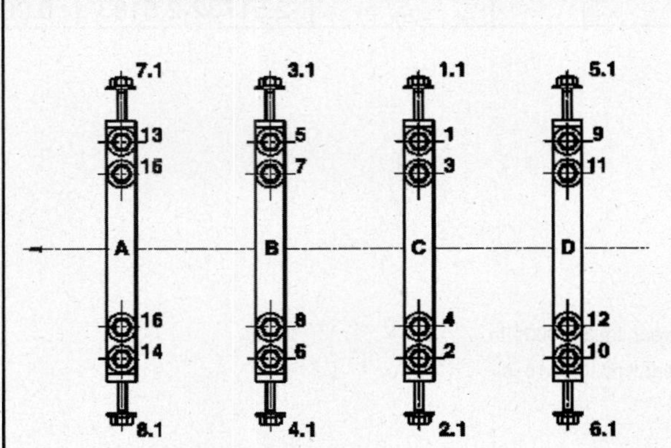

1. Lubricate bolts (1 to 16) for crankshaft bearing cap (A, B, C, D) on thread and the bolt head contact surface with engine oil.
2. Tighten bolts (1 to 16) for crankshaft bearing cap (A, B, C, D) as per tightening procedure.

i Observe tightening torque for bolts (1 to 16)

3. Tighten side bolts (1.1 to 8.1) for the crankshaft housing on crankshaft bearing cap (A, B, C, D) as per tightening procedure.

i Observe tightening torque for bolts (1.1 to 8.1)

4. Check crankshaft through turning freewheeling; remove crankshaft bearing cap (A, B, C, D) if necessary and determine error.

71112_MBSV_G0201

Fig. 1 Main bearing torque sequence

WHEEL ALIGNMENT

		Caster		Camber		
Year	Model	Range (+/-Deg.)	Preferred Setting (Deg.)	Range (+/-Deg.)	Preferred Setting (Deg.)	Toe (deg.) All +/-5'
2010	①	-35'/+5'	③	-35'/+5'	⑤	⑦
	②	-35'/+5'	④	-35'/+5'	⑥	⑧
2011	①	-35'/+5'	③	-35'/+5'	⑤	⑦
	②	-35'/+5'	④	-35'/+5'	⑥	⑧
2012	①	-35'/+5'	③	-35'/+5'	⑤	⑦
	②	-35'/+5'	④	-35'/+5'	⑥	⑧

* All dimensions +/-5'

① 906.11/131/133/135/21/23/61/63/71/73 exc. ZU7/ZU8 & 906.132/134/136 exc. code XB6 weight variant 4.2t

② 906.15/25/65 & 906.13/63/73 with ZU7/ZU8 & 906.132/134/136 with XB6 weight variant 4.2t

③ Rebound dimension:

227mm: 0
231mm: 0deg. 07'
235mm: 0deg.12'
238mm: 0deg.19'
242mm: 0deg.25'
246mm: 0deg.31'
250mm 0deg.39'
253mm: 0deg.44'
256mm: 0deg50'
257mm: 0deg.52'
260mm: 0deg.58'
261mm: 0deg.59'

④ Rebound dimension:

246mm: 0
250mm: 0deg.08'
253mm: 0deg.13'
254mm: 0deg.16'
256mm: 0deg.20'
257mm: 0deg.22'
260mm: 0deg.27'
261mm: 0deg.29'

⑤ Rebound dimension:

264mm: 1deg.05'
265mm: 1deg.07'
267mm: 1deg.12'
269mm: 1deg.14'
271mm: 1deg.19'
272mm: 1deg.23'
274mm: 1deg.26'
276mm: 1deg.31'
278mm: 1deg.34'
280mm: 1deg.39'
281mm: 1deg.42'
284mm: 1deg.48'
285mm: 1deg.50'

⑥ Rebound dimension:

264mm: 0deg.34'
265mm: 0deg.37'
267mm: 0deg.41'
269mm: 0deg.44'
271mm: 0deg.49'
272mm: 0deg.52'
274mm: 0deg.56'
276mm: 1deg.01'
278mm: 1deg.04'
280mm: 1deg.09'
281mm: 1deg.12'
284mm: 1deg.17'
285mm: 1deg.20'

⑦ Rebound dimension:

227mm: 0deg.02'
231mm: 0deg. 04'
235mm: 0deg.06'
238mm: 0deg.08'
242mm: 0deg.09'
246mm: 0deg.11'
250mm 0deg.13'
253mm: 0deg.14'
256mm: 0deg.15'
257mm: 0deg.16'
260mm: 0deg.17'
261mm: 0deg.17'

⑧ Rebound dimension:

246mm: 0deg.02'
250mm: 0deg.03'
253mm: 0deg.04'
254mm: 0deg.05'
256mm: 0deg.05'
257mm: 0deg.05'
260mm: 0deg.06'
261mm: 0deg.07'

TIRE, WHEEL, & BALL JOINT SPECIFICATIONS

Year	Model	OEM Tires		Tire Pressures (psi)		Wheel	Ball Joint	Wheel Bolts/Nuts
		Standard	Optional	Front	Rear	Size	Inspection	(ft. lbs.)
2010	2500	LT245/75R16 120/116	NA	①	①	NS	②	③
	3500	LT215/85R16 115/112	NA	①	①	NS	②	③
2011	2500	LT245/75R16 120/116	NA	①	①	NS	②	③
	3500	LT215/85R16 115/112	NA	①	①	NS	②	③
2012	2500	LT245/75R16 120/116	NA	①	①	NS	②	③
	3500	LT215/85R16 115/112	NA	①	①	NS	②	③

OEM: Original Equipment Manufacturer

PSI: Pounds Per Square Inch

NA: Not Applicable

NS: Not Specified

① See tire information label on the vehicle

② Permissible axial play of ball joints is 0

③ Wheel bolts: Model 906.11/13/21/23/61/63/71/73 & Model 906.15/25/65 w/code RH9 Super Single tires: Steel wheels: 177 ft. lbs.; Aluminum wheels: 132 ft. lbs.

Wheel nuts: Model 906.15/25/65 without code RH9 Super Single tires: 132 ft. lbs.

Tighten wheel bolts/nuts again after 31 miles (50 km)

When using new or newly painted rims, the wheel bolts/nuts must be retightened after 621-3106 miles (1000-5000km)

71112_MBSV_C0012

BRAKE SPECIFICATIONS

All measurements in inches unless noted

Year	Model	Position	Brake Disc			Minimum	Caliper
			Original Thickness	Minimum Thickness	Max. Runout	Pad Thickness	Bolts (ft. lbs.)
2010	2500	Front	1.102	0.984	0.0012	0.118	①
		Rear	0.623	0.551	0.0012	0.118	②
	3500	Front	1.102	0.984	0.0012	0.118	①
		Rear	1.102	0.984	0.0012	0.118	②
2011	2500	Front	1.102	0.984	0.0012	0.118	①
		Rear	0.623	0.551	0.0012	0.118	②
	3500	Front	1.102	0.984	0.0012	0.118	①
		Rear	1.102	0.984	0.0012	0.118	②
2012	2500	Front	1.102	0.984	0.0012	0.118	①
		Rear	0.623	0.551	0.0012	0.118	②
	3500	Front	1.102	0.984	0.0012	0.118	①
		Rear	1.102	0.984	0.0012	0.118	②

① M14x1.5 bolt: 59 ft. lbs. +40 degrees

M8 top guide pin/catch bolt to caliper support: 25 ft. lbs.

② Caliper support-to-axle tube

M14x1.5 bolts 59 ft. lbs. +30 degrees

M16x1.5 bolts: 59 ft. lbs. +40 degrees

Top section of caliper to caliper support guide pin/catch bolt

M8x1 bolt: 25 ft. lbs.

M10x1.25 bolt: 48 ft. lbs.

M14x1.5 bolts, caliper support to semi-trailing arm: 59 ft. lbs. +30 degrees

71112_MBSV_C0013

SCHEDULED MAINTENANCE INTERVALS
Sprinter

Maintenance – With ASSYST MAINTENANCE COMPUTER

ASSYST provides you with information on the best possible timing for maintenance work.
When the next maintenance service is due, this will be indicated in the multifunction display with a symbol.
You should have the maintenance performed within the stated period/distance.
The service indicator should be reset after an oil service and/or maintenance service has been performed.
To reset the ASSYST MAINTENANCE COMPUTER, perform the procedure below.

TO BE SERVICED	TYPE OF SERVICE	VEHICLE MILEAGE INTERVAL (x1000)												
		10	20	30	40	50	60	70	80	90	100	110	120	130
Engine oil & filter	R	✓	✓	✓	✓	✓	✓	✓	✓	✓	✓	✓	✓	✓
Tires	Rotate	✓	✓	✓	✓	✓	✓	✓	✓	✓	✓	✓	✓	✓
Power steering fluid	S/I	✓	✓	✓	✓	✓	✓	✓	✓	✓	✓	✓	✓	✓
Windshield washer system	S/I	✓	✓	✓	✓	✓	✓	✓	✓	✓	✓	✓	✓	✓
Brake hoses & linings	S/I			✓			✓			✓			✓	
Engine air filter	I	✓	✓	✓	✓	✓	✓	✓	✓	✓	✓	✓	✓	✓
Engine air filter	R		✓		✓		✓		✓		✓		✓	
Cabin Air Filter	R			✓			✓			✓			✓	
Battery	S/I			✓			✓			✓			✓	
Fuel Filter	R	✓	✓	✓	✓	✓	✓	✓	✓	✓	✓	✓	✓	✓
Parking Brake adjustment	S/I	✓	✓	✓	✓	✓	✓	✓	✓	✓	✓	✓	✓	✓
Chassis & Body bolts	S/I			✓										
Accessory drive belt	I/R						✓						✓	
Diesel Particle Filter (3.0L)	R									✓				
Tire pressures	S/I	✓	✓	✓	✓	✓	✓	✓	✓	✓	✓	✓	✓	✓
Automatic trans. fluid and filter	R						✓						✓	
Engine coolant	R	Every 180,000 miles												

R: Replace S/I: Service or Inspect C/L: Clean and lubricate I/R: Inspect and rerplace if necessary

In addition to the above maintenance work, the following should be performed:

Change the brake fluid every 2 years

Engine coolant every 10 years (if 180,000 miles has not already been achieved)

Change the rear axle fluid every 180,000 miles or 10 years

To reset the ASSYST MAINTENANCE COMPUTER, perform the following procedure:

Without Steering Wheel Buttons

1. Turn key to the ON/RUN position.
2. Within one second press the M button repeatedly until the service symbol and the current remaining distance, the remaining time or service exceeded is displayed.
3. Within 10 seconds turn the key to OFF/LOCK while still holding the M button.
4. Turn the key to ON/RUN again. The present status for days or distance is displayed once more.

Continue to hold the M button.

After approximately 10 seconds, a signal sounds and the display shows 16 000 km (10,000 miles) for approximately 10 seconds.

Release the M button.

With Steering Wheel Buttons

1. Turn key to the ON/RUN position.

Within one second press the service selection button repeatedly until the instrument cluster display shows the "Total and trip odometer" basic display.

3. Press the scroll forward/back button until the service symbol and the current remaining distance, the remaining time or service exceeded is displayed.
4. Press the reset button on the instrument cluster until the display on the instrument cluster shows the message "Reset service interval?"
5. Confirm the message "Reset service interval?" with the reset button on the instrument cluster.

If the reset button on the instrument cluster is pressed again, the message "Service interval was reset" is shown.

If the ASSYST counter was inadvertently reset, have an authorized dealer correct it.

71112_MBSV_C0014

PRECAUTIONS

Before servicing any vehicle, please be sure to read all of the following precautions, which deal with personal safety, prevention of component damage, and important points to take into consideration when servicing a motor vehicle:

- Never open, service or drain the radiator or cooling system when the engine is hot; serious burns can occur from the steam and hot coolant.
- Observe all applicable safety precautions when working around fuel. Whenever servicing the fuel system, always work in a well-ventilated area. Do not allow fuel spray or vapors to come in contact with a spark, open flame, or excessive heat (a hot drop light, for example). Keep a dry chemical fire extinguisher near the work area. Always keep fuel in a container specifically designed for fuel storage; also, always properly seal fuel containers to avoid the possibility of fire or explosion. Refer to the additional fuel system precautions later in this section.
- Fuel injection systems often remain pressurized, even after the engine has been turned **OFF**. The fuel system pressure must be relieved before disconnecting any fuel lines. Failure to do so may result in fire and/or personal injury.
- Brake fluid often contains polyglycol ethers and polyglycols. Avoid contact with the eyes and wash your hands thoroughly after handling brake fluid. If you do get brake fluid in your eyes, flush your eyes with clean, running water for 15 minutes. If eye irritation persists, or if you have taken brake fluid internally, IMMEDIATELY seek medical assistance.
- The EPA warns that prolonged contact with used engine oil may cause a number of skin disorders, including cancer. You should make every effort to minimize your exposure to used engine oil. Protective gloves should be worn when changing oil. Wash your hands and any other exposed skin areas as soon as possible after exposure to used engine oil. Soap and water, or waterless hand cleaner should be used.
- All new vehicles are now equipped with an airbag system, often referred to as a Supplemental Restraint System (SRS) or Supplemental Inflatable Restraint (SIR) system. The system must be disabled before performing service on or around system components, steering column, instrument panel components, wiring and sensors. Failure to follow safety and disabling procedures could result in accidental airbag deployment, possible personal injury and unnecessary system repairs.
- Always wear safety goggles when working with, or around, the airbag system. When carrying a non-deployed airbag, be sure the bag and trim cover are pointed away from your body. When placing a non-deployed airbag on a work surface, always face the bag and trim cover upward, away from the surface. This will reduce the motion of the module if it is accidentally deployed. Refer to the additional airbag system precautions later in this section.
- Clean, high quality brake fluid from a sealed container is essential to the safe and proper operation of the brake system. You should always buy the correct type of brake fluid for your vehicle. If the brake fluid becomes contaminated, completely flush the system with new fluid. Never reuse any brake fluid. Any brake fluid that is removed from the system should be discarded. Also, do not allow any brake fluid to come in contact with a painted surface; it will damage the paint.
- Never operate the engine without the proper amount and type of engine oil; doing so WILL result in severe engine damage.
- Timing belt maintenance is extremely important. Many models utilize an interference-type, non-freewheeling engine. If the timing belt breaks, the valves in the cylinder head may strike the pistons, causing potentially serious (also time-consuming and expensive) engine damage. Refer to the maintenance interval charts for the recommended replacement interval for the timing belt, and to the timing belt section for belt replacement and inspection.
- Disconnecting the negative battery cable on some vehicles may interfere with the functions of the on-board computer system(s) and may require the computer to undergo a relearning process once the negative battery cable is reconnected.
- When servicing drum brakes, only disassemble and assemble one side at a time, leaving the remaining side intact for reference.
- Only an MVAC-trained, EPA-certified automotive technician should service the air conditioning system or its components.

BRAKES — ANTI-LOCK BRAKE SYSTEM (ABS)

GENERAL INFORMATION

PRECAUTIONS

- Certain components within the ABS system are not intended to be serviced or repaired individually.
- Do not use rubber hoses or other parts not specifically specified for and ABS system. When using repair kits, replace all parts included in the kit. Partial or incorrect repair may lead to functional problems and require the replacement of components.
- Lubricate rubber parts with clean, fresh brake fluid to ease assembly. Do not use shop air to clean parts; damage to rubber components may result.
- Use only DOT 4 brake fluid from an unopened container.
- If any hydraulic component or line is removed or replaced, it may be necessary to bleed the entire system.
- A clean repair area is essential. Always clean the reservoir and cap thoroughly before removing the cap. The slightest amount of dirt in the fluid may plug an orifice and impair the system function. Perform repairs after components have been thoroughly cleaned; use only denatured alcohol to clean components. Do not allow ABS components to come into contact with any substance containing mineral oil; this includes used shop rags.
- The Anti-Lock control unit is a microprocessor similar to other computer units in the vehicle. Ensure that the ignition switch is **OFF** before removing or installing controller harnesses. Avoid static electricity discharge at or near the controller.
- If any arc welding is to be done on the vehicle, the control unit should be unplugged before welding operations begin.

SPEED SENSORS

REMOVAL & INSTALLATION

Front Wheel Sensor

See Figure 2.

1. Before servicing the vehicle, refer to the Precautions section.
2. Raise and safely support the vehicle.
3. Unscrew nut (1).
4. Raise wheel well lining (2).
5. Disconnect left front rpm sensor connector (X62/26) or right front rpm sensor connector (X62/27).
6. Expose line of left front rpm sensor (L6/1) or right front rpm sensor (L6/2).
7. Unscrew bolt (3).
8. Remove left front rpm sensor (L6/1) or right front rpm sensor (L6/2).
9. Installation is the reverse of removal.
10. Connect STAR DIAGNOSIS, read out fault memory and erase if required. Stored faults which may be caused by assembly work, test work, removed lines or a simulation, must be processed and erased in fault memories after completing the work.

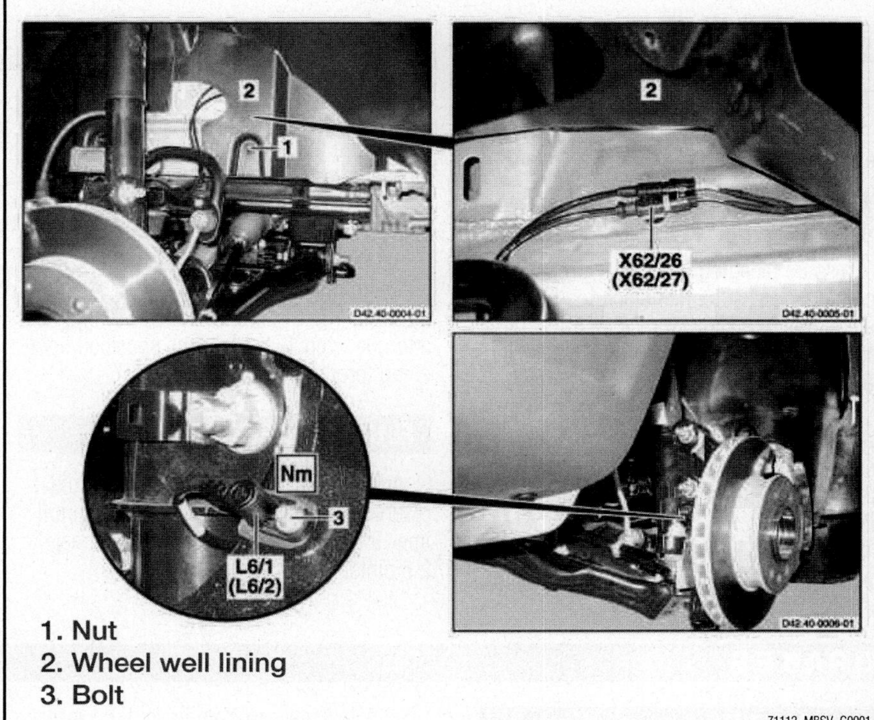

Fig. 2 Front wheel speed sensor removal sequence

Rear Wheel Sensor

See Figure 3.

1. Before servicing the vehicle, refer to the Precautions section.
2. Raise and safely support the vehicle.
3. Disconnect left rear rpm sensor connector (X62/28) or right rear rpm sensor connector (X62/29).
4. Expose line from left rear rpm sensor (L6/3) or right rear rpm sensor (L6/4).
5. Remove bolt (1).
6. Remove left rear rpm sensor (L6/3) or right rear rpm sensor (L6/4).

To install:

7. Grease sealing ring and place on left rear rpm sensor (L6/3) or right rear rpm sensor(L6/4). Apply MB high-temperature antifriction bearing grease (approx. 1g) to sealing ring. This prevents ingress of moisture and corrosion formation in the axle tube as well as on the left rear rpm sensor (L6/3) or right rear rpm sensor (L6/4).
8. Insert left rear rpm sensor (L6/3) or right rear rpm sensor (L6/4) straight into mounting hole until it makes contact.
9. Screw in bolt (1). Do not pull left rear rpm sensor (L6/3) or right rear rpm sensor (L6/4) into mounting hole with the bolt (1). Otherwise damage may occur, as the flange is not designed for this.
10. Spray left rear rpm sensor (L6/3) or right rear rpm sensor (L6/4) with sealing wax all around. Cover bore (2) during spraying so that spray mist cannot get to the brake disc and the brake pads. This would otherwise severely impair the braking effect.
11. Connect STAR DIAGNOSIS, read out fault memory and erase if required. Stored faults which may be caused by assembly work, test work, removed lines or a simulation, must be processed and erased in fault memories after completing the work.

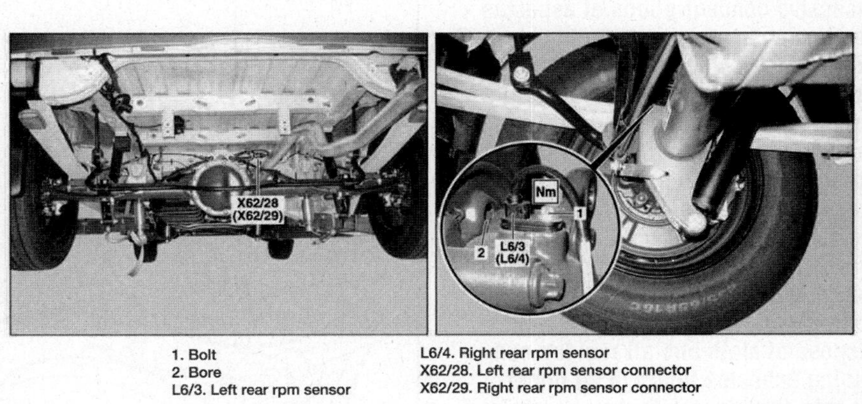

1. Bolt
2. Bore
L6/3. Left rear rpm sensor
L6/4. Right rear rpm sensor
X62/28. Left rear rpm sensor connector
X62/29. Right rear rpm sensor connector

71112_MBSV_G0002

Fig. 3 Rear wheel speed sensor removal sequence

BLEEDING PROCEDURE

See Figure 4.

1. Before servicing the vehicle, refer to the Precautions section.

➡Bleeder screw torque is 10 ft. lbs. (14 Nm).

Pressure bleeding is the only procedure recommended by the manufacturer. Follow the equipment manufacturer's instructions when using the equipment. Observe venting pressure.

2. Open right rear bleed valve (1). If the brake fluid that flows out is free of bubbles, close the right rear bleed valve (1) and use a torque wrench to apply the specified tightening torque.
3. Open left front bleed valve (2). If the brake fluid that flows out is free of bubbles, close the left front bleed valve (2) and use a torque wrench to apply the specified tightening torque.
4. Open left rear bleed valve (3). If the brake fluid that flows out is free of bubbles, close the left rear bleed valve (3) and use a torque wrench to apply the specified tightening torque.
5. Open right front bleed valve (4). If the brake fluid that flows out is free of bubbles, close the right front bleed valve (4) and use a torque wrench to apply the specified tightening torque.

FLUID FILL PROCEDURE

Add only DOT4 brake fluid to the fluid reservoir on the master cylinder, to the full line. Total system capacity is approximately 2.5 pints.

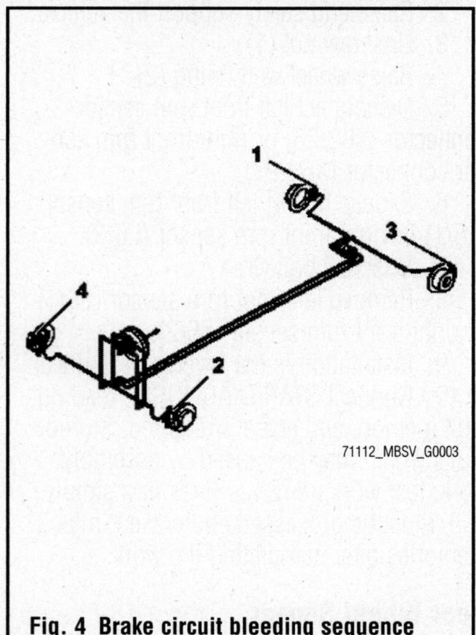

Fig. 4 Brake circuit bleeding sequence

⁂ CAUTION

Dust and dirt accumulating on brake parts during normal use may contain asbestos fibers from production or aftermarket brake linings. Breathing excessive concentrations of asbestos fibers can cause serious bodily harm. Exercise care when servicing brake parts. Do not sand or grind brake lining unless equipment used is designed to contain the dust residue. Do not clean brake parts with compressed air or by dry brushing. Cleaning should be done by dampening the brake components with a fine mist of water, then wiping the brake components clean with a dampened cloth. Dispose of cloth and all residue containing asbestos fibers in an impermeable container with the appropriate label. Follow practices prescribed by the Occupational Safety and Health Administration (OSHA) and the Environmental Protection Agency (EPA) for the handling, processing, and disposing of dust or debris that may contain asbestos fibers.

BRAKE CALIPER

REMOVAL & INSTALLATION

See Figure 5.

1. Before servicing the vehicle, refer to the Precautions section.
2. Unscrew cap from brake fluid reservoir.
3. Remove front wheels.
4. Unscrew screw (1) and remove left front brake pad contact sensor (S10/1) or right front brake pad contact sensor (S10/2) and wear indicator cable (2).
5. Remove brake hose (3). Seal line

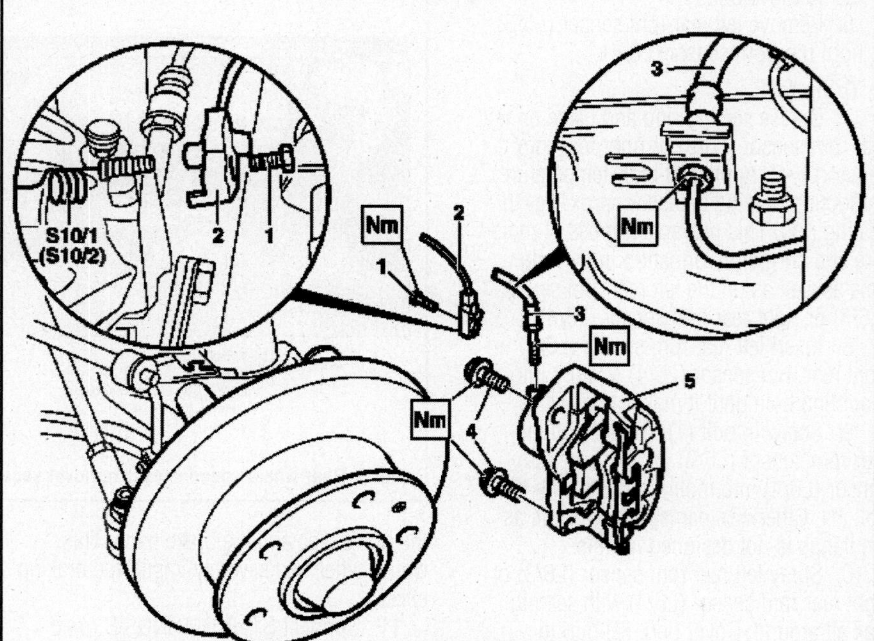

Fig. 5 Caliper removal/installation

ends and threaded stud on brake caliper (5) with plugs. Otherwise contamination may result in brake system failure.

6. Check the brake hose (3) for cracks and chafe marks. The brake hose (3) could start to leak causing the brake system to fail.

7. Unscrew screws (4) and remove brake caliper (5).

8. Install is the reverse of removal. Install new bolts (4). Torque the caliper bolts (M14x1.5) to 50 ft. lbs. (80 Nm) + 40 degrees. Torque the M8 top guide pin/catch bolt to caliper support: 25 ft. lbs. (33 Nm).

➡Make sure that the brake hose (3) is not installed twisted and that it has adequate clearance. The brake hose (3) can otherwise be damaged which could result in failure of the brake system.

9. Bleed brake system.

10. Check fluid level in reservoir; correct if necessary.

11. Check brake system for leaks.

BRAKE PADS

REMOVAL & INSTALLATION

See Figure 6.

1. Before servicing the vehicle, refer to the Precautions section.

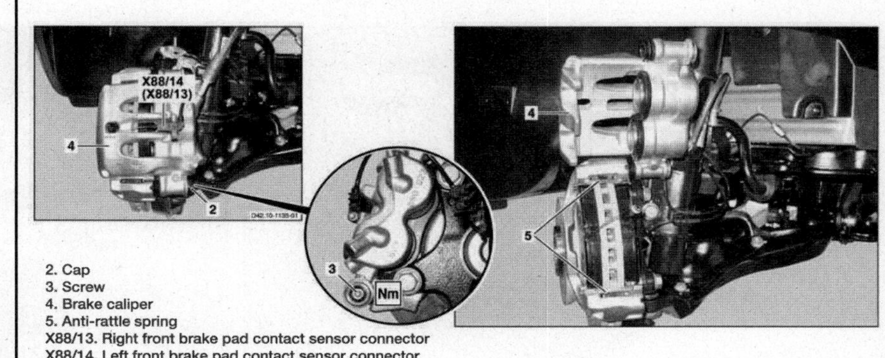

Fig. 6 Brake pad removal/installation

2. Unscrew lid from brake fluid reservoir.

3. Raise and safely support the vehicle.

4. Remove front wheels.

5. Detach left front brake pad contact sensor connector (X88/14) or right front brake pad contact sensor connector (X88/13). Use straight or angled needle nose pliers. Otherwise, damage may occur.

6. Remove cover (2).

7. Unscrew bolt (3).

8. Fold brake caliper (4) upwards, secure to protect it from falling down and remove brake pads. Do not use bushing seat as hooking- in point. Brake pads must be disposed of as special waste. The local authorities can provide information regarding whether disposal is also permitted as industrial waste similar to domestic waste.

9. Clean brake parts and check for wear and damage. Replace anti-rattle springs (5).

10. Push back piston. If the brake fluid level in the reservoir is too high, suction off a little brake fluid.

11. Installation is the reverse of removal.

12. Build up brake pressure by fully depressing brake pedal several times.

13. Check fluid level in reservoir; correct if necessary.

14. Check brake system for leaks.

BRAKES — REAR DISC BRAKES

⁂ CAUTION

Dust and dirt accumulating on brake parts during normal use may contain asbestos fibers from production or aftermarket brake linings. Breathing excessive concentrations of asbestos fibers can cause serious bodily harm. Exercise care when servicing brake parts. Do not sand or grind brake lining unless equipment used is designed to contain the dust residue. Do not clean brake parts with compressed air or by dry brushing. Cleaning should be done by dampening the brake components with a fine mist of water, then wiping the brake components clean with a dampened cloth. Dispose of cloth and all residue containing asbestos fibers in an impermeable container with the appropriate label. Follow practices prescribed by the Occupational Safety and Health Administration (OSHA) and the Environmental Protection Agency (EPA) for the handling, processing, and disposing of dust or debris that may contain asbestos fibers.

BRAKE CALIPER

REMOVAL & INSTALLATION

See Figures 7 and 8.

1. Before servicing the vehicle, refer to the Precautions section.

2. Remove rear wheels.

3. Detach left rear brake pad contact sensor connector (X88/16) or right rear brake pad contact sensor connector (X88/15).

4. Remove screw/bolt (3) and remove wear indicator cable (2).

5. Remove brake hose (4). Seal line ends and connection thread at brake caliper (5) with stop plug. Otherwise the brake system may fail due to contamination.

6. Check brake hose (4) for cracks and chafe marks, replace if necessary. If a damaged brake hose (4) continues to be used the brake system may fail.

7. Remove screws/bolts (6) and remove brake caliper (5).

8. Installation is the reverse of removal. Torque the caliper support-to-axle tube bolts as follows: M14x1.5 bolts 59 ft. lbs. (80 Nm) +30 degrees; M16x1.5 bolts: 59 ft. lbs. (80 Nm) +40 degrees; Top section of caliper to caliper support guide pin/catch bolt: M8x1 bolt: 25 ft. lbs. (34 Nm); M10x1.25 bolt: 48 ft. lbs. (65 Nm).

9. Bleed brake system.

10. Check fluid level in reservoir; correct if necessary.

11. Check brake system for leaks.

BRAKE PADS

REMOVAL & INSTALLATION

See Figures 9 and 10.

1. Before servicing the vehicle, refer to the Precautions section.

2. Unscrew lid of brake fluid reservoir.

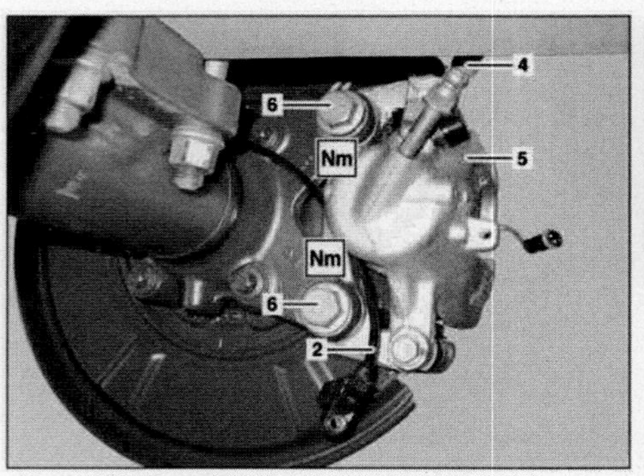

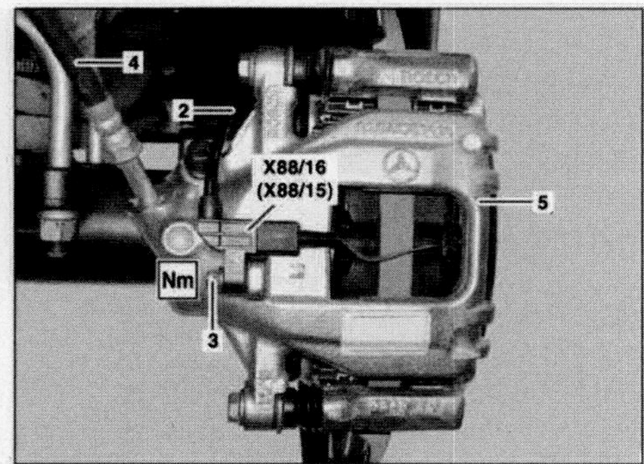

Model 900.63, model 906.11/13/21/23/61/63/71/73, shown on model 906.633 with rear axle 741.412

2. Wear indicator cable
3. Screw
4. Brake hose
5. Brake caliper
6. Bolts
X88/15. Right rear brake pad contact sensor connector
X88/16. Left rear brake pad contact sensor connector

71112_MBSV_G0006

Fig. 7 Brake caliper removal/installation model 906.11/13/21/23/61/63/71/73, shown on model 906.633 with rear axle 741.412

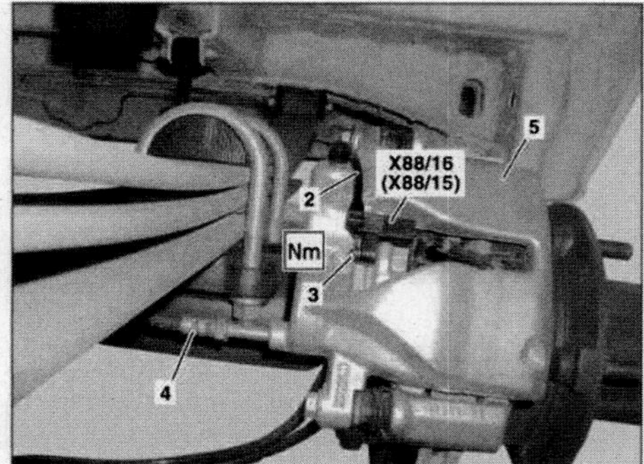

Model 900.65, model 906.15/25/65, Shown on model 906.15 with rear axle 741.414

2. Wear indicator cable
3. Screw
4. Brake hose
5. Brake caliper
6. Bolts
X88/15. Right rear brake pad contact sensor connector
X88/16. Left rear brake pad contact sensor connector

71112_MBSV_G0007

Fig. 8 Brake caliper removal/installation model 906.15/25/65, shown on model 906.15 with rear axle 741.414

3. Remove rear wheels.
4. Detach left rear brake pad contact sensor connector (X88/16) or right rear brake pad contact sensor connector (X88/15). Use straight or angled needle nose pliers. Otherwise, damage may occur.
5. Remove lower bolt (1) on brake caliper (2) In model 906.11/13/21/23/61/63/71/73. Undo bolt (1) on top of the brake caliper (2) In model 906.15/25/65.
6. Remove brake pads. On model 906.11/13/21/23/61/63/71/73, to do so, fold brake caliper (2) upwards. On model 906.15/25/65, to do so, fold the brake caliper (2) downward.

➡Brake pads are to be disposed of as special waste. The local authorities can provide information regarding whether disposal is also permitted as industrial waste similar to domestic waste.

7. Clean brake parts and check for wear and damage. On vehicles with Brembo brake caliper, replace anti-rattle springs (3). On vehicles with Bosch brake caliper, check anti-rattle springs (3) and replace if damaged or plastically deformed.
8. Push back brake piston. If the brake fluid level in the brake fluid reservoir is too high, extract some brake fluid.
9. Installation is the reverse of removal.
10. Build up brake pressure by fully depressing brake pedal several times.
11. Check fluid level in brake fluid reservoir, rectify if necessary.
12. Check brake system for leaks.

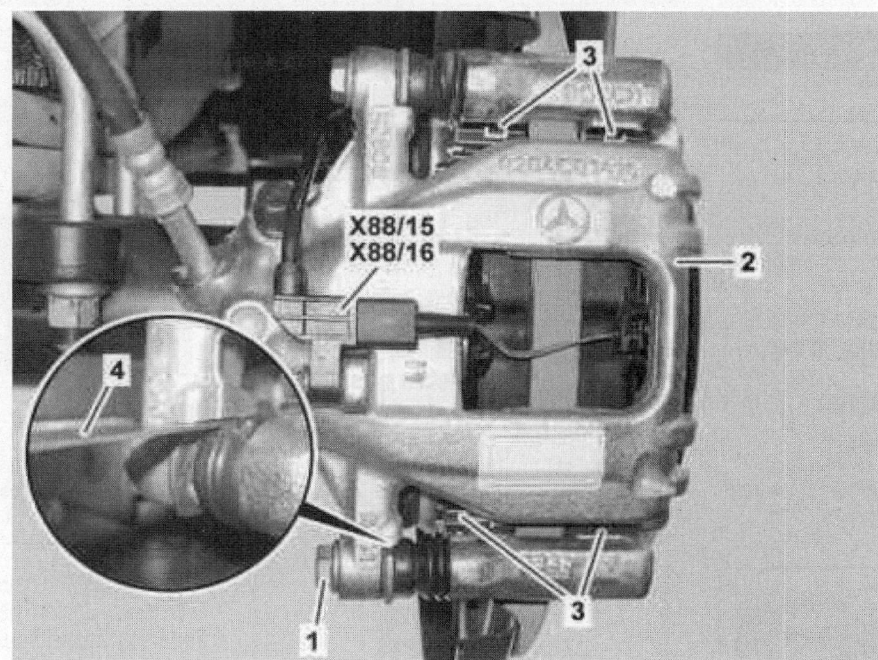

Model 900.63, 906.11/13/21/23/61/63/71/73, Shown on model 906.633 with rear axle 741.412

1. Screw
2. Brake caliper
3. Anti-rattle spring
4. Feeler gauge

X88/15. Right rear brake pad contact sensor connector
X88/16. Left rear brake pad contact sensor connector

71112_MBSV_G0008

Fig. 9 Brake pad removal/installation model 906.633 with rear axle 741.412

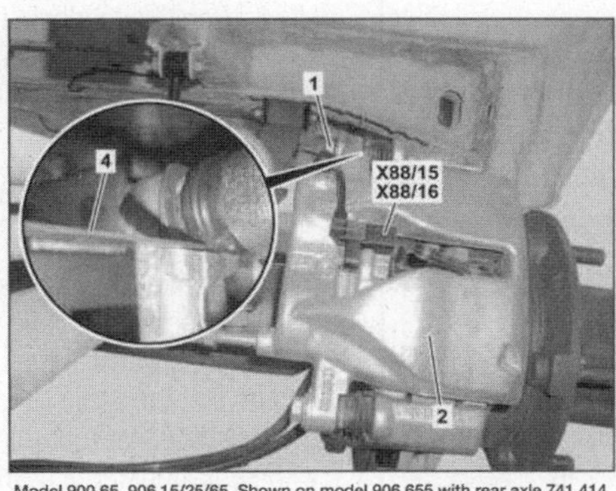

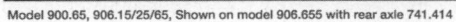

Model 900.65, 906.15/25/65, Shown on model 906.655 with rear axle 741.414

1. Screw
2. Brake caliper
3. Anti-rattle spring
4. Feeler gauge

X88/15. Right rear brake pad contact sensor connector
X88/16. Left rear brake pad contact sensor connector

71112_MBSV_G0009

Fig. 10 Brake pad removal/installation model 906.15/25/65, Shown on model 906.15 with rear axle 741.414

PARKING BRAKE CABLES

ADJUSTMENT

See Figures 11 through 15.

1. Before servicing the vehicle, refer to the Precautions section.
2. Loosen jam nut (33) and adjusting nut (30) and thus relieve parking brake cables (4) at cable adjuster (31).
3. Loosen nuts (34) and move cable adjuster (31) up to the end stop in the direction of travel.
4. On model 906.11/13/21/23/61/63/71/73:
   a. Turn the adjusting wheel (3) through the wheel bolt hole until the rear wheel can no longer be turned.
   b. Loosen adjusting wheel (3) by 3 to 4 teeth.
   c. Check freedom of movement of rear wheels.
5. On model 906.15/25/65:
   a. Tighten adjustment screw (1) to 89 inch lbs. (10 Nm).
   b. Turn back adjustment screw (1) two notches (approx. 2/3 revolution).
   c. Check freedom of movement of rear wheels.
6. Operate the hand brake lever several times with moderate force, then release and operate up to the third notch. Tighten adjusting nut (30) of cable adjuster (31) until the rear wheels can still just be turned by hand in the direction of travel.

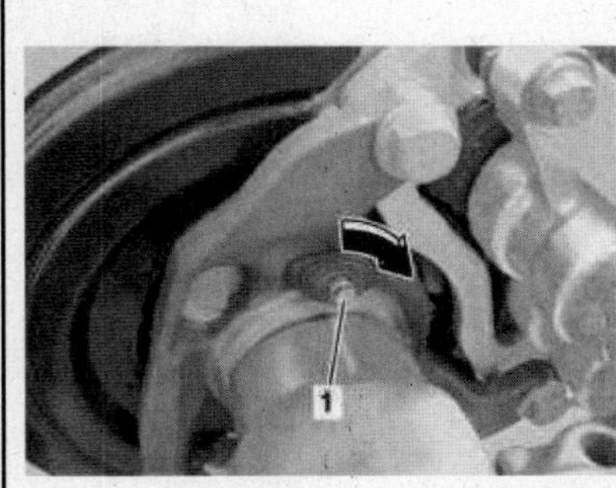

Fig. 15 Loosen adjusting wheel (3) by 3 to 4 teeth

7. Operate the hand brake lever 3 times and release again. The rear wheels must turn freely and without grinding the brake. If the rear wheels do not turn freely, the adjustment must be repeated.
8. Tighten lock nut (33).

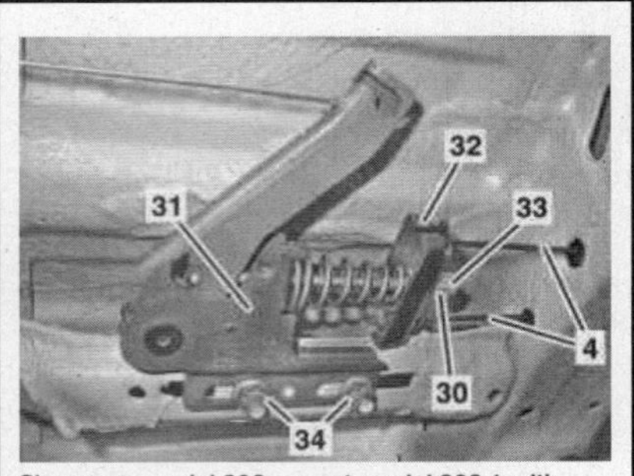

Fig. 11 Adjusting points

Fig. 13 Loosen adjusting wheel (3) by 3 to 4 teeth

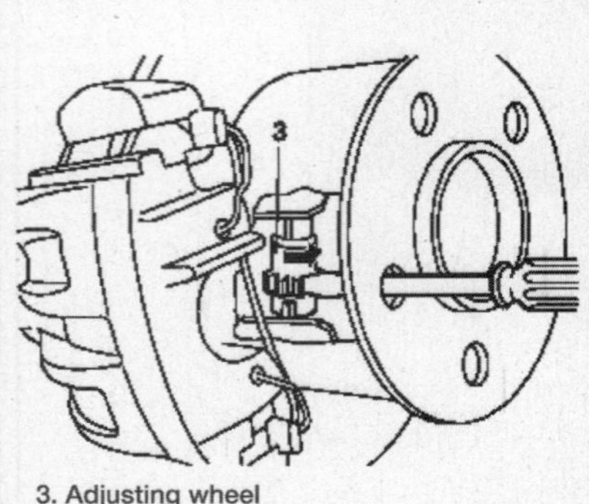

Fig. 12 Turn the adjusting wheel (3) through the wheel bolt hole until the rear wheel can no longer be turned.

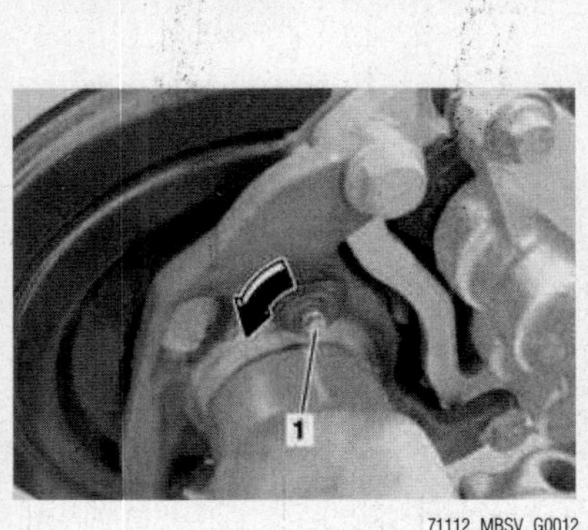

Fig. 14 Loosen adjusting wheel (3) by 3 to 4 teeth

PARKING BRAKE SHOES

REMOVAL & INSTALLATION

See Figure 16.

1. Before servicing the vehicle, refer to the Precautions section.
2. Remove rear wheels.
3. Remove rear axle brake disc.
4. Detach front brake cable from cable adjustment device. Do not detach the rear brake cables.
5. Release springs (2).
6. Unhook rear retracting spring (5).
7. Pull brake shoes (1) apart at the bottom and remove using brake shoe adjuster (6).
8. Check brake shoe (1) for wear.
9. Installation is the reverse of removal. Ensure that the cable lock (4) moves easily. Preassemble the front retracting spring (3) with short hook eyes from inside together with the brake shoe adjuster (6). The gear wheel of the brake shoe adjuster (6) is positioned at the bottom. Fit preassembled brake shoes (1) on to brake carrier.
10. Adjust parking brake
11. Build up brake pressure by operating brake pedal several times.
12. Check fluid level in reservoir; correct if necessary.
13. Check brake system for leaks.

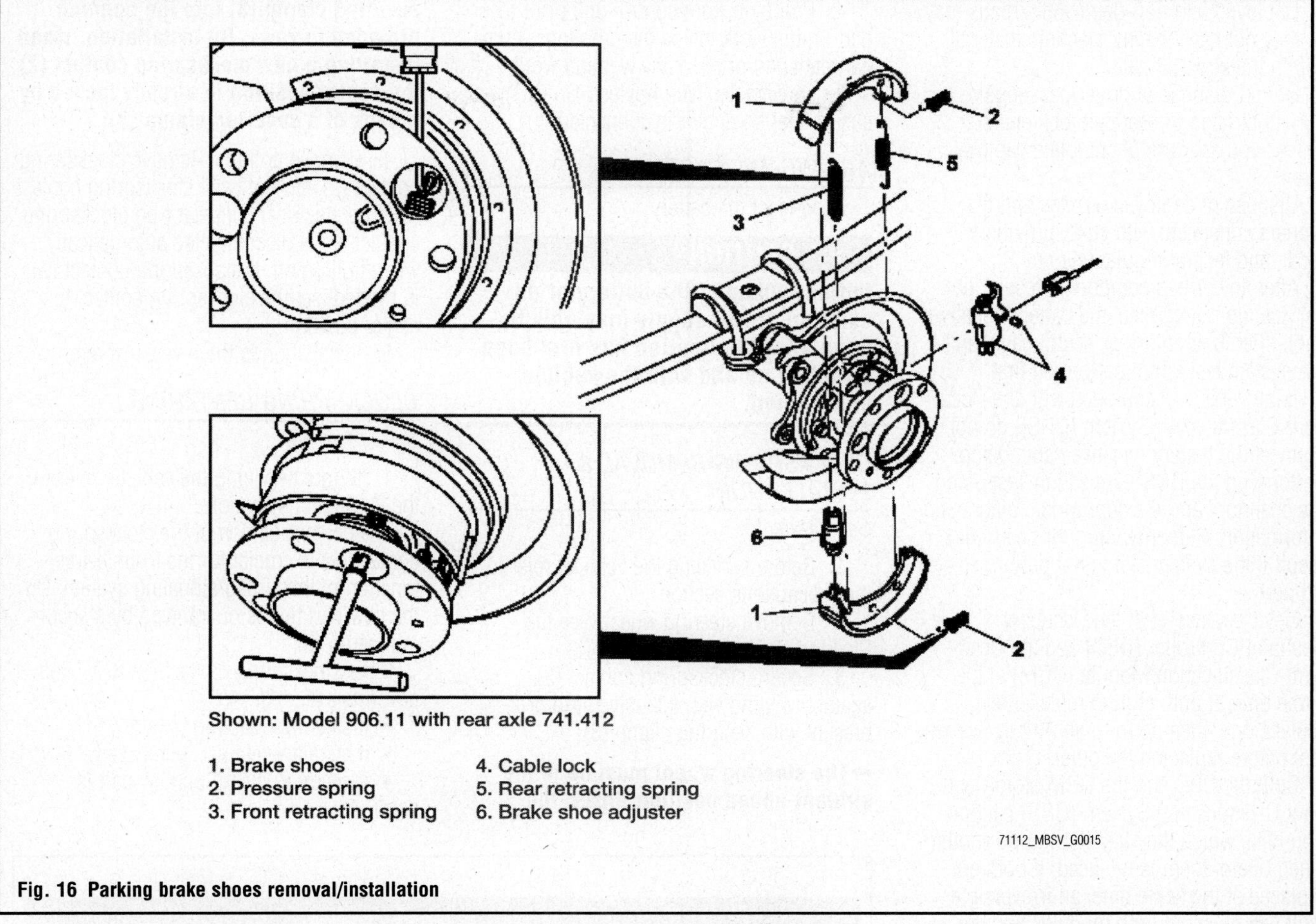

Fig. 16 Parking brake shoes removal/installation

CHASSIS ELECTRICAL

AIRBAG (SUPPLEMENTAL RESTRAINT SYSTEM)

GENERAL INFORMATION

CAUTION

These vehicles are equipped with an airbag system. The system must be disarmed before performing service on, or around, system components, the steering column, instrument panel components, wiring and sensors. Failure to follow the safety precautions and the disarming procedure could result in accidental airbag deployment, possible injury and unnecessary system repairs.

SERVICE PRECAUTIONS

Disconnect and isolate the battery negative cable before beginning any airbag system component diagnosis, testing, removal, or installation procedures. Allow system capacitor to discharge for two minutes before beginning any component service. This will disable the airbag system. Failure to disable the airbag system may result in accidental airbag deployment, personal injury, or death.

Do not place an intact undeployed airbag face down on a solid surface. The airbag will propel into the air if accidentally deployed and may result in personal injury or death.

When carrying or handling an undeployed airbag, the trim side (face) of the airbag should be pointing away from the body to minimize possibility of injury if accidental deployment occurs. Failure to do this may result in personal injury or death.

Replace airbag system components with OEM replacement parts. Substitute parts may appear interchangeable, but internal differences may result in inferior occupant protection. Failure to do so may result in occupant personal injury or death.

Wear safety glasses, rubber gloves, and long sleeved clothing when cleaning powder residue from vehicle after an airbag deployment. Powder residue emitted from a deployed airbag can cause skin irritation. Flush affected area with cool water if irritation is experienced. If nasal or throat irritation is experienced, exit the vehicle for fresh air until the irritation ceases. If irritation continues, see a physician.

Do not use a replacement airbag that is not in the original packaging. This may result in improper deployment, personal injury, or death.

The factory installed fasteners, screws and bolts used to fasten airbag components have a special coating and are specifically designed for the airbag system. Do not use substitute fasteners. Use only original equipment fasteners listed in the parts catalog when fastener replacement is required.

During, and following, any child restraint anchor service, due to impact event or vehicle repair, carefully inspect all mounting hardware, tether straps, and anchors for proper installation, operation, or damage. If a child restraint anchor is found damaged in any way, the anchor must be replaced. Failure to do this may result in personal injury or death.

Deployed and non-deployed airbags may or may not have live pyrotechnic material within the airbag inflator.

Do not dispose of driver/passenger/ curtain airbags or seat belt tensioners unless you are sure of complete deployment.

Dispose of deployed airbags and tensioners consistent with state, provincial, local, and federal regulations.

After any airbag component testing or service, do not connect the battery negative cable. Personal injury or death may result if the system test is not performed first.

If the vehicle is equipped with the Occupant Classification System (OCS), do not connect the battery negative cable before performing the OCS Verification Test using the scan tool and the appropriate diagnostic information. Personal injury or death may result if the system test is not performed properly.

Never replace both the Occupant Restraint Controller (ORC) and the Occupant Classification Module (OCM) at the same time. If both require replacement, replace one, then perform an Airbag System test before replacing the other.

Both the ORC and the OCM store Occupant Classification System (OCS) calibration data, which they transfer to one another when one of them is replaced. If both are replaced at the same time, an irreversible fault will be set in both modules and the OCS may malfunction and cause personal injury or death.

If equipped with OCS, the Seat Weight Sensor is a sensitive, calibrated unit and must be handled carefully. Do not drop or handle roughly. If dropped or damaged, replace with another sensor. Failure to do so may result in occupant injury or death.

If equipped with OCS, the front passenger seat must be handled carefully as well. When removing the seat, be careful when setting on floor not to drop. If dropped, the sensor may be inoperative, could result in occupant injury, or possibly death.

If equipped with OCS, when the passenger front seat is on the floor, no one should sit in the front passenger seat. This uneven force may damage the sensing ability of the seat weight sensors. If sat on and damaged, the sensor may be inoperative, could result in occupant injury, or possibly death.

DISARMING THE SYSTEM

1. Remove ignition key.
2. Disconnect external power sources (e.g. charger).
3. Disconnect and insulate battery ground cable.
4. Pull plug from control unit prior to performing work inside the passenger compartment and prior to any welding work.
5. On vehicles with Keyless-Go (KG), ensure that no circuit is connected.

ARMING THE SYSTEM

Reconnect the battery.

CAUTION

Initial hookup of the battery or an external power supply may only be done after the ignition has first been switched on and with the vehicle unoccupied.

CLOCKSPRING REMOVAL & INSTALLATION

See Figure 17.

1. Before servicing the vehicle, refer to the Precautions section.
2. Remove steering wheel. See the Steering section.
3. Secure clockspring contact (2) against twisting with adhesive strip or if present with securing clamp (3).

➡The steering wheel must be in the straight-ahead position. Insert the securing clamp (3) into the opening provided (arrow). On installation, when installing a new clockspring contact (2) the center position is already locked by means of a securing clamp (3).

4. Remove bolt (1). Remove clockspring contact (2). Do not twist clockspring contact (2). The electrical connector on clockspring contact (2) is disconnected automatically when pulling off. If clockspring contact (2) is twisted, set the clockspring contact to center position.
5. Installation is the reverse of removal.

CLOCKSPRING CENTERING

See Figure 18.

1. Before servicing the vehicle, refer to the Precautions section.

The center position of the clockspring contact (2) is crucial for the trouble-free function of the airbag/signaling system. On the new part this is guaranteed by a securing clamp (3).

If the clockspring contact (2) is twisted nevertheless, e. g.

- if steering coupling is removed,
- if auxiliary retainer is released,
- if securing clamp on new part is detached,

1. Bolts
2. Clock spring contact
3. Securing clamp

71112_MBSV_G0189

Fig. 17 Clockspring removal/installation

Shown on engine 642 in model 639

1. Pulley
2. Timing case cover
3. Fitting sleeves
4. Bolts

71112_MBSV_G0190

Fig. 18 Clockspring centering

The center position is to be determined as follows:

2. Remove clockspring contact (2).
3. Remove all mounting bolts.
4. Turn clockspring contact (2) to the left until a slight resistance is detectable.

➡The clockspring contact (2) is rolled up completely.

5. Turn (turn back) clockspring contact (2) approx. 2.5 revolutions clockwise until the opening (arrow) for the securing clamp (3) as well as the bolt holes (4) overlap.

➡The entire rotation range of the clockspring contact (2) is approx. 5.5 revolutions.

6. Secure clockspring contact (2) in this position using securing clamp (3) or an auxiliary retainer (adhesive strip, Allen wrench SW3 or suitable sheet metal screw).

➡The securing clamp (3) is only supplied together with a new clockspring contact (2).

DRIVETRAIN

AUTOMATIC TRANSMISSION FLUID

DRAIN & REFILL

See Figure 19.

1. Before servicing the vehicle, refer to the Precautions section.
2. Raise and safely support the vehicle.
3. Clean working area surrounding oil pan oil drain screw (6).
4. Remove oil drain screw from oil pan (6). Allow the oil to drain completely in the hot condition.
5. Replace sealing ring (7) and screw in oil drain screw (6) then tighten to 16 ft. lbs. (22 Nm).
6. Fill with transmission with the correct amount of oil. Fill it gradually until the level reaches the full hot level with the fluid hot.
7. Check transmission for leaks. Check oil pan (3), oil pan drain screw (6) and torque converter drain screw (8) for leaks.

FILTER REPLACEMENT

See Figure 19.

1. Before servicing the vehicle, refer to the Precautions section.
2. Raise and safely support the vehicle.
3. Clean working area surrounding oil pan oil drain screw (6).
4. Remove oil pan drain screw (6). Allow the oil to drain completely.
5. Remove oil pan (3):
   a. Support engine using suitable piece of wood placed onto crossmember over front spring.
   b. Remove both rear engine suspension bolts on transmission housing.
   c. Remove crossmember below automatic transmission at rear engine mount.
   d. Detach oil pan (1) with oil pan gasket (2). To do so, raise transmission slightly.
6. Pull oil filter (1) down and off.
7. Insert new oil filter (1).
8. Install oil pan (3):
   a. Replace oil pan gasket (2). Attach oil pan (1). First screw in screws manually and then tighten crosswise uniformly

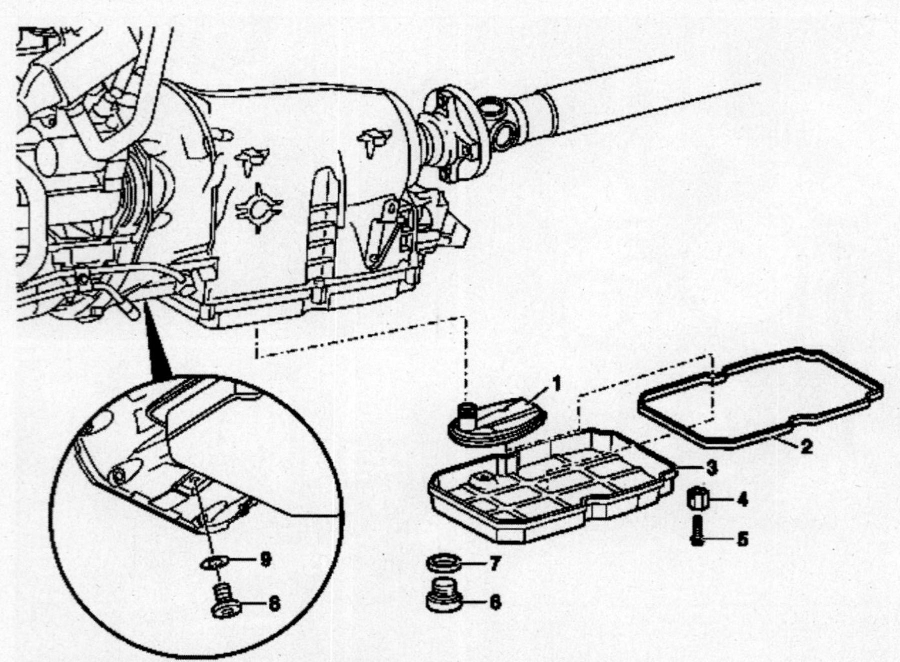

Fig. 19 Transmission oil pan and filter

from center. Torque is 79 inch lbs. (9 Nm).

b. Replace sealing ring (6). Screw in oil drain screw (5) and then tighten to 16 ft. lbs. (22 Nm).

c. Mount crossmember below automatic transmission with rear engine mount. Torque the rear engine mount-to-transmission to 29 ft. lbs. (40 Nm).

d. Remove support on crossmember over front spring.

9. Fill with transmission oil.

10. Check transmission for leaks. Check oil pan (3), oil pan drain screw (6) and torque converter drain screw (8) for leaks.

DRIVESHAFT

REMOVAL & INSTALLATION

See Figure 20.

1. Before servicing the vehicle, refer to the Precautions section.
2. Raise and safely support the vehicle.
3. Remove safety bracket (2).
4. Remove driveshaft (1) together with propeller shaft center support bearing (10).

➡Have the propeller shaft (1) held by a second person. For variant B (picture B) the flexible coupling (8) remains on the drive shaft (1).

5. Check flexible coupling (8) for signs of wear. If necessary replace flexible coupling (8).
6. Installation is the reverse of removal. Observe the following torques:
   - Safety bracket bolt: 74 ft. lbs. (100 Nm)
   - Support bearing frame-to-floor: 99 ft. lbs. (135 Nm)
   - Driveshaft-to-rear axle: M10x1 bolts, 11 ft. lbs. (15 Nm) + 90 degrees; E14 screw head, 11 ft. lbs. (15 Nm) + 70 degrees
   - Driveshaft-to-transmission, Variant A: M10x1 bolts, 11 ft. lbs. (15 Nm) + 90 degrees; E14 screw head, 11 ft. lbs. (15 Nm) + 70 degrees; E18 screw head, 44 ft. lbs. (60 Nm) +60 degrees
   - Flexible coupling-to-transmission, Variant B: 44 ft. lbs. (60 Nm) +60 degrees

REAR AXLE FLUID

DRAIN & REFILL

See Figure 21.

1. Before servicing the vehicle, refer to the Precautions section.
2. Raise and safely support the vehicle. Place a drain pan under the axle.
3. Remove the filler plug.
4. On axles with a drain plug (1), remove it. On axles with a stop plug, remove that. On metal plugs, clean the magnet.
5. Replace the plug. On screw-type drain plugs, torque them to:
   - Axle 741.130/131/407/408/409: 74 ft. lbs. (100 Nm)
   - Axle 741.980: 22 ft. lbs. (30 Nm)
   - Axle 741.412/413/414/415/416/429: Step 1, 44 ft. lbs. (60 Nm), Step 2, 66 ft. lbs. (90 Nm)
6. Fill the axle to the bottom edge of the filler opening.
7. Install the filler plug. Torque the screw type plug to:

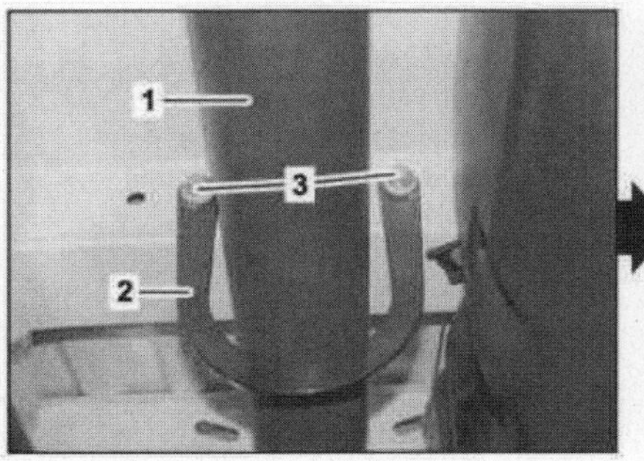

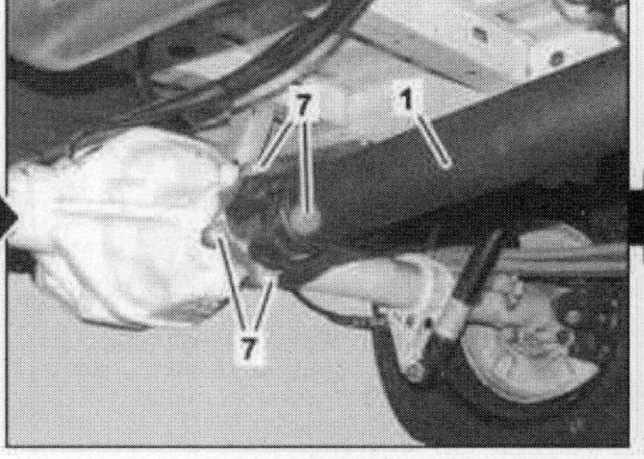

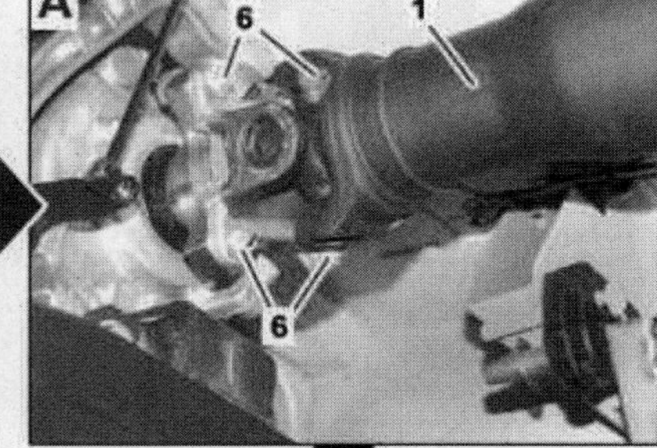

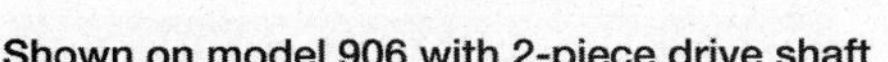

Shown on model 906 with 2-piece drive shaft
1. Propeller shaft
2. Securing clip
3. Bolts
4. Bolts
5. Bolts
6. Bolts Figure A Variant A
7. Bolts (without flexible coupling (8))
8. Flex disk Figure B Variant B
9. Bolts (with flexible coupling (8))
10. Propeller shaft center support bearing

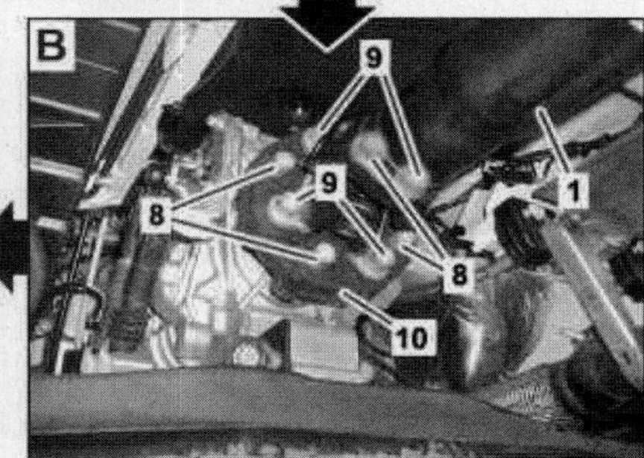

71112_MBSV_G0022

Fig. 20 Driveshaft removal/installation

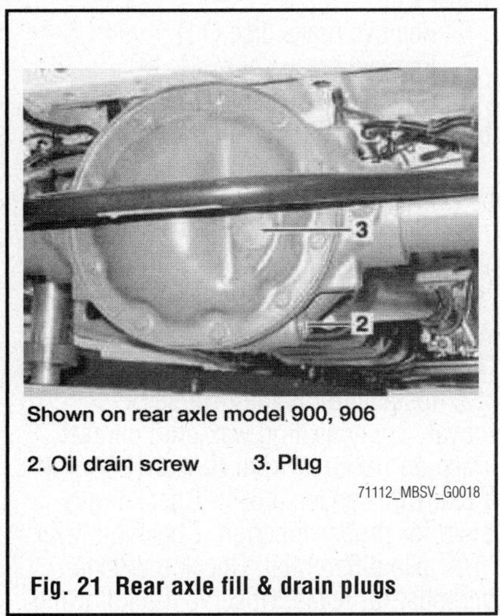

Shown on rear axle model 900, 906

2. Oil drain screw 3. Plug

71112_MBSV_G0018

Fig. 21 Rear axle fill & drain plugs

- Axle 741.130/131/407/408/409: 74 ft. lbs. (100 Nm)
- Axle 741.980: 22 ft. lbs. (30 Nm)

REAR AXLE HOUSING

REMOVAL & INSTALLATION

See Figures 22 and 23.

1. Before servicing the vehicle, refer to the Precautions section.

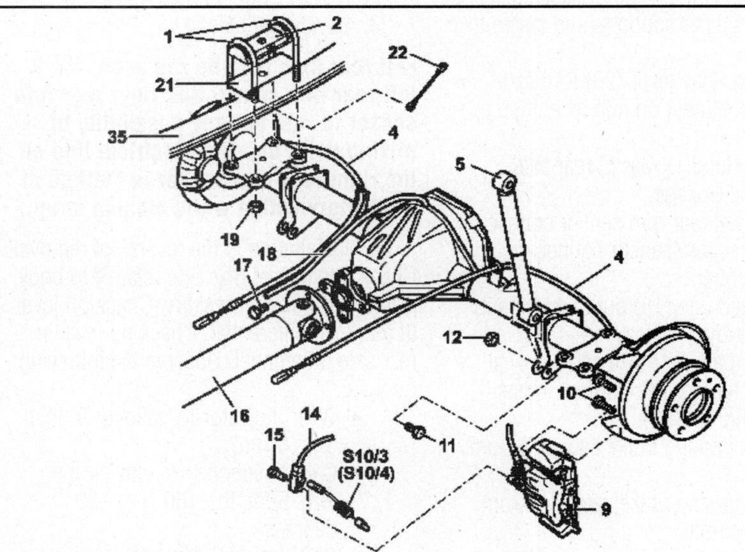

Shown on model 906.633 with rear axle 741.412

1. Spring U-bolt
2. Spring plate
4. Parking brake cable
5. Shock absorber
9. Brake caliper
10. Screw
11. Screw
12. Nut
14. Wiring harness
15. Screw
16. Propeller shaft
17. Screw
18. Vent line
19. Nut
21. Plate (with code (PL9) Air suspension from VB Air suspension)
22. Link rod (with code (PL9) Air suspension from VB-Air suspension)
35. Spring
S10/3. Left rear brake pad contact sensor
S10/4. Right rear brake pad contact sensor

71112_MBSV_G0019

Fig. 22 Rear axle removal/installation

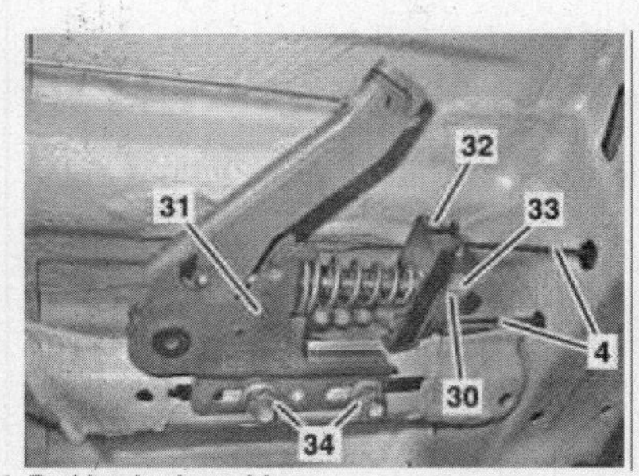

4. Parking brake cable
20. Relay lever (with code (LG0) Bi-xenon headlamp or code (LG1) Bi-xenon headlamp with cornering lights and without code (PL9) Air suspension from VB-Air suspension)
30. Nut
31. Cable adjustment device
32. Bracket
33. Jam nut
34. Nut

71112_MBSV_G0020

Fig. 23 Parking brake adjuster and air suspension relay lever

2. Release compressed air from air suspension, if so equipped.
3. Raise and safely support the vehicle.
4. Remove rear wheels.
5. Disconnect electrical connector on left rear brake pad contact sensor (S10/3) and on right rear brake pad contact sensor (S10/4).
6. Unscrew bolts (15) and remove electrical wiring harnesses (14) from right and left brake caliper (9).
7. Remove left and right brake caliper (9) with brake caliper supports and fasten to body.
8. Unscrew relay lever (20) for headlamp range adjustment on rear axle, if so equipped.
9. Detach stabilizer bar of rear axle from connecting linkage.
10. Detach left rear rpm sensor connector and right rear rpm sensor connector from frame member.
11. Pull bleed line (18) out of frame support on underbody.
12. Release parking brake cables (4) at the cable adjuster (31). To do this, loosen jam nut (33) and nut (30).
13. Unhook parking brake cable (4) from bracket (32).
14. Unclip parking brake cable (4) from frame floor assembly.
15. Unhook parking brake cable (4) from brackets on frame floor assembly.
16. Unscrew propeller shaft (16) from rear axle. In addition, secure rear axle to transmission jack using tensioning strap.
17. Fasten right and left spring (35) using tensioning straps to body. With code (PL9) Air suspension, VB-Air suspension company, fasten springs (35) using tensioning strap to body so that the springs (35) cannot move downwards. Otherwise the air spring bellows may be damaged.
18. Remove off both shock absorbers (5) at rear axle.
19. Support the axle with a floor jack.
20. Release right and left link rod (22) and unclip from plates (21).
21. Unscrew nuts (19) on left and right side, and then remove spring U-bolts (1) with spring plates (2).
22. Remove right and left plate (21).
23. Lower rear axle

➡If rear axle is to be replaced. Mark left rear rpm sensor and right rear rpm sensor to rule out any possibility of mixing them up. The electrical line on the right rear rpm sensor is marked at the factory with a white closing strap.

24. Installation is the reverse of removal. Check position of rear axle relative to body. Adjust bar link if necessary. Check oil level in rear axle differential. Check oil level in rear axle differential. Observe the following torques:
    - Wear indicator-to-caliper: 72 inch lbs. (8 Nm)
    - Caliper support-to-semi-trailing arm: 59 ft. lbs. (80 Nm) +30 degrees
    - Connecting rod-to-stabilizer & longitudinal frame member, with air suspension: 78 ft. lbs. (106 Nm)
    - Link rod-to-longitudinal frame member, with air suspension: 59 ft. lbs. (80 Nm)
    - Link rod-to-stabilizer bar, with air suspension: 76 ft. lbs. (104 Nm)
    - Driveshaft-to-rear axle: M10x1 bolts, 11 ft. lbs. (15 Nm) + 90 degrees; E14 screw head, 11 ft. lbs. (15 Nm) + 70 degrees
    - Shock absorber-to-axle: axle 741.412/413/415/428, 78 ft. lbs. (106 Nm)
    - Shock absorber-to-axle: axle 741.41/420/429 without air suspension, 99 ft. lbs. (135 Nm)
    - Shock absorber-to-axle: axle 741.41/420 with air suspension, 118 ft. lbs. (160 Nm)
    - Spring U-bolt nuts: 118 ft. lbs. (160 Nm)

REAR AXLE SHAFT, BEARING & SEAL

REMOVAL & INSTALLATION

See Figure 24.

1. Before servicing the vehicle, refer to the Precautions section.
2. Raise and safely support the vehicle.
3. Remove wheel from rear axle.
4. Loosen parking brake cables. To do so, release nut on relay lever until the parking brake cables are loose.
5. Remove bolts (17) and remove brake caliper (16) with brake caliper support. Fasten brake caliper (16) to the body using a suitable wire.
6. Remove brake disc (11).
7. Remove brake shoes (3, 14).
8. Unhook brake cable (8) from brake cable lock (9) and remove brake cable lock.
9. Pull brake cable (8) out of rear axle tube (2).
10. Remove bolts (1) from rear axle tube (2). Replace bolts (1).
11. Pull rear axle shaft (5) out of rear axle tube (2).
12. Remove anchor plate (20).
13. Installation is the reverse of removal. Spray sealing wax onto contact surface on right rear rpm sensor (L6/4) or left rear rpm sensor (L6/3). Check brake system for proper function. Check oil level in rear axle differential. Check rear axle differential for leaks. Observe the following torques:
    - Brake caliper support-to-rear axle tube: M14x1.5 bolts, 59 ft. lbs. (80 Nm) +30 degrees; M16x1.5 bolts, 59 ft. lbs. (80 Nm) +40 degrees
    - Rear axle shaft-to-axle tube bolts: Step 1, 22 ft. lbs. (30 Nm), Step 2, 74 ft. lbs. (100 Nm), Step 3, back off completely, Step 4, 22 ft. lbs. (30 Nm), Step 5, +45 degrees.

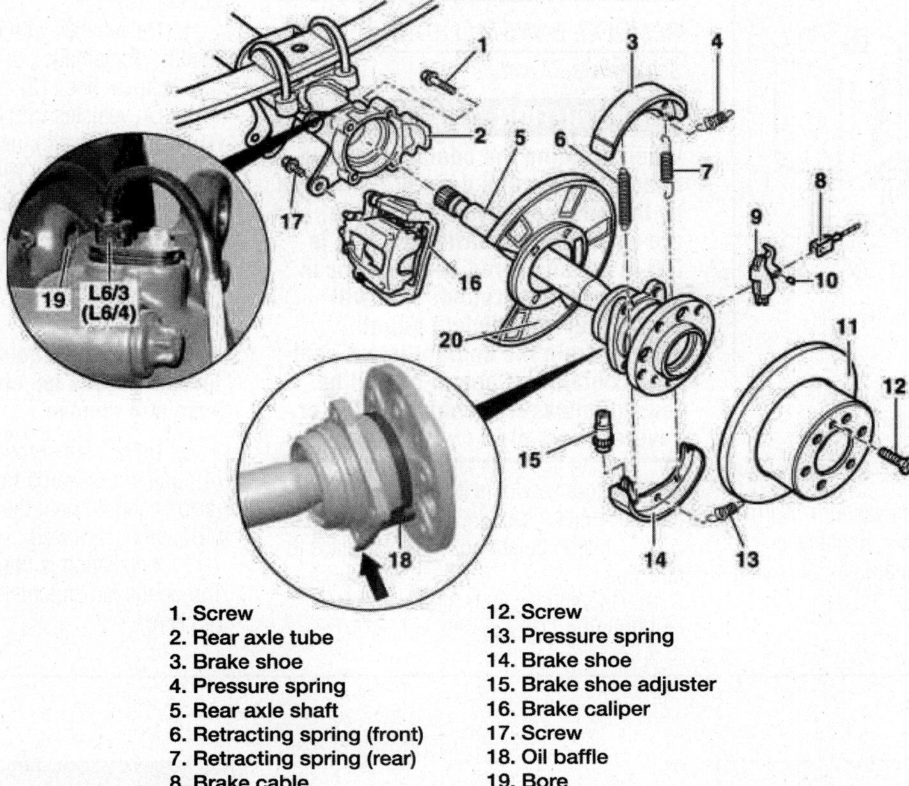

1. Screw
2. Rear axle tube
3. Brake shoe
4. Pressure spring
5. Rear axle shaft
6. Retracting spring (front)
7. Retracting spring (rear)
8. Brake cable
9. Brake cable lock
10. Pin
11. Brake disk
12. Screw
13. Pressure spring
14. Brake shoe
15. Brake shoe adjuster
16. Brake caliper
17. Screw
18. Oil baffle
19. Bore
20. Anchor plate
L6/3. Left rear rpm sensor
L6/4. Right rear rpm sensor

71112_MBSV_G0021

Fig. 24 Rear axle shaft removal/installation

ENGINE COOLING

ENGINE COOLANT

DRAIN & REFILL PROCEDURE

See Figures 25 and 26.

CAUTION

When draining the coolant, keep in mind that cats and dogs are attracted by the ethylene glycol antifreeze, and are quite likely to drink any that is left in an uncovered container or in puddles on the ground. This will prove fatal in sufficient quantity. Always drain the coolant into a sealable container. Coolant should be reused unless it is contaminated or several years old.

1. Before servicing the vehicle, refer to the Precautions section.
2. Unscrew cap (1).
3. Set heater control to maximum heat output.
4. Raise and safely support the vehicle.
5. Drain coolant at the radiator drain plug (2).
6. Check cooling system for contamination. The old coolant and the corrosion residues must be completely flushed out.
7. Close radiator drain screw (2), bleed cooling system by applying vacuum and fill.
8. Start engine and bleed cooling and

Shown on engine 646

1. Cap
2. Drain plug for radiator

71112_MBSV_G0023

Fig. 25 Cooling system drain/refill points

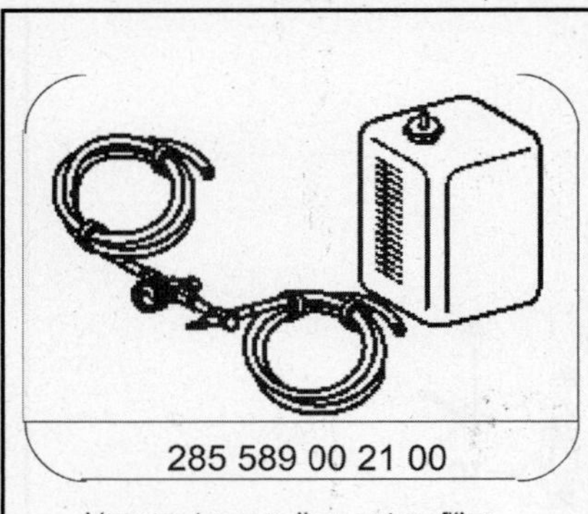

Fig. 26 Vacuum-type cooling system filler. Follow the manufacturer's instructions.

heating system by applying vacuum. Warm up engine at varying speeds. Replace coolant up to the "Max." mark.

9. Turn off engine.
10. Screw on cap (1).

ENGINE FAN

REMOVAL & INSTALLATION

See Figures 27 and 28.

***** CAUTION**

When draining the coolant, keep in mind that cats and dogs are attracted by the ethylene glycol antifreeze, and are quite likely to drink any that is left in an uncovered container or in puddles on the ground. This will prove fatal in sufficient quantity. Always drain the coolant into a sealable container. Coolant should be reused unless it is contaminated or several years old.

1. Before servicing the vehicle, refer to the Precautions section.
2. Unclip coolant hose (3) and place to one side.
3. On vehicles with Regulated air conditioning (Tempmatic), disconnect electrical connector (14) from viscous fan clutch (10).
4. On vehicles with Regulated air conditioning (Tempmatic), unscrew bolt (13) and lay electrical line (12) down to side.
5. On vehicles with Regulated air conditioning (Tempmatic), unscrew bolt (15) and turn torque support (16).
6. Unclip cover (2) at fan shroud (1).
7. Remove viscous fan clutch (10) with open end wrench (11) and counter-holder (8) from fan drive (9) and lay in fan shroud (1).

➡ Place counter-holder (8) on bolt (7), loosen viscous fan clutch (10) clockwise and remove.

8. Unlock fan shroud (1) at catch hooks (4), pull out upwards from guides (5, 6) (arrow) and lift until the viscous fan clutch (10) can be removed.
9. Installation is the reverse of removal. Torque the fan clutch nut to 33 ft. lbs. (45 Nm).

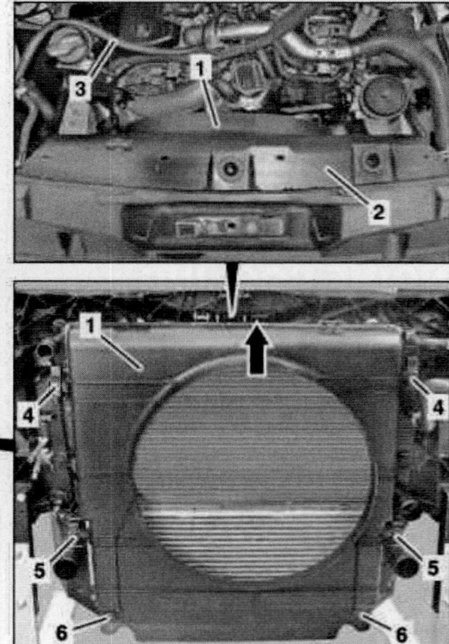

Shown on engine 642.992

1. Fan shroud
2. Cover
3. Coolant hose (on engine 642)
4. Catch hook
5. Guide
6. Guide (on engine 642)
7. Screw
8. Counter-holder
9. Fan drive (on engine 642)
10. Viscous fan clutch
11. Open end wrench

71112_MBSV_G0025

Fig. 27 Engine fan removal/installation

Only on engine 642.896/898 with code (HH9) Regulated air conditioning (Tempmatic)

10. Viscous fan clutch
12. Electrical line
13. Screw
14. Electrical connector
15. Screw
16. Torque support

71112_MBSV_G0026

Fig. 28 Engine fan with Tempmatic

FAN SHROUD

REMOVAL & INSTALLATION

See Figures 29 and 30.

1. Before servicing the vehicle, refer to the Precautions section.

⁂ CAUTION

When draining the coolant, keep in mind that cats and dogs are attracted by the ethylene glycol antifreeze, and are quite likely to drink any that is left in an uncovered container or in puddles on the ground. This will prove fatal in sufficient quantity. Always drain the coolant into a sealable container. Coolant should be reused unless it is contaminated or several years old.

2. Drain coolant.
3. Unclip coolant hose (3) and place to one side.
4. On vehicles with Code (HH9) Regulated air conditioning (Tempmatic), disconnect electrical connector (14) from viscous fan clutch (10).
5. On vehicles with Code (HH9) Regulated air conditioning (Tempmatic), unscrew bolt (13) and lay electrical line (12) down to side.
6. On vehicles with Code (HH9)

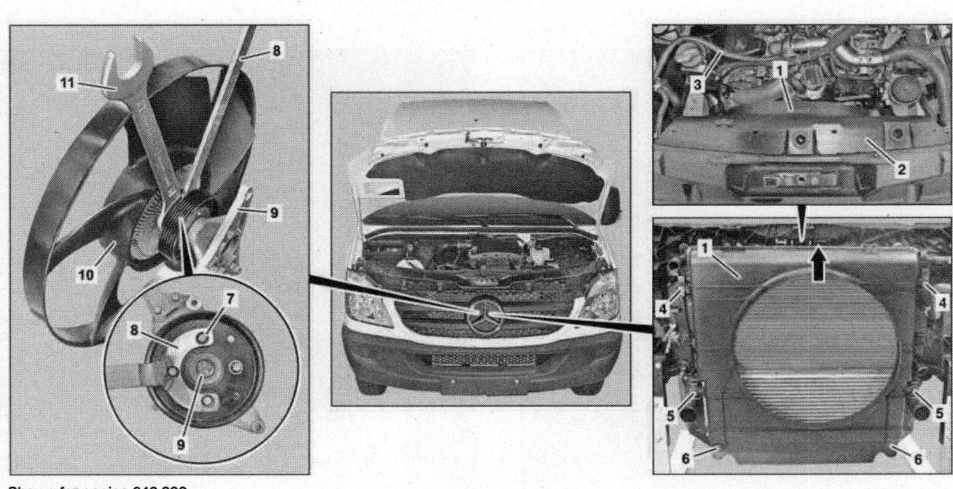

Shown for engine 642.992

1. Fan shroud
2. Cover
3. Coolant hose (on engine 642)
4. Catch hook
5. Guide
6. Guide (on engine 642)
7. Screw
8. Counter-holder
9. Fan drive (on engine 642)
10. Viscous fan clutch
11. Open end wrench

71112_MBSV_G0199

Fig. 29 Engine fan shroud removal/installation

Only on engine 642.896/898 with code (HH9) Regulated air conditioning (Tempmatic)

10. Viscous fan clutch
12. Electrical line
13. Screw
14. Electrical connector
15. Screw
16. Torque support

71112_MBSV_G0200

Fig. 30 Tempmatic components

Regulated air conditioning (Tempmatic), unscrew bolt (15) and turn torque support (16).

7. Unclip cover (2) at fan shroud (1).
8. Remove viscous fan clutch (10) with open end wrench (11) and counter-holder (8) from fan drive (9) and lay in fan shroud (1).
9. Unlock fan shroud (1) at catch hooks (4), pull out upwards from guides (5, 6) (arrow) and lift until the viscous fan clutch (10) can be removed.
10. Take out fan shroud (1).
11. Installation is the reverse of removal. Torque the viscous clutch on fan drive to 33 ft. lbs. (45 Nm).

RADIATOR

REMOVAL & INSTALLATION

See Figure 31.

1. Before servicing the vehicle, refer to the Precautions section.

CAUTION

When draining the coolant, keep in mind that cats and dogs are attracted by the ethylene glycol antifreeze, and are quite likely to drink any that is left in an uncovered container or in puddles on the ground. This will prove fatal in sufficient quantity. Always drain the coolant into a seal-

1. Condenser (for code (HH9) Regulated air conditioning, (Tempmatic)
2. Radiator
3. Steering oil cooler

71112_MBSV_G0027

Fig. 31 Radiator removal/installation

able container. Coolant should be reused unless it is contaminated or several years old.

2. Drain coolant.
3. Disconnect coolant hoses
4. Disconnect automatic transmission oil lines on cooler (2).
5. Remove A/T oil cooler on cooler (2) and swivel to one side with lines attached.
6. Remove fan shroud. See the engine fan removal procedure.
7. On vehicles with Regulated air conditioning (Tempmatic), remove additional fan unit.
8. On vehicles without Regulated air conditioning (Tempmatic), remove plate under front grille.
9. On vehicles without Regulated air conditioning (Tempmatic), remove front grille.
10. Unclip radiator (2) on front module (arrows A).
11. On vehicles with Regulated air conditioning (Tempmatic), push back radiator (2) with condenser (1) in direction of engine.

WARNING

Carefully push back cooler (2) with condenser (1). Damage to the cooler (2), hoses and lines can occur otherwise.

12. On vehicles with Regulated air -conditioning (Tempmatic), press locks, unclip condenser (1) on radiator (2) and lift until the bolts (arrows B) are accessible.
13. On vehicles without Regulated air conditioning (Tempmatic), remove steering oil cooler (3) on cooler (2).
14. Unscrew screw/bolts (arrows B).
15. On vehicles with Regulated air conditioning (Tempmatic), unclip condenser (1) at radiator (2).
16. With a helper, take out radiator (2). On vehicles with Regulated air conditioning (Tempmatic), fasten condenser (1) using cable ties. Damage to the refrigerant lines can occur otherwise.
17. Installation is the reverse of removal. Check transmission oil level.

THERMOSTAT

REMOVAL & INSTALLATION

See Figure 32.

1. Before servicing the vehicle, refer to the Precautions section.

CAUTION

When draining the coolant, keep in mind that cats and dogs are attracted by the ethylene glycol antifreeze, and are quite likely to drink any that is left in an uncovered container or in puddles on the ground. This will prove fatal in sufficient quantity. Always drain the coolant into a sealable container. Coolant should be reused unless it is contaminated or several years old.

2. Drain coolant.
3. Remove air filter housing.
4. Unclip vacuum line (4) from cover on left cylinder head cover.
5. Remove bracket (1) with glow output stage (N14/3) and lay down to side. Unclip coolant hose (2) from bracket (1). Do not disconnect electrical connectors from glow output stage (N14/3).
6. Unclip coolant hose (2) from bracket (3).
7. Open Henn coupling and remove coolant hose (6) on coolant thermostat (5). Replace sealing ring.
8. Unclip leak oil line (8) from coolant thermostat (5).
9. Unscrew bolts (7) and remove

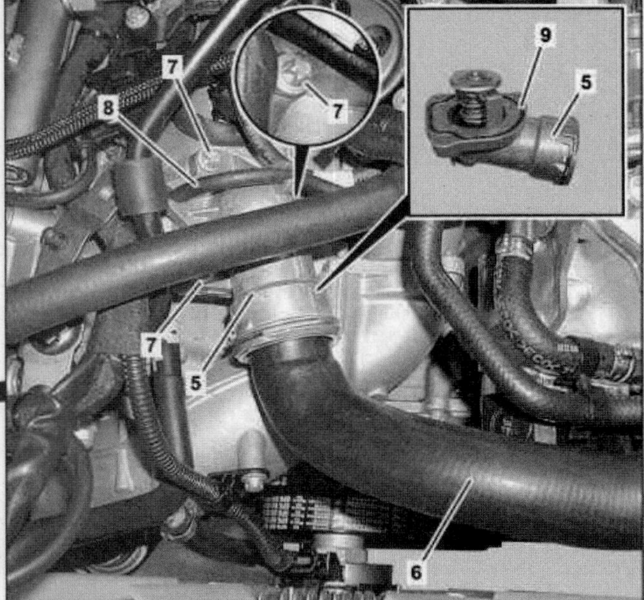

1. Bracket
2. Coolant hose
3. Bracket
4. Vacuum line
5. Coolant thermostat
6. Coolant hose
7. Screw
8. Leak oil line
9. Gasket
N14/3. Glow output stage

71112_MBSV_G0028

Fig. 32 Thermostat removal/installation

coolant thermostat (5) from charge air manifold.

10. Installation is the reverse of removal. Check seal (9) on coolant thermostat (5), if applicable replace seal and clean sealing surface on charge air manifold. Torque the bolts to 79 inch lbs. (9 Nm).

WATER PUMP

REMOVAL & INSTALLATION

See Figures 33 and 34.

1. Before servicing the vehicle, refer to the Precautions section.

**** CAUTION**

When draining the coolant, keep in mind that cats and dogs are attracted by the ethylene glycol antifreeze, and are quite likely to drink any that is left in an uncovered container or in puddles on the ground. This will prove fatal in sufficient quantity. Always drain the coolant into a sealable container. Coolant should be reused unless it is contaminated or several years old.

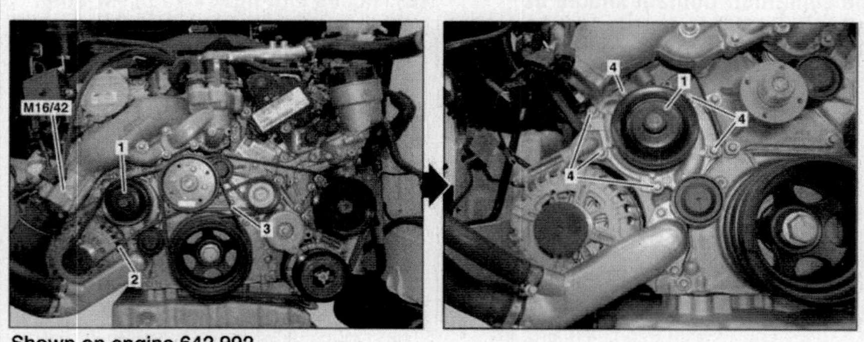

Shown on engine 642.992

1. Coolant pump
2. Poly-V belt
3. Poly-V belt
4. Bolts

M16/42. Throttle valve actuator (engine 642.992)

71112_MBSV_G0030

Fig. 33 Water pump removal/installation

2. Drain coolant.
3. On vehicles without high performance A/C, remove fan poly-V belt (3). See the engine fan procedure.
4. On vehicles with high performance A/C, remove poly-V belt for 2nd refrigerant compressor on air conditioning system.
5. Remove poly-V belt (2). See the engine fan procedure.
6. Remove mixing chamber:
   a. Raise and safely support the vehicle.
   b. Open coupling and remove charge air hose and remove charge air hose (1) from fitting (2). On installation, coat a

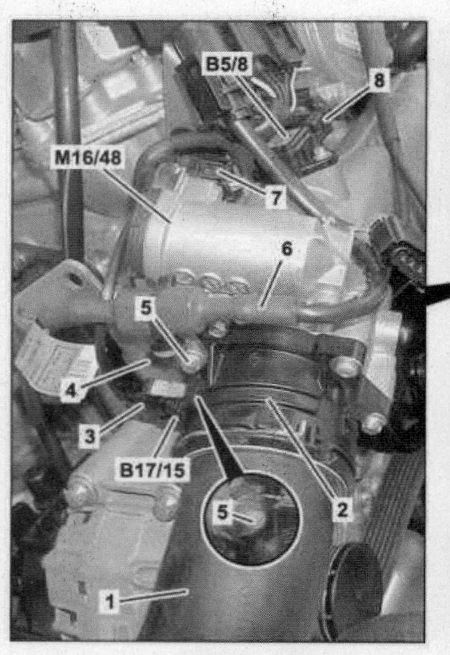

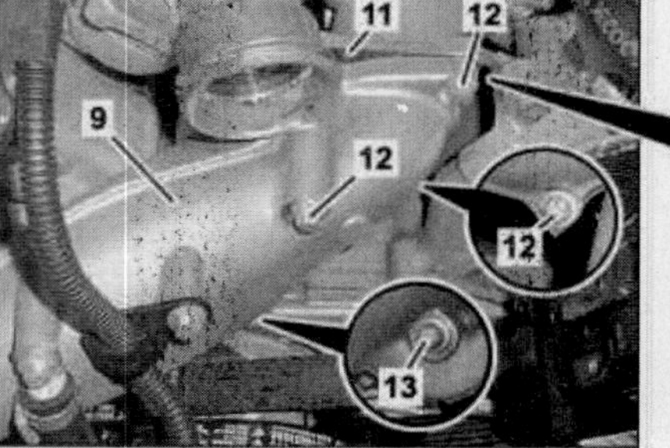

1. Charge air hose
2. Fitting
3. Electrical connector
4. Bracket
5. Screw
6. Wiring harness
7. Electrical connector
8. Electrical connector
9. Mixing chamber
10. Exhaust gas recirculation pipe
11. Gasket
12. Screw
13. Screw
14. Sealing ring
15. Charge air manifold

B5/8. Boost pressure sensor
B17/15. Charge air temperature sensor
M16/48. Throttle valve positioner

71112_MBSV_G0029

Fig. 34 Mixing chamber removal/installation

new seal with anti-friction paste, DB specification 6867.00, or equivalent.

c. Unscrew bolts (5) from bracket (4), unscrew fittings (2) and throttle valve actuator (M16/48).

d. Remove electrical wiring harness (6) from bracket (4) and unclip throttle valve actuator (M16/48).

e. Disconnect electrical connector (3) at charge air temperature sensor (B17/15).

f. Lower the vehicle.

g. Remove air filter housing.

h. Remove exhaust gas recirculation pipe (10) from exhaust gas recirculation valve to mixing chamber (9).

i. Remove viscous fan clutch.

j. Unscrew bolts (12).

k. Unscrew bolt (13) and remove mixing chamber (9) toward front. On installation, replace the sealing ring (14) on the charge air manifold (15) and seal (11).

l. Lift out mixing chamber (9) and disconnect electrical connector (7) from throttle valve actuator (M16/48).

m. Disconnect electrical connector (8) at boost pressure sensor (B5/8).

n. Clean sealing surfaces on charge air manifold (15), charge air hose (1) and fittings (2).

o. Clean sealing surfaces on mixing chamber (9).

7. Remove bolts (4) and remove coolant pump (1).

8. Installation is the reverse of removal. Clean sealing surface on timing case cover and coolant pump (1). Replace seal. Inspect cooling system for leaks. Observe the following torques:

- Water pump bolts to 88 inch lbs. (10 Nm).
- Throttle valve actuator and bracket: 79 inch lbs. (9 Nm)
- Mixing chamber-to-charge air manifold: 79 inch lbs. (9 Nm)
- Mixing chamber-to-support brace: 15 ft. lbs. (20 Nm)

ENGINE ELECTRICAL

BATTERY SYSTEM

BATTERY

REMOVAL & INSTALLATION

See Figure 35.

1. Before servicing the vehicle, refer to the Precautions section.
2. The battery is located under the floor pan on the driver's side.
3. Disconnect ground cable (1) from the battery (G1).
4. Detach positive pole cover (2).
5. Disconnect positive line (3) from battery (G1).
6. Detach vent line (4) from battery (G1).
7. Remove bracket (5).
8. Remove battery (G1).
9. Installation is the reverse of removal. When replacing the battery (G1) observe disposal regulations.

BATTERY RECONNECT/RELEARN PROCEDURE

The reconnect/relearn normalization is accomplished automatically when there is an error in the power window position recognition, for example, if the position counter indicates a negative status.

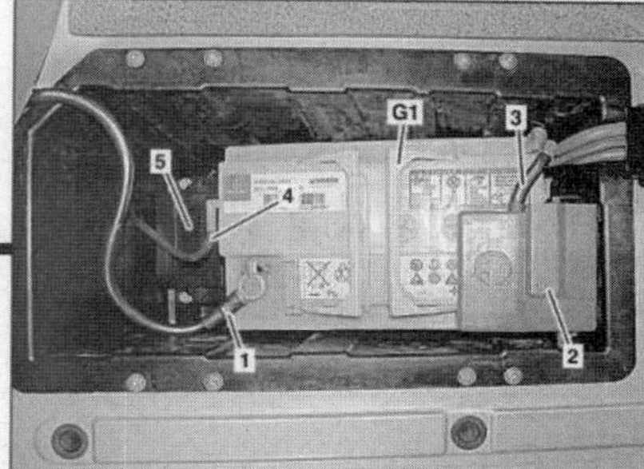

1. Ground cable
2. Positive terminal cover
3. Positive line
4. Vent line
5. Bracket
G1. Battery

71112_MBSV_G0031

Fig. 35 Battery removal/installation

ALTERNATOR

REMOVAL & INSTALLATION

See Figure 36.

1. Before servicing the vehicle, refer to the Precautions section.
2. Disconnect battery ground cable.
3. Loosen poly-V belt and remove from AC generator belt pulley with the LIN bus (G2/7).
4. Remove contact protection (1).
5. Remove electrical cables (2, 3) from AC generator with the LIN bus (G2/7).
6. Disconnect electrical connector (4) from AC generator at the LIN bus (G2/7).
7. Raise and safely support the vehicle.
8. Remove lower bolts (5).
9. Unscrew upper bolts (5) and remove alternator with LIN bus (G2/7).
10. Installation is the reverse of removal. Torque the bolts to 15 ft. lbs. (20 Nm).

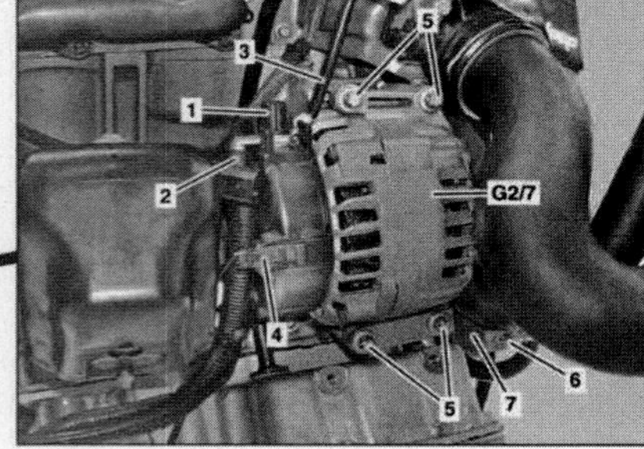

1. Contact protection
2. Electrical line
3. Electrical line
4. Electrical connector
5. Bolts
6. Bolt (engine 642.896)
7. Bracket (engine 642.896)
G2/7. Alternator with LIN bus

71112_MBSV_G0032

Fig. 36 Alternator removal/installation

STARTER

REMOVAL & INSTALLATION

See Figure 37.

1. Before servicing the vehicle, refer to the Precautions section.
2. Raise and safely support the vehicle.
3. Disconnect battery ground cable.
4. Detach electrical line for circuit 30 (1) and electrical line for circuit 50 (2) on starter (M1).
5. Remove bolts (3).
6. Remove starter (M1).
7. Installation is the reverse of removal. Torque the starter mounting bolts to 29 ft. lbs. (40 Nm) and the wire nuts to 12 ft. lbs. (16 Nm).

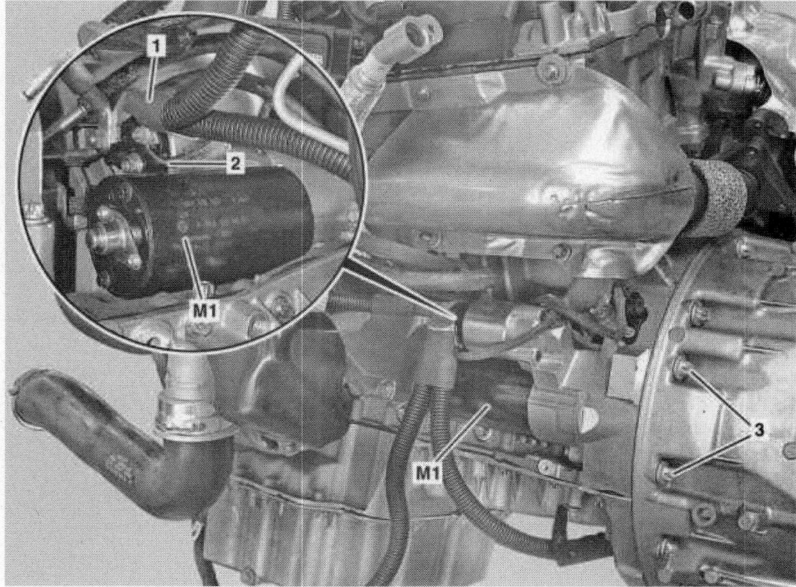

1. Electric line circuit 30
2. Electric cable circuit 50
3. Bolts
M1. Starter

71112_MBSV_G0033

Fig. 37 Starter removal/installation

ENGINE MECHANICAL

➡Disconnecting the negative battery cable may interfere with the functions of the on board computer systems and may require the computer to undergo a relearning process, once the negative battery cable is reconnected.

ACCESSORY DRIVE BELTS

ACCESSORY BELT ROUTING

For drive belt routings, see the illustrations in the Removal & Installation procedure.

INSPECTION

See Figure 38.

ADJUSTMENT

Drive belt tension is maintained automatically with the tensioner.

REMOVAL & INSTALLATION

See Figures 39 and 40.

1. Before servicing the vehicle, refer to the Precautions section.
2. With heavy duty air conditioning, remove poly-V belt for 2nd refrigerant compressor on air conditioning system:
    a. Remove fan shroud.
    b. Turn clamping device (5) on the Torx® insert (arrow A) in the direction of the arrow (arrow B).
    c. Remove poly-V belt (1) from belt pulley for the 2nd refrigerant compressor (A9/7).
    d. Turn detention clamping device (5) against the direction of the arrow (arrow B).
    e. Remove poly-V belt (1) completely.
3. Remove poly-V belt (1).
4. Check poly-V belt (1) for wear and damage.
5. Installation is the reverse of removal.

AIR CLEANER

HOUSING REMOVAL & INSTALLATION

See Figure 41.

1. Before servicing the vehicle, refer to the Precautions section.
2. Remove air intake hose downstream of air filter (2) on air filter housing (1).
3. Unclip electrical line on air filter housing (1).
4. Disconnect electrical connectors (3, 4).
5. Unhook jump-start connection point connector (X4/43) on air filter housing (1) and place to one side.

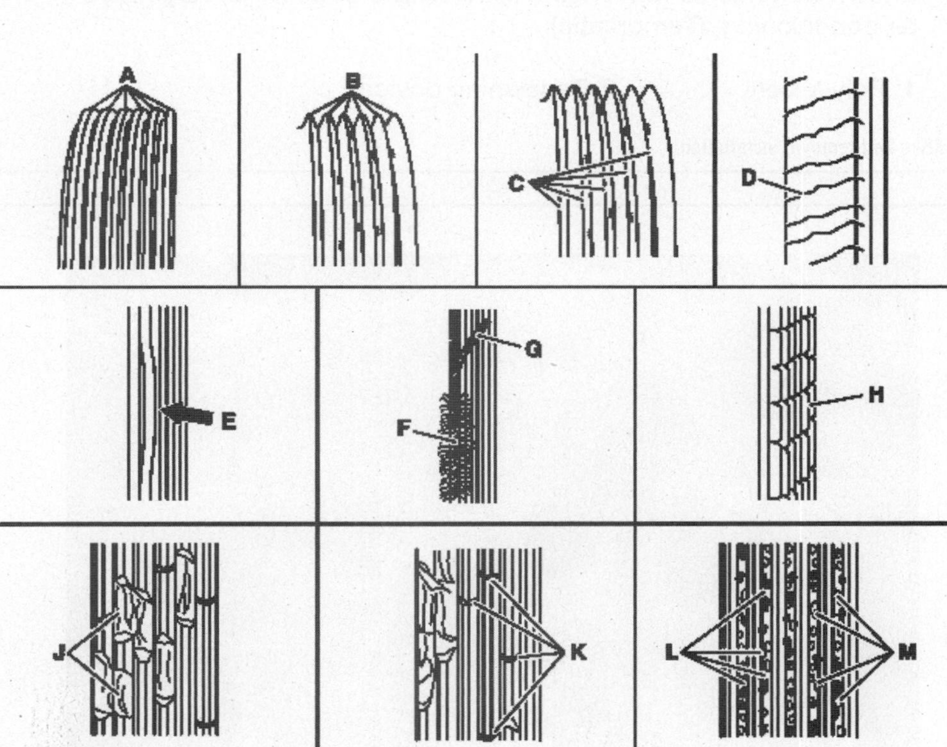

Damage profiles
A. Poly-V new - ribs are trapezoidal
B. Flank wear - ribs are tipped
C. Cord visible in base of rib (lighter points)
D. Transverse cracks across the back
E. Rib detached from base of belt (arrow)
F. Fraying of outer cords
G. Cord torn out at the side
H. Transverse cracks across several ribs
J. Missing chunks of rib
K. Individual transverse cracks across ribs
L. Dirt or stones embedded in ribs
M. Lumps of rubber in base of rib

71112_MBSV_G0036

Fig. 38 Drive belt inspection

Fig. 39 Typical single drive belt removal/installation

Fig. 40 Dual drive belt removal/installation

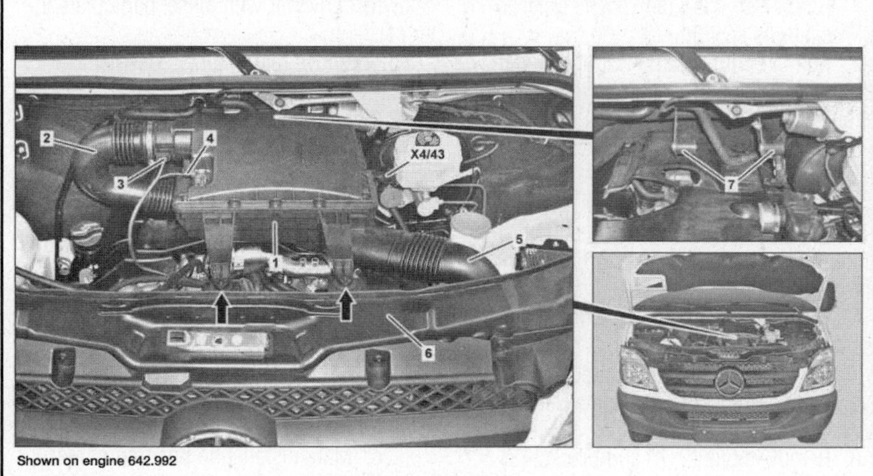

Shown on engine 642.992

1. Air cleaner housing
2. Air intake hose downstream of air filter
3. Electrical connector
4. Electrical connector
5. Air intake hose upstream of air filter
6. Front Module
7. Guides
X4/43. Jump-starting point connector

71112_MBSV_G0037

Fig. 41 Air filter housing removal/installation

6. Pull out air intake hose upstream of air filter (5) on front module (6).
7. Pry off air filter housing (1) at front from front module (6) (arrows) and pull out at rear from guides (7).
8. Take out air filter housing (1).
9. Installation is the reverse of removal.

CAMSHAFTS

REMOVAL & INSTALLATION

See Figure 42.

1. Before servicing the vehicle, refer to the Precautions section.

CAUTION

When draining the coolant, keep in mind that cats and dogs are attracted by the ethylene glycol antifreeze, and are quite likely to drink any that is left in an uncovered container or in puddles on the ground. This will prove fatal in sufficient quantity. Always drain the coolant into a sealable container. Coolant should be reused unless it is contaminated or several years old.

2. See Timing Chain in this section and remove the chain.
3. Detach bracket (6).
4. Remove hold-down device (5).
5. Lift camshafts (4) from cylinder head.
6. Push down hydraulic valve play compensation element by hand. Do not use a steel tool otherwise the hydraulic valve play compensation element can be damaged. Lower hydraulic valve play compensation element using normal force of the hand. If excessive pressure is supplied, the hydraulic valve play compensation element

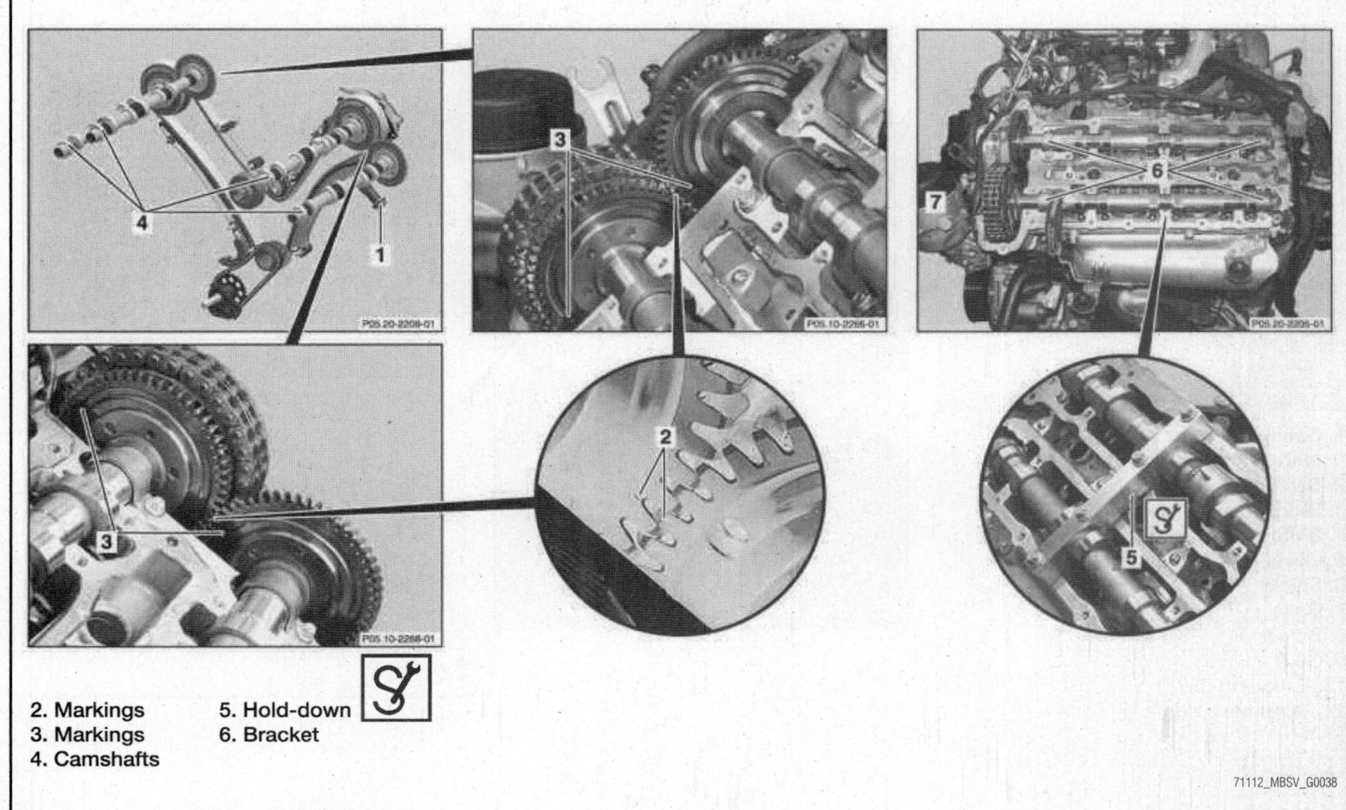

2. Markings
3. Markings
4. Camshafts
5. Hold-down
6. Bracket

71112_MBSV_G0038

Fig. 42 Camshaft removal/installation

will appear to drop, but in reality the valve opens. If many hydraulic valve play compensating element drop, check oil duct and oil feed bores on compensating elements for contamination; clean if necessary. If one hydraulic valve play compensation element drops much more than others then this must be replaced.

To install:

7. Lubricate hydraulic valve play compensation element and camshaft bearing point Insert camshaft (4) in the cylinder head.

➡Do not mix up camshafts (4). Markings (2) on camshafts (4) must be aligned with each other and markings (3) on camshafts, seen in the direction of travel, must be aligned on the left side to the cylinder head upper edge.

8. Install hold-down device (5).
9. Install bracket (6).
10. The remainder of installation will be found in the Timing Chain procedure.

CATALYTIC CONVERTER

REMOVAL & INSTALLATION

See Figures 43 through 45 and 63

1. Before servicing the vehicle, refer to the Precautions section.
2. Remove trim panel on right cylinder head cover. See the procedure in this section.
3. Unscrew bolts (7, 8) and remove shield (6).
4. Remove clamp (9).
5. Remove oxygen sensor. See the procedure in Engine Performance & Emission Controls.
6. Remove temperature sensor upstream of catalytic converter.
7. Remove exhaust gas recirculation valve. See the procedure in Engine Performance & Emission Controls.
8. Remove bolts (2, 4) and bracket (3).
9. Raise and safely support the vehicle.
10. Remove NOx sensor (18) and NOx sensor control unit. See the procedure in Engine Performance & Emission Controls.
11. Remove clamp (16) from catalytic converter with diesel particulate filter (1).
12. Unscrew pressure lines (12) from catalytic converter with diesel particulate filter (1).
13. Unscrew temperature sensor upstream of diesel particulate filter (B19/19).
14. Remove tensioning strap (13) from catalytic converter with diesel particulate filter (1).
15. Remove rear engine crossmember (17):
    a. Lift transmission (5) with the transmission jack (3) and transmission plate until engine mount (4) is relieved

➡In the case of transmission 722.6, the transmission jack (3) with transmission plate may only be placed on the outer edges of the transmission oil pan into to avoid damaging the transmission oil pan and underlying components. Underlay with suitable wooden blocks.

    b. Remove bolts (6)
    c. Mark installation position of rear engine crossmember (1). The mounting holes are arranged asymmetrically.
    d. Unscrew bolts (2) and remove left rear engine crossmember (1)
    e. Remove engine mount (4)
16. Carefully pull catalytic converter with diesel particulate filter (1) toward rear to prevent damaging detachable parts around.
17. Slightly push heat shield (15) upward. Do not deform heat shield (15) when pushing up.
18. Installation is the reverse of removal. Observe the following torques:

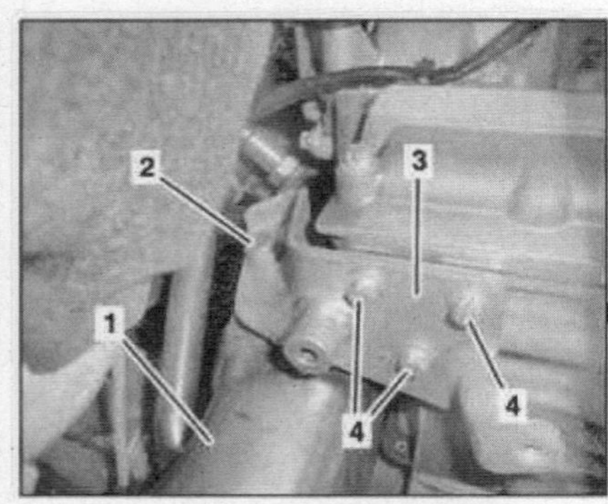

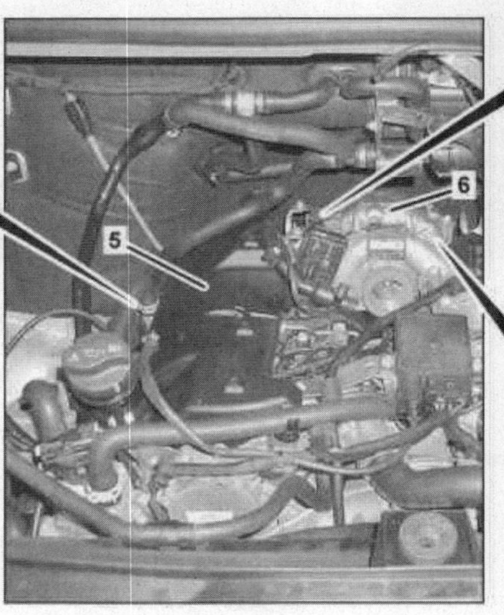

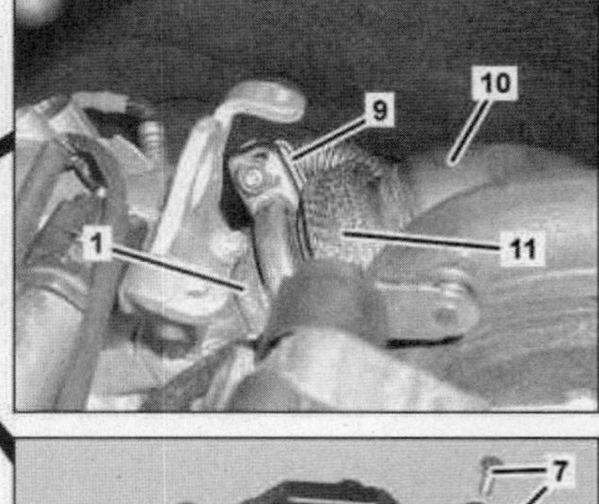

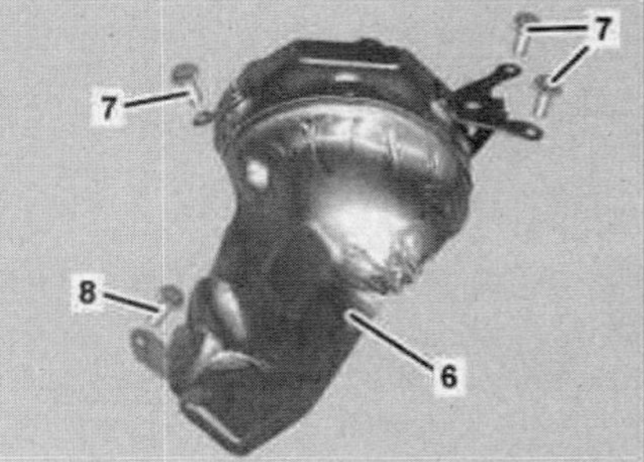

1. Catalytic converter with diesel particulate filter
2. Screw
3. Bracket
4. Bolts
5. Cover
6. Shield
7. Bolts
8. Screw
9. Clip
10. Exhaust pipe
11. Wire mesh ring

71112_MBSV_G0039

Fig. 43 Catalytic converter removal/installation, 1 of 2

1. Catalytic converter with diesel particulate filter
12. High pressure line
13. Tensioning strap
14. Electrical line
15. Heat shield
16. Clip
17. Rear engine crossmember
18. NOx sensor
B19/19. Temperature sensor upstream of diesel particulate filter

71112_MBSV_G0040

Fig. 44 Catalytic converter removal/installation, 2 of 2

Shown on engine 272.979

1. Rear engine crossmember
2. Bolts
3. Transmission jack
4. Engine mount
5. Transmission
6. Bolts

71112_MBSV_G0041

Fig. 45 Typical rear crossmember removal/installation

- Heat shield-to-holder: 72 inch lbs. (8 Nm)
- Heat shield-to-exhaust collector pipe: 106 inch lbs. (12 Nm)
- Particulate filter-to-converter clamp: 26 ft. lbs. (35 Nm)
- Particulate filter strap-to-holder: 18 ft. lbs. (25 Nm)
- Particulate filter-to-cylinder head holder: 17 ft. lbs. (23 Nm)
- Particulate filter clamp-to-exhaust pipe: 13 ft. lbs. (18 Nm)
- Particulate filter temperature sensor: 33 ft. lbs. (45 Nm)
- Rear crossmember-to-engine mount: M8 bolts 22 ft. lbs. (30 Nm), M10 bolts 43 ft. lbs. (58 Nm)
- Transmission-to-frame type integral support 43 ft. lbs. (58 Nm)
- Rear engine mount-to-transmission: 29 ft. lbs. (40 Nm)

CRANKSHAFT FRONT SEAL

REMOVAL & INSTALLATION

See Figures 46 through 48.

1. Before servicing the vehicle, refer to the Precautions section.
2. Remove belt pulley/vibration damper:
   a. Remove bottom engine compartment paneling.
   b. Remove the drive belt(s).
   c. Install retaining lock on starter ring gear.
   d. Unscrew center bolt (4).
   e. Remove vibration damper (1) from crankshaft.
3. Pry radial shaft sealing ring (1) out of timing case cover with suitable tool.

**** WARNING**

Do not damage mounting hole for radial shaft sealing ring (1); use clean rag as base to ensure that the radial shaft sealing ring (1) is tight.

To install:

4. Install radial shaft sealing ring (1):
   a. Place radial shaft sealing ring-crankshaft (8) on timing case cover (10) and press on lightly. Do not lubricate or grease crankshaft journal and sealing lip of radial shaft sealing ring-crankshaft (8). Grease on the tilted stays of sealing lip of radial shaft sealing ring crankshaft (8) prevents back transport of engine oil into the crankcase.
   b. Push centering sleeve (9) onto the crankshaft. Turn centering sleeve (9) to ensure that the groove on the centering sleeve (9) is aligned with the parallel key (7) in crankshaft.

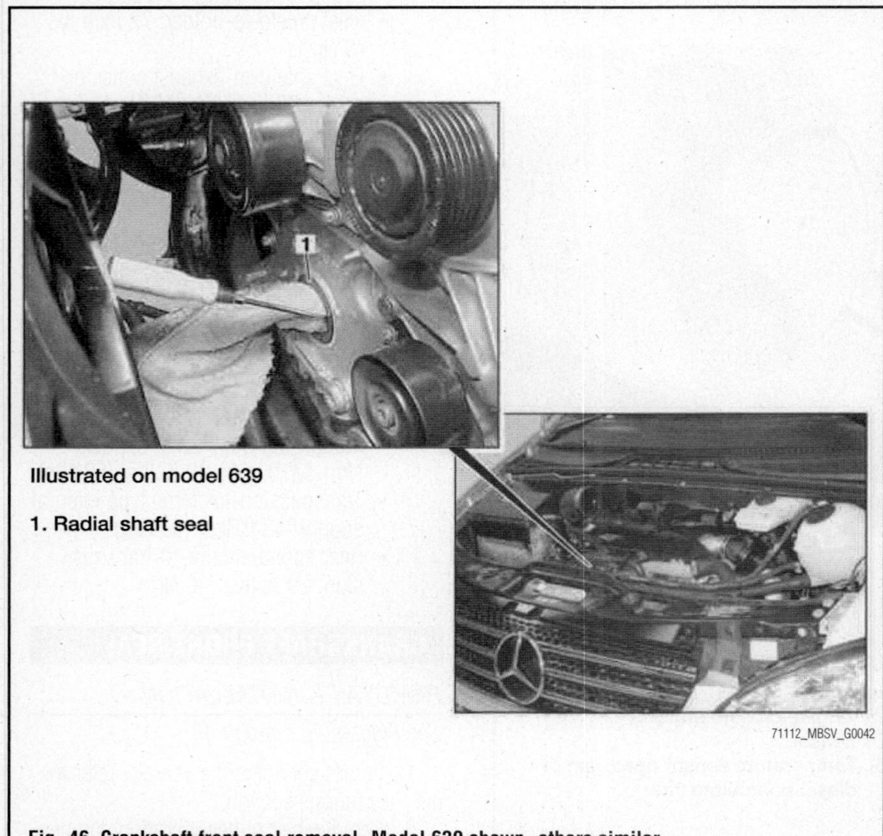

Fig. 46 Crankshaft front seal removal. Model 639 shown, others similar

Fig. 47 Damper removal/installation

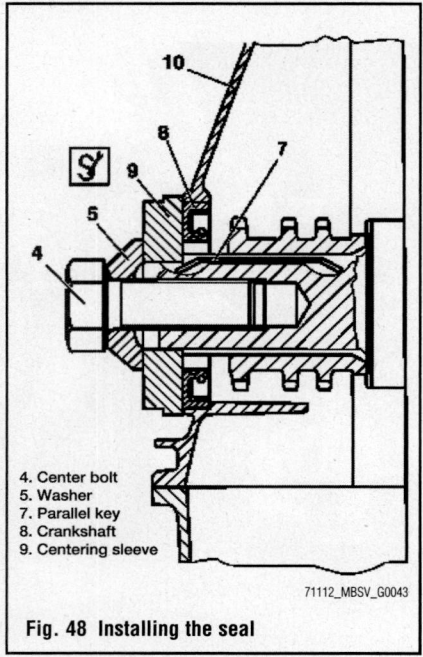

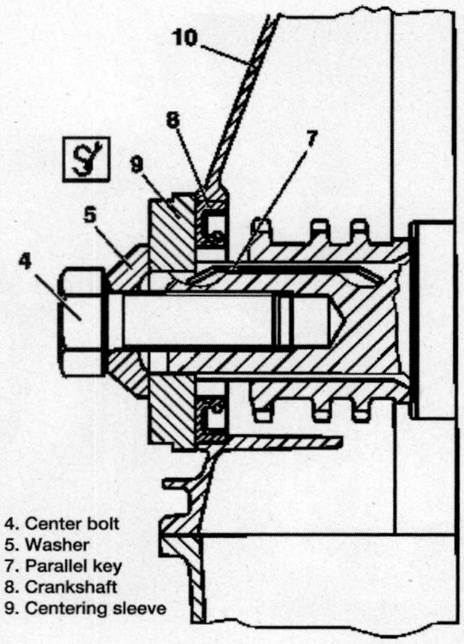

4. Center bolt
5. Washer
7. Parallel key
8. Crankshaft
9. Centering sleeve

71112_MBSV_G0043

Fig. 48 Installing the seal

c. Pull radial shaft sealing ring-crankshaft (8) over the centering sleeve (9) using the center bolt (4) and washer (5).

5. Install belt pulley/vibration damper. Torque the damper center bolt to 155 ft. lbs. (210 Nm) +180 degrees.

CYLINDER HEAD

REMOVAL & INSTALLATION

Right Side

See Figures 34, 47 49 through 52.

1. Before servicing the vehicle, refer to the Precautions section.

⁑ CAUTION

When draining the coolant, keep in mind that cats and dogs are attracted by the ethylene glycol antifreeze, and are quite likely to drink any that is left in an uncovered container or in puddles on the ground. This will prove fatal in sufficient quantity. Always drain the coolant into a sealable container. Coolant should be reused unless it is contaminated or several years old.

2. Remove mixing chamber:

a. Raise and safely support the vehicle.

b. Open coupling and remove charge air hose and remove charge air hose (1) from fitting (2). On installation, coat a new seal with anti-friction paste DB specification 6867.00, or equivalent.

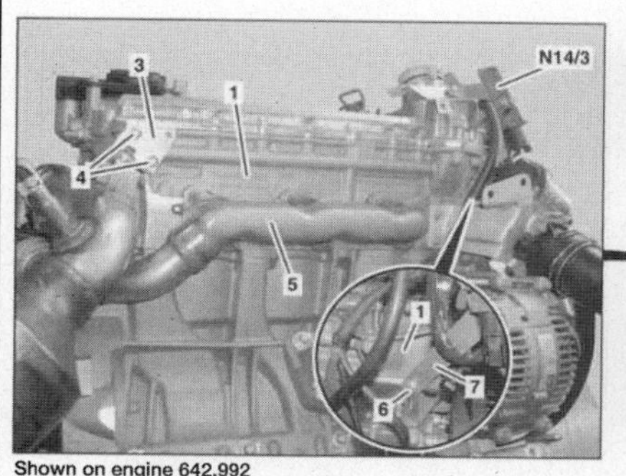

Shown on engine 642.992

1. Right cylinder head
3. Bracket
4. Bolts
5. Exhaust manifold
6. Screw
7. Bracket
8. Engine wiring harness
9. Mixing chamber
N14/3. Glow output stage

71112_MBSV_G0045

Fig. 49 Right cylinder head and related parts

c. Unscrew bolts (5) from bracket (4), unscrew fittings (2) and throttle valve actuator (M16/48).

d. Remove electrical wiring harness (6) from bracket (4) and unclip throttle valve actuator (M16/48).

e. Disconnect electrical connector (3) at charge air temperature sensor (B17/15).

f. Lower the vehicle.

g. Remove air filter housing.

h. Remove exhaust gas recirculation pipe (10) from exhaust gas recirculation valve to mixing chamber (9).

i. Remove viscous fan clutch.

j. Unscrew bolts (12).

k. Unscrew bolt (13) and remove mixing chamber (9) toward front. On installation, replace the sealing ring (14) on the charge air manifold (15) and seal (11).

l. Lift out mixing chamber (9) and disconnect electrical connector (7) from throttle valve actuator (M16/48).

Shown on engine 642.896

5. Exhaust manifold
8. Engine wiring harness
16. Mount (engine 642.896/898/993)
17. Mount (engine 642.896/898/993)
18. Ground line (engine 642.896/898/993)

71112_MBSV_G0046

Fig. 50 Right exhaust manifold and related parts

m. Disconnect electrical connector (8) at boost pressure sensor (B5/8).

n. Clean sealing surfaces on charge air manifold (15), charge air hose (1) and fittings (2).

o. Clean sealing surfaces on mixing chamber (9).

3. Remove the charge air manifold. See that procedure in this section.

4. Remove exhaust gas recirculation valve.

5. Remove bracket (16) on exhaust gas recirculation valve from right cylinder head (1).

6. Remove ground cable (18) from right cylinder head (1).

7. Remove bracket (17) on exhaust pipe from right cylinder head (1).

8. Remove exhaust manifold (5) from right cylinder head (1) and lay down to side.

9. Remove camshafts from right cylinder head (1).

10. Remove hydraulic valve play compensation element from right cylinder head (1).

11. Disconnect electrical connector to glow plugs (arrows) and expose engine wiring harness (8) on right cylinder head (1).

12. Pull out slide rail bolt (1) at right cylinder head. On installation, screw a suitable bolt into the slide rail bolt, drive the slide rail bolt into the head and remove it again.

13. Loosen and remove cylinder head bolts (13, 14) in stages and in reverse order of the tightening procedure, on a cooled engine.

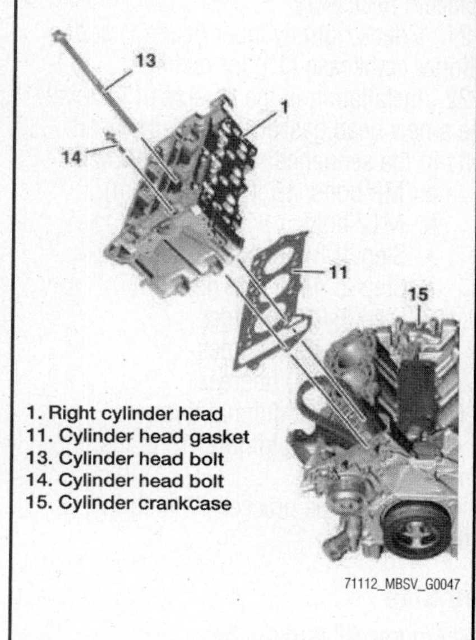

1. Right cylinder head
11. Cylinder head gasket
13. Cylinder head bolt
14. Cylinder head bolt
15. Cylinder crankcase

71112_MBSV_G0047

Fig. 51 Right cylinder head, bolts, and gasket

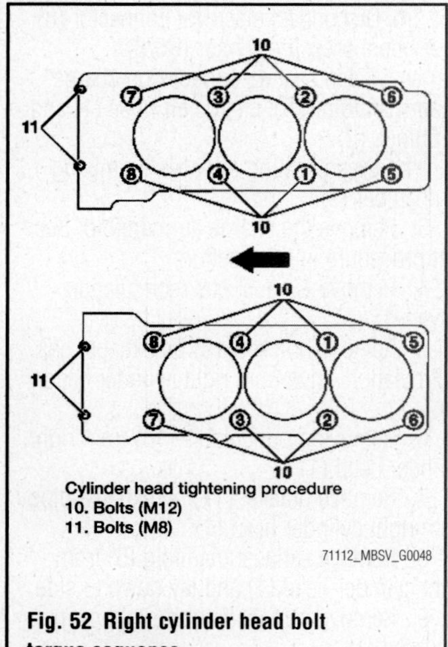

Fig. 52 Right cylinder head bolt torque sequence

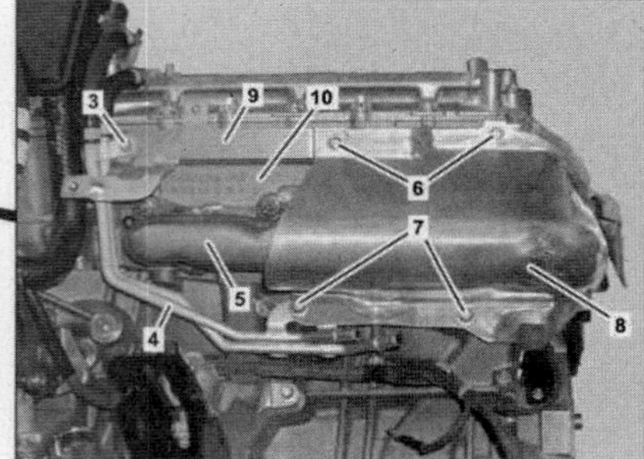

Shown on engine 642.992

2. Oil filter housing
3. Screw
4. Fuel lines
5. Exhaust manifold
6. Bolts
7. Bolts
8. Shield
9. Bracket
10. Left cylinder head
16. High-pressure pump

71112_MBSV_G0049

Fig. 53 Left cylinder head and related parts

14. Remove right cylinder head (1) and cylinder head gasket (11) from crankcase (15).

15. Cover cylinder bores and contact surface on cylinder crankcase (15).

16. Clean threaded holes for cylinder head bolts. Blow dirt or fluid out of the threaded (13, 14) crankcase holes.

17. Clean sealing surfaces at right cylinder head (1) and at crankcase (15).

18. Check stud bolts on exhaust manifold (5) on right cylinder head (1) for damage.

19. Check exhaust manifold (5) for crack formation and damage.

20. Inspect cylinder head bolts (13), replace if necessary.

21. Check right cylinder head (1) and cylinder crankcase (15) for damage.

22. Installation is the reverse of removal. Use a new head gasket. Tighten the head bolts in the sequence shown, as follows:

a. M8 bolts: 15 ft. lbs. (20 Nm)

b. M12 bolts:

- Step 1: 84 inch lbs. (10 Nm)
- Step 2: 44 ft. lbs. (60 Nm)
- Step 3: +90 degrees
- Step 4: +90 degrees
- Step 5: +90 degrees

Observe these additional torques:

- Exhaust manifold nuts: 18 ft. lbs. (25 Nm)
- Exhaust pipe bracket: 72 inch lbs. (8 Nm)

Left Side

See Figures 53 through 55.

1. Before servicing the vehicle, refer to the Precautions section.

**** CAUTION**

When draining the coolant, keep in mind that cats and dogs are attracted by the ethylene glycol antifreeze, and are quite likely to drink any that is left in an uncovered container or in puddles on the ground. This will prove fatal in sufficient quantity. Always drain the coolant into a sealable container. Coolant should be reused unless it is contaminated or several years old.

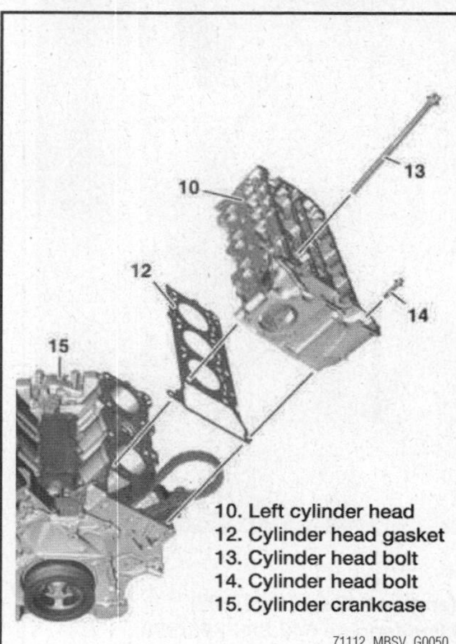

10. Left cylinder head
12. Cylinder head gasket
13. Cylinder head bolt
14. Cylinder head bolt
15. Cylinder crankcase

71112_MBSV_G0050

Fig. 54 Left cylinder head, bolts, and gasket

2. Remove the charge air manifold. See that procedure in this section.

3. Remove oil filter housing (2).

4. Remove high-pressure pump (16).

5. Remove camshafts from left cylinder head (10).

6. Remove hydraulic valve play compensation element in left cylinder head (10).

7. Remove bolts (6, 7) and shield (8). On installation, note that there are different sizes of bolts (6, 7).

8. Remove bolt (3) and lay fuel lines (4) to one side.

9. Pull out slide rail bolt from left cylinder head (10). On installation, screw a suitable bolt into the slide rail bolt, drive the slide rail bolt into the head and remove it again.

10. Loosen and remove cylinder head bolts (13, 14) in stages and in reverse order of the tightening procedure, on a cooled engine.

11. Remove left cylinder head (10) and cylinder head gasket (12) from crankcase (15).

12. Remove exhaust manifold (5) from cylinder head (10).

13. Cover cylinder bores and contact surface on cylinder crankcase (15).

14. Clean cylinder head bolt holes (13, 14) in crankcase (15).

15. Check stud bolts on exhaust manifold (5) on left cylinder head (10) for damage.

16. Inspect cylinder head bolts (13), replace if necessary.

17. Check right cylinder head (10) and cylinder crankcase (15) for damage.

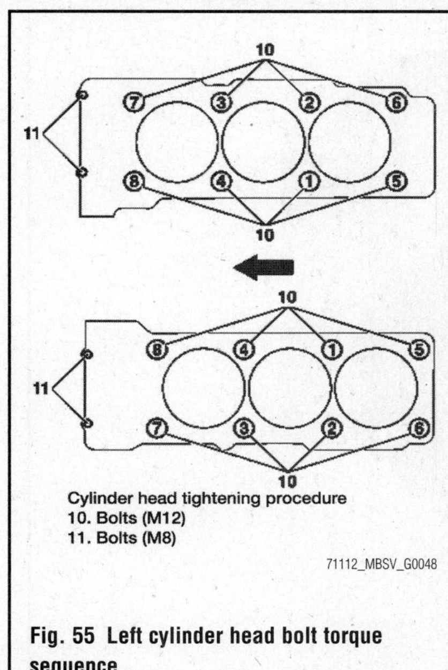

Fig. 55 Left cylinder head bolt torque sequence

18. Installation is the reverse of removal. Use a new head gasket. Tighten the head bolts in the sequence shown, as follows:
   a. M8 bolts: 15 ft. lbs. (20 Nm)
   b. M12 bolts:
   - Step 1: 84 inch lbs. (10 Nm)
   - Step 2: 44 ft. lbs. (60 Nm)
   - Step 3: +90 degrees
   - Step 4: +90 degrees
   - Step 5: +90 degrees

Observe these additional torques:

- Exhaust manifold nuts: 18 ft. lbs. (25 Nm)
- Exhaust pipe bracket: 72 inch (8 Nm)

CYLINDER HEAD (VALVE) COVERS

REMOVAL & INSTALLATION

Right Side

See Figures 89 through 91 and 56.

1. Before servicing the vehicle, refer to the Precautions section.
2. Remove rail (4) on right cylinder head (18). See the Fuel Systems section.
3. Remove injectors from right cylinder head (18). See the Fuel Systems section.
4. Disconnect electrical connector (5) from camshaft sensor (B6/20 or B6/24).
5. Remove vacuum pump (7):
   a. Remove air filter housing.
   b. Remove exhaust gas recirculation valve.
   c. Remove vacuum line (3) and place to one side.
   d. Unscrew bolts (4) from bracket (1).
   e. Detach engine wiring harness from fixture (1).
   f. Remove bolts (5) and upper bolt (7) and remove holder (1)
   g. Remove bolt (7) and vacuum pump (6). On installation use a new gasket. Align drive plate of vacuum pump (6).
6. Pull drain hose out of drain line (8), with code (KL5) Fuel filter with water separator.
7. Remove bolt (9), remove drain pipe (8) from holder (10) and swivel to the side, with code (KL5) Fuel filter with water separator.
8. Remove bolt (11) and turn oil dipstick guide tube (12) to the side.
9. Remove engine wiring harness (6) to cylinder head cover (1) and move out of the way.
10. Unscrew bolts (14), remove oil separator (20) and vent hose (21) from cylinder head.

➡On installation, clean sealing surfaces on oil separator (20) and vent hose (21) and replace sealing ring (16). Check radial shaft sealing ring (17) for damage, if applicable, replace oil separator (20).

11. Loosen and remove bolts (13) in stages and in reverse order of the tightening procedure, on a cooled engine.

➡On installation, pay attention to tightening procedure and tightening instructions for bolts (13) so that cylinder head cover (1) is not warped and camshafts are not damaged.

12. Press off cylinder head cover (1) to the corners (arrows) carefully from the cylinder head (18) using a suitable tool.

✲✲ WARNING

Press off cylinder head cover (1) from cylinder head (18) with the greatest of care. If cylinder head cover (1) is damaged then it can only be replaced in combination with the cylinder head (18).

➡On installation, replace cover (19). Remove sealant residue from sealing surfaces on cylinder head cover (1) and cylinder head (18). Lubricate bearing points on camshaft bearing. Use Loctite sealant 5970.

To install:

13. Fit right cylinder head cover. Torque the cover bolts in the sequence shown, in 3 steps:
   - Step 1, bolts 8-11: 36 inch lbs. (4 Nm)
   - Step 2, bolts 1-30: 53 inch lbs. (6 Nm)
   - Step 3, bolts 1-30: 72 inch lbs. (8 Nm)
14. Attach glow output stage.
15. Attach viscous fan clutch.
16. Observe the following torques:
   - Glow output stage-to-bracket: 72 inch lbs. (8 Nm)
   - Vacuum pump-to-cylinder head: 84 inch lbs. (9 Nm)
   - Oil dipstick tube: 106 inch lbs. (12 Nm)
   - Oil separator-to-cylinder head: 84 inch lbs. (9 Nm)

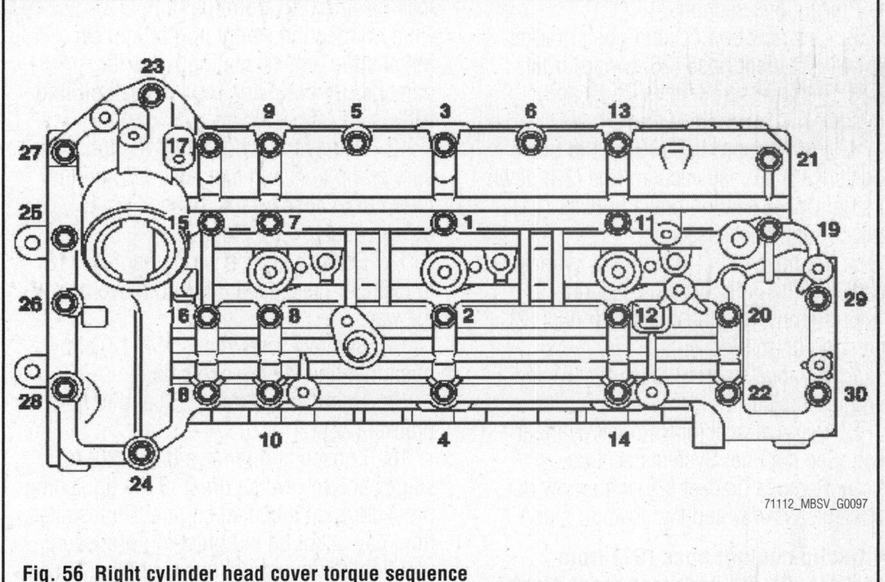

Fig. 56 Right cylinder head cover torque sequence

Shown on engine 642.992

1. Cylinder head cover
2. Engine charge air duct
3. Screw/bolt
4. Bracket
5. Screw/bolt
6. Steering reservoir
7. Screw/bolt
8. Coolant pipe (engine 642.992/993)
9. Screw/bolt (engine 642.992/993)
10. Rail

71112_MBSV_G0105

Fig. 57 Left cylinder head cover removal/installation, 1 of 4

- Oil separator connection fitting: 84 inch lbs. (9 Nm)

Left Side

See Figures 57 through 62.

1. Before servicing the vehicle, refer to the Precautions section.
2. Unscrew bolt (7) and push bracket (25) with coolant hose (26) toward front.
3. Remove screw/bolts (3, 5) and bracket (4).
4. Pull vacuum line (30) out of brake booster (31) and lay vacuum line (30) down to side. Check seal on brake booster (31), replace seal if necessary.
5. Remove rail (10) from left cylinder head. See the Fuel Systems section.
6. Remove engine charge air duct (2) and hang up to side.
7. Remove steering reservoir (6) and hang up to side.
8. Remove injector from left cylinder head. See the Fuel Systems section.
9. Remove bracket (29) with glow output stage (N14/3) and lay down to side.

➡ Unclip coolant hose (27) from bracket (28). Do not disconnect electrical connectors from glow output stage (N14/3).

10. Remove pressure line (13) from cylinder head cover (1) and high-pressure pump (19).
11. Pull retainer (33) and disconnect leak oil line (32) from fuel line (12). Plug connections with stop plugs. On installation, check sealing rings for damage, if necessary, replace leak oil line (32).
12. Remove fuel hose (14) to high pressure pump (19) and fuel hose (15) on fuel filter (16). Close off fuel hoses (14, 15) using suitable stop plugs.
13. Remove engine wiring harness (18) to cylinder head cover (1) and move out of the way.
14. Remove screw/bolts (11, 17) and push fuel line (12) to one side.
15. Undo screw/bolts (23) and remove bracket (22).
16. Loosen and remove bolts (20) in stages and in reverse order of the tightening procedure, on a cooled engine. On installation, pay attention to tightening procedure and tightening instructions for bolts (20) so that cylinder head cover (1) is not warped and camshafts are not damaged.
17. Press off cylinder head cover (1) at the corners (arrows) carefully from the cylinder head using a suitable tool.

⁂ WARNING

Press off cylinder head cover (1) from cylinder head with the greatest of care. If cylinder head cover (1) is damaged then it can only be replaced in combination with the cylinder head.

➡On installation, replace cover (1). Remove sealant residue from sealing surfaces on cylinder head cover (1) and cylinder head. Lubricate bearing points on camshaft bearing. Use Loctite sealant 5970.

18. Installation is the reverse of removal. Torque the cover bolts in the sequence shown, in 3 steps:
    - Step 1, bolts 8-11: 36 inch lbs. (4 Nm)
    - Step 2 bolts 1-28: 53 inch lbs. (6 Nm)

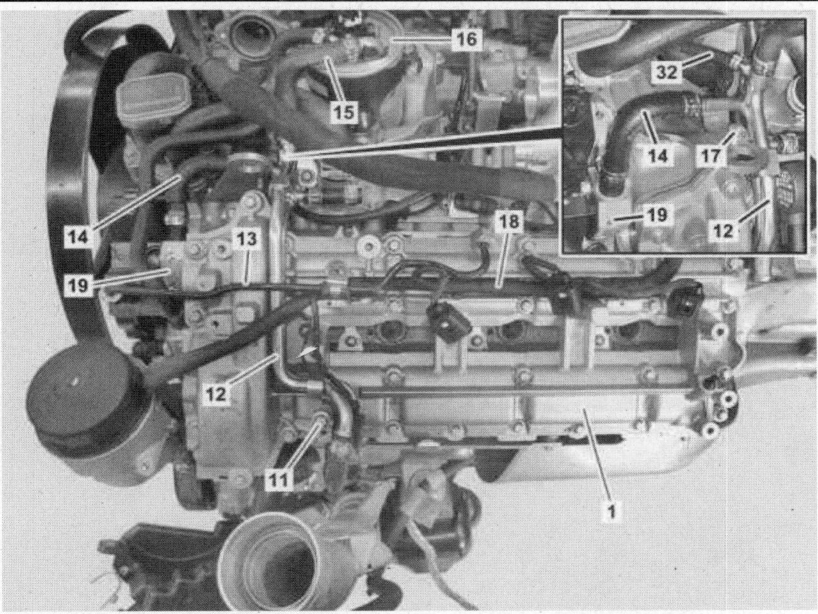

Shown on engine 642.992

1. Cylinder head cover
11. Screw/bolt
12. Fuel line
13. Pressure line
14. Fuel hose
15. Fuel hose
16. Fuel filter
17. Screw/bolt
18. Engine wiring harness
19. High-pressure pump
32. Leak oil line

71112_MBSV_G0106

Fig. 58 Left cylinder head cover removal/installation, 2 of 4

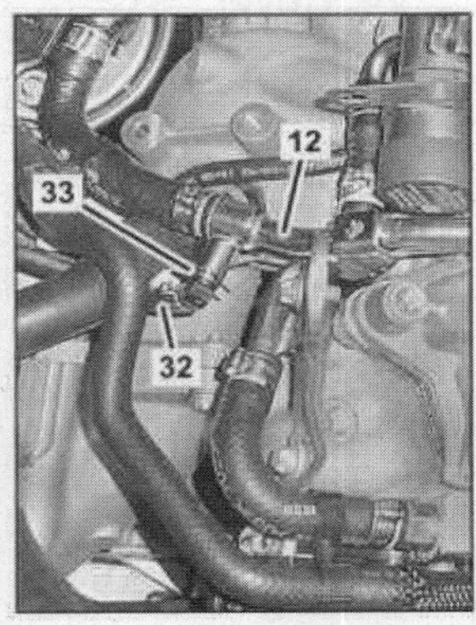

Shown on engine 642.896

7. Screw/bolt
12. Fuel line
22. Bracket
25. Mount (engine 642.896/898)
26. Coolant hose (engine 642.896/898)
27. Coolant hose (engine 642.896/898)
28. Mount (engine 642.896/898)
29. Mount (engine 642.896/898)
30. Vacuum line
31. Brake booster
32. Leak oil line
33. Retainer (engine 642.896/898/993)
N14/3. Glow output stage

71112_MBSV_G0107

Fig. 59 Left cylinder head cover removal/installation, 3 of 4

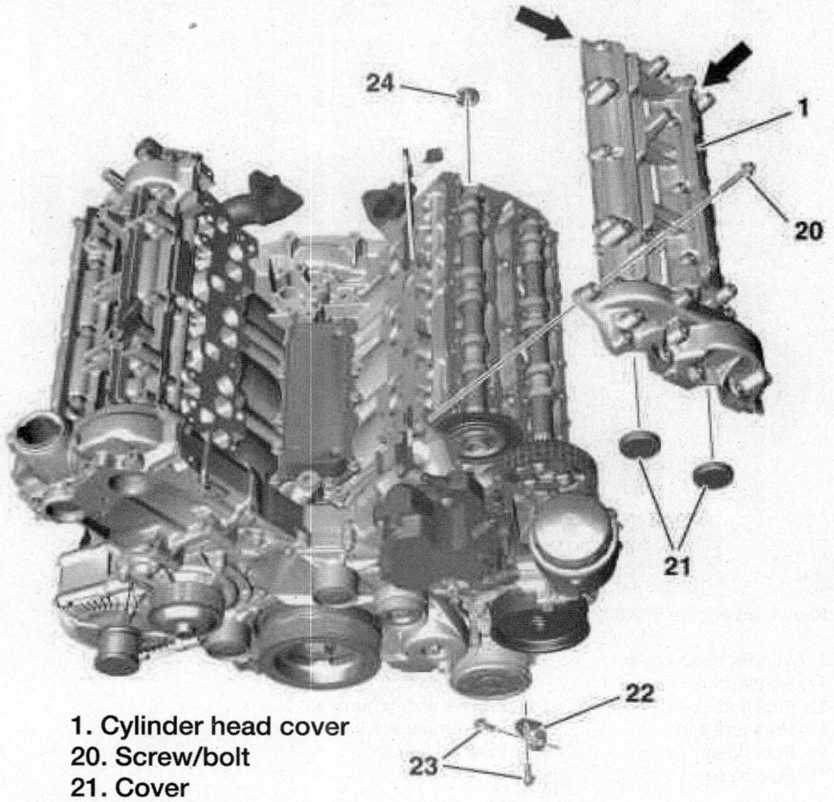

24

1

20

21

22

23

1. Cylinder head cover
20. Screw/bolt
21. Cover
22. Bracket
23. Bolts
24. Cover

71112_MBSV_G0108

Fig. 60 Left cylinder head cover removal/installation, 4 of 4

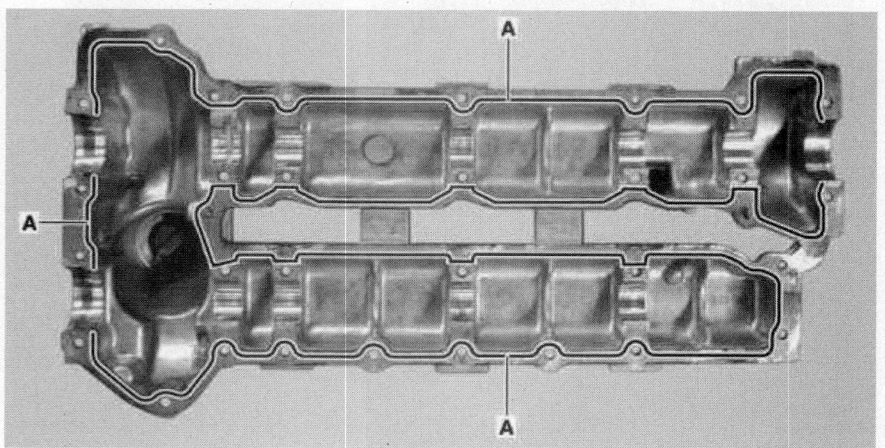

The sealing surfaces must be free of oil and grease. Leaks can occur otherwise.

The traced lines (A) identify the sealant path.
Apply sealant evenly in the form of a bead (A) with a height and width of 1.5 mm (+/-0.5 mm) on the lines (A) of the cylinder head cover.
The sealing compound must be applied within 10 min.

71112_MBSV_G0109

Fig. 61 Left cylinder head cover sealant application

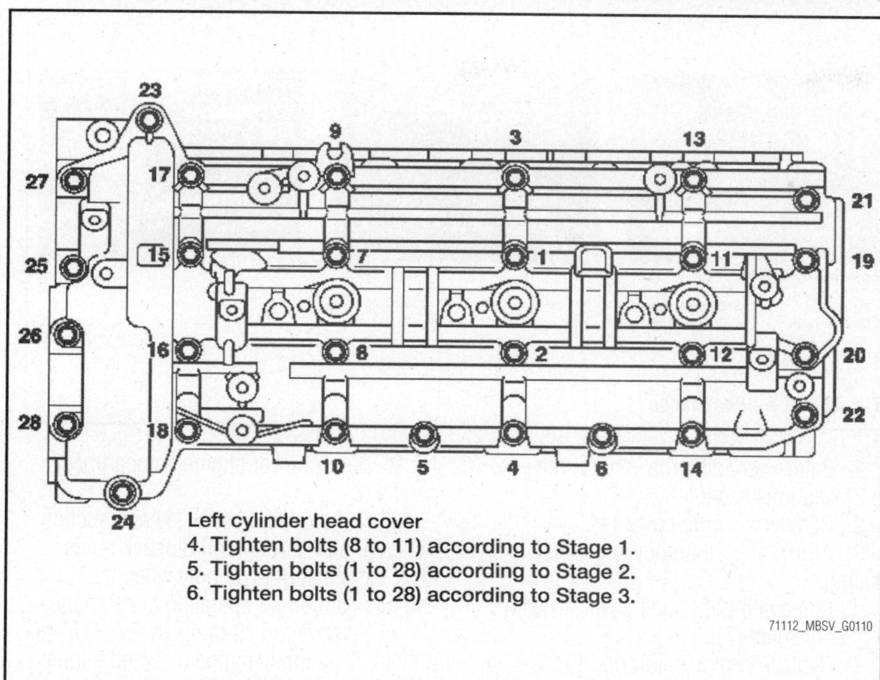

Fig. 62 Left cylinder head cover bolt torque sequence

- Step 3 bolts 1-28: 72 inch lbs. (8 Nm)

19. Observe the following torques:
    - Charge air duct to holder: 79 inch lbs. (9 Nm)
    - Power steering reservoir-to-head: 10 ft. lbs. (14 Nm)
    - Holder-to-charge air distribution line: 79 inch lbs. (9 Nm)
    - Pressure line-to-high pressure pump: 15 ft. lbs. (20 Nm) +60 degrees
    - Retaining clamp on high pressure line-to-cover: 10 ft. lbs. (14 Nm)

CYLINDER HEAD TRIM PANELS

REMOVAL & INSTALLATION

Right Side

See Figure 63.

1. Unclip electric wiring harness (7).
2. Remove bolt (2).
3. Turn oil filler neck (1) anticlockwise and remove upwards.

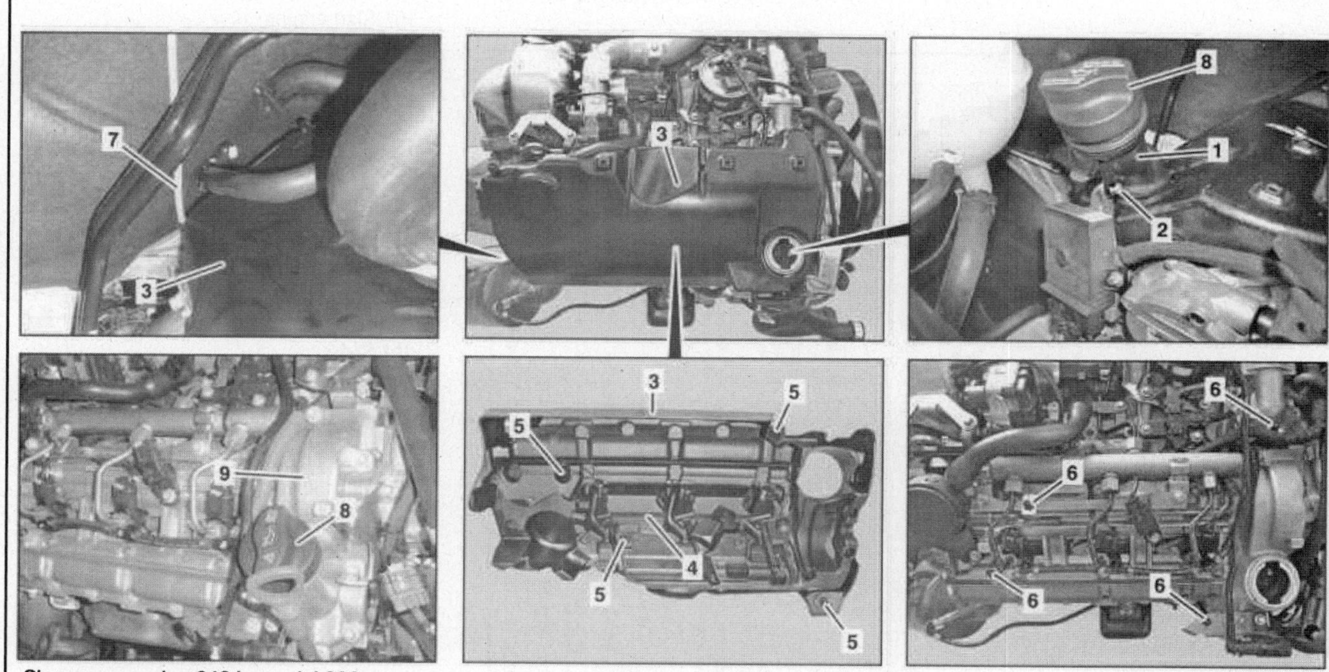

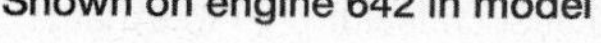
Shown on engine 642 in model 906

1. Oil filler neck
2. Screw
3. Cover
4. Soundproofing
5. Support
6. Ball head
7. Wiring harness
8. Oil filler cap
9. Cylinder head cover

71112_MBSV_G0053

Fig. 63 Right side trim panel removal/installation

4. Unclip cover (3) upward.
5. Unscrew oil filler cover (8) on oil filler neck (1).
6. Insert oil filler cover (8) into the opening on the cylinder head cover (9).

Left Side

See Figure 64.

1. Remove the windshield washer reservoir.
2. Remove turbocharger (1) noise damper.
3. Remove bolts (3, 4).
4. Undo screw (5) by about 3 revolutions.
5. Push engine charge air duct (6) to one side. Carefully push engine charge duct (6) to side to prevent damaging adjacent components.
6. Unclip cover (2) upward. On installation, the sound dampening (9) must be correctly positioned in the cover (2). Mounts (8) on cover (2) must engage in ball heads (7).

ENGINE OIL & FILTER

REPLACEMENT

See Figure 65.

Shown on engine 646

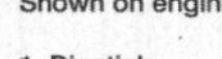
1. Dipstick
2. Oil filler neck

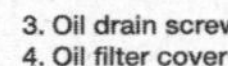
3. Oil drain screw
4. Oil filter cover

71112_MBSV_G0058

Fig. 65 Oil & filter change

1. Before servicing the vehicle, refer to the Precautions section.
2. Remove oil filter cover (4).
3. Allow oil to drain out of oil filter housing.
4. Remove oil filter bolt cover (1) with oil filter element (2).
5. Replace compression ring (3).
6. Insert new oil filter element (2) into oil filter housing.
7. Screw on and tighten oil filter screw cap (1).
8. Raise and safely support the vehicle.
9. Detach lower engine compartment paneling.
10. Remove oil dipstick (1) and suction out engine oil through oil dipstick guide tube. Extract engine oil only when the engine is at normal operating temperature.
11. Remove the oil drain screw (3) from oil pan. Only drain engine oil when engine is at normal operating temperature.
12. Install the drain screw.
13. Pour in engine oil at oil filler neck (2).
14. Install the filter.
15. Start engine.
16. Check oil filter cover (4) and oil drain screw (3) for leak tightness.
17. Observe the following torques:
    - Oil filter cap: 18 ft. lbs. (25 Nm)
    - Oil pan drain screw: 22 ft. lbs. (30 Nm)

EXHAUST MANIFOLD

REMOVAL & INSTALLATION

Right Side

See Figures 66 and 67.

1. Before servicing the vehicle, refer to the Precautions section.
2. Disconnect battery ground cable.
3. Remove trim panel on right cylinder head cover. See the procedure in this section.
4. Remove bolts (1, 2, 4) and shield (3).
5. Remove exhaust gas recirculation pipe from exhaust collector pipe to exhaust gas recirculation bypass flap and press to side.
6. Unbolt exhaust manifold (15) at exhaust collector pipe (9). Replace bolts (17) & seal (16).
7. Unscrew nuts (14) and remove exhaust manifold (15). Replace nuts (14) and seal (13).
8. Check stud bolts (18) on cylinder

Shown on engine 642.992 in model 906

1. Turbocharger silencer
2. Cover
3. Screw/bolt
4. Screw/bolt
5. Screw/bolt
6. Engine charge air duct
7. Ball head
8. Support
9. Soundproofing

71112_MBSV_G0054

Fig. 64 Left side trim panel removal/installation

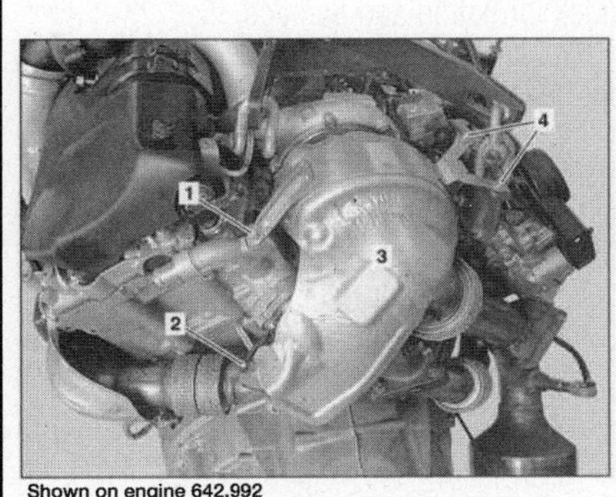

Shown on engine 642.992

1. Screw
2. Screw
3. Shield
4. Bolts
5. Turbocharger
9. Exhaust collector pipe
10. Exhaust pipe
11. Cylinder head

71112_MBSV_G0059

Fig. 66 Right side exhaust manifold removal/installation, 1 of 2

head (11) for damage. Replace damaged stud bolts.

9. Check exhaust manifold (15) for crack formation and damage.

10. Clean sealing surfaces on cylinder head (11).

11. Clean sealing surfaces on exhaust manifold.

12. Installation is the reverse of removal. Observe the following torques:

- Shield-to-holder bolts: 72 inch lbs. (8 Nm)
- Shield-to-collector pipe bolts: 106 inch lbs. (12 Nm)
- Manifold-to-cylinder head nuts: 18 ft. lbs. (25 Nm)
- Manifold-to-collector pipe flange: 15 ft. lbs. (20 Nm) +90 degrees

Left Side

See Figures 64, 68 through 70.

1. Before servicing the vehicle, refer to the Precautions section.
2. Disconnect battery ground cable.
3. Remove trim panel on left cylinder head cover. See the procedure in this section.
4. Remove engine charge air channel upstream of charge air cooler:
   a. Raise and safely support the vehicle.
   b. Open Henn coupling and remove charge air hose (8) from engine charge air duct (3). Plug connections with protective hoods. On installation, replace sealing ring.
   c. Lower vehicle.
   d. Remove air filter housing.
   e. Remove windshield fluid reservoir windshield washer system (1) and hand up to side. Do not detach lines connected.
   f. Remove electrical line (6) from engine charge air duct (3).
   g. Unscrew bolt (4) and pull out bracket (5).
   h. Remove bolts (7). On installation, screw all bolts (7) finger-tight, then tighten.
   i. Detach engine charge air duct (3) from noise damper (2) downwards and take out. On installation, replace sealing ring on noise damper (2). Install new cable tie for electrical line (6) before installing engine charge air duct (3).
5. Remove bolts (1, 2, 4) and shield (3).
6. Remove catalytic converter exhaust pipe to exhaust pipe to exhaust gas turbocharger (5).
7. Unbolt exhaust manifold (18) at exhaust collector pipe (9).
8. Remove bolts (15, 16) and shield (17).

➡The bolts are different.

9. Unscrew bolt (13), press fuel line (19) to side and remove bracket (14).
10. Unscrew nuts (22) and remove exhaust manifold (18). Replace nuts (22) and seal (23).
11. Check stud bolts (21) on left cylinder head (20) for damage. Replace damaged stud bolts.

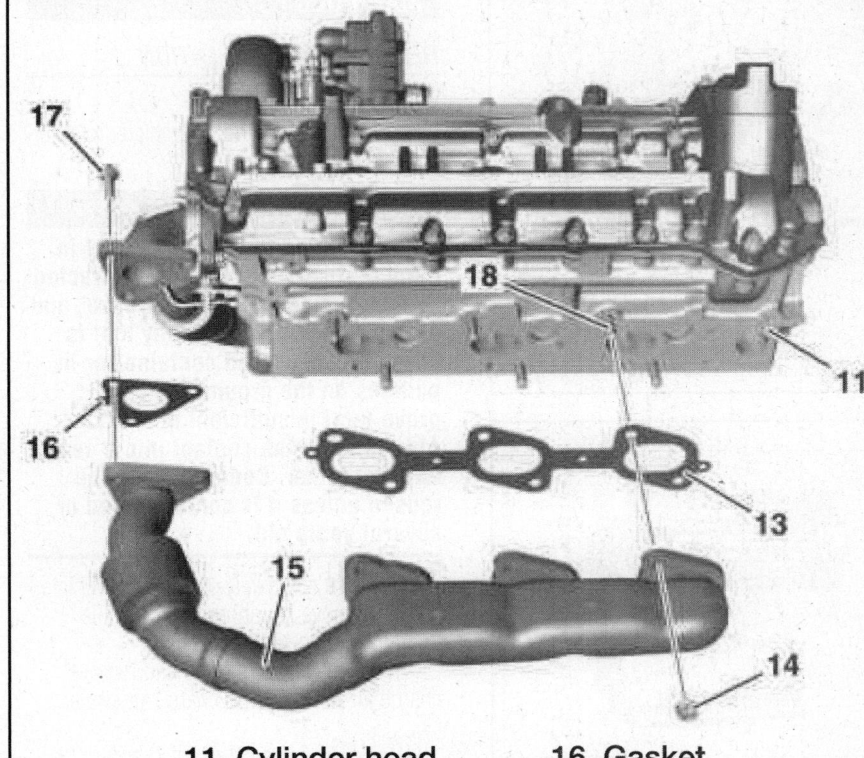

11. Cylinder head
13. Gasket
14. Nut
15. Exhaust manifold
16. Gasket
17. Screw
18. Stud bolt

71112_MBSV_G0060

Fig. 67 Right side exhaust manifold removal/installation, 2 of 2

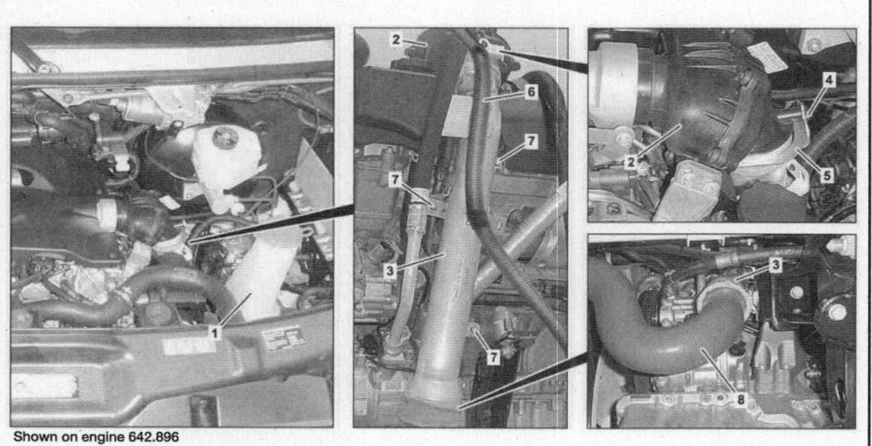

Shown on engine 642.896

1. Windshield washer system washer fluid reservoir
2. Noise damper
3. Engine charge air duct
4. Screw
5. Bracket
6. Electrical line
7. Screw
8. Charge air hose

71112_MBSV_G0063

Fig. 68 Charge air duct removal/installation

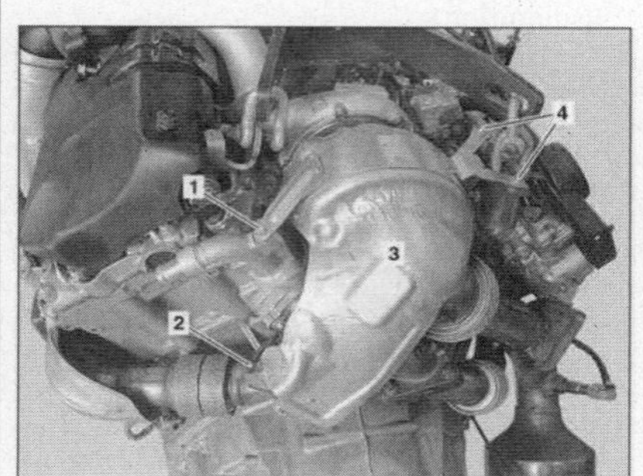

Shown on engine 642.992

1. Screw
2. Screw
3. Shield
4. Bolts)
5. Turbocharger
6. Bolts (engine 642.992)
7. Exhaust gas recirculation pipe (engine 642.992)
8. Bolts (engine 642.992)
9. Exhaust collector pipe
10. Exhaust pipe
11. Right cylinder head
12. Seal (engine 642.992)

71112_MBSV_G0061

Fig. 69 Left side exhaust manifold removal/installation, 1 of 2

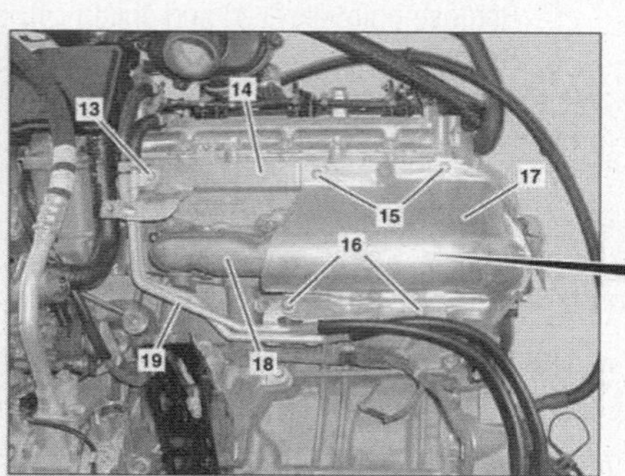

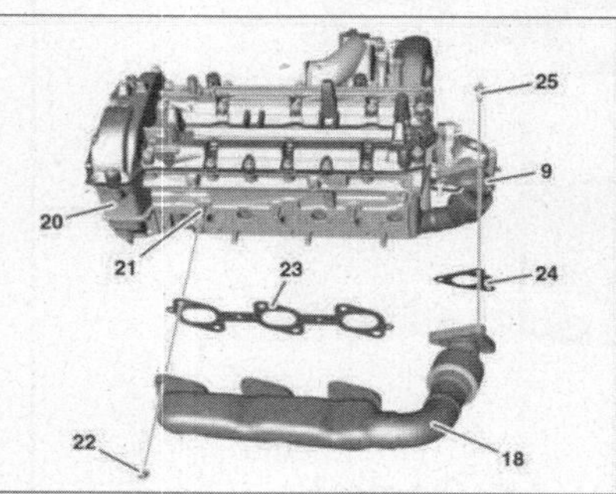

Shown on engine 642.992

9. Exhaust collector pipe
13. Screw
14. Bracket
15. Bolts
16. Bolts
17. Shield
18. Exhaust manifold
19. Fuel pipe
20. Left cylinder head
21. Stud bolt
22. Nut
23. Gasket
24. Gasket
25. Screw

71112_MBSV_G0062

Fig. 70 Left side exhaust manifold removal/installation, 2 of 2

12. Check exhaust manifold (18) for crack formation and damage.
13. Clean sealing surfaces on left cylinder head (20).
14. Clean sealing surfaces on exhaust manifold.
15. Installation is the reverse of removal. Observe the following torques:
    - Charge air duct upstream of charge air cooler-to-holder: 79 inch lbs. (9 Nm)
    - Charge air duct upstream of charge air cooler-to-engine support: 79 inch lbs. (9 Nm)
    - Shield-to-holder bolts: 72 inch lbs. (8 Nm)
    - Shield-to-collector pipe bolts: 106 inch lbs. (12 Nm)
    - EGR pipe-to-charge air distribution line: 115 inch lbs. (13 Nm)
    - EGR pipe-to-collector pipe: 84 inch lbs. (10 Nm) +90 degrees
    - Manifold-to-collector pipe flange: 15 ft. lbs. (20 Nm) +90 degrees
    - Manifold-to-cylinder head nuts: 18 ft. lbs. (25 Nm)

CHARGE AIR (INTAKE) MANIFOLD

REMOVAL & INSTALLATION

See Figures 71 through 74.

1. Before servicing the vehicle, refer to the Precautions section.

⁂ CAUTION

When draining the coolant, keep in mind that cats and dogs are attracted by the ethylene glycol antifreeze, and are quite likely to drink any that is left in an uncovered container or in puddles on the ground. This will prove fatal in sufficient quantity. Always drain the coolant into a sealable container. Coolant should be reused unless it is contaminated or several years old.

2. Raise and safely support the vehicle.
3. Remove fan shroud (1). See the Engine Cooling section.
4. Open Henn coupling and remove charge air hoses (2) on charge air cooler (3).
    a. Slide nose (2) of catch spring (3) into position (B). Never pull on the eyelet (1).
    b. The catch spring (3) will lose its pretension if one does that.
    c. Detach hose on component.
    d. Replace seal.

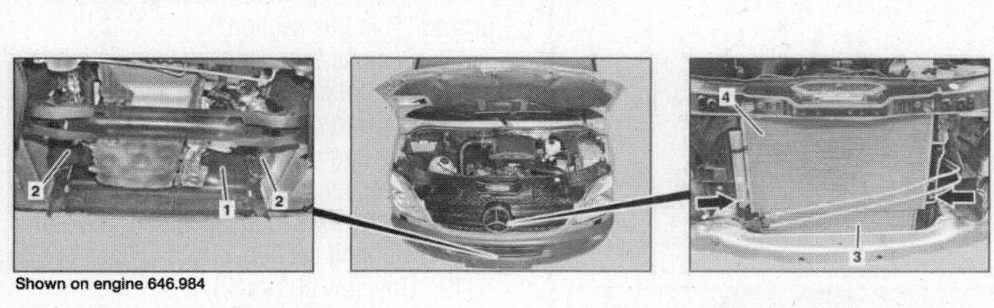

Shown on engine 646.984

1. Fan shroud
2. Charge air hose
3. Charge air cooler
4. Condenser (for code (HH9) Regulated air conditioning, (Tempmatic)

71112_MBSV_G0064

Fig. 71 Charge air cooler removal/installation

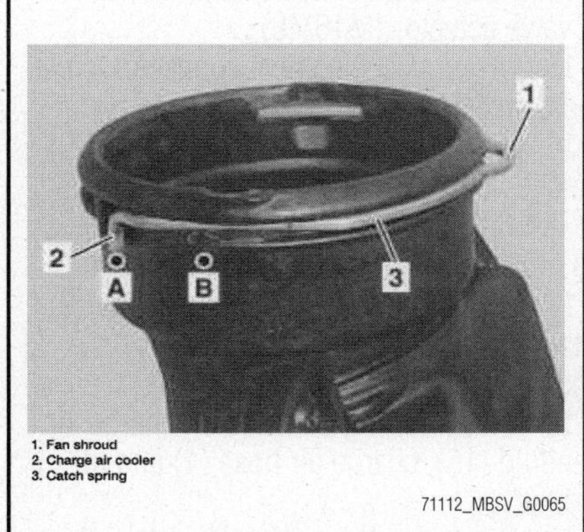

1. Fan shroud
2. Charge air cooler
3. Catch spring

71112_MBSV_G0065

Fig. 72 Henn coupling removal/installation

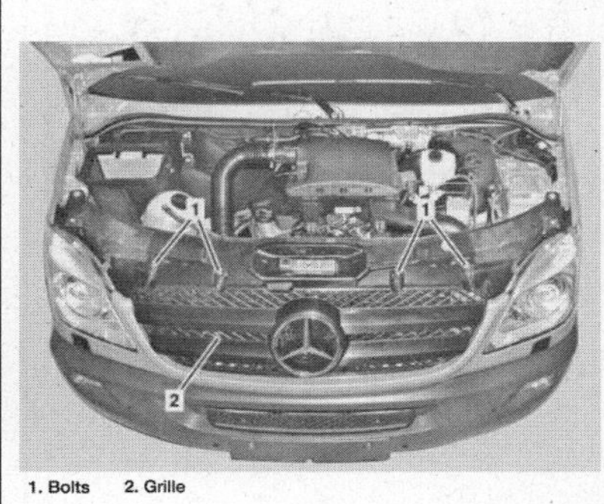

1. Bolts 2. Grille

71112_MBSV_G0066

Fig. 73 Front grille removal/installation

5. For vehicles with code (ZX8) Trademark scope-Dodge or with code (ZX9) Trademark scope-Freightliner (FTL) and without code (HH9) Regulated air conditioning, (Tempmatic), remove front grille:
    a. Remove bolts (1).
    b. Remove front grill (2) upward. On installation, ensure that front grill (2) is seated correctly.
6. For vehicles without code (ZX8) Trademark scope-Dodge or without code (ZX9) Trademark scope-Freightliner (FTL) and without code (HH9) Regulated air conditioning, (Tempmatic), remove plate under front grille:
    - Unscrew bolts (3, 4).
    - On vehicles with code (F46) Headlamp cleaning system, pull covers (2) toward front and unclip.
    - Slightly pull front cover (1) toward front (arrow), carefully insert removal tool (5) at side of fender (7) and unclip front cover (1) from fender (7) on both sides.
    - Unclip front covering (1) from bumper (6).
    - Remove front cover (1).
7. For vehicles with code (HH9) Regulated air conditioning, (Tempmatic), unclip condenser (4) at front module and raise until bolts are accessible (arrows).
8. Unscrew bolts (arrows).
9. Remove charge air cooler (3) downwards.
10. Installation is the reverse of removal. Observe the following torques:
    - Charge air hose-to-cooler clamp: 48 inch lbs. (5.5 Nm)

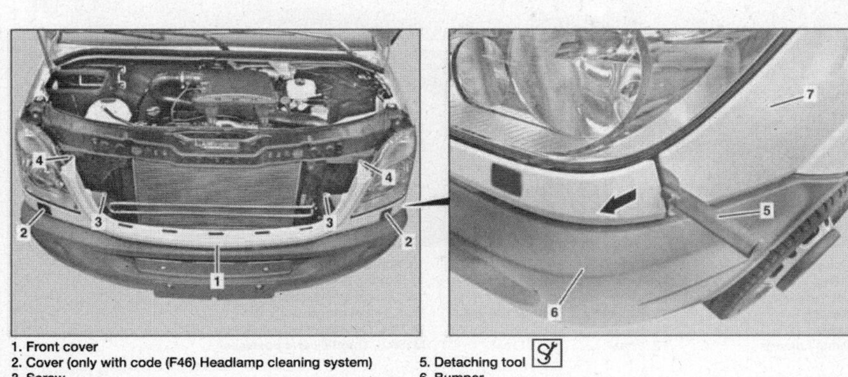

1. Front cover
2. Cover (only with code (F46) Headlamp cleaning system)
3. Screw
4. Screw
5. Detaching tool
6. Bumper
7. Fenders

71112_MBSV_G0067

Fig. 74 Front grille lower covering removal/installation

HYDRAULIC VALVE CLEARANCE COMPENSATING ELEMENTS (LIFTERS)

REMOVAL & INSTALLATION

See Figure 75.

1. Remove camshafts. See the procedure in this section.
2. Pry off clamps (2).
3. Detach compensating elements (1) from roller-type cam follower (3).
4. Remove roller drag lever (3).
5. Remove compensating elements (1).

➡Do not use magnets. This would magnetize the contact surfaces of the compensation element (1) and the roller drag lever (3). Tiny iron filings could gather in this way which could lead to damage on the compensating element (1), the roller-type cam follower (3) and the camshaft.

6. Installation is the reverse of removal. Compensating elements (1) which were not replaced must be installed again at the same installation location.

MIXING CHAMBER

REMOVAL & INSTALLATION

See Figure 76.

1. Before servicing the vehicle, refer to the Precautions section.

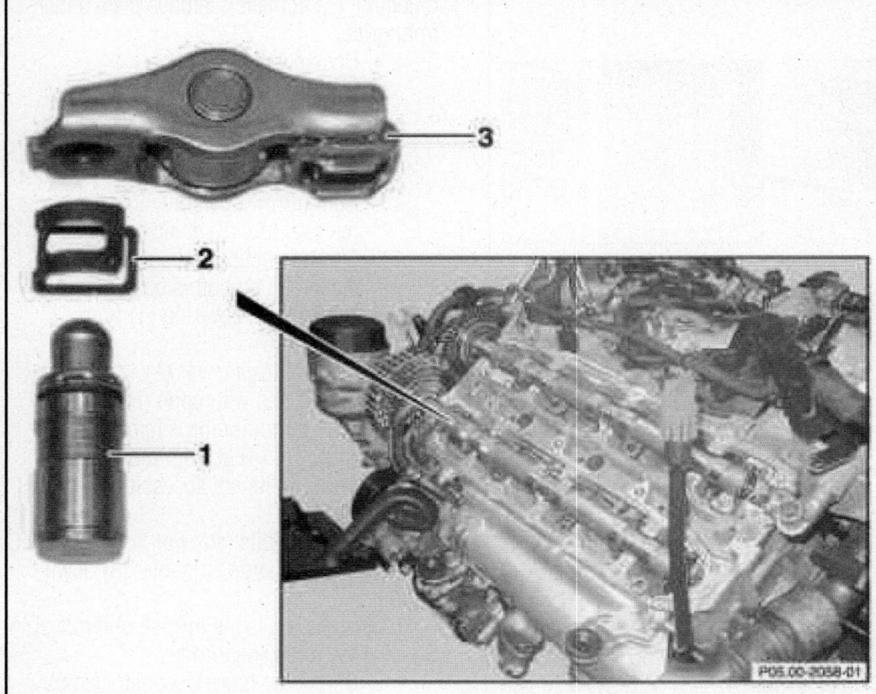

Shown on engine 642 in model 639

1. Compensating element
2. Clamp
3. Roller-type cam follower

71112_MBSV_G0202

Fig. 75 Lifter removal/installation

CAUTION

When draining the coolant, keep in mind that cats and dogs are attracted by the ethylene glycol antifreeze, and are quite likely to drink any that is left in an uncovered container or in puddles on the ground. This will prove fatal in sufficient quantity. Always drain the coolant into a sealable container. Coolant should be reused unless it is contaminated or several years old.

2. Disconnect the battery ground.
3. Raise and safely support the vehicle.
4. Open coupling and remove charge air hose (1) from fitting (2).
5. Unscrew bolts (5) from bracket (4), unscrew fittings (2) and throttle valve actuator (M16/48).
6. Remove electrical wiring harness (6) from bracket (4) and unclip throttle valve actuator (M16/48).
7. Disconnect electrical connector (3) at charge air temperature sensor (B17/15).
8. Lower the vehicle.
9. Remove air filter housing. See the procedure in this section.
10. Remove exhaust gas recirculation pipe (10) from exhaust gas recirculation valve to mixing chamber (9). See the procedure in the Engine Performance & Emission Controls section.
11. Remove viscous fan clutch. See the Engine Cooling section.
12. Unscrew bolts (12).
13. Unscrew bolt (13) and remove mixing chamber (9) toward front. On installation, replace sealing ring (14) on charge air manifold (15) and seal (11). Install mixing chamber (9) free of tension.
14. Lift out mixing chamber (9) and disconnect electrical connector (7) from throttle valve actuator (M16/48).
15. Disconnect electrical connector (8) at boost pressure sensor (B5/8).
16. If installing new mixing chamber (9), remove fittings (2) and throttle valve actuator (M16/48) from mixing chamber (9). See the procedure in the Fuel Systems section.
17. If installing new mixing chamber (9), detach boost pressure sensor (B5/8) on mixing chamber (9).
18. Clean sealing surfaces on charge air manifold (15), charge air hose (1) and fittings (2).
19. If re-using the mixing chamber, clean sealing surfaces on mixing chamber.
20. Installation is the reverse of removal. Observe the following torques:

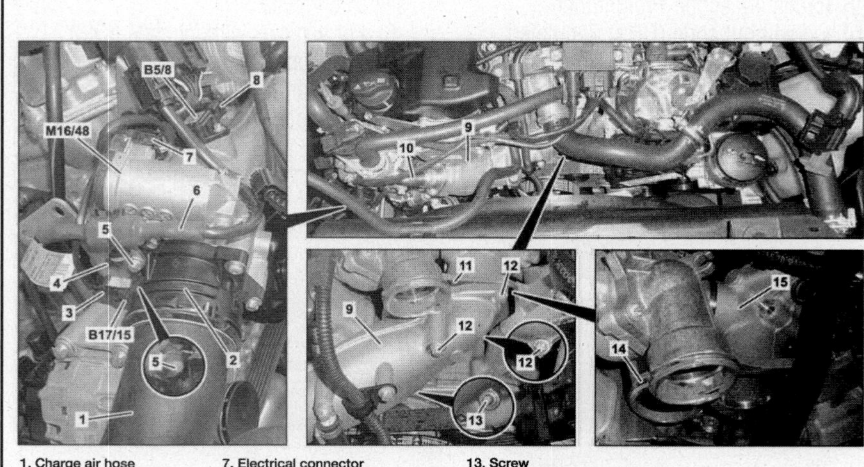

1. Charge air hose
2. Fitting
3. Electrical connector
4. Bracket
5. Screw
6. Wiring harness
7. Electrical connector
8. Electrical connector
9. Mixing chamber
10. Exhaust gas recirculation pipe
11. Gasket
12. Screw
13. Screw
14. Sealing ring
15. Charge air manifold

B5/8. Boost pressure sensor
B17/15. Charge air temperature sensor
M16/48. Throttle valve positioner

71112_MBSV_G0193

Fig. 76 Mixing chamber removal/installation

- Bolt, engine charge air duct downstream of charge air cooler to throttle valve actuator: 79 inch lbs. (9 Nm)
- Bolt, throttle valve actuator holder to cylinder head: 79 inch lbs. (9 Nm)
- Bolt, boost air pressure sensor to mixing chamber: 53 inch lbs. (6 Nm)
- Bolt of mixing chamber to charge air manifold: 79 inch lbs. (9 Nm)
- Bolt, mixing chamber to support brace: 15 ft. lbs. (20 Nm)

OIL PAN

REMOVAL & INSTALLATION

See Figures 77 through 80.

1. Before servicing the vehicle, refer to the Precautions section.
2. Remove the oil dipstick guide tube.
3. For code (HH9) Regulated air conditioning, (Tempmatic), remove refrigerant compressor (A9) and hang up to the side with connected lines.
4. Remove electrical wiring harness (6) with holder (7) from oil pan (1) and move out of the way.
5. Remove electrical wiring harness (6) and electrical line (13) from bracket (12) and move out of the way.
6. Detach the bracket (12) at the oil pan (1).
7. Remove oil pan bottom section (2):
   a. Raise and safely support the vehicle.
   b. Drain the oil.
   c. Only for code (H08) Heavy duty air conditioning, remove carrier from 2nd refrigerant compressor. See the HVAC section.
   d. Disconnect electrical connector (3) from engine oil sensor (B40 or B40/8).
   e. Remove bolts (2).
   f. Pry off oil pan bottom section (1) in the area of the cutouts (arrow). On installation, clean sealing surfaces of oil pan (1) and oil pan bottom section and apply sealant. Use Loctite sealant 5970.
8. Remove bolts (3, 5) and oil intake tube (4). On installation, clean oil strainer in oil intake tube (4). Replace sealing ring on oil intake tube (4).
9. Remove end cover (9) with radial shaft sealing ring.
10. Attach supports (11) to both sides of crankcase (8) and remove wooden block (10) under the oil pan (1).

➡The supports (11) serve as stop for the oil pan (1). They must not get bent and must lie evenly on the crankcase (8).

11. Remove bolts from oil pan (1).

➡The bolts are different lengths& diameters.

12. Pry off oil pan (1) at the cutouts (arrows) and remove. On installation, clean sealing surfaces to oil pan (1) and on crankcase (8). Apply sealing compound. Lay oil pan (1) on both supports (11). Center on the left and right on crankcase (8) and push upwards to crankcase (8). A helper is required. Use Loctite sealant 5970.
13. Installation is the reverse of removal. Observe the following torques:
    - Lower pan to upper pan bolts: 106 inch lbs. (12 Nm)
    - Top oil pan bracket: 72 inch lbs. (8 Nm)

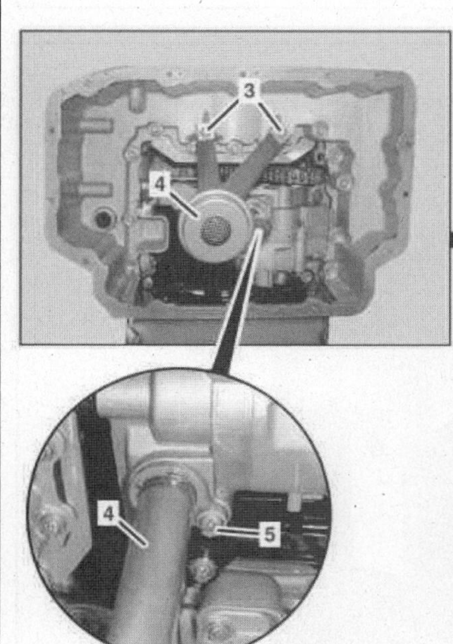

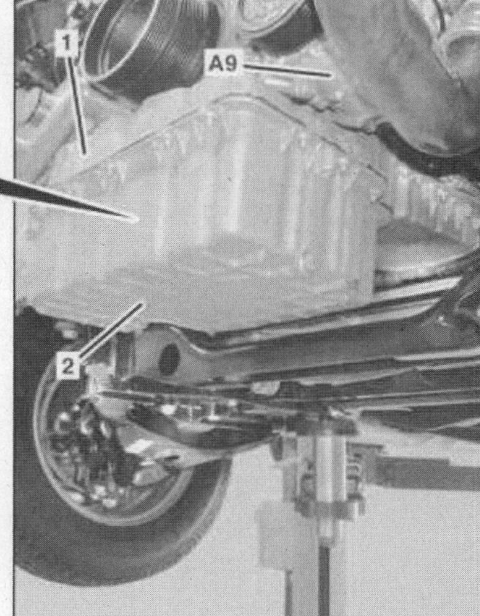

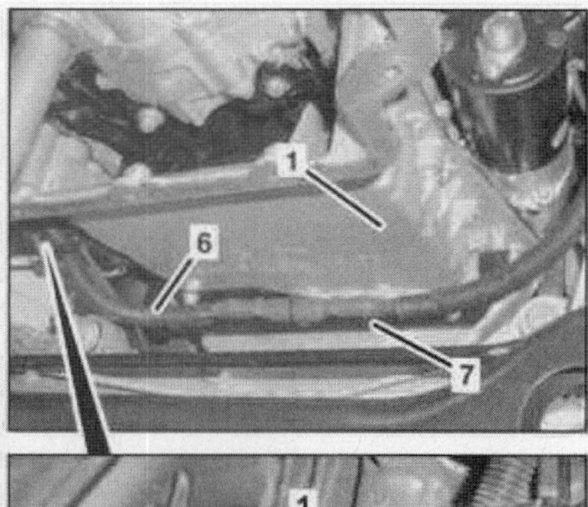

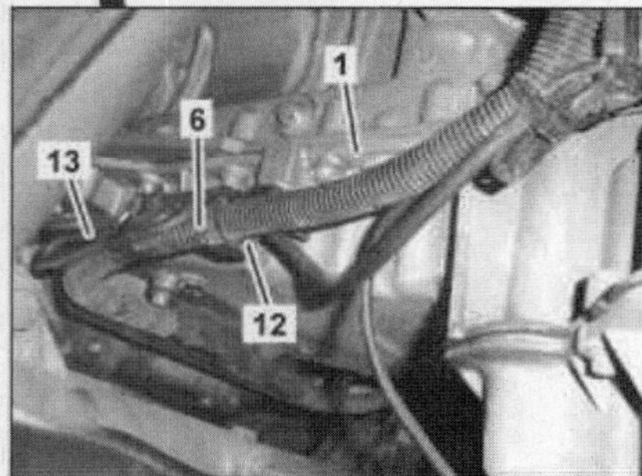

1. Oil pan
2. Oil pan bottom section
3. Bolts
4. Oil intake tube
5. Screw
6. Wiring harness
7. Bracket
12. Bracket
13. Electrical line
A9. Refrigerant compressor (for code (HH9) Regulated air conditioning,(Tempmatic)

71112_MBSV_G0068

Fig. 77 Oil pan removal/installation, 1 of 2

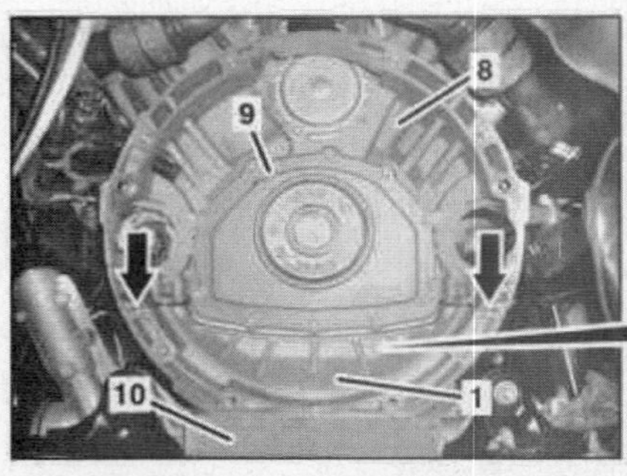

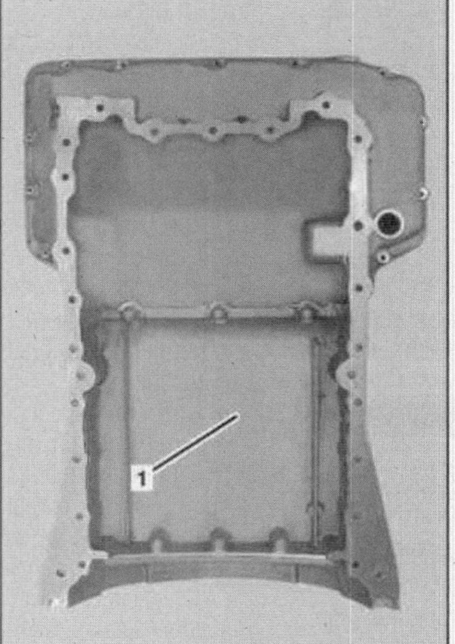

1. Oil pan
8. Cylinder crankcase
9. End cover
10. Wooden block
11. Support

71112_MBSV_G0069

Fig. 78 Oil pan removal/installation, 2 of 2

1. Oil pan bottom section
2. Screw
3. Electrical connector
B40. Engine oil sensor (engine 642.992/993)
B40/8. Engine oil sensor (engine 642.896/898)

71112_MBSV_G0070

Fig. 79 Lower oil pan removal/installation, 1 of 2

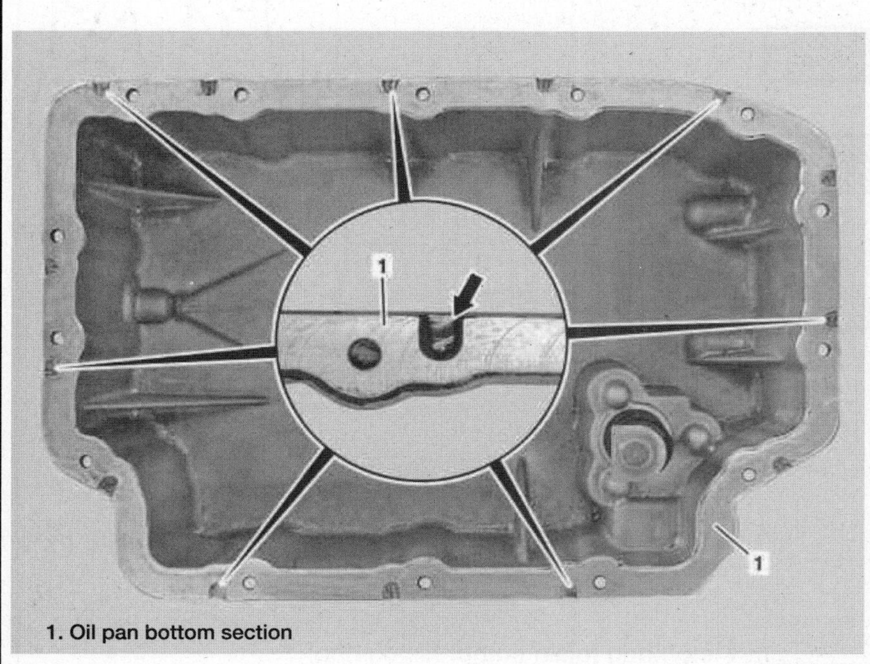

Fig. 80 Lower oil pan removal/installation, 2 of 2

- Oil pan-to-crankcase M6 bolts: 10 ft. lbs. (14 Nm)
- Oil pan-to-crankcase M8 bolts: 15 ft. lbs. (20 Nm)
- Oil pan-to-timing case cover bolts: 10 ft. lbs. (14 Nm)

OIL PUMP

REMOVAL & INSTALLATION

See Figure 81.

1. Before servicing the vehicle, refer to the Precautions section.
2. Remove oil pan.
3. Unscrew bolts (2) and remove oil deflector (1).
4. Remove bolts (5).
5. Remove bolts (4).
6. Push clamping bracket (8) in direction of arrow, unhook oil pump (3) from oil pump chain (7) and remove. On installation, before installing fill oil pump (3) with engine oil. Replace seal on oil pump.
7. Installation is the reverse of removal. Remove the bracket if installing a new pump. Observe the following torques:
    - Oil pump bolts: 14 ft. lbs. (19 Nm)
    - Bracket-to-oil pump M6 8.8 bolts: 72 inch lbs. (8 Nm)

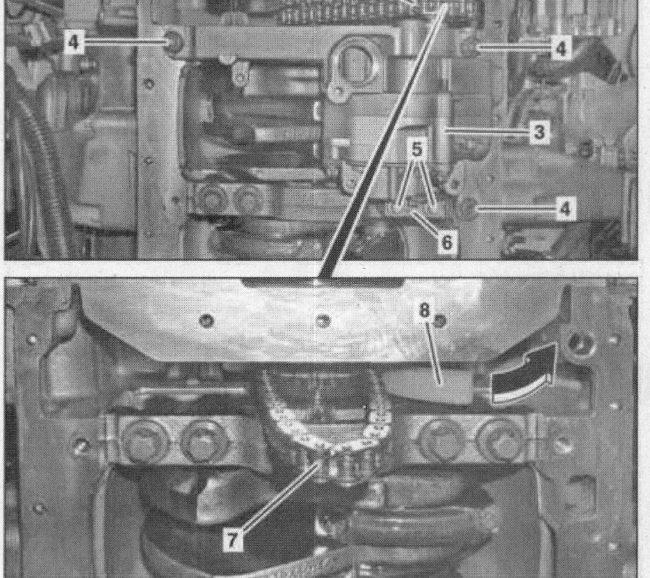

1. Oil deflector
2. Bolts
3. Oil pump
4. Screw
5. Bolts
6. Bracket
7. Oil pump chain
8. Retaining clamp

71112_MBSV_G0072

Fig. 81 Oil pump removal/installation

- Bracket-to-oil pump M6 10.9 bolts: 106 inch lbs. (12 Nm)
- Oil deflector-to-crankcase: 106 inch lbs. (12 Nm)

PISTON & RING

POSITIONING

See Figures 82 and 83.

REAR MAIN SEAL

REMOVAL & INSTALLATION

See Figure 84.

1. Before servicing the vehicle, refer to the Precautions section.
2. Remove transmission with torque converter.
3. Install retaining lock on crankshaft or starter ring gear.
4. Unscrew bolts and remove flexplate.
5. Remove flexplate.
6. Unscrew bolts (1) at end cover (2).
7. Use a hot air blower. Warm up end cover (2) and remove.

To install:

8. Apply sealant on the end cover (2) and install end cover (2) with radial shaft sealing ring-crankshaft (3). Torque to:
   - Step 1: 72 inch lbs. (8 Nm)
   - Step 2: 84 inch lbs. (10 Nm)
9. Install flexplate. Torque the bolts to 33 ft. lbs. (45 Nm) +90 degrees.
10. Install the transmission.

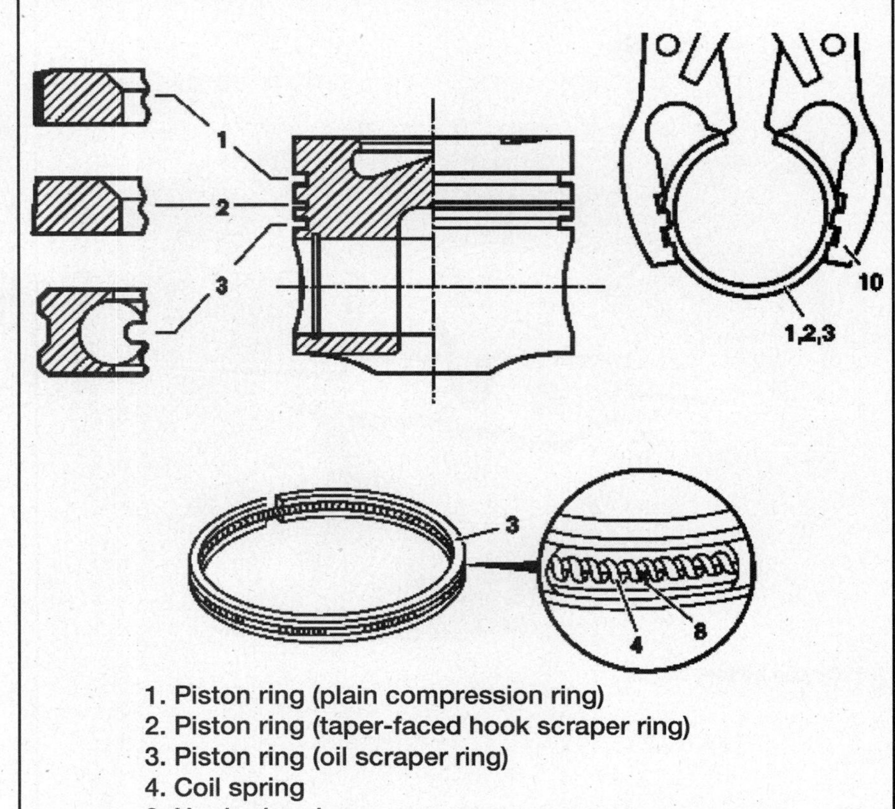

Fig. 83 Piston ring installation

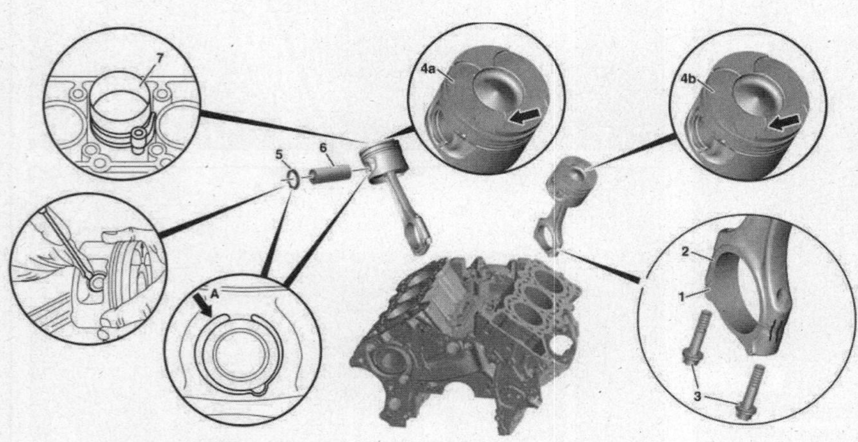

1. Connecting rod bearing cap
2. Connecting rod
3. Connecting rod bolts
4a Piston
4b Piston
5. Circlip
6. Piston pin
7. Tensioning strap

71112_MBSV_G0073

Fig. 82 Piston & connecting rod installation

TIMING CASE COVER

REMOVAL & INSTALLATION

See Figures 85 through 87.

1. Before servicing the vehicle, refer to the Precautions section.
2. Remove viscous fan clutch. See the Engine Cooling section.
3. Crank engine by hand at the vibration damper and place piston of cylinder 1 to ignition TDC.

➡The top dead center marking on the vibration damper must be flush with the stay on the timing case cover (2).

4. Remove front radial shaft sealing ring. See the Crankshaft Front Oil Seal procedure in this section. On installation, only install front radial shaft sealing ring after installing timing case cover (2).
5. Remove fan drive:
   a. For vehicle without code (H08) High performance air conditioning

Fig. 84 Rear main seal removal/installation

Fig. 85 Timing case cover removal/installation

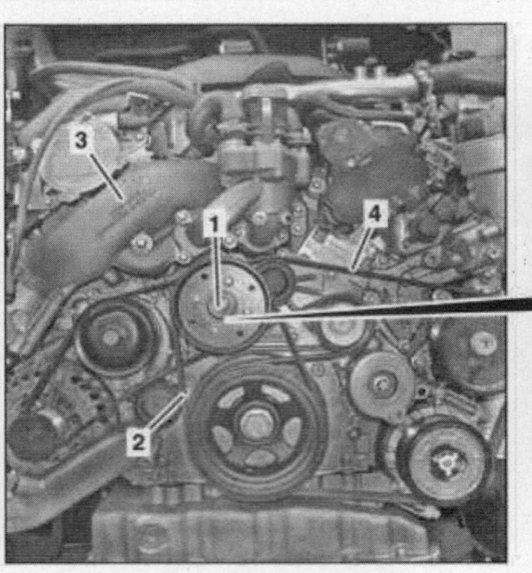

Shown on engine 642.992

1. Fan drive
2. Poly-V belt
3. Mixing chamber
4. Poly-V belt
5. Bolts
6. Bracket

71112_MBSV_G0191

Fig. 86 Fan drive removal/installation

system, remove poly-V belt from fan. See the procedure in this section.

b. For vehicle with code (H08) High performance air conditioning system, Remove poly-V belt from 2nd refrigerant compressor on air conditioning system.

c. Remove poly-V belt (4).

d. Remove mixing chamber (3). See the procedure in this section.

e. Remove bolts (5) and fan drive (1).

6. Remove poly-V belt tensioning device.

7. Remove guide pulley (1).

8. Remove oil pan bottom section. See the procedure in this section.

9. Remove timing case cover (2) with fitting sleeves (3) and sealing surfaces. The fitting sleeves (3) are no longer required. On installation, apply sealant, then place timing case cover (2) in place and tighten bolts (4) on timing case cover (2) finger-tight. Loosen lower bolts (4) again and insert centering sleeve in the timing case cover (2). Tighten all bolts on timing case cover (2) and remove centering sleeve.

➡See the accompanying illustration for correct sealant path on the timing case cover.

10. Installation is the reverse of removal. Observe the following torques:

- Guide pulley bolt: 20 ft. lbs. (28 Nm)
- Oil pan to timing case cover: 10 ft. lbs. (14 Nm)
- Timing case cover to crankcase: 88 inch lbs. (10 Nm)
- V-belt tensioner bolt: 43 ft. lbs. (58 Nm)

TIMING CHAIN

REMOVAL & INSTALLATION

See Figures 88 through 108 and 56.

1. Before servicing the vehicle, refer to the Precautions section.

⁂ CAUTION

When draining the coolant, keep in mind that cats and dogs are attracted by the ethylene glycol antifreeze, and are quite likely to drink any that is left in an uncovered container or in puddles on the ground. This will prove fatal in sufficient quantity. Always drain the coolant into a sealable container. Coolant should be reused unless it is contaminated or several years old.

Sealant path on timing case cover

At sealing surfaces and transitions between the oil pan and crankcase, it is particularly important to pay attention to cleanliness. The sealing surfaces must be oil and grease-free otherwise leaks can occur.

The superimposed line (A) shows the sealant path. Apply sealant evenly in the form of a bead with a height and width of 1.5 mm (+/-0.5) mm on the line (A) of the timing case cutout. The sealant must be applied within 10 min. The sealant must be applied in the upper area of the timing case cutout in the center area of the sealing surface because the sealant slides downwards due to placement of the timing case cover.

71112_MBSV_G0192

Fig. 87 Sealer application on timing case

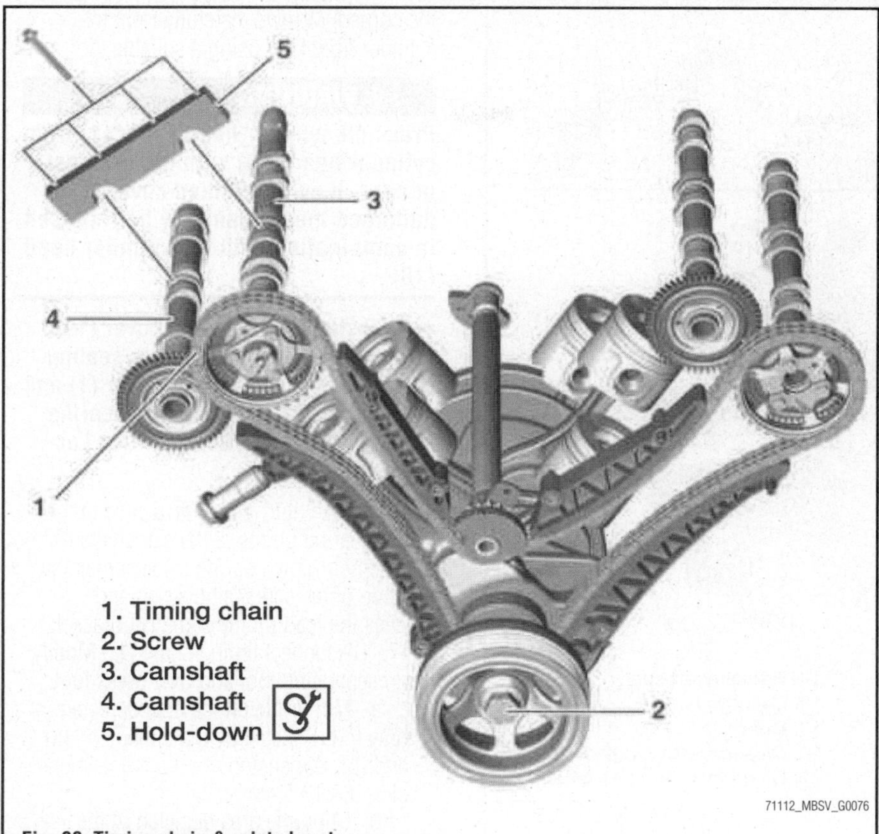

Fig. 88 Timing chain & related parts

2. Turn transmitter key in EIS control unit to position **"0"** and remove.
3. Remove viscous fan clutch and lay in fan shroud. See Engine Cooling.
4. Remove glow output stage and place to the side with lines connected. See the Fuel System section.
5. Remove rail (4) on right cylinder head (18). See the Fuel Systems section.
6. Remove injectors from right cylinder head (18). See the Fuel Systems section.
7. Disconnect electrical connector (5) from camshaft sensor (B6/20 or B6/24).
8. Remove vacuum pump (7):
    a. Remove air filter housing.
    b. Remove exhaust gas recirculation valve.
    c. Remove vacuum line (3) and place to one side.
    d. Unscrew bolts (4) from bracket (1).
    e. Detach engine wiring harness from fixture (1).
    f. Remove bolts (5) and upper bolt (7) and remove holder (1)
    g. Remove bolt (7) and vacuum pump (6). On installation use a new gasket. Align drive plate of vacuum pump (6).
9. Pull drain hose out of drain line (8),

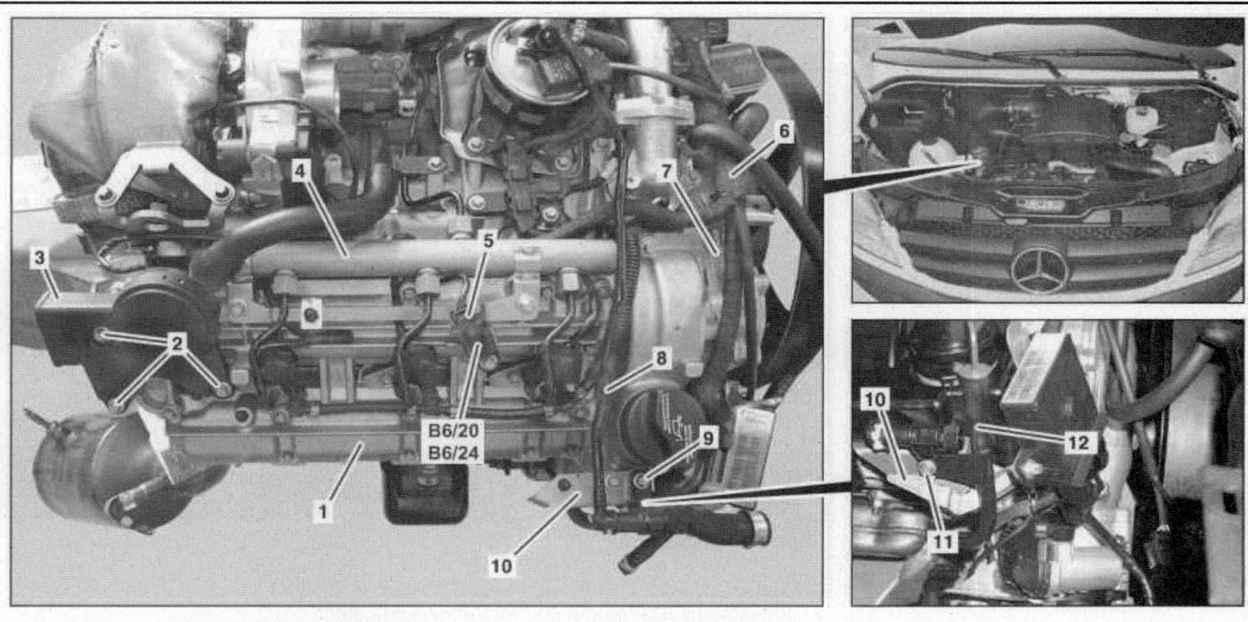

Fig. 89 Right cylinder head cover removal, 1 of 2

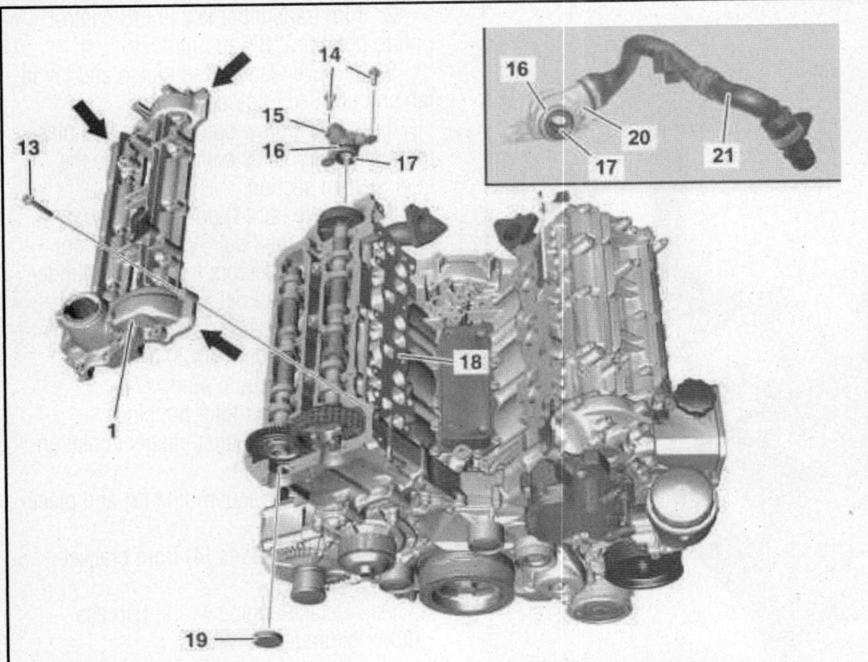

1. Cylinder head cover
13. Screw
14. Bolts
15. Connection fittings (engine 642.896/992/993)
16. Sealing ring
17. Radial shaft seal
18. Cylinder head
19. Cover
20. Oil separator (engine 642.898)
21. Bleed hose (engine 642.898)

71112_MBSV_G0078

Fig. 90 Right cylinder head cover removal, 2 of 2

with code (KL5) Fuel Filter with water separator.

10. Remove bolt (9), remove drain pipe (8) from holder (10) and swivel to the side, with code (KL5) Fuel filter with water separator.

11. Remove bolt (11) and turn oil dipstick guide tube (12) to the side.

12. Remove engine wiring harness (6) to cylinder head cover (1) and move out of the way.

13. Unscrew bolts (14), remove oil separator (20) and vent hose (21) from cylinder head.

➡On installation, clean sealing surfaces on oil separator (20) and vent hose (21) and replace sealing ring (16). Check radial shaft sealing ring (17) for damage, if applicable, replace oil separator (20).

14. Loosen and remove bolts (13) in stages and in reverse order of the tightening procedure, on a cooled engine.

➡On installation, pay attention to tightening procedure and tightening instructions for bolts (13) so that cylinder head cover (1) is not warped and camshafts are not damaged.

15. Press off cylinder head cover (1) to the corners (arrows) carefully from the cylinder head (18) using a suitable tool.

WARNING

Press off cylinder head cover (1) from cylinder head (18) with the greatest of care. If cylinder head cover (1) is damaged then it can only be replaced in combination with the cylinder head (18).

➡On installation, replace cover (19). Remove sealant residue from sealing surfaces on cylinder head cover (1) and cylinder head (18). Lubricate bearing points on camshaft bearing. Use Loctite sealant 5970.

16. Attach hold-down device (5) to the center bearing points of the camshafts (3, 4). The hold-down device (5) assumes the function of the camshaft bearing and relieves the load on the camshaft brackets.

17. Disconnect timing chain (1). Modify chain separating tool and rivet press tool:

a. Mill or file off the area depicted in gray in the sketch by the dimension (a) and (b). Dimension a = 6.5mm; Dimension b = 13.5mm

b. Grind the area depicted in the sketch by the dimension (c). Dimension

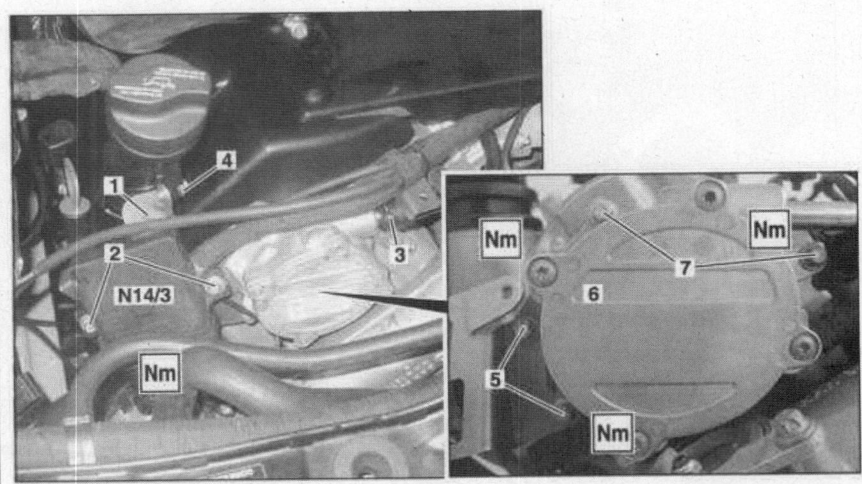

Shown on model 639

1. Bracket
2. Bolts (model 639, model 906 with engine 642.992)
3. Vacuum line
4. Screw
5. Bolts
6. Vacuum pump
7. Bolts
N14/3. Glow output stage (model 639, model 906 with engine 642.992)

71112_MBSV_G0096

Fig. 91 Vacuum pump removal/installation

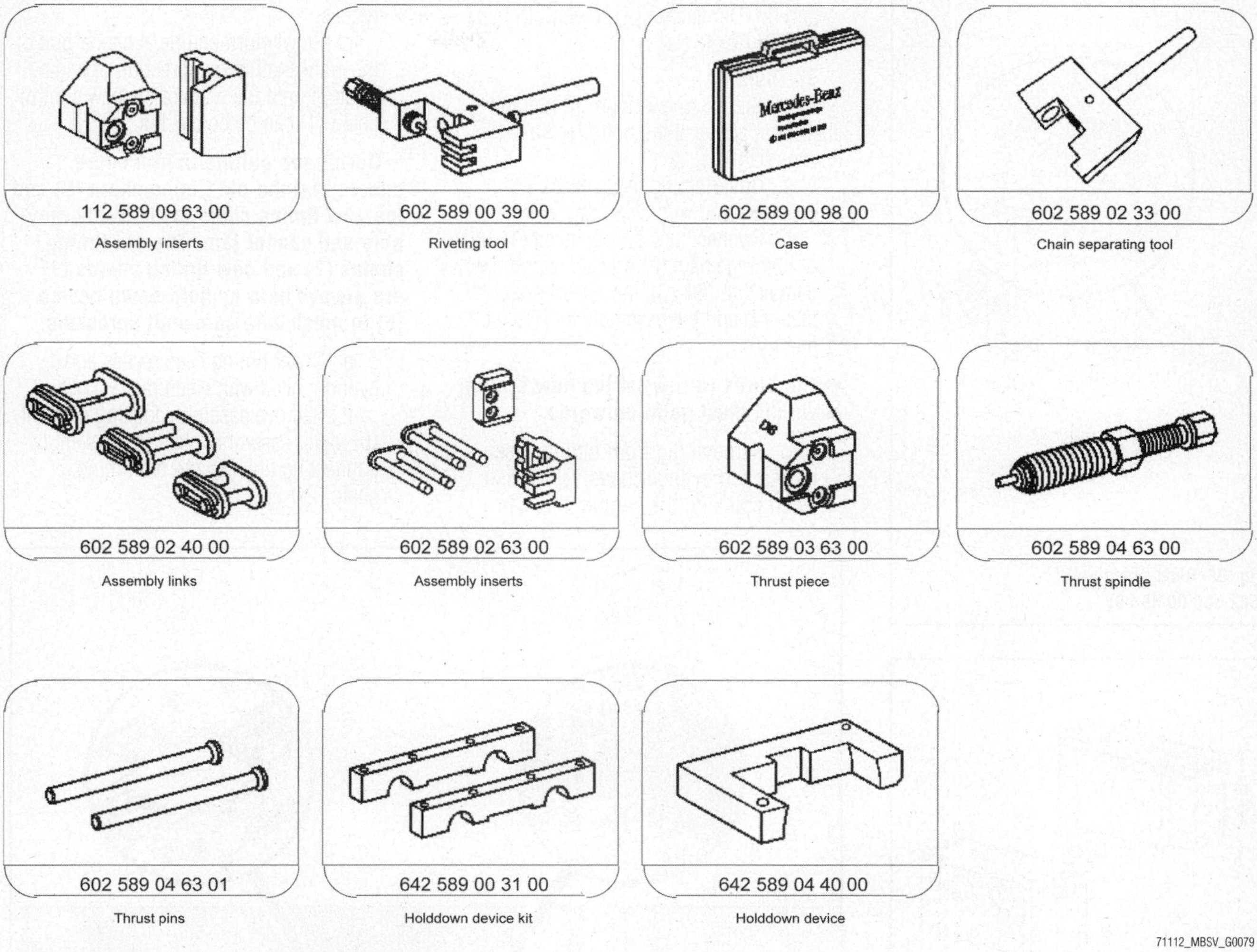

112 589 09 63 00
Assembly inserts
602 589 00 39 00
Riveting tool
602 589 00 98 00
Case
602 589 02 33 00
Chain separating tool
602 589 02 40 00
Assembly links
602 589 02 63 00
Assembly inserts
602 589 03 63 00
Thrust piece
602 589 04 63 00
Thrust spindle
602 589 04 63 01
Thrust pins
642 589 00 31 00
Holddown device kit
642 589 04 40 00
Holddown device
71112_MBSV_G0079

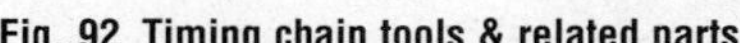

Fig. 92 Timing chain tools & related parts

b
a
602 589 02 33 00
71112_MBSV_G0080

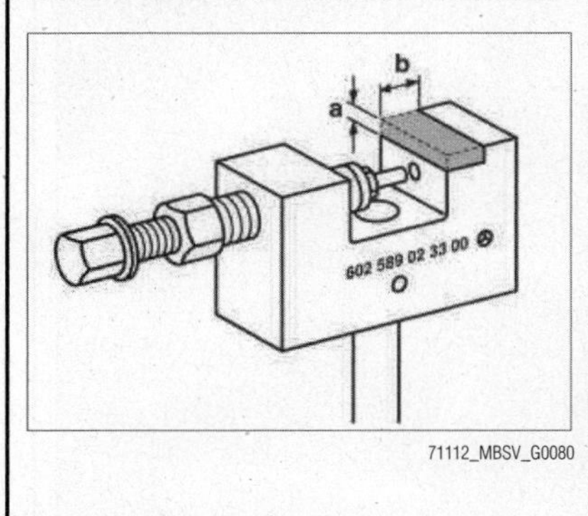

Fig. 93 Chain separating tool (602 589 02 33 00)

c
d
71112_MBSV_G0081

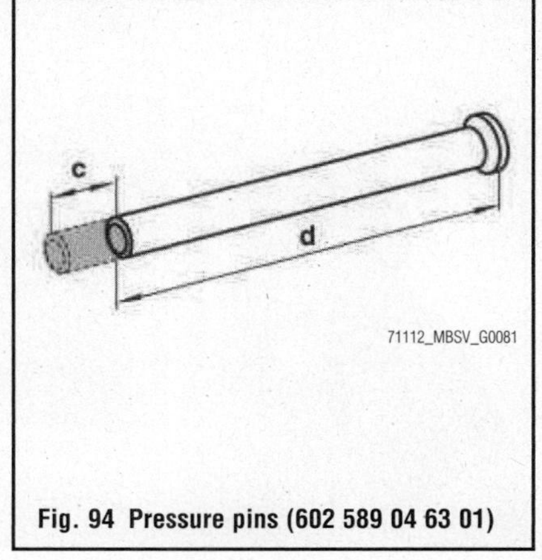

Fig. 94 Pressure pins (602 589 04 63 01)

e
f
602 589 00 39 00
71112_MBSV_G0082

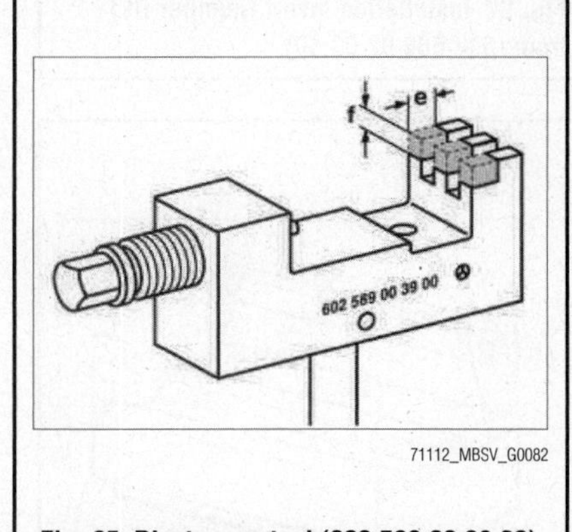

Fig. 95 Rivet press tool (602 589 00 39 00)

c = 6.5mm; Reference dimension d = 43.5mm

c. Mill or file off the area depicted in gray in the sketch by the dimension (e) and (f). Dimension e = 8.5mm; Dimension f = 7.2mm

d. Mill or file off the area depicted in gray in the sketch by the dimension (h) and (i). Dimension h = 11.5mm; Dimension i = 14mm

e. Mill or grind off the area depicted in gray in the sketch by the dimension (e). Dimension c =13.8mm; Chamfer the edges depicted in gray in the sketch by the dimension (n) for identifying the installation position. Dimension n = 3mm x 45 deg.

f. Mill or grind off the area depicted

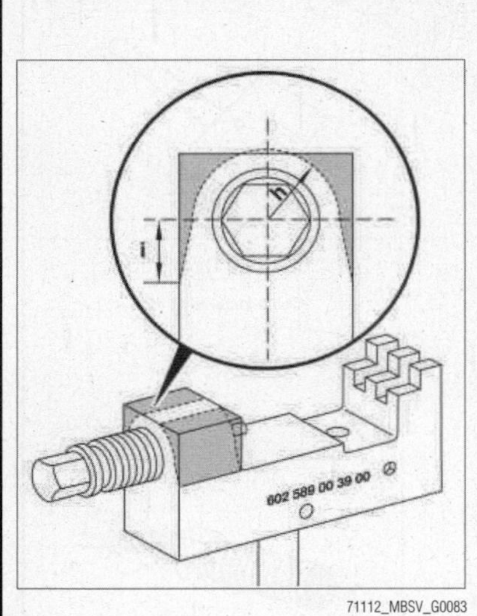

Fig. 96 Rivet press tool (602 589 00 39 00)

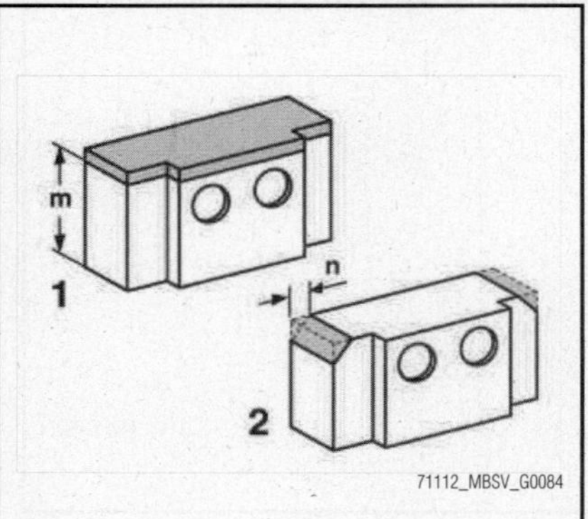

Fig. 97 Installation insert (number D9) from (602 589 02 63 00)

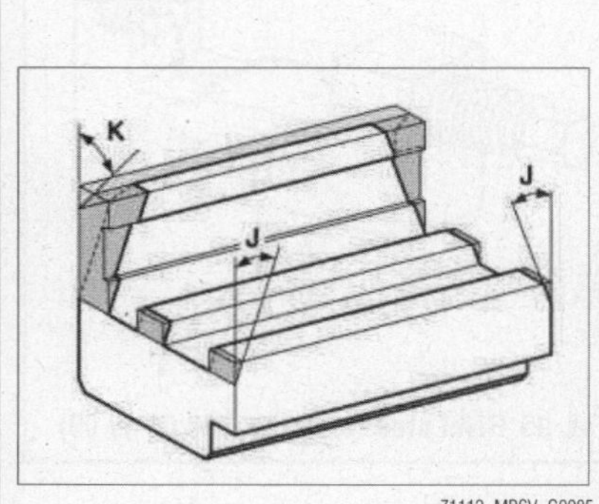

Fig. 98 Installation insert (number F1) from (112 589 09 63 00)

in gray in the sketch by the dimension (j) and (k). Dimension j = 20 deg.; Dimension k = 2X45 deg.

To install:

18. Position a new chain. Turn crankshaft from above at the bolt (2) to draw in timing chain (1):
    a. Cover timing case recess and cylinder head with clean rag.
    b. Connect new timing chain (1) and old timing chain (2) with the assembly connecting link (3), the outer assembly plate (4) and the assembly locking element (5).

➡The bores (arrow) of the new timing chain (1) must point outwards.

    c. Remove rag from timing case recess and cylinder head. Otherwise when cranking the engine, this can be drawn into the timing case recess.
    d. Slowly turn engine at center bolt of the crankshaft in the direction of engine rotation until the ends of the new control chain (1) can be connected.

➡During the pulling in procedure ensure that the old timing chain (2) and the new timing chain (1) is freely movable and cannot jam. The old timing chains (2) and new timing chains (1) are always held by hold-down device (6) in mesh with camshaft sprockets.

    e. Cover timing case recess and cylinder head with clean rag.
    f. Remove assembly locking element (5), outer assembly plate (4), assembly connecting link (3) and old timing chain (2).

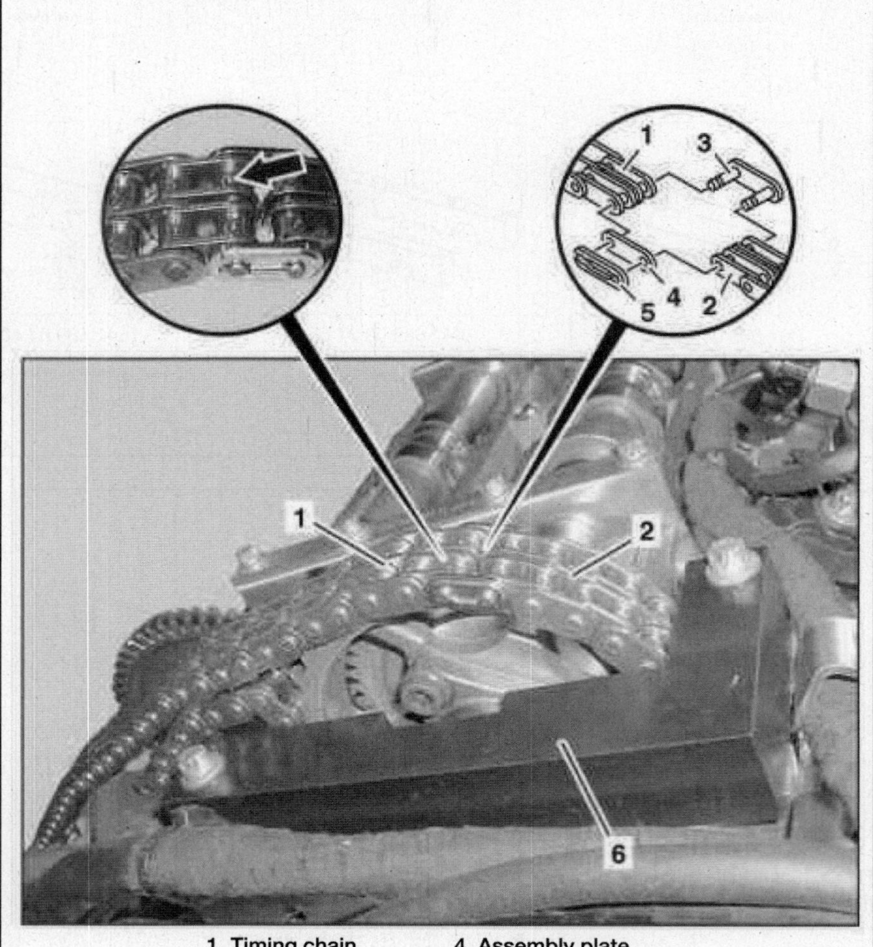

Fig. 99 Installing the chain

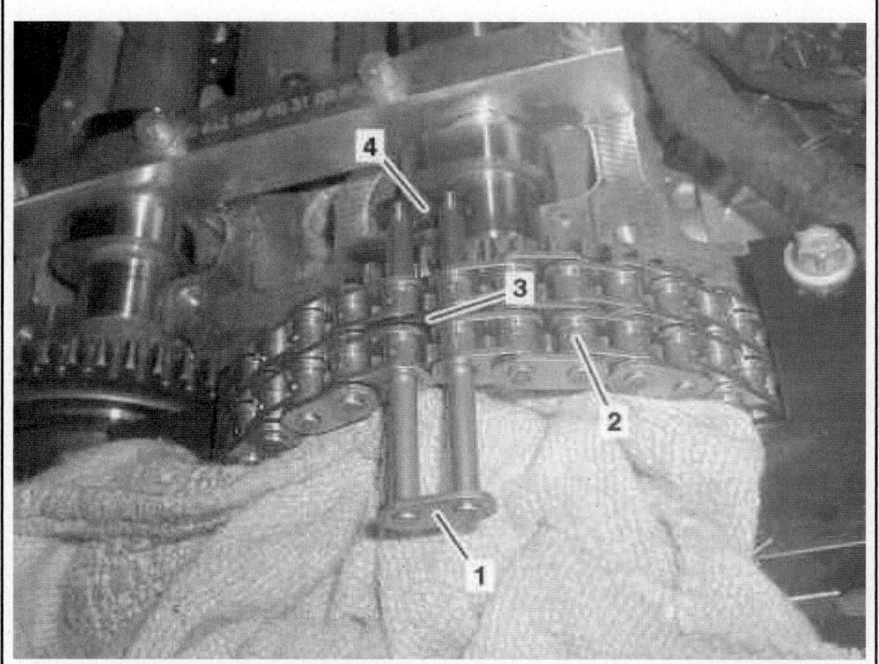

1. Centering fork
2. New timing chain
3. Middle plate
4. Riveted link

71112_MBSV_G0087

Fig. 100 Riveting the chain, 1 of 9

➡The engine does not start with the assembly locking element (5), the outer assembly plate (4) and the assembly connecting link (3) otherwise this can lead to engine damage. They are just assembly helpers and are not suitable for a running engine.

19. Rivet the timing chain:
   a. Cover timing case recess and cylinder head with shop towels.

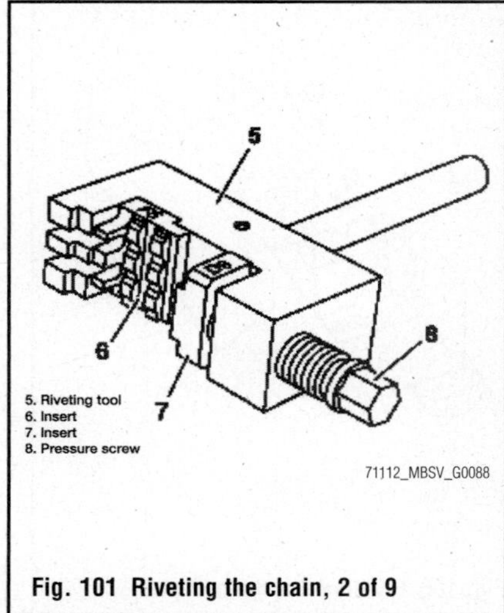

71112_MBSV_G0088

Fig. 101 Riveting the chain, 2 of 9

   b. Insert new riveted link (4) and new middle plate (3) together with centering fork (1) into the ends of the new timing chain (2). The new center axle (3) is secured with the centering fork (1).
   c. Insert and tighten assembly insert (6) with the digit F5 into the riveting tool (5).
   d. Place assembly insert (7) with the digit D9 into the riveting tool (5). The assembly insert (7) is able to move on pressure screw (8) and is loosely mounted.
   e. Bottom rivet press tool (5) in such a way that the new timing chain (2) that the assembly insert (7) touches the new riveted link and the centering fork (1) can be pressed out.
   f. Screw in thrust spindle (8) and press in new riveted link up to the stop. Remove centering fork (1). Ensure that riveted link and assembly insert (7) are aligned. Do not allow the centering fork (1) which is pressed out to drop into the timing case recess.
   g. Remove pressure screw (8) and rivet press tool (5).
   h. Remove assembly inserts (6, 7) from rivet press tool (5).

1. Centering fork
2. New timing chain
5. Press tool
6. Insert
7. Insert
8. Pressure screw

71112_MBSV_G0089

Fig. 102 Riveting the chain, 3 of 9

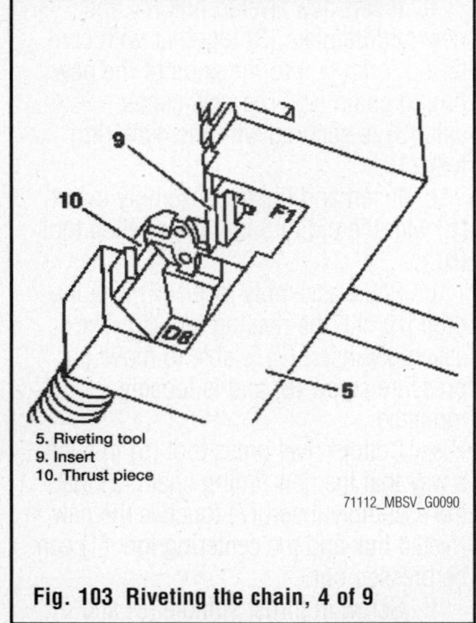

Fig. 103 Riveting the chain, 4 of 9

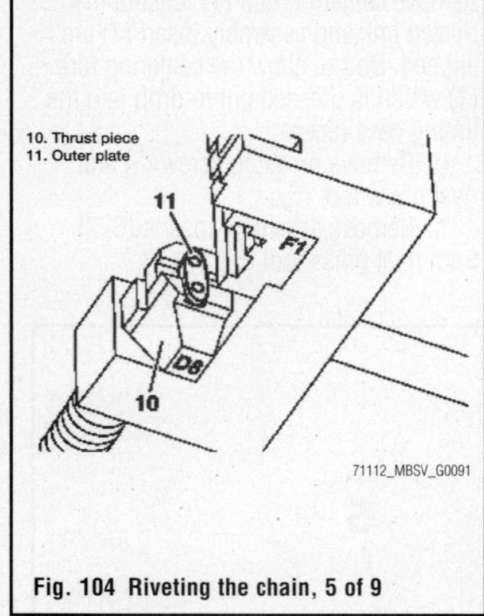

Fig. 104 Riveting the chain, 5 of 9

i. Insert and tighten assembly insert (9) with the digit F1 into the riveting tool (5).

j. Insert thrust piece (10) with digit D8 into the riveting tool (5).

k. Insert new outer plate (11) into the thrust piece (10). The new outer plate (11) is held firmly by the magnetic thrust piece (10).

l. Place rivet press tool (5) in such a way that the spacer bushing of the assembly insert (9) lies on the roll of the timing chain (2) (arrows). Ensure that riveted link and new outer plate are aligned.

m. Screw in pressure screw (8) on rivet press tool (5) until there is firm resistance. While pressing on ensure that the bolt of the new rivet link in the bores break in the new outer plate.

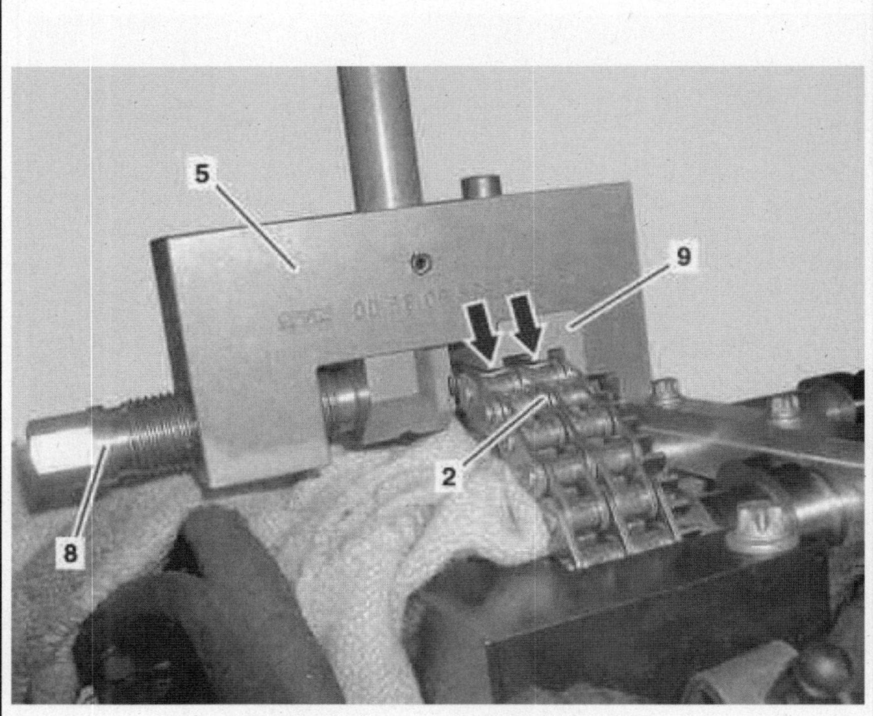

Fig. 105 Riveting the chain, 6 of 9

n. Remove pressure screw (8) and rivet press tool (5).

o. Turn thrust piece (10) in the rivet press tool (5) on the rivet profile (arrow).

p. Fit rivet press tool (5) at the center onto one of both timing chain pins of the new riveted link (arrow).

q. Tighten thrust spindle (8) of the rivet press tool (5) and rivet first timing chain bolt for the new riveted link. Observe tightening torque.

r. Loosen pressure screw (8) by turning and place rivet press tool (5) on second first timing chain bolt for the new riveted link.

s. Tighten pressure screw (8) on rivet press tool (5) and rivet second timing chain bolt. Observe tightening torque.

t. Loosen pressure screw (8) and remove rivet press tool (5).

u. Check both rivets (arrow) on the new timing chain (2); re-rivet if necessary.

v. Remove rag from timing case recess and cylinder head.

20. Remove hold-down device (5).
21. Fit right cylinder head cover. Torque the cover bolts in the sequence shown, in 3 steps:
    - Step 1 bolts 8-11: 36 inch lbs. (4 Nm)
    - Step 2 bolts 1-30: 53 inch lbs. (6 Nm)
    - Step 3 bolts 1-30: 72 inch lbs. (8 Nm)
22. Attach glow output stage.

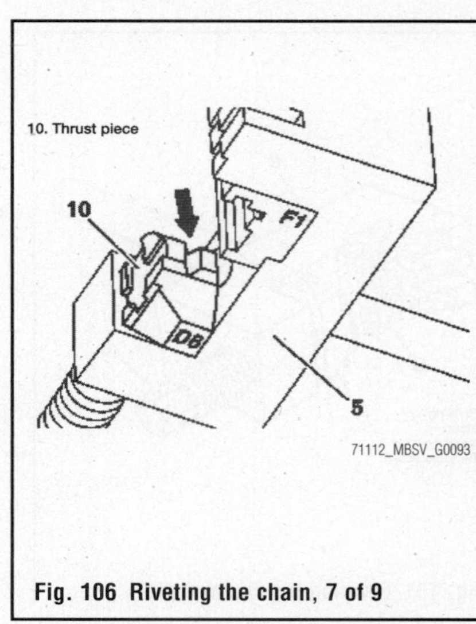

Fig. 106 Riveting the chain, 7 of 9

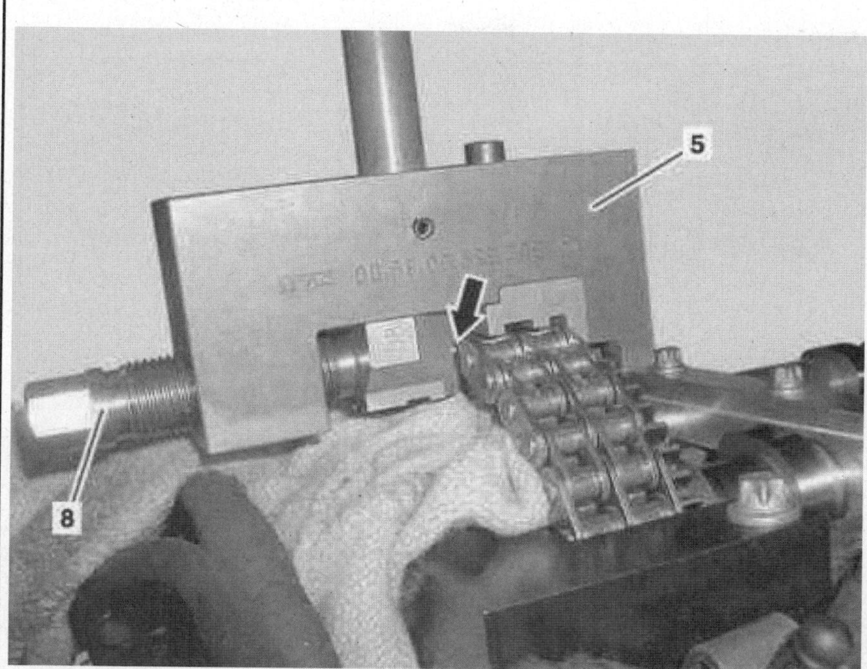

Fig. 107 Riveting the chain, 8 of 9

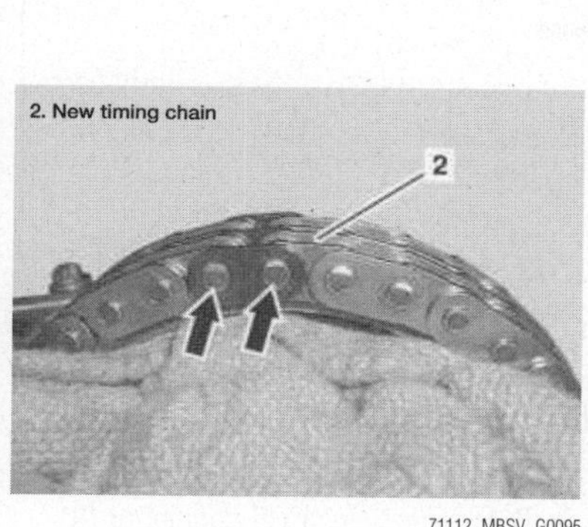

Fig. 108 Riveting the chain, 9 of 9

23. Attach viscous fan clutch.
24. Observe the following torques:
   - Glow output stage-to-bracket: 72 inch lbs. (8 Nm)
   - Vacuum pump-to-cylinder head: 84 inch lbs. (9 Nm)
   - Oil dipstick tube: 106 inch lbs. (12 Nm)
   - Oil separator-to-cylinder head: 84 inch lbs. (9 Nm)
   - Oil separator connection fitting: 84 inch lbs. (9 Nm)

TURBOCHARGER

REMOVAL & INSTALLATION

See Figures 63 and 109 through 115.

1. Before servicing the vehicle, refer to the Precautions section.

**** CAUTION**

When draining the coolant, keep in mind that cats and dogs are attracted by the ethylene glycol antifreeze, and are quite likely to drink any that is left in an uncovered container or in puddles on the ground. This will prove fatal in sufficient quantity. Always drain the coolant into a sealable container. Coolant should be reused unless it is contaminated or several years old.

2. Remove trim panel on right cylinder head cover. See the procedure in this section.
3. Remove the right side air filter housing bracket from the firewall:
   a. Unclip coolant hose (4) from bracket (5).
   b. Detach rubber mount (6) with circulation pump (M13/4) or heater circulation pump (M13/51) on bracket (7).
   c. Remove bracket (7) from firewall.
   d. Attach coolant hose (4) and circulation pump (M13/4) or heater circulation pump (M13/51) upwards.
4. Remove noise damper on turbocharger (6):
   a. Remove air intake hose downstream of air filter.
   b. Unscrew bolt from bracket (7) and pull out bracket (7).
   c. Unscrew bolts (10) from tensioning shackle (9) and engine charge air duct (1).
   d. Remove bolts (6, 8) on noise damper (5).
   e. Unscrew bolts (3) from tensioning shackle (2) and engine charge air duct (1).
   f. Unclip vacuum line (4) from cover on left cylinder head cover.
   g. Remove noise damper (5) with engine charge air duct (1). Clean open connections on charge air system and close. On installation, replace seal rings and coat with antifriction paste DB specification 6867.00, or equivalent.
   h. Remove noise damper (5) from engine charge air duct (1). On installation, replace seal ring and coat with antifriction paste, DB specification 6867.00, or equivalent.
5. Remove rear exhaust gas recirculation pipe (9) from exhaust recirculation pipe (10) to exhaust gas recirculation bypass flap.
   a. Remove exhaust gas recirculation pipe (6).
   b. Remove catalytic converter exhaust pipe (1) to exhaust gas turbocharger.
   c. Remove rear exhaust gas recirculation pipe (3) from exhaust collector pipe (2). On installation, replace seal (10).
   d. Remove clamp (4) on rear exhaust gas recirculation pipes (3) from bracket.
   e. Unscrew bolt (8) on exhaust pipe (9) from bracket (7).
   f. Remove bracket (7) at cylinder head. On installation, screw in bolt (8) on exhaust pipe (9) before tightening bracket (7).

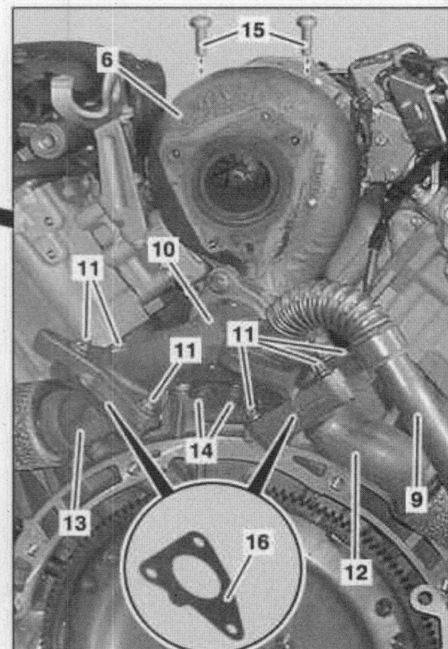

Shown on engine 642.896

1. Rail
2. Bracket
3. Electrical connector (engine 642.896/898)
4. Electrical connector
5. Electrical line (engine 642.896/898)
6. Turbocharger
7. Support brace
8. Bolts
9. Rear exhaust gas recirculation pipe
10. Exhaust collector pipe
11. Bolts
12. Exhaust manifold on the right
13. Exhaust manifold on the left
14. Bolts
15. Bolts
16. Gasket

Y77/1. Charge air actuator (engine 642.993)
Y77/8. Charge air actuator (engine 642.896/898)

71112_MBSV_G0098

Fig. 109 Turbocharger removal/installation

g. Disconnect oxygen sensor connector (B85/3x1) and expose electrical line.

h. Disconnect electrical connector (20) from temperature sensor upstream of CAT (B19/18) and expose electrical line.

i. Remove pressure hose (21) from pressure lines (12).

j. Remove clamp (5) on rear exhaust gas recirculation pipes (3) from bracket.

k. Remove clamp (17) from catalytic converter with diesel particulate filter (16).

l. Remove tensioning strap (15) from catalytic converter with diesel particulate filter (16).

m. Expose electrical line on temperature sensor upstream of diesel particulate filter (B19/19).

n. Press off catalytic converter with diesel particulate filter (16) and pull at side toward rear.

WARNING

Carefully pull catalytic converter with diesel particulate filter (16) toward rear to prevent damaging electrical line (18), oxygen sensor (B85/3), temperature sensor upstream of diesel particulate filter (B19/19) and pressure lines (12). Do not damage temperature sensor upstream of diesel particulate filter (B19/19), NOx sensor (19) and pressure hoses (21).

o. Turn rear exhaust gas recirculation pipe (3) and remove.

p. Clean sealing surfaces on exhaust collector pipe (2).

➡Press rear exhaust gas recirculation pipe (9) toward rear only; do not remove.

6. Remove bracket (2) from rail (1).
7. Disconnect electrical connector (3) from temperature sensor upstream of exhaust gas turbocharger (B16/11). Expose electrical line (5) from temperature sensor upstream of exhaust gas turbocharger (B16/11).
8. Disconnect electrical connector (4) from charge air actuator (Y77/1, Y77/8).
9. Unscrew bolts (8) and remove support (7).
10. Remove bolts (11). On installation, replace seals (16) and bolts (11).
11. Remove bolts (14) from bottom. Use new bolts (14).

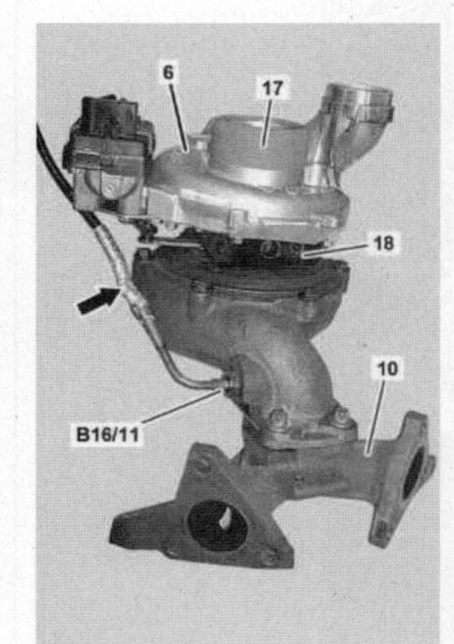

6. Turbocharger
10. Exhaust collector pipe
17. Sealing ring
18. Gasket
B16/11. Temperature sensor upstream of exhaust gas turbocharger (engine 642.896/898)

71112_MBSV_G0099

Fig. 110 Turbocharger disassembled

12. Remove bolts (15). Use new bolts.

13. Lift turbocharger (6) up and out. To prevent damage, close off openings on turbocharger (6), left exhaust manifold (12), right exhaust manifold (13) and on oil supply connection fitting, using suitable stop plugs. Collect escaping engine oil and remove dirt if necessary. On installation, install a new sealing ring (17) and seal (18). Replace seals (16) and fix seals (16) in place with four new bolts (11) on exhaust collector pipe (10) before inserting exhaust gas turbocharger (6).

14. If a new turbocharger is being installed, unscrew temperature sensor upstream of exhaust gas turbocharger (B16/11) from exhaust gas turbocharger (6).

➡On installation, when tightening temperature sensor upstream of exhaust gas turbocharger (B16/11), ensure that electrical line (5) is routed correctly. The heat protection hose (arrow) must be located in the area of the exhaust gas turbocharger (6).

15. If a new turbocharger is being installed, or in the case of leakage between exhaust collector pipe (10) and turbocharger (6), replace seal between turbocharger (6) and exhaust collector (10).

16. Clean sealing surfaces on right exhaust manifold (12), left exhaust manifold (13) and exhaust collector pipe (10).

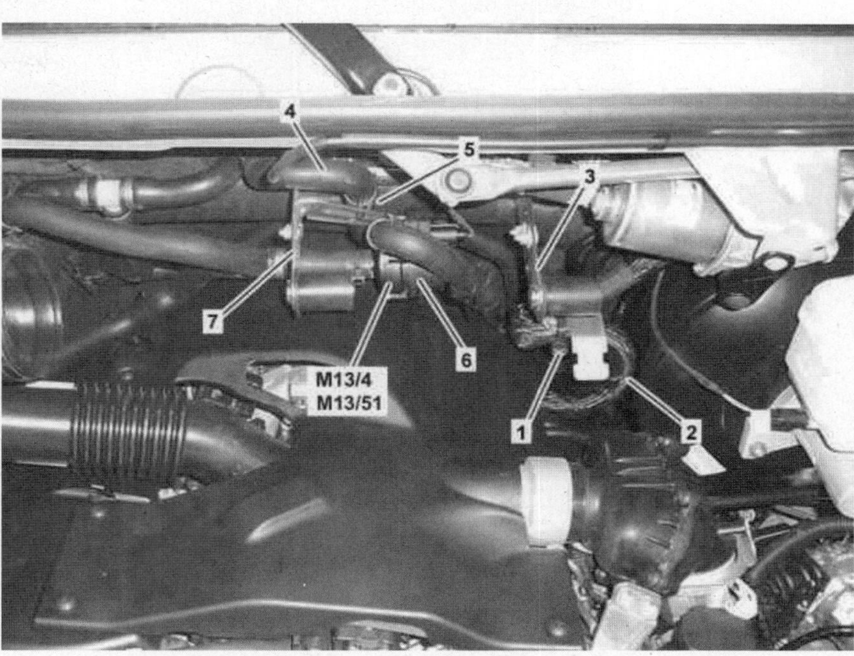

Shown on engine 642 with code (HH9) Regulated air conditioning, (Tempmatic)

1. Cable tie
2. Engine wiring harness
3. Bracket
4. Coolant hose
5. Bracket
6. Rubber bushing
7. Bracket

Circulation pump (for code (H12) Auxiliary heater (hot water)
Or for code (H13) Additional heat exchanger in cargo area
Or for code (H13) Additional heat exchanger in cargo area
Or for code (HH9) Regulated air conditioning, (Tempmatic)
Or for code (HZ5) 10 kW auxiliary water heater with timer
Or for code (HZ9) Heater booster, diesel)
M13/51. Heater circulation pump (for code (ZL9) Motor home "James Cook"
Or for code (ZO1) Camper James Cook Compact
Or for code for code (ZO2) Camper James Cook Classic
Or for code (ZO3) Camper James Cook Comfort)

71112_MBSV_G0100

Fig. 111 Right side air cleaner bracket removal/installation

17. Clean sealing surfaces on exhaust gas turbocharger (6).

18. Installation is the reverse of removal. Observe the following torques:

- Turbocharger-to-charge air manifold: 84 inch lbs. (10 Nm)
- Exhaust manifold-to-collector connection: 15 ft. lbs. (20 Nm) +90degrees
- Support brace-to-collector: 22 ft. lbs. (30 Nm)
- Turbocharger-to-collector: 15 ft. lbs. (20 Nm) +90 degrees
- Exhaust temperature sensor: 33 ft. lbs. (45 Nm)
- Charge air duct-to-holder: 79 inch lbs. (9 Nm)
- Noise damper-to-holder: 79 inch lbs. (9 Nm)
- Turbocharger-to-charge air manifold: 84 inch lbs. (10 Nm)
- Turbocharger-to-oil fed fitting: Step 1, 84 inch lbs. (10 Nm); Step 2, 22 ft. lbs. (30 Nm)

VALVE LASH (CLEARANCE)

ADJUSTMENT

Valve lash is maintained by hydraulic valve play compensation elements No adjustment is necessary.

Shown on engine 642.896

1. Engine charge air duct
2. Tensioning shackle
3. Screw
4. Vacuum line
5. Noise damper
6. Screw
7. Bracket
8. Bolts
9. Tensioning shackle
10. Bolts

71112_MBSV_G0101

Fig. 112 Turbocharger noise damper removal/installation

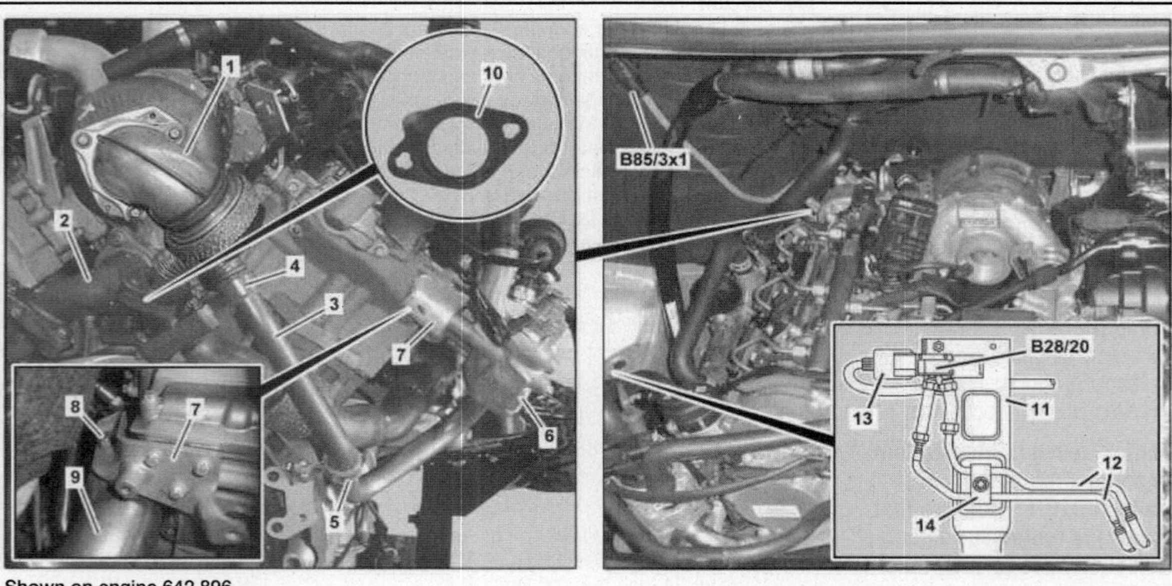

Shown on engine 642.896

1. Catalytic converter exhaust pipe
2. Exhaust collector pipe
3. Rear exhaust gas recirculation pipe
4. Clip
5. Clip
6. Exhaust gas recirculation
7. Bracket
8. Screw
9. Exhaust pipe
10. Gasket
11. Bracket
12. Pressure lines
13. Electrical connector
14. Bracket
B28/20. Diesel particulate filter differential pressure sensor
B85/3x1. Oxygen sensor connector

71112_MBSV_G0102

Fig. 113 Rear exhaust gas recirculation pipe removal/installation, 1 of 3

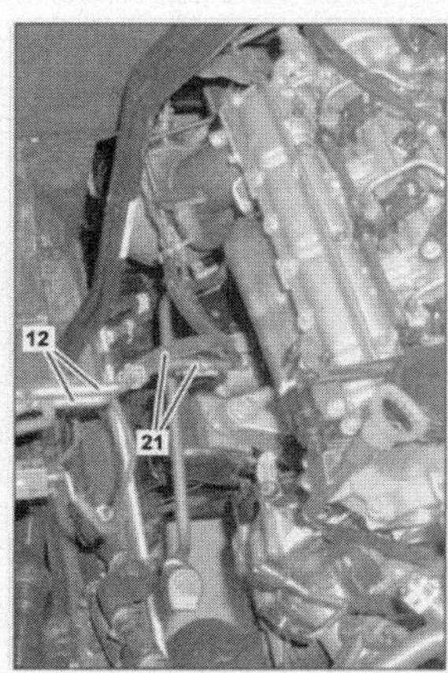

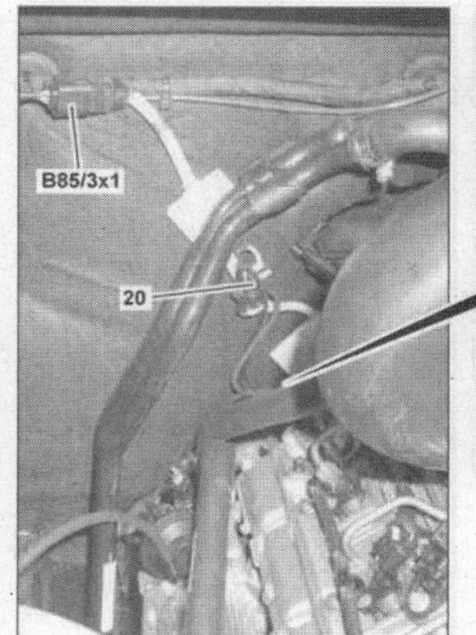

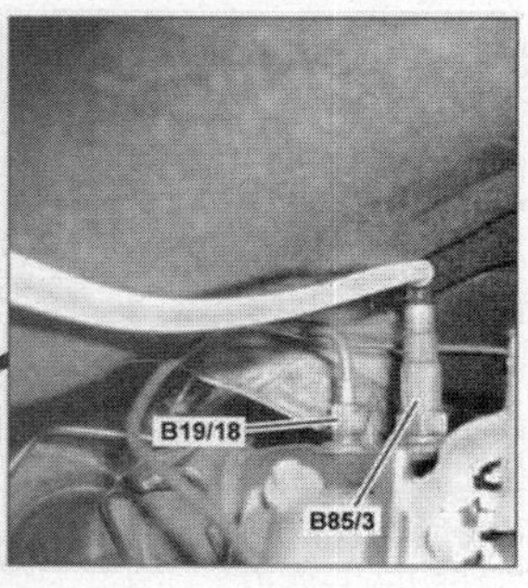

Shown on engine 642.898

12. Pressure lines
20. Electrical connector (engine 642.898)
21. Pressure hoses
B19/18. Temperature sensor upstream of CAT (Engine 642.898)
B85/3x1. Oxygen sensor connector
B85/3. Oxygen sensor

71112_MBSV_G0103

Fig. 114 Rear exhaust gas recirculation pipe removal/installation, 2 of 3

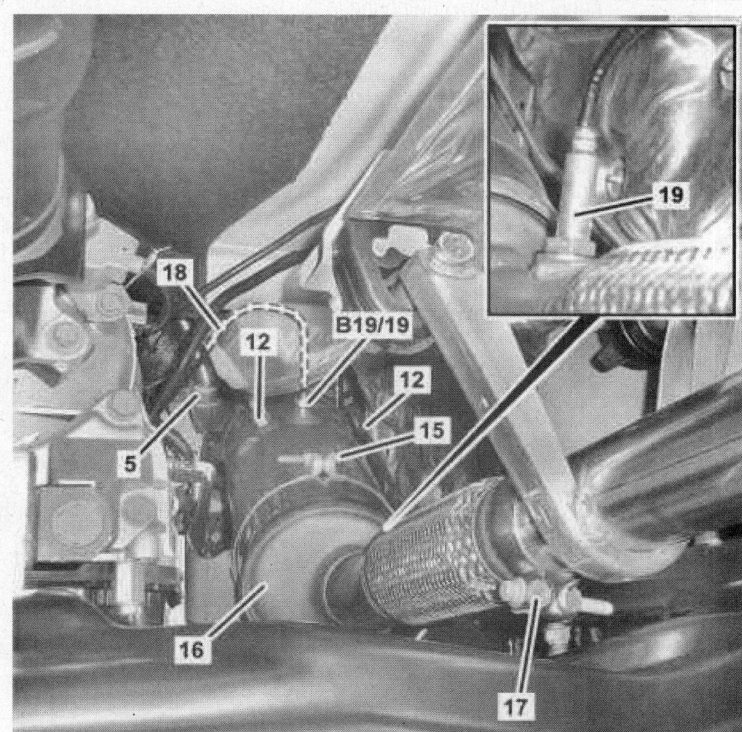

Shown on engine 642.898

5. Clip
12. High pressure line
15. Tensioning strap
16. Catalytic converter with diesel particulate filter
17. Clip
18. Electrical line
19. NOx sensor (engine 642.898)
B19/19. Temperature sensor upstream of diesel particulate filter

71112_MBSV_G0104

Fig. 115 Rear exhaust gas recirculation pipe removal/installation, 3 of 3

ENGINE PERFORMANCE & EMISSION CONTROLS

CAMSHAFT POSITION SENSOR

LOCATION

See Figure 89

The sensor is located on the right side cylinder head cover.

REMOVAL & INSTALLATION

Disconnect the wiring and unbolt it from the cover. On installation, torque the bolt to 72 inch lbs. (8 Nm).

CATALYTIC CONVERTER TEMPERATURE SENSOR

LOCATION

The sensor is located in the catalytic converter.

REMOVAL & INSTALLATION

See Figure 116.

1. Before servicing the vehicle, refer to the Precautions section.
2. Expose electrical connector (1) and disconnect.
3. Unscrew union nut on temperature sensor upstream of CAT (B19/18) from catalytic converter exhaust pipe (2).
4. Pull temperature sensor upstream CAT (B19/18) out catalytic converter exhaust pipe (2).
5. Installation is the reverse of removal. Apply anti-seize compound to the threads. Torque the sensor to 33 ft. lbs. (45 Nm).

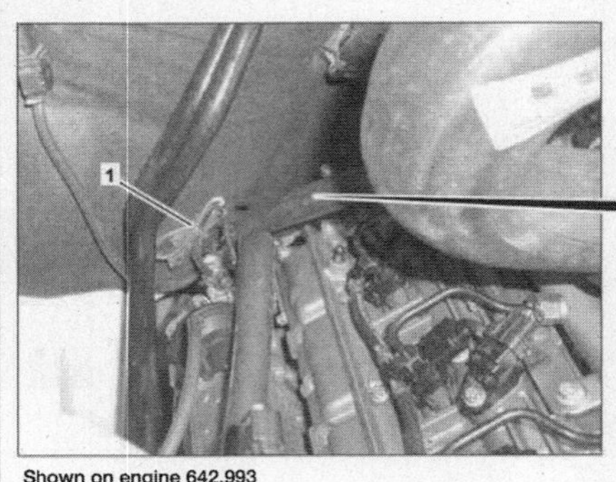

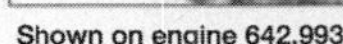

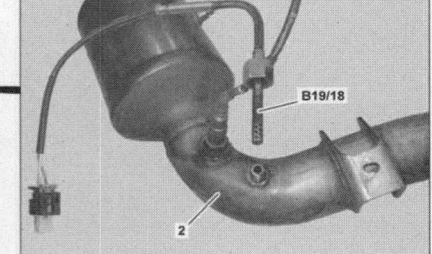

Shown on engine 642.993

1. Electrical connector
2. Catalytic convert exhaust pipe
B19/18. Temperature sensor upstream of TWC [KAT]

71112_MBSV_G0117

Fig. 116 Catalytic converter temperature sensor

CATALYTIC CONVERTER PARTICULATE FILTER

LOCATION

See the illustrations in the Removal & Installation procedure.

REMOVAL & INSTALLATION

See Figures 45, 63 117 and 118.

1. Before servicing the vehicle, refer to the Precautions section.
2. Remove trim panel on right cylinder head cover. See the procedure in this section.
3. Unscrew bolts (7, 8) and remove shield (6).
4. Remove clamp (9). On installation, push wire mesh ring (11) upward onto exhaust pipe (10) and install clamp (9).

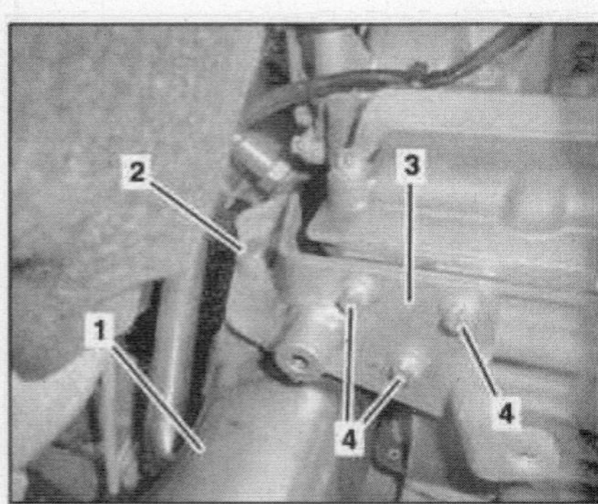

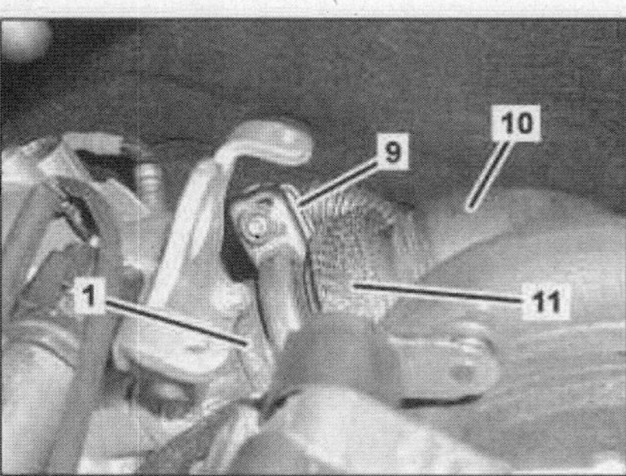

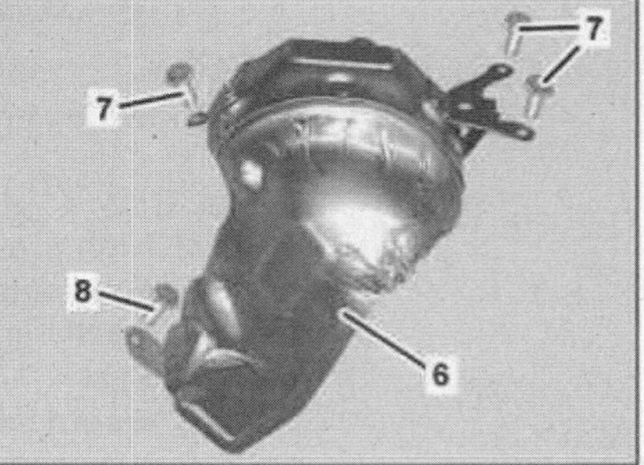

1. Catalytic converter with diesel particulate filter
2. Screw
3. Bracket
4. Bolts
5. Cover
6. Shield
7. Bolts
8. Screw
9. Clip
10. Exhaust pipe
11. Wire mesh ring

71112_MBSV_G0123

Fig. 117 Particulate filter removal/installation, 1 of 2

5. Position exhaust pipe of catalytic converter with diesel particulate filter (1) and push back wire mesh ring (11).

6. Remove oxygen sensor. See the procedure in this section.

7. Remove catalytic converter temperature sensor upstream of catalytic converter. See the procedure in this section.

8. Remove exhaust gas recirculation valve. See the procedure in this section.

9. Remove bolts (2, 4) and bracket (3). On installation, screw exhaust pipe on catalytic converter with diesel particulate filter (1) to bracket (3) with bolt (2) and then tighten bracket (3) to cylinder head with bolts (4). Tighten bolts (2) fully.

10. Raise and safely support the vehicle.

11. Remove NOx sensor (18) with NOx sensor control unit. See the procedure in this section.

12. Remove clamp (16) from catalytic converter with diesel particulate filter (1).

13. Unscrew pressure lines (12) from catalytic converter with diesel particulate filter (1).

14. Unscrew temperature sensor upstream of diesel particulate filter (B19/19). On installation, coat threads with temperature upstream of diesel particulate filter (B19/19) with paste DB specification 6867.00, or equivalent. Ensure that the electrical line (14) is routed correctly.

15. Remove tensioning strap (13) from catalytic converter with diesel particulate filter (1).

16. Remove rear engine crossmember (17):

a. Lift transmission (5) with the transmission jack (3) and transmission plate until engine mount (4) is relieved.

➡In the case of transmission 722.6, the transmission jack (3) with transmission plate may only be placed on the outer edges of the transmission oil pan into to avoid damaging the transmission oil pan and underlying components. Underlay with suitable wooden blocks.

b. Remove bolts (6).

c. Mark installation position of rear engine crossmember (1). The mounting holes are arranged asymmetrically.

d. Unscrew bolts (2) and remove left rear engine crossmember (1).

e. Remove engine mount (4).

- Rear crossmember-to-engine mount: M8 bolts 22 ft. lbs. (30 Nm), M10 bolts 43 ft. lbs. (58 Nm).
- Transmission-to-frame type integral support 43 ft. lbs. (58 Nm).

1. Catalytic converter with diesel particulate filter
12. High pressure line
13. Tensioning strap
14. Electrical line
15. Heat shield
16. Clip
17. Rear engine crossmember
18. NOx sensor
B19/19. Temperature sensor upstream of diesel particulate filter

71112_MBSV_G0124

Fig. 118 Particulate filter removal/installation, 2 of 2

17. Pull out catalytic converter with diesel particulate filter (1) toward rear.

⁂ WARNING

Carefully pull catalytic converter with diesel particulate filter (1) toward rear to prevent damaging detachable parts. Slightly push heat shield (15) upward. Do not deform heat shield (15) when pushing up.

18. Clean sealing surface on exhaust system.

19. Installation is the reverse of removal. Observe the following torques:

- Rear crossmember-to-engine mount: M8 bolts 22 ft. lbs. (30 Nm), M10 bolts 43 ft. lbs. (58 Nm)
- Transmission-to-frame type integral support 43 ft. lbs. (58 Nm)
Shield-to-bolder bolts: 72 inch lbs. (8 Nm)
- Shield-to-collector pipe: 106 inch lbs. (12 Nm)
- Particulate filter strap-to-holder: 18 ft. lbs. (25 Nm)
- Particulate filter-to-cylinder head holder: 17 ft. lbs. (23 Nm)
- Particulate filter clamp-to-exhaust pipe: 13 ft. lbs. (18 Nm)
- Bracket-to-cylinder head: 79 inch lbs. (9 Nm)
- Particulate filter-to-converter: 26 ft. lbs. (35 Nm)
- Pressure line-to-particulate filter: 33 ft. lbs. (45 Nm)
- Temperature sensor on particulate filter: 33 ft. lbs. (45 Nm)

CRANKSHAFT POSITION SENSOR

LOCATION

See the illustration in the Removal & Installation procedure.

REMOVAL & INSTALLATION

See Figure 119.

1. Before servicing the vehicle, refer to the Precautions section.

2. Raise and safely support the vehicle.

3. Disconnect electrical connector (1) from crankshaft sensor (B70/1 or L5).

4. Unscrew bolt (2) and remove crankshaft sensor (B70/1 or L5).

5. Installation is the reverse of removal. Torque the sensor to 79 inch lbs. (9 Nm).

1. Electrical connector
2. Screw

B70/1. Crankshaft sensor (on engine 642.896/898)
L5. Crankshaft sensor (on engine 642.992/993)

71112_MBSV_G0131

Fig. 119 Crankshaft position sensor

EXHAUST GAS RECIRCULATION VALVE

LOCATION

See the illustrations in the Removal & Installation procedure.

REMOVAL & INSTALLATION

See Figures 136 through 137, 120 through 123.

1. Before servicing the vehicle, refer to the Precautions section.
2. Disconnect battery ground cable.
3. Drain coolant.

**** CAUTION**

When draining the coolant, keep in mind that cats and dogs are attracted by the ethylene glycol antifreeze, and are quite likely to drink any that is left in an uncovered container or in puddles on the ground. This will prove fatal in sufficient quantity. Always drain the coolant into a sealable container. Coolant should be reused unless it is contaminated or several years old.

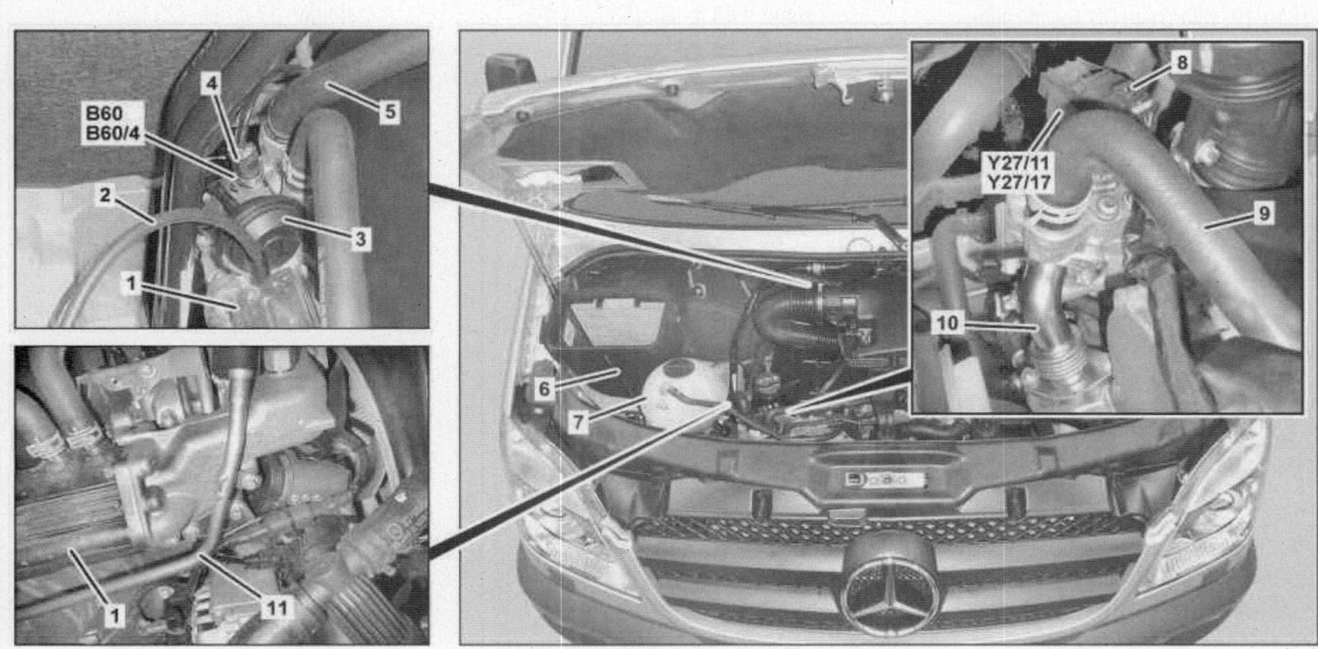

1. Exhaust gas recirculation
2. Vacuum line
3. Aneroid capsule
4. Electrical connector
5. Coolant hose
6. Ventilation box
7. Expansion reservoir
8. Electrical connector
9. Coolant hose
10. Front exhaust gas recirculation pipe
11. Oil filler line (transmission 722)

B60. Exhaust back pressure sensor (engine 642.993)
B60/4. Exhaust back pressure sensor (engine 642.898/ 989)
Y27/11. Exhaust gas recirculation positioner (engine 642.993)
Y27/17. Exhaust gas recirculation positioner (engine 642.898/ 989)

71112_MBSV_G0127

Fig. 120 EGR removal/installation, 1 of 2

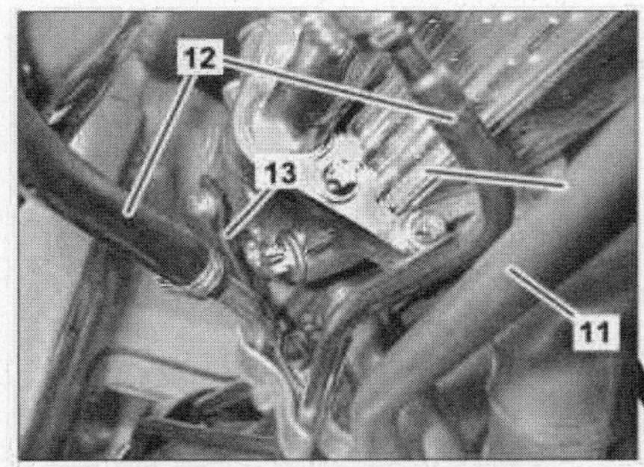

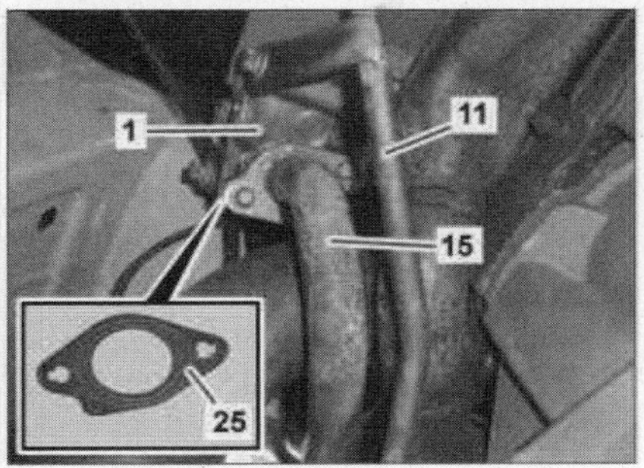

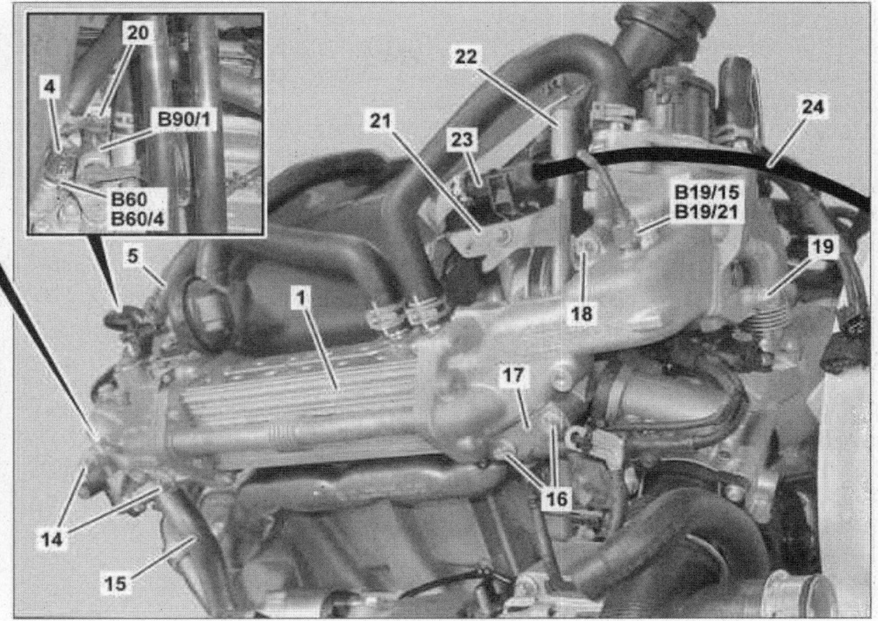

1. Exhaust gas recirculation
4. Electrical connector
5. Coolant hose
11. Oil filler line (transmission 722)
12. Pressure lines
13. Bracket
14. Bolts
15. Rear exhaust gas recirculation pipe
16. Bolts
17. Bracket
18. Screw
19. Screw
20. Electrical connector
21. Bracket
22. Oil dipstick guide tube
23. Drain pipe Fuel filter with water deflector (engine 642.898/993 with code (KL5)
24. Drain pipe (engine 642.898/993 with code (KL5) Fuel filter with water deflector)
25. Gasket

B19/15. Exhaust gas recirculation cooler temperature sensor (engine 642.993)
B19/21. Exhaust gas recirculation cooler temperature sensor (engine 642.898)
B60. Exhaust back pressure sensor (engine 642.993)
B60/4. Exhaust back pressure sensor (engine 642.896/898)
B90/1. End position sensor for exhaust gas recirculation cooler (engine 642.993)

71112_MBSV_G0128

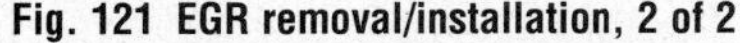

Fig. 121 EGR removal/installation, 2 of 2

4. Remove expansion reservoir (1) and lay down to side. Do not detach electrical connector and coolant hose:
    a. Unscrew cap from expansion reservoir (1). Draw off coolant from the expansion reservoir (1) using the hand pump.
    b. Remove bolts (7) and bracket (8) with AdBlue® filler neck from expansion reservoir (1). Lift bracket (8) until the expansion reservoir (1) can be taken out of the guide.
    c. Detach coolant hoses (2, 3) at expansion reservoir (1).
    d. Lift expansion reservoir (1) and disconnect electrical connector (6) at coolant level indicator switch (S41) 8 Take out expansion reservoir (1).
5. Remove ventilation box (6):
    a. Unscrew nuts (2).
    b. Pull ventilation box (1) away from bulkhead and remove upwards from guide (arrow).

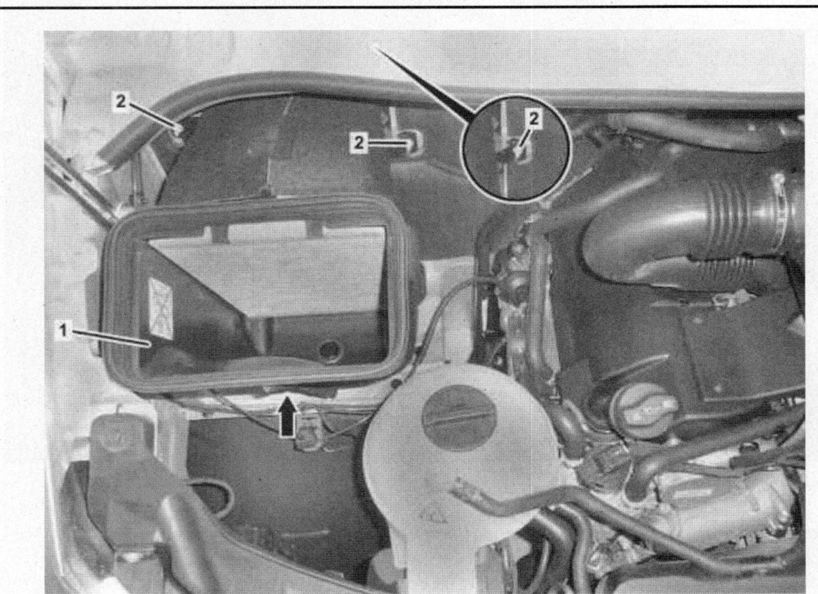

71112_MBSV_G0129

Fig. 122 Ventilation box removal/installation

6. Raise and safely support the vehicle.

7. Remove rear exhaust gas recirculation pipe (15) from exhaust gas recirculation valve (1). On installation, replace seal (25).

8. Lower the vehicle.

9. Disconnect electrical connector (8) from exhaust gas recirculation positioner (Y27/11 or Y27/17).

10. Unscrew exhaust gas recirculation cooler temperature sensor (B19/15 or B19/21), pull out of exhaust gas recirculation (1) and expose electrical line. On installation, apply paste DB specification 6879.20, or equivalent, to thread on exhaust gas recirculation cooler temperature sensor (B19/15 or B19/21).

11. Remove coolant hoses (5, 9) from exhaust gas recirculation valve (1).

12. Remove front exhaust gas recirculation pipe (10) from exhaust gas recirculation valve to mixing chamber:

a. Unscrew bolts (3) and remove exhaust gas recirculation pipe (4). Turn exhaust gas recirculation pipe (4) counterclockwise when removing mixing chamber (5). On installation, unscrew bolts (2, 3) by hand until flange surface make uniform contact.

b. Remove gaskets (6). On installation, replace seals (6).

c. Clean sealing surfaces on mixing chamber (5) and clean housing of exhaust gas recirculation valve (1).

d. Clean sealing surfaces on exhaust gas recirculation pipe (4).

13. Remove drain hose (24) from drain pipe (23).

14. Remove vacuum line (2) from aneroid capsule (3).

15. Disconnect electrical connector (4) from exhaust back pressure sensor (B60 or B60/4).

16. Remove oil dipstick guide tube (22) from bracket (21) and press to side.

17. Remove oil filler line (11) from bracket (13) and press to side.

18. Remove bracket (13) on pressure lines (12) from exhaust gas recirculation (1) and press to side.

19. Unscrew bolts (14) from exhaust gas recirculation valve (1).

20. Unscrew bolts (16) from bracket (17) and exhaust gas recirculation (1).

21. Unscrew bolt (19). The bolt (19) cannot be pulled out.

22. Unscrew bolt (18) and remove exhaust gas recirculation (1) upward. On installation, before positioning exhaust gas recirculation (1), insert bolt (19) into hole on flange of exhaust gas recirculation (1).

23. Clean sealing surfaces on rear exhaust gas recirculation pipe (15).

24. Clean sealing surfaces on exhaust gas recirculation (1).

25. Installation is the reverse of removal. Observe the following torques:

- EGR pipe-to-valve housing: 115 ft. lbs. (13 Nm)
- EGR pipe-to-mixing chamber: 79 inch lbs. (9 Nm)
- EGR pipe-to-bypass flap: 79 inch lbs. (9 Nm)
- EGR valve housing-to-bracket, M8x20 bolt: 21 ft. lbs. (28 Nm)
- EGR valve housing-to-bracket M8x80 bolt: 15 ft. lbs. (20 Nm)
- EGR bypass flap-to-bracket: 15 ft. lbs. (20 Nm)
- Temperature sensor-to-EGR valve: 33 ft. lbs. (45 Nm)

EXHAUST GAS RECIRCULATION COOLANT TEMPERATURE SENSOR

LOCATION

The sensor is located in the coolant manifold.

REMOVAL & INSTALLATION

See Figure 124.

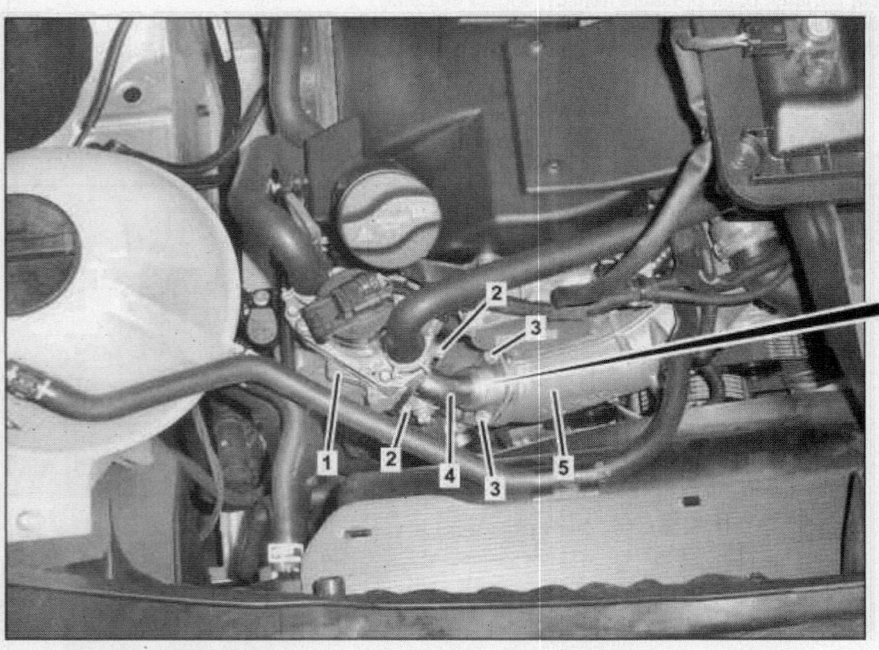

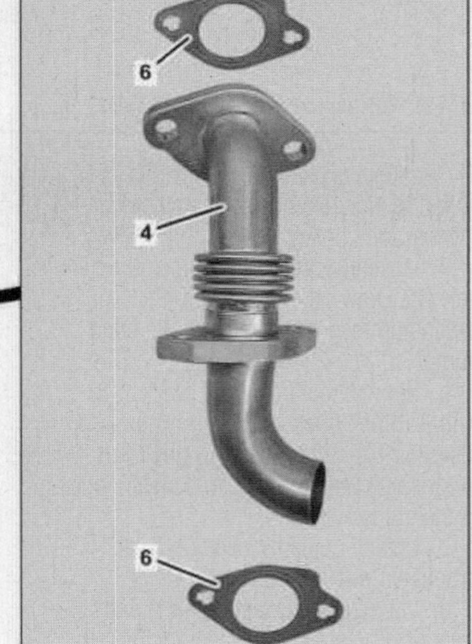

Shown on engine 642.896

1. Exhaust gas recirculation valve housing pipe
2. Screw
3. Screw
4. Exhaust gas recirculation
5. Mixing chamber
6. Gasket

71112_MBSV_G0130

Fig. 123 Front EGR pipe removal/installation

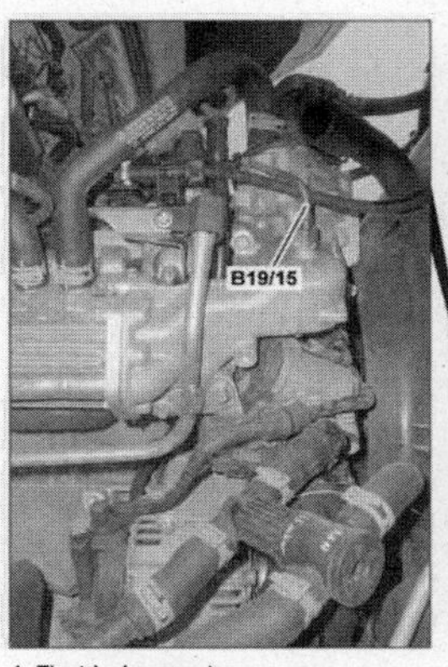

1. Electrical connector
2. Electrical line
B19/15. Exhaust gas recirculation cooler temperature sensor

71112_MBSV_G0118

Fig. 124 EGR Coolant temperature sensor

1. Before servicing the vehicle, refer to the Precautions section.
2. Expose electrical line (2) on exhaust gas recirculation cooler temperature sensor (B19/15).
3. Disconnect electrical connector (1).
4. Unscrew exhaust gas recirculation cooler temperature sensor (B19/15).
5. Installation is the reverse of removal. Apply sealer to the threads. Torque the sensor to 33 ft. lbs. (45 Nm).

INTAKE MANIFOLD PRESSURE SENSOR

LOCATION

See Figure 125.

The sensor is located in the air cleaner housing.

REMOVAL & INSTALLATION

See Figure 125.

1. Before servicing the vehicle, refer to the Precautions section.
2. Disconnect electrical connector (1) from intake manifold pressure sensor (B28, B28/17 or B28/19).
3. Unscrew bolts from intake manifold pressure sensor (B28, B28/17 or B28/19).
4. Pull intake manifold pressure sensor (B28, B28/17 or B28/19) out of air filter housing (2).
5. Installation is the reverse of removal. Use a new O-ring, if necessary.

MASS AIR FLOW SENSOR (HOT FILM)

LOCATION

The sensor is located in the air inlet tube at the air cleaner housing.

REMOVAL & INSTALLATION

See Figure 126.

1. Before servicing the vehicle, refer to the Precautions section.
2. Remove intake hose downstream of air filter (1) from hot film MAF sensor (B2/5, B2/7, B2/12 or B2/14).
3. Disconnect electrical connector (3) from hot film MAF sensor (B2/5, B2/7, B2/12 or B2/14).
4. Unscrew bolts from hot film MAF sensor (B2/5, B2/7, B2/12 or B2/14).
5. Pull hot film MAF sensor (B2/5, B2/7, B2/12 or B2/14) out of air filter housing (2). On installation, inspect O-ring, install new ring if necessary.
6. Installation is the reverse of removal.

NITROGEN OXIDE SENSOR

LOCATION

See the illustrations in the Removal & Installation procedure.

REMOVAL & INSTALLATION

See Figure 127.

1. Before servicing the vehicle, refer to the Precautions section.
2. Raise and safely support the vehicle.
3. Disconnect electrical connector (3).
4. Remove NOx sensor, upstream of SCR-CAT control unit (A97/1), from frame.
5. Expose electrical line (4).
6. Unscrew NOx sensor (1), upstream of SCR-CAT control unit (A97/1), from exhaust pipe (2).
7. Clean thread and sealing surfaces on exhaust pipe (2).
8. Installation is the reverse of removal. Torque the sensor to 44 ft. lbs. (60 Nm).

OXYGEN SENSOR

LOCATION

The sensor is located in the catalytic converter exhaust pipe.

REMOVAL & INSTALLATION

See Figures 63 and 128.

1. Before servicing the vehicle, refer to the Precautions section.
2. Remove air intake hose downstream of air filter.
3. Remove trim panel on right cylinder head cover. See the procedure in this section.
4. Disconnect lambda sensor connector (B85/3x1).
5. Expose electric wiring harness (1).
6. Unscrew oxygen sensor (B85/3) from catalytic converter exhaust pipe (3). On installation, coat thread of oxygen sensor (B85/3) with lubricant, DB specification 6869.20, or equivalent.

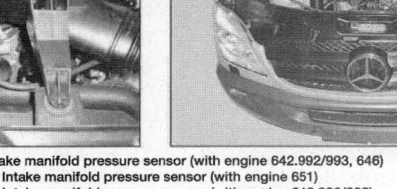

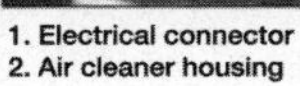
1. Electrical connector
2. Air cleaner housing

B28. Intake manifold pressure sensor (with engine 642.992/993, 646)
B28/17. Intake manifold pressure sensor (with engine 651)
B28/19. Intake manifold pressure sensor (with engine 642.896/898)

71112_MBSV_G0116

Fig. 125 Intake Manifold Pressure Sensor

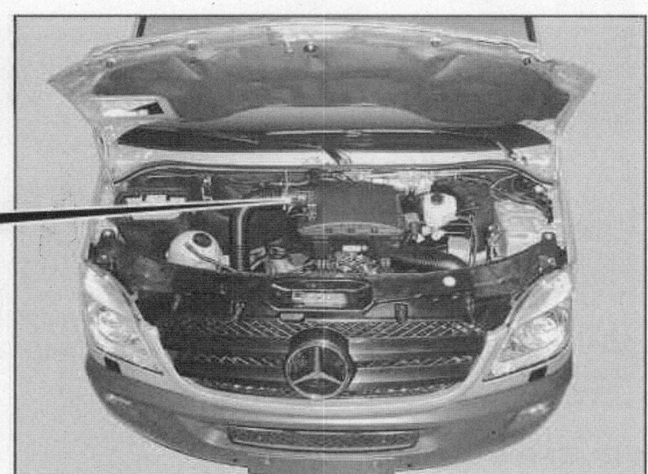

1. Intake hose downstream of air filter
2. Air cleaner housing
3. Electrical connector

B2/5. Hot film MAF sensor (with engine 646)
B2/7. Hot film MAF sensor (with engine 642.992/993)
B2/12. Hot film MAF sensor (with engine 651)
B2/14. Hot film MAF sensor (with engine 642.896/898)

71112_MBSV_G0132

Fig. 126 Mass air flow sensor

1. NOx sensor
2. Exhaust pipe
3. Electrical connector
4. Electrical line
A97/1. Control unit for NOx sensor upstream of SCR-CAT

71112_MBSV_G0126

Fig. 127 Nitrogen oxide sensor removal/installation

7. Installation is the reverse of removal. Torque the sensor to 33 ft. lbs. (45 Nm).

PARAMETERIZABLE SPECIAL MODULE (PSM)

LOCATION

See Figure 129.

The module is located under the driver's seat.

REMOVAL & INSTALLATION

See Figures 130 and 131.

1. Before servicing the vehicle, refer to the Precautions section.
2. Remove driver seat:
   a. Remove screw/bolt (1) and remove seat belt from driver seat (3).
   b. Remove screws/bolts (2) and remove driver seat (3).
3. Disconnect plug (1) and then plug (2) from PSM control unit (N26/15).

⁂ WARNING

It is essential to observe the specified sequence when disconnecting the plugs from the PSM control unit (N26/15) since failure to do so could result in damage to the PSM control unit (N26/15) and connected peripheral devices. On installation, connect the plugs (1, 2) in the reverse order. Failure to observe this point could result in damage to the PSM control unit (N26/15) and connected peripheral devices.

4. Unbolt PSM control unit (N26/15) inside seat frame.
5. Installation is the reverse of removal. Torque the seat belt bolts and seat bolts to 27 ft. lbs. (37 Nm). Recode PSM control unit (N26/15).

Shown on engine 642.896

1. Wiring harness
2. Cover
3. Catalytic converter exhaust pipe

B85/3. Oxygen sensor
B85/3x1. Oxygen sensor connector

71112_MBSV_G0125

Fig. 128 Oxygen sensor removal/installation

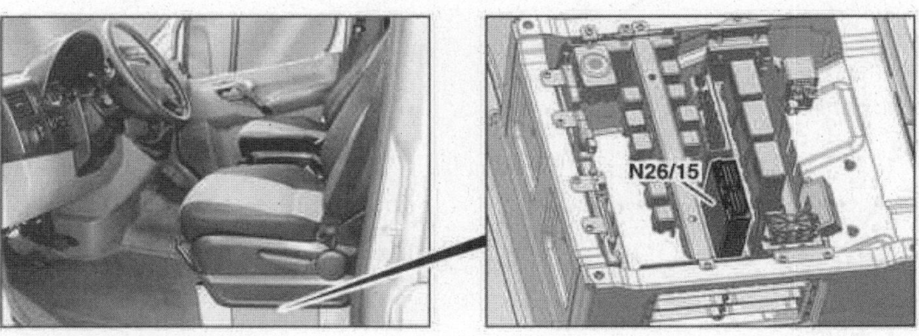

N26/15. PSM control unit

71112_MBSV_G0111

Fig. 129 PSM location

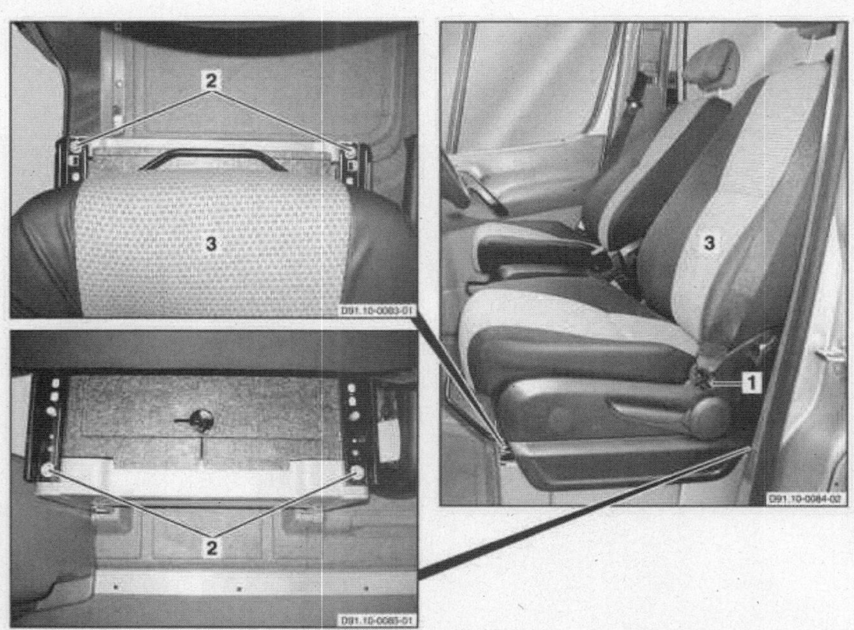

Shown on vehicle without code ZO1 James Cook Compact Camper and without code (ZO2) James Cook Classic Camper

1. Screw
2. Bolts
3. Driver seat

71112_MBSV_G0113

Fig. 130 Driver's seat removal/installation

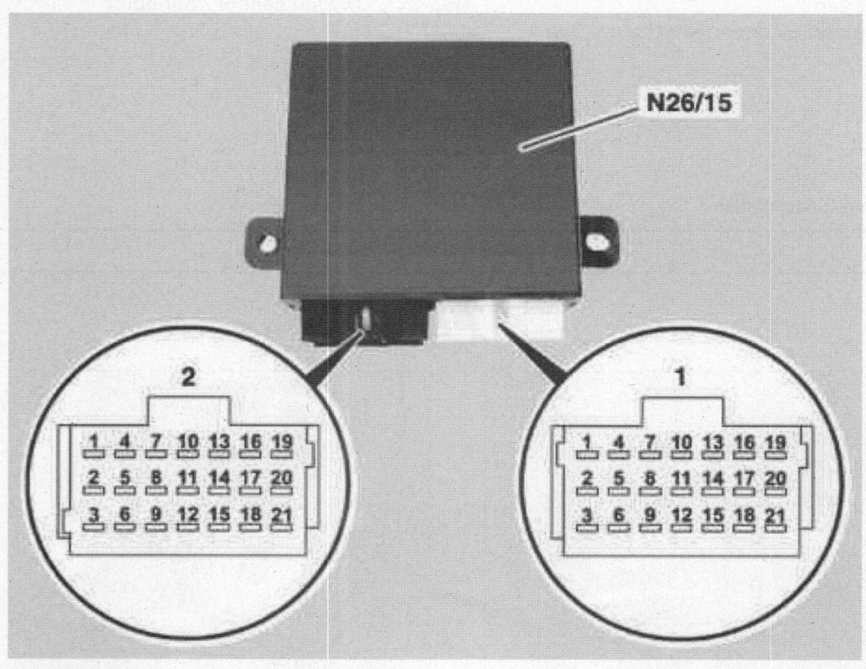

1. Plug 1
2. Plug 2
N26/15. PSM control unit

71112_MBSV_G0112

Fig. 131 PSM connectors

RECODING

See Figures 132 and 133.

PRESSURE DIFFERENTIAL SENSOR

LOCATION

See Figure 134.

The sensors are located at the expansion reservoir.

REMOVAL & INSTALLATION

See Figures 135 through 137.

1. Before servicing the vehicle, refer to the Precautions section.
2. Remove expansion reservoir (1) and lay down to side. Do not detach electrical connector and coolant hose:
   a. Unscrew cap from expansion reservoir (1). Draw off coolant from the expansion reservoir (1) using the hand pump.
   b. Remove bolts (7) and bracket (8) with AdBlue® filler neck from expansion reservoir (1). Lift bracket (8) until the

OPEN Body electronics *N26/15 PSM control unit* *X11 Diagnostic socket, 16-pin*

The PSM control unit forms the interface between the vehicle and the body manufacturer electronics.
Thanks to the body manufacturer electronics vehicle information can be read in by means of the PSM control unit via the Controller Area Network bus class B (interior) (CAN-B) and vehicle functions controlled (e.g. the central locking system (CL)).
For this there are digital and analog inputs and outputs (10 discrete inputs and 20 discrete outputs; the latter can likewise be used as inputs). For complex bodies, which require more inputs or outputs, the Controller Area Network-Bus Class C (body manufacturer) (body manufacturer CAN) is available as a further interface. A multitude of vehicle signals are transmitted on this. In addition there are some "free messages" which can be freely assigned with arbitrary contents.

The PSM control unit can thus convert information, which it receives via Controller Area Network (data bus/CAN bus) (CAN) messages, to discrete outputs or the body manufacturer CAN. In exactly the same way the PSM control unit can pass on discrete inputs or information from body manufacturer CAN to CAN B.
Over and above the interfaces internal functional units are available in the PSM control unit, e.g.:

- Access to motor functions (working speed control, engine start/stop)
- Programmable logic controller (PLC) functionality (logic operations AND, OR etc. of signals)
- Undervoltage detection

The type and direction of information and interfaces with the aid of STAR DIAGNOSIS. Only through this parameterization is the usability of the PSM control unit established and adapted to the corresponding body. For SA codes available from the plant, parameterization of the PSM control unit can be performed at the touch of a button via the menu standard coding. Parameterization via the expert coding is required for all other adjustments.

The SA codes available from the plant are:

- Retarder with code (BR9) Preinstallation for Telma retarder
- Working speed control:
  - with code (MT4) Electronic variable rpm regulator
  - with code (MT4) Electronic variable rpm regulator and with code (N05) Power take-off countershaft (2c) without flange
  - with code (MT4) Electronic variable rpm regulator and with code (N07) Power take-off countershaft (2b) with flange
  - with code (M53) Constant rpm control
  - with code (M53) Constant rpm control and with code (N05) Power take-off countershaft (2c) without flange
  - with code (M53) Constant rpm control and with code (N07) Power take-off countershaft (2b) with flange
- Preinstallation for crash data recorder with code (JV5)

71112_MBSV_G0114

Fig. 132 PSM recoding general information

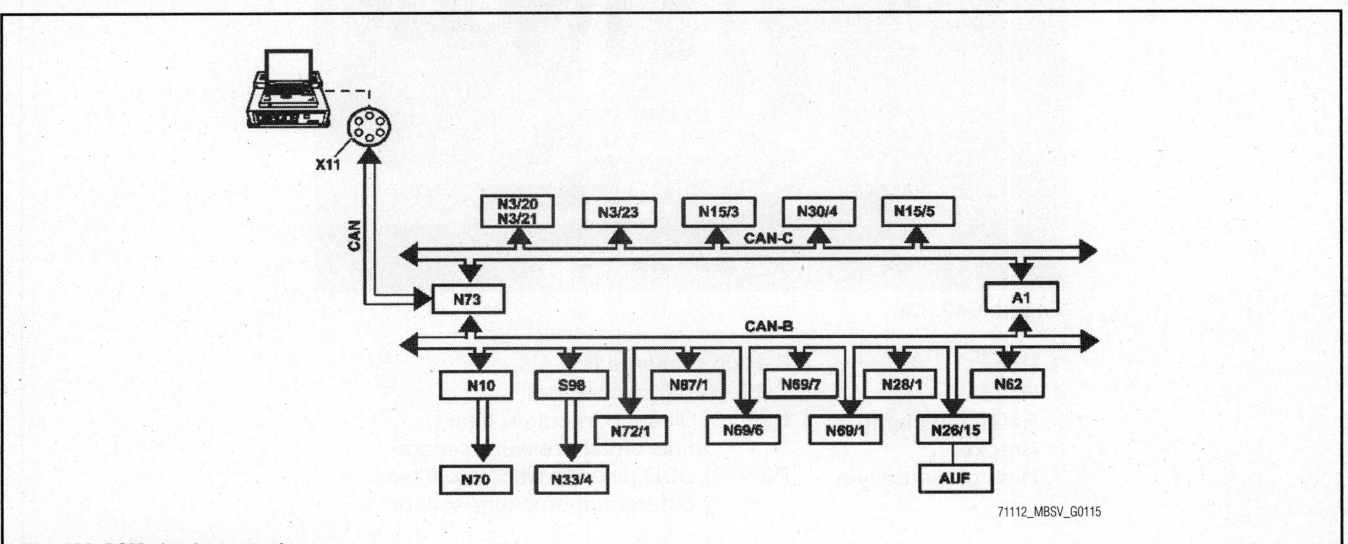

Fig. 133 PSM circuit connection

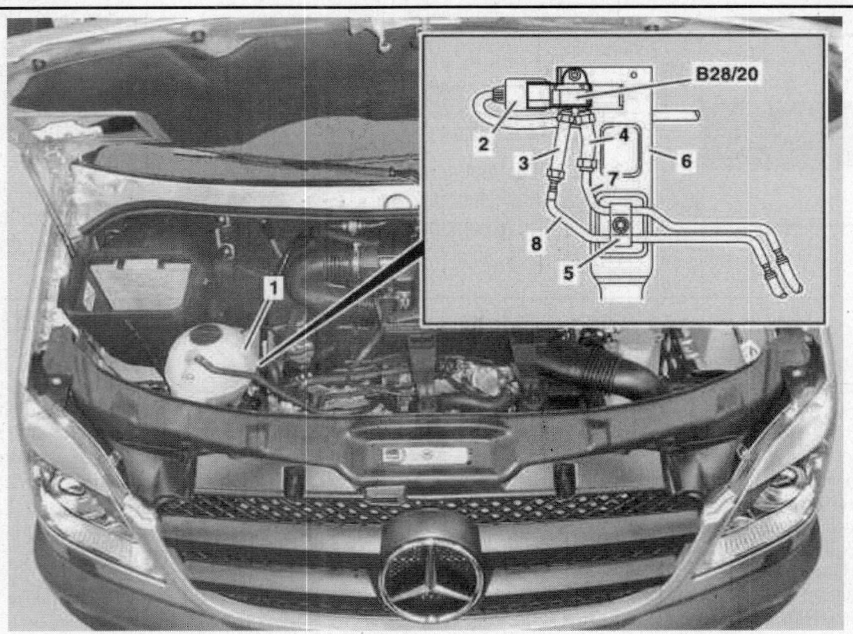

Shown for engine 642.896

1. Expansion reservoir
2. Electrical connector
3. Hose
4. Hose
5. Retaining clamp
6. Bracket
7. High pressure line
8. High pressure line

B28/20. Diesel particulate filter differential pressure sensor

71112_MBSV_G0119

Fig. 134 Pressure differential sensor location

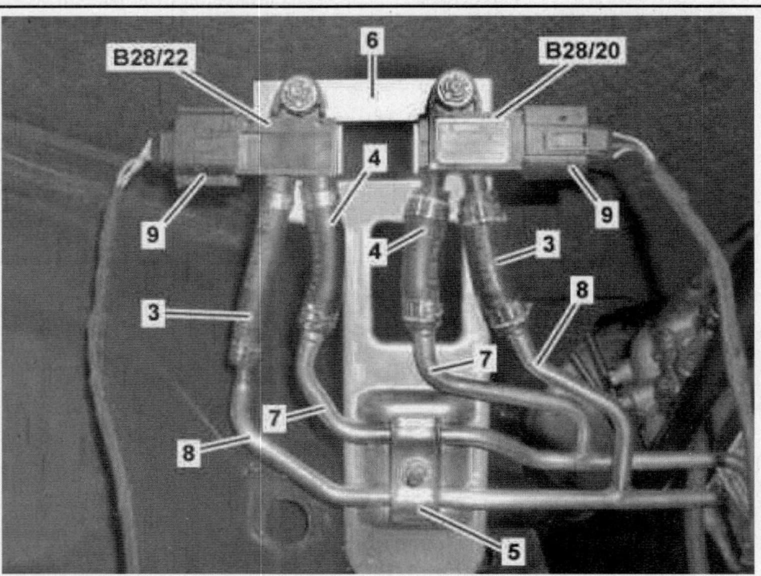

Engine 642.898

3. Hose
4. Hose
5. Retaining clamp
6. Bracket
7. High pressure line
8. High pressure line
9. Electrical connector

B28/20. Diesel particulate filter differential pressure sensor

B28/22. OBD diesel particulate filter differential pressure sensor

71112_MBSV_G0120

Fig. 135 Pressure differential sensor removal/installation

Shown on engine 642.898

1. Expansion reservoir
7. Bolts (on engine 642.898)
8. Bracket (on ENGINE 642.898)

71112_MBSV_G0121

Fig. 136 Expansion reservoir removal/installation, 1 of 2

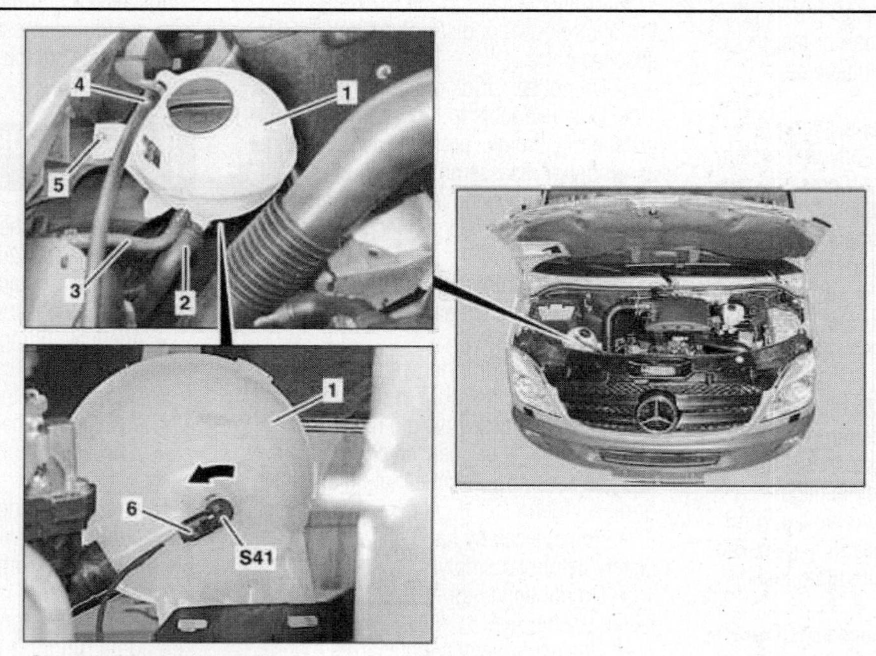

Shown on engine 646.985

1. Expansion reservoir
2. Coolant hose
3. Coolant hose
4. Coolant hose (with engine 271, 642, 646, 651)
5. Bolt (not for engine 642.989)
6. Electrical connector
S41. Coolant level indicator switch

71112_MBSV_G0122

Fig. 137 Expansion reservoir removal/installation, 2 of 2

expansion reservoir (1) can be taken out of the guide.

c. Detach coolant hoses (2, 3) at expansion reservoir (1).

d. Lift expansion reservoir (1) and disconnect electrical connector (6) at coolant level indicator switch (S41) 8 Take out expansion reservoir (1).

3. Disconnect electrical connector (9) from diesel particulate filter differential pressure sensor (B28/20) and OBD diesel particulate filter differential pressure sensor (B28/22).

➡Mark electrical connectors (9) to prevent mix-up when installing.

4. Remove diesel particulate filter differential pressure sensor (B28/20) and OBD diesel particulate filter differential pressure sensor (B28/22) from bracket (6).

5. Remove retaining clamp (5) from bracket (6).

6. Remove pressure lines (7, 8) with diesel particulate filter differential pressure sensor (B28/20) and OBD diesel particulate filter differential pressure sensor (B28/22) from bracket (6).

7. Remove hoses (3, 4) from pressure lines (7, 8) and remove diesel particulate filter differential pressure sensor (B28/20) and OBD diesel particulate filter differential pressure sensor (B28/22).

➡Do not remove hoses (3, 4) from diesel particulate filter differential pressure sensor (B28/20) and OBD diesel particulate filter differential pressure sensor (B28/22) to prevent damage. On installation, use new hose clamps.

8. Installation is the reverse of removal. Torque the sensor to 72 inch lbs. (8 Nm).

FUEL SYSTEM — DIESEL FUEL INJECTION SYSTEM

FUEL SYSTEM SERVICE PRECAUTIONS

Safety is the most important factor when performing not only fuel system maintenance but any type of maintenance. Failure to conduct maintenance and repairs in a safe manner may result in serious personal injury or death. Maintenance and testing of the vehicle's fuel system components can be accomplished safely and effectively by adhering to the following rules and guidelines.

- To avoid the possibility of fire and personal injury, always disconnect the negative battery cable unless the repair or test procedure requires that battery voltage be applied.
- Always relieve the fuel system pressure prior to disconnecting any fuel system component (injector, fuel rail, pressure regulator, etc.), fitting or fuel line connection. Exercise extreme caution whenever relieving fuel system pressure to avoid exposing skin, face and eyes to fuel spray. Please be advised that fuel under pressure may penetrate the skin or any part of the body that it contacts.
- Always place a shop towel or cloth around the fitting or connection prior to loosening to absorb any excess fuel due to spillage. Ensure that all fuel spillage (should it occur) is quickly removed from engine surfaces. Ensure that all fuel soaked cloths or towels are deposited into a suitable waste container.
- Always keep a dry chemical (Class B) fire extinguisher near the work area.
- Do not allow fuel spray or fuel vapors to come into contact with a spark or open flame.
- Always use a back-up wrench when loosening and tightening fuel line connection fittings. This will prevent unnecessary stress and torsion to fuel line piping.
- Always replace worn fuel fitting O-rings with new. Do not substitute fuel hose or equivalent where fuel pipe is installed.

Before servicing the vehicle, make sure to also refer to the precautions in the beginning of this section as well.

The following procedures and notes must be observed for removal/installation of common-rail components:

- Carefully clean the working area on engine and required tools before beginning removal of common-rail components to be free of dirt and fluid.
- Arrange access to the working area through removal of disturbing engine attached parts.
- Do not eat, drink or smoke.
- Only use tools to loosen and tighten fasteners and high- pressure lines. All other assembly or disassembly procedures must be performed by hand and without an aid.
- Close off opened connections using suitable caps.
- Keep container for assembly aid materials clean and seal or cover if not used.
- Mount sealing ring while moist (use assembly or engine oil). For vacuum and water hose use assembly aid material
- Palatinol N or soap water; for leak oil line use assembly aid material Palatinol N or diesel fuel.
- Remove cap by hand and only immediately before assembly.
- Do not bend high-pressure lines and install unstressed.
- Observe assembly notes from manufacturer and specified torques.
- Disassembly of common-rail components is not permissible. In the case of failure, completely replace the respective components with the exception of the fuel distribution rail.
- When replacing common-rail components use the caps from the new part on the removed part as soon as the new part is built-in.
- Do not lay any objects on the common-rail components; there is danger of unnoticed damage.
- After installing common-rail components, all connections are to be checked for leak tightness and the leak oil line possibly by hand for tight seating.
- When observing the detailed procedures common-rail components, apart from high-pressure lines on some engines, can be installed a number of times. Nevertheless, avoid unnecessary disassembly. Sealing rings and stretch bolts must always be replaced.

RELIEVING FUEL SYSTEM PRESSURE

Before starting the engine after assembly operations on the fuel system, or, after driving until the fuel tank is empty, the following should be observed:

- Adequate filling of the fuel filter housing.
- Do not bleed the fuel system at the high-pressure connection.
- If necessary run the starter continuously.

For a running engine and within the first 30 seconds after switching off, no assembly operation should be conducted on the fuel system. There is a danger of fuel escaping under high pressure. The engine should be run for a few minutes at a medium rotational speed for the subsequent leak test and then switched off again. Visually inspect the fuel system afterwards for leak tightness. In the case of leaks, despite a correct tightening torque, the common-rail components involved should be replaced.

FUEL INJECTORS

REMOVAL & INSTALLATION

See Figure 138.

1. Before servicing the vehicle, refer to the Precautions section.
2. Remove injection line (1) from injectors (Y76/1, Y76/2, Y76/3, Y76/4, Y76/5 or Y76/6) to be removed.
3. Disconnect electrical connector from injectors (Y76/1, Y76/2, Y76/3, Y76/4, Y76/5 or Y76/6) to be removed.
4. Remove screw (2) on injector (Y76/1, Y76/2, Y76/3, Y76/4, Y76/5 or Y76/6) to be removed. On installation, install new bolt (2).
5. Remove clamping claw (3) on injector (Y76/1, Y76/2, Y76/3, Y76/4, Y76/5 or Y76/6) to be removed.
6. Remove injector (Y76/1, Y76/2, Y76/3, Y76/4, Y76/5 or Y76/6). When removing a number of injectors, mark these assigned to the cylinders. On installation, grease stem on injector (Y76/1, Y76/2, Y76/3, Y76/4, Y76/5, Y76/6).
7. Remove sealing ring (4) from removed injector (Y76/1, Y76/2, Y76/3, Y76/4, Y76/5 or Y76/6). On installation, install new sealing ring (4).
8. Clean removed injectors.
9. Clean cylinder head of injector well of removed injector (Y76/1, Y76/2, Y76/3, Y76/4, Y76/5 or Y76/6) using a brush.
10. Installation is the reverse of removal. Torque the tensioning claw to injector to 60 inch lbs. (7 Nm) +180 degrees.

FUEL RAIL

REMOVAL & INSTALLATION

See Figures 139 and 140.

1. Before servicing the vehicle, refer to the Precautions section.
2. Remove injection lines (2 or 13) from corresponding rail (1 or 12). See the procedure in this section.
3. Detach connecting line (6) on rail (1 or 12) and charge air manifold. On installation, check connecting line (6) sealing cone for damage; replace connecting line (6) if necessary.

On the left side:

4. Unscrew bolt (4).
5. Remove pressure line (3) on rail (1). On installation, check pressure line (3) sealing cone for damage; replace pressure line (3) if necessary.
6. Disconnect electrical connector (5) at the pressure regulating valve (Y74/1 or Y74/6).
7. Remove cable tie (7) and expose engine wiring harness (8). On installation, replace cable ties (7).
8. Open clamp (10) and detach rail (1) from return hose (9).
9. Remove rail (1).

On the right side:

10. Unclip bracket with electrical connector on temperature sensor upstream of exhaust gas turbocharger from rail (12).
11. Disconnect electrical connector (11) at the rail pressure sensor (B4/6 or B4/17).
12. Remove rail (12).

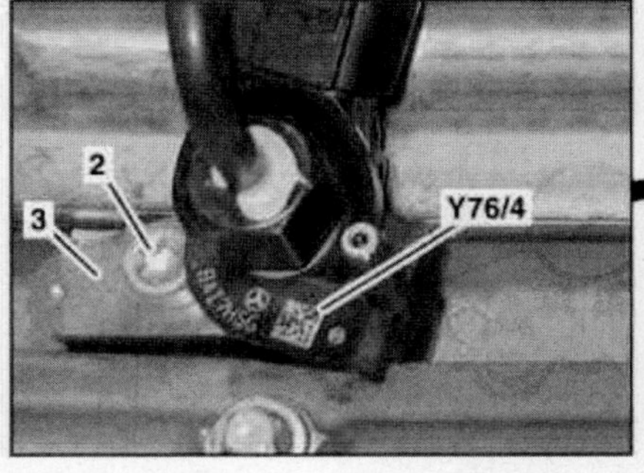

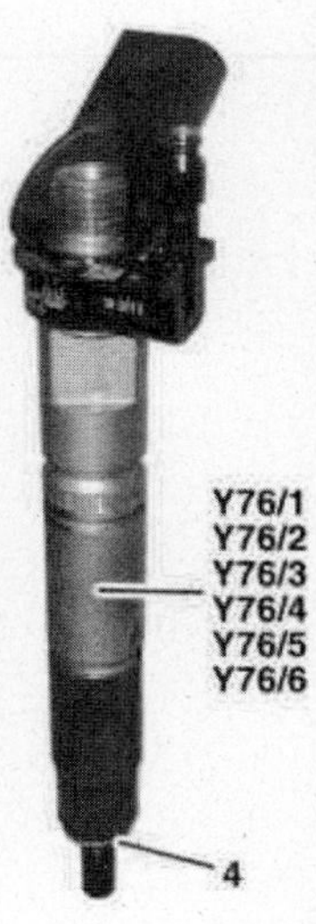

Shown on engine 642.992 and injector, cylinder 4

1. Injection line
2. Bolt
3. Clamping claw
4. Sealing ring
Y76/1. Injector, cylinder 1
Y76/2. Injector, cylinder 2
Y76/3. Injector, cylinder 3
Y76/4. Injector, cylinder 4
Y76/5. Injector, cylinder 5
Y76/6. Injector, cylinder 6

71112_MBSV_G0141

Fig. 138 Fuel injector removal/installation

Shown on rail (1) on left cylinder head

1. Rail
2. Injection lines
3. High pressure line
4. Screw
5. Electrical connector
6. Connecting line
7. Cable tie
8. Engine wiring harness
9. Return hose
10. Clip

71112_MBSV_G0137

Fig. 139 Left side fuel rail removal/installation

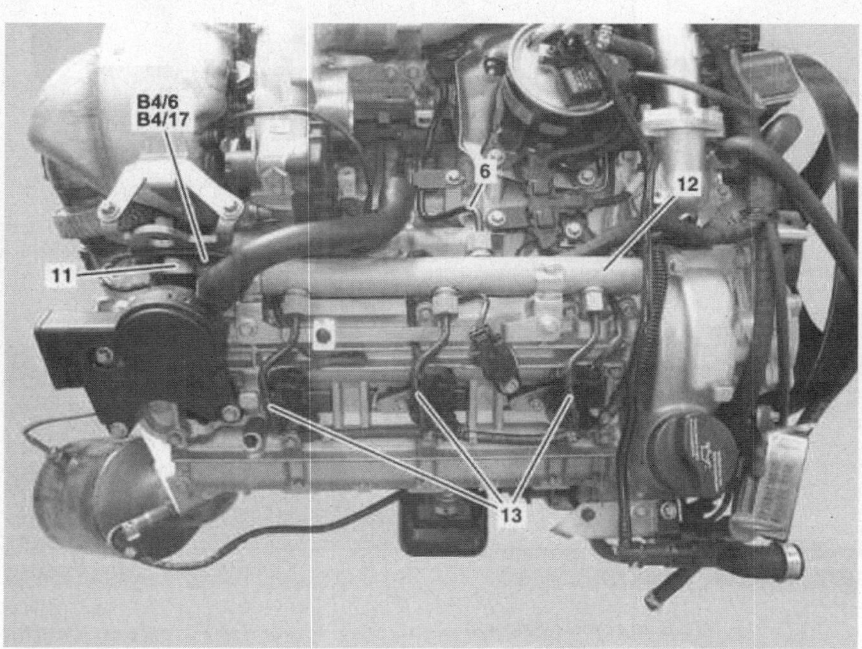

Shown on rail (12) on right cylinder head

6. Connecting line
11. Electrical connector
12. Rail
13. Injection lines
B4/6. Rail pressure sensor (engine 642.992/993)
B4/17. Rail pressure sensor (engine 642.896/898)

71112_MBSV_G0138

Fig. 140 Right side fuel rail removal/installation

13. Installation is the reverse of removal. Observe the following torques:

- Connecting line between left and right rail: 15 ft. lbs. (20 Nm) +60 degrees
- Pressure line to high-pressure pump to rail: 15 ft. lbs. (20 Nm) +60 degrees
- Bolt, retaining clamp of high-pressure line to cylinder head cover: 10 ft. lbs. (14 Nm)

FUEL RAIL PRESSURE SENSOR

REMOVAL & INSTALLATION

See Figure 141.

1. Before servicing the vehicle, refer to the Precautions section.
2. Remove oil separator (2).
3. Remove shield (4).
4. Remove lifting eye (3).
5. Disconnect electrical connector on rail pressure sensor (B4/6 or B4/17).
6. Unscrew rail pressure sensor (B4/6 or B4/17) on rail (1).
7. Close off connection on rail (1) using suitable stop plugs.
8. Installation is the reverse of removal. Torque the rail pressure sensor-to-rail to 52 ft. lbs. (70 Nm).

FUEL TANK

DRAINING

1. Before servicing the vehicle, refer to the Precautions section.

There is no drain plug. Fuel can be siphoned out of the filler neck. If the tank must be completely drained, the tank must be removed.

REMOVAL & INSTALLATION

See Figures 142 and 143.

1. Before servicing the vehicle, refer to the Precautions section.

Shown on engine 642.992

1. Rail
2. Oil separator
3. Lifting eye
4. Shield
B4/6. Rail pressure sensor (engine 642.992/993)
B4/17. Rail pressure sensor (engine 642.896/898)

71112_MBSV_G0145

Fig. 141 Fuel rail pressure sensor removal/installation

2
3
2
4
5

2. Screw/bolts
3. Cover
4. Screw/bolt
5. Filler neck

71112_MBSV_G0133

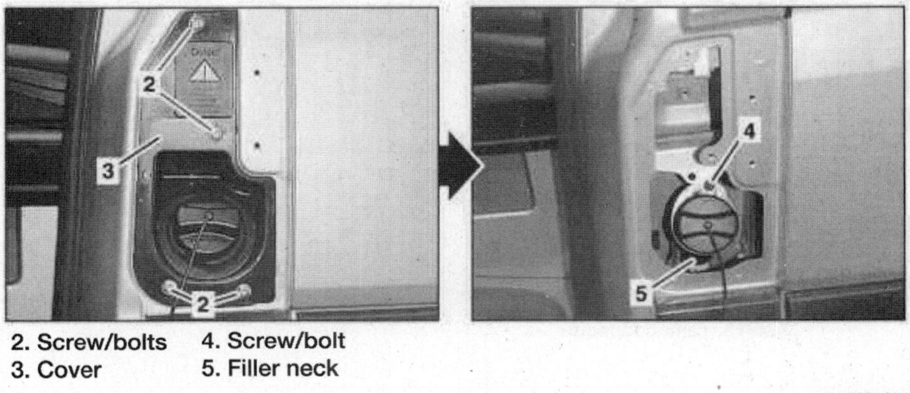

Fig. 142 Fuel tank removal/installation, 1of 2

2. Raise and safely support the vehicle.
3. Drain fuel tank (1).
4. Remove tank flap.
5. Remove screws/bolts (2) and remove panel (3).
6. Remove screw/bolt (4) on filler neck (5).
7. Remove cable ties (6).
8. Disconnect electrical tank connector (X25/16).
9. Remove seal (7).
10. Unclip electrical tank connector (X25/15) from under-floor and disconnect.
11. On vehicles with auxiliary heater, disconnect fuel line (arrow). Collect escaping fuel.
12. Release and disconnect fuel feed line (8) and fuel return line (9). Collect escaping fuel. On installation, do not mix up fuel feed line (8) and fuel return line (9). The connectors are color-coded.
13. Remove tensioning strap (10).
14. Support fuel tank (1) in the middle with a transmission jack.
15. Remove tensioning straps (11, 12).
16. Lower transmission jack with fuel tank (1) until vent line (13) is accessible.
17. Unclip vent line (13) on fuel tank (1) and detach.
18. Lower transmission jack with fuel tank (1) and suction off remaining fuel from fuel tank.
19. Remove fuel pump with fuel level sensor and lines on fuel tank (1).
20. Installation is the reverse of removal. Torque the straps to 41 ft. lbs. (56 Nm).

GLOW PLUGS

REMOVAL & INSTALLATION

See Figure 144.

1. Before servicing the vehicle, refer to the Precautions section.
2. Bring engine to operating temperature (approx. 176 deg. F [80 deg. C]).
3. Remove trim panel on right cylinder head cover. See the procedure in this section.
4. Remove trim panel on left cylinder head cover. See the procedure in this section.
5. Loosen engine wiring harness duct (2) on left cylinder head cover from charge air manifold and push to side.
6. Unclip left EKAS end position switch connector (X156/1) from left rail and lay to side.
7. Remove leak oil line distributor (1) from charge air manifold.
8. Disconnect electrical connectors from glow plugs (R9/1, R9/2, R9/3, R9/4, R9/5, R9/6) using pliers.
9. Remove glow plugs (R9/1, R9/2, R9/3, R9/4, R9/5, R9/6).
10. Clean glow plug bay using a cylinder brush.
11. Installation is the reverse of removal. Torque the glow plugs to 96 inch lbs. (11 Nm) and the oil line to 106 inch lbs. (12 Nm).

HIGH PRESSURE FUEL PUMP

REMOVAL & INSTALLATION

See Figure 145.

1. Before servicing the vehicle, refer to the Precautions section.

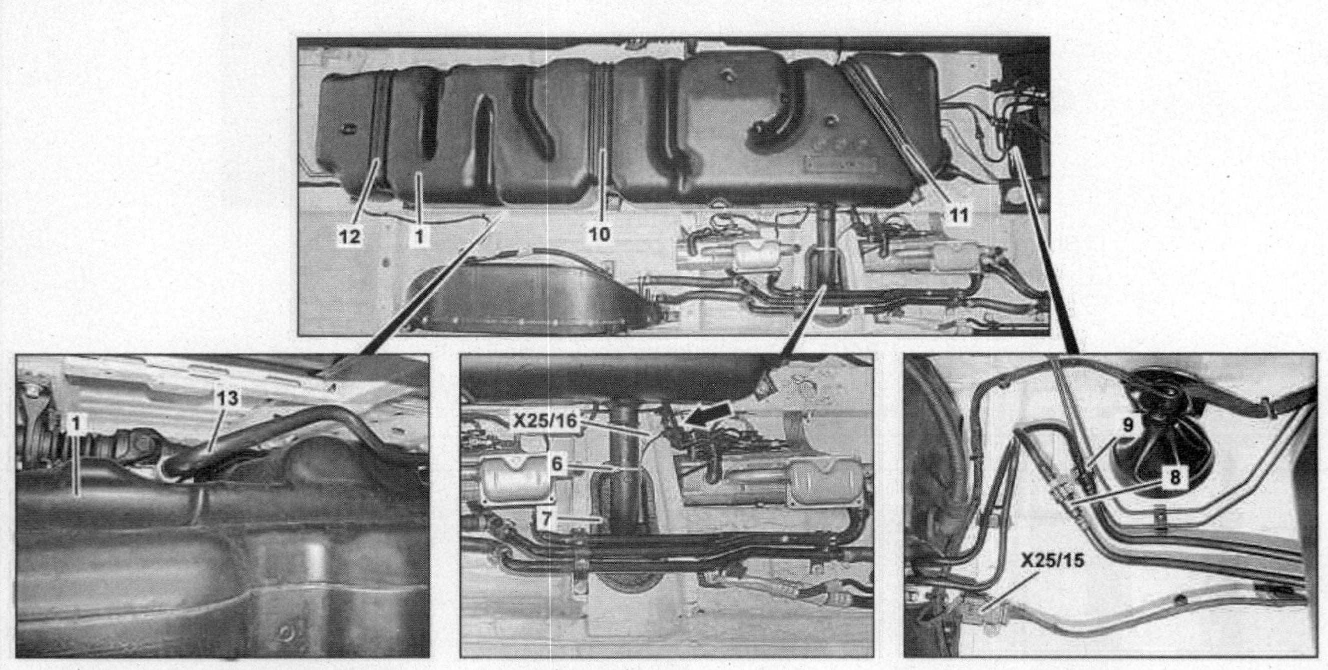

Fig. 143 Fuel tank removal/installation, 2of 2

Shown on ENGINE 642 in MODEL 906

1. Distributor leak oil line
2. Engine wiring harness duct
R9/1. Cylinder 1 glow plug
R9/2. Cylinder 2 glow plug
R9/3. Cylinder 3 glow plug
R9/4. Cylinder 4 glow plug
R9/5. Cylinder 5 glow plug
R9/6. Cylinder 6 glow plug
X156/1. Left EKAS end position switch connector (on engine 642.896/898 in model 906)

71112_MBSV_G0135

Fig. 144 Glow plug removal/installation

2. Remove fan shroud. See the Engine Cooling section.

3. Remove coolant hose (9) from bracket (10) and press toward rear.

4. Expose electrical line and disconnect electrical connector (7) from quantity control valve (Y94 or Y94/4).

5. Disconnect electrical connector (4) from fuel temperature sensor (B50 or B50/6).

6. Remove fuel hoses (2, 3) from high-pressure pump (1). Close off fuel hose (2, 3) using suitable stop plug. Collect escaping fuel.

7. Unscrew pressure line (5) from high-pressure fitting (6) on high-pressure pump (1) and push up slightly. Counterhold high-pressure fitting (6) when loosening pressure line (5) Do not crimp or bend pressure line (5). Plug pressure line (5) and high-pressure fitting (6) in high-pressure pump (1) with suitable stop plug. On installation, check pressure line (5) sealing cone; replace pressure line (5) if necessary. Ensure correct seating of the pressure line (5).

8. Unscrew bolts (8) from high pressure pump (1).

9. Remove high-pressure pump (1).

10. Installation is the reverse of removal.

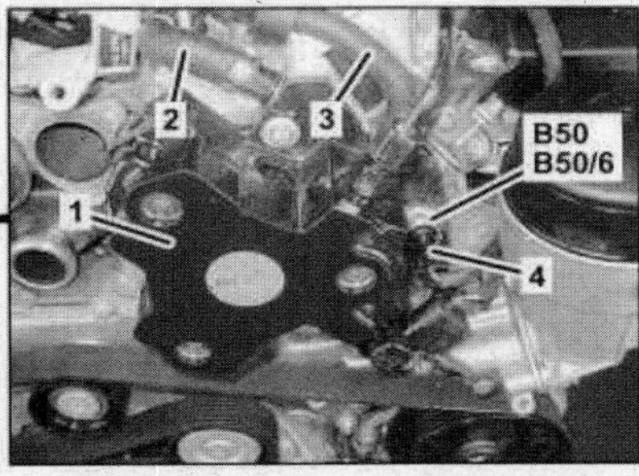

1. High-pressure pump
2. Fuel hose
3. Fuel hose
4. Electrical connector
5. High pressure line
6. High-pressure fitting
7. Electrical connector
8. Screw
9. Coolant hose (engine 642.896/898)
10. Mount (engine 642.896/898)
11. Sealing ring
12. Drive gear
B50. Fuel temperature sensor (engine 642.992/993)
B50/6. Fuel temperature sensor (engine 642.896/898)
Y94. Quantity control valve (engine 642.992/993)
Y94/4. Quantity control valve (engine 642.896/898)

71112_MBSV_G0142

Fig. 145 High pressure fuel pump removal/installation

If the pump is being replaced, remove the drive gear. Observe the following torques:

- Bolt, high-pressure pump to cylinder head: 10 ft. lbs. (14 Nm)
- Pressure line to high-pressure pump: 15 ft. lbs. (20 Nm) +60 degrees
- High pressure fitting on the high pressure pump: 40 ft. lbs. (55 Nm)

HIGH PRESSURE FUEL PUMP DRIVE GEAR

REMOVAL & INSTALLATION

See Figure 146.

1. Before servicing the vehicle, refer to the Precautions section.
2. Remove high-pressure pump (1).
3. Place a counter-holder wrench on drive gear (3) and unscrew nut (2).

➡Do not tilt counter-holder to prevent damage to tooth flanks.

4. Detach drive gear (3) using a 2-jawed puller.
5. Remove Woodruff key (4) from driveshaft on high-pressure pump (1). Check Woodruff key (4), replace if necessary.
6. Installation is the reverse of removal. Torque the nut to 52 ft. lbs. (70 Nm).

MAIN FUEL FILTER

REMOVAL & INSTALLATION

See Figures 147 and 148.

1. Before servicing the vehicle, refer to the Precautions section.
2. Remove air intake hose downstream of air filter.
3. Unclip vacuum line from cover on left cylinder head cover. Push vacuum line to side.

1. High-pressure pump
2. Nut
3. Drive gear
4. Woodruff key

71112_MBSV_G0144

Fig. 146 High pressure fuel pump gear removal/installation

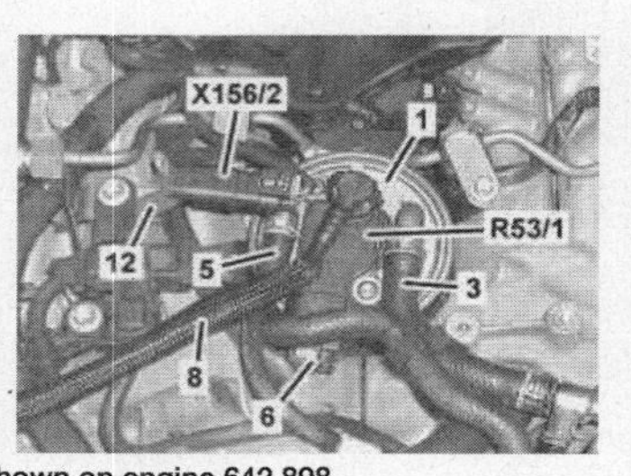

Shown on engine 642.898

1. Fuel filter
3. Fuel hose
5. Fuel hose
6. Electrical connector (for code (KL5) Fuel filter with water separator)
8. Drain pipe (with code (KL5) Fuel filter with water separator)
12. Bracket

R53/1. Fuel filter heater with water level sensor (engine 642.896/898 with code (KL5) with water separator)
X156/2. EKAS end position switch connector/right

71112_MBSV_G0136

Fig. 147 Fuel filter removal/installation

4. Remove glow output stage and lay down to side. See the procedure in this section.
5. Remove right EKAS end position switch connector (X156/2) from bracket (12).
6. Open clamps (2, 4). On installation, replace clamps (2, 4).
7. Detach fuel hoses (3, 5) from fuel filter (1) and close off using suitable stop plugs.
8. Loosen screw/bolt (7).
9. Lift out fuel filter (1) until electrical connector (6) and drain pipe (8) can be unclipped.
10. Disconnect electrical connector (6) from fuel filter water level sensor (B76) or fuel filter heater with water level sensor (R53/1).
11. Pull out safety clamp (10) (arrow), unlock catch hooks using suitable pliers (9) and detach drain pipe (8). On installation, check O-ring (11) and replace if necessary.
12. Remove fuel filter water level sensor (B76) or fuel filter heater with water level sensor (R53/1).
    a. Remove air filter
    b. Remove electrical connector and drain pipe from fuel filter water level sensor (B76) or on the fuel filter heater with water level sensor (R53/1). Do not remove the fuel filter.
    c. Unscrew screw/bolts (1) and remove fuel filter water level sensor (B76) or fuel filter heater with water level sensor (R53/1). Clean fuel filter (3) in area of fuel filter. water level sensor (B76) or fuel filter heater with water level sensor (R53/1). On installation, install new O-rings (2) and moisten with fuel. Torque the water level sensor-to-filter to 18 inch lbs. (2 Nm).
13. Installation is the reverse of removal. Before initially starting engine, fill fuel filter (1) by switching ignition on and off several times to prevent damaging high pressure pump.

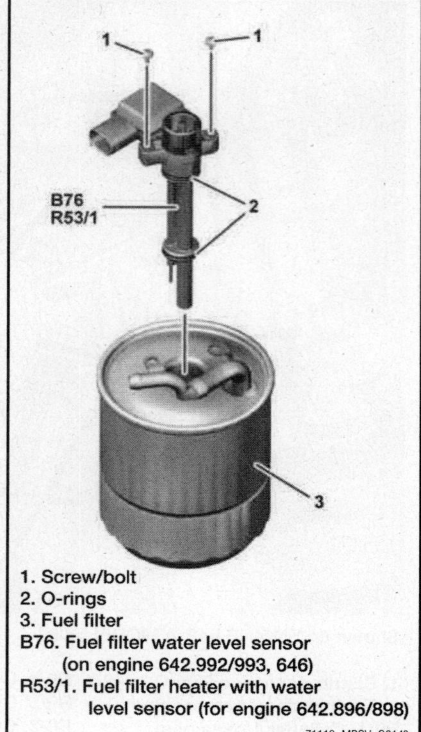

1. Screw/bolt
2. O-rings
3. Fuel filter

B76. Fuel filter water level sensor (on engine 642.992/993, 646)
R53/1. Fuel filter heater with water level sensor (for engine 642.896/898)

71112_MBSV_G0143

Fig. 148 Fuel/water separator removal/installation

THROTTLE VALVE ACTUATOR

REMOVAL & INSTALLATION

See Figure 149.

1. Before servicing the vehicle, refer to the Precautions section.
2. Remove mixing chamber (1). See the procedure in the Engine Mechanical section.
3. Unscrew bolts (3, 4) and remove fitting (2). On installation, replace sealing ring.
4. Unscrew bolts (5) and remove throttle valve actuator (M16/42 or M16/48). On installation, replace gasket (6).
5. If fitting (2) is replaced, pull out charge air temperature sensor (B17/9 or B17/15).
6. Clean sealing surface on mixing chamber (1).

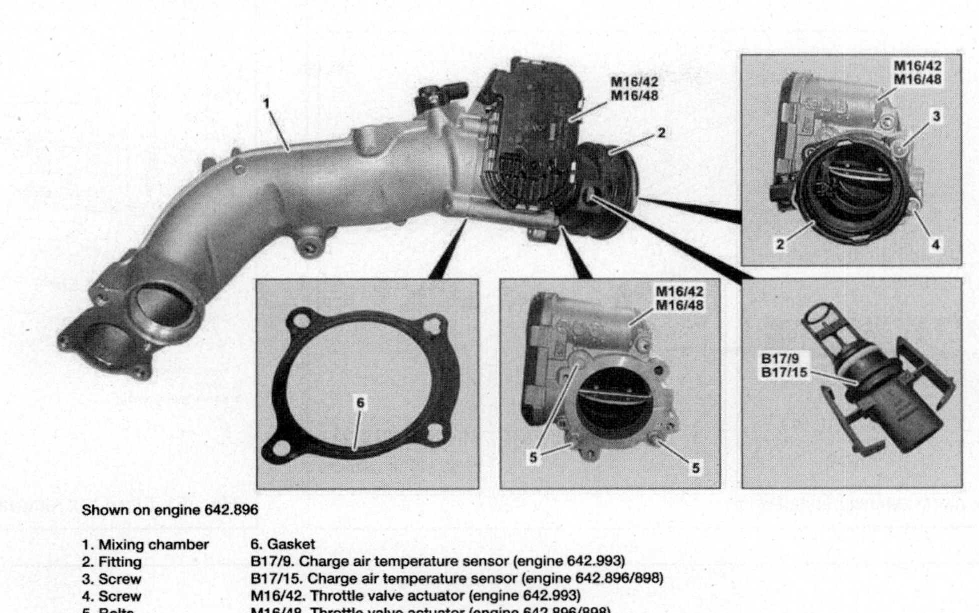

Fig. 149 Throttle valve actuator removal/installation

7. If fitting (2) and throttle valve actuator (M16/42 or M16/48) are not replaced, clean sealing surfaces on fittings (2) and throttle valve actuator (M16/42 or M16/48).
8. Installation is the reverse of removal. Observe the following torques:
   - Bolt, engine charge air duct downstream of charge air cooler to throttle valve actuator: 79 inch lbs. (9 Nm)
   - Bolt, throttle valve actuator to mixing chamber: 44 inch lbs. (5 Nm)

HEATING & AIR CONDITIONING SYSTEM

FRONT BLOWER MOTOR

REMOVAL & INSTALLATION

See Figures 150 and 151.

1. Before servicing the vehicle, refer to the Precautions section.
2. Remove glove box.
   a. Remove paneling below air vent (2).
   b. Open glove compartment (3), unlock and fold downward.
   c. Remove glove compartment (3).
   d. Remove glove box (1).
   e. Disconnect connector from glove compartment illumination.
   f. With Tempmatic A/C, remove coolant air hose from glove compartment (1).
3. Detach plug from connection line (2).
4. Unscrew bolt (1) to plastic strip behind the blower motor (M2).
5. Rotate the blower motor (M2) counterclockwise until it is detached from the blower housing.
6. Pull plastic strip to rear and remove blower motor (M2) from blower housing.
7. Installation is the reverse of removal.

HEATER CORE (HEAT EXCHANGER)

REMOVAL & INSTALLATION

See Figures 152 through 163.

1. Before servicing the vehicle, refer to the Precautions section.

⁂ CAUTION

When draining the coolant, keep in mind that cats and dogs are attracted by the ethylene glycol antifreeze, and are quite likely to drink any that is left in an uncovered container or in puddles on the ground. This will prove fatal in sufficient quantity. Always drain the coolant into a sealable container. Coolant should be reused unless it is contaminated or several years old.

2. Safely discharge the air conditioning system using an approved recovery station. On installation, evacuate air conditioning and then fill.
3. Disconnect ground cable from battery.
4. On model 906.1/2/ 6/7, remove headliner.
   a. Unclip paneling from A-pillars (6).
   b. On models without code (FF5) Stowage box/tray above windshield, remove sun visors (4).
   c. On models with code (FF5) Stowage box/tray above windshield, remove sun visors (4) and boxes. On installation, replace self-tapping bolts (2, 5).
   d. Pull out front dome lamp with switch (E15/1) and remove connector.
   e. Remove paneling from B-pillars (7).
   f. Unclip headliner (1).
5. Remove cover below steering wheel:
   a. Remove bolt on paneling (1) below air vent and pull off paneling.
   b. Remove bolt on cover (2) below steering wheel and pull off cover.
   c. Remove glove box.
   d. Remove paneling below air vent (2).

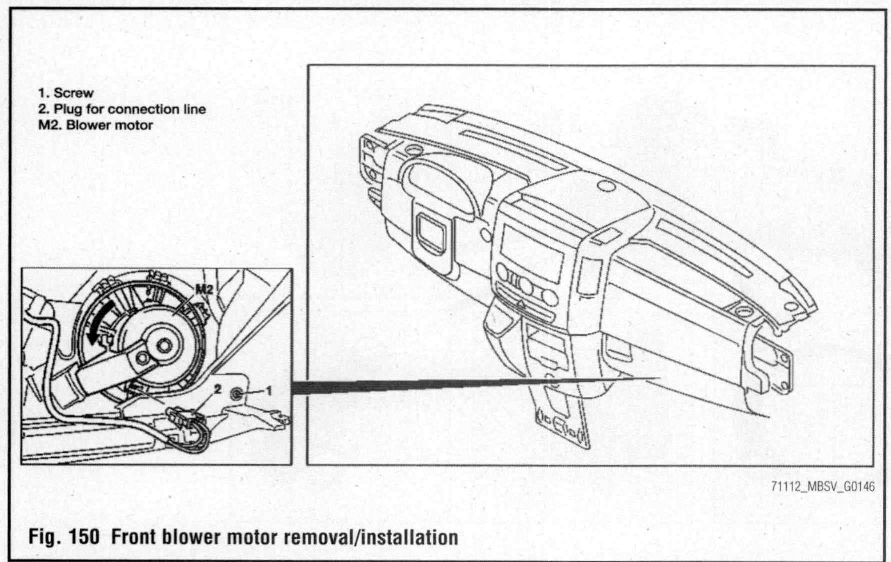

Fig. 150 Front blower motor removal/installation

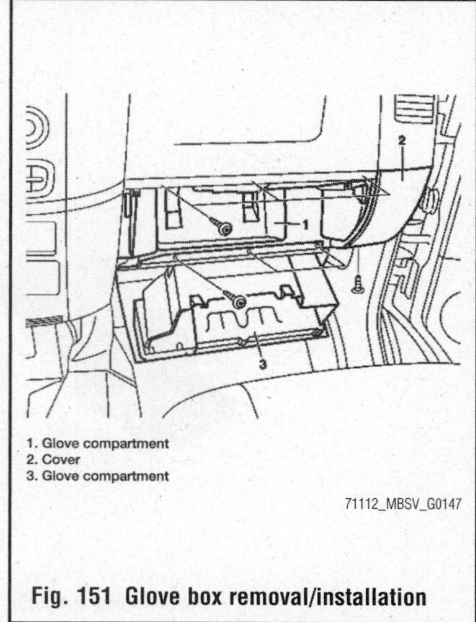

Fig. 151 Glove box removal/installation

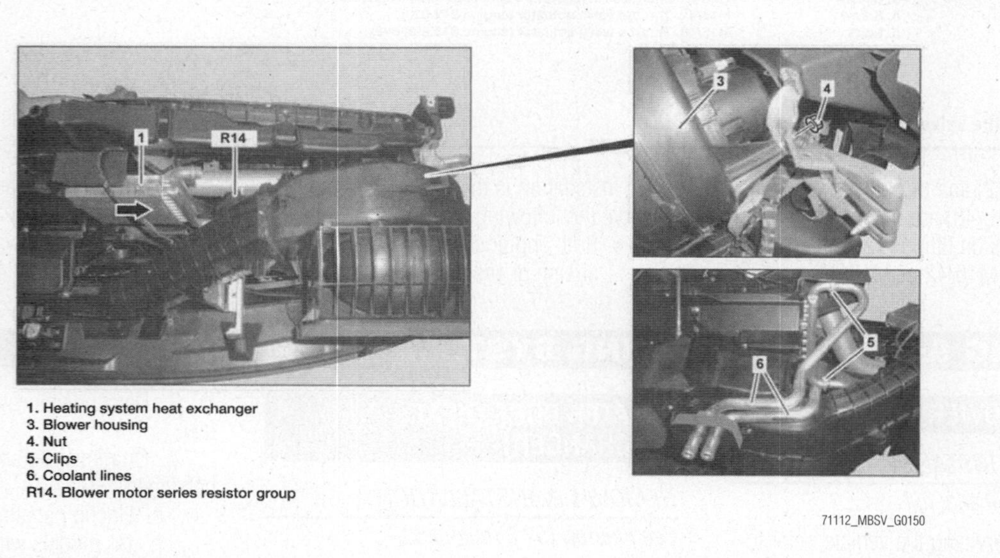

Fig. 152 Heat exchanger removal/installation

e. Open glove compartment (3), unlock and fold downward.

f. Remove glove compartment (3).

g. Remove glove box (1).

h. Disconnect connector from glove compartment illumination.

i. With Tempmatic A/C, remove coolant air hose from glove compartment (1).

6. Remove air outlet covers from dashboard center section:

a. Unclip covering from instrument panel center part.

b. Unscrew bolts from air vent covering (1) and remove air vent covering.

7. Remove cover on gearshift lever.

a. Remove vehicle tool kit cover from front passenger footwell.

b. Remove cover strips of floor covering from left and right entrance.

c. Fold floor covering back.

d. Unscrew bolts and remove center footwell cover (1).

8. Remove the selector lever:

a. Place the selector lever in the **P** position.

b. Unclip boot (1) upwards.

c. Put boot (1) upwards over the selector lever handle (2).

d. Turn clamping piece (3) in counterclockwise direction (arrow B). On installation: rotate clamping piece (3) clockwise (arrow A).

e. Pull selector lever handle (2) off selector lever (4).

f. Unclip cover (5) upwards.

g. Detach electrical connector (6) and remove cover (5).

h. If equipped, remove tachograph.

i. Unscrew bolts from cover (2).

j. Pull cover (2) toward rear and disconnect connectors at rear of cover (2).

k. Remove cover (2) upward.

9. Remove electronic selector lever module:

a. Disconnect electrical connector (4)
9 Remove bolts (1) and pull out electronic selector lever module control unit (N15/5) at both sides from the brackets (arrow).

b. Detach ball head (5) from electronic selector lever module control unit (N15/5). On installation, grease ball head (5). Pull sliding piece (6) with mounted

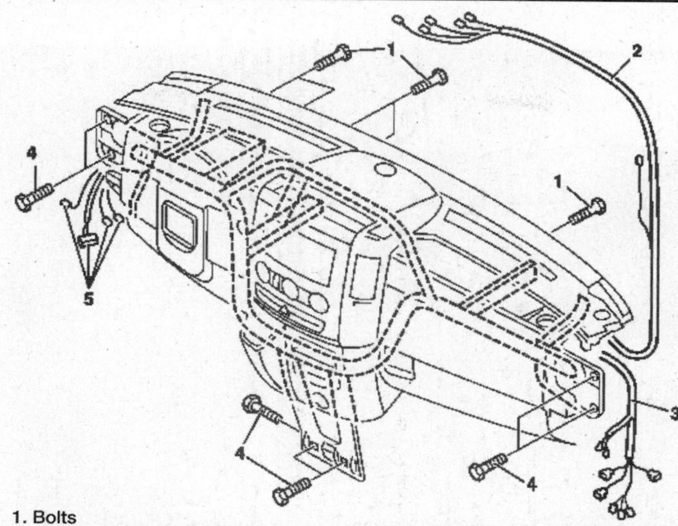

1. Bolts
2. Wiring harness (with code) (ED3) Antenna for GSM, GPS, UMTS network or code (EF9) Radio Sound 20 or code (EH3) Universal preinstallation for mobile phone interlinked or code (EH4) Comfort telephone or code (EJ2) Audio 20 or code (EJ3) Audio 20 with CD changer or code (EJ4) Audio 50 APS or code (EJ5) Audio 50 APS with DVD changer or code (EJ6) Command APS or code (EJ7) Command APS with DVD changer or code (EN0) Radio Sound 5 or code (EN4) Command with TMC interface or code (EN8) Radio Sound 50 APS or code (ER0) Radio preinstallation with antenna and 2 speaker or code (JV4) Universal preinstallation for mobile phone
3. Wiring harness
4. Bolts
5. Electrical connectors

71112_MBSV_G0151

Fig. 153 Dashboard removal/installation

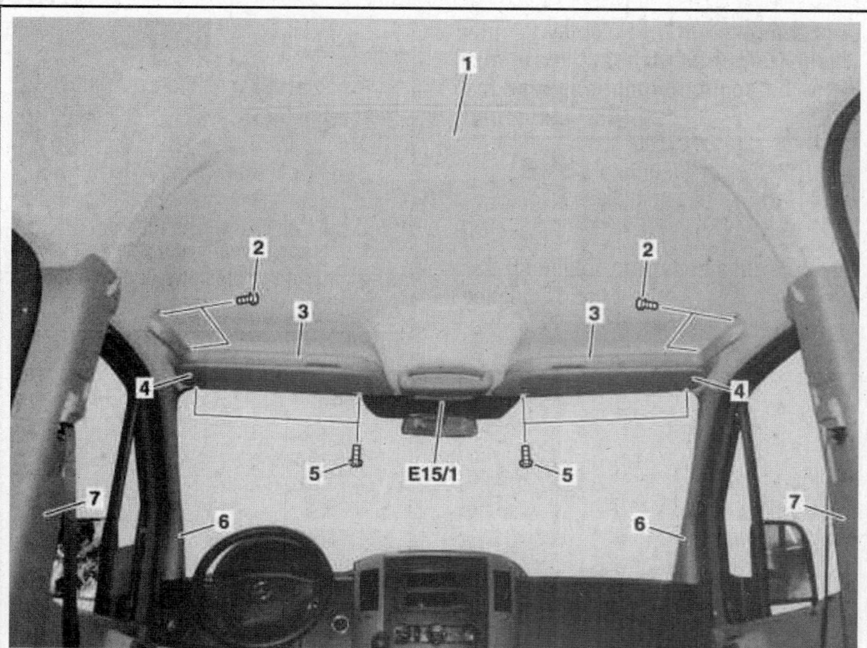

Shown on model 906 with code (FF5) Stowage box/tray above windshield

1. Headliner
2. Screw
3. Stowage box/tray (with code (FF5), Stowage box/tray above windshield)
4. Sun visor
5. Screw
6. A-pillar paneling
7. Lining on B-pillar
E15/1. Front dome lamp with switch

71112_MBSV_G0152

Fig. 154 Headliner removal/installation

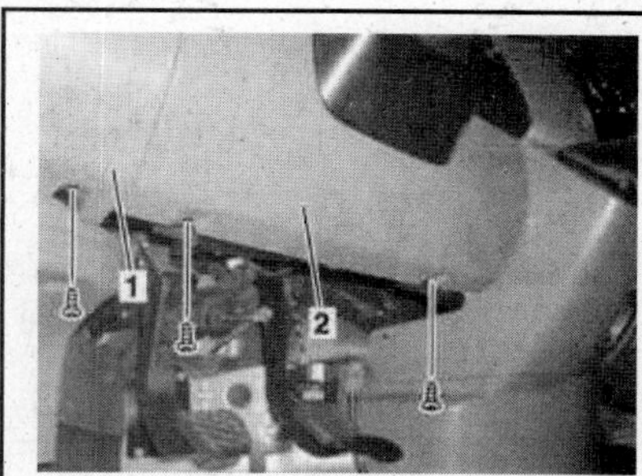

1. Cover
2. Cover

71112_MBSV_G0153

Fig. 155 Remove cover below steering wheel

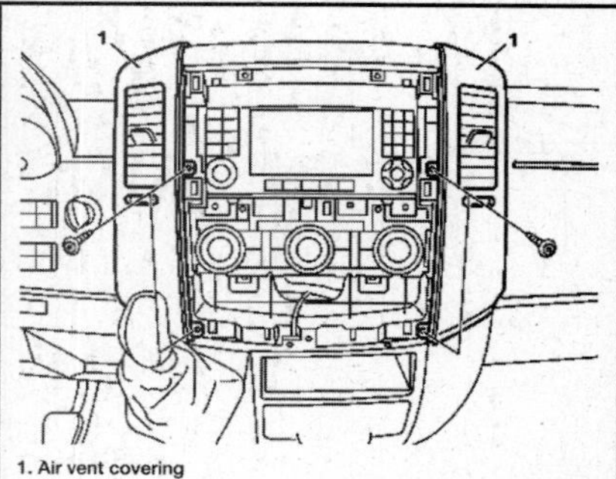

1. Air vent covering

71112_MBSV_G0154

Fig. 156 Air outlet covers removal/installation

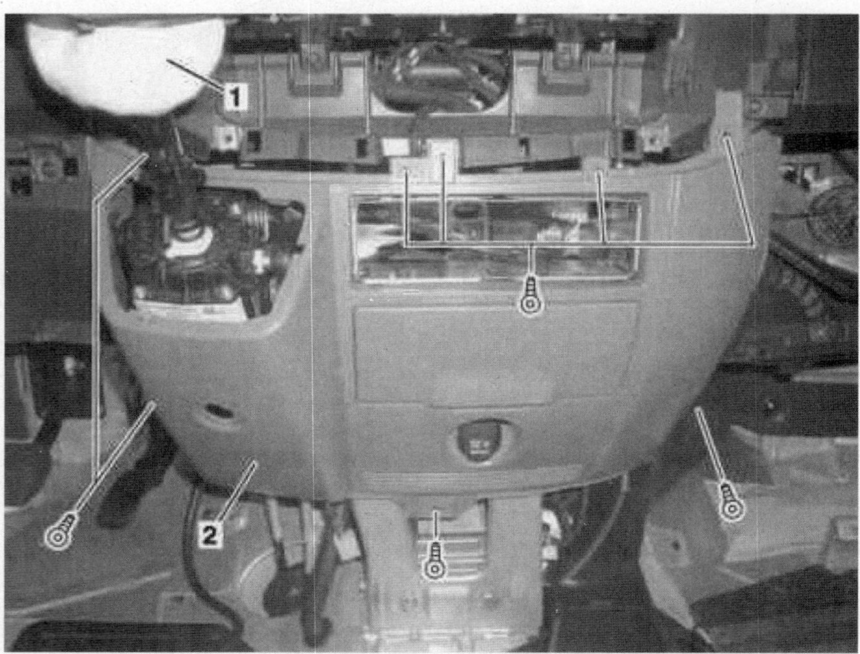

Fig. 157 Gearshift cover removal/installation

ball head (5) downwards towards locking plate (7) and allow to spring back again. This adjusts the selector lever Bowden cable (2).

c. Remove tab washer (7).

d. Detach selector lever Bowden cable (2) from electronic selector lever module control unit (N15/5)

e. Lift shackle (9), turn sleeve (8) through 90° to the left and detach Bowden cable from parking lock shift lock (3).

10. Remove side air outlet:

a. Unclip paneling from A-pillar.

b. Remove paneling below air vent (1).

c. Unscrew bolts from air vent (1) and remove air vent.

d. Only on driver side, disconnect connector (2) from rotary light switch (S1).

e. Only on driver side, except with code (LG0), bi-xenon headlamp and code (CE2) Rear air suspension,

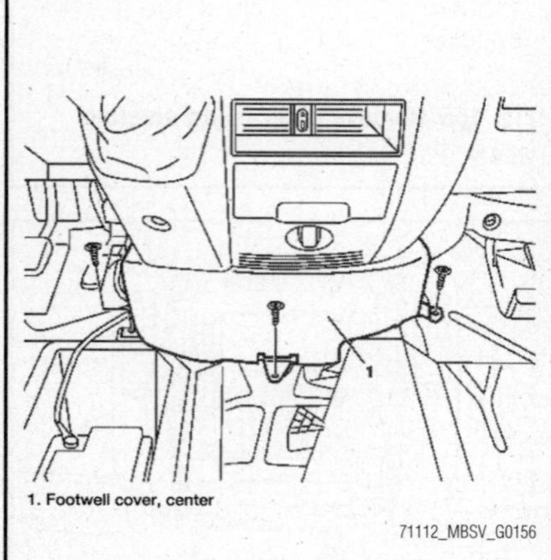

Fig. 158 Center footwell cover removal/installation

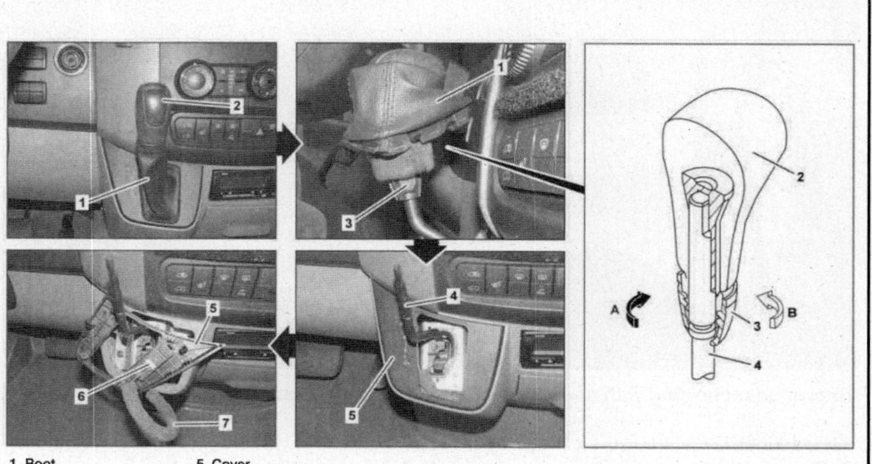

Fig. 159 Selector lever removal/installation

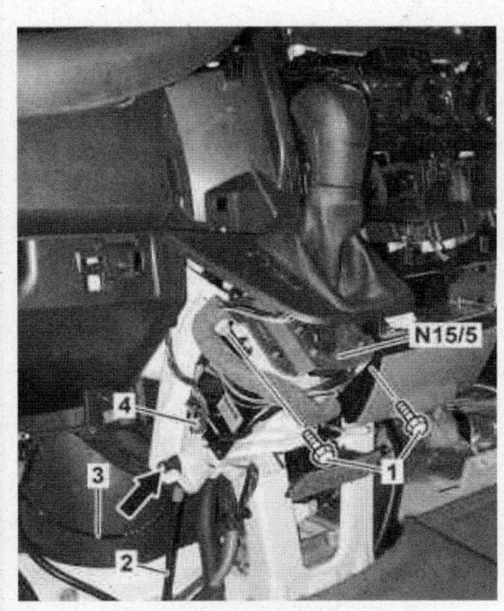

Shown with mounted selector lever handle with cover

1. Bolts
2. Selector lever Bowden cable
3. Parking shift lock Bowden cable
4. Electrical connector
N15/5. EWM control unit

71112_MBSV_G0158

Fig. 160 Selector lever module removal/installation, 1 of 2

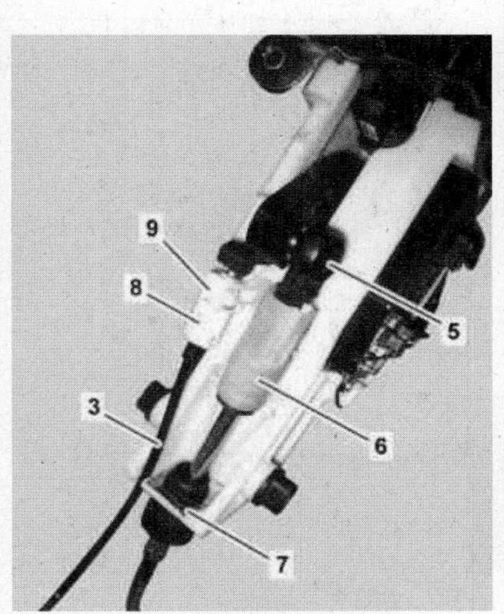

3. Parking shift lock Bowden cable
5. Ball head
6. Sliding piece
7. Locking plate
8. Sleeve
9. Tab

71112_MBSV_G0159

Fig. 161 Selector lever module removal/installation, 2 of 2

1. Air vent
2. Connector
S1. Exterior lamp switch

71112_MBSV_G0160

Fig. 162 Side outlet removal/installation

disconnect connector from headlamp range controller.

11. Turn steering wheel to center position and lock steering. See the Steering section.

➡**Wheels must be in straight-ahead position. Remove transmitter key from EZS control unit to lock.**

12. Disconnect all electrical connectors from wiring harness (2) in area of A-pillar and roof and remove wiring harness.

13. Disconnect all electrical connectors from wiring harness (3) in passenger footwell.

14. Disconnect all electrical connectors (5) on dashboard in driver footwell.

15. Disconnect connections and li nes of dashboard in interior compartment.

16. With code (HH9) Regulated air, conditioning (Tempmatic) or with code (HH7) Additional air conditioning in rear, disconnect connections and lines of dashboard in engine compartment. Seal openings on expansion valve and refrigerant lines with stop plug. On installation, use new O-rings coated with clean refrigerant oil.

17. Unscrew bolts (1) from firewall.

18. Remove screws/bolts (4).

19. Lift out dashboard support with dashboard. Place instrument panel onto a soft base. Otherwise the instrument panel may be scratched.

20. Remove blower motor series resistor group (R14):

a. Remove plug from connection line (1).

b. Rotate blower motor series resistor group (R14) far enough in clockwise direction, until the blower motor series resistor group (R14) is released from the air duct.

c. Remove blower motor series resistor group (R14).

21. Detach coolant lines (6) from heater heat exchanger (1). On installation, replace sealing rings.

22. Unscrew nut (4) from bracket of blower housing (3).

➡**Counterhold grub screw on the end of the shaft when unscrewing the nut (4). Otherwise the removal of the grub screw will destroy the connection between the grub screw and the blower housing (3). The blower housing (3) then needs to be replaced, because it can no longer be reliably secured.**

1. Plug for connection line
R14. Blower motor series resistor group

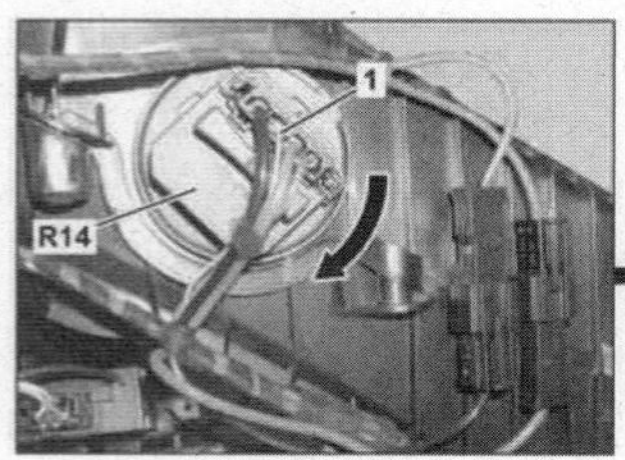

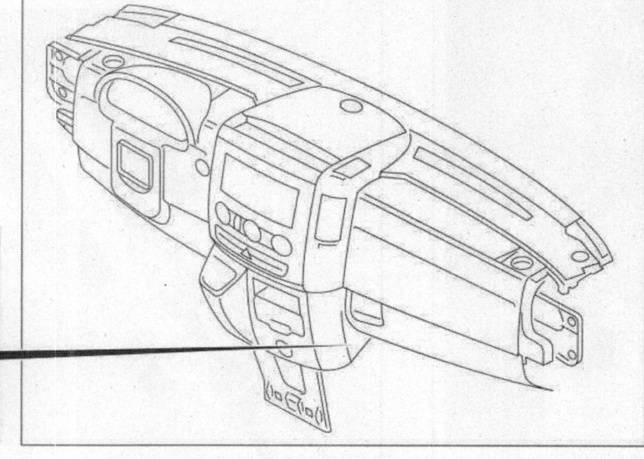

71112_MBSV_G0161

Fig. 163 Blower regulator removal/installation

23. Pull heater heat exchanger (1) out of its support in direction of arrow, push blower housing (3) to one side and remove heater heat exchanger (1).

24. Installation is the reverse of removal. Observe the following torques:

- Bolt, dashboard support to body: 15 ft. lbs. (20 Nm)
- Nut, refrigerant lines to expansion valve: 53 inch lbs. (6 Nm)
- Bolt, stowage box/tray to bracket: 44 inch lbs. (5 Nm)

STEERING

POWER STEERING GEAR

REMOVAL & INSTALLATION

See Figures 164 and 165.

1. Before servicing the vehicle, refer to the Precautions section.
2. Using a hand pump, suction off steering oil.
3. Raise and safely support the vehicle.
4. Remove front wheels.
5. Unscrew nut (2) at tie rod end (3).
6. Detach tie rod end (3) at left front and right front on steering knuckle using puller.
7. Turn steering (14) to right stop.
8. Remove bolt, (7) and loosen universal joint (6) on steering (14).
9. Remove nuts (10, 11) and loosen retaining clamps (8) at pressure line (9).
10. Remove bolt, (15) and detach pressure line (12) and return line (13) from steering (14).

➡Seal line bores on steering (14), pressure line (12) and return line (13) with stop plugs. This prevents dirt from entering. Replace seals on pressure line (12) and return line (13). This prevents leaks.

11. Mark installation position and loosen jam nut just enough that the tie rod end (3) can be screwed out. Remove left tie rod end (3).
12. Remove bolts (17) and remove left and right spring clamp plates (16).

➡Loosen bolts (17) uniformly in stages. Otherwise the spring clamp plates (16) will be pressed downwards approx. 10mm when loosened. This can cause damage to the threads.

➡Pay attention to different lengths of bolts.

13. Remove bolts (18) and steering (14).

⁂ WARNING

Carefully remove steering (14). Damage to the housing can result in leakage and malfunctions.

➡During installation, the universal joint (6) must first be inserted and then the bolts (18) fitted.

14. Installation is the reverse of removal. Observe the following torques:

- M12x1.5 bolt, lower spring clamp plate to front axle beam: 78 ft. lbs. (106 Nm) +90 degrees
- M8 bolt, lower spring clamp plate

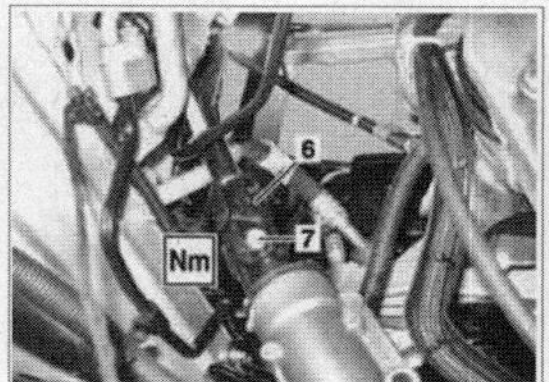

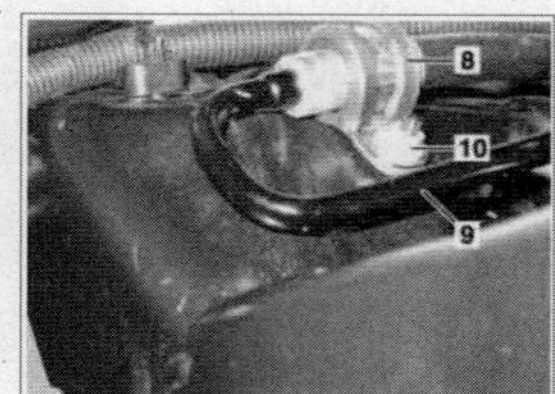

1. Brake disk
2. Nut
3. Tie rod end
4. Heat shield
5. Screw
6. Universal joint
7. Screw
8. Retaining clamp
9. Pressure line
10. Nut

71112_MBSV_G0164

Fig. 164 Steering gear removal/installation, 1 of 2

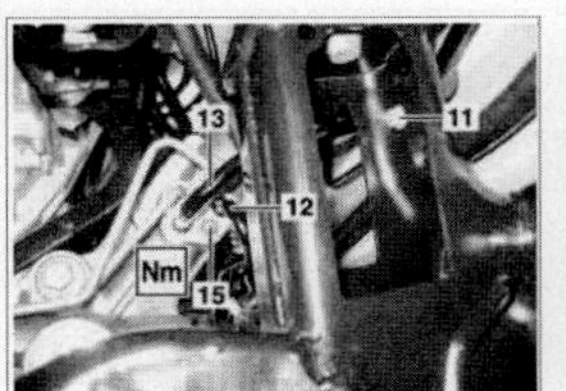

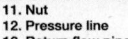

11. Nut
12. Pressure line
13. Return flow pipe
14. Steering
15. Screw
16. Spring clamp plates
17. Bolts
18. Bolts

71112_MBSV_G0165

Fig. 165 Steering gear removal/installation, 2 of 2

to front axle beam: 21 ft. lbs. (29 Nm)

- Universal joint to steering gear shaft: 20 ft. lbs. (28 Nm)
- High-pressure expansion hose to steering gear: 13 ft. lbs. (18 Nm)
- Return flow line to steering gear: 13 ft. lbs. (18 Nm)
- Bolt, steering gear to front axle: Step 1, 18 ft. lbs. (25 Nm); Step 2, 59 ft. lbs. (80 Nm); Step 3, +90 degrees
- M14x1.5 nut on ball head: 37 ft. lbs. (50 Nm) +60 degrees
- Lock nut at ball head: 48 ft. lbs. (65 Nm)

15. Torque the wheel as follows:
    - Model 906.11/13/21/23/61/63/71/73, Model 906.15/25/65 with code RH9 super single tires with steel rims: 177 ft. lbs. (240 Nm)
    - Model 906.11/13/21/23/61/63/71/73, Model 906.15/25/65 with code RH9 super single tires with aluminum rims: 133 ft. lbs. (180 Nm)
    - Model 906.15/25/65 without code RH9 super single tires: 133 ft. lbs. (180 Nm)

POWER STEERING PUMP

REMOVAL & INSTALLATION

See Figure 166.

1. Before servicing the vehicle, refer to the Precautions section.
2. Release washer fluid reservoir for windshield washer system, remove upwards and out of the guide and place to one side with lines and hoses attached.
3. Remove fan shroud. See the Engine Cooling section.
4. Release load on poly-V belt and remove from power steering pump (1). See the Engine Mechanical section.
5. Clamp off hose with clamp (2).
6. Disassemble hose (2) from power steering pump (1).
7. Position a catch container and disassemble high-pressure hose (3) from the power steering pump (1) and seal using a suitable stop plug.
8. Unscrew bolts (4, 5).
9. Take out power steering pump (1).
10. Installation is the reverse of removal. Observe the following torques:
    - High pressure expansion hose to power steering pump: 28 ft. lbs. (38 Nm)
    - Bolt, power steering pump to crankcase: 15 ft. lbs. (20 Nm)

FILLING & BLEEDING

See Figure 167.

1. Before servicing the vehicle, refer to the Precautions section.
2. Fill reservoir (1) of power steering pump. Fill up to approx. 10 mm below top edge of reservoir.
3. Start and shut off engine 2 to 3 times. The steering system bleeds itself automatically.
4. When the engine is running, turn the steering wheel several times from end stop to end stop. The power steering pump must not suction any air. Refill as necessary.

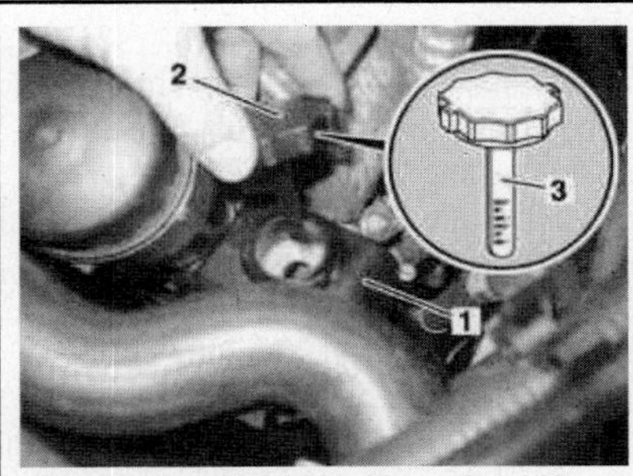

Shown on model 639 with engine 112
1. Reservoir
2. Reservoir cap
3. Dipstick

71112_MBSV_G0167

Fig. 167 Filling and bleeding the steering pump

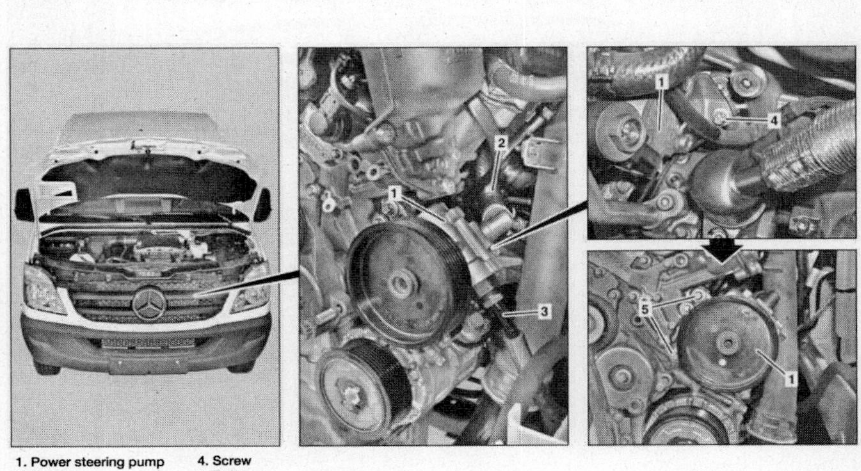

1. Power steering pump
2. Hose
3. High pressure hose
4. Screw
5. Bolts

71112_MBSV_G0166

Fig. 166 Steering pump removal/installation

LEAF SPRING

REMOVAL & INSTALLATION

See Figures 168 through 170.

1. Before servicing the vehicle, refer to the Precautions section.
2. Raise and safely support the vehicle.
3. Remove spring clamp plate (2). The spring clamp plates are spring loaded. To avoid damage to the thread, undo all bolts (1) by approx. 10 mm to relieve the spring pressure.
4. Detach left and right torsion bar linkage (7) from torsion bar.
5. Detach left and right stop plate (8) from transverse control arm (10).
6. With code (LG0) bi-xenon headlamp or code (LG1) bi-xenon headlamp with corner illuminating fog lamps, remove ball head of link rod (11) from transverse control arm (10).
7. Unscrew left transverse control arm (10) from front axle and pry out of place. See the procedure in this section.
8. Remove front spring (3) Check rubber bushings for signs of wear and damage, replace if necessary.
9. Installation is the reverse of removal. Check for correct seating of rubber bushings in front spring (3) and in the transverse control arm (10). Observe the following torques:
   - M12x1.5 Bolt, lower spring clamp plate to front axle beam: 78 ft. lbs. (106 Nm) +90 degrees
   - M8 Bolt, lower spring clamp plate to front axle beam: 21 ft. lbs. (29 Nm)
   - Nut, torsion bar linkage to torsion bar: 78 ft. lbs. (106 Nm)
   - Nut, transverse control arm to front axle housing: 127 ft. lbs. (172 Nm) +90 degrees
   - M10 Bolt, stop plate to transverse control arm/bump stop: 43 ft. lbs. (58 Nm)
   - M12x1.5 Bolt, stop plate to transverse control arm/bump stop: 78 ft. lbs. (106 Nm) +90 degrees
   - Nut (transverse control arm), supporting joint to steering knuckle: 125 ft. lbs. (170 Nm)

1. Bolts
2. Spring clamp plates
3. Front spring

71112_MBSV_G0168

Fig. 168 Leaf spring removal/installation, part 1 of 3

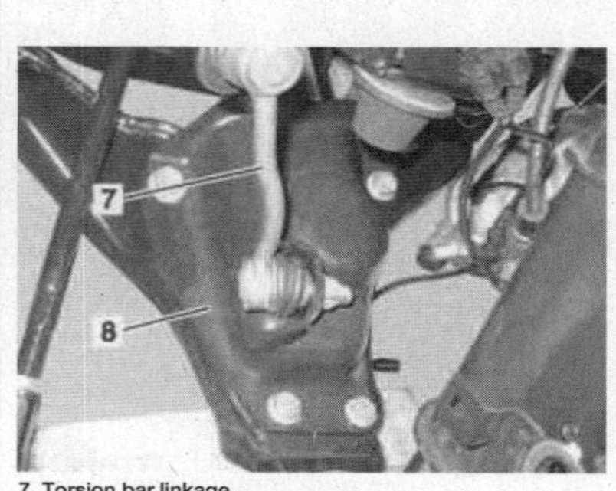

7. Torsion bar linkage
8. Stop plate

71112_MBSV_G0169

Fig. 169 Leaf spring removal/installation, part 2 of 3

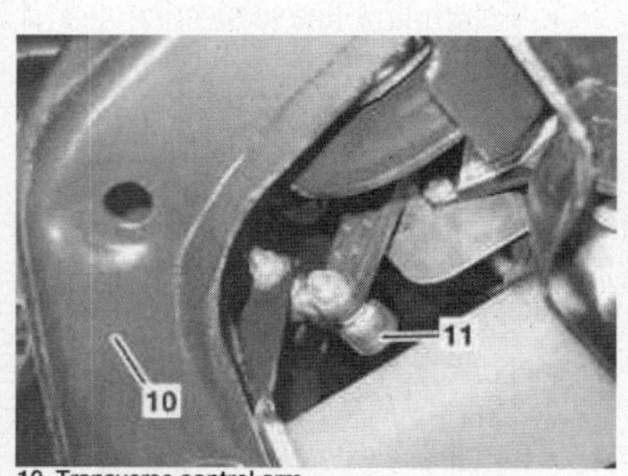

10. Transverse control arm
11. Link rod (with code (LG0) Bi-Xenon headlamp or code (LG1) Bi-xenon headlamp with cornering lights)

71112_MBSV_G0170

Fig. 170 Leaf spring removal/installation, part 3 of 3

STABILIZER BAR & LINKS

REMOVAL & INSTALLATION

See Figures 171 through 174.

1. Before servicing the vehicle, refer to the Precautions section.
2. Raise and safely support the vehicle.
3. Remove left and right spring clamp plates.
   a. Remove spring clamp plate (2).

✲✲ WARNING

The spring clamp plates are spring loaded. To avoid damage to the thread, undo all bolts (1) by approx. 10 mm to relieve the spring pressure.

   b. Detach left and right torsion bar linkage (4) from stabilizer bar (6).

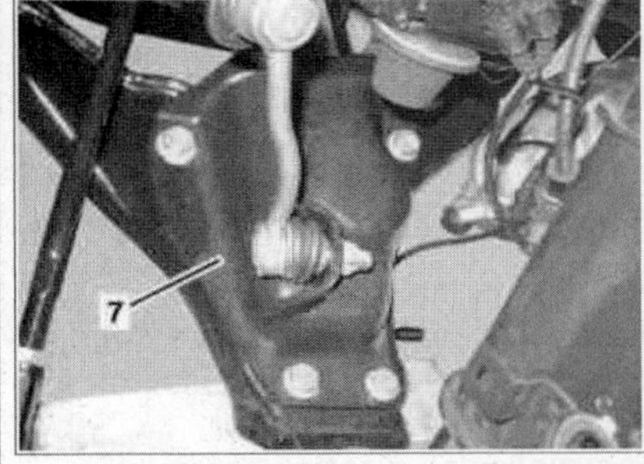

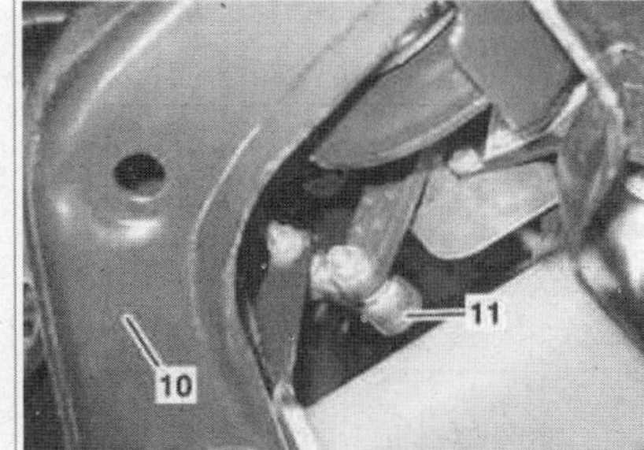

Shown on vehicle without code (ZG1/ZG2/ZG3/ZG4) All-wheel drive

3. Nut
4. Torsion bar linkage
5. Bolts
6. Stabilizer bar
7. Stop plate
10. Transverse control arm
11. Link rod (with code (LG0) Bi-xenon headlamp or code (LG1) Bi-xenon headlamp with cornering lights)

71112_MBSV_G0175

Fig. 171 Stabilizer bar & links removal/installation

1. Bolts
2. Spring clamp plates
3. Front spring

71112_MBSV_G0177

Fig. 172 Spring clamp plate removal/installation

c. Detach left and right stop plate (8) from transverse control arm (10).

d. With code (LG0) bi-xenon headlamp or code (LG1) bi-xenon headlamp with corner illuminating fog lamps, remove ball head of link rod (11) from transverse control arm (10).

e. Unscrew left transverse control arm (10) from front axle and pry out. See the procedure in this section.

4. Remove bearing shells and rubber mount from torsion bar (6).

5. Remove left stop plate (7) from transverse control arm (10).

6. With code (LG0) bi-xenon headlamp or code (LG1) bi-xenon headlamp with corner illuminating fog lamps, remove ball head of link rod (11) from transverse control arm (10).

7. Remove torsion bar (6) at left side.

To install:

8. Install torsion bar (6) on left side.

9. Bolt left transverse control arm (10) to front axle. See the procedure in this section.

10. With code (LG0) bi-xenon headlamp or code (LG1) bi-xenon headlamp with corner illuminating fog lamps, install ball head of link rod (11) to transverse control arm (10).

11. Mount left stop plate (7) onto transverse control arm (10).

12. Mount bearing shells and rubber mount to torsion bar (6). Check rubber mount for wear and damage, replace if necessary. For torsion bar with torsion rubber mounts: Tighten bolts (5) of mount after adjusting the torque.

➡See the accompanying illustration for modified rubber mount on front axle stabilizer bar.

13. Adjust and tighten stabilizer bar (6). For torsion bar (6) with torsion rubber mounts, measured from the lower edge of the front axle to the center of the mounting hole in the torsion bar (6), the installed dimension should be 2.34 inches (59.5mm)

14. Mount left and right torsion bar linkage (4) onto torsion bar (6).

15. Mount left and right spring clamp plates.

16. Observe the following torques:

- Bolt, stabilizer bar to frame-type integral support: 43 ft. lbs. (58 Nm)
- Nut, stabilizer bar linkage to stabilizer bar: 78 ft. lbs. (106 Nm)
- M10 Bolt, stop plate to transverse control arm/bump stop: 43 ft. lbs. (58 Nm)
- M12x1.5 Bolt, stop plate to trans-

Picture A: New version
1. Rubber bushing
2. Stabilizer bar
As of production period 07/2010 a modified rubber mount (1) to the stabilizer bar on the front axle. In contrast to the old rubber mount (3) this is a torsion bearing, which has to be installed and bolted at the zero position. The stabilizer bar (2) is then hooked into the link rods.

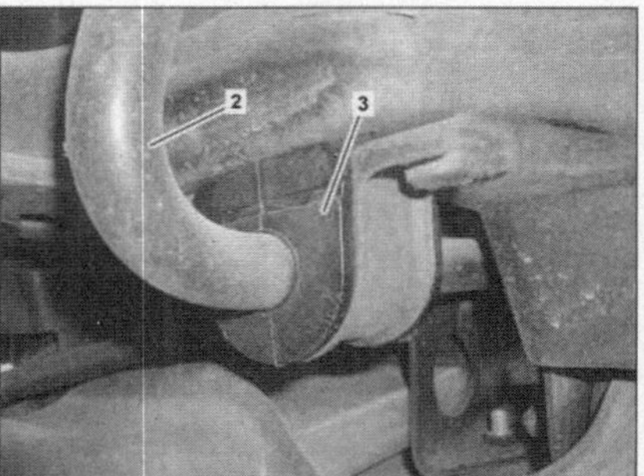

Picture B: Old version
2. Stabilizer bar
3. Rubber bushing
In a repair instance, care must be taken to ensure that only the rubber mounts (1) are installed. Both sides must always be processed. The bearing shells with bolts are also to be replaced during the change, because the geometry of the bearing shells was changed.

71112_MBSV_G0178

Fig. 173 Modified rubber mount on front axle stabilizer bar

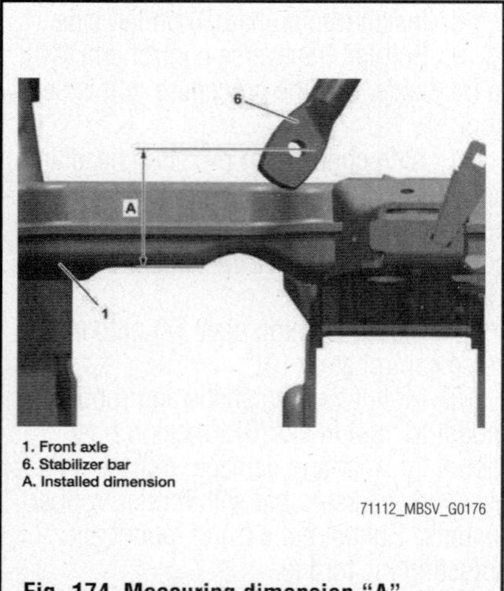

1. Front axle
6. Stabilizer bar
A. Installed dimension

71112_MBSV_G0176

Fig. 174 Measuring dimension "A"

verse control arm/bump stop: 78 ft. lbs. (106 Nm) +90 degrees

- Bolt, reinforcement plate to frame-type integral support: 21 ft. lbs. (29 Nm)

17. Lower the vehicle.

STEERING KNUCKLE

REMOVAL & INSTALLATION

See Figure 175.

1. Before servicing the vehicle, refer to the Precautions section.
2. Raise and safely support the vehicle.
3. Remove front wheel.
4. Remove brake disc (1). See the Brake section.

➡Unscrew brake carrier complete with brake pads and brake caliper and suspend in fender liner using binding wire.

5. Remove tie rod end (7) from steering knuckle (6).
6. Unscrew bolt (12) and remove left front rpm sensor (L6/1)/right front rpm sensor (L6/2).
7. Unscrew nut (3) from supporting joint (13).

⁂ CAUTION

Risk of injury caused by pinching or crushing when working on springs or spring bodies that are under tension. Use only approved tensioning devices; shield off hazard area if necessary. Inspect special tools for damage and proper operation (visual inspection). Wear protective gloves.

8. Remove steering knuckle (6) from suspension strut (4) and supporting joint (13) with a puller. On installation, replace bolts and nuts (2). Always mount the nuts (2) on the brake caliper side. Tighten nuts (2) only slightly. The final tightening torque takes place after the wheel alignment check.

➡The steering knuckle (6) and transverse control arm (8) are spring-loaded. Support transverse control arm (8) using a telescopic lifter, remove/install steering knuckle (6), and then slowly relieve transverse control arm (8).

9. Installation is the reverse of removal.
10. Perform wheel alignment check.
11. Observe the following torques:

1. Brake disk
2. Nuts
3. Nut
4. Suspension strut
5. Nut
6. Steering knuckle
7. Tie rod end
8. Transverse control arm
9. Screw
10. Heat shield
12. Screw
13. Supporting joint
L6/1. Left front rpm sensor
L6/2. Right front rpm sensor

71112_MBSV_G0181

Fig. 175 Steering knuckle removal/installation

- Bolt, suspension strut to steering knuckle: 110 ft. lbs. (140 Nm) +120 degrees
- Nut (transverse control arm), supporting joint to steering knuckle: 125 ft. lbs. (170 Nm)
- Bolt, ABS sensor to steering knuckle: 72 inch lbs. (8 Nm)
- Nut on ball head: 37 ft. lbs. (50 Nm) +60 degrees

SUSPENSION STRUT ASSEMBLY

REMOVAL & INSTALLATION

See Figure 176.

1. Before servicing the vehicle, refer to the Precautions section.
2. On passenger's side, remove cover from tools.
3. On driver's side, remove the cover strip (4).
4. Remove floor covering (5) on the driver' side.
5. Raise and safely support the vehicle.
6. Remove front wheel.
7. Remove wheel well cover.
8. Unclip cable on suspension strut (1).
9. Raise transverse control arm approx. 10mm using vehicle jack. This removes the tractive force from the suspension strut (1). This serves to prevent tearing the thread.
10. Remove flange bolt (3) of support bushing on suspension strut (1) at top. On installation, replace flange bolts (3). Only tighten the flange bolts (3) when the suspension strut (1) is screwed onto the steering knuckle.
11. Remove suspension strut (1) from steering knuckle. On installation, replace bolts and nuts (2). Always mount the nuts (2) on the brake caliper side. Pre-tighten nuts (2) slightly only. The final tightening torque takes place after the wheel alignment check.

➡Check suspension strut (1) for damage and leaks. If defects are detected, the suspension strut (1) must be replaced.

12. Installation is the reverse of removal.
13. Perform wheel alignment check.
14. Observe the following torques:
    - Bolt, suspension strut to steering knuckle: 103 ft. lbs. (140 Nm) + 120 degrees
    - Flange bolt, support bearing to body: 21 ft. lbs. (28 Nm) +60 degrees)

TORSION BAR LINKAGE

REMOVAL & INSTALLATION

See Figure 177.

1. Before servicing the vehicle, refer to the Precautions section.
2. Raise and safely support the vehicle.
3. Unscrew nuts (2).
4. Remove torsion bar linkage (1). Observe installation position as the torsion bar linkage (1) only has sufficient clearance in the correct installation position.
5. Installation is the reverse of removal. Observe the following torques:
    - Nut, torsion bar linkage to torsion bar: 78 ft. lbs. (106 Nm)
    - Nut, torsion bar linkage to transverse control arm: 78 ft. lbs. (106 Nm)

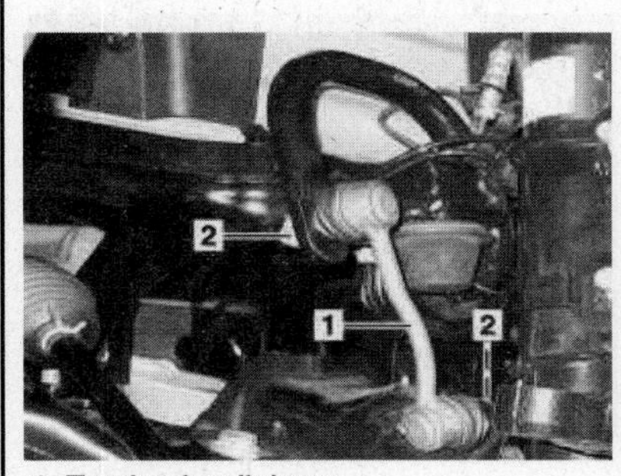

1. Torsion bar linkage
2. Nut

71112_MBSV_G0179

Fig. 177 Torsion Bar linkage

TRANSVERSE CONTROL ARM

REMOVAL & INSTALLATION

See Figures 178 through 181.

1. Before servicing the vehicle, refer to the Precautions section.
2. Unscrew left transverse control arm (10) from front axle and pry out of place.
    a. Remove stop plate (1) from transverse control arm (2) and turn up to top.
    b. Unscrew nut (7) from supporting joint.
    c. Support transverse control arm (2) using transmission jack.
    d. Unscrew transverse control arm (2) from front axle (6) and pry out. On installation, ensure correct seating of rubber bushings in front spring and in the transverse control arm (2). Tighten bolts (4) only with suspension compressed.

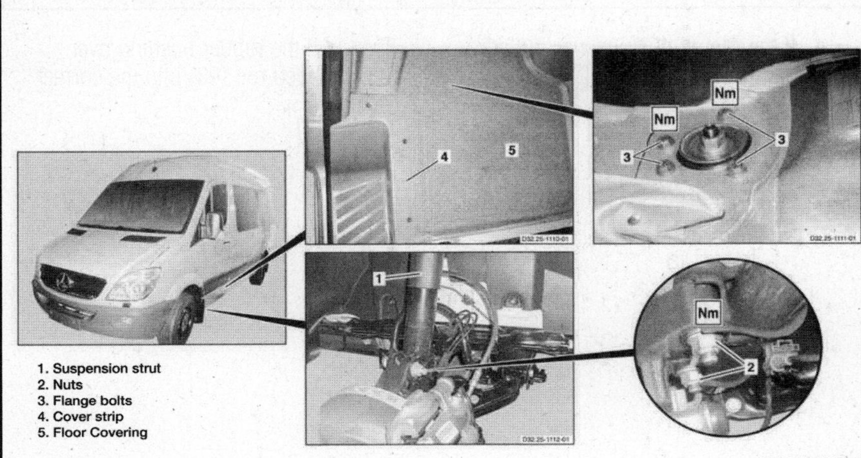

1. Suspension strut
2. Nuts
3. Flange bolts
4. Cover strip
5. Floor Covering

71112_MBSV_G0180

Fig. 176 Suspension strut removal/installation

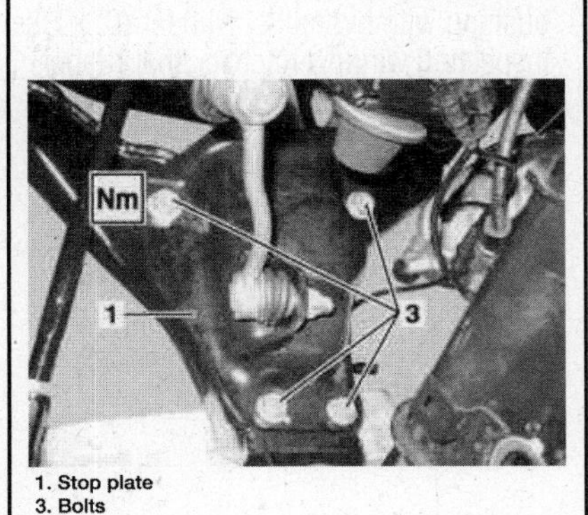

1. Stop plate
3. Bolts

71112_MBSV_G0171

Fig. 178 Transverse control arm removal/installation, part 1 of 4

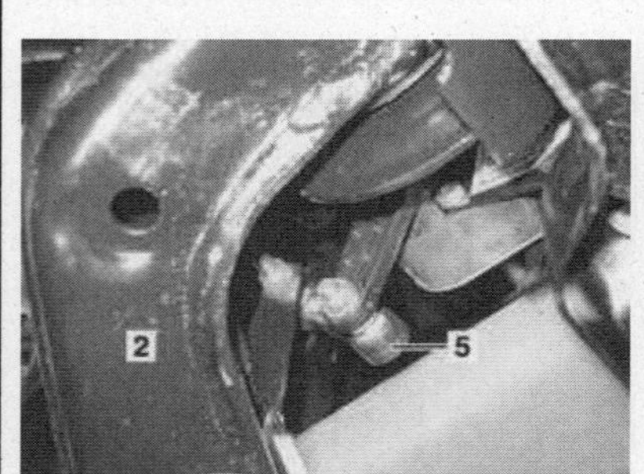

Shown on code (LG0) Bi-xenon headlamp

2. Transverse control arm
5. Link rod

71112_MBSV_G0172

Fig. 179 Transverse control arm removal/installation, part 2 of 4

2. Transverse control arm
4. Bolts
6. Front axle

71112_MBSV_G0173

Fig. 180 Transverse control arm removal/installation, part 3 of 4

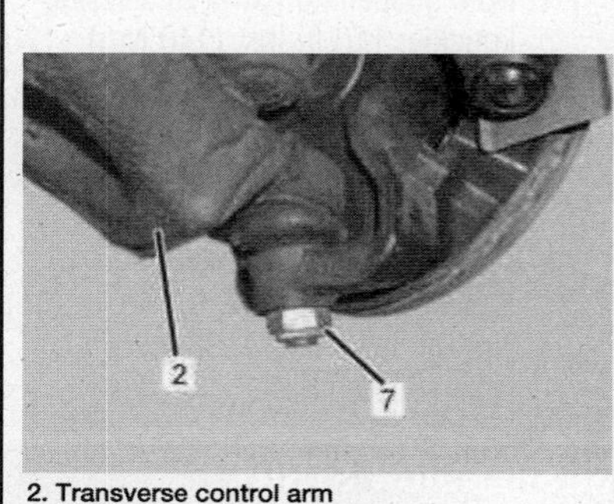

2. Transverse control arm
7. Nut

71112_MBSV_G0174

Fig. 181 Transverse control arm removal/installation, part 4 of 4

e. Detach supporting joint from steering knuckle and remove transverse control arm (2).

BUSHING REPLACEMENT

See Figure 182.

1. Before servicing the vehicle, refer to the Precautions section.
2. Remove transverse control arm (1).
3. Using a hydraulic press, press out rubber bushing from transverse control arm (1).
4. Follow the press instructions and press in a new bushing coated with silicone grease:
   a. Fit remover (02) on transverse control arm (1).
   b. Fit on hydraulic cylinder (01) with threaded rod (03) and from the other side push insertion sleeve (04) with new rubber bushing and friction discs (05) on to threaded rod (03).
   c. Screw on nut (06) until it is flush in insertion sleeve (04). Pull in rubber bushing with hydraulic cylinder (01). Use inspection window to check that rubber bushing is positioned centrally through in remover (02).

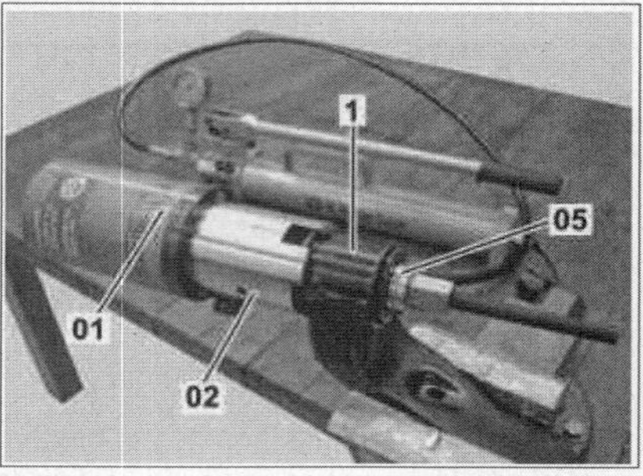

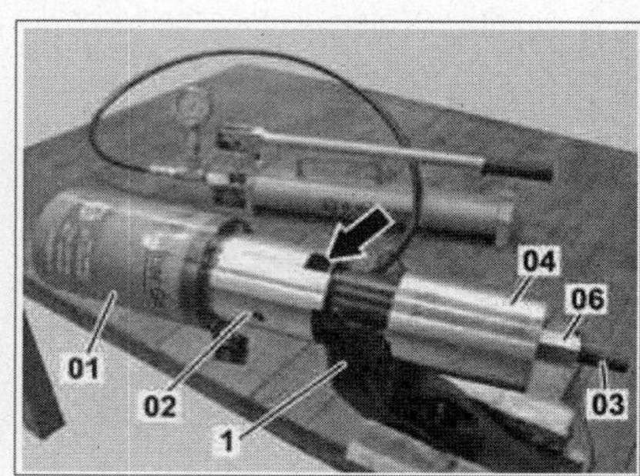

01. Hydraulic cylinder symbol can't be copied.
02. Remover symbol can't be copied.
03. Threaded rod symbol can't be copied.
04. Insertion sleeve symbol can't be copied.
05. Friction disks symbol can't be copied.
06. Nut symbol can't be copied.
1. Transverse control arm

71112_MBSV_G0182

Fig. 182 Bushing replacement

   d. If the rubber bushing was pulled in too far, fit the remover (02) on the opposite side as a counter support and then pull the rubber bushing over the threaded rod (03) into the correct position.

LEAF SPRINGS

REMOVAL & INSTALLATION

See Figures 183 and 184.

1. Before servicing the vehicle, refer to the Precautions section.
2. Raise and safely support the vehicle.
3. Support the rear axle using transmission jack and transmission plate.
4. When removing left rear spring (4) on vehicles with code (LG0) Bi-xenon headlamp or with code (LG1) Bi-xenon headlamp with cornering lights, use suitable tool to pry off ball head of link rod (9) from relay lever of rear axle sensor for headlamp range adjustment.
5. Detach spring U-bolt (1).
6. Remove spring plate (2).
7. Remove rear spring (4) from front spring bracket.
8. Remove rear spring (4) with spring shackle (7) from rear spring bracket.
9. Lower rear axle using transmission jack and remove rear spring (4). Take care to not stretch the brake hoses.
10. Detach spring shackle (7) from rear spring (4).
11. Check rubber mounts in rear spring (4) and spring shackle (7). If necessary, replace rubber mounts.

To install:

12. Mount spring shackle (7) onto rear bearing eye of rear spring (4). Replace nut (3). Adjust the installed dimension before tightening the nut (3). The correct dimension is 57.8 inches (146.75cm).
13. Mount rear spring (4) onto front spring bracket. Do not yet tighten screw/bolt (5) of front spring mounting. This prevents the spring bushings from tightening. Make sure that the rear spring (A) is at the correct installation position.
14. Install with the larger bearing eye (arrow) towards the front. Replace nut (3).
15. Mount rear spring (4) with spring shackle (7) to rear spring bracket. Do not yet tighten screw/bolt (8) of rear spring mounting. This prevents the spring bushings from tightening. Replace nut (3).
16. Raise rear axle using transmission jack Pay attention to correct seat of

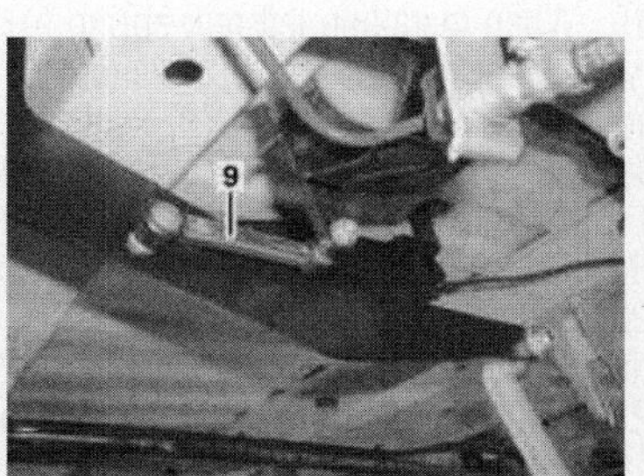

9. Link rod (with code (LG0) Bi-xenon headlamp or code (LG1) Bi-xenon headlamp with cornering lights)

71112_MBSV_G0187

Fig. 184 Link rod with codes LG0 or LG1

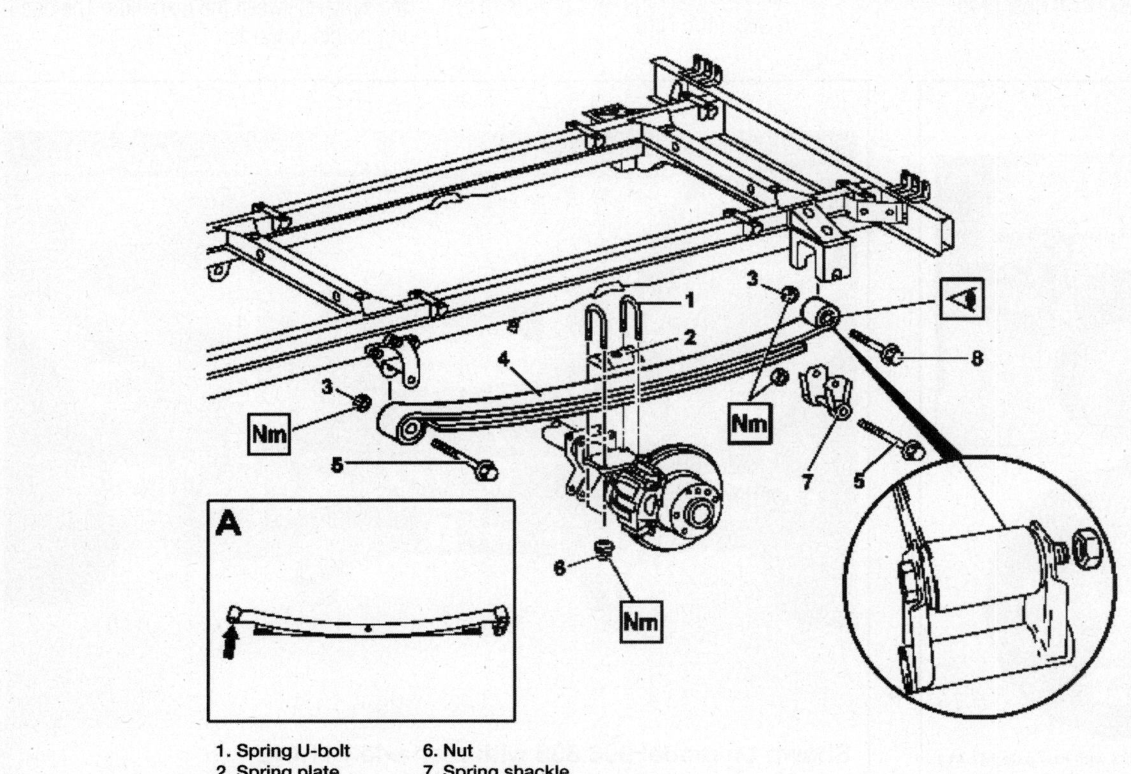

Fig. 183 Rear spring and related parts

center bolt in the mounting hole of the rear axle.

17. Mount spring plate (2).

18. Mount spring U-bolt (1) Replace nuts (6).

19. When installing left rear spring (4) on vehicles with code (LG0) Bi-xenon headlamp or with code (LG1) Bi-xenon headlamp with cornering lights, mount link rod (9) onto relay lever of rear axle sensor on headlamp range adjustment.

20. Lower the vehicle and remove supports.

21. Tighten bolts (5, 8) of spring attachments The screws/bolts (5, 8) should only be tightened with the rear spring (4) in its compressed state.

22. Observe the following torques:

- M12x1.5 bolt, rear spring to front spring bracket: 44 ft. lbs. (60 Nm) +180 degrees
- M16x1.5 bolt, rear spring to front spring bracket: 177 ft. lbs. (240 Nm)
- M12x1.5 bolt, rear spring to rear spring bracket: 52 ft. lbs. (70 Nm) +180 degrees
- M16x1.5 bolt, rear spring to rear spring bracket: 177 ft. lbs. (240 Nm)
- M12x1.5 bolt, spring shackle to rear spring bracket: 52 ft. lbs. (70 Nm) +180 degrees
- M16x1.5 bolt, spring shackle to rear spring bracket: 177 ft. lbs. (240 Nm)

SHOCK ABSORBERS

REMOVAL & INSTALLATION

See Figure 185.

1. Before servicing the vehicle, refer to the Precautions section.

2. Raise and safely support the vehicle.

3. Unscrew nut (2), pull out bolt and release damper (1) from lower mount.

4. Unscrew bolt (3) and remove shock absorber (1).

5. Check shock absorber (1) for damage and leaks. If damaged or leaking, the shock absorber (1) must be replaced.

6. Installation is the reverse of removal. Observe the following torques:

- M12x1.5 nut/bolt, shock absorber to rear axle, on Model 906.11/13/21/23/61/63/71/73 with rear axle 741.412/413/415/428: 78 ft. lbs. (106 Nm)
- M14x1.5 nut/bolt, shock absorber to rear axle, on Model 906.15/25/65 with rear axle 741.41/420/429 without code PL9: 99 ft. lbs. (135 Nm)

STABILIZER BAR (SWAY BAR) & LINKS

REMOVAL & INSTALLATION

See Figures 186 through 188.

1. Before servicing the vehicle, refer to the Precautions section.

2. Raise and safely support the vehicle.

3. Mark assembly position of the bushing on stabilizer bar.

4. Remove bolts (2).

5. Remove bolts (3) and remove stabilizer bar (1) on the link rods (4).

6. Remove clamps (5) and rubber bushing (6). Clean all parts, check for wear and replace if necessary Bushing points must be free of grease.

To install:

7. Mount rubber bushing (6). Only use rubber bushing. Align rubber bushing (6) in the center between the markings. The opening points upwards.

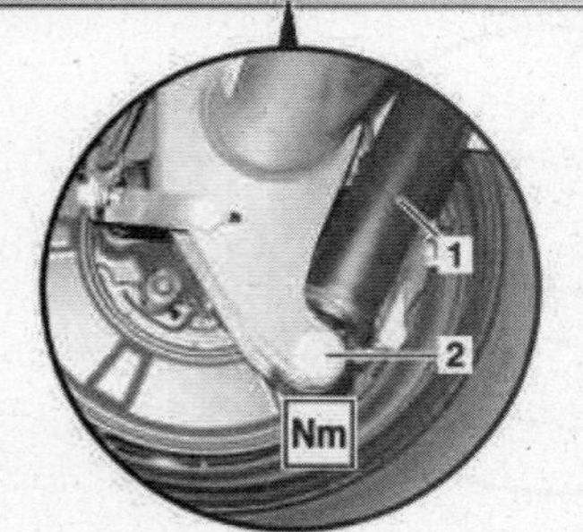

Shown on model 906.633 with rear axle 741.412

1. Shock absorber
2. Nut
3. Screw

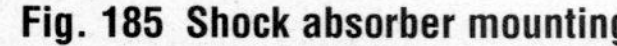

71112_MBSV_G0188

Fig. 185 Shock absorber mounting

Shown on model 906.633 with rear axle 741.412

1. Stabilizer bar
2. Bolts
3. Screw
4. Link rod

71112_MBSV_G0183

Fig. 186 Stabilizer bar removal/installation, 1 of 2

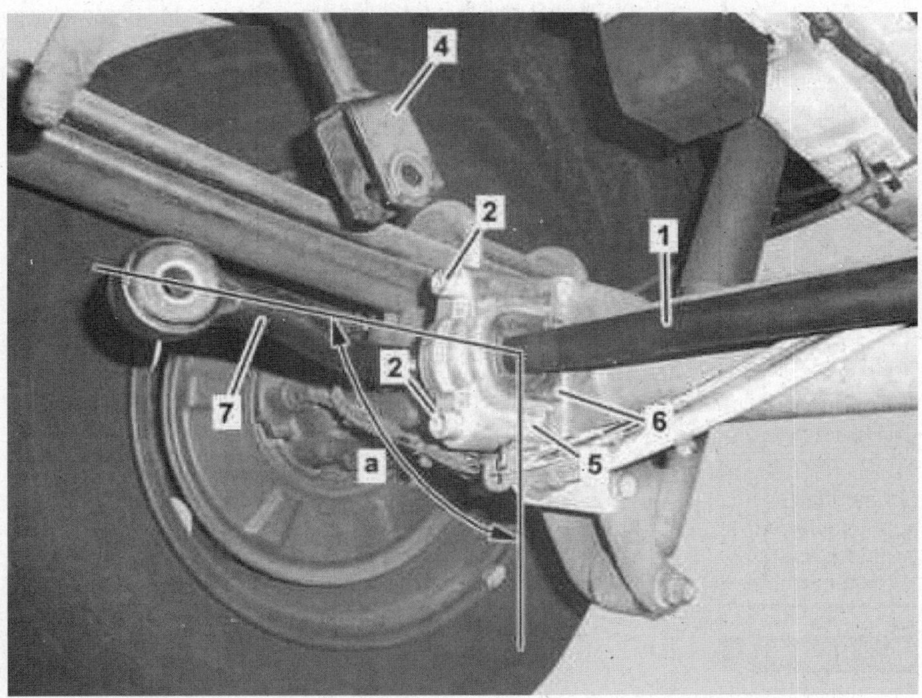

1. Stabilizer bar
2. Bolts
4. Link rod
5. Clip
6. Rubber bushing
7. Stabilizer bar arm

71112_MBSV_G0184

Fig. 187 Stabilizer bar removal/installation, 2 of 2

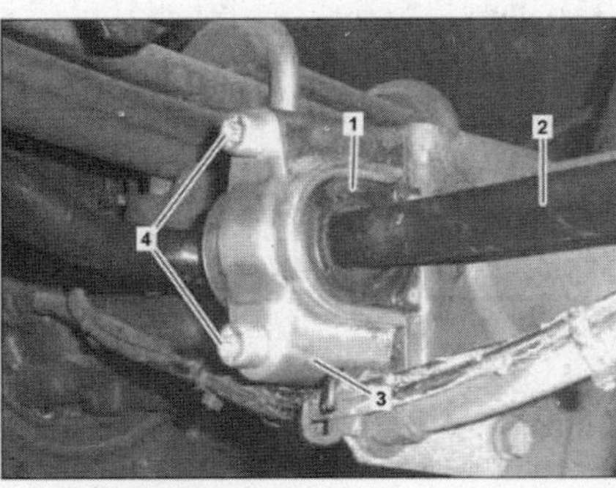

Illustrated on model 906.633

Picture A: New version
1. Rubber bushing
2. Stabilizer bar
3. Bearing shell
4. Bolts

As of production period 07/2012 a modified rubber bushing (1) to the stabilizer bar on the rear axle. In contrast to the old rubber bushing (5), this is a torsion bearing, which has to be installed and bolted at the zero position. The stabilizer bar (2) is then hooked into the link rods.

Picture B: Old version
2. Stabilizer bar
3. Bearing shell
4. Bolts
5. Rubber bushing

In a repair instance, care must be taken to ensure that only the new rubber bushings (1) are installed from now on. Both sides must always be processed. With the change in rubber bushings, the bearing shells (3) with bolts (4) have also changed, and therefore also need to be replaced.

71112_MBSV_G0185

Fig. 188 Modified rubber bushing on rear axle stabilizer bar

➡See the accompanying illustrations for modified rubber bushing on rear axle stabilizer bar:

8. Install clamps (5). Replace clamps if bushing has not been changed over to torsion bushing. For easy mounting, wet the rubber bushing (6) on the outside.
9. Adjust bushing so that the contact surfaces on the rear axle are at a 90° angle to the stabilizer bar arms (7).
10. Position stabilizer bar (1) on axle housing.
11. Adjust assembly position of stabilizer bar (dimension a). Dimension "a" should be 3.4 inches (86.7mm).
12. Tighten clamps (5).
13. Install stabilizer bar (1) on the link rods (4).
14. Observe the following torques:
    - Screw, connecting rod to stabilizer and longitudinal frame member (rear axle): 78 ft. lbs. (106 Nm)
    - Screw, stabilizer clamp to rear axle tube: 44 ft. lbs. (60 Nm)

MERCEDES-BENZ

Diagnostic Trouble Codes

DIAGNOSTIC TROUBLE CODES

OBD II VEHICLE APPLICATIONS

MERCEDES-BENZ

C/CLS
2011–2012
- 1.8L L4 SEFI. . .Engine Code: 271.860
- 1.8L L4, 3.0L V6 SEFI . .Engine Code: 272.947
- 1.8L L4, 3.0L V6 SEFI . .Engine Code: 272.948
- 3.5L V6 SEFI . .Engine Code: 272.961
- 3.5L V6 SEFI . .Engine Code: 272.957
- 4.7L V8 SEFI . .Engine Code: 278.922
- 5.5L V8, 6.2L V8 SEFI . .Engine Code: 273.960
- 5.5L V8, 6.2L V8 SEFI . .Engine Code: 157.981
- 6.2L V8 SEFI . .Engine Code: 156.985

E/SLK
2011–2012
- 1.8L L4 SEFI. . .Engine Code: 271.861
- 1.8L L4, 3.0L V6 CDI . . .Engine Code: 642.850
- 1.8L L4, 3.0L V6 SEFI . .Engine Code: 272.942
- 3.5L V6 SEFI . .Engine Code: 272.969
- 3.5L V6 SEFI . .Engine Code: 272.977
- 3.5L V6 SEFI . .Engine Code: 272.980
- 3.5L V6 SEFI . .Engine Code: 276.952
- 3.5L V6 SEFI . .Engine Code: 276.956
- 4.7L V8 SEFI . .Engine Code: 278.922
- 5.5L V8, 6.2L V8 SEFI . .Engine Code: 152.980
- 5.5L V8, 6.2L V8 SEFI . .Engine Code: 157.981
- 5.5L V8, 6.2L V8 SEFI . .Engine Code: 273.970
- 5.5L V8, 6.2L V8 SEFI . .Engine Code: 273.971
- 6.2L V8 SEFI . .Engine Code: 156.985

ML 450 hybrid
2011
- 3.5L L5 MFI . . .Engine Code: 272.973

Sprinter Van
2011–2012
- 3.0L V6 CDI . Engine Code: 642.898/C

OBD II Trouble Code List (P0XXX Codes)

DTC	Trouble Code Title, Conditions, Possible Causes
DTC: P0010 **T ECM, MIL: Yes** **Year:** 2011, 2012 **Model:** C250, C250, C300, C350, E350, E550, SLK350 **Engine:** 1.8L L4, 3.0L V6, 3.5L V6, 4.7L V8, 5.5L V8, 6.2L V8 **Transmission:** All	**Incorrect Camshaft Position Solenoid Circuit:** Continuous camshaft adjustment (Right Bank): Incorrect position of the intake camshaft. Intake CMP solenoid has an open or short circuit in the wiring.
DTC: P0011 **T ECM, MIL: Yes** **Year:** 2011, 2012 **Model:** C250, C250, C300, E350, E550 **Engine:** 1.8L L4, 3.0L V6, 3.5L V6, 4.7L V8, 4.7L V8, 5.5L V8, 6.2L V8 **Transmission:** All	**Incorrect Position of Intake Camshaft (Right Bank):** Engine output affected. Continuous camshaft adjustment (right side): incorrect position of the intake camshaft.
DTC: P0012 **T ECM, MIL: Yes** **Year:** 2011, 2012 **Model:** C250, C300, C350, E350, E550, SLK350 **Engine:** 1.8L L4, 3.0L V6, 3.5L V6, 4.7L V8, 5.5L V8, 6.2L V8 **Transmission:** All	**Incorrect Position of Intake Camshaft (Right Bank):** Engine output is affected. Continuous camshaft adjustment (right bank): incorrect position of the intake camshaft.
DTC: P0013 **T ECM, MIL: Yes** **Year:** 2011, 2012 **Model:** C250, C300, C350, E350, E550, SLK350 **Engine:** 1.8L L4, 3.0L V6, 3.5L V6, 4.7L V8, 5.5L V8, 6.2L V8 **Transmission:** All	**Camshaft Exhaust Solenoid (Left or Right Bank) :** No signal detected from the camshaft exhaust solenoids.
DTC: P0014 **T ECM, MIL: Yes** **Year:** 2011, 2012 **Model:** C250, C300, C350, E350, E550, SLK350 **Engine:** 1.8L L4, 3.0L V6, 3.5L V6, 4.7L V8, 5.5L V8, 6.2L V8 **Transmission:** All	**Incorrect Position of the Exhaust Camshaft :** Engine output is affected. Continuous camshaft adjustment (right bank).
DTC: P0015 **T ECM, MIL: Yes** **Year:** 2011, 2012 **Model:** C250, C300, C350, E350, E550, SLK350 **Engine:** 1.8L L4, 3.0L V6, 3.5L V6, 4.7L V8, 5.5L V8, 6.2L V8 **Transmission:** All	**Incorrect Position of the Exhaust Camshaft:** Engine output is affected. Continuous camshaft adjustment (right bank).
DTC: P0016 **T ECM, MIL: Yes** **Year:** 2011, 2012 **Model:** C250, C300, C350, E350, E550, SLK350 **Engine:** 1.8L L4, 3.0L V6, 3.5L V6, 4.7L V8, 5.5L V8, 6.2L V8 **Transmission:** All	**Constant Adjustment of Intake Camshaft (Right Bank) :** Constant adjustment of intake camshaft of right cylinder bank in direction of Advanced or Retarded.

DTC	Trouble Code Title, Conditions, Possible Causes
DTC: P0017 **T ECM, MIL: Yes** **Year:** 2011, 2012 **Model:** C250, C300, C350, E350, E550, SLK350 **Engine:** 1.8L L4, 3.0L V6, 3.5L V6, 4.7L V8, 5.5L V8, 6.2L V8 **Transmission:** All	**Constant Adjustment of Exhaust Camshaft (Right Bank) :** Constant adjustment of exhaust camshaft of right cylinder bank in direction of Advanced or Retarded.
DTC: P0018 **T ECM, MIL: Yes** **Year:** 2011, 2012 **Model:** C250, C300, C350, E350, E550, SLK350 **Engine:** 1.8L L4, 3.0L V6, 3.5L V6, 4.7L V8, 5.5L V8, 6.2L V8 **Transmission:** All	**Constant Adjustment of Intake Camshaft (Left Bank):** Constant adjustment of intake camshaft of left cylinder bank in direction of Advanced or Retarded.
DTC: P0019 **T ECM, MIL: Yes** **Year:** 2011, 2012 **Model:** C250, C300, C350, E350, E550, SLK350 **Engine:** 1.8L L4, 3.0L V6, 3.5L V6, 4.7L V8, 5.5L V8, 6.2L V8 **Transmission:** All	**Constant Adjustment of Exhaust Camshaft (Left Bank):** Constant adjustment of exhaust camshaft of left cylinder bank in the direction of Advanced or Retarded.
DTC: P0020 **T ECM, MIL: Yes** **Year:** 2011, 2012 **Model:** C250, C300, C350, E350, E550, SLK350 **Engine:** 1.8L L4, 3.0L V6, 3.5L V6, 4.7L V8, 5.5L V8, 6.2L V8 **Transmission:** All	**Continuous Camshaft Adjustment or Camshaft Intake Solenoid (Left Bank):** Left camshaft intake solenoid has an open circuit in the wiring. No signal from intake solenoid. Continuous camshaft adjustment (Left Bank): Incorrect position of the intake camshaft. Engine output is affected.
DTC: P0021 **T ECM, MIL: Yes** **Year:** 2011, 2012 **Model:** C250, C300, C350, E350, E550, SLK350 **Engine:** 1.8L L4, 3.0L V6, 3.5L V6, 4.7L V8, 5.5L V8, 6.2L V8 **Transmission:** All	**Incorrect Position of Intake Camshaft (Left Bank):** Continuous camshaft adjustment (Left Bank): Incorrect position of the intake camshaft. Engine output is affected.
DTC: P0022 **T ECM, MIL: Yes** **Year:** 2011, 2012 **Model:** C250, C300, C350, E350, E550, SLK350 **Engine:** 1.8L L4, 3.0L V6, 3.5L V6, 4.7L V8, 5.5L V8, 6.2L V8 **Transmission:** All	**Incorrect Position of the Intake Camshaft :** Continuous Camshaft Adjustment (Left Bank) Incorrect position of the intake camshaft. Engine output is affected
DTC: P0024 **T ECM, MIL: Yes** **Year:** 2011, 2012 **Model:** C250, C300, C350, E350, E550, SLK350 **Engine:** 1.8L L4, 3.0L V6, 3.5L V6, 4.7L V8, 5.5L V8, 6.2L V8 **Transmission:** All	**Incorrect Position of the Left Bank Exhaust Camshaft :** Continuous camshaft adjustment (left bank). Engine output is affected.

DTC	Trouble Code Title, Conditions, Possible Causes
DTC: P0025 **T ECM, MIL: Yes** **Year:** 2011, 2012 **Model:** C250, C300, C350, E350, E550, SLK350 **Engine:** 1.8L L4, 3.0L V6, 3.5L V6, 4.7L V8, 5.5L V8, 6.2L V8 **Transmission:** All	**Incorrect Position of the Left Bank Exhaust Camshaft :** Incorrect position of the exhaust camshaft (left bank). Engine output is affected.
DTC: P0030 **T ECM, MIL: Yes** **Year:** 2011, 2012 **Model:** C250, C300, C350, E350, E550, SLK350 **Engine:** 1.8L L4, 3.0L V6, 3.5L V6, 4.7L V8, 5.5L V8, 6.2L V8 **Transmission:** All	**HO2S Heater Control Circuit Sensor (Right Bank):** Heating of component G3/4 (Right O2 sensor, before TWC [KAT]) : Open circuit
DTC: P0031 **T ECM, MIL: Yes** **Year:** 2011, 2012 **Model:** C250, C300, C350, E350, E550, SLK350 **Engine:** 1.8L L4, 3.0L V6, 3.5L V6, 4.7L V8, 5.5L V8, 6.2L V8 **Transmission:** All	**HO2S Heater Control Circuit Short to Ground (Right Bank):** Heating of right O2 sensor, before TWC: Short circuit to ground
DTC: P0032 **T ECM, MIL: Yes** **Year:** 2011, 2012 **Model:** C250, C300, C350, E350, E550, SLK350 **Engine:** 1.8L L4, 3.0L V6, 3.5L V6, 4.7L V8, 5.5L V8, 6.2L V8 **Transmission:** All	**HO2S Heater Control Circuit Short to Positive:** Heating of component G3/4 (Right O2 sensor, before TWC [KAT]) : Short circuit to positive
DTC: P0036 **T , MIL: Yes** **Year:** 2011, 2012 **Model:** C250, C300, C350, E350, E550, SLK350 **Engine:** 1.8L L4, 3.0L V6, 3.5L V6, 4.7L V8, 5.5L V8, 6.2L V8 **Transmission:** All	**HO2S Open Circuit (Right Bank):** Heating of the right O2 sensor, after TWC: Open circuit
DTC: P0037 **T ECM, MIL: Yes** **Year:** 2011, 2012 **Model:** C250, C300, C350, E350, E550, SLK350 **Engine:** 1.8L L4, 3.0L V6, 3.5L V6, 4.7L V8, 5.5L V8, 6.2L V8 **Transmission:** All	**HO2S Heater Circuit Short (Right Bank):** Heating of right O2 sensor, after TWC: Short circuit to ground.
DTC: P0038 **T ECM, MIL: Yes** **Year:** 2011, 2012 **Model:** C250, C300, C350, E350, E550, SLK350 **Engine:** 1.8L L4, 3.0L V6, 3.5L V6, 4.7L V8, 5.5L V8, 6.2L V8 **Transmission:** All	**Heated Oxygen Sensor (Left Bank) Insufficient Heat:** Heating of component G3/5 (Left O2 sensor, after TWC [KAT]) : Heating capacity is too low.

DTC	Trouble Code Title, Conditions, Possible Causes
DTC: P0040 **T ECM, MIL: Yes** **Year:** 2011, 2012 **Model:** C250, C300, C350, E350, E550, SLK350 **Engine:** 1.8L L4, 3.0L V6, 3.5L V6, 4.7L V8, 5.5L V8, 6.2L V8 **Transmission:** All	**HO2S Sensors Improperly Connected:** Plug connections of the O2 sensors are wrongly connected. **NOTE: Check assignment of plug connections to O2 sensors.**
DTC: P0041 **T ECM, MIL: Yes** **Year:** 2011, 2012 **Model:** C250, C300, C350, E350, E550, SLK350 **Engine:** 1.8L L4, 3.0L V6, 3.5L V6, 4.7L V8, 5.5L V8, 6.2L V8 **Transmission:** All	**HO2S Sensors Downstream of TWC Improperly Connected:** O2 sensors downstream TWC : * Plug connections of the O2 sensors are wrongly connected. The ECM does not detect proper signal from sensor.
DTC: P0050 **T ECM, MIL: Yes** **Year:** 2011, 2012 **Model:** C250, C300, C350, E350, E550, SLK350 **Engine:** 1.8L L4, 3.0L V6, 3.5L V6, 4.7L V8, 5.5L V8, 6.2L V8 **Transmission:** All	**HO2S Sensor Open Circuit (Left Bank):** The ECM does not receive proper heat signal from O2 sensor (left bank, before TWC)
DTC: P0051 **T ECM, MIL: Yes** **Year:** 2011, 2012 **Model:** C250, C300, C350, E350, E550, SLK350 **Engine:** 1.8L L4, 3.0L V6, 3.5L V6, 4.7L V8, 5.5L V8, 6.2L V8 **Transmission:** All	**HO2S Circuit Short to Ground (Left Bank):** The ECM does not receive proper sensor heating signal.
DTC: P0052 **T ECM, MIL: Yes** **Year:** 2011, 2012 **Model:** C250, C300, C350, E350, E550, SLK350 **Engine:** 1.8L L4, 3.0L V6, 3.5L V6, 4.7L V8, 5.5L V8, 6.2L V8 **Transmission:** All	**HO2S Sensor Circuit Short to Positive (Left Bank):** The ECM does not receive proper heating signal from left forward O2 sensor.
DTC: P0056 **T ECM, MIL: Yes** **Year:** 2011, 2012 **Model:** C250, C300, C350, E350, E550, SLK350 **Engine:** 1.8L L4, 3.0L V6, 3.5L V6, 4.7L V8, 5.5L V8, 6.2L V8 **Transmission:** All	**HO2S Open Circuit (Left O2 Sensor, After TWC):** Exhaust system malfunction: * ECM does not receive proper signal from left O2 sensor. * Heating of left O2 sensor, after TWC open circuit
DTC: P0057 **T ECM, MIL: Yes** **Year:** 2011, 2012 **Model:** C250, C300, C350, E350, E550, SLK350 **Engine:** 1.8L L4, 3.0L V6, 3.5L V6, 4.7L V8, 5.5L V8, 6.2L V8 **Transmission:** All	**HO2S (Left O2 Sensor, After TWC) Short Circuit to Ground :** Exhaust system malfunction: * ECM does not receive proper signal from O2 sensor. * Left O2 sensor circuit short to ground

DTC	Trouble Code Title, Conditions, Possible Causes
DTC: P0058 **T ECM, MIL: Yes** **Year:** 2011, 2012 **Model:** C250, C300, C350, E350, E550, SLK350 **Engine:** 1.8L L4, 3.0L V6, 3.5L V6, 4.7L V8, 5.5L V8, 6.2L V8 **Transmission:** All	**HO2S Circuit (Left O2 Sensor, After TWC) Short to Positive:** Exhaust system malfunction: * ECM does not receive proper signal from left O2 sensor. * Left O2 sensor, after TWC [KAT]) Short circuit to positive.
DTC: P0068 **T ECM, MIL: Yes** **Year:** 2011, 2012 **Model:** C250, C300, C350, E350, E550, SLK350 **Engine:** 1.8L L4, 3.0L V6, 3.5L V6, 4.7L V8, 5.5L V8, 6.2L V8 **Transmission:** All	**MAF Signal Implausible:** The measured air mass is implausible compared to the position of the throttle valve. Irrational MAF and/or throttle valve position signal received. Engine output affected.
DTC: P0071 **T ECM, MIL: Yes** **Year:** 2011, 2012 **Model:** C250, C300, C350, E350, E550, SLK350 **Engine:** 1.8L L4, 3.0L V6, 3.5L V6, 4.7L V8, 5.5L V8, 6.2L V8 **Transmission:** All	**IAT Sensor Signal Outside Temperature Sensor Signal Improbable:** Plausibility error between signal of temperature sensor in intake pipe and signal of outside temperature sensor.
DTC: P0072 **T ECM, MIL: Yes** **Year:** 2011, 2012 **Model:** C250, C300, C350, E350, E550, SLK350 **Engine:** 1.8L L4, 3.0L V6, 3.5L V6, 4.7L V8, 5.5L V8, 6.2L V8 **Transmission:** All	**Ambient Temperature Sensor Short Circuit to Ground:** Incorrect ambient temperature display. Ambient temperature display temperature sensor has a short circuit to ground.
DTC: P0073 **T ECM, MIL: Yes** **Year:** 2011, 2012 **Model:** C250, C300, C350, E350, E550, SLK350 **Engine:** 1.8L L4, 3.0L V6, 3.5L V6, 4.7L V8, 5.5L V8, 6.2L V8 **Transmission:** All	**Ambient Temperature Sensor Circuit Short to Positive:** Improper ambient temperature display. Ambient temperature display temperature sensor has a short circuit to positive. Power generation is affected.
DTC: P0100 **2T ECM, MIL: Yes** **Year:** 2012 **Model:** CLS550, E550 **Engine:** 4.6L V8 **Transmission:** All	**Hot Film MAF Sensor:** Hot film MAF sensor signal threshold values and plausibility (air flow after air cleaner element) . Threshold values of voltage supply
DTC: P0101 **T ECM, MIL: Yes** **Year:** 2011, 2012 **Model:** C250, C300, C350, CLS550, E350, E550, SLK350 **Engine:** 1.8L L4, 3.0L V6, 3.5L V6, 4.7L V8, 4.6L V8, 5.5L V8, 6.2L V8 **Transmission:** All	**MAF Sensor:** Measured air mass is implausible compared to the position of the throttle valve. Air mass measured by hot film MAF sensor is too low. The cycle duration of the HFM signal is too long. **NOTE: Check sensor signal and voltage.**

DTC	Trouble Code Title, Conditions, Possible Causes
DTC: P0102 **T ECM, MIL: Yes** **Year:** 2011, 2012 **Model:** C250, C300, C350, CLS550, E350, E550, SLK350 **Engine:** 1.8L L4, 3.0L V6, 3.5L V6, 4.7L V8, 4.6L V8, 5.5L V8, 6.2L V8 **Transmission:** All	**MAF Sensor Circuit:** Hot film mass air flow sensor open circuit or short circuit to ground or to positive.
DTC: P0103 **T ECM, MIL: Yes** **Year:** 2011, 2012 **Model:** CLS550, E350, E550 **Engine:** 3.5L V6, 4.7L V8, 4.6L V8 **Transmission:** All	**MAF Sensor Circuit:** Hot film mass air flow sensor: Short circuit to positive. Short circuit to battery or reference voltage.
DTC: P0104 **T ECM, MIL: Yes** **Year:** 2011, 2012 **Model:** C250, C300, C350, CLS550, E350, E550, SLK350 **Engine:** 1.8L L4, 3.0L V6, 3.5L V6, 4.7L V8, 4.6L V8, 5.5L V8, 6.2L V8 **Transmission:** All	**Hot Film Mass Air Flow Sensor:** Engine output is affected. Hot film mass air flow sensor, loose contact with low frequency.
DTC: P0106 **2T ECM, MIL: Yes** **Year:** 2011, 2012 **Model:** C250, C300, C350, CLS550, E350, E550, SLK350 **Engine:** 1.8L L4, 3.0L V6, 3.5L V6, 4.7L V8, 4.6L V8, 5.5L V8, 6.2L V8 **Transmission:** All	**Pressure Sensor Implausible Value :** Engine output is affected . Pressure sensor may have failed . Signal of pressure sensor not equal to signal of altitude pressure sensor when engine not running.
DTC: P0107 **2T ECM, MIL: Yes** **Year:** 2011, 2012 **Model:** C250, C300, C350, CLS550, E350, E550, SLK350 **Engine:** 1.8L L4, 3.0L V6, 3.5L V6, 4.7L V8, 4.6L V8, 5.5L V8, 6.2L V8 **Transmission:** All	**Manifold Absolute Pressure/Barometric Pressure Circuit - Low Input:** Engine output is affected. Pressure sensor may have short circuit to ground, or an open circuit.
DTC: P0108 **2T ECM, MIL: Yes** **Year:** 2011, 2012 **Model:** C250, C300, C350, CLS550, E350, E550, SLK350 **Engine:** 1.8L L4, 3.0L V6, 3.5L V6, 4.7L V8, 4.6L V8, 5.5L V8, 6.2L V8 **Transmission:** All	**Manifold Absolute Pressure/Barometric Pressure Circuit - High Input:** Engine output is affected. Pressure sensor has short circuit to positive or open circuit.
DTC: P0110 **2T ECM, MIL: Yes** **Year:** 2011, 2012 **Model:** CLS550, E350, E550 **Engine:** 3.5L V6, 4.7L V8, 4.6L V8 **Transmission:** All	**Intake Air Temperature Circuit Malfunction:** The engine control module checks the current voltage at the IAT sensor to the voltage threshold values. If the threshold values are exceeded, an alternate value is established.

DTC	Trouble Code Title, Conditions, Possible Causes
DTC: P0111 **T ECM, MIL: Yes** **Year:** 2011, 2012 **Model:** C250, C300, C350, CLS550, E350, E550, SLK350 **Engine:** 1.8L L4, 3.0L V6, 3.5L V6, 4.7L V8, 4.6L V8, 5.5L V8, 6.2L V8 **Transmission:** All	**IAT Sensor Implausible or Does Not Change:** Intake air temperature sensor) is implausible.
DTC: P0112 **2T ECM, MIL: Yes** **Year:** 2011, 2012 **Model:** C250, C300, C350, CLS550, E350, E550, SLK350 **Engine:** 1.8L L4, 3.0L V6, 3.5L V6, 4.7L V8, 4.6L V8, 5.5L V8, 6.2L V8 **Transmission:** All	**Intake Air Temperature Circuit Low Input:** IAT sensor has a short circuit to ground, or short circuit to positive or open circuit.
DTC: P0113 **2T ECM, MIL: Yes** **Year:** 2011, 2012 **Model:** C250, C300, C350, CLS550, E350, E550, SLK350 **Engine:** 1.8L L4, 3.0L V6, 3.5L V6, 4.7L V8, 4.6L V8, 5.5L V8, 6.2L V8 **Transmission:** All	**Intake Air Temperature Circuit High Input:** Intake air temperature sensor has a short circuit to positive or ground; or an open circuit.
DTC: P0114 **2T ECM, MIL: Yes** **Year:** 2011, 2012 **Model:** C250, C300, C350, CLS550, E350, E550, SLK300, SLK350 **Engine:** 1.8L L4, 3.0L V6, 3.5L V6, 4.7L V8, 4.6L V8, 5.5L V8, 6.2L V8 **Transmission:** All	**Intake Air Temperature Circuit Intermittent:** Intake air temperature sensor has a short circuit to positive or ground; or an open circuit.
DTC: P0115 **2T ECM, MIL: Yes** **Year:** 2012 **Model:** CLS550, E550 **Engine:** 4.6L V8 **Transmission:** All	**Engine Coolant Temperature Circuit Malfunction:** If the internal time span has elapsed and the coolant temperature has not attained 41oF or has not increased to 104oC, the is then recognized as defective.
DTC: P0115 **T ECM, MIL: Yes** **Year:** 2011, 2012 **Model:** C250, C300, C350, E350, E550, SLK350 **Engine:** 1.8L L4, 3.0L V6, 3.5L V6, 4.7L V8, 5.5L V8, 6.2L V8 **Transmission:** All	**Heating System Shutoff Valve Circuit Malfunction:** Heating system shutoff valve circuit short to positive or to ground. Heating system shutoff valve circuit open.
DTC: P0116 **2T ECM, MIL: Yes** **Year:** 2011, 2012 **Model:** C250, C300, C350, CLS550, E350, E550, SLK350 **Engine:** 1.8L L4, 3.0L V6, 3.5L V6, 4.7L V8, 4.6L V8, 5.5L V8, 6.2L V8 **Transmission:** All	**Coolant Temperature Sensor Improper Signal:** Coolant temperature sensor shunt fault (improper sensor characteristic curve). Coolant temperature is too high or low. Engine temperature signal voltage from the ECM is implausible. Engine temperature signal from the ECM is implausible (shunt fault; improper sensor characteristic curve). The cooling performance of the engine cooling system is poor. Short circuit in wiring.

DTC	Trouble Code Title, Conditions, Possible Causes
DTC: P0117 **T ECM, MIL: Yes** **Year:** 2011, 2012 **Model:** C250, C300, C350, CLS550, E350, E550, SLK350 **Engine:** 1.8L L4, 3.0L V6, 3.5L V6, 4.7L V8, 4.6L V8, 5.5L V8, 6.2L V8 **Transmission:** All	**Coolant Temperature Sensor or Circuit:** Engine cooling malfunction. Coolant temperature sensor circuit short to positive or open circuit.
DTC: P0118 **T ECM, MIL: Yes** **Year:** 2011, 2012 **Model:** C250, C300, C350, CLS550, E350, E550, SLK350 **Engine:** 1.8L L4, 3.0L V6, 3.5L V6, 4.7L V8, 4.6L V8, 5.5L V8, 6.2L V8 **Transmission:** All	**Coolant Temperature Sensor or Circuit:** Cooling system malfunction: * The coolant temperature sensor circuit short to ground, short to positive, or an open circuit. * Coolant temperature sensor.
DTC: P0119 **2T ECM, MIL: Yes** **Year:** 2011, 2012 **Model:** CLS550, E550 **Engine:** 4.6L V8, 5.5L V8, 6.2L V8 **Transmission:** All	**Engine Coolant Temperature Circuit Intermittent:** Indicates the ECT circuit became intermittently open or shorted while the engine was running.
DTC: P0120 **2T ECM, MIL: Yes** **Year:** 2012 **Model:** CLS550, E550 **Engine:** 4.6L V8 **Transmission:** All	**Throttle Pedal Position Sensor/Switch A Circuit Malfunction:** Actual value potentiometers 1 and 2: signal voltage implausible or adaptation error. Deflection of throttle valve actuator.
DTC: P0121 **2T ECM, MIL: Yes** **Year:** 2012 **Model:** CLS550, E550 **Engine:** 4.6L V8 **Transmission:** All	**Throttle/Pedal Position Sensor/Switch A Circuit Range/Performance Problem:** Voltage of Hall sensor 1 does not agree with voltage of Hall sensor 2.
DTC: P0122 **2T ECM, MIL: Yes** **Year:** 2011, 2012 **Model:** C250, C300, C350, CLS550, E350, E550, SLK350 **Engine:** 1.8L L4, 3.0L V6, 3.5L V6, 4.7L V8, 4.6L V8, 5.5L V8, 6.2L V8 **Transmission:** All	**Throttle/Pedal Position Sensor/Switch A Circuit Low Input :** Throttle valve actuator (actual value potentiometer 1 - short circuit to ground).
DTC: P0123 **2T ECM, MIL: Yes** **Year:** 2011, 2012 **Model:** C250, C300, C350, CLS550, E350, E550, SLK350 **Engine:** 1.8L L4, 3.0L V6, 3.5L V6, 4.7L V8, 4.6L V8, 5.5L V8, 6.2L V8 **Transmission:** All	**Throttle/Pedal Position Sensor/Switch A Circuit Low Input:** Throttle valve actuator (actual value potentiometer 1 - short circuit to positive or open circuit).
DTC: P0125 **T ECM, MIL: Yes** **Year:** 2012 **Model:** CLS550, E550 **Engine:** 4.6L V8 **Transmission:** All	**Coolant Temperature Sensor:** Coolant temperature sensor: minimum engine temperature for lambda control has not been reached.

DTC	Trouble Code Title, Conditions, Possible Causes
DTC: P0126 **2T ECM, MIL: Yes** **Year:** 2011, 2012 **Model:** CLS550, E550 **Engine:** 4.6L V8, 5.5L V8, 6.2L V8 **Transmission:** All	**Insufficient Coolant Temperature for Stable Operation:** This DTC indicates that an ECT sensor range performance concern has been detected.
DTC: P0128 **T ECM, MIL: Yes** **Year:** 2011, 2012 **Model:** C250, C300, C350, E350, E550, SLK350 **Engine:** 1.8L L4, 3.0L V6, 3.5L V6, 4.7L V8, 5.5L V8, 6.2L V8 **Transmission:** All	**Thermostat:** Three-disk thermostat valve jams in opened position: Coolant temperature rises too slowly. Engine coolant temperature malfunction: * Thermostat valve jams in opened position. * Coolant temperature rises too slowly.
DTC: P0130 **2T ECM, MIL: Yes** **Year:** 2011, 2012 **Model:** C250, C300, C350, CLS550, E350, E550, SLK350 **Engine:** 1.8L L4, 3.0L V6, 3.5L V6, 4.7L V8, 4.6L V8, 5.5L V8, 6.2L V8 **Transmission:** All	**Right O2 Sensor Voltage :** Exhaust system malfunction ; * Right O2 sensor, before TWC, voltage is too high or too low * Open circuit * Sensor signal in the case of inertia fuel shutoff implausible.
DTC: P0131 **2T ECM, MIL: Yes** **Year:** 2012 **Model:** CLS550, E550 **Engine:** 4.6L V8 **Transmission:** All	**O2 Sensor Upstream of Catalytic Converter:** O2 sensor upstream of converter: Short circuit to ground.
DTC: P0132 **2T ECM, MIL: Yes** **Year:** 2012 **Model:** CLS550, E550 **Engine:** 4.6L V8 **Transmission:** All	**O2 Sensor Upstream of Catalytic Converter:** O2 sensor upstream of catalytic converter: Short circuit to positive.
DTC: P0133 **2T ECM, MIL: Yes** **Year:** 2011, 2012 **Model:** C250, C300, C350, CLS550, E350, E550, SLK350 **Engine:** 1.8L L4, 3.0L V6, 3.5L V6, 4.7L V8, 4.6L V8, 5.5L V8, 6.2L V8 **Transmission:** All	**Right HO2S Sensor (Before TWC) Aging: Sensor Too Sluggish :** Exhaust system malfunction. Operational fault of right O2 sensor, before TWC, aging - O2 sensor too sluggish. Slow response time.
DTC: P0134 **2T ECM, MIL: Yes** **Year:** 2012 **Model:** CLS550, E550 **Engine:** 4.6L V8 **Transmission:** All	**O2 Sensor Circuit No Activity Detected (Bank 1 Sensor 1):** Engine started, engine runtime over 140 seconds, vehicle driven at a steady speed of 25-81 mph at over 1500 rpm with the throttle valve open, and the ECM detected the HO2S-11 signal did not indicate rich (more than 450 mv) after 65 seconds under these conditions.
DTC: P0135 **2T ECM, MIL: Yes** **Year:** 2011, 2012 **Model:** C250, C300, C350, CLS550, E350, E550, SLK350 **Engine:** 1.8L L4, 3.0L V6, 3.5L V6, 4.7L V8, 4.6L V8, 5.5L V8, 6.2L V8 **Transmission:** All	**O2 Sensor Heater Circuit Malfunction (Bank 1 Sensor 1):** Exhaust system malfunction: * Right O2 sensor, before TWC, heating capacity is too low. * Right O2 sensor, before TWC, short or open circuit to positive/resistance of sensor heater too low.

DTC	Trouble Code Title, Conditions, Possible Causes
DTC: P0136 **2T ECM, MIL: Yes** **Year:** 2011, 2012 **Model:** C250, C300, C350, CLS550, E350, E550, SLK350 **Engine:** 1.8L L4, 3.0L V6, 3.5L V6, 4.7L V8, 4.6L V8, 5.5L V8, 6.2L V8 **Transmission:** All	**O2 Sensor Circuit Malfunction (Bank 1 Sensor 2):** Exhaust system malfunction Right O2 sensor, after TWC: * Short circuit to ground * Short circuit between signal line and line to sensor heater * Open circuit * Sensor signal in the case of inertia fuel shutoff implausible.
DTC: P0137 **T ECM, MIL: Yes** **Year:** 2012 **Model:** CLS550, E550 **Engine:** 4.6L V8 **Transmission:** All	**O2 Sensor Downstream of TWC:** Exhaust system malfunction: * O2 sensor downstream TWC: Short circuit to ground. * O2 sensor downstream TWC: Short circuit to positive.
DTC: P0138 **T ECM, MIL: Yes** **Year:** 2011, 2012 **Model:** C250, C300, C350, CLS550, E350, E550, SLK350 **Engine:** 1.8L L4, 3.0L V6, 3.5L V6, 4.7L V8, 4.6L V8, 5.5L V8, 6.2L V8 **Transmission:** All	**Right O2 Sensor Circuit:** Exhaust system malfunction: * Right O2 sensor, after TWC, short circuit to positive * Resistance of sensor heater too low
DTC: P0139 **2T ECM, MIL: Yes** **Year:** 2011, 2012 **Model:** C250, C300, C350, CLS550, E350, E550, SLK350 **Engine:** 1.8L L4, 3.0L V6, 3.5L V6, 4.7L V8, 4.6L V8, 5.5L V8, 6.2L V8 **Transmission:** All	**O2 Sensor Circuit Slow Response (Bank 1 Sensor 2) :** Exhaust system malfunction: Right O2 sensor, after TWC, aging
DTC: P0140 **2T ECM, MIL: Yes** **Year:** 2011, 2012 **Model:** C250, C300, C350, CLS550, E350, E550, SLK350 **Engine:** 1.8L L4, 3.0L V6, 3.5L V6, 4.7L V8, 4.6L V8, 5.5L V8, 6.2L V8 **Transmission:** All	**O2 Sensor Circuit No Activity Detected (Bank 1 Sensor 2):** Exhaust system malfunction: * Right O2 sensor, after TWC, discontinuity of signal line * Aging signal implausible * Open circuit
DTC: P0141 **2T ECM, MIL: Yes** **Year:** 2011, 2012 **Model:** C250, C300, C350, E350, E550, SLK350 **Engine:** 1.8L L4, 3.0L V6, 3.5L V6, 4.7L V8, 5.5L V8, 6.2L V8 **Transmission:** All	**O2 Sensor Heater Circuit Malfunction (Bank 1 Sensor 2):** Exhaust system malfunction: * Right O2 sensor, after TWC, heating capacity is too low. * Right O2 sensor, after TWC, short circuit to positive or open in circuit
DTC: P0142 **2T ECM, MIL: Yes** **Year:** 2011, 2012 **Model:** C250, C300, C350, CLS550, E350, E550, SLK300, SLK350 **Engine:** 1.8L L4, 3.0L V6, 3.5L V6, 4.7L V8, 4.6L V8, 5.5L V8, 6.2L V8 **Transmission:** All	**O2 Sensor Circuit Malfunction (Bank 1 Sensor 3):** Exhaust system malfunction: * O2 sensor, heating capacity is too low. * O2 sensor, short circuit to positive or open in circuit.

DTC	Trouble Code Title, Conditions, Possible Causes
DTC: P0143 **2T ECM, MIL: Yes** **Year:** 2011, 2012 **Model:** C250, C300, C350, CLS550, E350, E550 **Engine:** 1.8L L4, 3.0L V6, 3.5L V6, 4.7L V8, 4.6L V8, 5.5L V8, 6.2L V8 **Transmission:** All	**O2 Sensor Circuit Low Voltage (Bank 1 Sensor 3):** Exhaust system malfunction: * O2 sensor, heating capacity is too low. * O2 sensor, short circuit to positive or open in circuit.
DTC: P0144 **2T ECM, MIL: Yes** **Year:** 2011, 2012 **Model:** CLS550, E550 **Engine:** 4.6L V8, 5.5L V8, 6.2L V8 **Transmission:** All	**O2 Sensor Circuit High Voltage (Bank 1 Sensor 3):** The ECM monitors input voltage from rear HO2S. If the input voltage from the rear HO2S sensor is to high, the ECM determines that circuit input is high.
DTC: P0145 **2T ECM, MIL: Yes** **Year:** 2011, 2012 **Model:** C250, C300, C350, CLS550, E350, E550, SLK300, SLK350 **Engine:** 1.8L L4, 3.0L V6, 3.5L V6, 4.7L V8, 4.6L V8, 5.5L V8, 6.2L V8 **Transmission:** All	**O2 Sensor Circuit Slow Response (Bank 1 Sensor 3):** The ECM monitors inversion cycle period, Rear HO2S output voltage inclination. The ECM detects that the voltage inclinations are below threshold.
DTC: P0146 **2T ECM, MIL: Yes** **Year:** 2011, 2012 **Model:** C250, C300 **Engine:** 1.8L L4, 3.0L V6 **Transmission:** All	**O2 Sensor Circuit No Activity Detected (Bank 1 Sensor 3):** The ECM monitors input voltage from HO2S, the ECM determines that circuit input is faulty.
DTC: P0147 **2T ECM, MIL: Yes** **Year:** 2011, 2012 **Model:** C250, C300, C350, CLS550, E350, E550, SLK300, SLK350 **Engine:** 1.8L L4, 3.0L V6, 3.5L V6, 4.7L V8, 4.6L V8, 5.5L V8, 6.2L V8 **Transmission:** All	**O2 Sensor Heater Circuit Malfunction (Bank 1 Sensor 3):** The ECM monitors input voltage from HO2S, the ECM determines that circuit input is faulty.
DTC: P0150 **T ECM, MIL: Yes** **Year:** 2011, 2012 **Model:** C250, C300, C350, CLS550, E350, E550, SLK350 **Engine:** 1.8L L4, 3.0L V6, 3.5L V6, 4.7L V8, 4.6L V8, 5.5L V8, 6.2L V8 **Transmission:** All	**Left O2 Sensor Voltage Too High or Too Low:** Exhaust system malfunction: * Left O2 sensor, before TWC, voltage is too high or too low.
DTC: P0151 **T ECM, MIL: Yes** **Year:** 2012 **Model:** CLS550, E550 **Engine:** 4.6L V8 **Transmission:** All	**Left O2 Sensor (Before TWC) Circuit:** Left O2 sensor, before TWC: Short circuit in the signal line.
DTC: P0152 **T ECM, MIL: Yes** **Year:** 2012 **Model:** CLS550, E550 **Engine:** 4.6L V8 **Transmission:** All	**Left O2 Sensor (Before TWC) Circuit:** Left O2 sensor circuit short to positive.

DTC	Trouble Code Title, Conditions, Possible Causes
DTC: P0153 **2T ECM, MIL: Yes** **Year:** 2011, 2012 **Model:** C250, C300, C350, CLS550, E350, E550, SLK350 **Engine:** 1.8L L4, 3.0L V6, 3.5L V6, 4.7L V8, 4.6L V8, 5.5L V8, 6.2L V8 **Transmission:** All	**Left HO2S Sensor (Before TWC) Aging - Sensor Too Sluggish :** Operational fault of left O2 sensor, before TWC. Sensor aging - O2 sensor too sluggish: response time too long or too short.
DTC: P0154 **T ECM, MIL: Yes** **Year:** 2012 **Model:** CLS550, E550 **Engine:** 4.6L V8 **Transmission:** All	**Left O2 Sensor (Before TWC) Circuit:** Left O2 sensor circuit open.
DTC: P0155 **T ECM, MIL: Yes** **Year:** 2011, 2012 **Model:** C250, C300, C350, CLS550, E350, E550, SLK350 **Engine:** 1.8L L4, 3.0L V6, 3.5L V6, 4.7L V8, 4.6L V8, 5.5L V8, 6.2L V8 **Transmission:** All	**Heating Capacity of Left HO2S Too Low or Short Circuit:** Exhaust system malfunction: * Left O2 sensor, before TWC, heating capacity is too low. * Left O2 sensor, before TWC, short circuit to positive/resistance of sensor heater too low.
DTC: P0156 **T ECM, MIL: Yes** **Year:** 2011, 2012 **Model:** C250, C300, C350, CLS550, E350, E550, SLK350 **Engine:** 1.8L L4, 3.0L V6, 3.5L V6, 4.7L V8, 4.6L V8, 5.5L V8, 6.2L V8 **Transmission:** All	**Left O2 Sensor (After TWC) Circuit :** Exhaust system malfunction: * Left O2 sensor, after TWC, short circuit to ground or short circuit between signal line and line to sensor heater.
DTC: P0157 **T ECM, MIL: Yes** **Year:** 2012 **Model:** CLS550, E550 **Engine:** 4.6L V8 **Transmission:** All	**Left O2 Sensor (After TWC) Circuit:** Left O2 sensor circuit short to signal line.
DTC: P0158 **T ECM, MIL: Yes** **Year:** 2011, 2012 **Model:** C250, C300, C350, CLS550, E350, E550, SLK350 **Engine:** 1.8L L4, 3.0L V6, 3.5L V6, 4.7L V8, 4.6L V8, 5.5L V8, 6.2L V8 **Transmission:** All	**Left O2 Sensor (After TWC) Circuit:** Exhaust system malfunction: * Left O2 sensor, after TWC, short circuit to positive; resistance of sensor heater too low.
DTC: P0159 **T ECM, MIL: Yes** **Year:** 2011, 2012 **Model:** C250, C300, C350, CLS550, E350, E550, SLK350 **Engine:** 1.8L L4, 3.0L V6, 3.5L V6, 4.7L V8, 4.6L V8, 5.5L V8, 6.2L V8 **Transmission:** All	**Left HO2S Sensor Aging :** Exhaust system malfunction: Left O2 sensor, after TWC, aging

DTC	Trouble Code Title, Conditions, Possible Causes
DTC: P0160 **T ECM, MIL: Yes** **Year:** 2011, 2012 **Model:** C250, C300, C350, CLS550, E350, E550, SLK350 **Engine:** 1.8L L4, 3.0L V6, 3.5L V6, 4.7L V8, 4.6L V8, 5.5L V8, 6.2L V8 **Transmission:** All	**Left O2 Sensor (After TWC) Circuit:** Exhaust system malfunction: * Left O2 sensor, after TWC, discontinuity of signal line. * Open circuit.
DTC: P0161 **T ECM, MIL: Yes** **Year:** 2012 **Model:** CLS550, E550 **Engine:** 4.6L V8 **Transmission:** All	**Left O2 Sensor Heater (After TWC):** Left O2 sensor, after TWC: Heating capacity is too low.
DTC: P0162 **2T ECM, MIL: Yes** **Year:** 2011, 2012 **Model:** C250, C300, C350, CLS550, E350, E550, SLK300, SLK350 **Engine:** 1.8L L4, 3.0L V6, 3.5L V6, 4.7L V8, 4.6L V8, 5.5L V8, 6.2L V8 **Transmission:** All	**O2 Sensor Circuit Malfunction (Bank 2 Sensor 3):** Left O2 sensor, before TWC: Circuit malfunction detected.
DTC: P0163 **2T ECM, MIL: Yes** **Year:** 2011, 2012 **Model:** C250, C300, C350, CLS550, E350, E550, SLK300, SLK350 **Engine:** 1.8L L4, 3.0L V6, 3.5L V6, 4.7L V8, 4.6L V8, 5.5L V8, 6.2L V8 **Transmission:** All	**O2 Sensor Circuit Low Voltage (Bank 2 Sensor 3):** Left O2 sensor, before TWC: Circuit malfunction detected.
DTC: P0164 **2T ECM, MIL: Yes** **Year:** 2011, 2012 **Model:** C250, C300, C350, CLS550, E350, E550, SLK300, SLK350 **Engine:** 1.8L L4, 3.0L V6, 3.5L V6, 4.7L V8, 4.6L V8, 5.5L V8, 6.2L V8 **Transmission:** All	**O2 Sensor Circuit High Voltage (Bank 2 Sensor 3):** Left O2 sensor, before TWC: Circuit malfunction detected. O2 sensor circuit short to positive.
DTC: P0165 **2T ECM, MIL: Yes** **Year:** 2011, 2012 **Model:** C250, C300, C350, CLS550, E350, E550, SLK300, SLK350 **Engine:** 1.8L L4, 3.0L V6, 3.5L V6, 4.7L V8, 4.6L V8, 5.5L V8, 6.2L V8 **Transmission:** All	**O2 Sensor Circuit Slow Response (Bank 2 Sensor 3) :** The ECM monitors inversion cycle period, Rear HO2S output voltage inclination. The ECM detects that the voltage inclinations are below threshold.
DTC: P0166 **2T ECM, MIL: Yes** **Year:** 2011, 2012 **Model:** C250, C300, C350, CLS550, E350, E550, SLK300, SLK350 **Engine:** 1.8L L4, 3.0L V6, 3.5L V6, 4.7L V8, 4.6L V8, 5.5L V8, 6.2L V8 **Transmission:** All	**O2 Sensor Circuit No Activity Detected (Bank 2 Sensor 3):** The ECM monitors input voltage from HO2S, the ECM determines that circuit input is faulty.

DTC	Trouble Code Title, Conditions, Possible Causes
DTC: P0167 **2T ECM, MIL: Yes** **Year:** 2011, 2012 **Model:** C250, C300, C350, CLS550, E350, E550 **Engine:** 1.8L L4, 3.0L V6, 3.5L V6, 4.7L V8, 4.6L V8, 5.5L V8, 6.2L V8 **Transmission:** All	**O2 Sensor Heater Circuit Malfunction (Bank 2 Sensor 3):** O2 sensor circuit short to signal line.
DTC: P0170 **2T ECM, MIL: Yes** **Year:** 2011, 2012 **Model:** C250, C300, C350, CLS550, E350, E550, SLK350 **Engine:** 1.8L L4, 3.0L V6, 3.5L V6, 4.7L V8, 4.6L V8, 5.5L V8, 6.2L V8 **Transmission:** All	**Lambda Control (Fuel Trim) Malfunction-Bank 1):** Exhaust system malfunction. Engine output is affected. Lambda (fuel system) control, before right TWC, control implausible.
DTC: P0171 **2T ECM, MIL: Yes** **Year:** 2011, 2012 **Model:** C250, C300, C350, CLS550, E350, E550, SLK350 **Engine:** 1.8L L4, 3.0L V6, 3.5L V6, 4.7L V8, 4.6L V8, 5.5L V8, 6.2L V8 **Transmission:** All	**Lean Mixture Condition-System Too Lean (Bank 1):** Engine output is affected by: * Self-adaptation of mixture formation for enrichment at partial load or at idle for the right cylinder bank is above the permissible limit. * Lambda control, before right TWC, Lambda control is at rich stop.
DTC: P0172 **2T ECM, MIL: Yes** **Year:** 2011, 2012 **Model:** C250, C300, C350, CLS550, E350, E550, SLK350 **Engine:** 1.8L L4, 3.0L V6, 3.5L V6, 4.7L V8, 4.6L V8, 5.5L V8, 6.2L V8 **Transmission:** All	**Rich Mixture Condition-System Too Rich (Bank 1):** Engine output is affected by: * Self-adaptation of mixture formation for enrichment at partial load or at idle for the right cylinder bank is below the permissible limit. * Lambda control, before right TWC, Lambda control is at lean stop
DTC: P0173 **2T ECM, MIL: Yes** **Year:** 2011, 2012 **Model:** C250, C300, C350, CLS550, E350, E550, SLK350 **Engine:** 1.8L L4, 3.0L V6, 3.5L V6, 4.7L V8, 4.6L V8, 5.5L V8, 6.2L V8 **Transmission:** All	**Lambda Control (Fuel Trim) Implausible-(Bank 2):** Exhaust system malfunction: * Lambda control, before TWC left, control implausible
DTC: P0174 **2T ECM, MIL: Yes** **Year:** 2011, 2012 **Model:** C250, C300, C350, CLS550, E350, E550, SLK350 **Engine:** 1.8L L4, 3.0L V6, 3.5L V6, 4.7L V8, 4.6L V8, 5.5L V8, 6.2L V8 **Transmission:** All	**Improper/Lean Mixture Formation-System Too Lean (Bank 2):** Engine output is affected by: * Self-adaptation of mixture formation for enrichment at partial load or at idle for the left cylinder bank is below the permissible limit. * Lambda control, before left TWC, Lambda control is at lean stop.
DTC: P0175 **2T ECM, MIL: Yes** **Year:** 2011, 2012 **Model:** C250, C300, C350, CLS550, E350, E550, SLK350 **Engine:** 1.8L L4, 3.0L V6, 3.5L V6, 4.7L V8, 4.6L V8, 5.5L V8, 6.2L V8 **Transmission:** All	**Improper/Rich Mixture-System Too Rich (Bank 2):** Engine output is affected by: * Self-adaptation of mixture formation for enrichment at partial load or at idle, for the left cylinder bank is above the permissible limit. * Lambda control, before left TWC, Lambda control is at rich stop.

DTC	Trouble Code Title, Conditions, Possible Causes
DTC: P0176 **2T ECM, MIL: Yes** **Year:** 2011, 2012 **Model:** CLS550, E350, E550, SLK350 **Engine:** 3.5L V6, 4.7L V8, 4.6L V8, 5.5L V8, 6.2L V8 **Transmission:** All	**Fuel Composition Sensor Circuit Malfunction :** Composition failure detected.
DTC: P0201 **T ECM, MIL: Yes** **Year:** 2011, 2012 **Model:** C250, C300, C350, E350, E550, SLK350 **Engine:** 1.8L L4, 3.0L V6, 3.5L V6, 4.7L V8, 5.5L V8, 6.2L V8 **Transmission:** All	**Injection Valve Output Stage (Cyl. 1) Circuit :** Engine runs improperly. Injection valve output stage of cylinder 1 detects a line discontinuity (open)
DTC: P0202 **T ECM, MIL: Yes** **Year:** 2011, 2012 **Model:** C250, C300, C350, E350, E550, SLK350 **Engine:** 1.8L L4, 3.0L V6, 3.5L V6, 4.7L V8, 5.5L V8, 6.2L V8 **Transmission:** All	**Injection Valve Output Stage (Cyl. 2) Circuit Discontinuity:** Engine runs improperly. Injection valve output stage of cylinder 2 detects a line discontinuity
DTC: P0203 **T ECM, MIL: Yes** **Year:** 2011, 2012 **Model:** C250, C300, C350, E350, E550, SLK350 **Engine:** 1.8L L4, 3.0L V6, 3.5L V6, 4.7L V8, 5.5L V8, 6.2L V8 **Transmission:** All	**Injection Valve Output Stage (Cyl. 3) Circuit Discontinuity:** Engine runs improperly. Injection valve output stage of cylinder 3 detects a line discontinuity.
DTC: P0205 **T ECM, MIL: Yes** **Year:** 2011, 2012 **Model:** C250, C300, C350, E350, E550, SLK350 **Engine:** 3.0L V6, 3.5L V6, 4.7L V8, 5.5L V8, 6.2L V8 **Transmission:** All	**Injection Valve Output Stage (Cyl. 5) Circuit Discontinuity:** Engine runs improperly. Injection valve output stage of cylinder 4 detects a line discontinuity.
DTC: P0206 **T ECM, MIL: Yes** **Year:** 2011, 2012 **Model:** C250, C300, C350, E350, E550, SLK350 **Engine:** 3.0L V6, 3.5L V6, 4.7L V8, 5.5L V8, 6.2L V8 **Transmission:** All	**Injection Valve Output Stage (Cyl. 6) Circuit Discontinuity:** Engine runs improperly. Injection valve output stage of cylinder 61 detects a line discontinuity.
DTC: P0207 **T ECM, MIL: Yes** **Year:** 2011 **Model:** E550 **Engine:** 5.5L V8, 6.2L V8 **Transmission:** All	**Injection Valve (Cyl. 7) Circuit:** Engine output affected. The injection valve output stage of cylinder 7 detects a line discontinuity.

DTC	Trouble Code Title, Conditions, Possible Causes
DTC: P0208 **T ECM, MIL: Yes** **Year:** 2011 **Model:** E550 **Engine:** 5.5L V8, 6.2L V8 **Transmission:** All	**Injection Valve (Cyl. 8) Circuit:** Engine output affected. The injection valve output stage of cylinder 8 detects a line discontinuity.
DTC: P0219 **T TCM, TCIL: Yes** **Year:** 2011, 2012 **Model:** C250, C300, C350, E350, E550, SLK350 **Engine:** 1.8L L4, 3.0L V6, 3.5L V6, 4.7L V8, 5.5L V8, 6.2L V8 **Transmission:** All	**TCM Fault:** Transmission operation is affected. Fault in the transmission control unit.
DTC: P0222 **T ECM, MIL: Yes** **Year:** 2011, 2012 **Model:** C250, C300, C350, E350, E550, SLK350 **Engine:** 1.8L L4, 3.0L V6, 3.5L V6, 4.7L V8, 5.5L V8, 6.2L V8 **Transmission:** All	**Throttle Valve Actuator:** Engine output is affected. Throttle valve actuator actual value potentiometer 2 may have a short circuit to ground. Hall sensor 2, Short circuit to ground or open circuit in wiring.
DTC: P0223 **T ECM, MIL: Yes** **Year:** 2011, 2012 **Model:** C250, C300, C350, E350, E550, SLK350 **Engine:** 1.8L L4, 3.0L V6, 3.5L V6, 4.7L V8, 5.5L V8, 6.2L V8 **Transmission:** All	**Throttle Valve Actuator:** Engine output is affected. Throttle valve actuator actual value potentiometer 2 may have short circuit to positive or open. Hall sensor 2, short circuit to positive. The supply voltage of the sensors at the control module is not within the permissible range (over voltage or under voltage).
DTC: P0261 **T ECM, MIL: Yes** **Year:** 2011, 2012 **Model:** C250, C300, C350, E350, E550, SLK350 **Engine:** 1.8L L4, 3.0L V6, 3.5L V6, 4.7L V8, 5.5L V8, 6.2L V8 **Transmission:** All	**Injection Valve Output Stage (Cyl. 1) Detects Short Circuit to Ground:** Engine runs improperly. Injection Valve Output Stage (Cyl. 1) Detects Short Circuit to Ground.
DTC: P0262 **T ECM, MIL: Yes** **Year:** 2011, 2012 **Model:** C250, C300, C350, E350, E550, SLK350 **Engine:** 1.8L L4, 3.0L V6, 3.5L V6, 4.7L V8, 5.5L V8, 6.2L V8 **Transmission:** All	**Injection Valve Output Stage (Cyl. 1) Circuit:** Engine runs improperly. Injection valve output stage of cylinder 1 detects a short circuit to positive.
DTC: P0264 **T ECM, MIL: Yes** **Year:** 2011, 2012 **Model:** C250, C300, C350, E350, E550, SLK350 **Engine:** 1.8L L4, 3.0L V6, 3.5L V6, 4.7L V8, 5.5L V8, 6.2L V8 **Transmission:** All	**Injection Valve Output Stage (Cyl. 2) Detects Short Circuit to Ground:** Engine runs improperly. Injection valve output stage of cylinder 1 detects a short circuit to ground.

DTC	Trouble Code Title, Conditions, Possible Causes
DTC: P0265 **T ECM, MIL: Yes** **Year:** 2011, 2012 **Model:** C250, C300, C350, E350, E550, SLK350 **Engine:** 1.8L L4, 3.0L V6, 3.5L V6, 4.7L V8, 5.5L V8, 6.2L V8 **Transmission:** All	**Injection Valve Output Stage (Cyl. 2) Detects Short Circuit to Positive:** Engine runs improperly. Injection valve output stage of cylinder 1 detects a short circuit to positive.
DTC: P0267 **T ECM, MIL: Yes** **Year:** 2011, 2012 **Model:** C250, C300, C350, E350, E550, SLK350 **Engine:** 1.8L L4, 3.0L V6, 3.5L V6, 4.7L V8, 5.5L V8, 6.2L V8 **Transmission:** All	**Injection Valve Output Stage (Cyl. 3) Detects Short Circuit to Ground:** Engine runs improperly. Injection valve output stage of cylinder 1 detects a short circuit to ground.
DTC: P0268 **T ECM, MIL: Yes** **Year:** 2011, 2012 **Model:** C250, C300, C350, E350, E550, SLK350 **Engine:** 1.8L L4, 3.0L V6, 3.5L V6, 4.7L V8, 5.5L V8, 6.2L V8 **Transmission:** All	**Injection Valve Output Stage (Cyl. 3) Detects Short Circuit to Positive:** Engine runs improperly. Injection valve output stage of cylinder 1 detects a short circuit to positive.
DTC: P0270 **T ECM, MIL: Yes** **Year:** 2011, 2012 **Model:** C250, C300, C350, E350, E550, SLK350 **Engine:** 1.8L L4, 3.0L V6, 3.5L V6, 4.7L V8, 5.5L V8, 6.2L V8 **Transmission:** All	**Injection Valve Output Stage (Cyl. 4) Detects Short Circuit to Ground:** Engine runs improperly. Injection valve output stage of cylinder 1 detects a short circuit to ground.
DTC: P0271 **T ECM, MIL: Yes** **Year:** 2011, 2012 **Model:** C250, C300, C350, E350, E550, SLK350 **Engine:** 1.8L L4, 3.0L V6, 3.5L V6, 4.7L V8, 5.5L V8, 6.2L V8 **Transmission:** All	**Injection Valve Output Stage (Cyl. 4) Detects Short Circuit to Positive:** Engine runs improperly. Injection valve output stage of cylinder 1 detects a short circuit to positive.
DTC: P0273 **T ECM, MIL: Yes** **Year:** 2011, 2012 **Model:** C250, C300, C350, E350, E550, SLK350 **Engine:** 3.0L V6, 3.5L V6, 4.7L V8, 5.5L V8, 6.2L V8 **Transmission:** All	**Injection Valve Output Stage (Cyl. 5) Detects Short Circuit to Ground:** Engine runs improperly. Injection valve output stage of cylinder 1 detects a short circuit to ground.
DTC: P0274 **T ECM, MIL: Yes** **Year:** 2011, 2012 **Model:** C250, C300, C350, E350, E550, SLK350 **Engine:** 3.0L V6, 3.5L V6, 4.7L V8, 5.5L V8, 6.2L V8 **Transmission:** All	**Injection Valve Output Stage (Cyl. 5) Detects Short Circuit to Positive:** Engine runs improperly. Injection valve output stage of cylinder 1 detects a short circuit to positive.

DTC	Trouble Code Title, Conditions, Possible Causes
DTC: P0276 **T ECM, MIL: Yes** **Year:** 2011, 2012 **Model:** C250, C300, C350, E350, E550, SLK350 **Engine:** 3.0L V6, 3.5L V6, 4.7L V8, 5.5L V8, 6.2L V8 **Transmission:** All	**Injection Valve Output Stage (Cyl. 6) Detects Short Circuit to Ground:** Engine runs improperly. Injection valve output stage of cylinder 1 detects a short circuit to ground.
DTC: P0277 **T ECM, MIL: Yes** **Year:** 2011, 2012 **Model:** C250, C300, C350, E350, E550, SLK350 **Engine:** 3.0L V6, 3.5L V6, 4.7L V8, 5.5L V8, 6.2L V8 **Transmission:** All	**Injection Valve Output Stage (Cyl. 5) Detects Short Circuit to Positive:** Engine runs improperly. Injection valve output stage of cylinder 1 detects a short circuit to positive.
DTC: P0279 **T ECM, MIL: Yes** **Year:** 2011 **Model:** E550 **Engine:** 5.5L V8, 6.2L V8 **Transmission:** All	**Injector #7 Circuit:** Engine output affected. The injection valve output stage of cylinder 7 detects a short circuit to ground.
DTC: P0280 **T ECM, MIL: Yes** **Year:** 2011 **Model:** E550 **Engine:** 5.5L V8, 6.2L V8 **Transmission:** All	**Cylinder #7 Circuit:** Engine output affected. The injection valve output stage of cylinder 7 detects a short circuit to positive.
DTC: P0282 **T ECM, MIL: Yes** **Year:** 2011 **Model:** E550 **Engine:** 5.5L V8, 6.2L V8 **Transmission:** All	**Injector # 8 Circuit:** Engine output affected. The injection valve output stage of cylinder 8 detects a short circuit to ground.
DTC: P0283 **T ECM, MIL: Yes** **Year:** 2011 **Model:** E550 **Engine:** 5.5L V8, 6.2L V8 **Transmission:** All	**Injector #8 Circuit:** Engine output affected. The injection valve output stage of cylinder 8 detects a short circuit to positive.
DTC: P0300 **1T ECM, MIL: Yes** **Year:** 2011, 2012 **Model:** C350, CLS550, E350, E550, SLK350 **Engine:** 3.5L V6, 4.7L V8, 4.6L V8, 5.5L V8, 6.2L V8 **Transmission:** All	**Random/Multiple Cylinder Misfire Detected:** Engine output is affected and the vehicle runs rough. (Combustion misfiring) Any condition that causes abnormally high levels of unburned hydrocarbons, raw or partially burnt fuel will tend to significantly elevate its temperature, and cause damage. Vehicles equipped with OBD-II diagnostic systems are designed to alert the driver to a misfire condition by means of flashing the "check engine" light on the dashboard.
DTC: P0301 **1T ECM, MIL: Yes** **Year:** 2011, 2012 **Model:** C250, C300, C350, E350, E550, SLK350 **Engine:** 1.8L L4, 3.0L V6, 3.5L V6, 4.7L V8, 5.5L V8, 6.2L V8 **Transmission:** All	**Misfiring of Cylinder 1:** Engine output is affected and the vehicle runs rough. (Combustion misfiring) Any condition that causes abnormally high levels of unburned hydrocarbons, raw or partially burnt fuel will tend to significantly elevate its temperature, and cause damage. Vehicles equipped with OBD-II diagnostic systems are designed to alert the driver to a misfire condition by means of flashing the "check engine" light on the dashboard.

DTC	Trouble Code Title, Conditions, Possible Causes
DTC: P0302 **1T ECM, MIL: Yes** **Year:** 2011, 2012 **Model:** C250, C300, C350, E350, E550, SLK350 **Engine:** 1.8L L4, 3.0L V6, 3.5L V6, 4.7L V8, 5.5L V8, 6.2L V8 **Transmission:** All	**Misfiring of Cylinder 2:** Engine output is affected and the vehicle runs rough. (Combustion misfiring) Any condition that causes abnormally high levels of unburned hydrocarbons, raw or partially burnt fuel will tend to significantly elevate its temperature, and cause damage. Vehicles equipped with OBD-II diagnostic systems are designed to alert the driver to a misfire condition by means of flashing the "check engine" light on the dashboard.
DTC: P0303 **1T ECM, MIL: Yes** **Year:** 2011, 2012 **Model:** C250, C300, C350, E350, E550, SLK350 **Engine:** 1.8L L4, 3.0L V6, 3.5L V6, 4.7L V8, 5.5L V8, 6.2L V8 **Transmission:** All	**Misfiring of Cylinder 3:** Engine output is affected and the vehicle runs rough. (Combustion misfiring) Any condition that causes abnormally high levels of unburned hydrocarbons, raw or partially burnt fuel will tend to significantly elevate its temperature, and cause damage. Vehicles equipped with OBD-II diagnostic systems are designed to alert the driver to a misfire condition by means of flashing the "check engine" light on the dashboard.
DTC: P0304 **1T ECM, MIL: Yes** **Year:** 2011, 2012 **Model:** C250, C300, C350, E350, E550, SLK350 **Engine:** 1.8L L4, 3.0L V6, 3.5L V6, 4.7L V8, 5.5L V8, 6.2L V8 **Transmission:** All	**Misfiring of Cylinder 4:** Engine output is affected and the vehicle runs rough. (Combustion misfiring) Any condition that causes abnormally high levels of unburned hydrocarbons, raw or partially burnt fuel will tend to significantly elevate its temperature, and cause damage. Vehicles equipped with OBD-II diagnostic systems are designed to alert the driver to a misfire condition by means of flashing the "check engine" light on the dashboard.
DTC: P0305 **1T ECM, MIL: Yes** **Year:** 2011, 2012 **Model:** C250, C300, C350, E350, E550, SLK350 **Engine:** 3.0L V6, 3.5L V6, 4.7L V8, 5.5L V8, 6.2L V8 **Transmission:** All	**Misfiring of Cylinder 5:** Engine output is affected and the vehicle runs rough. (Combustion misfiring) Any condition that causes abnormally high levels of unburned hydrocarbons, raw or partially burnt fuel will tend to significantly elevate its temperature, and cause damage. Vehicles equipped with OBD-II diagnostic systems are designed to alert the driver to a misfire condition by means of flashing the "check engine" light on the dashboard.
DTC: P0306 **1T ECM, MIL: Yes** **Year:** 2011, 2012 **Model:** C250, C300, C350, E350, E550, SLK350 **Engine:** 3.0L V6, 3.5L V6, 4.7L V8, 5.5L V8, 6.2L V8 **Transmission:** All	**Misfiring of Cylinder 6:** Engine output is affected and the vehicle runs rough. (Combustion misfiring) Any condition that causes abnormally high levels of unburned hydrocarbons, raw or partially burnt fuel will tend to significantly elevate its temperature, and cause damage. Vehicles equipped with OBD-II diagnostic systems are designed to alert the driver to a misfire condition by means of flashing the "check engine" light on the dashboard.
DTC: P0307 **1T ECM, MIL: Yes** **Year:** 2011 **Model:** E550 **Engine:** 5.5L V8, 6.2L V8 **Transmission:** All	**Misfiring of Cylinder 7:** Engine output is affected and the vehicle runs rough. (Combustion misfiring) Any condition that causes abnormally high levels of unburned hydrocarbons, raw or partially burnt fuel will tend to significantly elevate its temperature, and cause damage. Vehicles equipped with OBD-II diagnostic systems are designed to alert the driver to a misfire condition by means of flashing the "check engine" light on the dashboard.
DTC: P0308 **1T ECM, MIL: Yes** **Year:** 2011 **Model:** E550 **Engine:** 5.5L V8, 6.2L V8 **Transmission:** All	**Misfiring of Cylinder 8:** Engine output is affected and the vehicle runs rough. (Combustion misfiring) Any condition that causes abnormally high levels of unburned hydrocarbons, raw or partially burnt fuel will tend to significantly elevate its temperature, and cause damage. Vehicles equipped with OBD-II diagnostic systems are designed to alert the driver to a misfire condition by means of flashing the "check engine" light on the dashboard.

DTC	Trouble Code Title, Conditions, Possible Causes
DTC: P0324 **T ECM, MIL: Yes** **Year:** 2011, 2012 **Model:** C250, C300, C350, E350, E550, SLK350 **Engine:** 1.8L L4, 3.0L V6, 3.5L V6, 4.7L V8, 5.5L V8, 6.2L V8 **Transmission:** All	**Knock Sensor (KS) Malfunction:** Engine operation is affected. The knock control (Knock Sensor) has a malfunction.
DTC: P0325 **T ECM, MIL: Yes** **Year:** 2011, 2012 **Model:** C250, C300, C350, E350, E550, SLK350 **Engine:** 1.8L L4, 3.0L V6, 3.5L V6, 4.7L V8, 5.5L V8, 6.2L V8 **Transmission:** All	**Knock Sensor 1 (Right Side):** Engine operation is affected. Knock sensor 1 (right side) has an electrical fault.
DTC: P0327 **T ECM, MIL: Yes** **Year:** 2011, 2012 **Model:** C250, C300, C350, E350, E550, SLK350 **Engine:** 1.8L L4, 3.0L V6, 3.5L V6, 4.7L V8, 5.5L V8, 6.2L V8 **Transmission:** All	**Knock Sensor 1 Circuit:** Engine operation is affected. Knock sensor 1 (right side) has a short circuit to ground.
DTC: P0328 **T ECM, MIL: Yes** **Year:** 2011, 2012 **Model:** C250, C300, C350, E350, E550, SLK350 **Engine:** 1.8L L4, 3.0L V6, 3.5L V6, 4.7L V8, 5.5L V8, 6.2L V8 **Transmission:** All	**Knock Sensor 1 Circuit:** Engine operation is affected. Knock sensor 1 (right side) has a short circuit to positive.
DTC: P0330 **T ECM, MIL: Yes** **Year:** 2011, 2012 **Model:** C250, C300, C350, E350, E550, SLK350 **Engine:** 1.8L L4, 3.0L V6, 3.5L V6, 4.7L V8, 5.5L V8, 6.2L V8 **Transmission:** All	**Knock Sensor 2 Electrical Fault:** Engine operation is affected. Knock sensor 2 (left side) has an electrical fault.
DTC: P0332 **T ECM, MIL: Yes** **Year:** 2011, 2012 **Model:** C250, C300, C350, E350, E550, SLK350 **Engine:** 1.8L L4, 3.0L V6, 3.5L V6, 4.7L V8, 5.5L V8, 6.2L V8 **Transmission:** All	**Knock Sensor 2 (Left Side) Circuit:** Engine operation is affected. Knock sensor 2 (left side) has a short circuit to ground.
DTC: P0333 **T ECM, MIL: Yes** **Year:** 2011, 2012 **Model:** C250, C300, C350, E350, E550, SLK350 **Engine:** 1.8L L4, 3.0L V6, 3.5L V6, 4.7L V8, 5.5L V8, 6.2L V8 **Transmission:** All	**Knock Sensor 2 (Left Side) Circuit:** Engine operation is affected. Knock sensor 2 (left side) has a short circuit to positive.

DTC	Trouble Code Title, Conditions, Possible Causes
DTC: P0335 **T ECM, MIL: Yes** **Year:** 2011, 2012 **Model:** C250, C300, C350, E350, E550, SLK350 **Engine:** 1.8L L4, 3.0L V6, 3.5L V6, 4.7L V8, 5.5L V8, 6.2L V8 **Transmission:** All	**Crankshaft Position (Hall) Sensor or Circuit :** Crankshaft position (Hall) sensor or circuit failed. No signal. Tooth detection is faulty. Mechanical fault
DTC: P0336 **T ECM, MIL: Yes** **Year:** 2011, 2012 **Model:** C250, C300, C350, E350, E550, SLK350 **Engine:** 1.8L L4, 3.0L V6, 3.5L V6, 4.7L V8, 5.5L V8, 6.2L V8 **Transmission:** All	**Crankshaft Hall Sensor (Crankshaft Position Sensor) Rotor:** Crankshaft Hall Sensor (Crankshaft Position Sensor) rotor problems: Signal implausible.- Number of teeth on sensor rotor too high or too low or wiring error. * No tooth space on sensor rotor detected or wiring error. * Tooth space on sensor rotor temporarily not detected or wiring error.
DTC: P0339 **T ECM, MIL: Yes** **Year:** 2011, 2012 **Model:** C250, C300, C350, E350, E550, SLK350 **Engine:** 1.8L L4, 3.0L V6, 3.5L V6, 4.7L V8, 5.5L V8, 6.2L V8 **Transmission:** All	**Crankshaft Hall Sensor or Circuit:** Crankshaft Hall sensor or circuit malfunction.
DTC: P0340 **T ECM, MIL: Yes** **Year:** 2011, 2012 **Model:** C250, C300, C350, E350, E550, SLK350 **Engine:** 1.8L L4, 3.0L V6, 3.5L V6, 4.7L V8, 5.5L V8, 6.2L V8 **Transmission:** All	**Camshaft Position (Hall) Sensors Not Detected:** Engine output is affected. The camshaft Hall sensors were not detected. * Left intake camshaft Hall sensor * Right intake camshaft Hall sensor * Left exhaust camshaft Hall sensor * Right exhaust camshaft Hall sensor
DTC: P0341 **T ECM, MIL: Yes** **Year:** 2011, 2012 **Model:** C250, C300, C350, E350, E550, SLK350 **Engine:** 1.8L L4, 3.0L V6, 3.5L V6, 4.7L V8, 5.5L V8, 6.2L V8 **Transmission:** All	**Intake Camshaft Hall (CMP) Sensor (Right Bank):** Engine output is affected. * Right intake camshaft Hall (CMP) sensor: The alternation frequency of the signal value is implausible. * Right intake camshaft Hall (CMP) sensor: The time of the signal value change is Implausible.
DTC: P0342 **T ECM, MIL: Yes** **Year:** 2011, 2012 **Model:** C250, C300, C350, E350, E550, SLK350 **Engine:** 1.8L L4, 3.0L V6, 3.5L V6, 4.7L V8, 5.5L V8, 6.2L V8 **Transmission:** All	**Intake Camshaft Hall Sensor Circuit Short to Ground (Right Bank):** Right intake camshaft Hall sensor: Short circuit to ground.
DTC: P0343 **T ECM, MIL: Yes** **Year:** 2011, 2012 **Model:** C250, C300, C350, E350, E550, SLK350 **Engine:** 1.8L L4, 3.0L V6, 3.5L V6, 4.7L V8, 5.5L V8, 6.2L V8 **Transmission:** All	**Intake Camshaft Hall Sensor Short Circuit to Positive or Open Circuit :** Engine output is affected. * Right intake camshaft Hall sensor: Short circuit to positive or open circuit

DTC	Trouble Code Title, Conditions, Possible Causes
DTC: P0346 **T ECM, MIL: Yes** **Year:** 2011, 2012 **Model:** C250, C300, C350, E350, E550, SLK350 **Engine:** 1.8L L4, 3.0L V6, 3.5L V6, 4.7L V8, 5.5L V8, 6.2L V8 **Transmission:** All	**Intake Camshaft Hall Sensor (Left Bank):** Engine output is affected. * Left intake camshaft Hall sensor: The alternation frequency of the signal value is implausible. * Left intake camshaft Hall sensor: The time of the signal value change is implausible.
DTC: P0347 **T ECM, MIL: Yes** **Year:** 2011, 2012 **Model:** C250, C300, C350, E350, E550, SLK350 **Engine:** 1.8L L4, 3.0L V6, 3.5L V6, 4.7L V8, 5.5L V8, 6.2L V8 **Transmission:** All	**Intake Camshaft Hall Sensor Circuit (Left Bank):** Left intake camshaft Hall sensor: Short circuit to ground.
DTC: P0348 **T ECM, MIL: Yes** **Year:** 2011, 2012 **Model:** C250, C300, C350, E350, E550, SLK350 **Engine:** 1.8L L4, 3.0L V6, 3.5L V6, 4.7L V8, 5.5L V8, 6.2L V8 **Transmission:** All	**Intake Camshaft Hall Sensor Circuit:** Engine output is affected. Left intake camshaft Hall sensor: * Short circuit to positive or open circuit
DTC: P0350 **T ECM, MIL: Yes** **Year:** 2011 **Model:** E550 **Engine:** 5.5L V8, 6.2L V8 **Transmission:** All	**Ignition Output Stage 2 :** Engine running is affected. Ignition output stage 2.
DTC: P0351 **T ECM, MIL: Yes** **Year:** 2011, 2012 **Model:** C250, C300, C350, E350, E550, SLK350 **Engine:** 1.8L L4, 3.0L V6, 3.5L V6, 4.7L V8, 5.5L V8, 6.2L V8 **Transmission:** All	**Ignition Coil (Cyl. 1):** Engine operation affected. Ignition coil primary current, signal fault, open circuit, or electrical fault. Combustion period readout too small. * Ignition coil primary current of cylinder 1 is too high. * Ignition coil primary current of cylinder 1 is too low. * Signal fault of ignition coil diagnosis of cylinder 1. * Ignition coil primary current of cylinder 1 alternates between too high and too low. * The control line to the ignition coil of cylinder 1 has an open circuit. * The output stage to ignition coil of cylinder 1 detects an electrical fault.
DTC: P0352 **T ECM, MIL: Yes** **Year:** 2011, 2012 **Model:** C250, C300, C350, E350, E550, SLK350 **Engine:** 1.8L L4, 3.0L V6, 3.5L V6, 4.7L V8, 5.5L V8, 6.2L V8 **Transmission:** All	**Ignition Coil (Cyl. 2):** Engine operation affected. Ignition coil primary current, signal fault, open circuit, or electrical fault. Combustion period readout too small. * Ignition coil primary current of cylinder 2 is too high. * Ignition coil primary current of cylinder 2 is too low. * Signal fault of ignition coil diagnosis of cylinder 2. * Ignition coil primary current of cylinder 2 alternates between too high and too low. * The control line to the ignition coil of cylinder 2 has an open circuit. * The output stage to ignition coil of cylinder 2 detects an electrical fault.

DTC	Trouble Code Title, Conditions, Possible Causes
DTC: P0353 **T ECM, MIL: Yes** **Year:** 2011, 2012 **Model:** C250, C300, C350, E350, E550, SLK350 **Engine:** 1.8L L4, 3.0L V6, 3.5L V6, 4.7L V8, 5.5L V8, 6.2L V8 **Transmission:** All	**Ignition Coil (Cyl. 3):** Engine operation affected. Ignition coil primary current, signal fault, open circuit, or electrical fault. Combustion period readout too small. * Ignition coil primary current of cylinder 3 is too high. * Ignition coil primary current of cylinder 3 is too low. * Signal fault of ignition coil diagnosis of cylinder 3. * Ignition coil primary current of cylinder 3 alternates between too high and too low. * The control line to the ignition coil of cylinder 3 has an open circuit. * The output stage to ignition coil of cylinder 3 detects an electrical fault.
DTC: P0354 **T ECM, MIL: Yes** **Year:** 2011, 2012 **Model:** C250, C300, C350, E350, E550, SLK350 **Engine:** 1.8L L4, 3.0L V6, 3.5L V6, 4.7L V8, 5.5L V8, 6.2L V8 **Transmission:** All	**Ignition Coil (Cyl. 4):** Engine operation affected. Ignition coil primary current, signal fault, open circuit, or electrical fault. Combustion period readout too small. * Ignition coil primary current of cylinder 4 is too high. * Ignition coil primary current of cylinder 4 is too low. * Signal fault of ignition coil diagnosis of cylinder 4. * Ignition coil primary current of cylinder 4 alternates between too high and too low. * The control line to the ignition coil of cylinder 4 has an open circuit. * The output stage to ignition coil of cylinder 4 detects an electrical fault.
DTC: P0355 **T ECM, MIL: Yes** **Year:** 2011, 2012 **Model:** C250, C300, C350, E350, E550, SLK350 **Engine:** 3.0L V6, 3.5L V6, 4.7L V8, 5.5L V8, 6.2L V8 **Transmission:** All	**Ignition Coil (Cyl. 5):** Engine operation affected. Ignition coil primary current, signal fault, open circuit, or electrical fault. * Ignition coil primary current of cylinder 5 is too high. * Ignition coil primary current of cylinder 5 is too low. * Signal fault of ignition coil diagnosis of cylinder 5. * Ignition coil primary current of cylinder 5 alternates between too high and too low. * The control line to the ignition coil of cylinder 5 has an open circuit. * The output stage to ignition coil of cylinder 5 detects an electrical fault.
DTC: P0356 **T ECM, MIL: Yes** **Year:** 2011, 2012 **Model:** C250, C300, C350, E350, E550, SLK350 **Engine:** 3.0L V6, 3.5L V6, 4.7L V8, 5.5L V8, 6.2L V8 **Transmission:** All	**Ignition Coil (Cyl. 6):** Engine running is affected: * Ignition coil primary current of cylinder 6 is too high. * Ignition coil primary current of cylinder 6 is too low. * Signal fault of ignition coil diagnosis of cylinder 6. * Ignition coil primary current of cylinder 6 alternates between too high and too low. * The control line to the ignition coil of cylinder 6 has an open circuit. * The output stage to ignition coil of cylinder 6 detects an electrical fault.
DTC: P0357 **T ECM, MIL: Yes** **Year:** 2011 **Model:** E550 **Engine:** 5.5L V8, 6.2L V8 **Transmission:** All	**Ignition Coil (Cyl. 7):** Engine running is affected: * Ignition coil primary current of cylinder 7 is too high. * Ignition coil primary current of cylinder 7 is too low. * Signal fault of ignition coil diagnosis of cylinder 7. * Ignition coil primary current of cylinder 7 alternates between too high and too low. * The control line to the ignition coil of cylinder 7 has an open circuit. * The output stage to ignition coil of cylinder 7 detects an electrical fault.
DTC: P0358 **T ECM, MIL: Yes** **Year:** 2011 **Model:** E550 **Engine:** 5.5L V8, 6.2L V8 **Transmission:** All	**Ignition Coil (Cyl. 8):** Engine running is affected: * Ignition coil primary current of cylinder 8 is too high. * Ignition coil primary current of cylinder 8 is too low. * Signal fault of ignition coil diagnosis of cylinder 8. * Ignition coil primary current of cylinder 8 alternates between too high and too low. * The control line to the ignition coil of cylinder 8 has an open circuit. * The output stage to ignition coil of cylinder 8 detects an electrical fault.

DTC	Trouble Code Title, Conditions, Possible Causes
DTC: P0366 **T ECM, MIL: Yes** **Year:** 2011, 2012 **Model:** C250, C300, C350, E350, E550, SLK350 **Engine:** 1.8L L4, 3.0L V6, 3.5L V6, 4.7L V8, 5.5L V8, 6.2L V8 **Transmission:** All	**Right Exhaust Camshaft Hall Sensor Signal Value Implausible:** Engine output is affected. Right exhaust camshaft Hall sensor: * The alternation frequency of the signal value is implausible. * The time of the signal value change is implausible.
DTC: P0367 **T ECM, MIL: Yes** **Year:** 2011, 2012 **Model:** C250, C300, C350, E350, E550, SLK350 **Engine:** 1.8L L4, 3.0L V6, 3.5L V6, 4.7L V8, 5.5L V8, 6.2L V8 **Transmission:** All	**Right Exhaust Camshaft Hall Sensor:** Engine output is affected. Right exhaust camshaft Hall sensor circuit may be short to ground.
DTC: P0368 **T ECM, MIL: Yes** **Year:** 2011, 2012 **Model:** C250, C300, C350, E350, E550, SLK350 **Engine:** 1.8L L4, 3.0L V6, 3.5L V6, 4.7L V8, 5.5L V8, 6.2L V8 **Transmission:** All	**Right Exhaust Camshaft Hall Sensor:** Engine output is affected. Right exhaust camshaft Hall sensor circuit may be short to positive or open.
DTC: P0391 **T ECM, MIL: Yes** **Year:** 2011, 2012 **Model:** C250, C300, C350, E350, E550, SLK350 **Engine:** 1.8L L4, 3.0L V6, 3.5L V6, 4.7L V8, 5.5L V8, 6.2L V8 **Transmission:** All	**Left Exhaust Camshaft Hall Sensor Alternation Frequency Implausible:** Engine output is affected. Left exhaust camshaft Hall sensor - alternation frequency of the signal value is implausible.
DTC: P0392 **T ECM, MIL: Yes** **Year:** 2011, 2012 **Model:** C250, C300, C350, E350, E550, SLK350 **Engine:** 1.8L L4, 3.0L V6, 3.5L V6, 4.7L V8, 5.5L V8, 6.2L V8 **Transmission:** All	**Left Exhaust Camshaft Hall Sensor Circuit:** Engine output is affected. Left exhaust camshaft Hall sensor circuit may be short to ground.
DTC: P0393 **T ECM, MIL: Yes** **Year:** 2011, 2012 **Model:** C250, C300, C350, E350, E550, SLK350 **Engine:** 1.8L L4, 3.0L V6, 3.5L V6, 4.7L V8, 5.5L V8, 6.2L V8 **Transmission:** All	**Left Exhaust Camshaft Hall Sensor Circuit:** Engine output is affected. Left exhaust camshaft Hall sensor circuit may be short to positive or open circuit.
DTC: P0410 **T ECM, MIL: Yes** **Year:** 2011, 2012 **Model:** C250, C300, C350, E350, E550, SLK350 **Engine:** 1.8L L4, 3.0L V6, 3.5L V6, 4.7L V8, 5.5L V8, 6.2L V8 **Transmission:** All	**Secondary Air Injection (Right or Left Bank):** Malfunction of secondary air injection at right bank of cylinders (function chain). Air flow too low. Air pump relay.

DTC	Trouble Code Title, Conditions, Possible Causes
DTC: P0412 **T ECM, MIL: Yes** **Year:** 2011, 2012 **Model:** C250, C300, C350, E350, E550, SLK350 **Engine:** 1.8L L4, 3.0L V6, 3.5L V6, 4.7L V8, 5.5L V8, 6.2L V8 **Transmission:** All	**Air Pump Switchover Valve Circuit:** Short circuit to positive or open circuit.
DTC: P0413 **T ECM, MIL: Yes** **Year:** 2011, 2012 **Model:** C250, C300, C350, E350, E550, SLK350 **Engine:** 1.8L L4, 3.0L V6, 3.5L V6, 4.7L V8, 5.5L V8, 6.2L V8 **Transmission:** All	**Air Pump Switchover Valve Circuit:** Air pump switchover valve circuit shows short circuit to positive.
DTC: P0414 **T ECM, MIL: Yes** **Year:** 2011, 2012 **Model:** C250, C300, C350, E350, E550, SLK350 **Engine:** 1.8L L4, 3.0L V6, 3.5L V6, 4.7L V8, 5.5L V8, 6.2L V8 **Transmission:** All	**Air Pump Switchover Valve Circuit:** Air pump switchover valve circuit shows short circuit to ground.
DTC: P0415 **T ECM, MIL: Yes** **Year:** 2011, 2012 **Model:** C250, C300, C350, E350, E550, SLK350 **Engine:** 1.8L L4, 3.0L V6, 3.5L V6, 4.7L V8, 5.5L V8, 6.2L V8 **Transmission:** All	**Air Pump Switchover Valve:** Air pump switchover valve.
DTC: P0418 **T ECM, MIL: Yes** **Year:** 2011 **Model:** E550 **Engine:** 5.5L V8, 6.2L V8 **Transmission:** All	**Air Pump Relay:** Relay for air pump : Open circuit.
DTC: P0422 **T ECM, MIL: Yes** **Year:** 2011, 2012 **Model:** C250, C300, C350, E350, E550, SLK350 **Engine:** 1.8L L4, 3.0L V6, 3.5L V6, 4.7L V8, 5.5L V8, 6.2L V8 **Transmission:** All	**Right or Left Catalytic Converter is Insufficient:** Exhaust system malfunction. Right or left catalytic converter is insufficient
DTC: P0442 **T ECM, MIL: Yes** **Year:** 2011, 2012 **Model:** C250, C300, C350, E350, E550, SLK350 **Engine:** 1.8L L4, 3.0L V6, 3.5L V6, 4.7L V8, 5.5L V8, 6.2L V8 **Transmission:** All	**EVAP System Small Leak Detected:** Purge control system has slight leak: * Leak in hose connection or shutoff valve of activated charcoal canister.

DTC	Trouble Code Title, Conditions, Possible Causes
DTC: P0444 **T ECM, MIL: Yes** **Year:** 2011, 2012 **Model:** C250, C300, C350, E350, E550, SLK350 **Engine:** 1.8L L4, 3.0L V6, 3.5L V6, 4.7L V8, 5.5L V8, 6.2L V8 **Transmission:** All	**Purge Control Valve Circuit:** Purge control valve open circuit. Switchover valve permanently closed
DTC: P0446 **T ECM, MIL: Yes** **Year:** 2011, 2012 **Model:** C250, C300, C350, E350, E550, SLK350 **Engine:** 1.8L L4, 3.0L V6, 3.5L V6, 4.7L V8, 5.5L V8, 6.2L V8 **Transmission:** All	**Charcoal Canister Shut-Off Valve:** Activated charcoal canister shut-off valve: * open circuit in the wiring * Mechanical defect or component (permanently open)
DTC: P0447 **T ECM, MIL: Yes** **Year:** 2011, 2012 **Model:** C250, C300, C350, E350, E550, SLK350 **Engine:** 1.8L L4, 3.0L V6, 3.5L V6, 4.7L V8, 5.5L V8, 6.2L V8 **Transmission:** All	**Charcoal Canister Shut-Off Valve Circuit:** Activated charcoal canister shut-off valve has a short circuit to positive.
DTC: P0448 **T ECM, MIL: Yes** **Year:** 2011, 2012 **Model:** C250, C300, C350, E350, E550, SLK350 **Engine:** 1.8L L4, 3.0L V6, 3.5L V6, 4.7L V8, 5.5L V8, 6.2L V8 **Transmission:** All	**Charcoal Canister Shut-Off Valve Circuit:** Activated charcoal canister shut-off valve has a short circuit to ground.
DTC: P0451 **T ECM, MIL: Yes** **Year:** 2011, 2012 **Model:** C250, C300, C350, E350, E550, SLK350 **Engine:** 1.8L L4, 3.0L V6, 3.5L V6, 4.7L V8, 5.5L V8, 6.2L V8 **Transmission:** All	**Fuel Tank Pressure Sensor Circuit:** Fuel tank pressure sensor circuit: * Short circuit to positive * Short circuit to ground * Open circuit * Signal implausible
DTC: P0452 **T ECM, MIL: Yes** **Year:** 2011, 2012 **Model:** C250, C300, C350, E350, E550, SLK350 **Engine:** 1.8L L4, 3.0L V6, 3.5L V6, 4.7L V8, 5.5L V8, 6.2L V8 **Transmission:** All	**Fuel Tank Pressure Sensor Circuit:** Tank pressure sensor diagnosis shows short circuit to ground.
DTC: P0453 **T ECM, MIL: Yes** **Year:** 2011, 2012 **Model:** C250, C300, C350, E350, E550, SLK350 **Engine:** 1.8L L4, 3.0L V6, 3.5L V6, 4.7L V8, 5.5L V8, 6.2L V8 **Transmission:** All	**Fuel Tank Pressure Sensor Circuit:** Tank pressure sensor diagnosis shows short circuit to positive or open.

DTC	Trouble Code Title, Conditions, Possible Causes
DTC: P0455 **T ECM** **Year:** 2011, 2012 **Model:** C250, C300, C350, E350, E550, SLK350 **Engine:** 1.8L L4, 3.0L V6, 3.5L V6, 4.7L V8, 5.5L V8, 6.2L V8 **Transmission:** All	**EVAP System Major Leak Detected:** Major leak in purge system: Hose in system not connected or filler cap open.
DTC: P0456 **T ECM, MIL: Yes** **Year:** 2011, 2012 **Model:** C250, C300, C350, E350, E550, SLK350 **Engine:** 1.8L L4, 3.0L V6, 3.5L V6, 4.7L V8, 5.5L V8, 6.2L V8 **Transmission:** All	**EVAP System Minor Leak Detected:** Purge control system has a slight leak (minor leak).
DTC: P0458 **T ECM, MIL: Yes** **Year:** 2011, 2012 **Model:** C250, C300, C350, E350, E550, SLK350 **Engine:** 1.8L L4, 3.0L V6, 3.5L V6, 4.7L V8, 5.5L V8, 6.2L V8 **Transmission:** All	**Purge Control Valve Circuit:** Purge control valve) : Short circuit to ground / Switchover valve permanently open.
DTC: P0459 **T ECM, MIL: Yes** **Year:** 2011, 2012 **Model:** C250, C300, C350, E350, E550, SLK350 **Engine:** 1.8L L4, 3.0L V6, 3.5L V6, 4.7L V8, 5.5L V8, 6.2L V8 **Transmission:** All	**Purge Control Valve Circuit:** Purge control valve: Short circuit to positive (switchover valve permanently closed).
DTC: P0460 **T ECM** **Year:** 2011, 2012 **Model:** C250, C300, C350, E350, E550, SLK350 **Engine:** 1.8L L4, 3.0L V6, 3.5L V6, 4.7L V8, 5.5L V8, 6.2L V8 **Transmission:** All	**Fuel Level Sensor:** Fuel system operation affected.
DTC: P0506 **T ECM, MIL: Yes** **Year:** 2011, 2012 **Model:** C250, C300, C350, E350, E550, SLK350 **Engine:** 1.8L L4, 3.0L V6, 3.5L V6, 4.7L V8, 5.5L V8, 6.2L V8 **Transmission:** All	**Idle Speed Too Low:** Engine output is affected. The idle speed is too low during catalytic converter warm-up.
DTC: P0507 **T ECM, MIL: Yes** **Year:** 2011, 2012 **Model:** C250, C300, C350, E350, E550, SLK350 **Engine:** 1.8L L4, 3.0L V6, 3.5L V6, 4.7L V8, 5.5L V8, 6.2L V8 **Transmission:** All	**Idle Speed Too High:** The idle speed is too high during catalytic converter warm-up.

DTC	Trouble Code Title, Conditions, Possible Causes
DTC: P0513 **T ECM, MIL: Yes** **Year:** 2011, 2012 **Model:** C250, C300, C350, E350, E550, SLK350 **Engine:** 1.8L L4, 3.0L V6, 3.5L V6, 4.7L V8, 5.5L V8, 6.2L V8 **Transmission:** All	**Start Enable Signal Not Sent to EIS Control Unit:** Start enable of DAS not sent: see fault codes in injection control unit.
DTC: P0562 **T TCM, TCIL: Yes** **Year:** 2011, 2012 **Model:** C250, C300, C350, E350, E550, SLK350 **Engine:** 1.8L L4, 3.0L V6, 3.5L V6, 4.7L V8, 5.5L V8, 6.2L V8 **Transmission:** All	**Transmission Function - Battery Voltage Too Low:** Transmission function is affected. Low voltage supply to ME-SFI components. Fault present in transmission control module.
DTC: P0563 **T TCM, TCIL: Yes** **Year:** 2011, 2012 **Model:** C250, C300, C350, E350, E550, SLK350 **Engine:** 1.8L L4, 3.0L V6, 3.5L V6, 4.7L V8, 5.5L V8, 6.2L V8 **Transmission:** All	**Transmission Function - Battery Voltage Too High:** Transmission operation is affected. Voltage too high to ME-SFI control unit. Voltage too high to TCM.
DTC: P0597 **T ECM, MIL: Yes** **Year:** 2011, 2012 **Model:** C250, C300, C350, E350, E550, SLK350 **Engine:** 1.8L L4, 3.0L V6, 3.5L V6, 4.7L V8, 5.5L V8, 6.2L V8 **Transmission:** All	**Thermostat Valve Circuit Open:** Cooling system malfunction. Three-disk thermostat valve has an open circuit in the wiring.
DTC: P0598 **T ECM, MIL: Yes** **Year:** 2011, 2012 **Model:** C250, C300, C350, E350, E550, SLK350 **Engine:** 1.8L L4, 3.0L V6, 3.5L V6, 4.7L V8, 5.5L V8, 6.2L V8 **Transmission:** All	**Thermostat Valve Circuit Short:** Engine cooling affected. Thermostat valve has a short circuit to ground.
DTC: P0599 **T ECM, MIL: Yes** **Year:** 2011, 2012 **Model:** C250, C300, C350, E350, E550, SLK350 **Engine:** 1.8L L4, 3.0L V6, 3.5L V6, 4.7L V8, 5.5L V8, 6.2L V8 **Transmission:** All	**Thermostat Valve Circuit Short:** Engine cooling affected. Three-disk thermostat valve has a short circuit to positive.
DTC: P0604 **T ECM, MIL: Yes** **Year:** 2011, 2012 **Model:** C250, C300, C350, E350, E550, SLK350 **Engine:** 1.8L L4, 3.0L V6, 3.5L V6, 4.7L V8, 5.5L V8, 6.2L V8 **Transmission:** All	**Engine Control Module (ME-SFI Control Unit) Has an Internal Error:** Control module (ME-SFI control unit) has an internal error. Random access memory error.

DTC	Trouble Code Title, Conditions, Possible Causes
DTC: P0605 **T ECM, MIL: Yes** **Year:** 2011, 2012 **Model:** C250, C300, C350, E350, E550, SLK350 **Engine:** 1.8L L4, 3.0L V6, 3.5L V6, 4.7L V8, 5.5L V8, 6.2L V8 **Transmission:** All	**Engine Control Module (ME-SFI control Unit) Has an Internal Error:** Control module (ME-SFI control unit) has an internal error. EEPROM error of control unit.
DTC: P0606 **T ECM, MIL: Yes** **Year:** 2011, 2012 **Model:** C250, C300, C350, E350, E550, SLK350 **Engine:** 1.8L L4, 3.0L V6, 3.5L V6, 4.7L V8, 5.5L V8, 6.2L V8 **Transmission:** All	**Engine Control Module Has an Internal Error:** Control module has an internal error.
DTC: P0607 **T ECM, MIL: Yes** **Year:** 2011, 2012 **Model:** C250, C300, C350, E350, E550, SLK350 **Engine:** 1.8L L4, 3.0L V6, 3.5L V6, 4.7L V8, 5.5L V8, 6.2L V8 **Transmission:** All	**O2 Sensor Analysis Defective or Battery Too Low for ADC or Control Module Internal Error:** O2 sensor in the engine control unit is defective. Battery voltage too low for ADC. Control module has an internal error.
DTC: P0620 **T ECM, MIL: Yes** **Year:** 2011, 2012 **Model:** C250, C300, C350, E350, E550, SLK350 **Engine:** 1.8L L4, 3.0L V6, 3.5L V6, 4.7L V8, 5.5L V8, 6.2L V8 **Transmission:** All	**Generator Performance:** Battery charging fault. On-board electrical system malfunction.
DTC: P0638 **T ECM, MIL: Yes** **Year:** 2011, 2012 **Model:** C250, C300, C350, E350, E550, SLK350 **Engine:** 1.8L L4, 3.0L V6, 3.5L V6, 4.7L V8, 5.5L V8, 6.2L V8 **Transmission:** All	**Throttle Valve Actuator:** Engine running condition affected: * Throttle valve mechanical failure. * Throttle valve actuator adaptation not performed. * Throttle valve jams/ices up Throttle valve plausibility. PWM signal issue
DTC: P0642 **T TCM, MIL: Yes, TCIL: Yes** **Year:** 2011, 2012 **Model:** C250, C300, C350, E350, E550, SLK350 **Engine:** 1.8L L4, 3.0L V6, 3.5L V6, 4.7L V8, 5.5L V8, 6.2L V8 **Transmission:** All	**TCM Fault:** Transmission operation is affected. Fault is present in the transmission control module.
DTC: P0643 **T TCM, MIL: Yes, TCIL: Yes** **Year:** 2011, 2012 **Model:** C250, C300, C350, E350, E550, SLK350 **Engine:** 1.8L L4, 3.0L V6, 3.5L V6, 4.7L V8, 5.5L V8, 6.2L V8 **Transmission:** All	**TCM Fault:** Transmission operation is affected. Fault is present in the TCM.

DTC	Trouble Code Title, Conditions, Possible Causes
DTC: P0651 **T ECM, MIL: Yes** **Year:** 2011, 2012 **Model:** C250, C300, C350, E350, E550, SLK350 **Engine:** 1.8L L4, 3.0L V6, 3.5L V6, 4.7L V8, 5.5L V8, 6.2L V8 **Transmission:** All	**Accelerator Pedal Position Sensor Power Supply:** Engine output is affected. Accelerator pedal position sensor power supply faulty.
DTC: P0702 **T TCM, TCIL: Yes** **Year:** 2011, 2012 **Model:** C250, C300, C350, E350, E550, SLK350 **Engine:** 1.8L L4, 3.0L V6, 3.5L V6, 4.7L V8, 5.5L V8, 6.2L V8 **Transmission:** All	**TCM or ETC Fault:** Transmission operation affected. Transmission control system electrical. Fault present in transmission control module (TCM). Fault present in ETC control unit. Torque request from control module is implausible.
DTC: P0706 **T TCM, TCIL: Yes** **Year:** 2011, 2012 **Model:** C250, C300, C350, E350, E550, SLK350 **Engine:** 1.8L L4, 3.0L V6, 3.5L V6, 4.7L V8, 5.5L V8, 6.2L V8 **Transmission:** All	**TCM Fault:** Transmission operation is affected. Fault is present in the transmission control module.
DTC: P0716 **T TCM, TCIL: Yes** **Year:** 2011, 2012 **Model:** C250, C300, C350, E350, E550, SLK350 **Engine:** 1.8L L4, 3.0L V6, 3.5L V6, 4.7L V8, 5.5L V8, 6.2L V8 **Transmission:** All	**TCM Fault:** Transmission operation is affected. Fault in the transmission control unit.
DTC: P0717 **T TCM, TCIL: Yes** **Year:** 2011, 2012 **Model:** C250, C300, C350, E350, E550, SLK350 **Engine:** 1.8L L4, 3.0L V6, 3.5L V6, 4.7L V8, 5.5L V8, 6.2L V8 **Transmission:** All	**TCM Fault:** Transmission operation is affected. Fault in the transmission control unit.
DTC: P0718 **T TCM, TCIL: Yes** **Year:** 2011, 2012 **Model:** C250, C300, C350, E350, E550, SLK350 **Engine:** 1.8L L4, 3.0L V6, 3.5L V6, 4.7L V8, 5.5L V8, 6.2L V8 **Transmission:** All	**TCM Fault:** Transmission operation is affected. Fault in the transmission control unit.
DTC: P0722 **T TCM, TCIL: Yes** **Year:** 2011, 2012 **Model:** C250, C300, C350, E350, E550, SLK350 **Engine:** 1.8L L4, 3.0L V6, 3.5L V6, 4.7L V8, 5.5L V8, 6.2L V8 **Transmission:** All	**TCM Fault:** Transmission operation is affected. Fault in the transmission control module.

DTC	Trouble Code Title, Conditions, Possible Causes
DTC: P0723 **T TCM, TCIL: Yes** **Year:** 2011 **Model:** E550 **Engine:** 5.5L V8, 6.2L V8 **Transmission:** All	**TCM Fault - Internal Error:** Internal error in TCM
DTC: P0723 **T TCM, TCIL: Yes** **Year:** 2011, 2012 **Model:** C350, E350, SLK350 **Engine:** 3.5L V6 **Transmission:** All	**TCM Fault:** Read out fault memory of control unit Transmission.
DTC: P0726 **T ECM, MIL: Yes** **Year:** 2011, 2012 **Model:** C250, C300, C350, E350, E550, SLK350 **Engine:** 1.8L L4, 3.0L V6, 3.5L V6, 4.7L V8, 5.5L V8, 6.2L V8 **Transmission:** All	**Engine Speed Input Signal Performance:** Smooth engine running is affected. Input signal of the engine speed has a malfunction
DTC: P0730 **T TCM, TCIL: Yes** **Year:** 2011, 2012 **Model:** C250, C300, C350, E350, E550, SLK350 **Engine:** 1.8L L4, 3.0L V6, 3.5L V6, 4.7L V8, 5.5L V8, 6.2L V8 **Transmission:** All	**TCM Fault:** Transmission operation is affected. Fault in the transmission control unit.
DTC: P0748 **T TCM, TCIL: Yes** **Year:** 2011, 2012 **Model:** C250, C300, C350, E350, E550, SLK350 **Engine:** 1.8L L4, 3.0L V6, 3.5L V6, 4.7L V8, 5.5L V8, 6.2L V8 **Transmission:** All	**TCM or ETC Fault - Pressure Control Circuit:** Transmission operation affected. Pressure control circuit malfunction. Fault present in transmission control module. Fault stored in ETC control module.
DTC: P0778 **T TCM, TCIL: Yes** **Year:** 2011, 2012 **Model:** C250, C300, C350, E350, E550, SLK350 **Engine:** 1.8L L4, 3.0L V6, 3.5L V6, 4.7L V8, 5.5L V8, 6.2L V8 **Transmission:** All	**TCM or ETC Fault:** Transmission operation affected. Fault is present in the transmission control module. Fault stored in ETC control unit.
DTC: P0798 **T TCM, TCIL: Yes** **Year:** 2011, 2012 **Model:** C250, C300, C350, E350, E550, SLK350 **Engine:** 1.8L L4, 3.0L V6, 3.5L V6, 4.7L V8, 5.5L V8, 6.2L V8 **Transmission:** All	**TCM Fault:** Transmission operation is affected. Fault is present in the TCM.
DTC: P0801 **T ECM** **Year:** 2011, 2012 **Model:** C350, CLS550, E350, E550, SLK350 **Engine:** 3.5L V6, 4.7L V8, 4.6L V8, 5.5L V8, 6.2L V8 **Transmission:** All	**Reverse Inhibit Control Circuit Malfunction:** The control circuit is not in the expected state.

DTC	Trouble Code Title, Conditions, Possible Causes
DTC: P0803 **T ECM, MIL: Yes** **Year:** 2011, 2012 **Model:** C350, CLS550, E350, E550, SLK350 **Engine:** 3.5L V6, 4.7L V8, 4.6L V8, 5.5L V8, 6.2L V8 **Transmission:** All	**1-4 Upshift (Skip Shift) Solenoid Control Circuit Malfunction :** The 1-4 solenoid control circuit was detected a faulty.
DTC: P0804 **T ECM** **Year:** 2011, 2012 **Model:** CLS550, E350, E550, SLK350 **Engine:** 3.5L V6, 4.7L V8, 4.6L V8, 5.5L V8, 6.2L V8 **Transmission:** All	**1-4 Upshift (Skip Shift) Lamp Control Circuit Malfunction:** The 1-4 solenoid control circuit was detected a faulty.
DTC: P1999 **T ECM, MIL: Yes** **Year:** 2011, 2012 **Model:** C250, C300, C350, E350, E550, SLK350 **Engine:** 1.8L L4, 3.0L V6, 3.5L V6, 4.7L V8, 5.5L V8, 6.2L V8 **Transmission:** All	**Idle Speed Above or Below Limits:** Engine idle and running condition affected. Idle speed with warm engine is above the permissible range limit.
DTC: P2004 **T ECM, MIL: Yes** **Year:** 2011, 2012 **Model:** C250, C300, C350, E350, E550, SLK350 **Engine:** 1.8L L4, 3.0L V6, 3.5L V6, 4.7L V8, 5.5L V8, 6.2L V8 **Transmission:** All	**Intake Manifold Tumble Flap:** Engine output affected. Diagnosis of tumble flap Intake manifold: * Short circuit to ground of sensor lines * Tumble flap shafts stick in the actuated position
DTC: P2005 **T ECM, MIL: Yes** **Year:** 2011, 2012 **Model:** C250, C300, C350, E350, E550, SLK350 **Engine:** 1.8L L4, 3.0L V6, 3.5L V6, 4.7L V8, 5.5L V8, 6.2L V8 **Transmission:** All	**Intake Manifold Tumble Flap:** Engine output affected. Diagnosis of tumble flap Intake manifold: * Short or open circuit in sensor lines * Mechanical fault of one actuating lever * Sensor faulty, replace sensor
DTC: P2006 **T ECM, MIL: Yes** **Year:** 2011, 2012 **Model:** C250, C300, C350, E350, E550, SLK350 **Engine:** 1.8L L4, 3.0L V6, 3.5L V6, 4.7L V8, 5.5L V8, 6.2L V8 **Transmission:** All	**Intake Manifold Tumble Flap:** Engine output affected. Diagnosis of tumble flap intake manifold: * Open circuit of sensor lines * Tumble flap shafts stick in the non-actuated position * Vacuum supply to tumble valve interrupted
DTC: P2008 **T ECM, MIL: Yes** **Year:** 2011, 2012 **Model:** C250, C300, C350, E350, E550, SLK350 **Engine:** 1.8L L4, 3.0L V6, 3.5L V6, 4.7L V8, 5.5L V8, 6.2L V8 **Transmission:** All	**Intake Manifold Switchover Valve Circuit:** Engine output is affected by: * Variable intake manifold switchover valve: Open circuit * Intake manifold tumble flap switchover valve: Open circuit

DTC	Trouble Code Title, Conditions, Possible Causes
DTC: P2009 **T ECM, MIL: Yes** **Year:** 2011, 2012 **Model:** C250, C300, C350, E350, E550, SLK350 **Engine:** 1.8L L4, 3.0L V6, 3.5L V6, 4.7L V8, 5.5L V8, 6.2L V8 **Transmission:** All	**Intake Manifold Switchover Valve Circuit:** Engine output is affected by:- Variable intake manifold switchover valve: * Short circuit - Intake manifold tumble flap switchover valve: Short circuit
DTC: P2010 **T ECM, MIL: Yes** **Year:** 2011, 2012 **Model:** C250, C300, C350, E350, E550, SLK350 **Engine:** 1.8L L4, 3.0L V6, 3.5L V6, 4.7L V8, 5.5L V8, 6.2L V8 **Transmission:** All	**Intake Manifold Switchover Valve Circuit:** Engine output is affected by:- Variable intake manifold switchover valve: * Short circuit - Intake manifold tumble flap switchover valve: Short circuit
DTC: P2072 **T ECM, MIL: Yes** **Year:** 2011, 2012 **Model:** C250, C300, C350, E350, E550, SLK350 **Engine:** 1.8L L4, 3.0L V6, 3.5L V6, 4.7L V8, 5.5L V8, 6.2L V8 **Transmission:** All	**Throttle Valve Jamming (Iced Up):** Engine output affected.
DTC: P2088 **T ECM, MIL: Yes** **Year:** 2011, 2012 **Model:** C250, C300, C350, E350, E550, SLK350 **Engine:** 1.8L L4, 3.0L V6, 3.5L V6, 4.7L V8, 5.5L V8, 6.2L V8 **Transmission:** All	**Camshaft Intake Solenoid Circuit:** Engine output affected. Short to ground
DTC: P2089 **T ECM, MIL: Yes** **Year:** 2011, 2012 **Model:** C250, C300, C350, E350, E550, SLK350 **Engine:** 1.8L L4, 3.0L V6, 3.5L V6, 4.7L V8, 5.5L V8, 6.2L V8 **Transmission:** All	**Camshaft Intake Solenoid Circuit:** Engine output affected.
DTC: P2090 **T ECM, MIL: Yes** **Year:** 2011, 2012 **Model:** C250, C300, C350, E350, E550, SLK350 **Engine:** 1.8L L4, 3.0L V6, 3.5L V6, 4.7L V8, 5.5L V8, 6.2L V8 **Transmission:** All	**Right or Left Camshaft Exhaust Solenoid:** Engine output is affected. Right or left camshaft exhaust solenoid has a short circuit to ground.
DTC: P2091 **T ECM, MIL: Yes** **Year:** 2011, 2012 **Model:** C250, C300, C350, E350, E550, SLK350 **Engine:** 1.8L L4, 3.0L V6, 3.5L V6, 4.7L V8, 5.5L V8, 6.2L V8 **Transmission:** All	**Right or Left Camshaft Exhaust Solenoid Circuit:** Engine output is affected. Right or left camshaft exhaust solenoid has a short circuit to positive.

DTC	Trouble Code Title, Conditions, Possible Causes
DTC: P2092 **T ECM, MIL: Yes** **Year:** 2011, 2012 **Model:** C250, C300, C350, E350, E550, SLK350 **Engine:** 1.8L L4, 3.0L V6, 3.5L V6, 4.7L V8, 5.5L V8, 6.2L V8 **Transmission:** All	**Camshaft Intake Solenoid Circuit:** Engine output affected.
DTC: P2093 **T ECM, MIL: Yes** **Year:** 2011, 2012 **Model:** C250, C300, C350, E350, E550, SLK350 **Engine:** 1.8L L4, 3.0L V6, 3.5L V6, 4.7L V8, 5.5L V8, 6.2L V8 **Transmission:** All	**Camshaft Intake Solenoid Circuit:** Engine output affected.
DTC: P2101 **T ECM, MIL: Yes** **Year:** 2011, 2012 **Model:** C250, C300, C350, E350, E550, SLK350 **Engine:** 1.8L L4, 3.0L V6, 3.5L V6, 4.7L V8, 5.5L V8, 6.2L V8 **Transmission:** All	**Throttle Valve Actuator:** Engine running condition affected.
DTC: P2111 **T ECM, MIL: Yes** **Year:** 2011, 2012 **Model:** C250, C300, C350, E350, E550, SLK350 **Engine:** 1.8L L4, 3.0L V6, 3.5L V6, 4.7L V8, 5.5L V8, 6.2L V8 **Transmission:** All	**Throttle Valve Actuator Mechanical Fault:** Engine running condition affected.
DTC: P2112 **T ECM, MIL: Yes** **Year:** 2011, 2012 **Model:** C250, C300, C350, E350, E550, SLK350 **Engine:** 1.8L L4, 3.0L V6, 3.5L V6, 4.7L V8, 5.5L V8, 6.2L V8 **Transmission:** All	**Throttle Valve Actuator Mechanical Fault:** Engine running condition affected
DTC: P2122 **T ECM, MIL: Yes** **Year:** 2011, 2012 **Model:** C250, C300, C350, E350, E550, SLK350 **Engine:** 1.8L L4, 3.0L V6, 3.5L V6, 4.7L V8, 5.5L V8, 6.2L V8 **Transmission:** All	**Accelerator Pedal Position Sensor Circuit:** Engine output is affected. Accelerator pedal sensor (Hall sensor 1): Short circuit to ground or open circuit.
DTC: P2123 **T ECM, MIL: Yes** **Year:** 2011, 2012 **Model:** C250, C300, C350, E350, E550, SLK350 **Engine:** 1.8L L4, 3.0L V6, 3.5L V6, 4.7L V8, 5.5L V8, 6.2L V8 **Transmission:** All	**Accelerator Pedal Position Sensor Circuit:** Engine output is affected. Accelerator pedal sensor: Short circuit to positive.

DTC	Trouble Code Title, Conditions, Possible Causes
DTC: P2127 **T ECM, MIL: Yes** **Year:** 2011, 2012 **Model:** C250, C300, C350, E350, E550, SLK350 **Engine:** 1.8L L4, 3.0L V6, 3.5L V6, 4.7L V8, 5.5L V8, 6.2L V8 **Transmission:** All	**Accelerator Pedal Position Sensor 2:** Engine output is affected. Accelerator pedal sensor 2: Short circuit to ground or open circuit.
DTC: P2128 **T ECM, MIL: Yes** **Year:** 2011, 2012 **Model:** C250, C300, C350, E350, E550, SLK350 **Engine:** 1.8L L4, 3.0L V6, 3.5L V6, 4.7L V8, 5.5L V8, 6.2L V8 **Transmission:** All	**Accelerator Pedal Position Sensor 2:** Engine output is affected. Accelerator pedal sensor 2: Short circuit to positive.
DTC: P2135 **T ECM, MIL: Yes** **Year:** 2011, 2012 **Model:** C250, C300, C350, E350, E550, SLK350 **Engine:** 1.8L L4, 3.0L V6, 3.5L V6, 4.7L V8, 5.5L V8, 6.2L V8 **Transmission:** All	**Throttle Valve Actuator Malfunction:** Engine output is affected. Throttle valve actuator: * Actual value potentiometer 1 or 2 has failed * Comparison error between actual value potentiometers 1 and 2
DTC: P2138 **T ECM, MIL: Yes** **Year:** 2011, 2012 **Model:** C250, C300, C350, E350, E550, SLK350 **Engine:** 1.8L L4, 3.0L V6, 3.5L V6, 4.7L V8, 5.5L V8, 6.2L V8 **Transmission:** All	**Accelerator Pedal Position Sensor Disagreement:** Engine output is affected. Accelerator pedal position sensor 1 and sensor 2 voltages do not agree with each other.
DTC: P2158 **T BCM, MIL: Yes** **Year:** 2011, 2012 **Model:** C250, C300, C350, E350, E550, SLK350 **Engine:** 1.8L L4, 3.0L V6, 3.5L V6, 4.7L V8, 5.5L V8, 6.2L V8 **Transmission:** All	**Traction System CAN Signal Implausible:** Traction system operation affected. CAN signal 'Vehicle speed at front axle' from control unit traction systems is implausible.
DTC: P2176 **T ECM, MIL: Yes** **Year:** 2011, 2012 **Model:** C250, C300, C350, E350, E550, SLK350 **Engine:** 1.8L L4, 3.0L V6, 3.5L V6, 4.7L V8, 5.5L V8, 6.2L V8 **Transmission:** All	**Throttle Valve Actuator:** The safety fuel shutoff is active. The throttle valve is jamming or is stiff. Throttle valve adaptation needs to be performed.
DTC: P2195 **T ECM, MIL: Yes** **Year:** 2011, 2012 **Model:** C250, C300, C350, E350, E550, SLK350 **Engine:** 1.8L L4, 3.0L V6, 3.5L V6, 4.7L V8, 5.5L V8, 6.2L V8 **Transmission:** All	**Oxygen Sensor Signal Lean (Right Bank):** Power generation is affected. The signal of the oxygen sensor upstream of the catalytic converter of the right cylinder bank is shifted towards 'Lean'.

DTC	Trouble Code Title, Conditions, Possible Causes
DTC: P2196 **T ECM, MIL: Yes** **Year:** 2011, 2012 **Model:** C250, C300, C350, E350, E550, SLK350 **Engine:** 1.8L L4, 3.0L V6, 3.5L V6, 4.7L V8, 5.5L V8, 6.2L V8 **Transmission:** All	**Oxygen Sensor Signal Rich (Right Bank):** Power generation is affected. The signal of the oxygen sensor upstream of the catalytic converter of the right cylinder bank is shifted towards 'Rich'.
DTC: P2197 **T ECM, MIL: Yes** **Year:** 2011, 2012 **Model:** C250, C300, C350, E350, E550, SLK350 **Engine:** 1.8L L4, 3.0L V6, 3.5L V6, 4.7L V8, 5.5L V8, 6.2L V8 **Transmission:** All	**Oxygen Sensor Signal Lean (Left Bank):** Power generation is affected. The signal of the oxygen sensor upstream of the catalytic converter of the left cylinder bank is shifted towards 'Lean'.
DTC: P2198 **T ECM, MIL: Yes** **Year:** 2011, 2012 **Model:** C250, C300, C350, E350, E550, SLK350 **Engine:** 1.8L L4, 3.0L V6, 3.5L V6, 4.7L V8, 5.5L V8, 6.2L V8 **Transmission:** All	**Oxygen Sensor Signal Rick (Left Bank):** Power generation is affected. The signal of the oxygen sensor upstream of the catalytic converter of the left cylinder bank is shifted towards 'Rich'.
DTC: P2227 **T , MIL: Yes** **Year:** 2011, 2012 **Model:** C250, C300, C350, E350, E550, SLK350 **Engine:** 1.8L L4, 3.0L V6, 3.5L V6, 4.7L V8, 5.5L V8, 6.2L V8 **Transmission:** All	**Ambient Pressure Sensor in ECM Implausible Value:** Ambient pressure sensor in engine control module: implausible value.
DTC: P2228 **T ECM, MIL: Yes** **Year:** 2011, 2012 **Model:** C250, C300, C350, E350, E550, SLK350 **Engine:** 1.8L L4, 3.0L V6, 3.5L V6, 4.7L V8, 5.5L V8, 6.2L V8 **Transmission:** All	**Ambient Pressure Sensor in ECM:** Ambient pressure sensor in ECM improper signal.
DTC: P2229 **T ECM, MIL: Yes** **Year:** 2011, 2012 **Model:** C250, C300, C350, E350, E550, SLK350 **Engine:** 1.8L L4, 3.0L V6, 3.5L V6, 4.7L V8, 5.5L V8, 6.2L V8 **Transmission:** All	**Ambient Pressure Sensor in ECM:** Ambient pressure sensor in ECM improper signal.
DTC: P2237 **T ECM, MIL: Yes** **Year:** 2011, 2012 **Model:** C250, C300, C350, E350, E550, SLK350 **Engine:** 1.8L L4, 3.0L V6, 3.5L V6, 4.7L V8, 5.5L V8, 6.2L V8 **Transmission:** All	**Right HO2S Sensor Circuit:** Exhaust system malfunction. Right HO2S sensor, before TWC,: * Voltage is too high. * Open circuit. * Signal voltage is implausible.

DTC	Trouble Code Title, Conditions, Possible Causes
DTC: P2240 **T ECM, MIL: Yes** **Year:** 2011, 2012 **Model:** C250, C300, C350, E350, E550, SLK350 **Engine:** 1.8L L4, 3.0L V6, 3.5L V6, 4.7L V8, 5.5L V8, 6.2L V8 **Transmission:** All	**Left HO2S Sensor Circuit:** Exhaust system malfunction. Left HO2S sensor, before TWC: * Voltage is too high. * Circuit is open. * Signal voltage is implausible.
DTC: P2243 **T ECM, MIL: Yes** **Year:** 2011, 2012 **Model:** C250, C300, C350, E350, E550, SLK350 **Engine:** 1.8L L4, 3.0L V6, 3.5L V6, 4.7L V8, 5.5L V8, 6.2L V8 **Transmission:** All	**Left HO2S Sensor Circuit:** Exhaust system malfunction. Left HO2S sensor, before TWC: Open circuit.
DTC: P2247 **T ECM, MIL: Yes** **Year:** 2011, 2012 **Model:** C250, C300, C350, E350, E550, SLK350 **Engine:** 1.8L L4, 3.0L V6, 3.5L V6, 4.7L V8, 5.5L V8, 6.2L V8 **Transmission:** All	**Left HO2S Sensor Circuit:** Exhaust system malfunction. Left HO2S sensor, before TWC: Open circuit.
DTC: P2251 **T ECM, MIL: Yes** **Year:** 2011, 2012 **Model:** C250, C300, C350, E350, E550, SLK350 **Engine:** 1.8L L4, 3.0L V6, 3.5L V6, 4.7L V8, 5.5L V8, 6.2L V8 **Transmission:** All	**Right HO2S Sensor Circuit:** Exhaust system malfunction. Right HO2S sensor, before TWC: Open circuit.
DTC: P2254 **T ECM, MIL: Yes** **Year:** 2011, 2012 **Model:** C250, C300, C350, E350, E550, SLK350 **Engine:** 1.8L L4, 3.0L V6, 3.5L V6, 4.7L V8, 5.5L V8, 6.2L V8 **Transmission:** All	**Left HO2S Sensor Circuit:** Exhaust system malfunction. Left HO2S sensor, before TWC: open circuit.
DTC: P2257 **T ECM, MIL: Yes** **Year:** 2011, 2012 **Model:** C250, C300, C350, E350, E550, SLK350 **Engine:** 1.8L L4, 3.0L V6, 3.5L V6, 4.7L V8, 5.5L V8, 6.2L V8 **Transmission:** All	**Secondary Air Pump Relay Circuit:** Relay for air pump: Short circuit to ground.
DTC: P2258 **T ECM, MIL: Yes** **Year:** 2011, 2012 **Model:** C250, C300, C350, E350, E550, SLK350 **Engine:** 1.8L L4, 3.0L V6, 3.5L V6, 4.7L V8, 5.5L V8, 6.2L V8 **Transmission:** All	**Secondary Air Pump Relay Circuit:** Relay for air pump : Short circuit to positive.

DTC	Trouble Code Title, Conditions, Possible Causes
DTC: P2270 **T ECM, MIL: Yes** **Year:** 2011, 2012 **Model:** C250, C300, C350, E350, E550, SLK350 **Engine:** 1.8L L4, 3.0L V6, 3.5L V6, 4.7L V8, 5.5L V8, 6.2L V8 **Transmission:** All	**Right HO2S Sensor Aging :** Exhaust system malfunction. Right O2 sensor, after TWC, aging.
DTC: P2271 **T ECM, MIL: Yes** **Year:** 2011, 2012 **Model:** C250, C300, C350, E350, E550, SLK350 **Engine:** 1.8L L4, 3.0L V6, 3.5L V6, 4.7L V8, 5.5L V8, 6.2L V8 **Transmission:** All	**Right HO2S Sensor Aging :** Exhaust system malfunction. Right O2 sensor, after TWC, aging.
DTC: P2272 **T ECM, MIL: Yes** **Year:** 2011, 2012 **Model:** C250, C300, C350, E350, E550, SLK350 **Engine:** 1.8L L4, 3.0L V6, 3.5L V6, 4.7L V8, 5.5L V8, 6.2L V8 **Transmission:** All	**Left HO2S Sensor Aging :** Left O2 sensor, after TWC, aging.
DTC: P2273 **T ECM, MIL: Yes** **Year:** 2011, 2012 **Model:** C250, C300, C350, E350, E550, SLK350 **Engine:** 1.8L L4, 3.0L V6, 3.5L V6, 4.7L V8, 5.5L V8, 6.2L V8 **Transmission:** All	**Left HO2S Sensor Aging :** Left O2 sensor, after TWC, aging.
DTC: P2279 **T ECM, MIL: Yes** **Year:** 2011, 2012 **Model:** C250, C300, C350, E350, E550, SLK350 **Engine:** 1.8L L4, 3.0L V6, 3.5L V6, 4.7L V8, 5.5L V8, 6.2L V8 **Transmission:** All	**Intake Tract Air Malfunction:** Engine output affected. Check the intake tract for unmetered air.
DTC: P2300 **T ECM, MIL: Yes** **Year:** 2011, 2012 **Model:** C250, C300, C350, E350, E550, SLK350 **Engine:** 1.8L L4, 3.0L V6, 3.5L V6, 4.7L V8, 5.5L V8, 6.2L V8 **Transmission:** All	**Ignition Coil 1 Circuit:** The control line to the ignition coil of cylinder 1 has a short circuit to ground. Engine running is affected.
DTC: P2301 **T ECM, MIL: Yes** **Year:** 2011, 2012 **Model:** C250, C300, C350, E350, E550, SLK350 **Engine:** 1.8L L4, 3.0L V6, 3.5L V6, 4.7L V8, 5.5L V8, 6.2L V8 **Transmission:** All	**Ignition Coil 1 Circuit:** The control line to the ignition coil of cylinder 1 has a short circuit to positive. Engine running is affected.

DTC	Trouble Code Title, Conditions, Possible Causes
DTC: P2303 **T ECM, MIL: Yes** **Year:** 2011, 2012 **Model:** C250, C300, C350, E350, E550, SLK350 **Engine:** 1.8L L4, 3.0L V6, 3.5L V6, 4.7L V8, 5.5L V8, 6.2L V8 **Transmission:** All	**Ignition Coil 2 Circuit:** The control line to the ignition coil of cylinder 2 has a short circuit to ground. Engine running is affected.
DTC: P2304 **T ECM, MIL: Yes** **Year:** 2011, 2012 **Model:** C250, C300, C350, E350, E550, SLK350 **Engine:** 1.8L L4, 3.0L V6, 3.5L V6, 4.7L V8, 5.5L V8, 6.2L V8 **Transmission:** All	**Ignition Coil 2 Circuit:** The control line to the ignition coil of cylinder 2 has a short circuit to positive. Engine running is affected.
DTC: P2306 **T ECM, MIL: Yes** **Year:** 2011, 2012 **Model:** C250, C300, C350, E350, E550, SLK350 **Engine:** 1.8L L4, 3.0L V6, 3.5L V6, 4.7L V8, 5.5L V8, 6.2L V8 **Transmission:** All	**Ignition Coil 3 Circuit:** The control line to the ignition coil of cylinder 3 has a short circuit to ground. Engine running is affected.
DTC: P2307 **T ECM, MIL: Yes** **Year:** 2011, 2012 **Model:** C250, C300, C350, E350, E550, SLK350 **Engine:** 1.8L L4, 3.0L V6, 3.5L V6, 4.7L V8, 5.5L V8, 6.2L V8 **Transmission:** All	**Ignition Coil 3 Circuit:** The control line to the ignition coil of cylinder 3 has a short circuit to positive. Engine running is affected.
DTC: P2309 **T ECM, MIL: Yes** **Year:** 2011, 2012 **Model:** C250, C300, C350, E350, E550, SLK350 **Engine:** 1.8L L4, 3.0L V6, 3.5L V6, 4.7L V8, 5.5L V8, 6.2L V8 **Transmission:** All	**Ignition Coil 4 Circuit:** The control line to the ignition coil of cylinder 4 has a short circuit to ground. Engine running is affected.
DTC: P2310 **T ECM, MIL: Yes** **Year:** 2011, 2012 **Model:** C250, C300, C350, E350, E550, SLK350 **Engine:** 1.8L L4, 3.0L V6, 3.5L V6, 4.7L V8, 5.5L V8, 6.2L V8 **Transmission:** All	**Ignition Coil 4 Circuit:** The control line to the ignition coil of cylinder 4 has a short circuit to positive. Engine running is affected.
DTC: P2312 **T ECM, MIL: Yes** **Year:** 2011, 2012 **Model:** C250, C300, C350, E350, E550, SLK350 **Engine:** 1.8L L4, 3.0L V6, 3.5L V6, 4.7L V8, 5.5L V8, 6.2L V8 **Transmission:** All	**Ignition Coil 5 Circuit:** The control line to the ignition coil of cylinder 5 has a short circuit to ground. Engine running is affected.

DTC	Trouble Code Title, Conditions, Possible Causes
DTC: P2313 **T ECM, MIL: Yes** **Year:** 2011, 2012 **Model:** C250, C300, C350, E350, E550, SLK350 **Engine:** 1.8L L4, 3.0L V6, 3.5L V6, 4.7L V8, 5.5L V8, 6.2L V8 **Transmission:** All	**Ignition Coil 5 Circuit:** The control line to the ignition coil of cylinder 5 has a short circuit to positive. Engine running is affected.
DTC: P2315 **T ECM, MIL: Yes** **Year:** 2011, 2012 **Model:** C250, C300, C350, E350, E550, SLK350 **Engine:** 1.8L L4, 3.0L V6, 3.5L V6, 4.7L V8, 5.5L V8, 6.2L V8 **Transmission:** All	**Ignition Coil 6 Circuit:** The control line to the ignition coil of cylinder 6 has a short circuit to ground. Engine running is affected.
DTC: P2316 **T ECM, MIL: Yes** **Year:** 2011, 2012 **Model:** C250, C300, C350, E350, E550, SLK350 **Engine:** 1.8L L4, 3.0L V6, 3.5L V6, 4.7L V8, 5.5L V8, 6.2L V8 **Transmission:** All	**Ignition Coil 6 Circuit:** The control line to the ignition coil of cylinder 6 has a short circuit to positive. Engine running is affected.
DTC: P2318 **T ECM, MIL: Yes** **Year:** 2011 **Model:** E550 **Engine:** 5.5L V8, 6.2L V8 **Transmission:** All	**Ignition Coil 7 Circuit:** The control line to the ignition coil of cylinder 7 has a short circuit to positive. Engine running is affected.
DTC: P2319 **T ECM, MIL: Yes** **Year:** 2011 **Model:** E550 **Engine:** 5.5L V8, 6.2L V8 **Transmission:** All	**Ignition Coil 7 Circuit:** The control line to the ignition coil of cylinder 7 has a short circuit to ground. Engine running is affected.
DTC: P2321 **T ECM, MIL: Yes** **Year:** 2011 **Model:** E550 **Engine:** 5.5L V8, 6.2L V8 **Transmission:** All	**Ignition Coil 8 Circuit:** The control line to the ignition coil of cylinder 8 has a short circuit to ground. Engine running is affected.
DTC: P2322 **T ECM, MIL: Yes** **Year:** 2011 **Model:** E550 **Engine:** 5.5L V8, 6.2L V8 **Transmission:** All	**Ignition Coil 8 Circuit:** The control line to the ignition coil of cylinder 8 has a short circuit to positive. Engine running is affected.
DTC: P2414 **T ECM, MIL: Yes** **Year:** 2011, 2012 **Model:** C250, C300, C350, E350, E550, SLK350 **Engine:** 1.8L L4, 3.0L V6, 3.5L V6, 4.7L V8, 5.5L V8, 6.2L V8 **Transmission:** All	**Right HO2S Sensor Signal Error:** Exhaust system malfunction. Right O2 sensor, before TWC [KAT]) : Signal implausible.

DTC	Trouble Code Title, Conditions, Possible Causes
DTC: P2415 **T ECM, MIL: Yes** **Year:** 2011, 2012 **Model:** C250, C300, C350, E350, E550, SLK350 **Engine:** 1.8L L4, 3.0L V6, 3.5L V6, 4.7L V8, 5.5L V8, 6.2L V8 **Transmission:** All	**Left HO2S Sensor Signal Error:** Exhaust system malfunction. Left O2 sensor, before TWC: Signal implausible.
DTC: P2421 **T ECM, MIL: Yes** **Year:** 2011, 2012 **Model:** C250, C300, C350, E350, E550, SLK350 **Engine:** 1.8L L4, 3.0L V6, 3.5L V6, 4.7L V8, 5.5L V8, 6.2L V8 **Transmission:** All	**EVAP Purge Control Valve Permanently Open:** Fuel system operation is affected. Mechanical defect of purge control valve: permanently open.
DTC: P2422 **T ECM, MIL: Yes** **Year:** 2011, 2012 **Model:** C250, C300, C350, E350, E550, SLK350 **Engine:** 1.8L L4, 3.0L V6, 3.5L V6, 4.7L V8, 5.5L V8, 6.2L V8 **Transmission:** All	**EVAP Canister Shut Off Valve Closed:** Mechanical defect or activated charcoal canister shut-off valve permanently closed.
DTC: P2505 **T , MIL: Yes** **Year:** 2011, 2012 **Model:** C250, C300, C350, E350, E550, SLK350 **Engine:** 1.8L L4, 3.0L V6, 3.5L V6, 4.7L V8, 5.5L V8, 6.2L V8 **Transmission:** All	**Engine Relay Circuit Voltage Too High or Too Low:** Battery system affected. On-board electrical system(s) affected. The voltage at relay 'Circuit 87' is too high or too low.
DTC: P2539 **T ECM, MIL: Yes** **Year:** 2011, 2012 **Model:** C250, C300, C350, E350, E550, SLK350 **Engine:** 1.8L L4, 3.0L V6, 3.5L V6, 4.7L V8, 5.5L V8, 6.2L V8 **Transmission:** All	**Fuel Pressure Sensor Electrical Fault:** **NOTE: This fault can be ignored and erased.** The fuel pressure sensor has an electrical fault.
DTC: P2541 **T ECM, MIL: Yes** **Year:** 2011, 2012 **Model:** C250, C300, C350, E350, E550, SLK350 **Engine:** 1.8L L4, 3.0L V6, 3.5L V6, 4.7L V8, 5.5L V8, 6.2L V8 **Transmission:** All	**Fuel Tank Pressure Sensor Circuit:** Fuel tank pressure sensor circuit has a short to ground.
DTC: P2542 **T ECM, MIL: Yes** **Year:** 2011, 2012 **Model:** C250, C300, C350, E350, E550, SLK350 **Engine:** 1.8L L4, 3.0L V6, 3.5L V6, 4.7L V8, 5.5L V8, 6.2L V8 **Transmission:** All	**Fuel Tank Pressure Sensor Circuit:** Fuel system operation is affected. The fuel tank pressure sensor circuit has a short to positive.

DTC	Trouble Code Title, Conditions, Possible Causes
DTC: P2610 **T ECM, MIL: Yes** **Year:** 2011, 2012 **Model:** C250, C300, C350, E350, E550, SLK350 **Engine:** 1.8L L4, 3.0L V6, 3.5L V6, 4.7L V8, 5.5L V8, 6.2L V8 **Transmission:** All	**Engine OFF Time Implausible Value:** CAN communication is affected. The engine off time has an implausible value.
DTC: P2626 **T ECM, MIL: Yes** **Year:** 2011, 2012 **Model:** C250, C300, C350, E350, E550, SLK350 **Engine:** 1.8L L4, 3.0L V6, 3.5L V6, 4.7L V8, 5.5L V8, 6.2L V8 **Transmission:** All	**Right HO2S Sensor Circuit :** Exhaust manifold malfunction. Right HO2S sensor, before TWC, has open circuit.
DTC: P2629 **T ECM, MIL: Yes** **Year:** 2011, 2012 **Model:** C250, C300, C350, E350, E550, SLK350 **Engine:** 1.8L L4, 3.0L V6, 3.5L V6, 4.7L V8, 5.5L V8, 6.2L V8 **Transmission:** All	**Left HO2S Sensor Circuit:** Exhaust system malfunction. Left HO2S sensor, before TWC, open circuit.
DTC: P2716 **T TCM, TCIL: Yes** **Year:** 2011, 2012 **Model:** C250, C300, C350, E350, E550, SLK350 **Engine:** 1.8L L4, 3.0L V6, 3.5L V6, 4.7L V8, 5.5L V8, 6.2L V8 **Transmission:** All	**TCM Fault:** Transmission function affected. Fault present in TCM.
DTC: P2725 **T TCM, TCIL: Yes** **Year:** 2011, 2012 **Model:** C250, C300, C350, E350, E550, SLK350 **Engine:** 1.8L L4, 3.0L V6, 3.5L V6, 4.7L V8, 5.5L V8, 6.2L V8 **Transmission:** All	**TCM Fault:** Transmission operation affected Fault present in TCM
DTC: P2734 **T TCM, TCIL: Yes** **Year:** 2011, 2012 **Model:** C250, C300, C350, E350, E550, SLK350 **Engine:** 1.8L L4, 3.0L V6, 3.5L V6, 4.7L V8, 5.5L V8, 6.2L V8 **Transmission:** All	**TCM Fault:** Transmission operation affected. Fault present in TCM
DTC: P2757 **T TCM, TCIL: Yes** **Year:** 2011, 2012 **Model:** C250, C300, C350, E350, E550, SLK350 **Engine:** 1.8L L4, 3.0L V6, 3.5L V6, 4.7L V8, 5.5L V8, 6.2L V8 **Transmission:** All	**TCM Fault:** Transmission operation is affected. Fault is present in TCM.

DTC	Trouble Code Title, Conditions, Possible Causes
DTC: P2759 **T TCM, TCIL: Yes** **Year:** 2011, 2012 **Model:** C250, C300, C350, E350, E550, SLK350 **Engine:** 1.8L L4, 3.0L V6, 3.5L V6, 4.7L V8, 5.5L V8, 6.2L V8 **Transmission:** All	**TCM Fault:** Transmission operation affected. Fault is present in TCM.
DTC: P2766 **T TCM, TCIL: Yes** **Year:** 2011, 2012 **Model:** C250, C300, C350, E350, E550, SLK350 **Engine:** 1.8L L4, 3.0L V6, 3.5L V6, 4.7L V8, 5.5L V8, 6.2L V8 **Transmission:** All	**TCM Fault:** Transmission operation affected. Fault is present in TCM.
DTC: P2767 **T TCM, TCIL: Yes** **Year:** 2011, 2012 **Model:** C250, C300, C350, E350, E550, SLK350 **Engine:** 1.8L L4, 3.0L V6, 3.5L V6, 4.7L V8, 5.5L V8, 6.2L V8 **Transmission:** All	**TCM Fault:** Transmission operation affected. Fault is present in TCM.
DTC: P2768 **T TCM, TCIL: Yes** **Year:** 2011, 2012 **Model:** C250, C300, C350, E350, E550, SLK350 **Engine:** 1.8L L4, 3.0L V6, 3.5L V6, 4.7L V8, 5.5L V8, 6.2L V8 **Transmission:** All	**TCM Fault:** Transmission operation is affected. Fault is present in TCM.
DTC: P2810 **T TCM, TCIL: Yes** **Year:** 2011, 2012 **Model:** C250, C300, C350, E350, E550, SLK350 **Engine:** 1.8L L4, 3.0L V6, 3.5L V6, 4.7L V8, 5.5L V8, 6.2L V8 **Transmission:** All	**TCM Fault:** Transmission operation is affected. Fault present in TCM

VOLVO

C30 • C70

10

SPECIFICATIONS AND MAINTENANCE CHARTS

ENGINE AND VEHICLE IDENTIFICATION CHART

Engine						
Code	Liters (cc)	Cu. in.	Cyl.	Fuel Sys.	Type	Eng. Mfg.
B5254T7	2.5 (2521)	154	5	EFI	DOHC	Volvo

Model Year	
Code ①	Year
B	2011
C	2012

① 10th Digit of VIN

EFI: Electronic Fuel Injection

DOHC: Double Overhead Camshafts

71112_C3C7_C0001

GENERAL ENGINE SPECIFICATIONS

Year	Model	Engine Displ. Liters	Engine ID	Net Horsepower @ rpm	Net Torque @ rpm (ft. lbs.)	Bore x Stroke (in.)	Com-pression Ratio	Oil Pressure @ rpm
2011	C30	2.5	B5254T7	227@5000	236@5000	3.27 x 3.67	9.0:1	51@4000
	C70	2.5	B5254T7	227@5000	236@5000	3.27 x 3.67	9.0:1	51@4000
2012	C30	2.5	B5254T7	227@5000	236@5000	3.27 x 3.67	9.0:1	51@4000
	C70	2.5	B5254T7	227@5000	236@5000	3.27 x 3.67	9.0:1	51@4000

NA: Information not available

71112_C3C7_C0002

ENGINE TUNE-UP SPECIFICATIONS

	Engine Displacement Liters	Engine ID	Spark Plug Gap (in.) ①	Ignition Timing (deg.)		Fuel Pump (psi)	Idle Speed (rpm)		Valve Clearance (in.)	
				MT	AT		MT	AT	In.	Ex.
2011	2.5	B5254T7	0.027	NA	NA	43-58	720	720	.007-.009	.015-.017
2012	2.5	B5254T7	0.027	NA	NA	43-58	720	720	.007-.009	.015-.017

NA: Information not available

① The label figures must be used if they differ from those in this chart.

71112_C3C7_C0003

CAPACITIES

Year	Model	Engine Disp. Liters	Engine ID	Engine Oil with Filter (qts.) ①	Transmission (qts.) Man	Transmission (qts.) Auto.	Brake Fluid (pts.)	Power Steering Fluid (qts.)	Air Conditioning (lbs.)	Fuel Tank (gal.)	Cooling System (qts.) ②
2011	C30	2.5	B5245T7	6.1	2.0	8.2	1.26	1.3	1.2	15.9	10.5 ③
	C70	2.5	B5254T7	6.1		8.2	1.26	1.3	1.2	15.9	10.5
2012	C30	2.5	B5254T7	6.1	2.0	8.2	1.26	1.3	1.2	15.9	10.5 ③
	C70	2.5	B5254T7	6.1		8.2	1.26	1.3	1.2	15.9	10.5

NOTE: All capacities are approximate. Add fluid gradualy and check to be sure a proper fluid level is obtair

① On turbocharged engines, add 0.7 US qts. if the cooler is drained

② With automatic transaxle

③ With manual transaxle - 10 qts.

71112_C3C7_C0005

FLUID SPECIFICATIONS

Year	Model	Engine Size Liters	Engine ID	Engine Oil	Auto Transmission	Manual Transmission	Rear Axle	Power Steering Fluid	Engine Coolant	Brake Fluid
2011	C30	2.5	B5254T7	5W-30	Volvo	Volvo	Volvo	Volvo	Volvo	DOT 4+
	C70	2.5	B5254T7	5W-30	Volvo	Volvo	Volvo	Volvo	Volvo	DOT 4+
2012	C30	2.5	B5254T7	5W-30	Volvo	Volvo	Volvo	Volvo	Volvo	DOT 4+
	C70	2.5	B5254T7	5W-30	Volvo	Volvo	Volvo	Volvo	Volvo	DOT 4+

DOT: Department Of Transpotation

71112_C3C7_C0004

VALVE SPECIFICATIONS

Year	Engine Displacement Liters	Engine ID	Seat Angle (deg.)	Face Angle (deg.)	Spring Test Pressure (lbs. @ in.)	Spring Installed Height (in.)	Stem-to-Guide Clearance (in.) Intake	Stem-to-Guide Clearance (in.) Exhaust	Stem Diameter (in.) Intake	Stem Diameter (in.) Exhaust
2011	2.5	B5254T7	45.5 ± 0.17	45.5 ± 0.17	NA	NA	0.0020-0.0028	0.0020-0.0028	0.2311-0.2367	0.2311-0.2367
2012	2.5	B5254T7	45.5 ± 0.17	45.5 ± 0.17	NA	NA	0.0020-0.0028	0.0020-0.0028	0.2311-0.2367	0.2311-0.2367

NA: Information not available

71112_C3C7_C0006

CRANKSHAFT AND CONNECTING ROD SPECIFICATIONS

All measurements are given in inches.

	Engine		Crankshaft				Connecting Rod		
Year	Displacement Liters	Engine ID	Main Brg. Journal Dia.	Main Brg. Oil Clearance	Shaft End-play	Thrust on No.	Journal Diameter	Oil Clearance	Side Clearance
2011	2.5	B5254T7	2.5585 - 2.5592	NA	0.003-0.007	NA	NA	NA	NA
2012	2.5	B5254T7	2.5585 - 2.5592	NA	0.003-0.007	NA	NA	NA	NA

NA: Information not available

71112_C3C7_C0007

PISTON AND RING SPECIFICATIONS

All measurements are given in inches.

	Engine			Ring Gap			Ring Side Clearance		
Year	Displ. Liters	Engine ID	Piston Clearance	Top Compression	Bottom Compression	Oil Control	Top Compression	Bottom Compression	Oil Control
2011	2.5	B5254T7	0.0004-0.0012	0.047	0.059	0.079	NA	NA	NA
2012	2.5	B5254T7	0.0004-0.0012	0.047	0.059	0.079	NA	NA	NA

NA: Information not available

71112_C3C7_C0008

TORQUE SPECIFICATIONS

All readings in ft. lbs.

Year	Engine Displacement Liters	Engine ID	Cylinder Head Bolts	Main Bearing Bolts	Rod Bearing Bolts	Crankshaft Damper Bolts	Flywheel Bolts	Manifold Intake	Manifold Exhaust	Spark Plugs	Lug Nut
2011	2.5	B5254T7	①	②	③	133	④	⑤	18	21	⑥
2012	2.5	B5254T7	①	②	③	133	④	⑤	18	21	⑥

① Step 1: 15 ft. lbs.
Step 2: 44 ft. lbs.
Step 3: Plus 130 degrees

② Step 1: M10 bolts: 15 ft. lbs.
Step 2: M10 bolts: 33 ft. lbs.
Step 3: M8 bolts: 18 ft. lbs.
Step 4: M7 bolts: 13 ft. lbs.
Step 5: M10 bolts: Plus 90 degrees

③ Step 1: 11 ft. lbs.
Step 2: 18 ft. lbs.
Step 3: Plus 100 degrees

④ Step 1: 33 ft. lbs.
Step 2: Plus 65 degrees

⑤ Upper: 7 ft. lbs.
Lower: 14 ft. lbs.

⑥ Step 1: 15 ft. lbs.
Step 2: 96 ft. lbs.

71112_C3C7_C0009

WHEEL ALIGNMENT

			Caster		Camber		
Year	Model		Range (+/-Deg.) ①	Preferred Setting (Deg.) ①	Range (+/-Deg.) ①	Preferred Setting (Deg.) ①	Toe-in (in.) ①
2011	C30	F	1.50	+3.60	0.70	-0.60	0.20+/-0.10
		R	NA	NA	1.00	-1.52	0.30+/-0.10
	C70	F	1.50	+3.80	0.70	-0.75	0.20+/-0.10
		R	NA	NA	1.00	-1.72	0.30+/-0.10
2012	C30	F	1.50	+3.60	0.70	-0.60	0.20+/-0.10
		R	NA	NA	1.00	-1.52	0.30+/-0.10
	C70	F	1.50	+3.80	0.70	-0.75	0.20+/-0.10
		R	NA	NA	1.00	-1.72	0.30+/-0.10

F: Front

R: Rear

NA: Information not available

① Specifications provided by TSB 19674 dated 2-09-2010. Please check for updated TSB before performing alignment.

71112_C3C7_C0010

TIRE, WHEEL AND BALL JOINT SPECIFICATIONS

		OEM Tires		Tire Pressures (psi)		Wheel	Ball Joint
Year	Model	Standard	Optional	Front	Rear	Size	Inspection
2011	C30	205/50R17	NA	①	①	7	NA
		215/45R18				7.5	
	C70	235/45R17	NA	①	①	7.5	NA
		235/40R18				7.5	
2012	C30	205/50R17	NA	①	①	7.5	NA
		215/45R18				7.5 or 8.0	
	C70	235/45R17	NA	①	①	7.5	NA
		235/40R18				7.5 or 8.0	

OEM: Original Equipment Manufacturer

PSI: Pounds Per Square Inch

STD: Standard

NA: Information not available

OPT: Optional

① See the tire placard on the vehicle

71112_C3C7_C0011

BRAKE SPECIFICATIONS

All measurements in inches unless noted

Year	Model		Brake Disc Original Thickness	Brake Disc Minimum Thickness	Brake Disc Maximum Runout	Minimum Lining Thickness	Brake Caliper Bracket bolts (ft. lbs.)	Brake Caliper Mounting bolts (ft. lbs.)
2011	C30	F	0.975	①	0.003	0.141	89	22
		R	0.429	②	0.002	0.141	52	26
	C70	F	0.975	①	0.003	0.141	89	22
		R	0.429	②	0.002	0.141	52	26
2012	C30	F	0.975	①	0.003	0.141	89	22
		R	0.429	②	0.002	0.141	52	26
	C70	F	0.975	①	0.003	0.141	89	22
		R	0.429	②	0.002	0.141	52	26

NA: Information not available

F: Front

R: Rear

① Minumum disc thickness when replacing pads. (0.928)
Minumum disc thickness. (0.897)

② Minumum disc thickness when replacing pads. (0.382)
Minumum disc thickness. (0.351)

71112_C3C7_C0012

SCHEDULED MAINTENANCE INTERVALS

2011-12 Volvo C30/C70

TO BE SERVICED	TYPE OF SERVICE	7.5	15	22.5	30	37.5	45	52.5	60	67.5	75	82.5	90	97.5	105	112.5	120	127.5	135	142.5	150
		VEHICLE MILEAGE INTERVAL (x1000)																			
Engine oil & filter	R	✓	✓	✓	✓	✓	✓	✓	✓	✓	✓	✓	✓	✓	✓	✓	✓	✓	✓	✓	✓
Automatic transmission fluid	I/A		✓		✓		✓	✓	✓		✓		✓		✓		✓		✓		✓
Brake pads, discs & lines	I	✓	✓	✓	✓	✓	✓	✓	✓	✓	✓	✓	✓	✓	✓	✓	✓	✓	✓	✓	✓
Parking brake	I/A		✓		✓		✓		✓		✓		✓		✓		✓		✓		✓
Wheels & tires	S/I	✓	✓	✓	✓	✓	✓	✓	✓	✓	✓	✓	✓	✓	✓	✓	✓	✓	✓	✓	✓
Spare tire	S/I				✓				✓				✓				✓				✓
Drive shafts	S/I								✓	✓	✓	✓	✓	✓	✓	✓	✓	✓	✓	✓	✓
Cabin air filter	R		✓		✓		✓		✓		✓		✓		✓		✓		✓		✓
Engine coolant	S/I		✓		✓		✓		✓		✓		✓		✓		✓		✓		✓
Air cleaner filter	R					✓					✓					✓					✓
Spark plugs	R										✓										✓
Accessory drive belt ①	R																✓				
Timing belt ①	R																✓				
Fuel lines	I				✓				✓				✓				✓				✓
Exhaust system	S/I								✓	✓	✓	✓	✓	✓	✓	✓	✓	✓	✓	✓	✓
Check suspension	S/I								✓	✓	✓	✓	✓	✓	✓	✓	✓	✓	✓	✓	✓
Brake fluid ②	R					✓					✓					✓					✓
Windshield & headlamps wipers/ washers	S/I	✓	✓	✓	✓	✓	✓	✓	✓	✓	✓	✓	✓	✓	✓	✓	✓	✓	✓	✓	✓
Battery	S/I				✓		✓		✓		✓		✓		✓		✓		✓		✓
Convertible roof system (C70)	S/I		✓		✓		✓		✓		✓		✓		✓		✓		✓		✓
Service reminder indicator (SRI)	S/I	✓	✓	✓	✓	✓	✓	✓	✓	✓	✓	✓	✓	✓	✓	✓	✓	✓	✓	✓	✓

R: Replace S/I: Service or Inspect I/A: Inspect and adjust.

① Replace at a maximum of every 10 years or or according to chart.

② Replace every 2 years or 30,000 miles, whichever comes first under normal conditions, more frequently in mountainous areas or mois

FREQUENT OPERATION MAINTENANCE (SEVERE SERVICE)

If a vehicle is operated under any of the following conditions it is considered severe service:

- Extremely dusty areas.

- 50% or more of the vehicle operation is in 90°F (32°C) or higher temperatures, or constant operation in temperatures below 32°F (0°C).

- Prolonged idling (vehicle operation in stop and go traffic).

- Frequent short running periods (engine does not warm to normal operating temperatures).

- Police, taxi, delivery usage or trailer towing usage.

Air filter element: service or inspect every 15,000 miles.

Automatic transmission oil service every 52,500 miles.

71112_C3C7_C0013

PRECAUTIONS

Before servicing any vehicle, please be sure to read all of the following precautions, which deal with personal safety, prevention of component damage, and important points to take into consideration when servicing a motor vehicle:

- Never open, service or drain the radiator or cooling system when the engine is hot; serious burns can occur from the steam and hot coolant.
- Observe all applicable safety precautions when working around fuel. Whenever servicing the fuel system, always work in a well-ventilated area. Do not allow fuel spray or vapors to come in contact with a spark, open flame, or excessive heat (a hot drop light, for example). Keep a dry chemical fire extinguisher near the work area. Always keep fuel in a container specifically designed for fuel storage; also, always properly seal fuel containers to avoid the possibility of fire or explosion. Refer to the additional fuel system precautions later in this section.
- Fuel injection systems often remain pressurized, even after the engine has been turned **OFF**. The fuel system pressure must be relieved before disconnecting any fuel lines. Failure to do so may result in fire and/or personal injury.
- Brake fluid often contains polyglycol ethers and polyglycols. Avoid contact with the eyes and wash your hands thoroughly after handling brake fluid. If you do get brake fluid in your eyes, flush your eyes with clean, running water for 15 minutes. If eye irritation persists, or if you have taken brake fluid internally, IMMEDIATELY seek medical assistance.
- The EPA warns that prolonged contact with used engine oil may cause a number of skin disorders, including cancer. You should make every effort to minimize your exposure to used engine oil. Protective gloves should be worn when changing oil. Wash your hands and any other exposed skin areas as soon as possible after exposure to used engine oil. Soap and water, or waterless hand cleaner should be used.
- All new vehicles are now equipped with an air bag system, often referred to as a Supplemental Restraint System (SRS) or Supplemental Inflatable Restraint (SIR) system. The system must be disabled before performing service on or around system components, steering column, instrument panel components, wiring and sensors. Failure to follow safety and disabling procedures could result in accidental air bag deployment, possible personal injury and unnecessary system repairs.
- Always wear safety goggles when working with, or around, the air bag system. When carrying a non-deployed air bag, be sure the bag and trim cover are pointed away from your body. When placing a non-deployed air bag on a work surface, always face the bag and trim cover upward, away from the surface. This will reduce the motion of the module if it is accidentally deployed. Refer to the additional air bag system precautions later in this section.
- Clean, high quality brake fluid from a sealed container is essential to the safe and proper operation of the brake system. You should always buy the correct type of brake fluid for your vehicle. If the brake fluid becomes contaminated, completely flush the system with new fluid. Never reuse any brake fluid. Any brake fluid that is removed from the system should be discarded. Also, do not allow any brake fluid to come in contact with a painted surface; it will damage the paint.
- Never operate the engine without the proper amount and type of engine oil; doing so WILL result in severe engine damage.
- Timing belt maintenance is extremely important. Many models utilize an interference-type, non-freewheeling engine. If the timing belt breaks, the valves in the cylinder head may strike the pistons, causing potentially serious (also time-consuming and expensive) engine damage. Refer to the maintenance interval charts for the recommended replacement interval for the timing belt, and to the timing belt section for belt replacement and inspection.
- Disconnecting the negative battery cable on some vehicles may interfere with the functions of the on-board computer system(s) and may require the computer to undergo a relearning process once the negative battery cable is reconnected.
- When servicing drum brakes, only disassemble and assemble one side at a time, leaving the remaining side intact for reference.
- Only an MVAC-trained, EPA-certified automotive technician should service the air conditioning system or its components.

BRAKES

ANTI-LOCK BRAKE SYSTEM (ABS)

GENERAL INFORMATION

PRECAUTIONS

- Certain components within the ABS system are not intended to be serviced or repaired individually.
- Do not use rubber hoses or other parts not specifically specified for and ABS system. When using repair kits, replace all parts included in the kit. Partial or incorrect repair may lead to functional problems and require the replacement of components.
- Lubricate rubber parts with clean, fresh brake fluid to ease assembly. Do not use shop air to clean parts; damage to rubber components may result.
- Use only DOT 3 brake fluid from an unopened container.
- If any hydraulic component or line is removed or replaced, it may be necessary to bleed the entire system.
- A clean repair area is essential. Always clean the reservoir and cap thoroughly before removing the cap. The slightest amount of dirt in the fluid may plug an orifice and impair the system function. Perform repairs after components have been thoroughly cleaned; use only denatured alcohol to clean components. Do not allow ABS components to come into contact with any substance containing mineral oil; this includes used shop rags.
- The Anti-Lock control unit is a microprocessor similar to other computer units in the vehicle. Ensure that the ignition switch is **OFF** before removing or installing controller harnesses. Avoid static electricity discharge at or near the controller.
- If any arc welding is to be done on the vehicle, the control unit should be unplugged before welding operations begin.

SPEED SENSORS

REMOVAL & INSTALLATION

Front

See Figure 1.

1. Before servicing the vehicle, always refer to the precautions sections.
2. Disconnect the negative battery cable.
3. Raise and support the vehicle safely.
4. Remove the tire and wheel assembly.

➡Blow clean around the sensor using compressed air before removing.

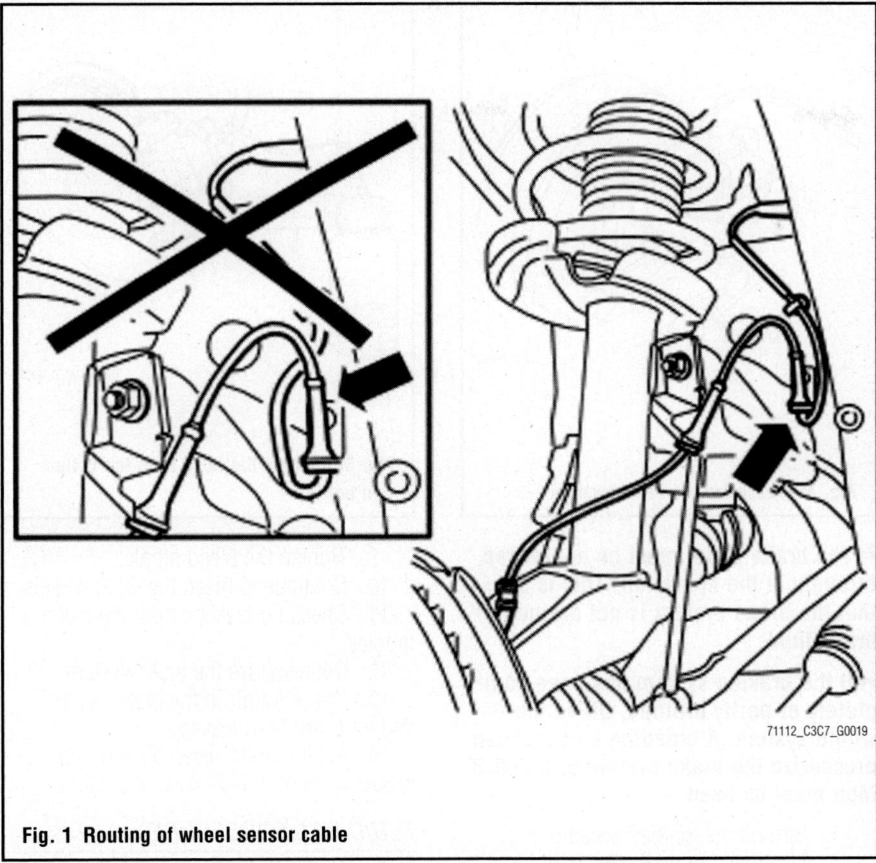
Fig. 1 Routing of wheel sensor cable

5. Remove the connector from the wheel sensor.
6. Remove the wheel sensor mounting screw.
7. Remove the wheel sensor.

To install:

8. Install the wheel sensor.
9. Install the wheel sensor mounting screw. Tighten to 44 inch lbs. (5 Nm)
10. Install the connector to the when sensor.
11. Make sure the wheel sensor cable is routed as illustrated.
12. Continue the installation in the reverse order of the removal procedure.

Rear

See Figure 2.

1. Before servicing the vehicle, always refer to the precautions sections.
2. Disconnect the negative battery cable.

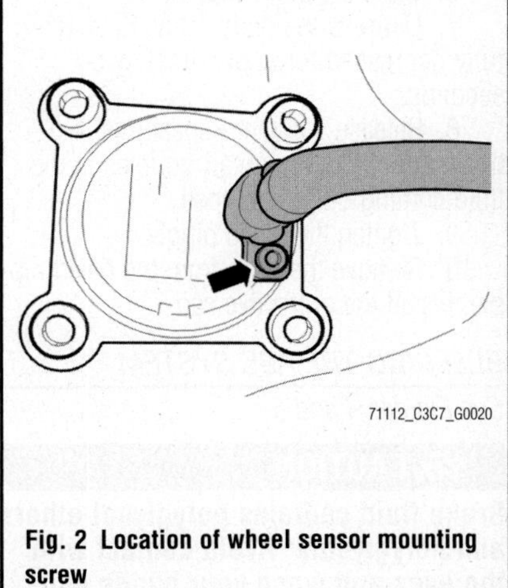
Fig. 2 Location of wheel sensor mounting screw

3. Raise and support the vehicle safely.
4. Remove the tire and wheel assembly.
5. For vehicles equipped with Nivomat, remove the shock absorber from the lateral link.

➡Blow clean around the sensor using compressed air before removing.

6. Remove the wheel sensor mounting screw, and pull out the connector.
7. Remove the wheel sensor.

To install:

8. Install the wheel sensor in the connector.
9. Install the connector and the wheel sensor mounting screw
10. Tighten the wheel sensor mounting screw to 44 inch lbs. (5 Nm)
11. For vehicles equipped with Nivomat, install the shock absorber to the lateral link.
12. Continue the installation in the reverse order of the removal procedure.

BRAKES — BLEEDING THE BRAKE SYSTEM

BLEEDING PROCEDURE

BLEEDING PROCEDURE

See Figure 3.

1. When reconditioning or replacing brake calipers bleed the relevant brake pipe as follows. The brake pedal must be depressed throughout the operation. This is so that the brake system is not drained of brake fluid. If the braking system has been completely or partly drained, bleed the whole system.
2. Perform the preparations as follows:
   a. Switch off the ignition
   b. Clean around the brake fluid reservoir filler cap
   c. Take out the container
   d. Remove the filler cap
   e. Fill the brake fluid reservoir completely.
3. Raise the vehicle.

➡While bleeding, check that there is sufficient brake fluid in the reservoir. Top up if necessary.

4. Remove the protective cap from the bleed nipple. Connect the hose from the collection bottle.
5. Depress the brake pedal a few times. Maintain pressure.

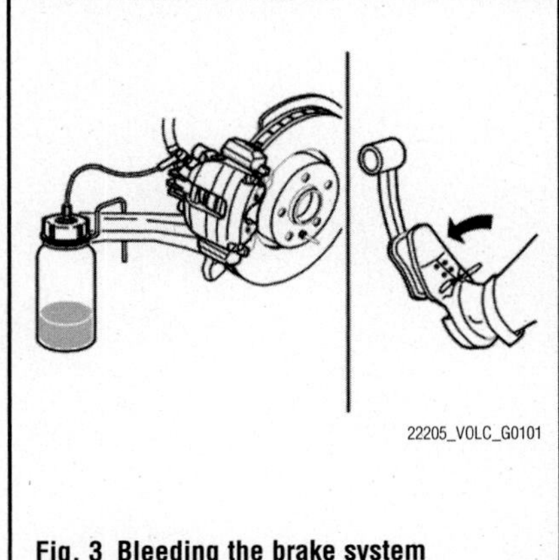
Fig. 3 Bleeding the brake system

6. Open the bleed nipple.
7. Depress the pedal fully. Keep it fully depressed for approximately 5 seconds.
8. Release it again. Repeat this 3–5 times until there are no air bubbles in the fluid coming out of the hose.
9. Tighten the bleed nipple.
10. Remove the hose from the bleed nipple. Install the protective cap.

BLEEDING THE ABS SYSTEM

See Figures 4 and 5.

⁂ CAUTION

Brake fluid contains polyglycol ethers and polyglycols. Avoid contact with the eyes and wash your hands thoroughly after handling brake fluid. If you do get brake fluid in your eyes, flush your eyes with clean, running water for 15 minutes. If eye irritation persists, or if you have taken brake fluid internally, IMMEDIATELY seek medical assistance.

⁂ WARNING

Clean, high quality brake fluid is essential to the safe and proper operation of the brake system. You should always buy the highest quality brake fluid that is available. If the brake fluid becomes contaminated, drain and flush the system, then refill the master cylinder with new fluid. Never reuse any brake fluid. Any brake fluid that is removed from the system should be discarded. Also, do not allow any brake fluid to come in contact with a painted surface; it will damage the paint.

When reconditioning or replacing brake calipers bleed the relevant brake pipe as follows.

Fig. 4 Pressurize the brake system

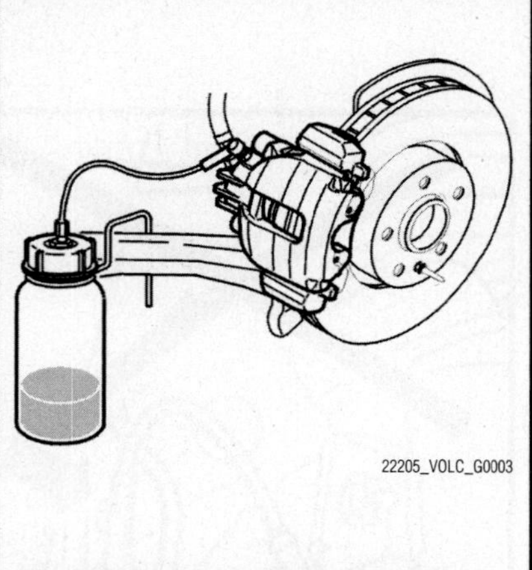

Fig. 5 Connect the hose from the collection bottle.

➡The brake pedal must be depressed throughout the operation. This is so that the brake system is not drained of brake fluid.

➡If the braking system has been completely or partly drained, bleed the whole system. A bleeding unit that can pressurize the brake system to 0.2–0.3 Mpa must be used.

1. Turn off the ignition switch.
2. Clean all around the brake fluid reservoir filler cap.
3. Take out the special brake fluid collection bottle.
4. Connect bleeding unit to the brake fluid reservoir. Follow manufacturer's instructions for connecting and using bleeding unit.
5. Pressurize the brake system. Check the brake fluid reservoir connector.
6. Raise the car and remove the wheels.
7. Remove the protective cap from the bleed nipple. Connect the hose from the collection bottle.
8. Open the bleed nipple. Close it when there are no more air bubbles in the fluid coming out of the hose.
9. Tighten the bleed nipple.
10. Continue to bleed the other wheels.
11. Check for leakage from the bleed nipples.
12. Depressurize the brake system.
13. Check for air in the brake system and for brake fluid leakage.
14. Fill the brake reservoir with the proper amount of DOT 4+ brake fluid.

FLUID FILL PROCEDURE

➡The brake fluid should always be between the mMIN and MAX marks on the side of the reservoir. Check, without removing the cap, that there is sufficient fluid in the reservoir.

➡Fluid type:DOT 4+ boiling point above 536°F (280 °C)

➡Replace:The fluid should be replaced according to the intervals specified in the scheduled maintenance. Noting that when the vehicle is driven under extremely hard conditions (mountain driving, etc.), it may be necessary to replace the fluid more often.

BRAKES

FRONT DISC BRAKES

⁂ CAUTION

Dust and dirt accumulating on brake parts during normal use may contain asbestos fibers from production or aftermarket brake linings. Breathing excessive concentrations of asbestos fibers can cause serious bodily harm. Exercise care when servicing brake parts. Do not sand or grind brake lining unless equipment used is designed to contain the dust residue. Do not clean brake parts with compressed air or by dry brushing. Cleaning should be done by dampening the brake components with a fine mist of water, then wiping the brake components clean with a dampened cloth. Dispose of cloth and all residue containing asbestos fibers in an impermeable container with the appropriate label. Follow practices prescribed by the Occupational Safety and Health Administration (OSHA) and the Environmental Protection Agency (EPA) for the handling, processing, and disposing of dust or debris that may contain asbestos fibers.

BRAKE CALIPER

REMOVAL & INSTALLATION

See Figure 6.

1. Before servicing the vehicle, always refer to the precautions sections.
2. Remove the wheel.
3. Secure the pedal in the depressed position using a pedal jack.
4. Remove the protective cap from the bleed nipple, connect a hose and open the nipple.

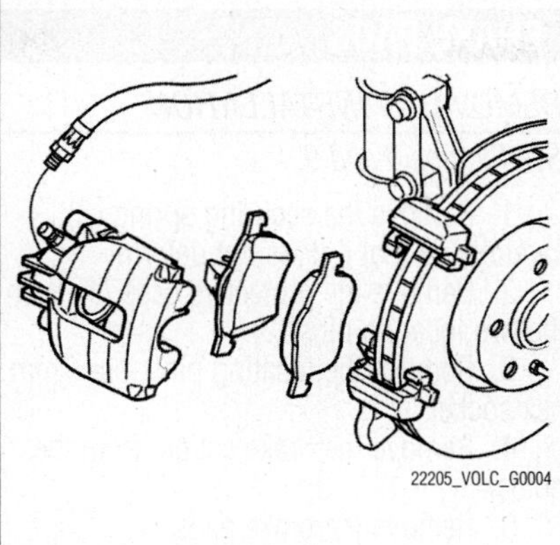

Fig. 6 Exploded view of the front brake caliper

5. Use a container to collect brake fluid.
6. Slacken off the brake hose half a turn.
7. Remove the following:
   - The spring
   - The protective caps
   - The locating pins, use a 7mm hex socket
   - The brake pads
   - The brake caliper (Unscrew the caliper from the brake hose)

To install:

8. Install the following.
   - The brake hose in the brake caliper (Do not tighten the hose fully yet.)
   - The brake pads
   - The locating pins, use a 7 mm hex socket and tighten to 22 ft. lbs. (30 Nm)
   - The protective caps
   - The spring
9. Tighten the brake hose to 17 ft. lbs. (23 Nm).
10. Bleed the brake system.
11. Install the wheel.
12. Depress the brake pedal a few times and check the brake fluid level.

BRAKE PADS

REMOVAL & INSTALLATION

1. Before servicing the vehicle, always refer to the Precautions Sections.
2. Remove the wheel.
3. Secure the pedal in the depressed position using a pedal jack.
4. Remove the protective cap from the bleed nipple, connect a hose and open the nipple.
5. Use a container to collect brake fluid.
6. Slacken off the brake hose half a turn.
7. Remove the following:
   - The spring
   - The protective caps
   - The locating pins, use a 7mm hex socket
   - The brake pads

To install:

8. Install the following.
   - The brake hose in the brake caliper (Do not tighten the hose fully yet.)
   - The brake pads
   - The locating pins, use a 7mm hex socket and tighten to 22 ft. lbs. (30 Nm)
   - The protective caps
   - The spring

BRAKES

REAR DISC BRAKES

⁂ CAUTION

Dust and dirt accumulating on brake parts during normal use may contain asbestos fibers from production or aftermarket brake linings. Breathing excessive concentrations of asbestos fibers can cause serious bodily harm. Exercise care when servicing brake parts. Do not sand or grind brake lining unless equipment used is designed to contain the dust residue. Do not clean brake parts with compressed air or by dry brushing. Cleaning should be done by dampening the brake components with a fine mist of water, then wiping the brake components clean with a dampened cloth. Dispose of cloth and all residue containing asbestos fibers in an impermeable container with the appropriate label. Follow practices prescribed by the Occupational Safety and Health Administration (OSHA) and the Environmental Protection Agency (EPA) for the handling, processing, and disposing of dust or debris that may contain asbestos fibers.

BRAKE CALIPERS

REMOVAL & INSTALLATION

See Figure 7.

1. Before servicing the vehicle, always refer to the Precautions Sections.
2. Remove the wheel.
3. Secure the pedal in the depressed position using a pedal jack.
4. Remove the protective cap from the bleed nipple, connect a hose and open the nipple.
5. Use a container to collect brake fluid.
6. Slacken off the brake hose half a turn.
7. Remove the following:
   - The spring
   - The protective caps
   - The locating pins, use a 7mm hex socket

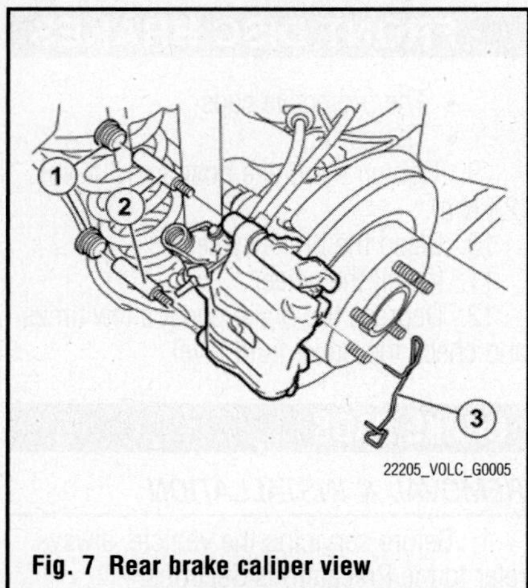

Fig. 7 Rear brake caliper view

- The brake pads
- The brake caliper (Unscrew the caliper from the brake hose.)

8. Remove the brake pads.
9. Remove the brake caliper.
10. Remove the parking brake cable.
11. Unscrew the caliper from the brake hose.

To install:

12. Install the following:
    - The brake hose in the brake caliper (Do not tighten the hose fully yet.)
    - The brake pads
    - The locating pins, use a 7 mm hex socket and tighten to 22 ft. lbs. (30 Nm)
    - The protective caps
    - The spring
13. Tighten the brake hose to 17 ft. lbs. (23 Nm).
14. Install the parking brake cable.
15. Bleed the brake system.
16. Install the wheel.
17. Depress the brake pedal a few times and check the brake fluid level.

BRAKE PADS

REMOVAL & INSTALLATION

See Figures 8 and 9.

1. Remove the securing spring (3) carefully so that it does not deform.
2. Remove the protective caps (1) from the two locating pins (2).
3. Remove the locating pins, use 7mm hex socket.
4. Remove the brake caliper from the holder.
5. Remove the brake pads.
6. Hang brake caliper from a steel wire from the spring so as not to damage brake hose.
7. Press the piston back into cylinder on brake caliper.
8. Check that the caliper dust boot is correctly positioned.

To install:

9. Install new brake pads.
10. Install the brake caliper.
11. Check the rubber sleeves of the locating pins. Replace if necessary.
12. Lubricate the locating pins with silicone brake grease. Insert the locating pins (2) into the rubber sleeves. The pins should slide into the sleeves easily.
13. Tighten the locating pins. Tighten to 22 ft. lbs. (30 Nm). Install protective caps (1).
14. Install the retaining spring (3).
15. Depress the brake pedal a few times.
16. Add brake fluid if necessary.
17. Adjust the parking brake as required.

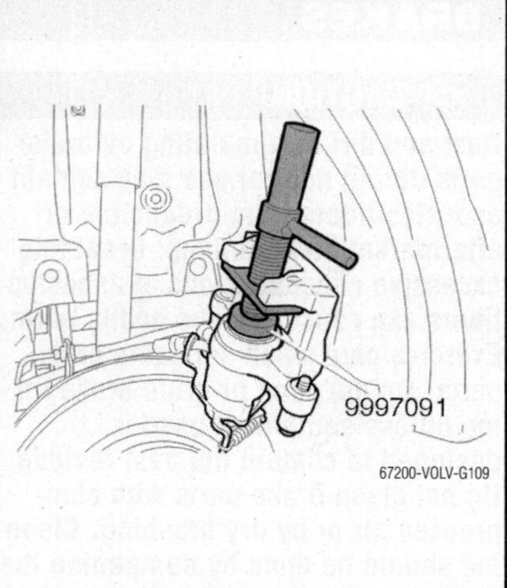

Fig. 8 Compressing the piston into the cylinder

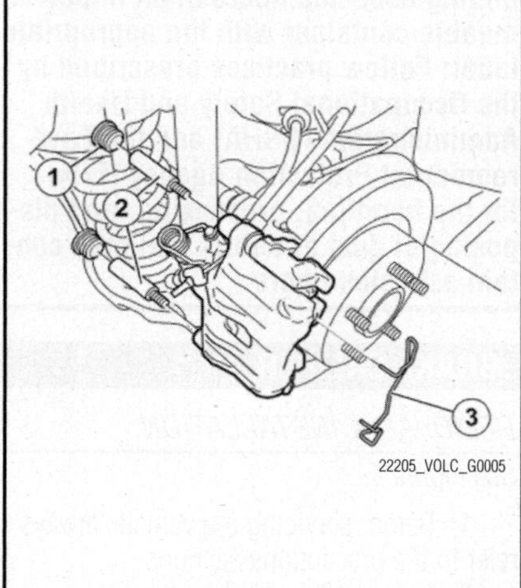

Fig. 9 Protective caps (1), locating pins (2), securing spring (3)

BRAKES — PARKING BRAKE

PARKING BRAKE CABLES

ADJUSTMENT

1. Before servicing the vehicle, refer to the Precautions Section.
2. Remove the panel for the center console or the panel in line with the parking brake cable.
3. Locate the adjustment for the parking brake.
4. Remove the retaining clip.
5. Turn the socket clockwise to increase tension on the parking brake cable.
6. Install the clip.
7. Depress the brake pedal to the 1st notch. Press out the adjustment using the adjustment rod: 951 2947.
8. Test the parking brake.

➡Full effect should be obtained between the 2nd and 5th ratchet teeth.

9. Install the panel that was removed.

GENERAL INFORMATION

⁂ CAUTION

These vehicles are equipped with an air bag system. The system must be disarmed before performing service on, or around, system components, the steering column, instrument panel components, wiring and sensors. Failure to follow the safety precautions and the disarming procedure could result in accidental air bag deployment, possible injury and unnecessary system repairs.

SERVICE PRECAUTIONS

Disconnect and isolate the battery negative cable before beginning any airbag system component diagnosis, testing, removal, or installation procedures. Allow system capacitor to discharge for two minutes before beginning any component service. This will disable the airbag system. Failure to disable the airbag system may result in accidental airbag deployment, personal injury, or death.

Do not place an intact undeployed airbag face down on a solid surface. The airbag will propel into the air if accidentally deployed and may result in personal injury or death.

When carrying or handling an undeployed airbag, the trim side (face) of the airbag should be pointing towards the body to minimize possibility of injury if accidental deployment occurs. Failure to do this may result in personal injury or death.

Replace airbag system components with OEM replacement parts. Substitute parts may appear interchangeable, but internal differences may result in inferior occupant protection. Failure to do so may result in occupant personal injury or death.

Wear safety glasses, rubber gloves, and long sleeved clothing when cleaning powder residue from vehicle after an airbag deployment. Powder residue emitted from a deployed airbag can cause skin irritation. Flush affected area with cool water if irritation is experienced. If nasal or throat irritation is experienced, exit the vehicle for fresh air until the irritation ceases. If irritation continues, see a physician.

Do not use a replacement airbag that is not in the original packaging. This may result in improper deployment, personal injury, or death.

The factory installed fasteners, screws and bolts used to fasten airbag components have a special coating and are specifically designed for the airbag system. Do not use substitute fasteners. Use only original equipment fasteners listed in the parts catalog when fastener replacement is required.

During, and following, any child restraint anchor service, due to impact event or vehicle repair, carefully inspect all mounting hardware, tether straps, and anchors for proper installation, operation, or damage. If a child restraint anchor is found damaged in any way, the anchor must be replaced. Failure to do this may result in personal injury or death.

Deployed and non-deployed airbags may or may not have live pyrotechnic material within the airbag inflator.

Do not dispose of driver/passenger/curtain airbags or seat belt tensioners unless you are sure of complete deployment. Refer to the Hazardous Substance Control System for proper disposal.

Dispose of deployed airbags and tensioners consistent with state, provincial, local, and federal regulations.

After any airbag component testing or service, do not connect the battery negative cable. Personal injury or death may result if the system test is not performed first.

If the vehicle is equipped with the Occupant Classification System (OCS), do not connect the battery negative cable before performing the OCS Verification Test using the scan tool and the appropriate diagnostic information. Personal injury or death may result if the system test is not performed properly.

Never replace both the Occupant Restraint Controller (ORC) and the Occupant Classification Module (OCM) at the same time. If both require replacement, replace one, then perform the Airbag System test before replacing the other.

Both the ORC and the OCM store Occupant Classification System (OCS) calibration data, which they transfer to one another when one of them is replaced. If both are replaced at the same time, an irreversible fault will be set in both modules and the OCS may malfunction and cause personal injury or death.

If equipped with OCS, the Seat Weight Sensor is a sensitive, calibrated unit and must be handled carefully. Do not drop or handle roughly. If dropped or damaged, replace with another sensor. Failure to do so may result in occupant injury or death.

If equipped with OCS, the front passenger seat must be handled carefully as well. When removing the seat, be careful when setting on floor not to drop. If dropped, the sensor may be inoperative, could result in occupant injury, or possibly death.

If equipped with OCS, when the passenger front seat is on the floor, no one should sit in the front passenger seat. This uneven force may damage the sensing ability of the seat weight sensors. If sat on and damaged, the sensor may be inoperative, could result in occupant injury, or possibly death.

DISARMING THE SYSTEM

1. Before servicing the vehicle, refer to the Precautions Section.
2. Disconnect and isolate the negative battery cable. Wait 3 minutes for the system capacitor to discharge before performing any service.

⁂ CAUTION

Wait at least 3 minutes before working on the vehicle. The air bag system is designed to retain enough power to deploy the air bag for a short time after the battery has been disconnected.

ARMING THE SYSTEM

1. Before servicing the vehicle, refer to the Precautions
2. After repairs are complete, connect the negative battery cable. Turn the ignition switch to the **ON** position and check the SRS light for proper operation.

DRIVE TRAIN

HALFSHAFT

REMOVAL & INSTALLATION

1. Before servicing the vehicle, refer to the Precautions Section.
2. Remove or disconnect the following:
   - Front wheel
   - Wheel speed sensor and wiring bracket
   - Brake hose bracket
   - Stabilizer bar link
   - Splash guards
   - Lower ball joint
   - Hub retainer nut
3. Pull the hub off of the stub shaft.
4. Pry the inner joint out of the transaxle and remove the axle halfshaft.

To install:

➡**Use new fasteners for assembly.**

5. Install the axle halfshaft so that the cir-clip is felt to seat in the retainer groove.
6. Guide the stub shaft into the hub.
7. Install or connect the following:
   - Hub retainer nut and tighten the nut to 89 ft. lbs. (120 Nm) plus 60°
   - Lower ball joint
   - Splash guards
   - Stabilizer bar link
   - Brake hose bracket
   - Wheel speed sensor and wiring bracket
   - Front wheel

ENGINE COOLING

ENGINE FAN

REMOVAL & INSTALLATION

See Figures 10 through 15.

1. Before servicing the vehicle, refer to the Precautions Section.
2. Disconnect ground cable of battery.
3. Remove the bumper cover.
4. Drain coolant:
5. Remove brake control module (BCM) cover.
6. Remove expansion tank cap.
7. Disconnect cooling fan electrical connector.
8. Remove 2 hose retaining clips.
9. Vehicles w/automatic transmission
   - Remove screws for transaxle oil cooler and place aside the cooler.
10. Vehicles w/premair sensors.
    - Remove connector for the premair sensor.
11. Remove 7 screws securing the splash guard.

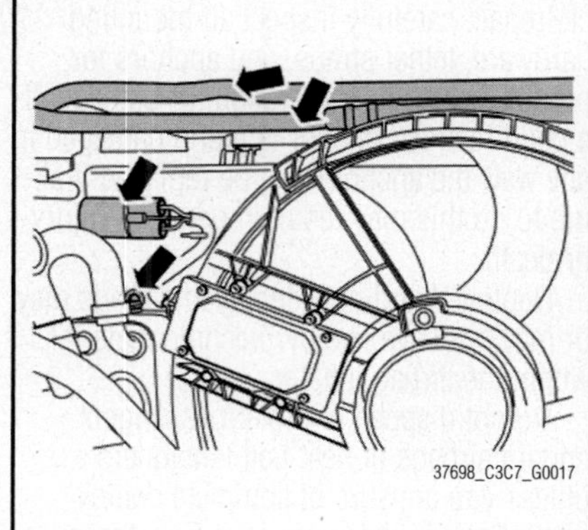

Fig. 11 Transaxle cooler screw locations.

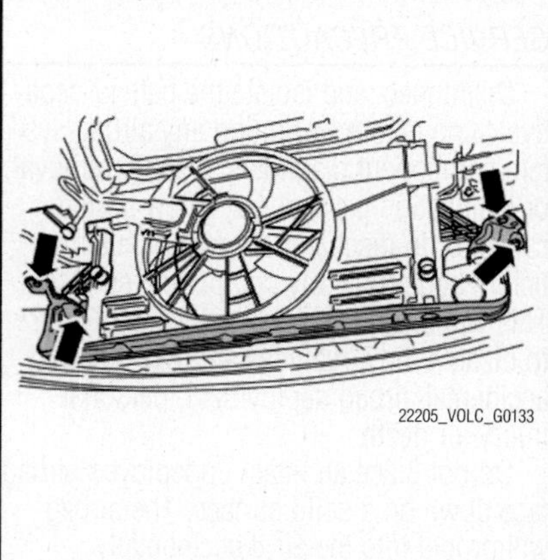

Fig. 13 A/C bracket screws location

12. Support the radiator assembly with jack stand.
13. Remove 4 screws for A/C brackets.
14. Remove coolant hoses.

➡**Be sure that when removing the cooling fan assembly that care is taken to prevent damage to the cables in the surrounding area.**

15. Press in both retaining clips at top of cooling fan shroud.

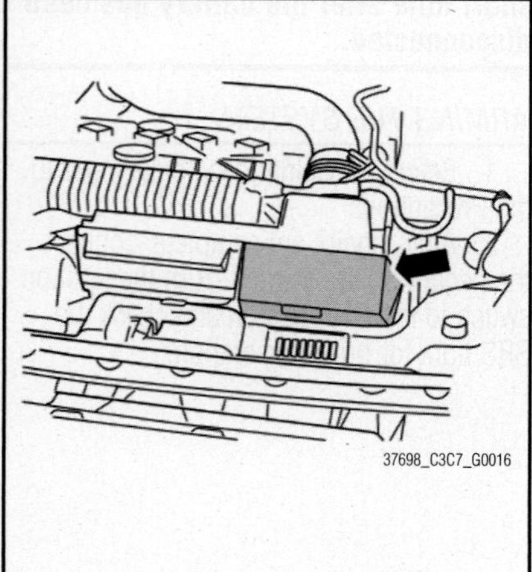

Fig. 10 Brake control module cover

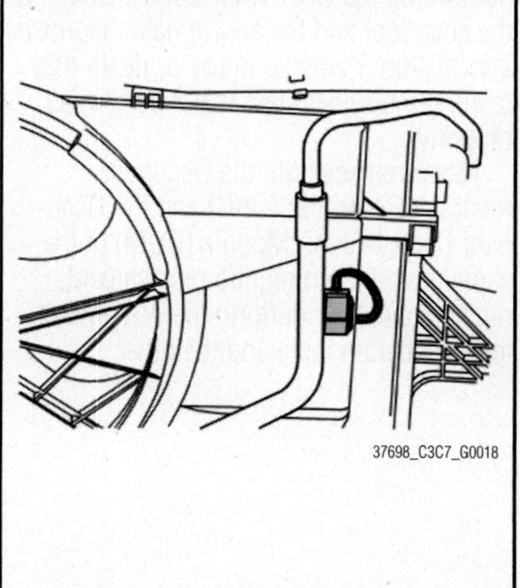

Fig. 12 Premair sensor location

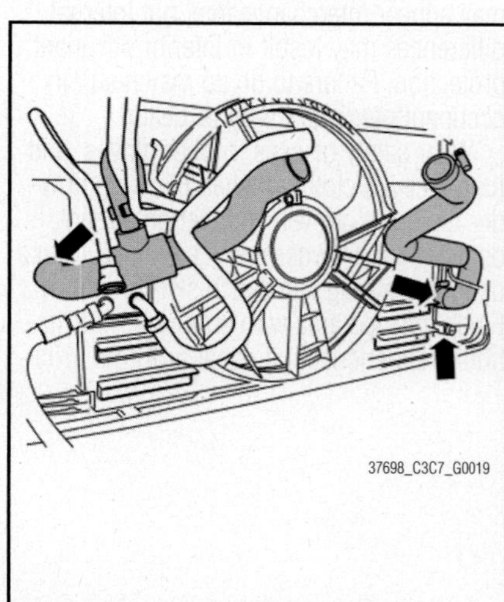

Fig. 14 Removal of 2 coolant hoses

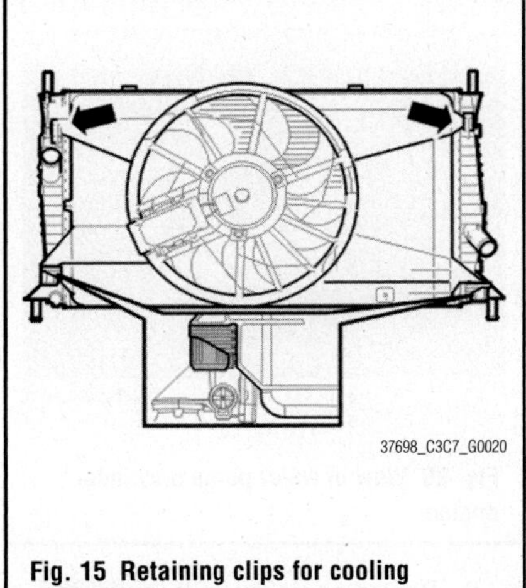

Fig. 15 Retaining clips for cooling fan shroud

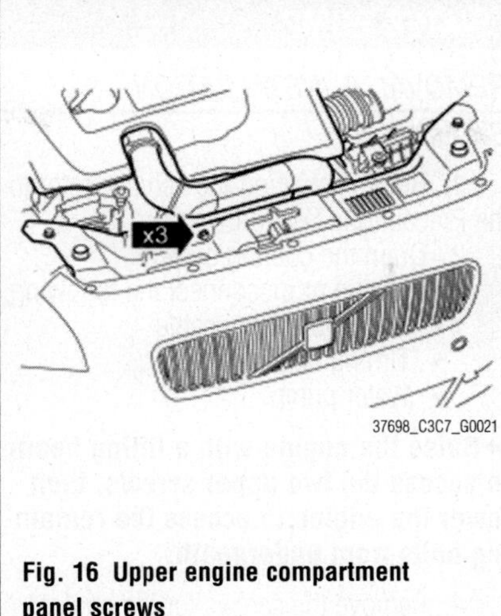

Fig. 16 Upper engine compartment panel screws

Fig. 18 Radiator and core support mounting bolts

16. Lift the cooling fan upwards to release from catches, then remove the assembly downwards.

To install:

17. Installation is the reverse of the removal process.

RADIATOR

REMOVAL & INSTALLATION

See Figures 16 through 18.

CAUTION

Never open, service or drain the radiator or cooling system when hot; serious burns can occur from the steam and hot coolant. Also, when draining engine coolant, keep in mind that cats and dogs are attracted to ethylene glycol antifreeze and could drink any that is left in an uncovered container or in puddles on the ground. This will prove fatal in sufficient quantities. Always drain coolant into a sealable container. Coolant should be reused unless it is contaminated or is several years old.

1. Be sure the engine is cold before removing the radiator.
2. Disconnect or remove:
   - Engine fan.

➡Once the engine fan is removed the radiator is now supported by reinstalling the radiator core support bracket.

   - Remove the charge air cooler.
   - Remove the 3 screws for the upper engine compartment panel and remove panel.
   - Remove the upper radiator mounts.
   - Slightly raise and suspend the A/C condenser.

➡Do not allow engine coolant to contact the accessory drive belt.

   - Disconnect and plug the oil cooler hoses from the automatic transaxle/transmission (if equipped).
   - The radiator mounting bolts.
   - Core support.
   - Remove radiator.

To install:

3. Lift radiator into position.
4. Install or connect the following:
   - Core support.
   - The radiator mounting bolts.
   - Install the charge air cooler (if equipped)
   - Oil cooler hoses from the automatic transaxle/transmission (if equipped)
   - Evacuation hose into expansion tank
   - Engine fan.
5. Be sure to refill the cooling system using the proper grade and type of engine coolant.
6. Start the engine and check for leaks.
7. Run engine and allow it to reach full operating temperature. Recheck the coolant level and transaxle/transmission fluid level. Fill as required.

THERMOSTAT

REMOVAL & INSTALLATION

See Figure 19.

1. Before servicing the vehicle, refer to the Precautions Section.
2. Drain the cooling system.
3. Remove air cleaner housing.
4. Disconnect or remove the following:

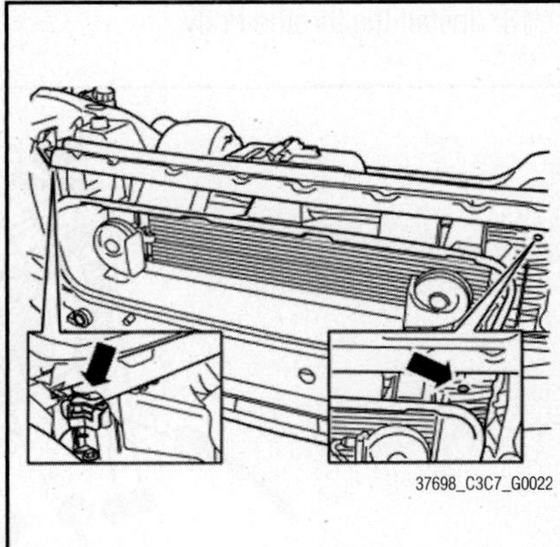

Fig. 17 Upper radiator mounts

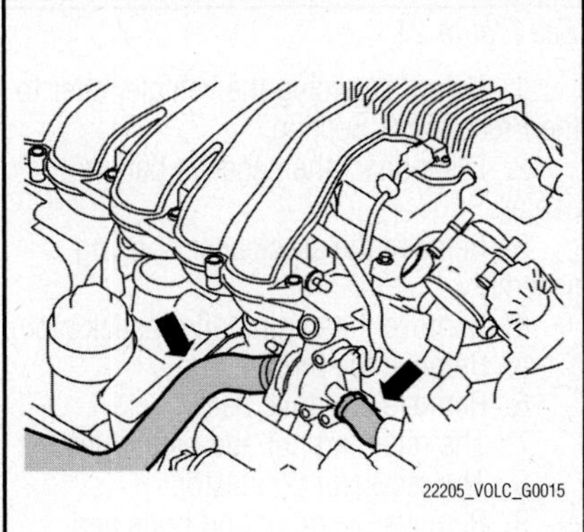

Fig. 19 Location of thermostat housing—5-Cylinder Engines

- Inlet and outlet hose from the thermostat housing.
- Connector from the temperature sensor
- Bolts for the thermostat housing
- Thermostat housing from cylinder head

To install:

5. Install or connect the following:
   - Thermostat housing assembly to cylinder head using new gasket and new hose clamp
   - Tighten thermostat housing to 16 ft. lbs. (22 Nm)
   - Inlet and outlet hose from the thermostat housing.
   - Connector for the temperature sensor
6. Reinstall air cleaner housing.
7. Refill the engine coolant.
8. Test drive the engine until the thermostat has opened.
9. Check for leaks, and proper thermostat operation. Fill fluid as necessary.

WATER PUMP

REMOVAL & INSTALLATION

See Figure 20.

1. Before servicing the vehicle, refer to the Precautions Section.
2. Drain the cooling system.
3. Remove or disconnect the following:
   - Negative battery cable
   - Timing belt
   - Water pump

➡Raise the engine with a lifting beam to access the two upper screws, then lower the engine to access the remaining bolts from underneath.

4. Remove the screws for the coolant pump.
5. Carefully tap the pump rotor with a plastic mallet and remove the pump.

To install:

6. Clean the engine surface.
7. Install a new gasket on water pump surface.

Fig. 20 View of water pump 5 cylinder engine

8. Tighten or reconnect the following:
   - Water pump
   - Timing belt
   - Negative battery cable
9. Refill the engine coolant and bleed cooling system.
10. Check for any signs of coolant leaks.

ENGINE ELECTRICAL — BATTERY SYSTEM

BATTERY

CHARGING

⁂ CAUTION

The chemical reaction which takes place in all batteries generates explosive hydrogen gas. A spark can cause the battery to explode and splash acid. To avoid personal injury, be sure there is proper ventilation and take appropriate fire safety precautions when working with or near a battery.

A battery should be charged at a slow rate to keep the plates inside from getting too hot. However, if some maintenance-free batteries are allowed to discharge until they are almost "dead," they may have to be charged at a high rate to bring them back to "life." Always follow the charger manufacturer's instructions on charging the battery.

ENGINE ELECTRICAL — CHARGING SYSTEM

ALTERNATOR

REMOVAL & INSTALLATION

See Figure 21.

1. Before servicing the vehicle, refer to the Precautions Section.
2. Disconnect the negative battery cable.
3. Remove the air cleaner housing assembly.
4. Remove the engine oil dipstick pipe.
5. Remove the throttle body.
6. Remove the drive belt.
7. The retaining nut and battery lead.
8. The regulator connector.
9. Remove the mounting bolts and remove alternator.

To install:

10. Install the alternator and tighten the mounting bolts to 18 ft. lbs. (25 Nm).
11. Install battery lead and tighten the retaining nut to 11 ft. lbs. (15 Nm).
12. Install the drive belt.
13. Install the throttle body.
14. Install the air cleaner housing assembly.
15. Connect the negative battery cable.
16. Test for proper operation.

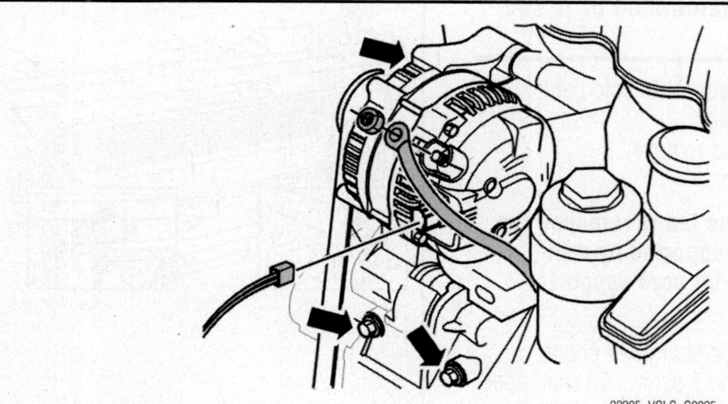

Fig. 21 Alternator removal components shown

FIRING ORDER

Firing order is: 1–2–4–5–3

IGNITION COIL PACK

REMOVAL & INSTALLATION

See Figures 22 and 23.

1. Before servicing the vehicle, refer to the Precautions Section.
2. Remove or disconnect the following:
   - Charge air pipe over the engine. Seal the openings.
   - Upper timing belt cover
   - Cover over the ignition coils
   - Ignition coil connector
   - Ignition coil mounting bolt
   - Carefully pull coil up and out

To install:

3. Align the coil and press it down.
4. Install ignition coil mounting bolt and tighten to 88 inch lbs. (10 Nm).
5. Press in the connector until a click sound is heard.
6. Install the cover over the ignition coil.
7. Replace the upper timing belt cover.
8. Remove the seals from the charge air pipe and reinstall over the engine.

Fig. 22 Charge Air Pipe Location—5-Cylinder Engine

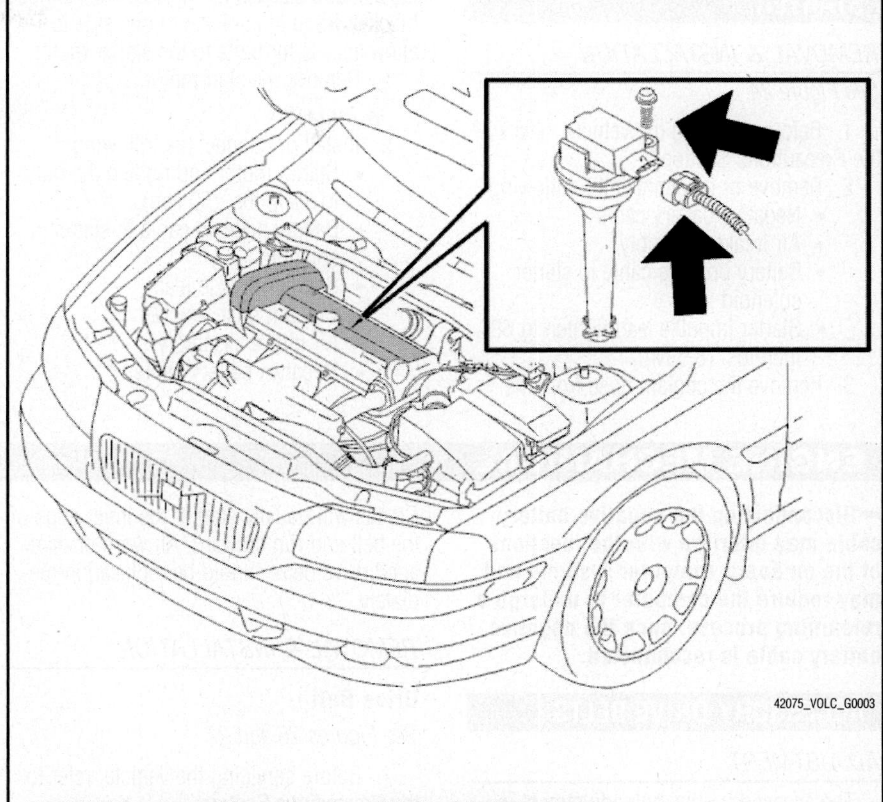

Fig. 23 Removing ignition coil and small bolt—5-Cylinder Engine

IGNITION TIMING

The ignition timing is controlled by the vehicles ECM.

SPARK PLUGS

REMOVAL & INSTALLATION

1. Before servicing the vehicle, refer to the Precautions Section.
2. Remove or disconnect the following:
   - Charge air pipe over the engine. Seal the openings.
   - Upper timing belt cover
   - Cover over the ignition coils
   - Ignition coil connector
   - Ignition coil mounting bolt
   - Carefully pull coil up and out
   - Remove spark plug

To install:

3. Install the spark plug and tighten to 22 ft. lbs. (30 Nm).
4. Align the coil and press it down.
5. Install ignition coil mounting bolt and tighten to 88 inch lbs. (10 Nm).
6. Press in the connector until a click sound is heard.
7. Install the cover over the ignition coil.
8. Replace the upper timing belt cover.
9. Remove the seals from the charge air pipe and reinstall over the engine.

ENGINE ELECTRICAL

STARTER

REMOVAL & INSTALLATION

See Figure 24.

1. Before servicing the vehicle, refer to the Precautions Section.
2. Remove or disconnect the following:
   - Negative battery cable
   - Air intake assembly
   - Battery positive cable to starter solenoid
   - Starter impulse lead tighten to 68 inch lbs. (8.5 Nm)
3. Remove the coolant hose from the bracket and slacken the nuts off for the hose bracket. Bend the bracket to one side to allow access for bolts to the starter motor.
4. Remove the start motor.

To install:

5. Install or connect the following:
   - Starter motor and tighten the bolts to 36 ft. lbs. (50 Nm).
   - Battery positive cable to starter solenoid
   - Starter impulse lead
   - Coolant hose bracket
   - Air intake assembly
   - Negative battery cable

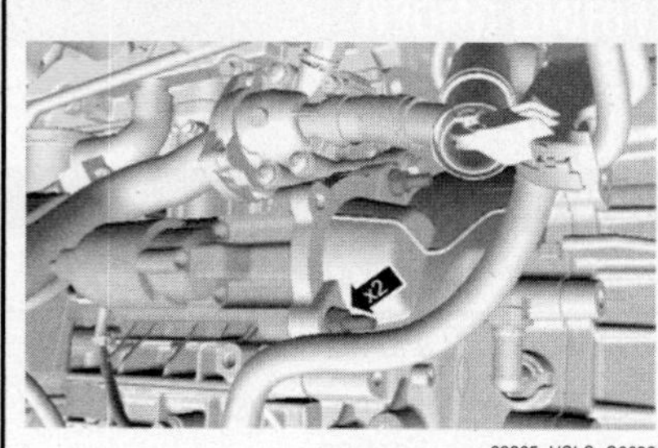

Fig. 24 Starter motor and mounting bolt view

ENGINE MECHANICAL

➡Disconnecting the negative battery cable may interfere with the functions of the on board computer systems and may require the computer to undergo a relearning process, once the negative battery cable is reconnected.

ACCESSORY DRIVE BELTS

ADJUSTMENT

The accessory drive belt adjustment is maintained by an automatic tensioner.

BELT ROUTINGS

See Figure 25.

INSPECTION

Inspect the drive belt for signs of glazing or cracking. A glazed belt will be perfectly smooth from slippage, while a good belt will have a slight texture of fabric visible. Cracks will usually start at the inner edge of the belt and run outward. All worn or damaged drive belts should be replaced immediately.

REMOVAL & INSTALLATION

Drive Belt

See Figures 26 and 27.

1. Before servicing the vehicle, refer to the Precautions Section.
2. Raise the vehicle.
3. Remove or disconnect the following:
   - Right front wheel
   - Right-hand fender liner. Slacken off the screws at the front edge and fold back the fender liner.
4. Remove the outer drive belt as follows:
   - Relieve the load from the belt tensioner. Use: 999-7109 or after market equivalent. Turn the belt tensioner **clockwise** as far as it will go. Remove the belt.
5. Remove the inner drive belt as follows:
   - Relieve the load from the belt tensioner using a Torx® wrench. Turn the belt tensioner **counter clockwise** as far as it will go. Remove the belt.

To install:

6. Installation is in the reverse of the removal procedure.

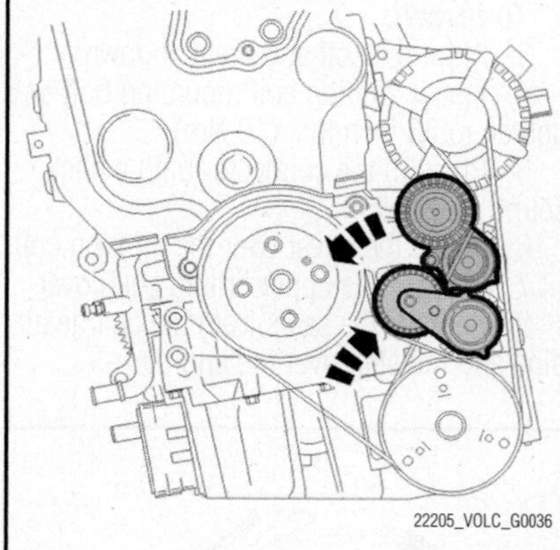

Fig. 27 Drive belt routing and tensioner view—2.5L engine

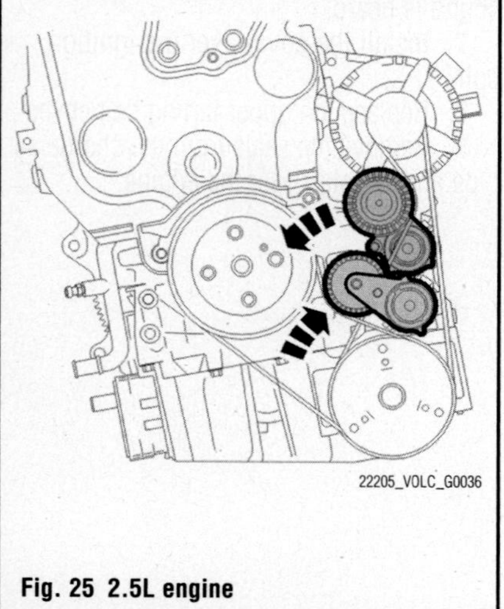

Fig. 25 2.5L engine

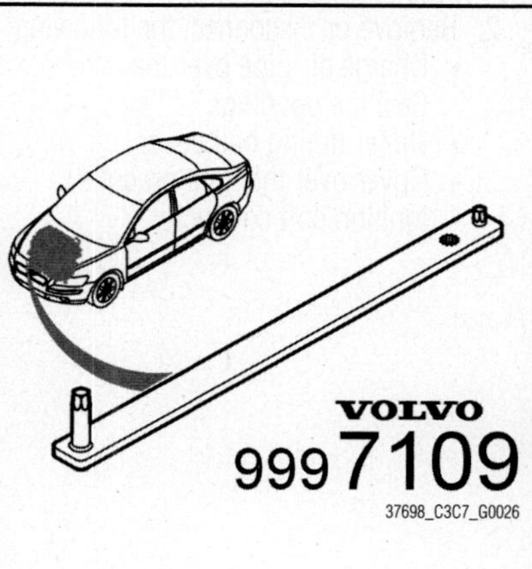

Fig. 26 Accessory drive belt tensioner tool

CRANKSHAFT DAMPER (BALANCER)

REMOVAL & INSTALLATION

See Figure 28.

1. Before servicing the vehicle, refer to the Precautions Section.

42075_VOLC_G0011

Fig. 28 Using Counterhold 999 5433 to remove crankshaft damper—5-Cylinder Engines

2. Remove or disconnect the following:
   - The cross stay between the suspension turrets
   - The servo reservoir and the expansion tank. Lift up and place on top of the engine.
   - The accessory drive belt
   - The upper timing belt cover
   - Remove the right front wheel
   - Remove the nut from the cover in the fender liner
3. Install counterhold 999 5433 on the crankshaft damper.
4. Remove crankshaft damper center nut.
5. Work the crankshaft damper loose and remove by hand.

To install:

6. Install the crankshaft damper and tighten the center nut to 133 ft. lbs. (180 Nm).
7. Remove the counterhold 999 5433 and install new bolts. Tighten to 18 ft. lbs. (25 Nm) and angle-tighten 30°.
8. Turn the crankshaft 2 turns. Check that the markings on the crankshaft damper and camshaft pulley correspond.
9. Install or connect the following:
   - Front timing belt cover. Tighten to 108 inch lbs. (12 Nm)
   - Upper timing belt cover
   - Accessory belt
   - Servo reservoir
   - Expansion tank

➡Ensure that the hoses are correctly positioned.

   - Engine stabilizer brace. Tighten the bolts at the suspension turrets to 37 ft. lbs. (50 Nm)
   - Tighten the engine bracket bolt to 59 ft. lbs. (80 Nm)
   - Fender liner cover
   - Front wheel and tighten lug nuts to 81–103 ft. lbs. (110–140 Nm)

CRANKSHAFT FRONT SEAL

REMOVAL & INSTALLATION

See Figure 29.

1. Before servicing the vehicle, refer to the Precautions Section.
2. Remove or disconnect the following:
   - Engine stabilizer brace
   - Upper timing belt cover
   - Servo reservoir
   - Expansion tank
   - Accessory drive belt
   - Front timing belt cover
   - Front wheel
   - Timing belt
   - Vibration damper
   - Crankshaft timing gear pulley
   - Front crankshaft seal

To install:

3. Install or connect the following:
   - Front crankshaft seal
   - Crankshaft timing gear pulley
   - Vibration damper and tighten nut to 133 ft. lbs. (180 Nm)
   - Timing belt
   - Front wheel
   - Front timing belt cover
   - Upper timing belt cover
   - Accessory drive belt
   - Expansion tank
   - Servo reservoir
   - Engine stabilizer brace. Tighten the bolts at the suspension turrets to 37 ft. lbs. (50 Nm). Tighten the engine bracket bolt to 59 ft. lbs. (80 Nm).
4. Start the engine and check for leaks.

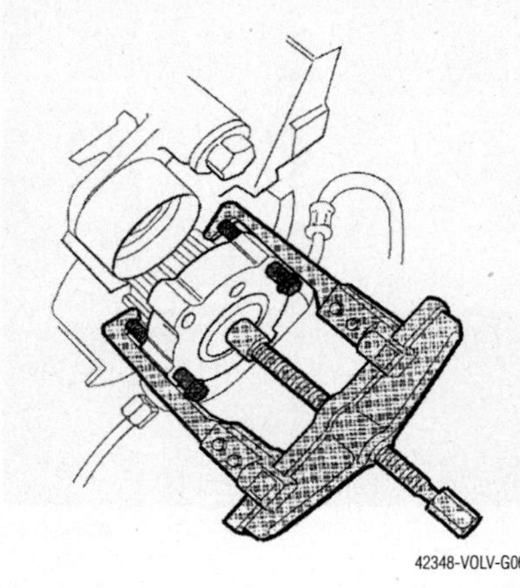

42348-VOLV-G06

Fig. 29 Removing crankshaft timing gear pulley

CYLINDER HEAD

REMOVAL & INSTALLATION

See Figures 30 through 33.

1. Before servicing the vehicle, refer to the Precautions Section.
2. Drain the cooling system.
3. Relieve the fuel pressure.
4. Remove or disconnect the following:
   - Negative battery cable
   - Engine appearance cover
   - Air cleaner housing
   - Ignition coils
   - Intake manifold
   - Fuel rail and injectors
   - O2 sensor connector
   - Front pipe at exhaust manifold
   - Exhaust manifold
   - Turbocharger, if equipped
5. Remove the screws for the bracket for the oil pipes for the power steering.
6. Remove the valve cover.

⁂ WARNING

Take extra care not to damage the mating faces.

7. Remove the tensioned mounting yoke.
8. Remove or disconnect the following:
   - Upper engine coolant hose
   - Accessory drive belt
   - Timing belt
   - Camshafts
   - Valve tappets (keep in their natural order)
   - Cylinder head

To install:

9. Clean the mating surfaces of cylinder head and engine block.
10. Install the cylinder head with a new

22205_VOLC_G0023

Fig. 30 Remove the valve cover

42348-VOLV-G21

Fig. 31 Cylinder head loosening sequence—5-cylinder engine

42348-VOLV-G03

Fig. 32 Cylinder head torque sequence

22205_VOLC_G0024

Fig. 33 Crankshaft adjustment tool 999-5451

gasket. Tighten the bolts in the following sequence:

a. Step 1: 15 ft. lbs. (20 Nm)
b. Step 2: 44 ft. lbs. (60 Nm)
c. Step 3: Plus 130°

11. Remove or disconnect the following:
    - Camshafts (Lubricate all components)
    - Valve tappets (in their natural order)
    - Camshafts
12. Remove the cover plug. Turn the crankshaft clockwise slightly. Install the crankshaft adjustment tool.
13. Install or connect the following:
    - Timing belt
    - Accessory drive belt
    - Intake manifold
    - Upper engine coolant hose
    - Valve cover (with new gasket)
    - Steering pipe bracket bolts
    - Turbocharger, if equipped
    - Exhaust manifold
    - Front pipe at exhaust manifold
    - O2 sensor connector
    - Fuel rail and injectors
    - Intake manifold
    - Ignition coils
    - Air cleaner housing
    - Engine appearance cover
14. Connect the negative battery cable.
15. Install new engine coolant and bleed the system.
16. Start the engine and check for leaks.

EXHAUST MANIFOLD

REMOVAL & INSTALLATION

See Figure 34.

1. Before servicing the vehicle, refer to the Precautions Section.
2. Remove or disconnect the following:

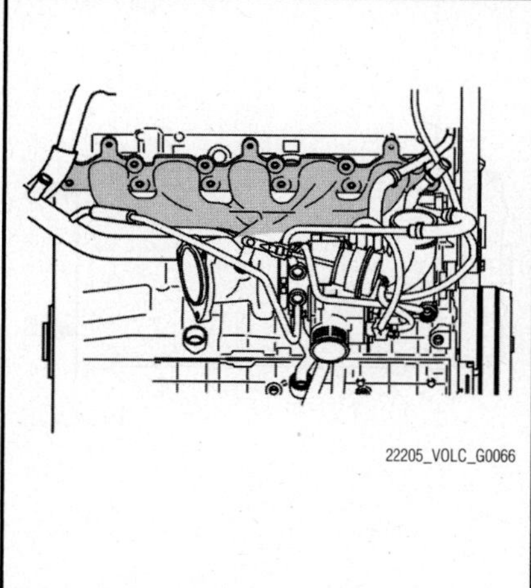

Fig. 34 Exhaust manifold view

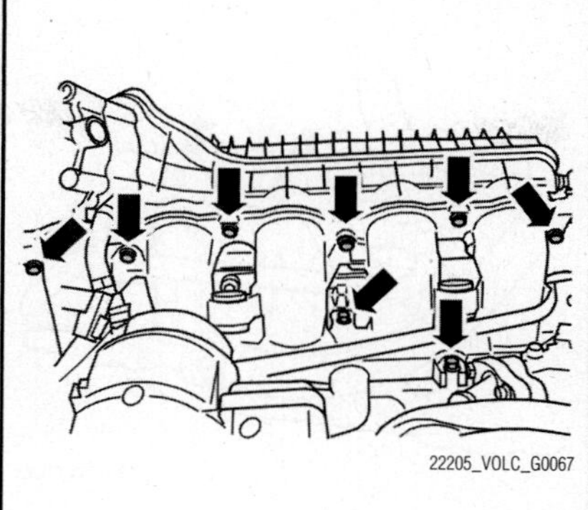

Fig. 35 Remove the 6 screws for the upper section of the intake

- Negative battery cable
- Exhaust manifold heat shield
- Exhaust front pipe
- Turbocharger
- Exhaust manifold

To install:

3. Install or connect the following:
   - Exhaust manifold and tighten the fasteners to 18 ft. lbs. (25 Nm)
   - Turbocharger, if equipped
   - Exhaust front pipe and tighten the fasteners to 44 ft. lbs. (60 Nm)
   - Exhaust manifold heat shield and tighten the fasteners to 88 inch lbs. (10 Nm)

4. Loosen the joint at the catalytic converter and re-tighten to 18 ft. lbs. (25 Nm). This is necessary to prevent stresses in the system.

5. Connect the negative battery cable.

6. Start the engine and check for leaks.

INTAKE MANIFOLD

REMOVAL & INSTALLATION

See Figures 35 and 36.

1. Before servicing the vehicle, refer to the Precautions Section.
2. Relieve the fuel system pressure.
3. Disconnect the negative battery cable.
4. Remove the brake vacuum hose.
5. Remove the hose for the throttle body.
6. Remove the intake manifold for the turbocharger. Remove the seals.
7. Remove the 6 screws for the upper section of the intake manifold.
8. Disconnect the vacuum hoses from the intake manifold. Put the pipe to one side.
9. Disconnect the connectors for the fuel pressure sensor and the connector for the injectors.
10. Remove the 2 fuel rail mounting screws.
11. Spray universal oil or similar around the injector nozzle at the terminal on the intake manifold.
12. Gently work the fuel rail and injector nozzles loose. Disconnect the fuel line to the fuel rail. Press in the two blue clips on the fuel rail. Pull the fuel line out of the fuel rail.
13. Place the fuel rail to one side.
14. Remove the hose from the oil trap to the timing belt cover at the terminal in the timing belt cover.
15. Remove the crankcase ventilation hoses from the intake manifold.
16. Remove the clamp for the fuel intake manifold.
17. Remove the lower screws for the intake manifold a few turns.
18. Remove the mounting screws in the upper row. Lift out the intake manifold.

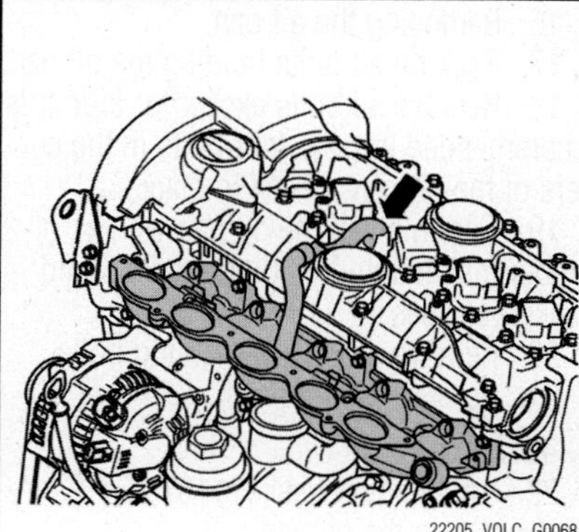

Fig. 36 Lower intake manifold view

19. Remove the screws in the lower row.
20. Remove the gasket for the intake manifold.

To install:

21. Install a new gasket held in position by the lower screws for the intake manifold the intake manifold.

➡Do not forget the crankcase ventilation hose. The hose must be inserted up through the gap between the second and third ducts.

22. Install the three upper screws. Tighten all the screws starting from the center to 13 ft. lbs. (17 Nm).
23. Install the clamp for the fuel line on the intake manifold.
24. Install the crankcase ventilation hoses on the intake manifold.
25. Install the hose from the oil trap to the camshaft cover. Use a new hose clamp.
26. Lubricate the injector O-rings using petroleum jelly. Depress the fuel rail. Ensure that all injectors sit correctly.
27. Press the quick-release connector together until a clicking sound is heard. Screw the fuel rail into place.
28. Connect the connector for the injectors and the fuel pressure sensors.
29. Install a new gasket for the intake manifold.
30. Install the vacuum hoses for the intake manifold.
31. Install the intake manifold. Align the guides with the lower section of the intake manifold.
32. Install the screws for the intake manifold and tighten to 13 ft. lbs. (17 Nm).
33. Install the intake manifold for the turbocharger. Install the seals.
34. Install the hose for the throttle body.
35. Install the brake vacuum hose.

MAIN BEARING TORQUE SEQUENCE

See Figure 37.

1. Tighten the screws in sequence from the center and outwards.
   - Step 1 M10 15 ft. lbs. (20 Nm)
   - Step 2 M10 33 ft. lbs. (45 Nm)
   - Step 3 M8 18 ft. lbs.(24 Nm)
   - Step 4 M7 13 ft. lbs. (17 Nm)
   - Step 5 M10 angle tighten to 90°

OIL PAN

REMOVAL & INSTALLATION

See Figures 38 through 41.

1. Before servicing the vehicle, refer to the Precautions Section.

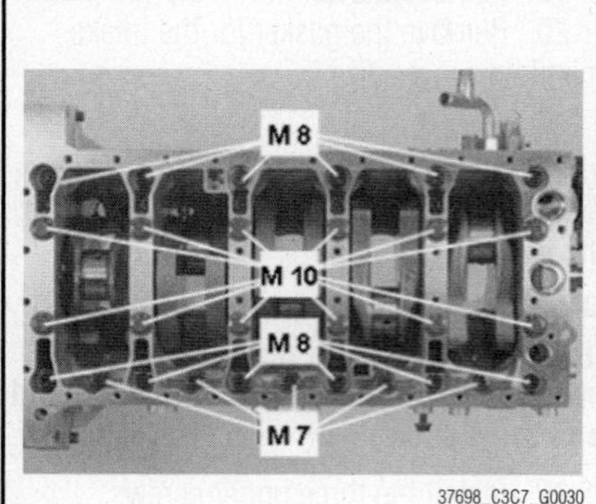

Fig. 37 Crankshaft intermediate torque sequence

Fig. 38 Power steering hose connections

2. Remove the oil dipstick and its pipe.
3. Remove the right hand front wheel.
4. Remove right hand fender apron panel by removing 6 screws at front edge and the plastic nut.
5. Bend the fender apron back and away.
6. Remove the splashguard under the engine.
7. Drain the engine oil and remove the oil filter.
8. Release the oil cooler from the oil pan. Hang up at the rear.
9. Remove the charge air pipe from under the engine.
10. Disconnect the power steering (P/S) pressure hose from P/S pump.

CAUTION

Seal P/S line/hoses to prevent contaminates.

11. Remove return hose from pump.

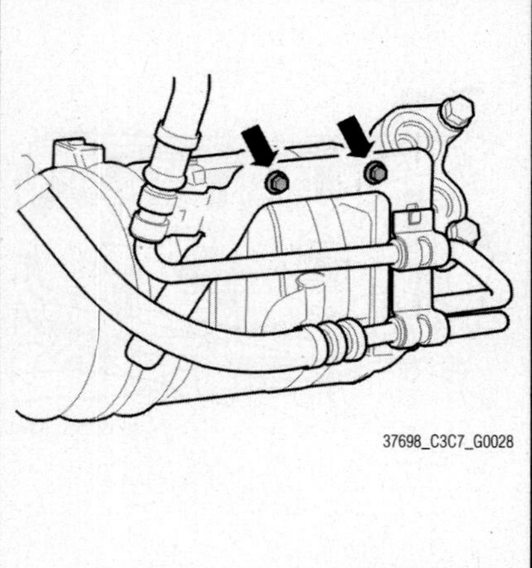

Fig. 39 Power steering hose bracket

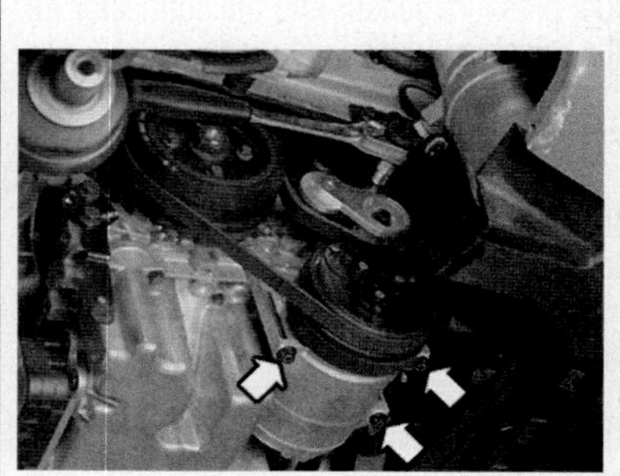

Fig. 40 Air conditioning compressor mounting

12. Remove the bracket for the P/S lines/hoses from the air conditioning (A/C) compressor.
13. Push aside and suspend the bracket from a suitable place.
14. Remove the accessory drive belts.
15. Remove the A/C compressor.
16. Removing the oil pan.
17. Back off all bolts holding the oil pan.
18. Remove all bolts except for four. It is recommended that the four bolts in the corners of the oil pan are left in place.
19. Carefully tap the oil pan with a rubber mallet until the joint and its liquid gasket releases.
20. Remove the four remaining bolts.
21. Remove the oil pan.

To install:

22. Apply liquid gasket 1161 059-9, or equivalent, to the oil pan.
23. Install new O-rings.
24. Position the oil pan. Secure it loosely with a few bolts.

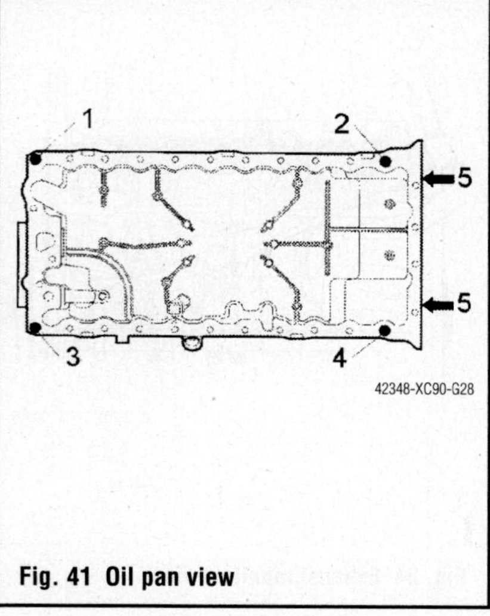

Fig. 41 Oil pan view

25. Install the remaining bolts loosely.
26. Press the oil pan against the transaxle. Tighten bolts 1, 2, 3 and 4 to 27 inch lbs. (3 Nm). Tighten bolt 5 to 18 ft. lbs. (25 Nm); then tighten to 35 ft. lbs. (48 Nm).
27. Tighten all bolts in the oil pan flange to 12 ft. lbs. (17 Nm). Start at the transaxle end and continue forwards in pairs.
28. Connect the oil cooler to the oil pan. Use new O-rings.
29. Install the A/C compressor.
30. Install the accessory drive belts.
31. Install P/S pressure line to P/S pump. Do not fully tighten line at this time.
32. Install P/S return hose to pump.
33. Install P/S line/hose bracket to the A/C compressor.
34. Tighten the P/S pressure line.
35. Install right fender panel and right front wheel.
36. Install splash guard.
37. Install the oil drain plug with a new gasket.
38. Install the oil dipstick and its pipe. Use a new O-ring.

➡Check that the O-ring is correctly positioned.

39. Install a new oil filter.
40. Fill with engine oil. Run the engine to operating temperature.
41. Check for oil leaks from the oil pan or oil cooler.
42. Check the oil level. Top up if required.

OIL PUMP

REMOVAL & INSTALLATION

See Figure 42.

1. Before servicing the vehicle, refer to the Precautions Section.

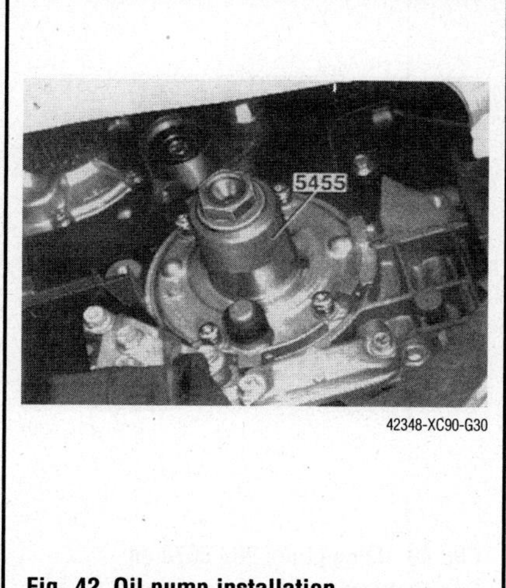

Fig. 42 Oil pump installation

2. Remove or disconnect the following:
   - Negative battery cable
   - Fuel line clips
   - Coolant recovery tank
   - Accessory drive belts
   - Right front wheel
   - Inner fender liner
   - Front cover
   - Timing belt
   - Crankshaft timing sprocket
   - Front crankshaft seal
   - Oil pump

To install:

3. Install the oil pump using special tool 999-5455. Use the oil pump bolts to guide the pump. Use the crankshaft nut to press the pump in until it is seated fully. Tighten the oil pump bolts to 88 inch lbs. (10 Nm).
4. Remove the crankshaft nut and the press tool.
5. Install or connect the following:
   - Front crankshaft seal
   - Crankshaft timing sprocket and tighten the nut to 133 ft. lbs. (180 Nm)
   - Timing belt
   - Front cover
   - Inner fender liner
   - Right front wheel
   - Accessory drive belts
   - Coolant recovery tank
   - Fuel line clips
   - Negative battery cable
6. Start the engine and check for leaks.

PISTONS & RINGS

POSITIONING

See Figures 43 and 44.

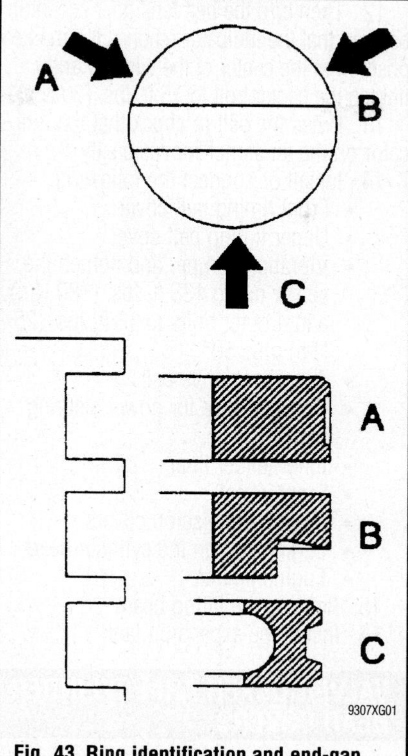

Fig. 43 Ring identification and end-gap spacing—all engines

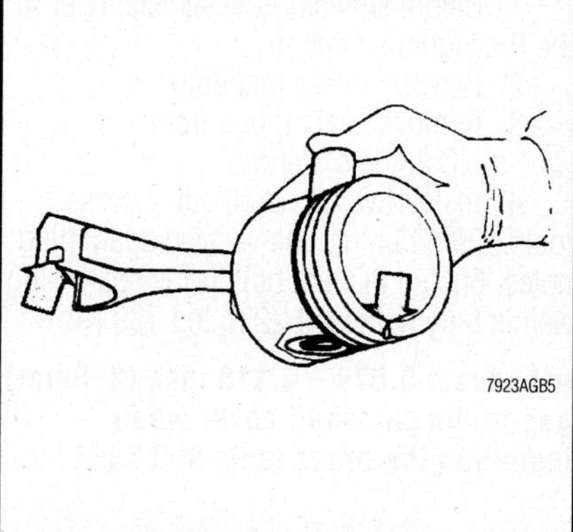

Fig. 44 Piston and rod positioning—all engines
The notch on the piston crown faces the front of the engine

TIMING BELT FRONT COVER

REMOVAL & INSTALLATION

1. Before servicing the vehicle, refer to the Precautions Section.
2. Remove or disconnect the following:
   - The cross stay between the suspension turrets
   - The servo reservoir and the expansion tank. Lift up and place on top of the engine.
   - The accessory drive belts
   - The upper timing belt cover

To install:

3. Install or connect the following:
   - Front timing belt cover. Tighten to 108 inch lbs. (12 Nm).
   - Upper timing belt cover
   - Accessory drive belts
   - Servo reservoir
   - Expansion tank

➡Ensure that the hoses are correctly positioned.

   - Cross stay brace and tighten the bolts at the suspension turrets to 37 ft. lbs. (50 Nm).
   - Tighten the engine bracket bolt to 59 ft. lbs. (80 Nm).
   - Fender liner cover
   - Front wheel and tighten the lug nuts to 81–103 ft. lbs. (110–140 Nm)

TIMING BELT & SPROCKETS

REMOVAL & INSTALLATION

See Figures 45 and 46.

1. Before servicing the vehicle, refer to the Precautions Section.
2. Lift the expansion tank and place it on top of the engine.
3. Install lifting beam 99-7103 or equivalent and tighten.
4. Remove or disconnect the following:
   - Engine limiter
   - Engine pad on the cylinder head
   - Front transmission covers

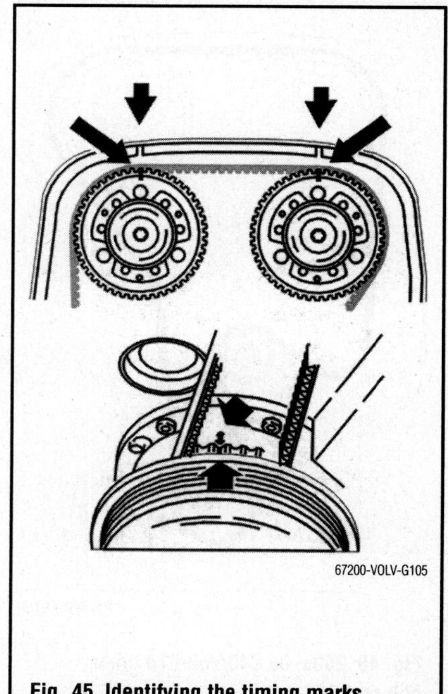

Fig. 45 Identifying the timing marks

- Right hand front wheel
- Inner fender liner
- Delivery line from the power steering pump
- Accessory drive belt
- Vibration damper
- Upper timing belt cover

5. Lower the engine slightly until the belt tensioner bolts can be accessed from beneath.
6. Turn the crankshaft clockwise until the markings on the crankshaft and camshaft pulleys correspond.
7. Slacken off the center bolt for the belt tensioner slightly and hold the center bolt still. Turn the tensioner clockwise to 10 o'clock.
8. Remove the timing belt.

To install:

9. Install the timing belt in the following order:
    a. Around the crankshaft
    b. Around the idler pulley
    c. Around the intake camshaft pulley
    d. Around the exhaust camshaft pulley
    e. Around the water pump
    f. Onto the belt tensioner
10. Carefully turn the crankshaft clockwise until the timing belt is tensioned. The belt must be tensioned between the intake camshaft pulley, the idler pulley and the crankshaft.
11. Hold the belt tensioner center bolt secure. Turn the belt tensioner eccentric counter-clockwise until the tensioner indicator passes the marked position.

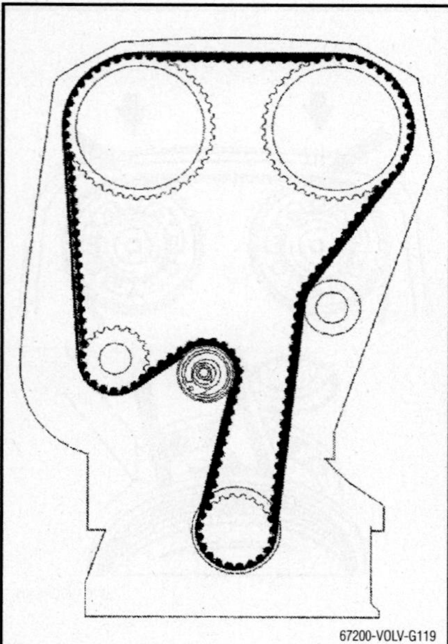

Fig. 46 2005–06 S40/V50/C70 timing belt routing

12. Then turn the belt tensioner eccentric back so that the indicator reaches the marked position in the center of the window and tighten the center bolt to 15 ft. lbs. (20 Nm).
13. Press the belt to check that the indicator on the tensioner moves easily.
14. Install or connect the following:
    - Front timing belt cover
    - Upper timing belt cover
    - Vibration damper and tighten the center nut to 133 ft. lbs. (180 Nm) and 4 outer bolts to 18 ft. lbs. (25 Nm) plus 60°
    - Accessory drive belt
    - Delivery hose for power steering pump
    - Inner fender liner
    - Front wheel
    - Front transmission covers
    - Engine pad on the cylinder head
    - Engine limiter
15. Remove the lifting beam.
16. Install the expansion tank.

VALVE/ROCKER ARM/CYLINDER HEAD COVERS

REMOVAL & INSTALLATION

See Figures 47 and 48.

1. Before servicing the vehicle, refer to the Precautions Section.
2. Remove intake manifold.
3. Remove spark plugs from:
    a. Cylinders 1 and 5
4. Install two camshaft cover press tools 999 5454 into the vacated spark plug holes. Ensure that the bolt in the spark plug well is fully tightened 22 ft. lbs. (30 Nm).

➡Leave a 0.079—0.118 inch (2–3mm) gap to the camshaft cover when installing the press tools 999 5454.

Fig. 47 Camshaft cover press tool 999 5454 installed

Fig. 48 Using pliers 999 5670 on Camshaft cover

5. Remove Variable Valve Timing (VVT) solenoid.
6. Remove all bolts securing the camshaft cover to cylinder head.
7. Use pliers 999 5670 to lift camshaft cover from cylinder head.
    a. Install pliers at the stop lugs. Start with cylinder 1 and work alternately backwards.
    b. Slacken off the wing nuts approximately 2 turns.
    c. Repeat the procedure working toward rear of engine.
8. Carefully press out the front and rear camshaft seals.
9. Remove the two press tools 999 5454 from spark plug holes.
10. Remove the camshaft cover.

To install:

11. Install new O-rings around spark plug wells at cylinder head.
12. Apply liquid gasket 1161 059 to the camshaft cover using roller 951 2767.

➡The surface must be covered without any excess. Ensure that no liquid gasket gets into the oil ducts.

13. Lubricate camshaft lobes, camshaft bearing surfaces, and valve lifters with clean engine oil.
14. Put camshaft cover in place.
15. Install the two press tools 999 5454.
16. Begin to tighten the camshaft cover bolts alternately, keeping camshaft cover parallel to the cylinder head using the press tools.
17. Tighten the bolts in sequence from the center and outwards to 88 inch lbs. (10 Nm).
18. Remove the press tools 999 5454.
19. Install:
    - Variable valve timing (VVT) solenoid.

Use a new gasket. Tighten center bolt to 89 ft. lbs. (120 Nm), center plug to 26 ft. lbs. (35 Nm)
- Spark plugs and tighten to 22 ft. lbs. (30 Nm)
- Intake manifold

VALVE LASH CLEARANCE

ADJUSTMENT

See Figures 49 through 56.

1. Remove the cable from the battery negative terminal.
2. Remove:
   - The cross stay between the suspension turrets
   - The ground strip from the cylinder head
   - The upper engine stabilizer brace
   - The cover in the cylinder head at the rear of the exhaust camshaft
   - The crankcase ventilation hose from the top of the camshaft cover
   - The radiator breather tube from the expansion tank. Install lock grip pliers.
3. Lift up the brake fluid reservoir.
4. Disconnect the ABS sensor connector.
5. Place the brake fluid reservoir over the engine.

WARNING

Ensure that no fluid is spilled on the engine. It is extremely flammable!

6. Disconnect the connector for the level sensor in the expansion tank.

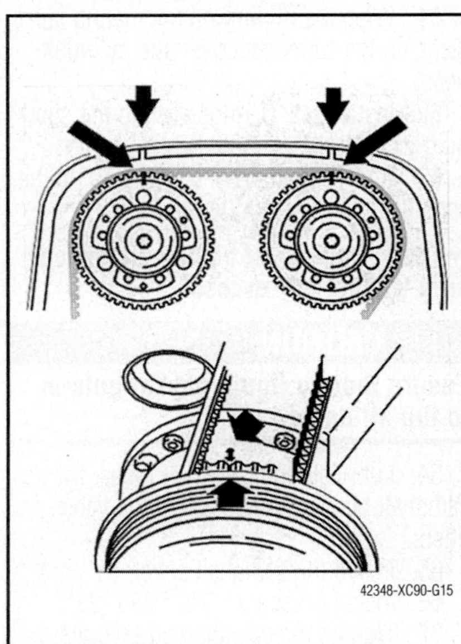

Fig. 49 Setting the timing marks—5 and 6-cylinder engines

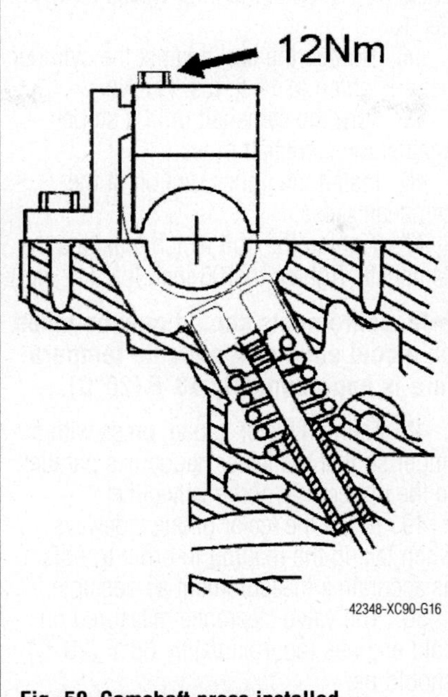

Fig. 50 Camshaft press installed—5-cylinder engines

7. Lift up and place the expansion tank on top of the engine.
8. Remove:
   - The accessory drive belt
   - The front timing cover
9. Position the upper timing cover.
10. Turn the crankshaft clockwise until the markings on the crankshaft belt pulley and the timing belt pulley are aligned with the markings on the oil pump and the upper timing cover.
11. Remove the upper timing cover.

CAUTION

Crankshaft and camshafts must not be turned more than is stated in the method description. If the shafts are turned in any other way the valves may be damaged.

12. Slacken off the center bolt for the belt tensioner slightly.
13. Hold the center bolt still. Turn the tensioner eccentric clockwise to 10 o'clock using a 6mm Allen key.
14. Remove the timing belt from the camshaft pulleys.
15. Install camshaft adjustment tool 999 5452 at the rear of the camshafts.
16. Check that the bolts securing the adjustment tool to the camshafts and the bolt holding the tool together are well tightened.
17. Remove: (timing gear pulley with variable valve timing unit)
   - The plug at the front of the variable valve timing unit
   - The center bolt in the variable valve timing unit. Carefully pull out the variable valve timing unit with the timing gear pulley.
18. Remove: (timing gear pulley without variable valve timing unit)
   - The bolts securing the timing gear pulley on the camshaft
   - The timing gear pulley.
19. Remove tool 999 5452.
20. Reinstall the expansion tank and the brake fluid reservoir at the fender liner.
21. Remove:
   - The variable valve timing (VVT) solenoid
   - spark plugs for cylinders 1 and 5.
22. Install 2 tools 999 5454. Leave a 0.079–0.118 inch (2–3mm) gap to the camshaft cover.
23. Ensure that the bolt in the spark plug well is fully tightened.
24. Remove all the bolts securing the camshaft cover to the cylinder head.
25. Use pliers 999 5670 to lift the cover from the cylinder head.
26. Install the pliers at the stop lugs. Start with cylinder 1 and work alternately backward.
27. Slacken off the wing nuts approximately 2 turns. Repeat the procedure with the pliers.
28. Carefully press the camshaft seals free.

➡Take care not to damage the sealing surfaces on the camshafts.

29. Remove:
   - Tool 999 5454
   - The camshaft cover
   - The camshafts.
30. Lift out the valve lifters. Mark up the valve lifters so that the original positions can be established.
31. Use a razor blade or a gasket scraper and gasket solvent on the camshaft cover.

WARNING

Use a fume hood or extractor when using gasket solvent.

32. Use only a gasket scraper or razor blade on the cylinder head.

CAUTION

Take great care around the oil ducts for the variable valve timing solenoid. This applies to both the camshaft cover and the cylinder head. The solenoid is extremely sensitive to contaminants.

33. Dry and blow all surfaces clean.

34. Carefully tap the end of the valve stem to ensure that the valve is correctly located in the seat.

35. Use a plastic, aluminum or brass drift to protect the valve and the surface of the valve lifter.

36. The sound made by tapping reveals if the valve is correctly seated.

37. Install both the valve lifters for the inlet valves at cylinder 1.

38. Check the notes made earlier. Select new valve lifters if necessary.

➡Only install two valve lifters. The valve lifters should be placed at the same cylinder.

39. Other valve lifters are available as replacement part/replacement part kits.

40. The valve clearance on a cold engine (approximately 20°C) should be:

- Inlet valve: 0.008 plus or minus 0.0010 inch (0.20 plus or minus 0.03mm).
- Exhaust valve: 0.016 plus or minus 0.0010 inch (0.40 plus or minus 0.03mm).

➡The tolerances are less at setting. When checking the valve clearance through the plug hole the tolerances are larger.

41. Position the intake camshaft. Ensure that the lobes at cylinder 1 point upwards.

42. Apply a little oil to the cam lobe and the upper side of the valve lifter to facilitate later measurement.

43. Install the lower section of camshaft

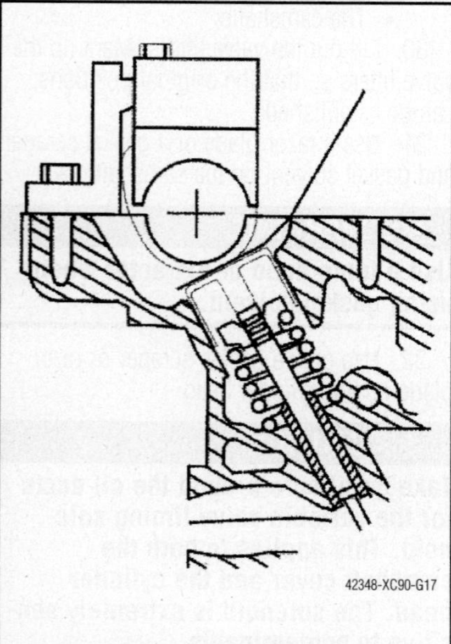

Fig. 51 Checking the valve clearance— 5 and 6-cylinder engines

press 999 5765 at the inlet valves for cylinder 1.

44. Tighten the tool against the cylinder head. Tighten to 13 ft. lbs. (17 Nm).

45. Turn the camshaft until it stops against the camshaft press.

46. Install the upper section of the camshaft press.

47. Tighten the bolt which tensions the camshaft. Tighten to 106 inch lbs. (12 Nm).

➡Measurements should only be taken on a cold engine. A suitable temperature is approximately 68°F (20°C).

48. Using a feeler gauge, press with a finger so that the feeler gauge lies parallel to the upper side of the valve lifter.

49. Move the feeler gauge sideways when taking the reading in order to obtain as accurate a measurement as possible.

50. The valve clearance measured on cold engines (approximately 68°F (20°C) should be:

- Intake valve: 0.008 inch plus or minus 0.001 inch (0.20mm plus or minus 0.03mm)
- Exhaust valve: 0.016 inch plus or minus 0.001 inch (0.30mm plus or minus 0.03mm)

➡The tolerances are less at setting. When checking the valve clearance through the plug hole the tolerances are larger.

51. Differences in valve clearance for different engines/ambient temperatures:

- -0.0004 inch (- 0.01mm) at 59°F (15°C)
- +0.0004 inch (+ 0.01mm) at 77°F (25°C)
- +0.0008 inch (+ 0.02mm) at 86°F (30°C)
- +0.0012 inch (+ 0.03mm) at 95°F (35°C)
- +0.0016 inch (+ 0.04mm) at 113°F (45°C)

52. Correcting measured clearance:

a. Lift out the upper section of the press tool.

b. Lift out the camshaft.

c. Adjust the play by replacing the valve lifters.

d. Other valve lifters are available as replacement part / replacement part kits.

e. Reinstall the camshaft and the upper section of the press tool. Tighten to 106 inch lbs. (12 Nm).

f. Take a new measurement.

53. When the correct valve clearance is reached, remove:

- The press tool 999 5765
- The camshaft

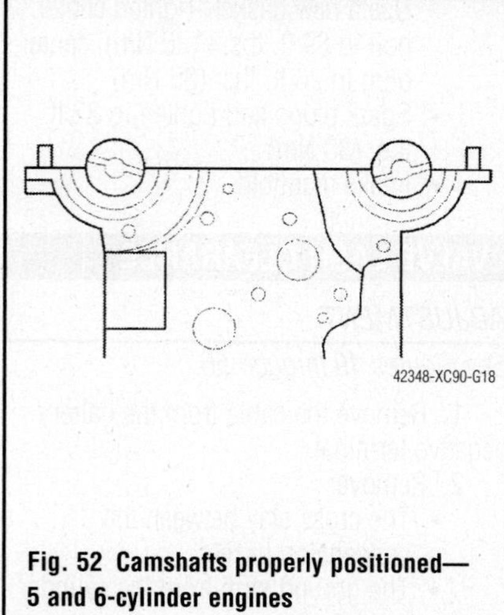

Fig. 52 Camshafts properly positioned— 5 and 6-cylinder engines

- The valve lifters

54. Carefully mark the valve lifters so that exact reinstallation can be carried out.
For example:
Intake side: I1, I2, I3 . . . I10.
Exhaust side: A1, A2, A3 . . . A10.

55. Repeat the procedure for measuring the valve clearance for all cylinders on both the intake and exhaust sides.

56. Lubricate the valve guide wells.

57. Install all the valve lifters.

58. Lubricate the camshaft bearing seats and the upper sides of the valve lifters.

59. Position the intake camshaft. Ensure that the groove at the rear edge of the camshaft is above an imaginary center line.

60. Position the exhaust camshaft. Ensure that the groove at the rear edge of the camshaft is below an imaginary center line.

61. Wipe the oil film off the mating surfaces on the camshaft cover and cylinder head.

62. Install new O-rings around the spark plug wells at the cylinder head.

63. Apply liquid gasket 1161 059 on the camshaft cover. Use roller 951 2767.

➡The surface must be completely covered without any excess.

CAUTION

Ensure that no liquid gasket gets in to the oil ducts.

64. Lubricate the camshaft lobes, the camshaft bearing surfaces and the valve lifters.

65. Install the camshaft cover.

66. Install press tool 999 5454 (2x).

67. Tighten the camshaft cover bolts alternately, keeping it parallel to the cylinder head using the press tools.

Fig. 53 Front seal installation tools—5 and 6-cylinder engines

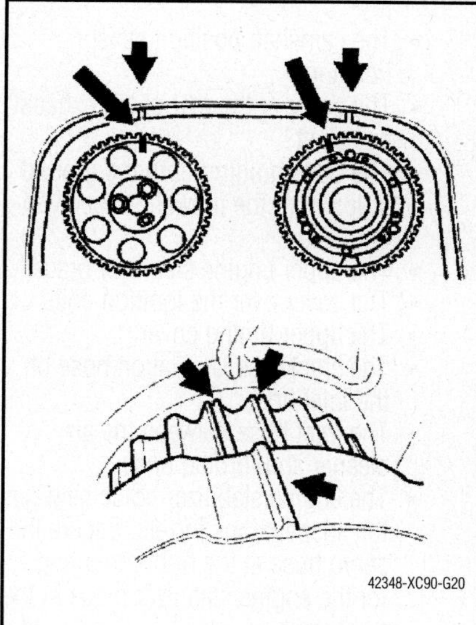

Fig. 54 Timing marks, with variable timing units—5 and 6-cylinder engines

68. Install all the bolts. Tighten the bolts from the middle and outwards.
69. Remove the press tool 999 5454
70. Install:
  - The Variable Valve Timing (VVT) solenoid. Use a new gasket.
  - The spark plugs. Tighten to 22 ft. lbs. (30 Nm)
  - The plugs for the test holes. Tighten to 15 ft. lbs. (20 Nm).
  - The crankcase ventilation hose to the top of the camshaft cover
  - The ignition coils according to the earlier marking
  - The ground terminals between the ignition coils
71. To clean the shaft journal and mating surface, use emery cloth.

➡When cleaning work around the shaft journal, not in and out. It is essential that any residue from the emery cloth and any other contaminants are completely removed before the new sealing ring is installed.

Fig. 55 Tensioning indicator at different temperatures—5 and 6-cylinder engines

72. Use drift 999 5450.
73. Lubricate the surface of the seal that the camshaft rotates against.
74. Press in the seal until the drift bottoms out.

➡If there are wear grooves on the camshaft, the seal can be pressed in a further 0.079 inch (2mm) by reversing the sleeve.

75. Install camshaft adjustment tool 999 5452 at the rear of the camshafts.
76. Check that the bolts securing the adjustment tool to the camshaft are tight.
77. Lift up and position the brake fluid reservoir and the expansion tank on top of the engine.
78. Use drift 999 5718 on camshafts with variable valve timing units. Use drift 999 5719 on camshafts without variable valve timing.
79. Use new seals and lubricate the surface of the seal that the camshaft rotates against.
80. Use the variable valve timing unit/timing belt pulley mounting bolts. Tighten the bolts until the drift bottoms out.
81. Remove the drift.
82. Remove:
  - The mounting bolts for the starter motor. Pull off the starter motor. Place the starter motor to one side
  - The blind cover plug and the seal washer.
83. Turn the crankshaft slightly clockwise.
84. Install the crankshaft stop 999 5451.

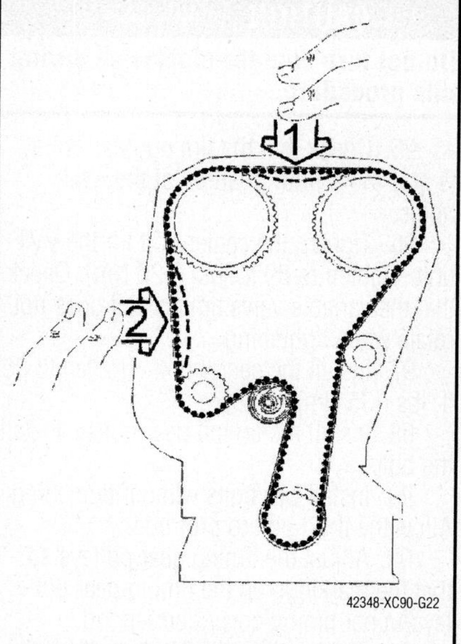

Fig. 56 Checking belt tension—5 and 6-cylinder engines

Ensure that it bottoms out against the cylinder block.
85. Turn the crankshaft counterclockwise until it stops against the crankshaft stop.
86. Check that the marking on the crankshaft timing gear pulley corresponds with the marking on the oil pump.

➡The purpose of the section is to ensure that the VVT unit is correctly positioned and to reset the camshaft timing gear pulley to the correct position using the markings made at the factory. This is to ensure that the conditions are correct for any later fault-tracing.

87. Slacken off, but do not remove the bolts which secure the timing gear pulley to the variable valve timing unit.
88. Press the variable valve timing unit/timing gear onto the camshaft.
89. Install the center bolt which secures the variable valve timing unit to the camshaft. Tighten slightly.
90. Turn the variable valve timing unit counter-clockwise as far as it will go.
91. Remove the center bolt.
92. Position the upper timing cover.
93. Turn the timing gear pulley clockwise until the bolts at the oval holes are in the limit position.
94. Continue turning clockwise until the timing gear pulley marking is 1 tooth before the marking on the upper timing cover.

CAUTION

Do not turn counter-clockwise during this procedure.

95. Check that the timing gear pulley is still in its limit position at the oval holes.
96. Tighten the center bolt for the VVT unit. Tighten to 89 ft. lbs. (120 Nm). Check that the variable valve timing unit does not rotate when tightening.
97. Install the center bolt. Tighten to 26 ft. lbs. (35 Nm).
98. Install the timing gear pulley. Install the bolts.
99. Install two bolts without tightening. Allow the third bolt to protrude.
100. Adjust the timing gear pulleys so that the markings on the timing gear pulleys/upper timing cover correspond.
101. Tighten the center bolt on the belt tensioner. Tighten to 44 inch lbs. (5 Nm).
102. Turn the variable valve timing unit clockwise to the stop.
103. Hold it secure in the limit position.
104. Install the belt in the following order:
    - Crankshaft
    - The idler pulley
    - Intake cam
    - Exhaust cam
    - Water pump
    - Belt tensioner

➡Adjust the timing gear pulleys so that the bolts are not at a limit position in the oval holes. Also check that the markings correspond.

➡This adjustment is always carried out on a cold engine. A suitable temperature is approximately 68°F (20°C).

At higher temperatures (with the engine at operating temperature or a high outside temperature for example) the indicator is further to the right.

The illustration shows the position of the indicator when aligning the timing belt tensioner at different temperatures.

105. Hold the center bolt secure and turn the belt tensioner eccentric counter-clockwise until the tensioner indicator passes the marked position.

➡Check that the variable valve timing unit is in its limit position.

106. Tighten the three bolts at the intake camshaft timing gear pulley. Tighten to 88 inch lbs. (10 Nm).
107. Tighten the three bolts at the exhaust camshaft timing gear pulley. Tighten to 15 ft. lbs. (20 Nm).
108. Turn the eccentric on the belt tensioner back so that the indicator reaches the marked position in the center of the window. Remember to hold the center bolt secure at the same time.
109. Hold the eccentric secure and tighten the center bolt. Tighten to 15 ft. lbs. (20 Nm).
110. Check that the indicator is in the correct position.
111. Remove camshaft adjustment tool 999 5451 and crankshaft stop 999 5452.
112. Install the plug with a new blind cover plug. Tighten to 30 ft. lbs. (40 Nm).
113. Press the timing belt to check that the indicator on the tensioner moves easily.
114. Turn the crankshaft two turns. Check that the markings on the crankshaft timing gear pulley and the camshaft timing gear pulley match up with the markings on the oil pump and upper timing cover respectively.
115. Check that the indicator on the belt tensioner is within the marked position.
116. Remove the upper timing cover.
117. Install:
    - Front timing cover
    - The accessory drive belt
    - The expansion tank
    - The servo oil reservoir
    - The bleed hose for the expansion tank
118. Close the clamp and check that the hoses lie correctly.
119. Connect the connectors for:
    - The ABS sensor by the right suspension turret
    - The coolant level sensor in the expansion tank
120. Install:
    - The starter motor
    - The plastic nuts for the cover in the fender liner
    - The right front wheel
121. Install:
    - The trigger wheel.

➡Ensure that the trigger wheel is correctly positioned against the camshaft.

- The camshaft position sensor housing
- The cover at the rear of the exhaust camshaft
- The bolts holding both the ground strips from the firewall to the cylinder head
- The upper engine stabilizer brace
- The cover over the ignition coils
- The upper timing cover
- The crankcase ventilation hose on the inlet hose
- The inlet hose between the air cleaner and throttle body
- The engine stabilizer brace between the suspensions turrets. Secure the servo hose at the right mounting for the engine stabilizer brace in the bodywork.
- The cable to the battery negative terminal.

122. Check the level in the expansion tank and the brake fluid reservoir.
123. Test drive the engine until the thermostat opens and check for any leakage.

ENGINE PERFORMANCE & EMISSION CONTROLS

COMPONENT LOCATIONS

See Figure 57.

The component location for 2.5L engines.

ACCELERATOR PEDAL POSITION (APP) SENSOR

LOCATION

The Accelerator Pedal Position (APP) sensor is located inside the vehicle and is integral to the accelerator pedal.

REMOVAL & INSTALLATION

See Figure 58.

1. Remove the Accelerator Pedal Position (APP) sensor connector.
2. Remove the 3 mounting nuts.
3. Remove the APP sensor.

To install:

4. Install the APP sensor and tighten the mounting nuts to 7 ft. lbs. (10 Nm).
5. Reconnect the APP sensor connector.

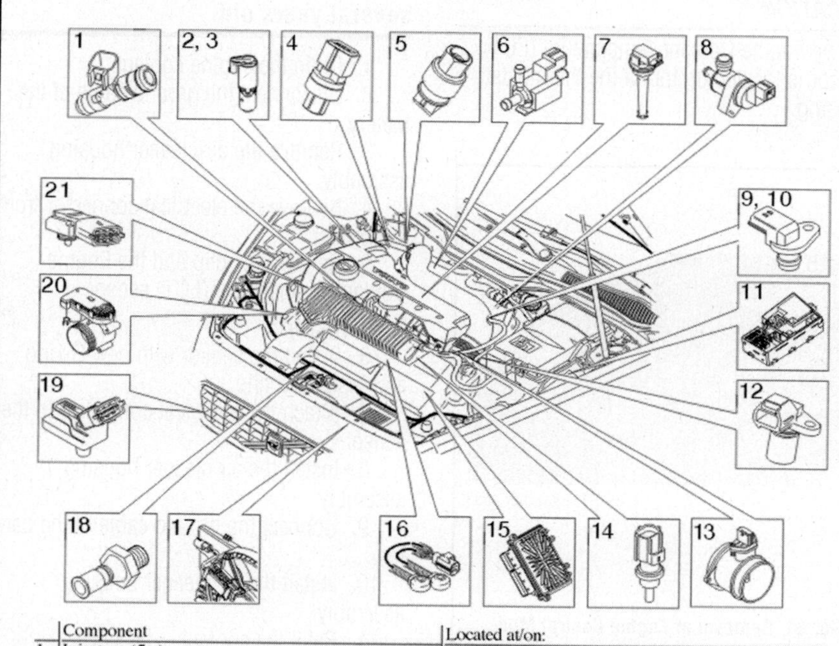

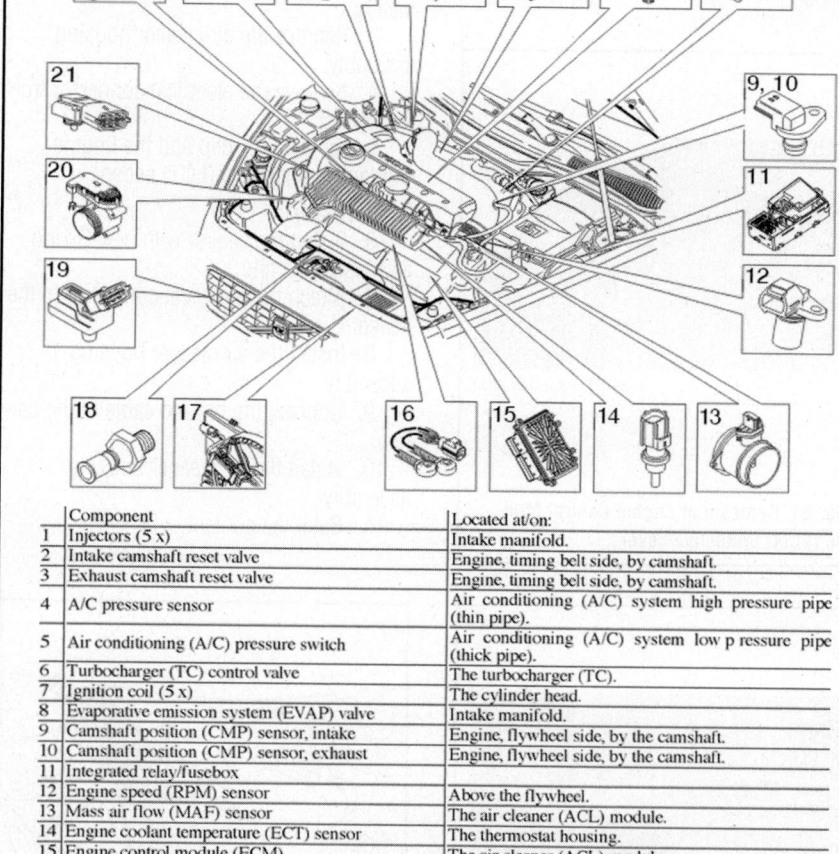

	Component	Located at/on:
1	Injectors (5 x)	Intake manifold.
2	Intake camshaft reset valve	Engine, timing belt side, by camshaft.
3	Exhaust camshaft reset valve	Engine, timing belt side, by camshaft.
4	A/C pressure sensor	Air conditioning (A/C) system high pressure pipe (thin pipe).
5	Air conditioning (A/C) pressure switch	Air conditioning (A/C) system low p ressure pipe (thick pipe).
6	Turbocharger (TC) control valve	The turbocharger (TC).
7	Ignition coil (5 x)	The cylinder head.
8	Evaporative emission system (EVAP) valve	Intake manifold.
9	Camshaft position (CMP) sensor, intake	Engine, flywheel side, by the camshaft.
10	Camshaft position (CMP) sensor, exhaust	Engine, flywheel side, by the camshaft.
11	Integrated relay/fusebox	
12	Engine speed (RPM) sensor	Above the flywheel.
13	Mass air flow (MAF) sensor	The air cleaner (ACL) module.
14	Engine coolant temperature (ECT) sensor	The thermostat housing.
15	Engine control module (ECM)	The air cleaner (ACL) module.
16	Knock sensor (KS)	The cylinder block under the air clean er (ACL) module.
17	Engine cooling fan (FC) control module	
18	Oil pressure switch	Lower front edge of the engine.
19	Boost pressure sensor	The charge air cooler (CAC) upper right-hand section.
20	Throttle unit	The engine intake manifold.
21	Fuel pressure sensor/fuel temperature sensor	Fuel rail right face.

22205_VOLC_G0081

Fig. 57 Engine component locations

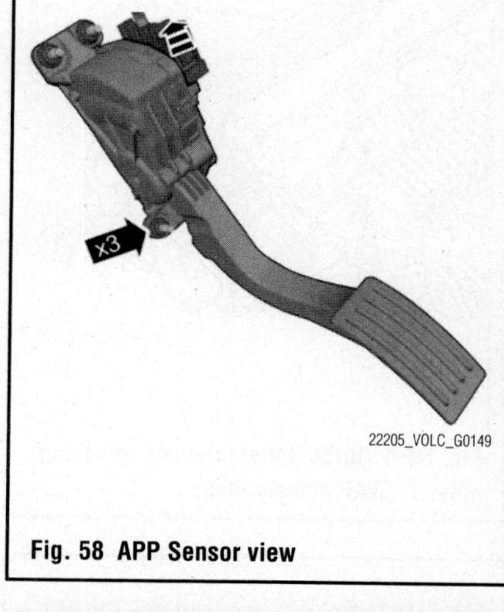

22205_VOLC_G0149

Fig. 58 APP Sensor view

CAMSHAFT POSITION (CMP) SENSOR

LOCATION

The Camshaft Position (CMP) sensor is located in the valve cover under the coil cover.

REMOVAL & INSTALLATION

1. Remove the intake manifold between the Manifold Absolute Pressure (MAF) sensor and the turbocharger. Slacken off the hose clamps and the screws. Place the manifold to one side.
2. Remove the cover over the ignition coils.
3. Remove the Camshaft Position (CMP) sensor.

To install:

4. Install the camshaft sensor.
5. Tighten the screw to 66 inch. lbs. (7.5 Nm)
6. Install the ignition coil cover.
7. Install intake manifold between MAF and turbo.

CRANKSHAFT POSITION (CKP) SENSOR

LOCATION

The Crankshaft Position (CKP) sensor is located under the upper intake manifold.

REMOVAL & INSTALLATION

See Figures 59 and 60.

1. Remove the air cleaner module assembly.
2. Remove turbo outlet air tube..
3. Remove EVAP canister hose from the intake manifold.

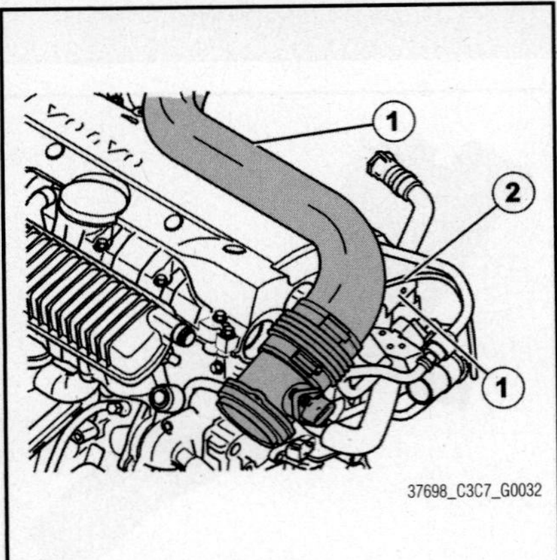

Fig. 59 1. Turbo outlet tube and attaching nuts. 2. EVAP canister hose.

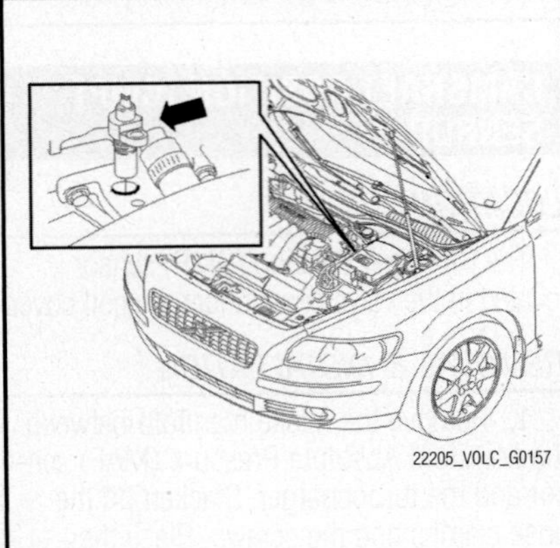

Fig. 60 Crankshaft position sensor location

4. Remove brake booster vacuum hose.
5. Remove nut for Crankshaft Position (CKP) sensor.
6. Hold the radiator hose aside and disconnect the electrical connector.
7. Lift up Crankshaft Position (CKP) sensor.

To install:

8. Install the CKP sensor and tighten the mounting nut to 77 inch lbs. (2 Nm).
9. Reverse the removal procedure to complete the installation.
10. Start the engine and check the function.

ELECTRONIC CONTROL MODULE (ECM)

LOCATION

The Engine Control Module (ECM) is mounted in the air cleaner module.

REMOVAL & INSTALLATION

See Figures 61 and 62.

1. Turn ignition switch to off position.
2. Disconnect negative battery terminal.
3. Remove Engine Control Module (ECM) protective cover.
4. Disconnect wire harness from (ECM).
5. Remove 4 bolts securing (ECM).

To install:

6. Reverse removal procedure to install.

ENGINE COOLANT TEMPERATURE (ECT) SENSOR

LOCATION

The Engine Coolant Temperature (ECT) sensor is located on top of the thermostat housing.

Fig. 61 Removal of Engine Control Module (ECM) protective cover

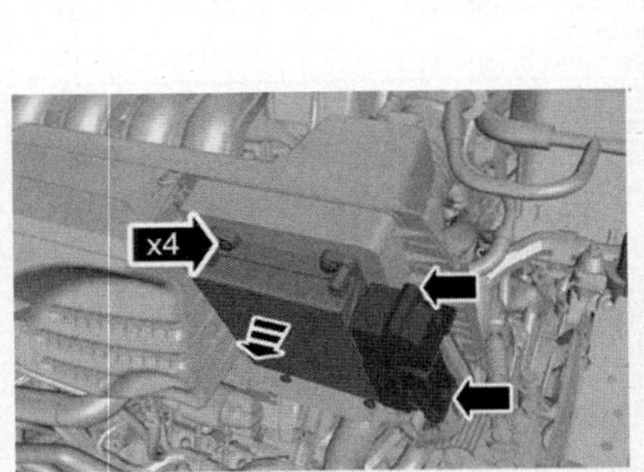

Fig. 62 Engine Control Module (ECM) view

REMOVAL & INSTALLATION

See Figure 63.

⁂ CAUTION

Never open, service or drain the radiator or cooling system when hot; serious burns can occur from the steam and hot coolant. Also, when draining engine coolant, keep in mind that cats and dogs are attracted to ethylene glycol antifreeze and could drink any that is left in an uncovered container or in puddles on the ground. This will prove fatal in sufficient quantities. Always drain coolant into a sealable container. Coolant should be reused unless it is contaminated or is several years old.

1. Drain the engine coolant.
2. Disconnect the ground cable of the battery.
3. Remove the air cleaner housing assembly.
4. Remove the electrical connector from the sensor.
5. Remove the clip and the Engine Coolant Temperature (ECT) sensor.

To install:

6. Install the sensor with new O-ring and install the clip.
7. Attach the electrical connector to the sensor.
8. Install the air cleaner housing assembly.
9. Connect the ground cable of the battery.
10. Install the air cleaner housing assembly.
11. Refill the coolant.

Fig. 63 Coolant temperature sensor

HEATED OXYGEN (HO2S) SENSOR

LOCATION

The front Heated Oxygen (HO2S) sensor is mounted in the exhaust manifold converter sub-assembly.

The rear HO2S sensor is mounted in the rear converter sub-assembly.

REMOVAL & INSTALLATION

Bank 1, Sensor 1

See Figure 64.

1. Slacken off and disconnect the connector for the front Heated Oxygen (HO2S) sensor.
2. Raise the vehicle.
3. Remove the lower engine cover.
4. Disconnect the sensor harness.
5. Remove the front HO2S. Use Proper tool.

To install:

6. Install the front HO2S. Tighten to 33 ft. lbs. (45 Nm).
7. Install the lower engine cover.
8. Reconnect the connector for the front HO2S.

Bank 1, Sensor 2

1. Raise the vehicle.
2. Remove the lower engine cover.
3. Raise the vehicle. Disconnect the Heated Oxygen (HO2S) sensor cable harness above the sub-frame.
4. Disconnect the cable harness from the SIPS member.
5. Remove the screw for the cable harness clamp in the three-way catalytic converter.
6. Remove the rear HO2S. Use Proper tool.

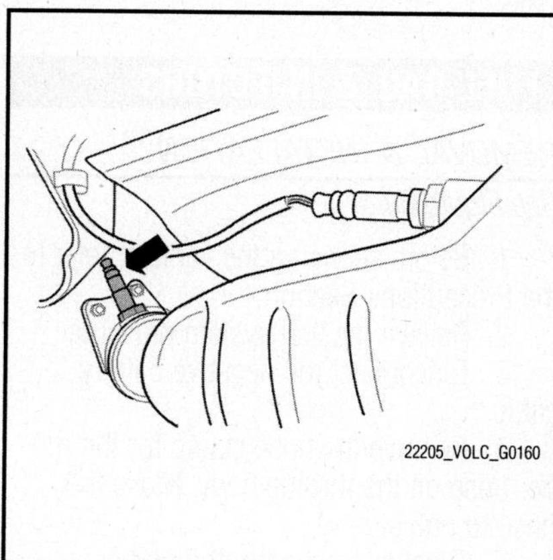

Fig. 64 Front Heated Oxygen (HO2S) sensor location view

To install:

7. Install the rear HO2S. Tighten to 33 ft. lbs. (45 Nm).
8. Reconnect the HO2S cable harness above the sub-frame.
9. Reconnect the cable harness from the SIPS member.
10. Install the lower engine cover.
11. Reconnect the cable harness clamp in the three-way catalytic converter. Tighten the screw.

KNOCK SENSOR (KS)

LOCATION

The Knock (KS) sensors are mounted on the left and the right front of the engine block.

REMOVAL & INSTALLATION

1. Remove the air filter module.
2. Remove the screws for the Knock (KS) sensor.
3. Remove KS.
4. Disconnect the KS connector.

To install:

5. Reconnect the KS connector.
6. Install the KS.
7. Tighten the mounting bolt to 15 ft. lbs. (20 Nm)

MALFUNCTION INDICATOR LIGHT

RESET PROCEDURE

1. Scan and check for any trouble codes present. Record present codes.
2. Disconnect the negative battery cable.
3. If the battery is disconnected or the power is cut and the vehicle is equipped with remote of the parking heater, the personal code is reset to the factory value (1234).

➡If the malfunction indicator light in the combined instrument panel illuminates, any diagnostic trouble codes for the engine management system must be read out and remedied before the battery is disconnected.

4. Initiate the central locking system and interior lighting by unlocking the vehicle with the remote control, key or via VIDA vehicle communication.
5. Initiate window positions. See: VIDA Car communication, Initiating the window position.

➡If the battery was disconnected, the engine may need to run for a few minutes before it runs smoothly.

MASS AIR FLOW SENSOR

REMOVAL & INSTALLATION

See Figure 65.

1. Loosen hose clamp on mass air flow.(MAF) sensor.
2. Remove EVAP canister hose from air inlet tube.
3. Remove 2 screws securing the air inlet tube and move tube aside.
4. Disconnect electrical connector from (MAF).
5. Remove screws for the (MAF) and pull out the (MAF).

To install:

6. Reverse removal procedure to install.

➡Lubricate the O–ring with petroleum jelly or an equivalent prior to installation.

THROTTLE POSITION SENSOR

LOCATION

The Throttle Position (TPS) sensor is an integral component of the Electronic Throttle Module (ETM) assembly.

REMOVAL & INSTALLATION

See Figure 66.

1. Disconnect the negative battery cable.
2. Detach and move aside the air inlet tube from the electronic throttle module (ETM).

Fig. 65 Removal of air tube screws

3. Disconnect the connector for the (ETM).
4. Remove the screws for the (ETM). Lift out the assembly.

To install:

5. Install the (ETM) assembly with a new gasket.
6. Install new screws and tighten the screws to 6 ft. lbs. (8 Nm).
7. Connect the negative battery cable.
8. Install the air inlet tube.

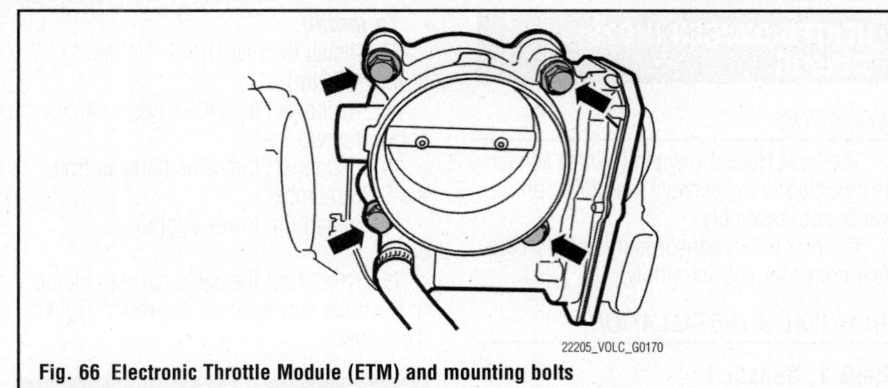

Fig. 66 Electronic Throttle Module (ETM) and mounting bolts

FUEL

GASOLINE FUEL INJECTION SYSTEM

FUEL SYSTEM SERVICE PRECAUTIONS

Safety is the most important factor when performing not only fuel system maintenance but any type of maintenance. Failure to conduct maintenance and repairs in a safe manner may result in serious personal injury or death. Maintenance and testing of the vehicle's fuel system components can be accomplished safely and effectively by adhering to the following rules and guidelines.

- To avoid the possibility of fire and personal injury, always disconnect the negative battery cable unless the repair or test procedure requires that battery voltage be applied.
- Always relieve the fuel system pressure prior to disconnecting any fuel system component (injector, fuel rail, pressure regulator, etc.), fitting or fuel line connection. Exercise extreme caution whenever relieving fuel system pressure to avoid exposing skin, face and eyes to fuel spray. Please be advised that fuel under pressure may penetrate the skin or any part of the body that it contacts.
- Always place a shop towel or cloth around the fitting or connection prior to loosening to absorb any excess fuel due to spillage. Ensure that all fuel spillage (should it occur) is quickly removed from engine surfaces. Ensure that all fuel soaked cloths or towels are deposited into a suitable waste container.
- Always keep a dry chemical (Class B) fire extinguisher near the work area.
- Do not allow fuel spray or fuel vapors to come into contact with a spark or open flame.
- Always use a back-up wrench when loosening and tightening fuel line connection fittings. This will prevent unnecessary stress and torsion to fuel line piping.
- Always replace worn fuel fitting O-rings with new Do not substitute fuel hose or equivalent where fuel pipe is installed.

Before servicing the vehicle, make sure to also refer to the precautions in the beginning of this section as well.

RELIEVING FUEL SYSTEM PRESSURE

1. Before servicing the vehicle, refer to the Precautions Section.
2. Remove the fuse or the fuel pump electrical connector.
3. Start the engine and allow it to idle until is stops.
4. Turn the engine using the starter motor for approximately 5 seconds until the pressure in the fuel rail has been released.

ADJUSTMENTS

IDLE SPEED

The Idle speed is controlled by the ECM.

FUEL FILTER

REMOVAL & INSTALLATION

See Figure 67.

➡The fuel filter is either on the left side of the firewall or next to the fuel pump near the left side of the fuel tank.

1. Before servicing the vehicle, refer to the Precautions Section.
2. Relieve the fuel system pressure.
3. Remove or disconnect the following:
   - Negative battery cable
   - Fuel filler cap
   - Fuel lines from the fuel filter
   - Fuel filter from the bracket

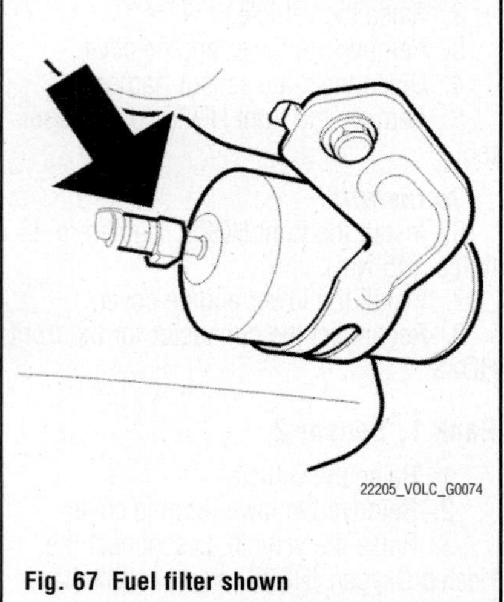

Fig. 67 Fuel filter shown

To install:

4. Install or connect the following:
   - Fuel filter to the bracket
   - Fuel lines to the fuel filter
   - Fuel filler cap
   - Negative battery cable
5. Start the engine and check for leaks.

FUEL RAIL & INJECTORS

REMOVAL & INSTALLATION

See Figure 68.

1. Before servicing the vehicle, refer to the Precautions Section.
2. Relieve the fuel system pressure.
3. Disconnect the negative battery cable.
4. Remove the hose clamp for the rubber hose on the throttle body. Move the hose to one side.
5. Disconnect the throttle body connector.
6. Remove the 6 screws for the upper

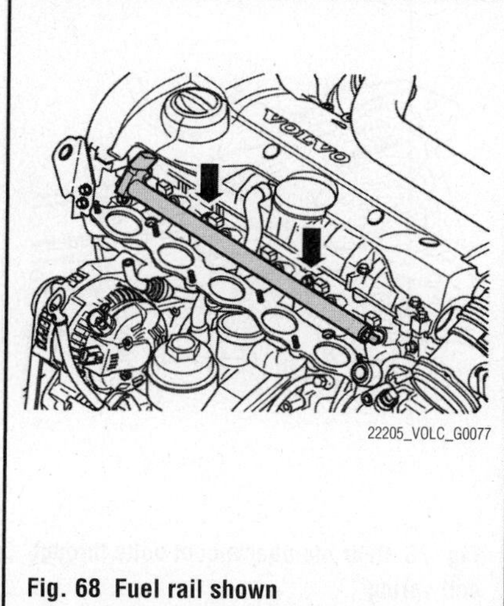

Fig. 68 Fuel rail shown

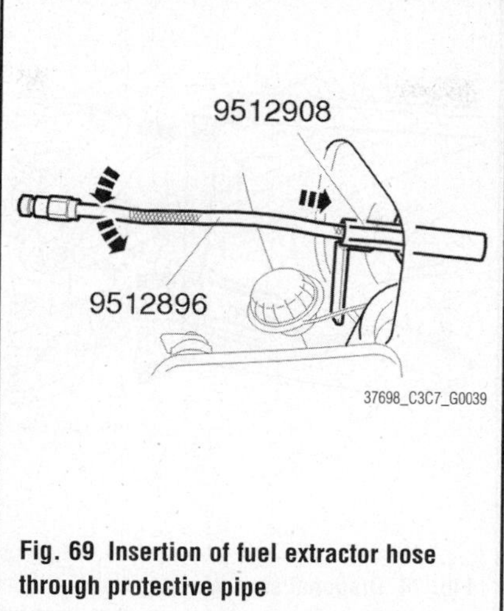

Fig. 69 Insertion of fuel extractor hose through protective pipe

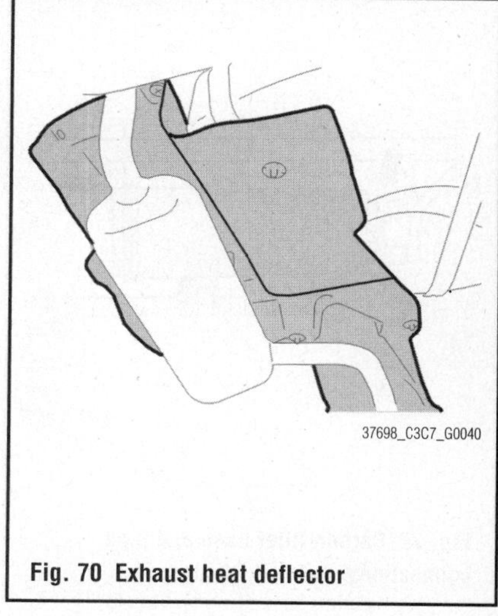

Fig. 70 Exhaust heat deflector

section of the intake manifold. Move the manifold to one side.

7. Disconnect the connector for the fuel pressure sensor and the connector for the injectors.
8. Remove the 2 fuel rail mounting screws.
9. Spray with universal oil or similar around the injector nozzle at the terminal on the intake manifold.
10. Gently work the fuel rail and injector nozzles loose. Disconnect the fuel line to the fuel rail.
11. Press in the two blue clips on the fuel rail.
12. Pull the fuel line out of the fuel rail.
13. Remove the screws holding the mounting rail to the fuel rail.
14. Remove the mounting rail.
15. Remove the injector.

To install:

16. Installation is in reverse of the removal procedure, note the following:
    a. Tighten the fuel rail bolts to 88 inch lbs. (10 Nm).
17. Start the engine and check for leaks.

FUEL TANK

DRAINING

See Figure 69.

✲✲ WARNING

Explosion risk. Use of a fresh air mask is highly recommended.

✲✲ WARNING

Always follow the safety recommendations of the fuel extractor you are using to avoid the potential of fire or explosion.

1. Disconnect negative battery cable from battery.
2. Insert drain hose through protective pipe in to fuel tank, using a twisting motion on hose while inserting to fuel filler.
3. Connect the hose to fuel extractor and drain fuel until air comes out.
4. Remove extractor hose and protective pipe.

➡Use care in removing the drain hose from the fuel fill to prevent damage to the evacuation valve.

REMOVAL & INSTALLATION

✲✲ CAUTION

Observe all applicable safety precautions when working around the fuel system. system. Whenever servicing the fuel system, always work in a well-ventilated area. Do not allow fuel spray or vapors to come in contact with a spark or open flame. Keep a dry chemical fire extinguisher near the work area. Always keep fuel in a container specifically designed for fuel storage; also, always properly seal fuel containers to avoid the possibility of fire or explosion.

C30 Models

See Figures 70 through 73.

1. Before servicing the vehicle, refer to the Precautions Section.
2. Relieve the fuel system pressure.
3. Drain the fuel tank.
4. Remove the seven plastic nuts securing the exhaust heat deflector and lower down the deflector.
5. Disconnect fuel filler and vent hose from the fuel tank.
6. Remove the carbon filter container hose and pipes.
7. Install suitable hydraulic jack under the fuel tank.
8. Disconnect fuel line from front of tank.
9. Remove 3 bolts securing the fuel tank straps then lower the tank slightly.
10. Disconnect fuel pump module electrical connector.
11. Lower the fuel tank and remove from hydraulic jack..
12. Remove fuel pump module from the tank.

To install:

13. Install or reconnect the following.
    - New O–ring.
    - Fuel pump module assembly.

➡Make sure the marking line on the fuel pump module is aligned with the marking on the tank.

- Large plastic retaining nut using Volvo special tool 999-7111 or equivalent.

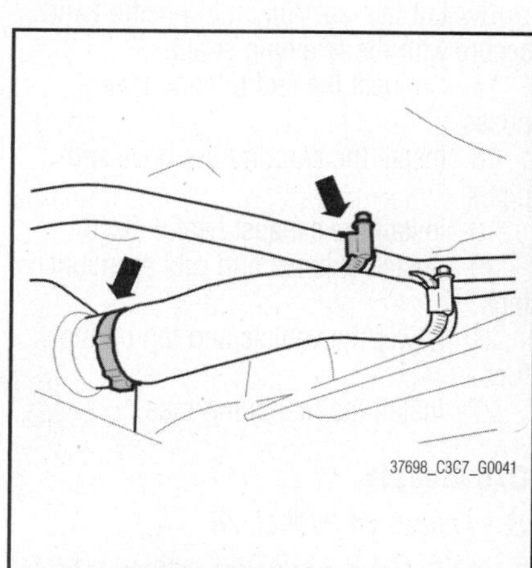

Fig. 71 Fuel filler and vent hose connections

Fig. 72 Carbon filter hose and pipe connections

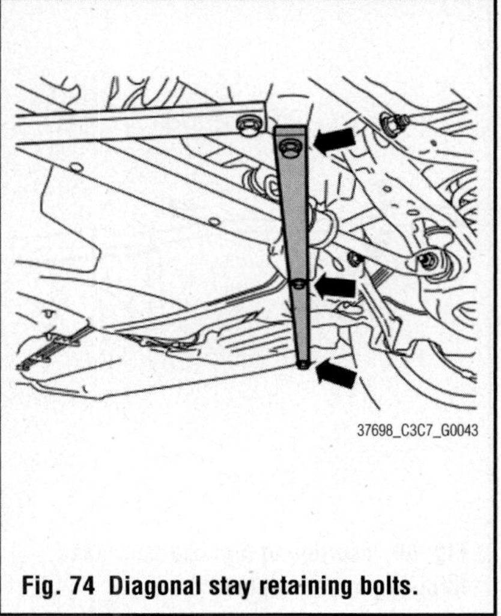

Fig. 74 Diagonal stay retaining bolts.

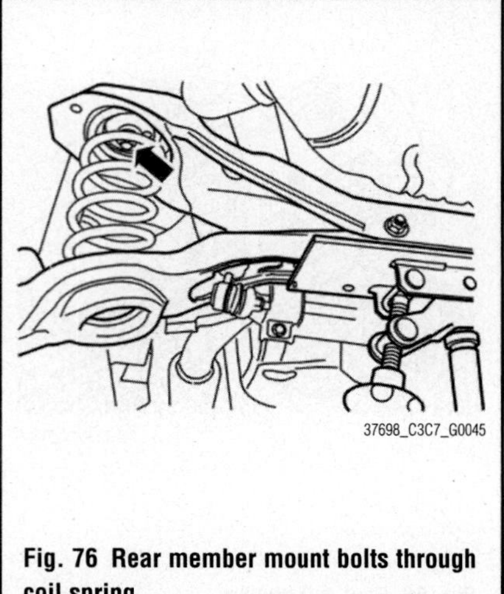

Fig. 76 Rear member mount bolts through coil spring

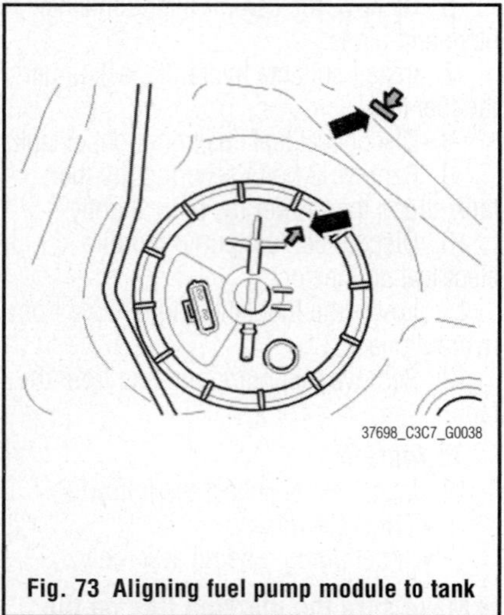

Fig. 73 Aligning fuel pump module to tank

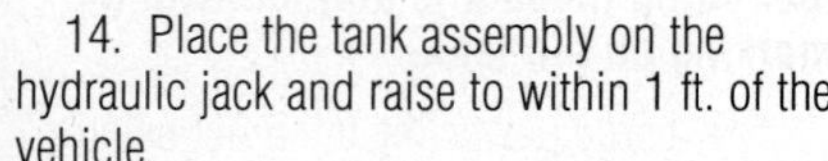

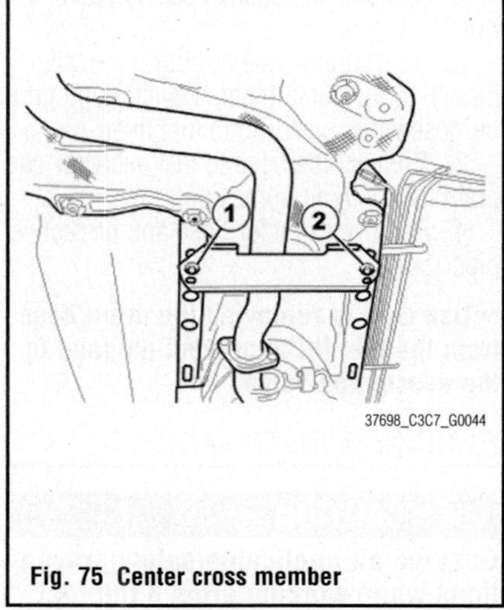

Fig. 75 Center cross member

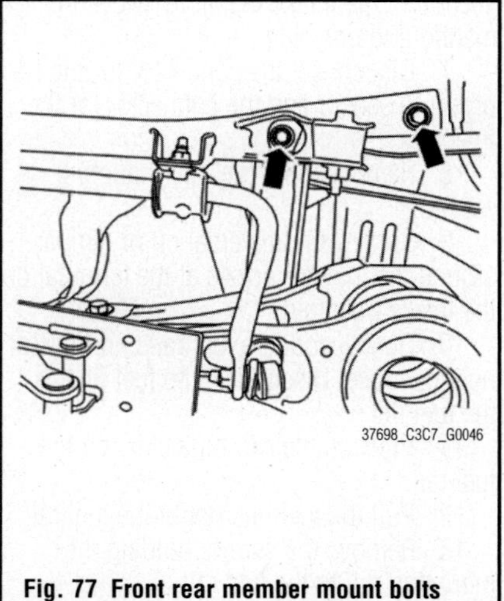

Fig. 77 Front rear member mount bolts

14. Place the tank assembly on the hydraulic jack and raise to within 1 ft. of the vehicle.
15. Connect the electrical connector to the fuel pump module.
16. Lift the tank fully into position and secure with the retaining straps.
17. Connect the fuel filler and vent hoses.
18. Install the carbon filter hose and pipes.
19. Install the exhaust heat deflector.
20. Install exhaust and rubber mountings.
21. Lower the vehicle and top up the fuel.
22. Install the fuel pump fuse.

C70 Models

See Figures 74 through 78.

1. Before servicing the vehicle, refer to the Precautions Section.
2. Relieve the fuel system pressure.
3. Drain the fuel tank.
4. Remove the diagonal stays under the sub-frame.
5. Remove two nuts for the front exhaust pipe.
6. Remove center cross member.
7. Remove rubber exhaust hanger from front side of rear suspension.
8. Remove rear muffler rubber hangers and position exhaust aside.
9. Remove left hand side air baffle.
10. Remove both rear shock absorber lower mounting bolts.
11. Position jack stand against rear member.
12. Pull brake hose out of its bracket on both sides.
13. Remove rear member mounting bolts on both sides.
14. Lower the rear member assembly approximately 2 in.

**** CAUTION**

Ensure that no cables or hoses are put under strain or trapped when lowering the rear member.

15. Remove the five plastic nuts retaining the exhaust heat shield
16. Remove fuel line from tank.
17. Remove the fuel filler hose.
18. Apply mobile jack under the fuel tank.
19. Remove three tank strap bolts.
20. Remove the tank straps and lower the tank slightly.
21. Disconnect the fuel level sensor wire connector.
22. Disconnect quick release the fuel line from the sender.
23. Lower the tank and remove the fuel pump module from tank.

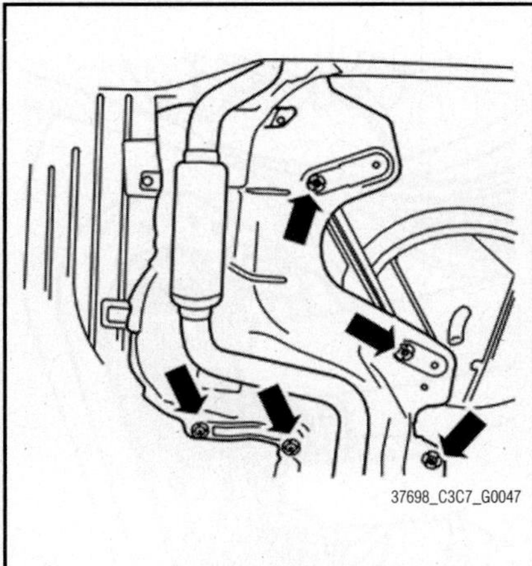

Fig. 78 Location of five plastic retaining nuts

To install:

24. Transfer the fuel pump module to the new tank.
   - New O-ring.
   - Fuel pump module assembly.

➡Make sure the marking line on the fuel pump module is aligned with the marking on the tank.

25. Raise fuel tank into place and reverse the removal procedures.
26. Top off the fuel tank.
27. Install the fuel pump fuse and check for any leaks and proper operation.

Fig. 79 Throttle body location—5-Cylinder Engines

THROTTLE BODY

REMOVAL & INSTALLATION

See Figure 79.

1. Before servicing the vehicle, refer to the Precautions Section.
2. Remove or disconnect the following:
   - The negative battery terminal.
   - The air intake between the front cover plate and the air cleaner housing.
   - The charge air pipe between the charge air cooler and the electronic throttle body.
3. Remove the throttle body:
   a. Disconnect the connector for the throttle body.
   b. Remove the 4 bolts from the throttle body.
   c. Lift out the throttle body and discard the gasket.

To install:

➡Ensure that the surfaces between the throttle body and the intake manifold are clean.

4. Install electronic throttle body using a new gasket. Tighten the 4 bolts to 88 inch lbs. (10 Nm).
5. Install the charge air pipe between the electronic throttle body module and the charge air cooler.

➡Heat the pipe at the connections to facilitate installation.

6. Install the intake pipe between the front cover plate and the air cleaner housing.
7. Start the engine and check the function of the electronic throttle body module.

➡After replacing the throttle unit, the throttle unit must be adapted using the vehicle communication input: Adaptation of the electronic throttle unit. Remedy as necessary.

HEATING & AIR CONDITIONING SYSTEM

BLOWER MOTOR

REMOVAL & INSTALLATION

See Figures 80 and 81.

1. Before servicing the vehicle, refer to the Precautions Section.
2. Remove or disconnect the following to gain access to blower motor:
   - The negative battery cable
   - The dashboard.
   - The rear air quality sensor (AQS)
   - The recirculation door actuator wire connector.
   - The recirculation door actuator.
   - The three screws for the air distribution damper cover.
   - The cover for the air distribution damper.
3. Removal of blower motor
   - The blower motor electrical connector.
   - Depress lock button and turn fan motor counter-clockwise approximately [[Q]] turn.
   - Remove blower motor from housing.

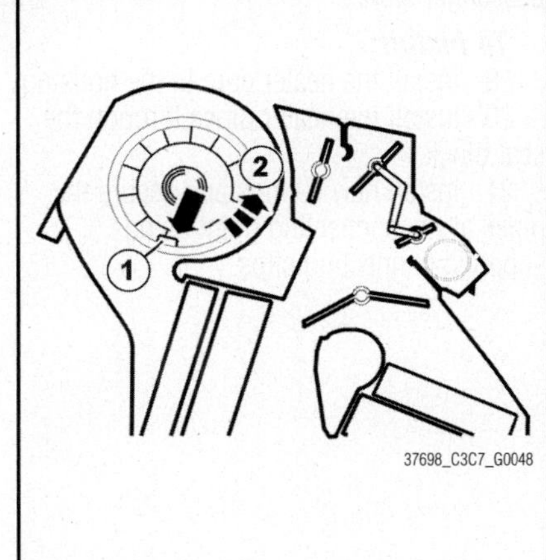

Fig. 80 Blower motor lock button.

To install:

4. Installation is the reverse of removal.

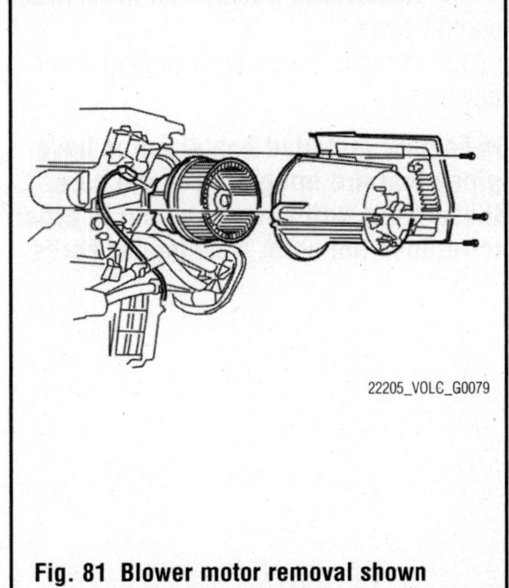

Fig. 81 Blower motor removal shown

HEATER CORE

REMOVAL & INSTALLATION

See Figures 82 through 84.

1. Before servicing the vehicle, refer to the Precautions Section.

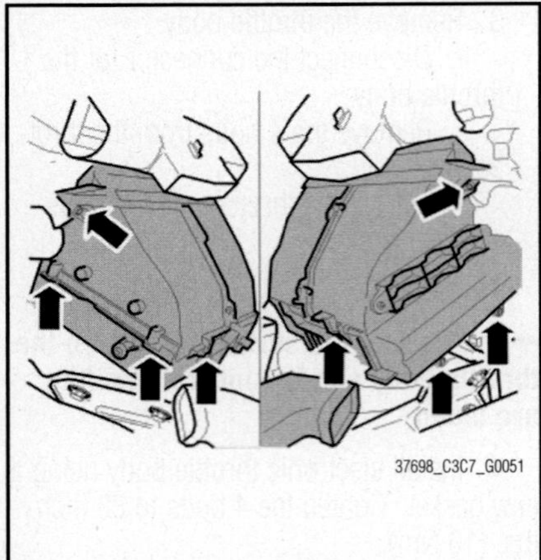

Fig. 82 Arrows indicate location of climate control cover attaching screws

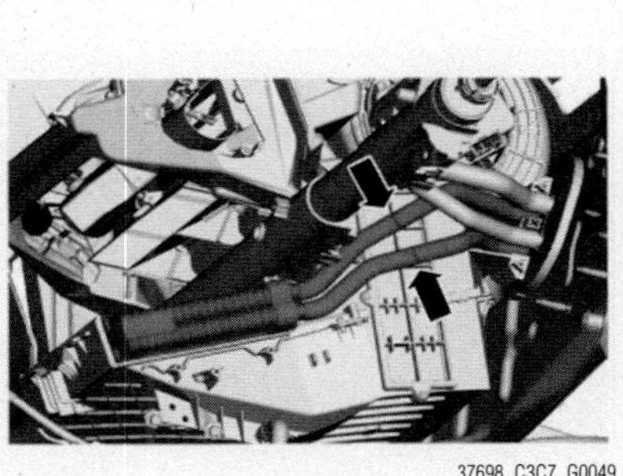

Fig. 83 Exploded view of the area to cut heater pipes

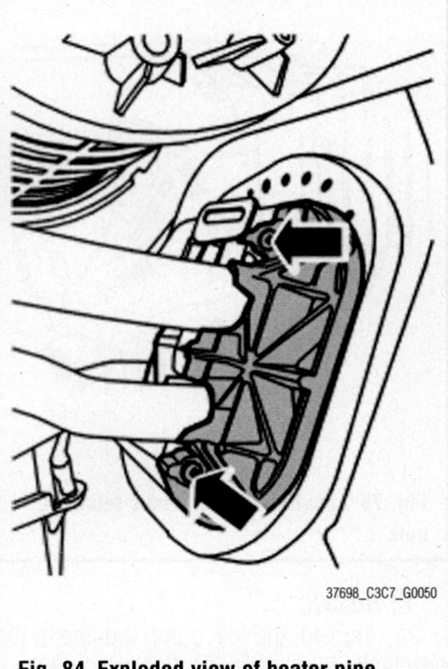

Fig. 84 Exploded view of heater pipe sealing block

2. Disconnect the negative battery cable.
3. Drain the cooling system into a clean container for reuse.
4. Disconnect the heater hoses from the heater core by turning each heater hose counter-clockwise and pulling the hose from the firewall connection.
5. Remove the center console.
6. Remove the glove box.
7. Remove the center control panel from its bracket but allow to hang from wiring harness.
8. Remove the brackets at both sides of the climate control unit and the three screws per bracket.
9. Remove the lower air duct.
10. Remove eight screws for the climate control cover.
11. Remove the cover by pulling cover downwards .

➡Factory installed heater cores have pipes that are integrated to the core. these pipes will need to be cut in order to remove the core. New heater cores are supplied with a service kit that has separate pipes for the installation process.

12. Place an absorbent towel to catch spilt coolant under the cutting area.
13. Cut or saw off heater pipes
14. Push the cut ends towards engine compartment.
15. Remove the two screws at the firewall to separate heater pipe sealing block.
16. Pull the heater pipes through the sealing block.
17. Plug /seal the heater core pipes at the heater core to avoid spilling of coolant when removing the core.
18. Angle the heater core up at the rear edge. Lift out the heater core towards the passenger side.

To install:

19. Install the heater core to the housing.
20. Install the heater pipes through the seal block.
21. Install new o-rings and secure the pipes at the connecting point using supplied connecting clips.

➡The clips only fit one way, when securing the clips a click noise must be heard

22. Install the climate control cover.
23. Install lower air duct.
24. Install the center control panel.
25. Install the center console.
26. Install heater hoses to the pipes.
27. Tighten the radiator drain plug.
28. Refill the cooling system.
29. Before installing the glove box check that the coupling does not leak.
30. Install the glove box.
31. Connect the negative battery cable.
32. Operate the engine to normal operating temperatures; then, check the climate control operation and double check for any leaks.

STEERING

POWER STEERING GEAR

REMOVAL & INSTALLATION

See Figure 85.

1. Before servicing the vehicle, refer to the precautions in the beginning of the section.

➡Ensure the steering wheel is set to the 'straight ahead' position and remove the key so the steering wheel lock engages.

2. Remove the left front wheel and measure and record the length of the tie rod in relation to the steering gear housing.
3. Remove or disconnect the following:
   - Left side soundproofing panel
   - Left front wheel
   - Steering shaft from the steering gear
   - Sub-frame
   - Powering steering hoses from the steering gear
4. Slacken off the nut for the outer steering arm. Press the steering arm out of the wheel spindle using special tool 951-2945 or equivalent.
5. Remove the steering gear.

To install:

6. Install or connect the following:
   - Steering gear
   - Outer steering arm; tighten nuts to 37 ft. lbs. (50 Nm)
   - Power steering hoses using new O-rings
   - Sub-frame
   - Steering shaft to the steering gear
   - Wheel
   - Soundproofing panel
7. Fill and bleed the power steering system.

POWER STEERING PUMP

BLEEDING

⁂ WARNING

Avoid skin contact with the oil.

1. Before servicing the vehicle, refer to the Precautions Section
2. With engine off, turn the steering wheel fully to the right and left several times.

➡Do not allow the fluid level in the reservoir tank to go below the MIN level line. Check and add fluid as needed.

3. Run the engine at idle speed. Turn the steering wheel fully to the right and then fully to the left. Hold for about three seconds. Check for fluid leakage.
4. Repeat the above step several times at three second intervals.

➡Do not hold the steering wheel in the locked position for more than ten seconds.

5. Check for air bubbles or cloudy fluid. If found, repeat the bleeding procedure.
6. Stop the engine and check the fluid level. Fill as required.

FLUID FILL PROCEDURE

See Figure 86.

⁂ WARNING

Avoid skin contact with the oil.

1. Remove the headlight.
2. Check the oil level by placing a work light above the power steering pump and check the oil level through the hole in the body, across from and above the power steering pump.
3. Remove steering reservoir cap.
4. Fill power steering fluid as needed.

To install:

5. Install steering reservoir cap.
6. Install the headlight.

REMOVAL & INSTALLATION

See Figures 87 and 88.

⁂ WARNING

Avoid skin contact with the oil.

➡The power steering pump is an integrated component of the electrical power steering module (EPS) and is not available as an individual component, and it requires programming for proper function.

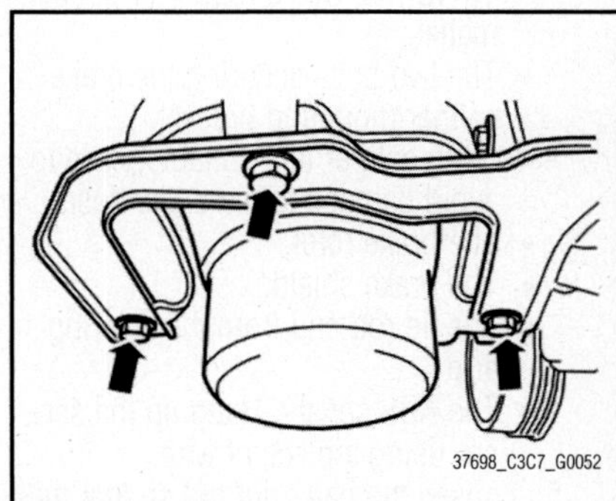

Fig. 87 Location of P/S pump/module mounting bolts.

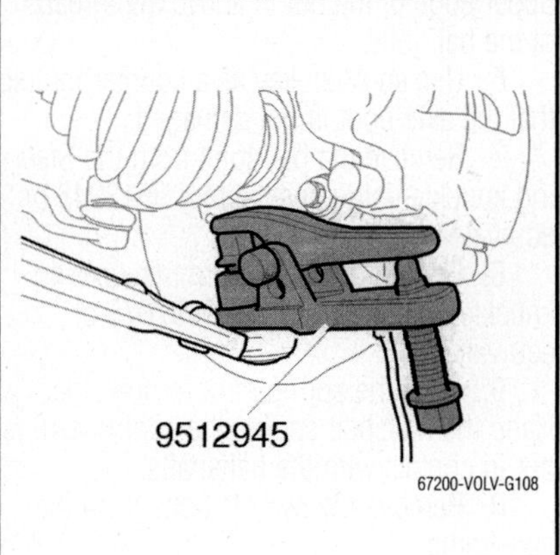

Fig. 85 Pull the steering arm from the wheel spindle.

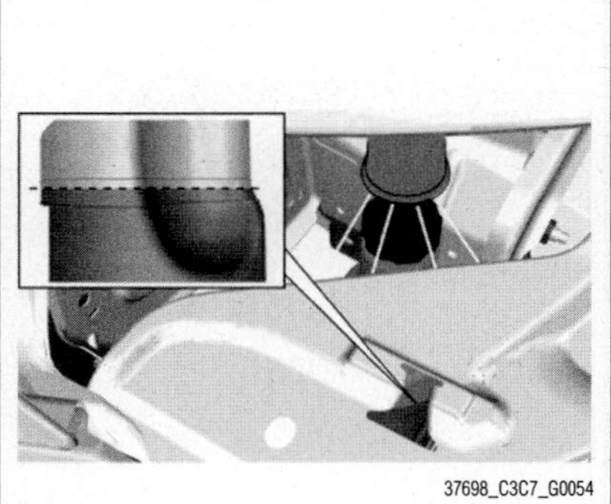

Fig. 86 Proper fill level as seen through headlamp opening

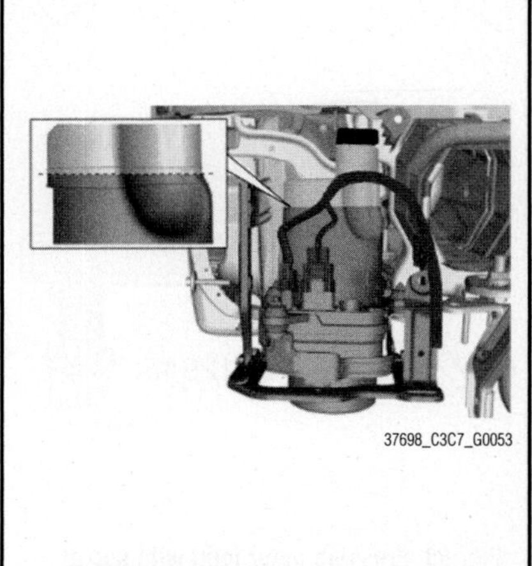

Fig. 88 Proper fill level

1. Before servicing the vehicle, refer to the Precautions Section.
2. Disconnect negative battery cable.
3. Remove right side headlamp assembly.
4. Remove bumper cover.
5. Siphon the P/S fluid from the reservoir into suitable drain pan.
6. Remove electrical connectors from pump motor.
7. Remove both pressure and return lines from pump.
8. Plug/seal lines to prevent fluid contamination.
9. Remove the three that secure pump to bracket.
10. Remove the pump.

To install:

11. Installation is the reversal of removal with the following.
12. Fill the power steering fluid .
13. Program electrical power steering module (EPS).
14. Bleed the steering system.

SUSPENSION

FRONT SUSPENSION

KNUCKLE & SPINDLE

REMOVAL & INSTALLATION

See Figures 89 and 90.

1. Before servicing the vehicle, refer to the Precautions Section.
2. Raise and support the vehicle safely.
3. Remove front wheel.
4. Remove or disconnect the following:
    - The halfshaft bolt. Use a counterhold.
    - Detach the halfshaft end at the hub Tap in the shaft end approximately 10-15mm. Use a rubber or copper mallet.
    - The two bolts securing the brake caliper mounting bracket.
    - Hang caliper in a suitable place to avoid damage to the brake hose.
    - The brake rotor.
    - The brake shield.
    - The tie rod end from the steering arm
    - The ABS sensor. Hang up the sensor using a piece of wire.
5. Loosen the ball joint nut so that the upper edge of the nut is above the threads of the ball joint.
6. Use an Allen key as a counterhold so that the axle boot is not damaged.
7. Remove the ball joint from the Steering knuckle using special tool 9512945 or equivalent.
8. Pry the ball joint from the steering knuckle using special tool 9997076 or equivalent.
9. Pull the halfshaft out of the hub and hang out of the way.
10. Remove strut pinch bolt.
11. Widen the steering knuckle pinch with special too 9997088 or an equivalent pry bar.
12. Tap on steering knuckle with a copper mallet to release from strut.

To install:

13. Install the steering knuckle to the strut.
14. Tighten pinch bolt to 66 ft. lbs. (90 Nm)
15. Insert halfshaft through hub.

➡Make sure that the mating surfaces on the ball joint and link are clean.

16. Install ball joint to the steering knuckle.
17. Tighten ball joint nut to 52 ft. lbs. (70 Nm)
18. Install the halfshaft bolt and tighten bolt to 27 ft. lbs. (35 Nm). Angle-tighten 90°. Counterhold the brake disc.
19. Install or connect the following:
    - The ABS sensor.
    - The tie rod end to the steering arm
    - The brake shield.
    - The brake rotor.
    - Install the brake caliper and tighten bolts to 86 ft. lbs. (120 Nm).
    - Install the wheel.

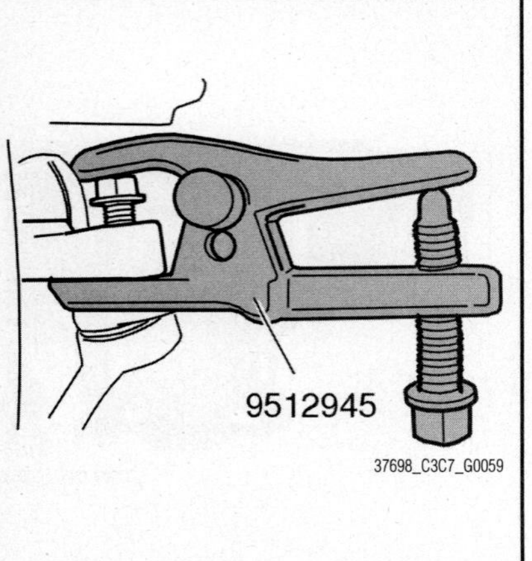

Fig. 89 Pressing outer joint with use of special tool 9512945

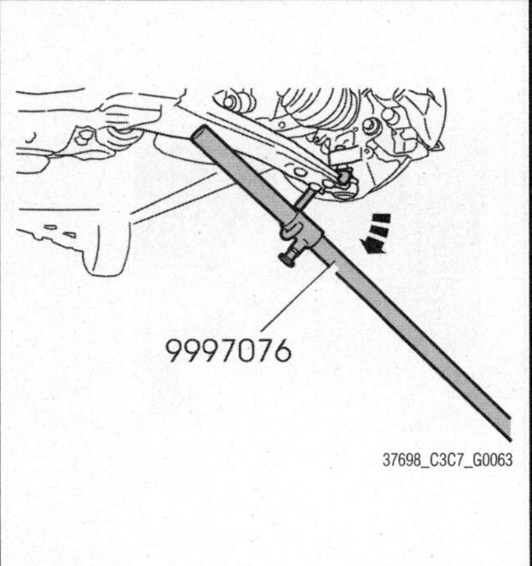

Fig. 90 Releasing of lower ball joint using 9997076

LOWER CONTROL ARMS

REMOVAL & INSTALLATION

See Figure 91.

1. Before servicing the vehicle, refer to the Precautions Section.
2. Remove the wheel
3. Remove the halfshaft bolt. Use a counterhold.
4. Detach the halfshaft end at the hub Tap in the shaft end approximately 10-15mm. Use a rubber or copper mallet.

➡It is not necessary to fully remove the halfshaft from the hub assembly. Loosening the shaft will allow for enough play when removing ball joint from steering knuckle.

5. Loosen the ball joint nut so that the upper edge of the nut is above the threads of the ball joint.
6. Use an Allen key as a counterhold so that the axle boot is not damaged.
7. Remove the ball joint from the Steering knuckle using special tool 9512945 or equivalent.
8. Pry the ball joint from the steering knuckle using special tool 9997076 or equivalent.
9. Twist the spring strut to one side. Hang the halfshaft so that the control arm is not in contact with the halfshafts.
10. Remove the two (1) bolts from the sub-frame.
11. Remove the bolt (2) from the sub-frame.
12. Remove the control arm.

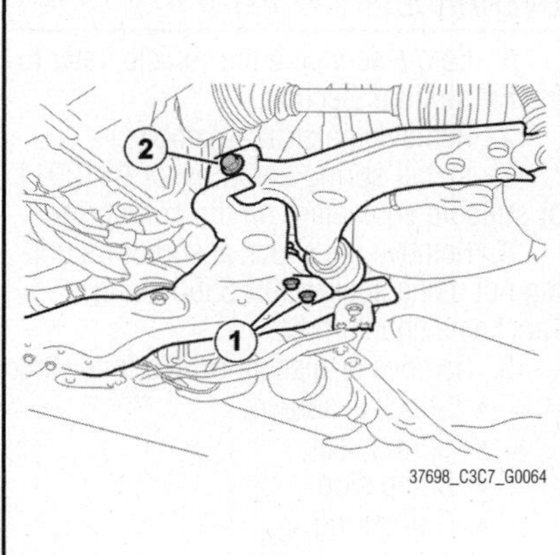

Fig. 91 View of attachment points (1, 2) of lower control arm

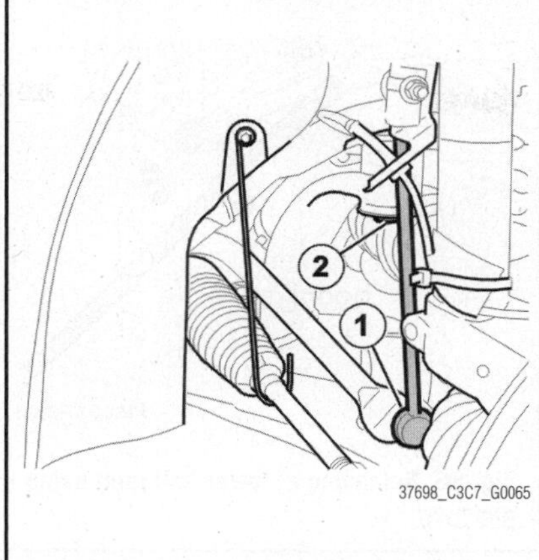

Fig. 92 Location of front sub-frame (2) bolts

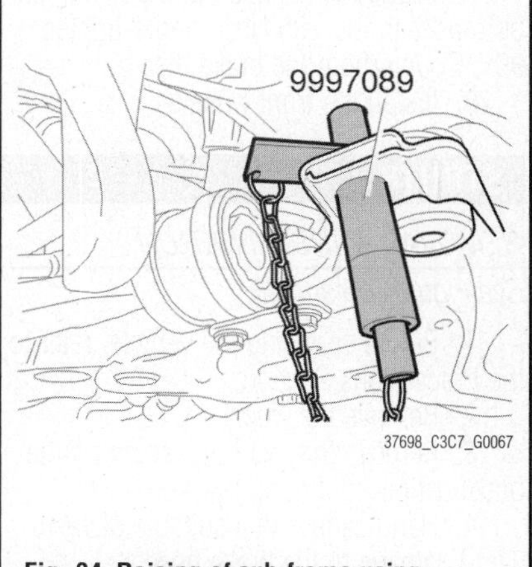

Fig. 94 Raising of sub-frame using alignment tool 9997089

To install:

13. Install the control arm on the sub-frame. Use new bolts. Tighten rear bolts to 36 ft. lbs. (60 Nm). Angle-tighten 90°. Front bolt to 129 ft. lbs. (175 Nm)
14. Install the bolts (1, 3). Tighten to 37 ft. lbs. (50 Nm).
15. Install the ball joint to the steering knuckle.
16. Install new nut and use Allen key as counterhold.
17. Tighten ball joint nut to 52 ft. lbs. (70 Nm)
18. Install a new halfshaft bolt. Tighten to 27 ft. lbs. (35 Nm). Angle-tighten 90°. Counterhold the brake disc.
19. Install the wheel.

STABILIZER BAR & LINKS

REMOVAL & INSTALLATION

Stabilizer Bar

See Figures 89 and 90, 92 through 94.

1. Before servicing the vehicle, refer to the Precautions Section.
2. Raise and support the vehicle safely.
3. Remove the front wheels.
4. Remove or disconnect the following:
   - The halfshaft bolt. Use a counter-hold.
   - Loosen the ball joint nut so that the upper edge of the nut is above the threads of the ball joint.
   - Use an Allen key as a counterhold so that the axle boot is not damaged.
   - Remove the ball joint from the Steering knuckle using special tool 9512945 or equivalent.
   - Pry the ball joint from the steering knuckle using special tool 9997076 or equivalent.
5. Remove the two bolts securing the steering rack.
6. Suspend the steering rack.
7. Remove both lower stabilizer bar link nuts.

➡Use a Torx® wrench as counterhold to avoid damage to the rubber bellows.

8. Slacken off both front sub-frame attaching bolts approx. 6 turns.
9. Remove the lower torque rod bolt.
10. Position and secure a transmission jack under sub-frame.
11. Remove or disconnect the following:
    - Rubber mountings (1).
    - Two screws (2).
    - Four bolts (3)
    - Heated oxygen sensor connector (4).
    - Sub-frame brackets.
12. Carefully lower the sub-frame enough for removal of stabilizer bar.
13. Remove the four bolts for stabilizer brackets.

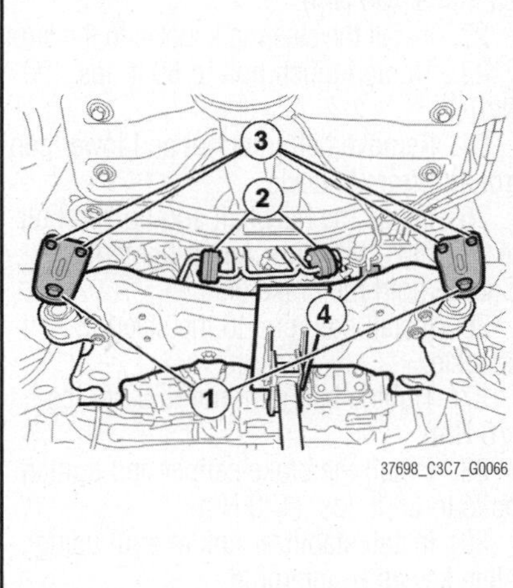

Fig. 93 Lowering of sub-frame

14. Remove the stabilizer bar.

To Install

15. Install the stabilizer bar .
16. Install the (M10) bolts for the anti-roll bar. Tighten to 37 ft. lbs. (50 Nm).
17. Install sub-frame alignment guides 9997089 or equivalent.
18. Carefully raise sub-frame so that the alignment tools meet the holes in the side members.

➡Make sure to keep from pinching steering gear when raise the sub-frame into place.

19. Install or connect the following:
    - Brackets to sub-frame.
    - The four bolts for brackets.

➡Using new bolts. Lube the bolts with oil. Tighten the sub-frame bolts starting on the left-hand side, then the right, using 2 steps: Step 1-78 ft. lbs. (105 Nm), Step 2-angle tighten 120°.

   - Tighten the M10 bolts for the brackets M10 to 37 ft. lbs. (50 Nm).
20. Install or connect the following:
    - The heated oxygen sensor connector (4).
    - The four bolts (3).
    - The two screws (2).
    - The rubber mountings (1).
    - Remove the transmission jack.
21. Install lower torque rod bolt.
22. Tighten two front sub-frame bolts.
23. Install and tighten lower stabilizer bar link nuts to 59 ft. lbs. (80 Nm).
24. Install the steering rack and tighten bolts to 37 ft. lbs. (50 Nm).
25. Install ball joint to the steering knuckle.
26. Tighten ball joint nut to 52 ft. lbs. (70 Nm)

27. Install the halfshaft bolt and tighten bolt to 27 ft. lbs. (35 Nm). Angle-tighten 90°. Counterhold the brake disc.
28. Install the front wheels.

STRUTS

REMOVAL & INSTALLATION

See Figures 95 and 96.

1. Before servicing the vehicle, refer to the Precautions Section.
2. Remove the wheel
3. Remove the two bolts securing the brake caliper mounting bracket.
4. Hang caliper in a suitable place to avoid damage to the brake hose.
5. Remove the halfshaft bolt. Use a counterhold.
6. Detach the halfshaft end at the hub Tap in the shaft end approximately 10-15mm. Use a rubber or copper mallet.
7. Loosen the ball joint nut so that the upper edge of the nut is above the threads of the ball joint.
8. Use an Allen key as a counterhold so that the axle boot is not damaged.
9. Remove the ball joint from the Steering knuckle using special tool 9512945 or equivalent.
10. Pry the ball joint from the steering knuckle using special tool 9997076 or equivalent.
11. Pull the halfshaft out of the hub and hang out of the way.
12. Hang the steering knuckle back on ball joint and loosely install nut.

➡This previous step is to support the knuckle while removing the knuckle from the strut.

13. Remove stabilizer link from strut using Allen key as counterhold.

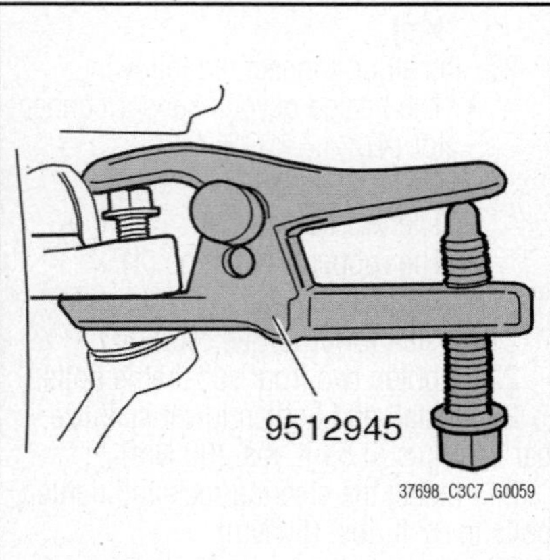

Fig. 95 Pressing outer joint with use of special tool 9512945

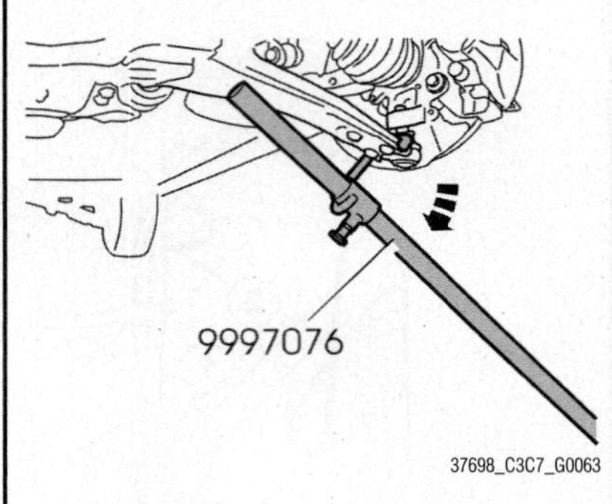

Fig. 96 Releasing of lower ball joint using 9997076

14. Remove strut pinch bolt.
15. Widen the steering knuckle pinch with special too 9997088 or an equivalent pry bar.
16. Tap on steering knuckle with a copper mallet to release from strut while having an assistant pry down on the lower control arm using special tool 9997076.
17. Remove the three upper mount bolts.
18. Remove the strut assembly and install spring compression tool..

➡Note the point of contact on the spring to help facilitate the installation of spring.

➡Ensure that the spring seat and the shock absorber bearing do not separate. The bearing comprises loose ball bearings in a frame. The ball bearings will fall out on separation.

19. Refer to overhaul below for further disassembly.

To install:

20. Install strut to the vehicle using new nuts and the new bolt.
21. Tighten upper mount bolts to 22 ft. lbs. (30 Nm).
22. Install the steering knuckle to the strut.
23. Tighten pinch bolt to 66 ft. lbs. (90 Nm)
24. Remove ball joint nut and lower control arm from knuckle.
25. Install the halfshaft and tighten bolt to 27 ft. lbs. (35 Nm). Angle-tighten 90°. Counterhold the brake disc.
26. Install ball joint to the steering knuckle.
27. Tighten ball joint nut to 52 ft. lbs. (70 Nm)
28. Install the brake caliper and tighten bolts to 86 ft. lbs. (120 Nm).
29. Install stabilizer link to strut using Allen key as counterhold.
30. Tighten nut to 37 ft. lbs. (50 Nm).
31. Install wheel.

OVERHAUL

1. Before servicing the vehicle, refer to the Precautions Section.
2. Remove the strut assembly.
3. Install spring compressor 9512911 or suitable equivalent on the coil spring.
4. Remove the shock absorber mounting nut using socket 999-5500 using a Torx® as a counterhold.
5. Remove or disconnect the following:
   - Shock absorber
   - Spring seat
   - Bump stop
   - Coil spring

To install:

6. Install spring compressor 9512911 or suitable equivalent on the coil spring.
7. Install or connect the following:
   - Bump stop
   - Coil spring
   - Spring seat
   - Shock absorber and tighten mounting nut to 52 ft. lbs. (70 Nm)
8. Remove the spring compressor.
9. Install the strut into the vehicle.
10. Check the wheel alignment and adjust as necessary.

WHEEL HUBS & BEARINGS

ADJUSTMENT

The front wheel bearings are not adjustable. If the lateral run-out on the hub with the disc removed exceeds 0.0007 in. (0.020mm), the hub must be replaced.

REMOVAL, PACKING, & INSTALLATION

See Figures 101 through 103.

1. Before servicing the vehicle, refer to the Precautions Section.
2. Remove the wheel.
3. Remove the steering knuckle. See: Steering Knuckle

Remove the hub and bearing as follows.

- Secure the steering knuckle in a hydraulic press.
- Using special tool 9997090 and drift 9991801 with 9995137 or equivalents to press out the bearing.

To install:

4. Install special tool 7090-1 or equivalent between the bearing and the hub
5. Position the bearing together with 7090-1 or equivalent on 9997090.
6. Position the steering knuckle and drift 7090-2.
7. Press in the bearing
8. Install the steering knuckle. See: Knuckle & Spindle.

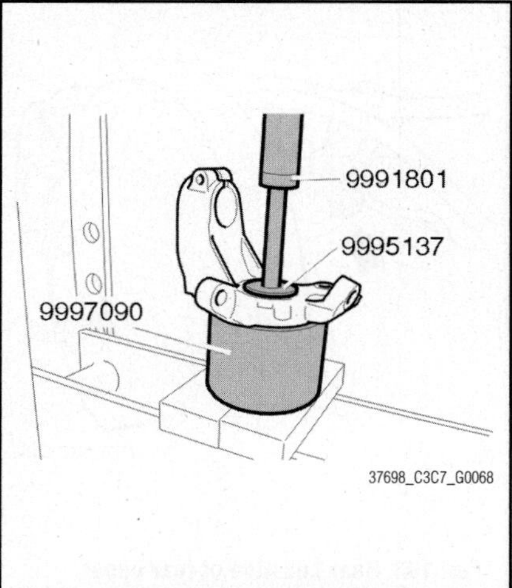

Fig. 97 Set up for pressing out the front wheel bearing

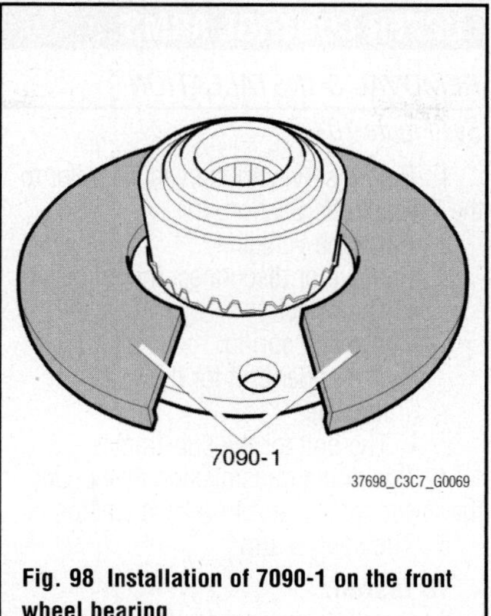

Fig. 98 Installation of 7090-1 on the front wheel bearing

Fig. 99 Set up for pressing in the front wheel bearing

SUSPENSION

REAR SUSPENSION

COIL SPRINGS

REMOVAL & INSTALLATION

See Figure 100.

1. Before servicing the vehicle, refer to the Precautions Section.
2. Remove the rear wheel.
3. For right-hand side spring only:
   a. Place a transmission jack under the control arm to relieve the tension on the shock absorber.
   b. Remove the shock absorber lower mounting bolt.
4. Install spring compressor 9512911 with claw 9512897 or suitable equivalent to compress the spring.

➡Note the position of spring for easier installation.

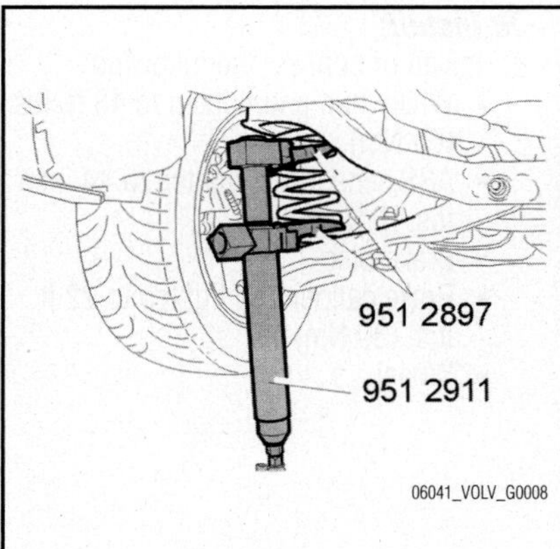

Fig. 100 Using spring compressor 951-2911 to remove the rear spring

5. Remove the spring.
6. For left-hand side spring only:
7. Install spring compressor 9512911 with claw 9512897 or suitable equivalents to compress the spring.
8. Compress the spring.

➡Note the position of spring for easier installation.

9. Remove the spring.

To install:

10. Install spring compressor 951-2911 with claw 9512897 or suitable equivalents to compress the spring.
11. Install the spring.

➡Ensure that the spring engages in the control arm grooves.

12. For right side spring only:
    a. Place a transmission jack under the control arm so the lower shock absorber mounting bolt can be installed.
13. Install the wheel.

LOWER CONTROL ARMS

REMOVAL & INSTALLATION

See Figures 101 and 102.

1. Before servicing the vehicle, refer to the Precautions Section.
2. Raise the vehicle.
3. Remove or disconnect the following:
   - The wheel
   - The coil spring.
   - The two nuts using a Torx® wrench counter hold to prevent damage to the boot.

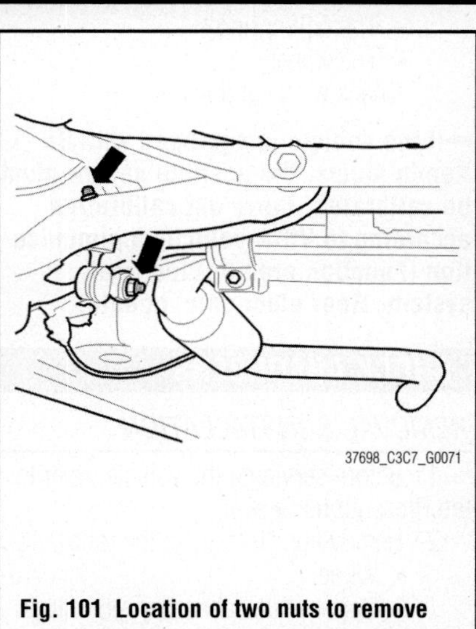

Fig. 101 Location of two nuts to remove

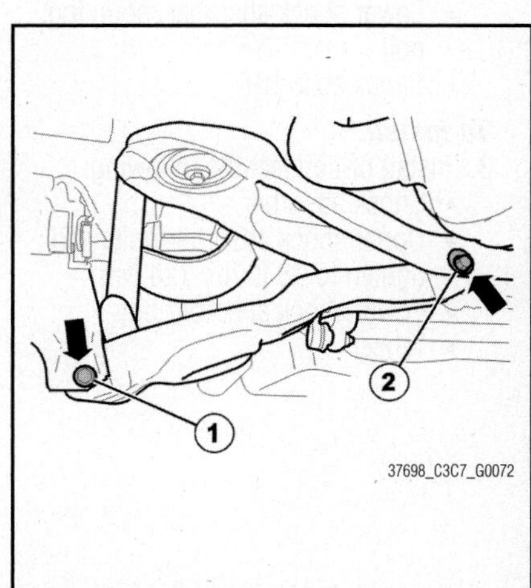

Fig. 102 Location of two bolts (1, 2) to remove from lower control arm

- The ball joints.
- The bolt for the wheel knuckle (1).
- The bolt for the sub frame (2).

4. Turn the rear stabilizer bar approximately 30° and remove the control arm.

To install:

➡Tighten all joints and rubber bushings with the rear suspension in the normal position.

5. Install or connect the following:
   - The control arm.
   - The control arm bolts. Do not tighten yet.
   - Position a transmission jack below the lower control arm. Press up until the measurement between the center of the wheel and the fender edge is approximately 350 mm.
6. Tighten the M12 bolt for the inner mounting for the control arm. Tighten to 59 ft. lbs. (80 Nm).
   - The ball joints
   - The coil spring
   - The wheel.
7. Check wheel alignment.

➡If the vehicle is equipped with Bi-Xenon lamps, the position sensor must be calibrated. Carry out calibration according to VIDA Vehicle communication (Function area 3, Electrical system, Rear electronic module).

SHOCK ABSORBERS

REMOVAL & INSTALLATION

1. Before servicing the vehicle, refer to the Precautions Section.
2. Remove or disconnect the following:
   - Wheel
   - Upper shock absorber mounting bolts
   - Lower shock absorber mounting bolt
   - Shock absorber

To install:

3. Install or connect the following:
   - Shock absorber
   - Upper shock absorber bolts and tighten to 18 ft. lbs. (24 Nm)
   - Lower shock absorber bolt
   - Wheel

UPPER CONTROL ARMS

REMOVAL & INSTALLATION

See Figure 103.

1. Before servicing the vehicle, refer to the Precautions Section.
2. Raise the vehicle.
3. Remove or disconnect the following:
   - The wheel.
   - The coil spring.
   - The upper bolt for the wheel knuckle.
   - The bolt for the sub-frame.
4. Position a transmission jack under the lower control arm to relieve tension.
5. The control arm

To install:

6. Install or connect the following:
   - The control arm
   - The bolts for the upper rear control arm mounting

➡Tighten the bolts when the rear suspension is in the normal position.

- Position a transmission jack below the lower control arm. Press up until the measurement between the center of the wheel and the fender edge is approximately 350 mm.
- Tighten the control arm bolts. to 85 ft. lbs. (115 Nm).
- The coil spring.
- The wheel

➡If the vehicle is equipped with Bi-Xenon lamps, the position sensor must be calibrated. Carry out calibration according to VIDA vehicle communication (Function area 3, Electrical system, Rear Electronic Module).

WHEEL HUBS & BEARINGS

ADJUSTMENT

The rear wheel bearings are sealed, pressed-in units, and no adjustment is possible.

REMOVAL, & INSTALLATION

See Figures 104.

1. Before servicing the vehicle, refer to the Precautions Section.
2. Raise the vehicle.

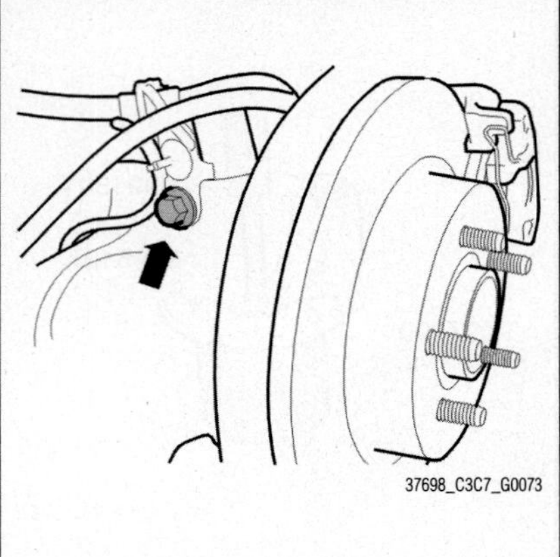

Fig. 103 Rear Location of rear upper knuckle bolt

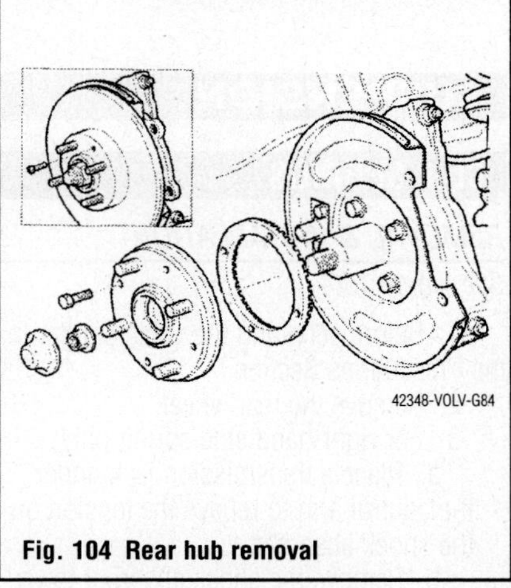

Fig. 104 Rear hub removal

3. Remove or disconnect the following:
   - Wheel
   - Brake caliper and hang with wire out of way
   - Brake disc.
   - ABS sensor
   - Wheel hub

To install:

4. Install or connect the following:
   - Wheel hub and tighten to 48 ft. lbs. (65 Nm).
   - ABS sensor and tighten to 44 inch lbs. (5 Nm).
   - Brake disc
   - Brake caliper and tighten to 22 ft. lbs. (30 Nm).
   - Wheel

VOLVO

S40 • S60

11

SPECIFICATIONS AND MAINTENANCE CHARTS

ENGINE AND VEHICLE IDENTIFICATION

Engine						
Code	Liters (cc)	Cu. In.	Cyl.	Fuel Sys.	Engine Type	Eng. Mfg.
B5254T5	2.5 (2,521)	154	5	EFI	DOHC	Volvo
B5254T7	2.5 (2,521)	154	5	EFI	DOHC	Volvo
B6304T4	3.0 (2,953)	175	6	EFI	DOHC	Volvo

Model Year	
Code ①	Year
B	2011
C	2012

① 10th position of VIN

EFI: Electronic Fuel Injection

DOHC: Dual Overhead Camshafts

71112_S4S6_C0001

GENERAL ENGINE SPECIFICATIONS

All measurements are given in inches.

Year	Model	Engine Displacemer Liters	Engine Series ID	Net Horsepower @ rpm	Net Torque @ rpm (ft. lbs.)	Bore x Stroke (in.)	Com-pression Ratio	Oil Pressure @ rpm
2011	S40	2.5	B5254T7	227@5000	236@1500	3.27 x 3.67	9.0:1	51@4000
	S60	3.0	B6304T4	300@5600	325@2100	3.23 x 3.67	9.3:1	51@4000
2012	S60	2.5	B5254T5	250@5500	266@1800	3.27 x 3.67	9.0:1	51@4000
		3.0	B6304T4	300@5600	325@2100	3.23 x 3.67	9.3:1	51@4000

71112_S4S6_C0002

GASOLINE ENGINE TUNE-UP SPECIFICATIONS

Year	Engine Displacement Liters	Engine ID	Spark Plug Gap (in.)	Ignition Timing (deg.)	Fuel Pump (psi)	Idle Speed (rpm)	Valve Lash Clearance	
							Intake	Exhaust
2011	2.5	B5254T7	0.028-0.032	①	44-58 ②	720	HYD	HYD
	3.0	B6304T4	0.028-0.032	①	55-58 ②	650	HYD	HYD
2012	2.5	B5254T5	0.028-0.032	①	58-69 ②	720	HYD	HYD
	3.0	B6304T4	0.028-0.032	①	55-58 ②	650	HYD	HYD

NOTE: The Vehicle Emission Control Information label often reflects specification changes made during production. The label figures must be used if they differ from those in this chart.

HYD: Hydraulic lash adjusters

① Ignition timing is controlled by the PCM and is not adjustable

② With key ON and engine OFF

71112_S4S6_C0003

CAPACITIES

Year	Model	Engine Displacement Liters	Engine ID	Engine Oil with Filter (qts.)	Transmission (pts.) Manual	Transmission (pts.) Auto. ①	Transfer Case (pts.)	Drive Axle Front (pts.)	Drive Axle Rear (pts.)	Fuel Tank (gal.)	Cooling System (qts.)
2011	S40	2.5	B5254T7	6.1	NA	16.2	NS	NS	NS	15.9	10.5
	S60	3.0	B6304T4	7.1	NA	11.6	NS	NS	NS	18.5	9.4
2012	S60	2.5	B5254T5	6.1	NA	16.2	NS	NS	NS	18.5	NS
		3.0	B6304T4	7.1	NA	11.6	NS	NS	NS	18.5	9.4

NA: Not Applicable

NS: Not specified by manufacturer at date of publication

NOTE: All capacities are approximate. Add fluid gradually and check to be sure a proper fluid level is obtained.

① Drain and refill

71112_S4S6_C0004

FLUID SPECIFICATIONS

Year	Model	Engine Displacement Liters	Engine ID	Engine Oil	Manual Trans.	Auto. Trans.	Power Steering Fluid	Brake Master Cylinder	Cooling System
2011	S40	2.5	B5254T7	5W-30	NA	Volvo	Volvo	DOT 4+	Volvo
	S60	3.0	B6304T4	5W-30	NA	Volvo	Volvo	DOT 4+	Volvo
2012	S60	2.5	B5254T5	5W-30	NA	Volvo	Volvo	DOT 4+	Volvo
		3.0	B6304T4	5W-30	NA	Volvo	Volvo	DOT 4+	Volvo

NA: Not Applicable

DOT: Department Of Transportation

71112_S4S6_C0005

VALVE SPECIFICATIONS

Year	Engine Displacement Liters	Engine ID	Seat Angle (deg.)	Face Angle (deg.)	Spring Test Pressure (lbs. @ in.)	Spring Installed Height (in.)	Stem-to-Guide Clearance (in.) Intake	Stem-to-Guide Clearance (in.) Exhaust	Stem Diameter (in.) Intake	Stem Diameter (in.) Exhaust
2011	2.5	B5254T7	45.33-45.67	45.33-45.67	NS	NS	0.0020-0.0028	0.0020-0.0028	0.2311-0.2366	0.2311-0.2366
	3.0	B6304T4	44.99-45.01	44.50	NS	①	0.0012-0.0024	0.0012-0.0028	0.2356-0.2344	0.2341-0.2350
2012	2.5	B5254T5	45.33-45.67	45.33-45.67	NS	NS	0.0020-0.0028	0.0020-0.0028	0.2311-0.2366	0.2311-0.2366
	3.0	B6304T4	44.99-45.01	44.50	NS	①	0.0012-0.0024	0.0012-0.0028	0.2356-0.2344	0.2341-0.2350

NS: Not specified by manufacturer at date of publication

① Height unloaded: 1.7677 - 1.8465 inches

71112_S4S6_C0006

CAMSHAFT AND BEARING SPECIFICATIONS CHART

All measurements are given in inches.

Year	Engine Displ. Liters	Engine ID	Journal Dia.	Brg. Oil Clearance	Shaft End-play	Runout	Journal Bore	Lobe Lift Intake	Lobe Lift Exhaust
2011	2.5	B5254T7	NS	NS	NS	NS	NS	0.3417	0.3563
	3.0	B6304T4	NS	NS	NS	NS	NS	0.3327	0.372
2012	2.5	B5254T5	NS	NS	NS	NS	NS	0.3417	0.3563
	3.0	B6304T4	NS	NS	NS	NS	NS	0.3327	0.372

NS: Not specified by manufacturer at date of publication

71112_S4S6_C0007

CRANKSHAFT AND CONNECTING ROD SPECIFICATIONS

All measurements are given in inches.

Year	Engine Displacement Liters	Engine ID	Crankshaft Main Brg. Journal Dia.	Crankshaft Main Brg. Oil Clearance	Crankshaft Shaft End-play	Crankshaft Thrust on No.	Connecting Rod Journal Diameter	Connecting Rod Oil Clearance	Connecting Rod Side Clearance
2011	2.5	B5254T7	2.5584-2.5592	0.0008-0.0021	0.0031-0.0075	NS	2.0866-2.0871	NS	NS
	3.0	B6304T4	2.5584-2.5592	NS	0.0031-0.0106	NS	2.0861-2.0866	NS	NS
2012	2.5	B5254T5	2.5584-2.5592	0.0008-0.0021	0.0031-0.0075	NS	2.0866-2.0871	NS	NS
	3.0	B6304T4	2.5584-2.5592	NS	0.0031-0.0106	NS	2.0861-2.0866	NS	NS

NS: Not specified by manufacturer at date of publication

71112_S4S6_C0008

PISTON AND RING SPECIFICATIONS

All measurements are given in inches.

Year	Engine Displ. Liters	Engine ID	Piston Clearance	Ring Gap Top Compression	Ring Gap Bottom Compression	Ring Gap Oil Control	Ring Side Clearance Top Compression	Ring Side Clearance Bottom Compression	Ring Side Clearance Oil Control
2011	2.5	B5254T7	0.0004-0.0012	0.0461-0.0469	0.0579-0.0587	0.0734-0.0783	NS	NS	NS
	3.0	B6304T4	0.0016-0.0024	0.0461-0.0469	0.0579-0.0587	0.0734-0.0783	0.0012-0.0028	0.0012-0.0028	0.0008-0.0065
2012	2.5	B5254T5	0.0004-0.0012	0.0461-0.0469	0.0579-0.0587	0.0734-0.0783	NS	NS	NS
	3.0	B6304T4	0.0016-0.0024	0.0461-0.0469	0.0579-0.0587	0.0734-0.0783	0.0012-0.0028	0.0012-0.0028	0.0008-0.0065

NS: Not specified by manufacturer at date of publication

71112_S4S6_C0009

TORQUE SPECIFICATIONS

All readings in ft. lbs.

Year	Engine Displacement Liters	Engine ID	Cylinder Head Bolts	Main Bearing Bolts	Rod Bearing Bolts	Crankshaft Damper Bolts	Flywheel Bolts	Manifold Intake	Manifold Exhaust	Spark Plugs	Oil Pan Drain Plug
2011	2.5	B5254T7	①	②	③	④	⑤	⑥	18	21	28
	3.0	B6304T2	⑦	⑧	⑨	⑩	59	13	18	21	28
2012	2.5	B5254T7	①	②	③	④	⑤	⑥	18	21	28
	3.0	B6304T2	⑦	⑧	⑨	⑩	59	13	18	21	28

NS: Not specified by manufacturer at date of publication

① Refer to procedure for torque sequence
- Step 1: 15 ft. lbs. (20 Nm)
- Step 2: 44 ft. lbs. (60 Nm)
- Step 3: plus 130 degrees

② See procedure for torque sequence/bolt identification
- Step 1: M10 bolts to 15 ft. lbs. (20 Nm)
- Step 2: M10 bolts to 33 ft. lbs. (45 Nm)
- Step 3: M8 bolts to 18 ft. lbs. (24 Nm)
- Step 4: M7 bolts to 13 ft. lbs. (17 Nm)
- Step 5: M10 bolts plus 90 degrees

③ Step 1: 11 ft. lbs. (15 Nm)
- Step 2: 18 ft. lbs. (25 Nm)
- Step 3: plus 100 degrees

④ Flanged screws
- Step 1: 18 ft. lbs. (25 Nm)
- Step 2: plus 60 degrees
- Center nut: 133 ft. lbs. (180 Nm)

⑤ Step 1: 33 ft. lbs. (45 Nm)
- Step 2: plus 65 degrees

⑥ Lower section: 14 ft. lbs. (19 Nm)
- Upper section: 89 inch lbs. (10 Nm)

⑦ Refer to procedure for torque sequence
- Step 1: 33 ft. lbs. (45 Nm)
- Step 2: 33 ft. lbs. (45 Nm)
- Step 3: plus 90 degrees
- Step 4: plus 180 degrees

⑧ Refer to procedure for torque sequence/bolt identification
- Step 1: M10 bolts to 44 inch lbs. (5 Nm)
- Step 2: M10 bolts to 22 ft. lbs. (30 Nm)
- Step 3: M8 bolts: 18 ft. lbs. (25 Nm)
- Step 4: M10 bolts plus 105 degrees
- Step 5: M8 bolts to 18 ft. lbs. (25 Nm)

⑨ Step 1: 106 inch lbs. (12 Nm)
- Step 2: 15 ft. lbs. (20 Nm)
- Step 3: plus 90 degrees

⑩ Step 1: 89 ft. lbs. (120 Nm)
- Step 2: Loosen 360 degrees
- Step 3: 37 ft. lbs. (50 Nm)
- Step 4: plus 90 degrees

71112_S4S6_C0010

TIRE, WHEEL AND BALL JOINT SPECIFICATIONS

Year	Model	OEM Tires Standard	OEM Tires Optional	Tire Pressures (psi) Front	Tire Pressures (psi) Rear	Wheel Size	Ball Joint Inspection	Lug Nut Torque (ft. lbs.)
2011	S40 T5	P205/50R17	NA	①	①	7.0 x 17	NS	②
	S40 T5 R	P205/50R17	P215/45R18	①	①	7.0 x 17 or 7.5 x 18	NS	②
	S60 T6	P235/45R17	NA	①	①	7.5 x 17	NS	③
2012	S60 T5	P235/45R17	NA	①	①	7.5 x 17	NS	③
	S60 T6	P235/40R18	NA	①	①	7.5 x 18	NS	③
	S60 T6 R	P235/40R18	NA	①	①	7.5 x 18	NS	③

OEM: Original Equipment Manufacturer
PSI: Pounds Per Square Inch
NA: Not Applicable
NS: Not specified by manufacturer at date of publication

① See the tire placard on the vehicle

② Tighten in a star pattern
- Steel wheels with low nut/small cone and locking wheel nuts:
  - Step 1: 15 ft. lbs. (20 Nm)
  - Step 2: 81 ft. lbs. (110 Nm)
- Aluminum and steel wheels with high nut/large cone:
  - Step 1: 15 ft. lbs. (20 Nm)
  - Step 2: 96 ft. lbs. (130 Nm)

③ Tighten in a star pattern
- Step 1: 15 ft. lbs. (20 Nm)
- Step 2: 103 ft. lbs. (140 Nm)

71112_S4S6_C0011

BRAKE SPECIFICATIONS

All measurements in inches unless noted

			Brake Disc			Minimum	Brake Caliper	
			Original	Minimum	Maximum	Lining	Bracket Bolts	Guide Pin Bolts
Year	Model		Thickness	Thickness	Runout	Thickness	(ft. lbs.)	(ft. lbs.)
2011	S40	F	0.984	0.906	0.003	①	89	22
		R	0.433	0.354	0.002	①	52	22
	S60	F	②	③	0.002	①	148	21
		R	④	⑤	0.002	①	81	26
2012	S60	F	②	③	0.002	①	148	21
		R	④	⑤	0.002	①	81	26

F: Front

R: Rear

① Replace the disc brake pads when the friction surface is worn to within 0.079 inch (2mm) of the mounting plates.

② 16/16.5/17 inch rotors: 1.102 inches (28mm)

③ 16/16.5/17 inch rotors: 1.023 inch (26mm)

④ 16 inch rotors: 0.472 inch (12mm)
17 inch solid rotors: 0.433 inch (11mm)
17 inch ventilated rotors: 0.866 inch (22mm)

⑤ 16 inch rotors: 0.393 inch (10mm)
17 inch solid rotors: 0.354 inch (9mm)
17 inch ventilated rotors: 0.787 inch (20mm)

71112_S4S6_C0012

SCHEDULED MAINTENANCE INTERVALS

2011-12 Volvo S40/S60

TO BE SERVICED	TYPE OF SERVICE	VEHICLE MILEAGE INTERVAL (x1000)																			
		7.5	15	22.5	30	37.5	45	52.5	60	67.5	75	82.5	90	97.5	105	112.5	120	127.5	135	142.5	150
Engine oil & filter	R	✓	✓	✓	✓	✓	✓	✓	✓	✓	✓	✓	✓	✓	✓	✓	✓	✓	✓	✓	✓
Automatic transmission fluid	I/A		✓		✓		✓	✓	✓		✓		✓		✓		✓		✓		✓
Brake pads, discs & lines	I	✓	✓	✓	✓	✓	✓	✓	✓	✓	✓	✓	✓	✓	✓	✓	✓	✓	✓	✓	✓
Parking brake	I/A		✓		✓		✓		✓		✓		✓		✓		✓		✓		✓
Wheels & tires	S/I	✓	✓	✓	✓	✓	✓	✓	✓	✓	✓	✓	✓	✓	✓	✓	✓	✓	✓	✓	✓
Spare tire	S/I				✓				✓				✓				✓				✓
Drive shafts	S/I								✓	✓	✓	✓	✓	✓	✓	✓	✓	✓	✓	✓	✓
Cabin air filter	R		✓		✓		✓		✓		✓		✓		✓		✓		✓		✓
Engine coolant	S/I		✓		✓		✓		✓		✓		✓		✓		✓		✓		✓
Air cleaner filter	R					✓					✓					✓					✓
Spark plugs	R										✓										✓
Accessory drive belt ①	R																✓				
Timing belt ①	R																✓				
Fuel lines	I				✓				✓				✓				✓				✓
Exhaust system	S/I								✓	✓	✓	✓	✓	✓	✓	✓	✓	✓	✓	✓	✓
Check suspension	S/I								✓	✓	✓	✓	✓	✓	✓	✓	✓	✓	✓	✓	✓
Brake fluid ②	R					✓					✓					✓					✓
Windshield & headlamps wipers/ washers	S/I	✓	✓	✓	✓	✓	✓	✓	✓	✓	✓	✓	✓	✓	✓	✓	✓	✓	✓	✓	✓
Battery	S/I				✓		✓		✓		✓		✓		✓		✓		✓		✓
Convertible roof system (C70)	S/I		✓		✓		✓		✓		✓		✓		✓		✓		✓		✓
Service reminder indicator (SRI)	S/I	✓	✓	✓	✓	✓	✓	✓	✓	✓	✓	✓	✓	✓	✓	✓	✓	✓	✓	✓	✓

R: Replace S/I: Service or Inspect I/A: Inspect and adjust.

① Replace at a maximum of every 10 years or or according to chart.

② Replace every 2 years or 30,000 miles, whichever comes first under normal conditions, more frequently in mountainous areas or mois

FREQUENT OPERATION MAINTENANCE (SEVERE SERVICE)

If a vehicle is operated under any of the following conditions it is considered severe service:

- Extremely dusty areas.

- 50% or more of the vehicle operation is in 90°F (32°C) or higher temperatures, or constant operation in temperatures below 32°F (0°C).

- Prolonged idling (vehicle operation in stop and go traffic).

- Frequent short running periods (engine does not warm to normal operating temperatures).

- Police, taxi, delivery usage or trailer towing usage.

Air filter element: service or inspect every 15,000 miles.

Automatic transmission oil service every 52,500 miles.

71112_S4S6_C0013

PRECAUTIONS

Before servicing any vehicle, please be sure to read all of the following precautions, which deal with personal safety, prevention of component damage, and important points to take into consideration when servicing a motor vehicle:

- Never open, service or drain the radiator or cooling system when the engine is hot; serious burns can occur from the steam and hot coolant.
- Observe all applicable safety precautions when working around fuel. Whenever servicing the fuel system, always work in a well-ventilated area. Do not allow fuel spray or vapors to come in contact with a spark, open flame, or excessive heat (a hot drop light, for example). Keep a dry chemical fire extinguisher near the work area. Always keep fuel in a container specifically designed for fuel storage; also, always properly seal fuel containers to avoid the possibility of fire or explosion. Refer to the additional fuel system precautions later in this section.
- Fuel injection systems often remain pressurized, even after the engine has been turned **OFF**. The fuel system pressure must be relieved before disconnecting any fuel lines. Failure to do so may result in fire and/or personal injury.
- Brake fluid often contains polyglycol ethers and polyglycols. Avoid contact with the eyes and wash your hands thoroughly after handling brake fluid. If you do get brake fluid in your eyes, flush your eyes with clean, running water for 15 minutes. If eye irritation persists, or if you have taken brake fluid internally, IMMEDIATELY seek medical assistance.
- The EPA warns that prolonged contact with used engine oil may cause a number of skin disorders, including cancer. You should make every effort to minimize your exposure to used engine oil. Protective gloves should be worn when changing oil. Wash your hands and any other exposed skin areas as soon as possible after exposure to used engine oil. Soap and water, or waterless hand cleaner should be used.
- All new vehicles are now equipped with an air bag system, often referred to as a Supplemental Restraint System (SRS) or Supplemental Inflatable Restraint (SIR) system. The system must be disabled before performing service on or around system components, steering column, instrument panel components, wiring and sensors. Failure to follow safety and disabling procedures could result in accidental air bag deployment, possible personal injury and unnecessary system repairs.
- Always wear safety goggles when working with, or around, the air bag system. When carrying a non-deployed air bag, be sure the bag and trim cover are pointed away from your body. When placing a non-deployed air bag on a work surface, always face the bag and trim cover upward, away from the surface. This will reduce the motion of the module if it is accidentally deployed. Refer to the additional air bag system precautions later in this section.
- Clean, high quality brake fluid from a sealed container is essential to the safe and proper operation of the brake system. You should always buy the correct type of brake fluid for your vehicle. If the brake fluid becomes contaminated, completely flush the system with new fluid. Never reuse any brake fluid. Any brake fluid that is removed from the system should be discarded. Also, do not allow any brake fluid to come in contact with a painted surface; it will damage the paint.
- Never operate the engine without the proper amount and type of engine oil; doing so WILL result in severe engine damage.
- Timing belt maintenance is extremely important. Many models utilize an interference-type, non-freewheeling engine. If the timing belt breaks, the valves in the cylinder head may strike the pistons, causing potentially serious (also time-consuming and expensive) engine damage. Refer to the maintenance interval charts for the recommended replacement interval for the timing belt, and to the timing belt section for belt replacement and inspection.
- Disconnecting the negative battery cable on some vehicles may interfere with the functions of the on-board computer system(s) and may require the computer to undergo a relearning process once the negative battery cable is reconnected.
- When servicing drum brakes, only disassemble and assemble one side at a time, leaving the remaining side intact for reference.
- Only an MVAC-trained, EPA-certified automotive technician should service the air conditioning system or its components.

BRAKES

ANTI-LOCK BRAKE SYSTEM (ABS)

GENERAL INFORMATION

PRECAUTIONS

- Certain components within the ABS system are not intended to be serviced or repaired individually.
- Do not use rubber hoses or other parts not specifically specified for and ABS system. When using repair kits, replace all parts included in the kit. Partial or incorrect repair may lead to functional problems and require the replacement of components.
- Lubricate rubber parts with clean, fresh brake fluid to ease assembly. Do not use shop air to clean parts; damage to rubber components may result.
- Use only DOT 3 brake fluid from an unopened container.
- If any hydraulic component or line is removed or replaced, it may be necessary to bleed the entire system.
- A clean repair area is essential. Always clean the reservoir and cap thoroughly before removing the cap. The slightest amount of dirt in the fluid may plug an orifice and impair the system function. Perform repairs after components have been thoroughly cleaned; use only denatured alcohol to clean components. Do not allow ABS components to come into contact with any substance containing mineral oil; this includes used shop rags.
- The Anti-Lock control unit is a microprocessor similar to other computer units in the vehicle. Ensure that the ignition switch is **OFF** before removing or installing controller harnesses. Avoid static electricity discharge at or near the controller.
- If any arc welding is to be done on the vehicle, the control unit should be unplugged before welding operations begin.

SPEED SENSORS

REMOVAL & INSTALLATION

Front

See Figure 1.

1. Before servicing the vehicle, refer to the Precautions Section.
2. Raise and safely support the vehicle.
3. Remove the tire and wheel assembly.
4. Remove the front brake rotor.
5. Remove the Wheel Speed Sensor (WSS) mounting bolt.
6. Pull the sensor out, being careful to turn it as little as possible. Do not pull on the sensor harness.

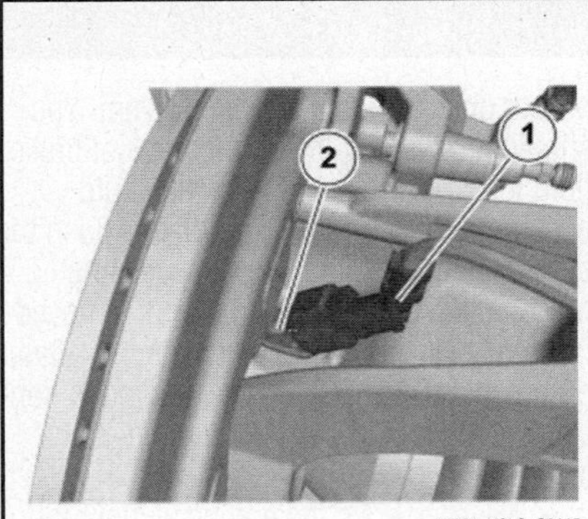

Fig. 1 View of ABS harness (1) and speed sensor (2)

7. Disconnect the WSS electrical connector.
8. Remove the harness from its mount.

To install:

9. Inspect the sensor O-ring, replace as required.
10. Before installing the sensor, be certain there are no foreign materials, like iron fragments adhering to:
    - The pick-up part of the sensor
    - The inside of the sensor mounting hole
    - The rotor mounting surface
11. Apply a thin coat of suitable grease to the wheel sensor O-ring and mounting hole.
12. Tighten the sensor mounting bolt:
    a. S40 vehicles to 44 inch lbs. (5 Nm).
    b. S60 vehicles to 89 inch lbs. (10 Nm).
13. Continue the installation in the reverse order of the removal procedure.

Rear

See Figure 2.

1. Before servicing the vehicle, always refer to the precautions sections.
2. Disconnect the negative battery cable.
3. Raise and support the vehicle safely.
4. Remove the tire and wheel assembly.
5. Remove the wheel speed sensor mounting bolt.
6. Pull the sensor out, being careful to turn it as little as possible. Do not pull on the sensor harness.
7. Disconnect the wheel speed sensor electrical connector.
8. Remove the harness from its mount.

To install:

9. Inspect the sensor O-ring, replace as required.
10. Before installing the sensor, be certain there are no foreign materials, like iron fragments adhering to:

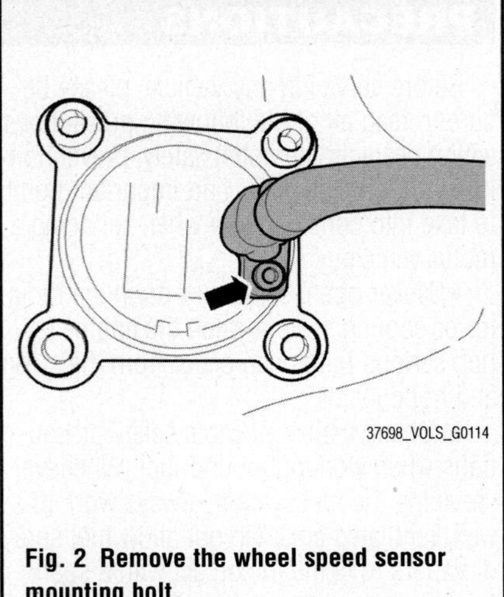

Fig. 2 Remove the wheel speed sensor mounting bolt

- The pick-up part of the sensor
- The inside of the sensor mounting hole
- The rotor mounting surface.

11. Apply a thin coat of suitable grease to the wheel sensor O-ring and mounting hole.
12. Tighten the sensor mounting bolt:
    a. S40 vehicles to 44 inch lbs. (5 Nm).
    b. S60 vehicles to 89 inch lbs. (10 Nm).
13. Continue the installation in the reverse order of the removal procedure.

BRAKES — BLEEDING THE BRAKE SYSTEM

BLEEDING PROCEDURE

BLEEDING PROCEDURE

⁂ CAUTION

Brake fluid contains polyglycol ethers and polyglycols. Avoid contact with the eyes and wash your hands thoroughly after handling brake fluid. If you do get brake fluid in your eyes, flush your eyes with clean, running water for 15 minutes. If eye irritation persists, or if you have taken brake fluid internally, IMMEDIATELY seek medical assistance.

⁂ WARNING

Clean, high quality brake fluid is essential to the safe and proper operation of the brake system. You should always buy the highest quality brake fluid that is available. If the brake fluid becomes contaminated, drain and flush the system, then refill the master cylinder with new fluid. Never reuse any brake fluid. Any brake fluid that is removed from the system should be discarded. Also, do not allow any brake fluid to come in contact with a painted surface; it will damage the paint.

When reconditioning or replacing brake calipers bleed the relevant brake pipe as follows.

➡If the braking system has been completely or partly drained, bleed the whole system.

1. Before servicing the vehicle, refer to the Precautions Section.
2. Turn the ignition switch OFF.
3. Clean all around the brake fluid reservoir filler cap.
4. Attach the special brake fluid collection bottle at the bleed nipple.
5. Remove the master cylinder filler cap.
6. Fill the brake fluid reservoir completely with genuine Volvo DOT 4+ brake fluid.
7. Raise and safely support the vehicle.

➡While bleeding, check that there is sufficient brake fluid in the reservoir. Top up, if necessary.

8. Remove the protective cap from the bleed nipple. Connect the hose from the collection bottle.
9. Depress the brake pedal a few times. Maintain pressure.
10. Open the bleed nipple.
11. Depress the pedal fully. Keep it fully depressed for approximately 5 seconds.
12. Release it again. Repeat this 3–5 times until there are no air bubbles in the fluid coming out of the hose.
13. Tighten the bleed nipple.
14. Remove the hose from the bleed nipple. Install the protective cap.
15. Continue to bleed the other wheels. Use the following wheel order:
    - Left front wheel

- Right front wheel
- Left rear wheel
- Right rear wheel

16. Check for leakage from the bleed nipples.
17. Check for air in the brake system and for brake fluid leakage.
18. Fill the brake reservoir with the proper amount of DOT 4+ brake fluid.
19. After completing the final wheel hydraulic circuit bleeding procedure, ensure that each of the 4 wheel hydraulic circuit bleeder valves are properly tightened.
20. Slowly depress and release the brake pedal. Observe the feel of the brake pedal.
21. If the brake pedal feels spongy, repeat the bleeding procedure again. If the brake pedal still feels spongy after repeating the bleeding procedure, perform the following steps:
    a. Inspect the brake system for external leaks.
    b. Pressure bleed the hydraulic brake system in order to purge any air that may still be trapped in the system.
22. Turn the ignition key ON, with the engine OFF. Check to see if the brake system warning lamp remains illuminated.

**** CAUTION**

If the brake system warning lamp remains illuminated, DO NOT allow the vehicle to be driven until it is diagnosed and repaired.

➡If the brake system warning lamp remains illuminated, refer to Diagnostic Trouble Codes.

BLEEDING THE ABS SYSTEM

See Figures 4 and 5.

**** CAUTION**

Brake fluid contains polyglycol ethers and polyglycols. Avoid contact with the eyes and wash your hands thoroughly after handling brake fluid. If you do get brake fluid in your eyes, flush your eyes with clean, running water for 15 minutes. If eye irritation persists, or if you have taken brake fluid internally, IMMEDIATELY seek medical assistance.

**** WARNING**

Clean, high quality brake fluid is essential to the safe and proper operation of the brake system. You should always buy the highest quality brake fluid that is available. If the brake fluid becomes contaminated, drain and flush the system, then refill the master cylinder with new fluid. Never reuse any brake fluid. Any brake fluid that is removed from the system should be discarded. Also, do not allow any brake fluid to come in contact with a painted surface; it will damage the paint.

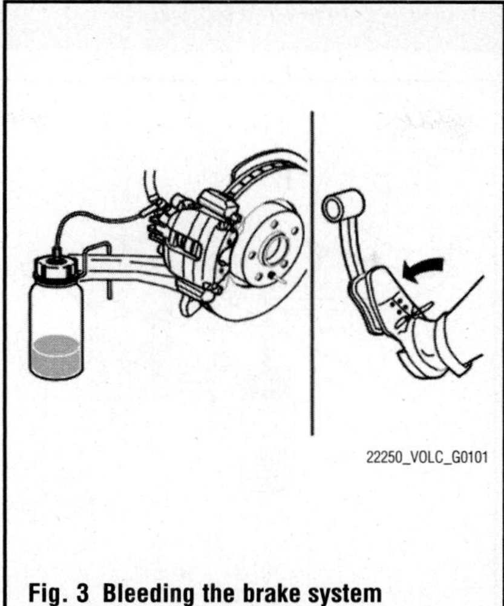

Fig. 3 Bleeding the brake system

When reconditioning or replacing brake calipers bleed the relevant brake pipe as follows.

➡The brake pedal must be depressed throughout the operation. This is so that the brake system is not drained of brake fluid.

➡If the braking system has been completely or partly drained, bleed the whole system. A bleeding unit that can pressurize the brake system to 0.2–0.3 Mpa must be used.

1. Before servicing the vehicle, refer to the Precautions Section.
2. Turn the ignition switch OFF.
3. Clean all around the brake fluid reservoir filler cap.
4. Take out the special brake fluid collection bottle.
5. Connect the bleeding unit to the brake fluid reservoir. Follow the manufacturer's instructions for connecting and using the bleeding unit.
6. Pressurize the brake system. Check the brake fluid reservoir connector.
7. Raise the car and remove the wheels.
8. Remove the protective cap from the bleed nipple. Connect the hose from the collection bottle.
9. Open the bleed nipple. Close it when there are no more air bubbles in the fluid coming out of the hose.

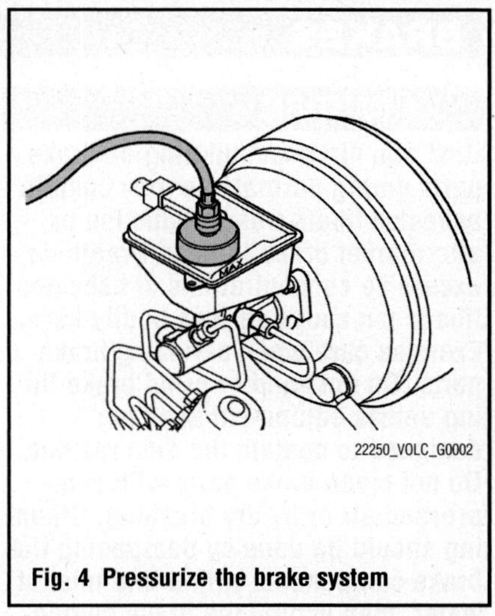

Fig. 4 Pressurize the brake system

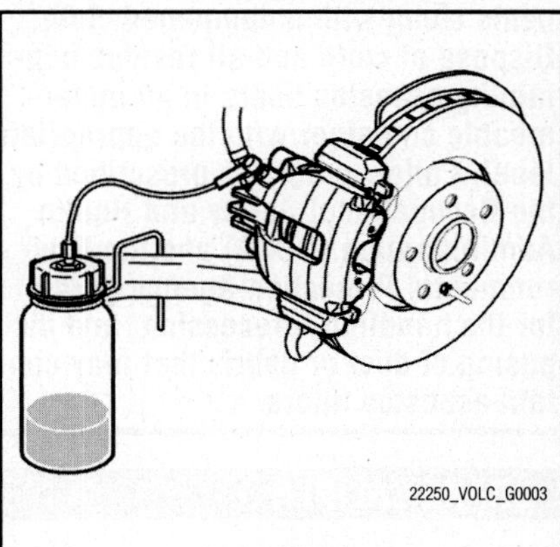

Fig. 5 Connect the hose from the collection bottle

10. Tighten the bleed nipple.
11. Continue to bleed the other wheels. Use the following wheel order:
    - Left front wheel
    - Right front wheel
    - Left rear wheel
    - Right rear wheel
12. Check for leakage from the bleed nipples.
13. Depressurize the brake system.
14. Check for air in the brake system and for brake fluid leakage.
15. Fill the brake reservoir with the proper amount of DOT 4+ brake fluid.

FLUID FILL PROCEDURE

Use DOT 4+ brake fluid. It provides protection with a boiling point above 536°F (280°C).

The brake fluid should always be between the MIN and MAX marks on the side of the reservoir. Check, without removing the cap, that there is sufficient fluid in the reservoir. Add or remove as necessary.

CAUTION

Dust and dirt accumulating on brake parts during normal use may contain asbestos fibers from production or aftermarket brake linings. Breathing excessive concentrations of asbestos fibers can cause serious bodily harm. Exercise care when servicing brake parts. Do not sand or grind brake lining unless equipment used is designed to contain the dust residue. Do not clean brake parts with compressed air or by dry brushing. Cleaning should be done by dampening the brake components with a fine mist of water, then wiping the brake components clean with a dampened cloth. Dispose of cloth and all residue containing asbestos fibers in an impermeable container with the appropriate label. Follow practices prescribed by the Occupational Safety and Health Administration (OSHA) and the Environmental Protection Agency (EPA) for the handling, processing, and disposing of dust or debris that may contain asbestos fibers.

BRAKE CALIPER

REMOVAL & INSTALLATION

S40

See Figures 6 and 7.

1. Before servicing the vehicle, refer to the Precautions Section.
2. Secure the brake pedal in the depressed position. Use a pedal jack.
3. Raise and safely support the vehicle.
4. Remove the tire and wheel assembly.
5. Clean the brake caliper thoroughly.
6. Remove the protective cap from the bleed nipple.
7. Install a plastic hose on the nipple.
8. Open the bleed nipple. Collect the brake fluid in a container (bottle). Close the bleed nipple.
9. Loosen the brake hose half a turn.
10. Remove the brake pads.
11. Remove the locating pins.
12. Unscrew the caliper from the brake hose.
13. Remove the brake caliper from the vehicle.

To install:

14. Install the brake hose to the brake caliper. Do not fully tighten the hose yet.
15. Install the brake pads.

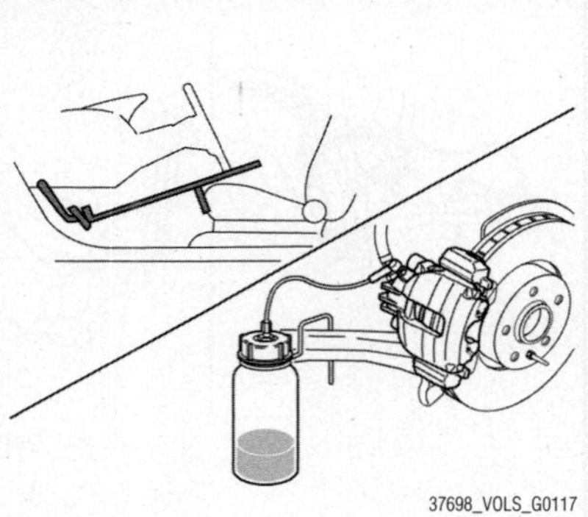

Fig. 6 Secure the brake pedal in the depressed position with a pedal jack

16. Tighten the brake hose to 17 ft. lbs. (23 Nm).

WARNING

Ensure that the brake hose is not twisted. If the brake hose is twisted, there is a risk of circuit failure.

17. Remove the pedal jack.
18. Fill and bleed the brake system.

➡Use only Volvo Genuine parts brake fluid, Volvo DOT 4+.

19. Check the function of the brakes after bleeding. Check that there is no leakage.
20. Install the wheel and tire assembly
21. Slowly depress and release the brake pedal. Observe the feel of the brake pedal.
22. If the brake pedal feels spongy, repeat the bleeding procedure again. If the brake pedal still feels spongy after repeating the bleeding procedure, perform the following steps:
    a. Inspect the brake system for external leaks.
    b. Pressure bleed the hydraulic brake system in order to purge any air that may still be trapped in the system.
23. Turn the ignition key ON, with the engine OFF. Check to see if the brake system warning lamp remains illuminated.

CAUTION

If the brake system warning lamp remains illuminated, DO NOT allow the vehicle to be driven until it is diagnosed and repaired.

➡If the brake system warning lamp remains illuminated, refer to Diagnostic Trouble Codes.

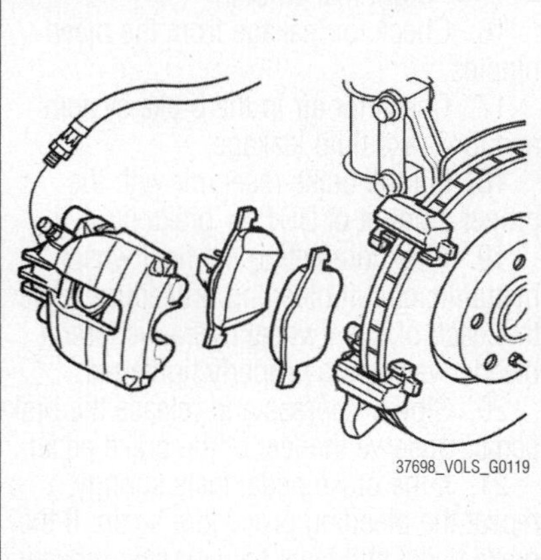

Fig. 7 View of front brake components—S40 vehicles

S60

See Figures 6 and 8.

1. Before servicing the vehicle, refer to the Precautions Section.
2. Secure the brake pedal in the depressed position. Use a pedal jack.
3. Raise and safely support the vehicle.
4. Remove the tire and wheel assembly.
5. Clean the brake caliper thoroughly.
6. Remove the protective cap from the bleed nipple.
7. Install a plastic hose on the nipple.
8. Open the bleed nipple. Collect the brake fluid in a container (bottle). Close the bleed nipple.
9. Loosen the brake hose from the brake caliper ½ turn.
10. Remove the securing spring carefully so that it does not deform.

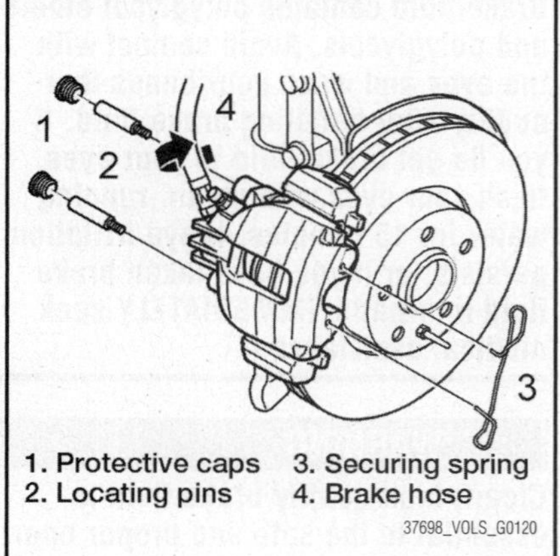

Fig. 8 View of front brake components—S60 vehicles

11. Remove the protective caps from the 2 locating pins.

12. Remove the locating pins, using a 7mm hex socket.

13. Remove the brake caliper from the holder.

14. Remove the brake hose from the brake caliper and drain the remaining brake fluid.

15. Remove the brake pads.

➡Do not depress the brake pedal while the brake pads are removed.

To install:

16. Install the brake hose in the brake caliper. Do not tighten the hose yet.

17. Install the brake pads.

18. Position the brake caliper in place.

19. Check the rubber sleeves of the locating pins. Replace if necessary.

20. Lubricate the locating pins using grease, P/N 1161325-4.

21. Insert the locating pins into the rubber sleeves. The pins should slide into the sleeves easily.

22. Tighten the locating pins to 21 ft. lbs. (28 Nm). Install the protective caps and the securing spring.

23. Tighten the brake hose in the caliper to 13 ft. lbs. (18 Nm).

24. Ensure that the brake hose is not twisted. If necessary alter the hose at the other end (brake pipe end).

✻✻ WARNING

If the brake hose is twisted it may rub against the tire, rim, or wheel arch. This could cause the circuit to fail.

25. Fill and bleed the brake system.

➡Use only Volvo Genuine parts brake fluid (Volvo DOT 4+).

26. Check the function of the brakes after bleeding. Check that there is no leakage.

27. Install the wheel and tire assembly.

28. Slowly depress and release the brake pedal. Observe the feel of the brake pedal.

29. If the brake pedal feels spongy, repeat the bleeding procedure again. If the brake pedal still feels spongy after repeating the bleeding procedure, perform the following steps:

a. Inspect the brake system for external leaks.

b. Pressure bleed the hydraulic brake system in order to purge any air that may still be trapped in the system.

30. Turn the ignition key ON, with the engine OFF. Check to see if the brake system warning lamp remains illuminated.

✻✻ CAUTION

If the brake system warning lamp remains illuminated, DO NOT allow the vehicle to be driven until it is diagnosed and repaired.

➡If the brake system warning lamp remains illuminated, refer to Diagnostic Trouble Codes.

BRAKE PADS

REMOVAL & INSTALLATION

S40

See Figures 9 and 10.

1. Before servicing the vehicle, refer to the Precautions Section.
2. Raise and safely support the vehicle.
3. Remove the tire and wheel assembly.
4. Remove the retaining spring.
5. Remove the protective caps from the locating pins.
6. Remove the locating pins using a 7mm hex socket.
7. Remove the brake caliper. Hang up the caliper in a suitable position to avoid damaging the brake hose.
8. Remove the brake pads.

➡Do not depress the brake pedal while the brake pads are removed.

To install:

9. Clean and check the brake caliper and dust cover.

10. Clean and check the brake pad mating surfaces in the brake caliper and caliper holder.

11. Clean the sliding pins using a steel brush.

➡If the dust boot is damaged, dirt may have penetrated the cylinder. If this is the case, the caliper must be replaced.

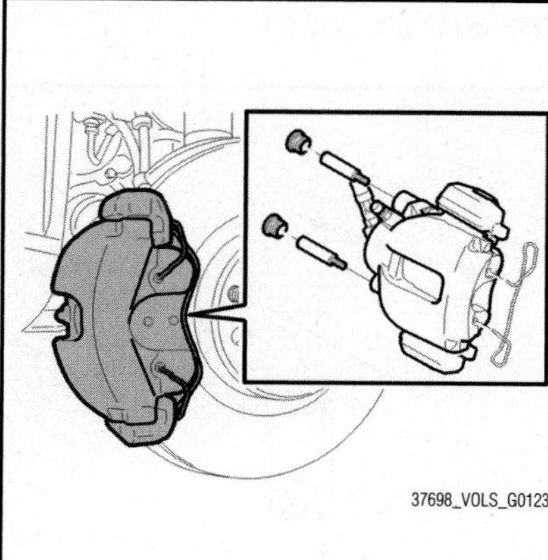

Fig. 9 Removing the brake caliper—S40 vehicles

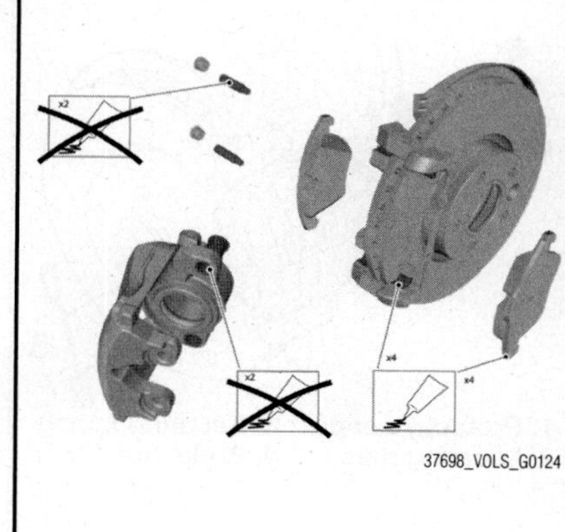

Fig. 10 Exploded view of brake components and lubrication points

12. Check brake disc friction surfaces.

a. If the brake disc displays signs of out-of-true, check its lateral run out.

b. Replace the brake disc if it displays signs of heavy wear or variable thickness.

13. Lubricate the contact surfaces of the brake pads using silicone grease.

➡Do not lubricate the sliding pins.

14. Press the brake piston back into the cylinder on the brake caliper. Check that the dust cover is correctly positioned.

15. Install new brake pads on both sides of the vehicle.

16. Install the brake caliper into position.

17. Install the locating pins and tighten to 22 ft. lbs. (30 Nm).

➡Check the rubber sleeves of the locating pins. Replace if necessary.

18. Install the protective caps on the locating pins.

19. Install the retaining spring.

20. Depress the brake pedal a few times. Check the brake fluid level in the reservoir. Top it up, if necessary.

21. Install the wheel and tire assembly.

S60

See Figures 11 and 12.

1. Before servicing the vehicle, refer to the Precautions Section.
2. Raise and safely support the vehicle.
3. Remove the tire and wheel assembly.
4. Remove the retaining spring carefully so that it does not deform.
5. Remove the protective caps from the locating pins.
6. Remove the locating pins using a 7mm hex socket.

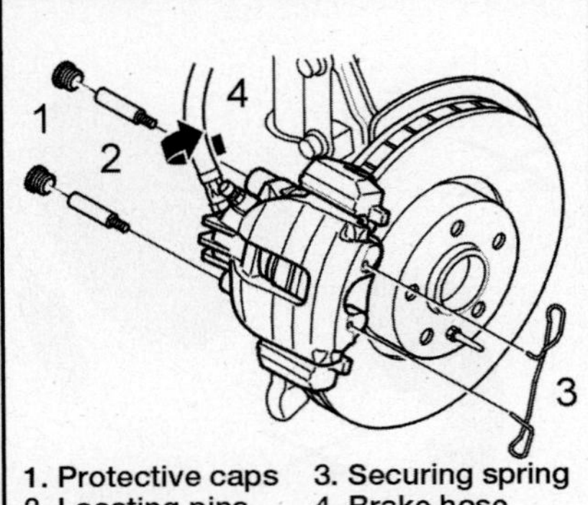

Fig. 11 View of front brake components—S60 vehicles

7. Remove the brake caliper from the holder. Hang the brake caliper by a steel wire from the front spring so as not to damage the brake hose.

8. Remove the brake pads.

➡Do not depress the brake pedal while the brake pads are removed.

To install:

9. Clean and check the brake pad mating surfaces in the brake caliper and caliper holder.

10. Clean the sliding pins using a steel brush.

11. Check the piston dust boot. Replace the dust boot if it is damaged.

➡If the dust boot is damaged, dirt may have penetrated the cylinder. The brake caliper must be reconditioned.

12. Check the brake disc friction surfaces.

a. If the brake disc displays signs of out-of-true, check its lateral run out.

b. Replace the brake disc if it displays signs of heavy wear or variable thickness.

13. Lubricate the contact surfaces of the brake pads using silicone grease.

➡Do not lubricate the sliding pins.

14. Press the piston back into the brake cylinder on the brake caliper. Check that the dust cover is correctly positioned.

15. Install new brake pads on both sides.

16. Install the brake caliper into position.

17. Check the rubber sleeves of the locating pins. Replace if necessary.

18. Insert the locating pins in the rubber sleeves. Tighten the locating pins to 21 ft. lbs. (28 Nm).

19. Install the protective caps on the locating pins.

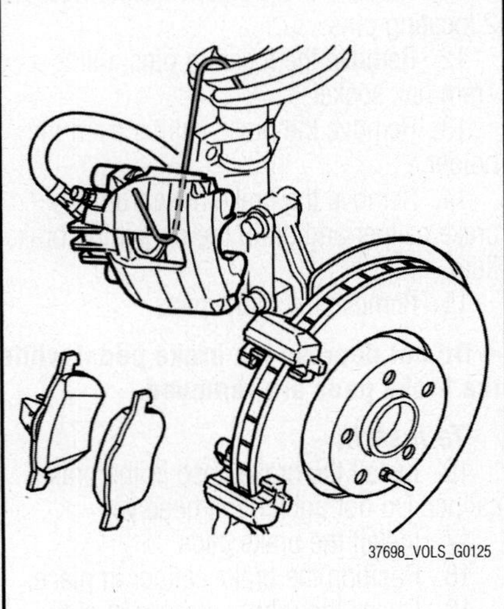

Fig. 12 Removing the front brake pads—S60 vehicles

20. Install the retaining spring.

21. Depress the brake pedal a few times. Check the level of the brake fluid reservoir, top up if necessary.

➡Use only Volvo Genuine parts brake fluid (Volvo DOT 4+).

22. Install the wheel and tire assembly.

CAUTION

Dust and dirt accumulating on brake parts during normal use may contain asbestos fibers from production or aftermarket brake linings. Breathing excessive concentrations of asbestos fibers can cause serious bodily harm. Exercise care when servicing brake parts. Do not sand or grind brake lining unless equipment used is designed to contain the dust residue. Do not clean brake parts with compressed air or by dry brushing. Cleaning should be done by dampening the brake components with a fine mist of water, then wiping the brake components clean with a dampened cloth. Dispose of cloth and all residue containing asbestos fibers in an impermeable container with the appropriate label. Follow practices prescribed by the Occupational Safety and Health Administration (OSHA) and the Environmental Protection Agency (EPA) for the handling, processing, and disposing of dust or debris that may contain asbestos fibers.

BRAKE CALIPER

REMOVAL & INSTALLATION

See Figures 13 and 14.

1. Before servicing the vehicle, refer to the Precautions Section.

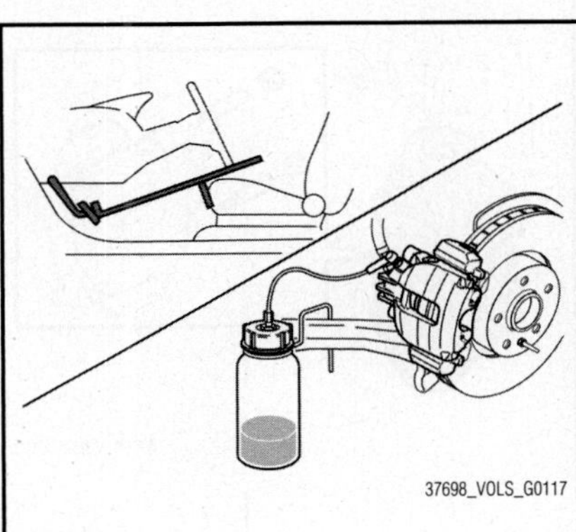

Fig. 13 Secure the brake pedal in the depressed position with a pedal jack

2. Remove the tire and wheel assembly.

3. Secure the pedal in the depressed position using a pedal jack.

4. Remove the protective cap from the bleed nipple, connect a hose and open the nipple.

5. Use a container to collect the brake fluid.

6. Loosen the brake hose ½ turn.

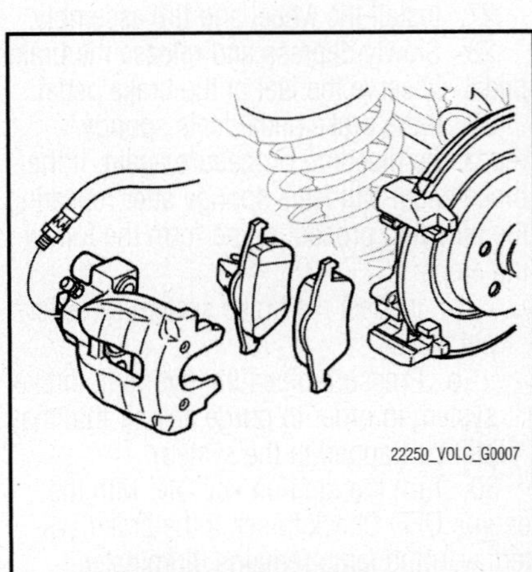

Fig. 14 Rear brake caliper view

7. Remove the retaining spring.
8. Remove the protective caps.
9. Remove the locating pins.
10. Remove the brake pads.
11. Remove the brake caliper.
12. Remove the brake hose from the brake caliper.

To install:

13. Install the brake hose in the brake caliper. Do not tighten the hose fully.
14. Install the brake pads.
15. Install the locating pins and tighten to 26 ft. lbs. (35 Nm).
16. Install the locating pin protective caps.
17. Install the retaining spring.
18. Tighten the brake hose to 17 ft. lbs. (23 Nm) on S40, 34 ft. lbs. (46Nm) on S60.
19. Bleed the brake system.
20. Depress the brake pedal a few times and check the brake fluid level.
21. Install the wheel and tire assembly.

BRAKE PADS

REMOVAL & INSTALLATION

See Figure 15.

1. Before servicing the vehicle, refer to the Precautions Section.
2. Remove the tire and wheel assembly.
3. Remove the caliper spring.
4. Remove the locating pin protective caps.
5. Remove the locating pins.
6. Remove the brake caliper and hang it in a suitable position.

⁂ WARNING

Make sure that no load is placed on the brake hose when the caliper is removed.

7. Remove the brake pads.

➡Do not depress the brake pedal while the brake pads are removed.

To install:

8. Check the rubber sleeves on the locating pins. Replace, if necessary.
9. Insert the locating pins in the rubber sleeves. The locating pins must slide into the sleeves easily.
10. Press the piston back into the cylinder using a C-clamp.
11. Install the brake pads.

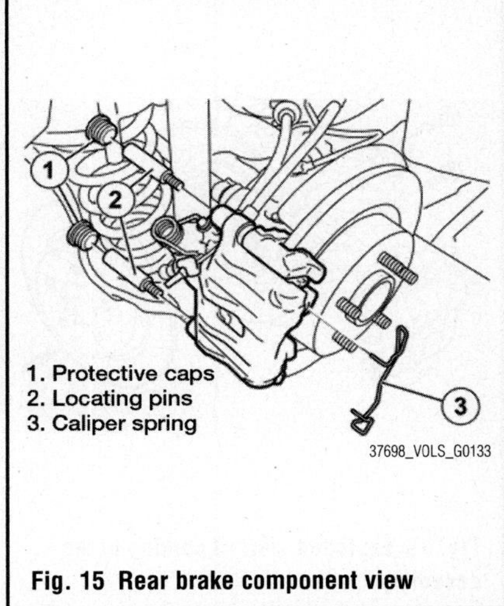

Fig. 15 Rear brake component view

12. Install the brake caliper.
13. Install the locating pins. Tighten to 26 ft. lbs. (35 Nm).
14. Install the protective caps.
15. Install the caliper spring.
16. Depress the brake pedal a few times and check the brake fluid level.
17. Install the wheel and tire assembly.

BRAKES — PARKING BRAKE

PARKING BRAKE CABLES

ADJUSTMENT

S40

See Figures 16 through 18.

1. Before servicing the vehicle, refer to the Precautions Section.
2. Remove the panel for the center console or the panel in line with the parking brake cable.
3. Locate the adjustment for the parking brake.
4. Remove the retaining clip.
5. Turn the socket clockwise to increase tension on the parking brake cable.
6. Install the clip.
7. Depress the brake pedal to the 1st notch. Press out the adjustment using the adjustment rod: 951-2947.
8. Test the parking brake.

Fig. 16 Remove the panel (cup holder) for the center console—S40 vehicles

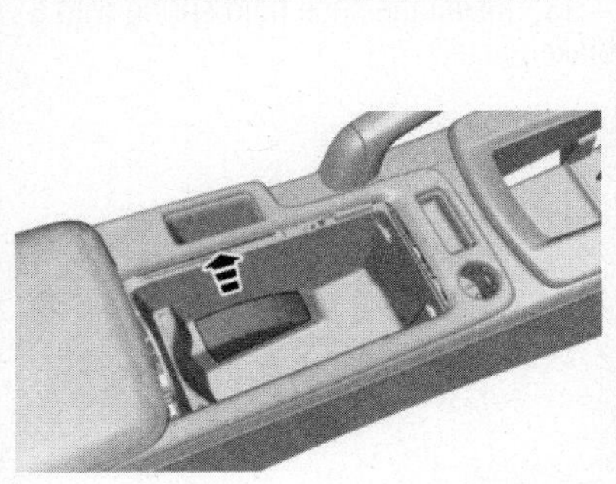

Fig. 17 Remove the parking brake adjustment cover—S40 vehicles

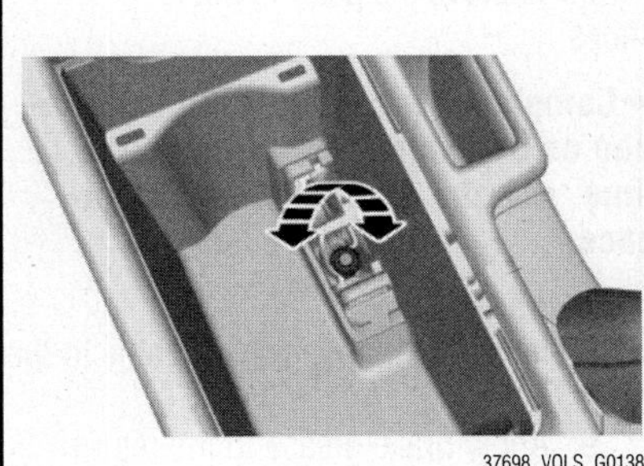

Fig. 18 Turn the socket clockwise to increase tension on the parking brake cable—S40 vehicles

➡Full effect should be obtained between the 2nd and 5th ratchet teeth.

9. Install the panel that was removed.

PARKING BRAKE SHOES

REMOVAL & INSTALLATION

See Figures 19 and 20.

1. Before servicing the vehicle, refer to the Precautions Section.
2. Remove the rear disc brake caliper assembly.

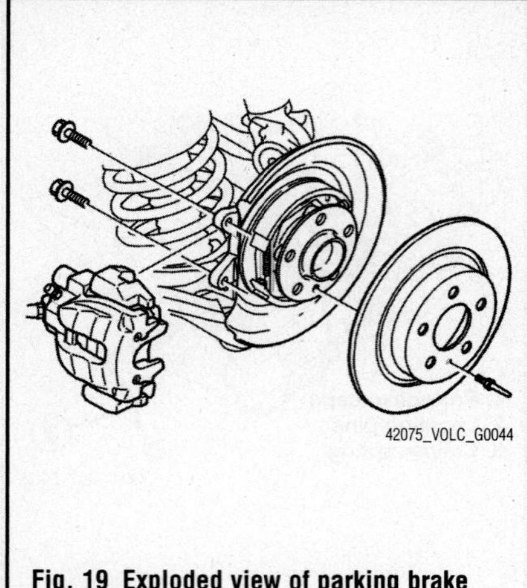

Fig. 19 Exploded view of parking brake assembly

➡Before removing the brake disc rotor, make a chalk marking by the bolts to aid in reassembly.

3. Remove the brake rotor.
4. Remove the shoe hold spring by turning the pin to coincide with the hole of the spring cap.
5. Remove the return spring.
6. For S40 and S60 vehicles, disconnect the cable end from the trailing shoe.
7. Remove the parking brake shoes.

➡Complete the removal and installation on one side of the vehicle at a time. Use the other side as a reference.

To install:

8. Install the parking brake cable to the operating lever.
9. Apply brake grease to the return spring and areas of movement on the mechanism, but do not apply grease to the brake shoe material.

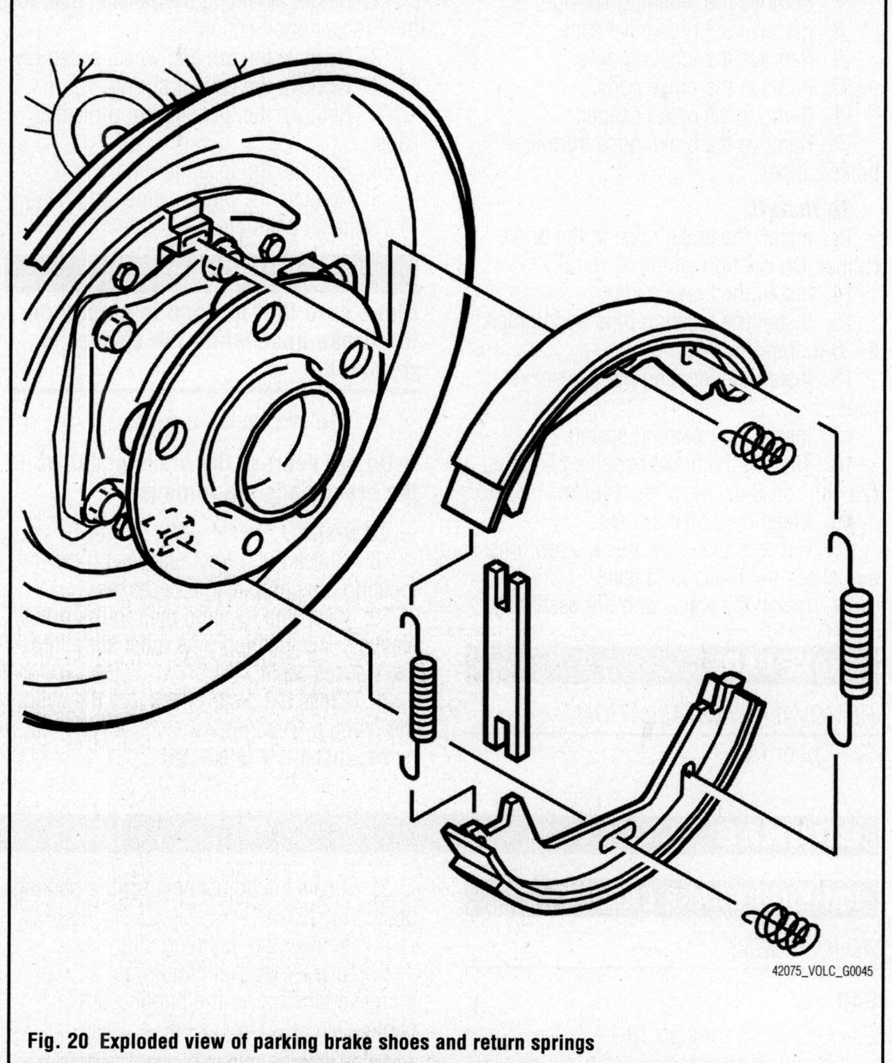

Fig. 20 Exploded view of parking brake shoes and return springs

10. Install the upper return spring and brake shoes.
11. Turn the adjuster in a counter clockwise direction and install.
12. Install the lower return spring.
13. Install the shoe hold spring with a brake pliers.
14. Install the disc brake and then align the marks while tightening the screw.
15. Check for proper operation of the parking brake assembly. Make adjustments as needed.

GENERAL INFORMATION

CAUTION

These vehicles are equipped with an air bag system. The system must be disarmed before performing service on, or around, system components, the steering column, instrument panel components, wiring and sensors. Failure to follow the safety precautions and the disarming procedure could result in accidental air bag deployment, possible injury and unnecessary system repairs.

SERVICE PRECAUTIONS

Disconnect and isolate the battery negative cable before beginning any airbag system component diagnosis, testing, removal, or installation procedures. Allow system capacitor to discharge for two minutes before beginning any component service. This will disable the airbag system. Failure to disable the airbag system may result in accidental airbag deployment, personal injury, or death.

Do not place an intact undeployed airbag face down on a solid surface. The airbag will propel into the air if accidentally deployed and may result in personal injury or death.

When carrying or handling an undeployed airbag, the trim side (face) of the airbag should be pointing towards the body to minimize possibility of injury if accidental deployment occurs. Failure to do this may result in personal injury or death.

Replace airbag system components with OEM replacement parts. Substitute parts may appear interchangeable, but internal differences may result in inferior occupant protection. Failure to do so may result in occupant personal injury or death.

Wear safety glasses, rubber gloves, and long sleeved clothing when cleaning powder residue from vehicle after an airbag deployment. Powder residue emitted from a deployed airbag can cause skin irritation. Flush affected area with cool water if irritation is experienced. If nasal or throat irritation is experienced, exit the vehicle for fresh air until the irritation ceases. If irritation continues, see a physician.

Do not use a replacement airbag that is not in the original packaging. This may result in improper deployment, personal injury, or death.

The factory installed fasteners, screws and bolts used to fasten airbag components have a special coating and are specifically designed for the airbag system. Do not use substitute fasteners. Use only original equipment fasteners listed in the parts catalog when fastener replacement is required.

During, and following, any child restraint anchor service, due to impact event or vehicle repair, carefully inspect all mounting hardware, tether straps, and anchors for proper installation, operation, or damage. If a child restraint anchor is found damaged in any way, the anchor must be replaced. Failure to do this may result in personal injury or death.

Deployed and non-deployed airbags may or may not have live pyrotechnic material within the airbag inflator.

Do not dispose of driver/passenger/curtain airbags or seat belt tensioners unless you are sure of complete deployment. Refer to the Hazardous Substance Control System for proper disposal.

Dispose of deployed airbags and tensioners consistent with state, provincial, local, and federal regulations.

After any airbag component testing or service, do not connect the battery negative cable. Personal injury or death may result if the system test is not performed first.

If the vehicle is equipped with the Occupant Classification System (OCS), do not connect the battery negative cable before performing the OCS Verification Test using the scan tool and the appropriate diagnostic information. Personal injury or death may result if the system test is not performed properly.

Never replace both the Occupant Restraint Controller (ORC) and the Occupant Classification Module (OCM) at the same time. If both require replacement, replace one, then perform the Airbag System test before replacing the other.

Both the ORC and the OCM store Occupant Classification System (OCS) calibration data, which they transfer to one another when one of them is replaced. If both are replaced at the same time, an irreversible fault will be set in both modules and the OCS may malfunction and cause personal injury or death.

If equipped with OCS, the Seat Weight Sensor is a sensitive, calibrated unit and must be handled carefully. Do not drop or handle roughly. If dropped or damaged, replace with another sensor. Failure to do so may result in occupant injury or death.

If equipped with OCS, the front passenger seat must be handled carefully as well. When removing the seat, be careful when setting on floor not to drop. If dropped, the sensor may be inoperative, could result in occupant injury, or possibly death.

If equipped with OCS, when the passenger front seat is on the floor, no one should sit in the front passenger seat. This uneven force may damage the sensing ability of the seat weight sensors. If sat on and damaged, the sensor may be inoperative, could result in occupant injury, or possibly death.

DISARMING THE SYSTEM

1. Before servicing the vehicle, refer to the Precautions Section.
2. Turn the ignition switch to **OFF**.
3. Disconnect the negative battery cable and isolate it from accidental reconnection. Insulate the cable end with high-quality electrical tape or a similar non-conductive wrapping.
4. Wait at least 3 minutes for the system capacitor to discharge before performing any service. The airbag system is designed to retain enough voltage to deploy the airbag for a short period of time after the battery has been disconnected.

➡DTC's will be lost when the negative battery cable is disconnected.

There are several reasons for disabling the SRS system, such as repairs to the SRS system or servicing a component near or attached to an SRS component. There are several ways to disable the SRS system depending on what type of service is being performed.

- If the vehicle was involved in an accident with an air bag deployment: Disconnect the negative battery cable
- When performing SRS diagnostics: Follow the appropriate SRS service manual diagnostic procedure(s)
- When removing or replacing an SRS component or a component attached to an SRS component: Disconnect the negative battery cable
- If the vehicle is suspected of having shorted electrical wires: Disconnect the negative battery cable
- When performing electrical diagnosis on components other than the SRS system: Remove the SRS/Airbag fuse(s) when indicated by the diagnostic procedure to disable the SRS system

ARMING THE SYSTEM

1. Before servicing the vehicle, refer to the Precautions Section.

2. Be sure the ignition switch is in the **OFF** position.
3. Install the fuses, if removed.
4. Connect the negative battery cable.

CAUTION

As an added precaution, make sure no one is in the vehicle when reconnecting the negative battery cable.

5. To confirm proper system operation, turn the ignition switch to the **ON** position. The SRS indicator light should light for at least 7 seconds and then go off.
6. If the AIR BAG warning indicator does not operate as described, perform a diagnostic system check.

CLOCKSPRING CENTERING

See Figures 21 and 22.

CAUTION

Models equipped with a Supplemental Restraint System (SRS), use an inflatable air bag. Whenever working near any of the SRS components, such as the impact sensors, the air bag module, steering column, and instrument panel, disable the SRS.

1. Before servicing the vehicle, refer to the Precautions.
2. Turn the contact reel (clockspring) clockwise to the limit position.
3. Turn the contact reel counter-clockwise 2 entire turns.

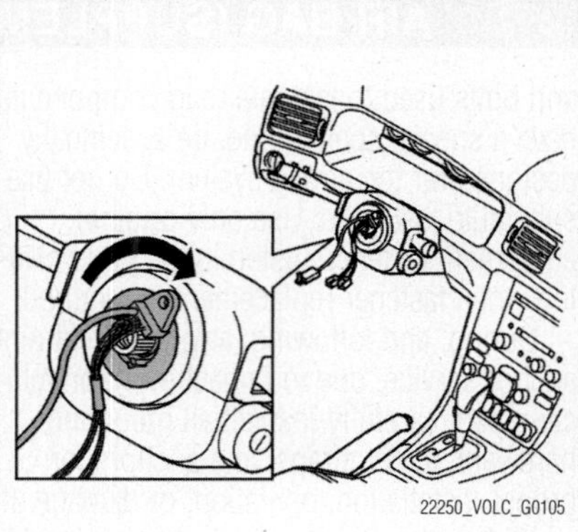

Fig. 21 Turn the contact reel counter-clockwise 2 entire turns

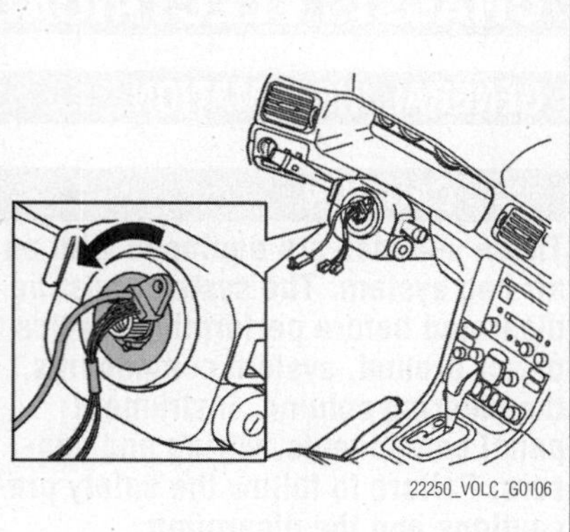

Fig. 22 Turn counter-clockwise further until the screw hole is at the "one o'clock" position

4. Turn the contact reel counter-clockwise further until the screw hole is at the "one o'clock" position.

➡On later models, the yellow marking must also be visible in the window.

5. Install the screw.
6. The contact reel (clockspring) is now reset and locked.

DRIVE TRAIN

DRIVESHAFT

REMOVAL & INSTALLATION

AWD Models

See Figures 23 and 24.

As the illustrations in this service information are used for different model years and/or models, some variation may occur. However, the essential information is always correct.

1. Before servicing the vehicle, refer to the Precautions Section.
2. Raise and safely support the vehicle.

➡If the same driveshaft, also called the propeller shaft, is to be reused when installing, mark the driveshaft CV-joint in relation to the drive flange.

3. Remove the screws for the driveshaft CV-joint. Use a counter-hold on the driveshaft, Special Tool: 951-2940.
4. Remove the screws for the driveshaft CV-joint.
   - For vehicles without a vibration damper on the Active On Demand Coupling (AOC) drive flange, use Special Tool: 999-7057, counter-hold.
   - For vehicles with a vibration damper on the AOC drive flange, use Special Tool: 951-2940, counter-hold.
5. Remove the screws for the propeller shaft center bearing front and rear.
6. Remove the rear screws for the front member for the center bearing.
7. Remove 3 of the 4 screws for the rear member for the center bearing.

CAUTION

Leave 1 screw in place for safety, so that the member does not fall.

8. Press the propeller shaft CV-joints together. Remove the propeller shaft from the flanges.
9. Remove the remaining screw in the rear member for the center bearing.

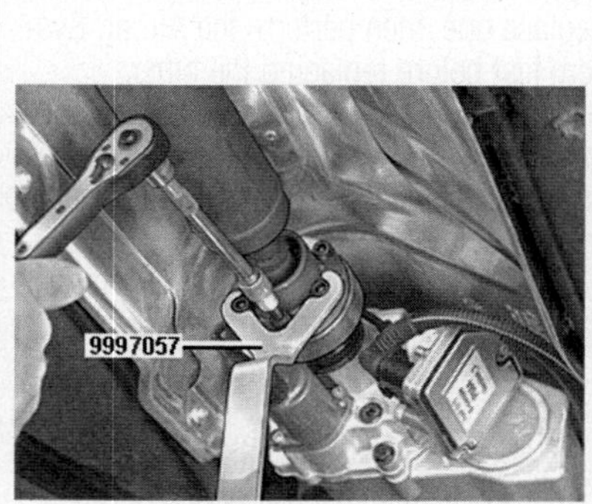

Fig. 23 Using Special Tool: 999-7057 to hold the driveshaft

Fig. 24 Using Special Tool: 951-2940 to hold the driveshaft

Allow the member to rest on the exhaust system.

10. Remove the propeller shaft. Pull the propeller shaft backwards.

⁂ WARNING

Be careful to avoid damaging the heated oxygen sensor or the heat shields.

11. Carefully pull the exhaust system down to free the center bearing.

To install:

12. Install the propeller shaft from behind.

⁂ WARNING

Be careful to avoid damaging the heated oxygen sensor or the heat shields.

13. Secure the propeller shaft by inserting at least 1 screw in the rear member for the center bearing.
14. Check carefully that the mating surfaces on the propeller shaft CV-joint and flange are clean.
15. If the same propeller shaft is to be reinstalled, install the propeller shaft using the marking made earlier.
16. Install the 2 M8 screws for the front member and tighten to 18 ft. lbs. (24 Nm).
17. Install the 4 M8 screws for the rear member and tighten to 18 ft. lbs. (24 Nm).
18. Install the 2 M8 screws for the propeller shaft center bearing front and rear and tighten to 18 ft. lbs. (24 Nm).
19. Install the driveshaft CV-joint front joint and then the rear joint.
    a. Use the appropriate counter-hold to keep the driveshaft from turning.
    b. Tighten the new screws at the CV-joint.
    - Step 1 to 89 inch lbs. (10 Nm)
    - Step 2 to 18 ft. lbs. (25 Nm)

FRONT HALFSHAFT

REMOVAL & INSTALLATION

See Figures 25 through 28.

1. Before servicing the vehicle, refer to the Precautions Section.
2. Remove the front wheel.
3. Remove the wheel speed sensor and wiring bracket.
4. Remove the brake hose bracket.
5. Remove the stabilizer bar link.
6. Remove the splash guards.

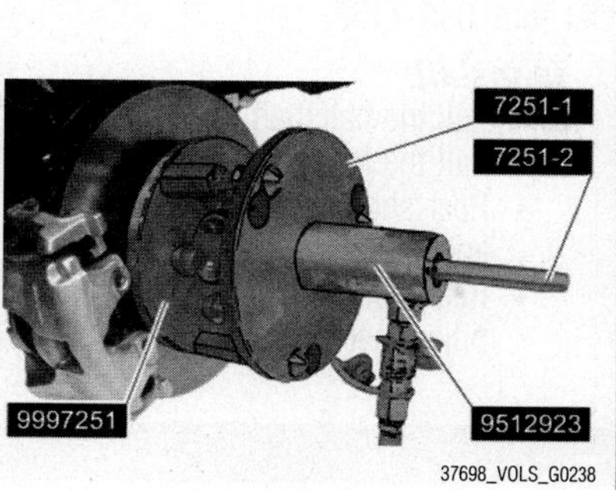

Fig. 25 Using special tools to pull the hub off of the stub shaft

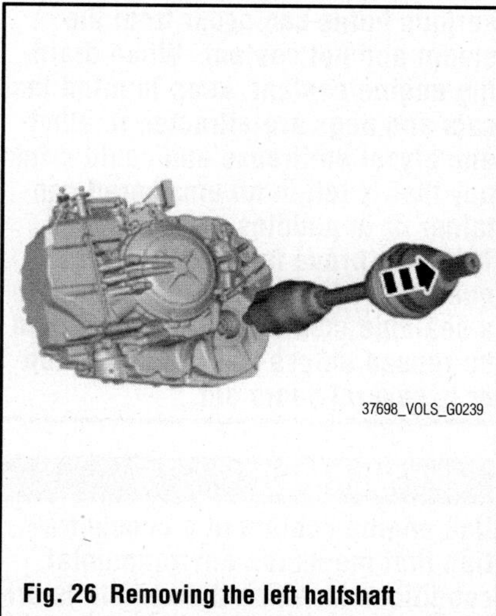

Fig. 26 Removing the left halfshaft

7. Remove the lower ball joint.
8. Remove the hub retainer nut.
9. Pull the hub off of the stub shaft.
10. Pry the inner joint out of the transaxle and remove the axle halfshaft.

To install:

➡Use new fasteners for assembly.

11. Install the axle halfshaft so that the cir-clip is felt to seat in the retainer groove.
12. Guide the stub shaft into the hub.
13. On the right side, tighten the 2 M8 bolts to 18 ft. lbs. (24 Nm).
14. Install the hub retainer nut and tighten the nut to 26 ft. lbs. (35 Nm) plus 90 degrees.
15. Install the lower ball joint.
16. Install the splash guards.
17. Install the stabilizer bar link.
18. Install the brake hose bracket.
19. Install the wheel speed sensor and wiring bracket.
20. Install the front wheel.

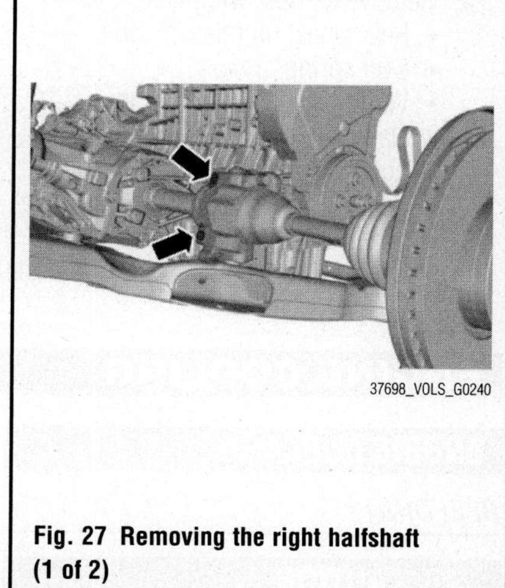

Fig. 27 Removing the right halfshaft (1 of 2)

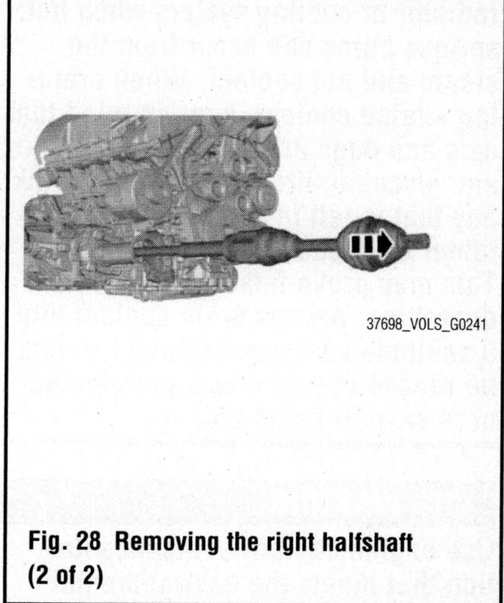

Fig. 28 Removing the right halfshaft (2 of 2)

REAR HALFSHAFT

REMOVAL & INSTALLATION

See Figure 29.

1. Before servicing the vehicle, refer to the Precautions Section.

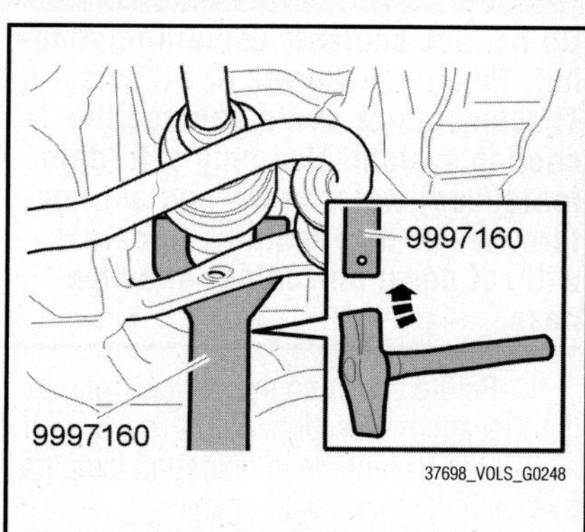

Fig. 29 Using Special Tool: 999-7160 to wedge out the rear halfshaft

2. Remove the following items:
   - Rear wheel on relevant side
   - Coil spring
   - Wheel knuckle rear to body
   - Halfshaft to wheel hub
   - Lower arm rear to sub-frame
   - Rear stabilizer bar link to lower stabilizer bar
   - Rear shock absorber to wheel knuckle

3. Remove the rear halfshaft using Special Tool: 999-7160.

To install:

4. Install the halfshaft.
5. Install the following items:
   - Rear shock absorber to wheel knuckle
   - Rear stabilizer bar link to lower stabilizer bar
   - Lower arm rear to subframe
   - Halfshaft to wheel hub. Tighten the nut to 26 ft. lbs. (35 Nm) plus 90 degrees
   - Wheel knuckle rear to body
   - Coil spring
   - Wheel

ENGINE COOLING

ENGINE COOLANT

BLEEDING

CAUTION

Never open, service, or drain the radiator or cooling system when hot; serious burns can occur from the steam and hot coolant. When draining engine coolant, keep in mind that cats and dogs are attracted to ethylene glycol antifreeze and could drink any that is left in an uncovered container or in puddles on the ground. This may prove fatal in sufficient quantities. Always drain coolant into a sealable container. Coolant should be reused unless it is contaminated or is several years old.

WARNING

Use engine coolant at a concentration that meets the environmental conditions in which the vehicle is driven, otherwise engine damage could occur. The engine has aluminum parts and must be protected by an ethylene-glycol-based coolant to prevent corrosion and freezing.

WARNING

Do not use coolants containing Alcohol, Methanol, Borate or Silicate. These coolants could damage the cooling system. Use only soft (demineralized) water in the coolant mixture. Water that contains minerals will cut down on coolant effectiveness.

1. Before servicing the vehicle, refer to the Precautions Section.
2. Run the engine to operating temperature until the thermostat opens.
3. Carefully open the coolant reservoir cap after the system cools.
4. Top off the coolant, as necessary.

DRAIN & REFILL

See Figures 30 through 32.

CAUTION

Never open, service, or drain the radiator or cooling system when hot; serious burns can occur from the steam and hot coolant. When draining engine coolant, keep in mind that cats and dogs are attracted to ethylene glycol antifreeze and could drink any that is left in an uncovered container or in puddles on the ground. This may prove fatal in sufficient quantities. Always drain coolant into a sealable container. Coolant should be reused unless it is contaminated or is several years old.

WARNING

Use engine coolant at a concentration that meets the environmental conditions in which the vehicle is driven, otherwise engine damage could occur. The engine has aluminum parts and must be protected by an ethylene-glycol-based coolant to prevent corrosion and freezing.

WARNING

Do not use coolants containing Alcohol, Methanol, Borate or Silicate. These coolants could damage the cooling system. Use only soft (demineralized) water in the coolant mixture. Water that contains minerals will cut down on coolant effectiveness.

1. Before servicing the vehicle, refer to the Precautions Section.
2. Remove the engine splashguard.
3. Release the cooling system pressure. Cover the coolant expansion tank cap with a thick cloth and remove the cap.

➡Be prepared to collect escaping fluid.

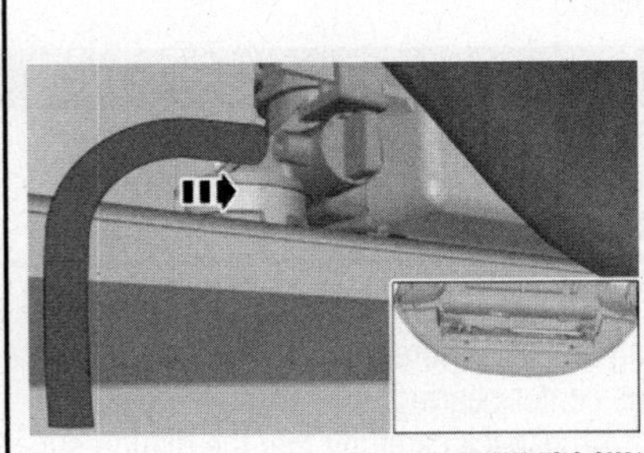

37698_VOLS_G0254

Fig. 30 Open the radiator drain valve and drain the coolant

4. Open the radiator drain valve and collect the coolant into a container.
5. Let the system drain completely.

To install:

6. Tighten the radiator drain plug securely.
7. Install the splash shield.
8. Fill the system with the specified quantity and strength of coolant using Special Tools: 951-2955 and 951-2957.

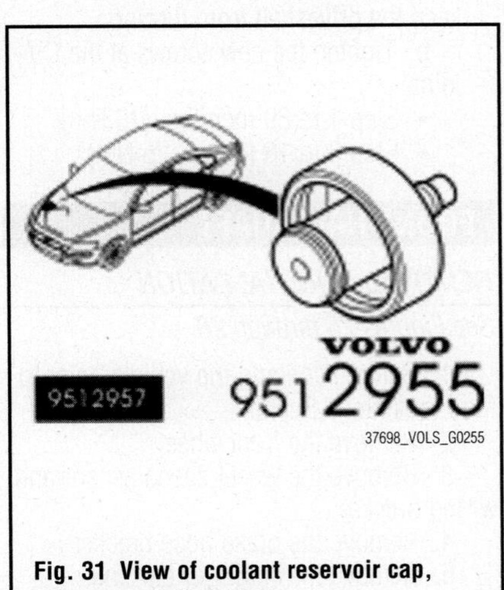

37698_VOLS_G0255

Fig. 31 View of coolant reservoir cap, Special Tool: 951-2955

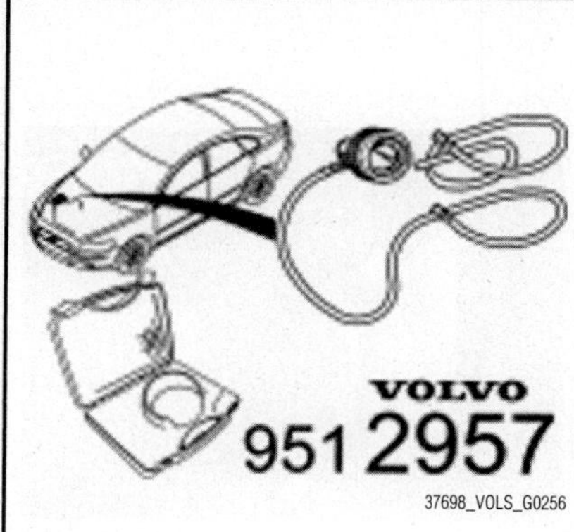

Fig. 32 View of coolant reservoir filling tool, Special Tool: 951-2957

9. Run the engine to operating temperature until the thermostat opens. Top off the coolant, as necessary.

ELECTRIC ENGINE FAN

REMOVAL & INSTALLATION

S40

See Figures 33 through 35.

Some variation in the illustrations may occur, but the essential information is always correct.

1. Disconnect the negative battery cable.
2. Before servicing the vehicle, refer to the Precautions Section.
3. Remove the bumper cover.
4. Drain the engine coolant.
5. Remove the cover for the Brake Control Module (BCM).
6. Remove the expansion tank cap.
7. Remove the connector for the engine cooling fan.

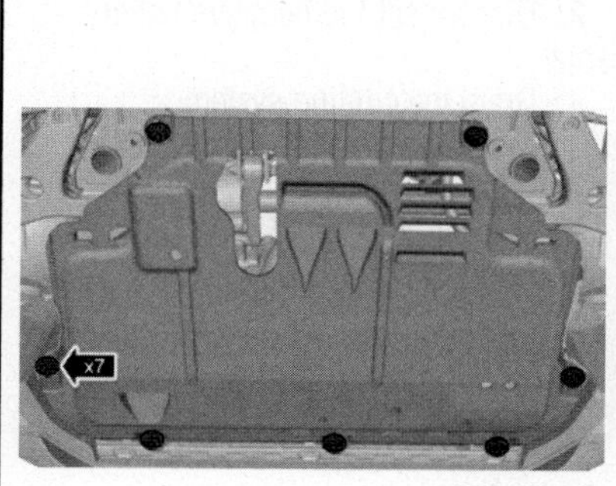

Fig. 33 Remove the lower engine splashguard

Fig. 34 Remove the bracket for the air conditioning aggregate

8. Remove the hoses from the clips of the cooling fan.
9. With automatic transaxle:
   a. Remove the screws for the transaxle oil cooler.
   b. Place the oil cooler to one side.
10. Remove the splash guard under the engine.
11. Install a mobile jack under the radiator.
12. Remove the 4 screws and the bracket for the air conditioning aggregate.
13. Remove the 2 coolant hoses.

⁂ WARNING

When removing the engine cooling fan, ensure that no cables are damaged.

14. Press in both clips on the upper section and lift the engine cooling fan from the catches.
15. Remove the engine fan downwards to remove from vehicle.

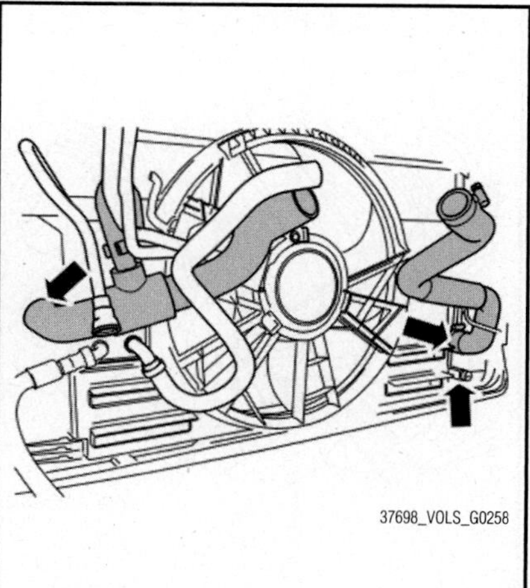
Fig. 35 Remove the 2 coolant hoses

To install:

16. Install the engine cooling fan from underneath.
17. Hook the engine cooling fan into the upper and lower mountings.
18. Install the 2 coolant hoses, close the drain screw.
19. Install the bracket for the air conditioning aggregate and the 4 M8 screws.
20. Install the splash guard under the engine.
21. With automatic transaxle, install the oil cooler to the transaxle.
22. Install the connector to the engine cooling fan.
23. Install the 2 hoses in the clips on the engine cooling fan assembly.
24. Install the cover for the BCM.
25. Check the engine coolant level..
26. Run the engine until the thermostat opens. Top up the coolant as needed.
27. Install the bumper cover.

S60

1. Disconnect the negative battery cable.
2. Before servicing the vehicle, refer to the Precautions Section.
3. Remove the intake pipe for the Air Cleaner Housing (ACL). Disconnect both the connectors for the engine cooling fan.
4. Remove the Evaporative Emission System (EVAP) valve from the engine cooling fan shroud.
5. Remove the hose clamps and charge air pipe/hose on the right-hand side.
6. Remove the tie straps that hold the cable harness secure at the fan shroud.
7. Lift out the hose for the expansion tank from the holders on top of the fan shroud.
8. Remove the cool box plastic hose from the fan shroud.
9. Remove the screws holding the fan shroud.
10. Release the hose for the coolant reservoir from the fan shroud.
11. Remove the engine cooling fan.

To install:

12. Carefully lower the fan shroud and align with the holders.
13. Route the cable harness behind the holder. Tighten the mounting screws.
14. Press the hose down from the expansion tank into the holder on the fan shroud.
15. Install the engine fan and attach the cable harness with clips and tie-straps
16. Install the canister purge valve.
17. Install the hose clamp and charge air pipe/hose on the right-hand side.

18. Install the intake manifold to the ACL housing.

19. Connect the engine cooling fan connectors.

20. Transfer the bracket to the new fan shroud.

21. Install the connectors for the fan on the bracket using the holder from the service kit.

22. Install the cover on the cool box.

RADIATOR

REMOVAL & INSTALLATION

See Figure 36.

CAUTION

Never open, service or drain the radiator or cooling system when hot; serious burns can occur from the steam and hot coolant. Also, when draining engine coolant, keep in mind that cats and dogs are attracted to ethylene glycol antifreeze and could drink any that is left in an uncovered container or in puddles on the ground. This will prove fatal in sufficient quantities. Always drain coolant into a sealable container. Coolant should be reused unless it is contaminated or is several years old.

1. Be sure the engine is cold before removing the radiator.
2. Disconnect or remove:
   - Engine fan.
   - Evacuation hose from the expansion tank
   - Upper and lower radiator hoses

➡Do not allow engine coolant to contact the accessory drive belt.

Fig. 36 Radiator and core support mounting bolts

   - Remove the charge air cooler
   - Disconnect and plug the oil cooler hoses from the automatic transaxle
   - The radiator mounting bolts
   - Core support
   - Remove the radiator

To install:

3. Lift radiator into position.
4. Install or connect the following:
   - The radiator mounting bolts. Tighten to 18 ft. lbs. (24 Nm)
   - Install the charge air cooler
   - Oil cooler hoses from the automatic transaxle
   - Upper and lower radiator hoses
   - Evacuation hose into expansion tank
   - Engine fan.
5. Be sure to refill the cooling system using the proper grade and type of engine coolant.
6. Start the engine and check for leaks.
7. Run the engine and allow it to reach full operating temperature. Recheck the coolant level and transaxle fluid level. Fill as required.

THERMOSTAT

REMOVAL & INSTALLATION

S40

See Figure 37.

1. Before servicing the vehicle, refer to the Precautions Section.
2. Drain the cooling system.
3. Disconnect or remove the following:
   - Hose clamp to the upper radiator hose
   - Hose from the thermostat housing
   - Connector from the temperature sensor

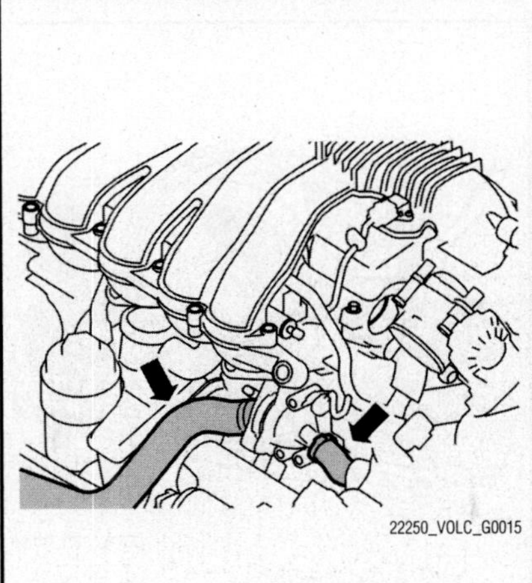

Fig. 37 Location of thermostat housing

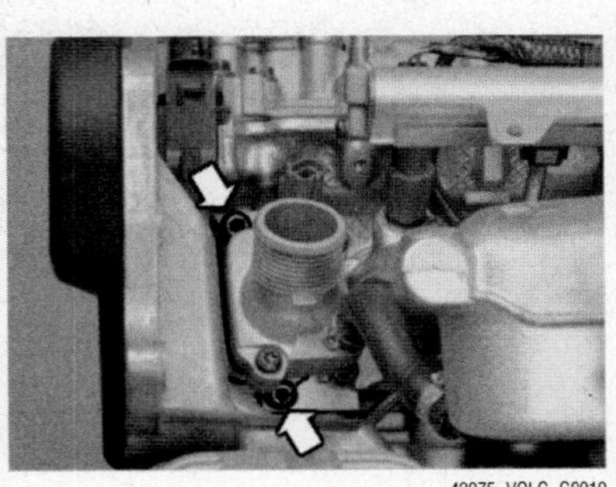

Fig. 38 Location of thermostat housing

   - Bolts for the thermostat housing
   - Thermostat housing from cylinder head

To install:

4. Install or connect the following:
   - Thermostat housing assembly to cylinder head using new gasket and new hose clamp
   - Tighten thermostat housing to 16 ft. lbs. (22 Nm)
   - Upper radiator hose and hose clamp
   - Connector for the temperature sensor
5. Refill the engine coolant.
6. Test drive the engine until the thermostat has opened.
7. Check for leaks, and proper thermostat operation. Fill fluid as necessary.

S60

See Figure 38.

1. Before servicing the vehicle, refer to the Precautions Section.
2. Disconnect the negative battery cable.
3. Drain the cooling system.
4. Disconnect or remove the following:
   - Control module cover
   - Insert tool 999-5722-7 to remove control module
   - Drive belt
   - Upper timing belt cover
   - Power steering pump
   - Hose clamp to the upper radiator hose
   - Hose from the thermostat housing
   - Connector from the temperature sensor
   - Bolts for the thermostat housing
   - Water hose for heating crankcase ventilation

- Thermostat housing from cylinder head

To install:

5. Install or reconnect the following:
   - Thermostat housing assembly to cylinder head using new gasket and new hose clamp
   - Tighten thermostat housing to 16 ft. lbs. (22 Nm)
   - Water hose for heating crankcase ventilation
   - Upper radiator hose and hose clamp
   - Connector for the temperature sensor
   - Power steering pump
   - Upper timing belt cover
   - Drive belt
   - Insert tool 999-5722-7 to remove control module
   - Control module cover
6. Connect the negative battery cable.
7. Refill engine with coolant and bleed the cooling system.
8. Test drive the engine until the thermostat has opened.
9. Check for coolant leaks and proper thermostat operation. Top off antifreeze as needed.

WATER PUMP

REMOVAL & INSTALLATION

See Figure 39.

1. Before servicing the vehicle, refer to the Precautions Section.
2. Drain the cooling system.
3. Remove the negative battery cable.
4. Remove the timing belt.
5. Remove the water pump:
   a. Raise the engine with a lifting beam to access and remove the 2 upper screws.
   b. Lower the engine to access and remove the remaining bolts from underneath the vehicle.
6. Carefully tap the pump rotor with a plastic mallet and remove the water pump.

To install:

7. Clean the engine surface.
8. Install a new gasket on water pump surface.

22250_VOLC_G0018

Fig. 39 View of water pump

9. Tighten the water pump bolts securely.
10. Install the timing belt.
11. Install the Negative battery cable.
12. Refill the engine coolant and bleed cooling system.
13. Check for any signs of coolant leaks.

ENGINE ELECTRICAL

BATTERY SYSTEM

BATTERY

REMOVAL & INSTALLATION

1. Before servicing the vehicle, refer to the Precautions Section.
2. Switch off the ignition and remove the key.
3. Wait at least 5 minutes after switching off the ignition before disconnecting the battery so that all information in the vehicle's electrical system can be stored in the control modules.
4. Remove the cover over the battery.
5. Disconnect the battery negative (ground) cable.
6. Disconnect the positive cable.
7. Remove the front side of the battery box with a screwdriver.
8. Release the clamp holding the battery.
9. Lift out the battery.
10. Installation is the reverse of removal. Be sure to connect the positive cable first.

BATTERY RECONNECT/RELEARN PROCEDURE

Vehicles equipped with engine and transaxle computers may require a relearn procedure after the vehicle battery has been disconnected. Most vehicle computers memorize and store vehicle operational patterns. When the battery is disconnected, the information may be cleared. If the information is cleared, the computer will go into default mode in order to operate the vehicle. The vehicle computer will relearn operational patterns each time the vehicle is restarted. The relearning process may take up to 40 or more key cycles.

When a specific engine component is replaced, a relearn procedure may be required. If the relearn procedure is not performed, the vehicle may exhibit the following:

- Harsh or poor shift quality
- Poor fuel mileage
- Hesitation or stumble
- Unstable idle or stalling
- Lean or rich running conditions

If an accessory component was replaced, a relearn procedure may also be required. The following systems and components may not work properly without a relearn procedure:

- Anti-theft system
- Steering system
- Power window system
- Power sunroof system

ENGINE ELECTRICAL — CHARGING SYSTEM

ALTERNATOR

REMOVAL & INSTALLATION

S40

See Figure 40.

1. Before servicing the vehicle, refer to the Precautions Section.
2. Disconnect the negative battery cable.
3. Remove the air intake resonator box.
4. Remove the drive belt.
5. The retaining nut and battery lead.
6. The regulator connector.
7. Remove the mounting bolts and remove the alternator.

To install:

8. Install the alternator and tighten the mounting bolts to 18 ft. lbs. (25 Nm).
9. Install battery lead and tighten the retaining nut to 11 ft. lbs. (15 Nm).
10. Install the drive belt.
11. Install the air intake resonator box.
12. Connect the negative battery cable.

S60

See Figure 41.

1. Before servicing the vehicle, refer to the Precautions Section.
2. Drain the cooling system.
3. Remove or disconnect the following:

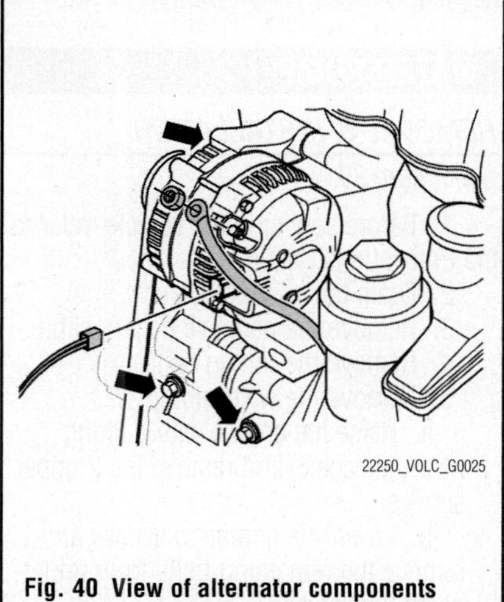

Fig. 40 View of alternator components

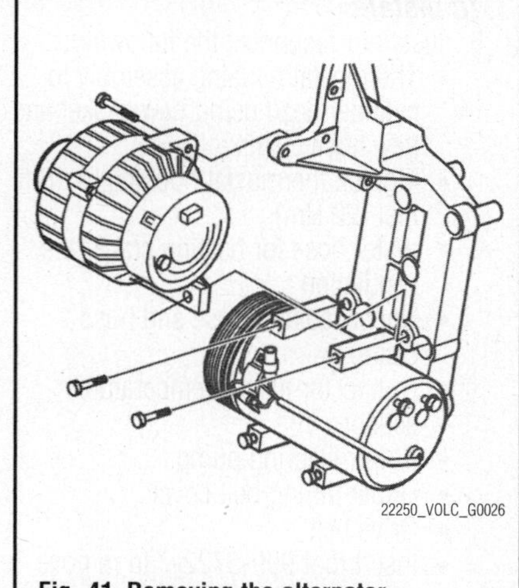

Fig. 41 Removing the alternator

- Negative battery cable
- Accessory drive belt
- Power steering pump
- Turbo hose from air conditioning assembly
- Radiator hose from radiator
- Mounting bolts common to alternator and compress
- Alternator connector and wiring
- Alternator mounting bolts
- Alternator

To install:

4. Install the alternator and tighten mounting bolts, and bolts common to the alternator and compressor, to 18 ft. lbs. (25 Nm).
5. Connect the alternator wiring.
6. Install the radiator hose to the radiator.
7. Install the turbo hose to the air conditioning assembly.
8. Install the power steering pump.
9. Install the accessory drive belt.
10. Install the negative battery cable.
11. Refill with engine coolant and bleed the cooling system.

ENGINE ELECTRICAL — IGNITION SYSTEM

FIRING ORDER

Firing order for the 5-cylinder engine: 1–2–4–5–3.

Firing order for the 6-cylinder engine: 1–5–3–6–2–4.

IGNITION COILS

REMOVAL & INSTALLATION

See Figures 42 and 43.

1. Before servicing the vehicle, refer to the Precautions Section.
2. Remove or disconnect the following:
   - Charge air pipe over the engine. Seal the openings
   - Upper timing belt cover
   - Cover over the ignition coils
   - Ignition coil connector
   - Ignition coil mounting bolt
   - Carefully pull coil up and out

To install:

3. Align the coil and press it down.
4. Install ignition coil mounting bolt and tighten to 89 inch lbs. (10 Nm).
5. Press in the connector until a click sound is heard.

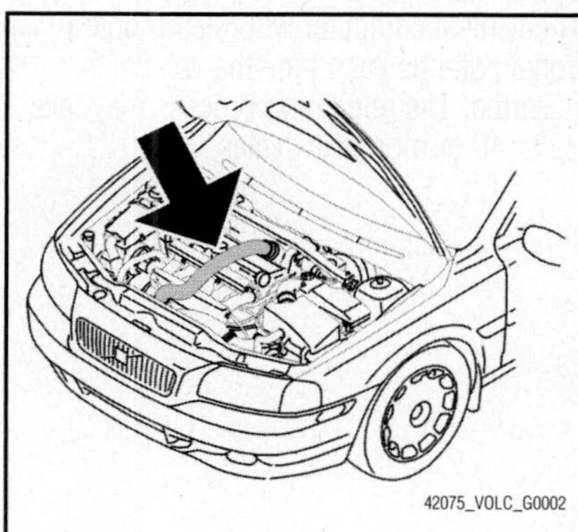

Fig. 42 Charge air pipe location

6. Install the cover over the ignition coil.
7. Replace the upper timing belt cover.
8. Remove the seals from the charge air pipe and reinstall over the engine.

SPARK PLUGS

REMOVAL & INSTALLATION

See Figure 44.

1. Before servicing the vehicle, refer to the Precautions Section.
2. Remove the ignition coil.
3. Use an appropriate spark plug wrench and socket to remove the spark plug.

To install:

4. Install the spark plug and tighten to 18 ft. lbs. (25 Nm).
5. Install the ignition coil.

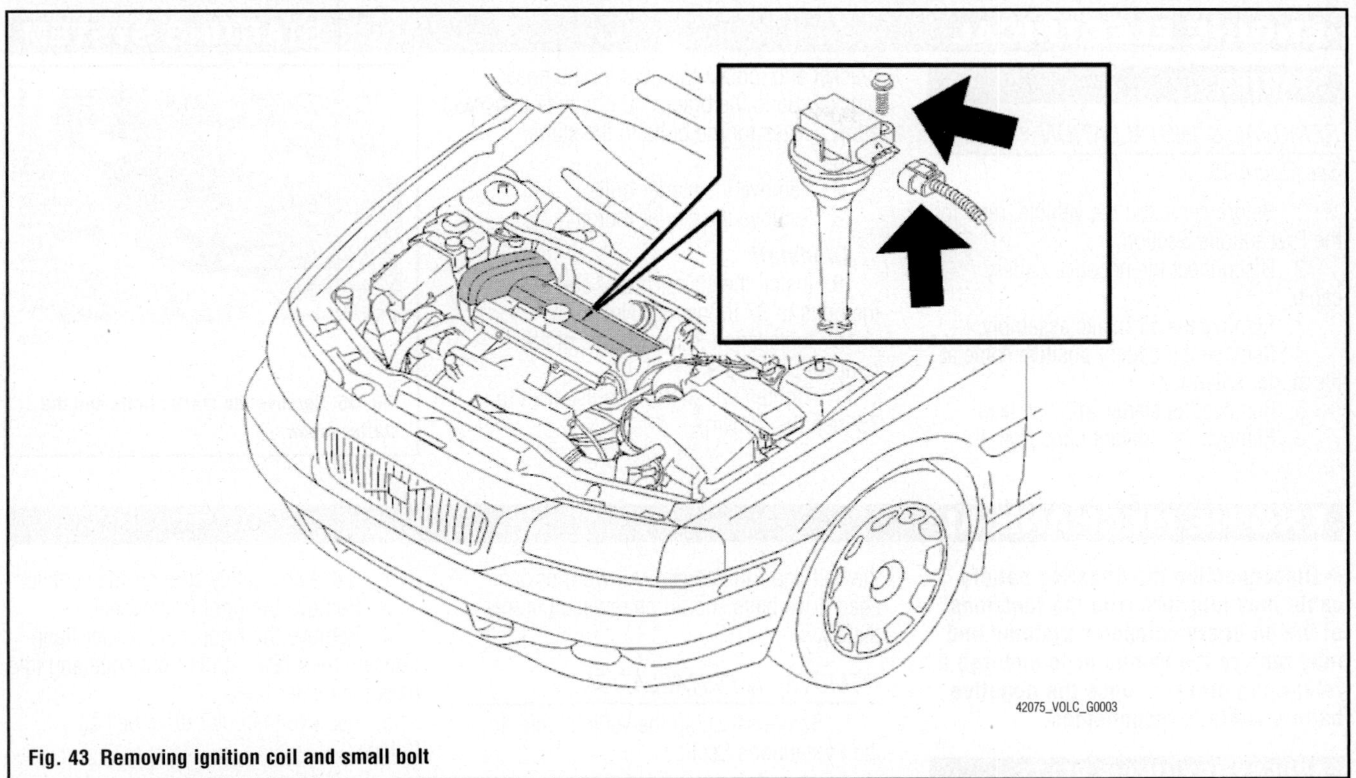

Fig. 43 Removing ignition coil and small bolt

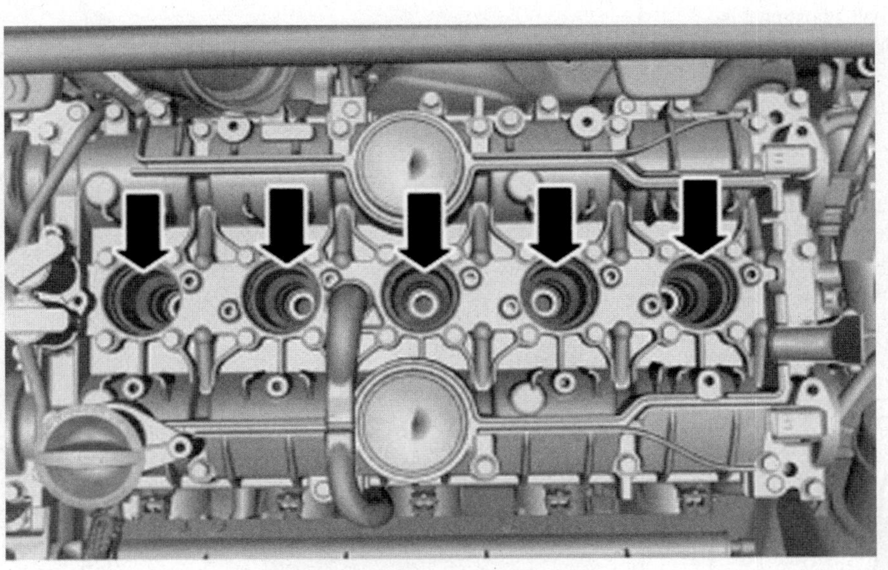

Fig. 44 View of spark plugs with ignition coils removed

ENGINE ELECTRICAL

STARTER

REMOVAL & INSTALLATION

See Figure 45.

1. Before servicing the vehicle, refer to the Precautions Section.
2. Disconnect the negative battery cable.
3. Remove the air intake assembly.
4. Remove the battery positive cable at the starter solenoid.
5. Remove the starter impulse lead.
6. Remove the coolant hose from the bracket and loosen the nuts for the hose bracket. Bend the bracket to one side to allow access for the bolts to the starter motor.
7. Remove the starter bolts.
8. Remove the starter motor.

To install:

9. Install the starter motor and tighten the bolts to 37 ft. lbs. (50 Nm).
10. Installation is the reverse of the removal procedure.
11. Tighten the starter impulse lead to 75 inch lbs. (9 Nm).

37698_VOLS_G0266

Fig. 45 Remove the starter bolts and the starter motor

ENGINE MECHANICAL

➡Disconnecting the negative battery cable may interfere with the functions of the on board computer systems and may require the computer to undergo a relearning process, once the negative battery cable is reconnected.

ACCESSORY DRIVE BELTS

ADJUSTMENT

The accessory drive belt adjustment is maintained by an automatic tensioner.

BELT ROUTINGS

See Figures 46 and 47.

INSPECTION

Inspect the drive belt for signs of glazing or cracking. A glazed belt will be perfectly smooth from slippage, while a good belt will have a slight texture of fabric visible. Cracks will usually start at the inner edge of the belt and run outward. All worn or damaged drive belts should be replaced immediately.

REMOVAL & INSTALLATION

1. Before servicing the vehicle, refer to the Precautions Section.
2. Raise and safely support the vehicle.
3. Remove the right front wheel.
4. Remove the right-hand fender liner. Loosen the screws at the front edge and fold back the fender liner.
5. Remove the outer drive belt as follows:

37698_VOLS_G0270

Fig. 46 Accessory drive belt routing—5 cylinder

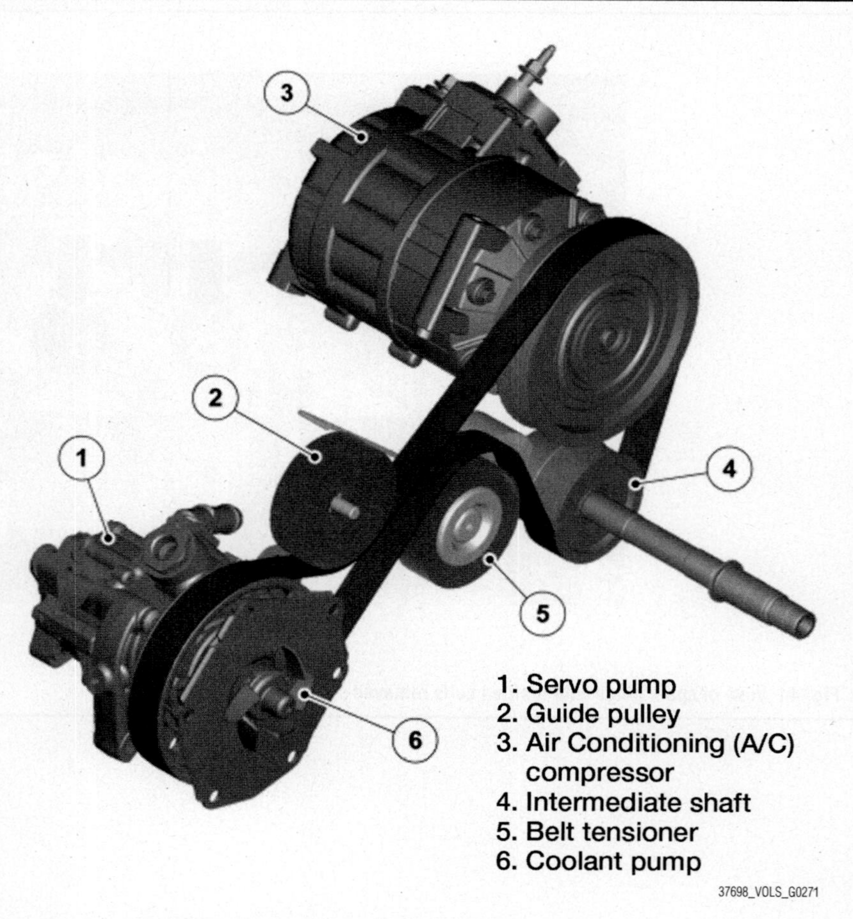

37698_VOLS_G0271

Fig. 47 Accessory drive belt routing—6 cylinder

a. Relieve the load from the belt tensioner. Using Special Tool: 999-7109, turn the belt tensioner.
b. Remove the belt.
6. Remove the inner drive belt as follows:
a. Relieve the load from the belt tensioner using a Torx® wrench.
b. Remove the belt.
7. Installation is in the reverse of the removal procedure.

AIR CLEANER

REMOVAL & INSTALLATION

S40 Vehicles

See Figures 48 and 49.

The illustrations in this service information are used for different model years and/or models. Some variation may occur. However, the essential information in the illustrations is always correct.

1. Before servicing the vehicle, refer to the Precautions Section.
2. Pull the protective cover on the Engine Control Module (ECM) straight up. Place the protective cover to one side.
3. Fold up the 2 red striker plates for the ECM connectors. Pull out the cable harness.
4. Remove the screws for the intake manifold and the resonator in the front cover plate.
5. Remove the intake manifold together with the resonator for the Air Cleaner (ACL) module.
6. Remove the hose for the Mass Air Flow (MAF) sensor.
7. Remove the brake vacuum hose from the ACL module. Disconnect the connector for the MAF sensor.
8. Cut the tie straps for the ACL module cable harness. Release the ACL module from the rubber mountings by lifting it straight up.
9. Pull the module towards the left front fender. Lift out the module.

To install:

10. Lubricate the mounting hooks on the ACL module using petroleum jelly or similar lubricant.
11. Install the ACL module. Turn the module downwards and pull it towards the right front fender. Push the module straight down so that the catches engage.
12. Install the hose on the MAF sensor. Tighten the hose clamp.
13. Install the brake vacuum hose to the ACL module. Use a new clamp.
14. Install the intake manifold together with the resonator for the ACL module. Connect the connector for the MAF sensor.
15. Connect the 2 connectors for the ECM. Lock with the 2 red striker plates.
16. Install the protective cover over the ECM.

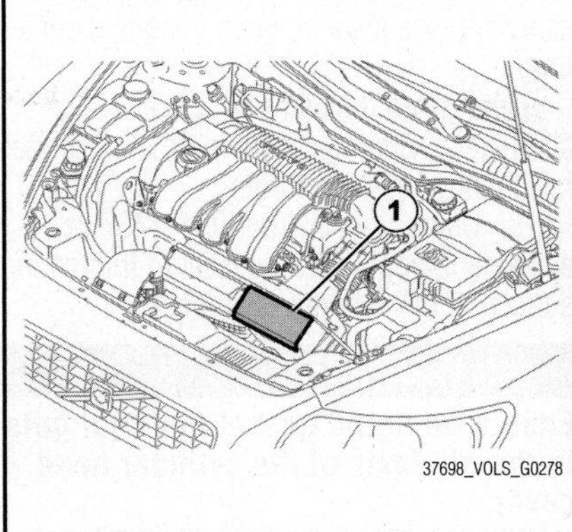

Fig. 48 Remove the protective cover (1) on the Engine Control Module (ECM)

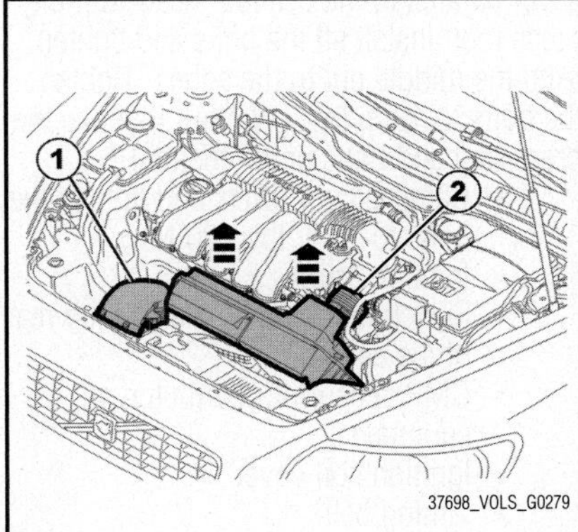

Fig. 49 Removing the resonator for the Air Cleaner (ACL) module (1) and the hose for the Mass Air Flow (MAF) sensor (2)

S60 Vehicles

See Figure 50.

1. Before servicing the vehicle, refer to the Precautions Section.
2. Remove the turbocharger control valve from the Air Cleaner (ACL) housing.
3. Remove the screws in the front panel for the inlet hose.
4. Remove the screws in the ACL housing for the inlet hose.
5. Remove the inlet hose.
6. Remove the nuts for the ACL housing.
7. Remove the hose clamp for the Mass Air Flow (MAF) sensor. Disconnect the connector for the MAF sensor.
8. Remove the ACL assembly.

Fig. 50 View of the Air Cleaner (ACL) housing—S60 vehicles

To install:

9. Install the ACL assembly.
10. Install the hose clamp for the MAF sensor.
11. Install the nuts for the ACL housing and tighten securely.
12. Install the inlet hose.
13. Install the screws for the inlet hose and tighten securely.
14. Install the turbocharger control valve on the ACL housing.
15. Connect the connector to the MAF sensor.

FILTER/ELEMENT REPLACEMENT

1. Before servicing the vehicle, refer to the Precautions Section.
2. Loosen the bolts, then open the Air Cleaner (ACL) housing cover.
3. Remove the ACL element from the ACL housing.

To install:

4. Check the ACL element for damage or clogging. If the ACL element is damaged or clogged with debris, replace it.

⁂ WARNING

Do not use compressed air to clean the ACL element.

5. Clean and remove any debris from inside the ACL housing.
6. Install the parts in the reverse order of removal.

CAMSHAFT & BEARINGS

INSPECTION

1. Check the camshaft journals for wear. If the journals are badly worn, replace the camshaft.
2. Check the cam lobes for damage. If

the lobe is damaged or excessively worn, replace the camshaft.

3. Measure the cam lift height.
4. Check the cam surface for abnormal wear or damage, and replace if necessary.
5. Check each bearing for damage. If the bearing surface is excessively damaged, replace the cylinder head assembly or the camshaft bearing cap, as necessary.

REMOVAL & INSTALLATION

5-Cylinder Engines

See Figures 51 and 52.

1. Before servicing the vehicle, refer to the Precautions Section.
2. Remove or disconnect the following:
   - Negative battery cable
   - Accessory drive belts
   - Front cover
   - Timing belt
   - Ignition coil cover
   - Switch holder and shield at left rear of the engine
   - Ignition coils
   - Camshaft sprockets
   - Cylinder head cover
   - Camshafts and lifters

➡Keep all valve train components in order for assembly.

To install:

3. Lubricate the valve lifters and camshaft bearing positions and lobes with clean engine oil.
4. Install the valve lifters in their original positions.
5. Install the intake camshaft. Make sure that the groove in the rear edge of the camshaft extends across an imagined center line.
6. Install the exhaust camshaft. Make sure that the groove in the rear edge of the camshaft extends across an imagined center line.
7. Tighten the camshaft cover bolts alternately, keeping it parallel to the cylinder head using the press tools.
8. Using Special Tool 951-2767 or equivalent, apply liquid gasket to the mating surface of the cylinder head cover.

⁂ WARNING

Ensure no liquid gasket material gets in the oil ducts of the cylinder head cover.

9. Position the Press Tool 999-5454 in the spark plug holes. Fit the 2 M6 bolts under each press tool to set the right height.
10. Crosswise tighten the cylinder head cover parallel to the cylinder head with the press tool. Install all the bolts and tighten from the middle out to the edges. Tighten the bolts to 13 ft. lbs. (17 Nm). Remove the press tool and bolts under the tool.
    - Camshaft sprockets and tighten the bolts to 15 ft. lbs. (20 Nm)
    - Ignition coils
    - Switch holder and shield at left rear of the engine
    - CMP sensor or distributor, as equipped
    - Ignition coil cover
    - Timing belt
    - Front cover
    - Accessory drive belts
    - Negative battery cable

6-Cylinder Engines

See Figures 53 and 54.

1. Before servicing the vehicle, refer to the Precautions Section.
2. Depressurize the fuel system.
3. Remove or disconnect the following:
   - Negative battery cable
   - Accessory drive belts
   - Front cover
   - Timing chain
   - Ignition coil cover
   - Ignition coils
   - Camshaft sprockets
   - Cylinder head cover
   - Camshafts and lifters

➡Mark the position of the components before removal.

To install:

4. Lubricate the valve lifters and camshaft bearing positions and lobes with clean engine oil.
5. Install the valve lifters in their original positions.
6. Install the intake camshaft. Make sure that the groove in the rear edge of the camshaft extends across an imagined center line.

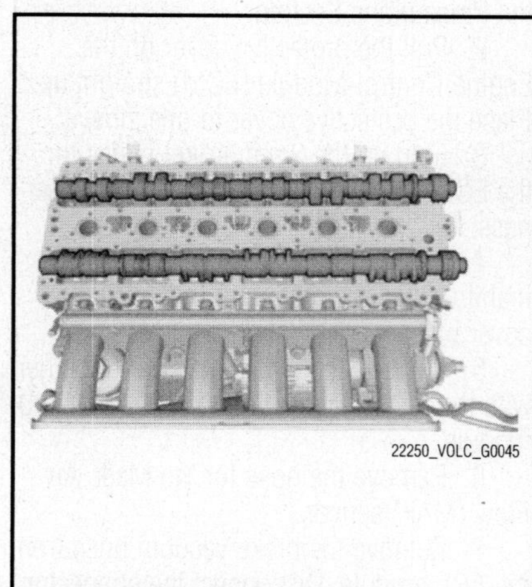

Fig. 53 Camshafts shown in cylinder head

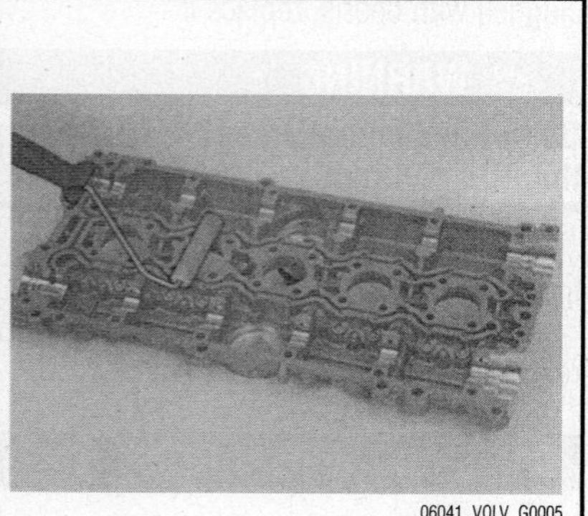

Fig. 51 Using Special Tool 951-2767 to apply the liquid gasket to the cylinder head cover

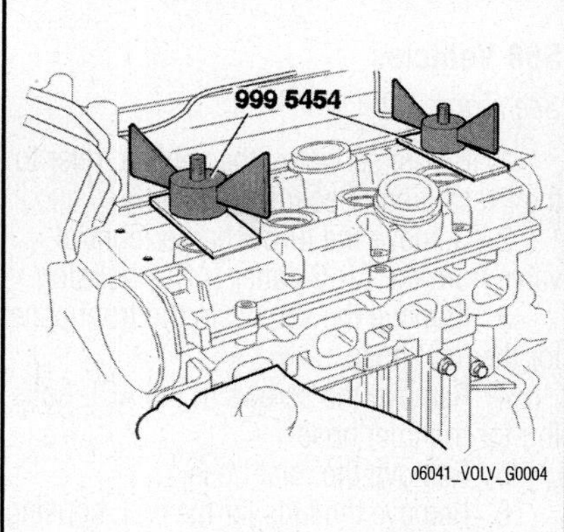

Fig. 52 Using Special Tool 999-5454 to install the cylinder head cover

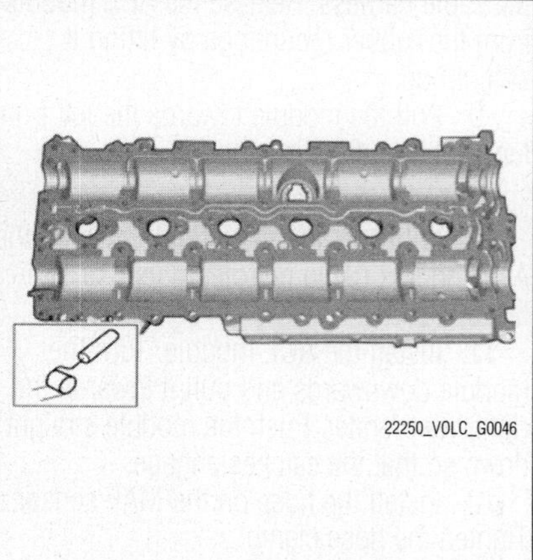

Fig. 54 Apply liquid gasket to the mating surface

7. Install the exhaust camshaft. Make sure that the groove in the rear edge of the camshaft extends across an imagined center line.

8. Tighten the camshaft cover bolts alternately, keeping it parallel to the cylinder head using the press tools.

9. Using Special Tool 951-2767 or equivalent, apply liquid gasket to the mating surface of the cylinder head cover.

⁂ WARNING

Ensure no liquid gasket material gets in the oil ducts of the cylinder head cover.

10. Position the Press Tool 999-5454 in the spark plug holes. Fit the 2 M6 bolts under each press tool to set the right height.

11. Crosswise tighten the cylinder head cover parallel to the cylinder head with the press tool. Install all the bolts and tighten from the middle out to the edges. Tighten the bolts to 13 ft. lbs. (17 Nm). Remove the press tool and bolts under the tool.

12. Install the camshaft sprockets and tighten the bolts to 15 ft. lbs. (20 Nm).

13. Install the ignition coils.
14. Install the ignition coil cover.
15. Install the timing chain.
16. Install the front cover.
17. Install the accessory drive belts.
18. Install the negative battery cable.

CRANKSHAFT DAMPER

REMOVAL & INSTALLATION

5-Cylinder Engines

See Figure 55.

1. Before servicing the vehicle, refer to the Precautions Section.
2. Remove the cross stay between the suspension turrets.
3. Remove the servo reservoir and the expansion tank. Lift it up and place it on top of the engine.
4. Remove the accessory drive belt.
5. Remove the upper timing belt cover.
6. Remove the right front wheel.
7. Remove the nut from the cover in the fender liner
8. Install Special Tool: 999-5433, counter-hold, on the crankshaft damper.
9. Remove the crankshaft damper center nut.
10. Work the crankshaft damper loose and remove by hand.

To install:

11. Install the crankshaft damper and tighten the center nut to 133 ft. lbs. (180 Nm).

Fig. 55 Using Special Tool: Counter-hold 999-5433 to remove crankshaft damper

12. Remove the counter-hold 999-5433 and install new bolts. Tighten the bolts to 18 ft. lbs. (25 Nm) plus 30°.
13. Turn the crankshaft 2 turns. Check that the markings on the crankshaft damper and camshaft pulley correspond.
14. Install or connect the following:
    - Front timing belt cover. Tighten to 106 inch lbs. (12 Nm)
    - Upper timing belt cover
    - Accessory belt
    - Servo reservoir
    - Expansion tank

➡Ensure that the hoses are correctly positioned.

- Engine stabilizer brace. Tighten the bolts at the suspension turrets to 37 ft. lbs. (50 Nm)
- Tighten the engine bracket bolt to 59 ft. lbs. (80 Nm)
- Fender liner cover
- Front wheel and tighten lug nuts to 103 ft. lbs. (140 Nm)

6-Cylinder Engines

See Figure 56.

1. Before servicing the vehicle, refer to the Precautions Section.
2. Disconnect the negative battery cable.
3. Remove the drive belt.
4. Remove the crank pulley cover.
5. Install the pulley removal tools 951-2926 bit Torx® 50 and counter-hold 999-5760.
6. Remove the crankshaft damper/pulley.

To install:

7. Install the crankshaft damper seal.
8. Install the crankshaft damper/pulley and tighten to 44 ft. lbs. (60 Nm).

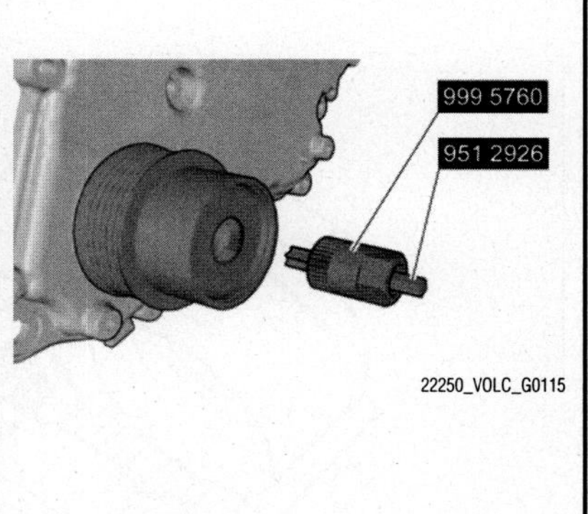

Fig. 56 Remove the crankshaft damper/pulley

9. Install a new pulley cover.
10. Install the drive belt.
11. Connect the negative battery cable.

CRANKSHAFT FRONT SEAL

REMOVAL & INSTALLATION

5-Cylinder Engines

See Figure 57.

1. Before servicing the vehicle, refer to the Precautions Section.
2. Remove or disconnect the following:
    - Engine stabilizer brace
    - Upper timing belt cover
    - Servo reservoir
    - Expansion tank
    - Accessory drive belt
    - Front timing belt cover
    - Front wheel
    - Timing belt
    - Vibration damper
    - Crankshaft timing gear pulley
    - Front crankshaft seal

To install:

3. Install or connect the following:
    - Front crankshaft seal
    - Crankshaft timing gear pulley
    - Vibration damper and tighten nut to 133 ft. lbs. (180 Nm)
    - Timing belt
    - Front wheel
    - Front timing belt cover
    - Upper timing belt cover
    - Accessory drive belt
    - Expansion tank
    - Servo reservoir
4. Install the engine stabilizer brace. Tighten the bolts at the suspension turrets to 37 ft. lbs. (50 Nm). Tighten the engine bracket bolt to 59 ft. lbs. (80 Nm).
5. Start the engine and check for leaks.

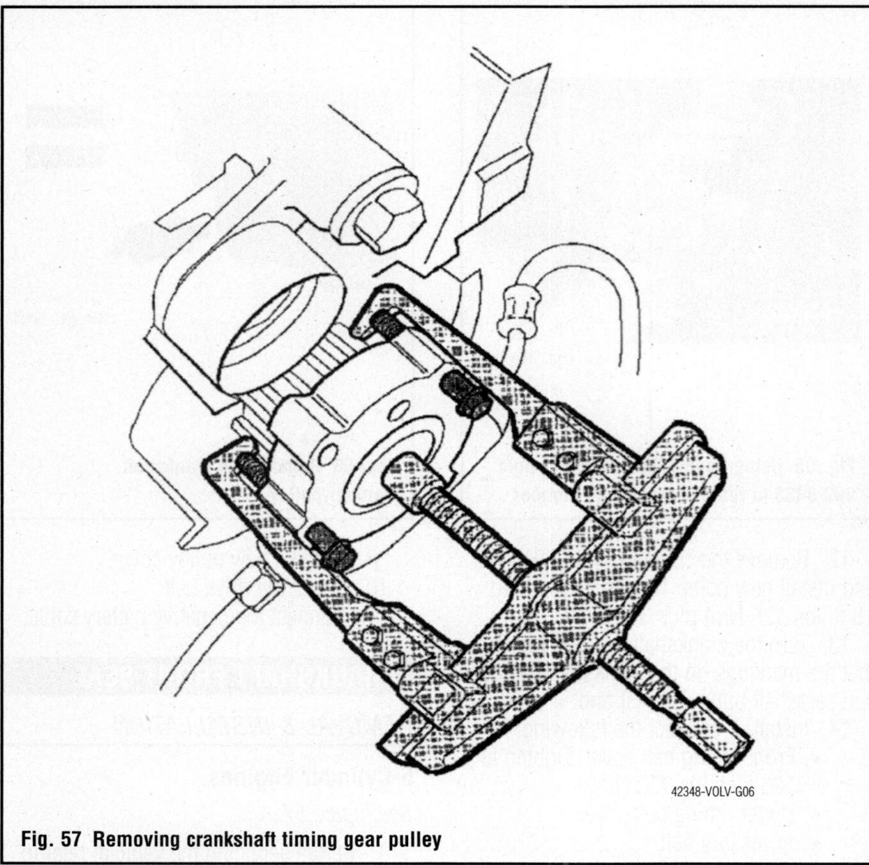

Fig. 57 Removing crankshaft timing gear pulley

6-Cylinder Engines

See Figure 58.

1. Before servicing the vehicle, refer to the Precautions Section.
2. Raise and safely support the vehicle.
3. Remove the right hand front wheel.
4. With a flat-head screwdriver, or similar tool, pry out the crankshaft front seal.

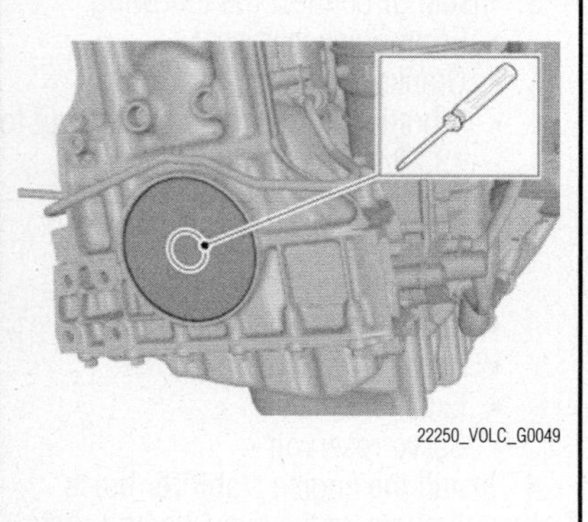

Fig. 58 Using a flat-head screwdriver to pry out the crankshaft front seal

To install:

5. Clean the surfaces of front seal area.
6. Install the front seal with a seal driver.

CYLINDER HEAD

REMOVAL & INSTALLATION

5-Cylinder Engines

See Figures 59 through 62.

1. Before servicing the vehicle, refer to the Precautions Section.

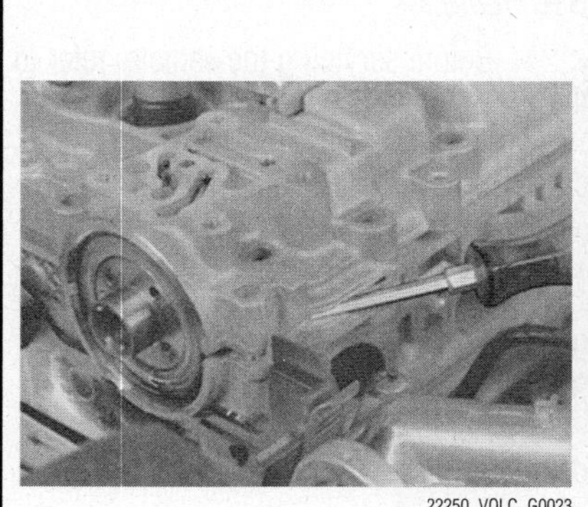

Fig. 59 Remove the valve cover

2. Drain the cooling system.
3. Relieve the fuel pressure.
4. Remove or disconnect the following:
   - Negative battery cable
   - Engine appearance cover
   - Air cleaner housing
   - Ignition coils
   - Intake manifold
   - Fuel rail and injectors
   - O2 sensor connector
   - Front pipe at exhaust manifold
   - Exhaust manifold
   - Turbocharger, if equipped
5. Remove the screws for the bracket for the oil pipes for the power steering.
6. Remove the valve cover.

WARNING

Take extra care not to damage the mating faces.

7. Remove the tensioned mounting yoke.
8. Remove or disconnect the following:
   - Upper engine coolant hose
   - Accessory drive belt

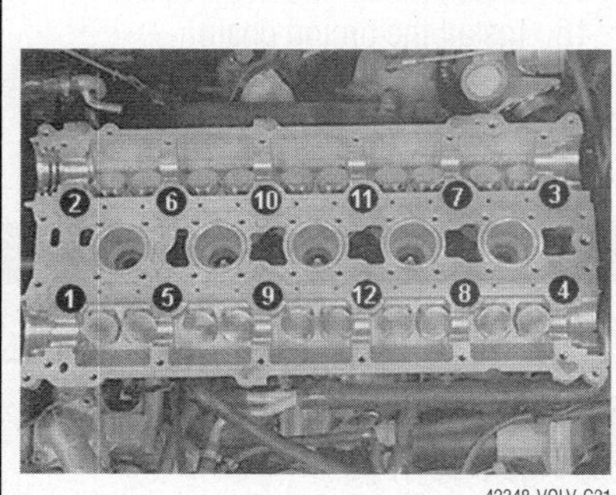

Fig. 60 Cylinder head loosening sequence

Fig. 61 Cylinder head torque sequence

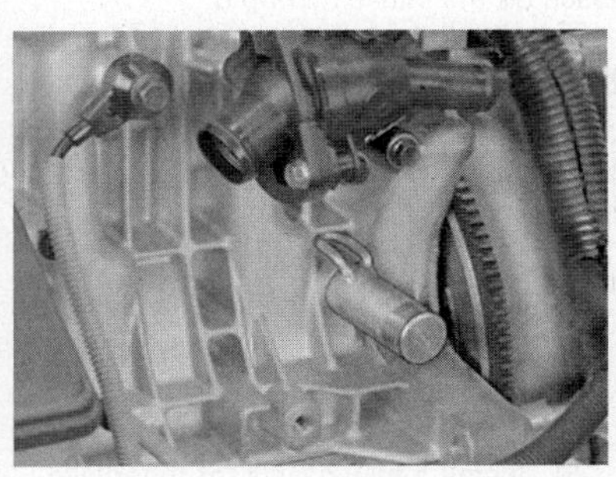

Fig. 62 Crankshaft adjustment tool 999-5451 installed

- Timing belt
- Camshafts
- Valve tappets (keep in order)
- Cylinder head

To install:

9. Clean the mating surfaces of cylinder head and engine block.
10. Install the cylinder head with a new gasket. Tighten the bolts in the following sequence:
    a. Step 1: 15 ft. lbs. (20 Nm)
    b. Step 2: 44 ft. lbs. (60 Nm)
    c. Step 3: Plus 130°
11. Install or connect the following:
    - Camshafts (Lubricate all components)
    - Valve tappets (in order)
    - Camshafts
12. Remove the cover plug. Turn the crankshaft clockwise slightly. Install the crankshaft adjustment tool.
13. Install or connect the following:
    - Timing belt
    - Accessory drive belt
    - Intake manifold
    - Upper engine coolant hose
    - Valve cover (with new gasket)
    - Steering pipe bracket bolts
    - Turbocharger, if equipped
    - Exhaust manifold
    - Front pipe at exhaust manifold
    - O2 sensor connector
    - Fuel rail and injectors
    - Intake manifold
    - Ignition coils
    - Air cleaner housing
    - Engine appearance cover
14. Connect the negative battery cable.
15. Install new engine coolant and bleed the system.
16. Start the engine and check for leaks.

6-Cylinder Engines

See Figures 63 and 64.

1. Before servicing the vehicle, refer to the Precautions Section.
2. Depressurize the fuel system.
3. Drain the cooling system.
4. Disconnect the negative battery cable.
5. Remove or disconnect the following:
    - Exhaust manifold
    - Intake manifold
    - Valve covers
    - Injectors and fuel rail

➡Mark the position of the components before removal.

6. Lift out the valve lifters. Use a suction cup tool.

⁂ WARNING

Take extra care not to damage the mating faces.

7. Remove the cylinder head bolts in sequence.

To install:

8. Make sure that the mating faces are clean and free of foreign material.
9. Make sure that the cylinder head thread holes in the engine block are free of fluid.
10. Check that the left-threaded sleeves go to the bottom.
11. Install a new head gasket.
12. Tighten the cylinder head as follows:
    - Stage 1: 33 ft. lbs. (45 Nm)
    - Stage 2: 33 ft. lbs. (45 Nm)
    - Stage 3: 90°
    - Stage 4: An additional 180°
13. Make sure that the choke valves are in place.

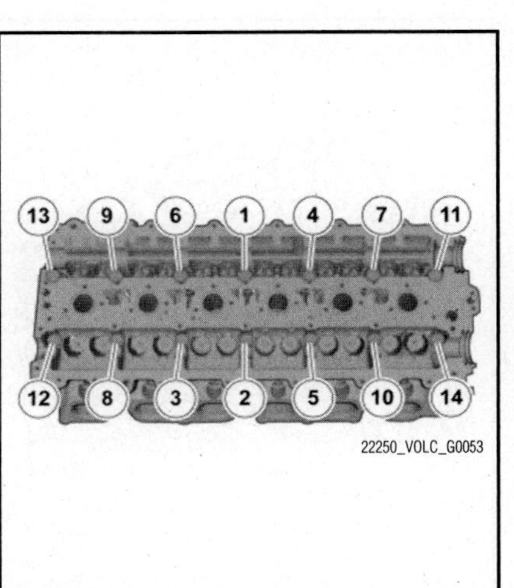

Fig. 63 Cylinder head torque sequence

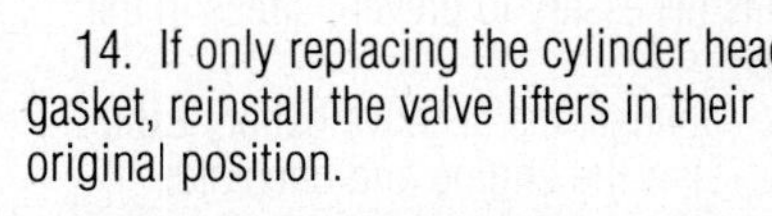

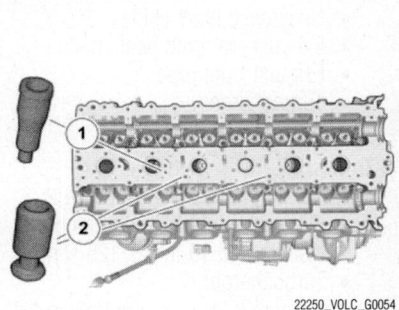

Fig. 64 Choke valves (1) and (2) location shown

14. If only replacing the cylinder head gasket, reinstall the valve lifters in their original position.

➡Valve clearance must be checked if the cylinder head is replaced.

15. Install or reconnect the following:
    - Injectors and fuel rail
    - Valve covers
    - Intake manifold
    - Exhaust manifold
16. Connect the negative battery cable.
17. Install new engine coolant and bleed the system.
18. Start the engine and check for leaks.

EXHAUST MANIFOLD

REMOVAL & INSTALLATION

See Figure 65.

1. Before servicing the vehicle, refer to the Precautions Section.

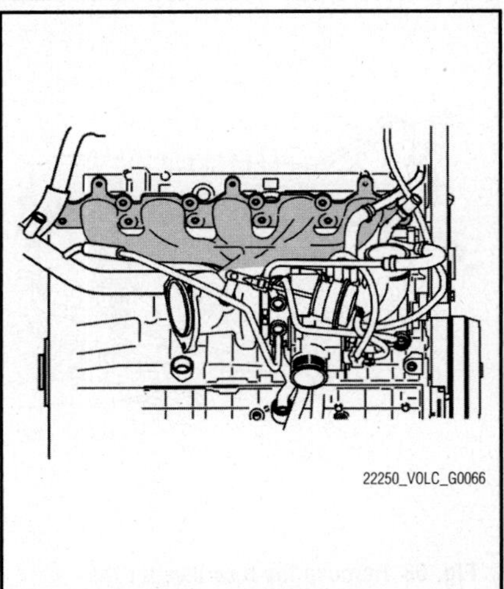

Fig. 65 Exhaust manifold view

2. Remove or disconnect the following:
   - Negative battery cable
   - Exhaust manifold heat shield
   - Exhaust front pipe
   - Turbocharger
   - Exhaust manifold

To install:

3. Install or connect the following:
   - Exhaust manifold and tighten the fasteners to 18 ft. lbs. (25 Nm)
   - Turbocharger
   - Exhaust front pipe and tighten the fasteners to 44 ft. lbs. (60 Nm)
   - Exhaust manifold heat shield and tighten the fasteners to 89 inch lbs. (10 Nm)
4. Loosen the joint at the catalytic converter and re-tighten to 18 ft. lbs. (25 Nm). This is necessary to prevent stress in the system.
5. Connect the negative battery cable.
6. Start the engine and check for leaks.

INTAKE MANIFOLD

REMOVAL & INSTALLATION

See Figures 66 and 67.

1. Before servicing the vehicle, refer to the Precautions Section.
2. Relieve the fuel system pressure.
3. Disconnect the negative battery cable.
4. Remove the brake vacuum hose.
5. Remove the hose for the throttle body.
6. Remove the intake manifold for the turbocharger. Remove the seals.
7. Remove the 6 screws for the upper section of the intake manifold.
8. Disconnect the vacuum hoses from the intake manifold. Put the pipe to one side.
9. Disconnect the connectors for the fuel pressure sensor and the connector for the injectors.
10. Remove the 2 fuel rail mounting screws.
11. Spray universal oil, or similar, around the injector nozzle at the terminal on the intake manifold.
12. Gently work the fuel rail and injector nozzles loose. Disconnect the fuel line to the fuel rail. Press in the 2 blue clips on the fuel rail. Pull the fuel line out of the fuel rail.
13. Place the fuel rail to one side.
14. Remove the hose from the oil trap to the timing belt cover at the terminal in the timing belt cover.
15. Remove the crankcase ventilation hoses from the intake manifold.
16. Remove the clamp for the fuel intake manifold.
17. Loosen the lower screws for the intake manifold a few turns.
18. Remove the mounting screws in the upper row. Lift out the intake manifold.
19. Remove the screws in the lower row.
20. Remove the intake manifold and gasket.

To install:

21. Install a new gasket held in position by the lower screws of the intake manifold.

➡Do not forget the crankcase ventilation hose. The hose must be inserted up through the gap between the second and third ducts.

22. Install the 3 upper screws. Tighten all the screws starting from the center to 13 ft. lbs. (17 Nm).
23. Install the clamp for the fuel line on the intake manifold.
24. Install the crankcase ventilation hoses on the intake manifold.
25. Install the hose from the oil trap to the camshaft cover. Use a new hose clamp.
26. Lubricate the injector O-rings using petroleum jelly. Depress the fuel rail. Ensure that all injectors seat correctly.
27. Press the quick-release connector together until a clicking sound is heard. Screw the fuel rail into place.
28. Connect the connector for the injectors and the fuel pressure sensors.
29. Install a new gasket for the intake manifold.
30. Install the vacuum hoses for the intake manifold.
31. Install the intake manifold. Align the guides with the lower section of the intake manifold.
32. Install the screws for the intake manifold and tighten to 13 ft. lbs. (17 Nm).
33. Install the intake manifold for the turbocharger. Install the seals.
34. Install the hose for the throttle body.
35. Install the brake vacuum hose.
36. Connect the negative battery cable.

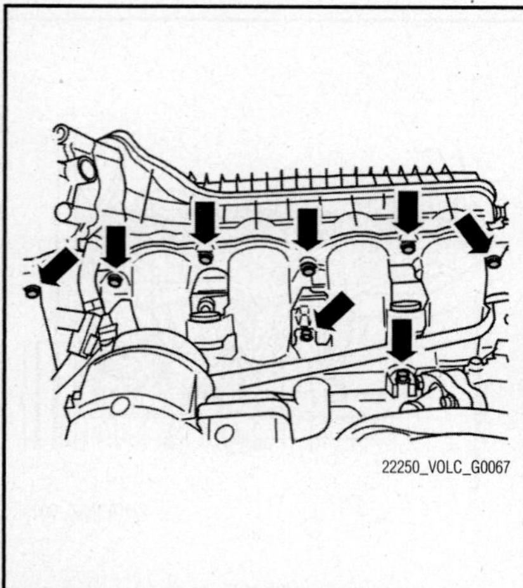

Fig. 66 Remove the 6 screws for the upper section of the intake manifold

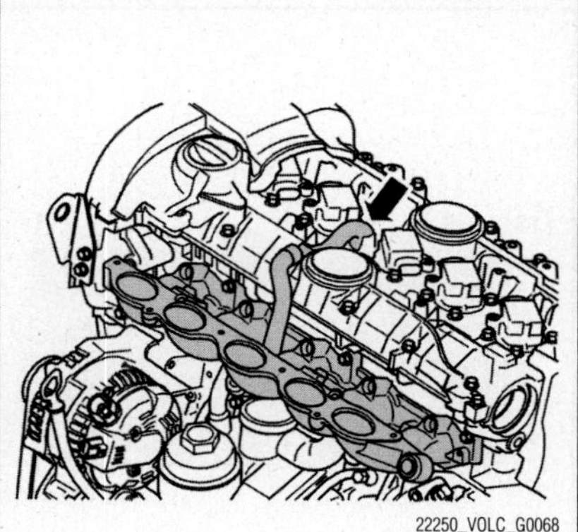

Fig. 67 Lower intake manifold view

OIL PAN

REMOVAL & INSTALLATION

S40

See Figure 68.

1. Before servicing the vehicle, refer to the Precautions Section.
2. Remove the oil dipstick and its pipe.
3. Remove the splashguard under the engine.
4. Drain the engine oil and remove the oil filter.
5. Release the oil cooler from the oil pan. Hang it up at the rear.
6. Remove the bolt from the bracket for the fuel line.
7. Back off all bolts holding the oil pan.
8. Remove all bolts except for 4. It is recommended that the 4 bolts in the corners of the oil pan are left in place.
9. Carefully tap the oil pan with a rubber mallet until the joint and its liquid gasket releases.
10. Remove the 4 remaining bolts.
11. Remove the oil pan.

To install:

12. Apply liquid gasket 1161 059-9, or equivalent, to the oil pan.
13. Install new O-rings.
14. Position the oil pan. Secure it loosely with a few bolts.
15. Install the remaining bolts loosely.
16. Press the oil pan against the

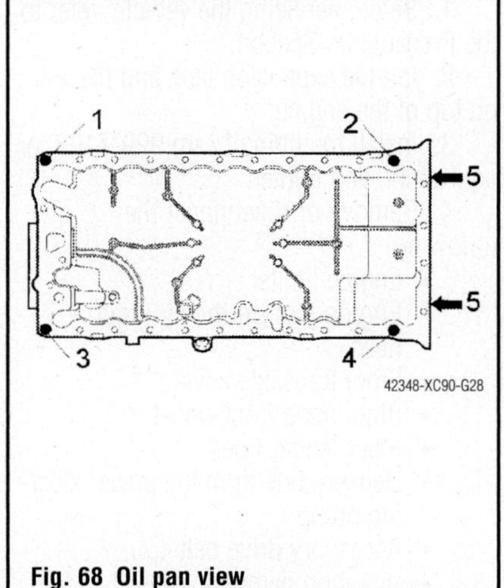

Fig. 68 Oil pan view

Fig. 69 Oil pump installation

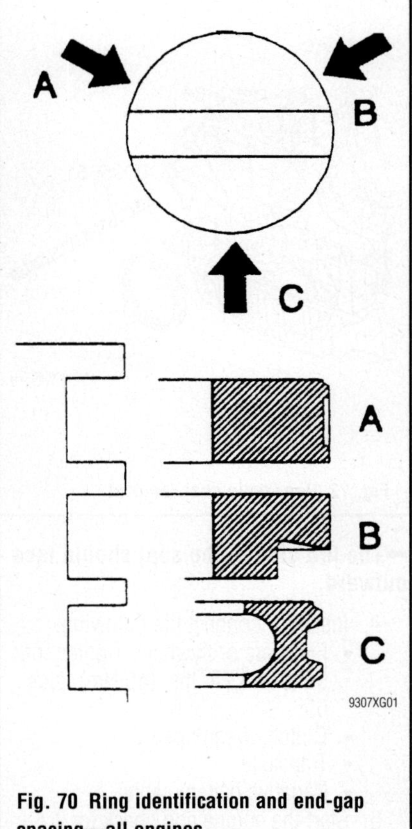

Fig. 70 Ring identification and end-gap spacing—all engines

transaxle. Tighten bolts 1, 2, 3, and 4 to 27 inch lbs. (3 Nm). Tighten bolt 5 to 18 ft. lbs. (25 Nm); then tighten to 35 ft. lbs. (48 Nm).

17. Tighten all bolts in the oil pan flange to 12 ft. lbs. (17 Nm). Start at the transaxle end and continue forwards in pairs.

18. Install the bolt for the bracket for the fuel line.

19. Connect the oil cooler to the oil pan. Use new O-rings. Reinstall the pipe on the sub-frame.

20. Install a new oil filter.

21. Install the oil drain plug with a new gasket.

22. Install the oil dipstick and its pipe. Use a new O-ring.

➡Check that the O-ring is correctly positioned.

23. Fill with engine oil. Run the engine to operating temperature.

24. Check for oil leaks from the oil pan or oil cooler.

25. Install the splashguard under the engine.

26. Check the oil level and adjust as needed.

OIL PUMP

REMOVAL & INSTALLATION

S40

See Figure 69.

1. Before servicing the vehicle, refer to the Precautions Section.
2. Remove or disconnect the following:
   - Negative battery cable
   - Fuel line clips
   - Coolant recovery tank
   - Accessory drive belts
   - Right front wheel
   - Inner fender liner
   - Front cover
   - Timing belt
   - Crankshaft timing sprocket
   - Front crankshaft seal
   - Oil pump

To install:

3. Install the oil pump using Special Tool 999-5455. Use the oil pump bolts to guide the pump. Use the crankshaft nut to press the pump in until it is seated fully. Tighten the oil pump bolts to 89 inch lbs. (10 Nm).
4. Remove the crankshaft nut and the press tool.
5. Install or connect the following:
   - Front crankshaft seal
   - Crankshaft timing sprocket and tighten the nut to 133 ft. lbs. (180 Nm)
   - Timing belt
   - Front cover
   - Inner fender liner
   - Right front wheel
   - Accessory drive belts
   - Coolant recovery tank
   - Fuel line clips
   - Negative battery cable
6. Start the engine and check for leaks.

PISTONS & RINGS

POSITIONING

See Figures 70 and 71.

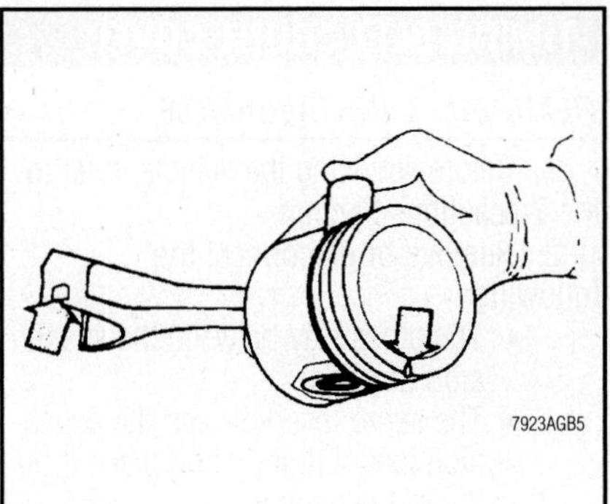

Fig. 71 Piston and rod positioning—all engines
The notch on the piston crown faces the front of the engine

REAR MAIN SEAL

REMOVAL & INSTALLATION

See Figure 72.

1. Before servicing the vehicle, refer to the Precautions Section.
2. Remove or disconnect the following:
   - Negative battery cable
   - Transaxle
   - Clutch, if equipped
   - Flexplate or flywheel
   - Rear main seal

To install:

3. Install the rear main seal using Special Tool 999-7174, or equivalent, so that the seal is flush with the cylinder block.

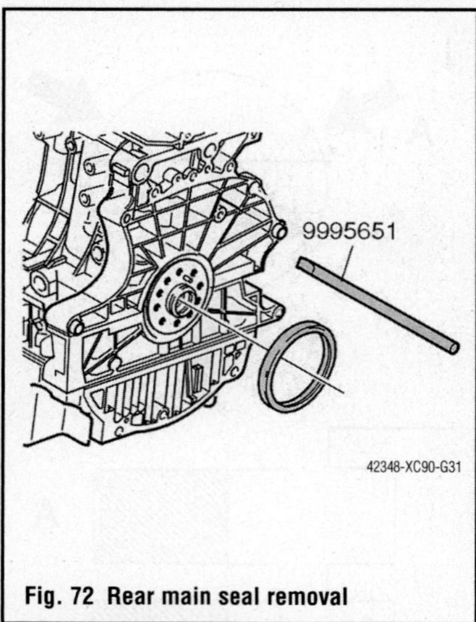

Fig. 72 Rear main seal removal

➡The felt side of the seal should face outward.

4. Install or connect the following:
   - Flexplate or flywheel. Tighten the bolts to 33 ft. lbs. (45 Nm), plus 65°.
   - Clutch, if equipped
   - Transaxle
   - Negative battery cable
5. Start the engine and check for leaks.

TIMING BELT FRONT COVER

REMOVAL & INSTALLATION

1. Before servicing the vehicle, refer to the Precautions Section.
2. Remove or disconnect the following:
   - The cross stay between the suspension turrets
   - The servo reservoir and the expansion tank. Lift it up and place it on top of the engine.
   - The accessory drive belt.
   - The upper timing belt cover

To install:

3. Install or connect the following:
   - Upper timing belt cover. Tighten to 106 inch lbs. (12 Nm).
   - Accessory drive belt
   - Servo reservoir
   - Expansion tank

➡Ensure that the hoses are correctly positioned.

   - Cross stay brace and tighten the bolts at the suspension turrets to 37 ft. lbs. (50 Nm).
   - Tighten the engine bracket bolt to 59 ft. lbs. (80 Nm).

TIMING BELT & SPROCKETS

REMOVAL & INSTALLATION

See Figures 73 through 75.

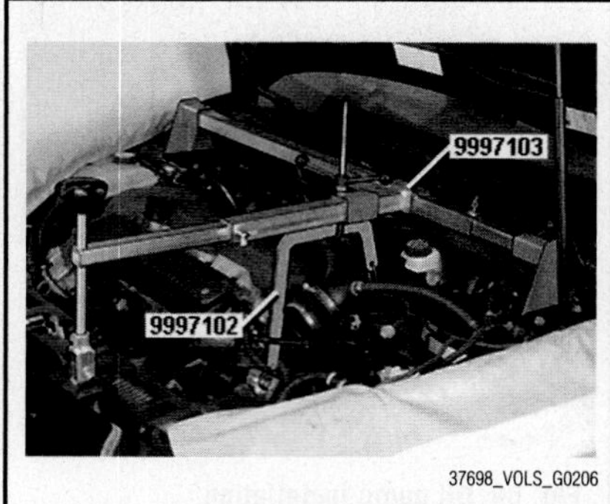

Fig. 73 Engine support system installed

1. Before servicing the vehicle, refer to the Precautions Section.
2. Lift the expansion tank and place it on top of the engine.
3. Install the lifting beam 999-7103, or equivalent, and tighten.
4. Remove or disconnect the following:
   - Engine limiter
   - Engine pad on the cylinder head
   - Front transaxle covers
   - Right hand front wheel
   - Inner fender liner
   - Delivery line from the power steering pump
   - Accessory drive belt
   - Vibration damper
   - Upper timing belt cover

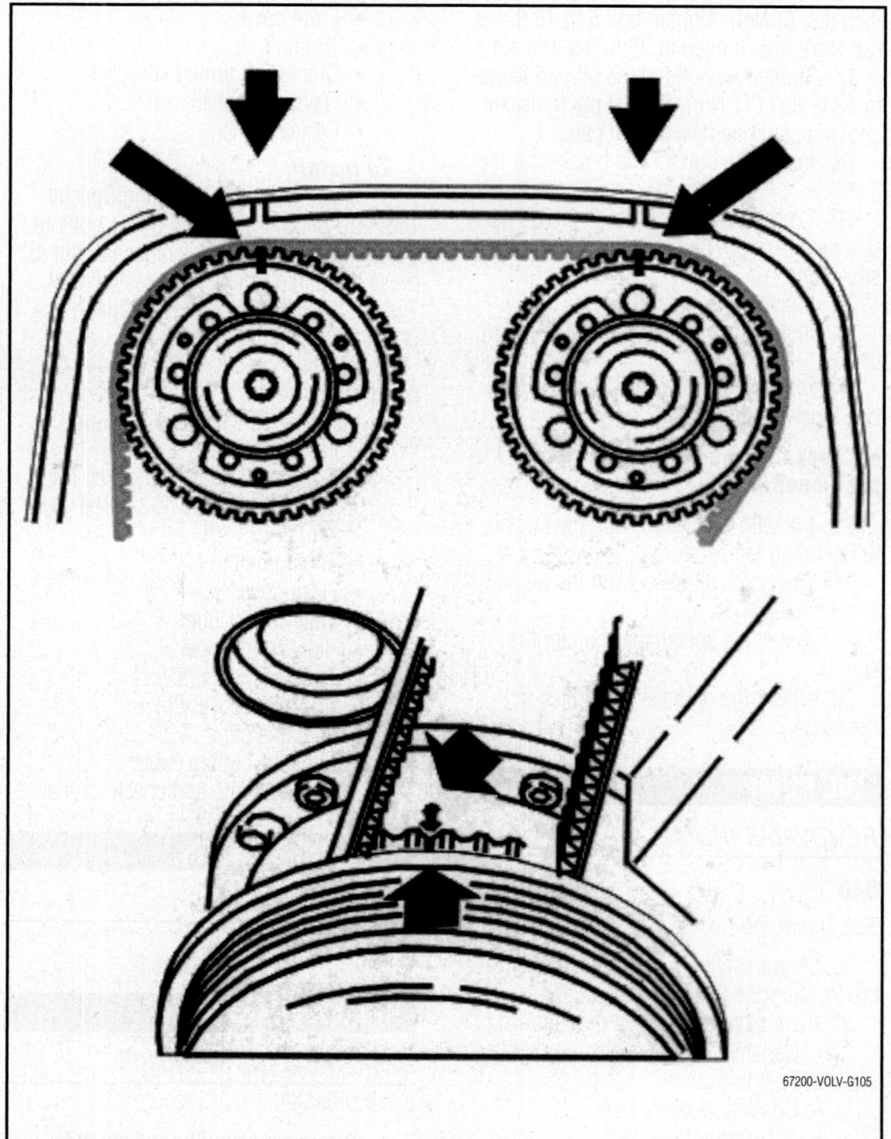

Fig. 74 Identifying the timing marks

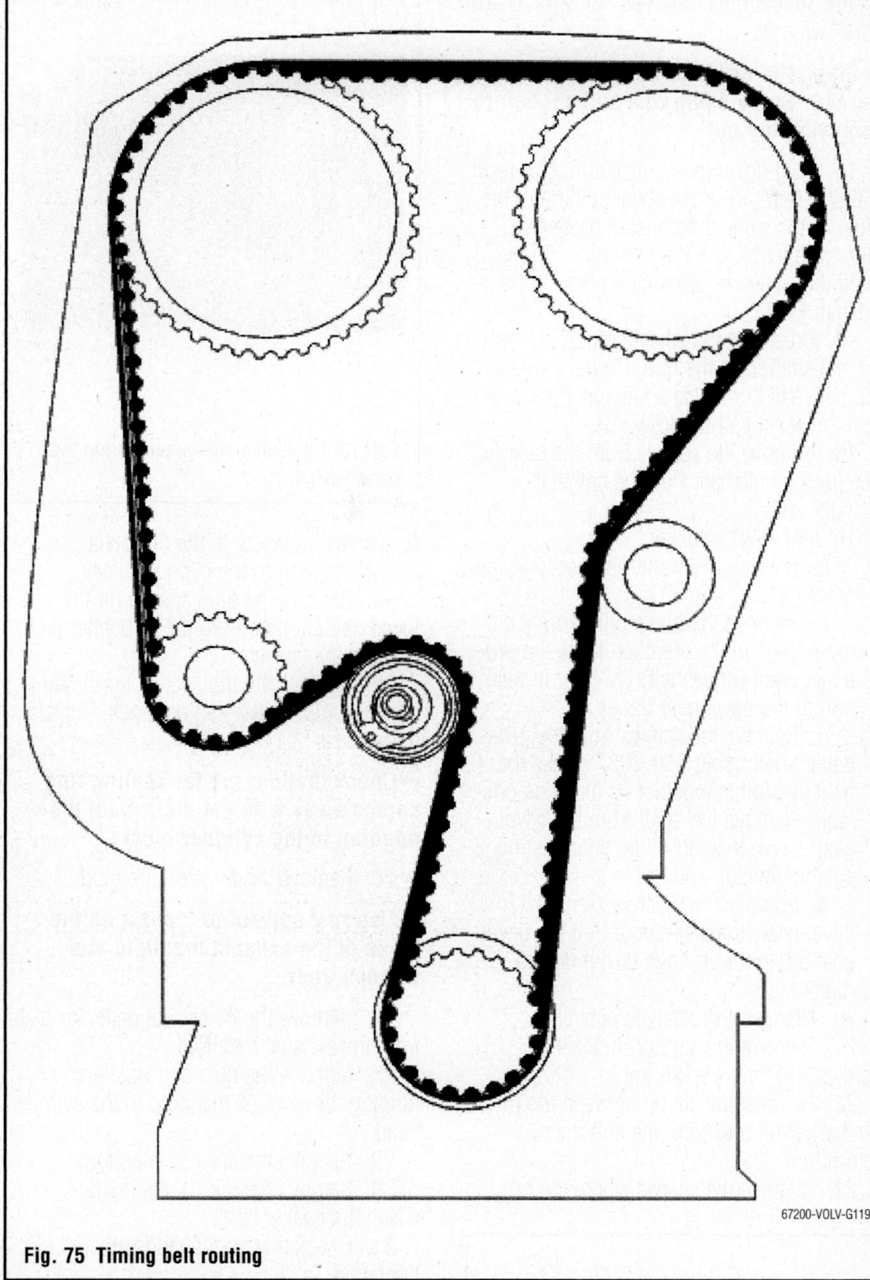

Fig. 75 Timing belt routing

5. Lower the engine slightly until the belt tensioner bolts can be accessed from beneath.
6. Turn the crankshaft clockwise until the markings on the crankshaft and camshaft pulleys correspond.
7. Loosen the center bolt for the belt tensioner slightly and hold the center bolt still. Turn the tensioner clockwise to 10 o'clock.
8. Remove the timing belt.

To install:

9. Install the timing belt in the following order:
   a. Around the crankshaft
   b. Around the idler pulley
   c. Around the intake camshaft pulley
   d. Around the exhaust camshaft pulley
   e. Around the water pump
   f. Onto the belt tensioner
10. Carefully turn the crankshaft clockwise until the timing belt is tensioned. The belt must be tensioned between the intake camshaft pulley, the idler pulley, and the crankshaft.
11. Hold the belt tensioner center bolt secure. Turn the belt tensioner eccentric counter-clockwise until the tensioner indicator passes the marked position.
12. Turn the belt tensioner eccentric back so that the indicator reaches the marked position in the center of the window and tighten the center bolt to 15 ft. lbs. (20 Nm).
13. Press the belt to check that the indicator on the tensioner moves easily.
14. Install or connect the following:
   - Front timing belt cover
   - Upper timing belt cover
   - Vibration damper and tighten the center nut to 133 ft. lbs. (180 Nm) and 4 outer bolts to 18 ft. lbs. (25 Nm) plus 60°
   - Accessory drive belt
   - Delivery hose for power steering pump
   - Inner fender liner
   - Front wheel
   - Front transaxle covers
   - Engine pad on the cylinder head
   - Engine limiter
15. Remove the lifting beam.
16. Install the expansion tank.

TURBOCHARGER

REMOVAL & INSTALLATION

S40

See Figure 76.

1. Before servicing the vehicle, refer to the Precautions Section.
2. Disconnect the negative battery cable.
3. Drain the cooling system.
4. Remove the catalytic converter.
5. Remove the clamps and brackets and the charge air pipe.

➡Make sure that the inside of the pipe ends are clean and free of oil residue.

6. Remove the coolant pipe at the turbocharger.
7. Remove the oil pressure pipe and crankcase connection from the turbocharger.
8. Remove the exhaust manifold and turbocharger.

To install:

9. Installation is the reverse of the removal procedure.
10. Tighten the M6 bolts to 89 inch lbs. (10 Nm).
11. Tighten the M8 bolts to 18 ft. lbs. (24 Nm).
12. Tighten the coolant pipe-to-turbocharger to 28 ft. lbs. (38 Nm).

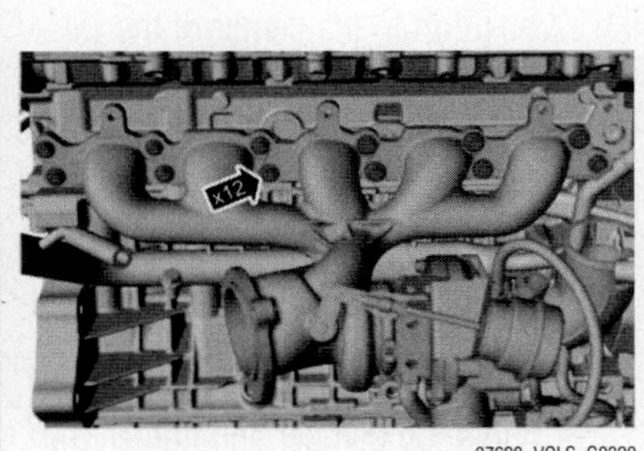

Fig. 76 View of exhaust manifold with turbocharger

13. Tighten the oil pressure pipe-to-turbocharger to 19 ft. lbs. (26 Nm).
14. Tighten the crankcase connection-to-turbocharger to 18 ft. lbs. (25 Nm).

S60 Vehicles

See Figures 77 and 78.

1. Before servicing the vehicle, refer to the Precautions Section.
2. Disconnect the negative battery cable.
3. Remove the cross stay between the suspension turrets.
4. Remove the charge air hose and the charge air pipe above the engine.
    a. Remove the hose clamps for the turbocharger intake pipe at the turbocharger.
    b. Pull off the pipe from the connector. Place the pipe to one side.
5. Raise and safely support the vehicle.
6. Drain the cooling system.
7. Mark the vacuum hose for the pressure regulator on the turbocharger.
8. Remove the vacuum hose from the pressure regulator on the turbocharger.
9. Remove the cable for the Heated Oxygen Sensors (HO2S) from the clips and clamps.
10. Remove the upper heat deflector plate from the turbocharger.
11. Remove the pipe screw for the oil pressure pipe in the turbocharger. Discard the gaskets.
12. Remove the pipe screws for the upper coolant pipe from the turbocharger. Discard the gaskets.
13. Remove the right-hand front wheel.
14. Remove the screw for the halfshaft/wheel hub.
15. Remove the nut for the ball joint and control arm. Counter-hold the ball joint pinion so that the boot does not twist. Use a Torx® wrench.

➡Clean the exposed threads outside the nut. Spray using rust solvent before removing the nut.

16. Fold down the control arm. Use lever 999-7076 to move the wheel spindle to the side. At the same time, install protective sleeve 999-5562 on the ball joint pinion. Hold the sleeve in place using the nut for the ball joint.
17. Press out the wheel spindle. Detach the halfshaft from the hub. Do not damage the halfshaft boot. Use a tensioner band to pull the spring strut backwards.
18. Remove the screws from the bearing cap for the halfshaft. Pull the halfshaft straight out.
19. For AWD vehicles:
    a. Remove the front member from the car body.
    b. Remove the brake pipe from the mountings in the member. Mark the propeller shaft (driveshaft) CV-joint in relation to the bevel gear flange.
    c. Remove the screws from the propeller shaft using 999-7057. Press the halfshaft joints together as much as possible. Remove the shaft from the bevel gear. Leave the end of the shaft resting against the anti-roll bar.
    d. Remove the 5 screws for the bevel gear (transfer case). Pull the bevel gear straight out. Then turn it during removal.
20. Remove the catalytic converter.
21. Remove the support bracket 3 screws and then the bracket.
22. Remove the clamp between the turbocharger oil pressure line and the oil return line.
23. Remove the screws where the oil return line connects to the turbocharger. Pull the pipe from the cylinder block.

Fig. 77 Remove the turbocharger support bracket

Fig. 78 Removing components from the turbocharger

24. Remove the pipe screws for the lower coolant pipe from the turbocharger. Discard the gaskets.
25. Remove the pipe screw for the oil pressure pipe in the engine block. Discard the gaskets.

➡Check that the rubber sealing ring comes away with the pipe. Seal the opening in the cylinder block.

26. Remove the oil pressure pipe.

➡Use rust solvent or similar on the studs of the exhaust manifold and turbocharger.

27. Remove the inner heat deflector plate from the exhaust manifold.
28. Remove the nuts and washers holding the exhaust manifold to the cylinder head.
29. Remove the exhaust manifold.
30. Remove the old gasket residue. Clean the gasket faces.
31. Check that all the studs are tightened.
32. Lower the turbocharger and exhaust manifold as one complete unit.

To install:

33. Install a new gasket between the turbocharger and exhaust manifold.
34. Install the turbocharger to the exhaust manifold using new screws and tighten to 28 ft. lbs. (37 Nm).
35. Install the hoses on the turbocharger according to the markings made at removal.
36. Raise the turbocharger and exhaust manifold as one complete unit.
37. Install new gaskets for the exhaust manifold.
38. Install the turbocharger and the

exhaust manifold. Use new nuts at the manifold.

39. Install the inner heat deflector plate.

40. Install the oil pressure pipe in the cylinder block with the pipe screw. Use new gaskets. Do not tighten.

41. Install the oil return line in the cylinder block with a new sealing ring.

42. Install the 2 screws for the oil return line in the turbocharger. Use a new gasket. Tighten.

43. Install the lower and upper coolant pipe and pipe screws. Tighten to 19 ft. lbs. (26 Nm).

44. Install the clamp between the oil pressure pipe and the return pipe. Tighten.

45. Install the attaching bracket.

46. For AWD vehicles:

a. Before installing the bevel gear, lubricate the spline joint between the transaxle and the bevel gear.

b. Ensure that the mating surfaces on the transaxle and bevel gear are clean. Install the bevel gear. Lightly tighten the M10 screws alternately. Tighten to 37 ft. lbs. (50 Nm).

c. Check that the mating surfaces of the propeller shaft and flange are clean. Install the propeller shaft using the marking made earlier. Use new screws. Tighten the screws.

47. Install the three-way catalytic converter (TWC).

48. Lubricate the mating surface at the end of the halfshaft. Use wheel bearing grease.

49. Install the halfshaft on the transaxle and the mounting for the pilot bearing with the bearing cap and the 2 M8 screws. Tighten to 18 ft. lbs. (24 Nm).

50. Press out the spring strut. Align the drive shaft in the hub. Remove the protective sleeve. Locate the control arm on the ball joint pinion. Use: 999-7076.

51. Install the nut for the ball joint and control arm. Tighten. Counter-hold so that the ball joint boot does not rotate. Use a Torx® wrench.

52. Install the halfshaft center screw. Use a new screw. Tighten. Use a screwdriver as a counter-hold on the brake disc.

53. Install the pipe screw together with new gaskets on the oil pressure pipe in the turbocharger. Tighten to 19 ft. lbs. (26 Nm).

54. Install the upper heat deflector plate. Tighten the screws.

55. Install the charge air pipe over the engine.

56. Install the cross stay between the suspension turrets.

57. Install the tie strap for the servo cable in the cross stay.

58. Raise the vehicle.

59. Install the pipe screws for the oil pressure pipe in the cylinder block. Tighten to 28 ft. lbs. (38 Nm).

60. Install the lower engine cover.

61. Install the right-hand front wheel.

62. Fill the engine with coolant.

63. Start the engine and run to a normal operating temperature.

64. Check for leaks. Fill the coolant if necessary.

ENGINE PERFORMANCE & EMISSION CONTROLS

COMPONENT LOCATIONS

See Figures 79 through 81.

ACCELERATOR PEDAL POSITION (APP) SENSOR

LOCATION

The Accelerator Pedal Position (APP) sensor is located inside the vehicle and is integral to the accelerator pedal.

REMOVAL & INSTALLATION

See Figure 82.

1. Remove the Accelerator Pedal Position (APP) sensor connector.
2. Remove the 3 mounting nuts.
3. Remove the APP sensor.

To install:

4. Install the APP sensor and tighten the mounting nuts to 89 inch lbs. (10 Nm).
5. Reconnect the APP sensor connector.

CAMSHAFT POSITION (CMP) SENSOR

LOCATION

The Camshaft Position (CMP) sensor is located in the valve cover under the coil cover.

REMOVAL & INSTALLATION

1. Before servicing the vehicle, refer to the Precautions Section.
2. Remove the intake manifold.
3. Loosen the hose clamps and the screws. Place the manifold to one side.
4. Remove the cover over the ignition coils.
5. Remove the Camshaft Position (CMP) sensor.

To install:

6. Install the CMP sensor.
7. Tighten the screw to 66 inch. lbs. (8 Nm).
8. Install the ignition coil cover.
9. Install intake manifold.

CRANKSHAFT POSITION (CKP) SENSOR

LOCATION

The Crankshaft Position (CKP) sensor is located under the upper intake manifold.

REMOVAL & INSTALLATION

See Figure 83.

1. Before servicing the vehicle, refer to the Precautions Section.
2. Remove the air cleaner module assembly.
3. Remove the upper intake manifold.
4. Loosen the 6 screws for the upper intake manifold, the 2 screws closest to the front cover plate, and the 2 screws against the firewall. Carefully bend up the intake manifold and hold it to one side.

➡Seal the openings in the lower part of the intake manifold with tape, or similar.

5. Remove the electrical connector to the Crankshaft Position (CKP) sensor.
6. Remove the mounting bolt and the CKP sensor.

To install:

7. Install the CKP sensor and tighten the mounting nut to 89 inch lbs. (10 Nm).
8. Install a new intake gasket.
9. Install the intake manifold and tighten the screws.
10. Tighten the screws alternately to 89 inch lbs. (10 Nm).
11. Install the electrical connector to the CKP sensor.
12. Install the air cleaner module assembly.
13. Start the engine and check for proper function.

ELECTRONIC CONTROL MODULE (ECM)

LOCATION

The Engine Control Module (ECM) is in the intake system. It is cooled by the engine intake air.

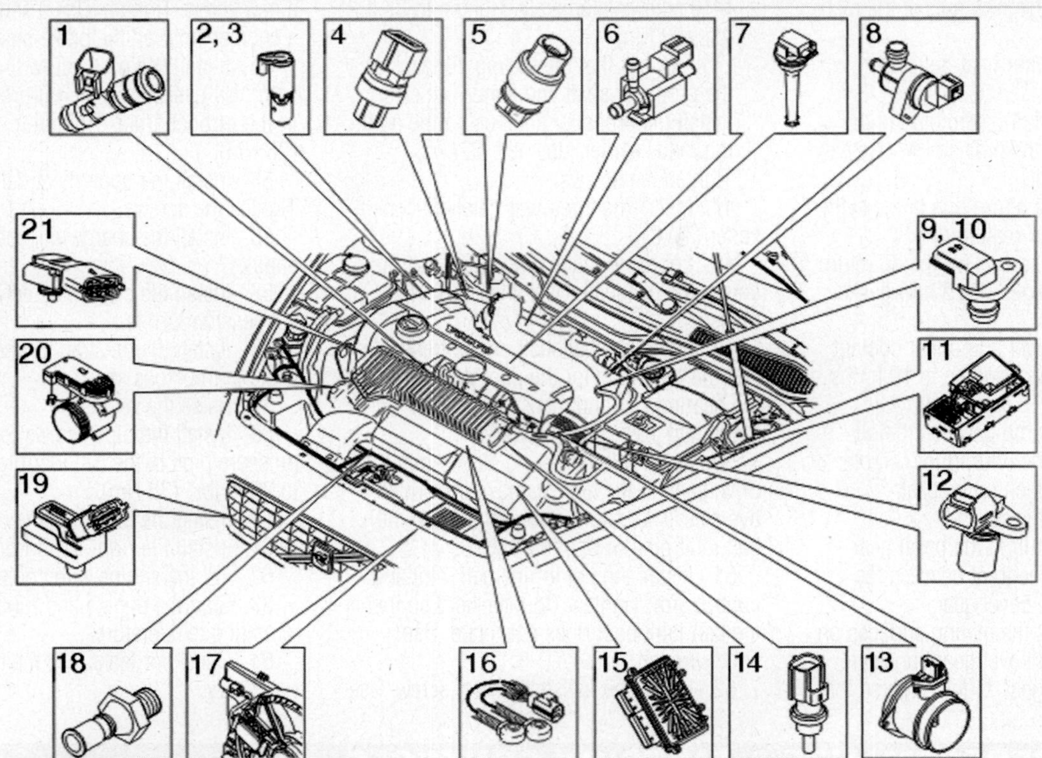

Not all the following components are necessarily in the car.

	Component	Located at/on:
1	Injectors (5x)	Intake manifold.
2	Intake camshaft reset valve	Engine, timing belt side, by camshaft.
3	Exhaust camshaft reset valve	Engine, timing belt side, by camshaft.
4	Air Conditioning (A/C) pressure sensor	A/C system high pressure pipe (thin pipe).
5	A/C pressure switch	A/C system low pressure pipe (thick pipe).
6	Turbocharger (TC) control valve	The Turbocharger (TC).
7	Ignition coil (5x)	The cylinder head.
8	Evaporative emission system (EVAP) valve	Intake manifold.
9	Camshaft Position (CMP) sensor, intake	Engine, flywheel side, by the camshaft.
10	Camshaft Position (CMP) sensor, exhaust	Engine, flywheel side, by the camshaft.
11	Integrated relay/fusebox	
12	Engine speed (RPM) sensor	Above the flywheel.
13	Mass Air Flow (MAF) sensor	The Air Cleaner (ACL) module.
14	Engine Coolant Temperature (ECT) sensor	The thermostat housing.
15	Engine Control Module (ECM)	The ACL module.
16	Knock Sensor (KS)	The cylinder block under the ACL module.
17	Engine Cooling Fan (FC) control module	
18	Oil pressure switch	Lower front edge of the engine.
19	Boost pressure sensor	The Charge Air Cooler (CAC) upper right-hand section.
20	Throttle unit	The engine intake manifold.
21	Fuel pressure sensor/fuel temperature sensor	Fuel rail right face.

37698_VOLS_G0323

Fig. 79 Engine component locations—B5254T7 engine

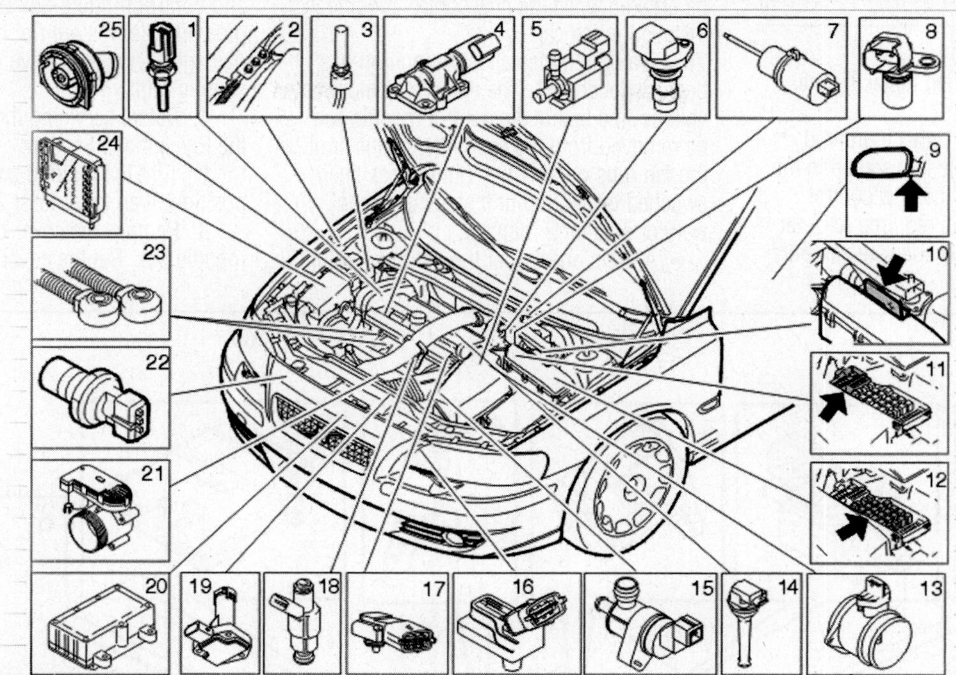

Not all the following components are necessarily in the car.

	Component	Remarks
1	Engine Coolant Temperature (ECT) sensor	
2	Ground terminal	
3	Coolant level sensor	
4	Reset valve, camshaft	Exhaust and intake camshafts.
5	Turbocharger (TC) control valve	Only Turbocharged (TC) engines
6	Camshaft sensor	Exhaust and intake camshafts.
7	Brake pedal sensor	
8	Engine speed (RPM) sensor	
9	Outer temperature sensor	
10	Power supply terminal	
11	Fusebox	
12	Relay box	
13	Mass Air Flow (MAF) sensor	
14	Ignition coil	
15	Canister Purge (CP) valve	
16	Boost pressure sensor	The Intake Air Temperature (IAT) sensor is integrated in the boost pressure sensor
17	Fuel pressure sensor	The fuel temperature sensor is integrated in the fuel pressure sensor
18	Injector	
19	Oil level sensor	Located in the oil trough
20	Engine Cooling Fan (FC) control module	
21	Throttle unit	Also includes the Throttle Position (TP) sensor
22	A/C pressure sensor	
23	Knock Sensor (KS)	
24	Engine control unit	
25	Engine Cooling Fan (FC) control modules	

37698_VOLS_G0324

Fig. 80 Engine component locations—B5254T5

REMOVAL & INSTALLATION

See Figures 84 and 85.

Points to observe when replacing the control module:

- New software can only be ordered when the control module is installed in the vehicle. VIDA reads off the new control module identity which is required to order the correct software. The software can only be ordered when the new control module is installed in the car.
- Wait 2 minutes after the ignition has been switched OFF. The main relay must be voltage-free before the control module can be removed from the car. If the engine cooling fan runs on after the ignition has been switched off, wait until it stops and then wait for another 2 minutes.
- Always check that the control module and control module box connector pins and sleeves are not bent or damaged. This may have caused the presenting fault.

1. Before servicing the vehicle, refer to the Precautions Section.
2. Turn the ignition switch to the OFF position. Wait for at least 2 minutes.
3. Remove the cover over the control module box. Put the cover to one side.

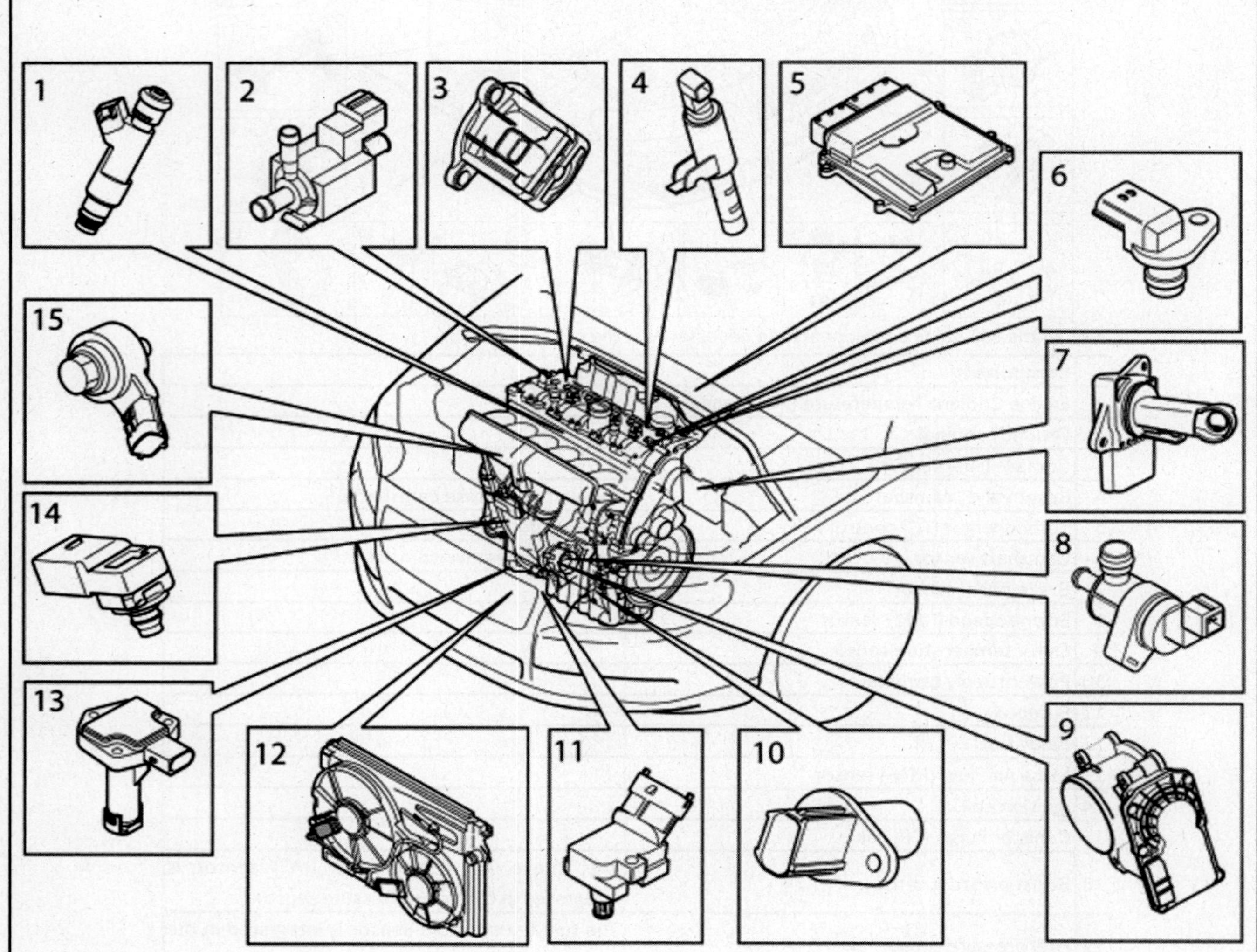

Fig. 81 Engine component locations—B6304T4 engine

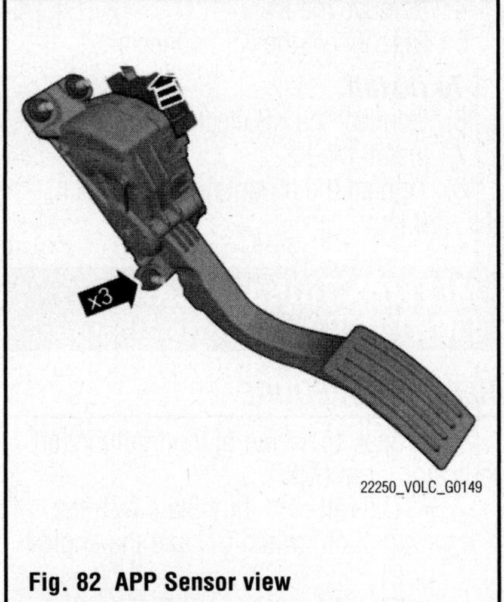

Fig. 82 APP Sensor view

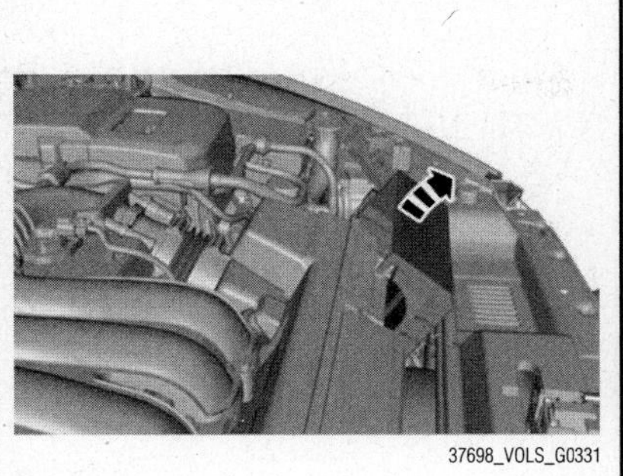

Fig. 84 Remove the cover over the Engine Control Module (ECM)

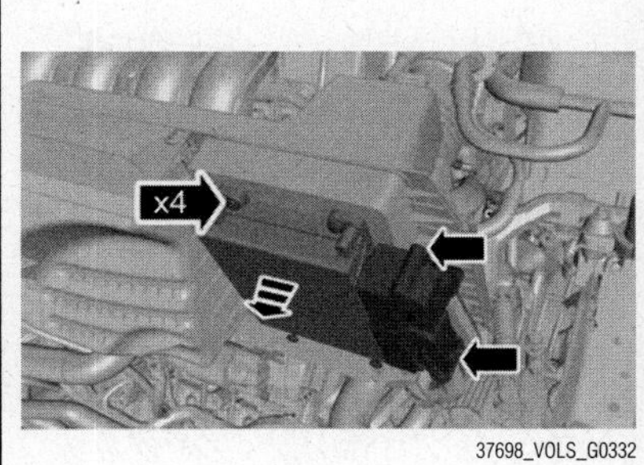

Fig. 85 Installing the Engine Control Module (ECM)

WARNING

Do not touch the control module terminal pins with your fingers. Static electricity may damage components in the control module.

4. Insert tool 999-5722 around the control module, as needed.
5. Move the upper section of the tool backwards as far as it will go. Pull up the tool.
6. Carefully pull up and remove the Engine Control Module (ECM).

To install:

7. Check that no pins or sockets are damaged on the connector.
8. Carefully press the control module down into the grooves on the inside of the control module box. Press to the limit position.
9. Insert tool 999-5722 around the control module, as needed.
10. Move the upper section of the tool forwards as far as it will go. Pull the tool upwards.
11. Press the cover into place over the control module.
12. Check that the air ducts are correctly positioned.

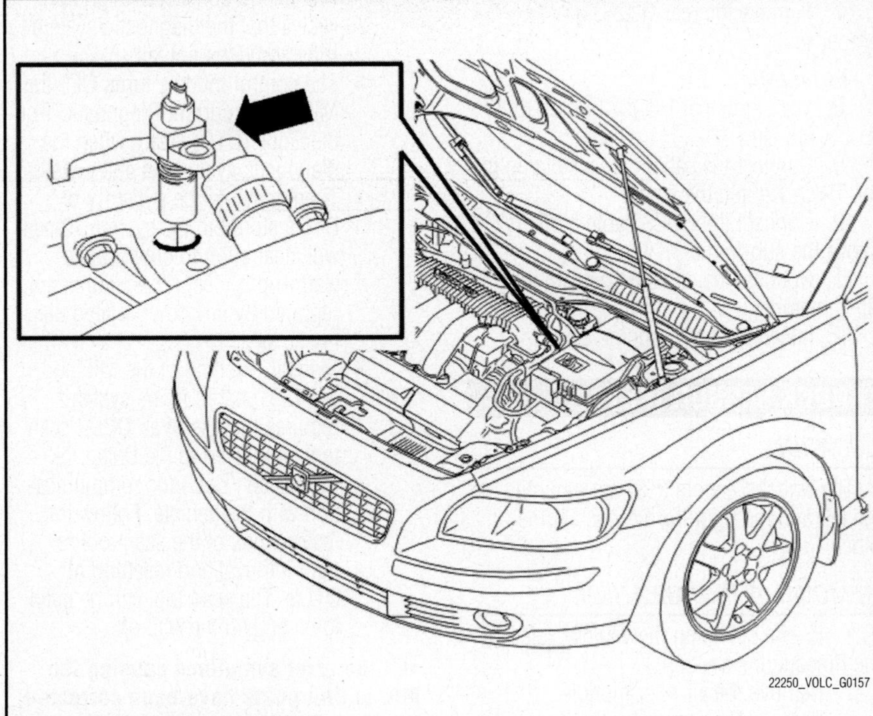

Fig. 83 Crankshaft position sensor

13. After downloading the software or replacing the ECM, the throttle unit must be adapted according to vehicle communication input: "Adapting the throttle unit."
14. Check that no Diagnostic Trouble Codes (DTC's) have been stored during the repair.
15. Test drive the vehicle and check the function of the engine.

ENGINE COOLANT TEMPERATURE (ECT) SENSOR

LOCATION

The Engine Coolant Temperature (ECT) sensor is located at the thermostat housing

REMOVAL & INSTALLATION

See Figure 86.

CAUTION

Never open, service or drain the radiator or cooling system when hot; serious burns can occur from the steam and hot coolant. Also, when draining engine coolant, keep in mind that cats and dogs are attracted to ethylene glycol antifreeze and could drink any that is left in an uncovered container or in puddles on the ground. This will prove fatal in sufficient quantities. Always drain coolant into a sealable container. Coolant should be reused unless it is contaminated or is several years old.

1. Before servicing the vehicle, refer to the Precautions Section.
2. Drain the engine coolant.
3. Disconnect the negative ground cable of the battery.

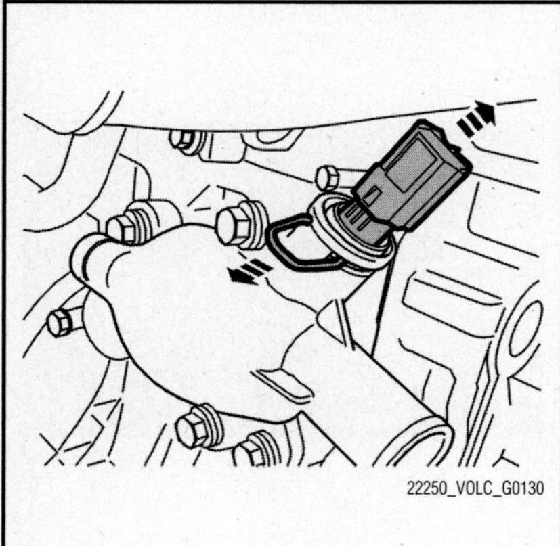

Fig. 86 Engine Coolant Temperature (ECT) sensor location

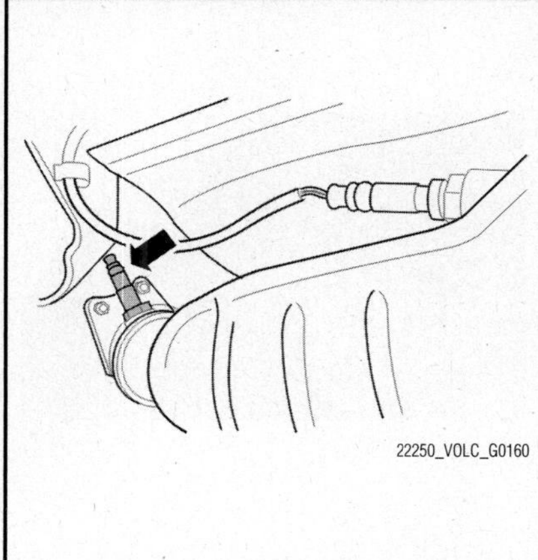

Fig. 87 Front Heated Oxygen (HO2S) sensor location view

4. Remove the electrical connector from the sensor.
5. Remove the clip from the Engine Coolant Temperature (ECT) sensor.

To install:

6. Install the sensor with a new O-ring and install the clip.
7. Attach the electrical connector to sensor.
8. Connect the ground cable of battery.
9. Fill the engine coolant with the proper type and amount of fluid.
10. Run the engine and check for leaks.

HEATED OXYGEN (HO2S) SENSOR

LOCATION

The front Heated Oxygen (HO2S) sensor is mounted in the exhaust manifold converter sub-assembly. The rear HO2S sensor is mounted in the rear converter sub-assembly.

REMOVAL & INSTALLATION

Upstream Sensor

See Figure 87.

1. Before servicing the vehicle, refer to the Precautions Section.
2. Loosen and disconnect the connector for the front Heated Oxygen Sensor (HO2S).
3. Raise and safely support the vehicle.
4. Remove the lower engine cover.
5. Disconnect the sensor harness.
6. Using an oxygen sensor socket, remove the front HO2S.

To install:

7. Install the front HO2S. Tighten to 33 ft. lbs. (45 Nm).
8. Reconnect the connector for the front HO2S.
9. Install the lower engine cover.

Downstream Sensor

1. Before servicing the vehicle, refer to the Precautions Section.
2. Raise and safely support the vehicle.
3. Remove the lower engine cover.
4. Disconnect the Heated Oxygen (HO2S) sensor cable harness above the sub-frame.
5. Disconnect the cable harness from the Side Impact Protection System (SIPS) member.
6. Remove the screw for the cable harness clamp in the Three-Way Catalytic Converter (TWC).
7. Remove the rear HO2S. Use the proper tool.

To install:

8. Install the rear HO2S. Tighten to 33 ft. lbs. (45 Nm).
9. Connect the cable harness clamp in the TWC. Tighten the screw.
10. Connect the HO2S cable harness above the sub-frame.
11. Connect the cable harness to the SIPS member.
12. Install the lower engine cover.

KNOCK SENSOR (KS)

LOCATION

The Knock Sensors (KS) are mounted on the left and the right front of the engine block.

REMOVAL & INSTALLATION

1. Before servicing the vehicle, refer to the Precautions Section.
2. Remove the air filter module.
3. Remove the screws for the Knock Sensor (KS).
4. Remove the KS.
5. Disconnect the KS connector.

To install:

6. Connect the KS electrical connector.
7. Install the KS.
8. Tighten the mounting bolt to 15 ft. lbs. (20 Nm).

MALFUNCTION INDICATOR LIGHT (MIL)

RESET PROCEDURE

1. Proper operation of the Malfunction Indicator Light (MIL):
   - The MIL will illuminate with the ignition switch ON and the engine OFF
   - The MIL will turn OFF when the engine is started
   - The MIL will remain ON if the self-diagnostic system has detected a malfunction
   - The MIL may turn OFF if the malfunction is no longer present
   - If the MIL is illuminated and then the engine stalls, the MIL will remain illuminated as long as the ignition switch is ON
   - If the MIL is not illuminated and the engine stalls, the MIL will not illuminate until the ignition switch is cycled OFF, then ON
2. Resetting the MIL:
   - The control module turns OFF the MIL after 3 consecutive ignition cycles that the diagnostic system runs and does not fail
   - The control module turns OFF the MIL after a current Diagnostic Trouble Code (DTC) clears when the diagnostic cycle runs and passes
   - There may still be a history of DTC's stored in the system. These will clear after 40 consecutive warm-up cycles, if no failures are reported by any other related diagnostic system
   - Manual resetting of the MIL and any DTC stored in the system, requires the use of an OBD2 scan tool connected to the Data Link Connector (DLC) for communication with the vehicle. Follow the instructions of the scan tool for both retrieval and resetting of DTC's. The scan tool can be used to command the MIL off.

➡If the error symptoms causing the MIL to illuminate have been corrected, the MIL will return to normal operation.

MANIFOLD ABSOLUTE PRESSURE (MAP) SENSOR

LOCATION

See Figure 88.

3>REMOVAL & INSTALLATION

1. Before servicing the vehicle, refer to the Precautions Section.
2. Cut the tie strap for the Manifold Absolute Pressure (MAP) sensor cable harness.
3. Disconnect the MAP sensor connector.
4. Remove the screws for the sensor.
5. Remove the MAP sensor.

To install:

6. Install the MAP sensor.
7. Install the screws for the pressure sensor. Tighten to 18 inch lbs. (2 Nm).
8. Connect the connector for the MAP sensor.
9. Install a new tie strap for the pressure sensor wiring.

MASS AIR FLOW SENSOR

LOCATION

The Mass Air Flow (MAF) sensor is located in the air cleaner housing or the air tube.

REMOVAL & INSTALLATION

1. Before servicing the vehicle, refer to the Precautions Section.
2. Remove the Mass Air Flow (MAF) sensor harness.
3. Remove the MAF sensor.
4. Installation is the reverse of removal.

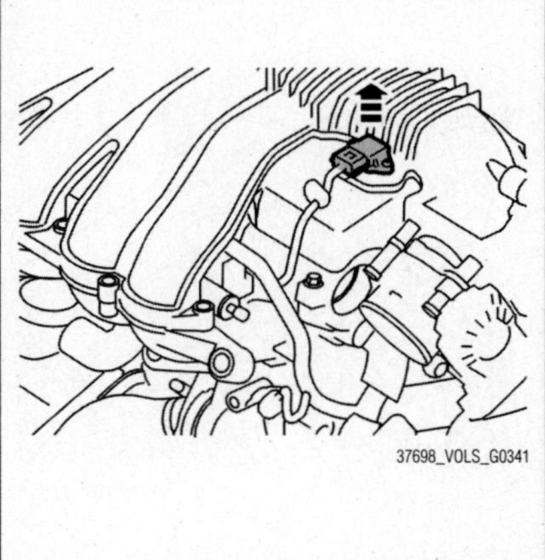

Fig. 88 Manifold Absolute Pressure (MAP) sensor location—S40 vehicles

THROTTLE POSITION SENSOR (TPS)

LOCATION

The Throttle Position Sensor (TPS) is mounted on the throttle body.

REMOVAL & INSTALLATION

The throttle body position sensor is not serviceable as a stand-alone part. The throttle body position sensor is an integral part of the throttle body. If the throttle position sensor requires replacement, replace the throttle body assembly.

VEHICLE SPEED SENSOR (VSS)

LOCATION

The Vehicle Speed Sensor (VSS) is located on the transaxle.

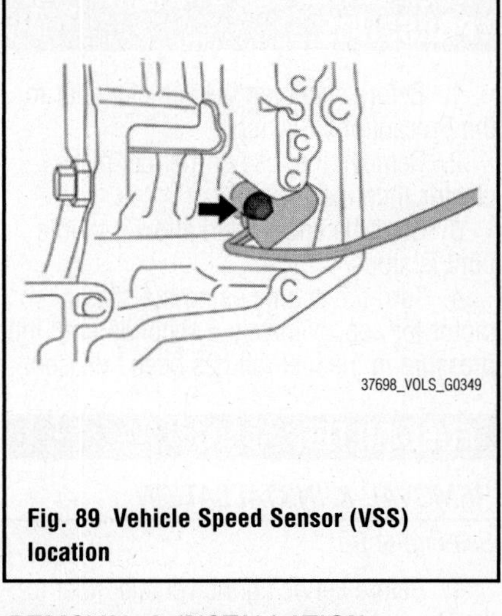

Fig. 89 Vehicle Speed Sensor (VSS) location

REMOVAL & INSTALLATION

See Figure 89.

Some variation in the illustrations may occur, but the essential information is correct.

1. Before servicing the vehicle, refer to the Precautions Section.
2. Disconnect the cable harness connector from the Transmission Control Module (TCM).
3. Clean around the sensors. Remove the sensors and the cable harness.

To install:

4. Install the new sensor(s). Apply a little automatic transmission fluid to the O-rings for the sensors. Tighten the M6 bolt to 89 inch lbs. (10 Nm).
5. Install the cable harness connector to the TCM.

FUEL — GASOLINE FUEL INJECTION SYSTEM

FUEL SYSTEM SERVICE PRECAUTIONS

Safety is the most important factor when performing not only fuel system maintenance but any type of maintenance. Failure to conduct maintenance and repairs in a safe manner may result in serious personal injury or death. Maintenance and testing of the vehicle's fuel system components can be accomplished safely and effectively by adhering to the following rules and guidelines.

- To avoid the possibility of fire and personal injury, always disconnect the negative battery cable unless the repair or test procedure requires that battery voltage be applied.
- Always relieve the fuel system pressure prior to disconnecting any fuel system component (injector, fuel rail, pressure regulator, etc.), fitting or fuel line connection. Exercise extreme caution whenever relieving fuel system pressure to avoid exposing skin, face and eyes to fuel spray. Please be advised that fuel under pressure may penetrate the skin or any part of the body that it contacts.
- Always place a shop towel or cloth around the fitting or connection prior to loosening to absorb any excess fuel due to spillage. Ensure that all fuel spillage (should it occur) is quickly removed from engine surfaces. Ensure that all fuel soaked cloths or towels are deposited into a suitable waste container.
- Always keep a dry chemical (Class B) fire extinguisher near the work area.
- Do not allow fuel spray or fuel vapors to come into contact with a spark or open flame.
- Always use a back-up wrench when loosening and tightening fuel line connection fittings. This will prevent unnecessary stress and torsion to fuel line piping.
- Always replace worn fuel fitting O-rings with new Do not substitute fuel hose or equivalent where fuel pipe is installed.

Before servicing the vehicle, make sure to also refer to the precautions in the beginning of this section as well.

RELIEVING FUEL SYSTEM PRESSURE

1. Before servicing the vehicle, refer to the Precautions Section.
2. Remove the fuse or the fuel pump electrical connector.
3. Start the engine and allow it to idle until is stops.
4. Turn the engine using the starter motor for approximately 5 seconds until the pressure in the fuel rail has been released.

FUEL FILTER

REMOVAL & INSTALLATION

See Figure 90.

1. Before servicing the vehicle, refer to the Precautions Section.
2. Relieve the fuel system pressure.
3. Remove or disconnect the following:
   - Negative battery cable
   - Fuel filler cap
   - Fuel lines from the fuel filter
   - Fuel filter from the bracket

To install:

4. Install or connect the following:
   - Fuel filter to the bracket
   - Fuel lines to the fuel filter
   - Fuel filler cap
   - Negative battery cable
5. Start the engine and check for leaks.

FUEL RAIL & INJECTORS

REMOVAL & INSTALLATION

See Figure 91.

1. Before servicing the vehicle, refer to the Precautions Section.
2. Relieve the fuel system pressure.
3. Disconnect the negative battery cable.

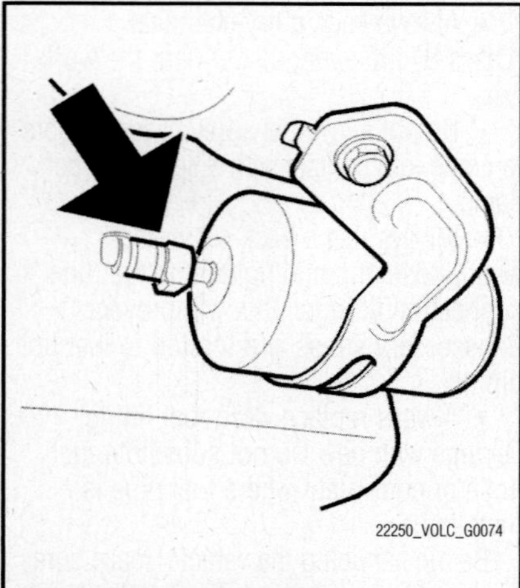

Fig. 90 Fuel filter mounting

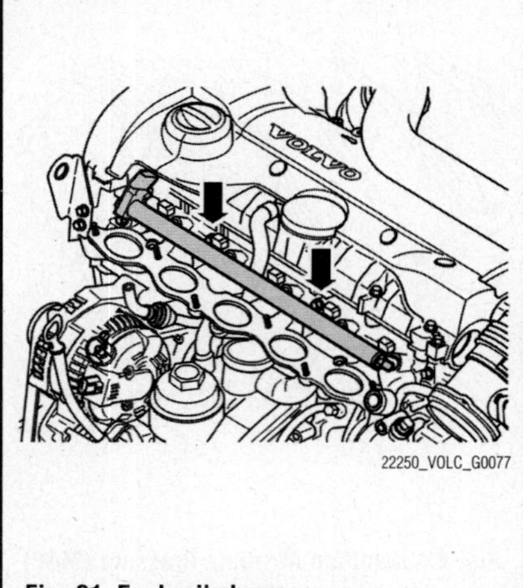

Fig. 91 Fuel rail shown

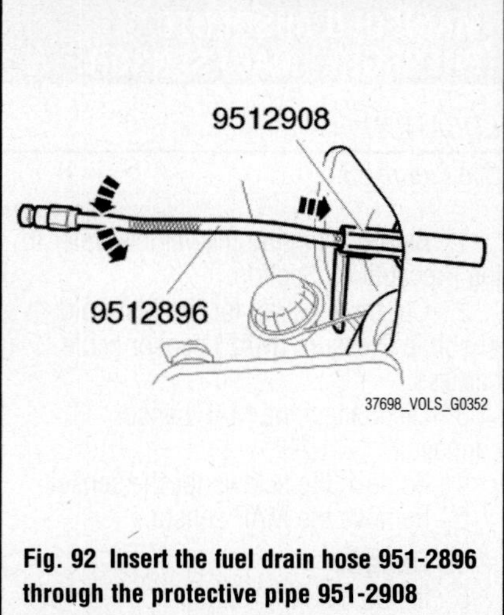

Fig. 92 Insert the fuel drain hose 951-2896 through the protective pipe 951-2908

4. Remove the hose clamp for the rubber hose on the throttle body. Move the hose to one side.
5. Disconnect the throttle body connector.
6. Remove the 6 screws for the upper section of the intake manifold. Move the manifold to one side.
7. Disconnect the connector for the fuel pressure sensor and the connector for the injectors.
8. Remove the 2 fuel rail mounting screws.
9. Spray with universal oil or similar around the injector nozzle at the terminal on the intake manifold.
10. Gently work the fuel rail and injector nozzles loose. Disconnect the fuel line to the fuel rail.
11. Press in the 2 blue clips on the fuel rail.
12. Pull the fuel line out of the fuel rail.
13. Remove the screws holding the mounting rail to the fuel rail.
14. Remove the mounting rail.
15. Remove the fuel injector(s).

To install:

16. Installation is in reverse of the removal procedure, note the following:
    a. Tighten the fuel rail bolts to 89 inch lbs. (10 Nm).
17. Start the engine and check for leaks.

FUEL TANK

DRAINING

See Figure 92.

Observe the following precautions:

- Observe all applicable safety precautions when working around the fuel system. Whenever servicing the fuel system, always work in a well-ventilated area. Do not allow fuel spray or vapors to come in contact with a spark or open flame
- Keep a dry chemical fire extinguisher near the work area
- Always keep fuel in a container specifically designed for fuel storage. Properly seal fuel containers to avoid the possibility of fire or explosion
- Use of a fresh air mask is highly recommended
- Always follow the safety recommendations of the fuel extractor you are using to avoid the potential of fire or explosion

1. Before servicing the vehicle, refer to the Precautions Section.
2. Disconnect the negative battery cable.
3. Insert the drain hose 95- 2896 through the protective pipe 951-2908 into the fuel tank. Use a twisting motion on the hose while inserting it into the fuel filler to clear any obstacles.
4. Connect the hose to the fuel extractor.
5. Pump the fuel out until only air is extracted.
6. Remove extractor hose and protective pipe.

✲✲ WARNING

Pull the hose out carefully to prevent damage to the evacuation valve.

REMOVAL & INSTALLATION

S40

See Figures 93 and 94.

Observe the following precautions:

- Observe all applicable safety precautions when working around the fuel system. Whenever servicing the fuel system, always work in a well-ventilated area. Do not allow

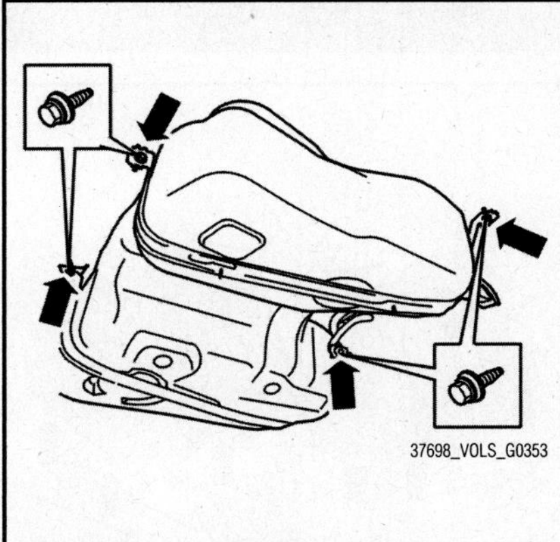

Fig. 93 Remove the tank retaining straps and lower the tank using a lift

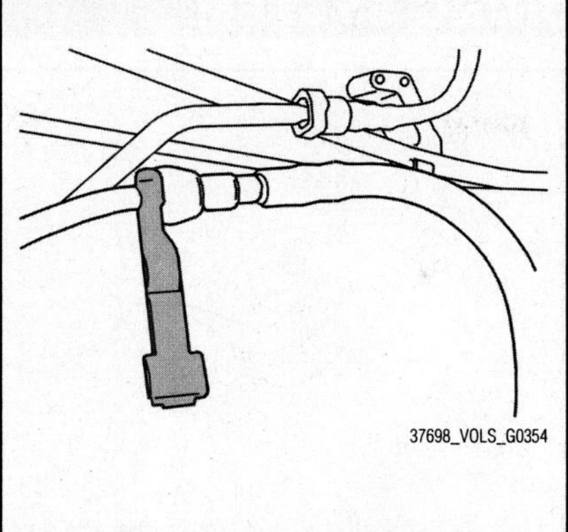

Fig. 94 Remove the fuel hose using tool 951-2666

fuel spray or vapors to come in contact with a spark or open flame

- Keep a dry chemical fire extinguisher near the work area
- Always keep fuel in a container specifically designed for fuel storage. Properly seal fuel containers to avoid the possibility of fire or explosion
- Use of a fresh air mask is highly recommended
- Always follow the safety recommendations of the fuel extractor you are using to avoid the potential of fire or explosion

The illustrations in this service information are used for different model years and/or models. Some variation may occur. However, the essential information in the illustrations is correct.

1. Before servicing the vehicle, refer to the Precautions Section.
2. Relieve the fuel pressure in the fuel system.
3. Disconnect the negative battery cable.
4. Drain the fuel tank.
5. Remove the middle muffler from the exhaust system.
6. Remove the plastic casing on the left and right side.
7. Remove the rear heat shield cover.
8. Place a suitable lift under the fuel tank.
9. Loosen the screws for the tank straps.
10. Remove the tank retaining straps. Lower the tank slightly using the lift.
11. Remove the hose clamp for the hose to the filler pipe.

CAUTION

Carefully loosen the hose from the fuel filler pipe as there may be fuel left in the tank.

12. Remove the hoses with quick-coupling fittings from the charcoal filter canister and evacuation pipe.
13. Remove the fuel hose using tool 951-2666.
14. Remove the level sensor connector and pull it from its bracket.
15. Carefully lower the tank and make sure that no cables or hoses are trapped.
16. Remove the fuel hose with the quick-coupling from the fuel pump module.
17. Drain any remaining fuel and remove the fuel tank.

To install:

18. Transfer any needed components if replacing the fuel tank.
19. Place the fuel tank on the mobile jack together with fixture 999-5972.
20. Raise the tank so that it is 12 inches (30cm) from the top position.
21. Install the hoses with the quick-coupling for the evacuation pipe and charcoal filter canister.
22. Install the fuel hose with the quick-coupling.
23. Install the connector for the level sensor.
24. Lift the fuel tank into position.
25. Install the filler pipe with the clamp.
26. Install the tank straps with screws and tighten the M8 bolts to 18 ft. lbs. (24 Nm).
27. Install the rear heat shield cover.
28. Install the plastic casing on both left and right sides.
29. Install the middle muffler to the exhaust system.
30. Top up the fuel.
31. Install the fuse for the fuel pump.
32. Check for leaks in the fuel system.

THROTTLE BODY

REMOVAL & INSTALLATION

See Figure 95.

1. Before servicing the vehicle, refer to the Precautions Section.
2. Remove the negative battery cable.
3. Remove the air intake between the front cover plate and the air cleaner housing.
4. With a turbocharger, remove the charge air pipe between the charge air cooler and the electronic throttle body.
5. Remove the throttle body:
   a. Disconnect the connector for the throttle body.
   b. Remove the 4 bolts from the throttle body.
   c. Lift out the throttle body and discard the gasket.

To install:

➡Ensure that the surfaces between the throttle body and the intake manifold are clean.

6. Install electronic throttle body using a new gasket. Tighten the 4 bolts to 89 inch lbs. (10 Nm).
7. With a turbocharger, install the charge air pipe between the electronic throttle body module and the charge air cooler.

➡Heat the pipe at the connections to facilitate installation.

8. Install the intake pipe between the front cover plate and the air cleaner housing.
9. Start the engine and check the function of the electronic throttle body module.

➡After replacing the throttle unit, the throttle unit must be adapted using the vehicle communication input: Adaptation of the electronic throttle unit. Remedy as necessary.

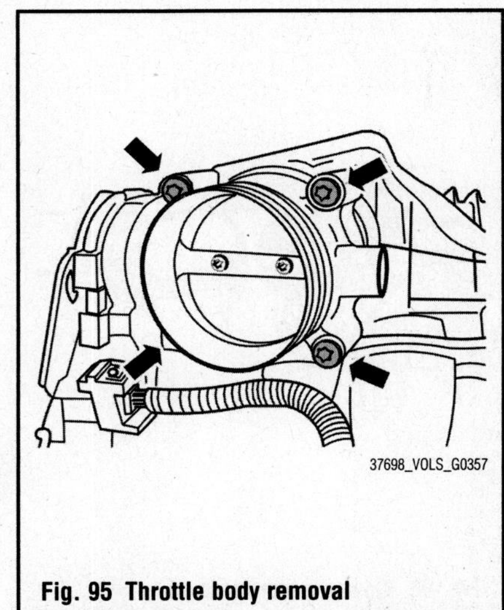

Fig. 95 Throttle body removal

HEATING & AIR CONDITIONING SYSTEM

BLOWER MOTOR

REMOVAL & INSTALLATION

See Figure 96.

1. Before servicing the vehicle, refer to the Precautions Section.
2. Remove the negative battery cable.
3. Remove the instrument panel.
4. Remove the rubber seals and the cable terminals.
5. Remove the bolts for the blower motor.
6. Remove the blower motor.

To install:

7. Install the blower motor using the M5 bolts. Tighten to 44 inch lbs. (5 Nm).
8. Install the cable terminals and the rubber seals.
9. Install the instrument panel.
10. Install the negative battery cable.

HEATER CORE

REMOVAL & INSTALLATION

S40

See Figures 97 through 99.

1. Before servicing the vehicle, refer to the Precautions Section.
2. Drain the engine coolant.
3. Detach the radiator hoses from the engine compartment. Turn the radiator hose connection counter-clockwise to the end position and then pull off the radiator hose.
4. Remove the center console.
5. Remove the glove compartment.
6. Detach the central electrical unit from its bracket, but allow it to hang from the wiring.

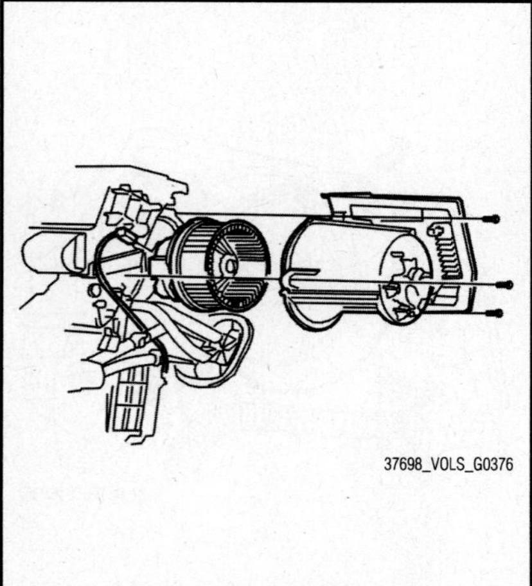

Fig. 96 Blower motor removal

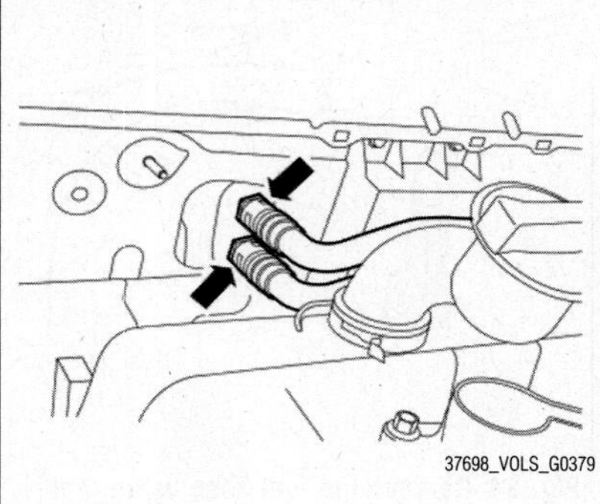

Fig. 97 Detach the radiator hoses from the engine compartment side of the heater core—S40 vehicles

7. Remove the brackets on both sides of the climate control unit and the screws, 3 per bracket.
8. Remove the air duct.
9. Remove the 8 screws from the heating unit cover.
10. Pull the cover at an angle downwards/backwards.
11. The heat exchanger has pipes that are factory integrated. These pipes must be cut in order to remove the unit. The heat exchanger in the service kit has separate pipes.
12. Place some paper below the pipe couplings to collect any spilled coolant and cut or saw off the pipes.
13. Press the pipes towards the firewall so that they protrude into the engine compartment.
14. Remove the 2 screws and the lead-in right half.
15. Remove the section that holds the heat exchanger and evaporator pipes apart.
16. Pull the heat exchanger pipes through the seal.
17. Seal the pipes to the heat exchanger so that the remaining coolant will not continue to run out.
18. Angle the heat exchanger up at the rear edge. Lift out the heat exchanger towards the passenger side.

➡Note how the seal is located on the heat exchanger.

To install:

19. Install a new seal carefully using the removed evaporator as a template.
20. Install the heat exchanger core.
21. Install the heat exchanger pipes through the seal.

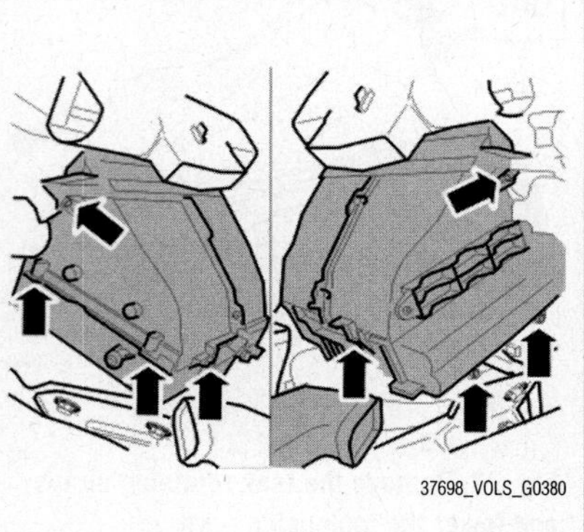

Fig. 98 Removing the heating unit cover—S40 vehicles

➡To facilitate assembling the pipes, lubricate the ends with a little oil. Use new O-rings for the pipe ends.

22. Install the pipes at the connection to the heat exchanger pipes.
23. Install the clips so that they lock securely. A click must be heard.

➡The clips only fit one way in the pipe connection.

24. Install the 8 screws for the cover and tighten.
25. Install the air duct.
26. Install the brackets on both sides of the climate control unit and the screws.
27. Install the central electrical unit in its bracket.
28. Install the center console.
29. Install the radiator hoses in the connections by the firewall.

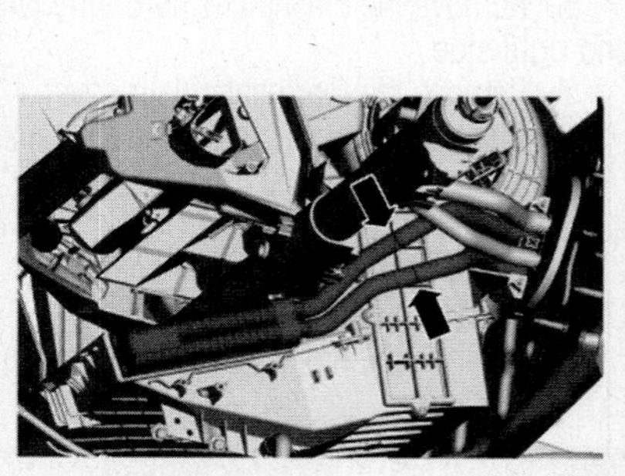

Fig. 99 The heater exchanger core pipes must be cut in order to remove the unit—S40 vehicles

30. Tighten the drain nipple on the radiator.
31. Fill the engine coolant.
32. Check that the pipe coupling does not leak.
33. Install the glove compartment.

S60

See Figure 100.

1. Before servicing the vehicle, refer to the Precautions Section.
2. Drain the engine coolant.
3. Detach the radiator hoses from the engine compartment. Turn the radiator hose connection counter-clockwise to the end position and then pull off the radiator hose.
4. Remove the seal and the plate.
5. Remove the soundproofing panel.
6. Remove the floor console.
7. Remove the tie strap for the pipes.
8. Remove the bolts for the heat exchanger.
9. Remove the mounting brackets for the pipes.
10. Position plenty of paper under the heat exchanger and around the pipes.

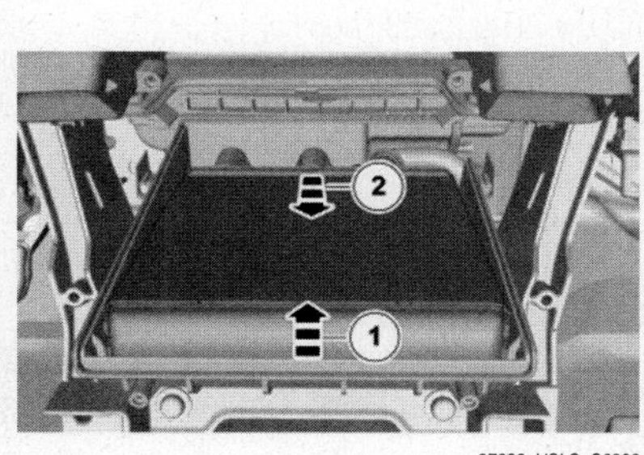

Fig. 100 Heat exchanger core removal

➡Be prepared to collect escaping fluid.

11. Drain the coolant into a suitable container.
12. Detach the pipes and position them out of the way.
13. Pull out the heat exchanger.

To install:

➡Always use new O-rings.

14. Install the heat exchanger carefully.
15. Bolt the heat exchanger into place.
16. Install the upper pipes.
17. Install the locking plate using round-nosed pliers.
18. Press in the pipes using a screwdriver. Press the catch using pliers.
19. Install the lower pipes.
20. Install the locking plate using round-nosed pliers.
21. Press in the pipe using a screwdriver. Press in the locking bracket using round-nosed pliers.
22. Install the tie strap for the pipes.
23. Install the seal and the plate.
24. Install the heating hoses in the engine compartment.
25. Fill the engine coolant.
26. Check that the pipe coupling does not leak.
27. Install the floor console.
28. Install the soundproofing panel.

STEERING

POWER STEERING GEAR

REMOVAL & INSTALLATION

S40

See Figure 101.

1. Before servicing the vehicle, refer to the Precautions Section.

➡Ensure the steering wheel is set to the straight ahead position and remove the key so the steering wheel lock engages.

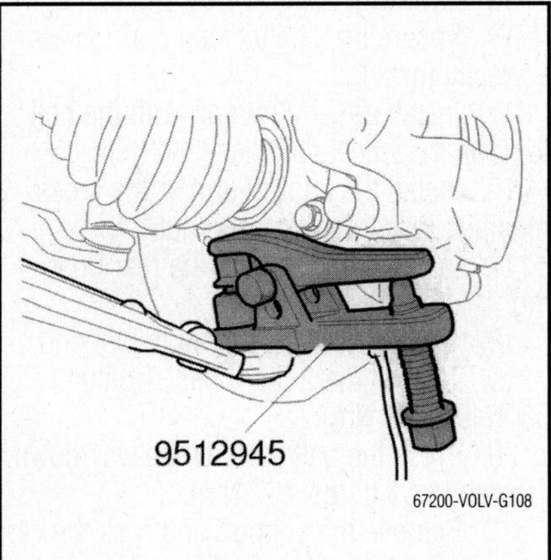

Fig. 101 Pull the steering arm from the wheel spindle

2. Remove the left front wheel and measure and record the length of the tie rod in relation to the steering gear housing.
3. Remove or disconnect the following:
   - Left side soundproofing panel
   - Left front wheel
   - Steering shaft from the steering gear
   - Sub-frame
   - Powering steering hoses from the steering gear
4. Loosen the nut for the outer steering arm. Press the steering arm out of the wheel spindle using Special Tool 951-2945 or equivalent.
5. Remove the steering gear.

To install:

6. Install or connect the following:
   - Steering gear
   - Outer steering arm; tighten nuts to 37 ft. lbs. (50 Nm)
   - Power steering hoses using new O-rings
   - Sub-frame
   - Steering shaft to the steering gear
   - Wheel
   - Soundproofing panel
7. Fill and bleed the power steering system.

POWER STEERING PUMP

BLEEDING

⁂ CAUTION

The fluid level should be checked with the engine OFF to prevent personal injury from moving parts and to assure an accurate fluid level reading.

⁂ WARNING

If the air is not purged from the power steering system correctly, pump failure could result.

1. Before servicing the vehicle, refer to the Precautions Section.
2. With engine OFF, turn the steering wheel fully to the right and left several times.

➡Do not allow the fluid level in the reservoir tank to go below the MIN level line. Check and add fluid as needed.

3. Run the engine at idle speed. Turn the steering wheel fully to the right and then fully to the left. Hold for about 3 seconds. Check for fluid leakage.

4. Repeat the above step several times at 3 second intervals.

❋❋ WARNING

Do not hold the steering wheel in the locked position for more than 10 seconds.

5. Check for air bubbles or cloudy fluid. If found, repeat the bleeding procedure.
6. Stop the engine and check the fluid level. Fill as required.

REMOVAL & INSTALLATION

See Figure 102.

❋❋ CAUTION

Used fluid is considerably more dangerous than new fluid. Avoid skin contact with the oil.

1. Before servicing the vehicle, refer to the Precautions Section.
2. Remove the accessory drive belt.
3. Drain the power steering pump oil:
   a. Install a lock-grip pliers on the hose from the fluid reservoir as close to the power steering pump as possible.
   b. Extract the oil.

➡Place a covering over the alternator as protection against oil.

4. Remove or disconnect the following:
   - The pressure hose
   - The feeder hose
5. Remove the mounting bolts from power steering pump.
6. Remove the power steering pump.

To install:

7. Installation is the reverse of the removal procedure.
8. Install the power steering pump with the M8 mounting bolts. Tighten to 18 ft. lbs. (24 Nm).
9. Install the pressure hose and feeder hose with the M6 bolts. Tighten to 89 inch lbs. (10 Nm).

➡Use a new O-ring.

10. Install the accessory drive belt.
11. Refill oil using Volvo power steering fluid.
12. Bleed the power steering system.

FLUID FILL PROCEDURE

Use Volvo power steering fluid, P/N 1161529.

❋❋ CAUTION

Used fluid is considerably more dangerous than new fluid. Avoid skin contact with the oil.

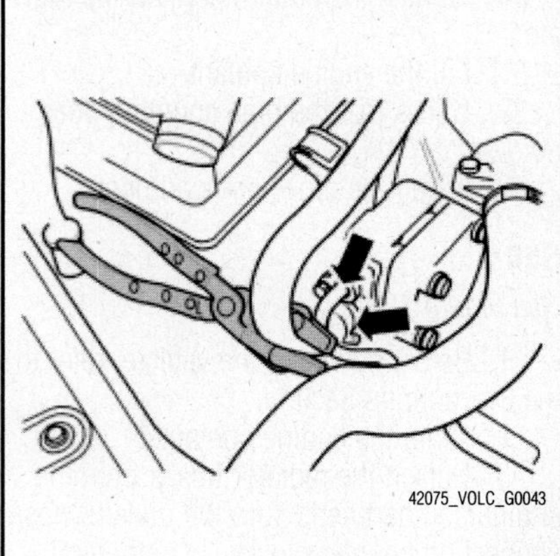

Fig. 102 Removing hoses from power steering pump with lock-grip pliers in place

1. Before servicing the vehicle, refer to the Precautions Section.
2. Inspect the power steering fluid level in the power steering reservoir. Do allow the fluid to drop below the MIN marking.
3. Remove the power steering reservoir cap.
4. Add fluid to the specified level, as necessary.

SUSPENSION

FRONT SUSPENSION

LOWER CONTROL ARMS

REMOVAL & INSTALLATION

See Figure 103.

1. Before servicing the vehicle, refer to the Precautions Section.
2. Raise and safely support the vehicle.
3. Loosen the ball joint nut as much as possible.

➡Clean the ball joint thread using a wire brush. Use rust penetrator. If the ball joint releases in the cone, position a transaxle jack under the control arm. Carefully lift (not more than so the front spring is in the resting position) until the cone jams. Remove the nut.

4. Remove the stud in the front edge.
5. Remove the 2 bolts at the rear edge.
6. Move the wheel to one side. Pull out the control arm from the cross member.

➡Ensure that the halfshaft is not pulled out of the transaxle.

7. Loosen the nut positioned on the ball joint as much as possible. Press the rubber down.

❋❋ WARNING

Secure the tool to prevent damage.

8. Press out the ball joint.

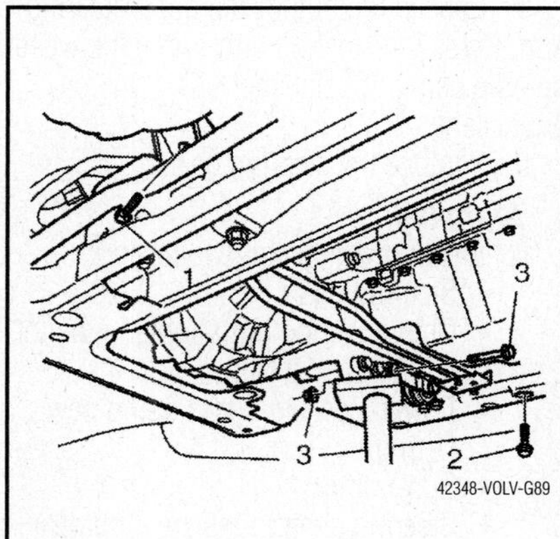

Fig. 103 Support the torque rod with a jack

9. Remove the nut and draw out the control arm.

To install:

10. Replace the ball joint rubber ring if it is worn or damaged.
11. Clean the area around the ball joint.
12. Remove the old rubber ring.
13. Lubricate the new ring and install it.
14. Ensure that the locking springs are correctly installed.
15. Install the control arm with the ball joint on the wheel spindle.
16. Install the control arm in the cross member. Install the bolt and nut.
17. Install the 2 bolts in the rear bushing.
18. Tighten all bolts and nuts by hand.
19. Tighten the 2 rear bolts. Tighten to 68 ft. lbs. (90 Nm).
20. Press the ball joint all the way down. Tighten to 51 ft. lbs. (67 Nm).
21. Remove the support and rock the car a few times so that the bushings come into the correct position.
22. Tighten the nut to 68 ft. lbs. (90 Nm), plus 60°.

23. Check the front mounting and wheel alignment.

STABILIZER BAR (SWAY BAR)

REMOVAL & INSTALLATION

See Figures 104 through 109.

1. Before servicing the vehicle, refer to the Precautions Section.

➡The anti-roll bar bushings and caps are vulcanized to the anti-roll bar and cannot be replaced separately.

2. Install the lifting tool 999-5716, modified according to the tool bulletin for version C, and lifting hooks 999-5460.
3. Lift the engine to relieve the load on the engine pads.
4. Remove the front wheels.
5. Loosen the right lower front part of the fender liner.
6. Remove or disconnect the following:
   - The plastic nuts on the fender liner
   - The protective plate
   - Bend out the fender liner
   - Bolts for the right-hand engine mounting
7. Remove or disconnect the following:
   - The splash guard under the engine
   - The skid guard, if equipped
   - The 4 mounting bolts for the Side Impact Protection System (SIPS) member
   - The brake pipe from the snap fastener on the member
   - The SIPS member
8. Remove or disconnect the following:
   - The rubber mountings for the exhaust pipe
   - The nuts and bolts holding the steering gear to the sub-frame
   - The power steering line from the clips on the sub-frame
   - The bracket for the Heated Oxygen Sensor (HO2S) from the sub-frame
   - The HO2S wiring from the right side of the sub-frame (only applies to 6-Cylinder engines)
9. Lower the sub-frame:
   a. Position a mobile jack with universal plate 999-5972 at the rear of the sub-frame.
   b. Remove the bolts holding the sub-frame bracket in the body.
   c. Remove the rear bolt for the sub-frame with the bracket and washer.
   d. Carefully lower the sub-frame until the clearance **A** between the sub-frame and the body is 4 ⅓ inches (110mm).
10. Remove the anti-roll bar on both sides. Use a Torx® wrench as a counter-hold so that the boot is not damaged.

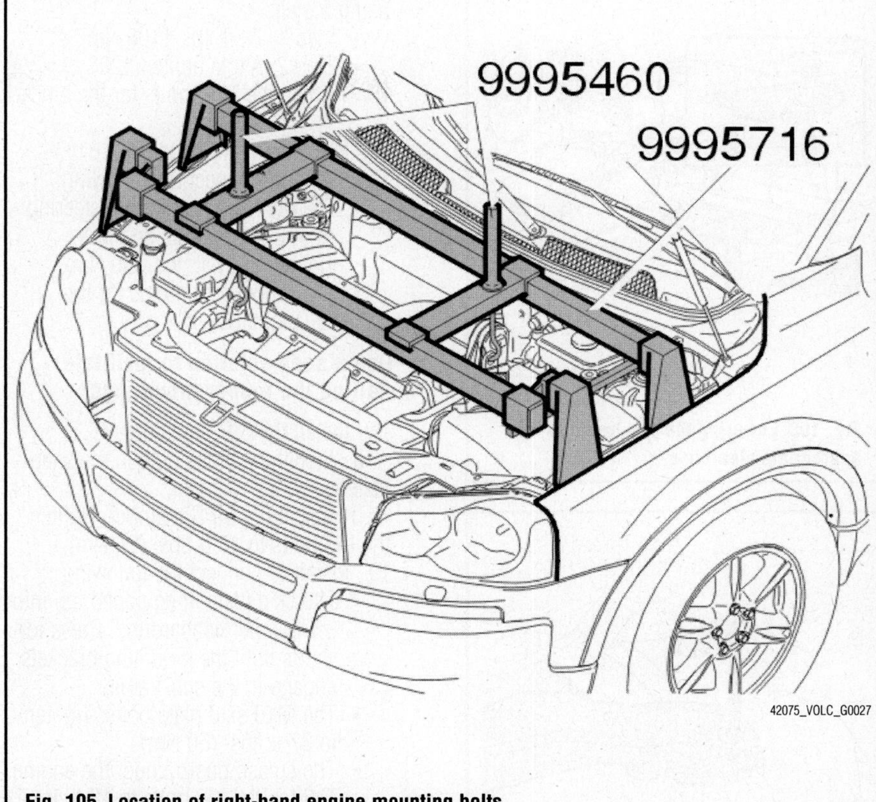

Fig. 105 Location of right-hand engine mounting bolts

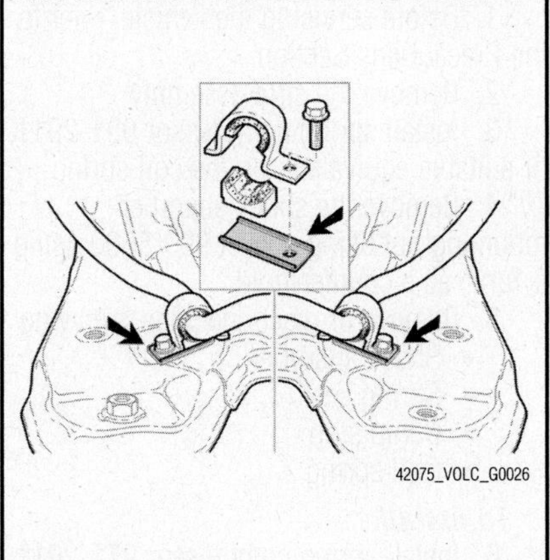

Fig. 104 Installation of lifting tool 999-5716 and lifting hooks 999-5460

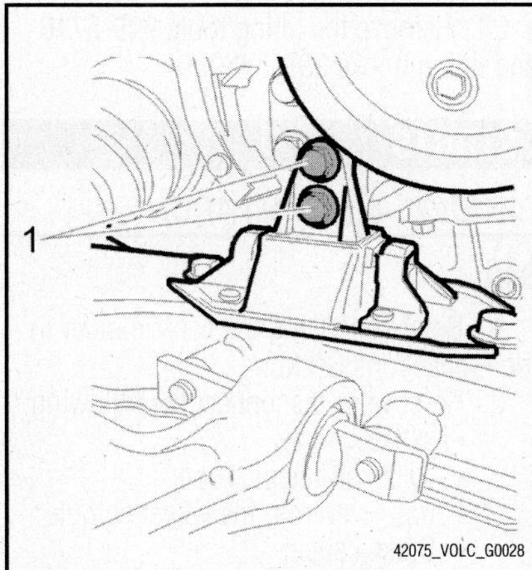

Fig. 106 Location and removal of the SIPS member

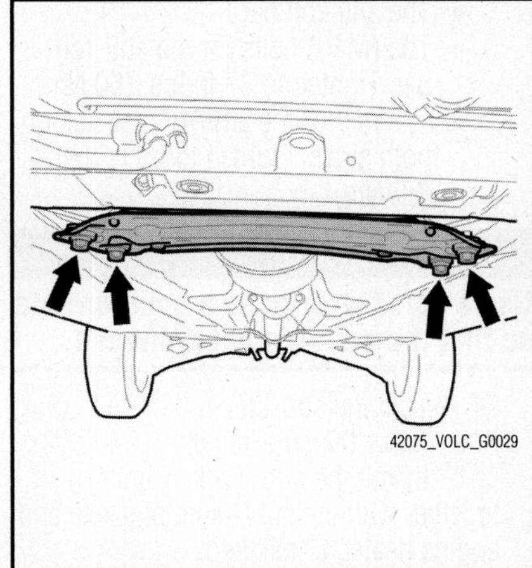

Fig. 107 Lowering the sub-frame using a mobile jack with universal plate 999-5972

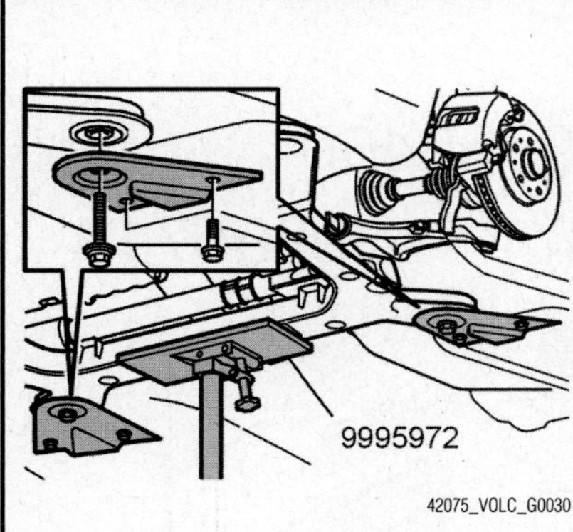

Fig. 108 Lowering the sub-frame to the appropriate clearance

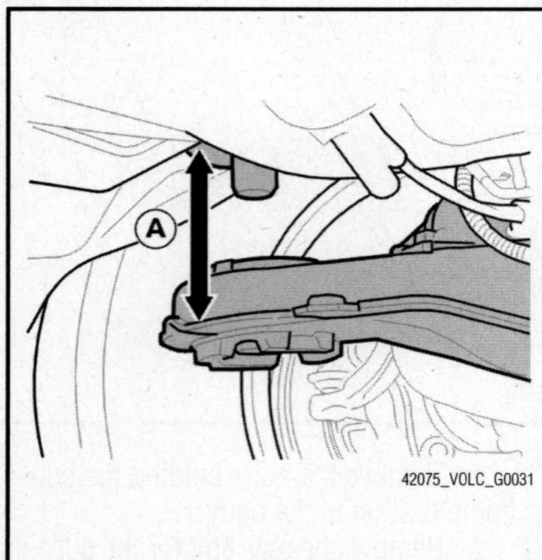

Fig. 109 Location and removal of anti-roll bar bolts

11. Remove the bolts for the anti-roll bar.
12. Remove the anti-roll bar.

To install:

13. Install or connect the following:
    - The anti-roll bar
    - The (M10) bolts for the anti-roll bar. Tighten to 37 ft. lbs. (50 Nm)
    - The nut for the anti-roll bar link on both sides. Tighten to 59 ft. lbs. (80 Nm)

WARNING

Use a Torx® wrench as a counter-hold so that the gaiter is not damaged.

14. Install the sub-frame:
    a. Raise the sub-frame.
    b. Install the sub-frame 4 bolts together with the sub-frame brackets and engine heater, if installed.
    c. Use new bolts. Lube the bolts with oil. Tighten the sub-frame bolts starting on the left-hand side, then the right, using 2 steps.
    - Step 1: 78 ft. lbs. (105 Nm)
    - Step 2: Angle tighten 120°
15. Tighten the M10 bolts for the brackets to 37 ft. lbs. (50 Nm).
16. Remove the lifting table.
17. Install or connect the following:
    - The nuts and bolt for the steering gear. Use new nuts and bolt. Tighten to 37 ft. lbs. (50 Nm).
    - The rubber mountings for the exhaust pipe

➡Use a soap solution to facilitate installing the rubber mountings.

18. Install the SIPS member:
    a. Install the brake pipe in the snap fastener on the member.
    b. Install the SIPS member. Tighten the M8 bolts to 18 ft. lbs. (24 Nm).
19. Install or connect the following:
    - The skid plate, if equipped, up into the bumper wraparound. Press forwards until the mounting brackets engage in the sub-frame.
    - The M10 skid plate bolts. Tighten to 37 ft. lbs. (50 Nm).
    - The splash guard under the engine. Tighten the M8 bolts to 18 ft. lbs. (24 Nm).
20. Install the right-hand engine mounting:
    a. Install the bolts for the right-hand engine mounting. Use new bolts. Tighten in 2 steps:
    - Step 1: 89 ft. lbs. (120 Nm)
    - Step 2: Angle-tighten 40°
21. Fold the fender liner back into position.
22. Install the plastic nuts.
23. Install the front wheels and tighten lug nuts to 81–103 ft. lbs. (110–140 Nm).
24. Remove the lifting tools 999-5716 and lifting hooks 999-5460.

STRUTS

REMOVAL & INSTALLATION

S40

1. Before servicing the vehicle, refer to the Precautions Section.
2. Remove or disconnect the following:
    - Wheel
    - Halfshaft retainer bolt
    - Ball joint from the wheel spindle
    - Brake caliper
    - Halfshaft from the wheel hub
    - Anti-roll bar link
3. Remove the lower strut mounting bolt and carefully tap the wheel spindle down until it releases from the strut assembly.
4. Remove the 3 top strut mounting bolts and remove the strut assembly.

To install:

5. Install or connect the following:
    - Strut assembly using new fasteners
    - Wheel spindle to strut assembly and tighten to 66 ft. lbs. (90 Nm)
    - Halfshaft into the wheel hub
    - Ball joint to the wheel spindle and tighten to 52 ft. lbs. (70 Nm)
    - Halfshaft retainer bolt
    - Brake caliper
    - Anti-roll bar link
    - Wheel

S60

1. Before servicing the vehicle, refer to the Precautions Section.
2. Remove or disconnect the following:
    - Wheel
    - Anti-roll bar link
    - ABS sensor
    - Bolts holding the strut in the wheel spindle
    - Strut assembly

To install:

➡Use new fasteners for safe assembly.

3. Install or connect the following:
    - Strut assembly and tighten the upper mount nuts to 18 ft. lbs. (25 Nm)
    - Strut assembly onto the wheel spindle and tighten to 77 ft. lbs. (105 Nm), plus 90°
    - Anti-roll bar link and tighten to 37 ft. lbs. (50 Nm)
    - ABS sensor
    - Wheel

OVERHAUL

1. Before servicing the vehicle, refer to the Precautions Section.
2. Remove the strut assembly.
3. Install spring compressor 951-2911, or suitable equivalent, on the coil spring.
4. Remove the shock absorber mounting nut using socket 999-5500 using a Torx® as a counter-hold.
5. Remove or disconnect the following:
    - Shock absorber
    - Spring seat
    - Bump stop
    - Coil spring

To install:

6. Install spring compressor 951-2911, or suitable equivalent, on the coil spring.
7. Install or connect the following:
    - Bump stop

- Coil spring
- Spring seat
- Shock absorber and tighten mounting nut to 52 ft. lbs. (70 Nm)

8. Remove the spring compressor.
9. Install the strut into the vehicle.
10. Check the wheel alignment and adjust as necessary.

WHEEL HUBS & BEARINGS

REMOVAL & INSTALLATION

S40

See Figure 110.

1. Before servicing the vehicle, refer to the Precautions Section.
2. Remove the wheel.
3. Loosen the center nut from the halfshaft.
4. Remove the 2 bolts from the brake caliper holder and hang them up to prevent damage to the brake hose.
5. Remove the brake disc.
6. Remove the brake backing plate.
7. Pull the steering arm out of the wheel spindle.
8. Remove the nut from the halfshaft.
9. Remove the ABS sensor and hang in a suitable position.
10. Remove the tie rod ball joint.
11. Remove the wheel spindle nut as much as possible.
12. Remove the ball-joint from the wheel spindle.
13. Press the halfshaft out of the wheel spindle.
14. Remove the wheel spindle from the spring strut.
15. Secure the wheel spindle in a hydraulic press using socket 999-7090 and drift 999-1801 to press out the bearing.

To install:

16. Press both halves of 7090-1 between the bearing and the hub on the press.
17. Press the bearing into the wheel spindle.
18. Install the wheel spindle on the strut assembly.
19. Press the halfshaft into the wheel spindle.
20. Install the ball-joint onto the wheel spindle and tighten the nut to 52 ft. lbs. (70 Nm).

Fig. 110 Securing the wheel spindle in a hydraulic press

21. Install the center nut for the halfshaft.
22. Install or connect the following:
    - ABS sensor
    - Steering arm to the wheel spindle
    - Brake backing plate
    - Brake disc
    - Brake caliper
    - Wheel

SUSPENSION

REAR SUSPENSION

COIL SPRINGS

REMOVAL & INSTALLATION

S40

See Figure 111.

1. Before servicing the vehicle, refer to the Precautions Section.
2. Remove the rear wheel.
3. For right-hand side spring only:
    a. Place a transaxle jack under the control arm to relieve the tension on the shock absorber.
    b. Remove the shock absorber lower mounting bolt.
4. Install spring compressor 951-2911 or suitable equivalent to compress the spring.
5. Remove the spring.

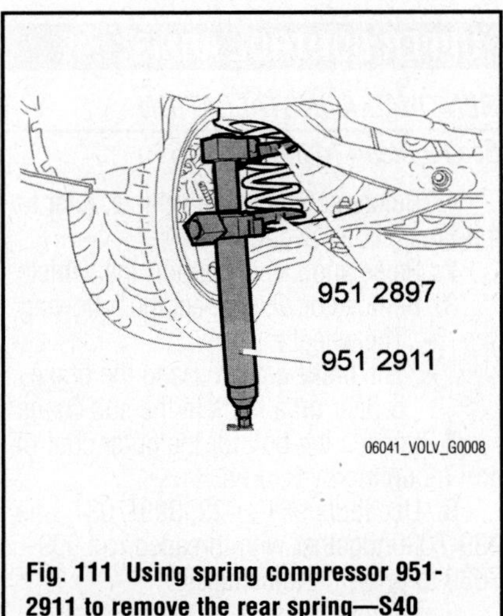

Fig. 111 Using spring compressor 951-2911 to remove the rear spring—S40

To install:

6. Install spring compressor 951-2911, or suitable equivalent, to compress the spring.
7. Install the spring.

➡Ensure that the spring engages in the control arm grooves.

8. For right side spring only:
    a. Place a transaxle jack under the control arm so the lower shock absorber mounting bolt can be installed.

S60

1. Before servicing the vehicle, refer to the Precautions Section.
2. Install plate 999-7079 to secure the spring.
3. Install a retaining strap between the control arms.
4. Remove or disconnect the following:
    - Brake caliper
    - Shock absorber
5. Install a spring compressor and tighten until the spring tension is relieved.
6. Remove or disconnect the following:
    - Grommet
    - Striker plate 999-7079
    - Coil spring

To install:

7. Install or connect the following:
    - Coil spring
    - Striker plate 999-7079 to secure the spring
    - Grommet
8. Remove the spring compressor.
9. Install or connect the following:
    - Shock absorber
    - Brake caliper
10. Remove striker plate 999-7079.

LOWER CONTROL ARMS

REMOVAL & INSTALLATION

See Figure 112.

1. Before servicing the vehicle, refer to the Precautions Section.
2. Raise and safely support the vehicle.
3. Remove or disconnect the following:
    - The wheel
    - The coil spring.

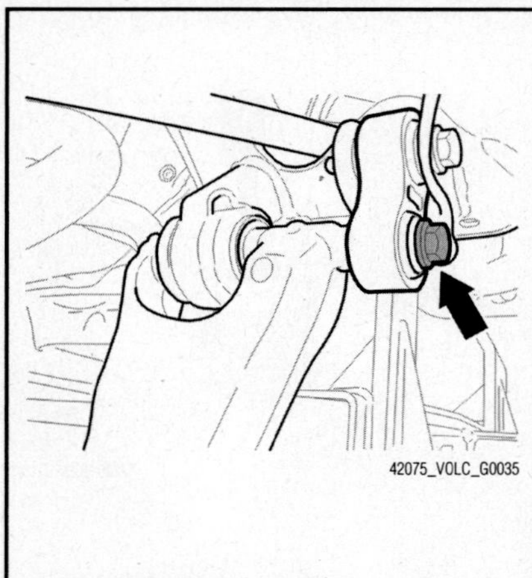

Fig. 112 Removal of rear lower control arm

- The bolt in the sub-frame for the lower control arm
- The control arm
- The control arm rail (5740-1)

To install:

➡Tighten all joints and rubber bushings with the rear suspension in the normal position.

4. Install or connect the following:
   - The control arm rail (5742-1) in the control arm
   - The control arm in the sub-frame. Do not tighten yet
   - The coil spring
5. Raise the control arms to their normal position using the tensioner 999-5659.
6. Tighten the M12 bolt for the inner mounting for the control arm. Tighten to 59 ft. lbs. (80 Nm).

➡If the vehicle is equipped with Bi-Xenon lamps, the position sensor must be calibrated. Carry out calibration according to VIDA Vehicle communication (Function area 3, Electrical system, Rear electronic module).

SHOCK ABSORBERS

REMOVAL & INSTALLATION

S40

1. Before servicing the vehicle, refer to the Precautions Section.
2. Raise and safely support the vehicle.
3. Remove or disconnect the following:
   - Wheel
   - Upper shock absorber mounting bolts
   - Lower shock absorber mounting bolt
   - Shock absorber

To install:

4. Install or connect the following:
   - Shock absorber
   - Upper shock absorber bolts and tighten to 18 ft. lbs. (24 Nm)
   - Lower shock absorber bolt
5. Install the wheel.

S60

1. Before servicing the vehicle, refer to the Precautions Section.
2. Fold the rear seat back forward.
3. Fold out the front edge of the side panel in the cargo compartment.
4. Remove the soundproofing panels.
5. Remove the upper shock absorber mounting nut using socket 999-5500 and a Torx® as a counter-hold.
6. Remove the lower shock absorber mounting bolt and remove the shock absorber.

To install:

7. Install or connect the following:
   - Shock absorber and tighten the lower bolt to 59 ft. lbs. (80 Nm)
   - Upper shock absorber nut using new nut and tighten to 44 ft. lbs. (60 Nm)
8. Install the soundproofing panels.
9. Install the side panel in the cargo compartment.
10. Install the rear seat back.

➡If the vehicle is equipped with Bi-Xenon lamps, the position sensor must be calibrated. Carry out calibration according to VIDA vehicle communication (Function area 3, Electrical system, Rear Electronic Module).

TESTING

See Figure 113.

The purpose of the shock absorber is simply to limit the motion of the spring during compression and rebound cycles. If the vehicle is not equipped with these motion dampers, the up and down motion would multiply until the vehicle was alternately trying to leap off the ground and to pound itself into the pavement.

Generally, the shocks do not affect the ride height of the vehicle. This is controlled by other suspension components such as springs and tires. Worn shock absorbers can affect handling; if the front of the vehicle is rising or falling excessively, the footprint of the tires changes on the pavement and the steering is affected.

The easiest test of the shock absorber is to simply push down on one corner of the unladen vehicle and release it. Observe the motion of the body as it is released. In most cases, it will come up beyond its original rest position, dip back below it, and settle quickly to rest. This shows that the damper is controlling the spring action. Any tendency to excessive pitch (up-and-down) motion or failure to return to rest within 2–3 cycles, is a sign of poor function within the shock absorber.

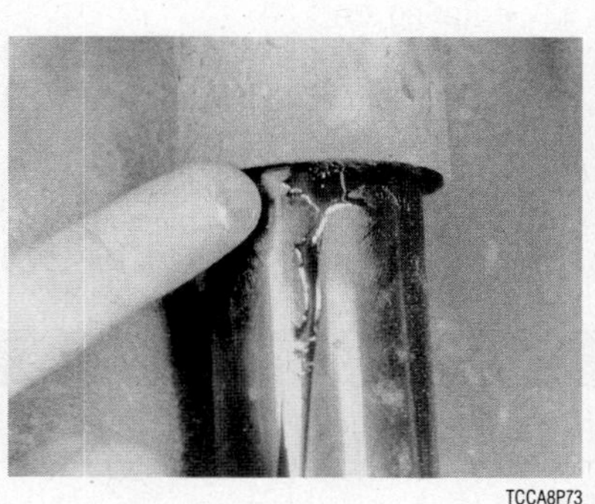

Fig. 113 When fluid is seeping out of the shock absorber, it's time to replace the shock

Oil-filled shocks may have a light film of oil around the seal, resulting from normal breathing and air exchange. This should NOT be taken as a sign of failure, but any sign of thick or running oil indicates failure. Gas-filled shocks may also show some film at the shaft; if the gas has leaked out, the shock will have almost no resistance to motion.

While each shock absorber can be replaced individually, it is recommended that they be changed as a pair (both front or both rear) to maintain equal response on both sides of the vehicle. If one side has failed, its mate may also be weak.

UPPER CONTROL ARMS

REMOVAL & INSTALLATION

See Figures 114 through 116.

1. Before servicing the vehicle, refer to the Precautions Section.
2. Raise and safely support the vehicle.
3. Remove or disconnect the following:
   - The wheel
   - The brake caliper. Hang the brake caliper on a hook in the sub-frame
4. Loosen the bolt for the outer control arm mounting by 3 turns.
5. Use tools 951-2923, 999-7031, and 999-7030 together with threaded rod 999-7039 to press off the knuckle.
6. Remove the bolt for the halfshaft.

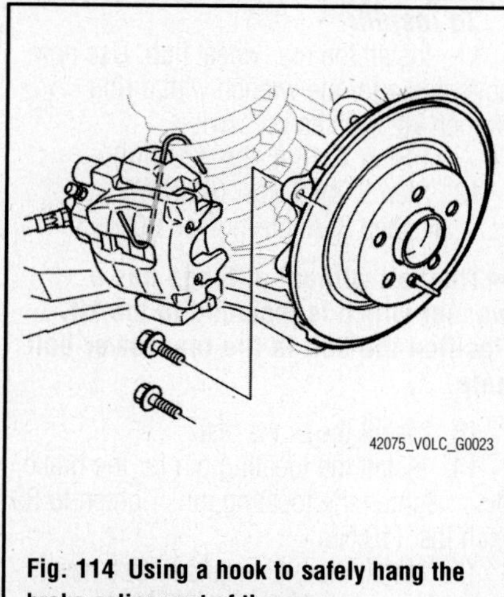

Fig. 114 Using a hook to safely hang the brake caliper out of the way

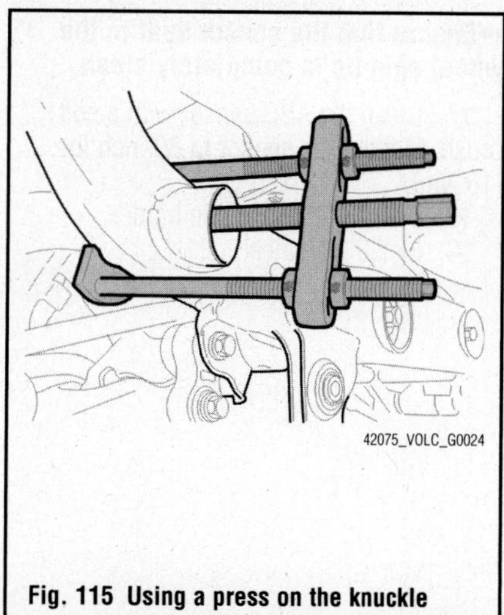

Fig. 115 Using a press on the knuckle

7. Press in the halfshaft and remove the spindle.

➡Only press until the bushing releases from the splined area.

8. Loosen the bolt 3 turns for the rear control arm mounting. Use puller 998-5434 with counter-hold 999-7074.
9. Remove or disconnect the following:
   - The bolt for the inner rear control arm mounting
   - The 2 bolts for the inner front control arm mounting
   - The control arm

To install:

10. Install or connect the following:
    - The bolts for the inner rear control arm mounting
    - The bolts for the front inner control arm mounting
    - The bolts for the outer control arm mounting
11. Install tensioner 999-5659.

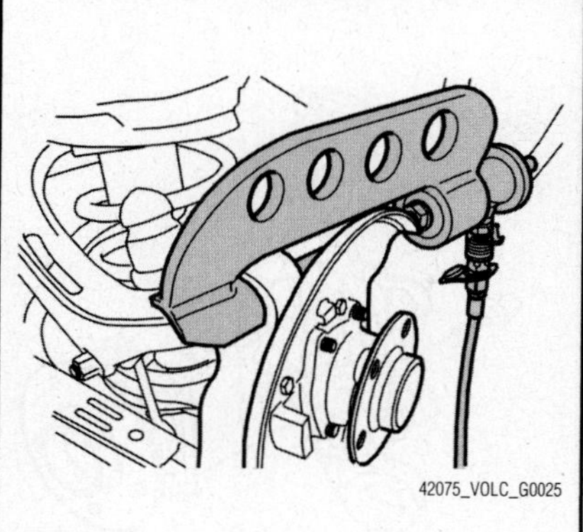

Fig. 116 Using puller 998-5434 with counter-hold 999-7074 on rear control arm mounting

➡The tensioner must be positioned as far out as possible on the tensioner plates to achieve the correct lifting force.

12. Tighten the M12 bolts for the inner rear control arm mounting to 59 ft. lbs. (80 Nm).
13. Tighten the M12 bolts for the front inner control arm mounting to 59 ft. lbs. (80 Nm).
14. Tighten the M12 bolts for the outer control arm mounting to 59 ft. lbs. (80 Nm).

➡Tighten the bolts when the rear suspension is in the normal position.

15. Remove tensioner 999-5659.
16. Install the wheel and tighten lug nuts to 81–103 ft. lbs. (110–140 Nm).

➡If the vehicle is equipped with Bi-Xenon lamps, the position sensor must be calibrated. Carry out calibration according to VIDA vehicle communication (Function area 3, Electrical system, Rear Electronic Module).

WHEEL HUBS & BEARINGS

REMOVAL & INSTALLATION

S40

See Figure 117.

1. Before servicing the vehicle, refer to the Precautions Section.
2. Remove or disconnect the following:
   - Wheel
   - Brake caliper
   - Brake disc
   - ABS sensor
   - Wheel hub

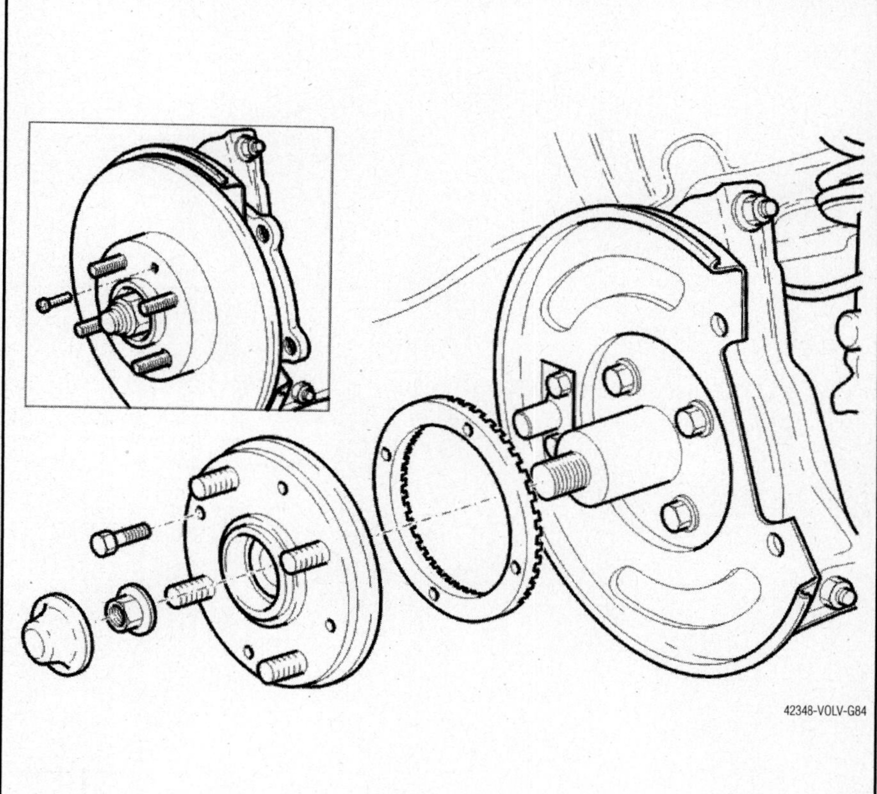

Fig. 117 Rear hub removal—S40

To install:

3. Install or connect the following:
   - Wheel hub and tighten to 41 ft. lbs. (55 Nm)
   - ABS sensor and tighten to 42 inch lbs. (5 Nm)
   - Brake disc
   - Brake caliper
4. Install the wheel.

S60

See Figure 118.

1. Before servicing the vehicle, refer to the Precautions Section.
2. Remove the wheel.
3. Remove ABS sensor and the cable from the wheel spindle.
4. Remove the brake caliper mounting bolts. Hang up the ABS line and the brake caliper. Use a piece of wire.
5. Remove the locating pin from the brake disc.
6. Remove the brake disc.
7. Remove the holder from the ABS line on the wheel spindle.
8. Press up the control arm slightly. Use a mobile jack.

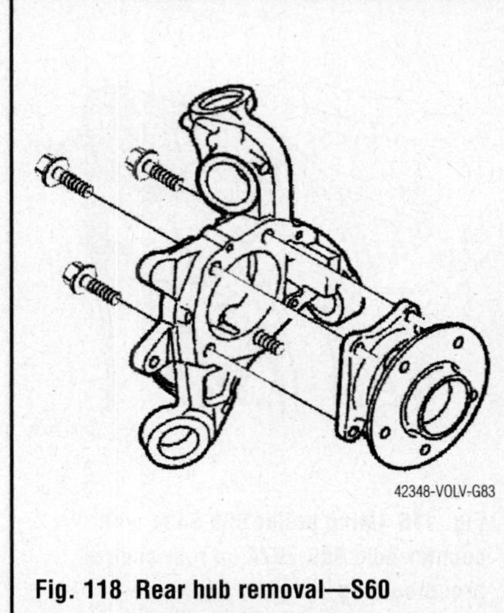

Fig. 118 Rear hub removal—S60

9. Remove the bolts from rear wheel hub.
10. Remove the rear wheel hub.

➡The flange on the lower rear bolt must be ground off before it can be removed from the wheel spindle.

To install:

11. Install the rear wheel hub. Use new bolts and a torque wrench with a ring wrench kit. Tighten crosswise.
    a. Step 1: 15 ft. lbs. (20 Nm).
12. Step 2: 49 ft. lbs. (65 Nm).
    a. Step 3: Angle-tighten 60°.

➡The bolt without a flange has a washer which is included in the kit. Position the bolt in the rear lower bolt hole.

13. Install the brake disc.
14. Install the locating pin for the brake disc. Tighten the locating pin. Tighten to 89 inch lbs. (10 Nm).
15. Install the brake caliper. Use new bolts. Tighten to 46 ft. lbs. (60 Nm).
16. Install the ABS sensor.

➡Ensure that the sensor seat in the wheel spindle is completely clean.

17. Clean the ABS sensor with a soft brush. Tighten the sensor to 89 inch lbs. (10 Nm).
18. Install the ABS-cable holder.
19. Install the wheel.

12

VOLVO

V50

SPECIFICATIONS AND MAINTENANCE CHARTS

ENGINE AND VEHICLE IDENTIFICATION CHART

Engine					Model Year	
Code	Liters (cc)	Fuel Sys.	Type	Eng. Mfg.	Code ①	Year
B5254T7	2.5 (2521)	EFI	DOHC	Volvo	B	2011

EFI: Electronic Fuel Injection

DOHC: Double Overhead Camshafts

① 10th Digit of VIN

71112_VV50_C0001

GENERAL ENGINE SPECIFICATIONS

Year	Model	Engine ID	Engine Displ. Liters	Net Horsepower @ rpm	Net Torque @ rpm (ft. lbs.)	Bore x Stroke (in.)	Com-pression Ratio	Oil Pressure @ rpm (psi)
2011	V50	B5254T7	2.5	227@5000	236@4800	3.27 x 3.67	9.0:1	51@4000

① Oil pressure should be between 35 and 54 psi at 2000 rpm

71112_VV50_C0002

ENGINE TUNE-UP SPECIFICATIONS

	Engine Displacement Liters	Engine ID	Spark Plug Gap (in.) ①	Ignition Timing (deg.)		Fuel Pump (psi)	Idle Speed (rpm)		Valve Clearance (in.)	
				MT	AT		MT	AT	In.	Ex.
2011	2.5	B5254T7	0.027	NA	NA	55-58	—	720	0.007	0.014

① The label figuires must be used if they differ from those in this chart.

NA: Information not available

71112_VV50_C0003

CAPACITIES

Year	Model	Engine Displacement (Liters)	Engine ID	Engine Oil with Filter (qts.)	Transmission (qts.)		Transfer Case (pts.)	Drive Axle		Fuel Tank (gal.)	Cooling System (qts.)
					Man	Auto.		Front (pts.)	Rear (pts.)		
2011	V50	2.5	B5254T7	6.1	—	8.14	NA	—	NA	15.9	10.5

NOTE: All capacities are approximate. Add fluid gradualy and check to be sure a proper fluid level is obtained.

71112_VV50_C0005

FLUID SPECIFICATIONS

Year	Model	Engine Size (Liters)	Engine ID	Engine Oil ①	Auto Transmission ②	Rear Axle	Power Steering	Engine Coolant	Brake Fluid
2011	V50	2.5	B5254T7	5W-30	1151 540/640	—	WSS M2C204-A	Volvo	DOT 4+

① API SL, GF-4, or ACEA A1/B1

② Volvo ATF Fluid

71112_VV50_C0004

VALVE SPECIFICATIONS

Year	Engine Displacement Liters	Engine ID	Seat Angle (deg.)	Face Angle (deg.)	Spring Test Pressure (lbs. @ in.)	Spring Installed Height (in.)	Stem-to-Guide Clearance (in.)		Stem Diameter (in.)	
							Intake	Exhaust	Intake	Exhaust
2011	2.5	B5254T7	45.5	45.5	NA	NA	0.0019-0.0027	0.0019-0.0027	0.2311-0.2366	0.2311-0.2366

NA: Information not available

71112_VV50_C0006

CRANKSHAFT AND CONNECTING ROD SPECIFICATIONS

All measurements are given in inches.

Year	Engine Displacement Liters	Engine ID	Crankshaft Main Brg. Journal Dia.	Crankshaft Main Brg. Oil Clearance	Crankshaft Shaft End-play	Crankshaft Thrust on No.	Connecting Rod Journal Diameter	Connecting Rod Oil Clearance	Connecting Rod Side Clearance
2011	2.5	B5254T7	2.5527 - 2.5602	NA	0.003-0.007	5	1.9324 1.9685	NA	NA

NA: Information not available

71112_VV50_C0007

PISTON AND RING SPECIFICATIONS

All measurements are given in inches.

Year	Engine Displ. Liters	Engine ID	Piston Clearance	Ring Gap Top Compression	Ring Gap Bottom Compression	Ring Gap Oil Control	Ring Side Clearance Top Compression	Ring Side Clearance Bottom Compression	Ring Side Clearance Oil Control
2011	2.5	B5254T7	0.0004-0.0012	0.047	0.059	NA	0.0012-0.0028	0.0012-0.0028	0.0015-0.0056

NA: Information not available

71112_VV50_C0008

TORQUE SPECIFICATIONS

All readings in ft. lbs.

Year	Engine Displacement Liters	Engine ID	Cylinder Head Bolts	Main Bearing Bolts	Rod Bearing Bolts	Crankshaft Damper Bolts	Flywheel Bolts	Manifold Intake	Manifold Exhaust	Spark Plugs	Lug Nut
2011	2.5	B5254T7	①	②	②	132-134	③	14	18	21	103

① Step 1: 15 ft. lbs.
Step 2: 44 ft. lbs.
Step 3: Plus 130 degrees

② Step 1: 11 ft. lbs.
Step 2: 18 ft. lbs.
Step 3: Plus 100 degrees

③ Step 1: 33 ft. lbs.
Step 2: Plus 65 degrees

71112_VV50_C0009

WHEEL ALIGNMENT

Year	Model		Caster Range (+/-Deg.)	Caster Preferred Setting (Deg.)	Camber Range (+/-Deg.)	Camber Preferred Setting (Deg.)	Toe-in (in.)
2011	V50	F	1.00	+4.00	0.90	-0.30	0.10+/-0.10
		R	—	—	1.00	0	0.20+/-0.20

F: Front

R: Rear

71112_VV50_C0010

TIRE, WHEEL AND BALL JOINT SPECIFICATIONS

Year	Model	OEM Tires Standard	OEM Tires Optional	Tire Pressures (psi) Front	Tire Pressures (psi) Rear	Wheel Size	Ball Joint Inspection
2011	V50	205/55VR17	None	①	①	7.5J	NA

OEM: Original Equipment Manufacturer

PSI: Pounds Per Square Inch

NA: Information not available

① See the tire placard on the vehicle

71112_VV50_C0011

BRAKE SPECIFICATIONS

All measurements in inches unless noted

Year	Model		Brake Disc Original Thickness	Brake Disc Minimum Thickness	Maximum Runout	Minimum Lining Thickness	Brake Caliper Bracket bolts (ft. lbs.)	Brake Caliper Mounting bolts (ft. lbs.)
2011	V50	F	NA	NA	0.003	0.118	88	22
		R	NA	NA	0.002	0.118	52	22

F: Front

R: Rear

NA: Information not available

71112_VV50_C0012

SCHEDULED MAINTENANCE INTERVALS
2011 VOLVO V50

TO BE SERVICED	TYPE OF SERVICE	VEHICLE MILEAGE INTERVAL (x1000)									
		7.5	15	22.5	30	37.5	45	52.5	60	67.5	75
Engine oil & filter	R	✓	✓	✓	✓	✓	✓	✓	✓	✓	✓
Underhood fluid levels	S/I	✓	✓	✓	✓	✓	✓	✓	✓	✓	✓
Brake pads	I	✓	✓	✓	✓	✓	✓	✓	✓	✓	✓
Collision warning camera (clean inside of windscreen)	S/I	✓	✓	✓	✓	✓	✓	✓	✓	✓	✓
Washer and wiper (windshield and headlights)	S/I	✓	✓	✓	✓	✓	✓	✓	✓	✓	✓
Wheels and tires	S/I	✓	✓	✓	✓	✓	✓	✓	✓	✓	✓
Cabin air filter	R		✓		✓		✓		✓		✓
Drivetrain fluid leaks	S/I		✓		✓		✓		✓		✓
Engine coolant	S/I		✓		✓		✓		✓		✓
Parking brake	A		✓		✓		✓		✓		✓
Brake and fuel lines	S/I				✓				✓		
Spare wheel/tire					✓				✓		
Air cleaner filter	R					✓					✓
Spark plugs	R										✓
Accessory drive belt and tensioner	R										✓
Automatic transmission fluid	Change if instructed by information display										
Temoprary tire sealing kit fluid	Replace fluid container every 4 years										
Driveshaft bellows and play	S/I								✓	✓	✓
Exhaust system	S/I								✓	✓	✓
Check suspension	S/I								✓	✓	✓
Brake fluid (1)	R										

R: Replace S/I: Service or Inspect A:Adjust

(1) Replace every 2 years or 30,000 miles, whichever comes first under normal conditions, more frequently in mountainous areas or moist climates.

FREQUENT OPERATION MAINTENANCE (SEVERE SERVICE)

If a vehicle is operated under any of the following conditions it is considered severe service:

- Extremely dusty areas.
- 50% or more of the vehicle operation is in 90°F (32°C) or higher temperatures, or constant operation in temperatures below 32°F (0°C).
- Prolonged idling (vehicle operation in stop and go traffic).
- Frequent short running periods (engine does not warm to normal operating temperatures).
- Police, taxi, delivery usage or trailer towing usage.

Oil & oil filter: change every 5000 miles.

Air filter element: service or inspect every 15,000 miles.

Automatic transmisson oil replace every 52,500 miles.

71112_VV50_C0013

PRECAUTIONS

Before servicing any vehicle, please be sure to read all of the following precautions, which deal with personal safety, prevention of component damage, and important points to take into consideration when servicing a motor vehicle:

- Never open, service or drain the radiator or cooling system when the engine is hot; serious burns can occur from the steam and hot coolant.
- Observe all applicable safety precautions when working around fuel. Whenever servicing the fuel system, always work in a well-ventilated area. Do not allow fuel spray or vapors to come in contact with a spark, open flame, or excessive heat (a hot drop light, for example). Keep a dry chemical fire extinguisher near the work area. Always keep fuel in a container specifically designed for fuel storage; also, always properly seal fuel containers to avoid the possibility of fire or explosion. Refer to the additional fuel system precautions later in this section.
- Fuel injection systems often remain pressurized, even after the engine has been turned **OFF**. The fuel system pressure must be relieved before disconnecting any fuel lines. Failure to do so may result in fire and/or personal injury.
- Brake fluid often contains polyglycol ethers and polyglycols. Avoid contact with the eyes and wash your hands thoroughly after handling brake fluid. If you do get brake fluid in your eyes, flush your eyes with clean, running water for 15 minutes. If eye irritation persists, or if you have taken brake fluid internally, IMMEDIATELY seek medical assistance.
- The EPA warns that prolonged contact with used engine oil may cause a number of skin disorders, including cancer. You should make every effort to minimize your exposure to used engine oil. Protective gloves should be worn when changing oil. Wash your hands and any other exposed skin areas as soon as possible after exposure to used engine oil. Soap and water, or waterless hand cleaner should be used.
- All new vehicles are now equipped with an air bag system, often referred to as a Supplemental Restraint System (SRS) or Supplemental Inflatable Restraint (SIR) system. The system must be disabled before performing service on or around system components, steering column, instrument panel components, wiring and sensors. Failure to follow safety and disabling procedures could result in accidental air bag deployment, possible personal injury and unnecessary system repairs.
- Always wear safety goggles when working with, or around, the air bag system. When carrying a non-deployed air bag, be sure the bag and trim cover are pointed away from your body. When placing a non-deployed air bag on a work surface, always face the bag and trim cover upward, away from the surface. This will reduce the motion of the module if it is accidentally deployed. Refer to the additional air bag system precautions later in this section.
- Clean, high quality brake fluid from a sealed container is essential to the safe and proper operation of the brake system. You should always buy the correct type of brake fluid for your vehicle. If the brake fluid becomes contaminated, completely flush the system with new fluid. Never reuse any brake fluid. Any brake fluid that is removed from the system should be discarded. Also, do not allow any brake fluid to come in contact with a painted surface; it will damage the paint.
- Never operate the engine without the proper amount and type of engine oil; doing so WILL result in severe engine damage.
- Timing belt maintenance is extremely important. Many models utilize an interference-type, non-freewheeling engine. If the timing belt breaks, the valves in the cylinder head may strike the pistons, causing potentially serious (also time-consuming and expensive) engine damage. Refer to the maintenance interval charts for the recommended replacement interval for the timing belt, and to the timing belt section for belt replacement and inspection.
- Disconnecting the negative battery cable on some vehicles may interfere with the functions of the on-board computer system(s) and may require the computer to undergo a relearning process once the negative battery cable is reconnected.
- When servicing drum brakes, only disassemble and assemble one side at a time, leaving the remaining side intact for reference.
- Only an MVAC-trained, EPA-certified automotive technician should service the air conditioning system or its components.

BRAKES — ANTI-LOCK BRAKE SYSTEM (ABS)

GENERAL INFORMATION

PRECAUTIONS

- Certain components within the ABS system are not intended to be serviced or repaired individually.
- Do not use rubber hoses or other parts not specifically specified for and ABS system. When using repair kits, replace all parts included in the kit. Partial or incorrect repair may lead to functional problems and require the replacement of components.
- Lubricate rubber parts with clean, fresh brake fluid to ease assembly. Do not use shop air to clean parts; damage to rubber components may result.
- Use only DOT 3 brake fluid from an unopened container.
- If any hydraulic component or line is removed or replaced, it may be necessary to bleed the entire system.
- A clean repair area is essential. Always clean the reservoir and cap thoroughly before removing the cap. The slightest amount of dirt in the fluid may plug an orifice and impair the system function. Perform repairs after components have been thoroughly cleaned; use only denatured alcohol to clean components. Do not allow ABS components to come into contact with any substance containing mineral oil; this includes used shop rags.
- The Anti-Lock control unit is a microprocessor similar to other computer units in the vehicle. Ensure that the ignition switch is **OFF** before removing or installing controller harnesses. Avoid static electricity discharge at or near the controller.
- If any arc welding is to be done on the vehicle, the control unit should be unplugged before welding operations begin.

SPEED SENSORS

REMOVAL & INSTALLATION

Front

See Figures 1 and 2.

1. Before servicing the vehicle, always refer to the Precautions Sections.
2. Disconnect the negative battery cable.
3. Raise and support the vehicle safely.
4. Remove the tire and wheel assembly.

➡Blow clean around the sensor using compressed air before removing.

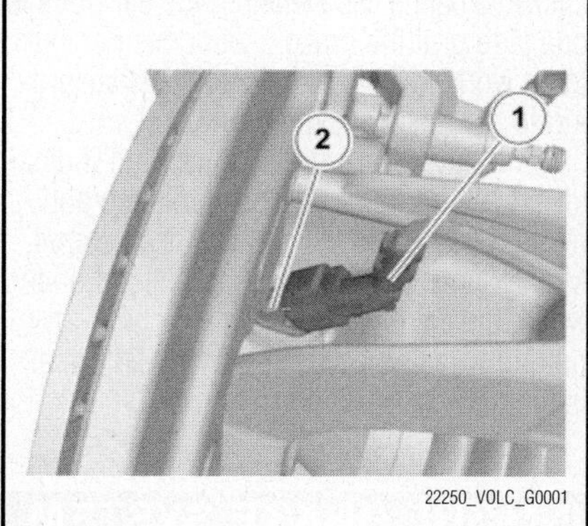

Fig. 1 ABS harness (1) and speed sensor (2) locations–front

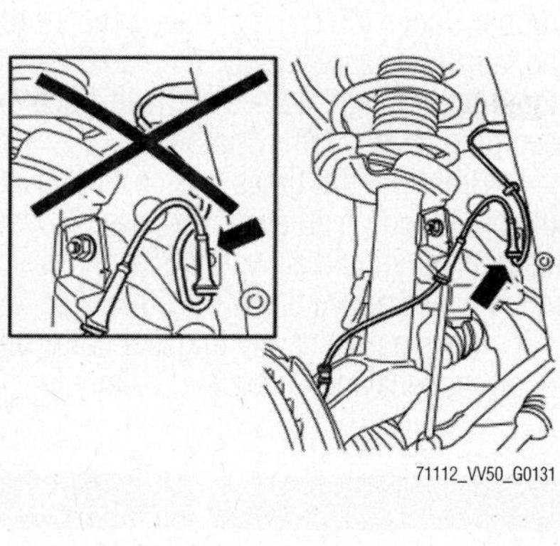

Fig. 2 Ensure that the wheel sensor cable is routed as shown

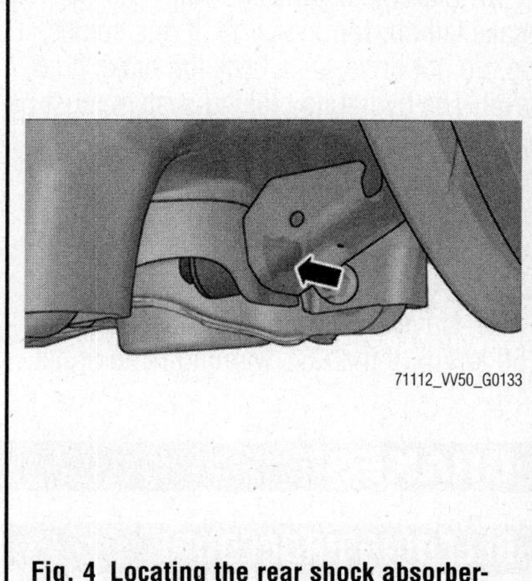

Fig. 4 Locating the rear shock absorber-to-wheel knuckle nut

5. Disconnect the wheel speed sensor electrical connector.
6. Remove the wheel speed sensor M5 mounting bolt.

➡Remove the rotor to gain access to the wheel sensor mounting bolt.

7. Pull the sensor out, being careful to turn it as little as possible. Do not pull on the sensor harness.
8. Remove the harness from its mount.

To install:

9. Inspect the sensor O-ring, and replace as required.
10. Before installing the sensor, be certain there are no foreign materials (like iron fragments) adhering to:
    - The pick-up part of the sensor
    - The inside of the sensor mounting hole
    - The rotor mounting surface.
11. Apply a thin coat of suitable grease to the wheel sensor O-ring and mounting hole.
12. Tighten the sensor mounting bolt to 44 inch lbs. (5 Nm).
13. Ensure that the wheel sensor cable is routed as shown.
14. To complete installation, reverse removal procedure.
15. Check for Diagnostic Trouble Codes (DTCs), and erase them from system.
16. Test drive vehicle.
17. Recheck for DTCs, and repair as necessary.

Rear

See Figures 3 through 5.

1. Before servicing the vehicle, always refer to the Precautions Sections.
2. Disconnect the negative battery cable.
3. Raise and support the vehicle safely.

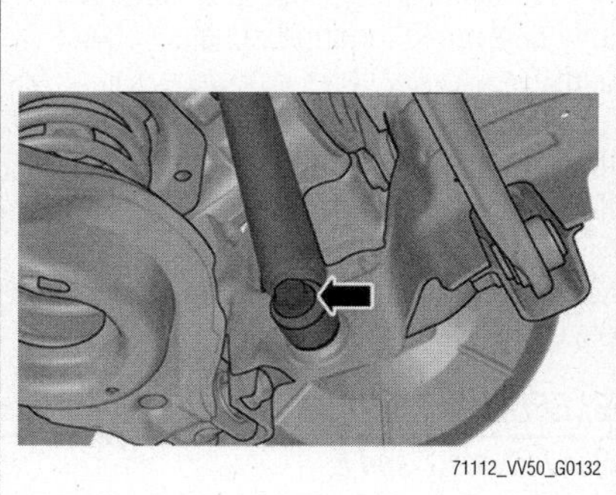

Fig. 3 Remove the lower shock absorber M5 mounting bolt

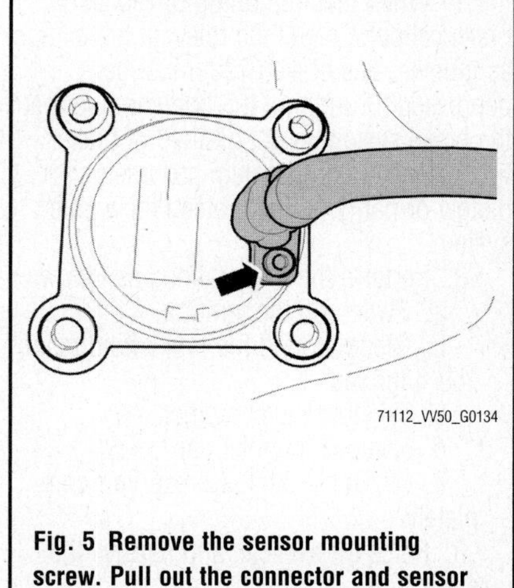

Fig. 5 Remove the sensor mounting screw. Pull out the connector and sensor

4. Remove the tire and wheel assembly.
5. Remove the lower shock absorber M5 mounting bolt.

➡Blow clean around the sensor using compressed air before removing.

6. Remove the sensor mounting screw. Pull out the connector and sensor.
7. Remove the wheel sensor from the connector.
8. Inspect the sensor O-ring, and replace as required.
9. Before installing the sensor, be certain there are no foreign materials (like iron fragments) adhering to:
    - The pick-up part of the sensor
    - The inside of the sensor mounting hole
    - The rotor mounting surface.
10. Apply a thin coat of suitable grease to the wheel sensor O-ring and mounting hole.
11. Tighten the sensor mounting bolt to 44 inch lbs. (5 Nm).
12. To complete installation, reverse removal procedure.
13. Check for Diagnostic Trouble Codes (DTCs), and erase them from system.
14. Test drive vehicle. Refer to Test Drive.
15. Recheck for DTCs, and repair as necessary.

TEST DRIVE—ABS

CAUTION

Problems with the brakes may make the vehicle difficult to maneuver. Always test drive cars under safe, controlled conditions. Follow the appropriate traffic and speed regulations.

1. Turn ignition off.

➡The ignition must be switched off so that the control module can engage the ABS system.

2. Start the engine and watch for the brake failure warning lamp. If this comes on, do not drive car. Check the brake fluid level. The hydraulic braking system must be checked for leaks if the brake fluid level is too low. Fault-trace according to the fault symptom "Brake circuit out of function, warning lamp lit" if the brake fluid level is OK.

3. Drive at a speed of at least 31 MPH (50 km/h). If the ABS warning lamp lights or does not go out, read off any Diagnostic Trouble Codes (DTCs) that have been stored and fault-trace accordingly. If no DTCs are stored but the light comes on, fault-trace according to the fault symptoms.

4. Brake several times to stop from a suitable speed on an even, dry road. At least one braking should activate ABS control from a speed above 31 MPH (50 km/h).

5. Make a note of any unusual noise or abnormal behavior. Listen particularly for clicks or bangs. See whether the car pulls to one side or if the brake pedal does not seem to be working normally. Fault-trace according to the relevant symptom.

6. If the ABS (Anti-spin) warning indicator comes on, return to the workshop and read off any DTCs which have been stored. Make a note of the driving conditions under which the warning lamp(s) came on. Carry out fault-tracing according to the DTC that is stored.

BRAKES — BLEEDING THE BRAKE SYSTEM

BLEEDING PROCEDURE

BLEEDING PROCEDURE

See Figure 6.

1. When reconditioning or replacing brake calipers, bleed the relevant brake pipe as follows. The brake pedal must be depressed throughout the operation so that the brake system is not drained of brake fluid. If the braking system has been completely or partly drained, bleed the whole system.

2. Perform the preparations as follows:
   a. Switch off the ignition.
   b. Clean around the brake fluid reservoir filler cap.
   c. Take out the container.
   d. Remove the filler cap.
   e. Fill the brake fluid reservoir completely.

3. Raise the vehicle, and remove the wheels.

➡While bleeding, check that there is sufficient brake fluid in the reservoir. Top up if necessary.

4. Remove the protective cap from the bleed nipple. Connect the hose from the collection bottle.

5. Depress the brake pedal a few times. Maintain pressure.

6. Open the bleed nipple.

7. Depress the pedal fully. Keep it fully depressed for approximately 5 seconds.

8. Release it again. Repeat this 3–5 times until there are no air bubbles in the fluid coming out of the hose.

9. Tighten the bleed nipple.

10. Remove the hose from the bleed nipple. Install the protective cap.

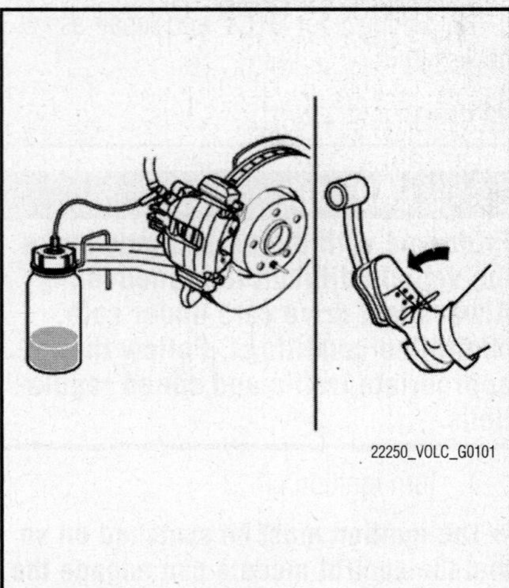

Fig. 6 Bleeding the brake system

BLEEDING THE ABS SYSTEM

See Figures 7 and 8.

CAUTION

Brake fluid contains polyglycol ethers and polyglycols. Avoid contact with the eyes and wash your hands thoroughly after handling brake fluid. If you do get brake fluid in your eyes, flush your eyes with clean, running water for 15 minutes. If eye irritation persists, or if you have taken brake fluid internally, IMMEDIATELY seek medical assistance.

WARNING

Clean, high quality brake fluid is essential to the safe and proper operation of the brake system. You should always buy the highest quality brake fluid that is available. If the brake fluid becomes contaminated, drain and flush the system, then refill the master cylinder with new fluid. Never reuse any brake fluid. Any brake fluid that is removed from the system should be discarded. Also, do not allow any brake fluid to come in contact with a painted surface; it will damage the paint.

➡The brake pedal must be depressed throughout the operation. This is so that the brake system is not drained of brake fluid.

➡If the braking system has been completely or partly drained, bleed the whole system. A bleeding unit that can pressurize the brake system to 0.2–0.3 Mpa must be used.

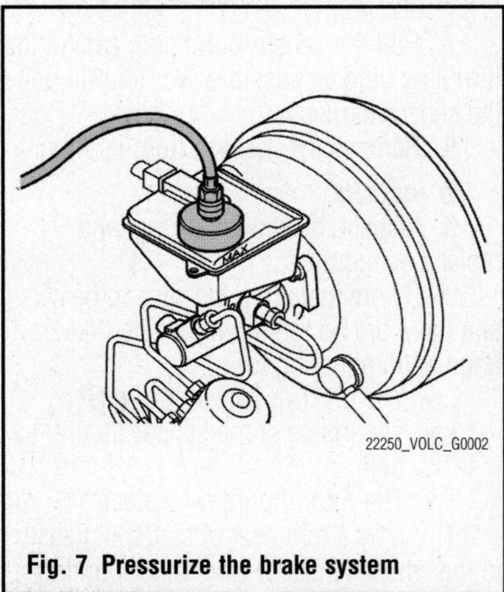

Fig. 7 Pressurize the brake system

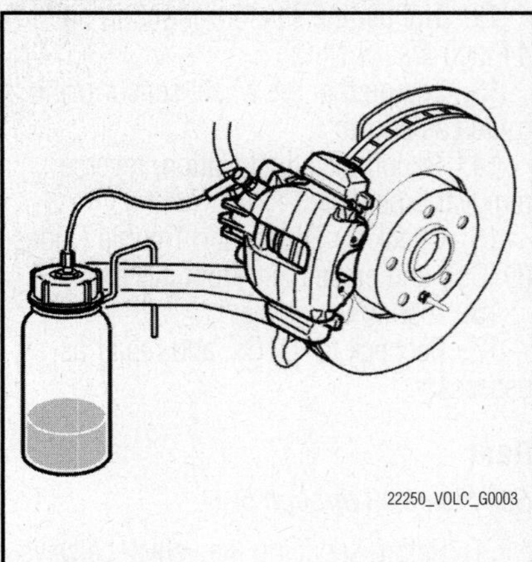

Fig. 8 Connect the hose from the collection bottle.

1. Turn off the ignition switch.
2. Clean all around the brake fluid reservoir filler cap.
3. Take out the special brake fluid collection bottle.
4. Connect bleeding unit to the brake fluid reservoir. Follow manufacturer's instructions for connecting and using bleeding unit.
5. Pressurize the brake system. Check the brake fluid reservoir connector.
6. Raise the car and remove the wheels.

➡The left front caliper must be the first one bled. Then the others progressing from front to rear.

7. Beginning with the left front brake caliper, remove the protective cap from the bleed nipple and connect the hose from the collection bottle.
8. Open the bleed nipple. Close it when there are no more air bubbles in the fluid coming out of the hose.
9. Tighten the bleed nipple.
10. Disconnect the hose from the collection bottle and replace the protective cap on the bleed nipple.
11. Continue to bleed the other wheels.
12. Check for leakage from the bleed nipples.
13. Depressurize the brake system.
14. Check for air in the brake system and for brake fluid leakage.
15. Fill the brake reservoir with the proper amount of DOT 4+ brake fluid.

BRAKES

FRONT DISC BRAKES

⁂ CAUTION

Dust and dirt accumulating on brake parts during normal use may contain asbestos fibers from production or aftermarket brake linings. Breathing excessive concentrations of asbestos fibers can cause serious bodily harm. Exercise care when servicing brake parts. Do not sand or grind brake lining unless equipment used is designed to contain the dust residue. Do not clean brake parts with compressed air or by dry brushing. Cleaning should be done by dampening the brake components with a fine mist of water, then wiping the brake components clean with a dampened cloth. Dispose of cloth and all residue containing asbestos fibers in an impermeable container with the appropriate label. Follow practices prescribed by the Occupational Safety and Health Administration (OSHA) and the Environmental Protection Agency (EPA) for the handling, processing, and disposing of dust or debris that may contain asbestos fibers.

BRAKE CALIPER

REMOVAL & INSTALLATION

See Figure 9.

1. Before servicing the vehicle, refer to the Precautions Section.
2. Secure the brake pedal in the depressed position. Use a pedal jack.
3. Raise and safely support the vehicle.
4. Remove the tire and wheel assembly.
5. Clean the brake caliper thoroughly.
6. Remove the protective cap from the bleed nipple.
7. Install a plastic hose on the nipple.
8. Open the bleed nipple. Collect the brake fluid in a container (bottle). Close the bleed nipple.
9. Loosen the brake hose half a turn.
10. Remove the brake pads.
11. Remove the locating pins.
12. Unscrew the caliper from the brake hose.
13. Remove the brake caliper from the vehicle.

To install:

14. Install the brake hose to the brake caliper. Do not fully tighten the hose yet.
15. Install the brake pads.
16. Tighten the brake hose to 17 ft. lbs. (23 Nm).

⁂ WARNING

Ensure that the brake hose is not twisted. If the brake hose is twisted, there is a risk of circuit failure.

17. Remove the pedal jack.
18. Fill and bleed the brake system.

➡Use only Volvo Genuine parts brake fluid, Volvo DOT 4+.

19. Check the function of the brakes after bleeding. Check that there is no leakage.
20. Install the wheel and tire assembly. Tighten the lug nuts in a star pattern.
    - Step 1: 15 ft. lbs. (20 Nm).
    - Step 2: 96 ft. lbs. (130 Nm).
21. Slowly depress and release the brake pedal. Observe the feel of the brake pedal.
22. If the brake pedal feels spongy, repeat the bleeding procedure again. If the brake pedal still feels spongy after repeating the bleeding procedure, perform the following steps:
    - Inspect the brake system for external leaks.
    - Pressure bleed the hydraulic brake system in order to purge any air that may still be trapped in the system.
23. Turn the ignition key **ON**, with the engine **OFF**. Check to see if the brake system warning lamp remains illuminated.

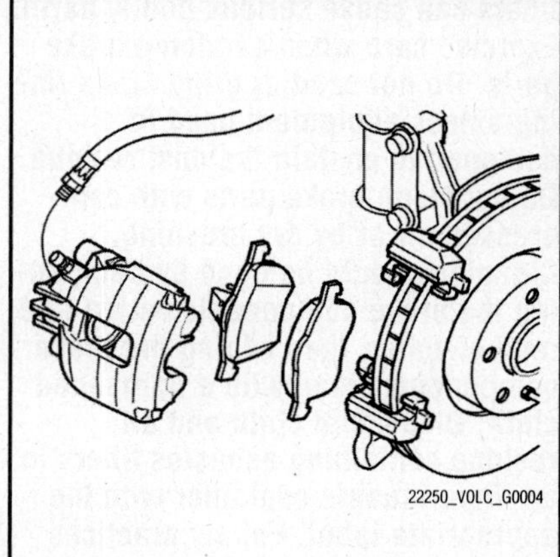

Fig. 9 Exploded view of the front brake caliper

⁂ CAUTION

If the brake system warning lamp remains illuminated, DO NOT allow the vehicle to be driven until it is diagnosed and repaired.

➡If the brake system warning lamp remains illuminated, refer to Diagnostic Trouble Codes.

BRAKE PADS

REMOVAL & INSTALLATION

1. Before servicing the vehicle, always refer to the Precautions Section.
2. Remove the wheel.
3. Secure the pedal in the depressed position using a pedal jack.
4. Remove the protective cap from the bleed nipple, connect a hose and open the nipple.
5. Use a container to collect brake fluid.
6. Slacken off the brake hose half a turn.
7. Remove the following:
    - The spring
    - The protective caps

- The locating pins (use a 7mm hex socket)
- The brake pads

To install:

8. Install the following.
   - The brake hose in the brake caliper (Do not tighten the hose fully yet.)
   - The brake pads
   - The locating pins (using 7mm hex socket, tighten to 22 ft. lbs. (30 Nm)
   - The protective caps
   - The spring

BRAKES

REAR DISC BRAKES

CAUTION

Dust and dirt accumulating on brake parts during normal use may contain asbestos fibers from production or aftermarket brake linings. Breathing excessive concentrations of asbestos fibers can cause serious bodily harm. Exercise care when servicing brake parts. Do not sand or grind brake lining unless equipment used is designed to contain the dust residue. Do not clean brake parts with compressed air or by dry brushing. Cleaning should be done by dampening the brake components with a fine mist of water, then wiping the brake components clean with a dampened cloth. Dispose of cloth and all residue containing asbestos fibers in an impermeable container with the appropriate label. Follow practices prescribed by the Occupational Safety and Health Administration (OSHA) and the Environmental Protection Agency (EPA) for the handling, processing, and disposing of dust or debris that may contain asbestos fibers.

BRAKE CALIPER

REMOVAL & INSTALLATION

See Figure 10.

1. Before servicing the vehicle, always refer to the Precautions Sections.
2. Remove the wheel.
3. Secure the pedal in the depressed position using a pedal jack.
4. Remove the protective cap from the bleed nipple, connect a hose and open the nipple.
5. Use a container to collect brake fluid.
6. Slacken off the brake hose half a turn.
7. Remove the following:
   - The spring
   - The protective caps
   - The locating pins (use a 7 mm hex socket)
   - The brake pads
   - The brake caliper (unscrew the caliper from the brake hose)
8. Remove the brake pads.
9. Remove the brake caliper.
10. Remove the parking brake cable.
11. Unscrew the caliper from the brake hose.

To install:

12. Install the following:
    - The brake hose in the brake caliper (Do not tighten the hose fully yet)
    - The brake caliper. Tighten the bolts to 52 ft. lbs. (70 Nm)
    - The brake pads
    - The locating pins–using a 7mm hex socket, tighten to 26 ft. lbs. (35 Nm)
    - The protective caps
    - The spring
13. Tighten the brake hose to 17 ft. lbs. (23 Nm).
14. Install the parking brake cable.
15. Fill and bleed the brake system.
16. Install the wheel.

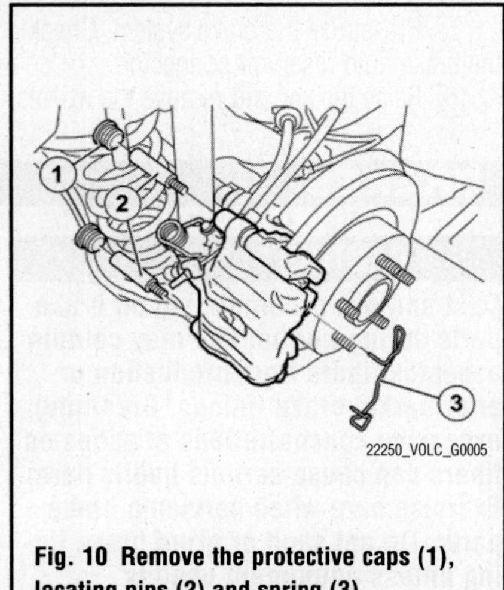

Fig. 10 Remove the protective caps (1), locating pins (2) and spring (3)

17. Depress the brake pedal a few times and check the brake fluid level.

BRAKE PADS

REMOVAL & INSTALLATION

See Figure 11.

1. Adjust parking brake.
2. Remove the wheel and tire assembly.
3. Remove the 2 caliper locating pins.
4. Using Press tool (999 5782) and Spanner (999 7091), remove brake pads.

To install:

5. Installation is the reverse of the removal procedure. Lubricate components as shown.
6. Depress the brake pedal a few times.
7. Add brake fluid if necessary.
8. Adjust the parking brake as required.

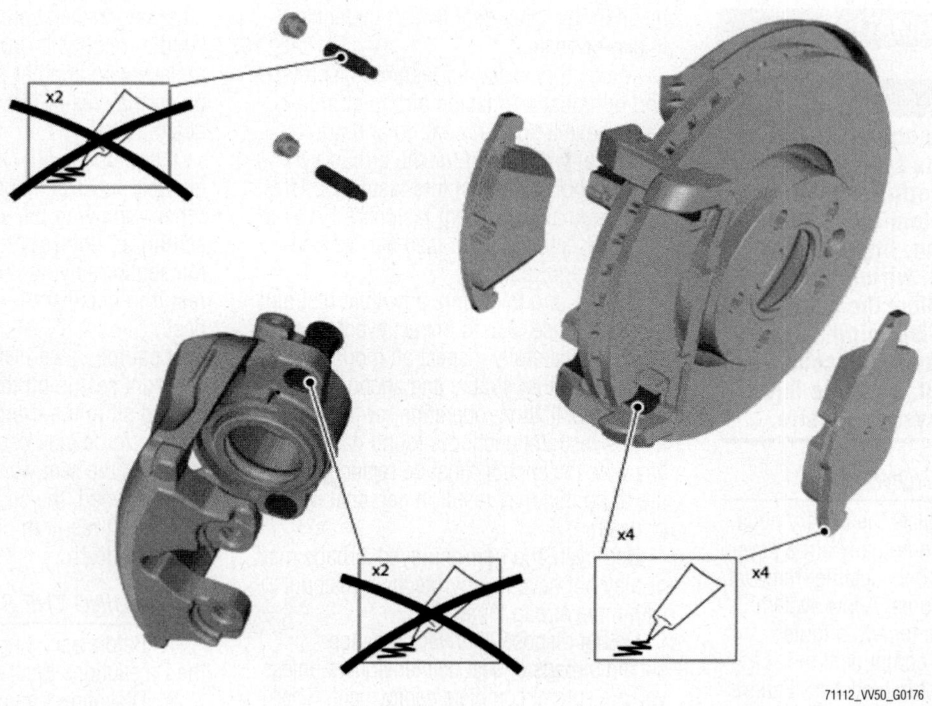

Fig. 11 Lubricate components as shown

PARKING BRAKE CABLES

ADJUSTMENT

See Figure 12.

1. Before servicing the vehicle, refer to the Precautions Section.
2. Apply the parking brake very hard 5 times.
3. Loosen the lever's rubber boot so that the adjusting nut is exposed.
4. Loosen the adjusting nut until the adjusting bolt's end is even with the nut, and apply the parking brake by pulling hard on the lever 5 times.
5. Make sure that the parking brake's lever is in resting position.

➡In the next step, the brakes should not be warmer than that they can be touched.

6. Adjust the brake caliper:
    a. Lift up the car so that the rear wheels can rotate freely.
    b. Check that the parking brake's lever is in resting position.
    c. Press 5 times on the brake pedal, so that the automatic adjustment in the brake caliper is activated.
    d. Rotate the rear wheels to check that there is no abnormal friction.

➡Always rotate 1 wheel at a time.

➡Friction may vary slightly between left and right side.

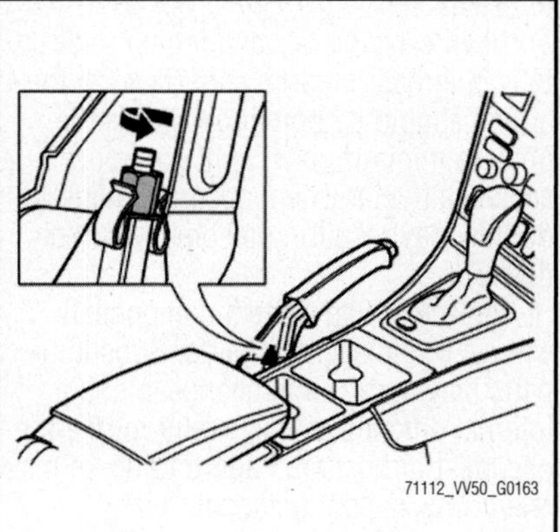

Fig. 12 Loosen the lever's rubber boot so that the adjusting nut is exposed

GENERAL INFORMATION

⁂ CAUTION

These vehicles are equipped with an air bag system. The system must be disarmed before performing service on, or around, system components, the steering column, instrument panel components, wiring and sensors. Failure to follow the safety precautions and the disarming procedure could result in accidental air bag deployment, possible injury and unnecessary system repairs.

SERVICE PRECAUTIONS

Disconnect and isolate the battery negative cable before beginning any airbag system component diagnosis, testing, removal, or installation procedures. Allow system capacitor to discharge for two minutes before beginning any component service. This will disable the airbag system. Failure to disable the airbag system may result in accidental airbag deployment, personal injury, or death.

Do not place an intact undeployed airbag face down on a solid surface. The airbag will propel into the air if accidentally deployed and may result in personal injury or death.

When carrying or handling an undeployed airbag, the trim side (face) of the airbag should be pointing towards the body to minimize possibility of injury if accidental deployment occurs. Failure to do this may result in personal injury or death.

Replace airbag system components with OEM replacement parts. Substitute parts may appear interchangeable, but internal differences may result in inferior occupant protection. Failure to do so may result in occupant personal injury or death.

Wear safety glasses, rubber gloves, and long sleeved clothing when cleaning powder residue from vehicle after an airbag deployment. Powder residue emitted from a deployed airbag can cause skin irritation. Flush affected area with cool water if irritation is experienced. If nasal or throat irritation is experienced, exit the vehicle for fresh air until the irritation ceases. If irritation continues, see a physician.

Do not use a replacement airbag that is not in the original packaging. This may result in improper deployment, personal injury, or death.

The factory installed fasteners, screws and bolts used to fasten airbag components have a special coating and are specifically designed for the airbag system. Do not use substitute fasteners. Use only original equipment fasteners listed in the parts catalog when fastener replacement is required.

During, and following, any child restraint anchor service, due to impact event or vehicle repair, carefully inspect all mounting hardware, tether straps, and anchors for proper installation, operation, or damage. If a child restraint anchor is found damaged in any way, the anchor must be replaced. Failure to do this may result in personal injury or death.

Deployed and non-deployed airbags may or may not have live pyrotechnic material within the airbag inflator.

Do not dispose of driver/passenger/curtain airbags or seat belt tensioners unless you are sure of complete deployment. Refer to the Hazardous Substance Control System for proper disposal.

Dispose of deployed airbags and tensioners consistent with state, provincial, local, and federal regulations.

After any airbag component testing or service, do not connect the battery negative cable. Personal injury or death may result if the system test is not performed first.

If the vehicle is equipped with the Occupant Classification System (OCS), do not connect the battery negative cable before performing the OCS Verification Test using the scan tool and the appropriate diagnostic information. Personal injury or death may result if the system test is not performed properly.

Never replace both the Occupant Restraint Controller (ORC) and the Occupant Classification Module (OCM) at the same time. If both require replacement, replace one, then perform the Airbag System test before replacing the other.

Both the ORC and the OCM store Occupant Classification System (OCS) calibration data, which they transfer to one another when one of them is replaced. If both are replaced at the same time, an irreversible fault will be set in both modules and the OCS may malfunction and cause personal injury or death.

If equipped with OCS, the Seat Weight Sensor is a sensitive, calibrated unit and must be handled carefully. Do not drop or handle roughly. If dropped or damaged, replace with another sensor. Failure to do so may result in occupant injury or death.

If equipped with OCS, the front passenger seat must be handled carefully as well. When removing the seat, be careful when setting on floor not to drop. If dropped, the sensor may be inoperative, could result in occupant injury, or possibly death.

If equipped with OCS, when the passenger front seat is on the floor, no one should sit in the front passenger seat. This uneven force may damage the sensing ability of the seat weight sensors. If sat on and damaged, the sensor may be inoperative, could result in occupant injury, or possibly death.

DISARMING THE SYSTEM

1. Before servicing the vehicle, refer to the Precautions Section.
2. Disconnect and isolate the negative battery cable. Wait 3 minutes for the system capacitor to discharge before performing any service.

⁂ CAUTION

Wait at least 3 minutes before working on the vehicle. The air bag system is designed to retain enough power to deploy the air bag for a short time after the battery has been disconnected.

ARMING THE SYSTEM

1. Before servicing the vehicle, refer to the Precautions Section.
2. After repairs are complete, connect the negative battery cable. Turn the ignition switch to the **ON** position and check the SRS light for proper operation.

CLOCKSPRING CENTERING

See Figures 13 and 14.

➡Make sure that the road wheels are in the straight ahead position.

⁂ WARNING

Make sure that the color marking is visible in the window.

Check that the SRS is functioning properly:

- Install the battery negative lead.
- Turn the ignition switch to Position II.

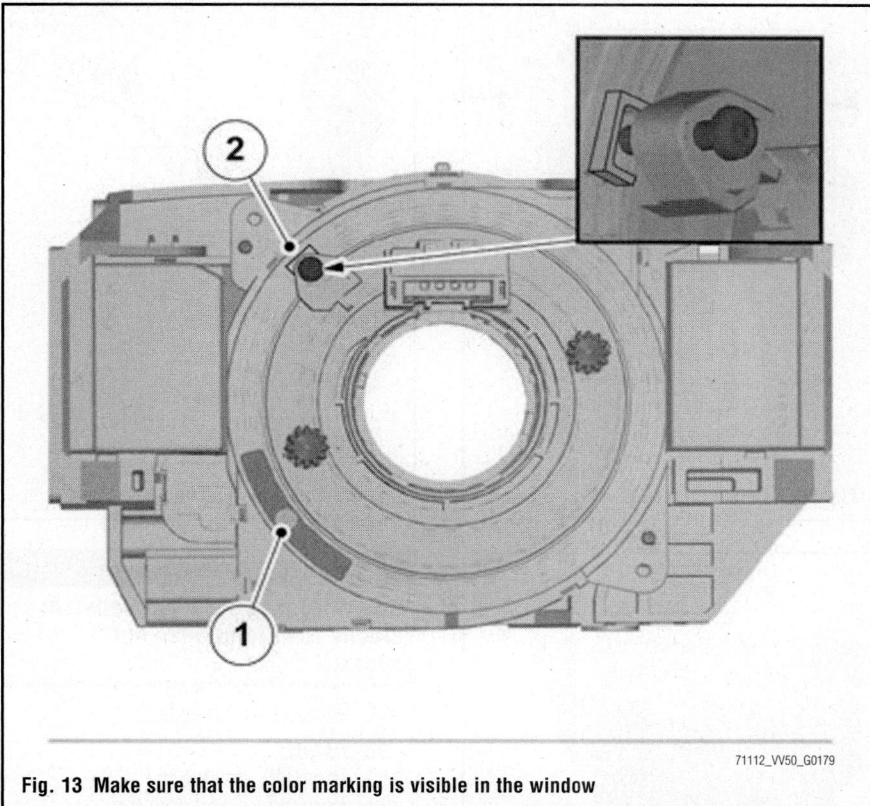

Fig. 13 Make sure that the color marking is visible in the window

• The SRS warning light in the instrument cluster must illuminate and go out after approximately 7 seconds.

• Check that the SRS warning light is not constantly lit. Fault-trace the SRS if the light is constantly lit.

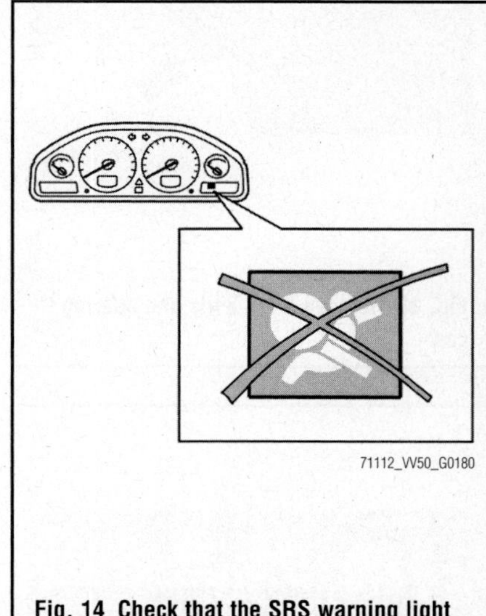

Fig. 14 Check that the SRS warning light in the instrument cluster is not constantly lit

DRIVE TRAIN

FRONT HALFSHAFT

REMOVAL & INSTALLATION

Right Halfshaft

See Figures 15 through 22.

WARNING

Do not use magnets or magnetic tools close to tooth wheels, drive shafts or wheel hubs. A magnetized tooth wheel will lose its function and generate incorrect signals, resulting in fault codes.

➡Any magnetized tooth wheel, drive shaft or wheel hub must be replaced with a new component.

1. Before servicing the vehicle, refer to the Precautions Section.
2. Raise and support vehicle.
3. Remove right front wheel.
4. Remove driveshaft-to-wheel hub bolt.
5. Install Hydraulic Hole Cylinder (951 2923) and Press Tool (999 7251) as shown.
6. Loosen wheel spindle.
7. Raise and support vehicle.
8. Remove 7 bolts and the engine splash plate.

Fig. 15 Remove driveshaft-to-wheel hub bolt

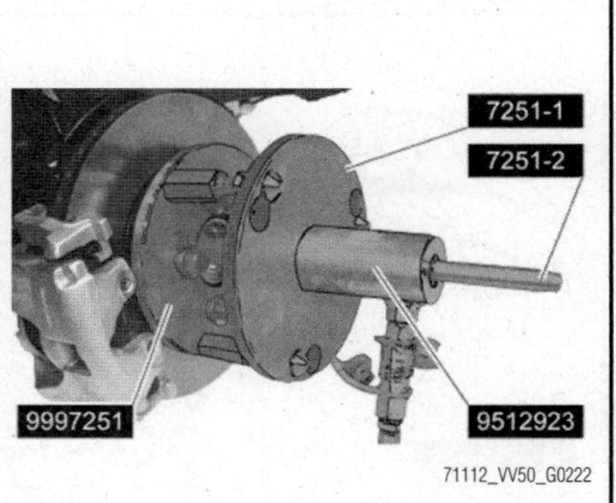

Fig. 16 Install Hydraulic Hole Cylinder (951 2923) and Press Tool (999 7251) as shown

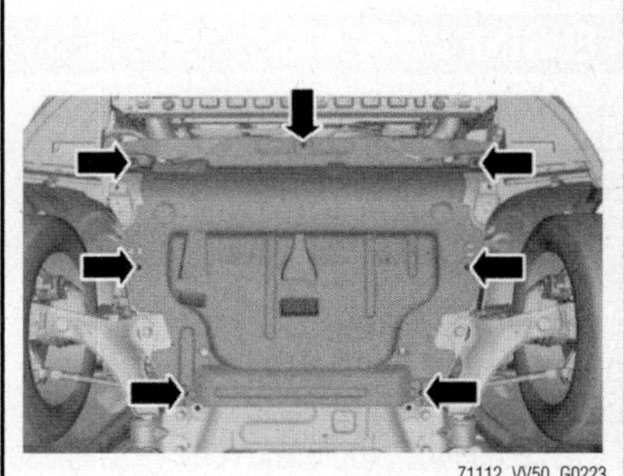

Fig. 17 Remove 7 bolts and the engine splash plate

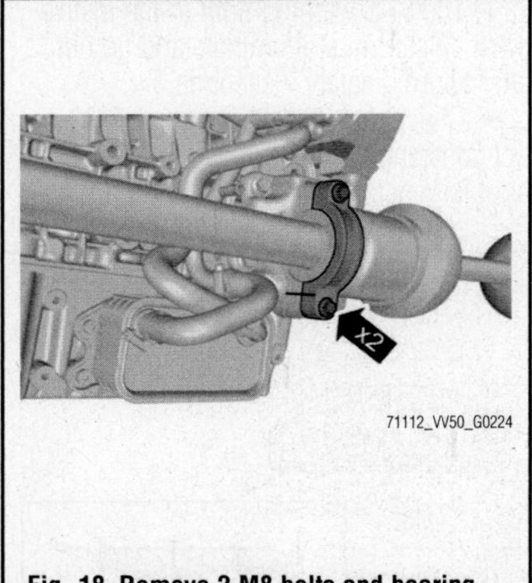

Fig. 18 Remove 2 M8 bolts and bearing cap

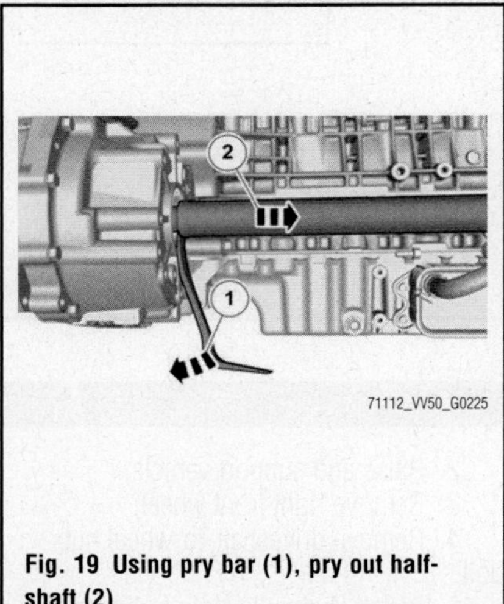

Fig. 19 Using pry bar (1), pry out half-shaft (2)

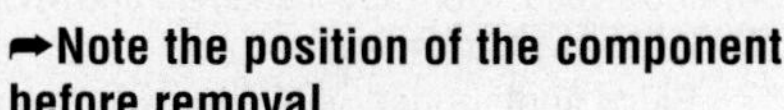

➡Note the position of the component before removal.

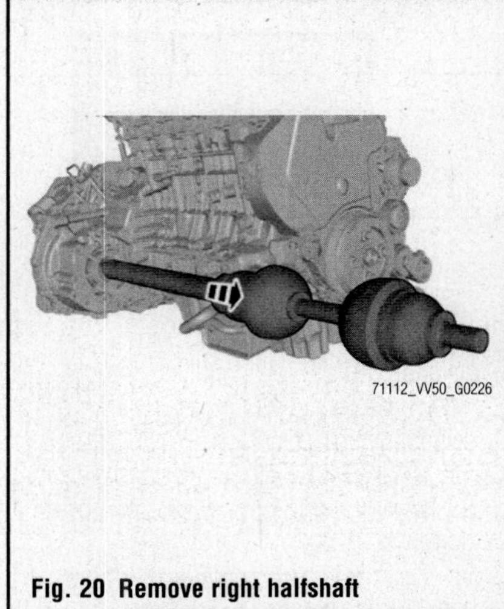

Fig. 20 Remove right halfshaft

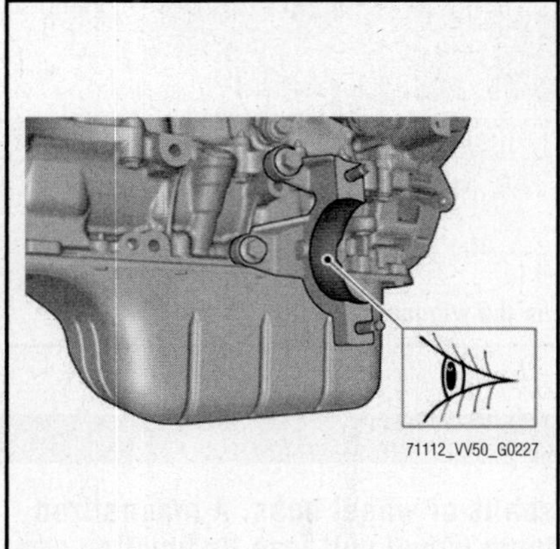

Fig. 21 Check surface of bearing saddle

9. Remove 2 M8 bolts and bearing cap.
10. Using pry bar, pry out halfshaft.

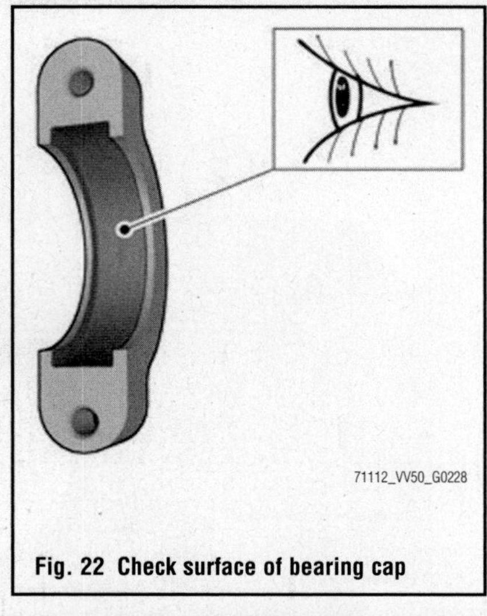

Fig. 22 Check surface of bearing cap

✲✲ WARNING

Make sure that the inner constant velocity (CV) joint does not separate.

11. Remove right halfshaft.

To install:

12. To install, reverse the removal procedure and note the following:
    - Tighten the driveshaft-to-wheel hub bolt to 26 ft. lbs. (35 Nm), plus 90°.
    - Tighten the M8 bolts to 18 ft. lbs. (24 Nm).

✲✲ WARNING

Make sure that the surfaces are clean and free of foreign material.

ENGINE COOLING

ENGINE COOLANT

DRAIN & REFILL

See Figures 23 and 24.

1. Raise the vehicle. Remove the splash guard under the engine.
2. Install a hose on the drain nipple and open the nipple, and drain the coolant in a container.
3. Close the nipple and remove the hose.
4. Refill drained coolant. Start the engine and warm up until the thermostat opens.
5. Check for leakage.
6. Install the protective cover under the engine. Lower the vehicle.

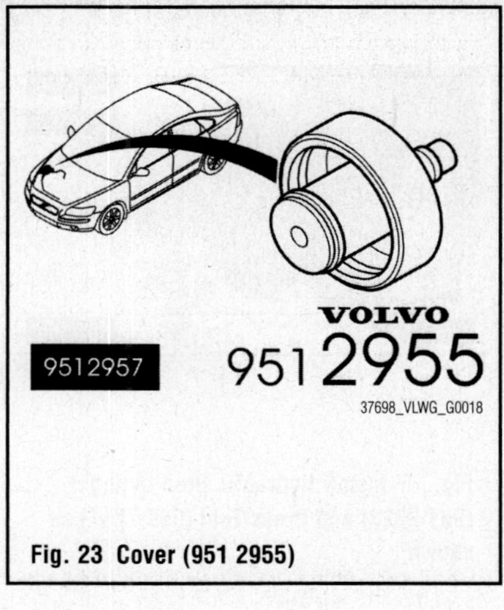

Fig. 23 Cover (951 2955)

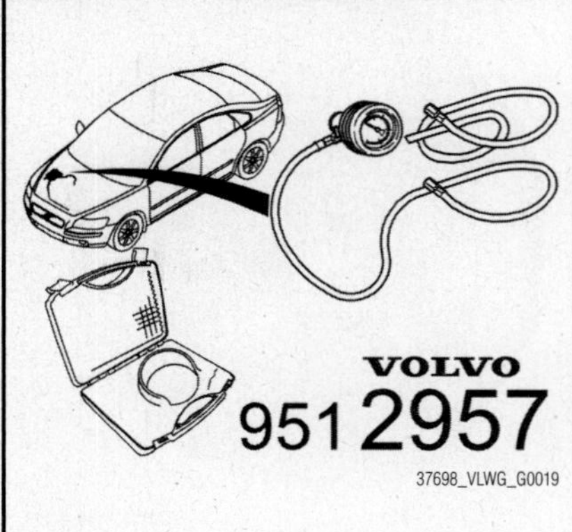

Fig. 24 Coolant reservoir pressure tester (951 2957)

7. Top up with coolant. Use filling equipment tools 951 2955 and 951 2957.

ELECTRIC ENGINE FAN

REMOVAL & INSTALLATION

See Figures 25 through 33.

1. Before servicing the vehicle, refer to the Precautions Section.
2. Disconnect negative battery cable.
3. Remove the front bumper cover.
4. Drain the cooling system.
5. Remove the cover for the Brake Control Module (BCM).
6. Remove the expansion tank cap.
7. Disconnect the connector for the engine cooling fan. Disengage hoses from the 2 clips.
8. Remove the bolts for the transmission's oil cooler. Place the oil cooler to one side.
9. Disconnect the connector for the premair sensor.
10. Remove 7 bolts and the engine splash plate.
11. Install a mobile jack under the radiator.
12. Remove the 4 bolts, and remove the bracket for the air conditioning aggregate.
13. Remove the 2 coolant hoses.

➡When removing the engine cooling fan, ensure that no cables are damaged.

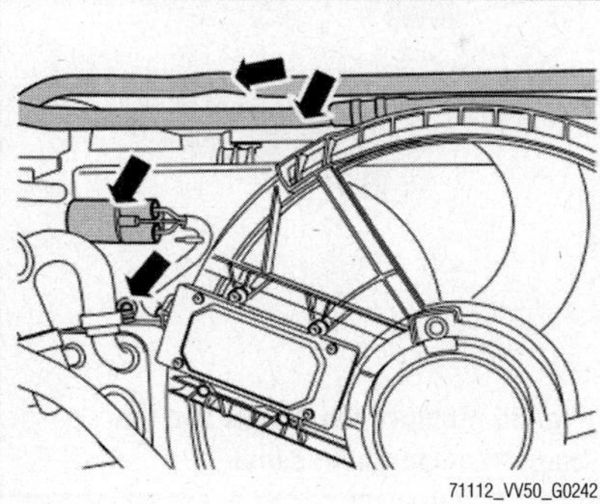

Fig. 27 Disconnect the connector for the engine cooling fan. Disengage hoses from the 2 clips

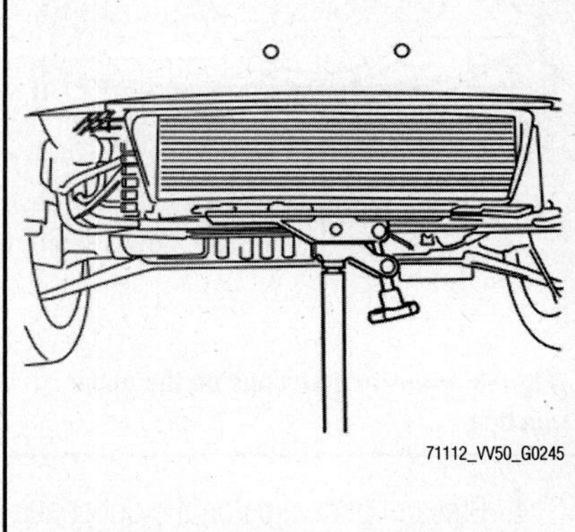

Fig. 30 Install a mobile jack under the radiator

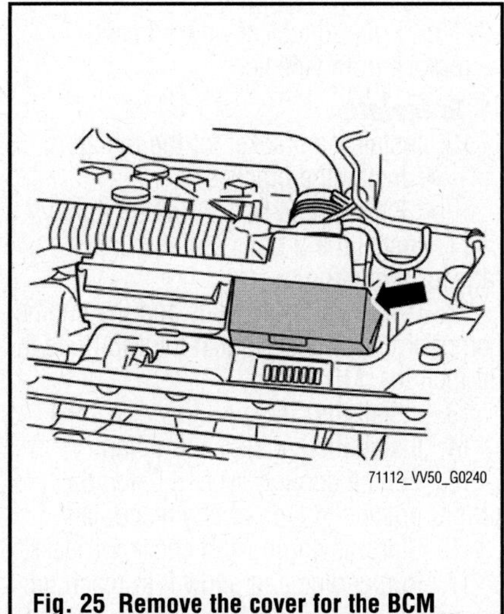

Fig. 25 Remove the cover for the BCM

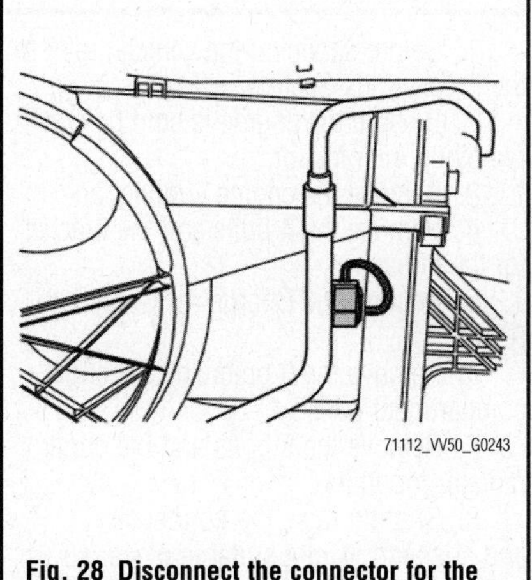

Fig. 28 Disconnect the connector for the premair sensor

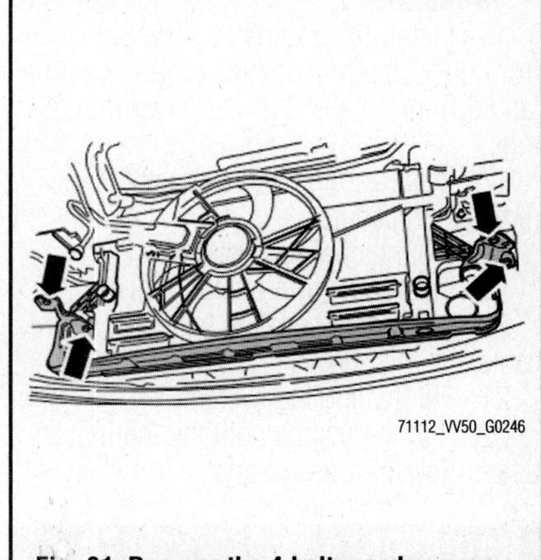

Fig. 31 Remove the 4 bolts, and remove the bracket for the air conditioning aggregate

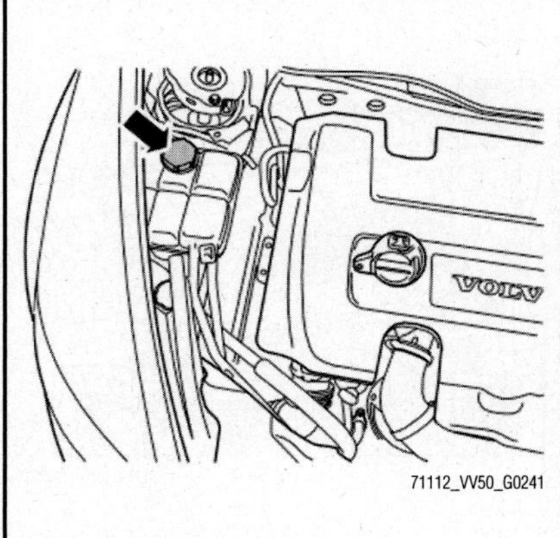

Fig. 26 Remove the expansion tank cap

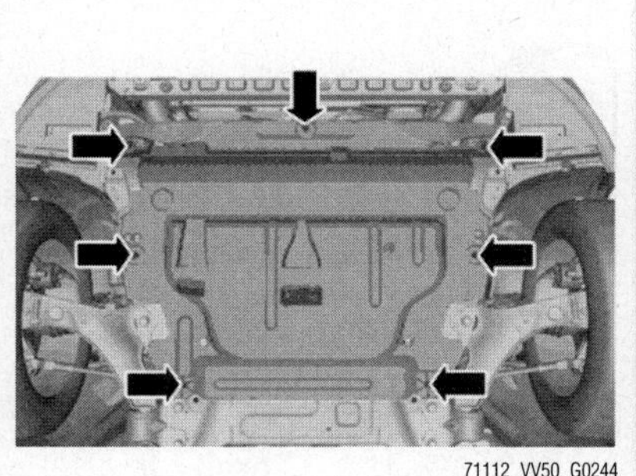

Fig. 29 Remove 7 bolts and the engine splash plate

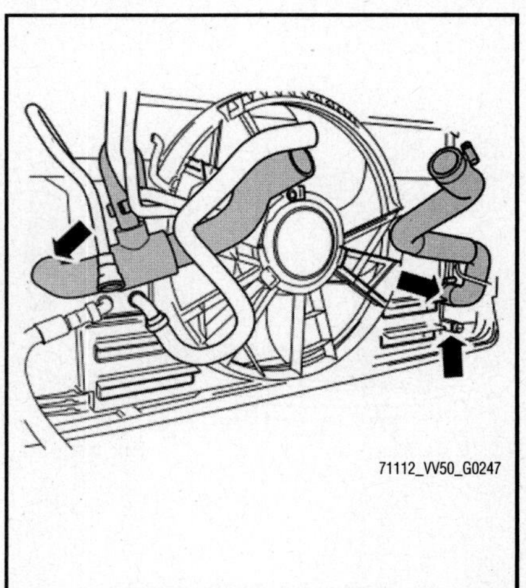

Fig. 32 Remove the 2 coolant hoses

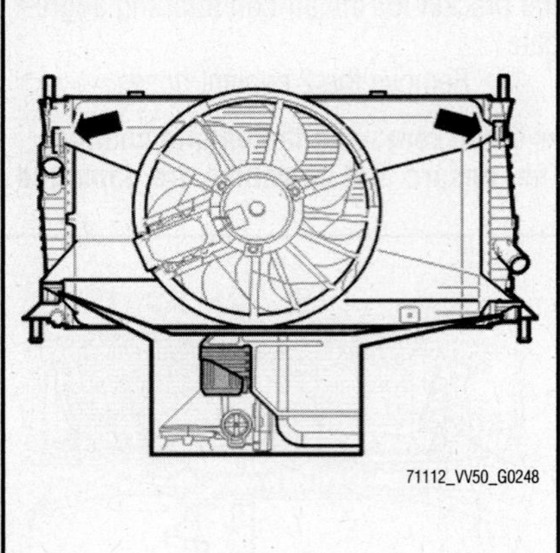

Fig. 33 Press in both clips on the upper section

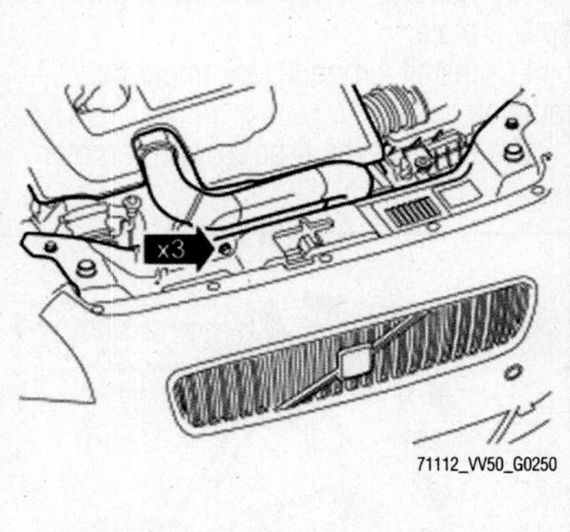

Fig. 35 Remove the 3 bolts and the engine compartment panel

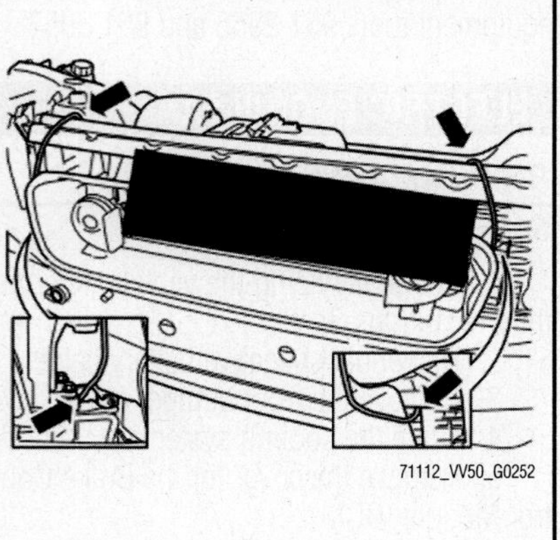

Fig. 37 Slightly raise the condenser and suspend from a suitable place

14. Press in both clips on the upper section, and lift the engine cooling fan from the catches.
15. Remove the fan downwards.

To install:

16. Install the engine cooling fan from underneath. Hook the engine cooling fan (FC) into the upper and lower mountings.
17. Installation is the reverse of the removal procedure.
18. Fill the cooling system.
19. Install the front bumper cover.
20. Reconnect negative battery cable.
21. Fill the cooling system.
22. Run the engine until the thermostat opens. Top up if necessary.

RADIATOR

REMOVAL & INSTALLATION

See Figures 34 through 38.

CAUTION

Never open, service or drain the radiator or cooling system when hot. Serious burns can occur from the steam and hot coolant.

1. Before servicing the vehicle, refer to the Precautions Section.
2. Be sure the engine is cold before removing the radiator.
3. Remove the engine cooling fan.
4. Remove the 4 bolts and the bracket for the radiator:
5. Remove the Charge Air Cooler (CAC).
6. Remove the 3 bolts and the engine compartment panel.
7. Remove the 2 bolts and the upper radiator mounting.
8. Slightly raise the condenser and suspend from a suitable place, so that the condenser is not put under any strain.
9. Remove the radiator:
   a. Remove the bolts for the upper radiator mounting (2 on both sides).
   b. Remove bracket under the air conditioning aggregate.
   c. Pull radiator downwards and remove from vehicle.

To install:

10. Install the bracket for the radiator:
    - Install the bracket.
    - Install the 4 bolts. Tighten lightly.
11. Install the 2 bolts and the upper radiator mounting.
12. Install the 3 M6 bolts and the engine compartment panel. Tighten the M6 bolts to 89 inch lbs. (10 Nm).
13. Install the CAC.
14. Install the engine cooling fan.
15. Fill the cooling system using the proper grade and type of engine coolant.
16. Start the engine and check for leaks.
17. Run engine and allow it to reach full operating temperature. Recheck the coolant

Fig. 34 Remove the 4 bolts and the bracket for the radiator

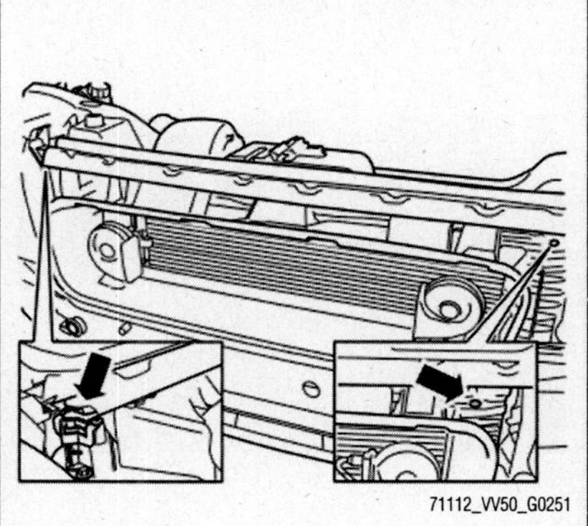

Fig. 36 Remove the 2 bolts and the upper radiator mounting

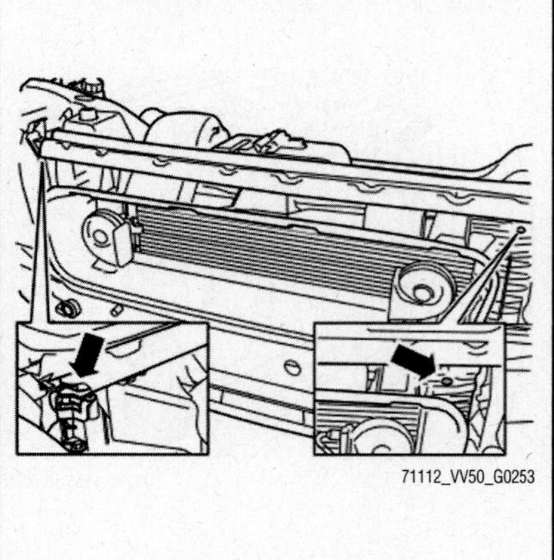

Fig. 38 Remove the radiator

level and transaxle fluid level. Fill as required.

THERMOSTAT

REMOVAL & INSTALLATION

See Figures 39 and 40.

1. Before servicing the vehicle, refer to the Precautions Section.
2. Drain the cooling system.
3. Remove the air cleaner housing.
4. Remove the 3 M6 bolts for the thermostat housing.
5. Disengage hose and cap from thermostat housing, and position aside.
6. Remove the thermostat.

➡Be prepared to collect escaping fluid.

To install:

7. Connect the hose and cap to thermostat housing assembly using new gasket and new hose clamp. Tighten the M6 bolts to 89 inch lbs. (10 Nm).
8. Fill the cooling system.
9. Test drive the engine until the thermostat has opened.
10. Check for leaks and proper thermostat operation. Fill fluid as necessary.

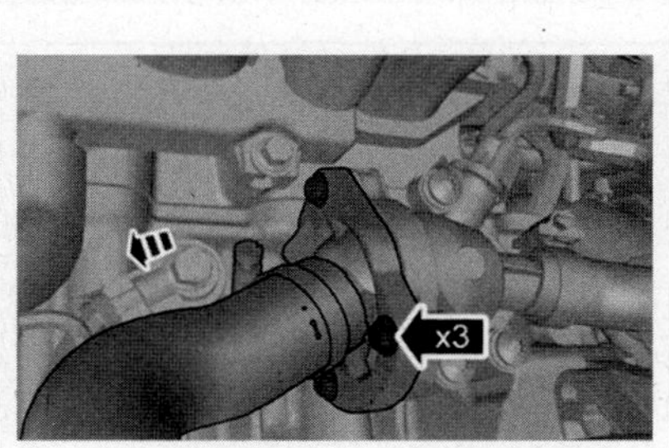

Fig. 39 Remove the 3 M6 bolts for the thermostat housing

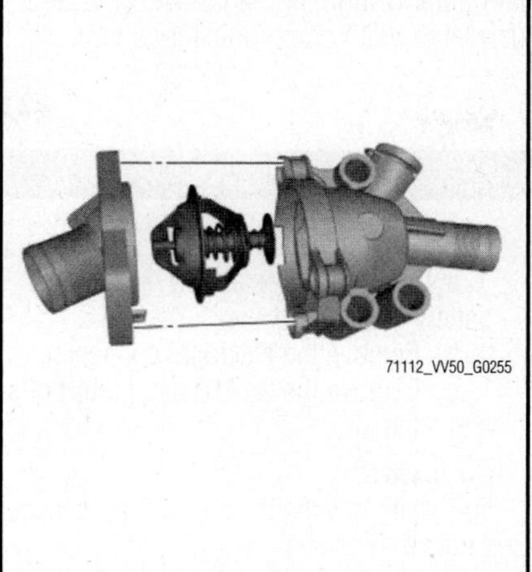

Fig. 40 Remove the thermostat

WATER PUMP

REMOVAL & INSTALLATION

See Figure 41.

➡The water pump may also be referred to as a coolant pump.

1. Before servicing the vehicle, refer to the Precautions Section.
2. Drain the cooling system.
3. Disconnect the negative battery cable.
4. Remove the timing belt. See Timing Belt, removal & installation.
5. Remove the 7 M7 bolts for the water pump.
6. Carefully tap the pump rotor with a plastic mallet to loosen, then remove the pump.

CAUTION

Be prepared to collect escaping fluid.

To install:

7. Clean the engine surface.
8. Install a new gasket on water pump surface.
9. Install the water pump with a new gasket. Tighten the M7 bolts to 13 ft. lbs. (17 Nm).
10. Install the timing belt. See Timing Belt, removal & installation.
11. Reconnect the negative battery cable.
12. Fill the cooling system.
13. Bleed system. Check for any signs of coolant leaks.

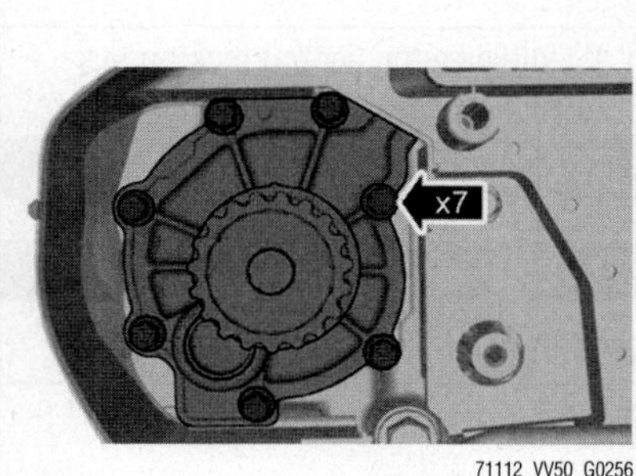

Fig. 41 Remove the 7 M7 bolts for the water pump

ENGINE ELECTRICAL — BATTERY SYSTEM

BATTERY

REMOVAL & INSTALLATION

See Figure 42.

➡On vehicles with Battery Monitoring Sensor (BMS), refer to Volvo central database when replacing battery (main battery).

1. Before servicing the vehicle, refer to the Precautions Section.
2. Turn ignition off.
3. Remove underhood cross bar cover. Remove 2 M8 bolts and cross bar over battery.
4. Remove battery cover.
5. Remove battery cables.
6. Remove side cover.
7. Remove bolts and battery hold-down.
8. Remove battery.

To install:

To install, reverse the removal procedure and note the following:

- Tighten the M6 bolts to 89 inch lbs. (10 Nm).
- Tighten the M8 bolts to 18 ft. lbs. (24 Nm).

WARNING

When switching the ignition on first time after a battery disconnect and connect, stand outside the vehicle and reach into the vehicle keeping clear of the air bag operating areas.

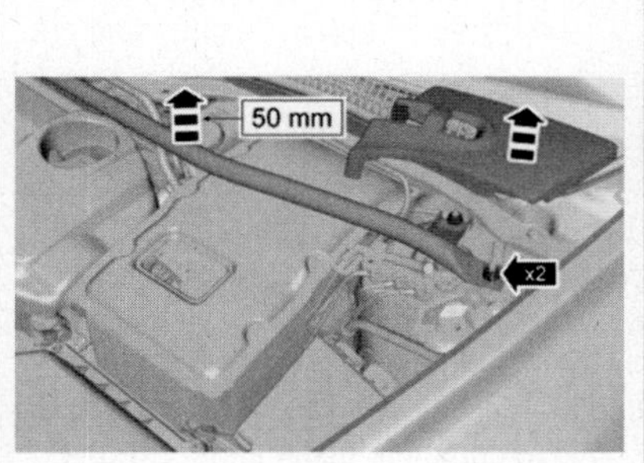

Fig. 42 Remove underhood cross bar cover. Remove 2 M8 bolts and cross bar over battery

BATTERY RECONNECT/RELEARN PROCEDURE

1. Initialize the central locking system, interior lighting and power windows using the VIDA communications tool.

➡**When the battery is disconnected, the engine may need to run for a few minutes before it runs smoothly.**

ENGINE ELECTRICAL — CHARGING SYSTEM

ALTERNATOR

REMOVAL & INSTALLATION

Alternator

See Figure 43.

1. Before servicing the vehicle, refer to the Precautions Section.
2. Turn ignition off.
3. Disconnect the negative battery cable.
4. Remove the air cleaner housing.
5. Remove the throttle body.
6. Remove the accessory drive belt.
7. Remove the M6 bolt and swivel the engine oil dipstick tube out of the way.
8. Remove the alternator:
    a. Remove the retaining nut and battery lead.
    b. Remove the electrical connector.
    c. Remove the 2 M10 mounting bolts and alternator.

To install:

To install, reverse the removal procedure and note the following:

- Tighten the M10 alternator bolts to 37 ft. lbs. (50 Nm).
- Tighten the alternator B+ terminal to 11 ft. lbs. (15 Nm).
- Tighten the M6 oil dipstick tube bolt to 88 inch lbs. (10 Nm).

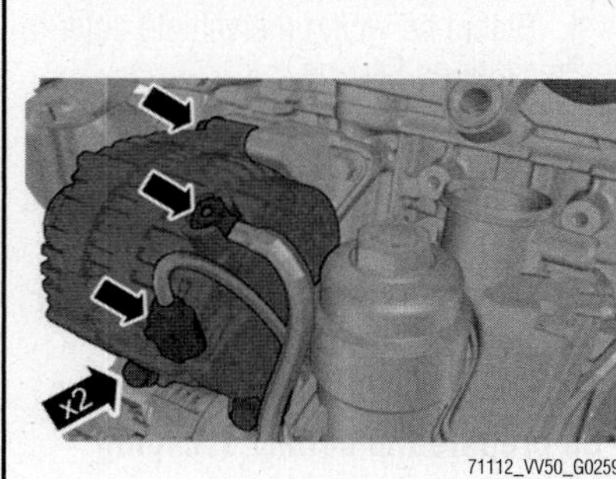

Fig. 43 Remove the alternator

ENGINE ELECTRICAL — IGNITION SYSTEM

FIRING ORDER

1—2—4—5—3

IGNITION COILS

REMOVAL & INSTALLATION

See Figure 44.

1. Before servicing the vehicle, refer to the Precautions Section.
2. Remove or disconnect the following:
    - Charge air pipe over the engine (M7 bolts). Seal the openings.
    - Upper timing belt covers (M6 bolts).
    - Cover over the ignition coils (M6 bolts).
    - Ignition coil connector.
    - Ignition coil mounting bolt.
    - Carefully pull the coil up and out.

To install:

3. Align the coil and press it down.
4. Install ignition coil mounting M6 bolt and tighten to 89 inch lbs. (10 Nm).
5. Press in the connector until a click sound is heard.
6. Install the cover over the ignition coil.
7. To complete installation, reverse the removal procedure and note the following:
    - Tighten the M6 bolts to 89 inch lbs. (10 Nm).
    - Tighten the M7 bolts to 13 ft. lbs. (17 Nm).

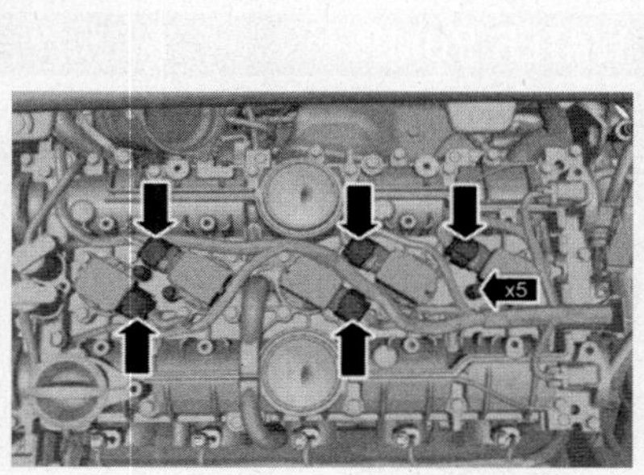

Fig. 44 Ignition coil locations

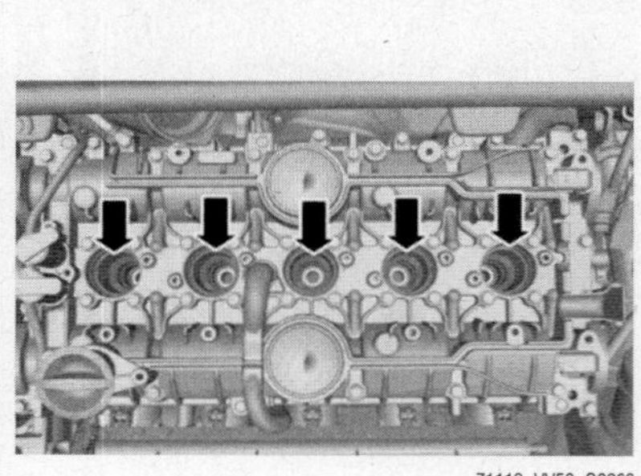

Fig. 45 Spark plug locations

IGNITION TIMING

INSPECTION & ADJUSTMENT

The ignition timing is controlled by the Powertrain Control Module (PCM). No adjustment is necessary or possible.

SPARK PLUGS

REMOVAL & INSTALLATION

See Figure 45.

1. Before servicing the vehicle, refer to the Precautions Section.
2. Remove the ignition coil.
3. Remove spark plug.

To install:

To install, reverse the removal procedure and note the following:

- Tighten the spark plug to 19 ft. lbs. (25 Nm).

STARTER

REMOVAL & INSTALLATION

See Figures 46 through 49.

1. Before servicing the vehicle, refer to the Precautions Section.
2. Disconnect the negative battery cable.
3. Remove the air cleaner housing.
4. Remove the coolant hose from the bracket.
5. Loosen the nuts securing the hose bracket. Bend the bracket to one side to allow access for bolts to the starter motor.
6. Remove the battery positive cable-to-starter solenoid.

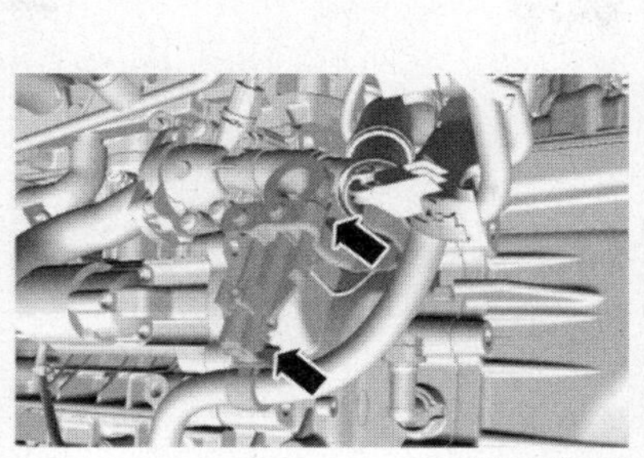

71112_VV50_G0268

Fig. 47 Loosen the nuts securing the hose bracket

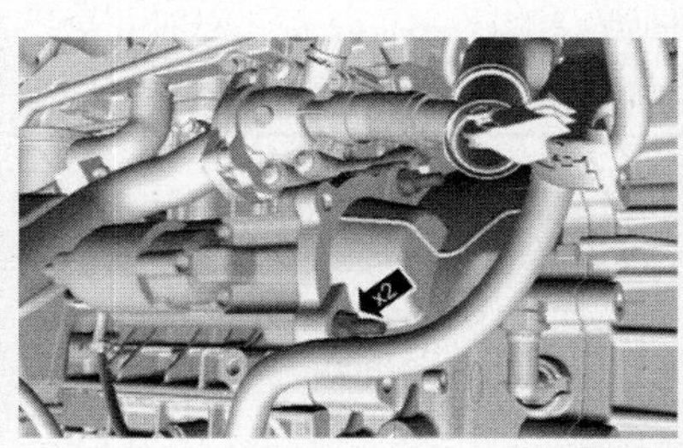

71112_VV50_G0270

Fig. 49 Remove the 2 M10 bolts and the starter motor

71112_VV50_G0267

Fig. 46 Remove coolant hose from bracket.

71112_VV50_G0269

Fig. 48 Remove the battery positive cable-to-starter solenoid. Remove the starter impulse lead

7. Remove the starter impulse lead.
8. Remove the 2 M10 bolts and the starter motor.

To install:

To install, reverse the removal procedure and note the following:

- Tighten the starter motor M10 bolts to 37 ft. lbs. (50 Nm).
- Tighten the start impulse lead to 75 inch lbs. (8.5 Nm).
- Tighten the battery positive cable-to-starter solenoid bolt to 98 inch lbs. (11 Nm).
- Tighten the coolant hose nuts to 89 inch lbs. (10 Nm).

ENGINE MECHANICAL

➡Disconnecting the negative battery cable may interfere with the functions of the on board computer systems and may require the computer to undergo a relearning process, once the negative battery cable is reconnected.

ACCESSORY DRIVE BELTS

ADJUSTMENT

The accessory drive belt adjustment is maintained by an automatic tensioner.

BELT ROUTINGS

See Figures 50 and 51.

INSPECTION

Inspect the drive belt for signs of glazing or cracking. A glazed belt will be perfectly smooth from slippage, while a good belt

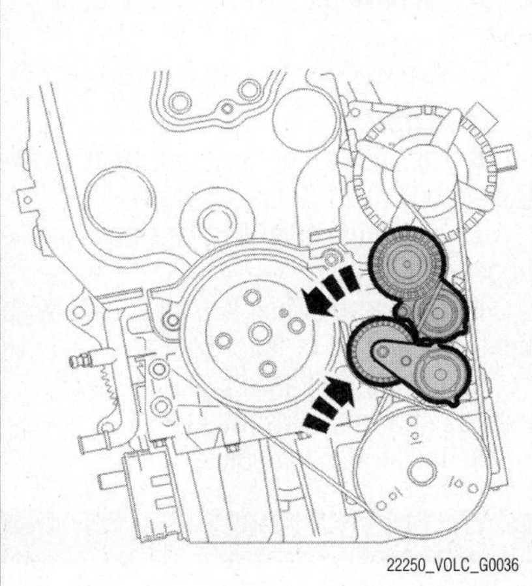

22250_VOLC_G0036

Fig. 50 Accessory drive belt routing and tensioner view

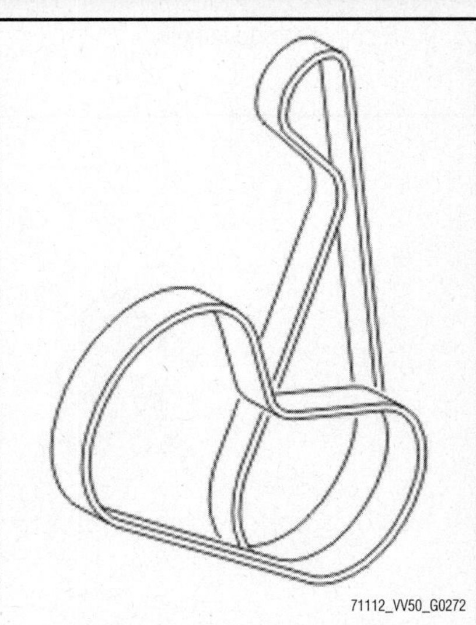

71112_VV50_G0272

Fig. 51 Accessory drive belt routing—without components

will have a slight texture of fabric visible. Cracks will usually start at the inner edge of the belt and run outward. All worn or damaged drive belts should be replaced immediately.

REMOVAL & INSTALLATION

Drive Belt

See Figure 52.

1. Before servicing the vehicle, refer to the Precautions Section.
2. Raise the vehicle.
3. Remove or disconnect the following:
   - Right front wheel
   - Right-hand fender liner. Slacken off the screws at the front edge and fold back the fender liner.
   - Engine splash plate.
4. Remove the outer drive belt as follows:
   - Relieve the load from the belt tensioner. Using 999 7109, turn the belt tensioner **clockwise** as far as it will go. Remove the belt.
5. Remove the inner drive belt as follows:
   - Relieve the load from the belt tensioner using a Torx® wrench. Turn the belt tensioner **counter-clockwise** as far as it will go. Remove the belt.

To install:

Installation is the reverse of the removal procedure.

Drive Belt Tensioner

See Figures 53 through 56.

1. Remove the drive belt.

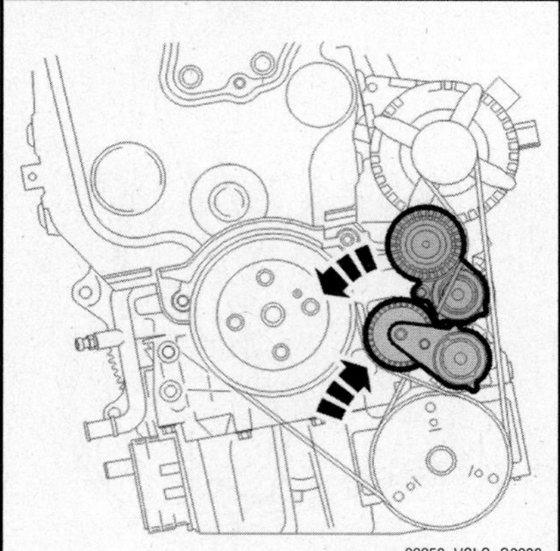

Fig. 52 Accessory drive belt routing and tensioner view

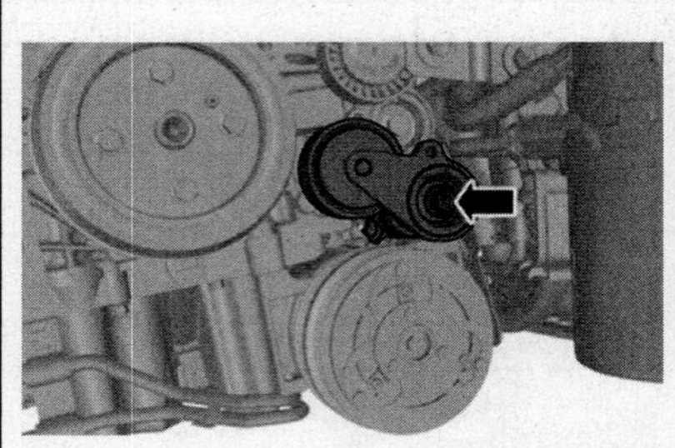

Fig. 53 Remove the outer belt tensioner bolt

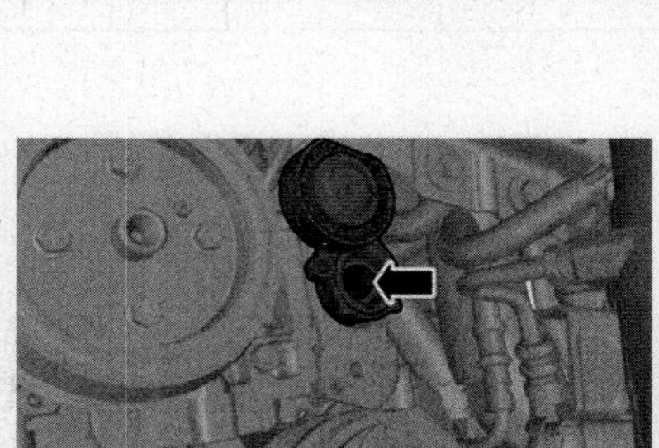

Fig. 54 Remove the inner belt tensioner bolt

2. Remove the outer belt tensioner bolt.
3. Remove the outer belt tensioner.
4. Remove the inner belt tensioner bolt.
5. Remove the inner belt tensioner.

To install:

6. Install the inner belt tensioner, and tighten bolt to 31 ft. lbs. (42 Nm).
7. Install the outer belt tensioner, and finger-tighten bolt.
8. Rotate outer belt tensioner clockwise, tighten bolt to 31 ft. lbs. (42 Nm).
9. Ensure clearance is 0.12 inch (3 mm) as shown in illustration.
10. Install the drive belt.

AIR CLEANER

REMOVAL & INSTALLATION

See Figures 57 through 60.

1. Remove the Engine Control Module (ECM).

Fig. 55 Rotate outer belt tensioner clockwise (1), and tighten bolt (2)

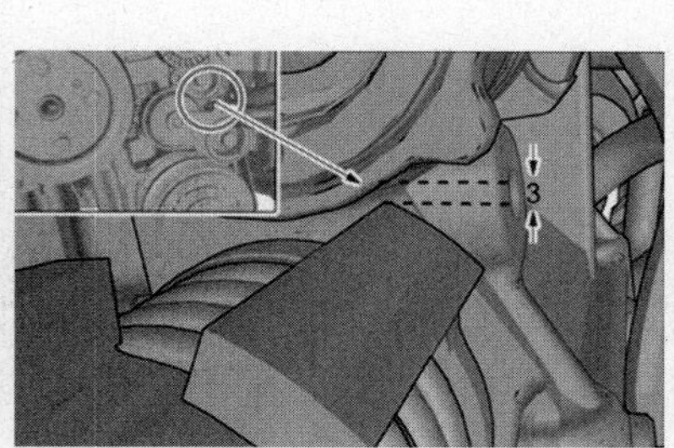

Fig. 56 Ensure clearance is 0.12 inch (3 mm) as shown

2. Disconnect hoses.
3. Disconnect the electrical connector.
4. Remove 2 M6 bolts securing the air cleaner assembly hose.

Fig. 57 Remove 2 M6 bolts securing the air cleaner assembly hose

CAUTION

Note the position of the component before removal.

5. Remove the 2 M12 bolts and the right engine mount.

➡This step requires considerable force.

6. Pushing engine rearward, remove the air cleaner assembly as shown.

To install:

To install, reverse the removal procedure and note the following:

- Tighten the M6 bolts to 89 inch lbs. (10 Nm).
- Tighten the M10 bolts to 37 ft. lbs. (50 Nm).

CAMSHAFTS

INSPECTION

1. Check the camshaft journals for wear. If the journals are badly worn, replace the camshaft.

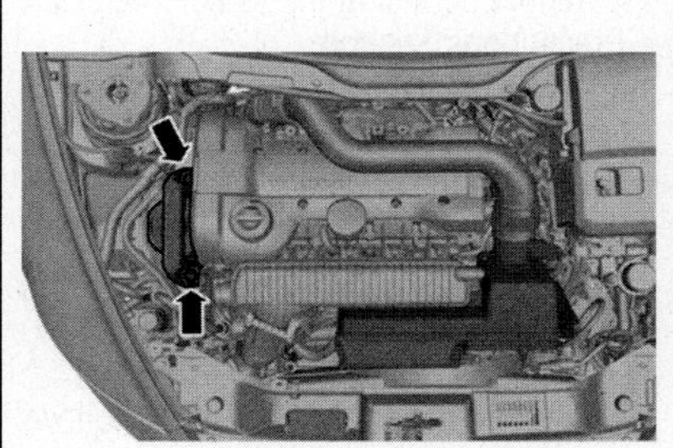

Fig. 58 Remove the 2 M12 bolts and the right engine mount

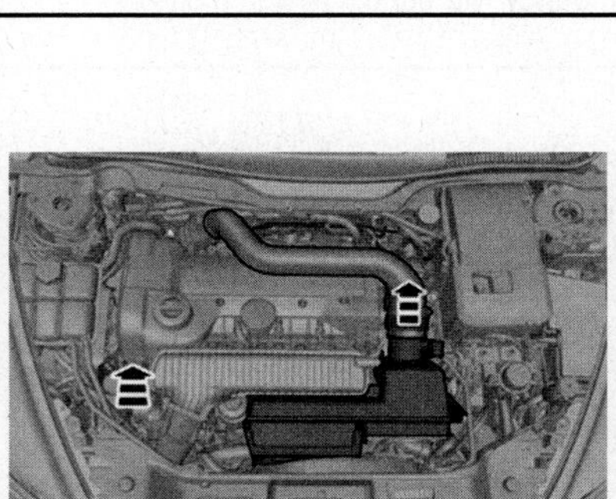

Fig. 59 Remove air cleaner assembly—step 1

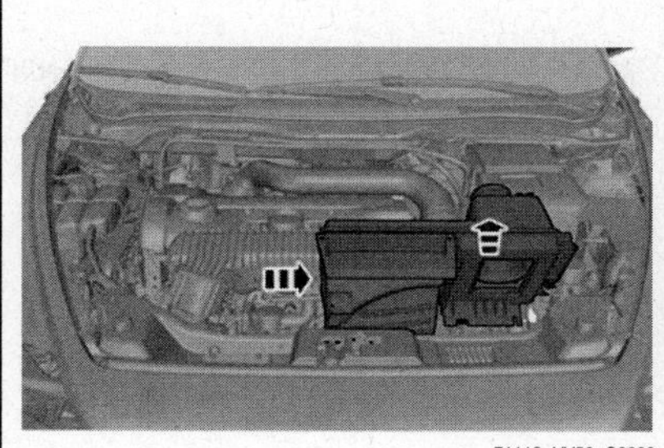

Fig. 60 Remove air cleaner assembly—step 2

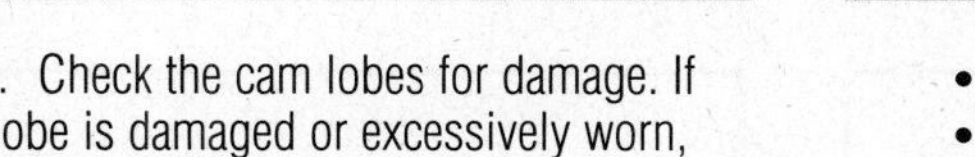

2. Check the cam lobes for damage. If the lobe is damaged or excessively worn, replace the camshaft.
3. Measure the cam lift height.
4. Check the cam surface for abnormal wear or damage, and replace if necessary.
5. Check each bearing for damage. If the bearing surface is excessively damaged, replace the cylinder head assembly or camshaft bearing cap, as necessary.

REMOVAL & INSTALLATION

See Figures 61 through 68.

1. Before servicing the vehicle, refer to the Precautions Section.
2. Install Support (999 7107) as shown.
3. Remove or disconnect the following:
   - Negative battery cable
   - Ignition coils
   - Spark plugs
   - Timing belt
   - VVT unit (camshaft sprocket)

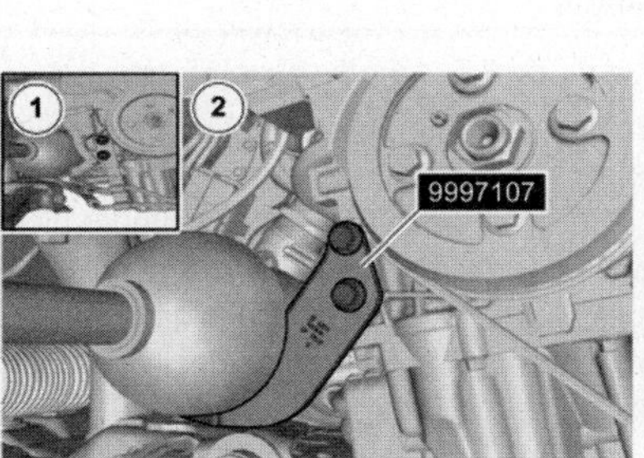

Fig. 61 Install Support (999 7107) as shown

9995454

71112_VV50_G0287

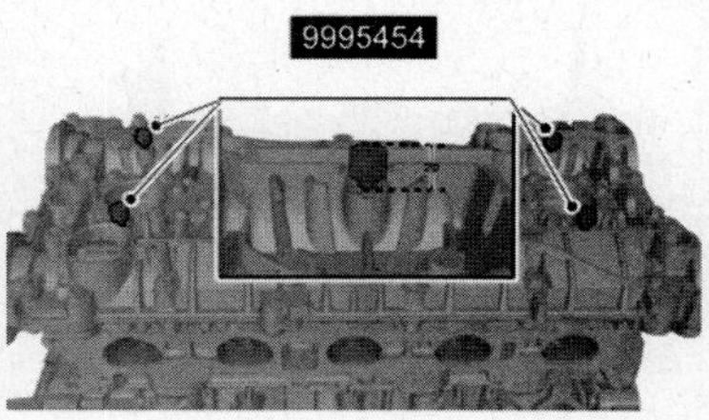

Fig. 62 Fit the 2 M6 bolts under each Press Tool

   - Camshaft seal
   - Oil filler tube
4. Install Press Tool (999 5454) in cylinder head:
   a. Fit the 2 M6 bolts under each Press Tool.
   b. Position the Press Tool in the spark plug holes.
5. Remove the 46 cylinder head cover bolts.

WARNING

Take extra care when handling the components.

6. Rotating Press Tool and using Pliers (999 5670), remove cylinder head cover.

WARNING

Note the position of the components before removal.

7. Remove the 2 camshafts.

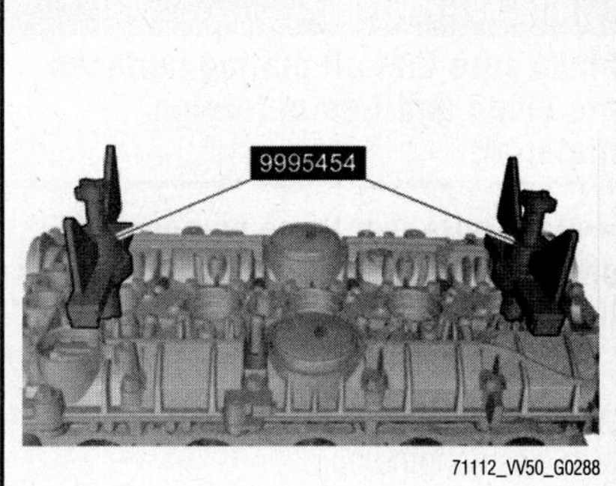

Fig. 63 Position the Press Tool in the spark plug holes

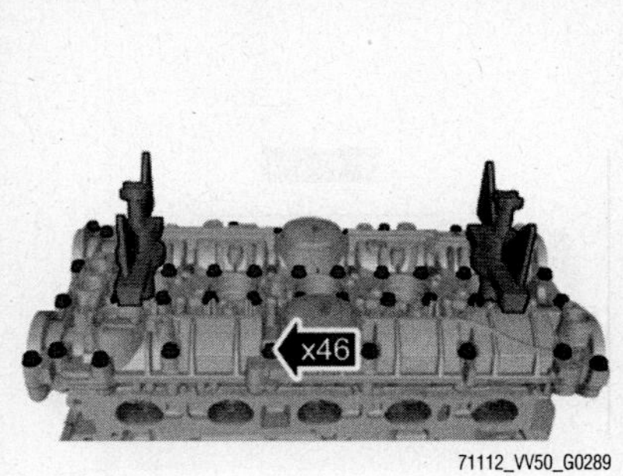

Fig. 64 Remove the 46 cylinder head cover bolts

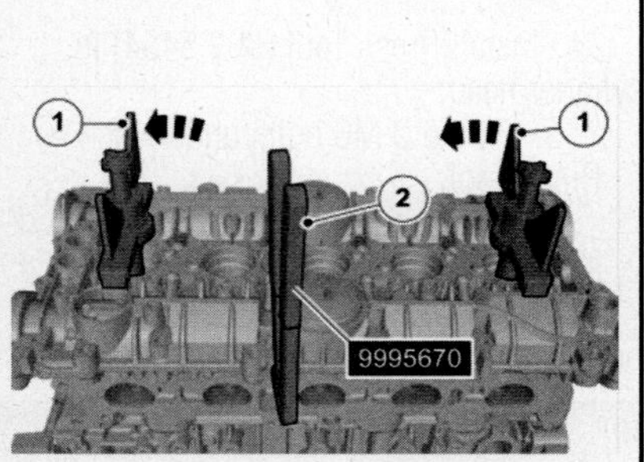

Fig. 65 Rotating Press Tool (1) and using Pliers (2), remove cylinder head cover

To install:

8. Perform valve clearance inspection.

➡This step is only necessary if adjustment is required.

⁂ WARNING

Make sure that all mating surfaces are clean and free of foreign material.

➡Make sure that these components are installed to the noted removal position.

9. Lubricate the tappets (valve lifters) and camshaft bearing positions and lobes with clean engine oil.
10. Install the tappets in their original positions.
11. Install the intake camshaft, then the exhaust camshaft. Ensure camshafts are aligned as shown.
12. Using Roller (951 2767) or equivalent, apply Liquid Gasket (116 1847) to the mating surface of the cylinder head cover.

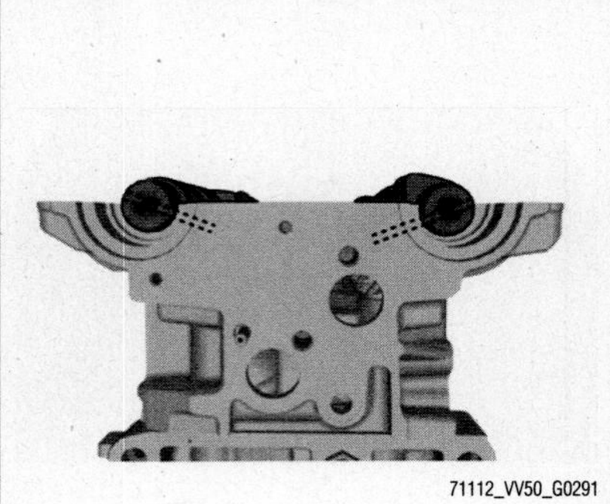

Fig. 66 Ensure camshafts are aligned as shown

Fig. 67 Apply the Liquid Gasket (116 1847) to the cylinder head cover

⁂ WARNING

Ensure no liquid gasket material gets in the oil ducts of the cylinder head cover.

13. Position the Press Tool (999 5454) in the spark plug holes. Fit the 2 M6 bolts under each press tool to set the right height.
14. Crosswise tighten the cylinder head cover parallel to the cylinder head with the press tool. Install all the bolts and tighten from the middle out to the edges. Tighten the bolts to 13 ft. lbs. (17 Nm). Remove the Press Tool and bolts under the tool.
15. Install or connect the following:
    - Oil filler tube
    - Camshaft seal
    - VVT unit
    - Timing belt
    - Spark plugs

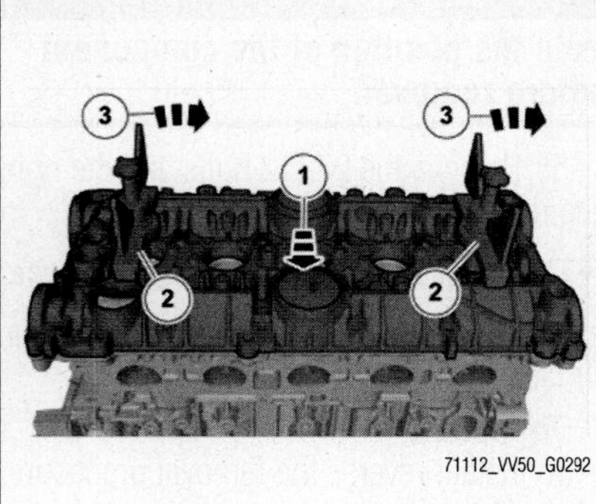

Fig. 68 Install the cylinder head cover

- Ignition coil
- Negative battery cable

CRANKSHAFT DAMPER

REMOVAL & INSTALLATION

See Figure 69.

1. Before servicing the vehicle, refer to the Precautions Section.
2. Raise the vehicle.
3. Remove or disconnect the following:
    - Right front wheel
    - Right-hand fender liner. Slacken off the screws at the front edge and fold back the fender liner.
    - Engine splash plate.
4. Remove the outer drive belt as follows:
    - Relieve the load from the belt tensioner. Using tool (999 7109), turn the belt tensioner **clockwise** as far as it will go. Remove the belt.
5. Remove the following:
    a. The 4 balancer-to-timing belt pulley M8 bolts.

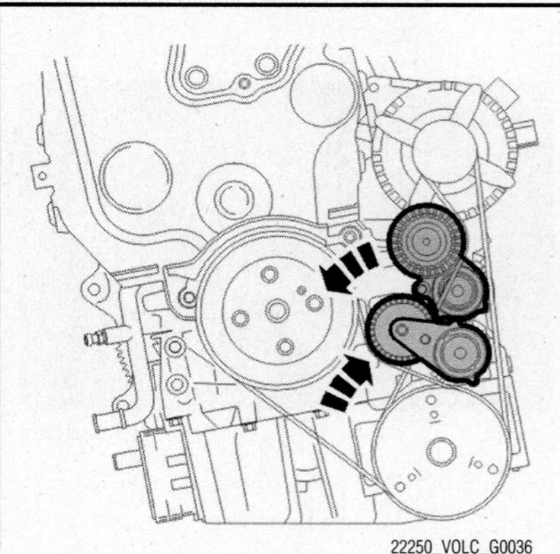

Fig. 69 Accessory drive belt routing and tensioner view

b. The balancer-to-crankshaft snout M8 nut.

c. The balancer.

To install:

To install, reverse the removal procedure and note the following:

- Tighten the 4 balancer-to-timing belt pulley bolts (M8) to:
- Step 1: 18 ft. lbs. (25 Nm).
- Step 2: Angle tighten 60°.
- Tighten the balancer-to-crankshaft snout M8 nut to 133 ft. lbs. (180 Nm).

CRANKSHAFT FRONT SEAL

REMOVAL & INSTALLATION

See Figures 70 through 73.

1. Before servicing the vehicle, refer to the Precautions Section.
2. Remove timing belt.
3. Install Drive Flange Separator (999 5304) onto timing belt crankshaft pulley.

Fig. 70 Install Drive Flange Separator (999 5304) onto crankshaft

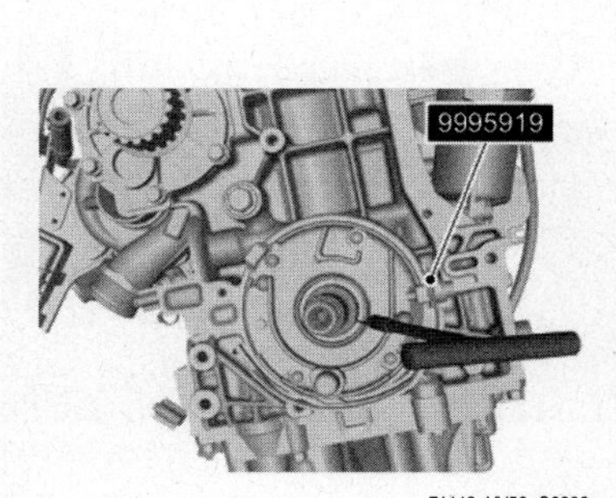

Fig. 71 Using Crankshaft Seal Puller (999 5919), remove seal

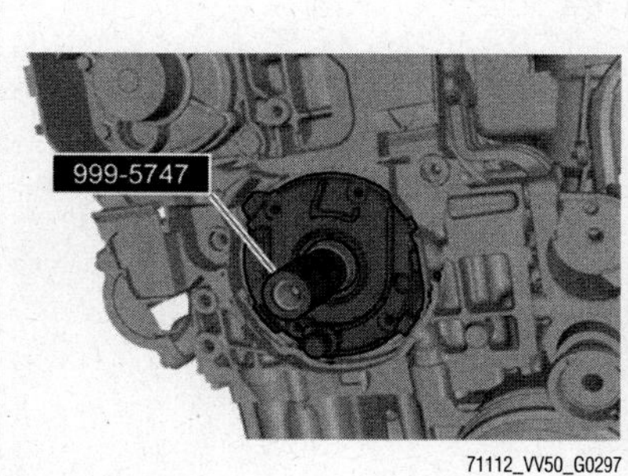

Fig. 72 Using Crankshaft Socket (999 5747), install seal

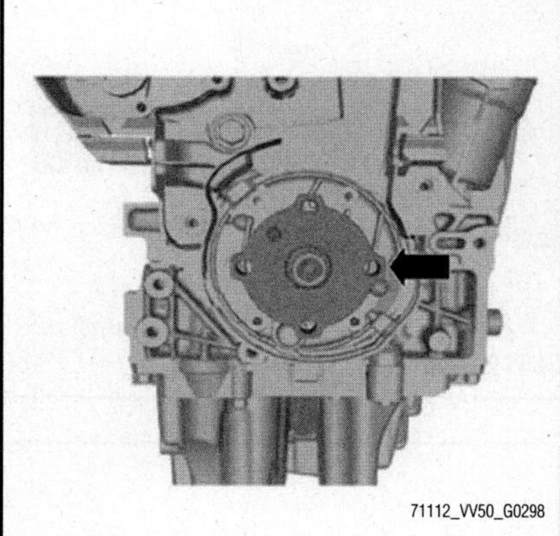

Fig. 73 Install plate

4. Using Crankshaft Seal Puller (999 5919), remove seal.

To install:

WARNING

Take extra care not to damage the seal.

5. Using Crankshaft Socket (999 5747), install seal.
6. Install plate. Tighten the M6 bolts to 89 inch lbs. (10 Nm).

➡The component can only be installed in 1 position.

7. Install timing belt.

CRANKSHAFT REAR SEAL

REMOVAL & INSTALLATION

See Figures 74 and 75.

1. Remove flexplate (also known as drive flange plate or carrier plate).

WARNING

Take extra care not to damage the mating faces.

2. Using Crankshaft Rear Seal Extractor (999 5651), remove seal.

To install:

WARNING

Make sure that the mating faces are clean and free of foreign material.

3. Using Drift (999 7174), install seal. Tighten bolt a quarter turn.
4. Install flexplate.

CYLINDER HEAD

REMOVAL & INSTALLATION

See Figures 76 through 91.

1. Before servicing the vehicle, refer to the Precautions Section.
2. Drain the cooling system.
3. Relieve the fuel pressure.
4. Install Support (999 7107) as shown in illustration.
5. Remove or disconnect the following:
   - Negative battery cable
   - Air cleaner housing
   - Fuel injectors
   - VVT solenoid
   - Spark plugs
   - Timing belt
   - VVT unit (camshaft sprocket)
   - Camshaft seal
   - Intake manifold
   - Exhaust manifold
6. Disconnect hose.
7. Remove engine cover M6 bolt.
8. Remove 3 M10 bolts, 3 M8 bolts and bracket.
9. Remove 2 bolts and oil filler tube.
10. Install Press Tool (999 5454) in cylinder head:
    a. Fit the 2 M6 bolts under each Press Tool.
    b. Position the Press Tool in the spark plug holes.
11. Remove the 46 cylinder head cover bolts.

WARNING

Take extra care when handling the components.

12. Rotating Press Tool and using Pliers (999 5670), remove cylinder head cover.

Fig. 74 Using Crankshaft Rear Seal Extractor (999 5651), remove seal

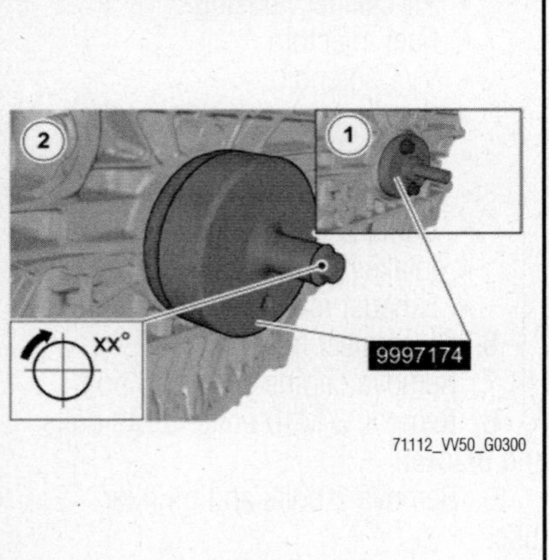

Fig. 75 Using Drift (999 7174), install seal. Tighten bolt a quarter turn

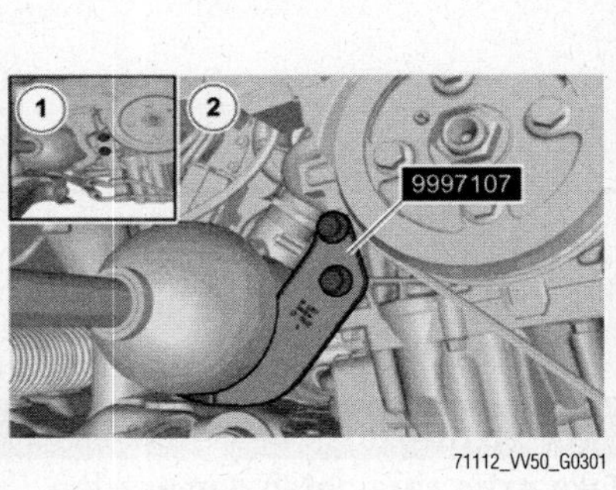

Fig. 76 Install Support (999 7107) as shown

WARNING

Note the position of the components before removal.

13. Remove the 2 camshafts.

WARNING

Take extra care when handling the components.

14. Remove cylinder head cover.

15. Remove the intake and exhaust camshafts.

WARNING

Note the location of the components before removal. Tappets must be reinstalled in original locations.

16. Using a magnet, remove the tappets.

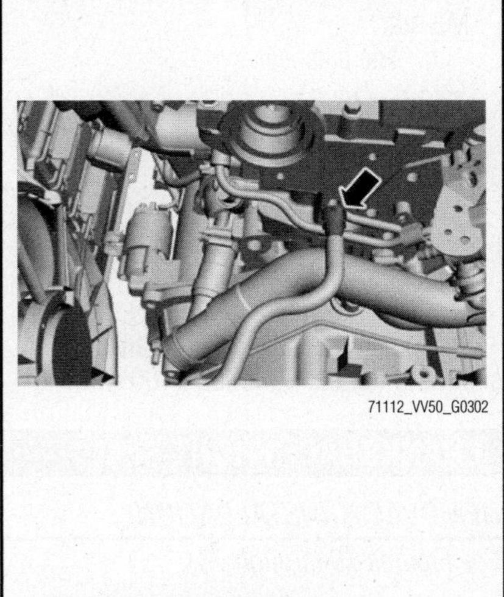

Fig. 77 Disconnect hose

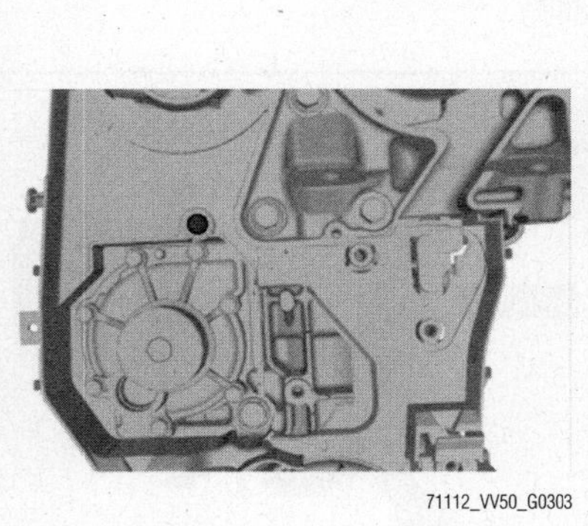

Fig. 78 Remove engine cover M6 bolt

Fig. 79 Remove 3 M10 bolts, 3 M8 bolts and bracket

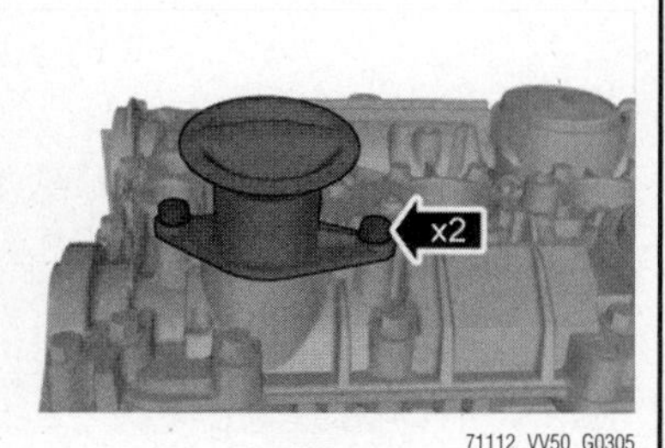

Fig. 80 Remove 2 bolts and oil filler tube

17. Remove cylinder head bolts in the specified sequence.

WARNING

Take extra care not to damage the mating faces.

18. Remove cylinder head.

To install:

WARNING

Take extra care when handling the component.

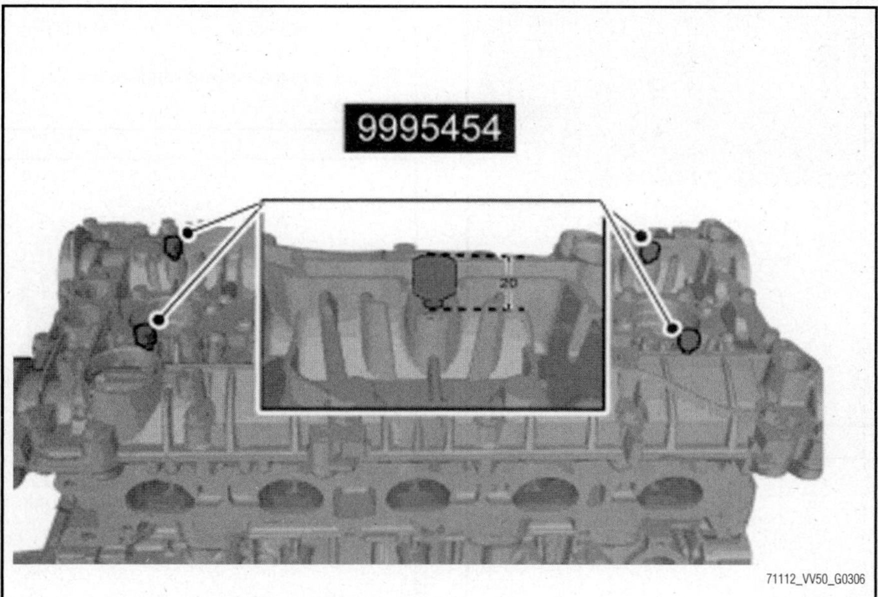

Fig. 81 Fit the 2 M6 bolts under each Press Tool

Fig. 82 Position the Press Tool in the spark plug holes

WARNING

Make sure that the mating faces are clean and free of foreign material.

WARNING

Make sure that no fluids are present in the cylinder head bolt threaded bores.

19. Using Liquid Gasket (116 1059), then Chemical Gasket (116 1847), install gasket.

20. Tighten cylinder head bolts in specified sequence:

a. Stage 1: 15 ft. lbs. (20 Nm).
b. Stage 2: 44 ft. lbs. (60 Nm).
c. Stage 3: Plus 130 degrees.

21. Perform valve clearance inspection.

➡This step is only necessary if adjustment is required.

WARNING

Make sure that all mating surfaces are clean and free of foreign material.

➡Make sure that these components are installed to the noted removal position.

22. Lubricate the tappets (valve lifters) and camshaft bearing positions and lobes with clean engine oil.

23. Install the tappets in their original positions.

24. Install the intake camshaft, then the exhaust camshaft. Ensure camshafts are aligned as shown.

25. Using Roller (951 2767) or equivalent, apply Liquid Gasket (116 1847) to the mating surface of the cylinder head cover.

WARNING

Ensure no liquid gasket material gets in the oil ducts of the cylinder head cover.

26. Position the Press Tool (999 5454) in the spark plug holes. Fit the 2 M6 bolts under each press tool to set the right height.

27. Crosswise tighten the cylinder head cover parallel to the cylinder head with the press tool. Install all the bolts and tighten from the middle out to the edges. Tighten the bolts to 13 ft. lbs. (17 Nm). Remove the Press Tool and bolts under the tool.

28. To install, reverse the removal procedure and note the following:

- Tighten the M10 bolts to 37 ft. lbs. (50 Nm).

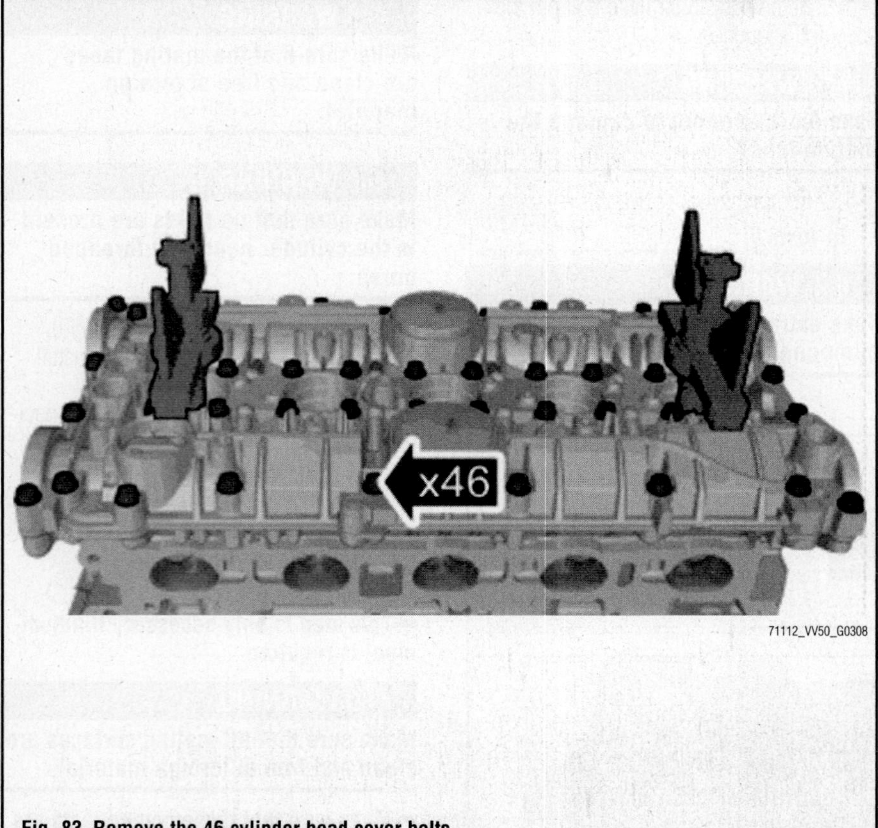

Fig. 83 Remove the 46 cylinder head cover bolts

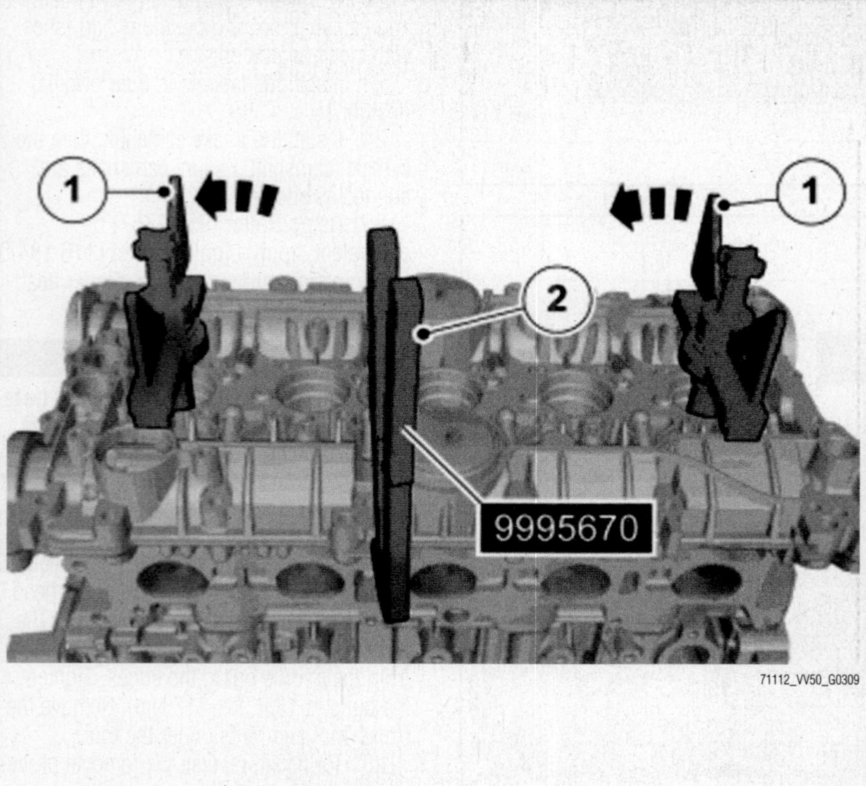

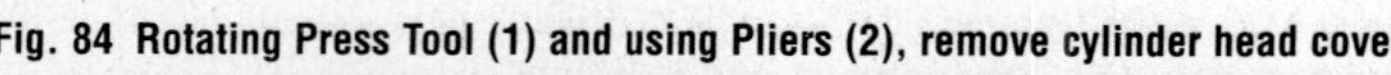

Fig. 84 Rotating Press Tool (1) and using Pliers (2), remove cylinder head cover

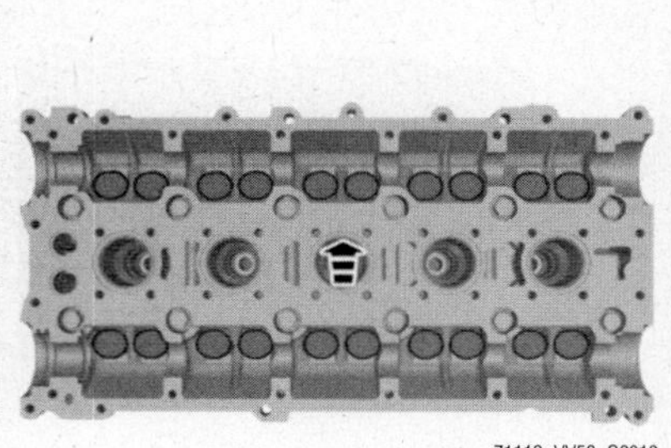

Fig. 85 Using a magnet, remove the tappets

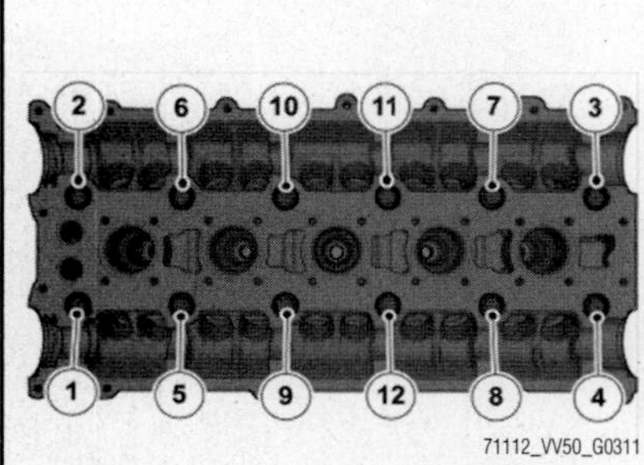

Fig. 86 Remove cylinder head bolts in the specified sequence

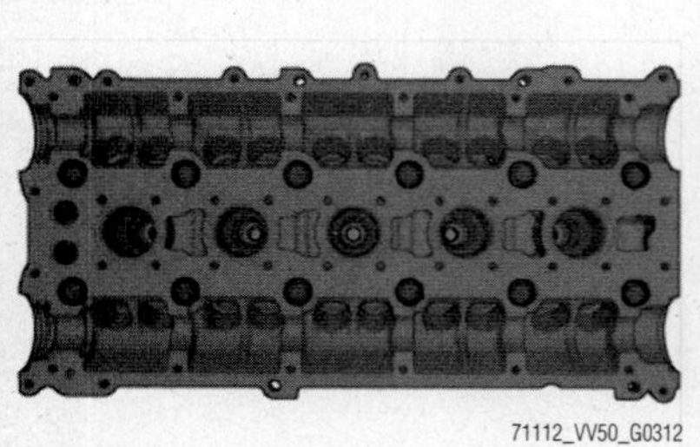

Fig. 87 Make sure that no fluids are present in the cylinder head bolt threaded bores

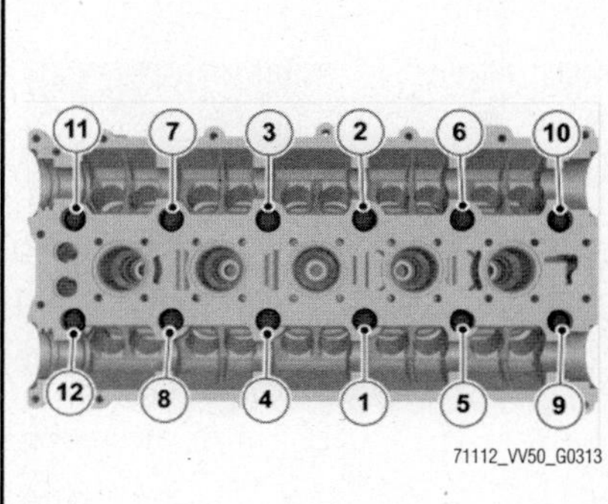

Fig. 88 Tighten cylinder head bolts in specified sequence

Fig. 89 Ensure camshafts are aligned as shown

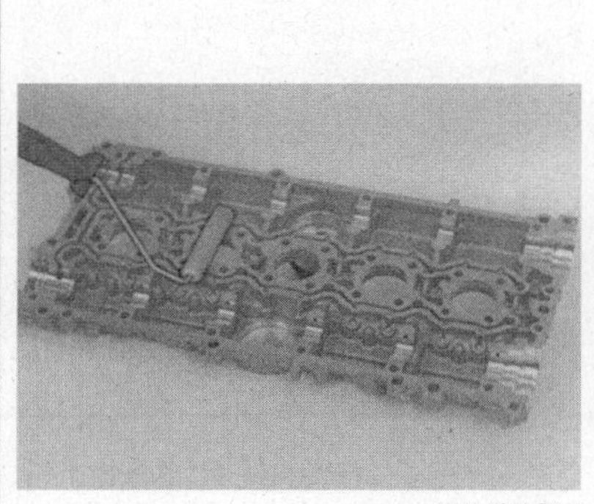

Fig. 90 Apply the Liquid Gasket (116 1847) to the cylinder head cover

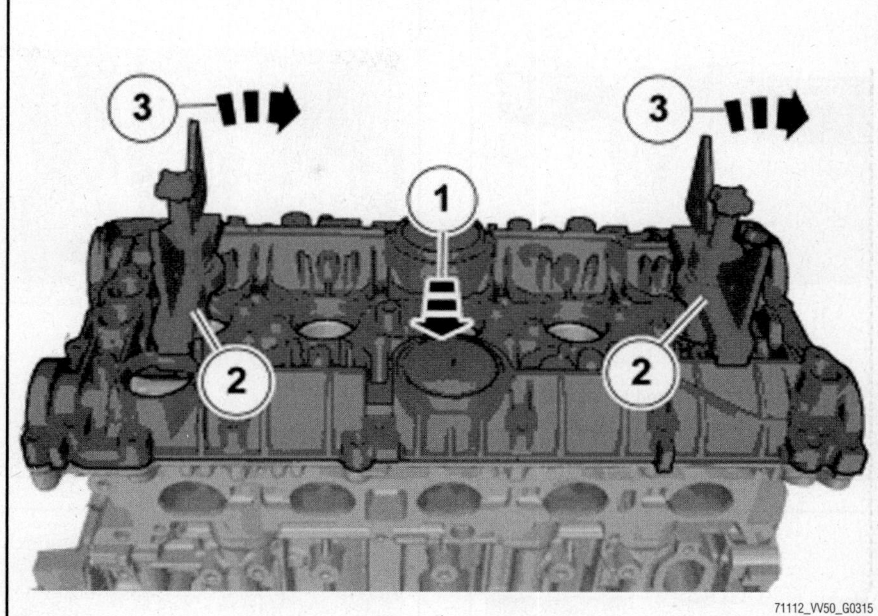

Fig. 91 Install the cylinder head cover

- Tighten the M8 bolts to 18 ft. lbs. (24 Nm).
- Tighten the M6 bolts to 89 inch lbs. (10 Nm).

29. Fill the cooling system.

EXHAUST MANIFOLD

REMOVAL & INSTALLATION

See Figures 92 through 103.

➡The exhaust manifold and turbocharger are a single unit.

1. Before servicing the vehicle, refer to the Precautions Section.
2. Disconnect the negative battery cable.
3. Drain the cooling system.
4. Remove the catalytic converter.
5. Disconnect electrical connector.
6. Remove vacuum hoses from inlet pipe.

⁂ WARNING

Make sure that the inside of the pipe ends are clean and free of oil residue.

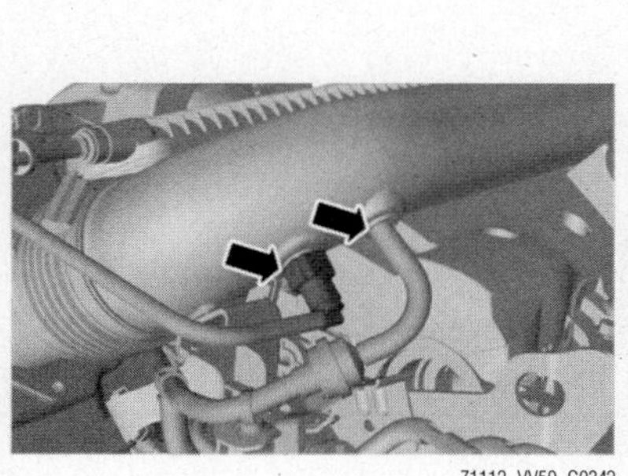

Fig. 92 Remove vacuum hoses from inlet pipe

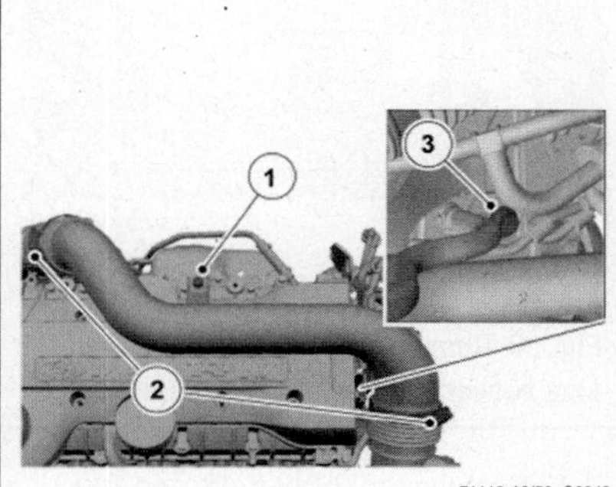

Fig. 93 Remove the 2 M6 bolts (1, 3) and 2 clamps (2) securing the air cleaner assembly hose

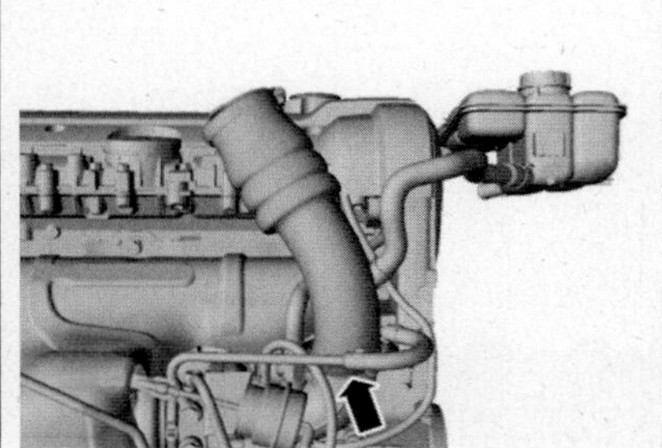

Fig. 94 Remove bolts and clamps, then pipe between intercooler and intake manifold

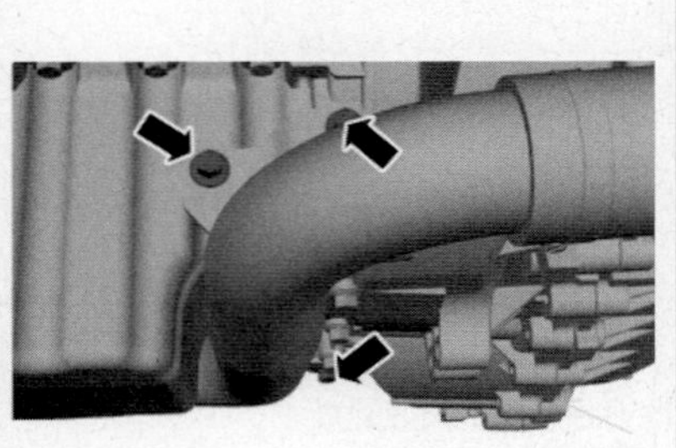

Fig. 95 Remove the 3 M6 bolts from pipe-to-oil pan brackets

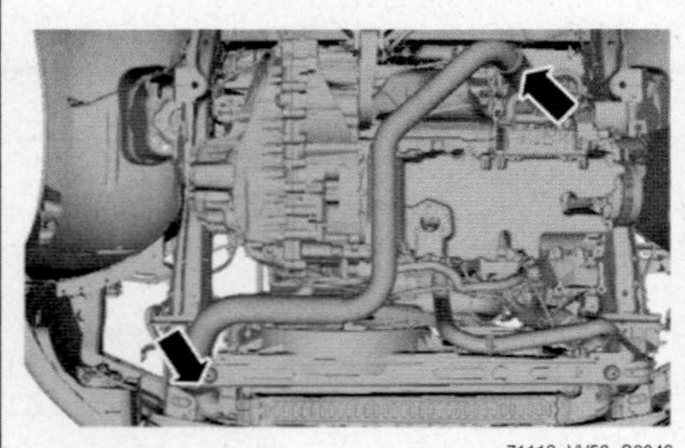

Fig. 96 Remove bolts and clamps, then pipe between turbocharger and intercooler

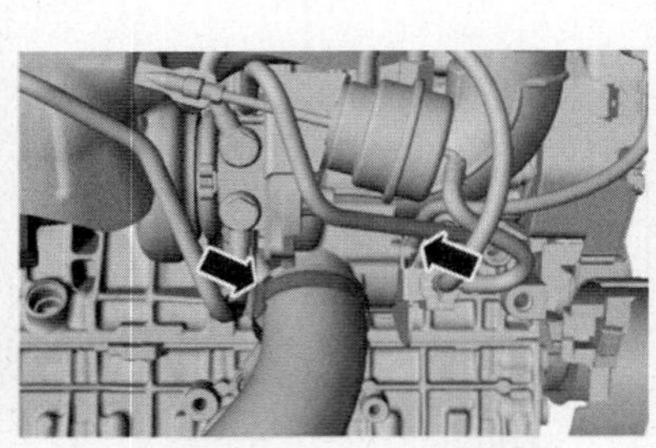

Fig. 97 Remove coolant pipes from turbocharger

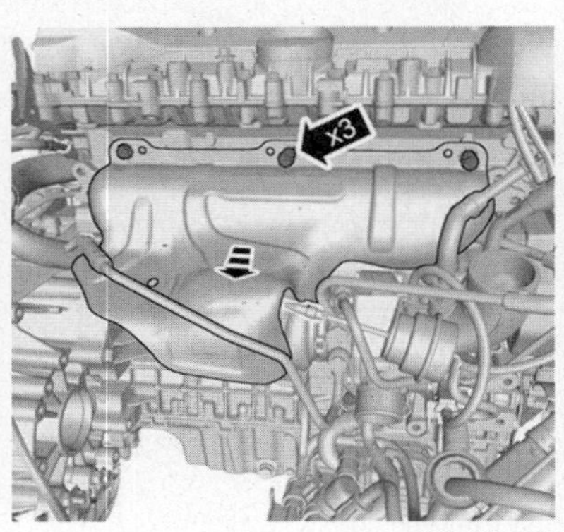

Fig. 98 Remove the 3 M8 bolts. Pull out and remove exhaust manifold heat shield

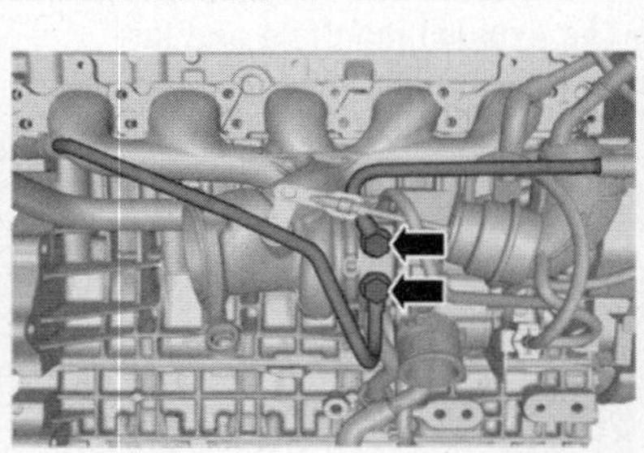

Fig. 99 Remove the coolant pipe to turbocharger

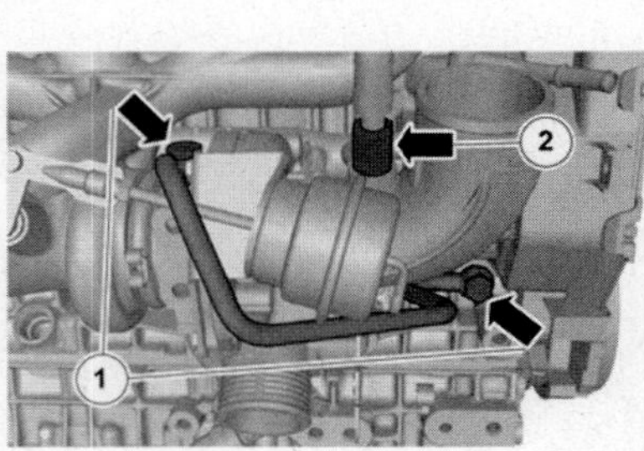

Fig. 100 Remove the oil pressure pipe (1) and crankcase ventilation pipe (2)

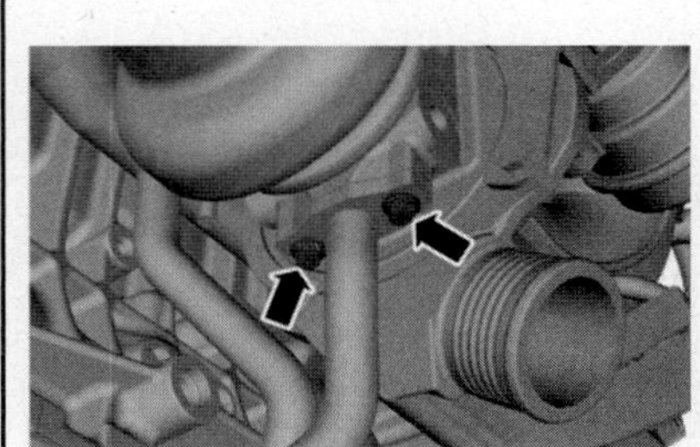

Fig. 101 Remove the 2 M6 bolts

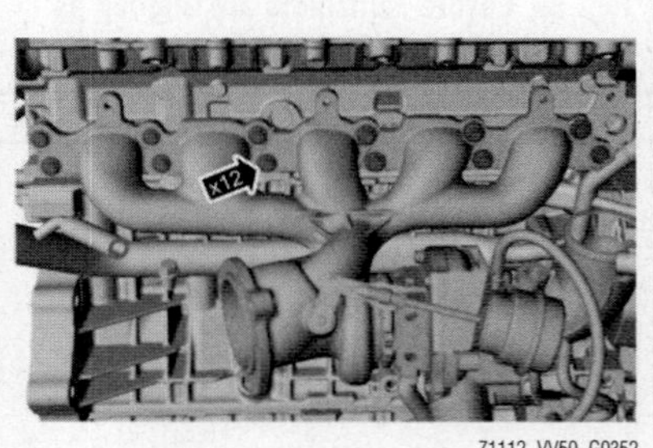

Fig. 102 Remove the 12 M8 bolts. Remove the exhaust manifold/turbocharger assembly

7. Remove the 2 M6 bolts and 2 clamps securing the air cleaner assembly hose.
8. Remove bolts and clamps, then pipe between intercooler and intake manifold.
9. Remove the 3 M6 bolts from pipe-to-oil pan brackets.
10. Remove bolts and clamps, then pipe between turbocharger and intercooler.
11. Remove coolant pipes from turbocharger.
12. Remove the 3 M8 bolts. Pull out and remove exhaust manifold heat shield.
13. Remove the coolant pipe to turbocharger.
14. Remove the oil pressure pipe and crankcase ventilation pipe to the turbocharger.
15. Remove the 2 M6 bolts.
16. Remove the 12 M8 bolts.
17. Remove the exhaust manifold/turbocharger assembly.
18. Disconnect 3 hose clamps, and remove vacuum hoses from turbocharger.

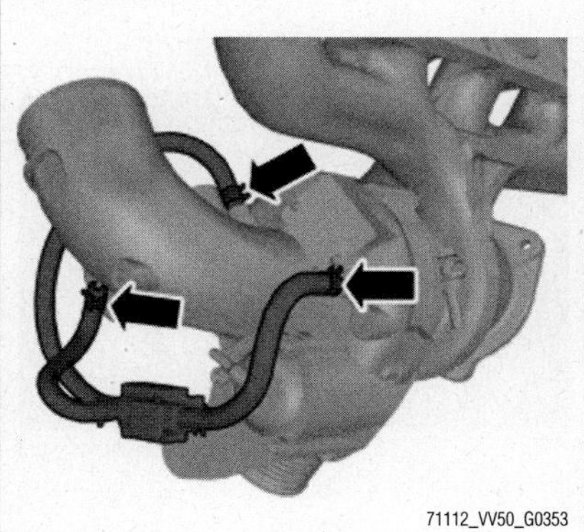
71112_VV50_G0353

Fig. 103 Disconnect 3 hose clamps, and remove vacuum hoses from turbocharger

To install:

19. To install, reverse the removal procedure and note the following:
   - Tighten the exhaust manifold/turbocharger M8 bolts to 18 ft. lbs. (24 Nm).
   - Tighten all M6 bolts to 89 inch lbs. (10 Nm).
   - Tighten the oil pressure pipe-to-turbocharger bolts to 19 ft. lbs. (26 Nm).
   - Tighten the crankcase ventilation pipe-to-turbocharger bolts to 18 ft. lbs. (25 Nm).
   - Tighten the coolant pipe-to-turbocharger bolts to 28 ft. lbs. (38 Nm).
   - Tighten the exhaust manifold heat shield M8 bolts to 18 ft. lbs. (24 Nm).

WARNING

Make sure that the inside of the pipe ends are clean and free of oil residue.

20. Connect the negative battery cable.
21. Start the engine and check for leaks.

INTAKE MANIFOLD

REMOVAL & INSTALLATION

Upper Manifold

See Figures 104 and 105.

➡This component is also referred to as an upper inlet pipe.

1. Before servicing the vehicle, refer to the Precautions Section.
2. Relieve the fuel system pressure.
3. Disconnect the negative battery cable.

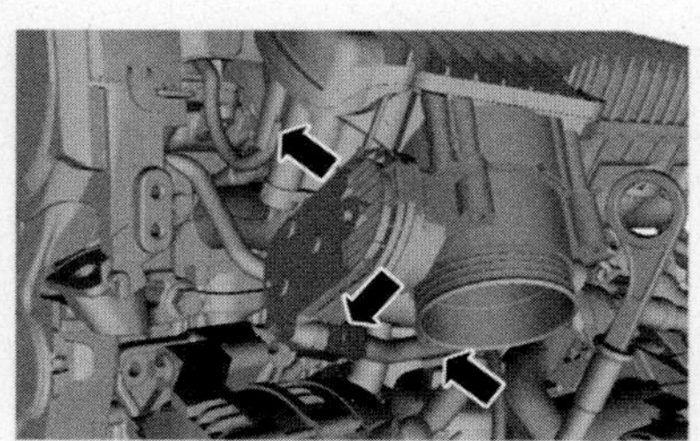
71112_VV50_G0368

Fig. 104 Disconnect the electrical connector, and remove hoses

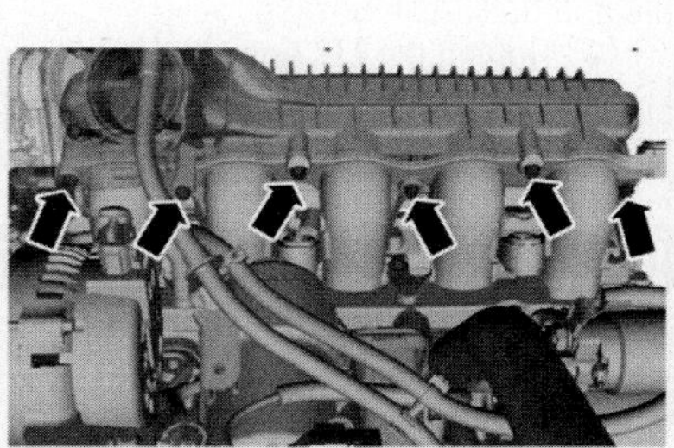
71112_VV50_G0369

Fig. 105 Remove the 6 M7 bolts for the upper sections of the intake manifold

4. Remove the air cleaner housing.
5. Remove the hose clamp for the rubber hose on the throttle body. Move the hose to one side.
6. Disconnect the throttle body connector.
7. Disconnect the electrical connector, and remove hoses.
8. Remove the 6 M7 bolts for the upper sections of the intake manifold. Move the manifold to one side.

To install:

➡Make sure that the mating faces are clean and free of foreign material.

9. To install, reverse the removal procedure and note the following:
   - Tighten all M6 bolts to 89 inch lbs. (10 Nm).
   - Tighten the intake manifold M7 bolts to 13 ft. lbs. (17 Nm).
10. Start the engine and check for leaks.

Lower Manifold

See Figures 106 through 108.

➡This component is also referred to as an "induction pipe".

1. Before servicing the vehicle, refer to the Precautions Section.

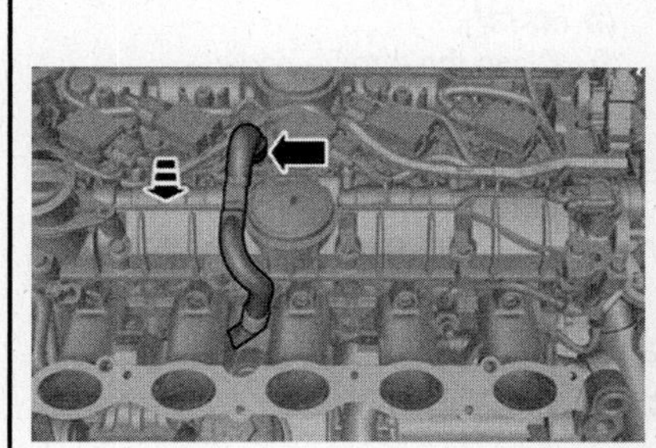
71112_VV50_G0370

Fig. 106 Disconnect hose and position aside

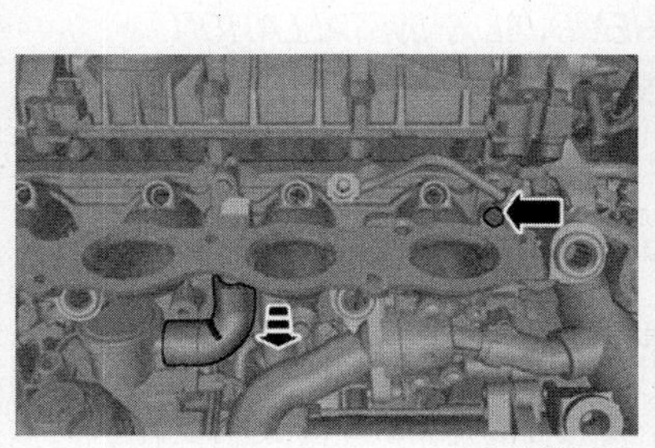
71112_VV50_G0371

Fig. 107 Remove the M6 bolt. Disconnect hose and position aside

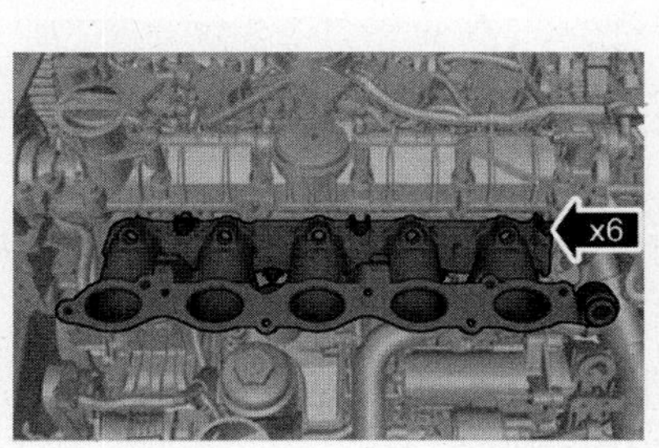

71112_VV50_G0372

Fig. 108 Remove the 6 M7 bolts and induction pipe

2. Relieve the fuel system pressure.
3. Disconnect the negative battery cable.
4. Remove the throttle body.
5. Remove the fuel injector.
6. Disconnect hose and position aside.
7. Remove the M6 bolt. Disconnect hose and position aside.
8. Remove the 6 M7 bolts and induction pipe.

To install:

9. Clean the throttle body:
   - Using brush, apply Cleaner (1161828), or equivalent into throttle body bore. Allow the cleaner to act for 5 minutes
   - Clean the throttle body

➡Make sure that the component is clean and free of foreign material.

10. To install, reverse the removal procedure and note the following:
   - Tighten the M7 bolts to 13 ft. lbs. (17 Nm).
   - Tighten the M6 bolts to 89 inch lbs. (10 Nm).

OIL COOLER

REMOVAL & INSTALLATION

See Figures 109 and 110.

1. Drain engine oil.
2. Apply hose clamp pliers to close off oil cooler hoses.
3. Remove the 2 hose clamps, and position hoses aside.
4. Remove the 4 M7 bolts.
5. Remove the oil cooler.

⁂ CAUTION

Be prepared to collect escaping fluid.

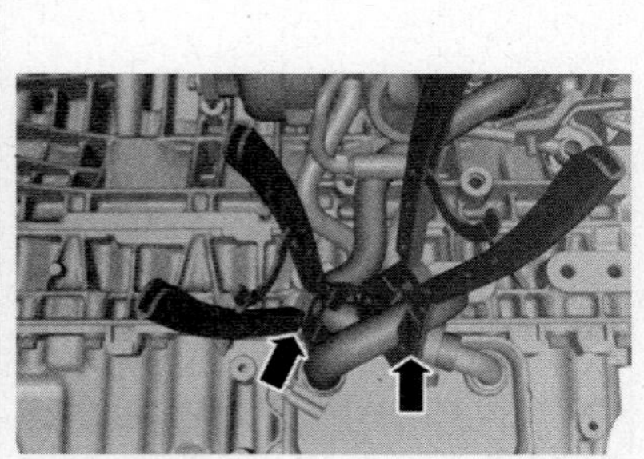

Fig. 109 Apply hose clamp pliers to close off oil cooler hoses

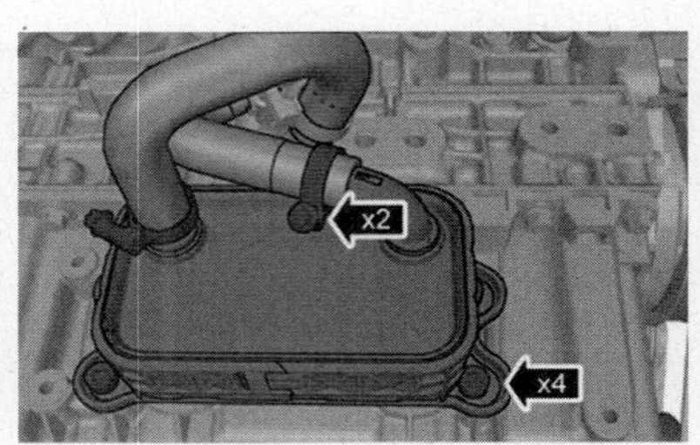

Fig. 110 Remove the 2 hose clamps. Remove the 4 M7 bolts

To install:

6. To install, reverse the removal procedure and note the following:
   - Tighten the M7 bolts to 13 ft. lbs. (17 Nm).
7. Fill the cooling system.

OIL PAN

REMOVAL & INSTALLATION

See Figures 111 through 120.

1. Before servicing the vehicle, refer to the Precautions Section.
2. Remove the oil dipstick and tube.
3. Remove the splash plate under the engine.
4. Drain the engine oil, and remove the oil filter.
5. Remove accessory drive belt.
6. Remove 3 bolts and A/C compressor.

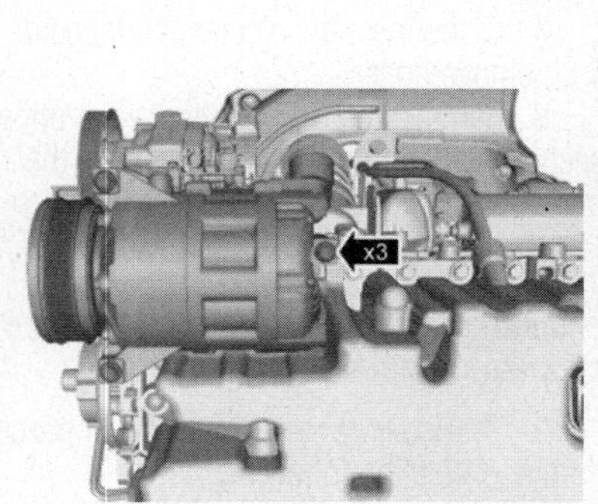

Fig. 111 Remove 3 bolts and A/C compressor

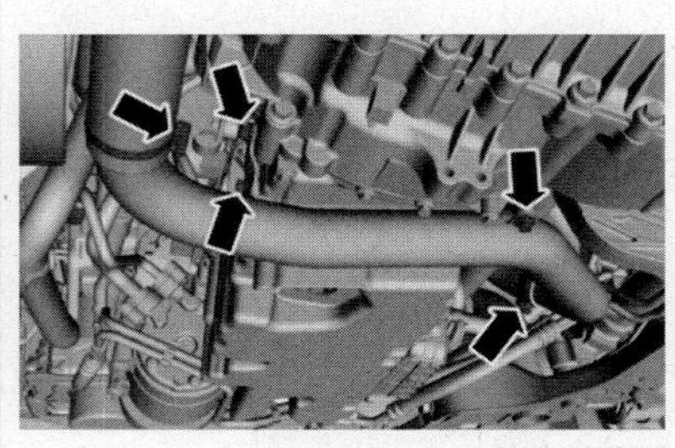

Fig. 112 Remove the air intake pipe

7. Remove air intake pipe retaining bolts and hose clamps.
8. Remove the air intake pipe.
9. Remove oil pan-to-transmission bolts as shown.
10. Remove the bolt from the bracket for the fuel line.
11. Remove 4 oil cooler bolts and detach the oil cooler from the oil pan.
12. Back off all bolts holding the oil pan.
13. Remove all but 4 bolts. It is recommended that the 4 bolts in the corners of the oil pan are left in place.
14. Carefully tap the oil pan with a rubber mallet until the joint and its liquid gasket releases.
15. Remove the 4 remaining bolts.
16. Remove the oil pan.

To install:

17. Install the 2 Guide Pins (999 7273) as shown.

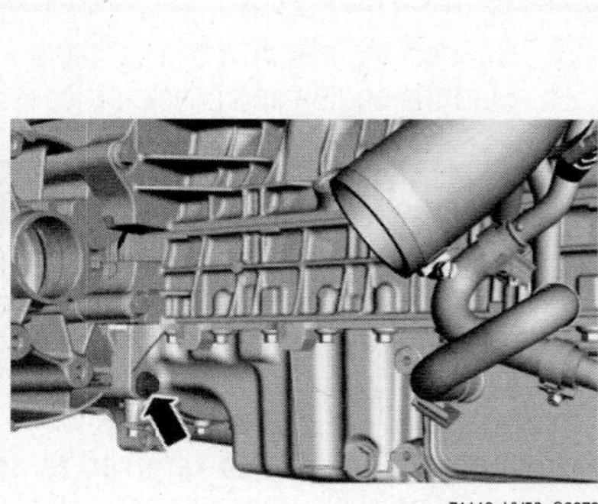

Fig. 113 Remove oil pan-to-transmission bolt—left side

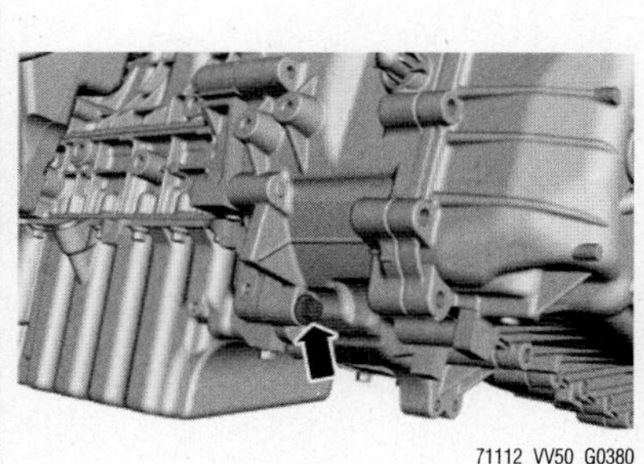

Fig. 114 Remove oil pan-to-transmission bolt—right side

Fig. 115 Remove the bolt from the bracket for the fuel line

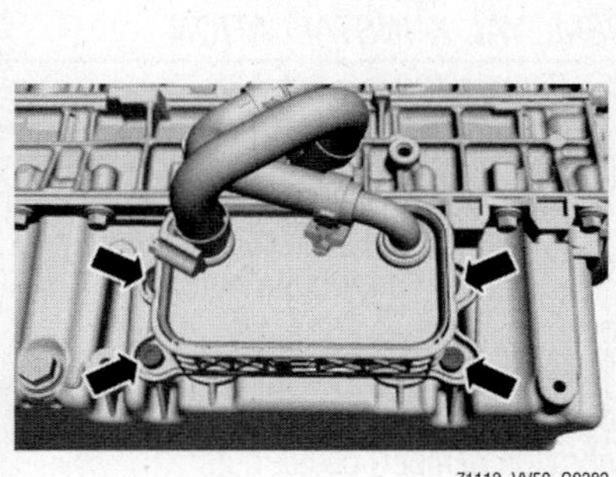

Fig. 116 Remove 4 oil cooler bolts

⁂ WARNING

Ensure the gaskets are correctly located.

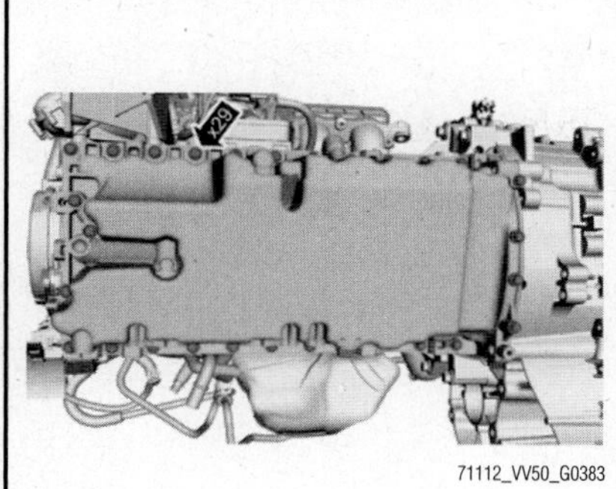

Fig. 117 Back off all bolts holding the oil pan

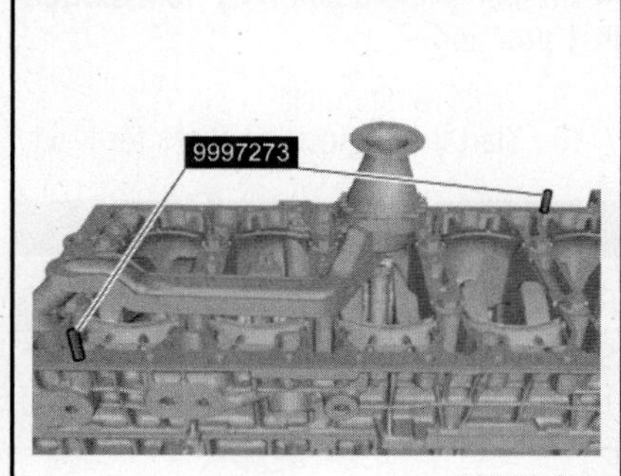

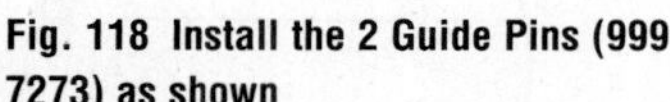

Fig. 118 Install the 2 Guide Pins (999 7273) as shown

Fig. 119 Ensure the gaskets are correctly located

⁂ WARNING

Ensure the mating faces are clean and free of foreign material.

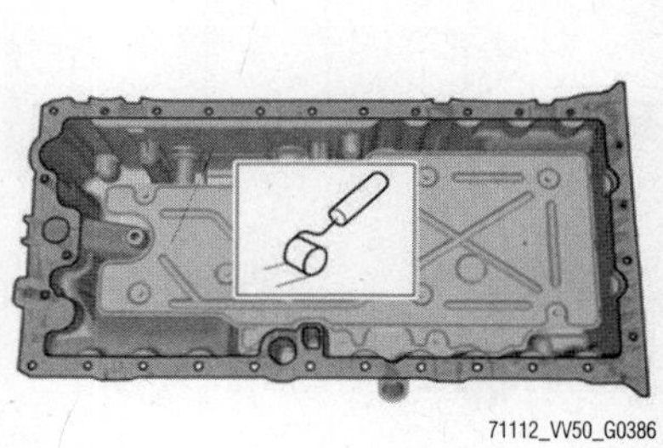

Fig. 120 Apply Liquid Gasket (116 1059) to the oil pan

18. Apply Liquid Gasket (116 1059) to the oil pan.
19. To install, reverse the removal procedure and note the following:
    - Tighten the M7 bolts to 13 ft. lbs. (17 Nm).
20. Install the oil drain plug with a new gasket.
21. Install the oil dipstick and its pipe. Use a new O-ring.

➡Check that the O-ring is correctly positioned.

22. Fill with engine oil. Run the engine to operating temperature.
23. Check for oil leaks.
24. Install the splash plate under the engine.
25. Check the oil level. Top up if required.

OIL PUMP

REMOVAL & INSTALLATION

See Figures 121 through 124.

1. Before servicing the vehicle, refer to the Precautions Section.
2. Remove timing belt.
3. Install Drive Flange Separator (999 5304) onto timing belt crankshaft pulley
4. Remove timing belt crankshaft pulley from crankshaft.
5. Remove 4 bolts and oil pump.

⁂ WARNING

Be prepared to collect escaping fluid.

To install:

6. Install oil pump.

⁂ WARNING

Take extra care not to damage the seal.

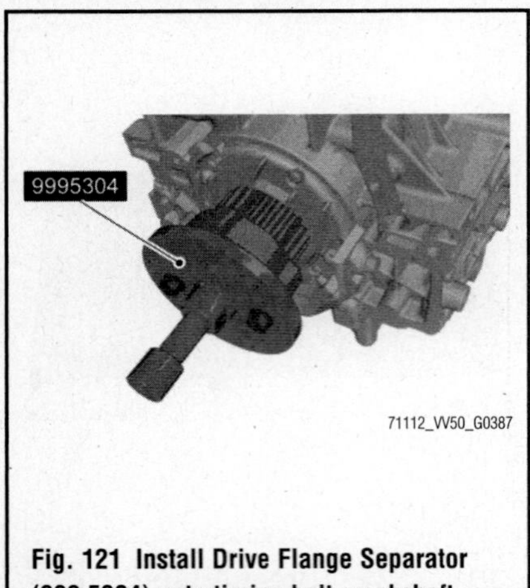

Fig. 121 Install Drive Flange Separator (999 5304) onto timing belt crankshaft pulley

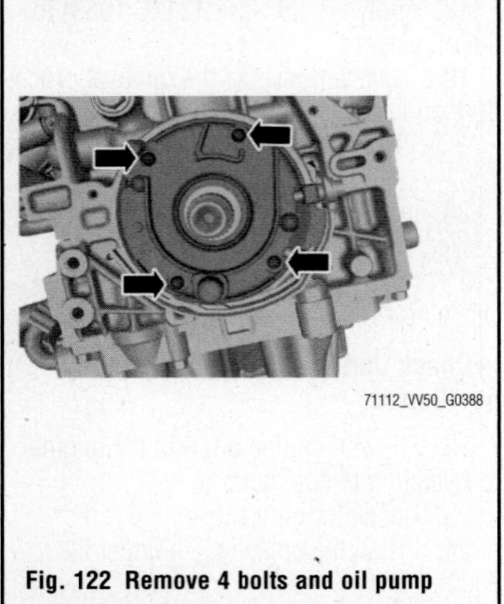

Fig. 122 Remove 4 bolts and oil pump

7. Using Crankshaft Socket (999 5747), install seal.
8. Install plate. Tighten the M6 bolts to 89 inch lbs. (10 Nm).

Fig. 123 Using Crankshaft Socket (999 5747), install seal

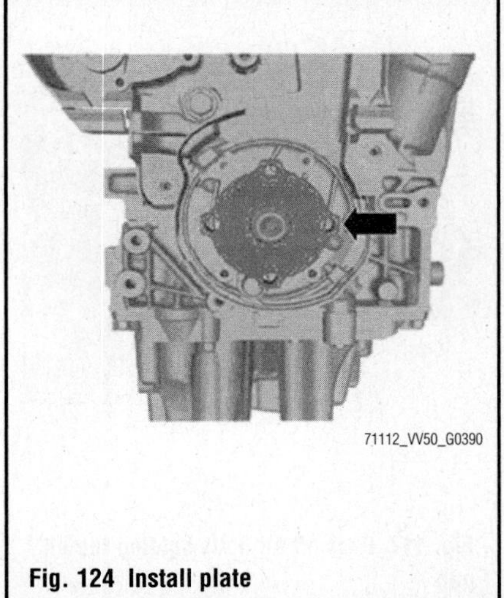

Fig. 124 Install plate

➡The component can only be installed in 1 position.

9. Install timing belt.
10. Start the engine and check for leaks.

PISTONS & RINGS

POSITIONING

See Figures 125 through 127.

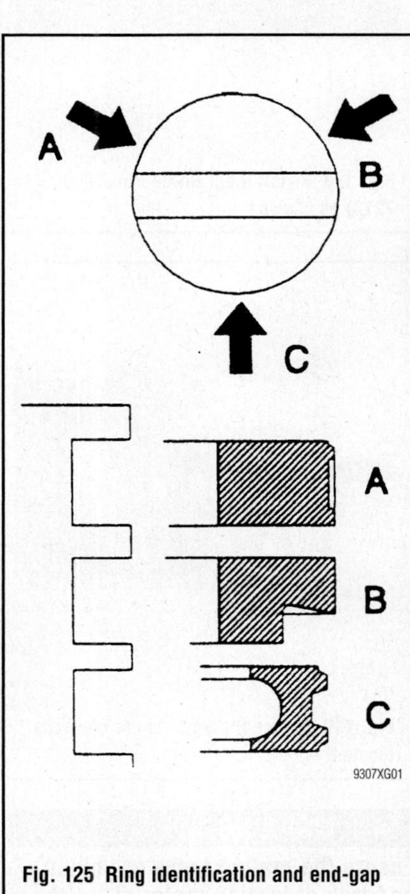

Fig. 125 Ring identification and end-gap spacing

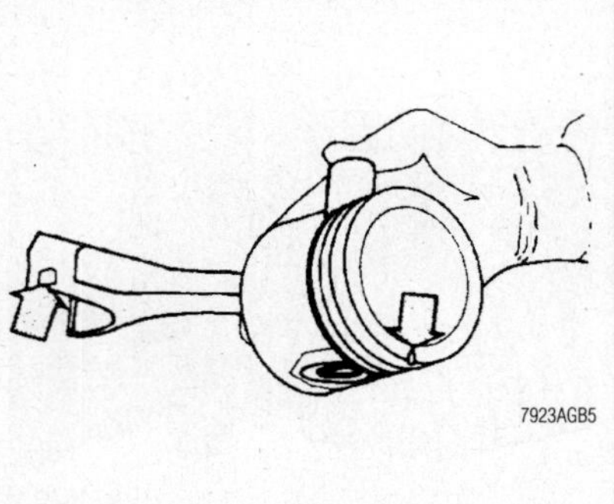

Fig. 126 Piston and rod positioning
The notch on the piston crown faces the front of the engine

TIMING BELT FRONT COVER

REMOVAL & INSTALLATION

See Figures 128 and 129.

1. Before servicing the vehicle, refer to the Precautions Section.

⁂ CAUTION

Remove the ignition key.

2. Remove the accessory drive belt.
3. Remove the hose bracket bolt.
4. Remove the M6 bolt, and remove upper cover.

To install:

To install, reverse the removal procedure and note the following:

- Tighten the M6 bolts to 89 inch lbs. (10 Nm).

TIMING BELT & SPROCKETS

REMOVAL & INSTALLATION

See Figures 130 through 136.

1. Before servicing the vehicle, refer to the Precautions Section.
2. Remove the right engine mount.
3. Remove the timing belt front cover.
4. Using Vibration Dampener Counterhold (999 5433), remove the 4 crankshaft (vibration damper) center nuts.
5. Using Vibration Dampener Counterhold, remove the 4 oscillation damper flange nuts.
6. Remove the crankshaft pulley cover.
7. Align the crankshaft timing marks as shown.
8. Align the camshaft sprockets (VVT units) timing marks as shown.
9. Rotate tensioner and insert pin.
10. Remove the 3 M8 bolts.

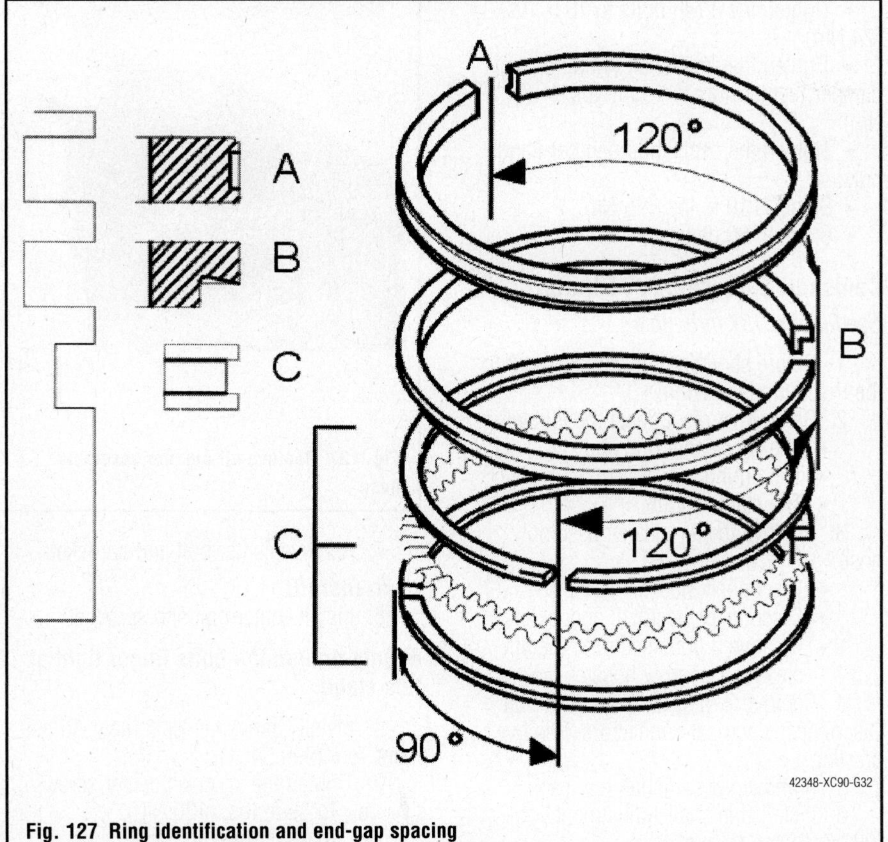

Fig. 127 Ring identification and end-gap spacing

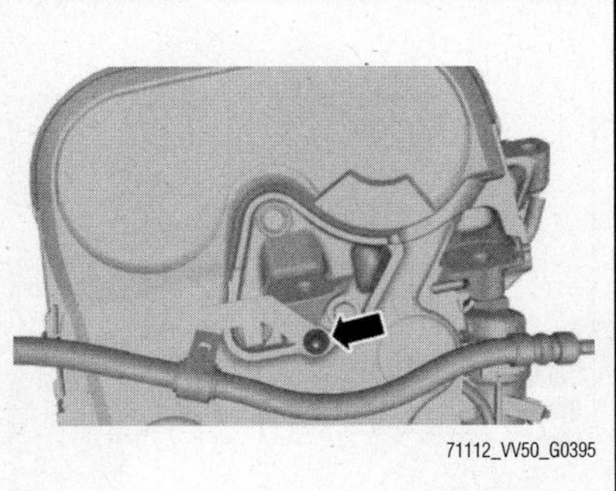

Fig. 128 Remove the hose bracket bolt

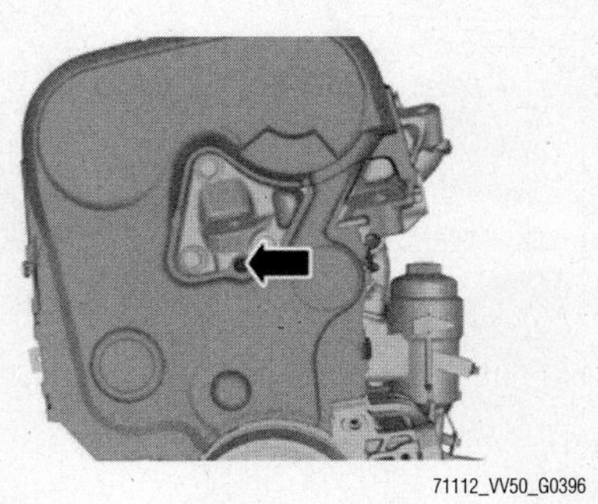

Fig. 129 Remove the M6 bolt, and remove upper cover

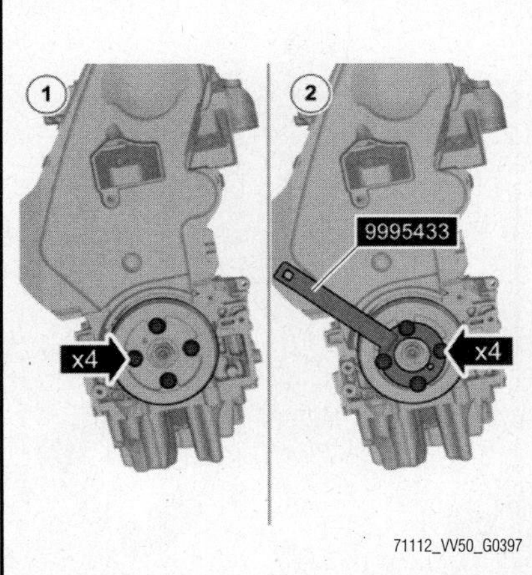

Fig. 130 Using Vibration Dampener Counterhold (999 5433), remove the 4 crankshaft (vibration damper) center nuts

➡The component can be reused unless it has been subjected to abnormal mechanical stress, damage or oil contamination.

11. Remove timing belt.

To install:

To install, reverse the removal procedure and note the following:

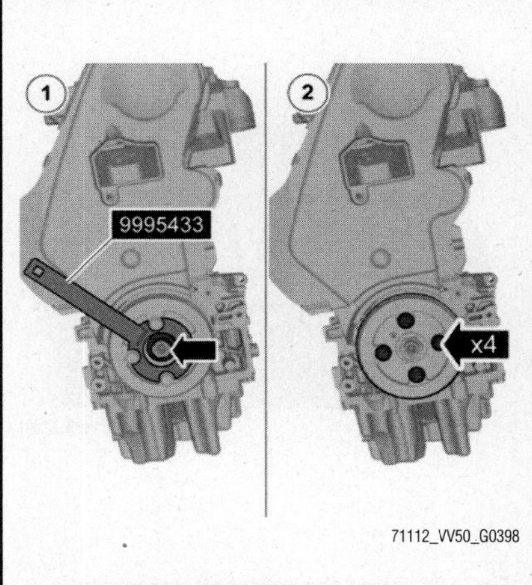

Fig. 131 Using Vibration Dampener Counterhold, remove the 4 oscillation damper flange nuts

Fig. 132 Remove the crankshaft pulley cover

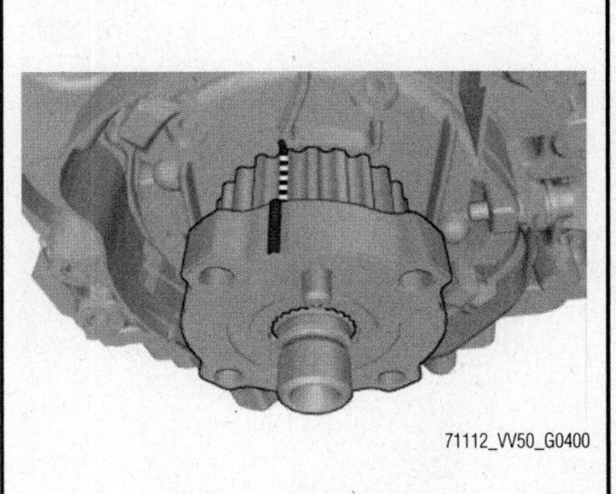

Fig. 133 Align the crankshaft timing marks as shown

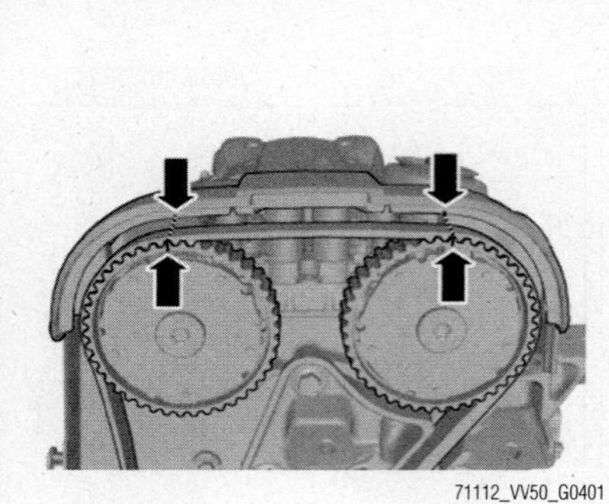

Fig. 134 Align the camshaft sprockets (VVT units) timing marks as shown

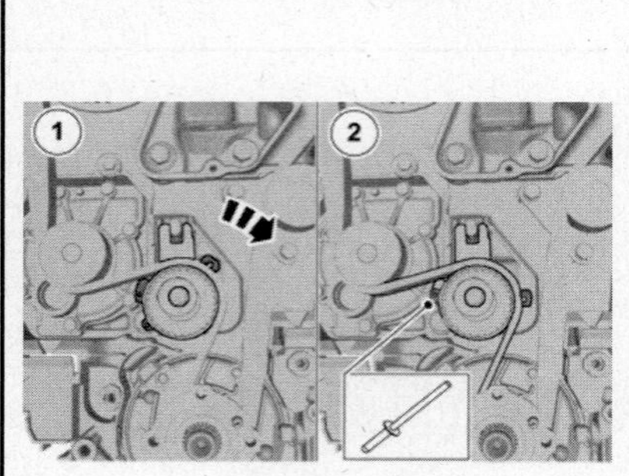

Fig. 135 Rotate tensioner and insert pin

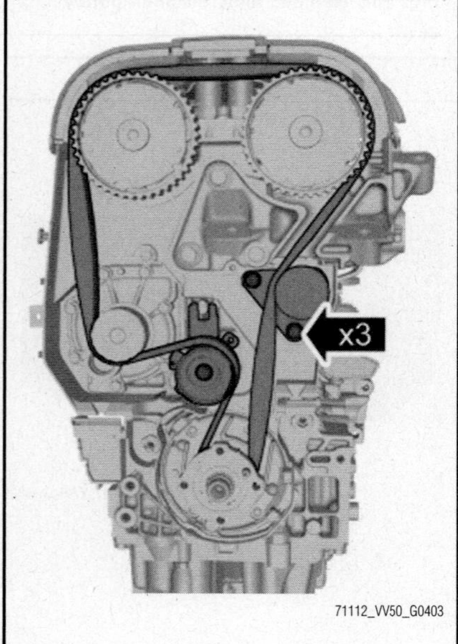

Fig. 136 Remove the 3 M8 bolts

- Tighten the 3 M8 bolts to 18 ft. lbs. (24 Nm).
- Tighten the crankshaft (vibration damper) center nuts to 133 ft. lbs. (180 Nm).
- Tighten the oscillation damper flange nuts:
  - Stage 1: 19 ft. lbs. (25 Nm).
  - Stage 2: 60 degrees.

Camshaft Sprockets (VVT Units)

See Figures 137 through 142.

1. Before servicing the vehicle, refer to the Precautions Section.
2. Remove or disconnect the following:
   - The air cleaner housing
   - The timing belt
   - The starter motor
3. Remove the air cleaner assembly hose:
   - Disconnect hoses.
   - Disconnect electrical connector.
   - Remove 2 bolts securing the air cleaner assembly hose.
4. Remove 2 M10 bolts and M6 bolt. Disconnect electrical connectors. Remove bracket.
5. Remove the camshaft rear caps.
6. Install Camshaft Adjustment Tool (999 5452) as shown.

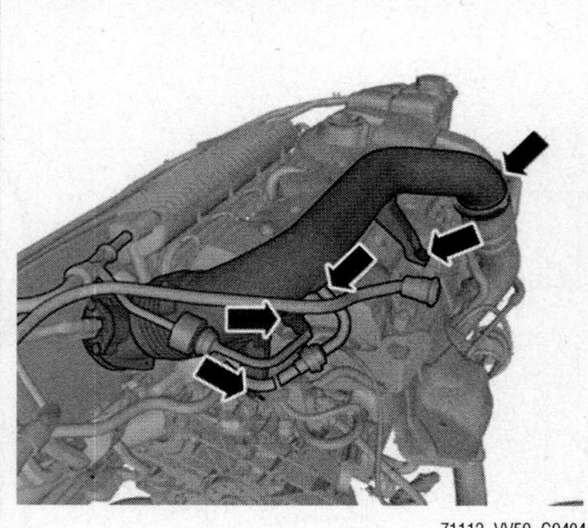

Fig. 137 Remove air cleaner assembly hose

7. Remove center bolt and sprocket.

To install:

8. Install center bolt and sprocket.

➡Only tighten the bolts finger tight at this stage.

9. Install Crankshaft Alignment Adjustment Tool (999 5451).
10. Tighten the sprocket center screw:
    a. To 89 ft. lbs. (120 Nm).
    b. To 26 ft. lbs. (35 Nm).

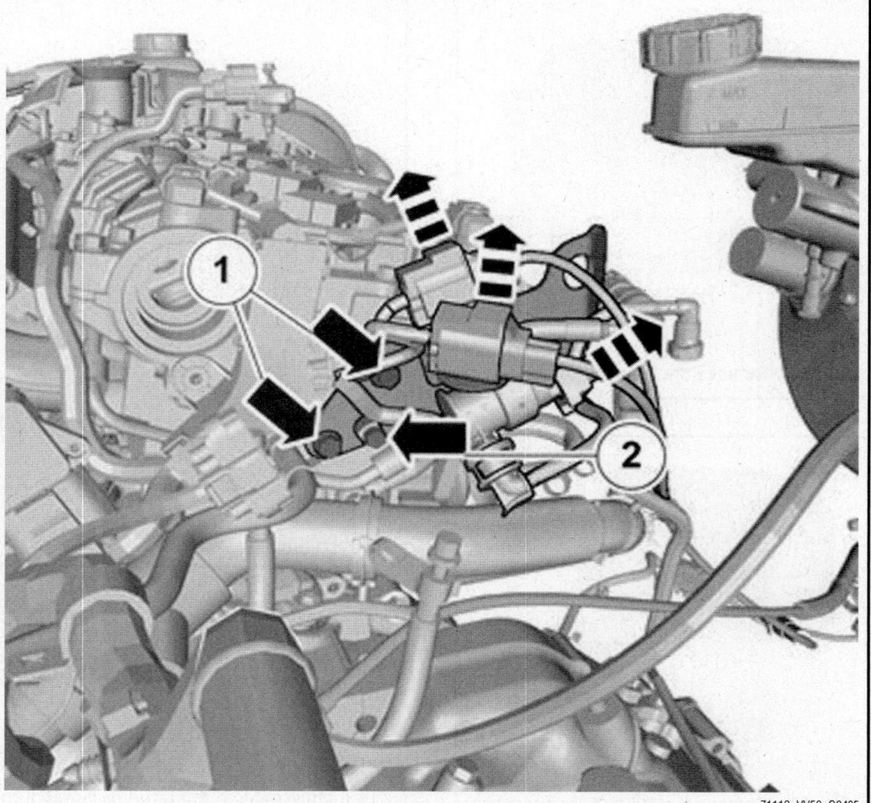

Fig. 138 Remove 2 M10 bolts (1) and M6 bolt (2). Disconnect electrical connectors

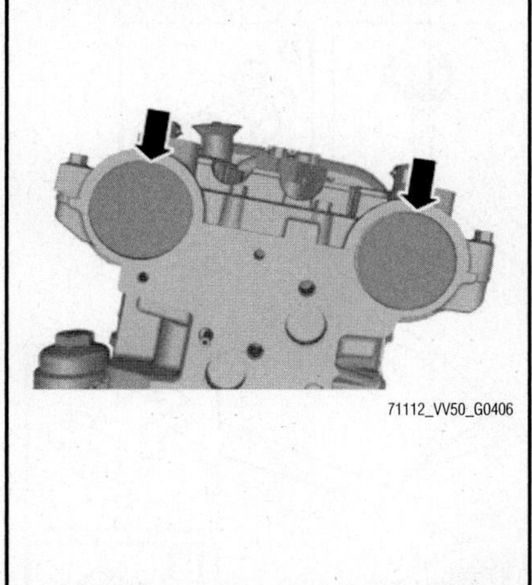

Fig. 139 Remove the camshaft rear caps

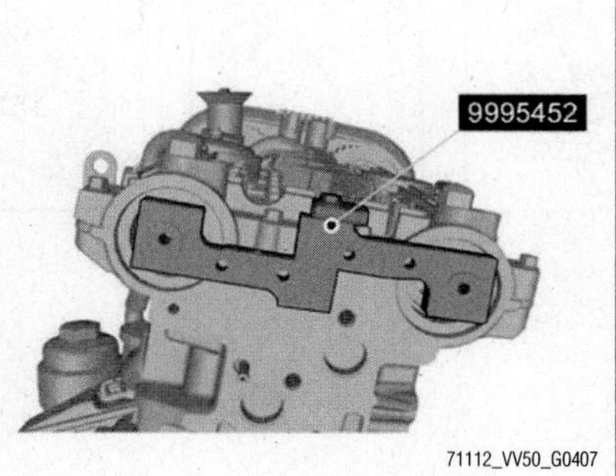

Fig. 140 Install Camshaft Adjustment Tool (999 5452) as shown

Fig. 141 Remove center bolt and sprocket

11. Install camshaft rear caps.
12. Install the bracket:
    - Tighten the M10 bolt to 37 ft. lbs. (50 Nm).
    - Tighten the M6 bolt to 89 inch lbs. (10 Nm).
13. Install the starter motor.
14. Install the timing belt.

WARNING

Ensure that the inside of the pipe ends are clean and free of oil residue.

15. Install the air cleaner assembly hose.

Tighten the M6 bolts to 89 inch lbs. (10 Nm).

16. Install the air cleaner housing.

VALVE LASH CLEARANCE

ADJUSTMENT

➡This step is only necessary when installing a new component.

Adjustment is done by replacing tappets as required to adjust valve clearance (lash).

- Measure the actual clearance between cam lobe and tappet by installing the tappet with the lowest height.

Fig. 142 Install Crankshaft Alignment Adjustment Tool (999 5451)

ENGINE PERFORMANCE & EMISSION CONTROLS

COMPONENT LOCATIONS

See Figure 143.

ACCELERATOR PEDAL POSITION (APP) SENSOR

LOCATION

The Accelerator Pedal Position (APP) sensor is located inside the vehicle and is integral to the accelerator pedal.

REMOVAL & INSTALLATION

See Figure 144.

1. Remove the Accelerator Pedal Position (APP) sensor connector.
2. Remove the 3 mounting nuts.
3. Remove the accelerator pedal assembly.

To install:

4. Install the accelerator pedal assembly and tighten the mounting nuts to 89 inch lbs. (10 Nm).
5. Reconnect the APP sensor connector.

CAMSHAFT POSITION (CMP) SENSOR

LOCATION

The Camshaft Position (CMP) sensor is located in the valve cover under the ignition coil cover.

REMOVAL & INSTALLATION

See Figures 145 through 148.

1. Remove the 2 M6 bolts securing the air cleaner assembly hose.
2. Remove clamp, and position the air cleaner assembly hose aside.
3. Remove the 6 M6 bolts, and remove ignition coil cover.
4. Remove the Camshaft Position (CMP) sensor from the exhaust camshaft:
    a. Disconnect the electrical connector.
    b. Remove the M6 bolt.
    c. Pull out and remove sensor.
5. Remove the Camshaft Position (CMP) sensor from the intake camshaft:
    a. Disconnect the electrical connector.
    b. Remove the M6 bolt.
    c. Pull out and remove sensor.

To install:

To install, reverse the removal procedure and note the following:

- Tighten the M6 bolts to 89 inch lbs. (10 Nm).

CRANKSHAFT POSITION (CKP) SENSOR

LOCATION

The Crankshaft Position (CKP) sensor is located above the flywheel.

REMOVAL & INSTALLATION

See Figure 149.

1. Remove the air cleaner housing.
2. Disconnect and position aside any hoses or lines obstructing access to the Crankshaft Position (CKP) sensor.
3. Remove the CKP sensor:

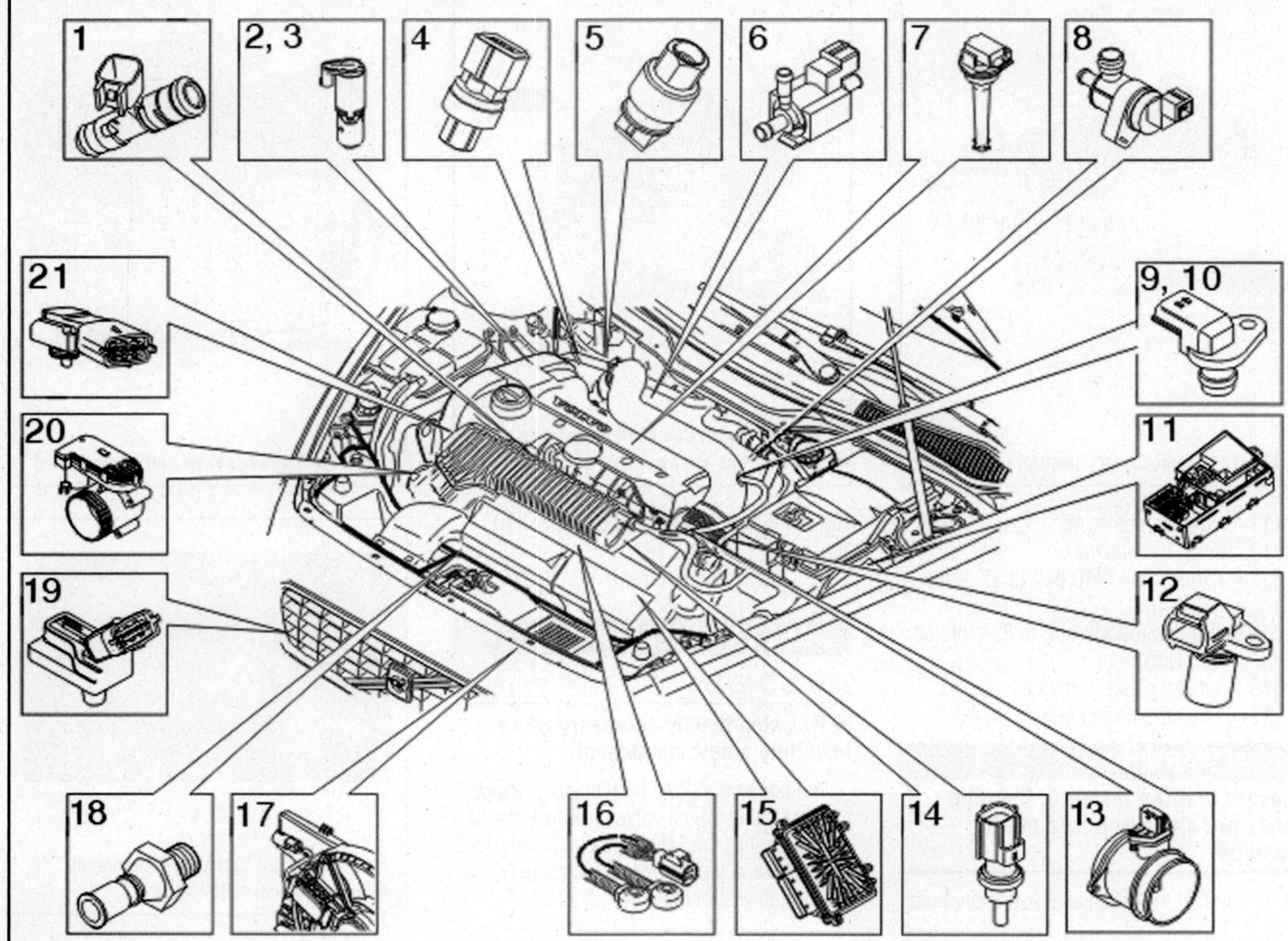

1. Injectors (5)-located on intake manifold
2. Intake camshaft reset valve-located on engine, timing belt side, by camshaft
3. Exhaust camshaft reset valve-located on engine, timing belt side, by camshaft
4. A/C pressure sensor-located on A/C system high pressure pipe (thin pipe)
5. A/C pressure switch-located on A/C system low pressure pipe (thick pipe)
6. Turbocharger (TC) control valve-located on the turbocharger
7. Ignition coil (5)-located on the cylinder head
8. Evaporative emission system (EVAP) valve-located on intake manifold
9. Camshaft Position (CMP) sensor, intake-located on engine, flywheel side, by the camshaft
10. Camshaft Position (CMP) sensor, exhaust-located on engine, flywheel side, by the camshaft
11. Integrated relay/fusebox
12. Engine speed (RPM) sensor-Above the flywheel
13. Mass Air Flow (MAF) sensor-located on the Air Cleaner (ACL) module
14. Engine Coolant Temperature (ECT) sensor-located on the thermostat housing
15. Engine Control Module (ECM)-located on the Air Cleaner (ACL) module
16. Knock Sensor (KS)-located on the cylinder block under the Air Cleaner (ACL) module
17. Engine cooling fan (FC) control module
18. Oil pressure switch-located on lower front edge of the engine
19. Boost pressure sensor-located on the Charge Air Cooler (CAC) upper right-hand section
20. Throttle unit-located on the engine intake manifold
21. Fuel pressure sensor/fuel temperature sensor-located on fuel rail right face

71112_VV50_G0424

Fig. 143 Engine compartment component locations

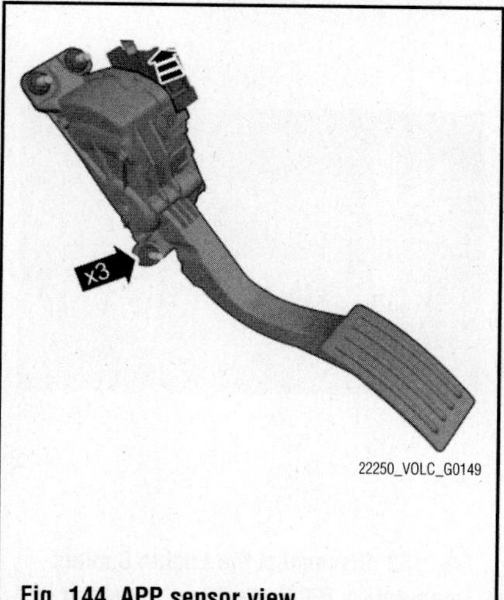

Fig. 144 APP sensor view

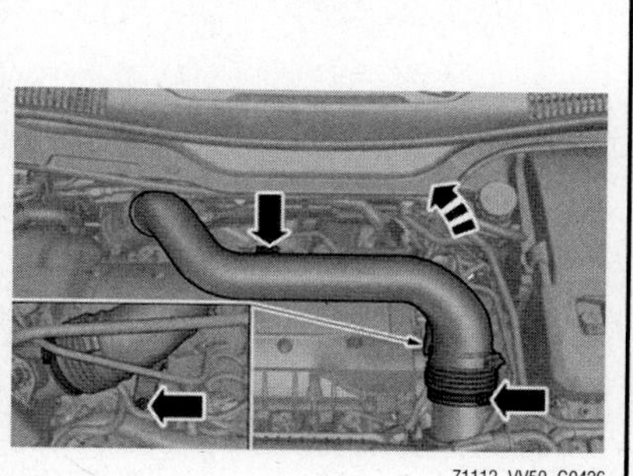

Fig. 145 Position the air cleaner assembly hose aside

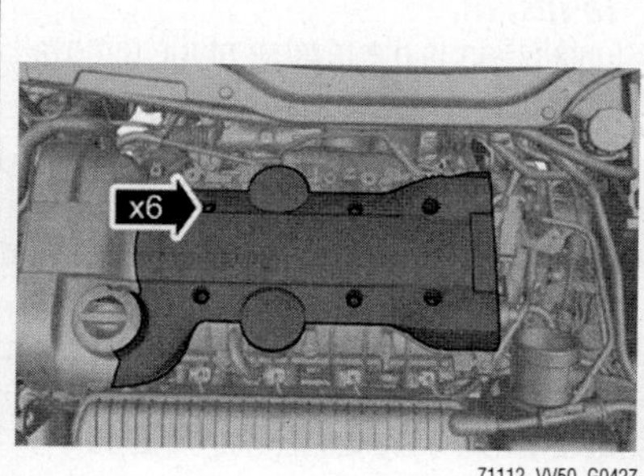

Fig. 146 Remove the 6 M6 bolts, and remove ignition coil cover

a. Disconnect the electrical connector.

b. Remove the bolts.

c. Pull out and remove sensor.

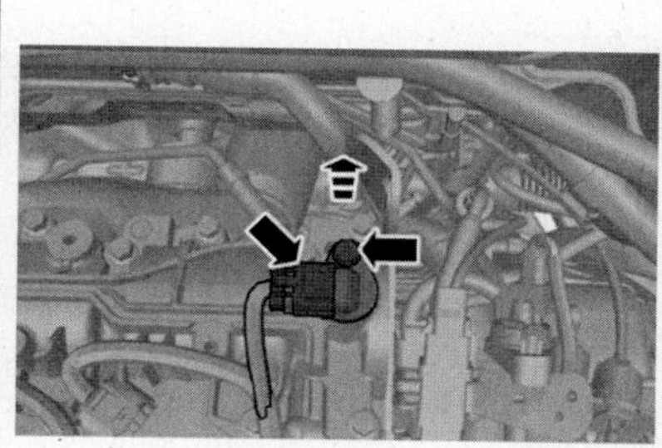

Fig. 147 Remove the Camshaft Position (CMP) sensor from the exhaust camshaft

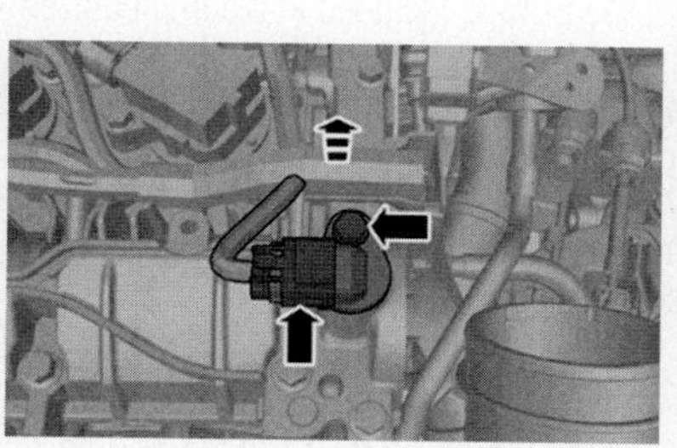

Fig. 148 Remove the Camshaft Position (CMP) sensor from the intake camshaft

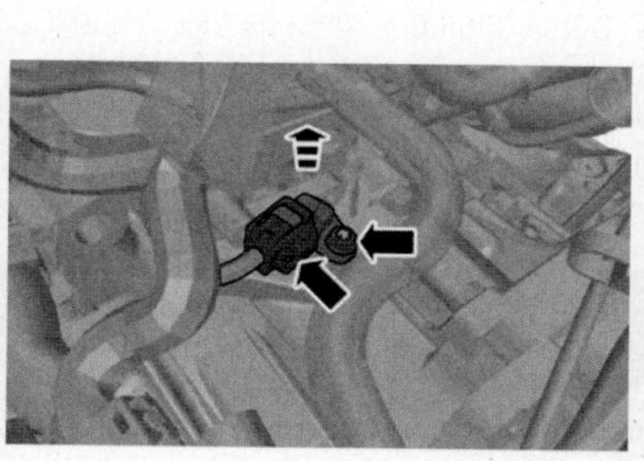

Fig. 149 Remove the Crankshaft Position (CKP) sensor

To install:

4. To install, reverse the removal procedure and note the following:
   - Tighten the M6 bolts to 89 inch lbs. (10 Nm).

5. Start the engine and check the function.

ENGINE CONTROL MODULE (ECM)

LOCATION

The Engine Control Module (ECM) is in the intake system. It is cooled by the engine intake air.

REMOVAL & INSTALLATION

See Figures 150 and 151.

WARNING

A VIDA communications tool will be needed to adapt the throttle body according to vehicle communication input.

Points to observe when replacing the control module:

- New software can only be ordered when the control module is installed in the vehicle. VIDA reads off the new control module identity which is required to order the correct software. The software can only be ordered when the new control module is installed in the car.
- Wait 2 minutes after the ignition has been turned off. The main relay must be voltage-free before the control module can be removed from the car. If the engine cooling fan runs on after the ignition has been switched off, wait until it stops and then wait for another 2 minutes.
- Always check that the control module and control module box connector pins and sleeves are not bent or damaged. This may have caused the presenting fault.

1. Before servicing the vehicle, refer to the Precautions Section.

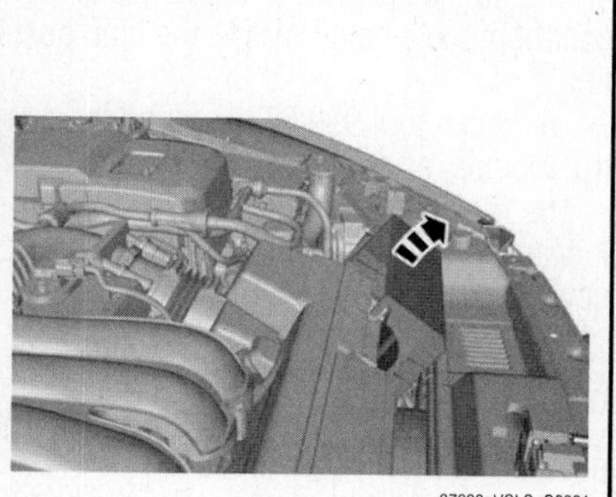

Fig. 150 Remove the cover over the Engine Control Module (ECM)

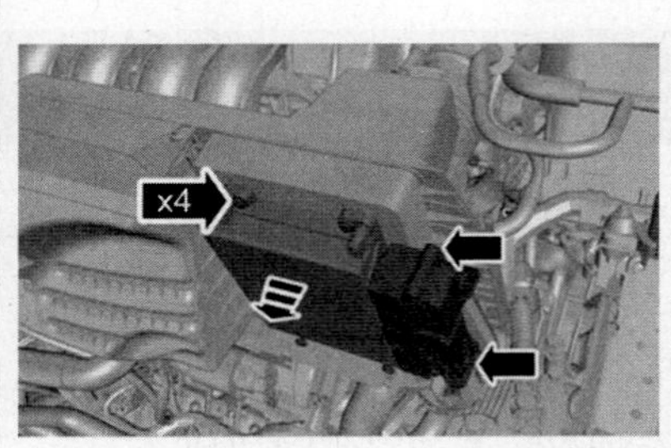

Fig. 151 **Installing the Engine Control Module (ECM)**

2. Turn ignition off. Wait for at least 2 minutes.
3. Remove the cover over the Engine Control Module (ECM). Put the cover to one side.

WARNING

Do not touch the control module terminal pins with your fingers. Static electricity may damage components in the control module.

4. Insert tool 999 5722 around the control module, as needed.
5. Move the upper section of the tool backwards as far as it will go. Pull up the tool.
6. Carefully pull up and remove the ECM.

To install:

7. Check that no pins or sockets are damaged on the connector.

➡Make sure that the seal is correctly located.

8. Carefully press the control module down into the grooves on the inside of the control module box. Press to the limit position.
9. Insert tool 999 5722 around the control module, as needed.
10. Move the upper section of the tool forwards as far as it will go. Pull the tool upwards.
11. Press the cover into place over the control module.
12. Check that the air ducts are correctly positioned.
13. Using VIDA, adapt the throttle body according to vehicle communication input.
14. Check that no Diagnostic Trouble Codes (DTCs) have been stored during the repair.
15. Test drive the vehicle and check the function of the engine.

RESET

When replacing the Engine Control Module (ECM), the hardware number on the control module is read and transmitted to the Volvo central database. The software is compiled depending on the configuration of the vehicle (for example, structure week and hardware number). The software is then transmitted to VIDA and downloading is carried out.

A vehicle identity check, a read off of the vehicles' new configuration for updating the Volvo central database and programming of codes are included in the download sequence. The procedure when updating software is identical except that the hardware number is not read but taken directly from the Volvo central database.

The ECM is included in the immobilizer system and a number of conditions must be met for the control module to approve a start.

Immobilizer code: During a start attempt, the Central Electronic Module (CEM) transmits its immobilizer code and the ECM compares this with its own programmed code. This condition is met if the codes correspond.

Serial number: The serial number for the brake control module (BCM) is programmed into the ECM. During a start attempt the engine control module (ECM) transmits a query to the Brake Control Module (BCM) about which serial number it has programmed in and then compares this with the serial number programmed into the ECM. This condition is met if the serial numbers correspond.

Both conditions must be met to allow a start. When replacing the ECM, both the immobilizer code and serial number are programmed in automatically when downloading software.

ENGINE COOLANT TEMPERATURE (ECT) SENSOR

LOCATION

The ECT sensor is located in the thermostat housing.

REMOVAL & INSTALLATION

See Figures 152 and 153.

1. Before servicing the vehicle, refer to the Precautions Section.
2. Drain the cooling system.
3. Remove the air cleaner housing.
4. Disconnect the Engine Coolant Temperature (ECT) electrical connector.

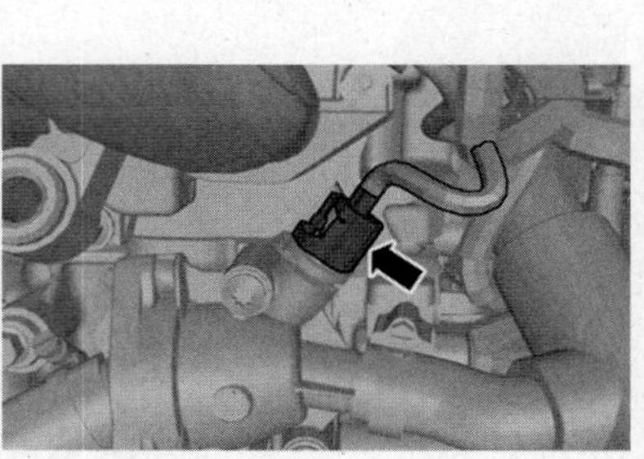

Fig. 152 Disconnect the Engine Coolant Temperature (ECT) electrical connector

Fig. 153 Remove clip and the ECT sensor

5. Remove clip and the ECT sensor.

To install:

Installation is the reverse of the removal procedure.

HEATED OXYGEN (HO2S) SENSOR

LOCATION

The front Heated Oxygen (HO2S) sensor is mounted in the exhaust manifold converter sub-assembly.

The rear HO2S sensor is mounted in the rear converter sub-assembly.

REMOVAL & INSTALLATION

See Figures 154 through 157.

➡The oxygen sensor is also referred to as catalyst monitor sensor.

1. Remove clip, and disconnect the electrical connector.

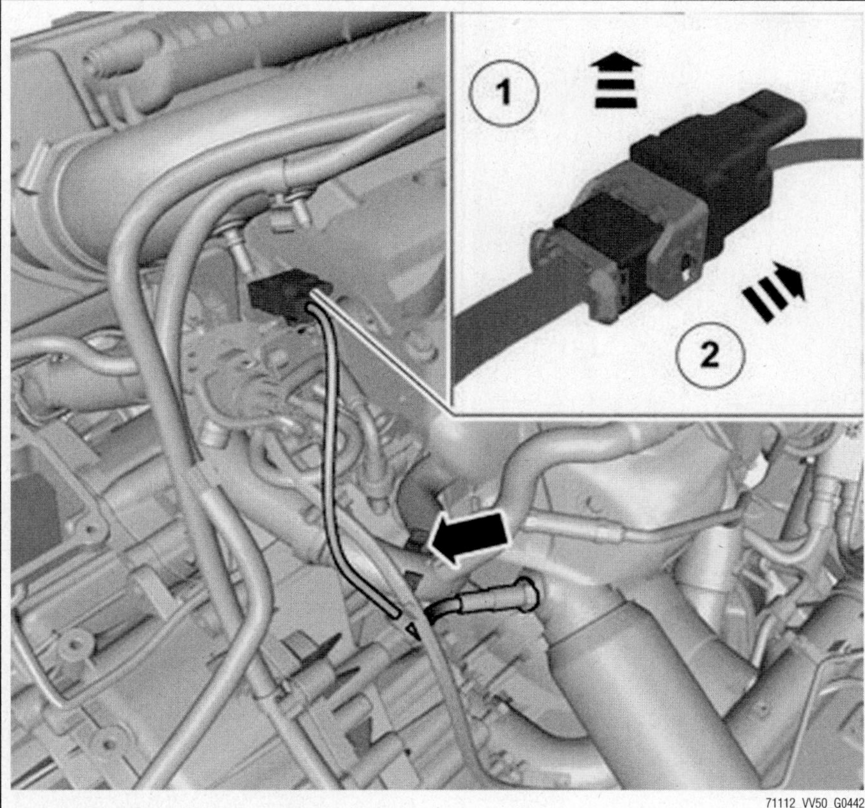

Fig. 154 Remove clip (1), and disconnect the electrical connector (2)

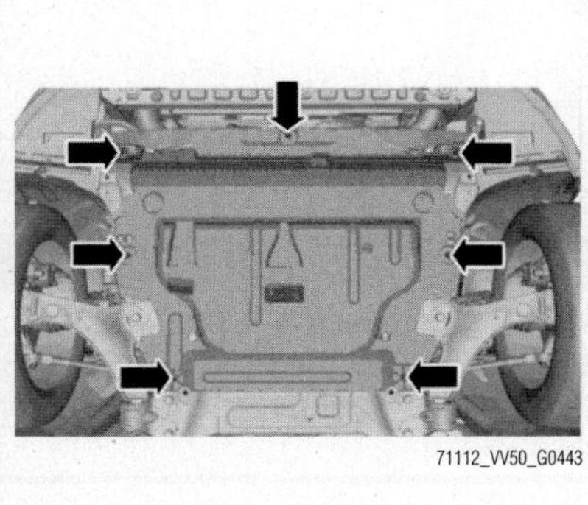

Fig. 155 Remove 7 bolts and the engine splash plate

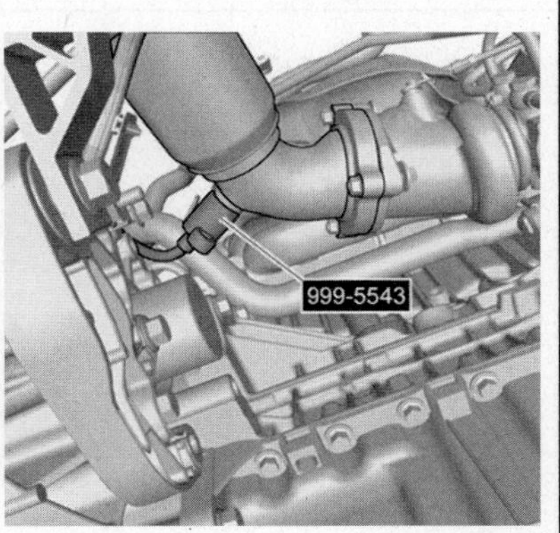

Fig. 156 Using Socket (999 5543), remove front oxygen sensor

2. Raise and support vehicle.
3. Remove 7 bolts and the engine splash plate.
4. Using Socket (999 5543), remove front oxygen sensor.
5. Using socket, remove rear oxygen sensor.

To install:

➡To ensure that there is no exhaust leakage, ensure flanged joint is assembled correctly.

➡All mating surfaces must be thoroughly cleaned. Always replace gaskets, nuts and screws with new ones.

6. When assembling a flanged joint, always ensure:
   - That all mating surfaces are thoroughly cleaned.
   - To replace gaskets, nuts and screws with new ones.
   - That there are not cracks or other damage at the mating surfaces which could result in leakage.
   - That all threads are working correctly.
   - That the gasket faces are flat.
   - Always use Copper Paste (1161 408) where necessary.
7. Installation is the reverse of the removal procedure.
8. Tighten the oxygen sensors to 33 ft. lbs. (45 Nm).

INTAKE AIR TEMPERATURE (IAT)/MANIFOLD ABSOLUTE PRESSURE (MAP) SENSOR

LOCATION

The Intake Air Temperature/Manifold Absolute Pressure (MAPT) sensor is located under the front bumper cover.

REMOVAL & INSTALLATION

See Figure 158.

1. Remove front bumper cover. See Bumper Covers, removal & installation.
2. Remove the Intake Air Temperature/ Manifold Absolute Pressure (MAPT) sensor:
   a. Disconnect the electrical connector.
   b. Remove the bolt.
   c. Remove sensor.

To install:

Installation is the reverse of the removal procedure.

KNOCK SENSOR (KS)

LOCATION

The Knock (KS) sensors are mounted on the left and the right front of the engine block below the intake manifold.

REMOVAL & INSTALLATION

1. Remove the air filter module.
2. Remove the screws for the Knock Sensor (KS).
3. Remove KS.
4. Disconnect the KS connector.

To install:

5. Reconnect the KS connector.
6. Install the KS.
7. Tighten the mounting bolt to 15 ft. lbs. (20 Nm).

MASS AIR FLOW (MAF) SENSOR

LOCATION

The Mass Air Flow (MAF) sensor is located on the air cleaner housing.

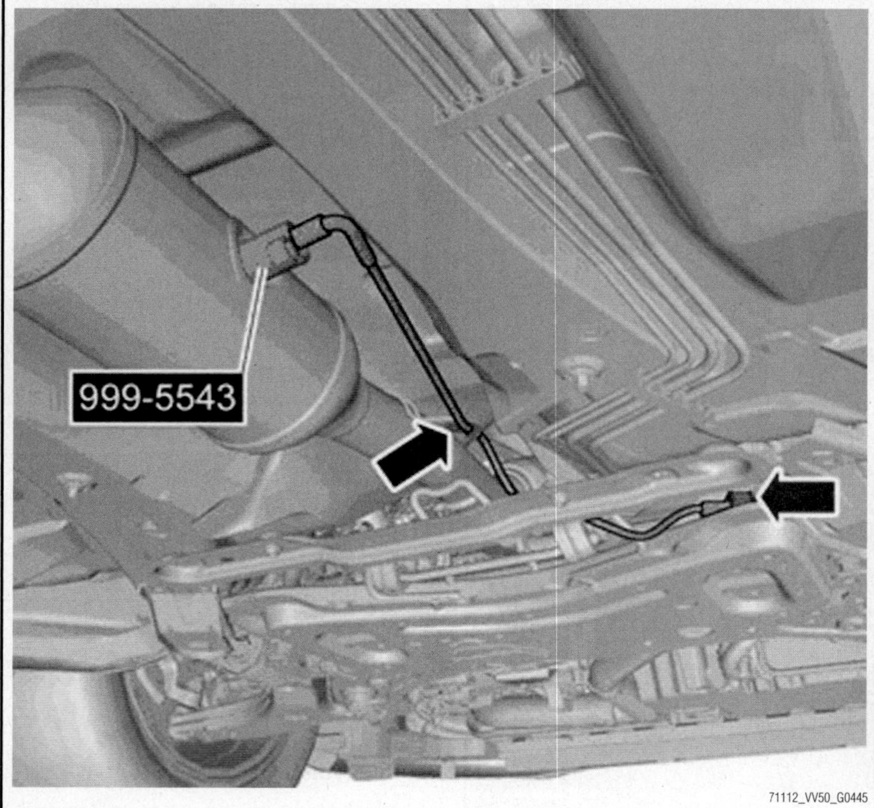

Fig. 157 Using socket, remove rear oxygen sensor

Fig. 158 Remove the Intake Air Temperature/Manifold Absolute Pressure (MAPT) sensor

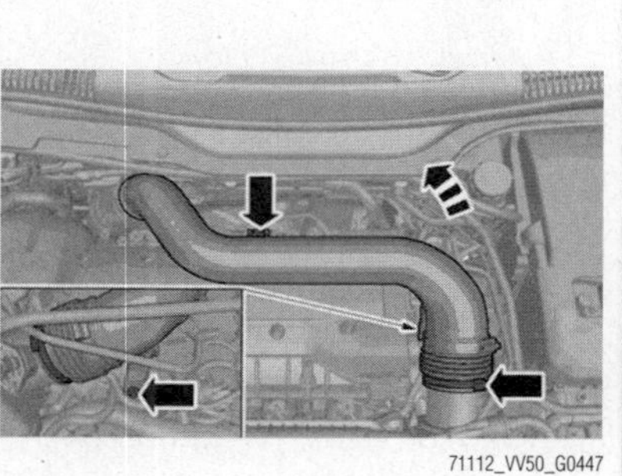

Fig. 159 Position the air cleaner assembly hose aside

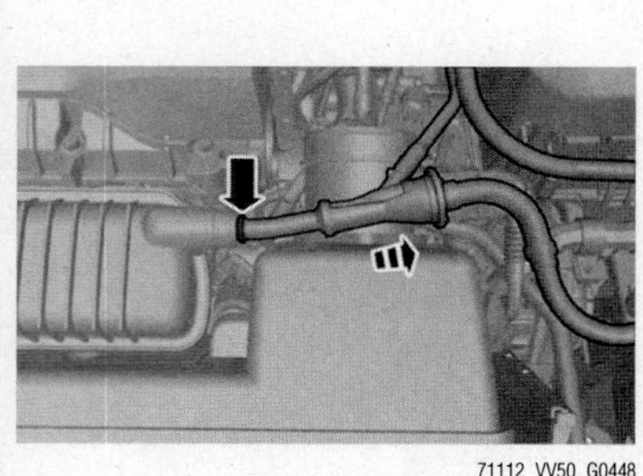

Fig. 160 Disconnect hoses from intake manifold, and position aside

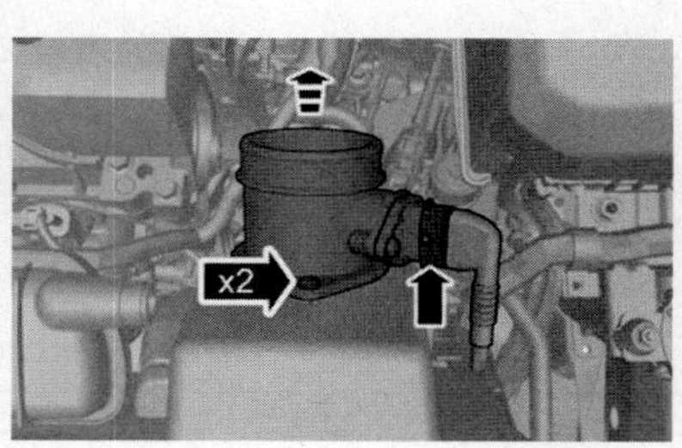

Fig. 161 Remove the Mass Air Flow (MAF) sensor

REMOVAL & INSTALLATION

See Figures 159 through 160.

1. Remove the 2 M6 bolts securing the air cleaner assembly hose.
2. Remove clamp, and position the air cleaner assembly hose aside.
3. Disconnect hoses from intake manifold, and position aside.
4. Remove the Mass Air Flow (MAF) sensor:
   a. Disconnect the electrical connector.
   b. Remove the 2 bolts.
   c. Pull out and remove sensor.

To install:

To install, reverse the removal procedure and note the following:

- Tighten the M6 bolts to 89 inch lbs. (10 Nm).

TRANSMISSION CONTROL MODULE (TCM)

REMOVAL & INSTALLATION

See Figures 162 and 163.

**** WARNING**

When this procedure is completed, software will be required to be downloaded from the Volvo central database.

**** WARNING**

The software can only be ordered when the control module is installed in the vehicle. VIDA reads off the new control module identity which is required to order the correct software.

**** WARNING**

Wait one minute after the ignition has been switched off. The main relay must be voltage free before the control module can be removed from the car. If the engine cooling fan runs on after the ignition has been

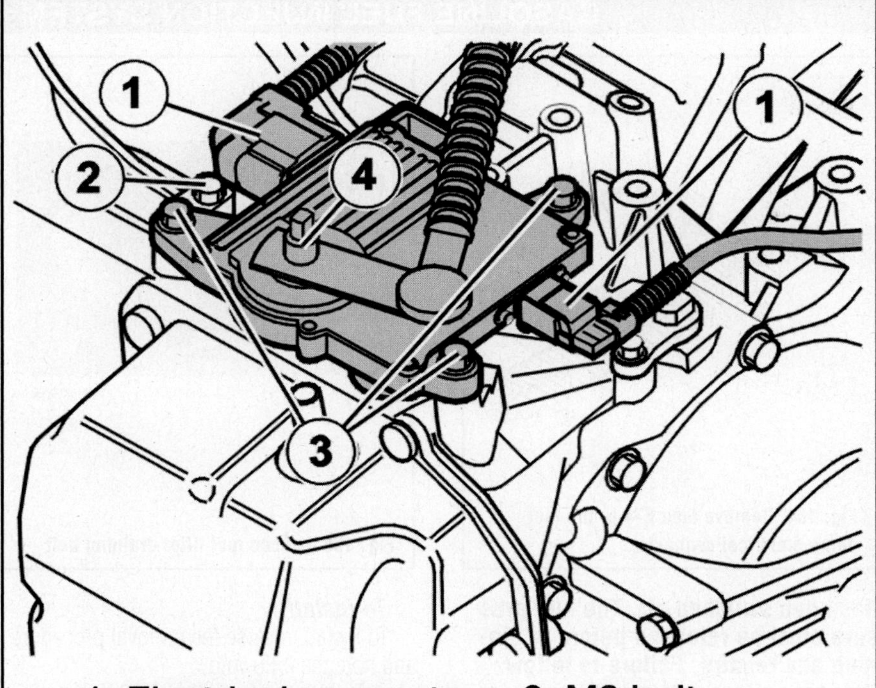

Fig. 162 Remove the Transmission Control Module (TCM)

switched off, wait until it stops. Then wait a further minute.

1. Turn ignition off.
2. Shift the gear selector lever to Neutral.
3. Disconnect the negative battery cable.
4. Remove the Air Cleaner (ACL) module.

WARNING

Do not touch the control module terminal pins with your fingers. Static electricity (electric static discharge - ESD) may damage components in the control module.

5. Remove the Transmission Control Module (TCM):
   a. Disconnet the 2 electrical connectors.
   b. Remove the M8 bolt for the bracket.
   c. Remove the bracket.
   d. Remove the 3 M8 bolts.
   e. Remove the nut.

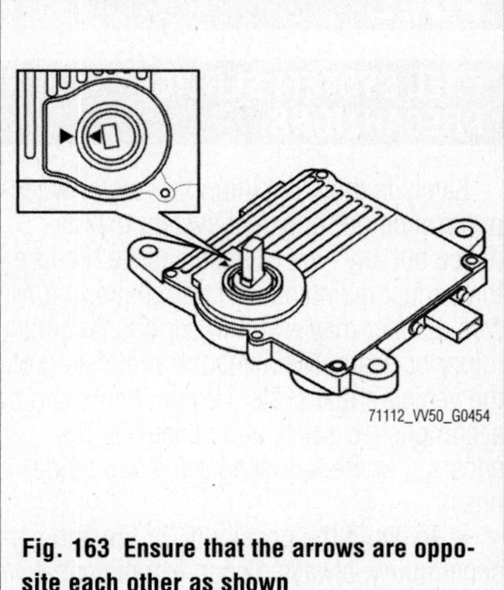

Fig. 163 Ensure that the arrows are opposite each other as shown

   f. Remove the lever.
   g. Remove the control module. Do not damage the terminal pins.

To install:

➡Ensure that the arrows are opposite each other as shown.

➡Shift the gear selector lever to Neutral.

6. To complete installation, reverse the removal procedure and note the following:
   - Do not damage the terminal pins of the module.
   - Tighten the M8 bolts to 18 ft. lbs. (24 Nm).
7. Order and download software 30667212 from the Volvo central database.
8. Check that no Diagnostic Trouble Codes (DTCs) have been stored during the repair.
9. Calibrate the gear-shift position sensor according to VIDA vehicle communication tool.

FUEL SYSTEM SERVICE PRECAUTIONS

Safety is the most important factor when performing not only fuel system maintenance but any type of maintenance. Failure to conduct maintenance and repairs in a safe manner may result in serious personal injury or death. Maintenance and testing of the vehicle's fuel system components can be accomplished safely and effectively by adhering to the following rules and guidelines.

- To avoid the possibility of fire and personal injury, always disconnect the negative battery cable unless the repair or test procedure requires that battery voltage be applied.
- Always relieve the fuel system pressure prior to disconnecting any fuel system component (injector, fuel rail, pressure regulator, etc.), fitting or fuel line connection. Exercise extreme caution whenever relieving fuel system pressure to avoid exposing skin, face and eyes to fuel spray. Please be advised that fuel under pressure may penetrate the skin or any part of the body that it contacts.
- Always place a shop towel or cloth around the fitting or connection prior to loosening to absorb any excess fuel due to spillage. Ensure that all fuel spillage (should it occur) is quickly removed from engine surfaces. Ensure that all fuel soaked cloths or towels are deposited into a suitable waste container.
- Always keep a dry chemical (Class B) fire extinguisher near the work area.
- Do not allow fuel spray or fuel vapors to come into contact with a spark or open flame.
- Always use a back-up wrench when loosening and tightening fuel line connection fittings. This will prevent unnecessary stress and torsion to fuel line piping.
- Always replace worn fuel fitting O-rings with new Do not substitute fuel hose or equivalent where fuel pipe is installed.

Before servicing the vehicle, make sure to also refer to the precautions in the beginning of this section as well.

RELIEVING FUEL SYSTEM PRESSURE

See Figure 164.

CAUTION

The fuel system remains under pressure for a long time after the ignition has been switched off. The fuel pressure must be released before beginning any repairs. Failure to follow the instructions can result in personal injury.

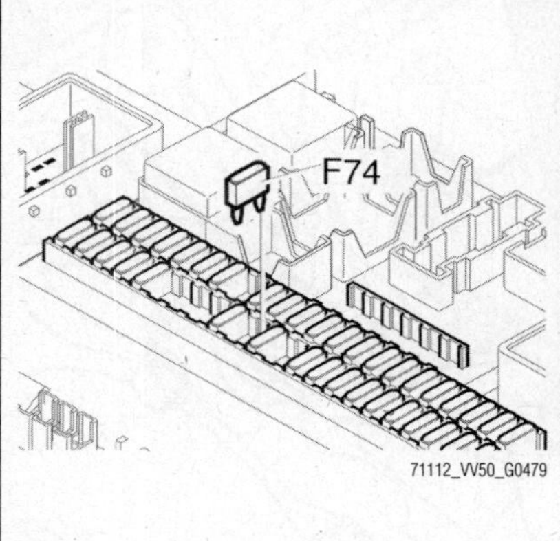

Fig. 164 Remove fuse F74 or the fuel pump electrical connector

1. Before servicing the vehicle, refer to the Precautions Section.
2. Remove fuse F74 or the fuel pump electrical connector.
3. Start the engine and allow it to idle until it stops.
4. Turn the engine using the starter motor for approximately 5 seconds until the pressure in the fuel rail has been released.

FUEL FILTER

REMOVAL & INSTALLATION

Standard Fuel Filter

See Figure 165.

WARNING

Make sure that the fuel tank is no more than 3/4 full.

1. Before servicing the vehicle, refer to the Precautions Section.
2. Relieve the fuel system pressure.

WARNING

Be prepared to collect escaping fluid.

➡Do not loosen the fuel filter draining bolt more than 4 turns.

3. Loosen fuel filter draining bolt.
4. Using Spanner (981 4098), remove fuel filter.

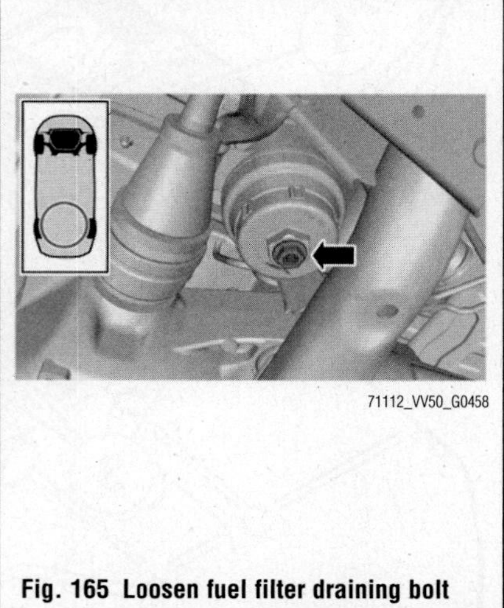

Fig. 165 Loosen fuel filter draining bolt

To install:

To install, reverse the removal procedure and note the following:

- Tighten the fuel filter to 18 ft. lbs. (25 Nm).
- Tighten the fuel filter draining bolt to 18 inch lbs. (2 Nm).

Extra Fuel Filter

See Figure 166.

1. Before servicing the vehicle, refer to the Precautions Section.
2. Relieve the fuel system pressure.

➡Place a tray or similar under the filter to capture any spillage.

WARNING

Extreme cleanliness must be exercised when handling these components.

Fig. 166 Remove the filter

3. Remove:
   - the M8 bolt for the clamp around the filter.
   - the quick-release connectors for the pipes.
   - the filter.

To install:

To install, reverse the removal procedure and note the following:

- Tighten the M8 bolt to 18 ft. lbs. (24 Nm).

FUEL PUMP MODULE

REMOVAL & INSTALLATION

See Figures 167 through 169.

1. Before servicing the vehicle, refer to the Precautions Section.
2. Relieve the fuel system pressure.
3. Remove the fuel tank.
4. Remove the level sensor on the left-hand side.

**** WARNING**

Ensure that the lever on the level sensor is not damaged when removing the pump.

**** WARNING**

When removing the plastic nut, ensure that the level sensor is not turned with it.

5. Release the 2 catches. Using Wrench (999 7111, 999 7093), remove the plastic nut.
6. Remove the fuel pump.

➡The following step applies to vehicles equipped with auxiliary heater.

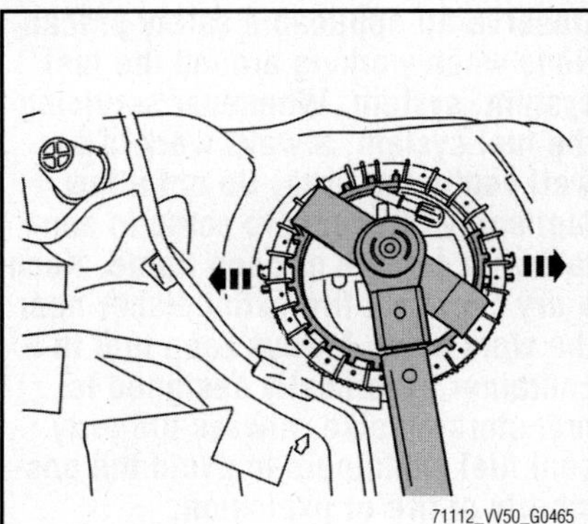

Fig. 167 Release the 2 catches. Using Wrench (999 7111, 999 7093), remove the plastic nut

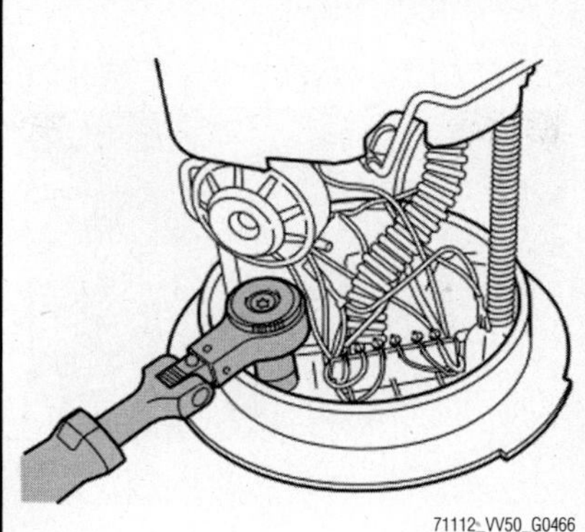

Fig. 168 Using a 9-mm socket, remove the plug for the suction line

7. Using a 9-mm socket, remove the plug for the suction line from the underside of the level sensor. Transfer the suction line to the new fuel pump.

To install:

**** WARNING**

Do not damage the lever on the level sensor during installation.

**** WARNING**

When installing the plastic nut, ensure that the level sensor is not turned with it.

8. Install a new O-ring.
9. Insert the hose for the fuel pump from the right-hand to the left-hand side of the tank.
10. Install the fuel pump.
11. Using Wrench (999 7111, 999 7093), tighten the plastic nut.

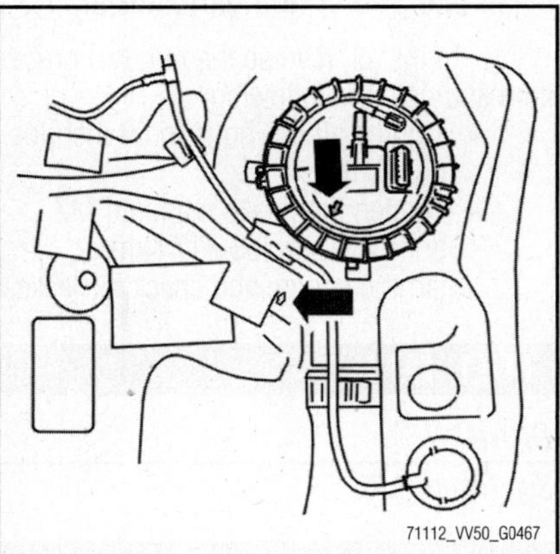

Fig. 169 The marking on the fuel pump must be opposite the marking on the fuel tank

➡The marking on the fuel pump must be opposite the marking on the fuel tank.

12. Install a new O-ring on the fuel level sending unit.
13. Install the level sensor on the left-hand side.
14. Install the fuel tank.
15. Start engine and check for leaks.

FUEL RAIL & INJECTORS

REMOVAL & INSTALLATION

See Figures 170 through 175.

1. Before servicing the vehicle, refer to the Precautions Section.
2. Relieve the fuel system pressure.
3. Disconnect the negative battery cable.
4. Remove the air cleaner housing.
5. Remove the hose clamp for the rubber hose on the throttle body. Move the hose to one side.

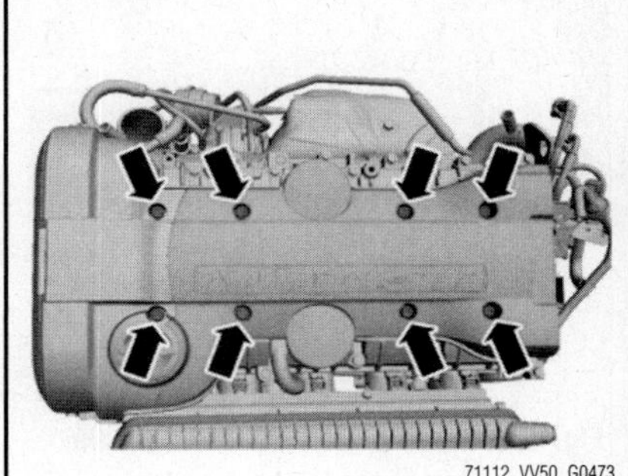

Fig. 170 Remove the 8 M6 bolts for the top timing belt and the ignition coil covers

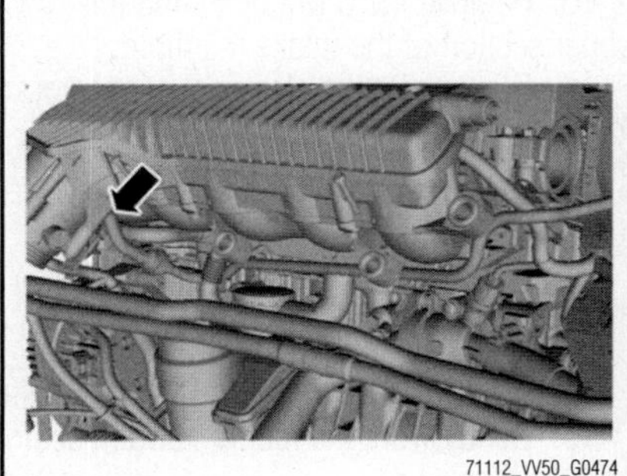

Fig. 171 Remove the fuel delivery pipe

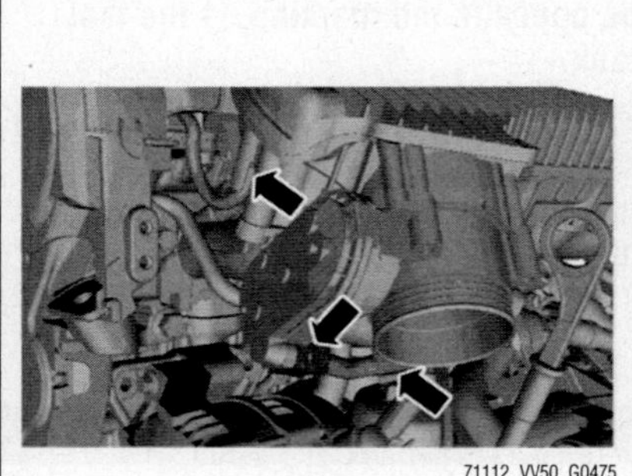

Fig. 172 Disconnect the electrical connector, and remove hoses

Fig. 173 Remove the 6 M7 bolts and the upper section of the intake manifold

6. Disconnect the throttle body connector.
7. Remove the 8 M6 bolts for the top timing belt and the ignition coil covers.
8. Remove the fuel delivery pipe.
9. Disconnect the electrical connector, and remove hoses.
10. Remove the 6 M7 bolts and the upper section of the intake manifold.
11. Disconnect the electrical connectors for the fuel pressure sensor and the 5 fuel injectors.
12. Remove the 2 fuel rail mounting bolts.
13. Spray with universal oil or similar around the injector nozzle where it seats into the intake manifold.
14. Disconnect the fuel line to the fuel rail.
15. Gently work the fuel rail and injector nozzles loose.
16. Press in the button, and pull out the 2 blue clips on the fuel rail.
17. Pull the fuel line out of the fuel rail.
18. Remove the screws holding the mounting rail to the fuel rail.

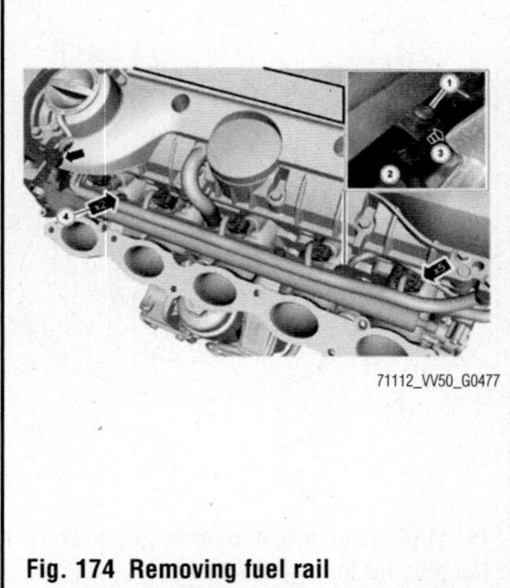

Fig. 174 Removing fuel rail

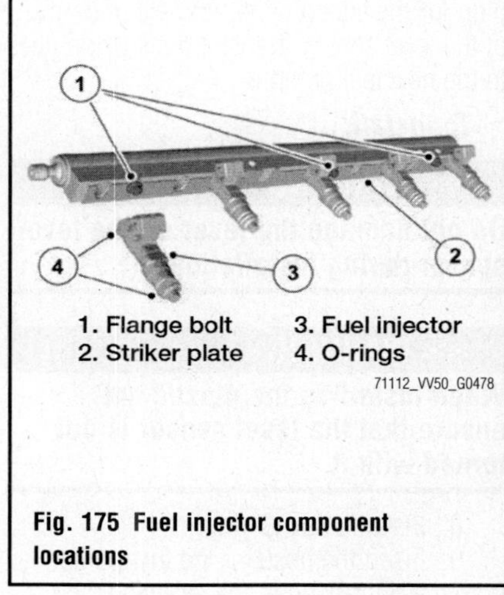

Fig. 175 Fuel injector component locations

19. Remove the mounting rail.
20. Remove the fuel injector.

To install:

➡Make sure that the mating faces are clean and free of foreign material.

21. To install, reverse the removal procedure and note the following:
    - Tighten all M6 bolts to 89 inch lbs. (10 Nm).
    - Tighten the intake manifold M7 bolts to 13 ft. lbs. (17 Nm).
22. Start the engine and check for leaks.

FUEL TANK

DRAINING

See Figure 176.

CAUTION

There is risk of explosion. Use a fresh air mask.

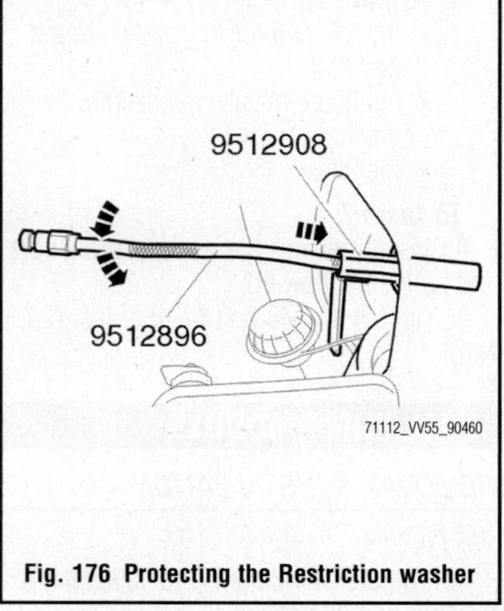

Fig. 176 Protecting the Restriction washer

1. Disconnect the battery negative cable.
2. Insert the Hose (951 2896) with Protective Pipe (to protect the restriction washer in the fuel filler pipe).
3. Turn the hose while sliding it downwards so that it clears any obstacles.
4. Connect the hose to a fuel extractor.
5. Pump until air comes out.

CAUTION

Always follow the instructions for the fuel extractor to avoid accidents.

6. Remove the hose.

WARNING

Carefully pull out the hose to prevent damage to the evacuation valve.

REMOVAL & INSTALLATION

See Figures 177 through 180.

CAUTION

Observe all applicable safety precautions when working around the fuel system. system. Whenever servicing the fuel system, always work in a well ventilated area. Do not allow fuel spray or vapors to come in contact with a spark or open flame. Keep a dry chemical fire extinguisher near the work area. Always keep fuel in a container specifically designed for fuel storage; also, always properly seal fuel containers to avoid the possibility of fire or explosion.

1. Before servicing the vehicle, refer to the Precautions Section.
2. Relieve the fuel system pressure.
3. Drain the fuel tank.

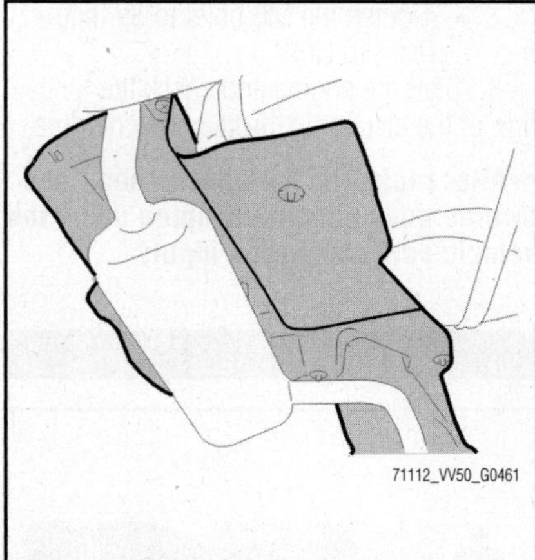

Fig. 177 Remove the 7 plastic nuts and the heat deflector plate

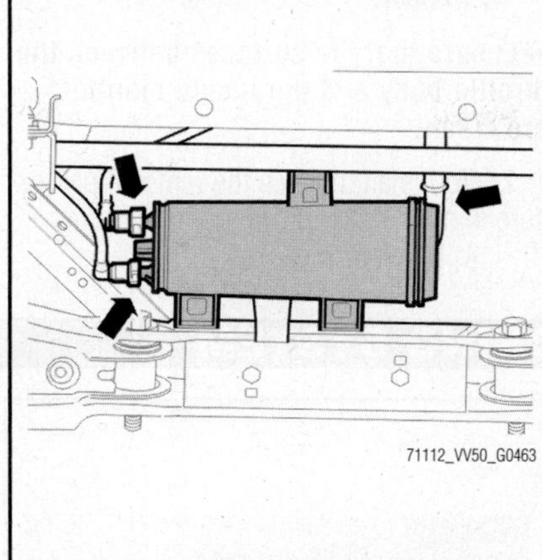

Fig. 179 Remove the carbon filter container

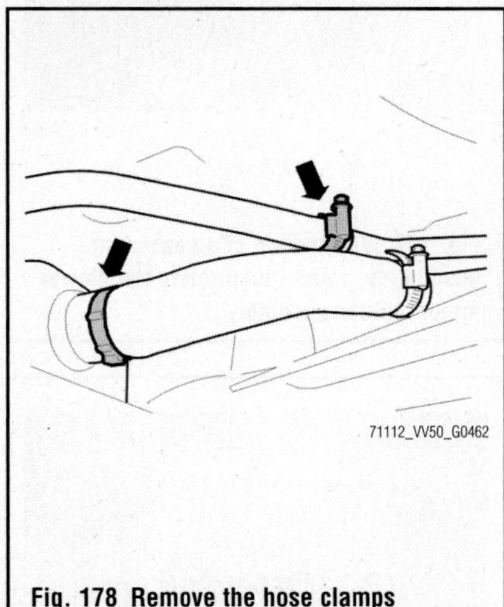

Fig. 178 Remove the hose clamps

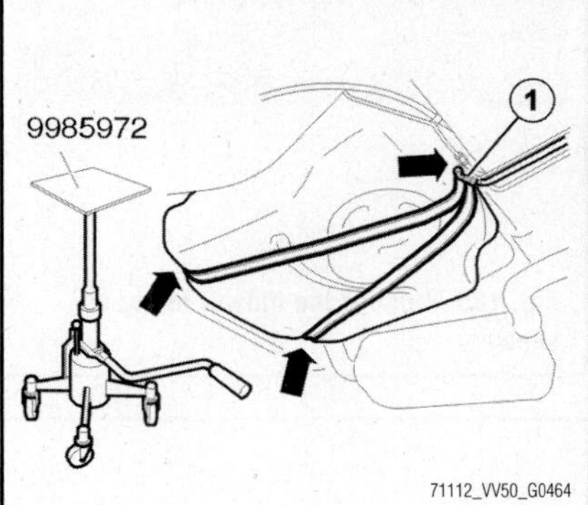

Fig. 180 Install a mobile jack with Fixture (999 5972) under the fuel tank. Disconnect the fuel connection (1)

4. Detach the exhaust system at the three-way catalytic converter (TWC) and at the rubber mountings.

➡Hang the exhaust system to one side.

➡Support the front section of the exhaust pipe so as not to put strain on the exhaust manifold.

5. Remove the 7 plastic nuts and the heat deflector plate.
6. Remove:
   - the hose clamp for the evacuation pipe at the fuel tank.
   - the hose clamp for the hose to the fuel filler pipe.

➡Carefully detach the hose from the fuel filler pipe, as there may be fuel left in the tank.

7. Remove or disconnect the following:
   - The hose
   - The 2 pipes, secured using quick-release connectors
   - The carbon filter container
8. Remove the fuel tank:
   a. Install a mobile jack with Fixture (999 5972) under the fuel tank.
   b. Disconnect the fuel connection.
   c. Remove the screws for the 3 fuel tank straps.
   d. Remove the tank retaining straps. Lower the tank slightly.
   e. Disconnect the level sensor connector.
   f. Lower the tank.
9. Remove the fuel pump.

To install:

10. Install the fuel pump.
11. Place the fuel tank on the mobile jack together with Fixture (999 5972).
12. Raise the tank so that it is 12 inches (30 cm) from the top.
13. Connect the connector for the level sensor.
14. Lift up the fuel tank.
15. Install or connect the following:
   - The tank retaining straps. Tighten the 3 M8 screws to 18 ft. lbs. (24 Nm).
   - The fuel connection.
   - The hose clamp for the evacuation pipe at the fuel tank
   - The hose clamp on the hose for the fuel filler pipe.
16. Install the hose, 2 pipes and carbon filter container.
17. Install the 7 plastic nuts and the heat deflector plate.
18. Attach the exhaust system at the three-way catalytic converter (TWC) and at the rubber mountings.
19. Top up the fuel.
20. Install the fuse for the fuel pump.

THROTTLE BODY

REMOVAL & INSTALLATION

See Figures 181 and 182.

⁂ WARNING

A VIDA communications tool will be needed to adapt the throttle body using the vehicle communication input.

1. Before servicing the vehicle, refer to the Precautions Section.
2. Disconnect the negative battery cable.

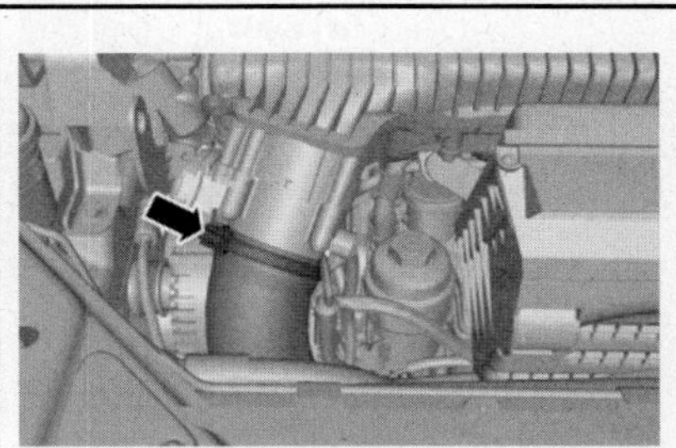

Fig. 181 Remove the clamp and the air inlet hose

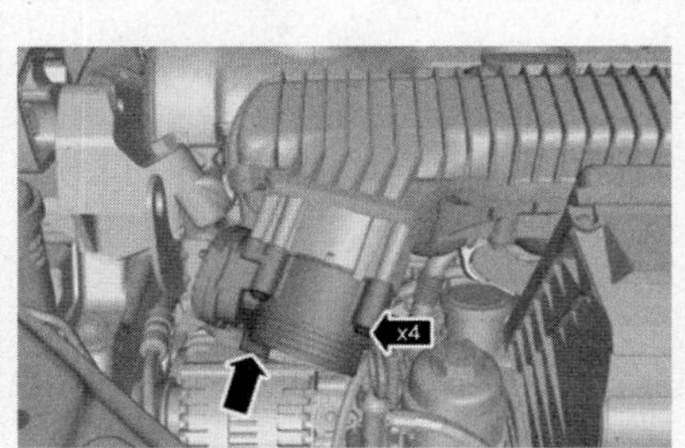

Fig. 182 Remove the 4 M6 bolts, then lift out and remove the throttle body

3. Remove the clamp and the air inlet hose.

4. Disconnect the connector for the throttle body.

5. Remove the 4 M6 bolts, then lift out and remove the throttle body.

6. Discard the gasket.

To install:

➡Ensure that the surfaces between the throttle body and the intake manifold are clean.

7. To install, reverse the removal procedure and note the following:

- Use a new gasket.
- Tighten the M6 bolts to 89 inch lbs. (10 Nm).

8. Start the engine and check the function of the electronic throttle body module.

➡After replacing the throttle body, the throttle body must be adapted using the vehicle communication input.

HEATING & AIR CONDITIONING SYSTEM

BLOWER MOTOR

REMOVAL & INSTALLATION

See Figures 183 through 188.

➡This procedure will require 2 or more

1. Before servicing the vehicle, refer to the Precautions Section.

2. Remove the glove compartment.

3. Remove the control module relay box.

4. Disconnect the 2 blower motor electrical connectors, and position aside.

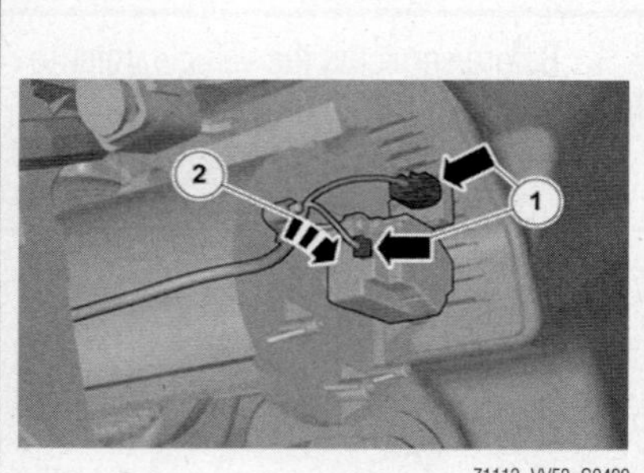

Fig. 183 Disconnect the 2 blower motor electrical connectors, and position aside

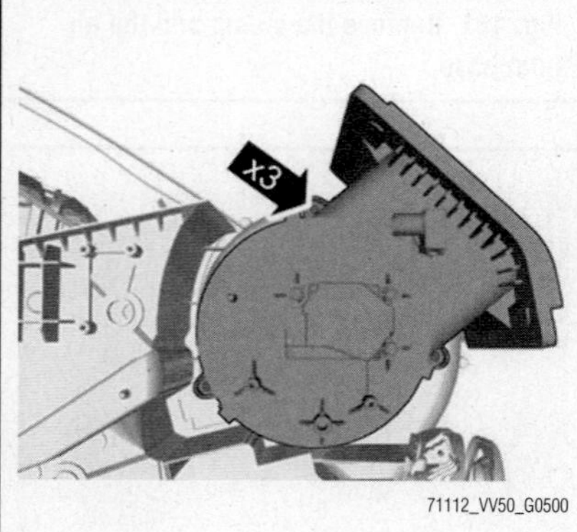

Fig. 184 Remove the 3 bolts securing the blower motor

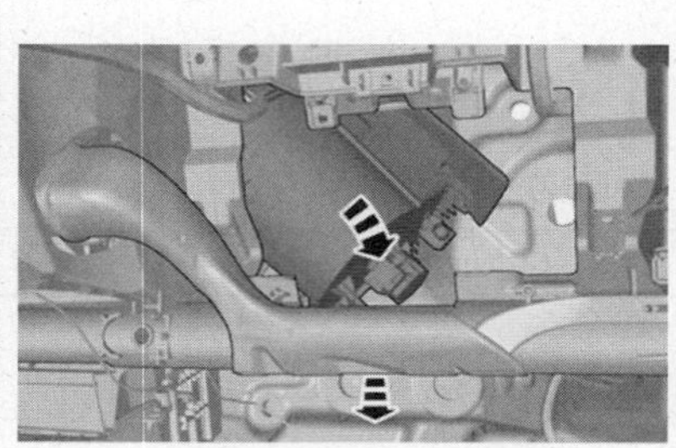

Fig. 185 Remove the blower motor as shown

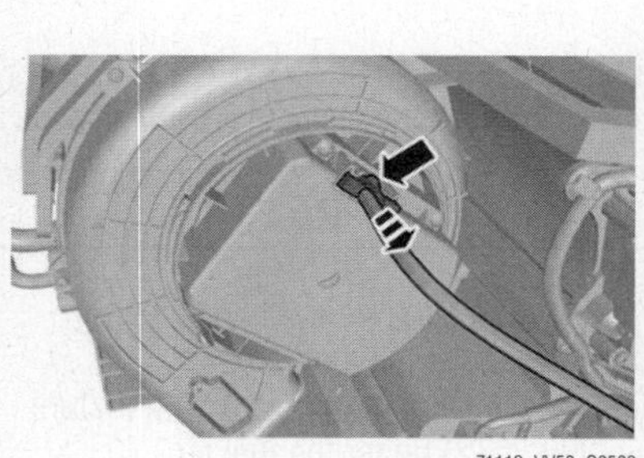

Fig. 186 Disconnect the blower motor electrical connector

5. Remove the 3 bolts securing the blower motor.

6. Remove the blower motor as shown.

7. Remove the lower instrument panel.

8. Disconnect the blower motor electrical connector.

9. With the aid of an assistant, push in tab, rotate, then rotate the blower motor and fan assembly.

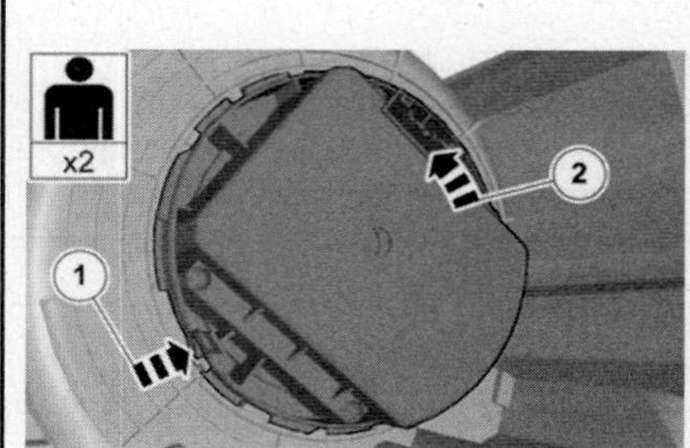

Fig. 187 With the aid of an assistant, push in tab, rotate, then rotate the blower motor and fan assembly

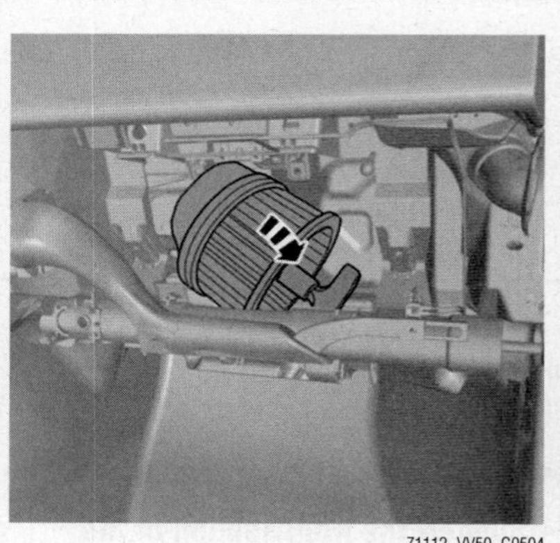

Fig. 188 Using Counterhold (999 7115), remove the blower motor and fan assembly

⁂ WARNING

Make sure that the blower motor and fan assembly is placed on the bench with the fan pointing upwards.

10. Using Counterhold (999 7115), remove the blower motor and fan assembly.

To install:

Installation is the reverse of the removal procedure.

HEATER CORE

REMOVAL & INSTALLATION

See Figures 00, 189 through 193.

➡This component may also be referred to as a heat exchanger.

1. Before servicing the vehicle, refer to the Precautions Section.
2. Turn ignition off.
3. Drain the refrigerant from the A/C system.
4. Remove the cover for the expansion tank and raise the vehicle.
5. Remove 7 bolts and the engine splash plate.
6. Attach a hose on the nipple at the radiator and lower the hose to a container.
7. Open the nipple and drain off the coolant.
8. Lower the vehicle.
9. Detach the radiator hoses from the engine compartment.

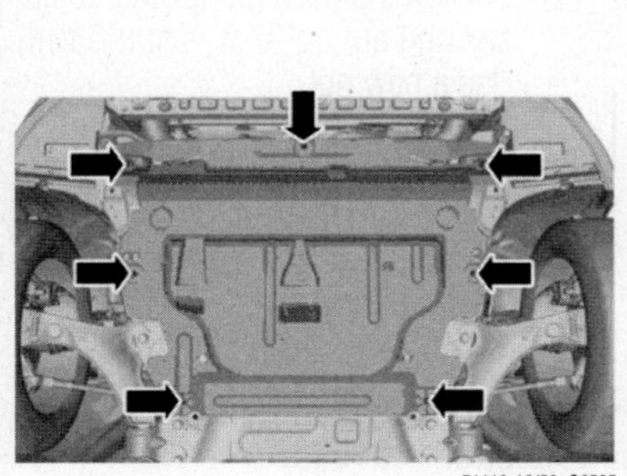

Fig. 189 Remove 7 bolts and the engine splash plate

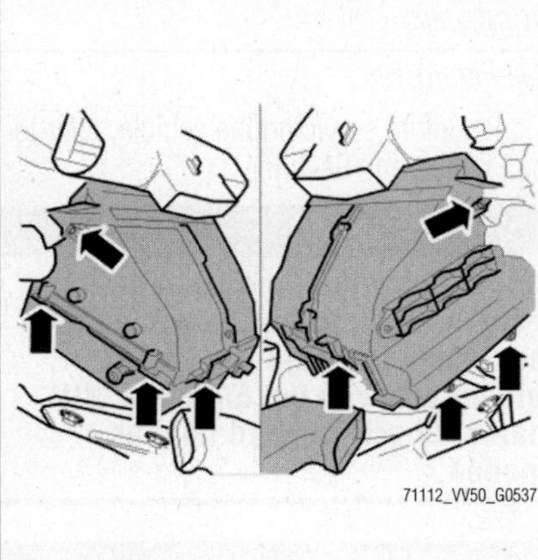

Fig. 190 Remove the 8 bolts for the heater core cover

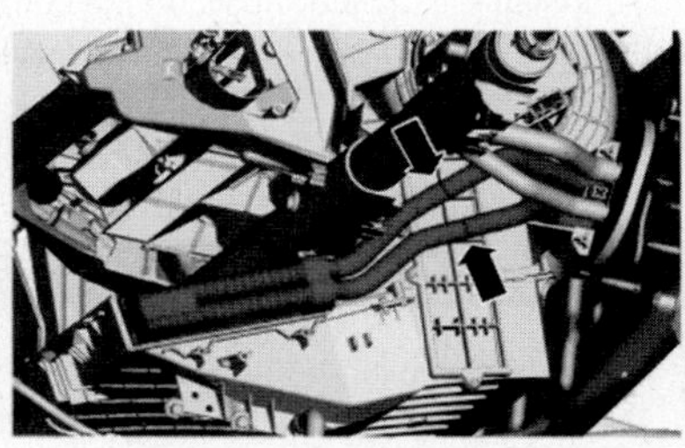

Fig. 191 The heater core has pipes that are factory integrated. These pipes must be cut in order to remove the unit

10. Turn the radiator hose connection counter-clockwise to the end position, and then pull off the radiator hose.
11. Remove the center console.
12. Remove the glove compartment.
13. Detach the control module relay box from its bracket, but allow it to hang from the wiring.
14. Perform the following:
    - Remove the 3 bolts and the bracket on both sides of the Climate Control Module (CCM)
    - Remove the air duct
    - Remove the 8 bolts for the heater core cover
    - Pull the cover at an angle downwards/backwards

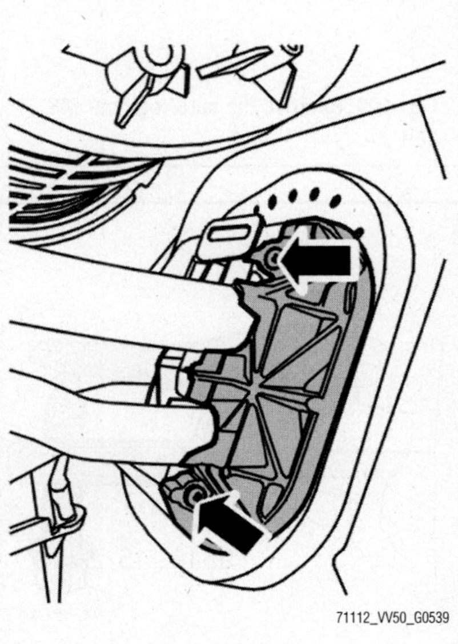

Fig. 192 Remove the 2 screws and the right-hand half of the lead-in

➡The heater core has pipes that are factory integrated. These pipes must be cut in order to remove the unit. The heater core in the service kit has separate pipes, however.

15. Place some paper below the pipe couplings to collect any spilled coolant.
16. Cut or saw off the pipes:
    - Press the pipes towards the firewall so that they protrude into the engine compartment.
    - To facilitate, also route the pipes from the engine compartment.
17. Remove the following:
    - The 2 screws and the right-hand half of the lead-in.
    - The spacer that holds the heater core and evaporator pipes apart.
18. Pull the heater core pipes through the seal.
19. Seal the pipes to the heater core so that the remaining coolant cannot run out.
20. Angle the heater core up at the rear edge. Lift out the heater core towards the passenger side.

➡Note how the seal is located on the heater core.

To install:

21. Install a new seal, using the removed heater core as a template.
22. Install the heater core
23. Install the heater core pipes through the seal (lubricate the ends with a little oil)

➡Use new O-rings for the pipe ends.

24. Install the pipes at the connection to the heater core pipes.

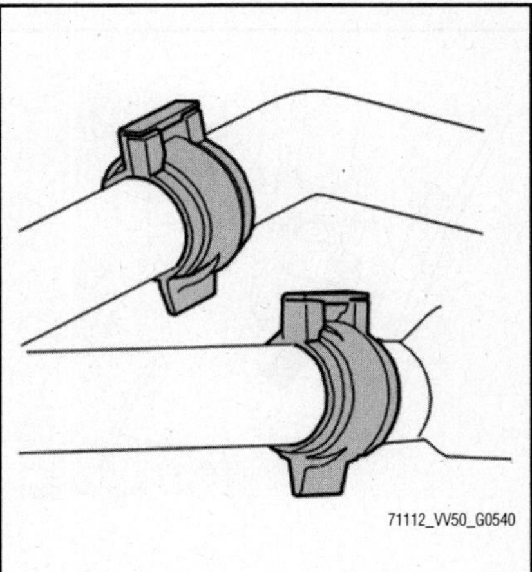

Fig. 193 Install the clips so that they lock securely

25. Install the clips so that they lock securely. A click must be heard.

➡**The clips only fit one way in the pipe connection.**

26. To complete installation, reverse the removal procedure.

27. Install the radiator hoses in the connections by the firewall.

28. Tighten the drain nipple on the radiator.

29. Fill with coolant and warm up the engine until the thermostat opens. Top up the coolant if necessary.

30. Check that the pipe coupling does not leak.

STEERING

POWER STEERING GEAR

REMOVAL & INSTALLATION

See Figures 194 through 197.

1. Before servicing the vehicle, refer to the Precautions Section.

➡**Ensure the steering wheel is set to the straight-ahead position, and remove the key so the steering wheel lock engages.**

2. Remove the left side soundproofing panel.

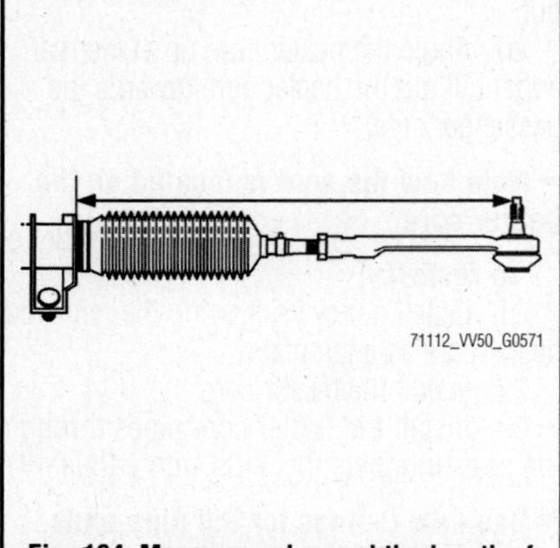

Fig. 194 Measure and record the length of the tie rod in relation to the steering gear housing

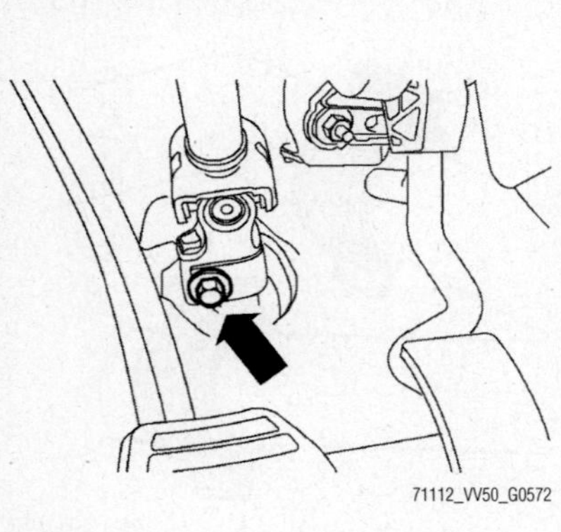

Fig. 195 Remove the bolt and the steering shaft from the steering gear

3. Remove the left front wheel.

4. Measure and record the length of the tie rod in relation to the steering gear housing.

5. Remove the M8 bolt and the steering shaft from the steering gear.

6. Remove the subframe.

➡**Place a little paper under the connection in the steering gear to absorb any oil spillage.**

7. Remove the steering gear M8 bolt.

8. Pull out and plug the pipes.

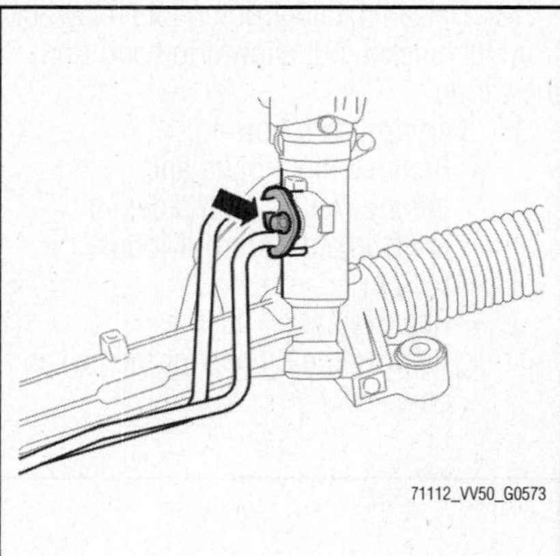

Fig. 196 Remove the steering gear M8 bolt

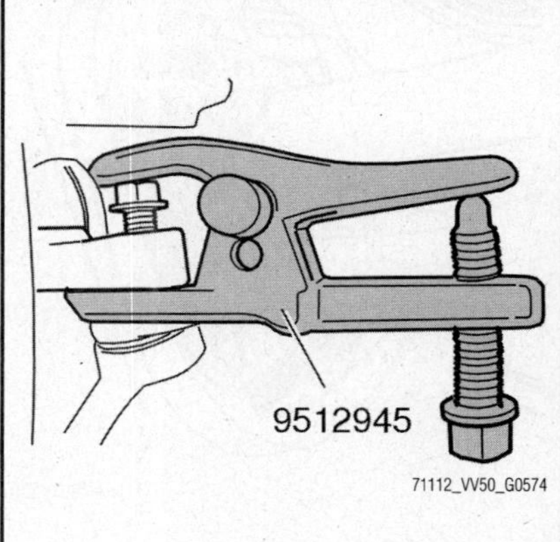

Fig. 197 Using Puller (951 2945), press the steering joint out of the wheel spindle

9. Slacken off the M10 nut for the outer steering arm so that the upper edge is above the screw.

10. Using Puller (951 2945), press the steering joint out of the wheel spindle.

➡**Be careful so that the steering joint's rubber gaiter is not damaged.**

11. Remove the steering gear.

To install:

12. To install, reverse the removal procedure and note the following:
    - Tighten all M8 bolts to 18 ft. lbs. (24 Nm).
    - Tighten the M10 nut for the outer steering arm to 37 ft. lbs. (50 Nm). Use a new nut.
    - Use new O-rings in the steering gear pipe.
    - Check that the position of the new steering gear is the same as the old steering gear.

13. Fill the power steering system.

➡**Use Volvo power steering fluid with part number 1161529.**

14. Bleed by turning the steering to full lock, alternately left and right, until the steering feels right.

15. Check/adjust the wheel alignment.

POWER STEERING PUMP

BLEEDING

See Figure 198.

1. Before servicing the vehicle, refer to the Precautions Section.

⁂ WARNING

Do not allow the fluid level in the reservoir tank to go below the MIN level line. The fluid level must remain between the MAX and MIN marks. Check and add fluid as needed.

⁂ CAUTION

Avoid skin contact with the specified material.

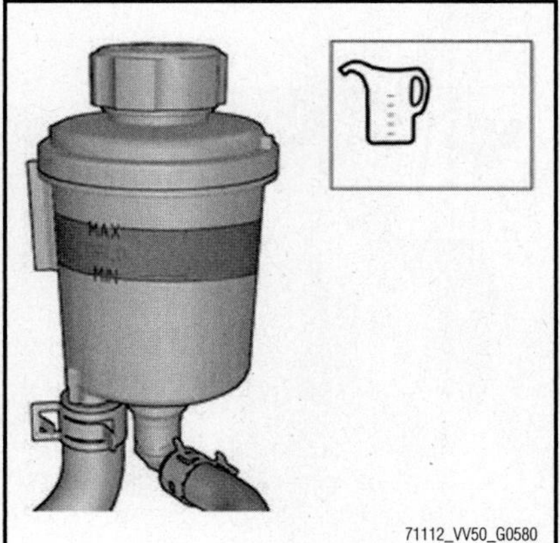

Fig. 198 The fluid level must remain between the MAX and MIN marks

WARNING

Do not hold the steering wheel in the locked position for more than 3–5 seconds. Damage to the power steering pump may occur.

2. With engine off and parking brake set, turn the steering wheel fully to the right and left at least 5 times. Hold in each position for about 3 seconds. Check for fluid leakage.
3. Start and run engine between 500–1000 RPM. Turn the steering wheel fully to the right and then fully to the left. Hold in each position for about 3 seconds. Check for fluid leakage.
4. Stop the engine and check the fluid level. Fill as required. Make sure that fluid level is to the MAX mark.
5. Let vehicle stand for 5 minutes.

WARNING

Make sure that the engine is switched off.

6. Start and run engine between 500–1000 RPM. Turn the steering wheel fully to the right and then fully to the left a total of 5 times. Hold in each position for about 3 seconds. Check for fluid leakage.
7. Stop the engine and check the fluid level. Fill as required. Make sure that fluid level is to the MAX mark.

WARNING

Make sure that the engine is switched off.

8. Let vehicle stand for 5 minutes.
9. Check the fluid level. Fill as required. Make sure that fluid level is to the MAX mark.
10. Start and run engine between 500–1000 RPM. Turn the steering wheel fully to the right and then fully to the left a total of 5 times. Hold in each position for about 3 seconds. Check for fluid leakage.
11. Stop the engine and check the fluid level. Fill as required. Make sure that fluid level is to the MAX mark.

WARNING

Make sure that the engine is switched off.

12. Check the fluid level. Fill as required. Make sure that fluid level is to the MAX mark.
13. Check for air bubbles or cloudy fluid. If found, repeat the bleeding procedure.

REMOVAL & INSTALLATION

See Figures 199 through 203.

WARNING

When this procedure is completed, software will be required to be downloaded from the Volvo central database.

➡The Electrical Power Steering (EPS) module is not available as an individual component, but is included in the power steering pump.

CAUTION

Used fluid is considerably more dangerous than new fluid. Avoid skin contact with the oil.

1. Before servicing the vehicle, refer to the Precautions Section.
2. Disconnect the negative battery cable.

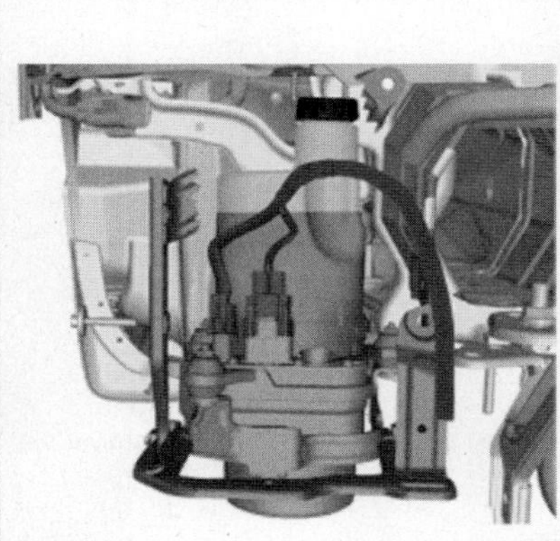

Fig. 199 Drain the fluid from the reservoir

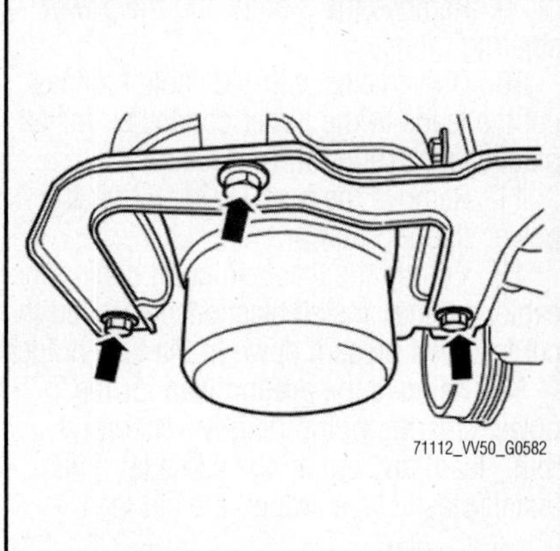

Fig. 200 Remove the 3 bolts and the power steering pump

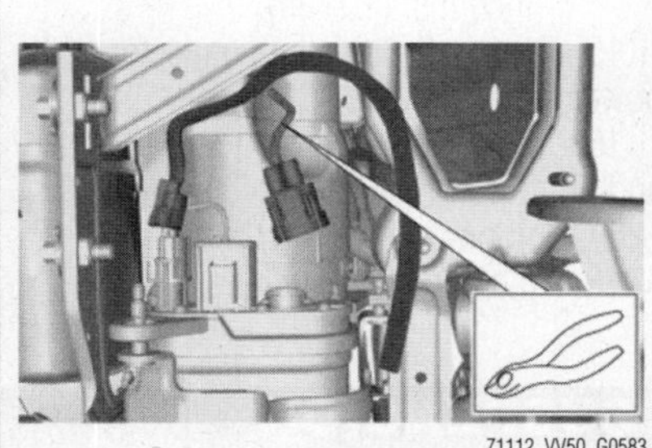

Fig. 201 On vehicles with old cable harness, cut the leads to the larger connector. Install plastic tape around the cut leads

3. Remove the headlight on the right side.
4. Remove the front bumper cover.
5. Using a suitable suction device, drain the fluid from the reservoir.
6. Remove the 2 connectors.

CAUTION

Be prepared to collect all escaping fluids.

➡Place a covering over the alternator as protection against oil.

7. Place an oil collection container under the pump.
8. Remove or disconnect the following:
   - The pressure hose
   - The feeder hose

WARNING

Make sure that all openings are sealed.

9. Remove the 3 bolts and the power steering pump.

10. On vehicles with old cable harness, cut the leads to the larger connector. Install plastic tape around the cut leads.

11. Remove the fuse 15/31: F2 for the power steering pump.

12. Pull up the lead and cut it behind the cable terminal. Install plastic tape around the cut lead and press it down in the fuse holder.

13. Remove the ground lead for the power steering pump (slightly coarser 4 mm_ lead) and cut off the cable terminal. Install plastic tape around the cut lead.

To install:

14. Install or connect the following:
- The cable harness.
- The lead and the fuse. Tighten the M5 bolt to 44 inch lbs. (5 Nm).
- The ground lead. Tighten to 89 inch lbs. (10 Nm).

15. Plug in the smaller connector to the power steering pump.

16. Install the 3 servo pump M8 bolts, and tighten to 18 ft. lbs. (24 Nm).

17. Fill power steering fluid.

18. To complete installation, reverse the removal procedure and note the following:

19. Re-program Electrical Power Steering (EPS) module. Order and download software 30667184 from the Volvo central database.

➡Move the vehicle a bit with some steering wheel movement so that the tires are not loaded too hard in one spot.

20. Start the engine and bleed the power steering system by steering to full lock, alternately left and right until the steering feels good.

21. Check the oil level again.

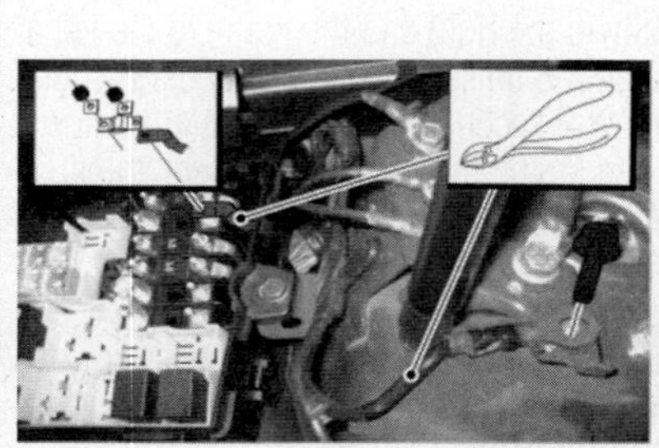

Fig. 202 Removing power steering pump electrical connections

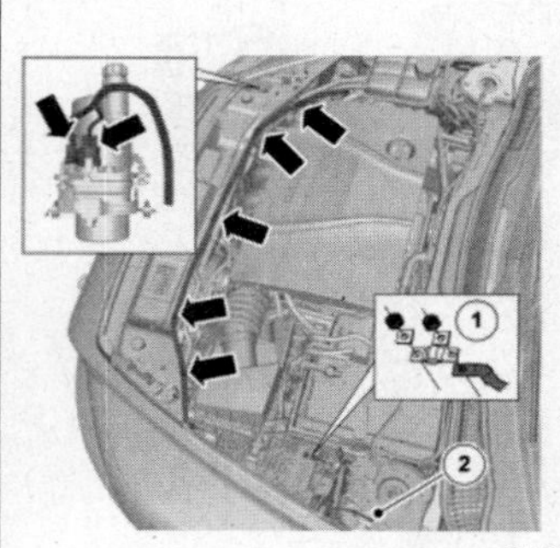

Fig. 203 Installing the lead (1) and the ground lead (2)

SUSPENSION

FRONT SUSPENSION

KNUCKLE & SPINDLE

REMOVAL & INSTALLATION

See Figures 204 through 208.

1. Before servicing the vehicle, refer to the Precautions Section.

2. Raise and support the vehicle safely.

3. Remove front wheel.

4. Remove the wheel hub-to-front axle bolt.

5. Disconnect the brake hose from the strut tube.

⁂ WARNING

Make sure that no load is placed on the brake hose.

6. Remove or disconnect the following:
- The brake caliper mounting bolts. Hang the caliper up using a piece of wire.
- The brake disc. Detach the end of the halfshaft in the hub by knocking the drive shaft into the hub approximately ⅓–½ inch (10–15 mm). Use a rubber or copper mallet.
- The wheel speed sensor wiring connector.

⁂ WARNING

Make sure that the ball joint ball does not rotate.

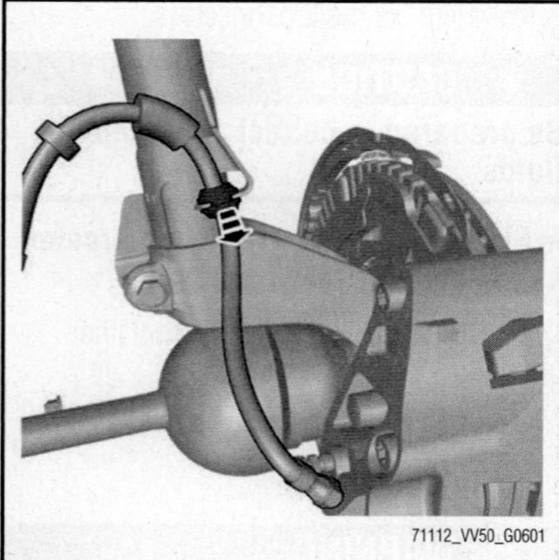

Fig. 204 Disconnect the brake hose from the strut tube

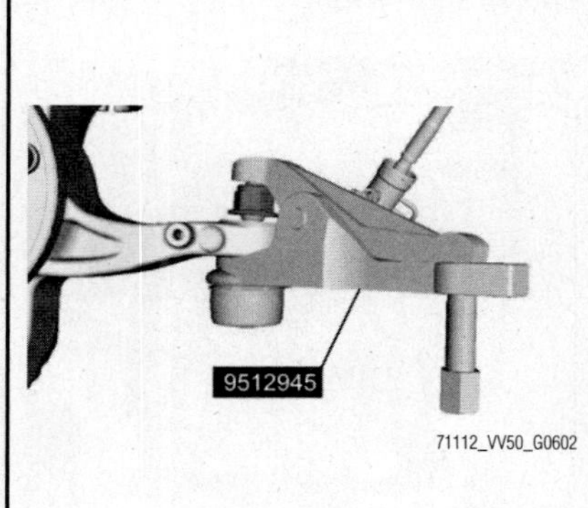

Fig. 205 Using Puller (951 2945), remove the ball joint

Fig. 206 Remove the wheel knuckle-to-strut bolt

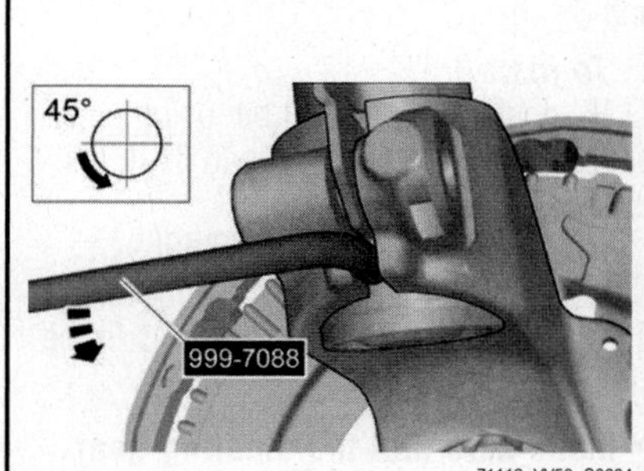

Fig. 207 Insert Expander (999 7088) in wheel knuckle and rotate 45° counterclockwise as shown

7. Remove the M10 nut.
8. Using Puller (951 2945), remove the ball joint.
9. Remove the wheel knuckle-to-strut bolt.
10. Insert Expander (999 7088) in wheel knuckle and rotate 45° counterclockwise as shown.
11. Pull down, and remove knuckle assembly.

To install:

To install, reverse the removal procedure and note the following:

- Tighten the wheel knuckle-to-strut bolt to 66 ft. lbs. (90 Nm).
- Tighten the ball joint M10 nut to 37 ft. lbs. (50 Nm).
- Tighten the brake caliper bolts to 88 ft. lbs. (120 Nm).
- Tighten the wheel hub-to-axle bolt: Step 1 = To 26 ft. lbs. (35 Nm); Step 2: = 90 degrees.

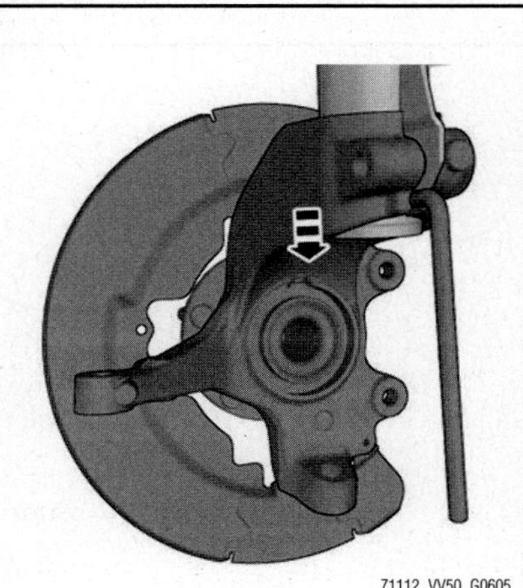

Fig. 208 Pull down, and remove knuckle assembly

LOWER CONTROL ARMS

REMOVAL & INSTALLATION

See Figures 209 through 212

1. Before servicing the vehicle, refer to the Precautions Section.

➡Perform the following steps on both sides of vehicle.

2. Remove the front wheel.
3. Remove the halfshaft to wheel hub bolt.
4. Slacken off the ball joint-to-wheel spindle nut so that the upper edge is above the screw. Use an Allen key as a counterhold so that the boot is not damaged.
5. Using Puller (951 2945), remove the ball joint from the control arm.
6. Using Lever (999 7076), pull the ball joint out of the wheel spindle.
7. Remove the 2 subframe bolts.
8. Remove the bolt and the control arm.

Fig. 209 Slacken off the ball joint-to-wheel spindle nut

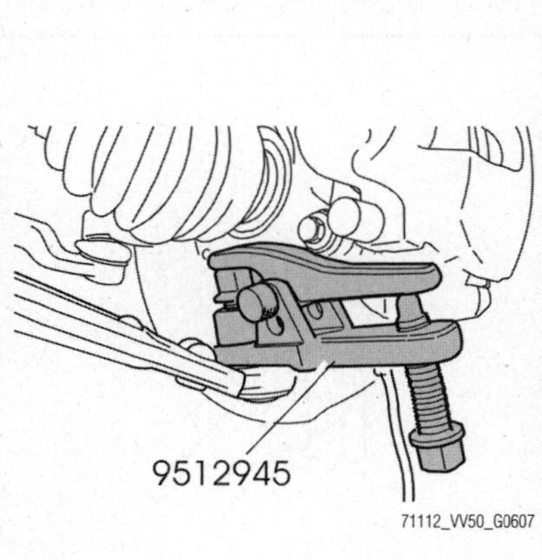

Fig. 210 Using Puller (951 2945), remove the ball joint from the control arm

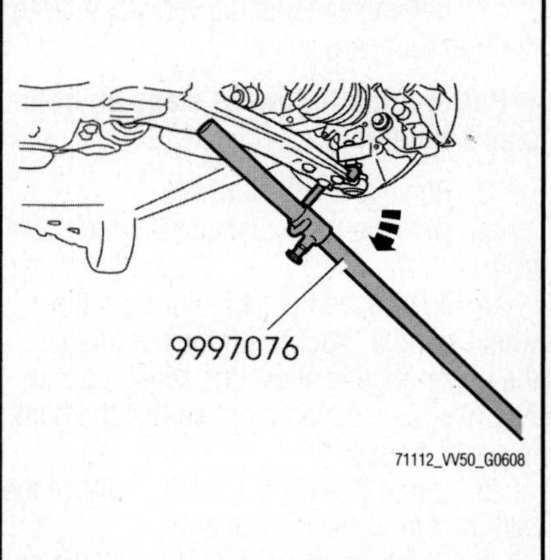

Fig. 211 Using Lever (999 7076), pull the ball joint out of the wheel spindle

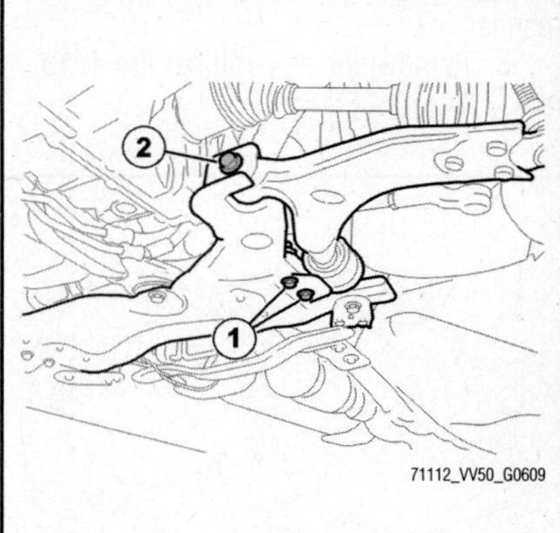

Fig. 212 Remove the 2 subframe bolts (1). Remove the bolt (2) and the control arm

To install:

10. Using new bolts, install the control arm.
11. Using the lever, install the ball joint in the wheel spindle. Use a new nut. Use an Allen key as a counterhold.
12. Install the ball joint-to-wheel spindle nut. Use an Allen key as a counterhold so that the boot is not damaged.
13. Install the halfshaft retainer bolt. Counterhold the brake disc. Use a screwdriver in the ventilation holes.
14. Install the front wheel.

STABILIZER BAR & LINKS

REMOVAL & INSTALLATION

Stabilizer Bar

See Figures 213 through 222.

➡This component may also be referred to as an anti-roll bar.

1. Before servicing the vehicle, refer to the Precautions Section.

➡**Perform the following steps on both sides of vehicle.**

2. Remove the front wheel.
3. Remove the halfshaft retainer bolt.
4. To remove the ball joint from the wheel spindle, slacken off the nut so that the upper edge is above the screw. Use an Allen key as a counterhold so that the boot is not damaged.
5. Using Puller (951 2945), remove the ball joint from the control arm.
6. Using Lever (999 7076), pull the ball joint out of the wheel spindle.
7. Remove the M12 bolt, and remove the steering gear from the subframe. Suspend the steering gear in an appropriate manner.
8. Remove the anti-roll bar link M10 nut.

➡**Use a Torx® wrench as a counterhold so as not to damage the rubber bellows.**

9. Slacken off the front screw of the subframe about 6 turns.
10. Remove M12 bolt and the lower torque rod.
11. Position a transmission jack under the subframe. Anchor the jack plate in the subframe in a suitable manner.
12. Remove or disconnect the following:
    - The rubber mountings for the exhaust pipe
    - The 2 rear subframe mounting bolts
    - The 4 M8 bracket bolts
    - The Heated Oxygen Sensor (HO2S) connector
    - The brackets
13. Carefully lower the rear edge of the subframe.
14. Remove the 4 M10 bolts and the anti-roll bar.

To install:

15. Install the anti-roll bar using new bolts. Tighten the M10 bolts to 37 ft. lbs. (50 Nm).
16. Install the Gauges (999 7089).
17. Carefully raise the subframe so that the adjustment tools meet the holes in the side members.

➡**Make sure that the steering gear is not pinched when raising the subframe.**

18. To complete installation, reverse the removal procedure and note the following:
    - Use 2 new rear subframe mounting bolts.
    - Tighten the 4 M8 bracket bolts to 18 ft. lbs. (24 Nm).
    - Tighten all M12 bolts to 59 ft. lbs. (80 Nm).

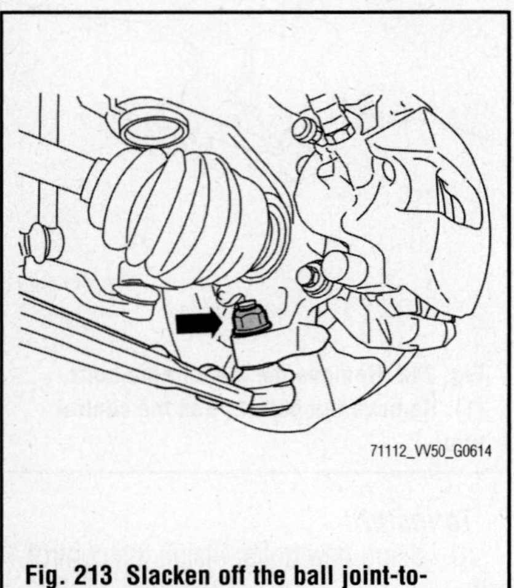

Fig. 213 Slacken off the ball joint-to-wheel spindle nut

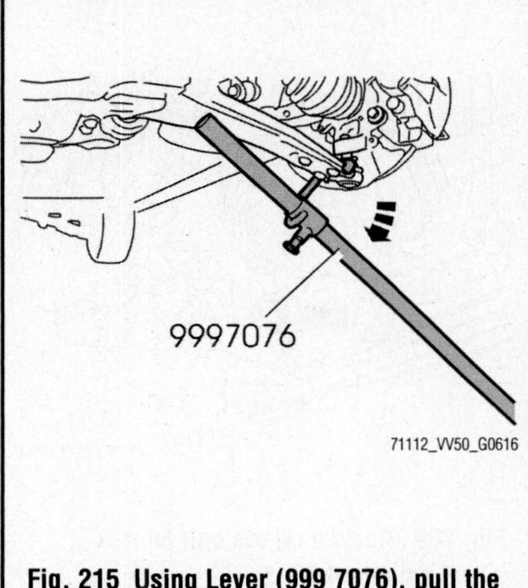

Fig. 215 Using Lever (999 7076), pull the ball joint out of the wheel spindle

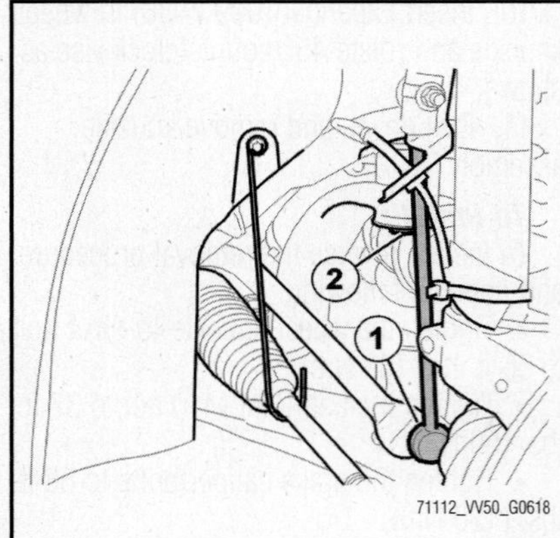

Fig. 217 Remove the anti-roll bar link nut (1). Slacken off the front screw (2) of the subframe about 6 turns

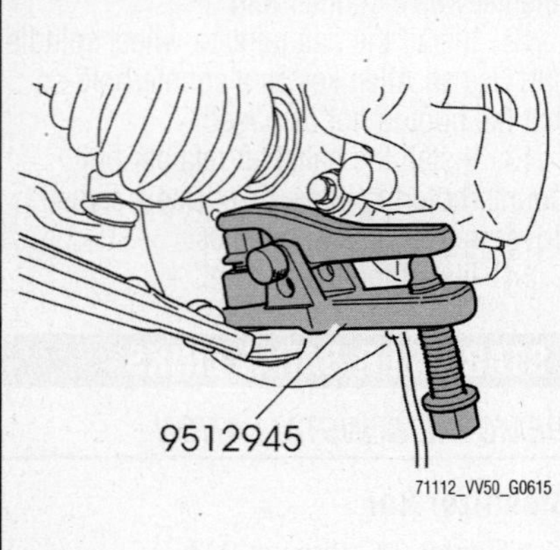

Fig. 214 Using Puller (951 2945), remove the ball joint from the control arm

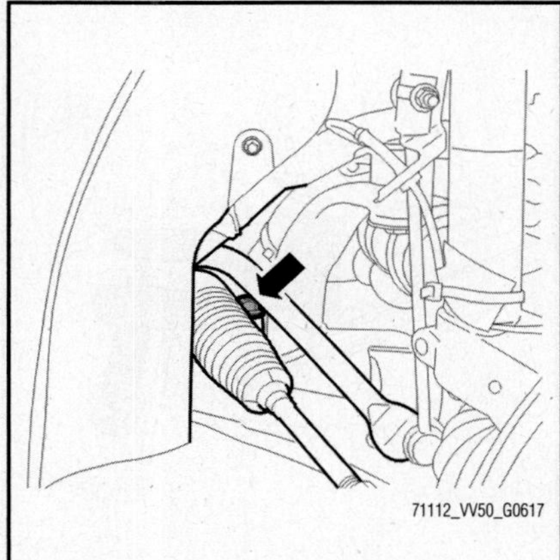

Fig. 216 Remove the bolt, and remove the steering gear from the subframe

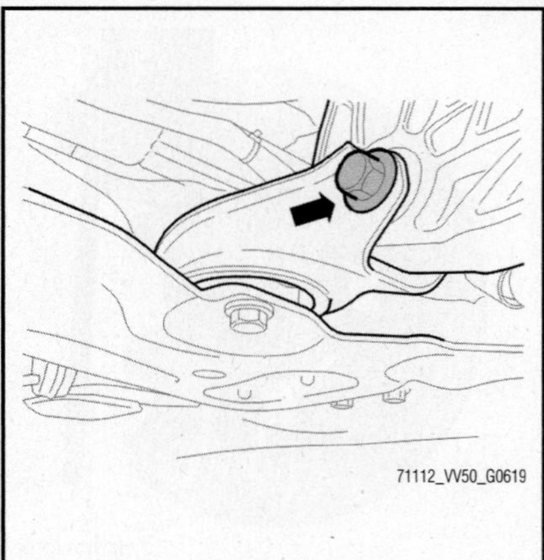

Fig. 218 Remove bolt and the lower torque rod

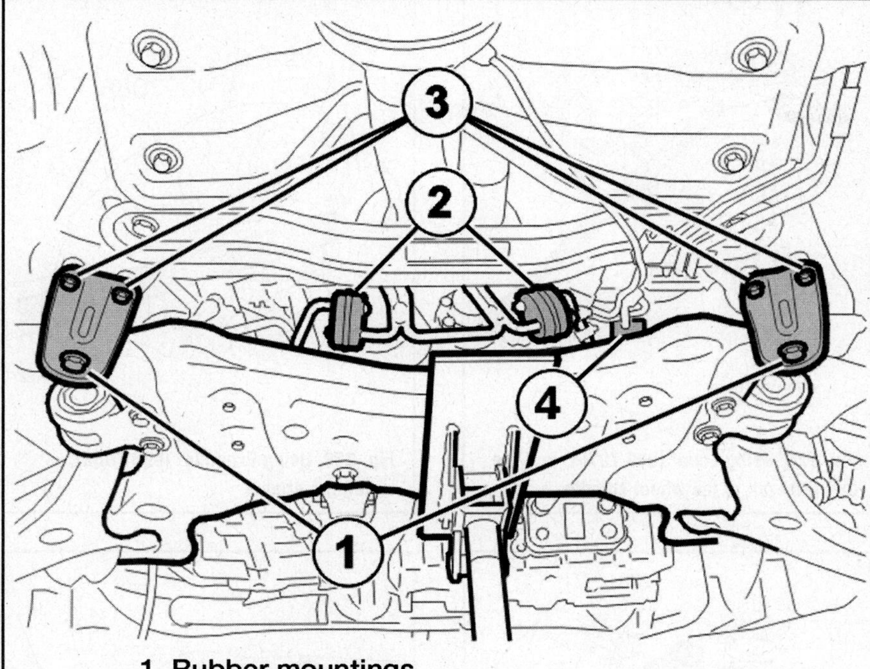

Fig. 219 Lowering the subframe

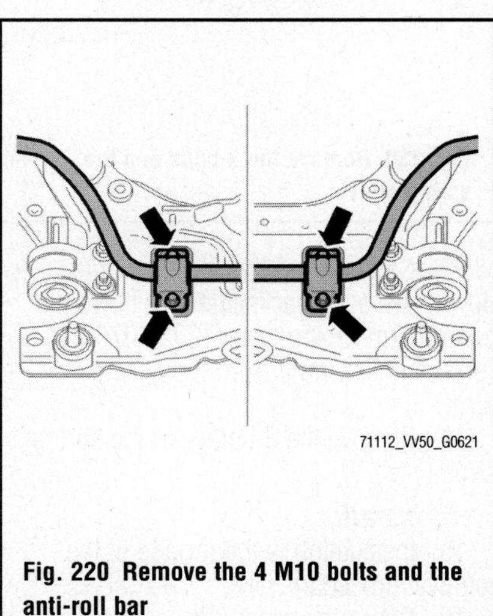

Fig. 220 Remove the 4 M10 bolts and the anti-roll bar

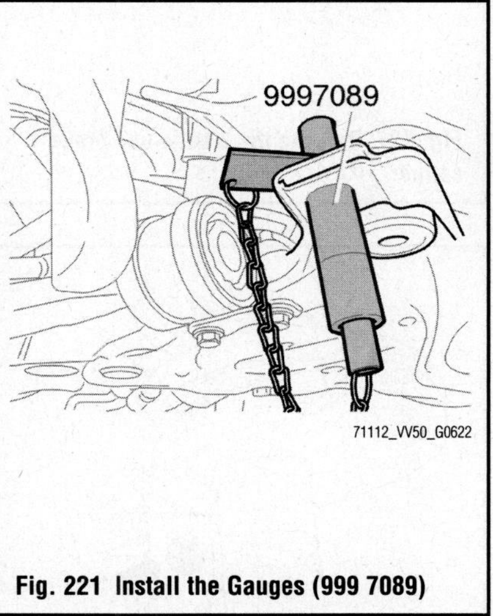

Fig. 221 Install the Gauges (999 7089)

- Tighten the 2 M10 anti-roll bar link bolts to 37 ft. lbs. (50 Nm).

➡Use a Torx® wrench as a counterhold so as not to damage the rubber bellows.

Stabilizer Bar Link

1. Before servicing the vehicle, refer to the Precautions Section.
2. Remove the front wheel.
3. Remove the 2 M10 bolts, and remove stabilizer bar link from the 2 mountings.

➡Use a Torx® wrench as a counterhold so as not to damage the rubber bellows.

To install:

To install, reverse the removal procedure and note the following:

- Use new M10 bolts.

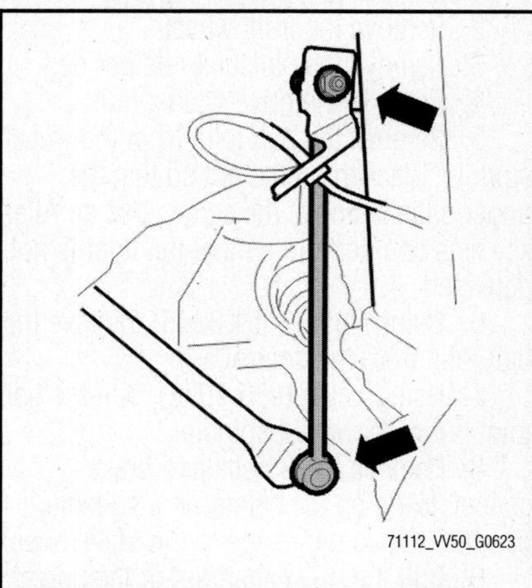

Fig. 222 Remove the stabilizer bar link from the 2 mountings

STRUT BAR

REMOVAL & INSTALLATION

See Figure 223.

1. Before servicing the vehicle, refer to the Precautions Section.
2. On both sides of vehicle, remove the 2 M8 nuts.
3. Remove the strut turret stabilizer bar.

To install:

4. To install, reverse the removal procedure and note the following:
   - Tighten the M8 nuts to 18 ft. lbs. (24 Nm).

STRUTS (MACPHERSON STRUTS)

REMOVAL & INSTALLATION

See Figures 224 through 230.

1. Before servicing the vehicle, refer to the Precautions Section.

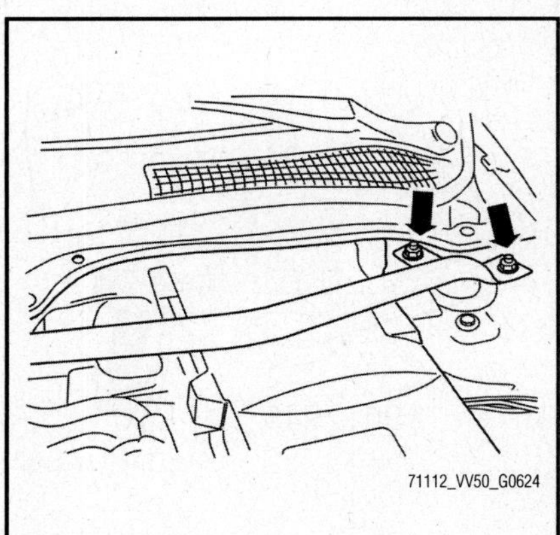

Fig. 223 Remove the strut turret stabilizer bar

2. Remove the front wheel.
3. Remove the halfshaft retainer bolt.
4. Press in the drive shaft a little.
5. Remove the ball joint from the wheel spindle. Slacken off the nut so that the upper edge is above the screw. Use an Allen key as a counterhold so that the boot is not damaged.
6. Using Puller (951 2945), remove the ball joint from the control arm.
7. Using Lever (999 7076), pull the ball joint out of the wheel spindle.
8. Remove the 2 bolts and brake caliper. Hang up the caliper in a suitable position to avoid damage to the brake hose.
9. Pull the drive shaft out of the hub. Hang up the drive shaft in an appropriate position. Hang up the wheel spindle on the ball joint. Using the lever, loosely install the nut.
10. Remove the nut, and the anti-roll bar link. Use an Allen key as a counterhold so that the boot is not damaged.

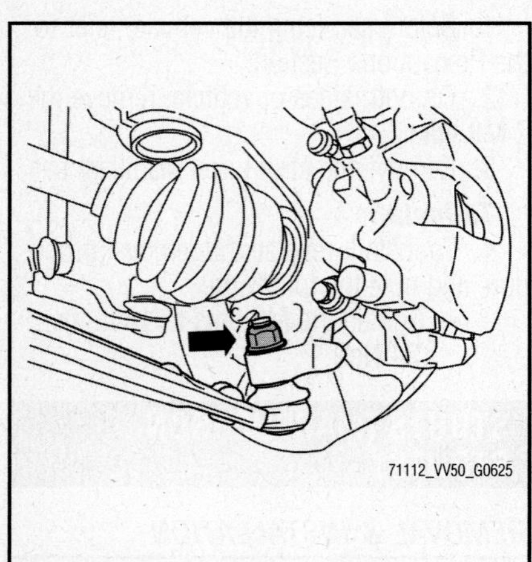

Fig. 224 Slacken off the ball joint-to-wheel spindle nut

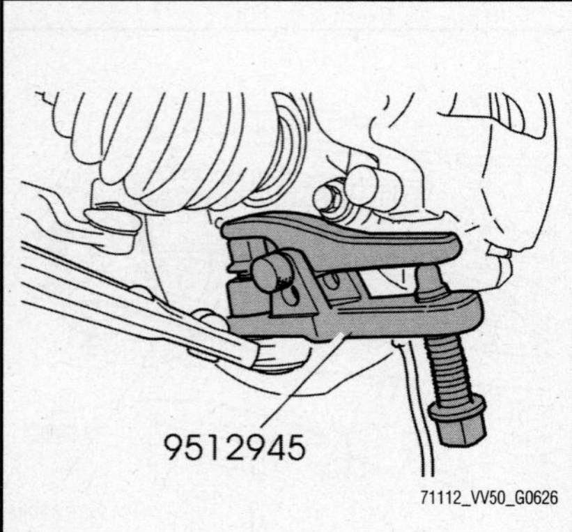

Fig. 225 Using Puller (951 2945), remove the ball joint from the control arm

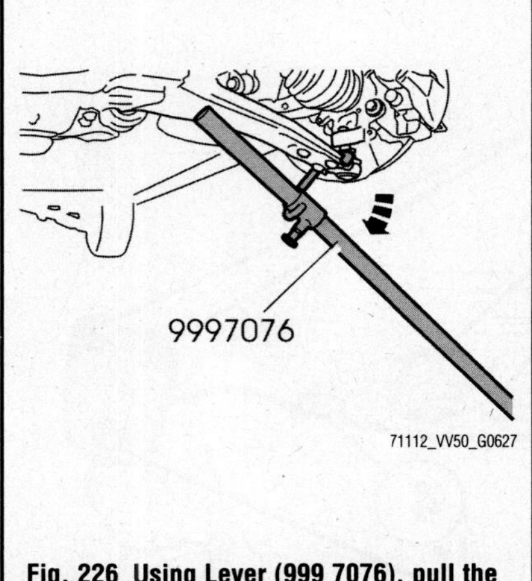

Fig. 226 Using Lever (999 7076), pull the ball joint out of the wheel spindle

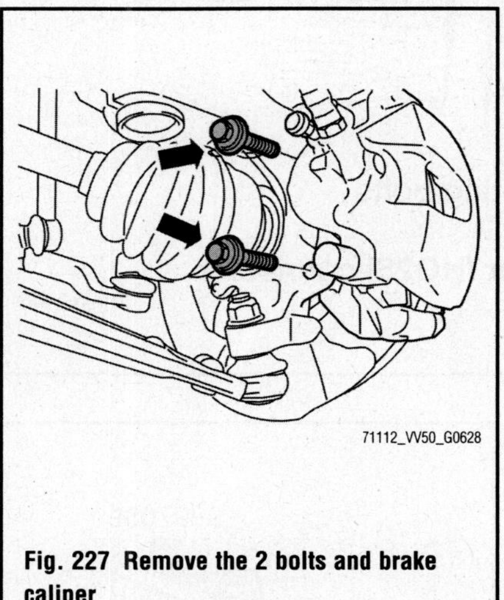

Fig. 227 Remove the 2 bolts and brake caliper

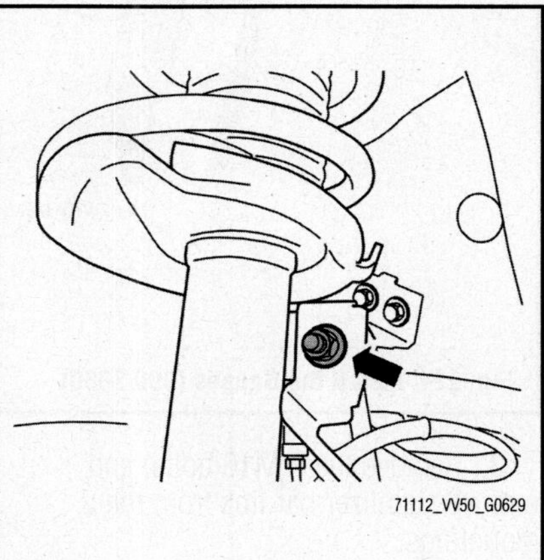

Fig. 228 Remove the nut, and the anti-roll bar link

11. Remove the bolt.
12. Using Expander (999 7088), widen the groove. Install the tool so that the flat sides run the length of the groove. Turn 45°.

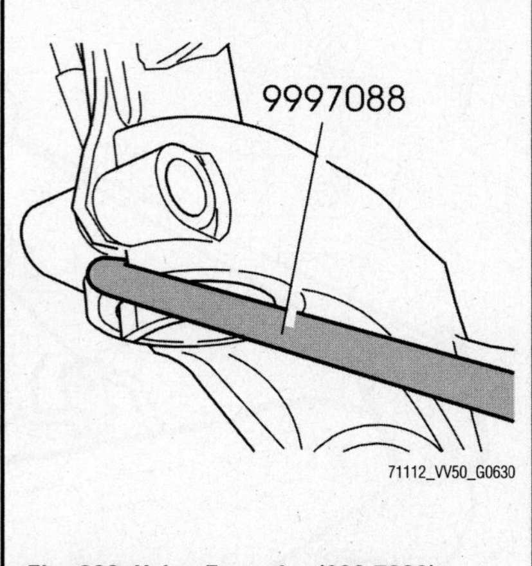

Fig. 229 Using Expander (999 7088), widen the groove

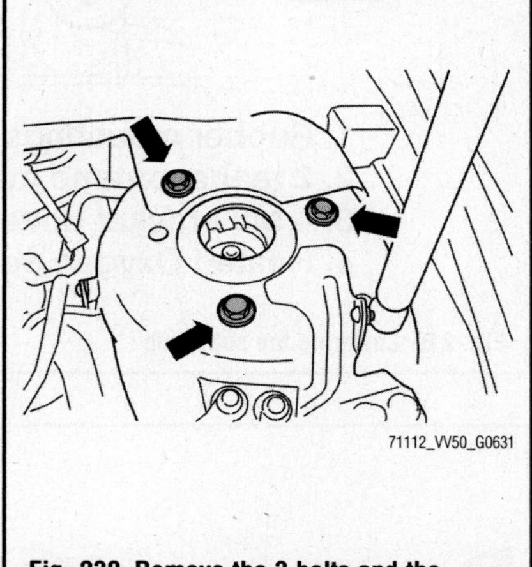

Fig. 230 Remove the 3 bolts and the spring strut

13. Carefully tap the wheel spindle down. Use a copper mallet. Pry down the control arm. Using Lever (999 7076), release the spindle from the spring strut.
14. Remove the 3 bolts and the spring strut.

To install:

15. Installation is the reverse of the removal procedure.
16. Check the headlights, and adjust if necessary.

OVERHAUL

See Figures 231 through 234.

1. Take the load off the springs. Use the hydraulic tool. Use Spring Compressor (951 2911) together with Claws (951 2914).
2. Remove or disconnect the following:
   - The nut on the shock absorber. Use Socket (999 5500) and a Torx-socket as a counterhold

- The spring seat
- The rubber bump stop and gaiter
- The spring

➡Note the point of contact on the spring to facilitate installation of a new spring.

➡Ensure that the spring seat and the shock absorber bearing do not separate. The bearing comprises loose balls in a frame. The balls will fall out on separation.

3. Check that the shock absorber bearing/spring seat, the rubber bump stop and boot are undamaged. Replace if necessary.

To install:

Installation is the reverse of the removal procedure.

➡Ensure that the spring seat marking is directly opposite the guide for the spring strut when installing the spring.

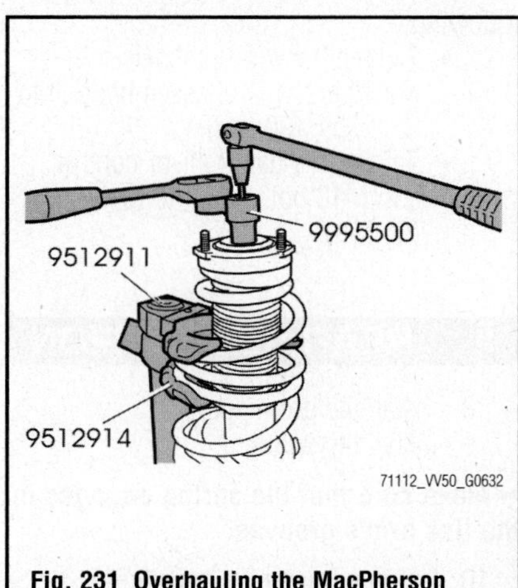

Fig. 231 Overhauling the MacPherson Strut

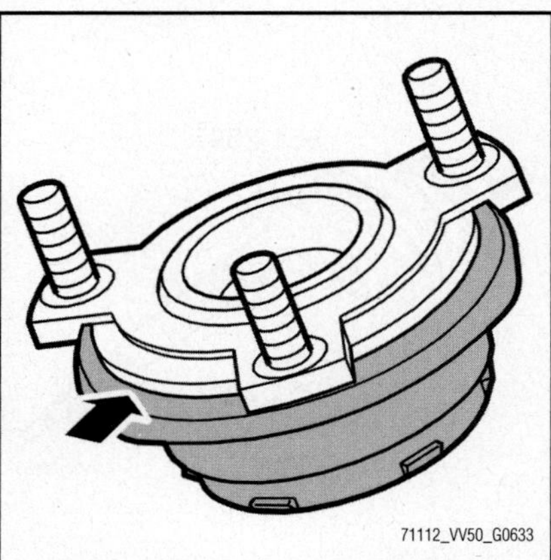

Fig. 232 Ensure that the spring seat and the shock absorber bearing do not separate

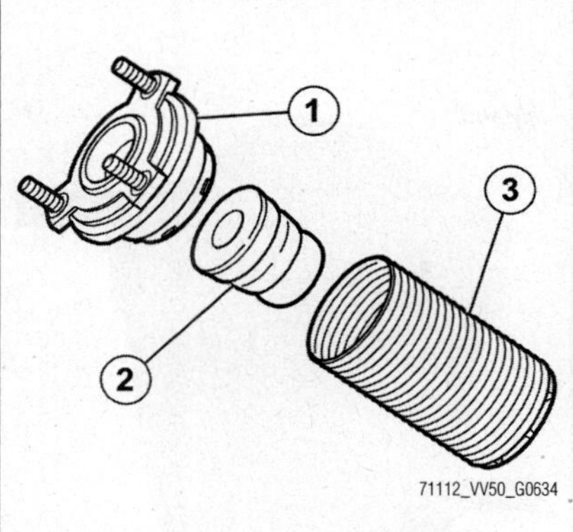

Fig. 233 Check that the shock absorber bearing/spring seat (1), the rubber bump stop (2) and boot (3) are undamaged

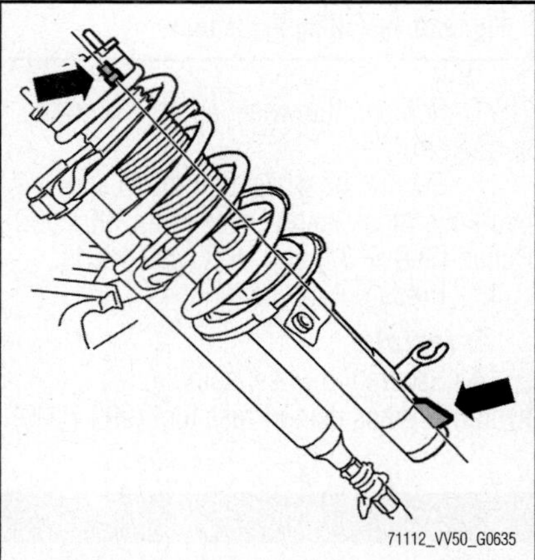

Fig. 234 Ensure that the spring seat marking is directly opposite the guide for the spring strut when installing the spring

WHEEL HUBS & BEARINGS

ADJUSTMENT

The front wheel bearings are not adjustable. If the lateral run-out on the hub with the disc removed exceeds 0.0007 inch (0.020mm), the hub must be replaced.

REMOVAL & INSTALLATION

See Figures 235 through 240.

1. Before servicing the vehicle, refer to the Precautions Section.
2. Remove the wheel.
3. Slacken off the center nut from the halfshaft.
4. Remove the 2 bolts from the brake caliper holder and hang them up to prevent damage to the brake hose.
5. Remove the brake disc.
6. Remove the brake rotor.

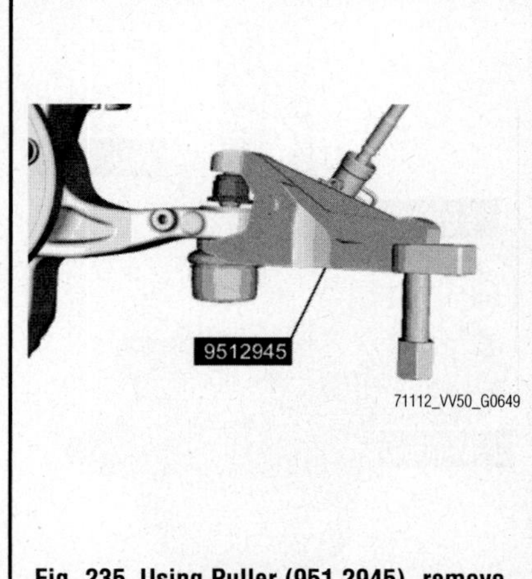

Fig. 235 Using Puller (951 2945), remove the ball joint

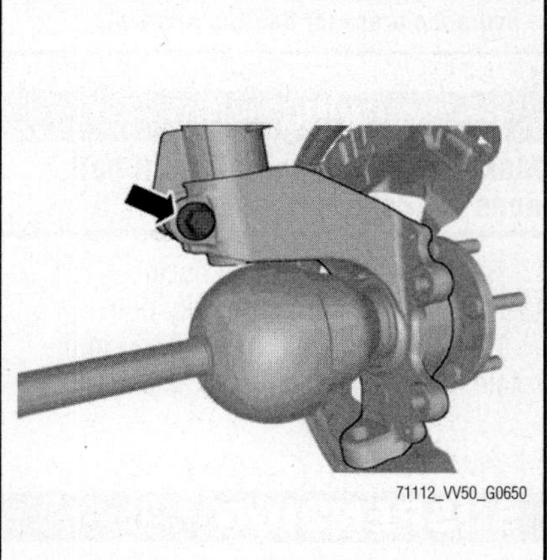

Fig. 236 Remove the wheel knuckle-to-MacPherson strut assembly bolt

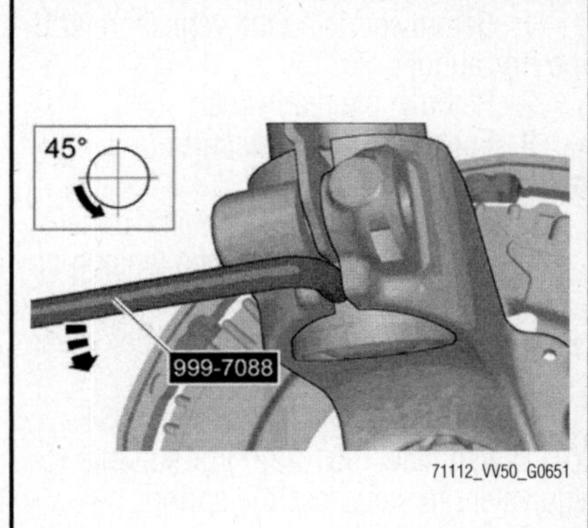

Fig. 237 Insert Expander (999 7088) and rotate 45° counterclockwise as shown

7. Remove the ABS sensor and hang in a suitable position.
8. Using Puller (951 2945), remove the ball joint.

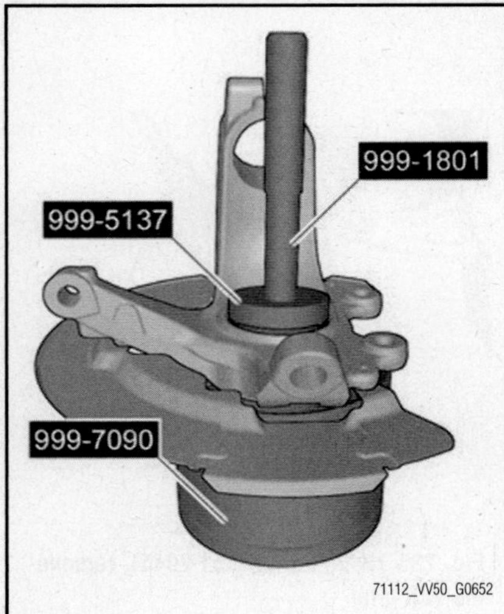

Fig. 238 Securing the wheel spindle in a hydraulic press for bearing removal

Fig. 239 Installing Press tool

Fig. 240 Securing the wheel spindle in a hydraulic press for bearing installation

WARNING

Make sure that the ball joint ball does not rotate.

9. Remove the wheel knuckle-to-MacPherson strut assembly bolt.
10. Insert Expander (999 7088) and rotate 45° counterclockwise as shown.
11. Remove the wheel spindle from the spring strut.
12. Secure the wheel spindle in a hydraulic press using Press tool (999 7090), Punch (999 5137) and Drift (999 1801).
13. Press out the bearing.

To install:

14. Secure the wheel spindle in a hydraulic press using Press tool (999 7090).
15. To complete installation, reverse the removal procedure and note the following:
    - Tighten the wheel knuckle-to-MacPherson strut assembly bolt to 66 ft. lbs. (90 Nm).
    - Tighten the ball joint-to-control arm M10 bolts to 37 ft. lbs. (50 Nm).

COIL SPRINGS

REMOVAL & INSTALLATION

See Figures 241 and 242.

1. Before servicing the vehicle, refer to the Precautions Section.
2. Remove the rear wheel.
3. For right-hand side spring only:
    a. Place a transmission jack under the control arm to relieve the tension on the shock absorber.
    b. Remove the shock absorber lower mounting bolt.
4. Install Spring Compressor (951 2911) with claw (951 2897) or suitable equivalent to compress the spring.
5. Remove the spring.

WARNING

It is essential that the correct claw for the vehicle model is used. Always check that the number punched on the claw matches the number indicated in the method.

➡Note the point of contact on the spring for easier installation.

6. Remove the grommet from the top of the spring.

To install:

7. Using the spring compresser and claw, compress the spring.
8. Install the grommet.
9. Install the spring.

➡Make sure that the spring engages in the link arm's grooves.

10. Using a transmission jack, carefully lift under the control arm so that

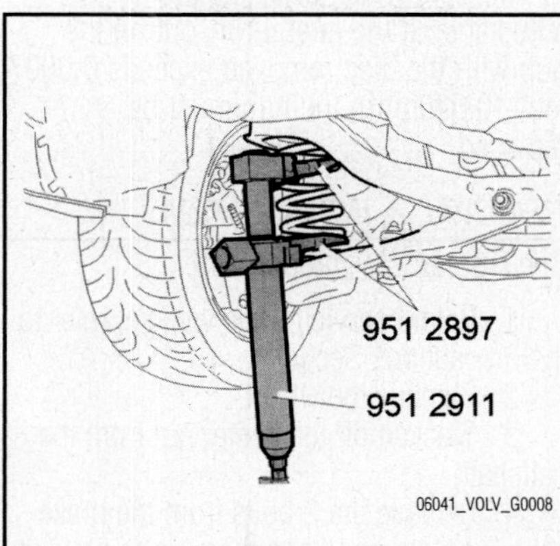

Fig. 241 Install Spring Compressor (951 2911) with claw (951 2897) to compress the spring

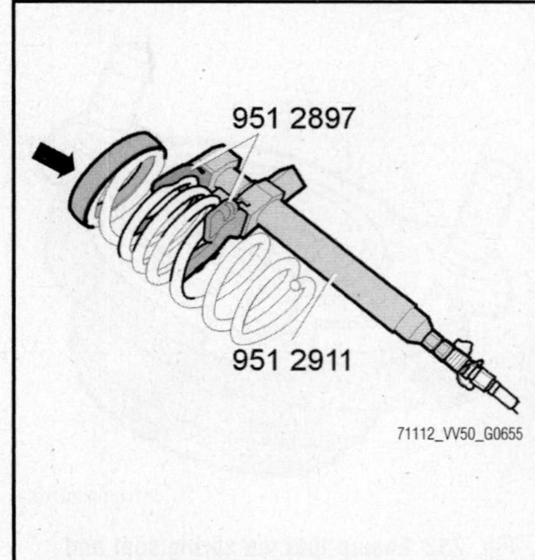

Fig. 242 Remove the grommet from the top of the spring

the bolt for the shock absorber can be installed.

➡Always make sure that the car is not lifted off the hoist when working with the transmission jack.

11. To complete installation, reverse the removal procedure.
12. Check headlights, and adjust as necessary.

KNUCKLES

REMOVAL & INSTALLATION

See Figures 243 through 251.

1. Before servicing the vehicle, refer to the Precautions Section.
2. Remove the coil spring.
3. Remove the rear wheel hub.
4. Remove the 2 plastic nuts, the bolt and the air baffle.

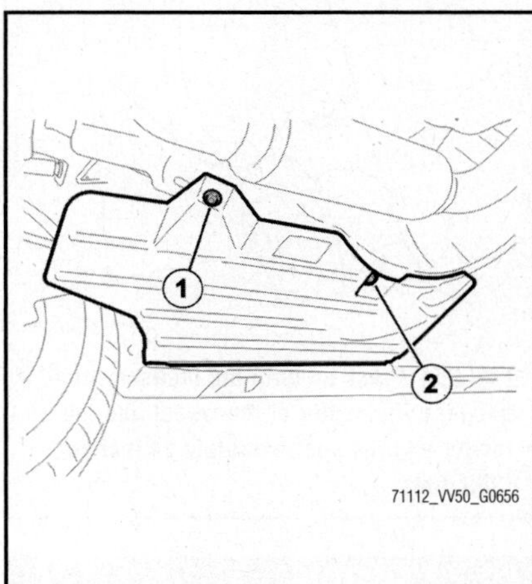

Fig. 243 Remove the 2 plastic nuts (1), the bolt (2) and the air baffle

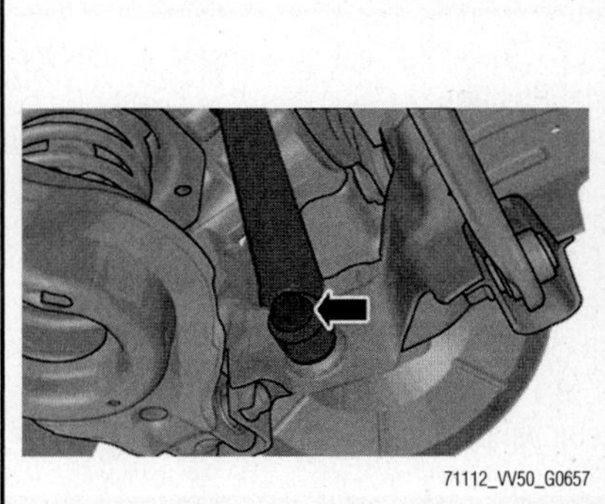

Fig. 244 Remove the lower shock absorber mounting bolt

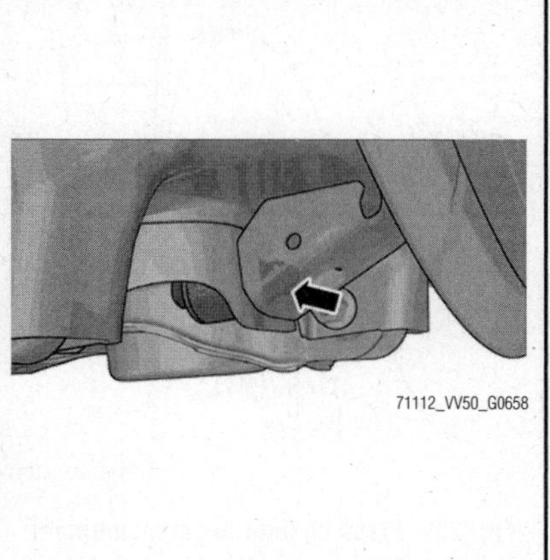

Fig. 245 Locating rear shock absorber-to-wheel knuckle nut

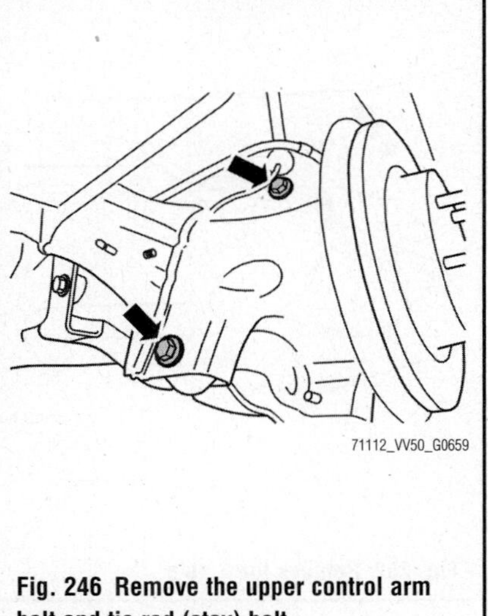

Fig. 246 Remove the upper control arm bolt and tie rod (stay) bolt

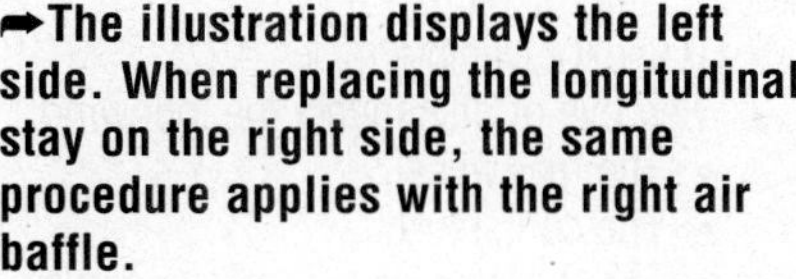
➡The illustration displays the left side. When replacing the longitudinal stay on the right side, the same procedure applies with the right air baffle.

5. Remove the lower shock absorber mounting bolt.
6. Remove the 2 bolts securing the upper control arm and the tie rod or stay.
7. Remove the bolt, and disconnect the control arm from the lateral link.
8. Remove the bolt and clip for the brake cable.
9. Remove the 3 clips, and disconnect the wheel sensor cable harness from the lateral link.
10. Remove the 2 bolts and the lateral link.

➡Note on which side of the lateral link the cable and cable harness must be positioned.

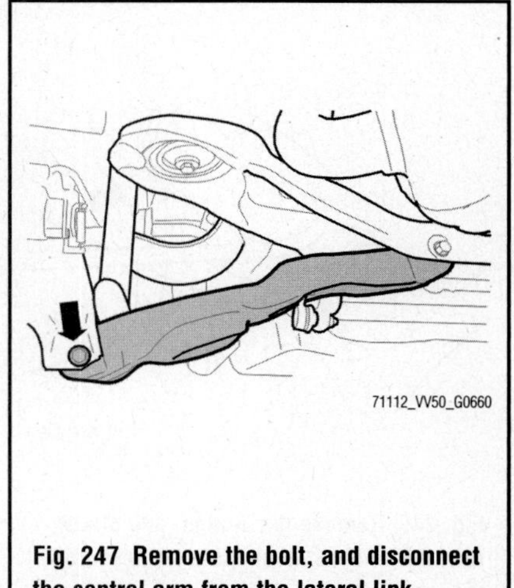

Fig. 247 Remove the bolt, and disconnect the control arm from the lateral link

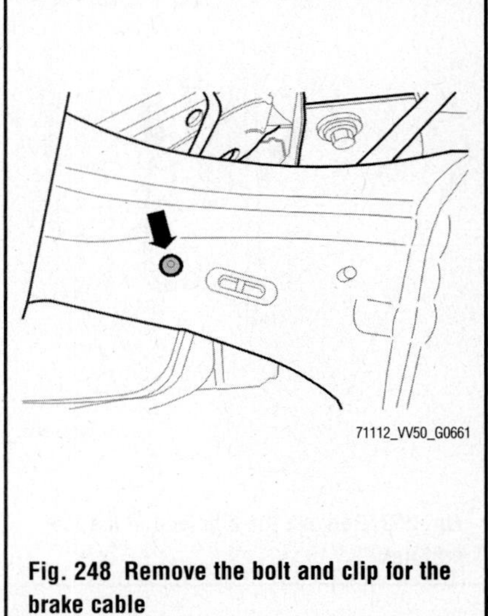

Fig. 248 Remove the bolt and clip for the brake cable

11. Remove the rear wheel knuckle.

To install:

12. Install the rear wheel knuckle.
13. Install the 2 bolts and the lateral link.
14. Install the 3 clips, and reconnect the wheel sensor cable harness to the lateral link.
15. Install the bolt and clip for the brake cable.
16. Install the upper control arm and tie rod bolts. Do not tighten yet.
17. Install the 2 bolts and lower control arm, but do not tighten yet.

➡The rear suspension must be in the Normal Position when tightening all the joints in the rear suspension where rubber bushings are involved.

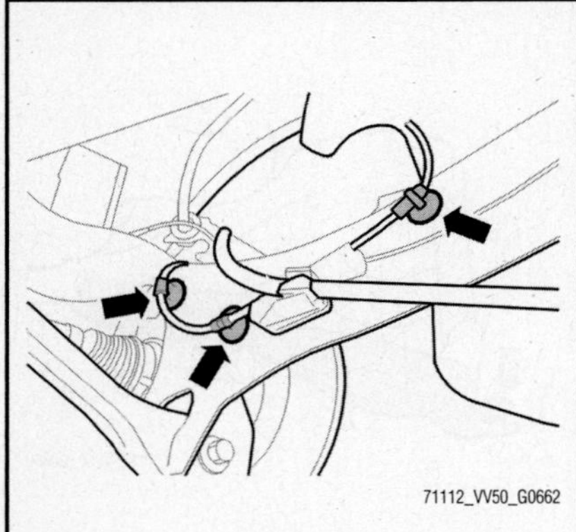

Fig. 249 Remove the 3 clips, and disconnect the wheel sensor cable harness from the lateral link

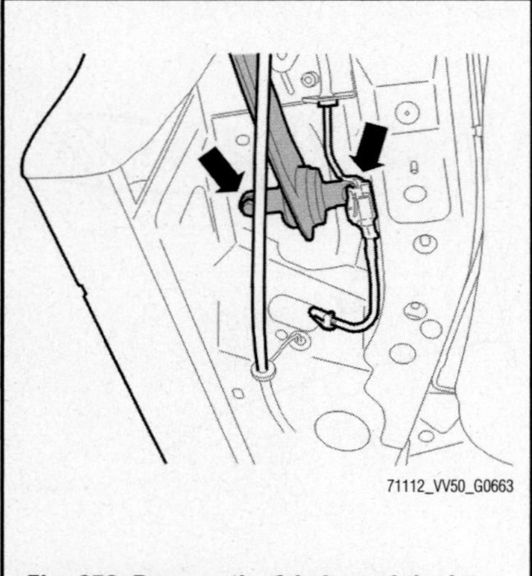

Fig. 250 Remove the 2 bolts and the lateral link

⁂ CAUTION

The work must always be carried out with the spring removed. Ensure that the car does not lift off the hoist when using the transmission jack.

18. To set the rear suspension in the Normal Position:
    a. Position a transmission jack below the lower control arm.
    b. Press up until the measurement between the center of the wheel and the fender edge is approximately 14 inches (350 mm).
19. To complete installation, reverse the removal procedure.
20. Check/adjust the wheel alignment.

LOWER CONTROL ARMS

REMOVAL & INSTALLATION

See Figures 252 through 254.

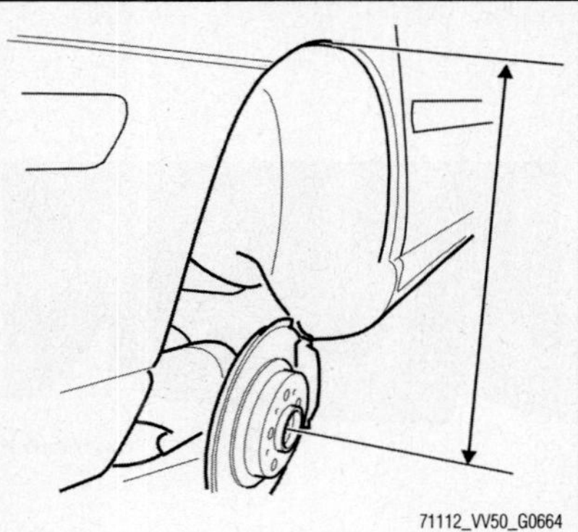

Fig. 251 Press up until the measurement between the center of the wheel and the fender edge is approximately 14 inches (350 mm)

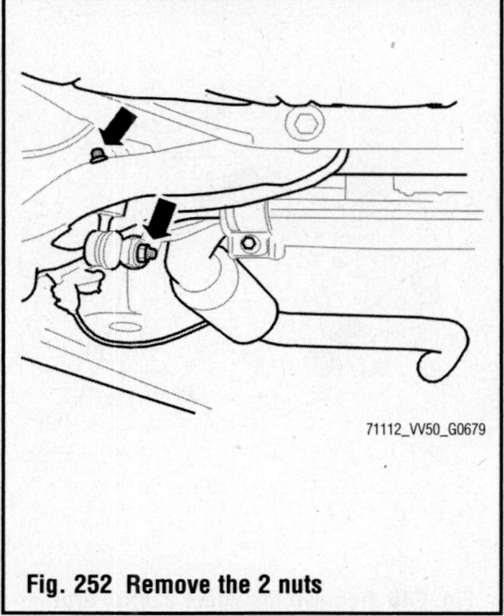

Fig. 252 Remove the 2 nuts

1. Before servicing the vehicle, refer to the Precautions Section.
2. Raise the vehicle.
3. Remove or disconnect the following:
    - The rear wheel
    - The coil spring.
    - The 2 nuts. Use a Torx® wrench as a counterhold so that the boot is not damaged
    - The ball joints
4. Remove the bolt for the wheel spindle and for the subframe.
5. Turn the anti-roll bar approximately 30°, and remove the control arm.

To install:

6. Install the 2 bolts and control arm, but do not tighten yet.

➡The rear suspension must be in the Normal Position when tightening all the joints in the rear suspension where rubber bushings are involved.

Fig. 253 Remove the bolt for the wheel spindle (1) and for the subframe (2)

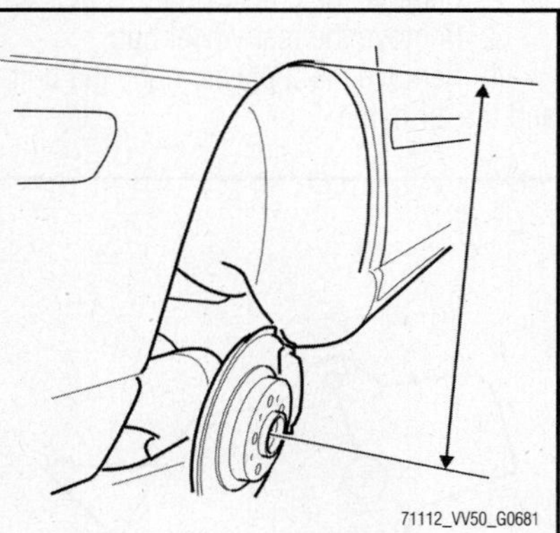

Fig. 254 Press up until the measurement between the center of the wheel and the fender edge is approximately 14 inches (350 mm)

⁂ CAUTION

The work must always be carried out with the spring removed. Ensure that the car does not lift off the hoist when using the transmission jack.

7. To set the rear suspension in the Normal Position:
    a. Position a transmission jack below the lower control arm.
    b. Press up until the measurement between the center of the wheel and the fender edge is approximately 14 inches (350 mm).
8. To complete installation, reverse the removal procedure.

SHOCK ABSORBERS

REMOVAL & INSTALLATION

Shock Absorber

See Figures 255 through 257.

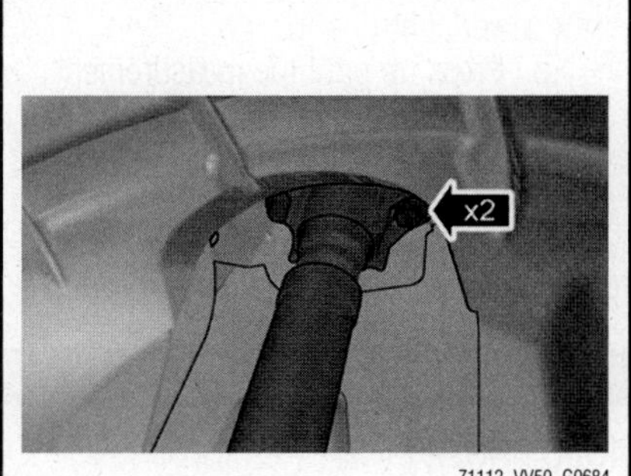

Fig. 255 Remove the 2 upper shock absorber mounting bolts

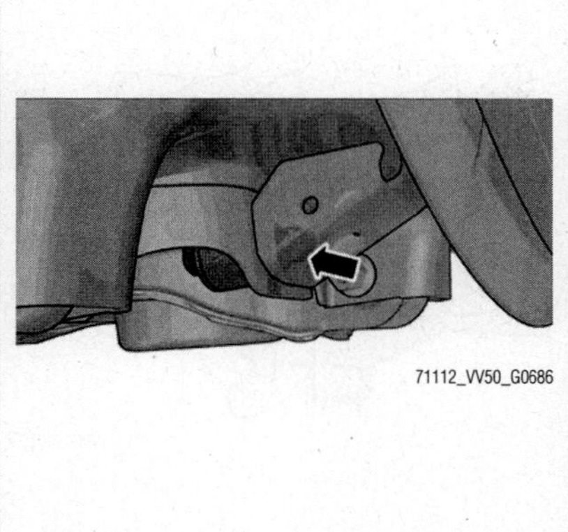

Fig. 257 Locating rear shock absorber-to-wheel knuckle nut

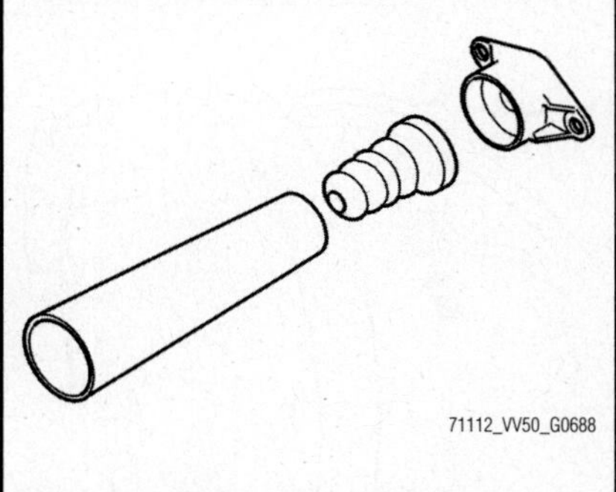

Fig. 259 Check the bump stop and dust boot for damage

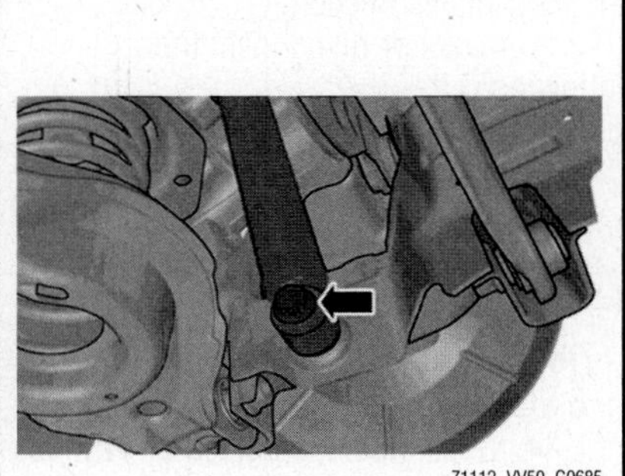

Fig. 256 Remove the lower shock absorber mounting bolt

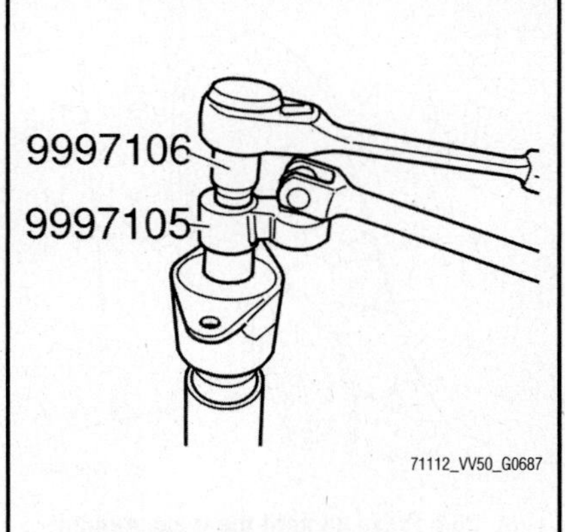

Fig. 258 Removing the shock absorber bushing on standard shock absorbers

1. Before servicing the vehicle, refer to the Precautions Section.
2. Remove the rear wheel.
3. Remove the 2 upper shock absorber mounting bolts.
4. Remove the lower shock absorber mounting bolt.

To install:

5. To install, reverse the removal procedure and note the following:
   - Tighten the rear shock absorber-to-wheel knuckle bolt to 85 ft. lbs. (115 Nm).
   - Tighten the upper shock absorber mounting bolts to 22 ft. lbs. (30 Nm).

Shock Absorber Upper Bushing

See Figures 258 and 259.

1. Before servicing the vehicle, refer to the Precautions Section.
2. Remove the shock absorber.
3. To remove the shock absorber bushing on standard shock absorbers:
   - Using Socket (999 7105) and Spanner (999 7106), remove the nut.
   - Remove the support plate.
   - Remove the bump stop and the dust boot.
4. To remove the shock absorber bushing on Nivomat shock absorbers:
   - Using Socket (999 5500) and Torx® socket, remove the nut.
   - Remove the support plate.
   - Remove the bump stop and the dust boot.

To install:

5. Check the bump stop and dust boot for damage. Replace if necessary.
6. To complete installation, reverse the removal procedure.

STABILIZER BAR

REMOVAL & INSTALLATION

Stabilizer Bar Link

See Figure 260.

1. Remove the nut.
2. Remove the screw with the bushings.

To install:

Installation is the reverse of the removal procedure.

UPPER CONTROL ARMS

REMOVAL & INSTALLATION

See Figures 261 through 264.

1. Before servicing the vehicle, refer to the Precautions Section.
2. Raise the vehicle.
3. Remove the rear wheel.
4. Remove the coil spring.
5. Remove the bolt for the wheel spindle.
6. Remove the subframe bolt.
7. Remove the control arm.

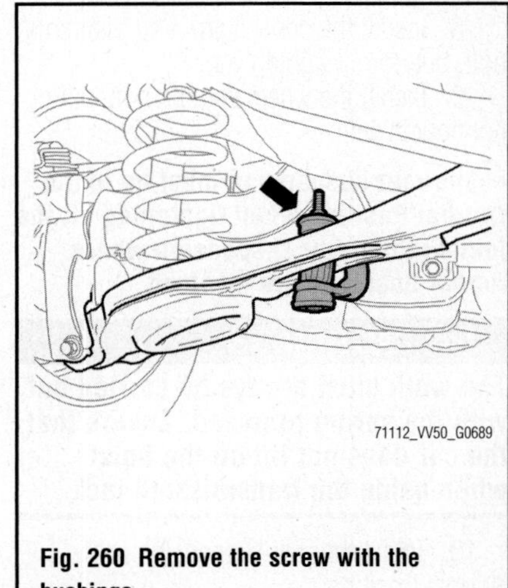

Fig. 260 Remove the screw with the bushings

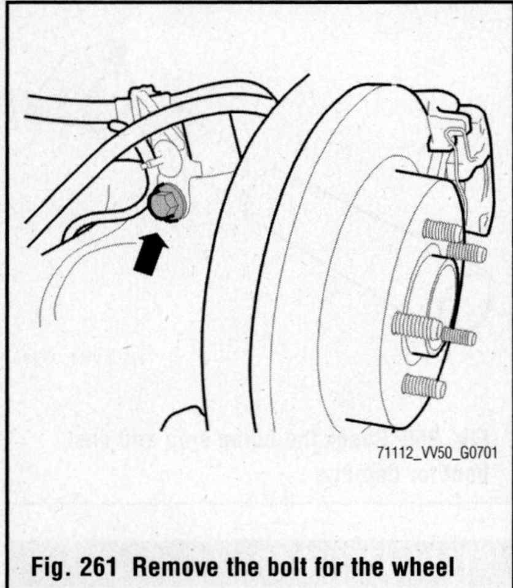

Fig. 261 Remove the bolt for the wheel spindle

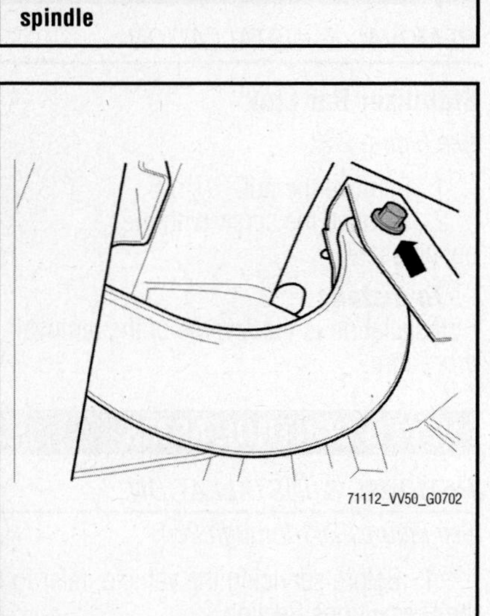

Fig. 262 Remove the subframe bolt

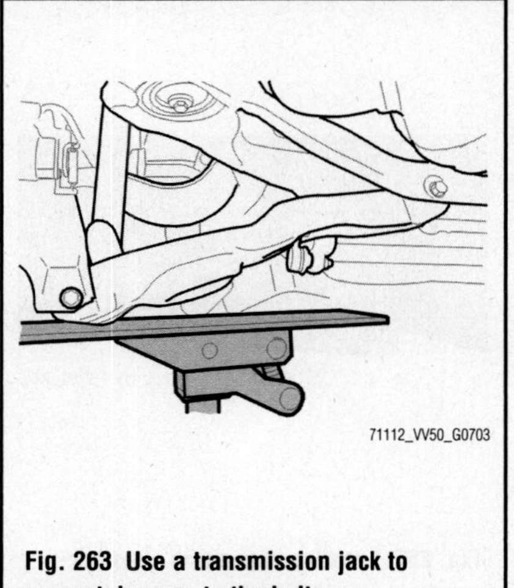

Fig. 263 Use a transmission jack to prevent damage to the bolts

Fig. 264 Press up until the measurement between the center of the wheel and the fender edge is approximately 14 inches (350 mm)

⁂ WARNING

Use a transmission jack to prevent damage to the bolts.

To install:

8. Install the control arm and subframe bolt, but do not tighten yet.
9. Install the wheel spindle bolt, but do not tighten yet.

➡The rear suspension must be in the Normal Position when tightening all the joints in the rear suspension where rubber bushings are involved.

⁂ CAUTION

The work must always be carried out with the spring removed. Ensure that the car does not lift off the hoist when using the transmission jack.

10. To set the rear suspension in the Normal Position:
    a. Position a transmission jack below the lower control arm.
    b. Press up until the measurement between the center of the wheel and the fender edge is approximately 14 inches (350 mm).
11. To complete installation, reverse the removal procedure.

WHEEL HUBS & BEARINGS

ADJUSTMENT

The rear wheel bearings are sealed, pressed-in units, and no adjustment is possible.

REMOVAL & INSTALLATION

See Figure 265.

1. Before servicing the vehicle, refer to the Precautions Section.
2. Remove or disconnect the following:
    - Wheel
    - Brake caliper
    - Brake disc
    - Wheel speed sensor
    - Wheel hub

To install:

3. Install or connect the following:
    - Wheel hub and tighten to 41 ft. lbs. (55 Nm)
    - ABS sensor and tighten to 42 inch lbs. (5 Nm)
    - Brake disc
    - Brake caliper
    - Wheel

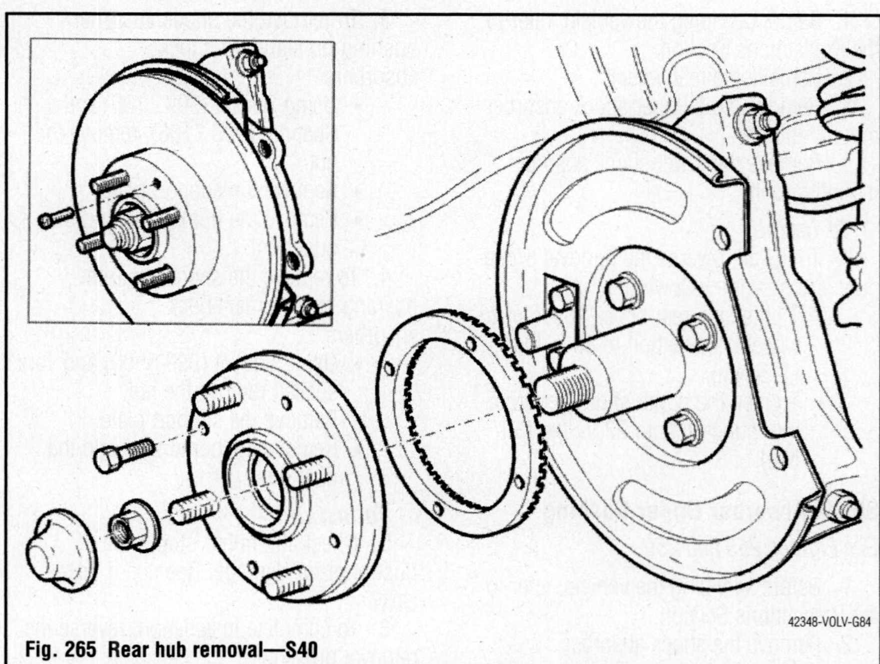

Fig. 265 Rear hub removal—S40

13

VOLVO

XC70

SPECIFICATIONS AND MAINTENANCE CHARTS

ENGINE AND VEHICLE IDENTIFICATION CHART

Engine				
Code	Liters (cc)	Fuel Sys.	Type	Eng. Mfg.
B6304T4	3.0 (3000)	EFI	DOHC	Volvo
B6324S4	3.2 (3200)	EFI	DOHC	Volvo
B6324S5	3.2 (3200)	EFI	DOHC	Volvo

Model Year	
Code ①	Year
B	2011
C	2012

EFI: Electronic Fuel Injection

DOHC: Double Overhead Camshafts

① 10th Digit of VIN

71112_XC70_C0001

GENERAL ENGINE SPECIFICATIONS

Year	Model	Engine ID	Engine Displ. Liters	Net Horsepower @ rpm	Net Torque @ rpm (ft. lbs.)	Bore x Stroke (in.)	Com-pression Ratio	Oil Pressure @ rpm (psi)
2011	XC70	B6304T4	3.0	300@5600	325@2100	3.23 x 3.67	9.3:1	51@4000
		B6324S4	3.2	230@6500	221@3300	3.31 x 3.78	10.3:1	51@4000
		B6324S5	3.2	240@6400	236@3200	3.31 x 3.78	10.8:1	51@4000
2012	XC70	B6304T4	3.0	300@5600	325@2100	3.23 x 3.67	9.3:1	51@4000
		B6324S4	3.2	230@6500	221@3300	3.31 x 3.78	10.3:1	51@4000
		B6324S5	3.2	240@6400	236@3200	3.31 x 3.78	10.8:1	51@4000

71112_XC70_C0002

ENGINE TUNE-UP SPECIFICATIONS

Year	Engine Displacement Liters	Engine ID	Spark Plug Gap (in.) ①	Ignition Timing (deg.)		Fuel Pump (psi)	Idle Speed (rpm)		Valve Clearance (in.)	
				MT	AT		MT	AT	In.	Ex.
2011	3.0	B6304T4	0.039	NA	NA	51-59	—	590	0.059-0.010	0.016-0.020
	3.2	B6324S4	0.039	NA	NA	51-59	—	590	0.059-0.010	0.016-0.020
	3.2	B6324S5	0.039	NA	NA	51-59	—	590	0.059-0.010	0.016-0.020
2012	3.0	B6304T4	0.039	NA	NA	51-59	—	590	0.059-0.010	0.016-0.020
	3.2	B6324S4	0.039	NA	NA	51-59	—	590	0.059-0.010	0.016-0.020
	3.2	B6324S5	0.039	NA	NA	51-59	—	590	0.059-0.010	0.016-0.020

NA: Information not available

① The label figures must be used if they differ from those in this chart.

71112_XC70_C0003

CAPACITIES

Year	Model	Engine Displacement (Liters)	Engine ID	Engine Oil with Filter (qts.)	Transmission (qts.) Man	Transmission (qts.) Auto.	Transfer Case (pts.)	Drive Axle Front (pts.)	Drive Axle Rear (pts.)	Fuel Tank (gal.)	Cooling System (qts.)
2011	XC70	3.0	B6304T4	7.18	—	5.8	①	—	②	18.5	9.4
		3.2	B6324S4	7.18	—	5.8	①	—	②	18.5	9.4
		3.2	B6324S5	7.18	—	5.8	①	—	②	18.5	9.4
2012	XC70	3.0	B6304T4	7.18	—	5.8	①	—	②	18.5	9.4
		3.2	B6324S4	7.18	—	5.8	①	—	②	18.5	9.4
		3.2	B6324S5	7.18	—	5.8	①	—	②	18.5	9.4

NOTE: All capacities are approximate. Add fluid gradualy and check to be sure a proper fluid level is obtained.

① Add fluid until fluid level reaches lower edge of fill hole.

② Add fluid until fluid level reaches lower edge of fill hole. Then suction out 50 ml.

71112_XC70_C0005

FLUID SPECIFICATIONS

Year	Model	Engine Size (Liters)	Engine ID	Engine Oil ①	Auto Transmission ②	Power Steering	Engine Coolant	Brake Fluid
2011	XC70	3.0	B6304T4	5W-30	BOT 341	WSS M2C204-A2	③	DOT 4+
		3.2	B6324S4	5W-30	BOT 341	WSS M2C204-A2	③	DOT 4+
		3.2	B6324S5	5W-30	BOT 341	WSS M2C204-A2	③	DOT 4+
2012	XC70	3.0	B6304T4	5W-30	BOT 341	WSS M2C204-A2	③	DOT 4+
		3.2	B6324S4	5W-30	BOT 341	WSS M2C204-A2	③	DOT 4+
		3.2	B6324S5	5W-30	BOT 341	WSS M2C204-A2	③	DOT 4+

① API SL, GF-4, or ACEA A1/B1; part number 1161754, -755, -756.

② Volvo ATF Fluid

③ Coolant with corrosion inhibitor mixed with water (50/50 mix)

71112_XC70_C0004

VALVE SPECIFICATIONS

Year	Engine Displacement Liters	Engine ID	Seat Angle (deg.)	Face Angle (deg.)	Spring Test Pressure (lbs. @ in.)	Spring Installed Height (in.)	Stem-to-Guide Clearance (in.) Intake	Stem-to-Guide Clearance (in.) Exhaust	Stem Diameter (in.) Intake	Stem Diameter (in.) Exhaust
2011	3.0	B6304T4	45	44.5	NA	1.768-1.846	0.0012-0.0024	0.0012-0.0028	0.235	0.2343-0.2346
	3.2	B6324S4	45	44.5	NA	1.768-1.846	0.0012-0.0024	0.0012-0.0028	0.235	0.2343-0.2346
	3.2	B6324S5	45	44.5	NA	1.768-1.846	0.0012-0.0024	0.0012-0.0028	0.235	0.2343-0.2346
2012	3.0	B6304T4	45	44.5	NA	1.768-1.846	0.0012-0.0024	0.0012-0.0028	0.235	0.2343-0.2346
	3.2	B6324S4	45	44.5	NA	1.768-1.846	0.0012-0.0024	0.0012-0.0028	0.235	0.2343-0.2346
	3.2	B6324S5	45	44.5	NA	1.768-1.846	0.0012-0.0024	0.0012-0.0028	0.235	0.2343-0.2346

NA: Information not available

71112_XC70_C0006

CAMSHAFT SPECIFICATIONS

All measurements in inches unless noted

Year	Engine Displacement Liters	Engine Code	Journal Diameter	Brg. Oil Clearance	Shaft End-play	Runout	Journal Bore	Lobe Height Intake	Lobe Height Exhaust
2011	3.0	B6304T4	NA	NA	NA	NA	NA	0.332	0.372
	3.2	B6324S4	NA	NA	NA	NA	NA	0.332	0.372
	3.2	B6324S5	NA	NA	NA	NA	NA	0.332	0.372
2012	3.0	B6304T4	NA	NA	NA	NA	NA	0.332	0.372
	3.2	B6324S4	NA	NA	NA	NA	NA	0.332	0.372
	3.2	B6324S5	NA	NA	NA	NA	NA	0.332	0.372

NA: Information not available

71112_XC70_C0007

CRANKSHAFT AND CONNECTING ROD SPECIFICATIONS

All measurements are given in inches.

Year	Engine Displacement Liters	Engine ID	Crankshaft Main Brg. Journal Dia.	Crankshaft Main Brg. Oil Clearance	Crankshaft Shaft End-play	Crankshaft Thrust on No.	Connecting Rod Journal Diameter	Connecting Rod Oil Clearance	Connecting Rod Side Clearance
2011	3.0	B6304T4	2.5591	NA	0.003-0.010	6	2.0866	NA	NA
	3.2	B6324S4	2.5591	NA	0.003-0.007	6	2.0866	NA	NA
	3.2	B6324S5	2.5591	NA	0.003-0.007	6	2.0866	NA	NA
2012	3.0	B6304T4	2.5591	NA	0.003-0.010	6	2.0866	NA	NA
	3.2	B6324S4	2.5591	NA	0.003-0.007	6	2.0866	NA	NA
	3.2	B6324S5	2.5591	NA	0.003-0.007	6	2.0866	NA	NA

NA: Information not available

71112_XC70_C0008

PISTON AND RING SPECIFICATIONS

All measurements are given in inches.

Year	Engine Displ. Liters	Engine ID	Piston Clearance	Ring Gap Top Compression	Ring Gap Bottom Compression	Ring Gap Oil Control	Ring Side Clearance Top Compression	Ring Side Clearance Bottom Compression	Ring Side Clearance Oil Control
2011	3.0	B6304T4	0.0016-0.0024	0.047	0.059	0.078	0.0012-0.0028	0.0012-0.0028	0.0008-0.0065
	3.2	B6324S4	0.0016-0.0024	0.047	0.059	0.078	0.0012-0.0028	0.0012-0.0028	0.0008-0.0065
	3.2	B6324S5	0.0016-0.0024	0.047	0.059	0.078	0.0012-0.0028	0.0012-0.0028	0.0008-0.0065
2012	3.0	B6304T4	0.0016-0.0024	0.047	0.059	0.078	0.0012-0.0028	0.0012-0.0028	0.0008-0.0065
	3.2	B6324S4	0.0016-0.0024	0.047	0.059	0.078	0.0012-0.0028	0.0012-0.0028	0.0008-0.0065
	3.2	B6324S5	0.0016-0.0024	0.047	0.059	0.078	0.0012-0.0028	0.0012-0.0028	0.0008-0.0065

NA: Information not available

71112_XC70_C0009

TIRE, WHEEL AND BALL JOINT SPECIFICATIONS

Year	Model	OEM Tires		Tire Pressures (psi)		Wheel	Ball Joint
		Standard	Optional	Front	Rear	Size	Inspection
2011	XC70	205/55VR17	None	①	①	7.5J	NA
2012	XC70	205/55VR17	None	①	①	7.5J	NA

OEM: Original Equipment Manufacturer

PSI: Pounds Per Square Inch

NA: Information not available

① See the tire placard on the vehicle

71112_XC70_C0011

BRAKE SPECIFICATIONS

All measurements in inches unless noted

Year	Model		Brake Disc			Minimum	Brake Caliper	
			Original Thickness	Minimum Thickness	Maximum Runout	Lining Thickness	Bracket bolts (ft. lbs.)	Mounting bolts (ft. lbs.)
2011	XC70	F	NA	NA	0.003	0.118	88	22
		R	NA	NA	0.002	0.118	52	22
2012	XC70	F	NA	NA	0.003	0.118	88	22
		R	NA	NA	0.002	0.118	52	22

F: Front

R: Rear

NA: Information not available

71112_XC70_C0012

SCHEDULED MAINTENANCE INTERVALS

2011-12 VOLVO XC70

TO BE SERVICED	TYPE OF SERVICE	VEHICLE MILEAGE INTERVAL (x1000)									
		7.5	15	22.5	30	37.5	45	52.5	60	67.5	75
Engine oil & filter	R	✓	✓	✓	✓	✓	✓	✓	✓	✓	✓
Underhood fluid levels	S/I	✓	✓	✓	✓	✓	✓	✓	✓	✓	✓
Brake pads	I	✓	✓	✓	✓	✓	✓	✓	✓	✓	✓
Collision warning camera (clean inside of windscreen)	S/I	✓	✓	✓	✓	✓	✓	✓	✓	✓	✓
Washer and wiper (windshield and headlights)	S/I	✓	✓	✓	✓	✓	✓	✓	✓	✓	✓
Wheels and tires	S/I	✓	✓	✓	✓	✓	✓	✓	✓	✓	✓
Cabin air filter	R		✓		✓		✓		✓		✓
Drivetrain fluid leaks	S/I		✓		✓		✓		✓		✓
Engine coolant	S/I		✓		✓		✓		✓		✓
Parking brake	A		✓		✓		✓		✓		✓
Brake and fuel lines	S/I				✓				✓		
Spare wheel/tire					✓				✓		
Air cleaner filter	R					✓					✓
Spark plugs	R										✓
Accessory drive belt and tensioner	R										✓
Automatic transmission fluid	Change if instructed by information display										
Temoprary tire sealing kit fluid	Replace fluid container every 4 years										
Driveshaft bellows and play	S/I								✓	✓	✓
Exhaust system	S/I								✓	✓	✓
Check suspension	S/I								✓	✓	✓
Brake fluid ①	R										

R: Replace S/I: Service or Inspect A:Adjust

① Replace every 2 years or 30,000 miles, whichever comes first under normal conditions, more frequently in mountainous areas or moist climates.

FREQUENT OPERATION MAINTENANCE (SEVERE SERVICE)

If a vehicle is operated under any of the following conditions it is considered severe service:

- Extremely dusty areas.
- 50% or more of the vehicle operation is in 90°F (32°C) or higher temperatures, or constant operation in temperatures below 32°F (0°C).
- Prolonged idling (vehicle operation in stop and go traffic).
- Frequent short running periods (engine does not warm to normal operating temperatures).
- Police, taxi, delivery usage or trailer towing usage.

Oil & oil filter: change every 5000 miles.

Air filter element: service or inspect every 15,000 miles.

Automatic transmisson oil replace every 52,500 miles.

71112_XC70_C0013

PRECAUTIONS

Before servicing any vehicle, please be sure to read all of the following precautions, which deal with personal safety, prevention of component damage, and important points to take into consideration when servicing a motor vehicle:

- Never open, service or drain the radiator or cooling system when the engine is hot; serious burns can occur from the steam and hot coolant.
- Observe all applicable safety precautions when working around fuel. Whenever servicing the fuel system, always work in a well-ventilated area. Do not allow fuel spray or vapors to come in contact with a spark, open flame, or excessive heat (a hot drop light, for example). Keep a dry chemical fire extinguisher near the work area. Always keep fuel in a container specifically designed for fuel storage; also, always properly seal fuel containers to avoid the possibility of fire or explosion. Refer to the additional fuel system precautions later in this section.
- Fuel injection systems often remain pressurized, even after the engine has been turned **OFF**. The fuel system pressure must be relieved before disconnecting any fuel lines. Failure to do so may result in fire and/or personal injury.
- Brake fluid often contains polyglycol ethers and polyglycols. Avoid contact with the eyes and wash your hands thoroughly after handling brake fluid. If you do get brake fluid in your eyes, flush your eyes with clean, running water for 15 minutes. If eye irritation persists, or if you have taken brake fluid internally, IMMEDIATELY seek medical assistance.
- The EPA warns that prolonged contact with used engine oil may cause a number of skin disorders, including cancer. You should make every effort to minimize your exposure to used engine oil. Protective gloves should be worn when changing oil. Wash your hands and any other exposed skin areas as soon as possible after exposure to used engine oil. Soap and water, or waterless hand cleaner should be used.
- All new vehicles are now equipped with an air bag system, often referred to as a Supplemental Restraint System (SRS) or Supplemental Inflatable Restraint (SIR) system. The system must be disabled before performing service on or around system components, steering column, instrument panel components, wiring and sensors. Failure to follow safety and disabling procedures could result in accidental air bag deployment, possible personal injury and unnecessary system repairs.
- Always wear safety goggles when working with, or around, the air bag system. When carrying a non-deployed air bag, be sure the bag and trim cover are pointed away from your body. When placing a non-deployed air bag on a work surface, always face the bag and trim cover upward, away from the surface. This will reduce the motion of the module if it is accidentally deployed. Refer to the additional air bag system precautions later in this section.
- Clean, high quality brake fluid from a sealed container is essential to the safe and proper operation of the brake system. You should always buy the correct type of brake fluid for your vehicle. If the brake fluid becomes contaminated, completely flush the system with new fluid. Never reuse any brake fluid. Any brake fluid that is removed from the system should be discarded. Also, do not allow any brake fluid to come in contact with a painted surface; it will damage the paint.
- Never operate the engine without the proper amount and type of engine oil; doing so WILL result in severe engine damage.
- Timing belt maintenance is extremely important. Many models utilize an interference-type, non-freewheeling engine. If the timing belt breaks, the valves in the cylinder head may strike the pistons, causing potentially serious (also time-consuming and expensive) engine damage. Refer to the maintenance interval charts for the recommended replacement interval for the timing belt, and to the timing belt section for belt replacement and inspection.
- Disconnecting the negative battery cable on some vehicles may interfere with the functions of the on-board computer system(s) and may require the computer to undergo a relearning process once the negative battery cable is reconnected.
- When servicing drum brakes, only disassemble and assemble one side at a time, leaving the remaining side intact for reference.
- Only an MVAC-trained, EPA-certified automotive technician should service the air conditioning system or its components.

BRAKES

ANTI-LOCK BRAKE SYSTEM (ABS)

GENERAL INFORMATION

PRECAUTIONS

- Certain components within the ABS system are not intended to be serviced or repaired individually.
- Do not use rubber hoses or other parts not specifically specified for and ABS system. When using repair kits, replace all parts included in the kit. Partial or incorrect repair may lead to functional problems and require the replacement of components.
- Lubricate rubber parts with clean, fresh brake fluid to ease assembly. Do not use shop air to clean parts; damage to rubber components may result.
- Use only DOT 3 brake fluid from an unopened container.
- If any hydraulic component or line is removed or replaced, it may be necessary to bleed the entire system.
- A clean repair area is essential. Always clean the reservoir and cap thoroughly before removing the cap. The slightest amount of dirt in the fluid may plug an orifice and impair the system function. Perform repairs after components have been thoroughly cleaned; use only denatured alcohol to clean components. Do not allow ABS components to come into contact with any substance containing mineral oil; this includes used shop rags.
- The Anti-Lock control unit is a microprocessor similar to other computer units in the vehicle. Ensure that the ignition switch is **OFF** before removing or installing controller harnesses. Avoid static electricity discharge at or near the controller.
- If any arc welding is to be done on the vehicle, the control unit should be unplugged before welding operations begin.

SPEED SENSORS

REMOVAL & INSTALLATION

Front

See Figure 1.

1. Before servicing the vehicle, refer to the Precautions Section.
2. Remove the front wheel.
3. Push in, then disconnect the electrical connector from the front wheel speed sensor.

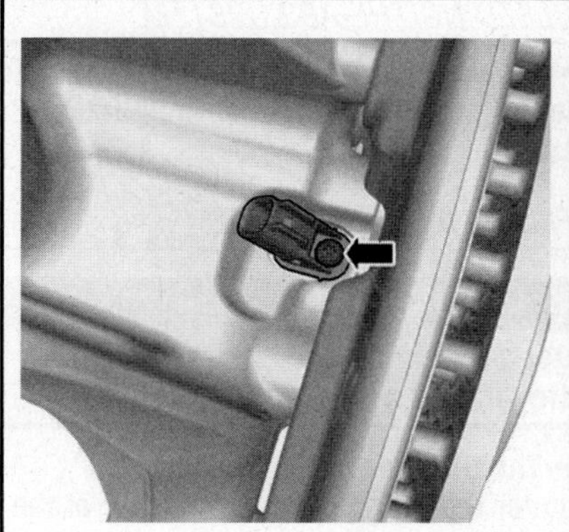

Fig. 1 Remove the screw, then remove the front wheel speed sensor

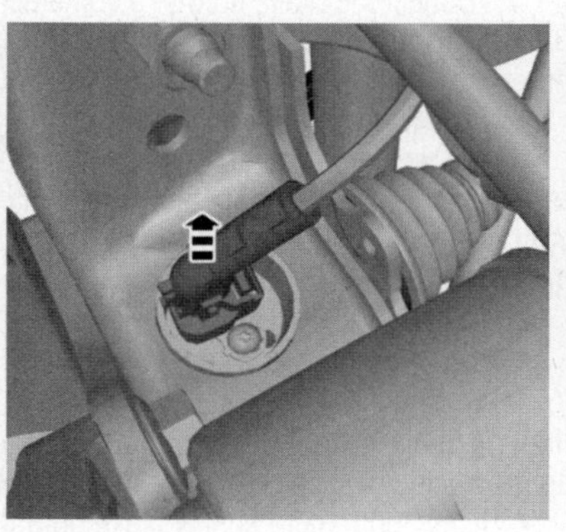

Fig. 2 Disconnect the electrical connector from the rear wheel speed sensor

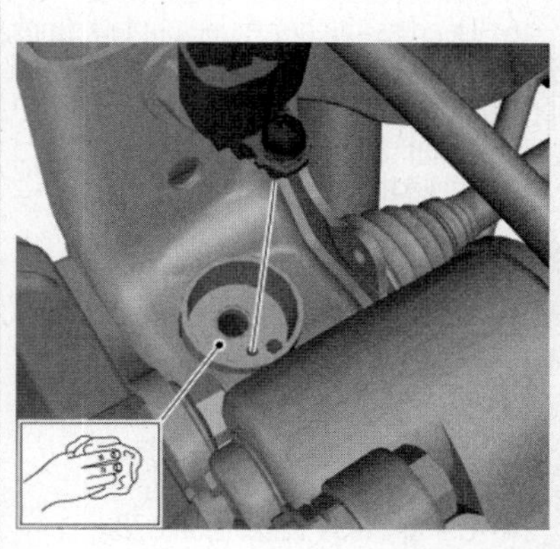

Fig. 3 Clean the area as shown

4. Remove the screw, then remove the front wheel speed sensor.

To install:

5. To install, reverse the removal procedure and note the following:
   - Tighten the front wheel speed sensor screw to 80 inch lbs. (9 Nm).

Rear

See Figures 2 and 3.

1. Before servicing the vehicle, refer to the Precautions Section.
2. Remove the rear wheel.
3. Disconnect the electrical connector from the rear wheel speed sensor.
4. Remove the screw, then remove the rear wheel speed sensor.

To install:

WARNING

Make sure that the area around the component is clean and free of foreign material.

To install, reverse the removal procedure and note the following:

- Clean the area as shown.

BRAKES — BLEEDING THE BRAKE SYSTEM

BLEEDING PROCEDURE

BLEEDING PROCEDURE

➡It is recommended that brake fluid is changed every other year. On cars that are exposed to heavy and frequent braking (for example, mountain driving or driving in tropical climates with high humidity), the brake fluid must be changed every year.

The oil must be replaced because it is hygroscopic (the fluid absorbs water molecules from the air). This absorption of water occurs through the brake hoses and brake fluid reservoir. These components are rubber and plastic respectively and are not completely sealed against water molecules. An increased water content in the brake fluid dramatically reduces its boiling point and causes corrosion in the brake system components. This results in damage to the brake system. Braking performance deteriorates markedly.

➡Use only Volvo Genuine Parts brake fluid designated DOT 4+. Never reuse brake fluid. Always keep the brake fluid sealed in the original packaging.

➡Continually check that there is sufficient brake fluid in the brake fluid reservoir when changing brake fluid.

Front

➡When reconditioning or replacing brake calipers, bleed the relevant brake line as follows. The brake pedal must be depressed throughout the operation. This is so that the brake system is not drained of brake fluid. If the braking system has been completely or partly drained, bleed the whole system.

➡Start the bleed procedure at the left front wheel, then bleed the right front, left rear and right rear wheels.

1. Turn off ignition.
2. Clean around the brake fluid reservoir filler cap.
3. Raise and support the vehicle.
4. Remove all 4 wheels.
5. Starting at the left front wheel, remove the protective cap from the bleed nipple.
6. Install a plastic hose on the nipple.
7. Depress the brake pedal a few times. Maintain pressure.
8. Open the bleed nipple. Collect the brake fluid in a container.
9. Press the brake caliper piston to the bottom of the caliper.
10. Install G-clamp as shown. Leave the G-clamp in pushed-in position.
11. Perform one of the following procedures:

Alternative 1:

- Connect the bleeding unit.
- Open the bleed nipple on the caliper. Wait until there is new oil in the plastic hose.
- Close the bleed nipple.

Alternative 2:

- Press down the brake pedal to the limit position.
- Keep it pressed down for approximately 2 seconds before releasing it.
- Repeat until there is new brake fluid in the plastic hose.
- Close the bleed nipple when the brake pedal is fully depressed.

12. Remove the hose. Install the protective cap.
13. Remove the G-clamp from the brake caliper.
14. Repeat the process on the other front wheel.

15. Adjust brake fluid level.
16. Depress the brake pedal a few times. Check the level of the brake fluid reservoir. Top up if necessary.
17. Install the front wheels.
18. Bleed the rear brake system.

Rear

➡Start the bleed procedure at the left rear wheel.

1. Turn off the ignition.
2. Raise and support the vehicle.
3. Remove the brake caliper.
4. Using Press Tools (999 5782, replace 5782-1 with 999 7091), press the piston into the brake caliper.
5. Remove the protective cap from the bleed nipple.
6. Install the plastic hose on the nipple. Open the bleed nipple.
7. Collect the brake fluid in a container.
8. Perform one of the following procedures:

Alternative 1:

- Connect the bleeding unit.
- Open the bleed nipple on the caliper. Wait until there is new oil in the plastic hose.
- Close the bleed nipple.

Alternative 2:

- Press down the brake pedal to the limit position. Keep it pressed down for approximately 2 seconds before releasing it.
- Repeat until there is new brake fluid in the plastic hose.
- Close the bleed nipple when the brake pedal is fully depressed.

9. Remove the hose and install the protective cap.
10. To complete installation, reverse the removal procedure.

BLEEDING THE ABS SYSTEM

➡Bleeding an ABS brake system takes longer than bleeding a normal brake system.

FLUID FILL PROCEDURE

**** WARNING**

Dot 4+ should never be mixed with any other type of brake fluid.

➡The fluid reservoir is concealed under the round cover at the rear of the engine compartment. The round cover must be removed first before the reservoir cap can be accessed.

1. Turn and open the cover.
2. Unscrew the reservoir cap, and fill with Dot 4+ brake fluid until the level is between the MIN and MAX marks.

BRAKES — FRONT DISC BRAKES

**** CAUTION**

Dust and dirt accumulating on brake parts during normal use may contain asbestos fibers from production or aftermarket brake linings. Breathing excessive concentrations of asbestos fibers can cause serious bodily harm. Exercise care when servicing brake parts. Do not sand or grind brake lining unless equipment used is designed to contain the dust residue. Do not clean brake parts with compressed air or by dry brushing. Cleaning should be done by dampening the brake components with a fine mist of water, then wiping the brake components clean with a dampened cloth. Dispose of cloth and all residue containing asbestos fibers in an impermeable container with the appropriate label. Follow practices prescribed by the Occupational Safety and Health Administration (OSHA) and the Environmental Protection Agency (EPA) for the handling, processing, and disposing of dust or debris that may contain asbestos fibers.

BRAKE CALIPER

REMOVAL & INSTALLATION

See Figure 4

➡The brake pedal must be depressed throughout the operation. This is so that the brake system is not drained of brake fluid.

1. Before servicing the vehicle, refer to the Precautions Section.
2. Remove the wheel and tire assembly.
3. Remove the front brake pads.
4. Remove the brake hose-to-front brake caliper.
5. Remove the 2 front brake caliper-to-slide rail bolts.
6. Remove the front brake caliper.
7. Remove the 2 bolts, then remove the front brake caliper bracket.

To install:

8. To install, reverse the removal procedure and note the following:

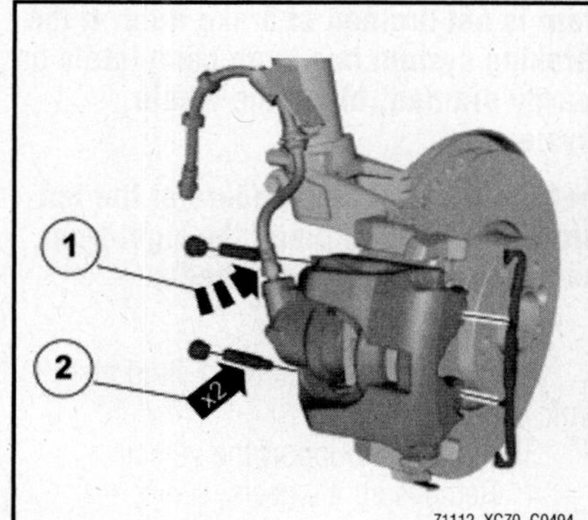

Fig. 4 Remove the brake hose-to-front brake caliper (1). Remove the 2 front brake caliper-to-slide rail bolts (2). Remove the front brake caliper

- Tighten the front brake caliper mount bolts to 148 ft. lbs. (200 Nm).
- Tighten the 2 front brake caliper-to-slide rail bolts to 21 ft. lbs. (28 Nm).
- Tighten the brake hose-to-front brake caliper to 13 ft. lbs. (18 Nm).

9. Fill and bleed the brake system.

➡Use only Volvo Genuine parts brake fluid (Volvo DOT 4+).

BRAKE PADS

REMOVAL & INSTALLATION

See Figure 5.

1. Before servicing the vehicle, refer to the Precautions Section.
2. Remove the wheel and tire assembly.
3. Remove the retaining clip.

**** WARNING**

The brake caliper housing Torx® bolts must not be removed.

**** WARNING**

Make sure that no load is placed on the brake hose.

4. Remove the caps, then remove the front brake caliper slide rails.
5. Push toward center, then remove brake pads.

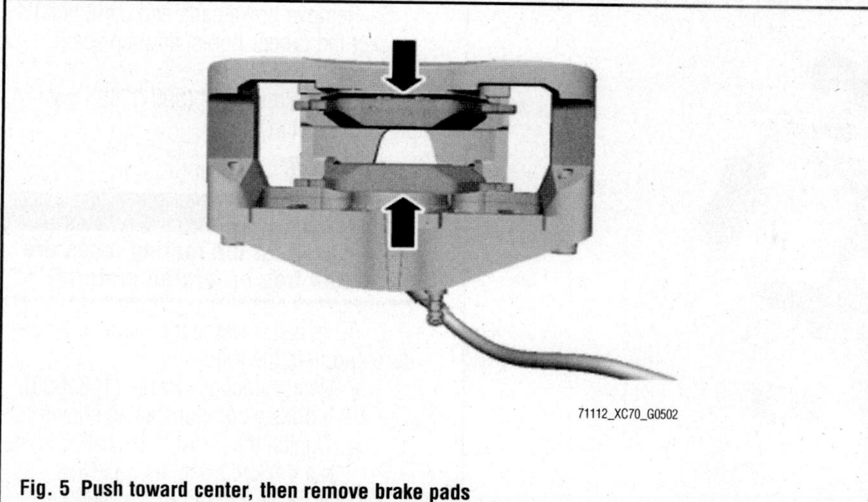

Fig. 5 Push toward center, then remove brake pads

To install:

WARNING

Make sure that the mating faces are clean and free of foreign material.

6. To install, reverse the removal procedure and note the following:
   - Using Silicone Grease (1161688), lubricate components as shown.
   - Tighten the front brake caliper slide rail to 21 ft. lbs. (28 Nm).
7. Depress the brake pedal a few times.
8. Add brake fluid if necessary.
9. Adjust the parking brake as required.

BRAKES

REAR DISC BRAKES

CAUTION

Dust and dirt accumulating on brake parts during normal use may contain asbestos fibers from production or aftermarket brake linings. Breathing excessive concentrations of asbestos fibers can cause serious bodily harm. Exercise care when servicing brake parts. Do not sand or grind brake lining unless equipment used is designed to contain the dust residue. Do not clean brake parts with compressed air or by dry brushing. Cleaning should be done by dampening the brake components with a fine mist of water, then wiping the brake components clean with a dampened cloth. Dispose of cloth and all residue containing asbestos fibers in an impermeable container with the appropriate label. Follow practices prescribed by the Occupational Safety and Health Administration (OSHA) and the Environmental Protection Agency (EPA) for the handling, processing, and disposing of dust or debris that may contain asbestos fibers.

BRAKE CALIPER

REMOVAL & INSTALLATION

See Figure 6.

➡The brake pedal must be depressed throughout the operation. This is so that the brake system is not drained of brake fluid.

1. Before servicing the vehicle, refer to the Precautions Section.
2. Adjust the parking brake.
3. Remove the wheel and tire assembly.
4. Disconnect the electrical connector.
5. Remove the brake hose-to-rear brake caliper bolt, and position hose aside.
6. Remove the 2 rear brake caliper slide rail bolts, then remove the rear brake caliper.

To install:

7. To install, reverse the removal procedure and note the following:
   - Tighten the 2 rear brake caliper slide rail bolts to 26 ft. lbs. (35 Nm).
   - Tighten the brake hose-to-rear brake caliper bolt to 34 ft. lbs. (46 Nm).
8. Bleed the brake system.
9. Adjust the parking brake.

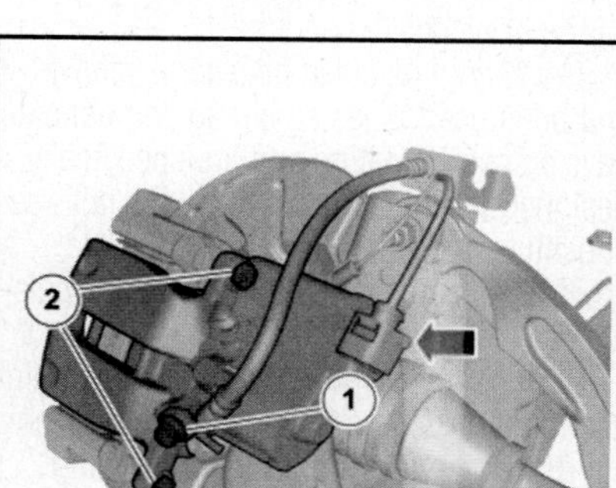

Fig. 6 Disconnect the electrical connector. Remove the brake hose-to-rear brake caliper bolt (1), and position hose aside. Remove the 2 rear brake caliper slide rail bolts (2), then remove the rear brake caliper

BRAKE PADS

REMOVAL & INSTALLATION

See Figures 7 and 8.

1. Before servicing the vehicle, refer to the Precautions Section.
2. Activate Parking Brake Module (PBM) service mode.
3. Remove the wheel and tire assembly.

WARNING

Make sure that no load is placed on the brake hose.

4. Remove the 2 rear brake caliper slide rail bolts, and position the caliper aside.

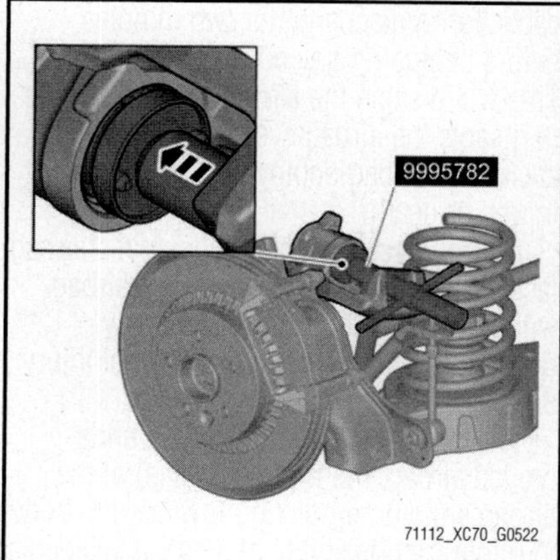

Fig. 7 Using Press Tool (999 5782), compress the piston.

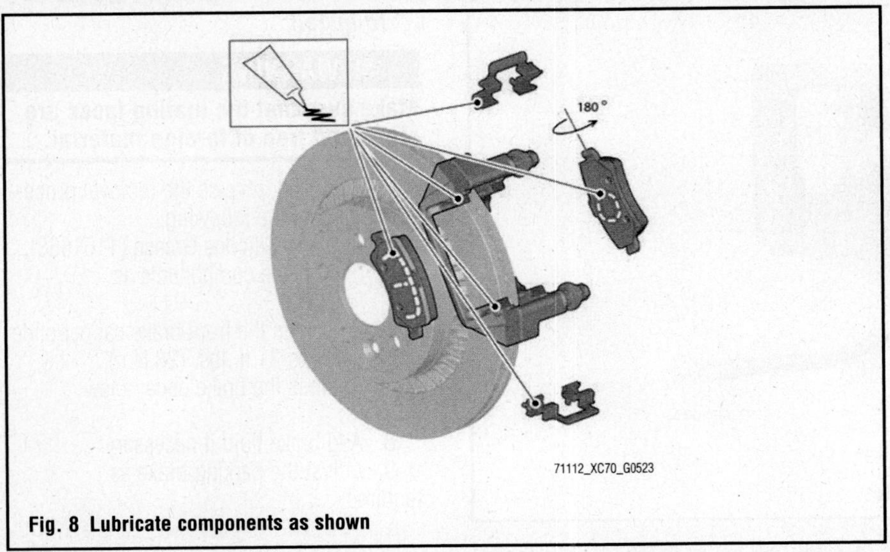

Fig. 8 Lubricate components as shown

5. Remove brake pads and components. Inspect the rubber boots, and replace if necessary.
6. Using Press Tool (999 5782), compress the piston.

To install:

WARNING

Make sure that the mating faces are clean and free of foreign material.

7. To install, reverse the removal procedure and note the following:
   - Using Silicone Grease (1161688), lubricate components as shown.
   - Tighten the 2 rear brake caliper slide rail bolts to 26 ft. lbs. (35 Nm).
8. Deactivate Parking Brake Module (PBM) service mode.

CHASSIS ELECTRICAL

AIR BAG (SUPPLEMENTAL RESTRAINT SYSTEM)

GENERAL INFORMATION

CAUTION

These vehicles are equipped with an air bag system. The system must be disarmed before performing service on, or around, system components, the steering column, instrument panel components, wiring and sensors. Failure to follow the safety precautions and the disarming procedure could result in accidental air bag deployment, possible injury and unnecessary system repairs.

SERVICE PRECAUTIONS

Disconnect and isolate the battery negative cable before beginning any airbag system component diagnosis, testing, removal, or installation procedures. Allow system capacitor to discharge for two minutes before beginning any component service. This will disable the airbag system. Failure to disable the airbag system may result in accidental airbag deployment, personal injury, or death.

Do not place an intact undeployed airbag face down on a solid surface. The airbag will propel into the air if accidentally deployed and may result in personal injury or death.

When carrying or handling an undeployed airbag, the trim side (face) of the airbag should be pointing towards the body to minimize possibility of injury if accidental deployment occurs. Failure to do this may result in personal injury or death.

Replace airbag system components with OEM replacement parts. Substitute parts may appear interchangeable, but internal differences may result in inferior occupant protection. Failure to do so may result in occupant personal injury or death.

Wear safety glasses, rubber gloves, and long sleeved clothing when cleaning powder residue from vehicle after an airbag deployment. Powder residue emitted from a deployed airbag can cause skin irritation. Flush affected area with cool water if irritation is experienced. If nasal or throat irritation is experienced, exit the vehicle for fresh air until the irritation ceases. If irritation continues, see a physician.

Do not use a replacement airbag that is not in the original packaging. This may result in improper deployment, personal injury, or death.

The factory installed fasteners, screws and bolts used to fasten airbag components have a special coating and are specifically designed for the airbag system. Do not use substitute fasteners. Use only original equipment fasteners listed in the parts catalog when fastener replacement is required.

During, and following, any child restraint anchor service, due to impact event or vehicle repair, carefully inspect all mounting hardware, tether straps, and anchors for proper installation, operation, or damage. If a child restraint anchor is found damaged in any way, the anchor must be replaced. Failure to do this may result in personal injury or death.

Deployed and non-deployed airbags may or may not have live pyrotechnic material within the airbag inflator.

Do not dispose of driver/passenger/curtain airbags or seat belt tensioners unless you are sure of complete deployment. Refer to the Hazardous Substance Control System for proper disposal.

Dispose of deployed airbags and tensioners consistent with state, provincial, local, and federal regulations.

After any airbag component testing or service, do not connect the battery negative cable. Personal injury or death may result if the system test is not performed first.

If the vehicle is equipped with the Occupant Classification System (OCS), do not connect the battery negative cable before performing the OCS Verification Test using the scan tool and the appropriate diagnostic information. Personal injury or death may result if the system test is not performed properly.

Never replace both the Occupant Restraint Controller (ORC) and the Occupant Classification Module (OCM) at the same time. If both require replacement, replace one, then perform the Airbag System test before replacing the other.

Both the ORC and the OCM store Occupant Classification System (OCS) calibration data, which they transfer to one another when one of them is replaced. If both are replaced at the same time, an irreversible fault will be set in both modules and the OCS may malfunction and cause personal injury or death.

If equipped with OCS, the Seat Weight Sensor is a sensitive, calibrated unit and must be handled carefully. Do not drop or handle roughly. If dropped or damaged, replace with another sensor. Failure to do so may result in occupant injury or death.

If equipped with OCS, the front passenger seat must be handled carefully as well. When removing the seat, be careful when setting on floor not to drop. If dropped, the sensor may be inoperative, could result in occupant injury, or possibly death.

If equipped with OCS, when the passenger front seat is on the floor, no one should sit in the front passenger seat. This uneven force may damage the sensing ability of the seat weight sensors. If sat on and damaged, the sensor may be inoperative, could result in occupant injury, or possibly death.

DISARMING THE SYSTEM

1. Before servicing the vehicle, refer to the Precautions Section.
2. Disconnect and isolate the negative battery cable. Wait 3 minutes for the system capacitor to discharge before performing any service.

CAUTION

Wait at least 3 minutes before working on the vehicle. The air bag system is designed to retain enough power to deploy the air bag for a short time after the battery has been disconnected.

ARMING THE SYSTEM

1. Before servicing the vehicle, refer to the Precautions Section.
2. After repairs are complete, connect the negative battery cable. Turn the ignition switch to the **ON** position and check the SRS light for proper operation.

CLOCKSPRING CENTERING

See Figure 9.

➡Make sure that the road wheels are in the straight-ahead position.

1. Remove steering the steering wheel.

WARNING

Make sure that the color marking is visible in the window.

2. Adjust the color marking as necessary using the screw.
3. Check that the SRS is functioning properly:
   - Install the battery negative lead.

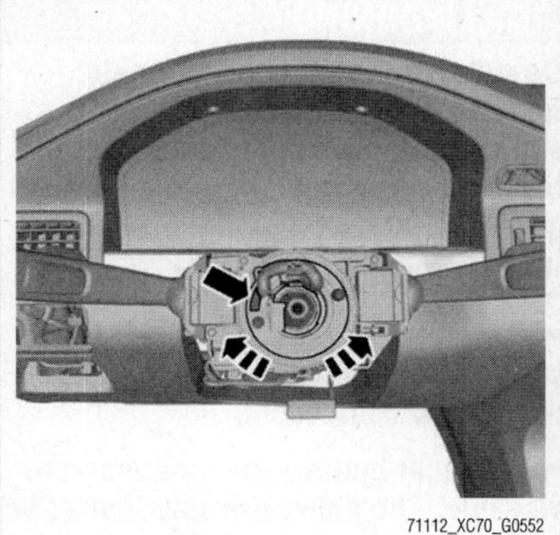

Fig. 9 Make sure that the color marking is visible in the window

- Turn the ignition switch to Position II.
- The SRS warning light in the instrument cluster must illuminate and go out after approximately 7 seconds.
- Check that the SRS warning light is not constantly lit. Fault-trace the SRS if the light is constantly lit.

DRIVE TRAIN

PROPELLER SHAFT

REMOVAL & INSTALLATION

See Figures 10 and 11.

1. Place gearshift selector lever in Neutral position.
2. Remove the 6 M8 bolts from the exhaust system.
3. Remove the 4 M8 bolts, then the 2 fasteners, and remove the front heat shield.

➡Note the position of the component before removal.

4. Using Counterhold (999 5743), remove the 6 front CV-joint-to-transfer case bolts.
5. Using Counterhold (999 5743), remove the 6 rear CV-joint-to-Active On-demand Coupling (AOC) input flange.
6. Noting alignment divets, remove the front crossmember.
7. Remove the 4 M8 bolts from the rear protecting plate and rear crossmember.
8. Remove the 2 bolts from the front and rear brackets.
9. Rotate and remove the propeller shaft.

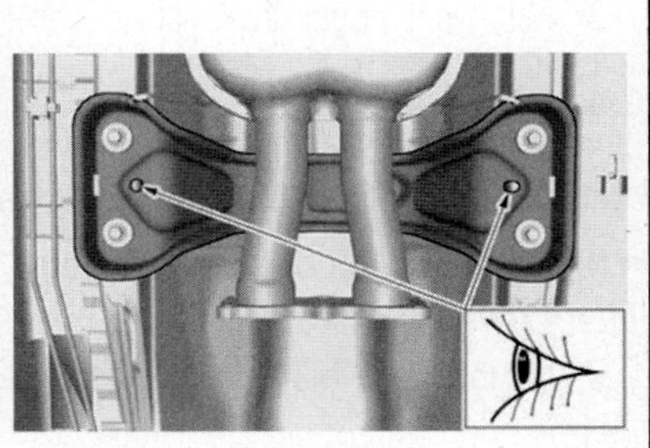

Fig. 10 Noting alignment divets, remove the front crossmember

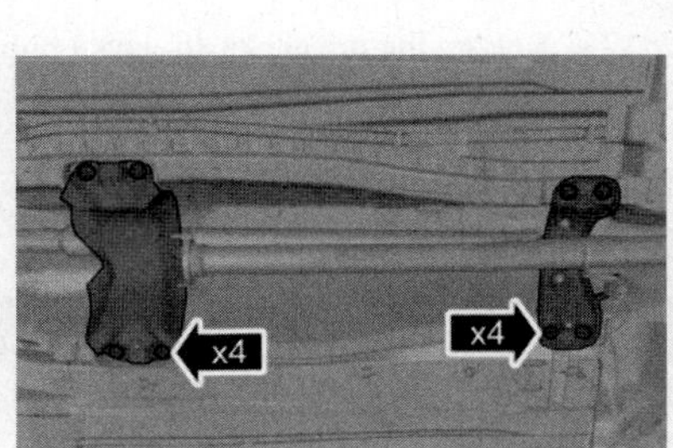

Fig. 11 Remove the 4 M8 bolts from the rear protecting plate and rear crossmember

To install:

To install, reverse the removal procedure and note the following:

- Tighten the propeller shaft center bearing to 22 ft. lbs. (30 Nm).
- Tighten the M8 bolts to 18 ft. lbs. (25 Nm).
- Tighten the front and rear propeller shaft CV-joint bolts:

Stage 1: Crosswise to 89 inch lbs. (10 Nm).

Stage 2: Crosswise to 18 ft. lbs. (25 Nm).

FRONT HALFSHAFT

REMOVAL & INSTALLATION

Left

See Figures 12 and 13.

***** WARNING**

Do not use magnets or magnetic tools close to tooth wheels, drive shafts or wheel hubs. A magnetized tooth wheel will lose its function and generate incorrect signals resulting in fault codes.

➡Any magnetized tooth wheel, drive shaft or wheel hub must be replaced with a new component.

➡The inner bellows kits are non-serviceable. The entire driveshaft must be replaced.

1. Remove the left front wheel.
2. Remove the front control arm.
3. Loosen the front link arm.
4. Remove the left driveshaft-to-wheel hub bolt.
5. Install Press Tool (999 7251) and Hydraulic Hole Cylinder (951 2923) as shown.
6. Using Key (999 7160), loosen the left front halfshaft.

***** WARNING**

Take extra care not to damage the seal.

7. Remove the left front halfshaft.

To install:

8. To install, reverse the removal procedure and note the following:
   - Tighten the driveshaft-to-wheel hub bolt to 26 ft. lbs. (35 Nm), then 90°.

Right

See Figure 14.

***** WARNING**

Do not use magnets or magnetic tools close to tooth wheels, drive shafts or wheel hubs. A magnetized tooth wheel will lose its function and generate incorrect signals resulting in fault codes.

Fig. 12 Remove the left driveshaft-to-wheel hub bolt

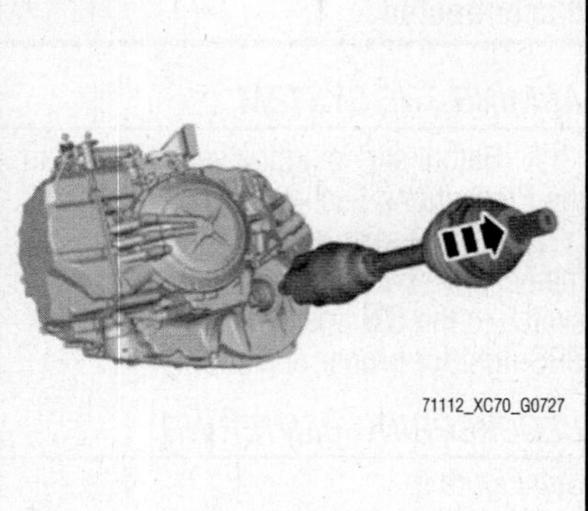

Fig. 13 Remove the left front halfshaft

➡Any magnetized tooth wheel, drive shaft or wheel hub must be replaced with a new component.

➡The inner bellows kits are non-serviceable. The entire driveshaft must be replaced.

1. Remove the right front wheel.
2. Remove the right engine rear lower support insulator.
3. Remove the right driveshaft-to-wheel hub bolt.
4. Loosen the wheel spindle.
5. Install Press Tool (999 7251) and Hydraulic Hole Cylinder (951 2923) as shown.

➡Note the position of the component before removal.

6. Remove the 2 M8 bolts and the bearing cap.

***** WARNING**

Make sure that the inner constant velocity (CV) joint does not separate.

7. Remove the right halfshaft.

***** WARNING**

Make sure that the surfaces are clean and free of foreign material.

To install:

8. To install, reverse the removal procedure and note the following:
   - Tighten the M8 bolts to 18 ft. lbs. (24 Nm).
   - Tighten the driveshaft-to-wheel hub bolt to 26 ft. lbs. (35 Nm), then 90°.

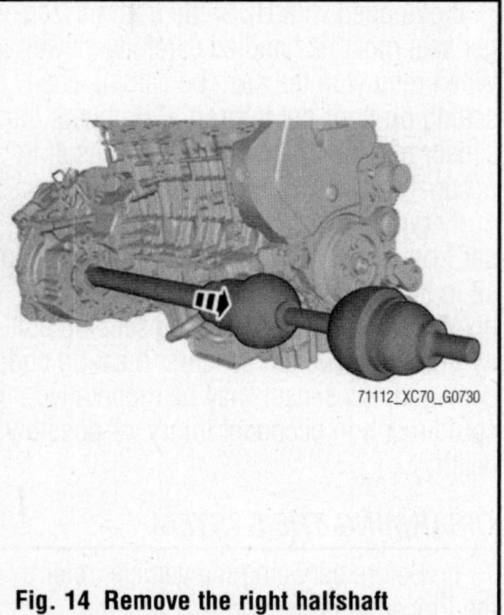

Fig. 14 Remove the right halfshaft

REAR HALFSHAFT

REMOVAL & INSTALLATION

See Figures 15 through 19.

➡This procedure applies to AWD vehicles only.

➡This procedure applies to removal of either the left or right-side rear halfshaft.

***** WARNING**

Do not use magnets or magnetic tools close to tooth wheels, drive shafts or wheel hubs. A magnetized tooth wheel will lose its function and generate incorrect signals resulting in fault codes.

➡Any magnetized tooth wheel, drive shaft or wheel hub must be replaced with a new component.

➡The inner bellows kits are non-serviceable. The entire driveshaft must be replaced.

1. Remove the rear spring.
2. Remove the rear shock absorber-to-wheel knuckle bolt.
3. Remove the rear lower arm-to-wheel knuckle bolt, and pivot lower arm out of the way.

***** WARNING**

Make sure that the ball joint ball does not rotate.

4. Remove the rear stabilizer bar link-to-lower stabilizer bar bolt, and position the link aside.
5. Remove the tie rod-to-longitudinal stay bolt, and position the component aside.

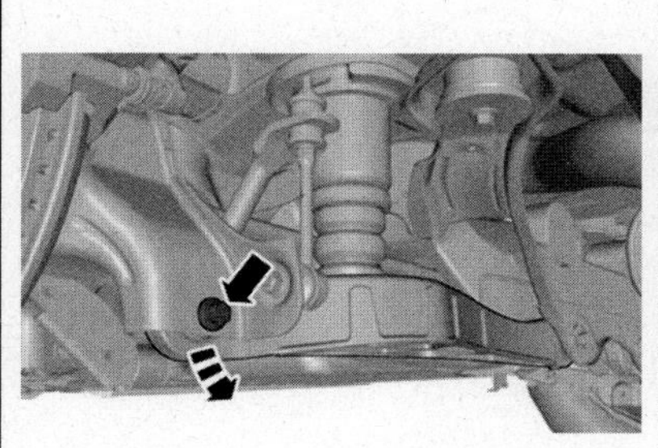

Fig. 15 Remove the rear lower arm-to-wheel knuckle bolt, and pivot lower arm out of the way

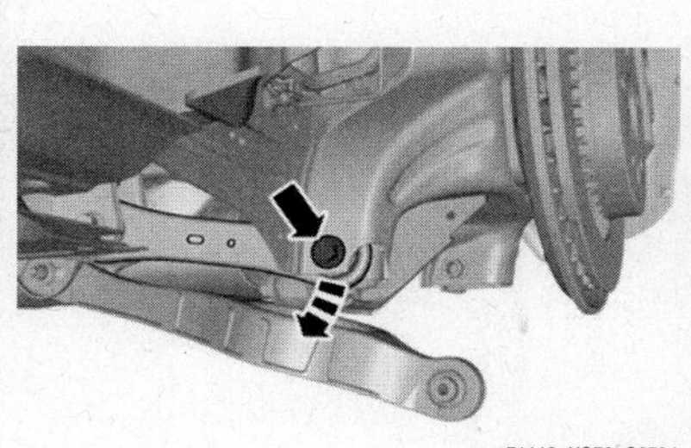

Fig. 16 Remove the tie rod-to-longitudinal stay bolt, and position the component aside

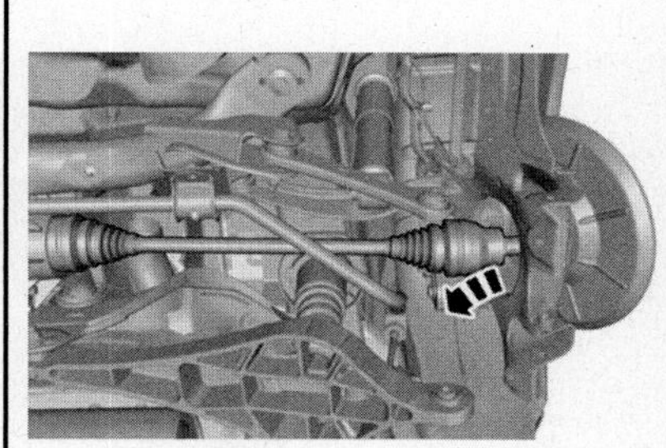

Fig. 17 Remove the rear halfshaft

6. Remove the rear driveshaft-to-wheel hub bolt.
7. On both sides of vehicle, remove the 4 bolts, then the splash plate.
8. Remove the rear driveshaft-to-wheel hub bolt.
9. Remove the clips.

➡This step requires the aid of another technician.

10. Pull the trailing arm and brake assembly aside.

➡This step requires the aid of another technician.

11. Remove the rear halfshaft.
12. Measure the CV-joint as shown. If the measurement is 3.2 inches (82 mm), vehicle is equipped with the early version. If the measurement is 2.8 inches (71 mm), vehicle is equipped with the late version.
13. If vehicle is equipped with the early version, use Puller (999 7399) to pry off the CV-joint.
14. If vehicle is equipped with the late version, install Counterhold (999 7398). Using Key (999 7397), remove the CV-joint.
15. On all vehicles, remove the rear half-shaft.

To install:

To install, reverse the removal procedure and note the following:

- Tighten the wheel knuckle-to-body bolt to 133 ft. lbs. (180 Nm).

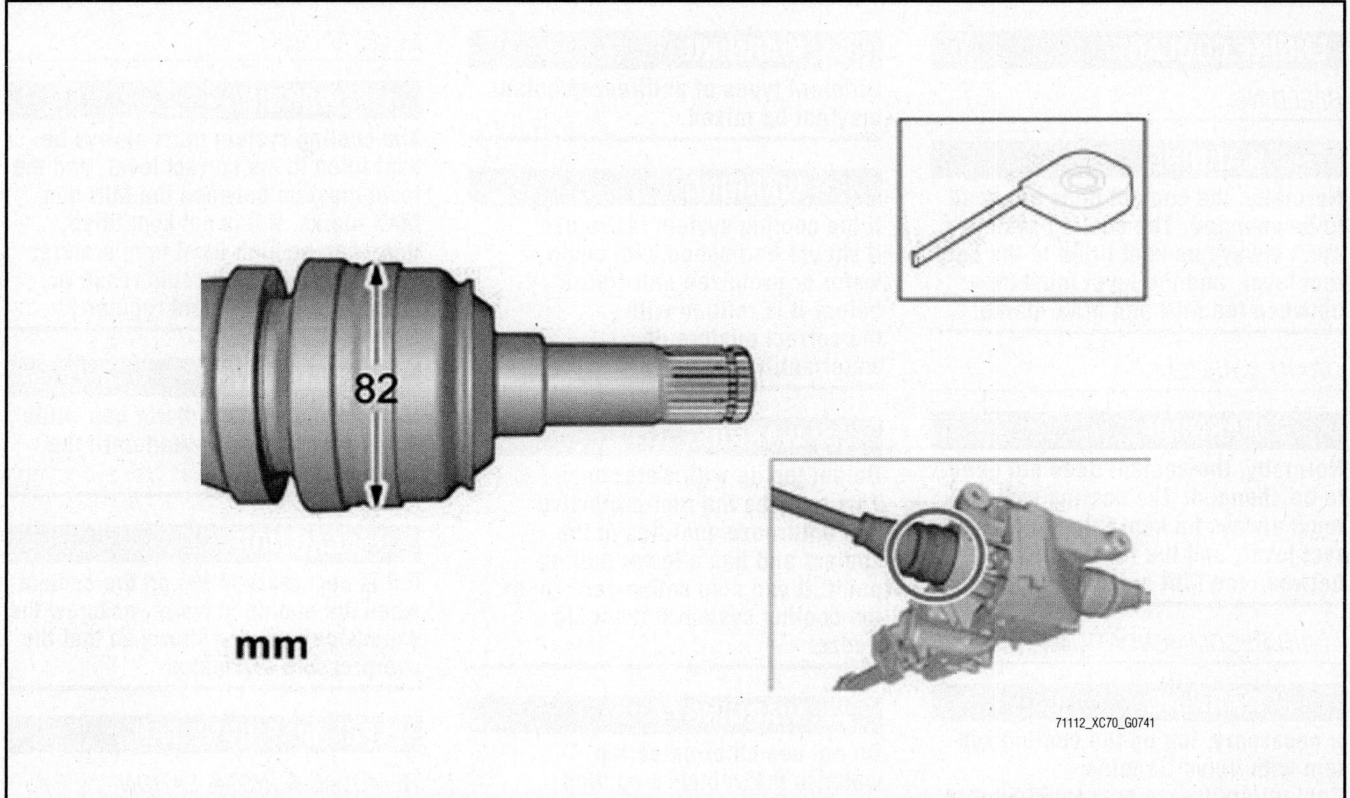

Fig. 18 Measure the CV-joint as shown. If the measurement is 3.2 inches (82 mm), vehicle is equipped with the early version

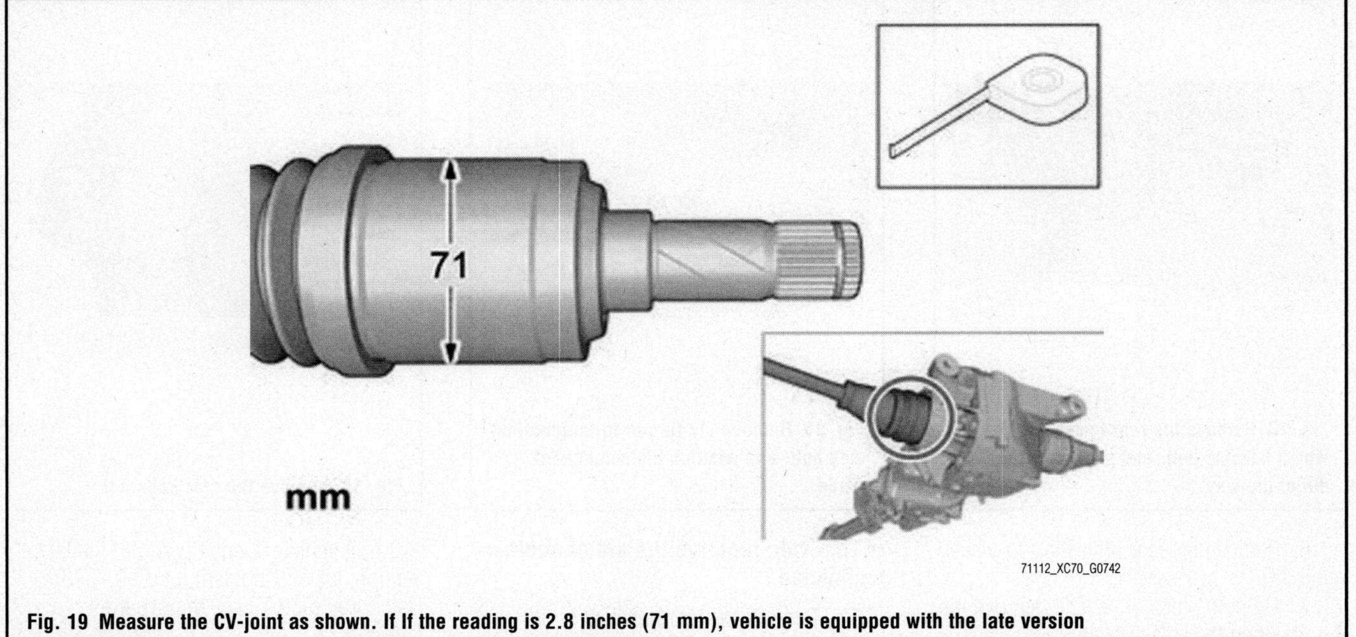

Fig. 19 Measure the CV-joint as shown. If If the reading is 2.8 inches (71 mm), vehicle is equipped with the late version

- Tighten the driveshaft-to-wheel hub to 26 ft. lbs. (35 Nm).
- Tighten the tie rod-to-longitudinal stay to 81 ft. lbs. (110 Nm).
- Tighten the rear stabilizer bar link-to-lower stabilizer bar bolt to 11 ft. lbs. (15 Nm).
- Tighten the rear lower arm-to-wheel knuckle bolt to 81 ft. lbs. (110 Nm).
- Tighten the rear shock absorber-to-wheel knuckle bolt:
  a. On vehicles without load-leveling shock absorbers, tighten to 129 ft. lbs. (175 Nm).
  b. On vehicles with load-leveling shock absorbers (Nivomat), tighten to 207 ft. lbs. (280 Nm).

ENGINE COOLING

ENGINE COOLANT

BLEEDING

⁂ WARNING

Normally, the coolant does not need to be changed. The cooling system must always be kept filled to the correct level, and the level must be between the MIN and MAX marks.

DRAIN & REFILL

⁂ WARNING

Normally, the coolant does not need to be changed. The cooling system must always be kept filled to the correct level, and the level must be between the MIN and MAX marks.

FLUID RECOMMENDATIONS

⁂ WARNING

If necessary, top up the cooling system with Volvo Genuine Coolant/Antifreeze only (a 50/50 mix of water and antifreeze).

⁂ WARNING

Different types of antifreeze/coolant may not be mixed.

⁂ WARNING

If the cooling system is drained, it should be flushed with clean water or premixed anti-freeze before it is refilled with the correct mixture of water/antifreeze.

⁂ WARNING

Do not top up with water only. This reduces the rust-protective and antifreeze qualities of the coolant and has a lower boiling point. It can also cause damage to the cooling system if it should freeze.

⁂ WARNING

Do not use chlorinated tap water in the vehicle's cooling system.

LEVEL CHECK

⁂ WARNING

The cooling system must always be kept filled to the correct level, and the level must be between the MIN and MAX marks. If it is not kept filled, there can be high local temperatures in the engine which could result in damage. Check coolant regularly.

⁂ CAUTION

Never remove the radiator cap while the engine is warm. Wait until the vehicle cools.

⁂ CAUTION

If it is necessary to top off the coolant when the engine is warm, unscrew the expansion tank cap slowly so that the overpressure dissipates.

ELECTRIC ENGINE FAN

REMOVAL & INSTALLATION

See Figures 20 through 23.

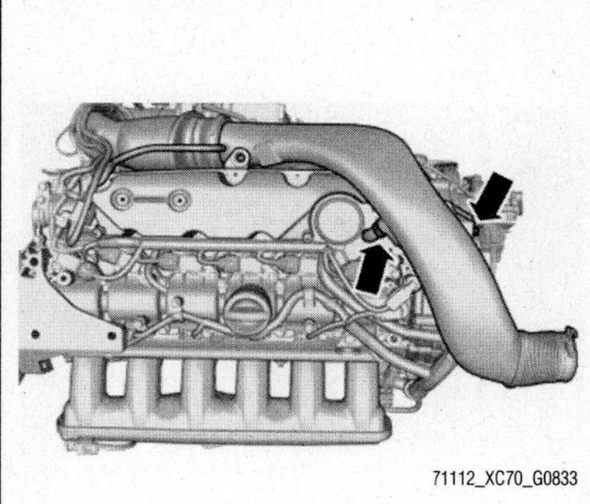
Fig. 20 **Remove the 2 clamps from the air duct as shown**

Fig. 22 **Remove the M8 bolts, the position the A/C compressor aside**

1. Remove the Air Cleaner (ACL) housing.
2. Remove the battery.
3. Remove the engine cover.
4. Remove the 2 clamps from the air duct as shown.
5. Remove the 4 M6 bolts, then remove the battery tray.

CAUTION

Be prepared to collect escaping fluid.

6. Remove the hose clamp and the 2 M6 nuts, then position the hose aside.
7. Remove the 2 M8 bolts, then remove the A/C compressor bracket.
8. Remove the M8 and M10 bolts, then remove the bracket.
9. Using a 19-mm Box wrench, pivot the drive belt tensioner down and insert a 3-mm pin into the hole to lock the tensioner.
10. Disconnect the 2 electrical connectors as shown.
11. Remove the M8 bolts, the position the A/C compressor aside.

CAUTION

Be prepared to collect escaping fluid.

12. Lift up and push in the fluid cooler, then remove the fluid cooler assembly and position aside.
13. Disconnect the electrical connector.
14. Remove the 2 M6 screws, then remove the bumper cover trim plates.
15. Pushing toward the engine, disengage the engine cooling fan.
16. On both sides of the engine cooling fan, disengage the hose.
17. Pulling up and out, remove the engine cooling fan.

To install:

18. To install, reverse the removal procedure and note the following:
    - Tighten the M6 fasteners to 89 inch lbs. (10 Nm).
    - Tighten the M8 bolts to 18 ft. lbs. (24 Nm).
    - Tighten the M10 bolts to 37 ft. lbs. (50 Nm).
19. Install the front bumper cover.
20. Reconnect negative battery cable.
21. Fill the cooling system.
22. Run the engine until the thermostat opens. Top up if necessary.

RADIATOR

REMOVAL & INSTALLATION

See Figures 24 through 27.

1. Remove the front cover bumper.
2. Remove the engine cooling fan.
3. Drain the cooling system.

CAUTION

Be prepared to collect escaping fluid.

4. Disengage the clips and clamp, and remove the hoses as shown.
5. Remove the right headlight.
6. Remove the M5 bolt and 6-point socket screw. Remove the fastener, then pull up to remove the belt guard.

CAUTION

Be prepared to collect escaping fluid.

7. Remove the hose clamp and the bolt. Lifting the fluid cooler up, remove the hose clamp, then remove the fluid cooler assembly.
8. Install In/Out Lift Fixture (999 5463) as shown.

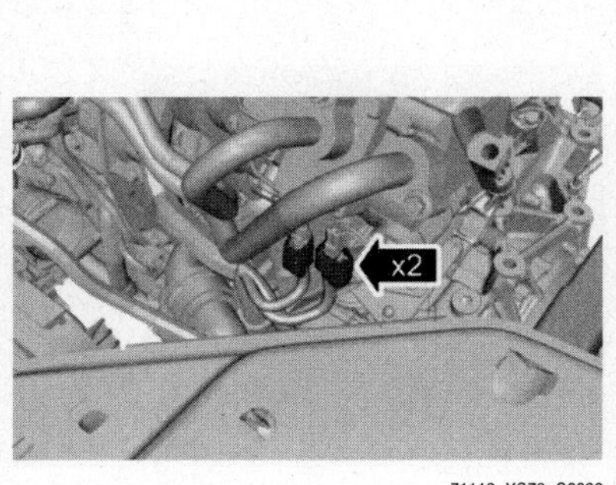

Fig. 21 **Disconnect the 2 electrical connectors as shown**

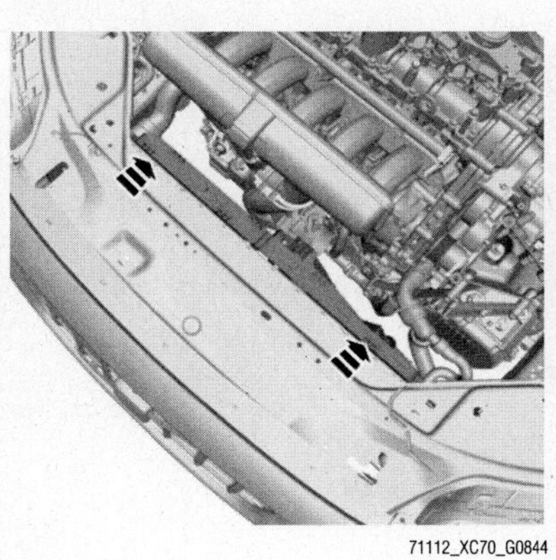
Fig. 23 **Pushing toward the engine, disengage the engine cooling fan**

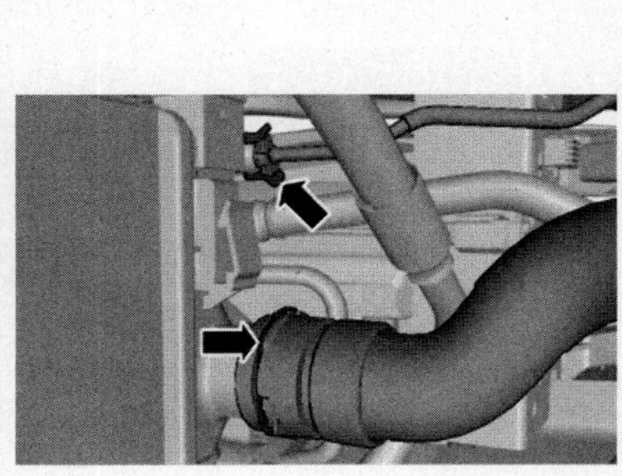
Fig. 24 **Disengage the clips and clamp, and remove the hoses as shown**

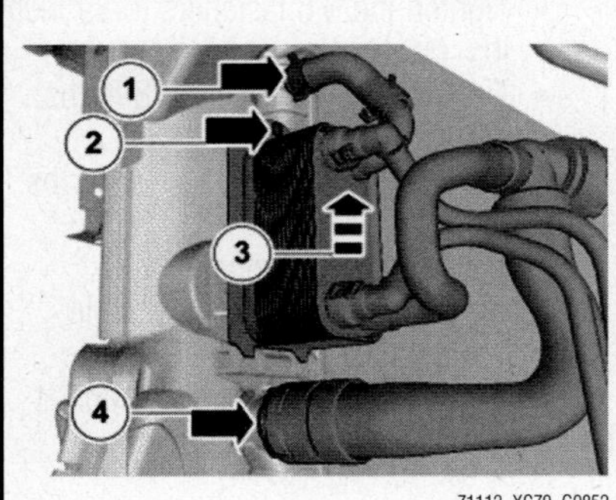

Fig. 25 Remove the hose clamp (1) and the bolt (2). Lifting the fluid cooler up (3), remove the hose clamp (4), then remove the fluid cooler assembly

Fig. 27 Pull down, then remove the radiator

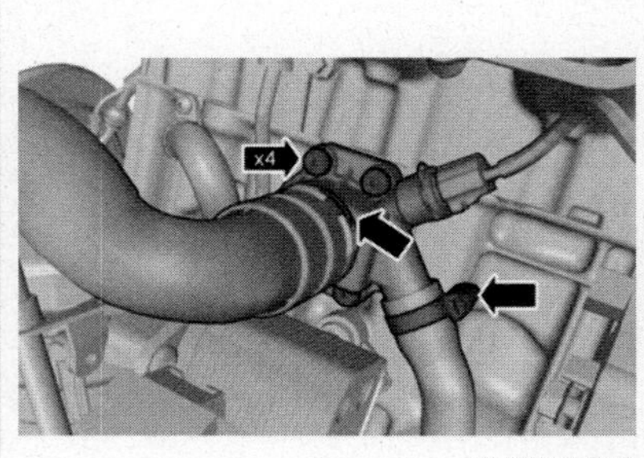

Fig. 28 Disconnect the electrical connector and remove the 2 hose clamps. Remove the 4 M6 bolts, then remove the thermostat

9. With the component supported, remove the power steering cooler.
10. With the condenser supported, disconnect the 4 clips
11. Remove the 4 M8 bolts, then remove the radiator support bracket.
12. Pull down, then remove the radiator.

To install:

13. To install, reverse the removal procedure and note the following:
    - Tighten the M5 bolts to 44 inch lbs. (5 Nm).
    - Tighten the M8 bolts to 18 ft. lbs. (24 Nm).
14. Fill the cooling system.

THERMOSTAT

REMOVAL & INSTALLATION

See Figure 28.

1. Drain the cooling system.
2. Remove the intake manifold.
3. Disconnect the electrical connector and remove the 2 hose clamps. Remove the 4 M6 bolts, then remove the thermostat.

To install:

4. To install, reverse the removal procedure and note the following:
    - Tighten the M6 bolts to 89 inch lbs. (10 Nm).
5. Fill the cooling system.

WATER PUMP

REMOVAL & INSTALLATION

See Figure 29.

1. Drain the cooling system.
2. Remove the Air Cleaner (ACL) housing.
3. Remove the battery.

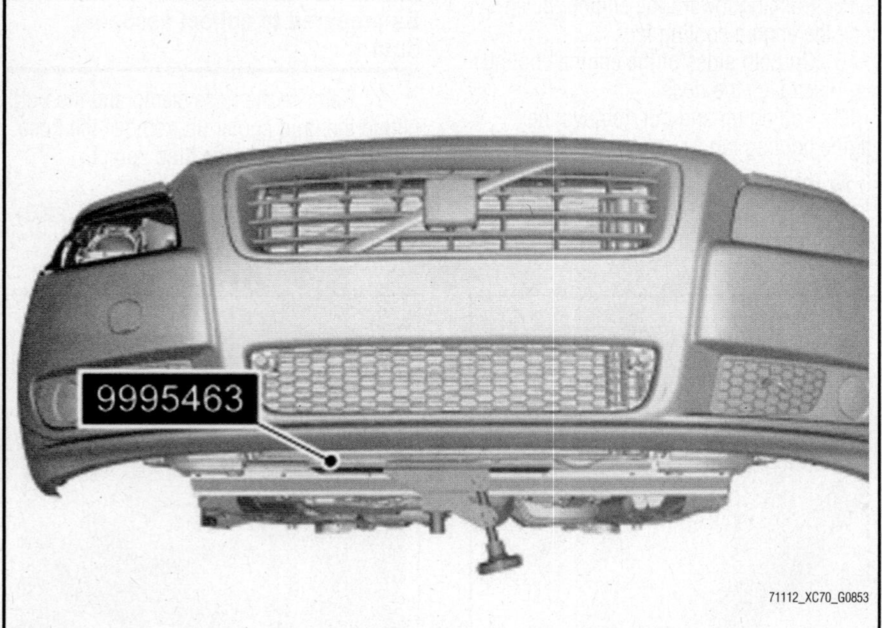

Fig. 26 Install In/Out Lift Fixture (999 5463) as shown

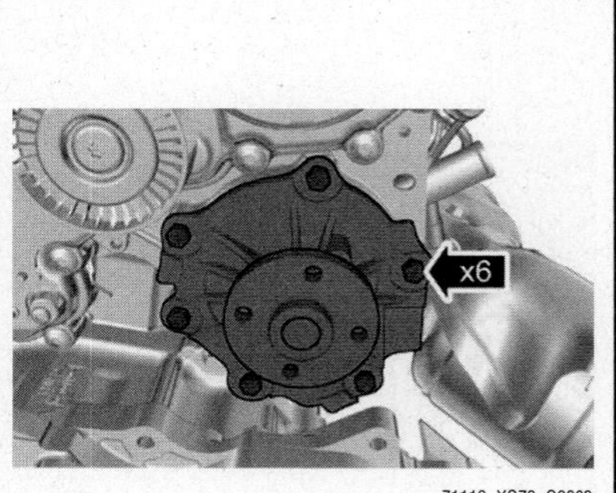

Fig. 29 Remove the 6 M6 bolts, then remove the water pump

➡**Do not loosen the bolts more than 2 turns.**

4. Loosen the 4 M6 bolts securing the pulley.
5. Loosen the accessory drive belt.
6. Remove the M6 bolt, then remove the bracket.
7. Remove the 4 M6 bolts, then remove the pulley.

➡**Use suitable paper to absorb any escaping fluid.**

8. Remove the 6 M6 bolts, then remove the water pump.

To install:

9. To install, reverse the removal procedure and note the following:
   - Tighten the M6 bolts to 89 inch lbs. (10 Nm).
10. Fill the cooling system.

ENGINE ELECTRICAL — BATTERY SYSTEM

BATTERY

REMOVAL & INSTALLATION

⁂ WARNING

When this procedure is completed, one or more components will require activation or calibration information.

1. Before servicing the vehicle, refer to the Precautions Section.
2. Turn the ignition off.
3. Disconnect the negative battery cable, then the positive battery cable.
4. Position the trim out of the way. Unlatch the 4 clips, and remove the battery lid.
5. Remove the cover.
6. Remove the 2 battery cables.
7. Remove the M6 bolt, then remove the bracket.

To install:

8. To install, reverse the removal procedure and note the following:
   - Tighten the M6 bolts to 89 inch lbs. (10 Nm).
   - Tighten the battery cables to 22 inch lbs. (2.5 Nm).
9. Reset the battery information.

ENGINE ELECTRICAL — CHARGING SYSTEM

ALTERNATOR

REMOVAL & INSTALLATION

See Figure 30.

1. Turn the ignition off.
2. Disconnect the battery.
3. Remove the intake manifold.
4. Disconnect the electrical and alternator B+ terminal connectors, remove the 4 M8 bolts, then remove the alternator.

To install:

➡**Only tighten the bolt finger tight at this stage.**

5. Install the alternator, and loosely install the top 2 M8 bolts.

⁂ WARNING

Make sure that the component is correctly located on the locating dowels.

6. Install 2 10mm locating dowels.
7. Reconnect the electrical and alternator B+ terminal connectors, and install the 4 M8 bolts. Tighten the bolts to 18 ft. lbs. (24 Nm). Tighten the alternator B+ terminal nut to 11 ft. lbs. (15 Nm).
8. Install the intake manifold.

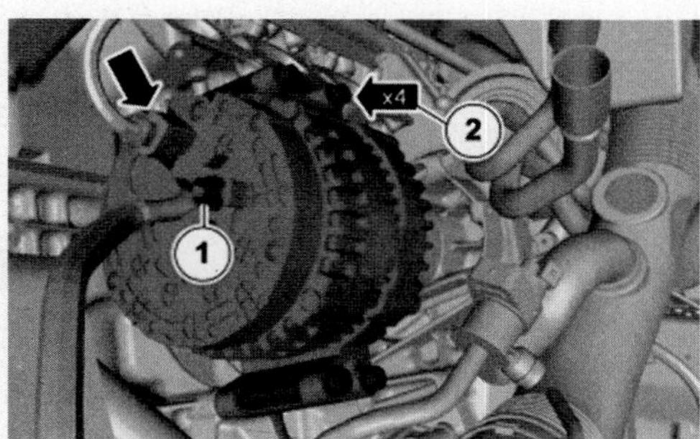

71112_XC70_G0885

Fig. 30 Disconnect the electrical and alternator B+ terminal connectors (1), remove the 4 M8 bolts (2), then remove the alternator

ENGINE ELECTRICAL — IGNITION SYSTEM

FIRING ORDER

The engine's firing order is 1-5-3-6-2-4. The firings occur every 120 degrees of crankshaft rotation.

IGNITION COIL

REMOVAL & INSTALLATION

See Figures 31 and 32.

1. Remove the engine cover.
2. Disconnect the 6 connectors, and remove the wiring harness.
3. Remove the 6 M6 bolts, then remove the ignition coils.

To install:

To install, reverse the removal procedure and note the following:

- Tighten the M6 bolts to 89 inch lbs. (10 Nm).

71112_XC70_G0904

Fig. 31 Disconnect the 6 connectors, and remove the wiring harness

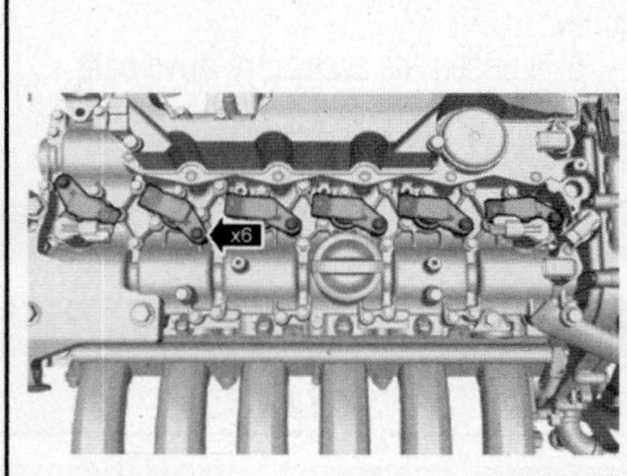

71112_XC70_G0905

Fig. 32 Remove the 6 M6 bolts, then remove the ignition coils

IGNITION TIMING

INSPECTION & ADJUSTMENT

The ignition timing is controlled by the Electronic Control Module (ECM) and is not adjustable.

SPARK PLUGS

REMOVAL & INSTALLATION

1. Remove the ignition coils.
2. Remove the 6 spark plugs.

To install:

To install, reverse the removal procedure and note the following:

- On B6304T4 and B6324S5 engines, tighten the spark plugs to 21 ft. lbs. (28 Nm).
- On B6324S4 engine, tighten the spark plugs to 18 ft. lbs. (25 Nm).

ENGINE ELECTRICAL — STARTING SYSTEM

STARTER

REMOVAL & INSTALLATION

See Figure 33.

1. Disconnect the battery.
2. Raise and support the vehicle.
3. Remove 7 bolts and the engine splash plate.
4. Remove the 2 M10 bolts.
5. Remove the battery positive cable-to-starter solenoid nut.
6. Remove the starter impulse lead nut.
7. Remove the starter.

To install:

To install, reverse the removal procedure and note the following:

- Tighten the starter impulse lead nut to 75 inch lbs (8.5 Nm).
- Tighten the battery positive cable-to-starter solenoid nut to 97 inch lbs. (11 Nm).
- Tighten the M10 bolts to 37 ft. lbs. (50 Nm).

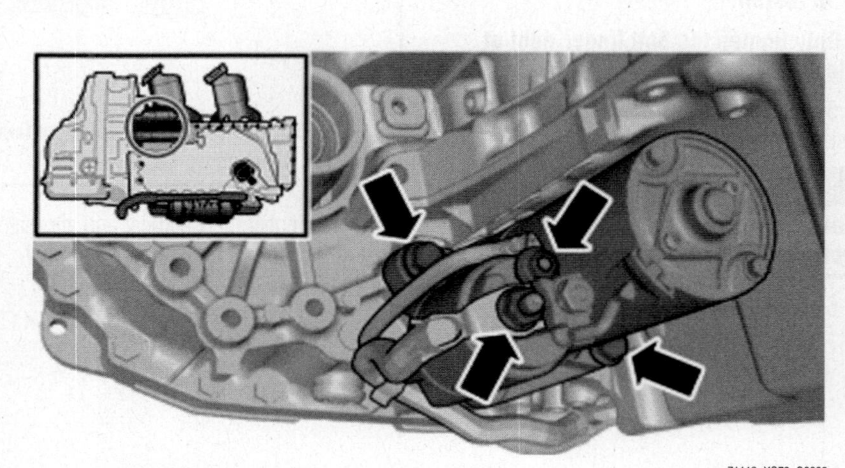

71112_XC70_G0909

Fig. 33 Removing the starter

ENGINE MECHANICAL

➡Disconnecting the negative battery cable may interfere with the functions of the on board computer systems and may require the computer to undergo a relearning process, once the negative battery cable is reconnected.

ACCESSORY DRIVE BELTS

ADJUSTMENT

The accessory drive belt system uses a tensioner pulley to automatically adjust the belt.

BELT ROUTINGS

See Figure 34.

INSPECTION

Inspect the drive belt for signs of glazing or cracking. A glazed belt will be perfectly smooth from slippage, while a good belt will have a slight texture of fabric visible. Cracks will usually start at the inner edge of the belt and run outward. All worn or damaged drive belts should be replaced immediately.

REMOVAL & INSTALLATION

See Figures 35 through 37.

1. Remove the battery.
2. Remove the Air Cleaner (ACL) housing.
3. Remove the engine cover.
4. Remove hose clamp and fasteners securing air duct.
5. Remove the battery.
6. Remove the 4 M6 bolts, then remove the battery box.
7. Remove the 2 M8 bolts, then remove the A/C compressor bracket.
8. Using a 19-mm Box wrench, pivot the drive belt tensioner down and insert a 3-mm pin into the hole to lock the tensioner.
9. Remove the 2 M8 bolts, then remove the A/C compressor bracket.
10. Remove the 3 M8 bolts, then position the A/C compressor aside.
11. Remove the M8 bolt, then remove the drive belt tensioner.
12. Remove the accessory drive belt.

To install:

To install, reverse the removal procedure and note the following:

- Tighten the M6 bolts to 89 inch lbs. (10 Nm).
- Tighten the M8 bolts to 18 ft. lbs. (24 Nm).

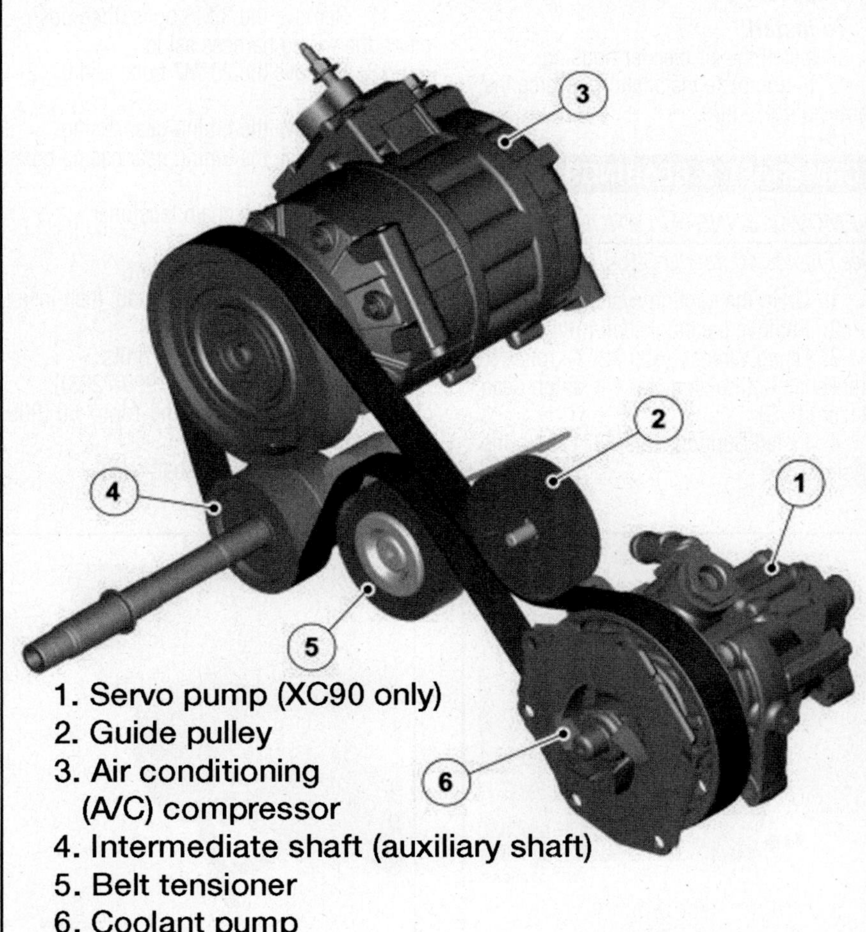

Fig. 34 Auxiliary drive system component locations

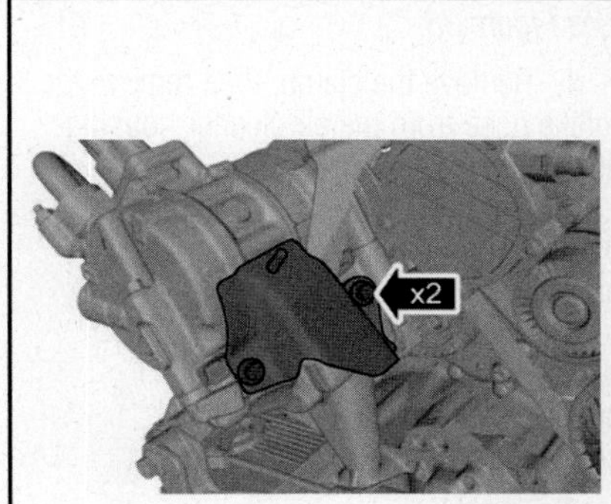

Fig. 35 Remove the 2 M8 bolts, then remove the A/C compressor bracket

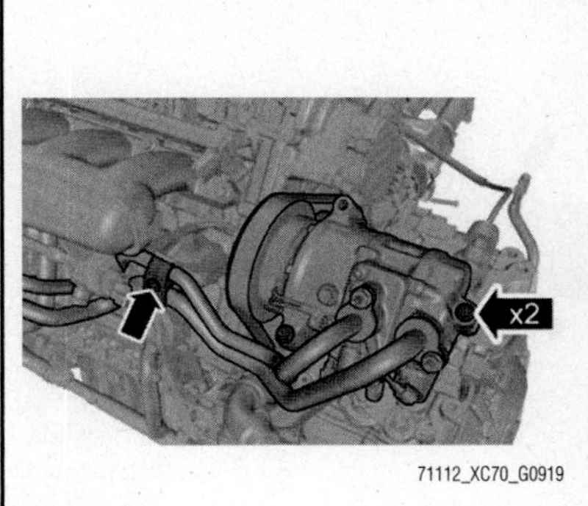

Fig. 36 Remove the 3 M8 bolts, then position the A/C compressor aside

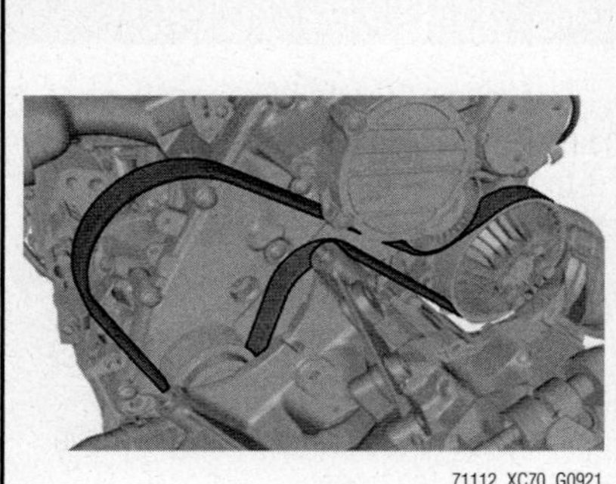

Fig. 37 Remove the accessory drive belt

AIR CLEANER

REMOVAL & INSTALLATION

3.0L Engines

See Figure 38.

1. Remove the clamp, then remove the intake hose from the air cleaner housing assembly.
2. Remove the air inlet and outlet ducts, them remove the air cleaner housing assembly.
3. Remove the 2 bolts, disengage the wiring from clamp, them remove the electrical connector.

To install:

Installation is the reverse of the removal procedure.

3.2L Engines

See Figure 39.

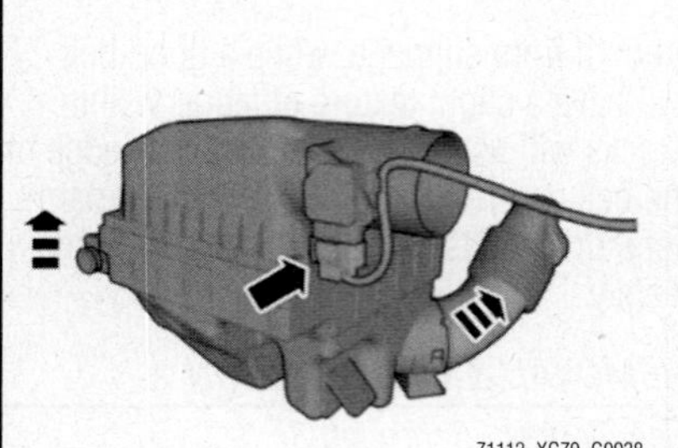

Fig. 39 Disconnect the electrical connector, remove the air duct, then remove the air cleaner housing

1. Remove the hose clamps, then disconnect the air duct from the air cleaner housing.
2. Disconnect the electrical connector, remove the air duct, then remove the air cleaner housing.

To install:

3. Install the air cleaner housing.
4. To complete installation, reverse the removal procedure.

CAMSHAFT & BEARINGS

REMOVAL & INSTALLATION

See Figures 40 through 49.

1. Drain the cooling system.
2. Remove the crankshaft front seal.
3. Using Wrench (999 7257), rotate the crankshaft until piston No. 1 is at top dead center (TDC).
4. Install Support (999 7271) onto the engine.
5. Remove the engine cover.
6. Remove hose clamp and fasteners securing air duct.
7. Remove bolt, then remove the coolant reservoir.
8. Remove the 7 bolts, then remove the torque rod and bracket.
9. Pry the plugs from the ends of the camshafts as shown.
10. Install the Camshaft Position Tool (999 7261) into the ends of the camshafts.
11. Remove the accessory drive belt.
12. Remove the hose clamp, then remove the return hose.
13. Remove the 3 M10 bolts, then remove the bracket.
14. Pry the plug from the auxiliary unit belt pulley as shown.
15. Install Counterhold (999 5760) and 50 Torx® Bit (951 2926) into the auxiliary unit belt pulley. Remove the belt pulley.
16. Remove the 2 bolts, then remove the inlet pipe. Remove the 3 bolts, disconnect the connector, and remove the water pump.
17. Remove the 3 M6 bolts, then position the wiring harness aside.
18. Remove the 20 M7 bolts and the 2 M8 bolts.
19. Remove the timing gear casing.
20. Remove the timing gear casing gasket.
21. Remove the chain tensioner:
    a. Slide tab to side.
    b. Press down on button.
    c. Using drift, depress tab, then insert a pin.
    d. Remove the 2 Torx® nuts.
22. Install Counterhold (999 7263), Counterhold (999 7264) and Torx ® 60 (999 7272) as shown.
23. Remove the camshaft chain.

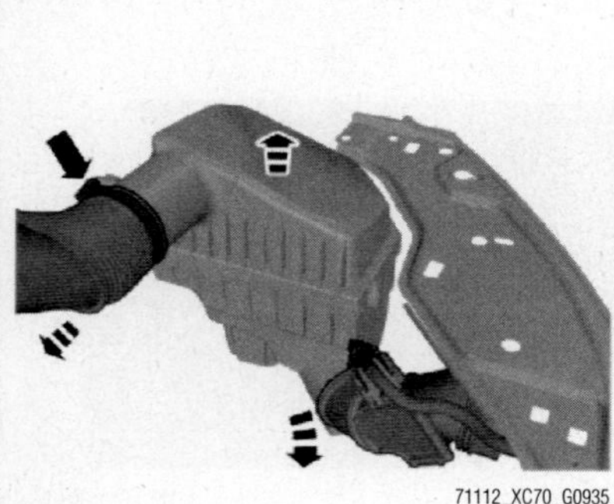

Fig. 38 Remove the air inlet and outlet ducts, them remove the air cleaner housing assembly

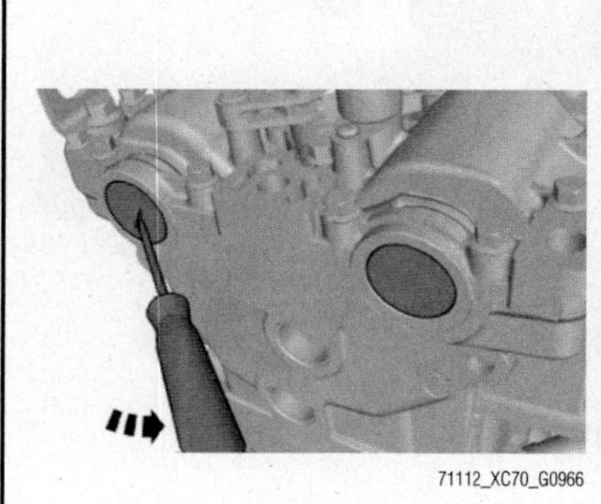

Fig. 40 Pry the plugs from the ends of the camshafts as shown

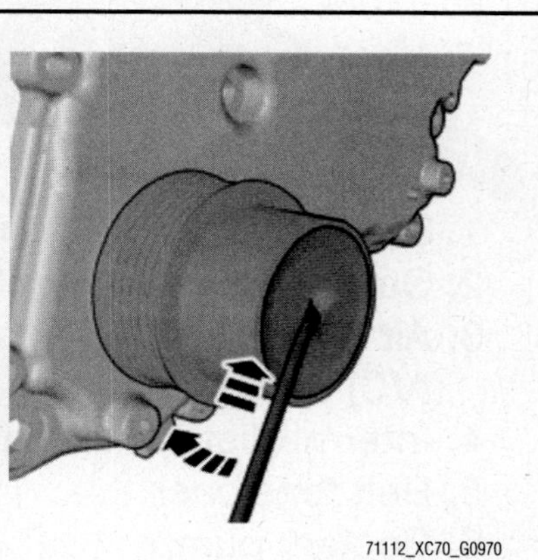

Fig. 41 Pry the plug from the auxiliary unit belt pulley as shown

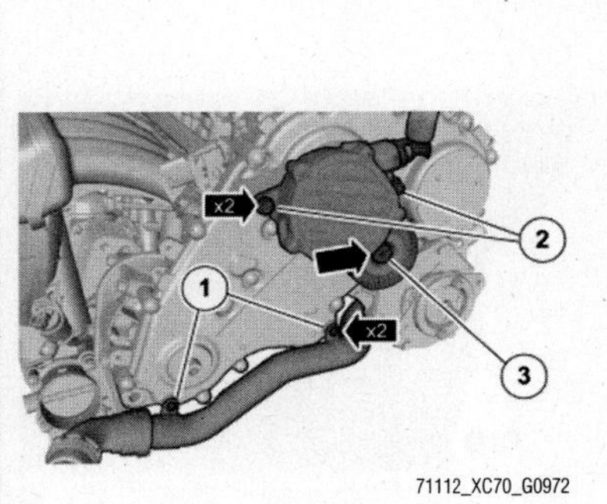

Fig. 42 Remove the 2 bolts, then remove the inlet pipe (1). Remove the 3 bolts, disconnect the connector, and remove the water pump (2, 3)

24. Remove the 3 M7 fasteners, then the coolant pipe.

CAUTION

Be prepared to collect escaping fluid.

25. Remove the 2 M7 bolts, then remove the cover.

26. Remove the cylinder head cover, then the camshafts.

To install:

27. Install the camshafts, then the cylinder head cover.

28. Install the Camshaft Position Tool (999 7261).

29. Install the gasket as shown.

➡Do not loosen the bolts more than 2 turns.

30. Loosen the 2 specified cover bolts.

31. Install the cover, then tighten the 2 M7 bolts to 13 ft. lbs. (17 Nm).

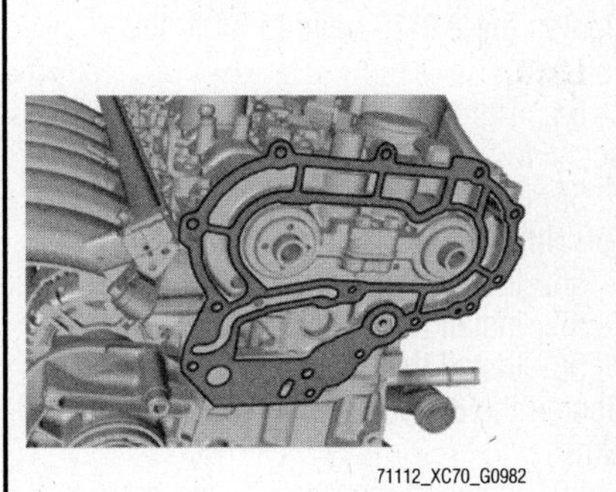

Fig. 44 Install the gasket as shown

32. Install the camshaft chain.

33. Remove the drift or pin from the chain tensioner, then tighten the 2 M6 bolts to 89 inch lbs. (10 Nm).

34. To install the camshaft center bolts, install Counterhold (999 7263), Counterhold (999 7264) and Torx® 60 (999 7272) as shown.

35. Tighten the exhaust camshaft center bolt:

a. Stage 1: 55 ft. lbs. (75 Nm)

b. Stage 2: 90 degrees

36. Tighten the intake camshaft center bolt to 81 ft. lbs. (110 Nm).

37. Remove the counterhold and Torx® tools.

38. Remove the Camshaft Position Tool (999 7261).

39. Using Wrench (999 7257), turn the crankshaft counterclockwise 2 complete rotations.

40. Remove the lip seal from the timing gear casing. Discard the lip seal.

➡Only tighten the bolt finger-tight at this stage.

41. Install Position Sensor (999 7266) and Position Sensor (999 7267) as shown.

42. Loosely install the 3 M7 bolts as specified.

43. Install the 3 M7 bolts into timing gear casing as specified, and tighten to 13 ft. lbs. (17 Nm).

44. Install the 17 M7 bolts into timing gear casing, and tighten in the order specified to 13 ft. lbs. (17 Nm).

45. Tighten the 2 9-mm adjuster screws to 27 inch lbs. (3 Nm).

46. Tighten the 2 M8 bolts to 18 ft. lbs. (24 Nm).

47. Install the wiring harness, then tighten the 3 M6 bolts to 89 inch lbs. (10 Nm).

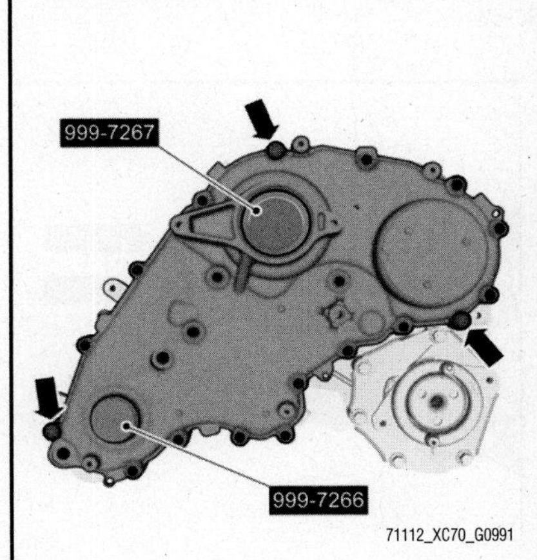

Fig. 46 Install Position Sensor (999 7266) and Position Sensor (999 7267) as shown. Loosely install the 3 M7 bolts as specified

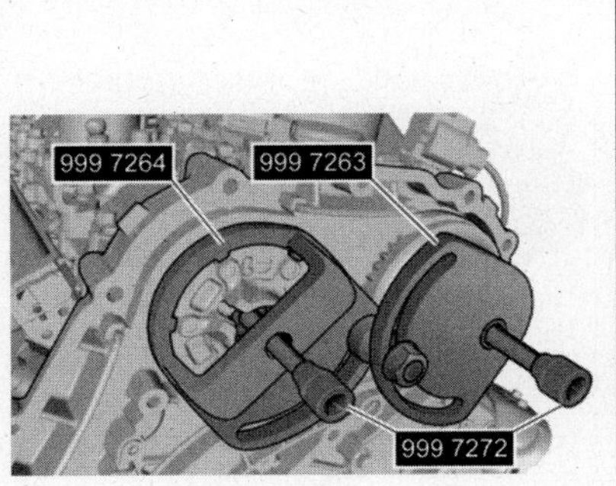

Fig. 43 Install Counterhold (999 7263), Counterhold (999 7264) and Torx® 60 (999 7272) as shown

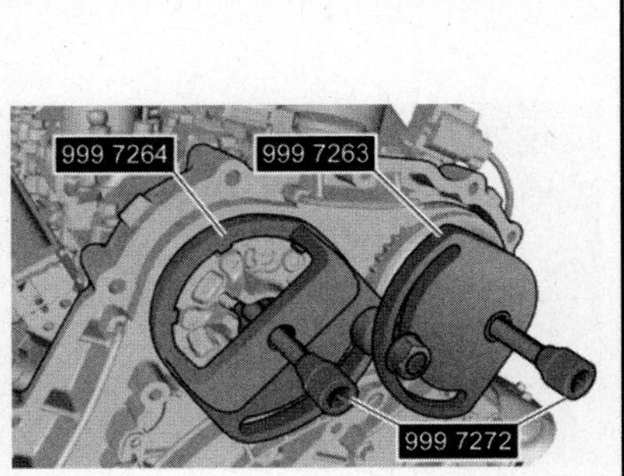

Fig. 45 Install Counterhold (999 7263), Counterhold (999 7264) and Torx® 60 (999 7272) as shown

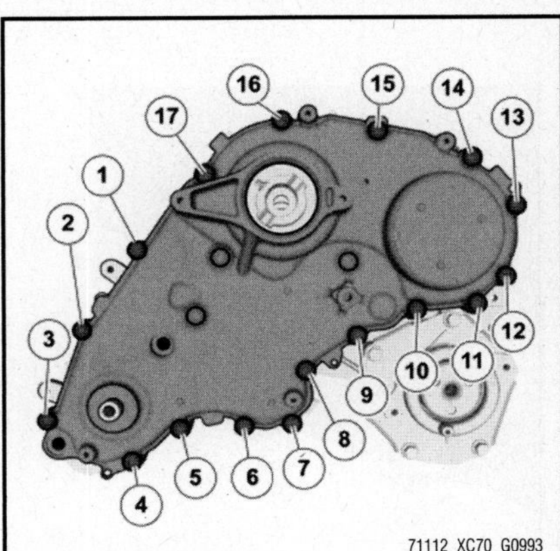

Fig. 47 Install the 17 M7 bolts into timing gear casing, and tighten in the order specified to 13 ft. lbs. (17 Nm)

48. Install the water pump and inlet pipe, and note the following:

- Tighten the M6 bolts to 89 inch lbs. (10 Nm).
- Tighten the M7 bolts to 13 ft. lbs. (17 Nm).
- Tighten the M8 bolts to 18 ft. lbs. (24 Nm).

➡**Make sure that a new component is installed.**

49. Using Drift (999 7265), insert the lip seal into the timing gear casing.

50. Install Counterhold (999 5760) and 50 Torx® Bit (951 2926) into the auxiliary unit belt pulley as shown.

Tighten to 44 ft. lbs. (60 Nm).

51. Install the auxiliary unit belt pulley plug as shown.

52. Install the torque rod adjusting screw.

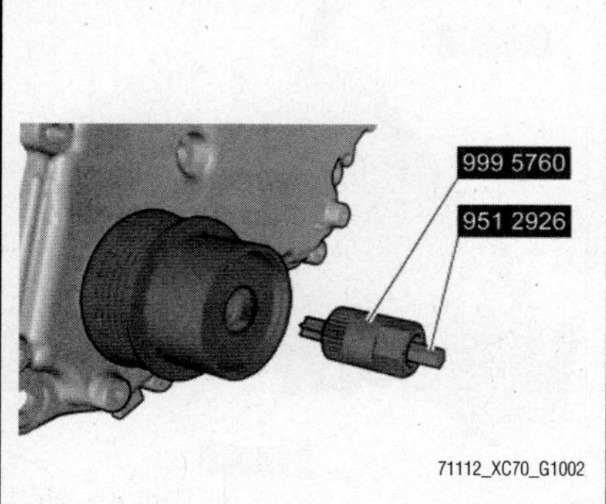

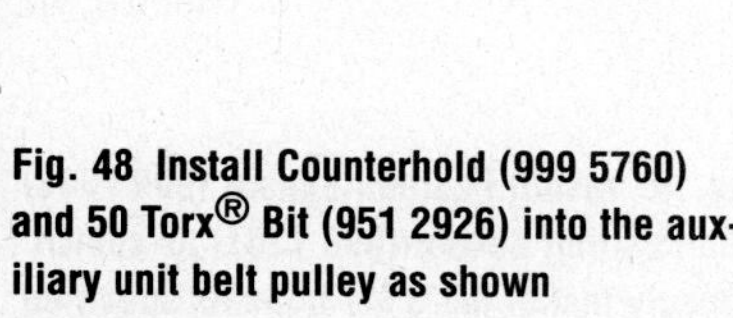

Fig. 48 Install Counterhold (999 5760) and 50 Torx® Bit (951 2926) into the auxiliary unit belt pulley as shown

53. Install the bracket, then tighten the 2 M10 bolts to 37 ft. lbs. (50 Nm).

54. Tighten the torque rod adjusting screw to 9 inch lbs. (1 Nm).

55. Tighten the M10 bolt to 37 ft. lbs. (50 Nm).

56. Install the return hose.

57. Install the accessory drive belt.

58. Install the coolant pipe, then tighten the 3 M7 fasteners to 13 ft. lbs. (17 Nm).

59. Install the torque rod and bracket using the 7 M12 bolts, then tighten the bolts to 59 ft. lbs. (80 Nm).

60. Install the coolant reservoir.

61. Remove Support (999 7271) from the engine.

62. Install the crankshaft front seal.

63. Fill the cooling system.

CAMSHAFT CHAIN & SPROCKETS

REMOVAL & INSTALLATION

See Figures 50 through 54.

1. Remove the crankshaft front seal.
2. Remove the 2 M6 nuts, and position the coolant pipe aside.
3. Using Wrench (999 7257), rotate the crankshaft until piston No. 1 is at top dead center (TDC).
4. Install Support (999 7271) onto the engine as shown.
5. Remove the 7 bolts, then remove the torque rod and bracket.
6. Pry the plugs from the ends of the camshafts as shown.
7. Install the Camshaft Position Tool (999 7261) into the ends of the camshafts as shown.

Fig. 51 Pry the plugs from the ends of the camshafts as shown

8. Remove the outer timing cover gasket.
9. Remove the chain tensioner:
   a. Slide tab to side
   b. Press down on button
   c. Using drift, depress tab, then insert a pin
   d. Remove the 2 Torx® nuts
10. Install Counterhold (999 7263), Counterhold (999 7264) and Torx ® 60 (999 7272) as shown.
11. Remove the camshaft chain.
12. Rotate each sprocket up and down, and remove the camshaft center bolts. Remove the camshaft sprockets.

To install:

13. Install the camshaft sprockets and chain. Do not allow the sprockets to rotate clockwise.
14. Remove the drift or pin from the chain tensioner, then tighten the 2 M6 bolts to 89 inch lbs. (10 Nm).

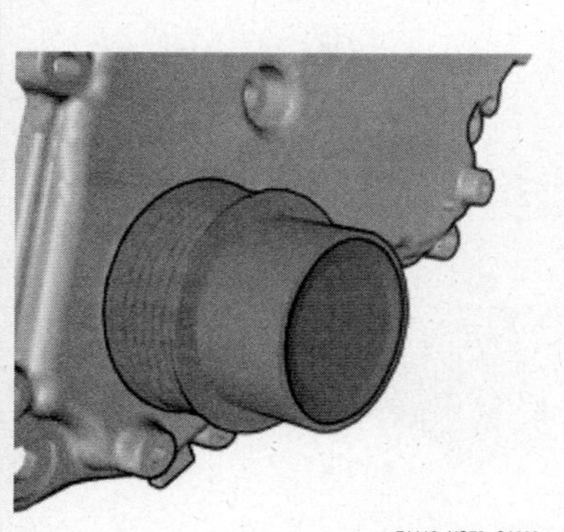

Fig. 49 Install the auxiliary unit belt pulley plug as shown

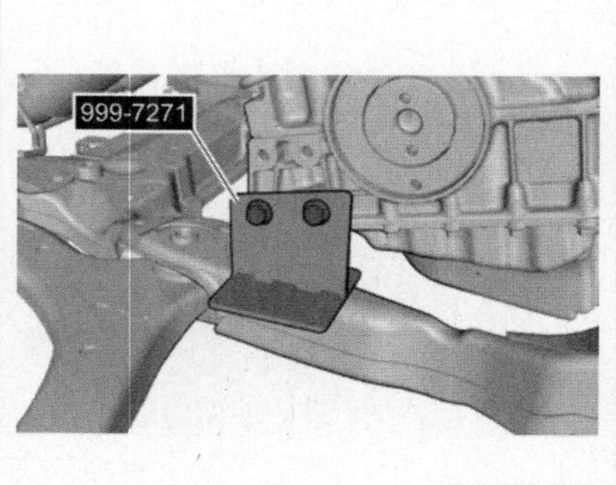

Fig. 50 Install Support (999 7271) onto the engine as shown

Fig. 52 Install the Camshaft Position Tool (999 7261) into the ends of the camshafts as shown

Fig. 53 Install Counterhold (999 7263), Counterhold (999 7264) and Torx® 60 (999 7272) as shown

15. To install the camshaft center bolts, install Counterhold (999 7263), Counterhold (999 7264) and Torx® 60 (999 7272) as shown.
16. Tighten the exhaust camshaft center bolt:
    a. Stage 1: 55 ft. lbs. (75 Nm)
    b. Stage 2: 90 degrees
17. Tighten the intake camshaft center bolt to 81 ft. lbs. (110 Nm).
18. Remove the counterhold and Torx® tools.
19. Remove the Camshaft Position Tool (999 7261).
20. Using Wrench (999 7257), turn the crankshaft counterclockwise 2 complete rotations.
21. Install the torque rod and bracket using the 7 M12 bolts, then tighten the bolts to 59 ft. lbs. (80 Nm).
22. Remove Support (999 7271).
23. To complete installation, reverse the removal procedure and note the following:
    - Tighten the M6 nuts to 89 inch lbs. (10 Nm).

CRANKSHAFT FRONT SEAL

REMOVAL & INSTALLATION

See Figures 55 through 57.

1. Remove the right front wheel.
2. Remove the 5 fasteners, then remove wheel well liner.
3. Using a punch tool, remove the crankshaft front seal.

To install:

4. Using Cleaning Agent (1161721), clean the seal surface as shown.
5. To complete installation, reverse the removal procedure.
6. Check the oil fluid level.

Fig. 55 Remove the 5 fasteners, then remove wheel well liner

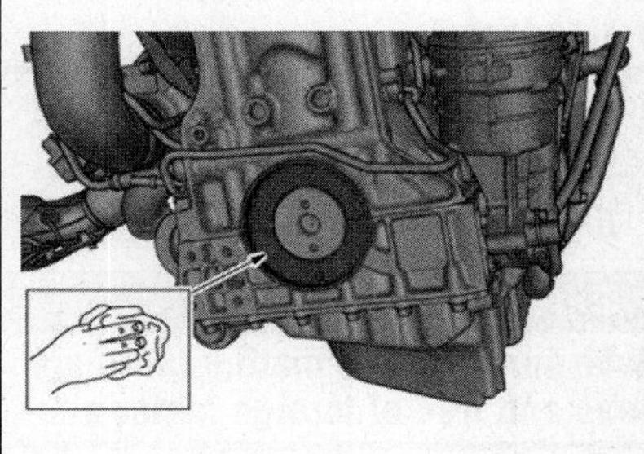

Fig. 57 Using Cleaning Agent (1161721), clean the seal surface as shown

CYLINDER HEAD

REMOVAL & INSTALLATION

See Figures 58 and 59.

1. Relieve the fuel system pressure.
2. Remove the following:
    - The exhaust manifold
    - The intake manifold
    - The camshafts

➡Note the position of each component before removal.

3. Using a suction cup and magnet, remove the valve tappets in the specified order.

WARNING

Note the position of the components before removal.

4. On B6304T4 and B6324S5 engines, remove the restricting orifices (chokes).

Fig. 54 Install Counterhold (999 7263), Counterhold (999 7264) and Torx® 60 (999 7272) as shown

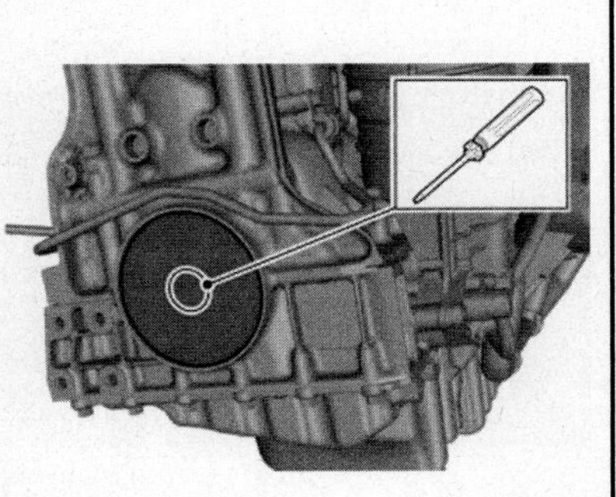

Fig. 56 Using a punch tool, remove the crankshaft front seal

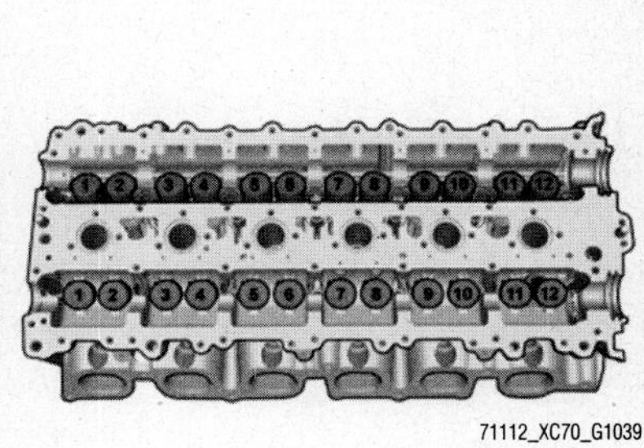

Fig. 58 Using a suction cup and magnet, remove the valve tappets in the specified order

✻✻ WARNING

Take extra care not to damage the mating faces.

5. Remove the 14 cylinder head bolts, then remove the cylinder head.

To install:

✻✻ WARNING

Make sure that the mating faces are clean and free of foreign material.

✻✻ WARNING

Make sure that no fluids are present in the cylinder head bolt threaded bores.

✻✻ WARNING

Make sure that the oil galleries are clean and free of foreign material.

6. Adjust the valve clearance.
7. Using Spanner (999 7300), tighten the cylinder head bolt sleeves to 90 inch lb (10 Nm).

➡Apply Gasket solution (1161847) to threads.

✻✻ WARNING

Take extra care not to damage the mating faces.

8. Install cylinder head bolts hand tight.

➡Apply Gasket solution, 1161847 to threads.

Tighten the cylinder head bolts in the specified order:

a. Stage 1: 33 ft. lbs. (45 Nm)
b. Stage 2: 33 ft. lbs. (45 Nm)
c. Stage 3: 90 degrees
d. Stage 4: 180 degrees

➡Make sure that these components are installed to the noted removal position.

9. On B6304T4 and B6324S5 engines, install the restricting orifices (chokes).

➡Make sure that these components are installed to the noted removal position.

10. Using a suction cup and magnet, install the valve tappets in the specified order.
11. Install the following:
   - The camshafts
   - The intake manifold
   - The exhaust manifold
12. Drain and fill the cooling system,

EXHAUST MANIFOLD

REMOVAL & INSTALLATION

B6304T4 (Turbocharged) Engine

See Figure 60.

1. Remove the turbocharger.
2. Remove the 14 M8 bolts, then remove the exhaust manifold.

To install:

To install, reverse the removal procedure and note the following:

- Tighten the M8 bolts to 18 ft. lbs. (24 Nm).

B6304S4 (Non-Turbocharged) Engine

See Figures 61 and 62.

1. Remove the catalytic converter.

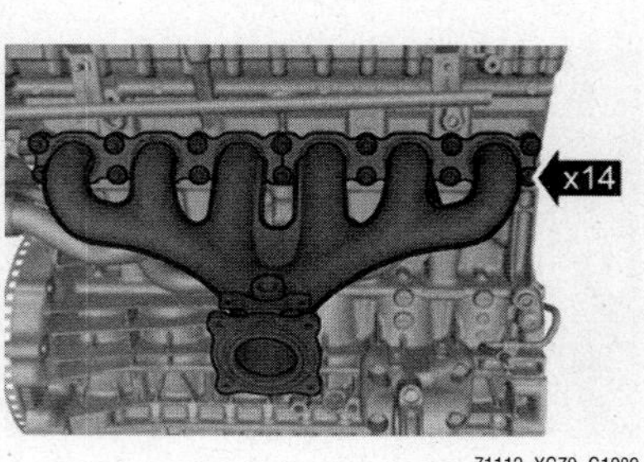

Fig. 61 Remove the 14 M8 bolts, then remove the exhaust manifold

2. Using Crow's Foot Socket (981 4102), remove the 3 M8 bolts from top of the protecting plate.
3. Remove the 2 M6 bolts from bottom of the protecting plate. Disconnect the electrical connector, and remove the protecting plate.
4. Remove the 14 M8 bolts, then remove the exhaust manifold.

To install:

5. Install the exhaust manifold, inserting Guide Pin (999 7269) in the 4 locations as shown.
6. Install 10 of the M8 bolts, and tighten to 18 ft. lbs. (24 Nm).
7. Install the remaining 4 M8 bolts, and tighten to 18 ft. lbs. (24 Nm).
8. Install the protecting plate, and tighten the top 3 M8 bolts to 18 ft. lbs. (24 Nm).
Tighten the bottom 2 M6 bolts to 89 inch lbs. (10 Nm). Connect the electrical connector.
9. Install the catalytic converter.

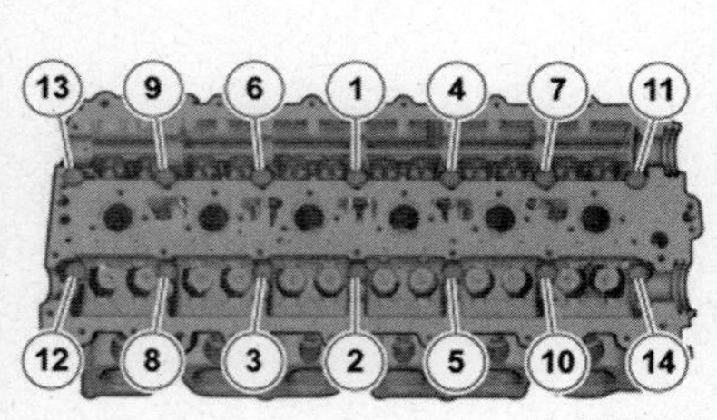

Fig. 59 Tighten the cylinder head bolts in the specified order

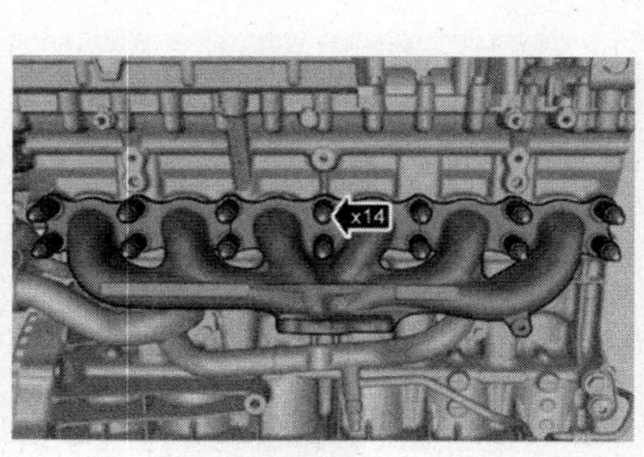

Fig. 60 Remove the 14 M8 bolts, then remove the exhaust manifold

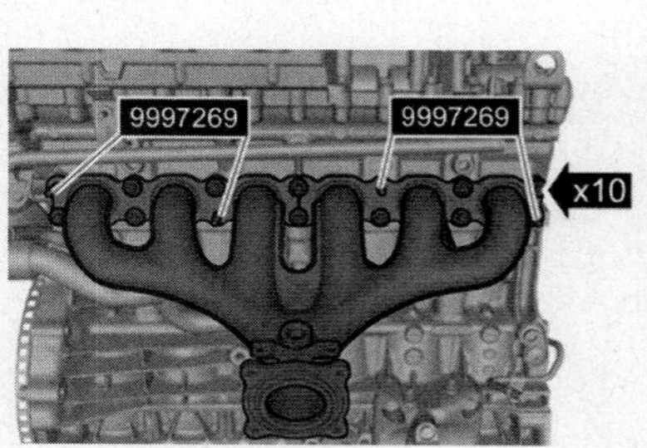

Fig. 62 Install the exhaust manifold inserting Guide Pin (999 7269) in the 4 locations as shown, then install 10 of the M8 bolts

B6304S5 (Lambda Sond) Engine

See Figures 63 through 65.

1. Remove the engine cover.
2. Disconnect the 2 electrical connectors.
3. Remove the catalytic converter.
4. Using Crow's Foot Socket (981 4102), remove the 3 M8 bolts from top of the protecting plate.
5. Remove the 2 M6 bolts from bottom of the protecting plate. Disconnect the 2 electrical connectors, and remove the protecting plate.
6. Remove the 14 M8 bolts, then remove the exhaust manifold.

To install:

7. Install the left exhaust manifold, inserting Guide Pin (999 7269) in the 2 locations as shown.
8. Install 4 of the M8 bolts, and tighten to 18 ft. lbs. (24 Nm).
9. Install the right exhaust manifold, inserting Guide Pin (999 7269) in the 2 locations as shown.
10. Install 4 of the M8 bolts, and tighten to 18 ft. lbs. (24 Nm).
11. Install the remaining 6 M8 bolts, and tighten to 18 ft. lbs. (24 Nm).
12. Install the protecting plate, and tighten the top 3 M8 bolts to 18 ft. lbs. (24 Nm).

Tighten the bottom 2 M6 bolts to 89 inch lbs. (10 Nm). Connect the electrical connectors.

13. Reconnect the 2 electrical connectors.
14. Install the engine cover.
15. Install the catalytic converter.

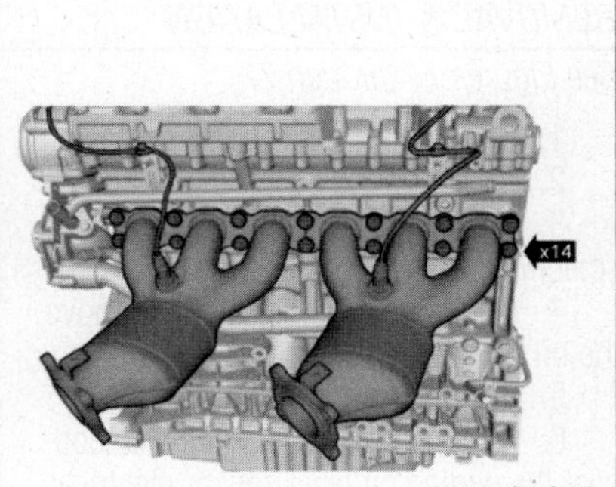

Fig. 63 Remove the 14 M8 bolts, then remove the exhaust manifold

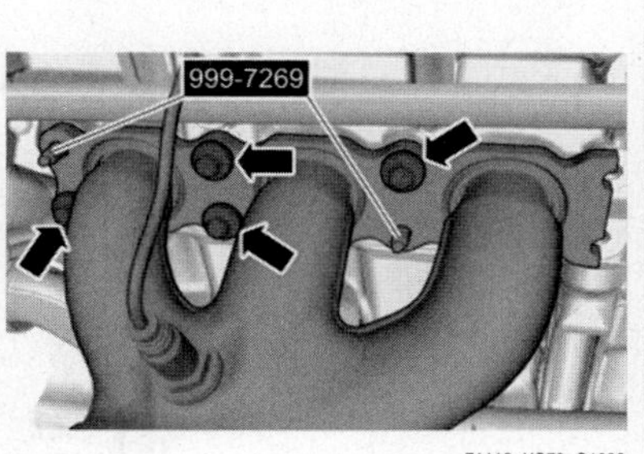

Fig. 64 Install the left exhaust manifold, insert Guide Pin (999 7269) in the 2 locations as shown, then install 4 of the M8 bolts

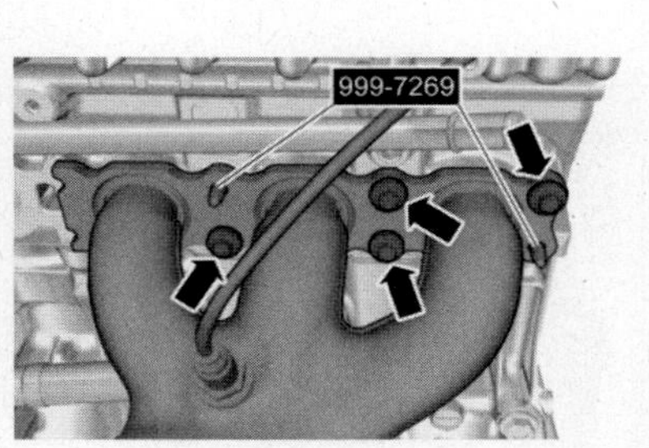

Fig. 65 Install the right exhaust manifold, insert Guide Pin (999 7269) in the 2 locations as shown, then install 4 of the M8 bolts

INTAKE MANIFOLD

REMOVAL & INSTALLATION

Turbocharged Engine (B6304T4)

See Figures 66 and 67.

1. Remove the engine cover.
2. Remove the hose clamp, then remove the air intake duct.
3. Disconnect the electrical connectors from the MAP sensor and throttle body, and remove the Evaporative emission system (EVAP) valve & hose.
4. Disconnect the vacuum line and the fuel pressure/temperature sensor wiring connector. Remove the 7 M7 bolts, then remove the intake manifold.
5. Remove the 4 bolts, then remove the throttle body from the intake manifold.

To install:

To install, reverse the removal procedure and note the following:

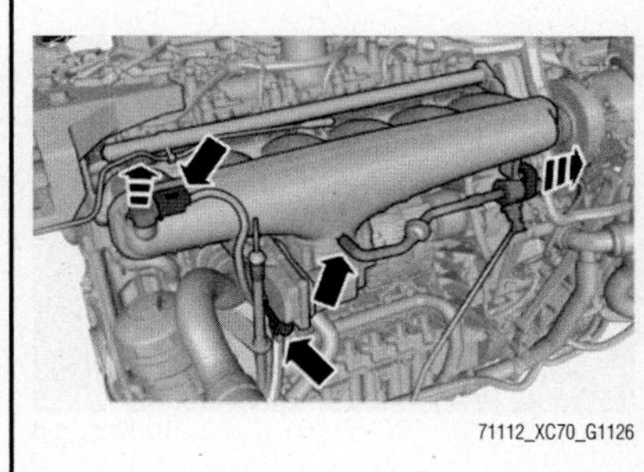

Fig. 66 Disconnect the electrical connectors from the MAP sensor and throttle body, and remove the Evaporative emission system (EVAP) valve & hose

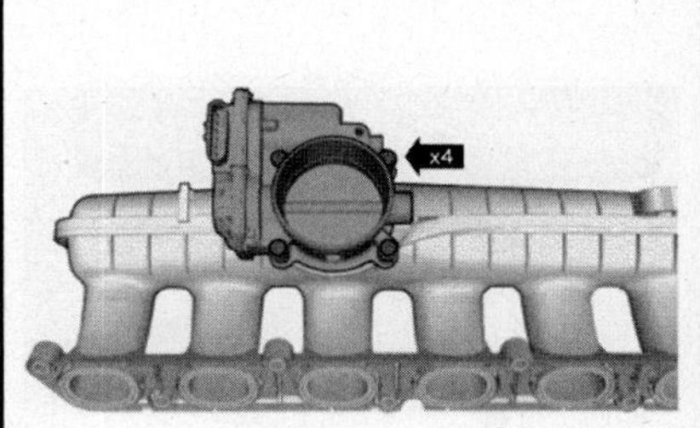

Fig. 67 Remove the 4 bolts, then remove the throttle body from the intake manifold

- Tighten the M7 bolts to 13 ft. lbs. (17 Nm).

Non-Turbocharged Engines (B6324S4 & B6324S5)

See Figures 68 through 70.

1. Remove the engine cover.
2. Raise and support the vehicle.
3. Remove 7 bolts and the engine splash plate.
4. Remove the hose clamps, then disconnect the air hose from the throttle body.
5. Remove the 2 M6 bolts securing the throttle body.
6. Remove the hose clamps, then disconnect the air duct from the air cleaner housing.
7. Disconnect the 5 electrical connectors from the intake manifold.
8. Disconnect Disconnect the vacuum line and the fuel pressure/temperature sensor electrical connector. Remove the 7 M7 bolts, then remove the intake manifold.

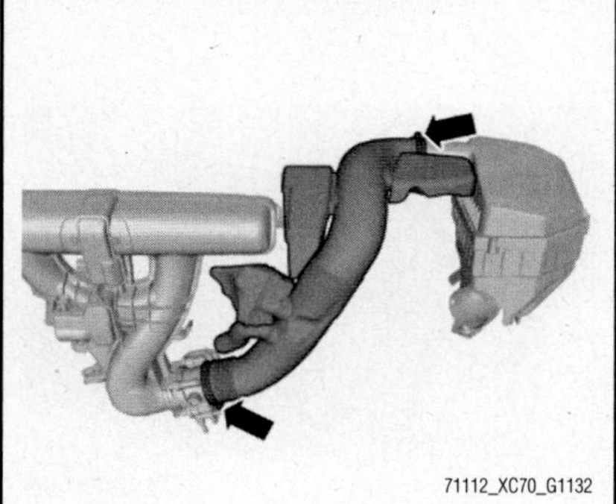

Fig. 68 Remove the hose clamps, then disconnect the air duct from the air cleaner housing

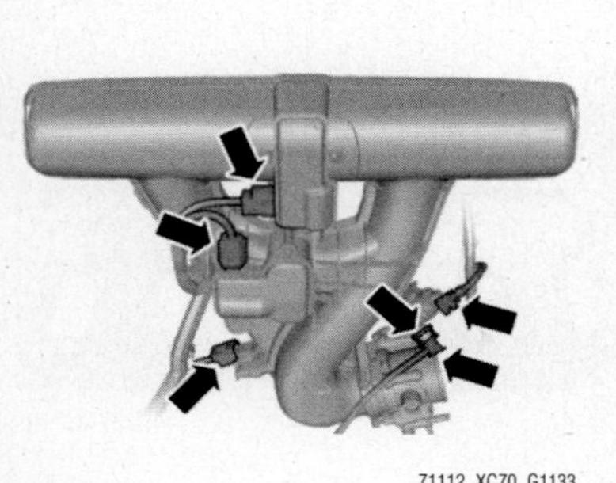

Fig. 69 Disconnect the 5 electrical connectors from the intake manifold

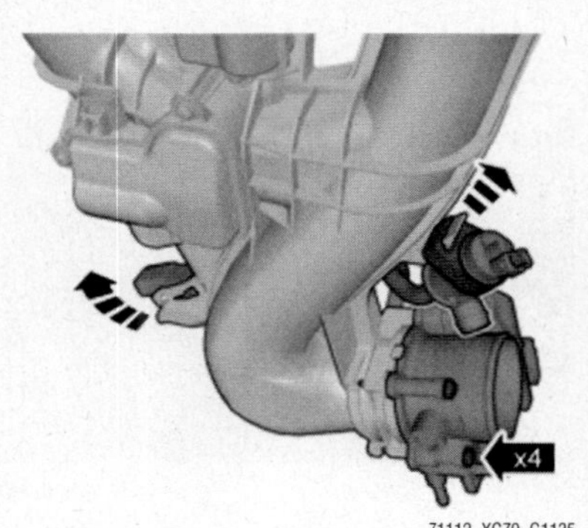

Fig. 70 Remove the MAP sensor and disconnect the EVAP valve from its bracket. Remove the 4 bolts, then remove the throttle body from the intake manifold

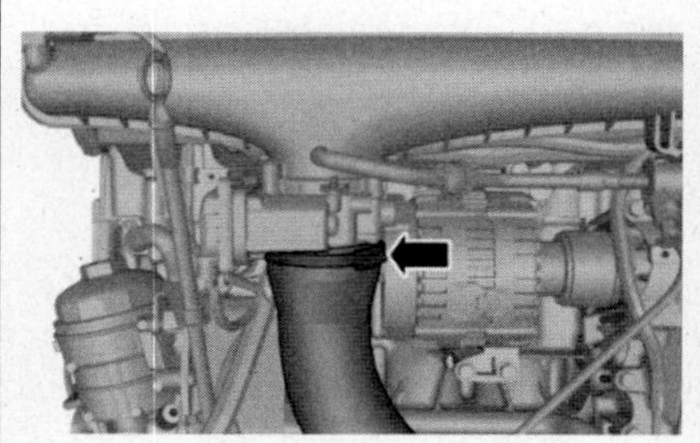

Fig. 71 Remove the hose clamp, then remove the charge air hose

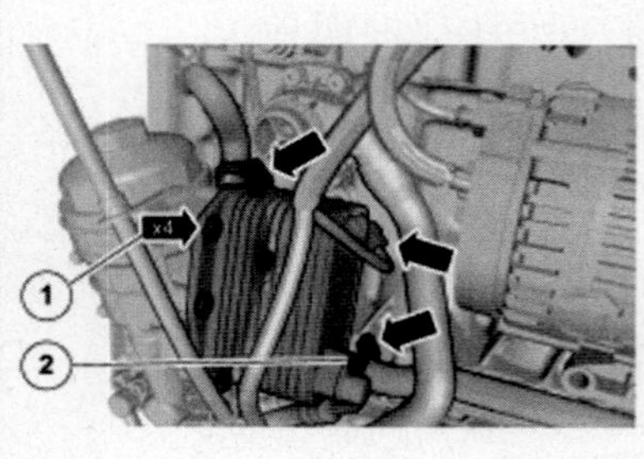

Fig. 72 Remove the 4 M6 bolts (1), then the M7 screws and clamps (2). Disconnect the electrical connector, then remove the oil cooler

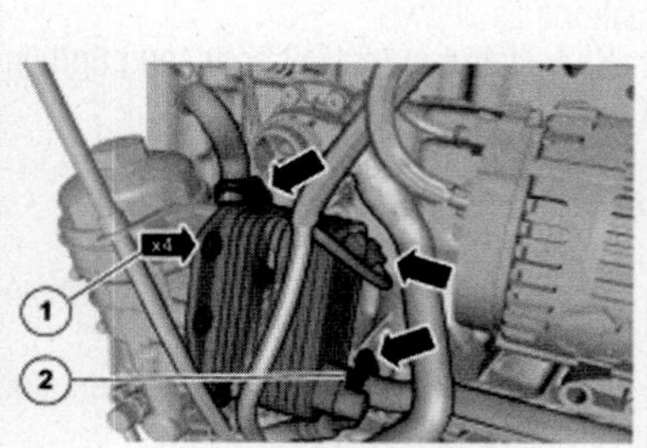

Fig. 73 Remove the 4 M6 bolts (1), then the M7 screws and clamps (2). Disconnect the electrical connector, then remove the oil cooler

9. Remove the MAP sensor and disconnect the EVAP valve from its bracket. Remove the 4 bolts, then remove the throttle body from the intake manifold

To install:

To install, reverse the removal procedure and note the following:

- Tighten the M6 bolts to 89 inch lbs. (10 Nm).
- Tighten the M7 bolts to 13 ft. lbs. (17 Nm).

OIL COOLER

REMOVAL & INSTALLATION

3.0L Engine

See Figures 71 and 72.

1. Drain the cooling system.
2. Remove the hose clamp, then remove the charge air hose.
3. Remove the 4 M6 bolts, then the M7 screws and clamps. Disconnect the electrical connector, then remove the oil cooler.

To install:

To install, reverse the removal procedure and note the following:

- Tighten the M6 bolts to 89 inch lbs. (10 Nm).
- Tighten the M7 screws to 13 ft. lbs. (17 Nm).

3.2L Engine

See Figure 73.

1. Drain the cooling system.
2. Remove the intake manifold.
3. Remove the 4 M6 bolts, then the M7 screws and clamps. Disconnect the electrical connector, then remove the oil cooler.

To install:

To install, reverse the removal procedure and note the following:

- Tighten the M6 bolts to 89 inch lbs. (10 Nm).
- Tighten the M7 screws to 13 ft. lbs. (17 Nm).

OIL PAN

REMOVAL & INSTALLATION

See Figures 74 through 77.

1. Drain the oil.
2. Raise and support the vehicle.
3. Remove 7 bolts and the engine splash plate.
4. Remove the M6 bolt, then remove the oil dipstick tube.
5. Remove the starter motor.
6. On turbocharged engines, disconnect the engine oil level sensor electrical connector, remove M6 bolts and hose clamps, then remove the charge air pipe.
7. On all models, remove the 2 end flange M10 screws.

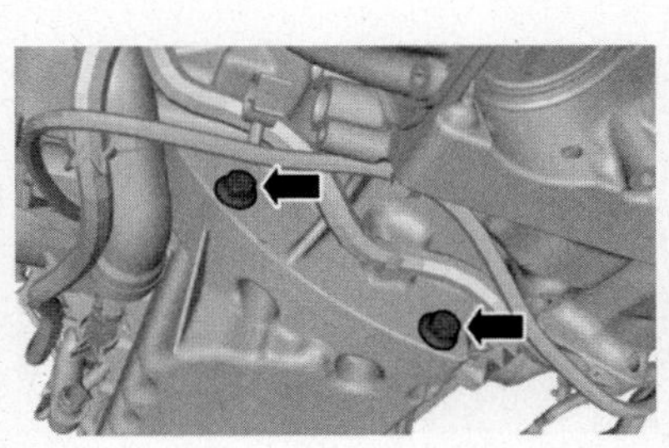

71112_XC70_G1154

Fig. 74 On all models, remove the 2 end flange M10 screws

8. Remove the 34 M7 bolts, then remove the oil pan.
9. Remove the engine oil level sensor from the bottom of the oil pan.

To install:

⁂ WARNING

Make sure that the mating faces are clean and free of foreign material.

⁂ WARNING

Take extra care not to damage the mating faces.

10. Install the engine oil level sensor, and tighten the fasteners to 75 inch lbs. (8.5 Nm).
11. Using Template (999 7270), apply Chemical Gasket (1161771) as shown.
12. Using Guide Pin (999 7273), install and tighten the specified 31 M7 oil pan bolts to 13 ft. lbs. (17 Nm). Install and tighten the remaining 3 M7 oil pan bolts to 13 ft. lbs. (17 Nm).
13. To complete installation, reverse the removal procedure and note the following:
    - Tighten the M6 bolts to 89 inch lbs. (10 Nm).
    - Tighten the M10 bolts to 37 ft. lbs. (50 Nm).
14. Fill the oil.

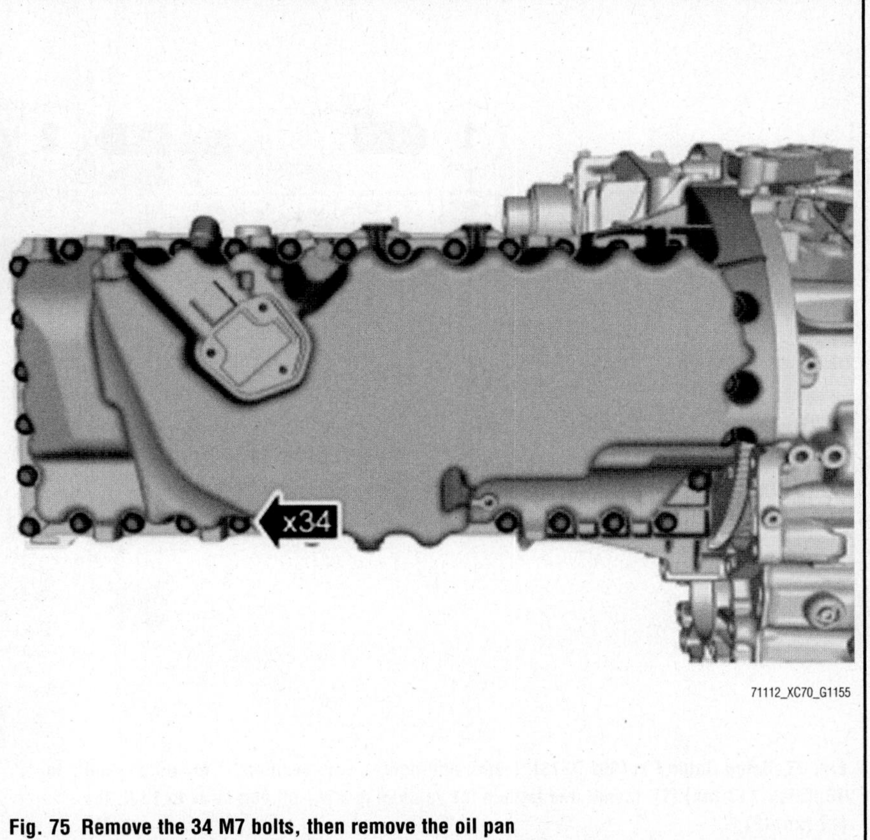

71112_XC70_G1155

Fig. 75 Remove the 34 M7 bolts, then remove the oil pan

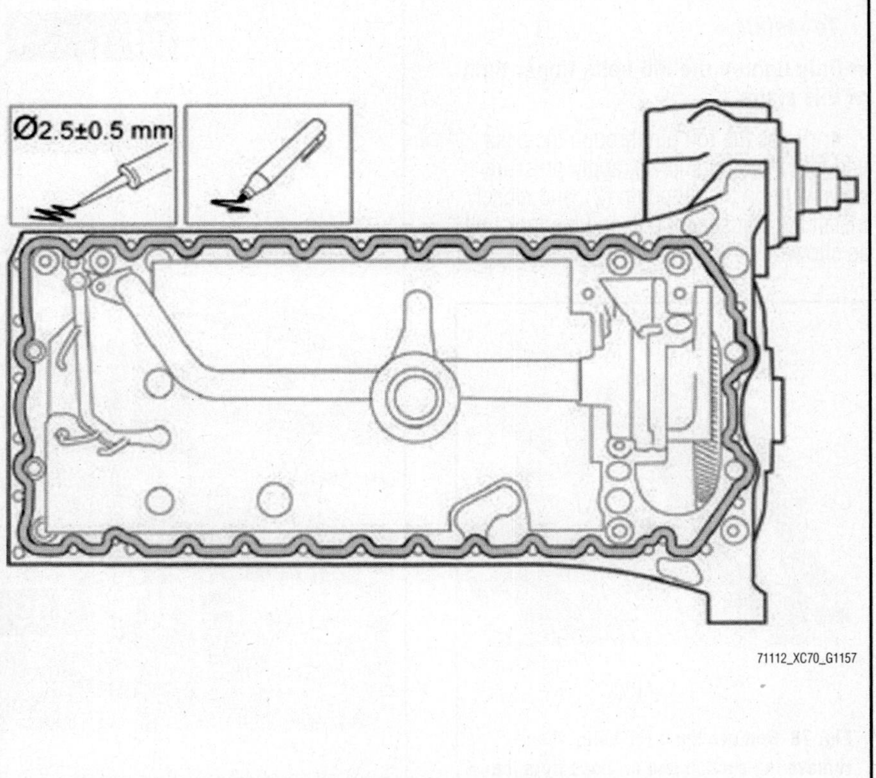

71112_XC70_G1157

Fig. 76 Using Template (999 7270), apply Chemical Gasket (1161771) as shown

OIL PUMP

REMOVAL & INSTALLATION

See Figures 78 through 80.

1. Remove the oil sump.
2. Remove the 3 M7 bolts, then remove the suction and oil lines from the oil pump.

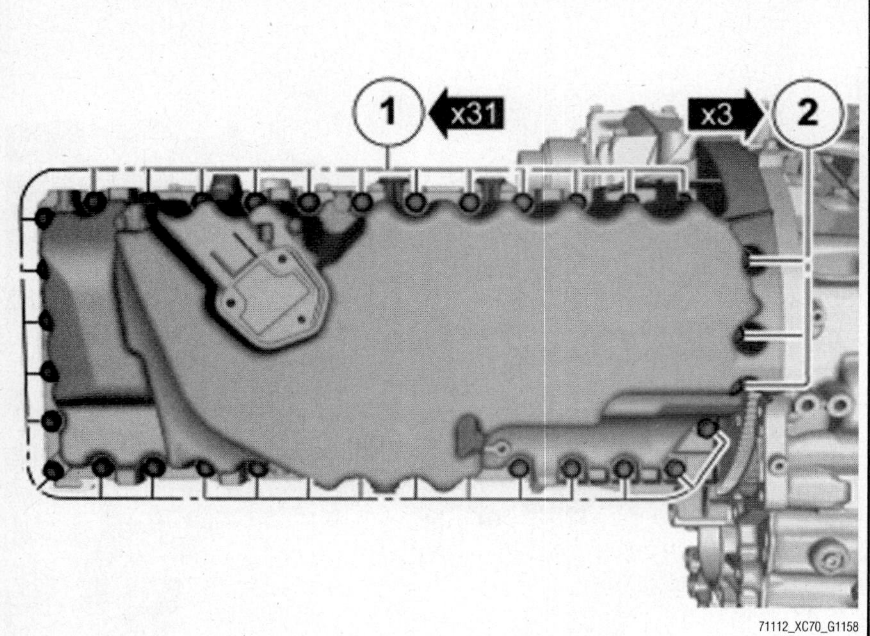

Fig. 77 **Using Guide Pin (999 7273), install and tighten the specified 31 M7 oil pan bolts to 13 ft. lbs. (17 Nm) (1). Install and tighten the remaining 3 M7 oil pan bolts to 13 ft. lbs. (17 Nm) (2)**

3. Install Puller (999 7313) into the oil pump and remove the 2 M6 bolts as shown.

To install:

➡Only tighten the M6 bolts finger tight at this stage.

4. Press the roll pin through the boss and into the oil pump (1), apply pressure downward on the oil pump (2), and loosely install the adjustment bolt and the lock bolt as shown.

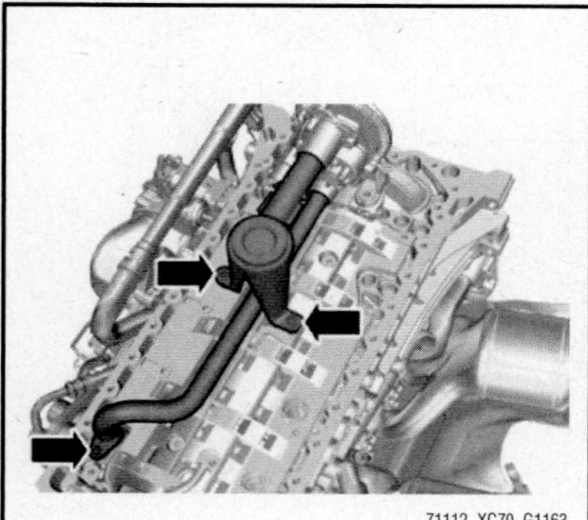

Fig. 78 Remove the 3 M7 bolts, then remove the suction and oil lines from the oil pump

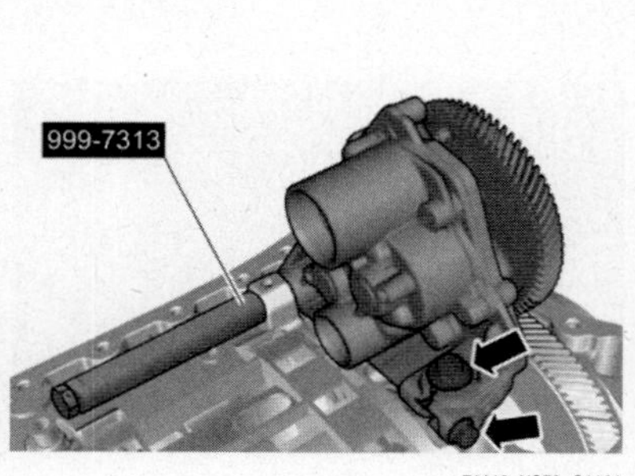

Fig. 79 Install Puller (999 7313) into the oil pump and remove the 2 M6 bolts as shown

5. Install following equipment onto the oil pan as shown:
- Dial Indicator (981 3134)
- Magnetic Base (999 9696)
- Magnetic Stand Plate (999 5971)

6. Adjust the top M6 bolt as necessary, then tighten the lock bolt to 89 inch lbs. (10 Nm).

7. Tighten the M6 lock bolt to 89 inch lbs. (10 Nm).

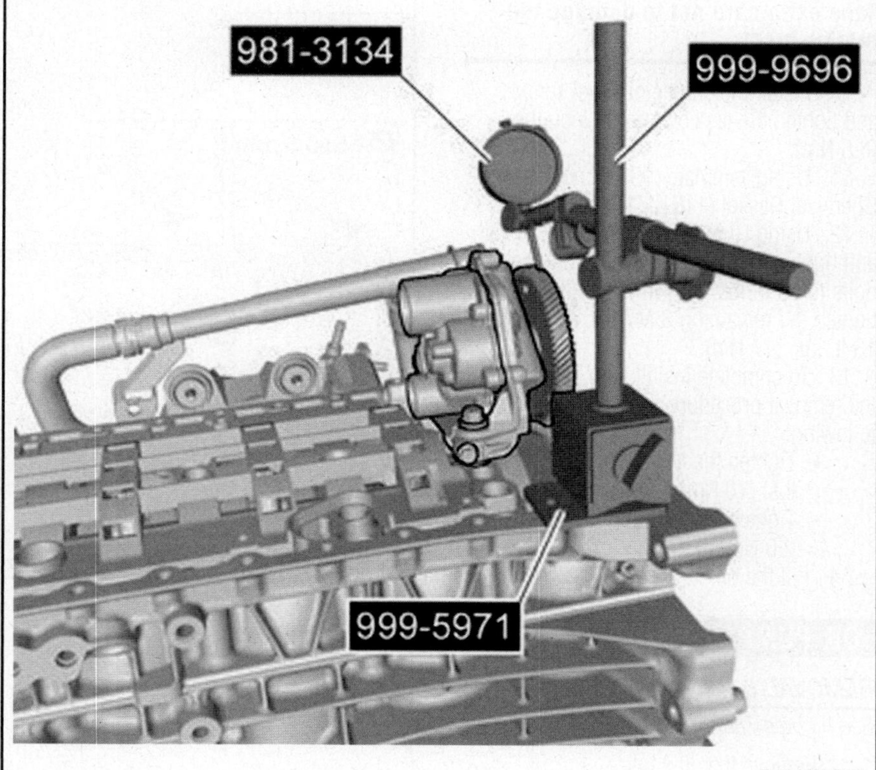

Fig. 80 Install equipment onto the oil pan as shown

8. To complete installation, reverse the removal procedure and note the following:

- Tighten the M7 bolts to 13 ft. lbs. (17 Nm).

PISTONS & RINGS

POSITIONING

See Figure 81.

➡The text on piston ring "A" must be face up.

1. Using piston ring pliers, position the rings as shown.

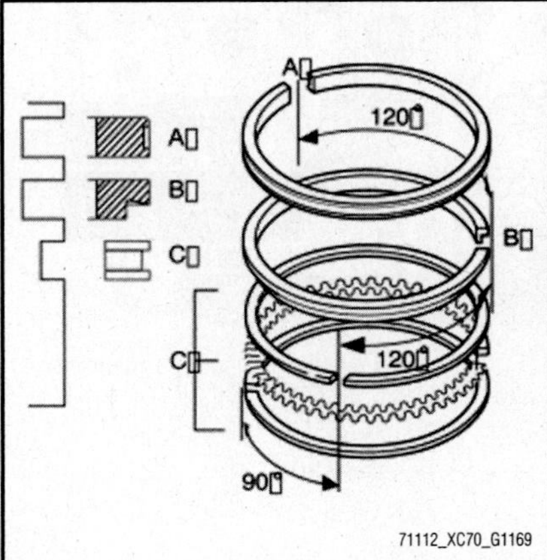

Fig. 81 Using piston ring pliers, position the rings as shown

TURBOCHARGER

REMOVAL & INSTALLATION

See Figures 82 through 86.

1. Drain the cooling system.
2. Remove the engine cover.
3. Remove hose clamp and fasteners securing air duct.
4. Remove the catalytic converter.
5. Remove the 2 hose clamps, then remove the charge air hose.
6. Remove the 2 M6 bolts, then remove the oil line.
7. Remove the hose clamp, then remove the resonator and air duct.

⁂ CAUTION

Be prepared to collect escaping fluid.

8. Remove the 2 coolant pipe-to-turbocharger bolts.
9. Move the coolant line aside and using a Crow's Foot Wrench (981 4102), remove the 4 M8 bolts, then remove the heat shield.

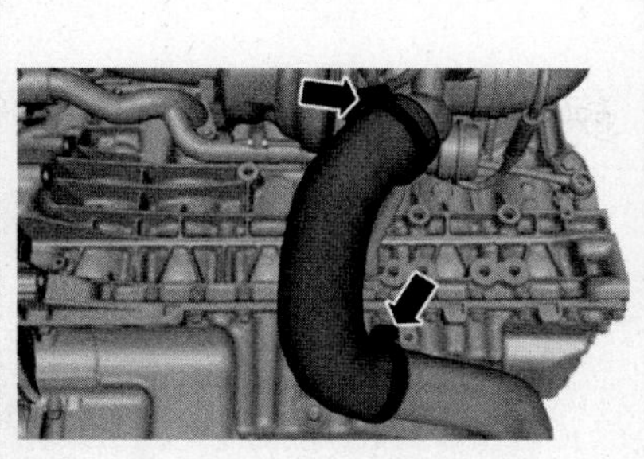

Fig. 82 Remove the 2 hose clamps, then remove the charge air hose

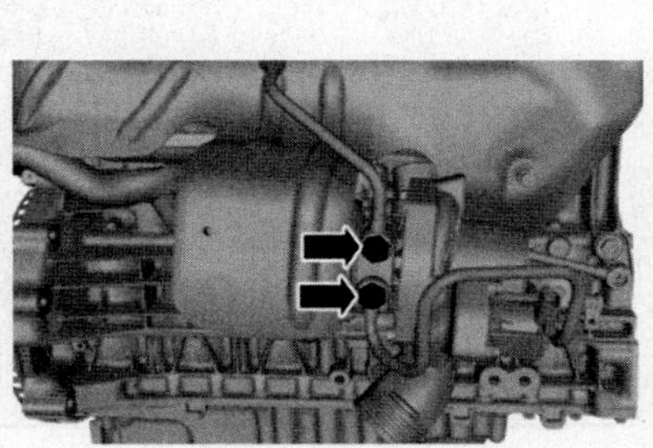

Fig. 83 Remove the 2 coolant pipe-to-turbocharger bolts

10. Remove the oil pressure pipe-to-turbocharger bolt.
11. Disconnect the electrical connector to the turbocharger. Remove the 2 hose clamps, then remove the hoses.
12. Remove the 3 turbocharger-to-exhaust manifold bolts.

To install:

To install, reverse the removal procedure and note the following:

- Tighten the 3 turbocharger-to-exhaust manifold bolts:
    a. Stage 1: 44 inch lbs. (5 Nm)
    b. Stage 2: 22 ft. lbs. (30 Nm)
- Tighten the oil pressure pipe-to-turbocharger bolt to 28 ft. lbs. (38 Nm).
- Tighten the M8 bolts to 18 ft. lbs. (24 Nm).
- Tighten the coolant pipe-to-turbocharger bolts to 28 ft. lbs. (38 Nm).
- Tighten the M6 bolts to 89 inch lbs. (10 Nm).

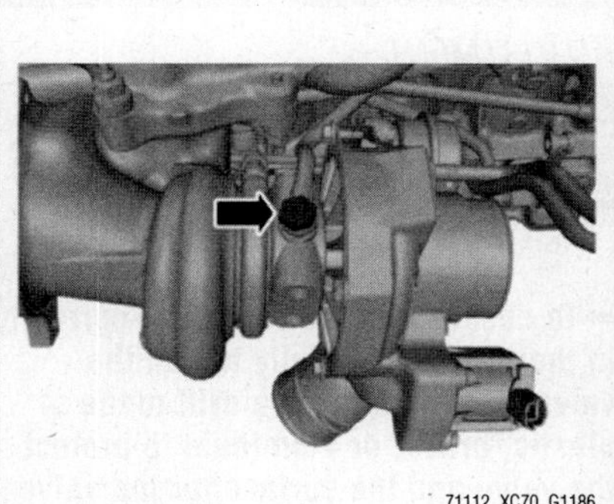

Fig. 84 Remove the oil pressure pipe-to-turbocharger bolt

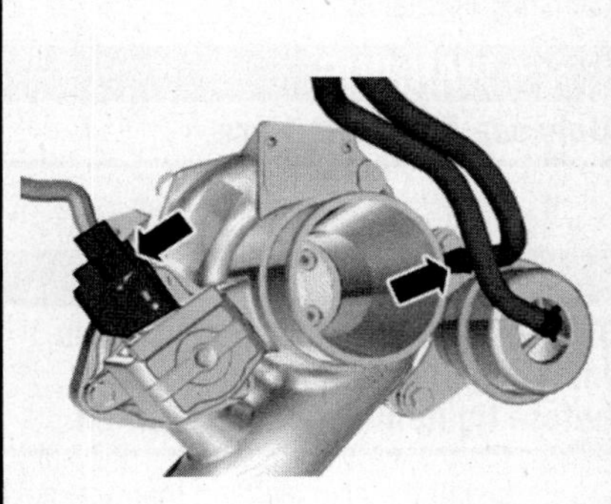

Fig. 85 Disconnect the electrical connector to the turbocharger. Remove the 2 hose clamps, then remove the hoses

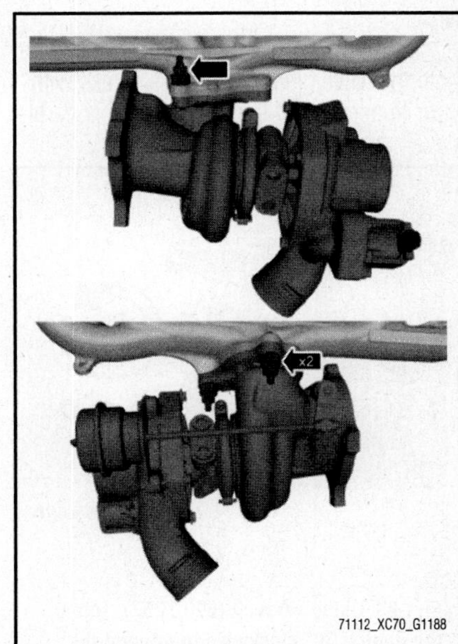

Fig. 86 Remove the 3 turbocharger-to-exhaust manifold bolts

VALVE LASH CLEARANCE

ADJUSTMENT

See Figures 87 through 92.

1. Before servicing the vehicle, refer to the Precautions Section.
2. Remove the camshafts.

➡To ensure that the valves lie correctly in their seats, carefully tap on the valve stem ends. Use a drift made of plastic, brass, or aluminum to protect the valve and the surface for the valve lifter. The sound made when tapping indicates whether the valve is correctly positioned.

3. Using Wrench (999 7257), rotate the engine 30° clockwise to prevent the valves from colliding with the pistons when the camshaft is rotated.

⁂ WARNING

Only use moderate force.

4. Install the exhaust camshaft.

⁂ WARNING

To avoid damage to the camshafts, install and hand tighten all caps before tightening to specification.

5. Install the camshafts in their journals using the special bearing caps (999 7281) to simulate the cam cover journals. Start in the middle and screw the bearing caps down alternating. Do not tighten.
6. Tighten the M7 bolts of the press tools in the order specified to 13 ft. lbs. (17 Nm).
7. Using a feeler gauge, measure and note the valve clearance values. Press with your finger so that the feeler gauge is paral-

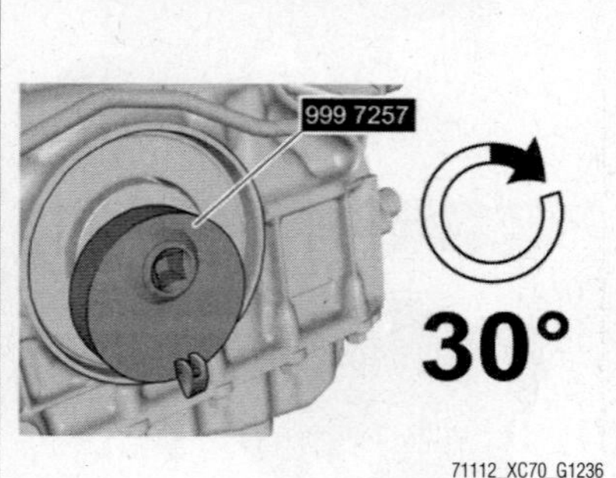

Fig. 87 Using Wrench (999 7257), rotate the engine 30° clockwise to prevent the valves from colliding with the pistons when the camshaft is rotated

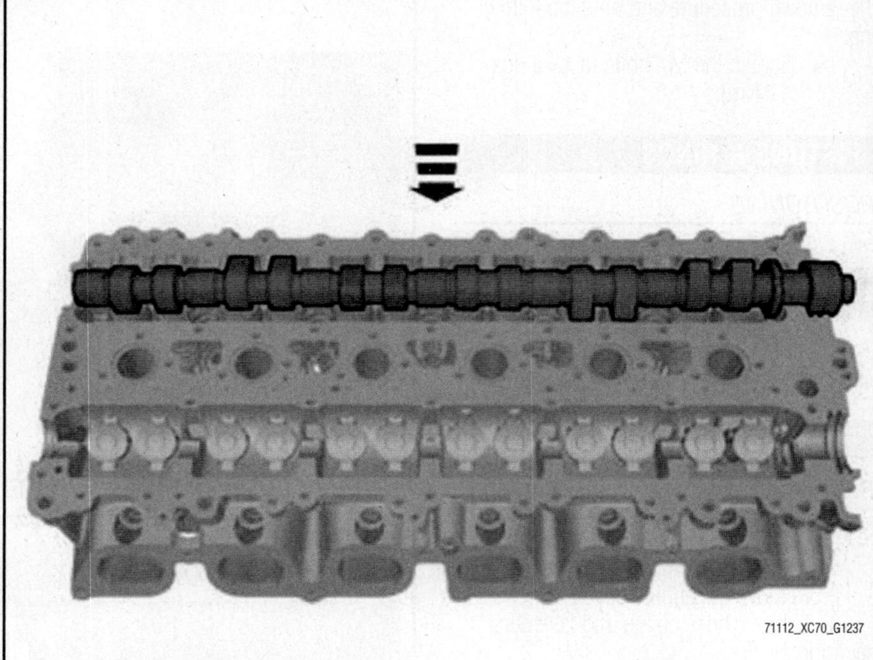

Fig. 88 Install the exhaust camshaft

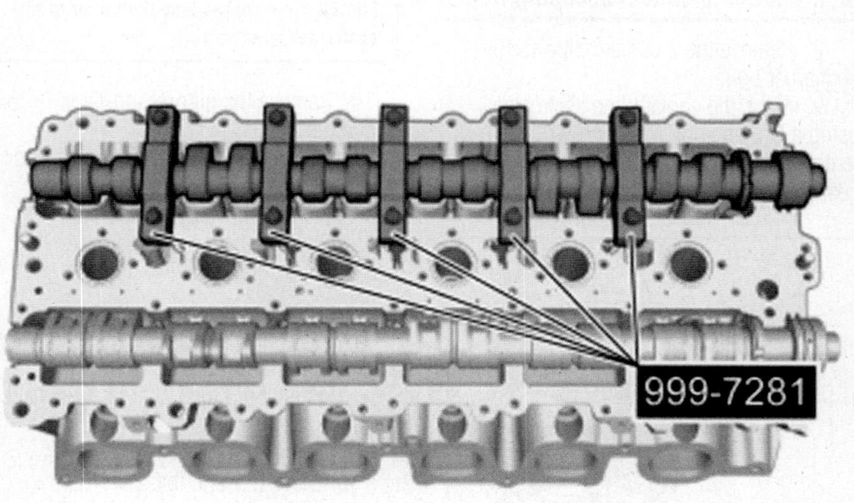

Fig. 89 Install the camshafts in their journals using the special bearing caps (999 7281) to simulate the cam cover journals

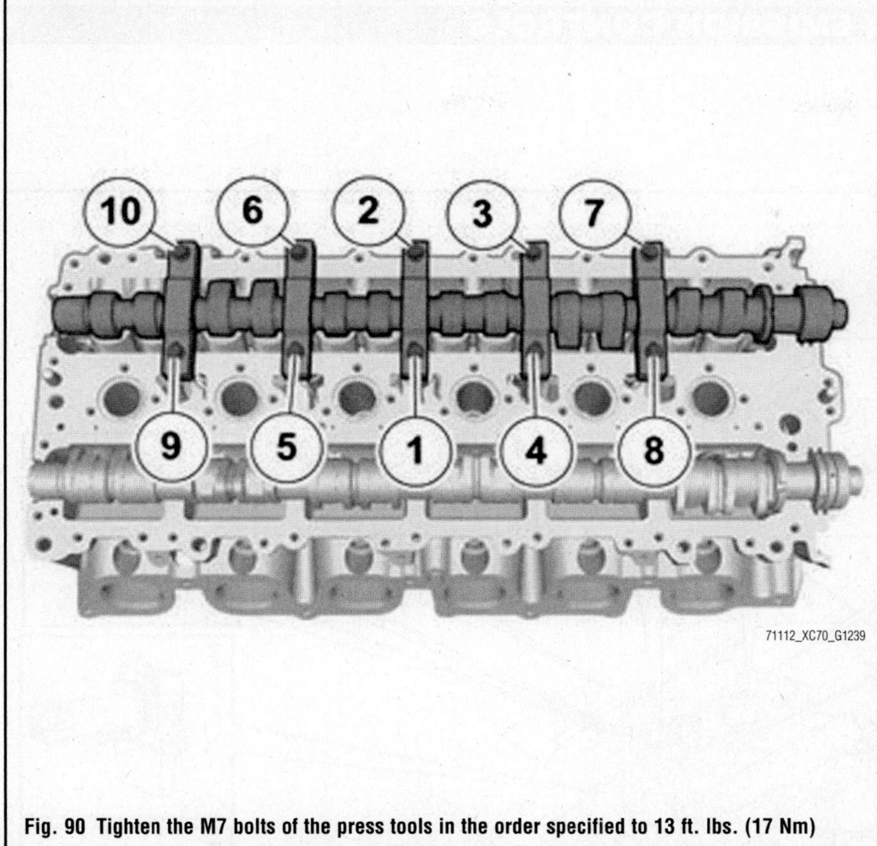

Fig. 90 Tighten the M7 bolts of the press tools in the order specified to 13 ft. lbs. (17 Nm)

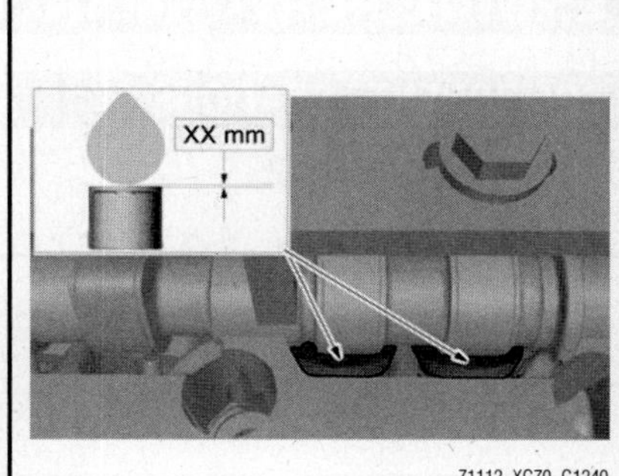

Fig. 91 Using a feeler gauge, measure and note the valve clearance values

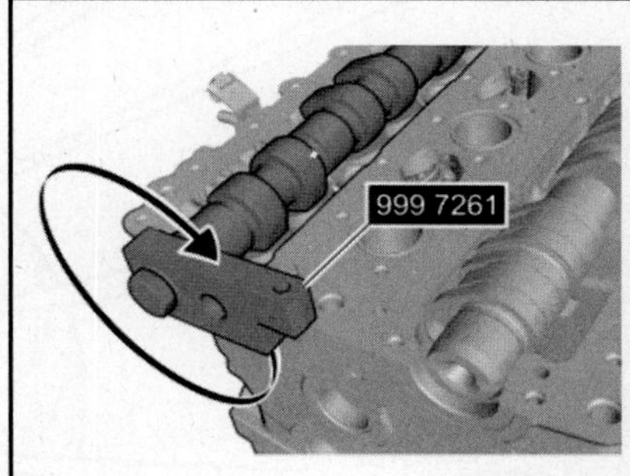

Fig. 92 Using Position Adjustment tool (999 7261), repeat the work by loosening the screws of the press tools and rotating the camshaft until the next node pair is in the correct position

lel to the top of the lifter. To ensure that measuring is as accurate as possible, move the feeler gauge laterally when measuring the clearance. Valve clearance as measured on a cold engine should be as follows:

- -0.0004 inch (-0.01mm) at 59° F (15° C)
- +0.0004 inch (+0.01mm) at 77° F (25° C)
- +0.0008 inch (+0.02mm) at 86° F (30° C)
- +0.0012 inch (+0.03mm) at 95° F (35° C)
- +0.0016 inch (+0.04mm) at 113° F (45° C)

8. Calculate the required thickness of the valve tappet with the following formula:
   - Measurement of existing valve clearance (actual value) =
   - Required thickness of valve tappet =
   - Compare the measured valve clearance(s) with the specifications.
9. Using Position Adjustment tool (999 7261), repeat the work by loosening the screws of the press tools and rotating the camshaft until the next node pair is in the correct position. Tighten and continue measuring until all exhaust valves have been measured.
10. Repeat the measurement for all cylinders.
11. If installing a new component, measure the actual clearance between cam lobe and tappet by installing the tappet with the lowest height.
12. Carefully note the results.
13. Correct measured clearance as necessary.
14. Remove the press tools. Lift off the camshaft. Adjust the clearance by replacing the lifter. Alternative lifters are available as a spare part/spare part kit. Reinstall the camshaft and press tools. Tighten to 13 ft. lbs. (17 Nm). Recheck the valve clearance on the adjusted valves.
15. When the correct valve clearance has been achieved, remove the press tools.
16. Remove the camshafts.
17. Test drive the engine until the thermostat opens and check for any leakage.

ENGINE PERFORMANCE & EMISSION CONTROLS

COMPONENT LOCATIONS

See Figures 93 through 95.

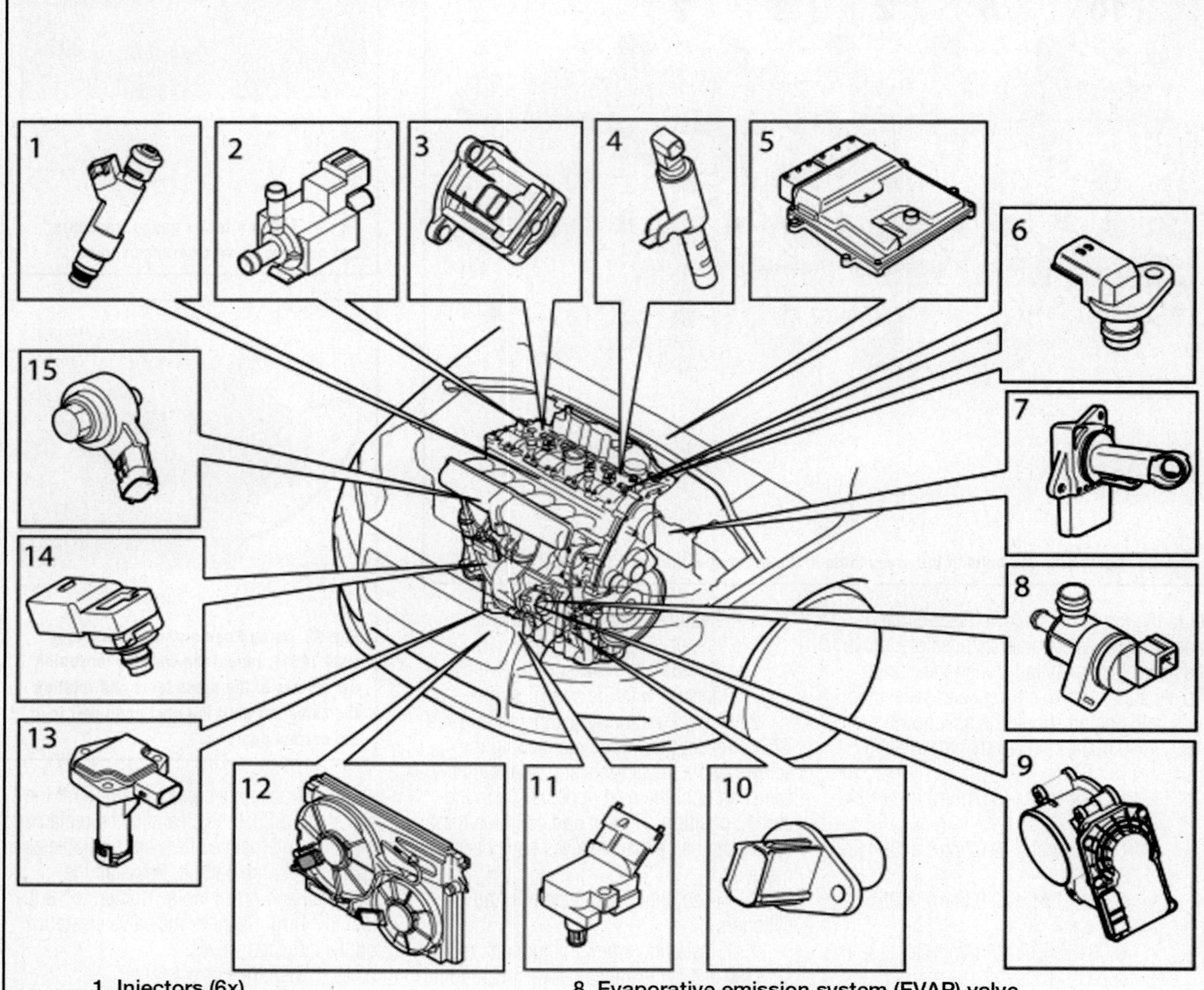

1. Injectors (6x)
2. Turbocharger (TC) control valve
3. Relief valve
4. Reset valve camshaft (CVVT)
5. Engine Control Module (ECM)
6. Camshaft sensor (2x)
7. Mass airflow sensor/air temperature sensor
8. Evaporative emission system (EVAP) valve
9. Throttle unit
10. Engine speed (RPM) sensor
11. Charge pressure sensor
12. Engine cooling fan (FC)
13. Oil level sensor
14. Intake pressure sensor
15. Knock Sensor (KS) (2x)

71112_XC70_G1258

Fig. 93 Engine performance and emission control component locations—B6304T4 engine

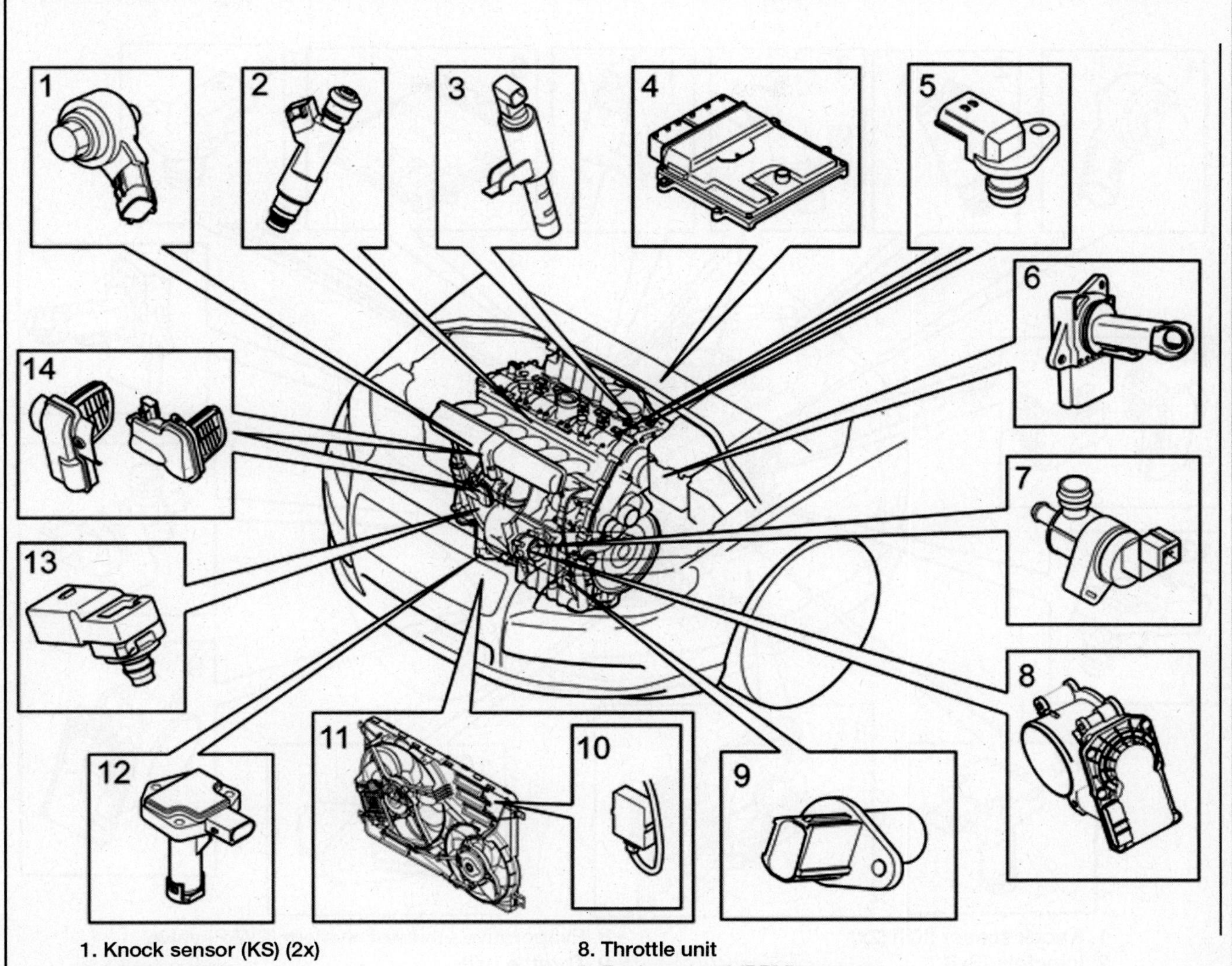

Fig. 94 Engine performance and emission control component locations—B6324S4 engine

CAMSHAFT POSITION (CMP) SENSOR

LOCATION

See Figure 96.

There is a Camshaft Position (CMP) sensor for each camshaft. The CMP sensors are located by the camshafts on the engine's right side.

REMOVAL & INSTALLATION

See Figure 97.

1. Before servicing the vehicle, refer to the Precautions Section.
2. Turn the ignition off.
3. Remove the engine cover.
4. Remove the 2 M6 bolts, then remove the Camshaft Position (CMP) sensors.

To install:

To install, reverse the removal procedure and note the following:

- Tighten the M6 bolts to 89 inch lbs. (10 Nm).

ELECTRONIC CONTROL MODULE (ECM)

LOCATION

See Figure 98.

The Engine Control Module (ECM) is located in the cold zone in front of the windshield.

REMOVAL & INSTALLATION

See Figures 99 through 101.

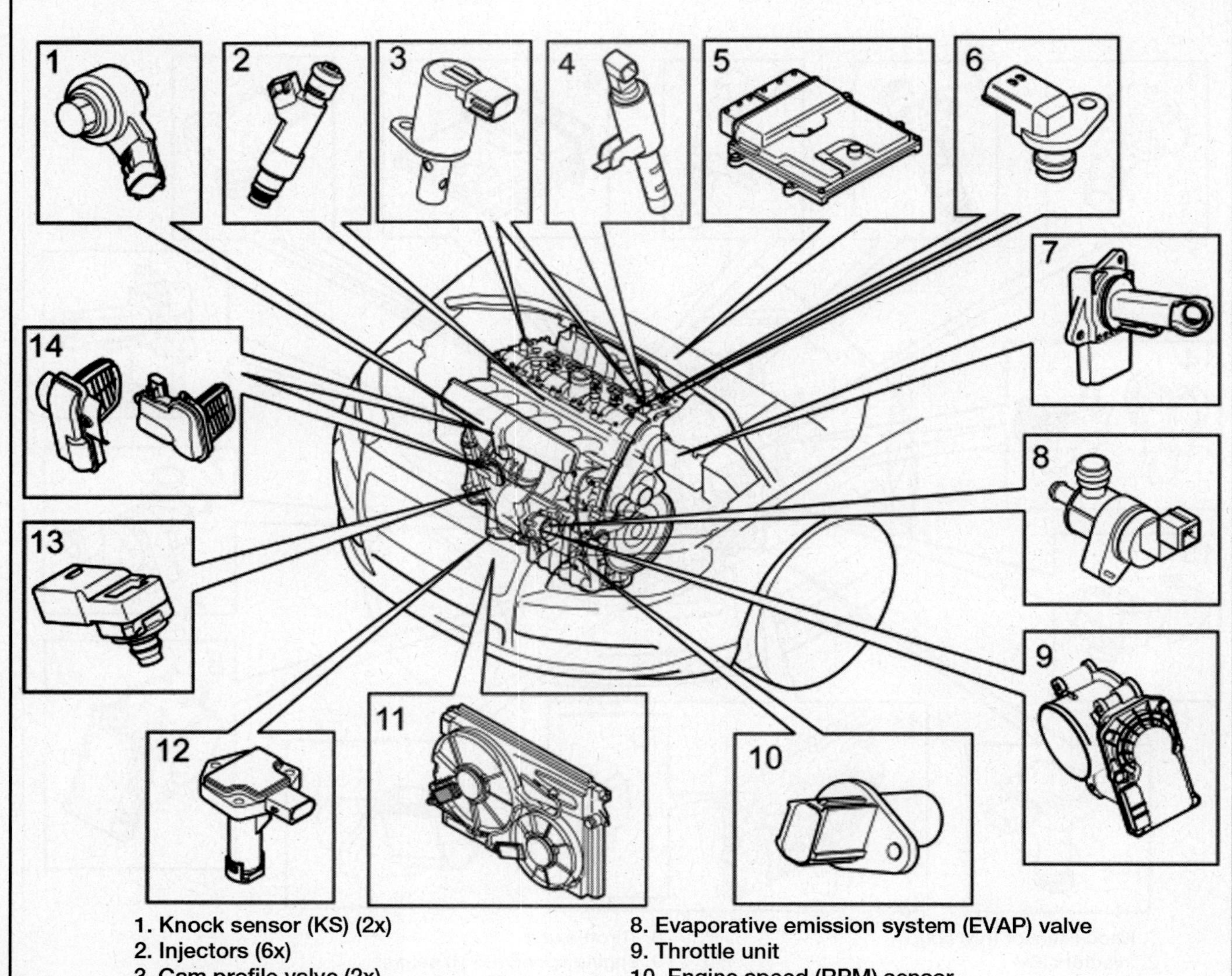

1. Knock sensor (KS) (2x)
2. Injectors (6x)
3. Cam profile valve (2x)
4. Reset valve camshaft (CVVT)
5. Engine Control Module (ECM)
6. Camshaft sensor (2x)
7. Mass airflow sensor/air temperature sensor
8. Evaporative emission system (EVAP) valve
9. Throttle unit
10. Engine speed (RPM) sensor
11. Engine cooling fan (FC)
12. Oil level sensor
13. Intake pressure sensor
14. Actuator variable intake (2x)

71112_XC70_G1260

Fig. 95 Engine performance and emission control component locations—B6324S5 engine

WARNING

When this procedure is completed, it will be required to download the designated software from the Volvo central database.

1. Before servicing the vehicle, refer to the Precautions Section.
2. Turn the ignition off.
3. Remove the cowl panel cover.
4. Remove the Engine Control Module (ECM).

➡Make sure that the component terminals are not bent or damaged.

5. Disengage the 2 tabs and pull the ECM out of the bracket.
6. Remove the 4 M6 bolts from the ECM as shown, then remove the ECM from backing plate.

To install:

To install, reverse the removal procedure and note the following:

7. Order and download software 30785202 from the Volvo central database.

RESET

New software can be downloaded into the Engine Control Module (ECM). When ordering software, the hardware and the software in the car is compared to the information in the Volvo central database. If the comparison is OK, the software is downloaded to the control module. If the comparison between the car and Volvo central database is not OK, the database is updated with the car configuration. When this is complete, the software is downloaded.

Fig. 96 Camshaft Position (CMP) sensor identification

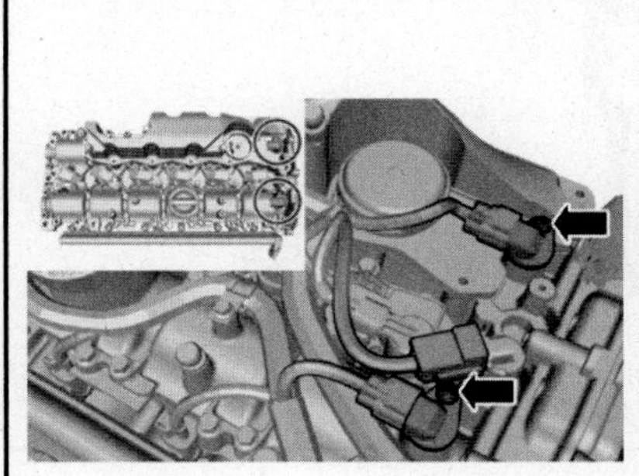

Fig. 97 Remove the 2 M6 bolts, then remove the Camshaft Position (CMP) sensors

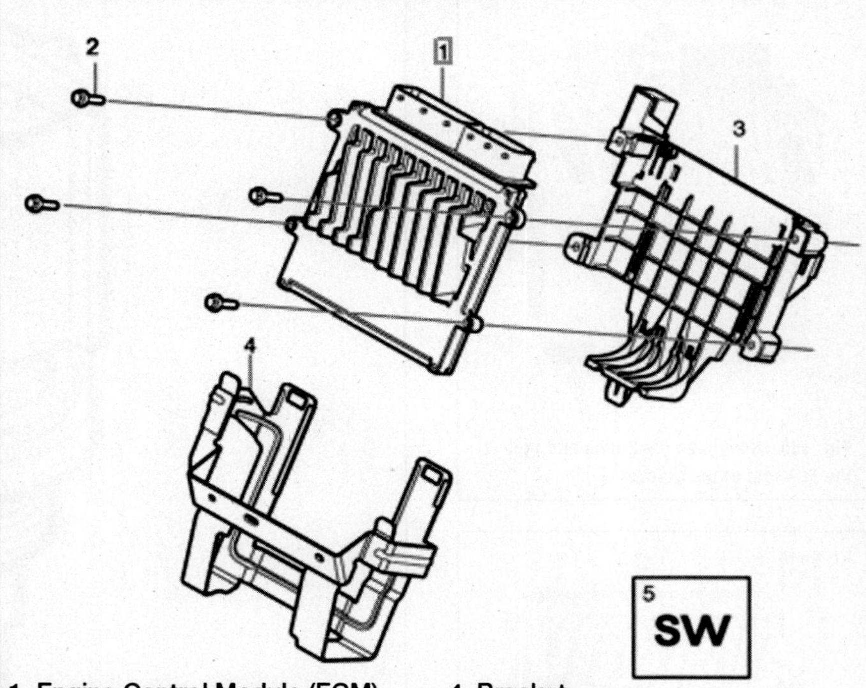

Fig. 98 Engine Control Module (ECM) component locations

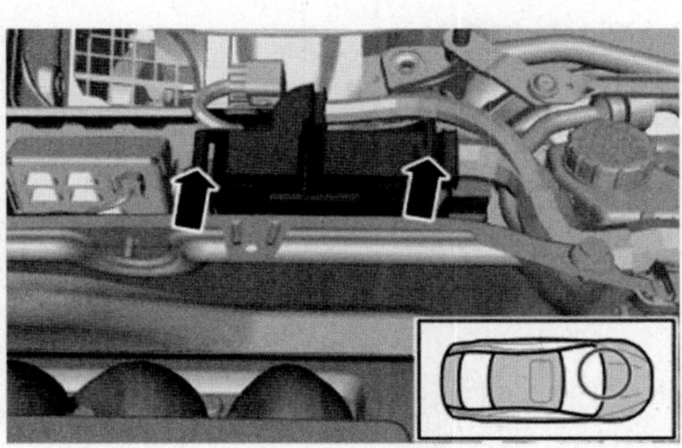

Fig. 99 Remove the Engine Control Module (ECM)

The ECM contains a unique code for each car for the immobilizer. The Central Electronic Module (CEM) checks this code at engine start up. The engine will not start if the CEM detects an incorrect code for the immobilizer. This means that the ECM cannot be switched from vehicle to vehicle.

The ECM must first be "unlocked" using a unique PIN for each car before it can be programmed with a code for the immobilizer. When the PIN has been approved by the ECM, the code for the immobilizer can be programmed.

The PIN and the code for the immobilizer are obtained from the Volvo central database and sent out with the software package when software for downloading has been ordered.

All new ECMs have the same PIN which is preprogrammed by the control module supplier. When the ECM has been programmed successfully, the original PIN for the car will be programmed in the ECM memory and will replace the pre-programmed PIN code.

ENGINE COOLANT TEMPERATURE (ECT) SENSOR

LOCATION

See Figure 102.

The Engine Coolant Temperature (ECT) sensor is located by the thermostat under the intake manifold.

REMOVAL & INSTALLATION

See Figures 103 and 104.

1. Drain the cooling system.
2. Remove the oil filter canister.
3. Disconnect the electrical connector, remove the cotter pin, then remove the Engine Coolant Temperature (ECT) sensor.

To install:

Installation is the reverse of the removal procedure.

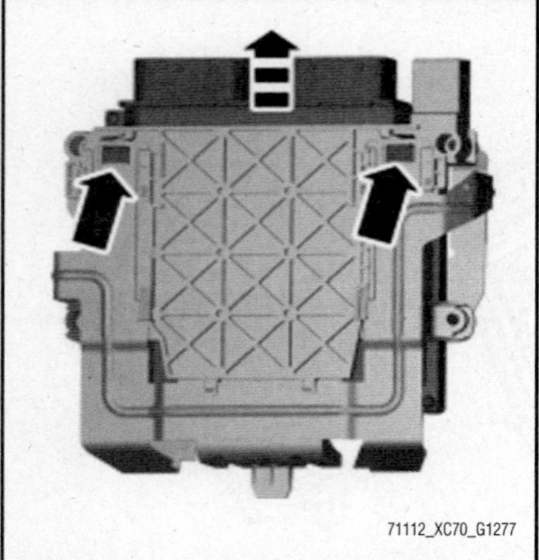

Fig. 100 Disengage the 2 tabs and pull the ECM out of the bracket

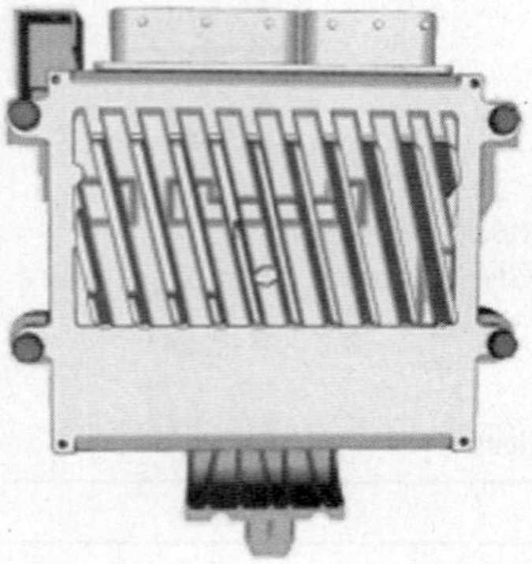

71112_XC70_G1278

Fig. 101 Remove the 4 M6 bolts from the ECM as shown, then remove the ECM from backing plate

ENGINE SPEED SENSOR

LOCATION

See Figure 105.

The engine speed (RPM) sensor is located on the engines flywheel side, pointing forward.

REMOVAL & INSTALLATION

See Figure 106.

➡This component may also be referred to as a Crankshaft Position (CKP) sensor.

1. Raise and support the vehicle.
2. Remove 7 bolts and the engine splash plate.
3. Remove the M6 bolt, then remove the engine speed (RPM) sensor.

To install:

To install, reverse the removal procedure and note the following:

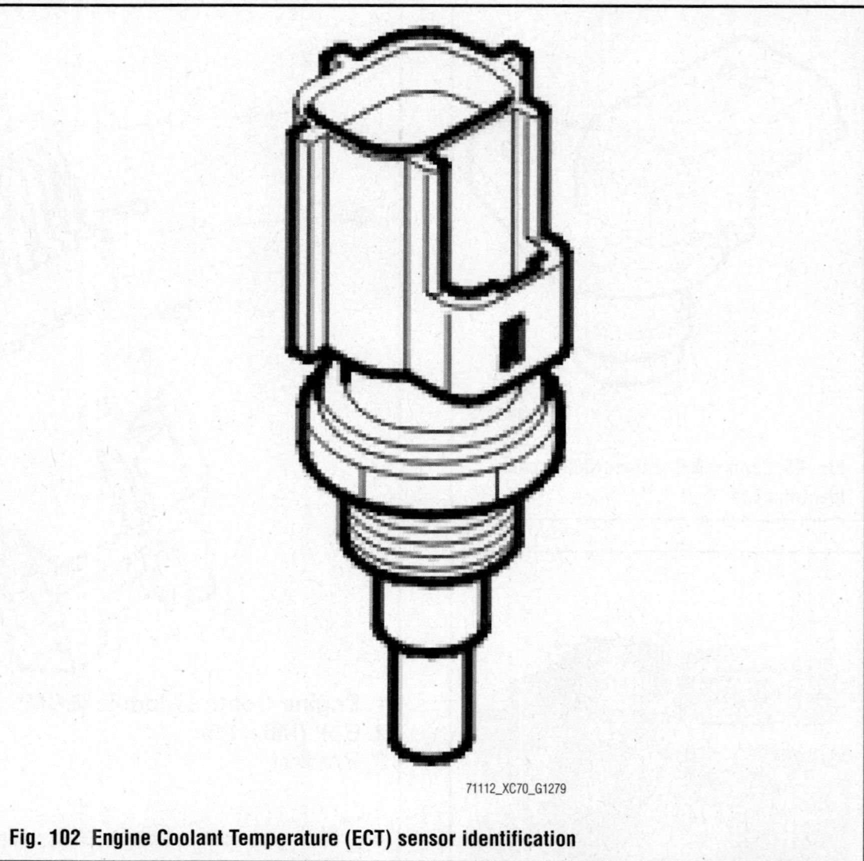

Fig. 102 Engine Coolant Temperature (ECT) sensor identification

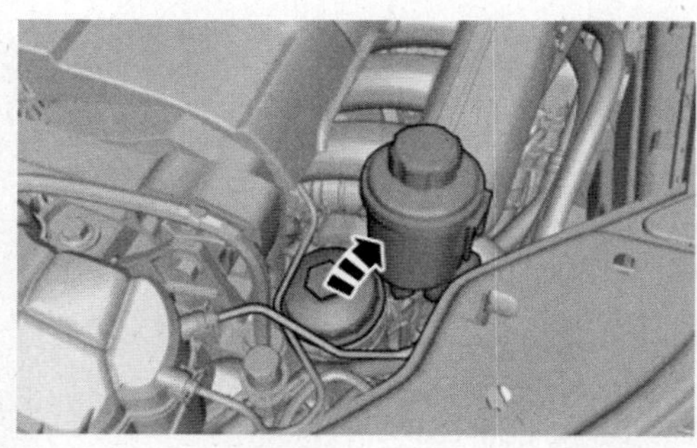

Fig. 103 Remove the oil filter canister

- Tighten the M6 bolt to 89 inch lbs. (10 Nm).

INPUT SPEED SENSOR

LOCATION

See Figure 107.

The transmission input speed sensor is located under the control system cover in the right front side of the engine compartment.

REMOVAL & INSTALLATION

See Figures 108 and 109.

1. Remove the control system cover.
2. Remove the M6 bolt, then remove the transmission input speed sensor.
3. Push in the tab, then pull out the sensor connector.

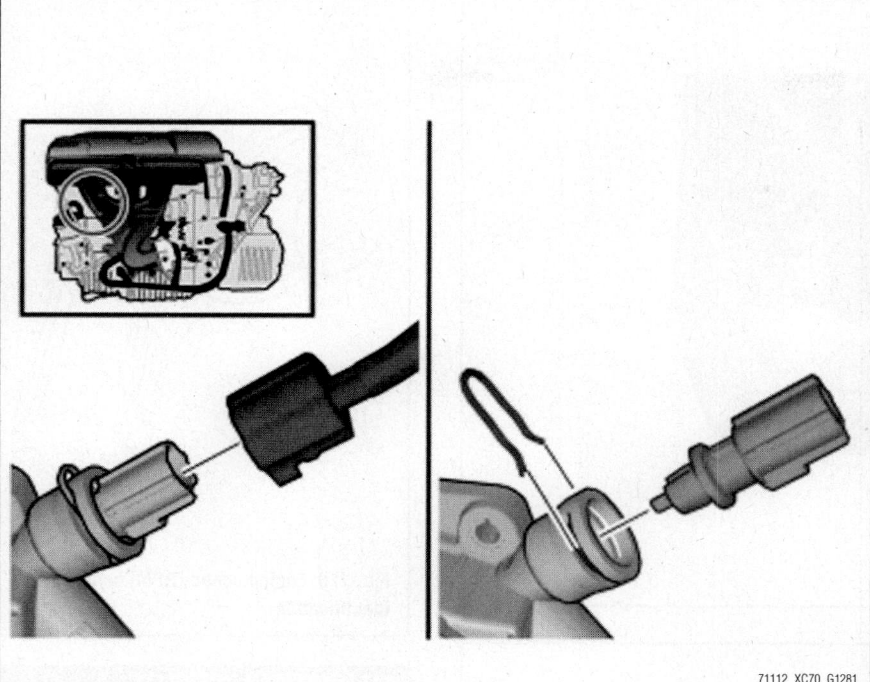

Fig. 104 Disconnect the electrical connector, remove the cotter pin, then remove the Engine Coolant Temperature (ECT) sensor

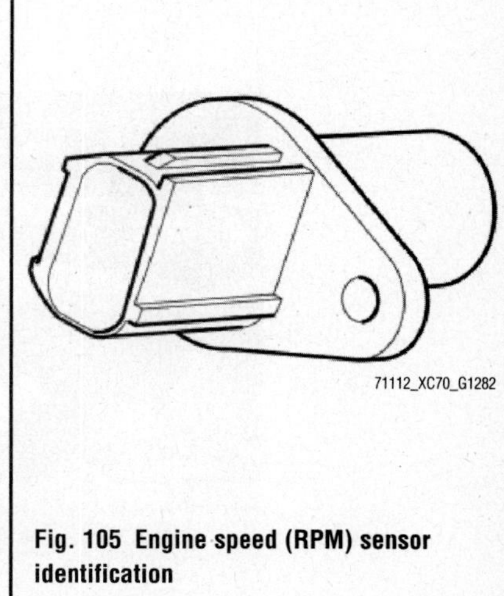

Fig. 105 Engine speed (RPM) sensor identification

To install:

Installation is the reverse of the removal procedure.

KNOCK SENSOR (KS)

LOCATION

See Figure 110.

The Knock Sensors (KS) are located on the cylinder block under the intake manifold.

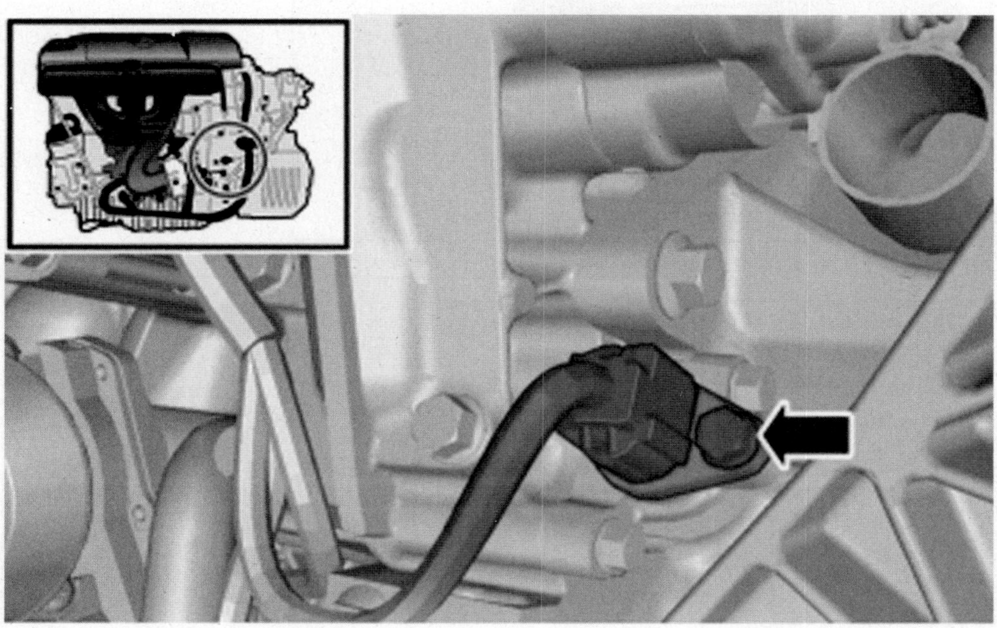

Fig. 106 Remove the M6 bolt, then remove the engine speed (RPM) sensor

Fig. 107 Transmission input speed sensor location

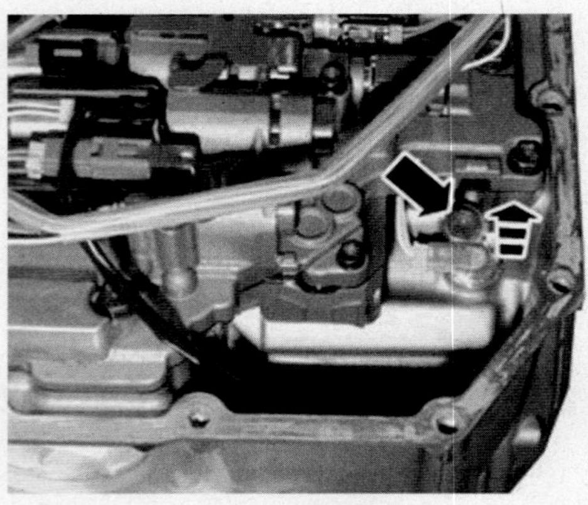

Fig. 108 Remove the M6 bolt, then remove the transmission input speed sensor

REMOVAL & INSTALLATION

See Figures 111 through 112

1. Remove the engine cover.
2. Remove the middle knock sensor as shown.
3. Remove the following:
   - The intake manifold
   - The engine oil cooler
4. Remove the rear knock sensor as shown.

To install:

To install, reverse the removal procedure and note the following:

- Tighten the knock sensors to 15 ft. lbs. (20 Nm).
- Tighten the M6 bolts to 89 inch lbs. (10 Nm).

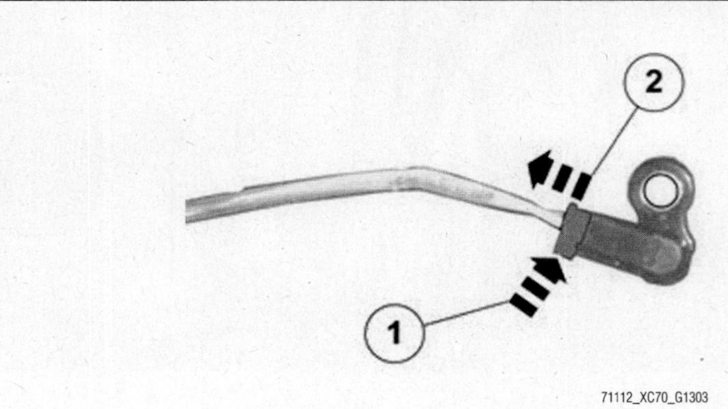

Fig. 109 Push in the tab (1), then pull out the sensor connector (2)

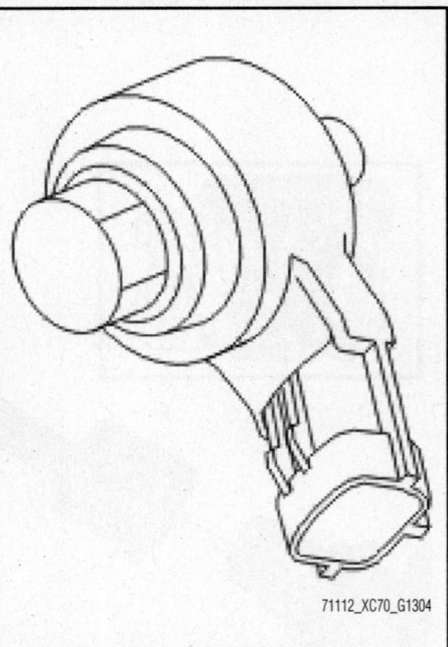

Fig. 110 Engine speed (RPM) sensor identification

MANIFOLD ABSOLUTE PRESSURE (MAP) SENSOR

LOCATION

The Manifold Absolute Pressure (MAP) sensor is located on the upper part of the intake manifold.

REMOVAL & INSTALLATION

See Figure 114.

1. Disconnect the electrical connector, then remove the Manifold Absolute Pressure (MAP) sensor.

To install:

Installation is the reverse of the removal procedure.

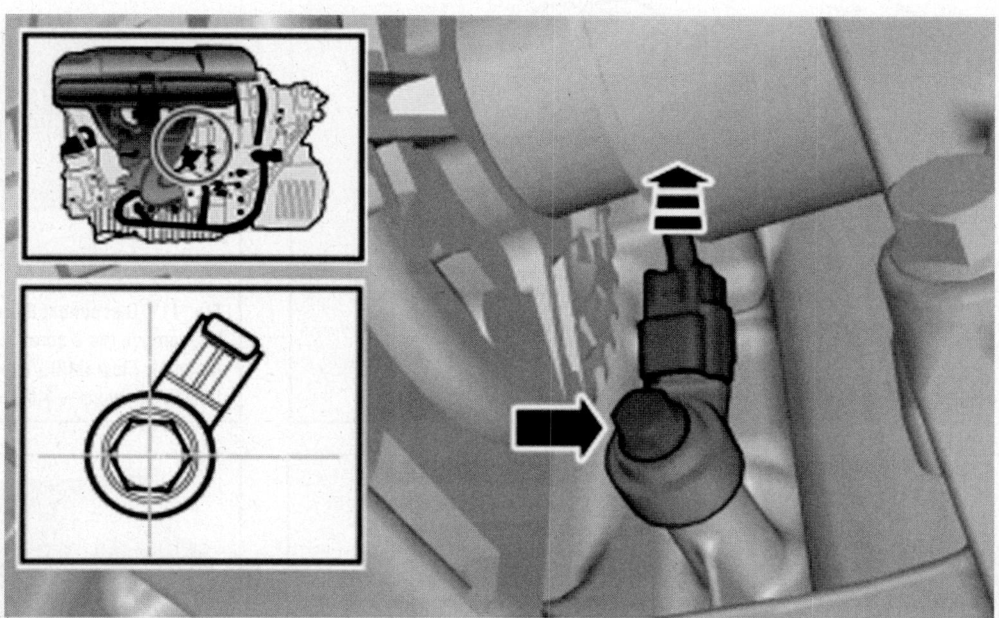

Fig. 111 Remove the middle knock sensor as shown.

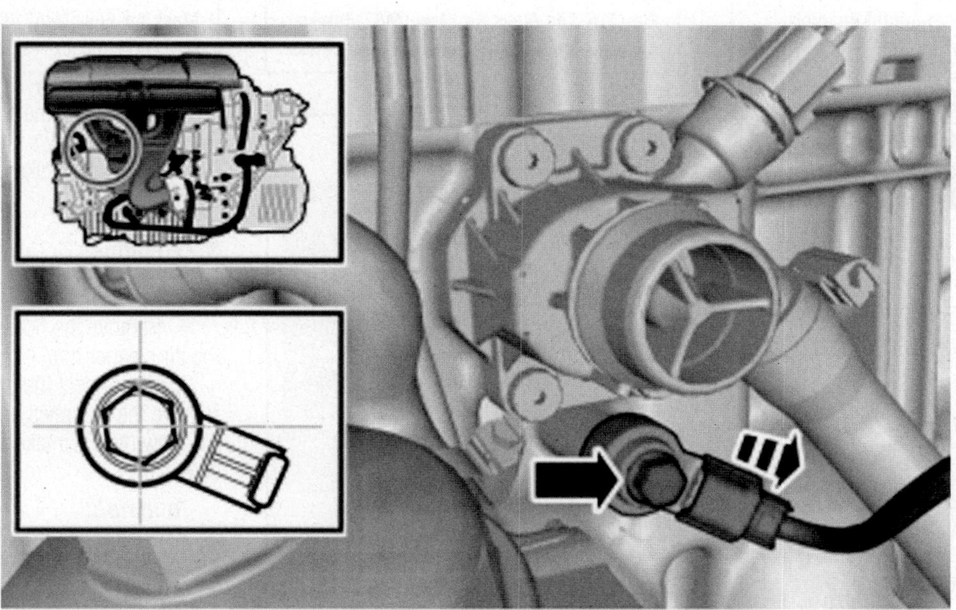

Fig. 112 Remove the rear knock sensor as shown.

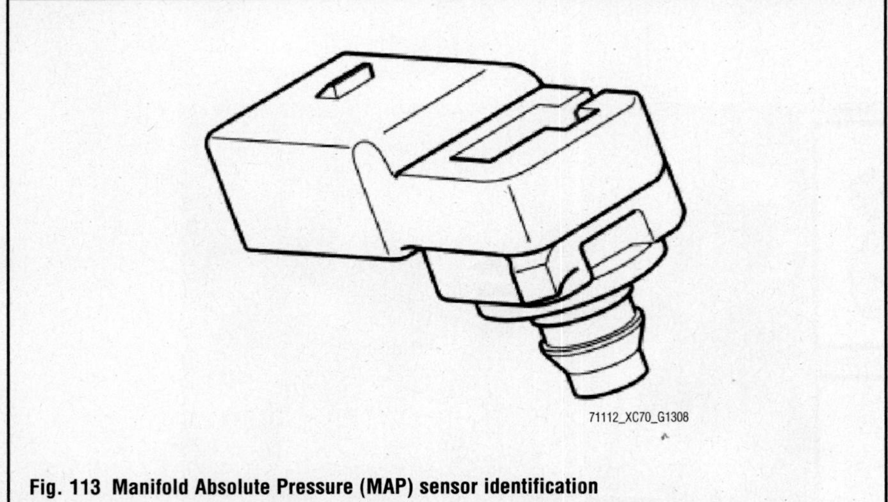
71112_XC70_G1308

Fig. 113 Manifold Absolute Pressure (MAP) sensor identification

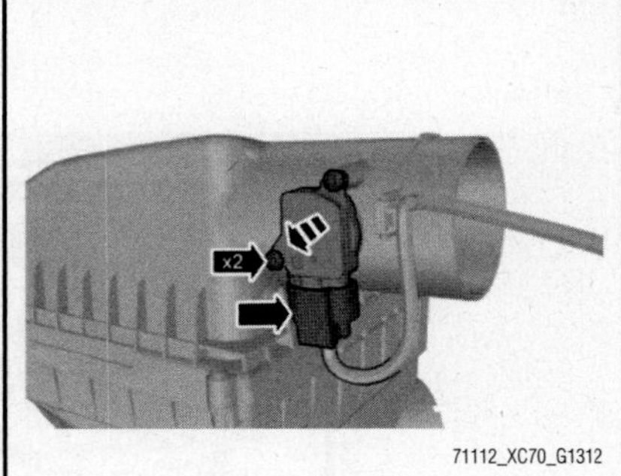

71112_XC70_G1312

Fig. 117 Disconnect the electrical connector, remove the 2 screws, then remove the Mass Air Flow (MAF)/Intake Air Temperature (IAT) sensor—3.0L engines

71112_XC70_G1309

Fig. 114 Disconnect the electrical connector, then remove the Manifold Absolute Pressure (MAP) sensor

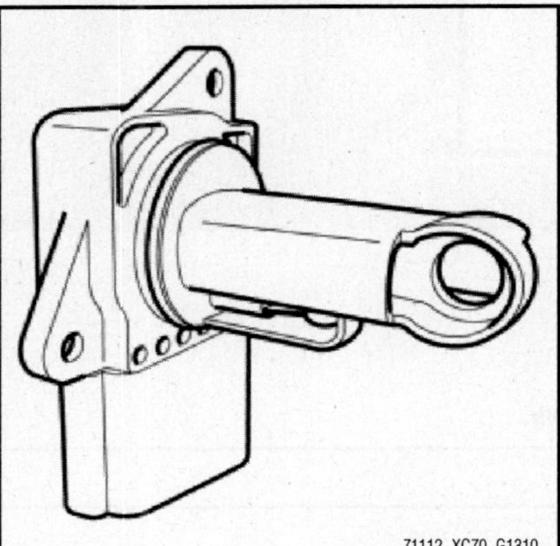
71112_XC70_G1310

Fig. 115 The Mass Air Flow (MAF)/Intake Air Temperature (IAT) sensor identification

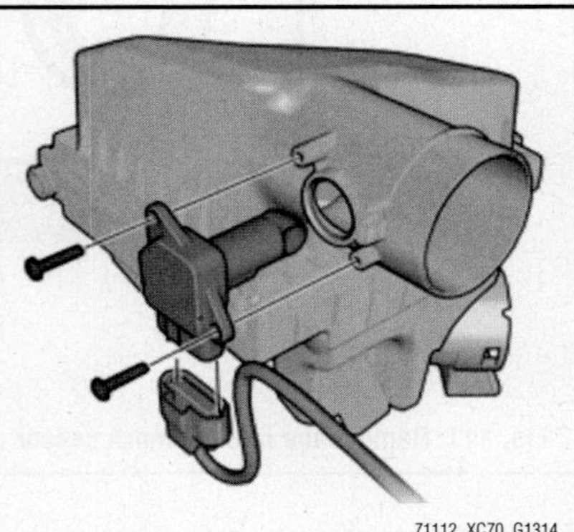
71112_XC70_G1314

Fig. 118 Disconnect the electrical connector, remove the 2 screws, then remove the Mass Air Flow (MAF)/Intake Air Temperature (IAT) sensor—3.2L engines

MASS AIR FLOW (MAF)/INTAKE AIR TEMPERATURE (IAT) SENSOR

LOCATION

See Figure 115

The Mass Air Flow (MAF)/Intake Air Temperature (IAT) sensor is located by the air filter housing.

REMOVAL & INSTALLATION

3.0L Engines

See Figures 116 and 117.

1. Remove the cover, then remove the air cleaner housing assembly.

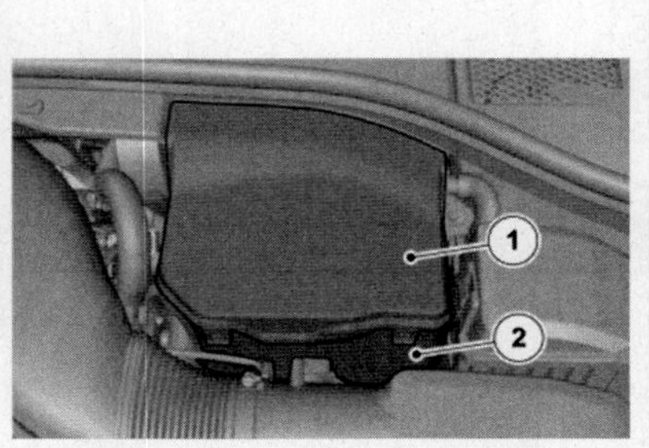

71112_XC70_G1311

Fig. 116 Remove the cover (1), then remove the air cleaner housing assembly (2)

2. Disconnect the electrical connector, remove the 2 screws, then remove the Mass Air Flow (MAF)/Intake Air Temperature (IAT) sensor.

3.2L Engines

See Figure 118.

1. Remove the hose clamp, then remove the air cleaner housing assembly.
2. Disconnect the electrical connector, remove the 2 screws, then remove the Mass Air Flow (MAF)/Intake Air Temperature (IAT) sensor.

To install:

Installation is the reverse of the removal procedure.

FUEL SYSTEM SERVICE PRECAUTIONS

Safety is the most important factor when performing not only fuel system maintenance but any type of maintenance. Failure to conduct maintenance and repairs in a safe manner may result in serious personal injury or death. Maintenance and testing of the vehicle s fuel system components can be accomplished safely and effectively by adhering to the following rules and guidelines.

- To avoid the possibility of fire and personal injury, always disconnect the negative battery cable unless the repair or test procedure requires that battery voltage be applied.
- Always relieve the fuel system pressure prior to disconnecting any fuel system component (injector, fuel rail, pressure regulator, etc.), fitting or fuel line connection. Exercise extreme caution whenever relieving fuel system pressure to avoid exposing skin, face and eyes to fuel spray. Please be advised that fuel under pressure may penetrate the skin or any part of the body that it contacts.
- Always place a shop towel or cloth around the fitting or connection prior to loosening to absorb any excess fuel due to spillage. Ensure that all fuel spillage (should it occur) is quickly removed from engine surfaces. Ensure that all fuel soaked cloths or towels are deposited into a suitable waste container.
- Always keep a dry chemical (Class B) fire extinguisher near the work area.
- Do not allow fuel spray or fuel vapors to come into contact with a spark or open flame.
- Always use a back-up wrench when loosening and tightening fuel line connection fittings. This will prevent unnecessary stress and torsion to fuel line piping.
- Always replace worn fuel fitting O-rings with new Do not substitute fuel hose or equivalent where fuel pipe is installed.

Before servicing the vehicle, make sure to also refer to the precautions in the beginning of this section as well.

RELIEVING FUEL SYSTEM PRESSURE

See Figure 119.

1. Access the fuse panel in the passenger side of the vehicle. Remove fuse No. 13.

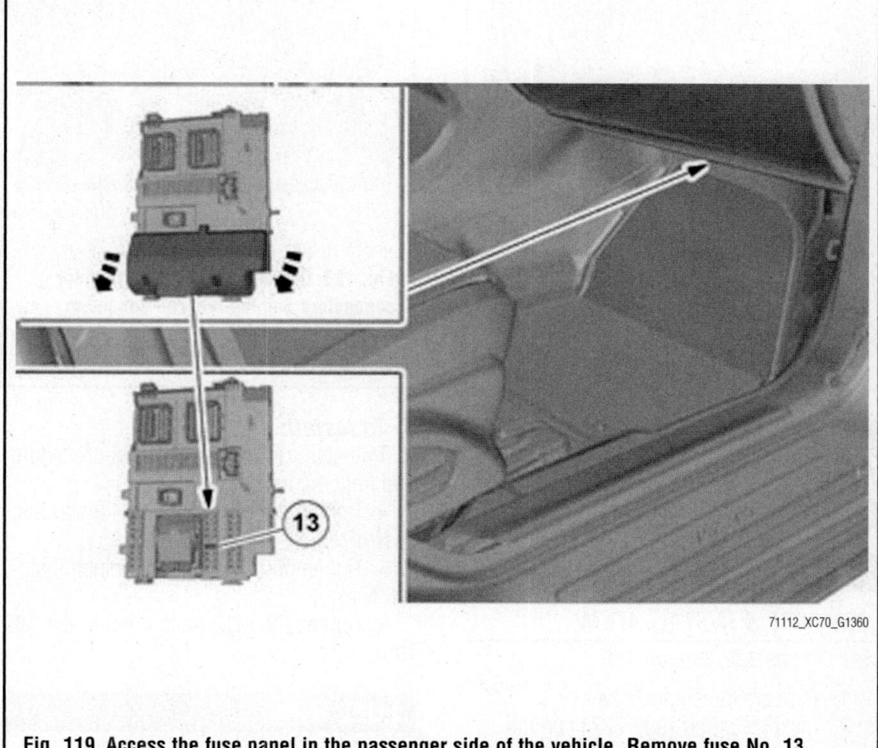

Fig. 119 Access the fuse panel in the passenger side of the vehicle. Remove fuse No. 13

2. Start and run the engine between 500–1000 RPM.

WARNING

Wait for a minimum of 1 minute after the engine has stopped before carrying out any repair to the fuel injection system.

To install:

Installation is the reverse of the removal procedure.

FUEL FILTER

REMOVAL & INSTALLATION

See Figures 120 and 121.

1. Before servicing the vehicle, refer to the Precautions Section.
2. Release the fuel pressure.

CAUTION

Be prepared to collect escaping fluid.

WARNING

Note the routing of the lines and hoses.

3. Release the 2 retainers, and disconnect fuel lines from the fuel filter.
4. Remove the M6 bolt, then remove the fuel filter.

To install:

To install, reverse the removal procedure and note the following:

- Tighten the M6 bolts to 89 inch lbs. (10 Nm).

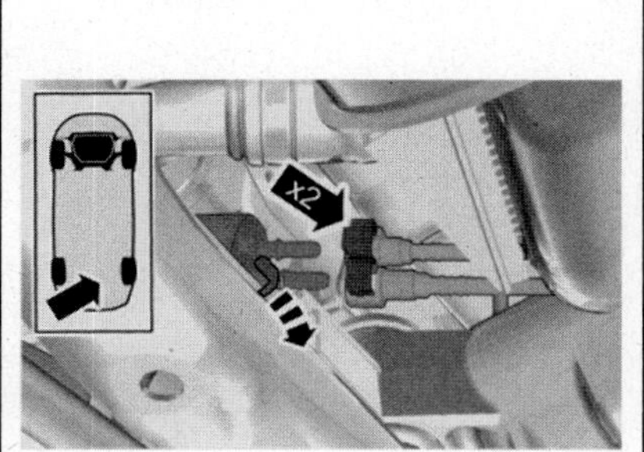

Fig. 120 Release the 2 retainers, and disconnect fuel lines from the fuel filter

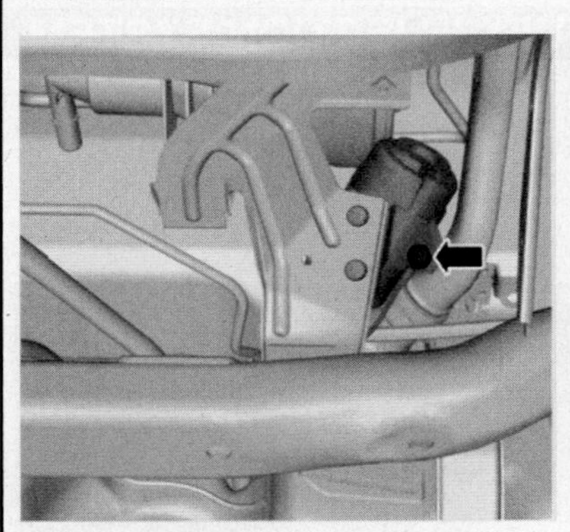
71112_XC70_G1337

Fig. 121 Remove the M6 bolt, then remove the fuel filter

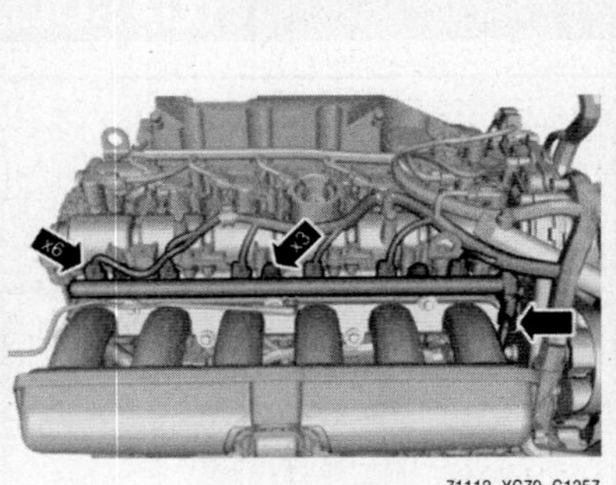
71112_XC70_G1357

Fig. 123 Disconnect the 6 fuel injector connectors and the fuel rail connector. Remove the 3 M6 bolts securing the fuel rail

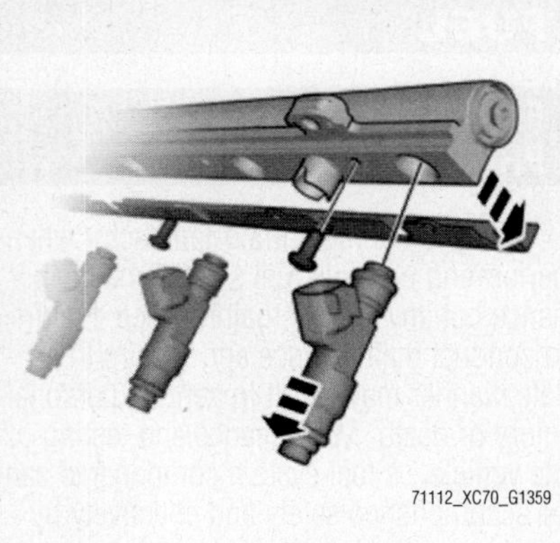
71112_XC70_G1359

Fig. 125 Remove the M5 screws, then remove the fuel injectors

WARNING

Make sure that the quick release couplings are correctly engaged.

FUEL RAIL & INJECTORS

REMOVAL & INSTALLATION

See Figures 122 through 125.

1. Remove the engine cover.
2. Install Support (999 7271) on the engine as shown.
3. Remove the 6 M12 bolts, then remove the torque rod and bracket.
4. Release the fuel pressure.
5. Disconnect the 6 fuel injector connectors and the fuel rail connector. Remove the 3 M6 bolts bolts securing the fuel rail.
6. Remove the fuel rail and injector assembly.
7. Remove the M5 screws, then remove the fuel injectors.

To install:

To install, reverse the removal procedure and note the following:

- Tighten the M5 screws to 44 inch lbs. (5 Nm).
- Tighten the M6 bolts to 89 inch lbs. (10 Nm).
- Tighten the M12 bolts to 59 ft. lbs. (80 Nm).

FUEL TANK

DRAINING

See Figures 126 and 127.

1. Remove the fuel filler cap.
2. Insert Hose (951 2896) into the fuel filler tube as shown.
3. Raise and support the vehicle.
4. Remove the hose clamp, then disconnect the fuel tank hose.
5. Insert Hose (999 7393) into the fuel tank as shown.
6. Drain the fuel tank.

REMOVAL & INSTALLATION

See Figures 128 through 131.

1. Drain the fuel tank.
2. Perform the Fuel System Pressure Release procedure.
3. Disconnect the battery lead.
4. Remove the front muffler.
5. On both sides of vehicle, remove the 4 bolts, then remove the splash plates.
6. Remove the rear propeller shaft.
7. Remove the 4 M8 bolts, then remove the bracket.
8. Remove the heat shield from the 4 clips.
9. Remove the fuel lines.

CAUTION

Fuel may still be present in the fuel tank after draining.

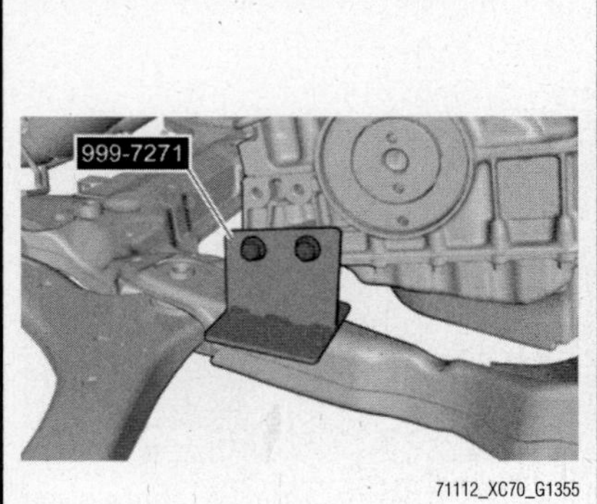

71112_XC70_G1355

Fig. 122 Install Support (999 7271) on engine as shown

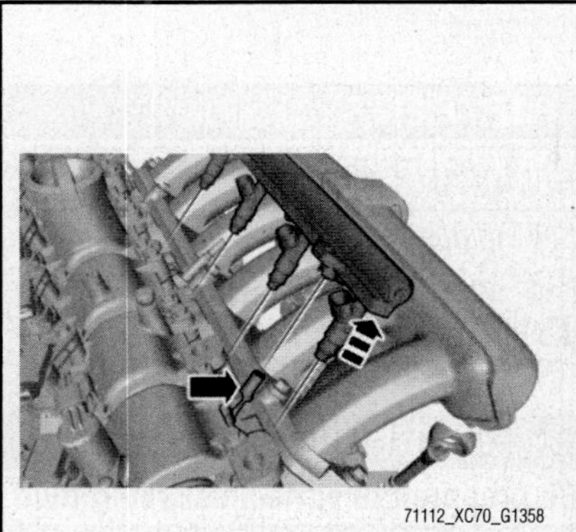
71112_XC70_G1358

Fig. 124 Remove the fuel rail and injector assembly

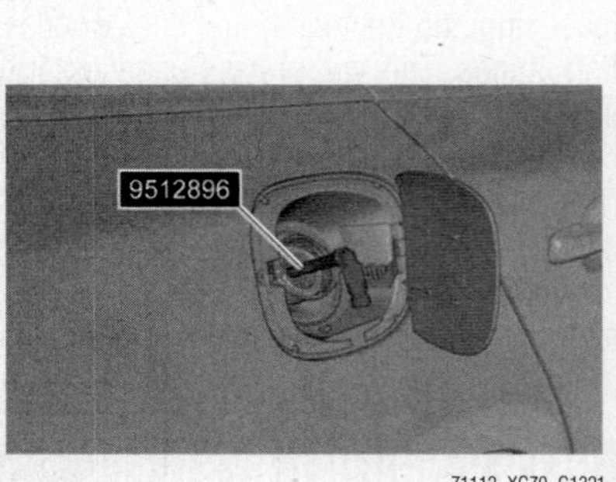

71112_XC70_G1321

Fig. 126 Insert Hose (951 2896) into the fuel filler tube as shown

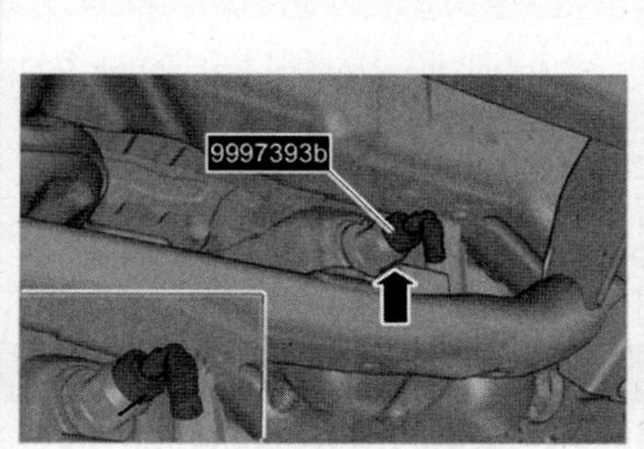

71112_XC70_G1323

Fig. 127 Insert Hose (999 7393) into the fuel tank as shown

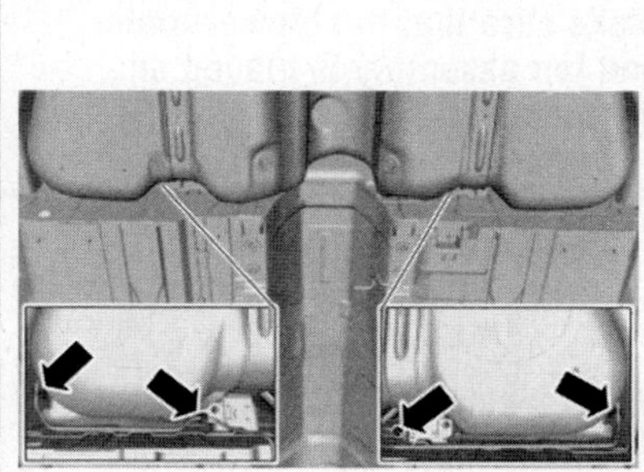
71112_XC70_G1327

Fig. 128 Remove the fuel lines

⁂ CAUTION

Be prepared to collect escaping fluids.

10. Disconnect the 2 electrical connectors to the fuel tank.

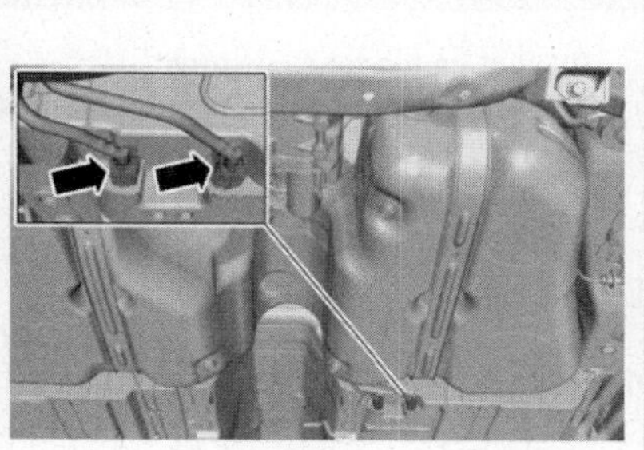
71112_XC70_G1328

Fig. 129 Disconnect the 2 electrical connectors to the fuel tank

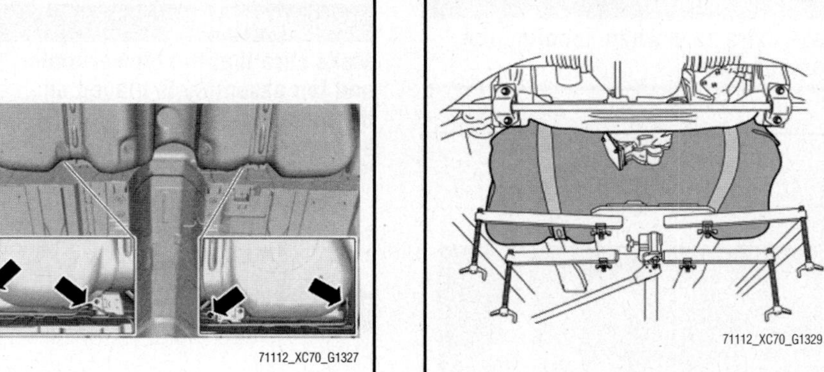
71112_XC70_G1329

Fig. 130 Using straps, attach the fuel tank to a unit lift as shown.

11. Using straps, attach the fuel tank to a unit lift as shown.
12. Remove the 4 M8 bolts, then remove the fuel tank straps.

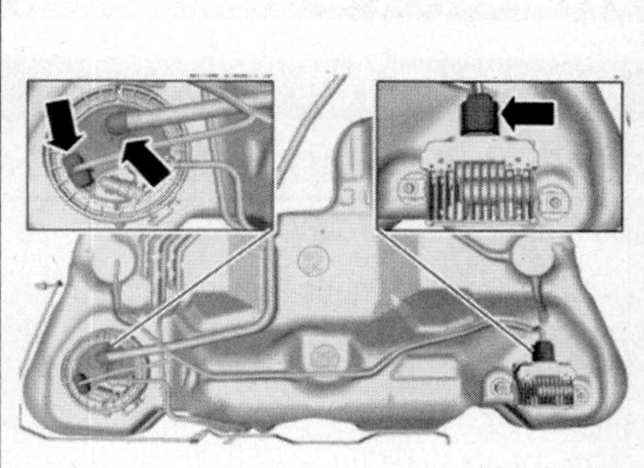
71112_XC70_G1331

Fig. 131 Disconnect the electrical connector and the hose from the fuel tank cover. Disconnect the electrical connector from the fuel pump control module

➡Make sure that no cables or hoses are trapped when lowering.

13. Disconnect the electrical connector and the hose from the fuel tank cover. Disconnect the electrical connector from the fuel pump control module.

⁂ CAUTION

Be prepared to collect escaping fluids.

14. Remove the hose clamp, then remove the filler pipe.
15. Drain the remaining fuel and remove the tank.
16. Remove the 2 bolts, then remove the fuel pump control module.
17. Remove the fuel pump.

To install:

To install, reverse the removal procedure and note the following:

- Tighten the M8 bolts to 18 ft. lbs. (24 Nm).

HEATING & AIR CONDITIONING SYSTEM

BLOWER MOTOR

REMOVAL & INSTALLATION

See Figures 132 through 137.

1. Make sure the the recirculated air system is turned off.
2. Remove the combined instrument panel.
3. Disconnect the electrical connector as shown.
4. Push in the 2 tabs, and disconnect the electrical connector from the fan motor.
5. Disengage the 3 clips, then remove the front door sill trim panel.
6. Move the passenger seat back. Remove the passenger s side front door sill trim panel.
7. Remove the passenger's side floor console panels as shown.
8. Pull up the molded carpet.
9. Remove the Central Electronic Module (CEM).
10. Remove the air duct.
11. Remove the 3 M8 bolts, then remove the bracket.
12. On vehicle with an air quality sensor, disconnect the electrical connector, rotate sensor as shown, then remove the air quality sensor.
13. On all vehicles, remove the electrical connector from the recirculation Damper Motor Module (DMM).
14. Remove the 3 screws, then remove the recirculation DMM.

✲✲ WARNING

Take extra care when handling the component.

15. Install the Removal/Installation Tools (999 7284) onto the blower motor cage fan as shown.
16. Using appropriate Torx® screwdriver, remove the screw securing the fan motor.

✲✲ WARNING

Take extra care when handling the component.

17. Push down on tab over fan motor.
18. With the help of an assistant, rotate the removal/installation tools 15 degrees counterclockwise. Remove the blower motor and fan assembly.

✲✲ WARNING

Make sure that the blower motor and fan assembly is placed on the bench with the fan pointing upwards.

To install:

To install, reverse the removal procedure and note the following:

➡Use a new fan motor screw if necessary.

19. Perform Climate Control System Check Procedure.

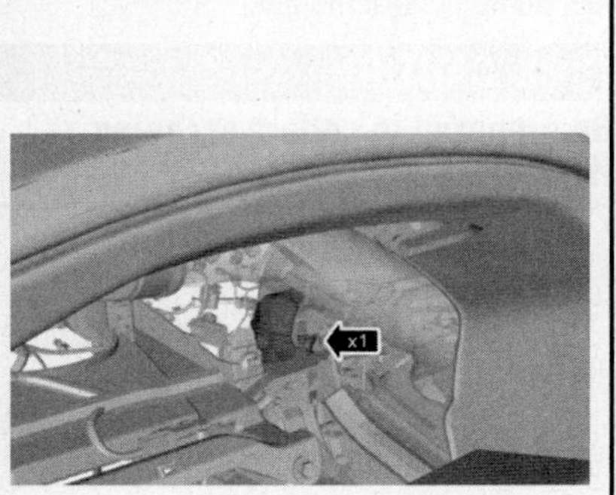

Fig. 132 Disconnect the electrical connector as shown

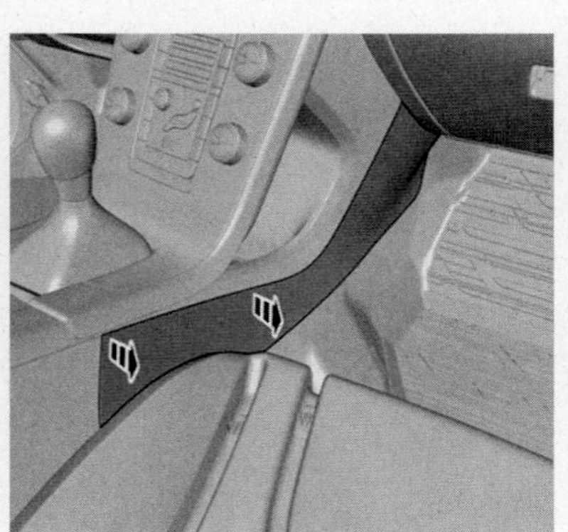

Fig. 133 Remove the passenger's side floor console panels as shown

Fig. 134 Remove the air duct

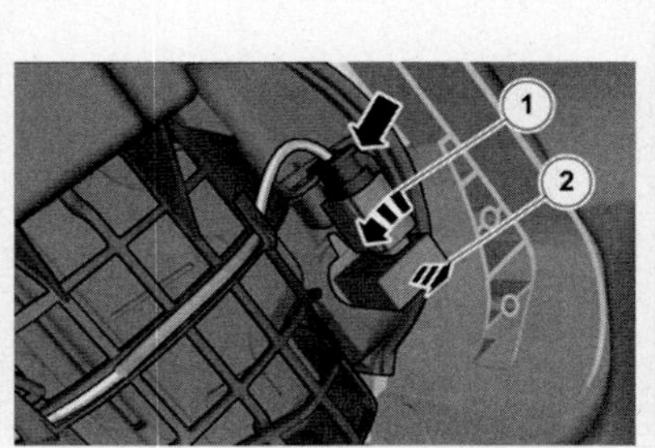

Fig. 135 On vehicle with an air quality sensor, disconnect the electrical connector, rotate sensor as shown (1), then remove the air quality sensor (2)

Fig. 136 Install the Removal/Installation Tools (999 7284) onto the blower motor cage fan as shown

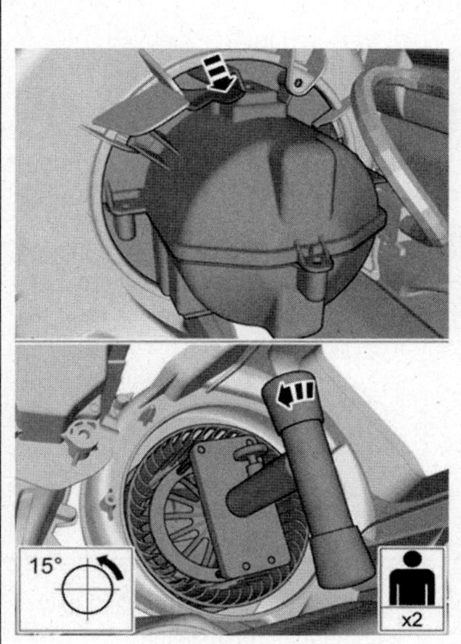

Fig. 137 Push down on tab over fan motor. With the help of an assistant, rotate the removal/installation tools 15 degrees counterclockwise. Remove the blower motor and fan assembly

HEATER CORE

REMOVAL & INSTALLATION

See Figures 138 through 140.

1. Drain the cooling system.
2. Remove the floor console.
3. Remove the duct assemblies from the console as shown.

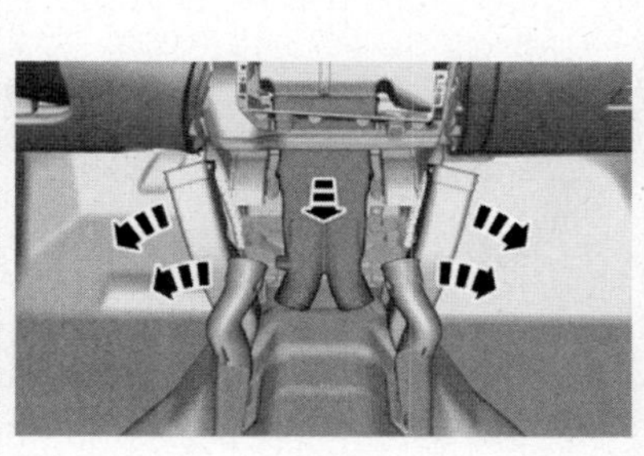

Fig. 138 Remove the duct assemblies from the console as shown

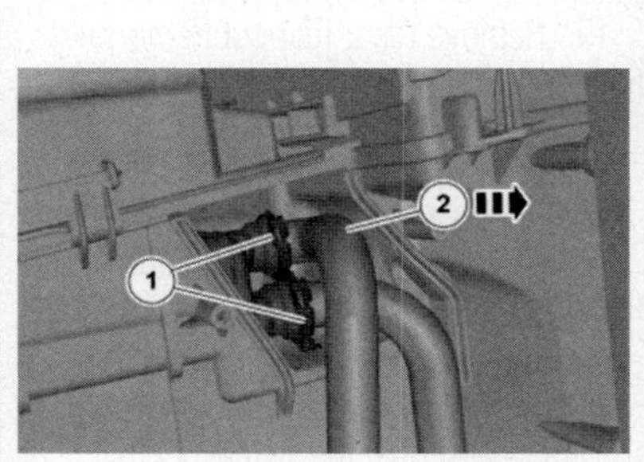

Fig. 139 Disengage the clips (1), then remove the hoses (2)

4. Remove the 4 bolts securing the front of the climate control unit.

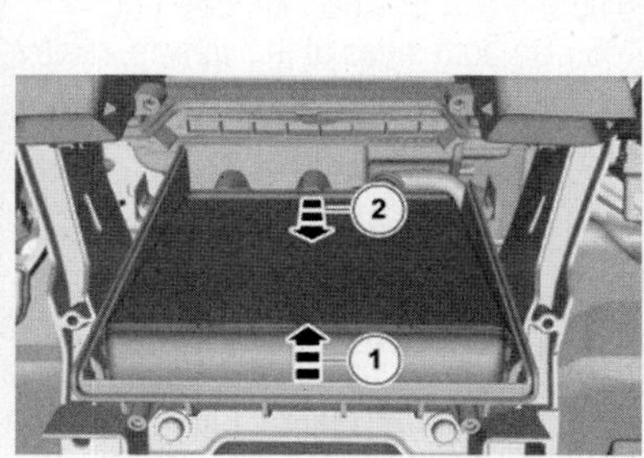

Fig. 140 Pushing the front up and the rear forward, remove the heater core

5. Remove the 2 bolts, then remove the damper actuator.

WARNING

Be prepared to collect escaping fluid.

6. Disengage the clips, then remove the hoses.

➡Note the position of each component before removal.

7. Pushing the front up and the rear forward, remove the heater core.

To install:

Installation is the reverse of the removal procedure.

➡Make sure that the seal is correctly located.

STEERING

POWER STEERING GEAR

REMOVAL & INSTALLATION

See Figures 141 through 145.

WARNING

Make sure that the steering column lock is engaged.

➡Make sure that the road wheels are in the straight-ahead position.

WARNING

Make sure that the ignition key is removed.

WARNING

Make sure that the steering column lock is engaged.

1. On vehicles without steering column lock, secure the steering wheel.
2. Remove the bolt, then remove the steering column-to-steering gear (steering shaft joint).
3. Drain the power steering fluid reservoir.
4. On both sides of the vehicle, remove:
   - The wheel
   - The wheel well housing

WARNING

Make sure that the ball joint ball does not rotate.

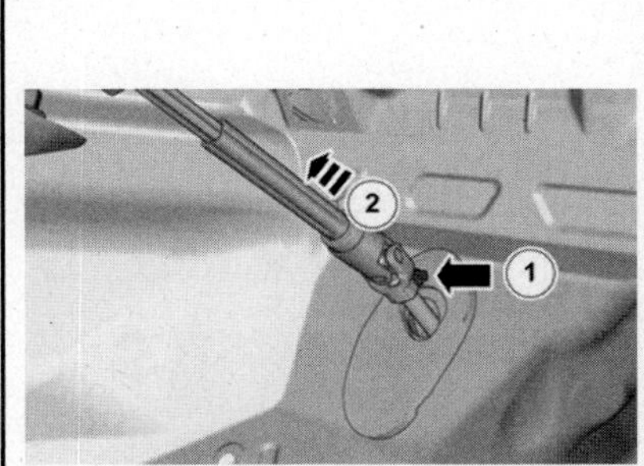

Fig. 141 Remove the bolt (1), then remove the steering column-to-steering gear (steering shaft joint) (2)

5. On both sides of the vehicle, remove the tie rod end-to-wheel knuckle nut.

6. On both sides of the vehicle, remove the nut and use Puller (951 2945) to remove the ball joint from the steering knuckle.

7. On both sides of the vehicle, measure and record the length of the tie rod.

8. On both sides of the vehicle, remove the front stabilizer bar link-to-stabilizer bar nut, and position the link aside.

9. Raise and support the vehicle.

10. Remove 7 bolts and the engine splash plate.

11. Remove the 2 M5 bolts, then remove the shield.

12. Remove the bolt, then disengage the lines from the steering gear assembly as shown.

CAUTION

Be prepared to collect escaping fluid.

CAUTION

Avoid skin contact with the fluid

13. Remove the bolt, then remove the steering gear delivery and return line assembly.

WARNING

Make sure that the exhaust flexible pipe is not forcibly bent.

14. Secure exhaust to keep it from bending.

15. Remove the 2 M8 bolt, then remove exhaust hangers and shackles.

16. Remove the 4 front lower arm-to-subframe (rear mounting) bolts.

17. Remove the 2 steering gear-to-subframe bolts.

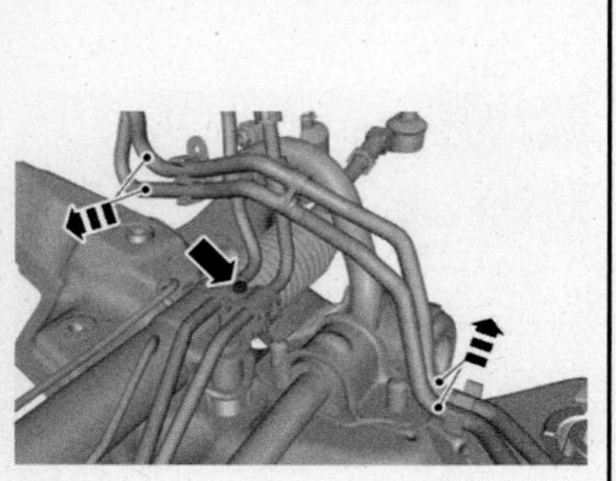

Fig. 142 Remove the bolt, then disengage the lines from the steering gear assembly as shown

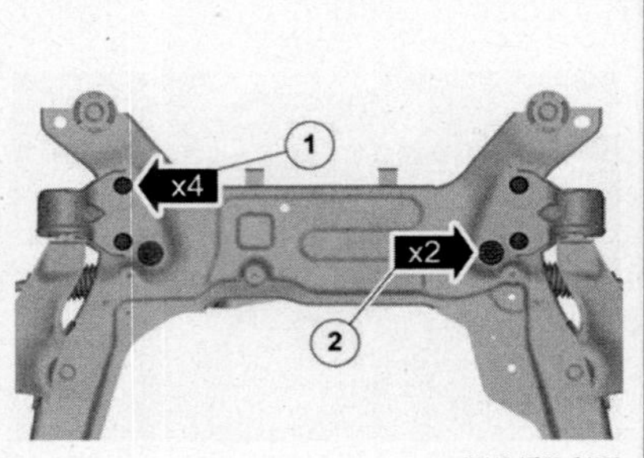

Fig. 143 Remove the 4 front lower arm-to-subframe (rear mounting) bolts (1). Remove the 2 steering gear-to-subframe bolts (2)

18. Remove the 4 M8 bolts and 2 M10 bolts, then remove the reinforcements.

19. Remove the 2 rear subframe-to-chassis bolts.

20. Lower the front subframe.

21. Remove the bracket.

22. Remove the power steering lines.

23. Remove the power rack and pinion steering gear assembly.

To install:

24. To install, reverse the removal procedure and note the following:

- Tighten the rear subframe-to-chassis bolts:
  a. Stage 1: 150 Nm
  b. Stage 2: 90 degrees
- Tighten the M10 bolts to 37 ft. lbs. (50 Nm).
- Tighten the 4 front lower arm-to-subframe (rear mounting) bolts to 129 ft. lbs. (175 Nm).
- Tighten the steering gear-to-subframe bolts to 103 ft. lbs. (140 Nm). Make sure that a new component is installed.
- Tighten the M8 bolts to 18 ft. lbs. (24 Nm).
- Tighten the steering gear delivery and return line bolt to 13 ft. lbs. (18 Nm).
- Tighten the M5 bolts to 44 inch lbs. (5 Nm).
- Tighten the front stabilizer bar link-to-stabilizer bar bolt to 52 ft. lbs. (70 Nm).
- Tighten the tie rod end-to-wheel knuckle nut to 59 ft. lbs. (80 Nm).
- Tighten the steering column-to-steering gear (steering shaft joint) bolt to 18 ft. lbs. (25 Nm). Make sure that a new component is installed.

25. Top up the power steering system.

26. Perform the Wheel Angles Check procedure in Wheel Alignment.

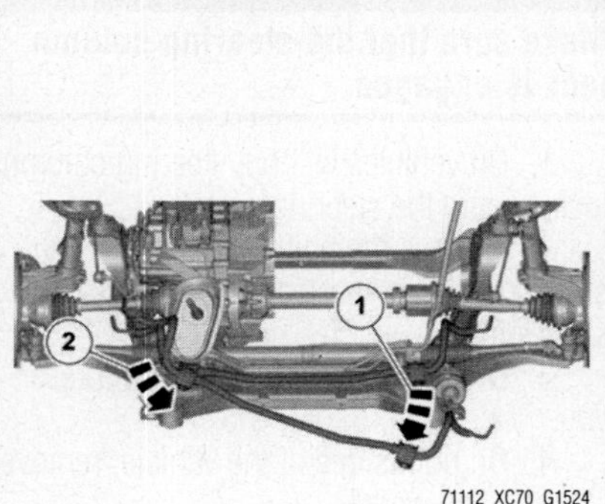

Fig. 144 Remove the power steering lines (1, 2)

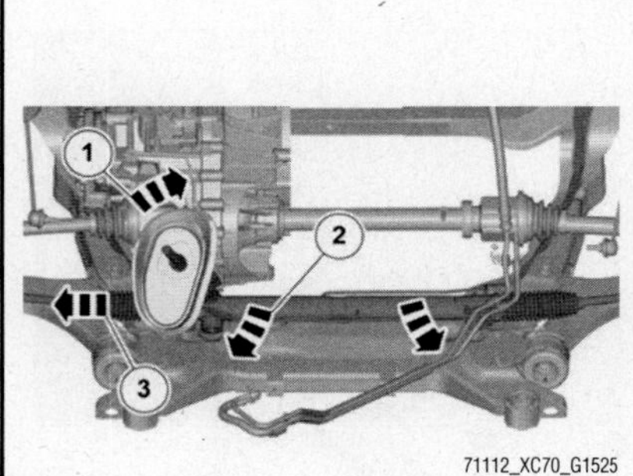

Fig. 145 Remove the power rack and pinion steering gear assembly (1, 2, 3)

POWER STEERING PUMP

BLEEDING

1. Before servicing the vehicle, refer to the Precautions Section.

WARNING

Do not allow the fluid level in the reservoir tank to go below the MIN level line. The fluid level must remain between the MAX and MIN marks. Check and add fluid as needed.

CAUTION

Avoid skin contact with the specified material.

WARNING

Do not hold the steering wheel in the locked position for more than 3–5 seconds. Damage to the power steering pump may occur.

2. With engine off and parking brake set, turn the steering wheel fully to the right and left at least 5 times. Hold in each position for about 3 seconds. Check for fluid leakage.
3. Start and run engine between 500–1000 RPM. Turn the steering wheel fully to the right and then fully to the left. Hold in each position for about 3 seconds. Check for fluid leakage.
4. Stop the engine and check the fluid level. Fill as required. Make sure that fluid level is to the MAX mark.
5. Let vehicle stand for 5 minutes.

WARNING

Make sure that the engine is switched off.

6. Start and run engine between 500–1000 RPM. Turn the steering wheel fully to the right and then fully to the left a total of 5 times. Hold in each position for about 3 seconds. Check for fluid leakage.
7. Stop the engine and check the fluid level. Fill as required. Make sure that fluid level is to the MAX mark.

WARNING

Make sure that the engine is switched off.

8. Let vehicle stand for 5 minutes.
9. Check the fluid level. Fill as required. Make sure that fluid level is to the MAX mark.
10. Start and run engine between 500–1000 RPM. Turn the steering wheel fully to the right and then fully to the left a total of 5 times. Hold in each position for about 3 seconds. Check for fluid leakage.
11. Stop the engine and check the fluid level. Fill as required. Make sure that fluid level is to the MAX mark.

WARNING

Make sure that the engine is switched off.

12. Check the fluid level. Fill as required. Make sure that fluid level is to the MAX mark.
13. Check for air bubbles or cloudy fluid. If found, repeat the bleeding procedure.

REMOVAL & INSTALLATION

See Figures 146 through 148.

WARNING

When this procedure is completed, software will be required to be downloaded from the Volvo central database.

1. Before servicing the vehicle, refer to the Precautions Section.
2. Drain the power steering fluid reservoir.
3. Remove the right front wheel.
4. Remove the right front wheel well housing.
5. Using Tensioner Band (999 5682) as shown, remove the right side casing.

CAUTION

Be prepared to collect escaping fluid.

WARNING

Make sure that all openings are sealed.

6. Remove the M8 bolt, then remove the pressure hose from the power steering pump.

CAUTION

Be prepared to collect escaping fluid.

7. Push in the tab, then disconnect the suction hose from the power steering pump.

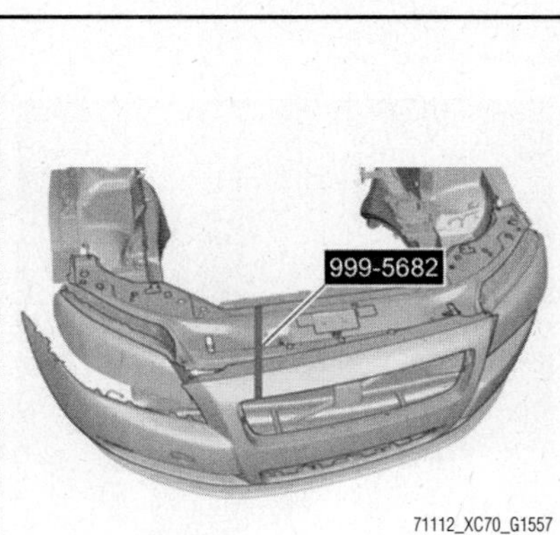

Fig. 146 Using Tensioner Band (999 5682) as shown, remove the right side casing

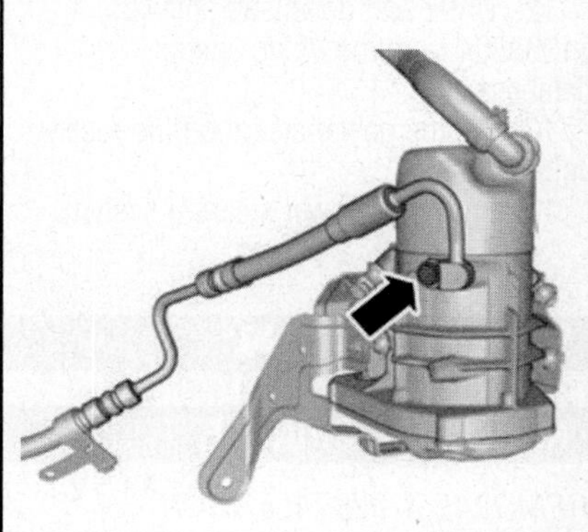

Fig. 147 Remove the M8 bolt, then remove the pressure hose from the power steering pump

WARNING

Make sure that all openings are sealed.

8. Remove the 4 M5 bolts securing the power steering pump.
9. Move the power steering pump forward and down to remove it from the bracket
10. Disconnect the 2 electrical connectors from the power steering pump.

To install:

11. To install, reverse the removal procedure and note the following:
    - Tighten the M5 bolts to 44 inch lbs. (5 Nm).

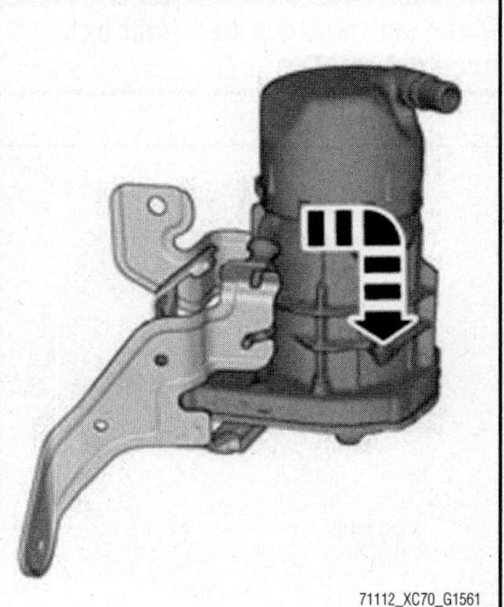

Fig. 148 Move the power steering pump forward and down to remove it from the bracket

12. Order and download software 31288804 from the Volvo central database.

13. Fill the power steering fluid reservoir.

14. Bleed the power steering system.

FLUID FILL PROCEDURE

WARNING

Keep the area around the power steering fluid reservoir clean when checking.

Check the level frequently. The fluid does not require changing. The fluid level must be between the MIN and MAX marks.

SUSPENSION

FRONT SUSPENSION

KNUCKLE & SPINDLE

REMOVAL & INSTALLATION

See Figures 149 through 151.

WARNING

Do not use magnets or magnetic tools close to tooth wheels, drive shafts or wheel hubs. A magnetized tooth wheel will lose its function and generate incorrect signals resulting in fault codes.

➡Any magnetized tooth wheel, drive shaft or wheel hub must be replaced with a new component.

1. Before servicing the vehicle, refer to the Precautions Section.
2. Remove the front brake disc.
3. Remove the M6 bracket-to-control arm bolt.
4. Remove the 3 M6 bolts, then remove the brake backing plate.
5. Remove the M5 bolt, then remove the wheel speed sensor.
6. Remove the front driveshaft-to-wheel hub bolt.

WARNING

Make sure that the ball joint ball does not rotate.

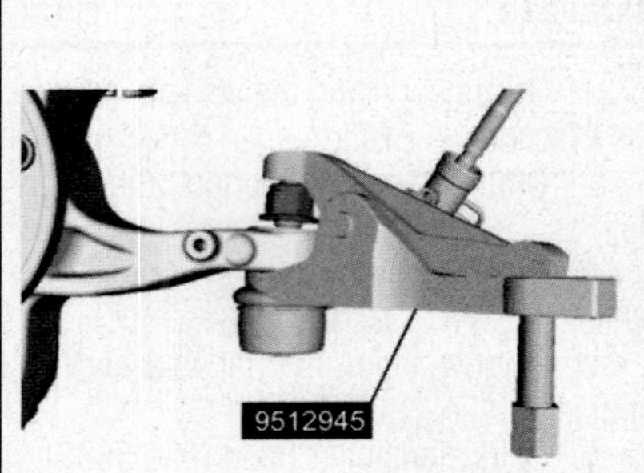

Fig. 150 Using Puller (951 2945), remove the tie rod end-to-wheel knuckle nut, then remove the ball joint from the steering knuckle

7. Using Puller (951 2945), remove the tie rod end-to-wheel knuckle nut, then remove the ball joint from the steering knuckle.
8. Remove the ball joint-to-wheel knuckle bolt.
9. Using Lever (999 7076), pull downward on the lower control to extract the ball joint out of the wheel spindle.
10. Remove the wheel knuckle-to-strut and spring assembly bolt.
11. Using Expander (999 7088), widen the groove. Install the tool so that the flat sides run the length of the groove. Turn 45°.
12. Carefully tap the wheel spindle down. Use a copper mallet. Pry down the control arm. Using Lever (999 7076), release the spindle from the spring strut.
13. Remove the spring strut.

To install:

To install, reverse the removal procedure and note the following:

- Tighten the wheel knuckle-to-strut and spring assembly bolt to 81 ft. lbs. (110 Nm).
- Tighten the ball joint-to-wheel knuckle bolt to 81 ft. lbs. (110 Nm).
- Tighten the tie rod end-to-wheel knuckle nut to 59 ft. lbs. (80 Nm).
- Tighten the driveshaft-to-wheel hub bolt.
  a. Stage 1: 26 ft. lbs. (35 Nm)
  b. Stage 2: 90 degrees
  - Tighten the M5 bolts to 44 inch lbs. (5 Nm).
  - Tighten the M6 bolts to 89 inch lbs. (10 Nm).

LOWER CONTROL ARMS

REMOVAL & INSTALLATION

See Figures 152 through 155.

1. Before servicing the vehicle, refer to the Precautions Section.

Fig. 149 Remove the front driveshaft-to-wheel hub bolt

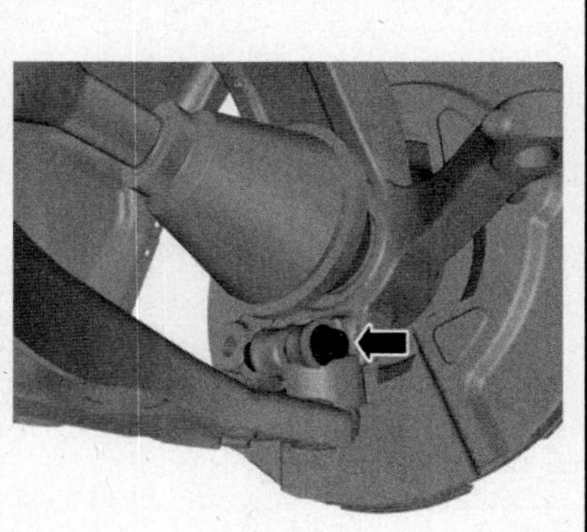

Fig. 151 Remove the ball joint-to-wheel knuckle bolt

Fig. 152 Remove the driveshaft-to-wheel hub bolt

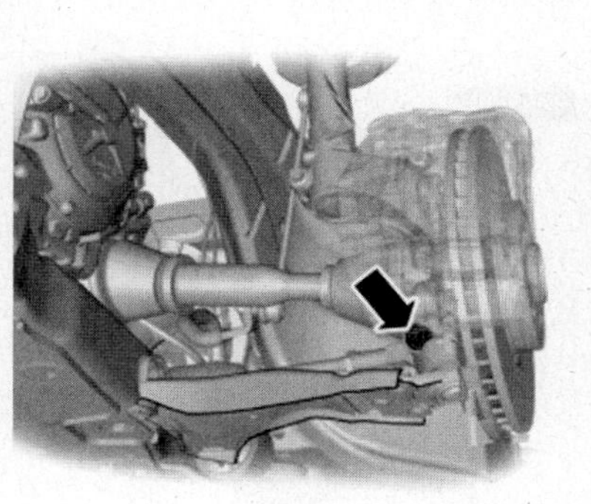

Fig. 153 Remove the ball joint-to-wheel knuckle bolt

2. Remove the front wheel.
3. Remove the driveshaft-to-wheel hub bolt.
4. Remove the ball joint-to-wheel knuckle bolt.
5. Using Lever (999 7076), apply enough pressure to pull the ball joint out of the wheel spindle.
6. Remove the lower control arm-to-subframe bolts in the order shown.
7. Remove the lower control arm.

To install:

To install, reverse the removal procedure and note the following:

- Tighten the front lower control arm-to-subframe bolt:
  a. Stage 1: 103 ft. lbs. (140 Nm)
  b. Stage 2: 45 degrees
- Tighten the 2 rear lower control arm-to-subframe bolts to 129 ft. lbs. (175 Nm).
- Tighten the ball joint-to-wheel knuckle bolt to 81 ft. lbs. (110 Nm).

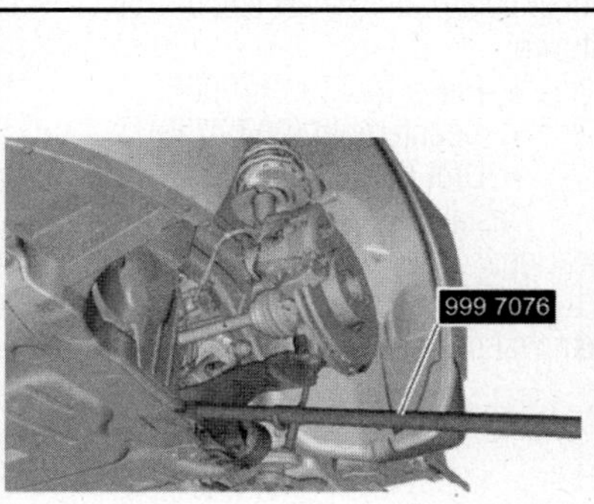

Fig. 154 Using Lever (999 7076), apply enough pressure to pull the ball joint out of the wheel spindle

Fig. 155 Remove the lower control arm-to-subframe bolts in the order shown

- Tighten the driveshaft-to-wheel hub bolt.
  a. Stage 1: 26 ft. lbs. (35 Nm)
  b. Stage 2: 90 degrees

STABILIZER BAR & LINKS

REMOVAL & INSTALLATION

Stabilizer Bar

See Figure 156.

1. Remove the front subframe.
2. Remove the front stabilizer bar.

To install:

3. Installation is the reverse of the removal procedure.

Stabilizer Links

See Figure 157.

1. Remove the front wheel.
2. Remove the front stabilizer bar link-to-strut and spring assembly bolt.

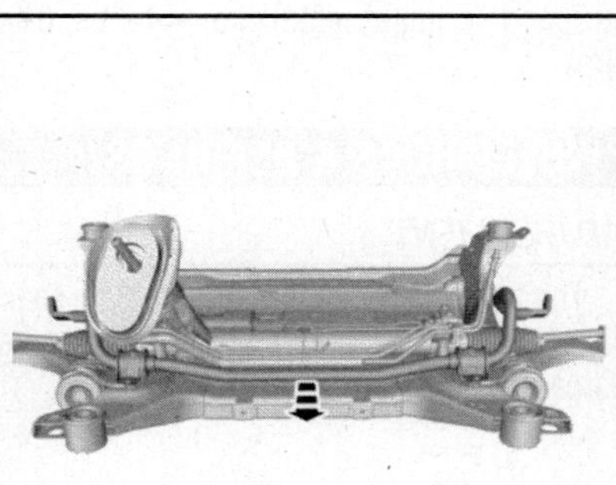

Fig. 156 Remove the front stabilizer bar

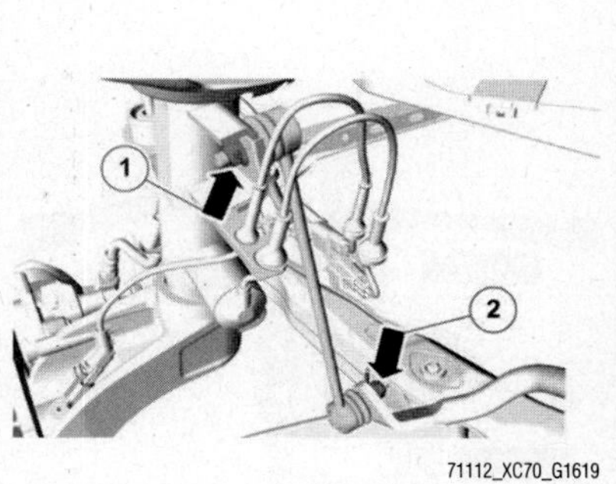

Fig. 157 Remove the front stabilizer bar link-to-strut and spring assembly bolt (1). Remove the front stabilizer bar link-to-stabilizer bar bolt (2)

3. Remove the front stabilizer bar link-to-stabilizer bar bolt.

To install:

4. To install, reverse the removal procedure and note the following:
   - Tighten the front stabilizer bar link-to-stabilizer bar bolt to 52 ft. lbs. (70 Nm).
   - Tighten the front stabilizer bar link-to-strut and spring assembly bolt to 44 ft. lbs. (60 Nm).

STRUTS (MACPHERSON STRUTS)

OVERHAUL

See Figure 158.

✲✲ WARNING

When this procedure is completed, vehicles with high intensity discharge headlights have one or more components that will require activation or calibration information.

1. Remove the front strut and spring assembly.
2. Using Spring Compressor (951 2911) together with Claw (951 2914, size 2), take the load off the spring.
3. Using Socket (999 5500) and a Torx® socket as a counterhold, remove the nut on the shock absorber.

➡Note the position of each component before removal.

To install:

4. To install, reverse the removal procedure and note the following:
   - Tighten the shock nut to 37 ft. lbs. (50 Nm).

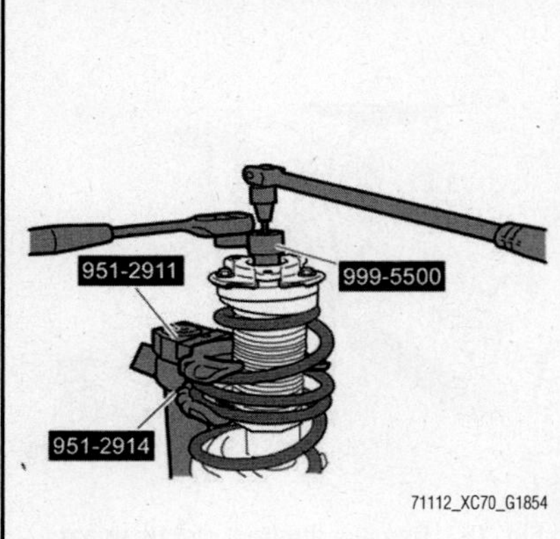

Fig. 158 Using Socket (999 5500) and a Torx® socket as a counterhold, remove the nut on the shock absorber

5. Calibrate the high intensity discharge headlights.

REMOVAL & INSTALLATION

See Figures 159 and 160.

1. Before servicing the vehicle, refer to the Precautions Section.
2. Remove the front wheel.
3. Remove the bolt, then remove the front stabilizer bar link-to-strut and spring assembly.

Fig. 159 Remove the bolt, then remove the front stabilizer bar link-to-strut and spring assembly

Fig. 160 Disengage the lower spring and strut assembly from the vehicle

4. Remove the ball joint-to-wheel knuckle bolt.
5. Using Expander (999 7088), widen the groove, then pull out the axle shaft using Lever (999 7076),
6. Disengage the lower spring and strut assembly from the vehicle.
7. Remove the 2 fasteners, then lift up the trim panel. Remove the 3 M8 bolts at the spring tower.

To install:

To install, reverse the removal procedure and note the following:

- Tighten the M8 bolts to 18 ft. lbs. (24 Nm).
- Tighten the ball joint-to-wheel knuckle bolt to 81 ft. lbs. (110 Nm).
- Tighten the front stabilizer bar link-to-strut and spring assembly, to 44 ft. lbs. (60 Nm).

WHEEL HUBS & BEARINGS

ADJUSTMENT

The wheel bearing and hub are non-serviceable (no repack). Replace when worn or damaged.

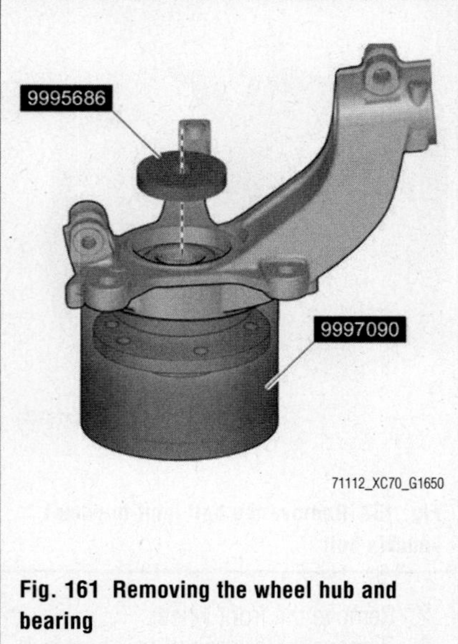

Fig. 161 Removing the wheel hub and bearing

REMOVAL & INSTALLATION

See Figure 161.

WARNING

The wheel bearings are sealed bearings and do not support repacking. Replace when damaged.

1. Remove the wheel spindle.
2. Install the following equipment on the wheel spindle as shown:
   - Press Tool (999 7090)
   - Drift (999 5686)
3. Remove the wheel hub and bearing.

To install:

4. Install the Counterhold (999 7296) on the wheel hub and bearing.
5. Install the following equipment on the wheel spindle as shown:
   - Press Tool (999 7090)
   - Counterhold (999 7296)
   - Drift (999 7295)
6. Install the wheel hub and bearing.
7. To complete installation, reverse the removal procedure.

COIL SPRINGS

REMOVAL & INSTALLATION

See Figures 162 and 163.

WARNING

When this procedure is completed, vehicles with high intensity discharge headlights have one or more components that will require activation or calibration information.

1. Before servicing the vehicle, refer to the Precautions Section.
2. Remove the rear wheel.
3. Remove the 3 inside and 3 outside screws, then remove the wheel well housing.
4. Remove the stabilizer bar link.
5. Compress the coil spring using the following equipment:
   - Hydraulic Piston (951 2911)
   - Extension Rod (951 2937)
   - Claw, size 1 (951 2913)

➡Note the position of each component before removal.

6. Remove the spring bracket and spacer.

To install:

7. Installation is the reverse of the removal procedure.
8. Calibrate the high intensity discharge headlights.

LATERAL LINK

REMOVAL & INSTALLATION

See Figure 164.

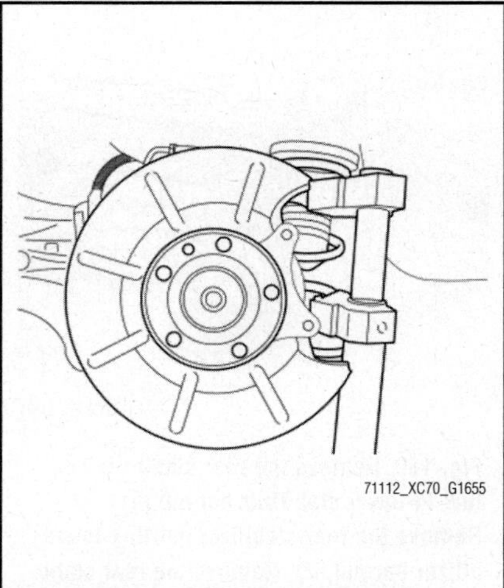

Fig. 162 Compressing the coil spring

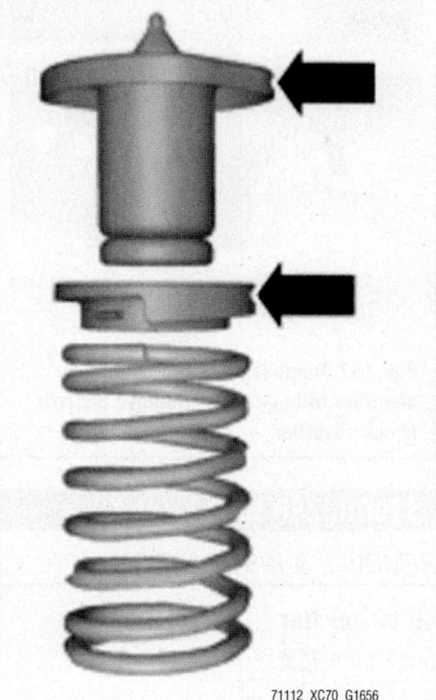

Fig. 163 Remove the spring bracket and spacer

WARNING

When this procedure is completed, vehicles with high intensity discharge headlights have one or more components that will require activation or calibration information.

1. Before servicing the vehicle, refer to the Precautions Section.
2. Remove the rear coil spring.
3. Remove the following:
   - The tie rod-to-subframe bolt
   - The tie rod-to-longitudinal stay bolt
   - The 2 M6 bolts
4. Remove the lower link.

To install:

➡Only tighten the nuts and bolts when the suspension is in the normal drive position.

5. To install, reverse the removal procedure and note the following:
   - Tighten the tie rod-to-subframe bolt to 81 ft. lbs. (110 Nm).
   - Tighten the tie rod-to-longitudinal stay bolt to 81 ft. lbs. (110 Nm).
   - Tighten the M6 bolts to 89 inch lbs. (10 Nm).
6. Perform the Service Position procedure.

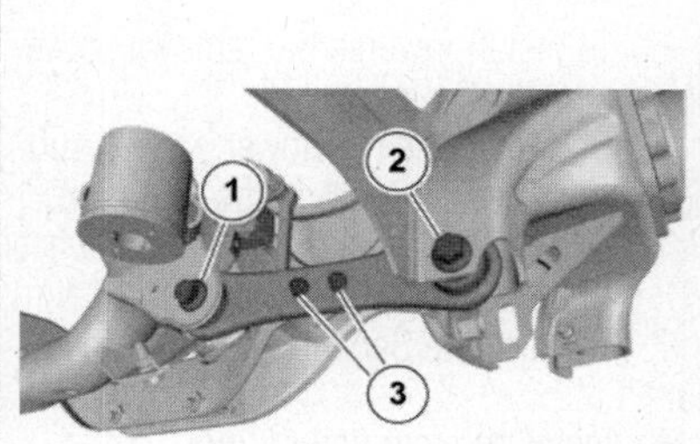

Fig. 164 Remove the tie rod-to-subframe bolt (1), the tie rod-to-longitudinal stay bolt (2), and the 2 M6 bolts (3). Remove the lower link

7. Install the coil spring.
8. Calibrate the high intensity discharge headlights.

LOWER CONTROL ARMS

REMOVAL & INSTALLATION

See Figure 165.

➡Some variation in the illustrations may occur, but the essential information is always correct.

1. Before servicing the vehicle, refer to the Precautions Section.
2. Remove the rear coil spring.
3. Remove the rear lower arm-to-wheel knuckle bolt.
4. Remove the rear lower arm-to-subframe bolt.
5. Remove the rear lower arm.

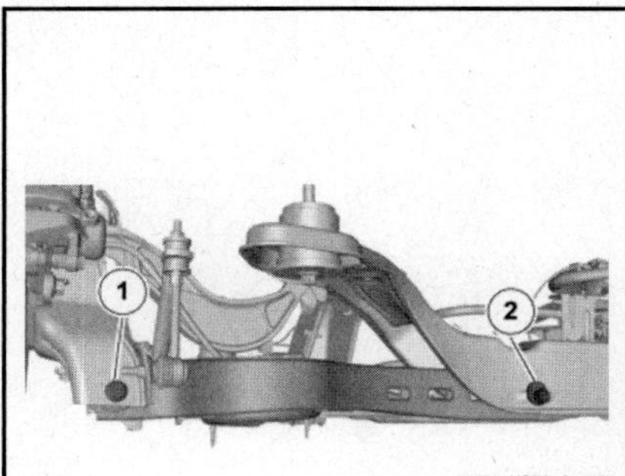

Fig. 165 Remove the rear lower arm-to-wheel knuckle bolt (1). Remove the rear lower arm-to-subframe bolt (2). Remove the rear lower arm

To install:

➡Only tighten the nuts and bolts when the suspension is in the normal drive position.

6. To install, reverse the removal procedure and note the following:
   - Tighten the rear lower arm-to-subframe bolt to 66 ft. lbs. (90 Nm).
   - Tighten the rear lower arm-to-wheel knuckle bolt to 81 ft. lbs. (110 Nm).
7. Perform the Service Position procedure.
8. Install the rear coil spring.
9. Check the wheel alignment.

SHOCK ABSORBERS

REMOVAL & INSTALLATION

See Figures 166 and 167.

1. Remove the rear shock absorber-to-wheel spindle bolt.
2. Remove the rear shock absorber-to-wheel knuckle bolt (Nivomat with M16 thread).
3. Remove the 2 rear shock absorber-to-body bolts.
4. Remove the rear shock absorber.

To install:

To install, reverse the removal procedure and note the following:

- Tighten the rear shock absorber-to-body bolts to 22 ft. lbs. (30 Nm).
- Tighten the rear shock absorber-to-wheel knuckle bolt to 207 ft. lbs. (280 Nm).
- Tighten the rear shock absorber-to-wheel spindle bolt:
  a. Early version (with M14-screw part number 999491): 129 ft. lbs. (175 Nm).
  b. Late version (with M14-screw part number 30624310): 111 ft. lbs. (150 Nm).

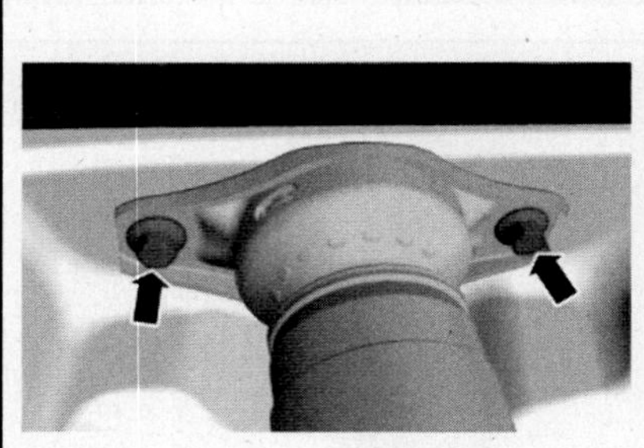

Fig. 167 Remove the 2 rear shock absorber-to-body bolts. Remove the rear shock absorber

STABILIZER BAR & LINKS

REMOVAL & INSTALLATION

Stabilizer Bar

See Figure 168.

1. Before servicing the vehicle, refer to the Precautions Section.
2. Raise and support the vehicle.
3. Remove the 2 rear stabilizer bar link-to-stabilizer bar bolts.
4. Remove the 4 stabilizer bar-to-rear subframe bolts.
5. Remove the stabilizer bar.

To install:

To install, reverse the removal procedure and note the following:

- Tighten the rear stabilizer bar link-to-stabilizer bar bolts to 44 ft. lbs. (60 Nm).
- Tighten the stabilizer bar-to-rear subframe bolts to 44 ft. lbs. (60 Nm).

Stabilizer Bar Link

See Figure 169.

1. Before servicing the vehicle, refer to the Precautions Section.

⁂ WARNING

Make sure that the ball joint ball does not rotate.

2. Remove the rear stabilizer bar link-to-lower stabilizer bar nut.
3. Remove the rear stabilizer bar link-to-stabilizer bar nut.
4. Remove the rear stabilizer bar link.

To install:

To install, reverse the removal procedure and note the following:

- Tighten the rear stabilizer bar link-to-lower stabilizer bar nut to 11 ft. lbs. (15 Nm).
- Tighten the rear stabilizer bar link-to-stabilizer bar nut to 44 ft. lbs. (60 Nm).

TRAILING ARMS

REMOVAL & INSTALLATION

See Figures 170 through 172.

1. Before servicing the vehicle, refer to the Precautions Section.
2. Raise and support the vehicle.
3. Remove the rear wheel hub.
4. Remove the rear coil spring.
5. Remove the brake disc backing plate.
6. Remove the brakeline from the 5 clips as shown.
7. Remove the rear shock absorber-to-wheel knuckle bolt.
8. Remove the rear stabilizer bar link-to-lower stabilizer bar nut.
9. Remove the upper arm-to-wheel knuckle bolt.

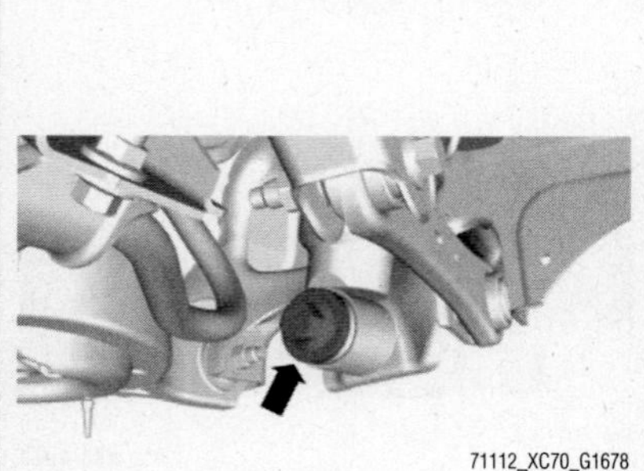

Fig. 166 Remove the rear shock absorber-to-wheel knuckle bolt (Nivomat with M16 thread)

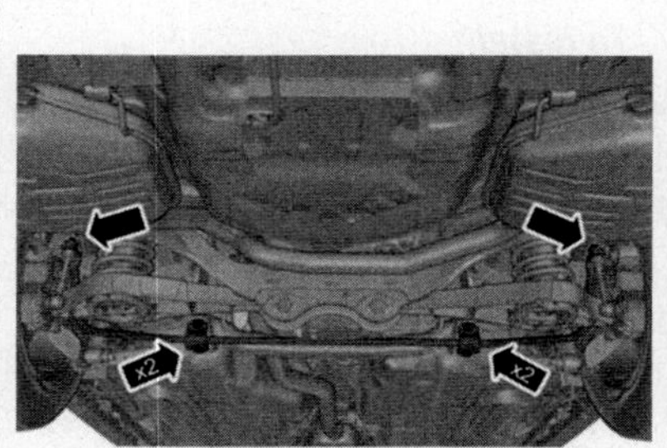

Fig. 168 Remove the 2 rear stabilizer bar link-to-stabilizer bar bolts. Remove the 4 stabilizer bar-to-rear subframe bolts. Remove the stabilizer bar

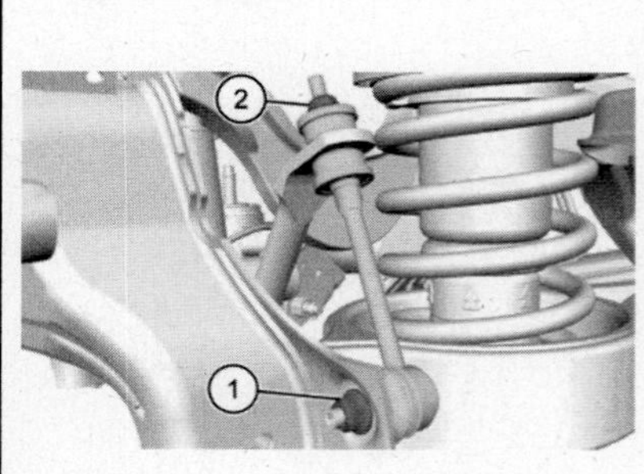

Fig. 169 Remove the rear stabilizer bar link-to-lower stabilizer bar nut (1). Remove the rear stabilizer bar link-to-stabilizer bar nut (2). Remove the rear stabilizer bar link

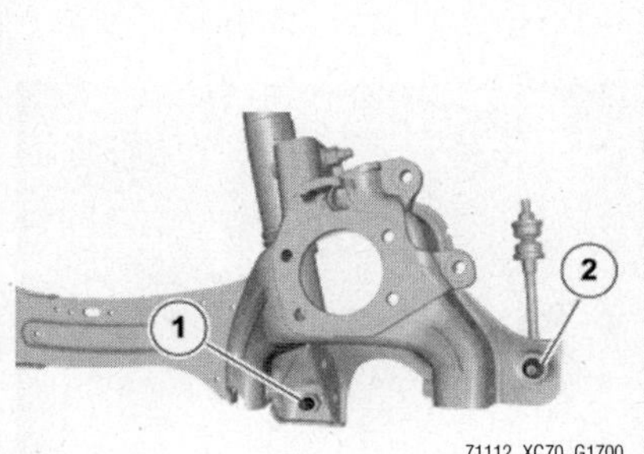

Fig. 170 Remove the rear shock absorber-to-wheel knuckle bolt (1). Remove the rear stabilizer bar link-to-lower stabilizer bar nut (2)

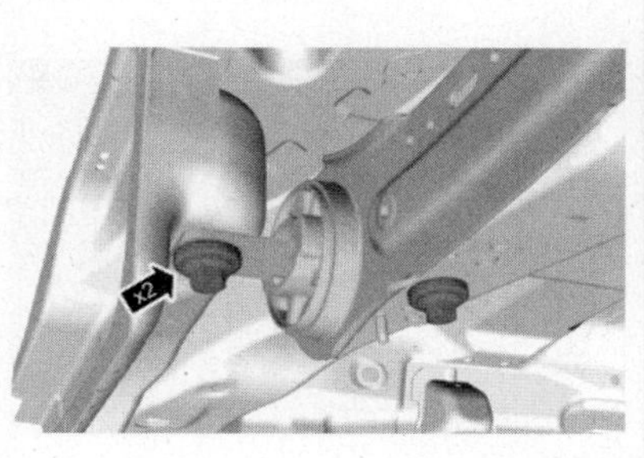

Fig. 172 Remove the 2 wheel knuckle-to-body bolts. Remove the trailing arm

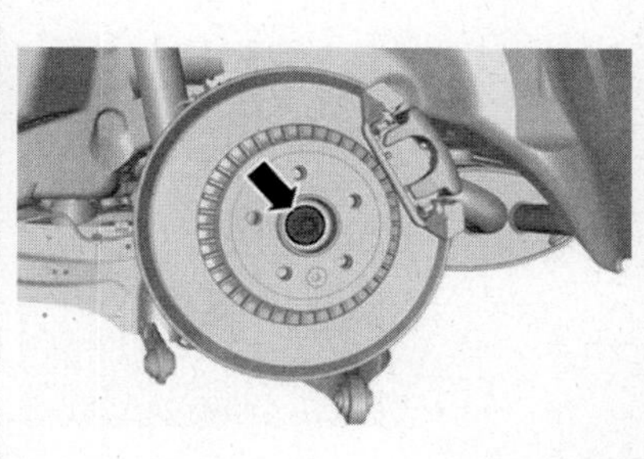

Fig. 173 Remove the rear driveshaft-to-wheel hub bolt

10. Remove the lower arm-to-wheel knuckle bolt.
11. Remove the 2 wheel knuckle-to-body bolts.
12. Remove the trailing arm.

To install:

➡Only tighten the nuts and bolts when the suspension is in the normal drive position.

13. To install, reverse the removal procedure and note the following:
    - Tighten the 2 wheel knuckle-to-body bolts to 133 ft. lbs. (180 Nm).
    - Tighten the lower arm-to-wheel knuckle bolt to 81 ft. lbs. (110 Nm).
    - Tighten the upper arm-to-wheel knuckle bolt to 81 ft. lbs. (110 Nm).
    - Tighten the rear stabilizer bar link-to-lower stabilizer bar nut to 11 ft. lbs. (15 Nm).
    - Tighten the rear shock absorber-to-wheel knuckle bolt to 129 ft. lbs. (175 Nm).
14. Perform the Service Position procedure.

WHEEL HUBS & BEARINGS

ADJUSTMENT

The wheel bearing and hub are non-serviceable (no repack). Replace when worn or damaged.

REMOVAL & INSTALLATION

AWD Vehicles

See Figures 173 through 176.

⁂ WARNING

The wheel bearings are sealed bearings and do not support repacking. Replace when damaged.

⁂ WARNING

Do not use magnets or magnetic tools close to tooth wheels, drive shafts or wheel hubs. A magnetized tooth wheel will lose its function and generate incorrect signals resulting in fault codes.

➡Any magnetized tooth wheel, drive shaft or wheel hub must be replaced with a new component.

1. Before servicing the vehicle, refer to the Precautions Section.
2. Remove the rear wheel.
3. Remove the rear driveshaft-to-wheel hub bolt.

⁂ WARNING

Make sure that no load is placed on the brake hose.

4. Remove the 2 bolts, then remove the rear brake caliper mount.
5. Remove the rear brake disc-to-wheel hub screw, then remove the brake disc.
6. Remove the rear stabilizer bar link-to-lower stabilizer bar nut, then position the stabilizer bar link aside.
7. Remove the 2 M10 bolts, then remove the stabilizer bar bracket.
8. Remove the 4 rear wheel bearing-to-wheel knuckle screws.
9. Remove the rear wheel hub and bearing assembly.

To install:

⁂ WARNING

Make sure that the component is positioned correctly.

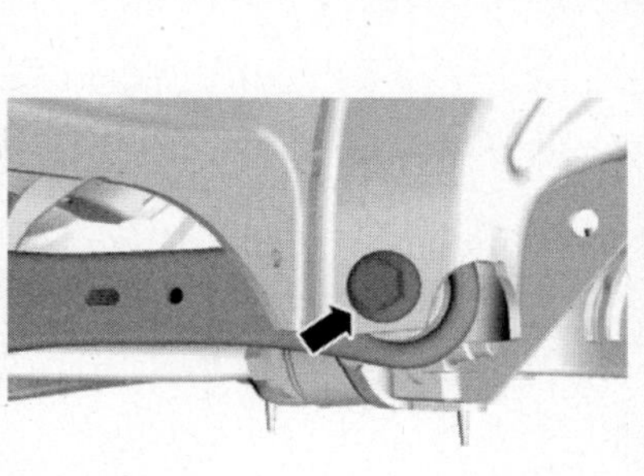

Fig. 171 Remove the lower arm-to-wheel knuckle bolt

Fig. 174 Remove the rear brake disc-to-wheel hub screw, then remove the brake disc

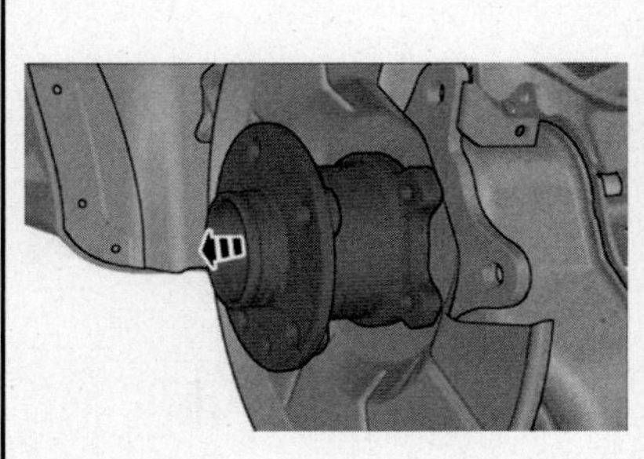

Fig. 175 Remove the rear wheel hub and bearing assembly

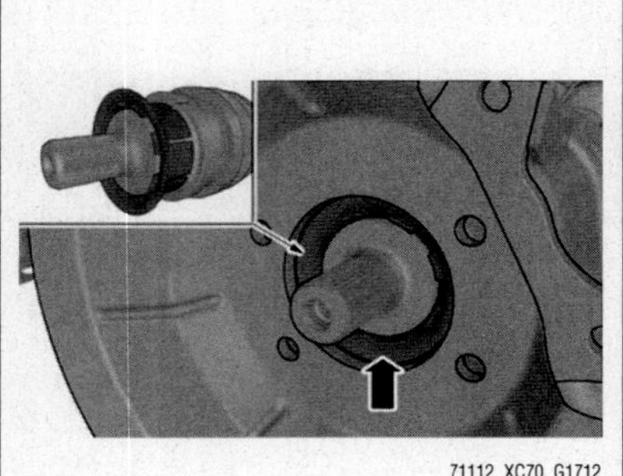

Fig. 176 Position the mudcap as shown

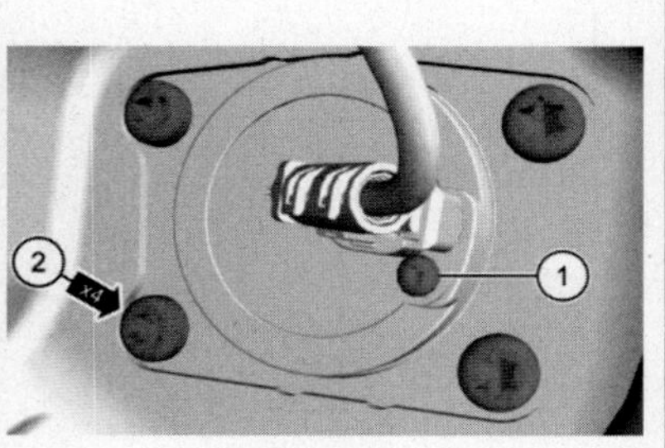

Fig. 177 Remove the M5 screw (1). Remove the 4 rear wheel bearing-to-wheel knuckle screws (2)

To install, reverse the removal procedure and note the following:

- Position the mudcap as shown.
- Tighten the rear wheel bearing-to-wheel knuckle screws to 81 ft. lbs. (110 Nm).
- Tighten the M10 bolts to 37 ft. lbs. (50 Nm).
- Tighten the rear stabilizer bar link-to-lower stabilizer bar nut to 11 ft. lbs. (15 Nm).
- Tighten the rear brake disc-to-wheel hub to 26 ft. lbs. (35 Nm).
- Tighten the rear brake caliper mount bolt to 81 ft. lbs. (110 Nm).
- Tighten the rear driveshaft-to-wheel hub to 26 ft. lbs. (35 Nm).

FWD Vehicles

See Figure 177.

⁂ WARNING

The wheel bearings are sealed bearings and do not support repacking. Replace when damaged.

⁂ WARNING

Do not use magnets or magnetic tools close to tooth wheels, drive shafts or wheel hubs. A magnetized tooth wheel will lose its function and generate incorrect signals resulting in fault codes.

➡Any magnetized tooth wheel, drive shaft or wheel hub must be replaced with a new component.

1. Before servicing the vehicle, refer to the Precautions Section.
2. Remove the rear brake disc.
3. Remove the M5 screw.
4. Remove the 4 rear wheel bearing-to-wheel knuckle screws.
5. Remove the rear wheel hub and bearing assembly.

To install:

To install, reverse the removal procedure and note the following:

- Tighten the 4 rear wheel bearing-to-wheel knuckle screws to 81 ft. lbs. (110 Nm).
- Tighten the M5 screw to 44 inch lbs. (5 Nm).

VOLVO

XC60 • XC90

14

SPECIFICATIONS AND MAINTENANCE CHARTS

ENGINE AND VEHICLE IDENTIFICATION

Engine							Model Year	
Code	Liters (cc)	Cu. In.	Cyl.	Fuel Sys.	Engine Type	Eng. Mfg.	Code ①	Year
B6304T4	3.0 (2,953)	175	6	EFI	DOHC	Volvo	B	2011
B6324S4	3.2 (3,192)	195	6	EFI	DOHC	Volvo	C	2012
B6324S5	3.2 (3,192)	195	6	EFI	DOHC	Volvo		
B8444S	4.4 (4,414)	269	8	EFI	DOHC	Volvo		

① 10th position of VIN
EFI: Electronic Fuel Injection
DOHC: Dual Overhead Camshafts

71112_X6X9_C0001

GENERAL ENGINE SPECIFICATIONS

All measurements are given in inches.

Year	Model	Engine Displacement Liters	Engine Series ID	Net Horsepower @ rpm	Net Torque @ rpm (ft. lbs.)	Bore x Stroke (in.)	Com-pression Ratio	Oil Pressure @ rpm
2011	XC60	3.0	B6304T4	300@5600	325@2100-4200	3.23 x 3.67	9.3:1	51@4000
		3.2	B6324S4	230@6500	221@3300	3.30 x 3.78	10.3:1	51@4000
		3.2	B6324S5	240@6400	236@3200	3.30 x 3.78	10.8:1	51@4000
	XC90	3.2	B6324S5	235@6200	235@3200	3.30 x 3.77	10.8:1	51@4000
		4.4	B8444S	311@6000	170@4400	3.70 x 3.13	10.4:1	33-54@2000
2012	XC60	3.0	B6304T4	300@5600	325@2100-4200	3.23 x 3.67	9.3:1	51@4000
		3.2	B6324S4	230@6500	221@3300	3.30 x 3.78	10.3:1	51@4000
		3.2	B6324S5	240@6400	236@3200	3.30 x 3.78	10.8:1	51@4000
	XC90	3.2	B6324S5	240@6400	236@3200	3.30 x 3.78	10.8:1	51@4000

71112_X6X9_C0002

GASOLINE ENGINE TUNE-UP SPECIFICATIONS

Year	Engine Displacement Liters	Engine ID	Spark Plug Gap (in.)	Ignition Timing (deg.)	Fuel Pump (psi)	Idle Speed (rpm)	Valve Lash Clearance	
							Intake	Exhaust
2011	3.0	B6304T4	0.028-0.032	①	51-59 ②	650	HYD	HYD
	3.2	B6324S4	0.028-0.032	①	51-59 B	650	HYD	HYD
	3.2	B6324S5	0.028-0.032	①	51-59 B	650	HYD	HYD
	4.4	B8444S	0.028-0.032	①	51-59 ②	675	.0067-.0091	.0106-.0130.
2012	3.0	B6304T4	0.028-0.032	①	51-59 ②	650	HYD	HYD
	3.2	B6324S4	0.028-0.032	①	51-59 B	650	HYD	HYD
	3.2	B6324S5	0.028-0.032	①	51-59 B	650	HYD	HYD

NOTE: The Vehicle Emission Control Information label often reflects specification changes made during production.
The label figures must be used if they differ from those in this chart.

HYD: Hydraulic lash adjusters

① Ignition timing is controlled by the PCM and is not adjustable

② With key ON and engine OFF

71112_X6X9_C0003

CAPACITIES

Year	Model	Engine Displacement Liters	Engine ID	Engine Oil with Filter (qts.)	Transmission (pts.) Manual	Transmission (pts.) Auto. ①	Transfer Case (pts.)	Drive Axle Front (pts.)	Drive Axle Rear (pts.)	Fuel Tank (gal.)	Cooling System (qts.)
2011	XC60	3.0	B6304T4	7.1	NA	14.8	NS	NS	NS	18.5	9.4
		3.2	B6324S4	7.1	NA	14.8	NS	NS	NS	18.5	9.4
		3.2	B6324S5	7.1	NA	14.8	NS	NS	NS	18.5	9.4
	XC90	3.2	B6324S5	7.2	NA	14.8	NS	NS	NS	21.1	7.9
		4.4	B8444S	7.1	NA	14.8	NS	NS	NS	21.1	10.7
2012	XC60	3.0	B6304T4	7.1	NA	14.8	NS	NS	NS	18.5	9.4
		3.2	B6324S4	7.1	NA	14.8	NS	NS	NS	18.5	9.4
	XC90	3.2	B6324S5	7.1	NA	14.8	NS	NS	NS	18.5	9.4
		3.2	B6324S5	7.2	NA	14.8	NS	NS	NS	21.1	7.9

NA: Not Applicable

NS: Not specified by manufacturer at date of publication

NOTE: All capacities are approximate. Add fluid gradually and check to be sure a proper fluid level is obtained.

① Drain and refill

71112_X6X9_C0004

FLUID SPECIFICATIONS

Year	Model	Engine Displacemen Liters	Engine ID	Engine Oil	Manual Trans.	Auto. Trans.	Power Steering Fluid	Brake Master Cylinder	Cooling System
2011	XC60	3.0	B6304T4	5W-30	Volvo	Volvo	Volvo	DOT 4+	Volvo
		3.2	B6324S4	5W-30	Volvo	Volvo	Volvo	DOT 4+	Volvo
		3.2	B6324S5	5W-30	Volvo	Volvo	Volvo	DOT 4+	Volvo
	XC90	3.2	B6324S5	5W-30	Volvo	Volvo	Volvo	DOT 4+	Volvo
		4.4	B8444S	5W-30	Volvo	Volvo	Volvo	DOT 4+	Volvo
2012	XC60	3.0	B6304T4	5W-30	Volvo	Volvo	Volvo	DOT 4+	Volvo
		3.2	B6324S4	5W-30	Volvo	Volvo	Volvo	DOT 4+	Volvo
		3.2	B6324S5	5W-30	Volvo	Volvo	Volvo	DOT 4+	Volvo
	XC90	3.2	B6324S5	5W-30	Volvo	Volvo	Volvo	DOT 4+	Volvo

NS: Not specified by manufacturer at date of publication

DOT: Department Of Transportation

71112_X6X9_C0005

VALVE SPECIFICATIONS

Year	Engine Displacement Liters	Engine ID	Seat Angle (deg.)	Face Angle (deg.)	Spring Test Pressure (lbs. @ in.)	Spring Installed Height (in.)	Stem-to-Guide Clearance (in.)		Stem Diameter (in.)	
							Intake	Exhaust	Intake	Exhaust
2011	3.0	B6304T4	44.99-45.01	18.75	NS	①	0.0012-0.0024	0.0012-0.0028	0.2350-0.2346	0.2346-0.2342
	3.2	B6324S4	44.99-45.01	18.75	NS	①	0.0012-0.0024	0.0012-0.0028	0.2350-0.2346	0.2346-0.2342
	3.2	B6324S5	44.99-45.01	18.75	NS	①	0.0012-0.0024	0.0012-0.0028	0.2350-0.2346	0.2346-0.2342
	4.4	B8444S	44.99-45.01	19.0	NS	NS	NS	NS	0.0067-0.0091	0.0106 0.0130
2012	3.0	B6304T4	44.99-45.01	18.75	NS	①	0.0012-0.0024	0.0012-0.0028	0.2350-0.2346	0.2346-0.2342
	3.2	B6324S4	44.99-45.01	18.75	NS	①	0.0012-0.0024	0.0012-0.0028	0.2350-0.2346	0.2346-0.2342
	3.2	B6324S5	44.99-45.01	18.75	NS	①	0.0012-0.0024	0.0012-0.0028	0.2350-0.2346	0.2346-0.2342

NS: Not specified by manufacturer at date of publication

① Height unloaded: 1.7677 - 1.8465 inches

71112_X6X9_C0006

CAMSHAFT AND BEARING SPECIFICATIONS CHART

All measurements are given in inches.

Year	Engine Displ. Liters	Engine ID	Journal Dia.	Brg. Oil Clearance	Shaft End-play	Runout	Journal Bore	Lobe Lift	
								Intake	Exhaust
2011	3.0	B6304T4	NS	NS	NS	NS	NS	0.3327	0.3720
	3.2	B6324S4	NS	NS	NS	NS	NS	0.3327	0.3720
	3.2	B6324S5	NS	NS	NS	NS	NS	0.3327	0.3720
	4.4	B8444S	NS	NS	NS	NS	NS	NS	NS
2012	3.0	B6304T4	NS	NS	NS	NS	NS	0.3327	0.3720
	3.2	B6324S4	NS	NS	NS	NS	NS	0.3327	0.3720
	3.2	B6324S5	NS	NS	NS	NS	NS	0.3327	0.3720

NS: Not specified by manufacturer at date of publication

① Lift height at high lift: 0.3937 inch

Lift height at how lift: 0.1417 inch

71112_X6X9_C0007

CRANKSHAFT AND CONNECTING ROD SPECIFICATIONS

All measurements are given in inches.

	Engine		Crankshaft				Connecting Rod		
Year	Displacement Liters	Engine ID	Main Brg. Journal Dia.	Main Brg. Oil Clearance	Shaft End-play	Thrust on No.	Journal Diameter	Oil Clearance	Side Clearance
2011	3.0	B6304T4	2.5584-2.5592	NS	0.0031-0.0106	NS	2.0861-2.0866	NS	NS
	3.2	B6324S4	2.5584-2.5592	NS	0.0031-0.0106	NS	2.0861-2.0866	NS	NS
	3.2	B6324S5	2.5584-2.5592	NS	0.0031-0.0106	NS	2.0861-2.0866	NS	NS
	4.4	B8444S	2.5591	NS	NS	NS	NS	NS	NS
2012	3.0	B6304T4	2.5584-2.5592	NS	0.0031-0.0106	NS	2.0861-2.0866	NS	NS
	3.2	B6324S4	2.5584-2.5592	NS	0.0031-0.0106	NS	2.0861-2.0866	NS	NS
	3.2	B6324S5	2.5584-2.5592	NS	0.0031-0.0106	NS	2.0861-2.0866	NS	NS

NS: Not specified by manufacturer at date of publication

71112_X6X9_C0008

PISTON AND RING SPECIFICATIONS

All measurements are given in inches.

	Engine			Ring Gap			Ring Side Clearance		
Year	Displ. Liters	Engine ID	Piston Clearance	Top Compression	Bottom Compression	Oil Control	Top Compression	Bottom Compression	Oil Control
2011	3.0	B6304T4	0.0016-0.0024	0.0461-0.0469	0.0579-0.0587	0.0734-0.0783	0.0012-0.0028	0.0012-0.0028	0.0008-0.0065
	3.2	B6324S4	0.0016-0.0024	0.0461-0.0469	0.0579-0.0587	0.0734-0.0783	0.0012-0.0028	0.0012-0.0028	0.0008-0.0065
	3.2	B6324S5	0.0016-0.0024	0.0461-0.0469	0.0579-0.0587	0.0734-0.0783	0.0012-0.0028	0.0012-0.0028	0.0008-0.0065
	4.4	B8444S	NS	0.0472	0.0472	0.0984	NS	NS	NS
2012	3.0	B6304T4	0.0016-0.0024	0.0461-0.0469	0.0579-0.0587	0.0734-0.0783	0.0012-0.0028	0.0012-0.0028	0.0008-0.0065
	3.2	B6324S4	0.0016-0.0024	0.0461-0.0469	0.0579-0.0587	0.0734-0.0783	0.0012-0.0028	0.0012-0.0028	0.0008-0.0065
	3.2	B6324S5	0.0016-0.0024	0.0461-0.0469	0.0579-0.0587	0.0734-0.0783	0.0012-0.0028	0.0012-0.0028	0.0008-0.0065

NS: Not specified by manufacturer at date of publication

71112_X6X9_C0009

TORQUE SPECIFICATIONS

All readings in ft. lbs.

Year	Engine Displacement Liters	Engine ID	Cylinder Head Bolts	Main Bearing Bolts	Rod Bearing Bolts	Crankshaft Damper Bolts	Flywheel Bolts	Manifold Intake	Manifold Exhaust	Spark Plugs	Oil Pan Drain Plug
2011	3.0	B6304T4	①	②	③	④	59	13	18	21	28
	3.2	B6324S4	①	②	③	④	59	13	18	21	28
	3.2	B6324S5	①	②	③	④	59	13	18	21	28
	4.4	B8444S	⑤	NS	NS	④	59	14	18	18	25
2012	3.0	B6304T4	①	②	③	④	59	13	18	21	28
	3.2	B6324S4	①	②	③	④	59	13	18	21	28
	3.2	B6324S5	①	②	③	④	59	13	18	21	28

NS: Not specified by manufacturer at date of publication

① Refer to procedure for torque sequence
- Step 1: 33 ft. lbs. (45 Nm)
- Step 2: 33 ft. lbs. (45 Nm)
- Step 3: plus 90 degrees
- Step 4: plus 180 degrees

② Refer to procedure for torque sequence/bolt identification
- Step 1: M10 bolts to 44 inch lbs. (5 Nm)
- Step 2: M10 bolts to 22 ft. lbs. (30 Nm)
- Step 3: M8 bolts: 18 ft. lbs. (25 Nm)
- Step 4: M10 bolts plus 105 degrees
- Step 5: M8 bolts to 18 ft. lbs. (25 Nm)

③ Step 1: 106 inch lbs. (12 Nm)
- Step 2: 15 ft. lbs. (20 Nm)
- Step 3: plus 90 degrees

④ Step 1: 89 ft. lbs. (120 Nm)
- Step 2: Loosen 360 degrees
- Step 3: 37 ft. lbs. (50 Nm)
- Step 4: plus 90 degrees

⑤ Refer to procedure for torque sequence
- Step 1: 30 ft. lbs. (40 Nm)
- Step 2: plus 90 degrees

71112_X6X9_C0010

TIRE, WHEEL AND BALL JOINT SPECIFICATIONS

Year	Model	OEM Tires Standard	OEM Tires Optional	Tire Pressures (psi) Front	Tire Pressures (psi) Rear	Wheel Size	Ball Joint Inspection	Lug Nut Torque (ft. lbs.)
2011	XC60 3.2	P235/65R17	P235/60R18	①	①	7.5 x 17 or 7.5 x 18	NS	103
	XC60 R-Design	P255/45R20	NA	①	①	8.0 x 20	NS	103
	XC60 T6 AWD	P235/60R18	NA	①	①	7.5 x 18	NS	103
	XC90 3.2	P235/60R18	NA	①	①	7.0 x 18	NS	103
	XC90 R-Design	P255/50R19	NA	①	①	8.0 x 19	NS	103
	XC90 V8	P235/65R18	NA	①	①	7.0 x 18	NS	103
2012	XC60 3.2	P235/65R17	P235/60R18	①	①	7.5 x 17 or 7.5 x 18	NS	103
	XC60 R-Design	P255/45R20	NA	①	①	8.0 x 20	NS	103
	XC60 T6 AWD	P235/60R18	NA	①	①	7.5 x 18	NS	103
	XC90 3.2	P235/60R18	NA	①	①	7.0 x 18	NS	103
	XC90 R-Design	P255/45R20	NA	①	①	8.0 x 20	NS	103

OEM: Original Equipment Manufacturer

PSI: Pounds Per Square Inch

NA: Not Applicable

NS: Not specified by manufacturer at date of publication

① See the tire placard on the vehicle

71112_X6X9_C0012

BRAKE SPECIFICATIONS

All measurements in inches unless noted

			Brake Disc			Minimum	Brake Caliper	
			Original	Minimum	Maximum	Lining	Bracket Bolts	Guide Pin Bolts
Year	Model		Thickness	Thickness	Runout	Thickness	(ft. lbs.)	(ft. lbs.)
2011	XC60	F	⑦	⑧	0.001	③	148	44
		R	0.866	⑨	0.001	③	81	26
	XC90	F	①	②	0.001	③	④	44
		R	0.787	0.709	0.001	③	⑤	⑥
2012	XC60	F	⑦	⑧	0.001	③	148	44
		R	0.866	⑨	0.001	③	81	26
	XC90	F	①	②	0.001	③	④	44
		R	0.787	0.709	0.001	③	⑤	⑥

F: Front

R: Rear

① 16 inch rotors: 1.102 inches (28mm)
17 inch rotors: 1.181 inches (30mm)

② 16 inch rotors: 0.984 inches (25mm)
17 inch rotors: 1.063 inches (27mm)

③ Replace the disc brake pads when the friction surface is worn to within 0.079 inch (2mm) of the mounting plates.

④ Caliper holder (steel spindle): 77 ft. lbs., plus 60 degrees

⑤ Caliper to wheel bearing housing: 26 ft. lbs., plus 60 degrees

⑥ Slide pin in brake caliper, wrench size 7mm: 20 ft. lbs.
Slide pin in brake caliper, wrench size 9 mm: 44 ft. lbs.

⑦ 16, 16.5, and 17.5 inch rotors: 1.102 inches (28mm)
17 inch rotors: 1.181 inches (30mm)

⑧ 16, 16.5, and 17.5 inch rotors: 1.024 inches (26mm)
17 inch rotors: 1.102 inches (28mm)

⑨ Solid disc: 0.354 inch (9mm)
Ventilated disc: 0.787 inch (20mm)

71112_X6X9_C0013

MAINTENANCE SERVICES

2011-12 VOLVO XC60 and XC90

TO BE SERVICED	TYPE OF SERVICE	VEHICLE MILEAGE INTERVAL (x1000)									
		7.5	15	22.5	30	37.5	45	52.5	60	67.5	75
Alignment wheel angles	S/I								✓	✓	✓
Alternator rubber connection (only B63x4x)	R	Every 15 years as a maximum interval									
Auxiliary drive belt, tensioner, idler pulleys (all except B63x4x) (10 year interval maximum)	R										
Auxiliary drive belt, tensioner, idler pulley, clutch, guide pins (B63x4x) (10 year interval maximum)	R										
Brake, clutch (if equipped), coolant, power steering, and washer fluids	S/I	✓	✓	✓	✓	✓	✓	✓	✓	✓	✓
Brake fluid ①	R					✓					✓
Brake line, fuel lines (for damage or leakage)	S/I				✓				✓		
Brake pads and rotors	S/I	✓	✓	✓	✓	✓	✓	✓	✓	✓	✓
Cabin air filter	R		✓		✓		✓		✓		✓
Collision warning camera windscreen cleaning (if equipped)	S/I	✓	✓	✓	✓	✓	✓	✓	✓	✓	✓
Engine air cleaner	R					✓					✓
Engine--check for oil/fluid leakage	S/I		✓		✓		✓		✓		✓
Engine coolant	S/I		✓		✓		✓		✓		✓
Engine oil and filter	R	✓	✓	✓	✓	✓	✓	✓	✓	✓	✓
Exhaust system	S/I								✓	✓	✓
Final drive, bevel gear oil leakage (AWD only)	S/I		✓		✓		✓		✓		✓
Front suspension/steering components	S/I								✓	✓	✓
Halfshaft joints and boots	S/I								✓	✓	✓
Parking Brake	S/I		✓		✓		✓		✓		✓
Propeller shaft, pilot bearing, universal joint (AWD only)	S/I								✓	✓	✓
Rear suspension	S/I								✓	✓	✓
Service Reminder Indicator (SRI) reset	S/I	✓	✓	✓	✓	✓	✓	✓	✓	✓	✓
Spare tire	S/I				✓				✓		
Spark Plugs	R										✓
Temporary tire sealing kit (if equipped)	R	Every 4th year									
Transmission--check for leakage ②	S/I		✓		✓		✓		✓		✓
Transmission oil change	R	Not normally required unless instructed in the information display									
Washer and wipers	S/I	✓	✓	✓	✓	✓	✓	✓	✓	✓	✓
Wheels and tires	S/I	✓	✓	✓	✓	✓	✓	✓	✓	✓	✓

R: Replace

S/I: Inspect and service, if necessary

① Replace every year if vehicle is used for mountain driving or mainly used in humid climates

② In event of leakage from the transmission, check the oil level

FREQUENT OPERATION MAINTENANCE (SEVERE SERVICE)

If a vehicle is operated under any of the following conditions, it is considered severe service:

- Extremely dusty areas

- 50% or more of the vehicle operation is in 90°F (32°C) or higher temperatures, or constant operation in temperatures below 32°F (0°C)

- Prolonged idling (vehicle operation in stop and go traffic)

- Frequent short running periods (engine does not warm to normal operating temperatures)

- Police, taxi, delivery usage, or trailer towing usage

- Driving in hilly or mountainous terrain

Oil & oil filter: change more frequently

Air filter element: service or inspect more frequently

Transmission oil: service more frequently

To reset the SERVICE REMINDER INDICATOR (SRI) light:

The SRI informs the driver that it is time for the vehicle to be serviced.

The text message is displayed for 120 seconds each time the ignition is switched ON.

The light can be reset using the Vehicle Information and Diagnostics for Aftersales (VIDA) vehicle communication equipment.

NOTE: If the light or message comes back on when starting the vehicle, the SRI has not reset. Repeat the procedure.

Resetting without VIDA equipment

1. Turn the ignition key to Position I.
2. Press and hold in the RESET button for the trip odometer.
3. Within 2 seconds of performing step 2, turn the ignition key to Position II.
4. Continue to hold the RESET button for the trip odometer until the original value has been reset.

NOTE: The information lamp will light when the reset button should be released.

5. Release the RESET button for the trip odometer within 4 seconds of the information lamp being illumined.
6. The instrument panel will give an audible signal when the resetting has succeeded.

NOTE: If the trip odometer has been reset prior to this procedure, the RESET button must be held in for a minimum of 10 seconds, maximum of 14 seconds.

NOTE: If the RESET button for the trip odometer is NOT released within 4 seconds (see step 5), the SRI will not reset.

NOTE: If the light or message comes back on when starting the vehicle, the SRI has not reset. Repeat the procedure.

ADDITIONAL MAINTENANCE SERVICES

2011-12 VOLVO XC60 and XC90

TO BE SERVICED	TYPE OF SERVICE	VEHICLE MILEAGE INTERVAL (x1000)									
		82.5	90	97.5	105	112.5	120	127.5	135	142.5	150
Alignment wheel angles	S/I	✓	✓	✓	✓	✓	✓	✓	✓	✓	✓
Alternator rubber connection (only B63x4x)	R	Every 15 years as a maximum interval									
Auxiliary drive belt, tensioner, idler pulley(s) (All except B63x4x) (10 year interval maximum)	R										✓
Auxiliary drive belt, tensioner, idler pulley, clutch, guide pins (B63x4x) (10 year interval maximum)	R										✓
Battery poles, electrolyte level, mounting	S/I		✓		✓		✓		✓		✓
Brake, clutch, coolant, power steering, and washer fluids	S/I	✓	✓	✓	✓	✓	✓	✓	✓	✓	✓
Brake fluid ①	R					✓					✓
Brake line, fuel lines (for damage or leakage)	S/I		✓				✓		✓		✓
Brake pads and rotors	S/I	✓	✓	✓	✓	✓	✓	✓	✓	✓	✓
Cabin air filter	R		✓		✓		✓		✓		✓
Collision warning camera windscreen cleaning (if equipped)	S/I	✓	✓	✓	✓	✓	✓	✓	✓	✓	✓
Engine air cleaner	R					✓					✓
Engine--check for oil/fluid leakage	S/I		✓		✓		✓		✓		✓
Engine coolant	S/I		✓		✓		✓		✓		✓
Engine oil and filter	R	✓	✓	✓	✓	✓	✓	✓	✓	✓	✓
Exhaust system	S/I	✓	✓	✓	✓	✓	✓	✓	✓	✓	✓
Final drive, bevel gear oil leakage (AWD only)	S/I		✓		✓		✓		✓		✓
Front suspension/steering components	S/I	✓	✓	✓	✓	✓	✓	✓	✓	✓	✓
Halfshaft joints and boots	S/I	✓	✓	✓	✓	✓	✓	✓	✓	✓	✓
Parking Brake	S/I		✓		✓		✓		✓		✓
Propeller shaft, pilot bearing, universal joint (AWD only)	S/I	✓	✓	✓	✓	✓	✓	✓	✓	✓	✓
Rear suspension	S/I	✓	✓	✓	✓	✓	✓	✓	✓	✓	✓
Service Reminder Indicator (SRI) reset	S/I	✓	✓	✓	✓	✓	✓	✓	✓	✓	✓
Spare tire	S/I		✓				✓				✓
Spark Plugs	R										✓
Temporary tire sealing kit (if equipped)	R	Every 4th year									
Transmission--check for leakage ②	S/I		✓		✓		✓		✓		✓
Transmission oil change	R	Not normally required unless instructed in the information display									
Washer and wipers	S/I	✓	✓	✓	✓	✓	✓	✓	✓	✓	✓
Wheels and tires	S/I	✓	✓	✓	✓	✓	✓	✓	✓	✓	✓

R: Replace

S/I: Inspect and service, if necessary

① Replace every year if vehicle is used for mountain driving or mainly used in humid climates

② In event of leakage from the transmission, check the oil level

71112_X6X9_C0015

PRECAUTIONS

Before servicing any vehicle, please be sure to read all of the following precautions, which deal with personal safety, prevention of component damage, and important points to take into consideration when servicing a motor vehicle:

- Never open, service or drain the radiator or cooling system when the engine is hot; serious burns can occur from the steam and hot coolant.
- Observe all applicable safety precautions when working around fuel. Whenever servicing the fuel system, always work in a well-ventilated area. Do not allow fuel spray or vapors to come in contact with a spark, open flame, or excessive heat (a hot drop light, for example). Keep a dry chemical fire extinguisher near the work area. Always keep fuel in a container specifically designed for fuel storage; also, always properly seal fuel containers to avoid the possibility of fire or explosion. Refer to the additional fuel system precautions later in this section.
- Fuel injection systems often remain pressurized, even after the engine has been turned **OFF**. The fuel system pressure must be relieved before disconnecting any fuel lines. Failure to do so may result in fire and/or personal injury.
- Brake fluid often contains polyglycol ethers and polyglycols. Avoid contact with the eyes and wash your hands thoroughly after handling brake fluid. If you do get brake fluid in your eyes, flush your eyes with clean, running water for 15 minutes. If eye irritation persists, or if you have taken brake fluid internally, IMMEDIATELY seek medical assistance.
- The EPA warns that prolonged contact with used engine oil may cause a number of skin disorders, including cancer. You should make every effort to minimize your exposure to used engine oil. Protective gloves should be worn when changing oil. Wash your hands and any other exposed skin areas as soon as possible after exposure to used engine oil. Soap and water, or waterless hand cleaner should be used.
- All new vehicles are now equipped with an air bag system, often referred to as a Supplemental Restraint System (SRS) or Supplemental Inflatable Restraint (SIR) system. The system must be disabled before performing service on or around system components, steering column, instrument panel components, wiring and sensors. Failure to follow safety and disabling procedures could result in accidental air bag deployment, possible personal injury and unnecessary system repairs.
- Always wear safety goggles when working with, or around, the air bag system. When carrying a non-deployed air bag, be sure the bag and trim cover are pointed away from your body. When placing a non-deployed air bag on a work surface, always face the bag and trim cover upward, away from the surface. This will reduce the motion of the module if it is accidentally deployed. Refer to the additional air bag system precautions later in this section.
- Clean, high quality brake fluid from a sealed container is essential to the safe and proper operation of the brake system. You should always buy the correct type of brake fluid for your vehicle. If the brake fluid becomes contaminated, completely flush the system with new fluid. Never reuse any brake fluid. Any brake fluid that is removed from the system should be discarded. Also, do not allow any brake fluid to come in contact with a painted surface; it will damage the paint.
- Never operate the engine without the proper amount and type of engine oil; doing so WILL result in severe engine damage.
- Timing belt maintenance is extremely important. Many models utilize an interference-type, non-freewheeling engine. If the timing belt breaks, the valves in the cylinder head may strike the pistons, causing potentially serious (also time-consuming and expensive) engine damage. Refer to the maintenance interval charts for the recommended replacement interval for the timing belt, and to the timing belt section for belt replacement and inspection.
- Disconnecting the negative battery cable on some vehicles may interfere with the functions of the on-board computer system(s) and may require the computer to undergo a relearning process once the negative battery cable is reconnected.
- When servicing drum brakes, only disassemble and assemble one side at a time, leaving the remaining side intact for reference.
- Only an MVAC-trained, EPA-certified automotive technician should service the air conditioning system or its components.

BRAKES — ANTI-LOCK BRAKE SYSTEM (ABS)

GENERAL INFORMATION

PRECAUTIONS

- Certain components within the ABS system are not intended to be serviced or repaired individually.
- Do not use rubber hoses or other parts not specifically specified for and ABS system. When using repair kits, replace all parts included in the kit. Partial or incorrect repair may lead to functional problems and require the replacement of components.
- Lubricate rubber parts with clean, fresh brake fluid to ease assembly. Do not use shop air to clean parts; damage to rubber components may result.
- Use only DOT 3 brake fluid from an unopened container.
- If any hydraulic component or line is removed or replaced, it may be necessary to bleed the entire system.
- A clean repair area is essential. Always clean the reservoir and cap thoroughly before removing the cap. The slightest amount of dirt in the fluid may plug an orifice and impair the system function. Perform repairs after components have been thoroughly cleaned; use only denatured alcohol to clean components. Do not allow ABS components to come into contact with any substance containing mineral oil; this includes used shop rags.
- The Anti-Lock control unit is a microprocessor similar to other computer units in the vehicle. Ensure that the ignition switch is **OFF** before removing or installing controller harnesses. Avoid static electricity discharge at or near the controller.
- If any arc welding is to be done on the vehicle, the control unit should be unplugged before welding operations begin.

SPEED SENSORS

REMOVAL & INSTALLATION

Front

See Figure 1.

1. Before servicing the vehicle, refer to the Precautions Section.
2. Disconnect the negative battery cable.
3. Raise and safely support the vehicle.
4. Remove the tire and wheel assembly.
5. Remove the front brake rotor.
6. Remove the wheel speed sensor mounting bolt.

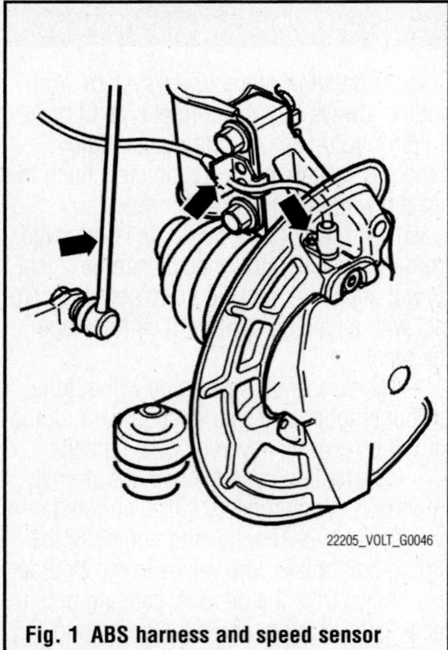

Fig. 1 ABS harness and speed sensor

➡Remove the rotor to gain access to the wheel sensor mounting bolt.

7. Remove the Wheel Speed Sensor (WSS) mounting bolt.
8. Pull the sensor out, being careful to turn it as little as possible. Do not pull on the sensor harness.
9. Disconnect the WSS electrical connector.
10. Remove the harness from its mount.

To install:

11. Installation is the reverse of removal.
12. Inspect the sensor O-ring, replace as required.
13. Before installing the sensor, be certain there are no foreign materials, like iron fragments adhering to:
    - The pick-up part of the sensor
    - The inside of the sensor mounting hole
    - The rotor mounting surface
14. Apply a thin coat of suitable grease to the wheel sensor O-ring and mounting hole.
15. Tighten the sensor mounting bolt to 44 inch lbs. (5 Nm).
16. Initialize the central locking system, interior lighting, and power windows using the VIDA communications tool.

➡When the battery is disconnected, the engine may need to run for a few minutes before it runs smoothly.

Rear

See Figure 2.

1. Before servicing the vehicle, always refer to the precautions sections.
2. Disconnect the negative battery cable.
3. Raise and support the vehicle safely.
4. Remove the tire and wheel assembly.
5. Remove the wheel speed sensor mounting bolt.
6. Pull the sensor out, being careful to turn it as little as possible. Do not pull on the sensor harness.
7. Disconnect the wheel speed sensor electrical connector.
8. Remove the harness from its mount.

To install:

9. Inspect the sensor O-ring, replace as required.

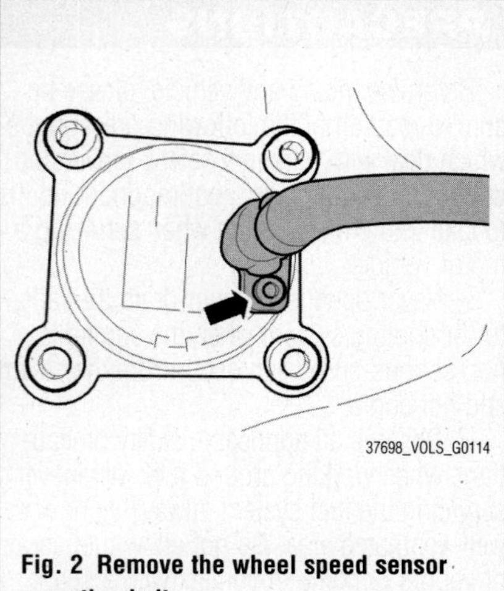

Fig. 2 Remove the wheel speed sensor mounting bolt

10. Before installing the sensor, be certain there are no foreign materials, like iron fragments adhering to:
    - The pick-up part of the sensor
    - The inside of the sensor mounting hole
    - The rotor mounting surface.
11. Apply a thin coat of suitable grease to the wheel sensor O-ring and mounting hole.
12. Tighten the sensor mounting bolt to 44 inch lbs. (5 Nm).
13. Initialize the central locking system, interior lighting, and power windows using the VIDA communications tool.

➡When the battery is disconnected, the engine may need to run for a few minutes before it runs smoothly.

BRAKES — BLEEDING THE BRAKE SYSTEM

BLEEDING PROCEDURE

BLEEDING THE ABS SYSTEM

✲✲ CAUTION

Brake fluid contains polyglycol ethers and polyglycols. Avoid contact with the eyes and wash your hands thoroughly after handling brake fluid. If you do get brake fluid in your eyes, flush your eyes with clean, running water for 15 minutes. If eye irritation persists, or if you have taken brake fluid internally, IMMEDIATELY seek medical assistance.

✲✲ WARNING

Clean, high quality brake fluid is essential to the safe and proper operation of the brake system. You should always buy the highest quality brake fluid that is available. If the brake fluid becomes contaminated, drain and flush the system, then refill the master cylinder with new fluid. Never reuse any brake fluid. Any brake fluid that is removed from the system should be discarded. Also, do not allow any brake fluid to come in contact with a painted surface; it will damage the paint.

When reconditioning or replacing brake calipers bleed the relevant brake pipe as follows.

➡The brake pedal must be depressed throughout the operation. This is so that the brake system is not drained of brake fluid.

➡If the braking system has been completely or partly drained, bleed the whole system. A bleeding unit that can pressurize the brake system to 0.2–0.3 Mpa must be used.

1. Before servicing the vehicle, refer to the Precautions Section.
2. Turn the ignition switch OFF.
3. Clean all around the brake fluid reservoir filler cap.
4. Take out the special brake fluid collection bottle.
5. Connect the bleeding unit to the brake fluid reservoir. Follow the manufacturer's instructions for connecting and using the bleeding unit.
6. Pressurize the brake system. Check the brake fluid reservoir connector.
7. Raise the car and remove the wheels.

8. Remove the protective cap from the bleed nipple. Connect the hose from the collection bottle.

9. Open the bleed nipple. Close it when there are no more air bubbles in the fluid coming out of the hose.

10. Tighten the bleed nipple.

11. Continue to bleed the other wheels. Use the following wheel order:

- Left front wheel
- Right front wheel
- Left rear wheel
- Right rear wheel

12. Check for leakage from the bleed nipples.

13. Depressurize the brake system.

14. Check for air in the brake system and for brake fluid leakage.

15. Fill the brake reservoir with the proper amount of DOT 4+ brake fluid.

FLUID FILL PROCEDURE

CAUTION

Brake fluid contains polyglycol ethers and polyglycols. Avoid contact with the eyes and wash your hands thoroughly after handling brake fluid. If you do get brake fluid in your eyes, flush your eyes with clean, running water for 15 minutes. If eye irritation persists, or if you have taken brake fluid internally, IMMEDIATELY seek medical assistance.

WARNING

Clean, high quality brake fluid is essential to the safe and proper operation of the brake system. You should always buy the highest quality brake fluid that is available. If the brake fluid becomes contaminated, drain and flush the system, then refill the master cylinder with new fluid. Never reuse any brake fluid. Any brake fluid that is removed from the system should be discarded. Also, do not allow any brake fluid to come in contact with a painted surface; it will damage the paint.

1. Before servicing the vehicle, refer to the Precautions Section.

2. Clean all around the brake fluid reservoir filler cap.

3. Remove the master cylinder filler cap.

4. Fill the brake fluid reservoir completely with genuine Volvo DOT 4+ brake fluid.

➡Use only Volvo Genuine Parts brake fluid designated DOT 4+. Never reuse brake fluid. Always keep the brake fluid sealed in the original packaging.

BRAKES

FRONT DISC BRAKES

CAUTION

Dust and dirt accumulating on brake parts during normal use may contain asbestos fibers from production or aftermarket brake linings. Breathing excessive concentrations of asbestos fibers can cause serious bodily harm. Exercise care when servicing brake parts. Do not sand or grind brake lining unless equipment used is designed to contain the dust residue. Do not clean brake parts with compressed air or by dry brushing. Cleaning should be done by dampening the brake components with a fine mist of water, then wiping the brake components clean with a dampened cloth. Dispose of cloth and all residue containing asbestos fibers in an impermeable container with the appropriate label. Follow practices prescribed by the Occupational Safety and Health Administration (OSHA) and the Environmental Protection Agency (EPA) for the handling, processing, and disposing of dust or debris that may contain asbestos fibers.

BRAKE CALIPER

REMOVAL & INSTALLATION

See Figure 3.

1. Before servicing the vehicle, refer to the Precautions Section.

2. Raise and safely support the vehicle.

3. Remove the tire and wheel assembly.

4. If the caliper is being replaced:

a. Secure the pedal in the depressed position. Use a pedal jack.

b. Clean the brake caliper thoroughly.

c. Remove the protective cap from the bleed nipple.

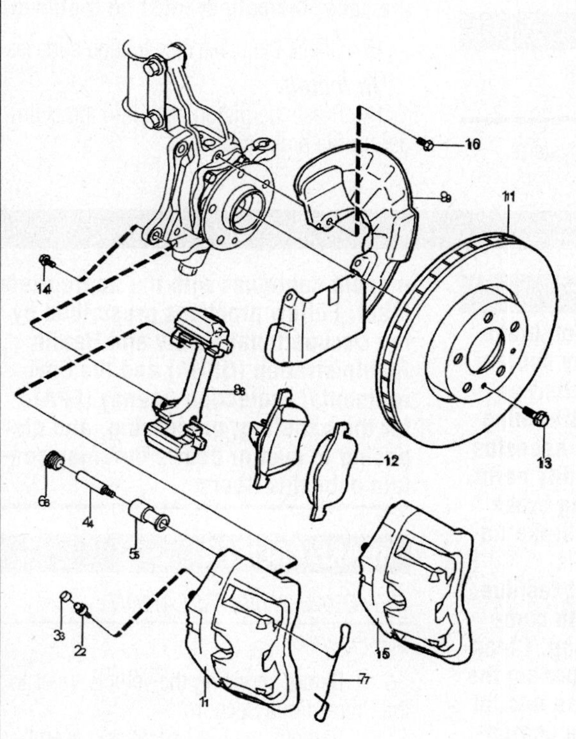

Fig. 3 Front brake exploded view

d. Install a plastic hose on the nipple.
e. Open the bleed nipple. Collect the brake fluid in a container. Shut the bleed nipple.
f. Loosen the brake hose approximately half a turn.
5. Remove the retaining spring carefully so as not to deform it.
6. Remove the protective caps from the 2 locating pins.
7. Remove the locating pins.
8. Remove the brake caliper from the holder.
9. Remove the brake pads.
10. Unscrew the brake caliper from the brake hose.
11. Drain the remaining brake fluid.

To install:

12. Clean the sliding pins using a steel brush. Lubricate the brake pad's friction surfaces. Insert the locating pins into the rubber sleeves. The pins should slide into the sleeves easily.
13. Install the brake pads.
14. Install the brake caliper in the holder.
15. Tighten the locating pins to 44 ft. lbs. (60 Nm).
16. Install the protective caps.
17. Install the securing spring.
18. Tighten the brake hose to 13 ft. lbs. (18 Nm).

⁂ WARNING

The brake hose must not be twisted.

19. Fill and bleed the brake system.

BRAKE PADS

REMOVAL & INSTALLATION

See Figure 4.

1. Before servicing the vehicle, refer to the Precautions Section.
2. Raise and safely support the vehicle.
3. Remove the tire and wheel assembly.
4. Remove the pad retaining spring carefully so as not to deform it.
5. Remove the protective caps from the 2 locating pins.
6. Remove the locating pins, using a 7mm hex socket.
7. Remove the brake caliper from the holder.
8. Remove the brake pads.
9. Hang brake caliper from a steel wire from the front spring so as not to damage brake hose.

➡Do not depress the brake pedal while the brake pads are removed.

10. Clean and check the brake caliper and dust cover.
11. Clean and check the brake pad mating surfaces in the brake caliper and caliper holder.
12. Check the piston dust boot.

➡If the dust boot is damaged, dirt may have penetrated the cylinder. If this is the case, the caliper must be replaced.

13. Check the brake disc friction surfaces.

To install:

14. Press the piston back into the cylinder on the brake caliper.

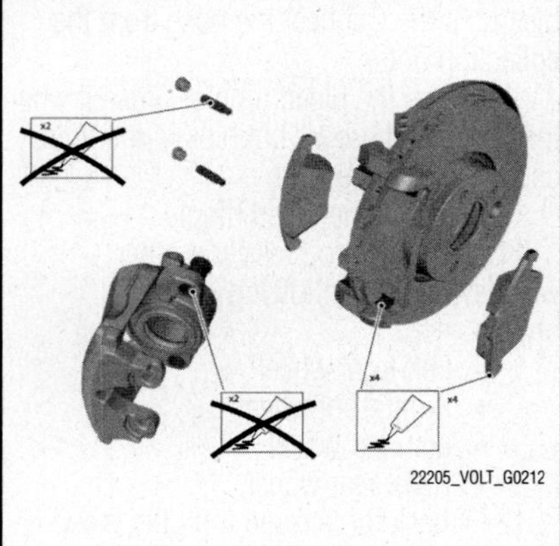

Fig. 4 Lubricate the locating pins using silicone caliper grease as illustrated

15. Check that the dust cover is correctly positioned.
16. Clean the sliding pins using a steel brush. Lubricate the brake pad friction surfaces, as illustrated. Insert the locating pins into the rubber sleeves. The pins should slide into the sleeves easily.
17. Install new brake pads.
18. Install the brake caliper.
19. Tighten the locating pins to 44 ft. lbs. (60 Nm).
20. Install the protective caps.
21. Install the securing spring.
22. Check the brake fluid level in the reservoir.
23. Depress the brake pedal a few times. Check the level of the brake fluid reservoir.
24. Install the wheels.

⁂ CAUTION

Dust and dirt accumulating on brake parts during normal use may contain asbestos fibers from production or aftermarket brake linings. Breathing excessive concentrations of asbestos fibers can cause serious bodily harm. Exercise care when servicing brake parts. Do not sand or grind brake lining unless equipment used is designed to contain the dust residue. Do not clean brake parts with compressed air or by dry brushing. Cleaning should be done by dampening the brake components with a fine mist of water, then wiping the brake components clean with a dampened cloth. Dispose of cloth and all residue containing asbestos fibers in an impermeable container with the appropriate label. Follow practices prescribed by the Occupational Safety and Health Administration (OSHA) and the Environmental Protection Agency (EPA) for the handling, processing, and disposing of dust or debris that may contain asbestos fibers.

BRAKE CALIPER

REMOVAL & INSTALLATION

See Figure 5.

1. Before servicing the vehicle, refer to the Precautions Section.
2. Remove the tire and wheel assembly.
3. If the caliper is being replaced:
a. Secure the pedal in the depressed position. Use a pedal jack.
b. Clean the brake caliper thoroughly.
c. Remove the protective cap from the bleed nipple.
d. Install a plastic hose on the nipple.
e. Open the bleed nipple. Collect the brake fluid in a container. Shut the bleed nipple.
f. Loosen the brake hose approximately half a turn.
4. Remove the brake caliper and brake pads.
5. Unscrew the brake caliper from the brake hose.
6. Drain the remaining brake fluid.

To install:

7. Clean the sliding pins using a steel brush. Lubricate the brake pad friction surfaces. Insert the locating pins into the rubber sleeves. The pins should slide into the sleeves easily.

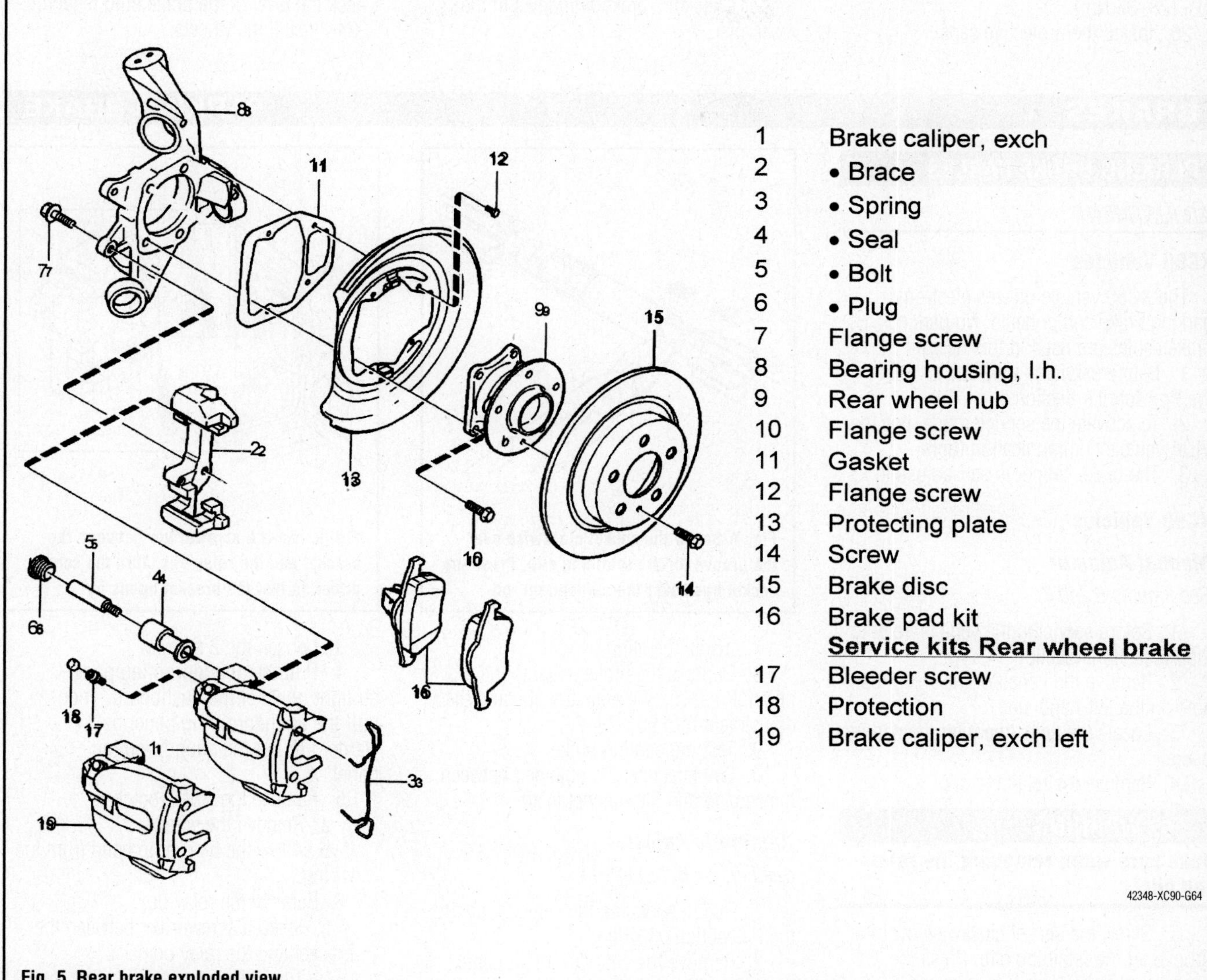

Fig. 5 Rear brake exploded view

8. Clean and install the brake pads and brake caliper.
9. Tighten the locating pins to 44 ft. lbs. (60 Nm).
10. Tighten the brake hose to 13 ft. lbs. (18 Nm).

WARNING

The brake hose must not be twisted.

11. Fill and bleed the brake system.
12. Depress the brake pedal a few times. Check the level of the brake fluid reservoir.

BRAKE PADS

REMOVAL & INSTALLATION

See Figure 4.

1. Before servicing the vehicle, refer to the Precautions Section.
2. Remove the tire and wheel assembly.
3. Remove the pad retaining spring carefully so as not to deform it.
4. Remove the protective caps from the two locating pins.
5. Remove the locating pins, using a 7mm hex socket.
6. Remove the brake caliper from the holder.
7. Remove the brake pads.
8. Hang brake caliper from a steel wire from the front spring so as not to damage brake hose.

➡Do not depress the brake pedal while the brake pads are removed.

9. Clean and check the brake caliper and dust cover.
10. Clean and check the brake pad mating surfaces in the brake caliper and caliper holder.
11. Check piston dust boot.

➡If the dust boot is damaged, dirt may have penetrated the cylinder. If this is the case, the caliper must be replaced.

12. Check brake disc friction surfaces.

To install:

13. Press the piston back into the cylinder on the brake caliper.
14. Check that the dust cover is correctly positioned.
15. Clean the sliding pins using a steel brush. Lubricate the brake pad friction surfaces.
16. Insert the locating pins into the rubber sleeves. The pins should slide into the sleeves easily.
17. Install new brake pads.
18. Install the brake caliper.

19. Tighten the locating pins to 20–26 ft. lbs. (28–35 Nm).

20. Install the protective caps.

21. Install the securing spring.

22. Check the brake fluid level in the reservoir.

23. Depress the brake pedal a few times. Check the level of the brake fluid reservoir.

24. Install the wheels.

PARKING BRAKE CABLES

ADJUSTMENT

XC60 Vehicles

The XC60 vehicle utilizes electronic parking brake components. No parking brake cables are used in this design.

1. Before servicing the vehicle, refer to the Precautions Section.
2. To activate the service mode, use the VIDA vehicle communication tools.
3. The brake caliper is self-adjusting.

XC90 Vehicles

Manual Adjuster

See Figures 6 and 7.

1. Before servicing the vehicle, refer to the Precautions Section.
2. Remove the panel for the center console on the left-hand side.
3. Locate the adjustment for the parking brake.
4. Remove the retaining clip.

⁂ WARNING

Take care when removing the retaining clip.

5. Screw the socket clockwise over the groove for the retaining clip. Press the socket back over the adjustment rod.
6. Screw the socket clockwise so that the groove for the clip emerges.

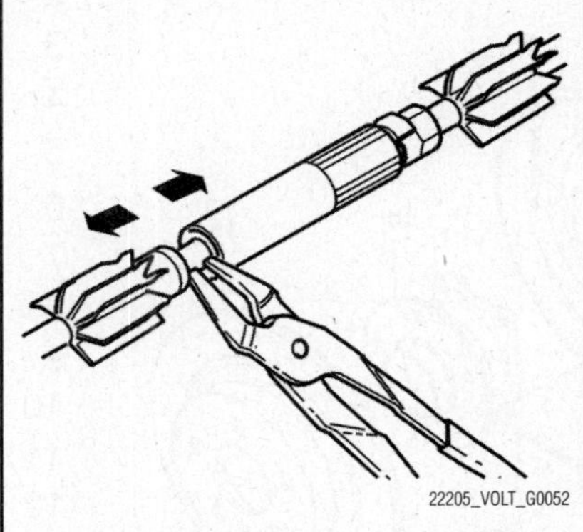

Fig. 7 Screw the socket clockwise over the groove for the retaining clip. Press the socket back over the adjustment rod

7. Install the clip.
8. Depress the brake pedal to the first notch. Press out the adjustment using the adjustment rod: 951-2947.
9. Test the parking brake.
10. Full effect can be obtained between the second and fifth ratchet teeth.

Automatic Adjuster

See Figures 8 through 11.

1. Before servicing the vehicle, refer to the Precautions Section.
2. Remove the soundproofing panels under the driver's side of the dash.

➡The soundproofing panel sits in grooves at the pedal box.

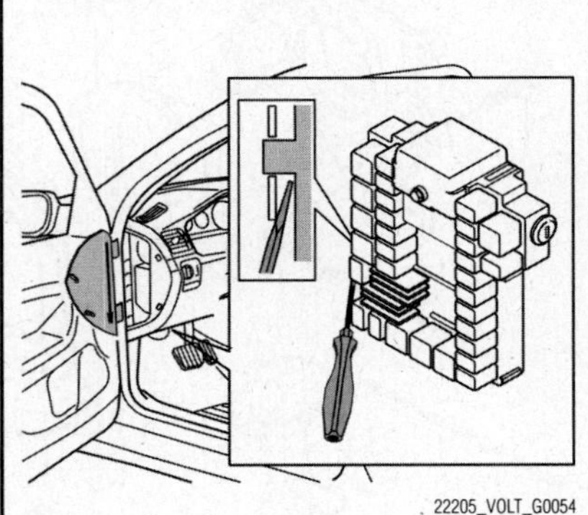

Fig. 9 Insert a screwdriver between the bracket and the relay box. Turn the screwdriver so that the bracket opens out

3. Loosen the 2 screws.
4. Pull the soundproofing panel straight down at the dashboard. Then pull the soundproofing panel backwards. Lift out the soundproofing panel.
5. Remove the OBD2 bracket.
   a. Remove the screws.
   b. Allow the bracket to hang from the wiring.
6. Remove the relay box.
   a. Insert a screwdriver between the bracket and the relay box.
   b. Turn the screwdriver so that the bracket opens out.
   c. At the same time, pull the relay box

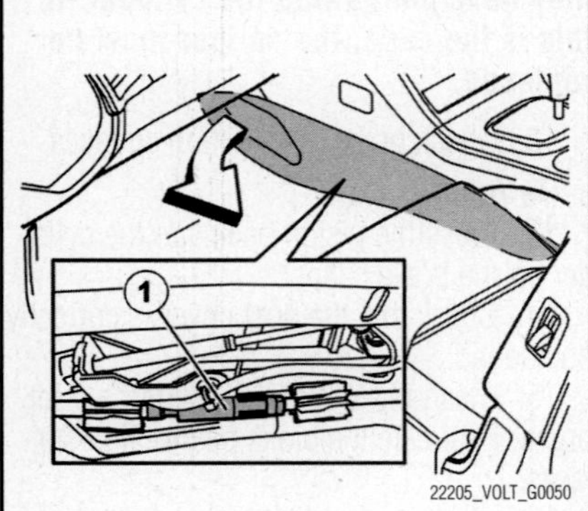

Fig. 6 Remove the panel for the center console on the left-hand side and locate the adjustment for the parking brake (1)

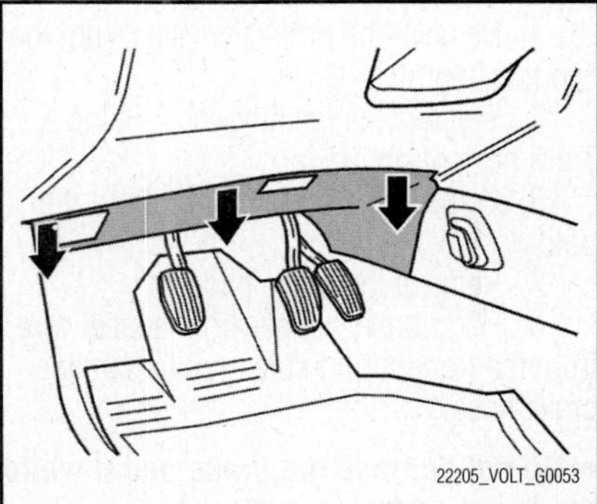

Fig. 8 Pull the soundproofing panel straight down at the dashboard. Then pull the soundproofing panel backwards and lift out

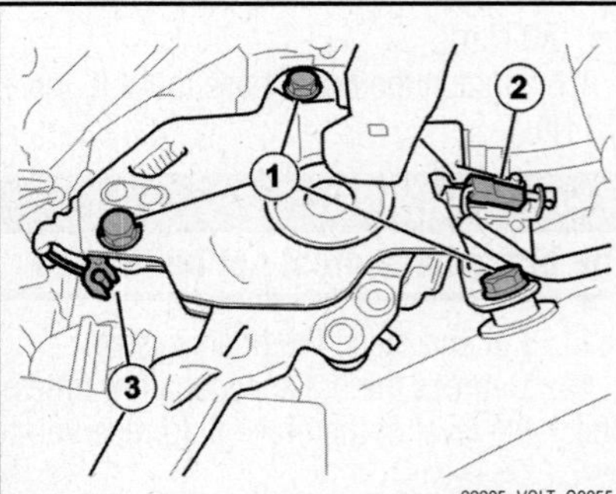

Fig. 10 Remove the pedal (1) from the body, screws, and pull/turn it diagonally backwards/inwards. Remove the wiring (2) for the pedal switch. Remove the disengagement cable (3) for the pedal

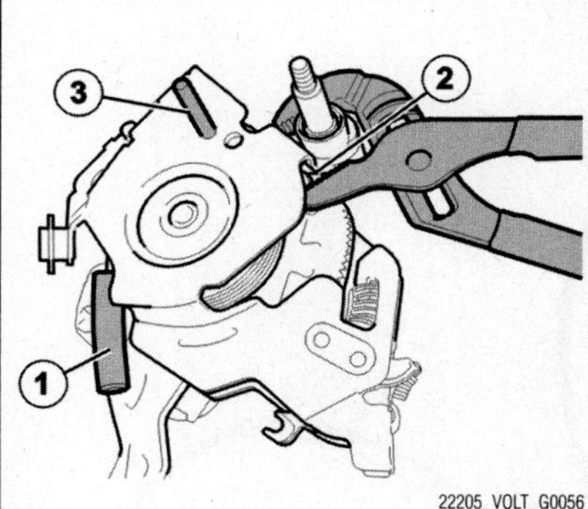

22205_VOLT_G0056

Fig. 11 Install a hose with an inner diameter of 5mm on the end of the friction spring (1). Open the friction spring so that the primary cable runs freely. Use a pipe wrench to push back the primary cable mounting (2). Insert a 6.5mm locking pin into the hole in the pedal (3) (it must pass through the bracket, cable pulley, pedal, and the other bracket)

out of the bracket towards the underside of the dashboard.

d. Lift the relay box off the bracket.

e. Pull the relay box downward under the dashboard.

7. Remove the parking brake pedal.

a. Remove the pedal from the body, screws, and pull/turn it diagonally backwards/inwards.

b. Remove the wiring for the pedal switch.

c. Remove the disengagement cable for the pedal.

8. Reset the parking brake to the zero position.

a. Install a hose with an inner diameter of 5mm on the end of the friction spring.

b. Open the friction spring so that the primary cable runs freely. Use a pipe wrench to push back the primary cable mounting.

c. Insert a 6.5mm locking pin into the hole in the pedal (it must pass through the bracket, cable pulley, pedal and the other bracket).

9. Resetting the parking brake.

a. Press the primary cable mounting back into place.

b. Remove the locking pin. Reset the primary cable mounting to the operating position.

c. Remove the hose from the friction spring.

10. Install the parking brake pedal.

11. Install the disconnecting cable for the pedal.

12. Install the cables for the switch before the pedal has been turned in.

13. Install the parking brake pedal and tighten the M8 screws to 18 ft. lbs. (24 Nm).

14. Check the function of the parking brake.

15. Press down and release the pedal 5 times.

16. Install the relay box on the bracket. Press the relay box forward so that the catches engage in the bracket and a click is heard.

17. Install the OBD2 bracket.

18. Install the soundproofing panel.

PARKING BRAKE SHOES

REMOVAL & INSTALLATION

XC60 Vehicles

See Figures 12 and 13.

1. Before servicing the vehicle, refer to the Precautions Section.

2. Remove the rear disc brake caliper assembly.

➡Before removing the brake disc rotor, make a chalk marking by the bolts to aid in reassembly.

3. Remove the brake rotor.

4. Remove the shoe hold spring by turning the pin to coincide with the hole of the spring cap.

5. Remove the return spring.

6. Disconnect the electrical connector from the actuator.

7. Remove the parking brake actuator.

8. Remove the parking brake shoes.

➡Complete the removal and installation on one side of the vehicle at a time. Use the other side as a reference.

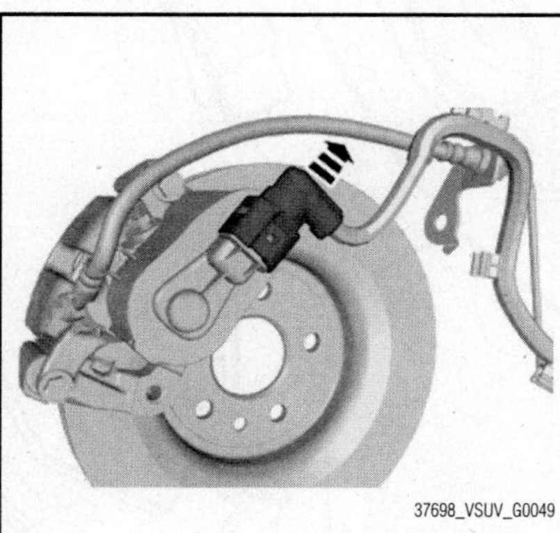
37698_VSUV_G0049

Fig. 12 Disconnect the electrical connector from the actuator—XC60 vehicles

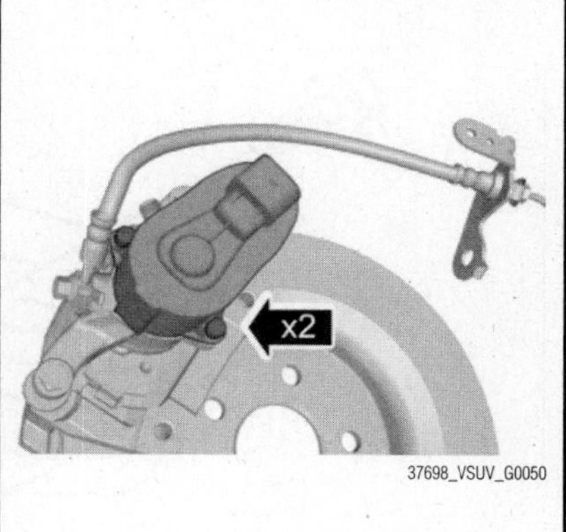

37698_VSUV_G0050

Fig. 13 Remove the parking brake actuator—XC60 vehicles

To install:

9. Apply brake grease to the return spring and areas of movement on the mechanism, but do not apply grease to the brake shoe material.

10. Install the upper return spring and brake shoes.

11. Turn the adjuster in a counter clockwise direction and install.

12. Install the lower return spring.

13. Install the shoe hold spring with a brake pliers.

14. Install the disc brake and then align the marks while tightening the screw.

15. Check for proper operation of the parking brake assembly. Make adjustments as needed.

XC90 Vehicles

See Figures 14 and 15.

1. Before servicing the vehicle, refer to the Precautions Section.

2. Remove rear disc brake caliper assembly.

➡Before removing the brake disc rotor, make a chalk marking by the bolts to aid in reassembly.

3. Remove the rotor.

4. Remove the shoe hold spring by turning the pin to coincide with hole of spring cap.

5. Remove the return spring.

6. Disconnect the cable end from the trailing shoe.

7. Remove the parking brake shoes.

➡Complete the removal and installation on one side of the vehicle at a time using the other side as a reference.

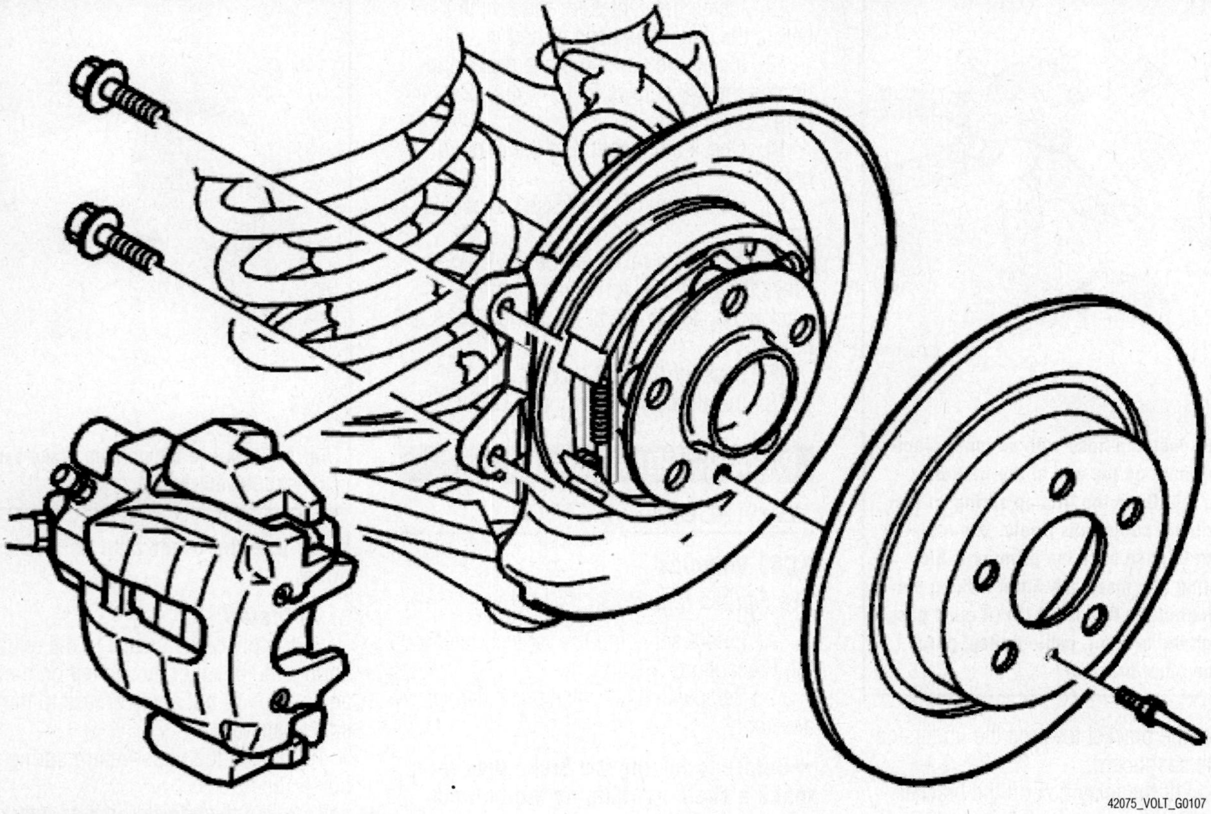

Fig. 14 Exploded view of parking brake assembly

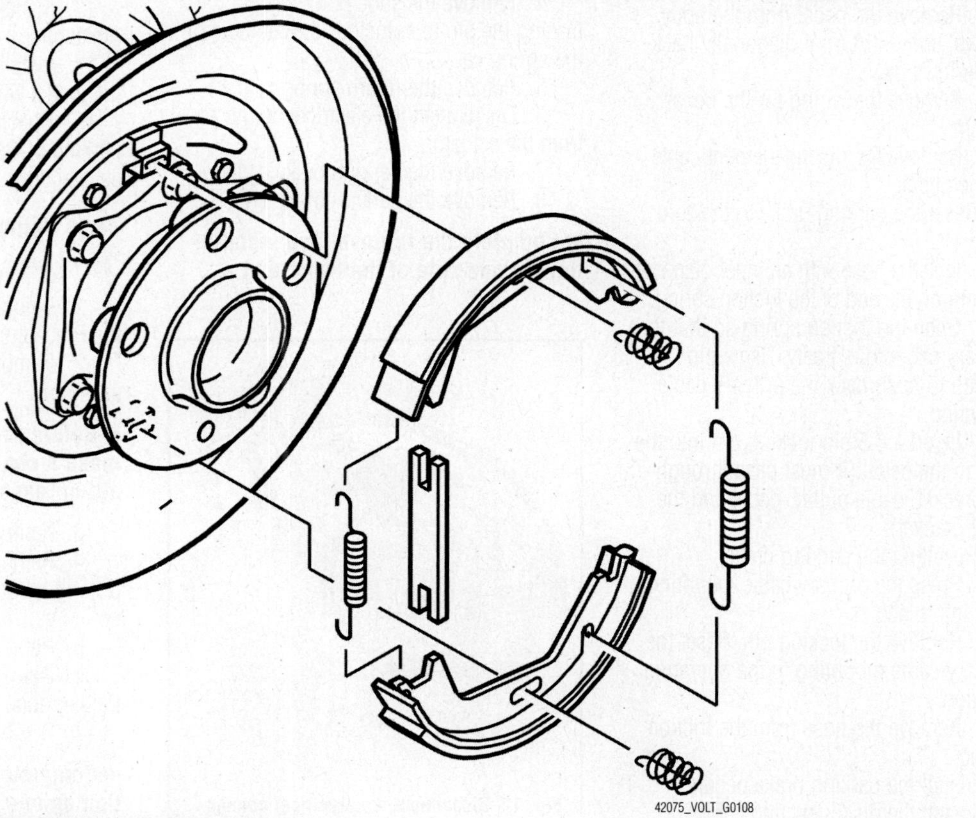

Fig. 15 Exploded view of parking brake shoes and return springs

To install:

8. Install the parking brake cable to the operating lever.
9. Apply brake grease to return spring and areas of movement on the mechanism, but do not apply grease to the brake shoe material.
10. Install the upper return spring and brake shoes.
11. Turn the adjuster in counter clockwise direction and install.
12. Install the lower return spring.
13. Install the shoe hold spring with a pliers.
14. Install the brake disc and then align the mark while tightening the screw.
15. Install the caliper.

CHASSIS ELECTRICAL — AIR BAG (SUPPLEMENTAL RESTRAINT SYSTEM)

GENERAL INFORMATION

**** CAUTION**

These vehicles are equipped with an air bag system. The system must be disarmed before performing service on, or around, system components, the steering column, instrument panel components, wiring and sensors. Failure to follow the safety precautions and the disarming procedure could result in accidental air bag deployment, possible injury and unnecessary system repairs.

SERVICE PRECAUTIONS

Disconnect and isolate the battery negative cable before beginning any airbag system component diagnosis, testing, removal, or installation procedures. Allow system capacitor to discharge for two minutes before beginning any component service. This will disable the airbag system. Failure to disable the airbag system may result in accidental airbag deployment, personal injury, or death.

Do not place an intact undeployed airbag face down on a solid surface. The airbag will propel into the air if accidentally deployed and may result in personal injury or death.

When carrying or handling an undeployed airbag, the trim side (face) of the airbag should be pointing towards the body to minimize possibility of injury if accidental deployment occurs. Failure to do this may result in personal injury or death.

Replace airbag system components with OEM replacement parts. Substitute parts may appear interchangeable, but internal differences may result in inferior occupant protection. Failure to do so may result in occupant personal injury or death.

Wear safety glasses, rubber gloves, and long sleeved clothing when cleaning powder residue from vehicle after an airbag deployment. Powder residue emitted from a deployed airbag can cause skin irritation. Flush affected area with cool water if irritation is experienced. If nasal or throat irritation is experienced, exit the vehicle for fresh air until the irritation ceases. If irritation continues, see a physician.

Do not use a replacement airbag that is not in the original packaging. This may result in improper deployment, personal injury, or death.

The factory installed fasteners, screws and bolts used to fasten airbag components have a special coating and are specifically designed for the airbag system. Do not use substitute fasteners. Use only original equipment fasteners listed in the parts catalog when fastener replacement is required.

During, and following, any child restraint anchor service, due to impact event or vehicle repair, carefully inspect all mounting hardware, tether straps, and anchors for proper installation, operation, or damage. If a child restraint anchor is found damaged in any way, the anchor must be replaced. Failure to do this may result in personal injury or death.

Deployed and non-deployed airbags may or may not have live pyrotechnic material within the airbag inflator.

Do not dispose of driver/passenger/curtain airbags or seat belt tensioners unless you are sure of complete deployment. Refer to the Hazardous Substance Control System for proper disposal.

Dispose of deployed airbags and tensioners consistent with state, provincial, local, and federal regulations.

After any airbag component testing or service, do not connect the battery negative cable. Personal injury or death may result if the system test is not performed first.

If the vehicle is equipped with the Occupant Classification System (OCS), do not connect the battery negative cable before performing the OCS Verification Test using the scan tool and the appropriate diagnostic information. Personal injury or death may result if the system test is not performed properly.

Never replace both the Occupant Restraint Controller (ORC) and the Occupant Classification Module (OCM) at the same time. If both require replacement, replace one, then perform the Airbag System test before replacing the other.

Both the ORC and the OCM store Occupant Classification System (OCS) calibration data, which they transfer to one another when one of them is replaced. If both are replaced at the same time, an irreversible fault will be set in both modules and the OCS may malfunction and cause personal injury or death.

If equipped with OCS, the Seat Weight Sensor is a sensitive, calibrated unit and must be handled carefully. Do not drop or handle roughly. If dropped or damaged, replace with another sensor. Failure to do so may result in occupant injury or death.

If equipped with OCS, the front passenger seat must be handled carefully as well. When removing the seat, be careful when setting on floor not to drop. If dropped, the sensor may be inoperative, could result in occupant injury, or possibly death.

If equipped with OCS, when the passenger front seat is on the floor, no one should sit in the front passenger seat. This uneven force may damage the sensing ability of the seat weight sensors. If sat on and damaged, the sensor may be inoperative, could result in occupant injury, or possibly death.

DISARMING THE SYSTEM

1. Before servicing the vehicle, refer to the Precautions Section.
2. Turn the ignition switch to **OFF**.
3. Disconnect the negative battery cable and isolate it from accidental reconnection. Insulate the cable end with high-quality electrical tape or a similar non-conductive wrapping.
4. Wait at least 3 minutes for the system capacitor to discharge before performing any service. The airbag system is designed to retain enough voltage to deploy the airbag for a short period of time after the battery has been disconnected.

➡DTC's will be lost when the negative battery cable is disconnected.

There are several reasons for disabling the SIR system, such as repairs to the SIR system or servicing a component near or attached to an SIR component. There are several ways to disable the SIR system depending on what type of service is being performed.

- If the vehicle was involved in an accident with an air bag deployment: Disconnect the negative battery cable
- When performing SIR diagnostics: Follow the appropriate SIR service manual diagnostic procedure(s)
- When removing or replacing an SIR component or a component attached to an SIR component: Disconnect the negative battery cable
- If the vehicle is suspected of having shorted electrical wires: Disconnect the negative battery cable
- When performing electrical diagnosis on components other than the SIR system: Remove the SIR/Airbag fuse(s) when indicated by the diagnostic procedure to disable the SIR system

ARMING THE SYSTEM

1. Before servicing the vehicle, refer to the Precautions Section.
2. Be sure the ignition switch is in the **OFF** position.
3. Install the fuses, if removed.
4. Connect the negative battery cable.

⁂ CAUTION

As an added precaution, make sure no one is in the vehicle when reconnecting the negative battery cable.

5. To confirm proper system operation, turn the ignition switch to the **ON** position. The SRS indicator light should light for at least 7 seconds and then go off.
6. If the AIR BAG warning indicator does not operate as described, perform a diagnostic system check.

CLOCKSPRING CENTERING

See Figures 16 and 17.

⁂ CAUTION

Models equipped with a Supplemental Restraint System (SRS), use an inflatable air bag. Whenever working near any of the SRS components, such as the impact sensors, the air bag module, steering column, and instrument panel, disable the SRS.

1. Before servicing the vehicle, refer to the Precautions.
2. Turn the contact reel (clockspring) clockwise to the limit position.
3. Turn the contact reel counter-clockwise 2 entire turns.
4. Turn the contact reel counter-clockwise further until the screw hole is at the "one o'clock" position.

➡**On later models, the yellow marking must also be visible in the window.**

5. Install the screw.
6. The contact reel (clockspring) is now reset and locked.

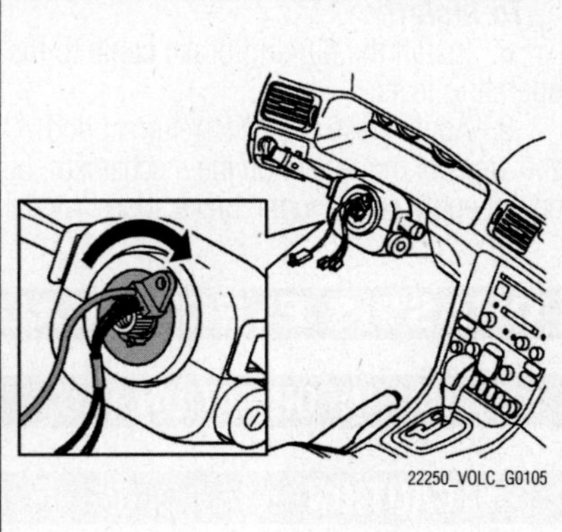

Fig. 16 Turn the contact reel counter-clockwise 2 entire turns

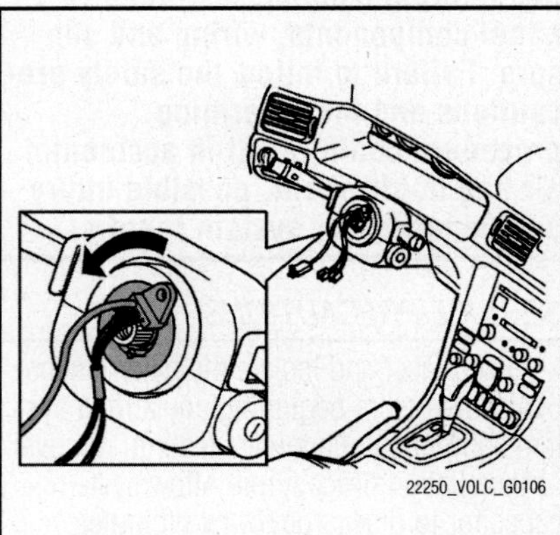

Fig. 17 Turn counter-clockwise further until the screw hole is at the "one o'clock" position

DRIVE TRAIN

HALFSHAFT

REMOVAL & INSTALLATION

Front

See Figures 18 through 21.

1. Before servicing the vehicle, refer to the Precautions Section.
2. Remove the front wheel.
3. Remove the wheel speed sensor and wiring bracket.
4. Remove the brake hose bracket.
5. Remove the stabilizer bar link.
6. Remove the splash guards.
7. Remove the lower ball joint.
8. Remove the hub retainer nut.
9. Pull the hub off of the stub shaft.
10. Pry the inner joint out of the transaxle and remove the axle halfshaft.

To install:

➡**Use new fasteners for assembly.**

11. Install the axle halfshaft so that the circlip is felt to seat in the retainer groove.
12. Guide the stub shaft into the hub.
13. On the right side, tighten the 2 M8 bolts to 18 ft. lbs. (24 Nm).
14. Install the hub retainer nut and tighten the nut to 26 ft. lbs. (35 Nm) plus 90°.

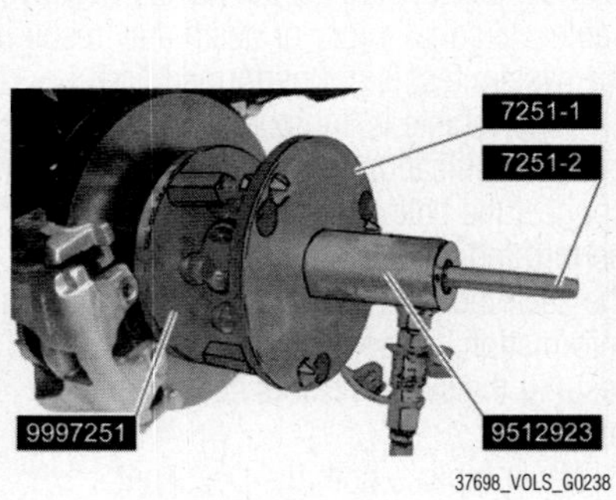

Fig. 18 Using special tools to pull the hub off of the stub shaft

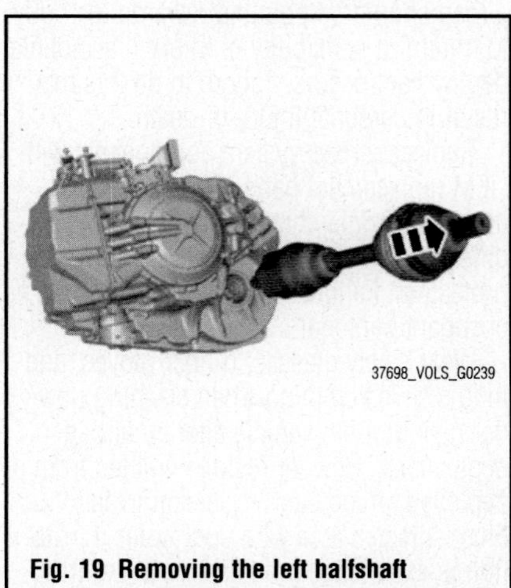

Fig. 19 Removing the left halfshaft

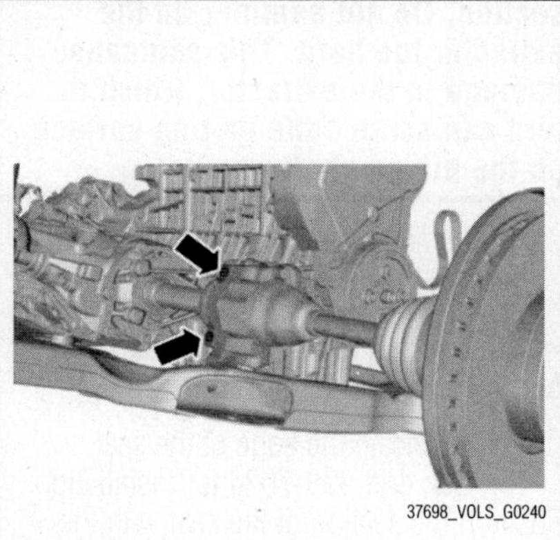

Fig. 20 Removing the right halfshaft (1 of 2)

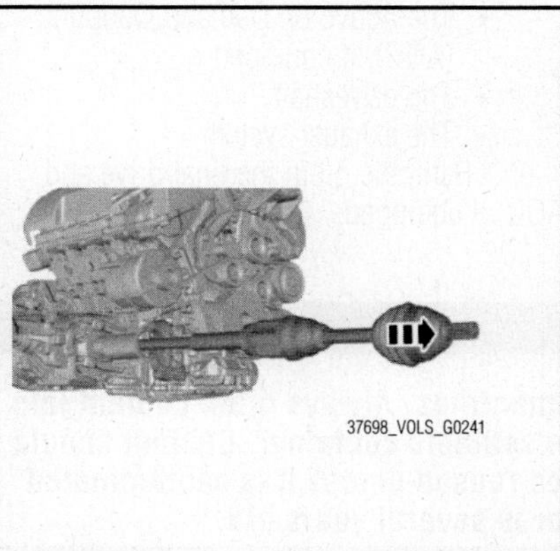

Fig. 21 Removing the right halfshaft (2 of 2)

15. Install the lower ball joint.
16. Install the splash guards.
17. Install the stabilizer bar link.
18. Install the brake hose bracket.
19. Install the wheel speed sensor and wiring bracket.
20. Install the front wheel.

Rear

See Figure 22.

1. Before servicing the vehicle, refer to the Precautions Section.
2. Remove the following items:
   - Rear wheel on relevant side
   - Coil spring
   - Wheel knuckle rear to body
   - Halfshaft to wheel hub
   - Lower arm rear to sub-frame
   - Rear stabilizer bar link to lower stabilizer bar
   - Rear shock absorber to wheel knuckle
3. Remove the rear halfshaft using Special Tool: 999-7160.

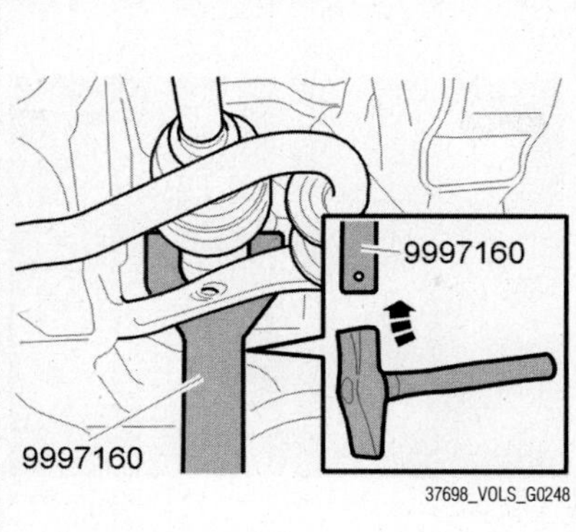

Fig. 22 Using Special Tool: 999-7160 to wedge out the rear halfshaft

To install:

4. Install the halfshaft.
5. Install the following items:
   - Rear shock absorber to wheel knuckle
   - Rear stabilizer bar link to lower stabilizer bar
   - Lower arm rear to sub-frame
   - Halfshaft to wheel hub. Tighten the nut to 26 ft. lbs. (35 Nm) plus 90°
   - Wheel knuckle rear to body
   - Coil spring
   - Wheel

REAR AXLE HOUSING

REMOVAL & INSTALLATION

See Figures 23 and 24.

1. Before servicing the vehicle, refer to the Precautions Section.
2. Raise and safely support the vehicle.
3. Remove the rear sub-frame.
   a. Remove the rear anti-roll bar.
   b. Remove the rear springs.
   c. Remove the driveshaft (propeller shaft) from the flange on the final drive.
   d. Remove the rear sub-frame.

⁂ WARNING

Make sure no components are stuck when removing the sub-frame.

4. Disconnect the upper control arm.
5. Remove the halfshafts.
6. Remove the final drive.

To install:

7. Installation is the reverse of removal.
8. Tighten bolts/nuts to specification as follows:
   - Final drive to rear sub-frame: 59 ft. lbs. (80 Nm)
   - Rear sub-frame to body: 82 ft. lbs. (110 Nm)

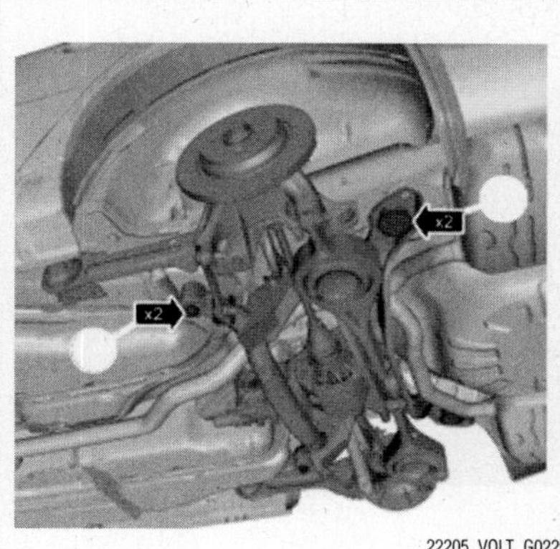

Fig. 23 View of rear sub-frame attaching bolts

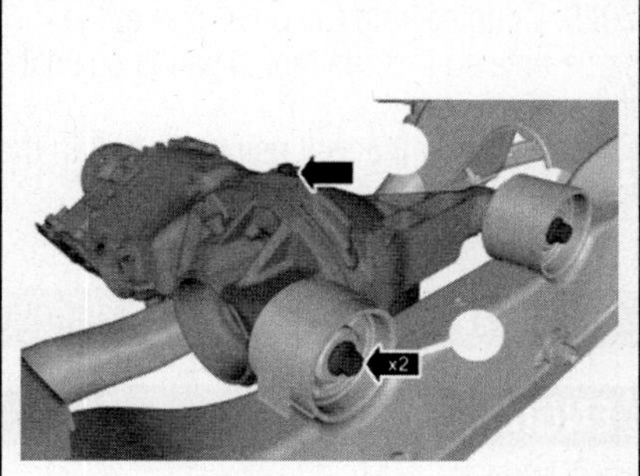

Fig. 24 View of final drive attaching bolts

9. Fill the final drive with oil. Check and adjust level.

PINION OIL SEAL

REMOVAL & INSTALLATION

See Figures 25 and 26.

1. Before servicing the vehicle, refer to the Precautions Section.
2. Remove or disconnect the following:
   - The exhaust system
   - The driveshaft.
   - The Active On Demand Coupling (AOC), if equipped

➡There are two parts to the pinion seal. Use extractor 999-7023 with care. The bolt and inner socket in the extractor must be unscrewed when tapping on the extractor to remove the pinion seal.

3. Tap the extractor tool 999-7023 onto the seal so that the flat end is against the seal.

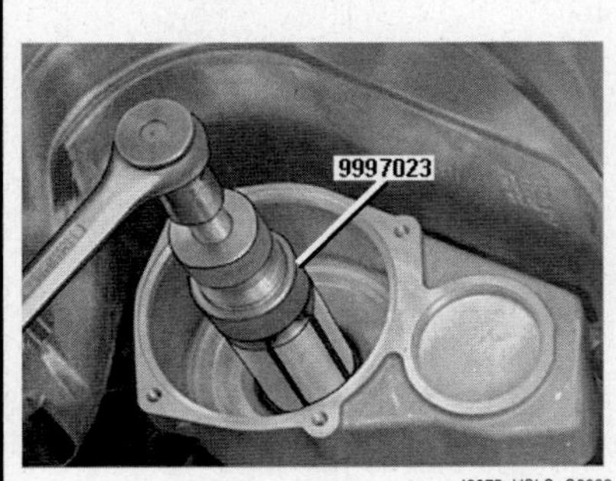

42075_VOLC_G0020

Fig. 25 Using extractor 999-7023 to remove the pinion seal

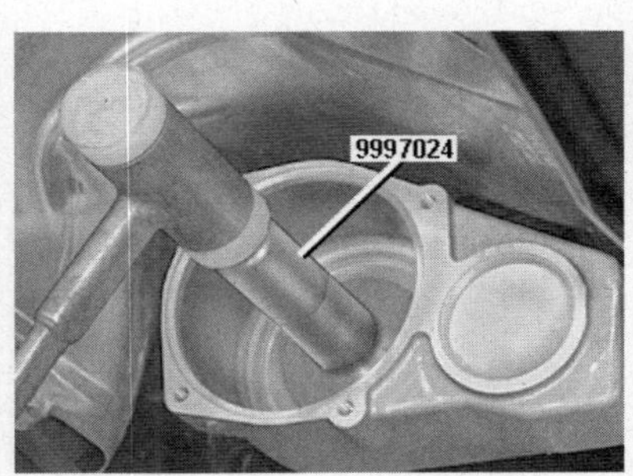

42075_VOLC_G0021

Fig. 26 Using drift 999-7024 to install the pinion seal

4. Tighten the inner socket of tool 999-7023. Counter-hold the outer part at the same time so that the tool expands against the seal.
5. Remove the seal using the bolt in the extractor.

WARNING

Check that no seal residue is left in the final drive. If the inner section of the seal remains in place, tap in the extractor again and pull out the inner section. Do not hammer on the extractor too hard. This can cause damage in the extractor, which in turn can scratch the mating surface on the pinion shaft.

6. Remove the pinion seal.

To install:

➡The seal consists of two sections, but is installed as one unit.

7. Lubricate the edge of the seal.
8. Use drift 999-7024 for installation. Position the section of the seal with the largest outer diameter against the drift.
9. Tap in the seal until the head of the drift is against the final drive housing.
10. Install or connect the following:
    - The Active on Demand Coupling (AOC), if equipped
    - The driveshaft
    - The exhaust system
11. Refill the oil in the final drive and AOC, if equipped.

ENGINE COOLING

ENGINE COOLANT

BLEEDING

CAUTION

Never open, service, or drain the radiator or cooling system when hot; serious burns can occur from the steam and hot coolant. When draining engine coolant, keep in mind that cats and dogs are attracted to ethylene glycol antifreeze and could drink any that is left in an uncovered container or in puddles on the ground. This may prove fatal in sufficient quantities. Always drain coolant into a sealable container. Coolant should be reused unless it is contaminated or is several years old.

WARNING

Use engine coolant at a concentration that meets the environmental conditions in which the vehicle is driven, otherwise engine damage could occur. The engine has aluminum parts and must be protected by an ethylene-glycol-based coolant to prevent corrosion and freezing.

WARNING

Do not use coolants containing Alcohol, Methanol, Borate or Silicate. These coolants could damage the cooling system. Use only soft (demineralized) water in the coolant mixture. Water that contains minerals will cut down on coolant effectiveness.

1. Before servicing the vehicle, refer to the Precautions Section.
2. Run the engine to operating temperature until the thermostat opens.
3. Carefully open the coolant reservoir cap after the system cools.
4. Top off the coolant, as necessary.

DRAIN & REFILL PROCEDURE

See Figures 27 through 29.

CAUTION

Never open, service, or drain the radiator or cooling system when hot; serious burns can occur from the steam and hot coolant. When draining engine coolant, keep in mind that cats and dogs are attracted to ethylene glycol antifreeze and could drink any that is left in an uncovered container or in puddles on the ground. This may prove fatal in sufficient quantities. Always drain coolant into a sealable container. Coolant should be reused unless it is contaminated or is several years old.

WARNING

Use engine coolant at a concentration that meets the environmental conditions in which the vehicle is driven, otherwise engine damage could occur. The engine has aluminum parts and must be protected by an ethylene-glycol-based coolant to prevent corrosion and freezing.

WARNING

Do not use coolants containing Alcohol, Methanol, Borate or Silicate. These coolants could damage the cooling system. Use only soft (demineralized) water in the coolant mixture. Water that contains minerals will cut down on coolant effectiveness.

1. Before servicing the vehicle, refer to the Precautions Section.
2. Remove the engine splashguard.
3. Release the cooling system pressure. Cover the coolant expansion tank cap with a thick cloth and remove the cap.

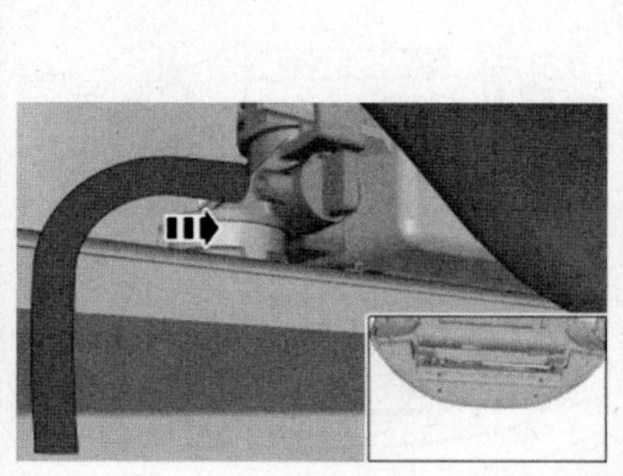

Fig. 27 Open the radiator drain valve and drain the coolant

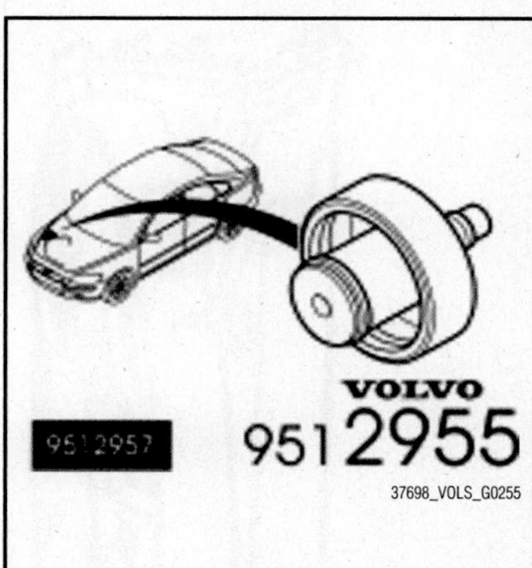

Fig. 28 View of coolant reservoir cap, Special Tool: 951-2955

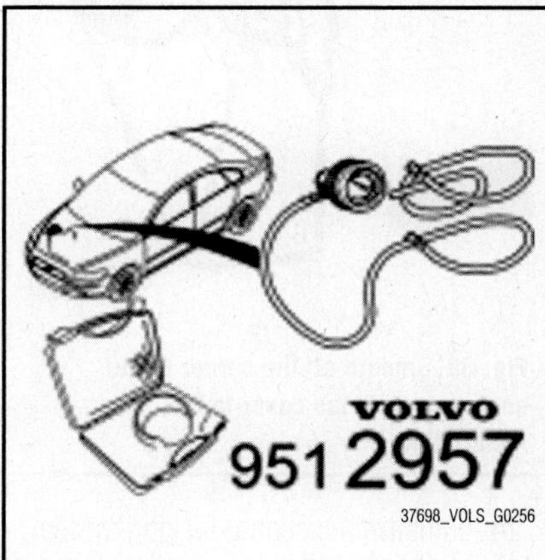

Fig. 29 View of coolant reservoir filling tool, Special Tool: 951-2957

➡Be prepared to collect escaping fluid.

4. Open the radiator drain valve and collect the coolant into a container.
5. Let the system drain completely.

To install:

6. Tighten the radiator drain plug securely.
7. Install the splash shield.
8. Fill the system with the specified quantity and strength of coolant using Special Tools: 951-2955 and 951-2957.
9. Run the engine to operating temperature until the thermostat opens. Top off the coolant, as necessary.

ENGINE FAN

REMOVAL & INSTALLATION

⁂ CAUTION

Never open, service or drain the radiator or cooling system when hot; serious burns can occur from the steam and hot coolant. Also, when draining engine coolant, keep in mind that cats and dogs are attracted to ethylene glycol antifreeze and could drink any that is left in an uncovered container or in puddles on the ground. This will prove fatal in sufficient quantities. Always drain coolant into a sealable container. Coolant should be reused unless it is contaminated or is several years old.

XC60 Vehicles

See Figures 30 and 31.

1. Before servicing the vehicle, refer to the Precautions Section.
2. Disconnect the negative battery cable.
3. Disconnect the electrical connection to the engine fan.
4. Remove the attaching screws.
5. Lift the engine fan assembly up to remove from the vehicle.
6. Installation is the reverse of the removal procedure.

XC90 Vehicle

See Figures 32 through 38.

1. Before servicing the vehicle, refer to the Precautions Section.
2. Disconnect the negative battery cable.
3. Drain the coolant, as necessary.
4. Remove the air cleaner inlet pipe.
   a. Remove the bolts.
   b. Lift the air cleaner inlet pipe out.
5. Remove the protective plate.

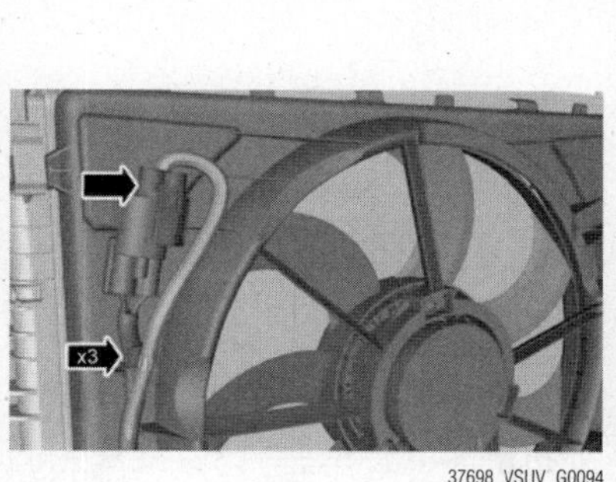

Fig. 30 Disconnect the electrical connection to the engine fan

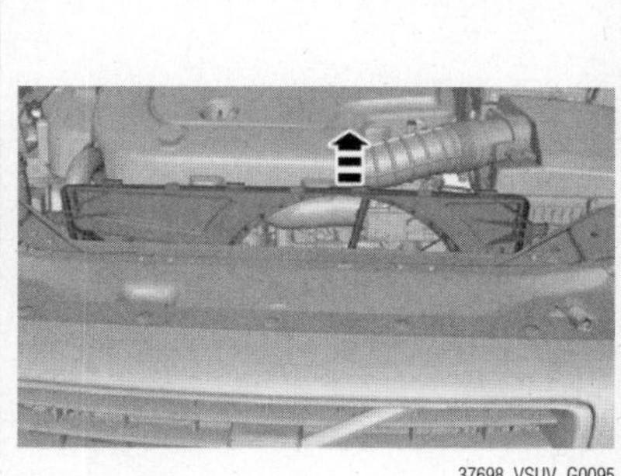

Fig. 31 Lift the engine fan assembly up to remove

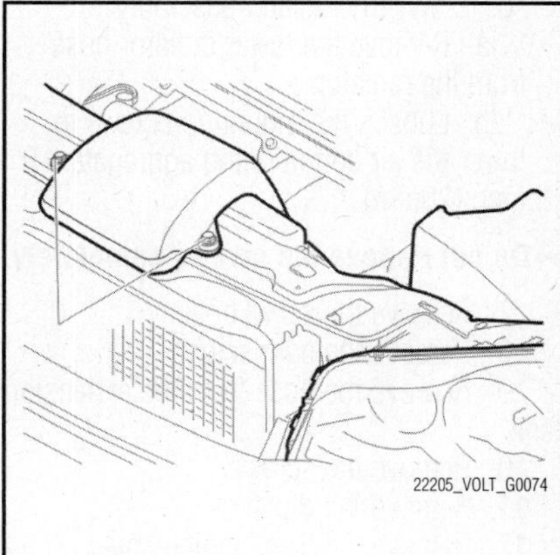

Fig. 32 Removing the air cleaner inlet pipe

➡There is a guide sleeve on the upper mounting for the plate. This must be lifted slightly so that the panel can be slid forward.

Fig. 33 Removing the protective plate

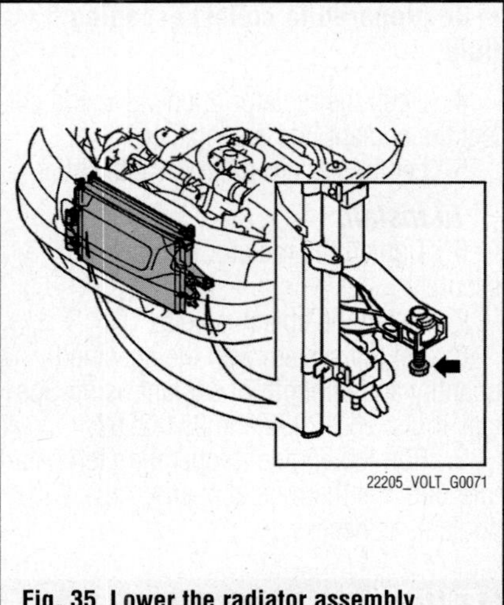
Fig. 35 Lower the radiator assembly

Fig. 37 Removing the hose from the expansion tank

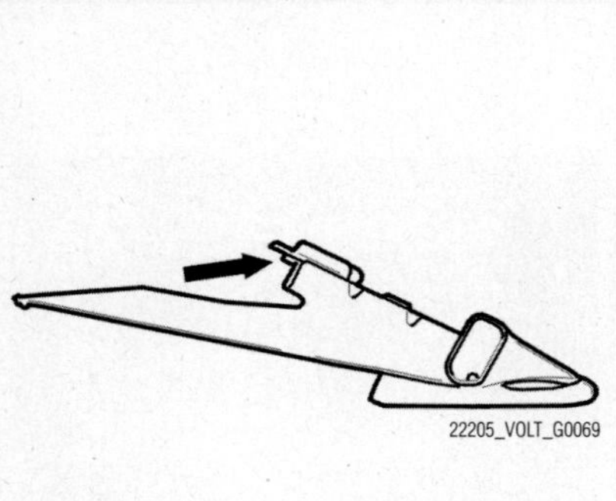
Fig. 34 There is a guide sleeve on the upper mounting for the plate. This must be lifted slightly so that the panel can be slid forward

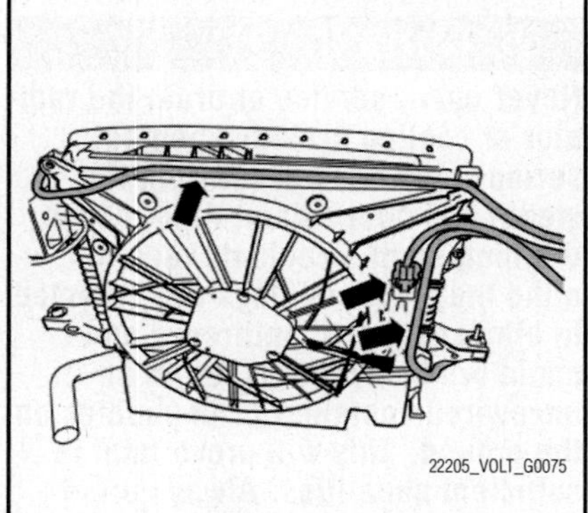
Fig. 36 Removing the hose from the expansion tank

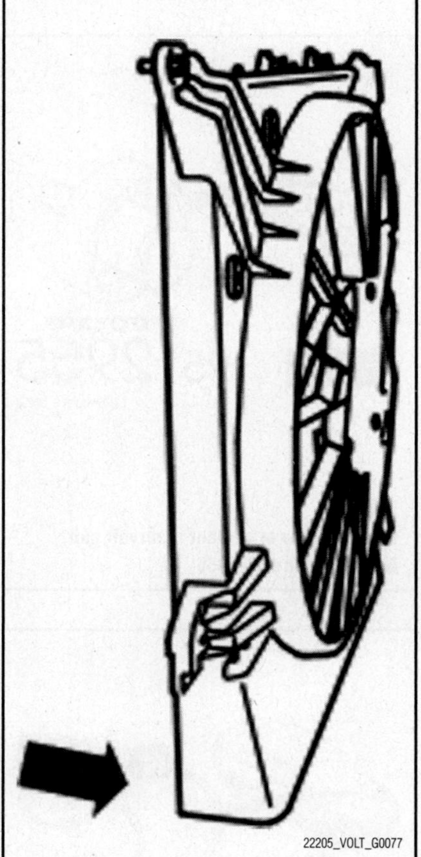
Fig. 38 Smooth off the corner of the engine cooling fan cover to facilitate installation

6. Lower the radiator assembly.
   a. Remove the lower radiator hose from the radiator.
   b. Loosen the mounting screws to lower the air conditioning aggregate 0.9 inch (20mm).

➡Do not remove the screws completely.

7. Remove the servo hose.
8. Remove the connector.
9. Remove the hose from the expansion tank.
10. Remove the screws.
11. Remove the dip stick.
12. Remove the front engine cover.
13. Lift off the engine cooling fan.

To install:

14. Install the engine cooling fan.

WARNING

Ensure that no hoses are trapped when installing the engine cooling fan.

➡Smooth off the corner of the engine cooling fan cover to facilitate installation.

15. Install the M6 screws and tighten to 89 inch lbs. (10 Nm).
16. Install the servo hose.
17. Install the connector.
18. Install the hose from the expansion tank.
19. Install the air cleaner intake pipe.
20. Install the M6 screws and tighten to 89 inch lbs. (10 Nm).
21. Install the radiator assembly. Tighten the M8 mounting screws to 18 ft. lbs. (24 Nm).
22. Install the protective plate.
    a. Move the protective plate up in the bumper cover.
    b. Press forward until the mounting brackets enter the sub-frame.
    c. Fit the M10 bolts and tighten to 37 ft. lbs. (50 Nm).
23. Connect the negative battery cable.
24. Initialize the central locking system, interior lighting, and power windows using the VIDA communications tool.

➡When the battery is disconnected, the engine may need to run for a few minutes before it runs smoothly.

RADIATOR

REMOVAL & INSTALLATION

XC60 Vehicle

See Figures 39 through 41.

CAUTION

Never open, service or drain the radiator or cooling system when hot; serious burns can occur from the steam and hot coolant. Also, when draining engine coolant, keep in mind that cats and dogs are attracted to ethylene glycol antifreeze and could drink any that is left in an uncovered container or in puddles on the ground. This will prove fatal in sufficient quantities. Always drain coolant into a sealable container. Coolant should be reused unless it is contaminated or is several years old.

1. Before servicing the vehicle, refer to the Precautions Section.
2. Remove the upper and lower screws attaching the front bumper cover.
3. Remove the front bumper cover.
4. Remove the engine cooling fan.
5. Drain the engine cooling system.

CAUTION

Be prepared to collect escaping fluid.

6. Remove the right headlight.
7. On turbocharged vehicles, detach the charge air cooler.
8. Remove the bolts connecting the A/C condenser to the radiator.
9. Remove the radiator bracket bolts.
10. Using Special Tool: 999-5463, lower the radiator from beneath the vehicle.

Fig. 39 Removing the front bumper cover

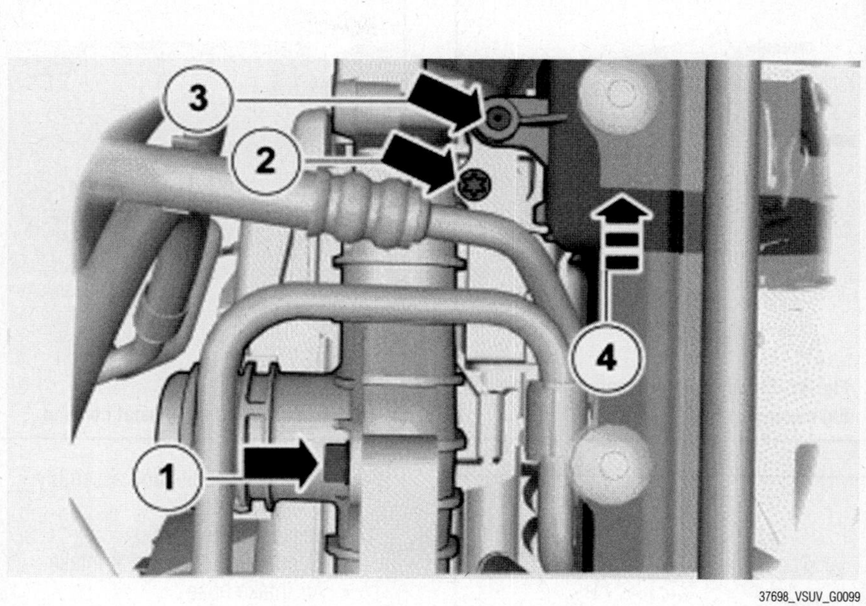

Fig. 40 Remove the bolts connecting the A/C condenser to the radiator

11. If replacing the radiator, remove any necessary components.

To install:

12. Installation is the reverse of the removal procedure.
13. Tighten the radiator-to-condenser bolts to 44 inch lbs. (5 Nm).
14. Tighten the M8 bolts to 18 ft. lbs. (24 Nm).

XC90 Vehicle

See Figures 42 and 43.

CAUTION

Never open, service or drain the radiator or cooling system when hot; serious burns can occur from the steam and hot coolant. Also, when draining engine coolant, keep in mind that cats and dogs are attracted to ethylene glycol antifreeze and could drink any that is left in an uncovered container or in puddles on the ground. This will prove fatal in sufficient quantities. Always drain coolant into a sealable container. Coolant should be reused unless it is contaminated or is several years old.

1. Before servicing the vehicle, refer to the Precautions Section.
2. Remove the engine cooling fan.
3. Remove the evacuation hose from the expansion tank.
4. Remove the bolts.
5. Remove the radiator.

To install:

6. Installation is the reverse of removal.

➡Ensure that the radiator is positioned correctly in the locating pins on top of the unit. Ensure that no hoses are trapped when installing the radiator.

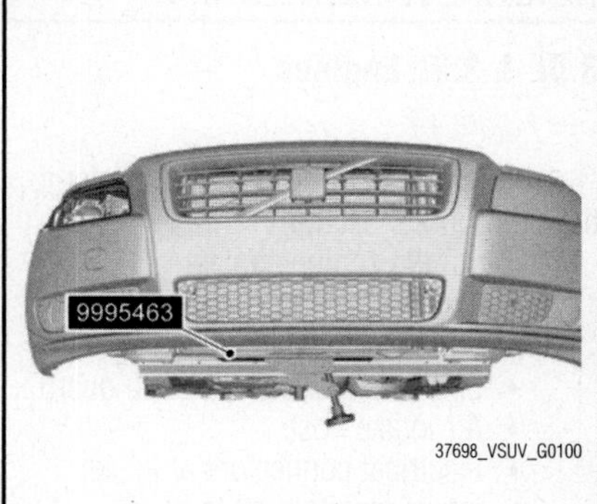

Fig. 41 Using Special Tool: 999-5463 to lower the radiator

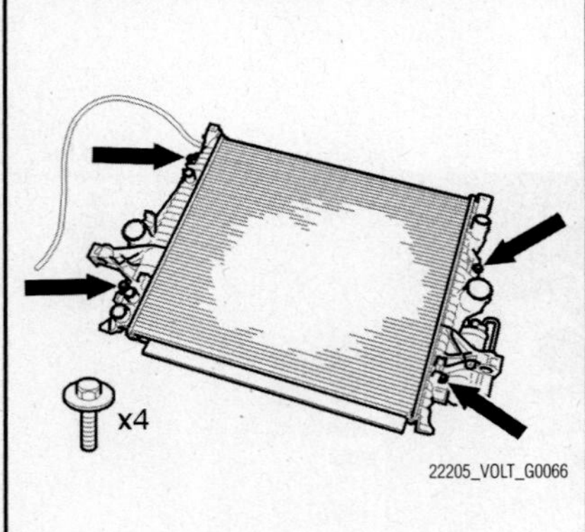

Fig. 42 Remove the evacuation hose from the expansion tank

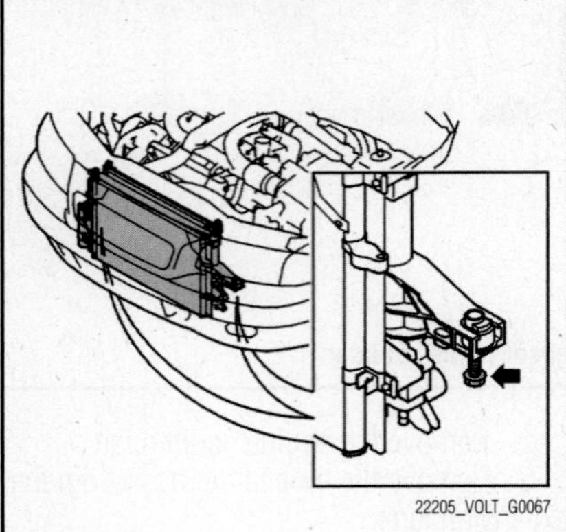

Fig. 43 Remove the radiator mounting bolts

7. Tighten the M6 screws to 89 inch lbs. (10 Nm).

THERMOSTAT

REMOVAL & INSTALLATION

3.0L & 3.2L Engines

See Figure 44.

1. Before servicing the vehicle, refer to the Precautions Section.
2. Drain the engine coolant.
3. Disconnect or remove the following:
   - Engine cover
   - Engine under cover splash guard
   - Air intake hose
   - Electrical connectors at intake
   - Intake manifold bolts
   - Intake manifold
   - Thermostat bolts and assembly

To install:

4. Disconnect or remove the following:

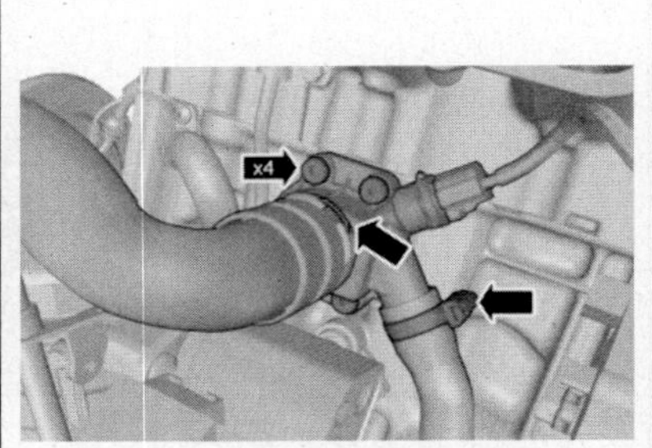

Fig. 44 Location of thermostat housing

   - Thermostat bolts and assembly
   - Intake manifold
   - Intake manifold bolts
   - Electrical connectors at intake
   - Air intake hose
   - Engine under cover splash guard
   - Engine cover
5. Install the engine coolant and bleed the cooling system.

4.4L Engine

See Figure 45.

1. Before servicing the vehicle, refer to the Precautions Section.
2. Raise and safely support the vehicle.
3. Drain the cooling system.
4. Remove the front engine cover.
5. Remove the thermostat housing bolts.
6. Remove the thermostat.

To install:

7. Install the thermostat.
8. Tighten the thermostat housing bolts to 89 inch lbs. (10 Nm).
9. Install the front engine cover.
10. Install engine coolant and bleed the cooling system.

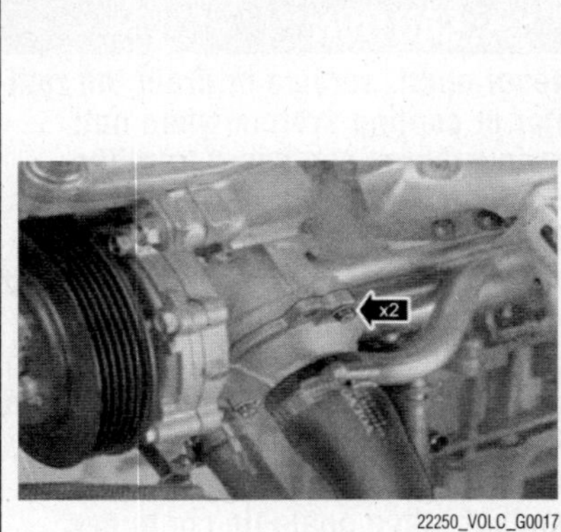

Fig. 45 Location of thermostat housing

WATER PUMP

REMOVAL & INSTALLATION

3.0L & 3.2L Engines

See Figure 46.

1. Before servicing the vehicle, refer to the Precautions Section.
2. Drain the cooling system.
3. Remove the air hose connection at the air filter assembly.
4. Disconnect the Mass Air Flow (MAF) sensor and remove the air filter box, if needed.
5. Remove the accessory drive belt.
6. Remove the power steering pressure hose and nuts holding the hose retainer brackets.
7. Plug the hose connector to reduce fluid loss.
8. Remove the power steering pump and set aside.
9. Plug the pressure hose to reduce fluid loss.
10. Remove the bolts to the water pump.
11. Remove the water pump by carefully taping on the pump shaft with a plastic mallet.

To install:

12. Clean the engine surface for the water pump.
13. Install the water pump and tighten the mounting bolts to 89 inch lbs. (10 Nm).
14. Make sure that the coupling spring clicks into place on the bonded part of the water pump.

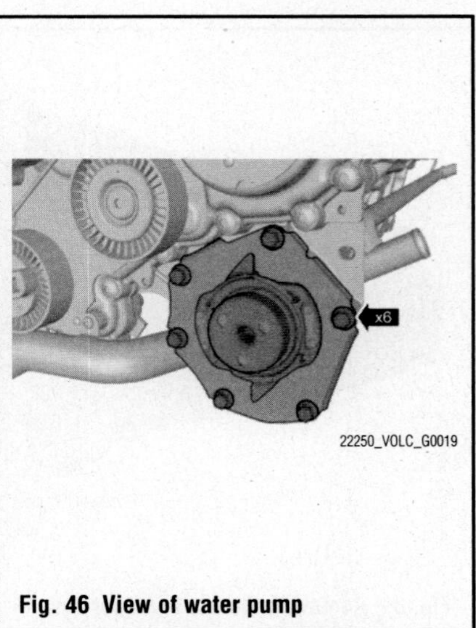

Fig. 46 View of water pump

15. Always use a new guide pin when installing.

16. Install power steering pump making sure that alignment is correct. Tighten the mounting bolts to 28 ft. lbs. (24 Nm).

17. Install the power steering pressure hose and tighten to 22 ft. lbs. (30 Nm). Make sure the brackets are aligned and tighten the retaining nuts to 18 ft. lbs. (24 Nm).

18. Install the accessory drive belt.

19. Install the air filter box and reconnect intake air hose.

20. Connect the MAF connector.

21. Install antifreeze and bleed the cooling system.

22. Top off the power steering fluid, bleed the system.

23. Check for leaks on the coolant system and power steering system.

4.4L Engine

See Figures 47 and 48.

1. Before servicing the vehicle, refer to the Precautions Section.
2. Raise and safely support the vehicle.
3. Drain the cooling system.
4. Loosen the water pump pulley bolts.
5. Remove the accessory drive belt.

Fig. 47 Remove the water pump pulley bolts

6. Completely remove the water pump pulley bolts.
7. Remove the water pump mounting bolts.

To install:

➡Make sure that the mating surfaces are clean and free of foreign objects.

8. Install the water pump and tighten the mounting bolts to 89 inch lbs. (10 Nm).

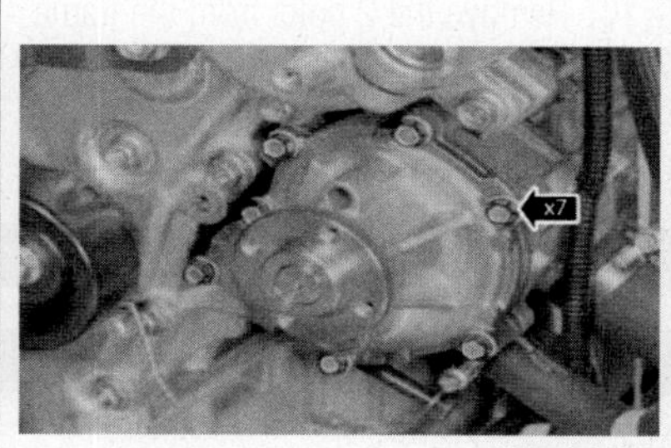

Fig. 48 View of water pump removal

9. Loosely install the water pump pulley and bolts.
10. Install the accessory drive belt.
11. Tighten the water pump pulley mounting bolts to 89 inch lbs. (10 Nm).
12. Install fresh engine coolant and bleed the cooling system.
13. Start the engine and check cooling system for leaks.

ENGINE ELECTRICAL

CHARGING SYSTEM

ALTERNATOR

REMOVAL & INSTALLATION

3.0L & 3.2L Engines

See Figure 49.

1. Before servicing the vehicle, refer to the Precautions Section.
2. Remove the negative battery cable.
3. Remove the intake manifold.
4. Remove the alternator regulator connector.
5. Remove the alternator B+ terminal.
6. Remove the alternator mounting bolts.
7. Remove the alternator from the vehicle.

To install:

8. Install the alternator into position.
9. Install the alternator mounting bolts. Tighten to 18 ft. lbs. (24 Nm).
10. Install the alternator B+ terminal. Tighten to 11 ft. lbs. (15 Nm).
11. Install the alternator regulator connector.
12. Install the intake manifold.
13. Connect the negative battery cable.

4.4L Engine

See Figure 50.

1. Before servicing the vehicle, refer to the Precautions Section.
2. Disconnect the negative battery cable.
3. Remove the drive belt.
4. Remove the rear engine cover.
5. Raise and safely support the vehicle.
6. Remove the alternator B+ terminal and regulator connector.
7. Remove the alternator mounting bolts.
8. Remove the right-hand halfshaft.

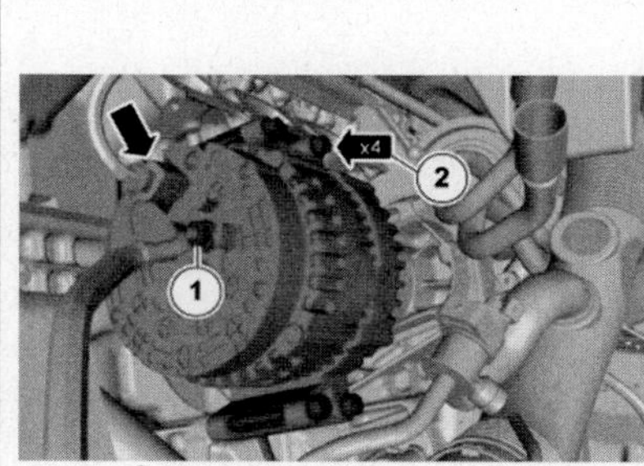

Fig. 49 Alternator removal—3.0L and 3.2L engines

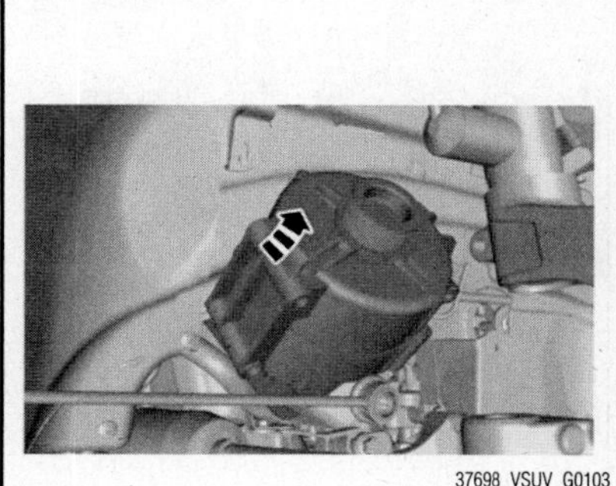

Fig. 50 Alternator removal—4.4L engine

9. Remove the right front stabilizer link from the strut.

10. Remove the 2 bolts from the frame bracket.

11. Remove the alternator.

➡**Ensure that the components are not bent.**

To install:

12. Installation is the reverse of the removal procedure.

13. Tighten the alternator mounting bolts to 18 ft. lbs. (24 Nm).

14. Tighten the alternator B+ terminal to 11 ft. lbs. (15 Nm).

ENGINE ELECTRICAL — IGNITION SYSTEM

FIRING ORDER

3.0L & 3.2L Engines

Firing order for the 6-cylinder engine: 1–5–3–6–2–4.

4.4L Engine

Firing order for the 8-cylinder engine: 1–8–4–3–6–5–7–2.

IGNITION COILS

REMOVAL & INSTALLATION

3.0L & 3.2L Engines

See Figures 51 and 52.

1. Before servicing the vehicle, refer to the Precautions Section.

2. Remove or disconnect the following:
   - Engine cover
   - Ignition coil electrical connector

➡**Seal the open ends of pipes.**

   - Ignition coil mounting bolt
   - Carefully pull coil up and out

To install:

3. Align the coil and press it down.

4. Install the ignition coil mounting bolt and tighten to 89 inch lbs. (10 Nm).

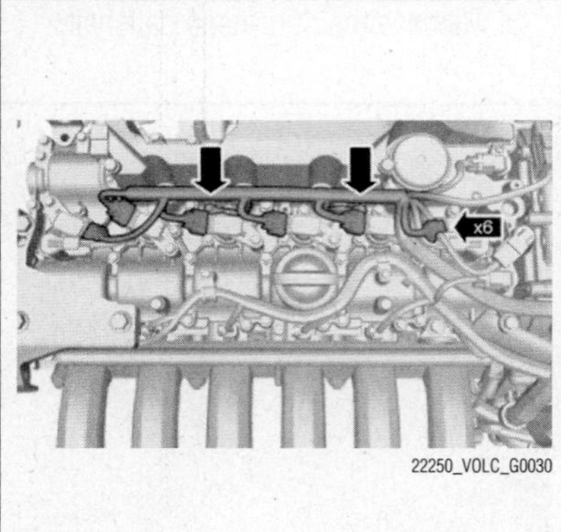

Fig. 51 Unplug the ignition coil electrical connectors

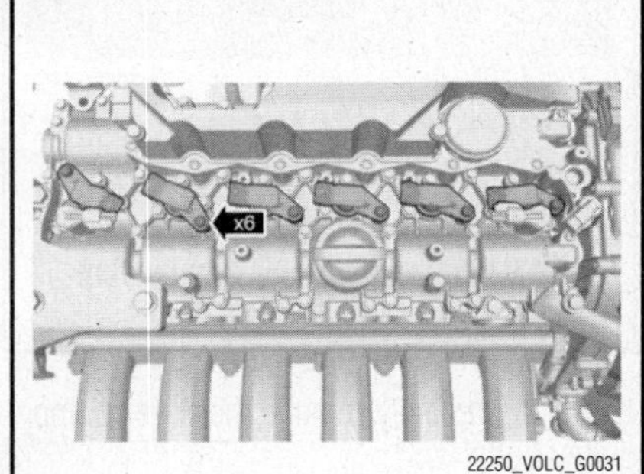
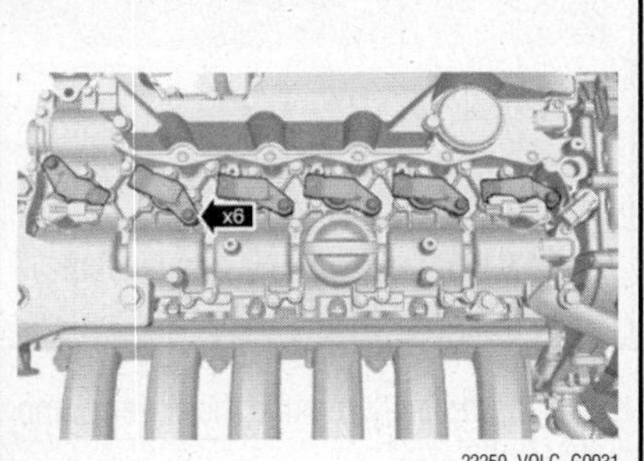

Fig. 52 Remove the ignition coil mounting bolts

5. Press in the connector until a click sound is heard.

6. Install the engine cover.

4.4L Engine

See Figure 53.

1. Before servicing the vehicle, refer to the Precautions Section.

2. Remove the left and right engine covers.

3. Remove the mounting bolt for the ignition coil.

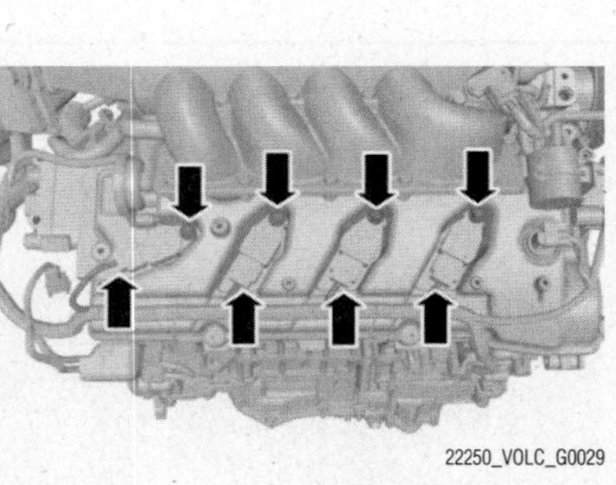

Fig. 53 Remove the mounting bolt for ignition coil

4. Lift up the ignition coil.

5. Remove the coil electrical connector.

6. Remove the ignition coil.

To install:

7. Installation is the reverse of the removal procedure.

8. Tighten the coil mounting bolt to 89 inch lbs. (10 Nm).

IGNITION TIMING

The ignition timing is controlled by the Engine Control Module (ECM). No adjustment is necessary or possible

All engines use a fixed ignition timing system. Basic ignition timing is not adjustable. All spark advance is determined by the Engine Control Module (ECM).

SPARK PLUGS

REMOVAL & INSTALLATION

3.0L & 3.2L Engines

See Figure 54.

1. Before servicing the vehicle, refer to the Precautions Section.

2. Remove the ignition coil.

3. Use an appropriate spark plug wrench and socket to remove the spark plug.

To install:

4. Install the spark plug and tighten to 18–21 ft. lbs. (25–28 Nm).

5. Install the ignition coil.

4.4L Engine

1. Before servicing the vehicle, refer to the Precautions Section.

2. Remove the ignition coil.

3. Use an appropriate spark plug wrench and socket to remove the spark plug.

To install:

4. Install the spark plug and tighten to 18–21 ft. lbs. (25–28 Nm).

5. Install the ignition coil.

Fig. 54 View of spark plugs with ignition coils removed

ENGINE ELECTRICAL

STARTING SYSTEM

STARTER

REMOVAL & INSTALLATION

3.0L & 3.2L Engines

See Figure 55.

1. Before servicing the vehicle, refer to the Precautions Section.
2. Disconnect the negative battery cable.
3. Raise the vehicle and remove the undercover splash guard.
4. Remove the battery positive cable from the starter solenoid.
5. Remove the starter impulse lead.
6. Remove the starter mounting bolts and the starter motor.

To install:

7. Install the starter motor and mounting bolts. Tighten the bolts to 37 ft. lbs. (50 Nm).
8. Install the starter impulse lead and tighten to 75 inch lbs. (9 Nm).
9. Install the battery positive cable to starter solenoid. Tighten the mounting nut to 97 inch lbs. (11 Nm).
10. Install the vehicle under cover splash guard.
11. Lower the vehicle and connect the negative battery cable.
12. Check for proper starter motor operation.

4.4L Engine

See Figures 56 and 57.

1. Before servicing the vehicle, refer to the Precautions Section.
2. Drain the engine cooling system.
3. Remove the air cleaner housing.
4. Remove the battery and battery box.

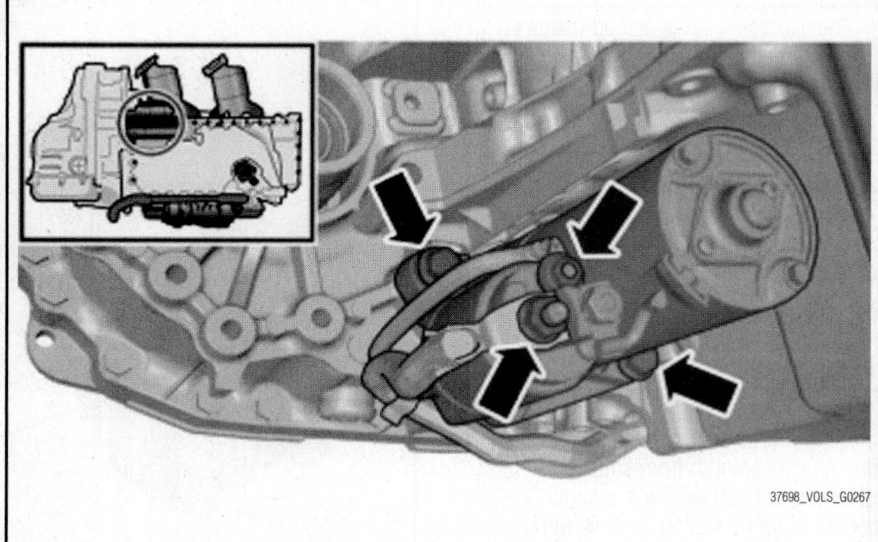

Fig. 55 Remove the starter bolts and the starter motor

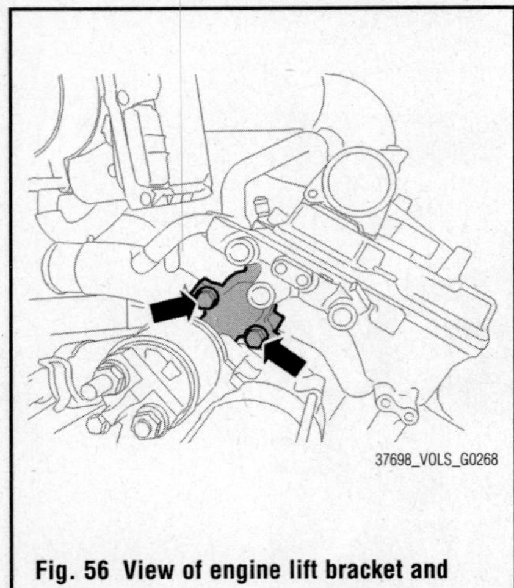

Fig. 56 View of engine lift bracket and bolts

5. Remove the battery positive cable from the starter solenoid.
6. Remove the starter impulse lead.

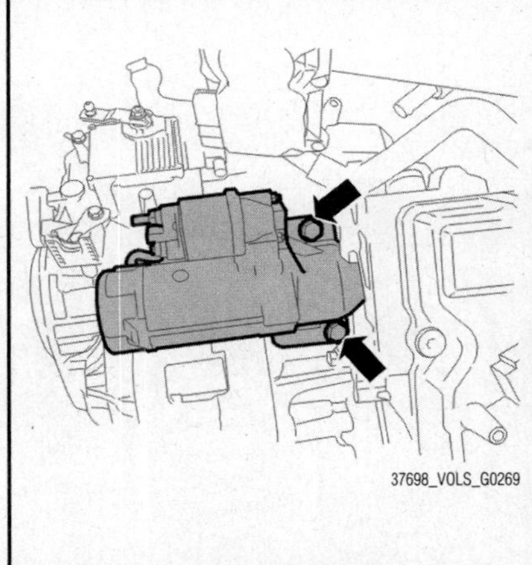

Fig. 57 Remove the starter bolts and the starter motor

7. Remove the coolant hose blocking access to starter mounting bolts.
8. Remove the engine lift bracket and bolts.
9. Remove the starter mounting bolts and the starter motor.

To install:

10. Install the starter motor and mounting bolts. Tighten the mounting bolts to 37 ft. lbs. (50 Nm).
11. Install the engine lift bracket and bolts. Tighten the bolts to 18 ft. lbs. (24 Nm).
12. Install the coolant hose that was removed.
13. Install the starter impulse lead.
14. Install the battery positive cable to starter solenoid. Tighten the cable mounting nut to 18 ft. lbs. (24 Nm).
15. Install the battery and battery box.
16. Install the air cleaner housin.
17. Fill the engine cooling system.

ENGINE MECHANICAL

➡Disconnecting the negative battery cable may interfere with the functions of the on board computer systems and may require the computer to undergo a relearning process, once the negative battery cable is reconnected.

ACCESSORY DRIVE BELT SYSTEM

ADJUSTMENT

The accessory drive belt adjustment is maintained by an automatic tensioner.

BELT ROUTINGS

3.0L & 3.2L Engines

See Figure 58.

4.4L Engine

See Figure 59.

INSPECTION

Inspect the drive belt for signs of glazing or cracking. A glazed belt will be perfectly smooth from slippage, while a good belt will have a slight texture of fabric visible. Cracks will usually start at the inner edge of the belt and run outward. All worn or damaged drive belts should be replaced immediately.

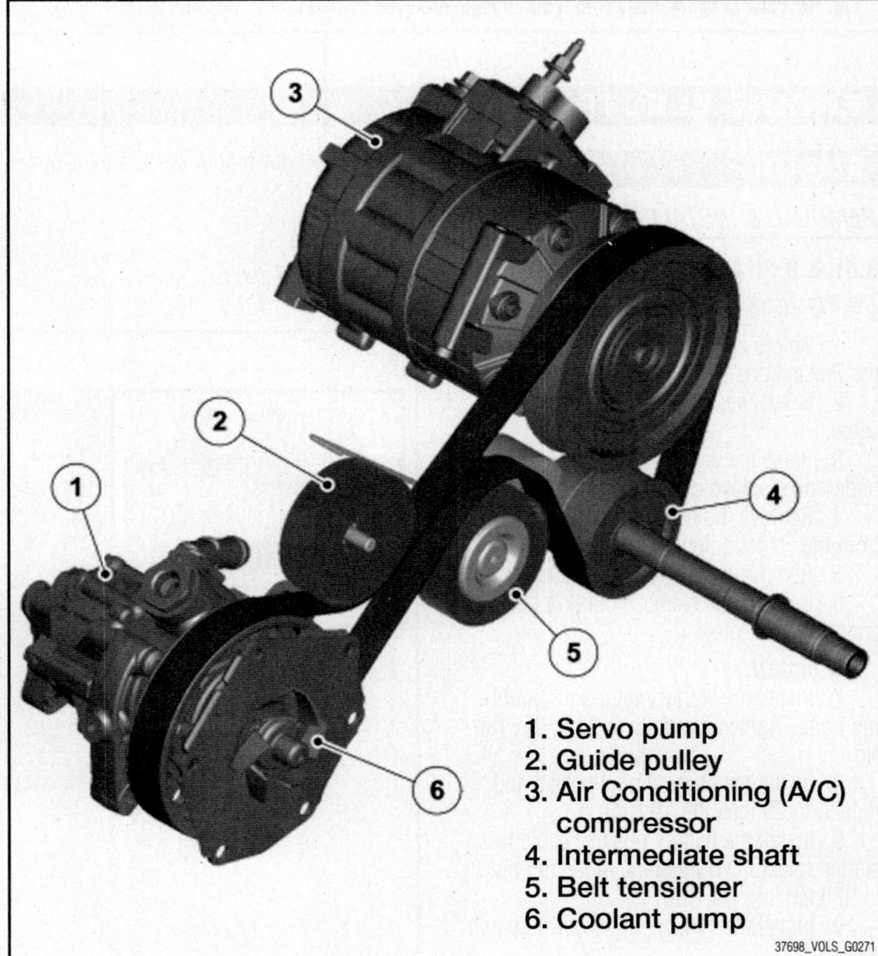

Fig. 58 Accessory drive belt routing—3.0L and 3.2L engines

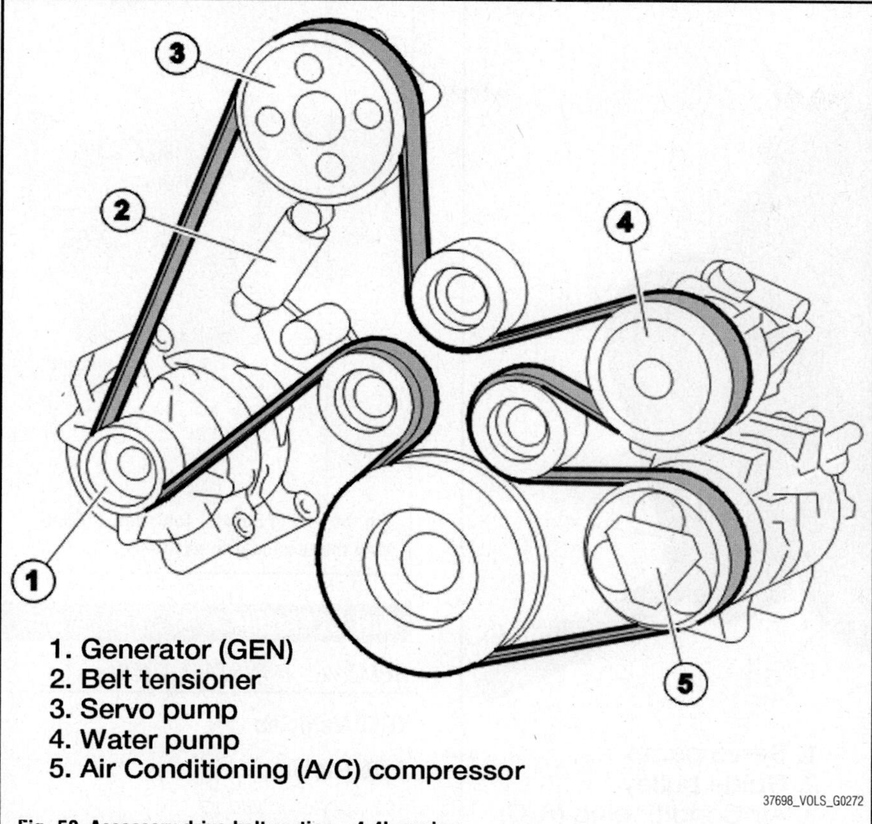

Fig. 59 Accessory drive belt routing—4.4L engine

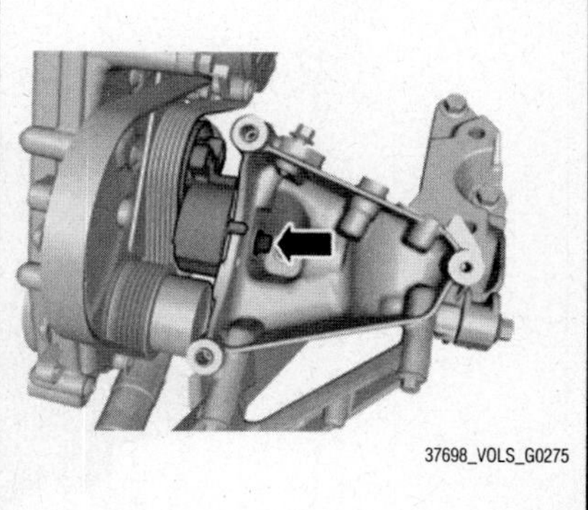

Fig. 62 Tensioner and mounting bolt shown

REMOVAL & INSTALLATION

Drive Belt

3.0L & 3.2L Engines

See Figures 60 through 64.

1. Before servicing the vehicle, refer to the Precautions Section.
2. Remove the engine cover.
3. Remove the battery and battery box.
4. Raise the vehicle and remove the engine under cover splash guard.
5. Remove the air intake clamp at the throttle body.
6. Lower the vehicle.
7. Remove the air intake at the air filter box.
8. Remove the air filter box.
9. Remove the power steering pressure line brackets at the A/C compressor.
10. Loosen the tensioner using a 19mm fixed wrench. Lock the tensioner in the loosened position using a 3mm pin.
11. Remove the engine support brackets at the A/C compressor.
12. Remove the power steering pump and set aside.
13. Remove the A/C compressor mounting bolts and line bracket retaining nuts. Do not remove the lines.
14. Remove the A/C compressor and set aside.
15. Remove the belt tensioner bolt.
16. Remove the drive belt. If needed, remove the belt tensioner bracket to remove the drive belt.

To install:

17. Installation is the reverse of the removal procedure.
18. Tighten the tensioner bolt to 18 ft. lbs. (24 Nm).
19. Tighten the A/C mounting bolts and bracket nuts to 18 ft. lbs. (24 Nm).
20. At installation, ensure that the

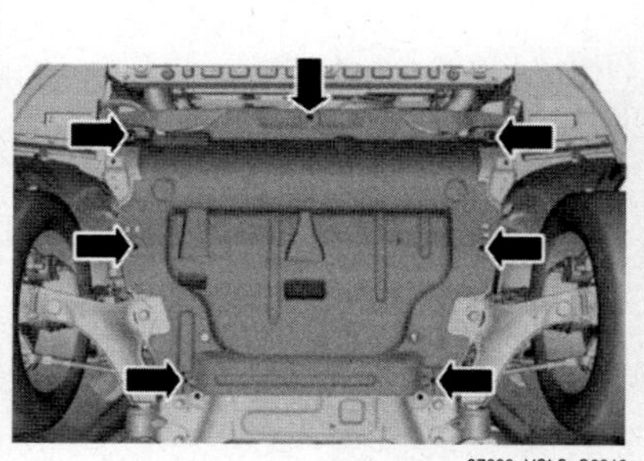

Fig. 60 Remove the splash guard from under the engine

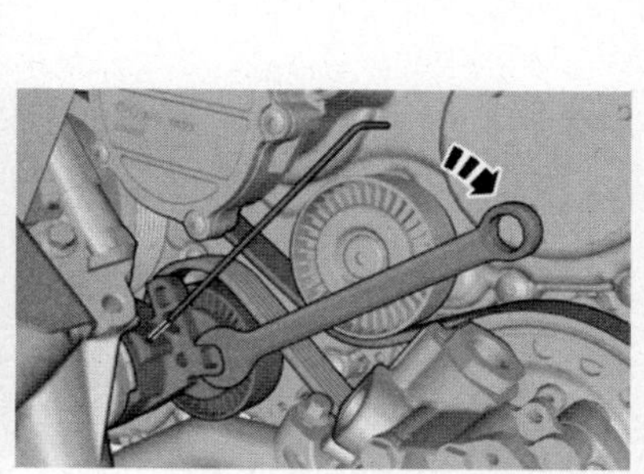

Fig. 61 Loosen the tensioner and lock it in position using a 3mm pin

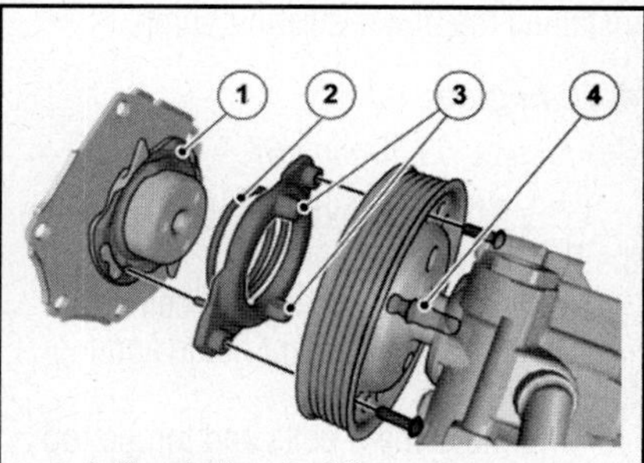

Fig. 63 Power steering pump and components

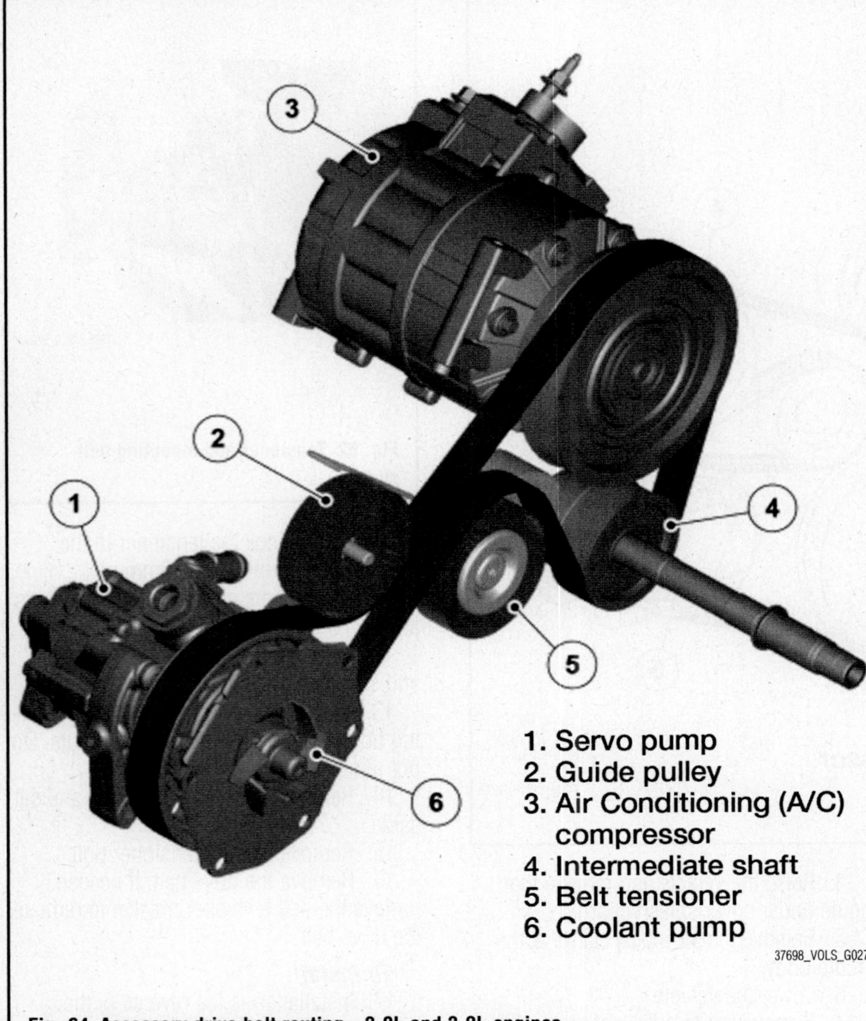

Fig. 64 Accessory drive belt routing—3.0L and 3.2L engines

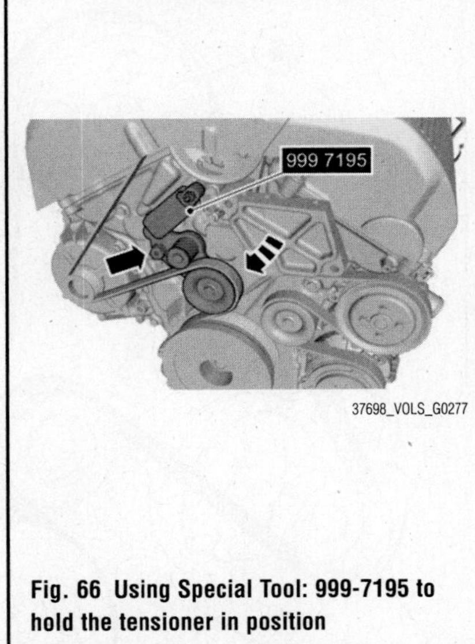

Fig. 66 Using Special Tool: 999-7195 to hold the tensioner in position

coupling spring clicks into position on the bonded section of the water pump and that the lugs meet the holes on the pulley.

21. Always use a new guide pin when installing the power steering pump.

4.4L Engine

See Figures 65 through 67.

1. Before servicing the vehicle, refer to the Precautions Section.
2. Remove the upper drive belt cover.
3. Remove the coolant bottle and the torque rod.
4. Remove the 3 bolts and torque rod bracket.
5. Remove the bracket for the torque rod bracket.
6. Remove the ground strap.
7. Remove the power steering pressure line and bracket retaining nut.
8. Relieve the load on the belt tensioner by turning it clockwise to a maximum 170 ft. lbs. (230 Nm) and lock the tensioner with a relevant tool.
9. Installation is the reverse of the removal procedure.

AIR CLEANER

REMOVAL & INSTALLATION

XC60 Vehicles

3.0L Engine

See Figures 68 and 69.

1. Before servicing the vehicle, refer to the Precautions Section.
2. Remove the clamps from the inlet hoses and disconnect the inlet hoses from the Air Cleaner (ACL) assembly.
3. Remove the attaching screws for the Mass Air Flow (MAF) sensor.
4. Disconnect the connector for the MAF sensor.
5. Remove the ACL assembly.
6. Installation is the reverse of the removal procedure.

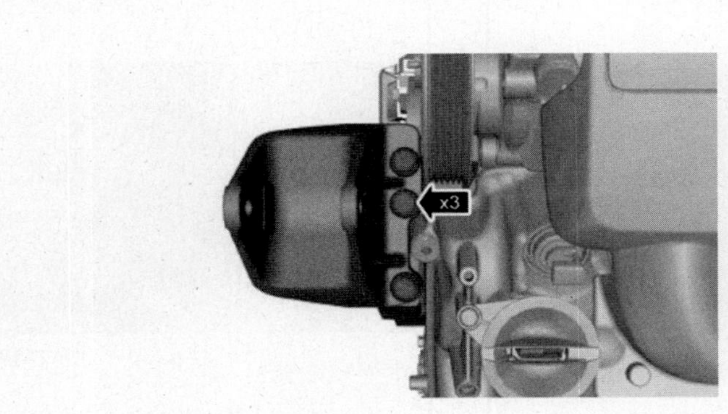

Fig. 65 Remove the 3 bolts and torque rod bracket

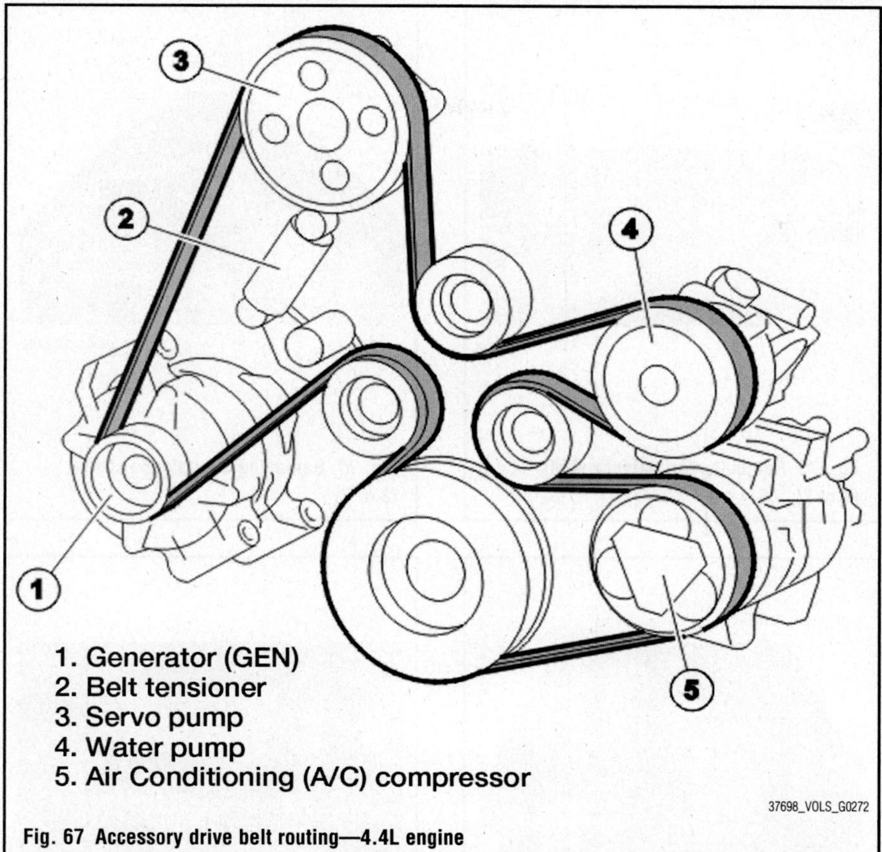

Fig. 67 Accessory drive belt routing—4.4L engine

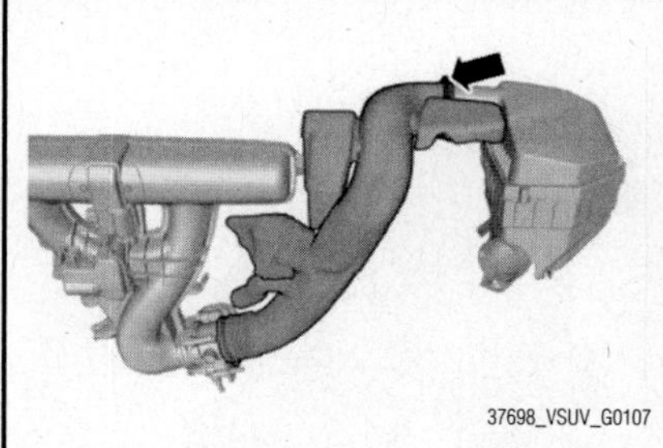

Fig. 70 Remove the clamps from the inlet hoses and disconnect the inlet hoses from the ACL assembly

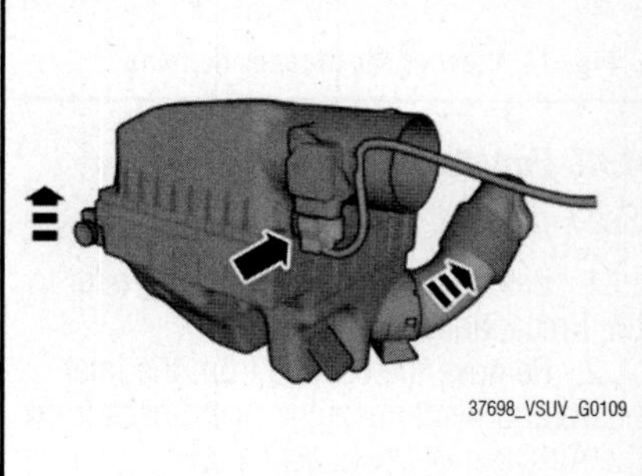

Fig. 71 Disconnect the connector for the Mass Air Flow (MAF) sensor

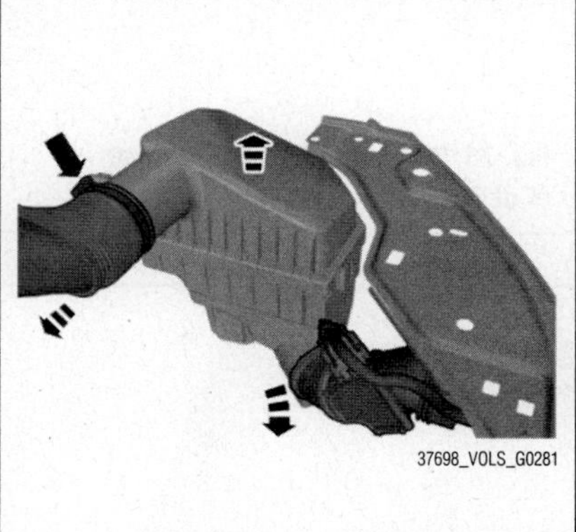

Fig. 68 Remove the Air Cleaner (ACL) assembly clamps from the inlet hoses

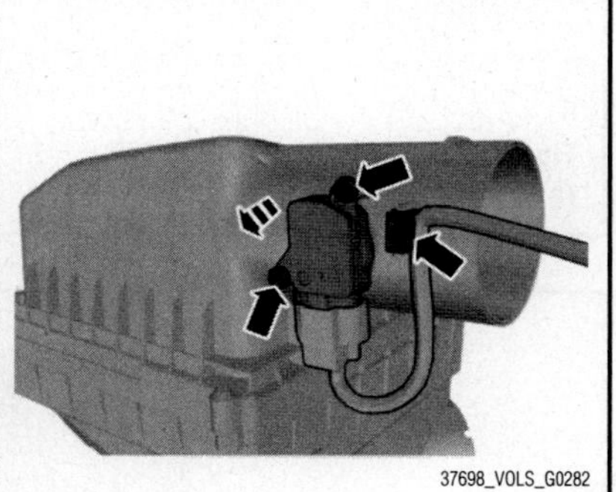

Fig. 69 Remove the Mass Air Flow (MAF) sensor

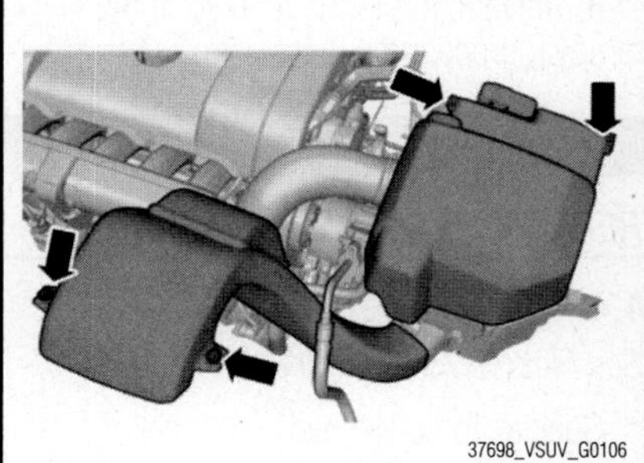

Fig. 72 Remove the screws attaching the Air Cleaner (ACL) housing

3.2L Engine

See Figures 70 and 71.

As the illustrations in this service information are used for different model years and/or models, some variation may occur. However, the essential information is correct.

1. Before servicing the vehicle, refer to the Precautions Section.
2. Remove the clamps from the inlet hoses and disconnect the inlet hoses from the Air Cleaner (ACL) assembly.
3. Disconnect the connector for the Mass Air Flow (MAF) sensor.
4. Remove the ACL assembly.
5. Installation is the reverse of the removal procedure.

XC90 Vehicles

3.2L Engine

See Figures 70, 72 and 73.

As the illustrations in this service information are used for different model years and/or models, some variation may occur. However, the essential information is correct.

1. Before servicing the vehicle, refer to the Precautions Section.
2. Disconnect the negative battery cable.
3. Remove the M6 screws attaching the Air Cleaner (ACL) housing.
4. Remove the clamps from the inlet hoses and disconnect the inlet hoses from the ACL assembly.

To install:

5. Installation is the reverse of the removal procedure.
6. Tighten the M6 screws to 89 inch lbs. (10 Nm).

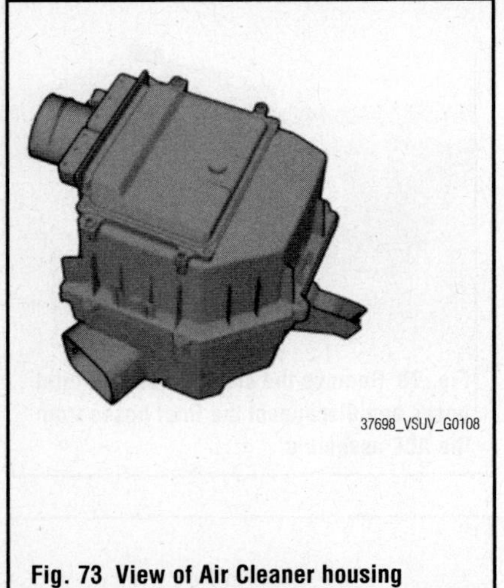

Fig. 73 View of Air Cleaner housing

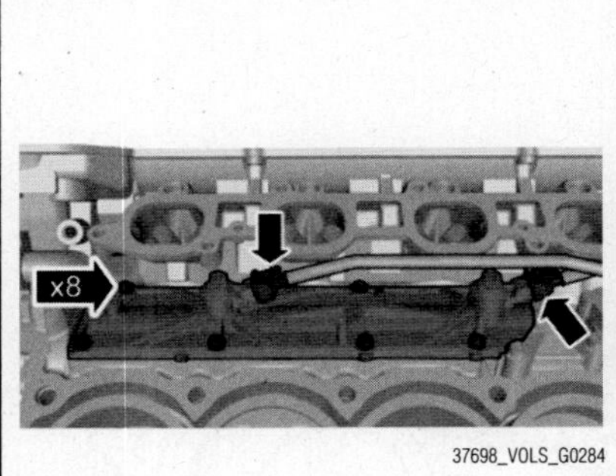

Fig. 75 Removing the balance shaft (1 of 7)

Fig. 77 Removing the balance shaft (3 of 7)

4.4L Engine

See Figure 74.

1. Before servicing the vehicle, refer to the Precautions Section.
2. Remove the clamps from the inlet hoses and disconnect the inlet hoses from the Air Cleaner (ACL) assembly.
3. Remove the attaching screws for the Mass Air Flow (MAF) sensor.
4. Disconnect the connector for the MAF sensor.
5. Lift up and remove the ACL assembly.
6. Installation is the reverse of the removal procedure.

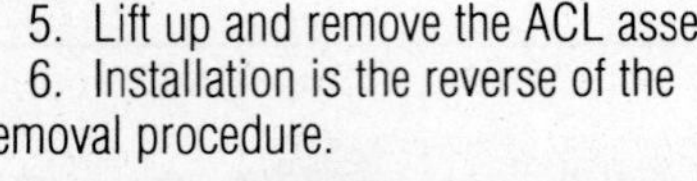

BALANCE SHAFT

REMOVAL & INSTALLATION

4.4L Engine

See Figures 75 through 81.

Special Tools Needed:

Fig. 74 Removing the Air Cleaner (ACL) assembly—4.4L engine

Fig. 76 Removing the balance shaft (2 of 7)

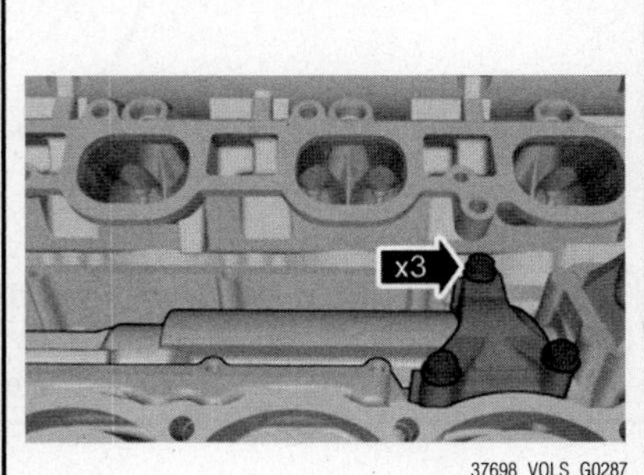

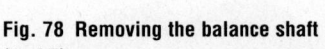

Fig. 78 Removing the balance shaft (4 of 7)

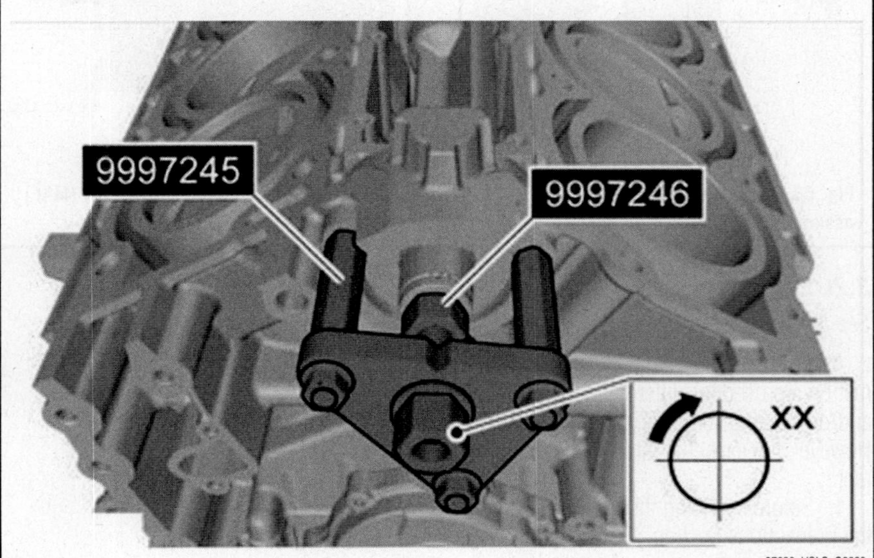

Fig. 79 Removing the balance shaft (5 of 7)

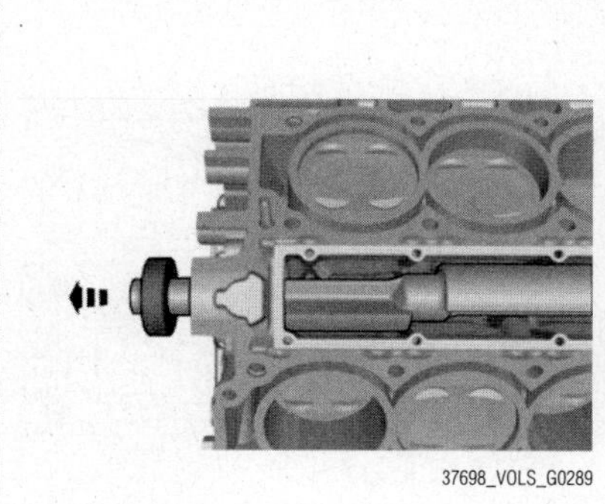
37698_VOLS_G0289

Fig. 80 Removing the balance shaft (6 of 7)

37698_VOLS_G0290

Fig. 81 Removing the balance shaft (7 of 7)

- 999-7245 Screw
- 999-7246 Press tool
- 999-7248 Position setter
- 999-7025 Drift Haldex coupling
- 999-7247 Drift

1. Before servicing the vehicle, refer to the Precautions Section.
2. Remove the left cylinder head.
3. Remove the balance shaft according to the following illustrations.

To install:

✲✲ WARNING

Make sure that the area around the component is clean and free of foreign material.

4. For vehicles with an engine serial number up to 6833, drill out an oil passage for the balance shaft prior to installation.
5. Install the balance shaft according to the following illustrations. Use the Special Tools as indicated.
6. Tighten the M10 bolts to 37 ft. lbs. (50 Nm).
7. Tighten the M8 bolts to 18 ft. lbs. (24 Nm).
8. Tighten the M6 bolts to 89 inch lbs. (10 Nm).
9. Install the left cylinder head.

CAMSHAFT & BEARINGS

INSPECTION

1. Check the camshaft journals for wear. If the journals are badly worn, replace the camshaft.
2. Check the cam lobes for damage. If the lobe is damaged or excessively worn, replace the camshaft.
3. Measure the cam lift height.
4. Check the cam surface for abnormal wear or damage, and replace if necessary.
5. Check each bearing for damage. If the bearing surface is excessively damaged, replace the cylinder head assembly or the camshaft bearing cap, as necessary.

REMOVAL & INSTALLATION

3.0L & 3.2L Engines

See Figures 82 and 83.

1. Before servicing the vehicle, refer to the Precautions Section.
2. Depressurize the fuel system.
3. Disconnect the negative battery cable.
4. Remove the accessory drive belts.
5. Remove the front cover.
6. Remove the timing chain.
7. Remove the ignition coil cover.
8. Remove the ignition coils.
9. Remove the camshaft sprockets.
10. Remove the cylinder head cover.
11. Remove the camshafts and lifters

➡Mark the position of the components before removal.

To install:

12. Lubricate the valve lifters and camshaft bearing positions and lobes with clean engine oil.
13. Install the valve lifters in their original positions.
14. Install the intake camshaft. Make sure that the groove in the rear edge of the camshaft extends across an imagined center line.
15. Install the exhaust camshaft. Make sure that the groove in the rear edge of the camshaft extends across an imagined center line.
16. Tighten the camshaft cover bolts alternately, keeping it parallel to the cylinder head using the press tools.
17. Using Special Tool 951-2767, or equivalent, apply liquid gasket to the mating surface of the cylinder head cover.

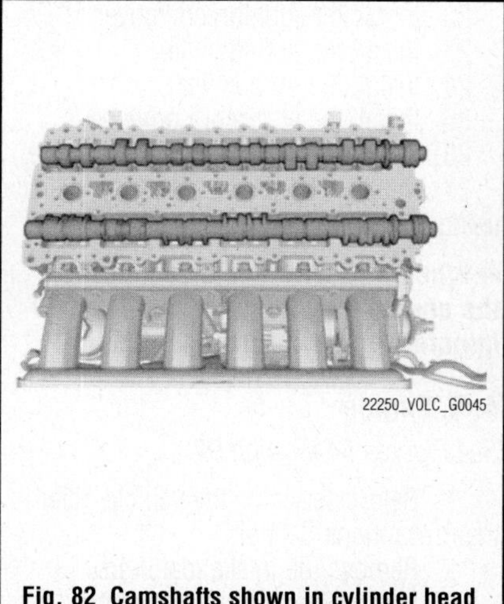
22250_VOLC_G0045

Fig. 82 Camshafts shown in cylinder head

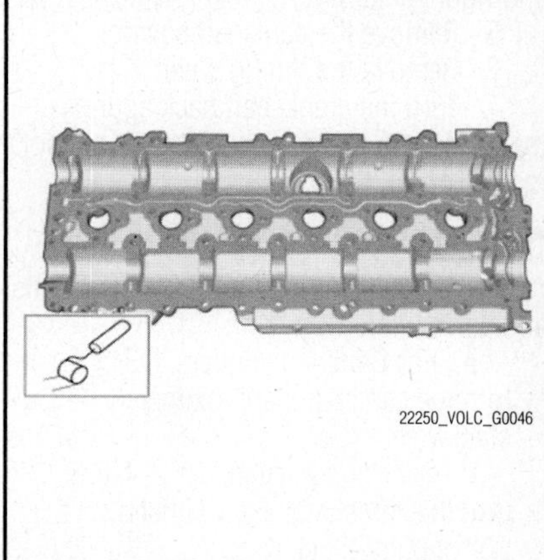
22250_VOLC_G0046

Fig. 83 Apply liquid gasket to the mating surface

✲✲ WARNING

Ensure no liquid gasket material gets in the oil ducts of the cylinder head cover.

18. Position the Press Tool 999-5454 in the spark plug holes. Fit the 2 M6 bolts under each press tool to set the right height.
19. Crosswise tighten the cylinder head cover parallel to the cylinder head with the press tool. Install all the bolts and tighten from the middle out to the edges. Tighten the bolts to 13 ft. lbs. (17 Nm). Remove the press tool and bolts under the tool.
20. Install the camshaft sprockets and tighten the bolts to 15 ft. lbs. (20 Nm).
21. Install the ignition coils.

22. Install the ignition coil cover.
23. Install the timing chain.
24. Install the front cover.
25. Install the accessory drive belts.
26. Connect the negative battery cable.
27. Initialize or calibrate affected systems using the VIDA diagnostic tool.

➡When the battery is disconnected, the engine may need to run for a few minutes before it runs smoothly.

4.4L Engine

See Figures 84 through 92.

1. Before servicing the vehicle, refer to the Precautions Section.
2. Remove the intake manifold.
3. Remove the air induction pipe.
4. Remove the ignition coils on the left and right banks.
5. Remove the camshaft covers.
6. Remove the timing chain.
7. Turn the crankshaft back approximately 45° so that the position setting tool is straight up.

➡The camshafts should rotate freely.

8. Remove the load from the camshafts and valve lifters:
   a. For Bank 1, cylinders 1-3-5-7, turn the camshafts approximately 45° clockwise.
   b. For Bank 2, cylinders 2-4-6-8, turn the camshafts approximately 10° counter-clockwise.
9. Remove the Variable Valve Timing (VVT) unit:
   a. Remove the 4 M6 bolts and the cap.

Fig. 84 Position setting tool installed backed off 45°

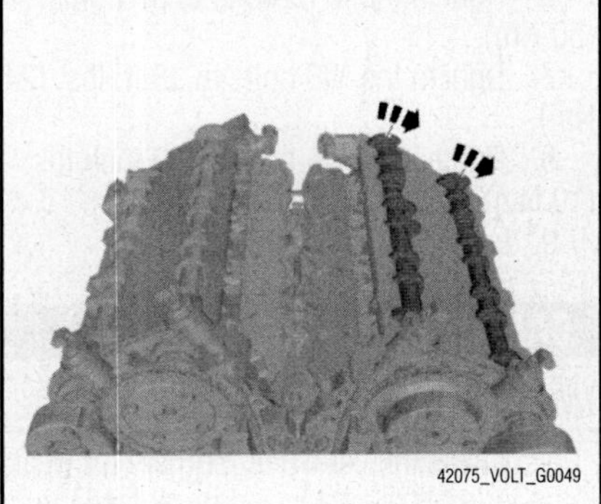

Fig. 85 Removing the load from Bank 1 camshafts

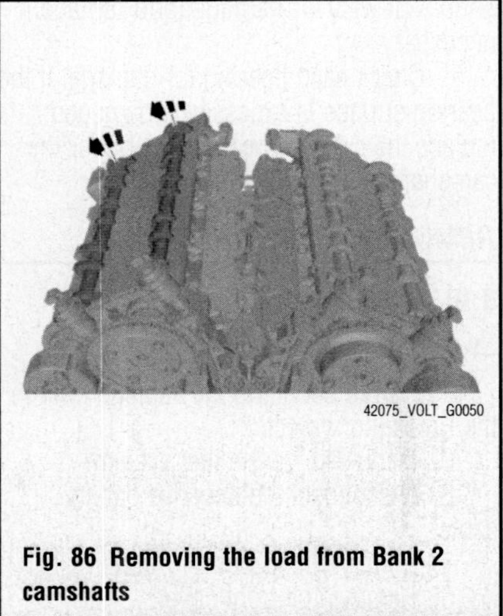

Fig. 86 Removing the load from Bank 2 camshafts

   b. Remove the 2 M6 bolts for the chain tensioner.
   c. Discard the 2 filters.
10. Remove the 8 M6 bolts holding the intake camshaft bearing caps.

➡Ensure that the camshaft is relieved from load against the valve lifters to prevent damaging the components. Note location of components.

11. Remove the chain tensioner.
12. Remove the camshaft.
13. To remove the exhaust camshaft, remove the 8 M6 bolts holding the exhaust camshaft bearing caps and remove exhaust camshaft.
14. Remove the valve lifters using a magnet or suction cup. Make note of the position of each lifter.

To install:

15. Install the valve lifters.
16. Install the VVT unit on the camshaft with 1 M10 bolt, but do not tighten.

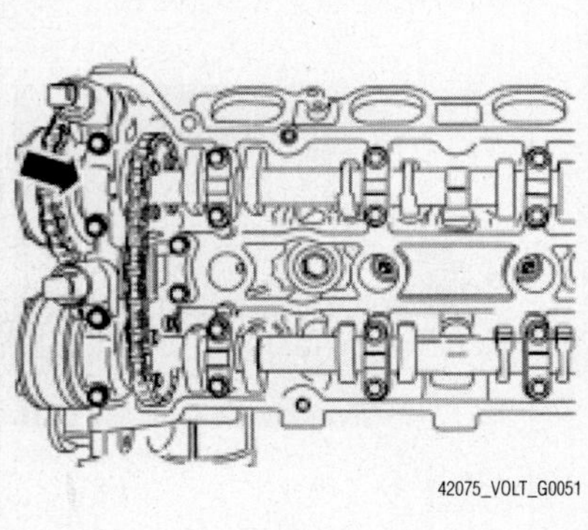

Fig. 87 Removing the Variable Valve Timing (VVT) unit

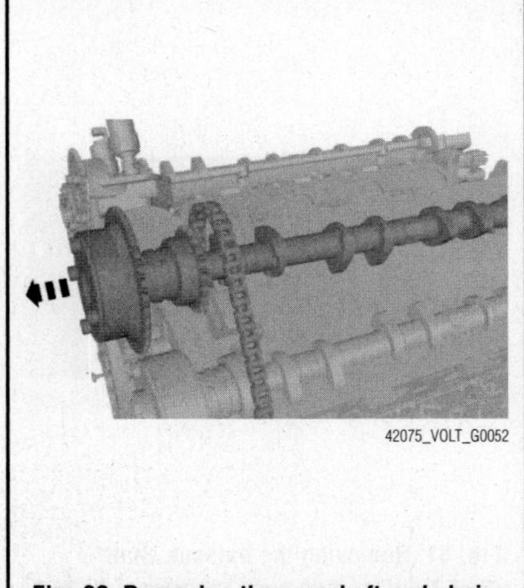

Fig. 88 Removing the camshaft and chain

17. Install the camshaft, chain, and chain tensioner.

➡Adjust the marking on the VVT unit to the color marking on the camshaft chain.

18. Install the camshaft bearing caps and tighten to 89 inch lbs. (10 Nm).
19. Install 2 new filters.
20. Install the 4 M6 bolts on the end cap of the camshafts and tighten to 18 inch lbs. (10 Nm).
21. Install the 2 M6 bolts for the chain tensioner and tighten to 18 inch lbs. (10 Nm).
22. Install tool 999-7236.
23. Minimize the slack of the camshaft chain.
   a. Use tool 999-7232.
   b. For cylinder head 1, 3, 5 and 7 (Bank 1), turn the VVT unit on the exhaust camshaft counter-clockwise, until the chain is tensioned underneath.

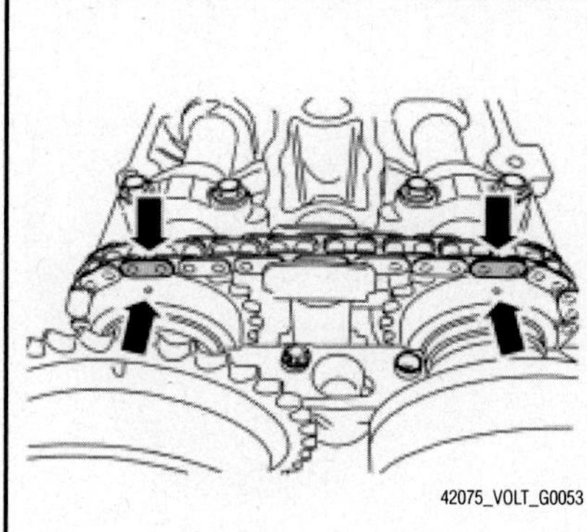

Fig. 89 Aligning timing marks on the VVT unit

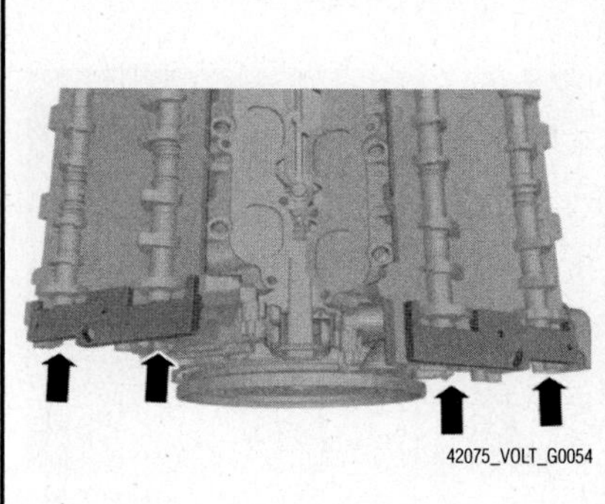

Fig. 90 Installation of the camshaft tool 999-7236

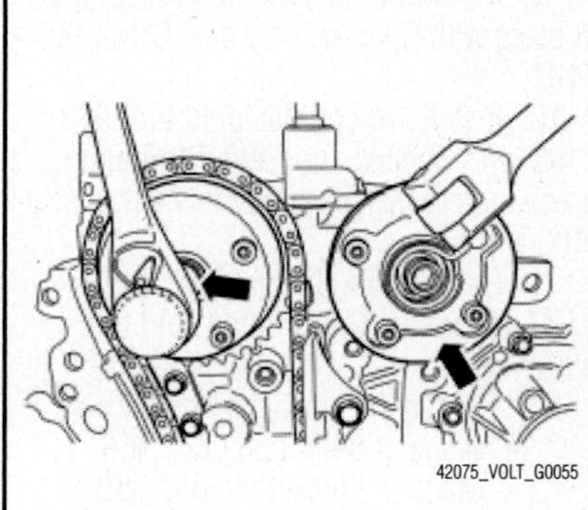

Fig. 91 Adjusting the camshaft chain tension

c. For cylinder head 2, 4, 6 and 8 (Bank 2), turn the VVT unit on the exhaust camshaft counter-clockwise, until the chain is tensioned on top.

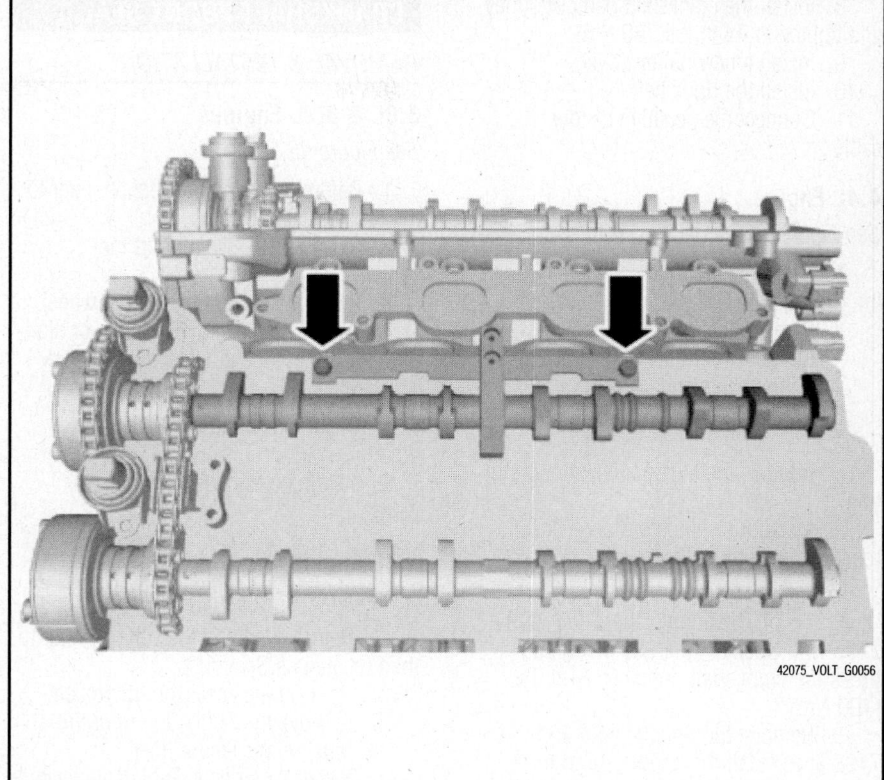

Fig. 92 Installation of the camshaft tool 999-7229

d. Tighten the bolt in the center of the intake camshaft VVT unit. Tighten to 15 ft. lbs. (20 Nm).

24. Install tool 999-7229 on the intake camshaft.

25. Tighten the center 1 M10 bolt on the camshaft to 37 ft. lbs. (50 Nm).

26. Remove the counter-hold.

27. Install the timing chain.

28. Install the camshaft covers.

29. Install the ignition coils on the left and right banks.

30. Install the air induction pipe.

31. Install the intake manifold.

32. Connect the negative battery cable.

33. Initialize or calibrate affected systems using the VIDA diagnostic tool.

➡When the battery is disconnected, the engine may need to run for a few minutes before it runs smoothly.

CRANKSHAFT DAMPER

REMOVAL & INSTALLATION

3.0L & 3.2L Engines

See Figure 93.

1. Before servicing the vehicle, refer to the Precautions Section.

2. Disconnect the negative battery cable.

3. Remove the accessory drive belt.

4. Remove the crank pulley cover.

5. Install the pulley removal tools 951-2926 bit Torx® 50 and counter-hold 999-5760.

6. Remove the crankshaft damper/pulley.

To install:

7. Install the crankshaft damper seal.

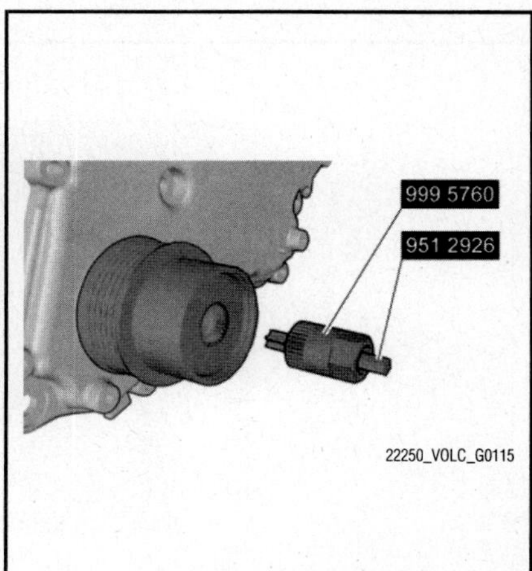

Fig. 93 Remove the crankshaft damper/pulley

8. Install the crankshaft damper/pulley and tighten to 44 ft. lbs. (60 Nm).
9. Install a new pulley cover.
10. Install the drive belt.
11. Connect the negative battery cable.

4.4L Engine

See Figure 94.

1. Before servicing the vehicle, refer to the Precautions Section.
2. Remove the drive belt.
3. Remove the right hand front tire.
4. Remove the fender liner.
5. Install the counter-hold tool 999-7196.
6. Remove the crank pulley mounting bolt.
7. Install the separator flange and remove the crank pulley.

To install:

8. Install the counter-hold tool 999-7196 with Special Tool 999-7198 and press the crankshaft pulley to 74 ft. lbs. (100 Nm).
9. Remove the Special Tool 999-7198 and install the counter-hold tool 999-7196.
10. Tighten the crankshaft pulley bolt as follows:
    - Stage 1: 89 ft. lbs. (120 Nm)
    - Stage 2: Loosen the bolt 360°
    - Stage 3: 37 ft. lbs. (50 Nm)
    - Stage 4: Additional 90°
11. Remove the counter-hold tool.
12. Install the drive belt.
13. Install the fender liner.
14. Install the wheel and tire assembly. Tighten the lug nuts in a star pattern.
    a. Step 1: 15 ft. lbs. (20 Nm).
    b. Step 2: 103 ft. lbs. (140 Nm).

CRANKSHAFT FRONT SEAL

REMOVAL & INSTALLATION

3.0L & 3.2L Engines

See Figure 95.

1. Before servicing the vehicle, refer to the Precautions Section.
2. Raise and safely support the vehicle.
3. Remove the right hand front wheel.
4. With a flat-head screwdriver, or similar tool, pry out the crankshaft front seal.

To install:

5. Clean the surfaces of front seal area.
6. Install the front seal with a seal driver.

4.4L Engine

See Figures 94, 96 and 97.

1. Before servicing the vehicle, refer to the Precautions Section.
2. Remove the accessory drive belt.
3. Remove the right hand front tire.
4. Remove the fender liner.
5. Install the Special Tool: Counter-hold 999-7196.
6. Remove the crank pulley mounting bolt.
7. Install the separator flange and remove the crank pulley.
8. Install seal puller 999-5069 and remove the front crankshaft seal.

To install:

➡Clean the surrounding area and around the crankshaft journal. Make sure that all residue from emery cloth and other foreign substances is completely removed before installing a new crankshaft seal.

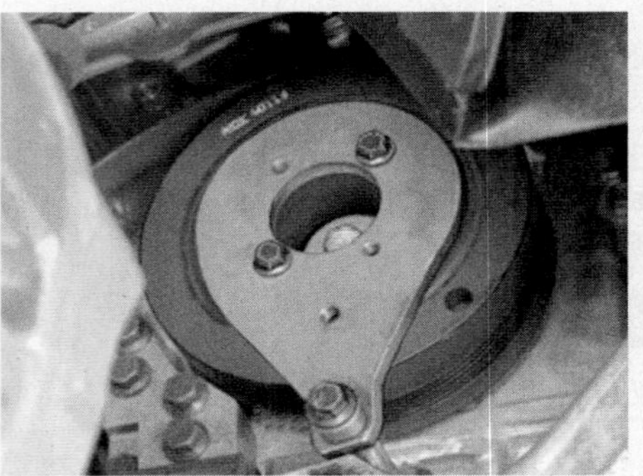

22250_VOLC_G0050

Fig. 94 Install the counter-hold tool 999-7196

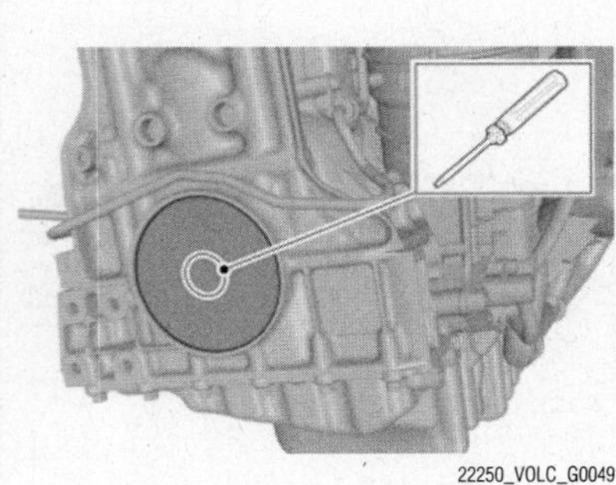

22250_VOLC_G0049

Fig. 95 Using a flat-head screwdriver to pry out the crankshaft front seal

22250_VOLC_G0051

Fig. 96 Install seal puller 999-5069 and remove the front crankshaft seal

9. Install the front crank seal and press in place with Special Tool: Seal Driver 999-7197.
10. Install the counter-hold tool 999-7196 with Special Tool 999-7198 and press the crankshaft pulley to 74 ft. lbs. (100 Nm).
11. Remove the Special Tool 999-7198 and install the counter-hold tool 999-7196.
12. Tighten the crankshaft pulley:
    - Stage 1: 89 ft. lbs. (120 Nm)
    - Stage 2: Loosen the bolt 360°
    - Stage 3: 37 ft. lbs. (50 Nm)
    - Stage 4: Additional 90°
13. Remove the counter-hold tool.
14. Install the accessory drive belt.
15. Install the fender liner.
16. Install the right front tire and tighten the lug nuts in a star pattern:
    - Step 1: 15 ft. lbs. (20 Nm)
    - Step 2: 103 ft. lbs. (140 Nm)

Fig. 97 Install front crank seal and press in place with Special Tool: Seal Driver 999-7197

CYLINDER HEAD

REMOVAL & INSTALLATION

3.0L & 3.2L Engines

See Figures 98 and 99.

1. Before servicing the vehicle, refer to the Precautions Section.
2. Depressurize the fuel system.
3. Drain the cooling system.
4. Disconnect the negative battery cable.
5. Remove or disconnect the following:
    - Exhaust manifold
    - Intake manifold
    - Valve covers
    - Injectors and fuel rail

➡Mark the position of the components before removal.

6. Lift out the valve lifters. Use a suction cup tool.

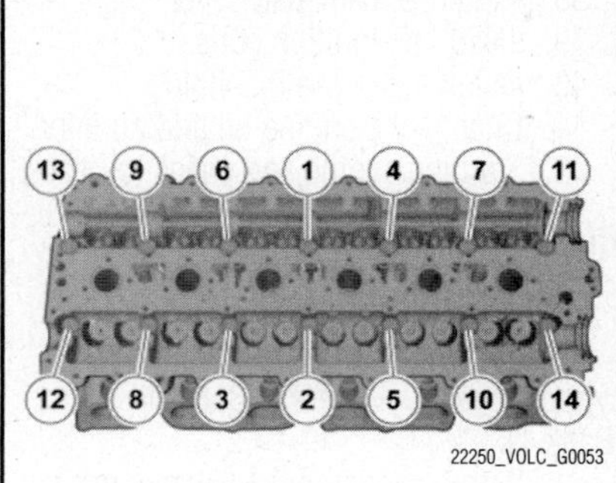

Fig. 98 Cylinder head torque sequence

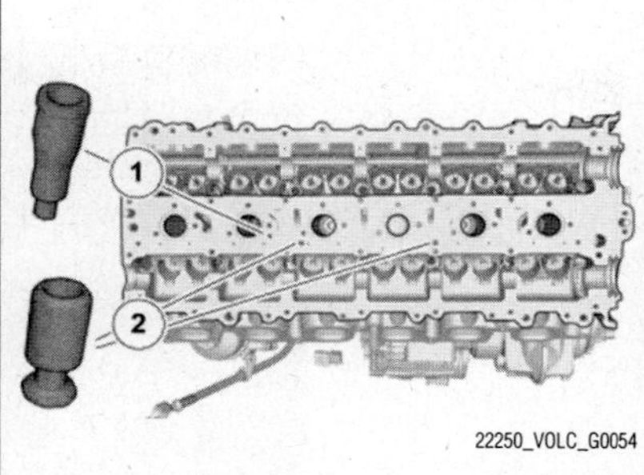

Fig. 99 Choke valves (1) and (2) location shown

⁂ WARNING

Take extra care not to damage the mating faces.

7. Remove the cylinder head bolts in sequence.

To install:

8. Make sure that the mating faces are clean and free of foreign material.
9. Make sure that the cylinder head thread holes in the engine block are free of fluid.
10. Check that the left-threaded sleeves go to the bottom.
11. Install a new head gasket.
12. Tighten the cylinder head as follows:
    - Stage 1: 33 ft. lbs. (45 Nm)
    - Stage 2: 33 ft. lbs. (45 Nm)
    - Stage 3: 90°
    - Stage 4: An additional 180°
13. Make sure that the choke valves are in place.
14. If only replacing the cylinder head gasket, reinstall the valve lifters in their original position.

➡Valve clearance must be checked if the cylinder head is replaced.

15. Install or reconnect the following:
    - Injectors and fuel rail
    - Valve covers
    - Intake manifold
    - Exhaust manifold
16. Connect the negative battery cable.
17. Install new engine coolant and bleed the system.
18. Start the engine and check for leaks.

4.4L Engine

Left Cylinder Head

See Figures 100 through 105.

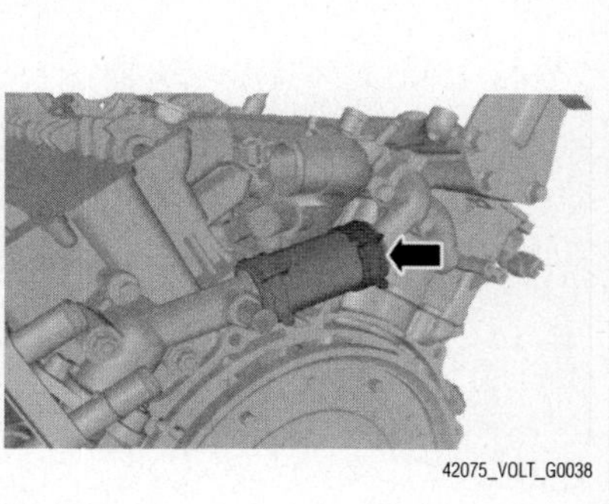

Fig. 100 Hose clamp location for removal

This procedure will expose the left cylinder head, cylinders 2, 4, 6 and 8 (Bank 2).

1. Before servicing the vehicle, refer to the Precautions Section.
2. Disconnect the negative battery cable.
3. Remove the intake manifold.
4. Remove the air induction pipe.
5. Remove the ignition coils on the left and right banks.
6. Remove the camshaft covers.
7. Remove the timing chain and sprockets.
8. Remove the camshafts.
9. Remove the cable harness from the engine bracket.
10. Remove the connector for the camshaft position sensor.
11. Remove the vacuum valve.
12. Remove the hose clip for the coolant hose.
13. Remove M6 bolt and heat shield around connector.

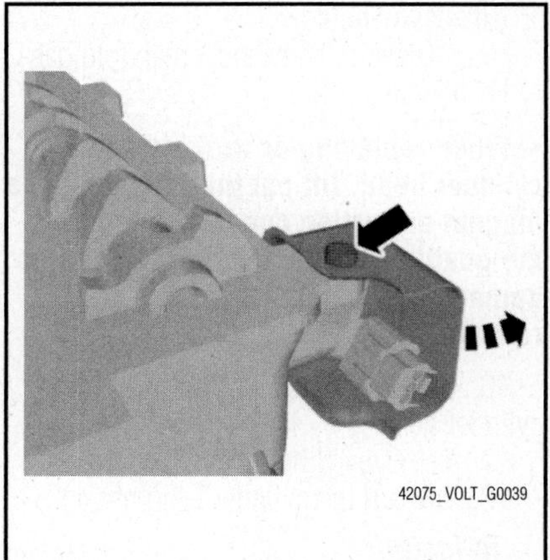

Fig. 101 Heat shield location

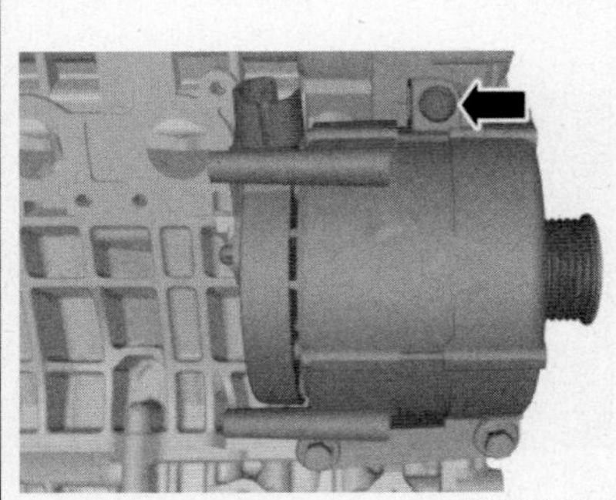

Fig. 102 Alternator upper mounting bolt location

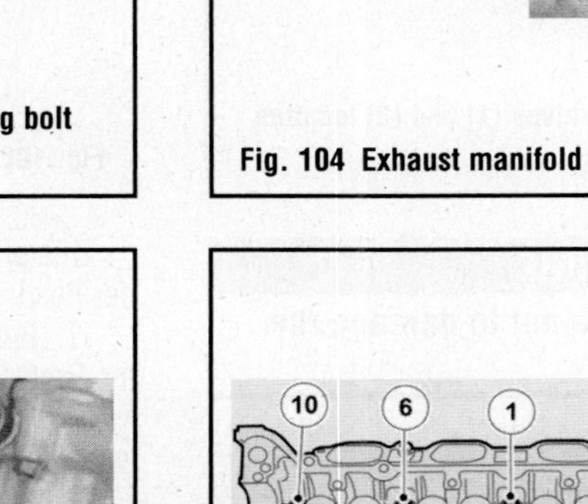

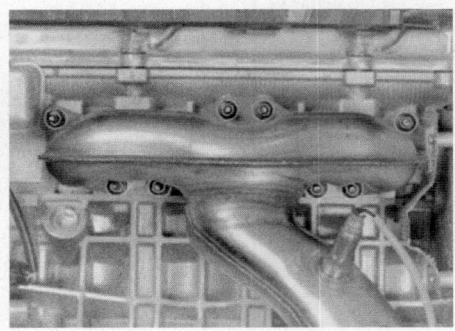

Fig. 104 Exhaust manifold bolt removal (Bank 2)

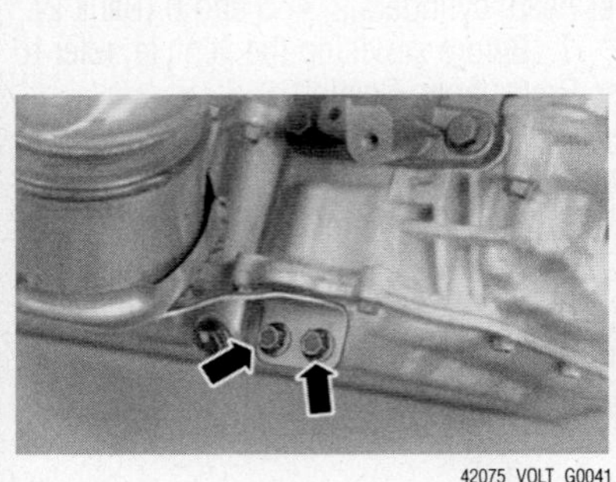

Fig. 103 Exhaust bracket and bolt location for removal (Bank 2)

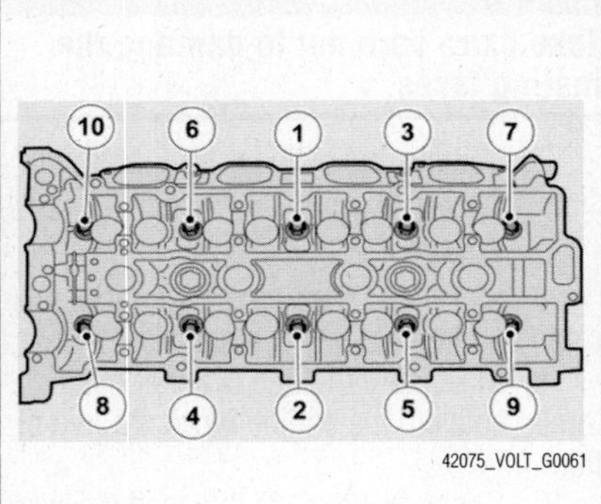

Fig. 105 Cylinder head torque sequence

14. Remove the M8 upper mounting bolt from the alternator.
15. To remove the exhaust manifold:
    a. Remove the 2 M8 bracket bolts.
    b. Remove the 8 M8 nuts from the exhaust manifold.
    c. Discard the exhaust manifold gasket.

➡When replacing or working on the cylinder head, lift out the lifters using a magnet or suction cup. Make note of the positions. Also, take care not to damage the mating surfaces when removing the cylinder head.

16. Remove the 10 M12 bolts in the cylinder head.
17. Remove cylinder head.
18. Discard the cylinder head gasket.

To install:

19. Clean and check:
    - The coolant bypass channel
    - The intake manifold
    - The cylinder block
    - The camshaft cover
    - All gasket faces
20. Carefully blow the oil ducts clean.

➡Check that all studs at the exhaust ports are tightened.

21. Install a new exhaust manifold gasket. Lubricate the studs using paste 116 1408.
22. Install a new cylinder head gasket. Apply sealing compound 307 57050 to both sides.
23. Install the cylinder head.
24. Install new bolts in the cylinder head. Lubricate the bolts.
25. Tighten the cylinder head bolts in a circle from the inside and outwards. Use protractor 951-2050. Tighten in 2 steps:
    - Step 1: 30 ft. lbs. (40 Nm)
    - Step 2: angle tighten to 90°
26. Install the valve lifters.

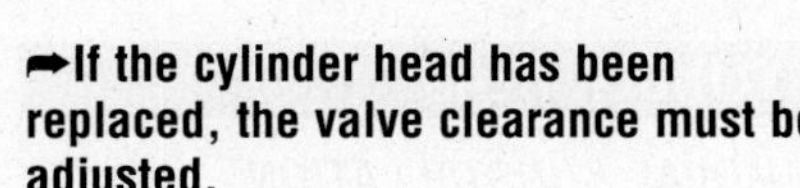

➡If the cylinder head has been replaced, the valve clearance must be adjusted.

27. Lubricate and install the valve lifters.
28. Install the exhaust manifold and tighten the 8 M8 nuts to 18 ft. lbs. (24 Nm).
29. Install the 2 M8 bolts for the exhaust manifold bracket and tighten to 18 ft. lbs. (24 Nm).
30. Install the M8 upper mounting bolt from the alternator and tighten to 18 ft. lbs. (24 Nm).
31. Install the heat shield and M6 bolt, tighten to 89 inch lbs. (10 Nm).
32. Install the connector for the camshaft position sensor.
33. Install the cable harness on the engine bracket.
34. Install the vacuum valve.
35. Install the hose clip for the coolant hose.
36. Install the camshafts.
37. Install the timing chain and sprockets.
38. Install the camshaft cover.
39. Install the ignition coils.
40. Install the intake manifold.
41. Change the engine oil and oil filter.
42. Start the engine and check for leaks.

Right Cylinder Head

See Figures 105 through 110.

This procedure will expose the right cylinder head, cylinders 1, 3, 5 and 7 (Bank 1).

1. Before servicing the vehicle, refer to the Precautions Section.
2. Remove the intake manifold.
3. Remove the air induction pipe.
4. Remove the ignition coils on the left and right banks.
5. Remove the camshaft covers.

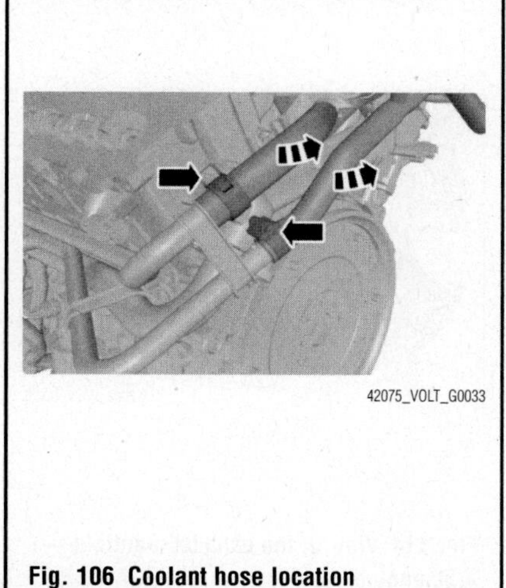

Fig. 106 Coolant hose location

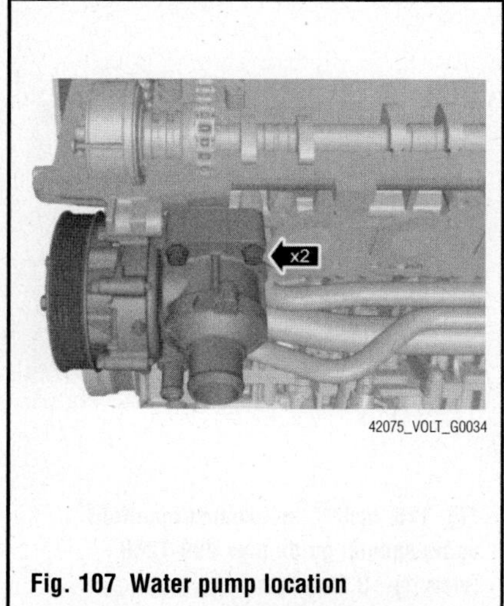

Fig. 107 Water pump location

6. Remove the timing chain and sprockets.
7. Remove the camshafts.
8. Remove the hose clamp for the upper coolant hose.
9. Remove the electrical connectors for the camshaft position sensors.
10. Remove the coolant hoses and place them to one side.
11. Remove the 2 M8 upper bolts holding the water pump.
12. Remove the M8 bolt and 2 M8 nuts attaching coolant pipes.
13. Remove exhaust manifold:
    a. Remove the 2 M8 bolts holding the bracket to the manifold.
    b. Remove the 8 M8 nuts holding the flanged joint to the manifold.
14. Discard the exhaust manifold gasket.

➡When replacing or working on the cylinder head, lift out the lifters using a magnet or suction cup. Make note of the positions. Also, take care not to damage the mating surfaces when removing the cylinder head.

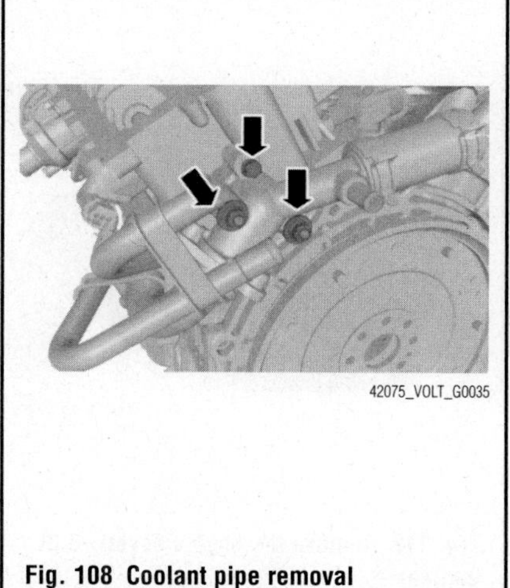

Fig. 108 Coolant pipe removal

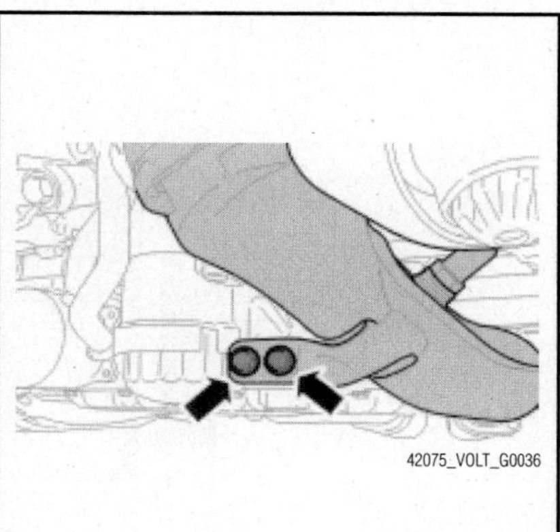

Fig. 109 Bracket bolt removal on exhaust manifold

15. Remove the 10 M12 bolts in the cylinder head.
16. Remove the cylinder head.
17. Discard the cylinder head gasket.

To install:

18. Clean and check:
    - The coolant bypass channel
    - The intake manifold
    - The cylinder block
    - The camshaft cover
    - All gasket faces
19. Carefully blow the oil ducts clean.

➡Check that all studs at the exhaust ports are tightened.

20. Install the new exhaust manifold gasket. Lubricate the studs using paste 116 1408.

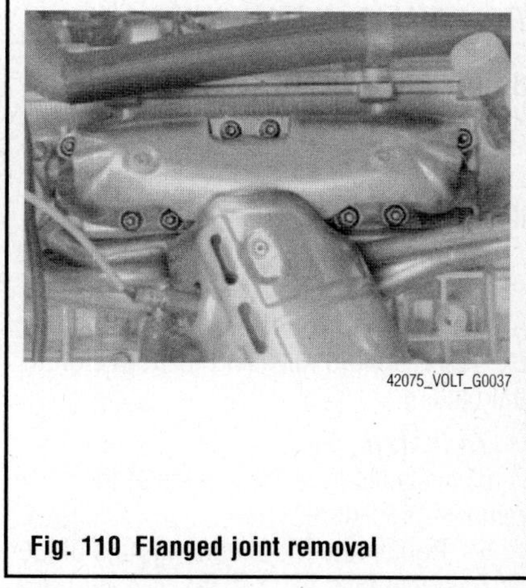

Fig. 110 Flanged joint removal

21. Install the new cylinder head gasket. Apply sealing compound 307 57050 to both sides.
22. Install the cylinder head.
23. Install the new bolts in the cylinder head. Lubricate the bolts.
24. Tighten the cylinder head bolts in a circle from the inside and outward. Use protractor 951-2050. Tighten in 2 steps:
    - Step 1: to 30 ft. lbs. (40 Nm)
    - Step 2: angle tighten to 90°
25. Install the valve lifters.

➡If the cylinder head has been replaced, the valve clearance must be adjusted.

26. Lubricate and install valve lifters.
27. Install the exhaust manifold flanged joint and tighten the 8 M8 nuts to 18 ft. lbs. (24 Nm).
28. Install the 2 M8 bolts for the exhaust manifold bracket and tighten to 18 ft. lbs. (24 Nm).
29. Install the M8 bolt and 2 M8 nuts attaching coolant pipes and tighten to 18 ft. lbs. (24 Nm).
30. Install the 2 M8 upper bolts holding the water pump and tighten to 18 ft. lbs. (24 Nm).
31. Install the coolant hoses and clamps.
32. Install the camshafts.
33. Install the timing chain and sprockets.
34. Install the camshaft cover.
35. Install the ignition coils.
36. Install the air induction pipe.
37. Install the intake manifold.
38. Change the oil and oil filter.
39. Install new engine coolant and bleed the cooling system.
40. Start the engine and check for leaks.

EXHAUST MANIFOLD

REMOVAL & INSTALLATION

3.0L Engine

See Figure 111.

1. Before servicing the vehicle, refer to the Precautions Section.
2. Disconnect the negative battery cable.
3. Remove the turbocharger.
4. Remove the 14 nuts attaching the exhaust manifold releasing them in a gradual pattern.

To install:

5. Installation is the reverse of the removal procedure.
6. Tighten the M8 mounting nuts of the exhaust manifold to 18 ft. lbs. (24 Nm) in a normal torque sequence.
7. Install the turbocharger.

3.2L Engine

See Figures 112 through 116.

1. Before servicing the vehicle, refer to the Precautions Section.
2. Remove the engine cover.
3. Disconnect the oxygen sensor connectors.
4. Remove the exhaust manifold shield.
5. Remove the catalytic converter(s).
6. Remove the 14 mounting bolts from the exhaust manifold in a gradual sequence.
7. Remove the exhaust manifold.

To install:

8. Install Special Tool: 999-7269, guide pins into the exhaust manifold sections.
9. Tighten the exhaust manifold M8 bolts to 18 ft. lbs. (24 Nm) in a normal torque sequence.

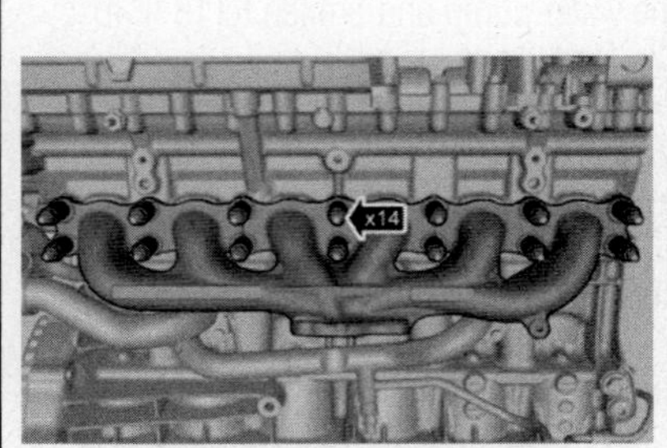

Fig. 111 View of exhaust manifold—3.0L engine

Fig. 112 Remove the engine cover—3.2L engine

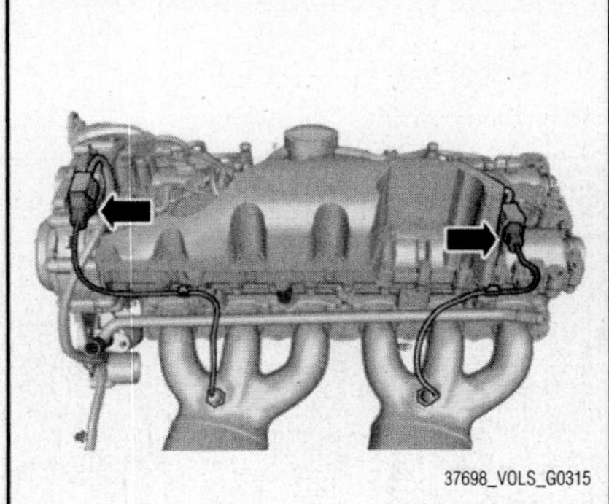

Fig. 113 Disconnect the oxygen sensor connectors—3.2L engine

10. Installation continues in the reverse of the removal procedure.

4.4L Engine

See Figures 117 through 120.

1. Before servicing the vehicle, refer to the Precautions Section.
2. Relieve the fuel system pressure.
3. Drain the cooling system.
4. Disconnect the negative battery cable.
5. Install the engine support system.
6. Remove the control arms on both sides.
7. Remove the front stabilizer bar link to stabilizer bar.
8. Remove the engine under cover.
9. Remove the catalytic converter.
10. Right-hand engine pad to sub-frame.
11. Remove the flex pipe heat shield near rack and pinion unit.
12. Remove the right lower torque mount.

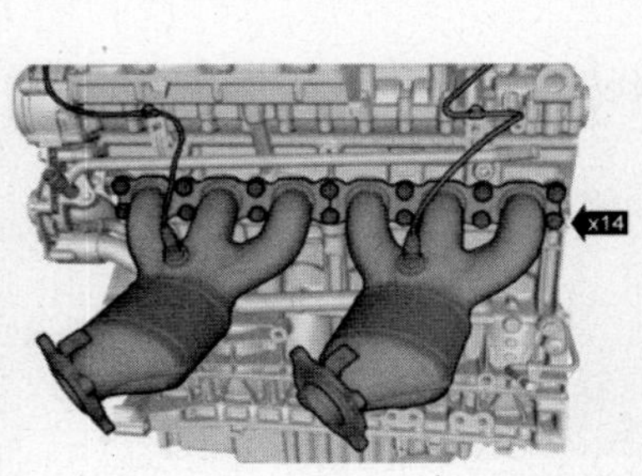

Fig. 114 View of the exhaust manifold—3.2L engine

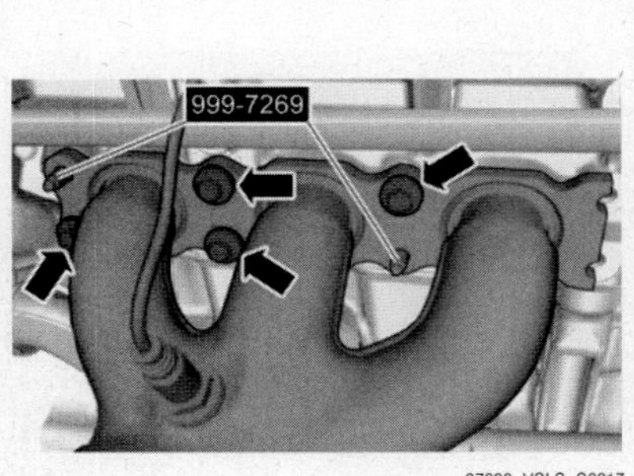

Fig. 115 Install the exhaust manifold using special guide pins 999-7269 (view 1)—3.2L engine

13. Remove the right lower torque rod bracket.
14. Remove the rack and pinion mounting bolts.
15. Support the steering rack with tie straps or mechanics wire.
16. Remove the collision member to sub-frame bracket.
17. Install a transaxle jack with adapters and support the sub-frame.
18. Remove the sub-frame mounting bolts and carefully lower the sub-frame.
19. Remove the right halfshaft.
20. Disconnect the O2 sensor electrical connectors.
21. Remove the bolts holding the exhaust bracket to the oil pan.
22. Remove the right or left exhaust manifold as needed.

To install:

23. Clean the mating surface and install new gasket.

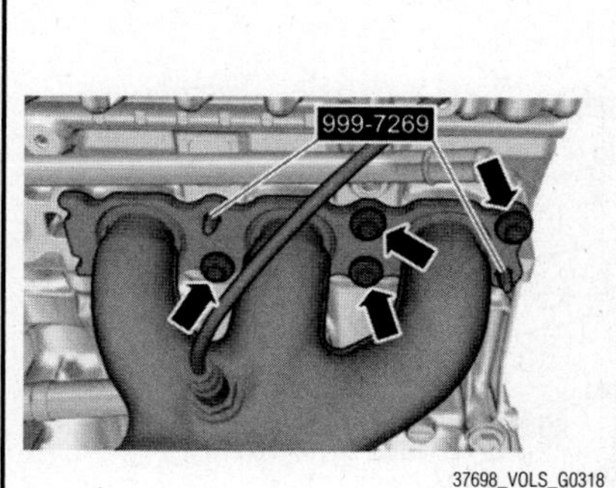

Fig. 116 Install the exhaust manifold using special guide pins 999-7269 (view 2)—3.2L engine

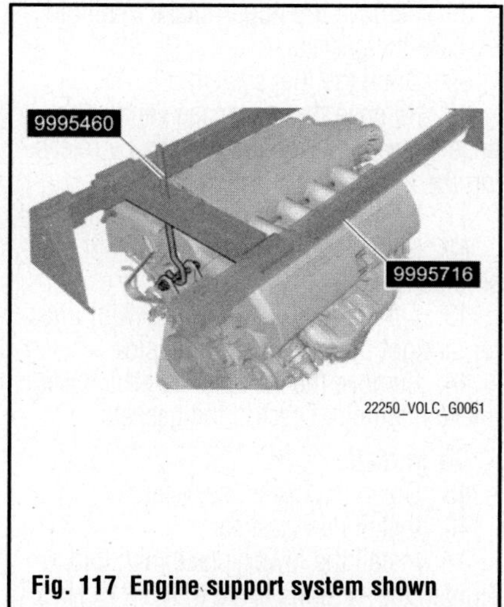

Fig. 117 Engine support system shown

24. Install the right or left manifold as needed. Tighten to 18 ft. lbs. (24 Nm).
25. Install the bolts holding the exhaust bracket to the oil pan. Tighten to 18 ft. lbs. (24 Nm).
26. Reconnect the O2 sensor electrical connectors.
27. Install the right halfshaft.
28. Install the sub-frame alignment tools 999-7089 and carefully raise the sub-frame.
29. Install a transaxle jack with adapters and support the sub-frame.
30. Install the sub frame mounting bolts and tighten in 2 stages:
    - Stage 1: 111 ft. lbs. (150 Nm)
    - Stage 2: Additional 90°
31. Install the collision member to sub-frame bracket.
32. Install the steering rack and tighten mounting bolts.
33. Install the right lower torque rod bracket and to 37 ft. lbs. (50 Nm).

Fig. 118 View of transaxle jack with adapters

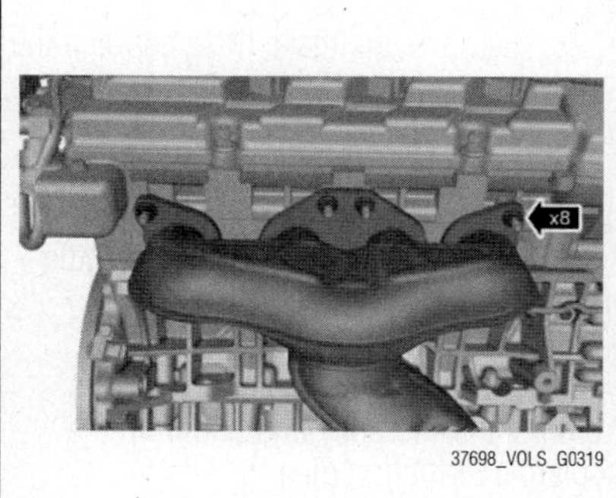

Fig. 119 Removing the exhaust manifold (right side shown)—4.4L engine

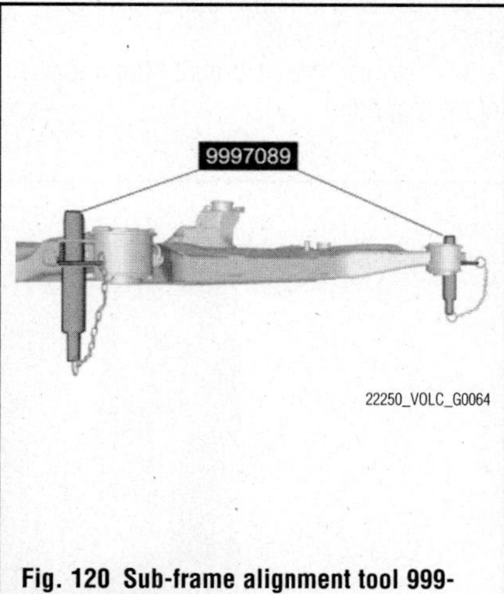

Fig. 120 Sub-frame alignment tool 999-7089 installed

34. Install the right lower torque mount and to 59 ft. lbs. (80 Nm).
35. Install the flex pipe heat shield near the rack and pinion unit.
36. Right-hand engine pad to sub-frame.
37. Install the catalytic converter.
38. Install the engine under cover.
39. Install the front stabilizer bar link to stabilizer bar.
40. Install the control arms on both sides.
41. Remove the engine support system.
42. Check for exhaust leaks.

INTAKE MANIFOLD

REMOVAL & INSTALLATION

Lower Manifold

3.0L & 3.2L Engines

See Figure 121.

1. Before servicing the vehicle, refer to the Precautions Section.
2. Disconnect the negative battery cable.
3. Remove the engine cover.
4. Remove the engine under cover.
5. Remove the intake hose at the intake manifold and air filter housing.
6. Remove all the electrical connectors at the intake manifold.
7. Remove the intake manifold bolts and manifold.
8. Installation is the reverse of the removal procedure. Note the following:
    - Clean mating surfaces and install a new gasket
    - Tighten the intake manifold bolts to 13 ft. lbs. (17 Nm)

4.4L Engine

See Figures 122 through 124.

1. Before servicing the vehicle, refer to the Precautions Section.
2. Disconnect the negative battery cable.

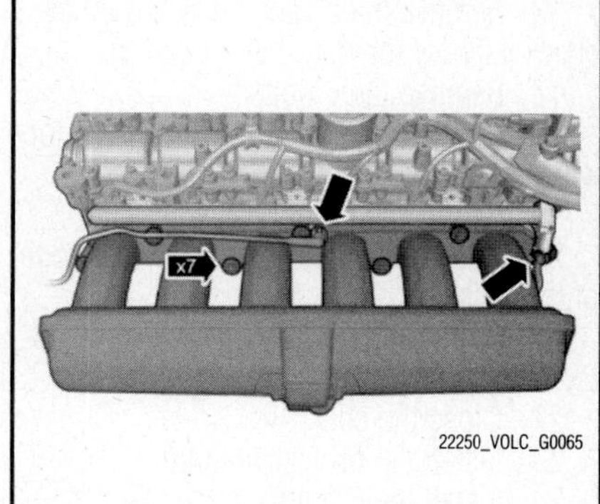

Fig. 121 Intake manifold bolts and manifold shown

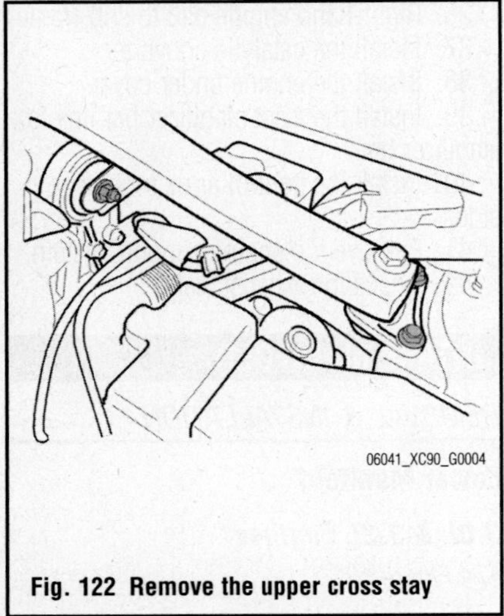

Fig. 122 Remove the upper cross stay

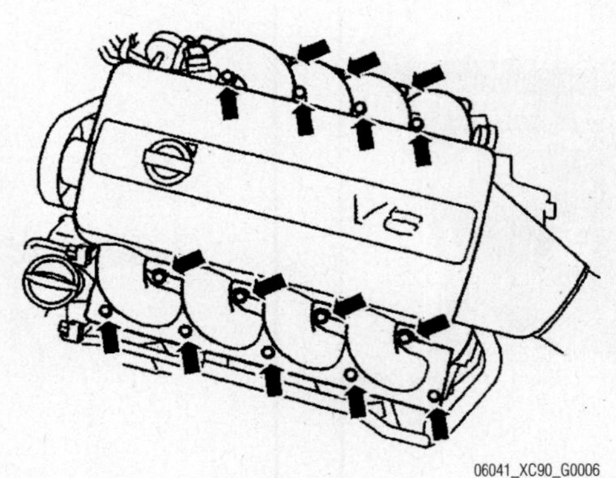

Fig. 123 Remove the 21 bolts of the upper intake manifold.

3. Remove the 4 bolts at the suspension turrets.
4. Remove the bolts of the upper engine mount on the engine.
5. Remove the upper cross stay.
6. Remove the air cleaner cover by pulling it straight up.
7. Remove the 2 connectors from the Engine Control Module (ECM); clip the band clamp to the cable harness.
8. Remove the connector from the mass air flow sensor.
9. Remove the brake vacuum hose from the vacuum pump.
10. Remove the 2 bolts of the fresh air hose in the front plate.
11. Remove the fresh air hose.
12. Remove the air cleaner by pulling it straight up.
13. Remove the upper engine covers by pulling them straight up.
14. Remove the cover over the servo pump.
15. Detach the connector of the pressure and temperature sensor.
16. Remove the 2 vacuum hoses of the check valve of the distribution damper.
17. Remove the 6 bolts.
18. Lift and slide the protective plate forward.
19. Remove the protective plate.
20. Open the cock on the lower left edge of the radiator.
21. Drain the coolant into a clean receptacle.
22. Close the cock.
23. Install the protective plate.
24. Install the 6 bolts.
25. Lower the vehicle.
26. Remove the 4 bolts and the upper engine mount.
27. Remove the brake vacuum hose from the intake manifold by releasing the clamp.
28. Remove the intake hose between the air cleaner and throttle body by releasing the 2 clamps.
29. Remove the 2 nuts on the throttle body.
30. Remove the 2 bolts on the throttle body.
31. Position aside the throttle body.
32. Detach the 2 coolant hoses, one from the throttle body and one from the coolant distribution pipe.
33. Remove the hose clip on the vacuum hose.
34. Remove the vacuum hose.
35. Remove the 2 M6 bolts on the non-return valve for crankcase ventilation.
36. Remove the non-return valve for crankcase ventilation.
37. Remove the 21 bolts of the upper intake manifold.
38. Remove the upper intake manifold. Discard the gaskets.
39. Drain the fuel system.
40. Remove the crankcase ventilation hose between the cylinder heads by releasing the 2 clamps.
41. Remove the 3 bolts from the fuel rail.
42. Remove the 2 bolts on the fuel pressure sensor.
43. Lift the fuel rail assembly with injector straight up and position it aside.
44. Remove the 12 bolts and the lower intake manifold. Discard the gaskets.

To install:

45. Clean the gasket surfaces.
46. Install new gaskets.
47. Install the lower intake manifold. Tighten the 12 bolts to 14 ft. lbs. (19 Nm).
48. Lubricate the O-rings on the injectors with petroleum jelly.
49. Install the fuel rail assembly with injectors.
50. Install the 3 bolts of the fuel rail.

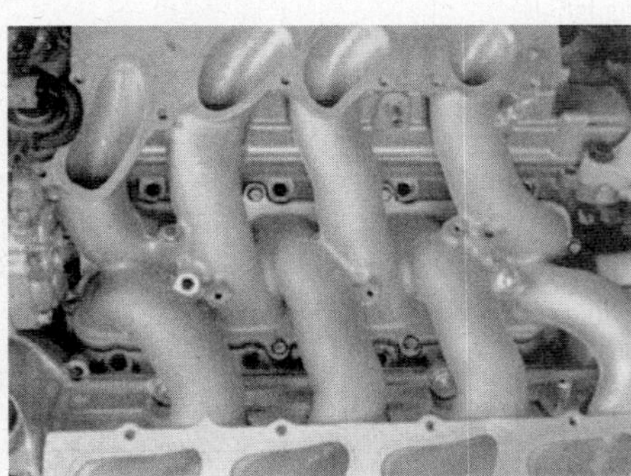

Fig. 124 Remove the 12 bolts and the lower intake manifold

51. Install the 2 bolts on the fuel pressure sensor.
52. Install the crankcase ventilation hose and 2 clamps.
53. Connect the fuel supply line and secure the line in the clamp.
54. Install new gaskets.
55. Install the upper intake manifold. Tighten the 21 bolts to 14 ft. lbs. (19 Nm).
56. Install the hoses to the intake manifold.
57. Install the non-return valve for crankcase ventilation.
58. Install the connector to the pressure and temperature sensor.
59. Install the 2 vacuum hoses of the check valve of the distribution damper.
60. Install the upper engine mount. Tighten the 4 M10 bolts.
61. Install the cover over the servo pump.
62. Position the engine covers and press them into the retainers.
63. Install the upper cross stay between the suspension turrets. Tighten the 4 bolts.
64. Install the bolt of the cross stay mount on the engine.
65. Install the air cleaner.
66. Install the brake vacuum hose on the brake pump.
67. Install the fresh air hose.
68. Install the 2 bolts of the fresh air hose in the front plate.
69. Install the 2 connectors to the ECM.
70. Install the connector to the mass air flow sensor.
71. Install the band clamp on the cable harness in the air cleaner housing.
72. Install the cover over the air cleaner.
73. Fill the engine with the proper type and amount of coolant.
74. Start the engine and allow it to warm to normal operating temperature. Check for leaks and proper function. Fill fluids as necessary.

Upper Manifold

4.4L Engine

See Figures 122 and 123.

1. Before servicing the vehicle, refer to the Precautions Section.
2. Disconnect the negative battery cable.
3. Remove the 4 bolts at the suspension turrets.
4. Remove the bolts of the upper engine mount on the engine.
5. Remove the upper cross stay.
6. Remove the air cleaner cover by pulling it straight up.
7. Remove the 2 connectors from the Engine Control Module (ECM); clip the band clamp to the cable harness.
8. Remove the connector from the mass air flow sensor.
9. Remove the brake vacuum hose from the vacuum pump.
10. Remove the 2 bolts of the fresh air hose in the front plate.
11. Remove the fresh air hose.
12. Remove the air cleaner by pulling it straight up.
13. Remove the upper engine covers by pulling them straight up.
14. Remove the cover over the servo pump.
15. Detach the connector of the pressure and temperature sensor.
16. Remove the 2 vacuum hoses of the check valve of the distribution damper.
17. Remove the 6 bolts.
18. Lift and slide the protective plate forward.
19. Remove the protective plate.
20. Open the cock on the lower left edge of the radiator.
21. Drain the coolant into a clean receptacle.
22. Close the cock.
23. Install the protective plate.
24. Install the 6 bolts.
25. Lower the vehicle.
26. Remove the 4 bolts and the upper engine mount.
27. Remove the brake vacuum hose from the intake manifold by releasing the clamp.
28. Remove the intake hose between the air cleaner and throttle body by releasing the 2 clamps.
29. Remove the 2 nuts on the throttle body.
30. Remove the 2 bolts on the throttle body.
31. Position aside the throttle body.
32. Detach the 2 coolant hoses, one from the throttle body and one from the coolant distribution pipe.
33. Remove the hose clip on the vacuum hose.
34. Remove the vacuum hose.
35. Remove the 2 M6 bolts on the non-return valve for crankcase ventilation.
36. Remove the non-return valve for crankcase ventilation.
37. Remove the 21 bolts of the upper intake manifold.
38. Remove the upper intake manifold. Discard the gaskets.

To install:

39. Clean the gasket surfaces.
40. Install new gaskets.
41. Install the upper intake manifold. Tighten the 21 bolts to 14 ft. lbs. (19 Nm).
42. Install the hoses to the intake manifold.
43. Install the non-return valve for crankcase ventilation.
44. Install the connector to the pressure and temperature sensor.
45. Install the 2 vacuum hoses of the check valve of the distribution damper.
46. Install the upper engine mount. Tighten the 4 M10 bolts.
47. Install the cover over the servo pump.
48. Position the engine covers and press them into the retainers.
49. Install the upper cross stay between the suspension turrets. Tighten the 4 bolts.
50. Install the bolt of the cross stay mount on the engine.
51. Install the air cleaner.
52. Install the brake vacuum hose on the brake pump.
53. Install the fresh air hose.
54. Install the 2 bolts of the fresh air hose in the front plate.
55. Install the 2 connectors to the ECM.
56. Install the connector to the mass air flow sensor.
57. Install the band clamp on the cable harness in the air cleaner housing.
58. Install the cover over the air cleaner.
59. Fill the engine with the proper type and amount of coolant.
60. Start the engine and allow it to warm to normal operating temperature. Check for leaks and proper function. Fill fluids as necessary.

OIL PAN

REMOVAL & INSTALLATION

3.0L & 3.2L Engines

See Figures 125 and 126.

1. Before servicing the vehicle, refer to the Precautions Section.
2. Raise the vehicle and remove the engine under cover.
3. Remove the dipstick.
4. Remove the starter motor.
5. Remove the level sensor electrical connector at oil pan.
6. Remove all bolts except for 4. It is recommended that the 4 bolts in the corners of the oil pan are left in place.
7. Carefully tap the oil pan with a rubber mallet until the joint and its liquid gasket releases.
8. Remove the 4 remaining bolts.
9. Remove the oil pan.

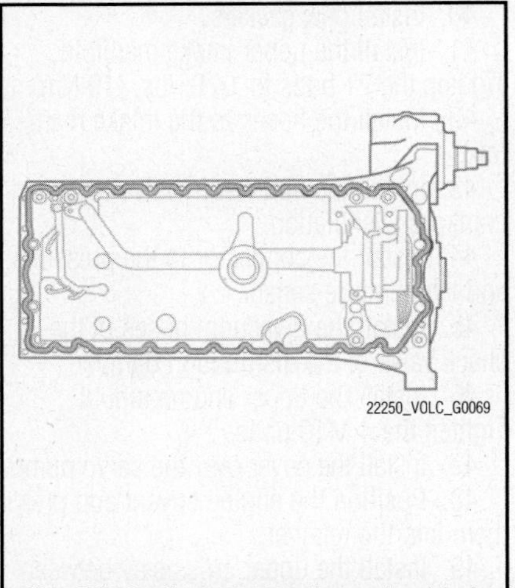
Fig. 125 Apply sealant to the engine block

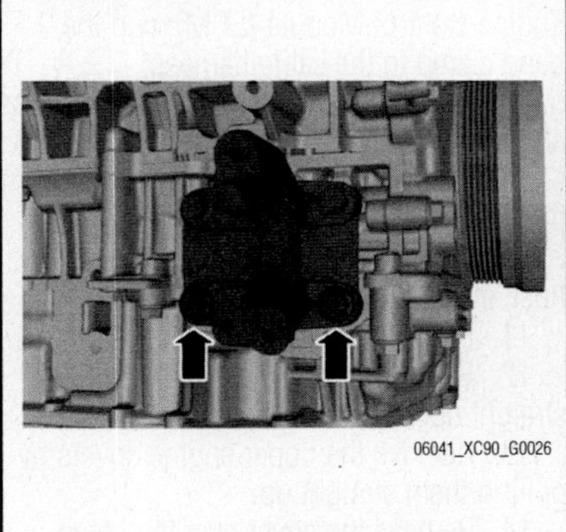
Fig. 127 View of right side engine mount—4.4L engine

Fig. 129 View of transaxle bolts—4.4L engine

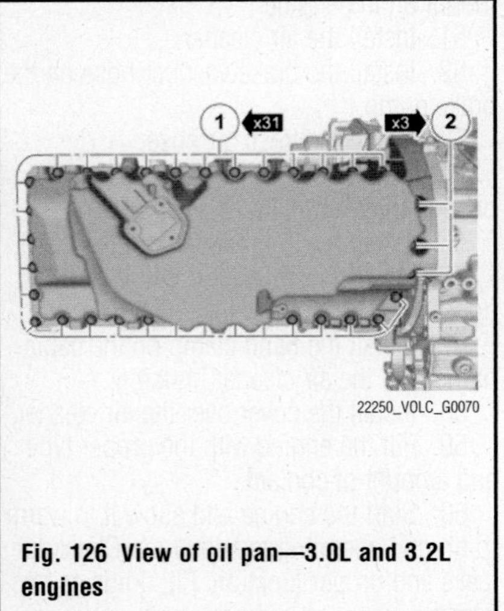

Fig. 126 View of oil pan—3.0L and 3.2L engines

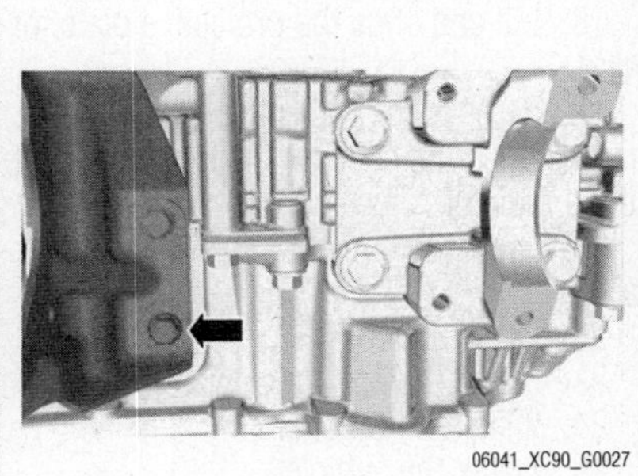
Fig. 128 View of M10 bracket bolt—4.4L engine

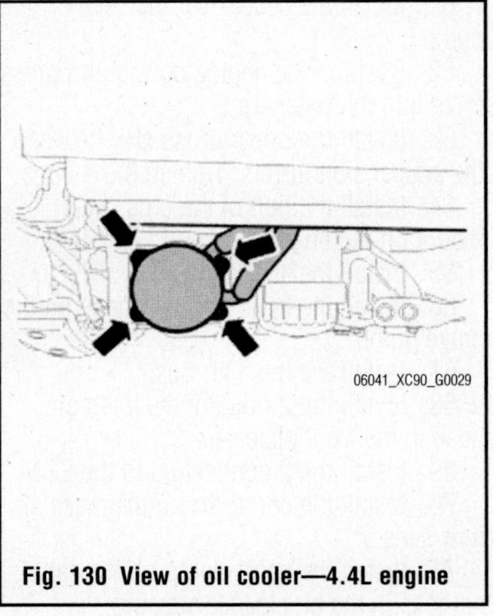
Fig. 130 View of oil cooler—4.4L engine

To install:

10. Make sure that the mating surfaces are clean and free of foreign material.
11. Apply a 2–3mm bead of sealant to the engine block.
12. Install the oil pan.
13. To ensure sealing in the joint, tighten all bolts:
    - Step 1: 13 ft. lbs. (17 Nm)
    - Step 2: 13 ft. lbs. (17 Nm) again

4.4L Engine

See Figures 127 through 133.

1. Before servicing the vehicle, refer to the Precautions Section.
2. Drain the engine oil, remove the oil filter.
3. Remove the exhaust manifolds.
4. Remove the right-hand engine mounting.
5. Remove the M10 bolt for the bracket.
6. Remove the 4 M10 bolts for the transaxle.
7. Remove the oil cooler. Discard the O-ring.
8. Remove the 20 M6 bolts.
9. Remove the oil level sensor.
10. Remove the 17 M8 bolts and the 1 M6 bolt securing the intermediate section.
11. Carefully tap the side of the oil pan using a rubber mallet. Lift out the oil pan.
12. Discard the O-rings.

To install:

➡Clean the surface, using a razor blade or a plastic scraper.

13. Apply liquid gasket 307 57050 as illustrated.

➡Use a minimum bead width of 0.039 inch (1mm).

➡Install the oil pan within 5 minutes (curing time for liquid gasket).

14. Install the oil pan, use new O-rings.
15. Install the 17 M8 bolts.
16. Install the bolt securing the intermediate section.

➡Clean the surface, using a razor blade or plastic scraper.

17. Apply liquid gasket 307 57050 as illustrated.

➡Use a minimum bead width of 0.039 inch (1mm).

➡Install the oil pan within 5 minutes (cure time for liquid gasket).

18. Install the 20 M6 bolts.
19. Install the oil level sensor.
20. Install the oil filter, using a new O-ring.
21. Install the oil cooler. Use new O-ring.
22. The remainder of installation is the reverse of removal.
23. Fill the crankcase with the proper type and amount of oil.
24. Run the engine and check for leakage.

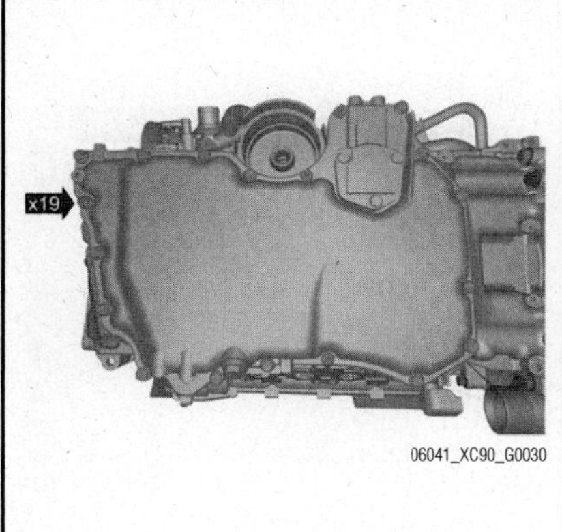

Fig. 131 Oil pan bolts shown—4.4L engine

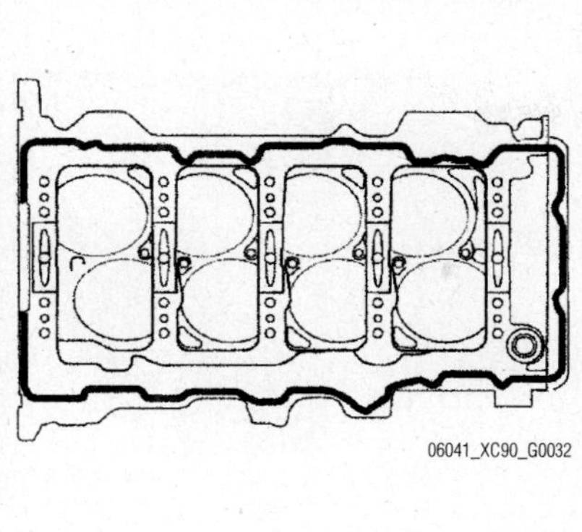

Fig. 133 Liquid gasket application—4.4L engine

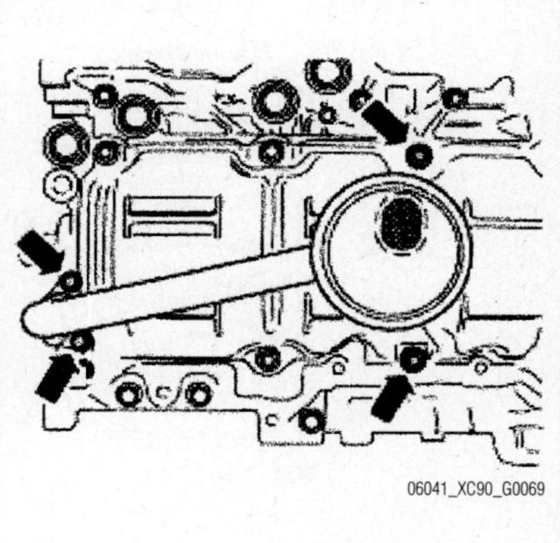

Fig. 134 Oil delivery pipe location—4.4L engine

Fig. 132 Intermediate section bolts shown—4.4L engine

OIL PUMP

REMOVAL & INSTALLATION

3.0L & 3.2L Engines

1. Before servicing the vehicle, refer to the Precautions Section.
2. Remove the timing belt.
3. Check the tensioner and idler pulleys.
4. Carefully pull the crankshaft timing gear pulley free. Remove the 4 oil pump bolts.
5. Carefully pry upward diagonally between the stop lugs and the cylinder block.
6. Lift out and remove the oil pump.

To install:

7. Install a new gasket.
8. Carefully insert the oil pump over the end of the crankshaft.

➡The sealing ring in the oil pump is very easy to damage if not installed correctly.

9. Install 4 new bolts as a guide.
10. Pull in the oil pump with tool 999-5455, or equivalent, and the crankshaft center nut.
11. Tighten the oil pump bolt. Tighten to 89 inch lbs. (10 Nm).
12. Install the timing gear pulley. Carefully tap alternately around the timing gear pulley until reaching its end position.

➡The timing gear pulley can only be in one position on the crankshaft end splines.

13. Install a new timing belt.
14. Install the pulley for the auxiliary belt. Locate the steering gear on the locating pin in the timing gear pulley.
15. Install the auxiliary belt.
16. Install counter-hold 999-5433.
17. Tighten crankshaft center nut.
18. Install the crankshaft damper. Use the crankshaft center nut as a counter-hold.
19. Check the engine oil level.

4.4L Engine

See Figures 134 and 135.

1. Before servicing the vehicle, refer to the Precautions Section.
2. Remove the timing chain.
3. Install the front engine bracket.
4. Remove the oil pan.
5. Remove the oil delivery pipe. Discard the gasket.
6. Remove the 3 M7 bolts and the oil pump.

Fig. 135 Oil pump mounting—4.4L engine

7. Discard the O-ring and the gasket for the oil delivery pipe.

To install

8. Install a new O-ring and the oil pump.
9. Install the oil delivery pipe using a new gasket.
10. Install the oil pan.
11. Install the timing chain.
12. Fill the crankcase with the proper type and amount of oil.
13. Run the engine and check for leakage.

PISTONS & RINGS

POSITIONING

3.0L & 3.2L Engines

See Figure 136.

4.4L Engine

See Figure 137.

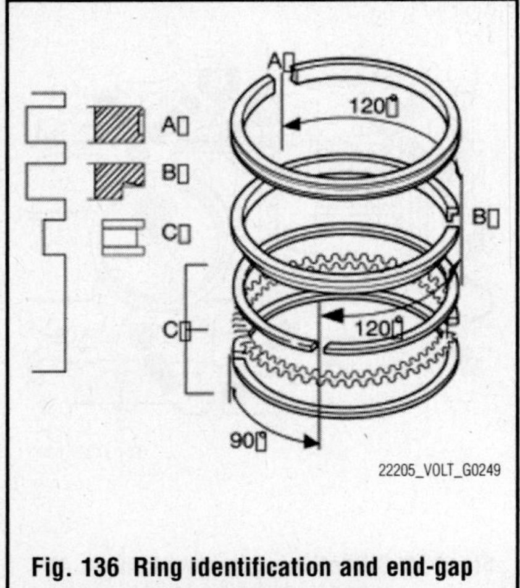

Fig. 136 Ring identification and end-gap spacing—3.0L and 3.2L engines

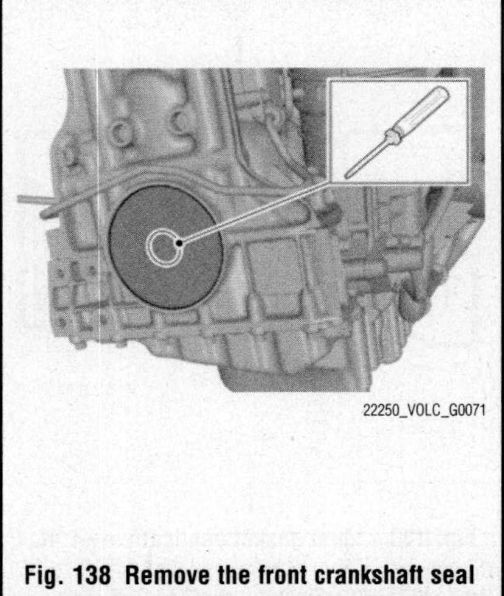

Fig. 138 Remove the front crankshaft seal

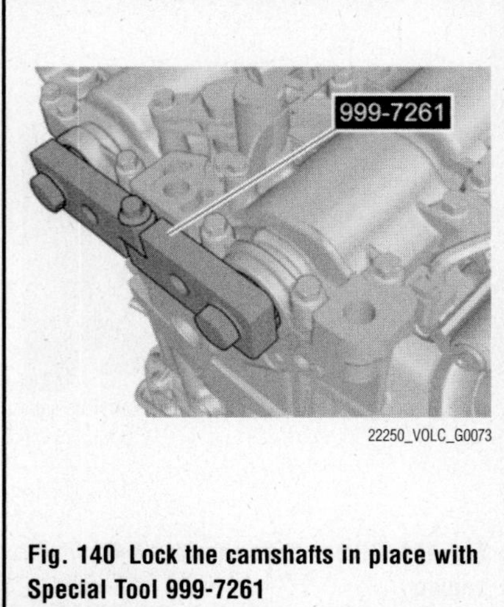

Fig. 140 Lock the camshafts in place with Special Tool 999-7261

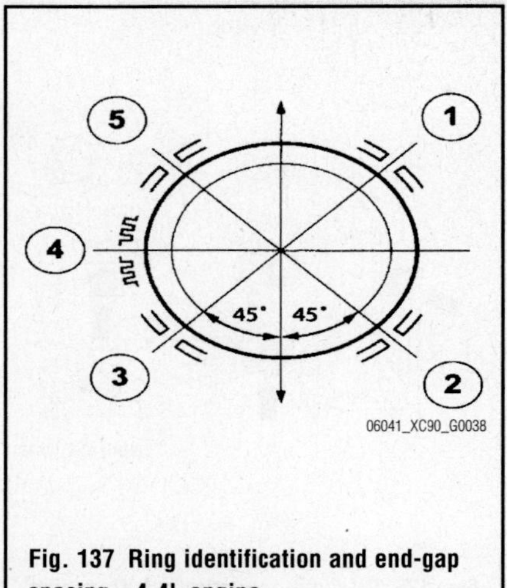

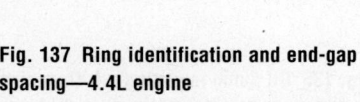

Fig. 137 Ring identification and end-gap spacing—4.4L engine

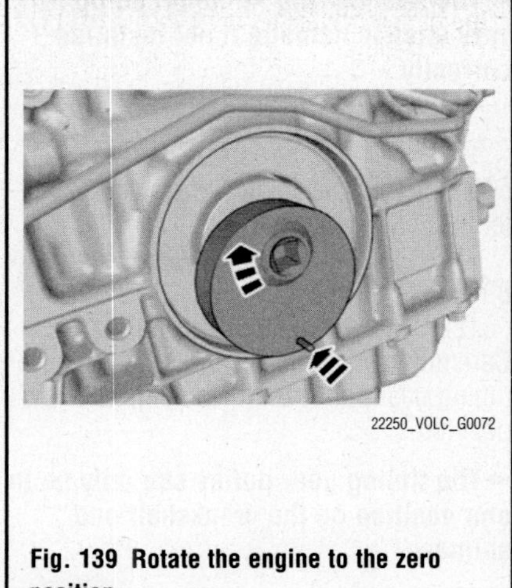

Fig. 139 Rotate the engine to the zero position

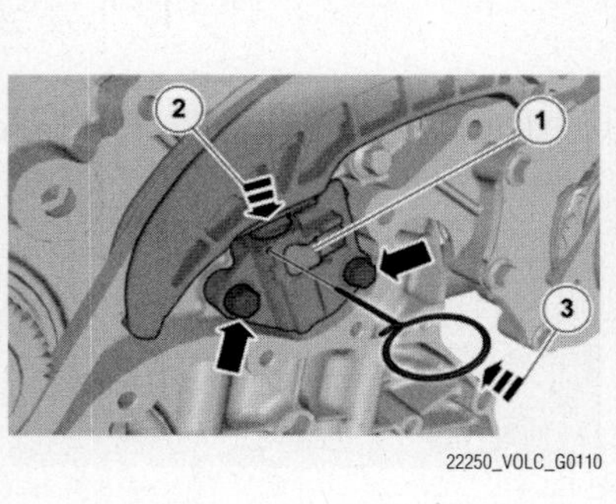

Fig. 141 View of tensioner lock tab (1), tensioner (2), and tensioner locking pin hole (3)

TIMING CHAIN COVER, CHAIN, TENSIONER, & SPROCKETS

REMOVAL & INSTALLATION

3.0L & 3.2L Engines

See Figures 138 through 146.

1. Before servicing the vehicle, refer to the Precautions Section.
2. Disconnect the negative battery cable.
3. Drain the cooling system.
4. Remove the front crankshaft seal.
5. Rotate the engine to the zero position.
6. Lock the camshafts in place with Special Tool 999-7261.
7. Remove the drive belt.
8. Remove the crank pulley cover.
9. Install the pulley removal tools 951-2926 bit Torx®50 and counter-hold 999-5760.
10. Remove the pulley.
11. Remove the components mounted to the front cover and the cover.
12. Slightly lift the tensioner lock tab.
13. Press together the tensioner.
14. Lock the tensioner with a steel wire, drill bit, or similar tool, in the tensioner hole.
15. Remove the tensioner bolts.
16. Install the special cam gear removing tools and remove the gears and timing chain.

To install:

17. Install the timing chain and camshaft gears.
18. Install the tensioner and tighten the mounting bolts to 89 inch lbs. (10 Nm).
19. Use the special cam gear tools and tighten as follows:
    - Stage 1: Center bolt, exhaust camshaft, 55 ft. lbs. (75 Nm)
    - Stage 2: Center bolt, exhaust camshaft, plus 90°
    - Center bolt, intake camshaft, 81 ft. lbs. (110 Nm)
20. Remove the rear camshaft holding tool.
21. Remove the special camshaft gear tools: 997-7264, 997-7263, and 997-7262.
22. Rotate the engine twice using the 999-7257 wrench.
23. Install a new cover seal, and intermediate shaft seal.
24. Use the tool and 3 screws in the indicated spot to guide the cover and gasket into the right position.

➡Install all bolts finger-tight before they are tightened.

25. Tighten the 3 inner M7 bolts to 13 ft. lbs. (17 Nm).
26. Tighten the outer M7 bolts in the sequence to 13 ft. lbs. (17 Nm).
27. Tighten the 2 remaining M8 bolts to 18 ft. lbs. (24 Nm).

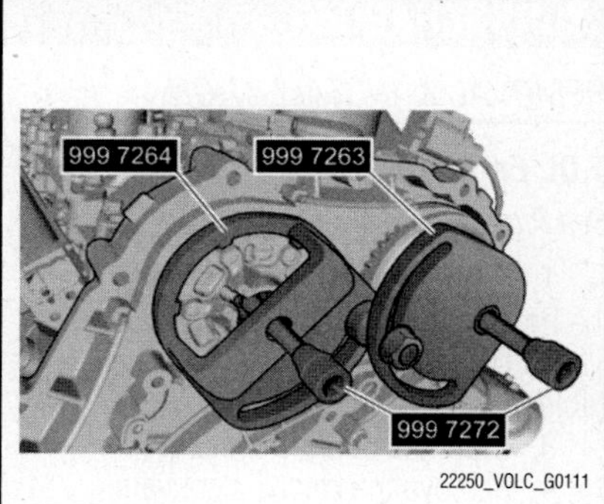

Fig. 142 View of special camshaft removal tools: 997-7264, 997-7263, and 997-7262

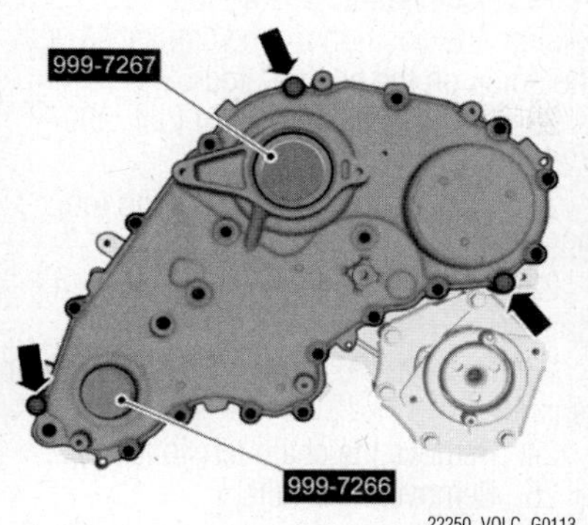

Fig. 144 Use the tool and 3 screws in the indicated spot to guide the cover and gasket into the right position

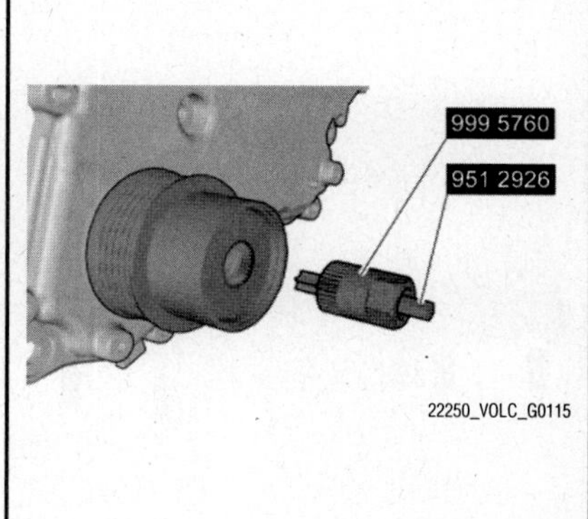

Fig. 146 Install the auxiliary pulley with special tools shown

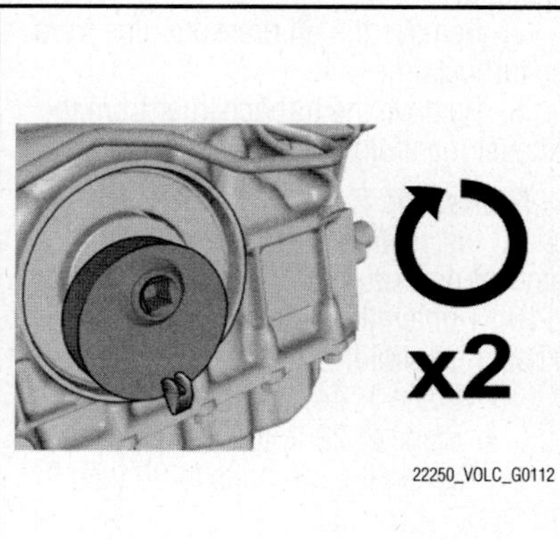

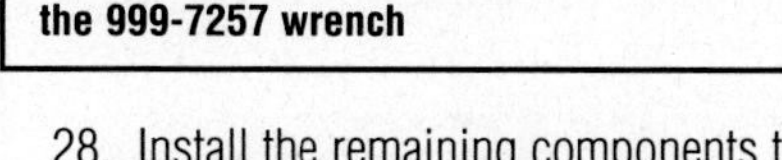

Fig. 143 Rotate the engine twice using the 999-7257 wrench

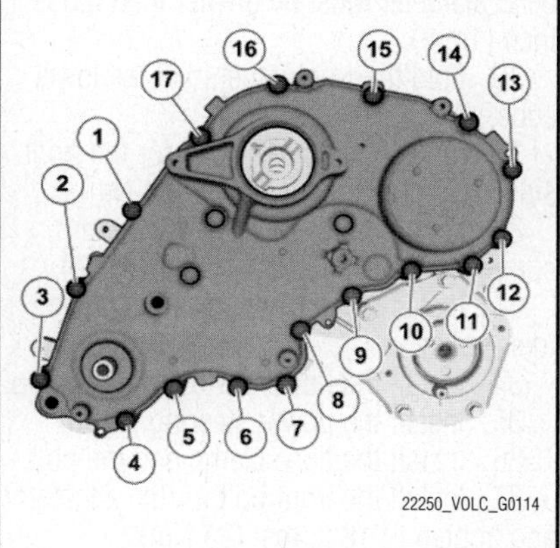

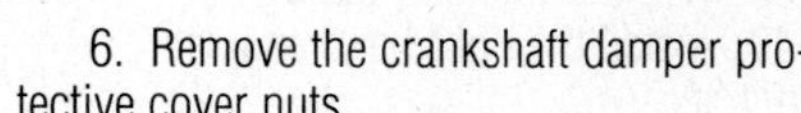

Fig. 145 Tighten the outer M7 bolts in sequence

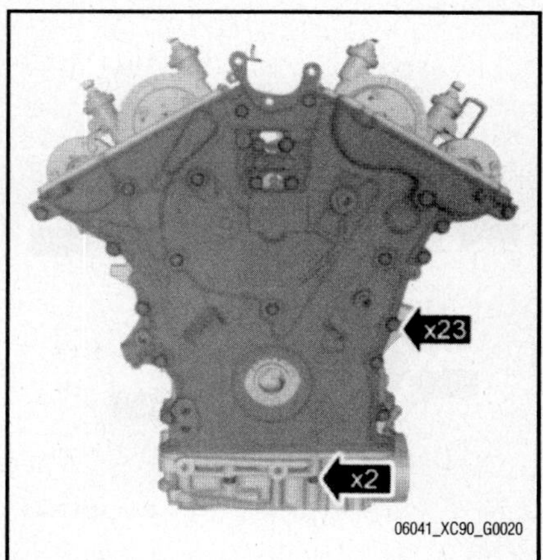

Fig. 147 Remove the front cover bolts—4.4L engine

28. Install the remaining components to the timing cover.
29. Install the auxiliary belt pulley seal.
30. Install the auxiliary pulley and tighten to 44 ft. lbs. (60 Nm).
31. Install a new pulley cover.
32. Install a new front crankshaft seal.
33. Install the drive belt.
34. Connect the negative battery cable.
35. Fill the engine cooling system and bleed the cooling system.
36. Run the engine and check for leakage.

4.4L Engine

See Figures 147 through 151.

1. Before servicing the vehicle, refer to the Precautions Section.
2. Disconnect the battery negative cable.
3. Raise and safely support the vehicle.
4. Remove the accessory drive belt.
5. Remove the right front wheel.
6. Remove the crankshaft damper protective cover nuts.
7. Push the protection towards the crankshaft damper.
8. Remove the center bolt using Special Tool 999-7196.
9. Install 999-7198 in the center hole of the crankshaft.
10. Pull off the crankshaft damper.
11. Remove the alternator.
12. Remove right engine pad.
13. Remove the right-hand engine pad/bracket.
14. Disconnect the power steering pump. Place the power steering pump to one side.
15. Remove the bolt and clamp for the power steering hose.
16. Remove the pulley from the water pump.
17. Remove the engine bracket and idler pulley
18. Remove the 25 bolts and the front cover. Discard the gaskets.

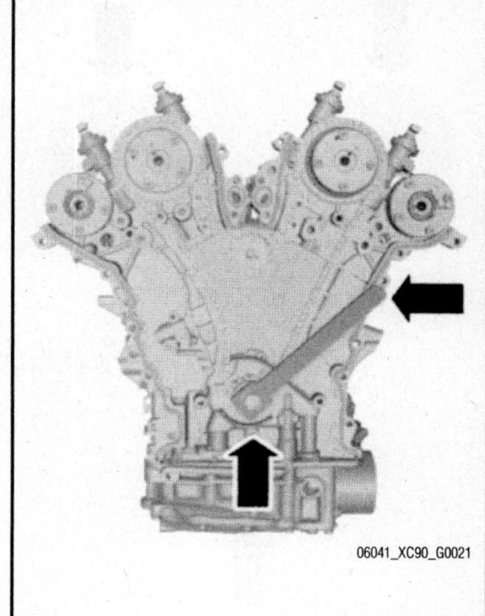

Fig. 148 Install position setting tool 999-7235—4.4L engine

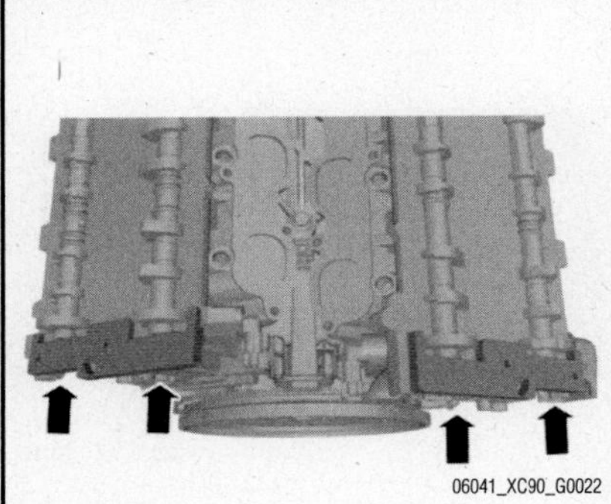

Fig. 149 Install position setting tool 999-7235—4.4L engine

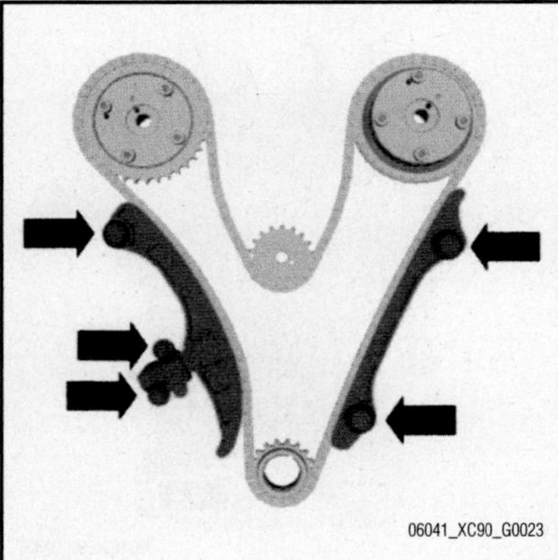

Fig. 150 View of timing chain tensioners—4.4L engine

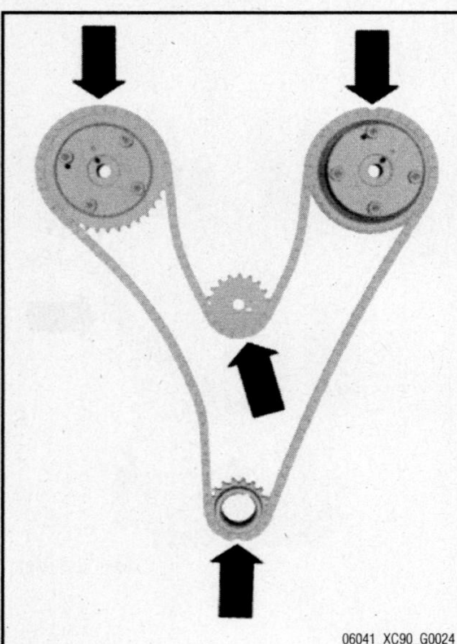

Fig. 151 View of timing chain alignment marks—4.4L engine

19. Use position setting tool 999-7235 to align the position on the crankshaft with the guide on the engine block.
20. Install position setting tool: 999-7236.
21. Remove the position setting tool: 999-7235.
22. Lock the chain tensioner using a drift.
23. Remove the 2 M6 bolts for the chain tensioner.
24. Remove the chain tensioner.
25. Remove the 2 rails.
26. Remove the timing chain.
27. Remove worn chain sprockets.

To install:

28. Adjust the color marking on the timing chain to the marking on the gears.
29. Apply liquid gasket 307 57050. The bead diameter must be greater than 0.039 inch (1mm).
30. Fold the front panel in at the lower edge.
31. Install the 23 M8 bolts for the front side and tighten to 18 ft. lbs. (24 Nm).
32. Install the 2 M8 bolts for the oil sump and tighten to 18 ft. lbs. (24 Nm).
33. Install the engine bracket and the idler pulley.
34. Install the pulley for the water pump.
35. Install the power steering pump.
36. Install the hose clamp and the bolt.
37. Install the front bolt for the alternator and tighten to 18 ft. lbs. (24 Nm).
38. Install lifting beam tool 999-5716, converted with the addition of 999-7070 and 999-5460.
39. Remove tool 999-5550.
40. Install the right-hand engine pad/brace.
41. Clean the surface for the sealing ring on the crankshaft damper with cloth 951 10.
42. Install tool 999-7196, drift 999-7198, and press in the crankshaft damper to its limit. Position using the old center bolt.
43. Remove the center bolt.
44. Insert a new bolt for the crankshaft damper and tighten 133 ft. lbs. (180 Nm).
45. Remove the tool 999-7196.
46. Install the protective cover.
47. Install the camshaft covers.
48. Install the accessory drive belt tensioner.
49. Install the wheel and tire assembly. Tighten the lug nuts in a star pattern.
    a. Step 1: 15 ft. lbs. (20 Nm).
    b. Step 2: 103 ft. lbs. (140 Nm).
50. Start the engine and run to normal operating temperature.
51. Check for leakage. Fill fluids as necessary.

TURBOCHARGER

REMOVAL & INSTALLATION

3.0L Engine

See Figure 152.

1. Before servicing the vehicle, refer to the Precautions Section.
2. Disconnect the negative battery cable.
3. Drain the cooling system.
4. Remove the catalytic converter.
5. Remove the clamps and brackets and the charge air pipe.

➡Make sure that the inside of the pipe ends are clean and free of oil residue.

6. Remove the coolant pipe at the turbocharger.
7. Remove the oil pressure pipe from the turbocharger.
8. Remove the turbocharger from the exhaust manifold.

To install:

9. Installation is the reverse of the removal procedure.
10. Tighten the turbocharger to the exhaust manifold:
    - Stage 1: 44 inch lbs. (5 Nm)
    - Stage 2: 22 ft. lbs. (30 Nm)
11. Tighten the M6 bolts to 89 inch lbs. (10 Nm).
12. Tighten the M8 bolts to 18 ft. lbs. (24 Nm).

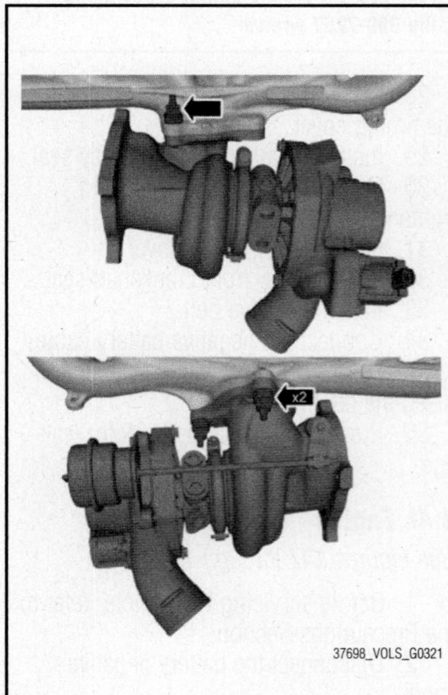

Fig. 152 Remove the turbocharger from the exhaust manifold

13. Tighten the coolant pipe-to-turbocharger to 28 ft. lbs. (38 Nm).
14. Tighten the oil pressure pipe-to-turbocharger to 28 ft. lbs. (38 Nm).
15. Tighten the crankcase connection-to-turbocharger to 18 ft. lbs. (25 Nm).

VALVE COVERS

REMOVAL & INSTALLATION

3.0L & 3.2L Engines

See Figures 153 through 161.

1. Before servicing the vehicle, refer to the Precautions Section.
2. Disconnect the negative battery cable.
3. Drain the cooling system.
4. Remove the timing cover and timing chain.
5. Remove the rear cover.
6. Remove the electrical harness connectors.
7. Remove the sensors.
8. Remove the ignition coils, lift brackets, and cover bolts.
9. Remove the camshaft cover (valve cover) assembly.

⁂ WARNING

Take extra care not to damage the mating faces.

To install:

10. Make sure that the mating faces are clean and free of foreign material.
11. Make sure that the threaded holes for the cylinder head screws are free of fluid. Use gasket solution, 1161 440. Ensure that no liquid gasket gets into the oil ducts.
12. Fit new O-rings around the spark plug sockets using Special Tool: 951-2767.

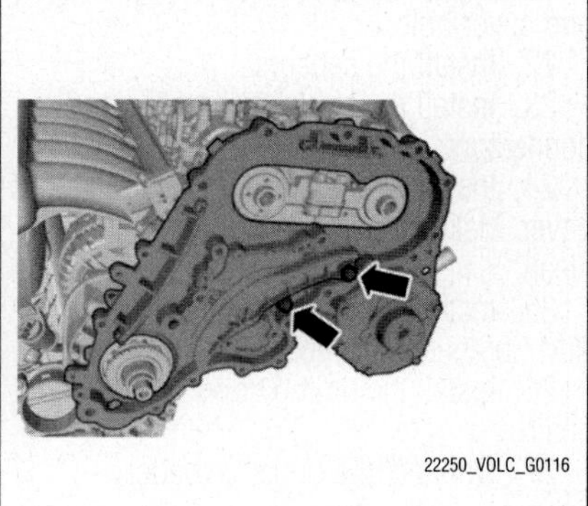

Fig. 153 Remove the rear cover and bolts

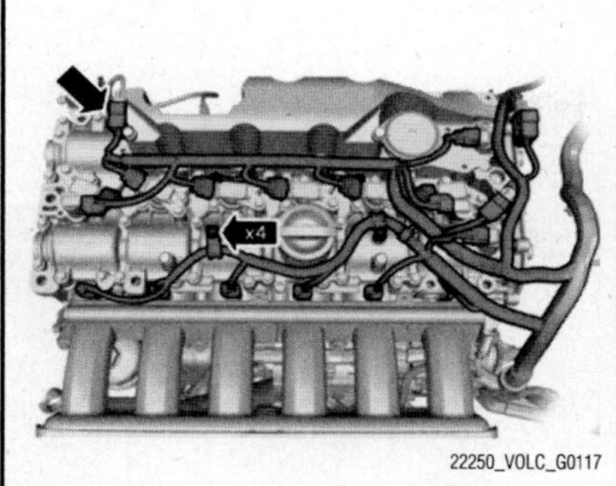

Fig. 154 Remove the electrical harness connectors

Fig. 155 Remove the ignition coils, lift brackets, and cover bolts

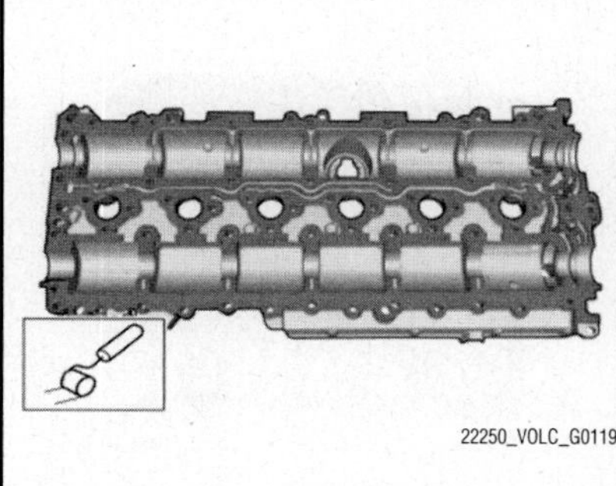

Fig. 156 Apply fluid gasket to the camshaft cover

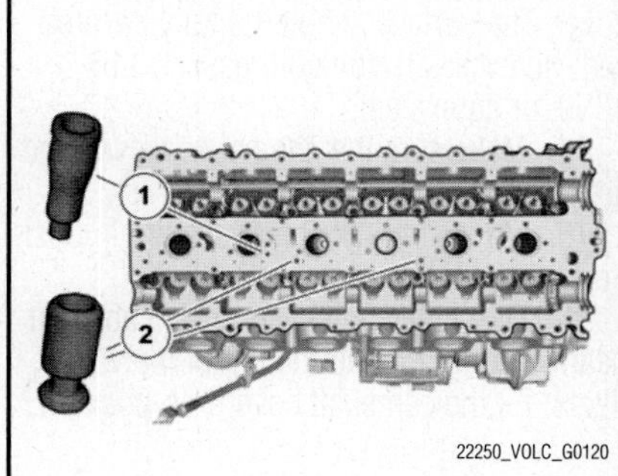

Fig. 157 Make sure that the choke valves (1) and (2) are in place

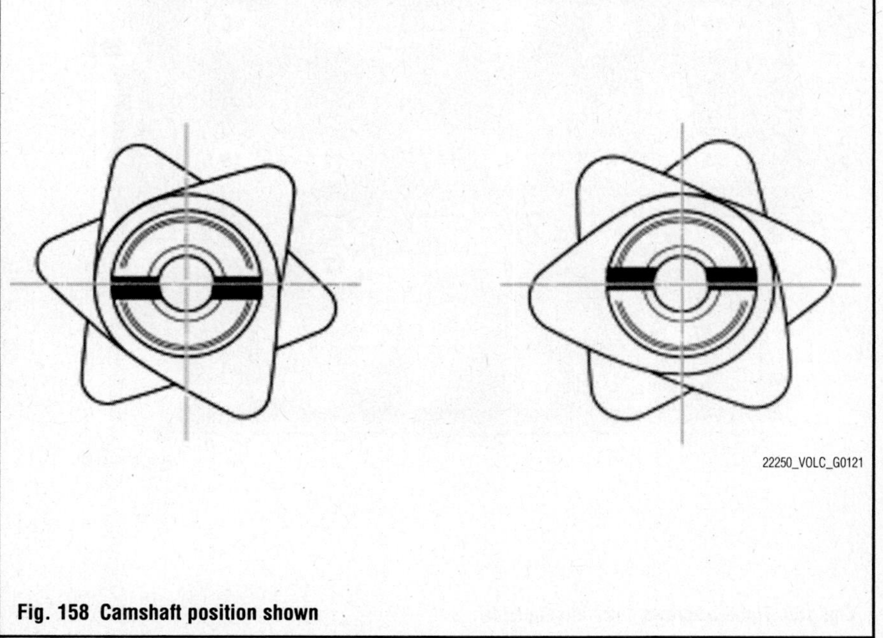

Fig. 158 Camshaft position shown

Fig. 159 Use the sequence 1–9 and tighten camshaft cover

13. Apply fluid gasket to the camshaft cover. The surface should be fully covered with no excess. Use liquid gasket, 116 1059, or equivalent.
14. Make sure that the choke valves and are in place.
15. Make sure the camshafts are in position.
16. Oil in the camshaft nodes, camshaft bearing surfaces, and the top of the valve lifters. Fit the camshaft cover into position.

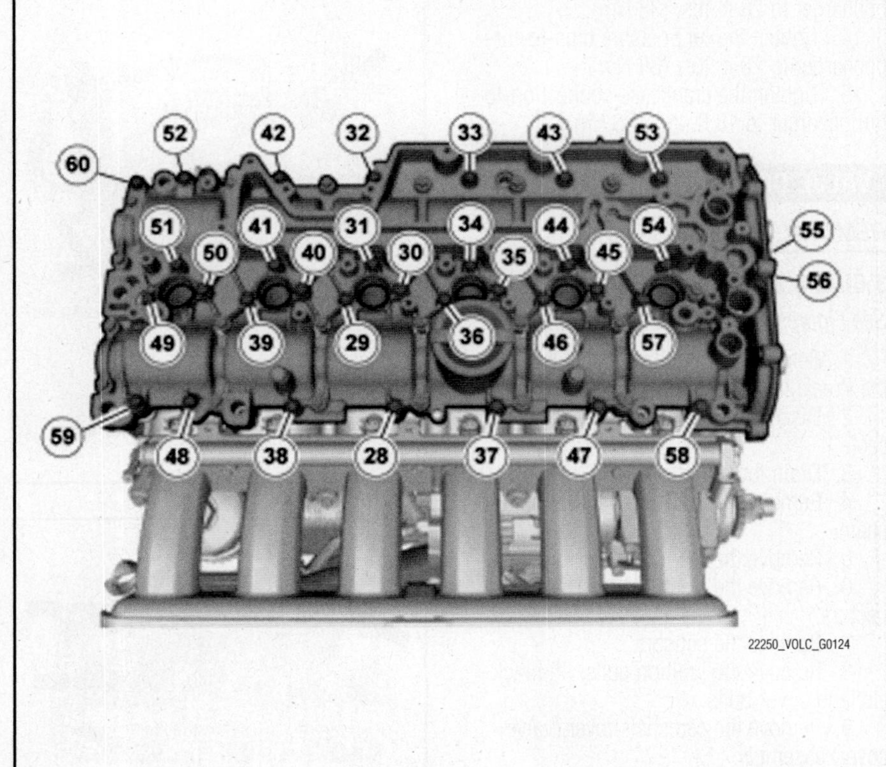

Fig. 161 Tighten screws 28–60 in sequence

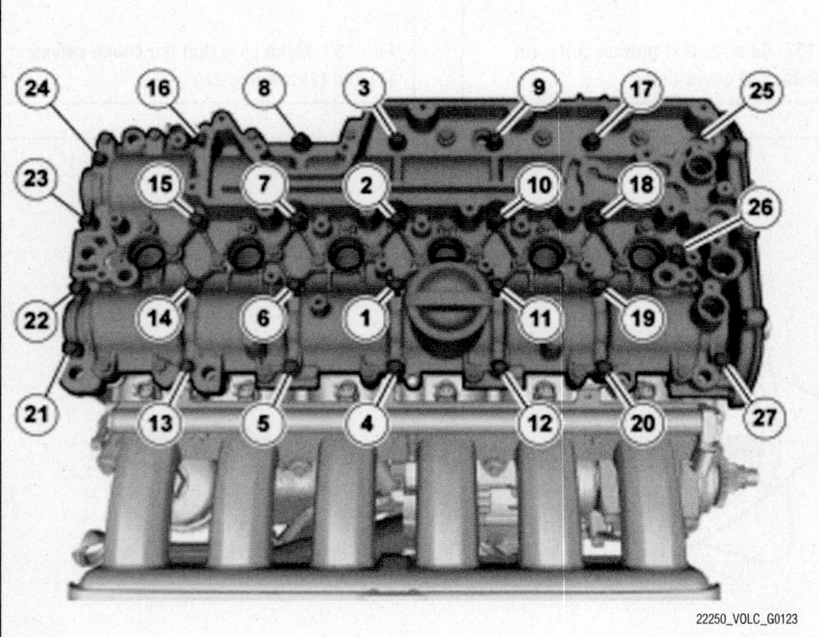

Fig. 160 Tighten screws 1–27 in sequence

17. Screw in all screws in a manner that the cover remains parallel to the cylinder head.
18. Using the torque sequence, tighten the camshaft cover to the cylinder head alternating a few turns at a time until there is full contact. Tighten other screws by hand.
19. Tighten screws 1–27, as illustrated, to 13 ft. lbs. (17 Nm).
20. Tighten screws 28–60 in sequence to 13 ft. lbs. (17 Nm).
21. Install the ignition coils, lift brackets, and cover bolts.
22. Install the sensors.
23. Install the electrical harness and connectors.
24. Install a new gasket for the rear cover. Make sure the contact surface is clean.
25. Install the rear cover and tighten the 2 M7 bolts to 13 ft. lbs. (17 Nm).
26. Install the timing cover and timing chain.
27. Connect the negative battery cable.
28. Fill the engine coolant and bleed the cooling system.
29. Start the vehicle and check for leaks.

4.4L Engine

See Figures 162 through 164.

1. Before servicing the vehicle, refer to the Precautions Section.
2. Release the fuel pressure.
3. Remove the engine covers.
4. Drain the cooling system.
5. Disconnect the negative battery cable.
6. Remove the following for the left valve cover:
   - Upper and lower intake manifold
   - Electrical connections
   - Ignition coils
   - Engine harness and bracket nuts
   - Valve cover mounting bolts
   - Valve cover
7. Remove the following for the right valve cover:
   - Fuel lines and mounting brackets
   - Sensor connectors
   - Ignition coils
   - Valve cover mounting bolts
   - Valve cover

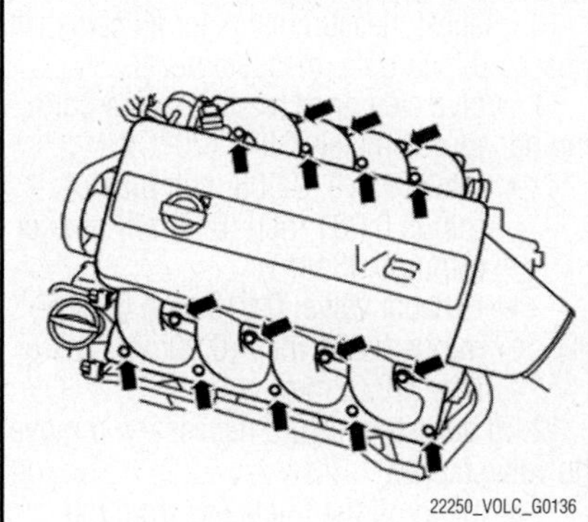

Fig. 162 Upper intake manifold and mounting bolts shown

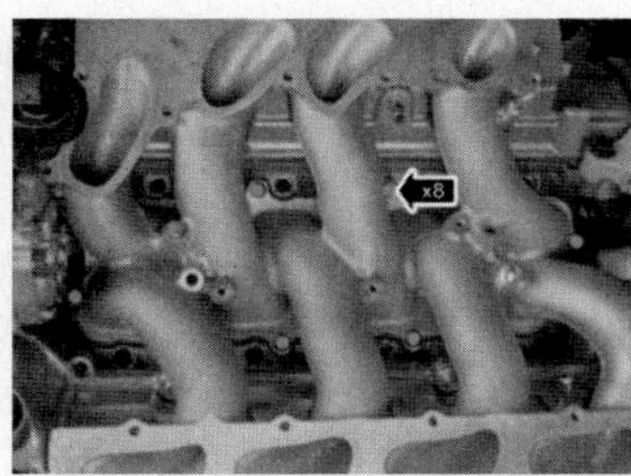

Fig. 163 Lower intake manifold and mounting bolts shown

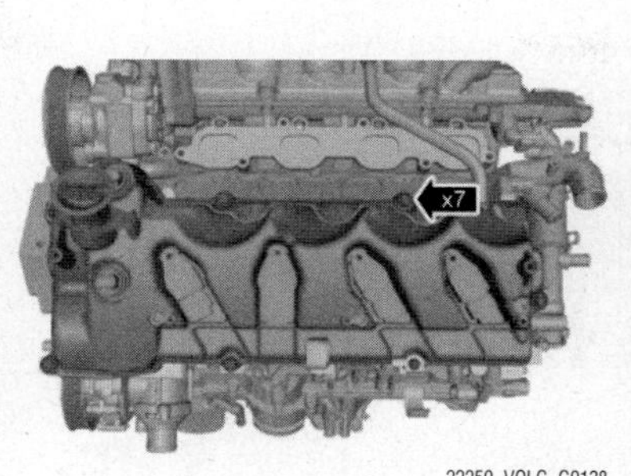

Fig. 164 Right valve cover and mounting bolts shown

To install:

8. Clean the mating surface and install new gaskets.
9. Reverse the removal procedure and note the following:
   - Tighten the valve cover mounting bolts to 89 inch lbs. (10 Nm)
   - Tighten the ignition coil mounting bolts to 89 inch lbs. (10 Nm)
   - Tighten all bracket nuts to 89 inch lbs. (10 Nm)
   - Tighten the intake manifold bolts to 14 ft. lbs. (19 Nm).

VALVE LASH CLEARANCE

ADJUSTMENT

3.0L & 3.2L Engines

See Figures 165 through 167.

1. Before servicing the vehicle, refer to the Precautions Section.

➡To ensure that the valves lie correctly in their seats, carefully tap on the valve stem ends. Use a drift made of plastic, brass, or aluminum to protect the valve and the surface for the valve lifter. The sound made when tapping indicates whether the valve is correctly positioned.

2. Using special tool 999-7257, rotate the engine 30° clockwise to prevent the valves from colliding with the pistons when the camshaft is rotated.
3. Refit all exhaust valve lifters following the markings made during removal.
4. If the markings have disappeared or if adjustments are to be made on a new cylinder head, use valve lifters of 0.113 inch (2.905mm) in thickness as a base.
5. Using special tool 999-7281, position the exhaust camshaft and screw it down towards its bearing mounting. Start in the middle and screw the bearing caps down alternating. Do not tighten

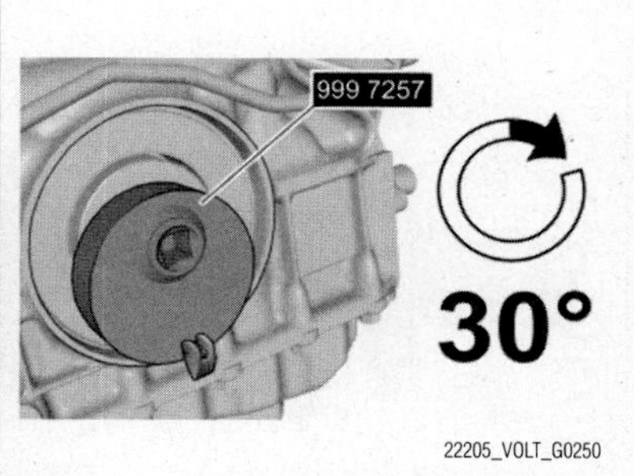

Fig. 165 Using special tool 999-7257, rotate the engine 30 degrees clockwise to prevent the valves from colliding with the pistons when the camshaft is rotated

6. Valve clearance measurements should only be taken on a cold engine. A suitable temperature is approximately 68°F (20°C).
7. The camshaft nodes on the cylinder whose valves are to be measured should point straight up in the direction of the valve.
8. Tighten the M7 screws of the press tools to 13 ft. lbs. (17 Nm).
9. Press with your finger so that the feeler gauge is parallel to the top of the lifter. To ensure that measuring is as accurate as possible, move the feeler gauge laterally when measuring the clearance.

Valve clearance as measured on a cold engine should be as follows:

- -0.0004 inch (-0.01mm) at 59°F (15°C)
- +0.0004 inch (+0.01mm) at 77°F (25°C)
- +0.0008 inch (+0.02mm) at 86°F (30°C)
- +0.0012 inch (+0.03mm) at 95°F (35°C)
- +0.0016 inch (+0.04mm) at 113°F (45°C)

10. Using special tool 999-7261, repeat the work by loosening the screws of the press tools and rotating the camshaft until the next node pair is in the correct position. Tighten and continue measuring until all exhaust valves have been measured.
11. Carefully note the results.
12. Correcting measured clearance as necessary.
13. Remove the press tools. Lift off the camshaft. Adjust the clearance by replacing

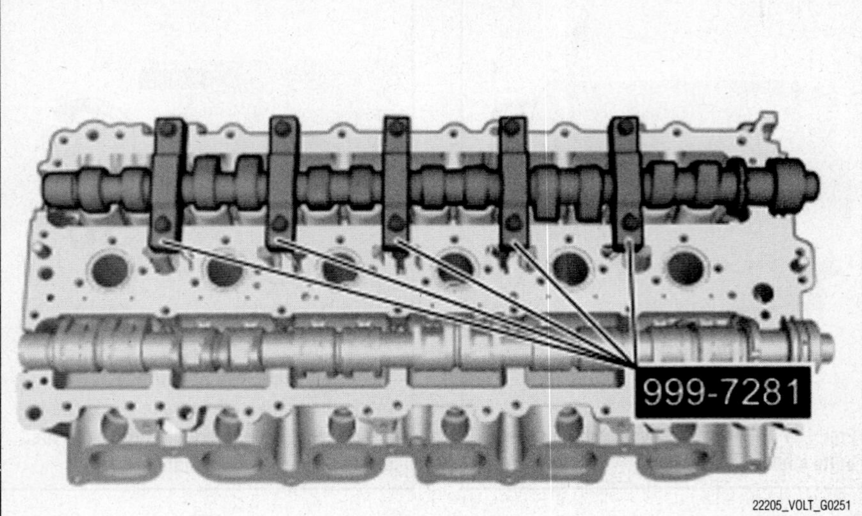

Fig. 166 Using special tool 999-7281 position the exhaust camshaft and screw it down towards its bearing mounting

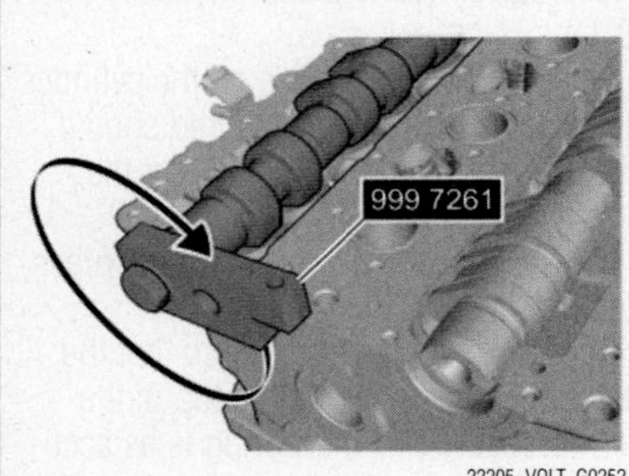

Fig. 167 Using special tool 999-7261, repeat the work by loosening the screws of the press tools and rotating the camshaft until the next node pair is in the correct position

the lifter. Alternative lifters are available as a spare part/spare part kit. Reinstall the camshaft and press tools. Tighten to 13 ft. lbs. (17 Nm). Recheck the valve clearance on the adjusted valves.

14. When the correct valve clearance has been achieved, remove the press tools.
15. Install the valve cover.
16. Test drive the engine until the thermostat opens and check for any leakage.

4.4L Engine

See Figure 168.

1. Before servicing the vehicle, refer to the Precautions Section.
2. Remove intake manifold.
3. Remove air induction pipe.
4. Remove ignition coils on the left and right banks.
5. Remove camshaft covers.

➡**Measurements should only be taken on a cold engine. A suitable temperature is approximately 68°F (20°C).**

6. Turn the crankshaft until the cam lobe is 180° to the valve lifter.
7. Measure the valve clearance between the camshaft and the valve lifter using a feeler gauge 999-5752.

⁂ WARNING

Only turn the crankshaft in normal rotational direction (clockwise).

8. Using a feeler gauge 999-5752,

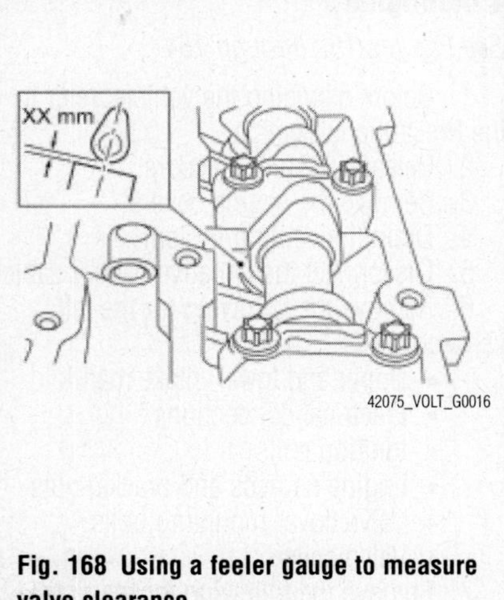

Fig. 168 Using a feeler gauge to measure valve clearance

press with a finger so that the feeler gauge lies parallel to the upper side of the valve lifter.

9. Move the feeler gauge sideways when taking the reading in order to obtain an accurate measurement.
10. Repeat measurements for all camshaft lobes and record the measurements.
11. Valve clearance readings on a cold engine, approximately 68°F (20°C):
    - Intake valve: 0.008 inch plus or minus 0.001 inch (0.20mm plus or minus 0.03mm)
    - Exhaust valve: 0.016 inch plus or minus 0.001 inch (0.30mm plus or minus 0.03mm)
12. If adjustments are necessary, remove the valve tappet:
    a. Read off the thickness from the underside of tappet.
    b. Calculate the required thickness of the valve lifter to be used.

➡**The thickness of the existing valve lifter plus the measured valve clearance equals the required value of new tappet minus the cold engine tolerance.**

    c. Install the correct valve tappet and measure the clearance again.

13. Install the camshaft covers.
14. Install intake manifold.
15. Test drive the vehicle until the thermostat opens and check for any leakage.

ENGINE PERFORMANCE & EMISSION CONTROLS

COMPONENT LOCATIONS

3.0L Engine

See Figure 169.

3.2L Engine

See Figures 170 and 171.

4.4L Engine

See Figure 172.

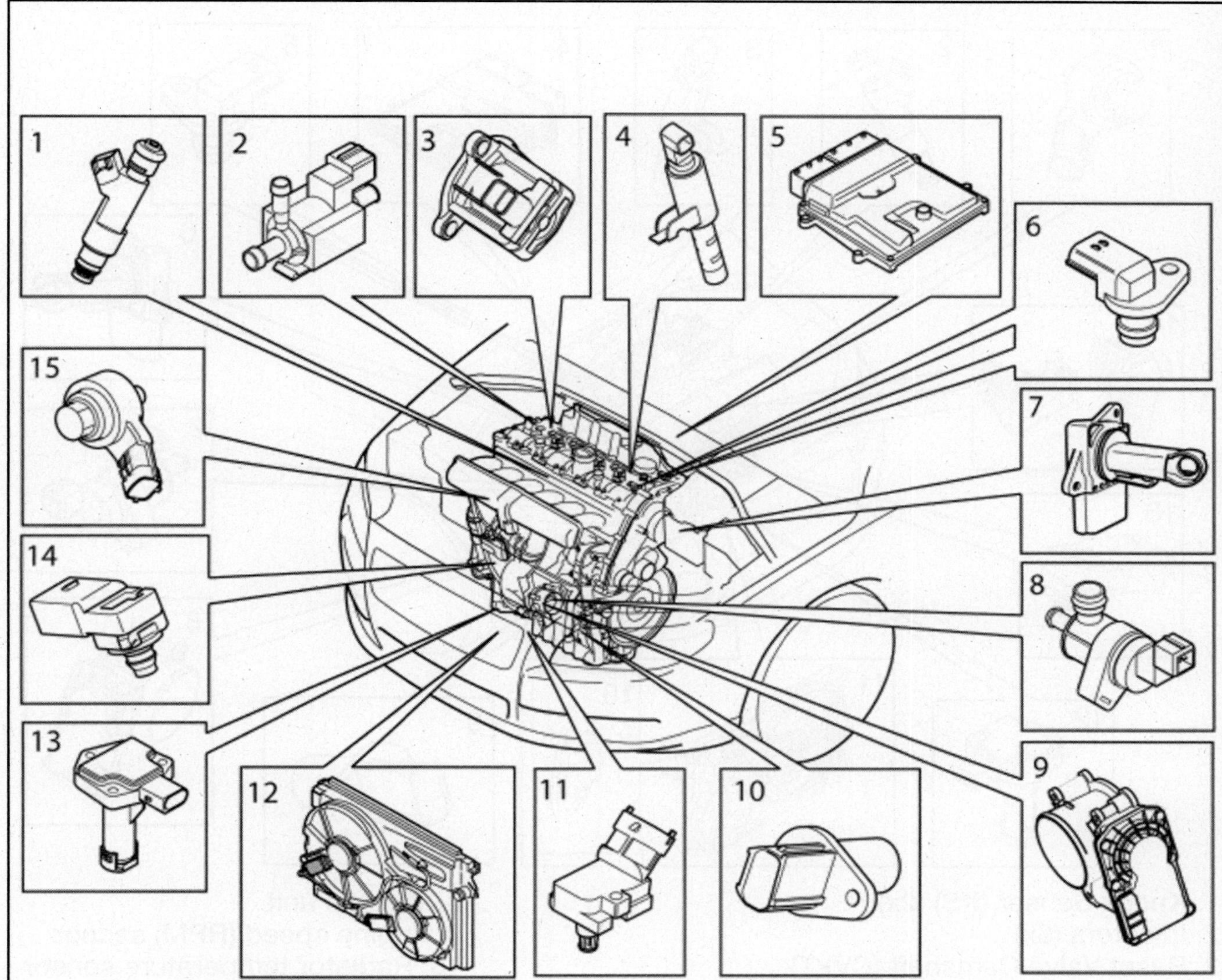

1. Injectors (6x)
2. Turbocharger (TC) control valve
3. Relief valve
4. Reset Valve Camshaft (CVVT)
5. Engine Control Module (ECM)
6. Camshaft sensor (2x)
7. Mass Air Flow (MAF) sensor/air temperature sensor
8. Evaporative emission system (EVAP) valve
9. Throttle unit
10. Engine speed (RPM) sensor
11. Charge pressure sensor
12. Engine Cooling Fan (FC)
13. Oil level sensor
14. Intake pressure sensor
15. Knock sensor (2x)

37698_VOLS_G0325

Fig. 169 Engine component locations—B6304T4 engine

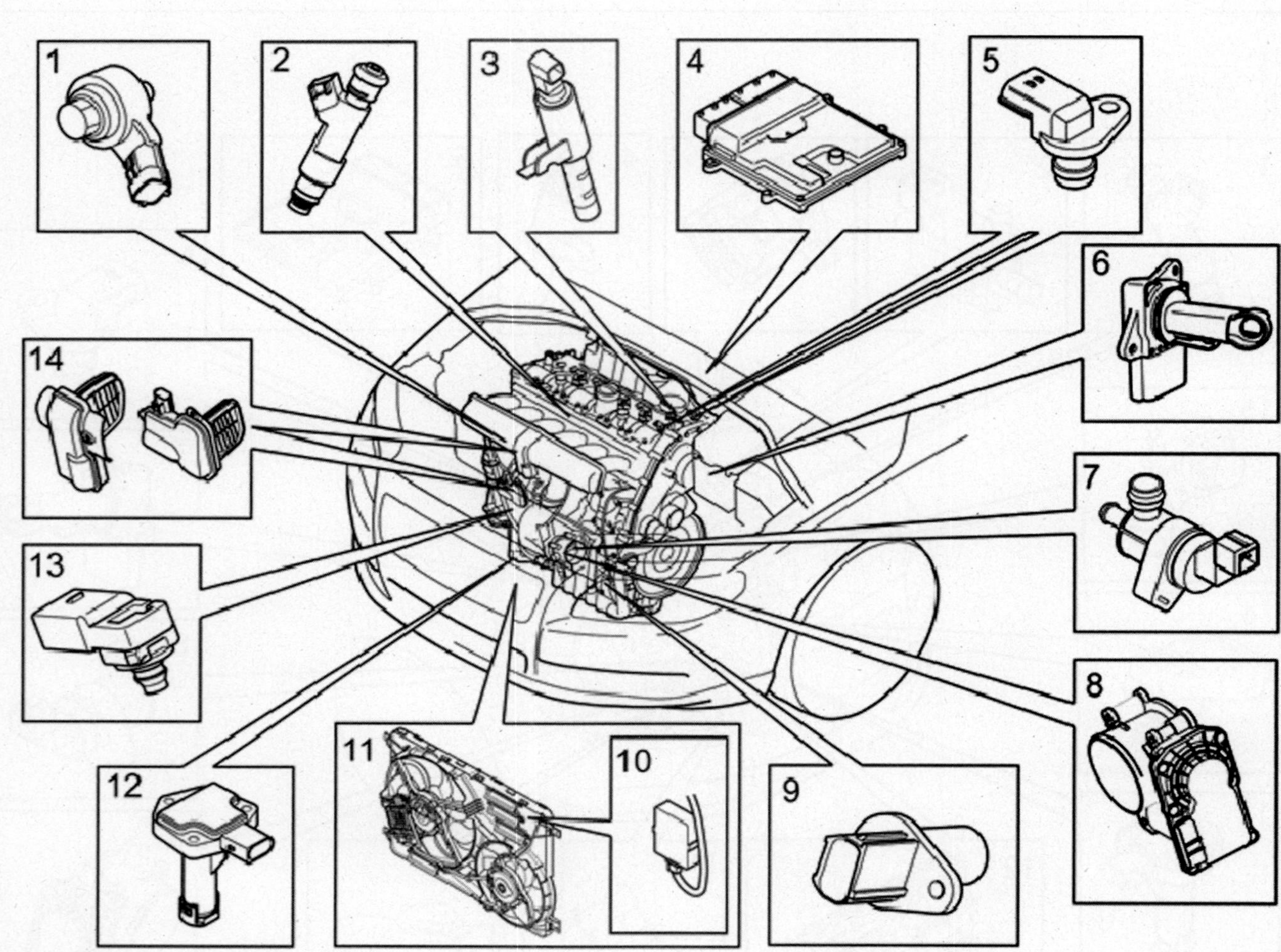

1. Knock Sensor (KS) (2x)
2. Injectors (6x)
3. Reset Valve Camshaft (CVVT)
4. Engine control module (ECM)
5. Camshaft sensor (2x)
6. Mass Air Flow (MAF) sensor/air temperature sensor
7. Evaporative emission system (EVAP) valve
8. Throttle unit
9. Engine speed (RPM) sensor
10. Radiator temperature sensor
11. Engine Cooling Fan (FC)
12. Oil level sensor
13. Intake pressure sensor
14. Actuator variable intake (2x)

37698_VOLS_G0327

Fig. 170 Engine component locations—B6324S4 engine

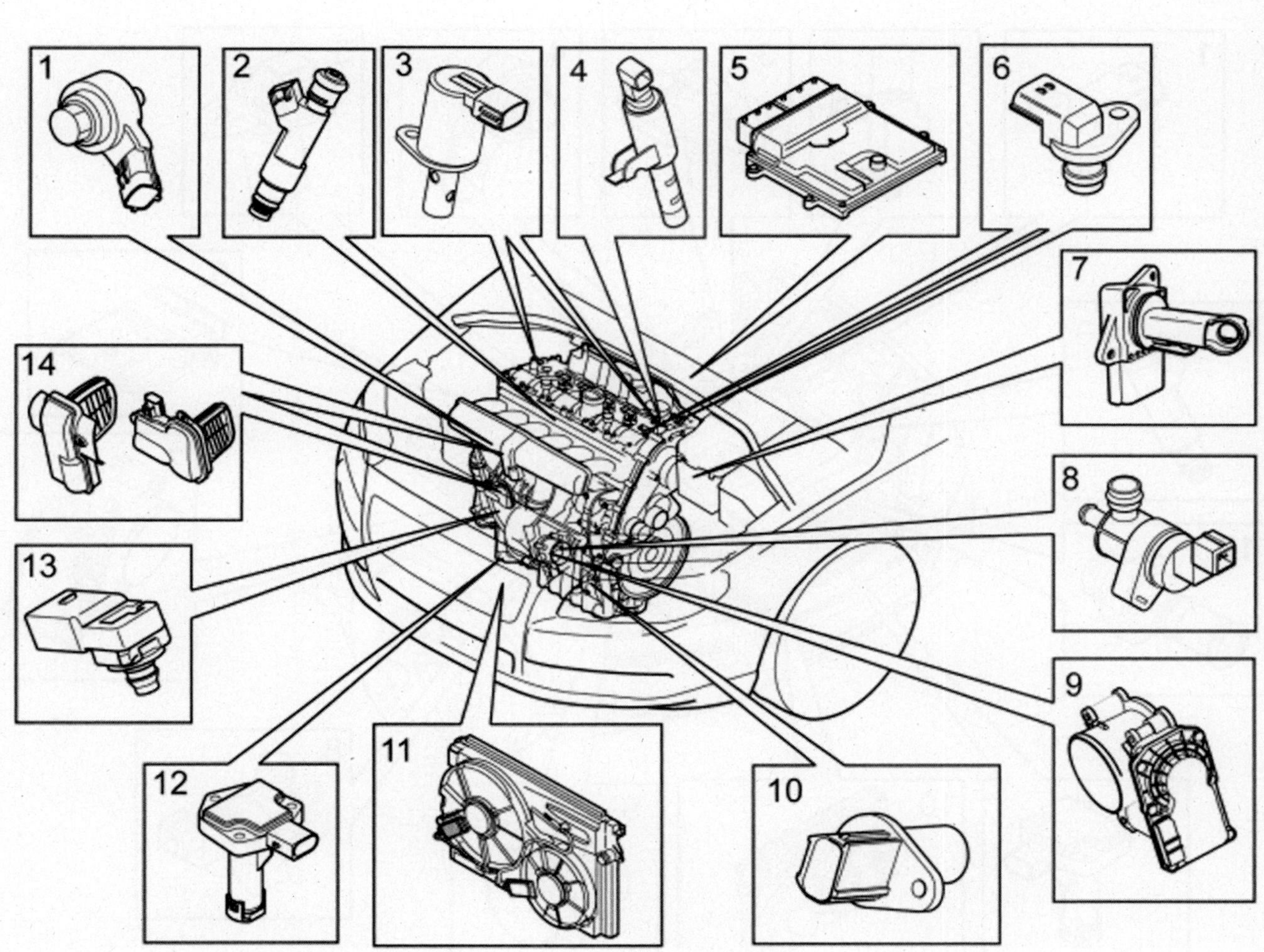

1. Knock Sensor (KS) (2x)
2. Injectors (6x)
3. Cam profile valve (2x)
4. Reset Valve Camshaft (CVVT)
5. Engine Control Module (ECM)
6. Camshaft sensor (2x)
7. Mass Air Flow (MAF) sensor/air temperature sensor
8. Evaporative emission system (EVAP) valve
9. Throttle unit
10. Engine speed (RPM) sensor
11. Engine Cooling Fan (FC)
12. Oil level sensor
13. Intake pressure sensor
14. Actuator variable intake (2x)

37698_VOLS_G0326

Fig. 171 Engine component locations—B6324S5 engine

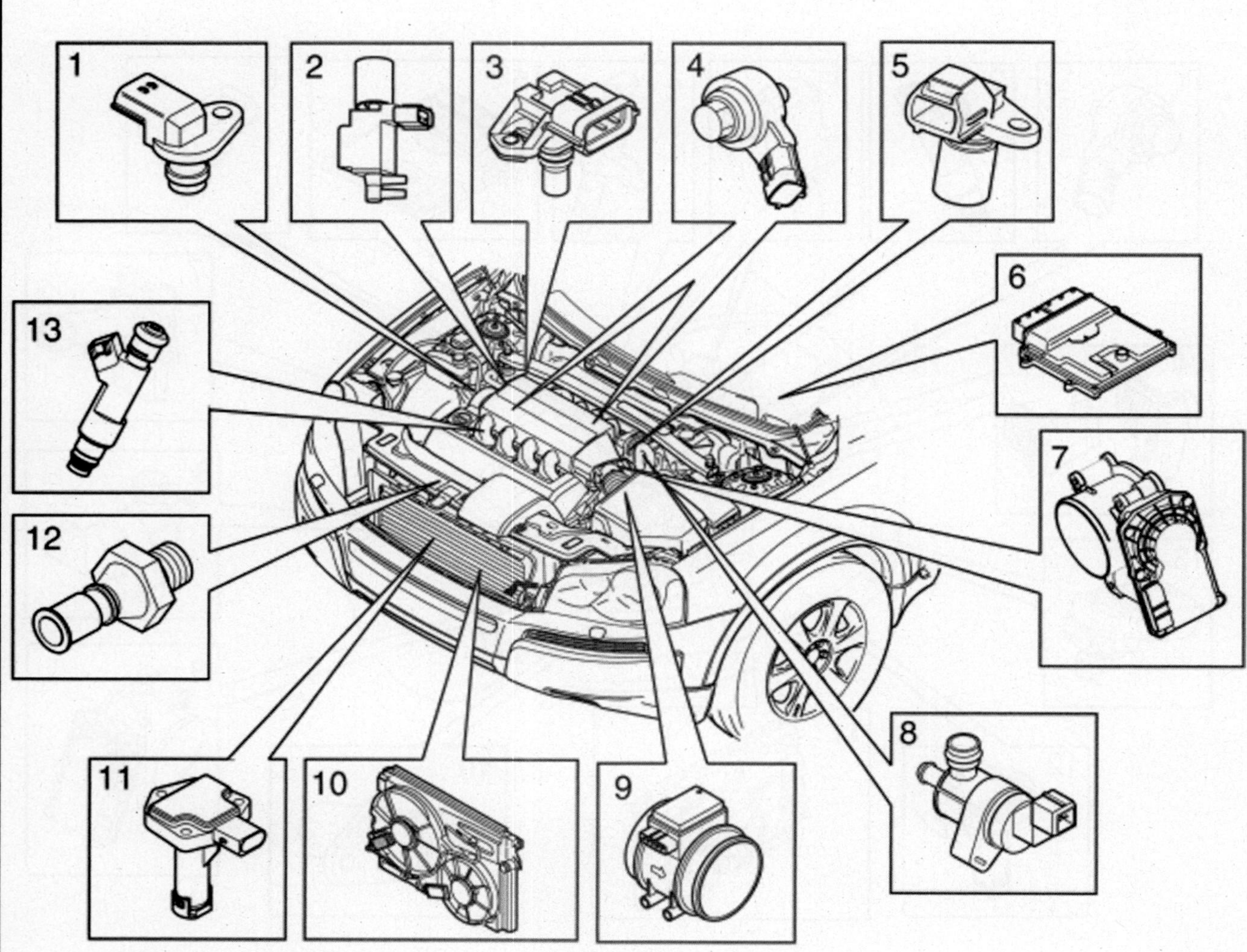

1. Camshaft sensors (4x)
2. Variable inlet, solenoid valve (TST)
3. Air pressure sensor inlet
4. Knock Sensor (KS)
5. Engine speed (RPM) sensor
6. Engine Control Module (ECM)
7. Throttle unit
8. EVAP valve
9. Mass Air Flow sensor/air temperature sensor
10. Engine Cooling Fan (FC)
11. Oil level sensor
12. Oil pressure monitor
13. Injector

37698_VOLS_G0328

Fig. 172 Engine component locations—B8444S engine

ACCELERATOR PEDAL POSITION (APP) SENSOR

LOCATION

See Figure 173.

The Accelerator Pedal Position (APP) sensor is located inside the vehicle and is integral to the accelerator pedal.

REMOVAL & INSTALLATION

See Figure 174.

1. Remove the Accelerator Pedal Position (APP) sensor connector.
2. Remove the 3 mounting nuts.
3. Remove the APP sensor.

To install:

4. Install the APP sensor and tighten the mounting nuts to 89 inch lbs. (10 Nm).
5. Reconnect the APP sensor connector.

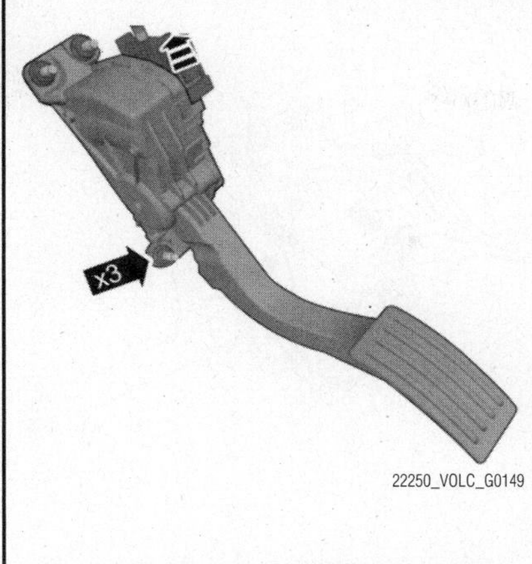

Fig. 174 Accelerator Pedal Position (APP) sensor view

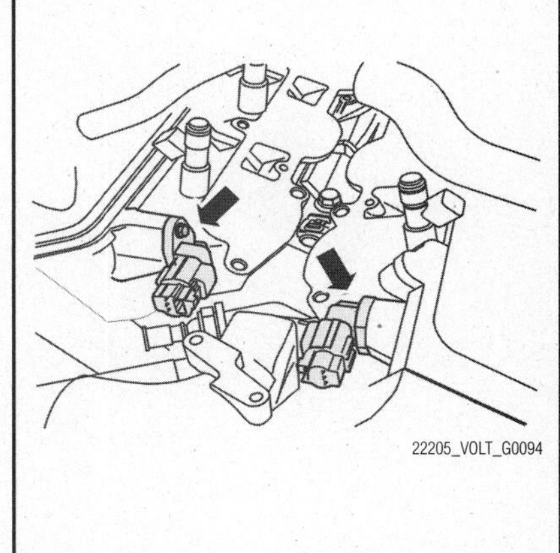

Fig. 176 Intake Camshaft Position (CMP) sensor location—4.4L engine

CAMSHAFT POSITION (CMP) SENSOR

LOCATION

3.0L & 3.2L Engines

See Figure 175.

The Camshaft Position (CMP) sensor is located in the valve cover under the engine cover.

4.4L Engine

See Figures 176 and 177.

The Camshaft Position (CMP) sensors are located under the intake manifold.

REMOVAL & INSTALLATION

3.0L & 3.2L Engines

1. Before servicing the vehicle, refer to the Precautions Section.
2. Remove the engine cover.
3. Remove the camshaft sensor.

To install:

4. Install the Camshaft Position (CMP) sensor.

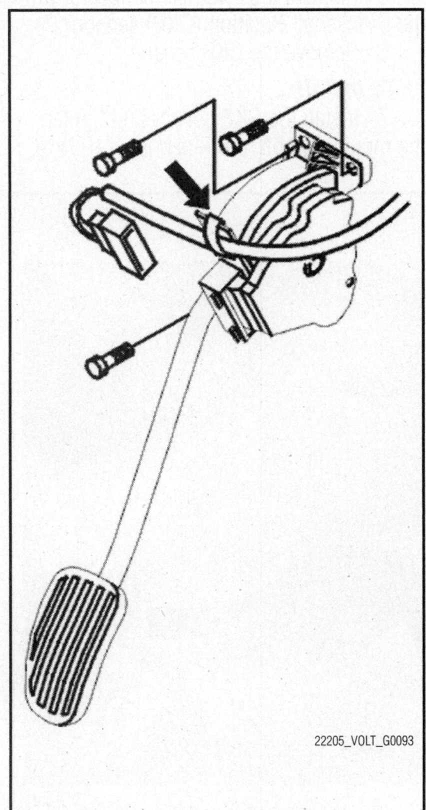

Fig. 173 Accelerator Pedal Position (APP) sensor location

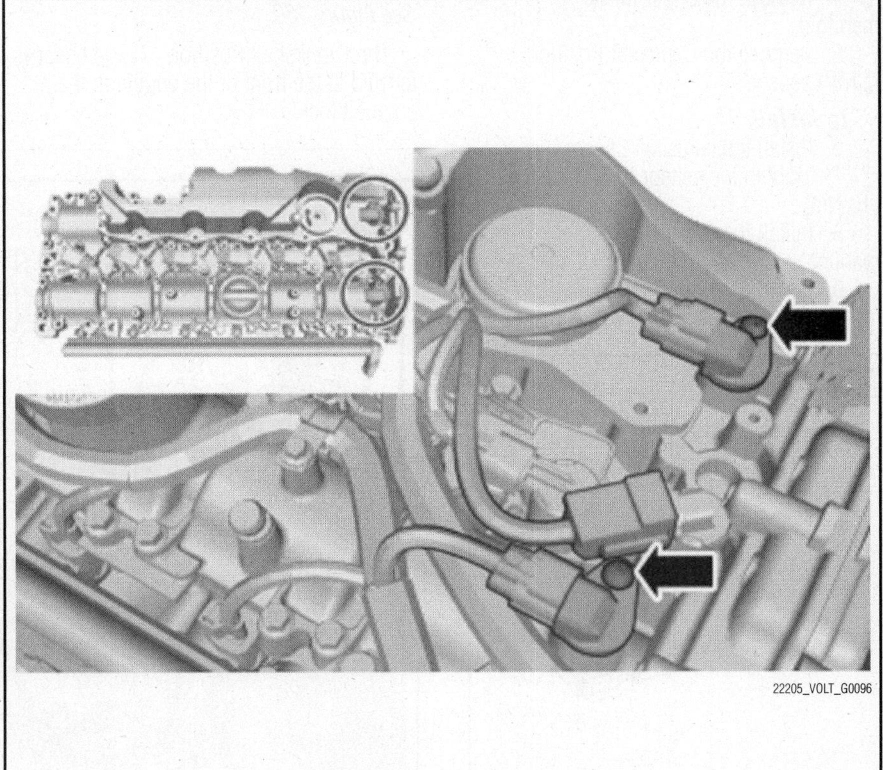

Fig. 175 Camshaft Position (CMP) sensor location—3.0L and 3.2L engines

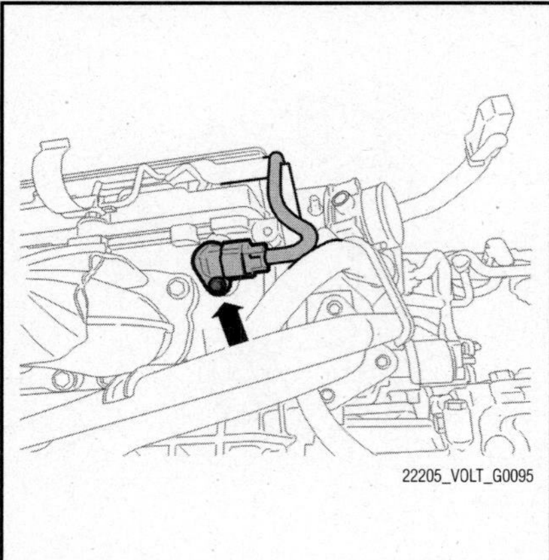
Fig. 177 Exhaust Camshaft Position (CMP) sensor location—4.4L engine

5. Tighten the screw to 66 inch. lbs. (8 Nm).
6. Install the engine cover.

4.4L Engine

See Figures 178 and 179.

1. Before servicing the vehicle, refer to the Precautions Section.
2. Remove the engine covers.
3. Remove the Mass Air Flow (MAF) connector and air hose.
4. Remove the upper intake manifold.
5. Remove the Camshaft Position (CMP) sensor.

To install:

6. Install the camshaft sensor.
7. Tighten the sensor to 89 inch lbs. (10 Nm).
8. Install the upper intake manifold.
9. Install a new gasket.

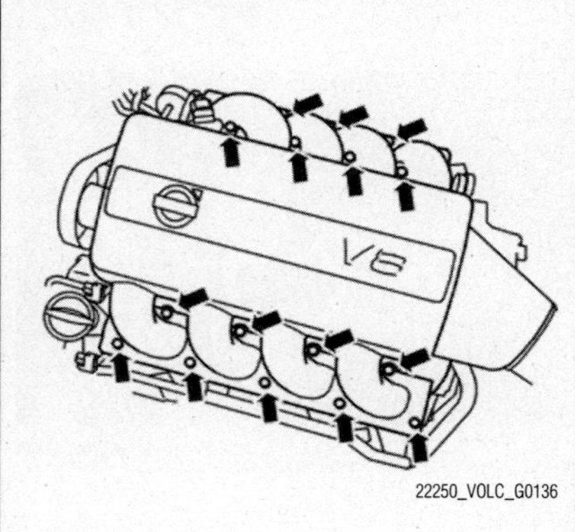
Fig. 178 Upper intake manifold and mounting bolt view

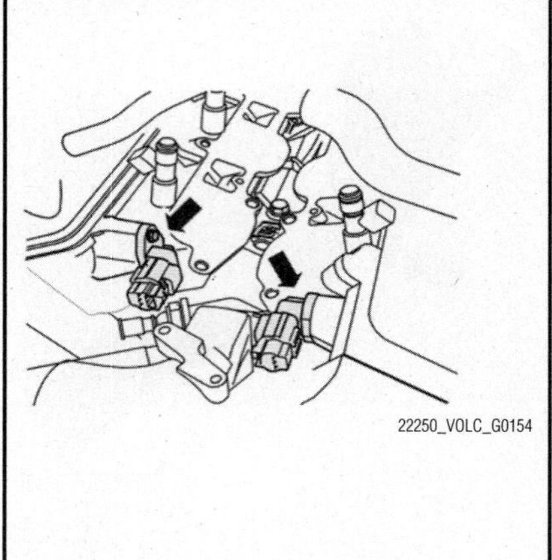
Fig. 179 Camshaft sensor view

10. Tighten the mounting bolts to 18 ft. lbs. (24 Nm).
11. Install the MAF connector and air hose.
12. Install the engine covers.

CRANKSHAFT POSITION (CKP) SENSOR

LOCATION

3.0L & 3.2L Engines

See Figure 180.

The Crankshaft Position (CKP) sensor is located at the front of the engine in the engine block.

4.4L Engine

See Figure 181.

The Crankshaft Position (CKP) sensor is located at the back of the engine facing the firewall.

REMOVAL & INSTALLATION

3.0L & 3.2L Engines

1. Before servicing the vehicle, refer to the Precautions Section.
2. Remove the engine under cover.
3. Remove the electrical connector to the Crankshaft Position (CKP) sensor.
4. Remove the mounting bolt and CKP sensor.

To install:

5. Install the CKP sensor and tighten the mounting bolt to 89 inch lbs. (10 Nm).
6. Install the electrical connector.
7. Install the engine under cover.

4.4L Engine

1. Before servicing the vehicle, refer to the Precautions Section.
2. Remove the battery.
3. Remove the air cleaner housing and holding bracket.
4. Remove the rear engine cover.
5. Remove the electrical connector to the Crankshaft Position (CKP) sensor.
6. Remove the CKP sensor.

To install:

7. Install the CKP sensor and tighten the mounting bolt to 89 inch lbs. (10 Nm).

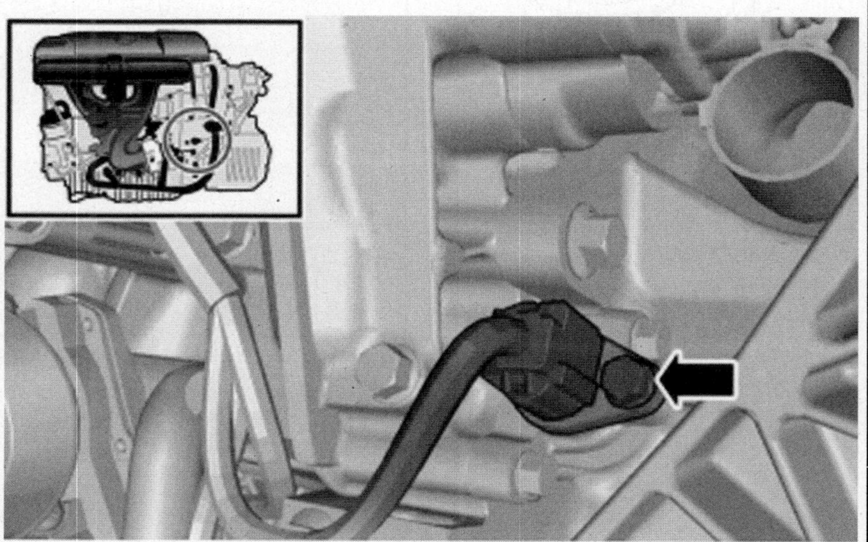
Fig. 180 Crankshaft Position (CKP) sensor—3.0L and 3.2L engines

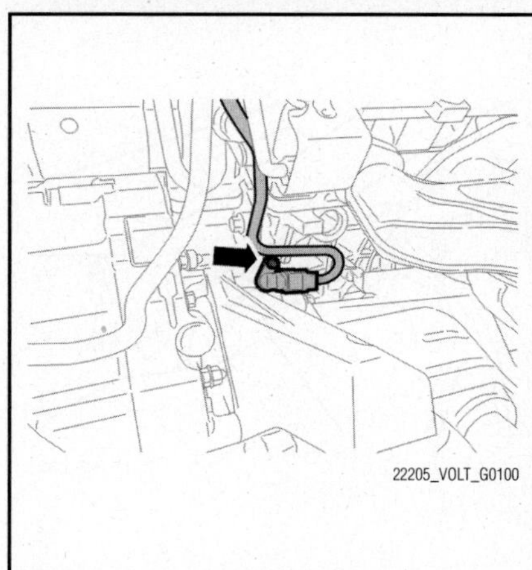

Fig. 181 Crankshaft Position (CKP) sensor—4.4L engine

8. Install the electrical connector to the CKP sensor.
9. Install the rear engine cover.
10. Install the air cleaner housing and tighten the holding bracket to 89 inch lbs. (10 Nm).
11. Install the battery.

ELECTRONIC CONTROL MODULE (ECM)

LOCATION

The Engine Control Module (ECM) is mounted in the intake cowl system under the wiper arms.

REMOVAL & INSTALLATION

See Figure 182.

Points to observe when replacing the control module:

- New software can only be ordered when the control module is installed in the vehicle. VIDA reads off the new control module identity which is required to order the correct software. The software can only be ordered when the new control module is installed in the car.
- Wait 2 minutes after the ignition has been switched OFF. The main relay must be voltage-free before the control module can be removed from the car. If the engine cooling fan runs on after the ignition has been switched off, wait until it stops and then wait for another 2 minutes.
- Always check that the control module and control module box connector pins and sleeves are not bent or damaged. This may have caused the presenting fault.

1. Before servicing the vehicle, refer to the Precautions Section.
2. Turn the ignition switch to the OFF position. Wait for at least 2 minutes.
3. Remove the wiper arm assembly.
4. Remove the 4 retaining clips. To remove press the center pin down onto the clips.
5. Turn the 2 catches counterclockwise ¼ turn.
6. Lift out the cowl.
7. Remove the old protective cover from under the cowl using a screwdriver or similar tool.
8. Remove the residue from the protective cover plastic welds using a small chisel.
9. Remove the ECM.

⁂ WARNING

Do not touch the control module terminal pins with your fingers. Static electricity may damage components in the control module.

To install:

10. Install the ECM into position.
11. Install the retaining screws and tighten to 89 inch lbs. (10 Nm).
12. Apply butyl tape to the protective cover. Press the tape out slightly before securing to the vehicle.
13. Install the protective cover by sliding it towards and under the windshield.
14. Press the front edge of the protective cover firmly so that the butyl tape adheres to the plate.
15. Install the cowl in the correct position. Ensure that the rubber seal is correctly located against the fender and windshield. Check that the guide clips underneath the cowl are in the correct position in relation to the windshield.
16. Turn the 2 catches clockwise ¼ turn. Check that the marking on the relevant catch is turned toward the windshield.
17. Install the wiper arm assembly.
18. After downloading the software or replacing the ECM, the throttle unit must be adapted according to vehicle communication input: Adapting the throttle unit.
19. Check that no Diagnostic Trouble Codes (DTC's) have been stored during the repair.
20. Test drive the vehicle and check the function of the engine.

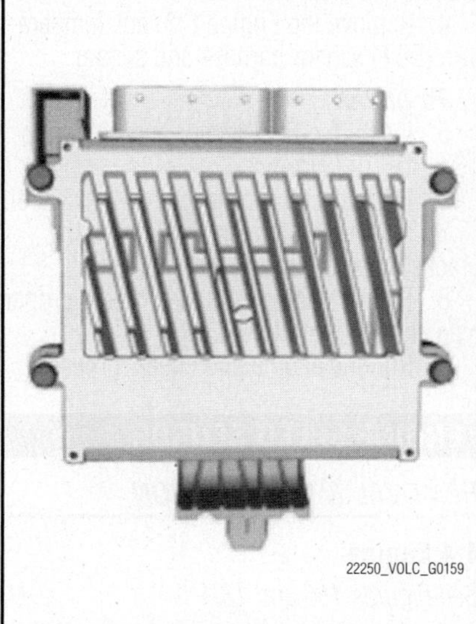

Fig. 182 Engine Control Module (ECM) view

ENGINE COOLANT TEMPERATURE (ECT) SENSOR

LOCATION

3.0L & 3.2L Engines

See Figure 183.

The Engine Coolant Temperature (ECT) sensor is located behind the power steering reservoir in the coolant housing.

4.4L Engine

See Figure 184.

The Engine Coolant Temperature (ECT) sensor is located at the rear of the engine above the transaxle, in the coolant housing.

Fig. 183 Engine Coolant Temperature (ECT) sensor location—3.0L and 3.2L engines

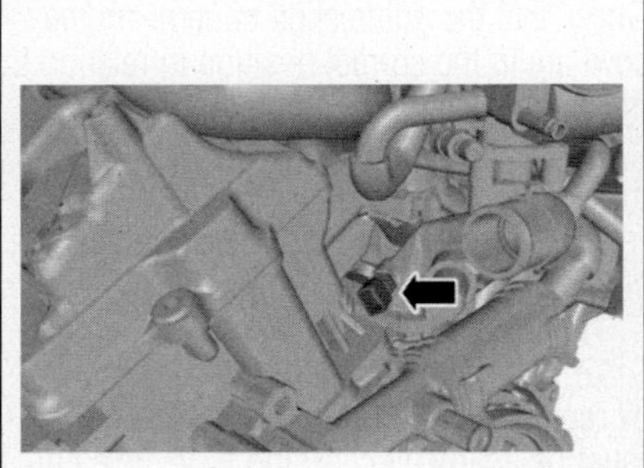

Fig. 184 Engine Coolant Temperature (ECT) sensor location—4.4L engine

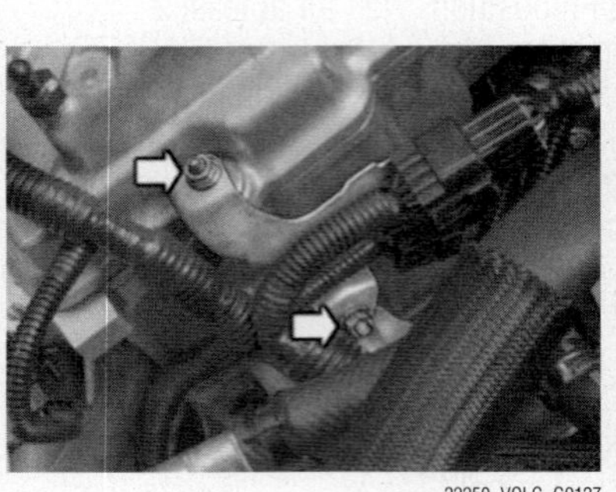

Fig. 185 Engine harness and bracket shown

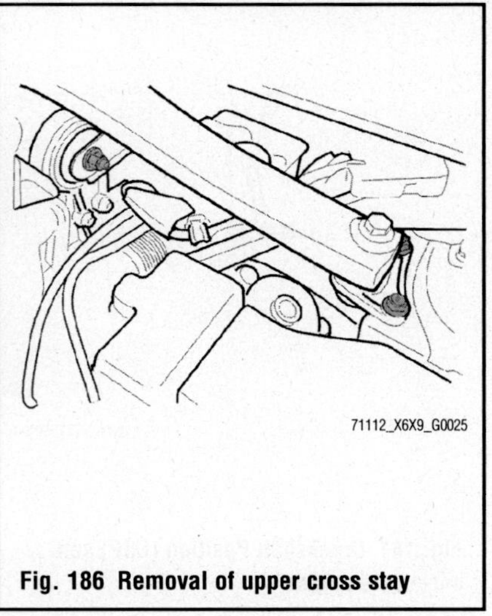

Fig. 186 Removal of upper cross stay

REMOVAL & INSTALLATION

3.0L & 3.2L Engines

CAUTION

Never open, service or drain the radiator or cooling system when hot; serious burns can occur from the steam and hot coolant. Also, when draining engine coolant, keep in mind that cats and dogs are attracted to ethylene glycol antifreeze and could drink any that is left in an uncovered container or in puddles on the ground. This will prove fatal in sufficient quantities. Always drain coolant into a sealable container. Coolant should be reused unless it is contaminated or is several years old.

1. Before servicing the vehicle, refer to the Precautions Section.
2. Remove the power steering reservoir and set it aside.
3. Remove the connector harness.
4. Remove the clip that retains the Engine Coolant Temperature (ECT) sensor.
5. Remove the ECT sensor.

To install:

6. Install the ECT sensor. Use a new O-ring.
7. Install the clip that retains the ECT sensor.
8. Install the connector harness.
9. Install the power steering reservoir.
10. Fill the engine coolant with the proper type and amount of fluid.
11. Run the engine and check for leaks.

4.4L Engine

See Figure 185.

CAUTION

Never open, service or drain the radiator or cooling system when hot; serious burns can occur from the steam and hot coolant. Also, when draining engine coolant, keep in mind that cats and dogs are attracted to ethylene glycol antifreeze and could drink any that is left in an uncovered container or in puddles on the ground. This will prove fatal in sufficient quantities. Always drain coolant into a sealable container. Coolant should be reused unless it is contaminated or is several years old.

1. Before servicing the vehicle, refer to the Precautions Section.
2. Remove the front engine cover.
3. Remove the engine harness and bracket, set it aside.
4. Remove the Engine Coolant Temperature (ECT) sensor harness and sensor.

To install:

5. Install the ECT sensor and tighten to 16 ft. lbs. (22 Nm).
6. Reconnect the connector at the sensor.
7. Install the harness and tighten the bracket nuts to 89 inch lbs. (10 Nm).
8. Fill the engine coolant with the proper type and amount of fluid.
9. Run the engine and check for leaks.

ENGINE SPEED SENSOR

REMOVAL & INSTALLATION

4.4 Engine

See Figures 186 and 187.

1. Remove the four screws at the suspension turrets.

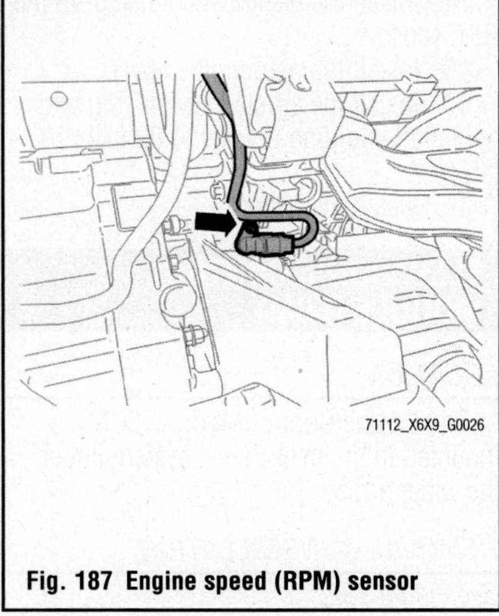

Fig. 187 Engine speed (RPM) sensor

2. Remove the screws of the upper engine mount on the engine
3. Remove the upper cross stay.
4. Pull upward on the rear engine cover to gain access to sensor.
5. Remove the 1 M6 screw of the engine speed sensor; pull out the sensor.
6. Remove the connector from the engine speed sensor.

To install:

7. Installation is the reverse of the removal.

HEATED OXYGEN (HO2S) SENSOR

LOCATION

3.0L & 3.2L Engines

See Figures 188 and 189.

The front Heated Oxygen (HO2S) sensor is mounted in the exhaust manifold con-

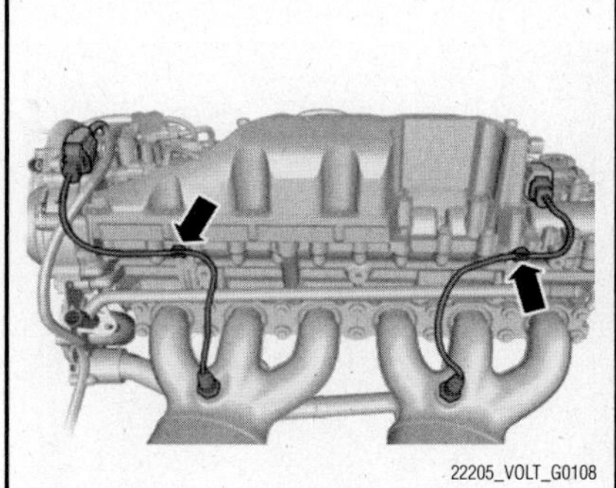

Fig. 188 Front Heated Oxygen (HO2S) sensor locations—3.0L and 3.2L engines

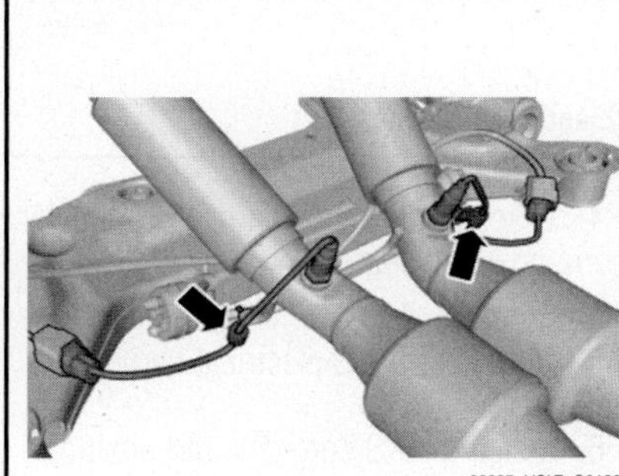

Fig. 189 Rear Heated Oxygen (HO2S) sensor locations—3.0L and 3.2L engines

verter sub-assembly. The rear HO2S sensor is mounted in the rear converter sub-assembly.

4.4L Engine

See Figures 190 and 191.

The front Heated Oxygen (HO2S) sensor is mounted in the exhaust manifold converter sub-assembly. The rear HO2S sensor is mounted in the rear of exhaust manifold converter sub-assembly.

REMOVAL & INSTALLATION

3.0L & 3.2L Engines

Front Sensor

1. Before servicing the vehicle, refer to the Precautions Section.
2. Remove the engine cover.
3. Remove the clip and harness connector.
4. Remove the front Heated Oxygen (HO2S) sensor. Use the proper tool.

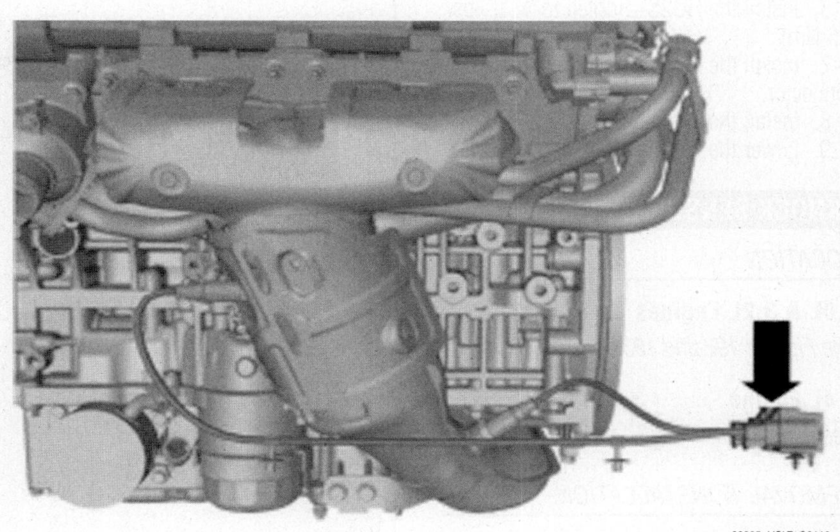

Fig. 190 Front Heated Oxygen (HO2S) sensor locations—4.4L engine

To install:

5. Install the front HO2S. Tighten to 33 ft. lbs. (45 Nm).
6. Connect the clip and harness connector.

Rear Sensor

1. Before servicing the vehicle, refer to the Precautions Section.
2. Raise and safely support the vehicle.
3. Remove the clip and harness connector from the frame.
4. Remove the rear Heated Oxygen (HO2S) sensor. Use the proper tool.

To install:

5. Install the rear HO2S. Tighten to 33 ft. lbs. (45 Nm).
6. Install the clip and harness connector from the frame.
7. Lower the vehicle.

4.4L Engine

Bank 1, Sensors 1 & 2

➡Bank 1 (cylinder row nearest the front): cylinders 1, 3, 5, and 7.

1. Before servicing the vehicle, refer to the Precautions Section.
2. Raise and safely support the vehicle.
3. Remove the engine undercover.
4. Remove the retaining clip and harness connector.
5. Remove the Heated Oxygen (HO2S) sensor.

To install:

6. Install the HO2S. Tighten to 33 ft. lbs. (45 Nm).
7. Install the retaining clip and harness connector.
8. Install the engine under cover.
9. Lower the vehicle.

Bank 2, Sensors 1 & 2

➡Bank 2 (cylinder row nearest the rear and the passenger compartment): cylinders 2, 4, 6, and 8.

1. Before servicing the vehicle, refer to the Precautions Section.
2. Raise and safely support the vehicle.
3. Remove the engine undercover.
4. Remove the retaining clip and harness connector.
5. Remove the Heated Oxygen (HO2S) sensor.

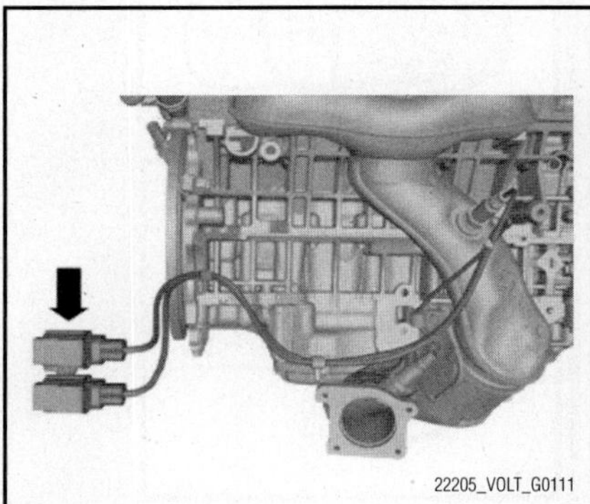

Fig. 191 Rear Heated Oxygen (HO2S) sensor locations—4.4L engine

To install:

6. Install the HO2S. Tighten to 33 ft. lbs. (45 Nm).
7. Install the retaining clip and harness connector.
8. Install the engine under cover.
9. Lower the vehicle.

KNOCK SENSOR (KS)

LOCATION

3.0L & 3.2L Engines

See Figures 192 and 193.

4.4L Engine

See Figure 194.

REMOVAL & INSTALLATION

3.0L & 3.2L Engines

1. Before servicing the vehicle, refer to the Precautions Section.
2. Remove the engine cover.
3. Remove the intake manifold.
4. Remove the mounting bolt and harness connector.
5. Remove the right Knock Sensor (KS).
6. Remove the oil cooler to remove the left side KS.

To install:

7. Installation is the reverse of the removal procedure.
8. Tighten the KS mounting bolts to 15 ft. lbs. (20 Nm).

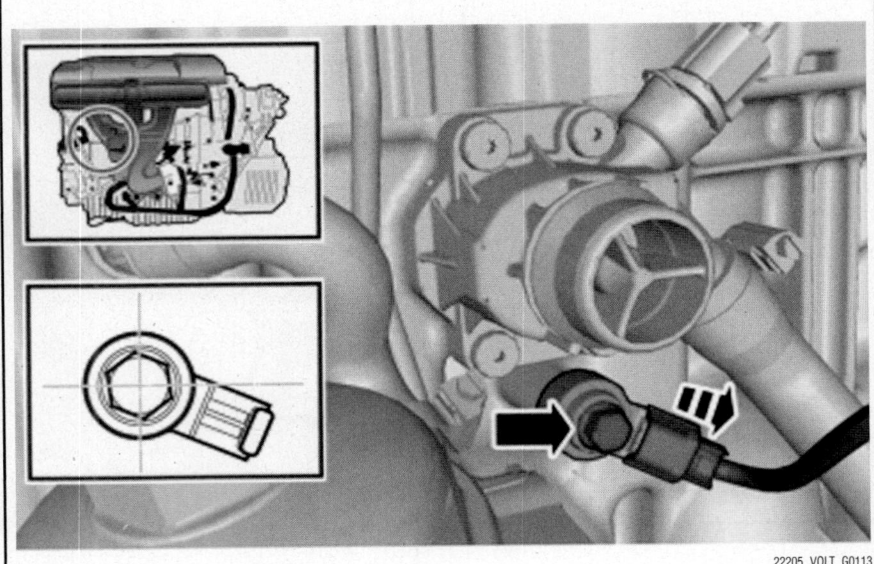

Fig. 193 Knock Sensor (KS) location (left side)—3.0L and 3.2L engines

4.4L Engine

➡Knock (KS) sensor 1 detects knocking on cylinders 5, 6, 7, and 8. KS 2 detects knocking on cylinders 1, 2, 3, and 4.

1. Before servicing the vehicle, refer to the Precautions Section.
2. Remove the upper and lower intake manifold.
3. Remove the mounting bolt of the Knock Sensor (KS).
4. Disconnect the KS harness connector and remove the sensor.

To install:

5. Connect the KS electrical harness connector.
6. Install the KS correctly into position, to avoid damage to the sensor.
7. Tighten the mounting bolt to 15 ft. lbs. (20 Nm).
8. Install the upper and lower intake manifold.

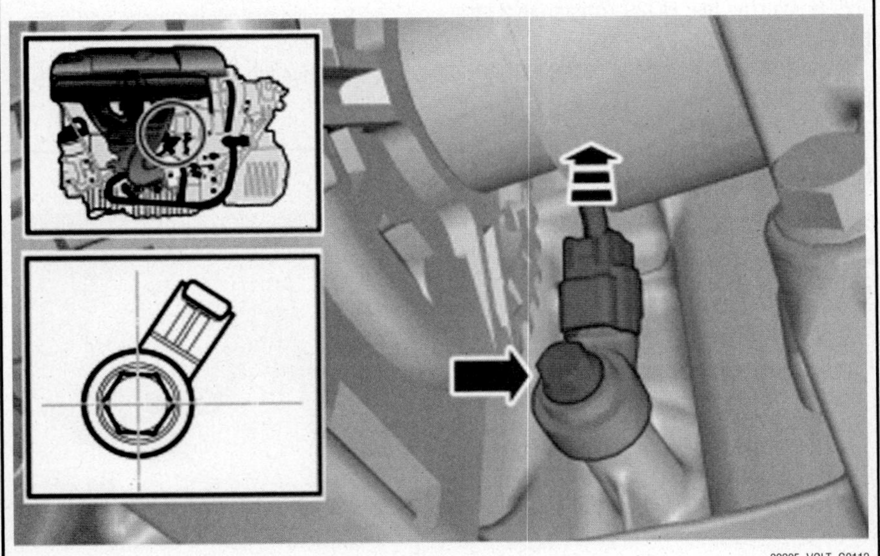

Fig. 192 Knock Sensor (KS) location (right side)—3.0L and 3.2L engines

MALFUNCTION INDICATOR LIGHT (MIL)

RESET PROCEDURE

Proper operation of the Malfunction Indicator Light (MIL):

- The MIL will illuminate with the ignition switch ON and the engine OFF

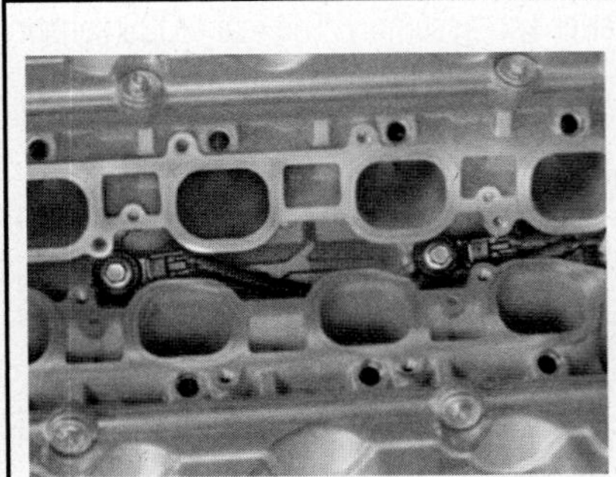

Fig. 194 Knock Sensor (KS) locations—4.4L engine

- The MIL will turn OFF when the engine is started
- The MIL will remain ON if the self-diagnostic system has detected a malfunction
- The MIL may turn OFF if the malfunction is no longer present
- If the MIL is illuminated and then the engine stalls, the MIL will remain illuminated as long as the ignition switch is ON
- If the MIL is not illuminated and the engine stalls, the MIL will not illuminate until the ignition switch is cycled OFF, then ON

1. Before servicing the vehicle, refer to the Precautions Section.
2. Resetting the MIL:
    - The control module turns OFF the MIL after 3 consecutive ignition cycles that the diagnostic system runs and does not fail
    - The control module turns OFF the MIL after a current Diagnostic Trouble Code (DTC) clears when the diagnostic cycle runs and passes
    - There may still be a history of DTC's stored in the system. These will clear after 40 consecutive warm-up cycles, if no failures are reported by any other related diagnostic system
    - Manual resetting of the MIL and any DTC stored in the system, requires the use of an OBD2 scan tool connected to the Data Link Connector (DLC) for communication with the vehicle. Follow the instructions of the scan tool for both retrieval and resetting of DTC's. The scan tool can be used to command the MIL off.

➡If the error symptoms causing the MIL to illuminate have been corrected, the MIL will return to normal operation.

3. If a DTC is present, record the code.
4. Disconnect the negative battery cable.

➡If the battery is disconnected or the power is cut and the vehicle is equipped with a remote parking heater, the personal code is reset to the factory value (1234).

➡If the MIL in the combined instrument panel illuminates, any DTC's for the engine management system must be read out and remedied before the battery is disconnected.

5. Initiate the central locking system and interior lighting by unlocking the vehicle with the remote control, key, or via VIDA vehicle communication.
6. Initiate window positions using VIDA Car communication.

➡If the battery was disconnected, the engine may need to run for a few minutes before it runs smoothly.

MANIFOLD ABSOLUTE PRESSURE (MAP) SENSOR

LOCATION

3.0L & 3.2L Engines

See Figure 195.

4.4L Engine

See Figure 196.

REMOVAL & INSTALLATION

3.0L & 3.2L Engines

The illustrations in this service information are used for different model years and/or models. Some variation may occur. However, the essential information in the illustrations is always correct.

1. Before servicing the vehicle, refer to the Precautions Section.
2. Disconnect the Manifold Absolute Pressure (MAP) sensor connector.
3. Remove the MAP sensor.

To install:

4. Install the MAP sensor.
5. Connect the connector for the MAP sensor.

4.4L Engine

1. Before servicing the vehicle, refer to the Precautions Section.
2. Disconnect the Manifold Absolute Pressure (MAP) sensor connector.
3. Remove the screws from the MAP sensor.
4. Remove the MAP sensor.

To install:

5. Install the MAP sensor.
6. Install the screws from the MAP sensor. Tighten the M5 screws to 44 inch lbs. (5 Nm).
7. Connect the connector for the MAP sensor.

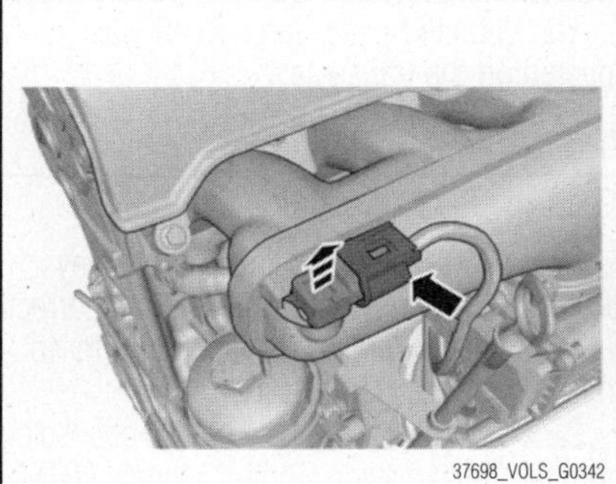

Fig. 195 Manifold Absolute Pressure (MAP) sensor location—3.0L and 3.2L engines

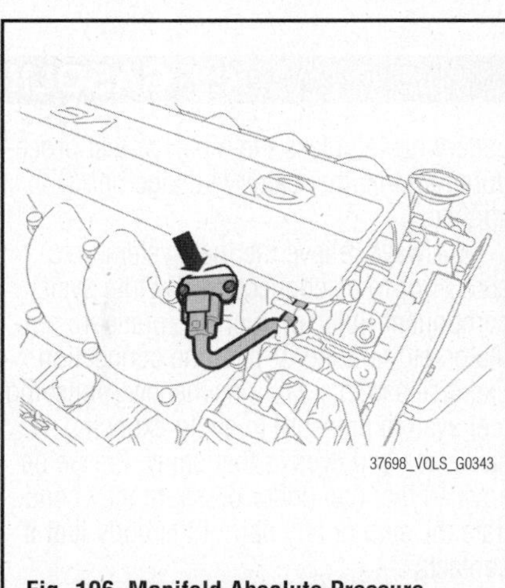

Fig. 196 Manifold Absolute Pressure (MAP) sensor location—4.4L engine

MASS AIR FLOW (MAF) SENSOR

LOCATION

3.0L & 3.2L Engines

See Figure 197.

The Mass Air Flow (MAF) sensor is located in the air cleaner housing or the air tube.

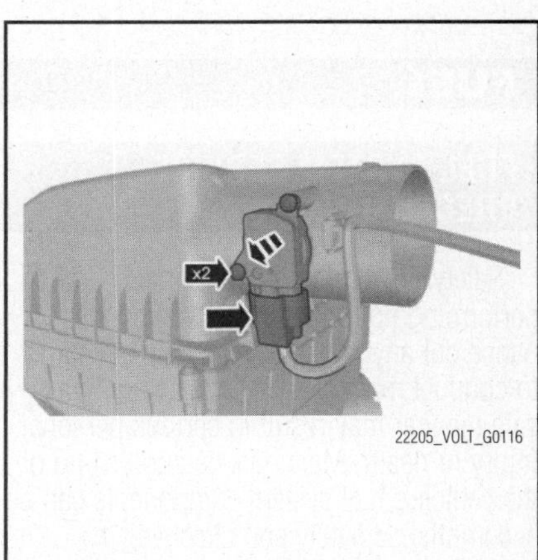

Fig. 197 Typical Mass Airflow (MAF) sensor location

4.4L Engine

See Figure 198.

The Mass Air Flow (MAF) sensor is located in the air cleaner housing or the air tube.

REMOVAL & INSTALLATION

3.0L & 3.2L Engines

1. Before servicing the vehicle, refer to the Precautions Section.
2. Remove the Mass Air Flow (MAF) sensor harness.
3. Remove the MAF sensor.

To install:

4. Install the MAF sensor.
5. Install the MAF sensor harness.

4.4L Engine

1. Before servicing the vehicle, refer to the Precautions Section.
2. Remove the Mass Air Flow (MAF) sensor harness.
3. Remove the MAF sensor.

To install:

4. Install the MAF sensor.
5. Install the MAF sensor harness.

THROTTLE POSITION SENSOR (TPS)

LOCATION

See Figure 199.

The Throttle Position (TPS) sensor is mounted on the throttle body.

REMOVAL & INSTALLATION

The Throttle Position Sensor (TPS) is not serviceable as a stand-alone part. The TPS is an integral part of the throttle body. If the TPS requires replacement, replace the throttle body assembly.

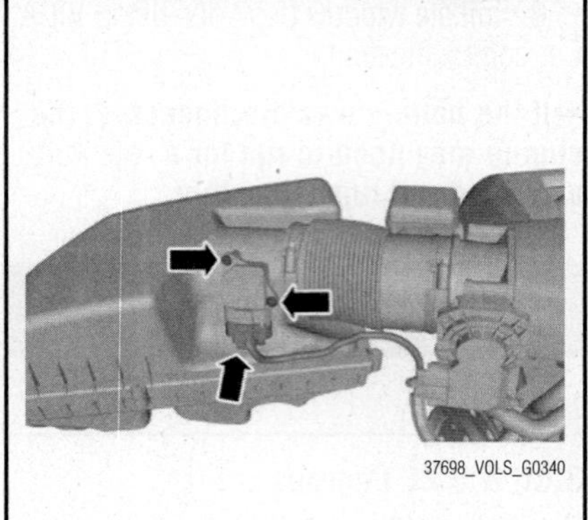

Fig. 198 Mass Air Flow (MAF) sensor location—4.4L engine

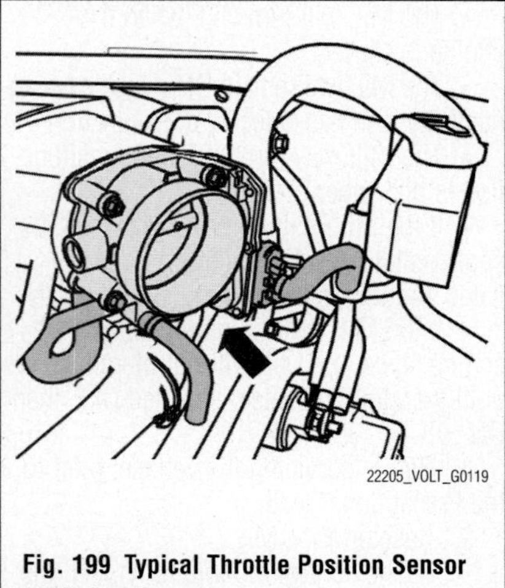

Fig. 199 Typical Throttle Position Sensor (TPS) location

VEHICLE SPEED SENSOR (VSS)

LOCATION

The Vehicle Speed Sensor (VSS) is located on the transaxle.

REMOVAL & INSTALLATION

See Figure 200.

Some variation in the illustrations may occur, but the essential information is correct.

1. Before servicing the vehicle, refer to the Precautions Section.
2. Disconnect the cable harness connector from the Transmission Control Module (TCM).
3. Clean around the sensors. Remove the sensors and the cable harness.

To install:

4. Install the new sensor(s). Apply a little automatic transaxle fluid to the O-rings for the sensors. Tighten the M6 bolt to 89 inch lbs. (10 Nm).
5. Install the cable harness connector to the TCM.

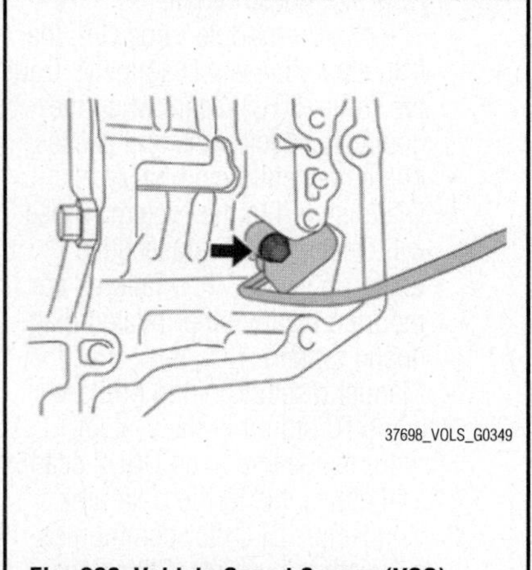

Fig. 200 Vehicle Speed Sensor (VSS) location—TF-80SC

FUEL SYSTEM SERVICE PRECAUTIONS

Safety is the most important factor when performing not only fuel system maintenance but any type of maintenance. Failure to conduct maintenance and repairs in a safe manner may result in serious personal injury or death. Maintenance and testing of the vehicle's fuel system components can be accomplished safely and effectively by adhering to the following rules and guidelines.

- To avoid the possibility of fire and personal injury, always disconnect the negative battery cable unless the repair or test procedure requires that battery voltage be applied.
- Always relieve the fuel system pressure prior to disconnecting any fuel system component (injector, fuel rail, pressure regulator, etc.), fitting or fuel line connection. Exercise extreme caution whenever relieving fuel system pressure to avoid exposing skin, face and eyes to fuel spray. Please be advised that fuel under pressure may penetrate the skin or any part of the body that it contacts.
- Always place a shop towel or cloth around the fitting or connection prior to loosening to absorb any excess fuel due to spillage. Ensure that all fuel spillage (should it occur) is quickly removed from engine surfaces. Ensure that all fuel soaked cloths or towels are deposited into a suitable waste container.
- Always keep a dry chemical (Class B) fire extinguisher near the work area.
- Do not allow fuel spray or fuel vapors to come into contact with a spark or open flame.
- Always use a back-up wrench when loosening and tightening fuel line connection fittings. This will prevent unnecessary stress and torsion to fuel line piping.

• Always replace worn fuel fitting O-rings with new Do not substitute fuel hose or equivalent where fuel pipe is installed.

Before servicing the vehicle, make sure to also refer to the precautions in the beginning of this section as well.

RELIEVING FUEL SYSTEM PRESSURE

WITHOUT FUEL PRESSURE RELIEF UNIT

1. Before servicing the vehicle, refer to the Precautions Section.
2. Remove the fuse or the fuel pump electrical connector.
3. Start the engine and allow it to idle until is stops.
4. Turn the engine using the starter motor for approximately 5 seconds until the pressure in the fuel rail has been released.

WITH FUEL PRESSURE RELIEF UNIT

See Figures 201 and 202.

1. Before servicing the vehicle, refer to the Precautions Section.
2. Remove the cover on the valve which is positioned on the fuel rail.
3. Connect adapter 999-5484 to the fuel pressure relief unit 981-2270, 981-2273, and 981-2282.
4. Connect the adapter to the valve on the fuel rail in the locked position.
5. Unlock the adapter.
6. Raise and safely support the vehicle.
7. Remove the cover on the valve cap positioned at the fuel filter.
8. Connect venting hose 999-5480 to the valve prior to the fuel filter.

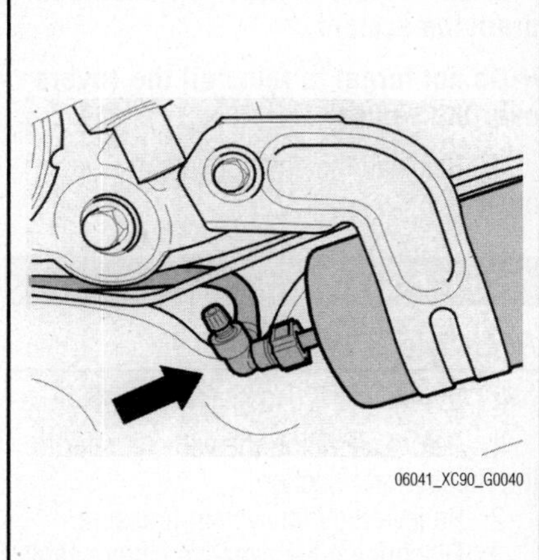

Fig. 202 Connect venting hose 999-5480 to the valve prior to the fuel filter

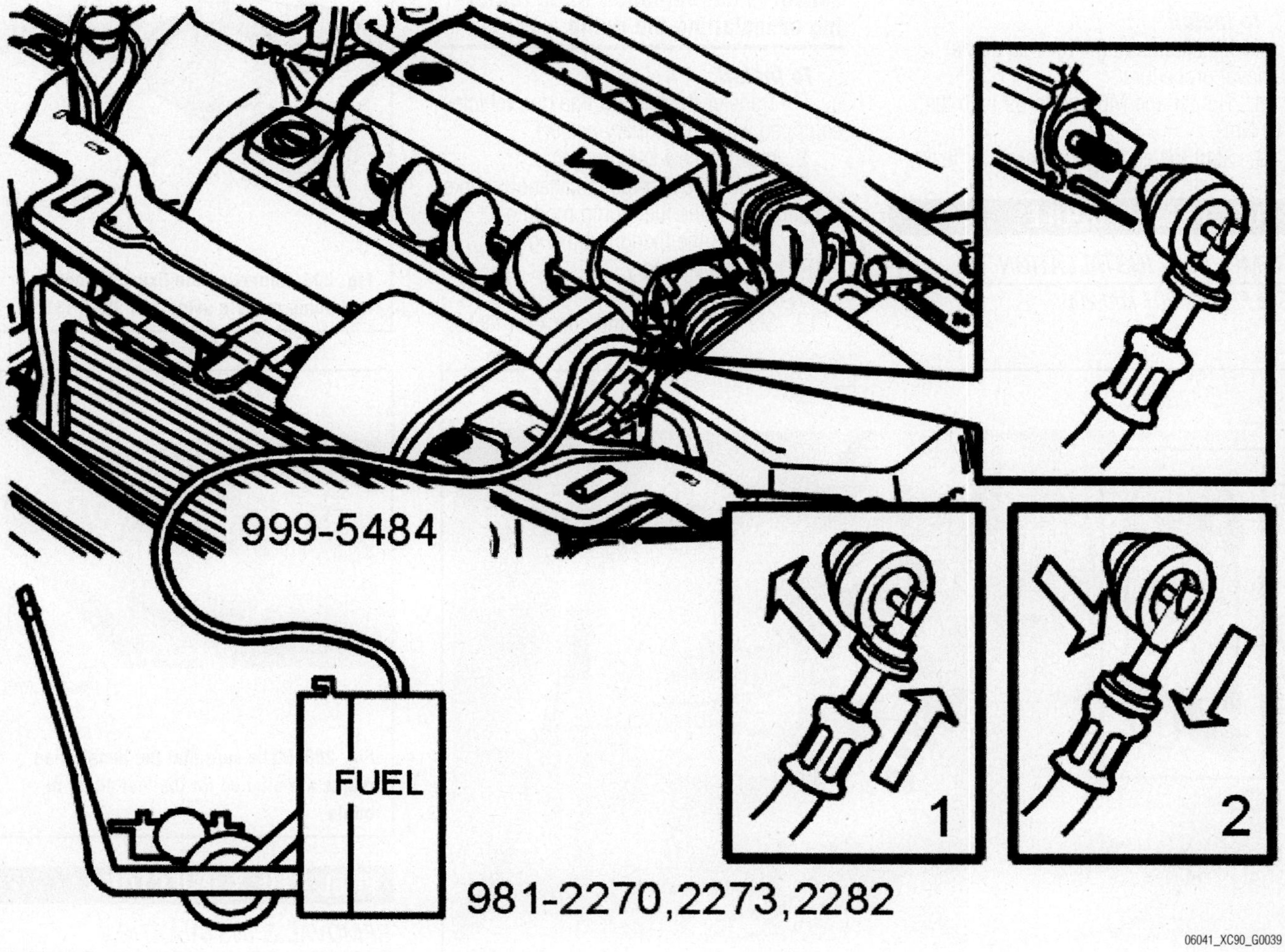

Fig. 201 Connect adapter 999-5484 to the fuel draining unit 981-2270, 981-2273, and 981-2282

➡It takes approximately 2 minutes to drain the system.

➡Do not forget to reinstall the covers over the valves.

9. Reinstall the components in reverse order

FUEL FILTER

REMOVAL & INSTALLATION

See Figures 203 and 204.

1. Before servicing the vehicle, refer to the Precautions Section.
2. Relieve the fuel system pressure.
3. Disconnect the negative battery cable.
4. Remove the fuel filler cap.
5. Remove the fuel lines from the fuel filter.
6. Remove the fuel filter from the bracket.

✲✲ CAUTION

Be prepared to collect escaping fluid.

To install:

7. Installation is the reverse of the removal procedure.
8. Tighten the M6 bolt to 89 inch lbs. (10 Nm).
9. Start the engine and check for leaks.

FUEL PUMP MODULE

REMOVAL & INSTALLATION

See Figures 205 and 206.

✲✲ CAUTION

Gasoline and gasoline vapors are highly flammable. A fire could occur if an ignition source is present. Never drain or store gasoline in an open container, due to the possibility of fire or explosion. Have a dry chemical (Class B) fire extinguisher nearby.

1. Before servicing the vehicle, refer to the Precautions Section.
2. Properly relieve the fuel system pressure.
3. Disconnect the negative battery cable.
4. Remove the fuel tank.
5. Remove the fixing nut on the fuel pump module using tool 999-7111, as necessary.
6. Remove the fuel pump module.

✲✲ WARNING

Ensure that the lever on the level sensor is not damaged when removing or installing the pump.

To install:

7. Transfer the suction line (for vehicles equipped with an auxiliary heater).
8. Install a new O-ring.
9. Make sure that the installation marks are aligned for the fuel pump module.
10. Tighten the fixing nut using tool 999-7111, as necessary.
11. Install the fuel tank.
12. Start the engine and check for leaks.

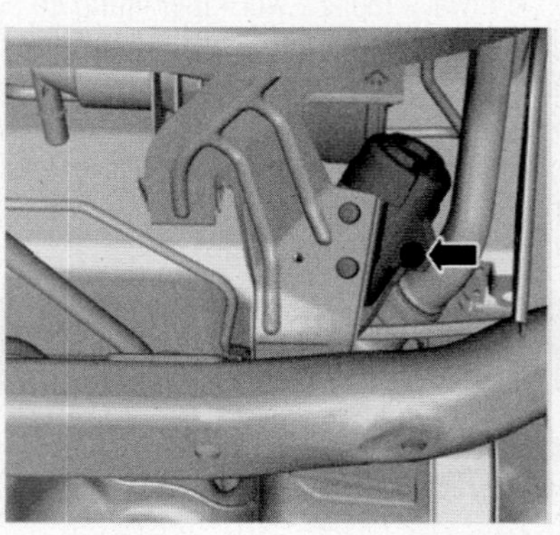

37698_VSUV_G0114

Fig. 204 Remove the fuel filter from the bracket

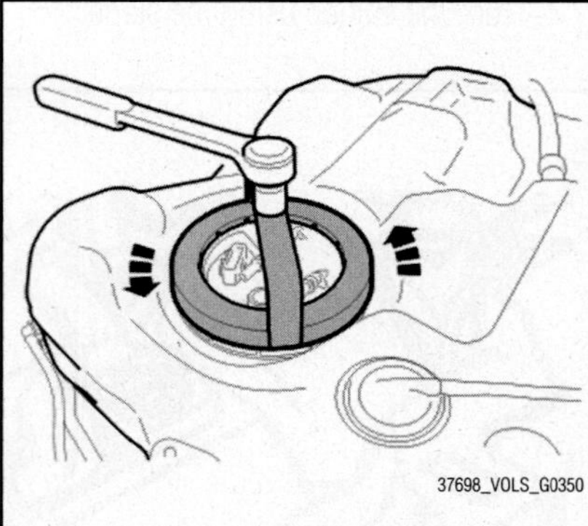

37698_VOLS_G0350

Fig. 205 Removing the fixing nut on the fuel pump module using tool 999-7111

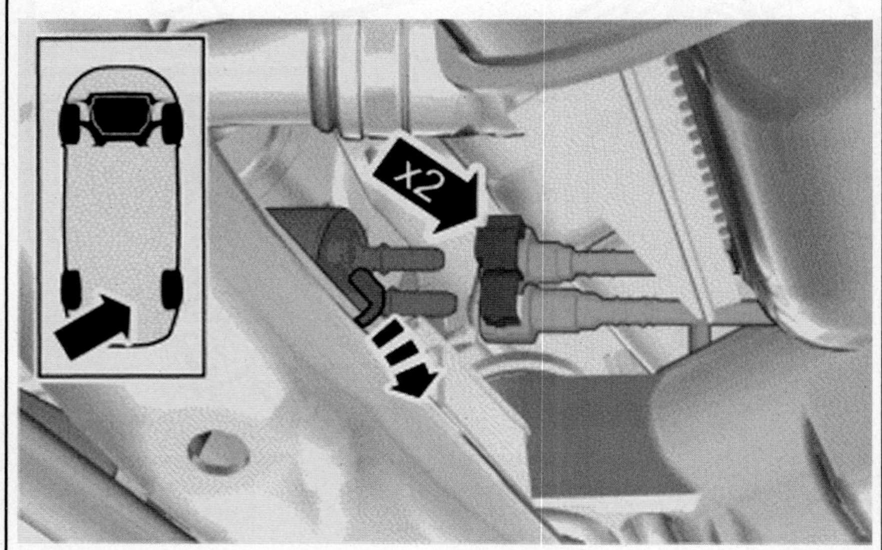

37698_VSUV_G0113

Fig. 203 Remove the fuel lines from the fuel filter

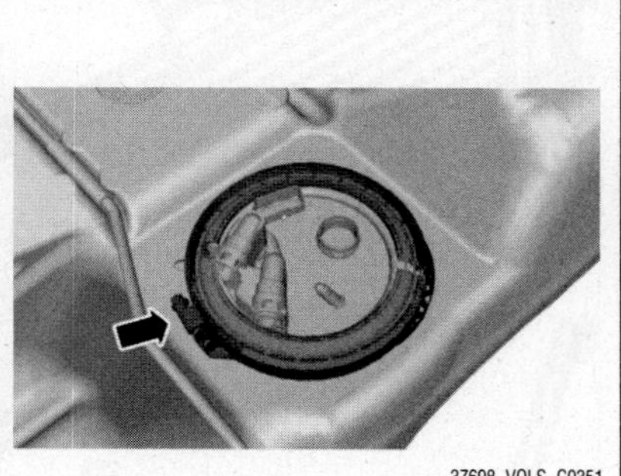

37698_VOLS_G0351

Fig. 206 Make sure that the installation marks are aligned for the fuel pump m odule

FUEL RAIL & INJECTORS

REMOVAL & INSTALLATION

3.0L & 3.2L Engines

See Figure 207.

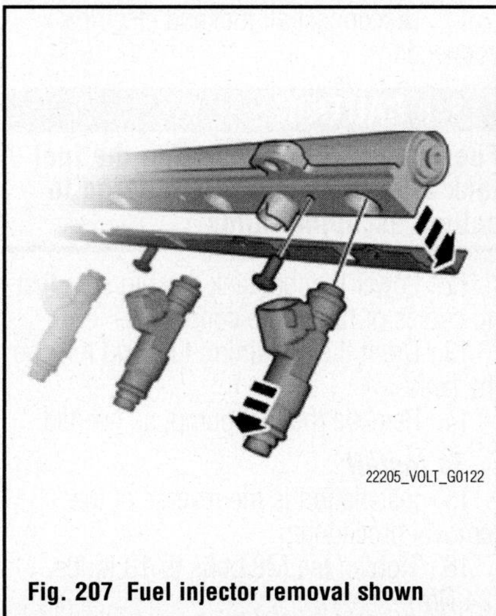
Fig. 207 Fuel injector removal shown

1. Before servicing the vehicle, refer to the Precautions Section.
2. Relieve the fuel system pressure.
3. Disconnect the negative battery cable.
4. Remove the engine cover.
5. Remove the engine torque mount and bracket.
6. Remove the fuel rail electrical connector.
7. Remove the fuel supply line.
8. Remove the fuel rail mounting bolts.
9. Carefully remove the fuel rail with the injectors.
10. Remove the screws that retain the bracket for the fuel injectors.
11. Remove the fuel injector(s).

To install:

12. Installation is the reverse of the removal procedure.
13. Lubricate the O-ring for the new injector using petroleum jelly.
14. Tighten bolts/nuts to specification as follows:
    - The fuel injector retaining screws: 44 inch lbs. (5 Nm)
    - The fuel rail mounting bolts: 44 inch lbs. (5 Nm)
    - The engine torque mount and bracket: 59 ft. lbs. (80 Nm)
15. Connect the negative battery cable.
16. Start the engine and check for leaks.

➡When the battery is disconnected, the engine may need to run for a few minutes before it runs smoothly.

17. Initialize the central locking system, interior lighting, and power windows using the VIDA communications tool.

4.4L Engine

See Figures 208 and 209.

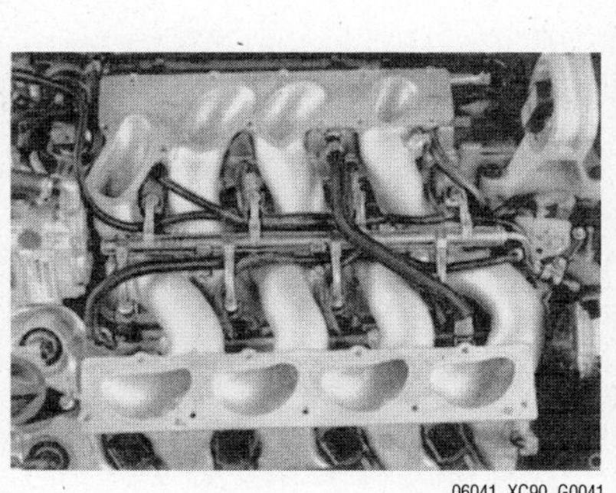
Fig. 208 View of fuel rail assembly—4.4L engine

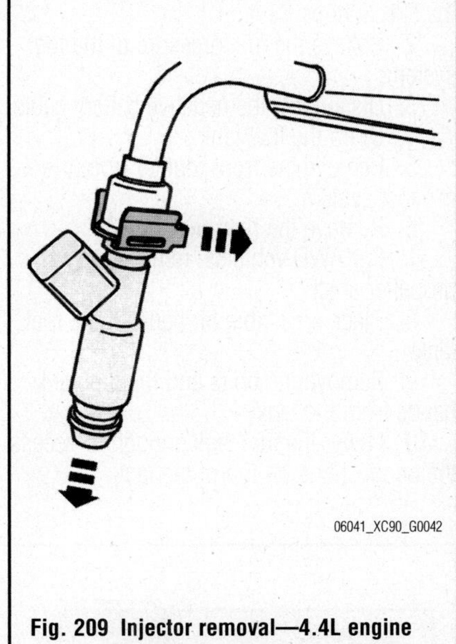
Fig. 209 Injector removal—4.4L engine

1. Before servicing the vehicle, refer to the Precautions Section.
2. Relieve the fuel system pressure.
3. Disconnect the negative battery cable.
4. Remove the engine cover.
5. Remove the upper intake manifold.
6. Remove the crankcase ventilation hose between the cylinder heads by releasing the 2 clamps.
7. Remove the 3 bolts from the fuel rail.
8. Remove the 2 bolts on the fuel pressure sensor.
9. Lift the fuel rail assembly with injectors straight up and move it aside.
10. Unplug the connector of the injector.
11. Remove the cir-clip of the injector; pull the clip laterally.
12. Remove the injector; jiggle and pull it straight out.

To install:

➡Lubricate the O-rings on the injectors with petroleum jelly, or similar product.

13. Install the injector(s).
14. Install the cir-clip.
15. Plug in the connector to the fuel injector.
16. Install the fuel rail assembly with injector.
17. Install the 3 bolts of the fuel rail.
18. Install the 2 bolts on the fuel pressure sensor.
19. Install the crankcase ventilation hose and 2 clamps.

⁂ WARNING

Make sure there is an audible click during connection.

20. Connect the fuel supply line and secure the line in the clamp.
21. Install the upper intake manifold.
22. Connect the negative battery cable.
23. Start the engine and check for leaks.
24. Install the engine cover.

➡When the battery is disconnected, the engine may need to run for a few minutes before it runs smoothly.

25. Initialize the central locking system, interior lighting, and power windows using the VIDA communications tool.

FUEL TANK

DRAINING

See Figure 210.

Observe the following precautions:

- Observe all applicable safety precautions when working around the fuel system. Whenever servicing the fuel system, always work in a well-ventilated area. Do not allow fuel spray or vapors to come in contact with a spark or open flame
- Keep a dry chemical fire extinguisher near the work area
- Always keep fuel in a container specifically designed for fuel storage. Properly seal fuel containers to avoid the possibility of fire or explosion
- Use of a fresh air mask is highly recommended
- Always follow the safety recommendations of the fuel extractor you are using to avoid the potential of fire or explosion

1. Before servicing the vehicle, refer to the Precautions Section.
2. Disconnect the negative battery cable.
3. Insert the drain hose 95- 2896

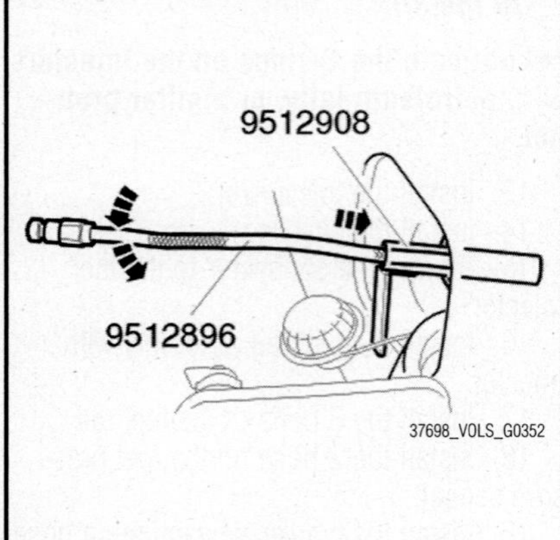

Fig. 210 Insert the fuel drain hose 951-2896 through the protective pipe 951-2908

through the protective pipe 951-2908 into the fuel tank. Use a twisting motion on the hose while inserting it into the fuel filler to clear any obstacles.

4. Connect the hose to the fuel extractor.
5. Pump the fuel out until only air is extracted.
6. Remove the extractor hose and the protective pipe.

WARNING

Pull the hose out carefully to prevent damage to the evacuation valve.

REMOVAL & INSTALLATION

XC60 Vehicles

See Figures 211 and 212.

Observe the following precautions:

- Observe all applicable safety precautions when working around the fuel system. Whenever servicing the fuel system, always work in a well-ventilated area. Do not allow fuel spray or vapors to come in contact with a spark or open flame
- Keep a dry chemical fire extinguisher near the work area
- Always keep fuel in a container specifically designed for fuel storage. Properly seal fuel containers to avoid the possibility of fire or explosion
- Use of a fresh air mask is highly recommended
- Always follow the safety recommendations of the fuel extractor you are using to avoid the potential of fire or explosion

The illustrations in this service information are used for different model years and/or models. Some variation may occur. However, the essential information in the illustrations is correct.

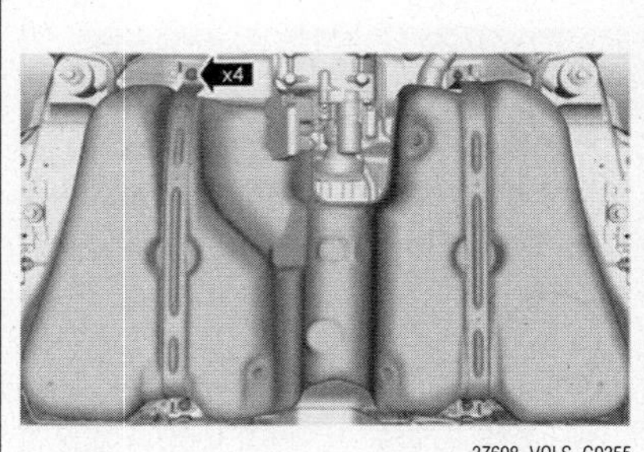

Fig. 211 Remove the fuel tank bands from the tank

1. Before servicing the vehicle, refer to the Precautions Section.
2. Relieve the fuel pressure in the fuel system.
3. Disconnect the negative battery cable.
4. Drain the fuel tank.
5. Remove the front muffler from the exhaust system.
6. Remove the rear heat shields.
7. For AWD vehicles, remove the rear propeller shaft.
8. Place a suitable lift beneath the fuel tank.
9. Remove the bolts and the fuel tank bands from the tank.
10. Lower the fuel tank enough to access the connections on top of the tank.
11. Disconnect all fuel and electrical connections.

CAUTION

Fuel may still be present in the fuel tank after draining. Be prepared to collect escaping fluids.

12. Lower the fuel tank making sure that no cables or hoses are connected.
13. Drain the remaining fuel and remove the tank.
14. Remove the fuel pump, as needed.

To install:

15. Installation is the reverse of the removal procedure.
16. Tighten the M8 bolts to 18 ft. lbs. (24 Nm).

XC90 Vehicles

See Figures 213 and 214.

Observe the following precautions:

- Observe all applicable safety precautions when working around the fuel system. Whenever servicing the fuel system, always work in a well-ventilated area. Do not allow fuel spray or vapors to come in contact with a spark or open flame
- Keep a dry chemical fire extinguisher near the work area
- Always keep fuel in a container specifically designed for fuel storage. Properly seal fuel containers to avoid the possibility of fire or explosion
- Use of a fresh air mask is highly recommended

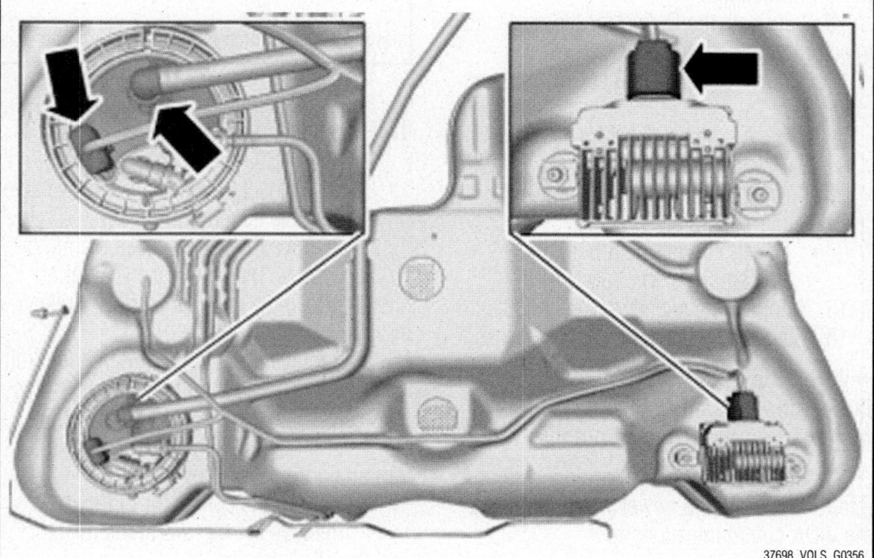

Fig. 212 Disconnect all fuel and electrical connections from the fuel tank

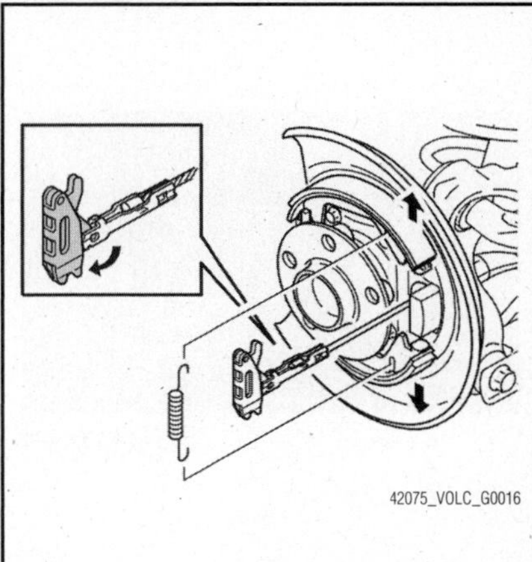

Fig. 213 Removing the expansion spring from rear brake

- Always follow the safety recommendations of the fuel extractor you are using to avoid the potential of fire or explosion

The illustrations in this service information are used for different model years and/or models. Some variation may occur. However, the essential information in the illustrations is correct.

1. Before servicing the vehicle, refer to the Precautions Section.
2. Relieve the fuel pressure in the fuel system.
3. Disconnect the negative battery cable.
4. Drain the fuel tank.
5. Block the parking brake pedal in the neutral position.
6. Remove or disconnect the following on both sides:
   - Rear wheels
   - Rear brake calipers
   - Rear brake discs
   - Rear tension spring and expander
7. Lift the brake shoe slightly. Grip the expander. Pull the expander outwards.
8. Unhook the expander from the metal bracket.
9. Remove or disconnect the following on both sides:
   - The guide sleeve for the cable sleeve. Apply a screwdriver between the guide sleeve lug and wheel arch. Pry apart slightly to remove the sleeve.
   - The parking brake cable from the tie rod and the sub-frame
10. Remove 2 bolts from the cable clips and 2 bolts from the front mounting for the heat deflector plate.
11. Fold out the cables from the heat deflector plate. Hang the cables up at the front of the car.
12. Remove the exhaust system from the three-way catalytic converter and backwards.

➡Hang up the three-way catalytic converter to prevent damaging the flex boot.

13. Remove the rear driveshaft:
    a. Mark up the position of the joint on the flange on the final drive and at the center bearing.
    b. Remove bolts from the joints. Use counter-hold 999-7057.
    c. Remove the rear section of the driveshaft.
14. Lower the rear suspension:
    a. Place the mobile jack: 999-5972 with plate: 999-5972 under the rear suspension.
    b. Raise to light contact.
15. Remove or disconnect the following on both sides:
    - The 2 bolts for the mounting bracket
    - The mounting bolt for the sub frame bushing
    - The brake pipe on both sides from the plastic clips on the bracket
16. Lower the rear suspension carefully.
17. Place a lifting table under the fuel tank.
18. Remove or disconnect the following:
    - The upper quick-release connector plastic pipe on the carbon filter container
    - The 4 bolts for the fuel tank securing strap
    - Remove the clamp for the fuel filler pipe
    - Remove the clamp for the bleed pipe
19. Lower the lifting table to access the plastic pipes on top of the tank.

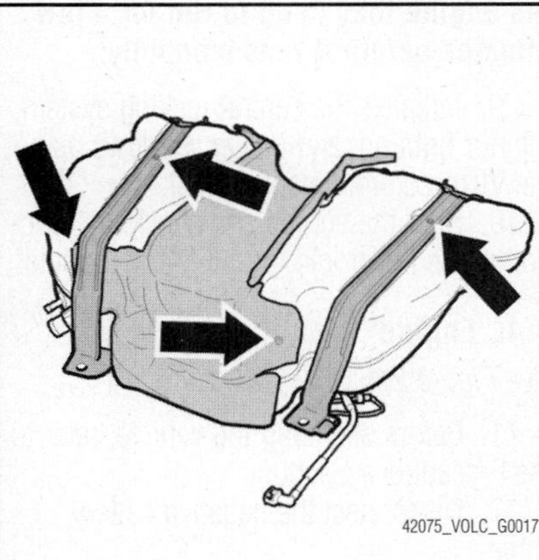

Fig. 214 Removing the fuel tank straps and heat shield

20. Remove the plastic pipe.
21. Remove the ABS cable harness from the clips on both sides of the fuel tank.
22. Remove the fuel tank.

To install:

23. Place the fuel tank on the lifting table.
24. Raise the lifting table to install the plastic hoses on the right-hand level sensor and in the grooves in the tank.
25. Secure the hoses in place using silver tape.
26. Install the ABS cable harnesses in the clips on both sides of the tank.
27. Align the fuel filler pipe and the bleed pipe.
28. Insert the cable harnesses for the level sensor and the fuel tank pressure sensor through the inspection holes in the floor.
29. Raise the fuel tank to the installation position.

➡Ensure that the fuel filler pipe and bleed pipe slide into position while raising the fuel tank.

30. Install the 4 bolts for the fuel tank securing strap. Tighten to 18 ft. lbs. (24 Nm).
31. Remove the lifting table.
32. Install or connect the following:
    - The clamp for the fuel filler pipe
    - The clamp for the bleed pipe
    - The upper plastic pipe in the quick-release connector for the carbon filter container
33. Install the rear suspension:
    a. Place the mobile jack: 999-5972 and plate: 999-5972 under the rear suspension.
    b. Carefully raise the rear suspension.

➡Ensure that no cable harnesses or brake lines are trapped while raising the rear suspension.

34. Install or connect the following on both sides:
    - The 2 bolts for the mounting bracket. Tighten to 59 ft. lbs. (80 Nm)
    - The bolt for the sub frame mounting. Tighten to 59 ft. lbs. (80 Nm)
    - The brake line in the plastic clip and bracket
35. Install the brakes.
36. Install the parking brake cable along the heat shields.
37. Install the bolts in the center and front mountings for the heat shield.
38. Install or connect the following:
    - The parking brake cables on the wheel units

- The parking brake cable mountings in the sub-frame. Tighten bolts to 19 ft. lbs. (25 Nm).
- The mounting for the parking brake cable on the tie rods

39. Press the guide sleeves for the parking brake cables into place on the wheel units.

➡Lubricate the O-rings on the guide sleeves. Use lubricant 1161580, or silicon grease.

40. Install or connect the following:
    - The expander on the cable. Press the mounting together to lock the cable in the expander.
    - The expander between the brake shoes
    - The return spring
41. Install the brake disc and the locating pin. Tighten to 89 inch lbs. (10 Nm).
42. Install the brake caliper. Use new bolts. Tighten to 44 ft. lbs. (60 Nm).

➡Activate parking brake adjuster.

43. Install the rear drive shaft.
    a. Position the propeller shaft as marked previously.
    b. Install new bolts for the joints. Use counter-hold 999-7057. Tighten all bolts to 22 ft. lbs. (30 Nm).
44. Install the exhaust system. Use a new flange gasket. Tighten the bolts to 18 ft. lbs. (25 Nm).
45. Install the cover over the level sensor.
46. Connect the wiring and the connectors.
47. Install the wheel and tire assembly. Tighten the lug nuts in a star pattern.
    a. Step 1: 15 ft. lbs. (20 Nm).
    b. Step 2: 103 ft. lbs. (140 Nm).

THROTTLE BODY

REMOVAL & INSTALLATION

3.0L & 3.2L Engines

See Figure 215.

1. Before servicing the vehicle, refer to the Precautions Section.
2. Remove the negative battery cable.
3. If equipped with a turbocharger:
    a. Remove the charge air cooler.
    b. Remove the hose between the turbocharger and the charge air cooler at its upper end. Push it to one side.
    c. Remove the pipe between the throttle body and the charge air cooler.

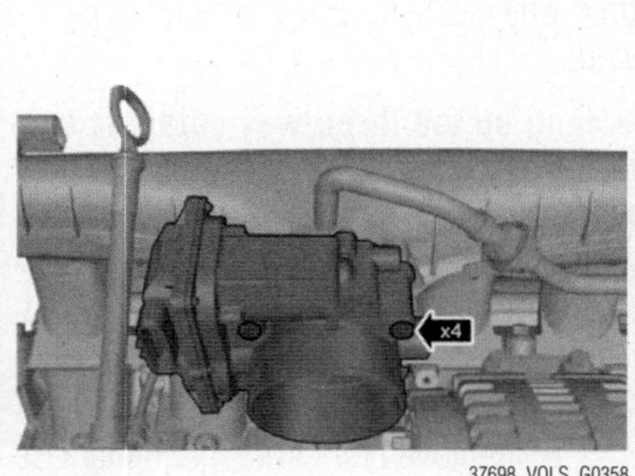

Fig. 215 Throttle body removal—3.0L and 3.2L engines

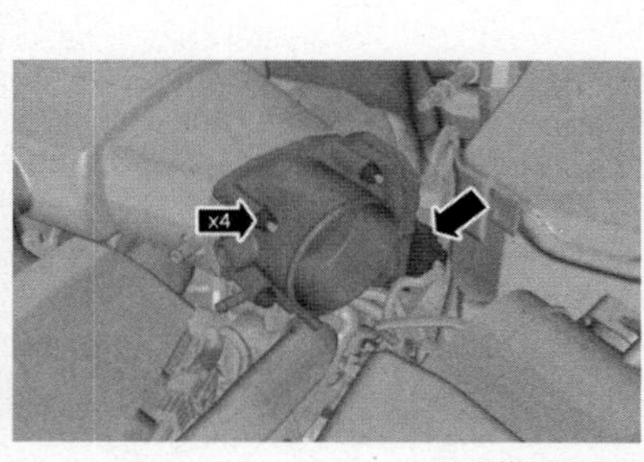

Fig. 216 Throttle body removal—4.4L engine

4. Remove the intake pipes between the front cover plate and air cleaner housing.
5. Removing the throttle body:
    a. Disconnect the throttle body connector.
    b. Remove the mounting bolts from the throttle body.
    c. Lift up and remove the throttle body. Discard the gasket.

To install:

6. Installation is the reverse of the removal procedure.
7. Clean the mating surfaces thoroughly.
8. Install the throttle body using a new gasket. Tighten the 4 bolts to 89 inch lbs. (10 Nm).

➡After replacing the throttle unit, the throttle unit must be adapted using the vehicle communication input: Adaptation of the electronic throttle unit. Remedy as necessary.

➡When the battery is disconnected, the engine may need to run for a few minutes before it runs smoothly.

9. Initialize the central locking system, interior lighting, and power windows using the VIDA communications tool.
10. Start the engine and check the function of the electronic throttle body module.

4.4L Engine

See Figure 216.

1. Before servicing the vehicle, refer to the Precautions Section.
2. Disconnect the negative battery cable.
3. Remove the intake hose by removing the 2 hose clips and bending aside the intake hose.
4. Remove the connector from the electronic throttle body module.
5. Remove the 2 coolant hoses attached to the throttle body and seal off the ends with a locking pliers.
6. Remove the 2 nuts and the 2 bolts holding the throttle body against the intake manifold.
7. Remove the throttle body.

To install:

8. Scrap the old gasket material to ensure a clean surface.
9. Install a new throttle body gasket.
10. Install the throttle body.
11. Install the 2 nuts and 2 bolts. Tighten to 88 inch lbs. (10 Nm).
12. Install the 2 coolant hoses secure to throttle body with hose clips.
13. Install the connector to the electronic throttle body module.
14. Install the intake hose. Tighten the 2 hose clips.

➡After replacing the throttle unit, the throttle unit must be adapted using the vehicle communication input: Adaptation of the electronic throttle unit. Remedy as necessary. If the throttle body was replaced, initialize the throttle unit, using the VIDA communications tool.

15. Initialize the central locking system, interior lighting, and power windows using the VIDA communications tool.

➡When the battery is disconnected, the engine may need to run for a few minutes before it runs smoothly.

16. Start the engine and check the function of the electronic throttle body module.

HEATING & AIR CONDITIONING SYSTEM

BLOWER MOTOR

REMOVAL & INSTALLATION

XC90 Vehicles

See Figures 217 and 218.

1. Before servicing the vehicle, refer to the Precautions Section.
2. Remove the rear left side panel.
3. Remove the rear blower fan motor.
4. Remove the rubber seals and the cable terminals.
5. Remove the 3 screws for the blower fan motor.
6. Remove the rear blower motor from the vehicle.

To install:

7. Install the rear blower fan motor.
8. Install the blower fan motor using the M5 screws and tighten to 44 inch lbs. (5 Nm).
9. Install the cable terminals and the rubber seals.
10. Check the function.
11. Install the rear left side panel.

Fig. 217 Rear left side panel attaching screws

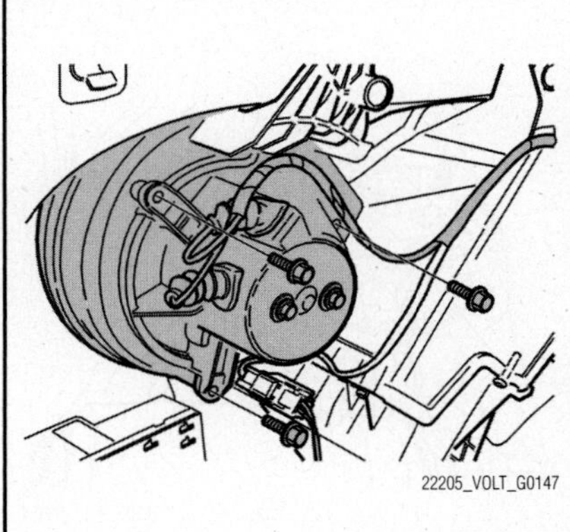

Fig. 218 Rear blower fan motor mounting screws

HEATER CORE

REMOVAL & INSTALLATION

XC60 Vehicles

See Figures 219 and 220.

The illustrations in this service information are used for different model years and/or models. Some variation may occur. However, the essential information in the illustrations is correct.

1. Before servicing the vehicle, refer to the Precautions Section.
2. Drain the engine coolant.
3. Detach the radiator hoses from the engine compartment. Turn the radiator hose connection counter-clockwise to the end position and then pull off the radiator hose.

➡Note the position of each component before removal.

4. Remove the seal and the plate.
5. Remove the soundproofing panel.
6. Remove the floor console.
7. Remove the tie strap for the pipes.
8. Remove the bolts for the heat exchanger.
9. Remove the mounting brackets for the pipes.
10. Position plenty of paper under the heat exchanger and around the pipes.

➡Be prepared to collect escaping fluid.

11. Drain the coolant into a suitable container.
12. Detach the pipes and position them out of the way.
13. Pull out the heat exchanger.

To install:

➡Always use new O-rings.

14. Install the heat exchanger carefully.
15. Bolt the heat exchanger into place.
16. Install the upper pipes.
17. Install the locking plate using round-nosed pliers.
18. Press in the pipes using a screwdriver. Press the catch using pliers.
19. Install the lower pipes.
20. Install the locking plate using round-nosed pliers.
21. Press in the pipe using a screwdriver. Press in the locking bracket using round-nosed pliers.
22. Install the tie strap for the pipes.
23. Install the seal and the plate.
24. Install the heating hoses in the engine compartment.
25. Fill the engine coolant.
26. Check that the pipe coupling does not leak.
27. Install the floor console.
28. Install the soundproofing panel.

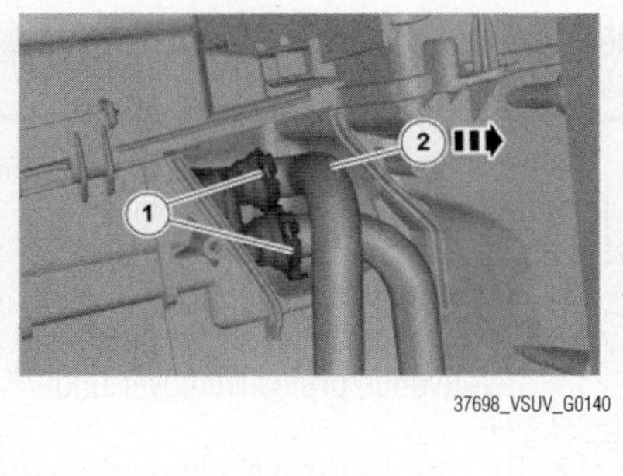

Fig. 219 Removing the heater hoses

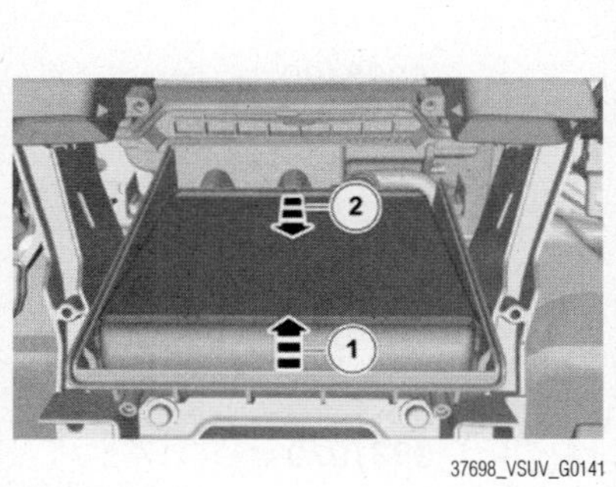

Fig. 220 Heat exchanger core removal

XC90 Vehicles

See Figures 221 and 222.

The illustrations in this service information are used for different model years and/or models. Some variation may occur. However, the essential information in the illustrations is correct.

1. Before servicing the vehicle, refer to the Precautions Section.

2. Drain the engine coolant.
3. Remove the hoses from the heater core pipes in the engine compartment.
4. Remove the seal and the plate.
5. Remove the soundproofing panel.
6. Remove the bolts for the heat exchanger.
7. Remove the mounting brackets for the pipes.
8. Position plenty of paper under the heat exchanger and around the pipes.
9. Drain the coolant into a suitable container.
10. Detach the pipes and move them out of the way.
11. Pull out the heat exchanger.

To install:

12. Install the upper pipe.
13. Install the striker plate using round-nosed pliers.
14. Install the catch using a pair of pliers.
15. Install the lower pipe.

Fig. 221 Remove the hoses from the heater core pipes in the engine compartment

16. Install the striker plate using round-nosed pliers.
17. Install the seal and the plate.
18. Install the heating hoses in the engine compartment.

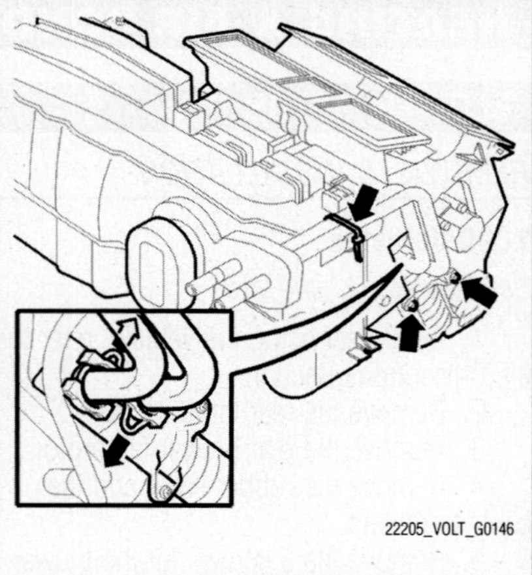

Fig. 222 Remove the bolts for the heat exchanger

19. Fill the engine coolant.
20. Start the engine and check that the pipe coupling does not leak.
21. Install the soundproofing panel.

STEERING

POWER STEERING GEAR

REMOVAL & INSTALLATION

See Figures 223 through 226.

The illustrations in this service information are used for different model years and/or models. Some variation may occur. However, the essential information in the illustrations is correct.

1. Before servicing the vehicle, refer to the Precautions Section.
2. Set the steering wheel to the straight ahead position. Remove the key so that the steering wheel lock engages.
3. Disconnect the negative battery cable.
4. Remove the front wheels.
5. Drain the power steering fluid reservoir.
    a. Lift up the oil reservoir.
    b. Place paper under the oil reservoir for any oil spillage. Position a container under the oil reservoir.
    c. Remove the hose with the clamp from the oil reservoir.
    d. Drain the oil.
6. Remove the bolts at the suspension turrets on both sides.
7. Install the lifting tool.

⁂ WARNING

When raising the engine make sure that the lifting eye does not scratch the torque rod. Tape the torque rod at the lifting eye.

8. Remove the oil filler cap. Remove the upper front engine casing by pulling it straight up. Reinstall the oil filler cap.
9. Removing the fender liner.
10. Remove the bolts to the engine pad.
11. Remove the protective cover under the engine.
12. Remove the exhaust pipes between front and rear catalytic converters.
13. Remove the lower bolt to the rear engine pad.
14. Disconnect the Heated Oxygen (HO2S) sensor connectors from the sub-frame. Fold aside the protective plate under the steering gear to gain access to the engine pad lower bolt. Remove the engine pad bolt.
15. Turn the steering wheel until optimum access to the bolt is achieved. Lock the steering wheel and take out the ignition key, so that the steering wheel lock is activated.
16. Remove the lower steering shaft joint.
17. On one side, measure the length of the track rod in relation to the steering gear housing. Make a note of the measurement, then remove the lower steering shaft joint.

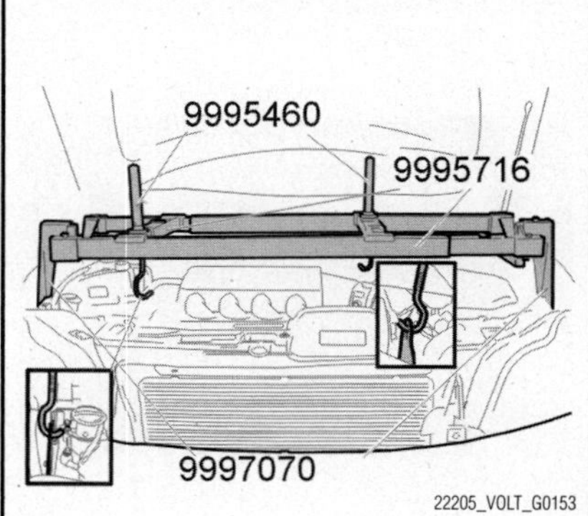

Fig. 223 View of lifting tool 999-5716 converted with kit 999-7070 and the lifting hooks 999-5460

Fig. 224 View of lower steering shaft joint

18. Remove the bolt to the lower steering shaft joint.
19. Remove the connector to the solenoid.
20. If replacing the steering gear, remove the tie rod ends.

⁂ WARNING

Do not turn the front wheels so that the position of the steering gear is changed. This could damage the SRS system contact reel.

21. Remove the track rod ends. Counter-hold with a wrench so that the gaiter is not damaged.
22. Lower the sub-frame at the rear edge.
23. Press the lower steering shaft joint up from the steering gear. Make sure that no pipes or lines are loaded or trapped when lowering.
24. Position a mobile jack at the rear end of the sub-frame.
25. Remove the bolts to the sub-frame brackets at the rear edge.
26. Remove the bolts to the sub-frame in the rear edge.
27. Remove the sub-frame brackets.
28. Release the HO2S lines from the anti-roll bar. Lower the sub-frame carefully.
29. Remove the pressure pipe and return pipe from the steering gear.
30. Remove the bolt to the bracket holding the pipe to the sub-frame.
31. Release the pipes from the clips.
32. Place a container under the steering gear.
33. Remove the bolt from the pipe on the valve housing.
34. Remove the pipes.

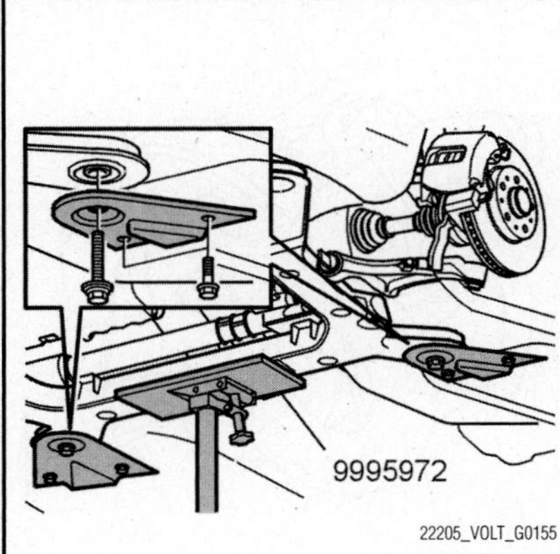

Fig. 225 View of sub-frame mounting bolts

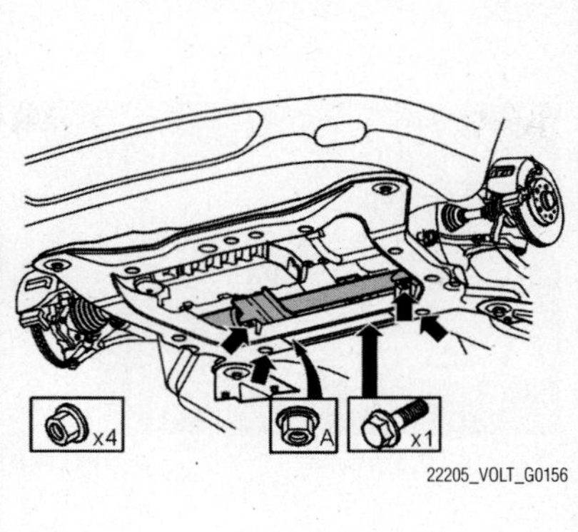

Fig. 226 View of power steering gear mounting nuts/bolts

35. Remove the metal protective cover.
36. Remove the bolt holding the protective plate on the steering gear.
37. Remove the bolt holding the protective plate to the sub-frame.
38. Remove the protective plate.
39. Remove the steering gear through the left-hand side of the vehicle.

To install:

40. Installation is the reverse of the removal procedure.

➡Replace bolts and nuts as specified.

41. Tighten bolts/nuts to specification as follows:
    - Power steering gear M10: 37 ft. lbs. (50 Nm)
    - Protective plate to steering gear M5: 44 inch lbs. (5 Nm)
    - Protective plate to sub-frame M6: 89 inch lbs. (10 Nm)
    - Oil pipe bracket to sub-frame M6: 89 inch lbs. (10 Nm)
    - Oil pipe to steering gear: 89 inch lbs. (10 Nm)
    - Sub-frame to body: Use new screws. Lube the screws with oil: 74 ft. lbs. (100 Nm)

➡First tighten the screws on the sub-frame left side, then on the right.

- Sub-frame brackets M10: 37 ft. lbs. (50 Nm)
- Rear engine pad lower bolt M10: 37 ft. lbs. (50 Nm)

➡Unscrew the upper nut engine pad bolt in order to facilitate fitting the lower bolt.

- Steering arms to the wheels spindles: Use new lock nuts: 52 ft. lbs. (70 Nm)

➡Always check carefully that the joint screw hole is aligned with the slot in the steering gear shaft.

- Lower steering shaft joint bolt: 18 ft. lbs. (24 Nm)
- Exhaust pipe nuts: 18 ft. lbs. (24 Nm)
- Protective engine under cover: 18 ft. lbs. (24 Nm)
- Right engine pad bolt M10: 37 ft. lbs. (50 Nm)
- Torque rod to suspension turret M10: 37 ft. lbs. (50 Nm)

42. Connect the negative battery cable.
43. Fill and bleed the power steering system.

➡For the correct oil grade, use Volvo power steering fluid, part number: 116 1529-1.

44. Initialize the central locking system, interior lighting, and power windows using the VIDA communications tool.

➡When the battery is disconnected, the engine may need to run for a few minutes before it runs smoothly.

45. Check the wheel alignment, adjust if necessary.

POWER STEERING PUMP

BLEEDING

⁂ CAUTION

The fluid level should be checked with the engine OFF to prevent personal injury from moving parts and to assure an accurate fluid level reading.

⁂ WARNING

If the air is not purged from the power steering system correctly, pump failure could result.

1. Before servicing the vehicle, refer to the Precautions Section.
2. With the engine OFF, turn the steering wheel fully to the right and to the left several times.

➡Do not allow the fluid level in the reservoir tank to go below the MIN level line. Check and add fluid as needed.

3. Run the engine at idle speed. Turn the steering wheel fully to the right and then fully to the left. Hold for about 3 seconds. Check for fluid leakage.

4. Repeat the above step several times at 3 second intervals.

WARNING

Do not hold the steering wheel in the locked position for more than 10 seconds.

5. Check for air bubbles or cloudy fluid. If found, repeat the bleeding procedure.
6. Stop the engine and check the fluid level. Fill as required.

FLUID FILL PROCEDURE

CAUTION

Used fluid is considerably more dangerous than new fluid. Avoid skin contact with the oil.

1. Before servicing the vehicle, refer to the Precautions Section.
2. Inspect the power steering fluid level in the power steering reservoir. Do allow the fluid to drop below the MIN marking.
3. Remove the power steering reservoir cap.
4. Add fluid to the specified level, as necessary.

➡Use Volvo power steering fluid, P/N 1161529.

REMOVAL & INSTALLATION

3.0L & 3.2L Engines

See Figures 227 through 229.

1. Before servicing the vehicle, refer to the Precautions Section.
2. Disconnect the negative battery cable.
3. Remove the relay and fuse box in the engine compartment.
4. Remove the air cleaner assembly.
5. Lift up the power steering pump oil reservoir. Place paper under the oil reservoir for any oil spillage.
6. Position a container under the oil reservoir. Remove the hose with the clamp from the oil reservoir.
7. Drain the power steering system.
8. Remove the pump bracket.
9. Disconnect the pressure hose at the pump.
10. Disconnect the transaxle selector cable from the lever and remove the attaching bracket.
11. Loosen the ABS hydraulic unit bolts and lift the unit 1.2 inches (30mm).

➡Do not loosen the bolt more than 4 turns.

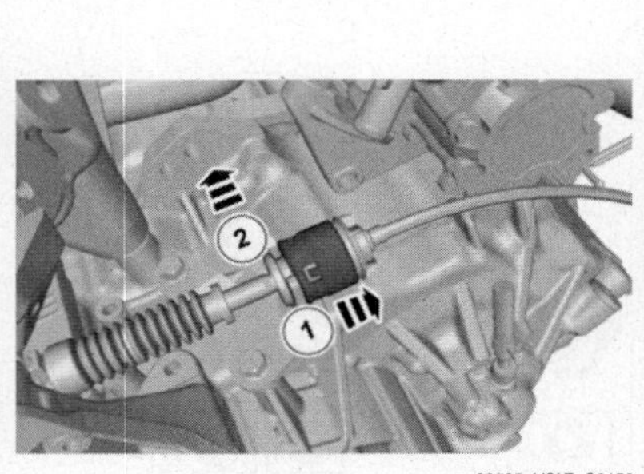

Fig. 227 Disconnecting the transaxle selector cable

Fig. 228 Remove the pump mounting bolts and move the pump out and up to remove

12. Remove the accessory drive belt.
13. Remove the stabilizer brackets at the pump.
14. Remove the pump mounting bolts and move the pump out and up to remove.

To install:

15. Installation is the reverse of the removal procedure.
16. Replace the centering pin prior to installing the pump.
17. Tighten the bolts/nuts to specification as follows:
    - Pump mounting bolts M8: 18 ft. lbs. (24 Nm)
    - Pump bracket bolts M8: 18 ft. lbs. (24 Nm)
    - ABS hydraulic unit bolts M6: 89 inch lbs. (10 Nm)
18. Fill and bleed the power steering system.
19. Connect the negative battery cable.

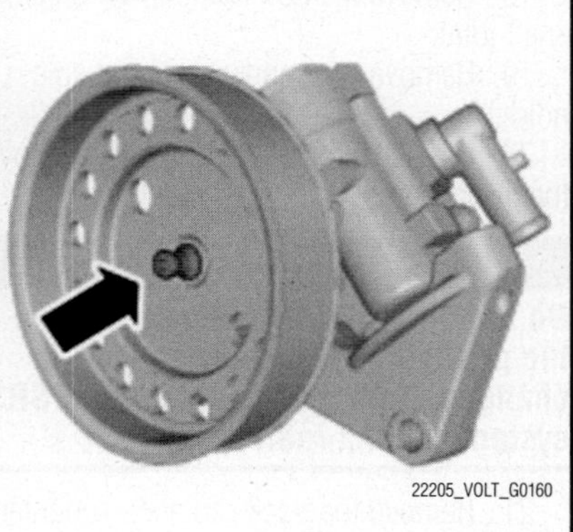

Fig. 229 Replace the centering pin prior to installing the pump

➡When the battery is disconnected, the engine may need to run for a few minutes before it runs smoothly.

20. Initialize the central locking system, interior lighting, and power windows using the VIDA communications tool.

4.4L Engine

See Figure 230.

1. Before servicing the vehicle, refer to the Precautions Section.
2. Lift up the oil reservoir. Place paper under the oil reservoir for any oil spillage.
3. Position a container under the oil reservoir. Remove the hose with the clamp from the oil reservoir.
4. Drain the power steering system.
5. Remove the intake manifold.
6. Remove the auxiliary drive belt.
7. Remove the bolt to the pressure pipe.
    a. Remove the pressure pipe.

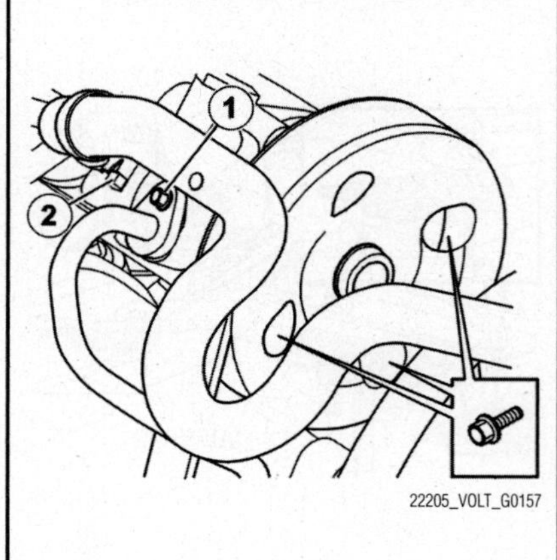

Fig. 230 View of power steering pressure pipe (1) and delivery hose (2)

b. Remove the delivery hose with the clamp.

c. Remove the 3 screws for the power steering pump.

d. Remove the power steering pump.

To install:

8. Install the power steering pump and tighten bolts to 18 ft. lbs. (24 Nm).

9. Install the pressure pipe. Use a new O-ring.

10. Install the screw for the pressure pipe. Tighten to 24 ft. lbs. (32 Nm).

11. Install the delivery hose with the clamp. Tighten to 24 ft. lbs. (32 Nm).

12. Install the auxiliary belt.

13. Install the intake manifold.

14. Install the hose with the clamp to the oil reservoir.

15. Install the oil reservoir.

16. Fill and bleed the power steering system.

SUSPENSION

FRONT SUSPENSION

KNUCKLE & SPINDLE

REMOVAL & INSTALLATION

See Figures 231 through 233.

1. Before servicing the vehicle, refer to the Precautions Section.

2. Raise and safely support the vehicle.

3. Remove the front wheel and tire assembly.

4. Remove the anti-roll bar link from the spring strut. Use a fixed wrench as a counter-hold.

5. Remove the ABS sensor. Hang up the sensor using a piece of wire.

6. Remove the ABS sensor cable from the spring strut.

7. Remove the brake caliper mounting bolts. Hang the caliper up using a piece of wire.

8. Remove the halfshaft bolt. Use a screwdriver as a counter-hold on the brake disc.

9. Remove the locating pin holding the brake disc.

10. Remove the brake disc. Detach the end of the halfshaft in the hub by knocking the halfshaft into the hub approximately ⅓–½ inch (10–15mm). Use a rubber or copper mallet.

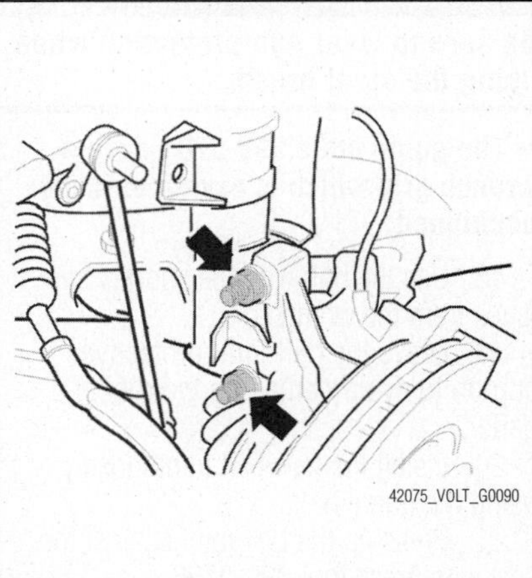

Fig. 231 Location of bolt removal of steering knuckle

11. Remove the tie rod ends from the steering arm.

12. Matchmark the position of the steering knuckle and spring strut for installation purposes.

13. Remove the bolts retaining the spring strut and the steering knuckle.

14. Press out the steering knuckle. At the same time, pull the halfshaft from the transaxle.

15. Suspend the halfshaft from a hook 999-5045.

➡Take care not to damage the halfshaft boot.

16. Disconnect the ball joint pinion from the control arm. Use tool 999-7062.

17. Install cap nut 7062-1 on the ball joint pinion.

18. Tighten the nut against the control arm.

19. Turn back 1 turn to form a gap between the cap nut and the control arm.

20. Position the extractor on the control arm. Detach the ball joint from the control arm.

21. Remove the steering knuckle.

To install:

22. Install the steering knuckle on the trailing arm.

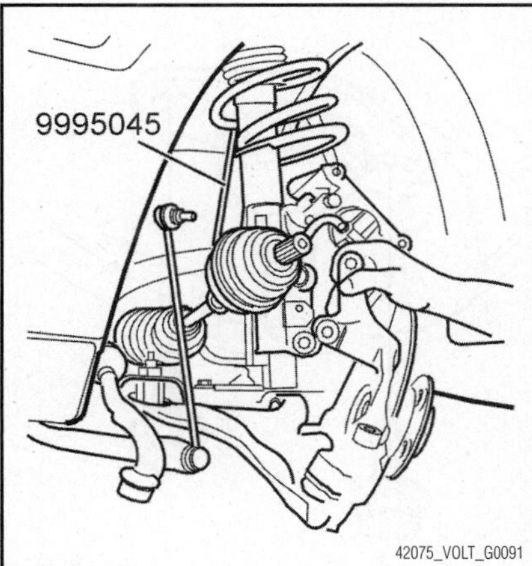

Fig. 232 Suspending halfshaft from hook 999-5045

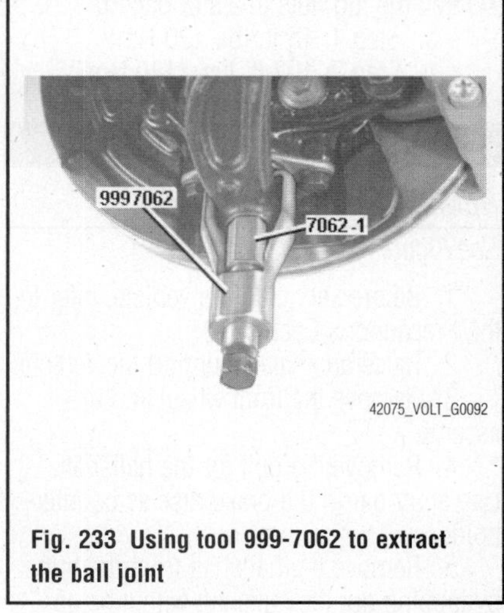

Fig. 233 Using tool 999-7062 to extract the ball joint

23. Install a new nut on the ball joint. Tighten to 59 ft. lbs. (80 Nm). Use a Torx® wrench as counter-hold.

➡Make sure that the mating surfaces on the ball joint and link are clean.

24. Clean the splines on the halfshaft.

25. Turn the steering knuckle and bring the halfshaft into the hub.

26. Install the halfshaft bolt. Lubricate the bolt.

27. Install bolts retaining the spring strut in the steering knuckle. Use new bolts and nuts. Tighten to 78 ft. lbs. (105 Nm), plus 60°.

28. Install the anti-roll bar link to the spring strut. Use a new nut. Counter-hold using a Torx® wrench so that the boot is not damaged. Tighten to 37 ft. lbs. (50 Nm).

29. Install the ABS sensor cable.

30. Install the ABS sensor onto the steering knuckle. Tighten the ABS sensor to 88 inch lbs. (10 Nm).

➡Ensure that the sensor seat in the steering knuckle is absolutely clean. Clean the ABS sensor with a soft brush.

31. Install the tie rod end onto the steering knuckle. Use a new nut. Tighten to 59 ft. lbs. (80 Nm).

32. Install the brake disc. Tighten the

brake disc locating pin to 89 inch lbs. (10 Nm).

➡**Ensure that the brake disc and wheel rim hub mating surfaces are clean.**

33. Tighten the halfshaft bolt. Use a screwdriver as a counter-hold on the brake disc. Tighten to 26 ft. lbs. (35 Nm), plus 120°.
34. Install the brake caliper. Use new bolts.
35. Install the wheel and tire assembly. Tighten the lug nuts in a star pattern.
    a. Step 1: 15 ft. lbs. (20 Nm).
    b. Step 2: 103 ft. lbs. (140 Nm).

LOWER BALL JOINTS

REMOVAL & INSTALLATION

See Figures 234 through 243.

1. Before servicing the vehicle, refer to the Precautions Section.
2. Raise and safely support the vehicle.
3. Remove the front wheel and tire assembly.
4. Remove the bolt for the halfshaft. Use a pry bar in the brake disc as counter-hold.
5. Remove the halfshaft from the hub by tapping out the halfshaft with a brass drift.
6. Move the spring strut aside.
7. Loosen the ball joint pin from the link arm. Use tool 999-7062.
8. Install the cap nut for the ball joint pinion. For earlier versions (deep thread pitch) use 999-7062 and for later versions (closer thread pitch) use 999-7231.
9. Tighten the nut against the link arm.
10. Turn back 1 turn so that clearance is created between the cap nut and link arm.

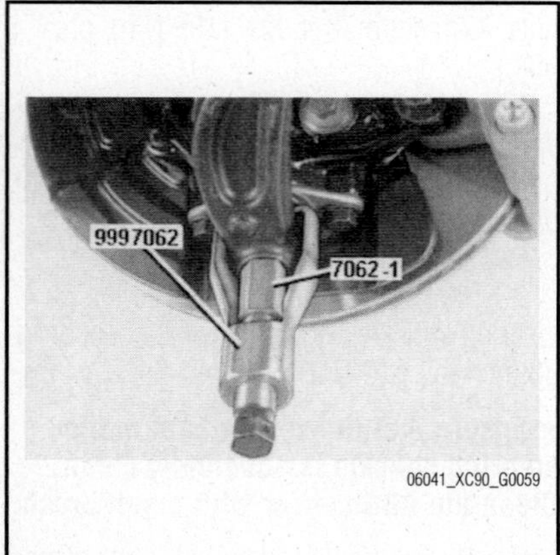

Fig. 234 Loosen the ball joint pin from the link arm

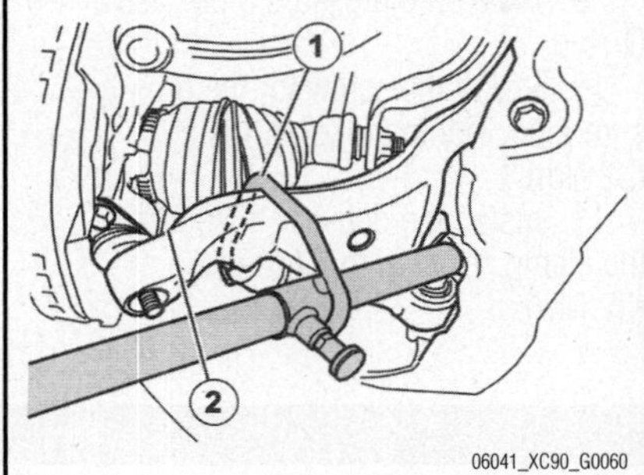

Fig. 235 If the catch is placed by this area (2), the rubber gaiter on the ball joint may be damaged. Press the control arm down using lever 999-7076. Position the hook here (1)

11. Place the puller on the link arm and loosen the ball joint from the link arm.

⁂ WARNING

Be careful not to damage the rubber gaiter on the ball joint.

12. Press the control arm down using lever 999-7076. Position the hook.
13. Disconnect the spring strut from the link arm.
14. Remove the ball joint bolts.
15. Install the nut on the ball joint. Use 999-7149 for earlier versions (deep thread pitch) and for later versions (closer thread pitch) use 999-7230.
16. Tap loose the ball joint and remove.

To install:

17. Clean both in the seat for the ball joint and the contact surfaces with a steel brush. Grease the seat with wheel bearing grease.

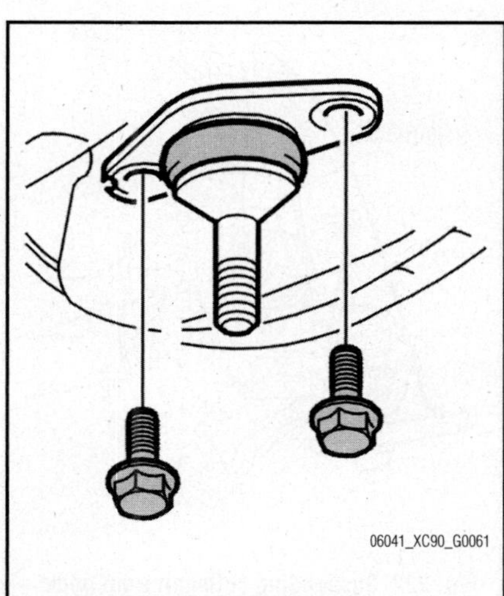

Fig. 236 View of ball joint bolts

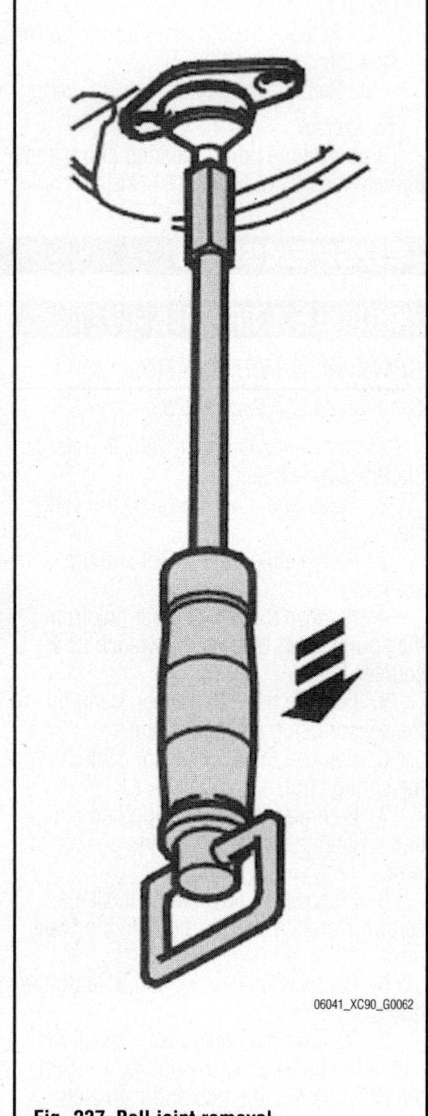

Fig. 237 Ball joint removal

⁂ CAUTION

Be sure to wear eye protection when using the steel brush.

➡**The guide bolts 999-5781 have a wrench grip which is asymmetrically positioned.**

18. Use the bolt with the shortest distance from the wrench grip.
19. Leave the ball joint protective cup on to avoid damaging the rubber gaiter.
20. Install the new ball joint loosely using the guide bolts.
21. Press up the ball joint against the seat with press tool 999-5796.
22. Check that the ball joint is centered in the seat.

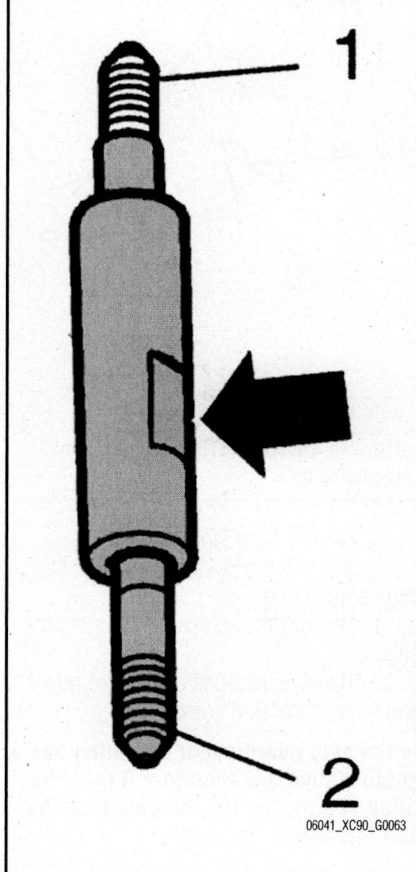

Fig. 238 The guide bolts 999-5781 (1) have a wrench grip (see arrow) which is asymmetrically positioned. Use the bolt (2) with the shortest distance from the wrench grip

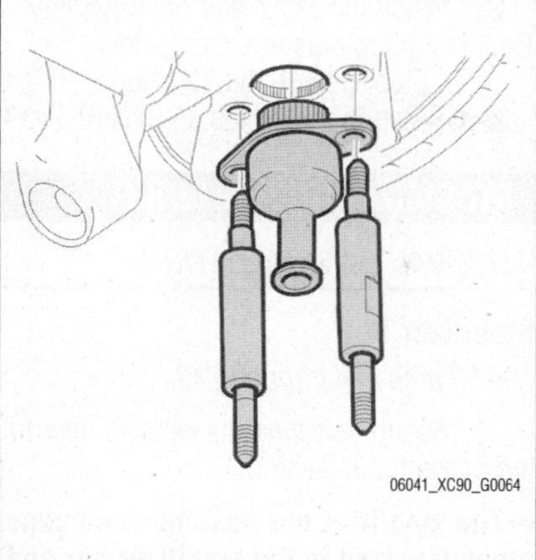

Fig. 239 Install the new ball joint loosely using the guide bolts

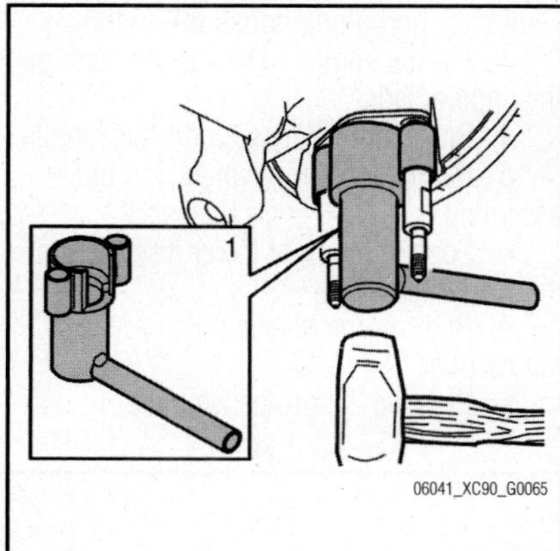

Fig. 240 Drive in the ball joint with a copper hammer

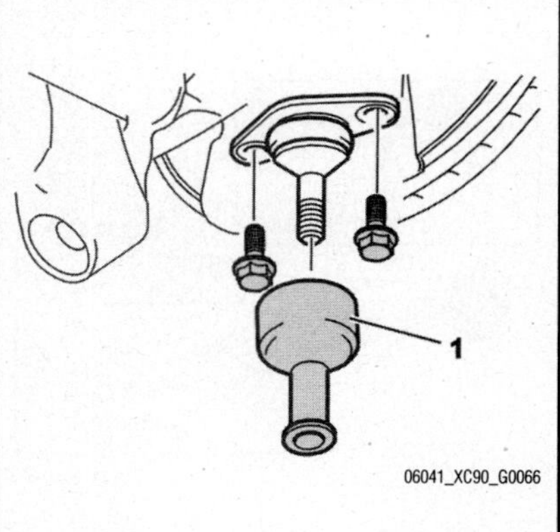

Fig. 241 Tighten down the ball joint with the new bolts. Ensure the rubber gaiter (1) on the ball joint is not damaged

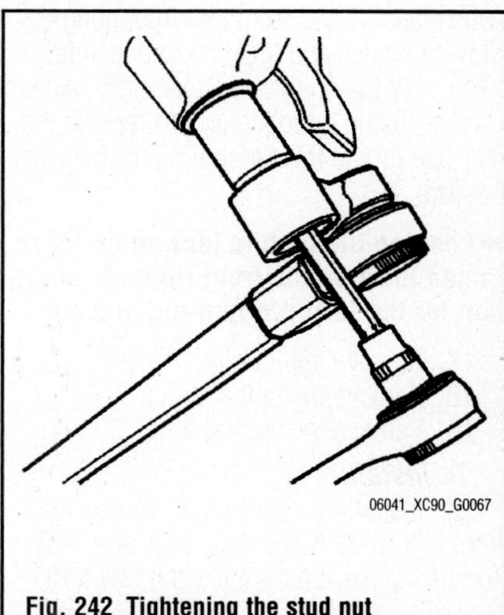

Fig. 242 Tightening the stud nut

23. Drive in the ball joint with a copper hammer.
24. Remove the guide bolts.
25. Tighten down the ball joint with the new bolts. Tighten to 74 ft. lbs. (100 Nm).
26. Remove the protective cup.
27. Install the halfshaft.
28. Press down the link with lever 999-7076.
29. Install the spring strut in the link arm.

➡The ball joint pin may not rotate. Use a bit Torx® as a counter-hold in order to prevent damaging the rubber gaiter.

30. Use 999-5500 as an adapter for the torque wrench.
31. Install the nut to 37 ft. lbs. (50 Nm), plus 35°.
32. Install the wheel and tire assembly. Tighten the lug nuts in a star pattern.
    a. Step 1: 15 ft. lbs. (20 Nm).
    b. Step 2: 103 ft. lbs. (140 Nm).

LOWER CONTROL ARMS

REMOVAL & INSTALLATION

See Figure 243.

1. Before servicing the vehicle, refer to the Precautions Section.
2. Raise and safely support the vehicle.
3. Remove the front wheel and tire assembly.
4. Disconnect the ball joint pinion from the control arm.
5. Install cap nut 7062-1 on the ball joint pinion.
6. Tighten the nut against the control arm.
7. Turn back 1 turn to form a gap between the cap nut and the control arm.
8. Position the extractor on the control arm. Detach the ball joint from the control arm.
9. Pull down the control arms using a tension strap.
10. Release the spring strut from the control arm.

✲✲ WARNING

Ensure that the tension strap is correctly secured in the control arms.

11. Remove the bolt for the halfshaft. Use a pry bar as a counter-hold on the brake disc.
12. Remove the halfshaft from the hub. Knock the halfshaft out using a brass drift.
13. Push the spring strut to one side. Remove the tensioning strap between the control arms.

✲✲ WARNING

Ensure that the tensioning strap does not get trapped when releasing.

14. Remove the splash guard under the engine.
15. Applies to the right-hand side only: Remove the hose for the EVAP canister and the fuel line for the engine block heater

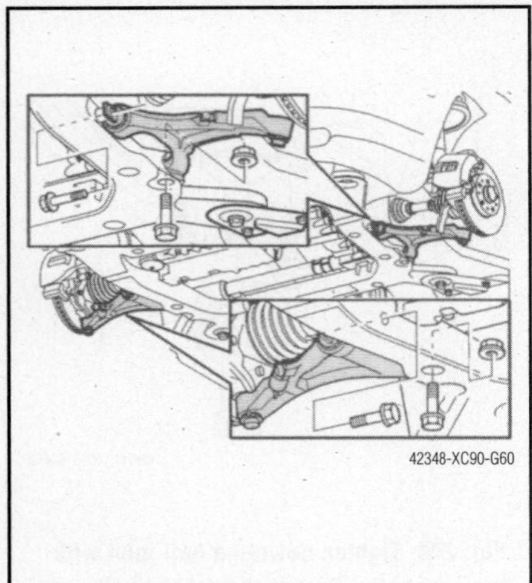

Fig. 243 Removing the lower control arm

(where applicable) from their mountings. Move the hose and fuel line to one side.

16. Lift the engine approximately ⅓ inch (10mm) using a mobile jack to remove the rear bolt on the front mounting for the control arm.

➡Position the mobile jack so that it is raised towards the front right mounting bolt for the lower torque rod bracket.

17. Remove the 2 bolts.
18. Remove the bolt and nut.
19. Remove the control arm.

To install:

20. Install the control arm. Torque the front bolt to 48 ft. lbs. (65 Nm), plus 120°. Torque the rear bolt/nut to 78 ft. lbs. (105 Nm), plus 120°.

➡Use new bolts.

21. Install the bolt for the front engine pad.
22. On the right-hand side only, install the hose for the EVAP canister and the fuel line for the engine block heater (if applicable) in their mountings.
23. Install the tensioning strap.
24. Insert the halfshaft in the hub.
25. Position the spring strut over the ball joint. Release the tensioning strap so that the control arm meets the ball joint.

***** WARNING**

Ensure that the tensioning strap does not get trapped when releasing.

26. Install the halfshaft in the hub. Install a new bolt. Use a pry bar as a counter-hold.
27. Install the upper ball joint nut. Tighten to 59 ft. lbs. (80 Nm).
28. Install the splashguard under the engine.
29. Install the wheel and tire assembly. Tighten the lug nuts in a star pattern.
    a. Step 1: 15 ft. lbs. (20 Nm).
    b. Step 2: 103 ft. lbs. (140 Nm).

STABILIZER BAR & LINKS

REMOVAL & INSTALLATION

Stabilizer Bar

See Figures 244 through 249.

1. Before servicing the vehicle, refer to the Precautions Section.

➡The stabilizer bar bushings and caps are vulcanized to the stabilizer bar and cannot be replaced separately.

2. Install the lifting tool 999-5716, modified according to the tool bulletin for version C, and lifting hooks 999-5460.
3. Lift the engine to relieve the load on the engine pads.
4. Raise and safely support the vehicle.
5. Remove the front wheel and tire assembly.
6. Loosen the right lower front part of the fender liner.
7. Remove the plastic nuts on the fender liner.
8. Remove the protective plate.

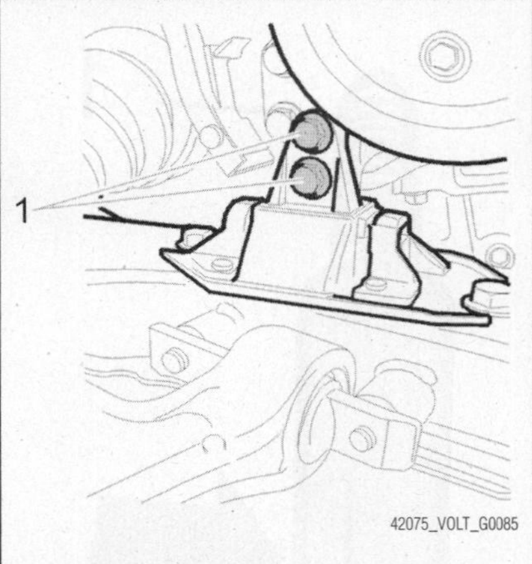

Fig. 245 Location of right-hand engine mounting bolts

9. Bend out the fender liner.
10. Remove the bolts for the right-hand engine mounting.
11. Remove the splash guard under the engine.
12. Remove the bolts of the skid guard and remove the skid guard.

➡The skid guard upper mounting has a guide sleeve and therefore it must be lifted slightly so that the panel can be slid forward.

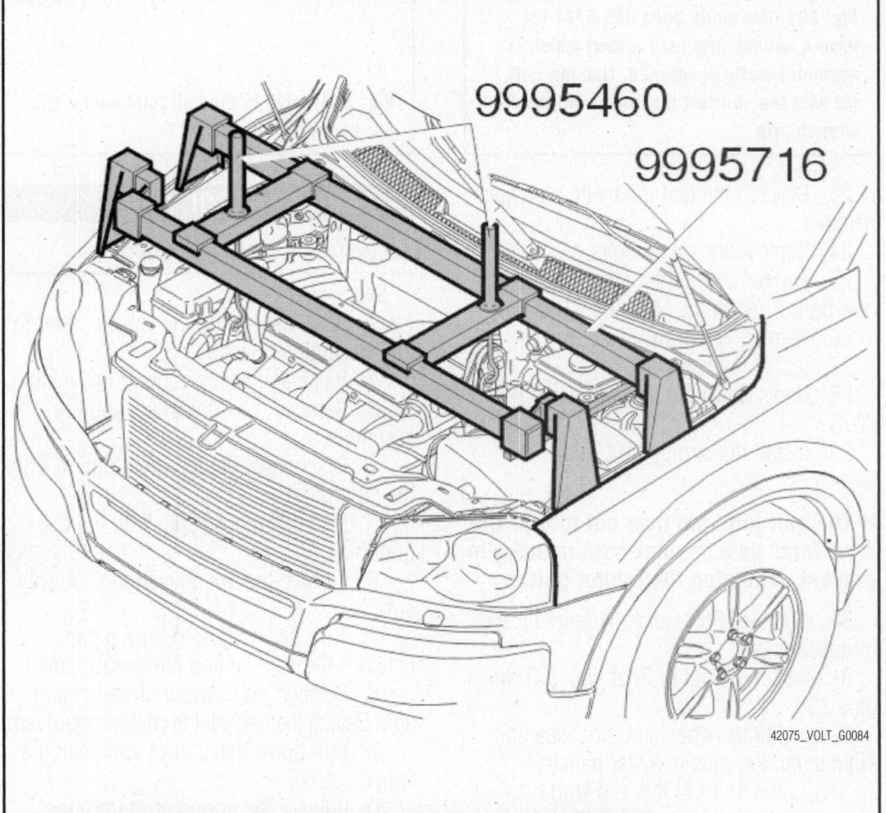

Fig. 244 Installation of lifting tool 999-5716 and lifting hooks 999-5460

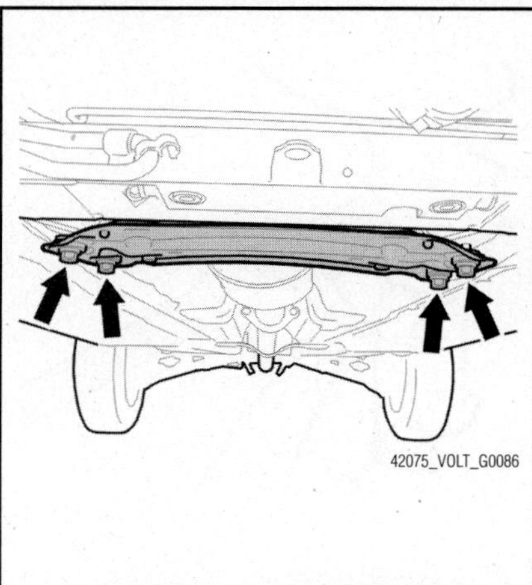

Fig. 246 Location and removal of the SIPS member

13. Remove the 4 mounting bolts for the Side Impact Protection System (SIPS) member.

14. Remove the brake pipe from the snap fastener on the member.

15. Remove the SIPS member.

16. Remove the rubber mountings for the exhaust pipe.

17. Remove the nuts and bolts holding the steering gear to the sub-frame.

18. Remove the power steering line from the clips on the sub-frame.

19. Remove the bracket for the Heated Oxygen (HO2S) sensor from the sub-frame.

20. Lower the sub-frame:

a. Position a mobile jack with universal plate 999-5972 at the rear of the sub-frame.

b. Remove the bolts holding the sub-frame bracket in the body.

c. Remove the rear bolt for the sub-frame with the bracket and washer.

d. Carefully lower the sub-frame until

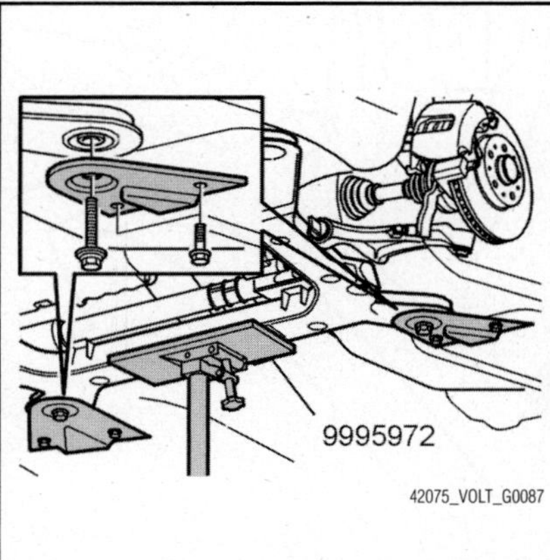

Fig. 247 Lowering the sub-frame using a mobile jack with a universal plate 999-5972

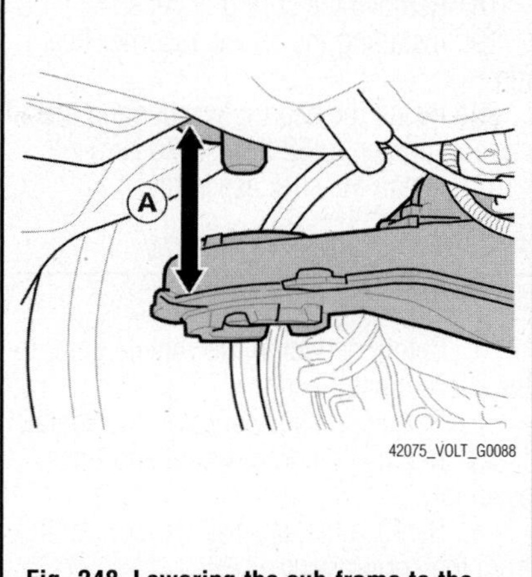

Fig. 248 Lowering the sub-frame to the appropriate clearance

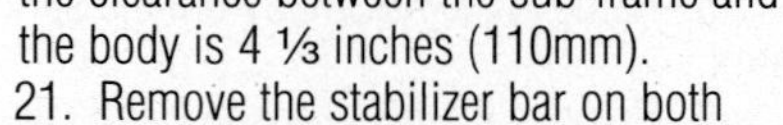

the clearance between the sub-frame and the body is 4 ⅓ inches (110mm).

21. Remove the stabilizer bar on both sides. Use a Torx® wrench as a counter-hold so that the boot is not damaged.

22. Remove the bolts for the stabilizer bar.

23. Remove the stabilizer bar.

To install:

24. Install the stabilizer bar.

25. Install the M10 bolts for the stabilizer bar. Tighten to 37 ft. lbs. (50 Nm).

26. Install the nut for the stabilizer bar link on both sides. Tighten to 59 ft. lbs. (80 Nm).

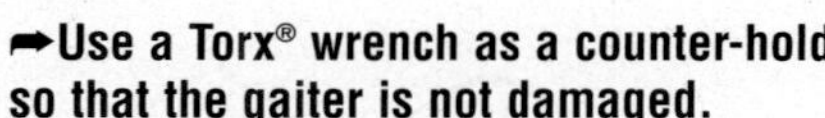

➡Use a Torx® wrench as a counter-hold so that the gaiter is not damaged.

27. Install the sub-frame:

a. Raise the sub-frame.

b. Install the sub-frame bolts together with the sub-frame brackets and engine heater, if installed.

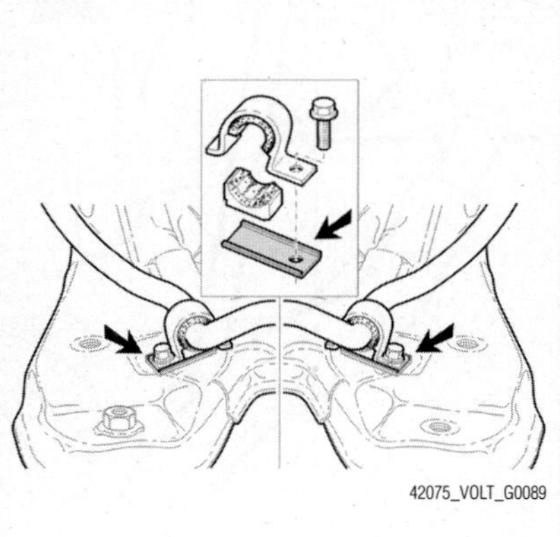

Fig. 249 Location and removal of stabilizer bar bolts

c. Use new bolts. Lube the bolts with oil. Tighten the sub-frame bolts starting on the left-hand side, then the right. Tighten to 78 ft. lbs. (105 Nm), plus 120°.

28. Tighten the M10 bolts for the brackets to 37 ft. lbs. (50 Nm).

29. Remove the lifting table.

30. Install the nuts and bolt for the steering gear. Use new nuts and bolt. Tighten to 37 ft. lbs. (50 Nm).

31. Install the rubber mountings for the exhaust pipe.

➡Use soap solution to facilitate installing the rubber mountings.

32. Install the SIPS member:

a. Install the brake pipe in the snap fastener on the member.

b. Install the SIPS member. Tighten the M8 bolts to 18 ft. lbs. (24 Nm).

33. Install the protective plate up into the bumper wrap-around. Press forwards until the mounting brackets engage in the sub-frame.

34. Install the M10 protective plate bolts. Tighten to 37 ft. lbs. (50 Nm).

35. Install the splash guard under the engine. Tighten the M8 bolts to 18 ft. lbs. (24 Nm).

36. Install the right-hand engine mounting and the bolts. Use new bolts. Tighten to 89 ft. lbs. (120 Nm), plus 40°.

37. Fold the fender liner back into position.

38. Install the plastic nuts.

39. Install the wheel and tire assembly. Tighten the lug nuts in a star pattern.

a. Step 1: 15 ft. lbs. (20 Nm).

b. Step 2: 103 ft. lbs. (140 Nm).

40. Remove the lifting tools 999-5716 and lifting hooks 999-5460.

Stabilizer Links

See Figure 250.

The illustrations in this service information are used for different model years and/or models. Some variation may occur. However, the essential information in the illustrations is correct.

1. Before servicing the vehicle, refer to the Precautions Section.

2. Raise and safely support the vehicle.

3. Remove the tire and wheel assembly.

4. Using the proper size wrench, hold the link stud while removing the link nut.

5. Remove the retaining nut from the stabilizer rod shaft and the strut.

6. Remove the stabilizer control link from the vehicle.

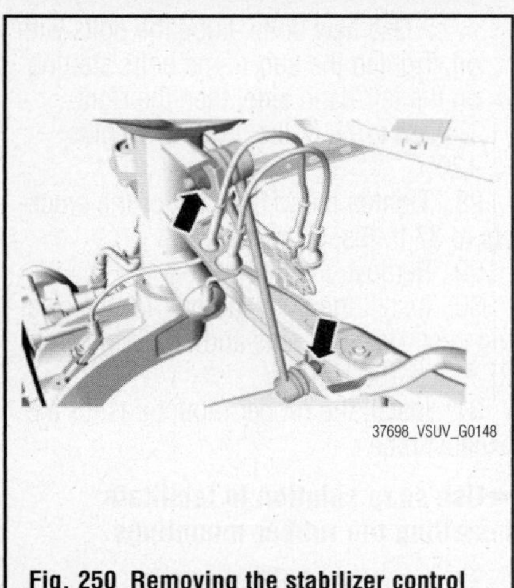

Fig. 250 Removing the stabilizer control link

To install:

7. Installation is the reverse of the removal procedure.
8. Tighten the control link at the strut to 44 ft. lbs. (60 Nm).
9. Tighten the control link at the stabilizer bar to 52 ft. lbs. (70 Nm).

STRUTS (MACPHERSON STRUTS)

OVERHAUL

1. Before servicing the vehicle, refer to the Precautions Section.
2. Remove the strut assembly.
3. Secure the spring strut in a vise.
4. Remove the nut for the shock absorber bearing. Use socket 999-5467 and a 3⁄8 inch Torx® wrench as a counter-hold.
5. Remove the washer.
6. Remove the support.
7. Take the load off the spring seat using a spring compressor.
8. Remove the fixing nut on the shock absorber. Use socket 999-5469 and a 3⁄8 inch Torx® wrench as a counter-hold.
9. Remove the spring seat.
10. Remove the spring.
11. Remove the rubber bump stop and gaiter.
12. Check that the shock absorber support plate, the spring seat, and the rubber bump stop with boot are undamaged. Replace if necessary.

To assemble:

13. Compress the new spring to a length of approximately 10 inches (260mm).
14. Install the bump stop with the boot.
15. Install the spring.
16. Install the spring seat.
17. Install the fixing nut. Tighten to 52 ft. lbs. (70 Nm).
18. Remove the spring clamps.
19. Installing the shock absorber bearing.
20. Install the bearing washer and the nut and tighten to 52 ft. lbs. (70 Nm).
21. Install the strut assembly.

REMOVAL & INSTALLATION

See Figures 251 through 253.

1. Before servicing the vehicle, refer to the Precautions Section.
2. Raise and safely support the vehicle.
3. Remove the front wheel and tire assembly.
4. Remove the anti-roll bar control link from the spring strut.

➡Use a Torx® wrench as a counter-hold so that the boot is not damaged.

5. Remove the ABS line from the spring strut.
6. Remove the ABS sensor. Hang up the sensor using a piece of wire.
7. Matchmark/measure the steering knuckle and spring strut at the upper bolt. Before measuring, clean off any dirt from the measuring surfaces. Note the measurement.
8. Remove both the bolts retaining the spring strut in the steering knuckle.

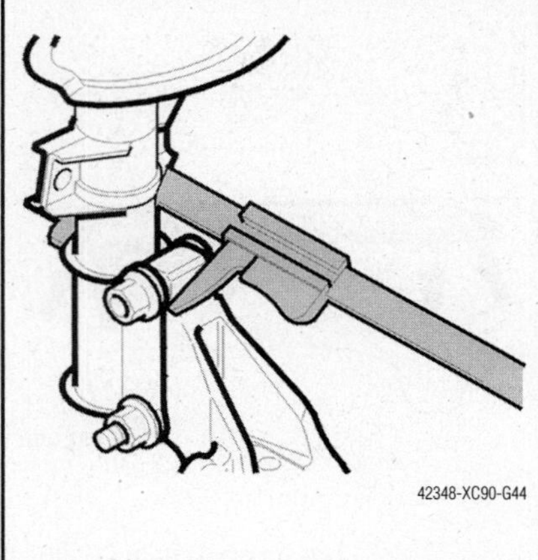

Fig. 251 Measuring over the spindle and strut

9. Remove the 3 nuts holding the spring strut in the bodywork.
10. Remove the spring strut.

To install:

11. Install the spring strut in the bodywork using new nuts. Tighten to 18 ft. lbs. (25 Nm).
12. Install the spring strut on the steering knuckle. Use new bolts and new nuts.
13. Adjust the spring strut and steering

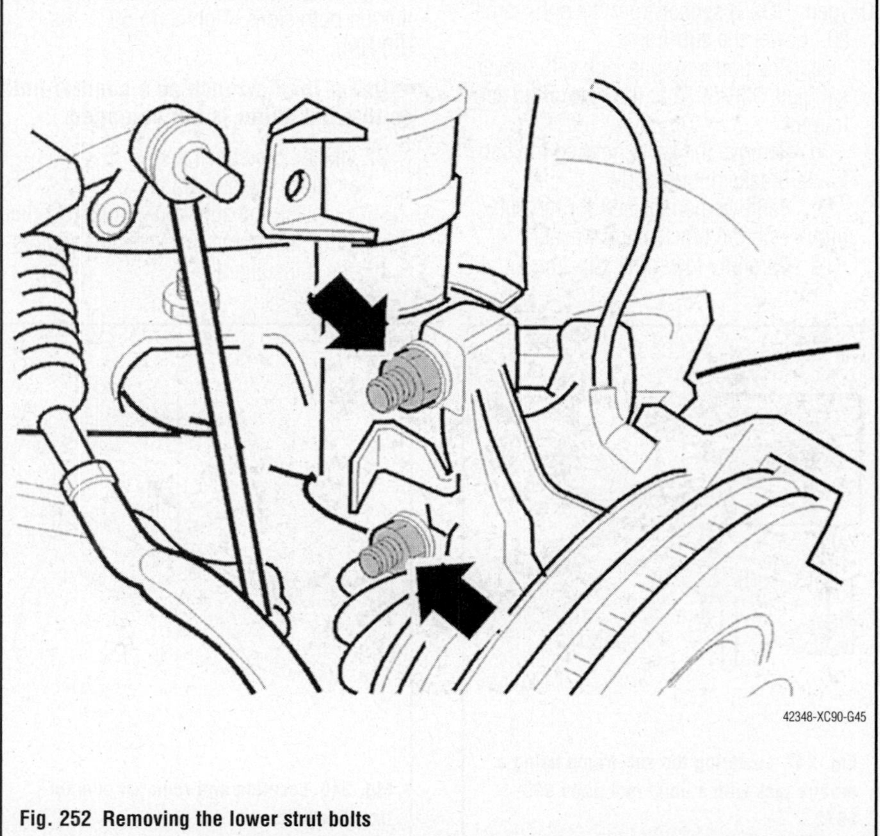

Fig. 252 Removing the lower strut bolts

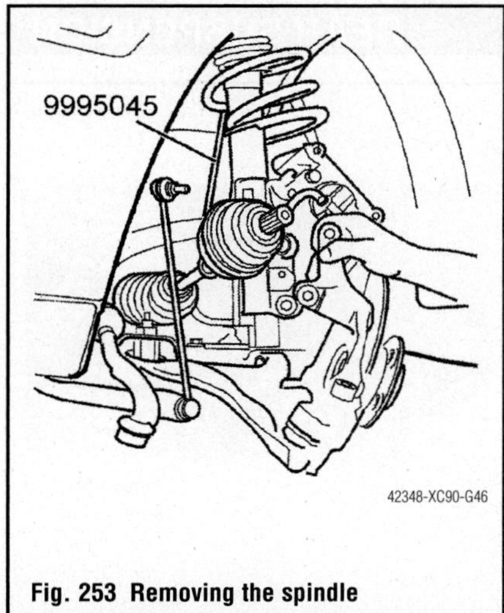

Fig. 253 Removing the spindle

knuckle to the measured value. Tighten to 77 ft. lbs. (105 Nm), plus 75°.

14. Install the anti-roll bar control link to the spring strut. Use a new nut. Tighten to 37 ft. lbs. (50 Nm). Counter-hold using a Torx® wrench to prevent damage to the boot.

15. Install the ABS sensor. Tighten to 89 inch lbs. (10 Nm).

➡Ensure that the ABS sensor seat in the steering knuckle is absolutely clean. Clean the ABS sensor with a soft brush.

16. Install the ABS sensor cable in the bracket.

17. Install the wheel and tire assembly. Tighten the lug nuts in a star pattern.
   a. Step 1: 15 ft. lbs. (20 Nm).
   b. Step 2: 103 ft. lbs. (140 Nm).

WHEEL HUBS & BEARINGS

ADJUSTMENT

The front wheel bearings are not adjustable. If the lateral run-out on the hub with the disc removed exceeds 0.0008 inch (0.020mm), the hub must be replaced.

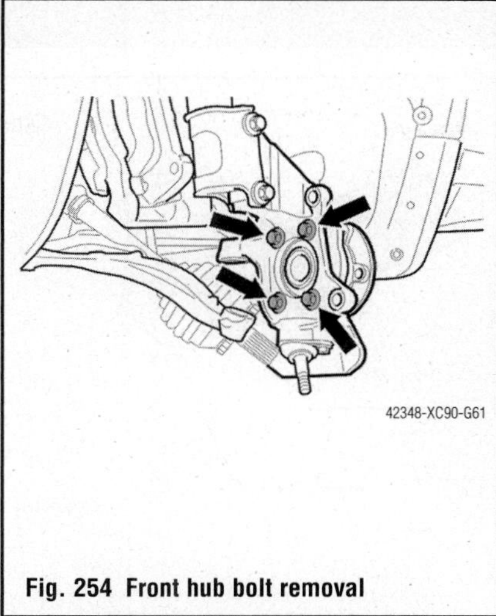

Fig. 254 Front hub bolt removal

REMOVAL & INSTALLATION

See Figure 254.

1. Before servicing the vehicle, refer to the Precautions Section.
2. Raise and safely support the vehicle.
3. Remove the front wheel and tire assembly.
4. Remove the brake caliper.
5. Hang up the caliper in a suitable position.
6. Remove the halfshaft bolt. Use a pry bar as a counter-hold on the brake disc.
7. Detach the end of the halfshaft in the hub by knocking the halfshaft into the hub approximately ⅓–½ inch (10–15mm). Use a rubber or copper mallet.
8. Remove the halfshaft bolt.
9. Remove the brake disc.
10. Remove the nut from the control link. Pull the control link out of its mounting.

➡Counter-hold using a Torx® wrench so that the boot for the link is not damaged.

11. Remove the ABS cable harness from its brackets.
12. Remove the nut from the ball joint. Counter-hold using a Torx® wrench so that the ball joint boot is not damaged.
13. Press out the ball joints.
14. Pull down the control arm using a tension strap.
15. Release the spring strut from the control arm and halfshaft.

⁂ WARNING

Ensure that the tension strap is correctly secured in the control arms.

16. Remove the bolts and remove the wheel hub/bearing assembly.

To install:

17. Install the hub.
18. Install the bolts and tighten the bolts:
   a. Step 1: to 15 ft. lbs. (20 Nm).
   b. Step 2: to 33 ft. lbs. (45 Nm).
   c. Step 3: plus 60°.
19. Install the halfshaft in the hub. Align the ball joint against the control arm.
20. Release the tensioning strap between the control arms.
21. Install a nut on the ball joint. Tighten to 59 ft. lbs. (80 Nm).

➡Counter-hold using a Torx® wrench to avoid damage to the boot.

22. Remove the tensioner strap.
23. Install the ABS cable harness in the brackets.
24. Install the stabilizer bar control link. Install the M12 nut and tighten to 44 ft. lbs. (60 Nm).
25. Install the steering arm. Install the nut and tighten to 52 ft. lbs. (70 Nm).
26. Install the brake disc.
27. Install a new halfshaft bolt and tighten.
28. Install the brake caliper.
29. Install the wheel and tire assembly. Tighten the lug nuts in a star pattern.
   a. Step 1: 15 ft. lbs. (20 Nm).
   b. Step 2: 103 ft. lbs. (140 Nm).

COIL SPRINGS

REMOVAL & INSTALLATION

See Figures 255 and 256.

1. Before servicing the vehicle, refer to the Precautions Section.
2. Raise and safely support the vehicle.
3. Remove the rear wheels.
4. Install tensioner 999-5659, or equivalent.
5. If equipped with Bi-Xenon headlamps, remove the position sensor.
6. Remove the bolt for the mounting of the stabilizer control link.
7. Remove the bolt holding the control arm in the steering knuckle.
8. Lower the control arm with the tensioner. The spring is now unloaded.
9. Lower the tensioner. Twist the tensioner so that it is positioned along the length of the car.
10. Press the control arm down by hand. Remove the spring.

To install:

11. Install the rear spring.
12. Check that the spring is correctly installed in the lower spring seat.
13. Lift the removed control arm by hand. Position the tensioner in the rails.

➡The tensioner must be positioned as far out as possible on the tensioner plates to achieve the correct lifting force.

14. Lift the control arms so that the bolt for the control arm and stabilizer control link can be installed. Align the bolt. Tighten by hand only.
15. Lower the tensioner. Install the bolt in the lower mounting for the shock absorber. Do not tighten yet.

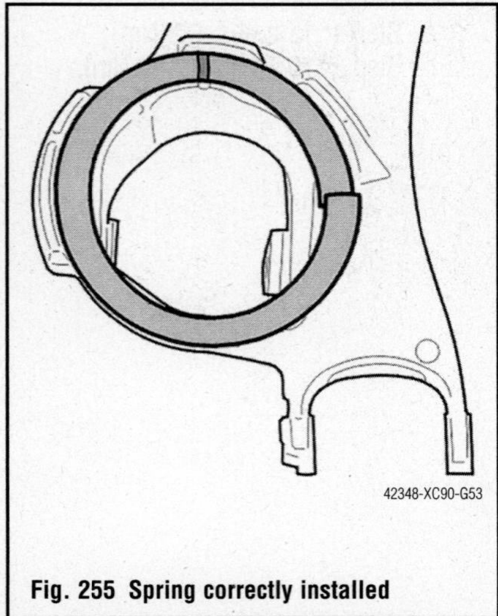
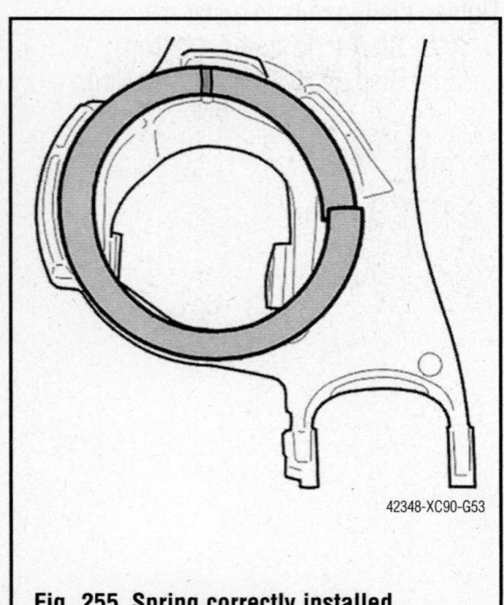

Fig. 255 Spring correctly installed

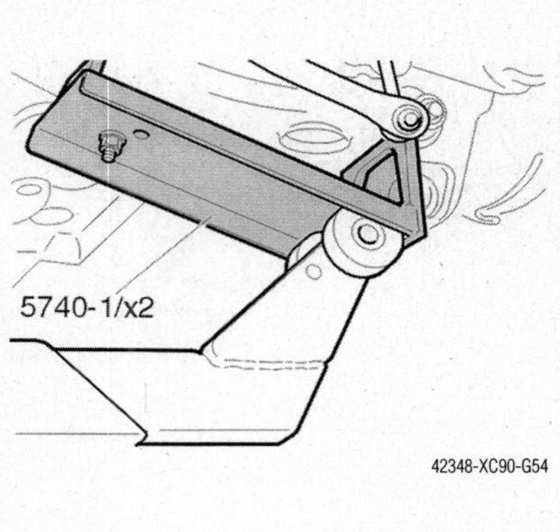

Fig. 256 Tensioner positioned on control arm

16. Tension the control arms to the normal position.
17. Tighten the bolts for the control arm, lateral link, and shock absorber.
18. Install the position sensor for Bi-Xenon lamps, if equipped.
19. Remove the tensioner.
20. Install the wheel and tire assembly. Tighten the lug nuts in a star pattern.
    a. Step 1: 15 ft. lbs. (20 Nm).
    b. Step 2: 103 ft. lbs. (140 Nm).

➡If the car is equipped with Bi-Xenon lamps, the position sensor must be calibrated using VIDA vehicle communication tools.

CONTROL LINKS

REMOVAL & INSTALLATION

XC60 Vehicles

See Figure 257.

The illustrations in this service information are used for different model years and/or models. Some variation may occur. However, the essential information in the illustrations is correct.

1. Before servicing the vehicle, refer to the Precautions Section.
2. Raise and safely support the vehicle.
3. Remove the tire and wheel assembly.
4. Using the proper size wrench, hold the link stud while removing the link nut.

⁂ WARNING

Make sure that the ball joint ball does not rotate.

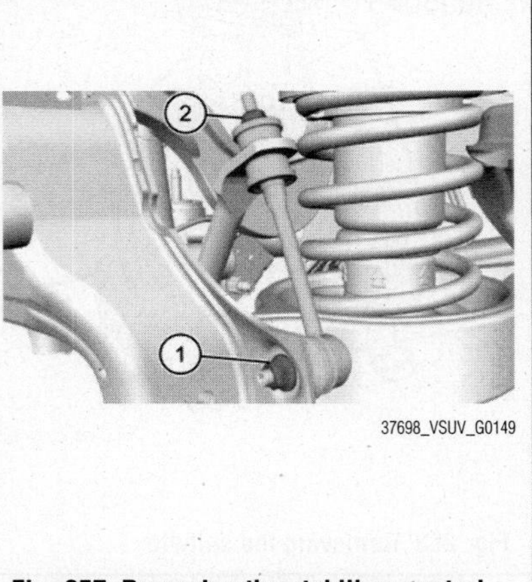

Fig. 257 Removing the stabilizer control link—XC60 vehicles

5. Remove the retaining nut from the stabilizer rod shaft and the control arm.
6. Remove the stabilizer control link from the vehicle.

To install:

7. Installation is the reverse of the removal procedure.
8. Tighten the control link at the control arm to 44 ft. lbs. (60 Nm).
9. Tighten the control link at the stabilizer bar to 11 ft. lbs. (15 Nm).

LATERAL LINK

REMOVAL & INSTALLATION

XC90 Vehicles

See Figure 258.

As the illustrations in this service information are used for different model years and/or models, some variation may occur. However, the essential information in the illustrations is correct.

1. Before servicing the vehicle, refer to the Precautions Section.
2. Raise and safely support the vehicle.
3. Remove the rear wheel and tire assembly.
4. Install tensioner 999-5659. Set the rear suspension to the normal position.
5. Remove the upper and lower bolts from the lateral link.
6. Remove the lateral link.

To install:

7. Install the lateral link into position.
8. Install new upper and lower bolts in the lateral link and tighten to 59 ft. lbs. (80 Nm).
9. Remove the tensioner.
10. Lower the vehicle.

Fig. 258 Removing the lateral link—XC90 vehicles

LOWER CONTROL ARMS

REMOVAL & INSTALLATION

XC60 VEHICLES

See Figure 259.

As the illustrations in this service information are used for different model years and/or models, some variation may occur. However, the essential information in the illustrations is correct.

1. Before servicing the vehicle, refer to the Precautions Section.
2. Raise and safely support the vehicle.
3. Remove the rear wheel and tire assembly.
4. Remove the rear spring.
5. Remove the lower arm rear-to-wheel knuckle bolt.
6. Remove the lower arm rear-to-sub-frame bolt.
7. Remove the lower control arm.

To install:

8. Install the lower control arm into position.
9. Install the coil spring.
10. Place the rear suspension into normal position.
11. Install the lower arm rear-to-sub-frame bolt and tighten to 66 ft. lbs. (90 Nm).
12. Install the lower arm rear-to-wheel knuckle bolt and tighten to 81 ft. lbs. (110 Nm).
13. Check the wheel alignment, adjust as necessary.

XC90 Vehicles

See Figure 260.

1. Before servicing the vehicle, refer to the Precautions Section.
2. Raise and safely support the vehicle.
3. Remove the rear wheel and tire assembly.
4. Remove the coil spring.
5. Remove the bolt in the sub-frame for the lower control arm.
6. Remove the control arm.
7. Remove the control arm rail (5740-1).

To install:

➡Tighten all joints and rubber bushings with the rear suspension in the normal position.

8. Install the control arm rail (5742-1) in the control arm.
9. Install the control arm in the sub-frame. Do not tighten yet.
10. Install the coil spring.
11. Raise the control arms to their normal position using the tensioner 999-5659.
12. Tighten the M12 bolt for the inner mounting for the control arm to 59 ft. lbs. (80 Nm).

➡If the vehicle is equipped with Bi-Xenon lamps, the position sensor must be calibrated using VIDA vehicle communication tools.

SHOCK ABSORBERS

REMOVAL & INSTALLATION

XC60 Vehicles

See Figures 261 and 262.

1. Before servicing the vehicle, refer to the Precautions Section.
2. Raise and safely support the vehicle.
3. Remove the rear wheel and tire assembly.
4. Support the rear suspension in normal position.
5. Remove the rear shock absorber-to-wheel knuckle bolt.
6. Remove the rear shock absorber-to-body bolts.

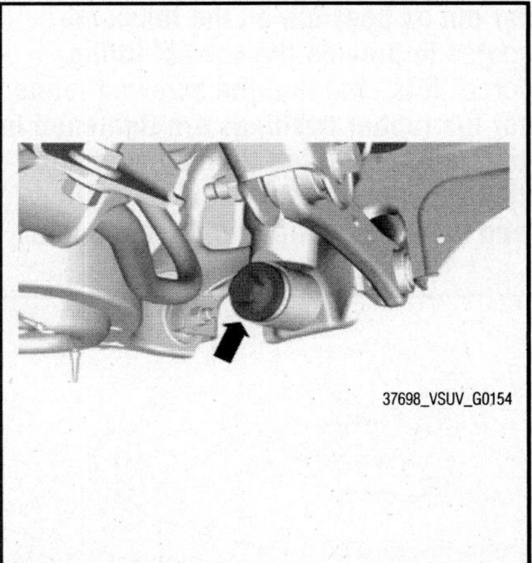

Fig. 261 Remove the rear shock absorber-to-wheel knuckle bolt

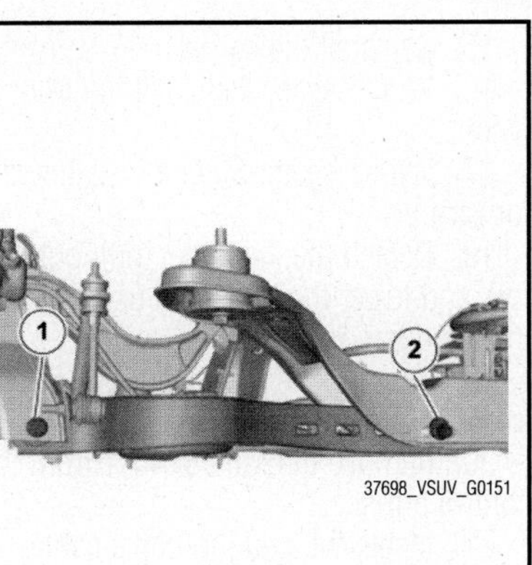

Fig. 259 Removing the lower control arm

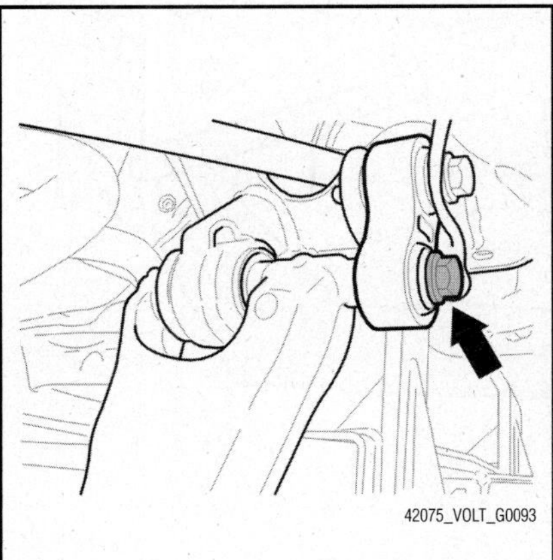

Fig. 260 Removal of rear lower control arm

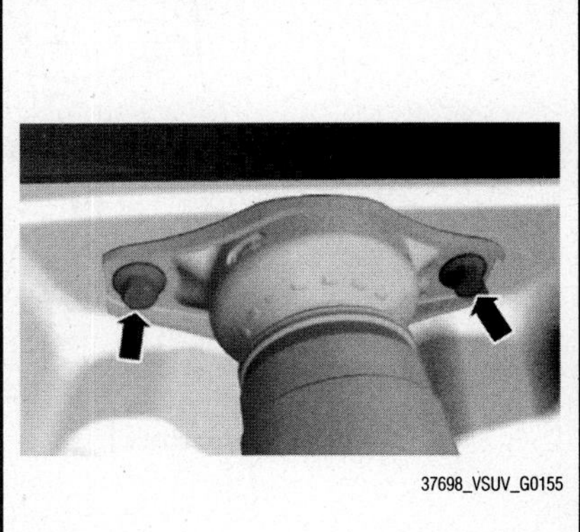

Fig. 262 Remove the rear shock absorber-to-body bolts

7. Remove the rear shock absorber.

To install:

8. Install the rear shock absorber to the vehicle.
9. Tighten the shock absorber-to-wheel knuckle bolt to 129 ft. lbs. (175 Nm).
10. Tighten the shock absorber-to-body bolts to 22 ft. lbs. (30 Nm).

XC90 Vehicles

See Figures 263 through 266.

1. Before servicing the vehicle, refer to the Precautions Section.
2. Raise and safely support the vehicle.
3. Remove the rear wheel and tire assembly.
4. Install tensioner 999-5659 as follows:
   a. Remove the parking brake cable mountings from the sub-frame.
   b. Install the tensioner.

➡The tensioner must be positioned as far out as possible on the tensioner plates to provide the correct lifting force. It is vital that the screwed joints for the rubber bushings are tightened in the normal position (in the same position as when the car is on the ground and has three people in the car and a full fuel tank). The tensioner relieves the pressure on the components in the suspension when removing and installing.

   c. The tool is secured to the sub-frame with mounting 999-7061. This means that the lift stability is not affected during work.
   d. Install the thread bar on the tensioner 999-5659.
   e. Lift up the tensioner with the threaded bar 999-5659.
   f. Insert the threaded bar in the mounting 999-7061 from underneath.
   g. Insert the locking washer with the handle in from the side in mounting 999-7061 under the threaded bolt.
   h. Lock the bolt in the locking washer. Align the locking washer in the mounting.

➡The locking washer has a locating pin which must be aligned with the bolt.

   i. Install the 2 bolts (5740-36) from kit 998-9761 in the control arm holes.
   j. Install the rails 5740-1 modified according to WG-276 on the control arms.
   k. Ensure that the rollers lie against the rails on both sides of the control arms.

➡The tensioner must be positioned as far out as possible on the tensioner plates to provide the correct lifting force.

   l. Raise the control arms to their normal position using the tensioner. The normal position of the rear suspension is 18 inches (453mm) from the fender edge to the center of the wheel.

5. On vehicles equipped with 5 seats, remove the front floor hatch and the form-molded floor mat.
6. Fold the soundproofing over the shock absorber mounting out of the way.
7. On vehicles equipped with 7 seats, slide the seat cushion back on the rear row of seats, lift up the carpet and cut the soundproofing as illustrated.
8. Fold up the soundproofing. Remove the cover on the splash guard.
9. Remove the shock absorber nut. Use socket 999-5500 and a Torx® wrench as a counter-hold.
10. Remove the bolt in the lower mounting for the shock absorber.
11. Remove the shock absorber.

To install:

12. Insert the new shock absorber through the control arm to the upper mounting.
13. Install the new nut loosely.

➡Ensure that the bushing seats correctly in the opening in the rear suspension.

14. Fix the shock absorber in the lower mounting. Tighten the upper nut for the shock absorber. Tighten to 44 ft. lbs. (60 Nm). Tighten the lower bolt to 59 ft. lbs. (80 Nm).
15. Reinstall the carpet.
16. With 5 seats: Reinstall the front floor hatch.
17. With 7 seats: Slide the seat cushion forward.
18. Detach the tensioner, pull out the fork and lower the tensioner using the threaded bar.
19. Remove the mounting 999-5659 from the sub-frame.
20. Remove the rails 5740-1 from the control arms.
21. Install the parking brake cable mountings in the sub-frame.
22. Install the wheel and tire assembly. Tighten the lug nuts in a star pattern.
   a. Step 1: 15 ft. lbs. (20 Nm).
   b. Step 2: 103 ft. lbs. (140 Nm).

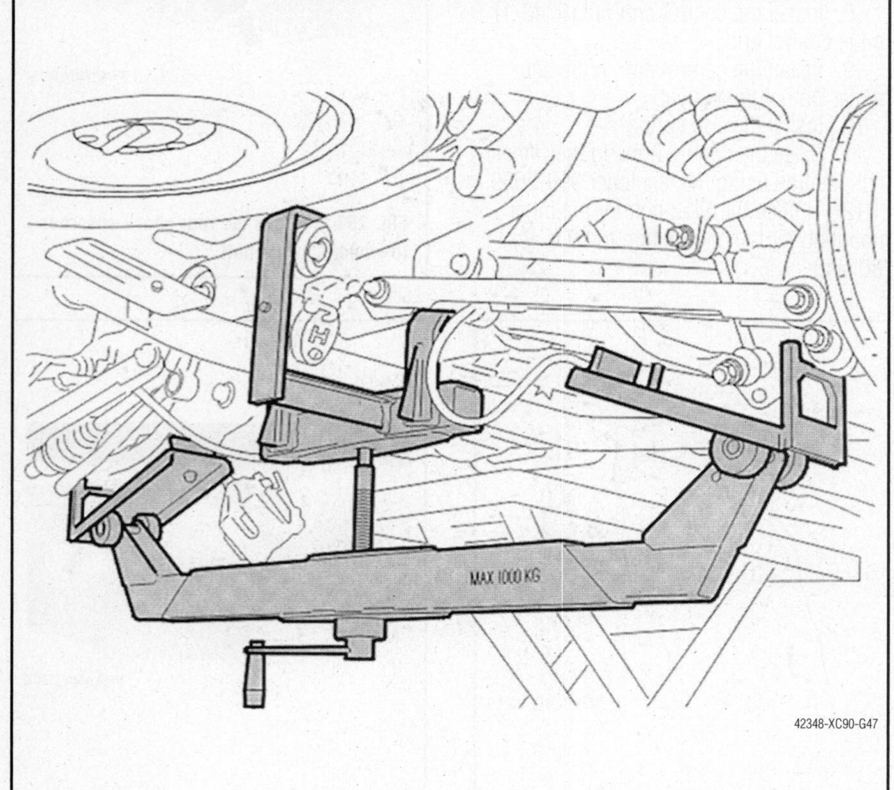

Fig. 263 Tensioner installed

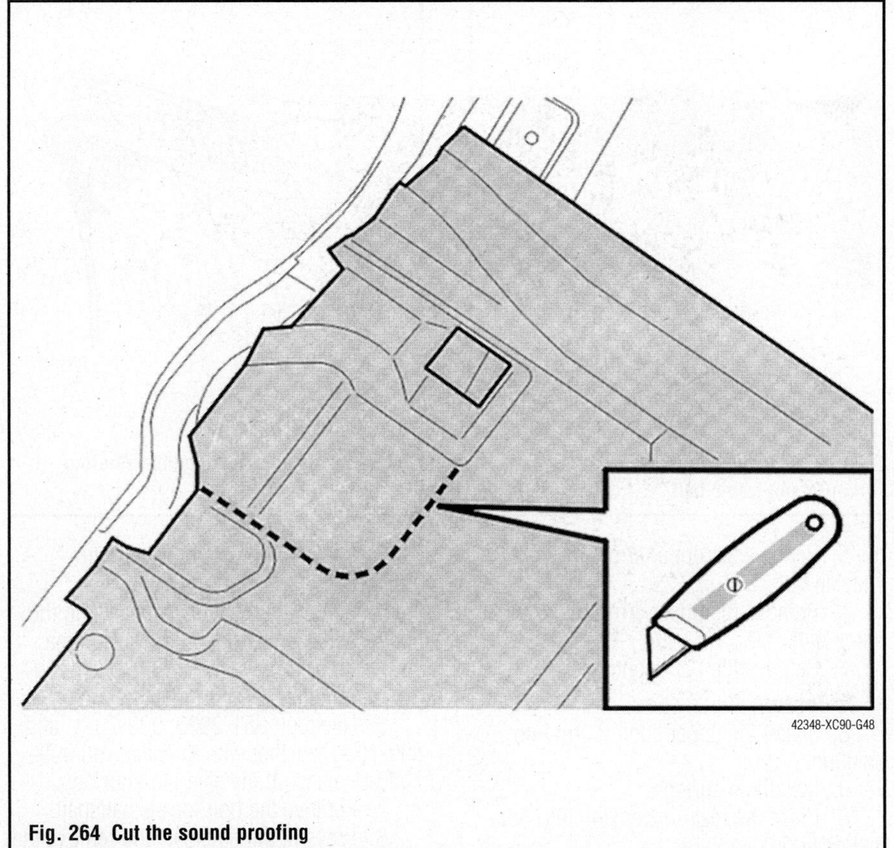

Fig. 264 Cut the sound proofing

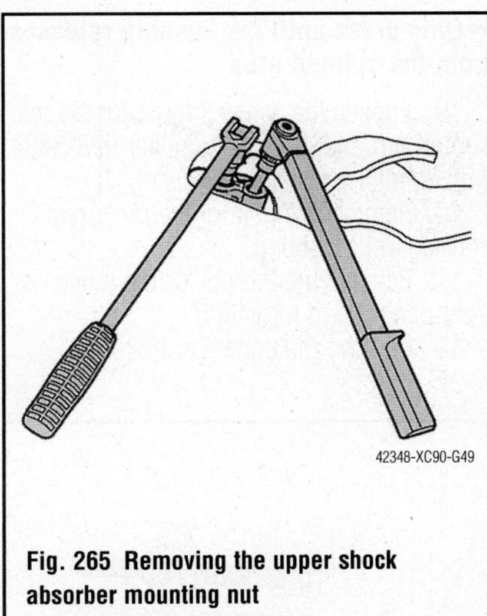

Fig. 265 Removing the upper shock absorber mounting nut

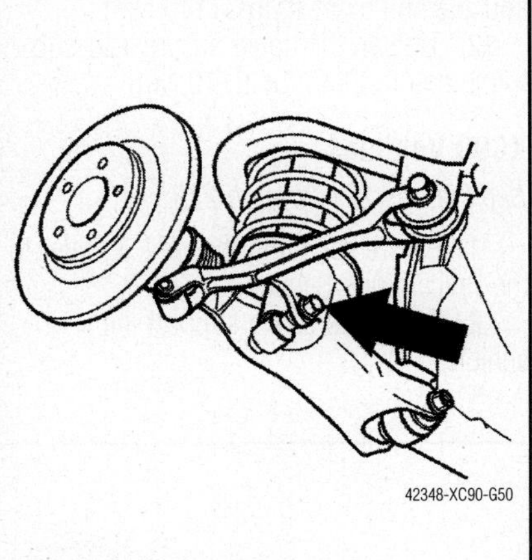

Fig. 266 Removing the lower shock absorber mounting bolt

➡If the vehicle is equipped with Bi-Xenon lamps, the position sensor must be calibrated. Carry out calibration according to VIDA vehicle communication.

STABILIZER BAR

REMOVAL & INSTALLATION

XC60 Vehicles

See Figure 267.

1. Before servicing the vehicle, refer to the Precautions Section.
2. Raise and safely support the vehicle.
3. Remove the rear wheel and tire assembly.
4. Disconnect the bar from the stabilizer control links.
5. Remove the stabilizer bar clamps from the suspension member.
6. Remove the rear stabilizer bar.

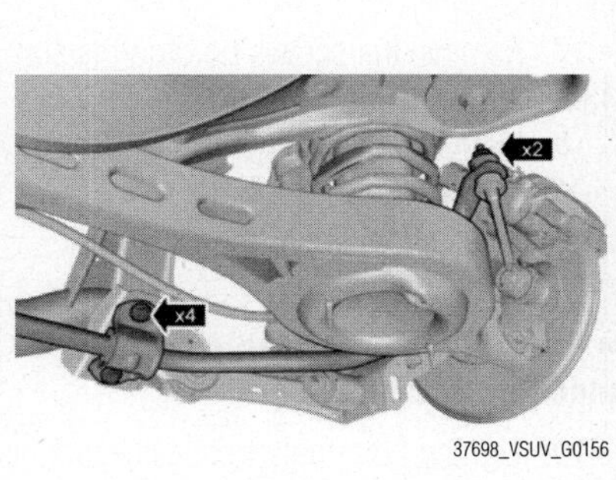

Fig. 267 Removing the rear stabilizer bar—XC60 vehicles

To install:

7. Installation is the reverse of the removal procedure.
8. Tighten bolts/nuts to specification as follows:
    - Stabilizer bar clamps to the suspension member: 37 ft. lbs. (50 Nm)
    - Rear stabilizer bar link to stabilizer bar: 11 ft. lbs. (15 Nm)

XC90 Vehicles

See Figure 268.

1. Before servicing the vehicle, refer to the Precautions Section.
2. Raise and safely support the vehicle.
3. Remove the rear wheel and tire assembly.
4. Remove the exhaust system.
5. Remove the rear spring and shock absorber.
6. Remove the stabilizer (anti-roll) bar from the outer mountings. Use a Torx®

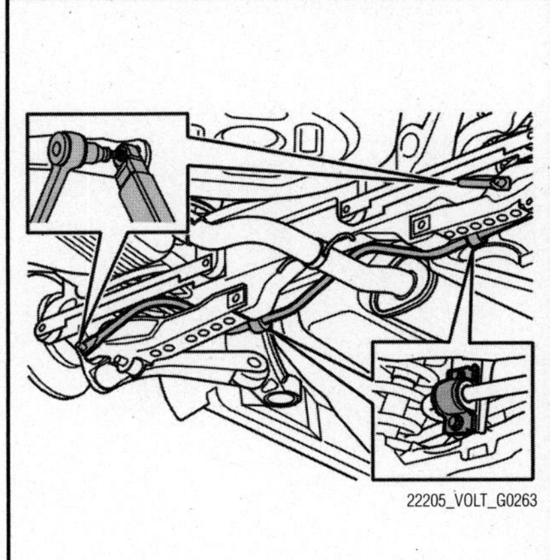

Fig. 268 Rear stabilizer bar removal—XC90 vehicles

wrench as a counter-hold so that the boot is not damaged.

7. Remove the screws holding the stabilizer bar in the sub-frame.

8. Remove the rear stabilizer bar.

To install:

9. Installation is the reverse of the removal procedure.

➡The parking brake cable must be under the stabilizer bar.

10. Tighten bolts/nuts to specification as follows:

- Stabilizer bar link in shock absorber front M12: 67 ft. lbs. (90 Nm)
- Stabilizer bar link in stabilizer bar front M10: 45 ft. lbs. (60 Nm)
- Stabilizer bar link to spring strut: 37 ft. lbs. (50 Nm)

➡Use a Torx® wrench as a counter-hold so that the boot is not damaged.

UPPER CONTROL ARMS

REMOVAL & INSTALLATION

XC60 Vehicles

See Figures 269 and 270.

As the illustrations in this service information are used for different model years and/or models, some variation may occur. However, the essential information in the illustrations is correct.

1. Before servicing the vehicle, refer to the Precautions Section.

2. Raise and safely support the vehicle.

3. Remove the rear wheel and tire assembly.

4. Remove the rear spring.

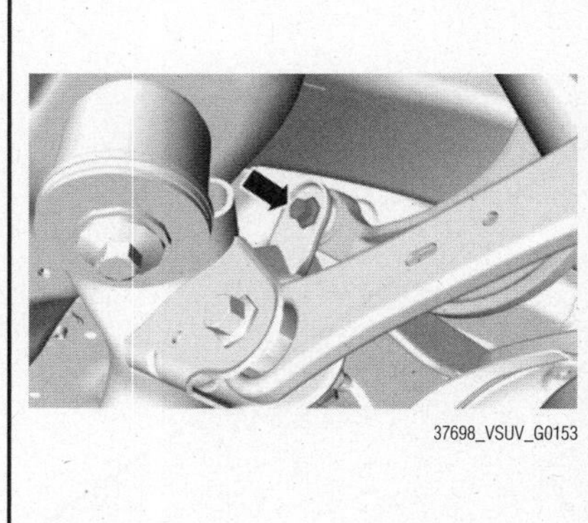

Fig. 270 Remove the upper arm rear-to-sub-frame bolt

5. Remove the upper arm rear-to-wheel knuckle bolt.

6. Remove the upper arm rear-to-sub-frame bolt.

7. Remove the upper control arm.

To install:

8. Install the upper control arm into position.

9. Install the spring.

10. Place the rear suspension into normal position.

11. Tighten the upper arm rear-to-wheel knuckle bolt to 81 ft. lbs. (110 Nm).

12. Tighten the upper arm rear-to-sub-frame bolt to 81 ft. lbs. (110 Nm).

XC90 Vehicles

See Figures 271 through 273.

1. Before servicing the vehicle, refer to the Precautions Section.

2. Raise and safely support the vehicle.

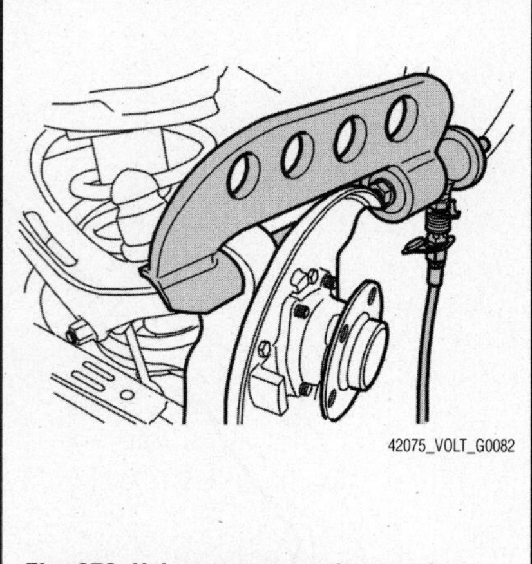

Fig. 272 Using a press on the steering knuckle

3. Remove the rear wheel and tire assembly.

4. Remove the brake caliper. Hang the brake caliper on a hook in the sub-frame.

5. Loosen the screw for the outer control arm mounting by 3 turns.

6. Use tool: 951-2923, 999-7031, and 999-7030 together with threaded rod 999-7039 to press off the steering knuckle.

7. Remove the bolt for the halfshaft.

8. Press in the halfshaft and remove the spindle.

➡Only press until the bushing releases from the splined area.

9. Loosen the screw 3 turns for the rear control arm mounting. Use puller 998-5434 with counter-hold 999-7074.

10. Remove the bolt for the inner rear control arm mounting.

11. Remove the 2 bolts for the inner front control arm mounting.

12. Remove the upper control arm.

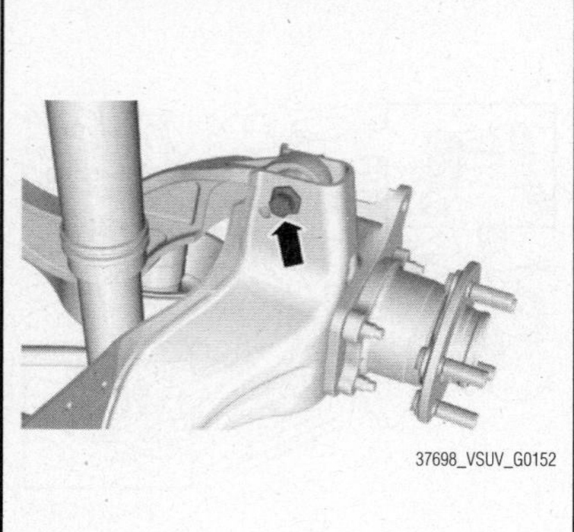

Fig. 269 Remove the upper arm rear-to-wheel knuckle bolt

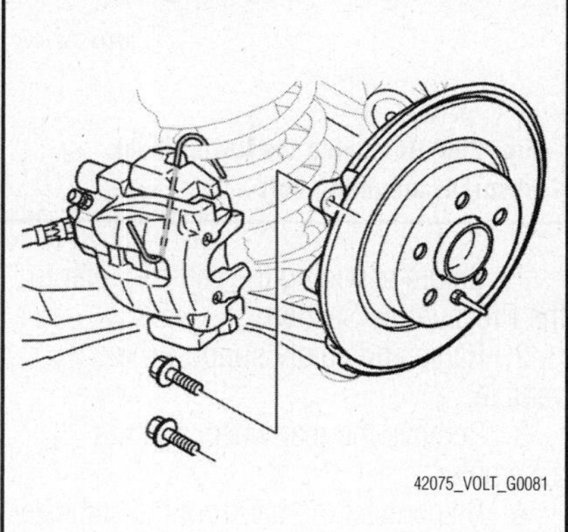

Fig. 271 Using a hook to safely hang the brake caliper out of the way

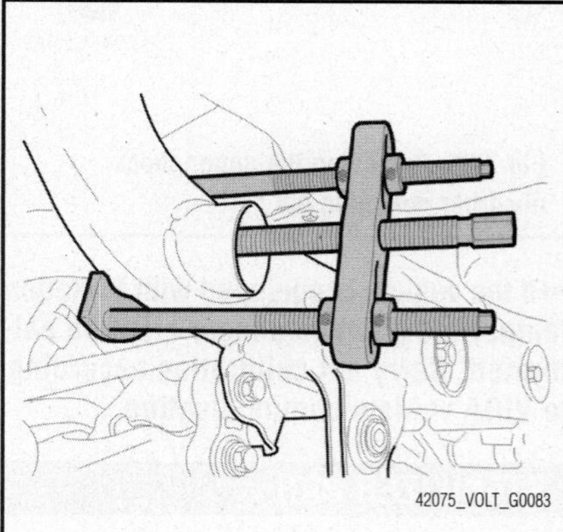

Fig. 273 Using puller 998-5434 with counter-hold 999-7074 on the rear control arm mounting

To install:

13. Install the bolts for the inner rear control arm mounting.
14. Install the bolts for the front inner control arm mounting.
15. Install the bolts for the outer control arm mounting.
16. Install tensioner 999-5659.

➡The tensioner must be positioned as far out as possible on the tensioner plates to achieve the correct lifting force.

17. Tighten the M12 bolts for the inner rear control arm mounting to 59 ft. lbs. (80 Nm).
18. Tighten the M12 bolts for the front inner control arm mounting to 59 ft. lbs. (80 Nm).
19. Tighten the M12 bolts for the outer control arm mounting to 59 ft. lbs. (80 Nm).

➡Tighten the bolts when the rear suspension is in the normal position.

20. Remove tensioner 999-5659.
21. Install the wheel and tire assembly. Tighten the lug nuts in a star pattern.
    a. Step 1: 15 ft. lbs. (20 Nm).
    b. Step 2: 103 ft. lbs. (140 Nm).

➡If the vehicle is equipped with Bi-Xenon lamps, the position sensor must be calibrated. Carry out calibration according to VIDA vehicle communication.

WHEEL HUBS & BEARINGS

ADJUSTMENT

The rear wheel bearings are sealed, pressed-in units, and no adjustment is possible.

REMOVAL & INSTALLATION

XC60 Vehicles

See Figure 274.

1. Before servicing the vehicle, refer to the Precautions Section.
2. Raise and safely support the vehicle.
3. Remove the rear wheel and tire assembly.
4. Remove the brake disc.
5. Disconnect the speed sensor and remove.
6. Remove the hub-to-halfshaft bolt.
7. Remove the hub mounting bolts.
8. Remove the hub from the wheel knuckle.

To install:

9. Installation is the reverse of the removal procedure.

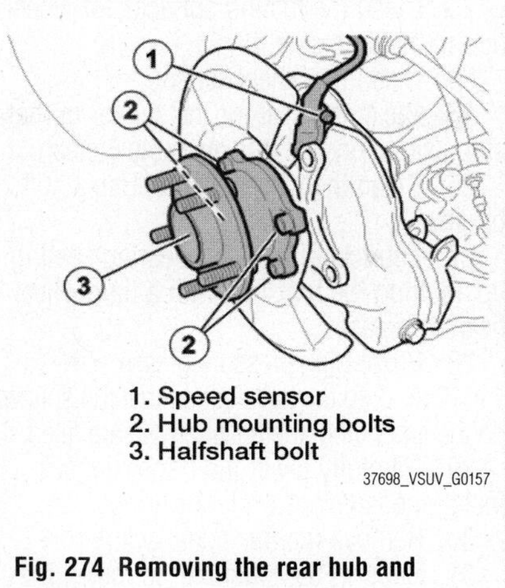

Fig. 274 Removing the rear hub and bearing

10. Tighten bolts/nuts to specification as follows:
    - M5 bolts: 44 inch lbs. (5 Nm)
    - Wheel bearing-to-wheel knuckle: 81 ft. lbs. (110 Nm)
    - Halfshaft-to-wheel hub (rear): 26 ft. lbs. (35 Nm)

XC90 Vehicles

See Figures 275 through 277.

As the illustrations in this service information are used for different model years and/or models, some variation may occur. However, the essential information in the illustrations is correct.

1. Before servicing the vehicle, refer to the Precautions Section.
2. Raise and safely support the vehicle.
3. Lock the self-adjuster unit for the parking brake.
4. Remove the rear wheel and tire assembly.
5. Remove the bolt for the rear halfshaft.
6. Remove the wheel sensor lead from the holder on the brake hose.
7. Remove the brake caliper mounting bolts. Hang the caliper up using a piece of wire.
8. Remove the brake disc locating pin/bolt.
9. Remove the brake disc.
10. Install tensioner 999-5659.
11. Support the rear suspension 20 inches (500mm) up between the fender edge and the center of the wheel.
12. Remove the bolt in the mounting for the tie rod.
13. Remove the bolt in the mounting for the control arm.
14. Remove the nut in the mounting for the stabilizer bar control link. Counter-hold using a wrench so that the boot does not rotate.
15. Remove the bolt for the mounting of the lateral link.
16. Position a transaxle jack under the steering knuckle and carefully raise.

➡Pull the halfshaft from the hub while raising the steering knuckle.

17. Release the tensioner so that the control arm hangs in the shock absorber.
18. Remove the 4 bolts attaching the hub assembly.
19. Remove the hub assembly.

⁂ WARNING

Make sure the halfshaft comes free from the rear wheel hub. There must not be any axial forces acting on the halfshaft joints.

To install:

20. Install the hub into position.

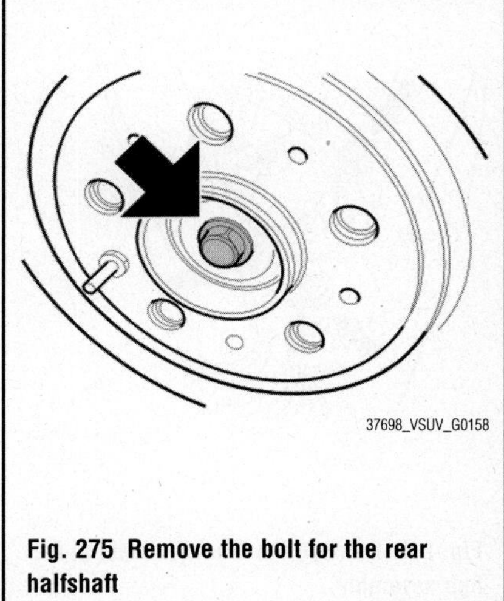

Fig. 275 Remove the bolt for the rear halfshaft

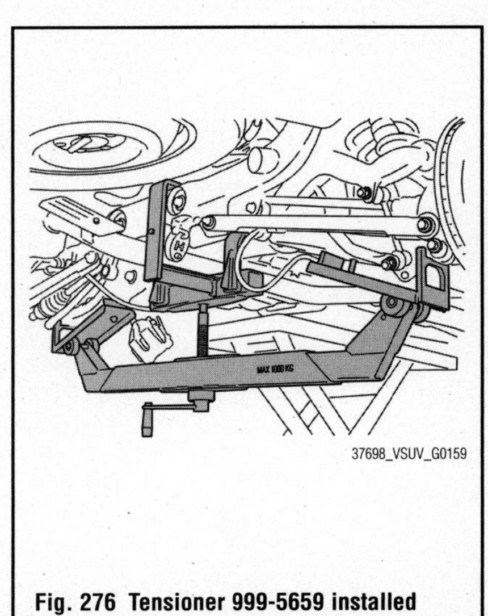

Fig. 276 Tensioner 999-5659 installed

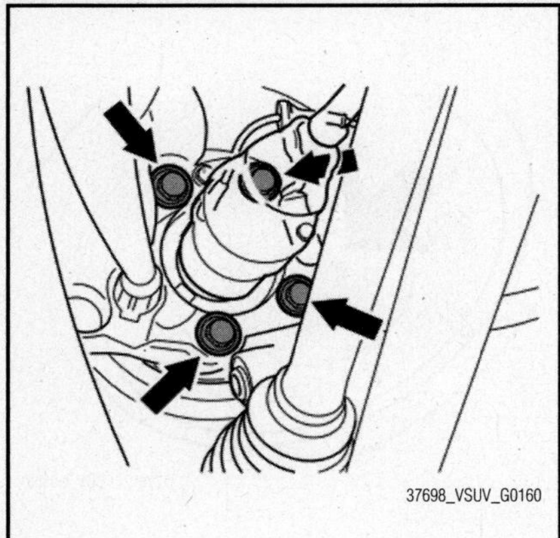

Fig. 277 Remove the 4 bolts attaching the hub assembly

21. Install the 4 bolts and tighten:
    a. Step 1: 15 ft. lbs. (20 Nm).
    b. Step 2: 33 ft. lbs. (45 Nm).
    c. Step 3: Angle tighten 60°.
22. Clean the halfshaft end, especially the rust on the edges. The outer wheel hub sealing ring will rest against this surface.
23. Clean the mating surfaces for wheel hub in the stub axle.
24. Clean the wheel sensor.
25. Clean the seat for the sensor in the stub axle to ensure it is absolutely clean.
26. Clean the wheel sensor. Use a soft brush.
27. Lubricate the wheel bearing sealing lip abutting the halfshaft with a little wheel bearing grease.
28. Brush high pressure grease, P/N 1161246, onto the halfshaft so that the splines on the rear half of the halfshaft pin are filled.
29. Carefully lower the transaxle jack. Install the halfshaft while lowering.
30. Remove the transaxle jack.
31. Support the tensioner to install the bolts for the control arm and lateral link.

⁂ WARNING

Lower the vehicle to normal ride height before tightening the bolts to proper torque.

32. Install the bolt for mounting the lateral link.
33. Install the nut in the mounting for the stabilizer bar link. Counter-hold using a wrench so that the boot does not rotate. Torque to 59 ft. lbs. (80 Nm).
34. Install the bolt for the mounting of the control arm.
35. Install the bolt for the mounting for the tie rod.
36. Remove tensioner 999-5659.
37. Install the brake disc.
38. Install the brake disc locating pin/bolt and tighten to 89 inch lbs. (10 Nm).
39. Install the brake caliper.
40. Install the brake caliper mounting bolts.
41. Install a new bolt for the halfshaft.
42. Install the wheel and tire assembly. Tighten the lug nuts in a star pattern.
    a. Step 1: 15 ft. lbs. (20 Nm).
    b. Step 2: 103 ft. lbs. (140 Nm).
43. Activate the self-adjuster for the parking brake.
44. Adjust the parking brake as necessary.

VOLVO

Diagnostic Trouble Codes

DIAGNOSTIC TROUBLE CODES

OBD II VEHICLE APPLICATIONS

VOLVO

C30
2011–2012
- 2.5L L5 EFI . . . Engine Code: B5254T7

C70
2011–2012
- 2.5L L5 EFI . . . Engine Code: B5254T7

S40
2011
- 2.5L L5 EFI . . . Engine Code: B525427

S60
2011–2012
- 2.5L L5 EFI . . . Engine Code: B5244T5
- 3.0L L6 EFI . . . Engine Code: B6304T4

S80
2011–2012
- 3.0L L6 EFI . . . Engine Code: B6304T4
- 3.2L L6 EFI . . . Engine Code: B6324S4
- 3.2L L6 EFI . . . Engine Code: B6324S5

V50
2011–2012
- 2.5L L5 EFI . . . Engine Code: B525427

XC60
2011–2012
- 3.0L L6 EFI . . . Engine Code: B6304T4
- 3.2L L6 EFI . . . Engine Code: B6324S4
- 3.2L L6 EFI . . . Engine Code: B6324S5

XC70
2011–2012
- 3.0L L6 EFI . . . Engine Code: B6304T4
- 3.2L L6 EFI . . . Engine Code: B6324S4
- 3.2L L6 EFI . . . Engine Code: B6324S5

XC90
2011–2012
- 3.2L L6 EFI . . . Engine Code: B6324S5
- 4.4L V8 EFI . . . . Engine Code: B8444S

OBD II Trouble Code List (P Codes) Differential Electronic Module (DEM)

DTC	Trouble Code Title and Conditions
DTC: DEM-P056017 T **Year:** 2011, 2012 **Model:** XC90 **Engine:** 4.4L V8	**System Voltage. General Electrical Failures. Circuit Voltage Above Threshold :** The Differential electronic module (DEM) continuously checks that the power supply to the control module is within its permitted range. The Differential electronic module (DEM) compares the power supply (signal) to the predefined parameters. The diagnostic trouble code (DTC) is stored if the control module detects that: The power supply is higher than 18.5 V. Incorrect value lasts longer than 3 seconds. The control module's test for the diagnostic trouble code (DTC) starts in the event of: * Ignition switch position II.
DTC: DEM-P060254 T **Year:** 2011, 2012 **Model:** XC90 **Engine:** 4.4L V8	**Powertrain Control Module Programming Error. System Programming Failures. Missing Calibration :** The differential electronic module (DEM) checks the software calibration. The control module has a number of parameters that can be calibrated. The parameters must have a default value. The parameters value is checked internally in the control module. The diagnostic trouble code (DTC) is stored if the control module detects that: The default values are missing or incorrect. The control module's test for the diagnostic trouble code (DTC) starts in the event of: Ignition switch position II. **Note! The control module is calibrated together with the control valve/the axial solenoid during production. This cannot be carried out on the after-market.**
DTC: DEM-P060749 T **Year:** 2011, 2012 **Model:** XC90 **Engine:** 4.4L V8	**Control Module Performance. System Internal Failures. Internal Electronic Failure :** The Differential electronic module (DEM) checks the internal components in the control module. The control module checks the function of the AC/DC converter, among other things. The control module compares the signal from the AC/DC converter to the predefined parameters. The diagnostic trouble code (DTC) is stored if the control module detects that: The signal from the AC/DC converter is outside the parameters. Incorrect value lasts longer than 3 seconds. The control module's test for the diagnostic trouble code (DTC) starts in the event of: Ignition switch position II.
DTC: DEM-P063468 T **Year:** 2011, 2012 **Model:** XC90 **Engine:** 4.4L V8	**PCM/ECM/TCM Internal Temperature Sensor Circuit. Algorithm Based Failures. Event Information :** The Differential Electronic Module (DEM) has a temperature sensor fitted on the control module's circuit board. The sensor provides the Differential Electronic Module (DEM) with information about the temperature in the control module. If the temperature exceeds a preset value all wheel drive is disabled. This is to protect the components from a too high load, which can result in internal mechanical faults. The diagnostic trouble code (DTC) is stored if the control module detects that: The temperature is higher than 110 °C. Incorrect value lasts longer than 3 seconds. The control module's test for the diagnostic trouble code (DTC) starts in the event of: Ignition switch position II.
DTC: DEM-P064F05 T **Year:** 2011, 2012 **Model:** XC90 **Engine:** 4.4L V8	**Unauthorized Software/Calibration Detected. General Failure Information. System Programming Failures :** Information about the vehicle configuration is sent on the CAN network. Depending on the model and equipment, the vehicle can be configured in different ways. The central electronic module (CEM) sends the applicable signal ID for the vehicle. The differential electronic module (DEM) compares its configuration ID with the signal configuration transmitted on the network by the central electronic module (CEM). The diagnostic trouble code (DTC) is stored if the control module detects that: These do not correspond, which means that the wrong software is programmed in Differential electronic module (DEM). The control module's test for the diagnostic trouble code (DTC) starts in the event of: Ignition switch position II.
DTC: DEM-P066611 T **Year:** 2011, 2012 **Model:** XC90 **Engine:** 4.4L V8	**PCM/ECM/TCM Internal Temperature Sensor Circuit. General Electrical Failures. Circuit Short To Ground :** The Differential Electronic Module (DEM) has a temperature sensor fitted on the control module's circuit board. If the temperature exceeds a preset value all wheel drive is disabled. This is to protect the control module. The diagnostic trouble code (DTC) is stored if the control module detects that: The temperature exceeds 193.2 °C. Incorrect value lasts longer than 3 seconds. The control module's test for the diagnostic trouble code (DTC) starts in the event of: Ignition on. **Note! The control module can only detect the fault once the test has been started and the diagnostic trouble code (DTC) is stored when the conditions are met.**

DTC	Trouble Code Title and Conditions
DTC: DEM-P066615 T **Year:** 2011, 2012 **Model:** XC90 **Engine:** 4.4L V8	**PCM/ECM/TCM Internal Temperature Sensor Circuit. General Electrical Failures. Circuit Short To Battery Or Open :** The Differential Electronic Module (DEM) has a temperature sensor fitted on the control module's circuit board. If the temperature is lower than a preset value, then the four-wheel drive is turned off. The diagnostic trouble code (DTC) is stored if the control module detects that: The temperature is lower than -53.7 °C. Incorrect value lasts longer than 3 seconds. The control module's test for the diagnostic trouble code (DTC) starts in the event of: Ignition on.
DTC: DEM-P066727 T **Year:** 2011, 2012 **Model:** XC90 **Engine:** 4.4L V8	**PCM/ECM/TCM Internal Temperature Sensor Range/Performance. General Signal Failures. Signal Rate Of Change Above Threshold :** The Differential Electronic Module (DEM) has a temperature sensor fitted on the control module's circuit board. If the temperature rises too quickly, four-wheel drive disengages. This is to protect the control module. The diagnostic trouble code (DTC) is stored if the control module detects that: The temperature increases at a speed greater than 10 °C/s. Incorrect value lasts longer than 50 ms. The control module's test for the diagnostic trouble code (DTC) starts in the event of: Engine running. **Note! The control module can only detect the fault once the test has been started and the diagnostic trouble code (DTC) is stored when the conditions are met.**
DTC: DEM-P074812 T **Year:** 2011, 2012 **Model:** XC90 **Engine:** 4.4L V8	**Pressure Control Solenoid A Electrical. General Electrical Failures. Circuit Short To Battery :** The Differential electronic module (DEM) checks the performance of the control valve/the axial solenoid. The control module controls the solenoid by controlling the current via an internal control circuit. The control module checks the solenoid by comparing the current to the predefined parameters. The diagnostic trouble code (DTC) is stored if the control module detects that: The current to the control valve/the axial solenoid is outside the predefined parameters. Incorrect value runs longer than 1 second. The control module's test for the diagnostic trouble code (DTC) starts in the event of: Ignition switch position II.
DTC: DEM-P07481D T **Year:** 2011, 2012 **Model:** XC90 **Engine:** 4.4L V8	**Pressure Control Solenoid A Electrical. General Electrical Failures. Circuit Current Out Of Range :** The Differential electronic module (DEM) checks the performance of the control valve/the axial solenoid. The control module controls the solenoid by controlling the current via an internal control circuit. The control module checks the solenoid by comparing the current to the predefined parameters. The diagnostic trouble code (DTC) is stored if the control module detects that: The amperage to the control valve/the axial solenoid deviates more than 0.2 A from the desired value. Incorrect value runs longer than 1 second. The control module's test for the diagnostic trouble code (DTC) starts in the event of: Normal driving.
DTC: DEM-P096162 T **Year:** 2011, 2012 **Model:** XC90 **Engine:** 4.4L V8	**Pressure Control Solenoid A Control Circuit Range/Performance. Algorithm Based Failures. Signal Compare Failure :** Differential Electronic Module (DEM) calculates an expected oil pressure increase in the AOC-unit (the mechanical clutch) during driving. The control module checks reasonableness of the oil pressure change. The diagnostic trouble code (DTC) is stored if the control module detects that: The signal from the oil pressure sensor deviates too much from the predefined value. Incorrect value lasts longer than 5 minutes. The control module's test for the diagnostic trouble code (DTC) starts when: The oil temperature is between -40 °C and 120 °C. 30 seconds since the test was run the last time. The torque transfer is below a certain level that can be calibrated. The lateral acceleration is below a certain level that can be calibrated. No ABS engagement. No antispin engagement.

DTC	Trouble Code Title and Conditions
DTC: DEM-P163568 T **Year:** 2011, 2012 **Model:** XC90 **Engine:** 4.4L V8	**Tire/Axle Out of Acceptable Range. Algorithm Based Failures. Event Information :** Differential electronic module (DEM) checks engagement and disengagement of four-wheel drive. The control module controls engagement and disengagement using a number of parameters, among others, by comparing speed of the wheels. If the vehicle's tires are worn unevenly (compared front and rear, or if a tire with incorrect dimension is installed (compared with the vehicle's other tires) on the vehicle's front or rear axle, this may result in incorrect engagement of four-wheel drive. The diagnostic trouble code (DTC) is stored if the control module detects that: Any of the wheels on the front or rear axle rotate faster than other wheels when driving on straight road with constant throttle application. The control module's test for the diagnostic trouble code (DTC) starts in the event of: * Constant vehicle speed (above 20 km/h). * Constant engine rpm. * Only small steering adjustments. * Brake pedal released (no braking). * The parking brake is not applied. * Engine brake not active (accelerator pedal pressed down).
DTC: DEM-P188912 T **Year:** 2011, 2012 **Model:** XC90 **Engine:** 4.4L V8	**Oil Pressure Pump Performance. General Electrical Failures. Circuit Short To Battery :** The Differential electronic module (DEM) checks the performance of the oil pressure pump. The control module compares the current strength from the oil pressure pump to the predefined parameters. The diagnostic trouble code (DTC) is stored if the control module detects that: The amperage from the oil pressure pump is greater than 9 A. Incorrect value lasts longer than 10 minutes. The control module's test for the diagnostic trouble code (DTC) starts in the event of: Ignition switch position II.
DTC: DEM-P188914 T **Year:** 2011, 2012 **Model:** XC90 **Engine:** 4.4L V8	**Oil Pressure Pump Performance. General Electrical Failures. Circuit Short To Ground Or Open :** The Differential electronic module (DEM) checks the performance of the oil pressure pump. The control module compares the signal from the oil pump to the predefined parameters. The diagnostic trouble code (DTC) is stored if the control module detects that: * The amperage from the oil pressure pump is less than 0.3 A. * Incorrect value lasts longer than 30 seconds. * The control module's test for the diagnostic trouble code (DTC) starts when: * The oil pressure pump voltage is 4.8 V or greater.
DTC: DEM-P188918 T **Year:** 2011, 2012 **Model:** XC90 **Engine:** 4.4L V8	**Oil Pressure Pump Performance. General Electrical Failures. Circuit Current Below Threshold :** The Differential electronic module (DEM) checks the performance of the oil pressure pump. The control module compares the signal from the oil pump to the predefined parameters. The current that goes through the oil pressure pump is dependent on the temperature of the oil. The diagnostic trouble code (DTC) is stored if the control module detects that: The amperage through the oil pressure pump is too low. Incorrect value has been registered at 30 on each following operating cycle. The control module's test for the diagnostic trouble code (DTC) starts when: * The oil temperature is above 0 °C. * The voltage across the oil pressure pump is greater than 11.5 V.
DTC: DEM-P188919 T **Year:** 2011, 2012 **Model:** XC90 **Engine:** 4.4L V8	**Oil Pressure Pump Performance. General Electrical Failures. Circuit Current Above Threshold :** The Differential electronic module (DEM) checks the performance of the oil pump. The current that goes through the oil pressure pump is dependent on the temperature of the oil. The diagnostic trouble code (DTC) is stored if the control module detects that: The amperage through the oil pressure pump is too high. Incorrect value lasts longer than 5.5 minutes. The control module's test for the diagnostic trouble code (DTC) starts when: The oil temperature is greater than 20 °C. The amperage is greater than 7.0 A.
DTC: DEM-P188949 T **Year:** 2011, 2012 **Model:** XC90 **Engine:** 4.4L V8	**Oil Pressure Pump Performance. System Internal Failures. Internal Electronic Failure :** The Differential electronic module (DEM) checks the performance of the oil pressure pump. The control module compares the current strength from the oil pressure pump to the predefined parameters. The diagnostic trouble code (DTC) is stored if the control module detects that: The amperage through the oil pressure pump is greater than 0.5 A when the pump is off. Incorrect value lasts longer than 30 seconds. The control module's test for the diagnostic trouble code (DTC) starts in the event of: Ignition switch position II. The oil pressure pump is switched off.

DTC	Trouble Code Title and Conditions
DTC: DEM-P18897A **T** **Year:** 2011, 2012 **Model:** XC90 **Engine:** 4.4L V8	**Oil Pressure Pump Performance. Mechanical Failures. Fluid Leak Or Seal Failure :** The Differential electronic module (DEM) checks the performance of the oil pressure pump. The control module compares the current strength from the oil pressure pump to the predefined parameters. The diagnostic trouble code (DTC) is stored if the control module detects that: The oil pressure pump runs for longer than 20 seconds. The control module's test for the diagnostic trouble code (DTC) starts in the event of: Engine running. 1 second after the accumulator has been topped up. The test is performed during a four second period but is cancelled if the accumulator requires topping up. The oil temperature is between 0 - 80 °C.

OBD II Trouble Code List (P Codes) Engine Control Module (ECM)

DTC	Trouble Code Title and Conditions
DTC: ECM-1000/P0107/P0108 **1T ECM, MIL: Yes** Years: 2011, 2012 Model: C30, S40, V50 **Engine:** 2.5L L5	**Engine Control Module (ECM) Signal Too High / Signal Too Low:** The diagnostic trouble code (DTC) is stored if the engine control module (ECM) registers an internal fault indicating that the signal from the internal atmospheric pressure sensor is incorrect. The diagnostic trouble code (DTC) can be diagnosed when the ignition has been on for, at least 15 seconds.
DTC: ECM-100A/P2227 **1T ECM, MIL: Yes** **Years:** 2011, 2012 **Model:** C30, S40, V50 **Engine:** 2.5L L5	**Engine Control Module (ECM) Faulty Signal:** The engine control module (ECM) compares the filtered signal from the pressure sensor to the inlet manifold with the signal from the atmospheric pressure sensor in the engine control module (ECM). The diagnostic trouble code is generated if the it registers that the deviation is greater than 70 hPa. The diagnostic trouble code can be diagnosed 15 seconds after the ignition is switched.
DTC: ECM-1100/P0070-73 **1T ECM** **Years:** 2011, 2012 **Model:** C30, S40, V50 **Engine:** 2.5L L5	**Outside Temperature Sensor (Faulty Signal):** A fault message is transmitted to the engine control module (ECM) and the diagnostic trouble code (DTC) is stored if a fault in the outside temperature sensor is detected by the central electronic module (CEM). The diagnostic trouble code (DTC) can be diagnosed when the ignition is switched on. **NOTE: This temperature is used if no fault has been detected on the intake temperature sensor. The constant 20 °C is used if a fault has also been detected on the intake temperature sensor.**
DTC: ECM-110A/P0071 **1T ECM** **Years:** 2011, 2012 **Model:** C30, S40, V50 **Engine:** 2.5L L5	**Outside temperature sensor. Faulty signal:** The central electronic module (CEM) transmits the signal from the outside temperature sensor via CAN to the engine control module (ECM). The diagnostic trouble code (DTC) is stored if the engine control module (ECM) detects that the value from the outside temperature sensor deviates too much from the values for intake and engine coolant temperature (ECT) after the engine has been allowed to cool from operating temperature for at least 8 hours. The diagnostic trouble code (DTC) can be diagnosed at ignition after the engine has been allowed to cool for at least 8 hours. **NOTE: This temperature is used if no fault has been detected on the intake temperature sensor. The constant 20 °C is used if a fault has also been detected on the intake temperature sensor.**
DTC: ECM-112C/P2229 **1T ECM, MIL: Yes** **Years:** 2011, 2012 **Model:** C30, C70, S40, V50 **Engine:** 2.5L L5	**Atmospheric Pressure Sensor (Signal Too High) :** The engine control module (ECM) checks the signal from the internal atmospheric pressure sensor. The diagnostic trouble code (DTC) is stored if the signal from the internal atmospheric pressure sensor is higher than a certain value for a certain amount of time. The diagnostic trouble code (DTC) can be diagnosed when the engine is running.
DTC: ECM-112D/P2228 **1T ECM, MIL: Yes** **Years:** 2011, 2012 **Model:** C30, C70, S40, V50 **Engine:** 2.5L L5	**Atmospheric Pressure Sensor (Signal Too Low):** The engine control module (ECM) checks the signal from the internal atmospheric pressure sensor. The diagnostic trouble code (DTC) is stored if the signal from the internal atmospheric pressure sensor is lower than a certain value for a certain amount of time. The diagnostic trouble code (DTC) can be diagnosed when the engine is running.
DTC: ECM-1130/P2227 **1T ECM, MIL: Yes** **Years:** 2011, 2012 **Model:** C30, C70, S40, V50 **Engine:** 2.5L L5	**Atmospheric Pressure Sensor (Faulty Signal):** The engine control module (ECM) checks the signal from the internal atmospheric pressure sensor. The diagnostic trouble code (DTC) is stored if the engine control module (ECM) detects a faulty signal from the internal atmospheric pressure sensor. The diagnostic trouble code (DTC) can be diagnosed when the ignition has been on for at least 20 seconds.
DTC: ECM-113B/P2227 **1T ECM, MIL: Yes** **Years:** 2011, 2012 **Model:** C30, C70, S40, V50 **Engine:** 2.5L L5	**Atmospheric Pressure Sensor (Signal Missing):** The engine control module (ECM) checks the signal from the internal atmospheric pressure sensor. The diagnostic trouble code (DTC) is stored if the engine control module (ECM) detects a faulty signal from the internal atmospheric pressure sensor. The diagnostic trouble code (DTC) can be diagnosed when the ignition has been on for at least 20 seconds

DTC	Trouble Code Title and Conditions
DTC: ECM-113C/P2227 **1T ECM, MIL: Yes** **Years:** 2011, 2012 **Model:** C30, C70, S40, V50 **Engine:** 2.5L L5	**Atmospheric Pressure Sensor (Signal Too High):** The engine control module (ECM) checks the signal from the internal atmospheric pressure sensor. The diagnostic trouble code (DTC) is stored if the engine control module (ECM) detects a faulty signal from the internal atmospheric pressure sensor. The diagnostic trouble code (DTC) can be diagnosed when the ignition has been on for at least 20 seconds.
DTC: ECM-113D/P2227 **1T ECM, MIL: Yes** **Years:** 2011, 2012 **Model:** C30, C70, S40, V50 **Engine:** 2.5L L5	**Atmospheric Pressure Sensor (Signal Too Low):** The engine control module (ECM) checks the signal from the internal atmospheric pressure sensor. The diagnostic trouble code (DTC) is stored if the engine control module (ECM) detects a faulty signal from the internal atmospheric pressure sensor. The diagnostic trouble code (DTC) can be diagnosed when the ignition has been on for at least 20 seconds.
DTC: ECM-1200/P0112-114 **1T ECM, MIL: Yes** **Years:** 2011, 2012 **Model:** C30, S40, V50 **Engine:** 2.5L L5	**Intake Air Temperature (IAT) sensor (Signal Too High Or Too Low):** This diagnostic trouble code (DTC) is stored if the engine control module (ECM) detects a short circuit to ground or supply voltage or an open-circuit in the intake air temperature (IAT) sensor. The diagnostic trouble code (DTC) can be diagnosed when the ignition is switched on. **NOTE: The value for the intake air temperature (IAT) is set at 30 °C.**
DTC: ECM-120A/P0111 **1T ECM, MIL: Yes** **Years:** 2011, 2012 **Model:** C30, S40, V50 **Engine:** 2.5L L5	**Intake Air Temperature (IAT) Sensor. Faulty Signal:** The engine control module (ECM) checks the signal from the intake air temperature (IAT) sensor in the intake manifold. The diagnostic trouble code (DTC) is stored if the engine control module (ECM) detects that the value from the intake air temperature (IAT) sensor deviates too much from the value of the engine coolant temperature (ECT) sensor after the engine has been switched off for an extended period. The diagnostic trouble code (DTC) is diagnosed once per operating cycle when the ignition is switched on, but only when the engine temperature has dropped by approximately 55 °C from operating temperature since the previous operating cycle.
DTC: ECM-120C/P0100 **1T ECM, MIL: Yes** **Years:** 2011, 2012 **Model:** C30, S40, V50 **Engine:** 2.5L L5	**Mass Air Flow, Signal Too High:** The engine control module (ECM) calculates the expected mass air flow. The calculation is based on a number of different parameters. The calculated value for mass air flow is divided (/) by the measured value from the mass air flow (MAF) sensor (= correction value, mass air flow). The diagnostic trouble code (DTC) is stored if the correction value deviates from 1 (higher than 1) i.e. the calculated air mass is higher than the measured air mass. The diagnostic trouble code (DTC) can be diagnosed when the engine is running.
DTC: ECM-120D/P0100 **1T ECM, MIL: Yes** **Years:** 2011, 2012 **Model:** C30, S40, V50 **Engine:** 2.5L L5	**Intake air temperature (IAT) sensor. Faulty signal:** The engine control module (ECM) checks the signal from the intake air temperature (IAT) sensor under two different driving conditions. First at a high air flow with vehicle speed, then at idle speed and a stationary vehicle. The diagnostic trouble code (DTC) is stored if the engine control module (ECM) registers that the temperature difference at these two measurement points is implausibly similar.
DTC: ECM-120D/P0111 **1T ECM, MIL: Yes** **Years:** 2011, 2012 **Model:** C30, S40, V50 **Engine:** 2.5L L5	**Intake air temperature (IAT) sensor. Faulty signal:** The engine control module (ECM) checks the signal from the intake air temperature (IAT) sensor under two different driving conditions. First at a high air flow with vehicle speed, then at idle speed and a stationary vehicle. The diagnostic trouble code (DTC) is stored if the engine control module (ECM) registers that the temperature difference at these two measurement points is implausibly similar.
DTC: ECM-122C/P0103 **1T ECM, MIL: Yes** **Years:** 2011, 2012 **Model:** C30, C70, S40, V50 **Engine:** 2.5L L5	**Mass Air Flow (MAF) Sensor (Flow Too high) :** The engine control module (ECM) calculates the anticipated mass air flow. The calculation is based on a number of parameters. The calculated value for mass air flow is then compared with the measured value from the mass air flow (MAF) sensor. The diagnostic trouble code (DTC) is stored if the engine control module (ECM) detects that the value for the measured air mass is higher than the calculated value for air mass. The diagnostic trouble code (DTC) can be diagnosed when the engine is running.
DTC: ECM-122D/P0102 **1T ECM, MIL: Yes** **Years:** 2011, 2012 **Model:** C30, C70, S40, V50 **Engine:** 2.5L L5	**Mass Air Flow (MAF) Sensor (Flow Too Low):** The engine control module (ECM) calculates the anticipated mass air flow. The calculation is based on a number of parameters. The calculated value for mass air flow is then compared with the measured value from the mass air flow (MAF) sensor. The diagnostic trouble code (DTC) is stored if the engine control module (ECM) detects that the value for the measured air mass is lower than the calculated value for air mass. The diagnostic trouble code (DTC) can be diagnosed when the engine is running.
DTC: ECM-1230/P0101 **1T ECM, MIL: Yes** **Years:** 2011, 2012 **Model:** C30, C70, S40, V50 **Engine:** 2.5L L5	**Mass Air Flow (MAF) (Signal Too Low):** The engine control module (ECM) calculates the anticipated mass air flow. The calculation is based on a number of parameters. The calculated value for mass air flow is then compared with the measured value from the mass air flow (MAF) sensor. The diagnostic trouble code (DTC) is stored if the engine control module (ECM) detects that the correction factor for the air mass (measured air mass/desired air mass value) is too low, while the long-term fuel trim is above or below a set value. The diagnostic trouble code (DTC) can be diagnosed when the engine is running.

DTC	Trouble Code Title and Conditions
DTC: ECM-123B/P0101 **1T ECM, MIL: Yes** **Years:** 2011, 2012 **Model:** C30, C70, S40, V50 **Engine:** 2.5L L5	**Mass Air Flow (MAF) Signal Too High):** The engine control module (ECM) calculates the anticipated mass air flow. The calculation is based on a number of parameters. The calculated value for mass air flow is then compared with the measured value from the mass air flow (MAF) sensor. The diagnostic trouble code (DTC) is stored if the engine control module (ECM) detects that the correction factor for the air mass (measured air mass/desired air mass value) is too high, while the long-term fuel trim is above or below a set value. The diagnostic trouble code (DTC) can be diagnosed when the engine is running
DTC: ECM-123C/P0101 **1T ECM, MIL: Yes** **Years:** 2011, 2012 **Model:** C30, C70, S40, V50 **Engine:** 2.5L L5	**Air Mass. (Signal Too High) :** The engine control module (ECM) calculates the anticipated mass air flow. The calculation is based on a number of parameters. The calculated value for mass air flow is then compared with the measured value from the mass air flow (MAF) sensor. The diagnostic trouble code (DTC) is stored if the engine control module (ECM) detects that the correction factor for the air mass (measured air mass/desired air mass value) is too high, while the long-term fuel trim is above or below a set value. The diagnostic trouble code (DTC) can be diagnosed when the engine is running.
DTC: ECM-123D/P0101 **1T ECM, MIL: Yes** **Years:** 2011, 2012 **Model:** C30, C70, S40, V50 **Engine:** 2.5L L5	**Air Mass. (Signal Too Low):** The engine control module (ECM) calculates the anticipated mass air flow. The calculation is based on a number of parameters. The calculated value for mass air flow is then compared with the measured value from the mass air flow (MAF) sensor. The diagnostic trouble code (DTC) is stored if the engine control module (ECM) detects that the correction factor for the air mass (measured air mass/desired air mass value) is too low, while the long-term fuel trim is above or below a set value. The diagnostic trouble code (DTC) can be diagnosed when the engine is running.
DTC: ECM-125C/P0238 **1T ECM, MIL: Yes** **Years:** 2011, 2012 **Model:** C30, C70, S40, V50 **Engine:** 2.5L L5	**Boost Pressure Sensor (Signal Too High):** The engine control module (ECM) checks the signal from the boost pressure sensor. The diagnostic trouble code (DTC) is stored if the signal from the boost pressure sensor is higher than a certain value for a certain amount of time. The diagnostic trouble code (DTC) can be diagnosed at ignition on and with the engine running.
DTC: ECM-125D/P0237 **1T ECM, MIL: Yes** **Years:** 2011, 2012 **Model:** C30, C70, S40, V50 **Engine:** 2.5L L5	**Boost Pressure Sensor (Signal Too Low):** The engine control module (ECM) checks the signal from the boost pressure sensor. The diagnostic trouble code (DTC) is stored if the signal from the boost pressure sensor is lower than a certain value for a certain amount of time. The diagnostic trouble code (DTC) can be diagnosed at ignition on and with the engine running.
DTC: ECM-1260/P0236/P0240 **1T ECM, MIL: Yes** **Years:** 2011, 2012 **Model:** C30, C70, S40, V50 **Engine:** 2.5L L5	**Boost Pressure Sensor (Signal Too High):** The engine control module (ECM) checks the signal from the boost pressure sensor. The diagnostic trouble code (DTC) is stored if the boost pressure sensor signal is within its normal range but is higher than a calculated value for the boost pressure. The diagnostic trouble code (DTC) is diagnosed by the control module when the engine is running.
DTC: ECM-126B/P0236/P0240 **1T ECM, MIL: Yes** **Years:** 2011, 2012 **Model:** C30, C70, S40, V50 **Engine:** 2.5L L5	**Boost Pressure Sensor (Signal Too Low) :** The engine control module (ECM) checks the signal from the boost pressure sensor. The diagnostic trouble code (DTC) is stored if the boost pressure sensor signal is within its normal range but the signal is lower than a calculated value from the atmospheric pressure sensor. The diagnostic trouble code (DTC) can be diagnosed at ignition on and with the engine running
DTC: ECM-126C/P0236/P0240 **1T ECM, MIL: Yes** **Years:** 2011, 2012 **Model:** C30, C70, S40, V50 **Engine:** 2.5L L5	**Boost Pressure Sensor (Signal Too High):** The engine control module (ECM) checks the signal from the boost pressure sensor. The diagnostic trouble code (DTC) is stored if the signal from the boost pressure sensor is higher than a certain value for a certain amount of time. The diagnostic trouble code (DTC) can be diagnosed at ignition on and with the engine running.
DTC: ECM-126D/P0236/P0240 **1T ECM, MIL: Yes** **Years:** 2011, 2012 **Model:** C30, C70, S40, V50 **Engine:** 2.5L L5	**Boost Pressure Sensor (Signal Too Low):** The engine control module (ECM) checks the signal from the boost pressure sensor. The diagnostic trouble code (DTC) is stored if the signal from the boost pressure sensor is lower than a certain value for a certain amount of time. The diagnostic trouble code (DTC) can be diagnosed at ignition on and with the engine running.
DTC: ECM-1300/P0102-104 **1T ECM, MIL: Yes** **Years:** 2011, 2012 **Model:** C30, S40, V50 **Engine:** 2.5L L5	**Mass Air Flow (MAF) Sensor (Signal Too High Or Too Low):** This diagnostic trouble code (DTC) is stored if the engine control module (ECM) detects a short circuit to ground or supply voltage or an open-circuit in the mass air flow (MAF) sensor circuit. The diagnostic trouble code (DTC) can be diagnosed when the ignition is switched on. **NOTE: A value calculated from engine speed (RPM) and pressure in the intake manifold is used.**

DTC	Trouble Code Title and Conditions
DTC: ECM-130A/P0101 **1T ECM, MIL: Yes** **Years:** 2011, 2012 **Model:** C30, S40, V50 **Engine:** 2.5L L5	**Mass Air Flow (MAF) Sensor. Faulty Signal:** The engine control module (ECM) measures the air mass through the intake manifold using a sensor. The diagnostic trouble code (DTC) is stored if the engine control module (ECM) detects that the sensor value deviates too much from a calculated value. The diagnostic trouble code (DTC) can be diagnosed when: Engine coolant temperature (ECT) is higher than or equal to 70 °C Engine speed (RPM) is approximately 700-5500 rpm Throttle angle is approximately 2-60°. **NOTE: This code can cause a jerky operation.**
DTC: ECM-130B **1T ECM, MIL: Yes** **Years:** 2011, 2012 **Model:** C30, S40, V50 **Engine:** 2.5L L5	**Mass Air Flow (MAF) Sensor (Signal Too High Or Too Low):** This diagnostic trouble code (DTC) is stored if the engine control module (ECM) detects a short circuit to ground or supply voltage or an open-circuit in the mass air flow (MAF) sensor circuit. The diagnostic trouble code (DTC) can be diagnosed when the ignition is switched on.
DTC: ECM-131C/P0113 **1T ECM, MIL: Yes** **Years:** 2011, 2012 **Model:** C30, C70, S40, V50 **Engine:** 2.5L L5	**Intake Air Temperature (IAT) Sensor (Signal Too High):** The engine control module (ECM) checks the signal for the intake air temperature. The diagnostic trouble code (DTC) is stored if the engine control module (ECM) detects that the signal for the intake air temperature corresponds to a temperature that is higher than a certain value. The diagnostic trouble code (DTC) can be diagnosed when the engine is running.
DTC: ECM-131D/P0112 **1T ECM, MIL: Yes** **Years:** 2011, 2012 **Model:** C30, C70, S40, V50 **Engine:** 2.5L L5	**Intake Air Temperature (IAT) Sensor (Signal Too Low):** The engine control module (ECM) checks the signal for the intake air temperature. The diagnostic trouble code (DTC) is stored if the engine control module (ECM) detects that the signal for the intake air temperature corresponds to a temperature that is lower than a certain value. The diagnostic trouble code (DTC) can be diagnosed when the engine is running.
DTC: ECM-1320/P0110 **1T ECM, MIL: Yes** **Years:** 2011, 2012 **Model:** C30, C70, S40, V50 **Engine:** 2.5L L5	**Intake Air Temperature (IAT) Sensor (Faulty Signal):** The engine control module (ECM) checks the signal for the intake air temperature. The diagnostic trouble code (DTC) is stored if the engine control module (ECM) detects that the signal does not follow a certain characteristics over a period of time. The diagnostic trouble code (DTC) can be diagnosed under specific driving conditions.
DTC: ECM-132C/P0111 **1T ECM, MIL: Yes** **Years:** 2011, 2012 **Model:** C30, C70, S40, V50 **Engine:** 2.5L L5	**Intake Air Temperature (IAT) Sensor (Signal Too High):** The engine control module (ECM) checks the signal for the intake air temperature. The diagnostic trouble code (DTC) is stored if the engine control module (ECM) detects that the signal from the intake air temperature (IAT) sensor is higher than a calculated desired value. The diagnostic trouble code (DTC) can be diagnosed under specific driving conditions.
DTC: ECM-132D/P0110 **1T ECM, MIL: Yes** **Year:** 2011, 2012 **Model:** V50 **Engine:** 2.5L L5	**Intake Air Temperature (IAT) Sensor, Signal Too Low:** The engine control module (ECM) checks the signal for the intake air temperature. The diagnostic trouble code (DTC) is stored if the engine control module (ECM) detects that the difference between the signals from the intake air temperature (IAT) sensor and the engine coolant temperature (ECT) sensor is more than 50 °C after the engine has been off for a certain amount of time. The diagnostic trouble code (DTC) can be diagnosed when the engine is running.
DTC: ECM-133C/P0111 **1T ECM, MIL: Yes** **Years:** 2011, 2012 **Model:** C30, C70, S40, V50 **Engine:** 2.5L L5	**Intake Air Temperature (IAT) Sensor Inlet (Signal Too High) :** Engine Control Module (ECM) checks the signal for inlet temperature at start. This is done by the control module saving the values from inlet, fuel and engine temperature sensors at the moment of start. Then the control module compares the values. If the signal from the air temperature sensor matches a temperature that exceeds a certain limit in relation to the other, the control module interprets this as a malfunction and the diagnostic trouble code (DTC) is generated. The diagnostic trouble code (DTC) can be diagnosed after approx. 10 minutes with the engine running.
DTC: ECM-133D/P0111 **1T ECM, MIL: Yes** **Years:** 2011, 2012 **Model:** C30, C70, S40, V50 **Engine:** 2.5L L5	**Intake Air Temperature (IAT) Sensor Inlet (Signal Too Low):** Engine Control Module (ECM) checks the signal for inlet temperature at start. This is done by the control module saving the values from inlet, fuel and engine temperature sensors at the moment of start. Then the control module compares the values. If the signal from the air temperature sensor matches a temperature that is below a certain limit in relation to the other, the control module interprets this as a malfunction and the diagnostic trouble code (DTC) is generated. The diagnostic trouble code (DTC) can be diagnosed after approx. 10 minutes with the engine running.
DTC: ECM-1400/P0107-109 **1T ECM, MIL: Yes** **Years:** 2011, 2012 **Model:** C30, S40, V50 **Engine:** 2.5L L5	**Intake Pressure Sensor (Signal Too High Or Too Low):** This diagnostic trouble code (DTC) is stored if the engine control module (ECM) detects a short circuit to ground or supply voltage or an open-circuit in the manifold absolute pressure (MAP) sensor circuit. The diagnostic trouble code (DTC) can be diagnosed when the ignition is switched on. **NOTE: The value from the mass air flow (MAF) sensor is substituted.**

DTC	Trouble Code Title and Conditions
DTC: ECM-140A/P0106 **1T ECM, MIL: Yes** **Years:** 2011, 2012 **Model:** C30, S40, V50 **Engine:** 2.5L L5	**Intake Pressure Sensor. Faulty Signal:** The engine control module (ECM) measures the pressure in the intake manifold using a sensor. The diagnostic trouble code (DTC) is stored if the engine control module (ECM) detects that the sensor value deviates too much from a calculated model. The diagnostic trouble code (DTC) is diagnosed at a fixed engine speed above 1100 rpm and with the engine at operating temperature (>70 °C). **NOTE: The value from the mass air flow (MAF) sensor is substituted.**
DTC: ECM-1410/P0071 **1T ECM, MIL: Yes** **Years:** 2011, 2012 **Model:** C30, C70, S40, V50 **Engine:** 2.5L L5	**Outside Temperature Sensor (Signal Missing):** The central electronic module (CEM) transmits the signal from the outside temperature sensor via CAN to the engine control module (ECM). The diagnostic trouble code (DTC) is stored in the engine control module (ECM) if the signal from the outside temperature sensor is within its normal range but deviates from the calculated temperature. The diagnostic trouble code (DTC) can be diagnosed after 5 minutes driving at an engine speed above 1700 rpm and a speed above 50 km/h.
DTC: ECM-141B/P0071 **1T ECM, MIL: Yes** **Years:** 2011, 2012 **Model:** C30, C70, S40, V50 **Engine:** 2.5L L5	**Outside Temperature Sensor (Signal Missing):** The central electronic module (CEM) transmits the signal from the outside temperature sensor via CAN to the engine control module (ECM). The diagnostic trouble code (DTC) is stored in the engine control module (ECM) if the signal from the outside temperature sensor is within its normal range but deviates from the calculated temperature. The diagnostic trouble code (DTC) can be diagnosed after 5 minutes driving at an engine speed above 1700 rpm and a speed above 50 km/h.
DTC: ECM-160A/P2175 **1T ECM, MIL: Yes** **Years:** 2011, 2012 **Model:** C30, S40, V50 **Engine:** 2.5L L5	**Electronic Throttle Unit. Faulty Signal :** The engine control module (ECM) checks the difference between the requested throttle position and the actual position. The diagnostic trouble code (DTC) is stored if the engine control module (ECM) registers that the difference was sufficiently great to affect emissions during warming up of the catalytic converter. The diagnostic trouble code (DTC) can be diagnosed when the engine is running and the three-way catalytic converter is being heated up.
DTC: ECM-2000/P0116-119 **1T ECM, MIL: Yes** **Years:** 2011, 2012 **Model:** C30, S40, V50 **Engine:** 2.5L L5	**Engine Coolant Temperature (ECT) Sensor (Signal Too High Or Too Low):** This diagnostic trouble code (DTC) is stored if the engine control module (ECM) registers a short circuit to ground or supply voltage or an open-circuit in the engine coolant temperature (ECT) sensor circuit. The diagnostic trouble code (DTC) can be diagnosed when the ignition is switched on. Substitute value: When starting: The intake air temperature (IAT) is used if no fault has been detected on the intake temperature sensor Otherwise the constant 20 °C is used After starting: The engine coolant temperature (ECT) is calculated based on a model The engine cooling fan (FC) is activated at the predefined speed.
DTC: ECM-200A/P0116 **1T ECM, MIL: Yes** **Years:** 2011, 2012 **Model:** C30, S40, V50 **Engine:** 2.5L L5	**Engine Coolant Temperature (ECT) Sensor. Faulty Signal:** The diagnostic trouble code (DTC) is stored if the engine control module (ECM) detects that the value from the engine coolant temperature (ECT) sensor deviates too much from the values for intake and outside temperatures after the engine has been switched off for an extended period. The diagnostic trouble code (DTC) is diagnosed once per operating cycle, with the ignition on, but only when the temperature in the intake manifold has dropped by approximately 35 °C, or to within several degrees of the calculated ambient temperature, from engine operating temperature since the previous operating cycle. Substitute value: When starting: The intake air temperature (IAT) is used if no fault has been detected on the intake temperature sensor. Otherwise the constant 20 °C is used After starting: The engine coolant temperature (ECT) is calculated based on a model Engine cooling fan (FC) is activated at the predefined speed.
DTC: ECM-200B/P0201 **1T ECM, MIL: Yes** **Years:** 2011, 2012 **Model:** C30, C70, S40, V50 **Engine:** 2.5L L5	**Injector Cylinder 1. (Signal Missing):** The engine control module (ECM) checks the circuit for the injectors. The diagnostic trouble code (DTC) is stored if the engine control module (ECM) detects that the signal for one of the injector circuits is missing. The diagnostic trouble code (DTC) indicates which injector is being referred to. ECM-200B/P0201: injector 1 The diagnostic trouble code (DTC) can be diagnosed when the engine is running.

DTC	Trouble Code Title and Conditions
DTC: ECM-200C/P0262 **1T ECM, MIL: Yes** **Years:** 2011, 2012 **Model:** C30, C70, S40, V50 **Engine:** 2.5L L5	**Injector Cylinder 1. (Signal too High):** The engine control module (ECM) checks the circuit for the injectors. The diagnostic trouble code (DTC) is stored if the engine control module (ECM) detects that the signal for one of the injector circuits is too high. The diagnostic trouble code (DTC) indicates which injector is being referred to. ECM-200C: injector 1 The diagnostic trouble code (DTC) can be diagnosed at ignition on and with the engine running.
DTC: ECM-200D/P0261 **1T ECM, MIL: Yes** **Years:** 2011, 2012 **Model:** C30, C70, S40, V50 **Engine:** 2.5L L5	**Injector Cylinder 1. (Signal Too Low):** The engine control module (ECM) checks the circuit for the injectors. The diagnostic trouble code (DTC) is stored if the engine control module (ECM) detects that the signal for one of the injector circuits is too low. The diagnostic trouble code (DTC) indicates which injector is being referred to. ECM-200D/P0261: injector 1 The diagnostic trouble code (DTC) can be diagnosed at ignition on and with the engine running.
DTC: ECM-201A/P0128 **1T ECM, MIL: Yes** **Years:** 2011, 2012 **Model:** C30, S40, V50 **Engine:** 2.5L L5	**Thermostat. Faulty Signal:** During the engine warm-up phase, the way the temperature increases is checked. This is compared with the expected temperature increase, calculated for example according to load conditions and starting temperature. The diagnostic trouble code (DTC) is stored if the engine control module (ECM) registers that the measured engine coolant temperature (ECT) deviates too much from a calculated temperature. The diagnostic trouble code (DTC) is diagnosed with the engine running, at an engine coolant temperature (ECT) above 80 °C, after the engine has first been allowed to cool from operating temperature for at least 8 hours.
DTC: ECM-201B/P0202 **1T ECM, MIL: Yes** **Years:** 2011, 2012 **Model:** C30, C70, S40, V50 **Engine:** 2.5L L5	**Injector Cylinder 2. (Signal Missing) :** The engine control module (ECM) checks the circuit for the injectors. The diagnostic trouble code (DTC) is stored if the engine control module (ECM) detects that the signal for one of the injector circuits is missing. The diagnostic trouble code (DTC) indicates which injector is being referred to. ECM-201B/P0202: injector 2 The diagnostic trouble code (DTC) can be diagnosed when the engine is running.
DTC: ECM-201C/P0265 **1T ECM, MIL: Yes** **Years:** 2011, 2012 **Model:** C30, C70, S40, V50 **Engine:** 2.5L L5	**Cylinder 2. (Signal Too High):** The engine control module (ECM) checks the circuit for the injectors. The diagnostic trouble code (DTC) is stored if the engine control module (ECM) detects that the signal for one of the injector circuits is too high. The diagnostic trouble code (DTC) indicates which injector is being referred to. ECM-201C/P0265: injector 2 The diagnostic trouble code (DTC) can be diagnosed at ignition on and with the engine running.
DTC: ECM-201D/P0264 **1T ECM, MIL: Yes** **Years:** 2011, 2012 **Model:** C30, C70, S40, V50 **Engine:** 2.5L L5	**Injector Cylinder 2. (Signal Too Low) :** The engine control module (ECM) checks the circuit for the injectors. The diagnostic trouble code (DTC) is stored if the engine control module (ECM) detects that the signal for one of the injector circuits is too low. The diagnostic trouble code (DTC) indicates which injector is being referred to. ECM-201D/P0264: injector 2 The diagnostic trouble code (DTC) can be diagnosed at ignition on and with the engine running.
DTC: ECM-202B/P0203 **1T ECM, MIL: Yes** **Years:** 2011, 2012 **Model:** C30, C70, S40, V50 **Engine:** 2.5L L5	**Injector Cylinder 3. (Signal Missing) :** The engine control module (ECM) checks the circuit for the injectors. The diagnostic trouble code (DTC) is stored if the engine control module (ECM) detects that the signal for one of the injector circuits is missing. The diagnostic trouble code (DTC) indicates which injector is being referred to. ECM-202B/P0203: injector 3 The diagnostic trouble code (DTC) can be diagnosed when the engine is running
DTC: ECM-202C/P0268 **1T ECM, MIL: Yes** **Years:** 2011, 2012 **Model:** C30, C70, S40, V50 **Engine:** 2.5L L5	**Injector Cylinder 3. (Signal Too High) :** The engine control module (ECM) checks the circuit for the injectors. The diagnostic trouble code (DTC) is stored if the engine control module (ECM) detects that the signal for one of the injector circuits is too high. The diagnostic trouble code (DTC) indicates which injector is being referred to. ECM-202C/P0268: injector 3 The diagnostic trouble code (DTC) can be diagnosed at ignition on and with the engine running.

DTC	Trouble Code Title and Conditions
DTC: ECM-202D/P0267 **1T ECM, MIL: Yes** **Years:** 2011, 2012 **Model:** C30, C70, S40, V50 **Engine:** 2.5L L5	**Injector Cylinder 3. (Signal Too Low):** The engine control module (ECM) checks the circuit for the injectors. The diagnostic trouble code (DTC) is stored if the engine control module (ECM) detects that the signal for one of the injector circuits is too low. The diagnostic trouble code (DTC) indicates which injector is being referred to. ECM-202D/P0267: injector 3 The diagnostic trouble code (DTC) can be diagnosed at ignition on and with the engine running.
DTC: ECM-203B/P0204 **1T ECM, MIL: Yes** **Years:** 2011, 2012 **Model:** C30, C70, S40, V50 **Engine:** 2.5L L5	**Injector Cylinder 4. (Signal Missing):** The engine control module (ECM) checks the circuit for the injectors. The diagnostic trouble code (DTC) is stored if the engine control module (ECM) detects that the signal for one of the injector circuits is missing. The diagnostic trouble code (DTC) indicates which injector is being referred to. ECM-203B/P0204: injector 4 The diagnostic trouble code (DTC) can be diagnosed when the engine is running.
DTC: ECM-203C/P0271 **1T ECM, MIL: Yes** **Years:** 2011, 2012 **Model:** C30, C70, S40, V50 **Engine:** 2.5L L5	**Injector Cylinder 4. (Signal Too High):** The engine control module (ECM) checks the circuit for the injectors. The diagnostic trouble code (DTC) is stored if the engine control module (ECM) detects that the signal for one of the injector circuits is too high. The diagnostic trouble code (DTC) indicates which injector is being referred to. ECM-203C/P0271: injector 4 The diagnostic trouble code (DTC) can be diagnosed at ignition on and with the engine running.
DTC: ECM-203D/P0270 **1T ECM, MIL: Yes** **Years:** 2011, 2012 **Model:** C30, C70, S40, V50 **Engine:** 2.5L L5	**Injector Cylinder 4. (Signal Too Low) :** The engine control module (ECM) checks the circuit for the injectors. The diagnostic trouble code (DTC) is stored if the engine control module (ECM) detects that the signal for one of the injector circuits is too low. The diagnostic trouble code (DTC) indicates which injector is being referred to. ECM-203DP0270: injector 4 The diagnostic trouble code (DTC) can be diagnosed at ignition on and with the engine running.
DTC: ECM-204B/P0205 **1T ECM, MIL: Yes** **Years:** 2011, 2012 **Model:** C30, C70, S40, V50 **Engine:** 2.5L L5	**Injector Cylinder 5. (Signal Missing):** The engine control module (ECM) checks the circuit for the injectors. The diagnostic trouble code (DTC) is stored if the engine control module (ECM) detects that the signal for one of the injector circuits is missing. The diagnostic trouble code (DTC) indicates which injector is being referred to. ECM-204B/P0205: injector 5. The diagnostic trouble code (DTC) can be diagnosed when the engine is running.
DTC: ECM-204C/P0274 **1T ECM, MIL: Yes** **Years:** 2011, 2012 **Model:** C30, C70, S40, V50 **Engine:** 2.5L L5	**Injector Cylinder 5. (Signal Too High):** The engine control module (ECM) checks the circuit for the injectors. The diagnostic trouble code (DTC) is stored if the engine control module (ECM) detects that the signal for one of the injector circuits is too high. The diagnostic trouble code (DTC) indicates which injector is being referred to. ECM-204C/P0274: injector 5. The diagnostic trouble code (DTC) can be diagnosed at ignition on and with the engine running.
DTC: ECM-204D/P0273 **1T ECM, MIL: Yes** **Years:** 2011, 2012 **Model:** C30, C70, S40, V50 **Engine:** 2.5L L5	**Injector Cylinder 5. (Signal Too Low):** The engine control module (ECM) checks the circuit for the injectors. The diagnostic trouble code (DTC) is stored if the engine control module (ECM) detects that the signal for one of the injector circuits is too low. The diagnostic trouble code (DTC) indicates which injector is being referred to. ECM-204D/P0273: injector 5. The diagnostic trouble code (DTC) can be diagnosed at ignition on and with the engine running.
DTC: ECM-210A/P0133 **1T ECM, MIL: Yes** **Years:** 2011, 2012 **Model:** C30, S40, V50 **Engine:** 2.5L L5	**Front Heated Oxygen Sensor (HO2S). Faulty Signal:** The engine control module (ECM) checks the signal from the heated oxygen sensor (HO2S). The diagnostic trouble code (DTC) is stored if the engine control module (ECM) registers that the heated oxygen sensor (HO2S) is not activated or is activated too slowly. The diagnostic trouble code (DTC) can be diagnosed when the engine is running.

DTC	Trouble Code Title and Conditions
DTC: ECM-2110/P0031/P0032 **1T ECM, MIL: Yes** **Years:** 2011, 2012 **Model:** C30, S40, V50 **Engine:** 2.5L L5	**Front Heated Oxygen Sensor (HO2S) (Signal Too High Or Too Low) :** This diagnostic trouble code (DTC) is stored if the engine control module (ECM) registers a short-circuit to ground or supply voltage or an open-circuit in the preheating circuit for the front heated oxygen sensor (HO2S). The diagnostic trouble code (DTC) can be diagnosed when the ignition is switched on. **NOTE: Fuel trim switched off and front heated oxygen sensor (HO2S) preheating switched off.**
DTC: ECM-2120/P0131/P0132 **1T ECM, MIL: Yes** **Years:** 2011, 2012 **Model:** C30, S40, V50 **Engine:** 2.5L L5	**Front Heated Oxygen Sensor (HO2S) (Signal Too High or Too Low):** This diagnostic trouble code (DTC) is stored if the engine control module (ECM) registers a short-circuit to ground or supply voltage in the signal cable for the front heated oxygen sensor (HO2S) or if there is an open-circuit. The diagnostic trouble code (DTC) can be diagnosed when the ignition is switched on.
DTC: ECM-2140/P1179 **T ECM, MIL: Yes** **Year:** 2011, 2012 **Model:** C70, S40 **Engine:** 2.5L L5	**Long-Term Fuel Trim, Bank 1:** This diagnostic trouble code can only be stored during lambda regulation quick tests. This is a workshop test, for detecting air leaks or low fuel pressure. During the quick test, the Engine control module (ECM) receives information from the heated oxygen sensor about the fuel/air mixture with reset fuel adaptations. If the fuel/air mixture is outside certain parameters, this means that there is a fault that can cause diagnostic trouble codes related to lambda regulation to be stored during normal operation. I.e. diagnostic trouble codes ECM-21AC, ECM-21AD, ECM-21CC or ECM-21DD. The diagnostic trouble code (DTC) is stored if the control module detects that: * Fuel/air mixture (lambda) deviates abnormally from the expected ($\lambda=1$). The control module's test for the diagnostic trouble code (DTC) starts in the event of: * Activate quick test
DTC: ECM-2140/P1179 **1T ECM** **Year:** 2011, 2012 **Model:** V50 **Engine:** 2.5L L5	**Long-Term Fuel Trim - (Bank 1):** This diagnostic trouble code can only be stored during lambda regulation quick tests. This is a workshop test, for detecting air leaks or low fuel pressure. During the quick test, the Engine control module (ECM) receives information from the heated oxygen sensor about the fuel/air mixture with reset fuel adaptations. If the fuel/air mixture is outside certain parameters, this means that there is a fault that can cause diagnostic trouble codes related to lambda regulation to be stored during normal operation. I.e. diagnostic trouble codes ECM-21AC, ECM-21AD, ECM-21CC or ECM-21DD. The diagnostic trouble code (DTC) is stored if the control module detects that: Fuel/air mixture (lambda) deviates abnormally from the expected ($\lambda=1$). The control module's test for the diagnostic trouble code (DTC) starts in the event of: Activate quick test
DTC: ECM-214C/P1177 **1T ECM** **Year:** 2011, 2012 **Model:** V50 **Engine:** 2.5L L5	**Long-Term Fuel Trim - (Bank 1):** This diagnostic trouble code can only be stored during lambda regulation quick tests. This is a workshop test, for detecting air leaks or low fuel pressure. During the quick test, the Engine control module (ECM) receives information from the heated oxygen sensor about the fuel/air mixture with reset fuel adaptations. If the fuel/air mixture is outside certain parameters, this means that there is a fault that can cause diagnostic trouble codes related to lambda regulation to be stored during normal operation. I.e. diagnostic trouble codes ECM-21AC, ECM-21AD, ECM-21CC or ECM-21DD. The diagnostic trouble code (DTC) is stored if the control module detects that: Fuel/air mixture (lambda) deviates abnormally from the expected ($\lambda=1$). The control module's test for the diagnostic trouble code (DTC) starts in the event of: Activate quick test
DTC: ECM-214C/P1177 **1T ECM, MIL: Yes** **Year:** 2011, 2012 **Model:** C70, S40 **Engine:** 2.5L L5	**Long-Term Fuel Trim, Bank 1:** This diagnostic trouble code can only be stored during lambda regulation quick tests. This is a workshop test, for detecting air leaks or low fuel pressure. During the quick test, the Engine control module (ECM) receives information from the heated oxygen sensor about the fuel/air mixture with reset fuel adaptations. If the fuel/air mixture is outside certain parameters, this means that there is a fault that can cause diagnostic trouble codes related to lambda regulation to be stored during normal operation. I.e. diagnostic trouble codes ECM-21AC, ECM-21AD, ECM-21CC or ECM-21DD. The diagnostic trouble code (DTC) is stored if the control module detects that: * Fuel/air mixture (lambda) deviates abnormally from the expected ($\lambda=1$). The control module's test for the diagnostic trouble code (DTC) starts in the event of: * Activate quick test

DTC	Trouble Code Title and Conditions
DTC: ECM-214D/P1178 **1T ECM, MIL: Yes** **Year:** 2011, 2012 **Model:** C70, S40 **Engine:** 2.5L L5	**Long-Term Fuel Trim, Bank 1:** This diagnostic trouble code can only be stored during lambda regulation quick tests. This is a workshop test, for detecting air leaks or low fuel pressure. During the quick test, the Engine control module (ECM) receives information from the heated oxygen sensor about the fuel/air mixture with reset fuel adaptations. If the fuel/air mixture is outside certain parameters, this means that there is a fault that can cause diagnostic trouble codes related to lambda regulation to be stored during normal operation. I.e. diagnostic trouble codes ECM-21AC, ECM-21AD, ECM-21CC or ECM-21DD. The diagnostic trouble code (DTC) is stored if the control module detects that: * Fuel/air mixture (lambda) deviates abnormally from the expected ($\lambda=1$). The control module's test for the diagnostic trouble code (DTC) starts in the event of: * Activate quick test
DTC: ECM-214D/P1178 **1T ECM** **Year:** 2011, 2012 **Model:** V50 **Engine:** 2.5L L5	**Long-Term Fuel Trim - (Bank 1):** This diagnostic trouble code can only be stored during lambda regulation quick tests. This is a workshop test, for detecting air leaks or low fuel pressure. During the quick test, the Engine control module (ECM) receives information from the heated oxygen sensor about the fuel/air mixture with reset fuel adaptations. If the fuel/air mixture is outside certain parameters, this means that there is a fault that can cause diagnostic trouble codes related to lambda regulation to be stored during normal operation. I.e. diagnostic trouble codes ECM-21AC, ECM-21AD, ECM-21CC or ECM-21DD. The diagnostic trouble code (DTC) is stored if the control module detects that: Fuel/air mixture (lambda) deviates abnormally from the expected ($\lambda=1$). The control module's test for the diagnostic trouble code (DTC) starts in the event of: Activate quick test **Note! The control module can only detect the fault once the test has been started and the diagnostic trouble code (DTC) is stored when the conditions are met.**
DTC: ECM-21AC/P2177 **1T ECM, MIL: Yes** **Years:** 2011, 2012 **Model:** C30, C70, S40, V50 **Engine:** 2.5L L5	**Long-Term Fuel Trim Load, Upper limit (Bank 1) :** The engine control module (ECM) receives information from the heated oxygen sensor (HO2S) about fuel / air mixture at both the upper and lower part-load range. If the fuel / air mixture deviates from $\lambda=1$, the short-term fuel trim will compensate for this by adjusting the injection time so that $\lambda=1$ is achieved. When the short-term fuel trim makes an adjustment, the integrator median must be adjusted by the long-term trim. The diagnostic trouble code (DTC) will be stored when the long-term trim must be adjusted almost to maximum in the upper and lower part-load ranges. The diagnostic trouble code (DTC) can be diagnosed when driving under specific driving conditions.
DTC: ECM-21AD/P2178 **1T ECM, MIL: Yes** **Years:** 2011, 2012 **Model:** C30, C70, S40, V50 **Engine:** 2.5L L5	**Long-Term Fuel Trim Load, Lower limit (Bank 1):** The engine control module (ECM) receives information from the heated oxygen sensor (HO2S) about fuel / air mixture at both the upper and lower part-load range. If the fuel / air mixture deviates from $\lambda=1$, the short-term fuel trim will compensate for this by adjusting the injection time so that $\lambda=1$ is achieved. When the short-term fuel trim makes an adjustment, the integrator median must be adjusted by the long-term trim. The diagnostic trouble code (DTC) will be stored when the long-term trim must be adjusted almost to maximum in the upper and lower part-load ranges. The diagnostic trouble code (DTC) can be diagnosed when driving under specific driving conditions.
DTC: ECM-21CC/P2187 **1T ECM, MIL: Yes** **Years:** 2011, 2012 **Model:** C30, C70, S40, V50 **Engine:** 2.5L L5	**Long-Term Fuel Trim, Idling, Upper Limit (Bank 1):** The engine control module (ECM) receives information from the heated oxygen sensor (HO2S) about the fuel / air mixture. If the fuel / air mixture deviates from $\lambda=1$, the short-term fuel trim will compensate for this by adjusting the injection time so that $\lambda=1$ is achieved. When the short-term fuel trim makes an adjustment, the integrator median must be adjusted by the long-term trim. The diagnostic trouble code (DTC) will be stored when the long-term trim must be adjusted almost to maximum in the idle range. The diagnostic trouble code (DTC) can be diagnosed when idling.
DTC: ECM-21CD/P2188 **1T ECM, MIL: Yes** **Years:** 2011, 2012 **Model:** C30, C70, S40, V50 **Engine:** 2.5L L5	**Long-Term Fuel Trim, Idling, Lower Limit (Bank 1) :** The engine control module (ECM) receives information from the heated oxygen sensor (HO2S) about the fuel / air mixture. If the fuel / air mixture deviates from $\lambda=1$, the short-term fuel trim will compensate for this by adjusting the injection time so that $\lambda=1$ is achieved. When the short-term fuel trim makes an adjustment, the integrator median must be adjusted by the long-term trim. The diagnostic trouble code (DTC) will be stored when the long-term trim must be adjusted almost to maximum in the idle range. The diagnostic trouble code (DTC) can be diagnosed when idling.
DTC: ECM-2200/P0141 **1T ECM, MIL: Yes** **Years:** 2011, 2012 **Model:** C30, S40, V50 **Engine:** 2.5L L5	**Rear Heated Oxygen Sensor (HO2S) (Signal Too High Or Too Low):** The engine control module (ECM) assumes two initial values for probe voltage, 0 V and 5 V. If probe preheating is active and at least one fuel shut-off has been made, the heated oxygen sensor (HO2S) maximum value must have exceeded 0.6 V and the minimum value must have been below 0.3 V. The diagnostic trouble code (DTC) is stored and the engine control module (ECM) interprets it as a fault if these limit values are not achieved after approximately 5 minutes and both the accumulated and actual heated oxygen sensor preheating have reached certain limit values. The diagnostic trouble code (DTC) can be diagnosed when the engine is running. **NOTE: The rear heated oxygen sensor (HO2S) control is shut off.**

DTC	Trouble Code Title and Conditions
DTC: ECM-220A/P0136 **1T ECM, MIL: Yes** **Years:** 2011, 2012 **Model:** C30, S40, V50 **Engine:** 2.5L L5	**Rear Heated Oxygen Sensor (HO2S). Faulty Signal:** The engine control module (ECM) measures the voltage difference between the rear heated oxygen sensor (HO2S) maximum and minimum values. The difference must be greater than 0.3 V. The diagnostic trouble code (DTC) is stored if the engine control module (ECM) registers that these parameters are not reached after approximately 5 minutes and the accumulated or actual probe preheating has reached its parameter. The diagnostic trouble code (DTC) can be diagnosed approximately 5 minutes after starting (if probe preheating is active and at least one fuel shut-off has been made).
DTC: ECM-220F/P0170 **1T ECM, MIL: Yes** **Years:** 2011, 2012 **Model:** C30, S40, V50 **Engine:** 2.5L L5	**Rear Heated Oxygen Sensor (HO2S) (Signal Too High Or Too Low):** The engine control module (ECM) compares the front and rear heated oxygen sensor (HO2S) adaptation values. In order to check front oxygen sensor regulation, check the engine control module (ECM) output signals from the rear oxygen sensor. If the control system for the heated oxygen sensors is working correctly, the control signals from the rear oxygen sensor must be within a predefined statistical interval. The diagnostic trouble code (DTC) is stored if the control module detects that: The measured signals from the rear oxygen sensor (bank 1) are over or under the permissible range for a long period of time. The diagnostic trouble code can be generated after 35 minutes of normal driving (not with heavy load). The control module's test for the diagnostic trouble code (DTC) starts in the event of: Engine running. **Note: This diagnostic trouble code (DTC) is only used for development purposes and is not to be fault-traced. This diagnostic trouble code (DTC) can be ignored and erased with no additional remedial action.**
DTC: ECM-2210/P0036-38 **1T ECM, MIL: Yes** **Years:** 2011, 2012 **Model:** C30, S40, V50 **Engine:** 2.5L L5	**Rear Heated Oxygen Sensor (HO2S) (Faulty Signal, Too High Or Too Low):** The engine control module (ECM) checks whether there is a short-circuit to ground or supply voltage in the preheating circuit heated oxygen sensor (HO2S). It also checks for an open-circuit or whether the heating resistor is faulty. The diagnostic trouble code (DTC) is stored if the engine control module (ECM) registers any of these. The diagnostic trouble code (DTC) can be diagnosed at ignition on and if the battery voltage is in the range 11-16 V.
DTC: ECM-2210/P0042-44 **1T ECM, MIL: Yes** **Years:** 2011, 2012 **Model:** C30, S40, V50 **Engine:** 2.5L L5	**Rear Heated Oxygen Sensor (HO2S) (Faulty Signal, Too High Or Too Low):** The engine control module (ECM) checks whether there is a short-circuit to ground or supply voltage in the preheating circuit heated oxygen sensor (HO2S). It also checks for an open-circuit or whether the heating resistor is faulty. The diagnostic trouble code (DTC) is stored if the engine control module (ECM) registers any of these. The diagnostic trouble code (DTC) can be diagnosed at ignition on and if the battery voltage is in the range 11-16 V.
DTC: ECM-221B/P0140 **1T ECM, MIL: Yes** **Years:** 2011, 2012 **Model:** C30, C70, S40, V50 **Engine:** 2.5L L5	**Rear Heated Oxygen Sensor (HO2S) ageing, Signal missing, (Bank 1):** The engine control module (ECM) monitors the operation of the rear heated oxygen sensor (HO2S) by checking its signal. The engine control module (ECM) checks that the probe has registered both rich and lean fuel/air mixtures. If this is not the case, the engine control module (ECM) changes the fuel/air mixture. The diagnostic trouble code (DTC) is stored if the rear probe has still not registered a lean or rich fuel / air mixture. **NOTE: At fuel shut-off, the probe must show a lean fuel/air mixture. The diagnostic trouble code (DTC) is stored if the switch-over time to a lean fuel/air mixture is too long.**
DTC: ECM-221C/P0140 **1T ECM, MIL: Yes** **Years:** 2011, 2012 **Model:** C30, C70, S40, V50 **Engine:** 2.5L L5	**Rear Heated Oxygen Sensor (HO2S) Ageing, Signal Too High (Bank 1):** The engine control module (ECM) monitors the operation of the rear heated oxygen sensor (HO2S) by checking its signal. The engine control module (ECM) checks that the probe has registered a rich fuel/air mixture. If this is not the case, the engine control module (ECM) changes the fuel/air mixture. The diagnostic trouble code (DTC) is stored if the rear probe has still not registered a rich fuel / air mixture. **NOTE: At fuel shut-off, the probe must show a lean fuel/air mixture. The diagnostic trouble code (DTC) is stored if the switch-over time to a lean fuel/air mixture is too long.**
DTC: ECM-221D/P0140 **1T ECM, MIL: Yes** **Years:** 2011, 2012 **Model:** C30, C70, S40, V50 **Engine:** 2.5L L5	**Rear Heated Oxygen Sensor (HO2S) Ageing, Signal Too Low (Bank 1) :** The engine control module (ECM) monitors the operation of the rear heated oxygen sensor (HO2S) by checking its signal. The engine control module (ECM) checks that the probe has registered a lean fuel/air mixture. If this is not the case, the engine control module (ECM) changes the fuel/air mixture. The diagnostic trouble code (DTC) is stored if the rear probe has still not registered a lean fuel / air mixture. **NOTE: At fuel shut-off, the probe must show a lean fuel/air mixture. The diagnostic trouble code (DTC) is stored if the switch-over time to a lean fuel/air mixture is too long.**
DTC: ECM-2220/P2232 **1T ECM, MIL: Yes** **Years:** 2011, 2012 **Model:** C30, C70, S40, V50 **Engine:** 2.5L L5	**Rear Heated Oxygen Sensor (HO2S), Faulty signal (Bank 1):** The engine control module (ECM) monitors the operation of the rear heated oxygen sensor (HO2S) by checking its signal. The diagnostic trouble code (DTC) is stored if the engine control module (ECM) registers that the signal deviates from its permitted operational range or if the voltage for the heated oxygen sensor (HO2S) preheating disrupts the heated oxygen sensor (HO2S) signal.

DTC	Trouble Code Title and Conditions
DTC: ECM-222B/P0136 **1T ECM, MIL: Yes** **Years:** 2011, 2012 **Model:** C30, C70, S40, V50 **Engine:** 2.5L L5	**Rear Heated Oxygen Sensor (HO2S), Signal Missing (Bank 1):** The engine control module (ECM) monitors the operation of the rear heated oxygen sensor (HO2S) by checking its signal. The diagnostic trouble code (DTC) is stored if the engine control module (ECM) registers that the signal deviates from its permitted operational range or if the voltage for the heated oxygen sensor (HO2S) preheating disrupts the heated oxygen sensor (HO2S) signal.
DTC: ECM-222C/P0138 **1T ECM, MIL: Yes** **Years:** 2011, 2012 **Model:** C30, C70, S40, V50 **Engine:** 2.5L L5	**Rear Heated Oxygen Sensor (HO2S), Signal Too High (Bank 1):** The engine control module (ECM) monitors the operation of the rear heated oxygen sensor (HO2S) by checking its signal. The diagnostic trouble code (DTC) is stored if the engine control module (ECM) registers that the signal deviates from its permitted operational range or if the voltage for the heated oxygen sensor (HO2S) preheating disrupts the heated oxygen sensor (HO2S) signal.
DTC: ECM-222D/P0137 **1T ECM, MIL: Yes** **Years:** 2011, 2012 **Model:** C30, C70, S40, V50 **Engine:** 2.5L L5	**Rear Heated Oxygen Sensor (HO2S), Signal Too Low (Bank 1):** The engine control module (ECM) monitors the operation of the rear heated oxygen sensor (HO2S) by checking its signal. The diagnostic trouble code (DTC) is stored if the engine control module (ECM) registers that the signal deviates from its permitted operational range or if the voltage for the heated oxygen sensor (HO2S) preheating disrupts the heated oxygen sensor (HO2S) signal.
DTC: ECM-223B/P0036 **1T ECM, MIL: Yes** **Years:** 2011, 2012 **Model:** C30, C70, S40, V50 **Engine:** 2.5L L5	**Rear Heated Oxygen Sensor (HO2S), Signal Missing (Bank 1):** The engine control module (ECM) controls preheating by pulsing the current to the positive temperature coefficient (PTC) element in the rear heated oxygen sensor (HO2S). Pulse lengths are dependent on the temperature of the heated oxygen sensor (HO2S). The diagnostic trouble code (DTC) is stored if the engine control module (ECM) registers that the signal is lower than a certain value when preheating is deactivated.
DTC: ECM-223C/P0038 **1T ECM, MIL: Yes** **Years:** 2011, 2012 **Model:** C30, C70, S40, V50 **Engine:** 2.5L L5	**Rear Heated Oxygen Sensor (HO2S), Signal Too High (Bank 1) :** The engine control module (ECM) controls preheating by pulsing the current to the positive temperature coefficient (PTC) element in the rear heated oxygen sensor (HO2S). Pulse lengths are dependent on the temperature of the heated oxygen sensor (HO2S). The diagnostic trouble code (DTC) is stored if the engine control module (ECM) registers that the signal is higher than a certain value when preheating is active.
DTC: ECM-223D/P0037 **1T ECM, MIL: Yes** **Years:** 2011, 2012 **Model:** C30, C70, S40, V50 **Engine:** 2.5L L5	**Rear Heated Oxygen Sensor (HO2S), Signal Too Low (Bank 1):** The engine control module (ECM) controls preheating by pulsing the current to the positive temperature coefficient (PTC) element in the rear heated oxygen sensor (HO2S). Pulse lengths are dependent on the temperature of the heated oxygen sensor (HO2S). The diagnostic trouble code (DTC) is stored if the engine control module (ECM) registers that the signal is lower than a certain value when preheating is deactivated.
DTC: ECM-2250/P0136 **1T ECM, MIL: Yes** **Years:** 2011, 2012 **Model:** C30, C70, S40, V50 **Engine:** 2.5L L5	**Rear Heated Oxygen Sensor (HO2S) (Bank 1):** Engine control module (ECM) monitors rear heated oxygen sensor by, among others, checking it electrically. This diagnostic trouble code is a collective code for diagnoses regarding electrical malfunctions on the heated oxygen sensor and its heating. **NOTE: This diagnostic trouble code is stored as a result of any other diagnostic trouble code for rear heated oxygen sensor being stored in the control module. Therefore, perform troubleshooting based on the second diagnostic trouble code.**
DTC: ECM-23X0/P0201-205 **1T ECM, MIL: Yes** **Years:** 2011, 2012 **Model:** C30, S40, V50 **Engine:** 2.5L L5	**Injector Cylinder X. Faulty Signal:** The engine control module (ECM) checks the signal cable for the injector. The diagnostic trouble code (DTC) is stored if the engine control module (ECM) detects that the signal for the injector is too high, too low or missing. The diagnostic trouble code (DTC) can be diagnosed at ignition on and with the engine running.
DTC: ECM-2400/P0053 **1T ECM, MIL: Yes** **Years:** 2011, 2012 **Model:** C30, C70, S40, V50 **Engine:** 2.5L L5	**Front Heated Oxygen Sensor (HO2S), Heating. Faulty Signal (Bank 1):** The diagnostic trouble code (DTC) is stored if the engine control module (ECM) registers that the front heated oxygen sensor (HO2S) has not reached normal operating temperature.
DTC: ECM-240B/P0053 **1T ECM, MIL: Yes** **Years:** 2011, 2012 **Model:** C30, C70, S40, V50 **Engine:** 2.5L L5	**Front Heated Oxygen Sensor (HO2S), Heating, Signal Missing (Bank 1):** The diagnostic trouble code (DTC) is stored if the engine control module (ECM) registers that there has been no control of the heater element for the front heated oxygen sensor (HO2S) for a certain amount of time.
DTC: ECM-240C/P0053 **1T ECM, MIL: Yes** **Years:** 2011, 2012 **Model:** C30, C70, S40, V50 **Engine:** 2.5L L5	**Front Heated Oxygen Sensor (HO2S) Heating, Signal Too High (Bank 1):** The diagnostic trouble code (DTC) is stored if the engine control module (ECM) registers that the resistance is too high at the front heated oxygen sensor (HO2S).

DTC	Trouble Code Title and Conditions
DTC: ECM-242D/P0133 **1T ECM, MIL: Yes** **Years:** 2011, 2012 **Model:** C30, C70, S40, V50 **Engine:** 2.5L L5	**Front Heated Oxygen Sensor (HO2S) Signal Missing, (Bank 1):** The engine control module (ECM) monitors the aging of the front heated oxygen sensor (HO2S) by checking its ability to react to changes in the exhaust gases. The diagnostic trouble code (DTC) is stored if the engine control module (ECM) registers that the heated oxygen sensor (HO2S) reacts too slowly to changes in the fuel/air mixture.
DTC: ECM-243B/P2231 **1T ECM, MIL: Yes** **Years:** 2011, 2012 **Model:** C30, C70, S40, V50 **Engine:** 2.5L L5	**Front Heated Oxygen Sensor (HO2S) Signal Missing, (Bank 1):** The engine control module (ECM) monitors the operation of the front heated oxygen sensor (HO2S) by checking its signal. The diagnostic trouble code (DTC) is stored if the voltage for the heated oxygen sensor (HO2S) preheating disrupts the heated oxygen sensor (HO2S) signal.
DTC: ECM-243C/P0135 **1T ECM, MIL: Yes** **Years:** 2011, 2012 **Model:** C30, C70, S40, V50 **Engine:** 2.5L L5	**Front Heated Oxygen Sensor (HO2S) (Signal Too High) :** The engine control module (ECM) controls the resistance on the preheating circuit in the front lambda. The check is made by the control module measuring the current through the circuit and then converting the current to temperature. The diagnostic trouble code (DTC) is stored and it is interpreted as a fault if the control module detects that the resistance is unreasonably high, which results in a low temperature. The diagnostic trouble code (DTC) can be diagnosed when driving.
DTC: ECM-244B/P0030 **1T ECM, MIL: Yes** **Years:** 2011, 2012 **Model:** C30, C70, S40, V50 **Engine:** 2.5L L5	**Front Heated Oxygen Sensor (HO2S) Heating, Signal Missing, (Bank 1) :** The engine control module (ECM) controls preheating by pulsing the current to the positive temperature coefficient (PTC) element in the front heated oxygen sensor (HO2S). Pulse lengths are dependent on the temperature of the heated oxygen sensor (HO2S). The diagnostic trouble code (DTC) is stored if the engine control module (ECM) registers that the signal is lower than a certain value when preheating is deactivated.
DTC: ECM-244C/P0032 **1T ECM, MIL: Yes** **Years:** 2011, 2012 **Model:** C30, C70, S40, V50 **Engine:** 2.5L L5	**Front Heated Oxygen Sensor (HO2S) Heating, Signal Too High (Bank 1):** The engine control module (ECM) controls preheating by pulsing the current to the positive temperature coefficient (PTC) element in the front heated oxygen sensor (HO2S). Pulse lengths are dependent on the temperature of the heated oxygen sensor (HO2S). The diagnostic trouble code (DTC) is stored if the engine control module (ECM) registers that the signal is higher than a certain value when preheating is active.
DTC: ECM-244D/P0031 **1T ECM, MIL: Yes** **Years:** 2011, 2012 **Model:** C30, C70, S40, V50 **Engine:** 2.5L L5	**Front Heated Oxygen Sensor (HO2S), Heating Signal Too Low (Bank 1):** The engine control module (ECM) controls preheating by pulsing the current to the positive temperature coefficient (PTC) element in the front heated oxygen sensor (HO2S). Pulse lengths are dependent on the temperature of the heated oxygen sensor (HO2S). The diagnostic trouble code (DTC) is stored if the engine control module (ECM) registers that the signal is lower than a certain value when preheating is deactivated.
DTC: ECM-2450/P1646 **1T ECM, MIL: Yes** **Years:** 2011, 2012 **Model:** C30, C70, S40, V50 **Engine:** 2.5L L5	**Front Heated Oxygen Sensor (HO2S), Faulty Signal (Bank 1) :** The diagnostic trouble code (DTC) is stored if the engine control module (ECM) registers an internal fault in the control for the heated oxygen sensors (HO2S). The diagnostic trouble code (DTC) can be diagnosed when the ignition is switched on.
DTC: ECM-245B/P1646 **1T ECM, MIL: Yes** **Years:** 2011, 2012 **Model:** C30, C70, S40, V50 **Engine:** 2.5L L5	**Front Heated Oxygen Sensor (HO2S), Signal Missing (Bank 1):** The diagnostic trouble code (DTC) is stored if the engine control module (ECM) registers an internal fault in the control for the heated oxygen sensors (HO2S). The diagnostic trouble code (DTC) can be diagnosed when the ignition is switched on.
DTC: ECM-245C/P1646 **1T ECM, MIL: Yes** **Years:** 2011, 2012 **Model:** C30, C70, S40, V50 **Engine:** 2.5L L5	**Front Heated Oxygen Sensor (HO2S), Signal Too High (Bank 1) :** The diagnostic trouble code (DTC) is stored if the engine control module (ECM) registers an internal fault in the control for the heated oxygen sensors (HO2S). The diagnostic trouble code (DTC) can be diagnosed when the ignition is switched on.
DTC: ECM-245D/P1646 **1T ECM, MIL: Yes** **Years:** 2011, 2012 **Model:** C30, C70, S40, V50 **Engine:** 2.5L L5	**Front Heated Oxygen Sensor (HO2S), Signal Too Low (Bank 1) :** The diagnostic trouble code (DTC) is stored if the engine control module (ECM) registers an internal fault in the control for the heated oxygen sensors (HO2S). The diagnostic trouble code (DTC) can be diagnosed when the ignition is switched on.
DTC: ECM-246B/P2626 **1T ECM, MIL: Yes** **Years:** 2011, 2012 **Model:** C30, C70, S40, V50 **Engine:** 2.5L L5	**Front Heated Oxygen Sensor (HO2S), Signal Missing (Bank 1):** The diagnostic trouble code (DTC) is stored if the engine control module (ECM) registers that the calibration current has ceased and the front heated oxygen sensor (HO2S) signal is implausibly high at fuel shut-off.

DTC	Trouble Code Title and Conditions
DTC: ECM-2470/P2238 **1T ECM, MIL: Yes** **Years:** 2011, 2012 **Model:** C30, C70, S40, V50 **Engine:** 2.5L L5	**Front Heated Oxygen Sensor (HO2S), Faulty Signal (Bank 1):** The diagnostic trouble code (DTC) is stored if the engine control module (ECM) registers that the pump current has ceased and the front heated oxygen sensor (HO2S) signal has been set to a default value.
DTC: ECM-247B/P2237 **1T ECM, MIL: Yes** **Years:** 2011, 2012 **Model:** C30, C70, S40, V50 **Engine:** 2.5L L5	**Front Heated Oxygen Sensor (HO2S), Signal Missing (Bank 1):** The diagnostic trouble code (DTC) is stored if the engine control module (ECM) registers that the pump current has ceased and the front heated oxygen sensor (HO2S) signal has been set to a default value.
DTC: ECM-247C/P2239 **1T ECM, MIL: Yes** **Years:** 2011, 2012 **Model:** C30, C70, S40, V50 **Engine:** 2.5L L5	**Front Heated Oxygen Sensor (HO2S), Signal Too High (Bank 1):** The diagnostic trouble code (DTC) is stored if the engine control module (ECM) registers that the pump current has ceased and the front heated oxygen sensor (HO2S) signal has been set to a default value.
DTC: ECM-248C/P0132 **1T ECM, MIL: Yes** **Years:** 2011, 2012 **Model:** C30, C70, S40, V50 **Engine:** 2.5L L5	**Front Heated Oxygen Sensor (HO2S), Signal Too High (Bank 1):** The diagnostic trouble code (DTC) is stored if the engine control module (ECM) registers that there is a short-circuit to supply voltage or a short-circuit to ground in the signal cables for the front heated oxygen sensor (HO2S).
DTC: ECM-248D/P0131 **1T ECM, MIL: Yes** **Years:** 2011, 2012 **Model:** C30, C70, S40, V50 **Engine:** 2.5L L5	**Front Heated Oxygen Sensor (HO2S), Signal Too Low (Bank 1) :** The diagnostic trouble code (DTC) is stored if the engine control module (ECM) registers that there is a short-circuit to supply voltage or a short-circuit to ground in the signal cables for the front heated oxygen sensor (HO2S).
DTC: ECM-249B/P2243 **1T ECM, MIL: Yes** **Years:** 2011, 2012 **Model:** C30, C70, S40, V50 **Engine:** 2.5L L5	**Front Heated Oxygen Sensor (HO2S), Signal Missing (Bank 1):** The diagnostic trouble code (DTC) is stored if the engine control module (ECM) registers an open-circuit in the signal cable to the component of the front heated oxygen sensor (HO2S) that detects the oxygen content of the exhaust gases.
DTC: ECM-24AB/P2251 **1T ECM, MIL: Yes** **Years:** 2011, 2012 **Model:** C30, C70, S40, V50 **Engine:** 2.5L L5	**Front Heated Oxygen Sensor (HO2S), Signal Missing (Bank 1) :** The diagnostic trouble code (DTC) is stored if the engine control module (ECM) registers an open-circuit in the ground lead for the front heated oxygen sensor (HO2S).
DTC: ECM-24C0/P2195/P2414 **1T ECM, MIL: Yes** **Years:** 2011, 2012 **Model:** C30, C70, S40, V50 **Engine:** 2.5L L5	**Front Heated Oxygen Sensor (HO2S), Faulty Signal (Bank 1):** The engine control module (ECM) monitors the operation of the heated oxygen sensor (HO2S) by checking its signal. The diagnostic trouble code (DTC) is stored if the engine control module (ECM) registers any of the following. The engine control module (ECM) compares the front and rear heated oxygen sensor (HO2S) adaptation values. The diagnostic trouble code (DTC) is stored when the values deviate by more than 3%. **Note! The fault may be in the front or rear heated oxygen sensor (HO2S) circuit.** The signal from the front heated oxygen sensor (HO2S) indicates a lean fuel/air mixture. The signal from the rear heated oxygen sensor (HO2S) indicates a rich fuel/air mixture The signal from the front heated oxygen sensor (HO2S) indicates a rich fuel/air mixture. The signal from the rear heated oxygen sensor (HO2S) indicates a lean fuel/air mixture The signal from the heated oxygen sensor (HO2S) indicates an incorrectly rich/lean fuel/air mixture compared to what is expected by the engine control module (ECM).
DTC: ECM-24CB/P2196 **1T ECM, MIL: Yes** **Years:** 2011, 2012 **Model:** C30, C70, S40, V50 **Engine:** 2.5L L5	**Front Heated Oxygen Sensor (HO2S), Signal Missing (Bank 1):** The engine control module (ECM) monitors the operation of the heated oxygen sensor (HO2S) by checking its signal. The diagnostic trouble code (DTC) is stored if the engine control module (ECM) registers any of the following. The engine control module (ECM) compares the front and rear heated oxygen sensor (HO2S) adaptation values. The diagnostic trouble code (DTC) is stored when the values deviate by more than 3%. **Note! The fault may be in the front or rear heated oxygen sensor (HO2S) circuit.** The signal from the front heated oxygen sensor (HO2S) indicates a lean fuel/air mixture. The signal from the rear heated oxygen sensor (HO2S) indicates a rich fuel/air mixture The signal from the front heated oxygen sensor (HO2S) indicates a rich fuel/air mixture. The signal from the rear heated oxygen sensor (HO2S) indicates a lean fuel/air mixture The signal from the heated oxygen sensor (HO2S) indicates an incorrectly rich/lean fuel/air mixture compared to what is expected by the engine control module (ECM).

DTC	Trouble Code Title and Conditions
DTC: ECM-24CC/P2096 **1T ECM, MIL: Yes** **Years:** 2011, 2012 **Model:** C30, C70, S40, V50 **Engine:** 2.5L L5	**Front Heated Oxygen Sensor (HO2S), Signal Too High (Bank 1) :** The engine control module (ECM) monitors the operation of the heated oxygen sensor (HO2S) by checking its signal. The diagnostic trouble code (DTC) is stored if the engine control module (ECM) registers any of the following. The engine control module (ECM) compares the front and rear heated oxygen sensor (HO2S) adaptation values. The diagnostic trouble code (DTC) is stored when the values deviate by more than 3%. **NOTE: The fault may be in the front or rear heated oxygen sensor (HO2S) circuit.** The signal from the front heated oxygen sensor (HO2S) indicates a lean fuel/air mixture. The signal from the rear heated oxygen sensor (HO2S) indicates a rich fuel/air mixture. The signal from the front heated oxygen sensor (HO2S) indicates a rich fuel/air mixture. The signal from the rear heated oxygen sensor (HO2S) indicates a lean fuel/air mixture The signal from the heated oxygen sensor (HO2S) indicates an incorrectly rich/lean fuel/air mixture compared to what is expected by the engine control module (ECM).
DTC: ECM-24CD/P2097 **1T ECM, MIL: Yes** **Years:** 2011, 2012 **Model:** C30, C70, S40, V50 **Engine:** 2.5L L5	**Front Heated Oxygen Sensor (HO2S), Signal Too Low (Bank 1):** The engine control module (ECM) monitors the operation of the heated oxygen sensor (HO2S) by checking its signal. The diagnostic trouble code (DTC) is stored if the engine control module (ECM) registers any of the following. The engine control module (ECM) compares the front and rear heated oxygen sensor (HO2S) adaptation values. The diagnostic trouble code (DTC) is stored when the values deviate by more than 3%. **NOTE: The fault may be in the front or rear heated oxygen sensor (HO2S) circuit.** The signal from the front heated oxygen sensor (HO2S) indicates a lean fuel/air mixture. The signal from the rear heated oxygen sensor (HO2S) indicates a rich fuel/air mixture The signal from the front heated oxygen sensor (HO2S) indicates a rich fuel/air mixture. The signal from the rear heated oxygen sensor (HO2S) indicates a lean fuel/air mixture The signal from the heated oxygen sensor (HO2S) indicates an incorrectly rich/lean fuel/air mixture compared to what is expected by the engine control module (ECM).
DTC: ECM-24D0/P2414 **1T ECM, MIL: Yes** **Years:** 2011, 2012 **Model:** C30, C70, S40, V50 **Engine:** 2.5L L5	**Front Heated Oxygen Sensor (HO2S), Faulty Signal (Bank 1) :** The engine control module (ECM) monitors the operation of the front heated oxygen sensor (HO2S) by checking its signal. The diagnostic trouble code (DTC) is stored if the engine control module (ECM) registers that the heated oxygen sensor (HO2S) only indicates air and no fuel/air mixture.
DTC: ECM-24EB/P013E **1T ECM, MIL: Yes** **Years:** 2011, 2012 **Model:** C30, C70, S40, V50 **Engine:** 2.5L L5	**Rear Heated Oxygen Sensor (HO2S), Slow Regulation:** The engine control module (ECM) checks the signal from the rear heated oxygen sensor (HO2S). The diagnostic trouble code (DTC) is stored if the engine control module (ECM) registers that the heated oxygen sensor (HO2S)reacts too slowly for changes in the fuel/ air mixing and the control module interprets this as a fault. The diagnostic trouble code can be diagnosed when driving.
DTC: ECM-24EC/P013A **1T ECM, MIL: Yes** **Years:** 2011, 2012 **Model:** C30, C70, S40, V50 **Engine:** 2.5L L5	**Rear Heated Oxygen Sensor (HO2S), Slow Regulation:** The engine control module (ECM) checks the signal from the rear heated oxygen sensor (HO2S). The diagnostic trouble code (DTC) is stored if the engine control module (ECM) registers that the heated oxygen sensor (HO2S)reacts too slowly for changes in the fuel/ air mixing and the control module interprets this as a fault. The diagnostic trouble code can be diagnosed when driving.
DTC: ECM-250A/P0171/P0172 **1T ECM, MIL: Yes** **Years:** 2011, 2012 **Model:** C30, S40, V50 **Engine:** 2.5L L5	**Long-term Fuel Trim (Upper Limit Or Lower Limit):** Engine Control Module (ECM) receives information from the heated oxygen sensor about fuel/air mixture in different load areas. If Engine Control Module (ECM) registers that fuel/air mixture deviates too much from target lambda, so that adaptations end up in any of its end-positions, the diagnostic trouble code is generated
DTC: ECM-2600/P0192-194 **1T ECM, MIL: Yes** **Years:** 2011, 2012 **Model:** C30, S40, V50 **Engine:** 2.5L L5	**Fuel Pressure Sensor (Signal Too High Or Too Low):** The engine control module (ECM) checks the signal from the fuel pressure sensor. The diagnostic trouble code (DTC) is stored if the engine control module (ECM) registers a fault in the signal from the fuel pressure sensor. The diagnostic trouble code (DTC) can be diagnosed when the ignition is switched on. **NOTE: The fuel pressure is set to a constant. The control signal to the fuel pump (FP) control module is set to a calculated value.**
DTC: ECM-260A/P0191 **1T ECM, MIL: Yes** **Years:** 2011, 2012 **Model:** C30, S40, V50 **Engine:** 2.5L L5	**Fuel Pressure Sensor (Faulty Signal Or Too High):** The engine control module (ECM) checks the signal from the fuel pressure sensor. If the Engine control module (ECM) registers that the signal from the fuel pressure sensor does not change when the fuel pump activation changes, the diagnostic trouble code is generated. The diagnostic trouble code (DTC) can be diagnosed when starting the engine. **NOTE: The fuel pressure is set to a constant. The control signal to the fuel pump (FP) control module is set to a calculated value.**

DTC	Trouble Code Title and Conditions
DTC: ECM-2610/P0091/P0092 **1T ECM, MIL: Yes** **Years:** 2011, 2012 **Model:** C30, S40, V50 **Engine:** 2.5L L5	**Fuel Pump (FP) Control Module (Signal Too High Or Too Low):** The engine control module (ECM) checks the control signal to the fuel pump (FP) control module. The diagnostic trouble code (DTC) is stored if the engine control module (ECM) registers a fault in the control signal to the fuel pump (FP) control module. The diagnostic trouble code (DTC) can be diagnosed when the engine is running.
DTC: ECM-261A/P0089 **1T ECM, MIL: Yes** **Years:** 2011, 2012 **Model:** C30, S40, V50 **Engine:** 2.5L L5	**Fuel Pressure System (Faulty Signal, Too High Or Too Low):** The engine control module (ECM) controls the fuel pressure via the fuel pump (FP) control module using a PWM signal. The fuel pump (FP) control module then controls the fuel pump (FP) depending on the pressure requested by the engine control module (ECM). For information about fuel pressure regulation, see VIDA Design and Function. The diagnostic trouble code (DTC), signal too high/low, is stored if the actual pressure (measured by the fuel pressure sensor) becomes too high/low compared with the requested pressure (engine control module (ECM) target value) for a certain amount of time. The diagnostic trouble code (DTC) (incorrect signal) is stored if the actual pressure varies/pulses too much. The diagnostic trouble code (DTC) can be diagnosed when the engine is running. **NOTE: The fuel pump (FP) is controlled using a calculated value.**
DTC: ECM-261A/P0093 **1T ECM, MIL: Yes** **Years:** 2011, 2012 **Model:** C30, S40 **Engine:** 2.5L L5	**Fuel Pressure System (Faulty Signal, Too High Or Too Low):** The engine control module (ECM) controls the fuel pressure via the fuel pump (FP) control module using a PWM signal. The fuel pump (FP) control module then controls the fuel pump (FP) depending on the pressure requested by the engine control module (ECM). For information about fuel pressure regulation, see VIDA Design and Function. The diagnostic trouble code (DTC), signal too high/low, is stored if the actual pressure (measured by the fuel pressure sensor) becomes too high/low compared with the requested pressure (engine control module (ECM) target value) for a certain amount of time. The diagnostic trouble code (DTC) (incorrect signal) is stored if the actual pressure varies/pulses too much. The diagnostic trouble code (DTC) can be diagnosed when the engine is running. **NOTE: The fuel pump (FP) is controlled using a calculated value.**
DTC: ECM-270B/P0125 **1T ECM, MIL: Yes** **Year:** 2011, 2012 **Model:** C70, V50 **Engine:** 2.5L L5	**Engine Coolant Temperature (ECT) Sensor. Signal Missing:** The engine control module (ECM) checks the signal for engine coolant temperature (ECT). As soon as the engine is started the temperature is calculated theoretically. The diagnostic trouble code (DTC) is stored if the calculated temperature exceeds the engine coolant temperature (ECT) sensor signal. The diagnostic trouble code (DTC) can be diagnosed when the engine is running.
DTC: ECM-273C/P0118 **1T ECM, MIL: Yes** **Years:** 2011, 2012 **Model:** C30, C70, S40, V50 **Engine:** 2.5L L5	**Engine Coolant Temperature (ECT) Sensor, Signal Too High:** The engine control module (ECM) checks the signal for engine coolant temperature (ECT). A diagnostic trouble code (DTC) is stored if the engine control module (ECM) receives a signal from the engine coolant temperature (ECT) sensor corresponding to a temperature that is higher than a certain value. The diagnostic trouble code (DTC) can be diagnosed when the ignition is switched on.
DTC: ECM-273D/P0117 **1T ECM, MIL: Yes** **Years:** 2011, 2012 **Model:** C30, C70, S40, V50 **Engine:** 2.5L L5	**Engine Coolant Temperature (ECT) Sensor, Signal Too Low :** The engine control module (ECM) checks the signal for engine coolant temperature (ECT). A diagnostic trouble code (DTC) is stored if the engine control module (ECM) receives a signal from the engine coolant temperature (ECT) sensor corresponding to a temperature that is lower than a certain value. The diagnostic trouble code (DTC) can be diagnosed when the ignition is switched on.
DTC: ECM-2740/P0116 **1T ECM, MIL: Yes** **Years:** 2011, 2012 **Model:** C30, C70, S40, V50 **Engine:** 2.5L L5	**Engine Coolant Temperature (ECT) Sensor, Faulty Signal:** The engine control module (ECM) checks the signal for engine coolant temperature (ECT). After the engine is started, the engine control module (ECM) calculates the theoretical engine coolant temperature (ECT) based on factors such as time since start, engine speed (RPM) and load. The diagnostic trouble code (DTC) is stored if the signal from the engine coolant temperature (ECT) sensor is static and does not correspond to the calculated temperature. The diagnostic trouble code (DTC) is stored together with another diagnostic trouble code (DTC) for the engine coolant temperature (ECT) sensor. The diagnostic trouble code (DTC) can be diagnosed when the engine is running.
DTC: ECM-274C/P0116 **1T ECM, MIL: Yes** **Years:** 2011, 2012 **Model:** C30, C70, S40, V50 **Engine:** 2.5L L5	**Engine Coolant Temperature (ECT) Sensor, Signal Too High:** Engine Control Module (ECM) checks the signal for engine temperature. If the engine temperature (signal) exceeds a certain limit, the control module checks current operating condition and compares to a calculated engine temperature. Calculations are based on, among other things, speed and load. If the signal from the engine temperature sensor matches a temperature that is higher than a certain limit value and is not reduced within a certain time, the control module interprets this as a malfunction and the diagnostic trouble code (DTC) is generated. The diagnostic trouble code (DTC) can be diagnosed when the engine is running.

DTC	Trouble Code Title and Conditions
DTC: ECM-274D/P0116 **1T ECM, MIL: Yes** **Years:** 2011, 2012 **Model:** C30, C70, S40, V50 **Engine:** 2.5L L5	**Engine Coolant Temperature (ECT) Sensor, Signal Too Low :** The engine control module (ECM) checks the signal for engine coolant temperature (ECT). After the engine is started, the engine control module (ECM) calculates the theoretical engine coolant temperature (ECT) based on factors such as time since start, engine speed (RPM) and load. The diagnostic trouble code (DTC) is stored if the signal from the engine coolant temperature (ECT) sensor is lower than the calculated temperature. The diagnostic trouble code (DTC) can be diagnosed when the engine is running.
DTC: ECM-275C/P0116 **1T ECM, MIL: Yes** **Years:** 2011, 2012 **Model:** C30, C70, S40, V50 **Engine:** 2.5L L5	**Engine Coolant Temperature (ECT) Sensor, Signal Too High:** Engine Control Module (ECM) checks the signal for engine temperature at start. This is done by the control module saving the values from inlet, fuel and engine temperature sensors at the moment of start. Then the control module compares the values. If the signal from the engine temperature sensor matches a temperature that exceeds a certain limit in relation to the other, the control module interprets this as a malfunction and the diagnostic trouble code (DTC) is generated. The diagnostic trouble code (DTC) can be diagnosed after approx. 10 minutes with the engine running.
DTC: ECM-275D/P0116 **1T ECM, MIL: Yes** **Years:** 2011, 2012 **Model:** C30, C70, S40, V50 **Engine:** 2.5L L5	**Engine Coolant Temperature (ECT) Sensor, Signal Too Low:** Engine Control Module (ECM) checks the signal for engine temperature at start. This is done by the control module saving the values from inlet, fuel and engine temperature sensors at the moment of start. Then the control module compares the values. If the signal from the engine temperature sensor matches a temperature that is below a certain limit in relation to the other, the control module interprets this as a malfunction and the diagnostic trouble code (DTC) is generated. The diagnostic trouble code (DTC) can be diagnosed after approx. 10 minutes with the engine running.
DTC: ECM-2800/P0191 **1T ECM** **Years:** 2011, 2012 **Model:** C30, C70, S40, V50 **Engine:** 2.5L L5	**Fuel Pressure Sensor, Faulty Signal:** The engine control module (ECM) checks the signal from the fuel pressure sensor. The diagnostic trouble code (DTC) is stored if the engine control module (ECM) registers that the signal from the fuel pressure sensor is within the normal signal range of the sensor but that the signal is below a calculated desired value for the fuel pressure. The diagnostic trouble code (DTC) can be diagnosed when the engine is running.
DTC: ECM-280B/P0190 **1T ECM** **Years:** 2011, 2012 **Model:** C30, C70, S40, V50 **Engine:** 2.5L L5	**Fuel Pressure Sensor, Signal Missing:** The engine control module (ECM) checks the signal from the fuel pressure sensor. The diagnostic trouble code (DTC) is stored if the engine control module (ECM) registers that there is no signal from the fuel temperature sensor. The diagnostic trouble code (DTC) can be diagnosed when the engine is running.
DTC: ECM-280C/P0193 **1T ECM** **Years:** 2011, 2012 **Model:** C30, C70, S40, V50 **Engine:** 2.5L L5	**Fuel Pressure Sensor, Signal Too High:** The diagnostic trouble code (DTC) is stored if the engine control module (ECM) registers that the signal from the fuel pressure sensor is too high. The diagnostic trouble code (DTC) can be diagnosed at ignition on and with the engine running.
DTC: ECM-280D/P0192 **1T ECM** **Years:** 2011, 2012 **Model:** C30, C70, S40, V50 **Engine:** 2.5L L5	**Fuel Pressure Sensor. Signal Too Low:** The diagnostic trouble code (DTC) is stored if the engine control module (ECM) registers that the signal from the fuel pressure sensor is too low. The diagnostic trouble code (DTC) can be diagnosed at ignition on and with the engine running.
DTC: ECM-281C/P0230 **1T ECM, MIL: Yes** **Years:** 2011, 2012 **Model:** C30, C70, S40, V50 **Engine:** 2.5L L5	**Text Message. Pressure Too High:** The engine control module (ECM) controls the fuel pressure via the fuel pump (FP) control module using a pulse width modulation (PWM) signal. The fuel pump (FP) control module then controls the fuel pump (FP) depending on the pressure requested by the engine control module (ECM). The diagnostic trouble code (DTC) is stored if the actual pressure (measured pressure from the fuel pressure sensor) rises too high in comparison with the requested pressure (target pressure) during a certain time frame. Message in information display. The diagnostic trouble code (DTC) can be diagnosed when the engine is idling.
DTC: ECM-2900/P0089 **1T ECM, MIL: Yes** **Years:** 2011, 2012 **Model:** C30, C70, S40, V50 **Engine:** 2.5L L5	**Fuel Pressure, Faulty Signal:** The engine control module (ECM) controls the fuel pressure via the fuel pump (FP) control module using a pulse width modulation (PWM) signal. The fuel pump (FP) control module then controls the fuel pump (FP) depending on the pressure requested by the engine control module (ECM). The diagnostic trouble code (DTC) is stored if the control capacity of the engine control module (ECM) for fuel pressure reaches the highest or lowest value and the desired fuel pressure (target value) is not achieved. The diagnostic trouble code (DTC) can be diagnosed when the engine is idling.
DTC: ECM-290B/P0090 **1T ECM, MIL: Yes** **Years:** 2011, 2012 **Model:** C30, C70, S40, V50 **Engine:** 2.5L L5	**Fuel Pressure, Signal Missing :** The engine control module (ECM) controls the fuel pressure via the fuel pump (FP) control module using a pulse width modulation (PWM) signal. The fuel pump (FP) control module then controls the fuel pump (FP) depending on the pressure requested by the engine control module (ECM). The diagnostic trouble code (DTC) is stored If the actual pressure (measured pressure from the fuel pressure sensor) pulses too much. The diagnostic trouble code (DTC) can be diagnosed when the engine is idling.

DTC	Trouble Code Title and Conditions
DTC: ECM-290C/P0088 **1T ECM, MIL: Yes** **Years:** 2011, 2012 **Model:** C30, C70, S40, V50 **Engine:** 2.5L L5	**Fuel Pressure, Signal Too High:** The engine control module (ECM) controls the fuel pressure via the fuel pump (FP) control module using a pulse width modulation (PWM) signal. The fuel pump (FP) control module then controls the fuel pump (FP) depending on the pressure requested by the engine control module (ECM). The diagnostic trouble code (DTC) is stored if the actual pressure (measured pressure from the fuel pressure sensor) rises too high in comparison with the requested pressure (target pressure) during a certain time frame. The diagnostic trouble code (DTC) can be diagnosed when the engine is idling.
DTC: ECM-290D/P0087 **1T ECM, MIL: Yes** **Years:** 2011, 2012 **Model:** C30, C70, S40, V50 **Engine:** 2.5L L5	**Fuel Pressure, Signal Too Low:** The engine control module (ECM) controls the fuel pressure via the fuel pump (FP) control module using a pulse width modulation (PWM) signal. The fuel pump (FP) control module then controls the fuel pump (FP) depending on the pressure requested by the engine control module (ECM). The diagnostic trouble code (DTC) is stored if the actual pressure (measured pressure from the fuel pressure sensor) is too low in comparison with the requested pressure (target pressure) during a certain time frame. The diagnostic trouble code (DTC) can be diagnosed when the engine is idling.
DTC: ECM-291B/P0627 **T ECM** **Years:** 2011, 2012 **Model:** C30, C70, S40, V50 **Engine:** 2.5L L5	**Fuel Pump Control Module, Signal Missing:** The engine control module (ECM) controls the fuel pressure via the fuel pump (FP) control module using a pulse width modulation (PWM) signal. The fuel pump (FP) control module then controls the fuel pump (FP) depending on the pressure requested by the engine control module (ECM). The diagnostic trouble code (DTC) is stored if there is no PWM signal between the engine control module (ECM) and the fuel pump (FP) control module. The diagnostic trouble code (DTC) can be diagnosed when the engine is running.
DTC: ECM-291C/P0629 **T ECM** **Years:** 2011, 2012 **Model:** C30, C70, S40, V50 **Engine:** 2.5L L5	**Fuel Pump Control Module, Signal Too High:** The engine control module (ECM) controls the fuel pressure via the fuel pump (FP) control module using a pulse width modulation (PWM) signal. The fuel pump (FP) control module then controls the fuel pump (FP) depending on the pressure requested by the engine control module (ECM). The diagnostic trouble code (DTC) is stored if the PWM signal between the engine control module (ECM) and the fuel pump (FP) control module is too high. The diagnostic trouble code (DTC) can be diagnosed when the engine is running.
DTC: ECM-291D/P0628 **T ECM** **Years:** 2011, 2012 **Model:** C30, C70, S40, V50 **Engine:** 2.5L L5	**Fuel Pump Control Module, Signal Too Low:** The engine control module (ECM) controls the fuel pressure via the fuel pump (FP) control module using a pulse width modulation (PWM) signal. The fuel pump (FP) control module then controls the fuel pump (FP) depending on the pressure requested by the engine control module (ECM). The diagnostic trouble code (DTC) is stored if the PWM signal between the engine control module (ECM) and the fuel pump (FP) control module is too low. The diagnostic trouble code (DTC) can be diagnosed when the engine is running.
DTC: ECM-2A0C/P0183 **1T ECM** **Years:** 2011, 2012 **Model:** C30, C70, S40, V50 **Engine:** 2.5L L5	**Fuel Temperature Sensor, Signal Too High:** The engine control module (ECM) checks the signal from the fuel temperature sensor. The fuel temperature sensor is integrated in the fuel pressure sensor. The diagnostic trouble code (DTC) is stored if the engine control module (ECM) registers that the signal from the fuel temperature sensor is too high. The diagnostic trouble code (DTC) can be diagnosed at ignition on and with the engine running.
DTC: ECM-2A0D/P0182 **1T ECM** **Years:** 2011, 2012 **Model:** C30, C70, S40, V50 **Engine:** 2.5L L5	**Fuel Temperature Sensor, Signal Too Low:** The engine control module (ECM) checks the signal from the fuel temperature sensor. The fuel temperature sensor is integrated in the fuel pressure sensor. The diagnostic trouble code (DTC) is stored if the engine control module (ECM) detects that the signal from the engine coolant temperature (ECT) sensor is too low. The diagnostic trouble code (DTC) can be diagnosed at ignition on and with the engine running.
DTC: ECM-2A10/P0181 **1T ECM, MIL: Yes** **Years:** 2011, 2012 **Model:** C30, C70, S40, V50 **Engine:** 2.5L L5	**Fuel Temperature Sensor, Signal Too High:** The engine control module (ECM) controls the fuel temperature signal while driving. This is done through the control module comparing values from the intake, fuel and engine temperature sensors. If the signal from the fuel temperature sensor matches a temperature that exceeds a certain limit in relation to the other, the control module interprets this as a malfunction and the diagnostic trouble code (DTC) is generated. The diagnostic trouble code (DTC) can be diagnosed when the engine is idling.
DTC: ECM-2A1C/P0181 **1T ECM, MIL: Yes** **Years:** 2011, 2012 **Model:** C30, C70, S40, V50 **Engine:** 2.5L L5	**Fuel Temperature Sensor, Signal Too High:** Engine Control Module (ECM) checks the signal for fuel temperature at start. This is done by the control module saving the values from inlet, fuel and engine temperature sensors at the moment of start. Then the control module compares the values. If the signal from the fuel temperature sensor matches a temperature that exceeds a certain limit in relation to the other, the control module interprets this as a malfunction and the diagnostic trouble code (DTC) is generated. The diagnostic trouble code (DTC) can be diagnosed after approx. 10 minutes with the engine running.
DTC: ECM-2A1D/P0181 **1T ECM, MIL: Yes** **Years:** 2011, 2012 **Model:** C30, C70, S40, V50 **Engine:** 2.5L L5	**Fuel Temperature Sensor, Signal Too Low:** Engine Control Module (ECM) checks the signal for fuel temperature at start. This is done by the control module saving the values from inlet, fuel and engine temperature sensors at the moment of start. Then the control module compares the values. If the signal from the fuel temperature sensor matches a temperature that is below a certain limit in relation to the other, the control module interprets this as a malfunction and the diagnostic trouble code (DTC) is generated. The diagnostic trouble code (DTC) can be diagnosed after approx. 10 minutes with the engine running.

DTC	Trouble Code Title and Conditions
DTC: ECM-2B00/P0128 **1T ECM, MIL: Yes** **Years:** 2011, 2012 **Model:** C30, C70, S40, V50 **Engine:** 2.5L L5	**Thermostat, Faulty Signal:** During the engine warm up phase the way the engine temperature should increase is calculated. Factors such as engine load and the start temperature are taken into account. This test takes place during the engine warm-up phase (under "normal operation") and continues until the engine temperature has reached 84 °C. For the test to start, the starting temperature of the engine must be below 35 °C, the outside temperature must be between -7 and +35 °C and at least 15 minutes must have passed since the engine was last run. The diagnostic trouble code (DTC) is stored if the calculated increase in temperature does not correspond to the actual increase (measured by the engine coolant temperature (ECT) sensor). **NOTE: This diagnostic trouble code (DTC) can also be caused by faults that store diagnostic trouble codes (DTCs) for outside temperature sensors.**
DTC: ECM-2B00/P0182-184 **1T ECM, MIL: Yes** **Years:** 2011, 2012 **Model:** C30, S40, V50 **Engine:** 2.5L L5	**Fuel Temperature Sensor (Signal Too High Or Too Low):** The engine control module (ECM) checks the signal from the fuel temperature sensor. The diagnostic trouble code (DTC) is stored if the engine control module (ECM) registers a fault in the signal from the fuel temperature sensor. The diagnostic trouble code (DTC) can be diagnosed when the ignition is switched on. **NOTE: The fuel temperature is set to a calculated value.**
DTC: ECM-2B0A/P0181 **1T ECM, MIL: Yes** **Years:** 2011, 2012 **Model:** C30, S40, V50 **Engine:** 2.5L L5	**Fuel Temperature Sensor. Faulty Signal:** The engine control module (ECM) checks the signal from the fuel temperature sensor. The diagnostic trouble code (DTC) is stored if the engine control module (ECM) detects that the value from the fuel temperature sensor deviates too much from the values for engine coolant and intake temperature after the engine has been switched off for an extended period. The diagnostic trouble code (DTC) is diagnosed once per operating cycle when the ignition is switched on, but only when the engine temperature has dropped by approximately 60 °C from operating temperature (>70 °C) since the previous operating cycle. **NOTE: The fuel temperature is set to a calculated value.**
DTC: ECM-300A/P0341 **1T ECM, MIL: Yes** **Years:** 2011, 2012 **Model:** C30, S40, V50 **Engine:** 2.5L L5	**Camshaft Position (CMP) Sensor, Intake. Faulty Signal:** The engine control module (ECM) checks that 5 camshaft flanks are detected during 2 crankshaft revolutions (i.e. that all camshaft flanks are detected on one camshaft revolution). The diagnostic trouble code (DTC) is stored if fewer camshaft flanks are detected. The diagnostic trouble code (DTC) can be diagnosed when the engine speed (RPM) is higher than a set value and refers to the camshaft position (CMP) sensor for the intake camshaft. **NOTE: Substituted value signal from the engine speed (RPM) sensor is used.**
DTC: ECM-3010/P0365 **1T ECM, MIL: Yes** **Years:** 2011, 2012 **Model:** C30, S40, V50 **Engine:** 2.5L L5	**Camshaft Position (CMP) Sensor, Exhaust. Faulty Signal :** The diagnostic trouble code (DTC) is stored if the engine control module (ECM) detects that the signal from the camshaft position (CMP) sensor (exhaust) is missing, or if the engine control module (ECM) detects too few flank changes during a set number of crankshaft revolutions. The diagnostic trouble code (DTC) can be diagnosed when the starter motor is turning.
DTC: ECM-301A/P0366 **1T ECM, MIL: Yes** **Years:** 2011, 2012 **Model:** C30, S40, V50 **Engine:** 2.5L L5	**Camshaft Position (CMP) Sensor, Exhaust. Faulty Signal:** The engine control module (ECM) checks that 5 camshaft flanks are detected during 2 crankshaft revolutions (i.e. that all camshaft flanks are detected on one camshaft revolution). The diagnostic trouble code (DTC) is stored if fewer camshaft flanks are detected. The diagnostic trouble code (DTC) can be diagnosed when the engine speed (RPM) is higher than a set value and refers to the camshaft position (CMP) sensor for the exhaust camshaft. **NOTE: The signal from the engine speed (RPM) sensor is used.**
DTC: ECM-303C/P0328 **1T ECM** **Years:** 2011, 2012 **Model:** C30, C70, S40, V50 **Engine:** 2.5L L5	**Front Knock Sensor (KS), Signal Too High:** In certain operating conditions the engine control module (ECM) checks the signal from the front knock sensor (KS). The diagnostic trouble code (DTC) is stored if the signal from the front knock sensor (KS) is too high in these operating conditions. The diagnostic trouble code (DTC) can be diagnosed when the engine is running.
DTC: ECM-303D/P0327 **1T ECM** **Years:** 2011, 2012 **Model:** C30, C70, S40, V50 **Engine:** 2.5L L5	**Front Knock Sensor (KS), Signal Too Low:** In certain operating conditions the engine control module (ECM) checks the signal from the front knock sensor (KS). The diagnostic trouble code (DTC) is stored if the signal from the front knock sensor (KS) is too low in these operating conditions. The diagnostic trouble code (DTC) can be diagnosed when the engine is running.
DTC: ECM-304C/P0333 **1T ECM** **Years:** 2011, 2012 **Model:** C30, C70, S40, V50 **Engine:** 2.5L L5	**Rear Knock Sensor (KS), Signal Too High:** In certain operating conditions the engine control module (ECM) checks the signal from the rear knock sensor (KS). The diagnostic trouble code (DTC) is stored if the signal from the rear knock sensor (KS) is too high in these operating conditions. The diagnostic trouble code (DTC) can be diagnosed when the engine is running.

DTC	Trouble Code Title and Conditions
DTC: ECM-304D/P0332 **1T ECM** **Years:** 2011, 2012 **Model:** C30, C70, S40, V50 **Engine:** 2.5L L5	**Rear Knock Sensor (KS), Signal Too Low:** In certain operating conditions the engine control module (ECM) checks the signal from the rear knock sensor (KS). The diagnostic trouble code (DTC) is stored if the signal from the rear knock sensor (KS) is too low in these operating conditions. The diagnostic trouble code (DTC) can be diagnosed when the engine is running.
DTC: ECM-3050/P0324 **1T ECM, MIL: Yes** **Years:** 2011, 2012 **Model:** C30, C70, S40, V50 **Engine:** 2.5L L5	**Knock Control, Internal Fault:** The diagnostic trouble code (DTC) is stored if the engine control module (ECM) detects an internal fault in the knock control sensor. The diagnostic trouble code (DTC) is diagnosed when the ignition is on.
DTC: ECM-305C/P0324 **1T ECM, MIL: Yes** **Years:** 2011, 2012 **Model:** C30, C70, S40, V50 **Engine:** 2.5L L5	**Knock Control, Internal Fault :** The diagnostic trouble code (DTC) is stored if the engine control module (ECM) detects an internal fault in the knock control sensor. The diagnostic trouble code (DTC) is diagnosed when the ignition is on.
DTC: ECM-305D/P0324 **1T ECM, MIL: Yes** **Years:** 2011, 2012 **Model:** C30, C70, S40, V50 **Engine:** 2.5L L5	**Knock Control, Internal Fault :** The diagnostic trouble code (DTC) is stored if the engine control module (ECM) detects an internal fault in the knock control sensor. The diagnostic trouble code (DTC) is diagnosed when the ignition is on.
DTC: ECM-3060/P0324 **1T ECM, MIL: Yes** **Years:** 2011, 2012 **Model:** C30, C70, S40, V50 **Engine:** 2.5L L5	**Knock Control, Internal Fault :** The signal from the knock sensor (KS) is filtered in the engine control module (ECM). The diagnostic trouble code (DTC) is stored if the engine control module (ECM) detects an internal fault in the knock control circuit filter. The diagnostic trouble code (DTC) is diagnosed when starting the engine.
DTC: ECM-3100/P0300 **1T ECM, MIL: Yes** **Years:** 2011, 2012 **Model:** C30, C70, S40, V50 **Engine:** 2.5L L5	**Misfire, At Least One Cylinder, Start Up:** The diagnostic trouble code (DTC) is stored if the engine control module (ECM) detects a certain number of misfires during the first 1000 engine revolutions after the engine is started. This diagnostic trouble code (DTC) is stored together with other diagnostic trouble codes (DTCs) which indicate which cylinders are misfiring.
DTC: ECM-3100/P0337 **1T ECM, MIL: Yes** **Years:** 2011, 2012 **Model:** C30, S40, V50 **Engine:** 2.5L L5	**Engine Speed (RPM) Sensor. Faulty Signal:** The engine control module (ECM) counts the number of teeth on the flywheel / carrier plate using the engine speed (RPM) sensor signal. The diagnostic trouble code (DTC) is stored if an incorrect number of teeth are detected during a set number of crankshaft revolutions when starting the engine. The diagnostic trouble code (DTC) can be diagnosed by the engine control module (ECM) when the starter motor is working. **NOTE: Substituted value signal from camshaft position (CMP) sensor is used.**
DTC: ECM-310A/P0336 **1T ECM, MIL: Yes** **Years:** 2011, 2012 **Model:** C30, S40, V50 **Engine:** 2.5L L5	**Engine Speed (RPM) Sensor. Signal Faulty/Intermittent Fault:** The engine control module (ECM) counts the number of teeth on the flywheel / carrier plate using the engine speed (RPM) sensor signal. The diagnostic trouble code (DTC) for an intermittent fault is stored if an incorrect number of teeth are detected during a set number of crankshaft revolutions. The diagnostic trouble code (DTC) for a faulty signal is stored if the fault is detected during several consecutive operating cycles. The diagnostic trouble code (DTC) can be diagnosed when the engine speed (RPM) is higher than approximately 1000 rpm. **NOTE: Substituted value signal from camshaft position (CMP) sensor.**
DTC: ECM-310C/P0300 **1T ECM, MIL: Yes** **Years:** 2011, 2012 **Model:** C30, C70, S40, V50 **Engine:** 2.5L L5	**Misfire, At Least One Cylinder, Catalytic Converter Damage:** The diagnostic trouble code (DTC) is stored if the engine control module (ECM) detects misfires in more than one cylinder which could damage the catalytic converter. The diagnostic trouble code (DTC) can be diagnosed when the engine is running. This diagnostic trouble code (DTC) is stored together with other diagnostic trouble codes (DTCs) which indicate which cylinders are misfiring.
DTC: ECM-310D/P0300 **1T ECM, MIL: Yes** **Years:** 2011, 2012 **Model:** C30, C70, S40, V50 **Engine:** 2.5L L5	**Misfire, At Least One Cylinder, Affects Emissions:** The diagnostic trouble code (DTC) is stored if the engine control module (ECM) detects misfires in more than one cylinder which could affect emissions. The diagnostic trouble code (DTC) can be diagnosed when the engine is running. This diagnostic trouble code (DTC) is stored together with other diagnostic trouble codes (DTCs) which indicate which cylinders are misfiring.
DTC: ECM-3110/P0301 **1T ECM, MIL: Yes** **Years:** 2011, 2012 **Model:** C30, C70, S40, V50 **Engine:** 2.5L L5	**Misfire Cylinder 1, Start Up:** The diagnostic trouble code (DTC) is stored if the engine control module (ECM) detects misfiring during the first 1000 engine revolutions. The diagnostic trouble code (DTC) indicates which cylinder is misfiring. The diagnostic trouble code (DTC) can be diagnosed when the engine is running.

DTC	Trouble Code Title and Conditions
DTC: ECM-311C/P0301 **1T ECM, MIL: Yes** **Years:** 2011, 2012 **Model:** C30, S40, V50 **Engine:** 2.5L L5	**Misfire Cylinder 1, Start Up:** The diagnostic trouble code (DTC) is stored if the engine control module (ECM) detects misfiring during the first 1000 engine revolutions. The diagnostic trouble code (DTC) indicates which cylinder is misfiring. The diagnostic trouble code (DTC) can be diagnosed when the engine is running.
DTC: ECM-311D/P0301 **1T ECM, MIL: Yes** **Years:** 2011, 2012 **Model:** C30, C70, S40, V50 **Engine:** 2.5L L5	**Misfire Cylinder 1, Emissions Impact:** The diagnostic trouble code (DTC) is stored if the engine control module (ECM) detects misfiring during the first 1000 engine revolutions. The diagnostic trouble code (DTC) indicates which cylinder is misfiring. The diagnostic trouble code (DTC) can be diagnosed when the engine is running.
DTC: ECM-3120/P0302 **1T ECM, MIL: Yes** **Years:** 2011, 2012 **Model:** C30, C70, S40, V50 **Engine:** 2.5L L5	**Misfire Cylinder 2, Start Up:** The diagnostic trouble code (DTC) is stored if the engine control module (ECM) detects misfiring during the first 1000 engine revolutions. The diagnostic trouble code (DTC) indicates which cylinder is misfiring. The diagnostic trouble code (DTC) can be diagnosed when the engine is running.
DTC: ECM-312C/P0302 **1T ECM, MIL: Yes** **Years:** 2011, 2012 **Model:** C30, C70, S40, V50 **Engine:** 2.5L L5	**Misfire Cylinder 2, Catalytic Converter Damage :** The diagnostic trouble code (DTC) is stored if the engine control module (ECM) detects misfiring during the first 1000 engine revolutions. The diagnostic trouble code (DTC) indicates which cylinder is misfiring. The diagnostic trouble code (DTC) can be diagnosed when the engine is running.
DTC: ECM-312D/P0302 **1T ECM, MIL: Yes** **Years:** 2011, 2012 **Model:** C30, C70, S40, V50 **Engine:** 2.5L L5	**Misfire Cylinder 2, Emissions Impact:** The diagnostic trouble code (DTC) is stored if the engine control module (ECM) detects misfiring during the first 1000 engine revolutions. The diagnostic trouble code (DTC) indicates which cylinder is misfiring. The diagnostic trouble code (DTC) can be diagnosed when the engine is running.
DTC: ECM-3130/P0303 **1T ECM, MIL: Yes** **Years:** 2011, 2012 **Model:** C30, C70, S40, V50 **Engine:** 2.5L L5	**Misfire Cylinder 3, Start Up:** The diagnostic trouble code (DTC) is stored if the engine control module (ECM) detects misfiring during the first 1000 engine revolutions. The diagnostic trouble code (DTC) indicates which cylinder is misfiring. The diagnostic trouble code (DTC) can be diagnosed when the engine is running.
DTC: ECM-313C/P0303 **1T ECM, MIL: Yes** **Years:** 2011, 2012 **Model:** C30, C70, S40, V50 **Engine:** 2.5L L5	**Misfire Cylinder 3, Catalytic Converter Damage:** The diagnostic trouble code (DTC) is stored if the engine control module (ECM) detects misfiring during the first 1000 engine revolutions. The diagnostic trouble code (DTC) indicates which cylinder is misfiring. The diagnostic trouble code (DTC) can be diagnosed when the engine is running.
DTC: ECM-313D/P0303 **1T ECM, MIL: Yes** **Years:** 2011, 2012 **Model:** C30, C70, S40, V50 **Engine:** 2.5L L5	**Misfire Cylinder 3, Emissions Impact:** The diagnostic trouble code (DTC) is stored if the engine control module (ECM) detects misfiring during the first 1000 engine revolutions. The diagnostic trouble code (DTC) indicates which cylinder is misfiring. The diagnostic trouble code (DTC) can be diagnosed when the engine is running.
DTC: ECM-3140/P0304 **1T ECM, MIL: Yes** **Years:** 2011, 2012 **Model:** C30, C70, S40, V50 **Engine:** 2.5L L5	**Misfire Cylinder 4, Start Up:** The diagnostic trouble code (DTC) is stored if the engine control module (ECM) detects misfiring during the first 1000 engine revolutions. The diagnostic trouble code (DTC) indicates which cylinder is misfiring. The diagnostic trouble code (DTC) can be diagnosed when the engine is running.
DTC: ECM-314C/P0304 **1T ECM, MIL: Yes** **Years:** 2011, 2012 **Model:** C30, C70, S40, V50 **Engine:** 2.5L L5	**Misfire Cylinder 4, Catalytic Converter Damage:** The diagnostic trouble code (DTC) is stored if the engine control module (ECM) detects misfiring during the first 1000 engine revolutions. The diagnostic trouble code (DTC) indicates which cylinder is misfiring. The diagnostic trouble code (DTC) can be diagnosed when the engine is running.
DTC: ECM-314D/P0304 **1T ECM, MIL: Yes** **Years:** 2011, 2012 **Model:** C30, C70, S40, V50 **Engine:** 2.5L L5	**Misfire Cylinder 4, Emissions Impact:** The diagnostic trouble code (DTC) is stored if the engine control module (ECM) detects misfiring during the first 1000 engine revolutions. The diagnostic trouble code (DTC) indicates which cylinder is misfiring. The diagnostic trouble code (DTC) can be diagnosed when the engine is running.

DTC	Trouble Code Title and Conditions
DTC: ECM-3150/P0305 **1T ECM, MIL: Yes** **Years:** 2011, 2012 **Model:** C30, C70, S40, V50 **Engine:** 2.5L L5	**Misfire Cylinder 5, Start Up:** The diagnostic trouble code (DTC) is stored if the engine control module (ECM) detects misfiring during the first 1000 engine revolutions. The diagnostic trouble code (DTC) indicates which cylinder is misfiring. The diagnostic trouble code (DTC) can be diagnosed when the engine is running.
DTC: ECM-315C/P0305 **1T ECM, MIL: Yes** **Years:** 2011, 2012 **Model:** C30, C70, S40, V50 **Engine:** 2.5L L5	**Misfire Cylinder 5, Catalytic Converter Damage:** The diagnostic trouble code (DTC) is stored if the engine control module (ECM) detects misfiring during the first 1000 engine revolutions. The diagnostic trouble code (DTC) indicates which cylinder is misfiring. The diagnostic trouble code (DTC) can be diagnosed when the engine is running.
DTC: ECM-3200/P0350 **1T ECM, MIL: Yes** **Years:** 2011, 2012 **Model:** C30, S40, V50 **Engine:** 2.5L L5	**Ignition Coil. Faulty Signal:** The engine control module (ECM) counts the number of ignitions for all 5 cylinders during a specific time period. The diagnostic trouble code (DTC) is stored if the engine control module (ECM) detects that a certain number of ignitions are missing during this time period. This diagnostic trouble code (DTC) is always stored together with diagnostic trouble code (DTC) ECM-33X0. The diagnostic trouble code (DTC) can be diagnosed when the engine is running.
DTC: ECM-3300/P0728 **1T ECM** **Years:** 2011, 2012 **Model:** C30, C70, S40, V50 **Engine:** 2.5L L5	**Engine Speed (RPM) Sensor, Signal Missing:** The engine control module (ECM) checks the signal from the engine speed (RPM) sensor. The diagnostic trouble code (DTC) is stored in the engine control module (ECM) if it detects that the signal from the engine speed (RPM) sensor is lower than the calculated engine speed (RPM) from the camshaft position (CMP) sensor. The diagnostic trouble code (DTC) can be diagnosed when the engine is running.
DTC: ECM-330B/P0727 **1T ECM** **Years:** 2011, 2012 **Model:** C30, C70, S40, V50 **Engine:** 2.5L L5	**Engine Speed (RPM) Sensor, Signal Missing:** The engine control module (ECM) checks the signal from the engine speed (RPM) sensor. The diagnostic trouble code (DTC) is stored if the engine control module (ECM) detects that there is no signal from the engine speed (RPM) sensor. The diagnostic trouble code (DTC) can be diagnosed when the engine is running.
DTC: ECM-33X0/P0351-355 **1T ECM, MIL: Yes** **Years:** 2011, 2012 **Model:** C30, S40, V50 **Engine:** 2.5L L5	**Ignition Coil x. Faulty Signal:** The engine control module (ECM) checks the primary circuit for the ignition coils using a signal from the diagnostic lead from the ignition coils. The diagnostic trouble code (DTC) is stored if the control module detects that the signal for an ignition coil is faulty. The diagnostic trouble code (DTC) can be diagnosed when the engine is running.
DTC: ECM-3400/P0327/P0328 **1T ECM, MIL: Yes** **Year:** 2011, 2012 **Model:** S40, V50 **Engine:** 2.5L L5	**Knock sensor (KS) (Signal Too High Or Too Low):** The diagnostic trouble code (DTC) is stored if the engine control module (ECM) detects that the signal from the knock sensor (KS) is higher or lower than the normal range for a certain time. The diagnostic trouble code (DTC) can be diagnosed when the ignition is switched on. **NOTE: Safety retardation of ignition advance is commanded.**
DTC: ECM-3400/P0344 **1T ECM** **Years:** 2011, 2012 **Model:** C30, C70, S40, V50 **Engine:** 2.5L L5	**Camshaft Position (CMP) Sensor, Intake Faulty Signal:** Diagnostic trouble code (DTC) ECM-3400 covers camshaft position (CMP) sensor, intake. Diagnostic trouble code (DTC) ECM-3410 covers camshaft position (CMP) sensor, exhaust. The engine control module (ECM) checks the pulse width modulation (PWM) signal from the camshaft position (CMP) sensor. The diagnostic trouble code (DTC) is stored if the signal from the camshaft position (CMP) sensor is missing intermittently. This is interpreted by the engine control module (ECM) as a fault. The diagnostic trouble code (DTC) can be diagnosed when the engine is running.
DTC: ECM-340A/P0326 **1T ECM, MIL: Yes** **Years:** 2011, 2012 **Model:** C30, S40, V50 **Engine:** 2.5L L5	**Knock sensor (KS). (Too Little Roar Or Too Much Roar):** The signal from the knock sensor (KS) varies according to engine speed (RPM). The engine control module (ECM) checks that the knock sensor (KS) signal is within certain limits. These limits are dependent on engine speed (RPM) and load. The diagnostic trouble code (DTC) is stored if the signal from the knock sensor (KS) is higher or lower than the set limits. The diagnostic trouble code (DTC) can be diagnosed when driving. **NOTE: Safety retardation of ignition advance is commanded.**
DTC: ECM-340B/P0340 **1T ECM** **Years:** 2011, 2012 **Model:** C30, C70, S40, V50 **Engine:** 2.5L L5	**Camshaft Position (CMP) Sensor, Intake Signal Missing:** Diagnostic trouble code (DTC) ECM-340B is for the camshaft position (CMP) sensor, intake. Diagnostic trouble code (DTC) ECM-341B is for the camshaft position (CMP) sensor, exhaust. The engine control module (ECM) checks the pulse width modulation (PWM) signal from the camshaft position (CMP) sensor. The diagnostic trouble code (DTC) is stored if there is no signal from the camshaft position (CMP) sensor although it appears sporadically. This is interpreted by the engine control module (ECM) as a fault. The diagnostic trouble code (DTC) can be diagnosed when the engine is running.

DTC	Trouble Code Title and Conditions
DTC: ECM-340C/P0343 **1T ECM** **Years:** 2011, 2012 **Model:** C30, C70, S40, V50 **Engine:** 2.5L L5	**Camshaft Position Sensor, Intake Signal Too High:** Diagnostic trouble code (DTC) ECM-340C is for the camshaft position (CMP) sensor, intake. Diagnostic trouble code (DTC) ECM-341C is for the camshaft position (CMP) sensor, exhaust. The engine control module (ECM) checks the pulse width modulation (PWM) signal from the camshaft position (CMP) sensor. The diagnostic trouble code (DTC) is stored if the signal from the camshaft position (CMP) sensor is constantly high. This is interpreted by the engine control module (ECM) as a fault. The diagnostic trouble code (DTC) can be diagnosed when the engine is running.
DTC: ECM-340D/P0342 **1T ECM** **Years:** 2011, 2012 **Model:** C30, C70, S40, V50 **Engine:** 2.5L L5	**Camshaft Position Sensor, Intake Signal Too Low:** Diagnostic trouble code (DTC) ECM-340D is for the camshaft position (CMP) sensor, intake. Diagnostic trouble code (DTC) ECM-341D is for the camshaft position (CMP) sensor, exhaust. The engine control module (ECM) checks the pulse width modulation (PWM) signal from the camshaft position (CMP) sensor. The diagnostic trouble code (DTC) is stored if the signal from the camshaft position (CMP) sensor is constantly low. This is interpreted by the engine control module (ECM) as a fault. The diagnostic trouble code (DTC) can be diagnosed when the engine is running.
DTC: ECM-3410/P0349/P0369 **1T ECM** **Years:** 2011, 2012 **Model:** C30, C70, S40, V50 **Engine:** 2.5L L5	**Camshaft Position (CMP) Sensor, Exhaust Faulty Signal:** Diagnostic trouble code (DTC) ECM-3400 covers camshaft position (CMP) sensor, intake. Diagnostic trouble code (DTC) ECM-3410 covers camshaft position (CMP) sensor, exhaust. The engine control module (ECM) checks the pulse width modulation (PWM) signal from the camshaft position (CMP) sensor. The diagnostic trouble code (DTC) is stored if the signal from the camshaft position (CMP) sensor is missing intermittently. This is interpreted by the engine control module (ECM) as a fault. The diagnostic trouble code (DTC) can be diagnosed when the engine s running.
DTC: ECM-341B/P0345/P0365 **1T ECM** **Years:** 2011, 2012 **Model:** C30, C70, S40, V50 **Engine:** 2.5L L5	**Camshaft Position (CMP) Sensor, Exhaust Signal Missing:** Diagnostic trouble code (DTC) ECM-340B is for the camshaft position (CMP) sensor, intake. Diagnostic trouble code (DTC) ECM-341B is for the camshaft position (CMP) sensor, exhaust. The engine control module (ECM) checks the pulse width modulation (PWM) signal from the camshaft position (CMP) sensor. The diagnostic trouble code (DTC) is stored if there is no signal from the camshaft position (CMP) sensor although it appears sporadically. This is interpreted by the engine control module (ECM) as a fault. The diagnostic trouble code (DTC) can be diagnosed when the engine is running.
DTC: ECM-341C/P0368/P0348 **1T ECM** **Years:** 2011, 2012 **Model:** C30, C70, S40, V50 **Engine:** 2.5L L5	**Camshaft Position Sensor, Exhaust Signal Too High:** Diagnostic trouble code (DTC) ECM-340C is for the camshaft position (CMP) sensor, intake. Diagnostic trouble code (DTC) ECM-341C is for the camshaft position (CMP) sensor, exhaust. The engine control module (ECM) checks the pulse width modulation (PWM) signal from the camshaft position (CMP) sensor. The diagnostic trouble code (DTC) is stored if the signal from the camshaft position (CMP) sensor is constantly high. This is interpreted by the engine control module (ECM) as a fault. The diagnostic trouble code (DTC) can be diagnosed when the engine is running.
DTC: ECM-341D/P0367/P0347 **1T ECM** **Years:** 2011, 2012 **Model:** C30, C70, S40, V50 **Engine:** 2.5L L5	**Camshaft Position Sensor, Exhaust Signal Too Low:** Diagnostic trouble code (DTC) ECM-340D is for the camshaft position (CMP) sensor, intake. Diagnostic trouble code (DTC) ECM-341D is for the camshaft position (CMP) sensor, exhaust. The engine control module (ECM) checks the pulse width modulation (PWM) signal from the camshaft position (CMP) sensor. The diagnostic trouble code (DTC) is stored if the signal from the camshaft position (CMP) sensor is constantly low. This is interpreted by the engine control module (ECM) as a fault. The diagnostic trouble code (DTC) can be diagnosed when the engine is running.
DTC: ECM-342B/P2614 **1T ECM** **Years:** 2011, 2012 **Model:** C30, C70, S40, V50 **Engine:** 2.5L L5	**Camshaft Position (CMP) Sensor, Signal Missing:** The diagnostic trouble code (DTC) (Signal missing) is stored if the engine control module (ECM) detects that the signal from the camshaft position (CMP) sensor for both intake and exhaust sides is incorrect or missing. This diagnostic trouble code (DTC) is always stored along with another diagnostic trouble code (DTC) for signal error, camshaft position (CMP) sensor.
DTC: ECM-3502/P0300-305 **1T ECM, MIL: Yes** **Years:** 2011, 2012 **Model:** C30, S40, V50 **Engine:** 2.5L L5	**Misfire, Emission Effect. (Misfire Cylinder 1-5):** If the engine control module (ECM) detects a particular number of misfires during a set number of crankshaft revolutions, this will be interpreted as misfires which increase emissions The diagnostic trouble code (DTC) will be stored. In certain cases, the diagnostic trouble code (DTC) qualifier can also indicate which cylinder is misfiring.
DTC: ECM-3503/P0300-305 **1T ECM, MIL: Yes** **Years:** 2011, 2012 **Model:** C30, S40, V50 **Engine:** 2.5L L5	**Misfire, Catalytic Converter Damage. (Misfire Cylinder 1-5):** If the engine control module (ECM) detects a particular number of misfires during a set number of crankshaft revolutions, this will be interpreted as misfires that could damage the catalytic converter. The diagnostic trouble code (DTC) will be stored. In certain cases, the diagnostic trouble code (DTC) qualifier can also indicate which cylinder is misfiring. The misfire diagnostic is active after the engine is started. The malfunction indicator lamp (MIL) flashes.

DTC	Trouble Code Title and Conditions
DTC: ECM-360B/P0351 **1T ECM, MIL: Yes** **Years:** 2011, 2012 **Model:** C30, C70, S40, V50 **Engine:** 2.5L L5	**Ignition Coil Cylinder 1. Signal Missing:** The engine control module (ECM) checks the signal cable for the ignition coil primary winding. The diagnostic trouble code (DTC) is stored if the engine control module (ECM) detects that the signal for the primary winding for the ignition coil is missing. The diagnostic trouble code (DTC) can be diagnosed when the engine is running.
DTC: ECM-360C/P2301 **1T ECM, MIL: Yes** **Years:** 2011, 2012 **Model:** C30, C70, S40, V50 **Engine:** 2.5L L5	**Ignition Coil Cylinder 1. Signal Too High:** The engine control module (ECM) checks the signal cable for the ignition coil primary winding. The diagnostic trouble code (DTC) is stored if the engine control module (ECM) detects that the signal for the primary winding for the ignition coil is too high. The diagnostic trouble code (DTC) can be diagnosed when the engine is running.
DTC: ECM-360D/P2300 **1T ECM, MIL: Yes** **Years:** 2011, 2012 **Model:** C30, C70, S40, V50 **Engine:** 2.5L L5	**Ignition Coil Cylinder 1. Signal Too Low:** The engine control module (ECM) checks the signal cable for the ignition coil primary winding. The diagnostic trouble code (DTC) is stored if the engine control module (ECM) detects that the signal for the primary winding for the ignition coil is too low. The diagnostic trouble code (DTC) can be diagnosed when the engine is running.
DTC: ECM-361B/P0352 **1T ECM, MIL: Yes** **Years:** 2011, 2012 **Model:** C30, C70, S40, V50 **Engine:** 2.5L L5	**Ignition Coil Cylinder 2. Signal Missing:** The engine control module (ECM) checks the signal cable for the ignition coil primary winding. The diagnostic trouble code (DTC) is stored if the engine control module (ECM) detects that the signal for the primary winding for the ignition coil is missing. The diagnostic trouble code (DTC) can be diagnosed when the engine is running.
DTC: ECM-361C/P2304 **1T ECM, MIL: Yes** **Years:** 2011, 2012 **Model:** C30, C70, S40, V50 **Engine:** 2.5L L5	**Ignition Coil Cylinder 2. Signal Too High:** The engine control module (ECM) checks the signal cable for the ignition coil primary winding. The diagnostic trouble code (DTC) is stored if the engine control module (ECM) detects that the signal for the primary winding for the ignition coil is too high. The diagnostic trouble code (DTC) can be diagnosed when the engine is running.
DTC: ECM-361D/P2303 **1T ECM, MIL: Yes** **Years:** 2011, 2012 **Model:** C30, C70, S40, V50 **Engine:** 2.5L L5	**Ignition Coil Cylinder 2. Signal Too Low:** The engine control module (ECM) checks the signal cable for the ignition coil primary winding. The diagnostic trouble code (DTC) is stored if the engine control module (ECM) detects that the signal for the primary winding for the ignition coil is too low. The diagnostic trouble code (DTC) can be diagnosed when the engine is running.
DTC: ECM-362B/P0353 **1T ECM, MIL: Yes** **Years:** 2011, 2012 **Model:** C30, C70, S40, V50 **Engine:** 2.5L L5	**Ignition Coil Cylinder 3. Signal Missing:** The engine control module (ECM) checks the signal cable for the ignition coil primary winding. The diagnostic trouble code (DTC) is stored if the engine control module (ECM) detects that the signal for the primary winding for the ignition coil is missing. The diagnostic trouble code (DTC) can be diagnosed when the engine is running.
DTC: ECM-362C/P2307 **1T ECM, MIL: Yes** **Years:** 2011, 2012 **Model:** C30, C70, S40, V50 **Engine:** 2.5L L5	**Ignition Coil Cylinder 3. Signal Too High:** The engine control module (ECM) checks the signal cable for the ignition coil primary winding. The diagnostic trouble code (DTC) is stored if the engine control module (ECM) detects that the signal for the primary winding for the ignition coil is too high. The diagnostic trouble code (DTC) can be diagnosed when the engine is running.
DTC: ECM-362D/P2306 **1T ECM, MIL: Yes** **Years:** 2011, 2012 **Model:** C30, C70, S40, V50 **Engine:** 2.5L L5	**Ignition Coil Cylinder 3. Signal Too Low:** The engine control module (ECM) checks the signal cable for the ignition coil primary winding. The diagnostic trouble code (DTC) is stored if the engine control module (ECM) detects that the signal for the primary winding for the ignition coil is too low. The diagnostic trouble code (DTC) can be diagnosed when the engine is running.
DTC: ECM-363B/P0354 **1T ECM, MIL: Yes** **Years:** 2011, 2012 **Model:** C30, C70, S40, V50 **Engine:** 2.5L L5	**Ignition Coil Cylinder 4. Signal Missing:** The engine control module (ECM) checks the signal cable for the ignition coil primary winding. The diagnostic trouble code (DTC) is stored if the engine control module (ECM) detects that the signal for the primary winding for the ignition coil is missing. The diagnostic trouble code (DTC) can be diagnosed when the engine is running.
DTC: ECM-363C/P2310 **1T ECM, MIL: Yes** **Years:** 2011, 2012 **Model:** C30, C70, S40, V50 **Engine:** 2.5L L5	**Ignition Coil Cylinder 4. Signal Too High:** The engine control module (ECM) checks the signal cable for the ignition coil primary winding. The diagnostic trouble code (DTC) is stored if the engine control module (ECM) detects that the signal for the primary winding for the ignition coil is too high. The diagnostic trouble code (DTC) can be diagnosed when the engine is running.

DTC	Trouble Code Title and Conditions
DTC: ECM-363D/P2309 **1T ECM, MIL: Yes** **Years:** 2011, 2012 **Model:** C30, C70, S40, V50 **Engine:** 2.5L L5	**Ignition Coil Cylinder 4. Signal Too Low:** The engine control module (ECM) checks the signal cable for the ignition coil primary winding. The diagnostic trouble code (DTC) is stored if the engine control module (ECM) detects that the signal for the primary winding for the ignition coil is too low. The diagnostic trouble code (DTC) can be diagnosed when the engine is running.
DTC: ECM-364B/P0355 **1T ECM, MIL: Yes** **Years:** 2011, 2012 **Model:** C30, C70, S40, V50 **Engine:** 2.5L L5	**Ignition Coil Cylinder 5. Signal Missing:** The engine control module (ECM) checks the signal cable for the ignition coil primary winding. The diagnostic trouble code (DTC) is stored if the engine control module (ECM) detects that the signal for the primary winding for the ignition coil is missing. The diagnostic trouble code (DTC) can be diagnosed when the engine is running.
DTC: ECM-364C/P2313 **1T ECM, MIL: Yes** **Years:** 2011, 2012 **Model:** C30, C70, S40, V50 **Engine:** 2.5L L5	**Ignition Coil Cylinder 5. Signal Too High:** The engine control module (ECM) checks the signal cable for the ignition coil primary winding. The diagnostic trouble code (DTC) is stored if the engine control module (ECM) detects that the signal for the primary winding for the ignition coil is too high. The diagnostic trouble code (DTC) can be diagnosed when the engine is running.
DTC: ECM-364D/P2312 **1T ECM, MIL: Yes** **Years:** 2011, 2012 **Model:** C30, C70, S40, V50 **Engine:** 2.5L L5	**Ignition Coil Cylinder 5. Signal Too Low:** The engine control module (ECM) checks the signal cable for the ignition coil primary winding. The diagnostic trouble code (DTC) is stored if the engine control module (ECM) detects that the signal for the primary winding for the ignition coil is too low. The diagnostic trouble code (DTC) can be diagnosed when the engine is running.
DTC: ECM-365C/P050B **1T ECM, MIL: Yes** **Years:** 2011, 2012 **Model:** C30, C70, S40, V50 **Engine:** 2.5L L5	**Ignition Timing Control During Cold Start:** Engine control module (ECM) performs and monitors ignition control during cold-start. If the ignition cannot be controlled acc. to preset manner, the catalytic converter is not heated fast enough, which may lead to worse emissions. **NOTE: Not being able to perform control in the desired way always depends on another malfunction in the system. It is highly likely that this malfunction also causes idle control to not work as it should. Therefore, troubleshoot acc. to diagnostic trouble code for idle control.**
DTC: ECM-366C/P050B **1T ECM, MIL: Yes** **Years:** 2011, 2012 **Model:** C30, C70, S40, V50 **Engine:** 2.5L L5	**Ignition Timing Control During Cold Start:** Engine control module (ECM) performs and monitors ignition control during cold-start. If the ignition cannot be controlled acc. to preset manner, the catalytic converter is not heated fast enough, which may lead to worse emissions. **Note! Not being able to perform control in the desired way always depends on another malfunction in the system. It is highly likely that this malfunction also causes idle control to not work as it should. Therefore, troubleshoot acc. to diagnostic trouble code for idle control.**
DTC: ECM-4000/P0443-445 **1T ECM, MIL: Yes** **Years:** 2011, 2012 **Model:** C30, S40, V50 **Engine:** 2.5L L5	**Canister Purge (CP) Valve. (Signal Too High Or Too Low):** The diagnostic trouble code (DTC) is stored if the control module, when driving, registers a short circuit to ground or supply voltage in the EVAP valve signal cable or an open-circuit. The diagnostic trouble code (DTC) can be diagnosed when the ignition is switched on.
DTC: ECM-400A/P0441 **1T ECM, MIL: Yes** **Years:** 2011, 2012 **Model:** C30, S40, V50 **Engine:** 2.5L L5	**Canister Purge (CP) Valve. Faulty Signal:** The engine control module (ECM) detects a fault in the function of the EVAP valve by analyzing the signal from the manifold absolute pressure (MAP) sensor. The diagnostic trouble code (DTC) is stored if the engine control module (ECM) registers that the EVAP valve has stuck.
DTC: ECM-400D/P0420 **1T ECM, MIL: Yes** **Years:** 2011, 2012 **Model:** C30, C70, S40, V50 **Engine:** 2.5L L5	**Three-Way Catalytic Converter (TWC) Efficiency, (Bank 1) Signal Too Low:** The engine control module (ECM) continuously checks three-way catalytic converter (TWC) efficiency by comparing signals from the rear heated oxygen sensor (HO2S) with the front heated oxygen sensor (HO2S). The diagnostic trouble code (DTC) will be stored if the efficiency of the three-way catalytic converter (TWC) deviates too much. The diagnostic trouble code (DTC) is diagnosed when driving under specific driving conditions.
DTC: ECM-4050/P0460 **1T ECM** **Years:** 2011, 2012 **Model:** C30, S40, V50 **Engine:** 2.5L L5	**Fuel Level Sensor. Faulty Signal:** A fault message is transmitted to the engine control module (ECM) and the diagnostic trouble code (DTC) is stored if a fault in the fuel level sensor is detected by the central electronic module (CEM). The diagnostic trouble code (DTC) can be diagnosed when the ignition is switched on.

DTC	Trouble Code Title and Conditions
DTC: ECM-4201/P0420 **1T ECM, MIL: Yes** **Years:** 2011, 2012 **Model:** C30, S40, V50 **Engine:** 2.5L L5	**Three-Way Catalytic Converter (TWC) Efficiency. Faulty Signal:** The engine control module (ECM) checks the efficiency of the catalytic converter by switching between rich and lean fuel/air mixtures. When the change-over is made, the signal from the rear heated oxygen sensor (HO2S) is checked and the time taken for the probe to switch. The diagnostic trouble code (DTC) is stored if the engine control module (ECM) registers that the rear heated oxygen sensor (HO2S) switches too rapidly. The engine control module (ECM) interprets this as reduced catalytic converter efficiency. The diagnostic trouble code (DTC) can be diagnosed approximately 15 minutes after the engine is started and if the following requirements are met: Speed 50-120 km/h Even load, not driving in the city
DTC: ECM-420C/P0496 **1T ECM, MIL: Yes** **Years:** 2011, 2012 **Model:** C30, C70, S40, V50 **Engine:** 2.5L L5	**Evaporative Emission System (EVAP) Valve Open:** When the control module activates evaporative emission system (EVAP) control, the idle air trim or short-term fuel trim will change. The diagnostic trouble code (DTC) is stored if the engine control module (ECM) does not detect any change in the idle air trim or in the long term fuel trim when evaporative emission (EVAP) control is active. The engine control module (ECM) interprets this as a damaged evaporative emission (EVAP) system.
DTC: ECM-420D/P0497 **1T ECM, MIL: Yes** **Years:** 2011, 2012 **Model:** C30, C70, S40, V50 **Engine:** 2.5L L5	**Evaporative Emission System (EVAP) Valve Closed:** When the control module activates evaporative emission system (EVAP) control, the idle air trim or short-term fuel trim will change. The diagnostic trouble code (DTC) is stored if the engine control module (ECM) does not detect any change in the idle air trim or in the long term fuel trim when evaporative emission (EVAP) control is active. The engine control module (ECM) interprets this as a damaged evaporative emission (EVAP) system.
DTC: ECM-421B/P0443 **1T ECM, MIL: Yes** **Years:** 2011, 2012 **Model:** C30, C70, S40, V50 **Engine:** 2.5L L5	**Canister Purge (CP) Valve, Signal Missing:** The diagnostic trouble code (DTC) is stored if the engine control module (ECM) detects that there is no signal from the evaporative emission system (EVAP) valve. The diagnostic trouble code (DTC) can be diagnosed when the ignition is switched on.
DTC: ECM-421C/P0444 **1T ECM, MIL: Yes** **Years:** 2011, 2012 **Model:** C30, C70, S40, V50 **Engine:** 2.5L L5	**Evaporative Emission System (EVAP) Valve. Signal Too High:** The diagnostic trouble code (DTC) is stored if the engine control module (ECM) registers that the signal from the evaporative emission system (EVAP) valve is too high. The diagnostic trouble code (DTC) can be diagnosed when the ignition is switched on.
DTC: ECM-421D/P0445 **1T ECM, MIL: Yes** **Years:** 2011, 2012 **Model:** C30, C70, S40, V50 **Engine:** 2.5L L5	**Evaporative Emission System (EVAP) Valve, Signal Too Low:** The diagnostic trouble code (DTC) is stored if the engine control module (ECM) registers that the signal from the evaporative emission system (EVAP) valve is too low. The diagnostic trouble code (DTC) can be diagnosed when the ignition is switched on.
DTC: ECM-4308/P0442 **T ECM, MIL: Yes** **Years:** 2011, 2012 **Model:** C30, S40, V50 **Engine:** 2.5L L5	**Tank System, leak. (Large Or Small Leak):** The engine control module (ECM) checks for leaks in the fuel system by taking a reading of the power consumption of the leak diagnosis pump during pressurization. If a certain pressure is not achieved in the system within a reasonable time, the engine control module (ECM) interprets this as leakage from the fuel injection system. The diagnostic trouble code (DTC) can be diagnosed when the leak diagnostic system is run.
DTC: ECM-430C/P0457 **1T ECM** **Years:** 2011, 2012 **Model:** C30, C70, S40, V50 **Engine:** 2.5L L5	**Fuel Tank System, Leakage. Fuel Tank Filler Cap Missing:** If the engine control module (ECM) registers that fuel filling has been carried out through the fuel level being changed, the position and installation of the fuel tank filler cap is checked. This is carried out by quicker leak diagnostics. The check is carried out a few minutes after start if the vehicle speed is constant and exceeds 30 km/h and only if no fault is detected on the leak diagnostic unit. The diagnostic trouble code (DTC) is stored if the engine control module (ECM) detects a leak after filling. This is interpreted as fuel tank filler cap missing or loosely installed.
DTC: ECM-4310/P2401/P2402 **T ECM, MIL: Yes** **Years:** 2011, 2012 **Model:** C30, S40, V50 **Engine:** 2.5L L5	**Leak Diagnostic Unit, Pump. (Signal Too High Or Too Low):** The engine control module (ECM) checks the control signal to the leak diagnostic pump. The diagnostic trouble code (DTC) is stored if the engine control module (ECM) registers a fault in the control signal to leak diagnostic pump. The diagnostic trouble code (DTC) can be diagnosed when the leak diagnostic system is run.
DTC: ECM-431A/P2405-2407 **T ECM, MIL: Yes** **Years:** 2011, 2012 **Model:** C30, S40, V50 **Engine:** 2.5L L5	**Leak Diagnostic Unit, Pump. (Faulty Signal):** The engine control module (ECM) checks the function of the leak diagnostic unit by measuring the current through the leak diagnostic pump. A diagnostic trouble code (DTC) is stored if the engine control module (ECM) registers that the voltage curve is rough the engine control module (ECM) interprets this as an incorrect reference reading. The diagnostic trouble code (DTC) can be diagnosed when the leak diagnostic system is run.

DTC	Trouble Code Title and Conditions
DTC: ECM-431B/P240A **1T ECM** **Years:** 2011, 2012 **Model:** C30, C70, S40, V50 **Engine:** 2.5L L5	**Leak Diagnostic Unit, Preheating. Signal Missing:** The engine control module (ECM) checks the control signal to the heater element in the leak diagnostic unit. The diagnostic trouble code (DTC) is stored if the engine control module (ECM) detects that the signal is missing. The diagnostic trouble code (DTC) can be diagnosed when the engine is running.
DTC: ECM-431C/P240C **1T ECM** **Years:** 2011, 2012 **Model:** C30, C70, S40, V50 **Engine:** 2.5L L5	**Leak Diagnostic Unit, Preheating. Signal Too High:** The engine control module (ECM) checks the control signal to the heater element in the leak diagnostic unit. The diagnostic trouble code (DTC) is stored if the engine control module (ECM) detects that the signal is too high. The diagnostic trouble code (DTC) can be diagnosed when the leak diagnostic system is run.
DTC: ECM-431D/P240B **1T ECM** **Years:** 2011, 2012 **Model:** C30, C70, S40, V50 **Engine:** 2.5L L5	**Leak Diagnostic Unit, Preheating. Signal Too Low:** The engine control module (ECM) checks the control signal to the heater element in the leak diagnostic unit. The diagnostic trouble code (DTC) is stored if the engine control module (ECM) detects that the signal is too low. The diagnostic trouble code (DTC) can be diagnosed when the engine is running.
DTC: ECM-4320/P0444/P0445 **T ECM, MIL: Yes** **Years:** 2011, 2012 **Model:** C30, S40, V50 **Engine:** 2.5L L5	**Leak Diagnostic Unit, valve. (Signal Too High Or Too Low):** The engine control module (ECM) checks the control signal to the reset valve in the leak diagnostic pump. The diagnostic trouble code (DTC) is stored if the engine control module (ECM) registers a fault in the control signal to the reset valve in the leak diagnostic pump. The diagnostic trouble code (DTC) can be diagnosed when the leak diagnostic system is run.
DTC: ECM-432A/P2404 **T ECM, MIL: Yes** **Years:** 2011, 2012 **Model:** C30, S40, V50 **Engine:** 2.5L L5	**Diagnostic Unit, Valve. (Faulty Signal) :** The engine control module (ECM) checks the function of the valve in the leak diagnostic unit pump by measuring the current through the leak diagnostic pump. After the leading reference phase in the leak diagnostic the air flow is directed from the reference leak to the fuel tank system and begins to pressurize it. In this change there is a short lowering of power consumption before pressure builds up in the tank system. A diagnostic trouble code (DTC) is stored if the engine control module (ECM) registers that the power consumption falls too slowly or not at all and it is interpreted as damage to the valve in the pump. The diagnostic trouble code (DTC) can be diagnosed when the leak diagnostic system is run.
DTC: ECM-432B/P2418 **1T ECM, MIL: Yes** **Years:** 2011, 2012 **Model:** C30, C70, S40, V50 **Engine:** 2.5L L5	**Leak Diagnostic Unit, Valve. Signal Missing:** The diagnostic trouble code (DTC) is stored if the engine control module (ECM) registers that there is no signal from the valve in the pump for the leak diagnostic when the valve is activated. The diagnostic trouble code (DTC) can be diagnosed when the engine has been switched off for 8 hours and is then run for 20 minutes.
DTC: ECM-432C/P2420 **1T ECM, MIL: Yes** **Years:** 2011, 2012 **Model:** C30, C70, S40, V50 **Engine:** 2.5L L5	**Leak Diagnostic Unit, Preheating. Signal Too High:** The diagnostic trouble code (DTC) is stored if the engine control module (ECM) registers that the signal from the valve in the pump for the leak diagnostic is too high when the valve is activated. The diagnostic trouble code (DTC) can be diagnosed when the engine has been switched off for 8 hours and is then run for 20 minutes.
DTC: ECM-432D/P2419 **1T ECM, MIL: Yes** **Years:** 2011, 2012 **Model:** C30, C70, S40, V50 **Engine:** 2.5L L5	**Leak Diagnostic Unit, Preheating. Signal Too Low:** The diagnostic trouble code (DTC) is stored if the engine control module (ECM) registers that the signal from the valve in the pump for the leak diagnostic is too low when the valve is deactivated. The diagnostic trouble code (DTC) can be diagnosed when the engine has been switched off for 8 hours and is then run for 20 minutes.
DTC: ECM-433B/P2400 **1T ECM, MIL: Yes** **Years:** 2011, 2012 **Model:** C30, C70, S40, V50 **Engine:** 2.5L L5	**Leak Diagnostic Unit, Pump. Signal Missing:** The diagnostic trouble code (DTC) is stored if the engine control module (ECM) detects that there is no signal from the leak diagnostic pump. The diagnostic trouble code (DTC) can be diagnosed when the ignition is switched on.
DTC: ECM-433C/P2420 **1T ECM, MIL: Yes** **Years:** 2011, 2012 **Model:** C30, C70, S40, V50 **Engine:** 2.5L L5	**Leak Diagnostic Unit, Pump. Signal Too High:** The diagnostic trouble code (DTC) is stored if the engine control module (ECM) registers that the signal from the pump for the leak diagnostic unit is too high. The diagnostic trouble code (DTC) can be diagnosed when the ignition is switched on.
DTC: ECM-433D/P2401 **1T ECM, MIL: Yes** **Years:** 2011, 2012 **Model:** C30, C70, S40, V50 **Engine:** 2.5L L5	**Leak Diagnostic Unit, Pump. Signal Too Low:** The diagnostic trouble code (DTC) is stored if the engine control module (ECM) registers that the signal from the pump for the leak diagnostic unit is too low. The diagnostic trouble code (DTC) can be diagnosed when the ignition is switched on.

DTC	Trouble Code Title and Conditions
DTC: ECM-434C/P0456 **1T ECM, MIL: Yes** **Years:** 2011, 2012 **Model:** C30, C70, S40, V50 **Engine:** 2.5L L5	**Fuel Tank System, Leakage. Minor Leak:** If no fault has been detected in the leak diagnostic unit, the engine control module (ECM) carries out a leak diagnostic of the fuel tank system. The diagnostic trouble code (DTC) is stored if the engine control module (ECM) detects a leak which is 0.5-1.0 mm.
DTC: ECM-4350/P2401/P2402 **T ECM** **Years:** 2011, 2012 **Model:** C30, S40, V50 **Engine:** 2.5L L5	**Leak Diagnostic Unit, Heater Element. (Signal Too High Or Too Low):** The engine control module (ECM) checks the control signal to the heater element in the leak diagnostic pump. The diagnostic trouble code (DTC) is stored if the engine control module (ECM) registers a fault on the control signal. The diagnostic trouble code (DTC) can be diagnosed when the leak diagnostic system is run.
DTC: ECM-4360/P2404 **1T ECM, MIL: Yes** **Years:** 2011, 2012 **Model:** C30, C70, S40, V50 **Engine:** 2.5L L5	**Leak Diagnostic Unit. Faulty Signal:** The engine control module (ECM) monitors the power consumption of the pump for the leak diagnostic unit when the leak diagnostic is run. The power consumption of the pump must drop when the leak diagnostic pump valve moves from the reference check to pressurizing the fuel tank system. The diagnostic trouble code (DTC) is stored if the power consumption of the pump drops too quickly or slowly. The diagnostic trouble code (DTC) can be diagnosed when leak diagnostics is run.
DTC: ECM-436B/P2407 **1T ECM, MIL: Yes** **Years:** 2011, 2012 **Model:** C30, C70, S40, V50 **Engine:** 2.5L L5	**Leak Diagnostic Unit. Signal Missing:** The engine control module (ECM) monitors the power consumption of the pump for the leak diagnostic unit when the leak diagnostic is run. The diagnostic trouble code (DTC) is stored if the power consumption of the pump fluctuates too much during the reference stage. The diagnostic trouble code (DTC) can be diagnosed when leak diagnostics is run.
DTC: ECM-436C/P2406 **1T ECM, MIL: Yes** **Years:** 2011, 2012 **Model:** C30, C70, S40, V50 **Engine:** 2.5L L5	**Leak Diagnostic Unit. Signal Too High:** The engine control module (ECM) monitors the power consumption of the pump for the leak diagnostic unit when the leak diagnostic is run. The diagnostic trouble code (DTC) is stored if the power consumption of the pump is higher than a certain value during the reference phase. The diagnostic trouble code (DTC) can be diagnosed when leak diagnostics is run.
DTC: ECM-436D/P2405 **1T ECM, MIL: Yes** **Years:** 2011, 2012 **Model:** C30, C70, S40, V50 **Engine:** 2.5L L5	**Leak Diagnostic Unit. Signal Too Low:** The engine control module (ECM) monitors the power consumption of the pump for the leak diagnostic unit when the leak diagnostic is run. The diagnostic trouble code (DTC) is stored if the power consumption of the pump is lower than a certain value during the reference phase. The diagnostic trouble code (DTC) can be diagnosed when leak diagnostics is run.
DTC: ECM-4380/P0457 **1T ECM** **Years:** 2011, 2012 **Model:** C30, C70, S40, V50 **Engine:** 2.5L L5	**Fuel Tank Filler Cap Missing. Faulty Signal:** If the engine control module (ECM) registers that fuel filling has been carried out through the fuel level being changed, the position and installation of the fuel tank filler cap is checked. This is carried out by quicker leak diagnostics. The check is carried out a few minutes after start if the vehicle speed is constant and exceeds 30 km/h and only if no fault is detected on the leak diagnostic unit. The diagnostic trouble code (DTC) is stored if the engine control module (ECM) detects a leak after filling. This is interpreted as fuel tank filler cap missing or loosely installed. This diagnostic trouble code (DTC) cannot occur alone but follows another stored diagnostic trouble code (DTC) for the fuel tank filler cap. The diagnostic trouble code (DTC) only remains during one operating cycle and lights a message in the display indicating that the fuel tank filler cap is not correctly positioned.
DTC: ECM-439C/P0442 **1T ECM, MIL: Yes** **Years:** 2011, 2012 **Model:** C30, C70, S40, V50 **Engine:** 2.5L L5	**Fuel Tank System, Leakage. Major Leak:** If no fault has been detected in the leak diagnostic unit, the engine control module (ECM) carries out a leak diagnostic of the fuel tank system. The diagnostic trouble code (DTC) is stored if the engine control module (ECM) detects a leak which is larger than 1.0 mm.
DTC: ECM-5000/P0336 **1T ECM** **Years:** 2011, 2012 **Model:** C30, C70, S40, V50 **Engine:** 2.5L L5	**Engine Speed (RPM) Sensor Signal. Faulty Signal:** The engine control module (ECM) detects the flywheel position for TDC using the signal from the engine speed (RPM) sensor. The diagnostic trouble code (DTC) is stored if the position for TDC is missing sporadically. The diagnostic trouble code (DTC) can be diagnosed when the engine is running.

DTC	Trouble Code Title and Conditions
DTC: ECM-5000/P0532/P0533 **T ECM** **Years:** 2011, 2012 **Model:** C30, S40, V50 **Engine:** 2.5L L5	**Air Conditioning (A/C) Pressure Sensor. (Signal Too High Or Too Low):** This diagnostic trouble code (DTC) is stored if the engine control module (ECM) registers a short circuit to ground or supply voltage or an open-circuit in the signal cable for the air conditioning (A/C) pressure sensor. Substitute value: The engine cooling fan (FC) is activated at the predefined speed Air conditioning (A/C) shut off The A/C pressure is calculated at approximately 700 kPa.
DTC: ECM-500A/P0531 **1T ECM, MIL: Yes** **Years:** 2011, 2012 **Model:** C30, S40, V50 **Engine:** 2.5L L5	**Air Conditioning (A/C) Pressure Sensor. (Faulty Signal or Signal Missing) :** It is interpreted as a fault (fault signal) and the diagnostic trouble code (DTC) (faulty signal) is stored if the engine control module (ECM) detects that the air conditioning (A/C) pressure does not rise by at least 61 kPa within 12 seconds from the time the first compressor activation is carried out. The diagnostic trouble code (DTC) can be diagnosed once per operating cycle, provided at least 15 minutes have passed since the previous operating cycle. It is interpreted as a fault (missing signal) and the diagnostic trouble code (DTC) is stored if the engine control module (ECM) detects that the pressure is lower than 97 kPa for 4 minutes, while the outside temperature is above 15 °C and the vehicle speed is above 50 km/h. The diagnostic trouble code (DTC) can be diagnosed continually when the conditions for outside temperature and vehicle speed are met. Substitute value: The engine cooling fan (FC) is activated at the predefined speed Air conditioning (A/C) shut off The A/C pressure is calculated at approximately 700 kPa.
DTC: ECM-500B/P0335 **1T ECM** **Years:** 2011, 2012 **Model:** C30, C70, S40, V50 **Engine:** 2.5L L5	**Engine Speed (RPM) Sensor Signal. Signal Missing:** The engine control module (ECM) detects the flywheel position for TDC using the signal from the engine speed (RPM) sensor. The diagnostic trouble code (DTC) is stored is stored if the engine control module (ECM) is unable to detect TDC at the flywheel. The diagnostic trouble code (DTC) can be diagnosed when the engine is running.
DTC: ECM-500C/P0338 **1T ECM** **Years:** 2011, 2012 **Model:** C30, C70, S40, V50 **Engine:** 2.5L L5	**Engine Speed (RPM) Sensor Signal. Signal Too High:** The engine control module (ECM) counts the number of teeth on the flywheel using the signal for the engine speed (RPM) sensor. The diagnostic trouble code (DTC) is stored if the engine control module (ECM) detects at least one tooth too many during a certain number of engine revolutions. The diagnostic trouble code (DTC) can be diagnosed when the engine is running.
DTC: ECM-500D/P0337 **1T ECM** **Year:** 2011, 2012 **Model:** S40 **Engine:** 2.5L L5	**Engine Speed (RPM) Sensor Signal. Signal Too Low:** The engine control module (ECM) counts the number of teeth on the flywheel using the signal for the engine speed (RPM) sensor. The diagnostic trouble code (DTC) is stored if the engine control module (ECM) detects at least one tooth too few during a certain number of engine revolutions. The diagnostic trouble code (DTC) can be diagnosed when the engine is running.
DTC: ECM-5100/P0700 **1T ECM, MIL: Yes** **Years:** 2011, 2012 **Model:** C30, C70, S40, V50 **Engine:** 2.5L L5	**Malfunction Indicator Lamp (MIL), Transmission Control Module (TCM). Faulty Signal,:** The diagnostic trouble code (DTC) is stored in the engine control module (ECM) if the engine control module (ECM) registers that the transmission control module (TCM) has transmitted a request to the central electronic module (CEM) to light the malfunction indicator lamp (MIL). The diagnostic trouble code (DTC) can be diagnosed when the ignition is switched on.
DTC: ECM-510D/P0500 **1T ECM, MIL: Yes** **Years:** 2011, 2012 **Model:** C30, S40, V50 **Engine:** 2.5L L5	**Vehicle Speed Signal. (Faulty Signal):** A fault message is transmitted to the engine control module (ECM) and a diagnostic trouble code (DTC) is stored in engine control module (ECM) if a fault in the speed signal is detected in the brake control module (BCM). Diagnostic trouble codes (DTCs) for the vehicle speed sensor (VSS) signal are stored in the brake control module (BCM). Substitute value: Cruise control is switched off The speed signal from the transmission control module (TCM) is used (AUT) The speed signal from the brake control module (BCM) is set at 6 km/h (MAN). **NOTE: The cruise control does not function at all.**

DTC	Trouble Code Title and Conditions
DTC: ECM-511D/P0500 **1T ECM** **Years:** 2011, 2012 **Model:** C30, S40, V50 **Engine:** 2.5L L5	**Vehicle Speed Signal. (Faulty Signal Or Missing Signal):** The diagnostic trouble code (DTC) (signal missing) is stored in the engine control module (ECM) if the CAN communication between the brake control module (BCM) and the engine control module (ECM) is lost or disrupted. A fault message is transmitted to the engine control module (ECM) and a diagnostic trouble code (DTC) (faulty signal) is stored in engine control module (ECM) if a fault in the speed signal is detected in the brake control module (BCM). Diagnostic trouble codes (DTCs) for the vehicle speed sensor (VSS) signal are stored in the brake control module (BCM). Substitute value: Cruise control is switched off The speed signal from the transmission control module (TCM) is used. (AUT) The speed signal from the brake control module (BCM) is set at 6 km/h (MAN).
DTC: ECM-512B/P0863 **1T ECM, MIL: Yes** **Years:** 2011, 2012 **Model:** C30, C70, S40, V50 **Engine:** 2.5L L5	**Malfunction Indicator Lamp (MIL) Communication. Signal Missing:** The diagnostic trouble code (DTC) is stored if the engine control module (ECM) registers a fault in the CAN communication between the transmission control module (TCM) and the engine control module (ECM). The diagnostic trouble code (DTC) is diagnosed with the engine running and with battery voltage above 10.5 V
DTC: ECM-512D/P2162 **1T ECM, MIL: Yes** **Years:** 2011, 2012 **Model:** C30, S40, V50 **Engine:** 2.5L L5	**Vehicle Speed Signal. (Faulty Signal):** A fault message is transmitted to the engine control module (ECM) and a diagnostic trouble code (DTC) is stored in the engine control module (ECM) if a fault in the speed signal is detected in the brake control module (BCM). Diagnostic trouble codes (DTCs) for the vehicle speed sensor (VSS) signal are stored in the brake control module (BCM). Substitute value: Cruise control is switched off The speed signal from the transmission control module (TCM) is used. (AUT) The speed signal from the brake control module (BCM) is set at 6 km/h (MAN).
DTC: ECM-5200/P0512 **T ECM** **Years:** 2011, 2012 **Model:** C30, S40, V50 **Engine:** 2.5L L5	**Starter Motor Signal. (Signal Too High Or Too Low):** The diagnostic trouble code (DTC) is stored if the engine control module (ECM) registers engine speed (RPM) above approximately 600 rpm, speed 0 km/h, without the ignition key being in position 3 and it is interpreted as a fault (low signal). It is interpreted as a fault and the diagnostic trouble code (DTC) is stored if the engine control module (ECM) registers the ignition key in position 3 while driving.
DTC: ECM-5200/P0531 **1T ECM** **Years:** 2011, 2012 **Model:** C30, C70, S40, V50 **Engine:** 2.5L L5	**Air Conditioning (A/C) Pressure Sensor. Faulty Signal:** The diagnostic trouble code (DTC) is stored if the engine control module (ECM) detects that the pressure in the air conditioning (A/C) system has not increased for a certain time following activation of the air conditioning (A/C) compressor. The diagnostic trouble code (DTC) can be diagnosed while the engine is running and air conditioning (A/C) control is active.
DTC: ECM-520B/P0530 **1T ECM** **Years:** 2011, 2012 **Model:** C30, C70, S40, V50 **Engine:** 2.5L L5	**Air Conditioning (A/C) Pressure Sensor. Signal Missing:** The diagnostic trouble code (DTC) is stored if the engine control module (ECM) detects that there is no signal from the air conditioning (A/C) pressure sensor. The diagnostic trouble code (DTC) can be diagnosed while the engine is running and while air conditioning (A/C) control is active.
DTC: ECM-520C/P0533 **1T ECM** **Years:** 2011, 2012 **Model:** C30, C70, S40, V50 **Engine:** 2.5L L5	**Air Conditioning (A/C) Pressure Sensor. Signal Too High:** The diagnostic trouble code (DTC) is stored if the engine control module (ECM) detects that the signal from the air conditioning (A/C) pressure sensor is higher than the normal operating range. The diagnostic trouble code (DTC) can be diagnosed while the engine is running and while air conditioning (A/C) control is active.
DTC: ECM-520D/P0532 **1T ECM, MIL: Yes** **Years:** 2011, 2012 **Model:** C30, C70, S40, V50 **Engine:** 2.5L L5	**Air Conditioning (A/C) Pressure Sensor. Signal Too Low:** The diagnostic trouble code (DTC) is stored if the engine control module (ECM) detects that the signal from the air conditioning (A/C) pressure sensor is lower than the normal operating range. The diagnostic trouble code (DTC) can be diagnosed while the engine is running and while air conditioning (A/C) control is active.
DTC: ECM-530D/P1618 **2T ECM, MIL: Yes** **Years:** 2011, 2012 **Model:** C30, C70, S40, V50 **Engine:** 2.5L L5	**DTC In The Transmission Control Module (TCM). (Faulty signal):** This diagnostic trouble code (DTC) only indicates whether there is one or more emission-related diagnostic trouble codes (DTCs) registered in the transmission control module (TCM). The diagnostic trouble code (DTC) is stored in the engine control module (ECM) if the transmission control module (TCM) requests that the engine control module (ECM) should light the malfunction indicator lamp (MIL).
DTC: ECM-531C/P0500 **1T ECM, MIL: Yes** **Year:** 2011, 2012 **Model:** C70, V50 **Engine:** 2.5L L5	**Vehicle Speed Signal (VSS) Signal Missing:** Internal functions in the engine control module (ECM) check important parameters. The diagnostic trouble code (DTC) is stored if the engine control module (ECM) detects an incorrect parameter. The diagnostic trouble code (DTC) can be diagnosed when driving under specific driving conditions.

DTC	Trouble Code Title and Conditions
DTC: ECM-531D/P0502 **1T ECM, MIL: Yes** **Year:** 2011, 2012 **Model:** S40 **Engine:** 2.5L L5	**Vehicle speed signal (VSS). Signal too low:** Internal functions in the engine control module (ECM) check important parameters. The diagnostic trouble code (DTC) is stored if the engine control module (ECM) detects an incorrect parameter. The diagnostic trouble code (DTC) can be diagnosed when driving under specific driving conditions.
DTC: ECM-5320/P0501 **1T ECM, MIL: Yes** **Years:** 2011, 2012 **Model:** C30, C70, S40, V50 **Engine:** 2.5L L5	**Vehicle Speed Signal (VSS). Faulty Signal:** The Engine Control Module (ECM) monitors the engine's speed. Engine control module (ECM) receives information about the vehicle's speed from Brake control module (BCM) via the CAN-net. When the Engine control module (ECM) requests fuel shut-off, e.g. when engine braking, the speed signal from the Brake control module (BCM) and engine speed (rpm) signal are checked. The diagnostic is used to diagnose the speed signal from the Brake control module (BCM). The diagnostic trouble code (DTC) is stored if the control module detects that: The speed signal from the Brake control module (BCM) indicates that the vehicle speed has been lower than 4 km/h (2.5 mph) for too long at the same time that the engine speed has been greater than 1520 rpm and lower than 4520 rpm. **NOTE: The diagnostic trouble code (DTC) may also be stored if the speed signal from the Brake control module (BCM) is too low, e.g. if there is dirt on the wheel sensors.**
DTC: ECM-532D/P0501 **T ECM** **Year:** 2011, 2012 **Model:** S40 **Engine:** 2.5L L5	**Communication, central electronic module (CEM). Signal too high:** The diagnostic trouble code (DTC) (Signal too high) is stored in the engine control module (ECM) if the central electronic module (CEM) detects that the checksum calculated by the engine control module (ECM) does not correspond to the checksum stored in the central electronic module (CEM). The diagnostic trouble code (DTC) (Signal missing) is stored in the engine control module (ECM) if the engine control module (ECM) registers a fault in the CAN communication between the central electronic module (CEM) and the engine control module (ECM). The diagnostic trouble code (DTC) is diagnosed when the ignition is on
DTC: ECM-532D/P2177 **1T ECM, MIL: Yes** **Years:** 2011, 2012 **Model:** C30, S40, V50 **Engine:** 2.5L L5	**High Emissions. (Faulty Signal) :** Diagnostic functions in the engine control module (ECM) have activated substitute values that result in fuel shut-off. The diagnostic trouble code (DTC) is stored in the engine control module (ECM) if it detects that fuel shut-off has been activated by the diagnostic function to such an extent that emissions may be negatively affected.
DTC: ECM-540B/P250A **1T ECM** **Years:** 2011, 2012 **Model:** C30, C70, S40, V50 **Engine:** 2.5L L5	**Oil Quality, Level And Temp Sensor. Signal Missing:** The Engine control module (ECM) checks the signal from the oil level sensor. The diagnostic trouble code (DTC) is stored if the engine control module (ECM) registers that the signal from the oil level sensor is incorrect. The diagnostic trouble code (DTC) can be diagnosed when the engine is running.
DTC: ECM-540C/P250D **1T ECM, MIL: Yes** **Years:** 2011, 2012 **Model:** C30, C70, S40, V50 **Engine:** 2.5L L5	**Oil Quality, Level And Temp Sensor. Signal Too High:** The engine control module (ECM) checks the signal from the oil level sensor. The diagnostic trouble code (DTC) is stored if the engine control module (ECM) registers that the signal from the oil level sensor is too high. The diagnostic trouble code (DTC) can be diagnosed when the engine is running.
DTC: ECM-540D/P250C **1T ECM, MIL: Yes** **Years:** 2011, 2012 **Model:** C30, C70, S40, V50 **Engine:** 2.5L L5	**Oil Quality, Level And Temp Sensor. Signal Too Low:** The engine control module (ECM) checks the signal from the oil level sensor. The diagnostic trouble code (DTC) is stored if the engine control module (ECM) detects that there is no signal from the oil level sensor. The diagnostic trouble code (DTC) can be diagnosed when the engine is running.
DTC: ECM-5500/P250B **1T ECM** **Years:** 2011, 2012 **Model:** C30, C70, S40, V50 **Engine:** 2.5L L5	**Oil Level Sensor. Faulty Signal:** The engine control module (ECM) checks the signal from the oil level sensor. The diagnostic trouble code (DTC) is stored if the engine control module (ECM) registers that the signal from the oil level sensor is outside a reasonable operating range. The diagnostic trouble code (DTC) is diagnosed when the engine is idling.
DTC: ECM-552C/P0197 **1T ECM** **Years:** 2011, 2012 **Model:** C30, C70, S40, V50 **Engine:** 2.5L L5	**Oil Temperature Sensor. Signal Too High:** The Engine control module (ECM) compares the signal from the oil temperature sensor with the signal from the engine temperature sensor. The signal is used to calculating service interval indication. The diagnostic trouble code (DTC) is stored if the engine control module (ECM) detects that the temperature differs too much between the oil temperature sensor and the coolant temperature sensor. The diagnostic trouble code can be diagnosed after the vehicle has been parked for more than 8 hours and then driven for more than 10 minutes.
DTC: ECM-552D/P0198 **1T ECM** **Years:** 2011, 2012 **Model:** C30, C70, S40, V50 **Engine:** 2.5L L5	**Oil Temperature Sensor. Signal Too Low:** The Engine control module (ECM) compares the signal from the oil temperature sensor with the signal from the engine temperature sensor. The diagnostic trouble code (DTC) is stored if the engine control module (ECM) detects that the temperature differs too much between the oil temperature sensor and the coolant temperature sensor. The diagnostic trouble code (DTC) can be diagnosed after approx. 10 minutes with the engine running.

DTC	Trouble Code Title and Conditions
DTC: ECM-6000/P0645-647 **T ECM** **Years:** 2011, 2012 **Model:** C30, S40, V50 **Engine:** 2.5L L5	**A/C Relay. (Signal Too High Or Too Low):** This diagnostic trouble code (DTC) is stored if the engine control module (ECM) registers a short circuit to ground or supply voltage or an open-circuit in the control signal cable for the air conditioning (A/C) relay.
DTC: ECM-600B/P0243 **1T ECM, MIL: Yes** **Years:** 2011, 2012 **Model:** C30, C70, S40, V50 **Engine:** 2.5L L5	**Turbocharger (TC) Control Valve. Signal Missing:** The engine control module (ECM) checks the signal cable for the turbocharger (TC) control valve. The diagnostic trouble code (DTC) is stored if the engine control module (ECM) detects an open-circuit in the signal cable for the turbocharger (TC) control valve. The diagnostic trouble code (DTC) can be diagnosed during control of the boost pressure.
DTC: ECM-600C/P0246 **1T ECM, MIL: Yes** **Years:** 2011, 2012 **Model:** C30, C70, S40, V50 **Engine:** 2.5L L5	**Turbocharger (TC) Control Valve. Signal Too High:** The engine control module (ECM) checks the signal cable for the turbocharger (TC) control valve. The diagnostic trouble code (DTC) is stored if the engine control module (ECM) detects that the voltage in the signal cable for the turbocharger (TC) control valve is too high. The diagnostic trouble code (DTC) can be diagnosed during control of the boost pressure.
DTC: ECM-600D/P0245 **1T ECM, MIL: Yes** **Years:** 2011, 2012 **Model:** C30, C70, S40, V50 **Engine:** 2.5L L5	**Turbocharger (TC) Control Valve. Signal Too Low:** The engine control module (ECM) checks the signal cable for the turbocharger (TC) control valve. The diagnostic trouble code (DTC) is stored if the engine control module (ECM) detects that the voltage in the signal cable for the turbocharger (TC) control valve is too low. The diagnostic trouble code (DTC) can be diagnosed during control of the boost pressure.
DTC: ECM-603C/P0234 **1T ECM** **Years:** 2011, 2012 **Model:** C30, C70, S40, V50 **Engine:** 2.5L L5	**Turbocharger (TC) Control System. Signal Too High:** The engine control module (ECM) checks the boost pressure. The diagnostic trouble code (DTC) is stored if the measured boost pressure from the boost pressure sensor (actual value) is higher than the control module target value (desired value). The diagnostic trouble code (DTC) can be diagnosed when the engine speed (RPM) and load is above a certain value.
DTC: ECM-603D/P0299 **T ECM** **Years:** 2011, 2012 **Model:** C30, C70, S40, V50 **Engine:** 2.5L L5	**Turbocharger (TC) Control System. Signal Too Low:** The engine control module (ECM) checks the boost pressure. The diagnostic trouble code (DTC) is stored if the measured boost pressure from the boost pressure sensor (actual value) is lower than the control module target value (desired value). The diagnostic trouble code (DTC) can be diagnosed when the engine speed (RPM) and load is above a certain value.
DTC: ECM-6100/P0484 **1T ECM, MIL: Yes** **Years:** 2011, 2012 **Model:** C30, S40, V50 **Engine:** 2.5L L5	**Engine Cooling Fan (FC) (Faulty Signal, Too High Or Too Low):** The diagnostic trouble code (DTC) is stored if the engine control module (ECM) detects a short-circuit to supply voltage (high signal), short-circuit to ground or an open-circuit (low signal) in the control signal circuit between the engine cooling fan (FC) control module and the engine control module (ECM). The diagnostic trouble code (DTC) is stored if the engine cooling fan (FC) control module registers that the fan blades are obstructed or that there is no power supply.
DTC: ECM-6110/P000A **1T ECM, MIL: Yes** **Years:** 2011, 2012 **Model:** C30, C70, S40, V50 **Engine:** 2.5L L5	**Camshaft Position Control, Intake. Slow:** The engine control module (ECM) checks that control of the intake camshaft is quick enough. This means that the intake camshaft (actual value) reaches the position requested by the engine control module (ECM) quickly enough. The diagnostic trouble code (DTC) is stored if the requested position is not reached within a certain time. The diagnostic trouble code (DTC) can be diagnosed by the engine control module (ECM) when the engine is running and the camshaft control is active.
DTC: ECM-611B/P000A **1T ECM, MIL: Yes** **Years:** 2011, 2012 **Model:** C30, C70, S40, V50 **Engine:** 2.5L L5	**Camshaft Control, Intake. Faulty:** The engine control module (ECM) checks that the position of the intake camshaft (actual value) corresponds to the requested position (desired value). The diagnostic trouble code (DTC) is stored if the requested position is not reached. The diagnostic trouble code (DTC) can be diagnosed while the engine is running and while camshaft control is active.
DTC: ECM-612B/P0075 **1T ECM, MIL: Yes** **Years:** 2011, 2012 **Model:** C30, C70, S40, V50 **Engine:** 2.5L L5	**Camshaft Reset Valve, Intake. Signal Missing, :** The engine control module (ECM) checks the signal cable for the reset valve for the intake camshaft. The diagnostic trouble code (DTC) is stored if the engine control module (ECM) detects an open-circuit in the signal cable for the reset valve. The diagnostic trouble code (DTC) can be diagnosed at ignition on and with the engine running.
DTC: ECM-612C/P0077 **1T ECM, MIL: Yes** **Years:** 2011, 2012 **Model:** C30, C70, S40, V50 **Engine:** 2.5L L5	**Camshaft Reset Valve, Intake. Signal Too High:** The engine control module (ECM) checks the signal cable for the reset valve for the intake camshaft. The diagnostic trouble code (DTC) is stored if the engine control module (ECM) detects that the signal from the reset valve is too high. The diagnostic trouble code (DTC) can be diagnosed at ignition on and with the engine running

DTC	Trouble Code Title and Conditions
DTC: ECM-612D/P0076 **1T ECM, MIL: Yes** **Years:** 2011, 2012 **Model:** C30, S40, V50 **Engine:** 2.5L L5	**Camshaft Reset Valve, Intake. Signal Too Low:** The engine control module (ECM) checks the signal cable for the reset valve for the intake camshaft. The diagnostic trouble code (DTC) is stored if the engine control module (ECM) detects that the signal from the reset valve is too low. The diagnostic trouble code (DTC) can be diagnosed at ignition on and with the engine running.
DTC: ECM-6140/P000B **1T ECM, MIL: Yes** **Years:** 2011, 2012 **Model:** C30, C70, S40, V50 **Engine:** 2.5L L5	**Camshaft Control, Exhaust. Slow:** The engine control module (ECM) checks that control of the exhaust camshaft is quick enough. This means that the exhaust camshaft (actual value) reaches the position requested by the engine control module (ECM) quickly enough. The diagnostic trouble code (DTC) is stored if the requested position is not reached within a certain time. The diagnostic trouble code (DTC) can be diagnosed while the engine is running and while camshaft control is active.
DTC: ECM-614B/P000B **1T ECM, MIL: Yes** **Years:** 2011, 2012 **Model:** C30, C70, S40, V50 **Engine:** 2.5L L5	**Camshaft Control, Exhaust. Faulty:** The engine control module (ECM) checks that the position of the exhaust camshaft (actual value) corresponds to the requested position (desired value). The diagnostic trouble code (DTC) is stored if the requested position is not reached. The diagnostic trouble code (DTC) can be diagnosed while the engine is running and while camshaft control is active.
DTC: ECM-616B/P0078 **1T ECM, MIL: Yes** **Years:** 2011, 2012 **Model:** C30, C70, S40, V50 **Engine:** 2.5L L5	**Exhaust Camshaft Reset Valve, Signal Missing:** The engine control module (ECM) checks the signal cable for the reset valve for the exhaust camshaft. The diagnostic trouble code (DTC) is stored if the engine control module (ECM) detects an open-circuit in the signal cable for the reset valve. The diagnostic trouble code (DTC) can be diagnosed at ignition on and with the engine running.
DTC: ECM-616C/P0080 **1T ECM, MIL: Yes** **Years:** 2011, 2012 **Model:** C30, C70, S40, V50 **Engine:** 2.5L L5	**Camshaft Reset Valve, Intake. Signal Too High:** The engine control module (ECM) checks the signal cable for the reset valve for the exhaust camshaft. The diagnostic trouble code (DTC) is stored if the engine control module (ECM) detects that the signal from the reset valve is too high. The diagnostic trouble code (DTC) can be diagnosed at ignition on and with the engine running.
DTC: ECM-616D/P0079 **1T ECM, MIL: Yes** **Years:** 2011, 2012 **Model:** C30, C70, S40, V50 **Engine:** 2.5L L5	**Camshaft Reset Valve, Intake. Signal Too Low:** The engine control module (ECM) checks the signal cable for the reset valve for the exhaust camshaft. The diagnostic trouble code (DTC) is stored if the engine control module (ECM) detects that the signal from the reset valve is too low. The diagnostic trouble code (DTC) can be diagnosed at ignition on and with the engine running.
DTC: ECM-618C/P054A **1T ECM, MIL: Yes** **Years:** 2011, 2012 **Model:** C30, C70, S40, V50 **Engine:** 2.5L L5	**Exhaust Camshaft Control During Cold Start:** The engine control module (ECM) checks that control of the exhaust camshaft is quick enough. This means that the exhaust camshaft (actual value) reaches the position requested by the engine control module (ECM) quickly enough. The diagnostic trouble code (DTC) is stored if the requested position is not reached within a certain time. The diagnostic trouble code can be diagnosed at cold-start, with the engine running and camshaft control active. **NOTE: The term cold-start means that an engine starts when catalytic converter heating is requested by Engine control module (ECM). Catalytic converter heating is requested when the engine has been off and cooled for at least 15 minutes, and the engine temperature at start is lower than 70 °C.**
DTC: ECM-619C/P052A **1T ECM, MIL: Yes** **Years:** 2011, 2012 **Model:** C30, C70, S40, V50 **Engine:** 2.5L L5	**Inlet Camshaft Control During Cold Start:** The engine control module (ECM) checks that control of the intake camshaft is quick enough. This means that the intake camshaft (actual value) reaches the position requested by the engine control module (ECM) quickly enough. The diagnostic trouble code (DTC) is stored if the requested position is not reached within a certain time. The diagnostic trouble code can be diagnosed at cold-start, with the engine running and camshaft control active. **NOTE: The term cold-start means that an engine starts when catalytic converter heating is requested by Engine control module (ECM). Catalytic converter heating is requested when the engine has been off and cooled for at least 15 minutes, and the engine temperature at start is lower than 70 °C.**
DTC: ECM-620A/P0506/P0507 **1T ECM, MIL: Yes** **Years:** 2011, 2012 **Model:** C30, S40, V50 **Engine:** 2.5L L5	**Idling speed (Too High Or Too Low):** The diagnostic trouble code (DTC) is stored if the engine control module (ECM) registers that the idling speed is 100 rpm lower or 200 rpm higher than the nominal idling speed. There are diagnostics for the diagnostic trouble code (DTC) with the engine at operating temperature (>80 °C), the car stationary and idling.
DTC: ECM-620B/P0485/P1480 **1T ECM** **Years:** 2011, 2012 **Model:** C30, C70, S40, V50 **Engine:** 2.5L L5	**Engine Cooling Fan Control Module, Signal Missing:** The diagnostic trouble code (DTC) is stored in the engine control module (ECM) if the engine cooling fan control module registers that the temperature in the driver stage for the engine cooling fan control module is too high or if the fan blade is blocked. The diagnostic trouble code (DTC) can be diagnosed when the engine is running.

DTC	Trouble Code Title and Conditions
DTC: ECM-620C/P0484 **1T ECM** **Years:** 2011, 2012 **Model:** C30, C70, S40, V50 **Engine:** 2.5L L5	**Engine Cooling Fan (FC) Control Module, Signal Too High:** The diagnostic trouble code (DTC) is stored in the engine control module (ECM) if the engine cooling fan control module registers that the temperature in the driver stage for the engine cooling fan control module is too high or if the fan blade is blocked. The diagnostic trouble code (DTC) can be diagnosed during the engine start process.
DTC: ECM-621B/P0480 **1T ECM** **Years:** 2011, 2012 **Model:** C30, C70, S40, V50 **Engine:** 2.5L L5	**Engine Cooling Fan (FC), Signal Missing:** The engine control module (ECM) checks the control signal cable for the engine cooling fan (FC). The diagnostic trouble code (DTC) is stored if the engine control module (ECM) detects a fault in the engine cooling fan (FC) module. The diagnostic trouble code (DTC) can be diagnosed when the ignition is switched on.
DTC: ECM-621C/P0692 **1T ECM** **Years:** 2011, 2012 **Model:** C30, C70, S40, V50 **Engine:** 2.5L L5	**Engine Cooling Fan (FC), Signal Too High:** The engine control module (ECM) checks the control signal cable for the engine cooling fan (FC). The diagnostic trouble code (DTC) is stored if the engine control module (ECM) detects a fault in the engine cooling fan (FC) module. The diagnostic trouble code (DTC) can be diagnosed when the ignition is switched on.
DTC: ECM-621D/P0691 **1T ECM** **Years:** 2011, 2012 **Model:** C30, C70, S40, V50 **Engine:** 2.5L L5	**Engine Cooling Fan (FC), Signal Too Low:** The engine control module (ECM) checks the control signal cable for the engine cooling fan (FC). The diagnostic trouble code (DTC) is stored if the engine control module (ECM) detects a fault in the engine cooling fan (FC) module. The diagnostic trouble code (DTC) can be diagnosed when the ignition is switched on.
DTC: ECM-6220/P0494 **1T ECM, MIL: Yes** **Years:** 2011, 2012 **Model:** C30, C70, S40, V50 **Engine:** 2.5L L5	**Engine Cooling Fan (FC). Faulty Signal:** The engine control module (ECM) monitors the engine temperature under different running conditions. If the signal from the engine temperature sensor corresponds to a temperature that is higher than a specific limit value despite a low engine load and speed, the control module interprets this as a fault and the diagnostic trouble code is stored. The diagnostic trouble code (DTC) can be diagnosed when the engine is running.
DTC: ECM-630B/P0645 **1T ECM** **Years:** 2011, 2012 **Model:** C30, C70, S40, V50 **Engine:** 2.5L L5	**A/C Relay, Signal Missing:** The engine control module (ECM) checks the signal cable for controlling the air conditioning (A/C) relay. The diagnostic trouble code (DTC) is stored if the engine control module (ECM) detects an open-circuit in the signal cable for the air conditioning (A/C) relay. The diagnostic trouble code (DTC) can be diagnosed at ignition on and with the engine running.
DTC: ECM-630C/P647 **1T ECM** **Years:** 2011, 2012 **Model:** C30, C70, S40, V50 **Engine:** 2.5L L5	**A/C Relay, Signal Too High:** The engine control module (ECM) checks the signal cable for controlling the air conditioning (A/C) relay. The diagnostic trouble code (DTC) is stored if the engine control module (ECM) detects that the signal from the air conditioning (A/C) relay is too high. The diagnostic trouble code (DTC) can be diagnosed at ignition on and with the engine running.
DTC: ECM-630D/P0646 **1T ECM** **Years:** 2011, 2012 **Model:** C30, C70, S40, V50 **Engine:** 2.5L L5	**A/C Relay, Signal Too Low:** The engine control module (ECM) checks the signal cable for controlling the air conditioning (A/C) relay. The diagnostic trouble code (DTC) is stored if the engine control module (ECM) detects that the signal from the air conditioning (A/C) relay is too low. The diagnostic trouble code (DTC) can be diagnosed at ignition on and with the engine running.
DTC: ECM-6400/P0010 **1T ECM, MIL: Yes** **Years:** 2011, 2012 **Model:** C30, S40, V50 **Engine:** 2.5L L5	**Camshaft Reset Valve (Intake Signal Too High Too Low Or Missing):** The diagnostic trouble code (DTC) is stored if the engine control module (ECM) detects a short-circuit to supply voltage (high signal), short-circuit to ground (low signal) or an open-circuit (signal missing) in the signal circuit between the intake camshaft reset valve and the engine control module (ECM). The diagnostic trouble code (DTC) can be diagnosed when the engine is running.
DTC: ECM-6400/P075-77 **1T ECM, MIL: Yes** **Years:** 2011, 2012 **Model:** C30, S40, V50 **Engine:** 2.5L L5	**Camshaft Reset Valve (Intake Signal Too High Too Low Or Missing):** The diagnostic trouble code (DTC) is stored if the engine control module (ECM) detects a short-circuit to supply voltage (high signal), short-circuit to ground (low signal) or an open-circuit (signal missing) in the signal circuit between the intake camshaft reset valve and the engine control module (ECM). The diagnostic trouble code (DTC) can be diagnosed when the engine is running.
DTC: ECM-640A/P0011 **1T ECM, MIL: Yes** **Years:** 2011, 2012 **Model:** C30, S40, V50 **Engine:** 2.5L L5	**Inlet Camshaft Control (Signal Too High Or Too Low):** The engine control module (ECM) checks that control of the intake camshaft is rapid enough by measuring the time taken to deploy the camshaft to the requested angle. The diagnostic trouble code (DTC) is stored if the engine control module (ECM) detects that deployment of the camshaft is too slow (signal too high) or to slow when the camshaft returns (signal too low). The diagnostic trouble code is diagnosed by engine control module (ECM) when the engine is warm and engine speed is higher than 1300 rpm.

DTC	Trouble Code Title and Conditions
DTC: ECM-640C/P2281 **1T ECM** **Years:** 2011, 2012 **Model:** C30, C70, S40, V50 **Engine:** 2.5L L5	**Turbocharger (TC) Control System, Signal Too High:** The diagnostic trouble code (DTC) is stored if the ratio between the measured boost pressure (measured value from the boost pressure sensor before the throttle) and the calculated boost pressure (calculated value after the throttle) is incorrect. The diagnostic trouble code (DTC) can be diagnosed when the engine is running and the turbocharger (TC) control system is not active.
DTC: ECM-640D/P2281 **1T ECM** **Years:** 2011, 2012 **Model:** C30, C70, S40, V50 **Engine:** 2.5L L5	**Turbocharger (TC) Control System, Signal Too Low:** The diagnostic trouble code (DTC) is stored if the ratio between the measured boost pressure (measured value from the boost pressure sensor before the throttle) and the calculated boost pressure (calculated value after the throttle) is incorrect. The diagnostic trouble code (DTC) can be diagnosed when the engine is running and the turbocharger (TC) control system is active.
DTC: ECM-640F/P0011 **1T ECM, MIL: Yes** **Years:** 2011, 2012 **Model:** C30, S40, V50 **Engine:** 2.5L L5	**Camshaft Position, Inlet (Misaligned, Too High Or Too Low):** The engine control module (ECM) checks that the camshaft is in the correct position in relation to the position of the crankshaft. If the camshaft position is incorrect, the control module will adjust the adaptation for the camshaft position. The diagnostic trouble code (DTC) is stored if the adaptation is too great. The diagnosis is active when the engine is on and is warm.
DTC: ECM-6600/P0616 **T ECM** **Years:** 2011, 2012 **Model:** C30, C70, S40, V50 **Engine:** 2.5L L5	**Starter Motor Relay (Signal Too High Or Too Low):** The engine control module (ECM) checks the signal cable for the starter motor relay coil. The diagnostic trouble code (DTC) is stored (high signal) if the engine control module (ECM) detects that the signal is high despite the ignition switch being in position 2 (ignition position). The diagnostic trouble code (DTC) is stored (low signal) if the engine control module (ECM) detects that the signal is low despite the ignition switch being in position 3 (starting position).
DTC: ECM-6600/P0616/P0617 **T ECM** **Years:** 2011, 2012 **Model:** C30, C70, S40, V50 **Engine:** 2.5L L5	**Starter Motor Relay (Open Circuit):** The engine control module (ECM) checks the signal cable for the starter motor relay coil. (The starter motor does not turn) The diagnostic trouble code (DTC) is stored if the control module detects that: Open circuit on signal cable. The diagnostic trouble code (DTC) can be diagnosed when: Ignition on before start attempt.
DTC: ECM-673C/P0017 **1T ECM, MIL: Yes** **Years:** 2011, 2012 **Model:** C30, C70, S40, V50 **Engine:** 2.5L L5	**Camshaft Position, Exhaust. High:** The engine control module (ECM) checks the angle of the camshaft (its position in relation to the crankshaft). If the angle of the exhaust camshaft is too high (the camshaft is "in front of" the crankshaft), the engine control module (ECM) will adapt the angle of the camshaft. The diagnostic trouble code (DTC) is stored if the adaptation value is above a certain level. The diagnostic trouble code (DTC) can be diagnosed when the engine is at operating temperature and is idling.
DTC: ECM-673D/P0017 **1T ECM, MIL: Yes** **Years:** 2011, 2012 **Model:** C30, C70, S40, V50 **Engine:** 2.5L L5	**Camshaft Position, Exhaust. Low:** The engine control module (ECM) checks the angle of the camshaft (its position in relation to the crankshaft). If the angle of the exhaust camshaft is too low (the camshaft is "behind" the crankshaft), the engine control module (ECM) will adapt the angle of the camshaft. The diagnostic trouble code (DTC) is stored if the adaptation value is below a certain level. The diagnostic trouble code (DTC) can be diagnosed when the engine is at operating temperature and is idling.
DTC: ECM-674C/P0016 **1T ECM, MIL: Yes** **Years:** 2011, 2012 **Model:** C30, C70, S40, V50 **Engine:** 2.5L L5	**Camshaft Position, Intake. High:** The engine control module (ECM) checks the angle of the camshaft (its position in relation to the crankshaft). If the angle of the intake camshaft is too high (the camshaft is "in front of" the crankshaft), the engine control module (ECM) will adapt the angle of the camshaft. The diagnostic trouble code (DTC) is stored if the adaptation value is above a certain level. The diagnostic trouble code (DTC) can be diagnosed when the engine is at operating temperature and is idling.
DTC: ECM-674D/P0016 **1T ECM, MIL: Yes** **Years:** 2011, 2012 **Model:** C30, C70, S40, V50 **Engine:** 2.5L L5	**Camshaft Position, Intake. Low:** The engine control module (ECM) checks the angle of the camshaft (its position in relation to the crankshaft). If the intake camshaft's angle position deviates and is too low (the camshaft is "after" the crankshaft) during fuel trim, the Engine control module (ECM) interprets this as a fault and stores a DTC. The control module's test for the diagnostic trouble code (DTC) starts when: Engine idling, hot engine.
DTC: ECM-700C/P0669 **1T ECM** **Years:** 2011, 2012 **Model:** C30, C70, S40, V50 **Engine:** 2.5L L5	**Engine Control Module (ECM), Internal Fault. Signal Too High:** The diagnostic trouble code (DTC) is stored if the engine control module (ECM) detects a fault in the circuit for the internal temperature sensor in the control module. The diagnostic trouble code (DTC) can be diagnosed when the ignition is switched on.

DTC	Trouble Code Title and Conditions
DTC: ECM-700D/P0668 **1T ECM** **Years:** 2011, 2012 **Model:** C30, C70, S40, V50 **Engine:** 2.5L L5	**Engine Control Module (ECM), Internal Fault. Signal Too Low:** The diagnostic trouble code (DTC) is stored if the engine control module (ECM) detects a fault in the circuit for the internal temperature sensor in the control module. The diagnostic trouble code (DTC) can be diagnosed when the ignition is switched on.
DTC: ECM-7010/P0634 **1T ECM** **Years:** 2011, 2012 **Model:** C30, C70, S40, V50 **Engine:** 2.5L L5	**Engine Control Module (ECM), Temperature. Faulty Signal:** The diagnostic trouble code (DTC) is stored if the temperature in the engine control module (ECM) exceeds 95 °C. The diagnostic trouble code (DTC) can be diagnosed when the ignition is switched on.
DTC: ECM-7020/P0634 **1T ECM** **Years:** 2011, 2012 **Model:** C30, C70, S40, V50 **Engine:** 2.5L L5	**Engine Control Module (ECM), Temperature. Faulty Signal:** The diagnostic trouble code (DTC) is stored if the temperature in the engine control module (ECM) exceeds 105 °C. The diagnostic trouble code (DTC) can be diagnosed when the ignition is switched on.
DTC: ECM-7100/P0634/U0426 **1T ECM** **Years:** 2011, 2012 **Model:** C30, C70, S40, V50 **Engine:** 2.5L L5	**Immobilizer Communication. Faulty Signal:** The engine control module (ECM) contains a code for the immobilizer which is unique to each car. Before the engine can be started, the immobilizer code is checked to ensure that it corresponds to both the central electronic module (CEM) and the engine control module (ECM). The diagnostic trouble code (DTC) is stored if the immobilizer code does not correspond. The diagnostic trouble code (DTC) can be diagnosed when the ignition is switched on.
DTC: ECM-710C/P0633 **1T ECM** **Years:** 2011, 2012 **Model:** C30, C70, S40, V50 **Engine:** 2.5L L5	**Immobilizer Communication, Signal Too High:** The engine control module (ECM) contains a code for the immobilizer which is unique to each car. Before the engine can be started, the immobilizer code is checked to ensure that it corresponds to both the central electronic module (CEM) and the engine control module (ECM). The diagnostic trouble code (DTC) will be stored if the engine control module (ECM) is not programmed or if an internal fault is detected in the engine control module (ECM). The diagnostic trouble code (DTC) can be diagnosed when the ignition is switched on.
DTC: ECM-7140/P0668/P0669 **T ECM** **Years:** 2011, 2012 **Model:** C30, S40, V50 **Engine:** 2.5L L5	**Temperature Sensor Engine Control Module (ECM). (Signal Too High Or Too Low):** The diagnostic trouble code (DTC) is stored if the engine control module (ECM) registers a fault in the temperature sensor circuit inside the module. The diagnostic trouble code (DTC) can be diagnosed when the ignition is switched on.
DTC: ECM-715D/P1637/P1638 **1T ECM** **Years:** 2011, 2012 **Model:** C30, S40, V50 **Engine:** 2.5L L5	**Engine Control Module (ECM) (Faulty Signal):** The diagnostic trouble code (DTC) is stored if the engine control module (ECM) detects that the internal temperature in the engine control module (ECM) has exceeded 90 °C for longer than a total of 200 hours. The diagnostic trouble code (DTC) is diagnosed when the ignition is on.
DTC: ECM-716D/P1637 **T ECM** **Years:** 2011, 2012 **Model:** C30, S40, V50 **Engine:** 2.5L L5	**Engine Control Module (ECM) (Faulty Signal):** The diagnostic trouble code (DTC) is stored if the engine control module (ECM) detects that the internal temperature in the engine control module (ECM) has exceeded 120 °C for at least 30 minutes at a time. The diagnostic trouble code (DTC) is diagnosed when the ignition is on.
DTC: ECM-7300/P0607/U0103 **1T ECM** **Years:** 2011, 2012 **Model:** C30, C70, S40, V50 **Engine:** 2.5L L5	**Gear Position Sensor. Faulty Signal:** The engine control module (ECM) checks the signals for gear position sensor positions P and N. The diagnostic trouble code (DTC) (Faulty signal) is stored if the engine control module (ECM) detects that the signal for P and N via CAN communication is missing or is incorrect. The diagnostic trouble code (DTC) can be diagnosed when the ignition is switched on.
DTC: ECM-730B/P0850 **1T ECM** **Years:** 2011, 2012 **Model:** C30, C70, S40, V50 **Engine:** 2.5L L5	**Gear Position Sensor, Signal Missing:** The engine control module (ECM) checks the signals for gear position sensor positions P and N. The diagnostic trouble code (DTC) is stored if the engine control module (ECM) detects a difference between the directly connected signal and the signal via CAN communication for the gear position sensor position. The diagnostic trouble code (DTC) can be diagnosed when the ignition is switched on.
DTC: ECM-8000/P0603 **1T ECM, MIL: Yes** **Years:** 2011, 2012 **Model:** C30, S40, V50 **Engine:** 2.5L L5	**12 Volt Power Supply (Signal Too Low):** When the ignition is switched on, the 12 volt supply to the engine control module (ECM) is checked. The diagnostic trouble code (DTC) is stored if there is no voltage. The diagnostic trouble code (DTC) can be diagnosed when the ignition is switched on.

DTC	Trouble Code Title and Conditions
DTC: ECM-8010/P0562/P0563 **T ECM** **Years:** 2011, 2012 **Model:** C30, S40, V50 **Engine:** 2.5L L5	**Battery Voltage (Signal Too High Or Too Low):** The diagnostic trouble code (DTC) is stored if the engine control module (ECM) detects that the battery voltage exceeds 16 V (high signal) or is below 8 V (low signal) and it is interpreted as a fault. The diagnostic trouble code (DTC) is diagnosed at ignition on and with the engine running.
DTC: ECM-820A/P0685 **T ECM, MIL: Yes** **Years:** 2011, 2012 **Model:** C30, S40, V50 **Engine:** 2.5L L5	**System Relay (Faulty Signal):** The engine control module (ECM) performs internal checks after the ignition has been switched off. These checks are complete within 10 minutes. The engine control module (ECM) then cancels the activation of the system relay coil. The diagnostic trouble code (DTC) is stored if the control module registers that the system relay is still engaged after the activation is cancelled.
DTC: ECM-820C/P0563 **T ECM** **Years:** 2011, 2012 **Model:** C30, C70, S40, V50 **Engine:** 2.5L L5	**Battery Voltage, Signal Too High:** The engine control module (ECM) checks the power supply from the system relay. The diagnostic trouble code (DTC) is stored if the engine control module (ECM) detects that the voltage from the system relay is higher than a certain value. The diagnostic trouble code (DTC) can be diagnosed at ignition on or when the engine is running.
DTC: ECM-820D/P0562 **T ECM** **Years:** 2011, 2012 **Model:** C30, C70, S40, V50 **Engine:** 2.5L L5	**Battery Voltage, Signal Too Low:** The engine control module (ECM) checks the power supply from the system relay. The diagnostic trouble code (DTC) is stored if the engine control module (ECM) detects that the voltage from the system relay is lower than a certain value. The diagnostic trouble code (DTC) can be diagnosed at ignition on or when the engine is running.
DTC: ECM-8210/P2510 **T ECM** **Years:** 2011, 2012 **Model:** C30, C70, S40, V50 **Engine:** 2.5L L5	**System Relay, Faulty Signal:** The engine control module (ECM) checks the power supply from the system relay. The diagnostic trouble code (DTC) is stored if the engine control module (ECM) detects that the power supply from the engine control module (ECM) to the throttle unit is lower than 8 V. The diagnostic trouble code (DTC) can be diagnosed when the ignition is switched on.
DTC: ECM-8300/P0620 **T ECM** **Years:** 2011, 2012 **Model:** C30, C70, S40, V50 **Engine:** 2.5L L5	**Alternator Control Module (ACM), Faulty:** The engine control module (ECM) uses LIN communication to communicate with the alternator control module (ACM). The diagnostic trouble code (DTC) is stored if the alternator control module (ACM) transmits information to the engine control module (ECM) indicating that the temperature of the generator (GEN) is above or certain value of indicating a mechanical fault (the engine speed (rpm) is above a certain value but the generator (GEN) is stationary). The diagnostic trouble code (DTC) can be diagnosed when the engine speed (RPM) is 600 rpm or higher
DTC: ECM-830B/P2502 **1T ECM** **Years:** 2011, 2012 **Model:** C30, C70, S40, V50 **Engine:** 2.5L L5	**Alternator Control Module (ACM), Faulty Communication:** The engine control module (ECM) transmits and receives information via a standardized serial communication method - LIN (Local Interconnect Network). The diagnostic trouble code (DTC) is stored if the engine control module (ECM) detects interference in communication with the alternator control module (ACM). The diagnostic trouble code (DTC) can be diagnosed when the ignition is switched on.
DTC: ECM-830C/P2504 **T ECM** **Years:** 2011, 2012 **Model:** C30, C70, S40, V50 **Engine:** 2.5L L5	**Alternator Control Module (ACM), Faulty Signal:** The engine control module (ECM) uses CAN communication to communicate with the central electronic module (CEM). A diagnostic trouble code (DTC) is stored in the engine control module (ECM) if the central electronic module (CEM) detects over voltage in the power supply system. This diagnostic trouble code (DTC) is always stored along with another diagnostic trouble code (DTC) for the power supply system. The diagnostic trouble code (DTC) can be diagnosed when the engine is running.
DTC: ECM-830D/P2503 **1T ECM** **Years:** 2011, 2012 **Model:** C30, C70, S40, V50 **Engine:** 2.5L L5	**Alternator Control Module (ACM), Signal Too High:** The engine control module (ECM) uses LIN communication to communicate with the alternator control module (ACM). The diagnostic trouble code (DTC) is stored if the alternator control module (ACM) transmits information to the engine control module (ECM) about an electrical fault in the generator (GEN). The diagnostic trouble code (DTC) can be diagnosed when the engine is running.
DTC: ECM-8400/P0642/P0643 **1T ECM** **Years:** 2011, 2012 **Model:** C30, C70, S40, V50 **Engine:** 2.5L L5	**5 Volt Power Supply (Signal Too Low Or Too High):** The diagnostic trouble code (DTC) is stored if the engine control module (ECM) detects that the 5 volt supply circuit for sensors has a voltage higher than 6 V (high signal) or lower than 4 V (low signal) and it is interpreted as a fault.

DTC	Trouble Code Title and Conditions
DTC: ECM-8410/P0512 **T ECM** **Years:** 2011, 2012 **Model:** C30, C70, S40, V50 **Engine:** 2.5L L5	**Auto starting, Engine Speed. Signal Too Low:** Engine control module (ECM) checks the signal for engine speed at start. If the Engine control module (ECM) detects that the engine speed is lower than a certain value for a certain time, (depending on the temperature), the control module interprets this as a malfunction and the diagnostic trouble code is generated. The diagnostic trouble code (DTC) can be diagnosed when starting the engine.
DTC: ECM-841B/P0512 **T ECM** **Years:** 2011, 2012 **Model:** C30, C70, S40, V50 **Engine:** 2.5L L5	**Auto starting, Power Supply. Signal Too Low:** Engine control module (ECM) checks the voltage feed at start. If the Engine control module (ECM) detects that the voltage feed is lower than a certain value, during a certain time, the control module interprets this as a malfunction and the diagnostic trouble code is generated. The diagnostic trouble code (DTC) can be diagnosed when starting the engine.
DTC: ECM-842C/P0617 **T ECM** **Years:** 2011, 2012 **Model:** C30, C70, S40, V50 **Engine:** 2.5L L5	**Starter Motor Relay, Signal Too High:** Engine Control Module (ECM) checks the starter motor relay. If Engine Control Module (ECM) registers that the starter motor relay's signal cable has a voltage that is higher than a certain limit value for a certain time, this is interpreted as a malfunction and the diagnostic trouble code (DTC) is generated. The diagnostic trouble code (DTC) can be diagnosed when starting the engine.
DTC: ECM-842D/P0617 **T ECM** **Years:** 2011, 2012 **Model:** C30, C70, S40, V50 **Engine:** 2.5L L5	**Starter Motor Relay, Signal Too Low:** Engine Control Module (ECM) checks the starter motor relay. If Engine Control Module (ECM) registers that the starter motor relay's signal cable has a voltage that is lower than a certain limit value for a certain time, this is interpreted as a malfunction and the diagnostic trouble code (DTC) is generated. The diagnostic trouble code (DTC) can be diagnosed when starting the engine.
DTC: ECM-843B/P0616 **T ECM** **Years:** 2011, 2012 **Model:** C30, C70, S40, V50 **Engine:** 2.5L L5	**Starter Motor Relay, Open:** The engine control module (ECM) checks the signal from the starter motor relay via the ground cable. The diagnostic trouble code (DTC) is stored if the control module detects that: No or faulty signal. The control module's test for the diagnostic trouble code (DTC) starts in the event of: After start.
DTC: ECM-843C/P0616 **T** **Years:** 2011, 2012 **Model:** C30, C70, S40, V50 **Engine:** 2.5L L5	**Starter Motor Relay, Signal Too High:** Engine Control Module (ECM) checks the starter motor relay. If Engine Control Module (ECM) registers that the starter motor relay's signal cable has a voltage that is higher than a certain limit value for a certain time, this is interpreted as a malfunction and the diagnostic trouble code (DTC) is generated. The diagnostic trouble code (DTC) can be diagnosed when starting the engine.
DTC: ECM-843D/P0616 **T ECM** **Years:** 2011, 2012 **Model:** C30, C70, S40, V50 **Engine:** 2.5L L5	**Starter Motor Relay, Signal Too Low:** Engine Control Module (ECM) checks the starter motor relay. If Engine Control Module (ECM) registers that the starter motor relay's signal cable has a voltage that is lower than a certain limit value for a certain time, this is interpreted as a malfunction and the diagnostic trouble code (DTC) is generated. The diagnostic trouble code (DTC) can be diagnosed when starting the engine.
DTC: ECM-8500/P0641 **1T ECM** **Years:** 2011, 2012 **Model:** C30, C70, S40, V50 **Engine:** 2.5L L5	**5 Volt Power Supply, Faulty Signal,:** The engine control module (ECM) checks the internal circuits for the 5 volt supply to the components. The diagnostic trouble code (DTC) is stored if the engine control module (ECM) registers that the voltage in one of the circuits is too high, too low or missing. The diagnostic trouble code (DTC) can be diagnosed when the ignition is switched on.
DTC: ECM-850C/P0643 **1T ECM** **Years:** 2011, 2012 **Model:** C30, C70, S40, V50 **Engine:** 2.5L L5	**5 Volt Power Supply, Signal Too High:** The engine control module (ECM) checks the internal circuits for the 5 volt supply to the components. The diagnostic trouble code (DTC) is stored if the engine control module (ECM) registers that the voltage in one of the circuits is too high, too low or missing. The diagnostic trouble code (DTC) can be diagnosed when the ignition is switched on.
DTC: ECM-850D/P0642 **1T ECM** **Years:** 2011, 2012 **Model:** C30, C70, S40, V50 **Engine:** 2.5L L5	**5 Volt Power Supply, Signal Too Low:** The engine control module (ECM) checks the internal circuits for the 5 volt supply to the components. The diagnostic trouble code (DTC) is stored if the engine control module (ECM) registers that the voltage in one of the circuits is too high, too low or missing. The diagnostic trouble code (DTC) can be diagnosed when the ignition is switched on.
DTC: ECM-8510/P0651 **1T ECM** **Years:** 2011, 2012 **Model:** C30, C70, S40, V50 **Engine:** 2.5L L5	**5 Volt Power Supply, Faulty Signal:** The engine control module (ECM) checks the internal circuits for the 5 volt supply to the components. The diagnostic trouble code (DTC) is stored if the engine control module (ECM) registers that the voltage in one of the circuits is too high, too low or missing. The diagnostic trouble code (DTC) can be diagnosed when the ignition is switched on.

DTC	Trouble Code Title and Conditions
DTC: ECM-851C/P0653 **1T ECM** **Years:** 2011, 2012 **Model:** C30, C70, S40, V50 **Engine:** 2.5L L5	**5 Volt Power Supply, Signal Too High:** The engine control module (ECM) checks the internal circuits for the 5 volt supply to the components. The diagnostic trouble code (DTC) is stored if the engine control module (ECM) registers that the voltage in one of the circuits is too high, too low or missing. The diagnostic trouble code (DTC) can be diagnosed when the ignition is switched on.
DTC: ECM-851D/P0652 **T ECM** **Years:** 2011, 2012 **Model:** C30, C70, S40, V50 **Engine:** 2.5L L5	**5 Volt Power Supply, Signal Too Low:** The engine control module (ECM) checks the internal circuits for the 5 volt supply to the components. The diagnostic trouble code (DTC) is stored if the engine control module (ECM) registers that the voltage in one of the circuits is too high, too low or missing. The diagnostic trouble code (DTC) can be diagnosed when the ignition is switched on
DTC: ECM-8520/P0697 **1T ECM** **Years:** 2011, 2012 **Model:** C30, C70, S40, V50 **Engine:** 2.5L L5	**5 Volt Power Supply, Faulty Signal:** The engine control module (ECM) checks the internal circuits for the 5 volt supply to the components. The diagnostic trouble code (DTC) is stored if the engine control module (ECM) registers that the voltage in one of the circuits is too high, too low or missing. The diagnostic trouble code (DTC) can be diagnosed when the ignition is switched on.
DTC: ECM-852C/P0699 **1T ECM** **Years:** 2011, 2012 **Model:** C30, C70, S40, V50 **Engine:** 2.5L L5	**5 Volt Power Supply, Signal Too High:** The engine control module (ECM) checks the internal circuits for the 5 volt supply to the components. The diagnostic trouble code (DTC) is stored if the engine control module (ECM) registers that the voltage in one of the circuits is too high, too low or missing. The diagnostic trouble code (DTC) can be diagnosed when the ignition is switched on.
DTC: ECM-852D/P0698 **1T ECM, MIL: Yes** **Years:** 2011, 2012 **Model:** C30, C70, S40, V50 **Engine:** 2.5L L5	**5 Volt Power Supply, Signal Too Low:** The engine control module (ECM) checks the internal circuits for the 5 volt supply to the components. The diagnostic trouble code (DTC) is stored if the engine control module (ECM) registers that the voltage in one of the circuits is too high, too low or missing. The diagnostic trouble code (DTC) can be diagnosed when the ignition is switched on.
DTC: ECM-9000/P0571/P2131 **1T ECM** **Years:** 2011, 2012 **Model:** C30, C70, S40, V50 **Engine:** 2.5L L5	**Brake Pedal Sensor, Faulty Signal:** The engine control module (ECM) checks that the signal from the brake pedal position sensor and the signal from the stop lamp switch are reliable. The diagnostic trouble code (DTC) is stored if the engine control module (ECM) registers a fault in the circuit for the brake pedal position sensor, the circuit for the stop lamp switch or in the CAN communication between the brake control module (BCM) and the engine control module (ECM), when the engine is running. The diagnostic trouble code (DTC) can be diagnosed when the ignition is on and the brake pedal is depressed.
DTC: ECM-900C/P0573 **1T ECM** **Years:** 2011, 2012 **Model:** C30, C70, S40, V50 **Engine:** 2.5L L5	**Brake Pedal Sensor, Signal Too High or Too Low:** The engine control module (ECM) checks that the signal from the brake pedal position sensor and the signal from the stop lamp switch are reliable. The diagnostic trouble code (DTC) is stored if the engine control module (ECM) registers a fault in the circuit for the brake pedal position sensor, the circuit for the stop lamp switch or in the CAN communication between the brake control module (BCM) and the engine control module (ECM), when the engine is running. The diagnostic trouble code (DTC) can be diagnosed when the ignition is on and the brake pedal is depressed.
DTC: ECM-900C/P0607 **T ECM, MIL: Yes** **Year:** 2011, 2012 **Model:** S40, V50 **Engine:** 2.5L L5	**Engine Control Module (ECM) (Internal Fault):** The diagnostic trouble code (DTC) is stored if the engine control module (ECM) registers an internal fault. The diagnostic trouble code (DTC) can be diagnosed when the ignition is switched on.
DTC: ECM-900E/P0607 **T ECM, MIL: Yes** **Years:** 2011, 2012 **Model:** C30, S40, V50 **Engine:** 2.5L L5	**Engine Control Module (ECM) (Internal Fault):** The diagnostic trouble code (DTC) is stored if the engine control module (ECM) registers an internal malfunction. The diagnostic trouble code (DTC) can be diagnosed when the ignition is switched on.
DTC: ECM-9011/P0571 **1T ECM** **Years:** 2011, 2012 **Model:** C30, C70, S40, V50 **Engine:** 2.5L L5	**Brake Pedal Sensor, Signal Via CAN. Faulty Signal:** If the engine control module (ECM) registers that the signal it receives from the brake pedal sensor on the controller area network (CAN) via the brake control module (BCM) is faulty. The diagnostic trouble code (DTC) is also stored if there is a fault in the CAN communication. The diagnostic trouble code (DTC) can be diagnosed when the ignition is switched on.
DTC: ECM-901B/P0571 **1T ECM** **Years:** 2011, 2012 **Model:** C30, C70, S40, V50 **Engine:** 2.5L L5	**Brake Pedal Sensor, Signal Via CAN. Signal Missing:** If the engine control module (ECM) registers that the signal it receives from the brake pedal sensor on the controller area network (CAN) via the brake control module (BCM) is faulty. The diagnostic trouble code (DTC) is also stored if there is a fault in the CAN communication. The diagnostic trouble code (DTC) can be diagnosed when the ignition is switched on.

DTC	Trouble Code Title and Conditions
DTC: ECM-901D/P0571 **1T ECM** **Years:** 2011, 2012 **Model:** C30, C70, S40, V50 **Engine:** 2.5L L5	**Brake Pedal Sensor, Signal Via CAN. Signal Too Low:** The diagnostic trouble code (DTC) is stored if the engine control module (ECM) registers that the brake pedal position sensor signal, sent via the controller area network (CAN) from the brake control module (BCM) to the engine control module (ECM), is incorrect or that there is a fault in the CAN communication. The diagnostic trouble code (DTC) can be diagnosed when the ignition is switched on.
DTC: ECM-902C/P0574 **T ECM** **Years:** 2011, 2012 **Model:** C30, S40, V50 **Engine:** 2.5L L5	**Engine Control Module (ECM) (Internal Fault):** The diagnostic trouble code (DTC) is stored if the engine control module (ECM) registers an internal fault when the cruise control is active. The diagnostic trouble code (DTC) can be diagnosed when the ignition is switched on.
DTC: ECM-910C/P0808 **1T ECM** **Years:** 2011, 2012 **Model:** C30 **Engine:** 2.5L L5	**Clutch Pedal Switch, Signal Too High:** The engine control module (ECM) receives a signal from the clutch pedal switch via a direct connection. When the clutch pedal is pressed down, the clutch pedal switch closes and thus grounds an input on the Engine control module (ECM). The engine control module also receives information on clutch pedal position from the central electronic module (CEM) via the CAN network. The central electronic module receives this information from the clutch pedal sensor. The diagnostic trouble code (DTC) is stored if the control module detects that: The CAN signal from the central electronic module (CEM) indicates that the clutch pedal is not depressed, but the input on the engine control module (ECM) is grounded. The diagnostic trouble code (DTC) can be diagnosed when: Engine on and vehicle speed over 2 km/h.
DTC: ECM-910D/P0807 **T ECM, MIL: Yes** **Years:** 2011, 2012 **Model:** C30 **Engine:** 2.5L L5	**Clutch Pedal Switch, Signal Too Low:** The engine control module (ECM) receives a signal from the clutch pedal switch via a direct connection. When the clutch pedal is pressed down, the clutch pedal switch closes and thus grounds an input on the Engine control module (ECM). The engine control module also receives information on clutch pedal position from the central electronic module (CEM) via the CAN network. The central electronic module receives this information from the clutch pedal sensor. The diagnostic trouble code (DTC) is stored if the control module detects that: The CAN signal from the central electronic module (CEM) indicates that the clutch pedal is depressed, but that the clutch pedal switch has not closed and grounded the input on the engine control module (ECM). The diagnostic trouble code (DTC) can be diagnosed when: Engine on and vehicle speed over 2 km/h.
DTC: ECM-9110/P0805 **1T ECM** **Years:** 2011, 2012 **Model:** C30 **Engine:** 2.5L L5	**Clutch Pedal Position Sensor, Faulty Signal:** The diagnostic trouble code (DTC) is stored if the engine control module (ECM) receives a fault message from the central electronic module (CEM), via the controller area network (CAN), indicating a faulty signal from the clutch pedal position sensor or a fault in the CAN communication. The diagnostic trouble code (DTC) can be diagnosed when the ignition is switched on.
DTC: ECM-911B/P0805 **1T ECM** **Years:** 2011, 2012 **Model:** C30 **Engine:** 2.5L L5	**Clutch Pedal Sensor, Signal Missing,:** The diagnostic trouble code (DTC) is stored if the engine control module (ECM) receives a fault message from the central electronic module (CEM), via the controller area network (CAN), indicating a faulty signal from the clutch pedal position sensor or a fault in the CAN communication. The diagnostic trouble code (DTC) can be diagnosed when the ignition is switched on.
DTC: ECM-911C/P0805 **1T ECM** **Years:** 2011, 2012 **Model:** C30 **Engine:** 2.5L L5	**Clutch Pedal Sensor, Signal Too High:** The diagnostic trouble code (DTC) is stored if the engine control module (ECM) receives a fault message from the central electronic module (CEM), via the controller area network (CAN), indicating a faulty signal from the clutch pedal position sensor or a fault in the CAN communication. The diagnostic trouble code (DTC) can be diagnosed when the ignition is switched on.
DTC: ECM-911D/P0805 **1T ECM** **Years:** 2011, 2012 **Model:** C30 **Engine:** 2.5L L5	**Clutch Pedal Sensor, Signal Too Low:** The diagnostic trouble code (DTC) is stored if the engine control module (ECM) receives a fault message from the central electronic module (CEM), via the controller area network (CAN), indicating a faulty signal from the clutch pedal position sensor or a fault in the CAN communication. The diagnostic trouble code (DTC) can be diagnosed when the ignition is switched on.
DTC: ECM-91AC/P2103 **1T ECM** **Years:** 2011, 2012 **Model:** C30, S40, V50 **Engine:** 2.5L L5	**Throttle Unit (Throttle jammed, Faulty Signal Or Current Too High):** The engine control module (ECM) checks that the throttle follows the requested throttle angle from the engine control module (ECM). The diagnostic trouble code (DTC) is stored if a fault related to the engine or control of the engine in the throttle unit is detected. The diagnostic trouble code (DTC) can be diagnosed when the car has been test-driven in various driving conditions.

DTC	Trouble Code Title and Conditions
DTC: ECM-9200/P0579 **T ECM** **Year:** 2011, 2012 **Model:** S40, V50 **Engine:** 2.5L L5	**Cruise Control (Faulty Signal):** The steering wheel module (SWM) checks the signals from the buttons on the cruise control. The diagnostic trouble code (DTC) is stored in the engine control module (ECM) if the steering wheel module (SWM) registers a fault in one of the signals from the cruise control buttons or if one of the buttons has been pressed in for too long. The diagnostic trouble code (DTC) can be diagnosed when the engine is idling.
DTC: ECM-9200/P2135 **1T ECM, MIL: Yes** **Years:** 2011, 2012 **Model:** C30, C70, S40, V50 **Engine:** 2.5L L5	**Throttle Position (TP) Sensor, Faulty Signal:** This diagnostic trouble code (DTC) is never stored on its own. This diagnostic trouble code (DTC) will also be stored if the engine control module (ECM) registers that one of the diagnostic trouble codes (DTCs) for the throttle position sensor circuit is stored. The diagnostic trouble code (DTC) can be diagnosed when the ignition is switched on.
DTC: ECM-9210/P0121/P0221 **1T ECM, MIL: Yes** **Years:** 2011, 2012 **Model:** C30, C70, S40, V50 **Engine:** 2.5L L5	**Electronic Throttle Unit, Potentiometer 1. Faulty Signal:** The diagnostic trouble code (DTC) is stored if the engine control module (ECM) registers a fault in the signal from the throttle position (TP) sensor, potentiometer 1 (circuit 1) in the electronic throttle unit. The diagnostic trouble code (DTC) can be diagnosed when the ignition is switched on.
DTC: ECM-921C/P0123 **1T ECM, MIL: Yes** **Years:** 2011, 2012 **Model:** C30, C70, S40, V50 **Engine:** 2.5L L5	**Electronic Throttle Unit, Potentiometer 1. Signal Too High:** The diagnostic trouble code (DTC) is stored if the engine control module (ECM) registers a fault in the signal from the throttle position (TP) sensor, potentiometer 1 (circuit 1) in the electronic throttle unit. The diagnostic trouble code (DTC) can be diagnosed when the ignition is switched on.
DTC: ECM-921D/P0122/P0222 **1T ECM, MIL: Yes** **Years:** 2011, 2012 **Model:** C30, C70, S40, V50 **Engine:** 2.5L L5	**Electronic Throttle Unit, Potentiometer 1. Signal Too Low:** The diagnostic trouble code (DTC) is stored if the engine control module (ECM) registers a fault in the signal from the throttle position (TP) sensor, potentiometer 1 (circuit 1) in the electronic throttle unit. The diagnostic trouble code (DTC) can be diagnosed when the ignition is switched on.
DTC: ECM-9220/P0122 **1T ECM** **Years:** 2011, 2012 **Model:** C30, C70, S40, V50 **Engine:** 2.5L L5	**Electronic Throttle Unit, Potentiometer 2. Faulty Signal:** The diagnostic trouble code (DTC) is stored if the engine control module (ECM) registers a fault in the signal from the throttle position (TP) sensor, potentiometer 2 (circuit 2) in the electronic throttle unit. The diagnostic trouble code (DTC) can be diagnosed when the ignition is switched on.
DTC: ECM-922C/P0223 **1T ECM, MIL: Yes** **Years:** 2011, 2012 **Model:** C30, C70, S40, V50 **Engine:** 2.5L L5	**Electronic Throttle Unit, Potentiometer 2. Signal Too High:** The diagnostic trouble code (DTC) is stored if the engine control module (ECM) registers a fault in the signal from the throttle position (TP) sensor, potentiometer 2 (circuit 2) in the electronic throttle unit. The diagnostic trouble code (DTC) can be diagnosed when the ignition is switched on.
DTC: ECM-922C/P0575 **T ECM** **Year:** 2011, 2012 **Model:** S40, V50 **Engine:** 2.5L L5	**Cruise Control (Communication Fault):** The engine control module (ECM) checks the CAN communication to the steering wheel module (SWM). The diagnostic trouble code (DTC) is stored in the engine control module (ECM) if it receives an incorrect check sum or if the update bit from the steering wheel module (SWM) is missing. The diagnostic trouble code (DTC) can be diagnosed when the ignition is switched on.
DTC: ECM-922D/P0223 **1T ECM** **Years:** 2011, 2012 **Model:** C30, S40, V50 **Engine:** 2.5L L5	**Electronic Throttle Unit, Potentiometer 2. Signal Too Low:** The diagnostic trouble code (DTC) is stored if the engine control module (ECM) registers a fault in the signal from the throttle position (TP) sensor, potentiometer 2 (circuit 2) in the electronic throttle unit. The diagnostic trouble code (DTC) can be diagnosed when the ignition is switched on.
DTC: ECM-9240/P2101 **1T ECM, MIL: Yes** **Years:** 2011, 2012 **Model:** C30, C70, S40, V50 **Engine:** 2.5L L5	**Engine Control Module (ECM), Faulty Signal:** The diagnostic trouble code (DTC) is stored if the engine control module (ECM) registers an internal fault or a fault in the circuit for the throttle unit damper motor. The diagnostic trouble code (DTC) can be diagnosed when the engine is running.
DTC: ECM-925C/P2111 **1T ECM, MIL: Yes** **Years:** 2011, 2012 **Model:** C30, C70, S40, V50 **Engine:** 2.5L L5	**Electronic Throttle Unit, Signal Too High:** The diagnostic trouble code (DTC) is stored if the engine control module (ECM) registers that the movements of the throttle is impeded, or that the return spring in the throttle unit is not functioning correctly, when attempting to adapt the electronic throttle unit.

DTC	Trouble Code Title and Conditions
DTC: ECM-925D/P2111 **1T ECM, MIL: Yes** **Years:** 2011, 2012 **Model:** C30, C70, S40, V50 **Engine:** 2.5L L5	**Electronic Throttle Unit. Signal Too Low:** The diagnostic trouble code (DTC) is stored if the engine control module (ECM) registers that the movements of the throttle is impeded, or that the return spring in the throttle unit is not functioning correctly, when attempting to adapt the electronic throttle unit.
DTC: ECM-926C/P2112 **1T ECM, MIL: Yes** **Years:** 2011, 2012 **Model:** C30, C70, S40, V50 **Engine:** 2.5L L5	**Electronic Throttle Unit, Signal Too High:** The diagnostic trouble code (DTC) is stored if the engine control module (ECM), when attempting to adapt the throttle unit, registers that the movements of the throttle is impeded or that the opening spring in the electronic throttle unit is not functioning correctly.
DTC: ECM-926D/P2112 **1T ECM, MIL: Yes** **Years:** 2011, 2012 **Model:** C30, C70, S40, V50 **Engine:** 2.5L L5	**Electronic Throttle Unit, Signal Too Low:** The diagnostic trouble code (DTC) is stored if the engine control module (ECM), when attempting to adapt the throttle unit, registers that the movements of the throttle is impeded or that the opening spring in the electronic throttle unit is not functioning correctly.
DTC: ECM-9270/P0638 **1T ECM, MIL: Yes** **Years:** 2011, 2012 **Model:** C30, C70, S40, V50 **Engine:** 2.5L L5	**Throttle Unit, Faulty Signal:** The diagnostic trouble code (DTC) is stored if, when the engine is running, the engine control module (ECM) registers that the desired throttle angle (desired value) does not correspond to the actual throttle angle (actual value) in the electronic throttle unit. The diagnostic trouble code (DTC) can be diagnosed when the engine is running.
DTC: ECM-9280/P2119 **1T ECM** **Years:** 2011, 2012 **Model:** C30, C70, S40, V50 **Engine:** 2.5L L5	**Throttle Unit, Faulty Signal:** The diagnostic trouble code (DTC) is stored if the engine control module (ECM) registers that the throttle angle at the return limit position is outside the programmed parameter when trying to adapt the throttle unit.
DTC: ECM-929C/P2108 **1T ECM, MIL: Yes** **Years:** 2011, 2012 **Model:** C30, C70, S40, V50 **Engine:** 2.5L L5	**Engine Control Module (ECM), Signal Too High:** The diagnostic trouble code (DTC) is stored if the engine control module (ECM) registers that the internal governor for control of the throttle angle in the throttle unit is damaged or that the control signal for the governor is too low when controlling the throttle. The diagnostic trouble code (DTC) can be diagnosed when the engine is running.
DTC: ECM-929D/P2108 **1T ECM, MIL: Yes** **Years:** 2011, 2012 **Model:** C30, C70, S40, V50 **Engine:** 2.5L L5	**Engine Control Module (ECM), Signal Too Low:** The diagnostic trouble code (DTC) is stored if the engine control module (ECM) registers that the internal governor for control of the throttle angle in the throttle unit is damaged or that the control signal for the governor is too low when controlling the throttle. The diagnostic trouble code (DTC) can be diagnosed when the engine is running.
DTC: ECM-92B0/P1124 **1T ECM, MIL: Yes** **Years:** 2011, 2012 **Model:** C30, C70, S40, V50 **Engine:** 2.5L L5	**Electronic Throttle Unit, Faulty Signal:** The diagnostic trouble code (DTC) is stored if the engine control module (ECM) fails to carry out its first adaptation of the electronic throttle unit. This is because the programmed parameter for the stop position in the throttle position (TP) sensor has been exceeded. This adaptation is normally run during manufacture of the vehicle. However the electronic throttle unit must be adapted again if the software, the engine control module (ECM) or the throttle unit is replaced. If other diagnostic trouble codes (DTCs) are stored, these must be remedied first. These may have caused the adaptation to fail. The diagnostic trouble code (DTC) can be diagnosed when the ignition is switched on.
DTC: ECM-92CC/P1167 **1T ECM** **Years:** 2011, 2012 **Model:** C30, C70, S40, V50 **Engine:** 2.5L L5	**Electronic Throttle Unit, Signal Too High:** The diagnostic trouble code (DTC) is stored if the engine control module (ECM) detects that the basic conditions for adaptation are not met when trying to adapt the electronic throttle unit. If other diagnostic trouble codes (DTCs) are stored, these must be remedied first. These may have caused the adaptation to fail.
DTC: ECM-92CD/P1167 **1T ECM, MIL: Yes** **Years:** 2011, 2012 **Model:** C30, C70, S40, V50 **Engine:** 2.5L L5	**Electronic Throttle Unit, Signal Too Low:** The diagnostic trouble code (DTC) is stored if the engine control module (ECM) detects that the basic conditions for adaptation are not met when trying to adapt the electronic throttle unit. If other diagnostic trouble codes (DTCs) are stored, these must be remedied first. These may have caused the adaptation to fail.
DTC: ECM-92D0/P1124 **1T ECM** **Years:** 2011, 2012 **Model:** C30, C70, S40, V50 **Engine:** 2.5L L5	**Electronic Throttle Unit. Faulty Signal:** The diagnostic trouble code (DTC) is stored if the ignition has been left on for 30 seconds and the engine control module (ECM) has been unable to adapt the electronic throttle unit. This is because the programmed parameter for the stop position in the throttle position (TP) sensor has been exceeded. Adaptation is usually carried out to ensure that the throttle unit parameters are within the programmed values that are stored in the engine control module (ECM). If other diagnostic trouble codes (DTCs) are stored, these must be remedied first. These may have caused the adaptation to fail.

DTC	Trouble Code Title and Conditions
DTC: ECM-92E0/P2109 **1T ECM** **Years:** 2011, 2012 **Model:** C30, C70, S40, V50 **Engine:** 2.5L L5	**Engine Control Module (ECM). Internal Fault:** The diagnostic trouble code (DTC) is stored if the engine control module (ECM), when attempting to adapt the electronic throttle unit, registers an internal fault in the integrated amplifier for the signal from potentiometer 1 in throttle position sensor (circuit 1) in the electronic throttle unit.
DTC: ECM-9300/P0579 **1T ECM** **Years:** 2011, 2012 **Model:** C30, C70, S40, V50 **Engine:** 2.5L L5	**Control Module Communication Problems, Faulty Signal:** The diagnostic trouble code (DTC) is stored if the engine control module (ECM) registers a fault in the CAN communication or a fault in one of the following control modules: steering wheel module (SWM), central electronic module (CEM), brake control module (BCM) or transmission control module (TCM). The diagnostic trouble code (DTC) can be diagnosed when the ignition is switched on.
DTC: ECM-930B/P0564 **1T ECM** **Years:** 2011, 2012 **Model:** C30, C70, S40, V50 **Engine:** 2.5L L5	**Control Module Communication Problems, Signal Missing:** The diagnostic trouble code (DTC) is stored if the engine control module (ECM) registers a fault in the CAN communication or a fault in one of the following control modules: steering wheel module (SWM), central electronic module (CEM), brake control module (BCM) or transmission control module (TCM). The diagnostic trouble code (DTC) can be diagnosed when the ignition is switched on.
DTC: ECM-930C/P0581 **1T ECM** **Years:** 2011, 2012 **Model:** C30, C70, S40, V50 **Engine:** 2.5L L5	**Control Module, Communication Problems, Signal Too High:** The diagnostic trouble code (DTC) is stored if the engine control module (ECM) registers a fault in the CAN communication or a fault in one of the following control modules: steering wheel module (SWM), central electronic module (CEM), brake control module (BCM) or transmission control module (TCM). The diagnostic trouble code (DTC) can be diagnosed when the ignition is switched on.
DTC: ECM-930D/P0580 **1T ECM** **Years:** 2011, 2012 **Model:** C30, C70, S40, V50 **Engine:** 2.5L L5	**Control Module Communication Problems, Signal Too Low:** The diagnostic trouble code (DTC) is stored if the engine control module (ECM) registers a fault in the CAN communication or a fault in one of the following control modules: steering wheel module (SWM), central electronic module (CEM), brake control module (BCM) or transmission control module (TCM). The diagnostic trouble code (DTC) can be diagnosed when the ignition is switched on.
DTC: ECM-9400/P2126/P2138 **1T ECM** **Years:** 2011, 2012 **Model:** C30, C70, S40, V50 **Engine:** 2.5L L5	**Accelerator Pedal (AP) Position Sensor, Faulty Signal:** The diagnostic trouble code (DTC) is stored if the engine control module (ECM) registers that there is a fault in the PWM signal from the accelerator pedal (AP) position sensor, or that the difference between the analog signal and the PWM signal from the accelerator pedal (AP) position sensor to the engine control module (ECM) is too great. The diagnostic trouble code (DTC) can be diagnosed when the engine is running.
DTC: ECM-940C/P2123 **1T ECM** **Years:** 2011, 2012 **Model:** C30, C70, S40, V50 **Engine:** 2.5L L5	**Accelerator Pedal (AP) Position Sensor, Signal Too High:** The diagnostic trouble code (DTC) is stored if the engine control module (ECM) registers that there is a fault in the PWM signal from the accelerator pedal (AP) position sensor, or that the difference between the analog signal and the PWM signal from the accelerator pedal (AP) position sensor to the engine control module (ECM) is too great. The diagnostic trouble code (DTC) can be diagnosed when the engine is running.
DTC: ECM-940C/P2128 **T ECM** **Year:** 2011, 2012 **Model:** S40, V50 **Engine:** 2.5L L5	**Brake pedal sensor (Faulty Signal Or Signal Missing):** The diagnostic trouble code (DTC) (missing signal) is stored if the engine control module (ECM) cannot communicate with the brake control module (BCM) on the CAN network. The diagnostic trouble code (DTC) (faulty signal) is stored in the engine control module (ECM) if the brake control module (BCM) receives a faulty signal from the brake pedal position sensor. The diagnostic trouble code (DTC) can be diagnosed when the ignition is switched on.
DTC: ECM-940D/P2127/P2122 **1T ECM** **Years:** 2011, 2012 **Model:** C30, C70, S40, V50 **Engine:** 2.5L L5	**Accelerator Pedal (AP) Position Sensor, Signal Too Low:** The diagnostic trouble code (DTC) is stored if the engine control module (ECM) registers that there is a fault in the PWM signal from the accelerator pedal (AP) position sensor, or that the difference between the analog signal and the PWM signal from the accelerator pedal (AP) position sensor to the engine control module (ECM) is too great. The diagnostic trouble code (DTC) can be diagnosed when the engine is running.
DTC: ECM-941C/P2128 **1T ECM** **Years:** 2011, 2012 **Model:** C30, C70, S40, V50 **Engine:** 2.5L L5	**Accelerator Pedal (AP) Position Sensor, Analog Signal. Signal Too High:** The diagnostic trouble code (DTC) is stored if the engine control module (ECM) receives a fault message from the central electronic module (CEM), via the CAN network, indicating that the analog signal from the accelerator pedal (AP) position sensor is faulty. The diagnostic trouble code (DTC) can be diagnosed when the engine is running.
DTC: ECM-941D/P2127 **1T ECM** **Years:** 2011, 2012 **Model:** C30, C70, S40, V50 **Engine:** 2.5L L5	**Accelerator Pedal (AP) Position Sensor, Analog Signal. Signal Too Low:** The diagnostic trouble code (DTC) is stored if the engine control module (ECM) receives a fault message from the central electronic module (CEM), via the controller area network (CAN), indicating that the analog signal from the accelerator pedal (AP) position sensor is faulty. The diagnostic trouble code (DTC) can be diagnosed when the engine is running.

DTC	Trouble Code Title and Conditions
DTC: ECM-9430/P2125 **1T ECM** **Years:** 2011, 2012 **Model:** C30, C70, S40, V50 **Engine:** 2.5L L5	**Accelerator Pedal (AP) Position Sensor, Analog Signal. Faulty Signal:** The diagnostic trouble code (DTC) is stored if the engine control module (ECM), via the controller area network (CAN), receives a fault message from the central electronic module (CEM) indicating that the analog signal from the accelerator pedal (AP) position sensor is faulty or that there is a fault in the CAN communication. The diagnostic trouble code (DTC) can be diagnosed when the engine is running.
DTC: ECM-943B/P2125 **1T ECM** **Years:** 2011, 2012 **Model:** C30, C70, S40, V50 **Engine:** 2.5L L5	**Accelerator Pedal (AP) Position Sensor, Analog Signal. Signal Missing:** The diagnostic trouble code (DTC) is stored if the engine control module (ECM), via the controller area network (CAN), receives a fault message from the central electronic module (CEM) indicating that the analog signal from the accelerator pedal (AP) position sensor is faulty or that there is a fault in the CAN communication. The diagnostic trouble code (DTC) can be diagnosed when the engine is running.
DTC: ECM-943C/P2125 **1T ECM** **Years:** 2011, 2012 **Model:** C30, C70, S40, V50 **Engine:** 2.5L L5	**Accelerator Pedal (AP) Position Sensor, Analog Signal. Signal Too High:** The diagnostic trouble code (DTC) is stored if the engine control module (ECM), via the controller area network (CAN), receives a fault message from the central electronic module (CEM) indicating that the analog signal from the accelerator pedal (AP) position sensor is faulty or that there is a fault in the CAN communication. The diagnostic trouble code (DTC) can be diagnosed when the engine is running.
DTC: ECM-943D/P2125 **1T ECM** **Years:** 2011, 2012 **Model:** C30, C70, S40, V50 **Engine:** 2.5L L5	**Accelerator Pedal (AP) Position Sensor, Analog Signal. Signal Too Low:** The diagnostic trouble code (DTC) is stored if the engine control module (ECM), via the controller area network (CAN), receives a fault message from the central electronic module (CEM) indicating that the analog signal from the accelerator pedal (AP) position sensor is faulty or that there is a fault in the CAN communication. The diagnostic trouble code (DTC) can be diagnosed when the engine is running.
DTC: ECM-950C/P0507 **1T ECM, MIL: Yes** **Years:** 2011, 2012 **Model:** C30, C70, S40, V50 **Engine:** 2.5L L5	**Engine Control Module (ECM), Idle Speed Control. Signal Too High:** If Engine Control Module (ECM) registers that the actual idle rpm (actual value) is over the limit value for a certain time, the diagnostic trouble code (DTC) is generated.
DTC: ECM-950C/P2120 **1T ECM** **Years:** 2011, 2012 **Model:** C30, S40, V50 **Engine:** 2.5L L5	**Accelerator Pedal (AP) Position Sensor. (Malfunction):** The engine control module (ECM) checks the pulse width modulation (PWM) signal and the analog signal from the accelerator pedal (AP) position sensor. The analog signal from the accelerator pedal (AP) position sensor is connected directly to the central electronic module (CEM). The signal is transmitted via CAN communication from the central electronic module (CEM) to the engine control module (ECM). The PWM signal is connected directly to the engine control module (ECM). The diagnostic trouble code (DTC) is stored if the engine control module (ECM) registers a malfunction in the signals from the accelerator pedal (AP) position sensor. The diagnostic trouble code (DTC) can be diagnosed when the ignition is switched on.
DTC: ECM-950D/P0506 **1T ECM, MIL: Yes** **Years:** 2011, 2012 **Model:** C30, C70, S40, V50 **Engine:** 2.5L L5	**Engine Control Module (ECM), Idle Speed Control. Signal Too Low:** If Engine Control Module (ECM) registers that the actual idle rpm (actual value) is under the limit value for a certain time, the diagnostic trouble code (DTC) is generated.
DTC: ECM-951C/P0507/P2122 **1T ECM, MIL: Yes** **Years:** 2011, 2012 **Model:** C30, C70, S40, V50 **Engine:** 2.5L L5	**Engine Control Module (ECM), Idle Speed Control. Signal Too High:** To warm up the catalytic converter at cold-start the Engine Control Module (ECM) controls idle so that the engine runs at a higher idle rpm until the catalytic converter has reached its operating temperature. If Engine Control Module (ECM) registers that the actual idle rpm (actual value) is over the limit value for a certain time, the diagnostic trouble code (DTC) is generated.
DTC: ECM-951D/P0506 **1T ECM, MIL: Yes** **Years:** 2011, 2012 **Model:** C30, C70, S40, V50 **Engine:** 2.5L L5	**Engine Control Module (ECM), Idle Speed Control. Signal Too Low:** To warm up the catalytic converter at cold-start the Engine Control Module (ECM) controls idle so that the engine runs at a higher idle rpm until the catalytic converter has reached its operating temperature. If Engine Control Module (ECM) registers that the actual idle rpm (actual value) is under the limit value for a certain time, the diagnostic trouble code (DTC) is generated.
DTC: ECM-9700/P2121 **1T ECM** **Years:** 2011, 2012 **Model:** C30, C70, S40, V50 **Engine:** 2.5L L5	**Accelerator Pedal (AP) Position Sensor, Digital Signal. Faulty Signal:** The diagnostic trouble code (DTC) is stored if the engine control module (ECM) registers that the basic frequency of the PWM signal from the accelerator pedal (AP) position sensor deviates from the predefined values. The diagnostic trouble code (DTC) can be diagnosed when the ignition is switched on.

DTC	Trouble Code Title and Conditions
DTC: ECM-970B/P2121 **1T ECM** **Years:** 2011, 2012 **Model:** C30, C70, S40, V50 **Engine:** 2.5L L5	**Accelerator Pedal (AP) Position Sensor, Digital Signal. Signal Missing:** The diagnostic trouble code (DTC) is stored if the engine control module (ECM) registers that the basic frequency of the PWM signal from the accelerator pedal (AP) position sensor deviates from the predefined values. The diagnostic trouble code (DTC) can be diagnosed when the ignition is switched on.
DTC: ECM-970C/P2121 **1T ECM** **Years:** 2011, 2012 **Model:** C30, C70, S40, V50 **Engine:** 2.5L L5	**Accelerator Pedal (AP) Position Sensor, Digital Signal. Signal Too High:** The diagnostic trouble code (DTC) is stored if the engine control module (ECM) registers that the basic frequency of the PWM signal from the accelerator pedal (AP) position sensor deviates from the predefined values. The diagnostic trouble code (DTC) can be diagnosed when the ignition is switched on.
DTC: ECM-970D/P2121 **1T ECM** **Years:** 2011, 2012 **Model:** C30, C70, S40, V50 **Engine:** 2.5L L5	**Accelerator Pedal (AP) Position Sensor, Digital Signal. Signal Too Low:** The diagnostic trouble code (DTC) is stored if the engine control module (ECM) registers that the basic frequency of the PWM signal from the accelerator pedal (AP) position sensor deviates from the predefined values. The diagnostic trouble code (DTC) can be diagnosed when the ignition is switched on.
DTC: ECM-9800/P0607 **1T ECM, MIL: Yes** **Years:** 2011, 2012 **Model:** C30, C70, S40, V50 **Engine:** 2.5L L5	**Engine Control Module (ECM), Torque Signal. Internal Fault:** The diagnostic trouble code (DTC) is stored if the engine control module (ECM) registers an internal fault which indicates that the normal engine control functions are producing a higher torque than is within the maximum permitted range. The diagnostic trouble code (DTC) is diagnosed at ignition on or with the engine running.
DTC: ECM-9810/P0607 **1T ECM, MIL: Yes** **Years:** 2011, 2012 **Model:** C30, C70, S40, V50 **Engine:** 2.5L L5	**Engine Control Module (ECM), Engine Speed (RPM). Internal Fault:** The diagnostic trouble code (DTC) is stored if the engine control module (ECM) registers an internal fault indicating that the calculated engine speed (RPM) in the internal monitoring functions differs from the normal calculated engine speed (RPM) in the engine control functions. The diagnostic trouble code (DTC) is diagnosed with the engine running and at an engine speed (RPM) above 520 rpm.
DTC: ECM-9818/P2111 **T ECM** **Years:** 2011, 2012 **Model:** C30, S40, V50 **Engine:** 2.5L L5	**Brake Vacuum (Faulty Signal):** The diagnostic trouble code (DTC) is stored in the engine control module (ECM) if the engine control module (ECM) detects that the throttle cannot be closed but is stuck in the open position, resulting in poor brake vacuum. The diagnostic trouble code (DTC) can be diagnosed when the engine is running.
DTC: ECM-9820/P0607 **1T ECM, MIL: Yes** **Years:** 2011, 2012 **Model:** C30, C70, S40, V50 **Engine:** 2.5L L5	**Engine Control Module (ECM), Load Signal. Internal Fault:** The diagnostic trouble code (DTC) is stored if the engine control module (ECM) registers a fault indicating that the calculated load signals for the normal engine control functions are lower than calculated by the internal monitoring functions. The diagnostic trouble code (DTC) is diagnosed with the engine running and at an engine speed (RPM) of more than 1000 rpm.
DTC: ECM-9830/P0607 **1T ECM, MIL: Yes** **Years:** 2011, 2012 **Model:** C30, C70, S40, V50 **Engine:** 2.5L L5	**Engine Control Module (ECM). Internal Fault:** The diagnostic trouble code (DTC) is stored if the engine control module (ECM) registers a fault indicating that the internal monitoring functions have registered one or more present values that do not correspond with the complement value. The diagnostic trouble code (DTC) is diagnosed at ignition on or with the engine running.
DTC: ECM-983B/P0607 **1T ECM, MIL: Yes** **Years:** 2011, 2012 **Model:** C30, C70, S40, V50 **Engine:** 2.5L L5	**Engine Control Module (ECM). Internal Fault:** The diagnostic trouble code (DTC) is stored if the engine control module (ECM) registers a fault indicating that the internal monitoring functions have registered one or more present values that do not correspond with the complement value. The diagnostic trouble code (DTC) is diagnosed at ignition on or with the engine Running.
DTC: ECM-983C/P0607 **1T ECM, MIL: Yes** **Years:** 2011, 2012 **Model:** C30, C70, S40, V50 **Engine:** 2.5L L5	**Engine Control Module (ECM). Internal Fault:** The diagnostic trouble code (DTC) is stored if the engine control module (ECM) registers a fault indicating that the internal monitoring functions have registered one or more present values that do not correspond with the complement value. The diagnostic trouble code (DTC) is diagnosed at ignition on or with the engine running.
DTC: ECM-983D/P0607 **1T ECM, MIL: Yes** **Years:** 2011, 2012 **Model:** C30, C70, S40, V50 **Engine:** 2.5L L5	**Engine Control Module (ECM). Internal Fault:** The diagnostic trouble code (DTC) is stored if the engine control module (ECM) registers a fault indicating that the internal monitoring functions have registered one or more present values that do not correspond with the complement value. The diagnostic trouble code (DTC) is diagnosed at ignition on or with the engine running.

DTC	Trouble Code Title and Conditions
DTC: ECM-9840/P0607 **1T ECM, MIL: Yes** **Years:** 2011, 2012 **Model:** C30, C70, S40, V50 **Engine:** 2.5L L5	**Engine control module (ECM). Internal fault:** If the engine control module (ECM) registers a fault where the input signals from the throttle unit position sensor are interpreted by the normal engine control functions as having exceeded their minimum or maximum limits. While the internal monitoring function interprets the input signals from the electronic throttle unit position sensor differently. The diagnostic trouble code (DTC) is diagnosed at ignition on or with the engine running.
DTC: ECM-984B/P0607 **1T ECM, MIL: Yes** **Year:** 2011, 2012 **Model:** S40 **Engine:** 2.5L L5	**Engine control module (ECM). Internal fault:** If the engine control module (ECM) registers a fault where the input signals from the throttle unit position sensor are interpreted by the normal engine control functions as having exceeded their minimum or maximum limits. While the internal monitoring function interprets the input signals from the electronic throttle unit position sensor differently. The diagnostic trouble code (DTC) is diagnosed at ignition on or with the engine running.
DTC: ECM-984B/P0607 **1T ECM, MIL: Yes** **Year:** 2011, 2012 **Model:** V50 **Engine:** 2.5L L5	**Engine Control Module (ECM). Internal Fault:** The diagnostic trouble code (DTC) stored if the engine control module (ECM) registers a fault where the input signals from the throttle unit position sensor are interpreted by the normal engine control functions as having exceeded their minimum or maximum limits, while the internal monitoring function interprets the input signals from the electronic throttle unit position sensor differently. The diagnostic trouble code (DTC) is diagnosed at ignition on or with the engine running.
DTC: ECM-985C/P0607 **1T ECM, MIL: Yes** **Years:** 2011, 2012 **Model:** C30, C70, S40, V50 **Engine:** 2.5L L5	**Engine Control Module (ECM), Fuel Shut-Off System. Internal Fault:** The diagnostic trouble code (DTC) is stored if the engine control module (ECM) registers an internal fault indicating that the internal monitoring functions in the engine control module (ECM) have registered a fault in the analog / digital converter function. The diagnostic trouble code (DTC) can be diagnosed at ignition on or with the engine running.
DTC: ECM-9860/P0607 **1T ECM, MIL: Yes** **Years:** 2011, 2012 **Model:** C30, C70, S40, V50 **Engine:** 2.5L L5	**Engine Control Module (ECM). Internal Fault:** The diagnostic trouble code (DTC) is stored if the engine control module (ECM) registers a fault indicating that the normal engine control functions have not discovered a fault in the signals from the accelerator pedal (AP) position sensor, but that the internal monitoring function has detected a difference between the two signals. The diagnostic trouble code (DTC) is diagnosed at ignition on or with the engine running.
DTC: ECM-990F/P2172 **T ECM** **Years:** 2011, 2012 **Model:** C30, S40, V50 **Engine:** 2.5L L5	**Torque Monitoring (Faulty Signal):** The engine control module (ECM) checks the engine torque by reading off the acceleration of the flywheel. The diagnostic trouble code (DTC) is stored if the measured torque exceeds the requested torque, based on the pedal position and the engine speed (RPM). The diagnostic trouble code (DTC) can be diagnosed when the engine is idling.
DTC: ECM-9918/P2106 **1T ECM, MIL: Yes** **Years:** 2011, 2012 **Model:** C30, S40, V50 **Engine:** 2.5L L5	**Throttle Unit (Faulty Signal):** The diagnostic trouble code (DTC) is stored if the engine control module (ECM) switches off the supply to the damper motor in the throttle unit, causing the throttle to turn to the return position using the return spring in the throttle unit. The diagnostic trouble code (DTC) can be diagnosed when the engine is idling.
DTC: ECM-9970/P0604 **T ECM, MIL: Yes** **Years:** 2011, 2012 **Model:** C30, C70, S40, V50 **Engine:** 2.5L L5	**Memory Fault In RAM. Faulty Signal:** The engine control module (ECM) continuously checks the internal RAM (random access memory) functionality. The diagnostic trouble code (DTC) is stored if there is a fault in the RAM. The diagnostic trouble code (DTC) is diagnosed when the ignition is on.
DTC: ECM-9980/P0605 **1T ECM, MIL: Yes** **Years:** 2011, 2012 **Model:** C30, C70, S40, V50 **Engine:** 2.5L L5	**Memory Fault In ROM. Faulty Signal:** The engine control module (ECM) continuously checks the internal ROM (read only memory) functionality. The diagnostic trouble code (DTC) is stored if there is a fault in the ROM. The diagnostic trouble code (DTC) is diagnosed when the ignition is on.
DTC: ECM-9990/P0606 **1T ECM, MIL: Yes** **Years:** 2011, 2012 **Model:** C30, C70, S40, V50 **Engine:** 2.5L L5	**Engine Control Module (ECM). Faulty Signal:** The engine control module (ECM) continuously checks the internal reset functionality in the engine control module (ECM). The diagnostic trouble code (DTC) is stored in the event of a fault in the reset function. The diagnostic trouble code (DTC) is diagnosed when the ignition is on.
DTC: ECM-999B/P0606 **1T ECM, MIL: Yes** **Years:** 2011, 2012 **Model:** C30, C70, S40, V50 **Engine:** 2.5L L5	**Engine Control Module (ECM). Signal Missing:** The engine control module (ECM) continuously checks the internal reset functionality in the engine control module (ECM). The diagnostic trouble code (DTC) is stored in the event of a fault in the reset function. The diagnostic trouble code (DTC) is diagnosed when the ignition is on.

DTC	Trouble Code Title and Conditions
DTC: ECM-999D/P0606 **1T ECM, MIL: Yes** **Years:** 2011, 2012 **Model:** C30, C70, S40, V50 **Engine:** 2.5L L5	**Engine Control Module (ECM). Signal Too Low:** The engine control module (ECM) continuously checks the internal reset functionality in the engine control module (ECM). The diagnostic trouble code (DTC) is stored in the event of a fault in the reset function. The diagnostic trouble code (DTC) is diagnosed when the ignition is on.
DTC: ECM-9A0B/P0607 **1T ECM, MIL: Yes** **Years:** 2011, 2012 **Model:** C30, C70, S40, V50 **Engine:** 2.5L L5	**Engine Control Module (ECM). Internal Fault:** The engine control module (ECM) has integrated control systems for detecting internal faults. The diagnostic trouble code (DTC) is stored if the engine control module (ECM) registers a fault in the internal voltage references. The diagnostic trouble code (DTC) can be diagnosed when the ignition is switched on.
DTC: ECM-9A0C/P0563 **1T ECM, MIL: Yes** **Years:** 2011, 2012 **Model:** C30, C70, S40, V50 **Engine:** 2.5L L5	**Engine Control Module (ECM). Internal Fault:** The engine control module (ECM) has integrated control systems for detecting internal faults. The diagnostic trouble code (DTC) is stored if the engine control module (ECM) registers a fault in the internal voltage references. The diagnostic trouble code (DTC) can be diagnosed when the ignition is switched on.
DTC: ECM-9A0D/P0562 **T ECM, MIL: Yes** **Years:** 2011, 2012 **Model:** C30, C70, S40, V50 **Engine:** 2.5L L5	**Engine Control Module (ECM). Internal Fault:** The engine control module (ECM) has integrated control systems for detecting internal faults. The diagnostic trouble code (DTC) is stored if the engine control module (ECM) registers a fault in the internal voltage references. The diagnostic trouble code (DTC) can be diagnosed when the ignition is switched on.
DTC: ECM-A12B/P0503 **1T ECM, MIL: Yes** **Years:** 2011, 2012 **Model:** C30, S40, V50 **Engine:** 2.5L L5	**Speed Signal, Signal Missing:** A fault message is transmitted to the engine control module (ECM) and the diagnostic trouble code (DTC) is stored if a fault is detected in the brake control module (BCM). Diagnostic trouble codes (DTCs) for the vehicle speed sensor (VSS) signal are also stored in the brake control module (BCM).
DTC: ECM-A12C/P0503 **1T ECM, MIL: Yes** **Years:** 2011, 2012 **Model:** C30, S40, V50 **Engine:** 2.5L L5	**Speed Signal, Signal Too High:** A fault message is transmitted to the engine control module (ECM) and the diagnostic trouble code (DTC) is stored if a fault is detected in the brake control module (BCM). Diagnostic trouble codes (DTCs) for the vehicle speed sensor (VSS) signal are also stored in the brake control module (BCM).
DTC: ECM-A130/P0503/U0001 **1T ECM** **Years:** 2011, 2012 **Model:** C30, S40, V50 **Engine:** 2.5L L5	**Control Module Communication, Faulty Signal:** The control modules transmit and receive information via a standardized serial communication method - CAN (Control Area Network). The diagnostic trouble code (DTC) is stored if the engine control module (ECM) registers serious interference (CAN communication blocked). **NOTE: In the event of system communication problems, it is not possible to communicate with the engine control module (ECM). Therefore it will only be possible to read off the diagnostic trouble code (DTC) if the fault is intermittent.**
DTC: ECM-A20B/P2610 **1T ECM, MIL: Yes** **Years:** 2011, 2012 **Model:** C30, S40, V50 **Engine:** 2.5L L5	**Engine Control Module (ECM). Signal Missing:** The central electronic module (CEM) transmits a timer signal to the control modules in the car via the controller area network (CAN). This signal informs how many seconds have passed since the engine was last switched off. The signal is used for example by the engine control module (ECM) when restarting a warm engine. The diagnostic trouble code (DTC) is stored if the engine control module (ECM) registers that the timer signal transmitted by the central electronic module (CEM) is incorrect. The diagnostic trouble code (DTC) can be diagnosed when the ignition is switched on.
DTC: ECM-A20C/P2610 **1T ECM, MIL: Yes** **Years:** 2011, 2012 **Model:** C30, C70, S40, V50 **Engine:** 2.5L L5	**Engine Control Module (ECM). Signal Too High:** The central electronic module (CEM) transmits a timer signal to the control modules in the car via the controller area network (CAN). This signal informs how many seconds have passed since the engine was last switched off. The signal is used for example by the engine control module (ECM) when restarting a warm engine. The diagnostic trouble code (DTC) is stored if the engine control module (ECM) registers that the timer signal transmitted by the central electronic module (CEM) is incorrect. The diagnostic trouble code (DTC) can be diagnosed when the ignition is switched on.
DTC: ECM-P001100 **1T ECM, MIL: Yes** **Year:** 2011, 2012 **Model:** XC90 **Engine:** 4.4L V8	**Intake Camshaft Position Timing - Over-Advanced (Bank 1) :** The Engine control module (ECM) regulates the camshaft position (angle). If the control module detects a difference between the requested position and the actual position, the speed is measured as the camshaft moves to the requested position. The diagnostic trouble code (DTC) is stored if the control module detects that: The cam shaft moves too slowly (to the late position). The control module's test for the diagnostic trouble code (DTC) starts in the event of: Hot engine. Engine speed above 1000 rpm. Camshaft control is active.

DTC	Trouble Code Title and Conditions
DTC: ECM-P001200 **1T ECM** **Year:** 2011, 2012 **Model:** XC90 **Engine:** 4.4L V8	**Intake Camshaft Position Timing - Over-Retarded (Bank 1):** The Engine control module (ECM) regulates the camshaft position (angle). If the control module detects a difference between the requested position and the actual position, the speed is measured as the camshaft moves to the requested position. The diagnostic trouble code (DTC) is stored if the control module detects that: The camshaft moves too slowly (to the early position). The control module's test for the diagnostic trouble code (DTC) starts in the event of: Hot engine. Engine speed above 1000 rpm. Camshaft control is active. **Note! The control module can only detect the fault once the test has been started and the diagnostic trouble code (DTC) is stored when the conditions are met.**
DTC: ECM-P001268 **T** **Years:** 2011, 2012 **Model:** S60, XC60, XC90 **Engine:** 3.0L L6 VIN 90, 3.2L L6 VIN 94, 3.2L L6 VIN 95	**Intake Camshaft Position Timing - Over-Retarded (Bank 1):** **NOTE: This diagnostic trouble code (DTC) status is an event controlled diagnostic trouble code (DTC). An event controlled diagnostic trouble code (DTC) does not mean that there is a fault in the control module when it is active, but is designed as information.** Engine control module (ECM) monitors the induction side's VVT-valve (bank 1). If the control module detects that the induction side's VVT-valve is too far from desired target value for a certain time, the diagnostic trouble code is generated.
DTC: ECM-P001400 **1T ECM** **Year:** 2011, 2012 **Model:** XC90 **Engine:** 4.4L V8	**Exhaust Camshaft Position Timing - Over-Advanced (Bank 1). :** The engine control module (ECM) controls the position of the camshaft (angle). The engine control module (ECM) checks that the requested position is reached. If the control module detects a difference between the requested position and the actual position, the time taken for control to reach the requested position is measured. The maximum permitted time to reach the requested position varies depending on how much the camshaft is controlled outwards. The diagnostic trouble code (DTC) is stored if the control module detects that control is too slow during the return phase of the exhaust camshaft. The diagnostic trouble code (DTC) can be diagnosed when the engine is at operating temperature, the engine speed (RPM) is above a certain value and when camshaft control is active.
DTC: ECM-P001500 **1T ECM** **Year:** 2011, 2012 **Model:** XC90 **Engine:** 4.4L V8	**Exhaust Camshaft Position Timing - Over-Retarded (Bank 1) :** The engine control module (ECM) regulates the camshaft position (angle position) and checks that the requested position has been achieved. If the control module detects a difference between the requested position and the actual position, the time taken for regulation to achieve the requested position is measured. The length of time permitted to achieve the requested position varies depending on how much the camshaft is to be deflected at that moment. The diagnostic trouble code is generated if the control module detects that regulation is too slow during exhaust camshaft deflection. The diagnostic trouble code can be diagnosed when the engine is at operating temperature, engine speed exceeds a certain value and camshaft regulation is active.
DTC: ECM-P001600 **1T PCM, MIL: Yes** **Years:** 2011, 2012 **Model:** S60, XC60, XC90 **Engine:** 3.0L L6 VIN 90, 3.2L L6 VIN 94, 3.2L L6 VIN 95	**Crankshaft Position - Camshaft Position Correlation - Bank 1 Sensor A:** The engine control module (ECM) checks that the camshaft is in the correct position (angle) in relation to the position (angle) of the crankshaft using signals from the camshaft sensor and engine speed (RPM) sensor. If the camshaft position does not correspond to the crankshaft position, the control module adjusts the adaption for the camshaft position. The adaption value corresponds to the difference in position between the camshaft and crankshaft when the crankshaft is in its default position. The diagnostic trouble code (DTC) is stored when adaption is greater or less than a certain value. The diagnostic trouble code (DTC) can be diagnosed when adaption of the camshaft is carried out (adaption occurs during engine braking).
DTC: ECM-P001621 **1T ECM** **Year:** 2011, 2012 **Model:** XC90 **Engine:** 4.4L V8	**Crankshaft Position - Camshaft Position Correlation - Bank 1 Sensor A. (Signal Too Low) :** The engine control module (ECM) checks that the camshaft is in the correct position (angle) in relation to the position (angle) of the crankshaft using signals from the camshaft sensor and engine speed (RPM) sensor. If the camshaft position does not correspond to the crankshaft position, the control module adjusts the adaption for the camshaft position. The adaption value corresponds to the difference in position between the camshaft and crankshaft when the crankshaft is in its default position. The diagnostic trouble code (DTC) is stored when adaption is greater or less than a certain value. The diagnostic trouble code (DTC) can be diagnosed when adaption of the camshaft is carried out (adaption occurs during engine braking).
DTC: ECM-P001622 **1T ECM** **Year:** 2011, 2012 **Model:** XC90 **Engine:** 4.4L V8	**Crankshaft Position - Camshaft Position Correlation - Bank 1 Sensor A. (Signal Too High):** The engine control module (ECM) checks that the camshaft is in the correct position (angle) in relation to the position (angle) of the crankshaft using signals from the camshaft sensor and engine speed (RPM) sensor. If the camshaft position does not correspond to the crankshaft position, the control module adjusts the adaption for the camshaft position. The adaption value corresponds to the difference in position between the camshaft and crankshaft when the crankshaft is in its default position. The diagnostic trouble code (DTC) is stored when adaption is greater or less than a certain value. The diagnostic trouble code (DTC) can be diagnosed when adaption of the camshaft is carried out (adaption occurs during engine braking).

DTC	Trouble Code Title and Conditions
DTC: ECM-P001692 **1T ECM** **Year:** 2011, 2012 **Model:** XC90 **Engine:** 4.4L V8	**Crankshaft Position - Camshaft Position Correlation - Bank 1 Sensor A. (Performance Or Incorrect Operation) :** The engine control module (ECM) checks that the camshaft is in the correct position in relation to the position of the crankshaft. If the camshaft position does not match the crankshaft position, the control module will adjust the adaptation for the camshaft position. The adaptation value corresponds to the difference between the camshaft and crankshaft. The diagnostic trouble code (DTC) is stored if the control module detects that: Change in the adaptation value is larger than what corresponds to a tooth. The control module's test for the diagnostic trouble code (DTC) starts in the event of: Hot engine. During engine start-up.
DTC: ECM-P001800 **2T PCM** **Years:** 2011, 2012 **Model:** S60, XC60, XC90 **Engine:** 3.0L L6 VIN 90, 3.2L L6 VIN 94, 3.2L L6 VIN 95	**Crankshaft Position - Camshaft Position Correlation - Bank 2 Sensor A:** The engine control module (ECM) checks that the camshaft is in the correct position in relation to the position of the crankshaft. If the camshaft position does not match the crankshaft position, the control module will adjust the adaptation for the camshaft position. The adaptation value corresponds to the difference between the camshaft and crankshaft. The diagnostic trouble code (DTC) is stored if the control module detects that: * Change in the adaptation value is larger than what corresponds to a tooth. The control module's test for the diagnostic trouble code (DTC) starts in the event of: * Hot engine. * During engine start-up.
DTC: ECM-P001892 **1T ECM, MIL: Yes** **Year:** 2011, 2012 **Model:** XC90 **Engine:** 4.4L V8	**Crankshaft Position - Camshaft Position Correlation - Bank 2 Sensor A:** The engine control module (ECM) checks that the camshaft is in the correct position in relation to the position of the crankshaft. If the camshaft position does not match the crankshaft position, the control module will adjust the adaptation for the camshaft position. The adaptation value corresponds to the difference between the camshaft and crankshaft. The diagnostic trouble code (DTC) is stored if the control module detects that: The fuel trim value change is greater than 16 degrees. The control module's test for the diagnostic trouble code (DTC) starts in the event of: Hot engine. During engine start-up. **Note! The control module can only detect the fault once the test has been started and the diagnostic trouble code (DTC) is stored when the conditions are met.**
DTC: ECM-P001A00 **1T PCM, MIL: Yes** **Years:** 2011, 2012 **Model:** S60, XC60, XC90 **Engine:** 3.0L L6 VIN 90, 3.2L L6 VIN 94, 3.2L L6 VIN 95	**Intake (A) Cam Profile Control Circuit/Open (Bank 1):** The engine control module (ECM) regulates the variable cam profiles. The engine control module (ECM) checks the control signal for the cam profile valves. The diagnostic trouble code (DTC) is stored if the control module detects that: * Signal missing. The control module's test for the diagnostic trouble code (DTC) starts in the event of: * Ignition switch position II. * Battery voltage higher than 10.5 V. **NOTE: For this function, bank 1 consists of cylinders 1, 2 and 4. Bank 2 consists of cylinders 3, 5 and 6.**
DTC: ECM-P001B00 **1T PCM, MIL: Yes** **Years:** 2011, 2012 **Model:** S60, XC60, XC90 **Engine:** 3.0L L6 VIN 90, 3.2L L6 VIN 94, 3.2L L6 VIN 95	**Intake (A) Cam Profile Control Circuit Low (Bank 1):** The engine control module (ECM) regulates the variable cam profiles. The engine control module (ECM) checks the control signal for the cam profile valves. The diagnostic trouble code (DTC) is stored if the control module detects that: * Control signal is too low. The control module's test for the diagnostic trouble code (DTC) starts in the event of: * Ignition switch position II. * Battery voltage higher than 10.5 V. **NOTE: For this function, bank 1 consists of cylinders 1, 2 and 4. Bank 2 consists of cylinders 3, 5 and 6.**
DTC: ECM-P001C00 **1T PCM, MIL: Yes** **Years:** 2011, 2012 **Model:** S60, XC60, XC90 **Engine:** 3.0L L6 VIN 90, 3.2L L6 VIN 94, 3.2L L6 VIN 95	**Intake (A) Cam Profile Control Circuit High (Bank 1):** The engine control module (ECM) regulates the variable cam profiles. The engine control module (ECM) checks the control signal for the cam profile valves. The diagnostic trouble code (DTC) is stored if the control module detects that: * Control signal is too high. The control module's test for the diagnostic trouble code (DTC) starts in the event of: * Ignition switch position II. * Battery voltage higher than 10.5 V. **NOTE: For this function, bank 1 consists of cylinders 1, 2 and 4. Bank 2 consists of cylinders 3, 5 and 6.**

DTC	Trouble Code Title and Conditions
DTC: ECM-P001D00 **1T PCM, MIL: Yes** **Years:** 2011, 2012 **Model:** S60, XC60, XC90 **Engine:** 3.0L L6 VIN 90, 3.2L L6 VIN 94, 3.2L L6 VIN 95	**Intake (A) Cam Profile Control Circuit/Open (Bank 2):** The engine control module (ECM) regulates the variable cam profiles. The engine control module (ECM) checks the control signal for the cam profile valves. The diagnostic trouble code (DTC) is stored if the control module detects that: * Signal missing. The control module's test for the diagnostic trouble code (DTC) starts in the event of: * Ignition switch position II. * Battery voltage higher than 10.5 V. **NOTE: For this function, bank 1 consists of cylinders 1, 2 and 4. Bank 2 consists of cylinders 3, 5 and 6.**
DTC: ECM-P001E00 **1T PCM, MIL: Yes** **Years:** 2011, 2012 **Model:** S60, XC60, XC90 **Engine:** 3.0L L6 VIN 90, 3.2L L6 VIN 94, 3.2L L6 VIN 95	**Intake (A) Cam Profile Control Circuit Low (Bank 2) :** The engine control module (ECM) regulates the variable cam profiles. The engine control module (ECM) checks the control signal for the cam profile valves. The diagnostic trouble code (DTC) is stored if the control module detects that: * Control signal is too low. The control module's test for the diagnostic trouble code (DTC) starts in the event of: * Ignition switch position II. * Battery voltage higher than 10.5 V. **NOTE: For this function, bank 1 consists of cylinders 1, 2 and 4. Bank 2 consists of cylinders 3, 5 and 6.**
DTC: ECM-P001F00 **1T PCM, MIL: Yes** **Years:** 2011, 2012 **Model:** S60, XC60, XC90 **Engine:** 3.0L L6 VIN 90, 3.2L L6 VIN 94, 3.2L L6 VIN 95	**Intake (A) Cam Profile Control Circuit High (Bank 2) :** The engine control module (ECM) regulates the variable cam profiles. The engine control module (ECM) checks the control signal for the cam profile valves. The diagnostic trouble code (DTC) is stored if the control module detects that: * Control signal is too high. The control module's test for the diagnostic trouble code (DTC) starts in the event of: * Ignition switch position II. **NOTE: For this function, bank 1 consists of cylinders 1, 2 and 4. Bank 2 consists of cylinders 3, 5 and 6.**
DTC: ECM-P003100 **1T ECM, MIL: Yes** **Year:** 2011, 2012 **Model:** XC90 **Engine:** 4.4L V8	**HO2S Heater Control Circuit Low (Bank 1, Sensor 1). :** The diagnostic trouble code (DTC) is stored if the Engine Control Module (ECM) registers that the front heated oxygen sensor (HO2S) preheating circuit (bank 1) has a short-circuit to ground, or if there is an open-circuit. The engine cylinders are counted from the cylinder furthest away from the flywheel. The diagnostic trouble code can be diagnosed when the ignition is on.
DTC: ECM-P003200 **1T ECM, MIL: Yes** **Year:** 2011, 2012 **Model:** XC90 **Engine:** 4.4L V8	**HO2S Heater Control Circuit High (Bank 1, Sensor 1):** The diagnostic trouble code (DTC) is stored if the Engine Control Module (ECM) registers that the front heated oxygen sensor (HO2S) preheating circuit (bank 1) has a short-circuit to supply voltage. The engine cylinders are counted from the cylinder furthest away from the flywheel. The diagnostic trouble code can be diagnosed when the ignition is on.
DTC: ECM-P003300 **1T ECM** **Year:** 2011, 2012 **Model:** XC90 **Engine:** 4.4L V8	**Turbo/Super Charger Bypass Valve Control Circuit/Open:** The Engine control module (ECM) uses a relief valve to reduce noises that may occur when the accelerator pedal is released quickly. The engine control module (ECM) checks the control signal for the relief valve. The diagnostic trouble code (DTC) is stored if the control module detects that: Signal missing. The control module's test for the diagnostic trouble code (DTC) starts in the event of: Ignition switch position II. Battery voltage higher than 10.5 V.
DTC: ECM-P003400 **1T ECM** **Year:** 2011, 2012 **Model:** XC90 **Engine:** 4.4L V8	**Turbo/Super Charger Bypass Valve Control Circuit Low:** The Engine control module (ECM) uses a relief valve to reduce noises that may occur when the accelerator pedal is released quickly. The engine control module (ECM) checks the control signal for the relief valve. The diagnostic trouble code (DTC) is stored if the control module detects that: Control signal is too low. The control module's test for the diagnostic trouble code (DTC) starts in the event of: Ignition switch position II. Battery voltage higher than 10.5 V.

DTC	Trouble Code Title and Conditions
DTC: ECM-P003500 **1T ECM** **Year:** 2011, 2012 **Model:** XC90 **Engine:** 4.4L V8	**Turbo/Super Charger Bypass Valve Control Circuit High:** The Engine control module (ECM) uses a relief valve to reduce noises that may occur when the accelerator pedal is released quickly. The engine control module (ECM) checks the control signal for the relief valve. The diagnostic trouble code (DTC) is stored if the control module detects that: Control signal is too high. The control module's test for the diagnostic trouble code (DTC) starts in the event of: Ignition switch position II. Battery voltage higher than 10.5 V. **Note! The control module can only detect the fault once the test has been started and the diagnostic trouble code (DTC) is stored when the conditions are met.**
DTC: ECM-P003600 **1T ECM, MIL: Yes** **Year:** 2011, 2012 **Model:** XC90 **Engine:** 4.4L V8	**HO2S Heater Control Circuit (Bank 1, Sensor 2) :** Engine control module (ECM) monitors the centre heated oxygen sensor's heating coil and its capacity to warm the oxygen sensor. This is done to measure impedance across the heater circuit during the preheating sequence for the oxygen sensor. Hint: The engine cylinders are counted from the cylinder furthest away from the flywheel. The diagnostic trouble code (DTC) is stored if the control module detects that: Impedance in heater circuit exceeds 42.1 Ω. The control module's test for the diagnostic trouble code (DTC) starts in the event of: Ignition position II or engine running.
DTC: ECM-P003700 **1T ECM, MIL: Yes** **Year:** 2011, 2012 **Model:** XC90 **Engine:** 4.4L V8	**HO2S Heater Control Circuit Low (Bank 1, Sensor 2):** Engine Control Module (ECM) checks if the centre heated oxygen sensor's preheating circuit (bank 1) is short-circuited to ground, if there is an open circuit in the circuit or if the resistance in the heating resistor is incorrect. Hint: The engine cylinders are counted from the cylinder furthest away from the flywheel. The diagnostic trouble code (DTC) is stored if the engine control module (ECM) registers any of these. The diagnostic trouble code (DTC) can be diagnosed at ignition on and if the battery voltage is in the range 11-16 V.
DTC: ECM-P003800 **1T ECM, MIL: Yes** **Year:** 2011, 2012 **Model:** XC90 **Engine:** 4.4L V8	**HO2S Heater Control Circuit High (Bank 1, Sensor 2):** Engine Control Module (ECM) checks if the centre heated oxygen sensor's preheating circuit (bank 1) is short-circuited to voltage. Hint: The engine cylinders are counted from the cylinder furthest away from the flywheel. The diagnostic trouble code (DTC) is stored if the engine control module (ECM) registers any of these. The diagnostic trouble code (DTC) can be diagnosed at ignition on and if the battery voltage is in the range 11-16 V.
DTC: ECM-P003900 **1T ECM** **Year:** 2011, 2012 **Model:** XC90 **Engine:** 4.4L V8	**Turbo/Super Charger Bypass Valve Control Circuit Range/Performance:** The Engine control module (ECM) has built-in functions to check whether the relief valve has jammed in the closed position. The control module performs a number of internal tests using the turbo control signal (this is done during the time that the control module knows that the valve is open) to evaluate the function of the valve. The diagnostic trouble code (DTC) is stored if the control module detects that: The relief valve is closed when it should be open. The control module's test for the diagnostic trouble code (DTC) starts in the event of: Engine running. Boost pressure (approx. 30 kPa above atmospheric pressure). Activated relief valve.
DTC: ECM-P004500 **1T ECM** **Year:** 2011, 2012 **Model:** XC90 **Engine:** 4.4L V8	**Turbo/Super Charger Boost Control Solenoid Circuit/Open:** The Engine control module (ECM) regulates the turbo pressure using a turbo control valve. The control module has integrated functions to check the function of the turbo control valve. The diagnostic trouble code (DTC) is stored if the control module detects that: Signal missing. The control module's test for the diagnostic trouble code (DTC) starts in the event of: * Ignition switch position II. * Battery voltage higher than 10.5 V. *
DTC: ECM-P004700 **1T ECM** **Year:** 2011, 2012 **Model:** XC90 **Engine:** 4.4L V8	**Turbo/Super Charger Boost Control Solenoid Circuit Low:** The Engine control module (ECM) regulates the turbo pressure using a turbo control valve. The control module has integrated functions to check the function of the turbo control valve. The diagnostic trouble code (DTC) is stored if the control module detects that: Control signal is too low. The control module's test for the diagnostic trouble code (DTC) starts in the event of: Ignition switch position II. Battery voltage higher than 10.5 V.

DTC	Trouble Code Title and Conditions
DTC: ECM-P004800 **1T ECM** **Year:** 2011, 2012 **Model:** XC90 **Engine:** 4.4L V8	**Turbo/Super Charger Boost Control Solenoid Circuit High:** The Engine control module (ECM) regulates the turbo pressure using a turbo control valve. The control module has integrated functions to check the function of the turbo control valve. The diagnostic trouble code (DTC) is stored if the control module detects that: Control signal is too high. The control module's test for the diagnostic trouble code (DTC) starts in the event of: Ignition switch position II. Battery voltage higher than 10.5 V.
DTC: ECM-P006D00 **1T ECM** **Year:** 2011, 2012 **Model:** XC90 **Engine:** 4.4L V8	**Barometric Pressure - Turbocharger/Supercharger Inlet Pressure Correlation:** The Engine control module (ECM) continuously checks the plausibility of the signal from the built-in atmospheric pressure sensor. The diagnostic trouble code (DTC) is stored if the control module detects that: Control signal is too high. The control module's test for the diagnostic trouble code (DTC) starts in the event of: Ignition switch position II. Battery voltage higher than 10.5 V.
DTC: ECM-P007000 **1T ECM, MIL: Yes** **Year:** 2011, 2012 **Model:** XC90 **Engine:** 4.4L V8	**Ambient Air Temperature Sensor Circuit:** Engine control module (ECM) measures the ambient temperature using an outside temperature sensor. The sensor is located in the left external rear-view mirror. The control module checks the direct voltage from the sensor. The diagnostic trouble code (DTC) is stored if the control module detects that: * The direct voltage is higher than 4.951 V. * Incorrect value lasts longer than 9 seconds. * Incorrect value lasts for 2 or more subsequent driving cycles. The control module's test for the diagnostic trouble code (DTC) starts in the event of: * Ignition switch position II.
DTC: ECM-P007100 **1T ECM, MIL: Yes** **Year:** 2011, 2012 **Model:** XC90 **Engine:** 4.4L V8	**Ambient Air Temperature Sensor Range/Performance:** The engine control module (ECM) checks the signal from the outside temperature sensor in the left door mirror. The diagnostic trouble code is generated if the control module detects that the value for outside temperature deviates too much from the intake temperature, fuel temperature or coolant temperature after the engine has been warmed up and then allowed to cool for at least 8 hours. The diagnostic trouble code can be diagnosed once per operating cycle with the ignition on, but only once the engine temperature has fallen to approx. 50 °C from operating temperature since the previous operating cycle.
DTC: ECM-P007162 **1T ECM, MIL: Yes** **Year:** 2011, 2012 **Model:** XC90 **Engine:** 4.4L V8	**Ambient Air Temperature Sensor Range/Performance:** The engine control module (ECM) checks the signal from the outside temperature sensor in the left door mirror. The diagnostic trouble code is generated if the control module detects that the value for outside temperature deviates too much from the intake temperature, fuel temperature or coolant temperature after the engine has been warmed up and then allowed to cool for at least 8 hours. The diagnostic trouble code can be diagnosed once per operating cycle with the ignition on, but only once the engine temperature has fallen to approx. 50 °C from operating temperature since the previous operating cycle.
DTC: ECM-P007164 **1T ECM, MIL: Yes** **Year:** 2011, 2012 **Model:** XC90 **Engine:** 4.4L V8	**Ambient Air Temperature Sensor Range/Performance:** The engine control module (ECM) checks the signal from the outside temperature sensor in the left door mirror. The diagnostic trouble code is generated if the control module detects that the value for outside temperature deviates too much from the intake temperature, fuel temperature or coolant temperature after the engine has been warmed up and then allowed to cool for at least 8 hours. The diagnostic trouble code can be diagnosed once per operating cycle with the ignition on, but only once the engine temperature has fallen to approx. 50 °C from operating temperature since the previous operating cycle.
DTC: ECM-P007200 **2T ECM** **Year:** 2011, 2012 **Model:** XC90 **Engine:** 4.4L V8	**Ambient Air Temperature Sensor Circuit:** Engine control module (ECM) measures the ambient temperature using an outside temperature sensor. The sensor is located in the left external rear-view mirror. The control module checks the direct voltage from the sensor. The diagnostic trouble code (DTC) is stored if the control module detects that: The direct voltage is higher than 4.951 V. Incorrect value lasts longer than 9 seconds. Incorrect value lasts for 2 or more subsequent driving cycles. The control module's test for the diagnostic trouble code (DTC) starts in the event of: Ignition switch position II.

DTC	Trouble Code Title and Conditions
DTC: ECM-P007300 **2T ECM, MIL: Yes** **Year:** 2011, 2012 **Model:** XC90 **Engine:** 4.4L V8	**Ambient Air Temperature Sensor Circuit:** Engine control module (ECM) measures the ambient temperature using an outside temperature sensor. The sensor is located in the left external rear-view mirror. The control module checks the direct voltage from the sensor. The diagnostic trouble code (DTC) is stored if the control module detects that: The direct voltage is higher than 4.951 V. Incorrect value lasts longer than 9 seconds. Incorrect value lasts for 2 or more subsequent driving cycles. The control module's test for the diagnostic trouble code (DTC) starts in the event of: Ignition switch position II.
DTC: ECM-P007500 **1T ECM, MIL: Yes** **Year:** 2011, 2012 **Model:** XC90 **Engine:** 4.4L V8	**Intake Valve Control Circuit (Bank 1):** The engine control module (ECM) regulates the position of the camshaft (angle) by regulating the camshaft reset valve. The engine control module (ECM) checks the control signal for the camshaft reset valve. The diagnostic trouble code (DTC) is stored if the control module detects that: Signal missing. The control module's test for the diagnostic trouble code (DTC) starts in the event of: Ignition switch position II. Battery voltage higher than 10.5 V. **Note! The control module can only detect the fault once the test has been started and the diagnostic trouble code (DTC) is stored when the conditions are met.**
DTC: ECM-P007600 **1T ECM, MIL: Yes** **Year:** 2011, 2012 **Model:** XC90 **Engine:** 4.4L V8	**Intake Valve Control Circuit Low (Bank 1):** The engine control module (ECM) regulates the position of the camshaft (angle) by regulating the camshaft reset valve. The engine control module (ECM) checks the control signal for the camshaft reset valve. The diagnostic trouble code (DTC) is stored if the control module detects that: Control signal is too low. The control module's test for the diagnostic trouble code (DTC) starts in the event of: Ignition switch position II. Battery voltage higher than 10.5 V.
DTC: ECM-P007700 **1T ECM, MIL: Yes** **Year:** 2011, 2012 **Model:** XC90 **Engine:** 4.4L V8	**Intake Valve Control Circuit High (Bank 1) :** The engine control module (ECM) regulates the position of the camshaft (angle) by regulating the camshaft reset valve. The engine control module (ECM) checks the control signal for the camshaft reset valve. The diagnostic trouble code (DTC) is stored if the control module detects that: Control signal is too high. The control module's test for the diagnostic trouble code (DTC) starts in the event of: Ignition switch position II. Battery voltage higher than 10.5 V.
DTC: ECM-P008700 **1T ECM, MIL: Yes** **Year:** 2011, 2012 **Model:** XC90 **Engine:** 4.4L V8	**Fuel Rail/System Pressure (Too Low):** The engine control module (ECM) controls the fuel pressure via the fuel pump (FP) control module using a pulse width modulation (PWM) signal. The fuel pump (FP) control module then controls the fuel pump (FP) depending on the pressure requested by the engine control module (ECM). For information about fuel pressure control, see VIDA Design and function. The diagnostic trouble code (DTC) is stored if the control module detects that: Actual pressure (gauged pressure from the fuel pressure sensor) becomes too low compared with the requested pressure (engine control module (ECM) target value) for a certain amount of time. The control module's test for the diagnostic trouble code (DTC) starts in the event of: Engine running.
DTC: ECM-P008800 **1T ECM, MIL: Yes** **Year:** 2011, 2012 **Model:** XC90 **Engine:** 4.4L V8	**Fuel Rail/System Pressure (Too High):** The engine control module (ECM) controls the fuel pressure via the fuel pump (FP) control module using a pulse width modulation (PWM) signal. The fuel pump (FP) control module then controls the fuel pump (FP) depending on the pressure requested by the engine control module (ECM). For information about fuel pressure control, see VIDA Design and function. The diagnostic trouble code (DTC) is stored if the control module detects that: Actual pressure (gauged pressure from the fuel pressure sensor) becomes too high compared with the requested pressure (engine control module (ECM) target value) for a certain amount of time. The control module's test for the diagnostic trouble code (DTC) starts in the event of: Engine running.

DTC	Trouble Code Title and Conditions
DTC: ECM-P008968 **T ECM** **Year:** 2011, 2012 **Model:** XC90 **Engine:** 4.4L V8	**Fuel Pressure Regulator Performance:** Engine control module (ECM) monitors the fuel system. If the control module detects that the fuel pressure is too low for a certain time, the diagnostic trouble code is generated. The diagnostic trouble code (DTC) can be diagnosed when the engine is running.
DTC: ECM-P009500 **1T ECM, MIL: Yes** **Year:** 2011, 2012 **Model:** XC90 **Engine:** 4.4L V8	**Intake Air Temperature Sensor 2 Circuit:** Engine control module (ECM) checks the signal from the air temperature sensor (integrated in boost pressure sensor) which is located between the turbocharger and the throttle module. **Note! The boost pressure sensor and air temperature sensor are integrated in the same component, the boost pressure sensor.** The diagnostic trouble code (DTC) is stored if the control module detects that: Control signal is too high. The control module's test for the diagnostic trouble code (DTC) starts in the event of: Ignition on. Battery voltage higher than 10.5 V.
DTC: ECM-P009600 **1T ECM, MIL: Yes** **Year:** 2011, 2012 **Model:** XC90 **Engine:** 4.4L V8	**Intake Air Temperature Sensor 2 Circuit Range/Performance:** Engine control module (ECM) checks the signal from the air temperature sensor (integrated in boost pressure sensor) which is located between the turbocharger and the throttle module. **Note! The boost pressure sensor and air temperature sensor are integrated in the same component, the boost pressure sensor.** The diagnostic trouble code (DTC) is stored if the control module detects that: The temperature (measured in the boost pressure sensor) deviates too much from the coolant temperature, outdoor temperature, or air temperature in the mass air flow (MAF) sensor. The control module's test for the diagnostic trouble code (DTC) starts in the event of: Ignition on. Once per operating cycle, but only when the engine's temperature has dropped by approx 50°C (from operating temperature) since the previous operating cycle. **Note! The control module can only detect the fault once the test has been started and the diagnostic trouble code (DTC) is stored when the conditions are met.**
DTC: ECM-P009621 **1T ECM, MIL: Yes** **Year:** 2011, 2012 **Model:** XC90 **Engine:** 4.4L V8	**Intake Air Temperature Sensor 2 Circuit Range/Performance (Bank 1). :** Engine control module (ECM) checks the signal from the air temperature sensor (integrated in boost pressure sensor) which is located between the turbocharger and the throttle module. **Note! The boost pressure sensor and air temperature sensor are integrated in the same component, the boost pressure sensor.** The diagnostic trouble code (DTC) is stored if the control module detects that: The temperature (measured in the boost pressure sensor) deviates too much from the coolant temperature, outdoor temperature, or air temperature in the mass air flow (MAF) sensor. The control module's test for the diagnostic trouble code (DTC) starts in the event of: Ignition on. Once per operating cycle, but only when the engine's temperature has dropped by approx 50°C (from operating temperature) since the previous operating cycle.
DTC: ECM-P009622 **1T ECM, MIL: Yes** **Year:** 2011, 2012 **Model:** XC90 **Engine:** 4.4L V8	**Intake Air Temperature Sensor 2 Circuit Range/Performance (Bank 1). :** Engine control module (ECM) checks the signal from the air temperature sensor (integrated in boost pressure sensor) which is located between the turbocharger and the throttle module. **Note! The boost pressure sensor and air temperature sensor are integrated in the same component, the boost pressure sensor.** The diagnostic trouble code (DTC) is stored if the control module detects that: The temperature (measured in the boost pressure sensor) deviates too much from the coolant temperature, outdoor temperature, or air temperature in the mass air flow (MAF) sensor. The control module's test for the diagnostic trouble code (DTC) starts in the event of: Ignition on. Once per operating cycle, but only when the engine's temperature has dropped by approx 50°C (from operating temperature) since the previous operating cycle.

DTC	Trouble Code Title and Conditions
DTC: ECM-P009700 **1T ECM, MIL: Yes** **Year:** 2011, 2012 **Model:** XC90 **Engine:** 4.4L V8	**Intake Air Temperature Sensor 2 Circuit Low Input:** Engine control module (ECM) checks the signal from the air temperature sensor (integrated in boost pressure sensor) which is located between the turbocharger and the throttle module. **Note! The boost pressure sensor and air temperature sensor are integrated in the same component, the boost pressure sensor.** The control module checks the direct voltage from the sensor. The diagnostic trouble code (DTC) is stored if the control module detects that: The direct voltage is lower than 0.112 V. Incorrect value lasts longer than 9 seconds. Incorrect value lasts for 2 or more subsequent driving cycles. The control module's test for the diagnostic trouble code (DTC) starts in the event of: Ignition switch position II.
DTC: ECM-P009800 **1T ECM, MIL: Yes** **Year:** 2011, 2012 **Model:** XC90 **Engine:** 4.4L V8	**Intake Air Temperature Sensor 2 Circuit High Input:** Engine control module (ECM) checks the signal from the air temperature sensor (integrated in boost pressure sensor) which is located between the turbocharger and the throttle module. The control module checks the direct voltage from the sensor. The diagnostic trouble code (DTC) is stored if the control module detects that: The direct voltage is higher than 4.902 V. Incorrect value lasts longer than 9 seconds. Incorrect value lasts for 2 or more subsequent driving cycles. The control module's test for the diagnostic trouble code (DTC) starts in the event of: Ignition switch position II.
DTC: ECM-P010000 **1T ECM, MIL: Yes** **Year:** 2011, 2012 **Model:** XC90 **Engine:** 4.4L V8	**Mass or Volume Air Flow Circuit:** Engine control module (ECM) measures the amount of air that passes through the inlet manifold using a mass air flow sensor. The control module checks the direct voltage from the sensor. **Note! The mass air flow sensor and air temperature sensor are integrated in the same component.** The diagnostic trouble code (DTC) is stored if the control module detects that: * Ignition switch position II. * The direct voltage is lower than 0.049 V. * Incorrect value lasts longer than 9 seconds. * Incorrect value lasts for 2 or more subsequent driving cycles. * The control module's test for the diagnostic trouble code (DTC) starts in the event of:
DTC: ECM-P010100 **1T ECM, MIL: Yes** **Year:** 2011, 2012 **Model:** XC90 **Engine:** 4.4L V8	**Mass or Volume Air Flow Circuit Range/Performance:** The engine control module (ECM) measures the air mass through the intake manifold using a sensor. The diagnostic trouble code (DTC) is stored if the Engine Control Module (ECM) detects that the signal from the mass air flow (MAF) sensor is too low. The diagnostic trouble code can be diagnosed when the ignition is on.
DTC: ECM-P010192 **1T ECM, MIL: Yes** **Year:** 2011, 2012 **Model:** XC90 **Engine:** 4.4L V8	**Mass or Volume Air Flow Circuit Range/Performance:** The engine control module (ECM) measures the air mass through the intake manifold using a sensor. The diagnostic trouble code (DTC) is stored if the Engine Control Module (ECM) detects that the signal from the mass air flow (MAF) sensor is too low. The diagnostic trouble code can be diagnosed when the ignition is on.
DTC: ECM-P010200 **2T ECM, MIL: Yes** **Year:** 2011, 2012 **Model:** XC90 **Engine:** 4.4L V8	**Mass Or Volume Air Flow Circuit (Low Input):** Engine control module (ECM) measures the amount of air that passes through the inlet manifold using a mass air flow sensor. The control module checks the direct voltage from the sensor. **Note! The mass air flow sensor and air temperature sensor are integrated in the same component.** The diagnostic trouble code (DTC) is stored if the control module detects that: * The direct voltage is lower than 0.049 V. * Incorrect value lasts longer than 9 seconds. * Incorrect value lasts for 2 or more subsequent driving cycles. * The control module's test for the diagnostic trouble code (DTC) starts in the event of: * Ignition switch position II.

DTC	Trouble Code Title and Conditions
DTC: ECM-P010300 **2T ECM, MIL: Yes** **Year:** 2011, 2012 **Model:** XC90 **Engine:** 4.4L V8	**Mass Or Volume Air Flow Circuit (High Input):** Engine control module (ECM) measures the amount of air that passes through the inlet manifold using a mass air flow sensor. The control module checks the direct voltage from the sensor. **Note! The mass air flow sensor and air temperature sensor are integrated in the same component.** The diagnostic trouble code (DTC) is stored if the control module detects that: * Ignition switch position II. * The direct voltage is lower than 0.049 V. * Incorrect value lasts longer than 9 seconds. * Incorrect value lasts for 2 or more subsequent driving cycles.
DTC: ECM-P010500 **1T ECM, MIL: Yes** **Year:** 2011, 2012 **Model:** XC90 **Engine:** 4.4L V8	**Manifold Absolute Pressure/BARO Circuit:** The engine control module (ECM) measures the pressure in the intake manifold using an air pressure sensor. The control module checks the direct voltage from the sensor. The diagnostic trouble code (DTC) is stored if the control module detects that: * Ignition switch position II. * The direct voltage is higher than 4.951 V. * Incorrect value lasts longer than 9 seconds. * Incorrect value lasts for 2 or more subsequent driving cycles.
DTC: ECM-P010600 **1T ECM, MIL: Yes** **Year:** 2011, 2012 **Model:** XC90 **Engine:** 4.4L V8	**Manifold Absolute Pressure/BARO Sensor Range/Performance:** The engine control module (ECM) measures the air pressure in the intake manifold using an air pressure sensor. The diagnostic trouble code is generated if the control module detects that the air pressure sensor value deviates too much from the value calculated based on a model. The diagnostic trouble code can be diagnosed at a fixed engine speed over 1250 rpm when the engine is warm (at least 70 °C).
DTC: ECM-P010700 **2T ECM, MIL: Yes** **Year:** 2011, 2012 **Model:** XC90 **Engine:** 4.4L V8	**Manifold Absolute Pressure/BARO Sensor (Low Input):** The engine control module (ECM) measures the pressure in the intake manifold using an air pressure sensor. The control module checks the direct voltage from the sensor. The diagnostic trouble code (DTC) is stored if the control module detects that: * Ignition switch position II. * The direct voltage is higher than 4.951 V. * Incorrect value lasts longer than 9 seconds. * Incorrect value lasts for 2 or more subsequent driving cycles.
DTC: ECM-P010800 **2T ECM, MIL: Yes** **Year:** 2011, 2012 **Model:** XC90 **Engine:** 4.4L V8	**Manifold Absolute Pressure/BARO Sensor (High Input):** The engine control module (ECM) measures the pressure in the intake manifold using an air pressure sensor. The control module checks the direct voltage from the sensor. * The diagnostic trouble code (DTC) is stored if the control module detects that: * Ignition switch position II. * The direct voltage is higher than 4.951 V. * Incorrect value lasts longer than 9 seconds. * Incorrect value lasts for 2 or more subsequent driving cycles.
DTC: ECM-P011000 **1T ECM, MIL: Yes** **Year:** 2011, 2012 **Model:** XC90 **Engine:** 4.4L V8	**Intake Air Temperature Sensor 1 Circuit:** Engine control module (ECM) measures the temperature of the inducted air using an air temperature sensor in the inlet manifold. The control module checks the direct voltage from the sensor. **Note! The mass air flow sensor and air temperature sensor are integrated in the same component.** The diagnostic trouble code (DTC) is stored if the control module detects that: * Ignition switch position II. * The direct voltage is higher than 4.951 V. * Incorrect value lasts longer than 9 seconds. * Incorrect value lasts for 2 or more subsequent driving cycles.
DTC: ECM-P011100 **1T ECM, MIL: Yes** **Year:** 2011, 2012 **Model:** XC90 **Engine:** 4.4L V8	**Intake Air Temperature Sensor 1 Circuit Range/Performance.:** The engine control module (ECM) checks the signal from the air temperature sensor in the intake manifold. A DTC is stored if the control module detects that the air temperature (measured in the mass air flow (MAF) sensor) deviates too much from the coolant temperature, the temperature measured in the boost pressure sensor (between the turbo compressor and throttle) or the fuel temperature, after the engine has been switched off for a long time. The diagnostic trouble code can be diagnosed once per operating cycle with the ignition on, but only once the engine temperature has fallen to approx. 50 °C from operating temperature since the previous operating cycle. **Note! The mass air flow sensor and air temperature sensor are integrated in the same Component.**

DTC	Trouble Code Title and Conditions
DTC: ECM-P011123 **1T ECM, MIL: Yes** **Year:** 2011, 2012 **Model:** XC90 **Engine:** 4.4L V8	**Intake Air Temperature Sensor 1 Circuit Range/Performance (Signal Stuck Low):** The engine control module (ECM) checks the signal from the air temperature sensor in the intake manifold. The diagnostic trouble code is generated if the control module detects that the value from the air temperature sensor deviates too much from the engine temperature, outside temperature or fuel temperature after the engine has been off for a long period of time. The diagnostic trouble code can be diagnosed once per operating cycle with the ignition on, but only once engine temperature has fallen to approx. 55 °C from operating temperature since the previous operating cycle.
DTC: ECM-P011124 **1T ECM, MIL: Yes** **Year:** 2011, 2012 **Model:** XC90 **Engine:** 4.4L V8	**Intake Air Temperature Sensor 1 Circuit Range/Performance (Signal Stuck High) :** The engine control module (ECM) checks the signal from the air temperature sensor in the intake manifold. The diagnostic trouble code is generated if the control module detects that the value from the air temperature sensor deviates too much from the engine temperature, outside temperature or fuel temperature after the engine has been off for a long period of time. The diagnostic trouble code can be diagnosed once per operating cycle with the ignition on, but only once engine temperature has fallen to approx. 55 °C from operating temperature since the previous operating cycle.
DTC: ECM-P011126 **1T ECM, MIL: Yes** **Year:** 2011, 2012 **Model:** XC90 **Engine:** 4.4L V8	**Intake Air Temperature Sensor 1 Circuit Range/Performance (Signal Rate Below Threshold):** The engine control module (ECM) checks the signal from the temperature sensor in the intake manifold under two different driving conditions. The check is first made during high airflow while the vehicle is travelling and then while the vehicle is stationary and idling. The diagnostic trouble code is generated if the control module registers that the temperature difference between these two measurements is unreasonably similar.
DTC: ECM-P011200 **2T ECM, MIL: Yes** **Year:** 2011, 2012 **Model:** XC90 **Engine:** 4.4L V8	**Intake Air Temperature Sensor 2 Circuit (Low Input):** Engine control module (ECM) measures the temperature of the inducted air using an air temperature sensor in the inlet manifold. The control module checks the direct voltage from the sensor. **Note! The mass air flow sensor and air temperature sensor are integrated in the same component.** The diagnostic trouble code (DTC) is stored if the control module detects that: * Ignition switch position II * The direct voltage is higher than 4.951 V. * Incorrect value lasts longer than 9 seconds. * Incorrect value lasts for 2 or more subsequent driving cycles.
DTC: ECM-P011300 **2T ECM, MIL: Yes** **Year:** 2011, 2012 **Model:** XC90 **Engine:** 4.4L V8	**Intake Air Temperature Sensor 1 Circuit High Input:** Engine control module (ECM) measures the temperature of the inducted air using an air temperature sensor in the inlet manifold. The control module checks the direct voltage from the sensor. **Note! The mass air flow sensor and air temperature sensor are integrated in the same component.** The diagnostic trouble code (DTC) is stored if the control module detects that: The direct voltage is higher than 4.951 V. Incorrect value lasts longer than 9 seconds. Incorrect value lasts for 2 or more subsequent driving cycles. The control module's test for the diagnostic trouble code (DTC) starts in the event of: Ignition switch position II. **Note! The control module can only detect the fault once the test has been started and the diagnostic trouble code (DTC) is stored when the conditions are met.**
DTC: ECM-P011400 **1T ECM, MIL: Yes** **Year:** 2011, 2012 **Model:** XC90 **Engine:** 4.4L V8	**Intake Air Temperature Sensor 1 Intermittent/Erratic:** The engine control module (ECM) checks the signal from the temperature sensor in the intake manifold under two different driving conditions. The check is first made during high airflow while the vehicle is travelling and then while the vehicle is stationary and idling. The diagnostic trouble code is generated if the control module registers that the temperature difference between these two measurements is unreasonably similar. **Note! The mass air flow sensor and air temperature sensor are integrated in the same component.**
DTC: ECM-P011500 **1T ECM, MIL: Yes** **Year:** 2011, 2012 **Model:** XC90 **Engine:** 4.4L V8	**Engine Coolant Temperature Circuit:** Engine control module (ECM) measures the engine temperature using a coolant temperature sensor. The control module checks the direct voltage from the sensor. The diagnostic trouble code (DTC) is stored if the control module detects that: The direct voltage is higher than 4.951 V. Incorrect value lasts longer than 9 seconds. Incorrect value lasts for 2 or more subsequent driving cycles. The control module's test for the diagnostic trouble code (DTC) starts in the event of: Ignition switch position II. **Note! The control module can only detect the fault once the test has been started and the diagnostic trouble code (DTC) is stored when the conditions are met.**

DTC	Trouble Code Title and Conditions
DTC: ECM-P011600 **1T ECM, MIL: Yes** **Year:** 2011, 2012 **Model:** XC90 **Engine:** 4.4L V8	**Engine Coolant Temperature Circuit Range/Performance:** The engine control module (ECM) monitors the engine temperature using a sensor. A DTC is stored if the control module detects that the coolant temperature deviates too much from the air temperature, the air temperature (measured in the mass air flow (MAF) sensor), the temperature measured in the boost pressure sensor (between the turbo compressor and throttle) or the fuel temperature, after the engine has been switched off for a long time. The diagnostic trouble code is diagnosed at ignition on once per driving cycle, but only when the fuel temperature has dropped by at least 20 °C and has ended up near the outdoor temperature from the previous driving cycle.
DTC: ECM-P011621 **1T ECM, MIL: Yes** **Year:** 2011, 2012 **Model:** XC90 **Engine:** 4.4L V8	**Engine Coolant Temperature Circuit Range/Performance. Signal Too Low:** The engine control module (ECM) monitors the engine temperature using a sensor. The diagnostic trouble code is generated if the control module detects that the value from the engine temperature sensor deviates too much from the intake temperature, outside temperature or fuel temperature after the engine has been off for a long period of time. The diagnostic trouble code is diagnosed at ignition on once per driving cycle, but only when the fuel temperature has dropped by at least 20 °C and has ended up near the outdoor temperature from the previous driving cycle.
DTC: ECM-P011622 **1T ECM, MIL: Yes** **Year:** 2011, 2012 **Model:** XC90 **Engine:** 4.4L V8	**Engine Coolant Temperature Circuit Range/Performance. Signal Too High:** The engine control module (ECM) monitors the engine temperature using a sensor. The diagnostic trouble code is generated if the control module detects that the value from the engine temperature sensor deviates too much from the intake temperature, outside temperature or fuel temperature after the engine has been off for a long period of time. The diagnostic trouble code is diagnosed at ignition on once per driving cycle, but only when the fuel temperature has dropped by at least 20 °C and has ended up near the outdoor temperature from the previous driving cycle.
DTC: ECM-P011629 **1T ECM, MIL: Yes** **Year:** 2011, 2012 **Model:** XC90 **Engine:** 4.4L V8	**Engine Coolant Temperature Circuit Range/Performance. Signal Invalid:** The engine control module (ECM) monitors the engine temperature using a sensor. If the control module detects that the value from the engine temperature sensor does not change during engine warm-up phase, the diagnostic trouble code is generated. The control module for the diagnostic trouble code starts when the calculated engine temperature has increased by 20 °C and the fuel temperature by 5 °C since engine start, but only if the fuel temperature has dropped by at least 5 °C since the end of the previous driving cycle.
DTC: ECM-P011700 **2T ECM, MIL: Yes** **Year:** 2011, 2012 **Model:** XC90 **Engine:** 4.4L V8	**Engine Coolant Temperature Circuit Low Input:** Engine control module (ECM) measures the engine temperature using a coolant temperature sensor. The control module checks the direct voltage from the sensor. The diagnostic trouble code (DTC) is stored if the control module detects that: The direct voltage is higher than 4.951 V. Incorrect value lasts longer than 9 seconds. Incorrect value lasts for 2 or more subsequent driving cycles. The control module's test for the diagnostic trouble code (DTC) starts in the event of: Ignition switch position II. **Note! The control module can only detect the fault once the test has been started and the diagnostic trouble code (DTC) is stored when the conditions are met.**
DTC: ECM-P011800 **2T ECM, MIL: Yes** **Year:** 2011, 2012 **Model:** XC90 **Engine:** 4.4L V8	**Engine Coolant Temperature Circuit High Input:** Engine control module (ECM) measures the engine temperature using a coolant temperature sensor. The control module checks the direct voltage from the sensor. The diagnostic trouble code (DTC) is stored if the control module detects that: The direct voltage is higher than 4.951 V. Incorrect value lasts longer than 9 seconds. Incorrect value lasts for 2 or more subsequent driving cycles. The control module's test for the diagnostic trouble code (DTC) starts in the event of: Ignition switch position II. **Note! The control module can only detect the fault once the test has been started and the diagnostic trouble code (DTC) is stored when the conditions are met.**

DTC	Trouble Code Title and Conditions
DTC: ECM-P012023 **1T ECM** **Year:** 2011, 2012 **Model:** XC90 **Engine:** 4.4L V8	**Throttle/Pedal Position Sensor A Circuit:** The engine control module (ECM) checks the pulse width modulation (PWM) signal and the analog signal from the accelerator pedal (AP) position sensor. The analog signal is directly connected to the Central electronic module (CEM) and the signal is transmitted via CAN communication to the Engine control module (ECM). The pulse width modulation (PWM) signal is directly connected to the engine control module (ECM). The PWM signal is used to determine the current accelerator pedal position in a fault free system. The engine control module (ECM) checks the PWM signal. The diagnostic trouble code (DTC) is stored if the control module detects that: The PWM signal is too low. Incorrect value lasts longer than 16 seconds. The control module's test for the diagnostic trouble code (DTC) starts in the event of: Ignition switch position II. **Note! The control module can only detect the fault once the test has been started and the diagnostic trouble code (DTC) is stored when the conditions are met.**
DTC: ECM-P012024 **1T ECM** **Year:** 2011, 2012 **Model:** XC90 **Engine:** 4.4L V8	**Throttle/Pedal Position Sensor A Circuit. Signal Stuck High:** The engine control module (ECM) checks the pulse width modulation (PWM) signal and the analog signal from the accelerator pedal (AP) position sensor. The analog signal is directly connected to the Central electronic module (CEM) and the signal is transmitted via CAN communication to the Engine control module (ECM). The pulse width modulation (PWM) signal is directly connected to the engine control module (ECM). The PWM signal is used to determine the current accelerator pedal position in a fault free system. The engine control module (ECM) checks the PWM signal. The diagnostic trouble code (DTC) is stored if the control module detects that: The PWM signal is too high. Incorrect value lasts longer than 16 seconds. The control module's test for the diagnostic trouble code (DTC) starts in the event of: Ignition switch position II. **Note! The control module can only detect the fault once the test has been started and the diagnostic trouble code (DTC) is stored when the conditions are met.**
DTC: ECM-P012038 **1T ECM** **Year:** 2011, 2012 **Model:** XC90 **Engine:** 4.4L V8	**Throttle/Pedal Position Sensor A Circuit. FM (Frequency Modulated) / PWM (Pulse Width Modulated):** The engine control module (ECM) checks the pulse width modulation (PWM) signal and the analog signal from the accelerator pedal (AP) position sensor. The analog signal is directly connected to the Central electronic module (CEM) and the signal is transmitted via CAN communication to the Engine control module (ECM). The pulse width modulation (PWM) signal is directly connected to the engine control module (ECM). The PWM signal is used to determine the current accelerator pedal position in a fault free system. The engine control module (ECM) checks the PWM signal. The diagnostic trouble code (DTC) is stored if the control module detects that: Incorrect frequency on the PWM signal. Incorrect value lasts longer than 16 seconds. The control module's test for the diagnostic trouble code (DTC) starts in the event of: Ignition switch position II. **Note! The control module can only detect the fault once the test has been started and the diagnostic trouble code (DTC) is stored when the conditions are met.**
DTC: ECM-P012200 **1T ECM, MIL: Yes** **Year:** 2011, 2012 **Model:** XC90 **Engine:** 4.4L V8	**Throttle/Pedal Position Sensor A Circuit Low:** Engine control module (ECM) checks the signals from the electronic throttle unit's two position sensors. If engine control module (ECM) detects unreasonably low signal from any of the sensors, the diagnostic trouble code is generated. The diagnostic trouble code can be diagnosed when the ignition is on.
DTC: ECM-P012300 **1T ECM** **Year:** 2011, 2012 **Model:** XC90 **Engine:** 4.4L V8	**Throttle/Pedal Position Sensor A Circuit High:** Engine control module (ECM) checks the signals from the electronic throttle unit's two position sensors. If engine control module (ECM) detects unreasonably high signal from any of the sensors, the diagnostic trouble code is generated. The diagnostic trouble code can be diagnosed when the ignition is on.
DTC: ECM-P012800 **1T ECM, MIL: Yes** **Year:** 2011, 2012 **Model:** XC90 **Engine:** 4.4L V8	**Coolant Thermostat (Coolant Temp Below Thermostat Regulating Temperature):** Checking of how the temperature increase proceeds takes place during the engine's warm-up phase. It is compared to the expected temperature increase, calculated according to load conditions and start temperature, among others. If engine control module (ECM) registers that measured engine temperature deviates too much from the calculated, the diagnostic trouble code is generated. The diagnostic trouble code is diagnosed once per operating cycle, with the engine running, when calculated engine temperature reaches 80 °C, but only if engine start is performed when measured engine temperature is between -10 and 63 °C.

DTC	Trouble Code Title and Conditions
DTC: ECM-P013100 **2T ECM, MIL: Yes** **Year:** 2011, 2012 **Model:** XC90 **Engine:** 4.4L V8	**O2 Circuit Low Voltage (Bank 1, Sensor 1):** The Engine control module (ECM) measures the volume of oxygen in the exhaust gases before the three-way catalytic converter (TWC) using a front heated oxygen sensor (HO2S) (bank 1). The control module checks the direct voltage from the sensor. The diagnostic trouble code (DTC) is stored if the control module detects that: The direct voltage is lower than 1.8 V. Incorrect value lasts longer than 5 seconds. Incorrect value lasts for 2 or more subsequent driving cycles. The control module's test for the diagnostic trouble code (DTC) starts in the event of: Engine running for at least 2 minutes. **Note! The control module can only detect the fault once the test has been started and the diagnostic trouble code (DTC) is stored when the conditions are met.**
DTC: ECM-P013200 **2T ECM, MIL: Yes** **Year:** 2011, 2012 **Model:** XC90 **Engine:** 4.4L V8	**O2 Circuit High Voltage (Bank 1, Sensor 1) :** The Engine control module (ECM) measures the volume of oxygen in the exhaust gases before the three-way catalytic converter (TWC) using a front heated oxygen sensor (HO2S) (bank 1). The control module checks the direct voltage from the sensor. The diagnostic trouble code (DTC) is stored if the control module detects that: The direct voltage is higher than 3.8 V. Incorrect value lasts longer than 5 seconds. Incorrect value lasts for 2 or more subsequent driving cycles. The control module's test for the diagnostic trouble code (DTC) starts in the event of: Engine running for at least 2 minutes. **Note! The control module can only detect the fault once the test has been started and the diagnostic trouble code (DTC) is stored when the conditions are met.**
DTC: ECM-P013300 **1T ECM, MIL: Yes** **Year:** 2011, 2012 **Model:** XC90 **Engine:** 4.4L V8	**O2 Circuit Slow Response (Bank 1, Sensor 1):** Engine Control Module (ECM) checks the front heated oxygen sensor's signal (bank 1). The Engine control module (ECM) actively regulates between rich and lean fuel / air mixture and registers how well the front heated oxygen sensor (HO2S) signal follows these changes. The diagnostic trouble code (DTC) is stored if the engine control module (ECM) registers that the heated oxygen sensor (HO2S) is not activated or is activated too slowly. The diagnostic trouble code (DTC) can be diagnosed with the engine at operating temperature, approximately 20 minutes after the engine has first been started if the vehicle is driven (normal road load) at 70-90 km/h for 40-50 seconds.
DTC: ECM-P013323 **1T ECM, MIL: Yes** **Year:** 2011, 2012 **Model:** XC90 **Engine:** 4.4L V8	**O2 Sensor Circuit Slow Response (Bank 1 Sensor 1). Signal Stuck Low:** Engine Control Module (ECM) checks the front heated oxygen sensor's signal (bank 1). The Engine control module (ECM) actively regulates between rich and lean fuel / air mixture and registers how well the front heated oxygen sensor (HO2S) signal follows these changes. The diagnostic trouble code (DTC) is stored if the engine control module (ECM) registers that the heated oxygen sensor (HO2S) is not activated or is activated too slowly. The diagnostic trouble code (DTC) can be diagnosed with the engine at operating temperature, approximately 20 minutes after the engine has first been started if the vehicle is driven (normal road load) at 70-90 km/h for 40-50 seconds.
DTC: ECM-P013324 **1T ECM, MIL: Yes** **Year:** 2011, 2012 **Model:** XC90 **Engine:** 4.4L V8	**O2 Sensor Circuit Slow Response (Bank 1 Sensor 1). Signal Stuck High:** Engine Control Module (ECM) checks the front heated oxygen sensor's signal (bank 1). The Engine control module (ECM) actively regulates between rich and lean fuel / air mixture and registers how well the front heated oxygen sensor (HO2S) signal follows these changes. The diagnostic trouble code (DTC) is stored if the engine control module (ECM) registers that the heated oxygen sensor (HO2S) is not activated or is activated too slowly. The diagnostic trouble code (DTC) can be diagnosed with the engine at operating temperature, approximately 20 minutes after the engine has first been started if the vehicle is driven (normal road load) at 70-90 km/h for 40-50 seconds.
DTC: ECM-P013326 **1T ECM, MIL: Yes** **Year:** 2011, 2012 **Model:** XC90 **Engine:** 4.4L V8	**O2 Sensor Circuit Slow Response (Bank 1 Sensor 1). Signal Rate of Change Below Threshold:** Engine Control Module (ECM) checks the front heated oxygen sensor's signal (bank 1). The Engine control module (ECM) actively regulates between rich and lean fuel / air mixture and registers how well the front heated oxygen sensor (HO2S) signal follows these changes. The diagnostic trouble code (DTC) is stored if the engine control module (ECM) registers that the heated oxygen sensor (HO2S) is not activated or is activated too slowly. The diagnostic trouble code (DTC) can be diagnosed with the engine at operating temperature, approximately 20 minutes after the engine has first been started if the vehicle is driven (normal road load) at 70-90 km/h for 40-50 seconds.

DTC	Trouble Code Title and Conditions
DTC: ECM-P013400 **1T ECM, MIL: Yes** **Year:** 2011, 2012 **Model:** XC90 **Engine:** 4.4L V8	**O2 Circuit No Activity Detected (Bank 1, Sensor 1) :** Engine Control Module (ECM) checks the front heated oxygen sensor's signal (bank 1). The engine cylinders are counted from the cylinder furthest away from the flywheel. The diagnostic trouble code (DTC) is stored if the engine control module (ECM) registers that the heated oxygen sensor (HO2S) is not activated or is activated too slowly. The diagnostic trouble code (DTC) can be diagnosed when the engine is running.
DTC: ECM-P013700 **1T ECM, MIL: Yes** **Year:** 2011, 2012 **Model:** XC90 **Engine:** 4.4L V8	**O2 Circuit Low Voltage (Bank 1, Sensor 2) :** The engine control module (ECM) assumes two initial values for probe voltage, 0 V and 5 V. If probe preheating is active and if at least one fuel shut-off (accelerator pedal released for at least 3 seconds) has been made, the centre heated oxygen sensor (bank 1) maximum value must have exceeded 0.6 V and the minimum value must have been below 0.1 V. Hint: The engine cylinders are counted from the cylinder furthest away from the flywheel. The diagnostic trouble code (DTC) is stored and the engine control module (ECM) interprets it as a fault if these parameters are not achieved after approximately 5 minutes and both the accumulated and actual heated oxygen sensor preheating have reached certain parameters. The diagnostic trouble code (DTC) can be diagnosed when the engine is running.
DTC: ECM-P013800 **1T ECM, MIL: Yes** **Year:** 2011, 2012 **Model:** XC90 **Engine:** 4.4L V8	**O2 Circuit High Voltage (Bank 1, Sensor 2) :** The engine control module (ECM) assumes two initial values for probe voltage, 0 V and 5 V. If probe preheating is active and if at least one fuel shut-off (accelerator pedal released for at least 3 seconds) has been made, the centre heated oxygen sensor (bank 1) maximum value must have exceeded 0.6 V and the minimum value must have been below 0.1 V. Hint: The engine cylinders are counted from the cylinder furthest away from the flywheel. The diagnostic trouble code (DTC) is stored and the engine control module (ECM) interprets it as a fault if these parameters are not achieved after approximately 5 minutes and both the accumulated and actual heated oxygen sensor preheating have reached certain parameters. The diagnostic trouble code (DTC) can be diagnosed when the engine is running.
DTC: ECM-P013968 **1T ECM, MIL: Yes** **Year:** 2011, 2012 **Model:** XC90 **Engine:** 4.4L V8	**O2 Circuit Slow Response (Bank 1, Sensor 2):** **Note! This diagnostic trouble code (DTC) status is an event controlled diagnostic trouble code (DTC). An event controlled diagnostic trouble code (DTC) does not mean that there is a fault in the control module when it is active, but is designed as information.** Engine control module (ECM) monitors the engine's heated oxygen sensor control. A DTC is stored if the control module detects that the heated oxygen sensor (HO2S) during fuel shut-off reacts slower than expected. The diagnostic trouble code (DTC) can be diagnosed when the engine is running.
DTC: ECM-P013A00 **1T ECM, MIL: Yes** **Year:** 2011, 2012 **Model:** XC90 **Engine:** 4.4L V8	**O2 Sensor Slow Response - Rich to Lean (Bank 1 and Sensor 2) :** The engine control module (ECM) checks the centre heated oxygen sensor (HO2S) signal (bank 1). The Engine control module (ECM) actively regulates between rich and lean fuel/air mixture and registers how well the centre heated oxygen sensor (HO2S) signal follows these changes. Hint: The engine cylinders are counted from the cylinder furthest away from the flywheel. The diagnostic trouble code (DTC) is stored if the control module detects that: The heated oxygen sensor reacts too slowly at switch from rich to lean. The control module's test for the diagnostic trouble code (DTC) starts in the event of: Special driving cases with fuel shut-offs.
DTC: ECM-P013E00 **1T ECM, MIL: Yes** **Year:** 2011, 2012 **Model:** XC90 **Engine:** 4.4L V8	**O2 Sensor Slow Response - Rich to Lean (Bank 1 and Sensor 2) :** The engine control module (ECM) checks the centre heated oxygen sensor (HO2S) signal (bank 1). The Engine control module (ECM) actively regulates between rich and lean fuel/air mixture and registers how well the centre heated oxygen sensor (HO2S) signal follows these changes. Hint: The engine cylinders are counted from the cylinder furthest away from the flywheel. The diagnostic trouble code (DTC) is stored if the control module detects that: The heated oxygen sensor reacts too slowly at switch from rich to lean. The control module's test for the diagnostic trouble code (DTC) starts in the event of: Special driving cases with fuel shut-offs.

DTC	Trouble Code Title and Conditions
DTC: ECM-P014000 **1T ECM, MIL: Yes** **Year:** 2011, 2012 **Model:** XC90 **Engine:** 4.4L V8	**O2 Circuit No Activity Detected (Bank 1, Sensor 2). :** The Engine control module (ECM) uses the heated oxygen sensor (HO2S), among other things, to determine if fuel trim is working as it should. The control module uses the heated oxygen sensor's (HO2S) volt signal to determine whether there is a fault in the system. The diagnostic trouble code (DTC) is stored if the control module detects that: The rear heated oxygen sensor (HO2S) is activated unusually late during regulation. The control module's test for the diagnostic trouble code (DTC) starts in the event of: Start of engine. Cold engine. The probe should have been sufficiently heated up by exhaust gases and internal heating circuit. **Note! The control module can only detect the fault once the test has been started and the diagnostic trouble code (DTC) is stored when the conditions are met.**
DTC: ECM-P017068 **1T ECM** **Year:** 2011, 2012 **Model:** XC90 **Engine:** 4.4L V8	**Fuel Trim (Bank 1):** **Note! This diagnostic trouble code (DTC) status is an event controlled diagnostic trouble code (DTC). An event controlled diagnostic trouble code (DTC) does not mean that there is a fault in the control module when it is active, but is designed as information.** Engine control module (ECM) monitors the engine's heated oxygen sensor control. If the control module detects that heated oxygen sensor control is outside the limit values for a certain time when the engine is running, the diagnostic trouble code is generated. The diagnostic trouble code (DTC) can be diagnosed when the engine is running.
DTC: ECM-P017100 **1T ECM, MIL: Yes** **Year:** 2011, 2012 **Model:** XC90 **Engine:** 4.4L V8	**System Too Lean (Bank 1):** Engine Control Module (ECM) receives information from the heated oxygen sensor about fuel/air mixture in different load areas. If Engine Control Module (ECM) registers that fuel/air mixture deviates too much from target lambda, so that adaptations for bank 1 end up in any of its end-positions, the diagnostic trouble code is generated.
DTC: ECM-P017200 **1T ECM, MIL: Yes** **Year:** 2011, 2012 **Model:** XC90 **Engine:** 4.4L V8	**System Too Rich (Bank 1) :** Engine Control Module (ECM) receives information from the heated oxygen sensor about fuel/air mixture in different load areas. If Engine Control Module (ECM) registers that fuel/air mixture deviates too much from target lambda, so that adaptations for bank 1 end up in any of its end-positions, the diagnostic trouble code is generated.
DTC: ECM-P018000 **T ECM** **Year:** 2011, 2012 **Model:** XC90 **Engine:** 4.4L V8	**Fuel Temperature Sensor A Circuit:** Engine control module (ECM) measures the temperature of the fuel in the fuel rail using a fuel temperature sensor. The control module checks the direct voltage from the sensor. **Note! The fuel pressure sensor and fuel temperature sensor are integrated in the same component.** The diagnostic trouble code (DTC) is stored if the control module detects that: The direct voltage is higher than 4.951 V. Incorrect value lasts longer than 5 seconds. Incorrect value lasts for 2 or more subsequent driving cycles. The control module's test for the diagnostic trouble code (DTC) starts in the event of: Ignition switch position II. **Note! The control module can only detect the fault once the test has been started and the diagnostic trouble code (DTC) is stored when the conditions are met.**
DTC: ECM-P018100 **1T ECM** **Year:** 2011, 2012 **Model:** XC90 **Engine:** 4.4L V8	**Fuel Temperature Sensor A Circuit Range/Performance:** The engine control module (ECM) checks the signal from the fuel temperature sensor. A DTC is stored if the control module detects that the fuel temperature deviates too much from the coolant temperature, the air temperature (measured in the mass air flow (MAF) sensor) or the temperature measured in the boost pressure sensor (between the turbo compressor and throttle) after the engine has been switched off for a long time. The diagnostic trouble code can be diagnosed once per operating cycle with the ignition on, but only once the engine temperature has fallen to approx. 50 °C from operating temperature since the previous operating cycle.
DTC: ECM-P018121 **1T ECM, MIL: Yes** **Year:** 2011, 2012 **Model:** XC90 **Engine:** 4.4L V8	**Fuel Temperature Sensor A Circuit Range/Performance. Signal Too Low:** The engine control module (ECM) checks the signal from the fuel temperature sensor. If the control module detects that the value from the fuel temperature sensor deviates too much from the values for engine and intake temperature or outdoor temperature after the engine has been turned off a longer time, the diagnostic trouble code is generated. The diagnostic trouble code can be diagnosed at ignition on after the engine temperature has dropped by at least 55 °C from fully warm engine (higher than 70 °C).
DTC: ECM-P018122 **1T ECM, MIL: Yes** **Year:** 2011, 2012 **Model:** XC90 **Engine:** 4.4L V8	**Fuel Temperature Sensor A Circuit Range/Performance. Signal Too High:** The engine control module (ECM) checks the signal from the fuel temperature sensor. If the control module detects that the value from the fuel temperature sensor deviates too much from the values for engine and intake temperature or outdoor temperature after the engine has been turned off a longer time, the diagnostic trouble code is generated. The diagnostic trouble code can be diagnosed at ignition on after the engine temperature has dropped by at least 55 °C from fully warm engine (higher than 70 °C).

DTC	Trouble Code Title and Conditions
DTC: ECM-P018200 **2T ECM, MIL: Yes** **Year:** 2011, 2012 **Model:** XC90 **Engine:** 4.4L V8	**Fuel Temperature Sensor A Circuit Low Input:** Engine control module (ECM) measures the temperature of the fuel in the fuel rail using a fuel temperature sensor. The control module checks the direct voltage from the sensor. **Note! The fuel pressure sensor and fuel temperature sensor are integrated in the same component.** The diagnostic trouble code (DTC) is stored if the control module detects that: The direct voltage is higher than 4.951 V. Incorrect value lasts longer than 5 seconds. Incorrect value lasts for 2 or more subsequent driving cycles. The control module's test for the diagnostic trouble code (DTC) starts in the event of: Ignition switch position II.
DTC: ECM-P018300 **2T ECM, MIL: Yes** **Year:** 2011, 2012 **Model:** XC90 **Engine:** 4.4L V8	**Fuel Temperature Sensor A Circuit High Input:** Engine control module (ECM) measures the temperature of the fuel in the fuel rail using a fuel temperature sensor. The control module checks the direct voltage from the sensor. **Note! The fuel pressure sensor and fuel temperature sensor are integrated in the same component.** The diagnostic trouble code (DTC) is stored if the control module detects that: The direct voltage is higher than 4.951 V. Incorrect value lasts longer than 5 seconds. Incorrect value lasts for 2 or more subsequent driving cycles. The control module's test for the diagnostic trouble code (DTC) starts in the event of: Ignition switch position II. **Note! The control module can only detect the fault once the test has been started and the diagnostic trouble code (DTC) is stored when the conditions are met.**
DTC: ECM-P019000 **1T ECM, MIL: Yes** **Year:** 2011, 2012 **Model:** XC90 **Engine:** 4.4L V8	**Fuel Rail Pressure Sensor:** The Engine control module (ECM) measures the fuel pressure in the fuel rail using the fuel pressure sensor. The control module checks the direct voltage from the sensor. **Note! The fuel pressure sensor and fuel temperature sensor are integrated in the same component.** The diagnostic trouble code (DTC) is stored if the control module detects that: The direct voltage is higher than 4.951 V. Incorrect value lasts longer than 9 seconds. Incorrect value lasts for 2 or more subsequent driving cycles. The control module's test for the diagnostic trouble code (DTC) starts in the event of: Ignition switch position II.
DTC: ECM-P019100 **1T ECM, MIL: Yes** **Year:** 2011, 2012 **Model:** XC90 **Engine:** 4.4L V8	**Fuel Rail Pressure Sensor Range/Performance:** The engine control module (ECM) checks the signal from the fuel pressure sensor. The diagnostic trouble code (DTC) is stored if the control module registers that the signal from the fuel pressure sensor does not change when the fuel pump (FP) activation changes. The diagnostic trouble code can be diagnosed during normal driving for at least 15 minutes and preferably after a start and stop.
DTC: ECM-P019126 **1T ECM, MIL: Yes** **Year:** 2011, 2012 **Model:** XC90 **Engine:** 4.4L V8	**Fuel Rail Pressure Sensor Range/Performance. Signal Rate Below Threshold:** The engine control module (ECM) checks the signal from the fuel pressure sensor. The diagnostic trouble code (DTC) is stored if the control module registers that the signal from the fuel pressure sensor does not change when the fuel pump (FP) activation changes. The diagnostic trouble code (DTC) can be diagnosed under specific driving conditions.
DTC: ECM-P019200 **2T ECM, MIL: Yes** **Year:** 2011, 2012 **Model:** XC90 **Engine:** 4.4L V8	**Fuel Rail Pressure Sensor Low Input:** The Engine control module (ECM) measures the fuel pressure in the fuel rail using the fuel pressure sensor. The control module checks the direct voltage from the sensor. **Note! The fuel pressure sensor and fuel temperature sensor are integrated in the same component.** The diagnostic trouble code (DTC) is stored if the control module detects that: The direct voltage is higher than 4.951 V. Incorrect value lasts longer than 9 seconds. Incorrect value lasts for 2 or more subsequent driving cycles. The control module's test for the diagnostic trouble code (DTC) starts in the event of: Ignition switch position II.

DTC	Trouble Code Title and Conditions
DTC: ECM-P019300 **2T ECM, MIL: Yes** **Year:** 2011, 2012 **Model:** XC90 **Engine:** 4.4L V8	**Fuel Rail Pressure Sensor High Input:** The Engine control module (ECM) measures the fuel pressure in the fuel rail using the fuel pressure sensor. The control module checks the direct voltage from the sensor. **Note! The fuel pressure sensor and fuel temperature sensor are integrated in the same component.** The diagnostic trouble code (DTC) is stored if the control module detects that: The direct voltage is higher than 4.951 V. Incorrect value lasts longer than 9 seconds. Incorrect value lasts for 2 or more subsequent driving cycles. The control module's test for the diagnostic trouble code (DTC) starts in the event of: Ignition switch position II. **Note! The control module can only detect the fault once the test has been started and the diagnostic trouble code (DTC) is stored when the conditions are met.**
DTC: ECM-P020100 **2T ECM, MIL: Yes** **Year:** 2011, 2012 **Model:** XC90 **Engine:** 4.4L V8	**Cylinder 1 Injector Circuit / Open:** Engine control module (ECM) controls injection time and injection timing by controlling the injectors' opening and closing. Control is performed by pulsating grounding of the signal line to respective valve. The control module checks the signal's shape and amplitude at opening and closing. The diagnostic trouble code (DTC) is stored if the control module detects that: The signal's shape and amplitude do not follow expected signal. Incorrect value in more than 20 of 400 pulses. Incorrect value lasts for 2 or more subsequent driving cycles. The control module's test for the diagnostic trouble code (DTC) starts in the event of: Engine running. **Note! The control module can only detect the fault once the test has been started and the diagnostic trouble code (DTC) is stored when the conditions are met.**
DTC: ECM-P020200 **2T ECM, MIL: Yes** **Year:** 2011, 2012 **Model:** XC90 **Engine:** 4.4L V8	**Cylinder 2 Injector Circuit / Open:** Engine control module (ECM) controls injection time and injection timing by controlling the injectors' opening and closing. Control is performed by pulsating grounding of the signal line to respective valve. The control module checks the signal's shape and amplitude at opening and closing. The diagnostic trouble code (DTC) is stored if the control module detects that: The signal's shape and amplitude do not follow expected signal. Incorrect value in more than 20 of 400 pulses. Incorrect value lasts for 2 or more subsequent driving cycles. The control module's test for the diagnostic trouble code (DTC) starts in the event of: Engine running. **Note! The control module can only detect the fault once the test has been started and the diagnostic trouble code (DTC) is stored when the conditions are met.**
DTC: ECM-P020300 **2T ECM, MIL: Yes** **Year:** 2011, 2012 **Model:** XC90 **Engine:** 4.4L V8	**Cylinder 3 Injector Circuit / Open:** Engine control module (ECM) controls injection time and injection timing by controlling the injectors' opening and closing. Control is performed by pulsating grounding of the signal line to respective valve. The control module checks the signal's shape and amplitude at opening and closing. The diagnostic trouble code (DTC) is stored if the control module detects that: The signal's shape and amplitude do not follow expected signal. Incorrect value in more than 20 of 400 pulses. Incorrect value lasts for 2 or more subsequent driving cycles. The control module's test for the diagnostic trouble code (DTC) starts in the event of: Engine running. **Note! The control module can only detect the fault once the test has been started and the diagnostic trouble code (DTC) is stored when the conditions are met**
DTC: ECM-P020400 **2T ECM, MIL: Yes** **Year:** 2011, 2012 **Model:** XC90 **Engine:** 4.4L V8	**Cylinder 4 Injector Circuit / Open:** Engine control module (ECM) controls injection time and injection timing by controlling the injectors' opening and closing. Control is performed by pulsating grounding of the signal line to respective valve. The control module checks the signal's shape and amplitude at opening and closing. The diagnostic trouble code (DTC) is stored if the control module detects that: The signal's shape and amplitude do not follow expected signal. Incorrect value in more than 20 of 400 pulses. Incorrect value lasts for 2 or more subsequent driving cycles. The control module's test for the diagnostic trouble code (DTC) starts in the event of: Engine running.

DTC	Trouble Code Title and Conditions
DTC: ECM-P020500 **2T ECM, MIL: Yes** **Year:** 2011, 2012 **Model:** XC90 **Engine:** 4.4L V8	**Cylinder 5 Injector Circuit/Open:** Engine control module (ECM) controls injection time and injection timing by controlling the injectors' opening and closing. Control is performed by pulsating grounding of the signal line to respective valve. The control module checks the signal's shape and amplitude at opening and closing. The diagnostic trouble code (DTC) is stored if the control module detects that: The signal's shape and amplitude do not follow expected signal. Incorrect value in more than 20 of 400 pulses. Incorrect value lasts for 2 or more subsequent driving cycles. The control module's test for the diagnostic trouble code (DTC) starts in the event of: Engine running.
DTC: ECM-P020600 **2T ECM, MIL: Yes** **Year:** 2011, 2012 **Model:** XC90 **Engine:** 4.4L V8	**Cylinder 6 Injector Circuit/Open:** Engine control module (ECM) controls injection time and injection timing by controlling the injectors' opening and closing. Control is performed by pulsating grounding of the signal line to respective valve. The control module checks the signal's shape and amplitude at opening and closing. The diagnostic trouble code (DTC) is stored if the control module detects that: The signal's shape and amplitude do not follow expected signal. Incorrect value in more than 20 of 400 pulses. Incorrect value lasts for 2 or more subsequent driving cycles. The control module's test for the diagnostic trouble code (DTC) starts in the event of: Engine running.
DTC: ECM-P022023 **1T ECM** **Year:** 2011, 2012 **Model:** XC90 **Engine:** 4.4L V8	**Throttle/Pedal Position Switch B Circuit. Signal Stuck Low:** The engine control module (ECM) checks the pulse width modulation (PWM) signal and the analog signal from the accelerator pedal (AP) position sensor. The analog signal is directly connected to the Central electronic module (CEM) and the signal is transmitted via CAN communication to the Engine control module (ECM). The pulse width modulation (PWM) signal is directly connected to the engine control module (ECM). The PWM signal is used to determine the current accelerator pedal position in a fault free system. The Engine control module (ECM) checks the analog signal (via CAN). The diagnostic trouble code (DTC) is stored if the control module detects that: Analog signal (via CAN) is too low. Incorrect value lasts longer than 16 seconds. The control module's test for the diagnostic trouble code (DTC) starts in the event of: Ignition switch position II. (Text window and warning symbol/Text message)
DTC: ECM-P022024 **1T ECM** **Year:** 2011, 2012 **Model:** XC90 **Engine:** 4.4L V8	**Throttle/Pedal Position Switch B Circuit. Signal Stuck High:** The engine control module (ECM) checks the pulse width modulation (PWM) signal and the analog signal from the accelerator pedal (AP) position sensor. The analog signal is directly connected to the Central electronic module (CEM) and the signal is transmitted via CAN communication to the Engine control module (ECM). The pulse width modulation (PWM) signal is directly connected to the engine control module (ECM). The PWM signal is used to determine the current accelerator pedal position in a fault free system. The Engine control module (ECM) checks the analog signal (via CAN). The diagnostic trouble code (DTC) is stored if the control module detects that: Analog signal (via CAN) is too high. Incorrect value lasts longer than 16 seconds. The control module's test for the diagnostic trouble code (DTC) starts in the event of: Ignition switch position II. (Text window and warning symbol/Text message)

DTC	Trouble Code Title and Conditions
DTC: ECM-P022082 **1T ECM** **Year:** 2011, 2012 **Model:** XC90 **Engine:** 4.4L V8	**Throttle/Pedal Position Switch B Circuit. Bus Signal/Message Failures. Alive/sequence counter incorrect/Not Updated:** The engine control module (ECM) checks the pulse width modulation (PWM) signal and the analog signal from the accelerator pedal (AP) position sensor. The analog signal is directly connected to the Central electronic module (CEM) and the signal is transmitted via CAN communication to the Engine control module (ECM). The pulse width modulation (PWM) signal is directly connected to the engine control module (ECM). The PWM signal is used to determine the current accelerator pedal position in a fault free system. The control module checks the communication with the Central electronic module (CEM). The diagnostic trouble code (DTC) is stored if the control module detects that: No communication with the Central electronic module (CEM). The control module's test for the diagnostic trouble code (DTC) starts in the event of: Ignition switch position II. **Note! The control module can only detect the fault once the test has been started and the diagnostic trouble code (DTC) is stored when the conditions are met.**
DTC: ECM-P022200 **1T ECM** **Year:** 2011, 2012 **Model:** XC90 **Engine:** 4.4L V8	**Throttle/Pedal Position Sensor/Switch B Circuit Low:** Engine control module (ECM) checks the signals from the electronic throttle unit's two position sensors. If engine control module (ECM) detects unreasonably low signal from any of the sensors, the diagnostic trouble code is generated. The diagnostic trouble code can be diagnosed when the ignition is on.
DTC: ECM-P022300 **1T ECM** **Year:** 2011, 2012 **Model:** XC90 **Engine:** 4.4L V8	**Throttle/Pedal Position Sensor/Switch B Circuit High:** Engine control module (ECM) checks the signals from the electronic throttle unit's two position sensors. If engine control module (ECM) detects unreasonably high signal from any of the sensors, the diagnostic trouble code is generated. The diagnostic trouble code can be diagnosed when the ignition is on.
DTC: ECM-P023400 **1T ECM** **Year:** 2011, 2012 **Model:** XC90 **Engine:** 4.4L V8	**Turbo/Super Charger Over boost Condition:** The Engine control module (ECM) regulates the turbo pressure using a turbo control valve. The control module can detect small faults in boost pressure regulation over a longer period of time and larger faults in a shorter time. The diagnostic trouble code (DTC) is stored if the control module detects that: The actual turbo pressure is greater (approx. 20 kPa for 10 seconds) than what the Engine control module (ECM) regulated (maximum regulation achieved). The control module's test for the diagnostic trouble code (DTC) starts in the event of: Normal load (driving). Boost pressure (approx. 30 kPa above atmospheric pressure). **Note! The control module can only detect the fault once the test has been started and the diagnostic trouble code (DTC) is stored when the conditions are met.**
DTC: ECM-P023500 **1T ECM, MIL: Yes** **Year:** 2011, 2012 **Model:** XC90 **Engine:** 4.4L V8	**Turbo/Super Charger Boost Sensor A Circuit:** Engine control module (ECM) checks the signal from the boost pressure sensor which is located between the turbocharger and the throttle module. **Note! The boost pressure sensor and air temperature sensor are integrated in the same component, the boost pressure sensor.** The diagnostic trouble code (DTC) is stored if the control module detects that: Control signal is too low. The control module's test for the diagnostic trouble code (DTC) starts in the event of: Ignition switch position II. Battery voltage higher than 10.5 V.
DTC: ECM-P023600 **1T ECM** **Year:** 2011, 2012 **Model:** XC90 **Engine:** 4.4L V8	**Turbo/Super Charger Boost Sensor A Circuit Range/Performance:** The Engine control module (ECM) regulates the turbo pressure using a turbo control valve. The control module has integrated functions to check the function of the turbo control valve. The diagnostic trouble code (DTC) is stored if the control module detects that: The turbo pressure is too high, compared with the internal calculating models in the control model. The difference between the atmospheric pressure and the pressure in the intake manifold (before the throttle unit) at idle is greater than a value that can be calibrated. The difference in pressure before and after the throttle module, during large throttle openings, is greater than a value that can be calibrated. The control module's test for the diagnostic trouble code (DTC) starts in the event of: Normal load (driving). Intake pressure is greater than atmospheric pressure.

DTC	Trouble Code Title and Conditions
DTC: ECM-P023700 **1T ECM, MIL: Yes** **Year:** 2011, 2012 **Model:** XC90 **Engine:** 4.4L V8	**Turbo/Super Charger Boost Sensor A Circuit Low:** Engine control module (ECM) checks the signal from the boost pressure sensor which is located between the turbocharger and the throttle module. **Note! The boost pressure sensor and air temperature sensor are integrated in the same component, the boost pressure sensor.** The diagnostic trouble code (DTC) is stored if the control module detects that: The direct voltage is lower than 0.112 V. Incorrect value lasts longer than 9 seconds. Incorrect value lasts for 2 or more subsequent driving cycles. The control module's test for the diagnostic trouble code (DTC) starts in the event of: Ignition switch position II.
DTC: ECM-P023800 **1T ECM, MIL: Yes** **Year:** 2011, 2012 **Model:** XC90 **Engine:** 4.4L V8	**Turbo/Super Charger Boost Sensor A Circuit High:** Engine control module (ECM) checks the signal from the boost pressure sensor which is located between the turbocharger and the throttle module. **Note! The boost pressure sensor and air temperature sensor are integrated in the same component, the boost pressure sensor.** The diagnostic trouble code (DTC) is stored if the control module detects that: The direct voltage is higher than 4.902 V. Incorrect value lasts longer than 9 seconds. Incorrect value lasts for 2 or more subsequent driving cycles. The control module's test for the diagnostic trouble code (DTC) starts in the event of: Ignition switch position II.
DTC: ECM-P026100 **2T ECM, MIL: Yes** **Year:** 2011, 2012 **Model:** XC90 **Engine:** 4.4L V8	**Cylinder 1 Injector Circuit Low:** Engine control module (ECM) controls injection time and injection timing by controlling the injectors' opening and closing. Control is performed by pulsating grounding of the signal line to respective valve. The control module checks the signal's shape and amplitude at opening and closing. The diagnostic trouble code (DTC) is stored if the control module detects that: * The signal's shape and amplitude do not follow expected signal. * Incorrect value in more than 20 of 400 pulses. * Incorrect value lasts for 2 or more subsequent driving cycles. The control module's test for the diagnostic trouble code (DTC) starts in the event of: * Engine running.
DTC: ECM-P026200 **2T ECM, MIL: Yes** **Year:** 2011, 2012 **Model:** XC90 **Engine:** 4.4L V8	**Cylinder 1 Injector Circuit High:** Engine control module (ECM) controls injection time and injection timing by controlling the injectors' opening and closing. Control is performed by pulsating grounding of the signal line to respective valve. The control module checks the signal's shape and amplitude at opening and closing. * The diagnostic trouble code (DTC) is stored if the control module detects that: * The signal's shape and amplitude do not follow expected signal. * Incorrect value in more than 20 of 400 pulses. * Incorrect value lasts for 2 or more subsequent driving cycles. The control module's test for the diagnostic trouble code (DTC) starts in the event of: Engine running.
DTC: ECM-P026400 **2T ECM, MIL: Yes** **Year:** 2011, 2012 **Model:** XC90 **Engine:** 4.4L V8	**Cylinder 2 Injector Circuit Low:** Engine control module (ECM) controls injection time and injection timing by controlling the injectors' opening and closing. Control is performed by pulsating grounding of the signal line to respective valve. The control module checks the signal's shape and amplitude at opening and closing. The diagnostic trouble code (DTC) is stored if the control module detects that: * The signal's shape and amplitude do not follow expected signal. * Incorrect value in more than 20 of 400 pulses. * Incorrect value lasts for 2 or more subsequent driving cycles. The control module's test for the diagnostic trouble code (DTC) starts in the event of: * Engine running.

DTC	Trouble Code Title and Conditions
DTC: ECM-P026500 **2T ECM, MIL: Yes** **Year:** 2011, 2012 **Model:** XC90 **Engine:** 4.4L V8	**Cylinder 2 Injector Circuit High:** Engine control module (ECM) controls injection time and injection timing by controlling the injectors' opening and closing. Control is performed by pulsating grounding of the signal line to respective valve. The control module checks the signal's shape and amplitude at opening and closing. The diagnostic trouble code (DTC) is stored if the control module detects that: * The signal's shape and amplitude do not follow expected signal. * Incorrect value in more than 20 of 400 pulses. * Incorrect value lasts for 2 or more subsequent driving cycles. The control module's test for the diagnostic trouble code (DTC) starts in the event of: * Engine running.
DTC: ECM-P026700 **2T ECM, MIL: Yes** **Year:** 2011, 2012 **Model:** XC90 **Engine:** 4.4L V8	**Cylinder 3 Injector Circuit Low:** Engine control module (ECM) controls injection time and injection timing by controlling the injectors' opening and closing. Control is performed by pulsating grounding of the signal line to respective valve. The control module checks the signal's shape and amplitude at opening and closing. The diagnostic trouble code (DTC) is stored if the control module detects that: * The signal's shape and amplitude do not follow expected signal. * Incorrect value in more than 20 of 400 pulses. * Incorrect value lasts for 2 or more subsequent driving cycles. The control module's test for the diagnostic trouble code (DTC) starts in the event of: * Engine running.
DTC: ECM-P026800 **2T ECM, MIL: Yes** **Year:** 2011, 2012 **Model:** XC90 **Engine:** 4.4L V8	**Cylinder 3 Injector Circuit High:** Engine control module (ECM) controls injection time and injection timing by controlling the injectors' opening and closing. Control is performed by pulsating grounding of the signal line to respective valve. The control module checks the signal's shape and amplitude at opening and closing. The diagnostic trouble code (DTC) is stored if the control module detects that: * The signal's shape and amplitude do not follow expected signal. * Incorrect value in more than 20 of 400 pulses. * Incorrect value lasts for 2 or more subsequent driving cycles. The control module's test for the diagnostic trouble code (DTC) starts in the event of: * Engine running.
DTC: ECM-P027000 **2T ECM, MIL: Yes** **Year:** 2011, 2012 **Model:** XC90 **Engine:** 4.4L V8	**Cylinder 4 Injector Circuit Low:** Engine control module (ECM) controls injection time and injection timing by controlling the injectors' opening and closing. Control is performed by pulsating grounding of the signal line to respective valve. The control module checks the signal's shape and amplitude at opening and closing. The diagnostic trouble code (DTC) is stored if the control module detects that: * The signal's shape and amplitude do not follow expected signal. * Incorrect value in more than 20 of 400 pulses. * Incorrect value lasts for 2 or more subsequent driving cycles. The control module's test for the diagnostic trouble code (DTC) starts in the event of: * Engine running.
DTC: ECM-P027100 **2T ECM, MIL: Yes** **Year:** 2011, 2012 **Model:** XC90 **Engine:** 4.4L V8	**Cylinder 4 Injector Circuit High:** Engine control module (ECM) controls injection time and injection timing by controlling the injectors' opening and closing. Control is performed by pulsating grounding of the signal line to respective valve. The control module checks the signal's shape and amplitude at opening and closing. The diagnostic trouble code (DTC) is stored if the control module detects that: * The signal's shape and amplitude do not follow expected signal. * Incorrect value in more than 20 of 400 pulses. * Incorrect value lasts for 2 or more subsequent driving cycles. The control module's test for the diagnostic trouble code (DTC) starts in the event of: * Engine running.

DTC	Trouble Code Title and Conditions
DTC: ECM-P027300 **2T ECM, MIL: Yes** **Year:** 2011, 2012 **Model:** XC90 **Engine:** 4.4L V8	**Cylinder 5 Injector Circuit Low:** Engine control module (ECM) controls injection time and injection timing by controlling the injectors' opening and closing. Control is performed by pulsating grounding of the signal line to respective valve. The control module checks the signal's shape and amplitude at opening and closing. The diagnostic trouble code (DTC) is stored if the control module detects that: * The signal's shape and amplitude do not follow expected signal. * Incorrect value in more than 20 of 400 pulses. * Incorrect value lasts for 2 or more subsequent driving cycles. The control module's test for the diagnostic trouble code (DTC) starts in the event of: * Engine running.
DTC: ECM-P027400 **2T ECM, MIL: Yes** **Year:** 2011, 2012 **Model:** XC90 **Engine:** 4.4L V8	**Cylinder 5 Injector Circuit High:** Engine control module (ECM) controls injection time and injection timing by controlling the injectors' opening and closing. Control is performed by pulsating grounding of the signal line to respective valve. The control module checks the signal's shape and amplitude at opening and closing. The diagnostic trouble code (DTC) is stored if the control module detects that: * The signal's shape and amplitude do not follow expected signal. * Incorrect value in more than 20 of 400 pulses. * Incorrect value lasts for 2 or more subsequent driving cycles. The control module's test for the diagnostic trouble code (DTC) starts in the event of: * Engine running.
DTC: ECM-P027600 **2T ECM, MIL: Yes** **Year:** 2011, 2012 **Model:** XC90 **Engine:** 4.4L V8	**Cylinder 6 Injector Circuit Low:** Engine control module (ECM) controls injection time and injection timing by controlling the injectors' opening and closing. Control is performed by pulsating grounding of the signal line to respective valve. The control module checks the signal's shape and amplitude at opening and closing. The diagnostic trouble code (DTC) is stored if the control module detects that: * The signal's shape and amplitude do not follow expected signal. * Incorrect value in more than 20 of 400 pulses. * Incorrect value lasts for 2 or more subsequent driving cycles. The control module's test for the diagnostic trouble code (DTC) starts in the event of: * Engine running.
DTC: ECM-P027700 **2T ECM, MIL: Yes** **Year:** 2011, 2012 **Model:** XC90 **Engine:** 4.4L V8	**Cylinder 6 Injector Circuit High:** Engine control module (ECM) controls injection time and injection timing by controlling the injectors' opening and closing. Control is performed by pulsating grounding of the signal line to respective valve. The control module checks the signal's shape and amplitude at opening and closing. The diagnostic trouble code (DTC) is stored if the control module detects that: * The signal's shape and amplitude do not follow expected signal. * Incorrect value in more than 20 of 400 pulses. * Incorrect value lasts for 2 or more subsequent driving cycles. The control module's test for the diagnostic trouble code (DTC) starts in the event of: * Engine running.
DTC: ECM-P029900 **1T ECM** **Year:** 2011, 2012 **Model:** XC90 **Engine:** 4.4L V8	**Turbo/Super Charger Under-boost:** The Engine control module (ECM) regulates the turbo pressure using a turbo control valve. The control module can detect small faults in boost pressure regulation over a longer period of time and larger faults in a shorter time. The diagnostic trouble code (DTC) is stored if the control module detects that: The actual turbo pressure is less (approx. 15 kPa for 10 seconds) than what the Engine control module (ECM) regulated (maximum regulation achieved). The control module's test for the diagnostic trouble code (DTC) starts in the event of: * Normal load (driving). * Boost pressure (approx. 30 kPa above atmospheric pressure).
DTC: ECM-P029C68 **T ECM** **Year:** 2011, 2012 **Model:** XC90 **Engine:** 4.4L V8	**Cylinder 1 Balance - Injector Restricted:** The Engine control module (ECM) continually monitors the engine's exhaust gases from the oxygen content in the exhaust gases (the lambda value). Using the built-in functions, the control module can determine the lambda value for each cylinder individually. The diagnostic trouble code (DTC) is stored if the control module detects that: * The discrepancy in the lambda value between the cylinders in bank 1 (cyl. 1-3) is too great to be compensated using individual fuel trim. The control module's test for the diagnostic trouble code (DTC) starts in the event of: * Individual cylinder fuel trim active.

DTC	Trouble Code Title and Conditions
DTC: ECM-P02A068 **T ECM** **Year:** 2011, 2012 **Model:** XC90 **Engine:** 4.4L V8	**Cylinder 2 Balance - Injector Restricted:** The Engine control module (ECM) continually monitors the engine's exhaust gases from the oxygen content in the exhaust gases (the lambda value). Using the built-in functions, the control module can determine the lambda value for each cylinder individually. The diagnostic trouble code (DTC) is stored if the control module detects that: * The Engine control module (ECM) detects that the deviation in the lambda value between the cylinders in bank 2 (cyl. 4-6) is too great to compensate using individual fuel trim. The control module's test for the diagnostic trouble code (DTC) starts in the event of: * Individual cylinder fuel trim active.
DTC: ECM-P02A468 **T ECM** **Year:** 2011, 2012 **Model:** XC90 **Engine:** 4.4L V8	**Cylinder 3 Balance - Injector Restricted:** The Engine control module (ECM) continually monitors the engine's exhaust gases from the oxygen content in the exhaust gases (the lambda value). Using the built-in functions, the control module can determine the lambda value for each cylinder individually. The diagnostic trouble code (DTC) is stored if the control module detects that: 1). The front heated oxygen sensor (bank 1) has become too slow to be used in cylinder individual fuel trim. The control module's test for the diagnostic trouble code (DTC) starts in the event of: 2). Individual cylinder fuel trim active.
DTC: ECM-P02A868 **T ECM** **Year:** 2011, 2012 **Model:** XC90 **Engine:** 4.4L V8	**Cylinder 4 Balance - Injector Restricted:** The Engine control module (ECM) continually monitors the engine's exhaust gases from the oxygen content in the exhaust gases (the lambda value). Using the built-in functions, the control module can determine the lambda value for each cylinder individually. The diagnostic trouble code (DTC) is stored if the control module detects that: 1). The front heated oxygen sensor (bank 2) has become too slow to be used in cylinder individual fuel trim. 2). The control module's test for the diagnostic trouble code (DTC) starts in the event of: Individual cylinder fuel trim active.
DTC: ECM-P030000 **1T ECM, MIL: Yes** **Year:** 2011, 2012 **Model:** XC90 **Engine:** 4.4L V8	**Random Misfire Detected:** The engine control module (ECM) checks engine combustion regarding misfire by registering speed deviations in flywheel rotation. If a certain number of misfires are detected for several cylinders during a certain number of crankshaft rotations, the misfires are considered emission-related or capable of damaging the catalytic converter and the diagnostic trouble code is generated. The diagnostic trouble code can be diagnosed when the engine is running.
DTC: ECM-P030100 **1T ECM, MIL: Yes** **Year:** 2011, 2012 **Model:** XC90 **Engine:** 4.4L V8	**Cylinder 1 Misfire Detected:** The engine control module (ECM) checks engine combustion regarding misfire by registering speed deviations in flywheel rotation. If a certain number of misfires are detected for several cylinders during a certain number of crankshaft rotations, the misfires are considered emission-related or capable of damaging the catalytic converter and the diagnostic trouble code is generated. The diagnostic trouble code can be diagnosed when the engine is running. The trouble code indicates which cylinder is misfiring: ECM-P030100, cylinder 1 misfire.
DTC: ECM-P030200 **1T ECM, MIL: Yes** **Year:** 2011, 2012 **Model:** XC90 **Engine:** 4.4L V8	**Cylinder 2 Misfire Detected:** The engine control module (ECM) checks engine combustion regarding misfire by registering speed deviations in flywheel rotation. If a certain number of misfires are detected for several cylinders during a certain number of crankshaft rotations, the misfires are considered emission-related or capable of damaging the catalytic converter and the diagnostic trouble code is generated. The diagnostic trouble code can be diagnosed when the engine is running. The trouble code indicates which cylinder is misfiring: ECM-P030200, cylinder 2 misfire.
DTC: ECM-P030300 **1T ECM, MIL: Yes** **Year:** 2011, 2012 **Model:** XC90 **Engine:** 4.4L V8	**Cylinder 3 Misfire Detected :** The engine control module (ECM) checks engine combustion regarding misfire by registering speed deviations in flywheel rotation. If a certain number of misfires are detected for several cylinders during a certain number of crankshaft rotations, the misfires are considered emission-related or capable of damaging the catalytic converter and the diagnostic trouble code is generated. The diagnostic trouble code can be diagnosed when the engine is running. The trouble code indicates which cylinder is misfiring: ECM-P030300, cylinder 3 misfire.
DTC: ECM-P030400 **1T ECM, MIL: Yes** **Year:** 2011, 2012 **Model:** XC90 **Engine:** 4.4L V8	**Cylinder 4 Misfire Detected :** The engine control module (ECM) checks engine combustion regarding misfire by registering speed deviations in flywheel rotation. If a certain number of misfires are detected for several cylinders during a certain number of crankshaft rotations, the misfires are considered emission-related or capable of damaging the catalytic converter and the diagnostic trouble code is generated. The diagnostic trouble code can be diagnosed when the engine is running. The trouble code indicates which cylinder is misfiring: ECM-P030400, cylinder 4 misfire.

DTC	Trouble Code Title and Conditions
DTC: ECM-P030500 **1T ECM, MIL: Yes** **Year:** 2011, 2012 **Model:** XC90 **Engine:** 4.4L V8	**Cylinder 5 Misfire Detected:** The engine control module (ECM) checks engine combustion regarding misfire by registering speed deviations in flywheel rotation. If a certain number of misfires are detected for several cylinders during a certain number of crankshaft rotations, the misfires are considered emission-related or capable of damaging the catalytic converter and the diagnostic trouble code is generated. The diagnostic trouble code can be diagnosed when the engine is running. The trouble code indicates which cylinder is misfiring: ECM-P030500, cylinder 5 misfire.
DTC: ECM-P030600 **1T ECM, MIL: Yes** **Year:** 2011, 2012 **Model:** XC90 **Engine:** 4.4L V8	**Cylinder 6 Misfire Detected:** The engine control module (ECM) checks engine combustion regarding misfire by registering speed deviations in flywheel rotation. If a certain number of misfires are detected for several cylinders during a certain number of crankshaft rotations, the misfires are considered emission-related or capable of damaging the catalytic converter and the diagnostic trouble code is generated. The diagnostic trouble code can be diagnosed when the engine is running. The trouble code indicates which cylinder is misfiring: ECM-P030600, cylinder 6 misfire.
DTC: ECM-P032600 **1T ECM** **Year:** 2011, 2012 **Model:** XC90 **Engine:** 4.4L V8	**Knock Sensor 1 Circuit Range/Performance (Bank 1):** The knock sensor signal varies with engine speed. The engine control module (ECM) checks that the knock sensor signal is within certain limits, which are determined by engine speed. The diagnostic trouble code is generated if the signal from the knock sensor is not within the limit values. The diagnostic trouble code can be diagnosed during a road test. The diagnostic trouble code refers to knock sensor 1.
DTC: ECM-P032621 **1T ECM** **Year:** 2011, 2012 **Model:** XC90 **Engine:** 4.4L V8	**Knock Sensor 1 Circuit Range/Performance (Bank 1). Signal Too Low:** The knock sensor signal varies with engine speed. The engine control module (ECM) checks that the knock sensor signal is within certain limits, which are determined by engine speed. The diagnostic trouble code is generated if the signal from the knock sensor is not within the limit values. The diagnostic trouble code can be diagnosed during a road test. The diagnostic trouble code refers to knock sensor 1.
DTC: ECM-P032622 **1T ECM** **Year:** 2011, 2012 **Model:** XC90 **Engine:** 4.4L V8	**Knock Sensor 1 Circuit Range/Performance (Bank 1). Signal Too High:** The knock sensor signal varies with engine speed. The engine control module (ECM) checks that the knock sensor signal is within certain limits, which are determined by engine speed. The diagnostic trouble code is generated if the signal from the knock sensor is not within the limit values. The diagnostic trouble code can be diagnosed during a road test. The diagnostic trouble code refers to knock sensor 1.
DTC: ECM-P032700 **2T ECM** **Year:** 2011, 2012 **Model:** XC90 **Engine:** 4.4L V8	**Knock Sensor 1 Circuit Low Input (Bank1) :** Engine control module (ECM) monitors combustion knock from the engine to, when needed, adjust the ignition and thus prevent continued knock. Monitoring is performed with two knock sensors located on the engine block between the cylinder rows. The control module checks the direct voltage from the sensors. The diagnostic trouble code (DTC) is stored if the control module detects that: The direct voltage is lower than 1.25 V. Incorrect value lasts longer than 26 seconds. Incorrect value lasts for 2 or more subsequent driving cycles. The control module's test for the diagnostic trouble code (DTC) starts in the event of: Ignition switch position II.
DTC: ECM-P032800 **2T ECM** **Year:** 2011, 2012 **Model:** XC90 **Engine:** 4.4L V8	**Knock Sensor 1 Circuit High Input (Bank 1):** Engine control module (ECM) monitors combustion knock from the engine to, when needed, adjust the ignition and thus prevent continued knock. Monitoring is performed with two knock sensors located on the engine block between the cylinder rows. The control module checks the direct voltage from the sensors. The diagnostic trouble code (DTC) is stored if the control module detects that: The direct voltage is higher than 4.75 V. Incorrect value lasts longer than 26 seconds. Incorrect value lasts for 2 or more subsequent driving cycles. The control module's test for the diagnostic trouble code (DTC) starts in the event of: Ignition switch position II. **Note! The control module can only detect the fault once the test has been started and the diagnostic trouble code (DTC) is stored when the conditions are met.**
DTC: ECM-P033100 **1T ECM** **Year:** 2011, 2012 **Model:** XC90 **Engine:** 4.4L V8	**Knock Sensor 2 Circuit Range/Performance (Bank 2):** The knock sensor signal varies with engine speed. The engine control module (ECM) checks that the knock sensor signal is within certain limits, which are determined by engine speed. The diagnostic trouble code is generated if the signal from the knock sensor is not within the limit values. The diagnostic trouble code can be diagnosed during a road test. The diagnostic trouble code refers to knock sensor 2.

DTC	Trouble Code Title and Conditions
DTC: ECM-P033121 **1T ECM** **Year:** 2011, 2012 **Model:** XC90 **Engine:** 4.4L V8	**Knock Sensor 2 Circuit Range/Performance (Bank 2). Signal Too Low:** The knock sensor signal varies with engine speed. The engine control module (ECM) checks that the knock sensor signal is within certain limits, which are determined by engine speed. The diagnostic trouble code is generated if the signal from the knock sensor is not within the limit values. The diagnostic trouble code can be diagnosed during a road test. The diagnostic trouble code refers to knock sensor 2.
DTC: ECM-P033122 **1T ECM** **Year:** 2011, 2012 **Model:** XC90 **Engine:** 4.4L V8	**Knock Sensor 2 Circuit Range/Performance (Bank 2). Signal Too High:** The knock sensor signal varies with engine speed. The engine control module (ECM) checks that the knock sensor signal is within certain limits, which are determined by engine speed. The diagnostic trouble code is generated if the signal from the knock sensor is not within the limit values. The diagnostic trouble code can be diagnosed during a road test. The diagnostic trouble code refers to knock sensor 2.
DTC: ECM-P033200 **2T ECM** **Year:** 2011, 2012 **Model:** XC90 **Engine:** 4.4L V8	**Knock Sensor 2 Circuit Low Input (Bank 2):** Engine control module (ECM) monitors combustion knock from the engine to, when needed, adjust the ignition and thus prevent continued knock. Monitoring is performed with two knock sensors located on the engine block between the cylinder rows. The control module checks the direct voltage from the sensors. The diagnostic trouble code (DTC) is stored if the control module detects that: The direct voltage is lower than 1.25 V. Incorrect value lasts longer than 26 seconds. Incorrect value lasts for 2 or more subsequent driving cycles. The control module's test for the diagnostic trouble code (DTC) starts in the event of: Ignition switch position II. **Note! The control module can only detect the fault once the test has been started and the diagnostic trouble code (DTC) is stored when the conditions are met.**
DTC: ECM-P033300 **2T ECM** **Year:** 2011, 2012 **Model:** XC90 **Engine:** 4.4L V8	**Knock Sensor 2 Circuit High Input (Bank 2) :** Engine control module (ECM) monitors combustion knock from the engine to, when needed, adjust the ignition and thus prevent continued knock. Monitoring is performed with two knock sensors located on the engine block between the cylinder rows. The control module checks the direct voltage from the sensors. The diagnostic trouble code (DTC) is stored if the control module detects that: The direct voltage is higher than 4.75 V. Incorrect value lasts longer than 26 seconds. Incorrect value lasts for 2 or more subsequent driving cycles. The control module's test for the diagnostic trouble code (DTC) starts in the event of: Ignition switch position II. **Note! The control module can only detect the fault once the test has been started and the diagnostic trouble code (DTC) is stored when the conditions are met.**
DTC: ECM-P033500 **1T ECM** **Year:** 2011, 2012 **Model:** XC90 **Engine:** 4.4L V8	**Crankshaft Position Sensor A Circuit:** The signal sent by the engine speed sensor to the engine control module (ECM) provides information on the number of teeth in the flywheel/number of holes in the carrier plate that has passed the engine speed sensor. The control module uses the signal to calculate engine speed. The diagnostic code is generated if via the engine speed sensor signal the control module detects an incorrect number of teeth on the flywheel/holes in the carrier plate for a certain number of crankshaft revolutions. The diagnostic trouble code (DTC) can be diagnosed when the engine is running.
DTC: ECM-P033600 **1T ECM** **Year:** 2011, 2012 **Model:** XC90 **Engine:** 4.4L V8	**Crankshaft Position Sensor A Circuit Range/Performance:** The signal sent by the engine speed sensor to the engine control module (ECM) provides information on the number of teeth in the flywheel/number of holes in the carrier plate that has passed the engine speed sensor. The control module uses the signal to calculate engine speed. The diagnostic code is generated if via the engine speed sensor signal the control module detects an incorrect number of teeth on the flywheel/holes in the carrier plate for a certain number of crankshaft revolutions. The diagnostic trouble code can be diagnosed by the control module when engine speed exceeds 1000 rpm.
DTC: ECM-P033900 **1T ECM** **Year:** 2011, 2012 **Model:** XC90 **Engine:** 4.4L V8	**Crankshaft Position Sensor A Circuit Intermittent:** The signal sent by the engine speed sensor to the engine control module (ECM) provides information on the number of teeth in the flywheel/number of holes in the carrier plate that has passed the engine speed sensor. The control module uses the signal to calculate engine speed. The diagnostic code is generated if via the engine speed sensor signal the control module detects an incorrect number of teeth on the flywheel/holes in the carrier plate for a certain number of crankshaft revolutions. The diagnostic trouble code can be diagnosed by the control module when the starter motor is running.
DTC: ECM-P034000 **1T ECM** **Year:** 2011, 2012 **Model:** XC90 **Engine:** 4.4L V8	**Camshaft Position Sensor A Circuit (Bank 1 or single sensor). :** The camshaft is divided into a number of segments (flanks). The camshaft houses a gearwheel with a number of teeth (the teeth are positioned between each segment) that are read by the engine control module (ECM) via the camshaft position sensor. The diagnostic trouble code is generated if the control module detects too few segments for a certain number of crankshaft revolutions. The diagnostic trouble code (DTC) can be diagnosed when the engine is running.

DTC	Trouble Code Title and Conditions
DTC: ECM-P034100 **1T ECM** **Year:** 2011, 2012 **Model:** XC90 **Engine:** 4.4L V8	**Camshaft Position Sensor A Circuit Range/Performance (Bank 1 or single sensor):** The camshaft is divided into a number of segments (flanks). The camshaft houses a gearwheel with a number of teeth (the teeth are positioned between each segment) that are read by the engine control module (ECM) via the camshaft position sensor. The diagnostic trouble code can be diagnosed by the control module when the engine is running and engine speed exceeds a certain value.
DTC: ECM-P034400 **1T ECM** **Year:** 2011, 2012 **Model:** XC90 **Engine:** 4.4L V8	**Camshaft Position Sensor A Circuit Intermittent (Bank 1 or single sensor) :** The camshaft is divided into a number of segments (flanks). The camshaft houses a gearwheel with a number of teeth (the teeth are positioned between each segment) that are read by the engine control module (ECM) via the camshaft position sensor. The diagnostic trouble code is generated if the control module detects too few segments for a certain number of crankshaft revolutions. The diagnostic trouble code (DTC) can be diagnosed when starting the engine.
DTC: ECM-P034500 **1T ECM** **Year:** 2011, 2012 **Model:** XC90 **Engine:** 4.4L V8	**Camshaft Position Sensor A Circuit (Bank 2) :** The camshaft houses a gearwheel with a number of teeth (the teeth are positioned between each segment) that are read by the engine control module (ECM) via the camshaft position sensor. The diagnostic trouble code is generated if the control module detects too few segments for a certain number of crankshaft revolutions. The diagnostic trouble code (DTC) can be diagnosed when the engine is running.
DTC: ECM-P034600 **1T ECM** **Year:** 2011, 2012 **Model:** XC90 **Engine:** 4.4L V8	**Camshaft Position Sensor A Circuit Range/Performance (Bank 2) :** The camshaft is divided into a number of segments (flanks). The camshaft houses a gearwheel with a number of teeth (the teeth are positioned between each segment) that are read by the engine control module (ECM) via the camshaft position sensor. The diagnostic trouble code is generated if the control module detects too few segments for 2 crankshaft revolutions (one camshaft revolution). The diagnostic trouble code can be diagnosed by the control module when the engine is running and engine speed exceeds a certain value.
DTC: ECM-P034900 **1T ECM** **Year:** 2011, 2012 **Model:** XC90 **Engine:** 4.4L V8	**Camshaft Position Sensor A Circuit Intermittent (Bank 2):** The camshaft houses a gearwheel with a number of teeth (the teeth are positioned between each segment) that are read by the engine control module (ECM) via the camshaft position sensor. The diagnostic trouble code is generated if the control module detects too few segments for a certain number of crankshaft revolutions. The diagnostic trouble code can be diagnosed by the control module when the engine is running and engine speed exceeds a certain value.
DTC: ECM-P035100 **2T ECM** **Year:** 2011, 2012 **Model:** XC90 **Engine:** 4.4L V8	**Ignition Coil A Primary/Secondary Circuit:** Engine control module (ECM) controls the ignition coils so that spark occurs at the right time. The control module checks the ignition coils' function using a separate diagnostic line. The control module also checks the direct voltage on the signal line from the ignition coil. The diagnostic trouble code (DTC) is stored if the control module detects that: The signal in the diagnostics line indicates malfunction, or that direct voltage in the signal line is considered too high or too low. Incorrect value lasts longer than 9 seconds. Incorrect value lasts for 2 or more subsequent driving cycles. The control module's test for the diagnostic trouble code (DTC) starts in the event of: Engine running. **Note! The control module can only detect the fault once the test has been started and the diagnostic trouble code (DTC) is stored when the conditions are met.**
DTC: ECM-P035200 **2T ECM** **Year:** 2011, 2012 **Model:** XC90 **Engine:** 4.4L V8	**Ignition Coil B Primary/Secondary Circuit:** Engine control module (ECM) controls the ignition coils so that spark occurs at the right time. The control module checks the ignition coils' function using a separate diagnostic line. The control module also checks the direct voltage on the signal line from the ignition coil. The diagnostic trouble code (DTC) is stored if the control module detects that: The signal in the diagnostics line indicates malfunction, or that direct voltage in the signal line is considered too high or too low. Incorrect value lasts longer than 9 seconds. Incorrect value lasts for 2 or more subsequent driving cycles. The control module's test for the diagnostic trouble code (DTC) starts in the event of: Engine running. **Note! The control module can only detect the fault once the test has been started and the diagnostic trouble code (DTC) is stored when the conditions are met.**

DTC	Trouble Code Title and Conditions
DTC: ECM-P035300 **2T ECM** **Year:** 2011, 2012 **Model:** XC90 **Engine:** 4.4L V8	**Ignition Coil C Primary/Secondary Circuit:** Engine control module (ECM) controls the ignition coils so that spark occurs at the right time. The control module checks the ignition coils' function using a separate diagnostic line. The control module also checks the direct voltage on the signal line from the ignition coil. The diagnostic trouble code (DTC) is stored if the control module detects that: The signal in the diagnostics line indicates malfunction, or that direct voltage in the signal line is considered too high or too low. Incorrect value lasts longer than 9 seconds. Incorrect value lasts for 2 or more subsequent driving cycles. The control module's test for the diagnostic trouble code (DTC) starts in the event of: Engine running. **Note! The control module can only detect the fault once the test has been started and the diagnostic trouble code (DTC) is stored when the conditions are met.**
DTC: ECM-P035400 **2T ECM** **Year:** 2011, 2012 **Model:** XC90 **Engine:** 4.4L V8	**Ignition Coil D Primary/Secondary Circuit:** Engine control module (ECM) controls the ignition coils so that spark occurs at the right time. The control module checks the ignition coils' function using a separate diagnostic line. The control module also checks the direct voltage on the signal line from the ignition coil. The diagnostic trouble code (DTC) is stored if the control module detects that: The signal in the diagnostics line indicates malfunction, or that direct voltage in the signal line is considered too high or too low. Incorrect value lasts longer than 9 seconds. Incorrect value lasts for 2 or more subsequent driving cycles. The control module's test for the diagnostic trouble code (DTC) starts in the event of: Engine running. **Note! The control module can only detect the fault once the test has been started and the diagnostic trouble code (DTC) is stored when the conditions are met.**
DTC: ECM-P035500 **1T ECM** **Year:** 2011, 2012 **Model:** XC90 **Engine:** 4.4L V8	**Ignition Coil E Primary/Secondary Circuit:** Engine control module (ECM) controls the ignition coils so that spark occurs at the right time. The control module checks the ignition coils' function using a separate diagnostic line. The control module also checks the direct voltage on the signal line from the ignition coil. The diagnostic trouble code (DTC) is stored if the control module detects that: The signal in the diagnostics line indicates malfunction, or that direct voltage in the signal line is considered too high or too low. Incorrect value lasts longer than 9 seconds. Incorrect value lasts for 2 or more subsequent driving cycles. The control module's test for the diagnostic trouble code (DTC) starts in the event of: Engine running.
DTC: ECM-P035600 **2T ECM** **Year:** 2011, 2012 **Model:** XC90 **Engine:** 4.4L V8	**Ignition Coil F Primary/Secondary Circuit:** Engine control module (ECM) controls the ignition coils so that spark occurs at the right time. The control module checks the ignition coils' function using a separate diagnostic line. The control module also checks the direct voltage on the signal line from the ignition coil. The diagnostic trouble code (DTC) is stored if the control module detects that: The signal in the diagnostics line indicates malfunction, or that direct voltage in the signal line is considered too high or too low. Incorrect value lasts longer than 9 seconds. Incorrect value lasts for 2 or more subsequent driving cycles. The control module's test for the diagnostic trouble code (DTC) starts in the event of: Engine running.
DTC: ECM-P036500 **1T ECM, MIL: Yes** **Year:** 2011, 2012 **Model:** XC90 **Engine:** 4.4L V8	**Camshaft Position Sensor B Circuit (Bank 1):** The camshaft is divided into a number of segments (flanks). The camshaft houses a gearwheel with a number of teeth (the teeth are positioned between each segment) that are read by the engine control module (ECM) via the camshaft position sensor. The diagnostic trouble code is generated if the control module detects too few segments for a certain number of crankshaft revolutions. The diagnostic trouble code (DTC) can be diagnosed when starting the engine.
DTC: ECM-P036600 **1T ECM, MIL: Yes** **Year:** 2011, 2012 **Model:** XC90 **Engine:** 4.4L V8	**Camshaft Position Sensor B Circuit Range/Performance (Bank 1):** The camshaft is divided into a number of segments (flanks). The camshaft houses a gearwheel with a number of teeth (the teeth are positioned between each segment) that are read by the engine control module (ECM) via the camshaft position sensor. The diagnostic trouble code can be diagnosed by the control module when the engine is running and engine speed exceeds a certain value.
DTC: ECM-P036900 **1T ECM, MIL: Yes** **Year:** 2011, 2012 **Model:** XC90 **Engine:** 4.4L V8	**Camshaft Position Sensor B Circuit Intermittent (Bank 1):** The camshaft is divided into a number of segments (flanks). The camshaft houses a gearwheel with a number of teeth (the teeth are positioned between each segment) that are read by the engine control module (ECM) via the camshaft position sensor. The diagnostic trouble code is generated if the control module detects too few segments for a certain number of crankshaft revolutions. The diagnostic trouble code (DTC) can be diagnosed when starting the engine.

DTC	Trouble Code Title and Conditions
DTC: ECM-P042000 **1T ECM, MIL: Yes** **Year:** 2011, 2012 **Model:** XC90 **Engine:** 4.4L V8	**Catalyst System Efficiency Below Threshold (Bank 1):** Engine Control Module (ECM) checks the efficiency of catalytic converter (bank 1) by switching between rich and lean fuel/air mixture. When the change-over is made, the signal from the rear heated oxygen sensor (HO2S) is checked and the time taken for the probe to switch. The diagnostic trouble code (DTC) is stored if the engine control module (ECM) registers that the rear heated oxygen sensor (HO2S) switches too quickly and is interpreted as poor catalytic converter efficiency. The diagnostic trouble code (DTC) can be diagnosed with the engine at operating temperature, approximately 15 minutes after the engine has first been started if the vehicle is driven (normal road load) at 70-90 km/h for 30-40 seconds.
DTC: ECM-P042268 **1T ECM** **Year:** 2011, 2012 **Model:** XC90 **Engine:** 4.4L V8	**Main Catalyst Efficiency Below Threshold (Bank 1) :** **Note! This diagnostic trouble code (DTC) status is an event controlled diagnostic trouble code (DTC). An event controlled diagnostic trouble code (DTC) does not mean that there is a fault in the control module when it is active, but is designed as information.** Engine Control Module (ECM) checks the efficiency of catalytic converter (bank 1) by switching between rich and lean fuel/air mixture. When the change-over is made, the signal from the rear heated oxygen sensor (HO2S) is checked and the time taken for the probe to switch. The diagnostic trouble code (DTC) is stored if the control module detects that: The signal from the rear heated oxygen sensor (HO2S) changes too quickly and this is interpreted as poor catalytic converter efficiency. The diagnostic trouble code (DTC) can be diagnosed when: Idling with hot engine. The vehicle must have been in motion before idling.
DTC: ECM-P043E00 **1T ECM, MIL: Yes** **Year:** 2011, 2012 **Model:** XC90 **Engine:** 4.4L V8	**Evaporative Emission System Leak Detection Reference Orifice Low Flow:** The engine control module (ECM) checks the function of the leakage diagnosis unit by measuring the current through the leakage diagnosis pump. If the Engine control module (ECM) registers that the current curve is unreasonably high or noisy, the control module interprets that the reference measurement has produced a faulty result and the diagnostic trouble code is generated. The diagnostic trouble code can be diagnosed when leakage diagnosis is running.
DTC: ECM-P043F00 **1T ECM, MIL: Yes** **Year:** 2011, 2012 **Model:** XC90 **Engine:** 4.4L V8	**Evaporative Emission System Leak Detection Reference Orifice High Flow:** The engine control module (ECM) checks the function of the leakage diagnosis unit by measuring the current through the leakage diagnosis pump. If the Engine control module (ECM) registers that the current curve is unreasonably low or noisy, it determines that the reference measurement has produced a faulty result and the diagnostic trouble code is generated. The diagnostic trouble code can be diagnosed when leakage diagnosis is running.
DTC: ECM-P044100 **1T ECM, MIL: Yes** **Year:** 2011, 2012 **Model:** XC90 **Engine:** 4.4L V8	**Evaporative Emission System Incorrect Purge Flow:** The engine control module (ECM) detects a fault in the function of the EVAP valve by analyzing the signal from the pressure sensor in the induction pipe. The diagnostic trouble code is generated if the control module registers that the EVAP valve has seized. The diagnostic trouble code can be diagnosed during EVAP control.
DTC: ECM-P044200 **1T ECM, MIL: Yes** **Year:** 2011, 2012 **Model:** XC90 **Engine:** 4.4L V8	**Evaporative Emission System Leak Detected (small leak). :** The engine control module (ECM) checks for leaks in the fuel system by measuring the current consumption of the leakage diagnosis pump when pressure is applied. If the current consumption measured under pressure does not change in a specific way or a certain pressure is not obtained in the system within a reasonable amount of time, the control module assesses this as a small leak (leak between 0.5 mm and 1.0 mm) from the fuel system. The diagnostic trouble code can be diagnosed when leakage diagnosis is running.
DTC: ECM-P044400 **1T ECM, MIL: Yes** **Year:** 2011, 2012 **Model:** XC90 **Engine:** 4.4L V8	**Evaporative Emission System Purge Control Valve Circuit Open:** If the Engine control module (ECM) registers an open circuit on the signal line between the control module and the EVAP-valve, the diagnostic trouble code is generated. The diagnostic trouble code can be diagnosed when the ignition is on.
DTC: ECM-P045500 **1T ECM, MIL: Yes** **Year:** 2011, 2012 **Model:** XC90 **Engine:** 4.4L V8	**Evaporative Emission System Leak Detected (Gross Leak/No Flow). :** The engine control module (ECM) checks for leaks in the fuel system by measuring the current consumption of the leakage diagnosis pump when pressure is applied. If the current consumption measured under pressure does not change in a specific way or a certain pressure is not obtained in the system within a reasonable amount of time, the control module assesses this as a large leak (leak larger than 1.0 mm) from the fuel system. See Design and Function for more information. The diagnostic trouble code can be diagnosed when leakage diagnosis is running.

DTC	Trouble Code Title and Conditions
DTC: ECM-P045800 **1T ECM, MIL: Yes** **Year:** 2011, 2012 **Model:** XC90 **Engine:** 4.4L V8	**Evaporative Emission System Purge Control Valve Circuit Low:** The diagnostic trouble code is generated if the engine control module (ECM) registers that the EVAP valve signal cable is short-circuited to ground or that the circuit is open. The diagnostic trouble code can be diagnosed when the ignition is on.
DTC: ECM-P045900 **1T ECM, MIL: Yes** **Year:** 2011, 2012 **Model:** XC90 **Engine:** 4.4L V8	**Evaporative Emission System Purge Control Valve Circuit High:** The diagnostic trouble code is generated if the engine control module (ECM) registers that the EVAP valve signal cable is short-circuited to supply voltage. The diagnostic trouble code can be diagnosed when the ignition is on.
DTC: ECM-P046000 **1T ECM** **Year:** 2011, 2012 **Model:** XC90 **Engine:** 4.4L V8	**Fuel Level Sensor A Circuit:** If a malfunction of the fuel level sensor's pump part is detected by central electronic module (CEM), a malfunction message is sent to engine control module (ECM) and the diagnostic trouble code is generated. The diagnostic trouble code can be diagnosed when the ignition is on.
DTC: ECM-P046100 **1T ECM** **Year:** 2011, 2012 **Model:** XC90 **Engine:** 4.4L V8	**Fuel Level Sensor A Circuit Range/Performance:** The central electronic module (CEM) sends the engine control module (ECM) information on fuel level and the fault status of the fuel level sensor. The engine control module (ECM) compares engine fuel consumption with the change in the fuel level over a certain period of time. The diagnostic trouble code is generated if the engine control module (ECM) registers an unreasonably small reduction in the fuel level as compared to calculated fuel consumption. The diagnostic trouble code can be diagnosed when the ignition is on.
DTC: ECM-P046400 **1T ECM** **Year:** 2011, 2012 **Model:** XC90 **Engine:** 4.4L V8	**Fuel Level Sensor A Circuit Intermittent:** The central electronic module (CEM) sends the engine control module (ECM) information on fuel level and the fault status of the fuel level sensor. The engine control module (ECM) compares engine fuel consumption with the change in the fuel level over a certain period of time. The diagnostic trouble code is generated if the engine control module (ECM) registers great fluctuations in the fuel level while the vehicle is stationary. The diagnostic trouble code can be diagnosed when the ignition is on.
DTC: ECM-P048000 **1T ECM** **Year:** 2011, 2012 **Model:** XC90 **Engine:** 4.4L V8	**Fan 1 Control Circuit:** The engine control module (ECM) sends a signal (speed request to the cooling fan) to the cooling fan module. The cooling fan module then regulates voltage to the fan motor at an infinitely variable rate. The diagnostic trouble code is generated if the engine control module (ECM) detects that fan speed is low. The diagnostic trouble code can be diagnosed when the engine is running. **Note! The electric cooling fan may have a post-running time of up to approx. 6 minutes after the engine has been shut off. The time for the electric cooling fan's post-running depends on the engine's temperature, temperature in the engine compartment as well as the pressure level in the AC system.**
DTC: ECM-P048100 **1T ECM** **Year:** 2011, 2012 **Model:** XC90 **Engine:** 4.4L V8	**Fan 2 Control Circuit:** The engine control module (ECM) sends a signal (speed request to the cooling fan) to the cooling fan module. The cooling fan module then regulates voltage to the fan motor at an infinitely variable rate. The diagnostic trouble code is generated if the engine control module (ECM) detects that fan speed is low. The diagnostic trouble code can be diagnosed when the engine is running. **Note! The electric cooling fan may have a post-running time of up to approx. 6 minutes after the engine has been shut off. The time for the electric cooling fan's post-running depends on the engine's temperature, temperature in the engine compartment as well as the pressure level in the AC system.**
DTC: ECM-P048368 **1T ECM** **Year:** 2011, 2012 **Model:** XC90 **Engine:** 4.4L V8	**Fan Performance:** **Note! This diagnostic trouble code (DTC) status is an event controlled diagnostic trouble code (DTC). An event controlled diagnostic trouble code (DTC) does not mean that there is a fault in the control module when it is active, but is designed as information.** Engine control module (ECM) monitors the engine's cooling system. The diagnostic trouble code (DTC) is stored if the control module detects that: The electric cooling fan is blocked. The diagnostic trouble code (DTC) can be diagnosed when the engine is running.

DTC	Trouble Code Title and Conditions
DTC: ECM-P050086 **1T ECM** **Year:** 2011, 2012 **Model:** XC90 **Engine:** 4.4L V8	**Vehicle Speed Sensor A. Bus Signal / Message Failures. Signal Invalid:** Information about vehicle speed is sent on the CAN-network from brake control module (BCM) to engine control module (ECM). If brake control module (BCM) registers a malfunction of the speed signal, information about the malfunction is sent to engine control module (ECM) which generates the diagnostic trouble code. The diagnostic trouble code can be diagnosed when the ignition is on. Hint: If Engine control module (ECM) has been recharged or if the battery voltage has been interrupted, the brake pedal must be pressed down twice for approx. two seconds to activate the cruise control function.
DTC: ECM-P050087 **1T ECM** **Year:** 2011, 2012 **Model:** XC90 **Engine:** 4.4L V8	**Vehicle Speed Sensor A. Bus Signal / Message Failures. Missing Message:** Information about vehicle speed is sent on the CAN-network from brake control module (BCM) to engine control module (ECM). If communication between brake control module (BCM) and engine control module (ECM) is missing, the diagnostic trouble code is generated. The diagnostic trouble code can be diagnosed when the ignition is on. Hint: If Engine control module (ECM) has been recharged or if the battery voltage has been interrupted, the brake pedal must be pressed down twice for approx. two seconds to activate the cruise control function.
DTC: ECM-P050429 **1T ECM** **Year:** 2011, 2012 **Model:** XC90 **Engine:** 4.4L V8	**Brake Switch A / B Correlation. General Signal Failures / Signal Invalid:** The engine control module (ECM) checks the stop lamp switch by comparing the received signal with the brake pedal switch position. Information about the position of the brake pedal switch is transmitted from the brake control module (BCM) via CAN communication. The control module compares both the signals. The diagnostic trouble code (DTC) is stored if the control module detects that: The signals indicate different positions of the brake pedal at several times. The control module's test for the diagnostic trouble code (DTC) starts in the event of: Ignition switch position II. The brake pedal depressed several times. Hint: If Engine control module (ECM) has been recharged or if the battery voltage has been interrupted, the brake pedal must be pressed down twice for approx. two seconds to activate the cruise control function.
DTC: ECM-P050462 **1T ECM** **Year:** 2011, 2012 **Model:** XC90 **Engine:** 4.4L V8	**Brake Switch A / B Correlation. Algorithm Based Failures / Signal Compare Failure:** The engine control module (ECM) checks the stop lamp switch by comparing the received signal with the brake pedal switch position. Information about the position of the brake pedal switch is transmitted from the brake control module (BCM) via CAN communication. The control module compares both the signals. The diagnostic trouble code (DTC) is stored if the control module detects that: The signals indicate different positions on the brake pedal for a total of two minutes and at least 5 shifts. The control module's test for the diagnostic trouble code (DTC) starts in the event of: Ignition switch position II. The brake pedal depressed several times. Hint: If Engine control module (ECM) has been recharged or if the battery voltage has been interrupted, the brake pedal must be pressed down twice for approx. two seconds to activate the cruise control function.
DTC: ECM-P050465 **1T ECM** **Year:** 2011, 2012 **Model:** XC90 **Engine:** 4.4L V8	**Brake Switch A / B Correlation. Signal Has Too Few Transitions / Events:** The engine control module (ECM) checks the stop lamp switch by comparing the received signal with the brake pedal switch position. Information about the position of the brake pedal switch is transmitted from the brake control module (BCM) via CAN communication. The control module compares both the signals. The diagnostic trouble code (DTC) is stored if the control module detects that: The signals indicate one and the same position for an implausibly long time. The control module's test for the diagnostic trouble code (DTC) starts in the event of: Ignition switch position II. The brake pedal depressed several times. Hint: If Engine control module (ECM) has been recharged or if the battery voltage has been interrupted, the brake pedal must be pressed down twice for approx. two seconds to activate the cruise control function.
DTC: ECM-P050568 **1T ECM** **Year:** 2011, 2012 **Model:** XC90 **Engine:** 4.4L V8	**Idle Air Control System:** **Note! This diagnostic trouble code (DTC) status is an event controlled diagnostic trouble code (DTC). An event controlled diagnostic trouble code (DTC) does not mean that there is a fault in the control module when it is active, but is designed as information.** Engine control module (ECM) monitors the idle control. If the control module detects that idle control has been outside the limit value for a certain time, the diagnostic trouble code is generated. The diagnostic trouble code (DTC) can be diagnosed when the engine is running.
DTC: ECM-P050600 **1T ECM, MIL: Yes** **Year:** 2011, 2012 **Model:** XC90 **Engine:** 4.4L V8	**Idle Control RPM Lower Than Expected:** If engine control module (ECM) registers that idle rpm is 100 rpm lower than the nominal idle rpm, the diagnostic trouble code is generated. The diagnostic trouble code can be diagnosed with warm engine (higher than 80 °C), vehicle stationary and idling.

DTC	Trouble Code Title and Conditions
DTC: ECM-P050700 **1T ECM, MIL: Yes** **Year:** 2011, 2012 **Model:** XC90 **Engine:** 4.4L V8	**Idle Control RPM Higher Than Expected:** The diagnostic trouble code (DTC) is stored if the control module detects that: Idling speed is 200 rpm greater than the nominal idling speed. The control module's test for the diagnostic trouble code (DTC) starts in the event of: The vehicle is stationary. The engine is idling. The engine temperature shall be over 80 °C with warm engine (upper radiator hose shall be warm). **Note! The control module can only detect the fault once the test has been started and the diagnostic trouble code (DTC) is stored when the conditions are met.**
DTC: ECM-P050A00 **1T ECM, MIL: Yes** **Year:** 2011, 2012 **Model:** XC90 **Engine:** 4.4L V8	**Cold Start Idle Air Control System Performance:** The Engine control module (ECM) checks the function for quick catalytic converter warm-up. The catalytic converter can be warmed up quickly by increasing the throttle angle, changing the camshaft angle etc. for example. The Engine control module (ECM) checks the function for catalytic converter warm-up. The Engine control module (ECM) calculates the difference between the requested energy applied for catalytic converter warm-up and the actual excess energy for catalytic converter warm-up. The diagnostic trouble code (DTC) is stored if the control module detects that: The difference between applied energy for warm-up of the catalytic converter and the actual energy for warm-up of the catalytic converter is too great. The control module's test for the diagnostic trouble code (DTC) starts in the event of: When starting the engine. Cold engine. Warming-up of catalytic converter started. **Note! The control module can only detect the fault once the test has been started and the diagnostic trouble code (DTC) is stored when the conditions are met.**
DTC: ECM-P050B00 **1T ECM, MIL: Yes** **Year:** 2011, 2012 **Model:** XC90 **Engine:** 4.4L V8	**Cold Start Ignition Timing Performance:** The Engine control module (ECM) checks the function for catalytic converter warm-up. The Engine control module (ECM) calculates the difference between the requested energy applied for catalytic converter warm-up and the actual excess energy for catalytic converter warm-up. The diagnostic trouble code (DTC) is stored if the control module detects that: The difference between applied energy for warm-up of the catalytic converter and the actual energy for warm-up of the catalytic converter is too great. The control module's test for the diagnostic trouble code (DTC) starts in the event of: Cold engine. Warming-up of catalytic converter started. **Note! The control module can only detect the fault once the test has been started and the diagnostic trouble code (DTC) is stored when the conditions are met.**
DTC: ECM-P052548 **1T ECM** **Year:** 2011, 2012 **Model:** XC90 **Engine:** 4.4L V8	**Cruise Control Servo Control Circuit Range/Performance:** The diagnostic trouble code (DTC) is stored if the engine control module (ECM) registers an internal fault when the cruise control is active. The diagnostic trouble code (DTC) can be diagnosed when the ignition is switched on. Hint: If Engine control module (ECM) has been recharged or if the battery voltage has been interrupted, the brake pedal must be pressed down twice for approx. two seconds to activate the cruise control function.
DTC: ECM-P052A00 **1T ECM** **Year:** 2011, 2012 **Model:** XC90 **Engine:** 4.4L V8	**Cold Start Camshaft Position Timing Over-Advanced (Bank 1):** The Engine control module (ECM) regulates the camshaft position (angle). The difference between requested angle and actual angle is stored in the Engine control module (ECM) during warm-up of the catalytic converter. The diagnostic trouble code (DTC) is stored if the control module detects that: The camshaft angle is greater than the requested during warm-up of the catalytic converter. The control module's test for the diagnostic trouble code (DTC) starts in the event of: * Cold engine. * Warming-up of catalytic converter.
DTC: ECM-P052B00 **1T ECM** **Year:** 2011, 2012 **Model:** XC90 **Engine:** 4.4L V8	**Cold Start Camshaft Position Timing Over-Retarded (Bank 1):** The Engine control module (ECM) regulates the camshaft position (angle). The difference between requested angle and actual angle is stored in the Engine control module (ECM) during warm-up of the catalytic converter. The diagnostic trouble code (DTC) is stored if the control module detects that: The camshaft angle is less than the requested during warm-up of the catalytic converter. The control module's test for the diagnostic trouble code (DTC) starts in the event of: * Cold engine. * Warming-up of catalytic converter.

DTC	Trouble Code Title and Conditions
DTC: ECM-P053100 **1T ECM** **Year:** 2011, 2012 **Model:** XC90 **Engine:** 4.4L V8	**A/C Refrigerant Pressure Sensor A Circuit Range/Performance:** The engine control module (ECM) calculates when a certain pressure change should have been reached in the air conditioning (A/C) system. The control module also measures the actual pressure changes at the air conditioning (A/C) pressure sensor. The diagnostic trouble code (DTC) is stored if the control module detects that: The calculated A/C pressure value differs from the actual pressure value. The control module's test for the diagnostic trouble code (DTC) starts in the event of: * Engine running. * Air conditioning (A/C) control, active.
DTC: ECM-P053200 **1T ECM** **Year:** 2011, 2012 **Model:** XC90 **Engine:** 4.4L V8	**A/C Refrigerant Pressure Sensor A Circuit Low Input:** The engine control module (ECM) checks if the signal from the air conditioning (A/C) pressure sensor is within its permitted range. The diagnostic trouble code (DTC) is stored if the control module detects that: The signal from the pressure sensor corresponds to a lower pressure than the normal operating value. The control module's test for the diagnostic trouble code (DTC) starts in the event of: Ignition on.
DTC: ECM-P053300 **1T ECM** **Year:** 2011, 2012 **Model:** XC90 **Engine:** 4.4L V8	**A/C Refrigerant Pressure Sensor A Circuit High Input:** The engine control module (ECM) checks if the signal from the air conditioning (A/C) pressure sensor is within its permitted range. The diagnostic trouble code (DTC) is stored if the control module detects that: The signal from the pressure sensor corresponds to a higher pressure than the normal operating value. The control module's test for the diagnostic trouble code (DTC) starts in the event of: Ignition on.
DTC: ECM-P053400 **1T ECM** **Year:** 2011, 2012 **Model:** XC90 **Engine:** 4.4L V8	**A/C Refrigerant Charge Loss:** The air conditioning (A/C) system must have a certain basic pressure in order for it to function optimally. The diagnostic trouble code (DTC) is stored if the control module detects that: The basic pressure in the air conditioning (A/C) system is too low. The control module's test for the diagnostic trouble code (DTC) starts in the event of: Engine running. Air conditioning (A/C) control, active. **Note! The control module can only detect the fault once the test has been started and the diagnostic trouble code (DTC) is stored when the conditions are met.**
DTC: ECM-P056300 **1T ECM** **Year:** 2011, 2012 **Model:** XC90 **Engine:** 4.4L V8	**System Voltage High:** Engine control module (ECM) checks the voltage level in the system. If engine control module (ECM) detects that the voltage is above a certain level, this is interpreted as a malfunction and the diagnostic trouble code is generated. The diagnostic trouble code can be diagnosed when the ignition is on.
DTC: ECM-P057500 **1T ECM** **Year:** 2011, 2012 **Model:** XC90 **Engine:** 4.4L V8	**Cruise Control Input Circuit:** The Central electronic module (CEM) receives and checks the signals from the steering wheel buttons for cruise control. The information is transmitted via CAN to the Engine control module (ECM). The Engine control module (ECM) checks the received information. The diagnostic trouble code (DTC) is stored if the control module detects that: The information means that any of the steering wheel buttons have been depressed longer than 180 seconds. The control module's test for the diagnostic trouble code (DTC) starts in the event of: Engine running. Hint: If Engine control module (ECM) has been recharged or if the battery voltage has been interrupted, the brake pedal must be pressed down twice for approx. two seconds to activate the cruise control function.
DTC: ECM-P060704 **1T ECM, MIL: Yes** **Year:** 2011, 2012 **Model:** XC90 **Engine:** 4.4L V8	**Control Module Performance:** The diagnostic trouble code (DTC) is stored if the engine control module (ECM) registers an internal fault. The diagnostic trouble code can be diagnosed when the ignition is on.
DTC: ECM-P060708 **1T ECM, MIL: Yes** **Year:** 2011, 2012 **Model:** XC90 **Engine:** 4.4L V8	**Control Module Performance:** The diagnostic trouble code (DTC) is stored if the engine control module (ECM) registers an internal fault. The diagnostic trouble code can be diagnosed when the ignition is on.

DTC	Trouble Code Title and Conditions
DTC: ECM-P060741 **1T ECM, MIL: Yes** **Year:** 2011, 2012 **Model:** XC90 **Engine:** 4.4L V8	**Control Module Performance. System Internal Failures:** The diagnostic trouble code (DTC) is stored if the engine control module (ECM) registers an internal fault. The diagnostic trouble code can be diagnosed when the ignition is on.
DTC: ECM-P060742 **1T ECM, MIL: Yes** **Year:** 2011, 2012 **Model:** XC90 **Engine:** 4.4L V8	**Control Module Performance. System Internal Failures:** The diagnostic trouble code (DTC) is stored if the engine control module (ECM) registers an internal fault. The diagnostic trouble code can be diagnosed when the ignition is on.
DTC: ECM-P060743 **1T ECM, MIL: Yes** **Year:** 2011, 2012 **Model:** XC90 **Engine:** 4.4L V8	**Control Module Performance. System Internal Failures:** The diagnostic trouble code (DTC) is stored if the engine control module (ECM) registers an internal fault. The diagnostic trouble code can be diagnosed when the ignition is on.
DTC: ECM-P060744 **1T ECM, MIL: Yes** **Year:** 2011, 2012 **Model:** XC90 **Engine:** 4.4L V8	**Control Module Performance. System Internal Failures / Data memory failure:** The diagnostic trouble code (DTC) is stored if the engine control module (ECM) registers an internal fault. The diagnostic trouble code can be diagnosed when the ignition is on.
DTC: ECM-P060745 **1T ECM, MIL: Yes** **Year:** 2011, 2012 **Model:** XC90 **Engine:** 4.4L V8	**Control Module Performance. System Internal Failures / Program Memory Failure:** The diagnostic trouble code (DTC) is stored if the engine control module (ECM) registers an internal fault. The diagnostic trouble code can be diagnosed when the ignition is on.
DTC: ECM-P060747 **1T ECM, MIL: Yes** **Year:** 2011, 2012 **Model:** XC90 **Engine:** 4.4L V8	**Control Module Performance. System Internal Failures. Watchdog / Safety µC Failure:** The diagnostic trouble code (DTC) is stored if the engine control module (ECM) registers an internal fault The diagnostic trouble code can be diagnosed when the ignition is on.
DTC: ECM-P060748 **1T ECM, MIL: Yes** **Year:** 2011, 2012 **Model:** XC90 **Engine:** 4.4L V8	**Control Module Performance. System Internal Failures / Supervision Software Failure:** The diagnostic trouble code (DTC) is stored if the engine control module (ECM) registers an internal fault The diagnostic trouble code can be diagnosed when the ignition is on.
DTC: ECM-P061511 **T ECM** **Year:** 2011, 2012 **Model:** XC90 **Engine:** 4.4L V8	**Starter Relay Circuit. General Electrical Failures. Circuit Short To Ground:** The engine control module (ECM) checks the signal of the starter motor relay coil. The diagnostic trouble code (DTC) is stored if the engine control module (ECM) detects that the signal is low despite the ignition switch being in position III (start position). The diagnostic trouble code can be diagnosed when the engine is started.
DTC: ECM-P061512 **T ECM** **Year:** 2011, 2012 **Model:** XC90 **Engine:** 4.4L V8	**Starter Relay Circuit. General Electrical Failures. Circuit Short To Battery:** The engine control module (ECM) checks the signal of the starter motor relay coil. The diagnostic trouble code (DTC) is stored if the engine control module (ECM) detects that the signal is high despite the ignition switch being in position II (ignition position). The diagnostic trouble code can be diagnosed when the ignition is on.
DTC: ECM-P061513 **T ECM** **Year:** 2011, 2012 **Model:** XC90 **Engine:** 4.4L V8	**Starter Relay Circuit. General Electrical Failures. Circuit Open:** The engine control module (ECM) checks the signal of the starter motor relay coil. The diagnostic trouble code is generated if the engine control module (ECM) detects that there is no signal from the starter relay.
DTC: ECM-P061A00 **T ECM** **Year:** 2011, 2012 **Model:** XC90 **Engine:** 4.4L V8	**Internal Control Module Torque Performance:** Engine Control Module (ECM) monitors the torque in the engine by reading and interpreting signals from mass air flow sensor, electronic throttle unit and air pressure sensor in the inlet manifold. The diagnostic trouble code (DTC) is stored if the measured torque exceeds the requested torque, based on the pedal position and the engine speed (RPM). The diagnostic trouble code (DTC) can be diagnosed in specific driving conditions.

DTC	Trouble Code Title and Conditions
DTC: ECM-P061A62 **T ECM** **Year:** 2011, 2012 **Model:** XC90 **Engine:** 4.4L V8	**Internal Control Module Torque Performance:** Engine Control Module (ECM) monitors the torque in the engine by reading and interpreting signals from mass air flow sensor, electronic throttle unit and air pressure sensor in the inlet manifold. The diagnostic trouble code (DTC) is stored if the measured torque exceeds the requested torque, based on the pedal position and the engine speed (RPM). The diagnostic trouble code (DTC) can be diagnosed in specific driving conditions.
DTC: ECM-P061A64 **1T ECM** **Year:** 2011, 2012 **Model:** XC90 **Engine:** 4.4L V8	**Internal Control Module Torque Performance:** Engine Control Module (ECM) monitors the torque in the engine by reading and interpreting signals from mass air flow sensor, electronic throttle unit and air pressure sensor in the inlet manifold. The diagnostic trouble code (DTC) is stored if the measured torque exceeds the requested torque, based on the pedal position and the engine speed (RPM). The diagnostic trouble code (DTC) can be diagnosed in specific driving conditions.
DTC: ECM-P061A68 **T ECM** **Year:** 2011, 2012 **Model:** XC90 **Engine:** 4.4L V8	**Internal Control Module Torque Performance:** **Note! This diagnostic trouble code (DTC) status is an event controlled diagnostic trouble code (DTC). An event controlled diagnostic trouble code (DTC) does not mean that there is a fault in the control module when it is active, but is designed as information.** Engine Control Module (ECM) monitors the torque in the engine by reading and interpreting signals from mass air flow sensor, electronic throttle unit and air pressure sensor in the inlet manifold. The diagnostic trouble code (DTC) is stored if the measured torque exceeds the requested torque, based on the pedal position and the engine speed (RPM). The diagnostic trouble code (DTC) can be diagnosed in specific driving conditions.
DTC: ECM-P061B64 **T ECM** **Year:** 2011, 2012 **Model:** XC90 **Engine:** 4.4L V8	**Internal Control Module Torque Calculation Performance. Signal Plausibility Failure:** Engine Control Module (ECM) monitors the torque in the engine by reading and interpreting signals from mass air flow sensor, electronic throttle unit and air pressure sensor in the inlet manifold. Torque is calculated according to two separate methods. The control module checks and compares both results of the calculation. The diagnostic trouble code (DTC) is stored if the engine control module (ECM) detects that both results of the calculations deviate too much from each other. The diagnostic trouble code (DTC) can be diagnosed in specific driving conditions.
DTC: ECM-P061B68 **T ECM** **Year:** 2011, 2012 **Model:** XC90 **Engine:** 4.4L V8	**Internal Control Module Torque Calculation Performance:** **Note! This diagnostic trouble code (DTC) status is an event controlled diagnostic trouble code (DTC). An event controlled diagnostic trouble code (DTC) does not mean that there is a fault in the control module when it is active, but is designed as information.** Engine control module (ECM) monitors the torque model internally in the control module. If the control module detects that the torque model has been outside the limit value for a certain time, the diagnostic trouble code is generated. The diagnostic trouble code (DTC) can be diagnosed when the engine is running.
DTC: ECM-P061F00 **1T ECM** **Year:** 2011, 2012 **Model:** XC90 **Engine:** 4.4L V8	**Internal Control Module Throttle Actuator Controller Performance:** Engine control module (ECM) checks the signals from the electronic throttle unit. If engine control module (ECM) detects that feedback throttle position does not change, despite adjustment being performed, the diagnostic trouble code is generated. The diagnostic trouble code can be diagnosed in specific operation situations
DTC: ECM-P062001 **1T ECM** **Year:** 2011, 2012 **Model:** XC90 **Engine:** 4.4L V8	**Generator Control Circuit:** The engine control module (ECM) regulates the alternator charge voltage (via LIN communication) on request of the central electronic module (CEM) (via CAN communication). The alternator control module (ACM) sends information on the fault to the engine control module (ECM) (via LIN communication). The diagnostic trouble code is generated if the alternator control module (ACM) sends the engine control module (ECM) information on an electrical fault in the alternator. The diagnostic trouble code can be diagnosed when the engine is running.
DTC: ECM-P06204B **1T ECM** **Year:** 2011, 2012 **Model:** XC90 **Engine:** 4.4L V8	**Generator Control Circuit. Over Temperature:** The engine control module (ECM) regulates the alternator charge voltage (via LIN communication) on request of the central electronic module (CEM) (via CAN communication). The alternator control module (ACM) sends information on the fault to the engine control module (ECM) (via LIN communication). The diagnostic trouble code is generated if the alternator control module (ACM) sends the engine control module (ECM) information indicating that the alternator temperature exceeds a certain value. The diagnostic trouble code can be diagnosed when the engine is running.
DTC: ECM-P062074 **1T ECM** **Year:** 2011, 2012 **Model:** XC90 **Engine:** 4.4L V8	**Generator Control Circuit. Actuator Slipping:** The engine control module (ECM) regulates the alternator charge voltage (via LIN communication) on request of the central electronic module (CEM) (via CAN communication). The alternator control module (ACM) sends information on the fault to the engine control module (ECM) (via LIN communication). The diagnostic trouble code is generated if the alternator control module (ACM) sends the engine control module (ECM) information on a mechanical fault in the alternator (engine speed exceeds a certain value but the alternator is not operating). The diagnostic trouble code can be diagnosed when the engine is running.

DTC	Trouble Code Title and Conditions
DTC: ECM-P062800 **T ECM** **Year:** 2011, 2012 **Model:** XC90 **Engine:** 4.4L V8	**Fuel Pump A Control Circuit Low:** The engine control module (ECM) checks the control signal to the fuel pump. The diagnostic trouble code (DTC) is stored if the control module registers a fault in the control signal to the fuel pump. The diagnostic trouble code (DTC) can be diagnosed when the engine is running.
DTC: ECM-P062900 **T ECM** **Year:** 2011, 2012 **Model:** XC90 **Engine:** 4.4L V8	**Fuel Pump A Control Circuit High:** The engine control module (ECM) checks the control signal to the fuel pump. The diagnostic trouble code (DTC) is stored if the control module registers a fault in the control signal to the fuel pump. The diagnostic trouble code (DTC) can be diagnosed when the engine is running.
DTC: ECM-P063400 **T ECM** **Year:** 2011, 2012 **Model:** XC90 **Engine:** 4.4L V8	**PCM / ECM / TCM Internal Temperature Too High:** If engine control module (ECM) registers that internal temperature in engine control module (ECM) has exceeded 120 °C for a certain time, the diagnostic trouble code is generated. The diagnostic trouble code can be diagnosed when the engine is running.
DTC: ECM-P06344B **T ECM** **Year:** 2011, 2012 **Model:** XC90 **Engine:** 4.4L V8	**PCM / ECM / TCM Internal Temperature Too High:** If engine control module (ECM) registers that internal temperature in engine control module (ECM) has exceeded 105 °C for a certain time, the diagnostic trouble code is generated. The diagnostic trouble code can be diagnosed when the engine is running.
DTC: ECM-P063498 **T ECM** **Year:** 2011, 2012 **Model:** XC90 **Engine:** 4.4L V8	**PCM / ECM / TCM Internal Temperature Too High:** If engine control module (ECM) registers that the accumulated internal temperature in engine control module (ECM) has exceeded 105 °C for longer than a certain time, the diagnostic trouble code is generated. The diagnostic trouble code can be diagnosed when the engine is running.
DTC: ECM-P064200 **T ECM** **Year:** 2011, 2012 **Model:** XC90 **Engine:** 4.4L V8	**Sensor Reference Voltage A Circuit Low:** Engine control module motor (ECM) checks the internal end-stage for 5 volt feed. If voltage becomes too high or too low, the diagnostic trouble code is generated. The diagnostic trouble code can be diagnosed when the ignition is on.
DTC: ECM-P064300 **1T ECM** **Year:** 2011, 2012 **Model:** XC90 **Engine:** 4.4L V8	**Sensor Reference Voltage A Circuit High:** Engine control module motor (ECM) checks the internal end-stage for 5 volt feed. If voltage becomes too high or too low, the diagnostic trouble code is generated. The diagnostic trouble code can be diagnosed when the ignition is on.
DTC: ECM-P064500 **T ECM** **Year:** 2011, 2012 **Model:** XC90 **Engine:** 4.4L V8	**A/C Clutch Relay Control Circuit:** Engine control module (ECM) checks the signal for controlling the A/C relay. If engine control module (ECM) detects a signal that is too low, the control module interprets this as a malfunction and the diagnostic trouble code is generated. The diagnostic trouble code can be diagnosed when the ignition is on.
DTC: ECM-P064600 **T ECM** **Year:** 2011, 2012 **Model:** XC90 **Engine:** 4.4L V8	**A/C Clutch Relay Control Circuit Low:** Engine control module (ECM) checks the signal for controlling the A/C relay. If engine control module (ECM) detects a signal that is too low, the control module interprets this as a malfunction and the diagnostic trouble code is generated. The diagnostic trouble code can be diagnosed when the ignition is on.
DTC: ECM-P064700 **T ECM** **Year:** 2011, 2012 **Model:** XC90 **Engine:** 4.4L V8	**A/C Connection Relay Control Circuit High:** Engine control module (ECM) checks the signal for controlling the A/C relay. If engine control module (ECM) detects a signal that is too high, the control module interprets this as a malfunction and the diagnostic trouble code is generated. The diagnostic trouble code can be diagnosed when the ignition is on.
DTC: ECM-P065A00 **1T ECM** **Year:** 2011, 2012 **Model:** XC90 **Engine:** 4.4L V8	**Generator System Performance:** The engine control module (ECM) regulates the alternator charge voltage (via LIN communication) on request of the central electronic module (CEM) (via CAN communication). The alternator control module (ACM) sends information on the fault to the engine control module (ECM) (via LIN communication). The diagnostic trouble code is generated if the alternator control module (ACM) sends the engine control module (ECM) information on an electrical fault in the alternator. The diagnostic trouble code can be diagnosed when the engine is running.

DTC	Trouble Code Title and Conditions
DTC: ECM-P065C00 **T ECM** **Year:** 2011, 2012 **Model:** XC90 **Engine:** 4.4L V8	**Generator Mechanical Performance:** The engine control module (ECM) regulates the alternator charge voltage (via LIN communication) on request of the central electronic module (CEM) (via CAN communication). The alternator control module (ACM) sends information on the fault to the engine control module (ECM) (via LIN communication). The diagnostic trouble code is generated if the alternator control module (ACM) sends the engine control module (ECM) information on a mechanical fault in the alternator (engine speed exceeds a certain value but the alternator is not operating). The diagnostic trouble code can be diagnosed when the engine is running.
DTC: ECM-P066200 **1T ECM, MIL: Yes** **Year:** 2011, 2012 **Model:** XC90 **Engine:** 4.4L V8	**Intake Manifold Tuning Valve Control Circuit High - Bank 1:** The engine control module (ECM) regulates the variable intake system VIS) via the electric throttle unit. The engine control module (ECM) monitors the control signal for the throttle unit. The diagnostic trouble code (DTC) is stored if the control module detects that: Control signal is too high. The control module's test for the diagnostic trouble code (DTC) starts in the event of: Ignition switch position II. Battery voltage higher than 10.5 V. **Note! The control module can only detect the fault once the test has been started and the diagnostic trouble code (DTC) is stored when the conditions are met.**
DTC: ECM-P066400 **1T ECM, MIL: Yes** **Year:** 2011, 2012 **Model:** XC90 **Engine:** 4.4L V8	**Intake Manifold Tuning Valve Control Circuit Low - Bank 2:** The engine control module (ECM) regulates the variable intake system VIS) via the electric throttle unit. The engine control module (ECM) monitors the control signal for the throttle unit. The diagnostic trouble code (DTC) is stored if the control module detects that: Signal missing. Control signal is too low. The control module's test for the diagnostic trouble code (DTC) starts in the event of: Ignition switch position II. Battery voltage higher than 10.5 V. **Note! The control module can only detect the fault once the test has been started and the diagnostic trouble code (DTC) is stored when the conditions are met.**
DTC: ECM-P066500 **1T ECM, MIL: Yes** **Year:** 2011, 2012 **Model:** XC90 **Engine:** 4.4L V8	**Manifold Tuning Valve Control Circuit High - Bank 2:** The engine control module (ECM) regulates the variable intake system VIS) via the electric throttle unit. The engine control module (ECM) monitors the control signal for the throttle unit. The diagnostic trouble code (DTC) is stored if the control module detects that: Control signal is too high. The control module's test for the diagnostic trouble code (DTC) starts in the event of: Ignition switch position II. Battery voltage higher than 10.5 V. **Note! The control module can only detect the fault once the test has been started and the diagnostic trouble code (DTC) is stored when the conditions are met.**
DTC: ECM-P066800 **2T ECM** **Year:** 2011, 2012 **Model:** XC90 **Engine:** 4.4L V8	**PCM / ECM / TCM Internal Temperature Sensor Circuit Low:** Engine control module (ECM) measures the temperature internally in the control module using a temperature sensor. The control module checks the direct voltage from the sensor. **Note! The temperature sensor is integrated in the Engine control module (ECM).** The diagnostic trouble code (DTC) is stored if the control module detects that: The direct voltage is lower than 0.112 V. Incorrect value runs longer than 10 seconds. Incorrect value lasts for 2 or more subsequent driving cycles. The control module's test for the diagnostic trouble code (DTC) starts in the event of: Ignition switch position II. **Note! The control module can only detect the fault once the test has been started and the diagnostic trouble code (DTC) is stored when the conditions are met.**

DTC	Trouble Code Title and Conditions
DTC: ECM-P066900 **2T ECM** **Year:** 2011, 2012 **Model:** XC90 **Engine:** 4.4L V8	**PCM / ECM / TCM Internal Temperature Sensor Circuit High:** Engine control module (ECM) measures the temperature internally in the control module using a temperature sensor. The control module checks the direct voltage from the sensor. **Note! The temperature sensor is integrated in the Engine control module (ECM).** The diagnostic trouble code (DTC) is stored if the control module detects that: The direct voltage is higher than 4.496 V. Incorrect value runs longer than 10 seconds. Incorrect value lasts for 2 or more subsequent driving cycles. The control module's test for the diagnostic trouble code (DTC) starts in the event of: Ignition switch position II. **Note! The control module can only detect the fault once the test has been started and the diagnostic trouble code (DTC) is stored when the conditions are met.**
DTC: ECM-P068B00 **T ECM** **Year:** 2011, 2012 **Model:** XC90 **Engine:** 4.4L V8	**Control Module Internal Power +5V:** After the ignition has been turned off the engine control module (ECM) performs internal checks. Within 10 minutes the checks are completed. Then the control module cuts off the activation to the system relay's winding. If the control module registers that the system relay still is active after activation has been cut off, the diagnostic trouble code is generated.
DTC: ECM-P069100 **1T ECM** **Year:** 2011, 2012 **Model:** XC90 **Engine:** 4.4L V8	**Fan 1 Control Circuit Low:** The engine control module (ECM) sends a signal (speed request to the cooling fan) to the cooling fan module. The cooling fan module then regulates voltage to the fan motor at an infinitely variable rate. The diagnostic trouble code is generated if the engine control module (ECM) detects that the control signal between the cooling fan module and the engine control module (ECM) is too low. The diagnostic trouble code can be diagnosed when the engine is running. **Note! The electric cooling fan may have a post-running time of up to approx. 6 minutes after the engine has been shut off. The time for the electric cooling fan's post-running depends on the engine's temperature, temperature in the engine compartment as well as the pressure level in the AC system.**
DTC: ECM-P069200 **1T ECM** **Year:** 2011, 2012 **Model:** XC90 **Engine:** 4.4L V8	**Fan 1 Control Circuit High:** The engine control module (ECM) sends a signal (speed request to the cooling fan) to the cooling fan module. The cooling fan module then regulates voltage to the fan motor at an infinitely variable rate. The diagnostic trouble code is generated if the engine control module (ECM) detects that the control signal between the cooling fan module and the engine control module (ECM) is too high. The diagnostic trouble code can be diagnosed when the engine is running. **Note! The electric cooling fan may have a post-running time of up to approx. 6 minutes after the engine has been shut off. The time for the electric cooling fan's post-running depends on the engine's temperature, temperature in the engine compartment as well as the pressure level in the AC system.**
DTC: ECM-P06A000 **T ECM** **Year:** 2011, 2012 **Model:** XC90 **Engine:** 4.4L V8	**Variable A/C Compressor Control Circuit:** Engine control module (ECM) checks the signal for controlling the control valve (solenoid). If engine control module (ECM) detects an incorrect signal, the control module interprets this as a malfunction and the diagnostic trouble code is generated. The diagnostic trouble code can be diagnosed with the engine running and the A/C control active.
DTC: ECM-P06A100 **T ECM** **Year:** 2011, 2012 **Model:** XC90 **Engine:** 4.4L V8	**Variable A/C Compressor Control Circuit Low:** Engine control module (ECM) checks the signal for controlling the control valve (solenoid). If engine control module (ECM) detects an incorrect signal, the control module interprets this as a malfunction and the diagnostic trouble code is generated. The diagnostic trouble code can be diagnosed with the engine running and the A/C control active.
DTC: ECM-P06A200 **T ECM** **Year:** 2011, 2012 **Model:** XC90 **Engine:** 4.4L V8	**Variable A/C Compressor Control Circuit High:** Engine control module (ECM) checks the signal for controlling the control valve (solenoid). If engine control module (ECM) detects an incorrect signal, the control module interprets this as a malfunction and the diagnostic trouble code is generated. The diagnostic trouble code can be diagnosed with the engine running and the A/C control active.

DTC	Trouble Code Title and Conditions
DTC: ECM-P085023 **T ECM** **Year:** 2011, 2012 **Model:** XC90 **Engine:** 4.4L V8	**Park / Neutral Switch Input Circuit. Signal Stuck Low:** Engine control module (ECM) uses signals from Transmission control module (TCM) to decide which position the gear selector is in. This is done so that Engine control module (ECM) can decide if engine start is permitted or not. Engine control module (ECM) checks the CAN-signal from transmission control module (TCM) compared to the signal that passes via the direct-connected cable from the gear selector. The diagnostic trouble code (DTC) is stored if the control module detects that: The signal on the direct-connected cable indicates that start is allowed, but the signal coming via CAN indicates the opposite. The control module's test for the diagnostic trouble code (DTC) starts in the event of: Ignition switch position II. Hint: If Engine control module (ECM) has been recharged or if the battery voltage has been interrupted, the brake pedal must be pressed down twice for approx. two seconds to activate the cruise control function.
DTC: ECM-P085024 **T ECM** **Year:** 2011, 2012 **Model:** XC90 **Engine:** 4.4L V8	**Park / Neutral Switch Input Circuit. Signal Stuck High:** Engine control module (ECM) uses signals from Transmission control module (TCM) to decide which position the gear selector is in. This is done so that Engine control module (ECM) can decide if engine start is permitted or not. Engine control module (ECM) checks the CAN-signal from transmission control module (TCM) compared to the signal that passes via the direct-connected cable from the gear selector. The diagnostic trouble code (DTC) is stored if the control module detects that: The signal coming via CAN indicates that start is allowed, but the signal on the direct-connected cable indicates the opposite. The control module's test for the diagnostic trouble code (DTC) starts in the event of: Ignition switch position II. Hint: If Engine control module (ECM) has been recharged or if the battery voltage has been interrupted, the brake pedal must be pressed down twice for approx. two seconds to activate the cruise control function.
DTC: ECM-P085086 **T ECM** **Year:** 2011, 2012 **Model:** XC90 **Engine:** 4.4L V8	**Park / Neutral Switch Input Circuit. Bus Signal / Message Failures. Signal Invalid:** Engine control module (ECM) uses signals from Transmission control module (TCM) to decide which position the gear selector is in. This is done so that Engine control module (ECM) can decide if engine start is permitted or not. The diagnostic trouble code (DTC) is stored if the control module detects that: The quality of the signal coming via CAN is too low. The control module's test for the diagnostic trouble code (DTC) starts in the event of: Ignition switch position II. Hint: If Engine control module (ECM) has been recharged or if the battery voltage has been interrupted, the brake pedal must be pressed down twice for approx. two seconds to activate the cruise control function.
DTC: ECM-P0A3B00 **1T ECM, MIL: Yes** **Year:** 2011, 2012 **Model:** XC90 **Engine:** 4.4L V8	**Generator Over Temperature:** The engine control module (ECM) regulates the alternator charge voltage (via LIN communication) on request of the central electronic module (CEM) (via CAN communication). The alternator control module (ACM) sends information on the fault to the engine control module (ECM) (via LIN communication). The diagnostic trouble code is generated if the alternator control module (ACM) sends the engine control module (ECM) information indicating that the alternator temperature exceeds a certain value. The diagnostic trouble code can be diagnosed when the engine is running.
DTC: ECM-P112662 **T ECM** **Year:** 2011, 2012 **Model:** XC90 **Engine:** 4.4L V8	**Throttle Position (Narrow Range) Sensor Circuit:** If engine control module (ECM) registers an internal malfunction, the diagnostic trouble code is generated. Text window and warning symbol/Text message on. The diagnostic trouble code can be diagnosed when the ignition is on.
DTC: ECM-P117068 **T ECM** **Year:** 2011, 2012 **Model:** XC90 **Engine:** 4.4L V8	**Engine Shut Off Solenoid:** **Note! This diagnostic trouble code (DTC) status is an event controlled diagnostic trouble code (DTC). An event controlled diagnostic trouble code (DTC) does not mean that there is a fault in the control module when it is active, but is designed as information.** Engine Control Module (ECM) monitors the front heated oxygen sensor (bank 1). If the control module detects that the heated oxygen sensor value is below or above a certain level for a certain time, the diagnostic trouble code is generated. The diagnostic trouble code (DTC) can be diagnosed when the engine is running.
DTC: ECM-P117368 **T ECM** **Year:** 2011, 2012 **Model:** XC90 **Engine:** 4.4L V8	**Rotor Calibration:** **Note! This diagnostic trouble code (DTC) status is an event controlled diagnostic trouble code (DTC). An event controlled diagnostic trouble code (DTC) does not mean that there is a fault in the control module when it is active, but is designed as information.** Engine Control Module (ECM) monitors the front heated oxygen sensor (bank 2). If the control module detects that the heated oxygen sensor value is below or above a certain level for a certain time, the diagnostic trouble code is generated. The diagnostic trouble code (DTC) can be diagnosed when the engine is running.

DTC	Trouble Code Title and Conditions
DTC: ECM-P117A68 **1T ECM** **Year:** 2011, 2012 **Model:** XC90 **Engine:** 4.4L V8	**Engine Oil Over temperature - Forced Limited:** **Note! This diagnostic trouble code (DTC) status is an event controlled diagnostic trouble code (DTC). An event controlled diagnostic trouble code (DTC) does not mean that there is a fault in the control module when it is active, but is designed as information.** The Engine Control Module (ECM) monitors the temperature of the engine oil. If the control module detects that the oil temperature is above a certain level for a certain time, the diagnostic trouble code is generated. The diagnostic trouble code (DTC) can be diagnosed when the engine is running.
DTC: ECM-P122477 **1T ECM** **Year:** 2011, 2012 **Model:** XC90 **Engine:** 4.4L V8	**Throttle Position Sensor B Out Of Self Test Range. Mechanical Failures:** Engine control module (ECM) checks that the electronic throttle unit follows the requested throttle angle from engine control module (ECM). If engine control module (ECM) detects that the current throttle angle deviates from the requested, the diagnostic trouble code is generated. The diagnostic trouble code can be diagnosed in specific operation situations.
DTC: ECM-P125000 **1T ECM** **Year:** 2011, 2012 **Model:** XC90 **Engine:** 4.4L V8	**Throttle Valve Spring:** The engine control module (ECM) checks the function in the throttle unit When switching off the engine a mechanical function check of the electronic throttle module (ETM) is carried out where the throttle disc spring is moved to the open position (open throttle). When control has finished, the time it takes for the damper to return to the return rest position is measured. If Engine Control Module (ECM) detects that the throttle movement does not take place within reasonable time, the diagnostic trouble code is generated. The diagnostic trouble code can be diagnosed when function check is performed.
DTC: ECM-P126000 **1T ECM** **Year:** 2011, 2012 **Model:** XC90 **Engine:** 4.4L V8	**Theft Detected, Vehicle Immobilized:** The Engine control module (ECM) and the Central electronic module (CEM) contain a code for the immobilizer which is unique to each vehicle. In addition to this, each key for the vehicle is electronically coded for the intended vehicle only. Internal checks are made at the start to check that the key is the correct one for the vehicle and that the immobilizer codes in the Engine control module (ECM) and Central electronic module (CEM) correspond. Text window and warning symbol/Text message on. The diagnostic trouble code is stored if the engine control module (ECM) registers that voltage feed for engine control module (ECM) as well as central electronic module (CEM) is lost before immobilizer codes are verified. The diagnostic trouble code (DTC) can be diagnosed when the ignition is switched on.
DTC: ECM-P134600 **T ECM** **Year:** 2011, 2012 **Model:** XC90 **Engine:** 4.4L V8	**Fuel Level Sensor B Circuit:** If a malfunction of the fuel level sensor's ejector part is detected by central electronic module (CEM), a malfunction message is sent to engine control module (ECM) and the diagnostic trouble code is generated. The diagnostic trouble code can be diagnosed when the ignition is on.
DTC: ECM-P145C68 **T ECM** **Year:** 2011, 2012 **Model:** XC90 **Engine:** 4.4L V8	**Fan System Component Error A:** **Note! This diagnostic trouble code (DTC) status is an event controlled diagnostic trouble code (DTC). An event controlled diagnostic trouble code (DTC) does not mean that there is a fault in the control module when it is active, but is designed as information.** Engine control module (ECM) monitors the engine's cooling system. The diagnostic trouble code (DTC) is stored if the control module detects that: The temperature in the electric cooling fan module exceeds a specific value. The diagnostic trouble code (DTC) can be diagnosed when the engine is running.
DTC: ECM-P145D68 **T ECM** **Year:** 2011, 2012 **Model:** XC90 **Engine:** 4.4L V8	**Fan System Component Error B:** **Note! This diagnostic trouble code (DTC) status is an event controlled diagnostic trouble code (DTC). An event controlled diagnostic trouble code (DTC) does not mean that there is a fault in the control module when it is active, but is designed as information.** Engine control module (ECM) monitors the engine's cooling system. The diagnostic trouble code (DTC) is stored if the control module detects that: The temperature in the electric cooling fan module exceeds a specific value. The diagnostic trouble code (DTC) can be diagnosed when the engine is running.
DTC: ECM-P151B68 **T ECM** **Year:** 2011, 2012 **Model:** XC90 **Engine:** 4.4L V8	**Idle Speed Control - RPM Lower Than Expected:** **Note! This diagnostic trouble code (DTC) status is an event controlled diagnostic trouble code (DTC). An event controlled diagnostic trouble code (DTC) does not mean that there is a fault in the control module when it is active, but is designed as information.** The Engine Control Module (ECM) monitors the engine's speed. If the control module detects that the engine rpm has been outside the limit value for engine stop, the diagnostic trouble code is generated. The diagnostic trouble code (DTC) can be diagnosed when the engine is running.

DTC	Trouble Code Title and Conditions
DTC: ECM-P151C68 **T ECM** **Year:** 2011, 2012 **Model:** XC90 **Engine:** 4.4L V8	**Idle Speed Control - RPM Higher Than Expected:** **Note! This diagnostic trouble code (DTC) status is an event controlled diagnostic trouble code (DTC). An event controlled diagnostic trouble code (DTC) does not mean that there is a fault in the control module when it is active, but is designed as information.** The Engine Control Module (ECM) monitors the engine's start rpm. If the control module detects that the start rpm has been outside the limit value for a certain time, the diagnostic trouble code is generated. The diagnostic trouble code (DTC) can be diagnosed when the engine is running.
DTC: ECM-P157281 **T ECM** **Year:** 2011, 2012 **Model:** XC90 **Engine:** 4.4L V8	**Brake Pedal Switch Circuit. Bus Signal / Message Failures:** The control module is continuously supplied with information about the position and status of the brake pedal switch from the brake control module (BCM) via CAN communication. The control module checks the communication with the Brake control module (BCM). The diagnostic trouble code (DTC) is stored if the control module detects that: Information from Brake control module (BCM) is incorrect/unreasonable. The control module's test for the diagnostic trouble code (DTC) starts in the event of: Ignition switch position II. Hint: If Engine control module (ECM) has been recharged or if the battery voltage has been interrupted, the brake pedal must be pressed down twice for approx. two seconds to activate the cruise control function.
DTC: ECM-P157282 **T ECM** **Year:** 2011, 2012 **Model:** XC90 **Engine:** 4.4L V8	**Brake Pedal Switch Circuit. Bus Signal / Message Failures. Alive / Sequence Counter Incorrect / Not Updated,:** The control module is continuously supplied with information about the position and status of the brake pedal switch from the brake control module (BCM) via CAN communication. The control module checks the communication with the Brake control module (BCM). The diagnostic trouble code (DTC) is stored if the control module detects that: Information from Brake control module (BCM) is incorrect/unreasonable. The control module's test for the diagnostic trouble code (DTC) starts in the event of: Ignition switch position II. Hint: If Engine control module (ECM) has been recharged or if the battery voltage has been interrupted, the brake pedal must be pressed down twice for approx. two seconds to activate the cruise control function.
DTC: ECM-P157283 **T ECM** **Year:** 2011, 2012 **Model:** XC90 **Engine:** 4.4L V8	**Brake Pedal Switch Circuit. Bus Signal / Message Failures. Value Of Signal Protection Calculation Incorrect:** The control module is continuously supplied with information about the position and status of the brake pedal switch from the brake control module (BCM) via CAN communication. The control module checks the communication with the Brake control module (BCM). The diagnostic trouble code (DTC) is stored if the control module detects that: Information from Brake control module (BCM) is incorrect/unreasonable. The control module's test for the diagnostic trouble code (DTC) starts in the event of: Ignition switch position II. Hint: If Engine control module (ECM) has been recharged or if the battery voltage has been interrupted, the brake pedal must be pressed down twice for approx. two seconds to activate the cruise control function.
DTC: ECM-P157286 **T ECM** **Year:** 2011, 2012 **Model:** XC90 **Engine:** 4.4L V8	**Brake Pedal Switch Circuit. Bus Signal / Message Failures. Signal invalid:** The control module is continuously supplied with information about the position and status of the brake pedal switch from the brake control module (BCM) via CAN communication. The control module checks the communication with the Brake control module (BCM). The diagnostic trouble code (DTC) is stored if the control module detects that: Information from Brake control module (BCM) is incorrect/unreasonable. The control module's test for the diagnostic trouble code (DTC) starts in the event of: Ignition switch position II. Hint: If Engine control module (ECM) has been recharged or if the battery voltage has been interrupted, the brake pedal must be pressed down twice for approx. two seconds to activate the cruise control function.
DTC: ECM-P157287 **T ECM** **Year:** 2011, 2012 **Model:** XC90 **Engine:** 4.4L V8	**Brake Pedal Switch Circuit. Bus Signal / Message Failures. Missing message:** The control module is continuously supplied with information about the position and status of the brake pedal switch from the brake control module (BCM) via CAN communication. The control module checks the communication with the Brake control module (BCM). The diagnostic trouble code (DTC) is stored if the control module detects that: No communication with the Brake control module (BCM). The control module's test for the diagnostic trouble code (DTC) starts in the event of: Ignition switch position II. Hint: If Engine control module (ECM) has been recharged or if the battery voltage has been interrupted, the brake pedal must be pressed down twice for approx. two seconds to activate the cruise control function.

DTC	Trouble Code Title and Conditions
DTC: ECM-P157300 **T ECM** **Year:** 2011, 2012 **Model:** XC90 **Engine:** 4.4L V8	**Throttle Position Not Available:** Engine control module (ECM) checks the signals from the electronic throttle unit's two position sensors. The diagnostic trouble code (DTC) is stored if the engine control module (ECM) detects a fault in both sensors. The diagnostic trouble code can be diagnosed when the ignition is on.
DTC: ECM-P157462 **1T ECM, MIL: Yes** **Year:** 2011, 2012 **Model:** XC90 **Engine:** 4.4L V8	**Throttle Position Sensor Outputs Disagree:** Engine control module (ECM) checks the signals from the electronic throttle unit's two position sensors. If engine control module (ECM) detects that the difference between both sensors' signals is too great, the diagnostic trouble code is generated. The diagnostic trouble code can be diagnosed when the ignition is on.
DTC: ECM-P158900 **1T ECM, MIL: Yes** **Year:** 2011, 2012 **Model:** XC90 **Engine:** 4.4L V8	**Throttle Control Unable To Control To Desired Throttle Angle:** Engine control module (ECM) checks the signals from the electronic throttle unit. If engine control module (ECM) detects that feedback throttle position does not change, despite adjustment being performed, the diagnostic trouble code is generated. The diagnostic trouble code can be diagnosed in specific operation situations.
DTC: ECM-P177100 **1T ECM** **Year:** 2011, 2012 **Model:** XC90 **Engine:** 4.4L V8	**Throttle Position Sensor Circuit High Input:** Engine control module (ECM) checks the signals from the electronic throttle unit's two position sensors. If engine control module (ECM) detects unreasonably high signal from any of the sensors, the diagnostic trouble code is generated. The diagnostic trouble code can be diagnosed when the ignition is on.
DTC: ECM-P177200 **1T ECM** **Year:** 2011, 2012 **Model:** XC90 **Engine:** 4.4L V8	**Throttle Position Sensor Circuit Low Input:** Engine control module (ECM) checks the signals from the electronic throttle unit's two position sensors. If engine control module (ECM) detects unreasonably low signal from any of the sensors, the diagnostic trouble code is generated. The diagnostic trouble code can be diagnosed when the ignition is on.
DTC: ECM-P193400 **1T ECM, MIL: Yes** **Year:** 2011, 2012 **Model:** XC90 **Engine:** 4.4L V8	**Vehicle Speed Signal:** If a malfunction of the speed signal is detected in the brake control module (BCM), a malfunction message is sent to engine control module (ECM) and a diagnostic trouble code is stored in the engine control module (ECM). Diagnostic trouble codes (DTCs) for the vehicle speed sensor (VSS) signal are stored in the brake control module (BCM).
DTC: ECM-P209600 **1T ECM, MIL: Yes** **Year:** 2011, 2012 **Model:** XC90 **Engine:** 4.4L V8	**Post Catalyst Fuel Trim System Too Lean Bank 1:** Engine Control Module (ECM) receives information from the rear heated oxygen sensor about fuel/air mixture in different load areas. Internal functions in the control module detect faults in the lambda control. The diagnostic trouble code (DTC) is stored if the control module detects that: Large differences have been measured in fuel/air mixture between the front and rear heated oxygen sensors (HO2S). So large that the trims for the rear heated oxygen sensor are in one of their limit positions. The control module's test for the diagnostic trouble code (DTC) starts in the event of: Run the engine to operating temperature (coolant temperature greater than 80 °C). Normal load at engine speeds between 1500-2000 rpm in 20-30 minutes. **Note! The control module can only detect the fault once the test has been started and the diagnostic trouble code (DTC) is stored when the conditions are met.**
DTC: ECM-P209700 **1T ECM, MIL: Yes** **Year:** 2011, 2012 **Model:** XC90 **Engine:** 4.4L V8	**Post Catalyst Fuel Trim System Too Rich Bank 1:** Engine Control Module (ECM) receives information from the rear heated oxygen sensor about fuel/air mixture in different load areas. Internal functions in the control module detect faults in the lambda control. The diagnostic trouble code (DTC) is stored if the control module detects that: Large differences have been measured in fuel/air mixture between the front and rear heated oxygen sensors (HO2S). So large that the trims for the rear heated oxygen sensor are in one of their limit positions. The control module's test for the diagnostic trouble code (DTC) starts in the event of: Run the engine to operating temperature (coolant temperature greater than 80 °C). Normal load at engine speeds between 1500-2000 rpm in 20-30 minutes. **Note! The control module can only detect the fault once the test has been started and the diagnostic trouble code (DTC) is stored when the conditions are met.**

DTC	Trouble Code Title and Conditions
DTC: ECM-P209800 **1T ECM, MIL: Yes** **Year:** 2011, 2012 **Model:** XC90 **Engine:** 4.4L V8	**Post Catalyst Fuel Trim System Too Lean Bank 2:** Engine Control Module (ECM) receives information from the rear heated oxygen sensor about fuel/air mixture in different load areas. Internal functions in the control module detect faults in the lambda control. The diagnostic trouble code (DTC) is stored if the control module detects that: Large differences have been measured in fuel/air mixture between the front and rear heated oxygen sensors (HO2S). So large that the trims for the rear heated oxygen sensor are in one of their limit positions. The control module's test for the diagnostic trouble code (DTC) starts in the event of: Run the engine to operating temperature (coolant temperature greater than 80 °C). Normal load at engine speeds between 1500-2000 rpm in 20-30 minutes. **Note! The control module can only detect the fault once the test has been started and the diagnostic trouble code (DTC) is stored when the conditions are met.**
DTC: ECM-P209900 **1T ECM, MIL: Yes** **Year:** 2011, 2012 **Model:** XC90 **Engine:** 4.4L V8	**Post Catalyst Fuel Trim System Too Rich Bank 2:** Engine Control Module (ECM) receives information from the rear heated oxygen sensor about fuel/air mixture in different load areas. Internal functions in the control module detect faults in the lambda control. The diagnostic trouble code (DTC) is stored if the control module detects that: Large differences have been measured in fuel/air mixture between the front and rear heated oxygen sensors (HO2S). So large that the trims for the rear heated oxygen sensor are in one of their limit positions. The control module's test for the diagnostic trouble code (DTC) starts in the event of: Run the engine to operating temperature (coolant temperature greater than 80 °C). Normal load at engine speeds between 1500-2000 rpm in 20-30 minutes. **Note! The control module can only detect the fault once the test has been started and the diagnostic trouble code (DTC) is stored when the conditions are met.**
DTC: ECM-P210600 **1T ECM, MIL: Yes** **Year:** 2011, 2012 **Model:** XC90 **Engine:** 4.4L V8	**Throttle Actuator Control System - Forced Limited Power:** Diagnostic functions in the engine control module (ECM) have activated substitute values that result in fuel shut-off. If Engine Control Module (ECM) detects that fuel shut-off is activated by diagnostic function to such an extent that emissions can be affected negatively, the diagnostic trouble code is stored in the control module. The diagnostic trouble code (DTC) can be diagnosed in specific driving conditions.
DTC: ECM-P211100 **1T ECM** **Year:** 2011, 2012 **Model:** XC90 **Engine:** 4.4L V8	**Throttle Actuator Control System - Stuck Open:** Engine control module (ECM) checks the difference in requested electronic throttle unit position from actual position. If engine control module (ECM) detects that the electronic throttle unit cannot close, and jams in open position, which gives reduced brake vacuum, the diagnostic trouble code is generated. The diagnostic trouble code can be diagnosed when the engine is running. Hint: If Engine control module (ECM) has been recharged or if the battery voltage has been interrupted, the brake pedal must be pressed down twice for approx. two seconds to activate the cruise control function.
DTC: ECM-P211800 **1T ECM** **Year:** 2011, 2012 **Model:** XC90 **Engine:** 4.4L V8	**Throttle Actuator Control Motor Current Range/Performance.:** Engine control module (ECM) checks the signals from the electronic throttle unit. If engine control module (ECM) detects electrical malfunction of the electronic throttle unit, the diagnostic trouble code is generated. Text window and warning symbol/Text message on. The diagnostic trouble code can be diagnosed with the ignition on.
DTC: ECM-P212038 **1T ECM** **Year:** 2011, 2012 **Model:** XC90 **Engine:** 4.4L V8	**Throttle/Pedal Position Sensor/Switch D Circuit. FM (Frequency Modulated) / PWM (Pulse Width Modulated) :** The engine control module (ECM) checks the pulse width modulation (PWM) signal and the analog signal from the accelerator pedal (AP) position sensor. The analog signal is directly connected to the Central electronic module (CEM) and the signal is transmitted via CAN communication to the Engine control module (ECM). The pulse width modulation (PWM) signal is directly connected to the engine control module (ECM). The PWM signal is used to determine the current accelerator pedal position in a fault free system. The engine control module (ECM) checks the PWM signal. The diagnostic trouble code (DTC) is stored if the control module detects that: Incorrect frequency on the PWM signal. Incorrect value lasts longer than 16 seconds. The control module's test for the diagnostic trouble code (DTC) starts in the event of: Ignition switch position II. Message in information display.

DTC	Trouble Code Title and Conditions
DTC: ECM-P212200 **1T ECM** **Year:** 2011, 2012 **Model:** XC90 **Engine:** 4.4L V8	**Throttle/Pedal Position Sensor/Switch D Circuit Low:** The engine control module (ECM) checks the pulse width modulation (PWM) signal and the analog signal from the accelerator pedal (AP) position sensor. The analog signal is directly connected to the Central electronic module (CEM) and the signal is transmitted via CAN communication to the Engine control module (ECM). The pulse width modulation (PWM) signal is directly connected to the engine control module (ECM). The PWM signal is used to determine the current accelerator pedal position in a fault free system. The engine control module (ECM) checks the PWM signal. The diagnostic trouble code (DTC) is stored if the control module detects that: The PWM signal is too low. Incorrect value lasts longer than 16 seconds. The control module's test for the diagnostic trouble code (DTC) starts in the event of: Ignition switch position II. Message in information display on. **Note! The control module can only detect the fault once the test has been started and the diagnostic trouble code (DTC) is stored when the conditions are met.**
DTC: ECM-P212300 **1T ECM** **Year:** 2011, 2012 **Model:** XC90 **Engine:** 4.4L V8	**Throttle/Pedal Position Sensor/Switch D Circuit High:** The engine control module (ECM) checks the pulse width modulation (PWM) signal and the analog signal from the accelerator pedal (AP) position sensor. The analog signal is directly connected to the Central electronic module (CEM) and the signal is transmitted via CAN communication to the Engine control module (ECM). The pulse width modulation (PWM) signal is directly connected to the engine control module (ECM). The PWM signal is used to determine the current accelerator pedal position in a fault free system. The engine control module (ECM) checks the PWM signal.. The diagnostic trouble code (DTC) is stored if the control module detects that: The PWM signal is too high. Incorrect value lasts longer than 16 seconds. The control module's test for the diagnostic trouble code (DTC) starts in the event of: Ignition switch position II. Message in information display on.
DTC: ECM-P212582 **1T ECM, MIL: Yes** **Year:** 2011, 2012 **Model:** XC90 **Engine:** 4.4L V8	**Throttle/Pedal Position Sensor/Switch E Circuit. Bus Signal / Message Failures. Alive / Sequence Counter Incorrect / Not Updated:** The engine control module (ECM) checks the pulse width modulation (PWM) signal and the analog signal from the accelerator pedal (AP) position sensor. The analog signal is directly connected to the Central electronic module (CEM) and the signal is transmitted via CAN communication to the Engine control module (ECM). The pulse width modulation (PWM) signal is directly connected to the engine control module (ECM). The PWM signal is used to determine the current accelerator pedal position in a fault free system. The control module checks the communication with the Central electronic module (CEM). The diagnostic trouble code (DTC) is stored if the control module detects that: No communication with the Central electronic module (CEM). The control module's test for the diagnostic trouble code (DTC) starts in the event of: Ignition switch position II. Message in information display on.
DTC: ECM-P212700 **1T ECM** **Year:** 2011, 2012 **Model:** XC90 **Engine:** 4.4L V8	**Throttle/Pedal Position Sensor/Switch E Circuit Low:** The engine control module (ECM) checks the pulse width modulation (PWM) signal and the analog signal from the accelerator pedal (AP) position sensor. The analog signal is directly connected to the Central electronic module (CEM) and the signal is transmitted via CAN communication to the Engine control module (ECM). The pulse width modulation (PWM) signal is directly connected to the engine control module (ECM). The PWM signal is used to determine the current accelerator pedal position in a fault free system. The Engine control module (ECM) checks the analog signal (via CAN). The diagnostic trouble code (DTC) is stored if the control module detects that: Analog signal (via CAN) is too low. Incorrect value lasts longer than 16 seconds. The control module's test for the diagnostic trouble code (DTC) starts in the event of: Ignition switch position II

DTC	Trouble Code Title and Conditions
DTC: ECM-P212800 **1T ECM** **Year:** 2011, 2012 **Model:** XC90 **Engine:** 4.4L V8	**Throttle/Pedal Position Sensor/Switch E Circuit High:** The engine control module (ECM) checks the pulse width modulation (PWM) signal and the analog signal from the accelerator pedal (AP) position sensor. The analog signal is directly connected to the Central electronic module (CEM) and the signal is transmitted via CAN communication to the Engine control module (ECM). The pulse width modulation (PWM) signal is directly connected to the engine control module (ECM). The PWM signal is used to determine the current accelerator pedal position in a fault free system. The Engine control module (ECM) checks the analog signal (via CAN). The diagnostic trouble code (DTC) is stored if the control module detects that: Analog signal (via CAN) is too high. Incorrect value lasts longer than 16 seconds. The control module's test for the diagnostic trouble code (DTC) starts in the event of: Ignition switch position II.
DTC: ECM-P213800 **T ECM** **Year:** 2011, 2012 **Model:** XC90 **Engine:** 4.4L V8	**Throttle/Pedal Position Sensor/Switch D / E Voltage Correlation:** The engine control module (ECM) checks the pulse width modulation (PWM) signal and the analog signal from the accelerator pedal (AP) position sensor. The analog signal is directly connected to the Central electronic module (CEM) and the signal is transmitted via CAN communication to the Engine control module (ECM). The pulse width modulation (PWM) signal is directly connected to the engine control module (ECM). The PWM signal is used to determine the current accelerator pedal position in a fault free system. The Engine control module (ECM) compares both the signals to each other. The diagnostic trouble code (DTC) is stored if the control module detects that: Difference between PWM signal and analog signal (via CAN) is too great. Incorrect value lasts longer than 16 seconds. The control module's test for the diagnostic trouble code (DTC) starts in the event of: Ignition switch position II.
DTC: ECM-P215886 **1T ECM** **Year:** 2011, 2012 **Model:** XC90 **Engine:** 4.4L V8	**Vehicle Speed Sensor B. Bus Signal/Message Failures. Signal invalid:** If a malfunction of the speed signal is detected in the Transmission control module (TCM), a malfunction message is sent to engine control module (ECM) and a diagnostic trouble code is stored in the engine control module (ECM). Diagnostic trouble code for the speed sensor's signal is stored in the Transmission control module (TCM).
DTC: ECM-P215887 **1T ECM** **Year:** 2011, 2012 **Model:** XC90 **Engine:** 4.4L V8	**Vehicle Speed Sensor B. Bus Signal/Message Failures. Missing message:** If a malfunction of the speed signal is detected in the Transmission control module (TCM), a malfunction message is sent to engine control module (ECM) and a diagnostic trouble code is stored in the engine control module (ECM). Diagnostic trouble code for the speed sensor's signal is stored in the Transmission control module (TCM).
DTC: ECM-P216262 **1T ECM** **Year:** 2011, 2012 **Model:** XC90 **Engine:** 4.4L V8	**Vehicle Speed Sensor A / B Correlation:** Information about vehicle speed is sent on the CAN-network from brake control module (BCM) and from transmission control module (TCM) to engine control module (ECM). If engine control module (ECM) detects a deviation between the speed signals from brake control module (BCM) and transmission control module (TCM), the diagnostic trouble code is stored. Hint: If Engine control module (ECM) has been recharged or if the battery voltage has been interrupted, the brake pedal must be pressed down twice for approx. two seconds to activate the cruise control function.
DTC: ECM-P222600 **1T ECM, MIL: Yes** **Year:** 2011, 2012 **Model:** XC90 **Engine:** 4.4L V8	**Barometric Pressure Circuit:** The Engine control module (ECM) measures the atmospheric pressure using an atmospheric pressure sensor. The control module checks the direct voltage from the sensor. **Note! The atmospheric pressure sensor is integrated in the Engine control module (ECM).** The diagnostic trouble code (DTC) is stored if the control module detects that: The direct voltage is lower than approximately 0.01 V. The direct voltage is higher than approximately 6 V. Incorrect value lasts longer than 9 seconds. Incorrect value lasts for 2 or more subsequent driving cycles. The control module's test for the diagnostic trouble code (DTC) starts in the event of: Ignition switch position II.
DTC: ECM-P222700 **1T ECM, MIL: Yes** **Year:** 2011, 2012 **Model:** XC90 **Engine:** 4.4L V8	**Barometric Pressure Circuit Range/Performance:** The engine control module (ECM) compares the filtered signal from the pressure sensor in the intake manifold with the signal from the atmospheric pressure sensor in the engine control module (ECM). The diagnostic trouble code is generated if the control module registers that the deviation is greater than 100 hPa. The diagnostic trouble code can be diagnosed 15 seconds after the ignition is switched.

DTC	Trouble Code Title and Conditions
DTC: ECM-P222792 **1T ECM, MIL: Yes** **Year:** 2011, 2012 **Model:** XC90 **Engine:** 4.4L V8	**Barometric Pressure Circuit Range/Performance:** The engine control module (ECM) compares the filtered signal from the pressure sensor in the intake manifold with the signal from the atmospheric pressure sensor in the engine control module (ECM). The diagnostic trouble code is generated if the control module registers that the deviation is greater than 100 hPa. The diagnostic trouble code can be diagnosed 15 seconds after the ignition is switched.
DTC: ECM-P222800 **1T ECM, MIL: Yes** **Year:** 2011, 2012 **Model:** XC90 **Engine:** 4.4L V8	**Barometric Pressure Circuit Low Input:** The Engine control module (ECM) measures the atmospheric pressure using an atmospheric pressure sensor. The control module checks the direct voltage from the sensor. **Note! The atmospheric pressure sensor is integrated in the Engine control module (ECM).** The diagnostic trouble code (DTC) is stored if the control module detects that: The direct voltage is lower than approximately 0.01 V. The direct voltage is higher than approximately 6 V. Incorrect value lasts longer than 9 seconds. Incorrect value lasts for 2 or more subsequent driving cycles. The control module's test for the diagnostic trouble code (DTC) starts in the event of: Ignition switch position II.
DTC: ECM-P222900 **1T ECM** **Year:** 2011, 2012 **Model:** XC90 **Engine:** 4.4L V8	**Barometric Pressure Circuit High Input:** The Engine control module (ECM) measures the atmospheric pressure using an atmospheric pressure sensor. The control module checks the direct voltage from the sensor. **Note! The atmospheric pressure sensor is integrated in the Engine control module (ECM).** The diagnostic trouble code (DTC) is stored if the control module detects that: * The direct voltage is lower than approximately 0.01 V. * The direct voltage is higher than approximately 6 V. * Incorrect value lasts longer than 9 seconds. * Incorrect value lasts for 2 or more subsequent driving cycles.
DTC: ECM-P226368 **1T ECM** **Year:** 2011, 2012 **Model:** XC90 **Engine:** 4.4L V8	**Turbo/Super Charge Boost System Performance:** **Note! This diagnostic trouble code (DTC) status is an event controlled diagnostic trouble code (DTC). An event controlled diagnostic trouble code (DTC) does not mean that there is a fault in the control module when it is active, but is designed as information.** The Engine Control Module (ECM) monitors the engine's turbo control. A DTC is stored if the control module detects that the boost pressure deviates too much that it lies outside a limit value. The diagnostic trouble code (DTC) can be diagnosed when the engine is running.
DTC: ECM-P227000 **1T ECM, MIL: Yes** **Year:** 2011, 2012 **Model:** XC90 **Engine:** 4.4L V8	**O2 Sensor Signal Stuck Lean - Bank 1, Sensor 2:** Engine control module (ECM) continuously monitors centre heated oxygen sensor (bank 1) by checking the voltage across the sensor. Hint: The engine's cylinders are counted starting with the cylinder farthest from the engine's flywheel. If engine control module (ECM) detects that the voltage is not below or above a certain value, the engine control module (ECM) interprets this as a malfunction and generates diagnostic trouble code. The diagnostic trouble code can be diagnosed after approx. 3-5 minutes with the engine running.
DTC: ECM-P227100 **1T ECM, MIL: Yes** **Year:** 2011, 2012 **Model:** XC90 **Engine:** 4.4L V8	**O2 Sensor Signal Stuck Rich - Bank 1, Sensor 2:** Engine control module (ECM) continuously monitors centre heated oxygen sensor (bank 1) by checking the voltage across the sensor. Hint: The engine's cylinders are counted starting with the cylinder farthest from the engine's flywheel. If engine control module (ECM) detects that the voltage is not below or above a certain value, the engine control module (ECM) interprets this as a malfunction and generates diagnostic trouble code. The diagnostic trouble code can be diagnosed after approx. 3-5 minutes with the engine running.
DTC: ECM-P227400 **1T ECM, MIL: Yes** **Year:** 2011, 2012 **Model:** XC90 **Engine:** 4.4L V8	**O2 Sensor Signal Stuck Lean - Bank 1, Sensor 3:** The engine control module (ECM) continuously detects the voltage of the rear lambda (bank 1). The engine's cylinders are counted starting with the cylinder farthest from the engine's flywheel. If engine control module (ECM) detects that the voltage is not below or above a certain value, the engine control module (ECM) interprets this as a malfunction and generates diagnostic trouble code. The diagnostic trouble code can be diagnosed after approx. 3-5 minutes with the engine running.
DTC: ECM-P227500 **1T ECM, MIL: Yes** **Year:** 2011, 2012 **Model:** XC90 **Engine:** 4.4L V8	**O2 Sensor Signal Stuck Rich - Bank 1, Sensor 3:** The engine control module (ECM) continuously detects the voltage of the rear lambda (bank 1). The engine's cylinders are counted starting with the cylinder farthest from the engine's flywheel. If engine control module (ECM) detects that the voltage is not below or above a certain value, the engine control module (ECM) interprets this as a malfunction and generates diagnostic trouble code. The diagnostic trouble code can be diagnosed after approx. 3-5 minutes with the engine running.

DTC	Trouble Code Title and Conditions
DTC: ECM-P240100 **T ECM, MIL: Yes** **Year:** 2011, 2012 **Model:** XC90 **Engine:** 4.4L V8	**Evaporative Emission System Leak Detection Pump Control Circuit Low:** The engine control module (ECM) checks the control signal to the leakage diagnosis pump. The diagnostic trouble code is generated if the control module registers a fault in the control signal to the leakage diagnosis pump. The diagnostic trouble code can be diagnosed when the ignition is on.
DTC: ECM-P240200 **T ECM, MIL: Yes** **Year:** 2011, 2012 **Model:** XC90 **Engine:** 4.4L V8	**Evaporative Emission System Leak Detection Pump Control Circuit High:** The engine control module (ECM) checks the control signal to the leakage diagnosis pump. The diagnostic trouble code is generated if the control module registers a fault in the control signal to the leakage diagnosis pump. The diagnostic trouble code can be diagnosed when the ignition is on.
DTC: ECM-P240700 **T ECM, MIL: Yes** **Year:** 2011, 2012 **Model:** XC90 **Engine:** 4.4L V8	**Evaporative Emission System Leak Detection Pump Sense Circuit Intermittent/Erratic:** The engine control module (ECM) checks the function of the leakage diagnosis unit by measuring the current through the leakage diagnosis pump. If the Engine control module (ECM) registers that the current curve is unreasonably noisy, the control module interprets that the reference measurement has produced a faulty result and the diagnostic trouble code is generated. The diagnostic trouble code can be diagnosed when leakage diagnosis is running.
DTC: ECM-P240800 **1T ECM, MIL: Yes** **Year:** 2011, 2012 **Model:** XC90 **Engine:** 4.4L V8	**Fuel Cap Sensor/Switch Circuit:** The engine control module (ECM) receives confirmation from the central electronic module (CEM) as to whether the request for tank flap locking was sent to the locking relay. Locking should occur at 17 km/h. The diagnostic trouble code is generated if the engine control module (ECM) registers that vehicle speed has exceeded 17 km/h for at least 10 seconds without receipt of the central electronic module (CEM) signal.
DTC: ECM-P240B00 **1T ECM, MIL: Yes** **Year:** 2011, 2012 **Model:** XC90 **Engine:** 4.4L V8	**Evaporative Emission System Leak Detection Pump Heater Circuit Low:** The engine control module (EM) checks the control signal to the heating element in the leakage diagnosis pump. The diagnostic trouble code is generated if the control module registers a fault in the control signal. The diagnostic trouble code can be diagnosed when the ignition is on.
DTC: ECM-P240C00 **1T ECM, MIL: Yes** **Year:** 2011, 2012 **Model:** XC90 **Engine:** 4.4L V8	**Evaporative Emission System Leak Detection Pump Heater Circuit High.** The engine control module (EM) checks the control signal to the heating element in the leakage diagnosis pump. The diagnostic trouble code is generated if the control module registers a fault in the control signal. The diagnostic trouble code can be diagnosed when the ignition is on.
DTC: ECM-P241900 **1T ECM, MIL: Yes** **Year:** 2011, 2012 **Model:** XC90 **Engine:** 4.4L V8	**Evaporative Emission Control System Switching Valve Control Circuit Low:** The engine control module (EM) checks the control signal to the changeover valve in the leakage diagnosis pump. The diagnostic trouble code is generated if the control module registers a fault in the control signal. The diagnostic trouble code can be diagnosed when the ignition is on.
DTC: ECM-P242000 **1T ECM, MIL: Yes** **Year:** 2011, 2012 **Model:** XC90 **Engine:** 4.4L V8	**Evaporative Emission Control System Switching Valve Control Circuit High:** The engine control module (EM) checks the control signal to the changeover valve in the leakage diagnosis pump. The diagnostic trouble code is generated if the control module registers a fault in the control signal. The diagnostic trouble code can be diagnosed when the ignition is on.
DTC: ECM-P242100 **2T ECM, MIL: Yes** **Year:** 2011, 2012 **Model:** XC90 **Engine:** 4.4L V8	**Evaporative Emission Control System Vent Valve Stuck Open:** The engine control module (ECM) checks the function of the valve in the leakage diagnosis unit pump by measuring the current through the leakage diagnosis pump. After the initial reference phase of leakage diagnosis, the airflow is guided from the reference leak to the tank system and begins to pressurize it. During this shift, there is a short drop in current consumption before pressure is built up in the tank system. The control module registers that current consumption drops too slowly or not at all, it takes it as an indication that the valve in the pump is damaged and the diagnostic trouble code is generated. The diagnostic trouble code can be diagnosed when leakage diagnosis is running.
DTC: ECM-P242200 **1T ECM, MIL: Yes** **Year:** 2011, 2012 **Model:** XC90 **Engine:** 4.4L V8	**Evaporative Emission Control System Vent Valve Stuck Closed:** The engine control module (ECM) checks the function of the valve in the leakage diagnosis unit pump by measuring the current through the leakage diagnosis pump. After the initial reference phase in the leakage diagnosis, the air flow is directed over from the reference leak to the tank system and starts to pressurize it. If the control module registers that power consumption during the reference phase is unreasonable, it interprets this as the valve in the pump being damaged and the diagnostic trouble code is generated. The diagnostic trouble code can be diagnosed when leakage diagnosis is running.

DTC	Trouble Code Title and Conditions
DTC: ECM-P250D00 **1T ECM** **Year:** 2011, 2012 **Model:** XC90 **Engine:** 4.4L V8	**Engine Oil Level Sensor Circuit High:** The oil level sensor is housed in the oil pan and sends information on engine oil level and quality to the engine control module (ECM). The diagnostic trouble code is generated if the engine control module (ECM) detects that the oil level signal is abnormally high. The diagnostic trouble code can be diagnosed when the engine is running.
DTC: ECM-P250F68 **1T ECM** **Year:** 2011, 2012 **Model:** XC90 **Engine:** 4.4L V8	**Engine Oil Level Too Low:** **Note! This diagnostic trouble code (DTC) status is an event controlled diagnostic trouble code (DTC). An event controlled diagnostic trouble code (DTC) does not mean that there is a fault in the control module when it is active, but is designed as information.** The Engine Control Module (ECM) monitors the level of the engine oil. A DTC is stored if the control module detects that the oil level is above or below a certain level. The diagnostic trouble code (DTC) can be diagnosed when the engine is running.
DTC: ECM-P252C00 **1T ECM** **Year:** 2011, 2012 **Model:** XC90 **Engine:** 4.4L V8	**Engine Oil Quality Sensor Circuit Low.** The oil level sensor sends information on engine oil level and quality to the engine control module (ECM). The diagnostic trouble code is generated if the control module detects that the oil quality signal is too low. The diagnostic trouble code can be diagnosed when the engine is running.
DTC: ECM-P252D00 **1T ECM, MIL: Yes** **Year:** 2011, 2012 **Model:** XC90 **Engine:** 4.4L V8	**Engine Oil Quality Sensor Circuit High:** The oil level sensor sends information on engine oil level and quality to the engine control module (ECM). The diagnostic trouble code is generated if the control module detects that the oil quality signal is too high. The diagnostic trouble code can be diagnosed when the engine is running.
DTC: ECM-P256702 **1T ECM, MIL: Yes** **Year:** 2011, 2012 **Model:** XC90 **Engine:** 4.4L V8	**Direct Ozone Reduction Catalyst Temperature Sensor Circuit:** Engine control module (ECM) communicates continuously with the radiator temperature sensor, located on the radiator. Communication takes place via the LIN-net and is done to ensure that the radiator is of the intended type for the vehicle. The control module checks so that communication with the sensor is correct. The diagnostic trouble code (DTC) is stored if the control module detects that: The signal from the radiator temperature sensor is incorrect. The control module's test for the diagnostic trouble code (DTC) starts in the event of: Ignition on.
DTC: ECM-P256800 **1T ECM, MIL: Yes** **Year:** 2011, 2012 **Model:** XC90 **Engine:** 4.4L V8	**Direct Ozone Reduction Catalyst Temperature Sensor Circuit Range/Performance:** Engine control module (ECM) communicates continuously with the radiator temperature sensor, located on the radiator. Communication takes place via the LIN-net and is done to ensure that the radiator is of the intended type for the vehicle. The radiator temperature sensor's signal is compared to signals from ambient temperature sensor and coolant temperature sensor at specific times. Then the change of the radiator temperature should be reasonable in relation to the other temperatures, otherwise the control module considers the radiator to be faulty. The diagnostic trouble code (DTC) is stored if the control module detects that: Temperature change is unreasonable. The control module's test for the diagnostic trouble code (DTC) starts in the event of: Specific operating conditions.
DTC: ECM-P258382 **1T ECM** **Year:** 2011, 2012 **Model:** XC90 **Engine:** 4.4L V8	**Cruise Control Front Distance Range Sensor. Bus Signal/Message Failures. Alive/Sequence Counter Incorrect/Not Updated:** The control module is continually supplied with necessary information from the Forward Sensing Module (FSM) via CAN communication. The control module checks the communication with the Forward Sensing Module (FSM). The diagnostic trouble code (DTC) is stored if the control module detects that: No communication with the Forward Sensing Module (FSM). The control module's test for the diagnostic trouble code (DTC) starts in the event of: Ignition switch position II. Hint: If Engine control module (ECM) has been recharged or if the battery voltage has been interrupted, the brake pedal must be pressed down twice for approx. two seconds to activate the cruise control function
DTC: ECM-P261000 **1T ECM** **Year:** 2011, 2012 **Model:** XC90 **Engine:** 4.4L V8	**ECM/PCM Internal Engine Off Timer Performance:** Central electronic module (CEM) sends information via the CAN-net about how long time has passed since the engine was turned off the last time. The Engine control module (ECM) checks that the time display that the Central electronic module (CEM) transmitted at the last engine shut-off is not greater than the one transmitted at engine start-up. The diagnostic trouble code can be diagnosed when the ignition is on. Hint: If the time display is less at start than at the last engine shut-off, this means that the time has been reset.

DTC	Trouble Code Title and Conditions
DTC: ECM-P261085 **T ECM** **Year:** 2011, 2012 **Model:** XC90 **Engine:** 4.4L V8	**ECM/PCM Internal Engine Off Timer Performance. Bus Signal / Message Failures. Signal Above Allowable Range:** Central electronic module (CEM) sends information via the CAN-net about how long time has passed since the engine was turned off the last time. Engine control module (ECM) receives the signal and compares it to own calculated time (calculated based on temperature changes of engine temperature and outdoor temperature). If engine control module (ECM) detects that the received time differs too much from the calculated time, the diagnostic trouble code is generated. The diagnostic trouble code can be diagnosed when the ignition is on. Hint: The diagnostic trouble code can be incorrectly generated due to use of an engine heater or sudden external temperature changes.
DTC: ECM-P261086 **T ECM** **Year:** 2011, 2012 **Model:** XC90 **Engine:** 4.4L V8	**ECM/PCM Internal Engine Off Timer Performance. Bus Signal / Message Failures. Signal Invalid:** Central electronic module (CEM) sends information via the CAN-net about how long time has passed since the engine was turned off the last time. Engine control module (ECM) receives the signal and compares it to own calculated time (calculated based on temperature changes of engine temperature and outdoor temperature). If engine control module (ECM) detects that the received time differs too much from the calculated time, the diagnostic trouble code is generated. The diagnostic trouble code can be diagnosed when the ignition is on. Hint: The diagnostic trouble code can be incorrectly generated due to use of an engine heater or sudden external temperature changes.
DTC: ECM-P261087 **T ECM** **Year:** 2011, 2012 **Model:** XC90 **Engine:** 4.4L V8	**ECM/PCM Internal Engine Off Timer Performance. Bus Signal / Message Failures:** Central electronic module (CEM) sends information via the CAN-net about how long time has passed since the engine was turned off the last time. Engine control module (ECM) receives the signal and compares it to own calculated time (calculated based on temperature changes of engine temperature and outdoor temperature). If Engine control module (ECM) does not receive any time from Central electronic module (CEM), the diagnostic trouble code is generated. The diagnostic trouble code can be diagnosed when the ignition is on.
DTC: ECM-P2A0068 **1T ECM** **Year:** 2011, 2012 **Model:** XC90 **Engine:** 4.4L V8	**O2 Circuit Range/Performance (Bank 1, Sensor 1) :** **Note! This diagnostic trouble code (DTC) status is an event controlled diagnostic trouble code (DTC). An event controlled diagnostic trouble code (DTC) does not mean that there is a fault in the control module when it is active, but is designed as information.** Engine Control Module (ECM) checks the front heated oxygen sensor's signal (bank 1). The Engine control module (ECM) actively regulates between rich and lean fuel / air mixture and registers how well the front heated oxygen sensor (HO2S) signal follows these changes. The diagnostic trouble code (DTC) is stored if the control module detects that: The heated oxygen sensor (HO2S) is not activated or is activated too slowly. The diagnostic trouble code (DTC) can be diagnosed when: Idling with hot engine. The vehicle must have been in motion before idling.
DTC: ECM-P2A0168 **1T ECM** **Year:** 2011, 2012 **Model:** XC90 **Engine:** 4.4L V8	**O2 Circuit Range/Performance (Bank 1, Sensor 2) :** **Note! This diagnostic trouble code (DTC) status is an event controlled diagnostic trouble code (DTC). An event controlled diagnostic trouble code (DTC) does not mean that there is a fault in the control module when it is active, but is designed as information.** The engine control module (ECM) checks the rear heated oxygen sensor (HO2S) signal (bank 1). The control module actively regulates between rich and lean fuel / air mixture and registers how well the rear heated oxygen sensor (HO2S) signal follows these changes. The diagnostic trouble code (DTC) is stored if the control module detects that: The heated oxygen sensor (HO2S) is not activated or is activated too slowly. The diagnostic trouble code (DTC) can be diagnosed when: Idling with hot engine. The vehicle must have been in motion before idling.

Commonly Used Abbreviations

2

2WD Two Wheel Drive

4

4WD Four Wheel Drive

A

A/C Air Conditioning
ABDC After Bottom Dead Center
ABS Anti-lock Brakes
AC Alternating Current
ACL Air cleaner
ACT Air Charge Temperature
AIR Secondary Air Injection
ALCL Assembly Line Communications Link
ALDL Assembly Line Diagnostic Link
AT Automatic Transaxle/Transmission
ATDC After Top Dead Center
ATF Automatic Transmission Fluid
ATS Air Temperature Sensor
AWD All Wheel Drive

B

BAP Barometric Absolute Pressure
BARO Barometric Pressure
BBDC Before Bottom Dead Center
BCM Body Control Module
BDC Bottom Dead Center
BPT Backpressure Transducer
BTDC Before Top Dead Center
BVSV Bimetallic Vacuum Switching Valve

C

CAC Charge Air Cooler
CARB California Air Resources Board
CAT Catalytic Converter
CCC Computer Command Control
CCCC Computer Controlled Catalytic Converter
CCCI Computer Controlled Coil Ignition
CCD Computer Controlled Dwell
CDI Capacitor Discharge Ignition
CEC Computerized Engine Control
CFI Continuous Fuel Injection
CIS Continuous Injection System
CIS-E Continuous Injection System - Electronic
CKP Crankshaft Position
CL Closed Loop
CMP Camshaft Position
CPP Clutch Pedal Position
CTOX Continuous Trap Oxidizer System
CTP Closed Throttle Position
CVC Constant Vacuum Control
CYL Cylinder

D

DBC Dual Bed Catalyst
DC Direct Current
DFI Direct Fuel Injection
DIS Distributorless Ignition System
DLC Data Link Connector
DMM Digital Multimeter
DOHC Double Overhead Camshaft
DRB Diagnostic Readout Box
DTC Diagnostic Trouble Code
DTM Diagnostic Test Mode
DVOM Digital Volt/Ohmmeter

E

EBCM Electronic Brake Control Module
ECM Engine Control Module
ECT Engine Coolant Temperature
ECU Engine Control Unit or Electronic Control Unit
EDIS Electronic Distributorless Ignition System
EEC Electronic Engine Control
EEPROM Electrically Erasable Programmable Read Only Memory
EFE Early Fuel Evaporation
EGR Exhaust Gas Recirculation
EGRT Exhaust Gas Recirculation Temperature
EGRVC EGR Valve Control
EPROM Erasable Programmable Read Only Memory
EVAP Evaporative Emissions
EVP EGR Valve Position

F

FBC Feedback Carburetor
FEEPROM Flash Electrically Erasable Programmable Read Only Memory
FF Flexible Fuel
FI Fuel Injection
FT Fuel Trim
FWD Front Wheel Drive

G

GND Ground

H

HAC High Altitude Compensation
HEGO Heated Exhaust Gas Oxygen sensor
HEI High Energy Ignition
HO2 Sensor Heated Oxygen Sensor

I

IAC Idle Air Control
IAT Intake Air Temperature
ICM Ignition Control Module
IFI Indirect Fuel Injection
IFS Inertia Fuel Shutoff
ISC Idle Speed Control
IVSV Idle Vacuum Switching Valve

Commonly Used Abbreviations

K

KOEO	Key On, Engine Off
KOER	Key ON, Engine Running
KS	Knock Sensor

M

MAF	Mass Air Flow
MAP	Manifold Absolute Pressure
MAT	Manifold Air Temperature
MC	Mixture Control
MDP	Manifold Differential Pressure
MFI	Multiport Fuel Injection
MIL	Malfunction Indicator Lamp or Maintenance
MST	Manifold Surface Temperature
MVZ	Manifold Vacuum Zone

N

NVRAM	Nonvolatile Random Access Memory

O

O2 Sensor	Oxygen Sensor
OBD	On-Board Diagnostic
OC	Oxidation Catalyst
OHC	Overhead Camshaft
OL	Open Loop

P

P/S	Power Steering
PAIR	Pulsed Secondary Air Injection
PCM	Powertrain Control Module
PCS	Purge Control Solenoid
PCV	Positive Crankcase Ventilation
PIP	Profile Ignition Pick-up
PNP	Park/Neutral Position
PROM	Programmable Read Only Memory
PSP	Power Steering Pressure
PTO	Power Take-Off
PTOX	Periodic Trap Oxidizer System

R

RABS	Rear Anti-lock Brake System
RAM	Random Access Memory
ROM	Read Only Memory
RPM	Revolutions Per Minute
RWAL	Rear Wheel Anti-lock Brakes
RWD	Rear Wheel Drive

S

SBC	Single Bed Converter
SBEC	Single Board Engine Controller
SC	Supercharger
SCB	Supercharger Bypass
SFI	Sequential Multiport Fuel Injection
SIR	Supplemental Inflatible Restraint
SOHC	Single Overhead Camshaft
SPL	Smoke Puff Limiter
SPOUT	Spark Output
SRI	Service Reminder Indicator
SRS	Supplemental Restraint System
SRT	System Readiness Test
SSI	Solid State Ignition
ST	Scan Tool
STO	Self-Test Output

T

TAC	Thermostatic Air Clearner
TBI	Throttle Body Fuel Injection
TC	Turbocharger
TCC	Torque Converter Clutch
TCM	Transmission Control Module
TDC	Top Dead Center
TFI	Thick Film Ignition
TP	Throttle Position
TR Sensor	Transaxle/Transmission Range Sensor
TVV	Thermal Vacuum Valve
TWC	Three-way Catalytic Converter

V

VAF	Volume Air Flow, or Vane Air Flow
VAPS	Variable Assist Power Steering
VRV	Vacuum Regulator Valve
VSS	Vehicle Speed Sensor
VSV	Vacuum Switching Valve

W

WOT	Wide Open Throttle
WU-TWC	Warm Up Three-way Catalytic Converter

ENGLISH TO METRIC CONVERSION: TORQUE

To convert foot-pounds (ft. lbs.) to Newton-meters (Nm), multiply the number of ft. lbs. by 1.36
To convert Newton-meters (Nm) to foot-pounds (ft. lbs.), multiply the number of Nm by 0.7376

ft. lbs.	Nm	ft. lbs.	Nm	ft. lbs.	Nm	ft. lbs.	Nm
0.1	0.1	34	46.2	76	103.4	118	160.5
0.2	0.3	35	47.6	77	104.7	119	161.8
0.3	0.4	36	49.0	78	106.1	120	163.2
0.4	0.5	37	50.3	79	107.4	121	164.6
0.5	0.7	38	51.7	80	108.8	122	165.9
0.6	0.8	39	53.0	81	110.2	123	167.3
0.7	1.0	40	54.4	82	111.5	124	168.6
0.8	1.1	41	55.8	83	112.9	125	170.0
0.9	1.2	42	57.1	84	114.2	126	171.4
1	1.4	43	58.5	85	115.6	127	172.7
2	2.7	44	59.8	86	117.0	128	174.1
3	4.1	45	61.2	87	118.3	129	175.4
4	5.4	46	62.6	88	119.7	130	176.8
5	6.8	47	63.9	89	121.0	131	178.2
6	8.2	48	65.3	90	122.4	132	179.5
7	9.5	49	66.6	91	123.8	133	180.9
8	10.9	50	68.0	92	125.1	134	182.2
9	12.2	51	69.4	93	126.5	135	183.6
10	13.6	52	70.7	94	127.8	136	185.0
11	15.0	53	72.1	95	129.2	137	186.3
12	16.3	54	73.4	96	130.6	138	187.7
13	17.7	55	74.8	97	131.9	139	189.0
14	19.0	56	76.2	98	133.3	140	190.4
15	20.4	57	77.5	99	134.6	141	191.8
16	21.8	58	78.9	100	136.0	142	193.1
17	23.1	59	80.2	101	137.4	143	194.5
18	24.5	60	81.6	102	138.7	144	195.8
19	25.8	61	83.0	103	140.1	145	197.2
20	27.2	62	84.3	104	141.4	146	198.6
21	28.6	63	85.7	105	142.8	147	199.9
22	29.9	64	87.0	106	144.2	148	201.3
23	31.3	65	88.4	107	145.5	149	202.6
24	32.6	66	89.8	108	146.9	150	204.0
25	34.0	67	91.1	109	148.2	151	205.4
26	35.4	68	92.5	110	149.6	152	206.7
27	36.7	69	93.8	111	151.0	153	208.1
28	38.1	70	95.2	112	152.3	154	209.4
29	39.4	71	96.6	113	153.7	155	210.8
30	40.8	72	97.9	114	155.0	156	212.2
31	42.2	73	99.3	115	156.4	157	213.5
32	43.5	74	100.6	116	157.8	158	214.9
33	44.9	75	102.0	117	159.1	159	216.2

METRIC TO ENGLISH CONVERSION: TORQUE

To convert foot-pounds (ft. lbs.) to Newton-meters (Nm), multiply the number of ft. lbs. by 1.36

To convert Newton-meters (Nm) to foot-pounds (ft. lbs.), multiply the number of Nm by 0.7376

Nm	ft. lbs.	Nm	ft. lbs.	Nm	ft. lbs.	Nm	ft. lbs.	Nm	ft. lbs.
0.1	0.1	34	25.0	76	55.9	118	86.8	160	117.6
0.2	0.1	35	25.7	77	56.6	119	87.5	161	118.4
0.3	0.2	36	26.5	78	57.4	120	88.2	162	119.1
0.4	0.3	37	27.2	79	58.1	121	89.0	163	119.9
0.5	0.4	38	27.9	80	58.8	122	89.7	164	120.6
0.6	0.4	39	28.7	81	59.6	123	90.4	165	121.3
0.7	0.5	40	29.4	82	60.3	124	91.2	166	122.1
0.8	0.6	41	30.1	83	61.0	125	91.9	167	122.8
0.9	0.7	42	30.9	84	61.8	126	92.6	168	123.5
1	0.7	43	31.6	85	62.5	127	93.4	169	124.3
2	1.5	44	32.4	86	63.2	128	94.1	170	125.0
3	2.2	45	33.1	87	64.0	129	94.9	171	125.7
4	2.9	46	33.8	88	64.7	130	95.6	172	126.5
5	3.7	47	34.6	89	65.4	131	96.3	173	127.2
6	4.4	48	35.3	90	66.2	132	97.1	174	127.9
7	5.1	49	36.0	91	66.9	133	97.8	175	128.7
8	5.9	50	36.8	92	67.6	134	98.5	176	129.4
9	6.6	51	37.5	93	68.4	135	99.3	177	130.1
10	7.4	52	38.2	94	69.1	136	100.0	178	130.9
11	8.1	53	39.0	95	69.9	137	100.7	179	131.6
12	8.8	54	39.7	96	70.6	138	101.5	180	132.4
13	9.6	55	40.4	97	71.3	139	102.2	181	133.1
14	10.3	56	41.2	98	72.1	140	102.9	182	133.8
15	11.0	57	41.9	99	72.8	141	103.7	183	134.6
16	11.8	58	42.6	100	73.5	142	104.4	184	135.3
17	12.5	59	43.4	101	74.3	143	105.1	185	136.0
18	13.2	60	44.1	102	75.0	144	105.9	186	136.8
19	14.0	61	44.9	103	75.7	145	106.6	187	137.5
20	14.7	62	45.6	104	76.5	146	107.4	188	138.2
21	15.4	63	46.3	105	77.2	147	108.1	189	139.0
22	16.2	64	47.1	106	77.9	148	108.8	190	139.7
23	16.9	65	47.8	107	78.7	149	109.6	191	140.4
24	17.6	66	48.5	108	79.4	150	110.3	192	141.2
25	18.4	67	49.3	109	80.1	151	111.0	193	141.9
26	19.1	68	50.0	110	80.9	152	111.8	194	142.6
27	19.9	69	50.7	111	81.6	153	112.5	195	143.4
28	20.6	70	51.5	112	82.4	154	113.2	196	144.1
29	21.3	71	52.2	113	83.1	155	114.0	197	144.9
30	22.1	72	52.9	114	83.8	156	114.7	198	145.6
31	22.8	73	53.7	115	84.6	157	115.4	199	146.3
32	23.5	74	54.4	116	85.3	158	116.2	200	147.1
33	24.3	75	55.1	117	86.0	159	116.9	201	147.8

ENGLISH/METRIC CONVERSION: TEMPERATURE

To convert Fahrenheit (F°) to Celsius (C°), take F° temperature and subtract 32, multiply the result by 5 and divide the result by 9
To convert Celsius (C°) to Fahrenheit (F°), take C° temperature and multiply it by 9, divide the result by 5 and add 32

F°	C°	F°	C°	C°	F°	C°	F°
-40	-40.0	150	65.6	-38	-36.4	46	114.8
-35	-37.2	155	68.3	-36	-32.8	48	118.4
-30	-34.4	160	71.1	-34	-29.2	50	122
-25	-31.7	165	73.9	-32	-25.6	52	125.6
-20	-28.9	170	76.7	-30	-22	54	129.2
-15	-26.1	175	79.4	-28	-18.4	56	132.8
-10	-23.3	180	82.2	-26	-14.8	58	136.4
-5	-20.6	185	85.0	-24	-11.2	60	140
0	-17.8	190	87.8	-22	-7.6	62	143.6
1	-17.2	195	90.6	-20	-4	64	147.2
2	-16.7	200	93.3	-18	-0.4	66	150.8
3	-16.1	205	96.1	-16	3.2	68	154.4
4	-15.6	210	98.9	-14	6.8	70	158
5	-15.0	212	100.0	-12	10.4	72	161.6
10	-12.2	215	101.7	-10	14	74	165.2
15	-9.4	220	104.4	-8	17.6	76	168.8
20	-6.7	225	107.2	-6	21.2	78	172.4
25	-3.9	230	110.0	-4	24.8	80	176
30	-1.1	235	112.8	-2	28.4	82	179.6
35	1.7	240	115.6	0	32	84	183.2
40	4.4	245	118.3	2	35.6	86	186.8
45	7.2	250	121.1	4	39.2	88	190.4
50	10.0	255	123.9	6	42.8	90	194
55	12.8	260	126.7	8	46.4	92	197.6
60	15.6	265	129.4	10	50	94	201.2
65	18.3	270	132.2	12	53.6	96	204.8
70	21.1	275	135.0	14	57.2	98	208.4
75	23.9	280	137.8	16	60.8	100	212
80	26.7	285	140.6	18	64.4	102	215.6
85	29.4	290	143.3	20	68	104	219.2
90	32.2	295	146.1	22	71.6	106	222.8
95	35.0	300	148.9	24	75.2	108	226.4
100	37.8	305	151.7	26	78.8	110	230
105	40.6	310	154.4	28	82.4	112	233.6
110	43.3	315	157.2	30	86	114	237.2
115	46.1	320	160.0	32	89.6	116	240.8
120	48.9	325	162.8	34	93.2	118	244.4
125	51.7	330	165.6	36	96.8	120	248
130	54.4	335	168.3	38	100.4	122	251.6
135	57.2	340	171.1	40	104	124	255.2
140	60.0	345	173.9	42	107.6	126	258.8
145	62.8	350	176.7	44	111.2	128	262.4

LENGTH CONVERSION

To convert inches (in.) to millimeters (mm), multiply the number of inches by 25.4
To convert millimeters (mm) to inches (in.), multiply the number of millimeters by 0.04

Inches	Millimeters	Inches	Millimeters	Inches	Millimeters	Inches	Millimeters
0.0001	0.00254	0.005	0.1270	0.09	2.286	4	101.6
0.0002	0.00508	0.006	0.1524	0.1	2.54	5	127.0
0.0003	0.00762	0.007	0.1778	0.2	5.08	6	152.4
0.0004	0.01016	0.008	0.2032	0.3	7.62	7	177.8
0.0005	0.01270	0.009	0.2286	0.4	10.16	8	203.2
0.0006	0.01524	0.01	0.254	0.5	12.70	9	228.6
0.0007	0.01778	0.02	0.508	0.6	15.24	10	254.0
0.0008	0.02032	0.03	0.762	0.7	17.78	11	279.4
0.0009	0.02286	0.04	1.016	0.8	20.32	12	304.8
0.001	0.0254	0.05	1.270	0.9	22.86	13	330.2
0.002	0.0508	0.06	1.524	1	25.4	14	355.6
0.003	0.0762	0.07	1.778	2	50.8	15	381.0
0.004	0.1016	0.08	2.032	3	76.2	16	406.4

ENGLISH/METRIC CONVERSION: LENGTH

To convert inches (in.) to millimeters (mm), multiply the number of inches by 25.4
To convert millimeters (mm) to inches (in.), multiply the number of millimeters by 0.04

Inches		Millimeters	Inches		Millimeters	Inches		Millimeters
Fraction	Decimal	Decimal	Fraction	Decimal	Decimal	Fraction	Decimal	Decimal
1/64	0.016	0.397	11/32	0.344	8.731	11/16	0.688	17.463
1/32	0.031	0.794	23/64	0.359	9.128	45/64	0.703	17.859
3/64	0.047	1.191	3/8	0.375	9.525	23/32	0.719	18.256
1/16	0.063	1.588	25/64	0.391	9.922	47/64	0.734	18.653
5/64	0.078	1.984	13/32	0.406	10.319	3/4	0.750	19.050
3/32	0.094	2.381	27/64	0.422	10.716	49/64	0.766	19.447
7/64	0.109	2.778	7/16	0.438	11.113	25/32	0.781	19.844
1/8	0.125	3.175	29/64	0.453	11.509	51/64	0.797	20.241
9/64	0.141	3.572	15/32	0.469	11.906	13/16	0.813	20.638
5/32	0.156	3.969	31/64	0.484	12.303	53/64	0.828	21.034
11/64	0.172	4.366	1/2	0.500	12.700	27/32	0.844	21.431
3/16	0.188	4.763	33/64	0.516	13.097	55/64	0.859	21.828
13/64	0.203	5.159	17/32	0.531	13.494	7/8	0.875	22.225
7/32	0.219	5.556	35/64	0.547	13.891	57/64	0.891	22.622
15/64	0.234	5.953	9/16	0.563	14.288	29/32	0.906	23.019
1/4	0.250	6.350	37/64	0.578	14.684	59/64	0.922	23.416
17/64	0.266	6.747	19/32	0.594	15.081	15/16	0.938	23.813
9/32	0.281	7.144	39/64	0.609	15.478	61/64	0.953	24.209
19/64	0.297	7.541	5/8	0.625	15.875	31/32	0.969	24.606
5/16	0.313	7.938	41/64	0.641	16.272	63/64	0.984	25.003
21/64	0.328	8.334	21/32	0.656	16.669	1/1	1.000	25.400
			43/64	0.672	17.066			

CHILTON® LABOR GUIDE

Chilton's labor times are so trusted, even a competing publisher uses them!

The *Chilton 2013 Labor Guide* features new models and new labor operations in order to stay current with new technologies. Labor times have also been refined for normal and severe maintenance schedules, if applicable. The 2013 edition Labor Guide Manuals provide repair times for 1990-current import and domestic vehicles and the 2013 edition Labor Guide CD-ROM provides repair times for 1981-current import and domestic vehicles. Chilton's editors consider warranty times, component locations, component type, the environment in which technicians work, the training they receive, and the tools they use when calculating a labor time. To allow for vehicle age, operating conditions, and type of service, the *Chilton 2013 Labor Guide* provides standard and severe service times, plus OEM warranty times. Vehicle makes and models conform to current Automotive Aftermarket Industry Association (AAIA) standards.

Chilton 2013 Labor Guide Manual Set (Domestic & Import) ISBN 978-1-2851-9293-2, Part No. 209293

Chilton 2013 Labor Guide CD-ROM (Domestic & Import) ISBN 978-1-2851-9296-3, Part No. 209296

CD-ROM FEATURES

- Access labor times for 1981- current import and domestic vehicle models.
- Save time with automatically calculated labor charges, taxes, & parts as total job is estimated.
- Create professional estimates for your customer and worksheets for your technicians, printing them whenever needed.
- Keep track of customers, prior estimates, and your own parts or package jobs with less paper.
- Choose part names for estimates from an industry standard database to reduce typing.
- Estimate and track your work status with improved forms.
- Communicate easily with customers using re-designed printouts which show all labor and parts in an easy-to-read format.
- Simplify adding parts to your estimate or work order with a helpful parts list.
- Locate information quick with a keyword search engine.
- Quickly locate work requests by day, week and month using the calendar feature.

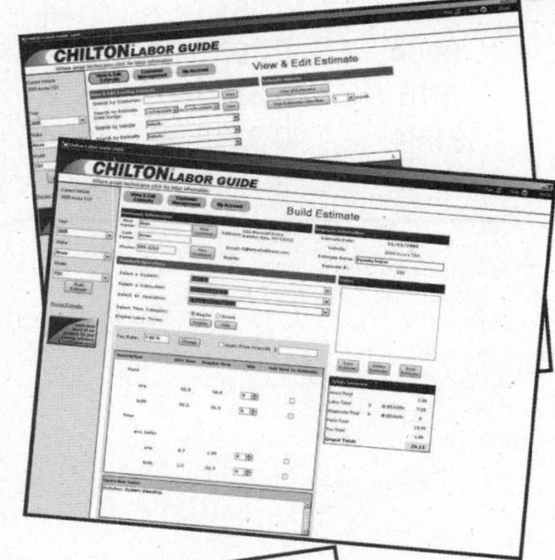

Manual FEATURES

- Nearly 4,000 pages of updated Chilton labor times split into two volumes includes vehicle information from 1990 to current models.
- Trusted by more service professionals than any other labor guide.
- Less flipping though pages with separate domestic and imported vehicle manuals and more specific vehicle groups.
- Convenient tabs display contents by manufacturer and model.
- Easy-to-find manufacturers are arranged alphabetically within each volume.
- Search using two-indexes - labor operations and systems - in each model group.
- Page numbers include manufacturer code so you know where you are in the book.

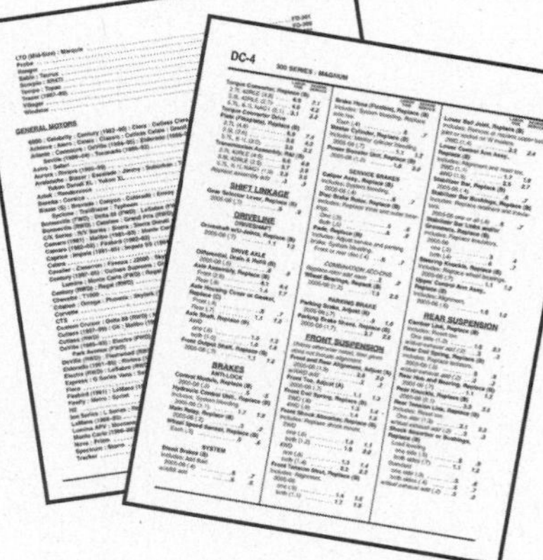